THE CLASSIC BIBLE COMMENTARY

THE CLASSIC BIBLE COMMENTARY

An Essential Collection of History's

Finest Commentaries in One Volume

EDITED AND COMPILED BY

OWEN COLLINS

CROSSWAY BOOKS • WHEATON, ILLINOIS
A DIVISION OF GOOD NEWS PUBLISHERS

The Classic Bible Commentary

Compilation copyright © 1999 by Owen Collins

Published by Crossway Books
 A division of Good News Publishers
 1300 Crescent Street
 Wheaton, Illinois 60187

First published in Great Britain in 1999 by HarperCollins*Religious* under the title: *The Definitive Bible Commentary.*

Owen Collins asserts the moral right to be identified as the editor of this work.

Cover design: Left Coast Design

Printed in the United States of America

ISBN 1-58134-124-5

CONTENTS

NEW TESTAMENT

INTRODUCTION

Charles Spurgeon's advice to aspiring preachers was, 'Read admirable commentaries.' He went on and told them, 'In order to expound the Scriptures, and as an aid to pulpit studies, you will need to be familiar with the commentaries: a glorious army, let me tell you, whose acquaintance will be your delight and profit. Of course, you are not such wiseacres as to think or say that you can expound Scripture without the assistance from the works of the divines and learned men who have laboured before you in the field of exposition. ... It seems odd, that certain men who talk so much about what the Holy Spirit reveals to themselves, should think so little of what he has revealed to others.'[1] This present one volume commentary on the 66 books of the Bible has a much wider purpose than being an aid to preachers. It is also intended for anyone who desires to study the Bible, either by themselves or with a group of people.

One of the advantages of having a one volume Bible commentary by a variety of authors is that the contributors who have written exceptionally good commentaries on particular Bible books can be selected. For example, Martin Luther's commentary on Galatians, and J.B. Lightfoot's commentaries on Colossians and Philemon remain in a class of their own. Genesis, 1 and 2 Timothy, Titus and 1 John are edited versions of Calvin's commentaries based on the first English translation of 1578. Calvin first published his commentary on Genesis in Latin in 1554 and his commentaries in this volume were written earlier than those of any of the other contributors, except for Martin Luther. Spurgeon wrote of Calvin, 'It would not be possible for me too earnestly to press upon you the importance of reading the expositions of that prince among men, John Calvin.' Calvin has been justly styled as the 'Bible teacher of the Reformation', mainly on account of his 51 volumes of Bible commentaries which he used to dictate to his five secretaries.

Three scholars

Robert Jamieson, A.R. Faussett and David Brown combined to write a one volume commentary on the Bible entitled *A Commentary, Critical, Explanatory, and Practical, on the Old and New Testaments* which was first published in 1871. Of this book C.H. Spurgeon wrote, 'It is to some extent a compilation and condensation of other men's thoughts, but it is sufficiently original to claim a place in every minister's library: indeed it contains so great a variety of information that if a man had no other exposition he would find himself at no great loss if he possessed this and used it diligently.'[2] David Brown's contributions to the

---

[1] C.H. Spurgeon, *Commenting and Commentaries*, Banner of Truth Trust, 1969, p. 1.
[2] C.H. Spurgeon, *Commenting and Commentaries*, Banner of Truth Trust, 1969, p. 20.

present volume are lists of the New Testament miracles and parables, a list of the principal events connected with the apostle Paul's life, and commentaries on Mark's gospel and John's gospel. Three introductions about groups of writings in the Old Testament by A.R. Faussett are included: 'Introduction to the prophetical books of the Old Testament', 'Introduction to the poetic books of the Old Testament' and 'Introduction to the prophets of the restoration'. Also Faussett's commentaries on the Song of Solomon, the twelve 'minor' prophets (Hosea, Joel, Amos, Obadiah, Jonah, Micah, Nahum, Habbakuk, Zephaniah, Haggai, Zechariah, and Malachi), Philippians, 1 and 2 Thessalonians, James, 1 and 2 Peter and Jude have been selected. Robert Jamieson's article on 'Introduction to the Pentateuch' and his commentaries on most of the historical books of the Old Testament, i.e. 1 and 2 Samuel, 1 and 2 Kings and 1 and 2 Chronicles are included.

The preacher

John Wesley, the founder of Methodism, rode over 10,000 miles each year, often preaching six times a day. But he also laboured in providing fellowship groups for Christians and his commentaries on all of the books of the Bible were intended to instruct Christians. His commentaries on Exodus, Leviticus, Numbers, Deuteronomy, Ezra, Nehemiah, Esther, Isaiah, Ezekiel and Daniel, from the Old Testament are included here. At the beginning of the New Testament section of this book all of Wesley's lists of contents of each New Testament book are grouped together. This provides a quick bird's eye view of each New Testament book. Wesley's commentaries on Matthew, and his commentaries on two letters from the New Testament, which often prove very hard to understand, Romans and Hebrews, are included here, as Wesley is one of the easiest writers to follow. J.C. Ryle, the first bishop of Liverpool, has his commentary on Luke included here.

The influence of Martin Luther's Bible commentaries is proverbial. John Wesley attended a small chapel in Aldersgate Street in the centre of London where he heard Martin Luther's *Preface to the Book of Romans* being read. It described exactly what John Wesley needed to know at that moment – real faith in Jesus Christ. It spoke about trusting in Jesus Christ for salvation and not trusting in any good deeds of our own. John Wesley's Journal entry for that night, 24 May 1738, read, 'About a quarter before nine, while he [the preacher at the chapel] was describing the change which God works in the heart through faith in Christ, I felt I did trust in Christ, Christ alone, for salvation, and an assurance was given me that He had taken away my sins, even mine, and saved me from the law of sin and death.'

John Wesley's brother, Charles, called 'the sweet singer of Methodism' on account of all the hymns he wrote, was also greatly influenced in his Christian life by one of Luther's commentaries, the one included in this volume – Galatians. After reading Luther's *Commentary on Galatians*, he wrote: 'The Spirit of God strove with my own and the evil spirit, till by degrees He chased away the darkness of my unbelief. I found myself convinced, I knew not how nor when, and immediately fell to intercession. I now found myself at peace with God, and rejoiced in hope of loving Christ. My temper for the rest of the day was mistrust of my own great, but before unknown, weakness. I saw that by faith I stood; by the continual support of faith, which kept me from falling, though of myself I am ever sinking into sin. I went to bed, still sensible of my own weakness, yet confident of Christ's protection.'

A 'landmark theologian'

Charles Hodge's commentaries on 1 and 2 Corinthians and Ephesians are included in this volume. J.I. Packer has written of Hodge, 'It can be safely said that most, if not all, of those today who know the name Charles Hodge think of him simply as the landmark English-speaking conservative Reformed theologian and churchman of the nineteenth-century.'[3] J.B. Lightfoot's commentaries on Colossians and Philemon have also been selected for this volume. Alister McGrath has written in his Introduction to a recently published edition of Lightfoot's commentaries on Colossians and Philemon, 'Joseph Barbour Lightfoot (1828–1889) is widely regarded as one of the finest nineteenth-century interpreters of Paul. ... There is enormous scholarly, spiritual, and theological wisdom packed into the pages of this commentary. It will bring new depth to your understanding of Colossians and its challenge for us today.'[4]

'First among the mighty'

The remainder of the Bible commentaries are by Matthew Henry. His commentaries on Joshua, Judges, Ruth, Job, Psalms, Proverbs, Ecclesiastes, Jeremiah and Lamentations, from the Old Testament; and Acts, 2 John, 3 John and Revelation, from the New Testament are included. C.H. Spurgeon had a high opinion of Henry's Bible commentaries: 'First among the mighty for general usefulness we are bound to mention the man whose name is a household word, Matthew Henry. He is most pious and pithy, sound and sensible, suggestive and sober, terse and trustworthy. ... His is the kind of commentary to be placed where I saw it, in the old meeting-house at Chester – chained in the vestry for anybody and everybody to read.'

The present volume

The above commentaries have not been added to in any way in this edition. For the sake of space some have needed to be cut down in size, and some of the Hebrew, Greek, Latin, German and French quotations have been cut out, and the occasional word which has now changed its meaning has been replaced. Most of the commentaries are based on the *Authorized Version/King James Version* (AV/KJV) of the Bible, since most of the writers had this in front of them when they wrote. However, Luke, 1 and 2 Corinthians, Ephesians, Colossians, 1 and 2 Timothy, Titus, Philemon and 1, 2, and 3 John use the *New Revised Standard Version* (NRSV). In the commentary parts of this book the **bold** typeface is used for the words from the Bible which are being commented upon. Very occasionally some of the words used differ from the AV and NRSV because the commentator is using his own translation of the Greek text.

'That he may read it with understanding'

It is useful to know how the Bible commentators included in this volume view the Bible themselves. They all believed that, 'All Scripture is inspired by God and is useful for teaching, for reproof, for correction, and for training in righteousness, so that everyone who belongs to

---

[3] J.I. Packer, introduction to *1 Corinthians, C.Hodge*, Crossway Books, 1995, p. ix.
[4] A.E. McGrath, introduction to *Colossians and Philemon*, Crossway Books, 1997, pp.xi-xii

God may be proficient, equipped for every good work' (2 Timothy 3:16–17, NRSV). All the commentators believed that the important thing for any commentary was to explain and apply the Bible text. John Wesley explains his approach to his Bible commentary in his own Introduction to *Notes on the Old Testament* as follows: 'Every thinking person will now easily discern my design in the following sheets. It is not, to write sermons, essays or set discourses, upon any part of scripture. It is not to draw inferences from the text, or to shew what doctrines may be proved thereby. It is this: To give the direct, literal meaning, of every verse, of every sentence, and as far as I am able, of every word in the oracles of God. I design only, like the hand of a dial, to point every man to This: not to take up his mind with something else, how excellent soever: but to keep his eye fixt upon the naked Bible, that he may read and hear it with understanding. I say again, (and desire it may be well observed, that none may expect what they will not find) It is not my design to write a book, which a man may read separate from the Bible: but barely to assist those who fear God, in hearing and reading the Bible itself, by showing the natural sense of every part, in as few and plain words as I can.

... My intention is, to make my readers think, and assist them in thinking. This is the way to understand the things of God; Meditate thereon day and night; So shall you attain the best knowledge; even to know the only true God and Jesus Christ whom He hath sent. And this knowledge will lead you, to love Him, because he hath first loved us: yea, to love the Lord your God with all your heart, and with all your soul, and with all your mind, and with all your strength. Will there not then be all that mind in you, which was also in Christ Jesus? And in consequence of this, while you joyfully experience all the holy tempers described in this book, you will likewise be outwardly holy as He that hath called you is holy, in all manner of conversation.'

Wesley then goes on to give this piece of advice to readers of the Bible: 'If you desire to read the scripture in such a manner as may most effectually answer this end, would it not be advisable, 1. To set apart a little time, if you can, every morning and evening for that purpose? 2. At each time if you have leisure, to read a chapter out of the Old, and one out of the New Testament: if you cannot do this, to take a single chapter, or a part of one? 3. To read this with a single eye, to know the whole will of God, and a fixt resolution to do it? In order to know his will, you should, 4. Have a constant eye to the analogy of faith; the connexion and harmony there is between those grand, fundamental doctrines, Original Sin, Justification by Faith, the New Birth, Inward and Outward Holiness. 5. Serious and earnest prayer should be constantly used, before we consult the oracles of God, seeing Scripture can only be understood through the same Spirit whereby it was given. Our reading should likewise be closed with prayer, that what we read may be written on our hearts. 6. It might also be of use, if while we read, we were frequently to pause, and examine ourselves by what we read, both with regard to our hearts, and lives. This would furnish us with matter of praise, where we found God had enabled us to conform to his blessed will, and matter of humiliation and prayer, where we were conscious of having fallen short. And whatever light you then receive, should be used to the uttermost, and that immediately. Let there be no delay. Whatever you resolve, begin to execute the first moment you can. So shall you find this word to be indeed the power of God unto present and eternal salvation.' EDINBURGH, *April 25, 1765.*

Owen Collins

THE OLD TESTAMENT

INTRODUCTION TO THE PENTATEUCH

Robert Jamieson

The Pentateuch, the name by which the first five books of the Bible are designated, is derived from two Greek words, *pente*, 'five,' and *teuchos*, a 'volume,' thus signifying the five-fold volume. Originally these books formed one continuous work, as in the Hebrew manuscripts they are still connected in one unbroken roll. At what time they were divided into five portions, each having a separate title, is not known, but it is certain that the distinction dates at or before the time of the Septuagint translation.

The names they bear in our English version are borrowed from the Septuagint, and they were applied by those Greek translators as descriptive of the principal subjects – the leading contents of the respective books. In the later Scriptures they are frequently comprehended under the general designation, The Law, The Book of the Law, since, to give a detailed account of the preparations for, and the delivery of, the divine code, with all the civil and sacred institutions that were peculiar to the ancient economy, is the object to which they are exclusively devoted. They have always been placed at the beginning of the Bible, not only on account of their priority in point of time, but as forming an appropriate and indispensable introduction to the rest of the sacred books.

The numerous and oft-recurring references made in the later Scriptures to the events, the ritual, and the doctrines of the ancient Church would have not only lost much of their point and significance, but have been absolutely unintelligible without the information which these five books contain. They constitute the groundwork or basis on which the whole fabric of revelation rests, and a knowledge of the authority and importance that is thus attached to them will sufficiently account for the determined assaults that infidels have made on these books, as well as for the zeal and earnestness which the friends of the truth have displayed in their defence.

Mosaic origin

The Mosaic origin of the Pentateuch is established by the concurring voices both of Jewish and Christian tradition; and their unanimous testimony is supported by the internal character and statements of the work itself. That Moses did keep a written record of the important transactions relative to the Israelites is attested by his own express affirmation. For in relating the victory over the Amalekites, which he was commanded by divine authority to record, the language employed, 'write this for a memorial in a book' [Hebrew, the book], (Ex 17:14), shows that that narrative was to form part of a register already in progress, and various circumstances combine to prove that this register was a continuous history of the special goodness and care of divine providence in the choice, protection, and guidance of the Hebrew nation.

First, there are the repeated assertions of Moses himself that the events which checkered the experience of that people were written down as they occurred (see Ex 24:4–7 34:27 Nu 33:2). Secondly, there are the testimonies borne in various parts of the later historical books to the Pentateuch as a work well known, and familiar to all the people (see Jos 1:8 8:34 23:6 24:26 1Ki 2:3, &c.) Thirdly, frequent references are made in the works of the prophets to the facts recorded in the books of Moses (compare Isa 1:9 with Ge 19:1; Isa 12:2 with Ex 15:2; Isa 51:2 with Ge 12:2; Isa 54:9 with Ge 8:21,22; compare Ho 9:10 with Nu 25:3; Ho 11:8 with Ge 19:24; Ho 12:4 with Ge 32:24,25; Ho 12:12 with Ge 28:5 29:20; compare Joe 1:9 with Nu 15:4–7 28:7–14 De 12:6,7 16:10,11; compare Am 2:9 with Nu 21:21; Am 4:4 with Nu 28:3; Am 4:11 with Ge 19:24; Am 9:13 with Le 26:5; compare Mic 6:5 with Nu 22:25; Mic 6:6 with Le 9:2; Mic 6:15 with Le 26:16, &c.) Fourthly, the testimony of Christ and the Apostles is repeatedly borne to the books of Moses (Mt 19:7 Lu 16:29 24:27 Joh 1:17 7:19 Ac 3:22 28:23 Ro 10:5).

Indeed the references are so numerous, and the testimonies so distinctly borne to the existence of the Mosaic books throughout the whole history of the Jewish nation, and the unity of character, design, and style pervading these books is so clearly perceptible, notwithstanding the rationalistic assertions of their forming a series of separate and unconnected fragments, that it may with all safety be said, there is immensely stronger and more varied evidence in proof of their being the authorship of Moses than of any of the Greek or Roman classics being the productions of the authors whose names they bear.

But admitting that the Pentateuch was written by Moses, an important question arises, as to whether the books which compose it have reached us in an authentic form; whether they exist genuine and entire as they came from the hands of their author. In answer to this question, it might be sufficient to state that, in the public and periodical rehearsals of the law in the solemn religious assemblies of the people, implying the existence of numerous copies, provision was made for preserving the integrity of 'The Book of the Law.' But besides this, two remarkable facts, the one of which occurred before and the other after the captivity, afford conclusive evidence of the genuineness and authenticity of the Pentateuch. The first is the discovery in the reign of Josiah of the autograph copy which was deposited by Moses in the ark of the testimony, and the second is the schism of the Samaritans, who erected a temple on Mount Gerizim, and who, appealing to the Mosaic law as the standard of their faith and worship equally with the Jews, watched with jealous care over every circumstance that could affect the purity of the Mosaic record.

There is the strongest reason, then, for believing that the Pentateuch, as it exists now, is substantially the same as it came from the hands of Moses. The appearance of a later hand, it is true, is traceable in the narrative of the death of Moses at the close of Deuteronomy, and some few interpolations, such as inserting the altered names of places, may have been made by Ezra, who revised and corrected the version of the ancient Scriptures. But, substantially, the Pentateuch is the genuine work of Moses, and many, who once impugned its claims to that character, and looked upon it as the production of a later age, have found themselves compelled, after a full and unprejudiced investigation of the subject, to proclaim their conviction that its authenticity is to be fully relied on.

Authenticity

The genuineness and authenticity of the Pentateuch being admitted, the inspiration and canonical authority of the work follow as a necessary consequence. The admission of Moses to the privilege of frequent and direct communion with God (Ex 25:22 33:3 Nu 7:89 9:8);

his repeated and solemn declarations that he spoke and wrote by command of God; the submissive reverence that was paid to the authority of his precepts by all classes of the Jewish people, including the king himself (De 17:18 27:3); and the acknowledgment of the divine mission of Moses by the writers of the New Testament, all prove the inspired character and authority of his books. The Pentateuch possessed the strongest claims on the attention of the Jewish people, as forming the standard of their faith, the rule of their obedience, the record of their whole civil and religious polity. But it is interesting and important to all mankind, inasmuch as besides revealing the origin and early development of the divine plan of grace, it is the source of all authentic knowledge, giving the true philosophy, history, geography, and chronology of the ancient world.

Finally, the Pentateuch is indispensable to the whole revelation contained in the Bible; for Genesis being the legitimate preface to the law; the law being the natural introduction to the Old Testament; and the whole a prelude to the gospel revelation, it could not have been omitted. What the four Gospels are in the New, the five books of Moses are in the Old Testament.

GENESIS

John Calvin

Introduction

Since the infinite wisdom of God is displayed in the admirable structure of heaven and earth, it is absolutely impossible to unfold The History of the Creation of the World in terms equal to its dignity. For while the measure of our capacity is too contracted to comprehend things of such magnitude, our tongue is equally incapable of giving a full and substantial account of them. As he, however, deserves praise, who, with modesty and reverence, applies himself to the consideration of the works of God, although he attain less than might be wished, so, if in this kind of employment, I endeavour to assist others according to the ability given to me, I trust that my service will be not less approved by pious men than accepted by God.

I have chosen to premise this, for the sake not only of excusing myself, but of admonishing my readers, that if they sincerely wish to profit with me in meditating on the works of God, they must bring with them a sober, docile, mild, and humble spirit. We see, indeed, the world with our eyes, we tread the earth with our feet, we touch innumerable kinds of God's works with our hands, we inhale a sweet and pleasant fragrance from herbs and flowers, we enjoy boundless benefits; but in those very things of which we attain some knowledge, there dwells such an immensity of divine power, goodness, and wisdom, as absorbs all our senses. Therefore, let men be satisfied if they obtain only a moderate taste of them, suited to their capacity. And it becomes us so to press towards this mark during our whole life, that (even in extreme old age) we shall not repent of the progress we have made, if only we have advanced ever so little in our course.

Moses' intention

The intention of Moses in beginning his Book with the creation of the world, is, to render God, as it were, visible to us in his works. But here presumptuous men rise up, and scoffingly inquire, whence was this revealed to Moses? They therefore suppose him to be speaking fabulously of things unknown, because he was neither a spectator of the events he records, nor had learned the truth of them by reading. Such is their reasoning; but their dishonesty is easily exposed. For if they can destroy the credit of this history, because it is traced back through a long series of past ages, let them also prove those prophecies to be false in which the same history predicts occurrences which did not take place till many centuries afterwards.

Those things, I affirm, are clear and obvious, which Moses testifies concerning the vocation of the Gentiles, the accomplishment of which occurred nearly two thousand years after his death. Was not he, who by the Spirit foresaw an event remotely future, and hidden at the time from the perception of mankind, capable of understanding whether the world was created by God, especially seeing that he was taught by a Divine Master? For he does not here put forward divinations of his own, but is the instrument of the Holy Spirit for the publication of those things which it was of importance for all men to know.

They greatly err in deeming it absurd that the order of the creation, which had been previously unknown, should at length have been described and explained by him. For he does not transmit to memory things before unheard of, but for the first time consigns to writing facts which the fathers had delivered as from hand to hand, through a long succession of years, to their children. Can we conceive that man was so placed in the earth as to be ignorant of his own origin, and of the origin of those things which he enjoyed? No sane person doubts that Adam was well-instructed respecting them all. Was he indeed afterwards dumb? Were the holy Patriarchs so ungrateful as to suppress in silence such necessary instruction? Did Noah, warned by a divine judgment so memorable, neglect to transmit it to posterity? Abraham is expressly honoured with this eulogy that he was the teacher and the master of his family, (Gen. 18: 19.) And we know that, long before the time of Moses, an acquaintance with the covenant into which God had entered with their fathers was common to the whole people. When he says that the Israelites were sprung from a holy race, which God had chosen for himself, he does not propound it as something new, but only commemorates what all held, what the old men themselves had received from their ancestors, and what, in short, was entirely uncontroverted among them.

Therefore, we ought not to doubt that the creation of the world, as here described was already known through the ancient and perpetual tradition of the Fathers. Yet, since nothing is more easy than that the truth of God should be so corrupted by men, that, in a long succession of time, it should, as it were, degenerate from itself, it pleased the Lord to commit the history to writing, for the purpose of preserving its purity. Moses, therefore, has established the credibility of that doctrine which is contained in his writings, and which, by the carelessness of men, might otherwise have been lost.

I now return to the design of Moses, or rather of the Holy Spirit, who has spoken by his mouth. We know God, who is himself invisible, only through his works. Therefore, the Apostle elegantly styles the worlds, *ta me ek fainomenoon blepomena*, as if one should say, 'the manifestation of things not apparent,' (Heb. 11: 3.) This is the reason why the Lord, that he may invite us to the knowledge of himself, places the fabric of heaven and earth before our eyes, rendering himself, in a certain manner, manifest in them. For his eternal power and Godhead (as Paul says) are there exhibited, (Rom. 1: 20.) And that declaration of David is most true, that the heavens, though without a tongue, are yet eloquent heralds of the glory of God, and that this most beautiful order of nature silently proclaims his admirable wisdom, (Ps. 19: 1.) This is the more diligently to be observed, because so few pursue the right method of knowing God, while the greater part adhere to the creatures without any consideration of the Creator himself. For men are commonly subject to these two extremes; namely, that some, forgetful of God, apply the whole force of their mind to the consideration of nature; and others, overlooking the works of God, aspire with a foolish and insane curiosity to inquire into his Essence. Both labour in vain.

The Author of nature

To be so occupied in the investigation of the secrets of nature, as never to turn the eyes to its Author, is a most perverted study; and to enjoy everything in nature without acknowledging the Author of the benefit, is the basest ingratitude. Therefore, they who assume to be philosophers without Religion, and who, by speculating, so act as to remove God and all sense of piety far from them, will one day feel the force of the expression of Paul, related by Luke, that God has never left himself without witness, (Acts 14: 17). For they shall not be permitted to escape with impunity because they have been deaf and insensible to testimonies so illustrious. And, in truth, it is the part of culpable ignorance, never to see God, who everywhere gives signs of his presence. But if mockers now escape by their cavils, hereafter their terrible destruction will bear witness that they were ignorant of God, only because they were willingly and maliciously blinded.

As for those who proudly soar above the world to seek God in his unveiled essence, it is impossible but that at length they should entangle themselves in a multitude of absurd figments. For God – by other means invisible – (as we have already said) clothes himself, so to speak, with the image of the world in which he would present himself to our contemplation. They who will not deign to behold him thus magnificently arrayed in the incomparable vesture of the heavens and the earth, afterwards suffer the just punishment of their proud contempt in their own ravings. Therefore, as soon as the name of God sounds in our ears, or the thought of him occurs to our minds, let us also clothe him with this most beautiful ornament; finally, let the world become our school if we desire rightly to know God.

Chapter 1

1. In the beginning. To expound the term **beginning**, of Christ, is altogether frivolous. For Moses simply intends to assert that the world was not perfected at its very commencement, in the manner in which it is now seen, but that it was created an empty chaos of heaven and earth. His language therefore may be thus explained. When God in the beginning created the heaven and the earth, the earth was empty and waste. He moreover teaches by the word **created**, that what before did not exist was now made; for he has not used the term *yatsar*, which signifies to frame or form but *bara*, which signifies to create. Therefore his meaning is, that the world was made out of nothing.

2. And the earth was without form and void. Were we now to take away from the earth all that God added after the time here alluded to, then we should have this rude and unpolished, or rather shapeless chaos.

And the Spirit of God. Moses asserts that this mass, however confused it might be, was rendered stable, for the time, by the secret efficacy of the Spirit. Now there are two significations of the Hebrew word which suit the present place; either that the spirit moved and agitated itself over the waters, for the sake of putting forth vigour; or that He brooded over them to cherish them.

3. And God said. Moses now, for the first time, introduces God in the act of speaking, as if he had created the mass of heaven and earth without the Word. Yet John testifies that 'without him was not any thing made that was made,' (John 1: 3.) And it is certain that the world had been begun by the same efficacy of the Word by which it was completed.

Let there be light. It be proper that the light, by means of which the world was to be adorned with such excellent beauty, should be first created.

4. And God saw the light. Here God is introduced by Moses as surveying his work, that he might take pleasure in it. But he does it for our sake, to teach us that God has made nothing without a certain reason and design. And we ought not so to understand the words of Moses as if God did not know that his work was good, till it was finished. But the meaning of the passage is, that the work, such as we now see it, was approved by God.

5. And God called the light. That is, God willed that there should be a regular vicissitude of days and nights; which also followed immediately when the first day was ended. For God removed the light from view, that night might be the commencement of another day.

6. Let there be a firmament. The work of the second day is to provide an empty space around the circumference of the earth, that heaven and earth may not be mixed together. Since, therefore, God has created the clouds, and assigned them a region above us, it ought not to be forgotten that they are restrained by the power of God, lest, gushing forth with sudden violence, they should swallow us up.

9. Let the waters … be gathered together. This also is an illustrious miracle, that the waters by their departure have given a dwelling-place to men. Let us, therefore, know that we are dwelling on dry ground, because God, by his command, has removed the waters that they should not overflow the whole earth.

11. Let the earth bring forth grass. Hitherto the earth was naked and barren, now the Lord fructifies it by his word. For though it was already destined to bring forth fruit, yet till new virtue proceeded from the mouth of God, it must remain dry and empty. If therefore we inquire, how it happens that the earth is fruitful, that the germ is produced from the seed, that fruits come to maturity, and their various kinds are annually reproduced; no other cause will be found, but that God has once spoken, that is, has issued his eternal decree; and that the earth, and all things proceeding from it, yield obedience to the command of God, which they always hear.

14. Let there be lights. Moses passes onwards to the fourth day, on which the stars were made. God had before created the light, but he now institutes a new order in nature, that the sun should be the dispenser of diurnal light, and the moon and stars should shine by night. And He assigns them this office, to teach us that all creatures are subject to his will, and execute what he enjoins upon them.

15. Let them be for lights. It is well again to repeat what I have said before, that it is not here philosophically discussed, how great the sun is in the heaven, and how great, or how little, is the moon; but how much light comes to us from them. For Moses here addresses himself to our senses, that the knowledge of the gifts of God which we enjoy may not glide away.

16. The greater light. Let the astronomers possess their more exalted knowledge; but, in the meantime, they who perceive by the moon the splendour of night, are convicted by its use of perverse ingratitude unless they acknowledge the beneficence of God.

20. Let the waters bring forth … the moving creature. On the fifth day the birds and fishes are created. The blessing of God is added, that they may of themselves produce offspring.

21. When he says that **the waters brought forth,** he proceeds to commend the efficacy of the word, which the waters hear so promptly, that, though lifeless in themselves, they suddenly teem with a living offspring, yet the language of Moses expresses more; namely, that fishes innumerable are daily produced from the waters, because that word of God, by which he once commanded it, is continually in force.

24. Let the earth bring forth. He descends to the sixth day, on which the animals were created, and then man. **Let the earth,** he says, **bring forth living creatures.** But whence has a dead element life? Therefore, there is in this respect a miracle as great as if God had begun to create out of nothing those things which he commanded to proceed from the earth.

26. Let us make man. Although the tense here used is the future, all must acknowledge that this is the language of one apparently deliberating. Hitherto God has been introduced simply as commanding; now, when he approaches the most excellent of all his works, he enters into consultation. God certainly might here command by his bare word what he wished to be done: but he chose to give this tribute to the excellency of man, that he would, in a manner, enter into consultation concerning his creation. This is the highest honour with which he has dignified us; to a due regard for which, Moses, by this mode of speaking would excite our minds. For God is not now first beginning to consider what form he will give to man, and with what endowments it would be fitting to adorn him, nor is he pausing as over a work of difficulty: but, just as we have before observed, that the creation of the world was distributed over six days, for our sake, to the end that our minds might the more easily be retained in the meditation of God's works: so now, for the purpose of commending to our attention the dignity of our nature, he, in taking counsel concerning the creation of man, testifies that he is about to undertake something great and wonderful.

In our image. Since the image of God had been destroyed in us by the fall, we may judge from its restoration what it originally had been. Paul says that we are transformed into the image of God by the gospel. And, according to him, spiritual regeneration is nothing else than the restoration of the same image. (Col. 3: 10, and Eph. 4: 23.) Therefore by this word the perfection of our whole nature is designated, as it appeared when Adam was endued with a right judgment, had affections in harmony with reason, had all his senses sound and well-regulated, and truly excelled in everything good. Thus the chief seat of the Divine image was in his mind and heart, where it was eminent.

And let them have dominion. Here he commemorates that part of dignity with which he decreed to honour man, namely, that he should have authority over all living creatures.

27. So God created man. The reiterated mention of the image of God is not a vain repetition. For it is a remarkable instance of the Divine goodness which can never be sufficiently proclaimed. And, at the same time, he admonishes us from what excellence we have fallen, that he may excite in us the desire of its recovery.

28. And God blessed them. This blessing of God may be regarded as the source from which the human race has flowed. And we must so consider it not only with reference to the whole, but also, as they say, in every particular instance.

31. And God saw everything. Once more, at the conclusion of the creation, Moses declares that God approved of everything which he had made. In speaking of God as seeing, he does it after the manner of men; for the Lord designed this his judgment to be as a rule and example to us; that no one should dare to think or speak otherwise of his works.

Chapter 2

1. Thus the heavens and the earth were finished. Moses summarily repeats that in six days the fabric of the heaven and the earth was completed.

2. And he rested on the seventh day. The question may not improperly be put, what kind of rest this was. For it is certain that inasmuch as God sustains the world by his power, governs it by his providence, cherishes and even propagates all creatures, he is constantly at work. God ceased from all his work, when he desisted from the creation of new kinds of things.

3. And God blessed the seventh day. He dedicated every seventh day to rest, that his own example might be a perpetual rule. The design of the institution must be always kept in memory: for God did not command men simply to keep holiday every seventh day, as if he delighted in their indolence; but rather that they, being released from all other business, might the more readily apply their minds to the Creator of the world.

4. These are the generations. The design of Moses was deeply to impress upon our minds the origin of the heaven and the earth, which he designates by the word generation.

7. And the Lord God formed man. He now explains what he had before omitted in the creation of man, that his body was taken out of the earth. He had said that he was formed after the image of God. This is incomparably the highest nobility; and, lest men should use it as an occasion of pride, their first origin is placed immediately before them; whence they may learn that this advantage was adventitious; for Moses relates that man had been, in the beginning, dust of the earth. Let foolish men now go and boast of the excellency of their nature!

8. And the Lord God planted. Moses now adds the condition and rule of living which were given to man. And he narrates in what part of the world he was placed, and what a happy and pleasant habitation was allotted to him.

9. Concerning **the tree of knowledge of good and evil**, we must hold, that it was prohibited to man, not because God would have him to stray like a sheep, without judgment and without

choice; but that he might not seek to be wiser than became him, nor by trusting to his own understanding, cast off the yoke of God, and constitute himself an arbiter and judge of good and evil. His sin proceeded from an evil conscience; whence it follows, that a judgment had been given him, by which he might discriminate between virtues and vices.

14. The simple meaning of Moses is, that the garden of which Adam was the possessor was well watered, the channel of a river passing that way, which was afterwards divided into four heads.

15. And the Lord God took the man. Moses now adds, that the earth was given to man, with this condition, that he should occupy himself in its cultivation. Whence it follows that men were created to employ themselves in some work, and not to lie down in inactivity and idleness.

16. And the Lord God commanded. Moses now teaches, that man was the governor of the world, with this exception, that he should, nevertheless, be subject to God.

17. Thou shalt surely die. But it is asked, what kind of death God means in this place? It appears to me, that the definition of this death is to be sought from its opposite; we must, I say, remember from what kind of life man fell. He was, in every respect, happy; his life, therefore, had alike respect to his body and his soul, since in his soul a right judgment and a proper government of the affections prevailed, there also life reigned; in his body there was no defect, wherefore he was wholly free from death. His earthly life truly would have been temporal; yet he would have passed into heaven without death, and without injury. Death, therefore, is now a terror to us; first, because there is a kind of annihilation, as it respects the body; then, because the soul feels the curse of God. We must also see what is the cause of death, namely alienation from God.

18. It is not good that the man should be alone. Moses now explains the design of God in creating the woman; namely, that there should be human beings on the earth who might cultivate mutual society between themselves.

21. And the Lord God caused a deep sleep to fall. Although to profane persons this method of forming woman may seem ridiculous, and some of these may say that Moses is dealing in fables, yet to us the wonderful providence of God here shines forth; for, to the end that the conjunction of the human race might be the more sacred he purposed that both males and females should spring from one and the same origin.

22. And brought her. Moses now relates that marriage was divinely instituted, which is especially useful to be known; for since Adam did not take a wife to himself at his own will, but received her as offered and appropriated to him by God, the sanctity of marriage hence more clearly appears, because we recognize God as its Author.

23. **This is now bone of.** In using the expression *hapa'am*, Adam indicates that something had been wanting to him; as if he had said, Now at length I have obtained a suitable companion, who is part of the substance of my flesh, and in whom I behold, as it were, another self.

24. **Therefore shall a man leave.** Among the offices pertaining to human society, this is the principal, and as it were the most sacred, that a man should cleave unto his wife.

25. **They were both naked.** That the nakedness of men should be deemed indecorous and unsightly, while that of cattle has nothing disgraceful, seems little to agree with the dignity of human nature. The cause of this sense of shame, to which we are now alluding, Moses will show in the next chapter. He now esteems it enough to say, that in our uncorrupted nature, there was nothing but what was honourable; whence it follows, that whatsoever is opprobrious in us, must be imputed to our own fault, since our parents had nothing in themselves which was unbecoming until they were defiled with sin.

Chapter 3

1. **Now the serpent was more subtil.** In this chapter, Moses explains, that man, after he had been deceived by Satan revolted from his Maker, became entirely changed and so degenerate, that the image of God, in which he had been formed, was obliterated. He then declares, that the whole world, which had been created for the sake of man, fell together with him from its primary original; and that in this way much of its native excellence was destroyed. But here many and arduous questions arise.

4. **And the serpent said unto the woman.** Satan now springs more boldly forward; and because he sees a breach open before him, he breaks through in a direct assault, for he is never wont to engage in open war until we voluntarily expose ourselves to him, naked and unarmed. He cautiously approaches us at first with blandishments; but when he has stolen in upon us, he dares to exalt himself petulantly and with proud confidence against God; just as he now seizing upon Eve's doubt, penetrates further, that he may turn it into a direct negative. It behoves us to be instructed, by much examples, to beware of his snares, and, by making timely resistance, to keep him far from us, that nearer access may not be permitted to him. He now, therefore, does not ask doubtingly, as before, whether or not the command of God, which he opposes, be true, but openly accuses God of falsehood, for he asserts that the word by which death was

denounced is false and delusive. Fatal temptation! when while God is threatening us with death, we not only securely sleep, but hold God himself in derision!

5. **For God does know.** Satan attempts to prove what he had recently asserted, reasoning, however, from contraries: God, he says, has interdicted to you the tree, that he may not be compelled to admit you to the participation of his glory; therefore, the fear of punishment is quite needless. In short, he denies that a fruit which is useful and salutary can be injurious. When he says, **God does know**, he censures God as being moved by jealousy: and as having given the command concerning the tree, for the purpose of keeping man in an inferior rank.

Ye shall be as gods. I have no doubt that Satan promises them divinity; as if he had said, For no other reason does God defraud you of the tree of knowledge, than because he fears to have you as companions.

6. **And when the woman saw.** This impure look of Eve, infected with the poison of concupiscence, was both the messenger and the witness of an impure heart. She could previously behold the tree with such sincerity, that no desire to eat of it affected her mind; for the faith she had in the word of God was the best guardian of her heart, and of all her senses. But now, after the heart had declined from faith, and from obedience to the word, she corrupted both herself and all her senses, and depravity was diffused through all parts of her soul as well as her body.

And gave also unto her husband with her. The reproof which soon afterwards follows 'Behold, Adam is as one of us,' clearly proves that he also foolishly coveted more than was lawful, and gave greater credit to the flatteries of the devil than to the sacred word of God.

7. **And the eyes of them both were opened.** It was necessary that the eyes of Eve should be veiled till her husband also was deceived; but now both, being alike bound by the chain of an unhappy consent, begin to be sensible of their wretchedness although they are not yet affected with a deep knowledge of their fault. They are ashamed of their nakedness, yet, though convinced, they do not humble themselves before God, nor fear his judgments as they ought; they even do not cease to resort to evasions.

8. **And they heard the voice of the Lord God.** As soon as the voice of God sounds, Adam and Eve perceive that the leaves by which they thought themselves well protected are of no avail. Moses here relates nothing which does not remain in human nature, and may be clearly discerned at the present day. The difference between good and evil is engraved on the hearts of all, as Paul teaches, (Rom. 2: 15;) but all bury the disgrace of their vices under flimsy leaves till

God, by his voice, strikes inwardly their consciences. Hence, after God had shaken them out of their torpor, their alarmed consciences compelled them to hear his voice.

10. And he said, I heard thy voice. Although this seems to be the confession of a dejected and humbled man, it will nevertheless soon appear that he was not yet properly subdued, nor led to repentance. He imputes his fear to the voice of God, and to his own nakedness, as, if he had never before heard God speaking without being alarmed, and had not been even sweetly exhilarated by his speech. His excessive stupidity appears in this, that he fails to recognize the cause of shame in his sin; he, therefore, shows that he does not yet so feel his punishment, as to confess his fault.

11. Who told thee that thou wast naked? An indirect reprimand to reprove the sottishness of Adam in not perceiving his fault in his punishment, as if it had been said, not simply that Adam was afraid at the voice of God, but that the voice of his judge was formidable to him because he was a sinner. Again, the atrocious nature of sin is marked in this transgression and rebellion; for, as nothing is more acceptable to God than obedience, so nothing is more intolerable than when men, having spurned his commandments, obey Satan and their own lust.

12. The woman whom thou gavest to be with me. The boldness of Adam now more clearly betrays itself; for, so far from being subdued, he breaks forth into coarser blasphemy. He had before been tacitly expostulating with God; now he begins openly to contend with him, and triumphs as one who has broken through all barriers. Whence we perceive what a refractory and indomitable creature man began to be when he became alienated from God; for a lively picture of corrupt nature is presented to us in Adam from the moment of his revolt.

13. And the Lord God said unto the woman. God contends no further with the man, nor was it necessary; for he aggravates rather than diminishes his crime, first by a frivolous defence, then by an impious disparagement of God, in short, though he rages he is yet held convicted. The Judge now turns to the woman, that the cause of both being heard, he may at length pronounce sentence.

The serpent beguiled me. Eve ought to have been confounded at the portentous wickedness concerning which she was admonished. Yet she is not struck dumb, but, after the example of her husband, transfers the charge to another; by laying the blame on the serpent, she foolishly, indeed, and impiously, thinks herself absolved.

14. And the Lord God said unto the serpent. He does not interrogate the serpent as he had done the man and the woman; because, in the animal itself there was no sense of sin, and because, to the devil he would hold out no hope of pardon.

Thou art cursed above all cattle. This curse of God has such force against the serpent as to render it despicable, and scarcely tolerable to heaven and earth, leading a life exposed to, and replete with, constant terrors.

15. I will put enmity. I interpret this simply to mean that there should always be the hostile strife between the human race and serpents, which is now apparent; for, by a secret feeling of nature, man abhors them.

16. Unto the woman he said. In order that the majesty of the judge may shine the more brightly, God uses no long disputation; whence also we may perceive of what avail are all our tergiversations with him. In bringing the serpent forward, Eve thought she had herself escaped. God, disregarding her cavils, condemns her. Let the sinner, therefore, when he comes to the bar of God, cease to contend, lest he should more severely provoke against himself the anger of him whom he has already too highly offended.

17. And unto Adam he said. It is to be observed, that punishment was not inflicted upon the first of our race so as to rest on those two alone, but was extended generally to all their posterity, in order that we might know that the human race was cursed in their person; we next observe, that they were subjected only to temporal punishment, that, from the moderation of the divine anger, they might entertain hope of pardon. God, by adducing the reason why he thus punishes the man, cuts off from him the occasion of murmuring.

18. Thorns also and thistles shall it bring forth. The participation of the fruits of the earth will be with labour and trouble. And he assigns as the reason, that the earth will not be the same as it was before, producing perfect fruits; for he declares that the earth would degenerate from its fertility, and bring forth briers and noxious plants. Therefore we may know, that whatsoever unwholesome things may be produced, are not natural fruits of the earth, but are corruptions which originate from sin.

21. Unto Adam also, and to his wife, did the Lord God make … The reason why the Lord clothed them with garments of skin appears to me to be this: because garments formed of this material would have a more degrading appearance than those made of linen or of woolen. God therefore designed that our first parents should, in such a dress, behold their own vileness.

22. Behold, the man is become as one of us. An ironical reproof, by which God would not only prick the heart of man, but pierce it through and through. He does not, however, cruelly triumph over the miserable and afflicted; but, according to the necessity of the disease, applies a more violent remedy. For, though Adam was confounded and astonished at his calamity, he yet did not so deeply reflect on its cause as to become weary of his pride, that he might learn to embrace true humility.

23. **Therefore the Lord God sent him forth.** Here Moses partly prosecutes what he had said concerning the punishment inflicted on man, and partly celebrates the goodness of God, by which the rigour of his judgment was mitigated. God mercifully softens the exile of Adam, by still providing for him a remaining home on earth, and by assigning to him a livelihood from the labourious culture of the ground; for Adam thence infers that the Lord has some care for him, which is a proof of paternal love. Moses, however, again speaks of punishment, when he relates that man was expelled and that cherubim were opposed with the blade of a turning sword, which should prevent his entrance into the garden. Adam was excommunicated from the tree of life, but a new remedy was offered him in sacrifices.

Chapter 4

1. **And Adam knew his wife Eve.** Moses now begins to describe the propagation of mankind; in which history it is important to notice that this benediction of God, **Increase and multiply,** was not abolished by sin; and not only so, but that the heart of Adam was divinely confirmed so that he did not shrink with horror from the production of offspring.

2. **And Abel was a keeper of sheep.** Since the Apostle refers the dignity of Abel's accepted sacrifice to faith, it follows, first, that he had not offered it without the command of God, (Heb. 11:4.) Secondly, it has been true from the beginning, of the world, that obedience is better than any sacrifices, (1 Sam. 15:22,) and is the parent of all virtues. Hence it also follows that man had been taught by God what was pleasing to Him. Thirdly, since God has been always like himself, we may not say that he was ever delighted with mere carnal and external worship. Yet he deemed those sacrifices of the first age acceptable. It follows, therefore, further, that they had been spiritually offered to him.

5. **But unto Cain and to his offering he had not respect.** It is not to be doubted, that Cain conducted himself as hypocrites are accustomed to do; namely, that he wished to appease God, as one discharging a debt, by external sacrifices, without the least intention of dedicating himself to God.

9. **Am I my brother's keeper?** Cain, in denying that he was the keeper of his brother's life, although, with ferocious rebellion, he attempts violently to repel the judgment of God, yet thinks to escape by this cavil, that he was not required to give an account of his murdered brother, because he had received no express command to take care of him.

10. **What hast thou done? The voice of thy brother's blood.** Moses shows that Cain gained nothing by his tergiversation. God first inquired where his brother was; he now more closely urges him, in order to extort an unwilling confession of his guilt; for in no racks or tortures of any kind is there so much force to constrain evildoers, as there was efficacy in the thunder of the Divine voice to cast down Cain in confusion to the ground. For God no longer asks whether he had done it; but, pronouncing in a single word that he was the doer of it, he aggravates the atrocity of the crime. We learn, then, in the person of one man, what an unhappy issue of their cause awaits those, who desire to extricate themselves by contending against God.

11. **And now art thou cursed from the earth.** Cain, having been convicted of the crime, judgment is now pronounced against him. And first, God constitutes the earth the minister of his vengeance, as having been polluted by the impious and horrible parricide: as if he had said, 'Thou didst just now deny to me the murder which thou hast committed, but the senseless earth itself will demand thy punishment.'

12. **A fugitive and a vagabond shalt thou be.** Another punishment is now also inflicted; namely, that he never could be safe, to whatever place he might come.

16. **And Cain went out from the presence of the Lord.** Cain is said to have departed from the presence of God, because, whereas he had hitherto lived in the earth as in an abode belonging to God, now, like an exile removed far from God's sight, he wanders beyond the limits of His protection.

19. **And Lamech took unto him two wives.** We have here the origin of polygamy in a perverse and degenerate race; and the first author of it, a cruel man, destitute of all humanity.

20. **Jabal; he was the father of such as dwell in tents.** Moses now relates that, with the evils which proceeded from the family of Cain, some good had been blended. For the invention of arts, and of other things which serve to the common use and convenience of life, is a gift of God by no means to be despised, and a faculty worthy of commendation. It is truly wonderful, that this race, which had most deeply fallen from integrity, should have excelled the rest of the posterity of Adam in rare endowments.

23. **Hear my voice, ye wives of Lamech.** The intention of Moses is to describe the ferocity of this man, who was, however, the fifth in descent from the fratricide Cain, in order to teach us, that, so far from being terrified by the example of divine judgment which he had seen in his ancestor, he was only the more hardened.

24. Cain shall be avenged sevenfold. God had intended that Cain should be a horrible example to warn others against the commission of murder; and for this end had marked him with a shameful stigma. Yet lest any one should imitate his crime, He declared whosoever killed him should be punished with sevenfold severity.

25. Adam knew his wife again. Our first parents, horror-struck at the impious slaughter, abstained for a while from the conjugal bed. Nor could it certainly be otherwise, than that they, in reaping this exceedingly sad and bitter fruit of their apostasy from God, should sink down almost lifeless. The reason why he now passes by others is that he designed to trace the generation of pious descendants through the line of Seth.

26. Then began men to call upon the name of the Lord. In the verb 'to call upon,' there is a synecdoche, for it embraces generally the whole worship of God. But religion is here properly designated by that which forms its principal part. For God prefers this service of piety and faith to all sacrifices, (Psalm 50: 14.) Yea, this is the spiritual worship of God which faith produces. This is particularly worthy of notice, because Satan contrives nothing with greater care than to adulterate, with every possible corruption, the pure invocation of God, or to draw us away from the only God to the invocation of creatures.

Chapter 5

1. This is the book of the generations of Adam. In this chapter Moses briefly recites the length of time which had intervened between the creation of the world and the deluge; and also slightly touches on some portion of the history of that period.

2. Male and female created he them. This clause commends the sacred bond of marriage, and the inseparable union of the husband and the wife. For when Moses has mentioned only one, he immediately afterwards includes both under one name. And he assigns a common name indiscriminately to both, in order that posterity might learn more sacredly to cherish this connection between each other, when they saw that their first parents were denominated as one person.

3. And begat a son in his own likeness. We have lately said that Moses traces the offspring of Adam only through the line of Seth, to propose for our consideration the succession of the Church. In saying that Seth begat a son after his own image, he refers in part to the first origin of our nature: at the same time its corruption and pollution is to be noticed, which having been contracted by Adam through the fall, has flowed down to all his posterity.

5. And he died. This clause, which records the death of each patriarch, is by no means superfluous. For it warns us that death was not in vain denounced against men; and that we are now exposed to the curse to which man was doomed, unless we obtain deliverance elsewhere.

22. And Enoch walked with God. Undoubtedly Enoch is honoured with peculiar praise among the men of his own age, when it is said that he walked with God. Yet both Seth and Enoch, and Cainan, and Mahalaleel, and Jared, were then living, whose piety was celebrated in the former part of the chapter. As that age could not be ruder or barbarous, which had so many most excellent teachers; we hence infer, that the probity of this holy man, whom the Holy Spirit exempted from the common order, was rare and almost singular.

24. And he was not, for God took him. He must be shamelessly contentious, who will not acknowledge that something extraordinary is here pointed out. All are, indeed, taken out of the world by death; but Moses plainly declares that Enoch was taken out of the world by an unusual mode, and was received by the Lord in a miraculous manner. That the translation of Enoch took place, which was to be as a visible representation of a blessed resurrection; by which, if Adam had been enlightened, he might have girded himself with equanimity for his own departure. His transition was by a peculiar privilege, such as that of other men would have been, if they had remained in their first state.

Chapter 6

1. And it came to pass, when men began to multiply. Moses, having enumerated in order, ten patriarchs, with whom the worship of God remained pure, now relates, that their families also were corrupted.

2. That they were fair. Moses does not deem it worthy of condemnation that regard was had to beauty, in the choice of wives; but that mere lust reigned. For marriage is a thing too sacred to allow that men should be induced to it by the lust of the eyes!

3. My Spirit shall not always strive. Although Moses had before shown that the world had proceeded to such a degree of wickedness and impiety, as ought not any longer to be borne; yet in order to prove more certainly, that the vengeance by which the whole world was drowned, was not less just than severe, he introduces God himself as the speaker.

4. There were giants in the earth. Among the innumerable kinds of corruptions with which the earth was filled, Moses especially records one in this place; namely that giants practised great violence and tyranny. I do not, however, suppose, that he speaks of all the men of this age; but of certain individuals, who, being stronger than the rest, and relying on their own might and power, exalted themselves unlawfully, and without measure.

5. And God saw that the wickedness of man was great. Moses prosecutes the subject to which he had just alluded, that God was neither too harsh, nor precipitate in exacting punishment from the wicked men of the world. And he introduces God as speaking after the manner of men, by a figure which ascribes human affections to God; because he could not otherwise express what was very important to be known; namely, that God was not induced hastily, or for a slight cause, to destroy the world. For by the word **saw,** he indicates long continued patience; as if he would say, that God had not proclaimed his sentence to destroy men, until after having well observed, and long considered, their case, he saw them to be past recovery.

6. And it repented the Lord that he had made man on the earth. The repentance which is here ascribed to God does not properly belong to him, but has reference to our understanding of him. For since we cannot comprehend him as he is, it is necessary that, for our sakes he should, in a certain sense, transform himself. That repentance cannot take place in God, easily appears from this single consideration that nothing happens which is by him unexpected or unforeseen. The same reasoning, and remark, applies to what follows, that God was affected with grief. Certainly God is not sorrowful or sad; but remains forever like himself in his celestial and happy repose: yet, because it could not otherwise be known how great is God's hatred and detestation of sin, therefore the Spirit accommodates himself to our capacity.

7. And the Lord said, I will destroy man whom I have created from the face of the earth, both man and beast. He again introduces God as deliberating, in order that we may the better know that the world was not destroyed without mature counsel on the part of God.

8. But Noah found grace in the eyes of the Lord. This is a Hebrew phrase, which signifies that God was propitious to him, and favoured him. For so the Hebrews are accustomed to speak:– 'If I have found grace in thy sight,' instead of, 'If I am acceptable to thee,' or, 'If thou wilt grant me thy benevolence or favour.' Which phrase requires to be noticed, because certain unlearned men infer with futile subtlety, that if men find grace in God's sight, it is because they seek it by their own industry and merits.

11. The earth also was corrupt before God. In the former clause of this verse Moses describes that impious contempt of God, which had left no longer any religion in the world; but the light of equity being extinct, all men had plunged into sin. In the second clause he declares, that the love of oppression, that frauds, injuries, and all kinds of injustice, prevailed.

13. And God said unto Noah. Here Moses begins to relate how Noah would be preserved. And first, he says, that the counsel of God respecting the destruction of the world was revealed to him. Secondly, that the command to build the ark was given. Thirdly, that safety was promised him, if, in obedience to God, he would take refuge in the ark.

14. Make thee an ark of gopher wood. Here follows the command to build the ark, in which God wonderfully proved the faith and obedience of his servant.

18. But with thee will I establish my covenant. Since the construction of the ark was very difficult, and innumerable obstacles might perpetually arise to break off the work when begun, God confirms his servant by a super added promise. Thus was Noah encouraged to obey God; seeing that he relied on the Divine promise, and was confident that his labour would not be in vain.

22. Thus did Noah. In a few words, but with great sublimity, Moses here commends the faith of Noah. Moses shows, that Noah obeyed God, not in one particular only, but in all. Which is diligently to be observed; because hence, chiefly, arises dreadful confusion in our life, that we are not able, unreservedly to submit ourselves to God; but when we have discharged some part of our duty, we often blend our own feelings with his word. But the obedience of Noah is celebrated on this account, that it was entire, not partial; so that he omitted none of those things which God had commanded.

Chapter 7

1. And the Lord said unto Noah. I have no doubt that Noah was confirmed, as he certainly needed to be, by oracles frequently repeated.

2. Of every clean beast. He again repeats what he had before said concerning animals, and not without occasion. For there was no little difficulty in collecting from woods, mountains, and caves, so great a multitude of wild beasts, many species of which were perhaps altogether unknown; and there was, in most of them, the same ferocity which we now perceive. Wherefore, God encourages the holy man, lest being alarmed with that difficulty, and having cast aside all hope of success, he should fail.

3. To keep seed alive upon the face of all the earth. That is, that hence offspring might be born. But this is referred to Noah; for although, properly speaking, God alone gives life, yet God here refers to those duties which he had enjoined upon his servant: and it is with respect to his appointed office, that God commands him to collect animals that he may keep seed alive.

5. And Noah did according to all that the Lord commanded. This is not a bare repetition of the former sentence; but Moses commends Noah's uniform tenor of obedience in keeping all God's commandments; as if he would say, that in whatever particular it pleased God to try his obedience, he always remained constant.

11. The same day were all the fountains of the great deep broken up. Moses recalls the period of the first creation to our memory; for the earth was originally covered with water; and by the singular kindness of God, they were made to recede, that some space should be left clear for living creatures.

12. And the rain was upon the earth. Although the Lord burst open the floodgates of the waters, yet he does not allow them to break forth in a moment, so as immediately to overwhelm the earth, but causes the rain to continue forty days; partly, that Noah, by long meditation, might more deeply fix in his memory what he had previously learned, by instruction, through the word; partly, that the wicked, even before their death, might feel that those warnings which they had held in derision, were not empty threats.

13. In the selfsame day entered Noah, and Shem … A repetition follows, sufficiently particular, considering the brevity with which Moses runs through the history of the deluge, yet by no means superfluous. For it was the design of the Spirit to retain our minds in the consideration of a vengeance too terrible to be adequately described by the utmost severity of language.

16. And the Lord shut him in. This is not added in vain, nor ought it to be lightly passed over. That door must have been large, which could admit an elephant. And truly, no pitch would be sufficiently firm and tenacious, and no joining sufficiently solid, to prevent the immense force of the water from penetrating through its many seams, especially in an irruption so violent, and in a shock so severe. Therefore, Moses, to cut off occasion for the vain speculations which our own curiosity would suggest, declares in one word, that the ark was made secure from the deluge, not by human artifice, but by divine miracle.

17. And the flood was forty days. Moses copiously insists upon this fact, in order to show that the whole world was immersed in the waters. Moreover, it is to be regarded as the special design of this narration that we should not ascribe to fortune, the flood by which the world perished; how ever customary it may be for men to cast some veil over the works of God, which may obscure either his goodness or his judgments manifested in them.

The Church is fitly, and justly, compared to the ark. But we must keep in mind the similitude by which they mutually correspond with each other; for that is derived from the word of God alone; because as Noah believing the promise of God, gathered himself his wife and his children together, in order that under a certain appearance of death, he might emerge out of death; so it is fitting that we should renounce the world and die, in order that the Lord may quicken us by his word. For nowhere else is there any security of salvation.

Chapter 8

1. And God remembered Noah. Moses now descends more particularly to that other part of the subject, which shows, that Noah was not disappointed in his hope of the salvation divinely promised to him. The remembrance of which Moses speaks, ought to be referred not only to the external aspect of things, (so to speak,) but also to the inward feeling of the holy man. Indeed it is certain, that God from the time in which he had once received Noah into his protection, was never unmindful of him; for, truly, it was by as great a miracle, that he did not perish through suffocation in the ark, as if he had lived without breath, submerged in the waters.

3. And after the end of the hundred and fifty days. Some think that the whole time, from the beginning of the deluge to the abatement of the waters, is here noted; and thus they include the forty days in which Moses relates that there was continued rain. But I make this distinction, that until the fortieth day, the waters rose gradually by fresh additions; then that they remained nearly in the same state for one hundred and fifty days; for both computations make the period a little more than six months and a half.

6. At the end of forty days. We may hence conjecture with what great anxiety the breast of the holy man was oppressed. After he had perceived the ark to be resting on solid ground, he yet did not dare to open the window till the fortieth day; not because he was stunned and torpid, but because an example, thus formidable, of the vengeance of God, had affected him with such fear and sorrow combined, that being deprived of all judgment, he silently remained in the chamber of his ark. At length he sends forth a raven, from which he might receive a more certain indication of the dryness of the earth. But the raven perceiving nothing but muddy marshes, hovers around, and immediately seeks to be readmitted.

The dove, in its first egress, imitated the raven, because it flew back to the ark; afterwards it brought a branch of olive in its bill; and at the third time, as if emancipated, it enjoyed the free air, and the free earth. Some writers exercise their ingenuity on the olive branch; because among the ancients it was the emblem of peace, as the laurel was of victory. But I rather think, that as the olive tree does not grow upon the mountains, and is not a very lofty tree, the Lord had given his servant some token whence he might infer, that pleasant regions, and productive of good fruits, were now freed from the waters.

15. And God spake unto Noah. Though Noah was not a little terrified at the judgment of God, yet his patience is commended in this respect, that having the earth, which offered him a home, before his eyes, he yet does not venture to go forth.

17. That they may breed abundantly. With these words the Lord would cheer the mind of Noah, and inspire him with confidence, that a seed had been preserved in the ark which should increase till it replenished the whole earth. In short, the renovation of the earth is promised to Noah; to the end that he may know that the world itself was inclosed in the ark, and that the solitude and devastation, at the sight of which his heart might faint, would not be perpetual.

20. And Noah builded an altar unto the Lord. As Noah had given many proofs of his obedience, so he now presents an example of gratitude. This passage teaches us that sacrifices were instituted from the beginning for this end, that men should habituate themselves, by such exercises, to celebrate the goodness of God, and to give him thanks.

21. And the Lord smelled a sweet savour. Moses calls that by which God was appeased, an odour of rest; as if he had said, the sacrifice had been rightly offered. Yet nothing can be more absurd than to suppose that God should have been appeased by the filthy smoke of entrails, and of flesh. But Moses here, according to his manner, invests God with a human character for the purpose of accommodating himself to the capacity of an ignorant people. For it is not even to be supposed, that the rite of sacrifice, in itself, was grateful to God as a meritorious act; but we must regard the end of the work, and not confine ourselves to the external form. For what else did Noah propose to himself than to acknowledge that he had received his own life, and that of the animals, as the gift of God's mercy alone?

And the Lord said in his heart. The meaning of the passage is, God had decreed that he would not hereafter curse the earth. And this form of expression has great weight: for although God never retracts what he has openly spoken with his mouth, yet we are more deeply affected when we hear, that he has fixed upon something in his own mind; because an inward decree of this kind in no way depends upon creatures. To sum up the whole, God certainly determined that he would never more destroy the world by a deluge.

22. While the earth remaineth. By these words the world is again completely restored. For so great was the confusion and disorder which had overspread the earth, that there was a necessity for some renovation.

Chapter 9

1. And God blessed Noah. We hence infer with what great fear Noah had been dejected, because God, so often and at such length, proceeds to encourage him. For when Moses here says, that God blessed Noah and his sons, he does not simply mean that the favour of fruitfulness was restored to them; but that, at the same time, the design of God concerning the new restitution of the world was revealed unto them. For to the blessing itself is added the voice of God by which he addresses them.

2. And the fear of you. This also has chiefly respect to the restoration of the world, in order that the sovereignty over the rest of animals might remain with men.

3. Every moving thing that liveth shall be meat for you. The Lord proceeds further, and grants animals for food to men, that they may eat their flesh. And because Moses now first relates that this right was given to men, nearly all commentators infer, that it was not lawful for man to eat flesh before the deluge, but that the natural fruits of the earth were his only food. But the argument is not sufficiently firm. For I hold to this principle; that God here does not bestow on men more than he had previously given, but only restores what had been taken away, that they might again enter on the possession of those good things from which they had been excluded.

5. And surely your blood of your lives will I require. In these words the Lord more explicitly declares that he does not forbid the use of blood out of regard to animals themselves, but because he accounts the life of men precious: and because the sole end of his law is, to promote the exercise of common humanity between them. The whole context is (in my opinion) to be thus read, 'And truly your blood, which is in your lives, or which is as your lives, that is which vivifies and quickens you, as it respects your body, will I require: from the hand of all animals will require it; from the hand of man, from the hand, I say, of man, his brother, will I require the life of man.'

6. Whoso sheddeth man's blood. This language expresses the atrociousness of the crime; because whosoever kills a man, draws down upon himself the blood and life of his brother. On the whole, they are deceived (in my judgment) who think that a political law, for the punishment of homicides, is here simply intended.

For in the image of God made he man. For the greater confirmation of the above doctrines God declares, that he is not thus solicitous respecting human life rashly, and for no purpose. Men are indeed unworthy of God's care, if respect be had only to themselves. But since they bear the image of God engraved on them, He deems himself violated in their person. Thus, although they have nothing of their own by which they obtain the favour of God, he looks upon his own gifts in them, and is thereby excited to love and to care for them.

7. **And you, be ye fruitful and multiply.** He again turns his discourse to Noah and his sons, exhorting them to the propagation of offspring: as if he would say, 'You see that I am intent upon cherishing and preserving mankind, do you therefore also attend to it.'

12. **This is the token of the covenant.** A sign is added to the promise, in which is exhibited the wonderful kindness of God; who, for the purpose of confirming our faith in his word, does not disdain to use such helps.

13. **I do set my bow in the cloud.** As it pleases the Lord to employ earthly elements, as vehicles for raising the minds of men on high, so I think the celestial arch which had before existed naturally, is here consecrated into a sign and pledge; and thus a new office is assigned to it; whereas, from the nature of the thing itself, it might rather be a sign of the contrary; for it threatens continued rain. Let this therefore be the meaning, of the words, 'As often as the rain shall alarm you, look upon the bow. For although it may seem to cause the rain to overflow the earth, it shall nevertheless be to you a pledge of returning dryness, and thus it will then become you to stand with greater confidence, than under a clear and serene sky.'

15. **And I will remember my covenant.** Moses, by introducing God so often as the speaker, teaches us that the word holds the chief place, and that signs are to be estimated by it.

18. **The sons of Noah.** Moses enumerates the sons of Noah, not only because he is about to pass on to the following history, but for the purpose of more fully illustrating the force of the promise, 'Replenish the earth.' For we may hence better conceive how efficacious the blessing of God has been, because an immense multitude of men proceeded in a short time from so small a number; and because one family, and that a little one, grew into so many, and such numerous nations.

22. **And Ham, the father of Canaan.** This circumstance is added to augment the sorrow of Noah, that he is mocked by his own son. For we must ever keep in memory, that this punishment was divinely inflicted upon him; partly,

because his fault was not a light one; partly that God in his person might present a lesson of temperance to all ages. Drunkenness in itself deserves as its reward, that they who deface the image of their heavenly Father in themselves, should become a laughingstock to their own children. For certainly, as far as possible, drunkards subvert their own understanding, and so far deprive themselves of reason as to degenerate into beasts.

23. **And Shem and Japheth took a garment.** Here the piety, as well as the modesty, of the two brothers is commended; who, in order that the dignity of their father might not be lowered in their esteem, but that they might always cherish and keep entire the reverence which they owed him, turned away their eyes from the sight of his disgrace.

26. **Blessed be the Lord God of Shem.** Noah places Shem in the highest post of honour. And this is the reason why Noah, in blessing him, breaks forth in the praise of God, without adhering to the person of man. For the Hebrews, when they are speaking of any rare and transcendent excellence, raise their thoughts to God. Therefore the holy man, when he perceived that the most abundant grace of God was destined for his son Shem, rises to thanksgiving. Whence we infer, that he spoke, not from carnal reason, but rather treated of the secret favours of God, the result of which was to be deferred to a remote period. Finally, by these words it is declared, that the benediction of Shem would be divine or heavenly.

28. **And Noah lived.** Although Moses briefly states the age of the holy man, and does not record his annals and the memorable events of his life, yet those things which are certain, and which Scripture elsewhere commemorates, ought to recur to our minds. Within one hundred and fifty years, the offspring of his three sons became so numerous, that he had sufficient and even abundant proof of the efficacy of the Divine benediction 'Increase and multiply.'

Chapter 10

1. **These are the generations.** First, in these bare names we have still some fragment of the history of the world; and the next chapter will show how many years intervened between the date of the deluge and the time when God made his covenant with Abraham. This second commencement of mankind is especially worthy to be known; and detestable is the ingratitude of those, who, when they had heard, from their fathers and grandfathers of the wonderful restoration of the world in so short a time, yet voluntarily became forgetful of the grace and the salvation of God. Even the memory of the deluge was by the greater part entirely lost. Very

few cared by what means or for what end they had been preserved.

8. And Cush begat Nimrod. It is certain that Cush was the prince of the Ethiopians. Moses relates the singular history of his son Nimrod, because he began to be eminent in an unusual degree. Moreover, I thus interpret the passage, that the condition of men was at that time moderate; so that if some excelled others, they yet did not on that account domineer, nor assume to themselves royal power; but being content with a degree of dignity, governed others by civil laws and had more of authority than power.

21. Unto Shem also, the father of all the children of Eber. Moses, being about to speak of the sons of Shem, makes a brief introduction, which he had not done in reference to the others. Nor was it without reason; for since this was the race chosen by God, he wished to sever it from other nations by some special mark. This also is the reason why he expressly styles him the **father of the sons of Eber,** and the elder brother of Japheth. For the benediction of Shem does not descend to all his grandchildren indiscriminately, but remains in one family. And although the grandchildren themselves of Eber declined from the true worship of God, so that the Lord might justly have disinherited them; yet the benediction was not extinguished, but only buried for a season, until Abraham was called, in honour of whom this singular dignity is ascribed to the race and name of Eber. For the same cause, mention is made of **Japheth,** in order that the promise may be confirmed, 'God shall speak gently unto Japheth, that he may dwell in the tents of Shem.'

Chapter 11

1. And the whole earth was of one language. Whereas mention had before been made of Babylon in a single word, Moses now more largely explains whence it derived its name. For this is a truly memorable history, in which we may perceive the greatness of men's obstinacy against God, and the little profit they receive from his judgments. And although at first sight the atrocity of the evil does not appear; yet the punishment which follows it, testifies how highly God was displeased with that which these men attempted.

4. Whose top may reach unto heaven. This is an hyperbolical form of speech, in which they boast as they extol the loftiness of the structure they are attempting to raise. And to the same point belongs what they immediately subjoin, **Let us make us a name;** for they intimate, that the work would be such as should not only be looked upon by the beholders as a kind of miracle, but should be celebrated everywhere to the utmost limits of the world. This is the perpetual infatuation of the world; to neglect heaven, and to seek immortality on earth, where every thing is fading and transient.

5. And the Lord came down. The remaining part of the history now follows, in which Moses teaches us with what ease the Lord could overturn their insane attempts, and scatter abroad all their preparations. There is no doubt that they strenuously set about what they had presumptuously devised. But Moses first intimates that God, for a little while, seemed to take no notice of them, in order that suddenly breaking off their work at its commencement, by the confusion of their tongues, he might give the more decisive evidence of his judgment. For he frequently bears with the wicked, to such an extent, that he not only suffers them to contrive many nefarious things, as if he were unconcerned, or were taking repose; but even further, their impious and perverse designs with animating success, in order that he may at length cast them down to a lower depth. The descent of God, which Moses here records, is spoken of in reference to men rather than to God; who, as we know, does not move from place to place. But he intimates that God gradually and as with a tardy step, appeared in the character of an Avenger. The Lord therefore descended that he might see; that is, he evidently showed that he was not ignorant of the attempt which the Babylonians were making.

7. Go to, let us go down. We have said that Moses has represented the case to us so that the judgments of God may be the more clearly illustrated. For which reason, he now introduces God as the speaker, who declares that the work which they supposed could not be retarded, shall, without any difficulty, be destroyed. The meaning of the words is of this kind, 'I will not use many instruments, I will only blow upon them, and they, through the confusion of tongues, shall be contemptibly scattered.'

9. Therefore is the name of it called Babel. Behold what they gained by their foolish ambition to acquire a name! They hoped that an everlasting memorial of their origin would be engraved on the tower; God not only frustrates their vain expectation, but brands them with eternal disgrace, to render them execrable to all posterity, on account of the great mischief indicted on the human race, through their fault. They gain, indeed, a name, but not each as they would have chosen: thus does God opprobriously cast down the pride of those who usurp to themselves honours to which they have no title.

10. These are the generations of Shem. Concerning the progeny of Shem, Moses had said something in the former chapter: but now he combines with the names of the men, the term of their several lives, that we might not be ignorant of the age of the world. For unless this brief description had been preserved, men at this day would not have known how much time intervened between the deluge and the day in which God made his covenant with Abraham. Moreover, it is to be observed, that God reckons the years of the world from the progeny of Shem, as a mark of honour: just as historians date their annals by the names of kings or consuls.

27. Terah begat Abram. Here also Abram is placed first among his brethren, not (as I suppose) because he was the firstborn; but because Moses, intent on the scope of his history, was not very careful in the arrangement of the sons of Tera.

28. And Haran died. Haran is said to have died before the face of his father; because he left his father the survivor.

30. But Sarai was barren. Not only does he say that Abram was without children, but he states the reasons namely, the sterility of his wife; in order to show that it was by nothing short of an extraordinary miracle that she afterwards bare Isaac, as we shall declare more fully in its proper place. Thus was God pleased to humble his servant; and we cannot doubt that Abram would suffer severe pain through this privation.

31. And Terah took Abram his son. Here the next chapter ought to commence; because Moses begins to treat of one of the principal subjects of his book; namely, the calling of Abram. For he not only relates that Terah changed his country, but he also explains the design and the end of his departure, that he left his native soils and entered on his journey, in order to come to the land of Canaan. Whence the inference is easily drawn, that he was not so much the leader or author of the journey, as the companion of his son.

Chapter 12

1. Now the Lord had said unto Abram. Moses had before said, that Terah and Abram had departed from their country to dwell in the land of Canaan. He now explains that they had not been impelled by levity as rash and fickle men are wont to be; nor had been drawn to other regions by disgust with their own country, as morose persons frequently are; nor were fugitives on account of crime; nor were led away by any foolish hope, or by any allurements, as many are hurried hither and thither by their own desires; but that Abram had been divinely commanded to go forth and had not moved a foot but as he was guided by the word of God.

Unto a land that I will show thee. This is another test to prove the faith of Abram. For why does not God immediately point out the land, except for the purpose of keeping his servant in suspense, that he may the better try the truth of his attachment to the word of God?

As if he would say, "I command thee to go forth with closed eyes, and forbid thee to inquire whither I am about to lead thee, until, having renounced thy country, thou shalt have given thyself wholly to me." And this is the true proof of our obedience, when we are not wise in our own eyes, but commit ourselves entirely unto the Lord.

2. And I will make of thee a great nation. Hitherto Moses has related what Abram had been commanded to do; now he annexes the promise of God to the command; and that for no light cause. For as we are slothful to obey, the Lord would command in vain, unless we are animated by a superadded confidence in his grace and benediction.

3. And I will bless them that bless thee. Here the extraordinary kindness of God manifests itself, in that he familiarly makes a covenant with Abram, as men are wont to do with their companions and equals. For this is the accustomed form of covenants between kings and others, that they mutually promise to have the same enemies and the same friends. This certainly is an inestimable pledge of special love, that God should so greatly condescend for our sake. For although he here addresses one man only, he elsewhere declares the same affection towards his faithful people.

In thee shall all families of the earth be blessed. God (in my judgment) pronounces that all nations should be blessed in his servant Abram because Christ was included in his loins. In this manner, he not only intimates that Abram would be an example, but a cause of blessing; so that there should be an understood antithesis between Adam and Christ. For whereas, from the time of the first man's alienation from God, we are all born accursed, here a new remedy is offered unto us.

7. And the Lord appeared unto Abram. He now relates that Abram was not left entirely destitute, but that God stretched forth his hand to help him. We must, however, mark, with what kind of assistance God succours him in his temptations. He offers him his bare word, and in such a way, indeed, that Abram might deem himself exposed to ridicule. For God declares he will give the land to his seed: but where is the seed, or where the hope of seed; seeing that he is childless and old, and his wife is barren? This was therefore an insipid consolation to the flesh. But faith has a different taste; the property of which is, to hold all the senses of the pious so bound by reverence to the word, that a single promise of God is quite sufficient.

And there builded he an altar. This altar was a token of gratitude. As soon as God appeared to him he raised an altar: to what end? That he might call upon the name of the Lord. We see, therefore, that he was intent upon giving of thanks; and that an altar was built by him in memory of kindness received.

15. And commended her before Pharaoh. Although Abram had sinned by fearing too much and too soon, yet the event teaches, that he had not feared without cause: for his wife was taken from him and brought to the king. At first Moses speaks generally of the Egyptians, afterwards he mentions the courtiers; by which course he intimates, that the rumour of Sara's beauty was everywhere spread abroad; but that it was more eagerly received by the courtiers who indulge themselves in greater license. Whereas he adds, that they told the king; we hence infer, how ancient is that corruption which now prevails immeasurably in the courts of kings.

And the woman was taken into Pharaoh's house. Since she was carried off, and dwelt for some time in the palace, many suppose that she was corrupted by the king. For it is not credible, that a lustful man, when he had her in his power, should have spared her modesty. This, truly, Abram had richly deserved, who had neither relied upon the grace of God, nor had committed the chastity of his wife to His faithfulness and care; but the plague which immediately followed, sufficiently proves that the Lord was mindful of her; and hence we may conclude, that she remained uninjured.

20. And Pharaoh commanded his men. In giving commandment that Abram should have a safe-conduct out of the kingdom, Pharaoh might seem to have done it, for the sake of providing against danger; because Abram had stirred up the odium of the nation against himself, as against one who had brought thither the scourge of God along with him; but as this conjecture has little solidity, I give the more simple interpretation, that leave of departure was granted to Abram with the addition of a guard, lest he should be exposed to violence. For we know how proud and cruel the Egyptians were; and how obnoxious Abram was to envy, because having there become suddenly rich, he would seem to be carrying spoil away with him.

Chapter 13

1. And Abram went up out of Egypt. In the commencement of the chapter, Moses commemorates the goodness of God in protecting Abram; whence it came to pass, that he not only returned in safety, but took with him great wealth. This circumstance is also to be noticed, that when he was leaving Egypt, abounding in cattle and treasures, he was allowed to pursue his journey in peace; for it is surprising that the Egyptians would suffer what Abram had acquired among them, to be transferred elsewhere.

5. And Lot also, which went with Abram. Next follows the inconvenience which Abram

suffered through his riches: namely, that he was torn from his nephew, whom he tenderly loved, as if it had been from his own heart.

8. And Abram said unto Lot. Moses first states, that Abram no sooner perceived the strifes which had arisen, than he fulfilled the duty of a good householder, by attempting to restore peace among his domestics; and that afterwards, by his moderation, he endeavoured to remedy the evil by removing it.

9. Is not the whole land before thee? Abram, for the sake of appeasing strife, voluntarily sacrifices his own right. For as ambition and the desire of victory is the mother of all contentions; so when every one meekly and moderately departs, in some degree, from his just claim, the best remedy is found for the removal of all cause of bitterness.

10. And Lot lifted up his eyes. As the equity of Abram was worthy of no little praise; so the inconsideration of Lot, which Moses here describes, is deserving of censure. He ought rather to have contended with his uncle for the palm of modesty; and this the very order of nature suggested; but just as if he had been, in every respect, the superior, he usurps for himself the better portion; and makes choice of that region which seemed the more fertile and agreeable.

13. But the men of Sodom. Lot thought himself happy that so rich a habitation had fallen to his share: but he learns at length, that the choice to which he had hastened, with a rashness equal to his avarice, had been unhappily granted to him; since he had to deal with proud and perverse neighbours, with whose conduct it was much harder to bear, than it was to contend with the sterility of the earth.

16. And I will make thy seed as the dust. The seed of Abram is compared to the dust, because of its immense multitude; and truly the sense of the term is to be sought for only in Moses' own words. It was, however, necessary to be here added, that God would raise up for him a seed, of which he was hitherto destitute. And we see that God always keeps him under the restraint of his own word; and will have him dependent upon his own lips. Abram is commanded to look at the dust; but when he turns his eyes upon his own family, what similitude is there between his solitariness and the countless particles of dust? This authority the Lord therefore requires us to attribute to his own word, that it alone should be sufficient for us.

18. And Abram removed his tent. Here Moses relates that the holy man, animated by the renewed promise of God traversed the land with great courage as if by a look alone he could subdue it to himself. Thus we see how greatly the oracle had profited him: not that he had heard anything from the mouth of God to which he had been unaccustomed, but because he had obtained a medicine so seasonable and suitable to his present grief, that he rose with collected energy towards heaven.

Chapter 14

1. **And it came to pass in the days of Amraphel.** The history related in this chapter is chiefly worthy of remembrance, for three reasons: first, because Lot, with a gentle reproof, exhorted the men of Sodom to repentance; they had, however, become altogether unteachable, and desperately perverse in their wickedness. But Lot was beaten with these scourges, because, having been allured and deceived by the richness of the soil, he had mixed himself with unholy and wicked men. Secondly, because God, out of compassion to him, raised up Abram as his avenger and liberator, to rescue him, when a captive, from the hand of the enemy; in which act the incredible goodness and benevolence of God towards his own people, is rendered conspicuous; since, for the sake of one man, he preserves, for a time, many who were utterly unworthy. Thirdly, because Abram was divinely honoured with a signal victory, and was blessed by the mouth of Melchizedek, in whose person, as appears from other passages of Scripture, the kingdom and priesthood of Christ was shadowed forth. As it respects the sum of the history, it is a horrible picture both of the avarice and pride of man.

10. **And the kings of Sodom and Gomorrah fled.** I understand the kings to have exchanged one kind of death for another, as is common in the moment of desperation; as if Moses had said, the swords of the enemy were so formidable to them, that, without hesitation, they threw themselves headlong into the pits.

12. **And they took Lot.** As Moses does not mention him till he speaks of the plundering of the city, the conjecture is probable, that at the conclusion of the battle, he was taken at home, unarmed. We here see, first, that sufferings are common to the good and the evil; then, that the more closely we are connected with the wicked and the ungodly, when God pours down his vengeance on them, the more quickly does the scourge come upon us.

13. **And there came one that had escaped.** This is the second part of the chapter, in which Moses shows, that when God had respect to his servant Lot, he gave him Abram as his deliverer, to rescue him from the hands of the enemy.

14. **When Abram heard that his brother was taken captive.** Moses briefly explains the cause of the war which was undertaken; namely, that Abram might rescue his relation from captivity.

18. **And Melchizedek king of Salem brought forth.** This is the last of the three principal points of this history, that Melchizedek, the chief father of the Church, having entertained Abram at a feast, blessed him, in virtue of his priesthood, and received tithes from him. There is no doubt that by the coming of this king to meet him, God also designed to render the victory of Abram famous and memorable to posterity. But a more exalted and excellent mystery was, at the same time, adumbrated: for seeing that the holy patriarch, whom God had raised to the highest rank of honour, submitted himself to Melchizedek, it is not to be doubted that God had constituted him the only head of the whole Church; for, without controversy, the solemn act of benediction, which Melchizedek assumed to himself, was a symbol of preeminent dignity.

19. **Blessed be Abram of the most high God.** The design of Melchizedek is to confirm and ratify the grace of the Divine vocation to holy Abram; for he points out the honour with which God had peculiarly dignified him by separating him from all others, and adopting him as his own son.

20. **And he gave him tithes of all.** Abram voluntarily gave tithes to Melchizedek, to do honour to his priesthood.

22. **And Abram said to the king of Sodom, I have lift up mine hand.** This ancient ceremony was very appropriate to give expression to the force and nature of an oath. For by raising the hand towards heaven, we show that we appeal to God as a witness, and also as an avenger, if we fail to keep our oath.

Chapter 15

1. **Fear not, Abram.** God exhorts Abram to be of a tranquil mind; but what foundation is there for such security, unless by faith we understand that God cares for us, and learn to rest in his providence? The promise, therefore, that God will be Abram's **shield** and his **exceeding great reward**, holds the first place; to which is added the exhortation, that, relying upon such a guardian of his safety, and such an author of his felicity, he should not fear.

2. **And Abram said, Lord God.** The Hebrew text has *Adonai Jehovah.* From which appellation it is inferred that some special mark of divine glory was stamped upon the vision; so that Abram, having no doubt respecting its author, confidently broke out in this expression.

6. **And he believed in the Lord.** None of us would be able to conceive the rich and hidden doctrine which this passage contains, unless Paul had borne his torch before us. (Rom. 4: 3.) However, it hence appears, that in all ages, Satan has laboured at nothing more assiduously than to extinguish, or to smother, the gratuitous justification of faith, which is here expressly

asserted. The words of Moses are, 'He believed in the Lord; and he counted it to him for righteousness.' In the first place, the faith of Abram is commended, because by it he embraced the promise of God; it is commended, in the second place, because hence Abram obtained righteousness in the sight of God, and that by imputation. Just as we understand that they to whom iniquity is imputed are guilty before God; so those to whom he imputes righteousness are approved by him as just persons; wherefore Abram was received into the number and rank of just persons by the imputation of righteousness.

7. I am the Lord that brought thee. Since it greatly concerns us, to have God as the guide of our whole life, in order that we may know that we have not rashly entered on some doubtful way, therefore the Lord confirms Abram in the course of his vocation, and recalls to his memory the original benefit of his deliverance; as if he had said, 'I, after I had stretched out my hand to thee, to lead thee forth from the labyrinth of death, have carried my favour towards thee thus far. Thou, therefore, respond to me in turn, by constantly advancing; and maintain steadfastly thy faith, from the beginning even to the end.'

11. And when the fowls came down. Although the sacrifice was dedicated to God, yet it was not free from the attack and the violence of birds. So neither are the faithful, after they are received into the protection of God, so covered with his hand, as not to be assailed on every side; since Satan and the world cease not to cause them trouble.

12. A deep sleep fell upon Abram. The vision is now mingled with a dream. Thus the Lord here joins those two kinds of communication together.

15. And thou shalt go to thy fathers in peace. Hitherto the Lord had respect to the posterity of Abram as well as to himself, that the consolation might be common to all; but now he turns his address to Abram alone, because he had need of peculiar confirmation. And the remedy proposed for alleviating his sorrow was, that he should die in peace, after he had attained the utmost limit of old age.

18. In the same day the Lord made a covenant. I willingly admit that the covenant was ratified by a solemn rite, when the animals were divided into parts. For there seems to be a repetition, in which he teaches what was the intent of the sacrifice which he has mentioned. Here, also, we may observe that the word is always to be joined with the symbols, lest our eyes be fed with empty and fruitless ceremonies. God has commanded animals to be offered to him; but he has shown their end and use, by a covenant appended to them. If, then, the Lord feeds us by sacraments, we infer, that they are

the evidences of his grace, and the tokens of those spiritual blessings which flow from it.

Chapter 16

1. Now Sarai, Abram's wife. Moses here recites a new history, namely, that Sarai, through the impatience of long delay, resorted to a method of obtaining seed by her husband, at variance with the word of God. She saw that she was barren, and had passed the age of bearing. And she inferred the necessity of a new remedy, in order that Abram might obtain the promised blessing. Moses expressly relates, that the design of marrying a second wife did not originate with Abram himself, but with Sarai, to teach us that the holy man was not impelled by lust to these nuptials; but that when he was thinking of no such thing, he was induced to engage in them, by the exhortation of his wife.

2. And Abram hearkened to the voice of Sarai. Truly the faith of Abram wavers, when he deviates from the word of God, and suffers himself to be borne away by the persuasion of his wife, to seek a remedy which was divinely prohibited.

3. And gave her to her husband Abram to be his wife. Moses states what was the design of Sarai; for neither did she intend to make her house a brothel, nor to be the betrayer of her maid's chastity, nor a pander for her husband. Yet Hagar is improperly called a wife; because she was brought into another person's bed, against the law of God.

4. Her mistress was despised in her eyes. Here Moses relates that the punishment of excessive precipitancy quickly followed. The chief blame, indeed, rested with Sarai; yet because Abram had proved himself too credulous, God chastises both as they deserve.

7. And the angel of the Lord found her. We are here taught with what clemency the Lord acts towards his own people, although they have deserved severe punishment. As he had previously mitigated the punishment of Abram and Sarai, so now he casts a paternal look upon Hagar, so that his favour is extended to the whole family.

10. I will multiply thy seed exceedingly. For the purpose of mitigating the offense, and of alleviating what was severe in the precept, by some consolation, he promises a blessing in the child which she should bear.

15. And Abram called. Hagar had been commanded to give that name to her son; but Moses follows the order of nature; because fathers, by the imposition of the name, declare the power which they have over their sons. We may easily gather, that Hagar, when she returned home, related the events which had occurred. Therefore, Abram shows himself to be obedient and grateful to God: because he both names his

son according to the command of the angel, and celebrates the goodness of God in having hearkened to the miseries of Hagar.

Chapter 17

1. And when Abram was ninety years old and nine. Moses passes over thirteen years of Abram's life, not because nothing worthy of remembrance had in the meantime occurred; but because the Spirit of God, according to his own will, selects those things which are most necessary to be known. He purposely points out the length of time which had elapsed from the birth of Ishmael to the period when Isaac was promised, for the purpose of teaching us that he long remained satisfied with that son who should, at length, be rejected, and that he was as one deluded by a fallacious appearance.

I am the Almighty God. The Hebrew noun *El*, which is derived from power, is here put for God. The same remark applies to the accompanying word *shaddai*, as if God would declare, that he had sufficient power for Abram's protection: because our faith can only stand firmly, while we are certainly persuaded that the defence of God is alone sufficient for use and can sincerely despise everything in the world which is opposed to our salvation. God, therefore, does not boast of that power which lies concealed within himself; but of that which he manifests towards his children; and he does so, in order that Abram might hence derive materials for confidence. Thus, in these words, a promise is included.

2. And I will make my covenant. The covenant of God with Abram had two parts. The first was a declaration of gratuitous love; to which was annexed the promise of a happy life. But the other was an exhortation to the sincere endeavour to cultivate uprightness.

3. And Abram fell on his face. We know that this was the ancient rite of adoration. Moreover, Abram testifies, first, that he acknowledges God, in whose presence all flesh ought to keep silence, and to be humbled; and, secondly that he reverently receives and cordially embraces whatever God is about to speak.

7. And thy seed after thee. There is no doubt that the Lord distinguishes the race of Abraham from the rest of the world. We must now see what people he intends. God made his covenant with those sons of Abraham who were naturally to be born of him.

To be a God unto thee. In this single word we are plainly taught that this was a spiritual covenant, not confirmed in reference to the present life only; but one from which Abraham might conceive the hope of eternal salvation so that being raised even to heaven, he might lay hold of solid and perfect bliss.

9. Thou shalt keep my covenant. As formerly, covenants were not only committed to public records, but were also wont to be engraved in brass, or sculptured on stones, in order that the memory of them might be more fully recorded, and more highly celebrated; so in the present instance, God inscribes his covenant in the flesh of Abraham. For circumcision was as a solemn memorial of that adoption, by which the family of Abraham had been elected to be the peculiar people of God. The pious had previously possessed other ceremonies which confirmed to them the certainty of the grace of God; but now the Lord attests the new covenant with a new kind of symbol.

10. Every man-child among you shall be circumcised. Although God promised alike to males and females, what he afterwards sanctioned by circumcision, he nevertheless consecrated, in one sex, the whole people to himself.

11. Ye shall circumcise the flesh of your foreskin. Very strange and unaccountable would this command at first sight appear. The subject treated of, is the sacred covenant, in which righteousness, salvation, and happiness are promised; whereby the seed of Abraham is distinguished from other nations, in order that it may be holy and blessed; and who can say that it is reasonable for the sign of so great a mystery to consist in circumcision? But as it was necessary for Abraham to become a fool, in order to prove himself obedient to God; so whosoever is wise, will both soberly and reverently receive what God seems to us foolishly to have commanded.

13. For an everlasting covenant. The meaning of this expression may be twofold: either that God promises that his grace, of which circumcision was a sign and pledge, should be eternal; or that he intended the sign itself to be perpetually observed. Indeed, I have no doubt that this perpetuity ought to be referred to the visible sign. But they who hence infer, that the use of it ought to flourish among the Jews even of the present time, are (in my opinion) deceived. For they swerve from that axiom which we ought to regard as fixed; that since Christ is the end of the law, the perpetuity which is ascribed to the ceremonies of the law, was terminated as soon as Christ appeared.

23. And Abraham took Ishmael. Moses now commends the obedience of Abraham because he circumcised the whole of his family as he had been commanded. For he must, of necessity, have been entirely devoted to God, since he did not hesitate to inflict upon himself a wound attended with acute pain, and not without danger of life. To this may be added the circumstance of the time; namely, that he does not defer the work to another day, but immediately obeys the Divine mandate.

Two things also here are worthy of observation. First, that Abraham was not deterred by the difficulty of the work from yielding to God the duty which he owed him. We know that he had a great multitude in his house, nearly equal to a people. It was scarcely credible that so many men would have suffered themselves to be wounded apparently to be made a laughing-stock. Therefore it was justly to be feared, that he would excite a great tumult in his tranquil family; yea, that, by a common impulse the major part of his servants would rise up against him; nevertheless, relying upon the word of God, he strenuously attempts what seemed impossible.

We next see, how faithfully his family was instructed; because not only his home-born slaves, but foreigners, and men bought with money, meekly receive the wound which was both troublesome, and the occasion of shame to carnal sense. It appears then that Abraham diligently took care to have them prepared for due obedience. And since he held them under holy discipline, he received the reward of his own diligence in finding them so tractable in a most arduous affair.

Chapter 18

2. And, lo, three men stood by him. Before Moses proceeds to his principal subject, he describes to us, the hospitality of the holy man; and he calls the angels men, because, being clothed with human bodies, they appeared to be nothing else than men. And this was done designedly, in order that he, receiving them as men, might give proof of his charity. For angels do not need those services of ours, which are the true evidences of charity.

6. And Abraham hastened into the tent. Abraham's care in entertaining his guests is here recorded; and Moses, at the same time, shows what a well-ordered house he had. In short, he presents us, in a few words, with a beautiful picture of domestic government. Abraham runs, partly, to command what he would have done; and partly, to execute his own duty, as the master of the house. Sarah keeps within the tent; not to indulge in sloth, but rather to take her own part also, in the labour.

11. Were old, and well stricken in age. Moses inserts this verse to inform us that what the angel was saying, justly appeared improbable to Sarah. For it is contrary to nature that children should be promised to decrepit old men.

12. Therefore Sarah laughed within herself. Abraham had laughed before, as appears in the preceding chapter: but the laughter of both was, by no means, similar. For Sarah is not transported with admiration and joy, on receiving the promise of God; but foolishly sets her own

age and that of her husband in opposition to the word of God; that she may withhold confidence from God, when he speaks.

13. And the Lord said. Because the majesty of God had now been manifested in the angels, Moses expressly mentions his Name. The word of the Lord is so precious to himself, that he would be regarded by us as present, whenever he speaks through his ministers.

15. Then Sarah denied. Another sin of Sarah's was, that she endeavoured to cover and hide her laughter by a falsehood.

18. Seeing that Abraham shall surely become a great and mighty nation. God continues his acts of kindness towards the faithful, yea, even increases them, and gradually heaps new favours upon those before granted. And he daily deals with us in the same manner. For what is the reason why he pours innumerable benefits upon us, in constant succession, unless that, having once embraced us with paternal love, he cannot deny himself?

19. For I know him, that he will command his children. The second reason why God chooses to make Abraham a partaker of his counsel is, because he foresees that this would not be done in vain, and without profit. And the simple meaning of the passage is, that Abraham is admitted to the counsel of God, because he would faithfully fulfill the office of a good householder, in instructing his own family.

20. The cry of Sodom. The Lord here begins more clearly to explain to Abraham his counsel concerning the destruction of the five cities; although he only names Sodom and Gomorrah, which were much more famous than the rest. But before he makes mention of punishment, he brings forward their iniquities, to teach Abraham that they justly deserved to be destroyed: otherwise the history would not tend to instruction.

25. Shall not the Judge of all the earth do right? He does not here teach God His duty, as if any one should say to a judge, 'See what thy office requires, what is worthy of this place, what suits thy character;' but he reasons from the nature of God, that it is impossible for Him to intend anything unjust.

27. Which am but dust and ashes. Abraham speaks thus for the sake of obtaining pardon. For what is mortal man when compared with God? He therefore confesses that he is too bold, in thus familiarly interrogating God; yet he desires that this favour may be granted unto him, by the Divine indulgence. It is to be noted, that the nearer Abraham approaches to God, the more fully sensible does he become of the miserable and abject condition of men. For it is only the brightness of the glory of God which covers with shame and thoroughly humbles men, when stripped of their foolish and intoxicated self-confidence. Whosoever, therefore, seems to himself to be something, let him turn his eyes to God, and immediately he will acknowledge himself to be nothing.

Chapter 19

4. Before they lay down. Here, in a single crime, Moses sets before our eyes a lively picture of Sodom. For it is hence obvious, how diabolical was their consent in all wickedness, since they all so readily conspired to perpetrate the most abominable crime. The greatness of their iniquity and wantonness, is apparent from the fact, that, in a collected troop, they approach, as enemies, to lay siege to the house of Lot. How blind and impetuous is their lust; since, without shame, they rush together like brute animals! How great their ferocity and cruelty; since they reproachfully threaten the holy man, and proceed to all extremities! Hence also we infer, that they were not contaminated with one vice only, but were given up to all audacity in crime, so that no sense of shame was left them.

6. And Lot went out at the door unto them. It appears from the fact that Lot went out and exposed himself to danger, how faithfully he observed the sacred right of hospitality. It was truly a rare virtue, that he preferred the safety and honour of the guests whom he had once undertaken to protect, to his own life: yet this degree of magnanimity is required from the children of God, that where duty and fidelity are concerned, they should not spare themselves.

8. I have two daughters. As the constancy of Lot, in risking his own life for the defence of his guests, deserves no common praise; so now Moses relates that a defect was mixed with this great virtue, which sprinkled it with some imperfection. For, being destitute of advice, he devises (as is usual in intricate affairs) an unlawful remedy. He does not hesitate to prostitute his own daughters, that he may restrain the indomitable fury of the people. But he should rather have endured a thousand deaths, than have resorted to such a measure. Yet such are commonly the works of holy men: since nothing proceeds from them so excellent, as not to be in some respect defective.

13. The Lord has sent us to destroy it. This place teaches us, that the angels are the ministers of God's wrath, as well as of his grace. Nor does it form any objection to this statement, that elsewhere the latter service is peculiarly ascribed to holy angels.

14. And Lot went out. The faith of the holy man, Lot, appeared first in this, that he was completely awed and humbled at the threatening of God; secondly, that in the midst of destruction, he yet laid hold of the salvation promised to him. In inviting his sons-in-law to join him, he manifests such diligence as becomes the sons of God; who ought to labour, by all means, to rescue their own families from destruction.

17. Escape for thy life. This was added by Moses, to teach us that the Lord not only stretches out his hand to us for a moment, in order to begin our salvation; but that without leaving his work imperfect, he will carry it on even to the end. It certainly was no common act of grace, that the ruin of Sodom was predicted to Lot himself, lest it should crush him unawares; next, that a certain hope of salvation was given him by the angels; and, finally, that he was led by the hand out of the danger.

19. Behold now, thy servant has found grace in thy sight. Lot commemorates the kindness of God, not so much for the sake of testifying his gratitude, as of acquiring thence greater confidence in asking for more. For since the goodness of God is neither exhausted, nor wearied, by bestowing; the more ready we find him to give, the more confident does it become us to be, in hoping for what is good. And this truly is the property of faith, to take encouragement for the future, from the experience of past favour. And Lot does not err on this point; but he acts rashly in going beyond the word for the sake of self-gratification. Therefore I have said, that his prayer, though it flowed from the fountain of faith, yet drew something turbid from the mire of carnal affection. Let us then, relying upon the mercy of God, not hesitate to expect all things from him; especially those which he himself has promised, and which he permits us to choose.

24. Then the Lord rained. Moses here succinctly relates in very unostentatious language, the destruction of Sodom and of the other cities. The atrocity of the case might well demand a much more copious narration, expressed in tragic terms; but Moses, according to his manner, simply recites the judgment of God, which no words would be sufficiently vehement to describe, and then leaves the subject to the meditation of his readers.

26. But his wife looked back. Moses here records the wonderful judgment of God, by which the wife of Lot was transformed into a statue of salt.

27. And Abraham got up early in the morning. Moses now reverts to Abraham, and shows that he, by no means, neglected what he had heard from the mouth of the angel; for he relates that Abraham came to a place where he might see the judgment of God.

29. God remembered Abraham. Although Moses does not assert that the deliverance of Abraham's nephew was made known to him; yet since he says, that Lot was saved from destruction for Abraham's sake, it is probable that he was not deprived of that consolation which he most needed; and that he was conscious of the benefit, for which it became him to give thanks. If it seems to any one absurd, that the holy man Lot should be granted for the sake of another; as if the Lord had not respect to his own piety: I answer, these two things well agree with each other; that the Lord, since he is wont to aid his own people, cared for Lot, whom he had chosen, and whom he governed by his Spirit; and yet that, at the same time, he would show, in the preservation of his life, how greatly he loved Abraham, to whom he not only granted personal protection, but also the deliverance of others.

35. And the younger arose, and lay with him. This place teaches us how dangerous it is, to fall in the snares of Satan. For, who once is caught therein, involves himself deeper and deeper in it. It is sure that Lot has been a modest man, but either, that the daughters have overtaken him while he was overcome with sadness, or that he allured by any other means to excessive drinking, once being decayed to excessiveness, he is again deceived the next day. We must therefore diligently resist the first beginning, for it is nearly impossible that they, who are once stupefied through its sweetness, totally lose themselves in the vices.

Chapter 20

1. And Abraham journeyed from thence. What Moses related respecting the destruction of Sodom, was a digression. He now returns to the continuation of his history, and proceeds to show what happened to Abraham; how he conducted himself, and how the Lord protected him; till the promised seed, the future source of the Church, should be born unto him.

3. But God came to Abimelech in a dream by night. Here Moses shows that the Lord acted with such gentleness, that in punishing his servant, he yet, as a father, forgave him: just as he deals with us, so that, while chastising us with his rod, his mercy and his goodness far exceed his severity.

12. And yet indeed she is my sister. Some suppose Sarah to have been Abraham's own sister, yet not by the same mother but born from a second wife. As, however, the name sister has a wider signification among the Hebrews, I willingly adopt a different conjecture; namely, that she was his sister in the second degree; thus it will be true that they had a common father, that is, a grandfather, from whom they had descended by brothers. Moreover, Abraham extenuates his offense, and draws a distinction between his silence and a direct falsehood; and certainly he professed with truth, that he was the brother of Sarah. Indeed it appears that he feigned nothing in words which differed from the facts themselves; yet when all things have been sifted, his

defence proves to be either frivolous, or, at least, too feeble. For since he had purposely used the name of sister as a pretext, lest men should have some suspicion of his marriage; he sophistically afforded them an occasion of falling into error.

14. And Abimelech took sheep. Abraham had before received possessions and gifts in Egypt; but with this difference, that whereas Pharaoh had commanded him to depart elsewhere; Abimelech offers him a home in his kingdom. It therefore appears that both kings were stricken with no common degree of fear. For when they perceived that they were reproved by the Lord, because they had been troublesome to Abraham; they found no method of appeasing God, except that of compensating, by acts of kindness, for the injury they had brought on the holy man.

17. So Abraham prayed. In two respects the wonderful favour of God towards Abraham was apparent; first that, with outstretched hand, He avenged the injury done to him; and, secondly, that, through Abraham's prayer, He became pacified towards the house of Abimelech.

Chapter 21

1. And the Lord visited Sarah. In this chapter not only is the nativity of Isaac related, but because, in his very birth, God has set before us a lively picture of his Church, Moses also gives a particular account of this matter. And first, he says that God visited Sarah, as he had promised. Because all offspring, flows from the kindness of God, therefore the Lord is said, not without reason, to visit those, to whom he gives children.

2. She bare Abraham a son. This is said according to the accustomed manner of speaking; because the woman is neither the head of a family, nor brings forth properly for herself, but for her husband. What follows, however, is more worthy of notice, **In his old age, at the set time,** which God had predicted: for the old age of Abraham does, not a little, illustrate the glory of the miracle. And now Moses, for the third time, recalls us to the word of God, that the constancy of his truth may always be present to our minds. And though the time had been predicted, alike to Abraham and to his wife, yet this honour is expressly attributed to the holy man; because the promise had been especially given on his account. Both, however, are distinctly mentioned in the context.

3. And Abraham called the name. Moses does not mean that Abraham was the inventor of the name; but that he adhered to the name which before had been given by the angel. This act of obedience, however, was worthy of commendation, since he not only ratified the word of God, but also executed his office as God's minister. For, as a herald, he proclaimed to all, that which the angel had committed to his trust.

4. And Abraham circumcised his son. Abraham pursued his uniform tenor of obedience, in not sparing his own son. For, although it would be painful for him to wound the tender body of the infant; yet, setting aside all human affection, he obeys the word of God. And Moses records that he did as the Lord had commanded him; because there is nothing of greater importance, than to take the pure word of God for our rule, and not to be wise above what is lawful. This submissive spirit is especially required, in reference to sacraments; lest men should either invent any thing for themselves, or should transfer those things which are commanded by the Lord, to any use they please.

8. And the child grew, and was weaned. Moses now begins to relate the manner in which Ishmael was rejected from the family of Abraham, in order that Isaac alone might hold the place of the lawful son and heir.

14. And Abraham rose up early. How painful was the wound, which the ejection of his first-born son inflicted upon the mind of the holy man, we may gather from the double consolation with which God mitigated his grief: He sends his son into banishments just as if he were tearing out his own heart. But being accustomed to obey God, he brings into subjection the paternal love, which he is not able wholly to cast aside. This is the true test of faith and piety, when the faithful are so far compelled to deny themselves, that they even resign the very affections of their original nature, which are neither evil nor vicious in themselves, to the will of God.

20. And God was with the lad. There are many ways in which God is said to be present with men. He is present with his elects whom he governs by the special grace of his Spirit; he is present also, sometimes, as it respects external life, not only with his elect, but also with strangers, in granting them some signal benediction: as Moses, in this place, commends the extraordinary grace by which the Lord declares that his promise is not void, since he pursues Ishmael with favour, because he was the son of Abraham. Hence, however, this general doctrine is inferred; that it is to be entirely ascribed to God that men grow up, that they enjoy the light and common breath of heaven, and that the earth supplies them with food. Only it must be remembered, the prosperity of Ishmael flowed from this cause, that an earthly blessing was promised him for the sake of his father Abraham.

33. And Abraham planted a grove. It hence appears that more rest was granted to Abraham, after the covenant was entered into, than he had hitherto enjoyed; for now he begins to plant trees, which is a sign of a tranquil and fixed habitation; for we never before read that he planted a single shrub. Wherefore, we see how far his condition was improved because he was

permitted to lead (as I may say) a settled life. The assertion, that he **called on the name of the Lord,** I thus interpret; he instituted anew the solemn worship of God, in order to testify his gratitude. Therefore God, after he had led his servant through continually winding paths, gave to him some relaxation in his extreme old age.

Chapter 22

1. And it came to pass. This chapter contains a most memorable narrative. For although Abraham, through the whole course of his life, gave astonishing proofs of faith and obedience, yet none more excellent can be imagined than the immolation of his son. For other temptations with which the Lord had exercised him, tended, indeed, to his mortification; but this inflicted a wound far more grievous than death itself. Here, however, we must consider something greater and higher than the paternal grief and anguish, which, being produced by the death of an only son, pierced through the breast of the holy man. It was sad for him to be deprived of his only son, sadder still that this son should be torn away by a violent death, but by far the most grievous that he himself should be appointed as the executioner to slay him with his own hand.

God did tempt Abraham. James, in denying that any one is tempted by God, (James 1:13,) refutes the profane calumnies of those who, to exonerate themselves from the blame of their sins, attempt to fix the charge of them upon God. Wherefore, James truly contends, that those sins, of which we have the root in our own concupiscence, ought not to be charged upon another. For though Satan instils his poison, and fans the flame of our corrupt desires within us, we are yet not carried by any external force to the commission of sin; but our own flesh entices us, and we willingly yield to its allurements. This, however is no reason why God may not be said to tempt us in his own way, just as he tempted Abraham, – that is, brought him to a severe test, – that he might make full trial of the faith of his servant.

And he said, Behold, here I am. It hence appears that the holy man was, in no degree, afraid of the wiles of Satan. For the faithful are not in such haste to obey God, as to allow a foolish credulity to carry them away, in whatever direction the breath of a doubtful vision may blow. But when it was once clear to Abraham, that he was called by God, he testified, by this answer, his prompt desire to yield obedience. For the expression before us is as much as if he said, Whatever God may have been pleased to command, I am perfectly ready to carry into effect. And, truly, he does not wait till God should expressly enjoin this or the other thing, but promises that he will be simply, and without exception, obedient in all things.

2. Take now thy son. Abraham is commanded to immolate his son.

Thine only son Isaac, whom thou lovest. As if it were not enough to command in one word the sacrifice of his son, he pierces, as with fresh strokes, the mind of the holy man. By calling him his **only** son, he again irritates the wound recently indicted, by the banishment of the other son; he then looks forward into futurity, because no hope of offspring would remain. If the death of a firstborn son is wont to be grievous, what must the mourning of Abraham be?

3. And Abraham rose up early in the morning. This promptitude shows the greatness of Abraham's faith.

7. My father. God produces here a new instrument of torture, by which he may, more and more, torment the breast of Abraham, already pierced with so many wounds. And it is not to be doubted, that God designedly both framed the tongue of Isaac to this tender appellation, and directed it to this question, in order that nothing might be wanting to the extreme severity of Abraham's grief. Yet the holy man sustains even this attack with invincible courage; and is so far from being disturbed in his proposed course, that he shows himself to be entirely devoted to God, hearkening to nothing which should either shake his confidence, or hinder his obedience. But it is important to notice the manner in which he unties this inextricable knot; namely, by taking refuge in Divine Providence, 'God will provide himself a lamb.' This example is proposed for our imitation.

11. And the angel of the Lord called unto him. The inward temptation had been already overcome, when Abraham intrepidly raised his hand to slay his son; and it was by the special grace of God that he obtained so signal a victory. But now Moses subjoins, that suddenly beyond all hope, his sorrow was changed into joy.

12. Now I know that thou fearest God. Truly, by condescending to the manner of men, God here says that what he has proved by experiment, is now made known to himself.

13. And, behold, behind him a ram. We need not doubt that it was presented there by miracle, whether it was then first created, or whether it was brought from some other place; for God intended to give that to his servant which would enable him, with joy and cheerfulness, to offer up a pleasant sacrifice: and at the same time he admonishes him to return thanks. Moreover, since a ram is substituted in the place of Isaac, God shows us, as in a glass, what is the design of our mortification; namely, that by the Spirit of God dwelling within us, we, though dead, may yet be living sacrifices.

17. Thy seed shall possess the gate of his enemies. He means that the offspring of Abraham should be victorious over their enemies; for in the gates were their bulwarks, and in them they administered judgment.

Chapter 23

1. And Sarah was an hundred and seven and twenty years old. It is remarkable that Moses, who relates the death of Sarah in a single word, uses so many in describing her burial.

3. And spake unto the sons of Heth. Moses is silent respecting the rite used by Abraham in the burial of the body of his wife: but he proceeds, at great length, to recite the purchasing of the sepulchre.

6. Thou art a mighty prince among us. The Hittites gratuitously offer a burying-place to Abraham wherever he might please to choose one. They testify that they do this, as a tribute to his virtues.

7. And Abraham stood up. Moses commends the modesty of the holy man, when he says that he rose up to do reverence to the people of the land.

8. If it be in your mind. Abraham constitutes them his advocates with Ephron, to persuade him to sell the double cave. Some suppose the cave to have been so formed that one part was above, and the other below. Let every one be at liberty to adopt what opinion he pleases; I, however, rather suppose, that there was one entrance, but that within, the cave was divided by a middle partition. It is more pertinent to remark that Abraham, by offering a full price, cultivated and maintained equity. Where is there one to be found, who, in buying, and in other business, does not eagerly pursue his own advantage at another's cost? For while the seller sets the price at twice the worth of a thing, that he may extort as much as possible from the buyer, and the buyer in return, by shuffling, attempts to reduce it to a low price, there is no end of bargaining. And although avarice has specious pretexts, it yet causes those who make contracts with each other, to forget the claims of equity and justice. This also, finally deserves to be noticed; that Abraham often declares that he was buying the field for a place of sepulture. And Moses is the more minute in this matter, that we may learn, with our father Abraham, to raise our minds to the hope of the resurrection. He saw the half of himself taken away; but because he was certain that his wife was not exiled from the kingdom of God, he hides her dead body in the tomb, until he and she should be gathered together.

11. Hear me. Although Ephron earnestly insisted upon giving the field freely to Abraham, the holy man adheres to his purpose, and at length compels him, by his entreaties, to sell the field. Ephron, in excusing himself, says that the price was too small for Abraham to insist upon giving; yet he estimates it at four hundred shekels. He had been presented with considerable gifts both by the king of Egypt and the king of Gerar, but he observed this rule; that he would neither receive all things, nor in all places, nor from all persons. He bought the field, in order that he might not possess a foot of land, by the gift of any man.

Chapter 24

1. And Abraham was old. Moses passes onwards to the relation of Isaac's marriage, because indeed Abraham, perceiving himself to be worn down by old age, would take care that his son should not marry a wife in the land of Canaan. In this place Moses expressly describes Abraham as an old man, in order that we may learn that he had been admonished, by his very age, to seek a wife for his son: for old age itself, which, at the most, is not far distant from death, ought to induce us so to order the affairs of our family, that when we die, peace may be preserved among our posterity, the fear of the Lord may flourish, and rightly-constituted order may prevail.

2. And Abraham said unto his eldest servant. Abraham here fulfils the common duty of parents, in labouring for and being solicitous about the choice of a wife for his son: but he looks somewhat further; for since God had separated him from the Canaanites by a sacred covenant, he justly fears lest Isaac, by joining himself in affinity with them, should shake off the yoke of God.

3. That thou shalt not take a wife. The kind of discipline which prevailed in Abraham's house is here apparent. Although this man was but a servant, yet, because he was put in authority by the master of the family, his servile condition did not prevent him from being next in authority to his lord; so that Isaac himself, the heir and successor of Abraham, submitted to his direction.

6. Beware that thou bring not my son thither again. If the woman should not be found willing, Abraham, commending the event to God, firmly adheres to the principal point, that his son Isaac should not return to his country, because in this manner he would have deprived himself of the promised inheritance. He therefore chooses rather to live by hope, as a stranger, in the land of Canaan, than to rest among his relatives in his native soil: and thus we see that, in perplexed and confused affairs, the mind of the holy man was not drawn aside from the command of God by any agitating cares; and we are taught, by his example, to follow God through every obstacle.

7. The Lord God of heaven. By a twofold argument Abraham infers, that what he is deliberating respecting the marriage of his son will, by the grace of God, have a prosperous issue. First, because God had not led him forth in vain from his own country into a foreign land; and secondly, because God had not falsely promised to give the land, in which he was dwelling as a stranger, to his seed. By calling God **the God of heaven,** he celebrates that divine power which was the ground of his confidence.

10. And the servant took ten camels. He takes the camels with him, to prove that Abraham is a man of great wealth, in order that he may the more easily obtain what he desires. For even an open-hearted girl would not easily suffer herself to be drawn away to a distant region, unless on the proposed condition of being supplied with the conveniences of life.

15. Before he had done speaking. This sufficiently demonstrates that his wish had not been foolishly conceived. For the quickness of the answer manifests the extraordinary indulgence of God, who does not suffer the man to be long harassed with anxiety. Rebekah had, indeed, left her house before he began to pray; but it must be maintained that the Lord, at whose disposal are both the moments of time and the ways of man, had so ordered it on both sides as to give clear manifestation of his Providence.

22. The man took a golden earring. His adorning the damsel with precious ornaments is a token of his confidence. For since it is evident by many proofs that he was an honest and careful servant, he would not throw away without discretion the treasures of his master.

26. And the man bowed down his head. When the servant of Abraham hears that he had alighted upon the daughter of Bethel, he is more and more elated with hope. Yet he does not exult, as profane men are wont to do, as if the occurrence were fortuitous; but he gives thanks to God, regarding it, as the result of Providence, that he had been thus opportunely led straight to the place he had wished.

33. I will not eat until I have told my errand. Moses begins to show by what means the parents of Rebekah were induced to give her in marriage to their nephew. That the servant, when food was set before him, should refuse to eat till he had completed his work is a proof of his diligence and fidelity; and it may with propriety be regarded as one of the benefits which God had vouchsafed to Abraham, that he should have a servant so faithful, and so intent upon his duty.

50. The thing proceedeth from the Lord. Whereas they are convinced by the discourse of the man, that God was the Author of this marriage, they avow that it would be unlawful for them to offer anything in the way of contradiction. They declare that the thing **proceedeth from the Lord;** because he had, by the clearest signs, made his will manifest. Hence we perceive, that although the true religion was in part observed among them, and in part infected with vicious errors, yet the fear of God was never so utterly extinguished, but this axiom remained firmly fixed in all their minds, that God must be obeyed.

52. **He worshipped.** Moses again repeats that Abraham's servant gave thanks to God; and it is not without reason that he so often inculcates this religious duty; because, since God requires nothing greater from us, the neglect of it betrays the most shameful indolence. The acknowledgment of God's kindness is a sacrifice of sweet-smelling savour; yea, it is a more acceptable service than all sacrifices.

67. **And Isaac brought her into his mother Sarah's tent.** He first brought her into the tent, then took her as his wife. By the very arrangement of his words, Moses distinguishes between the legitimate mode of marriage and barbarism. And certainly the sanctity of marriage demands that man and woman should not live together like cattle; but that, having pledged their mutual faith, and invoked the name of God, they might dwell with each other. Besides, it is to be observed, that Isaac was not compelled, by the tyrannical command of his father, to marry; but after he had given his mind to her he took her freely, and cordially gave her the assurance of conjugal fidelity.

And Isaac was comforted after his mother's death. Since his grief for the death of his mother was now first assuaged, we infer how great had been its vehemence; for a period sufficiently long had already elapsed. We may also hence infer, that the affection of Isaac was tender and gentle: and that his love to his mother was of no common kind, seeing he had so long lamented her death.

Chapter 25

6. **But unto the sons of the concubines.** Moses relates, that when Abraham was about to die, he formed the design of removing all cause of strife among his sons after his death, by constituting Isaac his sole heir, and dismissing the rest with suitable gifts. This dismissal was, indeed, apparently harsh and cruel; but it was agreeable to the appointment and decree of God, in order that the entire possession of the land might remain for the posterity of Isaac.

7. **And these are the days.** Moses now brings us down to the death of Abraham; and the first thing to be noticed concerning his age is the number of years during which he lived as a pilgrim; for he deserves the praise of wonderful and incomparable patience, for having wandered through the space of a hundred years, while God led him about in various directions, contented, both in life and death, with the bare promise of God.

8. **Then Abraham gave up the ghost.** They are mistaken who suppose that this expression denotes sudden death, as intimating that he had not been worn out by long disease, but expired without pain. Moses rather means to say that the father of the faithful was not exempt from the common lot of men, in order that our minds may not languish when the outward man is perishing; but that, by meditating on that renovation which is laid up as the object of our hope, we may, with tranquil minds, suffer this frail tabernacle to be dissolved. There is therefore no reason why a feeble, emaciated body, failing eyes, tremulous hands, and the lost use of all our members, should so dishearten us, that we should not hasten, after the example of our father, with joy and alacrity to our death.

9. **And his sons Isaac and Ishmael buried him.** Hence it appears, that although Ishmael had long ago been dismissed, he was not utterly alienated from his father, because he performed the office of a son in celebrating the obsequies of his deceased parent.

19. **These are the generations of Isaac.** Because what Moses has said concerning the Ishmaelites was incidental, he now returns to the principal subject of the history, for the purpose of describing the progress of the Church. And in the first place, he repeats that Isaac's wife was taken from Mesopotamia. He expressly calls her the sister of Laban the Syrian, who was hereafter to become the father-in-law of Jacob, and concerning whom he had many things to relate. But it is chiefly worthy of observation that he declares Rebekah to have been barren during the early years of her marriage. And we shall afterwards see that her barrenness continued, not for three or four, but for twenty years, in order that her very despair of offspring might give greater lustre to the sudden granting of the blessing. But nothing seems less accordant with reason, than that the propagation of the Church should be thus small and slow.

23. **Two nations.** In the first place, God answers that the contention between the twin-brothers had reference to something far beyond their own persons; for in this way he shows that there would be discord between their posterities. When he says, **there are two nations,** the expression is emphatic; for since they were brothers and twins, and therefore of one blood, the mother did not suppose that they would be so far disjoined as to become the heads of distinct nations; yet God declares that dissension should take place between those who were by nature joined together.

Secondly, he describes their different conditions, namely, that victory would belong to one of these nations, forasmuch as this was the cause of the contest, that they could not be equal, but one was chosen and the other rejected. For since the reprobate give way reluctantly, it follows of necessity that the children of God have to undergo many troubles and contests on account of their adoption.

Thirdly, the Lord affirms that the order of nature being inverted, the younger, who was inferior, should be the victor.

33. And Jacob said, Swear to me. Jacob did not act cruelly towards his brother, for he took nothing from him, but only desired a confirmation of that right which had been divinely granted to him; and he does this with a pious intention, that he may hereby the more fully establish the certainty of his own election. Meanwhile the infatuation of Esau is to be observed, who, in the name and presence of God, does not hesitate to set his birthright to sale. Although he had before rushed inconsiderately upon the food under the maddening impulse of hunger; now, at least, when an oath is exacted from him, some sense of religion should have stolen over him to correct his brutal cupidity. But he is so addicted to gluttony that he makes God himself a witness of his ingratitude.

34. Then Jacob gave. Esau having satisfied his appetite, did not consider that he had sacrificed a blessing far more valuable than a hundred lives, to purchase a repast which would be ended in half an hour. Thus are all profane persons accustomed to act: alienated from the celestial life, they do not perceive that they have lost anything, till God thunders upon them out of heaven. As long as they enjoy their carnal wishes, they cast the anger of God behind them; and hence it happens that they go stupidly forward to their own destruction. Wherefore let us learn, if, at any time, we, being deceived by the allurements of the world, swerve from the right way, quickly to rouse ourselves from our slumber.

Chapter 26

1. And there was a famine. Moses relates that Isaac was tried by nearly the same kind of temptation as that through which his father Abraham had twice passed. The condition in which it was the will of God to place his servants, as strangers and pilgrims in the land which he had promised to give them, seemed sufficiently troublesome and hard; but it appears still more intolerable, that he scarcely suffered them to exist in this wandering, uncertain, and changeable kind of life, but almost consumed them with hunger.

5. Because that Abraham obeyed my voice. Moses does not mean that Abraham's obedience was the reason why the promise of God was confirmed and ratified to him; but from chapter 22:18, where we have a similar expression, we

learn, that what God freely bestows upon the faithful is sometimes, beyond their desert, ascribed to themselves; that they, knowing their intention to be approved by the Lord, may the more ardently addict and devote themselves entirely to his service: so he now commends the obedience of Abraham, in order that Isaac may be stimulated to an imitation of his example.

14. And the Philistines envied him. We are taught by this history that the blessings of God which pertain to the present earthly life are never pure and perfect, but are mixed with some troubles, lest quiet and indulgence should render us negligent. Wherefore, let us all learn not too ardently to desire great wealth. If the rich are harassed by any cause of disquietude, let them know that they are roused by the Lord, lest they should fall fast asleep in the midst of their pleasures; and let the poor enjoy this consolation, that their poverty is not without its advantages.

23. And he went up from thence to Beersheba. Next follows a more abundant consolation, and one affording effectual refreshment to the mind of the holy man. In the tranquil enjoyment of the well, he acknowledges the favour which God had showed him: but forasmuch as one word of God weighs more with the faithful than the accumulated mass of all good things, we cannot doubt that Isaac received this oracle more joyfully than if a thousand rivers of nectar had flowed unto him: and truly Moses designedly commemorates in lofty terms this act of favour, that the Lord encouraged him by his own word, (verse 24;) whence we may learn, in ascribing proper honour to each of the other gifts of God, still always to give the palm to that proof of his paternal love which he grants us in his word. Food, clothing, health, peace, and other advantages, afford us a taste of the Divine goodness; but when he addresses us familiarly, and expressly declares himself to be our Father, then indeed it is that he thoroughly refreshes.

24. And the Lord appeared unto him. This vision was to prepare him to listen more attentively to God, and to convince him that it was God with whom he had to deal; for a voice alone would have had less energy. Therefore God appears, in order to produce confidence in and reverence towards his word. In short, visions were a kind of symbol of the Divine presence, designed to remove all doubt from the minds of the holy fathers respecting him who was about to speak.

25. And he builded an altar there. From other passages we are well aware that Moses here speaks of public worship; for inward invocation of God neither requires an altar; nor has any special choice of place; and it is certain that the saints, wherever they lived, worshipped. But because religion ought to maintain a testimony before men, Isaac, having erected and consecrated an altar, professes himself a worshipper of the true and only God, and by this method separates himself from the polluted rites of heathens.

28. We saw certainly that the Lord was with thee. By this argument they prove that they desired a compact with Isaac, not insidiously, but in good faith, because they acknowledge the favour of God towards him. For it was necessary to purge themselves from this suspicion, seeing that they now presented themselves so courteously to one against whom they had before been unreasonably opposed. This confession of theirs, however, contains very useful instruction. Profane men in calling one, whose affairs all succeed well and prosperously, the blessed of the Lord, bear testimony that God is the author of all good things, and that from him alone flows all prosperity. Exceedingly base, therefore, is our ingratitude, if, when God acts kindly towards us, we pass by his benefits with closed eyes.

Chapter 27

1. And it came to pass that when Isaac was old. In this chapter Moses prosecutes, in many words, a history which does not appear to be of great utility. It amounts to this; Esau having gone out, at his father's command, to hunt; Jacob, in his brother's clothing, was, by the artifice of his mother, induced to obtain by stealth the blessing due by the right of nature to the firstborn. It seems even like child's play to present to his father a kid instead of venison, to feign himself to be hairy by putting on skins, and, under the name of his brother, to get the blessing by a lie. But in order to learn that Moses does not in vain pause over this narrative as a most serious matter, we must first observe, that when Jacob received the blessing from his father, this token confirmed to him the oracle by which the Lord had preferred him to his brother. For the benediction here spoken of was not a mere prayer but a legitimate sanction, divinely interposed, to make manifest the grace of election. God had promised to the holy fathers that he would be a God to their seed for ever. They, when at the point of death, in order that the succession might be secured to their posterity, put them in possession, as if they would deliver, from hand to hand, the favour which they had received from God. So Abraham, in blessing his son Isaac, constituted him the heir of spiritual life with a solemn rite. With the same design, Isaac now, being worn down with age, imagines himself to be shortly about to depart this life, and wishes to bless his firstborn son, in order that the everlasting covenant of God may remain in his own family. The Patriarchs did not take this upon themselves rashly, or on their own private account, but were public and

divinely ordained witnesses. For even the faithful were accustomed to bless each other by mutual offices of charity; but the Lord enjoined this peculiar service upon the patriarchs, that they should transmit, as a deposit to posterity, the covenant which he had struck with them, and which they kept during the whole course of their life. The same command was afterwards given to the priests, as appears in Num. 6: 24, and other similar places. Therefore Isaac, in blessing his son, sustained another character than that of a father or of a private person, for he was a prophet and an interpreter of God, who constituted his son an heir of the same grace which he had received.

29. Cursed be every one that curseth thee. These are not bare wishes, such as fathers are wont to utter on behalf of their children, but that promises of God are included in them; for Isaac is the authorized interpreter of God, and the instrument employed by the Holy Spirit; and therefore, as in the person of God, he efficaciously pronounces those accursed who shall oppose the welfare of his son. This then is the confirmation of the promise, by which God, when he receives the faithful under his protection, declares that he will be an enemy to their enemies. The whole force of the benediction turns to this point, that God will prove himself to be a kind father to his servant Jacob in all things, so that he will constitute him the chief and the head of a holy and elect people, will preserve and defend him by his power, and will secure his salvation in the face of enemies of every kind.

37. Behold, I have made him thy Lord. Isaac now more openly confirms what I have before said, that since God was the author of the blessing, it could neither be vain nor evanescent. For he does not here magnificently boast of his dignity, but keeps himself within the bounds and measure of a servant, and denies that he is at liberty to alter anything. For he always considers, (which is the truth,) that when he sustains the character of God's representative, it is not lawful for him to proceed further than the command will bear him. Hence, indeed, Esau ought to have learned from whence he had fallen by his own fault, in order that he might have humbled himself, and might rather have joined himself with his brother, in order to become a partaker of his blessing, as his inferior, than have desired anything separately for himself. But a depraved cupidity carries him away, so that he, forgetful of the kingdom of God, pursues and cares for nothing except his own private advantage.

41. And Esau hated Jacob. It hence appears more clearly, that the tears of Esau were so far from being the effect of true repentance, that they were rather evidences of furious anger. For he is not content with secretly cherishing enmity against his brother, but openly breaks out in wicked threats. And it is evident how deeply malice had struck its roots, when he could indulge himself in the desperate purpose of murdering his brother. Even a profane and sacrilegious contumacy betrays itself in him, seeing that he prepares himself to abolish the decree of God by the sword. I will take care, he says, that Jacob shall not enjoy the inheritance promised to him. What is this but to annihilate the force of the benediction, of which he knew that his father was the herald and the minister?

Chapter 28

3. And God Almighty bless thee. He desires that Jacob should be blessed by God; that is, that he should be so increased and amplified in his own offspring, as to grow into a multitude of nations; or, in other words, that he should produce many people who might combine into one body under the same head; as if he had said, 'Let there arise from thee many tribes, who shall constitute one people.'

10. And Jacob went out. In the course of this history we must especially observe, how the Lord preserved his own Church in the person of one man. For Isaac, on account of his age, lay like a dry trunk; and although the living root of piety was concealed within his breast, yet no hope of further offspring remained in his exhausted and barren old age. Esau, like a green and flourishing branch, had much of show and splendour, but his vigour was only momentary. Jacob, as a severed twig, was removed into a far distant land; not that, being ingrafted or planted there, he should acquire strength and greatness, but that, being moistened with the dew of heaven, he might put forth his shoots as into the air itself. For the Lord wonderfully nourishes him, and supplies him with strength, until he shall bring him back again to his father's house. Meanwhile, let the reader diligently observe, that while he who was blessed by God is cast into exile; occasion of glorying was given to the reprobate Esau, who was left in the possession of everything, so that he might securely reign without a rival. Let us not, then, be disturbed, if at any time the wicked sound their triumphs, as having gained their wishes, while we are oppressed.

12. And he dreamed. Moses here teaches how opportunely, and in the critical moment, the Lord succoured his servant. Three things are here to be noticed in their order; first, that the Lord appeared unto Jacob in a dream; secondly, the nature of the vision as described by Moses; thirdly, the words of the oracle.

Jacob knew that this dream was divinely sent to him, as one differing from common dreams; and this is intimated in the words of Moses,

when he says that God appeared to him in a dream. For Jacob could not see God, nor perceive him present, unless his majesty had been distinguishable by certain marks.

And behold a ladder. Here the form of the vision is related, which is very pertinent to the subject of it; namely, that God manifested himself as seated upon a ladder, the extreme parts of which touched heaven and earth, and which was the vehicle of angels, who descended from heaven upon earth. The angels, to whom is committed the guardianship of the human race, while strenuously applying themselves to their office, yet do not communicate with us in such a way that we become conscious of their presence. It is Christ alone, therefore, who connects heaven and earth: he is the only Mediator who reaches from heaven down to earth: he is the medium through which the fulness of all celestial blessings flows down to us, and through which we, in turn, ascend to God. He it is who, being the head over angels, causes them to minister to his earthly members.

13. I am the Lord God of Abraham. This is the third point which, I said, was to be noticed: for mute visions are cold; therefore the word of the Lord is as the soul which quickens them. The figure, therefore, of the ladder was the inferior appendage of this promise; just as God illustrates and adorns his word by external symbols, that both greater clearness and authority may be added to it. We may therefore observe, that whenever God manifested himself to the fathers, he also spoke, lest a mute vision should have held them in suspense. Under the name 'Jehovah' God teaches that he is the only Creator of the world, that Jacob might not seek after other gods. But since his majesty is in itself incomprehensible, he accommodates himself to the capacity of his servant, by immediately adding, that he is the **God of Abraham and Isaac.** He made a special covenant with Abraham and Isaac, proclaiming himself their God, he recalls his servant Jacob to the true source of faith, and retains him also in his perpetual covenant.

14. And thy seed shall be as the dust of the earth. The sum of the whole is this, Whatever the Lord had promised to Abraham, Jacob transmitted to his sons. Meanwhile it behoved the holy man, in reliance on this divine testimony, to hope against hope; for though the promise was vast and magnificent, yet, wherever Jacob turned himself, no ray of good hope shone upon him. He saw himself a solitary man; no condition better than that of exile presented itself; his return was uncertain and full of danger; but it was profitable for him to be thus left destitute of all means of help, that he might learn to depend on the word of God alone.

15. I am with thee, and will keep thee. God now promptly anticipates the temptation which might steal over the mind of holy Jacob; for though he is, for a time, thrust out into a foreign land, God declares that he will be his keeper until he shall have brought him back again. He then extends his promise still further; saying, that he will never desert him till all things are fulfilled. There was a twofold use of this promise: first, it retained his mind in the faith of the divine covenant; and, secondly, it taught him that it could not be well with him unless he were a partaker of the promised inheritance.

20. And Jacob vowed a vow. The design of this vow was, that Jacob would manifest his gratitude, if God should prove favourable unto him. Thus they offered peace-offerings under the law, to testify their gratitude; and since thanksgiving is a sacrifice of a sweet odour, the Lord declares vows of this nature to be acceptable to him; and therefore we must also have respect to this point, when we are asked what and how it is lawful to vow to God; for some are too fastidious, who would utterly condemn all vows rather than open the door to superstitions.

21. Then shall the Lord be my God. In these words Jacob binds himself never to apostatize from the pure worship of the One God; for there is no doubt that he here comprises the sum of piety.

22. And this stone which I have set for a pillar. This ceremony was an appendage to divine worship; for external rites do not make men true worshippers of God, but are only aids to piety.

Chapter 29

1. Then Jacob went on his journey. Moses now relates the arrival of Jacob in Mesopotamia, and the manner in which he was received by his uncle; and although the narration may seem superfluous, it yet contains nothing but what is useful to be known; for he commends the extraordinary strength of Jacob's faith, when he says, that 'he lifted up his feet' to come into an unknown land. Again, he would have us to consider the providence of God, which caused Jacob to fall in with the shepherds, by whom he was conducted to the home he sought; for this did not happen accidentally, but he was guided by the hidden hand of God to that place; and the shepherds, who were to instruct and confirm him respecting all things, were brought thither at the same time. Therefore, whenever we may wander in uncertainty through intricate windings, we must contemplate, with eyes of faith, the secret providence of God which governs us and our affairs, and leads us to unexpected results.

13. And he told Laban all these things. Since Laban had previously seen one of Abraham's servants replenished with great wealth, an unfavourable opinion of his nephew might instantly enter into his mind: it was therefore necessary for holy Jacob to explain the causes of his own departure, and the reason why he had been sent away so contemptibly clothed. It is also probable that he had been instructed by his mother respecting the signs and marks by which he might convince them of his relationship: therefore Laban exclaims, 'Surely thou art my bone and my flesh;' intimating that he was fully satisfied, and that he was induced by indubitable tokens to acknowledge Jacob as his nephew. This knowledge inclines him to humanity; for the sense of nature dictates that they who are united by ties of blood should endeavour to assist each other; but though the bond between relatives is closer, yet our kindness ought to extend more widely, so that it may diffuse itself through the whole human race.

18. I will serve thee seven years. The iniquity of Laban betrays itself in a moment; for it is a shameful barbarity to give his daughter, by way of reward, in exchange for Jacob's services, making her the subject of a kind of barter. He ought, on the other hand, not only to have assigned a portion to his daughter, but also to have acted more liberally towards his future son-in-law. But under the pretext of affinity, he defrauds him of the reward of his labour, the very thing which he had before acknowledged to be unjust.

25. And he said to Laban. Jacob rightly expostulates respecting the fraud practised upon him. And the answer of Laban, though it is not without a pretext, yet forms no excuse for the fraud. It was not the custom to give the younger daughters in marriage before the elder: and injustice would have been done to the first-born by disturbing this accustomed order. But he ought not, on that account, craftily to have betrothed Rachel to Jacob, and then to have substituted Leah in her place. He should rather have cautioned Jacob himself, in time, to turn his thoughts to Leah, or else to refrain from marriage with either of them. But we may learn from this, that wicked and deceitful men, when once they have turned aside from truth, make no end of transgressing: meanwhile, they always put forward some pretext for the purpose of freeing themselves from blame.

31. And when the Lord saw. Moses here shows that Jacob's extravagant love was corrected by the Lord; as the affections of the faithful, when they become inordinate, are wont to be tamed by the rod. Rachel is loved, not without wrong to her sister, to whom due honour is not given. The Lord, therefore, interposes as her vindicator, and, by a suitable remedy, turns the mind of Jacob into that direction, to which it had been most averse. This passage teaches us, that offspring is a special gift of God; since the power of rendering one fertile, and of cursing the womb of the other with barrenness, is expressly ascribed to him.

32. She called his name Reuben. Moses relates that Leah was not ungrateful to God. And truly, I do not doubt, that the benefits of God were then commonly more appreciated than they are now. For a profane stupor so occupies the mind of nearly all men, that, like cattle, they swallow up whatever benefits God, in his kindness, bestows upon them. Further, Leah not only acknowledges God as the author of her fruitfulness; but also assigns as a reason, that her affliction had been looked upon by the Lord, and a son had been given her who should draw the affection of her husband to herself. Whence it appears probable, that when she saw herself despised, she had recourse to prayer, in order that she might receive more succour from heaven. For thanksgiving is a proof that persons have previously exercised themselves in prayer; since they who hope for nothing from God do, by their indolence, bury in oblivion all the favours he has conferred upon them. Therefore, Leah inscribed on the person of her son a memorial whereby she might stir herself up to offer praise to God. This passage also teaches, that they who are unjustly despised by men are regarded by the Lord.

Chapter 30

1. And when Rachel saw. Here Moses begins to relate that Jacob was distracted with domestic strifes. But although the Lord was punishing him, because he had been guilty of no light sin in marrying two wives, and especially sisters; yet the chastisement was paternal; and God himself, seeing that he is wont mercifully to pardon his own people, restrained in some degree his hand. Whence also it happened, that Jacob did not immediately repent, but added new offenses to the former. But first we must speak of Rachel. Whereas she rejoiced to see her sister subjected to contempt and grief, the Lord represses this sinful joy, by giving his blessing to Leah, in order to make the condition of both of them equal. She hears the grateful acknowledgment of her sister, and learns from the names given to the four sons, that God had pitied, and had sustained by his favour, her who had been unjustly despised by man. Nevertheless envy inflames her, and will not suffer anything of the dignity becoming a wife to appear in her. We see what ambition can do. For Rachel, in seeking preeminence, does not spare even her own sister; and scarcely refrains from venting her anger against God, for having honoured that sister with the gift of fruitfulness. Her emulation did not proceed from any injuries that she

had received, but because she could not bear to have a partner and an equal, though she herself was really the younger. What would she have done had she been provoked, seeing that she envies her sister who was contented with her lot? Now Moses, by exhibiting this evil in Rachel, would teach us that it is inherent in all; in order that each of us, tearing it up by the roots, may vigilantly purify himself from it. That we may be cured of envy, it behoves us to put away pride and self-love.

2. And Jacob's anger was kindled. The tenderness of Jacob's affection rendered him unwilling to offend his wife; yet her unworthy conduct compelled him to do so, when he saw her petulantly exalt herself, not only against her sister, who piously, homily, and thankfully was enjoying the gifts of God; but even against God himself.

5. And Bilhah conceived. It is wonderful that God should have deigned to honour an adulterous connexion with offspring: but he does sometimes thus strive to overcome by kindness the wickedness of men, and pursues the unworthy with his favour. Moreover, he does not always make the punishment equal to the offenses of his people, nor does he always rouse them, alike quickly, from their torpor, but waits for the matured season of correction.

15. Is it a small matter that thou hast taken my husband? Moses leaves more for his readers to reflect upon than he expresses in words; namely, that Jacob's house had been filled with contentions and strifes. For Leah speaks haughtily, because her mind had been long so exasperated that she could not address herself mildly and courteously to her sister. Perhaps the sisters were not thus contentious by nature; but God suffered them to contend with each other, that the punishment of polygamy might be exhibited to posterity.

17. And God hearkened unto Leah. Moses expressly declares this, in order that we may know how indulgently God dealt with that family. For who would have thought, that, while Leah was hatefully denying to her sister the fruits gathered by her boy, and was purchasing, by the price of those fruits, a night with her husband, there would be any place for prayers? Moses, therefore, teaches us, that pardon was granted for these faults, to prove that the Lord would not fail to complete his work notwithstanding such great infirmity.

22. And God remembered Rachel. Since with God nothing is either before or after, but all things are present, he is subject to no forgetfulness, so that, in the lapse of time, he should need to be reminded of what is past. But the Scripture describes the presence and memory of God from the effect produced upon ourselves, because we conceive him to be such as he appears to be by his acts. Moreover, whether Rachel's child was born the last of all, cannot with certainty be gathered from the words of Moses.

29. Thou knowest how I have served thee. This answer of Jacob is not intended to increase the amount of his wages; but he would expostulate with Laban, and would charge him with acting unjustly and unkindly in requiring a prolongation of the time of service. There is also no doubt that he is carried forth, with every desire of his mind, towards the land of Canaan. Therefore a return thither was, in his view, preferable to any kind of riches whatever. Yet, in the meantime, he indirectly accuses his father-in-law, both of cunning and of inhumanity, in order that he may extort something from him, if he must remain longer.

43. And the man increased exceedingly. Moses added this for the purpose of showing that he was not made thus suddenly rich without a miracle. We shall see hereafter how great his wealth was. For being entirely destitute, he yet gathered out of nothing, greater riches than any man of moderate wealth could do in twenty or thirty years. And that no one may deem this fabulous, as not being in accordance with the usual method, Moses meets the objection by saying, that the holy man was enriched in an extraordinary manner.

Chapter 31

1. And he heard the words. Although Jacob ardently desired his own country, and was continually thinking of his return to it; yet his admirable patience appears in this, that he suspends his purpose till a new occasion presents itself. I do not, however, deny that some imperfection was mixed with this virtue, in that he did not make more haste to return; but that the promise of God was always retained in his mind will shortly appear. In this respect, however, he showed something of human nature, that for the sake of obtaining wealth he postponed his return for six years: for when Laban was perpetually changing his terms, he might justly have bidden him farewell. But that he was detained by force and fear together, we infer from his clandestine flight. Now, at least, he has a sufficient cause for asking his dismissal; because his riches had become grievous and hateful to the sons of Laban: nevertheless he does not dare openly to withdraw himself from their enmity, but is compelled to flee secretly. Yet though his tardiness is in some degree excusable, it was probably connected with indolence; even as the faithful, when they direct their course towards God, often do not pursue it with becoming fervour. Wherefore, whenever the indolence of the flesh retards us, let us learn to fan the ardour of our spirits into a flame.

13. I am the God of Bethel. It is not wonderful that the angel should assume the person of God: either because God the Father appeared to the holy patriarchs in his own Word, as in a lively mirror, and that under the form of an angel; or because angels, speaking by the command of God, rightly utter their words, as from his mouth. For the prophets are accustomed to this form of speaking; not that they may exalt themselves into the place of God; but only that the majesty of God, whose ministers they are, may shine forth in his message. Now, it is proper that we should more carefully consider the force of this form of expression. He does not call himself **the God of Bethel,** because he is confined within the limits of a given place, but for the purpose of renewing to his servant the remembrance of his own promise; for holy Jacob had not yet attained to that degree of perfection which rendered the more simple rudiments unnecessary for him. But little light of true doctrine at that time prevailed; and even that was wrapped in many shadows. Nearly the whole world had apostatized to false gods; and that region, nay, even the house of his father-in-law, was filled with unholy superstitions. Therefore, amid so many hindrances, nothing was more difficult for him than to hold his faith in the one true God firm and invincible. Wherefore, pure religion is commended to him, in order that, among the various errors of the world, he may adhere to the obedience and worship of that God whom he had once known.

19. And Rachel had stolen. Although the Hebrews sometimes call those images 'seraphim,' which are not set forth as objects of worship: yet since this term is commonly used in an ill sense, I do not doubt that they were the household gods of Laban. Even he himself, shortly afterwards, expressly calls them his gods. It appears hence how great is the propensity of the human mind to idolatry: since in all ages this evil has prevailed; namely, that men seek out for themselves visible representations of God. From the death of Noah not yet two hundred years had elapsed; Shem had departed but a little while before; his teaching, handed down by tradition, ought most of all to have flourished among the posterity of Terah; because the Lord had chosen this family to himself, as the only sanctuary on earth in which he was to be worshipped in purity. The voice of Shem himself was sounding in their ears until the death of Abraham; yet now, from Terah himself, the common filth of superstition inundated this place, while the patriarch Shem was still living and speaking. And though there is no doubt that he endeavoured, with all his power, to bring back his descendants to a right mind, we see what was his success.

Why did she not, after her departure, explain to her husband what she had done? But there is no need of conjecture, since, from the sequel of the history, it is manifest that the house of Jacob was polluted with idols, even to the time of the violation of Dinah. It was not, then, the piety of Rachel, but her insane hankering after superstition which impelled her to the theft: because she thought that God could not be worshipped but through idols; for this is the source of the disease, that since men are carnal, they imagine God to be carnal too.

20. And Jacob stole away unawares to Laban. By the Hebrew form of expression, 'stole away the heart of Laban,' Moses shows that Jacob departed privately, or by stealth, unknown to his father-in-law.

32. That Rachel had stolen them. Moses relates the manner in which Rachel had concealed her theft; namely, by sitting on the idols, and pretending the custom of women as her excuse. It is a question, whether she did this through shame or pertinacity. It was disgraceful to be caught in the act of theft; she also dreaded the severe sentence of her husband. Yet to me it appears probable that fear did not so much influence her as the obstinate love of idolatry. For we know how greatly superstition infatuates the mind. Therefore, as if she had obtained an incomparable treasure, she thinks that she must attempt anything rather than allow herself to be deprived of it. Moreover, she chooses rather to incur the displeasure of her father and her husband, than to relinquish the object of her superstition. To her stratagem she also adds lying words, so that she deserves manifold censure.

44. Let us make a covenant, I and thou. Laban here acts as men conscious of guilt are wont to do, when they wish to guard themselves against revenge: and this kind of trepidation and anxiety is the just reward of evil deeds. Besides, wicked men always judge of others from their own disposition: whence it happens that they have fears on all sides.

53. The God of Abraham. It is indeed rightly and properly done, that Laban should adjure Jacob by the name of God. For this is the confirmation of covenants; to appeal to God on both sides, that he may not suffer perfidy to pass unpunished. But he sinfully blends idols with the true God, between whom there is nothing in common. Thus, truly, men involved in superstitions, are accustomed to confound promiscuously sacred things with profane, and the figments of men with the true God. He is compelled to give some honour to the God of Abraham, yet he lies plunged in his own idolatrous pollution; and, that his religion may not appear the worse, he gives it the colour of antiquity.

55. And blessed them. The character of the person is here to be noticed, because Laban, who had lapsed from true piety, and was a man of unholy and wicked manners, yet retained the habit of giving his blessing. For we are hereby taught, that certain principles of divine knowledge remain in the hearts of the wicked, so that no excuse may be left to them on the ground of ignorance; for the custom of pronouncing a blessing arises hence, that men are certainly persuaded that God alone is the author of all good things.

Chapter 32

1. And Jacob went on his way. After Jacob has escaped from the hands of his father-in-law, that is, from present death, he meets with his brother, whose cruelty was as much, or still more, to be dreaded; for by the threats of this brother he had been driven from his country; and now no better prospect lies before him. He therefore proceeds with trepidation, as one who goes to the slaughter. Seeing, however, it was scarcely possible but that he should sink oppressed by grief, the Lord affords him timely succour; and prepares him for this conflict, as well as for others, in such a manner that he should stand forth a brave and invincible champion in them all. Therefore, that he may know himself to be defended by the guardianship of God, angels go forth to meet him, arranged in ranks on both sides.

7. And he divided the people. Moses relates that Jacob formed his plans according to the existing state of affairs. He divides his family into two parts, and puts his maids in the foremost place, that they may bear the first assault, if necessary; but he places his free wives further from the danger. Hence indeed we gather, that Jacob was not so overcome with fear as to be unable to arrange his plans. We know that when a panic seizes the mind, it is deprived of discretion; and they who ought to look after their own concerns, become stupid and inanimate. Therefore it proceeded from the spirit of faith that Jacob interposed a certain space between the two parts of his family, in order that if any destruction approached, the whole seed of the Church might not perish. For by this scheme, he offered the half of his family to the slaughter, that, at length, the promised inheritance might come to the remainder who survived.

9. O God of my father Abraham. Having arranged his affairs as the necessity of the occasion suggested, he now retakes himself to prayer. And this prayer is evidence that the holy man was not so oppressed with fear as to prevent faith from proving victorious. For he does not, in a hesitating manner, commend himself and his family to God; but trusting both to God's promises and to the benefits already received, he casts his cares and his troubles into his heavenly Father's heart.

11. Deliver me. After he has declared himself to be bound by so many of God's benefits that he cannot boast of his own merits, and thus raised his mind to higher expectation, he now mentions his own necessity, as if he would say, 'O Lord, unless thou choosest to reduce so many excellent gifts to nothing, now is the time for thee to succour one, and to avert the destruction which, through my brother, is suspended over me.'

24. There wrestled a man with him. Although this vision was particularly useful to Jacob himself, to teach him beforehand that many conflicts awaited him, and that he might certainly conclude that he should be the conqueror in them all; there is yet not the least doubt that the Lord exhibited, in his person, a specimen of the temptations – common to all his people – which await them, and must be constantly submitted to, in this transitory life. Wherefore it is right to keep in view this design of the vision, which is to represent all the servants of God in this world as wrestlers; because the Lord exercises them with various kinds of conflicts. Moreover, it is not said that Satan, or any mortal man, wrestled with Jacob, but God himself: to teach us that our faith is tried by him; and whenever we are tempted, our business is truly with him, not only because we fight under his auspices, but because he, as an antagonist, descends into the arena to try our strength. This, though at first sight it seems absurd, experience and reason teaches us to be true. For as all prosperity flows from his goodness, so adversity is either the rod with which he corrects our sins, or the test of our faith and patience. And since there is no kind of temptations by which God does not try his faithful people, the similitude is very suitable, which represents him as coming, hand to hand, to combat with them. Therefore, what was once exhibited under a visible form to our father Jacob, is daily fulfilled in the individual members of the Church; namely, that, in their temptations, it is necessary for them to wrestle with God. He is said, indeed, to tempt us in a different manner from Satan; but because he alone is the Author of our crosses and afflictions, and he alone creates light and darkness, (as is declared in Isaiah,) he is said to tempt us when he makes a trial of our faith.

25. And when he saw that he prevailed not against him. Here is described to us the victory of Jacob, which, however, was not gained without a wound. In saying that the wrestling angel, or God, wished to retire from the contest, because he saw he should not prevail, Moses speaks after the manner of men. For we know that God, when he descends from his majesty to us, is wont to transfer the properties of human nature to himself.

28. Thy name shall be called no more Jacob. Jacob received his name from his mother's womb, because he had seized the heel of his brother's foot, and had attempted to hold him back. God now gives him a new and more honourable name; not that he may entirely abolish the other, which was a token of memorable grace, but that he may testify a still higher progress of his grace.

Chapter 33

1. And Jacob lifted up his eyes. We have said how greatly Jacob feared for himself from his brother; but now when Esau himself approaches, his terror is not only renewed, but increased. For although he goes forth like a courageous and spirited combatant to this contest, he is still not exempt from a sense of danger; whence it follows, that he is not free, either from anxiety or fear. For his cruel brother had still the same cause of hatred against him as before. And it was not probable, that, after he had left his father's house, and had been living as he pleased, he had become more mild. Therefore, as in a doubtful affair, and one of great danger, Jacob placed his wives and children in the order described; that, if Esau should attempt anything hostile, the whole seed might not perish, but part might have time for flight.

4. And Esau ran to meet him. That Esau meets his brother with unexpected benevolence and kindness, is the effect of the special favour of God. Therefore, by this method, God proved that he has the hearts of men in his hand, to soften their hardness, and to mitigate their cruelty as often as he pleases: in short, that he tames them as wild beasts are wont to be tamed; and then, that he hearkened to the prayers of his servant Jacob.

20. And he erected there an altar. Jacob having obtained a place in which he might provide for his family, set up the solemn service of God; as Moses before testified concerning Abraham and Isaac. For although, in every place, they gave themselves up to the pure worship of God in prayers and other acts of devotion; nevertheless they did not neglect the external confession of piety, whenever the Lord granted them any fixed place in which they might remain.

Chapter 34

1. And Dinah … went out. This chapter records a severe contest, with which God again exercised his servant. How precious the chastity of his daughter would be to him, we may readily conjecture from the probity of his whole life. When therefore he heard that she was violated, this disgrace would inflict the deepest wound of grief upon his mind: yet soon his grief is trebled, when he hears that his sons, from the desire of revenge, have committed a most dreadful crime. But let us examine everything in order. Dinah is ravished, because, having left her father's house, she wandered about more freely than was proper. She ought to have remained quietly at home.

3. And his soul clave unto Dinah. Moses intimates that she was not so forcibly violated, that Shechem having once abused her, treated her with contempt, as is usual with harlots; for he loved her as a wife; and did not even object to be circumcised that he might have her; but the fervour of lust had so prevailed, that he first subjected her to disgrace. And therefore although he embraced Dinah with real and sincere attachment, yet, in this want of self-government, he grievously sinned.

25. Simeon and Levi, Dinah's brethren. Although Moses names only two authors of the slaughter, it does not appear to me probable that they came alone, but that they were the leaders of the troop: for Jacob had a large family, and it might be that they called some of their brothers to join them; yet, because the affair was conducted by their counsel and direction, it is ascribed to them. There is no reader who does not readily perceive how dreadful and execrable was this crime. One man only had sinned, and he endeavoured to compensate for the injury, by many acts of kindness; but the cruelty of Simeon and Levi could only be satiated by the destruction of the whole city; and, under the pretext of a covenant, they form a design against friends and hospitable persons, in a time of peace, which would have been deemed intolerable against enemies in open war. Hence we perceive how mercifully God dealt with that people; seeing that, from the posterity of a sanguinary man, and even of a wicked robber, he raised up a priesthood for himself.

30. And Jacob said. Moses declares that the crime was condemned by the holy man, lest any one should think that he had participated in their counsel.

Chapter 35

1 And God said unto Jacob. Moses relates that when Jacob had been reduced to the last extremity, God came to his help in the right time, and as at the critical juncture. And thus he shows, in the person of one man, that God never deserts his Church which he has once embraced, but will procure its salvation. We must, however, observe the order of his procedure; for God did not immediately appear to his servant, but suffered him first to be tormented by grief and excessive cares, that he might learn patience, deferring his consolation to the time of extreme necessity. Certainly the condition of Jacob was then most miserable. For all, on every side, might be so incensed against him that he

would be surrounded with as many deaths as there were neighbouring nations: and he was not so stupid as to be insensible of his danger. God suffered the holy man to be thus tossed with cares and tormented with troubles, until, by a kind of resurrection, he restored him, as one half-dead.

5. And the terror of God was upon the cities. It now manifestly appears that deliverance was not in vain promised to the holy man by God; since, amidst so many hostile swords, he goes forth not only in safety but undisturbed. By the destruction of the Shechemites all the neighbouring people were inflamed with enmity against a single family; yet no one moves to take vengeance. The reason is explained by Moses, that the terror of God had fallen upon them, which repressed their violent assaults. Hence we may learn that the hearts of men are in the hands of God; that he can inspire those with fortitude who in themselves are weak; and, on the other hand, soften their iron-hardness whenever he pleases.

9. And God appeared unto Jacob. Moses, having introduced a few words on the death of Deborah, recites a second vision, by which Jacob was confirmed, after his return to Bethel. Once, in this place, God had appeared unto him, when he was on his way into Mesopotamia. In the meantime God had testified in various methods, as need required, that he would be present with him everywhere through his whole journey; but now he is brought back again to that very place where a more illustrious and memorable oracle had been given him, in order that he may receive again a new confirmation of his faith. The blessing of God here means nothing else than his promise; for though men pray for blessings on each other; God declares himself to be the sole Dispenser of perfect happiness.

10. Thy name shall not be called any more Jacob. We have before given the meaning of these words. The former name is not abolished, but the dignity of the other, which was afterwards put upon him, is preferred: for he was called Jacob from the womb, because he had strongly wrestled with his brother; but he was afterwards called Israel, because he entered into contest with God, and obtained the victory; not that he had prevailed by his own power, (for he had borrowed courage and strength and arms from God alone,) but because it was the Lord's will freely to confer upon him this honor. He therefore speaks comparatively, showing that the name Jacob is obscure and ignoble when compared with the name Israel.

11. I am God Almighty. God here, as elsewhere, proclaims his own might, in order that Jacob may the more certainly rely on his faithfulness. He then promises that he will cause

Jacob to increase and multiply, not only into one nation, but into a multitude of nations.

28. And the days of Isaac. When it is said, that he died old, and full of days, the meaning is, that, having fulfilled the course of his life, he departed by a mature death; this, therefore, is ascribed to the blessing of God. Nevertheless, I refer these words not merely to the duration of his life, but also to the state of his feelings; implying that Isaac, being satisfied with life, willingly and placidly departed out of the world. For we may see certain decrepit old men, who are not less desirous of life than they were in the flower of their age; and with one foot in the grave, they still have a horror of death. Therefore, though long life is reckoned among the blessings of God; yet it is not enough for men to be able to count up a great number of years; unless they feel that they have lived long, and, being satisfied with the favour of God and with their own age, prepare themselves for their departure.

Chapter 36

1. Now these are the generations of Esau. Though Esau was an alien from the Church in the sight of God; yet since he also, as a son of Isaac, was favored with a temporal blessing, Moses celebrates his race, and inscribes a sufficiently lengthened catalogue of the people born from him. This commemoration, however, resembles an honorable sepulture. For although Esau, with his posterity, took the precedence; yet this dignity was like a bubble, which is comprised under the figure of the world, and which quickly perishes.

9. And these are the generations of Esau, the father of the Edomites. Though Esau had two names, yet in this place the second name refers to his posterity, who are called Idumeans. For, to make it appear what God had bestowed upon him for the sake of his father Isaac, Moses expressly calls him the father of a celebrated and famous people. And certainly, it served this purpose not a little, to trace the effect and fulfillment of the prophecy in the progeny of Esau. For if the promise of God so mightily flourished towards a stranger, how much more powerfully would it put itself forth towards the children, to whom pertaineth the adoption, and consequently the inheritance of grace?

24. This was that Anah that found the mules. Mules are the adulterous offspring of the horse and the ass. Moses says that Anah was the author of this connection.

31. These are the kings that reigned. We must keep in memory that reprobates are suddenly exalted, that they may immediately fall, like the herb upon the roofs, which is destitute of root, and has a hasty growth, but withers the more quickly. To the two sons of Isaac had been promised the honour that kings should spring from them. The Idumeans first began to reign, and thus the condition of Israel seemed to be inferior. But at length, lapse of time taught how much better it is, by creeping on the ground, to strike the roots deep, than to acquire an extravagant pre-eminence for a moment, which speedily vanishes away.

Chapter 37

1. And Jacob dwelt. Moses confirms what he had before declared, that, by the departure of Esau, the land was left to holy Jacob as its sole possessor. Although in appearance he did not obtain a single clod; yet, contented with the bare sight of the land, he exercised his faith; and Moses expressly compares him with his father, who had been a stranger in that land all his life. Therefore, though by the removal of his brother to another abode, Jacob was no little gainer; yet it was the Lord's will that this advantage should be hidden from his eyes, in order that he might depend entirely upon the promise.

2. These are the generations of Jacob. By the word *toledoth* we are not so much to understand a genealogy, as a record of events, which appears more clearly from the context. For Moses having thus commenced, does not enumerate sons and grandsons, but explains the cause of the envy of Joseph's brethren, who formed a wicked conspiracy against him, and sold him as a slave: as if he had said 'Having briefly summed up the genealogy of Esau, I now revert to the series of my history, as to what happened to the family of Jacob.'

5. And Joseph dreamed a dream. Moses having stated what were the first seeds of this enmity, now ascends higher, and shows that Joseph had been elected, by the wonderful purpose of God, to great things; that this had been declared to him in a dream; and that, therefore, the hatred of his brethren broke forth into madness. God, however, revealed in dreams what he would do, that afterwards it might be known that nothing had happened fortuitously: but that what had been fixed by a celestial decree, was at length, in its proper time, carried forward through circuitous windings to its completion.

9. And he dreamed yet another dream. The scope of this dream is the same. The only difference is, that God, to inspire greater confidence in the oracle, presents him with a figure from heaven. The brethren of Joseph had despised what was said concerning the sheaves; the Lord now calls upon them to look towards heaven, where his august Majesty shines forth.

18. And when they saw him afar off. Here again Moses, so far from sparing the fame of his own family by adulation, brands its chiefs with a mark of eternal infamy, and exposes them to the hatred and execration of all nations. If, at any time, among heathens, a brother murdered his brother, such impiety was treated with the utmost severity in tragedies, that it might not pass into an example for imitation. But in profane history no such thing is found, as that nine brethren should conspire together for the destruction of an innocent youth, and, like wild beasts, should pounce upon him with bloody hands. Therefore a horrible, and even diabolical fury, took possession of the sons of Jacob, when, having cast aside the sense of nature, they were thus prepared cruelly to rage against their own blood.

20. And cast him into some pit. Before they perpetrate the murder, they seek a pretext whereby they may conceal their crime from men. Meanwhile, it never enters into their mind, that what is hidden from men cannot escape the eyes of God. But so stupid is hypocrisy, that while it flees from the disgrace of the world, it is careless about the judgment of God. But it is a disease deeply rooted in the human mind, to put some specious colour on every extreme act of iniquity. For although an inward judge convicts the guilty, they yet confirm themselves in impudence, that their disgrace may not appear unto others.

And we shall see what will become of his dreams. As if the truth of God could be subverted by the death of one man, they boast that they shall have attained their wish when they have killed their brother; namely, that his dreams will come to nothing.

21. And Reuben heard it. It may be well to observe, while others were hastening to shed his blood, by whose care Joseph was preserved. Reuben alone, having a regard to piety, and being mindful of fraternal duty, dissolves the impious conspiracy.

23. They stripped Joseph out of his coat. We see that these men are full of fictions and lies. They carelessly strip their brother; they feel no dread at casting him with their own hands into the pit, where hunger worse than ten swords might consume him; because they hope their crime will be concealed; and in taking home his clothes, no suspicion of his murder would be excited; because, truly, their father would believe that he had been torn by a wild beast.

36. And the Midianites sold him into Egypt. It was a sad spectacle, that Joseph should be thus driven from one hand to another. For it added no small indignity to his former suffering, that he is set to sale as a slave. The Lord, however, ceased not to care for him. He even suffered him to be transferred from hand to hand, in order that, at length, it might indeed appear, that he had come, by celestial guidance, to that very dominion which had been promised him in his dreams.

Chapter 38

1. And it came to pass at that time, that Judah. Before Moses proceeds in relating the history of Joseph, he inserts the genealogy of Judah, to which he devotes more labour, because the Redeemer was thence to derive his origin; for the continuous history of that tribe, from which salvation was to be bought, could not remain unknown, without loss. We may notice; first, that peculiar honour was given to the tribe of Judah, which had been divinely elected as the source whence the salvation of the world should flow; and secondly, that the narration of Moses is by no means honorable to the persons of whom he speaks; so that the Jews have no right to arrogate anything to themselves or to their fathers.

8. Go in unto thy brother's wife. Although no law had hitherto been prescribed concerning brother's marriages, that the surviving brother should raise up seed to one who was dead; it is, nevertheless, not wonderful that, by the mere instinct of nature, men should have been inclined to this course. For since each man is born for the preservation of the whole race, if any one dies without children, there seems to be here some defect of nature. It was deemed therefore an act of humanity to acquire some name for the dead, from which it might appear that they had lived.

13. And it was told Tamar. Moses relates how Tamar avenged herself for the injury done her. She did not at first perceive the fraud, but discovered it after a long course of time. When Shelah had grown up, finding herself deceived, she turned her thoughts to revenge. And it is not to be doubted that she had long meditated, and, as it were, hatched this design. For the message respecting Judah's departure was not brought to her accidentally; but, because she was intent upon her purpose, she had set spies who should bring her an account of all his doings. Now, although she formed a plan which was base, and unworthy of a modest woman, yet this circumstance is some alleviation of her crime, that she did not desire a connection with Judah, except while in a state of celibacy. In the meantime, she is hurried, by a blind error of mind, into another crime, not less detestable than adultery. For, by adultery, conjugal fidelity would have been violated; but, by this incestuous intercourse, the whole dignity of nature is subverted. This ought carefully to be observed, that they who are injured should not hastily rush to unlawful remedies.

24. And it came to pass about three months after. Tamar might sooner have exposed the crime; but she waited till she should be demanded for capital punishment; for then she would have stronger ground for expostulation.

The reason why Judah subjects his daughter-in-law to a punishment so severe, was, that he deemed her guilty of adultery: for what the Lord afterwards confirmed by his law, appears then to have prevailed by custom among men, that a maid, from the time of her espousals, should be strictly faithful to her husband.

Chapter 39

1. And Joseph was brought down. For the purpose of connecting it with the remaining part of the history, Moses repeats what he had briefly touched upon, that Joseph had been sold to Potiphar the Egyptian: he then subjoins that God was with Joseph, so that he prospered in all things. For although it often happens that all things proceed with wicked men according to their wish, whom God nevertheless does not bless with his favour; still the sentiment is true and the expression of it proper, that it is never well with men, except so far as the Lord shows himself to be gracious to them. For he vouchsafes his blessing, for a time, even to reprobates, with whom he is justly angry, in order that he may gently invite and even allure them to repentance; and may render them more inexcusable, if they remain obstinate; meanwhile, he curses their felicity.

3. And his master saw. The grace of God shone forth in Joseph, in no common or usual manner; since it became thus manifest to a man who was a heathen, and, in this respect, blind. **The Lord made all that he did to prosper in his hand.** This was a wonderful method of procedure, that the entire blessing by which the Lord was pleased to testify his paternal love towards Joseph, should turn to the gain of the Egyptians.

7. Lie with me. Moses only briefly touches upon the chief points, and the sum of the things he relates. For there is no doubt that this impure woman endeavoured, by various arts, to allure the pious youth, and that she insinuated herself by indirect blandishments, before she broke forth to such a shameless kind of license. But Moses, omitting other things, shows that she had been pushed so far by base lust, as not to shrink from openly soliciting a connection with Joseph. Now as this filthiness is a signal proof that carnal lust acts from blind and furious impulses; so, in the person of Joseph, an admirable example of fidelity and continence is set before us.

20. And put him into the prison. Though Moses does not state with what degree of severity Joseph was afflicted at the beginning of his imprisonment, yet we readily gather that he was not allowed any liberty, but was thrust into some obscure dungeon. The authority of Potiphar was paramount; he had the keeper of the prison under his power, and at his disposal. What clemency could be hoped for from a man who was jealous and carried away with the vehemence of his anger?

21. But the Lord was with Joseph. Moses says this because he extended this grace or mercy towards him; whence we may learn, that God, even when he delivers us from unjust violence, or when he assists us in a good cause, is yet induced to do so by his own goodness. For since we are unworthy that he should grant us his help, the cause of its communication must be in himself; seeing that he is merciful. Certainly if merits, which should lay God under obligation, are to be sought for in men, they would have been found in Joseph; yet Moses declares that he was assisted by the gratuitous favour of God.

Chapter 40

1. And it came to pass after these things. We have already seen, that when Joseph was in bonds, God cared for him. For whence arose the relaxation afforded him, but from the divine favour? Therefore, God, before he opened the door for his servant's deliverance, entered into the very prison to sustain him with his strength. But a far more illustrious benefit follows; for he is not only liberated from prison, but exalted to the highest degree of honour. In the meantime, the providence of God led the holy man through wonderful and most intricate paths. The butler and baker of the king are cast into the prison; Joseph expounds to them their dreams. Restoration to his office having been promised to the butler, some light of hope beams upon the holy captive; for the butler agreed, after he should have returned to his post, to become the advocate for Joseph's pardon. But, again, that hope was speedily cut off, when the butler failed to speak a word to the king on behalf of the miserable captive. Joseph, therefore, seemed to himself to be buried in perpetual oblivion, until the Lord again suddenly rekindles the light which had been smothered, and almost extinguished. Thus, when he might have delivered the holy man directly from prison, he chose to lead him around by circuitous paths, the better to prove his patience, and to manifest, by the mode of his deliverance, that he has wonderful methods of working, hidden from our view. He does this that we may learn not to measure, by our own sense, the salvation which he has promised us; but that we may suffer ourselves to be turned hither or thither by his hand, until he shall have performed his work.

5. And they dreamed a dream. Many frivolous things are presented to us, which pass away and are forgotten; some, however, have the force and significance of prophecy. Of this kind were these two dreams, by which God made known the hidden result of a future matter. For unless the mark of a celestial oracle had been engraven upon them, the butler and the baker would not have been in such consternation of mind.

23. Yet did not the chief butler remember. This was the most severe trial of Joseph's patience. For since he had obtained an advocate who, without trouble, was able to extricate him from prison, especially as the opportunity of doing so had been granted to him by God, he felt a certain assurance of deliverance, and earnestly waited for it every hour. But when he had remained to the end of the second year in suspense, not only did this hope vanish, but greater despair than ever rested upon his mind. Therefore, we are all taught, in his person, that nothing is more improper, than to prescribe the time in which God shall help us; since he purposely, for a long season, keeps his own people in anxious suspense, that, by this very experiment, they may truly know what it is to trust in Him. Besides, in this manner he designed openly to claim for himself the glory of Joseph's liberation.

Chapter 41

1. At the end of two full years. What anxiety oppressed the mind of the holy man during this time, each of us may conjecture from his own feeling; for we are so tender and effeminate, that we can scarcely bear to be put off for a short time. The Lord exercised his servant not only by a delay of long continuance, but also by another kind of temptation, because he took all human grounds of hope away from him. In the king's dream, this is worthy to be observed in the first place, that God sometimes deigns to present his oracles even to unbelieving and profane men. It was certainly a singular honour to be instructed concerning an event yet fourteen years future: for truly the will of God was manifested to Pharaoh, just as if he had been taught by the word, except that the interpretation of it was to be sought elsewhere. And although God designs his word especially for the Church, yet it ought not to be deemed absurd that he sometimes admits even aliens into his school, though for an inferior end. The doctrine which leads to the hope of eternal life belongs to the Church; while the children of this world are only taught, incidentally, concerning the state of the present life. If we observe this distinction, we shall not wonder that some oracles are common to profane and heathen men, though the Church possesses the spiritual doctrine of life, as the treasure of its own inheritance.

8. In the morning his spirit was troubled. A sting was left in Pharaoh's heart, that he might know that he had to deal with God; for this anxiety was as an inward seal of the Spirit of God, to give authenticity to the dream; although Pharaoh deserved to be deprived of the advantage of this revelation, when he resorted to magicians and soothsayers, who were wont to turn the truth of God into a lie.

14. Then Pharaoh sent and called Joseph. We see in the person of a proud king, as in a glass, what necessity can effect. They whose circumstances are happy and prosperous will scarcely condescend to hear those whom they esteem true prophets, still less will they listen to strangers. Wherefore it was necessary that the obstinacy of Pharaoh should be first subdued, in order that he might send for Joseph, and accept him as his master and instructor.

16. God shall give Pharaoh an answer of peace. Joseph added this from the kindly feeling of his heart; for he did not yet comprehend what the nature of the oracle would be. Therefore he could not, in his character as a prophet, promise a successful and desirable issue; but, as it was his duty sincerely to deliver what he received from the Lord, however sad and severe it might prove; so, on the other hand, this liberty presented no obstacle to his wishing a joyful issue to the king.

40. Thou shalt be over my house. Not only is Joseph made governor of Egypt, but is adorned also with the insignia of royalty, that all may reverence him, and may obey his command. The royal signet is put upon his finger for the confirmation of decrees. He is clothed in robes of fine linen, which were then a luxury, and were not to be had at any common price. He is placed in the most honorable chariot. It may, however, be asked, whether it was lawful for the holy man to appear with so great pomp? I answer, although such splendor can scarcely ever be free from blame, and therefore frugality in external ornaments is best; yet all kind of splendor in kings and other princes of the world is not to be condemned, provided they neither too earnestly desire it, nor make an ostentatious display of it.

50. And unto Joseph were born two sons. Although the names which Joseph gave his sons in consequence of the issue of his affairs, breathe somewhat of piety, because in them he celebrates the kindness of God: yet the oblivion of his father's house, which, he says, had been brought upon him, can scarcely be altogether excused. It was a pious and holy motive to gratitude, that God had caused him to 'forget' all his former miseries; but no honour ought to have been so highly valued, as to displace from his mind the desire and the remembrance of his father's house.

Chapter 42

1. Now when Jacob saw. Moses begins, in this chapter, to treat of the occasion which drew Jacob with his whole family into Egypt; and thus leaves it to us to consider by what hidden and unexpected methods God may perform whatever he has decreed. Though, therefore, the providence of God is in itself a labyrinth; yet when we connect the issue of things with their beginnings, that admirable method of operation shines clearly in our view, which is not generally acknowledged, only because it is far removed from our observation.

6. And Joseph was the governor over the land. Moses connects the honour of Joseph with his fidelity and diligence. For although he was possessed of supreme authority, he nevertheless submitted to every possible laborious service, just as if he had been a hired servant. From which example we must learn, that as any one excels in honour, he is bound to be the more fully occupied in business; but that they who desire to combine leisure with dignity, utterly pervert the sacred order of God.

21. And they said one to another. This is a remarkable passage, showing that the sons of Jacob, when reduced to the greatest straits, recall to memory a fratricide committed thirteen years previously. Before affliction pressed upon them, they were in a state of torpor. Moses relates that, even lately, they had spoken without agitation of Joseph's death, as if conscious to themselves of no evil. But now they are compelled to enter into their own consciences. We see then, how in adversity, God searches and tries men; and how, while dissipating all their flattering illusions, he not only pierces their minds with secret fear, but extorts a confession which they would gladly avoid.

28. What is this that God has done unto us? They do not expostulate with God, as if they thought this danger had come upon them without cause: but, perceiving that God was angry with them in many ways, they deplore their wretchedness. But why do they not rather turn their thoughts to Joseph? For the suspicion was natural, that this had been done by fraud, because he wished to lay new snares for them. How does it happen, then, that losing sight of man, they set God as an avenger directly before them? Truly, because this single thought possessed their minds, that a just reward, and such as their sins deserved, would be given them; and, from that time, they referred whatever evils happened to the same cause.

Chapter 43

1. And the famine was sore in the land. In this chapter is recorded the second journey of the sons of Jacob into Egypt, when the former supply of provision had been exhausted.

14. If I be bereaved. Jacob may seem here to be hardly consistent with himself; for, if the prayer which Moses has just related, was the effect of faith, he ought to have been more calm; and, at least, to have given occasion to the manifestation of the grace of God. But he appears to cut himself off from every ground of confidence, when he supposes that nothing is left for him but bereavement. It is like the speech of a man in despair, 'I shall remain bereaved as I am.' As if truly he had prayed in vain; or had feignedly professed that the remedy was in the hand of God. If, however, we observe to whom his speech was directed, the solution is easy. It is by no means doubtful that he stood firmly on the promise which had been given to him, and therefore he would hope for some fruit of his prayers; yet he wished deeply to affect his sons, in order that they might take greater care of their brother.

33. The first-born according to his birthright. The design of Moses was to show, that although Benjamin was the youngest, yet he was preferred to all the rest in honour; because Joseph could not refrain from giving him the principal token of his love. It was, indeed, his intention to remain unknown; but affection so far prevails, that, beyond the purpose of his mind, he suddenly breaks out into a declaration of his affection. From the concluding portion of the chapter we gather that the feast was unusually luxurious, and that they were received to it, in a liberal and joyful manner, beyond the daily custom.

Chapter 44

1. And he commanded the steward of his house. Here Moses relates how skilfully Joseph had contrived to try the dispositions of his brethren.

2. And put my cup, the silver cup. He commands the cup to be enclosed in Benjamin's sack, in order that he might claim him as his own, when convicted of the theft, and might send the rest away: however, he accuses all alike, as if he knew not who among them had committed the crime.

16. Behold, we are my lord's servants. They had before called themselves servants through modesty; now they consign themselves over to him as slaves. But in the case of Benjamin they plead for a mitigation of the severity of the punishment; and this is a kind of entreaty, that he might not be capitally punished, as they had agreed to, at the first.

18. Let thy servant, I pray thee, speak a word. Judah recites in what manner he and his brethren had departed from their father. There are two principal heads of his discourse; first, that they should be the means of bringing a sorrow upon their father which would prove fatal; and secondly, that he had bound himself individually, by covenant, to bring the youth back.

Chapter 45

1. Then Joseph could not refrain himself. Moses relates in this chapter the manner in which Joseph made himself known to his brethren. In the first place, he declares, that Joseph had done violence to his feelings, as long as he presented to them an austere and harsh countenance. At length the strong fraternal affection, which he had suppressed during the time that he was breathing severe threatening, poured itself forth with more abundant force: whence it appears that nothing severe or cruel had before been harbored in his mind. And whereas it thus bursts forth in tears, this softness or tenderness is more deserving of praise than if he had maintained an equable temper.

3. I am Joseph. Although he had given them the clearest token of his mildness and his love, yet, when he told them his name, they were terrified, as if he had thundered against them: for while they revolve in their minds what they have deserved, the power of Joseph seems so formidable to them, that they anticipate nothing for themselves but death. When, however, he sees them overcome with fear, he utters no reproach, but only labors to calm their perturbation. Nay, he continues gently to soothe them, until he has rendered them composed and cheerful. By this example we are taught to take heed lest sadness should overwhelm those who are truly and seriously humbled under a sense of shame.

8. So now, it was not you that sent me hither. This is a remarkable passage, in which we are taught that the right course of events is never so disturbed by the depravity and wickedness of men, but that God can direct them to a good end. We are also instructed in what manner and for what purpose we must consider the providence of God. When men of inquisitive minds dispute concerning it, they not only mingle and pervert all things without regard to the end designed, but invent every absurdity in their power, in order to sully the justice of God. And this rashness causes some pious and moderate men to wish this portion of doctrine to be concealed from view; for as soon as it is publicly declared that God holds the government of the whole world, and that nothing is done but by his will and authority, they who think with little reverence of the mysteries of God, break forth into various questions, not only frivolous but injurious. But, as this profane intemperance of mind is to be restrained, so a just measure is to

be observed on the other hand, lest we should encourage a gross ignorance of those things which are not only made plain in the word of God, but are exceedingly useful to be known.

24. See that ye fall not out by the way. Some explain the passage as meaning, that Joseph asks his brethren to be of tranquil mind, and not to disturb themselves with needless fear; he rather exhorts them, however, to mutual peace. Joseph was pacified towards his brethren; but at the same time he admonishes them not to stir up any strife among themselves. For there was reason to fear lest each, in attempting to excuse himself, should try to lay the blame on others, and thus contention would arise. We ought to imitate this kindness of Joseph; that we may prevent, as much as possible, quarrels and strifes of words; for Christ requires of his disciples, not only that they should be lovers of peace, but also that they should be peace-makers.

Chapter 46

1. And Israel took his journey. Because the holy man is compelled to leave the land of Canaan and to go elsewhere, he offers, on his departure, a sacrifice to the Lord, for the purpose of testifying that the covenant which God had made with his fathers was confirmed and ratified to himself. For, though he was accustomed to exercise himself in the external worship of God, there was yet a special reason for this sacrifice. And, doubtless, he had then peculiar need of support, lest his faith should fail: for he was about to be deprived of the inheritance promised to him, and of the sight of that land which was the type and the pledge of the heavenly country.

2. And God spake unto Israel. In this manner, God proves that the sacrifice of Jacob was acceptable to him, and again stretches out his hand to ratify anew his covenant. The vision by night availed for the purpose of giving greater dignity to the oracle. Jacob indeed, inasmuch as he was docile and ready to yield obedience to God, did not need to be impelled by force and terror; yet, because he was a man encompassed with flesh, it was profitable for him that he should be affected as with the glory of a present God, in order that the word might penetrate more effectually into his heart.

4. And Joseph shall put his hand upon thine eyes. This clause was added for the sake of showing greater indulgence. For though Jacob, in desiring that, when he died, his eyes should be closed by the hand of Joseph, showed that some infirmity of the flesh was involved in the wish; yet God is willing to comply with it, for the sake of moderating the grief of a fresh banishment. Moreover, we know that the custom of closing the eyes was of the greatest antiquity;

and that this office was discharged by one most closely connected with the deceased either by blood or affection.

31. I will go up and show Pharaoh. After Joseph had gone forth to meet his father for the purpose of doing him honour, he also provides what will be useful for him. On this account, he advises Jacob to declare that he and all his family were keepers of cattle, to the end that he might obtain, from the king, a dwelling-place for them, in the land of Goshen. Now although his moderation deserves commendation on the ground, that he usurps no authority to himself, but that, as one of the common people, he waits the pleasure of the king: he yet may be thought craftily to have devised a pretext, by which he might circumvent the king. We see what he desired. Seeing that the land of Goshen was fertile, and celebrated for its rich pastures; this advantage so allured his mind, that he wished to fix his father there: but then, keeping out of Pharaoh's sight the richness of the land, he puts forth another reason; namely, that Jacob with his sons, were men held in abomination, and that, therefore, he was seeking a place of seclusion, in which they might dwell apart from the Egyptians. It is not, however, very difficult to untie this knot. The fertility of the land of Goshen was so fully known to the king, that no room was left for fraud or calming, yea, Pharaoh, of his own accord, had offered them, unsolicited, the best and choicest place in the kingdom.

Chapter 47

7. And Joseph brought in Jacob his father. Although Moses relates, in a continuous narrative, that Jacob was brought to the king, yet I do not doubt that some time had intervened; at least, till he had obtained a place wherein he might dwell; and where he might leave his family more safely, and with a more tranquil mind; and also, where he might refresh himself, for a little while, after the fatigue of his journey. And whereas he is said to have blessed Pharaoh, by this term Moses does not mean a common and profane salutation, but the pious and holy prayer of a servant of God. For the children of this world salute kings and princes for the sake of honour, but, by no means, raise their thoughts to God. Jacob acts otherwise; for he adjoins to civil reverence that pious affection which causes him to commend the safety of the king to God.

9. Few and evil have the days of the years of my life been. Jacob may here seem to complain that he had lived but a little while, and that, in this short space of time, he had endured many and grievous afflictions. Why does he not rather recount the great and manifold favors of God which formed an abundant compensation for

every kind of evil? Besides, his complaint respecting the shortness of life seems unworthy of him; for why did he not deem a whole century and a third part of another sufficient for him? But if any one will rightly weigh his words, he rather expresses his own gratitude, in celebrating the goodness of God towards his fathers. For he does not so much deplore his own decrepitude, as he extols the vigor divinely afforded to his fathers. Certainly it was no new and unwonted thing to see a man, at his age, broken down and failing, and already near to the grave. Wherefore, this comparison was only intended to ascribe glory to God, whose blessing towards Abraham and Isaac had been greater than to himself.

13. And all the land of Canaan fainted. It was a memorable judgment of God, that the most fertile regions, which were accustomed to supply provisions for distant and transmarine nations, were reduced to such poverty that they were almost consumed. Moses pursues the history of the famine, with the intention of showing that the prediction of Joseph was verified by the event; and that, by his skill and industry, the greatest dangers were so well and dexterously provided against, that Egypt ought justly to acknowledge him as the author of its deliverance.

14. And Joseph gathered up all the money. Moses first declares that the Egyptian king had acted well and wisely, in committing the work of providing corn to the sole care and authority of Joseph. He then commends the sincere and faithful administration of Joseph himself. We know how few persons can touch the money of kings without defiling themselves by peculation. Amid such vast heaps of money, the opportunity of plundering was not less than the difficulty of self-restraint. But Moses says, that whatever money Joseph collected, he brought into the house of the king. It was a rare and unparalleled integrity, to keep the hands pure amidst such heaps of gold.

27. And Israel dwelt in the land. Moses does not mean that Jacob and his sons were proprietors of that land which Pharaoh had granted them as a dwelling-place, in the same manner in which the other parts of Egypt were given to the inhabitants for a perpetual possession: but that they dwelt there commodiously for a time, and thus were in possession by favour, provided they continued to be peaceable. Hence the cause that they so greatly increased, in a very short space of time. Therefore, what is here related by Moses belongs to the history of the following period; and he now returns to the proper thread of his narrative, in which he purposed to show how God protected his Church from many deaths; and not that only, but wonderfully exalted it by his own secret power.

29. And he called his son Joseph. Hence we infer, not only the anxiety of Jacob, but his invincible magnanimity. It is a proof of great courage, that none of the wealth or the pleasures of Egypt could so allure him, as to prevent him from sighing for the land of Canaan, in which he had always passed a painful and laborious life. But the constancy of his faith appeared still more excellent, when he, commanding his dead body to be carried back to Canaan, encouraged his sons to hope for deliverance. Thus it happened that he, being dead, animated those who were alive and remained, as with the sound of a trumpet. For, to what purpose was this great care respecting his sepulture, except that the promise of God might be confirmed to his posterity? Therefore, though his faith was tossed as upon the waves, yet it was so far from suffering shipwreck, that it conducted others into the haven. Moreover, he demands an oath from his son Joseph, not so much on account of distrust, as to show that a matter of the greatest consequence was in hand.

31. And Israel bowed himself upon the bed's head. By this expression, Moses again affirms that Jacob esteemed it a singular kindness, that his son should have promised to do what he had required respecting his burial. For he exerts his weak body as much as he is able, in order to give thanks unto God, as if he had obtained something most desirable. He is said to have worshipped towards the head of his bed: because, seeing he was quite unable to rise from the bed on which he lay, he yet composed himself with a solemn air in the attitude of one who was praying.

Chapter 48

1. After these things. Moses now passes to the last act of Jacob's life, which was especially worthy of remembrance. For, since he knew that he was invested by God with no common character, in being made the father of the fathers of the Church, he fulfilled, in the immediate prospect of death, the prophetic office, respecting the future state of the Church, which had been enjoined upon him. Private persons arrange their domestic affairs by their last wills; but very different was the method pursued by this holy man, with whom God had established his covenant, with this annexed condition, that the succession of grace should flow down to his posterity.

5. And now thy two sons. Jacob confers on his son the special privilege, that he, being one, should constitute two chiefs; that is, that his two sons should succeed to an equal right with their uncles, as if they had been heirs in the first degree. But what is this! that a decrepit old man assigns to his grandchildren, as a royal patrimony, a sixth part of the land in which he had entered as a stranger, and from which now again

he is an exile! Who would not have said that he was dealing in fables? It is a common proverb, that no one can give what he has not. What, therefore, did it profit Joseph to be constituted, by an imaginary title, lord of that land, in which the donor of it was scarcely permitted to drink the very water he had dug for with great labour, and from which, at length, famine expelled him? But it hence appears with what firm faith the holy fathers relied upon the word of the Lord, seeing they chose rather to depend upon his lips, than to possess a fixed habitation in the land. Jacob is dying an exile in Egypt; and meanwhile, calls away the governor of Egypt from his dignity into exile, that he may be well and happy. Joseph, because he acknowledges his father as a prophet of God, who utters no inventions of his own, esteems as highly the dominion offered to him, which has never yet become apparent, as if it were already in his possession.

17. And when Joseph saw. Because by crossing his arms, Jacob had so placed his hands as to put his left hand upon the head of the first-born, Joseph wished to correct this proceeding, as if it had been a mistake. He thought that the error arose from dimness of vision; but his father followed the Spirit of God as his secret guide, in order that he might transfer the title of honour, which nature had conferred upon the elder to the younger. For, as he did not rashly assume to himself the office of conveying the blessing; so was it not lawful for him to attempt anything according to his own will. And at length it was evident by the event, that whatever he had done had been dictated to him from heaven. Whereas Joseph took it amiss, that Manasseh, who by the right of nature was first, should be cast down to the second place, this feeling arose from faith and from holy reverence for the prophetic office. What shall we say was the cause, why he raised Ephraim above his own brother, to whom, according to usage, he was inferior? If any one should suppose that Ephraim had some hidden seed of excellence, he not only vainly trifles, but impiously perverts the counsel of God. For since God derives from himself and from his own liberality, the cause, why he prefers one of the two to the other: he confers the honour upon the younger, for the purpose of showing that he is bound by no claims of human merit; but that he distributes his gifts freely, as it seems good unto him.

Chapter 49

1. And Jacob called. In the former chapter, the blessing on Ephraim and Manasseh was related, because, before Jacob should treat of the state of the whole nation about to spring from him, it was right that these two grandsons should be inserted into the body of his sons. Now, as if carried above the heavens, he announces, not in the character of a man, but as from the mouth of God, what shall be the condition of them all, for a long time to come. And it will be proper first to remark, that as he had then thirteen sons, he sets before his view, in each of their persons, the same number of nations or tribes: in which act the admirable lustre of his faith is conspicuous. For since he had often heard from the Lord, that his seed should be increased to a multitude of people, this oracle is to him like a sublime mirror, in which he may perceive things deeply hidden from human sense. Moreover, this is not a simple confession of faith, by which Jacob testifies that he hopes for whatever had been promised him by the Lord; but he rises superior to men, at the interpreter and ambassador of God, to regulate the future state of the Church. Let us mark the design of the Holy Spirit. In the first place, the sons of Jacob are informed beforehand, of their future fortune, that they may know themselves to be objects of the special care of God; and that, although the whole world is governed by his providence, they, notwithstanding, are preferred to other nations, as members of his own household. It seems apparently a mean and contemptible thing, that a region productive of vines, which should yield abundance of choice wine, and one rich in pasturers, which should supply milk, is promised to the tribe of Judah. But if any one will consider that the Lord is hereby giving an illustrious proof of his own election, in descending, like the father of a family, to the care of food, and also showing, in minute things, that he is united by the sacred bond of a covenant to the children of Abraham, he will look for no deeper mystery. In the second place; the hope of the promised inheritance is again renewed unto them. And, therefore, Jacob, as if he would put them in possession of the land by his own hand, expounds familiarly, and as in an affair actually present, what kind of habitation should belong to each of them. Can the confirmation of a matter so serious, appear contemptible to sane and prudent readers? It is, however, the principal design of Jacob more correctly to point out from whence a king should arise among them, who should bring them complete felicity. And in this manner he explains what had been promised obscurely, concerning the blessed seed.

18. I have waited for thy salvation, O Lord. It may be asked, in the first place, what occasion induced the holy man to break the connection of his discourse, and suddenly to burst forth in this expression. I think, indeed, that when he perceived, as from a lofty watchtower, the condition of his offspring continually exposed to various changes, and even to be tossed by storms which would almost overwhelm them, he was moved with solicitude and fear; for he had not so put off all paternal affection, as to be entirely without care for those who were of his own blood. He, therefore, foreseeing many troubles, many dangers, many assaults, and even many slaughters, which threatened his seed with as many destructions, could not but condole with them, and, as a man, be troubled at the sight. But in order that he might rise against every kind of temptation with victorious constancy of mind, he commits himself unto the Lord, who had promised that he would be the guardian of his people.

29. And he charged them. Jacob especially commanded his son Joseph to take care that his body should be buried in the land of Canaan. Moses now repeats that the same command was given to all his sons, in order that they might go to that country with one consent; and might mutually assist each other in performing this office. Truly he did not wish to be carried into the land of Canaan, as if he would be the nearer heaven for being buried there: but that, being dead, he might claim possession of a land which he had held during his life, only by a precarious tenure. Not that any advantage would hence accrue to him privately, seeing he had already fulfilled his course; but because it was profitable that the memory of the promise should be renewed, by this symbol, among his surviving sons, in order that they might aspire to it. Meanwhile, we gather that his mind did not cleave to the earth; because, unless he had been an heir of heaven, he would never have hoped that God, for the sake of one who was dead, would prove so bountiful towards his children.

Chapter 50

1. And Joseph fell upon his father's face. In this chapter, what happened after the death of Jacob, is briefly related. Moses, however, states that Jacob's death was honoured with a double mourning – natural and ceremonial. That Joseph falls upon his father's face and sheds tears, flows from true and pure affection; that the Egyptians mourn for him seventy days, since it is done for the sake of honour, and in compliance with custom, is more from ostentation and vain pomp, than from true grief: and yet the dead are generally mourned over in this manner, that the last debt due to them may be discharged.

3. And forty days were fulfilled for him. Moses is speaking of a ceremonial mourning; and therefore he does not prescribe it as a law, or produce it as an example which it is right for us to follow.

4. Joseph spake unto the house of Pharaoh. A brief narration is here inserted of the permission obtained for Joseph, that, with the goodwill and leave of the king, he might convey his father's remains to the sepulchre.

7. And Joseph went up. Moses gives a full account of the burial. What he relates concerning the renewed mourning of Joseph and his brethren, as well as of the Egyptians, ought by no means to be established as a rule among ourselves. For we know, that since our flesh has no self government, men commonly exceed bounds both in sorrowing and in rejoicing.

20. Ye thought evil against me. Joseph well considers the providence of God; so that he imposes it on himself as a compulsory law, not only to grant pardon, but also to exercise beneficence. Seeing that, by the secret counsel of God, he was led into Egypt, for the purpose of preserving the life of his brethren, he must devote himself to this object, lest he should resist God. He says, in fact, by his action, 'Since God has deposited your life with me, I should be engaged in war against him, if I were not to be the faithful dispenser of the grace which he had committed to my hands.' Meanwhile, he skilfully distinguishes between the wicked counsels of men, and the admirable justice of God, by so ascribing the government of all things to God, as to preserve the divine administration free from contracting any stain from the vices of men. The selling of Joseph was a crime detestable for its cruelty and perfidy; yet he was not sold except by the decree of heaven. For neither did God merely remain at rest, and by conniving for a time, let loose the reins of human malice, in order that afterwards he might make use of this occasion; but, at his own will, he appointed the order of acting which he intended to be fixed and certain. Thus we may say with truth and propriety, that Joseph was sold by the wicked consent of his brethren, and by the secret providence of God.

25. God will surely visit you. By these words he intimates that they would be buried as in oblivion, so long as they remained in Egypt: and truly that exile was as if God had turned his back on them for a season. Nevertheless, Joseph does not cease to fix the eyes of his mind on God. This passage also clearly teaches what was the design of this anxious choice of his sepulchre, namely, that it might be a seal of redemption: for after he has asserted that God was faithful, and would, in his own time, grant what he had promised, he immediately adjures his brethren to carry away his bones. These were useful relics, the sight of which plainly signified that, by the death of men, the eternal covenant in which Joseph commands his posterity safely to rest, had by no means become extinct; for he deems it sufficient to adduce the oath of God, to remove all their doubts respecting their deliverance.

EXODUS

John Wesley

Introduction

Moses having in the first book of his history preserved the records of the church, while it existed in private families, comes, in the second book, to give us an account of its growth into a great nation. The beginning of the former book shows us how God formed the world for himself, the beginning of this shows us how he formed Israel for himself. There we have the creation of the world in history, here the redemption of the world in type. The Greek translators called this book Exodus, which signifies a going out, because it begins with the story of the going out of the children of Israel from Egypt.

This book gives us:
1. The accomplishment of the promise made before to Abraham, (1–19)
2. The establishment of the ordinances which were afterwards observed by Israel (20–36)

Moses in this book begins, like Caesar, to write his own commentaries; and gives us the history of those things which he was himself an eye and ear witness of. There are more types of Christ in this book than perhaps in any other book of the Old Testament. The way of man's reconciliation to God, and coming into covenant and communion with him by a Mediator, is here variously represented; and it is of great use to us for the illustration of the New Testament.

Chapter 1

God's kindness to Israel, in multiplying them exceedingly, (1–7)

1. Every man of his household – That is, children and grand-children.

3. And Benjamin – Who though youngest of all is placed before Dan, Naphtali, etc. because they were the children of the hand-maidens.

5. Seventy souls – This was just the number of the nations by which the earth was peopled, Gen 10:1–32, for when God separated the sons of Adam, he set the bounds of the people according to the number of the children of Israel, De 32:8.

7. And the children of Israel were fruitful, and increased abundantly – Like fishes or insects, so that they multiplied; and being generally healthful and strong, they waxed exceeding mighty, so that the land was filled with them, at least Goshen, their own allotment. This wonderful increase was the product of the promise long before made to the fathers. From the call of Abraham, when God first told him he would make him a great nation, to the deliverance of his seed out of Egypt, was 430 years; during the first 215 of which, they were increased to 70, but in the latter half, those 70 multiplied to 600,000 fighting men.

The Egyptians enslave them (8–14)

8. There arose a new king which knew not Joseph – All that knew him loved him, and were kind to his relations for his sake; but when he was dead he was soon forgotten, and the remembrance of the good offices he had done was either not retained or not regarded.

10. Come on, let us deal wisely with them, lest they multiply – When men deal wickedly it is common for them to imagine that they deal wisely, but the folly of sin will at last be manifested before all men.

11. They set over them task-masters, to afflict them – With this very design. They not only made them serve, which was sufficient for Pharaoh's profit, but they made them serve with rigour, so that their lives became bitter to them; intending hereby to break their spirits, and to rob them of every thing in them that was generous: to ruin their health, and shorten their days, and so diminish their numbers: to discourage them from marrying, since their children would be born to slavery; and to oblige them to desert the Hebrews, and incorporate with the Egyptians.

12. But the more they afflicted them, the more they multiplied – To the grief and vexation of the Egyptians. Times of affliction, have oft been the church's growing times: Christianity spread most when it was persecuted.

The Egyptians murder their children (15–22)

15. And the king spake to the Hebrew midwives – The two chief of them. They are called Hebrew midwives, probably not because they were themselves Hebrews; for sure Pharaoh could never expect they should be so barbarous to those of their own nation, but because they were generally made use of by the Hebrews, and being Egyptians he hoped to prevail with them.

17. But the midwives feared God – Dreaded his wrath more than Pharaoh's, and therefore saved the men-children alive.

Chapter 2

This chapter begins the story of Moses, the most remarkable type of Christ as prophet, Saviour, lawgiver, and mediator, in all the Old Testament.

The perils of his birth and infancy (1–4)

1. And there went a man – Amram, from the place of his abode to another place. **A daughter** – That is, grand-daughter of Levi.

2. Bare a son – It seems just at the time of his birth that cruel law was made for the murder of all the male-children of the Hebrews, and many no doubt perished by the execution of it. Moses's parents had Miriam and Aaron, both elder than he, born to them before that edit

came out. Probably his mother had little joy of her being with child of him, now this edict was in force. Yet this child proves the glory of his father's house. Observe the beauty of providence: just when Pharaoh's cruelty rose to this height, the deliverer was born. **She hid him three months** – In some private apartment of their own house, though probably with the hazard of their lives had he been discovered.

3. And when she could no longer hide him, she put him in an ark of bulrushes – By the river side. God put it into their hearts to do this, to bring about his own purposes: that Moses might by this means be brought into the hands of Pharaoh's daughter, and that by his deliverance, a specimen might be given of the deliverance of God's church.

His preservation through those perils, and the preferment of his childhood and youth (5–10)

5. And the daughter of Pharaoh came – Providence brings no less a person than Pharaoh's daughter just at that juncture, guides her to the place where this poor infant lay, inclines her heart to pity it, which she dares do, when none else durst. Never did poor child cry so seasonably, as this did; the babe wept, which moved her compassion, as no doubt his beauty did.

10. And he became her son – Moses, by having his education in a court, is the fitter to be a prince, and king in Jeshurun; by having his education in a learned court, is the fitter to be an historian; and by having his education in the court of Egypt, is the fitter to be employed as an ambassador to that court in God's name. The Jews tell us, that his father at his circumcision called him Joachim, but Pharaoh's daughter called him Moses, Drawn out of the water, so it signifies in the Egyptian language, The calling of the Jewish lawgiver by an Egyptian name is a happy omen to the Gentile world.

The pious choice of his riper years, which was to own the people of God: He offered them his service, so they would have accepted it (11–14)

11. When Moses was grown he went out unto his brethren, and looked on their burdens – He looked on their burdens as one that not only pitied them, but was resolved to venture with them, and for them.

12. He slew the Egyptian – Probably it was one of the Egyptian task-masters, whom he found abusing his Hebrew slave. By special warrant from heaven (which makes not a precedent in ordinary cases) Moses slew the Egyptian, and rescued his oppressed brother. The Jew's tradition is, that he did not slay him with any weapon, but as Peter slew Ananias and Sapphira, with the word of his mouth.

14. He said, Who made thee a prince? – He challengeth his authority; **Who made thee a prince?** – A man needs no great authority for giving a friendly reproof; it is an act of kindness; yet this man needs will interpret it an act of dominion, and represents his reprover as imperious and assuming. Thus, when people are sick of good discourse, or a seasonable admonition, they will call it preaching, as if a man could not speak a word for God, and against sin, but he took too much upon him. Yet Moses was indeed a prince, and a judge, and knew it, and thought the Hebrews would have understood it; but they stood in their own light, and thrust him away.

He retired, that he might reserve himself for farther service, (15–22)

15. Moses fled from Pharaoh – God ordered this for wise ends. Things were not yet ripe for Israel's deliverance. The measure of Egypt's iniquity was not yet full; the Hebrews were not sufficiently humbled, nor were they yet increased to such a multitude as God designed: Moses is to be farther fitted for the service, and therefore is directed to withdraw for the present, till the time to favour Israel, even the set time, come. God guided Moses to Midian, because the Midianites were of the seed of Abraham, and retained the worship of the true God; so that he might have not only a safe, but a comfortable settlement among them; and through this country he was afterwards to lead Israel, which, that he might do the better, he now had opportunity of acquainting himself with it. Hither he came, and sat down by a well; tired and thoughtful, waiting to see which way Providence would direct him. It was a great change with him, since he was but the other day at ease in Pharaoh's court.

22. Gershom – That is, A stranger there. Now this settlement of Moses in Midian was designed by Providence. To shelter him for the present; God will find hiding places for his people in the day of their distress. It was also designed to prepare him for the services he was farther designed to. His manner of life in Midian, where he kept the flock of his father-in-law would be of use to him, to inure him to hardship and poverty; and to inure him to contemplation and devotion. Egypt accomplished him for a scholar, a gentleman, a statesman, a soldier, all which accomplishments would be afterwards of use to him; but yet lacketh he one thing, in which the court of Egypt could not befriend him. He that was to do all by divine revelation must know, what it was to live a life of communion with God, and in this he would be greatly furthered by the retirement of a shepherd's life in Midian. By the former he was prepared to rule in Jeshurun, but by the latter he was prepared to converse with God in mount Horeb. Those that know what it is to be alone with God, are acquainted with better delights than ever Moses tasted in the court of Pharaoh.

The dawning of the day of Israel's deliverance (23–25)

23. The king of Egypt died – And after him, one or two more of his sons or successors. **And the children of Israel sighed by reason of bondage** – Probably the murdering of their infants did not continue, that part of their affliction only attended the birth of Moses, to signalize that. And now they were content with their increase, finding that Egypt was enriched by their labour; so they might have them for their slaves, they cared not how many they were. On this therefore they were intent, to keep them all at work, and make the best hand they could of their labour. When one Pharaoh died, another rose up in his place, that was as cruel to Israel as his predecessors.

24. And God heard their groaning – That is, he made it to appear that he took notice of their complaints. The groans of the oppressed cry loud in the ears of the righteous God, to whom vengeance belongs; especially the groans of God's children, the burdens they groan under, and the blessings they groan after.

Chapter 3

The discovery God was pleased to make of his glory to Moses at the bush, (1–5)

1. Now Moses – The years of Moses's life are remarkably divided into three forties; the first forty he spent as a prince in Pharaoh's court, the second a shepherd in Midian, the third a king in Jeshurun. He had now finished his second forty when he received his commission to bring Israel out of Egypt. Sometimes it is long before God calls his servants out to that work which of old he designed them for. Moses was born to be Israel's deliverer, and yet not a word is said of it to him till he is eighty years of age. **Even to Horeb** – Horeb and Sinai were two tops of the same mountain.

2. And the angel of the Lord appeared to him – It was an extraordinary manifestation of the divine glory; what was visible was produced by the ministry of an angel, but he heard God in it speaking to him. **In a flame of fire** – To shew that God was about to bring terror and destruction to his enemies, light and heat to his people, and to display his glory before all. **And the bush burned, and yet was not consumed** – An emblem of the church now in bondage in Egypt, burning in the brick-kilns, yet not consumed; cast down, but not destroyed.

3. **I will turn aside and see** – He speaks as one inquisitive, and bold in his inquiry; whatever it was, he would if possible know the meaning of it.

4. **When the Lord saw that he turned aside to see it, God called to him** – If he had carelessly neglected it, it is likely God had departed and said nothing to him. God called and said, **Moses, Moses** – This which he heard could not but surprise him much more than what he saw. Divine calls are then effectual, when the spirit of God makes them particular, and calls us as by name. **Here am I** – Not only to hear what is said, but to do what I am bidden.

5. **Put off thy shoes from off thy feet** – The putting off the shoe was then what the putting off the hat is now, a token of respect and submission. The ground is holy ground, made so by this special manifestation of the divine presence. We ought to approach to God with a solemn pause and preparation; and to express our inward reverence, by a grave and reverent behaviour in the worship of God, carefully avoiding every thing that looks light, or rude.

A general declaration of God's goodwill to his people, who were beloved for the Father's sake (6)

6. **I am the God of thy father** – He lets him know it is God that speaks to him, to engage his reverence, faith and obedience. **Thy father**, thy pious father Amram, and the God of Abraham, Isaac, and Jacob, thy ancestors. Engaged to them by solemn covenant, which I am now come to perform.

And Moses hid his face, for he was afraid to look upon God – The more we see of God, the more cause we shall see to worship him with reverence and godly fear. And even the manifestations of God's grace should increase our humble reverence of him.

A particular notification of God's purpose concerning the deliverance of Israel out of Egypt: He assures Moses it should now be done (7–9)

8. **I am come down to deliver them** – This deliverance was typical of our redemption by Christ, and in that the eternal Word did indeed come down from heaven to deliver us. A **large land** – So it was, according to its true and ancient bounds, as they are described, Gen 15:18, and not according to those narrow limits, to which they were afterwards confined for their unbelief and impiety. **A land flowing with milk and honey** – A proverbial expression, abounding with the choicest fruits, both for necessity and delight.

He gives him a commission to act in it as his ambassador and answers the objection Moses made of his own unworthiness (10–12)

10. **I will send thee** – And the same hand that now fetched a shepherd out of a desert to be the planter of the Jewish church, afterwards fetched fishermen from their ships to be the planters of the Christian church, that the excellency of the power might be of God.

11. **Who am I?** – He thinks himself unworthy of the honour and unable for the work.

He gives him full instructions what to say, both to Pharaoh and to Israel (13–18)

13. **When they shall say to me, What is his name? What shall I say unto them?** – What name shall I use, whereby thou mayest be distinguished from false gods, and thy people may be encouraged to expect deliverance from thee?

14. **And God said** – Two names God would now be known by.

1. A name that speaks what he is in himself, **I am that I am** – This explains his name Jehovah, and signifies, first, That he is self-existent; he has his being of himself, and has no dependence upon any other. And being self-existent he cannot but be self-sufficient, and therefore all-sufficient, and the inexhaustible fountain of being and bliss. Second, That he is eternal and unchangeable, always the same, yesterday to-day, and for ever: he will be what he will be, and what he is. Third, That he is faithful and true to all his promises, unchangeable in his word as well as in his nature, and not a man that he should lie. Let Israel know this, I am hath sent me unto you.

2. A name that speaks what he is to his people. Lest that name I am should puzzle them, he is farther directed to make use of another name of God, more familiar.

15. **The Lord God of our fathers hath sent me unto you** – Thus God made himself known, that he might revive among them the religion of their fathers, which was much decayed, and almost lost. And that he might raise their expectations of the speedy performance of the promises made unto their fathers: Abraham, Isaac, and Jacob are particularly named, because with Abraham the covenant was first made, and with Isaac and Jacob oft expressly renewed, and these three were distinguished from their brethren, and chosen to be the trustees of the covenant. This God will have to be his name for ever, and it has been, is, and will be his name, by which his worshippers know him, and distinguish him from all false gods.

He tells him before-hand what the issue would be, (19–22)

18. Hath met with us – Hath appeared to us, declaring his will, that we should do what follows.

19. I am sure he will not let you go – God sends his messengers to those whose obstinacy he foresees, that it may appear he would have them turn and live.

Chapter 4

This chapter continues and concludes God's discourse with Moses, concerning bringing Israel out of Egypt.

God gives Moses power to work miracles (1–9)

1. They will not hearken to my voice – That is, they would not take his bare word, unless he shewed them some sign. He remembered how they had once rejected him, and feared it would be so again.

2. A rod – Or staff.

5. That they may believe – An imperfect sentence to be thus compleated, This thou shalt do, before them, that they may believe.

6. His hand was leprous, as snow – For whiteness. This signified that Moses, by the power of God, should bring sore diseases upon Egypt, that at his prayer they should be removed. And that whereas the Israelites in Egypt were become leprous, polluted by sin, and almost consumed by oppression, by being taken into the bosom of Moses they should be cleansed and cured.

8. The voice of the first sign – God's works have a voice to speak to us, which we must diligently observe.

Moses objects his own slowness of speech so God promises his presence and commissions Aaron to be with him (10–17)

10. O my Lord, I am not eloquent – He was a great philosopher, statesman, and divine, and yet no orator; a man of a clear head, great thought and solid judgment, but had not a voluble tongue, nor ready utterance; and therefore he thought himself unfit to speak before great men, and about great affairs.

14. And the anger of the Lord was kindled against him – Even self-diffidence when it grows into an extreme, when it either hinders us from duty, or clogs us in duty, is very displeasing to him.

15. I will be with thy mouth and with his mouth – Even Aaron that could speak well, yet could not speak to purpose, unless God were with his mouth; without the constant aids of divine grace, the best gifts will fail.

Moses's execution of his commission (18–31)

19. The Lord said unto Moses – This seems to have been a second vision, whereby God calls him to the present execution of the command given before.

20. The rod of God – His shepherd's crook so called, as it was God's instrument in so many glorious works.

21. In thy hand – in thy power: I will harden his heart – After he has frequently hardened it himself, wilfully shutting his eyes against the light, I will at last permit Satan to harden it effectually.

22. Thus saith the Lord – This is the first time that preface is used by any man, which afterwards is used so frequently by all the prophets: **Israel is my son, my first-born** – Precious in my sight, honourable, and dear to me.

Chapter 5

Moses and Aaron here deal with Pharaoh to get leave of him to go to worship in the wilderness.

They demand to leave (1–3)

1. Thus saith the Lord God of Israel, Let my people go – Moses, in treating with the elders of Israel, is directed to call God the God of their fathers; but, in treating with Pharaoh, they call him the God of Israel, and it is the first time we find him called so in scripture. He is called the God of Israel, the person, Gen 33:20, but here it is Israel the people. They are just beginning to be formed into a people when God is called their God. **Let my people go** – They were God's people, and therefore Pharaoh ought not to detain them in bondage.

2. Who is the Lord that I should obey his voice? – Being summoned to surrender, he thus hangs out the flag of defiance. Who is Jehovah? I neither know him nor care for him; neither value nor fear him.

3. We pray thee, let us go three days journey into the desert – And that on a good errand, and unexceptionable: we will sacrifice to the Lord our God.

Pharaoh answers with further oppression (4–9)

5. The people are many – Therefore your injury to me is the greater, in attempting to make them rest from their labours.

7. Straw – To mix with the clay, or to burn the brick with.

8. They are idle – The cities they built for Pharaoh, were witnesses for them that they were not idle; yet he thus basely misrepresents them, that he might have a pretence to increase their burdens.

The cruel task-masters, (10–14)

14. In thy own people – For if they had given us straw, we should have fulfilled our task.

Complaints to Pharaoh, Moses and God (15–23)

21. The Lord look upon you, and judge – They should have humbled themselves before God, but instead of that they fly in the face of their best friends. Those that are called to public service for God and their generation, must expect to be tried not only by the threats of proud enemies, but by the unjust and unkind censures of unthinking friends. **To put a sword in their hand to slay us** – To give them the occasion they have long sought for.

Chapter 6

God gives him fuller instructions what to say to the children of Israel (1–9)

1. With a strong hand – That is, being forced to it by a strong hand, he shall let them go.

2. I am Jehovah – The same with I am that I am, the fountain of being and blessedness, and infinite perfection. The patriarchs knew this name, but they did not know him in this matter by that which this name signifies. God would now be known by his name Jehovah.

5. I have heard the groaning of the children of Israel – He means their groaning on occasion of the late hardships put upon them. God takes notice of the increase of his people's calamities, and observes how their enemies grow upon them.

6. I will bring you out: I will rid you: I will redeem you: I will bring you into the land of Canaan; and, I will give it you – Let man take the shame of his unbelief which needs such repetitions, and let God have the glory of his condescending grace which gives us such repeated assurances. **With a stretched out arm** – With almighty power: A metaphor taken from a man that stretches out his arm, to put forth all his strength.

7. I will take you to me for a people – A peculiar people, and I will be to you a God.

8. I am the Lord – And therefore have power to dispose of lands and kingdoms as I please.

9. But they hearkened not to Moses for anguish of spirit – That is, They were so taken up with their troubles that they did not heed him.

He sends him again to Pharaoh, (10–13)

11. That he let the children of Israel go – God repeats his precepts, before he begins his punishments. Those that have oft been called in vain to leave their sins, yet must be called again, and again.

12. Behold, the children of Israel have not hearkened to me; they gave no heed to what I have said, how then shall Pharaoh hear me? – If the anguish of their spirit makes them deaf to that which would compose and comfort them, much more will his pride and insolence, make him deaf to that which will but exasperate him. **Who am of uncircumcised lips** – He was conscious to himself that he had not the gift of utterance.

13. The Lord gave them a charge, both to the children of Israel, and to Pharaoh – God's authority is sufficient to answer all objections, and binds us to obedience without murmuring or disputing.

An abstract of the genealogy of the tribes of Reuben and Simeon, to introduce that of Levi, that the pedigree of Moses and Aaron might be cleared, (14–27)

14. This genealogy ends in those two great patriots, Moses and Aaron; and comes in here to shew that they were Israelites, bone of their bone, and flesh of their flesh, whom they were sent to deliver, raised up unto them of their brethren, as Christ also should be, who was to be the prophet and priest, the Redeemer and lawgiver of the house of Israel, and whose genealogy also like this was to be carefully preserved.

A repetition of the preceding story, (28–30)

In the close of the chapter, he returns to his narrative, from which he had broken off somewhat abruptly ver.13, and repeats, the charge God had given him to deliver his message to Pharaoh, ver.29.

29. Speak all that I say unto thee – As a faithful ambassador. Those that go on God's errand must not shun to declare the whole counsel of God.

Chapter 7

Moses applies himself to the execution of his commission, (1–7)

1. have made thee a god to Pharaoh – That is, my representative in this affair, as magistrates are called gods, because they are God's vicegerents. He was authorized to speak and act in God's name, and endued with a divine power, to do that which is above the ordinary course of nature. **And Aaron shall be thy prophet** – That is, he shall speak from thee to Pharaoh, as prophets do from God to the children of men.

7. Moses was fourscore years old – Joseph, who was to be only a servant to Pharaoh, was preferred at thirty years old; but Moses, who was to be a god to Pharaoh, was not so dignified till he was eighty years old. It is fit he should long wait for such an honour, and be long in preparing for such a service.

Moses confirms the demand he made to Pharaoh by a miracle, turning his rod into a serpent, but Pharaoh hardens his heart, (8–13)

9. Say unto Aaron, Take thy rod – This Moses ordinarily held in his hand, and delivered it to Aaron upon occasion, for the execution of his commands.

10. And Aaron cast his rod down, and it became a serpent – This was proper not only to affect Pharaoh with wonder, but to strike a terror upon him. This first miracle, though it was not a plague, yet amounted to the threatening of a plague; if it made not Pharaoh feel, it made him fear; this is God's method of dealing with sinners he comes upon them gradually.

11. Moses had been originally instructed in the learning of the Egyptians, and was suspected to have improved in magical arts in his long retirement. The magicians are therefore sent for to vie with him. The two chief of them were Jannes and Jambres. Their rods became serpents; probably by the power of evil angels artfully substituting serpents in the room of the rods, God permitting the delusion to be wrought for wise and holy ends. But the serpent which Aaron's rod was turned into, swallowed up the others, which was sufficient to have convinced Pharaoh on which side the right lay.

13. And he harden'd Pharaoh's heart – That is, permitted it to be hardened.

He chastiseth his disobedience by a plague, the first of ten, turning the waters into blood; but Pharaoh hardens his heart again, (14–25)

20. The waters that were in the river were turned into blood – This was a plague justly inflicted upon the Egyptians; for Nilus the river of Egypt was their idol; they and their land had so much benefit by that creature, that they served and worshipped it more than the creator.

22. And the magicians did so – By God's permission with their enchantments; and this served Pharaoh for an excuse not to set his heart to this also, (Ex 7:23,) and a poor excuse it was. Could they have turned the river of blood into water again, it had been something; then they had proved their power, and Pharaoh had been obliged to them as his benefactors.

Chapter 8

Three more of the plagues of Egypt are related in this chapter.

The plague of frogs (1–15)

2. All thy borders – All the land that is within thy borders.

3. The River – Nile. Under which are comprehended all other rivers and waters.

9. Glory over me – That is, I yield to thee.

15. But when Pharaoh saw that there was respite, he hardened his heart – Observe he did it himself, not God, any otherwise than by not hindering.

The plague of lice, (16–19)

17. The frogs were produced out of the waters, but the lice out of the dust of the earth; for out of any part of the creation God can fetch a scourge wherewith to correct those that rebel against him.

18. And the magicians did so – That is, endeavoured to do so.

19. This is the finger of God – The power of God. The devil's agents, when God permitted them, could do great things; but when he laid an embargo upon them, they could do nothing. The magicians inability in this instance shewed whence they had their ability in the former instances, and that they had no power against Moses but what was given them from above.

The plague of flies (20–32)

20. Rise up early – Those that would bring great things to pass for God and their generation must rise early, and redeem time in the morning.

21. Flies – Or insects of various kinds; not only flies, but gnats, wasps, hornets; and those probably more pernicious than the common ones were.

22. Know that I am the Lord in the midst of the earth – In every part of it.

24. There came a grievous swarm of flies – The prince of the power of the air has gloried in being Beel-zebub, the god of flies; but here it is proved that even in that he is a pretender, and an usurper; for even with swarms of flies God fights against his kingdom and prevails.

26. The abomination of the Egyptians – That which they abominate to see killed, because they worshipped them as gods.

27. As he shall command us – For he has not yet told us what sacrifices to offer.

Chapter 9

In this chapter we have an account of three more plagues.

Murrain among the cattle, (1–7)

3. The hand of the Lord – Immediately, without the stretching out of Aaron's hand, is upon the cattle, many of which, some of all kinds, shall die by a sort of pestilence. The hand of God is to be acknowledged even in the sickness and death of cattle, or other damage sustained in them; for a sparrow falls not to the ground without our father. And his providence is to be acknowledged with thankfulness in the life of the cattle, for he preserveth man and beast, Psa 36:6.

6. All the cattle died – All that were in the field. The creature is made subject to vanity by the sin of man, being liable, according to its capacity, both to serve his wickedness, and to share in his punishment. The Egyptians worshipped their cattle; it was among them that the Israelites learned to make a god of a calf; in that therefore this plague meets with them. But not one of the cattle of the Israelites died.

Boils upon man and beast, (8–12)

9. A boil breaking forth with blains – A burning scab, which quickly raised blisters and blains.

10. Ashes of the furnace – Sometimes God shows men their sin in their punishment: they had oppressed Israel in the furnaces, and now the ashes of the furnace are made as much a terror to them as ever their task-masters had been to the Israelites.

Hail, with thunder and lightning (13–26)

16. For this cause have I raised thee up – A most dreadful message Moses is here ordered to deliver to him, whether he will hear, or whether he will forbear. He must tell him, that he is marked for ruin: that he now stands as the butt at which God would shoot all the arrows of his wrath.

17. As yet exaltest thou thyself against my people – Wilt thou not yet submit?

18. Since the foundation thereof – Since it was a kingdom.

Pharaoh renews his treaty with Moses, but instantly breaks his word, (27–35)

29. The earth – The world, the heaven and the earth.

31. Bolled – Grown up into a stalk.

33. Moses went out of the city – Not only for privacy in his communion with God, but to shew that he durst venture abroad into the field, notwithstanding the hail and lightning, knowing that every hail-stone had its direction from God. The prayer of Moses opened and shut heaven, like Elijah's.

35. Pharaoh was frighted into compliance by the judgment, but, when it was over, his convictions vanished.

Chapter 10

The eighth and ninth plagues are recorded in this chapter.

The plague of locusts (1–20)

1. These plagues are standing monuments of the greatness of God, the happiness of the church, and the sinfulness of sin; and standing monitors to the children of men in all ages, not to provoke the Lord to jealousy, nor to strive with their Maker. The benefit of these instructions to the world doth sufficiently balance the expense.

3. Thus saith the Lord God of the Hebrews, How long wilt thou refuse to humble thyself before me? – It is justly expected from the greatest of men, that they humble themselves before the great God, and it is at their peril if they refuse to do it. Those that will not humble themselves, God will humble.

10. Let the Lord be so with you, as I will let you go, and your little ones – He now curses and threatens them, in case they offered to remove their little ones, telling them it was at their peril. Satan doth all he can to hinder those that serve God themselves, from bringing their children in to serve him. He is a sworn enemy to early piety, knowing how destructive it is to the interests of his kingdom.

13. The east-wind brought the locusts – From Arabia, where they are in great numbers: And God miraculously increased them.

15. They covered the face of the earth, and eat up the fruit of it – The earth God has given to the children of men; yet when God pleaseth he can disturb his possession even by locusts or caterpillars.

19. An east-wind brought the locusts and now a **west-wind** carried them off. Whatever point of the compass the wind is in, it is fulfilling God's word, and turns about by his counsel.

The plague of darkness (21–23)

23. But the children of Israel had light in their dwellings – Not only in the land of Goshen, where most of them inhabited, but in the particular dwellings which in other places the Israelites had dispersed among the Egyptians, as it appears they had by the distinction afterwards appointed to be put on their door-posts. And during these three days of darkness to the Egyptians, if God had so pleased, the Israelites by the light which they had, might have made their escape, and have asked Pharaoh no leave; but God would bring them out with a high hand, and not by stealth or in haste.

Pharaoh again treats with Moses, but the treaty breaks off, (24–29)

29. I will see thy face no more – Namely, after this time, for this conference did not break off till Ex 11:8, when Moses went out in great anger and told Pharaoh how soon his proud stomach would come down; which was fulfilled Ex 12:31, when Pharaoh became an humble supplicant to Moses to depart. So that after this interview Moses came no more till he was sent for.

Chapter 11

Pharaoh had bid Moses get out of his presence, 10:28, and Moses had promised this should be the last time he would trouble him, yet he refuses to say out what he had to say, before he left him.

The instructions God had given to Moses, which he was now to pursue (1–3)

2. Let every man ask of his neighbour jewels – This was the last day of their servitude, when they were to go away, and their masters, who had abused them in their work, would now have defrauded them of their wages, and have sent them away empty, and the poor Israelites were so fond of liberty that they themselves would be satisfied with that, without pay: but he that executeth righteousness and judgment for the oppressed, provided that the labourers should not lose their hire. God ordered them to demand it now at their departure, in jewels of silver, and jewels of gold; to prepare for which, God had now made the Egyptians as willing to part with them upon any terms, as before the Egyptians had made them willing to go upon any terms.

The last message Moses delivered to Pharaoh, concerning the death of the first-born, (48)

5. The death of the first-born had been threatened, Exo 4:23, but is last executed, and less judgments tried, which, if they had done the work, would have prevented this. See how slow God is to wrath, and how willing to be met in the way of his judgments, and to have his anger turned away! The maid-servant behind the mill – The poor captive slave, employed in the hardest labour.

8. All these thy servants – Thy courtiers and great officers: The people that follow thee – That are under thy conduct: and command. When Moses had thus delivered his message, he went out from Pharaoh in great anger, though he was the meekest of all the men of the earth. Probably he expected that the very threatening of the death of the first-born should have wrought upon Pharaoh to comply; especially he having complied so far already, and having seen how exactly all Moses's predictions were fulfilled. But it had not that effect; his proud heart would not yield, no not to save all the first-born of his kingdom.

A repetition of the prediction of Pharaoh's hardening his heart (9–10)

Chapter 12

This chapter gives an account of one of the most memorable ordinances, and one of the most memorable providences of all that are recorded in the Old Testament.

Instructions for the first Passover (1–20)

1. The Lord spake – Had spoken, before the three days darkness. But the mention of it was put off to this place, that the history of the plagues might not be interrupted.

2. This shall be to you the beginning of months – They had hitherto begun their year from the middle of September, but hence-forward they were to begin it from the middle of March, at least in all their ecclesiastical computations.

3. Take every man a lamb – In each of their families, or two or three families, if they were small, join for a lamb. The lamb was to be got ready four days before, and that afternoon they went, they were to kill it, (Ex 12:6,) as a sacrifice, not strictly, for it was not offered upon the altar, but as a religious ceremony, acknowledging God's goodness to them, not only in preserving them from, but in delivering them by the plagues inflicted on the Egyptians. The lamb so slain they were to eat roasted with unleavened bread and bitter herbs; they were to eat it in haste, Ex 12:11, and to leave none of it until the morning; for God would have them to depend upon him for their daily bread. Before they eat the flesh of the lamb, they were to sprinkle the blood upon the door-posts; by which their houses were to be distinguished from the houses of the Egyptians, and so their first-born secured from the sword of the destroying angel. Dreadful work was to be made this night in Egypt; all the first-born both of man and beast were to be slain; and judgment executed upon the gods of Egypt, Num 33:4. This was to be annually observed as a feast of the Lord in their generations, to which the feast of unleavened bread was annexed, during which, for seven days, they were to eat no bread but what was unleavened, in remembrance of their being confined to such bread for many days after they came out of Egypt, Ex 12:14–20.

There was much of the gospel in this ordinance:
1. The paschal lamb was typical.

Christ is our Passover, 1Cor 5:7, and is the Lamb of God, John 1:29.

1. It was to be a male of the first year; in its prime. Christ offered up himself in the midst of his days. It notes the strength and sufficiency of the Lord Jesus, on whom our help was laid.

2. It was to be without blemish, noting the purity of the Lord Jesus, a lamb without spot, 1Pet 1:19.

3. It was to be set apart four days before, noting the designation of the Lord Jesus to be a Saviour, both in the purpose and in the promise. It is observable, that as Christ was crucified at the passover, so he solemnly entered into Jerusalem four days before, the very day that the paschal lamb was set apart.

4. It was to be slain and roasted with fire, noting the exquisite sufferings of the Lord Jesus, even unto death, the death of the cross.

5. It was to be killed by the whole congregation between the two evenings, that is, between three o'clock and six. Christ suffered in the latter end of the world, Heb 9:26, by the hand of the Jews, the whole multitude of them, Luke 23:18.

6. Not a bone of it must be broken, Ex 12:46, which is expressly said to be fulfilled in Christ, John 19:33,36.

2. The sprinkling of the blood was typical.

1st, It was not enough that the blood of the lamb was shed, but it must be sprinkled, noting the application of the merits of Christ's death to our souls;

2dly, It was to be sprinkled upon the doorposts, noting the open profession we are to make of faith in Christ, and obedience to him. The mark of the beast may be received in the forehead, or in the right hand, but the seal of the lamb is always in the forehead, Rev 7:3.

3dly, The blood thus sprinkled was a means of the preservation of the Israelites from the destroying angel. If the blood of Christ be sprinkled upon our consciences, it will be our protection from the wrath of God, the curse of the law, and the damnation of hell.

3.The solemn eating of the lamb was typical of our gospel duty to Christ.

1st, The paschal lamb was killed not to be looked upon only, but to be fed upon; so we must by faith make Christ ours, as we do that which we eat, and we must receive spiritual strength and nourishment from him, as from our food, and have delight in him, as we have in eating and drinking when we are hungry or thirsty.

2dly, It was to be all eaten: those that, by faith, feed upon Christ, must feed upon a whole Christ. They must take Christ and his yoke, Christ and his cross, as well as Christ and his crown.

3dly, It was to be eaten with bitter herbs, in remembrance of the bitterness of their bondage in Egypt; we must feed upon Christ with brokenness of heart, in remembrance of sin.

4thly, It was to be eaten in a departing posture Ex 12:11, when we feed upon Christ by faith, we must sit loose to the world, and every thing in it.

4. The feast of unleavened bread was typical of the Christian life, 1Cor 5:7,8.

Having received Christ Jesus the Lord,

1st. We must keep a feast, in holy joy, continually delighting ourselves in Christ Jesus; If true believers have not a continual feast, it is their own fault.

2dly, It must be a feast of unleavened bread, kept in charity, without the leaven of malice, and in sincerity, without the leaven of hypocrisy. All the old leaven of sin must be put far from us, with the utmost caution, if we would keep the feast of a holy life to the honour of Christ.

9. **Raw** – Half roasted, but throughly drest.

10. **Ye shall burn with fire** – To prevent the profane abuse of it.

11. **The Lord's Passover** – A sign of his passing over you, when he destroyed the Egyptians.

16. **An holy convocation** – A solemn day for the people to assemble together.

19. **A stranger** – A proselyte. Heathens were not concerned in the Passover.

Taking part in the first Passover (21–28)

22. **Out of the door of his house** – Of that house, wherein he ate the passover: **Until the morning** – That is, till towards morning, when they would be called for to march out of Egypt. They went out very early in the morning.

23. **The destroyer** – The destroying angel, whether this was a good or an evil angel, we have not light to determine.

27. **The people bowed the head and worshipped** – They hereby signified their submission to this institution as a law, and their thankfulness for it as a favour and privilege.

The deliverance of the children of Israel out of Egypt (29–42)

31. **Rise up, and get you forth** – Pharaoh had told Moses he should see his face no more, but now he sent for him; those will seek God in their distress, who before had set him at defiance.

33. **We be all dead men** – When death comes unto our houses, it is seasonable for us to think of our own mortality.

37. **About six hundred thousand men** – The word means strong and able men fit for wars, beside women and children, which we cannot suppose to make less than twelve hundred thousand more. What a vast increase was this to arise from seventy souls, in little more than two hundred years.

40. It was just four hundred and thirty years from the promise made to Abraham (as the Apostle explains it, Gal 3:17,) at his first coming into Canaan, during all which time the Hebrews, were sojourners in a land that was not theirs, either Canaan or Egypt. So long the promise God made to Abraham lay dormant and unfulfilled, but now, it revived, and things began to work towards the accomplishment of it. The first day of the march of Abraham's seed

towards Canaan was four hundred and thirty years, from the promise made to Abraham, Gen 12:2, 'I will make of thee a great nation.'

42. This first passover night was a night of the Lord, much to be observed; but the last passover night, in which Christ was betrayed, was a night of the Lord, much more to be observed, when a yoke heavier than that of Egypt was broke from off our necks, and a land better than that of Canaan set before us. That was a temporal deliverance, to be celebrated in their generations; this an eternal redemption to be celebrated world without end.

A recapitulation (43–51)

47. All the congregation of Israel must keep it – Though it was observed in families apart, yet it is looked upon as the act of the whole congregation. And so the New Testament Passover, the Lord's Supper, ought not to be neglected by any that are capable of celebrating it.

Chapter 13

The commands God gave to Israel, (1–16)

2. Sanctify to me all the first-born – The parents were not to look upon themselves as interested in their first-born, till they had first solemnly presented them to God, and received them back from him again.

5. When the lord shall bring you into the land, thou shalt keep this service – Until then they were not obliged to keep the passover, without a particular command from God.

7. There shall no leavened bread be seen in all thy quarters – Accordingly the Jews usage was, before the feast of the passover, to cast all the leavened bread out of their houses; either they burnt it, or buried it, or broke it small, and threw it into the wind; they searched diligently with lighted candles in all the corners of their houses, lest any leaven should remain. The strictness enjoined in this matter was designed, to teach us how solicitous we should be to put away from us all sin.

9. Upon thy hand, between thine eyes – Proverbial expressions; denoting things which are never out of our thoughts.

13. Thou shalt redeem – The price of the redemption was fixed by the law.

16. For frontlets between thine eyes – As conspicuous as any thing fixt to thy forehead, or between thine eyes.

The care God took of Israel when he had brought them out of Egypt (17–22)

18. There were many reasons why God led them through the way of the wilderness of the Red-sea. The Egyptians were to be drowned in the Red-sea, the Israelites were to be humbled, and proved in the wilderness. God had given it to Moses for a sign, Ex 3:12, 'ye shall serve God in this mountain.'

21. And the Lord went before them in a pillar – In the two first stages, it was enough that God directed Moses whither to march; he knew the country, and the road; but now they are come to the edge of the wilderness, they would have occasion for a guide, and a very good guide they had, infinitely wise, kind, and faithful, the Lord went up before them. The Shechinah or appearance of the divine Majesty, which was a precious manifestation of the eternal Word, who in the fulness of time was to be made flesh, and dwell among us. Christ was with the church in the wilderness, 1Cor 10:9. What a satisfaction to Moses and the pious Israelites, to be sure that they were under a divine conduct? They need not fear missing their way who were thus led, nor being lost who were thus directed; they need not fear being benighted, who were thus illuminated, nor being robbed, who were thus protected. And they who make the glory of God their end, and the word of God their rule, the spirit of God the guide of their affections, and the providence of God the guide of their affairs, may be confident that the Lord goes before them, as truly as he went before Israel in the wilderness, though not so sensibly. They had sensible effects of God's going before them in this pillar. For, it led them the way in that vast howling wilderness, in which there was no road and no track. When they marched, this pillar went before them, at the rate that they could follow, and appointed the place of their encampment, as infinite Wisdom saw fit; which eased them from care, and secured them from danger, both in moving, and in resting. It sheltered them from the heat by day, which at sometimes of the year was extreme: And it gave them light by night when they had occasion for it.

22. He took not away the pillar of the cloud – No not when they seemed to have less occasion for it: it never left them until it brought them to the borders of Canaan. It was a cloud which the wind could not scatter. There was something spiritual in this pillar of cloud and fire.

1.The children of Israel were baptized unto Moses in this cloud, 1Cor 10:2. By coming under this cloud they signified their putting themselves under the conduct and command of Moses. Protection draws allegiance; this cloud was the badge of God's protection, and so became the bond of their allegiance. Thus they were initiated, and admitted under that government, now when they were entering upon the wilderness.

2.And it signifies the special conduct and protection which the church of Christ is under in this world.

Chapter 14

The extreme distress that Israel was in at the Red-sea (1–14)

2. They were got to the edge of the wilderness, Ex 13:20, and one stage or two would have brought them to Horeb, the place appointed for their serving God, but instead of going forward, they are ordered to turn short off, on the right-hand from Canaan, and to march towards the Red-sea.

3. They are entangled – Inclosed with mountains, and garrisons, and deserts.

5. And it was told the king that the people fled – He either forgot, or would not own that they had departed with his consent; and therefore was willing it should be represented to him as a revolt from their allegiance.

8. With an high hand – Boldly, resolutely.

9. Chariots and horsemen – It should seem he took no foot-soldiers with him, because the king's business required haste.

10. They were sore afraid – They knew the strength of the enemy, and their own weakness; numerous indeed they were, but all foot, unarmed, undisciplined, dispirited, by long servitude, and now pent up, so that they could not escape. On one hand was Pi-hahiroth, a range of craggy rocks unpassable; on the other hand were Migdol and Baal-zephon, forts upon the frontiers of Egypt; before them was the sea, behind them were the Egyptians; so that there was no way open for them but upwards, and thence their deliverance came.

13. Moses answered not these fools according to their folly. Instead of chiding he comforts them, and with an admirable pretence of mind, not disheartened either by the threatenings of Egypt, or the tremblings of Israel, stills their murmuring, **Fear ye not.** It is our duty, when we cannot get out of our troubles, yet to get above our fears, so that they may only serve to quicken our prayers and endeavours, but may not prevail to silence our faith and hope. Stand still, and think not to save yourselves either by fighting or flying; wait God's orders, and observe them; Compose yourselves, by an entire confidence in God, into a peaceful prospect of the great salvation God is now about to work for you. Hold your peace, you need not so much as give a shout against the enemy: the work shall be done without any concurrence of yours. In times of great difficulty, it is our wisdom to keep our spirits calm, quiet, and sedate, for then we are in the best frame both to do our own work, and to consider the work of God.

The wonderful deliverance that God wrought for them (15–28)

15. Wherefore criest thou unto me? – Moses though he was assured of a good issue, yet did not neglect prayer. We read not of one word he said in prayer, but he lifted up his heart to God, and God well understood, and took notice of. Moses's silent prayer prevailed more with God, than Israel's loud out-cries. But is God displeased with Moses for praying? No, he asks this question, **Wherefore criest thou unto me?** Wherefore shouldst thou press thy petition any farther, when it is already granted? Moses has something else to do besides praying, he is to command the hosts of Israel. **Speak to them that they go forward** – Some think Moses had prayed not so much for their deliverance, he was assured of that; as for the pardon of their murmurings, and God's ordering them to go forward, was an intimation of the pardon. Moses bid them stand still and expect orders from God: and now orders are given. They thought they must have been directed either to the right hand, or to the left; no, saith God, speak to them to go forward, directly to the sea-side; as if there had lain a fleet of transport ships ready for them to embark in. Let the children of Israel go as far as they can upon dry ground, and then God will divide the sea. The same power could have congealed the waters for them to pass over, but infinite wisdom chose rather to divide the waters for them to pass through, for that way of salvation is always pitched upon which is most humbling.

19. The angel of God – Whose ministry was made use of in the pillar of cloud and fire, went from before the camp of Israel, where they did not now need a guide; there was no danger of missing their way through the sea, and came behind them, where now they needed a guard, the Egyptians being just ready to seize the hindmost of them. There it was of use to the Israelites, not only to protect them, but to light them through the sea; and at the same time it confounded the Egyptians, so that they lost sight of their prey, just when they were ready to lay hands on it. The word and providence of God have a dark side towards sin and sinners, but a bright and pleasant side towards those that are Israelites indeed.

21. We have here the history of that work of wonder which is so often mentioned both in the Old and New Testament. An instance of God's almighty power in dividing the sea, and opening a passage through the waters. It was a bay, or gulf, or arm of the sea. The God of nature has not tied himself to its laws, but when he pleases dispenseth with them, and then the fire doth not burn, nor the water flow. They went through the sea to the opposite shore; they walked upon dry land in the midst of the sea; the waters were a wall to them on their right hand, and on their left. Moses and Aaron it is likely ventured first, into this untrodden path, and then all Israel after them; and this march through the paths of the great waters would make their march afterwards through the wilderness less formidable. This march through the sea was in the night, and not a moon-shine night, for it was seven days after the full moon, so that they had no light but what they had from the pillar of fire. This made it the more awful, but where God leads us, he will light us; while we follow his conduct we shall not want his comforts.

23. **And the Egyptians went in after them into the midst of the sea** – They thought, why might they not venture where Israel did? They were more advantageously provided with chariots and horses, while the Israelites were on foot.

25. They had driven furiously, but now they drove heavily, and found themselves embarrassed at every step; the way grew deep, their hearts grew sad, their wheels dropt off.

26. **And the Lord said unto Moses, Stretch out thy hand over the sea** – And give a signal to the waters to close again, as before upon the word of command they had opened to the right and the left. He did so, and immediately the waters returned to their place, and overwhelmed all the host of the Egyptians.

The impressions this made upon the Israelites (30–31)

30. **And Israel saw the Egyptians dead upon the shore** – The Egyptians were very curious in preserving the bodies of their great men, but here the utmost contempt is poured upon all the grandees of Egypt.

31. **And Israel feared the Lord, and believed the Lord, and his servant Moses** – Now they were ashamed of their distrusts and murmurings; and in the mind they were in, they would never again despair of help from heaven; no not in the greatest straits! They would never again quarrel with Moses; nor talk of returning to Egypt. How well were it for us, if we were, always in as good a frame, as we are in sometimes!

Chapter 15

Israel looks back upon Egypt with a song of praise for their deliverance (1–21)

1. **Then sang Moses** – Moses composed this song, and sang it with the children of Israel. Doubtless he wrote it by inspiration, and sang it on the spot. By this instance it appears that the singing of psalms, as an act of religious worship, was used in the church of Christ before the giving of the ceremonial law, therefore it is no part of it, nor abolished with it: singing is as much the language of holy joy, as praying is of holy desire. **I will sing unto the Lord** – All our joy must terminate in God, and all our praises be

offered up to him. **For he hath triumphed** – All that love God triumph in his triumphs.

2. Israel rejoiceth in God, as their **strength, song, and salvation** – Happy therefore the people whose God is the Lord: They are weak themselves, but he strengthens them, his grace is their strength: they are oft in sorrow, but in him they have comfort, he is their song: sin and death threaten them, but he is, and will be, their salvation. He is their **fathers God** – This they take notice of, because being conscious of their own unworthiness, they had reason to think that what God had now done for them was for their fathers sake.

3. **The Lord is a man of war** – Able to deal with all those that strive with their maker.

4. **He hath cast** – With great force, as an arrow out of a bow, so the Hebrew word signifies.

7. **In the greatness of thine excellency** – By thy great and excellent power.

8. **With the blast of thy nostrils** – By thine anger: **The depths were congealed** – Stood still, as if they had been frozen: **In the heart of the sea** – The midst of it.

9. **My lust** – My desire both of revenge and gain.

12. **The earth swallowed them** – Their dead bodies sunk into the sands on which they were thrown, which sucked them in.

13. **Thou in thy mercy hast led forth the people** – Out of the bondage of Egypt, and out of the perils of the Red-sea. **Thou hast guided them to thy holy habitation** – Thou hast put them into the way to it, and wilt in due time bring them to the end of that way.

18. **The Lord shall reign for ever and ever** – They had now seen an end of Pharaoh's reign, but time itself shall not put a period to Jehovah's reign, which like himself is eternal.

20. **Miriam** presided in an assembly of the women, who with timbrels and dances, sung this song. Moses led the psalm, and gave it out for the men, and then Miriam for the women.

21. **And Miriam answered them** – The men: They sung by turns, or in parts.

Israel marches forward in the wilderness (22–27)

23. **The name of it was called Marah** – That is, Bitterness.

25. **And he cried unto the Lord** – It is the greatest relief of the cares of magistrates and ministers, when those under their charge make them uneasy, that they may have recourse to God by prayer; he is the guide of the church's guides, and to the chief shepherd, the under shepherds must on all occasions apply themselves: And the Lord directed Moses to a tree, which he cast into the waters, and they were **made sweet** – Some think this wood had a

peculiar virtue in it for this purpose, because it is said, God **shewed him** the **tree.** God is to be acknowledged, not only in the creating things useful for man, but in discovering their usefulness. But perhaps this was only a sign, and not a means of the cure, no more than the brazen serpent. **There he made a statute and an ordinance, and there he proved them** – That is, there he put them upon trial, admitted them as probationers for his favour.

Chapter 16

This chapter gives us an account of the victualling of the camp of Israel.

Their complaint for want of bread, (1–3)

1. A month's provision, it seems, the host of Israel took with them out of Egypt, when they came thence on the fifteenth day of the first month, which, by the fifteenth day of the second month, was all spent.

2. **Then the whole congregation murmured against Moses and Aaron** – God's viceregents among them.

3. They so undervalue their deliverance, that they wish, they had died in Egypt, nay, and died by the hand of the Lord too.

The notice God gave them of the provision he intended to make for them, (4–12)

4. Man being made out of the earth, his Maker has wisely ordered him food out of the earth, Psa 104:14. But the people of Israel typifying the church of the first-born that are written in heaven, receiving their charters, laws and commissions from heaven, from heaven also they received their food. See what God designed in making this provision for them, **that I may prove them whether they will walk in my law or no** – Whether they will trust me, and whether they would serve him, and be ever faithful to so good a master.

5. **They shall prepare** – Lay up, grind, bake or boil.

6. **The Lord** – And not we, by our own counsel.

10. **The glory of the Lord** – An extraordinary and sudden brightness.

12. **And ye shall know that I am the Lord your God** – This gave proof of his power as the Lord, and his particular favour to them as their God; when God plagued the Egyptians, it was to make them know that he is the Lord; when he provided for the Israelites, it was to make them know that he was their God.

The sending of the manna, (13–15)

13. **The quails came up, and covered the camp** – So tame that they might take up as many of them as they pleased. Next morning he rained manna upon them, which was to be continued to them for their daily bread.

15. What is this? **Manna** descended from the clouds. It came down in dew melted, and yet was itself of such a consistency as to serve for nourishing strengthening food, without any thing else. It was pleasant food; the Jews say it was palatable to all, according as their tastes were. It was wholesome food, light of digestion. By this spare and plain diet we are all taught a lesson of temperance, and forbidden to desire dainties and varieties.

The laws and orders concerning the manna (16–32)

19. **Let no man leave of it till the morning** – But let them learn to go to bed and sleep quietly, though they had not a bit of bread in their tent, nor in all their camp, trusting God with the following day to bring them their daily bread. Never was there such a market of provisions as this, where so many hundred thousand men were daily furnished without money, and without price: never was there such an open house kept as God kept in the wilderness for 40 years together, nor such free and plentiful entertainment given. And the same wisdom, power and goodness that now brought food daily out of the clouds, doth in the constant course of nature bring food yearly out of the earth, and gives us all things richly to enjoy.

23. Here is a plain intimation of the observing a seventh day sabbath, not only before the giving of the law upon mount Sinai, but before the bringing of Israel out of Egypt and therefore from the beginning.

24. An omer of this manna was laid up in a golden pot as we are told, Heb 9:4, and kept before the testimony, or the ark, when it was afterwards made, The preservation of this manna from waste and corruption, was a standing miracle; and therefore the more proper memorial of this miraculous food. The manna is called spiritual meat, 1Cor 10:3, because it was typical of spiritual blessings. Christ himself is the true manna, the bread of life, of which that was a figure, John 6:49–51. The word of God is the manna by which our souls are nourished, Mt 4:4. The comforts of the Spirit are hidden manna, Rev 2:17. These comforts from heaven as the manna did, are the support of the divine life in the soul while we are in the wilderness of this world: it is food for Israelites, for those only that follow the pillar of cloud and fire: it is to be gathered; Christ in the word is to be applied to the soul, and the means of grace used: we must every one of us gather for ourselves. There was manna enough for all, enough for each, and none had too much; so in Christ there is a compleat sufficiency, and no superfluity. But they

that did eat manna hungered again, died at last, and with many of them God was not well pleased: whereas they that feed on Christ by faith shall never hunger, and shall die no more, and with them God will be for ever well pleased. The Lord evermore give us this bread!

Chapter 17

The watering of the host of Israel (1–7)

1. They **journeyed according to the commandment of the Lord,** led by the pillar of cloud and fire, and yet they came to a place where **there was no water for them to drink –** We may be in the way of our duty, and yet meet with troubles, which Providence brings us into for the trial of our faith.

5. **Go on before the people** – Though they spake of stoning him. He must take his rod with him, not to summon some plague to chastise them, but to fetch water for their supply. O the wonderful patience and forbearance of God towards provoking sinners! He maintains those that are at war with him, and reaches out the hand of his bounty to those that lift up the heel against him. If God had only shewed Moses a fountain of water in the wilderness, as he did to Hagar, not far from hence, Gen 21:19, that had been a great favour; but that he might shew his power as well as his pity, and make it a miracle of mercy, he gave them water out of a rock. He directed Moses whither to go, appointed him to take of the elders of Israel with him, to be witnesses of what was done, ordered him to smite the rock, which he did, and immediately water came out of it in great abundance, which ran throughout the camp in streams and rivers, Psa 78:15,16, and followed them wherever they went in that wilderness: God shewed his care of his people in giving them water when they wanted it; his own power in fetching it out of a rock, and put an honour upon Moses in appointing the water to flow out upon his smiting of the rock. This fair water that came out of the rock is called honey and oil, Deu 32:13, because the people's thirst made it doubly pleasant; coming when they were in extreme want.

The defeating of the host of Amalek (8–16)

8. **Then Amalek came and fought with Israel** – The Amalekites were the posterity of Esau, who hated Jacob because of the birth-right and blessing. They did not boldly front them as a generous enemy, but without any provocation given, basely fell upon their rear, and smote them that were faint and feeble.

9. **I will stand on the top of the hill with the rod of God in my hand** – See how God qualifies his people for, and calls them to various services for the good of his church; Joshua fights, Moses prays, and both minister to Israel. This rod Moses held up, not so much to Israel as to animate them; as to God by way of appeal to him; Is not the battle the Lord's? Is not he able to help, and engaged to help? Witness this rod! Moses was not only a standard-bearer, but an intercessor, pleading with God for success and victory.

11. **And when Moses held up his hand** in prayer **Israel prevailed, but when he let down his hand** from prayer, **Amalek prevailed** – To convince Israel that the hand of Moses contributed more to their safety than their own hands; the success rises and falls, as Moses lifts up or lets down his hand. The church's cause is ordinarily more or less successful, according as the church's friends are more or less fervent in prayer.

13. Though God gave the victory, yet it is said **Joshua discomfited Amalek,** because Joshua was a type of Christ, and of the same name, and in him it is that we are more than conquerors.

15. **And Moses built an altar, and called it Jehovah-niffi** – The Lord is my banner. The presence and power of Jehovah was the banner under which they were lifted, by which they were animated, and kept together, and therefore which they erected in the day of their triumph. In the name of our God we must always lift up our banners: He that doth all the work should have all the praise.

Chapter 18

This chapter is concerning Moses himself, and the affairs of his own family.

Jethro his father-in-law brings him his wife and children, (1–6)

1. **Jethro** to congratulate the happiness of Israel, and particularly the honour of Moses his son-in-law; comes to rejoice with them, as one that had a true respect both for them and for their God. And also to bring Moses's wife and children to him.

3. **The name of one was Gershom** – A stranger, designing thereby not only a memorial of his own condition, but a memorandum to this son of his, for we are all strangers upon earth.

4. **The name of the other was Eliezer** – My God a help.

Moses entertains his father-in-law (7–12)

11. **Now know I that JEHOVAH is greater than all gods** – That the God of Israel is greater than all pretenders; all deities, that usurp divine honours: he silenceth them, subdues them all, and is himself the only living and true God. He is also higher than all princes and potentates, who also are called gods, and has both an

incontestable authority over them, and an irresistible power to control them; he manages them all as he pleaseth, and gets honour upon them how great soever they are. **Now know I:** he knew it before, but now he knew it better; his faith grew up to a full assurance, upon this fresh evidence; **for wherein they dealt proudly** –- The magicians or idols of Egypt, or Pharaoh and his grandees, opposing God, and setting up in competition with him, he was above them. The magicians were baffled, Pharaoh humbled, his powers broken, and Israel rescued out of their hands.

12. **And Jethro took a burnt offering for God** – And probably offered it himself, for he was a priest in Midian, and a worshipper of the true God, and the priesthood was not yet settled in Israel. And they did **eat bread before God** – Soberly, thankfully, in the fear of God; and their talk such as became saints. Thus we must eat and drink to the glory of God; as those that believe God's eye is upon us.

Jethro adviseth him about the management of his business as a judge in Israel (13–27)

13. **Moses sat to judge the people** – To answer enquiries; to acquaint them with the will of God in doubtful cases, and to explain the laws of God that were already given.

15. **The people came to enquire of God** – And happy was it for them that they had such an oracle to consult. Moses was faithful both to him that appointed him, and to them that consulted him, and made them know the statutes of God, **and his laws** – His business was not to make laws, but to make known God's laws: his place was but that of a servant.

16. **I judge between one and another** – And if the people were as quarrelsome one with another as they were with God, he had many causes brought before him, and the more because their trials put them to no expense.

17. **Not good** – Not convenient either for thee or them.

19. **Be thou for them to God-ward** – That was an honour which it was not fit any other should share with him in. Also whatever concerned the whole congregation must pass through his hand, Ex 18:20. But, he appointed judges in the several tribes and families, which should try causes between man and man, and determine them, which would be done with less noise, and more dispatch than in the general assembly. Those whose gifts and stations are most eminent may yet be greatly furthered in their work by the assistance of those that are every way their inferiors. This is Jethro's advice; but he adds two qualifications to his counsel.

1. That great care should be taken in the choice of the persons who should be admitted into this trust; it was requisite that they should be men of the best character.

2. That he should attend God's direction in the case.

24. **So Moses hearkened unto the voice of his father-in-law.** When he came to consider the thing, he saw the reasonableness of it, and resolved to put it in practice, which he did soon after, when he had received directions from God. Those are not so wise as they would be thought to be, who think themselves too wise to be counselled; for a wise man will hear, and will increase learning, and not slight good counsel, though given by an inferior.

Chapter 19

This chapter introduces the giving of the law upon Mount Sinai, which was one of the most sensible appearances of the divine glory that ever was in this lower world.

The circumstances of time and place, (1–2)

1. **In the third month** after they came out of Egypt. It is computed that the law was given just fifty days after their coming out of Egypt, in remembrance of which the feast of Pentecost was observed the fiftieth day after the Passover, and in compliance with which the spirit was poured out upon the apostles, at the feast of Pentecost, fifty days after the death of Christ. Mount Sinai was a place which nature, not art, had made conspicuous, for it was the highest in all that range of mountains. Thus God put contempt upon cities and palaces, setting up his pavilion on the top of a mountain, in a barren desert. It is called Sinai, from the multitude of thorny bushes that over-spread it.

The covenant between God and Israel settled in general (3–8)

3. **Thus shalt thou say to the house of Jacob, and the children of Israel** – The people are called by the names both of Jacob and Israel, to mind them that they who had lately been as low as Jacob when he went to Padan-aram, were now grown as great as God made him when he came from thence, and was called Israel.

4. **Ye have seen what I did unto the Egyptians, and how I bare you on eagles' wings** – An high expression of the wonderful tenderness God showed for them. It notes great speed; God not only came upon the wing for their deliverance, but he hastened them out, as it were upon the wing. Also that he did it with great ease, with the strength as well as with the swiftness of an eagle. They that faint not, nor are weary, are said to mount up with wings as

eagles, Isa 40:31. Especially it notes God's particular care of them, and affection to them. Even Egypt was the nest in which these young ones were first formed as the embryo of a nation: when by the increase of their numbers they grew to some maturity, they were carried out of that nest. **I brought you unto myself** – They were brought not only into a state of liberty, but into covenant and communion with God. This, God aims at in all the gracious methods of his providence and grace, to bring us back to himself, from whom we have revolted, and to bring us home to himself, in whom alone we can be happy.

5. Then ye shall be a peculiar treasure to me – He doth not instance in any one particular favour, but expresses it in that which was inclusive of all happiness, that he would be to them a God in covenant, and they should be to him a people. Nay you shall be a peculiar treasure: not that God was enriched by them, as a man is by his treasure, but he was pleased to value and esteem them as a man doth his treasure; they were precious in his sight. He took them under his special care and protection, as a treasure that is kept under lock and key. He distinguished them from, and dignified them above all people, as a people devoted to him, and to his service.

6. A kingdom of priests, a holy nation – All the Israelites, if compared with other people, were priests unto God, so near were they to him, so much employed in his immediate service, and such intimate communion they had with him. The tendency of the laws given them was to distinguish them from others, and engage them for God as a holy nation. Thus all believers are, through Christ, made to our God kings and priests, Rev 1:6, a chosen generation, a royal priesthood, 1Pet 2:9.

7. And Moses laid before their faces all these words – He not only explained to them what God had given him in charge, but put it to their choice, whether they would accept these promises upon these terms or no. His laying it to their faces speaks his laying it to their consciences.

8. And they answered together; all that the Lord hath spoken we will do – Thus accepting the Lord to be to them a God, and giving up themselves to be to him a people.

Notice given three days before of God's design to give the law out of a thick cloud, (9–15)

10. Sanctify the people – As Job before sent and sanctified his sons, Job 1:5. Sanctify them, that is, call them off from their worldly business, and call them to religious exercises, meditation and prayer, that they may receive the law from God's mouth with reverence and devotion. Two things particularly were prescribed as instances of their preparation. 1st, In token of cleansing of themselves from all sinful pollutions, they must wash their clothes. Not that God regards our clothes, but while they were washing their clothes, he would have them think of washing their souls by repentance. It becomes us to appear in clean clothes when we wait upon great men; so clean hearts are required in our attendance on the great God. 2dly, In token of their devoting themselves entirely to religious exercises upon this occasion they must abstain even from lawful enjoyments during these three days, and not come at their wives.

11. In the sight of all the people – Though they should see no manner of similitude, yet they should see so much as would convince them, that God was among them of a truth. And so high was the top of Mount Sinai, that it is supposed not only the camp of Israel, but even the countries about might discern some extraordinary appearance of glory upon it.

12. Set bounds – Probably he drew a ditch round at the foot of the hill, which none were to pass upon pain of death. This was to intimate, 1st, That awful reverence which ought to possess the minds of all that worship God. 2dly, The distance which worshippers were kept at under that dispensation, which we ought to take notice of, that we may the more value our privilege under the gospel, having boldness to enter into the holiest by the blood of Jesus, Heb 10:19.

13. When the trumpet soundeth long – Then let them take their places at the foot of the mount. Never was so great a congregation called together and preached to at once as this was here. No one man's voice could have reached so many, but the voice of God did.

A terrible appearance of God's glory, (16–25)

16. Now at length is come that memorable day, in which Israel heard the voice of the Lord God speaking to them out of the midst of the fire and lived, Deu 4:33. Never was there such a sermon preached before or since, as this, which was here preached to the church in the wilderness. For, the preacher was God himself, Ex 19:17.

20. The Lord came down upon mount Sinai – The Shechinah, or glory of the Lord, appeared in the sight of all the people; he shined forth from mount Paran with ten thousand of his saints, attended with a multitude of the holy angels. Hence the law is said to be given by the disposition of angels, Acts 7:53.

Chapter 20

The ten commandments as God himself spake them upon Mount Sinai, (1–17)

1. God spake all these words – The law of the ten commandments is a law of God's making; a law of his own speaking. God has many ways of speaking to the children of men by his spirit, conscience, providences; his voice in all which we ought carefully to attend to: but he never spake at any time upon any occasion so as he spake the ten commandments, which therefore we ought to hear with the more earnest heed. This law God had given to man before, it was written in his heart by nature; but sin had so defaced that writing, that it was necessary to revive the knowledge of it.

2. I am the Lord thy God – Herein, God asserts his own authority to enact this law; and proposeth himself as the sole object of that religious worship which is enjoined in the four first commandments. They are here bound to obedience.

1. Because God is the Lord, Jehovah, self-existent, independent, eternal, and the fountain of all being and power; therefore he has an incontestable right to command us.

2. He was their God; a God in covenant with them; their God by their own consent.

3. He had brought them **out of the land of Egypt** – Therefore they were bound in gratitude to obey him, because he had brought them out of a grievous slavery into a glorious liberty. By redeeming them, he acquired a farther right to rule them; they owed their service to him, to whom they owed their freedom. And thus, Christ, having rescued us out of the bondage of sin, is entitled to the best service we can do him.

The four first commandments, concern our duty to God (commonly called the first-table.) It was fit those should be put first, because man had a Maker to love before he had a neighbour to love, and justice and charity are then only acceptable to God when they flow from the principles of piety.

3. The first commandment is concerning the object of our worship, Jehovah, and him only, **Thou shalt have no other gods before me** – The Egyptians, and other neighbouring nations, had many gods, creatures of their own fancy. This law was pre-fixed because of that transgression; and Jehovah being the God of Israel, they must entirely cleave to him, and no other, either of their own invention, or borrowed from their neighbours. The sin against this commandment, which we are most in danger of, is giving that glory to any creature which is due to God only. Pride makes a God of ourselves, covetousness makes a God of money, sensuality makes a God of the belly. Whatever is loved, feared, delighted in, or depended on, more than God,

that we make a god of. This prohibition includes a precept which is the foundation of the whole law, that we take the Lord for our God, accept him for ours, adore him with humble reverence, and set our affections entirely upon him. There is a reason intimated in the last words **before me**. It intimates:

1. That we cannot have any other god but he will know it.

2. That it is a sin that dares him to his face, which he cannot, will not, overlook. The second commandment is concerning the ordinances of worship, or the way in which God will be worshipped, which it is fit himself should appoint. Here is the prohibition; we are forbidden to worship even the true God by images. Our religious worship must be governed by the power of faith, not by the power of imagination.

5. Secondly, They must **not bow down to them** – Shew any sign of honour to them, much less serve them by sacrifice, or any other act of religious worship. When they paid their devotion to the true God, they must not have any image before them for the directing, exciting, or assisting their devotion. **For I the Lord Jehovah, thy God, am a jealous God**, especially in things of this nature. It intimates the care he has of his own institutions, his displeasure against idolaters, and that he resents every thing in his worship that looks like, or leads to, idolatry: **visiting the iniquity of the fathers upon the children unto the third and fourth generation** – Severely punishing.

6. Nor is it an unrighteous thing with God if the parents died in their iniquity, and the children tread in their steps, when God comes, by his judgments, to reckon with them, to bring into the account the idolatries their fathers were guilty of. **Keeping mercy for thousands** of persons, thousands of generations, **of them that love me and keep my commandments** – This intimates, that the second commandment, though in the letter of it is only a prohibition of false worship, yet includes a precept of worshipping God in all those ordinances which he hath instituted. As the first commandment requires the inward worship of love, desire, joy, hope, so this the outward worship of prayer and praise, and solemn attendance on his word. This mercy shall extend to thousands, much further than the wrath threatened to those that hate him, for that reaches but to the third or fourth generation.

7. The third commandment is concerning the manner of our worship; Where we have:

A strict prohibition. **Thou shalt not take the name of the Lord thy God in vain** – Supposing that, having taken Jehovah for their God, they would make mention of his name, this command gives a caution not to mention it in vain.

We take God's name in vain, first, By hypocrisy, making profession of God's name, but not living up to that profession. Secondly, By covenant breaking. If we make promises to God, and perform not to the Lord our vows, we take his name in vain. Thirdly, By rash swearing, mentioning the name of God, or any of his attributes, in the form of an oath, without any just occasion for it, but to no purpose, or to no good purpose. Fourthly, By false-swearing, which some think is chiefly intended in the letter of the commandment. Fifthly, By using the name of God lightly and carelessly. The profanation of the form of devotion is forbidden, as well as the profanation of the forms of swearing; as also, the profanation of any of those things whereby God makes himself known. **For the Lord will not hold him guiltless** – Magistrates that punish other offences, may not think themselves concerned to take notice of this; but God, who is jealous for his honour, will not connive at it. The sinner may perhaps hold himself guiltless, and think there is no harm in it; to obviate which suggestion, the threatening is thus expressed, God will **not hold him guiltless** – But more is implied, that God will himself be the avenger of those that take his name in vain; and they will find it a fearful thing to fall into the hands of the living God.

8. The fourth commandment concerns the time of worship; God is to be served and honoured daily; but one day in seven is to be particularly dedicated to his honour, and spent in his service. **Remember the sabbath day, to keep it holy; in it thou shalt do no manner of work** – It is taken for granted that the sabbath was instituted before. We read of God's blessing and sanctifying a seventh day from the beginning, Gen 2:3, so that this was not the enacting of a new law, but the reviving of an old law.

First, they are told what is the day, they must observe, a seventh after six days labour. Second, they are told how it must be observed:

1. As a day of rest; they were to do no manner of work on this day, in their worldly business.

2. As a holy day, set apart to the honour of the holy God, and to be spent in holy exercises. God, by his blessing it, had made it holy; they, by solemn blessing him, must keep it holy, and not alienate it to any other purpose than that for which the difference between it and other days was instituted.

10. Thirdly, they are told, who must observe it? Thou and **thy son** and **thy daughter** – The wife is not mentioned, because she is supposed to be one with the husband, and present with him, and if he sanctify the sabbath, it is taken for granted she will join with him; but the rest of the family is instanced in it, children and servants must keep it according to their age and capacity. In this, as in other instances of religion, it is expected that masters of families should take care, not only to serve the Lord themselves, but that their houses also should

serve him. Even the proselyted strangers must observe a difference between this day and other days, which, if it laid some restraint upon them then, yet proved a happy indication of God's gracious design, to bring the Gentiles into the church. By the sanctification of the sabbath, the Jews declared that they worshipped the God that made the world, and so distinguished themselves from all other nations, who worshipped gods which they themselves made.

12. We have here the laws of the second table, as they are commonly called; the six last commandments which concern our duty to ourselves, and one another, and are a comment upon the second great commandment, Thou shalt love thy neighbour as thyself. As religion towards God is, an essential branch of universal righteousness, so righteousness towards men is an essential branch of true religion: godliness and honesty must go together. The fifth commandment is concerning the duties we owe to our relations; that of children to their parents is only instanced in, **honour thy father and thy mother**. This includes:

1. An inward esteem of them, outwardly expressed upon all occasions in our carriage towards them; fear them, Lev 19:3, give them reverence, Heb 12:9. The contrary to this is mocking at them or despising them.

2. Obedience to their lawful commands; so it is expounded, Eph 6:1–3.

13. **Thou shalt not kill** – Thou shalt not do any thing hurtful to the health, or life of thy own body, or any other's. This doth not forbid our own necessary defence, or the magistrates putting offenders to death; but it forbids all malice and hatred to any, for he that hateth his brother is a murderer, and all revenge arising therefrom; likewise anger and hurt said or done, or aimed to be done in a passion; of this our Saviour expounds this commandment, Mt 5:22.

14. **Thou shalt not commit adultery** – This commandment forbids all acts of uncleanness, with all those desires, which produce those acts and war against the soul.

15. **Thou shalt not steal** – This command forbids us to rob ourselves of what we have, by sinful spending, or of the use and comfort of it by sinful sparing; and to rob others by invading our neighbour's rights, taking his goods, or house, or field, forcibly or clandestinely, overreaching in bargains, not restoring what is borrowed or found, with-holding just debts, rents or wages; and, which is worst of all, to rob the public in the coin or revenue, or that which is dedicated to the service of religion.

16. **Thou shalt not bear false witness** – This forbids:

1. Speaking falsely in any matter, lying, equivocating, and any way devising and designing to deceive our neighbour.

2. Speaking unjustly against our neighbour, to the prejudice of his reputation.

3. Bearing false witness against him, laying to his charge things that he knows not, either upon oath, by which the third commandment, the sixth or eighth, as well as this, are broken, or in common converse, slandering, backbiting, tale-bearing, aggravating what is done amiss, and any way endeavouring to raise our own reputation upon the ruin of our neighbour's.

17. **Thou shalt not covet** – The foregoing commands implicitly forbid all desire of doing that which will be an injury to our neighbour, this forbids all inordinate desire of having that which will be a gratification to ourselves. O that such a man's house were mine! such a man's wife mine! such a man's estate mine! This is certainly the language of discontent at our own lot, and envy at our neighbour's, and these are the sins principally forbidden here. God give us all to see our face in the glass of this law, and to lay our hearts under the government of it!

The impressions made upon the people, thereby, (18–21)

18. **They removed and stood afar off** – Before God began to speak, they were thrusting forward to gaze, but now they were effectually cured of their presumption, and taught to keep their distance.

19. **Speak thou with us** – Hereby they obliged themselves to acquiesce in the mediation of Moses, they themselves nominating him as a fit person to deal between them and God, and promising to hearken to him as to God's messenger.

20. **Fear not** – That is, Think not that this thunder and fire is, designed to consume you. No; it was intended:

1. To prove them, to try how they could like dealing with God immediately, without a mediator, and so to convince them how admirably well God had chosen for them in putting Moses into that office. Ever since Adam fled upon hearing God's voice in the garden, sinful man could not bear either to speak to God, or hear from him immediately.

2. To keep them to their duty, and prevent their sinning against God. We must not fear with amazement; but we must always have in our minds a reverence of God's majesty, a dread of his displeasure, and an obedient regard to his sovereign authority.

21. **While the people continued to stand afar off** – Afraid of God's wrath, Moses drew near unto the thick darkness; he was made to draw near, so the word is: Moses of himself durst not have ventured into the thick darkness if God had not called him, and encouraged him, and, as some of the Rabbins suppose, sent an angel to take him by the hand, and lead him up.

Some particular instructions which God gave to Moses, relating to his worship, (22–26)

22. Moses being gone into the thick darkness where God was, God there spoke in his hearing only, all that follows from hence to the end of chapter 23, which is mostly an exposition of the ten commandments; and he was to transmit it to the people. The laws in these verses relate to God's worship. **Ye have seen that I have talked with you from heaven** – Such was his wonderful condescension.

23. **Ye shall not make gods of silver** – This repetition of the second commandment comes in here, because they were more addicted to idolatry than to any other sin.

24. **An altar of earth** – It is meant of occasional altars, such as they reared in the wilderness before the tabernacle was erected, and afterwards upon special emergencies, for present use. They are appointed to make these very plain, either of earth or of unhewn stones. That they might not be tempted to think of a graven image, they must not so much as hew the stones into shape, that they made their altars of, but pile them up as they were in the rough. **In all places where I record my name** – Or where my name is recorded, that is, where I am worshipped in sincerity, I will come unto thee, and will bless thee.

26. **Neither shalt thou go up by steps unto mine altar** – Indeed afterwards God appointed an altar ten cubits high. But it is probable, they went not up to that by steps, but by a sloping ascent.

Chapter 21

The laws recorded in this chapter relate to the fifth and sixth commandments; and though not accommodated to our constitution, especially in point of servitude yet are of great use for the explanation of the moral law, and the rules of natural justice.

The duty of masters towards their servants (1–11)

1. The first verse is the general title of the laws contained in this and the two following chapters. Their government being purely a theocracy; that which in other states is to be settled by human prudence, was directed among them by a divine appointment. These laws are called judgments; because their magistrates were to give judgment according to them. In the doubtful cases that had hitherto occurred, Moses had particularly enquired of God, but now God gave him statutes in general, by which to determine particular cases. He begins with the laws concerning servants, commanding

mercy and moderation towards them. The Israelites had lately been servants themselves, and now they were become not only their own masters, but masters of servants too; lest they should abuse their servants as they themselves had been abused, provision was made for the mild and gentle usage of servants.

2. If thou buy an Hebrew servant – Either sold by him or his parents through poverty, or by the judges for his crimes, yet even such a one was to continue in slavery but seven years at the most.

6. For ever – As long as he lives, or till the year of Jubilee.

8. Who hath betrothed her to himself – For a concubine, or secondary wife. Not that masters always took maid-servants on these terms.

9. After the manner of daughters – He shall give her a portion, as to a daughter.

Various punishments (12–36)

20. Direction is given what should be done, if a servant died by his master's correction. This servant must not be an Israelite, but a Gentile slave, and it is supposed that he smite him with a rod, and not with any thing that was likely to give a mortal wound, yet if he died under his hand, he should be punished for his cruelty, at the discretion of the judges, upon consideration of circumstances.

24. Eye for eye – The execution of this law is not put into the hands of private persons, as if every man might avenge himself, which would introduce universal confusion. The tradition of the elders seems to have put this corrupt gloss upon it. But magistrates had an eye to this rule in punishing offenders, and doing right to those that are injured.

Chapter 22

Further commandments (1–31)

1. Five oxen for an ox, and four sheep for a sheep – More for an ox than for a sheep, because the owner, besides all the other profit, lost the daily labour of his ox. If he were not able to make restitution, he must be sold for a slave: the court of judgment was to do it, and it is likely the person robbed received the money.

2. If a thief broke a house in the night, and was killed in the doing it, his blood was upon his own head. But if it were in the day-time that the thief was killed, he that killed him was accountable for it, unless it were in the necessary defence of his own life.

3. For he should make full restitution – This the law determined: not that he should die.

4. In his hand alive – Not killed, nor sold, as Ex 22:1, so that the owner recover it with less charge and trouble.

5. He that wilfully put his cattle into his neighbour's field, must make restitution of the best of his own. The Jews hence observed it as a general rule, that restitution must always be made of the best; and that no man should keep any cattle that were likely to trespass upon his neighbour, or do him any damage.

6. He that designed only the burning of **thorns** might become accessary to the burning of corn, and should not be held guiltless. If the fire did mischief, he that kindled it must answer for it, though it could not be proved that he designed the mischief. Men must suffer for their carelessness, as well as for their malice. It will make us very careful of ourselves, if we consider that we are accountable not only for the hurt we do, but for the hurt we occasion through inadvertency.

7. If a man deliver goods, suppose to a carrier to be conveyed, or to a warehouse-keeper to be preserved, or cattle to a farmer to be fed upon a valuable consideration, and a special confidence reposed in the person they are lodged with; in case these goods be stolen or lost, perish or be damaged, if it appear that it was not by any fault of the trustee, the owner must stand to the loss, otherwise he that has been false to his trust must be compelled to make satisfaction.

14. If a man lent his team to his neighbour, if the owner were with it, or were to receive profit for the loan of it, whatever harm befell the cattle the owner must stand to the loss of it: but if the owner were so kind to the borrower as to lend it him gratis, and put such a confidence in him as to trust it from under his own eye, then, if any harm happened, the borrower must make it good. Learn hence to be very careful not to abuse any thing that is lent to us; it is not only unjust but base and disingenuous, we should much rather choose to lose ourselves, than that any should sustain loss by their kindness to us.

18. Witchcraft not only gives that honour to the devil which is due to God alone, but bids defiance to the divine providence, wages war with God's government, puts his work into the devil's hand expecting him to do good and evil.

21. A stranger must not be abused, not wronged in judgment by the magistrates, not imposed upon in contracts, nor any advantage taken of his ignorance or necessity, no, nor must he be taunted, or upbraided with his being a stranger; for all these were vexations. **For ye were strangers in Egypt** – and knew what it was to be vexed and oppressed there. Those that have themselves been in poverty and distress, if Providence enrich and enlarge them, ought to shew a particular tenderness towards those that are now in such circumstances as they were in formerly, now doing to them as they then wished to be done by.

22. Ye shall not afflict the widow, or fatherless child – That is, ye shall comfort and assist them, and be ready upon all occasions to shew them kindness. In making just demands from them, their condition must be considered who have lost those that should protect them: they are supposed to be unversed in business, destitute of advice, timorous, and of a tender spirit; and therefore must be treated with kindness and compassion, and no advantage taken against them, nor any hardship put upon them, which a husband or a father would have sheltered them from.

25. If thou lend –

1. They must not receive use for money from any that borrowed for necessity. And such provision the law made for the preserving estates to their families by the year of Jubilee, that a people who had little concern in trade could not be supposed to borrow money but for necessity; therefore it was generally forbidden among themselves; but to a stranger they were allowed to lend upon usury. This law therefore in the strictness of it seems to have been peculiar to the Jewish state; but in the equity of it, it obligeth us to shew mercy to those we have advantage against, and to be content to share with those we lend to in loss as well as profit, if Providence cross them: and upon this condition it seems as lawful to receive interest for my money, which another takes pains with, and improves, as it is to receive rent for my land, which another takes pains with, and improves, for his own use.

2. They must not take a poor man's bed-clothes in pawn; but if they did, must restore them by bed-time.

28. Thou shalt not revile the gods – That is, the judges and magistrates. Princes and magistrates are our fathers, whom the fifth commandment obligeth us to honour, and forbids us to revile. St. Paul applies this law to himself, and owns that he ought not to speak evil of the ruler of his people, no, not though he was then his most unrighteous persecutor, Acts 23:5.

29. The first-born of thy sons shalt thou give unto me – And much more reason have we to give ourselves and all we have to God, who spared not his own Son, but delivered him up for us all. The first ripe of their corn they must not delay to offer; there is danger if we delay our duty, lest we wholly omit it; and by slipping the first opportunity in expectation of another, we suffer Satan to cheat us of all our time.

31. Ye shall be holy unto me – And one mark of that honourable distinction is appointed in their diet, which was, that they should not **eat any flesh that was torn of beasts** – Both because the blood was not duly taken out of it, and because the clean beast was ceremonially defiled, by the touch of the unclean.

Chapter 23
Laws concerning justice (1–9)

1. Thou shalt not raise, the margin reads, Thou shalt not receive a false report, for sometimes the receiver in this case is as bad as the thief; and a backbiting tongue would not do so much mischief, if it were not countenanced. Sometimes we cannot avoid hearing a false report, but we must not receive it, we must not hear it with pleasure, nor easily give credit to it.

2. Thou shalt not follow a multitude to do evil – General usage will never excuse us in any ill practice; nor is the broad way ever the safer for its being crowded. We must inquire what we ought to do, not what the most do; because we must be judged by our master, not our fellow servants; and it is too great a compliment, to be willing to go to hell for company.

7. Keep thee far from a false matter – From assisting or abetting an ill thing. Yea, keep thee far from it, dread it as a dangerous snare. **I will not justify the wicked** – That is, I will condemn him that unjustly condemns others.

9. Thou shalt not oppress the stranger – Though aliens might not inherit lands among them; yet they must have justice done them. It was an instance of the equity of our law, that if an alien be tried for any crime except treason, the one half of his jury, if he desire it, shall be foreigners; a kind provision that strangers may not be oppressed. **For ye know the heart of a stranger** – You know something of the griefs and fears of a stranger by sad experience.

The Sabbatical Year (10–13)

10. The institution of the sabbatical year was designed

1. To shew what a plentiful land that was, into which God was bringing them, that so numerous a people could have rich maintenance out of the products of so small a country, without foreign trade, and yet could spare the increase of every seventh year.

2. To teach them a confidence in the Divine Providence, while they did their duty, that as the sixth day's manna served for two days meat, so the sixth year's increase should serve for two years subsistence.

13. In all things that I have said unto you be circumspect – We are in danger of missing our way on the right hand and on the left, and it is at our peril if we do, therefore we have need to look about us. A man may ruin himself through mere carelessness, but he cannot save himself without great care and circumspection; particularly since idolatry was a sin they were much addicted to, and would be greatly tempted to, they must endeavour to blot out the remembrance of the gods of the heathen, and must disuse all their superstitious forms of speech, and never mention them but with detestation.

The three annual feasts, (14–19)

14. The Passover, Pentecost, and feast of Tabernacles, in spring, summer, and autumn, were the three times appointed for their attendance; not in winter, because travelling was then uncomfortable; nor in the midst of their harvest.

17. All thy males – All that were of competent years, and health and strength, and at their own disposal. It is probable, servants were exempt: for none was to appear without an offering: but most of these had nothing to offer.

Gracious promises that God would conduct them through the wilderness, (20–33)

19. Some of the Gentiles, at the end of their harvest, seethed a kid in it's dam's milk, and sprinkled that milk-pottage in a magical way upon their gardens and fields, to make them fruitful. But Israel must abhor such foolish customs. Is not this rather forbidden, as having some appearance of cruelty?

20. Behold, I send an Angel before thee – The angel of the covenant: Accordingly the Israelites in the wilderness are said to tempt Christ. It is promised that this blessed anger should keep them in the way, though it lay through a wilderness first, and afterwards through their enemies country; and thus Christ has prepared a place for his followers.

21. Beware of him, and obey his voice; provoke him not – It is at your peril if you do; **for my name** – My nature, my authority is in him.

25. He shall bless thy bread, and thy water – And God's blessing will make bread and water more refreshing and nourishing, than a feast of fat things, and wines on the lees, without that blessing. **And I will take sickness away** – Either prevent it or remove it. Thy land shall not be visited with epidemical diseases, which are very dreadful, and sometimes have laid countries waste.

26. The number of thy days I will fulfill – And they shall not be cut off in the midst by untimely deaths. Thus hath godliness the promise of the life that now is.

27. I will send my fear before thee – And they that fear will soon flee. Hosts of hornets also made way for the hosts of Israel; such mean creatures can God make use of for the chastising of his people's enemies.

Chapter 24

The covenant is ratified (1–11)

1. Worship ye afar off – Before they came near, they must worship. Thus we must enter into God's gates with humble and solemn adorations.

2. And Moses alone shall come near – Being therein a type of Christ, who as the high priest entered alone into the most holy place. In the following verses we have the solemn covenant made between God and Israel and the exchanging of the ratifications: typifying the covenant of grace between God and believers through Christ.

3. Moses told the people all the words of the Lord – He laid before them all the precepts, in the foregoing chapters, and put it to them, whether they were willing to submit to these laws or no? **And all the people answered, All the words which the Lord hath said we will do** – They had before consented in general to be under God's government; here they consent in particular to these laws now given.

4. And Moses wrote the words of the Lord – That there might be no mistake; as God dictated them on the mount, where, it is highly probable, God taught him the use of letters. These Moses taught the Israelites, from whom they afterwards travelled to Greece and other nations. As soon as God had separated to himself a peculiar people, he governed them by a written word, as he has done ever since, and will do while the world stands. **Pillars** according to **the number of the tribes** – These were to represent the people, the other party to the covenant; and we may suppose they were set up over against the altar, and that Moses as mediator passed to and fro between them. Probably each tribe set up and knew its own pillar, and their elders stood by it. He then appointed sacrifices to be offered upon the altar. The blood of the sacrifice which the people offered was (part of it) sprinkled upon the altar, which signified the people's dedicating themselves to God, and his honour. In the blood of the sacrifices, all the Israelites were presented unto God as living sacrifices, Rom 12:1. 2. The blood of the sacrifice which God had owned and accepted was (the remainder of it) sprinkled, either upon the people themselves, or upon the pillars that represented them, which signified God's conferring his favour upon them, and all the fruits of that favour, and his giving them all the gifts they could desire from a God reconciled to them, and in covenant with them. This part of the ceremony was thus explained, Behold the blood of the covenant; see here how God sealed to you to be a God, and you seal to be to him a people; his promises to you, and yours to him, are yea and amen. Thus our Lord Jesus, the Mediator of the new covenant (of whom Moses was a type) having offered up himself a sacrifice upon the cross, that his blood might be indeed the blood of the covenant, sprinkled it upon the altar in his intercession (Heb 9:12,) and sprinkles it upon his church by his word and ordinances, and the influences and operations of the Spirit of promise by whom we are sealed.

10. They saw the God of Israel – That is, they had some glimpse of his glory, in light and fire, though they saw no manner of similitude. They saw the place where the God of Israel stood, so the seventy, something that came near a similitude, but was not; whatever they saw it was certainly something of which no image or picture could be made, and yet enough to satisfy them that God was with them of a truth. Nothing is described but that which was under his feet, for our conceptions of God are all below him. They saw not so much as God's feet, but at the bottom of the brightness they saw (such as they never saw before or after, and as the foot-stool or pedestal of it) a most rich and splendid pavement, as it had been of sapphires, azure, or sky-coloured. The heavens themselves are the pavement of God's palace, and his throne is above the firmament.

11. Upon the nobles or elders of Israel he laid not his hand – Though they were men, the splendour of his glory did not overwhelm them, but it was so moderated (Job 36:9,) and they were so strengthened (Dan 10:19,) that they were able to bear it: nay, though they were sinful men, and obnoxious to God's justice, yet he did not lay his avenging hand upon them, as they feared he would. When we consider what a consuming fire God is, and what stubble we are before him, we shall have reason to say, in all our approaches to him, It is of the Lord's mercies we are not consumed. They saw God, and did eat and drink; They had not only their lives preserved, but their vigour, courage, and comfort; it cast no damp upon their joy, but rather increased it. They feasted upon the sacrifice before God, in token of their cheerful consent to the covenant, their grateful acceptance of the benefits of it, and their communion with God in pursuance of that covenant.

The revelation from Mount Sinai (12–18)

12. Come up to the mount and be there – Expect to continue there for some time.

13. Joshua was **his minister** or servant, and it would be a satisfaction to him to have him with him as a companion during the six days that he tarried in the mount before God called to him. Joshua was to be his successor, and therefore thus he was honoured before the people, and thus he was prepared by being trained up in communion with God.

16. A cloud covered the mount six days – A visible token of God's special presence there, for he so shows himself to us, as at the same time to conceal himself from us, he lets us know so much as to assure us of his power and grace, but intimates to us that we cannot find him out to

perfection. During these six days Moses stayed waiting upon the mountain, for a call into the presence-chamber. And on **the seventh day** – Probably the sabbath-day, he called unto Moses. Now the thick cloud opened in the sight of all Israel, and the glory of the Lord broke forth like devouring fire.

18. Moses went into the midst of the cloud – It was an extraordinary presence of mind, which the grace of God furnished him with, else he durst not have ventured into the cloud, especially when it broke out in devouring fire. **And Moses was in the mount forty days and forty nights** – It should seem the six days, were not part of the forty; for during those six days, Joshua was with Moses, who did eat of the manna, and drink of the brook mentioned, Deu 9:21, and while they were together, it is probable Moses did eat and drink with him; but when Moses was called into the midst of the cloud, he left Joshua without, who continued to eat and drink daily while he waited for Moses's return, but from thenceforward Moses fasted.

Chapter 25

At this chapter begins an account of the instructions God gave Moses for erecting and furnishing the tabernacle.

A collection to be made among the people, (1–9)

1. Doubtless when Moses went into the midst of the cloud, and abode there so long, he saw and heard glorious things, but they were things which were not lawful or possible to utter; and therefore, in the records he kept of the transactions there, he saith nothing to satisfy curiosity, but writes that only which he was to speak to the children of Israel. Probably there never was any house or temple built for sacred uses, before this tabernacle was erected by Moses. In this God kept his court, as Israel's king, and it was intended for a sign or token of his presence, that while they had that in the midst of them they might never again ask, Is the Lord among us or not? And because in the wilderness they dwelt in tents, even this royal palace was ordered to be a tabernacle too, that it might move with them. And these holy places made with hands were the figures of the true, Heb 9:24. The gospel-church is the true tabernacle which the Lord pitched, and not man, Heb 8:2. The body of Christ, in and by which he made atonement, was the greater and more perfect tabernacle, Heb 9:11, 'The Word was made flesh, and dwelt among us, as in a tabernacle.'

2. Speak unto the children of Israel that they bring me an offering – This offering was to be given willingly, and with the heart. It was not prescribed to them what or how much they must give, but it was left to their generosity, that they might shew their good-will to the house of God, and the offices thereof.

4. Blue, and purple, and scarlet – Materials of those colours.

5. Shittim-wood – A kind of wood growing in Egypt and the deserts of Arabia, very durable and precious.

8. A sanctuary – A place of public and solemn worship; **that I may dwell among them.** Not by my essence, which is everywhere; but by my grace and glorious operations.

9. According to all that I shew thee – God showed him an exact plan of it in little, which he must conform to in all points. And God did not only shew him the model, but gave him also particular directions how to frame the tabernacle, according to that model, in all the parts of it. When Moses was to describe the creation of the world, though it be such a stately and curious fabric, yet he gave a very short and general account of it; but when he comes to describe the tabernacle, he doth it with the greatest niceness and accuracy imaginable: for God's church and instituted religion is more precious to him than all the rest of the world. And the scriptures were written not to describe to us the works of nature, but to acquaint us with the methods of grace, and those things which are purely matters of revelation.

The ark of the covenant, (10–22)

10. The **ark** was a chest or coffer, in which the two tables of the law, written with the finger of God, were to be deposited. This chest or cabinet was overlaid within and without with thin plates of gold; it had a crown, or cornish of gold round it; rings and staves to carry it with; and in it he must put the testimony. The tables of the law are called the testimony, because God did in them testify his will; his giving them that law was in token of his favour to them, and their acceptance of it was in token of their subjection to him. This law was a testimony to them to direct them in their duty, and would be a testimony against them if they transgressed. The ark is called the ark of the testimony, Exo 30:6, and the tabernacle, the tabernacle of the testimony, Num 10:11. The tables of the law were carefully preserved in the ark, to teach us to make much of the word of God, and to hide it in our inmost thoughts, as the ark was placed in the holy of holies. It intimates likewise the care which divine providence ever did, and ever will take to preserve the records of divine revelation in the church, so that even in the latter days there shall be seen in his temple the ark of his testament. See Rev 11:19.

17. The **mercy seat** was the covering of the ark, made exactly to fit the dimensions of it. This propitiatory covering, as it might well be translated, was a type of Christ the great propitiation, whose satisfaction covers our transgressions, and comes between us and the curse we deserve.

18. The cherubim (Cherubim is the plural of Cherub, not Cherubims) were fixed to the mercy-seat, and of a piece with it, and spread their wings over it. It is supposed these were designed to represent the holy angels, (who always attend the Shechinah, or divine majesty,) not by any effigies of an angel, but some emblem of the angelical nature, probably one or more of those four faces spoken of Eze 1:10. Whatever the faces were, they looked one towards another, and both downwards towards the ark, while their wings were stretched out so as to touch one another. It notes their attendance upon the Redeemer, their readiness to do his will, their presence in the assemblies of saints, Psa 68:17 1Cor 11:10, and their desire to look into the mysteries of the gospel, which they diligently contemplate, 1Pet 1:12. God is said to dwell or sit between the cherubim, on the mercy-seat, Psa 80:1, and from thence he here promiseth for the future to meet with Moses, and to commune with him. Thus he manifests himself, willing to keep up communion with us, by the mediation of Christ.

The table of shew-bread, (23–30)

23. This **table** was to stand not in the holy of holies, (nothing was in that but the ark with its appurtenances) but in the outer part of the tabernacle, called the sanctuary or holy place. This table was to be always furnished with the shew-bread, or bread of faces, twelve loaves, one for each tribe, set in two rows, six in a row. As the ark signified God's being present with them, so the twelve loaves signified their being presented to God. This bread was designed to be, a thankful acknowledgment of God's goodness to them in giving them their daily bread, a token of their communion with God; this bread on God's table being made of the same corn as the bread on their own tables. And a type of the spiritual provision which is made in the church, by the gospel of Christ, for all that are made priests to our God.

The golden candlestick, (31–40)

31. This **candlestick** had many branches drawn from the main shaft, which had not only bowls to put the oil and the kindled wick in for necessity, but knops made in the form of a pomegranate and flowers for ornament. The tabernacle had no windows, all its light was candle-light, which notes the comparative darkness of that dispensation, while the sun of righteousness was not as yet risen, nor had the day-star from on high visited his church. Yet God left not himself without witness, nor them without instruction; the commandment was a lamp, and the law a light, and the prophets were branches from that lamp, which gave light in their several ages. The church is still dark, as the tabernacle was, in comparison with what it will be in heaven: but the word of God is the candle-stick, a light burning in a dark place.

Chapter 26

These particulars seem of little use to us now, yet having been of great use to Moses and Israel, and God having thought fit to preserve to us the remembrance of them, we ought not to over-look them.

Instructions concerning the curtains, (1–14)

1. The curtains were to be embroidered with cherubim, to intimate that the angels of God pitched their tents round about the church, Psa 34:7. As there were cherubim over the mercy-seat, so there were round the tabernacle. There were to be two hangings, five breadths to each, sewed together, and the two hangings coupled together with golden clasps or tacks, so that it might be all one tabernacle, Ex 26:6. Thus the churches of Christ, though they are many, yet are one, being fitly joined together in holy love and by the unity of the Spirit, so growing into one holy temple in the Lord.

14. **Badgers' skins** – So we translate it, but it should rather seem to have been some strong sort of leather, (but very fine) for we read of the best sort of shoes made of it, Eze 16:10.

Instructions concerning boards and sockets (15–30)

15. Very particular directions are here given about the **boards** of the tabernacle, which were to bear up the curtains. These had tenons which fell into the mortices that were made for them in silver bases. The boards were coupled togeth-er with gold rings at top and bottom, and kept firm with bars that run through golden staples in every board. Thus every thing in the taberna-cle was very splendid, agreeable to that infant state of the church, when such things were proper to possess the minds of the worshippers with a reverence of the divine glory. In allusion to this, the new Jerusalem is said to be of pure gold, Rev 21:18. But the builders of the gospel church said, Silver and gold have we none; and yet the glory of their building far exceeded that of the tabernacle.

Instructions concerning the veils (31–37)

31. **A vail** – The veils are here ordered to be made, one for a partition between the holy place and the most holy, which not only forbad any to enter, but so much as to look into the holiest of all. Under that dispensation divine grace was veiled, but now we behold it with open face. The apostle tells us, this veil, intimated that the cere-monial law could not make the comers thereun-to perfect. The way into the holiest was not made manifest while the first tabernacle was standing; life and immortality lay concealed till they were brought to light by the gospel, which was therefore signified by the rending of this veil at the death of Christ. We have now bold-ness to enter into the holiest in all acts of devo-tion by the blood of Jesus; yet such as obliges us to a holy reverence, and a humble sense of our distance. Another veil was for the outward door of the tabernacle. Through this the priests went in every day to minister in the holy-place, but not the people, Heb 9:6.

Chapter 27

Concerning the brazen altar, (1–8)

1. As God intended in the tabernacle to man-ifest his presence among his people, so there they were to pay their devotions to him; not in the tabernacle itself, into that only the priests entered as God's domestic servants, but in the court before the tabernacle, where, as common subjects they attended. There an altar was ordered so be set up, to which they must bring their sacrifices; and this altar was to sanctify their gifts; from hence they were to present their services to God, as from the mercy-seat he gave his oracles to them; and thus a communion was settled between God and Israel.

2. **The horns of it,** were for ornament and for use; the sacrifices were bound with cords to the horns of the altar, and to them malefactors fled for refuge.

4. The **grate** was set into the hollow of the altar, about the middle of it, in which the fire was kept, and the sacrifice burnt; it was made of net-work like a sieve, and hung hollow, that the fire might burn the better, and that the ashes might fall through. Now, this brazen altar was a type of Christ dying to make atonement for our sins. Christ sanctified himself for his church as their altar, John 17:19, and by his mediation sanctifies the daily services of his people. To the horns of this altar poor sinners fly for refuge, and are safe in virtue of the sacrifice there offered.

Concerning the court of the tabernacle, (9–19)

9. Before the tabernacle there was to be a **court,** enclosed with **hangings of fine linen.** This court, according to the common computa-tion, was 50 yards long, and 25 broad. Pillars were set up at convenient distances, in sockets of brass, the pillars filleted with silver, and silver

tenterhooks in them, on which the linen hangings were fastened: the hanging which served for the gate was finer than the rest. This court was a type of the church, enclosed, and distinguished from the rest of the world; the inclosure supported by pillars, noting the stability of the church hung with the clean linen, which is said to be the righteousness of saints, Rev 19:8. Yet this court would contain but a few worshippers; thanks be to God, now the inclosure is taken down; and there is room for all that in every place call on the name of Christ.

Concerning the oil for the lamp, (20–21)

20. We read of the candlestick in the 25th chapter; here is order given for the keeping of the lamps constantly burning in it. The pure oil signified the gifts and graces of the Spirit, which are communicated to all believers from Christ the good olive, of whose fulness we receive, Zech 4:11–12. The priests were to light the lamps, and to tend them; to cause the lamp to burn always, night and day. Thus it is the work of ministers to preach and expound the scriptures, which are as a lamp to enlighten the church. This is to be a statute for ever, that the lamps of the word be lighted as duly as the incense of prayer and praise is offered.

Chapter 28

In this and the following chapter care is taken about the priests that were to minister in this holy place.

The command to make the priest's holy garments (1–5)

1. Aaron and his sons – Hitherto every master of a family was priest to his own family. But now the families of Israel began to be incorporated into a nation, and a tabernacle of the congregation was to be erected, as a visible centre of their unity, it was requisite there should be a public priesthood instituted. Moses, who had hitherto officiated, and is therefore reckoned among the priests of the Lord, Psa 99:6, had enough to do as their prophet, to consult the oracle for them, and as their prince, to judge among them. Nor was he desirous to engross all the honours to himself, or to entail that of the priesthood, which alone was hereditary, upon his own family; but was very well pleased to see his brother Aaron invested with this office, and his sons after him; while his sons after him would be but common Levites. It is an instance of the humility of that great man, and an evidence of his sincere regard to the glory of God, that he had so little regard to the preferment of his own family. Aaron, that had humbly served as a prophet to his younger brother Moses, and did not decline the office, is now advanced to be a priest to God. God had said to Israel in general, that they should be to him a kingdom of priests; but because it was requisite that those who ministered at the altar should give themselves wholly to the service, God here chose from among them one to be a family of priests, the father and his four sons; and from Aaron's loins descended all the priests of the Jewish church, whom we read of both in the Old Testament and in the New.

2. The priests' garments were made **for glory and beauty** – Some of the richest materials were to be provided, and the best artists employed in making them, whose skill God, by a special gift, would improve to a very high degree. Eminency, even in common arts, is a gift of God; it comes from him, and, ought to be used for him. The garments appointed were:

1. Four, which both the high-priest and the inferior priests wore, viz. The linen breeches, the linen coat, the linen girdle which fastened it to them, and the bonnet; that which the high-priest wore is called a mitre.

2. Four more which were peculiar to the high-priest, the ephod, with the curious girdle of it, the breast-plate of judgment, the long robe, and the golden plate on his forehead.

These glorious garments, were appointed:

1. That the priests themselves might be minded of the dignity of their office.

2. That the people might thereby be possessed with a holy reverence of that God whose ministers appeared in such grandeur.

3. That the priests might be types of Christ, and of all Christians who have the beauty of holiness put upon them.

The ephod (6–14)

6. The ephod, was the outmost garment of the high-priest; linen ephods were worn by the inferior priests, but this, which the high-priest wore, was called a golden ephod, because there was a great deal of gold woven into it. It was a short coat without sleeves, buttoned close to him with a curious girdle of the same stuff. The shoulder pieces were buttoned together with two precious stones set in gold, one on each shoulder. In allusion to this, Christ our high priest appeared to John, girt about the paps with a golden girdle, such as was the curious girdle of the ephod, Rev 1:13. Righteousness is the girdle of his loins. He is girt with strength for the work of our salvation. And as Aaron had the names of all Israel upon his shoulders in precious stones, so He presents to himself and to his Father a glorious church, Eph 5:27. He bears them before the Lord for a memorial, in token of his appearing before God as the representative of all Israel, and an advocate for them.

11. Ouches – Hollow places, such as are made in gold rings, to receive and hold the precious stones.

The breast-plate of judgement, (15–29)

15. The most considerable of the ornaments of the high priest was this **breast-plate**, a rich piece of cloth curiously wrought with gold and purple, two spans long, and a span broad; so that, being doubled, it was a span square. In this breast-plate, the tribes of Israel were recommended to God's favour in twelve precious stones. Some question whether Levi had a precious stone with his name on or no; if not Ephraim and Manasseh were reckoned distinct, as Jacob had said they should be, and the high priest himself being head of the tribe of Levi, sufficiently represented that tribe. Aaron was to bear their names for a memorial before the Lord continually, being ordained for men, to represent them in things pertaining to God; herein typifying our great High Priest, who always appears in the presence of God for us. The name of each tribe was engraved in a precious stone, to signify how precious, in God's sight, believers are, and how honourable, Isa 43:4. The high priest had the names of the tribes both on his shoulders and on his breast, noting both the power and the love with which our Lord Jesus intercedes for us. How near should Christ's name lie to our hearts, since he is pleased to lay our names so near his? And what a comfort is it to us, in all our addresses to God, that the great High Priest of our profession has the names of all his Israel upon his breast, before the Lord, for a memorial, presenting them to God?

The Urim and Thummim, (30)

30. The Urim and Thummim – By which the will of God was made known in doubtful cases, was put in this breast-plate, which is therefore called the breast-plate of judgment. Urim and Thummim signify light and integrity: many conjectures there are among the learned what they were: we have no reason to think they were any thing that Moses was to make, more than what was before ordered; so that either God made them himself, and gave them to Moses, for him to put into the breast-plate when other things were prepared; or, no more is meant but a declaration of the farther use of what was already ordered to be made. The words may be read thus, And thou shalt give, or add, to the breast-plate of judgment, the illuminations and perfections, and **they shall be upon the heart of Aaron** – That is, he shall be endued with a power of knowing and making known the mind of God in all difficult cases relating either to the civil or ecclesiastical state. Their government was a theocracy; God was their king, the high priest was, under God, their ruler, this Urim and Thummim were his cabinet council: probably Moses wrote upon the breast-plate, or wove into it, these words, Urim and Thummim, to signify, that the high-priest, having on him this breast-plate, and asking council of God in any emergency, should be directed to those measures, which God would own. If he were standing before the ark, probably he received instructions from off the mercy-seat, as Moses did, Ex 25:22. If he were at a distance from the ark, as Abiathar was when he enquired of the Lord for David, 1Sam 23:6, then the answer was given either by a voice from heaven, or by an impulse upon the mind of the high priest, which last is perhaps intimated in that expression, he shall bear the judgment of the children of Israel upon his heart. This oracle was of great use to Israel. Joshua consulted it, Num 27:21, and it is likely, the judges after him. It was lost in the captivity, and never retrieved after. It was a shadow of good things to come, and the substance is Christ. He is our oracle; by him God in these last days, makes known himself and his mind to us. Divine revelation centres in him, and comes to us through him; he is the light, the true light, the faithful witness; and from him we receive the Spirit of truth, who leads into all truth. The joining of the breast-plate to the ephod notes, that his prophetical office was founded on his priesthood; and it was by the merit of his death that he purchased this honour for himself, and this favour for us. It was the Lamb that had been slain that was worthy to take the book and to open the seals. Rev 5:9.

The judgment – The breast-plate of judgment: That breast-plate which declared the judgment or mind of God to the Israelites.

The robe of the ephod, (31–35)

31. The robe of the ephod – This was next under the ephod, and reached down to the knees, without sleeves, and was put on over their head, having holes on the sides to put the arms through, or, as Maimonides describes it, was not sewn together on the sides at all. The hole on the top through which the head was put was carefully bound about, that it might not tear in the putting on. The bells gave notice to the people in the outer court, when he went into the holy place to burn incense, that they might then apply themselves to their devotions at the same time, Luke 1:10, in token of their concurrence with him, and their hopes of the ascent of their prayers to God in the virtue of the incense he offered. Aaron must come near to minister in the garments that were appointed him, that he die not. 'Tis at his peril if he attend otherwise than according to the institution.

32. An habergeon – A coat of armour.

33. Pomegranates – The figures of Pomegranates, but flat and embroidered.

The mitre, (36–39)

36. On the golden plate fixed upon Aaron's forehead, like an half coronet, reaching, as the Jews say, from ear to ear, must be engraved, **Holiness to the Lord** – Aaron must hereby be minded, that God is holy, and that his priests must be holy. The high priest must be consecrated to God, and so must all his ministrations. All that attend in God's house must have holiness to the Lord engraved upon their foreheads, that is, they must be holy, devoted to the Lord, and designing his glory in all they do. This must appear in their forehead, in an open profession of their relation to God, as those that are not ashamed to own it, and in a conversation answerable to it. It must likewise be engraved like the engravings of a signet, so deep, so durable; not painted, so as it may be washed off, but sincere and lasting.

38. Aaron must have this upon his **forehead**, that he may **bear the iniquity of the holy things, and that they may be accepted before the Lord** – Herein he was a type of Christ, the great Mediator between God and man. Through him what is amiss in our services is pardoned: even this would be our ruin, if God should enter into judgment with us: but Christ our high priest bears this iniquity; bears it for us, so as to bear it from us. Through him likewise what is good is accepted; our persons, our performances are pleasing to God upon the account of Christ's intercession, and not otherwise. His being holiness to the Lord, recommends all those to the divine favour that believe in him. Having such a high priest, we come boldly to the throne of grace.

39. Embroidered the coat of fine linen – Was the innermost of the priestly garments, it reached to the feet, and the sleeves to the wrists, and was bound to the body with a girdle or sash of needlework. The mitre or diadem was of linen, such as kings anciently wore in the east, typifying the kingly office of Christ.

The garments of the inferior priests, (40–43)

43. It shall be a statute for ever – That is, It is to continue as long as the priesthood continues. And it is to have its perpetuity in the substance, of which these things were the shadows.

Chapter 29

Orders concerning the consecration of the priests, and the sanctification of the altar, (1–37)

4. They were to be consecrated at **the door of the tabernacle** – God was pleased to dwell in the tabernacle, the people attending in the courts, so that the door between the court and the tabernacle was the fittest place for them to be consecrated in, who were to mediate between God and man, and to stand between both, and lay their hands upon both. Here they were to be washed, signifying that they must be clean who bear the vessels of the Lord, Isa 52:11. And they were to be clothed with the holy garments, to signify that it was not sufficient for them to put away the pollutions of sin, but they must put on the graces of the Spirit, be clothed with righteousness, Psa 132:9. They must be girded, as men prepared and strengthened for their work; and they must be robed and crowned, as men that counted their work and office their true honour.

7. The high priest was to be anointed with the holy **anointing oil** – That the church might be filled with the sweet favour of his administrations, and in token of the pouring out of the Spirit upon him, to qualify him for his work.

10. There must be a sin-offering, to make atonement for them. The law made them priests that had infirmity; and therefore they must first offer for their own sin, before they could make atonement for the people, Heb 7:27,28. They were to put their hand on the head of their sacrifice; confessing that they deserved to die for their own sin, and desiring that the killing of the beast might be accepted as a vicarious satisfaction. It was used as other sin-offerings were; only, whereas the flesh of other sin-offerings was eaten by the priests, in token of the priests taking away the sin of the people, this was appointed to be all burnt without the camp, to signify the imperfection of the legal dispensation, for the sins of the priests themselves could not be taken away by those sacrifices, but they must expect a better high priest, and a better sacrifice.

15. There must be a burnt-offering, a ram wholly burnt, in token of the dedication of themselves wholly to God, as living sacrifices, kindled with the fire, and ascending in the flame of holy love. This sin-offering must be offered, and then the burnt-offering, for till guilt be removed no acceptable service can be performed.

19. There must be a peace-offering; it is called the ram of consecration, because there was more in this, peculiar to the occasion, than in the other two. In the burnt-offering God had the glory of their priesthood, in this they had the comfort of it. And in token of a mutual covenant between God and them, the blood of this sacrifice was divided between God and them, part of the blood was sprinkled upon the altar round about, and part upon them, upon their bodies, and upon their garments. Thus the benefit of the expiation made by the sacrifice was applied and assured to them, and their whole selves from head to foot sanctified to the service of God. The blood was put upon the extreme parts of the body, to signify, that it was all as it were enclosed and taken in for God, the tip of the ear, and the great toe not excepted. And the blood and oil signified the blood of Christ, and the graces of the Spirit, which constitute the beauty of holiness, and recommend us to God. The flesh of the sacrifice, with the meat-offering annexed to it, was likewise divided between God and them, that God and they might feast together, in token of friendship and fellowship.

22. Part of it was to be first waved before the Lord, and then burnt upon the altar, these were first put into the hands of Aaron to be waved to and fro in token of their being offered to God, and then they were to be burnt upon the altar, for the altar was to devour God's part of the sacrifice. Thus God admitted Aaron and his sons to wait at his table, taking the meat of his altar from their hands. Here, in a parenthesis as it were, comes in the law concerning the priests part of the peace-offerings afterwards, the breast and shoulder, which were now divided; Moses had the breast, and the shoulder was burnt on the altar with God's part.

31. The other part of the flesh of the ram, and of the bread, Aaron and his sons were to eat at the door of the tabernacle, to signify that he not only called them servants but friends. He supped with them, and they with him. Their eating of the things wherewith the atonement was made, signified their receiving the atonement, their thankful acceptance of the benefit of it, and their joyful communion with God thereupon.

35. **Seven days shalt thou consecrate them** – Though all the ceremonies were performed on the first day, yet, they were not to look upon their consecration as completed till the seven days end, which put a solemnity upon their admission, and a distance between this and their former state, and obliged them to enter upon their work with a pause, giving them time to consider the weight of it. This was to be observed in after ages: he that was to succeed Aaron in the high priesthood, must put on the holy garments seven days together, in token of a deliberate advance into his office, and that one sabbath might pass over him, in his consecration. Every day of the seven, in this first consecration, a bullock was to be offered for a sin-offering, which was to intimate:

1. That though atonement was made, yet they must still keep up a penitent sense of sin, and often repeat the confession of it.

2. That those sacrifices which were thus offered day by day, could not make the comers there unto perfect, for then they would have ceased to be offered; Heb 10:1,2. They must therefore expect the bringing in of a better hope. Now this consecration of the priests was a shadow of good things to come.

1. Our Lord Jesus is the great high priest of our profession, called of God to be so consecrated for evermore, anointed with the Spirit above his fellows, whence he is called Messiah, the Christ; clothed with the holy garments, even with glory and beauty; sanctified by his own blood, not that of bullocks and rams.

2. All believers are spiritual priests, to offer spiritual sacrifices, 1 Pet 2:5, washed in the blood of Christ, and so made to our God priests, Rev 1:5,6. They also are clothed with the beauty of holiness, and have received the anointing, 1 John 2:27. His blood sprinkled upon the conscience, purgeth it from dead works, that they may, as priests, serve the living God. The Spirit of God is called the finger of God (Lu 11:20, compared with Mt 12:28,) and by him the merit of Christ is effectually applied to our souls, as here Moses with his finger was to put the blood upon Aaron. It is likewise intimated that gospel ministers are to be solemnly set apart to the work of the ministry with great deliberation and seriousness, both in the ordainers, and in the ordained, as those that are employed in a great work, and intrusted with a great charge.

36. The consecration of the altar, seems to have been coincident with that of the priests; and the sin-offerings, which were offered every day for seven days together, had reference to the altar, as well as the priests. And atonement was made for the altar. The altar was also sanctified, not only set apart itself to a sacred use, but made so holy as to sanctify the gifts that were offered upon it, Mt 23:19. Christ is our altar, for our sakes he sanctified himself, that we and our performances might be sanctified and recommended to God, John 17:19.

Orders concerning the daily sacrifice, (38–46)

38. This daily service, a lamb offered upon the altar every morning, and every evening, typified the continual intercession which Christ ever lives to make in the virtue of his satisfaction for the continual sanctification of his church: though he offered himself once for all, yet that one offering thus becomes a continual offering. And this teaches us to offer up to God the spiritual sacrifices of prayer and praise every day, morning and evening, in humble acknowledgment of our dependence upon him, and our obligations to him.

Chapter 30

The altar of incense, (1–10)

1. The altar of incense was to be about a yard high, and half a yard square, with horns at the corners, a golden cornish round it, with rings and staves of gold for the convenience of carrying it,

Ex 30:1-5. It doth not appear that there was any grate to this altar for the ashes to fall into, that they might be taken away; but when they burn incense, a golden censer was brought, with coals in it, and placed upon the altar, and in that censer the incense was burnt, and with it all the coals were taken away, so that no coals or ashes fell upon the altar. The altar of incense in Ezekiel's temple is double to what it is here, Eze 41:22, and it is there called an altar of wood, and there is no mention of gold, to signify that the incense in gospel times should be spiritual, the worship plain, and the service of God enlarged. It was placed before the veil, on the outside of that partition, but before the mercy-seat, which was within the veil. For though he that ministered at that altar could not see the mercy-seat, the veil interposing, yet he must look towards it, and direct his incense that way, to teach us, that though we cannot with our bodily eyes see the throne of grace, that blessed mercy-seat, yet we must in prayer by faith set ourselves before it, direct our prayer and look up.

7. Aaron was to burn sweet incense upon this altar every morning and every evening, which was intended not only to take away the ill smell of the flesh that was burnt daily on the brazen altar, but for the honour of God, and to shew the acceptableness of his people's services to him. As by the offerings on the brazen altar satisfaction was made for what had been done displeasing to God, so by the offering on this what they did well was, as it were, recommended to the divine acceptance.

10. This altar was purified with the blood of the sin-offering put upon the horns of it every year, upon the day of atonement. See Lev 16:18,19. The high priest was to take this in his way as he came out from the holy of holies. This was to intimate, that the sins of the priests who ministered at this altar, and of the people for whom they ministered, put a ceremonial impurity upon it, from which it must be cleansed by the blood of atonement. This altar typified the mediation of Christ: the brazen altar in the court was a type of Christ dying on earth; the golden altar in the sanctuary was a type of Christ interceding in heaven. This altar was before the mercy-seat, for Christ always appears in the presence of God for us; and his intercession is unto God of a sweet smelling savour. And it typified the devotions of the saints, whose prayers are said to be set forth before God as incense, Psa 141:2. As the smoke of the incense ascended, so must our desires, being kindled with the fire of holy love. When the priest was burning incense the people were praying, Luke 1:10, to signify that prayer is the true incense. This incense was a perpetual incense, for we must pray always. The lamps were dressed or lighted at the same time that the incense was

burnt, to teach us that the reading of the scriptures (which are our light and lamp) is a part of our daily work, and should ordinarily accompany our prayers and praises. The devotions of sanctified souls are well-pleasing to God, of a sweet-smelling savour; the prayers of saints are compared to sweet odours, Rev 5:8, but it is the incense which Christ adds to them that makes them acceptable; and his blood that atones for the guilt which cleaves to our best services. Yet if the heart and life be not holy, even incense is an abomination, Isa 1:13.

The ransom money, which the Israelites were to pay when they were numbered, (11–16)

11. Perhaps the repetition of those words, **the Lord spake unto Moses**, here and afterwards, Ex 30:17,22,34, intimates, that God did not deliver these precepts to Moses, in a continued discourse, but with many intermissions, giving him time either to write what was said to him, or at least to charge his memory with it.

12. Some think this refers only to the first numbering of them, when the tabernacle was set up, and that this tax was to make up what was wanting in the voluntary contributions. Others think it was to be always when the people were numbered; and that David offended in not demanding it when he numbered the people. But many of the Jewish writers are of opinion, it was to be an annual tribute; only it was begun when Moses first numbered the people. This was that tribute-money which Christ paid lest he should offend his adversaries. The tribute to be paid was half a shekel, about fifteen-pence of our money. In other offerings men were to give according to their ability, but this, which was the ransom of the soul, must be alike for all; for the rich have as much need of Christ as the poor, and the poor are as welcome to him as the rich. And this was to be paid as a ransom of the soul, that there might be **no plague among them** – Hereby they acknowledged that they received their lives from God, that they had forfeited their lives to him, and that they depended upon his power and patience for the continuance of them; and thus they did homage to the God of their lives, and deprecated those plagues which their sins had deserved. This money was employed in the service of the tabernacle; with it they bought sacrifices, flour, incense, wine, oil, fuel, salt, priests garments, and all other things which the whole congregation was interested in.

The laver of brass, (17–21)

18. The **laver**, or font was a large vessel, that would contain a good quantity of water. The foot of brass, it is supposed, was so contrived as to receive the water, which was let out of the

laver, by spouts. They then had a laver for the priests only to wash in, but to us now there is a fountain opened for Judah and Jerusalem, Zech 13:1, an inexhaustible fountain of living water, so that it is our own fault if we remain in our pollution. Aaron and his sons were to wash their hands and feet at this laver every time they went in to minister. For this purpose clean water was put into the laver, fresh every day. This was designed, to teach them purity in all their ministrations, and to possess them with a reverence of God's holiness, and a dread of the pollutions of sin. They must not only wash and be made clean when they were first consecrated, but they must wash and be kept clean, whenever they went in to minister. He only shall stand in God's holy place that hath clean hands and a pure heart, Psa 24:3,4. And it was to teach us, who are daily to attend upon God, daily to renew our repentance for sin, and our believing application of the blood of Christ to our souls for remission.

The anointing oil, (22–33)

23. Interpreters are not agreed concerning these ingredients: the spices, which were in all near half a hundred weight, were to be infused in the oil, which was to be about five or six quarts, and then strained out, leaving an admirable smell in the oil. With this oil God's tent and all the furniture of it were to be anointed; it was to be used also in the consecration of the priests. It was to be continued throughout their generations, Ex 30:31. Solomon was anointed with it, 1Kings 1:39, and some other of the kings, and all the high priests, with such a quantity of it, as that it ran down to the skirts of the garments; and we read of the making it up, 1Chron 9:30. Yet all agree that in the second temple there was none of this holy oil, which was probably owing to a notion they had, that it was not lawful to make it up; Providence overruling that want as a presage of the better unction of the Holy Ghost in gospel-times, the variety of whose gifts was typified by these sweet ingredients.

The incense and perfume, which was to be burned on the golden altar, (34–38)

34. The incense which was burned upon the golden altar was prepared of sweet spices likewise, though not so rare and rich as those which the anointing oil was compounded of. This was prepared once a year, (the Jews say) a pound for each day of the year, and three pound over for the day of atonement. When it was used it was to be beaten very small; thus it pleased the Lord to bruise the Redeemer, when he offered himself for a sacrifice of a sweet smelling savour. Concerning both these preparations the same

law is here given, that the like should not be made for any common use. Thus God would preserve in the peoples minds a reverence for his own institutions, and teach us not to profane or abuse any thing whereby God makes himself known.

Chapter 31
God appoints what workmen should be employed in the building and furnishing the tabernacle, (1–11)

2. See I have called Bezaleel, the grandson of Hur, probably that Hur who had helped to hold up Moses's hand, Ex 17:10–12, and was at this time in commission with Aaron for the government of the people in the absence of Moses. Aholiab of the tribe of Dan is appointed next to Bezaleel, and partner with him. Hiram, who was the head-workman in the building of Solomon's temple, was also of the tribe of Dan, 2Chron 2:14.

3. And I have filled him with the spirit of God; and Ex 31:6. In the hearts of all that are wise-hearted I have put wisdom. Skill in common employments is the gift of God; It is he that puts even this wisdom into the inward parts, Job 38:36. He teacheth the husbandman discretion, Isa 28:26, and the tradesman too, and he must have the praise of it.

13. It is a sign between me and you – The institution of the sabbath was a great instance of God's favour, and a sign that he had distinguished them from all other people: and their religious observance of it, was a great instance of their duty to him. God, by sanctifying this day among them, let them know that he sanctified them, and set them apart for his service, otherwise he would not have revealed to them his holy Sabbaths to be the support of religion among them. The Jews by observing one day in seven, after six days labour, testified that they worshipped the God that made the world in six days, and rested the seventh; and so distinguished themselves from other nations, who having first lost the sabbath, the memorial of the creation, by degrees lost the knowledge of the creator, and gave the creature the honour due to him alone.

14. It is holy unto you – That is, it is designed for your benefit as well as for God's honour; it shall be accounted holy by you.

15. It is the sabbath of rest, holy to the Lord – It is separated from common use, for the service of God; and by the observance of it we are taught to rest from worldly pursuits, and devote ourselves, and all we are, have, and can do, to God's glory.

16. It was to be observed throughout their generations, in every age, for a perpetual

covenant – This was to be one of the most lasting tokens of the covenant between God and Israel.

17. On the seventh day he rested – And as the work of creation is worthy to be thus commemorated, so the great Creator is worthy to be thus imitated, by a holy rest the seventh day.

18. These **tables of stone**, were not prepared by Moses, but probably by the ministry of angels. **They were written with the finger of God** – That is, by his will and power immediately, without the use of any instrument. They were written in two tables, being designed to direct us in our duty, towards God, and towards man. And they were called **tables of testimony**, because this written law testified the will of God concerning them, and would be a testimony against them if they were disobedient.

Chapter 32

The sin of Israel, and Aaron particularly in making the golden calf, and worshipping it, (1–6)

1. Up, make us gods, which shall go before us. They were weary of waiting for the promised land. They thought themselves detained too long at mount Sinai. They had a God that stayed with them, but they must have a God to go before them to the land flowing with milk and honey. They were weary of waiting for the return of Moses: **As for this Moses, the man that brought us up out of Egypt, we know not what is become of him** – Observe how slightly they speak of his person, **this Moses:** And how suspiciously of his delay, **we know not what is become of him.** And they were weary of waiting for a divine institution of religious worship among them, so they would have a worship of their own invention, probably such as they had seen among the Egyptians. They say, make us gods which shall go before us. Gods! How many would they have? Is not one sufficient? And what good would gods of their own making do them? They must have such Gods to go before them as could not go themselves farther than they were carried!

2. And Aaron said break off the golden earrings – We do not find that he said one word to discountenance their proposal.

3. And all the people brake off their ear-rings – Which Aaron melted down, and, having a mould prepared, poured the melted gold into it, and then produced it in the shape of an ox or calf, giving it some finishing strokes with a graving tool.

5. And Aaron built an altar before it, and proclaimed a **feast** – A feast of dedication; yet he calls it a feast to Jehovah; for, as brutish as they were, they did not design to terminate their adoration in the image; but they made it for a representation of the true God, whom they intended to worship in and through this image. And yet this did not excuse them from gross idolatry, whose plea it is, that they do not worship the image, but God by the image; so making themselves just such idolaters as the worshippers of the golden calf, whose feast was a feast to Jehovah, and proclaimed to be so, that the most ignorant and unthinking might not mistake it.

6. And they rose up early on the morrow, and offered sacrifice to this new made deity. And **the people sat down to eat and drink** of the remainder of what was sacrificed, and then **rose up to play** – To play the fool, to play the wanton. It was strange that any of the people, especially so great a number of them, should do such a thing. Had they not, but the other day, in this very place, heard the voice of the Lord God speaking to them out of the midst of the fire, Thou shalt not make to thyself any graven image? – Yet they made a calf in Horeb, the very place where the law was given. It was especially strange that Aaron should be so deeply concerned, should make the calf and proclaim the feast! Is this Aaron the saint of the Lord! Is this he that had not only seen, but had been employed in summoning the plagues of Egypt, and the judgments executed upon the gods of the Egyptians? What! And yet himself copying out the abandoned idolatries of Egypt? How true is it, that the law made them priests which had infirmity, and needed first to offer for their own sins?

God's wrath against Israel (7–10)

8. They have turned aside quickly – Quickly after the law was given them, and they had promised to obey it; quickly after God had done such great things for them, and declared his kind intentions to do greater.

9. It is a stiff-necked people – Unapt to come under the yoke of the divine law, averse to all good, and prone to evil, obstinate to the methods of cure.

10. Let me alone – What did Moses, or what could he do, to hinder God from consuming them? When God resolves to abandon a people, and the decree is gone forth, no intercession can prevent it. But God would thus express the greatness of his displeasure, after the manner of men, who would have none to intercede for those they resolve to be severe with. Thus also he would put an honour upon prayer, intimating, that nothing but the intercession of Moses could save them from ruin, that he might be a type of Christ, by whose mediation alone God would reconcile the world unto himself.

The intercession which Moses made for them, (11–14)

11. And Moses besought the Lord his God – If God would not be called the God of Israel, yet he hoped he might address him as his own God. Now Moses is standing in the gap to turn away the wrath of God, Psa 106:23. He took the hint which God gave him when he said, Let me alone, which, though it seemed to forbid his interceding, did really encourage it, by showing what power the prayer of faith hath with God.

12. Turn from thy fierce wrath – Not as if he thought God were not justly angry, but he begs that he would not be so greatly angry as to consume them. Let mercy rejoice against judgment; **repent of this evil** – Change the sentence of destruction into that of correction, against thy people which thou broughtest up out of Egypt. For whom thou hast done so many great things? Wherefore should the **Egyptians** say, **For mischief did he bring them out** – Israel is dear to Moses, as his kindred, as his charge; but it is the glory of God that he is most concerned for. If Israel could perish without any reproach to God's name, Moses could persuade himself to sit down contented; but he cannot bear to hear God reflected on; and therefore this he insists upon, Lord, What will the Egyptians say? They will say, God was either weak, and could not, or fickle, and would not complete the salvation he begun.

13. Remember Abraham – Lord, if Israel be cut off, what will become of the promise?

14. And the Lord repented of the evil which he thought to do – Though he designed to punish them, yet he would not ruin them. See here, the power of prayer, God suffers himself to be prevailed with by humble believing importunity. And see the compassion of God towards poor sinners, and how ready he is to forgive.

Moses comes down from the mount, and burns the golden calf, (15–20)

19. He saw the calf, and the dancing, and his anger waxed hot – It is no breach of the law of meekness to shew our displeasure at wickedness. Those are angry and sin not, that are angry at sin only. Moses showed himself angry, both by breaking the tables, and burning the calf, that he might by these expressions of a strong passion awaken the people to a sense of the greatness of their sin. He broke the tables before their eyes, as it is Deu 9:17, that the sight of it might fill them with confusion when they saw what blessings they had lost. The greatest sign of God's displeasure against any people is his taking his law from them.

20. He burnt the calf – Melted it down, and then filed it to dust; and that the powder to which it was reduced might be taken notice of throughout the camp, he strawed it upon the water which they all drank of. That it might appear that an idol is nothing in the world, he reduced this to atoms, that it might be as near nothing as could be.

The examination of Aaron about it, (21–24)

21. What did this people unto thee – He takes it for granted that it must needs be something more than ordinary that prevailed with Aaron to do such a thing? Did they overcome thee by importunity, and hadst thou so little resolution as to yield to popular clamour! Did they threaten to stone thee, and couldest not thou have opposed God's threatenings to theirs?

23. They said, make us gods – It is natural to us to endeavour thus to transfer our guilt.

Execution done upon the ringleaders in the idolatry, (25–29)

26. Then Moses stood in the gate of the camp, the place of judgment; **and said, Who is on the Lord's side?** – The idolaters had set up the golden calf for their standard, and now Moses sets up his in opposition to them.

27. Slay every man his brother – That is, Slay all those that you know to have been active for the making and worshipping of the golden calf, though they were your nearest relations or dearest friends. Yet it should seem they were to slay those only whom they found abroad in the street of the camp; for it might be hoped that those who were retired into their tents were ashamed of what they had done.

28. And there fell of the people that day about three thousand men – Probably these were but few in comparison with the many that were guilty; but these were the men that headed the rebellion, and were therefore picked out to be made examples of; for terror to others.

The further intercession Moses made, to turn away the wrath of God from them, (30–35)

31. Oh, this people have sinned a great sin – God had first told him of it, Ex 32:7, and now he tells God of it by way of lamentation. He doth not call them God's people, he knew they were unworthy to be called so, but this people. This treacherous ungrateful people, they have made them gods of gold.

32. If not – If the decree be gone forth, and there is no remedy but they must be ruined, **blot me, I pray thee out of the book which thou hast written** – That is, out of the book of life. If all Israel must perish, I am content to perish with them. This expression may be illustrated from Rom 9:3. For I could wish myself to be an anathema from Christ, for my brethren's sake. Does this imply no more than not enjoying Canaan? Not that Moses absolutely desired this, but only comparatively expresses his vehement zeal for God's glory, and love to his people, signifying, that the very thought of their destruction, and the dishonour of God, was so intolerable to him, that he rather wishes, if it were possible, that God would accept of him, as a sacrifice in their stead, and by his utter destruction, prevent so great a mischief.

33. Whosoever hath sinned, him will I blot out of my book – The soul that sins shall die, and not the innocent for the guilty.

35. And the Lord plagued the people – Probably by the pestilence, or some other infectious disease. Thus Moses prevailed for a mitigation of the punishment, but could not wholly turn away the wrath of God.

Chapter 33

In this chapter we have a further account of the mediation of Moses between God and Israel.

Moses brings a very humbling message from God to them, (1–6)

5. I will come up – As if he had said, ye deserve that I should do so. **Put off thine ornaments, that I may know what to do with thee** – That is, put thyself into the posture of a penitent, that the dispute may be determined in thy favour, and mercy may rejoice against judgment.

6. And Israel stript themselves of their ornaments, by the mount – God bid them lay aside their ornaments, and they did so; both to shew in general their deep mourning, and in particular to take a holy revenge upon themselves for giving their ear-rings to make the golden calf of.

God descends in a cloudy pillar, and the people worship at the tent-doors, (7–11)

7. And Moses took the tabernacle – The tent wherein he gave audience, heard causes, and inquired of God, and pitched it without, **afar off from the camp** – To signify to them that they were unworthy of it. Perhaps this tabernacle was a model of the tabernacle that was afterwards to be erected, a hasty draught from the pattern showed him in the mount, designed for direction to the workman, and used in the mean time as a tabernacle of meeting between God and Moses about public affairs.

8. And when Moses went out unto the tabernacle, the people looked after him – In token of their respect to him whom before they had slighted, and their dependence upon his mediation. By this it appeared, that they were full of concern what would be the issue.

10. And when they saw the cloudy pillar, that symbol of God's presence, they all **worshipped, every man at his tent door** – Thereby they signified, their humble adoration of the divine

majesty. Their thankfulness to God, that he was pleased to shew them this token for good, for if he had been pleased to kill them he would not have showed them such things as these. And their hearty concurrence with Moses as their advocate, in every thing he should promise for them.

11. And the Lord spake to Moses face to face, as a man speaketh unto his friend – Which intimates not only that God revealed himself to Moses with greater clearness than to any other of the prophets, but also with greater expressions of particular kindness than to any other. He spake not as a prince to a subject, but as a man to his friend, whom he loves, and with whom he takes sweet counsel. **And he turned again into the camp** – To tell the people what hopes he had of bringing this business to a good issue. But because he intended speedily to return to the tabernacle, he left Joshua there.

Moses is earnest with God in prayer, and prevails (12–13)

12. Moses now returned to the door of the tabernacle, as an important supplicant for two favours, and prevails for both: herein he was a type of Christ the great intercessor, whom the Father heareth always. He is earnest with God for a grant of his presence with Israel in the rest of their march to Canaan. **Thou sayest, bring up this people** – Lord, it is thou thyself that employest me, and wilt thou not own me? I am in the way of my duty, and shall I not have thy presence with me in that way? Yet, Thou hast said, I know thee by name, as a particular friend, and thou hast also found grace in my sight, above any other.

13. Now therefore, if I have found grace in thy sight, shew me thy way – What favour God had expressed to the people they had forfeited the benefit of; and therefore Moses lays the stress of his plea upon what God had said to him. By this therefore he takes hold on God, Lord, if thou wilt do any thing for me, do this for the people. Thus our Lord Jesus, in his intercession, presents himself to the Father, as one in whom he is always well-pleased, and so obtains mercy for us with whom he is justly displeased.

17. I will do this thing also that thou hast spoken – See the power of prayer! See the riches of God's goodness! See in type the prevalency of Christ's intercession, which he ever lives to make for all those that come to God by him! And the ground of that prevalency, is purely in his own merit, it is because **thou hast found grace in my sight.** And now God is perfectly reconciled to them, and his presence in the pillar of cloud returns to them.

18. I beseech thee shew me thy glory – Moses had lately been in the mount with God, and had had as intimate communion with God, as ever any man had on this side heaven, and yet he is still desiring a farther acquaintance. **Shew me thy glory** – Make me to see it; so the word is: make it some way or other visible, and enable me to bear the sight of it. Not that he was so ignorant as to think God's essence could be seen with bodily eyes, but having hitherto only heard a voice out of a pillar of cloud or fire, he desired to see some representation of the divine glory, such as God saw fit to gratify him with.

20. Thou canst not see my face – A full discovery of the glory of God would quite overpower the faculties of any mortal man. **I will make all my goodness pass before thee** – He had given him wonderful instances of his goodness in being reconciled to Israel; but that was only goodness in the stream, he would shew him goodness in the spring. This was a sufficient answer to his request: Shew me thy glory, saith Moses; I will shew thee my goodness, saith God. God's goodness is his glory; and he will have us to know him by the glory of his mercy, more than by the glory of his majesty. **And I will be gracious to whom I will be gracious** – In bestowing his gifts, and is not debtor to any, nor accountable to any; all his reasons of mercy are fetched from within himself, not from any merit in his creatures, and **I will shew mercy on whom I will shew mercy** – For his grace is always free. He never damns by prerogative, but by prerogative he saves.

22. I will put thee in a cleft of the rock – In that he was to be sheltered from the dazzling light, and devouring fire of God's glory. This was the rock in Horeb, out of which water was brought, of which it is said, that rock was Christ, 1Cor 10:4. 'Tis in the clefts of this rock that we are secured from the wrath of God, which otherwise would consume us: God himself will protect those that are thus hid: and it is only through Christ that we have the knowledge of the glory of God. None can see that to their comfort, but those that stand upon this rock, and take shelter in it.

23. And I will take away my hand – Speaking after the manner of men. **And thou shalt see my back-parts** – The face in man is the seat of majesty, and men are known by their faces, in them we take a full view of men; that sight of God Moses might not have, but such a sight as we have of a man who is gone past us, so that we only see his back. Now Moses was allowed to see this only, but when he was a witness to Christ's transfiguration, he saw his face shine as the sun.

Chapter 34

Four instances of the return of God's favour we have in this chapter. In all which God dealt with Moses as a mediator between him and Israel, and a type of the great Mediator.

God orders Moses to come up to the mount the next morning, and bring two tables of stone with him, (1–4)

1. Moses must prepare for the renewing of the tables.

5. The Lord descended – By some sensible token of his presence, and manifestation of his glory. He descended **in the cloud** – Probably that pillar of cloud which had hitherto gone before Israel, and had the day before met Moses at the door of the tabernacle.

God meeting Moses, and the proclamation of his name, (6–9)

6. And the Lord passed by before him – Fixed views of God are reserved for the future state; the best we have in this world are transient. **And proclaimed** the name of **the Lord** – By which he would make himself known. He had made himself known to Moses in the glory of his self-existence, and self-sufficiency, when he proclaimed that name, I am that I am; now he makes himself known in the glory of his grace and goodness, and all-sufficiency to us. The proclaiming of it notes the universal extent of God's mercy; he is not only good to Israel, but good to all. The God with whom we have to do is a great God.

8. And Moses made haste, and bowed his head – Thus he expressed his humble reverence and adoration of God's glory, together with his joy in this discovery God had made of himself, and his thankfulness for it. Then likewise he expressed his holy submission to the will of God made known in this declaration, subscribing to his justice as well as mercy, and putting himself and his people Israel under the government of such a God as Jehovah had now proclaimed himself to be. Let this God be our God for ever and ever!

9. And he said, I pray thee, go among us – For thy presence is all to our safety and success. **And pardon our iniquity and our sin** – Else we cannot expect thee to go among us. **And take us for thine inheritance** – Which thou wilt have a particular eye to, and concern for. These things God had already promised Moses; and yet he prays for them, not as doubting the sincerity of God's grants, but as one solicitous for the ratification of them. But it is a strange plea he urges, **for it is a stiff-necked people** – God had given this as a reason why he would not go along with them, Ex 33:3. Yea, saith Moses, the rather go along with us; for the worse they are, the more need they have of thy presence. Moses sees them so stiff-necked, that he has neither patience nor power enough to deal with them; therefore, Lord, do thou go among us; else they will never be kept in awe; thou wilt spare, and bear with them, for thou art God and not man.

The instructions God gave Moses, and his converse with him forty days, (10–28)

10. Behold I make a covenant – When the covenant was broke, it was Israel that broke it; now it comes to be renewed, it is God that makes it. If there be quarrels, we must bear all the blame; if there be peace, God must have all the glory. **Before all thy people I will do marvels** – Such as the drying up of Jordan, the standing still of the sun. Marvels indeed, for they were without precedent, such as have not been done in all the earth; the people shall see, and own the work of the Lord; and they were the terror of their enemies: it is a terrible thing that I will do.

11. Observe that which I command thee – We cannot expect the benefit of the promises, unless we make conscience of the precepts.

12. Take heed to thyself – It is a sin thou art prone to, and that will easily beset thee; carefully abstain from all advances towards it, **make no covenant with the inhabitants of the land** – If God in kindness to them drove out the Canaanites, they ought in duty to God not to harbour them: If they espoused their children they would be in danger of espousing their gods. That they might not be tempted to make molten gods, they must utterly destroy those they found, and all that belonged to them, the altars and groves, lest, if they were left standing, they should be brought in process of time either to use them, or to take pattern by them.

21. Here is a repetition of several appointments made before, especially relating to their solemn feasts.

24. Neither shall any man desire thy land – Not only they shall not invade it, but they shall not so much as think of invading it. What a standing miracle was this, for so many generations?

28. He wrote – God.

The honour he put upon him when he sent him down with his face shining, (29–35)

29. The skin of his face shone – This time of his being in the mount he heard only the same he had heard before. But he saw more of the glory of God, which having with open face beheld, he was in some measure changed into the same image. This was a great honour done to Moses, that the people might never again question his mission, or think or speak slightly of him. He carried his credentials in his very countenance, some think as long as he lived, he retained some remainders of this glory, which perhaps contributed to the vigour of his old age; that eye could not wax dim which had seen God, nor that face wrinkle which had shone with his glory.

30. And Aaron and the children of Israel saw Moses, and were afraid – It not only dazzled their eyes, but struck such an awe upon them as

obliged them to retire. Probably they doubted whether it was a token of God's favour, or of his displeasure.

33. And Moses put a vail upon his face – This veil signified the darkness of that dispensation; the ceremonial institutions had in them much of Christ and the gospel, but a veil was drawn over it, so that the children of Israel could not distinctly and steadfastly see those good things to come which the law had a shadow of. It was beauty veiled, gold in the mine, a pearl in the shell; but thanks be to God, by the gospel, the veil is taken away from off the old testament; yet still it remains upon the hearts of those who shut their eyes against the light.

34. When he went before the Lord, he put off the vail – Every veil must be thrown aside when we go to present ourselves unto the Lord. This signified also, as it is explained, 2Cor 3:16, that when a soul turns to the Lord, the veil shall be taken away, that with open face it may behold his glory.

Chapter 35

The great affair of setting up God's worship is now upon its former channel again.

Moses gives Israel those instructions he had received (1–19)

2. Six days shall work be done – Work for the tabernacle, **but on the seventh day** – You must not strike a stroke, no not at the tabernacle-work; the honour of the sabbath was above that of the sanctuary.

3. Ye shall kindle no fire – For any servile work, as that of smiths or plumbers. We do not find that ever this prohibition extended farther.

The people bring in their contributions, (20–29)

21. Every one whom his spirit made willing – What they did they did cheerfully. They were willing; and it was not any external inducement that made them so, but their spirits. It was from a principle of love to God, and his service; a desire of his presence with them by his ordinances; gratitude for the great things he had done for them; and faith in his promises of what he would do further.

The head workmen are nominated, (30–35)

30. The Lord hath called Bezaleel – And those whom God called by name to this service, he filled with the spirit of God, to qualify them for it. The work was extraordinary which Bezaleel was designed for, and therefore he was qualified in an extraordinary manner for it. Thus when the apostles were appointed to be master-builders in setting up the gospel-tabernacle, they were filled with the spirit of God in wisdom and understanding.

Chapter 36

The work of the tabernacle is begun, (1–4)

2. **And Moses called Bezaleel** – Even those whom God has qualified for, and inclined to the service of the tabernacle, yet must wait for a call to it, either extraordinary, as that of preachers and apostles, or ordinary, as that of pastors and teachers. And observe who they were that Moses called; those in whose heart God had put wisdom for this purpose, beyond their natural capacity, and whose heart stirred him up to come to the work in good earnest. Those are to be called to the building of the gospel tabernacle, whom God has by his grace made in some measure fit for the work, and free to it: ability and willingness, with resolution, are the two things to be regarded in the call of ministers.

A stop put to the people's contributions, (5–7)

The curtains, (8–19)

The boards and bars, (20–34)

The partition veil, (35, 36)

35. **The vail** made for a partition between the holy place and the most holy, signified the darkness and distance of that dispensation compared with the New Testament, which shows us the glory of God more clearly, and invites us to draw near to it; and the darkness and distance of our present state in comparison with heaven, where we shall be ever with the Lord, and see him as he is.

The hangings of the door, (37, 38)

37. **An hanging** – Which divided the holy place from the court.

Chapter 37

Bezaleel and his workmen are still busy.

The ark with the mercy-seat and the cherubim, (1–9)

1–9. These several ornaments where with the tabernacle was furnished, the people were not admitted to see, but the priests only; and therefore it was requisite they should be thus largely described, particularly to them. And Moses would thus shew the great care which he and his workmen took to make every thing exactly according to the pattern showed him in the mount. Thus he appeals to every reader concerning his fidelity to him that appointed him, in all his house. And thus he teacheth us to have respect to all God's commandments, even to every jot and tittle of them. In these verses we have an account of the making of the ark with its glorious and significant appurtenances, the mercy-seat and the cherubim. Consider these three together, and they represent the glory of a holy God, the sincerity of a holy heart, and the communion that is between them by a Mediator. It is the glory of a holy God that he dwelleth between the cherubim, that is, is continually attended by the blessed angels, whose swiftness was signified by the wings of the cherubim, and their unanimity in their services, by their faces being one towards another. It is the character of an upright heart, that, like the ark of the testimony, it hath the law of God hid and kept in it. By Jesus Christ the great propitiation there is reconciliation made, and a communion settled, between us and God: he interposeth between us and God's displeasure; and through him we become entitled to God's favour.

The table with its vessels, (10–16)

10. Observe how much the dispensation of the gospel exceeds that of the law. Tho' here was a table furnished, it was only with shew-bread, bread to be looked upon, not to be fed upon, while it was on the table, and afterwards only by the priests: but to the table Christ has spread in the new covenant all good Christians are invited guests, and to them it is said, Eat, O friends, come eat of my bread. What the law gave but a sight of at a distance, the gospel gives the enjoyment of.

The candle-stick with its appurtenances, (17–24)

17. This candlestick, which was not of wood overlaid with gold, but all beaten-work of pure gold only, signified that light of divine revelation with which God's church upon earth hath always been enlightened, being always supplied with fresh oil from Christ the good olive, Zech 4:2,3. The bible is a golden candlestick, it is of pure gold; from it light is diffused to every part of God's tabernacle, that by it the spiritual priests may see to do the service of his sanctuary. The candlestick has not only its bowls for necessary use, but its knops and flowers for ornament; many things which God saw fit to beautify his word with, which we can no more give a reason for than for these knops and flowers, and yet must be sure they were added for good purpose. Let us bless God for this candlestick, have an eye to it continually, and dread the removal of it out of its place!

The golden altar for incense and the holy oil and incense, (25–29)

25. The incense burnt on this altar daily, signified both the prayers of saints, and the intercession of Christ, to which is owing the acceptableness of them.

Chapter 38

The brazen altar and laver, (1–8)

1. The altar of burnt-offering – On this all their sacrifices were offered. Christ was himself the altar to his own sacrifice of atonement, and so he is to all our sacrifices of acknowledgment. We must have an eye to him in offering them, as God hath in accepting them.

8. This **laver** signified the provision that is made in the gospel for cleansing our souls from the pollution of sin by the merit of Christ, that we may be fit to serve the holy God in holy duties.

The preparing of the hangings for the inclosing of the court in which the tabernacle was to stand, (9–20)

9. And he made the court – The walls of the court, were like the rest, curtains, or hangings. This represented the state of the Old Testament church, it was a garden enclosed; the worshippers were then confined to a little compass. But the inclosure being of curtains only, intimated that that confinement of the church to one particular nation was not to be perpetual. The dispensation itself was a tabernacle-dispensation, moveable and mutable, and in due time to be taken down and folded up, when the place of the tent should be enlarged, and its cords lengthened, to make room for the Gentile world.

A summary account of the gold, silver and brass that was contributed to, and, used in the preparing of the tabernacle, (21–31)

21. By the hand of Ithamar – Here we have a brief account which by Moses's appointment the Levites took and kept of the gold, silver, and brass, that was brought in for the tabernacle's use, and how it was employed. Ithamar the son of Aaron was appointed to draw up this account.

Chapter 39

This chapter gives us an account of the finishing of the work of the tabernacle. The last thing prepared was the holy garments.

Clothes for the priests, (1–31)

1. The priests garments are called here **clothes of service** –- Those that wear robes of honour must look upon them as clothes of service; for those upon whom honour is put, from

them service is expected. Holy garments were not made for men to sleep in, but to do service in, and then they are indeed for glory and beauty. These also were shadows of good things to come, but the substance is Christ. He is our great high priest; he put upon him the clothes of service when he undertook the work of our redemption; arrayed himself with the gifts and graces of the Spirit, which he received not by measure; charged himself with all God's spiritual Israel, bare them on his shoulder, carried them in his bosom, and presented them in the breast-plate of judgment unto his Father. And, lastly, he crowned himself with holiness to the Lord, consecrated his whole undertaking to the honour of his Fathers holiness. And all true believers are spiritual priests. The clean linen with which all their clothes of service must be made, is the righteousness of saints: and holiness to the Lord must be so written upon their foreheads, that all who converse with them may see they bear the image of God's holiness.

A summary account of the whole work, (32–43)

32. Thus was all the work finished – In not much more than five months. Though there was a great deal of fine work, such as used to be the work of time, embroidering, and engraving, not only in gold, but in precious stones, yet they went through with it in a little time, and with the greatest exactness imaginable. The workmen were taught of God, and so were kept from making blunders, which would have retarded them. And the people were hearty and zealous in the work, and impatient till it was finished. God had prepared their hearts, and then the thing was done suddenly, 2Chr 29:36.

43. And Moses did look upon all the work – Piece by piece, and behold they had done it according to the pattern showed him – For the same that showed him the pattern, guided their hand in the work. **And Moses blessed them** – He not only praised them, but prayed for them: he blessed them as one having authority. We read not of any wages Moses paid them for their work, but his blessing he gave them. For though ordinarily the labourer be worthy of his hire, yet in this case, they wrought for themselves. The honour and comfort of God's tabernacle among them would be recompense enough. And they had their meat from heaven on free-cost, for themselves and their families, and their raiment waxed not old upon them; so that they neither needed wages, nor had reason to expect any. But indeed this blessing in the name of the Lord was wages enough for all their work. Those whom God employs he will bless, and those whom he blesseth, they are blessed indeed. The blessing he commands is life for evermore.

Chapter 40

The tabernacle is erected (1–33)

2. The time for doing this is, **On the first day of the first month** – This wanted but fourteen days of a year since they came out of Egypt. Probably the work was made ready just at the end of the year, so that the appointing this day gave no delay. In Hezekiah's time they began to sanctify the temple on the first day of the first month, 2Chr 29:17. The new moon (which by their computation was the first day of every month) was observed by them with some solemnity; and therefore this first new moon of the year was thus made remarkable.

15. **Their anointing shall surely be an everlasting priesthood** – A seal that their priesthood shall continue as long as the Jewish polity lasts. He signifies that this unction should be sufficient for all succeeding priests. None were afterwards anointed but the high-priests.

God's glory fills the tabernacle (34–38)

34. As when God had finished this earth, which he designed for man's habitation, he made man, and put him in possession of it; so when Moses had finished the tabernacle, which was designed for God's dwelling-place among men, God came and took possession of it. By these visible tokens of his coming among them, he testified both the return of his favour, which they had forfeited by the golden calf, and his gracious acceptance of their care and pains about the tabernacle. Thus God showed himself well-pleased with what they had done, and abundantly rewarded them. **A cloud covered the tent** – The same cloud which, as the chariot or pavilion of the Shechinah, had come up before them out of Egypt, now settled upon the tabernacle, and hovered over it, even in the hottest and clearest day; for it was none of those clouds which the sun scatters. This cloud was intended to be a token of God's presence, constantly visible day and night to all Israel. A protection of the tabernacle: they had sheltered it with one covering upon another, but after all, the cloud that covered it was its best guard: And a guide to the camp of Israel in their march through the wilderness. While the cloud continued on the tabernacle, they rested; when it removed, they removed and followed it, as being purely under a divine conduct. **And the glory of the Lord filled the tabernacle** – The Shechinah now made an awful entry into the tabernacle, passing through the outer part of it into the most holy place, and there seating itself between the cherubim. It was in light and fire, and, for ought we know, no other-wise, that the Shechinah made itself visible. With these the tabernacle was now filled; yet as before the bush, so now the curtains were not consumed, for, to those that have received the anointing, the majesty of God is not destroying. Yet now so dazzling was the light, and so dreadful was the fire, that Moses was not able to enter into the tent of the congregation, at the door of which he attended, till the splendour was a little abated, and the glory of the Lord retired within the veil. But what Moses could not do, our Lord Jesus has done, whom God caused to draw near and approach, and as the fore-runner he is for us entered, and has invited us to come boldly even to the mercy-seat. He was able to enter into the holy place not made with hands; he is himself the true tabernacle, filled with the glory of God, even with that divine grace and truth which were figured by this fire and light. In him the Shechinah took up its rest for ever, for in him dwells all the fulness of the Godhead bodily.

LEVITICUS

John Wesley

Introduction

This book, containing the actions of about one month's space, acquaint us with the Levitical ceremonies used after the tabernacle was erected in the wilderness, and is therefore called Leviticus: It treats of laws concerning persons, and things, clean and unclean; as also purifyings in general once a year, and divers particular cleansings, with a brief repetition of divers laws, together with certain feasts, of seven years rest, of the jubilee, and the redemption of things consecrated to God; but especially of such ceremonies as were used about offerings and sacrifices, which were both expiatory for trespasses committed, whether by the People or the priests; and also eucharistic in the owning of God's blessings. Here are declared also laws for the regulating of these, and prescribing the lawful time for marriages; here is set down how several abominable sins are punishable by the magistrate; and how these things are to be managed by certain persons appropriated to the tribe of Levi, whose office is confirmed from heaven, and the male-administration of it threatened, and the judgment particularly inflicted on Nadab and Abihu for an example. Here are promises, and threatenings, to the observers, or breakers of this law. The records of even these abrogated laws are of use to us, for the strengthening of our faith in it, as the lamb slain from the foundation of the world; and for the increase of our thankfulness to God, for freeing us from that heavy yoke.

Chapter 1

Directions concerning burnt-offerings:
A bullock (1–9)

1. Moses – Stood without, Ex 40:35, waiting for God's call. **The tabernacle** – From the mercy-seat in the tabernacle.

2. There are divers kinds of sacrifices here prescribed, some by way of acknowledgment to God for mercies either desired or received; others by way of satisfaction to God for men's sins; others were mere exercises of devotion. And the reason why there were so many kinds of them was, partly a respect to the childish state of the Jews, who by the custom of nations, and their own natural inclinations were much addicted to outward rites and ceremonies, that they might have full employment of that kind in God's service, and thereby be kept from temptations to idolatry; and partly to represent as well the several perfections of Christ, the true sacrifice, and the various benefits of his death, as the several duties which men owe to their Creator and Redeemer, all which could not be so well expressed by one sort of sacrifice. **Of the flock** – Or, **Of the sheep;** though the Hebrew word contains both the sheep and goats.

4. He shall put his hand – Both his hands, Lev 8:14,18, and Lev 16:21. Whereby he signified,

1. That he willingly gave it to the Lord.

2. That he judged himself worthy of that death which it suffered in his stead; and that he laid his sins upon it with an eye to him upon whom God would lay the iniquity of us all, Isa 53:6, and that together with it he did freely offer up himself to God. **To make atonement** –

Sacramentally; as directing his faith and thoughts to that true propitiatory sacrifice which in time was to be offered up for him. And although burnt-offerings were commonly offered by way of thanksgiving; yet they were sometimes offered by way of atonement for sin, that is, for sins in general, as appears from Job 1:5, but for particular sins there were special sacrifices.

6. **Pieces** – Namely, the head, and fat, and inwards, and legs, Lev 1:8,9.

7. **Put fire** – Or, dispose the fire, that is, blow it up, and put it together, so as it might be fit for the present work. For the fire there used and allowed came down from heaven, Lev 9:24, and was to be carefully preserved there, and all other fire was forbidden, Lev 10:1.

8. **The fat** – All the fat was to be separated from the flesh, and to be put together, to increase the flame, and to consume the other parts of the sacrifice more speedily.

9. **But the inwards shall he wash** – To signify the universal and perfect purity both of the inwards, or the heart, and of the legs, or ways or actions, which was in Christ, and which should be in all Christians. And he washed not only the parts now mentioned, but all the rest, the trunk of the body, and the shoulders. **A sweet savour** – Not in itself, for so it rather caused a stink, but as it represented Christ's offering up himself to God as a sweet smelling savour.

A sheep, goat, lamb, or kid (10–13)

11. **North-ward** – Here this and other kinds of sacrifices were killed, Lev 6:25, and Lev 7:2, because here seems to have been the largest and most convenient place for that work, the altar being probably near the middle of the east-end of the building, and the entrance being on the south-side. Besides this might design the place of Christ's death both more generally, in Jerusalem, which was in the sides of the north, Psa 48:2, and more specially, on mount Calvary, which was on the north-west side of Jerusalem.

A turtle dove, or young pigeon (14–17)

14. **Turtledoves** – These birds were appointed for the poor who could not bring better. And these birds are preferred before others, partly because they were easily gotten, and partly because they are fit representations of Christ's chastity, and meekness, and gentleness, for which these birds are remarkable. The pigeons must be young, because then they are best; but the turtle-doves are better when they are grown up, and therefore they are not confined to that age.

15. **His head** – From the rest of the body; as sufficiently appears, because this was to be burnt by itself, and the body afterwards, Lev 1:17.

16. **With its feathers** – Or, with its dung or filth, contained in the crop and in the guts. **On the east** – Of the Tabernacle. Here the filth was cast, because this was the remotest place from the holy of holies, which was in the west-end; to teach us, that impure things and persons should not presume to approach to God, and that they should be banished from his presence. **The place of the ashes** – Where the ashes fell down and lay, whence they were afterwards removed without the camp.

17. He shall cleave the bird through the whole length, yet so as not to separate the one side from the other. **A sweet savour unto the Lord** – Yet after all, to love God with all our hearts, and to love our neighbour as ourselves, is better than all burnt-offerings and sacrifices.

Chapter 2

Directions concerning the meal-offerings.

Of fine flour with oil and frankincense (1–11)

1. **A meal-offering** – (Not meat-offering, an ancient false print, which has run through many editions of our bible.) This was of two kinds, the one joined with other offerings, Num 15:4,7,10, which was prescribed, together with the measure or proportion of it: the other, of which this place speaks, was left to the offerer's good will both for the thing, and for the quantity. And the matter for this offering was things without life, as meal, corn, or cakes.

2. **He shall take** – That priest to whom he brought it, and who is appointed to offer it. **The memorial** – That part thus selected and offered; which is called a memorial, either

1. to the offerer, who by offering this part is minded, that the whole of that he brought, and of all which he hath of that kind, is God's to whom this part was paid as an acknowledgment. Or

2. to God, whom (to speak after the manner of men) this did put in mind of his gracious covenant and promises of favour, and acceptance of the offerer and his offering. **A sweet savour unto the Lord** – And so are our spiritual offerings, which are made by the fire of holy love, particularly that of almsgiving. With such sacrifices God is well-pleased.

3. **Sons** – To be eaten by them, Lev 6:16. **Most holy** – Or such as were to be eaten only by the priests, and that only in the holy place near the altar.

4. **In the oven** – Made in the sanctuary for that use.

6. **In pieces** – Because part of it was offered to God, and part given to the priests.

11. **No leaven** – Namely, in that which is offered of free-will; for in other offerings it might be used, Lev 7:13, 23:17. This was forbidden, partly to mind them of their deliverance

out of Egypt, when they were forced through haste to bring away their meal or dough (which was the matter of this oblation) unleavened; partly to signify what Christ would be, and what they should be, pure and free from all error in the faith and worship of God, and from all hypocrisy, and malice or wickedness, all which are signified by leaven.

Of the first fruits (12–16)

12. Ye may offer them – Or either of them, leaven or honey. **They shall not be burnt** – But reserved for the priests.

13. Salt – To signify that incorruption of mind, and sincerity of grace, which in scripture is signified by salt, Mark 9:49, Col 4:6, and which is necessary in all them that would offer an acceptable offering to God. Or in testimony of that communion which they had with God in these exercises of worship; salt being the great symbol of friendship in all nations is called, either,

1. because it represented the perpetuity of God's covenant with them, which is designed by salt, Num 18:19, 2Chr 13:5. Or,

2. because it was so particularly required as a condition of their covenant with God; this being made absolutely necessary in all their offerings; and as the neglect of sacrifices was a breach of covenant on their part, so also was the neglect of salt in their sacrifices.

14. First-fruits – Of thine own free-will; for there were other first-fruits, and that of several sorts, which were prescribed, and the time, quality, and proportion of them appointed by God.

16. Made by fire – The fire denotes that fervency of spirit, which ought to be in all our religious services. Holy love is the fire, by which all our offerings must be made: else they are not of a sweet savour to God.

Chapter 3

Directions concerning peace-offerings.

A bullock or an heifer (1–5)

1. A peace-offering – This was an offering for peace and prosperity, and the blessing of God, either,

1. obtained, and so it was a thank-offering, or,

2. desired; and so it was a kind of supplication to God.

2. At the door – Not on the north-side of the altar, where the burnt-offering was killed, as also the sin-offering, and the trespass-offering, but in the very entrance of the court where the brazen altar stood, which place was not so holy as the other; as appears both because it was more remote from the holy of holies, and because the ashes of the sacrifices were to be laid here. And the reason of this difference is not obscure, both because part of this sacrifice was to be waved by the hands of the offerer, Lev 7:30, who might not come into the court; and because this offering was not so holy as the others, which were to be eaten only by the priest, whereas part of these were eaten by the offerer.

5. Upon the burnt sacrifice – Either,

1. Upon the remainders of it, which were yet burning; or rather,

2. After it; for the daily burnt-offering was first to be offered, both as more eminently respecting God's honour; and as the most solemn and stated sacrifice, which should take place of all occasional oblations, and as a sacrifice of an higher nature, being for atonement, without which no peace could be obtained, nor peace offering offered with acceptance.

A lamb (6–11)

9. The rump – Which in sheep is fat, and sweet, and in these parts was very much larger and better than ours.

11. Burnt it – The parts now mentioned; the rest fell to the priest, Lev 7:31. **The food** – That is, the fuel of the fire, or the matter of the offering. It is called food, Heb. bread, to note God's acceptance of it, and delight in it; as men delight in their food.

A goat (12–16)

16. Shall burn them – The parts mentioned, among which the tail is not one, as it was in the sheep, because that in goats is a refuse part. **All the fat** – This is to be limited,

1. To those beasts, which were offered or offerable in sacrifice, as it is explained, Lev 7:23,25.

2. To that kind of fat which is above-mentioned, and required to be offered, which was separated, or easily separable from the flesh for the fat which was here and there mixed with the flesh they might eat.

No fat or blood to be eaten (17)

17. All your dwellings – Not only at or near the tabernacle, not only of those beasts which you actually sacrifice, but also in your several dwellings, and of all that kind of beasts. **Fat** – Was forbidden,

1. To preserve the reverence of the holy rites and sacrifices.

2. That they might be taught hereby to acknowledge God as their Lord, and the Lord of all the creatures, who might reserve what he pleased to himself.

3. To exercise them in obedience to God, and self-denial and mortification of their appetites, even in those things which probably many of them would much desire. **Blood** – Was forbidden partly to maintain reverence to God and his worship; partly out of opposition to idolaters,

who used to drink the blood of their sacrifices; partly with respect to Christ's Blood, thereby manifestly signified. God would not permit the very shadows of this to be used as a common thing. Nor will he allow us, tho' we have the comfort of the atonement made, to assume to ourselves any share in the honour of making it.

Chapter 4

Directions concerning sin-offerings; which were intended for sins committed through ignorance.

The priest himself (1–12)

1. The Lord spake unto Moses – The laws contained in the three first chapters, seem to have been delivered to Moses at one time. Here begin the laws of another day, which God delivered from between the Cherubim.

2. If a soul sin – This must necessarily be understood of more than common daily infirmities; for if every such sin had required an offering, it had not been possible either for most sinners to bear such a charge, or for the altar to receive so many sacrifices, or for the priests to manage so infinite a work. And for ordinary sins, they were ceremonially expiated by the daily offering, and by that on the great day of atonement, Lev 16:30. **Through ignorance** – Or, error, either not knowing his act to be sinful, as appears by comparing Lev 4:13,14, or not considering it, but falling into sin through the power of some sudden passion or temptation, as the Hebrew word signifies, Psa 119:67. **Things which ought not to be done** – The words may be rendered, in or about every, or any of the commandments of the Lord which should not be done; or, which concern things that should not be done, namely, in any negative commands. Then he shall offer according to his quality, which is here to be understood out of the following verses.

3. If the priest – That is, the high-priest, who only was anointed after the first time.

4. On the head – To testify both his acknowledgment of his sin, and faith in God's promise for the expiation of his sins through Christ, whom that sacrifice typified. **Kill the bullock** – By one of the priests, whom he should cause to do it.

5. To the tabernacle – Into the tabernacle; which was not required nor allowed in any other sacrifice, possibly to show the greatness of the high-priest's sin, which needed more than ordinary diligence in him, and favour from God to expiate it.

6. Seven times – A number much used in scripture, as a number of perfection; and here prescribed, either to shew that his sins needed more than ordinary purgation, and more exercise of his faith and repentance, both which

graces he was obliged to join with that ceremonial rite. **Before the vail** – The second veil dividing between the holy of holies, which is generally called the veil of the sanctuary.

7. All the blood – All the rest; for part was disposed elsewhere.

12. The whole bullock – So no part of this was to be eaten by the priests, as it was in other sin-offerings. The reason is plain, because the offerer might not eat of his own sin-offering, and the priest was the offerer in this case, as also in the sin-offering for the whole congregation below, of which the priest himself was a member. **Shall be carried forth** – Not himself, which would have defiled him, but by another whom he shall appoint for that work. **Without the camp** – To signify either,

1. The abominable nature of sin, especially in high and holy persons, or when it overspreads a whole people.

2. The removing of the guilt or punishment of that sin from the people.

3. That Christ should suffer without the camp or gate.

Where the ashes are – For the ashes, though at first they were thrown down near the altar, Lev 1:16, yet afterwards they, together with the filth of the sacrifices, were carried into a certain place without the camp.

The whole congregation (13–21)

13. The whole congregation – The body of the people, or the greater part of them, their rulers concurring with them.

14. A bullock – But if the sin of the congregation was only the omission of some ceremonial duty, a kid of the goats was to be offered, Num 15:24.

15. The elders – Who here acted in the name of all the people, who could not possibly perform this act in their own persons.

17. And sprinkle it – It was not to be poured out there, but sprinkled only; for the cleansing virtue of the blood of Christ was sufficiently represented by sprinkling. It was sprinkled seven times: seven is a number of perfection; because God made the world in six days, and rested the seventh. This signified the perfect satisfaction Christ made, and the complete cleansing of our souls thereby.

18. The altar – Of incense: **Which is before the Lord** – That is, before the holy of holies, where the Lord was in a more special manner present.

20. For a sin-offering – That is, for the priest's sin-offering, called the first bullock, Lev 4:21.

A ruler (22–26)

24. The burnt-offering – So called by way of eminency, to wit, the daily burnt-offering. **It is a**

sin-offering – And therefore to be killed where the burnt-offering is killed; whereby it is distinguished from the peace-offering, which were killed elsewhere.

26. It shall be forgiven – Both judicially, as to all ecclesiastical censures or civil punishment; and really, upon condition of repentance and faith in the Messiah to come.

A private person (27–35)

28. A female – Which here was sufficient, because the sin of one of those was less than the sin of the ruler, for whom a male was required.

33. He shall slay it – Not by himself, but by the hands of the priest.

35. Burn them – The fat; but he useth the plural number, because the fat was of several kinds, as we saw Lev 4:8,9, Heb. upon the offerings, together with them, or after them; because the burnt-offerings were to have the first place.

Chapter 5

Directions concerning trespass-offerings. Both this and the sin-offering were intended to make atonement for sin, but the former was more general: The latter was to be offered only in some particular cases.

Hearing and concealing blasphemy (1)

1. And hear – This declares in particular what the sin was. Or, namely, that of cursing, or blasphemy, as the word commonly signifies, and that either against one's neighbour, or against God. This may seem to be principally intended here, because the crime spoken of is of so high a nature, that he who heard it, was obliged to reveal it, and prosecute the guilty. **He hath seen** – Been present when it was said. **Or known** – By sufficient information from others. **His iniquity** – That is, the punishment of it; so that word is oft used, as Gen 19:15, Num 18:1.

Touching an unclean thing (2, 3)

2. If it be hidden from him – If he do it unawares, yet that would not excuse him, because he should have been more circumspect to avoid all unclean things. Hereby God designed to awaken men to watchfulness against, and repentance for, their unknown, or unobserved sins. **He shall be clean** – Not morally, for the conscience was not directly polluted by these things, but ceremonially.

3. When he knoweth – As soon as he knoweth it, he must not delay to make his peace with God. **Otherwise he shall be guilty** – For his violation and contempt of God's authority and command.

Swearing (4)

4. If a soul swear – Rashly, without consideration either of God's law, or his own power or right, as David did, 1Sam 25:22. **To do evil** – To himself, to punish himself either in his body, or estate, or something else which is dear to him. Or rather to his neighbour. **And it be hid from him** – That is, he did not know, or not consider, that what he swore to do, was or would be impossible, or unlawful: When he discovers it to be so, either by his own consideration, or by information from others, whether it was good or evil which he swore to do.

Offer a lamb or kid (5–6)

5. In one of these things – In one of the three fore-mentioned cases, either by sinful silence, or by an unclean touch, or by rash swearing. **He shall confess** – Before the Lord in the place of public worship. And this confession is not to be restrained to the present case, but by a parity of reason, and comparing of other scriptures, to be extended to other sacrifices for sin, to which this was a constant companion.

6. His trespass-offering – But how comes confession and a sacrifice to be necessary for him that touched an unclean thing, when such persons were cleansed with simple washing, as appears from Lev 11:25,28,32,40,43, and Num 19:7,8,10,19? This place speaks of him that being so unclean did come into the tabernacle, as may be gathered by comparing this place with Num 19:13, which if any man did, knowing himself to be unclean, which was the case there, he was to be cut off for it; and if he did it ignorantly, which is the case here, he was upon discovery of it to offer this sacrifice.

Offer two young pigeons (7–10)

7. Not able – Through poverty. And this exception was allowed also in other sin-offerings. **For a sin-offering** – Which was for that particular sin, and therefore offered first: before the **burnt-offering**, which was for sins in general; to teach us not to rest in general confessions and repentance, but distinctly and particularly, as far as we can, to search out, and confess, and loath, and leave our particular sins, without which God will not accept our other religious services.

9. It is a sin-offering – This is added as the reason why its blood was so sprinkled and spilt.

10. According to the manner – Or order appointed by God. **The priest shall make an atonement** – Either declaratively, he shall pronounce him to be pardoned; or typically, with respect to Christ.

Offer fine flour (11–13)

11. The tenth part of an ephah – About six pints. He shall put no **oil**, neither **frankincense** –

Either to distinguish these from the meal-offerings, Lev 2:1, or as a fit expression of their sorrow for their sins, in the sense whereof they were to abstain from things pleasant; or to signify that by his sins he deserved to be utterly deprived both of the oil of gladness, the gifts, graces and comforts of the Holy Ghost; and of God's gracious acceptance of his prayers and sacrifices, which is signified by incense, Psa 141:2.

13. **As a meal offering** – As it was in the meal-offering, where all, except one handful, fell to the share of the priests. And this is the rather mentioned here, because in the foregoing sacrifices, Lev 4:3, &c. Lev 4:13, &c. the priest had no part reserved for him.

Offer a ram, if he had embezzled holy things (14–19)

15. **A trespass** – Against the Lord and his priests. **Through ignorance** – For if a man did it knowingly, he was to be cut off, Num 15:30. **In the holy things** – In things consecrated to God, and to holy uses; such as tithes and first-fruits, or any things due, or devoted to God, which possibly a man might either with-hold, or employ to some common use. **A ram** – A more chargeable sacrifice than the former, as the sin of sacrilege was greater. **With thy estimation** – As thou shalt esteem or rate it, thou, O priest; and at present, thou, O Moses, for he as yet performed the priest's part. And this was an additional charge and punishment to him; besides the ram, he was to pay for the holy thing which he had with-held or abused, so many shekels of silver as the priest should esteem proportionable to it.

17. The former law concerns the alienation of holy things from sacred to common use; this may concern other miscarriages about holy things, and holy duties, as may be gathered from Lev 5:19, where this is said to be a trespass against the Lord, not in a general sense, for so every sin was; but in a proper and peculiar sense.

Chapter 6

Further directions concerning trespass-offerings (1–7)

2. **If a soul sin** – This sin, though directly committed against man, is emphatically said to be done against the Lord, not only in general, for so every sin against man is also against the Lord, but in a special sense, because this was a violation of human society, whereof God is the author, and president, and defender: and because it was a secret sin, of which God alone was the witness and judge: and because God's name was abused in it by perjury. **To keep** – In

trust. **Or in fellowship** – This Hebrew phrase means, Or in putting of the hand: that is, commerce or fellowship in trading, which is very usual when one man puts any thing into another's hand, not to keep it, but to improve it for the common benefit of them both, in which cases of partnership it is easy for one to deceive the other, and therefore provision is made against it. And this is called a putting of the hand, because such agreements used to be confirmed by giving or joining their hands together. **By violence** – Secretly; for he seems to speak here of such sins as could not be proved by witness. **Or hath deceived** – Got any thing from him by fraud; so the word signifies.

3. **Swear falsely** – His oath being required, seeing there was no other way of discovery left.

4. **Is guilty** – This guilt being manifested by his voluntary confession upon remorse, whereby he reapeth this benefit, that he only restores the principal with the addition of a fifth part; whereas if he were convicted of his fault, he was to pay double, Exo 22:9.

5. **In the day** – It must not be delayed, but restitution to man must accompany repentance towards God. Wherever wrong has been done, restitution must be made, and till it is made to the utmost of our power we cannot look for forgiveness; for the keeping of what is unjustly got, avows the taking: And both together make but one continued act of unrighteousness.

Concerning the burnt-offerings (8–13)

9. **And the Lord spake** – Hitherto he hath prescribed the sacrifices themselves; now he comes to the manner of them. **The burnt-offering** – The daily one, which Exo 29:38, Num 28:3, as the following words shew. This was to be so managed and laid on piece after piece, that the fire might be constantly maintained by it.

10. **The ashes which the fire hath consumed** – That is, the wood consumed into ashes.

11. **Other garments** – Because this was no sacred, but a common work. **A clean place** – Where no dung or filth was laid. The priest himself was to do all this. God's servants must think nothing below them but sin.

12. **It shall not be put out** – The fire coming down from heaven, was to be perpetually preserved, and not suffered to go out, partly that there might be no occasion or temptation to offer strange fire; and partly to teach them whence they were to expect the acceptance of all their sacrifices, even from the divine mercy, signified by the fire that came down from heaven which was an usual token of God's favourable acceptance.

13. Thus should we keep the fire of holy love ever burning in our hearts.

Concerning the meal-offerings (14–18)

14. Of the meal-offering – Of that which was offered alone, and that by any of the people, not by the priest, for then it must have been all burnt. This law before delivered, is here repeated for the sake of some additions made to it.

16. His sons – The males only might eat these, because they were most holy things; whereas the daughters of Aaron might eat other holy things.

17. It – That part which remains to the priest; for the part offered to God seems not to have been baked at all.

18. Every one – That is, none should touch, or eat them, but consecrated persons, priests, or their sons.

Particularly that at the consecration of the priests (19–23)

20. When he is anointed – For high-priest for he only of all the priests was to be anointed in future ages. This law of his consecration was delivered before, and is here repeated because of some additions made to it. **Perpetual** – Whensoever any of them shall be so anointed. **At night** – Or, in the evening; the one to be annexed to the morning-sacrifice, the other to the evening-sacrifice, over and besides that meal-offering which every day was to be added to the daily morning and evening sacrifices.

21. Thou – Who art so anointed and consecrated.

23. It shall not be eaten – No part of it shall be eaten by the priest, as it was when the offering was for the people. The reason of the difference is, partly because when he offered it for the people, he was to have some recompense for his pains; partly to signify the imperfection of the Levitical priest, who could not bear their own iniquity; for the priest's eating part of the people's sacrifices did signify his typical bearing of the people's iniquity; and partly to teach the priests and ministers of God, that it is their duty to serve God with singleness of heart, and to be content with God's honour though they have no present advantage by it.

Concerning the sin-offering (24–30)

26. For sin – For the sins of the rulers, or of the people, or any of them, but not for the sins of the priests; for then its blood was brought into the tabernacle, and therefore it might not be eaten.

27. Upon any garment – Upon the priest's garment; for it was he only that sprinkled it, and in so doing he might easily sprinkle his garments. **In the holy place** – Partly out of reverence to the blood of sacrifices, which hereby was kept from a profane or common touch; and partly that such garments might be decent, and fit for sacred administrations.

28. Broken – Because being full of pores, the liquor in which it was sodden might easily sink into it, whereby it was ceremonially holy, and therefore was broken, lest afterwards it should be abused to common uses. **Rinsed** – And not broken, as being of considerable value, which therefore God would not have unnecessarily wasted. And this being of a more solid substance than an earthen vessel, was not so apt to drink in the moisture.

Chapter 7

The trespass-offering (1–7)

7. So is – In the matter following, for in other things they differed. **The priests shall have it** – That part of it, which was by God allowed to the priest.

The burnt-offering and meal-offering (8–10)

9. All the meal-offering – Except the part reserved by God, Lev 2:2,9. Because these were ready drest and hot, and to be presently eaten.

10. Dry – Without oil, or drink-offering, as those Lev 5:11, Num 5:15. **All the sons of Aaron** – These were to be equally divided among all the priests. And there was manifest reason for this difference, because these were in greater quantity than the former; and being raw, might more easily be reserved for the several priests to dress it in that way which each of them liked.

The peace-offering (11–21)

13. Leavened bread – Because this was a sacrifice of another kind than those in which leaven was forbidden, this being a sacrifice of thanksgiving for God's blessings, among which leavened bread was one. Leaven indeed was universally forbidden, Lev 2:11. But that prohibition concerned only things offered and burnt upon the altar, which this bread was not.

16. A vow – Offered in performance of a vow, the man having desired some special favour from God, and vowed the sacrifice to God if he would grant it. **On the morrow also** – Which was not allowed for the thank-offering.

18. Neither shall it be imputed – For an acceptable service to God.

19. And the flesh – Namely of the holy offering, of which he is here treating; and therefore the general word is to be so limited; for other flesh one might eat in this case.

20. That eateth – Knowingly; for if it were done ignorantly, a sacrifice was accepted for it.

21. Of man – Or, of women, for the word signifies both.

Fat and blood again forbidden (22–27)

23. The general prohibition of eating fat, Lev 3:17, is here explained of those kind of creatures which were sacrificed. The fat of others they might eat.

The priest's share of it (28–34)

29. Shall bring – Not by another, but by himself, that is, those parts of the peace-offering, which are in a special manner offered to God. **His oblation unto the Lord** – That is, to the tabernacle, where the Lord was present in a special manner. Though part of such offerings might be eaten in any clean place, Lev 10:14, yet not till they had been killed, and part of them offered to the Lord in the place appointed by him for that purpose.

30. His own hands – After the beast was killed, and the parts of it divided, the priest was to put the parts mentioned into the hands of the offerer. **Offerings made by fire** – So called, not strictly, as burnt-offerings are, because some parts of these were left for the priest, but more largely, because even these peace-offerings were in part, tho' not wholly, burnt. **Waved** – To and fro, by his hands, which were supported and directed by the hands of the priest.

34. The wave-breast and heave-shoulder – The breast or heart is the seat of wisdom, and the shoulder of strength for action; and these two may denote that wisdom, and power, which were in Christ our high-priest, and which ought to be in every priest.

The conclusion of these instructions (35–38)

35. Of the anointing of Aaron – That is, of the priesthood; the sign put for the thing signified; and the anointing by a like figure is put for the part of the sacrifices belonging to the priest by virtue of his anointing. This was their portion appointed them by God in that day, and therefore to be given to them in after ages.

Chapter 8

This chapter gives an account of the consecration of Aaron and his sons before the congregation.

Moses washes and dresses them (1–9)

3. All the congregation – The elders who represented all, and as many of the people as would, and could get thither, that all might be witnesses both of Aaron's commission from God, and of his work and business.

Anoints the tabernacle with its utensils (10–13)

12. He poured – In a plentiful manner, as appears from Psa 133:2, whereas other persons and things were only sprinkled with it: because his unction was to typify the anointing of Christ with the Spirit, which was not given by measure

to him. A measure of the same anointing is given to all believers.

Offers for them a sin-offering (14–17)

14. The bullock – There were indeed seven bullocks to be offered at his consecration, one every day; but here he mentions only one, because he here describes only the work of the first day.

A burnt-offering (18–21)

18. He brought the ram – Hereby they gave to God the glory of this great honour which was put upon them: and also signified the devoting themselves and all their service to God.

The ram of consecration (22–30)

29. Moses's part – Who at this time administering the priest's office was to receive the priest's wages.

Declares to them God's charge, which they perform (31–36)

31. The flesh – That which was left of the ram, and particularly the breast, which was said to be Moses's part, Lev 8:29, and by him was given to Aaron, that he and his sons might eat of it, in token that they and only they should have the right to do so for the future.

33. Seven days – In each of which the same ceremonies were to be repeated, and other rites to be performed. **He** – Either God or Moses; for the words may be spoken by Moses, either in God's name or in his own; Moses speaking of himself in the third person, which is very common in scripture.

36. So Aaron and his sons did all things – And thus the covenant of life and peace, Mal 2:5, was made with them.

Chapter 9

Moses appoints Aaron to offer various sacrifices (1–7)

1. On the eighth day – Namely, from the day of his consecration, or when the seven days of his consecration were ended. The eighth day is famous in scripture for the perfecting and purifying both of men and beasts. See Lev 12:2,3 14:8,9,10 15:13,14 22:27. **And the elders of Israel** – All the congregation were called to be witnesses of Aaron's installment into his office, to prevent their murmurings and contempt; which being done, the elders were now sufficient to be witnesses of his first execution of his office.

2. For a sin-offering – For himself and his own sins, which was an evidence of the imperfection of that priesthood, and of the necessity of a better.

3. A sin-offering – For the people, for whose sin a young bullock was required, Lev 4:15, but that was for some particular sin; this was more general for all their sins.

4. The Lord will appear – The Hebrew has 'Hath appeared.' He speaks of the thing to come as if it were past, which is frequent in scripture, to give them the more assurance of the thing.

6. The glory of the Lord – The glorious manifestation of God's powerful and gracious presence.

7. Go and offer – Moses had hitherto sacrificed, but now he resigns his work to Aaron, and actually gives him that commission which from God he had received for him.

Aaron offers for himself (8–14)

9. The altar – Of burnt-offering, of which alone he speaks both in the foregoing and following words; and the blood was poured out at the bottom of this altar only, not of the altar of incense, as appears from Lev 4:7, where indeed there is mention of putting some of the blood upon the horns of the altar of incense, in this case of the priest's sacrificing for his own sins.

Offers for, and blesses the people (15–22)

17. Besides the burnt-sacrifice – Which was to be first offered every morning; for God will not have his ordinary and stated service swallowed up by extraordinary.

22. Aaron lifted up his hands – Which was the usual rite of blessing. By this posture he signified both whence he expected the blessing, and his hearty desire of it for them. **And blessed them** – And herein was a type of Christ, who came into the world to bless us, and when he was parting from his disciples, lifted up his hands and blessed them: yea, and in them his whole church, of which they were the elders and representatives.

God signifies his acceptance of their persons and of their sacrifices (23–24)

23. And Moses – Went in with Aaron to direct him, and to see him perform those parts of his office which were to be done in the holy place, about the lights, and the table of shewbread, and the altar of incense, upon which part of the blood of the sacrifices now offered was to be sprinkled, Lev 4:7,16. **And the glory of the Lord** – Either a miraculous brightness shining from the cloudy pillar, as Exo 16:10, or a glorious and visible discovery of God's gracious presence and acceptance of the present service.

24. And there came a fire – In token of God's approbation of the priesthood now instituted, and the sacrifices offered, and consequently of others of the like nature. And this fire now given was to be carefully kept, and not suffered to go out, Lev 6:13, and therefore was carried in a peculiar vessel in their journeys in the wilderness. **They shouted** – As wondering at, rejoicing in, and blessing God for this gracious discovery of himself, and his favour. This also was a figure of good things to come. Thus the Spirit descended in fire upon the apostles, so ratifying their commission, as this does that of the priests. And the descent of this holy fire into our souls, to kindle in them devout affections, and such an holy zeal as burns up all unholiness, is a certain token of God's gracious acceptance.

Chapter 10

The death of Nadab and Abihu, and quieting of Aaron (1–3)

1. Strange fire – Fire so called, because not taken from the altar, as it ought, but from some common fire.

2. From the Lord – From heaven, or rather from the sanctuary. **Devoured them** – Destroyed their lives; for their bodies and garments were not consumed. Thus the sword is said to devour, 2Sam 2:26.

3. That come nigh me – Who draw near to me, or to the place where I dwell, and are admitted into the holy place, whence others are shut out. It is a description of the priests. **I will be glorified** – As they have sinned publically and scandalously, so I will vindicate my honour in a public and exemplary manner, that all men may learn to give me the glory of my holiness by an exact conformity to my laws. **And Aaron held his peace** – In acknowledgment of God's justice and submission to it. He murmured not, nor replied against God.

Orders given to bury them, and not to mourn (4–7)

4. Moses called Mishael – For Aaron and his sons were employed in their holy ministrations, from which they were not called for funeral solemnities. **Out of the camp** – Where the burying-places of the Jews were, that the living might neither be annoyed by the unwholesome scent of the dead, nor defiled by the touch of their graves.

6. Uncover not your head – That is, give no signification of your sorrow; mourn not for them; partly lest you should seem to justify your brethren, and tacitly reflect upon God as too severe; and partly lest thereby you should be diverted from, or disturbed in your present service, which God expects to be done cheerfully. **But bewail the burning** – Not so much in compassion to them, as in sorrow for the tokens of divine displeasure.

7. Ye shall not go from the tabernacle – Where at this time they were, because this happened within seven days of their consecration.

A command not to drink wine or strong drink, and to distinguish between holy and unholy (8–11)

9. Drink not wine – it is not improbable, that the sin of Nadab and Abihu was owing to this very thing.

11. Ye may teach – Which drunken persons are very unfit to do.

Directions concerning the parts of the burnt-offerings which were to be eaten (12–15)

12. Eat it – Moses repeats the command, partly lest their grief should cause them to neglect their meat prescribed by God, and partly to encourage them to go on in their holy services, and not to be dejected, as if God would no more accept them or their sacrifices.

13. In the holy place – in the court, near the altar of burnt-offerings.

Moses reproves the priests, but is pacified by Aaron (16–20)

16. He was angry with Eleazar – He spares Aaron at this time, as overwhelmed with sorrow, and because the rebuking him before his sons might have exposed him to some contempt; but he knew that the reproof though directed to them, would concern him too.

17. God hath given it to you – As a reward of your service, whereby you expiate, bear, and take away their sins, by offering those sacrifices, by which God through Christ is reconciled to the penitent and believing offerers.

20. He rested satisfied with his answer. It appeared, that Aaron sincerely aimed at pleasing God: and those who do so, will find he is not extreme to mark what is done amiss.

Chapter 11

Of clean and unclean beasts (1–8)

1. From the laws concerning the priests, he now comes to those which belong to all the people.

2. These are the beasts – Though every creature of God be good and pure in itself, yet it pleased God to make a difference between clean and unclean, which he did in part before the flood, Gen 7:2., but more fully here for many reasons; as:

1. To assert his own sovereignty over man, and all the creatures which men may not use but with God's leave.

2. To keep up the wall of partition between the Jews and other nations, which was very necessary for many great and wise purposes.

3. That by bridling their appetite in things in themselves lawful, and some of them very

desirable, they might be better prepared and enabled to deny themselves in things simply and grossly sinful.

4. For the preservation of their health, some of the creatures forbidden being, though used by the neighbouring nations, of unwholesome nourishment, especially to the Jews, who were very obnoxious to leprosies. To teach them to abhor that filthiness, and all those ill qualities for which some of these creatures are noted.

3. Cloven-footed – That is, divided into two parts only. **And cheweth the cud** – Heb. and bringeth up the cud, that is, the meat once chewed, out of the stomach in the mouth again, that it may be chewed a second time for better concoction.

4. The camel – An usual food in Arabia, but yielding bad nourishment.

Fishes (9–12)

9. Fins and scales – Both of them; such fishes being more cleanly, and more wholesome food than others.

11. Unto you – This clause is added to shew that they were neither abominable in their own nature, nor for the food of other nations; and consequently when the partition-wall between Jews and Gentiles was taken away, these distinctions of meat were to cease.

Fowls (13–19)

13. Among the fowls – The fowls forbidden in diet, are all either ravenous and cruel, or such as delight in the night and darkness, or such as feed upon impure things; and so the signification of these prohibitions is manifest, to teach men to abominate all cruelty or oppression, and all works of darkness and filthiness.

Creeping things, flying (20–28)

20. All fowls – Flying things that crawl or creep upon the earth, and so degenerate from their proper nature, and are of a mongrel kind, which may intimate that apostates and mongrels in religion are abominable in the sight of God.

22. The locust – Locusts, though unusual in our food, were commonly eaten by the Ethiopians, Lybians, Parthians, and other eastern people bordering upon the Jews.

27. Upon his paws – Heb. upon his hands, that is, which hath feet divided into several parts like fingers, as dogs, cats, apes, and bears.

Creeping things, upon the earth (29–43)

34. That on which such water cometh – That flesh or herbs or other food which is dressed in water, in a vessel so polluted, shall be unclean; not so, if it be food which is eaten dry, as bread, or fruits; the reason of which difference seems to be this, that the water did sooner receive the pollution in itself, and convey it to the food so dressed.

37. Seed – Partly because this was necessary provision for man; and partly because such seed would not be used for man's food till it had received many alterations in the earth whereby such pollution was taken away.

39. If any beast die – Either of itself, or being killed by some wild beast, in which cases the blood was not poured forth, as it was when they were killed by men either for food or sacrifice.

41. Every creeping thing – Except those expressly excepted, Lev 11:29,30.

42. Upon the belly – As worms and snakes. **Upon all four** – As toads and divers serpents.

An exhortation to holiness (44, 45)

44. Ye shall be holy – By this he gives them to understand, that all these cautions about eating or touching these creatures was not for any real uncleanness in them, but only that by diligent observation of these rules they might learn with greater care to avoid all moral pollutions, and to keep themselves from all filthiness of flesh and spirit, and from all familiar and intimate converse with notorious sinners.

The conclusion (46, 47)

46. This is the law – It was so, as long the Mosaic dispensation lasted. But under the gospel we find it expressly repealed by a voice from heaven, Acts 10:15. Let us therefore bless God, that to us every creature of God is good, and nothing to be refused.

Chapter 12
Laws concerning the uncleanness of women in child-birth (1–5)

1. From uncleanness contracted by the touching or eating of external things, he now comes to that uncleanness which ariseth from ourselves.

2. Seven days – Not for any filthiness which was either in the conception, or in bringing forth, but to signify the universal and deep pollution of man's nature, even from the birth, and from the conception. Seven days or thereabouts, nature is employed in the purgation of most women. **Her infirmity** – Her monthly infirmity. And it may note an agreement therewith not only in the time, Lev 15:19, but in the degree of uncleanness.

4. In the blood of her purifying – In her polluted and separated estate; for the word blood or bloods signifies both guilt, and uncleanness, as here and elsewhere. And it is called the blood of her purifying, because by the expulsion or purgation of that blood, which is done by degrees, she is purified.

Concerning their purification (6–8)

6. For a son or a daughter – For the birth of a son, or of a daughter: but the purification was for herself, as appears from the following verses.

8. The morality of this law obliges women who have received mercies from God in child-bearing, with all thankfulness to acknowledge his goodness to them, owning themselves unworthy of it, and to continue in faith, and love, and holiness, with sobriety.

Chapter 13
Rules whereby the priest was to judge of the leprosy (1–44)

2. In the skin – For there is the first seat of the leprosy, the bright spot shining like the scale of a fish, as it is in the beginning of a leprosy. **The priest** – The priest was to admit to, or exclude from, the sanctuary, and therefore to examine who were to be excluded.

3. When the hair is turned white – This change of colour was an evidence both of the abundance of excrementous humours, and of the weakness of nature, as we see in old and sick persons. **His flesh** – For the leprosy consumed both the skin and the flesh.

4. Seven days – For greater assurance; to teach ministers not to be hasty in their judgments, but diligently to search and examine all things before-hand.

13. All his flesh – When it appeared in some one part it discovered the ill humour which lurked within, and withal the inability of nature to expel it; but when it overspread all, it manifested the strength of nature conquering the distemper, and purging out the ill humours into the outward parts.

33. He shall be shaven – For the more certain discovery of the growth or stay of the plague.

42. It is a leprosy – It is a sign that such baldness came not from age, or any accident, but from the leprosy.

Directions concerning the leper (45, 46)

45. His clothes shall be rent – In the upper and fore parts, which were most visible. This was done partly as a token of sorrow, because though this was not a sin, yet it was an effect of sin, and a sore punishment, whereby he was cut off both from converse with men, and from the enjoyment of God in his ordinances; partly as a warning to others to keep at a due distance from him wheresoever he came. **And his head bare** – Another sign of mourning. God would have men though not overwhelmed with, yet deeply sensible of his judgments. **A covering on his upper lip** – Partly as another badge of his sorrow and shame, and partly for the preservation of others from his breath or touch.

Unclean, unclean – As begging the pity and prayers of others, and confessing his own infirmity, and cautioning those who came near him, to keep at a distance from him.

46. He shall dwell alone – Partly for his humiliation; partly to prevent the infection of others; and partly to shew the danger of converse with spiritual lepers, or notorious sinners.

Concerning the leprosy in garments (47–59)

47. Leprosy in garments and houses is unknown in these times and places, which is not strange, there being some diseases peculiar to some ages and countries.

Chapter 14

Cleansing a leper (1–9)

2. He shall be brought to the priest – Not into the priest's house, but to some place without the camp or city, which the priest shall appoint.

3. Healed by God – For God alone did heal or cleanse him really, the priest only declaratively.

4. Two birds – The one to represent Christ as dying for his sins, the other to represent him as rising again for his purification or justification.

8. All his hair – Partly to discover his perfect soundness; partly to preserve him from a relapse through any relics of it which might remain in his hair or in his clothes. **Out of his tent** – Out of his former habitation, in some separate place, lest some of his leprosy yet lurking in him should break forth to the infection of his family.

9. All his hair – Which began to grow again, and now for more caution is shaved again.

The sacrifices to be offered for him (10–32)

10. Oil is added as a fit sign of God's grace and mercy, and of the leper's healing.

11. Maketh him clean – The healing is ascribed to God, Lev 14:13, but the ceremonial cleansing was an act of the priest using the rites which God had prescribed.

12. A trespass-offering – To teach them, that sin was the cause of leprosy, and of all diseases, and that these ceremonial observations had a farther meaning, to make them sensible of their spiritual diseases, that they might fly to God in Christ for the cure of them.

14. The priest shall put it – To signify, that he was now free to hear God's word in the appointed places, and to touch any person or thing without defiling it, and to go whither he pleased.

15. The oil – As the blood signified Christ's blood by which men obtained remission of sins, so the oil noted the graces of the spirit by which they are renewed.

25. The priest shall put the blood – Upon the extremities of the body, to include the whole. And some of the oil was afterwards put in the same places upon the blood. That blood seems to have been a token of forgiveness, the oil of healing: For God first forgiveth our iniquities, and then healeth our diseases. When the leper was anointed, the oil must have blood under it, to signify that all the graces and comforts of the spirit, all his sanctifying influences are owing to the death of Christ. It is by his blood alone that we are sanctified.

The management of an house suspected of leprosy (33–53)

37. In the walls of the house – This was an extraordinary judgment of God peculiar to this people, either as a punishment of their sins, which were much more sinful and inexcusable than the sins of other nations; or as a special help to repentance, which God afforded them above other people; or as a token of the mischievous nature of sin, typified by leprosy, which did not only destroy persons, but their habitations also: **Hollow streaks** – Such as were in the bodies of leprous persons.

40. An unclean place – Where they used to cast dirt and filthy things.

Summary (54–57)

57. To teach – To direct the priest when to pronounce a person or house clean or unclean. So it was not left to the priests power or will, but they were tied to plain rules, such as the people might discern no less than the priest.

Chapter 15

This chapter contains laws concerning other ceremonial uncleannesses, contracted either by bodily disease, or some natural incidents.

In men (1–18)

7. The flesh – That is, any part of his body.

11. And hath not rinsed – That is, the person touched, to whom the washing of his hands is prescribed, if speedily done; but if that was neglected, a more labourious course was enjoined.

15. An atonement – Not as if this was in itself a sin, but only a punishment of sin; though oft-times it was sinful, as being a fruit of intemperance.

In women (19–33)

19. And if a woman – Heb. And a woman when she shall have an issue of blood, and her issue shall be in her flesh, that is, in her secret parts, as flesh is taken, Lev 15:2. So it notes her monthly disease. **Put apart** – Not out of the camp, but from converse with her husband and others, and from access to the house of God. **Seven days** – For sometimes it continues so long; and it was decent to allow some time for purification after the ceasing of her issue.

31. **When they defile my tabernacle** – Both ceremonially, by coming into it in their uncleanness, and morally by the contempt of God's express command to cleanse themselves. The grand reason of all these laws was, to separate the children of Israel from their uncleanness. Hereby they were taught their privilege and honour, that they were purified unto God, a peculiar people; for that was a defilement to them, which was not so to others. They were also taught their duty, which was to keep themselves clean from all pollutions.

Chapter 16

The institution of the yearly day of atonement for the whole nation. The whole service is committed to the high-priest.

Entering the holy of holies (1–4)

2. **At all times** – Not whensoever he pleaseth, but only when I shall appoint him, namely, to take down the parts and furniture of it upon every removal, and to minister unto me once in the year. **Lest he die** – For his irreverence and presumption. **In the cloud** – In a bright and glorious cloud, over the mercy-seat, as a token when I would have him come.

3. **With a young bullock** – That is, with the blood of it; the body of it was to be offered upon the altar of burnt-offerings. **A sin-offering** – For his own and family's sins; for a goat was offered for the sins of the people.

4. **The linen coat** – It is observable, the high-priest did not now use his peculiar and glorious robes, but only his linen garments, which were common to him with the ordinary priests. The reason whereof was, because this was not a day of feasting and rejoicing, but of mourning and humiliation, at which times people were to lay aside their ornaments. **These are holy** – Because appropriated to an holy and religious use.

Offering a goat, and a bullock for a sin-offering (5–13)

8. **For the Lord** – For the Lord's use by way of sacrifice. Both this and the other goat typified Christ; this in his death and passion for us; that in his resurrection for our deliverance.

12. **Within the vail** – That is, into the holy of holies, Lev 16:2.

13. **Upon the fire** – Which was in the censer, Lev 16:12.

Sprinkling the blood before the mercy seat, and upon the altar (13–19)

14. **Upon the mercy-seat** – To teach us, that God is merciful to sinners only through and for the blood of Christ. With his face **east-ward**, or upon the eastern part, towards the people, who were in the court which lay east-ward from the holy of holies, which was the most western part of the tabernacle. This signified that the high-priest in this act represented the people, and that God accepted it on their behalf.

15. **Then shall he kill the goat** – He went out of the holy of holies, and killed it, and then returned thither again with its blood. And whereas the high-priest is said to be allowed to enter into that place but once in a year, that is to be understood, but one day in a year, though there was occasion of going in and coming out more than once upon that day.

16. **Because of the uncleannesses of Israel** – For though the people did not now enter into that place, yet their sins entered thither, and would hinder the effects of the high-priest's mediation on their behalf if God was not reconciled to them.

18. **The altar before the Lord** – That is, the altar of incense, where the blood of sacrifices was to be put, particularly the blood of the sin-offerings offered upon this day of atonement, and which is most properly said to be before the Lord, that is, before the place where God in a special manner dwelt. His going out relates to the holy of holies, into which he was said to go in, Lev 16:17.

19. **Seven times** – To signify its perfect cleansing, (seven being a number of perfection) and our perfect reconciliation by the blood of Christ.

Confessing over the scape-goat, the sins of the people, and then send him into the wilderness (20–23)

21. **All the iniquities** – He mentions iniquities, transgressions, and sins, to note sins of all sorts, and that a free and full confession was to be made, and that the smallest sins needed, and the greatest sins were not excluded from, the benefit of Christ's death here represented. **On the head** – Charging all their sins and the punishment due to them upon the goat, which tho' only a ceremony, yet being done according to God's appointment and manifestly pointing at Christ upon whom their iniquities and punishments were laid, Isa 53:5,6, it was available for this end.

Offering the burnt-offerings (24–28)

24. **He shall put on his linen garments** – Not his ordinary priestly linen garments, for he was

to leave them in the tabernacle, Lev 16:23, but the high-priestly garments, called his garments properly, and by way of distinction. And this change of his garments was not without cause. For the common priestly garments were more proper for him in the former part of his ministration, both because he was to appear before the Lord in the most holy place to humble himself and make atonement for his own and for the people's sins, and therefore his meanest attire was most fit, and because he was to lay his hands upon that goat on which all their sins were put, by which touch both he and his garments would be in some sort defiled, and therefore as he washed himself, so we may presume his linen garments were laid by for the washing, as the clothes of him who carried away the scape-goat were washed, Lev 16:26. And the high-priestly garments were most proper for the latter part of his work, which was of another nature.

Appointing this day to be a solemn fast, by a statute for ever (29–34)

29. Your souls – Yourselves, both your bodies, by abstinence from food and other delights, and your minds by grief for former sins, which though bitter, yet is voluntary in all true penitents, who are therefore here said to afflict themselves, or to be active in the work.

31. A sabbath – Observed as a sabbath-day from all servile works, and diligent attendance upon God's worship.

34. This shall be an everlasting statute – By which were typified the two great gospel privileges; remission of sins, and access to God, both which we owe to the mediation of the Lord Jesus.

Chapter 17

No sacrifice be offered by any but the priests (1–9)

3. That killeth – Not for common use, for such beasts might be killed by any person or in any place but for sacrifice. **In the camp, or out of the camp** – That is, anywhere.

4. The tabernacle – This was appointed in opposition to the Heathens, who sacrificed in all places; to cut off occasions of idolatry; to prevent the people's usurpation of the priest's office, and to signify that God would accept of no sacrifices but through Christ and in the Church; (of both which the tabernacle was a type.) But though men were tied to this law, God was free to dispense with his own law, which he did sometimes to the prophets, as 1Sam 7:9, 11:15.

7. A whoring – Idolatry, especially in God's people, is commonly called whoredom, because

it is a violation of that covenant by which they were peculiarly betrothed or married to God.

No blood be eaten (10–16)

10. I will set my face – I will be an enemy to him, and execute vengeance upon him immediately; because such persons probably would do this in private, so that the magistrate could not know nor punish it. Write that man undone, for ever undone, against whom God sets his face.

15. That eateth – Through ignorance or inadvertency; for if it was done knowingly, it was more severely punished. **A stranger** – Who is a proselyte to the Jewish religion: other strangers were allowed to eat such things, Deu 14:21, out of which the blood was either not drawn at all, or not regularly.

16. His iniquity – The punishment of it, and therefore must offer a sacrifice for it.

Chapter 18

A prohibition of conformity to the heathens (1–5)

2. Your God – Your sovereign, and lawgiver. This is often repeated because the things here forbidden were practised and allowed by the gentiles, to whose custom he opposes divine authority and their obligation to obey his commands.

3. Egypt and Canaan – These two nations he mentions, because their habitation and conversation among them made their evil example in the following matters more dangerous. But under them he includes all other nations.

4. My judgments – Though you do not see the particular reason of some of them, and though they be contrary to the laws and usages of the other nations.

Particular laws against incest (6–18)

16. Thy brother's wife – God afterwards commanded, that in one case, a man should marry his brother's widow.

18. Thou shalt not take a wife to her sister – Perhaps this text doth not simply forbid the taking one wife to another, but the doing it in such a manner or for such an end, that he may vex or punish, or revenge himself of the former; which probably was a common motive amongst that hardhearted people to do so.

Against unnatural lusts and barbarous idolatries (19–23)

19. As long as she is set apart – No not to thy own wife. This was not only a ceremonial pollution, but an immorality also, whence it is put amongst gross sins, Eze 18:6. And therefore it is now unlawful under the gospel.

21. Pass through fire – This was done, either by burning them in the fire, or by making them pass between two great fires, which was a kind of consecration of them to that God. **Moloch –** Called also Milcom, was an idol chiefly of the Ammonites.

Enforced from the destruction of the Canaanites (24–30)

25. I visit – I am about to visit, that is, to punish.

29. Cut off – This phrase therefore of cutting off, is to be understood variously, either of ecclesiastical, or civil punishment, according to the differing natures of the offences for which it is inflicted.

Chapter 19

Various Precepts to be holy (1, 2)

2. Be ye holy – Separated from all the afore-mentioned defilements, and entirely consecrated to God and obedient to all his laws. **I am holy –** Both in my essence, and in all my laws, which are holy and just and good.

To honour parents and Sabbaths (3)

3. His mother – The mother is put first, partly because the practice of this duty begins there, mothers, by perpetual converse, being sooner known to their children than their fathers; and partly because this duty is commonly neglected to the mother, upon whom children have not so much dependence as they have upon their father. And this fear includes the two great duties of reverence and obedience. **And keep my Sabbaths –** This is added, to shew, that, whereas it is enjoined to parents that they should take care the sabbath be observed both by themselves and their children, it is the duty of children to fear and obey their parents in this matter.

To shun idolatry (4)

4. Idols – The word signifies such as are no gods, or nothings, as they are called, 1Cor 8:4, many idols having no being, but in the fancy of their worshippers, and all of them having no virtue or power to do good or evil, Isa 41:23.

Duty to eat their peace-offering (5–8)

5. At your own will – Or, according to your own pleasure, what you think fit: For though this in general was required, yet it was left to their choice to determine the particulars.

To leave gleanings for the poor (9, 10)

10. I am the Lord your God – Who gave you all these things with a reservation of my right in them, and with a charge of giving part of them to the poor.

Not to steal, lie, swear falsely, or defraud (11–13)

12. Ye shall not swear falsely – This is added, to shew how one sin draws on another, and that when men will lie for their own advantage, they will easily be induced to perjury.

Not to curse the deaf, or put a stumbling-block before the blind (14)

14. Before the blind – To make them fall. Under these two particulars are manifestly forbidden all injuries done to such as are unable to right or defend themselves; of whom God here takes the more care, because they are not able to secure themselves.

Not to judge unjustly, carry tales, or bear false witness (15, 16)

15. The poor – So as through pity to him to give an unrighteous sentence.

16. Stand against the blood – In judgment as a false accuser or false witness, for accusers and witnesses used to stand, whilst the judges sit in courts of judicature.

To reprove sinners, not to revenge themselves; to love their neighbours (17, 18)

17. Thou shalt not hate – As thou dost, in effect, if thou dost not rebuke him. **Thy brother** – The same as thy neighbour, that is, every man.

18. Thy neighbour – Every man.

Not to mix different things (19)

19. Thou shalt not let thy cattle gender – This was prohibited, partly to restrain the curiosity and boldness of men, who might attempt to amend or change the works of God, partly that by the restraint here laid even upon brute-creatures men might be taught to abhor all unnatural lusts, partly to teach the Israelites to avoid mixtures with other nations, either in marriage or in religion, which also may be signified by the following prohibitions.

Not to lie with their bond-maids (20–22)

20. She shall be scourged – Heb. There shall be a scourging, which probably may belong to both of them.

Not to eat of the fruit of the land for four years (23–25)

23. As uncircumcised – That is, as unclean, not to be eaten but cast away.

24. Holy – Consecrated to the Lord, as the first-fruits and tithes were, and therefore given to the priests and Levites, Num 18:12,13 Deu 18:4 yet so that part of them were communicated to the poor widows and fatherless and strangers.

Not to eat blood, use enchantments, or heathen customs (26–28)

26. Any thing with the blood – Any flesh out of which the blood is poured. **Neither shall ye use enchantments** – It was unpardonable in them, to whom were committed the oracles of God, to ask counsel of the devil. **Nor observe times** – Superstitiously, esteeming some days lucky, others unlucky.

27. The corners of your heads – That is your temples, ye shall not cut off the hair of your heads round about your temples. This the Gentiles did, either for the worship of their idols, to whom young men used to consecrate their hair, being cut off from their heads, as Homer, Plutarch and many others write; or in funerals or immoderate mournings, as appears from Isa 15:2 Jer 48:37. And the like is to be thought concerning the beard or the hair in the corner, that is, corners of the beard. The reason then of this prohibition is because God would not have his people agree with idolaters, neither in their idolatries, nor in their excessive sorrowing, no nor so much as in the appearances of it.

Not to prostitute their daughters (29–30)

29. Do not prostitute – As the Gentiles frequently did for the honour of some of their idols, to whom women were consecrated, and publically prostituted.

Not to regard wizards (31)

31. Wizards – Them that have entered into covenant with the devil, by whose help they foretell many things to come, and acquaint men with secret things. See Lev 20:27 Deu 18:11 1Sam 28:3,7,9 2Kings 21:6.

To honour the aged (32)

32. Rise up – To do them reverence when they pass by, for which end they were obliged, as the Jews say, presently to sit down again when they were past, that it might be manifest they arose out of respect to them.

Love the stranger (33, 34)

33. Vex him – Either with opprobrious expressions, or grievous exactions.

Do no injustice (34–36)

34. Ye were strangers – And therefore are sensible of the fears, distresses, and miseries of such, which call for your pity, and you ought to do to them, as you desired others should do to you, when you were such.

37. Therefore – Because my blessings and deliverances are not indulgences to sin, but greater obligations to all duties to God and men.

Chapter 20

Prohibitions against offering children to Moloch (1–5)

2. The people – Here follow the punishments of the crimes forbidden in the former chapters.

3. I will set my face against that man – Deal with him as an enemy, and make him a monument of my justice. **To defile my sanctuary** – Because the sanctuary was defiled by gross abominations committed in that city or land where God's sanctuary was: or because by these actions they declared to all men that they esteemed the sanctuary and service of God abominable and vile, by preferring such odious idolatry before it. **And to profane my name** – Partly by despising it themselves, partly by disgracing it to others, and giving them occasion to blaspheme it, and to abhor the true religion.

4. Hide their eyes – Wink at his fault, and forbear to accuse and punish him.

Against consulting wizards (6)

6. To go a whoring – To seek counsel or help from them.

Holiness enjoined (7, 8)

8. Who sanctify you – Who separate you from all nations, and from their impurities and idolatries, to be a peculiar people to myself; and who give you my grace to keep my statutes.

Against cursing parents and against adultery (9–10)

9. Curseth – This is not here meant of every perverse expression, but of bitter reproaches or imprecations. **His blood shall be upon him** – He is guilty of his own death: he deserves to die for so unnatural a crime.

Against incestuous mixtures (11–21)

12. Confusion – By perverting the order which God hath appointed, and making the same off-spring both his own child and his grandchild.

13. Put to death – Except the one party was forced by the other. See Deu 22:25.

14. They – All who consented to it.

15. Slay the beast – Partly for the prevention of monstrous births, partly to blot out the memory of so loathsome a crime.

17. See her nakedness – In this and several of the following verses, uncovering nakedness plainly appears to mean not marriage, but fornication or adultery.

20. They shall die childless – Either shall be speedily cut off ere they can have a child by that incestuous conjunction; if this seem a less crime than most of the former incestuous mixtures, and therefore the magistrate forbear to punish it with death; yet they shall either have no children from such an unlawful bed, or their children shall die before them.

21. His brother's wife – Except in the case allowed by God, Deu 25:5.

Holiness again enjoined; soothsayers to be stoned (22–27)

27. A man or a woman that hath a familiar spirit, shall surely be put to death – They that are in league with the devil, have in effect made a covenant with death: and so shall their doom be.

Chapter 21

Directions to the priests (1–9)

1. Among his people – None of the priests shall touch the dead body, or assist at his funeral, or eat of the funeral feast. The reason of this law is evident, because by such pollution they were excluded from converse with men, to whom by their function they were to be serviceable upon all occasions, and from the handling of holy things. And God would hereby teach them, and in them all successive ministers, that they ought entirely to give themselves to the service of God. Yea, to renounce all expressions of natural affection, and all worldly employments, so far as they are impediments to the discharge of their holy services.

2. Near to him – Under which general expression his wife seems to be comprehended, though she be not expressed. And hence it is noted as a peculiar case, that Ezekiel, who was a priest, was forbidden to mourn for his wife, Eze 24:16, &c. These exceptions God makes in condescension to human infirmity, because in such cases it was very hard to restrain the affections. But this allowance concerns only the inferior priest, not the high-priest.

3. That is nigh him – That is, by nearness not of relation, (for that might seem a needless addition) but of habitation, one not yet cut off from the family. For if she was married, she was now of another family, and under her husband's care in those matters.

4. Being – Or, seeing he is a chief man, for such not only the high-priest, but others also of the inferior priests were. He shall not defile himself for any other person whatsoever. **To profane himself** – Because such defilement for the dead did profane him, or make him as a common person, and consequently unfit to manage his sacred employment.

5. They shall not make baldness – In funerals, as the Heathens did. Though I allow them to defile themselves for some of the dead, yet in no case shall they use these superstitious rites, which also the people were forbidden to do; but the priests in a more peculiar manner, because

they are by word and example to teach the people their duty.

6. Holy unto their God – Devoted to God's service, and always prepared for it, and therefore shall keep themselves from all defilements. **The name of their God** – Which they especially bear. **The bread of their God** – That is, the shew-bread: or rather, all the other offerings, besides burnt-offerings: which are called bread, because bread is commonly put for all food.

7. Profane – Or defiled, or deflowered, though it were done secretly, or by force: because the priest must take care that all the members of his family be free not only from gross wickedness, but from all suspicions of evil.

9. And the daughter – And by analogy his son also, and his wife, because the reason of the law here added, concerns all. And nothing is more common than to name one kind for the rest of the same nature, as also is done Lev 18:6. **She profaneth her father** – Exposeth his person and office, and consequently religion, to contempt.

To the high-priest (10–15.)

10. The garments – Those holy garments, which were peculiar to him. **Shall not uncover his head** – This being then the posture of mourners, Lev 10:6, though afterwards the custom was changed and mourners covered their heads, 2Sam 15:30, Esth 6:12. **Nor rent his clothes** – Another expression of mourning.

11. Go in – Into the chamber or house where they lie. This and divers other rites here prescribed were from hence translated by the Heathens into their use, whose priests were put under the same obligations.

12. Out of the sanctuary – To attend the funerals of any person: for upon other occasions he might and did commonly go out. **Nor profane the sanctuary** – Either by the performance of a civility, or by entering into the sanctuary before the seven days allotted for his cleansing, Num 19:11, were expired. **The crown of the anointing oil** – Or, the crown, the golden plate, which is called the holy crown, Exo 29:6, and the anointing oil of his God are upon him. So there is only an ellipsis of the conjunction and, which is frequent. And these two things, being most eminent, are put for the rest, as the sign is put for the thing signified, that is, for he is God's high-priest.

13. In her virginity – Or, a virgin, partly because as he was a type of Christ, so his wife was a type of the church, which is compared to a virgin, and partly for greater caution and assurance that his wife was not a defiled or deflowered person. Most of these things are forbidden to all the priests; and here to the high-priest, to shew that he also, and he especially is obliged to the same cautions.

15. I the Lord sanctify him – I have separated him from all other men for my immediate service, and therefore will not have that race corrupted.

None of these must have any blemish (16–24)

17. Of thy seed – Whether the high priest, or the inferior ones. **That hath** – In all successive ages, any defect or excess of parts, any notorious deformity or imperfection in his body. The reason hereof is partly typical, that he, might more fully represent Christ, the great high-priest, who was typified both by the priest and sacrifice, and therefore both were to be without blemish; partly moral, to teach all Christians and especially ministers of holy things, what purity and perfection of heart and life they should labour after, and that notorious blemishes in the mind or conversation, render a man unfit for the ministry of the gospel; and partly prudential, because such blemishes were apt to breed contempt of the person; and consequently, of his function, and of the holy things wherein he ministered. For which reason, such persons as have notorious defects or deformities, are still unfit for the ministry except where there are eminent gifts and graces, which vindicate a man from the contemptibleness of his bodily presence.

18. A flat nose – Most restrain this word to the nose, and to some great deformity relating to it. But according to others, it signifies more generally, a person that wants some member or members, because the next word, to which it is opposed, signifies one that hath more members than he should.

21. A blemish – Any notorious blemish whereby he is disfigured, though not here mentioned.

22. He shall eat – Which a priest having any uncleanness might not do whereby God would shew the great difference between natural infirmities sent upon a man by God, and moral defilements which a man brought upon himself.

23. To the vail – To the second veil which was between the holy and the most holy place, to burn incense, to order the shew-bread, and to dress the lamps, which were nigh unto that veil though without. **My altar** – The altar of burnt-offering, which was without the sanctuary. The sense is, he shall not execute the priest's office, which was to be done in those two places.

Chapter 22

A priest, having any uncleanness, must not eat of the holy things (1–7)

2. Separate themselves – When any uncleanness is upon them, as appears from Lev 22:3,4. **From the holy things** – From eating of those parts of the offerings, which belong to them. Only of the tithes they might eat. **They** – The children of Israel. And it ill became the

priests to profane or pollute what the people did hallow.

3. Goeth unto the holy things – To eat them, or to touch them; for if the touch of one of the people having his uncleanness upon him defiled the thing he touched, much more was it so in the priest. **Cut off** – From my ordinances by excommunication: He shall be excluded both from the administration, and from the participation of them.

7. His food – His portion, the means of his subsistence. This may be added, to signify why there was no greater nor longer a penalty put upon the priests than upon the people in the same case, because his necessity craved some mitigation: tho' otherwise the priests being more sacred persons, deserved a greater punishment.

No priest must eat that which dies of itself, or is torn (8, 9)

9. Lest they bear sin – Incur guilt and punishment. **For it** – For the neglect or violation of it.

No stranger must eat of holy things (10–13)

10. No stranger – Of a strange family, who is not a priest; but there is an exception to this rule, Lev 22:11. **A sojourner** – One that comes to his house and abides there for a season, and eats at his table.

12. A stranger – To one of another family, who is no priest. Yet the priest's wife, though of another family, might eat. The reason of which difference is, because the wife passeth into the name, state and privileges of her husband, from whom the family is denominated.

Of them that do it ignorantly (14–16)

14. Unto it – Over and above the principle, and besides the ram to be offered to God, Lev 5:15. **And shall give unto the priest the holy thing** – That is, the worth of it, which the priest was either to take to himself or to offer to God, as the nature of the thing was.

15. They – The people shall not profane them, by eating them: or the priests shall not profane them, that is, suffer the people to profane them, without censure and punishment.

16. They – That is, the priests, shall not **suffer them** – That is, the people, **to bear the iniquity of trespass** – That is, the punishment of their sin, which they might expect from God, and for the prevention whereof the priest was to see restitution made.

Sacrifices must be without blemish, and of a due age (17–27)

18. Strangers – Such as were proselytes.

19. A male – For a burnt-offering, which was always of that kind: but the females were accepted in peace-offerings, and sin-offerings.

25. **A stranger's hand** – From proselytes: even from those, such should not be accepted, much less from the Israelites. **The bread of your God** – That is, the sacrifices.

Thank offerings must be eaten the same day (29, 30)

28. **In one day** – Because it favoured of cruelty.

An exhortation to obedience (31–33)

32. **Hallowed**, or sanctified, either by you in keeping my holy commands, or upon you in executing my holy and righteous judgments. I will manifest myself to be an holy God that will not bear the transgression of my laws.

Chapter 23

Directions concerning the sabbath (1–3)

2. **Ye shall proclaim** – Cause to be proclaimed, by the priests. **Holy convocations** – Days for your assembling together to my worship in a special manner.

3. **Ye shall do no work therein** – So it runs in the general for the sabbath day, and for the day of expiation, Lev 23:28, excluding all works about earthly employments whether of profit or of pleasure; but upon other feast days he forbids only servile works, as Lev 23:7,21,36, for surely this manifest difference in the expressions used by the wise God must needs imply a difference in the things. **In all your dwellings** – Other feasts, were to be kept before the Lord in Jerusalem only, whither all the males were to come for that end; but the sabbath was to be kept in all places, both in synagogues, and in their private houses.

The Passover (4–8)

4. **These are the feasts of the Lord** – Or rather, the solemnities: (for the day of atonement was a fast:) and so the word is used, Isa 33:20, where Zion is called the city of our solemnities.

The first fruits (9–14)

10. **An omer** – They did not offer this corn in the ear, or by a sheaf or handful, but, as Josephus, 3. 10 affirms, and may be gathered from Lev 2:14,15,16, purged from the chaff, and dried, and beaten out.

11. **He shall wave the sheaf before the Lord** – In the name of the whole congregation, which as it were sanctified to them the whole harvest, and gave them a comfortable use of all the rest. For then we may eat our bread with joy, when God hath accepted our works. And thus should we always begin with God; begin our lives with him, begin every day with him, begin every work and business with him: seek ye first the kingdom of God. **The morrow after the sabbath** – After the first day of the feast of unleavened bread, which was a sabbath or day of rest, as appears from Lev 23:7, or upon the sixteenth day of the month. And this was the first of those fifty days, in the close whereof was the feast of Pentecost.

13. **Two tenth deals** – Or, parts, of an ephah, that is, two omers, whereas in other sacrifices of lambs there was but one tenth deal prescribed. The reason of which disproportion may be this, that one of the tenth deals was a necessary attendant upon the lamb, and the other was peculiar to this feast, and was an attendant upon that of the corn, and was offered with it in thanksgiving to God for the fruits of the earth.

14. **Bread** – Made of new wheat. **Nor green ears** – Which were usual, not only for offerings to God, but also for man's food.

The feast of Pentecost (15–22)

15. **From the morrow** – From the sixteenth day of the month, and the second day of the feast of unleavened bread inclusively.

16. **A new meal-offering** – Of new corn made into loaves.

18. **One bullock and two rams** – In Num 28:11,19, it is two young bullocks and one ram. Either therefore it was left to their liberty to choose which they would offer, or one of the bullocks there, and one of the rams here, were the peculiar sacrifices of the feast day, and the other were attendants upon the two loaves, which were the proper offering at this time. And the one may be mentioned there, and the other here, to teach us, that the addition of a new sacrifice did not destroy the former, but both were to be offered, as the extraordinary sacrifices of every feast did not hinder the oblation of the daily sacrifice.

19. **One kid** – In Lev 4:14, the sin-offering for the sin of the people is a bullock, but here a kid; the reason of the difference may be this, because that was for some particular sin of the people, but this only in general for all their sins.

20. **Wave them** – Some part of them in the name of the whole; and so for the two lambs, otherwise they had been too big and too heavy, to be waved. **For the priests** – Who had to themselves not only the breast and shoulder as in others, which belonged to the priest, but also the rest which belonged to the offerer; because the whole congregation being the offerer here, it could neither be distributed to them all, nor given to some without offence to the rest.

21. **An holy convocation** – A sabbath or day of rest, called Pentecost; which was instituted, partly in remembrance of the consummation of their deliverance out of Egypt by bringing them thence to the mount of God, or Sinai, as God had promised, and of that admirable blessing of

giving the law to them on the 50th day, and forming them into a commonwealth under his own immediate government; and partly in gratitude for the farther progress of their harvest, as in the Passover they offered a thank-offering to God for the beginning of their harvest. The perfection of this feast, was the pouring out of the holy spirit upon the apostles on this very day, in which the law of faith was given, fifty days after Christ our Passover was sacrificed for us. And on that day the apostles, having themselves received the first-fruits of the spirit, begat three thousand souls through the word of truth, as the first-fruits of the Christian church.

22. When ye reap, thou – From the plural, ye, he comes to the singular, thou, because he would press this duty upon every person who hath an harvest to reap, that none might plead exemption from it. And it is observable, that though the present business is only concerning the worship of God, yet he makes a kind of excursion to repeat a former law of providing for the poor, to shew that our devotion to God is little esteemed by him if it be not accompanied with acts of charity to men.

The feast of trumpets (23–25)

24. A sabbath – Solemnized with the blowing of trumpets by the priests, not in a common way, as they did every first day of every month, but in an extraordinary manner, not only in Jerusalem, but in all the cities of Israel. They began to blow at sun-rise, and continued blowing till sun-set. This seems to have been instituted:

1. To solemnize the beginning of the new year, whereof as to civil matters and particularly as to the Jubilee, this was the first day; concerning which it was fit the people should be admonished, both to excite their thankfulness for God's blessings in the last year, and to direct them in the management of their civil affairs.

2. To put a special honour upon this month. For as the seventh day was the sabbath, and the seventh year was a sabbatical year, so God would have the seventh month to be a kind of sabbatical month, for the many Sabbaths and solemn feasts which were observed in this more than in any other month. And by this sounding of the trumpets in its beginning, God would quicken and prepare them for the following Sabbaths, as well as that of atonement and humiliation for their sins, as those of thanksgiving for God's mercies.

Of atonement (26–32)

27. Afflict your souls – With fasting, and bitter repentance for all, especially their national sins, among which no doubt God would have them remember their sin of the golden calf. For as God had threatened to remember it in after times to punish them for it, so there was great

reason why they should remember it to humble themselves for it.

28. Whatsoever soul – Either of the Jewish nation, or religion. Hereby God would signify the absolute necessity which every man had of repentance and forgiveness of sin, and the desperate condition of all impenitent persons.

32. From even to even – The day of atonement began at the evening of the ninth day, and continued till the evening of the tenth day. **Ye shall celebrate your sabbath** – This particular sabbath is called your sabbath, possibly to note the difference between this and other Sabbaths: for the weekly sabbath is oft called the sabbath of the Lord. The Jews are supposed to begin every day, and consequently their Sabbaths, at the evening, in remembrance of the creation, as Christians generally begin their days and Sabbaths with the morning in memory of Christ's resurrection.

Of tabernacles (33–44)

34. Of tabernacles – Of tents or booths or arbours. This feast was appointed to remind them of that time when they had no other dwellings in the wilderness, and to stir them up to bless God, as well for the gracious protection then afforded them, as for the more commodious habitations now given them; and to excite them to gratitude for all the fruits of the year newly ended, which were now completely brought in.

36. Ye shall offer – A several-offering each day. **The eighth day** – Which though it was not one of the days of this feast strictly taken. Yet in a larger sense it belonged to this feast, and is called the great day of the feast, John 7:37. And so indeed it was, as for other reasons, so because, by their removal from the tabernacles into fixed habitations, it represented that happy time wherein their 40 years tedious march in the wilderness was ended with their settlement in the land of Canaan, which it was most fit they should acknowledge with such a solemn day of thanksgiving as this was.

37. A sacrifice – A sin-offering, called by the general name, a sacrifice, because it was designed for that which was the principal end of all sacrifices, the expiation of sin.

38. Beside the Sabbaths – The offerings of the weekly sabbaths. God will not have any sabbath-sacrifice diminished because of the addition of others, proper to any other feast. And it is here to be noted, that though other festival days are sometimes called sabbaths, yet these are here called the sabbaths of the Lord, in way of contradistinction, to shew that this was more eminently such than other feast-days. **Your gifts** – Which being here distinguished from the free-will-offerings made to the Lord, may note what they freely gave to the priests over and above their first-fruits and tithes or other things which they were enjoined to give.

40. Of goodly trees – Namely, olive, myrtle and pine, mentioned, Neh 8:15,16, which were most plentiful there, and which would best preserve their greenness. **Thick trees** – Fit for shade and shelter. **And willows** – To mix with the other, and in some sort bind them together. And as they made their booths of these materials, so they carried some of these boughs in their hands.

42. In booths – Which were erected in their cities or towns, either in their streets, or gardens, or the tops of their houses. These were made flat, and therefore were fit for the use.

44. The feasts of the Lord – We have reason to be thankful, that the feasts of the Lord, now are not so numerous, nor the observance of them so burdensome and costly; but more spiritual and significant, and surer and sweeter earnests of the everlasting feast, at the last ingathering, which we hope to be celebrating to eternity.

Chapter 24

Laws concerning the lamps (1–4)

2. To cause the lamps to burn – Heb. the lamp: yet Lev 24:4, it is the lamps: The seven lamps made all one lamp. In allusion to which, the Blessed Spirit is represented, Rev 4:5, by seven lamps of fire before the throne. For there are diversities of gifts, but one spirit.

3. Aaron – Either by himself, or by his sons, Exo 25:37.

4. The pure candlestick – So called, partly because it was made of pure gold, partly because it was to be always kept clean.

The shew-bread (5–9)

5. Thou – By the priests or Levites, whose work it was to prepare them, 1Chr 9:32. **Twelve cakes** – Representing the twelve tribes.

6. Two rows – Not one above another, but one beside another, as the frankincense put upon each, Lev 24:7, shows.

7. Pure frankincense – Unmixed and uncorrupted, or of the best sort, to be burnt before the Lord. **On the bread** – And this was done every time that the bread was changed. **For a memorial** – For that part which properly belonged to God, whereas the rest belonged to the priests.

8. From the children of Israel – And these cakes are said to be received from or offered by the children of Israel, bought with the money which they contributed. **By an everlasting covenant** – By virtue of that compact made between me and them, by which they were obliged to keep this amongst other commands, and, they so doing, I am obliged to be their God

and to bless them. And this may be here called an everlasting covenant, not only because it was to endure as long as the Jewish polity stood, but also because this was to stand everlastingly, or continually, and therefore the new cakes were first brought before the old were taken away.

9. It – The old bread now to be taken away. **Made by fire** – The incense was offered by fire, and that for or instead of the bread, and therefore the bread was reputed as if it had been so offered.

10. Whose father was an Egyptian – This circumstance seems noted, partly to shew the danger of marriages with persons of wicked principles, and partly by this severity against him who was a stranger by the father, and an Israelite by the mother, to shew that God would not have this sin go unpunished amongst his people, what-soever he was that committed it. **Went out** – Out of Egypt, being one of that mixed multitude, which came out with the Israelites, Exo 12:32. It is probable, this was done when the Israelites were near Sinai.

Blasphemy occasioned by that of Shelomith's son (10–16)

11. The name of the Lord – The words of the Lord, or of Jehovah, are supplied out of Lev 24:16, where they are expressed; here they are omitted perhaps for the aggravation of his crime. He blasphemed the name so called by way of eminency; that name which is above every name; that name which a man should in some sort tremble to mention; which is not to be named without cause or without reverence. **And cursed** – Not the Israelite only, but his God also, as appears from Lev 24:15,16. **And they brought him** – Either the people who heard him, or the inferior magistrate, to whom he was first brought.

12. That the mind of the Lord might be showed – For God had only said in general, that he would not hold such guiltless, that is, he would punish them, but had not declared how he would have them punished by men.

14. Lay their hands upon his head – Whereby they gave public testimony that they heard this person speak such words, and did in their own and all the peoples names, demand justice to be executed upon him, that by this sacrifice God might be appeased, and his judgments turned away from the people, upon whom they would certainly fall if he were unpunished. **Stone him** – The same punishment which was before appointed for those who cursed their parents.

15. Whosoever curseth his God – Speaketh of him reproachfully. **Shall bear his sin** – That is, the punishment of it; shall not go unpunished.

16. He that blasphemeth the name of the Lord – This is a repetition of the same sin in other words, which is common. As this law is laid down in general terms, Lev 24:15, so both the sin and the punishment are particularly expressed, Lev 24:16. **All the congregation** – To shew their zeal for God, and to beget in them the greater dread and abhorrence of blasphemy.

The law of retaliation (17–22)

17. He that killeth – This law is repeated here, to prevent the mischievous effects of men's striving together, which as here it caused blasphemy, so it might in others lead to murder.

22. One law – That is, in matters of common right, but not as to church privileges.

The blasphemer stoned (23)

23. Stone him with stones – This blasphemer was the first that died by the law of Moses. Stephen the first that died for the gospel, died by the abuse of the law. The martyr and the malefactor suffered the same death; but how vast the difference between them.

Chapter 25

In token of his peculiar right to the land of Canaan, God in this chapter appoints certain regulations.

Every seventh year should be a year of rest (1–7)

1. In mount Sinai – That is, near mount Sinai. So the Hebrew particle beth is sometimes used. So there is no need to disturb the history in this place.

2. When ye come into the land – So as to be settled in it; for the time of the wars was not to be accounted, nor the time before Joshua's distribution of the land among them. **Keep a sabbath** – That is, enjoy rest and freedom from plowing, and tilling. **Unto the Lord** – In obedience and unto the honour of God. This was instituted:

1. For the assertion of God's sovereign right to the land, in which the Israelites were but tenants at God's will.

2. For the trial of their obedience.

3. For the demonstration of his providence as well in general towards men, as especially towards his own people.

4. To wean them from inordinate love, and pursuit of worldly advantages, and to inure them to depend upon God alone, and upon God's blessing for their subsistence.

5. To put them in mind of that blessed and eternal rest provided for all good men.

4. A sabbath of rest to the land – They were neither to do any work about it, nor expect any harvest from it. All yearly labours were to be intermitted in the seventh year, as much as daily labours on the seventh day.

5. Of its own accord – From the grains that fell out of the ears the last reaping time. **Thou shalt not reap** – That is, as thy own peculiarly, but only so as others may reap it with thee, for present food. **Undressed** – Not cut off by thee, but suffered to grow for the use of the poor.

6. The sabbath of the land – That is, the growth of the sabbath, or that fruit which groweth in the sabbatical year. **For thy servant** – For all promiscuously, to take food from thence as they need it.

Every fiftieth year should be a year of jubilee (8–17)

9. The jubilee – Signified the true liberty from our spiritual debts and slaveries to be purchased by Christ, and to be published to the world by the sound of the gospel. **The seventh month** – Which was the first month of the year for civil affairs; the jubilee therefore began in that month; and, as it seems, upon this very tenth day, when the trumpet sounded, as other feasts generally began when the trumpet sounded. **In the day of atonement** – A very fit time, that when they fasted and prayed for God's mercy to them in the pardon of their sins, then they might exercise their charity to men in forgiving their debts; and to teach us, that the foundation of all solid comfort must be laid in repentance and atonement for our sins through Christ.

10. The fiftieth year – The year of jubilee was not the forty and ninth year, as some learned men think, but precisely the fiftieth. The old weekly sabbath is called the seventh day, because it truly was so, being next after the six days of the week and distinct from them all: and the year of release is called the seventh year, Lev 25:4, as immediately following the six years, Lev 25:3, and distinct from them all. And in like manner the jubilee is called the fiftieth year, because it comes next after seven tines seven or forty-nine years, Lev 25:8, and is distinct from them all. **Unto all the inhabitants** – Understand such as were Israelites; principally to all servants, even to such as would not and did not go out at the seventh year, and to the poor, who now were acquitted from all their debts, and restored to their possessions. **Jubilee** – So called either from the Hebrew word Jobel which signifies first a ram, and then a ram's horn, by the sound whereof it was proclaimed; or from Jubal the inventor of musical instruments, Gen 4:21, because it was celebrated with music and all expressions of joy. **Unto his possession** – Which had been sold or otherwise alienated from him. This law was not at all unjust, because all buyers and sellers had an eye to this condition in their bargains; but it was expedient in many regards, as:

1. To mind them that God alone was the Lord and proprietor both of them and of their lands,

and they only his tenants; a point which they were very apt to forget.

2. That hereby inheritances, families, and tribes, might be kept entire and clear until the coming of the Messiah, who was to be known as by other things, so by the tribe and family out of which he was to come. And this accordingly was done by the singular providence of God until the Lord Jesus did come. Since which time those characters are miserably confounded: which is no small argument that the Messiah is come.

3. To set bounds both to the insatiable avarice of some, and the foolish prodigality of others, that the former might not wholly and finally swallow up the inheritances of their brethren, and the latter might not be able to undo themselves and their posterity for ever, which was a singular privilege of this law and people. His family – From whom he was gone, being sold to some other family either by himself or by his father.

12. It shall be holy – So it was, because it was sequestered in great part from worldly employments and dedicated to God, and to the exercise of holy joy and thankfulness; and because it was a type of that holy and happy jubilee which they were to expect and enjoy under the Messiah. The increase thereof – Such things as it produced of itself. Out of the field – Whence they in common with others might take it as they needed it; but must not put it into barns, See Lev 25:5, and Exo 23:11.

14. Ye shall not oppress – Neither the seller by requiring more, nor the buyer by taking the advantage from his brother's necessities to give him less than the worth of it.

15. Years of fruits – Or, fruitful years; for there were some unfruitful years; those wherein they were not allowed to sow or reap.

16. Years of fruits – Or, For the number of the fruits. The meaning is, he selleth not the land, but only the fruits thereof, and that for a certain time.

21. For three years – Not compleatly, but in great part, namely, for that part of the 6th year which was between the beginning of harvest and the beginning of the 7th year, for the whole 7th year, and for that part of the 8th year which was before the harvest, which reached almost until the beginning of the ninth year. This is added to shew the equity of this command. As God would hereby try their faith and obedience, so he gave them an eminent proof of his own exact providence and tender care over them in making provisions suitable to their necessities.

A peculiar blessing added (18–22)

22. Old fruit – Of the sixth year principally, if not solely.

23. For ever – So as to be for ever alienated from the family of him that sells it. Or, absolutely and properly, so as to become the property of the buyer: Or, to the extermination or utter cutting off, namely, of the seller, from all hopes and possibility of redemption. The land is mine – Procured for you by my power, given to you by my grace and bounty, and the right of propriety reserved by me. With me – That is, in my land or houses: thus he is said to sojourn with another that dwells in his house. Howsoever in your own or other mens opinions you pass for lords and proprietors, yet in truth, ye are but strangers and sojourners, not to possess the land for ever, but only for a season, and to leave it to such as I have appointed for it.

The land sold may be redeemed (23–34)

24. A redemption – A right of redemption in the time and manner following.

25. If any of his kin come – Or, If the redeemer come, being near akin to him, who in this was an eminent type of Christ, who was made near akin to us by taking our flesh, that he might perform the work of redemption for us.

27. The years of the sale – That is, from the time of the sale to the jubilee. See above, Lev 25:15,16. The overplus – That is, a convenient price for the years from this redemption to the jubilee.

28. Go out – That is, out of the buyer's hand, without any redemption money.

30. It shall not go out – The reasons before alledged for lands do not hold in such houses; there was no danger of confusion in tribes or families by the alienation of houses. The seller also had a greater propriety in houses than in lands, as being commonly built by the owner's cost and diligence, and therefore had a fuller power to dispose of them. Besides, God would hereby encourage persons to buy and possess houses in such places, as frequency and fulness of inhabitants in cities, was a great strength, honour and advantage to the whole land.

31. In the villages – Because they belonged to and were necessary for the management of the lands.

34. May not be sold – Not sold at all, partly, because it was of absolute necessity for them for the keeping of their cattle, and partly because these were no enclosures, but common fields, in which all the Levites that lived in such a city had an interest, and therefore no particular Levite could dispose of his part in it.

Usury forbidden (35–38)

35. A sojourner – Understand it of proselytes only, for of other strangers they were permitted to take usury, Deu 23:20.

36. Of him – That is, of thy brother, whether he be Israelite, or proselyte. Or increase – All

kinds of usury are in this case forbidden, whether of money, or of victuals, or of any thing that is commonly lent by one man to another upon usury, or upon condition of receiving the thing lent with advantage and overplus. If one borrow in his necessity, there can be no doubt but this law is binding still. But it cannot be thought to bind, where money is borrowed for purchase of lands, trade, or other improvements. For there it is reasonable, that the lender share with the borrower in the profit.

Jewish servants to be released at the jubilee but heathens might be retained (39–46)

39. As a bond-man – Neither for the time, for ever, nor for the manner, with the hardest and vilest kinds of service, rigorously and severely exacted.

41. Then shall he depart – Thou shalt not suffer him or his to abide longer in thy service, as thou mightest do in the year of release, Exo 21:2,6.

42. They are my servants – They, no less than you, are members of my church and people; such as I have chosen out of all the world to serve me here, and to enjoy me hereafter, and therefore are not to be oppressed, neither are you absolute lords over them to deal with them as you please.

43. Fear thy God – Though thou dost not fear them who are in thy power, and unable to right themselves, yet fear that God who hath commanded thee to use them kindly, and who can and will avenge their cause, if thou oppress them.

Of an Israelite that sold himself to a stranger (47–55)

47. The flock – Heb. root, that is, one of the root or flock. So the word root is elsewhere used for the branch or progeny growing from it. He seems to note one of a foreign race and country, transplanted into the land of Israel, and there having taken root amongst the people of God, yet even such an one, though he hath some privilege by it, shall not have power to keep an Hebrew servant from the benefit of redemption.

50. According to the time of an hired servant – Allowance shall be made for the time wherein he hath served, proportionable to that which is given to an hired servant for so long service, because his condition is in this like theirs; it is not properly his person, but his work and labour that was sold.

53. In thy sight – Thou shalt not suffer this to be done, but whether thou art a magistrate, or a private person, thou shalt take care according to thy capacity to get it remedied.

Chapter 26

A general enforcement of the preceding laws, by promises of reward, and threats of punishment.

A repetition of some principal commandments (1, 2)

1. An image – Or pillar, that is, to worship it, or bow down to it, as it follows. Otherwise this was not simply prohibited, being practised by holy men, both before and after this law.

2. My sanctuary – By purging and preserving it from all uncleanness, by approaching to it and managing all the services of it with reverence, and in such manner only as God hath appointed.

A promise of all good to the obedient (3–13)

4. Rain – Therefore God placed them not in a land where there were such rivers as the Nile, to water it and make it fruitful, but in a land which depended wholly upon the rain of heaven, the key whereof God kept in his own hand, that so he might the more effectually oblige them to obedience, in which their happiness consisted.

5. The vintage – That is, you shall have so plentiful an harvest, that you shall not be able to thresh out your corn in a little time, but that work will last till the vintage.

6. The sword – That is, war, as the sword is oft taken. It shall not enter into it, nor have passage through it, much less shall your land be made the seat of war.

8. Five – A small number; a certain number for an uncertain.

9. Establish my covenant – That is, actually perform all that I have promised in my covenant made with you.

10. Bring forth – Or, cast out, throw them away as having no occasion to spend them, or give them to the poor, or even to your cattle, that you may make way for the new corn, which also is so plentiful, that of itself it will fill up your barns.

11. I will set – As I have placed it, so I will continue it among you, and not remove it from you, as once I did upon your miscarriage, Exo 33:7.

12. I will walk among you – As I have hitherto done, both by my pillar of cloud and fire, and by my tabernacle, which have walked or gone along with you in all your journeys, and staid among you in all your stations, to protect, conduct, instruct, and comfort you. And I will own you for that peculiar people which I have singled out of mankind, to bless you here and to save you hereafter.

13. Upright – With heads lifted up, not pressed down with a yoke. It notes their liberty, security, confidence and glory.

A threatening of terrible judgments to the disobedient (14–39)

15. Break my covenant – Break your part of that covenant made between me and you, and thereby discharge me from the blessings promised on my part.

16. That shall consume the eyes, and cause sorrow of heart – Two remarkable effects of this distemper, when it continues long. It eminently weakens the sight, and sinks the spirit. All chronical diseases are here included in the consumption, all acute in the burning ague or fever.

19. The pride of your power – That is, your strength of which you are proud, your numerous and united forces, your kingdom, yea, your ark and sanctuary. **I will make your heaven as iron** – The heavens shall yield you no rain, nor the earth fruits.

20. In vain – in plowing, and sowing, and tilling the ground.

25. The quarrel of my covenant – That is, my quarrel with you for your breach of your covenant made with me.

26. When I have broken the staff of your bread – By sending a famine or scarcity of bread, which is the staff and support of man's present life. **Ten women** – That is, ten or many families, for the women took care for the bread and food of all the family. **By weight** – This is a sign and consequence both of a famine, and of the baking of the bread of several families together in one oven, wherein each family took care to weigh their bread, and to receive the same proportion which they put in.

29. The flesh of your sons – Through extreme hunger. See Lam 4:10.

30. High places – In which you will sacrifice after the manner of the Heathens. **The carcases of your idols** – So he calls them, either to signify that their idols how specious soever or glorious in their eyes, were in truth but lifeless and contemptible carcases; or to shew that their idols should be so far from helping them, that they should be thrown down and broken with them, and both should lie together in a forlorn and loathsome state.

31. Sanctuaries – God's sanctuary, called sanctuaries here, as also Psa 73:17 74:7 Jer 51:51 Eze 28:18, because there were divers apartments in it, each of which was a sanctuary, or, which is all one, an holy place, as they are severally called. And yours emphatically, not mine, for I disown and abhor it, and all the services you do in it, because you have defiled it. **I will not smell** – Not own or accept them. **Your sweet odours** – Either of the incense, or of your sacrifices, which when offered with faith and obedience, are sweet and acceptable to me.

32. Who dwell therein – Having driven you out and possessed your places.

33. After you – The sword shall follow you into strange lands, and you shall have no rest there.

34. The land shall enjoy her Sabbaths – It shall enjoy those sabbatical years of rest from tillage, which you through covetousness would not give it.

37. When none pursueth – Your guilt and fear causing you to imagine that they do pursue when indeed they do not.

39. Pine away – Be consumed and melt away by degrees through diseases, oppressions, griefs, and manifold miseries.

A promise of mercy to the penitent (40–46)

40. If they shall confess their iniquity, and the iniquity of their fathers, with their trespass which they have trespassed against me – That is, with their prevarication with me and defection from me to idolatry, which by way of eminency he calls their trespass: and that also they have walked contrary to me, Lev 26:41, and that I also have walked contrary unto them, and **have brought them into the land of their enemies** – That is, that they are not come into these calamities by chance, nor by the misfortune of war, but by my just judgment upon them. And, if then their uncircumcised, that is, impure, carnal, profane, and impenitent hearts be humbled, that is, subdued, purged, reformed: if to this confession they add sincere humiliation and reformation, I will do what follows.

41. If they accept of – The meaning is, if they sincerely acknowledge the righteousness of God and their own wickedness, and patiently submit to his correcting hand; if with David they are ready to say, it is good for them that they are afflicted, that they may learn God's statutes, and yield obedience to them for the future, which is a good evidence of true repentance.

42. I will remember my covenant – So as to make good all that I have promised in it. For words of knowledge or remembrance in scripture, commonly denote affection and kindness. **I will remember the land** – Which now seems to be forgotten and despised, as if I had never chosen it to be the peculiar place of my presence and blessing.

44. For I am the Lord their God – Therefore neither the desperateness of their condition, nor the greatness of their sins, shall make me wholly make void my covenant with them and their ancestors, but I will in due time remember them for good, and for my covenant's sake return to them in mercy. From this place the Jews take great comfort, and assure themselves of deliverance out of their present servitude and misery.

And from this, and such other places, St. Paul concludes, that the Israeli nation, tho' then rejected and ruined, should be gathered again and restored.

46. These are the laws which the Lord made between him and the children of Israel – Hereby his communion with his church is kept up. He manifests not only his dominion over them, but his favour to them, by giving them his law. And they manifest not only their holy fear, but their holy love by the observance of it. And thus it is made between them rather as a covenant than as a law: for he draws them with the cords of a man.

Chapter 27

Laws concerning persons sanctified to God (1–8)

2. A singular vow – Or, an eminent, or hard vow, not concerning things, which was customary, but concerning persons, which he devoted to the Lord, which was unusual and difficult: yet there want not instances of persons who devoted either themselves or their children, and that either more strictly, as the Nazarites, and the Levites, 1Sam 1:11, and for these there was no redemption admitted, but they were in person to perform the service to which they were devoted: or more largely, as some who were not Levites, might yet through zeal to God, or to obtain God's help, which they wanted or desired, devote themselves or their children to the service of God and of the sanctuary, tho' not in such a way as the Levites, which was forbidden, yet in some kind of subserviency to them. And because there might be too great a number of persons thus dedicated, which might be burdensome to the sanctuary, an exchange is allowed, and the priests are directed to receive a tax for their redemption. **By thy estimation** – Thine, O man that vowest, as appears from Lev 27:8, where his estimation is opposed to the priest's valuation. Nor was there any fear of his partiality in his own cause, for the price is particularly limited. But where the price is undetermined, there, to avoid that inconvenience, the priest is to value it, as Lev 27:8,12.

3. Unto sixty years – Which is the best time for strength and service, and therefore prized at the highest rate.

4. Thirty shekels – Less than the man's price, because she is inferior to him both in strength and serviceableness.

5. Five years old – At which age they might be vowed by their parents, as appears from 1Sam 1:11–28, tho' not by themselves; and the children were obliged by their parents vow, which is not strange considering the parents right to dispose of their children so far as is not contrary to the mind of God.

8. Than thy estimation – If he be not able to pay the price which thou, according to the rules here given, requirest of him.

Concerning cattle (9–13)

9. Whereof men bring an offering – That is, a clean beast. **Giveth** – Voweth to give: **Shall be holy** – Consecrated to God, either to be sacrificed, or to be given to the priest, according to the manner of the vow, and the intention of him that voweth.

10. He shall not alter it, nor change it – Two words expressing the same thing more emphatically, that is, he shall in no wise change it, neither for one of the same, nor of another kind: partly because God would preserve the reverence of consecrated things, and therefore would not have them alienated, and partly to prevent abuses of them who on this pretence might exchange it for the worse. **It and the exchange** – That is, both the thing first vowed, and the thing offered or given in exchange. This was inflicted upon him as a just penalty for his levity in such weighty matters.

11. Unclean – Either for the kind, or for the quality of it; if it were such an one as might not be offered.

Concerning houses and lands (14–25)

14. Sanctify his house – By a vow, for of that way and manner of sanctification he speaks in this whole chapter.

15. The fifth part – Which he might the better do, because the priests did usually put a moderate rate upon it.

16. Of his possession – That is, which is his by inheritance, because particular direction is given about purchased lands, Lev 27:22. And he saith, part of it, for it was unlawful to vow away all his possessions, because thereby he disabled himself from the performance of divers duties, and made himself burdensome to his brethren. **According to the seed** – That is, according to the quantity and quality of the land, which is known by the quantity of seed which it can receive and return.

17. From the year of jubilee – That is, immediately after the year of jubilee is past. **According to thy estimation** – Now mentioned, of fifty shekels for an omer of barley seed. **It shall stand** – That is, that price shall be paid without diminution.

18. After the jubilee – That is, some considerable time after. The defalcation from the full price of fifty shekels shall be more or less as the years are more or fewer.

20. If he will not redeem it – When the priest shall set a price upon it, and offer it to him in the first place to redeem it: or, rather and, for this seems to be added by way of accumulation, if he, that is, the priest, of whom he might have redeemed it, upon his refusal, offers it to sale, and **have sold the field to another man** – He shall for ever lose the benefit of redemption.

21. **When it goeth out** – That is, out of the possession of the other man to whom the priest sold it. **The possession shall be the priests** – For their maintenance. Nor is this repugnant to that law, that the priests should have no inheritance in the land, Num 18:20, for that is only spoken of, the tribe of Levi in general, in reference to the first division of the land, wherein the Levites were not to have a distinct part of land, as other tribes had; but this doth not hinder, but some particular lands might be vowed and given to the priests, either for their own benefit, or for the service of the sanctuary.

22. **His possession** – His patrimony or inheritance.

23. **Thy estimation** – That is, the price which thou, O Moses, by my direction hast set in such cases. **To the jubilee** – As much as it is worth, for that space of time between the making of the vow and the year of jubilee: for he had no right to it for any longer time, as the next verse tells us. **As an holy thing** – As that which is to be consecrated to God instead of the land redeemed by it.

An exception concerning firstlings (26–27)

26. **No man shall sanctify it** – By vow; because it is not his own, but the Lord's already, and therefore to vow such a thing to God is a tacit derogation from, and an usurpation of the Lord's right, and a mocking of God by pretending to give what we cannot withhold from him. **Or ox or sheep** – Under these two eminent kinds he comprehends all other beasts which might be sacrificed to God, the firstlings whereof could not be redeemed but were to be sacrificed; whereas the firstlings of men were to be redeemed, and therefore were capable of being vowed, as we see, 1Sam 1:11.

27. **An unclean beast** – That is, if it be the first-born of an unclean beast, as appears from Lev 27:26, which could not be vowed, because it was a first-born, nor offered, because it was unclean, and therefore is here commanded to be redeemed or sold. **It shall be sold** – And the price thereof was given to the priests, or brought into the Lord's treasury.

Concerning what was devoted (28, 29)

28. **No devoted thing** – That is, nothing which is absolutely devoted to God with a curse upon themselves or others, if they disposed not of it according to their vow; as the Hebrew word implies. **Most holy** – That is, only to be touched or employed by the priests, and by no other persons; no not by their own families, for that was the state of the most holy things.

29. **Devoted of men** – Not by men, as some would elude it; but of men, for it is manifest both from this and the foregoing verses, that men are here not the persons devoting, but devoted to destruction, either by God's sentence, as idolaters, Exo 22:20 Deu 23:15, the Canaanites, Deu 20:17, the Amalekites, Deu 25:19, and 1Sam 15:3,26, Benhaded, 1Kings 20:42, or by men, in pursuance of such a sentence of God, as Num 21:2,3 31:17, or for any crime of an high nature, as Jud 21:5 Jos 17:15.

Concerning tithes (30–34)

30. **The tithe** – There are divers sorts of tithes, but this seems to be understood only of the ordinary and yearly tithes belonging to the Levites, as the very expression intimates, and the addition of the fifth part in case of redemption thereof implies.

34. **These are the commandments which the Lord commanded Moses for the children of Israel in mount Sinai** – This has reference to the whole book. Many of these commandments are moral: others ceremonial and peculiar to the Jewish economy: Which yet are instructive to us, who have a key to the mysteries that are contained in them. Upon the whole, we have cause to bless God, that we are not come to mount Sinai, that we are not under the dark shadows of the law, but enjoy the clear light of the gospel. The doctrine of our reconciliation to God by a Mediator, is not clouded with the smoke of burning sacrifices, but cleared by the knowledge of Christ, and him crucified. And we may praise him, that we are not under the yoke of the law, but under the sweet and easy instructions of the gospel, which pronounces those the true worshippers, that worship the Father in spirit and in truth, by Christ only, who is our priest, temple, altar, sacrifice, purification and all.

NUMBERS

John Wesley

Introduction

This book is thus entitled, because of the numbers of the children of Israel, so often mentioned therein, an eminent accomplishment of God's promise to Abraham, that his seed should be as the stars of heaven for multitude. It also relates two numberings of them, one at mount Sinai, chap. 1, the other, thirty-nine years after. And there are not three men of the same in the last account that were in the first. The book is almost equally divided, between histories and laws intermixed. An abstract of much of this book we have in a few words, Psa 95:10. Forty years long was I grieved with this generation: and an application of it to ourselves, Heb 4:1. Let us fear lest we come short!

Chapter 1

Orders given to Moses to number the people (1–4)

1. In the wilderness – Where now they had been a full year or near it, as may be gathered by comparing this place with Exo 19:1 40:17.

2. Take the sum – This is not the same muster with that Exo 38:26, as plainly appears, because that was before the building of the tabernacle, which was built and set up on the first day of the first month, Exo 40:2, but this was after it, on the first day of the second month. And they were for different ends; that was to tax them for the charges of the tabernacle; but this was for other ends, partly that the great number of the people might be known to the praise of God's faithfulness, in making good his promises of multiplying them, and to their own encouragement: partly for the better ordering their camp and march, for they were now beginning their journey; and partly that this account might be compared with the other in the close of the book, where we read that not one of all this vast number, except Caleb and Joshua were left alive; a fair warning to all future generations to take heed of rebelling against the Lord. It is true, the sums and num-

bers agree in this and that computation, which is not strange, because there was not much time between the two numberings, and no eminent sin among the people in that interval, whereby God was provoked to diminish their numbers. Some conceive that in that number, Exo 30:11–16 and 38:25,26, the Levites were included, which are here excepted, Num 1:47, and that in that interval of time, there were grown up as many more men of those years as there were Levites of the same age. **Israel** – So the strangers mixed with them, were not numbered. **Their fathers** – The people were divided into twelve tribes, the tribes into great families, Num 26:5, these great families into lesser families called the houses of their fathers, because they were distinguished one from another by their fathers.

Persons named to assist him therein (5–16)

5. Reuben – The tribes are here numbered according to the order or quality of their birth, first the children of Leah, then of Rachel, and then of the handmaids.

The particular number of each tribe (17–43)

19. He numbered them – For ought that appears in one day.

20. By their generations – That is, the persons begotten of Reuben's immediate children, who are here subdivided into families, and they into houses, and they into particular persons.

27. Threescore and fourteen thousand – Far more than any other tribe, in accomplishing Jacob's prophecy, Gen 49:8-12.

33. Ephraim – Above 8000 more than Manasseh, towards the accomplishment of that promise, Gen 48:20, which the devil in vain attempted to defeat by stirring up the men of Gath against them, 1Chr 7:21,22.

37. Thirty five thousand – The smallest number, except one, though Benjamin had more immediate children than any of his brethren, Gen 46:21, whereas Dan had but one immediate son, Gen 46:23, yet now his number is the biggest but one of all the tribes, and is almost double to that of Benjamin. Such great and strange changes God easily can, and frequently doth make in families, 1Sam 2:5. And therefore let none boast or please themselves too much in their numerous offspring.

Summary; the Levites excepted (44–54)

49. Levi – Because they were not generally to go out to war, which was the thing principally eyed in this muster, Nu 1:3,20,45, but were to attend upon the service of the tabernacle. They that minister upon holy things, should not entangle themselves in secular affairs. The ministry itself is work enough for a whole man, and all little enough to be employed in it.

50. The tabernacle of testimony – So called here, and Exo 38:21, because it was made chiefly for the sake of the ark of the testimony, which is often called the testimony.

51. That cometh nigh – The stranger elsewhere is one of another nation, here one of another tribe. So as to do the offices mentioned, Nu 1:50.

53. No wrath – From God, who is very tender of his worship, and will not suffer the profaners of it go unpunished! whose wrath is called simply wrath by way of eminency, as the most terrible kind of wrath.

Chapter 2

Orders concerning the camp.

A general order (1, 2)

2. His own standard – It is manifest there were four great standards or ensigns, which here follow, distinguished by their colours or figures; also there were other particular ensigns belonging to each of their fathers houses or families. **Far off** – Partly out of reverence to God and his worship,

and the portion, allotted to it, and partly for caution, lest their vicinity to it might tempt them to make too near approaches to it. It is supposed they were at 2000 cubits distance from it, which was the space between the people and the ark; and it is not improbable, because the Levites encamped round about it, between them and the tabernacle. It is observable, those tribes were placed together, that were nearest of kin to each other. Judah, Issachar, and Zebulun were the three youngest sons of Leah, and Issachar and Zebulun would not grudge to be under Judah, their elder brother. Reuben and Simeon would not be content with their place. Therefore Reuben, Jacob's eldest son, is chief of the next squadron. Simeon doubtless is willing to be under him. And Gad, the son of Leah's handmaid, is fitly added to him, in Levi's room. Ephraim, Manasseh, and Benjamin are all the posterity of Rachel. Dan the eldest son of Bilhah leads the rest; to them are added the two younger sons of the handmaids. So much of the wisdom of God appears even in these smaller circumstances!

The vanguard, on the east, Judah, Issachar, and Zebulun (3–9)

3. Judah – This tribe was in the first post, and in their marches led the van, not only because it was the most numerous, but chiefly because Christ, the Lion of the tribe of Judah, was to descend from it: Yea, from the loins of Nahshon, who is here appointed the chief captain of it.

In the right wing, southward, Reuben, Simeon, and Gad (10–16)

The tabernacle in the midst (17)

17. In the midst – This is not to be understood strictly, but largely; for in their march they were divided, and part of that tribe marched next after Judah, Num 10:17, and the other part exactly in the midst of the camp.

In the rear, westward, Ephraim, Manasseh, and Benjamin (18–24)

18. Ephraim – Who is here preferred before his brother, according to the prophecy, Gen 48:19,20.

In the left wing, northward, Dan, Asher, and Naphtali (25-31)

31. The Camp of Dan – The strongest camp next after Judah, and therefore he comes in the rear, as Judah marched in the front, that the tabernacle might be best guarded where there was most danger.

The conclusion of the appointment (32–34)

Chapter 3
An account of the priests (1–4)

1. These – Which follow in this chapter. **The generations** – The kindred or family. Moses his family and children are here included under the general name of the Amramites, Nu 3:27, which includes all the children and grand-children of Amram, the persons only of Aaron and Moses being excepted. And the generations of Moses are thus obscurely mentioned, because they were but common Levites, the priesthood being given solely to Aaron's posterity, whence Aaron is here put before Moses, who elsewhere is commonly named after him. **In Sinai** – Nadab and Abihu, were then alive, though dead at the time of taking this account.

4. In the sight of Aaron – Under his inspection and direction, and as their father's servants or ministers in the priest's office.

The work of the Levites, taken instead of the first-born (5–13)

6. Present them – Offer them to the Lord for his special service. This was promised to them before, and now actually conferred.

7. His charge – That is, Aaron's, or those things which are committed principally to Aaron's care and oversight. **Of the congregation** – That is, of all the sacrifices and services which are due to the Lord from all the people, because the people might not perform them, in their own persons, therefore they were to be performed by some particular persons in their stead; formerly by the first-born, Num 8:16, and now by the Levites. **Before the tabernacle** – Not within the tabernacle, for the care of the things within the holy place was appropriated to the priests, as the care of the most holy place was to the high-priest.

8. Of the children of Israel – Those things which all the children of Israel are in their several places and stations obliged to take care of, though not in their persons, yet by others in their stead.

9. Given to him – To attend upon him and observe his orders, and ease him of his burden.

10. The stranger – That is, every one who is of another family than Aaron's; yea, though he be a Levite. **That cometh nigh** – To execute any part of the priest's office.

12. The first-born – Who were God's property, Exo 13:12, and to whom the administration of holy things was formerly committed, which now was taken away from them, either because they had forfeited this privilege by joining with the rest of their brethren in the idolatrous worship of the calf, or because they were to be mainly concerned in the distribution and management of the inheritances which now they were going to possess, and therefore could not be at leisure to attend upon the service of the sanctuary: and God would not commit it to some other persons in each tribe, which might be an occasion of idolatry, confusion, division, and contempt of sacred things, but to one distinct tribe, which might be entirely devoted to that service, and particularly to the tribe of Levi; partly out of his respect to Moses and Aaron, branches of this tribe; partly as a recompence of their zeal for God against idolaters, and partly because it was the smallest of the tribes, and therefore most likely to find both employment in, and maintenance for the work.

Of the number, place and charge of each family; the Gershonites (14–26)

15. From a month old – Because at that time the first-born, in whose stead the Levites came, were offered to God. And from that time the Levites were consecrated to God, and were, as soon as capable, instructed in their work. Elsewhere they are numbered from twenty-five years old, when they were entered as novices into part of their work, Num 8:24, and from thirty years old, when they were admitted to their whole office.

25. The tabernacle – Not the boards, which belonged to Merari, Nu 3:36, but the ten curtains. **The tent** – The curtains of goats hair. **The coverings** – That is, the coverings of rams-skins and badgers-skins.

26. The cords – By which the tabernacle was fastened to the pins, and stretched out, Exo 35:18.

27. Of Kohath – This family had many privileges above the others: of that were Moses and Aaron, and all the priests: they had the chief place about the tabernacle, and the care of the most holy things here, and in the land of Canaan they had twenty three cities, which were almost as many as both their brethren received. Yet the posterity of Moses were not at all dignified or distinguished from other Levites. So far was he from seeking any advantage or honour for his own family.

The Kohathites (27–32)

28. Keeping – That is, appointed for that work, as soon as they were capable of it. **Of the sanctuary** – That is, of the holy things contained in or belonging to the sanctuary.

31. The hanging – Which covered the most holy place, for all other hangings belonged to the Gershonites. **The service** – That is, all the other furniture belonging to it.

32. Chief – Next under the high-priest;

whence he is called the second priest, 2Kings 25:18, and in case of the high-priest's absence by sickness or other necessary occasions, he was to perform his work, and he had a superiority over all the rest of the priests and Levites. **The chief of the Levites** – That is, over those three persons, who were each the chief of their several families, Num 3:24,31,34.

The Merarites (33–39)

38. For the charge – Either in their stead, that charge which they were obliged to keep, if God had not committed it to those: or for their benefit; for their preservation, as the word may be rendered.

39. Two and twenty thousand – If the particular numbers mentioned Num 3:22,28,34, be put together, they make 22,300. But the odd 300 are omitted here, either according to the use of the holy scripture, where in so great numbers small sums are commonly neglected, or, because they were the first-born of the Levites, and therefore belonged to God already, and so could not be given to him again instead of the other first-born. If this number of first-born seem small to come from 22,000 Levites, it must be considered, that only such first-born are here named as were males, and such as continued in their parents families, not such as had erected new families of their own. Add to this, that God so ordered things by his wise providence for divers weighty reasons, that this tribe should be much the least of all the tribes, as is evident by comparing the numbers of the other tribes, from twenty years old, Num 1:3-49, with the number of this from a month old; and therefore it is not strange if the number of their first-born be less than in other tribes.

Of the first-born (40–51)

41. Instead of the first-born – Such as are now alive of them, but those which should be born of them hereafter are otherwise disposed. **Of the Levites** – Not that they were to be taken from the Levites, or to be sacrificed to God, any more than the Levites themselves were; but they together with the Levites were to be presented before the Lord by way of acknowledgment, that the Levites might be set apart for God's service, and their cattle for themselves as God's ministers, and for their support in God's work.

46. For those that are to be redeemed – 'Tis probable, in the exchange they began with the eldest of the first-born, and so downwards, so that those were to be redeemed, who were the two hundred, seventy three youngest of them.

47. Five shekels – Which was the price paid for the redemption of a first-born a month old.

Chapter 4

A command to number the Levites from thirty to fifty years old (1–3)

3. From thirty – This age was prescribed, as the age of full strength of body, and therefore most proper for their labourious work of carrying the parts and vessels of the tabernacle, and of maturity of judgment, which is necessary for the right management of holy services. Whence even John and Christ entered not upon their ministry till that age. Indeed their first entrance upon their work was at their 25th year, when they began as learners, and acted under the inspection and direction of their brethren; but in their 30th year they were completely admitted to a full discharge of their whole office. But David, being a prophet, and particularly directed by God in the affairs of the temple, made a change in this matter, because the magnificence of the temple, and the great multitude of sacred utensils and sacrifices, required a greater number of attendants than formerly was necessary. **Until fifty** – When they were exempted from the toilsome work of carrying burdens, but not discharged from the honourable and easy work done within the tabernacle, Num 8:26. **All that enter** – That is, that do and may enter, having no defect, nor other impediment.

The charge of the Kohathites (4–20)

5. They shall take down – For upon this necessary occasion the inferior priests are allowed to come into the holy of holies, which otherwise was peculiar to the high-priest. **The covering vail** – The second veil, wherewith the ark was covered while the tabernacle stood, Exo 40:3. **Cover the ark** – Because the Levites, who were to carry the ark, might neither see, nor immediately touch it.

6. Badgers' skins – Whereby the ark was secured from the injuries of the weather.

7. The dishes – Upon which the shew-bread was put. **Continual bread** – So called because it was continually to be there, even in the wilderness; where though they had only manna for themselves, yet they reserved corn for the weekly making of these loaves, which they might with no great difficulty procure from some of the people bordering upon the wilderness.

11. The golden altar – All covered with plates of gold.

12. The instruments of ministry – The sacred garments used by the priests in their holy ministrations. **Cover them** – All these coverings were designed:

1. For safety, that these holy things might not be filled by rain, or tarnished by the sun.

2. For decency, most of them had a cloth of blue, or purple, or scarlet over them; the ark, a

cloth wholly of blue, perhaps an emblem of the azure skies, which are spread between us and the Majesty on high.

3. For concealment. It was a fit sign of the darkness of that dispensation. The holy things were then covered. But Christ hath now destroyed the face of the covering.

13. The altar – Hence we may conclude, that they did offer sacrifices at other times, though not so constantly and diligently, as they did in Canaan. Moreover the taking away of the ashes only doth sufficiently imply that the fire was preserved, which as it came down from heaven, Lev 9:24. So it was by God's command to be continually fed, and kept burning, and therefore doubtless was put into some vessel, which might be either fastened to the altar and put within this covering, or carried by some person appointed thereunto.

15. Bear it – Upon their shoulders. Afterward the priests themselves, being multiplied, carried these things, though the Levites also were not excluded. They shall not touch – Before they are covered.

16. Eleazar – He himself is to carry these things, and not to commit them to the sons of Kohath. The oversight – The care that all the things above mentioned be carried by the persons and in the manner expressed.

18. Cut not off – Do not by your neglect provoke God to cut them off for touching the holy things.

19. To his service – To that which is peculiarly allotted to him, the services, and burdens being equally distributed among them.

Of the Gershonites (21–28)

25. The curtains – The curtains or covering of goats-hair. The tabernacle – The ten curtains which covered the boards of the tabernacle; for the boards themselves were carried by the Merarites. His covering – The covering of rams-skins which was put next over those ten curtains.

26. Which is round about – Which court compassed both the tabernacle and the altar.

28. Under the hand – Under his conduct and direction.

Of the Merarites (29–33)

31. The sockets – Which were as the feet upon which the pillars stood.

32. Ye shall reckon – Every part and parcel shall be put in an inventory; which is required here rather than in the fore-going particulars; because these were much more numerous than the former; because being meaner things, they might otherwise have been neglected; and also to teach us, that God esteems nothing small in his service, and that he expects his will should be observed in the minutest circumstances. The death of the

saints is represented as the taking down of the tabernacle. The immortal soul, like the most holy things, is first covered and taken away, carried by angels unseen, and care is taken also of the body, the skin and flesh, which are as the curtains, the bones and sinews, which are as the bars and pillars. None of these shall be lost. Commandment is given concerning the bones, a covenant made with the dust. They are in safe custody, and shall be produced in the great day, when this tabernacle shall be set up again, and these vile bodies made like the glorious body of Jesus Christ.

The number of each and of all in general (34–49)

44. Three thousand – Here appears the wisdom of Divine Providence, that whereas in the Kohathites and Gershonites, whose burdens were fewer and easier, there were but about a third part of them fit for service; the Merarites, whose burdens were more and heavier, had above half of them fit for this work.

Chapter 5

A command to remove the unclean out of the camp (1–4)

3. That they defile not the camp – By which God would intimate the danger of being made guilty by other mens sins, and the duty of avoiding intimate converse with wicked men. I dwell – By my special and gracious presence.

Laws concerning restitution (5–10)

6. Any sin that men commit – Heb. any sins of men, that is, sins against men, as deceits or wrongs, whereby other men are injured, of which he manifestly speaks. Against the Lord – Which words may be added, to shew that such injuries done to men are also sins against God, who hath commanded justice to men, as well as religion to himself. Guilty – That is, shall be sensible of his guilt, convicted in his conscience.

7. They shall confess their sin – They shall not continue in the denial of the fact, but give glory to God, and take shame to themselves by acknowledging it. The principal – That is, the thing he took away, or what is equivalent to it. And add – Both as a compensation to the injured person for the want of his goods so long, and as a penalty upon the injurious dealer, to discourage others from such attempts.

8. No kinsman – This supposes the person injured to be dead or gone, into some unknown place, and the person injured to be known to the injurer. To the priest – Whom God appointed as his deputy to receive his dues, and take them to his own use, that so he might more cheerfully and entirely devote himself to the ministration

of holy things. This is an additional explication to that law, Lev 6:2, and for the sake thereof it seems here to be repeated.

9. Unto the priest – To offer by his hands.

10. Every man's hallowed things – Understand this not of the sacrifices, because these were not the priest's peculiar, but part of them was offered to God, and the remainder was eaten by the offerer as well as by the priest; but of such other things as were devoted to God, and could not be offered in sacrifice; as suppose a man consecrated an house to the Lord, this was to be the priest's.

The law concerning a woman suspected of adultery (11–31)

12. If a man's wife – This law was given partly to deter wives from adulterous practices, and partly to secure wives against the rage of their hard-hearted husbands, who otherwise might upon mere suspicions destroy them, or at least put them away. There was not like fear of inconveniences to the husband from the jealousy, of the wife, who had not that authority and power, and opportunity for the putting away or killing the husband, as the husband had over the wife. **Go aside** – From the way of religion and justice, and that either in truth, or in her husband's opinion.

15. The man shall bring her to the priest – Who first strove to persuade her to own the truth. If she did, she was not put to death, but only was divorced and lost her dowry. **Her offering** – By way of solemn appeal to God, whom hereby she desired to judge between her and her husband, and by way of atonement to appease God, who had for her sins stirred up her husband against her. **He shall pour no oil** – Both because it was a kind of sin-offering, from which these were excluded, and because she came thither as a delinquent, or suspected of delinquency, unpleasing both to God and men; as one that wanted that grace and amiableness and joy which oil signified, and that acceptance with God which frankincense denoted, Psa 141:2. **Bringing iniquity to remembrance** – Both to God before whom she appeared as a sinner, and to her own conscience, if she was guilty; and, if she were not guilty of this, yet it reminded her of her other sins, for which this might be a punishment.

16. Before the Lord – That is, before the sanctuary where the ark was.

17. Holy water – Water of purification appointed for such uses. This was used, that if she were guilty, she might be afraid to add profaneness to her other crime. **An earthen vessel** – Because, after this use, it was to be broken in pieces, that the remembrance of it might be blotted out as far as was possible. **Dust** – An emblem of vileness and misery. **From the floor of the tabernacle** – Which made it holy dust,

and struck the greater terror into the woman, if she were guilty.

18. Before the Lord – Before the tabernacle with her face towards the ark. **Uncover her head** – Partly that she might be made sensible how manifest she and all her ways were to God; partly in token of her sorrow for her sin, or at least for any cause of suspicion which she had given. **In her hands** – That she herself might offer it, and thereby call God to be witness of her innocency. **Bitter** – So called either from the bitter taste which the dust gave it, or from the bitter effects of it upon her, if she were guilty. **That causeth the curse** – Not by any natural power, but by a supernatural efficacy.

19. By an oath – To answer truly to his question, or to declare whether she be guilty or no, and after such oath shall say as follows.

21. An oath – That is, a form of cursing, that when they would curse a person, they may wish that they may be as miserable as thou wast. **Thy thigh** – A modest expression, used both in scripture, as Gen 46:26, Exo 1:5, and other authors. **To rot** – Heb. to fall, that is, to die or waste away. **To swell** – Suddenly and violently till it burst, which the Jews note was frequent in this case. And it was a clear evidence of the truth of their religion.

22. Amen, amen – That is, so let it be if I be guilty. The word is doubled by her as an evidence of her innocency, and ardent desire that God would deal with her according to her desert.

23. In a book – That is, in a scroll of parchment, which the Hebrews commonly call a book. **Blot them out** – Or scrape them out and cast them into the bitter water. Whereby it was signified, that if she was innocent, the curses should be blotted out and come to nothing; and, if she were guilty, she should find in her the effects of this water which she drank, after the words of this curse had been scraped and put in.

24. To drink – That is, after the jealousy-offering was offered.

28. Conceive seed – That is, shall bring forth children, as the Jews say, in case of her innocency, she infallibly did, yea though she was barren before.

31. Guiltless – Which he should not have been, if he had either indulged her in so great a wickedness, and not endeavoured to bring her to repentance or punishment, or cherished suspicions in his breast, and thereupon proceeded to hate her or cast her off. Whereas now, whatsoever the consequence is, the husband shall not be censured for bringing such curses upon her, or for defaming her, if she appear to be innocent. **Her iniquity** – That is, the punishment of her iniquity, whether she was false to her husband, or by any light carriage gave him occasion to suspect her.

Chapter 6

The law of the Nazarites. What they were to abstain from (1–8)

2. Man or woman – For both sexes might make this vow, if they were free and at their own disposal: otherwise their parents or husbands could disannul the vow. **A vow of a Nazarite** – Whereby they sequestered themselves from worldly employments and enjoyments, that they might entirely consecrate themselves to God's service, and this either for their whole lifetime, or for a less and limited space of time.

3. Nor eat grapes – Which was forbidden him for greater caution to keep him at the farther distance from wine.

4. All the days of his separation – Which were sometimes more, sometimes fewer, as he thought fit to appoint.

5. No razor – Nor scissors, or other instrument to cut off any part of his hair. This was appointed, partly as a sign of his mortification to worldly delights and outward beauty; partly as a testimony of that purity which hereby he professed, because the cutting off the hair was a sign of uncleanness, as appears from Num 6:9, partly that by the length of his hair he might be constantly minded of his vow; and partly that he might reserve his hair entirely for God, to whom it was to be offered. **Holy** – That is, wholly consecrated to God and his service, whereby he shows that inward holiness was the great thing which God required and valued in these, and consequently in other rites and ceremonies.

7. His father – Wherein he was equal to the high-priest, being, in some sort, as eminent a type of Christ, and therefore justly required to prefer the service of God, to which he had so fully given himself, before the expressions of his affections to his dearest and nearest relations. **The consecration** – That is, the token of his consecration, namely, his long hair.

9. He shall shave his head – Because his whole body, and especially his hair was defiled by such an accident, which he ought to impute either to his own heedlessness, or to God's providence so ordering the matter, possibly for the punishment of his other sins, or for the quickening him to more purity and detestation of all dead works, whereby he would be defiled.

How to be cleansed from casual uncleanness (9–12)

11. A sin-offering – Because such a pollution was, though not his sin, yet the chastisement of his sin. **He sinned** – That is, contracted a ceremonial uncleanness, which is called sinning, because it was a type of sin, and a violation of a law, tho' through ignorance and inadvertency.

Hallow – Begin again to hallow or consecrate it.

12. The days of his separation – As many days as he had before vowed to God. **Lost** – Heb. fall, to the ground, that is, be void or of none effect.

14. A sin-offering – Whereby he confessed his miscarriages, notwithstanding the strictness of his vow and all the diligence which he could use, and consequently acknowledged his need of the grace of God in Christ Jesus the true Nazarite. **For peace-offerings** – For thankfulness to God, who had given him grace to make and in some measure to keep such a vow. So he offered all the three sorts of offerings, that he might so far fulfil all righteousness and profess his obligation to observe the will of God in all things.

How to be discharged from their vow (13–21)

15. Their meal-offering – Such as generally accompanied the sacrifices.

18. At the door – Publically, that it might be known that his vow was ended, and therefore he was at liberty as to those things from which he had restrained himself for a season, otherwise some might have been scandalized at his use of his liberty. **The fire** – Upon which the flesh of the peace-offerings was boiled.

19. The shoulder – The left-shoulder, as it appears from Num 6:20, where this is joined with the heave-shoulder, which was the right-shoulder, and which was the priests due in all sacrifices, Lev 7:32, and in this also. But here the other shoulder was added to it, as a special token of thankfulness from the Nazarites for God's singular favours vouchsafed unto them. **The hands** – That he may give them to the priest, as his peculiar gift.

20. May drink wine – And return to his former manner of living.

21. That his hand shall get – Besides what he shall voluntarily give according to his ability.

The form of blessing the people (22–27)

23. On this wise – Heb. Thus, or in these words: yet they were not tied to these very words; because after this we have examples of Moses and David and Solomon, blessing the people in other words.

24. Bless thee – Bestow upon you all manner of blessings, temporal and spiritual. **Keep thee** – That is, continue his blessings to thee, and preserve thee in and to the use of them; keep thee from sin and its bitter effects.

25. Shine upon thee – Alluding to the shining of the sun upon the earth, to enlighten, and warm, and renew the face of it. The Lord love thee, and make thee know that he loves thee. We cannot but be happy, if we have God's love;

and we cannot but be easy, if we know that we have it.

26. Lift up his countenance – That is, look upon thee with a cheerful and pleasant countenance, as one that is well pleased with thee and thy services. **Peace** – Peace with God, with thy own conscience, and with all men; all prosperity is comprehended under this word.

27. Put my name – Shall call them by my name, shall recommend them to me as my own people, and bless them and pray unto me for them as such; which is a powerful argument to prevail with God for them.

Chapter 7

The offerings of the princes upon the dedication of the tabernacle (1–9)

1. On the day – It seems day is for time, and on the day, for about the time. For all the princes did not offer these things upon one and the same day, but on several days, as here it follows. And so this chapter comes in its proper place, and those things were done in the second month of the second year after the tabernacle and altar, and all other instruments thereof were anointed, as is here expressed; and after the Levites were separated to the service of the tabernacle, and appointed to their several works, which was done about a month after the tabernacle was erected, and after the numbering of the people, Num 1: 2–49, when the princes here employed in the offerings were first constituted; and after the disposal of the tribes about the tabernacle, the order of which is here observed in the time of their offerings.

2. Offered – In the manner and days hereafter mentioned.

3. Waggons – For the more convenient and safe carriage of such things as were most cumbersome.

5. According to his service – More or fewer, as the nature of their service and of the things to be carried required.

9. Upon their shoulders – Because of the greater worth and holiness of the things which they carried.

The dedication of the altar (10–89)

10. The altar – Of burnt-offerings, and incense too, as appears from the matter of their offerings. Not for the first dedication of them, for it is apparent they were dedicated or consecrated before this time by Moses and Aaron: but for a farther dedication of them, these being the first offerings that were made for any particular persons or tribes. **In the day** – That is, about the time, as soon as it was anointed.

11. On his day – And in this offering they followed the order of their camp, and not of their birth.

13. Charger – A large dish or platter; to be employed about the altar of burnt-offering, or in the court; not in the sanctuary, for all its vessels were of gold.

17. Peace-offerings – Which are more numerous because the princes and priests, and some of the people made a feast before the Lord out of them.

87. Their meat-offering – Which was not mentioned before, because it was sufficiently understood from the law which required it.

88. After it was anointed – Which words are very conveniently added to explain in what sense he had so oft said, that this was done in the day when it was anointed, namely, not exactly, but in a latitude, a little after that it was anointed.

89. To speak with him – To consult God upon occasion. **The mercy-seat** – Which Moses standing without the veil could easily hear. And this seems to be added in this place, to shew that when men had done their part, God was not wanting in the performance of his part, and promise. God's speaking thus to Moses by an audible voice, as if he had been clothed with a body, was an earnest of the incarnation of the Son of God, when in the fulness of time the Word should be made flesh, and speak in the language of the sons of men. That he who spake to Moses was the Eternal Word, was the belief of many of the ancients. For all God's communion with man is by his Son, who is the same yesterday, to-day and for ever.

Chapter 8

Directions concerning the lamps (1–4)

2. When thou lightest the lamps – The priests lighted the middle lamp from the fire of the altar; and the rest one from another; signifying that all light and knowledge comes from Christ, who has the seven spirits of God, figured by the seven lamps of fire. **Over against the candlestick** – On that part which is before the candlestick, Heb. over against the face of the candlestick – That is, in that place towards which the candlestick looked, or where the candlestick stood in full view, that is, upon the north-side, where the table of shew-bread stood, as appears from hence, because the candlestick stood close to the boards of the sanctuary on the south-side, Exo 26:35. And thus the lights were on both sides of the sanctuary, which was necessary, because it was dark in itself, and had no window.

4. Of beaten gold – Not hollow, but solid gold, beaten out of one piece, not of several pieces joined or soldered together.

Concerning cleansing the Levites (5–8)

7. Of purifying – Heb. of sin, that is, for the expiation of sin. This water was mixed with the ashes of a red heifer, Num 19:9, which therefore may seem to have been prescribed before, though it be mentioned after; such kind of transplacings of passages being frequent in scripture. **Shave all their flesh** – This external rite signified the cutting off their inordinate desire of earthly things and that singular purity of heart and life which is required in the ministers of God.

8. A young bullock – The same sacrifice which was offered for a sin-offering for the whole congregation, because the Levites came in the stead of all the first-born, who did in a manner represent the whole congregation.

Concerning the presenting them to God (9–22)

10. The children of Israel – Not all of them, which was impossible, but some in the name of all the princes or chiefs of each tribe, who used to transact things in the name of their tribes. **Put their hands** – Whereby they signified their transferring that right of ministering to God from the first-born in whose hands it formerly was, to the Levites, and their entire resignation and dedication of them to God's service.

11. For an offering – Heb. for a wave-offering. Not that Aaron did so wave them, which he could not do, but that he caused them to imitate that motion, and to wave themselves toward the several parts of the world: whereby they might signify their readiness to serve God, according to their capacity wheresoever they should be.

12. Lay their hands – To signify that they were offered by them and for them.

13. Set the Levites before Aaron – Give the Levites to them, or to their service. **Unto the Lord** – For to him they were first properly offered, and by him given to the priests in order to his service.

15. Go in – Into the court, where they were to wait upon the priests at the altar of burnt-offering; and, at present, into the tabernacle, to take it down and set it up.

19. To do the service of Israel – To serve God in their stead, to do what otherwise they had been obliged to do in their own persons. **To make an atonement** – Not by offering sacrifices, which the priests alone might do, but by assisting the priests in that expiatory work, and by a diligent performance of all the parts of their office, whereby God was pleased both with them and with the people. **That there be no plague** – This is added as a reason why God appointed them to serve in the tabernacle, that they might guard it, and not suffer any of the people to come near it, or meddle with holy things, which if they did, it would certainly bring a plague upon them.

Concerning their age and service (23–26)

26. In the tabernacle – By way of advice, and assistance in lesser and easier works.

Chapter 9

Orders concerning eating the passover on the 14th day of the first month (1–5)

1. In the first month – And therefore before the numbering of the people, which was not till the second month, Num 1:1,2. But it is placed after it, because of a special case relating to the passover, which happened after it, upon occasion whereof he mentions the command of God for keeping the passover in the wilderness, which was done but once, and without this command they had not been obliged to keep it at all, till they came to the land of Canaan.

On the 14th day of the second month, by those who had been hindered (8–12)

6. They came – For resolution of their difficulty.

7. An offering – Which if we neglect, we must be cut off, and if we keep it in these circumstances, we must also be cut off. What shall we do?

10. Unclean or in a journey – Under these two instances the Hebrews think that other hindrances of like nature are comprehended; as if one be hindered by a disease, or by any other such kind of uncleanness; which may seem probable both from the nature of the thing, and the reason of the law which is the same in other cases.

Concerning the negligent and the stranger (13, 14)

14. A stranger – Who is a proselyte.

Concerning the pillar of cloud and fire (15–23)

15. Namely, the tent of the testimony – Or, the tabernacle above the tent of the testimony, that is, that part of the tabernacle in which was the testimony, or the ark of the testimony; for there the cloudy pillar stood. This was an evident token of God's special presence with, and providence over them. And this cloud was easily distinguished from other clouds, both by its peculiar figure and by its constant residence in that place. **Fire** – That they might better discern it and direct themselves and their journeys or stations by it. Had it been a cloud only, it had scarce been visible by night: And had it been a fire only, it would have been scarce discernable by day. But God was pleased to give them sensible demonstrations, that he kept them night and day.

17. Was taken up – Or, ascended on high, above its ordinary place, by which it became more visible to all the camp.

18. The motion or stay of the cloud is fitly called the command of God, because it was a signification of God's will and their duty.

19. The charge – That is, the command of God, that they should stay as long as the cloud stayed.

21. When the cloud abode – This is repeated again and again, because it was a constant miracle, and because it is a matter we should take particular notice of, as highly significant and instructive. It is mentioned long after by David, Psa 105:39, and by the people of God after their captivity, Neh 9:19. And the guidance of this cloud is spoken of, as signifying the guidance of the Blessed Spirit, Isa 63:14. The Spirit of the Lord caused him to rest, and so didst thou lead the people.

And thus, in effect, does he guide, all those, who commit their ways unto the Lord. So that they may well say, Father, thy will be done! Dispose of me and mine as thou pleasest. Here I am, waiting on my God, to journey and rest at the commandment of the Lord. What thou wilt, and where thou wilt: only let me be thine, and always in the way of my duty.

Chapter 10

Orders concerning the silver trumpets (1–10)

2. Two trumpets – For Aaron's two sons: though afterwards the number of the trumpets was much increased, as the number of the priests also was. These trumpets were ordained, both for signification of the great duty of ministers, to preach the word; and for use, as here follows.

6. For their journeys – As a sign for them to march forward, and consequently for the rest to follow them.

9. Ye shall be saved – If you use this ordinance of God with trust and dependance upon God for help.

10. In the days of your gladness – Days appointed for rejoicing and thanksgiving to God for former mercies, or deliverances. **Your solemn days** – Your stated festivals. **For a memorial** – That God may remember you for good to accept and bless you. God then takes pleasure in our religious exercises, when we take pleasure in them. Holy work should be done with holy joy.

The removal of the Israelites to Paran (11–28)

12. Paran – From which they travelled to other places, and then returned into it again, Num 12:16.

21. The others – The Gershonites, and Merarites, who therefore marched after the first camp, a good distance from, and before the Kohathites, that they might prepare the tabernacle for the reception of its utensils, which the Kohathites brought some time after them.

The treaty of Moses with Hobab (29–32)

29. Raguel – Called also Reuel, Exo 2:18, who seems to be the same with Jethro; it being usual in scripture for one person to have two or three names. And therefore this **Hobab** is not Jethro, but his son, which may seem more probable, because Jethro was old and unfit to travel, and desirous, as may well be thought, to die in his own country, whither he returned, Exo 18:27, but Hobab was young and fitter for these journeys, and therefore entreated by Moses to stay and bear them company.

30. I will not go – So he might sincerely say, though afterward he was overcome by the persuasions of Moses.

31. Thou mayest be to us instead of eyes – To direct and guide us: for though the cloud determined them to a general place, yet many particulars might be unknown to Moses, wherein Hobab, having long lived in those parts, might be able to advise him, as concerning the conveniences of water for their cattle, concerning the safety or danger of the several parts, by reason of serpents or wild-beasts, or enemies, in the parts adjoining to them, that so they might guard themselves better against them. Or, this is to be understood of his directing them not so much in their way. as about great and difficult matters, wherein the counsel he had from God did not exclude the advice of men, as we see in Hobab's father Jethro, Exo 18:19-27. And it is probable, this was the wise son of a wise father.

His prayer at the removal and resting of the ark (33–36)

33. Three days – With continued journeys; only it seems probable, that the cloud made little pauses that they might have time for sleep and necessary refreshments. **The ark went before them** – Although in their stations it was in the middle, yet in their marches it went before them; and the cloud was constantly over the ark whether it stood or went; therefore the ark is said to go before and direct them, not as if the ark could be seen of all the camps, which being carried only upon mens shoulders was impossible; but because the cloud, which always attended upon the ark, and did, together with the ark, constitute, in a manner, one sign of God's presence, did lead and direct them. **To search out** – A metaphorical expression, for discovering to them; for the ark could not search, and God, who knew all places and things, needed not to search.

34. By day – And by night too, as was expressed before. So we must learn to compare places of scripture, and to supply the defects of one out of another, as we do in all authors.

36. Return – Or, give rest, that is, a safe and quiet place, free from enemies and dangers.

Chapter 11

The punishment of the murmurers stopt by the prayer of Moses (1–3)

1. Complained – Or, murmured, the occasion whereof seems to be their last three days journey in a vast howling wilderness, and thereupon the remembrance of their long abode in the wilderness, and the fear of many other tedious journeys, whereby they were like to be long delayed before coming to the land of milk and honey, which they thirsted after. **The fire of the Lord** – A fire sent from God in an extraordinary manner, possibly from the pillar of cloud and fire, or from heaven. **The uttermost parts** – Either because the sin began there among the mixed multitude, or in mercy to the people, whom he would rather awaken to repentance than destroy; and therefore he sent it into the skirts and not the midst of the camp.

2. The people – The murmurers, being penitent; or others for fear.

3. Taberah – This fire; as it was called Kibroth-hattaavah from another occasion, Nu 11:34,35, and Num 33:16. It is no new thing in scripture for persons and places to have two names. Both these names were imposed as monuments of the peoples sin and of God's just judgment.

The fresh murmuring of the people (4–6)

4. Israel also – Whose special relation and obligation to God should have restrained them from such carriage. **Flesh** – This word is here taken generally so as to include fish, as the next words shew. They had indeed cattle which they brought out of Egypt, but these were reserved for breed to be carried into Canaan, and were so few that they would scarce have served them for a month.

5. Freely – Either without price, for fish was very plentiful, and fishing was there free, or with a very small price. And this is the more probable because the Egyptians might not taste of fish, nor of the leeks and onions, which they worshipped for Gods, and therefore the Israelites, might have them upon cheap terms.

6. Our soul – Either our life, as the soul signifies, Gen 9:5, or our body, which is often signified by the soul. **Dried away** – Is withered and pines away; which possibly might be true, through envy and discontent, and inordinate appetite.

The description of manna (7–9)

7. As coriander-seed – Not for colour, for that is black, but for shape and figure. **Bdellium** – Is either the gum of a tree, of a white and bright colour, or rather a gem or precious stone, as the Hebrew doctors take it; and particularly a pearl wherewith the Manna manifestly agrees both in its colour, which is white, Exo 16:14, and in its figure which is round.

8. Fresh oil – Or, of the most excellent oil; or of cakes made with the best oil, the word cakes being easily supplied out of the foregoing member of the verse; or, which is not much differing, like wafers made with honey, as it is said Exo 16:31. The nature and use of Manna is here thus particularly described, to shew the greatness of their sin in despising such excellent food.

The murmuring of Moses (10–15)

10. In the door of his tent – To note they were not ashamed of their sin.

11. Not found favour – Why didst thou not hear my prayer, when I desired thou wouldest excuse me, and commit the care of this unruly people to some other person.

12. Have I begotten them? – Are they my children, that I should be obliged to provide food and all things for their necessity and desire?

14. To bear – The burden of providing for and satisfying them. **Alone** – Others were only assistant to him in smaller matters; but the harder and greater affairs, such as this unquestionably was, were brought to Moses and determined by him alone.

15. My wretchedness – Heb. my evil, my torment, arising from the insuperable difficulty of my office and work of ruling this people, and from the dread of their utter extirpation, and the dishonour which thence will accrue to God and to religion, as if, not I only, but God also were an impostor.

God's answer (16–23)

16. To be elders – Whom thou by experience discernest to be elders not only in years, and name, but also in wisdom and authority with the people. And according to this constitution, the Sanhedrim, or great council of the Jews, which in after-ages sat at Jerusalem, and was the highest court of the judgment among them, consisted of seventy men.

17. I will come down – By my powerful presence and operation. **I will put it on them** – That is, I will give the same spirit to them which I have given to thee. But as the spirit was not conveyed to them from or through Moses, but immediately from God, so the spirit or its gifts were not by this means impaired in Moses. The spirit is here put for the gifts of the spirit, and particularly for the spirit of prophecy, whereby they were enabled, as Moses had been and still was, to discern hidden and future things, and resolve doubtful and difficult cases, which made them fit for government. It is observable, that God would not, and therefore men should not, call any persons to any office for which they were not sufficiently qualified.

18. Sanctify themselves – Prepare to meet thy God, O Israel, in the way of his judgments. Prepare yourselves by true repentance, that you may either obtain some mitigation of the plague, or, whilst your bodies are destroyed by the flesh you desire and eat, your souls may be saved from the wrath of God. Sanctifying is often used for preparing, as Jer 6:4 12:3. **In the ears of the Lord** – Not secretly in your closets, but openly and impudently in the doors of your tents, calling heaven and earth to witness.

20. At your nostrils – Which meat violently vomited up frequently doth. Thus God destroys them by granting their desires, and turns even their blessings into curses. **Ye have despised the Lord** – You have lightly esteemed his bounty and manifold blessings, you have slighted and distrusted his promises and providence after so long and large experience of it. **Who is among you** – Who is present and resident with you to observe all your carriage, and to punish your offences. This is added as a great aggravation of the crime, to sin in the presence of the judge. **Why came we forth out of Egypt?** – Why did God do us such an injury? Why did we so foolishly obey him in coming forth?

21. Six hundred thousand footmen – Fit for war, besides women and children. That Moses speaks this as distrusting God's word is evident; and that Moses was not remarkably punished for this as he was afterward for the same sin, Num 20:12, may be imputed to the different circumstances of this and that sin: this was the first offence of the kind, and therefore more easily passed by; that was after warning and against more light and experience. This seems to have been spoken secretly: that openly before the people; and therefore it was fit to be openly and severely punished to prevent the contagion of that example.

The appointment of the seventy elders (24–30)

24. Moses went out – Out of the tabernacle, into which he entered to receive God's answers from the mercy-seat. **The seventy men** – They are called seventy from the stated number, though two of them were lacking, as the Apostles are called the twelve, Mt 26:20, when one of that number was absent. **Round the tabernacle** – Partly that the awe of God might be imprinted upon their hearts, that they might more seriously undertake and more faithfully manage their high employment, but principally, because that was the place where God manifested himself, and therefore there he would bestow his spirit upon them.

25. Rested on them – Not only moved them for a time, but took up his settled abode with them, because the use and end of this gift was perpetual. **They prophesied** – Discoursed of the word and works of God in a marvellous manner, as the prophets did. So this word is used, 1Sam 10:5,6 Joel 2:28 1Cor 14:3. Yet were they not hereby constituted teachers, but civil magistrates, who together with the spirit of government, received also the spirit of prophesy, as a sign and seal both to themselves and to the people, that God had called them to that employment. **They did not cease** – Either for that day, they continued in that exercise all that day, and, it may be, all the night too, as it is said of Saul, 1Sam 19:24, or, afterwards also, to note that this was a continued gift conferred upon them to enable them the better to discharge their magistracy; which was more expedient for them than for the rulers of other people, because the Jews were under a theocracy or the government of God, and even their civil controversies were decided out of that word of God which the prophets expounded.

26. In the camp – Not going to the tabernacle, as the rest did, either not having seasonable notice to repair thither: or, being detained in the camp by sickness, or some urgent occasion, not without God's special providence, that so the miracle might be more evident. **Were written** – In a book or paper by Moses, who by God's direction nominated the fittest persons.

27. Told Moses – Fearing lest his authority should be diminished by their prophesying; and thereby taking authority to themselves without his consent.

28. One of his young men – Or, one of his choice ministers, which may be emphatically added, to note that even great and good men may mistake about the works of God. **Forbid them** – He feared either schism, or sedition, or that by their usurpation of authority, independently upon Moses, his power and esteem might be lessened.

29. Enviest thou for my sake – Art thou grieved because the gifts and graces of God are imparted to others besides me? **Prophets** – He saith prophets, not rulers, for that he knew was absurd and impossible. So we ought to be pleased, that God is glorified and good done, tho' to the lessening of our own honour.

30. Into the camp – Among the people, to exercise the gifts and authority now received.

Quails sent with a plague (31–35)

31. A wind from the Lord – An extraordinary and miraculous wind both for its vehemency and for its effects. **Quails** – God gave them quails once before, Exo 16:13, but neither in the same quantity, nor with the same design and effect as now. **From the sea** – Principally from the Red-sea, and both sides of it where, by the reports of ancient Heathen writers, they were then in great numbers, and, no doubt, were wonderfully increased by God's special providence for this very occasion. **Two cubits high** – Not as if the quails did cover all the ground two cubits high for a day's journey on each side of the camp, for then there had been no place left where they could spread them all abroad round about the camp; but the meaning is, that the quails came and fell down round about the camp for a whole day's journey on each side of it, and that in all that space they lay here and there in great heaps, which were often two cubits high.

32. Stood up – Or rather rose up, which word is often used for beginning to do any business. **All that night** – Some at one time, and some at the other, and some, through greediness or diffidence, at both times.

33. Chewed – Heb. cut off, namely from their mouths. **A very great plague** – Probably the pestilence. But the sense is, before they had done eating their quails, which lasted for a month. Why did God so sorely punish the peoples murmuring for flesh here, when he spared them after the same sin, Exo 16:12. Because this was a far greater sin, and aggravated with worse circumstances; proceeding not from necessity, as that did, when as yet they had no food, but from mere wantonness, when they had Manna constantly given them; committed after large experience of God's care and kindness, after God had pardoned their former sins, and after God had in a solemn and terrible manner made known his laws to them.

34. Kibroth-hattaavah – Heb. the graves of lust, that is, of the men that lusted, as it here follows. And it notes that the plague did not seize upon all that eat of the quails, for then all had been destroyed, but only upon those who were inordinate both in the desire and use of them.

Chapter 12

Miriam and Aaron murmur against Moses (1–3)

1. Miriam – Miriam seems to be first named, because she was the first mover of the sedition; wherefore she is more eminently punished. **The Ethiopian** – Either:

1. Zipporah, who is here called an Ethiopian, in the Hebrew a Cushite, because she was a Midianite: the word Cush being generally used in scripture, not for Ethiopia properly so called below Egypt, but for Arabia. If she be meant, probably they did not quarrel with him for marrying her, because that was done long since, but for being swayed by her and her relations, by whom they might think he was persuaded to choose seventy rulers, by which co-partnership in government they thought their authority and reputation diminished. And because they durst not accuse God, they charge Moses, his instrument, as the manner of men is. Or,

2. some other woman, whom he married either whilst Zipporah lived, or rather because she was now dead, though that, as many other things, be not recorded. For, as the quarrel seems to be about his marrying a stranger, it is probable it was a fresh occasion about which they contended. And it was lawful for him as well as any other to marry an Ethiopian or Arabian woman, provided she were, a sincere proselyte.

2. By us – Are not we prophets as well as he? So Aaron was made, Exo 4:15,16, and so Miriam is called, Exo 15:20. And Moses hath debased and mixed the holy seed, which we have not done. Why then should he take all power to himself, and make rulers as he pleaseth, without consulting us. **The Lord heard** – Observed their words and carriage to Moses.

3. Meek – This is added as the reason why Moses took no notice of their reproach, and why God did so severely plead his cause. Thus was he fitted for the work he was called to, which required all the meekness he had. And this is often more tried by the unkindness of our friends, than by the malice of our enemies. Probably this commendation was added, as some other clauses were, by some succeeding prophet. How was Moses so meek, when we often read of his anger? But this only proves, that the law made nothing perfect.

God calls them to an account for it (4–9)

4. Suddenly – To stifle the beginnings of the sedition, that this example might not spread amongst the people. **Come out** – Out of your private dwellings, that you may know my pleasure and your own doom.

5. In the door – While they stood without, not being admitted into the tabernacle, as Aaron used to be; a sign of God's displeasure.

6. Among you – if you be prophets, yet know there is a difference among prophets, nor do I put equal honour upon all of them.

7. In all my house – That is, whom I have set over all my house, my church and people, and therefore over you; and who hath discharged his office faithfully, and not partially as you falsely accuse him.

8. Mouth to mouth – That is, distinctly, by an articulate voice; immediately, not by an interpreter, nor by shadows and representations in his fancy, as it is in visions and dreams; and familiarly. **Apparently** – Plainly and certainly. **Dark speeches** – Not in parables, similitudes, dark resemblances; as by showing a boiling pot, an almond tree, to Jeremiah; a chariot with wheels to Ezekiel. **The similitude** – Not the face or essence of God, which no man can see and live, Exo 33:20, but some singular manifestation of his glorious presence, as Exo 33:11,20. Yea the Son of God appeared to him in an human shape, which he took up for a time, that he might give him a foretaste of his future incarnation. **My servant** – Who is so in such an eminent and extraordinary manner.

9. He departed – From the door of the tabernacle, in token of his great displeasure, not waiting for their answer. The removal of God's presence from us, is the saddest token of his displeasure. And he never departs, till we by our sin and folly drive him from us.

Miriam becoming leprous, Aaron humbles himself, and Moses prays for her (10–13)

10. From the tabernacle – Not from the whole tabernacle, but from that part, whither it was come, to that part which was directly over the mercy-seat, where it constantly abode. **Leprous** – She, and not Aaron, either because she was chief in the transgression or because God would not have his worship interrupted or dishonoured, which it must have been if Aaron had been leprous. **White** – This kind of leprosy was the most virulent and incurable of all. It is true, when the leprosy began in a particular part, and thence spread itself over all the flesh by degrees, and at last made it all white, that was an evidence of the cure of the leprosy, Lev 13:12,13. But it was otherwise when one was suddenly smitten with this universal whiteness.

11. Lay not the sin – Let not the guilt and punishment of this sin rest upon us, upon her in this kind, upon me in any other kind, but pray to God for the pardon and removal of it.

12. As one dead – Because part of her flesh was putrefied and dead, and not to be restored but by the mighty power of God. Like a stillborn child, that hath been for some time dead in the womb, which when it comes forth, is putrefied, and part of it consumed.

She is healed, but shut out of the camp for seven days (14–16)

14. Spit in her face – That is, expressed some eminent token of indignation and contempt, which was this, Job 30:10 Isa 50:6. **Ashamed** – And withdraw herself, from her father's presence, as Jonathan did upon a like occasion,

1Sam 20:34. So though God healed her according to Moses's request, yet he would have her publically bear the shame of her sin, and be a warning to others to keep them from the same transgression.

15. Journeyed not – Which was a testimony of respect to her both from God and from the people, God so ordering it, partly lest she should be overwhelmed by such a public rebuke from God, and partly lest, she being a prophetess, the gift of prophecy should come into contempt.

16. Paran – That is, in another part of the same wilderness.

Chapter 13

The sending of the spies into Canaan (1–17)

1. Speak unto Moses – In answer to the peoples petition about it, as is evident from Deu 1:22. And it is probable, the people desired it out of diffidence of God's promise.

2. A ruler – A person of wisdom and authority.

8. Oshea – Called also Joshua, Nu 13:16.

11. Of Joseph – The name of Joseph is elsewhere appropriated to Ephraim, here to Manasseh; possibly to aggravate the sin of the ruler of this tribe, who did so basely degenerate from his noble ancestor.

16. Jehoshua – Oshea notes a desire of salvation, signifying, Save we pray thee; but Jehoshua, or Joshua, includes a promise of salvation, He will save. So this was a prophecy of his succession to Moses in the government, and of the success of his arms. Joshua is the same name with Jesus, of whom Joshua was a type. He was the Saviour of God's people from the powers of Canaan, Christ from the powers of hell.

17. Southward – Into the southern part of Canaan, which was the nearest part, and the worst too, being dry and desert, and therefore fit for them to enter and pass through with less observation. **Into the mountain** – Into the mountainous country, and thence into the valleys, and so take a survey of the whole land.

The instructions given them (18–20)

18. What it is – Both for largeness, and for nature and quality.

19. In tents – As the Arabians did; or in unwalled villages, which, like tents, are exposed to an enemy.

20. Fat – Rich and fertile.

Their journey and return (21–25)

21. Zin – In the south of Canaan, differing from the wilderness of Sin, which was nigh unto Egypt. **To Hamath** – From the south they passed through the whole land to the northern parts of it; Rehob was a city in the north-west part, Hamath, a city in the north-east.

22. By the south – Moses having described their progress from south to north, more particularly relates some memorable places and passages. **They came** – Heb. He came, namely, Caleb, as appears from Jos 14:9,12,14. For the spies distributed their work among them, and went either severally, or by pairs; and it seems the survey of this part was left to Caleb. **Anak** – A famous giant, whose children these are called, either more generally, as all giants sometimes were, or rather more specially because Arbah, from whom Hebron was called Kiriath-arbah, was the father of Anak, Jos 15:13. And this circumstance is mentioned as an evidence of the goodness of that land, because the giants chose it for their habitation. **Before Zoan** – This seems to be noted to confront the Egyptians, who vainly boasted of the antiquity of their city Zoan above all places.

23. Upon a staff – Either for the weight of it, considering the length of the way they were to carry it, or for the preservation of it whole and entire. In those eastern and southern countries there are vines and grapes of an extraordinary bigness as Strabo and Pliny affirm.

24. Eschol – That is, a cluster of grapes.

25. They returned after forty days – 'Tis a wonder the people had patience to stay forty days, when they were just ready to enter Canaan, under all the assurances of success they could have from the Divine power, proved by a constant series of miracles, that had hitherto attended them. But they distrusted God, and chose to be held in suspense by their own counsels, rather than to rest upon God's promise! How much do we stand in our own light by unbelief?

Their report (26–33)

26. Kadesh – Kadesh-barnea, which some confuse with Kadesh in the wilderness of Sin, into which they came not 'till the fortieth year after their coming out of Egypt, as appears from Num 33:37,38, whereas they were in this Kadesh in the second year, and before they received the sentence of their forty years abode in the wilderness.

27. They told him – In the audience of the people.

29. The Amalekites in the south – Where we are to enter the land, and they who were so fierce against us that they came into the wilderness to fight with us, will, without doubt, oppose us when we come close by their land, the rather, to revenge themselves for their former loss. Therefore they mention them, though they were not Canaanites. **In the mountains** – In the mountainous country, in the south-east part of the land, so that you cannot enter there without great difficulty, both because of the noted strength and valour of those people, and

because of the advantage they have from the mountains. **By the sea** – Not the mid-land sea, which is commonly understood by that expression, but the salt or dead sea, as appears

1. Because it is that sea which is next to Jordan,

2. Because the Canaanites dwelt principally in those parts, and not near the mid-land sea. So these guard the entrance on the east-side, as the others do on the south.

30. Caleb – Together with Joshua, as is manifest from Nu 14:6,7,30, but Caleb alone is here mentioned, possibly because he spake first and most, which he might better do, because he might be presumed to be more impartial than Joshua, who being Moses's minister might be thought to speak only what he knew his master would like. **Stilled the people** – Which implies either that they had began to murmur, or that by their looks and carriage, they discovered the anger which boiled in their breasts. **Before Moses** – Or, towards Moses, against whom they were incensed, as the man who had brought them into such sad circumstances. **Let us go up and possess it** – He does not say, Let us go up and conquer it. He looks on that to be as good as done already: but, Let us go up and possess it! There is nothing to be done, but to enter without delay, and take the possession which our great Lord is now ready to give us! Thus difficulties that lie in the way of salvation, vanish away before a lively faith.

31. The men – All of them, Joshua excepted. **Stronger** – Both in stature of body and numbers of people. Thus they question the power, and truth, and goodness of God, of all which they had such ample testimonies.

32. Eateth up its inhabitants – Not so much by civil wars, for that was likely to make their conquest more easy; but rather by the unwholesomeness of the air and place, which they guessed from the many funerals, which, as some Hebrew writers, not without probability affirm, they observed in their travels through it: though that came to pass from another cause, even from the singular providence of God, which, to facilitate the Israelites conquest, cut off vast numbers of the Canaanites either by a plague, or by the hornet sent before them, as is expressed, Jos 24:12.

Chapter 14

The murmuring of the people against Moses and Aaron (1–4)

2. Against Moses and Aaron – As the instruments and occasions of their present calamity. That **we had died in this wilderness** – It was not long before they had their desire, and did die in the wilderness.

3. The Lord – From instruments they rise higher, and strike at God the cause and author of their journey: by which we see the prodigious growth and progress of sin when it is not resisted. **A prey** – To the Canaanites whose land we were made to believe we should possess.

4. A captain – Instead of Moses, one who will be more faithful to our interest than he. **Into Egypt** – Stupendous madness! Whence should they have protection against the hazards, and provision against all the wants of the wilderness? Could they expect either God's cloud to cover and guide them, or Manna from heaven to feed them? Who could conduct them over the Red-sea? Or, if they went another way, who should defend them against those nations whose borders they were to pass? What entertainment could they expect from the Egyptians, whom they had deserted and brought to so much ruin?

Their fruitless endeavour to still them (5–10)

5. Fell on their faces – As humble and earnest suppliants to God, the only refuge to which Moses resorted in all such straits, and who alone was able to govern this stiff-necked people. **Before all the assembly** – That they might awake to apprehend their sin and danger, when they saw Moses at his prayers, whom God never failed to defend, even with the destruction of his enemies.

6. Rent their clothes – To testify their hearty grief for the peoples blasphemy against God and sedition against Moses, and that dreadful judgment which they easily foresaw this must bring upon the congregation.

8. Delight in us – If by our rebellion and ingratitude we do not provoke God to leave and forsake us.

9. Bread – We shall destroy them as easily as we eat our bread. **Their defence** – Their conduct and courage, and especially God, who was pleased to afford them his protection 'till their iniquities were full, is utterly departed from them, and hath given them up as a prey to us. **With us** – By his special grace and almighty power, to save us from them and all our enemies. **Only rebel not against the Lord** – Nothing can ruin sinners but their own rebellion. If God leaves them, 'tis because they drive him from them, and they die, because they will die.

10. Appeared – Now in the extremity of danger to rescue his faithful servants, and to stop the rage of the people. **In the tabernacle** – Upon or above the tabernacle, where the cloud usually resided, in which the glory of God appeared now in a more illustrious manner. When they reflected upon God, his glory appeared not, to silence their blasphemies: but when they

threatened Caleb and Joshua, they touched the apple of his eye, and his glory appeared immediately. They who faithfully expose themselves for God, are sure of his special provision.

God's threatening utterly to destroy them (11–12)

12. I will smite them – This was not an absolute determination, but a commination, like that of Nineveh's destruction, with a condition implied, except there be speedy repentance, or powerful intercession.

The intercession of Moses (13–19)

16. Not able – His power was quite spent in bringing them out of Egypt, and could not finish the work he had begun and had sworn to do.

17. Be great – That is appear to be great, discover its greatness: namely, the power of his grace and mercy, or the greatness of his mercy, in pardoning this and their other sins: for to this the following words manifestly restrain it, where the pardon of their sins is the only instance of this power both described in God's titles, Nu 14:18, and prayed for by Moses Nu 14:19, and granted by God in answer to him, 14:20. Nor is it strange that the pardon of sin, especially such great sins, is spoken of as an act of power in God, because undoubtedly it is an act of omnipotent and infinite goodness.

18. Visiting the iniquity – These words may seem to be improperly mentioned, as being a powerful argument to move God to destroy this wicked people, and not to pardon them. It may be answered, that Moses useth these words together with the rest, because he would not sever what God had put together. But the truer answer seems to be, that these words are to be translated otherwise, And in destroying he will not utterly destroy, though he visit the iniquity of the fathers upon the children, unto the third and fourth generation.

The decree that all that generation should die in the wilderness (20–35)

20. I have pardoned – So far as not utterly to destroy them.

21. With the glory of the Lord – With the report of the glorious and righteous acts of God in punishing this rebellious people.

22. My glory – That is, my glorious appearances in the cloud, and in the tabernacle. **Ten times** – That is, many times. A certain number for an uncertain.

24. Caleb – Joshua is not named, because he was not now among the people, but a constant attendant upon Moses, nor was he to be reckoned as one of them, any more than Moses and Aaron were, because he was to be their chief commander. **He had another spirit** – Was a man of another temper, faithful and courageous, not acted by that evil spirit of cowardice, unbelief, disobedience, which ruled in his brethren but by the spirit of God. **Fully** – Universally and constantly, through difficulties and dangers, which made his partners halt. **Whereinto he went** – In general, Canaan, and particularly Hebron, and the adjacent parts, Jos 14:9.

25. In the valley – Beyond the mountain, at the foot whereof they now were, Num 14:40. And this clause is added, either

1. As an aggravation of Israel's misery and punishment, that being now ready to enter and take possession of the land, they are forced to go back into the wilderness or

2. As an argument to oblige them more willingly to obey the following command of returning into the wilderness, because their enemies were very near them, and severed from them only by that Idumean mountain, and, if they did not speedily depart, their enemies would fall upon them, and so the evil which before they causelessly feared would come upon them; they, their wives and their children, would become a prey to the Amalekites and Canaanites, because God would not assist nor defend them. **By the way of the Red-sea** – That leadeth to the Red-sea, and to Egypt, the place whither you desire to return.

28. As ye have spoken – When you wickedly wished you might die in the wilderness.

30. You – Your nation; for God did not swear to do so to these particular persons.

32. Your carcases – See with what contempt they are spoken of, now they had by their sin made themselves vile! The mighty men of valour were but carcases, now the Spirit of the Lord was departed from them! It was very probably upon this occasion, that Moses wrote the ninetieth psalm.

33. Forty years – So long as to make up the time of your dwelling in the wilderness forty years; one whole year and part of another were past before this sin or judgment. **Your whoredoms** – The punishment of your whoredoms, of your apostasy from, and perfidiousness against your Lord, who was your husband, and had married you to himself.

34. Each day for a year – So there should have been forty years to come, but God was pleased mercifully to accept of the time past as a part of that time. **Ye shall know my breach of promise** – That as you have first broken the covenant between you and me, by breaking the conditions of it, so I will make it void on my part, by denying you the blessings promised in that covenant. So you shall see, that the breach of promise wherewith you charged me, lies at your door, and was forced from me by your perfidiousness.

The immediate death of the spies (36–39)

37. By the plague – Either by the pestilence, or by some other sudden and extraordinary judgment, sent from the cloud in which God dwelt, and from whence he spake to Moses, and wherein his glory at this time appeared before all the people, Nu 14:10, who therefore were all, and these spies among the rest, before the Lord.

38. But Joshua and Caleb lived still – Death never misses his mark, nor takes any by oversight who are designed for life, tho' in the midst of those that are to die.

39. And the people mourned greatly – But it was now too late. There was now no place for repentance. Such mourning as this there is in hell; but the tears will not quench the flames.

The ill success of those who would go up notwithstanding (40–45)

40. Gat them up – Designed or prepared themselves to go up.

45. The Canaanites – Largely so called, but strictly the Amorites. **Hormah** – A place so called afterwards, Nu 21:3, from the slaughter or destruction of the Israelites at this time.

Chapter 15

Laws, concerning meal-offerings and drink offerings (1–16)

2. I give you – Will certainly give you, not withstanding this great provocation. And for their better assurance hereof he repeats and amplifies the laws of sacrifices, whereby through Christ he would be reconciled to them and theirs upon their repentance.

3. A sacrifice – A peace-offering.

8. Peace-offerings – Such as were offered either freely or by command, which may be called peace-offerings or thank-offerings, by way of eminency, because such are offered purely by way of gratitude to God, and with single respect to his honour, whereas the peace-offerings made in performance of a vow were made and offered, with design of getting some advantage by them.

12. Their number – As many cattle as ye sacrifice, so many meal and drink-offerings ye shall offer.

15. Before the Lord – As to the worship of God: his sacrifices shall be offered in the same manner and accepted by God upon the same terms, as yours: which was a presage of the future calling of the Gentiles. And this is added by way of caution, to shew that strangers were not upon this pretence to partake of their civil privileges.

Concerning dough for heave-offerings (17–21)

19. When ye eat – When you are about to eat it: for before they eat it, they were to offer this offering to God. **The bread** – That is, the bread-corn.

20. The threshing floor – That is, of the corn in the threshing floor, when you have gathered in your corn.

Sacrifices for sins of ignorance (22–29)

22. All these commandments – Those now spoken of, which concern the outward service of God, or the rites or ceremonies belonging to it. And herein principally this law may seem to differ from that Lev 4:13, which speaks of some positive miscarriage, or doing that which ought not to have been done, about the holy things of God; whereas this speaks only of an omission of something which ought to have been done about holy ceremonies.

Concerning presumptuous sinners (30, 31)

30. Reproacheth the Lord – He sets God at defiance, and exposes him to contempt, as if he were unable to punish transgressors.

An instance in the sabbath-breaker (32–36)

32. On the sabbath-day – This seems to be added as an example of a presumptuous sin: for as the law of the sabbath was plain and positive, so this transgression of it must needs be a known and wilful sin.

33. To all the congregation – That is, to the rulers of the congregation.

34. They – That is, Moses and Aaron, and the seventy rulers. **What should be done** – That is, in what manner he was to be cut off, or by what kind of death he was to die, which therefore God here particularly determines: otherwise it was known in general that sabbath-breakers were to be put to death.

Concerning fringes on the borders of their garments (37–41)

38. Fringes – These were certain threads or ends, standing out a little further than the rest of their garments, left there for this use. **In the borders** – That is, in the four borders or quarters, as it is, Deut 22:12. **Of their garments** – Of their upper garments. This was practised by the Pharisees in Christ's time, who are noted for making their borders larger than ordinary. A **ribband** – To make it more obvious to the sight, and consequently more serviceable to the use here mentioned. **Of blue** – Or, purple.

39. For a fringe – That is, the ribband, shall be unto you, shall serve you for a fringe, to render it more visible by its distinct colour, whereas the fringe without this was of the same piece and colour with the garment, and therefore less observeable. **That ye seek not** – Or, enquire not for other rules and ways of serving me than I have prescribed you. **Your own heart,**

and eyes – Neither after the devices of your own hearts, as Nadab and Abihu did when they offered strange fire; nor after the examples of others which your eyes see, as you did when you were set upon worshipping a calf after the manner of Egypt. The phylacteries worn by the Pharisees in our Lord's time, were a different thing from these. Those were of their own invention: these were a divine institution.

40. Be ye holy – Purged from sin and sincerely devoted to God.

41. I am the Lord your God – Though I am justly displeased with you for your frequent rebellions, for which also I will keep you forty years in the wilderness, yet I will not utterly cast you off, but will continue to be your God.

Chapter 16

Korah, Dathan and Abiram, rise up against Moses (1–4)

1. The son of Izhar – Amram's brother, Exo 6:18, therefore Moses and he were cousins. Moreover, Izhar was the second son of Kohath, whereas Elizaphan, whom Moses had preferred before him, and made prince or ruler of the Kohathites, Num 3:30, was the son of Aisle, the fourth son of Kohath. This, the Jewish writers say, made him malcontent, which at last broke forth into sedition. **Sons of Reuben** – These were drawn into confederacy with Korah, partly because they were his next neighbours, both being encamped on the south-side, partly in hopes to recover their rights of primogeniture, in which the priesthood was comprehended, which was given away from their father.

2. Rose up – That is, conspired together, and put their design in execution. **Before Moses** – Not obscurely, but openly and boldly, not fearing nor regarding the presence of Moses.

3. They – Korah, Dathan and Abiram, and the rest, who were all together when Moses spake those words, Nu 16:5–7, but after that, Dathan and Abiram retired to their tents, and then Moses sent for Korah and the Levites, who had more colourable pretences to the priesthood, and treats with them apart, and speaks what is mentioned, Nu 16:8–11. Having dispatched them, he sends for Dathan and Abiram, Nu 16:12, that he might reason the case with them also apart. **Against Aaron** – To whom the priesthood was confined, and **against Moses**, both because this was done by his order, and because before Aaron's consecration Moses appropriated it to himself. For whatever they intended, they seem not now directly to strike at Moses for his supreme civil government, but only for his influence in the disposal of the priesthood. **Ye take too much** – By perpetuating the priesthood in yourselves and family, with the exclusion of all others from it. **All are holy** –

A kingdom of priests, an holy nation, as they are called, Exo 19:6, a people separated to the service of God, and therefore no less fit to offer sacrifice and incense, than you are. **Among them** – By his tabernacle and cloud, the tokens of his gracious presence, and therefore ready to receive sacrifices from their own hands. **Ye** – Thou Moses, by prescribing what laws thou pleasest about the priesthood, and confining it to thy brother; and thou Aaron by usurping it as thy peculiar privilege.

4. On his face – Humbly begging that God would direct and vindicate him. Accordingly God answers his prayers, and strengthens him with new courage, and confidence of success.

Moses reasons with them (5–11)

5. To-morrow – Heb. In the morning, the time appointed by men for administering justice, and chosen by God for that work. Some time is allowed, partly that Korah and his company might prepare themselves and their censers, and partly to give them space for consideration and repentance. **He will cause him** – He will by some evident token declare his approbation of him and his ministry.

8. Ye sons of Levi – They were of his own tribe, nay, they were of God's tribe. It was therefore the worse in them thus to mutiny against God and against him.

9. To minister to them – So they were the servants both of God and of the church, which was an high dignity, though not sufficient for their ambitious minds.

11. Against the Lord – Whose chosen servant Aaron is. You strike at God through Aaron's sides.

Sends for Dathan and Abiram, who refuse to come (12–14)

12. Dathan and Abiram – To treat with them and give them, as he had done Korah and his company, a timely admonition. **Come up** – To Moses's tabernacle, whither the people used to go up for judgment. Men are said in scripture phrase to go up to places of judgment.

14. These men – Of all the people who are of our mind: wilt thou make them blind, or persuade them that they do not see what is visible to all that have eyes, to wit, that thou hast deceived them, and broken thy faith and promise given to them?

His proposal to Korah (15–19)

15. Respect not their offering – Accept not their incense which they are now going to offer, but shew some eminent dislike of it. He calls it their offering, though it was offered by Korah and his companions, because it was offered in the

name and by the consent of all the conspirators, for the decision of the present controversy between them and Moses. **I have not hurt one of them** – I have never injured them, nor used my power to defraud or oppress them, as I might have done; I have done them many good offices, but no hurt: therefore their crime is without any cause or provocation.

16. Before the Lord – Not in the tabernacle, which was not capable of so many persons severally offering incense, but at the door of the tabernacle, where they might offer it by Moses's direction upon this extraordinary occasion. This work could not be done in that place, which alone was allowed for the offering up of incense; not only for its smallness, but also because none but priests might enter to do this work. Here also the people, who were to be instructed by this experiment, might see the proof and success of it.

18. Fire – Taken from the altar which stood in that place, for Aaron might not use other fire. And it is likely the remembrance of the death of Nadab and Abihu deterred them from offering any strange fire.

19. Against them – That they might be witnesses of the event, and, upon their success, which they doubted not of, might fall upon Moses and Aaron. And it seems by this that the people were generally incensed against Moses, and inclined to Korah's side. **The glory appeared** – In the cloud, which then shone with greater brightness and majesty, as a token of God's approach and presence.

The punishment of the rebels (20–35)

22. The spirits – And this is no empty title here, but very emphatic. Thou art the maker of spirits, destroy not thy own workmanship! O thou who art the preserver of men, and of their spirits, the Lord of spirits, Job 12:10, who as thou mayst justly destroy this people, so thou canst preserve whom thou pleasest: the father of spirits, the souls. Deal mercifully with thy own children: the searcher of spirits, thou canst distinguish between those who have maliciously railed this tumult, and those whose ignorance and simple credulity hath made them a prey to crafty seducers. **Of all flesh** – Of all mankind: the word flesh is often put for men. **One man** – Korah, the ringleader of this sedition.

24. The congregation – Whom for your sakes I will spare upon the condition following.

25. Unto Dathan – Because they refused to come to him. **The elders** – The seventy rulers, whom he carried with him for the greater solemnity of the action, and to encourage them in their work, notwithstanding the obstinate nature of the people they were to govern.

27. Stood in the door – An argument of their foolish confidence, obstinacy and impenitency, whereby they declared that they neither feared God, nor reverenced man.

28. All these works – As the bringing of the people out of Egypt; the conducting of them through the wilderness; the exercising authority among them; and giving laws to them concerning the priesthood.

29. The death of all men – By a natural death. **The visitation of all men** – By plague, or sword, or some usual judgment. **The Lord hath not sent me** – I am content that you take me for an imposter, falsely pretending to be sent of God.

32. All that appertained unto Korah – That is, all his family which were there, women, children, and servants; but his sons, who were spared, Num 26:11,58 1Ch 6:22,37, were absent either upon some service of the tabernacle, or upon some other occasion, God so ordering it by his providence either because they disliked their fathers act, or upon Moses's intercession for them. This expression may intimate, that Korah himself was not here, but that he continued with his two hundred and fifty men before the Lord, where they were waiting for God's decision of the controversy. Nor is it probable that their chief captain would desert them, and leave them standing there without an head, especially, when Aaron his great adversary, abode there still, and did not go with Moses to Dathan. And Korah may seem to have been consumed with those two hundred and fifty. And so much is intimated, Nu 16:40, that no stranger come near to offer incense before the Lord, that he be not as Korah, and as his company, that is, destroyed, as they were, by fire from the Lord. And when the Psalmist relates this history, Psa 106:17-18, the earth's swallowing them up is confined to Dathan and Abiram, Psa 106:17, and for all the rest of that conspiracy it is added, Psa 106:18. And a fire was kindled in their company, the flame burnt up the wicked.

33. Into the pit – Into the earth, which first opened itself to receive them, and then shut itself to destroy them.

35. From the Lord – From the cloud, wherein the glory of the Lord appeared.

Their censers preserved for a memorial (36–40)

37. To Eleazer – Rather than to Aaron, partly because the troublesome part of the work was more proper for him, and partly lest Aaron should be polluted by going amongst those dead carcasses; for it is probable this fire consumed them, as lightning sometimes doth, others, by taking away their lives, and leaving their bodies dead upon the place. **Out of the burning** – From among the dead bodies of those men who were burnt. **Yonder** – Far from the altar and sanctuary, into an unclean place, where the ashes were wont to be cast: by which God shows his rejection of their services. **They are hallowed** – By God's appointment, because they were presented before the Lord by his express order, Nu 16:16,17.

38. Their own souls – That is, their own lives: who were the authors of their own destruction. **The altar** – Of burnt-offerings, which was made of wood, but covered with brass before this time, Exo 27:1,2, to which this other covering was added for farther ornament, and security against the fire, continually burning upon it. **A sign** – A warning to all strangers to take heed of invading the priesthood.

40. To him – To Eleazer. These words belong to Num 16:38, the meaning is, that Eleazer did as God bade him.

A new insurrection stopped by a plague (41–45)

41. On the morrow – Prodigious wickedness and madness so soon to forget such a terrible instance of Divine vengeance! **The people of the Lord** – So they call those wicked wretches, and rebels against God! Tho' they were but newly saved from sharing in the same punishment, and the survivors were as brands plucked out of the burning, yet they fly in the face of Moses and Aaron, to whose intercession they owe their preservation.

42. They – Moses and Aaron, who in all their distresses made God their refuge.

43. Moses and Aaron came – To hear what God, who now appeared, would say to them.

45. They fell upon their faces – To beg mercy for the people; thus rendering Good for Evil.

Aaron stays the plague (46–50)

46. Incense – Which was a sign of intercession, and was to be accompanied with it. **Go unto the congregation** – He went with the incense, to stir up the people to repentance and prayer, to prevent their utter ruin. This he might do upon this extraordinary occasion, having God's command for his warrant, though ordinarily incense was to be offered only in the tabernacle.

48. The living – Whereby it may seem that this plague, like that fire, Nu 11:1, began in the uttermost parts of the congregation, and so proceeded destroying one after another in an orderly manner, which gave Aaron occasion and direction so to place himself, as a mediator to God on their behalf.

Chapter 17

The blossoming of Aaron's rod (1–9)

2. Of every one – Not of every person, but of every tribe. **A rod** – That staff, or rod, which the princes carried in their hands as tokens of their dignity and authority. **Every man's name** – Every prince's: for they being the first-born, and the chief of their tribes might above all others pretend to the priesthood, if it was communicable to any of their tribes, and besides each prince represented all his tribe: so that this was a full decision of the question. And this place seems to confirm, that not only Korah and the Levites, but also those of other tribes contested with Moses and Aaron about the priesthood, as that which belonged to all the congregation they being all holy.

3. Aaron's name – Rather than Levi's, for that would have left the controversy undecided between Aaron and the other Levites, whereas this would justify the appropriation of the priesthood to Aaron's family. **One rod** – There shall be in this, as there is in all the other tribes, only one rod, and that for the head of their tribe, who is Aaron in this tribe: whereas it might have been expected that there should have been two rods, one for Aaron, and another for his competitors of the same tribe. But Aaron's name was sufficient to determine both the tribe, and that branch or family of the tribe, to whom this dignity should be affixed.

4. Before the testimony – That is, before the ark of the testimony, close by the ark. **I will meet with you** – And manifest my mind to you, for the ending of this dispute.

6. Among their rods – Was laid up with the rest, being either one of the twelve, as the Hebrews affirm, or the thirteenth, as others think.

8. Into the tabernacle – Into the most holy place, which he might safely do under the protection of God's command, though otherwise none but the high-priest might enter there, and that once in a year.

It is laid up for a memorial (10, 11)

10. To be kept for a token – it is probable, the buds and blossoms and fruit, all which could never have grown together, but by miracle, continued fresh, the same which produced them in a night preserving them for ages.

The people are terrified (12, 13)

12. We perish – Words of consternation, arising from the remembrance of these severe and repeated judgments, from the threatening of death upon any succeeding murmurings, and from the sense of their own guilt and weakness, which made them fear lest they should relapse into the same miscarriages, and thereby bring the vengeance of God upon themselves.

13. Near – Nearer than we should do; an error which we may easily commit. Will God proceed with us according to his strict justice, till all the people be cut off?

Chapter 18

The work of the priests and Levites (1–7)

1. Shall bear the iniquity of the sanctuary – Shall suffer the punishment of all the usurpations, or pollutions of the sanctuary, or the holy things, by the Levites, or any of the people, because you have power from me to keep them all within their bounds. Thus the people are in good measure secured against their fears. Also they are informed that Aaron's high dignity was attended with great burdens, having not only his own, but the people's sins to answer for; and therefore they had no such reason to envy him, if the benefits and dangers were equally considered. **The iniquity of your priesthood** – That is, of all the errors committed by yourselves, or by you permitted in others in things, belonging to your priesthood.

2. Unto thee – About sacrifices and offerings and other things, according to the rules I have prescribed them. The Levites are said to minister to Aaron here, to the church, Num 16:9, and to God, Deu 10:8. They shall not contend with thee for superiority, as they have done, but shall be subordinate to thee. **Thy sons with thee** – Or, both to thee, and to thy sons with thee: Which translation may seem to be favoured by the following words, before the tabernacle, which was the proper place where the Levites ministered. Besides, both the foregoing words, and the two following verses, entirely speak of the ministry of the Levites, and the ministry of the priests is distinctly spoken of, Nu 18:5.

3. They charge – That is, that which thou shalt command them and commit unto them.

5. The sanctuary – Of the holy, and of the most holy place.

6. To you they are given as a gift – We are to value it as a great gift of the divine bounty, to have those joined to us, that will be helpful and serviceable to us, in the service of God.

7. The altar – Of burnt-offering. **Within the vail** – This phrase here comprehends both the holy and the most holy place. As a gift which I have freely conferred upon you, and upon you alone; and therefore let no man henceforth dare either to charge you with arrogance in appropriating this to yourselves, or to invade your office.

The maintenance of the priests (8–20)

8. I have given them – Not only the charge, but the use of them for thyself and family. **By reason of the anointing** – That is, because thou art priest, and art to devote thyself wholly to my service.

9. Most holy – Such as were to be eaten only by the priests, and that in the sanctuary. **Reserved** – That is, such sacrifices or parts of sacrifices as were not burnt in the fire. **Render unto me** – By way of compensation for a trespass committed against me, in which case a ram was to be offered, which was a most holy thing, and may be particularly designed here.

10. In the most holy place – In the court of the priests, where there were places for this use, which is called the most holy place, not simply and absolutely, but in respect of the thing he speaks of because this was the most holy of all the places appointed for eating holy things, whereof some might be eaten in any clean place in the camp, or in their own house.

13. Whatsoever is first ripe – Not only the first-fruits of the oil and wine, and wheat now mentioned, but all other first-fruits of all other grains, and all fruit trees. **Clean** – And none else, because these were first offered to God, and by consequence given to priests; but for those which were immediately given to the priests, the clean and unclean might eat of them.

14. Devoted – Dedicated to God by vow or otherwise, provided it be such a thing as might be eaten: for the vessels or treasures of gold and silver which were dedicated by Joshua, David, or others, were not the priests, but appropriated to the uses of the temple.

15. Of men – Which were offered to God in his temple, and to his service and disposal.

16. Those that are to be redeemed – Namely, of men only, not of unclean beasts, as is manifest from the time and price of redemption here mentioned, both which agree to men; the time, Num 18:16, the price, Num 3:46,47, but neither agree to unclean beasts, which were to be redeemed with a sheep, Exo 13:13, and that after it was eight days old.

17. Holy – Namely, in a peculiar manner, consecrated to an holy use, even to be sacrificed to God. Deu 15:19.

18. The flesh – All the flesh of them, and not only some parts, as in other sacrifices.

19. A covenant of salt – A durable and perpetual covenant; so called here and 1Ch 13:5, either, because salt is a sign of incorruption, as being of singular use to preserve things from corruption: or, because it is ratified on their part by salt, which is therefore called the salt of the covenant, for which the priests were obliged to take care, that it should never be lacking from any meat-offering, Lev 2:13. And this privilege conferred upon the priests is called a covenant because it is given them conditionally, upon condition of their service, and care about the worship of God.

20. In their land – In the land of the children of Israel. You shall not have a distinct portion of land, as the other tribes shall. The reason of this law, was, partly because God would have them wholly devoted to his service, and therefore free from worldly incumbrance; partly, because God had abundantly provided for them otherwise, by tithes and first-fruits and oblations; and partly that by this means being dispersed among the several tribes, they might have the better opportunity for teaching and watching over the people. **I am thy part** – I have appointed thee a liberal maintenance out of my oblations.

Of the Levites (21–24)

21. The tenth – For the tithes were all given to the Levites, and out of their tithes the tenth was given to the priests.

22. Nigh – So nigh as to do any proper act to the priests or Levites.

23. Their iniquity – The punishment due not only for their own, but also for the people's miscarriage, if it be committed through their connivance or negligence. And this was the reason why the priests withstood King Uzziah, when he would have burnt incense to the Lord.

24. An heave-offering – An acknowledgment that they have all their land and the fruits of it from God's bounty. Note the word heave-offering, which is for the most part understood of a particular kind of offerings heaved or lifted up to the Lord, is here used for any offering.

The portion they are to pay to the priests (25–32)

26. Ye shall offer up an heave-offering – They who are employed in assisting the devotions of others, must be sure to pay their own as an heave-offering. Prayers and praises, or rather the heart lifted up in them, are now our heave-offerings.

27. As though it were the corn – It shall be accepted of you as much as if you offered it out of your own lands and labours.

28. To Aaron – And to his children, who were all to have their share herein.

29. Your gifts – Not only out of your tithes, but out of the other gifts which you receive from the people, and out of those fields which shall belong to your cities. **Offer** – To the priest. As many gifts, so many heave-offerings; you shall reserve a part out of each of them for the priest. **The hallowed part** – the tenth part, which was the part or proportion that God hallowed or sanctified to himself as his proper portion.

31. Every place – In every clean place, and not in the holy place only.

32. Neither shall ye pollute the holy things – As you will do, if you abuse their holy offerings, by reserving that entirely to yourselves, which they offer to God to be disposed as he hath appointed, namely, part to you, and part to the priests.

Chapter 19

The manner of preparing the water of purification (1–10)

2. Red – A fit colour to shadow forth the bloody nature of sin, and the blood of Christ, from which this water and all other rites had their purifying virtue. **No blemish** – A fit type of Christ. **Upon which never came yoke** – Whereby may be signified, either that Christ in himself was free from all the yoke or obligation of God's command, till for our sakes he put himself under the law; or that Christ was not forced to undertake our burden and cross, but did voluntarily choose it. He was bound and held with no other cords but those of his own love.

3. Eleazar – Who was the second priest, and in some cases, the deputy of the high-priest. To him, not to Aaron, because this service made him unclean for a season, and consequently unfit for holy ministrations, whereas the high-priest was, as far as possibly he could, to be preserved from all sorts of defilement, fit for his high and holy work. **Without the camp** – Partly because it was reputed an unclean and accursed thing, being laden with the sins of all the people; and partly to signify that Christ should suffer without the camp, in the place where malefactors suffered.

4. Before the tabernacle – Or, towards the tabernacle, standing at a good distance from it, even without the camp, yet turning and looking towards it. For here is no intimation that he went into the camp before this work was done, but rather the contrary is implied, Nu 19:7. And because being defiled by this work he could not come near the tabernacle, it was sufficient for him to turn and look towards it. This signified his presenting this blood before the Lord by way of atonement for his and the people's sins, and his expectation of acceptance and pardon only from God, and from his mercy-seat in the tabernacle. And this typified the satisfaction that was made to God, by the death of Christ, who by the eternal Spirit offered himself without spot to God, and did as it were sprinkle his own blood before the sanctuary, when he said, Into thy hands I commend my spirit!

5. Burn the heifer – To signify the sharp and grievous sufferings of Christ for our sins. **Her blood** – All of it, but what was spent in sprinkling.

6. Cedar-wood, hyssop, scarlet – All which are here burnt, and as it were offered to God, that they might be sanctified to this holy use for the future; for of these kinds of things was the sprinkle made wherewith the unclean were sprinkled, Lev 14:4.

7. Shall be unclean – Partly to teach us the imperfection of the Levitical priesthood, in which the priest himself was defiled by some parts of his work, and partly to shew that Christ himself, though he had no sin of his own, yet was reputed by men, and judged by God, as a sinful person, by reason of our sins which were laid upon him.

9. For a water – Or, to the water, that is, to be put to the water, or mixed with it. **Of separation** – Appointed for the cleansing of them that are in a state of separation, who for their uncleanness are separated from the congregation. **It is a purification for sin** – Heb. a sin, that is, an offering for sin, or rather a means for expiation or cleansing of sin. And this was a type of that purification for sin, which our Lord Jesus made by his death.

10. The stranger – A proselyte.

Of using it (11–22)

12. With it – With the water of separation. **On the third day** – To typify Christ's resurrection on that day by which we are cleansed or sanctified.

13. Whosoever toucheth – If this transgression be done presumptuously; for if it was done ignorantly, he was only to offer sacrifice. **Defiled** – By approaching to it in his uncleanness: for holy things or places were ceremonially defiled with the touch of any unclean person or thing. **Is upon him** – He continues in his guilt, not now to be washed away by this water, but to be punished by cutting off.

16. With a sword – Or by any other violent way.

17. Running water – Waters flowing from a spring or river, which are the purest. These manifestly signify God's spirit, which is oft compared to water, and by which alone true purification is obtained. Those who promise themselves benefit by the righteousness of Christ, while they submit not to the influence of his spirit, do but deceive themselves; for they cannot be purified by the ashes, otherwise than in the running water.

20. That shall not purify himself – Shall contemptuously refuse to submit to this way of purification.

21. Shall wash his clothes – Because he is unclean. It is strange, that the same water should cleanse one person, and defile another. But God would have it so, to teach us that it did not cleanse by any virtue in itself, or in the work done, but only by virtue of God's appointment: to mind the laws of the imperfection of their priesthood, and their ritual purifications and expiations, and consequently of the necessity of a better priest and sacrifice and way of purifying; and to shew that the efficacy of God's ordinances doth not depend upon the person or quality of his ministers, because the same person who was polluted himself could and did cleanse others. **He that toucheth the water** –

Either by sprinkling of it, or by being sprinkled with it; for even he that was cleansed by it, was not fully cleansed as soon as he was sprinkled, but only at the even of that day.

22. The unclean person – Not he who is so only by touching the water of separation, Nu 19:21, but he who is so by the greater sort of uncleanness, which lasted seven days, and which was not removed without the use of this water of purification.

Chapter 20

This chapter begins the history of the fortieth year of the Israelites wandering in the wilderness. Little is recorded of them from the beginning of their second year till this, which brought them to the borders of Canaan.

The death of Miriam (1)

1. Then – To wit, after many stations and long journeys here omitted, but particularly described, Num 33:1-49. **Zin** – A place near the land of Edom, distinct and distant from that Sin, Exo 16:1. **The first month** – Of the fortieth year, as is evident, because the next station to this was in mount Hor, where Aaron died, who died in the fifth month of the fortieth year, Num 33:38. Moses doth not give us an exact journal of all occurrences in the wilderness, but only of those which were most remarkable, and especially of those which happened in the first and second, and in the fortieth year. **Miriam died** – Four months before Aaron, and but a few more before Moses.

The fetching water out of the rock (2–13)

2. No water – Which having followed them through all their former journeys, began to fail them here, because they were now come near countries, where waters might be had by ordinary means, and therefore God would not use extraordinary, lest he should seem to prostitute the honour of miracles. This story, though like that, Exo 17:1-7, is different from it, as appears by divers circumstances. It is a great mercy, to have plenty of water; a mercy which if we found the want of, we should own the worth of.

3. Before the Lord – Suddenly, rather than to die such a lingering death. Their sin was much greater than that of their parents, because they should have taken warning by their miscarriages, and by the terrible effects of them, which their eyes had seen.

8. The rod – That which was laid up before the Lord in the tabernacle; whether it was Aaron's rod, which was laid up there, Num 17:10, or Moses's rod by which he wrought so many miracles. For it is likely, that wonderworking rod, was laid up in some part of the tabernacle, though not in or near the ark, where Aaron's blossoming rod was put.

9. From before the Lord – Out of the tabernacle.

12. Ye believed me not – But showed your infidelity: which they did, either by smiting the rock, and that twice, which is emphatically noted, as if he doubted whether once smiting would have done it, whereas he was not commanded to smite so much as once, but only to speak to it: or by the doubtfulness of these words, Num 20:10. Must we fetch water out of the rock? which implies a suspicion of it, whereas they should have spoken positively and confidently to the rock to give forth water. And yet they did not doubt of the power of God, but of his will, whether he would gratify these rebels with this farther miracle, after so many of the like kind. **To sanctify me** – To give me the glory of my power in doing this miracle, and of my truth in punctually fulfilling my promise, and of my goodness in doing it notwithstanding the peoples perverseness. **In the eyes of Israel** – This made their sin scandalous to the Israelites, who of themselves were too prone to infidelity; to prevent the contagion, God leaves a monument of his displeasure upon them, and inflicts a punishment as public as their sin.

13. Meribah – That is, strife. **In them** – Or, among them, the children of Israel, by the demonstration of his omnipotency, veracity, and clemency towards the Israelites, and of his impartial holiness and severity against sin even in his greatest friends and favourites.

The treaty with the Edomites (14–21)

14. All the travel – All the wanderings and afflictions of our parents and of us their children, which doubtless have come to thine ears.

16. An Angel – The Angel of the Covenant, who first appeared to Moses in the bush, and afterward in the cloudy pillar, who conducted Moses and the people out of Egypt, and through the wilderness. For though Moses may be called an angel or messenger yet it is not probable that he is meant, partly because Moses was the person that sent this message; and partly because another angel above Moses conducted them, and the mention hereof to the Edomites, was likely to give more authority to their present message. **In Kadesh** – Near, the particle in being so often used.

17. The wells – Or, pits, which any of you have dug for your private use, not without paying for it, Num 20:19, but only of the waters of common rivers, which are free to all passengers. No man's property ought to be invaded, under colour of religion. Dominion is founded in providence, not in grace.

18. By me – Through my country: I will not suffer thee to do so: which was an act of policy, to secure themselves from so numerous an host.

19. Said – That is, their messengers replied what here follows.

The death of Aaron and installment of Eleazar (22–29)

23. And the Lord spake unto Moses and Aaron – So these two dear brothers must part! Aaron must die first: but Moses is not likely to be long after him. So that it is only for a while, a little while, that they are separated.

24. Because they rebelled – This was one but not the only reason. God would not have Moses and Aaron to carry the people into Canaan, for this reason also, to signify the insufficiency of the Mosaic law and Aaronic priesthood to make them perfectly happy, and the necessity of a better, and to keep the Israelites from resting in them, so as to be taken off from their expectation of Christ.

26. His garments – His priestly garments, in token of his resignation of his office. **Put them on Eleazar** – By way of admission and inauguration to his office.

27. In the sight of all the congregation – That their hearts might be more affected with their loss of so great a pillar, and that they all might be witnesses of the translation of the priesthood from Aaron to Eleazar.

28. And Moses stript Aaron – And Death will strip us. Naked we came into the world: naked we must go out. We shall see little reason to be proud of our clothes, our ornaments, or marks of honour, if we consider how soon death will strip us of all our glory, and take the crown off from our head! **Aaron died there** – He died in Mosera, Deu 10:6. Mosera was the general name of the place where that station was, and mount Hor a particular place in it. Presently after he was stript of his priestly garments, he laid him down and died. A good man would desire, if it were the will of God, not to outlive his usefulness. Why should we covet to continue any longer in this world, than while we may do God and our generation some service?

29. Saw – Understood by the relation of Moses and Eleazar, and by other signs. **Thirty days** – The time of public and solemn mourning for great persons.

Chapter 21

The defeat of Arad (1–3)

1. King Arad – Or rather, the Canaanite King of Arad: for Arad is not the name of a man, but of a city or territory. And he seems to be called a Canaanite in a general sense, as the Amorites and others. **The south** – Of Canaan, towards the east, and near the dead sea. **Of the spies** – Not of those spies which Moses sent to spy the land, for that was done thirty eight years before this, and they went so privately, that the Canaanites took

no notice of them, nor knew which way they came or went; but of the spies which he himself sent out to observe the marches and motions of the Israelites. **Took some of them prisoners** – Which God permitted for Israel's humiliation, and to teach them not to expect the conquest of that land from their own wisdom or valour.

2. I will utterly destroy them – I will reserve no person or thing for my own use, but devote them all to total destruction.

3. They utterly destroyed them – Neither Moses nor the whole body of the people did this but a select number sent out to punish that king and people, who were so fierce and malicious that they came out of their own country to fight with the Israelites in the wilderness; and these, when they had done this work, returned to their brethren into the wilderness. But why did they not all now go into Canaan, and pursue this victory? Because God would not permit it, there being several works yet to be done, other people must be conquered, the Israelites must be farther humbled and tried and purged, Moses must die, and then they shall enter, and that in a more glorious manner, even over Jordan, which shall be miraculously dried up, to give them passage. **Hormah** – That is, utter destruction.

The people murmur and are plagued with fiery serpents (4–6)

4. By way of the Red-sea – Which leadeth to the Red-sea, as they must needs do to compass the land of Edom. **Because of the way** – By reason of this journey, which was long and troublesome, and unexpected, because the successful entrance and victorious progress which some of them had made in the borders of Canaan, made them think they might have speedily gone in and taken possession of it, and so have saved the tedious travels and farther difficulties, into which Moses had again brought them.

5. Against God – Against Christ, their chief conductor, whom they tempted, 1Cor 10:19. Thus contemptuously did they speak of Manna, whereas it appears it yielded excellent nourishment, because in the strength of it they were able to go so many and such tedious journeys.

6. Fiery serpents – There were many such in this wilderness, which having been hitherto restrained by God, are now let loose and sent among them. They are called fiery from their effects, because their poison caused an intolerable heat and burning and thirst, which was aggravated with this circumstance of the place, that here was no water, Num 21:5.

They are healed by looking on the brazen serpent (7–9)

8. A fiery serpent – That is, the figure of a serpent in brass, which is of a fiery colour. This would require some time: God would not speedily take off the judgment, because he saw they were not throughly humbled. **Upon a pole** – That the people might see it from all parts of the camp, and therefore the pole must be high, and the serpent large. **When he looketh** – This method of cure was prescribed, that it might appear to be God's own work, and not the effect of nature or art: and that it might be an eminent type of our salvation by Christ. The serpent signified Christ, who was in the likeness of sinful flesh, though without sin, as this brazen serpent had the outward shape, but not the inward poison, of the other serpents: the pole resembled the cross upon which Christ was lifted up for our salvation: and looking up to it designed our believing in Christ.

9. He lived – He was delivered from death, and cured of his disease.

They journey forward (10–20)

10. In Oboth – Not immediately, but after two other stations mentioned, Nu 33:43,44.

12. The valley of Zared – Or rather, by the brook of Zared, which ran into the dead sea.

13. On the other side – Or rather, on this side of Arnon, for so it now was to the Israelites, who had not yet passed over it. **Between Moab and the Amorites** – Though formerly it and the land beyond it belonged to Moab, yet afterwards it had been taken from them by Sihon. This is added to reconcile two seemingly contrary commands of God, the one that of not meddling with the land of the Moabites, Deu 2:9, the other that of going over Arnon and taking possession of the land beyond it, Deu 2:24, because, saith he, it is not now the land of the Moabites, but of the Amorites.

14. The book of the wars of the Lord – This seems to have been some poem or narration of the wars and victories of the Lord, either by: or relating to the Israelites: which may be asserted without any prejudice to the integrity of the holy scripture, because this book doth not appear to have been written by a prophet, or to be designed for a part of the canon, which yet Moses might quote, as St. Paul doth some of the heathen poets. And as St. Luke assures us, that many did write an history of the things done, and said by Christ, Luke 1:1, whose writings were never received as canonical, the like may be conceived concerning this and some few other books mentioned in the old testament. **The brooks** – The brook, the plural number for the singular, as the plural number rivers is used concerning Jordan, Psa 74:15, and concerning Tigris, Nah 2:6, and concerning Euphrates, Psa 137:1, all which may be so called because of the several little streams into which they were divided.

15. Ar – A chief city in Moab.

16. Beer – This place and Mattanah, Nahaliel, and Bamoth named here, Nu 21:19, are not mentioned among those places where they pitched or encamped, Nu 33:1-49. Probably they did not pitch or encamp in these places, but only pass by or through them. **I will give them water** – In a miraculous manner. Before they prayed, God granted, and prevented them with the blessings of goodness. And as the brazen serpent was the figure of Christ, so is this well a figure of the spirit, who is poured forth for our comfort, and from him flow rivers of living waters.

17. Spring up – Heb. ascend, that is, let thy waters, which now lie hid below in the earth, ascend for our use. It is either a prediction that it should spring up, or a prayer that it might.

18. With their staves – Probably as Moses smote the rock with his rod, so they struck the earth with their staves, as a sign that God would cause the water to flow out of the earth where they smote it, as he did before out of the rock. Perhaps they made holes with their staves in the sandy ground, and God caused the water immediately to spring up.

20. Pisgah – This was the top of those high hills of Abarim.

Conquer Sihon (21–32)

21. Sent messengers – By God's allowance, that so Sihon's malice might be the more evident and inexcusable, and their title to his country more clear in the judgment of all men, as being gotten by a just war, into which they were forced for their own defence.

22. Let me pass – They spoke what they seriously intended and would have done, if he had given them quiet passage.

24. From Arnon – Or, which reached from Arnon; and so here is a description or limitation of Sihon's conquest and kingdom, that is, extended only from Arnon, unto the children of Ammon; and then the following words, for the border of the children of Ammon was strong, come in very fitly, not as a reason why the Israelites did not conquer the Ammonites, for they were absolutely forbidden to meddle with them, Deu 3:8, but as a reason why Sihon could not enlarge his conquests to the Ammonites, as he had done to the Moabites. **Jabbok** – A river by which the countries of Ammon and Moab were in part bounded and divided. **Strong** – Either by the advantage of the river, or by their strong holds in their frontiers.

26. Was the city of Sihon – This is added as a reason why Israel took possession of this land, because it was not now the land of the Moabites, but in the possession of the Amorites. **The former king** – The predecessor of Balak, who was the present king. See the wisdom of providence, which prepares long before, for the accomplishing God's purposes in their season! This country being designed for Israel, is before-hand put into the hand of the Amorites, who little think they have it but as trustees, till Israel comes of age. We understand not the vast reaches of providence: but known unto God are all his works!

27. In proverbs – The poets or other ingenious persons, of the Amorites or Canaanites, who made this following song of triumph over the vanquished Moabites: which is here brought in, as a proof that this was now Sihon's land, and as an evidence of the just judgment of God in spoiling the spoilers, and subduing those who insulted over their conquered enemies. **Come into Heshbon** – These are the words either of Sihon speaking to his people, or of the people exhorting one another to come and possess the city which they had taken. **Of Sihon** – That which once was the royal city of the king of Moab, but now is the city of Sihon.

28. A fire – The fury of war, which is fitly compared to fire. **Out of Heshbon** – That city which before was a refuge and defence to all the country, now is turned into a great annoyance. **It hath consumed Ar** – This may be understood not of the city Ar, but of the people or the country subject or belonging to that great and royal city. **The lords of the high places** – The princes or governors of the strong holds, which were frequently in high places, especially in that mountainous country, and which were in divers parts all along the river Arnon. So the Amorites triumphed over the vanquished Moabites. But the triumphing of the wicked is short!

29. People of Chemosh – The worshippers of Chemosh: so the God of the Moabites was called. He, that is, their God, hath delivered up his own people to his and their enemies; nor could he secure even those that had escaped the sword, but suffered them to be carried into captivity. The words of this and the following verse seem to be not a part of that triumphant song made, by some Amoritish poet, which seems to be concluded, Nu 21:28, but of the Israelites making their observation upon it. And here they scoff at the impotency not only of the Moabites, but of their God also, who could not save his people from the sword of Sihon and the Amorites.

30. Though you feeble Moabites, and your God too, could not resist Sihon, we Israelites, by the help of our God, have shot, with success and victory, at them, at Sihon and his Amorites. **Heshbon** – The royal city of Sihon, and by him lately repaired. **Is perished** – Is taken away from Sihon, and so is all his country, even as far as Dibon.

32. Jaazer – One of the cities of Moab formerly taken from them by Sihon, and now taken from him by the Israelites.

And Og (33–35)

33. Og – Who also was a king of the Amorites. And it may seem that Sihon and Og were the leaders or captains of two great colonies which came out of Canaan, and drove out the former inhabitants of these places. **Bashan** – A rich country, famous for its pastures and breed of cattle, and for its oaks.

Chapter 22
Balak's fear of Israel (1–4)

1. The plains of Moab – Which still retained their ancient title, though they had been taken away from the Moabites by Sihon, and from him by the Israelites. **By Jericho** – That is, over against Jericho.

3. Sore afraid – As it was foretold both in general of all nations, Deu 2:25, and particularly concerning Moab, Exo 15:15.

4. The elders – Called the kings of Midian, Nu 31:8, and princes of Midian, Jos 13:21, who though divided into their kingdoms yet were now united upon the approach of the Israelites their common enemy, and being, as it seems, a potent and crafty people, and neighbours to the Moabites, these seek confederacy with them. We read of Midianites near mount Sinai, Exod. 2, and 3, which seem to have been a colony of this people, that went out to seek new quarters, as the manner of those times was, but the body of that people were seated in those parts. **Lick up** – That is, consume and utterly destroy, in which sense the fire is said to lick up the water and sacrifices, 1Ki 18:38. **All that are round about us** – All our people, who live in the country adjoining to each city, where the princes reside.

His message to Balaam, who refuses to come (5–14)

5. Balaam – Who is called a prophet, 2Pet 2:16, because God was pleased to inspire and direct him to speak the following prophecies. Indeed many of the Jewish writers say, that Balaam had been a great prophet, who for the accomplishment of his predictions, and the answers of his prayers, had been looked upon justly as a man of great interest with God. However it is certain, that afterwards for his covetousness, God departed from him. **Beor** – Or, Bosor, 2Pet 2:15, for he had two names, as many others had. **Pethor** – A city in Mesopotamia. **By the river** – By Euphrates, which is called the river, by way of eminency, and here the river of Balaam's land or country, to wit, of Mesopotamia.

6. Curse them for my sake and benefit; use thy utmost power, which thou hast with thy Gods, to blast and ruin them. **We may smite them** – Thou by thy imprecations, and I by my sword.

8. This night – The night was the time when God used to reveal his mind by dreams. **The Lord** – Heb. Jehovah, the true God, whom he here mentions, either for his own greater reputation, as if he consulted not with inferior spirits, but with the supreme God; or rather because this was Israel's God, and the only possible way of ruining them was by engaging their God against them: as the Romans and other Heathens, when they went to besiege any city, used enchantments to call forth that God under whose peculiar protection they were. **Of Moab** – And of Midian too.

9. What men are these – He asks this that Balaam by repeating the thing in God's presence might be convinced and ashamed of his sin and folly, in offering his service in such a business: and for a foundation to the following answer.

On the second message he goes (15–21)

20. If the men come – On this condition he was to go.

He is rebuked by an angel (22–35)

22. Because he went – Because he went of his own accord, with the princes of Moab, and did not wait till they came to call him, which was the sign and condition of God's permission, but rather himself rose and called them. The apostle describes Balaam's sin here to be, that he ran greedily into an error for reward, Jude 1:11. **For an adversary** – To oppose, if not to kill him. **His servants with him** – The rest of the company being probably gone before them. For in those ancient times there was more of simplicity, and less of ceremony, and therefore it is not strange that Balaam came at some distance, after the rest, and attended only by his own servants.

28. Opened the mouth – Conferred upon her the power of speech and reasoning for that time.

29. Balaam said – Balaam was not much terrified with the ass's speaking, because perhaps he was accustomed to converse with evil spirits, who appeared to him and discoursed with him in the shape of such creatures. Perhaps he was so blinded by passion, that he did not consider the strangeness of the thing.

31. On his face – In token of reverence and submission.

32. Thy way is perverse – Springing from covetousness.

33. I had slain thee – I had slain thee alone, and not her, therefore her turning aside and falling down was wholly for thy benefit, not for her own, and thy anger against her was unjust and unreasonable.

35. Go with the men – I allow thee to go, upon the following terms.

His interview with Balak (36–41)

36. In the utmost coast – Not far from the camp of the Israelites, whom he desired him to curse.

40. The princes – Whom the king had left to attend him.

41. The high places of Baal – Consecrated to the worship of Baal, that is, of Baal Peor, who was their Baal or God. **The utmost part** – That is, all that people, even to the utmost and remotest of them, as appears by comparing this with, Nu 23:13. He hoped that the sight of such a numerous host ready to break in upon his country would stir up his passion.

Chapter 23

Balaam's first attempt to curse Israel, turned into a blessing (1–10)

1. Build seven altars – To the true God, otherwise he would not have mentioned it to God, as an argument why he should grant his requests, as he doth, Nu 23:4. And though Balak was averse from God and his worship, yet he would be easily overruled by Balaam, who doubtless told him that it was in vain to make an address to any other than the God of Israel, who alone was able either to bless or curse them as he pleased. **Seven** – This being the solemn and usual number in sacrifices.

3. Stand by thy burnt-offering – As in God's presence, as one that offers thyself as well as thy sacrifices to obtain his favour. **I will go** – To some solitary and convenient place, where I may prevail with God to appear to me. **Sheweth me** – Reveals to me, either by word or sign. **An high place** – Or, into the plain, as that word properly signifies.

7. His parable – That is, his oracular and prophetical speech; which he calls a parable, because of the weightiness of the matter, and the liveliness of the expressions which is usual in parables. **Jacob** – The posterity of Jacob.

9. The rocks – Upon which I now stand. **I see him** – I see the people, according to thy desire, Nu 22:41, but cannot improve that sight to the end for which thou didst design it, to curse them. **The people shall dwell alone** – This people are of a distinct kind from others, God's peculiar people, separated from all other nations, as in religion and laws, so also in divine protection; and therefore enchantments cannot have that power against them which they have against other persons and people.

10. The dust – The numberless people of Jacob or Israel, who according to God's promise, are now become as the dust of the earth. **Of the righteous** – Of this righteous and holy people. The sense is, they are not only happy above other nations in this life, and therefore in vain should I curse them, but they have this peculiar privilege, that they are happy after death: their happiness begins where the happiness of other people ends; and therefore I heartily wish that my soul may have its portion with theirs when I die. Was not God now again striving with him, not only for the sake of Israel, but of his own soul?

Balaam's second attempt with like success (11–24)

12. Must I not – Ought I not? Is it not my duty? Canst thou blame me for it?

13. Thou shalt not see them all – Perhaps he thought the sight of all them might discourage him, or as it did before, raise his fancy to an admiration of the multitude and felicity of the people.

15. While I meet the Lord – To consult him, and to receive an answer from him.

18. Rise up – This word implies the diligent attention required; rouse up thyself and carefully mind what I say.

19. That he should lie – Break his promises made to his people for their preservation and benediction. **Repent** – Change his counsels or purposes; unless he see iniquity in Jacob.

21. Iniquity – Not such as in the Canaanites: Such as he will punish with a curse, with utter destruction. **The Lord is with him** – He hath a favour for this people, and will defend and save them. **The shout of a king** – That is, such joyful and triumphant shouts as those wherewith a people congratulate the approach and presence of their King: when he appears among them upon some solemn occasion, or when he returns from battle with victory. This expression implies God's being their King and ruler, and their abundant security and confidence in him.

22. Out of Egypt – Namely, by a strong hand, and in spite of all their enemies, and therefore it is in vain to seek or hope to overcome them. **He** – Israel, whom God brought out of Egypt, such change of numbers being very common in the Hebrew language. The sense is, Israel is not now what he was in Egypt, a poor, weak, dispirited, unarmed people, but high and strong and invincible. **An unicorn** – The word may mean either a rhinoceros, or a strong and fierce kind of wild goat. But such a creature as an unicorn, as commonly painted, has no existence in nature.

23. Against Jacob – Nor against any that truly believe in Christ. **What hath God wrought** – How wonderful and glorious are those works which God is now about to do for Israel! These things will be a matter of discourse and admiration to all ages.

24. As a great Lion – As a lion rouseth up himself to fight, or to go out to the prey, so shall Israel stir up themselves to warlike attempts

against their enemies. **He shall not lie down** – Not rest or cease from fighting and pursuing.

The preparation for a third attempt (25–30)

28. Peor – An high place called Beth-peor, Deu 3:29. That is, the house or temple of Peor, because there they worshipped Baal-peor.

Chapter 24
Balaam inspired by God, blesses Israel again (1–9)

1. At other times – In former times. **Toward the wilderness** – Where Israel lay encamped, expecting what God of his own accord would suggest to him concerning this matter.

2. Came upon him – Inspired him to speak the following words.

3. Whose eyes are open – Heb. Who had his eyes shut, but now open. The eyes of his mind, which God had opened in a peculiar and prophetical manner, whence prophets are called Seers, 1Sam 9:9. It implies that before he was blind and stupid, having eyes, but not seeing nor understanding.

4. The vision – So called properly, because he was awake when this was revealed to him: **A trance** – Or, fainting and falling upon the ground, as the prophets used to do.

6. As the valleys – Which often from a small beginning are spread forth far and wide. **As gardens** – Pleasant and fruitful and secured by a fence. **As lign-aloes** – An Arabian and Indian tree of a sweet smell, yielding shade and shelter both to man and beast; such is Israel, not only safe themselves, but yielding shelter to all that join themselves to them. **Which the Lord hath planted** – Nature, not art.

7. He shall pour the water – That is, God will abundantly water the valleys, gardens, and trees, which represent the Israelites; he will wonderfully bless his people, not only with outward blessings, of which a chief one in those parts was plenty of water, but also with higher gifts and graces, with his word and spirit, which are often signified by water, and at last with eternal life, the contemplation whereof made Balaam desire to die the death of the righteous. **His seed shall be in many waters** – This also may be literally understood of their seed, which shall be sown in waterish ground, and therefore bring forth a better increase. **His King** – That is, the King of Israel, or their chief governor. **Than Agag** – Than the King of the Amalekites, which King and people were famous and potent in that age, as may be guessed by their bold attempt upon so numerous a people as Israel. And it is probable, that Agag was the common name of the Amalekitish Kings, as Abimelech was of the Philistines, and Pharaoh of the Egyptians, and Caesar of the Romans.

9. He lay down – Having conquered his enemies the Canaanites, and their land, he shall quietly rest and settle himself there.

Answers Balak's reproof (10–13)

11. The Lord – Whose commands thou hast preferred before my desires and interest; and therefore seek thy recompense from him, and not from me.

Utters several prophecies (14–24)

17. I shall see him – Or, I have seen, or do see the star, and sceptre as it here follows, that is, a great and eminent prince, which was to come out of Israel's loins, the Messiah, as both Jewish and Christian interpreters expound it, who most eminently and fully performed what is here said, in destroying the enemies of Israel or of God's church, here described under the names of the nearest and fiercest enemies of Israel: And to him alone agrees the foregoing verb properly, I shall see him, in my own person, as every eye shall see him, when he comes to judgment. **Not now** – Not yet, but after many ages. **A star** – A title often given to, princes and eminent persons, and particularly to the Messiah, Rev 2:28 22:16. **A sceptre** – That is, a sceptre-bearer, a king or ruler, even that sceptre mentioned Gen 49:10. **The corners** – The borders, which are often used in scripture for the whole country to which they belong. **Of Sheth** – This seems to be the name of some then eminent, though now unknown place or prince in Moab; there being innumerable instances of such places or persons sometime famous, but now utterly lost as to all monuments and remembrances of them.

18. A possession – Which was also foretold, Gen 25:23, and in part fulfilled, 2Sam 8:14 1Chr 18:13, but more fully by Christ, Amos 9:12 Ob 1:18, who shall subdue and possess all his enemies; here signified by the name of Edom, as Jacob or Israel, his brother, signifies all his church and people. **Seir** – A part and, mountain of Edom.

19. Out of Jacob – Out of Jacob's loins. **He that shall have dominion** – David, and especially Christ. **Of the city** – Or from or out of this city, that is, the cities, the singular number for the plural. He shall not subdue those Moabites and Edomites which meet him in the field, but he shall pursue them even to their strongest holds and cities.

20. He looked on Amalek – From the top of Pisgah, which was exceeding high, and gave him the prospect of part of all these kingdoms. **The first** – Heb. the first fruits; so called either, because they were the first of all the neighbouring nations which were embodied together in one government: or, because he was the first

who fought against Israel and was vanquished by them. That victory was an earnest and first fruit of the large harvest of victories which the Israelites should in due time get over all their enemies. **He shall perish for ever** – He began with God and with Israel, but God will end with him, and the firm purpose of God is, that he shall be utterly destroyed; so that Saul lost his kingdom for not executing this decree, and God's command pursuant thereunto.

21. The Kenites – The posterity or kindred of Jethro; not that part of them which dwelt among the Israelites, to whom the following words do not agree, but those of them who were mingled with the Amalekites and Midianites. **Thy nest** – Thy dwelling-place, so called, either because it was in an high place, as nests commonly are: or in allusion to their name, for ken in Hebrew signifies a nest.

22. The Kenite – Heb. Kain, that is, the Kenite, so called, either by a transposition of letters, which is very usual in the Hebrew tongue; or from the name of some eminent place where they lived, or person from whom they were descended, though now the memory of them be utterly lost, as it hath fared with innumerable other places and persons, famous in their generations, mentioned in ancient Heathen writers. **Shall be wasted** – Shall be by degrees diminished by the incursions of divers enemies, till at last the Assyrian comes to complete the work and carries them into captivity. For the Kenites who lived partly among the ten tribes, and partly with the two tribes, were carried captive with them, part by Salmaneser, the King of Assyria, and part by Nebuchadnezzar, who also is called an Assyrian, Ezra 6:22 Isa 52:4.

23. Who shall live – How calamitous and miserable will the state of the world be, when the Assyrian, and after him the Chaldean, shall over-turn all these parts of the world? Who will be able to keep his heart from fainting under such grievous pressures? Nay, how few will escape the destroying sword?

24. Chittim – A place or people so called from Chittim the son of Javan, Gen 10:4, whose posterity were very numerous, and were first seated in the lesser Asia, and from thence sent forth colonies into the islands of the Aegean sea, and into Cyprus, afterwards into Macedonia and other parts of Greece, and then into Italy. Whence it comes to pass that by this name is understood sometimes Macedonia, as 1Mac. i. 1, and 1Mac. viii. 5, sometimes Italy, as Dan 11:29,30, and sometimes both, as in this place: for he speaks here of the scourge that God hath appointed for the Assyrian after he had done God's work in punishing of his people and the bordering nations. Now although the Assyrian and Chaldean empire was subdued by the

Medes and Persians, yet the chief afflictions of that people came from two hands, both beyond the sea and brought to them by ships; first from the Grecians under Alexander and his successors, by whom that people were grievously oppressed and wasted; then from the Romans, who subdued all the Grecian empire, one great part whereof were the Assyrians largely so called. **Eber** – The posterity of Eber, the Hebrews, who were the chief and flower of Eber's children. **He also** – Not the Hebrews: they shall have a better end; all Israel shall be saved; but the afflicter or scourge of Ashur and Eber, namely, the Grecian and Roman empire. Thus Balaam, instead of cursing the church, curses Amalek, the first, and Rome, the last enemy of it!

Goes home (25)

25. **To his place** – To Mesopotamia; tho' afterwards he returned to the Midianites, and gave them that devilish counsel which was put in practice, Num 25:16-18.

Chapter 25

The sin of Israel (1–3)

1. **Shittim** – And this was their last station, from whence they passed immediately into Canaan. This is noted as a great aggravation of their sin, that they committed it, when God was going to put them into the possession of their long-expected land. **The people** – Many of them. **Whoredom** – Either because they prostituted themselves to them upon condition of worshipping their God: or because their filthy God was worshipped by such filthy acts, as Priapus and Venus were. **The daughters of Moab** – And of Midian too; for both these people being confederated in this wicked design, the one is put for the other, and the daughters of Moab may be named, either because they began the transgression, or because they were the chief persons, possibly, the relations or courtiers of Balak.

2. **They** – The Moabites being now neighbours to the Israelites, and finding themselves unable to effect their design by war and witchcraft, fell another way to work, by contracting familiarity with them, and, perceiving their evil inclinations, they, that is, their daughters, invited them. **Unto the sacrifices** – Unto the feasts which were made of their parts of the sacrifices, after the manner of the Jews and Gentiles too, the participation whereof, was reckoned a participation in the worship of that God to whom the sacrifices were offered. **Of their gods** – Of their God, Baal-peor, the plural Elohim being here used, as commonly it is, for one God.

3. **Joined himself** – The word implies a forsaking God to whom they were joined and a turning to, and strict conjunction with, this false God. **Baal-peor** – Called Baal, by the name common to many false Gods, and especially to those that represented any of the heavenly bodies, and Peor, either from the hill Peor, where he was worshipped, Num 23:28, rather from a verb signifying to open and uncover, because of the obscene posture in which the idol was set, as Priapus was: or because of the filthiness which was exercised in his worship.

Their punishment (4, 5)

4. **Take all the heads** – Take, that is, apprehend, all the heads, that is, the chief, of the people, such as were chief in this transgression, and in place and power, who are singled out to this exemplary punishment for their concurrence with others in this wickedness, which was more odious and mischievous in them. **Hang them up before the Lord** – To the vindication of God's honour and justice. **Against the sun** – Publically, as their sin was public and scandalous, and speedily, before the sun go down.

5. **Every one his men** – Those under his charge, for as these seventy were chosen to assist Moses in the government, so doubtless the care and management of the people was distributed among them by just and equal proportions.

The zeal of Phinehas, with the promise added to it (6–15)

6. **One came** – This was done, when Moses had given the charge to the Judges, and, as it may seem, before the execution of it; otherwise it is probable he would not have been so foolish to have run upon certain ruin, when the examples were frequent before his eyes. **To his brethren** – Into the camp of the Israelites. **In the sight of Moses** – An argument of intolerable impudence and contempt of God and of Moses. **Weeping** – Bewailing the wickedness of the people, and the dreadful judgments of God, and imploring God's mercy and favour.

8. **Thrust them through** – Phinehas was himself a man in great authority, and did this after the command given by Moses to the rulers to slay these transgressors, and in the very sight, and no doubt by the consent of Moses himself, and also by the special direction of God's spirit.

9. **Twenty four thousand** – St. Paul says twenty three thousand, 1Cor 10:8. The odd thousand here added were slain by the Judges according to the order of Moses, the rest by the immediate hand of God, but both sorts died of the plague, the word being used, as often it is, for the sword, or hand, or stroke of God.

12. **My covenant of peace** – That is, the covenant of an everlasting priesthood, as it is expounded, Nu 25:13, which is called a covenant of peace, partly with respect to the happy effect of this heroical action of his,

whereby he made peace between God and his people; and partly with regard to the principal end of the priestly office, which was constantly to do that which Phinehas now did, even to mediate between God and men, to obtain and preserve his own and Israel's peace and reconciliation with God, by offering up sacrifices and incense, and prayers, to God on their behalf, as also by turning them away from iniquity, which is the only peace-breaker, and by teaching and pressing the observation of that law, which is the only bond of their peace.

13. An everlasting priesthood – To continue as long as the law and common-wealth of the Jews did. But this promise was conditional, and therefore might be made void, by the miscarriages of Phinehas's sons, as it seems it was, and thereupon a like promise was made to Eli of the line of Ithamar, that he and his should walk before the Lord, namely, in the office of high-priest, for ever, which also for his and their sins was made void, 1Sam 2:30. And the priesthood returned to Phinehas's line in the time of Solomon, 1Kings 2:26,27,34.

The command to slay the Midianites (16–18)

17. The Midianites – And why not the Moabites. It is probable the Midianites were most guilty, as in persuading Balak to send for Balaam, Nu 22:4,7. So in the reception of Balaam after Balak had dismissed him, Nu 31:8, and in farther consultation with him, and in contriving the means for the executing of this wicked plot.

18. With their wiles – For under pretence of kindred and friendship and leagues, which they offered to them, instead of that war which the Israelites expected, they sought only an opportunity to insinuate themselves into their familiarity, and execute their hellish plot of bringing that curse upon the Israelites, which they had in vain attempted to bring another way.

Chapter 26

Orders for numbering the people (1–4)

2. Take the sum – They were numbered twice before, Exo 30:11,12 Nu 1:1,2. Now they are numbered a third time, to demonstrate the faithfulness of God, both in cutting all those off whom he had threatened to cut off, Nu 14:29, and in a stupendous increase of the people according to his promise, notwithstanding all their sins, and the sweeping judgments inflicted upon them; and to prepare the way for the equal division of the land, which they were now going to possess.

Their families and number (5–51)

7. Families – The chief houses, which were subdivided into divers lesser families. **Forty three thousand seven hundred and thirty** – Whereas in their last numbering they were forty six thousand five hundred; for Korah's conspiracy, as well as other provocations of theirs, had cut off many of them.

10. With Korah – According to this translation Korah was not consumed by fire with his two hundred and fifty men, but swallowed up by the earth. But others rather think he was devoured by the fire, and render these words, and the things of Korah, or belonging to Korah, namely, his tent and goods, and family, children excepted, as here follows. **A sign** – God made them a monument or example, to warn others not to rebel against God, or magistracy, nor to usurp the priestly office.

11. Died not – God being pleased to spare them, because they disowned their father's fact, and separated themselves both from his tent and company. Hence the sons of Korah are mentioned, 1Chr 6:22,38, and often in the book of Psalms.

12. Jachin – Called also Jarib, 1Chr 4:24. And such names might be either added or changed upon some special occasion not recorded in scripture.

14. Twenty two thousand and two hundred – No tribe decreased so much as Simeon's. From fifty nine thousand and three hundred it sunk to twenty two thousand and two hundred, little more than a third part of what it was. One whole family of that tribe, (Ohad mentioned Exo 6:15) was extinct in the wilderness. Some think most of the twenty four thousand, cut off by the plague for the iniquity of Peor, were of that tribe. For Zimri, a ring-leader in that iniquity, was a prince of that tribe. Simeon is not mentioned in Moses's blessing, Deu 33:1-29. And the lot of that tribe in Canaan was inconsiderable, only a canton out of Judah's lot, Jos 19:9.

18. Children of Gad – Fewer by above five thousand than there were in their last numbering.

22. The families of Judah – About two thousand more than they were, Nu 1:27, whereas the foregoing tribes were all diminished.

34. Fifty two thousand and seven hundred – Whereas they were but thirty two thousand and two hundred, in Nu 1:35. So they are now increased above twenty thousand, according to that prophecy, Gen 49:22.

38. The sons of Benjamin – Who were ten, Gen 46:21, whereof only five are here mentioned, the rest probably, together with their families, being extinct.

43. Threescore and four thousand and four hundred – All from one son and family, whereas of Benjamin who had ten sons, and five families, there were only forty five thousand and six hundred, to shew that the increase of families depends singly upon God's blessing and good pleasure.

51. These were the numbered – Very nigh as many as there were before, Nu 1:46. So wisely and marvellously did God at the same time manifest his justice in cutting off so vast a number; his mercy in giving such a speedy and numerous supply; and his truth in both.

Directions for dividing the land between them (52–55)

53. The land shall be divided – The land was divided into nine parts and an half, respect being had in such division to the goodness as well as to the largeness of the several portions, and the lot gave each tribe their part. **Of names** – Of persons, the share of each tribe was divided amongst the several families, to some more, to some less, according to the number of the persons of each family. And withal, if one of the portions proved too large or too little for the families and persons of that tribe, they might give part of their portion to another tribe, (as Simeon and Dan had part of Judah's share) or take away a part from the portion belonging to another tribe.

55. By lot – For the tribes, not for the several families; for the distribution of it to them was left to the rulers wisdom according to the rule now given.

The families and number of the Levites (56–62)

56. Many and few – That share, which shall by lot fall to each tribe, shall be distributed to the several families and persons in such proportions as their numbers shall require.

Notice taken of the death of them that were first numbered (62–65)

65. Not left a man – Only of the Levites, who being not guilty of that sin did not partake of their judgment.

Chapter 27

The case of Zelophehad's daughters determined (1–11)

2. By the door of the tabernacle – Nigh unto which it seems was the place where Moses and the chief rulers assembled for the administration of public affairs, which also was very convenient, because they had frequent occasion of recourse to God for his direction.

3. In his own sin – For his own personal sins. It was a truth, and that believed by the Jews that death was a punishment for mens own sins.

4. Be done away – As it will be, if it be not preserved by an inheritance given to us in his name and for his sake. Hence some gather, that the first son of each of these heiresses was called by their father's name, by virtue of that law, Deu

25:6, whereby the brother's first son was to bear the name of his elder brother, whose widow he married. **Give us a possession** – In the land of Canaan upon the division of it, which though not yet conquered, they concluded would certainly be so, and thereby gave glory to God.

10. No brethren – Nor sisters, as appears from Nu 27:8.

11. A statute of judgment – A statute or rule, by which the magistrates shall give judgment in such cases.

Notice given to Moses of his death (12–14)

12. Abarim – The whole tract of mountains was called Abarim, whereof one of the highest was called Nebo, and the top of that Pisgah.

13. Thou shalt be gathered unto thy people – Moses must die: but death does not cut him off; it only gathers him to his people, brings him to rest with the holy patriarchs that were gone before him. Abraham, Isaac and Jacob were his people, the people of his choice, and to them death gathered him.

His successor provided (15–23)

15. And Moses spake unto the Lord – Concerning his successor. We should concern ourselves both in our prayers and in our endeavours for the rising generation, that God's kingdom may be advanced among men, when we are in our graves.

16. The Lord of the spirits of all flesh – God of all men: the searcher of spirits, that knowest who is fit for this great employment; the father and giver and governor of spirits, who canst raise and suit the spirits of men to the highest and hardest works.

17. Go out before them – That is, who may wisely conduct them in all their affairs, both when they go forth to war, or upon other occasions, and when they return home and live in peace. A metaphor from shepherds, who in those places used not to go behind their sheep, as ours now do, but before them, and to lead them forth to their pasture, and in due time to lead them home again.

18. The spirit – The spirit of government, of wisdom, and of the fear of the Lord. **Lay thy hand** – By which ceremony Moses did both design the person and confer the power, and by his prayers, which accompanied that rite, obtain from God all the spiritual gifts and graces necessary for his future employment.

19. Before all the congregation – That they may be witnesses of the whole action, and may acknowledge him for their supreme ruler. **Give him charge** – Thou shalt give him counsels and instructions for the right management of that great trust.

20. Put some of thine honour – Thou shalt not now use him as a servant, but as a brother and thy partner in the government, that the people being used to obey him while Moses lived, might do it afterward the more cheerfully.

21. Who shall ask counsel for him – When he requires him to do so, and in important and difficult matters. **Of Urim** – Urim is put for both Urim and Thummim. **Before the Lord** – Ordinarily in the tabernacle near the second veil setting his face to the ark. **At his word** – The word of the Lord, delivered to him by the high priest.

22. And Moses did as the Lord commanded him – It had been little to resign his honour to a son of his own. But with his own hands, first to ordain Eleazar high-priest, and now Joshua chief ruler, while his own children had no preferment at all, but were left in the rank of common Levites: this was more to his glory than the highest advancement of his family could have been. This shows him to have had a principle which raised him above all other lawgivers, who always took care to establish their families in some share of the greatness themselves possessed.

Chapter 28

Laws concerning the daily (1–8)

2. Command the children of Israel – God here repeats some of the former laws about sacrifices, not without great reason, partly because they had been generally discontinued for thirty eight years together; partly because the generation to which the former laws had been given about these things was wholly dead, and it was fit the new generation should be instructed about them, as their parents were; partly to renew their testimonies of God's grace and mercy, notwithstanding their frequent forfeitures thereof by their rebellion: and principally because they were now ready to enter into that land, in which they were obliged to put these things in practice.

7. In the holy place – Upon the altar of burnt offerings, which was in the court of the priests, nigh to the entrance into the sanctuary.

Weekly and monthly and yearly sacrifices (9–31)

17. The feast – Namely, of unleavened bread.

23. In the morning – And that in the evening too, as is evident from other scriptures; but the morning-sacrifice alone is mentioned, because the celebration of the feast began with it, and principally because this alone was doubtful, whether this might not be omitted when so many other sacrifices were offered in that morning, whereas there was no question but the evening sacrifice should be offered, when there were none other to be offered.

26. The day of the first fruits – In the feast of Pentecost, Acts 2:1. **Your weeks** – The seven weeks which you are to number from the Passover.

Chapter 29

Offerings to be made in the seventh month.

At the feast of trumpets (1–6)

6. Of the month – Belonging to every new moon.

In the day of atonement (7–11)

7. Afflict your souls – Yourselves, by fasting and abstinence from all delightful things, and by compunction for your sins, and the judgments of God, either deserved by you or inflicted upon you.

At the feast of tabernacles (12–40)

12. Seven days – Not by abstaining so long from all servile work, but by offering extraordinary sacrifices each day. This was the Feast of Tabernacles. And all the days of their dwelling in booths, they must offer sacrifices. While we are in these tabernacles, 'tis our interest as well as duty, to keep up our communion with God. Nor will the unsettledness of our outward condition, excuse our neglect of God's worship.

Chapter 30

Vows must be performed, and particular exceptions (1–5)

5. In the days – Speedily, or without delay, allowing only convenient time for deliberation. And it is hereby intimated, that the day or time he had for disallowing her vow, was not to be reckoned from her vowing, but from his knowledge of her vow. **The Lord shall forgive** – Or, will forgive her not performing it. But this should be understood only of vows which could not be performed without invading the father's right; for if one should vow to forbear such, or such a sin, and all occasions or means leading to it, and to perform such, or such duties, when he had opportunity, no father can discharge him from such vows. If this law does not extend to children's marrying without the parent's consent, so far as to put it in the power of the parent, to disannul the marriage, (which some think it does) yet certainly it proves the sinfulness of such marriages, and obliges those children to repent and humble themselves before God and their parents.

And the vow of a wife, not allowed by her husband (6–16)

9. Widow or divorced – Though she be in her father's house, whither such persons often returned.

10. If she vowed – If she that now a widow, or divorced, made that vow while her husband lived with her; as suppose she then vowed, that if she was a widow, she would give such a proportion of her estate to pious or charitable uses, of which vow she might repent when she came to be a widow, and might believe or repented she was free from it, because that vow was made in her husband's lifetime; this is granted, in case her husband then disallowed it; but denied, in case by silence, or otherwise he consented to it.

13. To afflict her soul – Herself by fasting, by watching, or the like. And these words are added to shew that the husband had this power not only in those vows which concerned himself or his estate, but also in those which might seem only to concern her own person, or body, and the reason is, because the wife's person or body being the husband's right; she might not do any thing to the injury of her body without his consent.

15. After he hath heard – And approved them by his silence from day to day, if after that time he shall hinder it, which he ought not to do: her non-performance of her vow shall be imputed to him, not to her.

Chapter 31

God commands Moses to avenge Israel of the Midianites (1–6)

3. Avenge ye the Lord – For the affront which they offered to God, by their own idolatry and lewdness, and by seducing God's people into rebellion against him. God's great care was to avenge the Israelites, Nu 31:2, and Moses's chief desire was to avenge God rather than himself or the people.

5. Twelve thousand – God would send no more, though it is apparent the Midianites were numerous and strong, because he would exercise their trust in him, and give them an earnest of their Canaanite conquests.

6. Them and Phinehas – Who had the charge not of the army, as general, (an office never committed to a priest in all the Old Testament) but of the holy instruments, and was sent to encourage, and quicken, them in their enterprise. **The holy instruments** – The holy breastplate, wherein was the Urim and Thummim, which was easily carried, and very useful in war upon many emergent occasions.

They slay the Midianites (7–12)

7. All the males – Namely all who lived in those parts, for colonies of them, were sent forth to remoter places, which therefore had no hand either in their former sin, or in this present ruling. And herein they did according to God's own order concerning such people, Deu 20:13, only their fault was, that they did not consider

the special reason which they had to involve the women in the destruction.

He reproves them for sparing the women (13–18)

13. Without the camp – Partly to put respect upon them, and congratulate with them for their happy success; and partly to prevent the pollution of the camp by the untimely entrance of the warriors into it.

17. The little ones – Which they were forbidden to do to other people, Deu 20:14, except the Canaanites, to whom this people had equalled themselves by their horrid crimes, and therefore it is not strange, nor unjust, that God, the supreme Lord of all mens lives, who as he gives them, so may take them away when he pleaseth, did equal them in the punishment. **Every woman** – Partly for punishment, because the guilt was general, and though some of them only did prostitute themselves to the Israelites, yet the rest made themselves accessary by their consent or approbation; and partly, for prevention of the like mischief from such an adulterous generation.

Directions for purifying themselves (19–24)

20. Your raiment – Namely, your spoil and prey. **All work** – All which had contracted some ceremonial uncleanness either from the dead bodies which wore them, or the tents or houses where they were, in which such dead bodies lay, or from the touch of the Israeli soldiers, who were legally defiled by the slaughters they made.

The distribution of the spirit (25–47)

27. Two parts – The congregation hath some share, because the warriors went in the name of all, and because all having been injured by the Midianites, all were to have some share in the reparations: but the warriors who were but 12000, have a far greater share than their brethren, because they underwent greater pains and dangers.

29. An heave-offering – In thankfulness to God for their preservation and good success.

30. One of fifty – Whereas the former part was one of five hundred; the reason of the difference is, partly, because this was taken out of the peoples portion, whose hazards being less than the others, their gains also in all reason were to be less: partly because this was to be distributed into more hands, the Levites being now numerous, whereas the priests were but few.

The free-will-offering of the officers (48–54)

50. An atonement – For their error noted, Nu 31:14,15,16, and withal for a memorial, or by way of gratitude for such a stupendous assistance and deliverance. We should never take any thing to ourselves in war or trade, of which we cannot in faith consecrate a part to God, who hates robbery for burnt-offerings. But when God has remarkably preserved and succeeded us, he expects we should make some particular return of gratitude to him.

Chapter 32

The request of Reuben and Gad for an inheritance on this side Jordan (1–5)

1. Jazer – A city and country of the Amorites; **Gilead** – A mountainous country, famous for pasturage.

Moses's misconstruction of it (6–15)

6. Ye sit here – In ease and peace, while your brethren are engaged in a bloody war.

12. The Kenezite – So called from Kenaz, his grand-father.

15. All this people – Who being moved by your counsel and example, will refuse to go over Jordan.

Their explication of it (16–19)

17. We ourselves – Either all, or as many as shall be thought necessary, leaving only so many as may be necessary to provide for the sustenance and defence of our wives and children here.

The grant of their petition (20–42)

20. Before the Lord – Before the ark, which was the token of God's presence. He alludes either to the order of the tribes in their march, whereby Reuben and Gad marched immediately before the ark, or to the manner of their passage over Jordan, wherein the ark went first into Jordan, and stood there while all the tribes marched over Jordan by and before it, and these amongst the rest, as is expressly noted in these very words, that they passed over before the Lord, Jos 4:13.

22. Before the Lord – By his presence and gracious and powerful assistance.

23. Your sin – The punishment of your sin. Sin will certainly find out the sinner sooner or later. It concerns us therefore to find our sins out, that we may repent of them and forsake them, lest our sins find us out, to our confusion and destruction.

30. They shall have possession – They shall forfeit their possessions in Gilead, and be constrained to go over Jordan, and to seek possessions there among their brethren.

31. As the Lord hath said – Either at this time by thy mouth: or formerly, where he commanded us, as well as our brethren to go into Canaan and possess it.

34. Built – Repaired and fortified. For they neither had need nor leisure as yet to do more, the old cities not being burnt and ruined, as divers in Canaan were.

38. Their names changed – Either because conquerors of places used to do so; or because the names of other gods were not to be mentioned, Exo 23:13.

40. Machir – Not to Machir himself, who doubtless was long since dead, but the family or posterity of Machir.

42. Nobah – Who, though not else where named, was doubtless an eminent person of the tribe of Manasseh. 'Tis observable, that these tribes, as they were placed before the other tribes, so they were displaced before them. They were carried captive by the king of Assyria, some years before the other tribes. Such a proportion does providence frequently observe, in balancing prosperity and adversity.

Chapter 33

An account of the marches and encampments of the Israelites, from Egypt to Canaan (1–49)

2. And Moses wrote their goings out – When they set out, God ordered him to keep a journal of all the remarkable occurrences in the way, that it might be a satisfaction to himself and an instruction to others. It may be of use to Christians, to preserve an account of the providences of God concerning them, the constant series of mercies they have experienced, and especially those turns which have made some days of their lives more remarkable.

4. On their gods – Their false gods, namely those beasts which the brutish Egyptians worshipped as gods, which were killed with the rest, for the first-born both of men and beasts were then killed. Probably their images likewise were thrown down, as Dagon afterward before the ark.

10. By the Red-sea – By another part of that sea which they passed over.

48. Shittim – The place where the people sinned in the matter of Peor, is here called Abel-Shittim – Abel signifies mourning; and probably this place was so called, from the mourning of Israel for that sin, and the heavy punishment inflicted on the sinners.

A strict command to drive out all the Canaanites (50–56)

52. Drive out – Not by banishing, but by destroying them. **Pictures** – Which seem to have been stones curiously engraved, and set up for worship. **High Places** – Chapels, altars, groves, or other means of worship there set up.

Chapter 34

Directions concerning the bounds of Canaan (1-15)

2. **Coasts** – Or limits or bounds, to wit, of the land beyond Jordan. Which are here particularly described:

1. to direct and bound them in their wars and conquests, that they might not seek the enlargement of their empire, after the manner of other nations, but be contented with their own portion.

2. To encourage them in their attempt upon Canaan, and assure them of their success. There was a much larger possession promised them, if they were obedient, even to the river Euphrates. But this, which is properly Canaan, lay in a very little compass. 'Tis but about an hundred and fifty miles in length, and about fifty in breadth. This was that little spot of ground, in which alone for many ages God was known! But its littleness was abundantly compensated by its fruitfulness: otherwise it could not have sustained so numerous a nation. See, how little a share of the world God often gives to his own people! But they that have their portion in heaven, can be content with a small pittance of this earth.

3. **Your fourth quarter** – Which is here described from east to west by divers windings and turnings, by reason of the mountains and rivers. **The salt sea** – So called from the salt and sulphurous taste of its waters. **Eastward** – That is, at the eastern part of that sea, where the eastern and southern borders meet.

4. **From the south** – Or, on the south, that is, proceeding onward towards the south. **Azmon** – Which is at the west-end of the mount of Edom.

5. **The river of Egypt** – Called Sihor, Jos 13:3, which divided Egypt from Canaan. **The sea** – The midland sea, called the sea emphatically, whereas the other seas, as they are called, are indeed but lakes.

6. **The great sea** – This midland sea from the south to the north, so far as it runs parallel with mount Libanus.

7. **Hor** – Not that Hor where Aaron died, which was southward, and bordering upon Edom, but another mountain, and, as it is conceived, the mountain of Libanus, which is elsewhere mentioned as the northern border of the land, and which, in regard of divers parts, or by divers names, and here Hor, which signifies a mountain, by way of eminency.

Concerning the division of it (16-29)

17. **Eleazar** – Who was to act in God's name, to cast lots, to prevent contentions, to consult with God in cases of difficulty, to transact the whole business in a solemn and religious manner.

19. **Judah** – The order of the tribes is here different from that, Nu 1:7.26, and in other places, being conformed to the order of their several inheritances, which afterwards fell to them by lots. Which is an evident demonstration of the infinite wisdom of God's providence, and of his peculiar care over his people.

Chapter 35

Forty eight cities assigned to the Levites, of which six were cities of refuge (1-15)

3. **For the cattle** – For pasturage for their cattle: where they might not build houses, nor plant gardens, orchards or vineyards, no nor sow corn, for which they were abundantly provided out of the first-fruits. And these suburbs did not belong to the Levites in common, but were distributed to them in convenient proportions.

4. **A thousand cubits** – In the next verse it is two thousand. But this verse and the next do not speak to the same thing; this speaks of the space from whence the suburbs shall be measured, the next speaks of the space unto which that measure shall be extended; and the words may very well be read thus. **And the suburbs** – Shall be from the wall of the city and from without it, or, from the outward parts of it, even from a thousand cubits round about. Which are mentioned not as the thing measured, but as the space from which the measuring line should begin. And then it follows, Nu 35:5. And ye shall measure from without the city, (not from the wall of the city, as said before Nu 35:4, but from without it, that is, from the said outward space of a thousand cubits without the wall of the city round about) on the east side two thousand cubits. So in truth there were three thousand cubits from the wall of the city, whereof one thousand probably were for out-houses, stalls for cattle, gardens, vineyards and olive-yards, and the other two thousand for pasture, which are therefore called the field of the suburbs, Lev 25:34, by way of distinction from the suburbs themselves, which consist of the first thousand cubits from the wall of the city.

6. **Cities for refuge** – Or, of escape for manslayers: And these cities are assigned among the Levites, partly because they might be presumed to be the most proper and impartial judges between man-slayers, and wilful murderers; partly because their presence and authority would more effectually bridle the passions of the avenger of blood who might pursue him thither; and perhaps to signify, that it is only in Christ (whom the Levitical priests represented) that sinners find refuge and safety from the destroyer.

11. **Unawares** – Not wilfully, designedly or maliciously, but through mistake or indiscretion.

12. From the avenger – Heb. from the redeemer, or, from the next kinsman, to whom by the law belonged the right of redemption of the lands of; and vindication of the injury done to, the person deceased. **Die not** – Be not killed by the avenger meeting him in some other place. **Before the congregation** – Before the judges or elders who were appointed in every city for the decision of criminal causes, who were to examine, and that publically before the people, whether the murder was wilful or casual.

14. On this side Jordan – Because that land was as long as Canaan, though not so broad, and besides these might be convenient for many of them that lived in Canaan.

In what cases it was not allowed to flee to these (16–21)

16. If he smite him – Wittingly and wilfully, though not with premeditated malice. **He shall be put to death** – Yea though he were fled into the city of refuge.

19. He shall slay him – Either by himself, as the following words shew; so it is a permission, that he may do it without offence to God or danger to himself: or by the magistrate, from whom he shall demand justice: so it is a command.

In what cases it was allowed (22–24)

24. Then – If the man-slayer flee to the city of refuge.

Laws concerning them (25–34)

26. He shall abide in it – Be confined to it, partly to shew the hatefulness of murder in God's account by so severe a punishment, inflicted upon the very appearance of it, and partly for the security of the man-slayer, lest the presence of such a person, and his conversation among the kindred of the deceased, might occasion reproach and blood-shed. **The death of the high-priest** – Perhaps to shew that the death of

Christ (the true High-priest, whom the others represented) is the only means whereby sins are pardoned and sinners set at liberty.

27. Not guilty – Not liable to punishment from men, though not free of guilt before God. This God ordained to oblige the man-slayer to abide in his city of refuge.

Chapter 36

An inconvenience if heiresses should marry into another tribe (1–4)

2. Our brother – Our kinsman.

An appointment that they should marry in their own tribe (5–9)

6. To the family – They seem hereby to be confined not only to the same tribe, but also to the family of their tribe, as appears from the reason of the law, for God would have the inheritance of families as well as tribes kept entire and unmixed.

8. The inheritance of his fathers – This law was not general to forbid every woman to marry into another tribe, as may be reasonably concluded from the practice of so many patriarchs, kings, priests, and other holy men, who have married women of other tribes, yea sometimes of other nations, but restrained to heiresses, or such as were likely to be so. But if they had brethren, they were free to marry into any tribe, yet so that, if their brethren died, the inheritance went from them to the next a-kin of their father's tribe and family. And the principal reason why God was solicitous to preserve tribes and families unmixed was, that the tribe and family too, out of which the Messiah was to come, and by which he should be known, might be evident and unquestionable.

Zelophehad's daughters marry their cousins (10–13)

DEUTERONOMY

John Wesley

Introduction

The Greek interpreters call this book Deuteronomy, that is, The second law, or a second edition of the law, because it is a repetition of many of the laws, as well as much of the history contained in the three foregoing books. They to whom the first law was given were all dead, and a new generation sprung up, to whom God would have it repeated by Moses himself, that it might make the deeper impression upon them. It begins with a brief rehearsal of the most remarkable events, that had befallen them since they came from mount Sinai. In the fourth chapter begins a pathetic exhortation to obedience: From the 12th to the 27th are repeated many particular laws, enforced in the 27th and 28th with promises and threatenings, which are formed into a covenant, chap. 29,30. Care is taken in chap. 31 to perpetuate the remembrance of these things among them, particularly by a song, chap. 32 concluded with a blessing, chap. 33. All this was delivered by Moses to Israel, in the last month of his life. See how busy this great and good man was to do good, when he knew his time was short.

Chapter 1

The preface, fixing the time and place (1–5)

1. All Israel – Namely, by the heads or elders of the several tribes, who were to communicate these discourses to all the people. **In the wilderness** – In the plain of Moab, as may appear by comparing this with Deu 1:5, and Num 22:1, and Deu 34:8. The word *Suph* here used does not signify the Red-Sea, which is commonly called Jam-suph, and which was at too great a distance, but some other place now unknown to us, (as also most of the following places are) so called from the reeds or flags, or rushes (which that word signifies) that grew in or near it. **Paran** – Not that Num 10:12, which there and elsewhere is called the Wilderness of Paran, and which was too remote, but some other place called by the same name. **Laban, Hazeroth, and Dizahab** – These places seem to be the several bounds, not of the whole country of Moab, but of the plain of Moab, where Moses now was.

2. There are eleven days journey – This is added to shew that the reason why the Israelites, in so many years were advanced no farther from Horeb, than to these plains, was not the distance of the places but because of their rebellions. **Kadesh-barnea** – Which was not far from the borders of Canaan.

3. The eleventh month – Which was but a little before his death. **All that the Lord had given him in commandment** – Which shows not only that what he now delivered was in substance the same with what had formerly been commanded, but that God now commanded him to repeat it. He gave this rehearsal and exhortation by divine direction: God appointed him to leave this legacy to the church.

4. Og – His palace or mansion-house was at Astaroth, and he was slain at Edrei.

Israel commanded to march (6–8)

7. To the mount of the Amorites – That is, to the mountainous country where the Amorites dwelt, which is opposed to the plain, where others of them dwelt. And this is the first mentioned, because it was in the borders of the land.

8. Before you – Heb. Before your faces; it is open to your view, and to your possession; there is no impediment in the way.

Judges provided (9–18)

9. At that time – That is, about that time, namely, a little before their coming to Horeb.

12. Your burden – The trouble of ruling and managing so perverse a people. **Your strife** – Your contentions among yourselves, for the determination whereof the elders were appointed.

15. Officers – Inferior officers, that were to attend upon the superior magistrates, and to execute their decrees.

16. The stranger – That converseth or dealeth with him. To such God would have justice equally administered as to his own people, partly for the honour of religion, and partly for the interest which every man hath in matters of common right.

17. Respect persons – Heb. Not know, or acknowledge faces, that is, not give sentence according to the outward qualities of the person, as he is poor or rich, your friend or enemy, but purely according to the merit of the cause. For which reason some of the Grecian lawgivers ordered that the judges should give sentence in the dark where they could not see mens faces. **The judgment is God's** – It is passed in the name of God, and by commission from him, by you as representing his person, and doing his work; who therefore will defend you therein against all your enemies, and to whom you must give an exact account.

18. All the things which ye shall do – I delivered unto you, and especially unto your judges, all the laws, statutes, and judgments revealed unto me by the lord in Horeb.

They come to Kadesh-barnea and spies sent, their report, the people's murmuring (19–33)

24. Eshcol – That is, of grapes, so called from the goodly cluster of grapes which they brought from thence.

28. Greater – In number and strength and valour.

31. Bare thee – Or, carried thee, as a father carries his weak and tender child in his arms, through difficulties and dangers, gently leading you according as you are able to go, and sustaining you by his power and goodness.

32. Ye did not believe the Lord –. So they could not enter in, because of unbelief. It was not any other sin shut them out of Canaan, but their disbelief of that promise, which was typical of gospel grace: to signify that no sin will

ruin us but unbelief, which is a sin against the remedy; and therefore without remedy.

33. Your words – That is to say, your murmurings, your unthankful, impatient, distrustful and rebellious speeches.

The sentence passed upon them (34–40)

36. Save Caleb – Under whom Joshua is comprehended, though not here expressed, because he was not now to be one of the people, but to be set over them as a chief governor.

37. For your sakes – Upon occasion of your wickedness and perverseness, by which you provoked me to speak unadvisedly.

38. Who standeth – Who is now thy servant.

They are smitten by the Amorites, and remain at Kadesh (41–46)

44. As bees – As bees which being provoked come out of their hives in great numbers, and with great fury pursue their adversary and disturber.

Chapter 2

Their march from Kadesh-barnea (1–3)

1. Mount Seir – The mountainous country of Seir or Edom. **Many days** – Even for thirty eight years.

3. Northward – Towards the land of the Amorites and Canaanites.

A charge not to trouble the Edomites or the Moabites (4–12)

6. Buy meat – For though the manna did yet rain upon them, they were not forbidden to buy other meats when they had opportunity, but only were forbidden greedily to hunger after them when they could not obtain them. **Buy water** – For water in those parts was scarce, and therefore private persons did severally dig pits for their particular use.

7. The Lord hath blessed thee – By God's blessing thou art able to buy thy conveniences, and therefore thy theft and rapine will be inexcusable, because without any pretence of necessity.

9. Ar – The chief city of the Moabites, here put for the whole country which depended upon it. **The children of Lot** – So called to signify that this preservation, was not for their sakes, for they were a wicked people, but for Lot's sake whose memory God yet honours.

10. The Emims – Men terrible for stature and strength, as their very name imparts, whose expulsion by the Moabites is here noted as a great encouragement to the Israelites, for whose sake he would much more drive out the wicked and accursed Canaanites.

12. Which the Lord gave – The past tense is here put for the future, will give after the manner of the prophets.

They pass the river Zered; a charge not to trouble the Ammonites (13–23)

23. The Caphtorim – A people a-kin to the Philistines, Gen 10:14, and confederate with them in this enterprise, and so dwelling together, and by degrees uniting together by marriages, they became one people. **Caphtor** – Which is by the learned thought to be Cappadocia: whither these people might make an expedition out of Egypt, either because of the report of the great riches of part of that country which drew others thither from places equally remote, or for some other reason now unknown.

A command to attack Sihon (24–26)

25. Under heaven – The following words restrain the sentence to those nations that heard of them.

The conquest of his kingdom (27–37)

28. On my feet – Or, with my company who are on foot: which is added significantly, because if their army had consisted as much of horsemen as many other armies did, their passage through his land might have been more mischievous and dangerous.

29. As the children of Esau did – They did permit them to pass quietly by the borders, though not through the heart of their land, and in their passage the people sold them meat and drink, being it seems more kind to them than their king would have had them; and therefore they here ascribe this favour not to the king, though they are now treating with a king, but to the people, the children of Esau.

30. Hardened his spirit – That is, suffered it to be hardened.

34. Utterly destroyed – By God's command, these being a part of those people who were devoted by the Lord of life and death, to utter destruction for their abominable wickedness.

37. Of Jabbok – That is, beyond Jabbok: for that was the border of the Ammonites.

Chapter 3

The conquest of Og and his country (1–11)

8. On this side Jordan – So it was when Moses wrote this book; but afterward when Israel passed over Jordan it was called the land beyond Jordan.

9. Sirion – Elsewhere called Mount Gilead, and Lebanon, and here Shenir, and Sirion, which several names are given to this one mountain partly by several people, and partly in regard of several tops and parts of it.

10. All Gilead – Gilead is sometimes taken for all the Israelites possessions beyond Jordan, and so it comprehends Bashan; but here for that part of it which lies in and near mount Gilead, and so it is distinguished from Bashan and Argob.

11. In Rabbath – Where it might now be, either because the Ammonites in some former battle with Og, had taken it as a spoil: or because after Og's death, the Ammonites desired to have this monument of his greatness, and the Israelites permitted them to carry it away to their chief city. **Nine cubits** – So his bed was four yards and an half long, and two yards broad.

The distribution of it to the two tribes and an half (12–17)

14. Unto this day – This must be put among those passages which were not written by Moses, but added by those holy men, who digested the books of Moses into this order, and inserted some few passages to accommodate things to their own time and people.

15. Gilead – That is, the half part of Gilead. **To Machir** – That is, unto the children of Machir, son of Manasseh, for Machir was now dead.

16. Half the valley – Or rather to the middle of the river: for the word rendered half signifies commonly middle, and the same Hebrew word means both a valley and a brook or river. And this sense is agreeable to the truth, that their land extended from Gilead unto Arnon, and, to speak exactly, to the middle of that river; for as that river was the border between them and others, so one half of it belonged to them, as the other half did to others, Jos 12:2. The same thing is expressed in the same words in the Hebrew which are here, though our translators render the self-same words there, from the middle of the river, which here they render, half of the valley. There the bounds of Sihon's kingdom, which was the same portion here mentioned as given to Reuben and Gad, are thus described, from Aroer, which is upon the bank of the river of Arnon, and from the middle of the river, and from half Gilead, even unto the river Jabbok, which is the border of the children of Ammon.

17. The plain – The low country towards Jordan. **The sea of the plain** – That is, that salt sea, which before that dreadful conflagration was a goodly plain.

On condition of assisting their brethren (18–22)

18. You – Namely, the Reubenites and Gadites. **All that are meet** – In such number as your our brethren shall judge necessary. They were in all above an hundred thousand. Forty thousand of them went over Jordan before their brethren.

Moses prays that he may go into Canaan (23–25)

23. I besought the Lord – We should allow no desire in our hearts, which we cannot in faith offer unto God by prayer.

24. Thou hast begun to shew thy servant thy greatness – Lord, perfect what thou hast begun. The more we see of God's glory in his works, the more we desire to see. And the more we are affected with what we have seen of God, the better we are prepared for farther discoveries.

25. Let me go over – For he supposed God's threatening might be conditional and reversible, as many others were. **That goodly mountain** – Which the Jews not improbably understood of that mountain on which the temple was to be built. This he seems to call that mountain, emphatically and eminently, that which was much in Moses's thoughts, though not in his eye.

But is refused, yet permitted to see it (26–29)

28. He shall go over – It was not Moses, but Joshua or Jesus that was to give the people rest, Heb 4:8. 'Tis a comfort to those who love mankind, when they are dying and going off, to see God's work likely to be carried on by other hands, when they are silent in the dust.

Chapter 4

An exhortation to obedience (1–13)

1. The statutes – The laws which concern the worship and service of God. **The judgments** – The laws concerning your duties to men. So these two comprehend both tables, and the whole law of God.

6. In the sight of the nations – For though the generality of Heathens in the latter ages, did through inveterate prejudices condemn the laws of the Hebrews, yet it is certain, the wisest Heathens did highly approve of them, so that they made use of divers of them, and translated them into their own laws and constitutions; and Moses, the giver of these laws, hath been mentioned with great honour for his wisdom and learning by many of them. And particularly the old Heathen oracle expressly said, that the Chaldeans or Hebrews, who worshipped the uncreated God, were the only wise men.

7. So nigh – By glorious miracles, by the pledges of his special presence, by the operations of his grace, and particularly by his readiness to hear our prayers, and to give us those succours which we call upon him for.

8. So righteous – Whereby he implies that the true greatness of a nation doth not consist in pomp or power, or largeness of empire, as commonly men think, but in the righteousness of its laws.

10. Thou stoodest – Some of them stood there in their own persons, though then they were but young, the rest in the loins of their parents.

11. The midst of heaven – Flaming up into the air, which is often called heaven.

12. No similitude – No resemblance or representation of God, whereby either his essence, or properties, or actions were represented, such as were usual among the Heathens.

A warning against idolatry (14–28)

14. Statutes and judgments – The ceremonial and judicial laws which are here distinguished from the moral, or the ten commandments.

15. In Horeb – God, who in other places and times did appear in a similitude in the fashion of a man, now in this most solemn appearance, when he comes to give eternal laws for the direction of the Israelites in the worship of God, and in their duty to men, purposely avoids all such representations, to shew that he abhors all worship of images, or of himself by images of what kind soever, because he is the invisible God, and cannot be represented by any visible image.

16. Lest ye corrupt yourselves – Your ways, by worshipping God in a corrupt manner.

19. Driven – Strongly inclined. **Which the Lord hath divided unto all nations** – Which are not Gods, but creatures, made not for the worship, but for the use of men; yea, of the meanest and most barbarous people under heaven, and therefore cannot without great absurdity be worshipped, especially by you who are so much advanced above other nations in wisdom and knowledge, and in this, that you are my peculiar people.

24. A consuming fire – A just and terrible God, who, notwithstanding his special relation to thee, will severely punish thee, if thou provoke him. **A jealous God** – Who being espoused to thee, will be highly incensed against thee, (if thou follow after other lovers, or commit whoredom with idols) and will bear no rival or partner.

28. Ye shall serve gods – You shall be compelled by men, and given up by me to idolatry. So that very thing which was your choice, shall be your punishment: it being just and usual for God to punish one sin by giving men up to another.

A promise upon repentance (29–40)

29. If from thence thou seek the Lord – Whatever place we are in, we may from thence seek him. There is no part of the earth which has a gulf fixt between it and heaven.

30. In the latter days – In succeeding ages.

32. The one side of heaven – That is, of the earth under heaven. Ask all the inhabitants of the world.

33. And live – And was not overwhelmed and consumed by such a glorious appearance.

34. By temptations – Temptations is the general title, which is explained by the following particulars, signs, and wonders which are called temptations, because they were trials both to the Egyptians and Israelites, whether they would be induced to believe and obey God or no. **By terrors** – Raised in the minds of the Egyptians, or, by terrible things done among them.

37. In his sight – Keeping his eye fixed upon him, as the father doth on his beloved child.

Cities of refuge appointed; and the place where Moses repeated the law (41–49)

44. This is the law – More punctually expressed in the following chapter, to which these words are a preface.

Chapter 5

The general intent of the Ten Commandments as a covenant between God and Israel (1–5)

1. All Israel – Namely by their elders, who were to impart it to the rest.

3. Not with our fathers – Only: but with us, **who are all alive** – He saith not, that all who made the covenant at Sinai are now alive, but this covenant was made with all that are now alive; which is most true, for it was made with the elders in their persons, and with the rest in their parents, who covenanted for them.

4. Face to face – Personally and immediately, not by the mouth or ministry of Moses; plainly and certainly, as when two men talk face to face; freely and familiarly, so as not to overwhelm and confound you.

5. Between the Lord and you – As a mediator between you, according to your desire. **The word of the Lord** – Not the ten commandments, which God himself uttered, but the following statutes and judgments.

The Commandments (6–21)

7. There being little said, concerning the spiritual sense of the Ten Commandments, in the notes on the twentieth of Exodus, I think it needful to add a few questions here, which the reader may answer between God and his own soul. Thou shalt have none other gods before me – Hast thou worshipped God in spirit and in truth? Hast thou proposed to thyself no end besides him? Hath he been the end of all thy actions? Hast thou sought for any other happiness, than the knowledge and love of God? Dost thou experimentally know the only true God, and Jesus Christ whom he hath sent? Dost thou love God? Dost thou love him with all thy heart, with all thy soul, and with all thy strength; so as to love nothing else but in that manner and degree which tends to increase thy love of him? Hast thou found happiness in God? Is he the desire of thine eyes, the joy of thy heart? If not, thou hast other gods before him.

8. Thou shalt not make any graven image – Hast thou not formed any gross image of God in thy mind? Hast thou always thought of him as a pure spirit, whom no man hath seen, nor can see? And hast thou worshipped him with thy body, as well as with thy spirit, seeing both of them are God's?

11. Thou shalt not take the name of the Lord thy God in vain – Hast thou never used the name of God, unless on solemn and weighty occasions? Hast thou then used it with the deepest awe? Hast thou duly honoured his word, his ordinances, his ministers? Hast thou considered all things as they stand in relation to him, and seen God in all? Hast thou looked upon heaven as God's throne? Upon earth as God's footstool? On every thing therein as belonging to the great king? On every creature as full of God?

12. Keep the sabbath-day, to sanctify it – Dost thou do no work on this day, which can be done as well on another? Art thou peculiarly careful on this day, to avoid all conversation, which does not tend to the knowledge and love of God? Dost thou watch narrowly over all that are within thy gates, that they too may keep it holy? And dost thou try every possible means, to bring all men, wherever you are, to do the same?

16. Honour thy father and mother – Hast thou not been irreverent or undutiful to either? Hast thou not slighted their advice? Hast thou cheerfully obeyed all their lawful commands? Hast thou loved and honoured their persons? Supplied their wants, and concealed their infirmities? Hast thou wrestled for them with God in prayer? Hast thou loved and honoured thy prince, and avoided as fire all speaking evil of the ruler of thy people? Have ye that are servants done all things as unto Christ? Not with eye-service, but in singleness of heart? Have ye who are masters, behaved as parents to your servants, with all gentleness and affection? Have ye all obeyed them that watch over your souls, and esteemed them highly in love for their work's sake?

17. Thou shalt not kill – Have you not tempted any one, to what might shorten his life? Have you tempted none to intemperance? Have you suffered none to be intemperate under your roof, or in your company? Have you done all you could in every place, to prevent intemperance of all kinds? Are you guilty of no degree of self-murder? Do you never eat or drink any thing because you like it, although you have reason to believe, it is prejudicial to your health? Have you constantly done whatever you had reason to believe was conducive to it? Have you not hated your neighbour in your heart? Have you reproved him that committed sin in your sight? If not, you have in God's account hated him, seeing you suffered sin upon him. Have you loved all men as your own soul? As Christ loved us? Have you done unto all men, as in like circumstances, you would they should do to you? Have you done all in your power to help your neighbours, enemies as well as friends? Have you laboured to deliver every soul you could from sin and misery? Have you showed that you loved all men as yourself, by a constant, earnest endeavour, to fill all places with holiness and happiness, with the knowledge and love of God?

18. Neither shalt thou commit adultery – If thou hast not been guilty of any act of uncleanness, hath thy heart conceived no unclean thought? Hast thou not looked on a woman so as to lust after her? Hast thou not betrayed thy own soul to temptation, by eating and drinking to the full, by needless familiarities, by foolish talking, by levity of dress or behaviour? Hast thou used all the means which scripture and reason suggest, to prevent every kind and degree of unchastity? Hast thou laboured, by watching, fasting, and prayer, to possess thy vessel in sanctification and honour?

19. Neither shalt thou steal – Have you seriously considered, that these houses, lands, money, or goods, which you are used to call your own, are not your own, but belong to another, even God? Have you ever considered, that God is the sole proprietor of heaven and earth? The true owner of every thing therein? Have you considered, that he has only lent them to you? That you are but a steward of your Lord's goods? And that he has told you expressly the uses and purposes for which he intrusts you with them? Namely, for the furnishing first yourselves, and then as many others as you can, with the things needful for life and godliness? Have you considered, that you have no right at all, to apply any part of them to any other purpose? And that if you do, you are as much a robber of God, as any can be a robber of you?

20. Neither shalt thou bear false witness against thy neighbour – Have you not been guilty of evil-speaking? Of needlessly repeating the real fault of your neighbour? If I see a man do an evil thing, and tell it to another, unless from a full and clear conviction, that it is necessary to mention it just then, for the glory of God, the safety or good of some other person, or for the benefit of him that hath done amiss; and unless I then do it only so far, as is necessary to these ends, that is evil-speaking. O beware of this! It is scattering abroad arrows, fire-brands, and death.

21. Neither shalt thou covet any thing that is thy neighbour's – The plain meaning of this is, thou shalt not desire any thing that is not thy own, any thing which thou hast not. Indeed why shouldst thou? God hath given thee whatever tends to thy one end, holiness. Thou canst not deny it, without making him a liar: and: when any thing else will tend thereto, he will give thee that also. There is therefore no room to desire any thing which thou hast not. Thou hast already every thing that is really good for thee, wouldst thou have more money, more pleasure, more praise still? Why this is not good for thee. God has told thee so, by withholding it from thee. O give thyself up to his wise and gracious disposal!

God writes them, and grants the people's request, that he would speak by Moses (22–28)

22. Out of the midst of the fire, of the cloud, and of the thick darkness – That was a dispensation of terror, designed to make the gospel of grace the more welcome, and to be a specimen of the terrors of the judgment-day. **He added no more** – He ceased for that time to speak immediately, and with that loud voice unto the people; for the rest were delivered to Moses, and by him communicated unto them. This he did to shew the preeminence of that law above the rest, and its everlasting obligation.

25. Why should we die? – For though God hath for this season kept us alive, yet we shall never be able to endure any farther discourse from him in such a terrible manner, but shall certainly sink under the burden of it.

26. Flesh – Is here put for man in his frail, corruptible, and mortal state.

Exhortations to obedience (29–33)

29. O that there were such an heart in them! – A heart to fear God, and keep his commandments forever! The God of heaven is truly and earnestly desirous of the salvation of poor sinners. He has given abundant proof that he is so: he gives us time and space to repent; by his mercies invites us to repentance, and waiteth to be gracious: has sent his son to redeem us, published a general offer of pardon, promised his spirit to those that pray for him; and has said, yea and sworn, that he hath no pleasure in the death of a sinner!

Chapter 6

A call to obedience, and the first truth, God is One, the first duty, to love him (1–5)

5. And thou shalt love the Lord thy God with all thine heart – And is this only an external commandment? Can any then say, that the Sinai-covenant was merely external? **With all thy heart** – With an entire love. He is One; therefore our hearts must be united in his love.

And the whole stream of our affections must run toward Him. O that this love of God may be shed abroad in our hearts.

The means hereto (6–9)

7. Teach them diligently – Heb. whet, or sharpen them, so as they may pierce deep into their hearts. This metaphor signifies the manner of instructing them, that it is to be done diligently, earnestly, frequently, discreetly.

8. Thou shalt bind them – Thou shalt give all diligence, and use all means to keep them in thy remembrance, as men often bind something upon their hands, or put it before their eyes to prevent forgetfulness of a thing which they much desire to remember.

A caution not to forget God in prosperity (10–13)

13. Shalt swear by his name – When thou hast a call and just cause to swear, not by idols, or any creatures.

Not to worship idols, or tempt God (14–16)

15. Among you – Heb. In the midst of you, to see and observe all your ways and your turnings aside to other Gods.

16. Ye shall not tempt – Not provoke him, as the following instance explains. Sinners, especially presumptuous sinners, are said to tempt God, that is, to make a trial of God, whether he be, so wise as to see their sins, so just and true and powerful as to take vengeance on them, concerning which they are very apt to doubt because of the present impunity and prosperity of many such persons.

Exhortation to obedience and to teach their children (17–25)

17. Ye diligently keep – Negligence will ruin us: but we cannot be saved without diligence.

25. It shall be our righteousness – Heb. Righteousness shall be to us. We shall be owned and pronounced by God to be righteous and holy persons, if we sincerely obey him, otherwise we shall be declared to be unrighteous and ungodly. Or, mercy shall be to us, or with us. For as the Hebrew word rendered righteousness is very often put for mercy, (as Psa 24:5 36:10 51:14 Pro 10:2 11:4 Dan 9:16) so this sense seems best to agree both with the scripture use of this phrase, (in which righteousness, seldom or never, but grace or mercy frequently, is said to be to us or with us) and with the foregoing verse and argument God, saith he, Deu 5:24, commanded these things for our good, that he might preserve us alive, as it is this day. And, saith he in this verse, this is not all; for as he hath done us good, so he will go on to do us more and

more good, and God's mercy shall be to us, or with us, in the remainder of our lives, and for ever, if we observe these commandments.

Chapter 7

A command to destroy the Canaanites, with all pertaining to their idols (1–5)

1. Seven nations – There were ten in Gen 15:19-21. But this being some hundreds of years after, it is not strange if three of them were either destroyed by foreign or domestick wars, or by cohabitation and marriage united with, and swallowed up in the rest.

4. To serve other gods – That is, there is manifest danger of apostasy and idolatry from such matches. Which reason doth both limit the law to such of these as are unconverted (otherwise Salmon married Rahab, Matt 1:5) and enlarge it to other idolatrous nations, as appears from 1Kin 11:2 Ezra 9:2 Neh 13:23.

5. Their graves – Which idolaters planted about the temples and altars of their Gods. Hereby God designed to take away whatsoever might bring their idolatry to remembrance, or occasion the reviving of it.

And to obey God, considering their relation to him (6–11)

7. The fewest – To wit, at that time when God first declared his choice of you for his peculiar people, which was done to Abraham. For Abraham had but one son concerned in this choice and covenant, namely, Isaac, and that was in his hundredth year; and Isaac was sixty years old ere he had a child, and then had only two children; and though Jacob had twelve sons, it was a long time before they made any considerable increase. Nor do we read of any great multiplication of them 'till after Joseph's death.

8. The Lord loved you – It was his free choice without any cause or motive on your part.

10. Them that hate him – Not only those who hate him directly and properly, (for so did few or none of the Israelites to whom he here speaks,) but those who hate him by construction and consequence; those who hate and oppose his people, and word, those who wilfully persist in the breach of God's commandments. **To their face** – That is, openly, and so as they shall see it, and not be able to avoid it. **Slack** – So as to delay it beyond the fit time or season for vengeance, yet withal he is long-suffering, and slow to anger.

Promises to the obedient (12–15)

12. The covenant and the mercy – That is, the covenant of mercy, which he out of his own mere grace made with them.

13. He will love thee – He will continue to love thee, and to manifest his love to thee.

15. The diseases of Egypt – Such as the Egyptians were infected with, either commonly, or miraculously. It seems to refer not only to the plagues of Egypt, but to some other epidemic disease, which they remembered to have prevailed among the Egyptians, and by which God had chastised them for their national sins. Diseases are God's servants, which go where he sends them, and do what he bids them.

A repetition of the command, utterly to destroy the Canaanites, with all the monuments of their idolatry (16–26)

19. The temptations – The trials and exercises of thy faith and obedience to my commands.

24. No man shall stand – This promise is made upon condition of their performance of their duty, which they neglecting, justly lose the benefit of it.

25. The silver or gold – Wherewith the idols are covered or adorned, nor consequently any other of their ornaments. This he commands to shew his utter detestation of idolatry, and to cut off all occasions of it.

Chapter 8

An exhortation to obedience, in consideration of past and promised mercies (1–9)

1. Live – Live comfortably and happily.

2. All the way – All the events which befell thee in the way, the miraculous protections, deliverances, provisions, instructions which God gave thee; and withal the frequent and severe punishments of thy disobedience. **To know** – That thou mightest discover to thyself and others that infidelity, inconstancy, hypocrisy, and perverseness, which lay hid in thy heart; the discovery whereof was of singular use both to them, and to the church of God in all succeeding ages. It is good for us likewise to remember all the ways both of God's providence and grace, by which he has led us hitherto through the wilderness, that we may trust him, and cheerfully serve him.

3. By every word – That is, by every or any thing which God appoints for this end, how unlikely so-ever it may seem to be for nourishment; seeing it is not the creature, but only God's command and blessing upon it, that makes it sufficient for the support of life.

5. As a man chastiseth his son – That is, unwillingly, being constrained by necessity; moderately, in judgment remembering mercy; and for thy reformation not thy destruction.

7. Depths – Deep wells or springs, or lakes, which were numerous and large.

9. Whose stones are iron – Where are mines of iron in a manner as plentiful as stones, and upon which travellers must tread, as in other parts they do upon stones.

10. Bless the Lord – Solemnly praise him for thy food; which is a debt both of gratitude and justice, because it is from his providence and favour that thou receivest both thy food and refreshment and strength by it. The more unworthy and absurd is that too common profaneness of them, who, professing to believe a God, from whom all their comforts come, grudge to own him at their meals, either by desiring his blessing before them, or by offering due praise to God after them.

14. Lifted up – As if thou didst receive and enjoy these things, either, by thy own wisdom, and valour, and industry, or for thy own merit.

16. That he might humble thee – By keeping thee in a constant dependence upon him for every day's food, and convincing thee what an impotent, helpless creature thou art, having nothing whereon to subsist, and being supported wholly by the alms of divine goodness from day to day. The mercies of God, if duly considered, are as powerful a mean to humble us as the greatest afflictions, because they increase our debts to God, and manifest our dependance upon him, and by making God great, they make us little in our own eyes. **To do thee good** – That is, that after he hath purged and prepared thee by afflictions, thou mayest receive and enjoy his blessings with less disadvantage, whilst by the remembrance of former afflictions. thou art made thankful for them, and more cautious not to abuse them.

Chapter 9

A promise of Canaan (1–3)

1. Hear, O Israel – This seems to be a new discourse, delivered at some distance of time from the former, probably on the next Sabbathday. **This day** – That is, shortly, within a little time, the word day being often put for time. **Nations** – That is, the land of those nations. **Mightier than thyself** – This he adds, that they might not trust to their own strength, but rely upon God's help for the destroying them, and, after the work was done, might ascribe the glory of it to God alone, and not to themselves.

2. Who can stand – This seems to be a proverb used in those times.

A caution, not to ascribe this to their own merit (4–6)

5. Not for thy righteousness – Neither for thy upright heart, nor holy life, which are the two things which God above all things regards. And consequently he excludes all merit. And surely they who did not deserve this earthly Canaan, could not merit the kingdom of glory. **To perform the word** – To shew my faithfulness in accomplishing that promise which I graciously made and confirmed with my oath.

6. Stiff-necked – Rebellious and perverse, and so destitute of all pretence of righteousness. And thus our gaining possession of the heavenly Canaan, must be ascribed to God's power, not our own might, and to God's Grace, not our own merit. In him we must glory.

A rehearsal of their various rebellions (7–24)

8. In Horeb – When your miraculous deliverance out of Egypt was fresh in memory; when God had but newly manifested himself to you in so stupendous and dreadful a manner, and had taken you into covenant with himself, when God was actually conferring farther mercies upon you.

10. With the finger of God – Immediately and miraculously, which was done not only to procure the greater reverence to the law, but also to signify, that it is the work of God alone to write this law upon the tables of men's hearts. **In the day of the assembly** – That is, when the people were gathered by God's command to the bottom of mount Sinai, to hear and receive God's ten commandments from his own mouth.

14. Let me alone! – Stop me not by thy intercession.

17. I brake them before your eyes – Not by an unbridled passion, but in zeal for God's honour, and by the direction of God's spirit, to signify to the people, that the covenant between God and them contained in those tables was broken and they were now cast out of God's favour, and could expect nothing from him but fiery indignation.

18. I fell down – In a way of humiliation and supplication, on your behalf.

21. Into the brook – That there might be no monument or remembrance of it left.

Moses's intercession for them (25–29)

25. I fell down forty days – The same as were mentioned before, Deu 9:18, as appears by comparing this with Exodus, where this history is more fully related, and where this is said to be done twice only.

26. Through thy greatness – Through the greatness of thy power, which appeared most eminently in that work.

27. Thy servants – That is, the promise made and sworn to thy servants.

29. Thy people – Whom thou hast chosen to thyself out of all mankind, and publically owned them for thine, and hast purchased and redeemed them from the Egyptians.

Chapter 10

God's mercy, in renewing the two tables (1–5)

2. I will write on the tables – Tho' the tables were broken, because they broke his commandment, they were now renewed, in proof that his wrath was turned away. And thus God's writing his law in our inward parts, is the surest proof of our reconciliation to him.

In leading Israel forward, and choosing the tribe of Levi for his own (6–9)

6. This following history comes in manifestly by way of parenthesis, as may appear from Deu 10:10, where he returns to his former discourse; and it seems to be here inserted as an evidence of God's gracious answer to Moses's prayers, and of his reconciliation to the people, notwithstanding their late and great provocation. For, saith he, after this they proceeded by God's guidance in their journeys, and though Aaron died in one of them, yet God made up that breach, and Eleazar came in his place, and ministered as priest, one branch of which office was to intercede for the people.

8. At that time – About that time, that is, when I was come down from the mount, as was said, Deu 10:5. **To stand before the Lord** – A phrase used concerning the prophets, 1Kings 17:1 18:15, this being the posture of ministers. Hence the angels are said to stand, 2Chr 18:18 Luke 1:19. **To bless** – The people, by performance of those holy ministrations for the people, and giving those instructions to them, to which God's blessing was promised; and this they did in God's name, that is, by command, and commission from him.

9. The Lord is his inheritance – That is, the Lord's portion, namely, tithes and offerings, which belong to God, are given by him to the Levites for their subsistence, from generation to generation.

In accepting the intercession as Moses (10–11)

11. Take thy journey before the people – 'Twas fit that he who had saved them from ruin by his intercession, should have the conduct and command of them. And herein he was a type of Christ, who, as he ever lives to make intercession for us, so has all power in heaven and in earth.

An exhortation to fear, love, and serve God (12–22)

12. What doth he require – By way of duty and gratitude for such amazing mercies.

14. The heaven – The airy and starry heaven. **The heaven of heavens** – The highest or third heaven, called the heaven of heavens for its eminency. **All that therein is** – With all creatures and all men, which being all his, he might have chosen what nation he pleased to be his people.

15. To love them – He shews that God had no particular obligation to their fathers, any more than to other persons or people, all being equally his creatures, and that his choice of them out of and above all others, proceeded only from God's good pleasure.

16. Circumcise – Rest not in your bodily circumcision, but seriously set upon that substantial work which is signified thereby: cleanse your hearts from all filthiness and superfluity of naughtiness, fitly compared to the foreskin, which if not cut off, made persons profane, unclean and odious in the sight of God.

17. Regardeth not persons – Whether Jews or Gentiles, but deals justly and equally with all sorts of men; and as whosoever fears and obeys him shall be accepted, so all incorrigible transgressors shall be severely punished, and you no less than other people: therefore do not flatter yourselves as if God would bear with your sins because of his particular kindness to you or to your fathers.

18. He doth execute – That is, plead their cause, and give them right against their potent adversaries, and therefore he expects you should do so too.

20. To him shalt thou cleave – With firm confidence, true affection, and constant obedience.

21. Thy praise – The object and matter of thy praise, as Exo 15:2, whom thou shouldest ever praise.

Chapter 11

Moses exhorts them to obedience by rehearsing God's works (1–7)

2. Know – That is, acknowledge and consider it with diligence and thankfulness.

4. Unto this day – The effect of which destruction continueth to this day, in their weakness and fear, and our safety from their farther attempts against us.

7. Your eyes have seen – All of them had seen some, and some of them had seen all the great things done in Egypt and at the Red-sea, and in the Wilderness. What our eyes have seen, especially in our early days, should be improved by us long after.

By describing the goodness of the land (8–12)

10. With thy foot – That is, with great pains and labour of thy feet, partly by going up and down to fetch water and disperse it, and partly by digging furrows with thy foot, and using engines for distributing the water, which engines

they thrust with their feet. For tho' the river Nile did once in a year overflow the grounds, and made them fruitful, yet often it failed them, at least in part, and then they were put to great pains about their ground. And when it did overflow sufficiently, and left its mud upon the earth, yet that mud was in a little time hardened, and needed another watering, and much digging and labour both of the hand and feet, especially in places more remote from that river; which inconvenience Canaan was free from.

11. Of hills and valleys – And therefore much more healthful than Egypt was, which as it was enriched, so it was annoyed with the Nile, which overflowed the land in summer time, and thereby made the country both unpleasant and unhealthful. And health being the greatest of all outward blessings, Canaan must therefore needs be a more desirable habitation than Egypt. **The rain of heaven** – Which is more easy, being given thee without thy charge or pains; more sweet and pleasant, not hindering thy going abroad upon thy occasions, as the overflow of the Nile did, whereby the Egyptians were confined in a great measure to their houses; more safe and healthful, being free from that mud which attends upon the waters of the Nile; and more certain too, the former and the latter rain being promised to be given to them in their several seasons, upon condition of their obedience, which condition, tho' it may seem a clog and inconvenience, yet indeed was a great benefit, that by their own necessities and interest they might be obliged to that obedience, upon which their happiness depended both for this life and the next.

12. Careth for – In a special manner watering it immediately as it were by his own hand, without man's help, and giving peculiar blessings to it, which Egypt enjoys not. **To the end of the year** – To give it the rain, and other blessings proper to the several seasons. But all these mercies, and the fruitfulness of the land consequent upon them, were suspended upon their disobedience. And therefore it is not at all strange that some later writers, describe the land of Canaan as a barren soil, which is, so far from affording ground to question the authority of the scriptures, that it doth much more confirm it, this, being an effect of that threatening that God would turn a fruitful land into barrenness for the wickedness of these that dwell in it, Psa 107:34.

By promises and threats (13–17)

14. The ruin of your land – Which is, proper to your land, not common to Egypt, where, as all authors agree, there is little rain. The first rain fell in seed time, to make the corn spring, the other a little before harvest, to ripen it.

15. I will send grass in thy fields – So godliness has here the promise of the life which now is. But the favour of God puts gladness into the heart, more than the increase of corn, wine and oil.

17. Shut up the heaven – Which is compared sometimes to a great store-house wherein God lays up his treasures of rain, Job 38:22, the doors whereof God is said to open when he gives rain, and to shut when he withholds it.

An exhortation to teach their children, closed with a promise (18–25)

21. As the days of heaven – As long as the heaven keeps its place and continues its influences upon earth.

24. Every place – Not absolutely, as the Rabbins fondly conceit, but in the promised land, as it is restrained in the following words; either by possession, or by dominion, namely, upon condition of your obedience. **The wilderness** – Of Sin, on the south-side. **To Lebanon** – Which was on the north border. **Euphrates** – On the east. So far the right of dominion extended, but that their sins cut them short: and so far Solomon extended his dominion. **The uttermost sea** – The western or midland sea.

A blessing and a curse (26–32)

26. I set before you – I propose them to your choice.

28. Which ye have not known – Which you have no acquaintance with, nor experience of their power, or wisdom, or goodness, as you have had of mine.

29. Put – Heb. Thou shalt give, that is, speak or pronounce, or cause to be pronounced. So the word to give is used, Deu 13:1,2 Job 36:3 Pro 9:9. This is, more particularly expressed, Deu 27:12,13.

30. Over against – Looking toward Gilgal, tho' at some considerable distance from it. **Beside the plains of Moreh** – This was one of the first places that Abram came to in Canaan. So that in sending them thither to hear the blessing and the curse, they were minded of the promise made to Abram in that very place, Gen 12:6,7.

Chapter 12

A command, to destroy all relics of idolatry (1–3)

2. All the places – Temples, chapels, altars, groves, as appears from other scriptures. **Green-tree** – As the Gentiles consecrated divers trees to their false gods, so they worshipped these under them.

3. Pillars – Upon which their images were set. **Names** – That is, all the memorials of them, and the very names given to the places from the idols.

To worship God in his own place, and according to his own appointment (4–14)

4. Not do so – That is, not worship him in several places, mountains, and groves.

5. To put his name there – That is, to set up his worship there, and which he shall call by his name, as his house, or his dwelling-place; namely, where the ark should be, the tabernacle, or temple: which was first Shiloh, and then Jerusalem. There is not one precept in all the law of Moses, so largely inculcated as this, to bring all their sacrifices to that one altar. And how significant is that appointment? They must keep to one place, in token of their belief. That there is one God, and one Mediator between God and man. It not only served to keep up the notion of the unity of the godhead, but the one only way of approach to God and communion with him in and by his son.

6. Thither bring your burnt-offerings – Which were wisely appropriated to that one place, for the security of the true religion, and for the prevention of idolatry and superstition, which might otherwise more easily have crept in: and to signify that their sacrifices were not accepted for their own worth, but by God's gracious appointment, and for the sake of God's altar, by which they were sanctified, and for the sake of Christ, whom the altar manifestly represented. **Your heave-offerings** – That is, your first-fruits, of corn, and wine, and oil, and other fruits. And these are called the heave-offerings of their hand, because the offerer was first to take these into his hands, and to heave them before the Lord, and then to give them to the priest. **Your free-will-offerings** – Even your voluntary oblations, which were not due by my prescription, but only by your own choice: you may choose what kind of offering you please to offer, but not the place where you shall offer them.

7. There – Not in the most holy place, wherein only the priests might eat, but in places allowed to the people for this, and in the holy city. **Ye shall eat** – Your part of the things mentioned, Deu 12:6. **Before the Lord** – In the place of God's presence, where God's sanctuary shall be.

8. Here – Where the inconveniency of the place, and the uncertainty of our abode, would not permit exact order in sacrifices and feasts and ceremonies, which therefore God was then pleased to dispense with; but, saith he, he will not do so there. **Right in his own eyes** – Not that universal liberty was given to all persons to worship how they listed; but in many things their unsettled condition gave opportunity to do so.

11. His name – His majesty and glory, his worship and service, his special and gracious presence. **Your choice vows** – Heb. the choice of your vows, that is, your select or chosen vows; so called, because things offered for vows, were to be perfect, whereas defective creatures were accepted in free-will-offerings.

12. Your daughters – Hence it appears, that though the males only were obliged to appear before God in their solemn feasts, yet the women also were permitted to come.

13. Thy burnt-offerings – Nor the other things mentioned above, this one and most eminent kind being put for all the rest.

A permission to eat flesh, but not blood; and directions to eat the tithe in the holy place, and to take care of the Levite (15–19)

17. Within thy gates – That is, in your private habitations, here opposed to the place of God's worship.

A farther permission to eat flesh, but not blood (20–25)

20. Enlarge thy border – Which will make it impossible to bring all the cattle thou usest to the tabernacle.

21. If the place be too far – Being obliged to carry their sacrifices to the place of worship, they might think themselves obliged to carry their other cattle thither to be killed. They are therefore released from all such obligations, and left at liberty to kill them at home, whether they lived nearer that place, or farther from it; only the latter is here mentioned, as being the matter of the scruple. **As I have commanded** – In such a manner as the blood may be poured forth.

22. As the roe-buck – As common or unhallowed food, tho' they be of the same kind with the sacrifices which are offered to God. **The unclean** – Because there was, no holiness in such meat for which the unclean might be excluded from it.

A direction to eat holy things in the holy place (26–28)

27. The flesh – Excepting what shall be burned to God's honour, and given to the priest according to his appointment.

Farther cautions against idolatry (29–32)

30. By following them – By following the example they left, when their persons are destroyed.

Chapter 13

Enticers to idolatry to be stoned (1–11)

1. A dreamer of dreams – One that pretends God hath revealed himself to him by visions or dreams. **Giveth a sign or wonder** – That is, shall foretell some strange and wonderful thing.

3. Thou shalt not hearken to that prophet – Not receive his doctrine, though the sign come

to pass. For although when such a sign or wonder foretold did not follow or come to pass, it was a sign of a false prophet, yet when it did come to pass, it was no sufficient sign of a true one, especially, in such a case. There are many things, which may be wrought by evil spirits, God so permitting it for wise and just reasons, not only for the trial of the good, but also for the punishment of ungodly men. **Proveth you** – That is, trieth your faith and love and obedience. **To know** – Namely, judicially, or in a public manner, so as both you and others may know and see it, that so the justice of his judgments upon you may be more evident and glorious.

5. To thrust – This phrase notes the great force and power of seducers to corrupt men's minds. **So shalt thou put the evil away** – Thou shalt remove the guilt, by removing the guilty.

6. The son of thy mother – This is added, to restrain the signification of the word brother, which is often used generally for one near a-kin, and to express the nearness of the relation, the mother's side being usually the ground of the most fervent affection. **Thy daughter** – Thy piety must overcome both thy affection, and thy compassion to the weaker sex. The father and mother are here omitted, because they are sufficiently contained in the former examples.

8. Conceal him – That is, smother his fault, hide or protect his person, but shalt accuse him to the magistrate, and demand justice upon him.

9. Thou shalt kill him – Not privately, which pretence would have opened the door to innumerable murders, but by procuring his death by the sentence of the magistrate. Thou shalt cast the first stone at him, as the witness was to do.

Idolatrous cities to be entirely destroyed (12–18)

13. Children of Belial – It signifies properly persons without yoke, vile and wretched miscreants, lawless and rebellious, that will suffer no restraint, that neither fear God, nor reverence man. **From among you** – That is, from your church and religion. It notes a separation from them, not in place (as appears by their partnership with their fellow citizens both in the sin and punishment) but in heart, doctrine and worship.

14. Enquire – This is, meant of the magistrate, to whose office this properly belongs, and of whom he continues to speak in the same manner, thou, Deu 13:15,16. The Jewish writers say, the defection of a city is to be tried by the great Sanhedrim. If it appear, that they are thrust away to idolatry, they send two learned men, to admonish them. If they repent, all is well: if not, all Israel must go up and execute this sentence. Tho' we do not find this law put in execution, in all the history of the Jewish church, yet for neglecting the execution of it on inferior cities, God himself by the army of the Chaldeans, executed it on Jerusalem, the head city, which was utterly destroyed, and lay in ruins for seventy years.

15. The inhabitants – Namely, all that are guilty, not the innocent part, such as disowned this apostasy, who doubtless by choice, at least upon warning, would come out of so wicked a place. **Utterly** – The very same punishment which was, inflicted upon the cities of the cursed Canaanites, to whom having made themselves equal in sin, it is but just God should equal them in punishment.

16. For the Lord – For the satisfaction of God's justice, the maintenance of his honour and authority, and the pacification of his offended majesty. **It shall not be built** – It shall be an eternal monument of God's justice, and terror to after ages.

17. Multiply thee – So thou shalt have no loss of thy numbers by cutting off so many people.

Chapter 14

Directions concerning mourning (1, 2)

1. Of the Lord – Whom therefore you must not disparage by unworthy or unbecoming practices. **Ye shall not cut yourselves** – Which were the practices of idolaters, both in the worship of their idols, in their funerals, and upon occasion of public calamities. Is not this like a parent's charge to his little children, playing with knives, 'Do not cut yourselves!' This is the intention of those commands, which obliges us to deny ourselves. The meaning is, Do yourselves no harm! And as this also is, the design of cross providences, to remove from us those things by which we are in danger of doing ourselves harm.

Concerning clean and unclean meats (3–21)

3. Abominable – Unclean and forbidden by me, which therefore should be abominable to you.

Concerning tithes (22–29)

22. All the increase – This is to be understood of the second tithes, which seem to be the same with the tithes of the first year, mentioned De 14:28.

25. In thine hand – That is, in a bag to be taken into thy hand and carried with thee.

27. Thou shalt not forsake him – Thou shalt give him a share in such tithes or in the product of them.

28. At the end of three years – That is, in the third year, as it is, expressed, Deu 26:12. **The same year** – This is added to shew that he speaks of the third year, and not of the fourth year, as

some might conjecture from the phrase, at the end of three years.

Chapter 15

Orders concerning the release of debts every seventh year (1–6)

1. At the end – That is, in the last year of the seven, as is, most evident from De 15:9. And this year of release, as it is, called below, De 15:9, is the same with the sabbatical year, Ex 23:11.

2. Every creditor – Here is, a law for poor, insolvent debtors. Every seventh year was a year of release, when among other acts of grace, this was one, that every Israelite, who had borrowed money, and had not been able to pay it before, should this year be released from it. And tho' if he was able, he was bound in conscience to pay it afterwards, yet it could not be recovered by law. **His brother** – This is added to limit the word neighbour, which is more general, unto a brother, in nation and religion, an Israelite. **The Lord's release** – Or, a release for the Lord, in obedience to his command, for his honour, and as an acknowledgment of his right in your estates, and of his kindness in giving and continuing them to you.

4. Save when there shall be no poor – The words may be rendered thus, as in the margin of our Bibles, To the end that there be no poor among you. And so they contain a reason of this law, namely, that none be impoverished and ruined by a rigid exaction of debts.

Concerning lending (7–11)

8. Open thine hand wide – That is, deal bountifully and liberally with him.

9. Beware – Suppress the first risings of such uncharitableness. **It be sin** – That is, it be charged upon thee as a sin.

10. Thine heart shall not be grieved – That is, thou shalt give, not only with an open hand, but with a willing and cheerful mind, without which thy very charity is uncharitable, and not accepted by God.

11. The poor shall never cease – God by his providence will so order it, partly for the punishment of your disobedience, and partly for the trial and exercise of your obedience to him and charity to your brother.

Concerning the release of servants (12–18)

12. If thy brother be sold – Either by himself, or his parents, or as a criminal. **Six years** – To be computed from the beginning of his servitude, which is every where limited to the space of six years.

15. The Lord redeemed thee – And brought thee out with riches, which because they would not, God gave thee as a just recompense for thy service; and therefore thou shalt follow his example, and send out thy servant furnished with all convenient provisions.

17. For ever – All the time of his life, or, at least, 'till the year of jubilee. **Likewise** – That is, either dismiss her with plenty, or engage her to perpetual servitude, in the same manner and by the same rites.

Concerning the firstlings (19–23)

19. All the firstling males thou shalt sanctify – Giving them to God on the eighth day. And thou shalt do no work with the female firstlings of the cow, nor shear those of the sheep. Even these must be offered to God as peace-offerings, or used in a religious feast.

20. Year by year – Namely, in the solemn feasts which returned upon them every year.

Chapter 16

A repetition of the laws concerning the Passover (1–8)

1. Observe the month of Abib – Or of new fruits, which answers to part of March and part of April, and was by a special order from God made the beginning of their year, in remembrance of their deliverance out of Egypt. **By night** – In the night Pharaoh was forced to give them leave to depart, and accordingly they made preparation for their departure, and in the morning they perfected the work.

2. The Passover – That is, the feast of the Passover, and so the place may be rendered, thou shalt therefore observe the feast of the Passover unto the Lord thy God, with sheep, and with oxen, as is prescribed, Num 28:18, &c.

3. With it – Or, in it, that is, during the time of the feast of the Passover. **Bread of affliction** – Bread which is not usual nor pleasant, to put thee in mind both of thy miseries endured in Egypt; and of thy hasty coming out of it, which allowed thee no time to leaven or prepare thy bread.

4. Any of the flesh – That is, of the Passover properly so called.

5. Of thy gates – That is, of thy cities.

6. There – Namely, in the court of the tabernacle or temple. This he prescribed, partly that this great work might be done with more solemnity in such manner as God required; partly, because it was not only a sacrament, but also a sacrifice, and because here was the sprinkling of blood, which is the essential part of a sacrifice; and partly to design the place where Christ, the true Passover or lamb of God, was to be slain. **At the season** – About the time you were preparing yourselves for it.

7. In the morning – The morning after the seventh day. **Thy tents** – That is, thy dwellings,

which he calls tents, as respecting their present state, and to put them in mind afterwards when they were settled in better habitations, that there was a time when they dwelt in tents.

8. Six days – Namely, besides the first day, on which the Passover was killed.

The feast of Pentecost (9–12)

9. To put the sickle – That is, to reap thy corn, thy barley, when the first-fruits were offered.

10. Of weeks – Of Pentecost. **Thou shalt give** – Over and besides what was appointed.

That of tabernacles, and all the males are to attend them (13–17)

17. Thou shalt rejoice – In God and the effects of his favour, praising him with a glad heart.

An appointment of judges and officers (18–20)

18. Judges – Chief magistrates to examine and determine causes and differences. **Officers** – Who were subordinate to the other to bring causes and persons before him, to acquaint people with the sentence of the judges, and to execute their sentence. **Thy gates** – Thy cities, which he here calls gates, because there were seats of judgment set. Pursuant to this law, in every town which contained above an hundred and twenty families, there was a court of twenty three judges; in the smaller towns, a court of three judges.

19. Wrest judgment – Not give an unjust sentence. **A gift doth blind the eyes** – Biasseth his mind, that he cannot discern between right and wrong. **The words** – That is, the sentence, of those judges who are used to do righteous things, it makes them give wrong judgment.

20. That which is altogether just – Heb. righteousness, righteousness, that is, nothing but righteousness in all causes and times, and to all persons equally.

A caution against groves and images (21, 22)

21. Thou shalt not plant – Because this was the practice of idolaters, and might be an occasion of reviving idolatry.

Chapter 17

A charge, concerning sacrifices.

Concerning putting idolaters to death (1–7)

1. Bullock or sheep – Either greater or smaller sacrifices, all being comprehended under the two most eminent kinds.

2. In transgressing his covenant – That is, in idolatry, as it is explained De 17:3, which is called a transgression of God's covenant made with Israel, both because it is a breach of their faith given to God and of that law which they covenanted to keep; and because it is a dissolution of that matrimonial covenant with God, a renouncing of God and his worship, and a choosing other gods.

3. The host of heaven – Those glorious creatures, which are to be admired as the wonderful works of God, but not to be set up in God's stead. By condemning the most specious of all idolaters, he intimates, how absurd a thing it is to worship stocks and stones, the works of men's hands. **I have not commanded** – That is, I have forbidden. Such negative expressions are emphatic.

6. Witnesses – Namely, credible and competent witnesses. The Jews rejected the testimonies of children, women, servants, familiar friends or enemies, persons of dissolute lives or evil fame.

7. First upon him – God thus ordered it, for the caution of witnesses, that, if they had through malice or wrath accused him falsely, they might now be afraid to imbrue their hands in innocent blood; and for the security and satisfaction of the people in the execution of this punishment.

Concerning the decision of cases by the Sanhedrim (8–13)

8. For thee – He speaks to the inferior magistrates, who were erected in several cities. If thou hast not skill to determine, **between blood and blood** – That is, in capital causes. **Between plea and plea** – In civil causes, about words or estates. **Between stroke and stroke** – In criminal causes, concerning blows, or wounds inflicted by one man upon another. **Matters of controversy** – That is, such things being doubtful, and the magistrates divided in their opinions about it.

9. Unto the priests – That is, unto the great council, which consisted chiefly of the priests and Levites, as being the best expositors of the laws of God, by which all those controversies were to be decided. And the high-priest was commonly one of that number, understood here under the priests, whereof he was the chief. **The judge** – Probably the high-priest, to whom it belonged to determine, some at least, of those controversies, and to expound the law of God. And he may be distinctly named, tho' he be one of the priests, because of his eminence, and to shew that amongst the priests, he especially was to be consulted in such cases. **The sentence of judgment** – Heb. The word, or matter of judgement, that is, the true state of the cause, and what judgment or sentence ought to be given in it.

10. Thou – Thou shalt pass sentence: he speaks to the inferior magistrates; who were to give sentence, and came hither to be advised about it.

11. Thou shalt do – In particular suits between man and man, although the judge be hereby confined to his rule in giving the sentence, yet it seems but fit and reasonable that people should be bound simply to acquiesce in the sentence of their last and highest judge, or else there would have been no end of strife.

12. Do presumptuously – That will proudly and obstinately oppose the sentence given against him. **The evil** – The evil thing, that scandal, that pernicious example.

13. When thou shalt – He only foresees and foretells what they would do, but doth not approve of it. Yea when they did this thing for this very reason, he declares his utter dislike of it, 1Sam 8:7.

Concerning the choice and duty of a king (14–20)

15. Thy God shall choose – Approve of, or appoint. So it was in Saul and David. God reserved to himself the nomination both of the family, and of the person. **Thy brethren** – Of the same nation and religion; because such a person was most likely to maintain true religion, and to rule with righteousness, gentleness, and kindness to his subjects; and that he might be a fit type of Christ their supreme king, who was to be one of their brethren.

16. He shall not multiply horses – Tho' he might have horses for his own use, yet he was not to have many horses for his officers and guard, much less for war, lest he should trust in them. The multiplying horses is also forbidden, lest it should raise too great a correspondence with Egypt which furnished Canaan with them. **The Lord hath said** – The Lord hath now said to me, and I by his command declare it to you. **Ye shall no more return that way** – Into Egypt, lest ye be again infected with her idolatries.

17. Turn away – From God and his law.

18. He shall write – With his own hand, as the Jews say. **Out of that** – Out of the original, which was carefully kept by the priests in the sanctuary, that it might be a perfect copy, and that it might have the greater influence upon him, coming to him as from the hand and presence of God.

19. All the days of his life – 'Tis not enough to have Bibles, but we must use them, yea, use them daily. Our souls must have constant meals of that manna, which if well digested, will afford them true nourishment and strength.

20. If his heart be not lifted up – He intimates, that the scriptures diligently read, are a powerful means to keep him humble, because they shew him in that, tho' a king, he is subject to an higher monarch, to whom he must give an account of all his administrations, and receive from him his sentence agreeable to their quality, which is sufficient to abate the pride of the haughtiest person in the world.

Chapter 18

Rules concerning priests and Levites (1–8)

1. His inheritance – The Lord's portion or inheritance, which God had reserved to himself, as tithes and first fruits, and other oblations distinct from those which were made by fire.

3. The maw – The Hebrew word here rendered maw or stomach, may have another signification, and some render it the breast, others take it for the part, which lies under the breast.

6. With all the desire of his mind – With full purpose to fix his abode, and to spend his whole time and strength in the service of God. It seems, the several priests were to come from their cities to the temple by turns, before David's time; and it is certain they did so after it. But if any of them were not contented with this attendance upon God in his tabernacle, or temple, and desired more entirely and constantly to devote himself to God's service there, he was permitted so to do, because this was an eminent act of piety joined with self-denial, to part with those great conveniences which he enjoyed in the city of his possession.

8. Like portions – With their brethren who were in actual ministration: as they share with them in the work, so shall they in the encouragements. **Beside that which cometh** – The reason of this law was, because he that waited on the altar, ought to live by the altar: and because it was fit he should keep his money, wherewith he might redeem what he sold, if afterwards he saw occasion for it. Mr. Henry adds a remarkable note here: especially considering he wrote threescore years ago. 'A hearty, pious zeal to serve God and his church, tho' it may a little encroach upon a settled order, and there may be somewhat in it that looks irregular, yet ought to be gratified, and not discouraged. He that loves dearly to be employed in the service of the sanctuary: in God's name let him minister. He shall be as welcome to God as the Levites, whose course it was to minister, and should be so to them.'

Cautions against witchcraft (9–14)

10. Useth divination – Foretelleth things secret or to come, by unlawful arts and practices. **An observer of times** – Superstitiously pronouncing some days lucky, and others unlucky. Or, an observer of the clouds or heavens, one that divineth by the motions of the clouds, by the stars, or by the flying or chattering of birds, all which Heathens used to observe. **An inchanter** – Or, a conjecturer, that discovers hidden things by a superstitious use of words or

ceremonies, by observation of water or smoke or any contingencies. **A witch** – One that is in covenant with the devil.

11. A charmer – One that charmeth serpents or other cattle. Or, a fortune-teller, that foretelleth the events of men's lives by the conjunctions of the stars. **Spirits** – Whom they call upon by certain words or rites. **A wizard** – Heb. a knowing man, who by any forbidden way's undertakes the revelation of secret things. **A necromancer** – One that calleth up and enquireth of the dead.

13. Perfect – Sincerely and wholly his, seeking him and cleaving to him and to his word alone, and therefore abhorring all commerce and conversations with devils.

14. Hath not suffered thee so to do – Hath not suffered thee to follow these superstitious and diabolical practices, as he hath suffered other nations to do, but hath instructed thee better by his word and spirit, and will more fully instruct thee by a great prophet.

A promise of Christ (15–19)

15. Will raise up – Will produce and send into the world in due time. **A prophet like unto me** – Christ was truly, and in all commendable parts like him, in being both a prophet and a king and a priest and mediator, in the excellency of his ministry and work, in the glory of his miracles, in his familiar and intimate converse with God.

19. I will require it – I will punish him severely for it. The sad effect of this threatening the Jews have felt for above sixteen hundred years together.

The punishment and mark of a false prophet (20–22)

22. If the thing – Which he gives as a sign of the truth of his prophecy. The falsehood of his prediction shows him to be a false prophet. **Presumptuously** – Impudently ascribing his own vain and lying fancies to the God of truth.

Chapter 19

Of the cities of refuge (1–10)

2. In the midst of the land – Namely, beyond Jordan, as there were three already appointed on this side Jordan: In the midst of the several parts of their land, to which they might speedily flee from all the parts of the land.

3. Prepare thee a way – Distinguish it by evident marks, and make it plain and convenient, to prevent mistakes and delays.

8. Enlarge thy coast – As far as Euphrates.

9. If thou shalt keep all these commandments – But the Jewish writers themselves own, that the condition not being performed, the

promise of enlarging their coast was not fulfilled, so that there was no need for three more
cities of refuge. Yet the holy, blessed God, say
they, did not command it in vain, for in the
day's of Messiah the Prince, they shall be added.
They expect it in the letter: but we know, it has
in Christ its spiritual accomplishment.

Of wilful murderers, removing land-marks and true witnesses (11–15)

15. Rise – Or be established, accepted, owned
as sufficient: it is the same word which in the
end of the verse is rendered, be established.

Of false witnesses (16–21)

16. A safe witness – A single witness, though
he speak truth, is not to be accepted for the condemnation of another man, but if he be convicted of false witness, this is sufficient for his own
condemnation.

21. Eye for eye – What punishment the law
allotted to the accused, if he had been convicted,
the same shall the false accuser bear.

Chapter 20

The exhortation of the priest to them who were going to battle (1–4)

2. Speak unto the people – Probably to one
regiment of the army after another.

The dismissing of them who were engaged in business, or faint-hearted (5–9)

5. What man – This and the following exceptions are to be understood only of a war allowed
by God, not in a war commanded by God, not
in the approaching war with the Canaanites,
from which even the bridegroom was not
exempted, as the Jewish writers note.

6. A vineyard – This and the former dispensation were generally convenient, but more
necessary in the beginning of their settlement in
Canaan, for the encouragement of those who
should build houses or plant vineyards, which
was chargeable to them, and beneficial to the
common-wealth. **Eaten of it** – Heb. made it common, namely, for the use of himself and family
and friends, which it was not, 'till the fifth year.

9. Make captains – Or rather, as the Hebrew
hath it, they shall set or place the captains of the
armies in the head or front of the people under
their charge, that they may conduct them, and
by their example encourage their soldiers. It is
not likely they had their captains to make when
they were just going to battle.

How they were to treat distant cities, and the cities of the Canaanites (10–18)

16. Nothing – No man. For the beasts, some
few excepted, were given them for a prey.

Fruit-trees not to be destroyed (19, 20)

19. Thou shalt not destroy – Which is to be
understood of a general destruction of them, not
of the cutting down some few of them, as the
conveniency of the siege might require. **Man's
life** – The sustenance or support of his life.

Chapter 21

The expiation of an uncertain murder (1–9)

1. The field – Or, in the city, or any place:
only the field is named, as the place where such
murders are most commonly committed.

2. Thy elders and judges – Those of thy elders
who are judges: the judges or rulers of all the
neighbouring cities. **Measure** – Unless it be evident which city is nearest; for then measuring
was superfluous.

3. Which hath not drawn in the yoke – A fit
representative of the murderer, in whose stead it
was killed, who would not bear the yoke of
God's laws. A type also of Christ, who was under
the yoke, but what he had voluntarily taken
upon himself.

4. A rough valley – That such a desert and
horrid place might beget an horror of murder
and of the murderer. **Strike off the neck** – To
shew what they would and should have done to
the murderer if they had found him.

5. Every controversy – Of this kind: every
controversy which shall rise about any stroke,
whether such a mortal stroke as is here spoken
of, or any other stroke or wound given by one
man to another.

7. They shall answer – To the priests who shall
examine them. **This blood** – This about which
the present enquiry is made: or this which is here
present: for it is thought the corps of the slain
man was brought into the same place where the
heifer was slain. Nor have we seen or understood
how or by whom this was done.

8. Forgiven – Though there was no mortal
guilt in this people, yet there was a ceremonial
uncleanness in the land, which was to be expiated and forgiven.

The usage of a captive taken to wife (10–14)

10. Enemies – Of other nations, but not of
the Canaanites.

11. Hast a desire unto her – Or, hast taken
delight in her: which may be a modest expression
for lying with her, and seems probable, because it
is said, De 21:14, that he had humbled her.

12. She shall shave her head – In token of her
renouncing her heathenish idolatry and superstition, and of her becoming a new woman, and
embracing the true religion.

13. Raiment of captivity – Those sordid rai-
ments which were put upon her when she was

taken captive. **Bewail her father and mother** – Either their death, or which was in effect the same, her final separation from them.

14. If thou have no delight in her – If thou dost not choose to marry her. **Thou shalt not make merchandise of her** – Make gain of her, either by using her to thy own servile works, or by prostituting her to the lusts or to the service of others.

The first-born to not to be disinherited (15–17)

15. Two wives – This practice, though tolerated, is not hereby made lawful; but only provision is made for the children in this case. **Hated** – Comparatively, that is, less loved.

A stubborn son to be put to death (18–21)

19. His father and mother – The consent of both is required to prevent the abuse of this law to cruelty. And it cannot reasonably be supposed that both would agree without the son's abominable and incorrigible wickedness, in which case it seems a righteous law, because the crime of rebellion against his own parents did so fully signify what a pernicious member he would be in the commonwealth of Israel, who had dissolved all his natural obligations. **Unto the elders** – Which was a sufficient caution to preserve children from the malice of any hardhearted parents, because these elders were first to examine the cause with all exactness, and then to pronounce the sentence.

20. A glutton and a drunkard – Under which two offences others of a like or worse nature are comprehended.

Bodies of malefactors to be buried (22–23)

22. On a tree – Which was done after the malefactor was put to death some other way, this public shame being added to his former punishment.

23. He is accursed of God – He is in a singular manner cursed and punished by God's appointment with a most shameful kind of punishment, as this was held among the Jews and all nations; and therefore this punishment may suffice for him, and there shall not be added to it that of lying unburied. And this curse is here appropriated to those that are hanged, to so signify that Christ should undergo this execrable punishment, and be made a curse for us, Gal 3:13, which though it was to come in respect to men, yet was present unto God. **Defiled** – Either by inhumanity towards the dead: or by suffering the monument of the man's wickedness, and of God's curse, to remain public a longer time than God would have it, whereas it should be put out of sight, and buried in oblivion.

Chapter 22

Laws for preserving stray or fallen cattle (1–4)

1. Thy brother's – Any man's. **Thou shalt not hide thyself** – Dissemble or pretend that thou dost not see them; or pass them by as if thou hadst not seen them.

2. To thine own house – To be used like thine own cattle.

3. Hide thyself – Dissemble that thou hast found it. Or, hide it, that is, conceal the thing lost.

Law of separation (5–12)

5. Shall not wear – Namely, ordinarily or unnecessarily, for in some cases this may be lawful, as to make an escape for one's life. Now this is forbidden, both for decency sake, that men might not confound those sexes which God hath distinguished, that all appearance of evil might be avoided, such change of garments carrying a manifest sign of effeminacy in the man, of arrogance in the woman, of lightness and petulance in both; and also to cut off all suspicions and occasions of evil, which this practice opens a wide door to.

7. Let the dam go – Partly for the bird's sake, which suffered enough by the loss of its young; for God would not have cruelty exercised towards the brute creatures: and partly for mens sake, to refrain their greediness, that, they should not monopolize all to themselves, but leave the hopes of a future seed for others.

8. A battlement – A fence or breastwork, because the roofs of their houses were made flat, that men might walk on them. **Blood** – The guilt of blood, by a man's fall from the top of thy house, through thy neglect of this necessary provision. The Jews say, that by the equity of this law, they are obliged, and so are we, to fence or remove every thing, whereby life may be endangered, as wells, or bridges, lest if any perish through our omission, their blood be required at our hand.

9. Divers seeds – Either:

1. With divers kinds of seed mixed and sowed together between the rows of vines in thy vineyard: which was forbidden to be done in the field, Lev 19:19, and here, in the vineyard. Or,

2. With any kind of seed differing from that of the vine, which would produce either herbs, or corn, or fruit-bearing trees, whose fruit might be mingled with the fruit of the vines.

10. An ox and an ass – Because the one was a clean beast, the other unclean whereby God would teach men to avoid polluting themselves by the touch of unclean persons or things.

12. Fringes – Or laces, or strings, partly to bring the commands of God to their remembrance, as it is expressed, Num 15:38, and partly as a public profession of their nation and religion, whereby they might be distinguished from strangers, that so they might be more circumspect to behave as became the people of God, and that they should own their religion before all the world. **Thou coverest thyself** – These words seem restrictive to the upper garment wherewith the rest were covered.

Law of marriage (13–30)

13. If any man take a wife – And afterward falsely accuse her. What the meaning of that evidence is, by which the accusation was proved false, the learned are not agreed. Nor is it necessary for us to know: they for whom this law was intended, undoubtedly understood it.

19. The father – Because this was a reproach to his family, and to himself, as such a miscarriage of his daughter would have been ascribed to his evil education.

24. She cried not – And therefore is justly presumed to have consented to it.

26. Even so – Not an act of choice, but of force and constraint.

27. The damsel cried – Which is in that case to be presumed; charity obliging us to believe the best, 'till the contrary be manifest.

29. Fifty shekels – Besides the dowry, as Philo, the learned Jew notes, which is here omitted, because that was customary, it being sufficient here to mention what was peculiar to this case. **His wife** – If her father consented to it.

30. Take – To wife. So this respects the state, and the next branch speaks of the act only.

Chapter 23

Who are to be excluded the congregation of rulers (1–6)

1. He that is wounded – A phrase denoting an eunuch. **Shall not enter into the congregation of the Lord** – Shall not be admitted to honours and offices either in the church or commonwealth of Israel; and so the congregation of the Lord doth not here signify, the body of the people, but the society of the elders or rulers of the people. Add to this, that the Hebrew word, *Kahal*, generally signifies a congregation or company of men met together; and therefore this cannot so conveniently be meant of all the body of the people, which could never meet in one place, but of the chief rulers, which frequently did so. Nor is it strange that eunuchs are excluded from government, both because such persons are commonly observed to want that courage which is necessary for a governor, because as such persons ordinarily were despicable, so the authority in their hands was likely to be exposed to the same contempt.

2. The congregation – Taking the word as in the former verse.

3. For ever – This seems to note the perpetuity of this law, that it should be inviolably observed in all succeeding ages.

4. They met you not with bread and water – As the manner of those times was to wait and provide for strangers and travellers, which was the more necessary, because in those times and countries, there were no public houses of entertainment. Their fault then was unmercifulness to strangers and afflicted persons, which was aggravated both by their relation to the Israelites, as being the children of Lot, and by the special kindness of God, and of the Israelites to them, in not fighting against them.

6. Thou shalt not seek their peace – That is, make no contracts either by marriages or leagues, or commerce with them, but rather constantly keep a jealous eye over them, as enemies who will watch every opportunity to ensnare or disturb thee. This counsel was now the more necessary, because a great part of the Israelites lived beyond Jordan in the borders of those people, and therefore God sets up this wall of partition betwixt them, as well knowing the mischief of bad neighbours, and Israel's proneness to receive infection from them. Each particular Israelite is not hereby forbidden to perform any office of humanity to them, but the body of the nation are forbidden all familiar conversation with them.

An Edomite and an Egyptian not to be abhorred (7, 8)

7. Thou wast a stranger – And didst receive habitation, protection and provision from them a long time, which kindness thou must not forget for their following persecution. It is ordinary with men, that one injury blots out the remembrance of twenty courtesies; but God doth not deal so with us, nor will he have us to deal so with others, but commands us to forget injuries, and to remember kindnesses.

8. In their third generation – Supposing their grandfather, or great-grandfather turned proselyte, and the children continue in that faith received by such ancestors.

No uncleanness to be in the camp (9–14)

9. Keep from every wicked thing – Then especially take heed, because that is a time of confusion and licentiousness; when the laws of God and man cannot be heard for the noise of arms; because the success of thy arms depends upon God's blessing, which wicked men have no reason to expect; and because thou dost carry thy life in thy hand, and therefore hast need to be well prepared for death and judgment.

13. **Cover** – To prevent the annoyance of ourselves or others; to preserve and exercise modesty and natural honesty; and principally that by such outward rites they might be inured to the greater reverence of the Divine Majesty, and the greater caution to avoid all real and moral uncleanness.

Of servants, escaped from their masters (15, 16)

15. **The servant** – Of such as belonged to the Canaanites, or other neighbouring nations, because if he had lived in remote countries, it is not probable that he would flee so far to avoid his master, or that his master would follow him so far to recover him. For the Canaanites this sentence was most just, because both they and theirs were all forfeited to God and Israel, and whatsoever they enjoyed was by special indulgence. And for the other neighbours it may seem just also, because both masters and servants of these and other nations are unquestionably at the disposal of the Lord their maker and sovereign ruler. Understand it likewise of such as upon enquiry appear to have been unjustly oppressed by their masters. Now it is not strange if the great God, who hates all tyranny, and styles himself the refuge of the oppressed doth interpose his authority to rescue such persons from their cruel masters.

Laws, against sodomy and whoredom (17, 18)

17. **No whore** – No common prostitute, such as were tolerated and encouraged by the Gentiles, and used even in their religious worship. Not that such practices were allowed to the strangers among them, as is evident from many scriptures and reasons, but that it was in a peculiar manner, and upon special reasons, forbidden to them, as being much more odious in them than in strangers.

18. **The hire of a whore** – This is opposed to the practice of the Gentiles, who allowed both such persons and the oblations they made out of their infamous gains; and some of them kept lewd women, who prostituted themselves in the temples, to the honour of their false Gods, and offered part of their profit to them. **Or the price of a dog** – It seems to mean, of a whoremonger or sodomite. Such are called dogs, Rev 22:15. And it is not improbable they are called so here. From these God would not accept of any offering.

Against usury (19, 20)

19. **Thou shalt not lend upon usury to thy brother** – To an Israelite. They held their estates immediately from God, who while he distinguished them from all other people, might have ordered, had he pleased, that they should have all things in common. But instead of that, and in token of their joint interest in the good land he had given them, he only appointed them, as there was occasion, to lend to one another without interest. This among them would be little or no loss to the lender, because their land was so divided, their estates so settled, and there was so little a merchandise among them, that it was seldom or never they had occasion to borrow any great sums, but only for the subsistence of their family, or some uncommon emergence. But they might lend to a stranger upon usury, who was supposed to live by trade, and therefore got by what he borrowed: in which case 'tis just, the lender should share in the gain. This usury therefore is not oppressive: for they might not oppress a stranger.

Against the breach of vows (21–23)

21. **Not slack** – Not delay: because delays may make them both unable to pay it, and unwilling too.

23. **A free-will-offering** – Which though thou didst really make, yet being made, thou art no longer free, but obliged to perform it.

The liberty which might be taken in another's field or vineyard (24, 25)

24. **At thy pleasure** – Which was allowed in those parts, because of the great plenty and fruitfulness of vines there.

Chapter 24

Divorce (1–4)

1. **Some uncleanness** – Some hateful thing, some distemper of body or quality of mind not observed before marriage: or some light carriage, as this phrase commonly signifies, but not amounting to adultery. **Let him write** – This is not a command as some of the Jews understood it, nor an allowance and approbation, but merely a permission of that practice for prevention of greater mischiefs, and this only until the time of reformation, till the coming of the Messiah when things were to return to their first institution and purest condition.

4. **May not** – This is the punishment of his levity and injustice in putting her away without sufficient cause, which by this offer he now acknowledgeth. **Defiled** – Not absolutely, as if her second marriage were a sin, but with respect to her first husband, to whom she is as a defiled or unclean woman, that is, forbidden things; forbidden are accounted and called unclean, Jud 13:7, because they may no more be touched or used than an unclean thing. **Thou shalt not cause the land to sin** – Thou shalt not suffer such lightness

to be practised, lest the people be polluted, and the land defiled and accursed by that means.

New-married men discharged from the war (5)

5. Business – Any public office or employment, which may cause an absence from or neglect of his wife. **One year** – That their affections may be firmly settled, so as there may be no occasions for the divorces last mentioned.

Pledges, man-stealers, and leprosy (6–9)

6. Mill-stone – Used in their hand-mills. Under this, he understands all other things necessary to get a livelihood, the taking away whereof is against the laws both of charity and prudence, seeing by those things alone he can be enabled both to subsist and to pay his debts. **Life** – His livelihood, the necessary support of his life.

More pledges (10–13)

10. Thou shalt not go in – To prevent both the poor man's reproach by having his wants exposed, and the creditor's greediness which might be occasioned by the sight of something which he desired, and the debtor could not spare.

11. The pledge – He shall choose what pledge he pleases, provided it be sufficient for the purpose.

12. Thou shalt not sleep – But restore it before night, which intimates that he should take no such thing for pledge, without which a man cannot sleep.

13. Bless thee – Bring down the blessing of God upon thee by his prayers: for though his prayers, if he be not a good man, shall not avail for his own behalf, yet they shall avail for thy benefit. **It shall be right** – Esteemed and accepted by God as a work of righteousness, or mercy.

Daily wages (14, 15)

15. At this day – At the time appointed, weekly or daily.

None to be punished for another's sin (16)

16. Not put to death – If the one be free from the guilt of the others sin, except in those cases where the sovereign Lord of life and death, before whom none is innocent, hath commanded it, as Deu 13:1-18 Jos 7:24. For though God do visit the father's sins upon the children, Exo 20:5, yet he will not suffer men to do so.

Of justice and mercy to the widow, fatherless and stranger (17–22)

17. Raiment – Not such as she hath daily and necessary use of, as being poor. But this concerns not rich persons, nor superfluous raiment.

Chapter 25

Stripes not to exceed forty (1–3)

1. Justify – Acquit him from guilt and false accusations, and free him from punishment.

2. Beaten – Which the Jews say was the case of all those crimes which the law commands to be punished, without expressing the kind or degree of punishment. **Before his face** – That the punishment may be duly inflicted, without excess or defect. And from this no person's rank or quality exempted him, if he was a delinquent.

3. Forty stripes – It seems not superstition, but prudent caution, when the Jews would not exceed thirty-nine stripes, lest through mistake or forgetfulness they should go beyond their bounds, which they were commanded to keep. **Should seem vile** – Should be made contemptible to his brethren, either by this cruel usage of him, as if he were a brute beast: or by the deformity or infirmity of body which excessive beating might produce.

The ox not to be muzzled (4)

4. He treadeth out the corn – Which they did in those parts, either immediately by their hoofs or by drawing carts or other instruments over the corn. Hereby God taught them humanity, even to their beasts that served them, and much more to their servants or other men who laboured for them, especially to their ministers, 1Cor 9:9.

Of marrying the brother's widow (5–10)

5. Together – In the same town, or at least country. For if the next brother had removed his habitation into remote parts, or were carried thither into captivity, then the wife of the dead had her liberty to marry the next kinsman that lived in the same place with her. **One** – Any of them, for the words are general, and the reason of the law was to keep up the distinction of tribes and families, that so the Messiah might be discovered by the family from which he was appointed to proceed; and also of inheritances, which were divided among all the brethren, the first-born having only a double portion. **A stranger** – To one of another family.

6. That his name be not put out – That a family be not lost. So this was a provision that the number of their families might not be diminished.

9. Loose his shoe – As a sign of his resignation of all his right to the woman, and to her husband's inheritance: for as the shoe was a sign of one's power and right, Psa 60:8 108:9, so the parting with the shoe was a token of the alienation of such right; and as a note of infamy, to signify that by this disingenuous action he was unworthy to be amongst freemen, and fit to be reduced to the condition of the meanest servants, who used to go barefoot, Isa 20:2,4.

10. His name – That is, his person, and his posterity also. So it was a lasting blot.

Of an immodest woman and of just weights and measures (11–16)

13. A great and a small – The great to buy with, the small for selling.

Amalek to be destroyed (17–19)

17. Out of Egypt – Which circumstance greatly aggravates their sin, that they should do thus to a people, who had been long exercised with sore afflictions, to whom pity was due by the laws of nature and humanity, and for whose rescue God had in so glorious a manner appeared, which they could not be ignorant of. So this was barbarousness to Israel, and setting the great Jehovah at defiance.

Chapter 26

A form of confession made by him that offered the first-fruits (1–11)

2. Thou shalt take – This seems to be required of each master of a family, either upon his first settlement, or once every year at one of their three feasts, when they were obliged to go up to Jerusalem.

5. A Syrian – So Jacob was, partly by his original, as being born of Syrian parents, as were Abraham and Rebecca, both of Chaldea or Mesopotamia, which was a part of Syria largely so called, partly by his education and conversation; and partly by his relations, his wives being such, and his children too by their mother's. **Ready to perish** – Either through want and poverty; (See Gen 28:11,20 32:10,) or through the rage of his brother Esau, and the treachery of his father-in-law Laban.

10. It – The basket of first-fruits, Deu 26:2.

11. Thou shalt rejoice – Thou shalt hereby be enabled to take comfort in all thy employments, when thou hast sanctified them by giving God his portion. It is the will of God, that we should be cheerful not only in our attendance upon his holy ordinances, but in our enjoyment of the gifts of his providence. Whatever good thing God gives us, we should make the most comfortable use of it we can, still tracing the streams to the fountain of all consolation.

A prayer to be made after the disposal of the third year's tithe (12–15)

13. Before the Lord – In thy private addresses to God; for this is to be said presently upon the distribution of these tithes, which was not done at Jerusalem, but in their own private gates or dwellings. And this is to be spoken before the Lord, that is, solemnly, seriously, and in a religious manner, with due respect to God's presence, and will, and glory.

14. In my mourning – In sorrow, or grieving that I was to give away so much of my profits to the poor, but I have cheerfully eaten and feasted with them, as I was obliged to do. **Unclean use** – For any common use; for any other use than that which thou hast appointed, which would have been a pollution of them. **For the dead** – For any funeral pomp or service; for the Jews used to send in provisions to feast with the nearest relations of the party deceased; and in that case both the guests and food were legally polluted, Num 19:11,14, and therefore the use of these tithes in such cases had been a double fault, both the defiling of sacred food, and the employing those provisions upon sorrowful occasions, which by God's express command were to be eaten with rejoicing.

15. Look down – After that solemn profession of their obedience to God's commands, they are taught to pray for God's blessing whereby they are instructed how vain and ineffectual the prayers of unrighteous or disobedient persons are.

He binds all these precepts upon them, by the divine authority, and the covenant between God and them (16–19)

17. Avouched – Or, declared, or owned.

18. Avouched thee – Hath owned thee for such before all the world by eminent and glorious manifestations of his power and favour, by a solemn entering into covenant with thee, and giving peculiar laws, promises, and privileges to thee above all mankind.

Chapter 27

A command to write all the law upon stones (1–8)

2. On that day – About that time, for it was not done 'till some days after their passing over.

3. This law – The law properly so called, that is, the sum and substance of the precepts or laws of Moses, especially such as were moral, particularly the decalogue. **Write it, that thou mayest go in** – As the condition of thy entering into the land. For since Canaan is given only by promise, it must be held by obedience.

4. Mount Ebal – The mount of cursing. Here the law is written, to signify that a curse was due to the violators of it, and that no man could expect justification from the works of the law, by the sentence whereof all men are justly accused, as being all guilty of the transgression of it in one kind and degree or other. Here the sacrifices are to be offered, to shew that there is no way to be delivered from this curse, but by the blood of Christ, which all these sacrifices did typify, and by Christ's being made a curse for us.

6. Whole stones – Rough, not hewed or polished. By the law written on the stones, God spake to them: by the altar and sacrifices upon it, they spake to God: and thus was communion kept up between them and God.

A charge to Israel, to obey God (9–10)

9. The people of the Lord – By thy solemn renewing of thy covenant with him.

To pronounce a blessing on mount Gerizzim, and a curse on mount Ebal (11–13)

12. Upon mount Gerizzim – These words may be rendered beside or near to mount Gerizzim. There were in Canaan two mountains that lay near together, with a valley between, one called Gerizzim, the other Ebal. On the sides of these which faced each other, all the tribes were to be drawn up, six on a side, so that in the valley they came near each other, so near that the priests standing between them, might be heard by them that were next them on both sides. Then one of the priests, or perhaps more, at some distance from each other, pronounced with a loud voice, one of the curses following. And all the people who stood on the foot and side of mount Ebal, (those farther off taking the signal from those who were nearer) said Amen! Then the contrary blessing was pronounced, 'Blessed is he that doth so or so:' To which all who stood on the foot and side of mount Gerizzim, said, Amen! **Simeon** – All these were the children of the free-women, Leah and Rachel, to shew both the dignity of the blessings above the curses, and that the blessings belong only to those who are evangelically such, as this is expounded and applied, Gal 4:22, even to those that receive the Spirit of adoption and liberty. Joseph is here put for both his sons and tribes Manasseh and Ephraim, which are reckoned as one tribe, because Levi is here numbered; but when Levi is omitted, as it is where the division of the land is made, there Manasseh and Ephraim pass for two tribes.

13. To curse – Of the former tribes, 'tis said, they stood to bless the people: of these, that they stood to curse. Perhaps the different way of speaking intimates, That Israel in general were an happy people, and should ever be so, if they were obedient. And to that blessing, they on mount Gerizzim said, Amen! But the curses come in, only as exceptions to the general rule: 'Israel is a blessed people: but if there be any even among them, that do such and such things, they have no part or lot in this matter, but are under a curse.' This shows how ready God is to bestow the blessing: if any fall under the curse,

they bring it on their own head. Four of these are children of the bond-woman, to shew that the curse belongs to those of servile and disingenuous spirits. With these are joined Reuben, who by his shameful sin fell from his dignity, and Zebulun, the youngest of Leah's children, that the numbers might be equal.

To the Levites, to pronounce the whole curse (14–26)

14. The Levites – Some of the Levites, namely, the priests, who bare the ark, as it is expressed Jos 8:33, for the body of the Levites stood upon mount Gerizzim, Deu 27:12. But these stood in the valley between Gerizzim and Ebal, looking towards the one or the other mountain as they pronounced either the blessings or the curses.

15. Cursed – The curses are expressed, but not the blessings. For as many as were under the law, were under the curse. But it was an honour reserved for Christ to bless us; to do that which the law could not do. So in his sermon on the mount, the true mount Gerizzim, we have blessings only. **The man** – Under this particular he understands all the gross violations of the first table, as under the following branches he comprehends all other sins against the second table. **Amen** – 'Tis easy to understand the meaning of Amen to the blessings. But how could they say it to the curses? It was both a profession of their faith in the truth of it, and an acknowledgment of the equity of these curses. So that when they said Amen, they did in effect say, not only, it is certain it shall be so, but it is just it should be so.

16. Light – Or, despiseth in his heart: or reproacheth or curseth, secretly: for if the fact was notorious, it was punished with death.

17. Out of the way – That misleadeth simple souls, giving them pernicious counsel, either for this life, or for the next.

24. Smiteth – That is, killeth. This includes murder under colour of law, which is of all others the greatest affront to God. Cursed therefore is he that any ways contributes to accuse, or convict, or condemn an innocent person.

26. Confirmeth not – Or, performeth not. To this we must all say, Amen! Owning ourselves to be under the curse, and that we must have perished for ever, if Christ had not redeemed us from the curse of the law, by being made a curse for us.

Chapter 28

The blessings of obedience, personal, family and national (1–14)

2. Overtake thee – Those blessings which others greedily follow after, and never overtake, shall follow after thee, and shall be thrown into thy lap by special kindness.

3. In the city, and in the field – Whether they were husbandmen or tradesmen, whether in the town or country, they should be preserved from the dangers of both, and have the comforts of both. How constantly must we depend upon God, both for the continuance and comfort of life! We need him at every turn: we cannot be safe, if he withdraw his protection, nor easy, if he suspends his favour: but if he bless us, go where we will, 'tis well with us.

5. Store – Store-house, it shall always be well replenished and the provision thou hast there shall be preserved for thy use and service.

6. Comest in – That is, in all thy affairs and administrations.

9. Establish thee – Shall confirm his covenant with thee, by which he separated thee to himself as an holy and peculiar people.

10. Of the Lord – That you are in truth his people and children: A most excellent and glorious people, under the peculiar care and countenance of the great God.

11. The same things which were said before are repeated, to shew that God would repeat and multiply his blessings upon them.

12. His treasure – The heaven or the air, which is God's storehouse, where he treasures up rain or wind for man's use.

13. The head – The chief of all people in power, or at least in dignity and privileges; so that even they that are not under thine authority shall reverence thy greatness and excellency. So it was in David's and Solomon's time, and so it should have been much oftner and much more, if they had performed the conditions.

The curses of the disobedient; their extreme vexation (15–44)

15. Overtake thee – So that thou shalt not be able to escape them, as thou shalt vainly hope and endeavour to do. There is no running from God, but by running to him; no flying from his justice, but by flying to his mercy.

20. Vexation – This seems chiefly to concern the mind, arising from the disappointment of hopes and the presages of its approaching miseries. **Rebuke** – Namely, from God, not so much in words as by his actions, by cross providences, by sharp and sore afflictions.

23. Brass – Like brass, hard and dry, and shut up from giving rain. **Iron** – Hard and barren.

24. Dust – Either thy rain shall be as unprofitable to thy ground and seed as if it were only so much dust. Or instead of rain shall come nothing but dust from heaven, which being raised and carried up by the wind in great abundance, returns, and falls upon the earth as it were in clouds or showers.

27. The botch of Egypt – Such boils and blains as the Egyptians were plagued with,

spreading from head to foot: **The emerodes** – Or piles.

28. Blindness – Of mind, so that they shall not know what to do: **Astonishment** – They shall be filled with wonder and horror because of the strangeness and soreness of their calamities.

29. Grope at noon day – In the most clear and evident matters thou shalt grossly mistake. **Thy ways** – Thy counsels and enterprises shall be frustrated and turn to thy destruction.

32. Unto another people – By those who have conquered them, and taken them captives, who shall give or sell them to other persons. **Fail** – Or, be consumed, partly with grief and plentiful tears; and partly with earnest desire, and vain and long expectation of their return. **No might** – No power to rescue, nor money to ransom them.

33. Which thou knowest not – Which shall come from a far country, which thou didst not at all expect or fear, and therefore will be the more dreadful when they come; a nation whose language thou understandest not, and therefore canst not plead with them for mercy, nor expect any favour from them.

34. Thou shalt be mad for the sight of thine eyes – Quite put out of the possession of their own souls; quite bereaved of all comfort and hope, and abandoned to utter despair. They that walk by sight, and not by faith, are in danger of losing reason itself, when all about them looks frightful; and their condition is bad indeed, who are mad for the sight of their eyes.

36. Thy king – The calamity shall be both universal, which even thy king shall not be able to avoid, much less the subjects, who have far less advantage and opportunity for escape; and irrecoverable, because he who should protect or rescue them is lost with them, Lam 4:10. **Wood and stone** – So what formerly was their choice and delight now becomes their plague and misery. And this doubtless was the condition of many Israelites under the Assyrian and Babylonia captivities.

43. Within thee – Within thy gates; who formerly honoured and served thee, and were some of them glad of the crumbs which fell from thy table.

Their utter ruin and destruction (45–68)

45. Moreover all these curses – It seems Moses has been hitherto foretelling their captivity in Babylon, by which even after their return, they were brought to the low condition mentioned, Deu 28:44. But in the following he foretells their last destruction by the Romans. And the present deplorable state of the Jewish nation, so exactly answers this prediction, that it is an incontestable proof of the truth of the prophecy, and consequently of the divine authority of the scriptures. And this destruction more dreadful than the former shows, that their sin in rejecting Christ, was more provoking to God than idolatry itself, and left them more under the power of Satan. For their captivity in Babylon cured them effectually of idolatry in seventy years. But under this last destruction, they continue above sixteen hundred years incurably averse to the Lord Jesus.

46. They – These curses now mentioned. **A wonder** – Signal and wonderful to all that hear of them. 'Tis amazing, a people so incorporated, should be so universally dispersed! And that a people scattered in all nations, should not mix with any, but like Cain, be fugitives and vagabonds, and yet so marked as to be known.

54. Evil – Unkind, envious, covetous to monopolize these dainty bits to themselves, and grudging that their dearest relations should have any part of them.

56. Evil – Unmerciful: she will desire or design their destruction for her food.

57. Her young one – Heb. after-birth: that which was loathsome to behold, will now be pleasant to eat; and together with it she shall eat the child which was wrapt up in it, and may be included in this expression. **Which she shall bear** – Or, which she shall have born, that is, her more grown children. **She shall eat them** – This was fulfilled more than once, to the perpetual reproach of the Jewish nation. Never was the like done either by Greek or Barbarian. See the fruit of being abandoned by God!

63. To destroy you – His just indignation against you will be so great, that it will be a pleasure to him to take vengeance on you. For though he doth not delight in the death of a sinner in itself, yet he doth delight in glorifying his justice upon incorrigible sinners, seeing the exercise of all his attributes must needs please him, else he were not perfectly happy.

65. Neither shall thy foot have rest – Ye shall have no settlement in the land whither you are banished, but there you shall be tossed about from place to place, and sold from person to person, or Cain-like, wander about.

66. Thy life shall hang in doubt – Either because thou art in the hands of thy enemies that have power, and want no will, to destroy thee: or because of the terrors of thy own mind, and the guilt of thy conscience making thee to fear, even where no fear is.

68. Into Egypt – Which was literally fulfilled under Titus, when multitudes of them were carried thither in ships, and sold for slaves. And this expression seems to mind them of that time when they went over the sea without ships, God miraculously drying up the sea before them, which now they would have occasion sadly to remember. **By the way** – Or, to the way. And the

way seems not to be meant here of the usual road-way from Canaan to Egypt, which was wholly by land, but to be put for the end of the way or journey, even the land of Egypt, for to this, and not to the road-way between Canaan and Egypt, agree the words here following, whereof I speak unto thee, thou shalt see it, (that is, Egypt) no more again. **No man shall buy you** – Either because the number of your captives shall be so great, that the market shall be glutted with you; or because you shall be so loathsome and contemptible that men shall not be willing to have you for slaves. And this was the condition of the Jews after the destruction of Jerusalem, as Josephus the Jew hath left upon record. Let us all learn hence, to stand in awe and not to sin. I have heard of a wicked man (says Mr. Henry) who on reading these threatenings, was so enraged, that he tore the leaf out of his bible. But to what purpose is it, to deface a copy, while the original remains unchangeable? By which it is determined, that the wages of sin is death: yea, a death more dreadful than all that is here spoken!

Chapter 29

The preface of God's covenant (1)

1. These are the terms or conditions upon which God hath made, that is renewed his covenant with you. The covenant was but one in substance, but various in the time and manner of its dispensation.

A recital of his dealings with them (2–8)

4. Yet the Lord – That is, you have perceived and seen them with the eyes of your body, but not with your minds and hearts; you have not yet learned rightly to understand the word and works of God, so as to know them for your good, and to make a right use of them, and to comply with them: which he expresseth thus, the Lord hath not given you, &c. not to excuse their wickedness, but to direct them to whom they must have recourse for a good understanding of God's works; and to intimate that although the hearing ear, and the seeing eye, be the workmanship of God, yet their want of his grace was their own fault, and the just punishment of their former sins; their present case being like theirs in Isaiah's time, who first shut their own eyes and ears that they might not see and hear, and would not understand, and then by the righteous judgment of God, had their eyes and ears closed that they should not see and hear, and understand. God's readiness to do us good in other things, is a plain evidence, that if we have not grace, that best of gifts, 'tis our own fault and not his: he would have gathered us, and we would not.

6. Ye have not eaten bread – Common bread purchased by your own money, or made by your own hands, but heavenly and angelical bread. **Neither drank wine** – But only water out of the rock. **The Lord** – Omnipotent and all-sufficient for your provision without the help of any creatures, and your God in covenant with you who hath a true affection to you, and fatherly care of you.

A solemn exhortation to keep covenant with God (9–17)

11. Thy stranger – Such strangers as had embraced their religion: all sorts of persons, yea, even the meanest of them.

12. Into covenant and into his oath – Into covenant, confirmed by a solemn oath.

13. That he may establish thee – Here is the summary of that covenant whereof Moses was the mediator, and in the covenant relation between God and them, all the precepts and promises of the covenant are included. That they should be established for a people to him, to fear, love, obey, and be devoted to him, and that he should be to them a God, to make them holy and happy; and a due sense of the relation we stand in to God as our God, and the obligation we are under to him as his people, is enough to bring us to all the duties, and all the comforts of the covenant. And does this covenant include nothing spiritual? nothing that refers to eternity?

15. So also – With your posterity. For so the covenant was made at first with Abraham and his seed, by which as God engaged himself to continue the blessing of Abraham upon his posterity, so he also engaged them to the same duties which were required of Abraham. So it is even among men, where a king confers an estate upon a subject and his heirs for ever, upon some certain conditions, all his heirs who enjoy that benefit, are obliged to the same conditions. It may likewise include those who were then constrained to be absent, by sickness, or any necessary occasion. Nay one of the Chaldee paraphrasts reads it, all the generations that have been from the first days of the world, and all that shall arise to the end of the whole world, stand with us here this day. And so taking this covenant as a typical dispensation of the covenant of grace, 'tis a noble testimony to the Mediator of that covenant, who is the same yesterday, to day, and for ever.

16. Egypt – Where you have seen their idolatries, and learned too much of them, as the golden calf showed, and therefore have need to renew your covenant with God; where also we were in dreadful bondage whence God alone hath delivered us, to whom therefore we are deeply obliged, and have all reason to renew our covenant with him. **Through the nations** – With what hazard, if God had not appeared for us!

A severe threatening to them that break it (18–28)

18. A root – An evil heart inclining you to such cursed idolatry, and bringing forth bitter fruits.

19. Of this curse – Of that oath where-in he swore he would keep covenant with God, and that with a curse pronounced against himself if he did not perform it. **Bless himself** – Flatter himself in his own eyes, with vain hopes, as if God did not mind such things, and either could not, or would not punish them. **Peace** – Safety and prosperity. **My own heart** – Though I do not follow God's command, but my own devices. **To add drunkenness to thirst** – The words may be rendered, to add thirst to drunkenness, and so the sense may be, that when he hath multiplied his sins, and made himself as it were drunk with them, yet he is not satisfied therewith, but still whets his appetite, and provokes his thirst after more, as drunkards often use means to make themselves thirst after more drink.

20. Shall smoke – Shall burn and break forth with flame and smoke as it were from a furnace.

21. Unto evil – Unto some peculiar and exemplary plague; he will make him a monument of his displeasure to the whole land.

23. Salt and burning – Is burnt up and made barren, as with brimstone and salt.

26. Whom God had not given to them – For their worship, but hath divided them unto all nations, for their use and service. So he speaks here of the sun and moon and stars, which were the principal gods worshipped by the neighbouring nations.

The end of the revealed will of God (29)

29. The secret things – Having mentioned the amazing judgments of God upon the whole land and people of Israel, and foreseeing the utter extirpation which would come upon them for their wickedness, he breaks out into this pathetic exclamation, either to bridle their curiosity, who would be apt to enquire into the time and manner of so great an event; or to quiet his own mind, and satisfy the scruples of others, who perceiving God to deal so severely with his own people, when in the meantime he suffered those nations which were guilty of grosser atheism and idolatry, might thence take occasion to deny his providence or question the equity of his proceedings. To this he answers, that the ways and judgments of God, tho' never unjust, are often times hidden from us, unsearchable by our shallow capacities, and matter for our admiration, not our enquiry. But the things which are revealed by God and his word, are the proper object of our enquiries, that thereby we may know our duty, and be kept from such terrible calamities as these now mentioned.

Chapter 30

Promises upon their repentance (1–10)

1. **The blessing** – When thou art obedient. **The curse** – When thou becomest rebellious.

6. **And the Lord** – Or, For the Lord will circumcise thine heart, will by his word and spirit change and purge thy heart from all thine idolatry and wickedness, and incline thy heart to love him. God will first convert and sanctify them, the fruit whereof shall be, that they shall return and obey God's commandments, Deu 30:8, and then shall prosper in all things, Deu 30:9. This promise principally respects the times of the gospel, and the grace which was to be then imparted to all Israel by Christ.

9. **For good** – Whereas thou didst formerly receive these mercies for thy hurt, now thou shalt have them for thy good, thy heart shall be so changed that thou shalt not now abuse them, but employ them to the service of God the giver. **Over thee for good** – To do thee good; as he did rejoice to destroy thee.

10. **If thou wilt hearken** – This is added to warn them that they should not receive the grace of God in vain, and to teach them that the grace of God doth not discharge man's obligation to his duty, nor excuse him for the neglect of it. It is observable, that Moses calls God, the Lord thy God twelve times in these ten verses. In the threatnings of the former chapter, he is all along called the Lord, a God of power, and the judge of all. But in the promises of this chapter, the Lord thy God, a God of grace, and in covenant with thee.

The righteousness of faith set before them (11–14)

11. **This commandment** – The great command of loving and obeying God, which is the sum of the law, of which yet he doth not here speak, as it is in itself, but as it is mollified and accompanied with the grace of the gospel. The meaning is, that tho' the practice of God's laws be now far from us, and above our strength, yet, considering the advantage of gospel grace, whereby God enables us to do our duty, it is near and easy to us, who believe. And so this well agrees with Rom 10:6, where St. Paul applies this place to the righteousness of faith. **Is not hidden** – Heb. Is not too wonderful for thee, not too hard for thee to know and do. The will of God, which is but darkly manifested to other nations, Acts 17:27, is clearly and fully revealed unto thee: thou canst not pretend ignorance or invincible difficulty.

12. **In heaven** – Shut up there, but it hath been thence delivered and published in thy hearing.

13. **Neither beyond the sea** – The knowledge of this commandment is not to be fetched from far distant places, to which divers of the wise Heathens travelled for their wisdom; but it was brought to thy very doors and ears, and declared to thee in this wilderness.

14. **In thy mouth** – Thou knowest it so well, that it is the matter of thy common discourse. **In thy heart** – In thy mind, (as the heart is very commonly taken) to understand and believe it. In a word, the Law is plain and easy: but the gospel is much more so.

Life and death offered to their choice (15–20)

19. **Choose life** – They shall have life that choose it: they that choose the favour of God, and communion with him, shall have what they choose. They that come short of life and happiness, must thank themselves only. They had had them, if they had chosen them, when they were put to their choice: but they die, because they will die.

20. **That thou mayest love the Lord thy God** – Here he shows them in short, what their duty is; To love God as the Lord, a being most amiable, and as their God, a God in covenant with them: as an evidence of their love, to obey his voice in every thing, and by constancy in this love and obedience, to cleave to him all their days. And what encouragement had they to do this? **For he is thy life and the length of thy days** – He gives life, preserves life, restores life, and prolongs it, by his power, tho' it be a frail life, and by his presence, tho' it be a forfeited life. He sweetens life by his comforts, and completes all in life everlasting.

Chapter 31

Moses encourages the people and Joshua (1–8)

1. **Went and spake** – Continued to speak, an usual Hebrew phrase.

2. **Go out and come in** – Perform the office of a leader or governor, because the time of my death approaches.

Delivers to the priests the law, to be read every seventh year (9–13)

9. **This law** – Largely so called, the whole law or doctrine delivered unto Moses contained in these five books. **To the priests** – That they might keep it carefully and religiously, and bring it forth upon occasion, and read it, and instruct the people out of it. **The elders** – Who were assistants to the priests, to take care that

the law should be kept, and read, and observed.

10. The year of release – When they were freed from debts and troubles, and cares of worldly matters, and thereby fitter to attend on God and his service.

11. Thou shalt read – Thou shalt cause it to be read by the priest or Levites; for he could not read it himself in the hearing of all Israel, but this was to be done by several persons, and so the people met in several congregations.

12. Together – Not in one place. But into divers assemblies or synagogues. **Women** who hereby are required to go to Jerusalem at this solemnity, as they were permitted to do in other solemnities. **Children** – Such of them as could understand, as appears from Neh 8:2,3, the pious Jews doubtless read it daily in their houses, and Moses of old time was read in the synagogues every Sabbath day. But once in seven years, the law was thus to be read in public, to magnify it and make it honourable.

God informs Moses of his approaching death, and the future apostasy of Israel (14–18)

14. Give him a charge – Immediately from myself for his greater encouragement, and to gain him more authority with the people.

16. The strangers of the land – That is, of the Canaanites, who will be turned out of their possessions, and become as strangers in their own land. This aggravates their folly to worship such gods as could neither preserve their friends, nor annoy their enemies.

17. Hide my face – Withdraw my favour and help. Whatever outward troubles we are in if we have but the light of God's countenance, we are safe. But if God hide his face from us then we are undone.

Orders him to write a song, which should be a testimony against them (19–22)

19. Write this song – Which is contained Deu 32:1-43, and is put into a song that it may be better learned, and more fixed in their minds and memories. **Put it in their mouths** – Cause them to learn it, and sing it one to another, to oblige them to more circumspection. **A witness** – Of my kindness in giving them so many blessings, of my patience in bearing so long with them, of my clemency in giving them such fair and plain warnings, and my justice in punishing such an incorrigible people.

21. Their imaginations – Inclinations to Idolatry, which they do not check, as they ought; and some of them do not only cherish it in their hearts, but as far as they can and dare, secretly practise it, as may be gathered from Amos 5:25 Acts 7:43.

Moses gives the law to the Levites to lay up beside the ark, and bids them assemble the people to hear his song (24–30)

25. The Levites – The priests, Deu 31:9, who also were Levites.

26. Take this book – Probably the very same book, which (after having been some way misplaced) was found in the house of the Lord, in the days of Josiah, and publically read by the king himself, for a witness against a people, who were then almost ripe for ruin. **In the side** – In the outside, in a little chest fixed to it, for nothing but the tables of stone were contained in the ark, 1Kings 8:9, here it was kept for greater security and reverence. **A witness against thee** – Against thy people, to whom he turns his speech that they might be the more affected with it.

Chapter 32

The song of Moses contains the preface (1, 2)

1. O heavens, O earth – You lifeless and senseless creatures, which he calls upon partly to accuse the stupidity of Israel, that were more dull of hearing than these: and partly as witnesses of the truth of his sayings and the justice of God's proceedings against them.

2. As the rain – Look what effect rain and dew have upon herbs and grass which they make fresh and fragrant and growing, the same effect may my discourse have upon your hearts, that is, to make them soft and pliable and fruitful.

A high character of God (3–6)

3. The name of the Lord – His glorious excellencies and righteous actions, by which he hath made himself known as a man is known by his name, and by which it will appear both that there is no blame to be laid upon him whatsoever befals you, and that it is gross madness to forsake such a God for dumb idols. **Ascribe ye** – As I am about to publish the majesty and glory of God, so do you also acknowledge it.

4. A rock – As for the stability of his nature, and invincibleness of his power, so also for his fixedness and immutability in his counsels and promises and ways; so that if there shall be a sad change in your affairs, remember that this proceeds from yourselves and from the change of your ways towards God, and not from God, in whom there is no variableness or shadow of change, Jam 1:17. **His work** – All his works and actions are unblameable, perfect, wise and righteous. **His ways** – All his administrations in the world and particularly with you are managed with wisdom and justice. **A God of truth** – Constant to his promises: you cannot accuse him of any unfaithfulness to this day.

5. They – The Israelites. **Their spot** – The wickedness with which they are stained, is **not**

of his children – Plainly shews they are not his children, but the devil's. God's children have no such spot. Indeed this text does not affirm, they have any spot at all. **Perverse** – Froward and untractable: **Crooked** – Irregular and disorderly.

6. **O foolish people and unwise!** – Fools and double fools! Fools indeed, to disoblige one, on whom you so entirely depend! Who hath bewitched you! To forsake your own mercies for lying vanities! **Bought thee** – That hath redeemed thee from Egyptian bondage. **Made thee** – Not only in a general by creation, but in a peculiar manner by making thee his peculiar people. **Established** – That is, renewed and confirmed his favour to thee, and not taken it away, which thou hast often provoked him to do.

A recital of the great things God had done for them, and of their carriage toward him (7–18)

7. **The days of old** – The events of ancient days or former ages, and thou wilt find that I had a respect unto thee not only in Abraham's time, but long before it.

8. **Their inheritance** – When God by his providence allotted the several parts of the world to several people, which was done Gen 10:1-32 Gen 11:1-9. **When he separated** – Divided them in their languages and habitations according to their families. **He set the bounds** – That is, he disposed of the several lands and limits of the people so as to reserve a sufficient place for the great numbers of the people of Israel. And therefore he so guided the hearts of several people, that the posterity of Canaan, which was accursed of God, and devoted to ruin, should be seated in that country which God intended for the children of Israel, that so when their iniquities were ripe, they might be rooted out, and the Israelites come in their stead.

9. **His people** – It is no wonder God had so great a regard to this people, for he chose them out of all mankind to be his peculiar portion.

10. **He found him** – Not by chance, but as it were looking out and seeking for him. He did indeed manifest himself to him in Egypt, but it was in the wilderness at Sinai, God found him in an eminent manner, and revealed his will to him, and entered into covenant with him, and imparted himself and his grace and blessing to him. By this word he also signifies both their lost condition in themselves, and that their recovery was not from themselves, but only from God who sought and found them out by his grace. **In the waste howling wilderness** – In a place destitute of all the necessaries and comforts of life, which also was a type of that desolate and comfortless condition in which all men are before the grace of God finds them out; where instead of the voices of men, is nothing heard but the howlings and yellings of ravenous birds and beasts. **He led them** – He conducted them from place to place by his cloudy pillar and providence. Or, he compassed him about, by his provident care, watching over him and preserving him on every side. **As the apple of his eye** – As men use to keep the apple of their eye, that is, with singular care and diligence, this being as a most tender, so a most useful part.

11. **Her nest** – Her young ones in the nest; which she by her cry and motion provoketh to fly. **Her wings** – As preparing herself to fly. **On her wings** – Or, as on her wings, that is, gently, and tenderly and safely too, as if she carried them not in her claws for fear of hurting them, but upon her wings. Some say, the eagle doth usually carry her young ones upon her wings.

12. **Did lead them** – When they were shut up in Egypt as in their nest whence they durst not venture to fly nor stir, he taught and encouraged and enabled them to fly out from that bondage, he dealt tenderly with them, bearing with their infirmities, keeping them from all harms. **With him** – To assist him at that work or to deliver them. The more unworthy they in giving to idols a share in that worship which they owe to God only.

13. **The high places** – To conquer their strongest holds, which often are in the mountains, and their cities fenced with walls of greatest height and strength. To ride upon, in scripture phrase, is to subdue or conquer. **Out of the rock** – This being a land flowing with honey, where the bees made honey in the holes of rocks, or in the trees that grew upon or among the rocks. **Out of the flinty rocks** – The olive-trees grow and bear most fruit in rocky or hilly places.

14. **Fat of lambs** – For though the fat wherewith the inward parts were covered was not to be eaten by them, but offered to God, yet that fat which was mixed with the flesh they might eat, as the Jewish doctors note. **Bashan** – A place famous for excellent cattle. **Fat of kidneys of wheat** – With the finest of the grains of wheat; compared to kidneys for their shape and largeness.

15. **Jeshurun** – Israel whom he calls right or upright, (as the word signifies) by way of instruction to mind them what they professed and ought to be; to shew them what a shame it was to degenerate so much from their name and profession. **Kicked** – As well fed cattle use to do: he grew insolent and rebellious against God and against his word and spirit.

16. **To jealousy** – To anger and fury, for jealousy is the rage of a man. And withal it implies the ground of his anger, their falseness to God whom they had accepted as their husband, and their spiritual whoredom with other gods.

17. Unto devils – Unto idols, which the devils brought into the world in opposition to God, in and by which the devils often manifested themselves to men, and gave them answers, and received their worship. The Gentiles pretended to worship God in those idols, and the devils which inspired them, deluded the nations with pretences that they were a sort of lower gods. Moses takes off this mark, and shows the Israelites that these pretended gods were really devils, and therefore that it was the height of madness to honour or worship them. **Not to God** – For God utterly rejected those sacrifices which they offered to him together with idols. **They knew not** – Or, who never knew them, that is, never showed any kindness to them, or did them any good: **New gods** – Not simply or absolutely, for some of these had been worshipped for many generations, but comparatively to the true God, who is the ancient of days, De 7:9, and who was worshipped from the beginning of the world. **Feared not** – Served not, worshipped not.

18. Of the rock – Of God, one of whose titles this is, or of Christ, who is called the rock, 1 Cor 10:4, whom the Israelites tempted.

A prediction of judgments for their aggravated impieties (19–35)

19. His sons and daughters – Such they were by calling and profession.

20. I will see – I will make them and others see, what the fruit of such actions shall be. **No faith** – No fidelity: perfidious, that have broken their covenant so solemnly made with me.

21. I will move them to jealousy with those that are not a people – With the Heathen nations, who are none of my people, who scarce deserve the name of a people, as being without the knowledge and fear of God, which is the foundation of all true policy and government, and many of them destitute of all government, laws and order. And yet these people I will take in your stead, receive them and reject you; which, when it came to pass how desperately did it provoke the Jews to jealousy? **A foolish nation** – So the Gentiles were both in the opinion of the Jews and in truth and reality, notwithstanding all their pretences to wisdom, there being nothing more foolish or brutish than the worship of idols.

22. A fire is kindled – Great and grievous judgments shall be inflicted, which often come under the name of fire. Are they proud of their plenty? It shall burn up the increase of the earth. Are they confident of their strength? It shall destroy the very foundations of the mountains. It shall burn unto the lowest hell: it shall bring them to the very depth of misery in this world, which yet will be but a faint resemblance of their endless misery in the next.

23. Spend mine arrows – Even empty my quiver, and send upon them all my plagues, which, like arrows shot by a skilful and strong hand, shall speedily reach and certainly hit and mortally wound them.

24. With hunger – With famine, which burns and parches the inward parts, and make the face black as a coal, Lam 4:8. **Burning heat** – From fevers or carbuncles, or other inflaming distempers.

27. The wrath – Their rage against me, as it is expressed, Isa 37:28,29, their furious reproaches against my name, as if I were cruel to my people or unable to deliver them. The fear hereof is ascribed to God after the manner of men. **Strangely** – Insolently and arrogantly above what they used to do.

28. Void of counsel – Their enemies are foolish people, and therefore make so false and foolish a judgment upon things.

29. They – Israel. **Latter end** – What their end will be, and that tho' God spare them long, yet at last judgment will certainly overtake them.

30. One – Israelite. **Their rock** – Their God, who was their refuge and defence. **Sold them** – Namely, for bond-slaves, had given themselves up into their enemies hands. **Shut them up** – As it were in the net which their enemies had laid for them.

31. Being judges – Who by their dear bought experience have been forced to acknowledge that our God was far stronger than they and their false gods together.

32. For – As if he had said, This is the reason why their rock hath shut them up. **Their vine is of the vine of Sodom** – The people of Israel, which I planted as a choice vine, are now degenerated and become like the vine of Sodom, their principles and practices are all corrupt and abominable. **Bitter** – Their fruits are loathsome to me, mischievous to others, and at last will be pernicious to themselves.

34. This – All their wickedness mentioned before. My long suffering towards them may make them think I have forgotten their sins, but I remember them punctually, they are sealed up as in a bag, Job 14:17, and as men seal up their treasures.

35. Their feet shall slide – They who now think they stand fast and unmoveable, shall fall into utter destruction. **In due time** – Though not so soon as some may expect, yet in that time when it shall be most proper, when they have filled up the measure of their sins. **At hand** – Heb. is near. So the scripture often speaks of those things which are at many hundred years distance, to signify, that though they may be afar off as to our measures of time, yet in God's account they are near, they are as near as may be, when the measure of their sins is once full, the judgment shall not be deferred.

A promise of vengeance upon their enemies, and deliverance for a remnant (36–43)

36. For – Or, nevertheless, having spoken of the dreadful calamity which would come upon his people, he now turns his discourse into a more comfortable strain, and begins to shew that after God had sorely chastised his people, he would have mercy upon them and turn their captivity. **Judge his people** – Shall plead their cause, shall protect and deliver them. **Repent** – Of the evils he hath brought upon them. **None shut up** – Either in their strong cities or castles or other hiding places, or in the enemies hands or prisons, whence there might be some hope or possibility of redemption; and none left, as the poor and contemptible people are neglected and usually left by the conquerors in the conquered land, but all seem to be cut off and destroyed.

37. He shall say – The Lord, before he deliver his people, will first convince them of their former folly in forsaking him and following idols.

38. Which did eat – That is, to whom you offered sacrifices and oblations after the manner of the Gentiles. **Help you** – If they can.

39. See now – Learn by your own sad experience what vain and impotent things idols are. **I am he** – The only true, omnipotent and irresistible God.

40. I lift up my hand – I solemnly swear, that I will do what here follows. **I live** – As sure as I live.

41. If I whet my sword – If once I begin to prepare for war and for the execution of my sentence. **Judgment** – Of the instruments of judgment, of the weapons of war. A metaphor from warriors, that take their weapons into their hand, when they intend to fight.

42. Captives – Whom my sword hath sorely wounded, though not utterly killed. **From the beginning** – When once I begin to revenge myself and my people upon mine and their enemies, I will go on and make a full end.

43. Rejoice – He calls upon the nations to rejoice and bless God for his favours, and especially for the last wonderful deliverance which shall be given to the Jews, when they shall be converted to the gospel in the last days; which they have all reason to do, because of that singular advantage which all nations will have at that time and upon that occasion.

An exhortation annexed (44–47)

44. He and Hoshea – Or Joshua. Probably Moses spoke it to as many as could hear him, while Joshua in another assembly at the same time delivered it to as many as his voice would reach. Thus Joshua, as well as Moses, would be a witness against them, if ever they forsook God.

47. Not vain – It is not an unprofitable or contemptible work I advise you to, but well worthy of your most serious care.

Orders given to Moses, to go up to the mount and die (48–52)

48. That self-same day – Now he had finished his work, why should he desire to live a day longer? He had indeed formerly desired and prayed, that he might go over Jordan: but now he is entirely satisfied, and saith no more of that matter.

49. Nebo – A ridge or top of the mountains of Abarim.

51. Because ye trespassed – God reminds him of the sin he had committed long before. It is good for the holiest of men to die repenting, even of their early sins.

52. Yet thou shalt see the land – And see it as the earnest of that better country, which is only seen with the eye of faith. What is death to him who has a believing prospect and a steadfast hope of eternal life?

Chapter 33

The blessing of Moses. He pronounces them all blessed, in what God had done for them, already (1–5)

1. Moses blessed Israel – He is said to bless them, by praying to God with faith for his blessing upon them; and by foretelling the blessings which God would confer upon them. And Moses calls himself here the man of God, that is, the servant or prophet of God, to acquaint them that the following prophecies were not his own inventions, but divine inspirations. **The children of Israel** – The several tribes: only Simeon is omitted, either in detestation of their parent Simeon's bloody carriage, for which Jacob gives that tribe a curse rather than a blessing, in Gen 49:5-7. Or, because that tribe had no distinct inheritance, but was to have its portion in the tribe of Judah, Jos 19:1.

2. The Lord came – Namely, to the Israelites, manifested himself graciously and gloriously among them. **From Sinai** – Beginning at Sinai, where the first appearance of God was, and so going on with them to Seir and Paran. **And rose up** – He appeared or showed himself, as the sun doth when it riseth. **From Seir** – From the mountain or land of Edom, to which place the Israelites came, Num 20:14, and from thence God led them on towards the land of promise, and then gloriously appeared for them in subduing Sihon and Og before them. But because the land of Edom is sometimes taken more largely, and so reacheth even to the Red-sea, and therefore mount Sinai was near to it, and because Paran was also near Sinai, being the next station into which they came from the wilderness of Sinai: all this verse may belong to God's appearance in mount Sinai, where that glorious light which shone upon mount Sinai directly, did in all probability scatter its beams into adjacent parts, such as Seir and Paran were. And if so, this is only a poetical expression of the same thing in divers words, and God coming or rising or shining from or to or in Sinai and Seir and Paran note one and the same illustrious action of God appearing there with ten thousands of his saints or holy angels, and giving a fiery law to them. **Paran** – A place where God eminently manifested his presence and goodness both in giving the people flesh which they desired, and in appointing the seventy elders and pouring forth his spirit upon them. **With ten thousands of saints** – That is, with a great company of holy angels, Psa 68:17 Dan 7:10, which attended upon him in this great and glorious work of giving the law, as may be gathered from Acts 7:53 Gal 3:19. **From his right hand** – Which both wrote the law and gave it to men. An allusion to men who ordinarily write and give gifts with their right hand. **A fiery law** – The law is called fiery, because it is of a fiery nature purging and searching and inflaming, to signify that fiery wrath which it inflicteth upon sinners for the violation of it, and principally because it was delivered out of the midst of the fire.

3. The people – The tribes of Israel. The sense is, this law, though delivered with fire and smoke and thunder, which might seem to portend nothing but hatred and terror, yet in truth was given to Israel, in great love, as being the great mean of their temporal and eternal salvation. Yea, he embraced the people, and laid them in his bosom! so the word signifies, which speaks not only the dearest love, but the most tender and careful protection. All God's saints or holy ones, that is, his people, were in thy hand, that is, under God's care to protect, direct and govern them. These words are spoken to God: the change of persons, his and thy, is most frequent in the Hebrew tongue. This clause may farther note God's kindness to Israel, in upholding them when the fiery law was delivered, which was done with so much terror that not only the people were ready to sink under it, but even Moses did exceedingly fear and quake. But God sustained both Moses and the people, in or by his hand, whereby he in a manner covered them, that no harm might come to them. **At thy feet** – Like scholars to receive instructions. He alludes to the place where the people waited when the law was delivered, which was at the foot of the mount. **Every one** – Of the people will receive or submit to thy instructions and commands. This may respect either, the peoples promise when they heard the law, that they

would hear and do all that was commanded. Or, their duty to do so.

4. Moses – He speaks this of himself in the third person, which is very usual in the Hebrew language. The law is called their inheritance, because the obligation of it was hereditary, passing from parents to their children, and because this was the best part of their inheritance, the greatest of all those gifts which God bestowed upon them.

5. He was king in Jeshurun – Moses was their king not in title, but in reality, being under God, their supreme governor, and law giver. **Gathered together** – When the princes and people met together for the management of public affairs, Moses was owned by them as their king and lawgiver.

He pronounces a blessing upon each tribe (6–25)

6. Let Reuben live – Though Reuben deserve to be cut off or greatly diminished and obscured, according to Jacob's prediction, Gen 49:4, yet God will spare them and give them a name and portion among the tribes of Israel, and bless them with increase of their numbers. All the ancient paraphrasts refer this to the other world, so far were they from expecting temporal blessings only. Let Reuben live in life eternal, says Onkelos, and not die the second death. Let Reuben live in this world, so Jonathan and the Jerusalem Targum, and not die that death which the wicked die in the world to come.

7. Hear, Lord – God will hear his prayer for the accomplishment of those great things promised to that tribe, Gen 49:8-12. This implies the delays and difficulties Judah would meet with, that would drive him to his prayers, which would be with success. **Unto his people** – When he shall go forth to battle against his enemies and shall fall fiercely upon them, as was foretold, Gen 49:8,9. Bring him back with honour and victory, to his people, to the rest of his tribe who were left at home when their brethren went to battle: and to his brethren the other tribes of Israel. **Let his hands be sufficient for him** – This tribe shall be so numerous and potent that it shall suffice to defend itself without any aid, either from foreign nations or from other tribes; as appeared when this tribe alone was able to grapple with nine or ten of the other tribes. **From his enemies** – Thou wilt preserve this tribe in a special manner, so that his enemies shall not be able to ruin it, as they will do other tribes, and that for the sake of the Messiah who shall spring out of it.

8. Let thy Urim – The Thummim and the Urim, which are thine, O Lord by special institution and consecration, (by which he understands the ephod in which they were put, and the high priesthood, to which they were appropriated, and withal the gifts and graces signified by the Urim and Thummim, and necessary for the discharge of that high-office) shall be with thy holy one, that is, with that priest, whom thou hast consecrated to thyself, and who is holy in a more peculiar manner than all the people were; that is, the priesthood shall be confined to and continued in Aaron's family. **Whom thou didst prove** – Although thou didst try him, and rebuke him, yet thou didst not take away the priesthood from him. **At Massah** – Not at that Massah mentioned Exo 17:7, which is also called Meribah, but at that other Meribah, Num 20:13. **Thou didst strive** – Whom thou didst reprove and chastise.

9. I have not seen him – That is, I have no respect unto them. The sense is, who followed God and his command fully, and executed the judgment enjoined by God without any respect of persons, Exo 32:26,27. **They kept thy covenant** – When the rest broke their covenant with God by that foul sin of idolatry with the calf, that tribe kept themselves pure from that infection, and adhered to God and his worship.

11. His substance – Because he hath no inheritance of his own and therefore wholly depends upon thy blessing. **The work of his hands** – All his holy administrations, which he fitly calls the work of his hands, because a great part of the service of the Levites and priests was done by the labour of their hand and body, whereas the service of evangelical ministers is more spiritual and heavenly. **Smite** – He prays thus earnestly for them, because he foresaw they who were to teach and reprove, and chastise others would have many enemies, and because they were under God, the great preservers and upholders of religion, and their enemies were the enemies of religion itself.

12. Of Benjamin – Benjamin is put next to Levi, because the temple, where the work of the Levites lay, was upon the edge of the lot of this tribe. And 'tis put before Joseph, because of the dignity of Jerusalem, (part of which was in this lot) above Samaria, which was in the tribe of Ephraim: likewise because Benjamin adhered to the house of David and to the temple of God, when the rest of the tribes deserted both. **The beloved of the Lord** – So called in allusion to their father Benjamin who was the beloved of his father Jacob; and because of the kindness of God to this tribe which appeared both in this, that they dwelt in the best part of the land, as Josephus affirms, and in the following privilege. **Shall dwell in safety by him** – Shall have his lot nigh to God's temple, which was both a singular comfort and safeguard to him. **Shall cover** – Shall protect that tribe continually while they cleave to him. **He** – The Lord shall dwell, that is, his temple shall be placed, between his shoulders, that is, in his portion, or between his borders as the word shoulder is often used. And this was truly the situation of the temple, on both sides whereof was Benjamin's portion. And though mount Sion was in the tribe of Judah, yet mount Moriah, on which the temple was built, was in the tribe of Benjamin.

13. And of Joseph – Including both Ephraim and Manasseh. In Jacob's blessing that of Joseph's is the largest. And so it is here. **His land** – His portion shall be endowed with choice blessings from God. **Of heaven** – That is, the precious fruits of the earth brought forth by the influences of heaven, the warmth of the sun, and the rain which God will send from heaven. **The deep** – The springs of water bubbling out of the earth: perhaps it may likewise refer to the great deep, the abyss of waters, which is supposed to be contained in the earth.

14. By the sun – Which opens and warms the earth, cherishes and improves and in due time ripens the seeds and fruits of it. **The moon** – Which by its moisture refreshes and promotes them. Heb. Of the moons, or months, that is, which it bringeth forth in the several months or seasons of the year.

15. The chief things – That is, the excellent fruits, as grapes, olives, figs, which delight in mountains, growing upon, or the precious minerals contained in, their mountains and hills called ancient and lasting, that is, such as have been from the beginning of the world, and are likely to continue to the end of it, in opposition to those hills or mounts which have been cast up by man.

16. And for – And in general for all the choice fruits which the land produceth in all the parts of it, whither hills or valleys. **Fulness thereof** – That is, the plants and cattle and all creatures that grow, increase, and flourish in it. **The good will** – For all other effects of the good will and kindness of God who not long since did for a time dwell or appear in the bush to me in order to the relief of his people, Ex 3:2. **Of Joseph** – That is, of Joseph's posterity. **Him that was separated from his brethren** – His brethren separated him from them by making him a slave, and God distinguished him from them by making him a prince. The preceding words might be rendered, My dweller in the bush. That was an appearance of the divine majesty to Moses only, in token of his particular favour. Many a time had God appeared to Moses; but now he is just dying, he seems to have the most pleasing remembrance, of the first time that he saw the visions of the Almighty. It was here God declared himself the God of Abraham, Isaac and Jacob, and so confirmed the promise made to the father, that promise which our Lord shows, reaches as far as the resurrection and eternal life.

17. His glory is like the firstling of his bullock – Or young bull, which is a stately creature, and was therefore formerly used as an emblem of royal majesty. This seems to note the kingdom which Ephraim should obtain in Jeroboam and his successors. **His horns** – His strength and power shall be very great. **The people** – All that shall oppose him, and particularly the Canaanites. **The ten thousands** – Of the land of Canaan. Though Manasseh be now more numerous, yet Ephraim shall shortly outstrip him, as was foretold Gen 48:17-19.

19. They – Zebulun of whom Moses takes more special notice. And so having dispatched Issachar in two words, he returns to Zebulun. **The people** – the Gentiles, either those of Galilee, which was called Galilee of the Gentiles, who were their neighbours; or people of other nations, with whom they had commerce, which they endeavoured to improve in persuading them to worship the true God. **The mountain** – That is, to the temple, which Moses knew was to be seated upon a mountain. **Sacrifices of righteousness** – Such as God requires. Their trafficking abroad with Heathen nations shall not make them forget their duty at home, nor shall their distance from the place of sacrifice hinder them from coming to it to discharge that duty. **Of the abundance of the sea** – They shall grow rich by the traffic of the sea, and shall consecrate themselves and their riches to God.

20. Enlargeth – That bringeth him out of his straits amid troubles, which he was often engaged in, because he was encompassed with potent enemies. **As a lion** – Safe and secure from his enemies, and terrible to them when they rouse and molest him. **Teareth the arm** – Utterly destroys his enemies, both the head, the seat of the crown, their dignity and principality, and the arm, the subject of strength and instrument of action; both chief princes, and their subjects.

21. The first part – The first fruits of the land of promise, the country of Sihon, which was first conquered, which he is said to provide for himself, because he desired and obtained it of Moses. **Of the law-giver** – Of Moses, whose portion this is called, either because this part of the land beyond Jordan was the only part of the land which Moses was permitted to enter upon: or because it was given him by Moses, whereas the portions beyond Jordan were given to the several tribes by Joshua according to the direction of the lot. **Seated** – Heb. hid or protected: for their wives and children were secured in their cities, while many of their men went over to the war in Canaan. **He came** – He went, or he will go, to the war in Canaan, with the princes, or captains, or rulers of the people of Israel, that is, under their command and conduct, as indeed they did; or with the first of the people; or, in the front of the people, as the Syriac renders it; for this tribe and their brethren whose lot fell beyond Jordan, were to march into Canaan

before their brethren. **He executed** – The just judgment of God against the Canaanites, as the rest of the Israelites did.

22. A lion's whelp – Courageous, and generous, and strong, and successful against his enemies. **Which leapeth** – From Bashan, because there were many and fierce lions in those parts, whence they used to come forth and leap upon the prey. Or this may refer either to the particular victories obtained by Samson, who was of the tribe of Dan, or to a more general achievement of that tribe, when a party of them surprised Laish, which lay in the farthest part of the land of Canaan from them. And the mountain of Bashan lying not far from that city, from whence they probably made their descent upon it, thus leaping from Bashan.

23. Satisfied with favour – With the favour of God. That only is the favour that satisfies the soul. They are happy indeed that have the favour of God; and they shall have it, that place their satisfaction in it. **And full with the blessing of the Lord** – Not only with corn, wine and oil, the fruit of the blessing, but with the blessing itself, the grace of God, according to his promise and covenant. **Possess thou the west and the south** – Or, the sea and the south. This is not to be understood of the place, that his lot should fall there, for he was rather in the east and north of the land; but of the pleasures and commodities of the west or of the sea, which were conveyed to him from his neighbour Zebulun; and of the south, that is, from the southern tribes and parts of Canaan, which were brought to him down the river Jordan, and both sorts of commodities were given him in exchange for the fruitful rich soil which he had in great abundance.

24. Let Asher – Who carries blessedness in his very name, **be blessed with children** – He shall have numerous, strong and healthful children. **Acceptable to his brethren** – By his sweet disposition and winning carriage. **In oil** – He shall have such plenty of oil that he may not only wash his face, but his feet also in it.

25. Iron and brass – The mines of iron and copper, which were in their portion, whence Sidon their neighbour was famous among the Heathens for its plenty of brass, and Sarepta is thought to have its name from the brass and iron which were melted there in great quantity. **Thy strength shall be** – Thy strength shall not be diminished with age, but thou shalt have the vigour of youth even in thine old age: thy tribe shall grow stronger and stronger.

He pronounces them all in general blessed, on account of what God would be to them, and do for them, if they were obedient (26–29)

26. There is none – These are the last words that ever Moses wrote, perhaps the greatest writer that ever lived upon the earth. And this man of God, who had as much reason to know both as ever any mere man had, with his last breath magnifies both the God of Israel, and the Israel of God. Unto the God of Jeshurun, who to help thee, rideth upon the heaven, and with the greatest state and magnificence, on the sky. Riding on the heaven denotes the greatness and glory, in which he manifests himself to the upper world, and the use he makes of the influences of heaven and the products of the clouds, in bringing to pass his own counsels in this lower world. All these he manages and directs, as a man doth the horse he rides on.

27. The eternal God – He who was before all worlds, and will be, when time shall be no more: **Is thy refuge** – Or, thy habitation or mansion-house (so the word signifies) in whom thou art safe, and easy, and at rest, as a man is in his own house. Every true Israelite is at home in God: the soul returns to him, and reposes in him. And they that make him their habitation shall have all the comforts and benefits of an habitation in him. **And underneath are the everlasting arms** – The almighty power of God, which protects and comforts all that trust in him, in their greatest straits and distresses. **He shall thrust out the enemy from before thee** – Shall make room for thee by his resistless power, and shall say, **Destroy them** – Giving thee not only a commission but strength to put it in execution. And, has he not given the same commission and the same strength to believers, to destroy all sin?

29. The shield of thy help – By whom thou art sufficiently guarded against all assailants; and **the sword of thy excellency** – Or, thy most excellent sword, that is, thy strength and the author of all thy past or approaching victories. Those in whose hearts is the excellency of holiness, have God himself for their shield and sword. They are defended by the whole armour of God: His word is their sword, and faith their shield. **And thine enemies shall be found liars unto thee** – Who said they would destroy thee: or at least, that they would never submit: **and thou shalt tread upon their high places** – Their strong holds, palaces and temples. Thus shall the God of peace tread Satan under the feet of all believers, and that shortly.

Chapter 34

Moses having finished his testimony, finishes his life. This chapter was probably added by Samuel, who wrote by divine authority what he found in the records of Joshua, and his successors the Judges.

The view Moses had of the land (1–4)

1. And Moses went up – When he knew the place of his death he cheerfully mounted a steep

hill to come to it. Those who are well acquainted with another world, are not afraid to leave this. When God's servants are sent for out of the world, the summons runs go up and die! **Unto Dan** – To that city which after Moses's death was called so.

2. All Naphtali – The land of Naphtali, which together with Dan, was in the north of Canaan, as Ephraim and Manasseh were in the midland parts, and Judah on the south, and the sea, on the west. So these parts lying in the several quarters are put for all the rest. He stood in the east and saw also Gilead, which was in the eastern part of the land, and thence he saw the north and south and west. **The utmost sea** – The midland sea, which was the utmost bound of the land of promise on the west.

3. The south – The south quarter of the land of Judah, which is towards the salt sea, **the city of palm-trees** – Jericho, so called from the multitude of palm-trees, which were in those parts, as Josephus and Strabo write. From whence and the balm there growing it was called Jericho, which signifies, odoriferous or sweet smelling.

4. I have caused thee to see it – For tho' his sight was good, yet he could not have seen all Canaan, an hundred and sixty miles in length, and fifty or sixty in breadth, if his sight had not been miraculously assisted and enlarged. He saw it at a distance. Such a sight the Old Testament believers had of the kingdom of the Messiah. And such a sight believers have now of the glory that shall be revealed. Such a sight have we now, of the knowledge of the glory of the Lord, which shall cover the earth. Those that come after us shall undoubtedly enter into that promised land: which is a comfort to us, when we find our own carcases falling in this wilderness.

Moses' death, burial, and age (5–7)

5. So Moses the servant of the Lord died – He is called **the servant of the Lord,** not only as a good man, (all such are his servants) but as a man eminently useful, who had served God's counsels in bringing Israel out of Egypt, and leading them through the wilderness. And it was more his honour, to be the servant of the Lord, than to be king in Jeshurun. Yet he dies. Neither his piety nor his usefulness would exempt him from the stroke of death. God's servants must die, that they may rest from their labours, receive their recompense, and make room for others. But when they go hence, they go to serve him better, to serve him day and night in his temple. The Jews say, God sucked his soul out of his body with a kiss. No doubt he died in the embraces of his love.

6. He – The Lord, buried him either immediately, or by the ministry of angels, whereof Michael was the chief or prince. **Of his sepulchre** – Of the particular place where he was buried:

which God hid from the Israelites, to prevent their superstition and idolatry, to which he knew their great proneness. And for this very reason the devil endeavoured to have it known and contended with Michael about it, Jude 1:9. God takes care even of the dead bodies of his servants. As their death is precious, so is their dust. Not one grain of it shall be lost, but the covenant with it shall be remembered.

7. **His eye was not dim** – By a miraculous work of God in mercy to his church and people.

Israel's mourning for Moses (8)

8. **Thirty days** – Which was the usual time of mourning for persons of high place and eminence. 'Tis a debt owing to the surviving honour of deceased worthies, to follow them with our tears, as those who loved and valued them, are sensible of the loss, and humbled for the sins which have provoked God to deprive us of them.

Moses' successor (9)

9. **Wisdom** – And other gifts and graces too, but wisdom is mentioned as being most necessary for the government to which he was now called. **Upon him** – And this was the thing which Moses at that time asked of God for him.

Moses' character (10–12)

10. **Whom the Lord** – Whom God did so freely and familiarly converse with.

12. Moses was greater than any other of the prophets of the Old Testament. By Moses God gave the law, and moulded and formed the Jewish church. By the other prophets he only sent particular reproofs, directions and predictions. But as far as the other prophets came short of him, our Lord Jesus went beyond him. Moses was faithful as a servant, but Christ as a son: his miracles more illustrious, his communion with the father more intimate: for he is in his bosom from eternity. Moses lies buried: but Christ is sitting at the right-hand of God, and of the increase of his government there shall be no end.

INTRODUCTION TO THE PROPHETICAL BOOKS OF THE OLD TESTAMENT

A.R. Faussett

This constitutes the second division, the others being the Law and Hagiographa (the writings). It included Joshua, Judges, First and Second Samuel, First and Second Kings, called the former prophets; and Isaiah, Jeremiah, Ezekiel, &c., to Malachi, the latter prophets. Daniel is excluded, because, though highly endowed with prophetic gifts, he had not filled the prophetic office: his book is therefore classed with the Hagiographa. Ezra probably commenced, and others subsequently completed, the arrangement of the canon. The prophets were not mere predictors. Their Hebrew name, *nabi*, comes from a root 'to boil up as a fountain' (GESENIUS); hence the fervour of inspiration (2Pe 1:21). Others interpret it as from an Arabic root (Ex 4:16, 'spokesman' of God, the Holy Ghost supplying him with words); communicated by dreams (Joe 2:28 Job 33:14-17); or visions, the scene being made to pass before their mind (Isa 1:1); or trance, ecstasy (Nu 24:4,16 Eze 1:3; 3:14); not depriving them, however, of free conscious agency (Jer 20:7,9 1Co 14:32).

Special forms of inspiration

These special forms of inspiration distinguish prophets, strictly so called, from Moses and others, though inspired (Nu 12:6-8). Hence their name seers. Hence, too, the poetical cast of their style, though less restricted, owing to their practical tendency, by the outward forms observed in strictly poetical books. Hence, too, the union of music with prophesying (1Sa 10:5). This ecstatic state, though exalted, is not the highest: for Jesus Christ was never in it, nor Moses. It was rendered necessary by the frailty of the prophets, and the spiritual obtuseness of the people. It accordingly predominates in the Old Testament, but is subordinate in the New Testament, where the Holy Ghost by the fulness of His ordinary gifts renders the extraordinary less necessary.

After the time of the Mosaic economy, the idea of a prophet was regularly connected with the prophetic office – not conferred by men, but by God. In this they differ from mystics whose pretended inspiration is for themselves: prophecy is practical, not dreamy and secluded; the prophet's inspiration is theirs only as God's messengers to the people. His ordinary servants and regular teachers of the people were the priests; the prophets distinguished from them by inspiration, were designed to rouse and excite. In Israel, however, as distinguished from Judah (as there was no true priesthood) the prophets were the regular and only ministers of God. Prophecy in Israel needed to be supported more powerfully: therefore the 'schools' were more established; and more striking prophetic deeds (for example, Elijah's and Elisha's) are recorded, than in Judah. The law was their basis (Isa 8:16,20), both its form and spirit (De 4:2 13:1–3); at times they looked forward to a day when its ever-living spirit would break its then imperfect form for a freer and more perfect development (Jer 3:16; 31:31); but they altered not a tittle in their own days. EICHORN well calls Moses' song (De 32:1–47) the Magna Charta of prophecy. The fulfilment of their predictions was to be the sign of their being real prophets of God (De 18:22); also, their speaking in the name of no other but the true God (De 18:20). Prophecy was the only sanctioned indulgence of the craving after knowledge of future events, which is so prevalent in the East (De 18:10,11). For a momentary inspiration the mere beginning of spiritual life sufficed, as in Balaam's case; but for a continuous mission, the prophet must be converted (Isa 6:7). In Samuel's days (1Sa 10:8 19:20) begin the prophetic 'schools.' These were associations of men, more or less endowed with the Spirit, in which the feebler were helped by those of greater spiritual powers: so at Beth-el and Gilgal (2Ki 2:3 4:38 6:21). Only the leaders stood in immediate communion with God, while the rest were joined to Him through their mediation (1Ki 19:15 2Ki 8:13); the former acted through the latter as their instruments (1Ki 19:16 2Ki 9:1,2). The bestowal of prophetic gifts was not, however, limited to these schools (Am 7:14,15).

Symbolic actions

As to symbolic actions, many of them are not actual but only parts of the prophetic visions, (Jer 13:1–10 25:12–38 Ho 1:2–11). Still the internal actions, when possible and proper, were often expressed externally (1Ki 22:11). Those purely internal express the subject more strikingly than a naked statement could.

Other criteria of a true prophet, besides the two above, were, the accordance of his addresses with the law; his not promising prosperity without repentance; his own assurance of his divine mission (sometimes received reluctantly, Jer 20:8,9 26:12), producing that inward assurance of the truth in others, which is to them a stronger proof from the Spirit of God, than even outward miracles and arguments: his pious life, fortitude in suffering, and freedom from fanaticism, confirm these criteria. Miracles, though proofs, are not to be trusted without the negative criteria (De 13:2). Predictions fulfilled in the prophet's lifetime established his authority thenceforth (1Sa 3:19 Jer 22:11–12 Eze 12:12–13 24:1–27).

Promulgation

As to their promulgation, it was usually oral, before the assembled people, and afterwards revised in writing. The second part of Isaiah and Ezekiel 40–48 were probably not given orally, but in writing. Before Isaiah's and his contemporaries' time, prophecies were not written, as not being intended for universal use. But now a larger field was opened. To the worldly power of heathen nations which threatened to destroy the theocracy is henceforth opposed the kingdom of God, about to conquer all through Messiah, whose coming concerns all ages. The lesser prophets give the quintessence of the prophecies of their respective authors. An instance of the mode of collecting and publishing prophecies occurs (Jer 36:4–14). Those of the later prophets rest on those of the earlier (Zec 1:4 7:7,12).

EWALD fancies that a great number of prophetic rolls have been lost. But the fact of the prophets often alluding to writings which we have, and never to those which it can be proved we have not, makes it likely that we have all those predictions which were committed to writing; the care bestowed on them as divine, and the exact knowledge of them long after (Jer 26:18,19), confirm this view.

Chronological order

The arrangement of the prophetic books is chronological; but as the twelve lesser prophets are regarded as one work, and the three last of them lived later than Jeremiah and Ezekiel, the former are put after the latter. The lesser prophets are arranged chronologically, except Hosea, who being the largest, is placed first, though some were earlier than he; also Jonah, who seems to have been the earliest of the latter prophets.

The Messiah

As to the Messiah, no single prophet gives a complete view of Him: this is made up of the various aspects of Him in different prophecies combined; just as His life in the Gospels is one under a fourfold aspect. In the first part of Isaiah, addressed to the whole people, the prominent idea is His triumph, as King, the design being there to remove their fears of the surrounding nations; in the second, addressed to the elect remnant, He is exhibited as Prophet and Priest, Himself being the sacrifice.

JOSHUA

Matthew Henry

Introduction

Here is the history of Israel's passing into the land of Canaan, conquering and dividing it, under the command of Joshua, and their history until his death. The power and truth of God in fulfilling his promises to Israel, and in executing his justly threatened vengeance on the Canaanites, are wonderfully displayed. This should teach us to regard the tremendous curses denounced in the word of God against impenitent sinners, and to seek refuge in Christ Jesus.

Chapter 1

The Lord appoints Joshua to succeed Moses (1–4)

God promises to assist Joshua (5–9)

Preparation to pass over Jordan (10–15)

The people promise to obey Joshua (16–18)

The Lord appoints Joshua to succeed Moses (1–4)

Joshua had attended upon Moses. He who was called to honour, had been long used to business. Our Lord Jesus took upon him the form of a servant. Joshua was trained up under command. Those are fittest to rule, who have learned to obey. The removal of useful men should quicken survivors to be the more diligent in doing good. Arise, go over Jordan. At this place and at this time the banks were overflowed. Joshua had no bridge or boats, and yet he must believe that God, having ordered the people over, would open a way.

God promises to assist Joshua (5–9)

Joshua is to make the law of God his rule. He is charged to meditate therein day and night, that he might understand it. Whatever affairs of this world we have to mind, we must not neglect the one thing needful. All his orders to the people, and his judgments, must be according to the law of God. Joshua must himself be under command; no man's dignity or dominion sets him above the law of God. He is to encourage himself with the promise and presence of God. Let not the sense of thine own infirmities dishearten thee; God is all-sufficient. I have commanded, called, and commissioned thee to do it, and will be sure to bear thee out in it. When we are in the way of duty, we have reason to be strong and very bold. Our Lord Jesus, as Joshua here, was borne up under his sufferings by a regard to the will of God, and the commandment from his Father.

Preparation to pass over Jordan (10–15)

Joshua says to the people, Ye shall pass over Jordan, and shall possess the land; because God had said so to him. We honour the truth of God, when we stagger not at the promise of God. The two tribes and a half were to go over Jordan with their brethren. When God, by his providence, has given us rest, we ought to consider what service we may do to our brethren.

The people promise to obey Joshua (16–18)

The people of Israel engage to obey Joshua. All that thou commandest us to do we will readily do, without murmuring or disputing, and whithersoever thou sendest us we will go. The best we can ask of God for our magistrates, is, that they may have the presence of God; that will make them blessings to us, so that in seeking this for them, we consult our own interest. May we be enabled to enlist under the banner of the Captain of our salvation, to be obedient to his commands, and to fight the good fight of faith, with all that trust in and love his name, against all who oppose his authority; for whoever refuses to obey him must be destroyed.

Chapter 2

Rahab receives and hides two Israelites (1–7)

Rahab and the spies (8–21)

The return of the spies (22–24)

Rahab receives and hides two Israelites (1–7)

Faith in God's promises ought not to do away, but to encourage our diligence in the use of proper means. The providence of God directed the spies to the house of Rahab. God knew where there was one that would be true to them, though they did not. Rahab appears to have been an innkeeper; and if she had formerly been one of bad life, which is doubtful, she had left her evil courses. That which seems to us most accidental, is often overruled by the Divine providence to serve great ends. It was by faith that Rahab received those with peace, against whom her king and country had war. We are sure this was a good work; it is so spoken of by the apostle, James 2:25; and she did it by faith, such a faith as set her above the fear of man. Those only are true believers, who find in their hearts to venture for God; they take his people for their people, and cast in their lot among them. The spies were led by the special providence of God, and Rahab entertained them out of regard to Israel and Israel's God, and not for lucre or for any evil purpose. Though excuses may be offered for the guilt of Rahab's falsehood, it seems best to admit nothing which tends to explain it away. Her views of the Divine law must have been very dim: a falsehood like this, told by those who enjoy the light of revelation, whatever the motive, would deserve heavy censure.

Rahab and the spies (8–21)

Rahab had heard of the miracles the Lord wrought for Israel. She believed that his promises would certainly be fulfilled, and his threatenings take effect; and that there was no way of escape but by submitting to him, and joining with his people. The conduct of Rahab proved that she had the real principle of Divine faith. Observe the promises the spies made to her. The goodness of God is often expressed by his kindness and truth, Psalm 117:2; in both these we must be followers of him. Those who will be conscientious in keeping promises, are cautious in making them. The spies make needful conditions. The scarlet cord, like the blood upon the doorpost at the Passover, recalls to remembrance the sinner's security under the atoning blood of Christ; and that we are to flee thereto for refuge from the wrath of a justly offended God. The same cord Rahab used for the saving of these Israelites, was to be used for her own safety. What we serve and honour God with, we may expect he will bless, and make useful to us.

The return of the spies (22–24)

The report the spies brought was encouraging. All the people of the country faint because of Israel; they have neither wisdom to yield, nor courage to fight. Those terrors of conscience, and that sense of Divine wrath, which dismay the ungodly, but bring not to repentance, are fearful forebodings of approaching destruction. But grace yet abounds to the chief of sinners. Let them, without delay, flee to Christ, and all shall be well.

Chapter 3

The Israelites come to Jordan (1–6)

The Lord encourages Joshua – Joshua encourages the people (7–13)

The Israelites pass through Jordan on dry land (14–17)

The Israelites come to Jordan (1–6)

The Israelites came to Jordan in faith, having been told that they should pass it. In the way of duty, let us proceed as far as we can, and depend on the Lord. Joshua led them. Particular notice is taken of his early rising, as afterwards upon other occasions, which shows how little he sought his own ease. Those who would bring great things to pass, must rise early. Love not sleep, lest thou come to poverty. All in public stations should always attend to the duty of their place. The people were to follow the ark. Thus must we walk after the rule of the word, and the direction of the Spirit, in everything; so shall peace be upon us as upon the Israel of God; but we must follow our ministers only as they follow Christ. All their way through the wilderness was an untrodden path, but most so this through Jordan. While we are here, we must expect and prepare to pass ways that we have not passed before; but in the path of duty we may proceed with boldness and cheerfulness. Whether we are called to suffer poverty, pain, labour, persecution, reproach, or death, we are following the Author and Finisher of our faith; nor can we set our feet in any dangerous or difficult spot, through our whole journey, but faith will there see the prints of the Redeemer's feet, who trod that very path to glory above, and bids us follow him, that where he is, we may be also. They were to sanctify themselves. Would we experience the effects of God's love and power, we must put away sin, and be careful not to grieve the Holy Spirit of God.

The Lord encourages Joshua – Joshua encourages the people (7–13)

The waters of Jordan shall be cut off. This must be done in such a way as never was done, but in the dividing of the Red sea. That miracle is here repeated; God has the same power to finish the salvation of his people, as to begin it; the Word of the Lord was as truly with Joshua as with Moses. God's appearances for his people ought to encourage faith and hope. God's work is perfect, he will keep his people. Jordan's flood cannot keep out Israel, Canaan's force cannot turn them out again.

The Israelites pass through Jordan on dry land (14–17)

Jordan overflowed all its banks. This magnified the power of God, and his kindness to Israel. Although those who oppose the salvation of God's people have all advantages, yet God can and will conquer. This passage over Jordan, as an entrance to Canaan, after their long, weary wanderings in the wilderness, shadowed out the believer's passage through death to heaven, after he has finished his wanderings in this sinful world. Jesus, typified by the ark, hath gone before, and he crossed the river when it most flooded the country around. Let us treasure up experiences of His faithful and tender care, that they may help our faith and hope in the last conflict.

Chapter 4

Stones taken out of Jordan (1–9)

The people pass through Jordan (10–19)

The twelve stones placed in Gilgal (20–24)

Stones taken out of Jordan (1–9)

The works of the Lord are so worthy of remembrance, and the heart of man is so prone to forget them, that various methods are needful to refresh our memories, for the glory of God,

our advantage, and that of our children. God gave orders for preparing this memorial.

The people pass through Jordan (10–19)

The priests with the ark did not stir till ordered to move. Let none be weary of waiting, while they have the tokens of God's presence with them, even the ark of the covenant, though it be in the depths of adversity. Notice is taken of the honour put upon Joshua. Those are feared in the best manner, and to the best purpose, who make it appear that God is with them, and that they set him before them.

The twelve stones placed in Gilgal (20–24)

It is the duty of parents to tell their children betimes of the words and works of God, that they may be trained up in the way they should go. In all the instruction parents give their children, they should teach them to fear God. Serious godliness is the best learning. Are we not called, as much as the Israelites, to praise the loving-kindness of our God? Shall we not raise a pillar to our God, who has brought us through dangers and distresses in so wonderful a way? For hitherto the Lord hath helped us, as much as he did his saints of old. How great the stupidity and ingratitude of men, who perceive not His hand, and will not acknowledge his goodness, in their frequent deliverances.

Chapter 5

The Canaanites are afraid; circumcision renewed (1–9)

The Passover at Gilgal, the manna ceases (10–12)

The Captain of the Lord's host appears to Joshua (13–15)

The Canaanites are afraid; circumcision renewed (1–9)

How dreadful is their case, who see the wrath of God advancing towards them, without being able to turn it aside, or escape! Such will be the horrible situation of the wicked; nor can words express the anguish of their feelings, or the greatness of their terror. Oh that they would now take warning, and before it be too late, flee for refuge to lay hold upon that hope set before them in the gospel! God impressed these fears on the Canaanites, and dispirited them. This gave a short rest to the Israelites, and circumcision rolled away the reproach of Egypt. They were hereby owned to be the free-born children of God, having the seal of the covenant. When God glorifies himself in perfecting the salvation of his people, he not only silences all enemies, but rolls back their reproaches upon themselves.

The Passover at Gilgal, the manna ceases (10–12)

A solemn Passover was kept, at the time appointed by the law, in the plains of Jericho, in defiance of the Canaanites round about them. It was a performance of the promise, that when they went up to keep the feasts, their land should be under the special protection of the Divine providence, Exodus 34:24 . Notice is taken of the ceasing of the manna as soon as they had eaten the old corn of the land. For as it came just when they needed, so it continued as long as they needed it. This teaches us not to expect supplies by miracles, when they may be had in a common way. The word and ordinances of God are spiritual manna, with which God nourishes his people in this wilderness. Though often forfeited, yet they are continued while we are here; but when we come to the heavenly Canaan, this manna will cease, for we shall no longer need it.

The Captain of the Lord's host appears to Joshua (13–15)

We read not of any appearance of God's glory to Joshua till now. There appeared to him one as a man to be noticed. This Man was the Son of God, the eternal Word. Joshua gave him Divine honours: he received them, which a created angel would not have done, and he is called Jehovah, 6:2. To Abraham he appeared as a traveller; to Joshua as a man of war. Christ will be to his people what their faith needs. Christ had his sword drawn, which encouraged Joshua to carry on the war with vigour. Christ's sword drawn in his hand, denotes how ready he is for the defence and salvation of his people. His sword turns every way. Joshua will know whether he is a friend or a foe. The cause between the Israelites and Canaanites, between Christ and Beelzebub, will not admit of any man's refusing to take one part or the other, as he may do in worldly contests. Joshua's inquiry shows an earnest desire to know the will of Christ, and a cheerful readiness and resolution to do it. All true Christians must fight under Christ's banner, and they will conquer by his presence and assistance.

Chapter 6

The siege of Jericho (1–5)

The city is compassed (6–16)

Jericho is taken; Rahab and her family are saved (17–27)

The siege of Jericho (1–5)

Jericho resolves Israel shall not be its master. It shut itself up, being strongly fortified both by art and nature. Thus were they foolish, and their hearts hardened to their destruction; the miserable case of all that strengthen themselves against the Almighty. God resolves Israel shall be its master, and that quickly. No warlike preparations were to be made. By the uncommon method of besieging the city, the Lord honoured the ark, as the symbol of his presence, and showed that all the victories were from him. The faith and patience of the people were proved and increased.

The city is compassed (6–16)

Wherever the ark went, the people attended it. God's ministers, by the trumpet of the everlasting gospel, which proclaims liberty and victory, must encourage the followers of Christ in their spiritual warfare. As promised deliverances must be expected in God's way, so they must be expected in his time. At last the people were to shout: they did so, and the walls fell. This was a shout of faith; they believed the walls of Jericho would fall. It was a shout of prayer; they cry to Heaven for help, and help came.

Jericho is taken; Rahab and her family are saved (17–27)

Jericho was to be a solemn and awful sacrifice to the justice of God, upon those who had filled up the measure of their sins. So He appoints, from whom, as creatures, they received their lives, and to whom, as sinners, they had forfeited them. Rahab perished not with them that believed not, Hebrews 11:31. All her kindred were saved with her; thus faith in Christ brings salvation to the house, Acts 14:31. She, and they with her, were plucked as brands from the burning. With Rahab, or with the men of Jericho; our portion must be assigned, as we possess or disregard the sign of salvation; even faith in Christ, which worketh by love. Let us remember what depends upon our choice, and let us choose accordingly. God shows the weight of a Divine curse; where it rests there is no getting from under it; for it brings ruin without remedy.

Chapter 7

The Israelites smitten at Ai (1–5)

Joshua's humiliation and prayer (6–9)

God instructs Joshua what to do (10–15)

Achan is detected, He is destroyed (16–26)

The Israelites smitten at Ai (1–5)

Achan took some of the spoil of Jericho. The love of the world is that root of bitterness, which of all others is most hardly rooted up. We should take heed of sin ourselves, lest by it many be defiled or disquieted, Hebrews 12:15; and take heed of having fellowship with sinners, lest we share their guilt. It concerns us to watch over one another to prevent sin, because others' sins may be to our damage. The easy conquest of Jericho excited contempt of the enemy, and a disposition to expect the Lord to do all for them without their using proper means. Thus men abuse the doctrines of Divine grace, and the promises of God, into excuses for their own sloth and self-indulgence. We are to work out our own salvation, though it is God that works in us. It was a dear victory to the Canaanites, whereby Israel was awakened and reformed, and reconciled to their God, and the people of Canaan hardened to their own ruin.

Joshua's humiliation and prayer (6–9)

Joshua's concern for the honour of God, more than even for the fate of Israel, was the language of the Spirit of adoption. He pleaded with God. He laments their defeat, as he feared it would reflect on God's wisdom and power, his goodness and faithfulness. We cannot at any time urge a better plea than this, Lord, what wilt thou do for thy great name? Let God be glorified in all, and then welcome his whole will.

God instructs Joshua what to do (10–15)

God awakens Joshua to inquiry, by telling him that when this accursed thing was put away, all would be well. Times of danger and trouble should be times of reformation. We should look at home, into our own hearts, into our own houses, and make diligent search to find out if there be not some accursed thing there, which God sees and abhors; some secret lust, some unlawful gain, some undue withholding from God or from others. We cannot prosper, until the accursed thing be destroyed out of our hearts, and put out of our habitations and our families, and forsaken in our lives. When the sin of sinners finds them out, God is to be acknowledged. With a certain and unerring judgment, the righteous God does and will distinguish between the innocent and the guilty; so that though the righteous are of the same tribe, and family, and household with the wicked, yet they never shall be treated as the wicked.

Achan is detected, He is destroyed (16–26)

See the folly of those that promise themselves secrecy in sin. The righteous God has many ways of bringing to light the hidden works of darkness. See also, how much it is our concern, when God is contending with us, to find out the cause that troubles us. We must pray with holy Job, Lord, show me wherefore thou contendest with me. Achan's sin began in the eye. He saw these fine things, as Eve saw the forbidden fruit. See what comes of suffering the heart to walk

after the eyes, and what need we have to make this covenant with our eyes, that if they wander they shall be sure to weep for it. It proceeded out of the heart. They that would be kept from sinful actions, must mortify and check in themselves sinful desires, particularly the desire of worldly wealth. Had Achan looked upon these things with an eye of faith, he would have seen they were accursed things, and would have dreaded them; but looking on them with an eye of sense only, he saw them as goodly things, and coveted them. When he had committed the sin, he tried to hide it. As soon as he had got this plunder, it became his burden, and he dared not to use his ill-gotten treasure. So differently do objects of temptation appear at a distance, to what they do when they have been gotten.

See the deceitfulness of sin; that which is pleasing in the commission, is bitter in the reflection. See how they will be deceived that rob God. Sin is a very troublesome thing, not only to a sinner himself, but to all about him. The righteous God will certainly recompense tribulation to them that trouble his people. Achan perished not alone in his sin. They lose their own, who grasp at more than their own. His sons and daughters were put to death with him. It is probable that they helped to hide the things; they must have known of them. What fatal consequences follow, even in this world, to the sinner himself, and to all belonging him! One sinner destroys much good. What, then, will be the wrath to come? Let us flee from it to Christ Jesus as the sinner's Friend. There are circumstances in the confession of Achan, marking the progress of sin, from its first entrance into the heart to its being done, which may serve as the history of almost every offence against the law of God, and the sacrifice of Jesus Christ.

Chapter 8

God encourages Joshua (1, 2)

The taking of Ai (3–22)

The destruction of Ai and its king (23–29)

The law read on Ebal and Gerizim (30–35)

God encourages Joshua (1, 2)

When we have faithfully put away sin, that accursed thing which separates between us and God, then, and not till then, we may look to hear from God to our comfort; and God's directing us how to go on in our Christian work and warfare, is a good evidence of his being reconciled to us. God encouraged Joshua to proceed. At Ai the spoil was not to be destroyed as at Jericho, therefore there was no danger of the people's committing such a trespass. Achan, who caught at forbidden spoil, lost that, and life, and all; but the rest of the people, who kept themselves from the accursed thing, were quickly rewarded for their obedience. The way to have the comfort of what God allows us, is, to keep from what he forbids us. No man shall lose by self-denial.

The taking of Ai (3–22)

Observe Joshua's conduct and prudence. Those that would maintain their spiritual conflicts must not love their ease. Probably he went into the valley alone, to pray to God for a blessing, and he did not seek in vain. He never drew back till the work was done. Those that have stretched out their hands against their spiritual enemies, must never draw them back.

The destruction of Ai and its king (23–29)

God, the righteous Judge, had sentenced the Canaanites for their wickedness; the Israelites only executed his doom. None of their conduct can be drawn into an example for others. Especial reason no doubt there was for this severity to the king of Ai; it is likely he had been notoriously wicked and vile, and a blasphemer of the God of Israel.

The law read on Ebal and Gerizim (30–35)

As soon as Joshua got to the mountains Ebal and Gerizim, without delay, and without caring for the unsettled state of Israel, or their enemies, he confirmed the covenant of the Lord with his people, as appointed, verse 27. We must not think to defer covenanting with God till we are settled in the world; nor must any business put us from minding and pursuing the one thing needful. The way to prosper is to begin with God, Matthew 6:33. They built an altar, and offered sacrifice to God, in token of their dedicating themselves to God, as living sacrifices to his honour, in and by a Mediator. By Christ's sacrifice of himself for us, we have peace with God. It is a great mercy to any people to have the law of God in writing, and it is fit that the written law should be in a known tongue, that it may be seen and read of all men.

Chapter 9

The kings combine against Israel (1, 2)

The Gibeonites apply for peace (3–13)

They obtain peace, but are soon detected (14–21)

The Gibeonites are to be bondmen (22–27)

The kings combine against Israel (1, 2)

Hitherto the Canaanites had defended themselves, but here they consult to attack Israel. Their minds were blinded, and their hearts hardened to their destruction. Though often at enmity with each other, yet they united against Israel. Oh that Israel would learn of Canaanites, to sacrifice private interests to the public welfare, and to lay aside all quarrels among themselves, that they may unite against the enemies of God's kingdom!

The Gibeonites apply for peace (3–13)

Other people heard these tidings, and were driven thereby to make war upon Israel; but the Gibeonites were led to make peace with them. Thus the discovery of the glory and the grace of God in the gospel, is to some a savour of life unto life, but 2 Corinthians softens wax and hardens clay. The falsehood of the Gibeonites cannot be justified. We must not do evil that good may come to the God of Israel. We have reason to think Joshua would have been directed by the oracle of God to spare their lives. But when they had once said, 'We are come from a far country,' they were led to say it accounted for their skins, and their clothes: one lie brings on another, and that a third, and so on. The way of that sin is especially down-hill. Yet their faith and prudence are to be commended. In submitting to Israel they submitted to the God of Israel, which implied forsaking their idolatries. And how can we do better than cast ourselves upon the mercy of a God of all goodness? The way to avoid judgment is to meet it by repentance. Let us do like these Gibeonites, seek peace with God in the rags of abasement, and godly sorrow; so our sin shall not be our ruin. Let us be servants to Jesus, our blessed Joshua, and we shall live.

They obtain peace, but are soon detected (14–21)

The Israelites, having examined the provisions of the Gibeonites, hastily concluded that they confirmed their account. We make more haste than good speed, when we stay not to take God with us, and do not consult him by the word and prayer. The fraud was soon found out. A lying tongue is but for a moment. Had the oath been in itself unlawful, it would not have been binding; for no obligation can render it our duty to commit a sin. But it was not unlawful to spare the Canaanites who submitted, and left idolatry, desiring only that their lives might be spared. A citizen of Zion swears to his own hurt, and changes not, Psalm 15:4. Joshua and the princes, when they found that they had been deceived, did not apply to Eleazar the high priest to be freed from their engagement, much less did they pretend that no faith is to be kept with those to whom they had sworn. Let this convince us how we ought to keep our promises, and make good our bargains; and what conscience we ought to make of our words.

The Gibeonites are to be bondmen (22–27)

The Gibeonites do not justify their lie, but plead that they did it to save their lives. And the fear was not merely of the power of man; one might flee from that to the Divine protection; but of the power of God himself, which they saw engaged against them. Joshua sentences them to perpetual bondage. They must be servants, but any work becomes honourable, when it is done for the house of the Lord, and the offices thereof. Let us, in like manner, submit to our Lord Jesus, saying, We are in thy hand, do unto us as seemeth good and right unto thee, only save our souls; and we shall not repent it. If He appoints us to bear his cross, and serve him, that shall be neither shame nor grief to us, while the meanest office in God's service will entitle us to a dwelling in the house of the Lord all the days of our life. And in coming to the Saviour, we do not proceed upon a peradventure. We are invited to draw nigh, and are assured that him that cometh to Him, he will in nowise cast out. Even those things which sound harsh, and are humbling, and form sharp trials of our sincerity, will prove of real advantage.

Chapter 10

Five kings war against Gibeon (1–6)

Joshua succours Gibeon; the sun and moon stand still (7–14)

The kings are taken, their armies defeated, and they are put to death (15–27)

Seven other kings defeated and slain (28–43)

Five kings war against Gibeon (1–6)

When sinners leave the service of Satan and the friendship of the world, that they make peace with God and join Israel, they must not marvel if the world hate them, if their former friends become foes. By such methods Satan discourages many who are convinced of their danger, and almost persuaded to be Christians, but fear the cross. These things should quicken us to apply to God for protection, help, and deliverance.

Joshua succours Gibeon; the sun and moon stand still (7–14)

The meanest and most feeble, who have just begun to trust the Lord, are as much entitled to be protected as those who have long and faithfully been his servants. It is our duty to defend the afflicted, who, like the Gibeonites, are brought into trouble on our account, or for the sake of the gospel. Joshua would not forsake his new vassals. How much less shall our true Joshua fail those who trust in Him! We may be wanting in our trust, but our trust never can want success. Yet God's promises are not to slacken and do away, but to quicken and encourage our endeavours. Notice the great faith of Joshua, and the power of God answering it by the miraculous staying of the sun, that the day of Israel's victories might be made longer. Joshua acted on this occasion by impulse on his mind from the Spirit of God. It was not necessary that Joshua should speak, or the miracle be recorded, according to the modern terms of astronomy. The sun appeared to the Israelites over Gibeon, and the moon over the valley of Ajalon, and there they appeared to be stopped on their course for one whole day. Is any thing too hard for the Lord? forms a sufficient answer to ten thousand difficulties, which objectors have in every age started against the truth of God as revealed in his written word. Proclamation was hereby made to the neighbouring nations, Behold the works of the Lord, and say, What nation is there so great as Israel, who has God so nigh unto them?

The kings are taken, their armies defeated, and they are put to death (15–27)

None moved his tongue against any of the children of Israel. This shows their perfect safety. The kings were called to an account, as rebels against the Israel of God. Refuges of lies will but secure for God's judgment. God punished the abominable wickedness of these kings, the measure of whose iniquity was now full. And by this public act of justice, done upon these ringleaders of the Canaanites in sin, he would possess his people with the greater dread and detestation of the sins of the nations that God cast out from before them. Here is a type and figure of Christ's victories over the powers of darkness, and of believers' victories through him. In our spiritual conflicts we must not be satisfied with obtaining some important victory. We must pursue our scattered enemies, searching out the remains of sin as they rise up in our hearts, and thus pursue the conquest. In so doing, the Lord will afford light until the warfare be accomplished.

Seven other kings defeated and slain (28–43)

Joshua made speed in taking these cities. See what a great deal of work may be done in a little time, if we will be diligent, and improve our opportunities. God here showed his hatred of the idolatries and other abominations of which the Canaanites had been guilty, and shows us how great the provocation was, by the greatness of the destruction brought upon them. Here also was typified the destruction of all the enemies of the Lord Jesus, who, having slighted the riches of his grace, must for ever feel the weight of his wrath. The Lord fought for Israel. They could not have gotten the victory, if God had not undertaken the battle. We conquer when God fights for us; if he be for us, who can be against us?

Chapter 11

Divers kings overcome at the waters of Merom (1–9)

Hazor is taken and burned (10–14)

All that country subdued; the Anakims cut off (15–23)

Divers kings overcome at the waters of Merom (1–9)

The wonders God wrought for the Israelites were to encourage them to act vigorously themselves. Thus the war against Satan's kingdom, carried on by preaching the gospel, was at first forwarded by miracles; but being fully proved to be of God, we are now left to the Divine grace in the usual course, in the use of the sword of the Spirit. God encouraged Joshua. Fresh dangers and difficulties make it necessary to seek fresh supports from the word of God, which we have nigh unto us for use in every time of need. God proportions our trials to our strength, and our strength to our trials. Joshua's obedience in destroying the horses and chariots, shows his self-denial in compliance with God's command. The possession of things on which the carnal heart is prone to depend, is hurtful to the life of faith, and the walk with God; therefore it is better to be without worldly advantages, than to have the soul endangered by them.

Hazor is taken and burned (10–14)

The Canaanites filled up the measure of their iniquity, and were, as a judgment, left to the pride, obstinacy, and enmity of their hearts, and to the power of Satan; all restraints being withdrawn, while the dispensations of Providence tended to drive them to despair. They brought on themselves the vengeance they justly merited, of which the Israelites were to be executioners, by the command the Lord gave to Moses.

All that country subdued; the Anakims cut off (15–23)

Never let the sons of Anak be a terror to the Israel of God, for their day to fall will come. The land rested from war. It ended not in a peace with the Canaanites, that was forbidden, but in a peace from them. There is a rest, a rest from war, remaining for the people of God, into

which they shall enter, when their warfare is accomplished. That which was now done, is compared with what had been said to Moses. God's word and his works, if viewed together, will be found mutually to set each other forth. If we make conscience of our duty, we need not question the performance of the promise. But the believer must never put off his armour, or expect lasting peace, till he closes his eyes in death; nay, as his strength and usefulness increase, he may expect more heavy trials; yet the Lord will not permit any enemies to assault the believer till he has prepared him for the battle. Christ Jesus ever lives to plead for his people, and their faith shall not fail, however Satan may be permitted to assault them. And however tedious, sharp, and difficult the believer's warfare, his patience in tribulation may be encouraged by the joyfulness of hope; for he will, ere long, rest from sin and from sorrow in the Canaan above.

Chapter 12

The two kings conquered by Moses (1–6)

The kings whom Joshua smote (7–24)

The two kings conquered by Moses (1–6)

Fresh mercies must not drown the remembrance of former mercies, nor must the glory of the present instruments of good to the church diminish the just honour of those who went before them, since God is the same who wrought by both. Moses gave to one part of Israel a very rich and fruitful country, but it was on the outside of Jordan. Joshua gave to all Israel the holy land, within Jordan. So the law has given to some few of God's spiritual Israel worldly blessings, earnests of good things to come; but our Lord Jesus, the true Joshua, provided for all the children of promise spiritual blessings, and the heavenly Canaan.

The kings whom Joshua smote (7–24)

We have here the limits of the country Joshua conquered. A list is given of the kings subdued by Israel: thirty-one in all. This shows how fruitful Canaan then was, in which so many chose to throng together. This was the land God appointed for Israel; yet in our day it is one of the most barren and unprofitable countries in the world. Such is the effect of the curse it lies under, since its possessors rejected Christ and his gospel, as was foretold by Moses, Deuteronomy 29:23. The vengeance of a righteous God, inflicted on all these kings and their subjects, for their wickedness, should make us dread and hate sin. The fruitful land bestowed on his chosen people, should fill our hearts with hope and confidence in his mercy, and with humble gratitude.

Chapter 13

Bounds of the land not yet conquered (1–6)
Inheritance of Reuben (7–33)

Bounds of the land not yet conquered (1–6)

At this chapter begins the account of the dividing of the land of Canaan among the tribes of Israel by lot; a narrative showing the performance of the promise made to the fathers, that this land should be given to the seed of Jacob. We are not to pass over these chapters of hard names as useless. Where God has a mouth to speak, and a hand to write, we should find an ear to hear, and an eye to read; and may God give us a heart to profit! Joshua is supposed to have been about one hundred years old at this time. It is good for those who are old and stricken in years to be put in remembrance of their being so. God considers the frame of his people, and would not have them burdened with work above their strength. And all people, especially old people, should set to do that quickly which must be done before they die, lest death prevent them, Ecclesiastes 9:10. God promised that he would make the Israelites masters of all the countries yet unsubdued, though Joshua was old, and not able to do it; old, and not likely to live to see it done. Whatever becomes of us, and however we may be laid aside as despised, broken vessels, God will do his own work in his own time. We must work out our salvation, then God will work in us, and work with us; we must resist our spiritual enemies, then God will tread them under our feet; we must go forth to our Christian work and warfare, then God will go forth before us.

Inheritance of Reuben (7–33)

The land must be divided among the tribes. It is the will of God that every man should know his own, and not take that which is another's. The world must be governed, not by force, but right. Wherever our habitation is placed, and in whatever honest way our portion is assigned, we should consider them as allotted of God; we should be thankful for, and use them as such, while every prudent method should be used to prevent disputes about property, both at present and in future. Joshua must be herein a type of Christ, who has not only conquered the gates of hell for us, but has opened to us the gates of heaven, and having purchased the eternal inheritance for all believers, will put them in possession of it. Here is a general description of the country given to the two tribes and a half, by Moses. Israel must know their own, and keep to it; and may not, under pretence of their being God's peculiar people, encroach on their neighbours. Twice in this chapter it is noticed, that to the tribe of Levi Moses gave no inheritance: see Numbers 18:20. Their maintenance must be brought out of all the tribes. The ministers of the Lord should show themselves indifferent about worldly interests, and the people should take care they want nothing suitable. And happy are those who have the Lord God of Israel for their inheritance, though little of this world falls to their lot. His providences will supply their wants, his consolations will support their souls, till they gain heavenly joy and everlasting pleasures.

Chapter 14

The nine tribes and a half to have their inheritance (1–5)
Caleb obtains Hebron (6–15)

The nine tribes and a half to have their inheritance (1–5)

The Israelites must occupy the new conquests. Canaan would have been subdued in vain, if it had not been inhabited. Yet every man might not go and settle where he pleased. God shall choose our inheritance for us. Let us survey our heritage of present mercy, our prospect for the land of promise, eternal in the heavens. Is God any respecter of persons? Is it not better that our place, as to earthly good or sorrow, should be determined by the infinite wisdom of our heavenly Father, than by our own ignorance? Should not those for whom the great mystery of godliness was exhibited, those whose redemption was purchased by Jesus Christ, thankfully refer their earthly concerns to his appointment?

Caleb obtains Hebron (6–15)

Caleb's request is, 'Give me this mountain,' (verse 12), or Hebron, because it was formerly in God's promise to him, and he would let Israel know how much he valued the promise. Those who live by faith value that which is given by God's promise, far above what is given by his providence only. It was now in the Anakims' possession, and Caleb would let Israel know how little he feared the enemy, and that he would encourage them to push on their conquests. Caleb answered to his name, which signifies 'all heart.' Hebron was settled on Caleb and his heirs, because he wholly followed the Lord God of Israel. Happy are we if we follow him. Singular piety shall be crowned with singular favour.

Chapter 15

The borders of the lot of Judah (1–12)

Caleb's portion, His daughter's blessing (13–19)

The cities of Judah (20–63)

The borders of the lot of Judah (1–12)

Joshua allotted to Judah, Ephraim, and the half of Manasseh, their inheritances before they left Gilgal. Afterwards removing to Shiloh, another survey was made, and the other tribes had their portion assigned. In due time all God's people are settled.

Caleb's portion, His daughter's blessing (13–19)

Achsah obtained some land by Caleb's free grant. He gave her a south land. Land indeed, but a south land, dry and apt to be parched. She obtained more, on her request, and he gave the upper and the nether springs. Those who understand it but of one field, watered both with the rain of heaven, and the springs that issued out of the earth, countenance the allusion commonly made to this, when we pray for spiritual and heavenly blessings which relate to our souls, as blessings of the upper springs, and those which relate to the body and the life that now is, as blessings of the nether springs. All the blessings, both of the upper and the nether springs, belong to the children of God. As related to Christ, they have them freely given of the Father, for the lot of their inheritance.

The cities of Judah (20–63)

Here is a list of the cities of Judah. But we do not here find Bethlehem, afterwards the city of David, and ennobled by the birth of our Lord Jesus in it. That city, which, at the best, was but little among the thousands of Judah, Micah 5:2, except that it was thus honoured, was now so little as not to be accounted one of the cities.

Chapter 16

The sons of Joseph (1–10)

This and the following chapter should not be separated. They give the lots of Ephraim and Manasseh, the children of Joseph, who, next to Judah, were to have the post of honour, and therefore had the first and best portion in the northern part of Canaan, as Judah in the southern part. God's people now, as of old, suffer his enemies to remain. These settled boundaries may remind us, that our situation and provision in this life, as well as our future inheritance, are appointed by the only wise and righteous God,

and we should be content with our portion, since he knows what is best for us, and all we have is more than we deserve.

Chapter 17

The lot of Manasseh (1–6)

The boundaries of Manasseh, The Canaanites not driven out (7–13)

Joseph desires a larger portion (14–18)

The lot of Manasseh (1–6)

Manasseh was but half of the tribe of Joseph, yet it was divided into two parts. The daughters of Zelophehad now reaped the benefit of their pious zeal and prudent forecast. Those who take care in the wilderness of this world, to make sure to themselves a place in the inheritance of the saints in light, will have the comfort of it in the other world; while those who neglect it now, will lose it for ever. Lord, teach us here to believe and obey, and give us an inheritance among thy saints, in glory everlasting.

The boundaries of Manasseh, The Canaanites not driven out (7–13)

There was great communication between Manasseh and Ephraim. Though each tribe had its inheritance, yet they should intermix one with another, to do good offices one to another, as became those, who, though of different tribes, were all one Israel, and were bound to love as brethren. But they suffered the Canaanites to live among them, against the command of God, to serve their own ends.

Joseph desires a larger portion (14–18)

Joshua, as a public person, had no more regard to his own tribe than to any other, but would govern without favour or affection; wherein he has left a good example to all in public trusts. Joshua tells them, that what was fallen to their share would be a sufficient lot for them, if they would but work and fight. Men excuse themselves from labour by any pretence; and nothing serves the purpose better than having rich and powerful relations, able to provide for them; and they are apt to desire a partial and unfaithful disposal of what is intrusted to those they think able to give such help. But there is more real kindness in pointing out the advantages within reach, and in encouraging men to make the best of them, than in granting indulgences to sloth and extravagance. True religion gives no countenance to these evils. The rule is, They shall not eat who will not work; and many of our 'cannots' are only the language of idleness, which magnifies every difficulty and danger.

This is especially the case in our spiritual work and warfare. Without Christ we can do nothing, but we are apt to sit still and attempt nothing. If we belong to Him, he will stir us up to our best endeavours, and to cry to him for help.

Chapter 18
The tabernacle set up at Shiloh (1)
The remainder of the land described and divided (2–10)
The boundaries of Benjamin (11–28)

The tabernacle set up at Shiloh (1)

Shiloh was in the lot of Ephraim, the tribe to which Joshua belonged, and it was proper that the tabernacle should be near the residence of the chief governor. The name of this city is the same as that by which Jacob prophesied of the Messiah, Ge 49:10. It is supposed by some that the city was thus called, when it was chosen for the resting-place of the ark, which typified our great Peace-maker, and the way by him to a reconciled God.

The remainder of the land described and divided (2–10)

After a year or more, Joshua blamed their slackness, and told them how to proceed. God, by his grace, has given us a title to a good land, the heavenly Canaan, but we are slack to take possession of it; we enter not into that rest, as we might by faith, and hope, and holy joy. How long shall it be thus with us? How long shall we thus stand in our own light, and forsake our own mercies for lying vanities? Joshua stirs the Israelites up to take possession of their lots. He is ready to do his part, if they will do theirs.

The boundaries of Benjamin (11–28)

The boundaries of each portion were distinctly drawn, and the inheritance of each tribe settled. All contests and selfish claims were prevented by the wise appointment of God, who allotted the hill and the valley, the corn and pasture, the brooks and rivers, the towns and cities. Is the lot of any servant of Christ cast in affliction and sorrow? It is the Lord; let him do what seemeth him good. Are we in prosperity and peace? It is from above. Be humbled when you compare the gift with your own unworthiness. Forget not Him that gave the good, and always be ready to resign it at his command.

Chapter 19
The lot of Simeon (1–9)
The lot of Zebulun (10–16)
The lot of Issachar, Asher, Naphtali, and Dan (17–51)

The lot of Simeon (1–9)

The men of Judah did not oppose taking away the cities within their border, when convinced that they had more than was right. If a true believer has obtained an unintended and improper advantage in any thing, he will give it up without murmuring. Love seeketh not her own, and doth not behave unseemly; it will induce those in whom it richly dwells, to part with their own to supply what is lacking to their brethren.

The lot of Zebulun (10–16)

In the division to each tribe of Israel, the prophetic blessings of Jacob were fulfilled. They chose for themselves, or it was divided to them by lot, in the manner and places that he foresaw. So sure a rule to go by is the word of prophecy: we see by it what to believe, and it proves beyond all dispute the things that are of God.

The lot of Issachar, Asher, Naphtali, and Dan (17–51)

Joshua waited till all the tribes were settled, before he asked any provision for himself. He was content to be unfixed, till he saw them all placed, and herein is an example to all in public places, to prefer the common welfare before private advantage. Those who labour most to do good to others, seek an inheritance in the Canaan above: but it will be soon enough to enter thereon, when they have done all the service to their brethren of which they are capable. Nor can any thing more effectually assure them of their title to it, than endeavouring to bring others to desire, to seek, and to obtain it. Our Lord Jesus came and dwelt on earth, not in pomp but poverty, providing rest for man, yet himself not having where to lay his head; for Christ pleased not himself. Nor would he enter upon his inheritance, till by his obedience to death he secured the eternal inheritance for all his people; nor will he account his own glory completed, till every ransomed sinner is put in possession of his heavenly rest.

Chapter 20

The law concerning the cities of refuge (1–6)

The cities appointed as refuges (7–9)

The law concerning the cities of refuge (1–6)

When the Israelites were settled in their promised inheritance, they were reminded to set apart the cities of refuge, whose use and typical meaning have been explained, Numbers 35; Deuteronomy 19. God's spiritual Israel have, and shall have in Christ and heaven, not only rest to repose in, but refuge to secure themselves in. These cities were designed to typify the relief which the gospel provides for penitent sinners, and their protection from the curse of the law and the wrath of God, in our Lord Jesus, to whom believers flee for refuge, Hebrews 6:18.

The cities appointed as refuges (7–9)

These cities, as those also on the other side Jordan, stood so that a man might in half a day reach one of them from any part of the country. God is ever a Refuge at hand. They were all Levites' cities. It was kindness to the poor fugitive, that when he might not go up to the house of the Lord, yet he had the servants of God with him, to instruct him, and pray for him, and to help to make up the want of public ordinances. Some observe a significance in the names of these cities with application to Christ our Refuge. Kedesh signifies holy, and our Refuge is the holy Jesus. Shechem, a shoulder, and the government is upon his shoulder. Hebron, fellowship, and believers are called into the fellowship of Christ Jesus our Lord. Bezer, a fortification, for he is a strong hold to all those that trust in him. Ramoth, high or exalted, for Him hath God exalted with his own right hand. Golan, joy or exultation, for in Him all the saints are justified, and shall glory.

Chapter 21

Cities for the Levites (1–8)

The cities allotted to the Levites (9–42)

God gave the land and rest to the Israelites, according to his promise (43–45)

Cities for the Levites (1–8)

The Levites waited till the other tribes were provided for, before they preferred their claim to Joshua. They build their claim upon a very good foundation; not their own merits or services, but the Divine precept. The maintenance of ministers is not a thing left merely to the will of the people, that they may let them starve if they please; they which preach the gospel should live by the gospel, and should live comfortably.

The cities allotted to the Levites (9–42)

By mixing the Levites with the other tribes, they were made to see that the eyes of all Israel were upon them, and therefore it was their concern to walk so that their ministry might not be blamed. Every tribe had its share of Levites' cities. Thus did God graciously provide for keeping up religion among them, and that they might have the word in all parts of the land. Yet, blessed be God, we have the gospel more diffused amongst us.

God gave the land and rest to the Israelites, according to his promise (43–45)

God promised to give to the seed of Abraham the land of Canaan for a possession, and now they possessed it, and dwelt therein. And the promise of the heavenly Canaan is as sure to all God's spiritual Israel; for it is the promise of Him that cannot lie. There stood not a man before them. The after-prevalence of the Canaanites was the effect of Israel's slothfulness, and the punishment of their sinful inclination to the idolatries and abominations of the heathen whom they harboured and indulged. There failed not aught of any good thing, which the Lord had spoken to the house of Israel. In due season all his promises will be accomplished; then will his people acknowledge that the Lord has exceeded their largest expectations, and made them more than conquerors, and brought them to their desired rest.

Chapter 22

Reuben and Gad, with the half tribe of Manasseh, dismissed to their homes (1–9)

They build an altar of testimony, The congregation offended thereat (10–20)

The answer of the Reubenites (21–29)

The children of Israel satisfied (30–34)

Reuben and Gad, with the half tribe of Manasseh, dismissed to their homes (1–9)

Joshua dismisses the tribes with good counsel. Those who have the commandment have it in vain, unless they do the commandment; and it will not be done aright unless we take diligent heed. In particular to love the Lord our God, as the best of beings, and the best of friends; and as far as that principle rules in the heart, there will be constant care and endeavour to walk in his ways, even those that are narrow and up-hill. In every instance to keep his commandments. At all times, and in all conditions, with purpose of heart to cleave unto the Lord, and to serve him and his kingdom among men, with all our heart, and with all our soul. This good counsel is given to all; may God give us grace to take it!

They build an altar of testimony, The congregation offended thereat (10–20)

Here is the care of the separated tribes to keep their hold of Canaan's religion. At first sight it seemed a design to set up an altar against the altar at Shiloh. God is jealous for his own institutions; we should be so too, and afraid of every thing that looks like, or leads to idolatry. Corruptions in religion are best dealt with at first. But their prudence in following up this zealous resolution is no less commendable. Many an unhappy strife would be prevented, or soon made up, by inquiries into the matter of the offence. The remembrance of great sins committed formerly, should engage us to stand on our guard against the beginnings of sin; for the way of sin is down-hill. We are all concerned to reprove our neighbour when he does amiss, lest we suffer sin upon him, Leviticus 19:17. The offer made that they should be welcome to come to the land where the Lord's tabernacle was, and settle there, was in the spirit of true Israelites.

The answer of the Reubenites (21–29)

The tribes took the reproofs of their brethren in good part. With solemnity and meekness they proceeded to give all the satisfaction in their power. Reverence of God is expressed in the form of their appeal. This brief confession of faith would remove their brethren's suspicion that they intended to worship other gods. Let us always speak of God with seriousness, and mention his name with a solemn pause. Those who make appeals to Heaven with a careless 'God knows,' take his name in vain: it is very unlike this. They express great confidence of their own uprightness in the matter of their appeal. 'God knows it,' for he is perfectly acquainted with the thoughts and intents of the heart. In every thing we do in religion, it highly concerns us to approve ourselves to God, remembering that he knows the heart. And if our sincerity be known to God, we should study likewise to let others know it by its fruits, especially those who, though they mistake us, show zeal for the glory of God. They disdained the design of which they were suspected to be guilty, and fully explained their true intent in building this altar. Those who have found the comfort and benefit of God's ordinances, cannot but desire to preserve them to their seed, and to use all possible care that their children may be looked upon as having a part in him. Christ is the great Altar that sanctifies every gift; the best evidence of our interest in him is the work of his Spirit in our hearts.

The children of Israel satisfied (30–34)

It is well that there was on both sides a disposition to peace, as there was a zeal for God; for quarrels about religion, for want of wisdom and love, often prove the most fierce and difficult to be made up. Proud and peevish spirits, when they have passed any unjust blame on their brethren, though full evidence be brought of its unfairness, can by no means be persuaded to withdraw it. But Israel was not so prejudiced. They looked upon their brethren's innocence as a token of God's presence. Our brethren's zeal for the power of godliness, and faith and love, notwithstanding the fears of their breaking the unity of the church, are things of which we should be very glad to be satisfied. The altar was called 'Ed', a witness. It was a witness of their care to keep their religion pure and entire, and would witness against their descendants, if they should turn from following after the Lord. Happy will it be when all professed Christians learn to copy the example of Israel, to unite zeal and steady adherence to the cause of truth, with candour, meekness, and readiness to understand each other, to explain and to be satisfied with the explanations of their brethren. May the Lord increase the number of those who endeavour to keep the unity of the Spirit in the bond of peace! may increasing grace and consolation be with all who love Jesus Christ in sincerity!

Chapter 23

Joshua's exhortation before his death (1–10)
Joshua warns the people of idolatry (11–16)

Joshua's exhortation before his death (1–10)

Joshua was old and dying, let them observe what he said now. He put them in mind of the great things God had done for them in his days. He exhorted them to be very courageous. Keep with care, do with diligence, and regard with sincerity what is written. Also, very cautiously to endeavour that the heathen idolatry may be forgotten, so that it may never be revived. It is sad that among Christians the names of the heathen gods are so commonly used, and made so familiar as they are. Joshua exhorts them to be very constant. There might be many things amiss among them, but they had not forsaken the Lord their God; the way to make people better, is to make the best of them.

Joshua warns the people of idolatry (11–16)

Would we cleave to the Lord, we must always stand upon our guard, for many a soul is lost through carelessness. Love the Lord your God, and you will not leave him. Has God been thus true to you? Be not you false to him. He is faithful that has promised, Hebrews 10:23. The experience of every Christian witnesses the same truth. Conflicts may have been severe and long, trials great and many; but at the last he will acknowledge that goodness and mercy followed him all the days of his life. Joshua states the fatal consequences of going back; know for a certainty it will be your ruin. The first step would be, friendship with idolaters; the next would be, marrying with them; the end of that would be, serving their gods. Thus the way of sin is down-hill, and those who have fellowship with sinners, cannot avoid having fellowship with sin. He describes the destruction he warns them of. The goodness of the heavenly Canaan, and the free and sure grant God has made of it, will add to the misery of those who shall for ever be shut out from it. Nothing will make them see how wretched they are, so much, as to see how happy they might have been. Let us watch and pray against temptation. Let us trust in God's faithfulness, love, and power; let us plead his promises, and cleave to his commandments, then we shall be happy in life, in death, and for ever.

Chapter 24

God's benefits to their fathers (1–14)

Joshua renews the covenant between the people and God (15–28)

Joshua's death, Joseph's bones buried, The state of Israel (29–33)

God's benefits to their fathers (1–14)

We must never think our work for God done, till our life is done. If he lengthen out our days beyond what we expected, like those of Joshua, it is because he has some further service for us to do. He who aims at the same mind which was in Christ Jesus, will glory in bearing the last testimony to his Saviour's goodness, and in telling to all around, the obligations with which the unmerited goodness of God has bound him. The assembly came together in a solemn religious manner. Joshua spake to them in God's name, and as from him. His sermon consists of doctrine and application. The doctrinal part is a history of the great things God had done for his people, and for their fathers before them. The application of this history of God's mercies to them, is an exhortation to fear and serve God, in gratitude for his favour, and that it might be continued.

Joshua renews the covenant between the people and God (15–28)

It is essential that the service of God's people be performed with a willing mind. For love is the only genuine principle whence all acceptable service of God can spring. The Father seeks only such to worship him, as worship him in spirit and in truth. The carnal mind of man is enmity against God, therefore, is not capable of such spiritual worship. Hence the necessity of being born again. But numbers rest in mere forms, as tasks imposed upon them. Joshua puts them to their choice; but not as if it were indifferent whether they served God or not. Choose you whom ye will serve, now the matter is laid plainly before you. He resolves to do this, whatever others did. Those that are bound for heaven, must be willing to swim against the stream. They must not do as the most do, but as the best do. And no one can behave himself as he ought in any station, who does not deeply consider his religious duties in family relations. The Israelites agree with Joshua, being influenced by the example of a man who had been so great a blessing to them; We also will serve the Lord. See how much good great men do, by their influence, if zealous in religion. Joshua brings them to express full purpose of heart to cleave to the Lord. They must come off from all confidence in their own sufficiency, else their purposes would be in vain. The service of God being made their deliberate choice, Joshua binds them to it by a solemn covenant. He set up a monument of it. In this affecting manner Joshua took his last leave of them; if they perished, their blood would be upon their own heads. Though the house of God, the Lord's table, and even the walls and trees before which we have uttered our solemn purposes of serving him, would bear witness against us if we deny him, yet we may trust in him, that he will put his fear into our hearts, that we shall not depart from him. God alone can give grace, yet he blesses our endeavours to engage men to his service.

Joshua's death, Joseph's bones buried, The state of Israel (29–33)

Joseph died in Egypt, but gave commandment concerning his bones, that they should not rest in their grave till Israel had rest in the land of promise. Notice also the death and burial of Joshua, and of Eleazar the chief priest. The most useful men, having served their generation, according to the will of God, one after another, fall asleep and see corruption. But Jesus, having spent and ended his life on earth more effectually than either Joshua or Joseph, rose from the dead, and saw no corruption. And the redeemed of the Lord shall inherit the kingdom he prepared for them from the foundation of the world. They will say in admiration of the grace of Jesus, Unto him that loved us, and washed us from our sins in his own blood, and hath made us kings and priests unto God and his Father, to him be glory and dominion for ever and ever. Amen.

JUDGES

Matthew Henry

Introduction

The book of Judges is the history of Israel during the government of the Judges, who were occasional deliverers, raised up by God to rescue Israel from their oppressors, to reform the state of religion, and to administer justice to the people. The state of God's people does not appear in this book so prosperous, nor their character so religious, as might have been expected; but there were many believers among them, and the tabernacle service was attended to. The history exemplifies the frequent warnings and predictions of Moses, and should have close attention. The whole is full of important instruction.

Chapter 1

Proceedings of the tribes of Judah and Simeon (1–8)

Hebron and other cities taken (9–20)

The proceedings of other tribes (21–36)

Proceedings of the tribes of Judah and Simeon (1–8)

The Israelites were convinced that the war against the Canaanites was to be continued; but they were in doubt as to the manner in which it was to be carried on after the death of Joshua. In these respects they inquired of the Lord. God appoints service according to the strength he has given. From those who are most able, most work is expected. Judah was first in dignity, and must be first in duty. Judah's service will not avail unless God give success; but God will not give the success, unless Judah applies to the service. Judah was the most considerable of all the tribes, and Simeon the least; yet Judah begs Simeon's friendship, and prays for aid from him. It becomes Israelites to help one another against Canaanites; and all Christians, even those of different tribes, should strengthen one another. Those who thus help one another in love, have reason to hope that God will graciously help both. Adoni-bezek was taken prisoner. This prince had been a severe tyrant. The Israelites, doubtless under the Divine direction, made him suffer what he had done to others; and his own conscience confessed that he was justly treated as he had treated others. Thus the righteous God sometimes, in his providence, makes the punishment answer the sin.

Hebron and other cities taken (9–20)

The Canaanites had iron chariots; but Israel had God on their side, whose chariots are thousands of angels, Psalms 68:17. Yet they suffered their fears to prevail against their faith. About Caleb we read in Joshua 15:16–19. The Kenites had settled in the land. Israel let them fix where they pleased, being a quiet, contented people. They that molested none, were molested by none. Blessed are the meek, for they shall inherit the earth.

The proceedings of other tribes (21–36)

The people of Israel were very careless of their duty and interest. Owing to slothfulness and cowardice, they would not be at the pains to complete their conquests. It was also owing to their covetousness: they were willing to let the Canaanites live among them, that they might make advantage of them. They had not the dread and detestation of idolatry they ought to have had. The same unbelief that kept their fathers forty years out of Canaan, kept them now out of the full possession of it. Distrust of the power and promise of God deprived them of advantages, and brought them into troubles. Thus many a believer who begins well is hindered. His graces languish, his lusts revive, Satan plies him with suitable temptations, the world recovers its hold; he brings guilt into his conscience, anguish into his heart, discredit on his character, and reproach on the gospel. Though he may have sharp rebukes, and be so recovered that he does not perish, yet he will have deeply to lament his folly through his remaining days; and upon his dying bed to mourn over the opportunities of glorifying God and serving the church he has lost. We can have no fellowship with the enemies of God within us or around us, but to our hurt; therefore our only wisdom is to maintain unceasing war against them.

Chapter 2

The angel of the Lord rebukes the people (1–5)

The wickedness of the new generation after Joshua (6–23)

The angel of the Lord rebukes the people (1–5)

It was the great Angel of the covenant, the Word, the Son of God, who spake with Divine authority as Jehovah, and now called them to account for their disobedience. God sets forth what he had done for Israel, and what he had promised. Those who throw off communion with God, and have fellowship with the unfruitful works of darkness, know not what they do now, and will have nothing to say for themselves in the day of account shortly. They must expect to suffer for this their folly. Those deceive themselves who expect advantages from friendship with God's enemies. God often makes men's sin their punishment; and thorns and snares are in the way of the froward, who will walk contrary to God. The people wept, crying out against their own folly and ingratitude. They trembled at the word, and not without cause. It is a wonder sinners can ever read the Bible with dry eyes. Had they kept close to God and their duty, no voice but that of singing had been heard in their congregation; but by their sin and folly they made other work for themselves, and nothing is to be heard but the voice of weeping. The worship of God, in its own nature, is joy, praise, and thanksgiving; our sins alone render weeping needful. It is pleasing to see men weep for their sins; but our tears, prayers, and even amendment, cannot atone for sin.

The wickedness of the new generation after Joshua (6–23)

We have a general idea of the course of things in Israel, during the time of the Judges. The nation made themselves as mean and miserable by forsaking God, as they would have been great and happy if they had continued faithful to him. Their punishment answered to the evil they had done. They served the gods of the nations round about them, even the meanest, and God made them serve the princes of the nations round about them, even the meanest. Those who have found God true to his promises, may be sure that he will be as true to his threatenings. He might in justice have abandoned them, but he could not for pity do it. The Lord was with the judges when he raised them up, and so they became saviours. In the days of the greatest distress of the church, there shall be some whom God will find or make fit to help it. The Israelites were not thoroughly reformed; so mad were they upon their idols, and so obstinately bent to backslide. Thus those who have forsaken the good ways of God, which they have once known and professed, commonly grow most daring and desperate in sin, and have their hearts hardened. Their punishment was, that the Canaanites were spared, and so they were beaten with their own rod. Men cherish and indulge their corrupt appetites and passions; therefore God justly leaves them to themselves, under the power of their sins, which will be their ruin. God has told us how deceitful and desperately wicked our hearts are, but we are not willing to believe it, until by making bold with temptation we find it true by sad experience. We need to examine how matters stand with ourselves, and to pray without ceasing, that we may be rooted and grounded in love, and that Christ may dwell in our hearts by faith. Let us declare war against every sin, and follow after holiness all our days.

Chapter 3

The nations left to prove Israel (1–7)

Othniel delivers Israel (8–11)

Ehud delivers Israel from Eglon (12–30)

Shamgar delivers and judges Israel (31)

The nations left to prove Israel (1–7)

As the Israelites were a type of the church on earth, they were not to be idle and slothful. The Lord was pleased to try them by the remains of the devoted nations they spared. Temptations and trials detect the wickedness of the hearts of sinners; and strengthen the graces of believers in their daily conflict with Satan, sin, and this evil world. They must live in this world, but they are not of it, and are forbidden to conform to it. This marks the difference between the followers of Christ and mere professors. The friendship of the world is more fatal than its enmity; the latter can only kill the body, but the former murders many precious souls.

Othniel delivers Israel (8–11)

The first judge was Othniel: even in Joshua's time Othniel began to be famous. Soon after Israel's settlement in Canaan their purity began to be corrupted, and their peace disturbed. But affliction makes those cry to God who before would scarcely speak to him. God returned in mercy to them for their deliverance. The Spirit of the Lord came upon Othniel. The Spirit of wisdom and courage to qualify him for the service, and the Spirit of power to excite him to it. He first judged Israel, reproved and reformed them, and then went to war. Let sin at home be conquered, that worst of enemies, then enemies abroad will be more easily dealt with. Thus let Christ be our Judge and Lawgiver, then he will save us.

Ehud delivers Israel from Eglon (12–30)

When Israel sins again, God raises up a new oppressor. The Israelites did ill, and the Moabites did worse; yet because God punishes the sins of his own people in this world, Israel is weakened, and Moab strengthened against them. If lesser troubles do not do the work, God will send greater. When Israel prays again, God raises up Ehud. As a judge, or minister of Divine justice, Ehud put to death Eglon, the king of Moab, and thus executed the judgments of God upon him as an enemy to God and Israel. But the law of being subject to principalities and powers in all things lawful, is the rule of our conduct. No such commissions are now given; to pretend to them is to blaspheme God. Notice Ehud's address to Eglon. What message from God but a message of vengeance can a proud rebel expect? Such a message is contained in the word of God; his ministers are boldly to declare it, without fearing the frown, or respecting the persons of sinners. But, blessed be God, they have to deliver a message of mercy and of free salvation; the message of vengeance belongs only to those who neglect the offers of grace. The consequence of this victory was, that the land had rest eighty years. It was a great while for the land to rest; yet what is that to the saints' everlasting rest in the heavenly Canaan.

Shamgar delivers and judges Israel (31)

The side of the country which lay south-west, was infested by the Philistines. God raised up Shamgar to deliver them; having neither sword nor spear, he took an ox-goad, the instrument next at hand. God can make those serviceable to his glory and to his church's good, whose birth, education, and employment, are mean and obscure. It is no matter what the weapon is, if God directs and strengthens the arm. Often he works by unlikely means, that the excellency of the power may appear to be of God.

Chapter 4

Israel again revolts, and is oppressed by Jabin (1–3)

Deborah concerts their deliverance with Barak (4–9)

Sisera defeated (10–16)

Sisera put to death by Jael (17–24)

Israel again revolts, and is oppressed by Jabin (1–3)

The land had rest for eighty years, which should have confirmed them in their religion; but it made them secure, and indulge their lusts. Thus the prosperity of fools destroys them. Jabin and his general Sisera, mightily oppressed Israel. This enemy was nearer than any of the former. Israel cried unto the Lord, when distress drove them to him, and they saw no other way of relief. Those who slight God in prosperity, will find themselves under a necessity of seeking him in trouble.

Deborah concerts their deliverance with Barak (4–9)

Deborah was a prophetess; one instructed in Divine knowledge by the inspiration of the Spirit of God. She judged Israel as God's mouth to them; correcting abuses, and redressing grievances. By God's direction, she ordered Barak to raise an army, and engage Jabin's forces. Barak insisted much upon her presence. Deborah promised to go with him. She would not send him where she would not go herself. Those who in God's name call others to their duty, should be ready to assist them in it. Barak values the satisfaction of his mind, and the good success of his enterprise, more than mere honour.

Sisera defeated (10–16)

Sisera's confidence was chiefly in his chariots. But if we have ground to hope that God goes before us, we may go on with courage and cheerfulness. Be not dismayed at the difficulties thou meetest with in resisting Satan, in serving God, or suffering for him; for is not the Lord gone before thee? Follow him then fully. Barak went down, though upon the plain the iron chariots would have advantage against him: he quitted the mountain in dependence on the Divine power; for in the Lord alone is the salvation of his people, Jeremiah 3:23. He was not deceived in his confidence. When God goes before us in our spiritual conflicts, we must bestir ourselves; and when, by his grace, he gives us some success against the enemies of our souls, we must improve it by watchfulness and resolution.

Sisera put to death by Jael (17–24)

Sisera's chariots had been his pride and his confidence. Thus are those disappointed who rest on the creature; like a broken reed, it not only breaks under them, but pierces them with many sorrows. The idol may quickly become a burden, Isa 46:1; what we were sick for, God can make us sick of. It is probable that Jael really intended kindness to Sisera; but by a Divine impulse she was afterwards led to consider him as the determined enemy of the Lord and of his people, and to destroy him. All our connexions with God's enemies must be broken off, if we would have the Lord for our God, and his people for our people. He that had thought to have destroyed Israel with his many iron chariots, is himself destroyed with one iron nail. Thus the weak things of the world confound the mighty. The Israelites would have prevented much mischief, if they had sooner destroyed the Canaanites, as God commanded and enabled them: but better be wise late, and buy wisdom by experience, than never be wise.

Chapter 5

Praise and glory ascribed to God (1–5)

The distress and deliverance of Israel (6–11)

Some commended, others censured (12–23)

Sisera's mother disappointed (24–31)

Praise and glory ascribed to God (1-5)

No time should be lost in returning thanks to the Lord for his mercies; for our praises are most acceptable, pleasant, and profitable, when they flow from a full heart. By this, love and gratitude would be more excited and more deeply fixed in the hearts of believers; the events would be more known and longer remembered. Whatever Deborah, Barak, or the army had done, the Lord must have all the praise. The will, the power, and the success were all from Him.

The distress and deliverance of Israel (6–11)

Deborah describes the distressed state of Israel under the tyranny of Jabin, that their salvation might appear more gracious. She shows what brought this misery upon them. It was their idolatry. They chose new gods, with new names. But under all these images, Satan was worshipped. Deborah was a mother to Israel, by diligently promoting the salvation of their souls.

She calls on those who shared the advantages of this great salvation, to offer up thanks to God for it. Let such as are restored, not only to their liberty as other Israelites, but to their rank, speak God's praises. This is the Lord's doing. In these acts of his, justice was executed on his enemies. In times of persecution, God's ordinances, the walls of salvation, whence the waters of life are drawn, are resorted to at the hazard of the lives of those who attend them. At all times Satan will endeavour to hinder the believer from drawing near to the throne of grace. Notice God's kindness to his trembling people. It is the glory of God to protect those who are most exposed, and to help the weakest. Let us notice the benefit we have from the public peace, the inhabitants of villages especially, and give God the praise.

Some commended, others censured (12–23)

Deborah called on her own soul to be in earnest. He that will set the hearts of other men on fire with the love of Christ, must himself burn with love. Praising God is a work we should awake to, and awake ourselves unto. She notices who fought against Israel, who fought for them, and who kept away. Who fought against them. They were obstinate enemies to God's people, therefore the more dangerous. Who fought for them. The several tribes that helped are here spoken of with honour; for though God is above all to be glorified, those who are employed must have their due praise, to encourage others. But the whole creation is at war with those to whom God is an enemy. The river of Kishon fought against their enemies. At most times it was shallow, yet now, probably by the great rain that fell, it was so swelled, and the stream so deep and strong, that those who attempted to pass, were drowned. Deborah's own soul fought against them. When the soul is employed in holy exercises, and heart-work is made of them, through the grace of God, the strength of our spiritual enemies will be trodden down, and will fall before us. She observes who kept away, and did not side with Israel, as might have been expected. Thus many are kept from doing their duty by the fear of trouble, the love of ease, and undue affection to their worldly business and advantage. Narrow, selfish spirits care not what becomes of God's church, so that they can but get, keep, and save money. All seek their own, Philippians 2:21. A little will serve those for a pretence to stay at home, who have no mind to engage in needful services, because there is difficulty and danger in them. But we cannot keep away from the contest between the Lord and his enemies; and if we do not actively endeavour to promote his cause in this wicked world, we shall fall under the curse against the workers of iniquity. Though He needs no human help, yet he is pleased to accept the services of those who improve their talents to advance his cause. He requires every man to do so.

Sisera's mother disappointed (24–31)

Jael had a special blessing. Those whose lot is cast in the tent, in a low and narrow sphere, if they serve God according to the powers he has given them, shall not lose their reward. The mother of Sisera looked for his return, not in the least fearing his success. Let us take heed of indulging eager desires towards any temporal good, particularly toward that which cherishes vain-glory, for that was what she here doted on. What a picture does she present of an ungodly and sensual heart! How shameful and childish these wishes of an aged mother and her attendants for her son! And thus does God often bring ruin on his enemies when they are most puffed up. Deborah concludes with a prayer to God for the destruction of all his foes, and for the comfort of all his friends. Such shall be the honour, and joy of all who love God in sincerity, they shall shine for ever as the sun in the firmament.

Chapter 6

Israel oppressed by Midianites (1–6)
Israel rebuked by a prophet (7–10)
Gideon set to deliver Israel (11–24)
Gideon destroys Baal's altar (25–32)
Signs given him (33–40)

Israel oppressed by Midianites (1–6)

Israel's sin was renewed, and Israel's troubles were repeated. Let all that sin expect to suffer. The Israelites hid themselves in dens and caves; such was the effect of a guilty conscience. Sin dispirits men. The invaders left no food for Israel, except what was taken into the caves. They prepared that for Baal with which God should have been served, now God justly sends an enemy to take it away in the season thereof.

Israel rebuked by a prophet (7–10)

They cried to God for a deliverer, and he sent them a prophet to teach them. When God furnishes a land with faithful ministers, it is a token that he has mercy in store for it. He charges them with rebellion against the Lord; he intends to bring them to repentance. Repentance is real when the sinfulness of sin, as disobedience to God, is chiefly lamented.

Gideon set to deliver Israel (11–24)

Gideon was a man of a brave, active spirit, yet in obscurity through the times: he is here stirred up to undertake something great. It was very sure that the Lord was with him, when his Angel was with him. Gideon was weak in faith, which made it hard to reconcile the assurances of the presence of God with the distress to which Israel was brought. The Angel answered his objections. He told him to appear and act as Israel's deliverer, there needed no more. Bishop Hall says, While God calls Gideon valiant, he makes him so. God delights to advance the humble. Gideon desires to have his faith confirmed. Now, under the influences of the Spirit, we are not to expect signs before our eyes such as Gideon here desired, but must earnestly pray to God, that if we have found grace in his sight, he would show us a sign in our heart, by the powerful working of his Spirit there, The Angel turned the meat into an offering made by fire; showing that he was not a man who needed meat, but the Son of God, who was to be served and honoured by sacrifice, and who in the fulness of time was to make himself a sacrifice. Hereby a sign was given to Gideon, that he had found grace in God's sight. Ever since man has by sin exposed himself to God's wrath and curse, a message from heaven has been a terror to him, as he scarcely dares to expect good tidings thence. In this world, it is very awful to have any converse with that world of spirits to which we are so much strangers. Gideon's courage failed him. But God spoke peace to him.

Gideon destroys Baal's altar (25–32)

See the power of God's grace, that he could raise up a reformer; and the kindness of his grace, that he would raise up a deliverer, out of the family of a leader in idolatry. Gideon must not think it enough not to worship at that altar; he must throw it down, and offer sacrifice on another. It was needful he should make peace with God, before he made war on Midian. Till sin be pardoned through the great Sacrifice, no good is to be expected. God, who has all hearts in his hands, influenced Joash to appear for his son against the advocates for Baal, though he had joined formerly in the worship of Baal. Let us do our duty, and trust God with our safety. Here is a challenge to Baal, to do either good or evil; the result convinced his worshippers of their folly, in praying to one to help them that could not avenge himself.

Signs given him (33–40)

These signs are truly miraculous, and very significant. Gideon and his men were going to fight the Midianites; could God distinguish between a small fleece of Israel, and the vast floor of Midian? Gideon is made to know that God could do so. Is Gideon desirous that the dew of Divine grace might come down upon himself in particular? He sees the fleece wet with dew to assure him of it. Does he desire that God will be as the dew to all Israel? Behold, all the ground is wet. What cause we sinners of the Gentiles have, to bless the Lord that the dew of heavenly blessings, once confined to Israel, is now sent to all the inhabitants of the earth! Yet still the means of grace are in different measures, according to the purposes of God. In the same congregation, one man's soul is like Gideon's moistened fleece, another like the dry ground.

Chapter 7

Gideon's army reduced (1–8)

Gideon is encouraged (9–15)

The defeat of the Midianites (16–22)

The Ephraimites take Oreb and Zeeb (23–25)

Gideon's army reduced (1–8)

God provides that the praise of victory may be wholly to himself, by appointing only three hundred men to be employed. Activity and prudence go with dependence upon God for help in our lawful undertakings. When the Lord sees that men would overlook him, and through unbelief, would shrink from perilous services, or that through pride they would vaunt themselves against him, he will set them aside, and do his work by other instruments. Pretences will be found by many, for deserting the cause and escaping the cross. But though a religious society may thus be made fewer in numbers, yet it will gain as to purity, and may expect an increased blessing from the Lord. God chooses to employ such as are not only well affected, but zealously affected in a good thing. They grudged not at the liberty of the others who were dismissed. In doing the duties required by God, we must not regard the forwardness or backwardness of others, nor what they do, but what God looks for at our hands. He is a rare person who can endure that others should excel him in gifts or blessings, or in liberty; so that we may say, it is by the special grace of God that we regard what God says to us, and not look to men what they do.

Gideon is encouraged (9–15)

The dream seemed to have little meaning in it; but the interpretation evidently proved the whole to be from the Lord, and discovered that the name of Gideon had filled the Midianites with terror. Gideon took this as a sure pledge of success; without delay he worshipped and praised God, and returned with confidence to his three hundred men. Wherever we are, we may speak to God, and worship him. God must have the praise of that which encourages our faith. And his providence must be acknowledged in events, though small and seemingly accidental.

The defeat of the Midianites (16–22)

This method of defeating the Midianites may be alluded to, as exemplifying the destruction of the devil's kingdom in the world, by the preaching of the everlasting gospel, the sounding that trumpet, and the holding forth that light out of earthen vessels, for such are the ministers of the gospel, 2Co 4:6,7. God chose the foolish things of the world to confound the wise, a barley-cake to overthrow the tents of Midian, that the excellency of the power might be of God only. The gospel is a sword, not in the hand, but in the mouth: the sword of the Lord and of Gideon; of God and Jesus Christ, of Him that sits on the throne and the Lamb. The wicked are often led to avenge the cause of God upon each other, under the power of their delusions, and the fury of their passions. See also how God often makes the enemies of the church instruments to destroy one another; it is a pity that the church's friends should ever act like them.

The Ephraimites take Oreb and Zeeb (23–25)

Two chief commanders of the host of Midian were taken and slain by the men of Ephraim. It were to be wished that we all did as these did, and that where help is needed, that it were willingly and readily performed by another. And that if there were any excellent and profitable matter begun, we were willing to have fellow-labourers to the finishing and perfecting the same, and not, as often, hinder one another.

Chapter 8

Gideon pacifies the Ephraimites (1–3)

Succoth and Penuel refuse to relieve Gideon (4–12)

Succoth and Penuel punished (13–17)

Gideon avenges his brethren (18–21)

Gideon declines the government, but given occasion for idolatry (22–28)

Gideon's death, Israel's ingratitude (29–35)

Gideon pacifies the Ephraimites (1–3)

Those who will not attempt or venture any thing in the cause of God, will be the most ready to censure and quarrel with such as are of a more zealous and enterprising spirit. And those who are the most backward to difficult services, will be the most angry not to have the credit of them. Gideon stands here as a great example of self-denial; and shows us that envy is best removed by humility. The Ephraimites had given vent to their passion in very wrong freedom of speech, a certain sign of a weak cause: reason runs low when chiding flies high.

Succoth and Penuel refuse to relieve Gideon (4–12)

Gideon's men were faint, yet pursuing; fatigued with what they had done, yet eager to do more against their enemies. It is many a time the true Christian's case, fainting, and yet pursuing. The world knows but little of the persevering and successful struggle the real believer maintains with his sinful heart. But he betakes himself to that Divine strength, in the faith of which he began his conflict, and by the supply of which alone he can finish it in triumph.

Succoth and Penuel punished (13–17)

The active servants of the Lord meet with more dangerous opposition from false professors than from open enemies; but they must not care for the behaviour of those who are Israelites in name, but Midianites in heart. They must pursue the enemies of their souls, and of the cause of God, though they are ready to faint through inward conflicts and outward hardships. And they shall be enabled to persevere. The less men help, and the more they seek to hinder, the more will the Lord assist. Gideon's warning being slighted, the punishment was just. Many are taught with the briers and thorns of affliction, who would not learn otherwise.

Gideon avenges his brethren (18–21)

The kings of Midian must be reckoned with. As they confessed themselves guilty of murder, Gideon acted as the avenger of blood, being the next of kin to the persons slain. Little did they think to have heard of this so long after; but murder seldom goes unpunished in this life. Sins long forgotten by man, must be accounted for to God. What poor consolation in death from the hope of suffering less pain, and of dying with less disgrace than some others! yet many are more anxious on these accounts, than concerning the future judgment, and what will follow.

Gideon declines the government, but given occasion for idolatry (22–28)

Gideon refused the government the people offered him. No good man can be pleased with any honour done to himself, which belongs only to God. Gideon thought to keep up the remembrance of this victory by an ephod, made of the choicest of the spoils. But probably this ephod had, as usual, a teraphim annexed to it, and Gideon intended this for an oracle to be consulted. Many are led into false ways by one false step of a good man. It became a snare to Gideon

himself, and it proved the ruin of the family. How soon will ornaments which feed the lust of the eye, and form the pride of life, as well as tend to the indulgences of the flesh, bring shame on those who are fond of them!

Gideon's death, Israel's ingratitude (29–35)

As soon as Gideon was dead, who kept the people to the worship of the God of Israel, they found themselves under no restraint; then they went after Baalim, and showed no kindness to the family of Gideon. No wonder if those who forget their God, forget their friends. Yet conscious of our own ingratitude to the Lord, and observing that of mankind in general, we should learn to be patient under any unkind returns we meet with for our poor services, and resolve, after the Divine example, not to be overcome of evil, but to overcome evil with good.

Chapter 9

Abimelech murders his brethren, and is made king (1–6)

Jotham rebukes the Shechemites (7–21)

The Shechemites conspire against Abimelech (22–29)

Abimelech destroys Shechem (30–49)

Abimelech slain (50–57)

Abimelech murders his brethren, and is made king (1–6)

The men of Shechem chose Abimelech king. God was not consulted whether they should have any king, much less who it should be. If parents could see what their children would do, and what they are to suffer, their joy in them often would be turned into sorrow: we may be thankful that we cannot know what shall happen. Above all, we should fear and watch against sin; for our evil conduct may produce fatal effects upon our families, after we are in our graves.

Jotham rebukes the Shechemites (7–21)

There was no occasion for the trees to choose a king, they are all the trees of the Lord which he has planted. Nor was there any occasion for Israel to set a king over them, for the Lord was their King. Those who bear fruit for the public good, are justly respected and honoured by all that are wise, more than those who merely make a figure. All these fruit-trees gave much the same reason for their refusal to be promoted over the trees; or, as the margin reads it, to go up and down for the trees. To rule, involves a man in a great deal both of toil and care. Those who are preferred to public trust and power, must forego all private interests and advantages, for the good of others. And those advanced to honour and dignity, are in great danger of losing their fruitfulness. For which reason, they that desire to do good, are afraid of being too great. Jotham compares Abimelech to the bramble or thistle, a worthless plant, whose end is to be burned. Such a one was Abimelech.

The Shechemites conspire against Abimelech (22–29)

Abimelech is seated in the throne his father refused. But how long does this glory last? Stay but three years, and see the bramble withered and burned. The prosperity of the wicked is short and fickle. The Shechemites are plagued by no other hand than Abimelech's. They raised him unjustly to the throne; they first feel the weight of his sceptre.

Abimelech destroys Shechem (30–49)

Abimelech intended to punish the Schechemites for slighting him now, but God punished them for their serving him formerly in the murder of Gideon's sons. When God uses men as instruments in his hand to do his work, he means one thing, and they another. That, which they hoped would have been for their welfare, proved a snare and a trap, as those will certainly find, who run to idols for shelter; such will prove a refuge of lies.

Abimelech slain (50–57)

The Shechemites were ruined by Abimelech; now he is reckoned with, who was their leader in villany. Evil pursues sinners, and sometimes overtakes them, when not only at ease, but triumphant. Though wickedness may prosper a while, it will not prosper always. The history of mankind, if truly told, would greatly resemble that of this chapter. The records of what are called splendid events present to us such contests for power. Such scenes, though praised of men, fully explain the Scripture doctrine of the deceitfulness and desperate wickedness of the human heart, the force of men's lust, and the effect of Satan's influence. Lord, thou hast given us thy word of truth and righteousness, O pour upon us thy spirit of purity, peace, and love, and write thy holy law in our hearts.

Chapter 10

Tola and Jair judge Israel (1–5)

The Philistines and Ammonites oppress Israel (6–9)

Israel's repentance (10–18)

Tola and Jair judge Israel (1–5)

Quiet and peaceable reigns, though the best to live in, yield least variety of matter to be spoken of. Such were the days of Tola and Jair. They were humble, active, and useful men, rulers appointed of God.

The Philistines and Ammonites oppress Israel (6–9)

Now the threatening was fulfilled, that the Israelites should have no power to stand before their enemies, Le 26:17,37. By their evil ways and their evil doings they procured this to themselves.

Israel's repentance (10–18)

God is able to multiply men's punishments according to the numbers of their sins and idols. But there is hope when sinners cry to the Lord for help, and lament their ungodliness as well as their more open transgressions. It is necessary, in true repentance, that there be a full conviction that those things cannot help us which we have set in competition with God. They acknowledged what they deserved, yet prayed to God not to deal with them according to their deserts. We must submit to God's justice, with a hope in his mercy. True repentance is not only for sin, but from sin. As the disobedience and misery of a child are a grief to a tender father, so the provocations of God's people are a grief to him. From him mercy never can be sought in vain. Let then the trembling sinner, and the almost despairing backslider, cease from debating about God's secret purposes, or from expecting to find hope from former experiences. Let them cast themselves on the mercy of God our Saviour, humble themselves under his hand, seek deliverance from the powers of darkness, separate themselves from sin, and from occasions of it, use the means of grace diligently, and wait the Lord's time, and so they shall certainly rejoice in his mercy.

Chapter 11

Jephthah and the Gileadites (1–11)

He attempts to make peace (12–28)

Jephthah's vow. He vanquishes the Ammonites (29–40)

Jephthah and the Gileadites (1–11)

Men ought not to be blamed for their parentage, so long as they by their personal merits roll away any reproach. God had forgiven Israel, therefore Jephthah will forgive. He speaks not with confidence of his success, knowing how justly God might suffer the Ammonites to prevail for the further punishment of Israel. Nor does he speak with any confidence at all in himself. If he succeed, it is the Lord delivers them into his hand; he thereby reminds his countrymen to look up to God as the Giver of victory. The same question as here, in fact, is put to those who desire salvation by Christ. If he save you, will ye be willing that he shall rule you? On no other terms will he save you. If he make you happy, shall he make you holy? If he be your helper, shall he be your Head? Jephthah, to obtain a little worldly honour, was willing to expose his life: shall we be discouraged in our Christian warfare by the difficulties we may meet with, when Christ has promised a crown of life to him that overcometh?

He attempts to make peace (12–28)

One instance of the honour and respect we owe to God, as our God, is, rightly to employ what he gives us to possess. Receive it from him, use it for him, and part with it when he calls for it. The whole of this message shows that Jephthah was well acquainted with the books of Moses. His argument was clear, and his demand reasonable. Those who possess the most courageous faith, will be the most disposed for peace, and the readiest to make advances to obtain; but rapacity and ambition often cloak their designs under a plea of equity, and render peaceful endeavours of no avail.

Jephthah's vow. He vanquishes the Ammonites (29–40)

Several important lessons are to be learned from Jephthah's vow.

1. There may be remainders of distrust and doubting, even in the hearts of true and great believers.

2. Our vows to God should not be as a purchase of the favour we desire, but to express gratitude to him.

3. We need to be very well-advised in making vows, lest we entangle ourselves.

4. What we have solemnly vowed to God, we must perform, if it be possible and lawful, though it be difficult and grievous to us.

5. It well becomes children, obediently and cheerfully to submit to their parents in the Lord. It is hard to say what Jephthah did in performance of his vow; but it is thought that he did not offer his daughter as a burnt-offering. Such a sacrifice would have been an abomination to the Lord; it is supposed she was obliged to remain unmarried, and apart from her family. Concerning this and some other such passages in the sacred history, about which learned men are divided and in doubt, we need not perplex ourselves; what is necessary to our salvation, thanks be to God, is plain enough. If the reader recollects the promise of Christ concerning the teaching of the Holy Spirit, and places himself under this heavenly Teacher, the Holy Ghost will guide to all truth in every passage, so far as it is needful to be understood.

Chapter 12

Ephraimites quarrel with Jephthah (1–7)

Ibzan, Elon, and Abdon judge Israel (8–15)

Ephraimites quarrel with Jephthah (1–7)

The Ephraimites had the same quarrel with Jephthah as with Gideon. Pride was at the bottom of the quarrel; only by that comes contention. It is ill to fasten names of reproach upon persons or countries, as is common, especially upon those under outward disadvantages. It often occasions quarrels that prove of ill consequence, as it did here. No contentions are so bitter as those between brethren or rivals for honour. What need we have to watch and pray against evil tempers! May the Lord incline all his people to follow after things which make for peace!

Ibzan, Elon, and Abdon judge Israel (8–15)

We have here a short account of three more of the judges of Israel. The happiest life of individuals, and the happiest state of society, is that which affords the fewest remarkable events. To live in credit and quiet, to be peacefully useful to those around us, to possess a clear conscience; but, above all, and without which nothing can avail, to enjoy communion with God our Saviour while we live, and to die at peace with God and man, form the substance of all that a wise man can desire.

Chapter 13

The Philistines, Samson announced (1–7)

The angel appears to Manoah (8–14)

Manoah's sacrifice (15–23)

Birth of Samson (24, 25)

The Philistines, Samson announced (1–7)

Israel did evil: then God delivered them again into the hands of the Philistines. When Israel was in this distress, Samson was born. His parents had been long childless. Many eminent persons were born of such mothers. Mercies long waited for, often prove signal mercies; and by them others may be encouraged to continue their hope in God's mercy. The angel notices her affliction. God often sends comfort to his people very seasonably, when they feel their troubles most. This deliverer of Israel must be devoted to God. Manoah's wife was satisfied that the messenger was of God. She gave her husband a particular account, both of the promise and of the precept. Husbands and wives should tell each other their experiences of communion with God, and their improvements in acquaintance with him, that they may help each other in the way that is holy.

The angel appears to Manoah (8–14)

Blessed are those who have not seen, and yet, as Manoah, have believed. Good men are more careful and desirous to know the duty to be done by them, than to know the events concerning them: duty is ours, events are God's. God will guide those by his counsel, who desire to know their duty, and apply to him to teach them. Pious parents, especially, will beg Divine assistance. The angel repeats the directions he had before given. There is need of much care for the right ordering both of ourselves and our children, that we may be duly separate from the world, and living sacrifices to the Lord.

Manoah's sacrifice (15–23)

What Manoah asked for instruction in his duty, he was readily told; but what he asked to gratify his curiosity, was denied. God has in his word given full directions concerning our duty, but never designed to answer other questionings. There are secret things which belong not to us, of which we must be quite contented to be ignorant, while in this world. The name of our Lord is wonderful and secret; but by his wonderful works he makes himself known as far as is needful for us. Prayer is the ascent of the soul to God. But without Christ in the heart by faith, our services are offensive smoke; in him, acceptable flame. We may apply this to Christ's sacrifice of himself for us; he ascended in the flame of his own offering, for by his own blood he entered in once into the holy place, Hebrews 9:12. In Manoah's reflections there is great fear; We shall surely die. In his wife's reflection there is great faith. As a help meet for him, she encouraged him. Let believers who have had communion with God in the word and prayer, to whom he has graciously manifested himself, and who have had reason to think God has accepted their works, take encouragement from thence in a cloudy and dark day. God would not have done what he has done for my soul, if he had designed to forsake me, and leave me to perish at last; for his work is perfect. Learn to reason as Manoah's wife; If God designed me to perish under his wrath, he would not give me tokens of his favour.

Birth of Samson (24, 25)

The Spirit of the Lord began to move Samson when a youth. This was evidence that the Lord blessed him. Where God gives his blessing, he gives his Spirit to qualify for the blessing. Those are blessed indeed in whom the Spirit of grace begins to work in the days of their childhood. Samson drank no wine or strong drink, yet excelled in strength and courage, for he had the Spirit of God moving him; therefore be not drunk with wine, but be filled with the Spirit.

Chapter 14

Samson desires a wife of the Philistines (1–4)

Samson kills a lion (5–9)

Samson's riddle (10–20)

Samson desires a wife of the Philistines (1–4)

As far as Samson's marriage was a common case, it was weak and foolish of him to set his affections upon a daughter of the Philistines. Shall one, not only an Israelite, but a Nazarite, devoted to the Lord, covet to become one with a worshipper of Dagon? It does not appear that he had any reason to think her wise or virtuous, or any way likely to be a help meet for him; but he saw something in her agreeable to his fancy. He that, in the choice of a wife, is only guided by his eye, and governed by his fancy, must afterwards thank himself if he find a Philistine in his arms. Yet it was well done not to proceed till Samson had made his parents acquainted with the matter. Children ought not to marry, nor to move towards it, without the advice and consent of their parents. Samson's parents did well to dissuade him from yoking himself unequally with unbelievers. It seems that it pleased God to leave Samson to follow his own inclinations, intending to bring out good from his conduct; and his parents consented, because he was bent upon it. However, his example is not recorded for us to do likewise.

Samson kills a lion (5–9)

By enabling him to kill a lion, God let Samson know what he could do in the strength of the Spirit of the Lord, that he might never be afraid to look the greatest difficulties in the face. He was alone in the vineyards, whither he had rambled. Young people consider not how they exposed themselves to the roaring lion that seeks to devour, when they wander from their prudent, pious parents. Nor do men consider what lions lurk in the vineyards, the vineyards of red wines. Our Lord Jesus having conquered Satan, that roaring lion, believers, like Samson, find honey in the carcass abundant strength and satisfaction, enough for themselves, and for all their friends.

Samson's riddle (10–20)

Samson's riddle literally meant no more than that he had got honey, for food and for pleasure, from the lion, which in its strength and fury was ready to devour him. But the victory of Christ over Satan, by means of his humiliation, agonies, and death, and the exaltation that followed to him, with the glory thence to the Father, and spiritual advantages to his people, seem directly alluded to. And even death, that devouring monster, being robbed of his sting, and stripped of his horror, forwards the soul to the realms of bliss. In these and other senses, out of the eater comes forth meat, and out of the strong, sweetness. Samson's companions obliged his wife to get the explanation from him. A worldly wife, or a worldly friend, is to a godly man as an enemy in the camp, who will watch every opportunity to betray him. No union can be comfortable or lasting, where secrets cannot be intrusted, without danger of being divulged. Satan, in his temptations, could not do us the mischief he does, if he did not plough with the heifer of our corrupt nature. His chief advantage against us arises from his correspondence with our deceitful hearts and inbred lusts. This proved an occasion of weaning Samson from his new relations. It were well for us, if the unkindness we meet with from the world, and our disappointments in it, obliged us by faith and prayer to return to our heavenly Father's house, and to rest there. See how little confidence is to be put in man. Whatever pretence of friendship may be made, a real Philistine will soon be weary of a true Israelite.

Chapter 15

Samson is denied his wife; he smites the Philistines (1–8)

Samson kills a thousand of the Philistines with a jaw-bone (9–17)

His distress from thirst (18–20)

Samson is denied his wife; he smites the Philistines (1–8)

When there are differences between relations, let those be reckoned the wisest and best, who are most forward to forgive or forget, and most willing to stoop and yield for the sake of peace. In the means which Samson employed, we must look at the power of God supplying them, and making them successful, to mortify the pride and punish the wickedness of the Philistines. The Philistines threatened Samson's wife that they would burn her and her father's house. She, to save herself and oblige her countrymen, betrayed her husband; and the very thing that she feared, and by sin sought to avoid, came upon her! She, and her father's house, were burnt with fire, and by her countrymen, whom she thought to oblige by the wrong she did to her husband. The mischief we seek to escape by any unlawful practices, we often pull down upon our own heads.

Samson kills a thousand of the Philistines with a jaw-bone (9–17)

Sin dispirits men, it hides from their eyes the things that belong to their peace. The Israelites blamed Samson for what he had done against the Philistines, as if he had done them a great injury. Thus our Lord Jesus did many good works, and for those the Jews were ready to stone him. When the Spirit of the Lord came upon Samson, his cords were loosed: where the Spirit of the Lord is, there is liberty, and those are free indeed who are thus set free. Thus Christ triumphed over the powers of darkness that shouted against him, as if they had him in their power. Samson made great destruction among the Philistines. To take the bone of an ass for this, was to do wonders by the foolish things of the world, that the excellency of the power might be of God, not of man. This victory was not in the weapon, was not in the arm; but it was in the Spirit of God, which moved the weapon by the arm. We can do all things through Him that strengtheneth us. Seest thou a poor Christian, who is enabled to overcome a temptation by weak, feeble counsel, there is the Philistine vanquished by a sorry jaw-bone.

His distress from thirst (18–20)

So little notice did the men of Judah take of their deliverer, that he was ready to perish for want of a draught of water. Thus are the greatest slights often put upon those who do the greatest services. Samson prayed to God in this distress. Those that forget to attend God with their praises, may be compelled to attend him with their prayers. Past experiences of God's power and goodness, are excellent pleas in prayer for further mercy. He pleads his being exposed to God's enemies; our best pleas are taken from God's glory. The Lord sent him seasonable relief. The place of this action was, from the jaw-bone, called Lehi. And in the place thus called, God caused a fountain suddenly and seasonably to open, close by Samson. We should be more thankful for the mercy of water, did we consider how ill we can spare it. Israel submitted to him whom they had betrayed. God was with him; henceforward they were directed by him as their judge.

Chapter 16

Samson's escape from Gaza (1–3)

Samson enticed to declare where his strength lay (4–17)

The Philistines take Samson, and put out his eyes (18–21)

Samson's strength is renewed (22–24)

He destroys many of the Philistines (25–31)

Samson's escape from Gaza (1–3)

Hitherto Samson's character has appeared glorious, though uncommon. In this chapter we find him behaving in so wicked a manner, that many question whether or not he were a godly man. But the apostle has determined this, Hebrews 11:32. By adverting to the doctrines and examples of Scripture, the artifices of Satan, the deceitfulness of the human heart, and the methods in which the Lord frequently deals with his people, we may learn useful lessons from this history, at which some needlessly stumble, while others cavil and object. The peculiar time in which Samson lived may account for many things, which, if done in our time, and without the special appointment of Heaven, would be highly criminal. And there might have been in him many exercises of piety, which, if recorded, would have reflected a different light upon his character. Observe Samson's danger. Oh that all who indulge their sensual appetites in drunkenness, or any fleshly lusts, would see themselves thus surrounded, way-laid, and marked for ruin by their spiritual enemies! The faster they sleep, the more secure they feel, the greater their danger. We hope it was with a pious resolution not to return to his sin, that he rose under a fear of the danger he was in. Can I be safe under this guilt? It was bad that he lay down without such checks; but it would have been worse, if he had laid still under them.

Samson enticed to declare where his strength lay (4–17)

Samson had been more than once brought into mischief and danger by the love of women, yet he would not take warning, but is again taken in the same snare, and this third time is fatal. Licentiousness is one of the things that take away the heart. This is a deep pit into which many have fallen; but from which few have escaped, and those by a miracle of mercy, with the loss of reputation and usefulness, of almost all, except their souls. The anguish of the suffering is ten thousand times greater than all the pleasures of the sin.

The Philistines take Samson, and put out his eyes (18–21)

See the fatal effects of false security. Satan ruins men by flattering them into a good opinion of their own safety, and so bringing them to mind nothing, and fear nothing; and then he robs them of their strength and honour, and leads them captive at his will. When we sleep our spiritual enemies do not. Samson's eyes were the inlets of his sin, (ver. 1,) and now his punishment began there. Now the Philistines blinded him, he had time to remember how his own lust had before blinded him. The best way to preserve the eyes, is, to turn them away from beholding vanity. Take warning by his fall, carefully to watch against all fleshly lusts; for all our glory is gone, and our defence departed from us, when our separation to God, as spiritual Nazarites, is profaned.

Samson's strength is renewed (22–24)

Samson's afflictions were the means of bringing him to deep repentance. By the loss of his bodily sight the eyes of his understanding were opened; and by depriving him of bodily strength, the Lord was pleased to renew his spiritual strength. The Lord permits some few to wander wide and sink deep, yet he recovers them at last, and marking his displeasure at sin in their severe temporal sufferings, preserves them from sinking into the pit of destruction. Hypocrites may abuse these examples, and infidels mock at them, but true Christians will thereby be rendered more humble, watchful, and circumspect; more simple in their dependence on the Lord, more fervent in prayer to be kept from falling, and in praise for being preserved; and, if they fall, they will be kept from sinking into despair.

He destroys many of the Philistines (25–31)

Nothing fills up the sins of any person or people faster than mocking and misusing the servants of God, even though it is by their own folly that they are brought low. God put it into Samson's heart, as a public person, thus to avenge on them God's quarrel, Israel's, and his own. That strength which he had lost by sin, he recovers by prayer. That it was not from passion or personal revenge, but from holy zeal for the glory of God and Israel, appears from God's accepting and answering the prayer. The house was pulled down, not by the natural strength of Samson, but by the almighty power of God. In his case it was right he should avenge the cause of God and Israel. Nor is he to be accused of self-murder. He sought not his own death, but Israel's deliverance, and the destruction of their enemies. Thus Samson died in bonds, and among the Philistines, as an awful rebuke for his sins; but he died repentant. The effects of his death typified those of the death of Christ, who, of his own will, laid down his life among transgressors, and thus overturned the foundation of Satan's kingdom, and provided for the deliverance of his people. Great as was the sin of Samson, and justly as he deserved the judgments he brought upon himself, he found mercy of the Lord at last; and every penitent shall obtain mercy, who flees for refuge to that Saviour whose blood cleanses from all sin. But here is nothing to encourage any to indulge sin, from a hope they shall at last repent and be saved.

Chapter 17
The beginning of idolatry in Israel, Micah and his mother (1–6)
Micah hires a Levite to be his priest (7–13)

The beginning of idolatry in Israel, Micah and his mother (1–6)

What is related in this, and the rest of the chapters to the end of this book, was done soon after the death of Joshua: see Judges 20:28. That it might appear how happy the nation was under the Judges, here is showed how unhappy they were when there was no Judge. The love of money made Micah so undutiful to his mother as to rob her, and made her so unkind to her son, as to curse him. Outward losses drive good people to their prayers, but bad people to their curses. This woman's silver was her god, before it was made into a graven or a molten image. Micah and his mother agreed to turn their money into a god, and set up idol worship in their family. See the cause of this corruption. Every man did that which was right in his own eyes, and then they soon did that which was evil in the sight of the Lord.

Micah hires a Levite to be his priest (7–13)

Micah thought it was a sign of God's favour to him and his images, that a Levite should come to his door. Thus those who please themselves with their own delusions, if Providence unexpectedly bring any thing to their hands that further them in their evil way, are apt from thence to think that God is pleased with them.

Chapter 18
The Danites seek to enlarge their inheritance, and rob Micah (1–31)

The Danites determined to take Micah's gods with them. Oh the folly of these Danites! How could they imagine those gods should protect them, that could not keep themselves from being stolen! To take them for their own use, was a double crime; it showed they neither feared God, nor regarded man, but were lost both to godliness and honesty. What a folly was it for Micah to call those his gods, which he had made, when He only is to be worshipped by us as God, that made us! That is put in God's place,

which we are concerned about, as if our all were bound up in it. If people will walk in the name of their false gods, much more should we love and serve the true God!

Chapter 19
The wickedness of the men of Gibeah (1–30)

The three remaining chapters of this book contain a very sad history of the wickedness of the men of Gibeah, in Benjamin. The righteous Lord permits sinners to execute just vengeance on one another, and if the scene here described is horrible, what will the discoveries of the day of judgment be! Let each of us consider how to escape from the wrath to come, how to mortify the sins of our own hearts, to resist Satan's temptations, and to avoid the pollutions there are in the world.

Chapter 20
The tribe of Benjamin nearly extirpated (1–48)

The Israelites' abhorrence of the crime committed at Gibeah, and their resolution to punish the criminals, were right; but they formed their resolves with too much haste and self-confidence. The eternal ruin of souls will be worse, and more fearful, than these desolations of a tribe.

Chapter 21
The Israelites lament for the Benjamites (1–25)

Israel lamented for the Benjamites, and were perplexed by the oath they had taken, not to give their daughters to them in marriage. Men are more zealous to support their own authority than that of God. They would have acted better if they had repented of their rash oaths, brought sin-offerings, and sought forgiveness in the appointed way, rather than attempt to avoid the guilt of perjury by actions quite as wrong. That men can advise others to acts of treachery or violence, out of a sense of duty, forms a strong proof of the blindness of the human mind when left to itself, and of the fatal effects of a conscience under ignorance and error.

RUTH

Matthew Henry

Introduction

We find in this book excellent examples of faith, piety, patience, humility, industry, and loving-kindness, in the common events of life. Also we see the special care which God's providence takes of our smallest concerns, encouraging us to full trust therein. We may view this book as a beautiful, because natural representation of human life; as a curious detail of important facts; and as a part of the plan of redemption.

Chapter 1

Elimelech and his sons die in the land of Moab (1–5)

Naomi returns home (6–14)

Orpah stays behind, but Ruth goes with Naomi (15–18)

They come to Bethlehem (19–22)

Elimelech and his sons die in the land of Moab (1–5)

Elimelech's care to provide for his family, was not to be blamed; but his removal into the country of Moab could not be justified. And the removal ended in the wasting of his family. It is folly to think of escaping that cross, which, being laid in our way, we ought to take up. Changing our place seldom is mending it. Those who bring young people into bad acquaintance, and take them out of the way of public ordinances, though they may think them well-principled, and armed against temptation, know not what will be the end. It does not appear that the women the sons of Elimelech married, were proselyted to the Jewish religion. Earthly trials or enjoyments are of short continuance. Death continually removes those of every age and situation, and mars all our outward comforts: we cannot too strongly prefer those advantages which shall last for ever.

Naomi returns home (6–14)

Naomi began to think of returning, after the death of her two sons. When death comes into a family, it ought to reform what is amiss there. Earth is made bitter to us, that heaven may be made dear. Naomi seems to have been a person of faith and piety. She dismissed her daughters-in-law with prayer. It is very proper for friends, when they part, to part with them thus in love. Did Naomi do well, to discourage her daughters from going with her, when she might save them from the idolatry of Moab, and bring them to the faith and worship of the God of Israel? Naomi, no doubt, desired to do that; but if they went with her, she would not have them to go upon her account. Those that take upon them a profession of religion only to oblige their friends, or for the sake of company, will be converts of small value. If they did come with her, she would have them make it their deliberate choice, and sit down first and count the cost, as it concerns those to do who make a profession of religion. And more desire 'rest in the house of a husband,' or some worldly settlement or earthly satisfaction, than the rest to which Christ invites our souls; therefore when tried they will depart from Christ, though perhaps with some sorrow.

Orpah stays behind, but Ruth goes with Naomi (15–18)

See Ruth's resolution, and her good affection to Naomi. Orpah was loth to part from her; yet she did not love her well enough to leave Moab for her sake. Thus, many have a value and affection for Christ, yet come short of salvation by him, because they will not forsake other things for him. They love him, yet leave him, because they do not love him enough, but love other things better. Ruth is an example of the grace of God, inclining the soul to choose the better part. Naomi could desire no more than the solemn declaration Ruth made. See the power of resolution; it silences temptation. Those that go in religious ways without a steadfast mind, stand like a door half open, which invites a thief; but resolution shuts and bolts the door, resists the devil and forces him to flee.

They come to Bethlehem (19–22)

Naomi and Ruth came to Bethlehem. Afflictions will make great and surprising changes in a little time. May God, by his grace, fit us for all such changes, especially the great change! Naomi signifies 'pleasant,' or 'amiable;' Mara, 'bitter,' or 'bitterness.' She was now a woman of a sorrowful spirit. She had come home empty, poor, a widow and childless. But there is a fulness for believers of which they never can be emptied; a good part which shall not be taken from those who have it. The cup of affliction is a 'bitter' cup, but she owns that the affliction came from God. It well becomes us to have our hearts humbled under humbling providences. It is not affliction itself, but affliction rightly borne, that does us good.

Chapter 2

Ruth gleans in the field of Boaz (1–3)

The kindness of Boaz to Ruth (4–16)

Ruth returns to her mother-in-law (17–23)

Ruth gleans in the field of Boaz (1–3)

Observe Ruth's humility. When Providence had made her poor, she cheerfully stoops to her lot. High spirits will rather starve than stoop; not so Ruth. Nay, it is her own proposal. She speaks humbly in her expectation of leave to glean. We may not demand kindness as a debt, but ask, and take it as a favour, though in a small matter. Ruth also was an example of industry. She loved not to eat the bread of idleness. This is an example to young people. Diligence promises well, both for this world and the other. We must not be shy of any honest employment. No labour is a reproach. Sin is a thing below us, but we must not think any thing else so, to which Providence

call us. She was an example of regard to her mother, and of trust in Providence. God wisely orders what seem to us small events; and those that appear altogether uncertain, still are directed to serve his own glory, and the good of his people.

The kindness of Boaz to Ruth (4–16)

The pious and kind language between Boaz and his reapers shows that there were godly persons in Israel. Such language as this is seldom heard in our field; too often, on the contrary, what is immoral and corrupt. A stranger would form a very different opinion of our land, from that which Ruth would form of Israel from the converse and conduct of Boaz and his reapers. But true religion will teach a man to behave aright in all states and conditions; it will form kind masters and faithful servants, and cause harmony in families. True religion will cause mutual love and kindness among persons of different ranks. It had these effects on Boaz and his men. When he came to them he prayed for them. They did not, as soon as he was out of hearing curse him, as some ill-natured servants that hate their master's eye, but they returned his courtesy. Things are likely to go on well where there is such good-will as this between masters and servants. They expressed their kindness to each other by praying one for another. Boaz inquired concerning the stranger he saw, and ordered her to be well treated. Masters must take care, not only that they do no hurt themselves, but that they suffer not their servants and those under them to do wrong. Ruth humbly owned herself unworthy of favours, seeing she was born and brought up a heathen. It well becomes us all to think humbly of ourselves, esteeming others better than ourselves. And let us, in the kindness of Boaz to Ruth, note the kindness of the Lord Jesus Christ to poor sinners.

Ruth returns to her mother-in-law (17–23)

It encourages industry, that in all labour, even that of gleaning, there is profit. Ruth was pleased with what she gained by her own industry, and was careful to secure it. Let us thus take care that we lose not those things which we have wrought, 2 John should examine their children, as Naomi did, not to frighten or discourage them, so as to make them hate home, or tempt them to tell a lie; but to commend them if they have done well, and with mildness to reprove and caution them if they have done otherwise. It is a good question for us to ask ourselves every night, Where have I gleaned to-day? What improvement have I made in knowledge and grace? What have I done that will turn to a good account? When the Lord deals bountifully with us, let us not be found in any other field, nor seeking for happiness and satisfaction in the creature. We lose Divine favours, if we slight them. Ruth dutifully observed her mother's directions. And when the harvest was ended, she kept her aged mother company at home. Dinah went out to see the daughters of the land; her vanity ended in disgrace, Genesis 34. Ruth kept at home, and helped to maintain her mother, and went out on no other errand than to get provision for her; her humility and industry ended in preferment.

Chapter 3

The directions given to Ruth by Naomi (1–5)

Boaz acknowledges the duty of a kinsman (6–13)

Ruth's return to her mother-in-law (14–18)

The directions given to Ruth by Naomi (1–5)

The married state should be a rest, as much as any thing upon earth can be so, as it ought to fix the affections and form a connexion for life. Therefore it should be engaged in with great seriousness, with earnest prayers for direction, for the blessing of God, and with regard to his precepts. Parents should carefully advise their children in this important concern, that it may be well with them as to their souls. Be it always remembered, That is best for us which is best for our souls. The course Naomi advised appears strange to us; but it was according to the laws and usages of Israel. If the proposed measure had borne the appearance of evil, Naomi would not have advised it. Law and custom gave Ruth, who was now proselyted to the true religion, a legal claim upon Boaz. It was customary for widows to assert this claim, Deuteronomy 25:5-10. But this is not recorded for imitation in other times, and is not to be judged by modern rules. And if there had been any evil in it, Ruth was a woman of too much virtue and too much sense to have listened to it.

Boaz acknowledges the duty of a kinsman (6–13)

What in one age or nation would be improper, is not always so in another age or another nation. Being a judge of Israel, Boaz would tell Ruth what she should do; also whether he had the right of redemption, and what methods must be taken, and what rites used, in order to accomplishing her marriage with him or another person. The conduct of Boaz calls for the highest praise. He attempted not to take advantage of Ruth; he did not disdain her as a poor, destitute stranger, nor suspect her of any ill intentions. He spoke honourably of her as a virtuous woman, made her a promise, and as soon as the morning arrived, sent her away with a present to her mother-in-law. Boaz made his promise conditional, for there was a kinsman nearer than he, to whom the right of redemption belonged.

Ruth's return to her mother-in-law (14–18)

Ruth had done all that was fit for her to do, she must patiently wait the event. Boaz, having undertaken this matter, would be sure to manage it well. Much more reason have true believers to cast their care on God, because he has promised to care for them. Our strength is to sit still, Isaiah 30:7. This narrative may encourage us to lay ourselves by faith at the feet of Christ: He is our near Kinsman; having taken our nature upon him. He has the right to redeem. Let us seek to receive from him his directions: Lord, what wilt thou have me to do? Acts 9:6. He will never blame us as doing this unseasonably. And let us earnestly desire and seek the same rest for our children and friends, that it may be well with them also.

Chapter 4

The kinsman refuses to redeem Ruth's inheritance (1–8)

Boaz marries Ruth (9–12)

Birth of Obed (13–22)

The kinsman refuses to redeem Ruth's inheritance (1–8)

This matter depended on the laws given by Moses about inheritances, and doubtless the whole was settled in the regular and legal manner. This kinsman, when he heard the conditions of the bargain, refused it. In like manner many are shy of the great redemption; they are not willing to espouse religion; they have heard well of it, and have nothing to say against it; they will give it their good word, but they are willing to part with it, and cannot be bound to it, for fear of marring their own inheritance in this world. The right was resigned to Boaz. Fair and open dealing in all matters of contract and trade, is what all must make conscience of, who would approve themselves true Israelites, without guile. Honesty will be found the best policy.

Boaz marries Ruth (9–12)

Men are ready to seize opportunities for increasing their estates, but few know the value of godliness. Such are the wise men of this world, whom the Lord charges with folly. They attend not to the concerns of their souls, but reject the salvation of Christ, for fear of marring their inheritance. But God did Boaz the honour to bring him into the line of the Messiah, while the kinsman, who was afraid of lessening himself, and marring his inheritance, has his name, family, and inheritance forgotten.

Birth of Obed (13–22)

Ruth bore a son, through whom thousands and myriads were born to God; and in being the lineal ancestor of Christ, she was instrumental in the happiness of all that shall be saved by him; even of us Gentiles, as well as those of Jewish descent. She was a witness for God to the Gentile world, that he had not utterly forsaken them, but that in due time they should become one with his chosen people, and partake of his salvation. Prayer to God attended the marriage, and praise to him attended the birth of the child. What a pity it is that pious language should not be more used among Christians, or that it should be let fall into formality! Here is the descent of David from Ruth. And the period came when Bethlehem-Judah displayed greater wonders than those in the history of Ruth, when the outcast babe of another forlorn female of the same race appeared, controlling the counsels of the Roman master of the world, and drawing princes and wise men from the east, with treasures of gold, and frankincense, and myrrh to his feet. His name shall endure for ever, and all nations shall call Him blessed. In that Seed shall all the nations of the earth be blessed.

1 SAMUEL

Robert Jamieson

Introduction to the first and second books of Samuel

The first and second books of Samuel were, by the ancient Jews, conjoined so as to make one book, and in that form could be called the Book of Samuel with more propriety than now, the second being wholly occupied with the relation of transactions that did not take place till after the death of that eminent judge. Accordingly, in the Septuagint and the Vulgate, it is called the First and Second Books of Kings. The early portion of the First Book, down to the end of the twenty-fourth chapter, was probably written by Samuel; while the rest of it and the whole of the Second, are commonly ascribed to Nathan and Gad, founding the opinion on 1Ch 29:29. Commentators, however, are divided about this, some supposing that the statements in 1Sa 2:26 3:1, indicate the hand of the judge himself, or a contemporary; while some think, from 1Sa 6:18 12:5 27:6, that its composition must be referred to a later age. It is probable, however, that these supposed marks of an after-period were interpolations of Ezra. This uncertainty, however, as to the authorship does not affect the inspired authority of the book, which is indisputable, being quoted in the New Testament (1Sa 13:14 in Ac 13:22, and 2Sa 7:14 in Heb 1:5), as well as in many of the Psalms.

Chapter 1

Of Elkanah and his two wives (1:1–8)

1-2. a certain man of Ramathaim-zophim – The first word being in the dual number, signifies the double city – the old and new town of Ramah (1Sa 1:19). Though a native of Ephratha or Beth-lehem-judah, Elkanah was a Levite (1Ch 6:33,34). Though of this order, and a good man, he practised polygamy. This was contrary to the original law, but it seems to have been prevalent among the Hebrews in those days, when there was no king in Israel, and every man did what seemed right in his own eyes (Jud 21:25).

3. this man went up out of his city yearly to worship in Shiloh – In that place was the 'earth's one sanctuary,' and thither he repaired at the three solemn feasts, accompanied by his family at one of them – probably the Passover.

Although a Levite, he could not personally offer a sacrifice – that was exclusively the office of the priests; and his piety in maintaining a regular attendance on the divine ordinances is the more worthy of notice because the character of the two priests who administered them was notoriously bad. But doubtless he believed, and acted on the belief, that the ordinances were 'effectual means of salvation, not from any virtue in them, or in those who administered them, but from the grace of God being communicated through them.'

4. when Elkanah offered, he gave to Peninnah portions – The offerer received back the greater part of the peace offerings, which he and his family or friends were accustomed to eat at a social feast before the Lord. It was out of these consecrated viands Elkanah gave portions to all the members of his family.

6. her adversary also provoked her sore – The conduct of Peninnah was most unbecoming. But domestic broils in the houses of polygamists are of frequent occurrence, and the most fruitful cause of them has always been jealousy of the husband's superior affection, as in this case of Hannah.

Hannah's prayer (1:9–18)

11. She prayed. She vowed a vow. Here is a specimen of the intense desire that reigned in the hearts of the Hebrew women for children. This was the burden of Hannah's prayer; and the strong preference she expressed for a male child originated in her purpose of dedicating him to the tabernacle service. The circumstance of his birth bound him to this; but his residence within the precincts of the sanctuary would have to commence at an earlier age than usual, in consequence of the Nazarite vow.

12–18. Eli marked her mouth – The suspicion of the aged priest seems to indicate that the vice of intemperance was neither uncommon nor confined to one sex in those times of disorder. This mistaken impression was immediately removed, and, in the words, 'God grant', or rather, 'will grant', was followed by an invocation which, as Hannah regarded it in the light of a prophecy pointing to the accomplishment of her earnest desire, dispelled her sadness, and filled her with confident hope (1Sa 1:18). The character and services of the expected child were sufficiently important to make his birth a fit subject for prophecy.

Samuel born (1:19–27)

20. called his name Samuel – doubtless with her husband's consent. The names of children were given sometimes by the fathers, and sometimes by the mothers (see Ge 4:1,26 5:29 19:37 21:3); and among the early Hebrews, they were commonly compound names, one part including the name of God.

21. the man Elkanah … went up to offer … his vow – The solemn expression of his concurrence in Hannah's vow was necessary to make it obligatory.

Chapter 2

Hannah's song in thankfulness to God (2:1–11)

1. Hannah prayed, and said – Praise and prayer are inseparably conjoined in Scripture (Col 4:2 1Ti 2:1). This beautiful song was her tribute of thanks for the divine goodness in answering her petition.

5. the barren hath born seven – that is, many children.

6. he bringeth down to the grave, and bringeth up – that is, He reduces to the lowest state of degradation and misery, and restores to prosperity and happiness.

10. the Lord shall judge the ends of the earth … exalt the horn of his anointed – This is the first place in Scripture where the word anointed, or Messiah, occurs; and as there was no king in Israel at the time, it seems the best interpretation to refer it to Christ. There is, indeed, a remarkable resemblance between the song of Hannah and that of Mary (Lu 1:46).

11. the child did minister unto the Lord before Eli the priest – He must have been engaged in some occupation suited to his tender age, as in playing upon the cymbals, or other instruments of music; in lighting the lamps, or similar easy and interesting services.

The sin of Eli's sons (2:12–17)

12. Now the sons of Eli were sons of Belial – not only careless and irreligious, but men loose in their actions, and vicious and scandalous in their habits. Though professionally engaged in sacred duties, they were not only strangers to the power of religion in the heart, but they had thrown off its restraints, and even ran, as is sometimes done in similar cases by the sons of eminent ministers, to the opposite extreme of reckless and open profligacy.

13–17. the priests' custom with the people – When persons wished to present a sacrifice of peace offering on the altar, the offering was brought in the first instance to the priest, and as the Lord's part was burnt, the parts appropriated respectively to the priests and offerers were to be sodden. But Eli's sons, unsatisfied with the breast and shoulder, which were the perquisites appointed to them by the divine law (Ex 29:27; Le 7:31,32), not only claimed part of the offerer's share, but rapaciously seized them previous to the sacred ceremony of heaving or waving; and moreover they committed the additional injustice of taking up with their fork those portions which they preferred, while still raw.

Samuel's ministry (2:18–26)

18. But Samuel ministered before the Lord, being a child – This notice of his early services in the outer courts of the tabernacle was made to pave the way for the remarkable prophecy regarding the high priest's family.

girded with a linen ephod – A small shoulder-garment or apron, used in the sacred service by the inferior priests and Levites; sometimes also by judges or eminent persons, and hence allowed to Samuel, who, though not a Levite, was devoted to God from his birth.

19. his mother made him a little coat, and brought it to him from year to year – Aware

that he could not yet render any useful service to the tabernacle, she undertook the expense of supplying him with wearing apparel. All weaving stuffs, manufacture of cloth, and making of suits were anciently the employment of women.

22–24. the women that assembled at the door of the tabernacle – This was an institution of holy women of a strictly ascetic order, who had relinquished worldly cares and devoted themselves to the Lord; an institution which continued down to the time of Christ (Lu 2:37).

25. the Lord would slay them – It was not God's preordination, but their own wilful and impenitent disobedience which was the cause of their destruction.

A prophecy against Eli's house (2:27–35)

27. there came a man of God unto Eli, and said … that there shall not be an old man in thine house – So much importance has always, in the East, been attached to old age, that it would be felt to be a great calamity, and sensibly to lower the respectability of any family which could boast of few or no old men. The prediction of this prophet was fully confirmed by the afflictions, degradation, poverty, and many untimely deaths with which the house of Eli was visited after its announcement (see 1Sa 4:11 14:3 22:18-23 1Ki 2:27).

31. I will cut off thine arm, and the arm of thy father's house – By the withdrawal of the high priesthood from Eleazar, the elder of Aaron's two sons, after Nadab and Abihu were destroyed, (Nu 3:4), that dignity had been conferred on the family of Ithamar, to which Eli belonged, and now that his descendants had forfeited the honor, it was to be taken from them and restored to the elder branch.

Chapter 3

The Lord appears to Samuel in a vision (3:1–21)

1. the word of the Lord was precious in those days – It was very rarely known to the Israelites; and in point of fact only two prophets are mentioned as having appeared during the whole administration of the judges (Jud 4:4 6:8).

there was no open vision – no publicly recognized prophet whom the people could consult, and from whom they might learn the will of God. There must have been certain indubitable evidences by which a communication from heaven could be distinguished. Eli knew them, for he may have received them, though not so frequently as is implied in the idea of an **open vision**.

3. ere the lamp of God went out in the temple of the Lord – The **temple** seems to have become the established designation of the tabernacle, and the time indicated was towards the morning

twilight, as the lamps were extinguished at sunrise (see Le 6:12,13).

5–18. he ran unto Eli, and said, Here am I; for thou calledst me – It is evident that his sleeping chamber was close to that of the aged high priest and that he was accustomed to be called during the night. The three successive calls addressed to the boy convinced Eli of the divine character of the speaker, and he therefore exhorted the child to give a reverential attention to the message. The burden of the Lord's message was an extraordinary premonition of the judgments that impended over Eli's house; and the aged priest, having drawn the painful secret from the child, exclaimed, **It is the Lord; let him do what seemeth him good.** Such is the spirit of meek and unmurmuring submission in which we ought to receive the dispensations of God, however severe and afflictive. In his personal character Eli seems to have been a good man, but his sons' conduct was flagrantly bad; and though his misfortunes claim our sympathy, it is impossible to approve or defend the weak and unfaithful course which, in the retributive justice of God, brought these adversities upon him.

Chapter 4

Israel overcome by the Philistines (4:1–11)

1. the word of Samuel came to all Israel – The character of Samuel as a prophet was now fully established. The want of an open vision was supplied by him, for 'none of his words were let fall to the ground' (1Sa 3:19); and to his residence in Shiloh all the people of Israel repaired to consult him as an oracle, who, by his gift of a prophet, could inform them what was the mind of God.

Israel went out against the Philistines to battle – that is, to resist this new incursion.

3–9. Let us fetch the ark of the covenant of the Lord out of Shiloh unto us – Strange that they were so blind to the real cause of the disaster and that they did not discern, in the great and general corruption of religion and morals (1Sa 2:22-25 7:3 Ps 78:58), the reason why the presence and aid of God were not extended to them. Their first measure for restoring the national spirit and energy ought to have been a complete reformation – a universal return to purity of worship and morals. But, instead of cherishing a spirit of deep humiliation and sincere repentance, instead of resolving on the abolition of existing abuses, and the re-establishing of the pure faith, they adopted what appeared an easier and speedier course – they put their trust in ceremonial observances, and doubted not but that the introduction of the ark into the battlefield would ensure their victory.

Eli hearing the tidings (4:12–22)

13–18. Eli sat upon a seat by the wayside – The aged priest, as a public magistrate, used, in dispensing justice, to seat himself daily in a spacious recess at the entrance gate of the city. Poor Eli! He was a good man, in spite of his unhappy weaknesses. So strongly were his sensibilities enlisted on the side of religion, that the news of the capture of the ark proved to him a knell of death; and yet his overindulgence, or sad neglect of his family – the main cause of all the evils that led to its fall – has been recorded, as a beacon to warn all heads of Christian families against making shipwreck on the same rock.

Chapter 5

The Philistines bring the ark into the house of Dagon (5:1–2)

2. the house of Dagon – Stately temples were erected in honour of this idol, which was the principal deity of the Philistines, but whose worship extended over all Syria, as well as Mesopotamia and Chaldea. It was represented under a monstrous combination of a human head, breast, and arms, joined to the belly and tail of a fish. The captured ark was placed in the temple of Dagon, right before this image of the idol.

Dagon falls down (5:3–5)

3–4. they of Ashdod arose early – the object of their stupid veneration prostrate before the symbol of the divine presence. Though set up, it fell again, and lay in a state of complete mutilation; its head and arms, severed from the trunk, were lying in distant and separate places, as if violently cast off, and only the fishy part remained. The degradation of their idol, though concealed by the priests on the former occasion, was now more manifest and infamous. It lay in the attitude of a vanquished enemy and a suppliant, and this picture of humiliation significantly declared the superiority of the God of Israel.

5. Therefore neither the priests … nor any … tread on the threshold of Dagon – A superstitious ceremony crept in, and in the providence of God was continued, by which the Philistines contributed to publish this proof of the helplessness of their god.

The Philistines are smitten with emerods (5:6–12)

6. the hand of the Lord was heavy upon them of Ashdod – The presumption of the Ashdodites was punished by a severe judgment that overtook them in the form of a pestilence.

smote them with emerods – bleeding piles, hemorrhoids (Ps 78:66), in a very aggravated form. As the heathens generally regarded diseases affecting the secret parts of the body as punishments from the gods for trespasses committed against themselves, the Ashdodites would be the more ready to look upon the prevailing epidemic as demonstrating the anger of God, already shown against their idol.

7. the ark of God shall not abide with us – It was removed successively to several of the large towns of the country, but the same pestilence broke out in every place and raged so fiercely and fatally that the authorities were forced to send the ark back into the land of Israel (1Sa 5:8-10).

Chapter 6

The Philistines counsel how to send back the ark (6:1–9)

1. the ark … was in the country of the Philistines seven months – Notwithstanding the calamities which its presence had brought on the country and the people, the Philistine lords were unwilling to relinquish such a prize, and tried every means to retain it with peace and safety, but in vain.

4. Five golden emerods – Votive or thank offerings were commonly made by the heathen in prayer for, or gratitude after, deliverance from lingering or dangerous disorders, in the form of metallic (generally silver) models or images of the diseased parts of the body.

five golden mice – This animal is supposed by some to be the jumping mouse of Syria and Egypt; by others, to be the short-tailed field mouse, which often swarms in prodigious numbers and commits great ravages in the cultivated fields of Palestine.

6. Wherefore then do ye harden your hearts, as the Egyptians and Pharaoh hardened their hearts? The memory of the appalling judgments that had been inflicted on Egypt was not yet obliterated. Whether preserved in written records, or in floating tradition, they were still fresh in the minds of men, and being extensively spread, were doubtless the means of diffusing the knowledge and fear of the true God.

7. two milch kine – Such untrained heifers, wanton and vagrant, would pursue no certain and regular path, like those accustomed to the yoke, and therefore were most unlikely of their own spontaneous motion to prosecute the direct road to the land of Israel.

8. take the ark of the Lord, and lay it upon the cart – This mode of carrying the sacred symbol was forbidden; but the ignorance of the Philistines made the indignity excusable.

put the jewels … in a coffer by the side thereof

– The way of securing treasure in the East is still in a chest, chained to the house wall or some solid part of the furniture.

The Philistines return the ark (6:10–21)

12. **the lords of the Philistines went after them** to give their tribute of homage, to prevent imposture, and to obtain the most reliable evidence of the truth. The result of this journey tended to their own deeper humiliation, and the greater illustration of God's glory.

14. **offered the kine** – Though contrary to the requirements of the law (Le 1:3 22:19), these animals might properly be offered, as consecrated by God Himself; and though not beside the tabernacle, there were many instances of sacrifices offered by prophets and holy men on extraordinary occasions in other places.

19. **he smote the men of Beth-shemesh, because they had looked into the ark** – In the ecstasy of delight at seeing the return of the ark, the Beth-shemesh reapers pried into it beneath the wagon cover; and instead of covering it up again, as a sacred utensil, they let it remain exposed to common inspection, wishing it to be seen, in order that all might enjoy the triumph of seeing the votive offerings presented to it, and gratify curiosity with the sight of the sacred shrine. This was the offense of those Israelites who had treated the ark with less reverence than the Philistines themselves.

21. **Kirjath-jearim** 'the city of woods'. This was the nearest town to Beth-shemesh; and being a place of strength, it was a more fitting place for the residence of the ark. Beth-shemesh being in a low plain, and Kirjath-jearim on a hill, explains the message, **Come ye down, and fetch it up to you.**

Chapter 7

The ark at Kirjath-Jearim (7:1–2)

1. **brought it into the house of Abinadab in the hill** – Why it was not transported at once to Shiloh where the tabernacle and sacred vessels were remaining, is difficult to conjecture.

2. **the ark abode in Kirjath-jearim … twenty years** – It appears, in the subsequent history, that a much longer period elapsed before its final removal from Kirjath-jearim (2Sa 6:1-19; 1Ch 13:1-14). But that length of time had passed when the Israelites began to revive from their sad state of religious decline. The capture of the ark had produced a general indifference either as to its loss or its recovery.

all the house of Israel lamented after the Lord – They were then brought, doubtless by the influence of Samuel's exhortations, to renounce idolatry, and to return to the national worship of the true God.

The Israelites, through Samuel's influence, solemnly repent at Mizpeh (7:3–6)

3–6. **Samuel spake unto all the house of Israel** – A great national reformation was effected through the influence of Samuel. Disgusted with their foreign servitude, and panting for the restoration of liberty and independence, they were open to salutary impressions; and convinced of their errors, they renounced idolatry. The re-establishment of the faith of their fathers was inaugurated at a great public meeting, held at Mizpeh in Judah, and hallowed by the observance of impressive religious solemnities. The drawing water, and pouring it out before the Lord, seems to have been a symbolical act by which, in the people's name, Samuel testified their sense of national corruption, their need of that moral purification of which water is the emblem, and their sincere desire to pour out their hearts in repentance before God.

While Samuel prays, the Philistines are discomfited (7:7–14)

7–11. **when the Philistines heard** – The character and importance of the national convention at Mizpeh were fully appreciated by the Philistines. They discerned in it the rising spirit of religious patriotism among the Israelites that was prepared to throw off the yoke of their domination. Anxious to crush it at the first, they made a sudden incursion while the Israelites were in the midst of their solemn celebration. Unprepared for resistance, they besought Samuel to supplicate the divine interposition to save them from their enemies. The prophet's prayers and sacrifice were answered by such a tremendous storm of thunder and lightning that the assailants, panic-struck, were disordered and fled. The Israelites, recognizing the hand of God, rushed courageously on the foe they had so much dreaded and committed such immense havoc, that the Philistines did not for long recover from this disastrous blow. This brilliant victory secured peace and independence to Israel for twenty years, as well as the restitution of the usurped territory.

12. **Samuel took a stone, and set it between Mizpeh and Shen** – A huge stone pillar was erected as a monument of their victory (Le 26:1).

Chapter 8

Because of the ill-government of Samuel's sons, the Israelites ask for a king (8:1–22)

1–5. **when Samuel was old** – He was now about fifty-four years of age, having discharged the office of sole judge for twelve years. Unable, from growing infirmities, to prosecute his circuit journeys through the country, he at length confined his magisterial duties to Ramah and its neighbourhood (1Sa 7:15), delegating to his sons as his deputies the administration of justice in the southern districts of Palestine, their provincial court being held at Beer-sheba. The young men, however, did not inherit the high qualities of their father. Having corrupted the fountains of justice for their own private aggrandizement, a deputation of the leading men in the country lodged a complaint against them in headquarters, accompanied with a formal demand for a change in the government. The limited and occasional authority of the judges, the disunion and jealousy of the tribes under the administration of those rulers, had been creating a desire for a united and permanent form of government; while the advanced age of Samuel, together with the risk of his death happening in the then unsettled state of the people, was the occasion of calling forth an expression of this desire now.

6–10. the thing displeased Samuel when they said, Give us a king to judge us – The appointment of a visible monarch would necessarily tend to throw out of view their unseen King and Head. God intimated, through Samuel, that their request would, in anger, be granted, while at the same time he apprised them of some of the evils that would result from their choice.

11. This will be the manner of the king – The following is a very just and graphic picture of the despotic governments which anciently and still are found in the East, and into conformity with which the Hebrew monarchy, notwithstanding the restrictions prescribed by the law, gradually slid.

19–22. Nevertheless the people refused to obey the voice of Samuel – They sneered at Samuel's description as a bugbear to frighten them. Determined, at all hazards, to gain their object, they insisted on being made like all the other nations, though it was their glory and happiness to be unlike other nations in having the Lord for their King and Lawgiver (Nu 23:9; De 33:28). Their demand was conceded, for the government of a king had been provided for in the law; and they were dismissed to wait the appointment, which God had reserved to Himself (De 17:14-20).

Chapter 9

Saul, despairing to find his father's asses, comes to Samuel (9:1–14)

1. a mighty man of power – that is, of great wealth and substance.

2. Saul, a choice young man, and a goodly – He had a fine appearance; for it is evident that he must have been only a little under seven feet tall. A gigantic stature and an athletic frame must have been a popular recommendation at that time in that country.

3. the asses of Kish Saul's father were lost. And Kish said to Saul . . . arise, go seek the asses – The probability is that the family of Kish, according to the immemorial usage of Oriental shepherds in the purely pastoral regions, had let the animals roam at large during the grazing season, at the close of which messengers were despatched in search of them. Such travelling searches are common; and, as each owner has his own stamp marked on his cattle, the mention of it to the shepherds he meets gradually leads to the discovery of the strayed animals. This ramble of Saul's had nothing extraordinary in it, except its superior directions and issue, which turned its uncertainty into certainty.

6. peradventure he can show us our way that we should go – It seems strange that a dignified prophet should be consulted in such an affair. But it is probable that at the introduction of the prophetic office, the seers had discovered things lost or stolen, and thus their power for higher revelations was gradually established.

7. Saul said to his servant, But, behold, if we go, what shall we bring the man? According to Eastern notions, it would be considered a want of respect for any person to go into the presence of a superior man of rank or of official station without a present of some kind in his hand, however trifling in value.

8. the fourth part of a shekel of silver – Contrary to our Western notions, money is in the East the most acceptable form in which a present can be made to a man of rank.

9. seer ... Prophet – The recognized distinction in latter times was, that a seer was one who was favored with visions of God – a view of things invisible to mortal sight; and a prophet foretold future events.

God reveals to Samuel Saul's coming, and his appointment to the kingdom (9:15–27)

15–16. Now the Lord had told Samuel in his ear a day before – The description of Saul, the time of his arrival, and the high office to which he was destined, had been secretly intimated to Samuel from heaven. The future king of Israel was to fight the battles of the Lord and protect His people. It would appear that they were at this time suffering great molestation from the Philistines, and that this was an additional reason of their urgent demands for the appointment of a king.

20–21. on whom is all the desire of Israel? Is it not on thee, and on all thy father's house? This was a covert and indirect premonition of the royal dignity that awaited him; and, though Saul's answer shows that he fully understood it, he affected to doubt that the prophet was in earnest.

21. And Saul answered and said, Am not I a Benjamite, of the smallest of the tribes of Israel

– By selecting a king from this least and nearly extinct tribe (Jud 20:46–48), divine wisdom designed to remove all grounds of jealousy among the other tribes.

22. Samuel took Saul and his servant, and brought them into the parlour – The toil-worn but noble-looking traveller found himself suddenly seated among the principal men of the place and treated as the most distinguished guest.

24. the cook took up the shoulder ... and set it before Saul. And Samuel said, Behold that which is left; set it before thee, and eat – This was, most probably, the right shoulder; which, as the perquisite of the sacrifice, belonged to Samuel, and which he had set aside for his expected guest. In the sculptures of the Egyptian shambles, also, the first joint taken off was always the right shoulder for the priest. The meaning of those distinguished attentions must have been understood by the other guests.

25–27. Samuel communed with Saul upon the top of the house – Saul was taken to lodge with the prophet for that night. Before retiring to rest, they communed on the flat roof of the house, the couch being laid there (Jos 2:6), when, doubtless, Samuel revealed the secret and described the peculiar duties of a monarch in a nation so related to the divine King as Israel.

Chapter 10

Samuel anoints Saul, and confirms him by the prediction of three signs (10:1–27)

1. Then Samuel took a vial of oil – This was the ancient (Jud 9:8) ceremony of investiture with the royal office among the Hebrews and other Eastern nations. But there were two unctions to the kingly office; the one in private, by a prophet (1Sa 16:13), which was meant to be only a prophetic intimation of the person attaining that high dignity – the more public and formal inauguration (2Sa 2:4; 5:3) was performed by the high priest, and perhaps with the holy oil, but that is not certain. The first of a dynasty was thus anointed, but not his heirs, unless the succession was disputed (1Ki 1:39; 2Ki 11:12; 23:30; 2Ch 23:11).

kissed him – This salutation, as explained by the words that accompanied it, was an act of respectful homage, a token of congratulation to the new king (Ps 2:12).

2. When thou art departed from me today – The design of these specific predictions of what should be met with on the way, and the number and minuteness of which would arrest attention, was to confirm Saul's reliance on the prophetic character of Samuel, and lead him to give full credence to what had been revealed to him as the word of God.

6. the Spirit of the Lord will come upon thee – literally, 'rush upon thee', suddenly endowing thee with a capacity to act in a manner far superior to thy previous character and habits; and instead of the simplicity, ignorance, and sheepishness of a peasant, thou wilt display an energy, wisdom, and magnanimity worthy of a prince.

9–11. when he had turned his back to go from Samuel, God gave him another heart – Influenced by the words of Samuel, as well as by the accomplishment of these signs, Saul's reluctance to undertake the onerous office was overcome. The fulfilment of the two first signs is passed over, but the third is specially described. The spectacle of a man, though more fit to look after his father's cattle than to take part in the sacred exercises of the young prophets – a man without any previous instruction, or any known taste, entering with ardor into the spirit, and skilfully accompanying the melodies of the sacred band, was so extraordinary a phenomenon, that it gave rise to the proverb, 'Is Saul also among the prophets?' (see 1Sa 19:24). The prophetic spirit had come upon him; and to Saul it was as personal and experimental an evidence of the truth of God's word that had been spoken to him, as converts to Christianity have in themselves from the sanctifying power of the Gospel.

17–25. Samuel called the people together ... at Mizpeh – a shaft-like hill near Hebron, five hundred feet in height. The national assemblies of the Israelites were held there. A day having been appointed for the election of a king, Samuel, after having charged the people with a rejection of God's institution and a superseding of it by one of their own, proceeded to the nomination of the new monarch. As it was of the utmost importance that the appointment should be under the divine direction and control, the determination was made by the miraculous lot, tribes, families, and individuals being successively passed until Saul was found. His concealment of himself must have been the result either of innate modesty, or a sudden nervous excitement under the circumstances. When dragged into view, he was seen to possess all those corporeal advantages which a rude people desiderate in their sovereigns; and the exhibition of which gained for the prince the favorable opinion of Samuel also. In the midst of the national enthusiasm, however, the prophet's deep piety and genuine patriotism took care to explain 'the manner of the kingdom', that is, the royal rights and privileges, together with the limitations to which they were to be subjected; and in order that the constitution might be ratified with all due solemnity, the charter of this constitutional monarchy was recorded and laid up 'before the Lord', that is, deposited in the custody of the priests, along with the most sacred archives of the nation.

27. the children of Belial said, How shall this man save us? And they despised him, and brought him no presents – In Eastern countries, the honor of the sovereign and the splendor of the royal household are upheld, not by a fixed rate of taxation, but by presents brought at certain seasons by officials, and men of wealth, from all parts of the kingdom, according to the means of the individual, and of a customary registered value. Such was the tribute which Saul's opponents withheld, and for want of which he was unable to set up a kingly establishment for a while. But **biding his time**, he bore the insult with a prudence and magnanimity which were of great use in the beginning of his government.

Chapter 11

Nahash offers them of Jabesh-Gilead a reproachful condition (11:1–4)

1. Then Nahash the Ammonite came up – Nahash ('serpent'); (see Jud 8:3). The Ammonites had long claimed the right of original possession in Gilead. Though repressed by Jephthah (Jud 11:33), they now, after ninety years, renew their pretensions; and it was the report of their threatened invasion that hastened the appointment of a king (1Sa 12:12).

Make a covenant with us, and we will serve thee – They saw no prospect of aid from the western Israelites, who were not only remote, but scarcely able to repel the incursions of the Philistines from themselves.

2. thrust out all your right eyes – literally, 'scoop' or 'hollow out' the ball. This barbarous mutilation is the usual punishment of usurpers in the East, inflicted on chiefs; sometimes, also, even in modern history, on the whole male population of a town. Nahash meant to keep the Jabeshites useful as tributaries, whence he did not wish to render them wholly blind, but only to deprive them of their right eye, which would disqualify them for war. Besides, his object was, through the people of Jabesh-gilead, to insult the Israelitish nation.

3–4. send messengers unto all the coasts of Israel – a curious proof of the general dissatisfaction that prevailed as to the appointment of Saul. Those Gileadites deemed him capable neither of advising nor succoring them; and even in his own town the appeal was made to the people – not to the prince.

They send to Saul, and are delivered (11:5–11)

7. he took a yoke of oxen, and hewed them in pieces – (see Jud 19:29). This particular form of war summons was suited to the character and habits of an agricultural and pastoral people. Solemn in itself, the denunciation that accompanied it carried a terrible threat to those that neglected to obey it. Saul conjoins the name of Samuel with his own, to lend the greater influence to the measure, and to strike greater terror unto all contemners of the order. The small contingent furnished by Judah suggests that the disaffection to Saul was strongest in that tribe.

11. on the morrow, that Saul put the people in three companies – Crossing the Jordan in the evening, Saul marched his army all night, and came at daybreak on the camp of the Ammonites, who were surprised in three different parts, and totally routed. This happened before the seven days' truce expired.

Saul confirmed king (11:12–15)

12–15. the people said ..., Who is he that said, Shall Saul reign over us? The enthusiastic admiration of the people, under the impulse of grateful and generous feelings, would have dealt summary vengeance on the minority who opposed Saul, had not he, either from principle or policy, shown himself as great in clemency as in valor. The call and sagacious counsel of Samuel directed the popular feelings into a right channel, by appointing a general assembly of the militia, the really effective force of the nation, at Gilgal, where, amid great pomp and religious solemnities, the victorious leader was confirmed in his kingdom (1Sa 11:15).

Chapter 12

Samuel testifies his integrity (12:1–5)

1–4. Samuel said unto all Israel – This public address was made after the solemn reinstalment of Saul, and before the convention at Gilgal separated. Samuel, having challenged a review of his public life, received a unanimous testimony to the unsullied honor of his personal character, as well as the justice and integrity of his public administration.

5. the Lord is witness against you, and his anointed is witness – that, by their own acknowledgment, he had given them no cause to weary of the divine government by judges, and that, therefore, the blame of desiring a change of government rested with themselves. This was only insinuated, and they did not fully perceive his drift.

Samuel reproves the people for ingratitude (12:6–16)

7–16. Now therefore stand still, that I may reason with you – The burden of this faithful and uncompromising address was to show them, that though they had obtained the change of government they had so importunely desired, their conduct was highly displeasing to their heavenly King; nevertheless, if they remained faithful to Him and to the principles of the theocracy, they might be delivered from many of the evils to which the new state of things would expose them. And in confirmation of those statements, no less than in evidence of the divine displeasure, a remarkable phenomenon, on the invocation of the prophet, and of which he gave due premonition, took place.

Samuel terrifies them with thunder in harvest-time (12:17–25)

17–25. Is it not wheat harvest to-day? That season in Palestine occurs at the end of June or beginning of July, when it seldom or never rains, and the sky is serene and cloudless. There could not, therefore, have been a stronger or more appropriate proof of a divine mission than the phenomenon of rain and thunder happening, without any prognostics of its approach, upon the prediction of a person professing himself to be a prophet of the Lord, and giving it as an attestation of his words being true. The people regarded it as a miraculous display of divine power, and, panic-struck, implored the prophet to pray for them. Promising to do so, he dispelled their fears. The conduct of Samuel, in this whole affair of the king's appointment, shows him to have been a great and good man who sank all private and personal considerations in disinterested zeal for his country's good and whose last words in public were to warn the people, and their king, of the danger of apostasy and disobedience to God.

Chapter 13

Saul's selected band (13:1–2)

2. Saul chose him three thousand men of Israel – This band of picked men was a bodyguard, who were kept constantly on duty, while the rest of the people were dismissed till their services might be needed. It seems to have been his tactics to attack the Philistine garrisons in the country by different detachments, rather than by risking a general engagement; and his first operations were directed to rid his native territory of Benjamin of these enemies.

Saul calls the Hebrews to Gilgal against the Philistines (13:3–4)

3–4. smote the garrison of the Philistines … in Geba – Geba and Gibeah were towns in Benjamin, very close to each other (Jos 18:24, 28). The word rendered 'garrison' is different from that of 1Sa 13:23; 14:1, and signifies, literally, something erected; probably a pillar or flagstaff, indicative of Philistine ascendency.

That the secret demolition of this standard, so obnoxious to a young and noble-hearted patriot, was the feat of Jonathan referred to, is evident from the words, **the Philistines heard of it,** which is not the way we should expect an attack on a fortress to be noticed.

Saul blew the trumpet throughout all the land – This, a well-known sound, was the usual Hebrew war summons; the first blast was answered by the beacon fire in the neighbouring places. A second blast was blown – then answered by a fire in a more distant locality, whence the proclamation was speedily diffused over the whole country. As the Philistines resented what Jonathan had done as an overt attempt to throw off their yoke, a levy of the people was immediately ordered, the rendezvous to be the old camping ground at Gilgal.

The Philistines' great host (13:5)

5. The Philistines gathered themselves together to fight with Israel, thirty thousand chariots, and six thousand horsemen – Either this number must include chariots of every kind – or the word **chariots** must mean the men fighting in them (2Sa 10:18; 1Ki 20:21; 1Ch 19:18); or, as some eminent critics maintain, Sheloshim (thirty), has crept into the text, instead of Shelosh (three).

The Israelites' distress (13:6–8)

6. When the men of Israel saw that they were in a strait – Though Saul's gallantry was unabated, his subjects displayed no degree of zeal and energy. Instead of venturing an encounter, they fled in all directions. Some, in their panic, left the country (1Sa 13:7), but most took refuge in the hiding-places which the broken ridges of the neighborhood abundantly afford. The rocks are perforated in every direction with **caves,** and **holes,** and **pits** – crevices and fissures sunk deep in the rocky soil, subterranean granaries or dry wells in the adjoining fields.

Saul, tired of waiting for Samuel, sacrifices (13:9–23)

9–14. Saul said, Bring hither a burnt offering to me, and peace offerings – Saul, though patriotic enough in his own way, was more ambitious of gaining the glory of a triumph to himself than ascribing it to God. He did not understand his proper position as king of Israel; and although aware of the restrictions under which he held the sovereignty, he wished to rule as an autocrat, who possessed absolute power both in civil and sacred things. This occasion was his first trial. Samuel waited till the last day of the seven, in order to put the constitutional character of the king to the test; and, as Saul, in his impatient and passionate haste knowingly transgressed (1Sa 13:12) by invading the priest's office and thus showing his unfitness for his high office (as he showed nothing of the faith of Gideon and other Hebrew generals), he incurred a threat of the rejection which his subsequent waywardness confirmed.

19–20. Now there was no smith found throughout … Israel – The country was in the lowest state of depression and degradation. The Philistines, after the great victory over the sons of Eli, had become the virtual masters of the land. Their policy in disarming the natives has been often followed in the East. For repairing any serious damage to their agricultural implements, they had to apply to the neighbouring forts.

Chapter 14

Jonathan and the defeat of the Philistines (14:1–46)

4. there was a sharp rock on the one side, and a sharp rock on the other side … Bozez – ('shining') from the aspect of the chalky rock.

Seneh – ('the thorn') probably from a solitary acacia on its top. They are the only rocks of the kind in this vicinity; and the top of the crag towards Michmash was occupied as the post of the Philistines. The two camps were in sight of each other; and it was up the steep rocky sides of this isolated eminence that Jonathan and his armorbearer (1Sa 14:6) made their adventurous approach. This enterprise is one of the most gallant that history or romance records. The action, viewed in itself, was rash and contrary to all established rules of military discipline, which do not permit soldiers to fight or to undertake any enterprise that may involve important consequences without the order of the generals.

6. it may be that the Lord will work for us – This expression did not imply a doubt; it signified simply that the object he aimed at was not in his own power – but it depended upon God – and that he expected success neither from his own strength nor his own merit.

9–10. if they say, Come up unto us; then we will go up – for the Lord hath delivered them into our hand – When Jonathan appears here to prescribe a sign or token of God's will, we may infer that the same spirit which inspired this enterprise suggested the means of its execution, and put into his heart what to ask of God.

11. Behold, the Hebrews come forth out of the holes – As it could not occur to the sentries that two men had come with hostile designs, it was a natural conclusion that they were Israelite deserters. And hence no attempt was made to hinder their ascent, or stone them.

14–15. that first slaughter, which Jonathan and his armour-bearer made, was about twenty men, within as it were an half acre of land, which a yoke of oxen might plow – This was a very ancient mode of measurement, and it still subsists in the East. The men who saw them scrambling up the rock had been surprised and killed, and the spectacle of twenty corpses would suggest to others that they were attacked by a numerous force. The success of the adventure was aided by a panic that struck the enemy, produced both by the sudden surprise and the shock of an earthquake. The feat was begun and achieved by the faith of Jonathan, and the issue was of God.

16. the watchmen of Saul … looked – The wild disorder in the enemies' camp was described and the noise of dismay heard on the heights of Gibeah.

17–19. Then said Saul unto the people that were with him, Number now, and see who is gone from us – The idea occurred to him that it might be some daring adventurer belonging to his own little troop, and it would be easy to discover him.

19. Withdraw thine hand – The priest, invested with the ephod, prayed with raised and extended hands. Saul perceiving that the opportunity was inviting, and that God appeared to have sufficiently declared in favor of His people, requested the priest to cease, that they might immediately join in the contest. The season for consultation was past – the time for prompt action was come.

20–22. Saul and all the people – All the warriors in the garrison at Gibeah, the Israelite deserters in the camp of the Philistines, and the fugitives among the mountains of Ephraim, now all rushed to the pursuit, which was hot and sanguinary.

23. So the Lord saved Israel that day: and the battle passed over unto Beth-aven – that is, 'Beth-el'. It passed over the forest, now destroyed, on the central ridge of Palestine, then over to the other side from the eastern pass of Michmash (1Sa 14:31), to the western pass of Aijalon, through which they escaped into their own plains.

24. Saul had adjured the people – Afraid lest so precious an opportunity of effectually humbling the Philistine power might be lost, the impetuous king laid an anathema on any one who should taste food until the evening. This rash and foolish denunciation distressed the people, by preventing them taking such refreshments as they might get on the march, and materially hindered the successful attainment of his own patriotic object.

25. all they of the land came to a wood; and there was honey – The honey is described as **upon the ground, dropping** from the trees, and in honeycombs – indicating it to be bees' honey. 'Bees in the East are not, as in England, kept in hives; they are all in a wild state. The forests

235

literally flow with honey; large combs may be seen hanging on the trees as you pass along, full of honey' (ROBERTS).

31–34. the people were very faint. And the people flew upon the spoil – at evening, when the time fixed by Saul had expired. Faint and famishing, the pursuers fell voraciously upon the cattle they had taken, and threw them on the ground to cut off their flesh and eat them raw, so that the army, by Saul's rashness, were defiled by eating blood, or living animals; probably, as the Abyssinians do, who cut a part of the animal's rump, but close the hide upon it, and nothing mortal follows from that wound. They were painfully conscientious in keeping the king's order for fear of the curse, but had no scruple in transgressing God's command. To prevent this violation of the law, Saul ordered a large stone to be rolled, and those that slaughtered the oxen to cut their throats on that stone. By laying the animal's head on the high stone, the blood oozed out on the ground, and sufficient evidence was afforded that the ox or sheep was dead before it was attempted to eat it.

45. the people rescued Jonathan, that he died not – When Saul became aware of Jonathan's transgression in regard to the honey, albeit it was done in ignorance and involved no guilt, he was, like Jephthah (Jud 11:31,35), about to put his son to death, in conformity with his vow (1Sa 14:44). But the more enlightened conscience of the army prevented the tarnishing the glory of the day by the blood of the young hero, to whose faith and valor it was chiefly due.

Chapter 15

Saul sent to destroy Amalek (15:1–6)

1. Samuel also said unto Saul, The Lord sent me to anoint thee … : now therefore hearken thou unto … the Lord. Several years had been passed in successful military operations against troublesome neighbours. During these Saul had been left to act in a great measure at his own discretion as an independent prince. Now a second test is proposed of his possessing the character of a theocratic monarch in Israel; and in announcing the duty required of him, Samuel brought before him his official station as the Lord's vicegerent, and the peculiar obligation under which he was laid to act in that capacity. He had formerly done wrong, for which a severe rebuke and threatening were administered to him (1Sa 13:13-14). Now an opportunity was afforded him of retrieving that error by an exact obedience to the divine command.

2–3. Amalek – the powerful tribe which inhabited the country immediately to the eastward of the northern Cushites. Their territory extended over the whole of the eastern portion of the desert of Sinai to Rephidim – the earliest opponent (De 25:18; Ex 17:8-16) – the hereditary and restless enemy of Israel (Nu 14:45; Jud 3:13 6:3), and who had not repented (1Sa 14:48) of their bitter and sleepless hatred during the five hundred years that had elapsed since their doom was pronounced. Being a people of nomadic habits, they were as plundering and dangerous as the Bedouin Arabs, particularly to the southern tribes. The national interest required, and God, as King of Israel, decreed that this public enemy should be removed. Their destruction was to be without reservation or exception.

I remember – I am reminded of what Amalek did – perhaps by the still remaining trophy or memorial erected by Moses (Ex 17:15-16).

4. Saul gathered the people together – The alacrity with which he entered on the necessary preparations for the expedition gave a fair, but delusive promise of faithfulness in its execution.

Telaim – or Telem, among the uttermost cities of the tribe of Judah towards the coast of Edom (Jos 15:21,24).

5. Saul came to a city of Amalek – probably their capital.

laid wait in the valley – following the strategic policy of Joshua at Ai (Jos 8:4).

6. Kenites. In consequence, probably, of the unsettled state of Judah, they seem to have returned to their old desert tracts. Though now intermingled with the Amalekites, they were not implicated in the offenses of that wicked race; but for the sake of their ancestors, between whom and those of Israel there had been a league of amity, a timely warning was afforded them to remove from the scene of danger.

He spares Agag and the best of the spoil (15:7–9)

7–9. Saul smote the Amalekites – His own view of the proper and expedient course to follow was his rule, not the command of God.

8–9. he took Agag … alive – This was the common title of the Amalekite kings. He had no scruple about the apparent cruelty of it, for he made fierce and indiscriminate havoc of the people. But he spared Agag, probably to enjoy the glory of displaying so distinguished a captive, and, in like manner, the most valuable portions of the booty, as the cattle. By this wilful and partial obedience to a positive command (1Sa 15:3), complying with it in some parts and violating it in others, as suited his own taste and humour, Saul showed his selfish, arbitrary temper, and his love of despotic power, and his utter unfitness to perform the duties of a delegated king in Israel.

God rejects Saul as king (15:10–35)

10–11. Then came the word of the Lord unto Samuel, saying, It repenteth me that I have set up Saul – Repentance is attributed in Scripture to Him when bad men give Him cause to alter His course and method of procedure, and to treat them as if He did repent of kindness shown. To the heart of a man like Samuel, who was above all envious considerations, and really attached to the king, so painful an announcement moved all his pity and led him to pass a sleepless night of earnest intercession.

12. Saul came to Carmel – in the south of Judah (Jos 15:55 1Sa 25:2).

he set him up a place – that is, a pillar (2Sa 18:18); literally, *a hand,* indicating that whatever was the form of the monument, it was surmounted, according to the ancient fashion, by the figure of a hand, the symbol of power and energy. The erection of this vainglorious trophy was an additional act of disobedience. His pride had overborne his sense of duty in first raising this monument to his own honour, and then going to Gilgal to offer sacrifice to God.

13–23. Saul said unto him, Blessed be thou of the Lord: I have performed the commandment of the Lord – Saul was either blinded by a partial and delusive self-love, or he was, in his declaration to Samuel, acting the part of a bold and artful hypocrite. He professed to have fulfilled the divine command, and that the blame of any defects in the execution lay with the people. Samuel saw the real state of the case, and in discharge of the commission he had received before setting out, proceeded to denounce his conduct as characterized by pride, rebellion, and obstinate disobedience. When Saul persisted in declaring that he had obeyed, alleging that the animals, whose bleating was heard, had been reserved for a liberal sacrifice of thanksgiving to God, his shuffling, prevaricating answer called forth a stern rebuke from the prophet. It well deserved it – for the destination of the spoil to the altar was a flimsy pretext – a gross deception, an attempt to conceal the selfishness of the original motive under the cloak of religious zeal and gratitude.

24–26. I have sinned … turn again with me, that I may worship the Lord – The erring, but proud and obstinate monarch was now humbled. He was conscience-smitten for the moment, but his confession proceeded not from sincere repentance, but from a sense of danger and desire of averting the sentence denounced against him. For the sake of public appearance, he besought Samuel not to allow their serious differences to transpire, but to join with him in a public act of worship. Under the influence of his painfully agitated feelings, he designed to offer sacrifice, partly to express his gratitude for the recent victory, and partly to implore mercy

and a reversal of his doom. It was, from another angle, a politic scheme, that Samuel might be betrayed into a countenancing of his design in reserving the cattle for sacrificing. Samuel declined to accompany him.

I feared the people, and obeyed their voice – This was a different reason from the former he had assigned. It was the language of a man driven to extremities, and even had it been true, the principles expounded by Samuel showed that it could have been no extenuation of the offense. The prophet then pronounced the irreversible sentence of the rejection of Saul and his family. He was judicially cut off for his disobedience.

27, 28. he laid hold upon the skirt of his mantle – the *moil,* upper tunic, official robe. In an agony of mental excitement, he took hold of the prophet's dress to detain him; the rending of the mantle (1Sa 15:27) was adroitly pointed to as a significant and mystical representation of his severance from the throne.

29. the Strength of Israel – *Hebrew,* 'He that gives a victory to Israel,' a further rebuke of his pride in rearing the Carmel trophy, and an intimation that no loss would be sustained in Israel by his rejection.

31. Samuel turned again after Saul – not to worship along with him; but first, that the people might have no ground, on pretense of Saul's rejection, to withdraw their allegiance from him; and secondly, to compensate for Saul's error, by executing God's judgment upon Agag.

32. Agag came unto him delicately – or cheerfully, since he had gained the favour and protection of the king.

33. Samuel hewed Agag – This cruel tyrant met the retribution of a righteous Providence. Never has it been unusual for great or official personages in the East to perform executions with their own hands. Samuel did it **before the Lord** in Gilgal, appointing that same mode of punishment (hitherto unknown in Israel) to be used towards him, which he had formerly used towards others.

Chapter 16

Samuel sent by God to Bethlehem (16:1–10)

1. the Lord said unto Samuel, How long wilt thou mourn for Saul – Samuel's grief on account of Saul's rejection, accompanied, doubtless, by earnest prayers for his restitution, showed the amiable feelings of the man; but they were at variance with his public duty as a prophet. The declared purpose of God to transfer the kingdom of Israel into other hands than Saul's was not an angry menace, but a fixed and immutable decree; so that Samuel ought to have sooner submitted to the peremptory manifestation of the divine will. But to leave him no longer room to doubt of its being unalterable, he was sent on a private mission to anoint a successor to Saul. The immediate designation of a king was of the greatest importance for the interests of the nation in the event of Saul's death, which, to this time, was dreaded; it would establish David's title and comfort the minds of Samuel and other good men with a right settlement, whatever contingency might happen.

I have provided me a king – The language is remarkable, and intimates a difference between this and the former king. Saul was the people's choice, the fruit of their wayward and sinful desires for their own honour and aggrandizement. The next was to be a king who would consult the divine glory, and selected from that tribe to which the pre-eminence had been early promised (Ge 49:10).

2. How can I go? – This is another instance of human infirmity in Samuel. Since God had sent him on this mission, He would protect him in the execution.

I am come to sacrifice – It seems to have been customary with Samuel to do this in the different circuits to which he went, that he might encourage the worship of God.

3. call Jesse to the sacrifice – that is, the social feast that followed the peace offering. Samuel, being the offerer, had a right to invite any guest he pleased.

4. the elders of the town trembled at his coming – Bethlehem was an obscure town, and not within the usual circuit of the judge. The elders were naturally apprehensive, therefore, that his arrival was occasioned by some extraordinary reason, and that it might entail evil upon their town, in consequence of the estrangement between Samuel and the king.

5. sanctify yourselves – by the preparations described (Ex 19:14,15). The elders were to sanctify themselves. Samuel himself took the greatest care in the sanctification of Jesse's family.

6–10. Samuel said, Surely the Lord's anointed is before him – Here Samuel, in consequence of taking his impressions from the external appearance, falls into the same error as formerly (1Sa 10:24).

Samuel anoints David (16:11–13)

11. There remaineth yet the youngest, and, behold, he keepeth the sheep – Jesse having evidently no idea of David's wisdom and bravery, spoke of him as the most unfit. God, in His providence, so ordered it, that the appointment of David might the more clearly appear to be a divine purpose, and not the design either of Samuel or Jesse. David having not been sanctified with the rest of his family, it is probable that he returned to his pastoral duties the moment the special business on which he had been summoned was done.

13. Then Samuel took the horn of oil, and anointed him – This transaction must have been strictly private.

God takes his spirit from Saul (16:14–23)

14–18. The Spirit of the Lord departed from Saul, and an evil spirit from the Lord troubled him – His own gloomy reflections, the consciousness that he had not acted up to the character of an Israelite king, the loss of his throne, and the extinction of his royal house, made him jealous, irritable, vindictive, and subject to fits of morbid melancholy.

19. Saul sent messengers unto Jesse, and said, Send me David – In the East the command of a king is imperative; and Jesse, however reluctant and alarmed, had no alternative but to comply.

20. Jesse took an ass laden with bread, and a bottle of wine, and a kid, and sent them … unto Saul – as a token of homage and respect.

21. David came to Saul – Providence thus prepared David for his destiny, by placing him in a way to become acquainted with the manners of the court, the business of government, and the general state of the kingdom.

became his armour-bearer – This choice, as being an expression of the king's partiality, shows how honourable the office was held to be.

23. David took an harp, and played with his hand: so Saul was refreshed, and was well – The ancients believed that music had a mysterious influence in healing mental disorders.

Chapter 17

The Israelites and Philistines being ready for battle (17:1–3)

1. the Philistines gathered together their armies – twenty-seven years after their overthrow at Michmash. Having now recovered their spirits and strength, they sought an opportunity of wiping out the infamy of that national disaster, as well as to regain their lost ascendency over Israel.

Goliath challenges a combat (17:4–11)

4–11. a champion – *Hebrew*, a 'man between two'; that is, a person who, on the part of his own people, undertook to determine the national quarrel by engaging in single combat with a chosen warrior in the hostile army.

5. helmet of brass – The Philistine helmet had the appearance of a row of feathers set in a tiara, or metal band, to which were attached scales of the same material, for the defence of the neck and the sides of the face.

a coat of mail – a kind of corslet, quilted with leather or plates of metal, reaching only to the chest, and supported by shoulder straps, leaving the shoulders and arms at full liberty.

6. greaves of brass – boots, terminating at the ankle, made in one plate of metal, but round to the shape of the leg, and often lined with felt or sponge. They were useful in guarding the legs, not only against the spikes of the enemy, but in making way among thorns and briers.

a target of brass – a circular frame, carried at the back, suspended by a long belt which crossed the breast from the shoulders to the loins.

7. staff of his spear – rather under five feet long, and capable of being used as a javelin (1Sa 19:10). It had an iron head.

one bearing a shield – In consequence of their great size and weight, the Oriental warrior had a trusty and skilful friend, whose office it was to bear the large shield behind which he avoided the missile weapons of the enemy. He was covered, cap-a-pie, with defensive armour, while he had only two offensive weapons – a sword by his side and a spear in his hand.

8–11. I defy the armies of Israel ...; give me a man, that we may fight together – In cases of single combat, a warrior used to go out in front of his party, and advancing towards the opposite ranks, challenge someone to fight with him. If his formidable appearance, or great reputation for physical strength and heroism, deterred any from accepting the challenge, he used to parade himself within hearing of the enemy's lines, specify in a loud, boastful, bravado style, defying them, and pouring out torrents of abuse and insolence to provoke their resentment.

David accepts the challenge and kills Goliath (17:12–58)

17. Take now for thy brethren an ephah of this parched corn, and these ten loaves – In those times campaigns seldom lasted above a few days at a time. The soldiers were volunteers or militia, who were supplied with provisions from time to time by their friends at home.

18. carry these ten cheeses to the captain – to enlist his kind attention. Oriental cheeses are very small; and although they are frequently made of so soft a consistence as to resemble curds, those which David carried seem to have been fully formed, pressed, and sufficiently dried to admit of their being carried.

take their pledge – Tokens of the soldiers' health and safety were sent home in the convenient form of a lock of their hair, or piece of their nail, or such like.

20. David left the sheep with a keeper – This is the only instance in which the hired shepherd is distinguished from the master or one of his family.

22. left his carriage in the hand of the keeper of the carriage – to make his way to the standard of Judah.

25. make his father's house free in Israel – His family should be exempted from the impositions and services to which the general body of the Israelites were subjected.

34–36. a lion, and a bear – The bear must have been a Syrian bear, which is believed to be a distinct species, or perhaps a variety, of the brown bear. The beard applies to the lion alone. Those feats seem to have been performed with no weapons more effective than the rude staves and stones of the field, or his shepherd's crook.

37. The Lord that delivered me – It would have been natural for a youth, and especially an Oriental youth, to make a parade of his gallantry. But David's piety sank all consideration of his own prowess and ascribed the success of those achievements to the divine aid, which he felt assured would not be withheld from him in a cause which so intimately concerned the safety and honour of His people.

Saul said unto David, Go, and the Lord be with thee – The pious language of the modest but valiant youth impressed the monarch's heart. He felt that it indicated the true military confidence for Israel, and, therefore, made up his mind, without any demur, to sanction a combat on which the fate of his kingdom depended, and with a champion supporting his interests apparently so unequal to the task.

38, 39. Saul armed David with his armour – The ancient Hebrews were particularly attentive to the personal safety of their warriors, and hence Saul equipped the youthful champion with his own defensive accoutrements, which would be of the best style. It is probable that Saul's coat of mail, or corslet, was a loose shirt, otherwise it could not have fitted both a stripling and a man of the colossal stature of the king.

40. brook – wady.

bag – or scrip for containing his daily food.

sling – The sling consisted of a double rope with a thong, probably of leather, to receive the stone. The slinger held a second stone in his left hand. David chose five stones, as a reserve, in case the first should fail. Shepherds in the East carry a sling and stones still, for the purpose of driving away, or killing, the enemies that prowl about the flock.

42–47. the Philistine said ... said David to the Philistine – When the two champions met, they generally made each of them a speech, and sometimes recited some verses, filled with allusions and epithets of the most opprobrious kind, hurling contempt and defiance at one another. This kind of abusive dialogue is common among the Arab combatants still. David's speech, however, presents a striking contrast to the usual strain of these invectives. It was full of pious trust, and to God he ascribed all the glory of the triumph he anticipated.

49. smote the Philistine in his forehead – At the opening for the eyes – that was the only exposed part of his body.

51. cut off his head – not as an evidence of the giant's death, for his slaughter had been effected in presence of the whole army, but as a trophy to be borne to Saul. The heads of slain enemies are always regarded in the East as the most welcome tokens of victory.

54. tent – the sacred tabernacle. David dedicated the sword of Goliath as a votive offering to the Lord.

55–58. Saul … said unto Abner … whose son is this youth? – A young man is more spoken of in many Eastern countries by his father's name than his own. The growth of the beard, and other changes on a now full-grown youth, prevented the king from recognizing his former favourite minstrel (1Sa 16:23).

Chapter 18

Jonathan loves David (18:1–4)

1. the soul of Jonathan was knit with the soul of David – They were nearly of an age. The prince had taken little interest in David as a minstrel; but his heroism and modest, manly bearing, his piety and high endowments, kindled the flame not of admiration only, but of affection, in the congenial mind of Jonathan.

2. Saul would let him go no more home – He was established as a permanent resident at court.

3. Then Jonathan and David made a covenant – Such covenants of brotherhood are frequent in the East. They are ratified by certain ceremonies, and in presence of witnesses, that the persons covenanting will be sworn brothers for life.

4. Jonathan stripped himself of the robe that was upon him, and gave it to David – To receive any part of the dress which had been *worn* by a sovereign, or his eldest son and heir, is deemed, in the East, the *highest* honour which can be conferred on a subject. The girdle, being connected with the sword and the bow, may be considered as being part of the military dress, and great value is attached to it in the East.

Saul envies David being praised (18:5–9)

6. the women came out of all cities of Israel – in the homeward march from the pursuit of the Philistines. This is a characteristic trait of Oriental manners. On the return of friends long absent, and particularly on the return of a victorious army, bands of women and children issue from the towns and villages, to form a triumphal procession, to celebrate the victory, and, as they go along, to gratify the soldiers with dancing, instrumental music, and extempore songs, in honour of the

generals who have earned the highest distinction by feats of gallantry. The Hebrew women, therefore, were merely paying the customary congratulations to David as the deliverer of their country, but they committed a great indiscretion by praising a subject at the expense of their sovereign.

9. Saul eyed David – that is, invidiously, with secret and malignant hatred.

Saul seeks to kill David (18:10–12)

10. on the morrow, that the evil spirit from God came upon Saul – This rankling thought brought on a sudden paroxysm of his mental malady.

he prophesied – The term denotes one under the influence either of a good or a bad spirit. In the present it is used to express that Saul was in a frenzy. David, perceiving the symptoms, hastened, by the soothing strains of his harp, to allay the stormy agitation of the royal mind. But before its mollifying influence could be felt, Saul hurled a javelin at the head of the young musician.

there was a javelin in Saul's hand – Had it been followed by a fatal result, the deed would have been considered the act of an irresponsible maniac. It was repeated more than once ineffectually, and Saul became impressed with a dread of David as under the special protection of Providence.

Saul fears David because of his good success (18:13–16)

13. Therefore Saul removed him from him – sent him away from the court, where the principal persons, including his own son, were spellbound with admiration of the young and pious warrior. **made him captain over a thousand** – gave him a military commission, which was intended to be an honourable exile. But this post of duty served only to draw out before the public the extraordinary and varied qualities of his character, and to give him a stronger hold of the people's affections.

Saul offers David his daughter as a trap (18:17–30)

17. Saul said to David, Behold my elder daughter Merab, her will I give thee to wife – Though bound to this already (1Sa 17:25), he had found it convenient to forget his former promise. He now holds it out as a new offer, which would tempt David to give additional proofs of his valour. But the fickle and perfidious monarch broke his pledge at the time when the marriage was on the eve of being celebrated, and bestowed Merab on another man; an indignity as well as a wrong, which was calculated deeply to wound the feelings and provoke the resentment of David. Perhaps it was intended to do so, that advantage might be taken of his indiscretion. But David was preserved from this snare.

20. Michal Saul's daughter loved David – This must have happened some time after.

they told Saul, and the thing pleased him – Not from any favour to David, but he saw that it would be turned to the advancement of his malicious purposes, and the more so when, by the artful intrigues and flattery of his spies, the loyal sentiments of David were discovered.

25. The king desireth not any dowry – In Eastern countries the husband *purchases* his wife either by gifts or services. As neither David nor his family were in circumstances to give a suitable dowry for a princess, the king intimated that he would be graciously pleased to accept some gallant deed in the public service.

a hundred foreskins of the Philistines – Such mutilations on the bodies of their slain enemies were commonly practised in ancient war, and the number told indicated the glory of the victory. Saul's willingness to accept a public service had an air of liberality, while his choice of so difficult and hazardous a service seemed only putting a proper value on gaining the hand of a king's daughter. But he covered unprincipled malice against David under this proposal, which exhibited a zeal for God and the covenant of circumcision.

26. the days were not expired – The period within which this exploit was to be achieved was not exhausted.

27. David ... slew of the Philistines two hundred men – The number was doubled, partly to show his respect and attachment to the princess, and partly to oblige Saul to the fulfilment of his pledge.

29. Saul was yet the more afraid of David – because Providence had visibly favoured him, by not only defeating the conspiracy against his life, but through his royal alliance paving his way to the throne.

Chapter 19

Jonathan discloses his father's purpose to kill David (19:1–7)

1. Saul spake to Jonathan his son, and to all his servants, that they should kill David – The murderous design he had secretly cherished he now reveals to a few of his intimate friends. Jonathan was among the number. He prudently said nothing at the time, but secretly apprised David of his danger; and waiting till the morning, when his father's excited temper would be cooled, he stationed his friend in a place of concealment, where, overhearing the conversation, he might learn how matters really stood and take immediate flight, if necessary.

4–7. Jonathan spake good of David – He told

his father he was committing a great sin to plot against the life of a man who had rendered the most invaluable services to his country and whose loyalty had been uniformly steady and devoted. The strong remonstrances of Jonathan produced an effect on the impulsive mind of his father. As he was still susceptible of good and honest impressions, he bound himself by an oath to relinquish his hostile purpose; and thus, through the intervention of the noble-minded prince, a temporary reconciliation was effected, in consequence of which David was again employed in the public service.

Saul's malicious rage breaks out against David (19:8–17)

8–10. David went out, and fought with the Philistines, and slew them with a great slaughter – A brilliant victory was gained over the public enemy. But these fresh laurels of David reawakened in the moody breast of Saul the former spirit of envy and melancholy. On David's return to court, the temper of Saul became more fiendish than ever; the melodious strains of the harp had lost all their power to charm; and in a paroxysm of uncontrollable frenzy he aimed a javelin at the person of David – the missile having been thrown with such force that it pierced the chamber wall. David providentially escaped; but the king, having now thrown off the mask and being bent on aggressive measures, made his son-in-law's situation everywhere perilous.

11, 12. Saul sent messengers unto David's house, to watch him, and to slay him – The fear of causing a commotion in the town, or favouring his escape in the darkness, seemed to have influenced the king in ordering them to patrol till the morning. This infatuation was overruled by Providence to favour David's escape; for his wife, secretly apprised by Jonathan, who was aware of the design, or by spying persons in court livery watching the gate, let him down through a window.

13, 14. And Michal took an image, and laid it in the bed – an image, literally, 'the teraphim,' and laid, not in the bed, but literally on the 'divan'; and **the pillows**, that is, the cushion, which usually lay at the back of the divan and was stuffed with **goat's hair,** she took from its bolster or heading at the upper part of the divan. This she placed lower down, and covered with a mantle, as if to foster a proper warmth in a patient; at the same time spreading the goat's hair skin, so as to resemble human hair in a dishevelled state. The pretext was that David lay there sick. The first messengers of Saul, keeping at a respectable distance, were deceived; but the imposition was detected on a closer inspection.

15. Bring him to me in the bed – a portable couch or mattress.

David flees to Samuel (19:18–23)

18–23. David fled, ... and came to Samuel to Ramah – Samuel was living in retirement, superintending the school of the prophets, established in the little hamlet of Naioth, in the neighbourhood of Ramah. It was a retreat congenial to the mind of David; but Saul, having found out his asylum, sent three successive bodies of men to apprehend him. The character of the place and the influence of the sacred exercises produced such an effect on them that they were incapable of discharging their commission, and were led, by a resistless impulse, to join in singing the praises of God. Saul, in a fit of rage and disappointment, determined to go himself. But, before reaching the spot, his mental susceptibilities were roused even more than his messengers, and he was found, before long, swelling the ranks of the young prophets. This singular change can be ascribed only to the power of Him who can turn the hearts of men even as the rivers of water.

Saul prophesies (19:24)

24. lay down naked – that is, divested of his armour and outer robes – in a state of trance. Thus God, in making the wrath of man to praise Him, preserved the lives of all the prophets, frustrated all the purposes of Saul, and preserved the life of His servant.

Chapter 20

David consults with Jonathan for his safety (1–10)

1–3. David fled from Naioth in Ramah, and came and said before Jonathan – He could not remain in Naioth, for he had strong reason to fear that when the religious fit, if we may so call it, was over, Saul would relapse into his usual fell and sanguinary temper. It may be thought that David acted imprudently in directing his flight to Gibeah. But he was evidently prompted to go thither by the most generous feelings – to inform his friend of what had recently occurred, and to obtain that friend's sanction to the course he was compelled to adopt. Jonathan could not be persuaded there was any real danger after the oath his father had taken; at all events, he felt assured his father would do nothing without telling him. Filial attachment naturally blinded the prince to defects in the parental character and made him reluctant to believe his father capable of such atrocity. David repeated his unshaken convictions of Saul's murderous purpose, but in terms delicately chosen (1Sa 20:3), not to wound the filial feelings of his friend; while Jonathan, clinging, it would seem, to a hope that the extraordinary scene enacted at Naioth might have wrought a

sanctified improvement on Saul's temper and feelings, undertook to inform David of the result of his observations at home.

5. David said unto Jonathan, Behold, to-morrow the new moon, and I should not fail to sit with the king at meat – The beginning of a new month or moon was always celebrated by special sacrifices, followed by feasting, at which the head of a family expected all its members to be present. David, both as the king's son-in-law and a distinguished courtier, dined on such occasions at the royal table, and from its being generally known that David had returned to Gibeah, his presence in the palace would be naturally expected. This occasion was chosen by the two friends for testing the king's state of feeling. As a suitable pretext for David's absence, it was arranged that he should visit his family at Bethlehem, and thus create an opportunity of ascertaining how his non-appearance would be viewed. The time and place were fixed for Jonathan reporting to David; but as circumstances might render another interview unsafe, it was deemed expedient to communicate by a concerted signal.

Their covenant renewed by oath (29:11–23)

11. Jonathan said to David, Come, let us go into the field – The private dialogue, which is here detailed at full length, presents a most beautiful exhibition of these two amiable and noble-minded friends. Jonathan was led, in the circumstances, to be the chief speaker. The strength of his attachment, his pure disinterestedness, his warm piety, his invocation to God, the calm and full expression he gave of his conviction that his own family were, by the divine will, to be disinherited, and David elevated to the possession of the throne, the covenant entered into with David on behalf of his descendants, and the imprecation (1Sa 20:16) denounced on any of them who should violate his part of the conditions, the reiteration of this covenant on both sides (1Sa 20:17) to make it indissoluble – all this indicates such a power of mutual affection, such magnetic attractiveness in the character of David, such susceptibility and elevation of feeling in the heart of Jonathan, that this interview for dramatic interest and moral beauty stands unrivalled in the records of human friendship.

19. when thou hast stayed three days – either with your family at Bethlehem, or wherever you find it convenient.

come to the place where thou didst hide thyself when the business was in hand – *Hebrew*, 'in the day,' or 'time of the business,' when the same matter was under inquiry formerly (1Sa 19:22).

remain by the stone Ezel – *Hebrew*, 'the stone of the way'; a sort of milestone which directed travellers. He was to conceal himself in some cave or hiding-place near that spot.

23. as touching the matter which thou and I have spoken of – The plan being concerted, the friends separated for a time, and the amiable character of Jonathan again peers out in his parting allusion to their covenant of friendship.

Saul, missing David, seeks to kill Jonathan (29:24–40)

25. the king sat upon his seat, as at other times … by the wall – The left-hand corner at the upper end of a room was and still is in the East, the most honourable place. The person seated there has his left arm confined by the wall, but his right hand is at full liberty. From Abner's position next the king, and David's seat being left empty, it would seem that a state etiquette was observed at the royal table, each of the courtiers and ministers having places assigned them according to their respective gradations of rank.

Jonathan arose – either as a mark of respect on the entrance of the king, or in conformity with the usual Oriental custom for a son to stand in presence of his father.

26. he is not clean – No notice was taken of David's absence, as he might be labouring under some ceremonial defilement.

27. on the morrow, which was the second day of the month – The time of the moon's appearance being uncertain – whether at midday, in the evening, or at midnight, the festival was extended over two days. Custom, not the law, had introduced this.

Saul said unto Jonathan his son, Wherefore cometh not the son of Jesse – The question was asked, as it were, casually, and with as great an air of indifference as he could assume. And Jonathan having replied that David had asked and obtained his permission to attend a family anniversary at Bethlehem (1Sa 20:28,29), the pent-up passions of the king burst out in a most violent storm of rage and invective against his son.

30. Thou son of the perverse rebellious woman – This is a striking Oriental form of abuse. Saul was not angry with his wife; it was the son alone, upon whom he meant, by this style of address, to discharge his resentment. The principle on which it is founded seems to be, that to a genuine filial instinct it is a more inexpiable offense to hear the name or character of a parent traduced, than any personal reproach. This was, undoubtedly, one cause of 'the fierce anger' in which the high-minded prince left the table without tasting a morsel.

33. Saul cast a javelin at him – This is a sad proof of the maniacal frenzy into which the unhappy monarch was transported.

35. Jonathan went out into the field at the time appointed – or, 'at the place appointed.'

36. he said unto his lad, Run, find out now the arrows which I shoot – The direction given aloud to the attendant was the signal preconcerted with David. It implied danger.

40. Jonathan gave his artillery unto his lad – that is, his missive weapons. The French word *artillerie*, signifies 'archery.' The term is still used in England, in the designation of the 'artillery company of London,' the association of archers, though they have long disused bows and arrows. Jonathan's boy being despatched out of the way, the friends enjoyed the satisfaction of a final meeting.

Jonathan and David lovingly part (20:41–42)

41–42. David … fell on his face to the ground, and bowed three times – a token of homage to the prince's rank; but on a close approach, every other consideration was sunk in the full flow of the purest brotherly affection.

42. Jonathan said to David, Go in peace – The interview being a stolen one, and every moment precious, it was kindness in Jonathan to hasten his friend's departure.

Chapter 21

David, at Nob, obtains from Ahimelech hallowed bread (21:1–7)

1. Then came David to Nob to Ahimelech – Nob, a city of the priests (1Sa 22:19), was in the neighbourhood of Jerusalem, on the Mount of Olives – a little north of the top, and on the northeast of the city. It is computed to have been about five miles distant from Gibeah. Ahimelech, the same as Ahiah, or perhaps his brother, both sons of Ahitub (compare 1Sa 14:3, with 1Sa 22:4–11,20). His object in fleeing to this place was partly for the supply of his necessities, and partly for comfort and counsel, in the prospect of leaving the kingdom.

Ahimelech was afraid at the meeting of David – suspecting some extraordinary occurrence by his appearing so suddenly, and in such a style, for his attendants were left at a little distance.

2. The king hath commanded me a business, and hath said unto me, Let no man know – This was a direct falsehood, extorted through fear. David probably supposed, like many other persons, that a lie is quite excusable which is told for the sole purpose of saving the speaker's life. But what is essentially sinful, can never, from circumstances, change its immoral character; and David had to repent of this vice of lying (Ps 119:29).

4. there is hallowed bread – There would be plenty of bread in his house; but there was no time to wait for it. The **hallowed bread** was the old shew-bread, which had been removed the previous day, and which was reserved for the use of the priests alone (Le 24:9). Before entertaining the idea that this bread could be lawfully given to David and his men, the high priest seems to have consulted the oracle (1Sa 22:10) as to the course to be followed in this emergency. A dispensation to use the hallowed bread was specially granted by God Himself.

5. these three days – as required by law (Ex 19:15). David and his attendants seem to have been lurking in some of the adjoining caves, to elude pursuit, and to have been, consequently, reduced to great extremities of hunger.

the bread is in a manner common – that is, now that it is no longer standing on the Lord's table. It is eaten by the priests, and may also, in our circumstances, be eaten by us.

yea, though it were sanctified this day in the vessel – that is, though the hallowed bread had been but newly placed on the vessel, the ritual ordinance would have to yield to the great law of necessity and mercy.

6. there was no bread there – in the tabernacle. The removal of the old and the substitution of the new bread was done on the Sabbath (Le 24:8), the loaves being kept warm in an oven heated the previous day.

7. Doeg, an Edomite – who had embraced the Hebrew religion.

detained before the Lord – at the tabernacle, perhaps, in the performance of a vow, or from its being the Sabbath, which rendered it unlawful for him to prosecute his journey.

the chiefest of the herdmen that belonged to Saul – Eastern monarchs anciently had large possessions in flocks and herds; and the office of the chief shepherd was an important one.

David takes Goliath's sword (21:8–9)

9. behind the ephod – in the place allowed for keeping the sacred vestments, of which the ephod is mentioned as the chief. The giant's sword was deposited in that safe custody as a memorial of the divine goodness in delivering Israel.

There is none like that – not only for its size and superior temper, but for its being a pledge of the divine favour to him, and a constant stimulus to his faith.

At Gath David pretends to be mad (21:10–15)

10. David ... fled ... to Achish the king of Gath – which was one of the five principalities of the Philistines. In this place his person must have been known, and to venture into that country, he their greatest enemy, and with the sword of Goliath in his hand, would seem to have been a perilous experiment; but, doubtless, the protection he received implies that he had been directed by the divine oracle. Achish was generous (1Sa 27:6). He might wish to weaken the resources of Saul, and it was common in ancient times for great men to be harbored by neighbouring princes.

13. feigned himself mad – It is supposed to have been an attack of epilepsy, real or perhaps only pretended. This disease is relieved by foaming at the mouth.

let his spittle fall down upon his beard – No wonder that Achish supposed him insane, as such an indignity, whether done by another, or one's self, to the beard, is considered in the East an intolerable insult.

Chapter 22

David's kindred and others resort to him at Adullam (22:1–8)

1. David ... escaped to the cave Adullam – supposed to be that now called Deir-Dubban, a number of pits or underground vaults, some nearly square, and all about fifteen or twenty feet deep, with perpendicular sides, in the soft limestone or chalky rocks. They are on the borders of the Philistine plain at the base of the Judea mountains, six miles southwest from Bethlehem, and well adapted for concealing a number of refugees.

his brethren and all his father's house ... went down – to escape the effects of Saul's rage, which seems to have extended to all David's family. From Bethlehem to Deir-Dubban it is, indeed, a descent all the way.

3. David went thence to Mizpeh of Moab – Mizpeh signifies a watchtower, and it is evident that it must be taken in this sense here, for it is called the 'hold' or fort (1Sa 22:4). The king of Moab was an enemy of Saul (1Sa 14:47), and the great-grandson of Ruth, of course, was related to the family of Jesse. David, therefore, had less anxiety in seeking an asylum within the dominions of this prince than those of Achish, because the Moabites had no grounds for entertaining vindictive feelings against him, and their enmity, to Saul rendered them the more willing to receive so illustrious a refugee from his court.

5. the prophet Gad said unto David, Abide not in the hold – This sound advice, no doubt, came from a higher source than Gad's own sagacity. It was right to appear publicly among the people of his own tribe, as one conscious of innocence and trusting in God; and it was expedient that, on the death of Saul, his friends might be encouraged to support his interest.

6. Saul abode ... under a tree in Ramah – literally, 'under a grove on a hill.' Oriental princes frequently sit with their court under some shady canopy in the open air. A spear was the early sceptre.

7-8. Hear now, ye Benjamites – This was an appeal to stimulate the patriotism or jealousy of his own tribe, from which he insinuated it was the design of David to transfer the kingdom to another. This address seems to have been made on hearing of David's return with his four hundred men to Judah. A dark suspicion had risen in the jealous mind of the king that Jonathan was aware of this movement, which he dreaded as a conspiracy against the crown.

Doeg accuses Ahimelech (22:9–16)

10. he inquired of the Lord for him – Some suppose that this was a malicious fiction of Doeg to curry favour with the king, but Ahimelech seems to acknowledge the fact. The poor simple-minded high priest knew nothing of the existing family feud between Saul and David. The informer, if he knew it, said nothing of the cunning artifice by which David obtained the aid of Ahimelech. The *facts looked* against him, and the whole priesthood along with him were declared abettors of conspiracy (1Sa 22:16,17).

Saul commands to kill the priests (22:17–19)

17–18. the footmen that stood about him – his bodyguard, or his runners (1Sa 8:11 2Sa 15:1 1Ki 1:5 1Ki 14:28), who held an important place at court (2Ch 12:10). But they chose rather to disobey the king than to offend God by imbruing their hands in the blood of his ministering servants. A foreigner alone (Ps 52:1-3) could be found willing to be the executioner of this bloody and sacrilegious sentence. Thus was the doom of the house of Eli fulfilled (1Sa 2:30–36).

19. Nob, the city of the priests, smote he with the edge of the sword – The barbarous atrocities perpetrated against this city seem to have been designed to terrify all the subjects of Saul from affording either aid or an asylum to David. But they proved ruinous to Saul's own interest, as they alienated the priesthood and disgusted all good men in the kingdom.

Abiathar escapes and flees after David (22:20–23)

20–23. one of the sons of Ahimelech … escaped – This was Abiathar, who repaired to David in the forest of Hareth, rescuing, with his own life, the high priest's vestments (1Sa 23:6,9). On hearing his sad tale, David declared that he had dreaded such a fatal result from the malice and intriguing ambition of Doeg; and, accusing himself as having been the occasion of all the disaster to Abiathar's family, David invited him to remain, because, firmly trusting himself in the accomplishment of the divine promise, David could guarantee protection to him.

Chapter 23

David rescues Keilah (23:1–6)

1. Then they told David – rather, 'now they had told'; for this information had reached him previous to his hearing (1Sa 23:6) of the Nob tragedy.

and they rob the threshing-floors – These were commonly situated on the fields and were open to the wind (Jud 6:11 Ru 3:2).

2–5. David inquired of the Lord – most probably through Gad (2Sa 24:11 1Ch 21:9), who was present in David's camp (1Sa 22:5), probably by the recommendation of Samuel. To repel unprovoked assaults on unoffending people who were engaged in their harvest operations, was a humane and benevolent service. But it was doubtful how far it was David's duty to go against a public enemy without the royal commission; and on that account he asked, and obtained, the divine counsel. A demur on the part of his men led David to renew the consultation for their satisfaction; after which, being fully assured of his duty, he encountered the aggressors and, by a signal victory, delivered the people of Keilah from further molestation.

6. an ephod – in which was the Urim and Thummim (Ex 28:30). It had, probably, been committed to his care, while Ahimelech and the other priests repaired to Gibeah, in obedience to the summons of Saul.

Saul's coming, and treachery of the Keilites (23:7–13)

7. it was told Saul that David was come to Keilah – Saul imagined himself now certain of his victim, who would be hemmed within a fortified town. The wish was father to the thought. How wonderfully slow and unwilling to be convinced by all his experience, that the special protection of Providence shielded David from all his snares!

8. Saul called all the people together to war – not the united tribes of Israel, but the inhabitants of the adjoining districts. This force was raised, probably, on the ostensible pretext of opposing the Philistines, while, in reality, it was secretly to arouse mischief against David.

9. he said to Abiathar the priest, Bring hither the ephod – The consultation was made, and the prayer uttered, by means of the priest. The alternative conditions here described have often been referred to as illustrating the doctrine of God's foreknowledge and preordination of events.

David escapes to Ziph (23:14–18)

16–17. Jonathan went to David into the wood, and strengthened his hand in God – by the recollection of their mutual covenant. What a victory over natural feelings and lower considerations must the faith of Jonathan have won, before he could seek such an interview and give utterance to such sentiments! To talk with calm and assured confidence of himself and family being superseded by the man who was his friend by the bonds of a holy and solemn covenant, could only have been done by one who, superior to all views of worldly policy, looked at the course of things in the spirit and through the principles of that theocracy which acknowledged God as the only and supreme Sovereign of Israel. Neither history nor fiction depicts the movements of a friendship purer, nobler, and more self-denying than Jonathan's!

Saul pursues David (23:19–29)

19–23. Then came up the Ziphites to Saul to Gibeah, saying, Doth not David hide himself with us? – From the tell of Ziph a panorama of the whole surrounding district is to be seen. No wonder, then, that the Ziphites saw David and his men passing to and fro in the mountains of the wilderness.

29. David went up from thence, and dwelt in strong holds at En-gedi – that is, 'the spring of the wild goats or gazelles' – a name given to it from the vast number of ibexes or Syrian chamois which inhabit these cliffs on the western shore of the Dead Sea (Jos 15:62). It is now called Ain Jiddy. On all sides the country is full of caverns, which might then serve as lurking places for David and his men, as they do for outlaws at the present day (ROBINSON).

Chapter 24

David in a cave at Engedi cuts of Saul's skirt, but spares his life (24:1–7)

2. Saul … went … to seek David … upon the rocks of the wild goats – Nothing but the blind infatuation of fiendish rage could have led the king to pursue his outlawed son-in-law among those craggy and perpendicular precipices, where were inaccessible hiding places. The large force he took with him seemed to give him every prospect of success. But the overruling providence of God frustrated all his vigilance.

3. he came to the sheepcotes – most probably in the upper ridge of Wady Chareitun. There a large cave – I am quite disposed to say the cave – lies hardly five minutes to the east of the village ruin, on the south side of the wady. It is high upon the side of the calcareous rock, and it has undergone no change since David's time. The same narrow natural vaulting at the entrance; the same huge natural chamber in the rock, probably the place where Saul lay down to rest in the heat of the day; the same side vaults, too, where David and his men were concealed. There, accustomed to the obscurity of the cavern, they saw Saul enter, while, blinded by the

glare of the light outside, he saw nothing of him whom he so bitterly persecuted.

4–7. the men of David said … Behold the day of which the Lord said unto thee, Behold, I will deliver thine enemy into thine hand – God had never made any promise of delivering Saul into David's hand; but, from the general and repeated promises of the kingdom to him, they concluded that the king's death was to be effected by taking advantage of some such opportunity as the present. David steadily opposed the urgent instigations of his followers to put an end to his and their troubles by the death of their persecutor; he, however, cut off a fragment from the skirt of the royal robe. It is easy to imagine how this dialogue could be carried on and David's approach to the king's person could have been effected without arousing suspicion. The bustle and noise of Saul's military men and their beasts, the number of cells or divisions in these immense caverns being enveloped in darkness, while every movement could be seen at the cave's mouth – the probability that the garment David cut from might have been a loose or upper cloak lying on the ground, and that Saul might have been asleep – these facts and presumptions will be sufficient to account for the incidents detailed.

David urges thereby his innocency (24:8–15)

8–15. David also arose … and went out of the cave, and cried after Saul – The closeness of the precipitous cliffs, though divided by deep wadies, and the transparent purity of the air enable a person standing on one rock to hear distinctly the words uttered by a speaker standing on another (Jud 9:7). The expostulation of David, followed by the visible tokens he furnished of his cherishing no evil design against either the person or the government of the king, even when he had the monarch in his power, smote the heart of Saul in a moment and disarmed him of his fell purpose of revenge. He owned the justice of what David said, acknowledged his own guilt, and begged kindness to his house. He seems to have been naturally susceptible of strong, and, as in this instance, of good and grateful impressions. The improvement of his temper, indeed, was but transient – his language that of a man overwhelmed by the force of impetuous emotions and constrained to admire the conduct, and esteem the character, of one whom he hated and dreaded. But God overruled it for ensuring the present escape of David. Consider his language and behaviour. This language – **a dead dog, a flea,** terms by which, like Eastern people, he strongly expressed a sense of his lowliness and the entire committal of his cause to Him who alone is the judge of human actions, and to whom vengeance belongs, his steady repulse of the vindictive counsels of his followers; the relentings of heart which he felt even for the apparent indignity he had done to the person of the Lord's anointed; and the respectful homage he paid the jealous tyrant who had set a price on his head – evince the magnanimity of a great and good man, and strikingly illustrate the spirit and energy of his prayer 'when he was in the cave' (Ps 142:1, title).

Chapter 25

Samuel dies (25:1–9)

1. Samuel died – After a long life of piety and public usefulness, he left behind him a reputation which ranks him among the greatest of Scripture worthies.

buried him in his house at Ramah – that is, his own mausoleum. The Hebrews took as great care to provide sepultures anciently as people do in the East still, where every respectable family has its own house of the dead. Often this is in a little detached garden, containing a small stone building (where there is no rock), resembling a house, which is called the sepulchre of the family – it has neither door nor window.

David arose, and went down to the wilderness of Paran – This removal had probably no connection with the prophet's death; but was probably occasioned by the necessity of seeking provision for his numerous followers.

2. the man was very great – His property consisted in cattle, and he was considered wealthy, according to the ideas of that age.

3. he was of the house of Caleb – of course, of the same tribe with David himself; but many versions consider Caleb ('dog') not as a proper, but a common noun, and render it, 'he was snappish as a dog.'

4–9. Nabal did shear his sheep, and David sent out ten young men – David and his men lurked in these deserts, associating with the herdsmen and shepherds of Nabal and others and doing them good offices, probably in return for information and supplies obtained through them. Hence when Nabal held his annual sheep-shearing in Carmel, David felt himself entitled to share in the festival and sent a message, recounting his own services and asking for a present. 'In all these particulars we were deeply struck with the truth and strength of the biblical description of manners and customs almost identically the same as they exist at the present day. On such a festive occasion, near a town or village, even in our own time, an Arab sheik of the neighbouring desert would hardly fail to put in a word either in person or by message; and his message, both in form and substance, would be only a transcript of that of David' (ROBINSON).

The churlish answer provokes David (25:10–13)

10–12. Nabal answered David's servants, … Who is David? – Nabal's answer seems to indicate that the country was at the time in a loose and disorderly state. David's own good conduct, however, as well as the important services rendered by him and his men, were readily attested by Nabal's servants. The preparations of David to chastise his insolent language and ungrateful requital are exactly what would be done in the present day by Arab chiefs, who protect the cattle of the large and wealthy sheep masters from the attacks of the marauding border tribes or wild beasts. Their protection creates a claim for some kind of tribute, in the shape of supplies of food and necessaries, which is usually given with great good will and gratitude; but when withheld, is enforced as a right. Nabal's refusal, therefore, was a violation of the established usages of the place.

Abigail pacifies David (25:14–35)

14–18. Then Abigail made haste – The prudence and address of Nabal's wife were the means of saving him and family from utter destruction. She acknowledged the demand of her formidable neighbours; but justly considering, that to atone for the insolence of her husband, a greater degree of liberality had become necessary, she collected a large amount of food, accompanying it with the most valued products of the country.

bottles – goatskins, capable of holding a great quantity.

parched corn – It was customary to eat parched corn when it was fully grown, but not ripe.

19. she said unto her servants, Go on before me; behold, I come after you – People in the East always try to produce an effect by their presents, loading on several beasts what might be easily carried by one, and bringing them forward, article by article, in succession. Abigail not only sent her servants in this way, but resolved to go in person, following her present, as is commonly done, to watch the impression which her munificence would produce.

23. she hasted, and lighted off the ass, and fell before David on her face – Dismounting in presence of a superior is the highest token of respect that can be given; and it is still an essential act of homage to the great. Accompanying this act of courtesy with the lowest form of prostration, she not only by her attitude, but her language, made the fullest amends for the disrespect shown by her husband, as well as paid the fullest tribute of respect to the character and claims of David.

25. Nabal – signifying *fool*, gave pertinence to his wife's remark.

26. let thine enemies … be as Nabal – be as foolish and contemptible as he.

29. the soul of my lord shall be bound in the bundle of life with the Lord thy God – An Orientalism, expressing the perfect security of David's life from all the assaults of his enemies, under the protecting shield of Providence, who had destined him for high things.

32–35. David said to Abigail, Blessed be the Lord – Transported by passion and blinded by revenge, he was on the eve of perpetrating a great injury. Doubtless, the timely appearance and prudent address of Abigail were greatly instrumental in changing his purpose. At all events, it was the means of opening his eyes to the moral character of the course on which he had been impetuously rushing; and in accepting her present, he speaks with lively satisfaction as well as gratitude to Abigail, for having relieved him from bloodshed.

Nabal's death (25:36–44)

36. he held a feast in his house, like the feast of a king – The sheep-shearing season was always a very joyous occasion. Masters usually entertained their shepherds; and even Nabal, though of a most niggardly disposition, prepared festivities on a scale of sumptuous liberality. The modern Arabs celebrate the season with similar hilarity.

37, 38. in the morning … his wife had told him these things, that his heart died within him – He probably fainted from horror at the perilous situation in which he had unconsciously placed himself; and such a shock had been given him by the fright to his whole system, that he rapidly pined and died.

39–42. the Lord hath returned the wickedness of Nabal upon his own head – If this was an expression of pleasure, and David's vindictive feelings were gratified by the intelligence of Nabal's death, it was an instance of human infirmity which we may lament; but perhaps he referred to the unmerited reproach (1Sa 25:10,11), and the contempt of God implied in it.

David sent and communed with Abigail, to take her to wife – This unceremonious proceeding was quite in the style of Eastern monarchs, who no sooner take a fancy for a lady than they despatch a messenger to intimate their royal wishes that she should henceforth reside in the palace; and her duty is implicitly to obey. David's conduct shows that the manners of the Eastern nations were already imitated by the great men in Israel; and that the morality of the times which God permitted, gave its sanction to the practice of polygamy. His marriage with Abigail brought him a rich estate.

44. Michal – By the unchallengeable will of her father, she who was David's wife was given to another. But she returned and sustained the character of his wife when he ascended the throne.

Chapter 26

Saul comes to the hill of Hachilah against David (26:1–5)

1–2. the Ziphites came unto Saul to Gibeah – This people seem to have thought it impossible for David to escape, and therefore recommended themselves to Saul, by giving him secret information (see on 1Sa 23:19). The knowledge of their treachery makes it appear strange that David should return to his former haunt in their neighbourhood; but, perhaps he did it to be near Abigail's possessions, and under the impression that Saul had become mollified. But the king had relapsed into his old enmity.

4, 5. David … sent out spies … and David arose, and came to the place where Saul had pitched – Having obtained certain information of the locality, he seems, accompanied by his nephew (1Sa 26:6), to have hid himself, perhaps disguised, in a neighbouring wood, or hill, on the skirts of the royal camp towards night, and waited to approach it under covert of the darkness.

David prevents Abishai from killing Saul, but takes his spear and cruse (26:5–25)

5. Saul lay in the trench, and the people pitched round about him – Among the nomad people of the East, the encampments are usually made in a circular form. The circumference is lined by the baggage and the men, while the chief's station is in the centre, whether he occupy a tent or not. His spear, stuck in the ground, indicates his position. Similar was the disposition of Saul's camp – in this hasty expedition he seems to have carried no tent, but to have slept on the ground. The whole troop was sunk in sleep around him.

8–12. Then said Abishai to David, God hath delivered thine enemy into thine hand – This midnight stratagem shows the activity and heroic enterprise of David's mind, and it was in unison with the style of warfare in ancient times.

11. the spear that is at his bolster, and the cruse of water – The Oriental spear had, and still has, a spike at the lower extremity, intended for the purpose of sticking the spear into the ground when the warrior is at rest. This common custom of Arab sheiks was also the practice of the Hebrew chiefs.

at his bolster – literally, 'at his head'; perhaps, Saul as a sovereign had the distinguished luxury of a bolster carried for him. A **cruse of water** is usually, in warm climates, kept near a person's couch, as a drink in the night time is found very refreshing. Saul's cruse would probably be of superior materials, or more richly ornamented than common ones, and therefore by its size or form be easily distinguished.

13–20. Then David … stood on the top of an hill afar off … and cried to the people – The extraordinary purity and elasticity of the air in Palestine enable words to be distinctly heard that are addressed by a speaker from the top of one hill to people on that of another, from which it is separated by a deep intervening ravine. Hostile parties can thus speak to each other, while completely beyond the reach of each other's attack. It results from the peculiar features of the country in many of the mountain districts.

15. David said to Abner, Art not thou a valiant man: … wherefore then hast thou not kept thy lord the king? – The circumstance of David having penetrated to the centre of the encampment, through the circular rows of the sleeping soldiers, constituted the point of this sarcastic taunt. This new evidence of David's moderation and magnanimous forbearance, together with his earnest and kindly expostulation, softened the obduracy of Saul's heart.

19. If the Lord have stirred thee up against me – By the evil spirit He had sent, or by any spiritual offenses by which we have mutually displeased Him.

let him accept an offering – that is, let us conjointly offer a sacrifice for appeasing His wrath against us.

if they be the children of men – The prudence, meekness, and address of David in ascribing the king's enmity to the instigations of some malicious traducers, and not to the jealousy of Saul himself, is worthy of notice.

saying, Go, serve other gods – This was the drift of their conduct. By driving him from the land and ordinances of the true worship, into foreign and heathen countries, they were exposing him to all the seductions of idolatry.

25. So David went on his way – Notwithstanding this sudden relenting of Saul, David placed no confidence in his professions or promises, but wisely kept at a distance and awaited the course of Providence.

Chapter 27

Saul hearing that David was fled to Gath, seeks him no more (27:1–4)

1. David said in his heart, … there is nothing better for me than that I should speedily escape into the land of the Philistines – This resolution of David's was, in every respect, wrong: (1) It was removing him from the place where the divine oracle intimated him to remain (1Sa 22:5); (2) It was rushing into the idolatrous land, for driving him into which he had denounced an imprecation on his enemies (1Sa 26:19); (3) It was a withdrawal of his counsel and aid from God's people. It was a movement,

however, overruled by Providence to detach him from his country and to let the disasters impending over Saul and his followers be brought on by the Philistines.

David begs Ziklag of Achish (27:5–12)

5. let them give me a place in some town in the country – It was a prudent arrangement on the part of David; for it would prevent him being an object of jealous suspicion, or of mischievous plots among the Philistines.

6. Ziklag – Though originally assigned to Judah (Jos 15:31), and subsequently to Simeon (Jos 19:5), this town had never been possessed by the Israelites. It belonged to the Philistines, who gave it to David.

10. Achish said, Whither have ye made a road to-day? – that is, *raid,* a hostile excursion for seizing cattle and other booty.

David said, Against the south of Judah, and against the south of the Jerahmeelites – Jerahmeel was the great-grandson of Judah, and his posterity occupied the southern portion of that tribal domain. **the south of the Kenites** – the posterity of Jethro, who occupied the south of Judah (Jud 1:16 Nu 24:21). The deceit practised upon his royal host and the indiscriminate slaughter committed, lest any one should escape to tell the tale, exhibit an unfavourable view of this part of David's history.

Chapter 28

Achish's confidence in David (28:1–6)

1. The Philistines gathered their armies together for warfare, to fight with Israel – The death of Samuel, the general dissatisfaction with Saul, and the absence of David, instigated the cupidity of those restless enemies of Israel.

Achish said to David, Know thou assuredly, that thou shalt go out with me to battle – This was evidently to try him. Achish, however, seems to have thought he had gained the confidence of David and had a claim on his services.

2. Surely thou shalt know what thy servant can do – This answer, while it seemed to express an apparent cheerfulness in agreeing to the proposal, contained a studied ambiguity – a wary and politic generality.

Therefore will I make thee keeper of mine head for ever – or, 'my life'; that is, 'captain of my bodyguard,' an office of great trust and high honour.

3. Now Samuel is dead, – This event is here alluded to as affording an explanation of the secret and improper methods by which Saul sought information and direction in the present crisis of his affairs. Overwhelmed in perplexity and fear, he yet found the common and legitimate channels of communication with Heaven shut against him. And so, under the impulse of that dark, distempered, superstitious spirit which had overmastered him, he resolved, in desperation, to seek the aid of one of those fortune telling impostors whom, in accordance with the divine command (Le 19:31; 20:6, 27; De 18:11), he had set himself formerly to exterminate from his kingdom.

Saul seeks a witch, who, being encouraged by him, raises up Samuel (28:7–25)

7–8. Then said Saul unto his servants, Seek me a woman that hath a familiar spirit – From the energetic measures which he himself had taken for extirpating the dealers in magical arts (the profession having been declared a capital offense), his most attached courtiers might have had reason to doubt the possibility of gratifying their master's wish. Anxious inquiries, however, led to the discovery of a woman living very secluded in the neighbourhood, who had the credit of possessing the forbidden powers. To her house he repaired by night in disguise, accompanied by two faithful servants.

En-dor – 'the fountain of the circle' (that figure being constantly affected by magicians) was situated directly on the other side of the Gilboa range, opposite Tabor; so that, in this midnight adventure, Saul had to pass over the shoulder of the ridge on which the Philistines were encamped.

8–14. bring me him up, whom I shall name unto thee – This pythoness united to the arts of divination a claim to be a necromancer (De 18:11); and it was her supposed power in calling back the dead of which Saul was desirous to avail himself. Though she at first refused to listen to his request, she accepted his pledge that no risk would be incurred by her compliance. It is probable that his extraordinary stature, the deference paid him by his attendants, the easy distance of his camp from En-dor, and the proposal to call up the great prophet and first magistrate in Israel (a proposal which no private individual would venture to make), had awakened her suspicions as to the true character and rank of her visitor. The story has led to much discussion whether there was a real appearance of Samuel or not. On the one hand, the woman's profession, which was forbidden by the divine law, the refusal of God to answer Saul by any divinely constituted means, the well-known age, figure, and dress of Samuel, which she could easily represent herself, or by an accomplice – his apparition being evidently at some distance, being muffled, and not actually seen by Saul, whose attitude of prostrate homage, moreover, must have prevented him distinguishing the person though he had been near, and the voice seemingly issuing out of the ground, and coming along to Saul – and the vagueness of the information, imparted much

which might have been reached by natural conjecture as to the probable result of the approaching conflict – the woman's representation – all of this has led many to think that this was a mere deception. On the other hand, many eminent writers (considering that the apparition came before her arts were put in practice; that she herself was surprised and alarmed; that the prediction of Saul's own death and the defeat of his forces was confidently made), are of opinion that Samuel really appeared.

25. Then they rose up, and went away that night – Exhausted by long abstinence, overwhelmed with mental distress, and now driven to despair, the cold sweat broke on his anxious brow, and he sank helpless on the ground. But the kind attentions of the woman and his servants having revived him, he returned to the camp to await his doom.

Chapter 29

David is spared from fighting Saul (29:1–11)

2. David and his men passed on in the rereward with Achish – as the commander of the lifeguards of Achish, who was general of this invading army of the Philistines.

3. these days, or these years – He had now been with the Philistines a full year and four months (1Sa 27:7), and also some years before. It has been thought that David kept up a private correspondence with this Philistine prince, either on account of his native generosity, or in the anticipation that an asylum in his territories would sooner or later be needed.

4. the princes of the Philistines were wroth with him – It must be considered a happy circumstance in the overruling providence of God to rescue David out of the dangerous dilemma in which he was now placed. But David is not free from censure in his professions to Achish (1Sa 29:8), to do what he probably had not the smallest purpose of doing – of fighting with Achish against his enemies. It is just an instance of the unhappy consequences into which a false step – a departure from the straight course of duty – will betray everyone who commits it.

Chapter 30

The Amalekites spoil Ziklag (30:1–5)

1. Amalekites had invaded the south, and Ziklag, and smitten Ziklag – While the strength of the Philistine forces was poured out of their country into the plain of Esdraelon, the Amalekite marauders seized the opportunity of the defenceless state of Philistia to invade the southern territory. Of course, David's town suffered from the ravages of these nomad plunderers, in revenge for his recent raid upon their territory.

2. they slew not any, either great or small, but carried them away – Their conduct seems to stand in favourable contrast to that of David (1Sa 27:11). But their apparent clemency did not arise from humane considerations. It is traceable to the ancient war usages of the East, where the men of war, on the capture of a city, were unsparingly put to death, but there were no warriors in Ziklag at the time. The women and boys were reserved for slaves, and the old people were spared out of respect to age.

But David, encouraged by God, pursues them (30:6–15)

6. David was greatly distressed – He had reason, not only on his own personal account (1Sa 30:5), but on account of the vehement outcry and insurrectionary threats against him for having left the place so defenceless that the families of his men fell an unresisting prey to the enemy. Under the pressure of so unexpected and widespread a calamity, of which he was upbraided as the indirect occasion, the spirit of any other leader guided by ordinary motives would have sunk;

but David encouraged himself in the LORD his God – His faith supplied him with inward resources of comfort and energy, and through the seasonable inquiries he made by Urim, he inspired confidence by ordering an immediate pursuit of the plunderers.

11–15. they found an Egyptian in the field, and brought him to David – Old and homeborn slaves are usually treated with great kindness. But a purchased or captured slave must look to himself; for, if feeble or sick, his master will leave him to perish rather than encumber himself with any additional burden. This Egyptian seems to have recently fallen into the hands of an Amalekite, and his master having belonged to the marauding party that had made the attack on Ziklag, he could give useful information as to the course taken by them on their return.

15. Swear unto me by God – Whether there was still among these idolatrous tribes a lingering belief in one God, or this Egyptian wished to bind David by the God whom the Hebrews worshipped, the solemn sanction of an oath was mutually recognized.

And recovers his two wives and all the spoil (30:16–31)

16. they were spread abroad upon all the earth – Believing that David and all his men of war were far away, engaged with the Philistine expedition, they deemed themselves perfectly secure and abandoned themselves to all manner of barbaric revelry. The promise made in answer to the devout inquiries of David (1Sa 30:8) was fulfilled. The marauders were surprised and panic-stricken. A great slaughter ensued – the people as well as the booty taken from Ziklag was recovered, besides a great amount of spoil which they had collected in a wide, freebooting excursion.

21. David came to the two hundred men, which were so faint that they could not follow – This unexpected accession of spoil was nearly proving an occasion of quarrel through the selfish cupidity of some of his followers, and serious consequences might have ensued had they not been prevented by the prudence of the leader, who enacted it as a standing ordinance – the equitable rule – that all the soldiers should share alike (see Nu 31:11).

26. when David came to Ziklag, he sent of the spoil to the elders of Judah – This was intended as an acknowledgment to the leading men in those towns and villages of Judah which had ministered to his necessities in the course of his various wanderings. It was the dictate of an amiable and grateful heart; and the effect of this well timed liberality was to bring a large accession of numbers to his camp (1Ch 12:22). The enumeration of these places shows what a numerous and influential party of adherents to his cause he could count within his own tribe (1Sa 30:27-31).

Chapter 31

Saul having lost his army at Gilboa, and his sons being killed, he and armour-bearer kill themselves (31:1–7)

3–5. the battle went sore against Saul, – He seems to have bravely maintained his ground for some time longer; but exhausted with fatigue and loss of blood, and dreading that if he fell alive into the enemy's hands, they would insolently maltreat him (Jos 8:29 10:24 Jud 8:21), he requested his armour bearer to despatch him. However, that officer refused to do so. Saul then falling on the point of his sword killed himself; and the armour bearer, who, according to Jewish writers, was Doeg, following the example of his master, put an end to his life also. They died by one and the same sword – the very weapon with which they had massacred the Lord's servants at Nob.

6. and his three sons – The influence of a directing Providence is evidently to be traced in permitting the death of Saul's three eldest and most energetic sons, particularly that of Jonathan, for whom, had he survived his father, a strong party would undoubtedly have risen and thus obstructed the path of David to the throne.

The Philistines triumph over their dead bodies (31:8–10)

8–9. on the morrow, when the Philistines came to strip the slain, that they found Saul and his three sons fallen – On discovering the corpses of the slaughtered princes on the battlefield, the enemy reserved them for special indignities. They consecrated the armour of the king and his sons to the temple of Ashtaroth and fastened their bodies on the temple of Shen, while they fixed the royal heads ignominiously in the temple of Dagon (1Ch 10:10); thus dividing the glory among their several deities.

The men of Jabeth-Gilead recover the bodies and bury them at Jabesh (31:11–13)

11–13. the inhabitants of Jabesh-gilead heard of that which the Philistines had done – Mindful of the important and timely services Saul had rendered them, they gratefully and heroically resolved not to suffer such indignities to be inflicted on the remains of the royal family.

12. valiant men arose, and went all night, and took the body of Saul and the bodies of his sons – Considering that Beth-shan is an hour and a half's distance, and by a narrow upland passage, to the west of the Jordan (the whole being a journey from Jabesh-gilead of about ten miles), they must have made all haste to travel thither to carry off the headless bodies and return to their own side of the Jordan in the course of a single night.

burnt them – This was not a Hebrew custom. It was probably resorted to on this occasion to prevent all risk of the Beth-shanites coming to disinter the royal remains for further insult.

2 SAMUEL

Robert Jamieson

Introduction

See 1 Samuel Introduction

Chapter 1

An Amalekite brings tidings of Saul's death (1:1–16)

1. David had abode two days in Ziklag – Though greatly reduced by the Amalekite incendiaries, that town was not so completely sacked and destroyed, but David and his six hundred followers, with their families, could still find some accommodation.

2. a man came out of the camp from Saul – As the narrative of Saul's death, given in the last chapter, is inspired, it must be considered the true account, and the Amalekite's story a fiction of his own, invented to ingratiate himself with David, the presumptive successor to the throne. David's question, 'How went the matter?' evinces the deep interest he took in the war, an interest that sprang from feelings of high and generous patriotism, not from views of ambition. The Amalekite, however, judging him to be actuated by a selfish principle, fabricated a story improbable and inconsistent, which he thought would procure him a reward. Having probably witnessed the suicidal act of Saul, he thought of turning it to his own account, and suffered the penalty of his grievously mistaken calculation.

10. the crown – a small metallic cap or wreath, which encircled the temples, serving the purpose of a helmet, with a very small horn projecting in front, as the emblem of power.

the bracelet that was on his arm – the armlet worn above the elbow; an ancient mark of royal dignity. It is still worn by kings in some Eastern countries.

13–15. David said unto the young man … Whence art thou? – The man had at the outset stated who he was. But the question was now formally and judicially put. The punishment inflicted on the Amalekite may seem too severe, but the respect paid to kings in the West must not be regarded as the standard for that which the East may think due to royal station. David's reverence for Saul, as the Lord's anointed, was in his mind a principle on which he had faithfully acted on several occasions of great temptation. In present circumstances it was especially important that his principle should be publicly known; and to free himself from the imputation of being in any way accessory to the execrable crime of regicide was the part of a righteous judge, no less than of a good politician.

David laments Saul and Jonathan (1:17–27)

17, 18. David lamented with this lamentation – It has always been customary for Eastern people, on the death of great kings and warriors, to celebrate their qualities and deeds in funeral songs.

19. The beauty of Israel is slain upon thy high places – literally, 'the gazelle' or 'antelope of Israel.' In Eastern countries, that animal is the chosen type of beauty and symmetrical elegance of form.

how are the mighty fallen! – This forms the chorus.

21. let there be no dew, neither let there be rain – To be deprived of the genial atmospheric influences which, in those anciently cultivated hills, seem to have reared plenty of first-fruits in the corn harvests, was specified as the greatest calamity the lacerated feelings of the poet could imagine. The curse seems still to lie upon them; for the mountains of Gilboa are naked and sterile.

the shield of the mighty is vilely cast away – To cast away the shield was counted a national disgrace. Yet, on that fatal battle of Gilboa, many of the Jewish soldiers, who had displayed unflinching valour in former battles, forgetful of their own reputation and their country's honour, threw away their shields and fled from the field. This dishonourable and cowardly conduct is alluded to with exquisitely touching pathos.

24–27. Ye daughters of Israel, weep over Saul, who clothed you in scarlet, with other delights, – The fondness for dress, which anciently distinguished Oriental women, is their characteristic still. It appears in their love of bright, and divers colours, in profuse display of ornaments, and in various other forms. The inmost depths of the poet's feeling are stirred, and his amiable disposition appears in the strong desire to celebrate the good qualities of Saul, as well as Jonathan. But the praises of the latter form the burden of the poem, which begins and ends with that excellent prince.

Chapter 2

David, by God's direction, goes up to Hebron, and is made king over Judah
(2:1–7)

1–4. David inquired of the Lord – By Urim. He knew his destination, but he knew also that the providence of God would pave the way. Therefore he would take no step in such a crisis of his own and the nation's history, without asking and obtaining the divine direction. He was told to go into Judah, and fix his headquarters in Hebron, whither he accordingly repaired with his now considerable force. There his interests were very powerful; for he was not only within his own tribe, and near chiefs with whom he had been long in friendly relations but Hebron was the capital and centre of Judah, and one of the Levitical cities; the inhabitants of which were strongly attached to him, both from sympathy with his cause ever since the massacre at Nob, and from the prospect of realizing in his person their promised pre-eminence among the tribes. The princes of Judah, therefore, offered him the crown over their tribe, and it was accepted. More could not, with prudence, be done in the circumstances of the country.

5–7. David sent messengers unto the men of Jabesh-gilead – There can be no doubt that this message of thanks for their bold and dangerous enterprise in rescuing the bodies of Saul and his sons was an expression of David's personal and genuine feeling of satisfaction. At the same time, it was a stroke of sound and timely policy. In this view the announcement of his royal power in Judah, accompanied by the pledge of his protection of the men of Jabesh-gilead, should they

be exposed to danger for their adventure at Beth-shan, would bear an important significance in all parts of the country and hold out an assurance that he would render them the same timely and energetic succour that Saul had done at the beginning of his reign.

Abner makes Ish-bosheth king over Israel
(2:8–18)

8–17. Abner the son of Ner, captain of Saul's host took Ish-bosheth – Here was the establishment of a rival kingdom, which, however, would probably have had no existence but for Abner. Abner – was first cousin of Saul, commander of the forces, and held in high respect throughout the country. Loyalty to the house of his late master was mixed up with opposition to David and views of personal ambition in his originating this factious movement.

9, 10. over Gilead – used in a loose sense for the land beyond Jordan.

Ashurites – the tribe of Asher in the extreme north.

Jezreel – the extensive valley bordering on the central tribes.

over all Israel … But Judah – David neither could nor would force matters. He was content to wait God's time and studiously avoided any collision with the rival king, till, at the lapse of two years, hostilities were threatened from that quarter.

12. Abner … and the servants of Ish-bosheth … went out from Mahanaim to Gibeon – This town was near the confines of Judah, and as the force with which Abner encamped there seemed to have some aggressive design, David sent an army of observation, under the command of Joab, to watch his movements.

14. Abner said to Joab, Let the young men now arise, and play before us – Some think that the proposal was only for an exhibition of a little tilting match for diversion. Others suppose that, both parties being reluctant to commence a civil war, Abner proposed to leave the contest to the decision of twelve picked men on either side. This fight by championship instead of terminating the matter, inflamed the fiercest passions of the two rival parties; a general engagement ensued, in which Abner and his forces were defeated and put to flight.

Asahel slain (2:19–32)

19–32. Asahel pursued after Abner – To gain the general's armour was deemed the grandest trophy. Asahel, ambitious of securing Abner's, had outstripped all other pursuers, and was fast gaining on the retreating commander. Abner, conscious of possessing more physical power, and unwilling that there should be 'blood' between himself and Joab, Asahel's brother, twice urged him to desist. The impetuous young soldier being deaf to the generous remonstrance, the veteran raised the pointed butt of his lance, as the modern Arabs do when pursued, and, with a sudden back thrust, transfixed him on the spot, so that he fell, and lay weltering in his blood. But Joab and Abishai continued the pursuit by another route till sunset. On reaching a rising ground, and receiving a fresh reinforcement of some Benjamites, Abner rallied his scattered troops and earnestly appealed to Joab's better feelings to stop the further effusion of blood, which, if continued, would lead to more serious consequences – a destructive civil war. Joab, while upbraiding his opponent as the sole cause of the fray, felt the force of the appeal and led off his men; while Abner probably dreading a renewal of the attack when Joab should learn his brother's fate, and vow fierce revenge, endeavoured, by a forced march, to cross the Jordan that night. On David's side the loss was only nineteen men, besides Asahel. But of Ish-bosheth's party there fell three hundred and sixty. This skirmish is exactly similar to the battles of the Homeric warriors, among whom, in the flight of one, the pursuit by another, and the dialogue held between them, there is vividly represented the style of ancient warfare.

Chapter 3

Six sons born to David (3:1–5)

1. there was long war between the house of Saul and the house of David – The rival parties had varying success, but David's interest steadily increased; less, however, by the fortunes of war, than a growing adherence to him as the divinely designated king.

2. unto David were sons born in Hebron – The six sons mentioned had all different mothers.

3. Chileab – ('his father's picture') – called also Daniel.

Maacah the daughter of Talmai king of Geshur – a region in Syria, north of Israel. This marriage seems to have been a political match, made by David, with a view to strengthen himself against Ish-bosheth's party, by the aid of a powerful friend and ally in the north. Piety was made to yield to policy, and the bitter fruits of this alliance with a heathen prince he reaped in the life of the turbulent Absalom.

5. Eglah David's wife – This addition has led many to think that Eglah was another name for Michal, the *first* and *proper* wife, who, though she had no family after her insolent ridicule of David, might have had a child before.

Abner revolts to David (3:6–12)

6-11. Abner made himself strong for the house of Saul – In the East, the wives and concubines of a king are the property of his successor to this extent, that for a private person to aspire to marry one of them would be considered a virtual advance of pretensions to the crown.

12, 13. Abner sent messengers to David – Though his language implied a secret conviction, that in supporting Ish-bosheth he had been labouring to frustrate the divine purpose of conferring the sovereignty of the kingdom on David, this acknowledgment was no justification either of the measure he was now adopting, or of the motives that prompted it. Nor does it seem possible to uphold the full integrity and honour of David's conduct in entertaining his secret overtures for undermining Ish-bosheth, except we take into account the divine promise of the kingdom, and his belief that the secession of Abner was a means designed by Providence for accomplishing it. The demand for the restoration of his wife Michal was perfectly fair; but David's insisting on it at that particular moment, as an indispensable condition of his entering into any treaty with Abner, seems to have proceeded not so much from a lingering attachment as from an expectation that his possession of her would incline some adherents of the house of Saul to be favourable to his cause.

17–21. Abner had communication with the elders of Israel – He spoke the truth in impressing their minds with the well-known fact of David's divine designation to the kingdom. But he acted a base and hypocritical part in pretending that his present movement was prompted by religious motives, when it sprang entirely from malice and revenge against Ish-bosheth. The particular appeal of the Benjamites was a necessary policy; their tribe enjoyed the honour of giving birth to the royal dynasty of Saul; they would naturally be disinclined to lose that *prestige*. They were, besides, a determined people, whose contiguity to Judah might render them troublesome and dangerous. The enlistment of their interest, therefore, in the scheme, would smooth the way for the adhesion of the other tribes; and Abner enjoyed the most convenient opportunity of using his great influence in gaining over that tribe while escorting Michal to David with a suitable equipage. The mission enabled him to cover his treacherous designs against his master – to draw the attention of the elders and people to David as uniting in himself the double recommendation of being the nominee of Jehovah, no less than a connection of the royal house of Saul, and, without suspicion of any dishonourable motives, to advocate policy of terminating the civil discord, by bestowing the sovereignty on the husband of Michal. In the same character of public ambassador, he was received and feted by David; and while, ostensibly, the restoration of Michal was the sole object of his visit, he busily employed himself in making private overtures to David for bringing over to his cause those tribes which he had artfully seduced. Abner pursued a course unworthy of an honourable man and though his offer was accepted by David, the guilt and infamy of the transaction were exclusively his.

Joab kills Abner (3:22–30)

24-27. Joab came to the king, and said, What hast thou done? – Joab's knowledge of Abner's wily character might have led him to doubt the sincerity of that person's proposals and to disapprove the policy of relying on his fidelity. But undoubtedly there were other reasons of a private and personal nature which made Joab displeased and alarmed by the reception given to Abner. The military talents of that general, his popularity with the army, his influence throughout the nation, rendered him a formidable rival. In the event of his overtures being carried out, the important service of bringing over all the other tribes to the king of Judah would establish so strong a claim on the gratitude of David, that his accession would inevitably raise a serious obstacle to the ambition of Joab.

31. David said to Joab, and to all the people that were with him, Rend your clothes, and gird you with sackcloth – David's sorrow was sincere and profound, and he took occasion to give it public expression by the funeral honours he appointed for Abner.

King David himself followed the bier – a sort of wooden frame, partly resembling a coffin, and partly a hand-barrow.

33, 34. the king lamented over Abner – This brief elegy is an effusion of indignation as much as of sorrow.

Chapter 4

Baanah and Rechab slay Ish-Bosheth, and bring his head to Hebron (4:1, 2)

4. Jonathan, Saul's son, had a son that was lame of his feet – This is mentioned as a reason why, according to Oriental notions, he was considered unfit for exercising the duties of sovereignty.

5, 6. Rechab and Baanah went and came about the heat of the day to the house of Ish-bosheth. – It is still a custom in the East to allow their soldiers a certain quantity of corn, together with some pay; and these two captains very naturally went to the palace the day before to fetch wheat, in order to distribute it to the soldiers, that it might be sent to the mill at the accustomed hour in the morning.

8. They brought the head of Ish-bosheth unto David … and said, Behold the head of Ish-bosheth – Such bloody trophies of rebels and conspirators have always been acceptable to princes in the East, and the carriers have been liberally rewarded. Ish-bosheth being a usurper,

the two assassins thought they were doing a meritorious service to David by removing the only existing obstacle to the union of the two kingdoms.

David causes them to be put to death (4:10–12)

12. slew them, and cut off their hands and their feet – as the instruments in perpetrating their crime. The exposure of the mutilated remains was intended as not only a punishment of their crime, but also the attestation of David's abhorrence.

Chapter 5

The tribes anoint David king over Israel (5:1–5)

1, 2. Then came all the tribes of Israel – a combined deputation of the leading authorities in every tribe. David possessed the first and indispensable qualification for the throne; namely, that of being an Israelite. Of his military talent he had furnished ample proof.

3. King David made a league with them in Hebron before the Lord – This formal declaration of the constitution was chiefly made at the commencement of a new dynasty, or at the restoration of the royal family after a usurpation (2Ki 11:17), though circumstances sometimes led to its being renewed on the accession of any new sovereign (1Ki 12:4). It seems to have been accompanied by religious solemnities.

He takes Zion from the Jebusites (5:6–12)

6. the king and his men went to Jerusalem unto the Jebusites – The first expedition of David, as king of the whole country, was directed against this place, which had hitherto remained in the hands of the natives. It was strongly fortified and deemed so impregnable that the blind and lame were sent to man the battlements, in derisive mockery of the Hebrew king's attack, and to shout, 'David cannot come in hither.' To understand the full meaning and force of this insulting taunt, it is necessary to bear in mind the depth and steepness of the valley of Gihon, and the lofty walls of the ancient Canaanite fortress.

7. the stronghold of Zion – Whether Zion be the southwestern hill commonly so-called, or the peak now level on the north of the temple mount, it is the towering height which catches the eye from every quarter – 'the hill fort,' 'the rocky hold' of Jerusalem.

8. Whosoever getteth up to the gutter – This is thought by some to mean a subterranean passage; by others a spout through which water was poured upon the fire which the besiegers often applied to the woodwork at the gateways, and by the projections of which a skilful climber might make his ascent good; a third class render the words, 'whosoever dasheth them against the precipice'.

9. David dwelt in the fort – Having taken it by storm, he changed its name to 'the city of David,' to signify the importance of the conquest, and to perpetuate the memory of the event.

David built round about from Millo and inward – probably a row of stone bastions placed on the northern side of Mount Zion, and built by David to secure himself on that side from the Jebusites, who still lived in the lower part of the city. The house of Millo was perhaps the principal corner tower of that fortified wall.

Eleven sons born to David (5:13–16)

13. David took him more concubines and wives – In this conduct David transgressed an express law, which forbade the king of Israel to multiply wives unto himself.

David smites the Philistines (5:17–25)

17. when the Philistines heard that they had anointed David king over Israel – During the civil war between the house of Saul and David, those restless neighbours had remained quiet spectators of the contest. But now, jealous of David, they resolved to attack him before his government was fully established.

22. the Philistines came up yet again – The next year they renewed their hostile attempt with a larger force, but God manifestly interposed in David's favour.

24. the sound of a going in the tops of the mulberry trees – now generally thought not to be mulberry trees, but some other tree, most probably the poplar, which delights in moist situations, and the leaves of which are rustled by the slightest movement of the air.

Chapter 6

David fetches the ark from Kirjath-Jearimon (6:1–5)

1. Again, David gathered together all the chosen men of Israel – The object of this second assembly was to commence a national movement for establishing the ark in Jerusalem, after it had continued nearly fifty years in the house of Abinada.

3. they set the ark of God upon a new cart – or a covered wagon. This was a hasty and inconsiderate procedure, in violation of an express statute.

Uzzah smitten (6:6–11)

6. the oxen shook it – or, 'stumbled'. Fearing that the ark was in danger of being overturned, Uzzah, under the impulse of momentary

feeling, laid hold of it to keep it steady. Whether it fell and crushed him, or some sudden disease attacked him, he fell dead upon the spot. This melancholy occurrence not only threw a cloud over the joyous scene, but entirely stopped the procession; for the ark was left where it then was, in the near neighbourhood of the capital. It is of importance to observe the proportionate severity of the punishments attending the profanation of the ark.

9, 10. David was afraid of the Lord that day – His feelings on this alarming judgment were greatly excited on various accounts, dreading that the displeasure of God had been provoked by the removal of the ark, that the punishment would be extended to himself and people, and that they might fall into some error or neglect during the further conveyance of the ark. He resolved, therefore, to wait for more light and direction as to the path of duty. An earlier consultation by Urim would have led him right at the first, whereas in this perplexity and distress, he was reaping the fruits of inconsideration and neglect.

David brings the ark to Zion (6:12–19)

12. it was told king David, saying, The Lord hath blessed the house of Obed-edom, and all that pertaineth unto him, because of the ark of God – The lapse of three months not only restored the agitated mind of the monarch to a tranquil and settled tone, but led him to a discovery of his former error. Having learned that the ark was kept in its temporary resting-place not only without inconvenience or danger, but with great advantage, he resolved forthwith to remove it to the capital, with the observance of all due form and solemnity. It was transported now on the shoulders of the priests, who had been carefully prepared for the work, and the procession was distinguished by extraordinary solemnities and demonstrations of joy.

14. David danced before the Lord – The Hebrews, like other ancient people, had their sacred dances, which were performed on their solemn anniversaries and other great occasions of commemorating some special token of the divine goodness and favour.

with all his might – intimating violent efforts of leaping, and divested of his royal mantle (in a state of undress), conduct apparently unsuitable to the gravity of age or the dignity of a king. But it was unquestionably done as an act of religious homage, his attitudes and dress being symbolic, as they have always been in Oriental countries, of penitence, joy, thankfulness, and devotion.

17. they brought in the ark of the Lord, and set it in his place, in the midst of the tabernacle that David had pitched for it – The old tabernacle remained at Gibeon. Probably it was not removed because it was too large for the temporary place the king had appropriated, and because he contemplated the building of a temple.

Michal's barrenness (6:20–23)

20–22. Michal … came out to meet David – Proud of her royal extraction, she upbraided her husband for lowering the dignity of the crown and acting more like a buffoon than a king. But her taunting sarcasm was repelled in a manner that could not be agreeable to her feelings while it indicated the warm piety and gratitude of David.

Chapter 7

Nathan approves the purpose of David to build God a house (7:1–3)

2. the king said unto Nathan the prophet, See now, I dwell in an house of cedar – The palace which Hiram had sent men and materials to build in Jerusalem had been finished. It was magnificent for that age, though made wholly of wood: houses in warm countries not being required to possess the solidity and thickness of walls which are requisite for dwellings in regions exposed to rain and cold. Cedar was the rarest and most valuable timber. The elegance and splendour of his own royal mansion, contrasted with the mean and temporary tabernacle in which the ark of God was placed, distressed the pious mind of David.

3. Nathan said to the king, Go, do all that is in thine heart – The piety of the design commended it to the prophet's mind, and he gave his hasty approval and encouragement to the royal plans. The prophets, when following the impulse of their own feelings, or forming conjectural opinions, fell into frequent mistakes.

God appoints his successor to build it (7:4–17)

4–17. it came to pass that night, that the word of the Lord came unto Nathan – The command was given to the prophet on the night immediately following; that is, before David could either take any measures or incur any expenses.

11. Also the Lord telleth thee that he will make thee an house – As a reward for his pious purpose, God would increase and maintain the family of David and secure the succession of the throne to his dynasty.

13. He shall build an house for my name, and I will establish the throne of his kingdom for ever – This declaration referred, in its primary application, to Solomon, and to the temporal kingdom of David's family. But in a larger and sublimer sense, it was meant of David's Son of another nature.

David's prayer and thanksgiving (7:18–29)

18. Then went king David in, and sat before the Lord – Sitting was anciently an attitude for worship.

19. is this the manner of man, O Lord God? – that is, is it customary for men to show such condescension to persons so humble as I am?

20. what can David say more unto thee? – that is, my obligations are greater than I can express.

Chapter 8

David subdues the Philistines (8:1–2)

1. David took Metheg-ammah out of the hand of the Philistines – that is, Gath and her suburban towns. That town had been 'a bridle' by which the Philistines kept the people of Judah in check. David used it now as a barrier to repress that restless enemy.

David smites Hadadezer and the Syrians (3–14)

3. Zobah – This kingdom was bounded on the east by the Euphrates, and it extended westward from that river, perhaps as far north as Aleppo. It was long the chief among the petty kingdoms of Syria, and its king bore the hereditary title of 'Hadadezer' or 'Hadarezer' ('Hadad,' that is, 'helped').

11. Which also king David did dedicate unto the Lord – Eastern princes have always been accustomed to hoard up vast quantities of gold. This is the first instance of a practice uniformly followed by David of reserving, after defraying expenses and bestowing suitable rewards upon his soldiers, the remainder of the spoil taken in war, to accumulate for the grand project of his life – the erection of a national temple at Jerusalem.

13. David gat him a name when he returned from smiting of the Syrians – Instead of Syrians, the *Septuagint* version reads 'Edomites,' which is the true reading. This conquest, made by the army of David, was due to the skilful generalship and gallantry of Abishai and Joab.

David's reign (8:15–18)

15. David executed judgment and justice unto all his people – Though involved in foreign wars, he maintained an excellent system of government at home, the most eminent men of the age composing his cabinet of ministers.

Chapter 9

David sends for Mephibosheth (9:1–12)

1–7. David said, Is there yet any that is left of the house of Saul – On inquiry, Saul's land steward was found, who gave information that there still survived Mephibosheth, a son of Jonathan who was five years old at his father's death, and whom David, then wandering in exile, had never seen. His lameness had prevented him from taking any part in the public contests of the time. Mephibosheth was invited to court, and a place at the royal table on public days was assigned him, as is still the custom with Eastern monarchs.

Chapter 10

David's messengers, sent to comfort Hanun, are treated disgracefully (10:1–5)

2. Then said David, I will show kindness unto Hanun the son of Nahash, as his father showed kindness unto me – David, on leaving Gath, where his life was exposed to danger, found an asylum with the king of Moab; and as Nahash, king of the Ammonites, was his nearest neighbours, it may be that during the feud between Saul and David, he, through enmity to the former, was kind and hospitable to David. **3. the princes of the children of Ammon said unto Hanun** – Their suspicion was not warranted either by any overt act or by any cherished design of David: it must have originated in their knowledge of the denunciations of God's law against them, and of David's policy in steadfastly adhering to it. **4. Hanun took David's servants, and shaved off the one half of their beards** – From the long flowing dress of the Hebrews and other Orientals, the curtailment of their garments must have given them an aspect of gross indelicacy and ludicrousness. Besides, a knowledge of the extraordinary respect and value which has always been attached, and the gross insult that is implied in any indignity offered, to the beard in the East, will account for the shame which the deputies felt, and the determined spirit of revenge which burst out in all Israel on learning the outrage.

The Ammonites overcome (10:6-14)

6–14. when the children of Ammon saw that they stank before David – To chastise those insolent and inhospitable Ammonites, who had violated the common law of nations, David sent a large army under the command of Joab, while they, informed of the impending attack, made energetic preparations to repel it by engaging the services of an immense number of Syrian mercenaries. **14. So Joab returned and came to Jerusalem** – Probably the season was too far advanced for entering on a siege.

The Syrians defeated (10:15–19)

16. Hadarezer sent and brought out the Syrians that were beyond the river – This prince had enjoyed a breathing time after his defeat. But alarmed at the increasing power and greatness of David, as well as being an ally of the

Ammonites, he levied a vast army not only in Syria, but in Mesopotamia, to invade the Hebrew kingdom. Shobach, his general, in pursuance of this design, had marched his troops as far as Kelam, a border town of eastern Manasseh, when David, crossing the Jordan by forced marches, suddenly surprised, defeated, and dispersed them. As a result of this great and decisive victory, all the petty kingdoms of Syria submitted and became his tributaries.

Chapter 11

Joab besieges Rabbah (11:1)

1. at the time when kings go forth to battle – The return of spring was the usual time of commencing military operations. This expedition took place the year following the war against the Syrians; and it was entered upon because the disaster of the former campaign having fallen chiefly upon the Syrian mercenaries, the Ammonites had not been punished for their insult to the ambassadors.

David sent Joab and his servants … they destroyed the children of Ammon – The powerful army that Joab commanded ravaged the Ammonite country and committed great havoc both on the people and their property, until having reached the capital, they besieged Rabbah. **Rabbah denotes a great city.** This metropolis of the Ammonites was situated in the mountainous tract of Gilead, not far from the source of the Arnon. Extensive ruins are still found on its site.

David commits adultery with Bathsheba (11:2–12)

2. it came to pass in an eveningtide, that David arose from off his bed – The Hebrews, like other Orientals, rose at daybreak, and always took a nap during the heat of the day. Afterwards they lounged in the cool of the evening on their flat-roofed terraces. It is probable that David had ascended to enjoy the open-air refreshment earlier than usual. **3. Is not this Bath-sheba?** – She seems to have been a celebrated beauty, whose renown had already reached the ears of David, as happens in the East, from reports carried by the women from harem to harem. **4. David sent messengers, and took her** – The despotic kings of the East, when they take a fancy for a woman, send an officer to the house were she lives, who announces it to be the royal pleasure she should remove to the palace. An apartment is there assigned to her; and if she is made queen, the monarch orders the announcement to be made that he has made choice of her to be queen.

5. the woman conceived, and sent and told David – Some immediate measures of concealing their sin were necessary, as well for the king's honour as for her safety, for death was the punishment of an adulteress.

8. David said to Uriah, Go down to thy house – This sudden recall, the manner of the king, his frivolous questions, and his urgency for Uriah to sleep in his own house, probably awakened suspicions of the cause of this procedure.

there followed him a mess of meat from the king – A portion of meat from the royal table, sent to one's own house or lodgings, is one of the greatest compliments which an Eastern prince can pay.

9. But Uriah slept at the door of the king's house – It is customary for servants to sleep in the porch or long gallery; and the guards of the Hebrew king did the same.

Uriah slain (11:14–27)

14, 15. David wrote a letter to Joab, and sent it by the hand of Uriah … Set ye Uriah in the forefront of the hottest battle – The various arts and stratagems by which the king tried to cajole Uriah, till at last he resorted to the horrid crime of murder – the cold-blooded cruelty of despatching the letter by the hands of the gallant but much-wronged soldier himself, the enlistment of Joab to be a partaker of his sin, the heartless affectation of mourning, and the indecent haste of his marriage with Bath-sheba – have left an indelible stain upon the character of David, and exhibit a painfully humiliating proof of the awful lengths to which the best of men may go when they forfeit the restraining grace of God.

Chapter 12

Nathan's parable (12:1–6)

1. the Lord sent Nathan unto David – The use of parables is a favourite style of speaking among Oriental people, especially in the conveyance of unwelcome truth. This exquisitely pathetic parable was founded on a common custom of pastoral people who have pet lambs, which they bring up with their children, and which they address in terms of endearment. The atrocity of the real, however, far exceeded that of the fictitious offense.

5. the man that hath done this thing shall surely die – This punishment was more severe than the case deserved, or than was warranted by the divine statute. The sympathies of the king had been deeply enlisted, his indignation aroused, but his conscience was still asleep; and at the time when he was most fatally indulgent to his own sins, he was most ready to condemn the delinquencies and errors of others.

Nathan applies it to David (12:7–23)

7. Nathan said to David, Thou art the man – These awful words pierced his heart, aroused his conscience, and brought him to his knees. He was pardoned, so far as related to the restoration of the divine favour. But as from his high character for piety, and his eminent rank in society, his deplorable fall was calculated to do great injury to the cause of religion, it was necessary that God should testify His abhorrence of sin by leaving even His own servant to reap the bitter temporal fruits.

8. I gave thee thy master's house, and thy master's wives – The phraseology means nothing more than that God in His providence had given David, as king of Israel, everything that was Saul's. The history furnishes conclusive evidence that he never actually married any of the wives of Saul. But the harem of the preceding king belongs, according to Oriental notions, as a part of the regalia to his successor.

15-23. the Lord struck the child … and it was very sick – The first visible chastisement inflicted on David appeared on the person of that child which was the evidence and monument of his guilt.

Solomon is born (12:24, 25)

24, 25. Bath-sheba … bare a son, and he called his name Solomon – that is, 'peaceable.' But Nathan gave him the name of Jedediah, by command of God, or perhaps only as an expression of God's love. This love and the noble gifts with which he was endowed, considering the criminality of the marriage from which he sprang, is a remarkable instance of divine goodness and grace.

Rabbah is taken (12:26–31)

26. Joab fought against Rabbah – The time during which this siege lasted, since the intercourse with Bath-sheba, and the birth of at least one child, if not two, occurred during the progress of it, probably extended over two years.

28. encamp against the city, and take it – It has always been characteristic of Oriental despots to monopolize military honours; and as the ancient world knew nothing of the modern refinement of kings gaining victories by their generals, so Joab sent for David to command the final assault in person. A large force was levied for the purpose. David without much difficulty captured the royal city and obtained possession of its immense wealth.

30. he took their king's crown from off his head – While the treasures of the city were given as plunder to his soldiers, David reserved to himself the crown, which was of rarest value. Its great weight makes it probable that it was like many ancient crowns, not worn, but suspended over the head, or fixed on a canopy on the top of the throne.

the precious stones – *Hebrew*, 'stone'; was a round ball composed of pearls and other jewels, which was in the crown, and probably taken out of it to be inserted in David's own crown.

Chapter 13

Amnon loves Tamar (13:1–5)

1. Tamar – daughter of David by Maachah.

2. for she was a virgin – Unmarried daughters were kept in close seclusion from the company of men; no strangers, nor even their relatives of the other sex, being permitted to see them without the presence of witnesses. Of course, Amnon must have seen Tamar, for he had conceived a violent passion for her. But he had no means of making it known to her, and the pain of that disappointment preying upon his mind produced a visible change in his appearance and health.

3. Jonadab, the son of Shimeah – or Shammah. By the counsel and contrivance of this scheming cousin a plan was devised for obtaining an unrestricted interview with the object of his attachment.

Amnon defiles Tamar (13:6–7)

6–8. Amnon lay down, and made himself sick – The Orientals are great adepts in feigning sickness, whenever they have any object to accomplish.

let Tamar my sister come and make me a couple of cakes – To the king Amnon spoke of Tamar as 'his sister,' a term artfully designed to hoodwink his father; and the request appeared so natural, the delicate appetite of a sick man requiring to be humoured, that the king promised to send her. The cakes seem to have been a kind of fancy bread, in the preparation of which Oriental ladies take great delight. Tamar, flattered by the invitation, lost no time in rendering the required service in the house of her sick brother.

12–14. do not force me – The remonstrances and arguments of Tamar were so affecting and so strong, that had not Amnon been violently goaded on by the lustful passion of which he had become the slave, they must have prevailed with him to desist from his infamous purpose. In bidding him, however, 'speak to the king, for he will not withhold me from thee,' it is probable that she urged this as her last resource, saying anything she thought would please him, in order to escape for the present out of his hands.

15. Then Amnon hated her exceedingly – It is not unusual for persons instigated by violent and irregular passions to go from one extreme to another. In Amnon's case the sudden revulsion is easily accounted for; the atrocity of his

conduct, with all the feelings of shame, remorse, and dread of exposure and punishment, now burst upon his mind, rendering the presence of Tamar intolerably painful to him.

20. So Tamar remained desolate in her brother Absalom's house – He was her natural protector, and the children of polygamists lived by themselves, as if they constituted different families.

Ammon is slain (13:28–36)

28. Absalom had commanded his servants, saying … when Amnon's heart is merry with wine … kill him, fear not – On a preconcerted signal from their master, the servants, rushing upon Amnon, slew him at the table, while the rest of the brothers, horror-struck, and apprehending a general massacre, fled in affrighted haste to Jerusalem.

30, 31. tidings came to David, saying, Absalom hath slain all the king's sons – It was natural that in the consternation and tumult caused by so atrocious a deed, an exaggerated report should reach the court, which was at once plunged into the depths of grief and despair. But the information of Jonadab, who seems to have been aware of the plan, and the arrival of the other princes, made known the real extent of the catastrophe.

Absalom flees to Talmai (13:37–39)

37. Absalom fled, and went to Talmai – The law as to premeditated murder gave him no hope of remaining with impunity in his own country. The cities of refuge could afford him no sanctuary, and he was compelled to leave the kingdom, taking refuge at the court of Geshur, with his maternal grandfather, who would, doubtless, approve of his conduct.

Chapter 14

Joab instructs a woman of Tekoah (14:1–21)

2-21. And Joab sent to Tekoah, and fetched thence a wise woman – The king was strongly attached to Absalom; and having now got over his sorrow for the violent death of Amnon, he was desirous of again enjoying the society of his favourite son, who had now been three long years absent. But a dread of public opinion and a regard to the public interests made him hesitate about recalling or pardoning his guilty son; and Joab, whose discerning mind perceived this struggle between parental affection and royal duty, devised a plan for relieving the scruples, and, at the same time, gratifying the wishes, of his master. Having procured a countrywoman of superior intelligence and address, he directed her to seek an audience of the king, and by soliciting his royal interposition in the settlement of a domestic grievance, convinced him that the life of a murderer might in some cases be saved. Tekoah was about twelve miles south of Jerusalem, and six south of Beth-lehem; and the design of bringing a woman from such a distance was to prevent either the petitioner being known, or the truth of her story easily investigated. Her speech was in the form of a parable – the circumstances – the language – the manner – well suited to the occasion, represented a case as like David's as it was policy to make it, so as not to be prematurely discovered. Having got the king pledged, she avowed it to be her design to satisfy the royal conscience, that in pardoning Absalom he was doing nothing more than he would have done in the case of a stranger, where there could be no imputation of partiality. The device succeeded; David traced its origin to Joab; and, secretly pleased at obtaining the judgment of that rough, but generally sound-thinking soldier, he commissioned him to repair to Geshur and bring home his exiled son.

Joab brings Absalom to Jerusalem (14:22–33)

22. To-day thy servant knoweth that I have found grace in thy sight – Joab betrayed not a little selfishness amid his professions of joy at this act of grace to Absalom, and flattered himself that he now brought both father and son under lasting obligations. In considering this act of David, many extenuating circumstances may be urged in favour of it; the provocation given to Absalom; his being now in a country where justice could not overtake him; the risk of his imbibing a love for heathen principles and worship; the safety and interests of the Hebrew kingdom; together with the strong predilection of the Hebrew people for Absalom, as represented by the stratagem of Joab – these considerations form a plausible apology for David's grant of pardon to his bloodstained son.

28. So Absalom dwelt two full years in Jerusalem, and saw not the king's face – Whatever error David committed in authorizing the recall of Absalom, he displayed great prudence and command over his feelings afterwards – for his son was not admitted into his father's presence but was confined to his own house and the society of his own family. This slight severity was designed to bring him to sincere repentance, on perceiving that his father had not fully pardoned him, as well as to convince the people of David 's abhorrence of his crime. Not being allowed to appear at court, or to adopt any state, the courtiers kept aloof; even his cousin did not deem it prudent to go into his society. For two full years his liberty was more restricted, and his life more apart from his countrymen while living in Jerusalem, than in Geshur; and he might have continued in this

disgrace longer, had he not, by a violent expedient, determined to force his case on the attention of Joab, through whose kind and powerful influence a full reconciliation was effected between him and his father.

Chapter 15

Absalom steals the hearts of Israel (15:1–9)

1. Absalom prepared him chariots and horses, and fifty men to run before him – This was assuming the state and equipage of a prince. The royal guards, called runners, avant couriers, amounted to fifty. The chariot, as the Hebrew indicates, was of a magnificent style; and the horses, a novelty among the Hebrew people, only introduced in that age as an appendage of royalty, formed a splendid retinue, which would make him 'the observed of all observers.'

2–6. Absalom rose up early, and stood beside the way of the gate – Public business in the East is always transacted early in the morning – the kings sitting an hour or more to hear causes or receive petitions, in a court held anciently, and in many places still, in the open air at the city gateway; so that, as those whose circumstances led them to wait on King David required to be in attendance on his morning levees, Absalom had to rise up early and stand beside the way of the gate. Through the growing infirmities of age, or the occupation of his government with foreign wars, many private causes had long lain undecided, and a deep feeling of discontent prevailed among the people. This dissatisfaction was artfully fomented by Absalom, who addressed himself to the various suitors; and after briefly hearing their tale, he gratified everyone with a favourable opinion of his case. Studiously concealing his ambitious designs, he expressed a wish to be invested with official power, only that he might accelerate the course of justice and advance the public interests. His professions had an air of extraordinary generosity and disinterestedness, which, together with his fawning arts in lavishing civilities on all, made him a popular favourite. Thus, by forcing a contrast between his own display of public spirit and the dilatory proceedings of the court, he created a growing disgust with his father's government, as weak, careless, or corrupt, and seduced the affections of the multitude, who neither penetrated the motive nor foresaw the tendency of his conduct.

Absalom forms a conspiracy (15:10–12)

10. Absalom sent spies throughout all the tribes of Israel – These emissaries were to sound the inclination of the people, to further interests of Absalom, and exhort all the adherents of his party to be in readiness to join his standard as soon as they should hear that he had been proclaimed king. As the summons was to be made by the sound of trumpets, it is probable that care had been taken to have trumpeters stationed on the heights, and at convenient stations – a mode of announcement that would soon spread the news over all the country of his inauguration to the throne.

12. Absalom sent for Ahithophel – who he knew was ready to join the revolt, through disgust and revenge, as Jewish writers assert, at David's conduct towards Bath-sheba, who was his granddaughter.

the conspiracy was strong – The rapid accession of one place after another in all parts of the kingdom to the party of the insurgents, shows that deep and general dissatisfaction existed at this time against the person and government of David. The remnant of Saul's partisans, the unhappy affair of Bath-sheba, the overbearing insolence and crimes of Joab, negligence and obstruction in the administration of justice – these were some of the principal causes that contributed to the success of this widespread insurrection.

David flees from Jerusalem (15:13–37)

14. David said … Arise, and let us flee – David, anxious for the preservation of the city which he had beautified, and hopeful of a greater support throughout the country, wisely resolved on leaving Jerusalem.

30. David went up by the ascent of mount Olivet – The same pathway over that mount has been followed ever since that memorable day.

had his head covered – with a mourning wrapper. The humility and resignation of David marked strongly his sanctified spirit, induced by contrition for his transgressions. He had fallen, but it was the fall of the upright; and he rose again, submitting himself meekly in the meantime to the will of God.

32. when David was come to the top of the mount, where he worshipped – looking towards Jerusalem, where were the ark and tabernacle.

Chapter 16

Ziba claims his master's inheritance (16:1–4)

1. Ziba the servant of Mephibosheth met him – This crafty man, anticipating the certain failure of Absalom's conspiracy, took steps to prepare for his future advancement on the restoration of the king.

3. To-day shall the house of Israel restore me the kingdom of my father – Such a hope might not unnaturally arise at this period of civil distraction, that the family of David would destroy themselves by their mutual broils, and the people reinstate the old dynasty. There was an air of plausibility in Ziba's story. Many, on whom the

king had conferred favours, were now deserting him. No wonder, therefore, that in the excitement of momentary feeling, believing, on the report of a slanderer, Mephibosheth to be among the number, he pronounced a rash and unrighteous judgment by which a great injury was inflicted on the character and interests of a devoted friend.

Shemei curses David (15:5–19)

13. threw stones at him – as a mark of contempt and insult.

cast dust – As if to add insult to injury, clouds of dust were thrown by this disloyal subject in the path of his unfortunate sovereign.

14. refreshed themselves there – that is, in the city of Bahurim.

15–19. Hushai said unto Absalom, God save the king – Hushai's devotion to David was so well-known, that his presence in the camp of the conspirators excited great surprise. Professing, however, with great address, to consider it his duty to support the cause which the course of Providence and the national will had seemingly decreed should triumph, and urging his friendship for the father as a ground of confidence in his fidelity to the son, he persuaded Absalom of his sincerity, and was admitted among the councillors of the new king.

Ahithophel's counsel (16:20–23)

20. Give counsel among you what we shall do – This is the first cabinet council on record, although the deference paid to Ahithophel gave him the entire direction of the proceedings.

21. Ahithophel said unto Absalom – This councillor saw that now the die was cast; half measures would be inexpedient. To cut off all possibility of reconciliation between the king and his rebellious son, he gave this atrocious advice regarding the treatment of the royal women who had been left in charge of the palace. Women, being held sacred, are generally left inviolate in the casualties of war. The history of the East affords only one parallel to this infamous outrage of Absalom.

Chapter 17

Ahithophel's counsel overthrown by Hushai (17:1–14)

1-11. Moreover Ahithophel said unto Absalom – The recommendation to take prompt and decisive measures before the royalist forces could be collected and arranged, evinced the deep political sagacity of this councillor. The adoption of his advice would have extinguished the cause of David; and it affords a dreadful proof of the extremities to which the heartless prince was, to secure his ambitious objects, prepared to go, that the counsel 'pleased Absalom well, and all the elders of Israel.' It was happily overruled, however, by the address of Hushai, who saw the imminent danger to which it would expose the king and the royal cause. He dwelt upon the warlike character and military experience of the old king – represented him and his adherents as mighty men, who would fight with desperation; and who, most probably, secure in some stronghold, would be beyond reach, while the smallest loss of Absalom's men at the outset might be fatal to the success of the conspiracy. But his dexterity was chiefly displayed in that part of his counsel which recommended a general levy throughout the country; and that Absalom should take command of it in person – thereby flattering at once the pride and ambition of the usurper. The bait was caught by the vainglorious and wicked prince.

14. The counsel of Hushai the Archite is better than the counsel of Ahithophel – The reasons specified being extremely plausible, and expressed in the strong hyperbolical language suited to dazzle an Oriental imagination, the council declared in favour of Hushai's advice; and their resolution was the immediate cause of the discomfiture of the rebellion, although the council itself was only a link in the chain of causation held by the controlling hand of the Lord.

Secret intelligence sent to David (17:15–22)

16. send quickly, and tell David – Apparently doubting that his advice would be followed, Hushai ordered secret intelligence to be conveyed to David of all that transpired, with an urgent recommendation to cross the Jordan without a moment's delay, lest Ahithophel's address and influence might produce a change on the prince's mind, and an immediate pursuit be determined on.

Ahithophel hangs himself (17:23–29)

23. when Ahithophel saw that his counsel was not followed – His vanity was wounded, his pride mortified on finding that his ascendency was gone; but that chagrin was aggravated by other feelings – a painful conviction that through the delay which had been resolved on, the cause of Absalom was lost. Hastening home, therefore, he arranged his private affairs, and knowing that the storm of retributive vengeance would fall chiefly upon him as the instigator and prop of the rebellion, he hanged himself. It may be remarked that the Israelites did not, at that time, refuse the rites of sepulture even to those who died by their own hands. He had an imitator in Judas, who resembled him in his treason, as well as in his infamous end.

27-29. when David was come to Mahanaim – The necessities of the king and his followers

were hospitably ministered to by three chiefs, whose generous loyalty is recorded with honour in the sacred narrative.

29. in the wilderness – spread out beyond the cultivated tablelands into the steppes of Hauran.

Chapter 18

David reviewing the armies (18:1–4)

1, 2. David numbered the people that were with him – The hardy mountaineers of Gilead came in great numbers at the call of their chieftains, so that, although without money to pay any troops, David soon found himself at the head of a considerable army. A pitched battle was now inevitable. But so much depending on the life of the king, he was not allowed to take the field in person; and he therefore divided his forces into three detachments under Joab, Abishai, and Ittai, the commander of the foreign guards.

David gives them charge of Absalom (18:5–13)

5. Deal gently for my sake with the young man, even with Absalom – This affecting charge, which the king gave to his generals, proceeded not only from his overwhelming affection for his children, but from his consciousness that this rebellion was the chastisement of his own crimes, Absalom being merely an instrument in the hand of retributive Providence; – and also from his piety, lest the unhappy prince should die with his sins unrepented of.

8. the wood devoured more people than the sword – The thick forest of oaks and terebinths, by obstructing the flight, greatly aided the victors in the pursuit.

9. Absalom met the servants of David – or was overtaken. 'It is necessary to be continually on one's guard against the branches of trees; and when the hair is worn in large locks floating down the back, as was the case with a young man of the party to which I belonged, any thick boughs interposing in the path might easily dislodge a rider from his seat, and catch hold of his flowing hair' [HARTLEY]. Some, however, think that the sacred historian points not so much to the hair, as to the *head* of Absalom, which, being caught while running between two branches, was enclosed so firmly that he could not disengage himself from the hold, nor make use of his hands.

11, 12. Joab said unto the man that told him, … I would have given thee ten shekels of silver, and a girdle – that is, would have raised him from the ranks to the status of a commissioned officer. Besides a sum of money, a girdle, curiously and richly wrought, was among the ancient Hebrews a mark of honour, and sometimes bestowed as a reward of military merit. This soldier, however, who may be taken as a fair sample of David's faithful subjects, had so great a respect for the king's wishes, that no prospect of reward would have tempted him to lay violent hands on Absalom.

Absalom is slain by Joab (18:14–32)

14. he took three darts … and thrust them through the heart of Absalom – The deed, partially done by Joab, was completed by his bodyguard. Being a violation of the expressed wish, as well as of all the fond paternal feelings of David, it must have been deeply offensive to the king, nor was it ever forgotten, and yet there is the strongest reason for believing that Joab, in doing it, was actuated by a sincere regard to the interests of David, both as a man and a monarch.

18. Absalom in his lifetime had reared up for himself a pillar – literally, 'hand.' In the valley of Jehoshaphat, on the east of Jerusalem, is a tomb or cenotaph, said to be this 'pillar' or monument: it is twenty-four feet square, dome-topped, and reaches forty feet in height. This may occupy the spot, but cannot itself be the work of Absalom, as it evidently bears the style of a later architecture.

24–32. David sat between the two gates – that is, in the tower-house on the wall that overhung the gate of Mahanaim. Near it was a watch-tower, on which a sentinel was posted, as in times of war, to notify every occurrence. The delicacy of Ahimaaz' communication was made up by the unmistakable plainness of Cushi's. The death of Absalom was a heavy trial, and it is impossible not to sympathize with the outburst of feeling by which David showed that all thoughts of the victory he had won as a king were completely sunk in the painful loss he had sustained as a father. The extraordinary ardour and strength of his affection for this worthless son break out in the redundancy and vehemence of his mournful ejaculations.

Chapter 19

Joab causes the king to cease mourning (19:1–8)

3. the people gat them by stealth … to the city – The rumour of the king's disconsolate condition spread a universal and unseasonable gloom. His troops, instead of being welcomed back (as a victorious army always was) with music and other demonstrations of public joy, slunk secretly and silently into the city, as if ashamed after the commission of some crime.

4. the king covered his face – one of the usual signs of mourning.

5. Thou hast shamed … the faces of all thy servants – by withdrawing thyself to indulge in grief, as if their services were disagreeable and their devotion irksome to thee. Instead of hailing their return with joy and gratitude, thou

hast refused them the small gratification of seeing thee. Joab's remonstrance was right and necessary, but it was made with harshness. He was one of those persons who spoil their important services by the insolence of their manners, and who always awaken a feeling of obligation in those to whom they render any services. He spoke to David in a tone of hauteur that ill became a subject to show towards his king.

7. Now … arise, go forth, and speak comfortably unto thy servants – The king felt the truth of Joab's reprimand; but the threat by which it was enforced, grounded as it was on the general's unbounded popularity with the army, showed him to be a dangerous person; and that circumstance, together with the violation of an express order to deal gently for his sake with Absalom, produced in David's mind a settled hatred, which was strongly manifested in his last directions to Solomon.

The Israelites bring the king back (19:9–43)

9–11. all the people were at strife throughout all the tribes of Israel – The kingdom was completely disorganized. The sentiments of three different parties are represented in the royalists, the adherents of Absalom who had been very numerous, and those who were indifferent to the Davidic dynasty. In these circumstances the king was right in not hastening back, as a conqueror, to reascend his throne. A re-election was, in some measure, necessary. He remained for some time on the other side of Jordan, in expectation of being invited back. That invitation was given without, however, the concurrence of Judah. David, disappointed and vexed by his own tribe's apparent lukewarmness, despatched the two high priests to rouse the Judahites to take a prominent interest in his cause. It was the act of a skilful politician. Hebron having been the seat of the rebellion, it was graceful on his part to encourage their return to allegiance and duty; it was an appeal to their honour not to be the last of the tribes. But this separate message, and the preference given to them, occasioned an outburst of jealousy among the other tribes that was nearly followed by fatal consequences.

24–30. Mephibosheth … came down to meet the king – The reception given to Mephibosheth was less creditable to David. The sincerity of that prince's grief for the misfortunes of the king cannot be doubted.

He had neither dressed his feet – not taken the bath,

nor trimmed his beard – The Hebrews cut off the hair on the upper lip and cheeks, but carefully cherished it on the chin from ear to ear. Besides dyeing it black or red colours, which, however, is the exception, and not the rule in the East, there are various modes of trimming it: they train it into a massy bushy form, swelling and round; or they terminate it like a pyramid, in a sharp point. Whatever the mode, it is always trimmed with the greatest care; and they usually carry a small comb for the purpose. The neglect of this attention to his beard was an undoubted proof of the depth of Mephibosheth's grief. The king seems to have received him upbraidingly, and not to have been altogether sure either of his guilt or innocence. It is impossible to commend the cavalier treatment, any more than to approve the partial award, of David in this case. If he were too hurried and distracted by the pressure of circumstances to inquire fully into the matter, he should have postponed his decision; for if by 'dividing the land' he meant that the former arrangement should be continued by which Mephibosheth was acknowledged the proprietor, and Ziba the farmer, it was a hardship inflicted on the owner to fix him with a tenant who had so grossly slandered him. But if by 'dividing the land,' they were now to share alike, the injustice of the decision was greatly increased. In any view, the generous, disinterested spirit displayed by Mephibosheth was worthy a son of the noble-hearted Jonathan.

40–43. the king went on to Gilgal, … and all the people of Judah conducted the king, and also half the people of Israel – Whether from impatience to move on or from some other cause, David did not wait till all the tribes had arrived to conduct him on his return to the capital. The procession began as soon as Amasa had brought the Judahite escort, and the preference given to this tribe produced a bitter jealousy, which was nearly kindling a civil war fiercer than that which had just ended. A war of words ensued between the tribes – Israel resting their argument on their superior numbers; 'they had ten parts in the king,' whereas Judah had no more than one. Judah grounded their right to take the lead, on the ground of their nearer relationship to the king. This was a claim dangerous to the house of David; and it shows the seeds were already sown for that tribal dissension which, before long, led to the dismemberment of the kingdom.

Chapter 20

Sheba makes a party in Israel (20:1–9)

1. Sheba … a Benjamite – Though nothing is known of this man, he must have been a person of considerable power and influence, before he could have raised so sudden and extensive a sedition. He belonged to the tribe of Benjamin, where the adherents of Saul's dynasty were still numerous; and perceiving the strong disgust of the other tribes with the part assumed by Judah in the restoration, his ill-designing heart

resolved to turn it to the overthrow of David's authority in Israel.

4. Then said the king to Amasa, Assemble me the men of Judah within three days – Amasa is now installed in the command which David had promised him. The revolt of the ten tribes, probably, hastened the public declaration of this appointment, which he hoped would be popular with them, and Amasa was ordered within three days to levy a force from Judah sufficient to put down the insurrection. The appointment was a blunder, and the king soon perceived his error. The specified time passed, but Amasa could not muster the men. Dreading the loss of time, the king gave the commission to Abishai, and not to Joab – a new affront, which, no doubt, wounded the pride of the stern and haughty old general. But he hastened with his attached soldiers to go as second to his brother, determined to take the first opportunity of wreaking his vengeance on his successful rival.

Amasa is slain (20:10–13)

10. smote him … in the fifth rib – the seat of the liver and bowels, where wounds are mortal. **struck him not again** – that is, despatched him at the first blow.

11–13. He that favoureth Joab, and he that is for David, let him go after Joab – It is a striking proof of Joab's unrivalled influence over the army, that with this villainous murder perpetrated before their eyes they unanimously followed him as their leader in pursuit of Sheba. A soldier conjoined his name with David's, and such a magic spell was in the word 'Joab,' that all the people 'went on' – Amasa's men as well as the rest. The conjunction of these two names is very significant. It shows that the one could not afford to do without the other – neither Joab to rebel against David, nor David to get rid of Joab, though hating him.

Joab pursues Sheba to Abel (20:1–15)

14. he went through all the tribes of Israel unto Abel – beating up for recruits. But there the prompt marches of Joab overtook and hemmed him in by a close siege of the place.

A wise woman saves the city by Sheba's head (20:16–22)

16. Then cried a wise woman – The appeal of this woman, who, like Deborah, was probably a judge or governess of the place, was a strong one. **18-20. They were wont to speak in old time** – The translation of the *Margin* gives a better meaning, which is to this effect: When the people saw thee lay siege to Abel, they said, Surely he will ask if we will have peace, for the law prescribes that he should offer peace to strangers, much more then to Israeli cities; and if he do this, we shall soon bring things to an amicable agreement, for we are a peaceable people. The answer of Joab brings out the character of that ruthless veteran as a patriot at heart, who, on securing the author of this insurrection, was ready to put a stop to further bloodshed and release the peaceable inhabitants from all molestation.

David's great officers (20:23–26)

23. **Now Joab was over all the host of Israel** – David, whatever his private wishes, found that he possessed not the power of removing Joab; so winking at the murder of Amasa, he re-established that officer in his former post of commander-in-chief. The enumeration of David's cabinet is here given to show that the government was re-established in its wonted course.

Chapter 21

The three years' famine for the Gibeonites (21:1–9)

1. **the Lord answered, It is for Saul, and for his bloody house, because he slew the Gibeonites** – The sacred history has not recorded either the time or the reason of this massacre. Some think that they were sufferers in the atrocity perpetrated by Saul at Nob, where many of them may have resided as attendants of the priests; while others suppose it more probable that the attempt was made afterwards, with a view to regain the popularity he had lost throughout the nation by that execrable outrage.

6. **Let seven men of his sons be delivered unto us, and we will hang them up unto the Lord in Gibeah of Saul** – The practice of the Hebrews, as of most Oriental nations, was to slay first, and afterwards to suspend on a gibbet, the body not being left hanging after sunset. The king could not refuse this demand of the Gibeonites, who, in making it, were only exercising their right as blood-avengers; and, although through fear and a sense of weakness they had not hitherto claimed satisfaction, yet now that David had been apprised by the oracle of the cause of the long-prevailing calamity, he felt it his duty to give the Gibeonites full satisfaction – hence their specifying the number seven, which was reckoned full and complete. And if it should seem unjust to make the descendants suffer for a crime which, in all probability, originated with Saul himself, yet his sons and grandsons might be the instruments of his cruelty, the willing and zealous executors of this bloody *raid*.

the king said, I will give them – David cannot be charged with doing this as an indirect way or ridding himself of rival competitors for the throne, for those delivered up were only collateral branches of Saul's family, and never set up any claim to the sovereignty. Moreover, David was only granting the request of the Gibeonites as God had bidden him do.

9. **they hanged them in the hill before the Lord** – Deeming themselves not bound by the criminal law of Israel, their intention was to let the bodies hang until God, propitiated by this offering, should send rain upon the land, for the want of it had occasioned the famine. It was a heathen practice to gibbet men with a view of appeasing the anger of the gods in seasons of famine, and the Gibeonites, who were a remnant of the Amorites, though brought to the knowledge of the true God, were not, it seems, free from this superstition. God, in His providence, suffered the Gibeonites to ask and inflict so barbarous a retaliation, in order that the oppressed Gibeonites might obtain justice and some reparation of their wrongs, especially that the scandal brought on the name of the true religion by the violation of a solemn national compact might be wiped away from Israel, and that a memorable lesson should be given to respect treaties and oaths.

Rizpah's kindness unto the dead (21:10–11)

10. **Rizpah … took sackcloth, and spread it for her upon the rock** – She erected a tent near the spot, in which she and her servants kept watch, as the relatives of executed persons were wont to do, day and night, to scare the birds and beasts of prey away from the remains exposed on the low-standing gibbets.

David buries the bones of Saul and Jonathan in their father's sepulchre (21:12–22)

12. **David went and took the bones of Saul and the bones of Jonathan his son** – Before long, the descent of copious showers, or perhaps an order of the king, gave Rizpah the satisfaction of releasing the corpses from their ignominious exposure; and, incited by her pious example, David ordered the remains of Saul and his sons to be transferred from their obscure grave in Jabesh-gilead to an honourable interment in the family vault at Zelah or Zelzah, now Beit-jala.

Chapter 22

David's psalm of thanksgiving for God's deliverance (22:1–55)

The song contained in this chapter is the same as the eighteenth Psalm. This inspired ode was manifestly the effusion of a mind glowing with the highest fervour of piety and gratitude, and it is full of the noblest imagery that is to be found within the range even of sacred poetry. It is David's grand tribute of thanksgiving for deliverance from his numerous and powerful enemies, and establishing him in the power and glory of the kingdom.

Chapter 23

David professes his faith in God's promises (23:1–7)

1. Now these be the last words of David – Various opinions are entertained as to the precise meaning of this statement, which, it is obvious, proceeded from the compiler or collector of the sacred canon. Some think that, as there is no division of chapters in the Hebrew Scriptures, this introduction was intended to show that what follows is no part of the king's poetical compositions; while still others consider it the last of his utterances as an inspired writer.

raised up on high – from an obscure family and condition to a throne.

the anointed of the God of Jacob – chosen to be king by the special appointment of that God, to whom, by virtue of an ancient covenant, the people of Israel owed all their peculiar destiny and distinguished privileges.

the sweet psalmist of Israel – that is, delightful, highly esteemed.

2. The Spirit of the Lord spake by me – Nothing can more clearly show that all that is excellent in spirit, beautiful in language, or grand in prophetic imagery, which the Psalms of David contain, were owing, not to his superiority in natural talents or acquired knowledge, but to the suggestion and dictates of God's Spirit.

3. the Rock of Israel – This metaphor, which is commonly applied by the sacred writers to the Almighty, was very expressive to the minds of the Hebrew people. Their national fortresses, in which they sought security in war, were built on high and inaccessible rocks.

6. But the sons of Belial shall be all of them as thorns – that is, the wicked enemies and persecutors of this kingdom of righteousness. They resemble those prickly, thorny plants which are twisted together, whose spires point in every direction, and which are so sharp and strong that they cannot be touched or approached without danger; but hard instruments and violent means must be taken to destroy or uproot them. So God will remove or destroy all who are opposed to this kingdom.

A catalogue of David's mighty men (23:8–39)

19–39. the first three – The mighty men or champions in David's military staff were divided into three classes – the highest, Jashobeam, Eleazar, and Shammah; the second class, Abishai, Benaiah, and Asahel; and the third class, the thirty, of which Asahel was the chief. There are thirty-one mentioned in the list, including Asahel; and these added to the two superior orders make thirty-seven.

Chapter 24

David numbers the people (24:1–9)

1–4. again the anger of the Lord was kindled against Israel, and he moved David against them to say, Go, number Israel and Judah – God, though He cannot tempt any man is frequently described in Scripture as doing what He merely permits to be done; and so, in this case, He permitted Satan to tempt David. Satan was the active mover, while God only withdrew His supporting grace, and the great tempter prevailed against the king. The order was given to Joab, who, though not generally restrained by religious scruples, did not fail to present, in strong terms, the sin and danger of this measure. He used every argument to dissuade the king from his purpose. The sacred history has not mentioned the objections which he and other distinguished officers urged against it in the council of David. But it expressly states that they were all overruled by the inflexible resolution of the king.

David repents and chooses three days' pestilence (24:10–14)

10–13. David's heart smote him after that he had numbered the people. And David said unto the Lord, I have sinned – The act of numbering the people was not in itself sinful; for Moses did it by the express authority of God. But David acted not only independently of such order of sanction, but from motives unworthy of the delegated king of Israel; from pride and vainglory; from self-confidence and distrust of God; and, above all, from ambitious designs of conquest, in furtherance of which he was determined to force the people into military service, and to ascertain whether he could muster an army sufficient for the magnitude of the enterprises he contemplated. It was a breach of the constitution, an infringement of the liberties of the people, and opposed to that divine policy which required that Israel should continue a separate people. His eyes were not opened to the heinousness of his sin till God had spoken unto him by His commissioned prophet.

13. Shall seven years of famine come unto thee – that is, in addition to the three that had been already, with the current year included.

14. David said, ... Let us fall now into the hand of the Lord – His overwhelming sense of his sin led him to acquiesce in the punishment denounced, notwithstanding its apparent excess of severity. He proceeded on a good principle in choosing the pestilence. In pestilence he was equally exposed, as it was just and right he should be, to danger as his people, whereas, in war and famine, he possessed means of protection superior to them. Besides, he thereby showed his trust, founded on long experience, in the divine goodness.

David's intercession to God (24:15–25)

16. the Lord repented him of the evil – God is often described in Scripture as repenting when He ceased to pursue a course He had begun.

17. David . . . said – or, 'had said,' **I have sinned … but these sheep, what have they done?** – The guilt of numbering the people lay exclusively with David. But in the body politic as well as natural, when the head suffers, all the members suffer along with it; and, besides, although David's sin was the immediate cause, the great increase of national offenses at this time had kindled the anger of the Lord.

21. to build an altar unto the Lord, that the plague may be stayed – It is evident that the plague was not stayed till after the altar was built, and the sacrifice offered, so that what is related was by anticipation. Previous to the offering of this sacrifice, he had seen the destroying angel as well as offered the intercessory prayer. This was a sacrifice of expiation; and the reason why he was allowed to offer it on Mount Moriah was partly in gracious consideration to his fear of repairing to Gibeon, and partly in anticipation of the removal of the tabernacle and the erection of the temple there.

25. David offered burnt offerings and peace offerings – There seem to have been two sacrifices; the first expiatory, the second a thanksgiving for the cessation of the pestilence.

1 KINGS

Robert Jamieson

Introduction

The first and second books of Kings, in the ancient copies of the Hebrew Bible, constitute one book. Various titles have been given them; in the Septuagint and the Vulgate they are called the Third and Fourth Books of Kings. The authorship of these books is unknown; but the prevailing opinion is that they were compiled by Ezra, or one of the later prophets, from the ancient documents that are so frequently referred to in the course of the history as of public and established authority. Their inspired character was acknowledged by the Jewish Church, which ranked them in the sacred canon; and, besides, it is attested by our Lord, who frequently quotes from them (compare 1Ki 17:9 2Ki 5:14 with Lu 4:24–27; 1Ki 10:1 with Mt 12:42).

Chapter 1

1Ki 1:1–4. Abishag cherishes David in his old age.

1, 2. Now king David was old – He was in the seventieth year of his age. But the wear and tear of a military life, bodily fatigue, and mental care, had prematurely, if we may say it, exhausted the energies of David's strong constitution.

3. a Shunammite – Shunem, in the tribe of Issachar (Jos 19:18), lay on an eminence in the plain of Esdraelon, five miles south of Tabor. It is now called Sulam.

1Ki 1:5–31. Adonijah usurps the kingdom

5, 6. Then Adonijah the son of Haggith exalted himself – Nothing is said as to the origin or rank of Haggith, so that it is probable she was not distinguished by family descent. Adonijah, though David's fourth son (2Sa 3:4 1Ch 3:2), was now the oldest alive; and his personal attractions and manners (1Sa 9:2) not only recommended him to the leading men about court, but made him the favourite of his father, who, though seeing him assume an equipage becoming only the heir-presumptive to the throne (2Sa 15:1), said nothing; and his silence was considered by many, as well as by Adonijah, to be equivalent to an expression of consent. The sinking health of the king prompted him to take a decisive step in furtherance of his ambitious designs.

7. he conferred with Joab – The anxiety of Adonijah to secure the influence of a leader so bold, enterprising, and popular with the army was natural, and the accession of the hoary commander is easily accounted for from his recent grudge at the king (see on 2Sa 19:13).

and with Abiathar the priest – His influence was as great over the priests and Levites – a powerful body in the kingdom – as that of Joab over the troops. It might be that both of them thought the crown belonged to Adonijah by right of primogeniture, from his mature age and the general expectations of the people (1Ki 2:15).

8. But Zadok the priest – He had been high priest in the tabernacle at Gibeon under Saul (1Ch 16:39). David, on his accession, had conjoined him and Abiathar equal in the exercise of their high functions (2Sa 8:17 15:24,29,35). But it is extremely probable that some cause of jealousy or discord between them had arisen, and hence each lent his countenance and support to opposite parties.

Benaiah – Distinguished for his bravery (1Sa 23:20), he had been appointed captain of the king's bodyguard (2Sa 8:18 20:23 1Ch 18:17), and was regarded by Joab as a rival.

Nathan the prophet – He was held in high estimation by David, and stood on the most intimate relations with the royal family (2Sa 12:25).

Shimei – probably the person of this name who was afterwards enrolled among Solomon's great officers (1Ki 4:18).

Rei – supposed to be the same as Ira (2Sa 20:26).

and the mighty men – the select band of worthies.

9, 10. En-rogel – situated (Jos 15:7–10) east of Jerusalem, in a level place, just below the junction of the valley of Hinnom with that of Jehoshaphat. It is a very deep well, measuring one hundred twenty-five feet in depth; the water is sweet, but not very cold, and it is at times quite full to overflowing. The Orientals are fond of enjoying festive repasts in the open air at places which command the advantage of shade, water, and verdure; and those *fetes champetres* are not cold collations, but magnificent entertainments, the animals being killed and dressed on the spot. Adonijah's feast at En-rogel was one of this Oriental description, and it was on a large scale (2Sa 3:4,5 5:14–16 1Ch 14:1–7). At the accession of a new king there were sacrifices offered (1Sa 11:15). But on such an occasion it was no less customary to entertain the grandees of the kingdom and even the populace in a public manner (1Ch 12:23–40). There is the strongest probability that Adonijah's feast was purely political, to court popularity and secure a party to support his claim to the crown.

11–27. Nathan spake unto Bath-sheba … let me … give thee counsel – The revolt was defeated by this prophet, who, knowing the Lord's will (2Sa 7:12 1Ch 22:9), felt himself bound, in accordance with his character and office, to take the lead in seeing it executed. Hitherto the succession of the Hebrew monarchy had not been settled. The Lord had reserved to Himself the right of nomination (De 17:15), which was acted upon in the appointments both of Saul and David; and in the case of the latter the rule was so far modified that his posterity were guaranteed the perpetual possession of the sovereignty (2Sa 7:12). This divine purpose was known throughout the kingdom; but no intimation had been made as to whether the right of inheritance was to belong to the oldest son. Adonijah, in common with the people generally, expected that this natural arrangement should be followed in the Hebrew kingdom as in all others. Nathan, who was aware of the old king's solemn promise to Solomon, and, moreover, that this promise was sanctioned by the divine will, saw that no time was to be lost. Fearing the effects of too sudden excitement in the king's

feeble state, he arranged that Bath-sheba should go first to inform him of what was being transacted without the walls, and that he himself should follow to confirm her statement. The narrative here not only exhibits the vivid picture of a scene within the interior of a palace, but gives the impression that a great deal of Oriental state ceremonial had been established in the Hebrew court.

20. the eyes of all Israel are upon thee, that thou shouldest tell them who shall sit on the throne – When the kings died without declaring their will, then their oldest son succeeded. But frequently they designated long before their death which of their sons should inherit the throne. The kings of Persia, as well as of other Eastern countries, have exercised the same right in modern and even recent times.

21. I and my son … shall be counted offenders – that is, slain, according to the barbarous usage of the East towards all who are rivals to the throne.

28–31. Then king David answered and said, Call me Bath-sheba – He renews to her the solemn pledge he had given, in terms of solemnity and impressiveness which show that the aged monarch had roused himself to the duty the emergency called for.

1Ki 1:32–49. Solomon, by David's appointment, is anointed king.

33. cause Solomon my son to ride upon mine own mule – Directions were forthwith given for the immediate coronation of Solomon. A procession was to be formed by the 'servants of their lord' – that is, the king's bodyguard. Mules were then used by all the princes (2Sa 13:29); but there was a state mule of which all subjects were forbidden, under pain of death, to make use, without special permission; so that its being granted to Solomon was a public declaration in his favour as the future king.

bring him down to Gihon – a pool or fountain on the west of Jerusalem (see on 2Ch 32:30), chosen as equally public for the counter proclamation.

34. anoint him – done only in the case of a new dynasty or disputed succession (see on 1Sa 16:13 and 2Sa 2:1).

35. Then ye shall come up after him, that he may come and sit upon my throne – The public recognition of the successor to the throne, during the old king's lifetime, is accordant with the customs of the East.

39. an horn of oil out of the tabernacle – It was the sacred oil (Ex 30:25) with which the kings were anointed.

40. all the people came up after him – that is, from the valley to the citadel of Zion.

41–49. Adonijah and all the guests that were with him heard it as they had made an end of eating – The loud shouts raised by the populace at the joyous proclamation at Gihon, and echoed by assembled thousands, from Zion to En-rogel, were easily heard at that distance by Adonijah and his confederates. The arrival of a trusty messenger, who gave a full detail of the coronation ceremony (1Ki 1:43–48), spread dismay in their camp. The wicked and ambitious plot they had assembled to execute was dissipated, and every one of the conspirators consulted his safety by flight.

1Ki 1:50–53. Adonijah, fleeing to the horns of the altar, is dismissed by Solomon

50–53. Adonijah ... went, and caught hold on the horns of the altar – most probably the altar of burnt offering which had been erected on Mount Zion, where Abiathar, one of his partisans, presided as high priest. The horns or projections at the four corners of the altar, to which the sacrifices were bound, and which were tipped with the blood of the victim, were symbols of grace and salvation to the sinner. Hence the altar was regarded as a sanctuary (Ex 21:14), but not to murderers, rebels, or deliberate perpetrators. Adonijah, having acted in opposition to the will of the reigning king, was guilty of rebellion, and stood self-condemned. Solomon spared his life on the express condition of his good behaviour – living in strict privacy, leading a quiet, peaceable life, and meddling with the affairs of neither the court nor the kingdom.

53. they brought him down from the altar – from the ledge around the altar on which he was standing.

he bowed himself – that is, did homage to Solomon as king.

Chapter 2

1Ki 2:1–11. David dies

1. David ... charged Solomon his son – The charge recorded here was given to Solomon just before his death and is different from the farewell address delivered in public some time before (1Ch 28:29). It is introduced with great solemnity.

2. I go the way of all the earth – a beautiful and impressive periphrasis for death.

be thou strong, ... show thyself a man – This counsel is similar to the apostolic direction (1Co 16:13) and refers to the fortitude or strength of mind that was required to discharge the onerous functions of king.

3. keep the charge of the Lord thy God – that is, the divine law in all its ceremonial as well as moral requirements. But particular reference was intended to its political institutions, as it was only by strictly maintaining the conduct that became the Hebrew monarch (De 17:10-20), that he would secure the blessing of peace and prosperity to his reign.

4. there shall not fail thee ... a man on the throne of Israel – a reference to the promise made to David of the sovereignty being vested perpetually in his lineage (2Sa 7:11–16), which was confirmed to Solomon afterwards (see 1Ki 9:5), and repeated with reference to its spiritual meaning long after (Jer 33:17).

5, 6. thou knowest also what Joab ... did – The insolent and imperious conduct of that general had not only been deeply offensive to the feelings (2Sa 18:5–15 19:5–7), but calculated to bring reproach on the character, to injure the prospects, and endanger the throne of David. Passing over the injuries committed directly against himself, David dwelt with strong feelings on the base assassination of Abner and Amasa.

shed the blood of war in peace, – The obvious meaning is, that in peace he acted towards them as if they had been in a state of warfare; but perhaps these graphic expressions might be designed to impress Solomon's mind more strongly with a sense of the malice, treachery, and cruelty by which those murders were characterized.

6. Do ... according to thy wisdom – Joab's immense popularity with the army required that any proceedings instituted against him should be taken with great prudence and deliberation.

8. thou hast with thee Shimei – Though David promised him a pardon, which being enforced by the presence of a thousand followers, could not have been well refused, he warned his son against Shimei as a turbulent and dangerous character. It must not be supposed that in these dying instructions David was evincing a fierce, vindictive spirit. He is rather to be considered as acting in the character of a king and magistrate, in noticing crimes which he had not been in a condition to punish, and pointing out persons of whom Solomon would be under a necessity to rid himself as dangerous to the state. The grateful mention of Barzillai's kindness [1Ki 2:7] was, however, a personal feeling that does honour to the warmth of his heart; and his silence as to Mephibosheth, the son of his beloved Jonathan, would imply the previous death of that prince.

9. for thou art a wise man – Solomon had given early indications of wisdom before his miraculous endowment with the heavenly gift (see 1Ki 3:11), and his own sagacity would dictate the course that should be followed in any new offense that Shimei might commit.

10. So David slept with his fathers – about six months after the coronation of Solomon (compare 2Sa 5:5, with 1Ch 29:27). The interval was spent in developing his ideas and plans for the future glory of the kingdom and providing for the permanent worship of God (see on 1Ch 22:1, and following). Sepulchres were not

allowed within the precincts of cities. Jerusalem, however, formed an exception; and yet, even there, the privilege was reserved chiefly for the royal family (Ac 2:29). Tradition says that the bones of David repose on Mount Zion, and the minaret of a small mosque points out the spot which tradition has fixed. His was a noble, a wondrous, and a humbling history. He was a good man, yet his life was deformed by various crimes of a very gross character. But there were many bright and noble traits in his character; he was an earnest lover of the divine law; his reign was signalized by many important services that contributed to the glory of God and the exaltation of His kingdom; and his name, as the sweet Psalmist of Israel, will be held in honour to the latest age of the Church.

1Ki 2:12–24. Solomon succeeds him

12. Then sat Solomon upon the throne of David his father – His ascension to the royal dignity was made under the happiest auspices. Having been born after his father became monarch of the *whole* kingdom, his claim, according to the notions of Oriental people, was preferable to that of all, *even* his elder brothers. The Hebrew kingdom enjoyed internal prosperity; it was respected and renowned abroad, and Solomon well knew how to improve these advantages.

13–18. Adonijah … came to Bath-sheba – Her question to him betrays an apprehension which his recent conduct might well warrant; but his pious acknowledgment of the divine will seemed apparently to indicate so entire an acquiescence in the settlement of the succession (1Ki 2:15), that, in her womanly simplicity, she perceived not the deep cunning and evil design that was concealed under his request and readily undertook to promote his wishes.

19, 20. Bath-sheba . . . went unto King Solomon – The filial reverence and the particular act of respect, which Solomon rendered, were quite in accordance with the sentiments and customs of the East. The right hand is the place of honour; and as it expressly said to have been assigned to 'the king's mother,' it is necessary to remark that, when a husband dies, his widow acquires a higher dignity and power, as a mother over her son, than she ever possessed before. Besides, the dignity of 'king's mother' is a state office, to which certain revenues are attached. The holder has a separate palace or court, as well as possesses great influence in public affairs; and as the dignity is held for life, it sometimes happens, in consequence of deaths, that the person enjoying it may not be related to the reigning sovereign by natural maternity. Bath-sheba had evidently been invested with this honourable office.

22. why dost thou ask Abishag … ask for him the kingdom also – (See on 2Sa 16:5; also see on 2Sa 12:8). Solomon's indignation was roused; he in a moment penetrated the artful scheme, and from his associating the names of Abiathar and Joab, he seems to have suspected or known that those deep schemers had been the prompters of Adonijah.

23–25. God do so to me, and more also – the common form of introducing a solemn oath.

if Adonijah have not spoken this word against his own life – Whether there was a treasonable design to conceal under this request or not, the act, according to Eastern notions, was criminal, and of dangerous consequence to the state. There is no ground of censure upon Solomon for cruelty or precipitation in this instance. He had pardoned Adonijah's former conspiracy; but this new attempt was rebellion against the viceroy appointed by the divine King and called for condign punishment. The office of executioner was among the Hebrews, as in other ancient countries of the East, performed unceremoniously and privately – often without any previous warning – by the captain of the guard, or one of his officers (Mt 14:10).

26, 27. unto Abiathar the priest said the king – This functionary, as the counsellor or accomplice of Adonijah, had deserved to share his fate. But partly from regard to his priestly dignity, and partly from his long associations with the late king, Solomon pronounced on him the mitigated sentence of banishment to his country estate at Anathoth, and thereby, as God's viceregent, deprived him of his office and its emoluments. The sacred writer notices the remarkable fulfilment. Abiathar's degradation from the high priesthood (see on 1Ki 4:4), of the doom denounced against the house of Eli (1Sa 2:30).

1Ki 2:28–45. Joab slain.

28. Then tidings came to Joab – The execution of these sentences respectively on Adonijah and Abiathar prepared Joab for his fate. Death, due to his great crimes (Nu 35:33), would long ago have been inflicted, had not his power and popularity with the army been too formidable for the old king. He now fled to the altar, which, though a recognized asylum, afforded no sanctuary to the rebel and murderer (Ex 21:14). And, as he refused to leave it, he seems to have cherished some faint hope that a religious scruple would have been felt at the thought of violating the sanctity of the place by bloodshed. Benaiah, not liking to assume any responsibility, referred the matter to Solomon, who determined that the law should take its course (De 19:13).

33. Their blood shall … return upon the head of Joab, – A reference is here made to the curse publicly and solemnly pronounced by King David (2Sa 3:28,29).

1Ki 2:34-46. Shimei put to death.

34. Benaiah … went up, and fell upon him – According to the terms of the statute (Ex 21:14), and the practice in similar cases (2Ki 11:15), the criminal was to be dragged from the altar and slain elsewhere. But the truth is, that the sanctity of the altar was violated as much by the violence used in forcing the criminal from the place as in shedding his blood there; the express command of God authorized the former and therefore by implication permitted the latter.

was buried in his own house – or family vault, at his property in the wilderness of Judah. His interment was included in the king's order, as enjoined in the divine law (De 21:23).

36. the king sent and called for Shimei – He was probably residing at Bahurim, his native place. But, as he was a suspicious character, Solomon condemned him henceforth to live in Jerusalem, on the penalty of death, for going without the gates. He submitted to this confinement for three years, when, violating his oath, he was arrested and put to death by Solomon for perjury, aggravated by his former crime of high treason against David [1Ki 2:42–44].

46. the kingdom was established in the hand of Solomon – Now, by the death of Shimei, *all* the leaders of the rival factions had been cut off.

Chapter 3

1Ki 3:1. Solomon marries Pharaoh's daughter.

1. Solomon made affinity with Pharaoh – This was a royal title, equivalent to 'sultan,' and the personal name of this monarch is said to have been Vaphres. The formation, on equal terms, of this matrimonial alliance with the royal family of Egypt, shows the high consideration to which the Hebrew kingdom had now arisen. Rosellini has given, from the Egyptian monuments, what is supposed to be a portrait of this princess. She was received in the land of her adoption with great eclat; for the Song of Solomon and the forty-fifth Psalm are supposed to have been composed in honour of this occasion, although they may both have a higher typical reference to the introduction of the Gentiles into the church.

and brought her into the city of David – that is, Jerusalem. She was not admissible into the stronghold of Zion, the building where the ark was (De 23:7,8). She seems to have been lodged at first in her mother's apartments (So 3:4 8:2), as a suitable residence was not yet provided for her in the new palace (1Ki 7:8 9:24 2Ch 8:11).

building … the wall of Jerusalem round about – Although David had begun (Ps 51:18), it was, according to Josephus, reserved for Solomon to extend and complete the fortifications of the city.

It has been questioned whether this marriage was in conformity with the law (see Ex 34:16 De 7:3 Ezr 10:1–10 Ne 13:26). But it is nowhere censured in Scripture, as are the connections Solomon formed with other foreigners (1Ki 11:1–3); whence it may be inferred that he had stipulated for her abandonment of idolatry, and conforming to the Jewish religion (Ps 45:10,11).

1Ki 3:2–5. High places being in use his sacrifices at Gibeon.

3. And Solomon loved the Lord – This declaration, illustrated by what follows, affords undoubted evidence of the young king's piety; nor is the word 'only,' which prefaces the statement, to be understood as introducing a qualifying circumstance that reflected any degree of censure upon him. The intention of the sacred historian is to describe the generally prevailing mode of worship before the temple was built.

high places were altars erected on natural or artificial eminences, probably from the idea that men were brought nearer to the Deity. They had been used by the patriarchs, and had become so universal among the heathen that they were almost identified with idolatry. They were prohibited in the law (Le 17:3,4 De 12:13,14 Jer 7:31 Eze 6:3,4 Ho 10:8). But, so long as the tabernacle was migratory and the means for the national worship were merely provisional, the worship on those high places was tolerated. Hence, as accounting for their continuance, it is expressly stated (1Ki 3:2) that God had not yet chosen a permanent and exclusive place for his worship.

4. the king went to Gibeon to sacrifice there – The old tabernacle and the brazen altar which Moses had made in the wilderness were there (1Ch 16:39 21:29 2Ch 1:3–6). The royal progress was of public importance. It was a season of national devotion. The king was accompanied by his principal nobility (2Ch 1:2); and, as the occasion was most probably one of the great annual festivals which lasted seven days, the rank of the offerer and the succession of daily oblations may help in part to account for the immense magnitude of the sacrifices.

5. In Gibeon the Lord appeared to Solomon in a dream – It was probably at the close of this season, when his mind had been elevated into a high state of religious fervour by the protracted services. Solomon felt an intense desire, and he had offered an earnest petition, for the gift of wisdom. In sleep his thoughts ran upon the subject of his prayer, and he dreamed that God appeared to him and gave him the option of every thing in the world – that he asked wisdom, and that God granted his request (1Ki 3:9-12). His dream was but an imaginary repetition of his former desire, but God's grant of it was real.

1Ki 3:6-15. He chooses wisdom.

6. Solomon said – that is, had dreamed that he said.

7. I am but a little child – not in age, for he had reached manhood (1Ki 2:9) and must have been at least twenty years old; but he was raw and inexperienced in matters of government.

10. the speech pleased the Lord – It was Solomon's waking prayers that God heard and requited, but the acceptance was signified in this vision.

15. behold, it was a dream – The vivid impression, the indelible recollection he had of this dream, together with the new and increased energy communicated to his mind, and the flow of worldly prosperity that rushed upon him, gave him assurance that it came by divine inspiration and originated in the grace of God. The wisdom, however, that was asked and obtained was not so much of the heart as of the head – it was wisdom not for himself personally, but for his office, such as would qualify him for the administration of justice, the government of a kingdom, and for the attainment of general scientific knowledge.

1Ki 3:16–28. His judgment between two harlots.

16. Then came there two women – Eastern monarchs, who generally administer justice in person, at least in all cases of difficulty, often appeal to the principles of human nature when they are at a loss otherwise to find a clue to the truth or see clearly their way through a mass of conflicting testimony. The modern history of the East abounds with anecdotes of judicial cases, in which the decision given was the result of an experiment similar to this of Solomon upon the natural feelings of the contending parties.

Chapter 4

1Ki 4:1–6. Solomon's princes.

1. So King Solomon was king over all Israel – This chapter contains a general description of the state and glory of the Hebrew kingdom during the more flourishing or later years of his reign.

2. these were the princes – or chief officers, as is evident from two of them marrying Solomon's daughters.

Azariah the son of Zadok the priest – rather, 'the prince,' as the Hebrew word frequently signifies (Ge 41:45 Ex 2:16 2Sa 8:18); so that from the precedency given to his person in the list, he seems to have been prime minister, the highest in office next the king.

3. scribes – that is, secretaries of state. Under David, there had been only one [2Sa 8:17 20:25]. The employment of three functionaries

in this department indicates either improved regulations by the division of labour, or a great increase of business, occasioned by the growing prosperity of the kingdom, or a more extensive correspondence with foreign countries.

recorder – that is, historiographer, or annalist – an office of great importance in Oriental courts, and the duties of which consisted in chronicling the occurrences of every day.

4. Benaiah – **was over the host** – formerly captain of the guard. He had succeeded Joab as commander of the forces.

Zadok and Abiathar were the priests – Only the first discharged the sacred functions; the latter had been banished to his country seat and retained nothing more than the name of high priest.

5. over the officers – that is, the provincial governors enumerated in 1Ki 4:17-19.

principal officer, and the king's friend – perhaps president of the privy council, and Solomon's confidential friend or favourite. This high functionary had probably been reared along with Solomon. That he should heap those honours on the sons of Nathan was most natural, considering the close intimacy of the father with the late king, and the deep obligations under which Solomon personally lay to the prophet.

6. Ahishar was over the household – steward or chamberlain of the palace.

Adoniram – or Adoram (2Sa 20:24 1Ki 12:18), or Hadoram (2Ch 10:18),

was over the tribute – not the collection of money or goods, but the levy of compulsory labourers (compare 1Ki 5:13,14).

1Ki 4:7–21. His twelve officers.

7. Solomon had twelve officers over all Israel – The royal revenues were raised according to the ancient, and still, in many parts, existing usage of the East, not in money payments, but in the produce of the soil. There would be always a considerable difficulty in the collection and transmission of these tithes (1Sa 8:15). Therefore, to facilitate the work, Solomon appointed twelve officers, who had each the charge of a tribe or particular district of country, from which, in monthly rotation, the supplies for the maintenance of the king's household were drawn, having first been deposited in 'the store cities' which were erected for their reception (1Ki 9:19 2Ch 8:4,6).

8. The son of Hur – or, as the *Margin* has it, *Benhur, Bendekar*. In the rural parts of Syria, and among the Arabs, it is still common to designate persons not by their own names, but as the sons of their fathers.

21. Solomon reigned over all kingdoms from the river – All the petty kingdoms between the Euphrates and the Mediterranean were tributary to him. Similar is the statement in 1Ki 4:24.

22, 23. Solomon's provision for one day – not for the king's table only, but for all connected with the court, including, besides the royal establishment, those of his royal consorts, his principal officers, his bodyguards, his foreign visitors, The quantity of fine flour used is estimated at two hundred forty bushels; that of meal or common flour at four hundred eighty. The number of cattle required for consumption, besides poultry and several kinds of game did not exceed in proportion what is needed in other courts of the East.

24. from Tiphsah – that is, Thapsacus, a large and flourishing town on the west bank of the Euphrates, the name of which was derived from a celebrated ford near it, the lowest on that river.

even to Azzah – that is, Gaza, on the southwestern extremity, not far from the Mediterranean.

25. every man under his vine and . . . fig tree – This is a common and beautiful metaphor for peace and security (Mic 4:4 Zec 3:10), founded on the practice, still common in modern Syria, of training these fruit trees up the walls and stairs of houses, so as to make a shady arbor, beneath which the people sit and relax.

26. forty thousand stalls – for the royal mews (see on 2Ch 9:25).

28. Barley . . . and straw – Straw is not used for litter, but barley mixed with chopped straw is the usual fodder of horses.

dromedaries – one-humped camels, distinguished for their great fleetness.

1Ki 4:29–34. His wisdom.

29. God gave Solomon wisdom and understanding exceeding much, and largeness of heart – that is, high powers of mind, great capacity for receiving, as well as aptitude for communicating, knowledge.

30. Solomon's wisdom excelled the wisdom of all the children of the east country – that is, the Arabians, Chaldeans, and Persians (Ge 25:6).

all the wisdom of Egypt – Egypt was renowned as the seat of learning and sciences, and the existing monuments, which so clearly describe the ancient state of society and the arts, show the high culture of the Egyptian people.

31. wiser than all men – that is, all his contemporaries, either at home or abroad.

than Ethan – or Jeduthun, of the family of Merari (1Ch 6:44).

Heman – (1Ch 15:17–19) – the chief of the temple musicians and the king's seers (1Ch 25:5); the other two are not known.

the sons of Mahol – either another name for Zerah (1Ch 2:6); or taking it as a common noun, signifying a dance, a chorus, 'the sons of Mahol' signify persons eminently skilled in poetry and music.

32. he spake three thousand proverbs – embodying his moral sentiments and sage observations on human life and character.

songs … a thousand and five – Psalm 72, 127, 132, and the Song of Songs are his.

33. he spake of trees, from the cedar . . . to the hyssop – all plants, from the greatest to the least. The Spirit of God has seen fit to preserve comparatively few memorials of the fruits of his gigantic mind. The greater part of those here ascribed to him have long since fallen a prey to the ravages of time, or perished in the Babylonian captivity, probably because they were not inspired.

Chapter 5

1Ki 5:1–6. Hiram sends to congratulate Solomon.

1. Hiram . . . sent his servants unto Solomon – the grandson of David's contemporary or the same Hiram. The friendly relations which the king of Tyre had cultivated with David are here seen renewed with his son and successor, by a message of condolence as well as of congratulation on his accession to the throne of Israel. The alliance between the two nations had been mutually beneficial by the encouragement of useful traffic. Israel, being agricultural, furnished corn and oil, while the Tyrians, who were a commercial people, gave in exchange their Phoenician manufactures, as well as the produce of foreign lands. A special treaty was now entered into in furtherance of that undertaking which was the great work of Solomon's splendid and peaceful reign.

6. command thou that they hew me cedar trees out of Lebanon – Nowhere else could Solomon have procured materials for the woodwork of his contemplated building. The forests of Lebanon, adjoining the seas in Solomon's time, belonged to the Phoenicians, and the timber being a lucrative branch of their exports, immense numbers of workmen were constantly employed in the felling of trees as well as the transportation and preparation of the wood. Hiram stipulated to furnish Solomon with as large a quantity of cedars and cypresses as he might require and it was a great additional obligation that he engaged to render the important service of having it brought down, probably by the Dog river, to the seaside, and conveyed along the coast in floats; that is, the logs being bound together, to the harbor of Joppa (2Ch 2:16), whence they could easily find the means of transport to Jerusalem.

my servants shall be with thy servants – The operations were to be on so extensive a scale that the Tyrians alone would be insufficient. A division of labour was necessary, and while the former would do the work that required skilful artisans, Solomon engaged to supply the labourers.

1Ki 5:7–12. Furnishes timber to build the temple.

7. Blessed be the Lord – This language is no decisive evidence that Hiram was a worshipper of the true God, as he might use it only on the polytheistic principle of acknowledging Jehovah as the God of the Hebrews (see on 2Ch 2:11).

8. Hiram sent to Solomon, saying, I have considered the things … and I will do – The contract was drawn out formally in a written document (2Ch 2:11), which, according to JOSEPHUS, was preserved both in the Jewish and Tyrian records.

10. fir trees – rather, the cypress.

11. food to his household – This was an annual supply for the palace, different from that mentioned in 2Ch 2:10, which was for the workmen in the forests.

1Ki 5:13–18. Solomon's workmen and labourers.

13. Solomon raised a levy out of all Israel – The renewed notice of Solomon's divine gift of wisdom (1Ki 5:12) is evidently introduced to prepare for this record of the strong but prudent measures he took towards the accomplishment of his work. So great a stretch of arbitrary power as is implied in this compulsory levy would have raised great discontent, if not opposition, had not his wise arrangement of letting the labourers remain at home two months out of three, added to the sacredness of the work, reconciled the people to this forced labour. The carrying of burdens and the irksome work of excavating the quarries was assigned to the remnant of the Canaanites (1Ki 9:20 2Ch 8:7–9) and war prisoners made by David – amounting to 153,600. The employment of persons of that condition in Eastern countries for carrying on any public work, would make this part of the arrangements the less thought of.

17. brought great stones – The stone of Lebanon is 'hard, calcareous, whitish and sonorous, like free stone' [SHAW]. The same white and beautiful stone can be obtained in every part of Syria and Palestine. **hewed stones** – or neatly polished, as the *Hebrew* word signifies (Ex 20:25). Both Jewish and Tyrian builders were employed in hewing these great stones.

18. and the stone squarers – The *Margin*, which renders it 'the Giblites' (Jos 13:5), has long been considered a preferable translation. This marginal translation also must yield to another which has lately been proposed, by a slight change in the *Hebrew* text, and which would be rendered thus: 'Solomon's builders, and Hiram's builders, did hew them and bevel them' [THENIUS]. These great bevelled or grooved stones, measuring some twenty, others thirty feet in length, and from five to six feet in breadth, are still seen in the substructures about the ancient site of the temple; and, in the judgment of the most competent observers, were those originally employed 'to lay the foundation of the house.'

Chapter 6

1Ki 6:1–4. The building of Solomon's temple.

2. the house which king Solomon built for the Lord – The dimensions are given in cubits, which are to be reckoned according to the early standard (2Ch 3:3), or holy cubit (Eze 40:5 43:13), a handbreadth longer than the common or later one. It is probable that the internal elevation only is here stated.

3. the porch – or portico, extended across the whole front (see on 2Ch 3:4).

4. windows of narrow lights – that is, windows with lattices, capable of being shut and opened at pleasure, partly to let out the vapour of the lamps, the smoke of the frankincense, and partly to give light [KEIL].

1Ki 6:5–10. The chambers thereof.

5. against the wall of the house he built chambers – On three sides, there were chambers in three stories, each story wider than the one beneath it, as the walls were narrowed or made thinner as they ascended, by a rebate being made, on which the beams of the side floor rested, without penetrating the wall. These chambers were approached from the right-hand side, in the interior of the under story, by a winding staircase of stone, which led to the middle and upper stories.

7. there was neither hammer nor axe nor any tool of iron heard in the house while it was in building – A subterranean quarry has been very recently discovered near Jerusalem, where the temple stones are supposed to have been hewn. There is unequivocal evidence in this quarry that the stones were dressed there; for there are blocks very similar in size, as well as of the same kind of stone, as those found in the ancient remains. Thence, probably, they would be moved on rollers down the Tyropean valley to the very side of the temple [PORTER, *Tent and Kahn*].

9, 10. built the house – The temple is here distinguished from the wings or chambers attached to it – and its roofing was of cedar-wood.

10. chambers … five cubits high – The height of the whole three stories was therefore about fifteen cubits.

they rested on the house with timber of cedar – that is, because the beams of the side stones rested on the ledges of the temple wall. The wing was attached to the house; it was connected with the temple, without, however, interfering injuriously with the sanctuary [KEIL].

1Ki 6:11–14. God's promises unto it.

11–13. the word of the Lord came to Solomon – probably by a prophet. It was very seasonable, being designed: first, to encourage him to go on with the building, by confirming anew the promise made to his father David (2Sa 7:12–16); and secondly, to warn him against the pride and presumption of supposing that after the erection of so magnificent a temple, he and his people would always be sure of the presence and favour of God. The condition on which that blessing could alone be expected was expressly stated. The dwelling of God among the children of Israel refers to those symbols of His presence in the temple, which were the visible tokens of His spiritual relation to that people.

1Ki 6:15–22. The ceiling and adorning of it.

15–21. he built the walls of the house within – The walls were wainscotted with cedar-wood; the floor, paved with cypress planks; the interior was divided (by a partition consisting of folding doors, which were opened and shut with golden chains) into two apartments – the back or inner room, that is, the most holy place, was twenty cubits long and broad; the front, or outer room, that is, the holy place, was forty cubits. The cedar-wood was beautifully embellished with figures in relievo, representing clusters of foliage, open flowers, cherubim, and palm trees. The whole interior was overlaid with gold, so that neither wood nor stone was seen; nothing met the eye but pure gold, either plain or richly chased.

31–35. for the entering of the oracle – The door of the most holy place was made of solid olive tree and adorned with figures. The door of the holy place was made of cypress wood, the sides being of olive wood.

36. the inner court – was for the priests. Its wall, which had a coping of cedar, is said to have been so low that the people could see over it.

1Ki 6:37, 38. The time taken to build it

37. In the fourth year was the foundation laid – The building was begun in the second month of the fourth year and completed in the eighth month of the eleventh year of Solomon's reign, comprising a period of seven and a half years, which is reckoned here in round numbers. It was not a very large, but a very splendid building, requiring great care, and ingenuity, and division of labour. The immense number of workmen employed, together with the previous preparation of the materials, serves to account for the short time occupied in the process of building.

Chapter 7

1Ki 7:1. Building of Solomon's house.

1. Solomon was building his own house

thirteen years – The time occupied in building his palace was nearly double that spent in the erection of the temple (1Ki 6:38), because neither had there been the same previous preparations for it, nor was there the same urgency as in providing a place of worship, on which the national well-being so much depended.

1Ki 7:2-7. Of the house of Lebanon.

2. He built also the house of the forest of Lebanon – It is scarcely possible to determine whether this was a different edifice from the former, or whether his house, the house of the forest of Lebanon, and the one for Pharaoh's daughter, were not parts of one grand palace. As difficult is it to decide what was the origin of the name; some supposing it was so called because built on Lebanon; others, that it was in or near Jerusalem, but contained such a profuse supply of cedar columns as to have occasioned this peculiar designation. We have a similar peculiarity of name in the building called the East India house, though situated in London. The description is conformable to the arrangement of Eastern palaces. The building stood in the middle of a great oblong square, which was surrounded by an enclosing wall, against which the houses and offices of those attached to the court were built. The building itself was oblong, consisting of two square courts, flanking a large oblong hall which formed the centre, and was one hundred cubits long, by fifty broad. This was properly the house of the forest of Lebanon, being the part where were the cedar pillars of this hall. In front was the porch of judgment, which was appropriated to the transaction of public business. On the one side of this great hall was the king's house; and on the other the harem or royal apartments for Pharaoh's daughter (Es 2:3,9). This arrangement of the palace accords with the Oriental style of building, according to which a great mansion always consists of three divisions, or separate houses – all connected by doors and passages – the men dwelling at one extremity, the women of the family at the other, while public rooms occupy the central part of the building.

10. the foundation was of costly stones, even great stones – Enormous stones, corresponding exactly with the dimensions given, are found in Jerusalem at this day. Not only the walls from the foundation to the roof beams were built of large hewn stones, but the spacious court around the palace was also paved with great square stones.

12. for the inner court of the house of the Lord – should be, *as in* the inner court of the house of the Lord; the meaning is, that in this palace, as in the temple, rows of hewed stones and the cedar beams formed the enclosing wall.

1Ki 7:13–51. Hiram's works.

13. Solomon sent and fetched Hiram out of Tyre – The Tyrians and other inhabitants on the Phoenician coast were the most renowned artists and workers in metal in the ancient world.

14. He was a widow's son of the tribe of Naphtali – In 2Ch 2:14 his mother is said to have been of the daughters of Dan. The apparent discrepancy may be reconciled thus: Hiram's mother, though belonging to the tribe of Dan, had been married to a Naphtalite, so that when married afterwards to a Tyrian, she might be described as a widow of the tribe of Naphtali. Or, if she was a native of the city Dan (Laish), she might be said to be of the daughters of Dan, as born in that place; and of the tribe of Naphtali, as really belonging to it.

a worker in brass – This refers particularly to the works described in this chapter. But in 2Ch 2:13 his artistic skill is represented as extending to a great variety of departments. In fact, he was appointed, from his great natural talents and acquired skill, to superintend the execution of all the works of art in the temple.

15–22. two pillars of brass of eighteen cubits high – They were made of the brass (bronze) which was taken from the king of Zobah (1Ch 18:8). In 2Ch 3:15 they are said to have been thirty-five cubits high. There, however, their joint lengths are given; whereas here the length of the pillars is given separately. Each pillar was seventeen and a half cubits long, which is stated, in round numbers, as eighteen. Their dimensions in American measure are as follows: The pillars without the capitals measured thirty-two and a half feet long, and seven feet diameter; and if hollow, as WHISTON, in his translation of JOSEPHUS, thinks (Jer 52:21), the metal would be about three and a half inches thick; so that the whole casting of one pillar must have been from sixteen to twenty tons. The height of the capitals was eight and three-fourths feet; and, at the same thickness of metal, would not weigh less than seven or eight tons each. The nature of the workmanship in the finishing of these capitals is described (1Ki 7:17–22). The pillars, when set up, would stand forty feet in height [NAPIER, *Metal*].

17, 18. nets of checker work – that is, branch-work, resembling the branches of palm trees, and **wreaths of chain-work** – that is, plaited in the form of a chain, composing a sort of crown or garland. Seven of these were wound in festoons on one capital, and over and underneath them were fringes, one hundred in a row. Two rows of pomegranates strung on chains (2Ch 3:16) ran round the capital (1Ki 7:42; compare 2Ch 4:12,13 Jer 52:23), which, itself, was of a bowl-like or globular form (1Ki 7:41).

These rows were designed to form a binding to the ornamental work – to keep it from falling asunder; and they were so placed as to be above the chain work, and below the place where the branch-work was.

19. lily work – beautiful ornaments, resembling the stalks, leaves, and blossoms of lilies – of large dimensions, as suited to the height of their position.

21. Jachin and … Boaz – These names were symbolical, and indicated the strength and stability – not so much of the material temple, for they were destroyed along with it (Jer 52:17), as of the spiritual kingdom of God, which was embodied in the temple.

23–26. he made a molten sea – In the tabernacle was no such vessel; the laver served the double purpose of washing the hands and feet of the priests as well as the parts of the sacrifices. But in the temple there were separate vessels provided for these offices. (See on 2Ch 4:6). The molten sea was an immense semicircular vase, measuring seventeen and a half feet in diameter, and being eight and three-fourths feet in depth. This, at three and a half inches in thickness, could not weigh less than from twenty-five to thirty tons in one solid casting – and held from sixteen thousand to twenty thousand gallons of water. (See on 2Ch 4:3.) The brim was all carved with lily work or flowers; and oxen were carved or cut on the outside all round, to the number of three hundred; and it stood on a pedestal of twelve oxen. These oxen must have been of considerable size, like the Assyrian bulls, so that their corresponding legs would give thickness or strength to support so great a weight for, when the vessel was filled with water, the whole weight would be about one hundred tons [NAPIER]. (See on 2Ch 4:3).

27–39. he made ten bases of brass – These were trucks or four-wheeled carriages, for the support and conveyance of the lavers. The description of their structure shows that they were elegantly fitted up and skilfully adapted to their purpose. They stood, not on the axles, but on four rests attached to the axles, so that the figured sides were considerably raised above the wheels. They were all exactly alike in form and size. The lavers which were borne upon them were vessels capable each of holding three hundred gallons of water, upwards of a ton weight. The whole, when full of water, would be no less than two tons [NAPIER].

40–45. And Hiram made the lavers, and the shovels, and the basins – These verses contain a general enumeration of Hiram's works, as well as those already mentioned as other minor things. The Tyrian artists are frequently mentioned by ancient authors as skilful artificers in fashioning and embossing metal cups and bowls; and we need not wonder, therefore, to find them employed by Solomon in making the golden and brazen utensils for his temple and palaces.

46. In the plain of Jordan did the king cast them – Zarthan, or Zaretan (Jos 3:16), or Zartanah (1Ki 4:12), or Zeredathah (2Ch 4:17), was on the bank of the Jordan in the territories of western Manasseh. Succoth was situated on the eastern side of Jordan, at the ford of the river near the mouth of the Jabbok. One reason assigned by commentators for the castings being made there is, that at such a distance from Jerusalem that city would not be annoyed by the smoke and noxious vapours necessarily occasioned by the process. [Note in *Bagster's Bible.*] But the true reason is to be found in the nature of the soil; *Margin*, 'the thickness of the ground.' That part of the Jordan valley abounds with marl. Clay and sand are the moulding material still used for bronze. Such large quantities of metal as one of these castings would contain could not be fused in one furnace, but would require a series of furnaces, especially for such a casting as the brazen sea – the whole series of furnaces being filled with metal, and fused at one time, and all tapped together, and the metal let run into the mould. Thus a national foundry was erected in the plain of Jordan [NAPIER].

48. the altar of gold – that is, the altar of incense.

49. candlesticks of pure gold – made, probably, according to the model of that in the tabernacle, which, along with the other articles of furniture, were deposited with due honour, as sacred relics, in the temple. But these seem not to have been used in the temple service; for Solomon made new lavers tables, and candlesticks, ten of each. (See further regarding the dimensions and furniture of the temple, in 2Ch 3:1–5:14).

Chapter 8

1Ki 8:1–12. The dedication of the temple.

2–6. at the feast in the month Ethanim – The public and formal inauguration of this national place of worship did not take place till eleven months after the completion of the edifice. The delay, most probably, originated in Solomon's wish to choose the most fitting opportunity when there should be a general rendezvous of the people in Jerusalem; and that was not till the next year. That was a jubilee year, and he resolved on commencing the solemn ceremonial a few days before the feast of tabernacles, which was the most appropriate of all seasons. That annual festival had been instituted in commemoration of the Israelites dwelling in booths during their stay in the wilderness, as well as of the tabernacle, which was then erected, in which

God promised to meet and dwell with His people, sanctifying it with His glory. As the tabernacle was to be superseded by the temple, there was admirable propriety in choosing the feast of tabernacles as the period for dedicating the new place of worship, and praying that the same distinguished privileges might be continued to it in the manifestation of the divine presence and glory. At the time appointed for the inauguration, the king issued orders for all the heads and representatives of the nation to repair to Jerusalem and take part in the August procession [1Ki 8:1]. The lead was taken by the king and elders of the people, whose march must have been slow, as priests were stationed to offer an immense number of sacrifices at various points in the line of road through which the procession was to go. Then came the priests bearing the ark and the tabernacle – the old Mosaic tabernacle which was brought from Gibeon. Lastly, the Levites followed, carrying the vessels and ornaments belonging to the old, for lodgment in the new, house of the Lord. There was a slight deviation in this procedure from the order of march established in the wilderness (Nu 3:31 4:15); but the spirit of the arrangement was duly observed. The ark was deposited in the oracle; that is, the most holy place, under the wings of the cherubim – not the Mosaic cherubim, which were firmly attached to the ark (Ex 37:7,8), but those made by Solomon, which were far larger and more expanded.

8. they drew out the staves – a little way, so as to project; and they were left in that position. The object was, that these projecting staves might serve as a guide to the high priest, in conducting him to that place where, once a year, he went to officiate before the ark; otherwise he might miss his way in the dark, the ark being wholly overshadowed by the wings of the cherubim.

9. There was nothing in the ark save the two tables of stone – Nothing else was ever in the ark, the articles mentioned (Heb 9:4) being not *in*, but *by* it, being laid in the most holy place before the testimony (Ex 16:33 Nu 17:10).

10, 11. the cloud filled the house of the Lord – The cloud was the visible symbol of the divine presence, and its occupation of the sanctuary was a testimony of God's gracious acceptance of the temple as of the tabernacle (Ex 40:34). The dazzling brightness, or rather, perhaps, the dense portentous darkness of the cloud, struck the minds of the priests, as it formerly had done Moses, which such astonishment and terror (Le 16:2–13 De 4:24 Ex 40:35) that they could not remain. Thus the temple became the place where the divine glory was revealed, and the king of Israel established his royal residence.

1Ki 8:12–21. Solomon's blessing.

12. Then spake Solomon – For the reassurance of the priests and people, the king reminded them that the cloud, instead of being a sign ominous of evil, was a token of approval.

The Lord said – not in express terms, but by a continuous course of action (Ex 13:21 24:16 Nu 9:15).

13. I have surely built thee an house – This is an apostrophe to God, as perceiving His approach by the cloud, and welcoming Him to enter as guest or inhabitant of the fixed and permanent dwelling-place, which, at His command, had been prepared for His reception.

14. the king turned his face about – From the temple, where he had been watching the movement of the mystic cloud, and while the people were standing, partly as the attitude of devotion, partly out of respect to royalty, the king gave a fervent expression of praise to God for the fulfilment of His promise (2Sa 7:6–16).

1Ki 8:22–61. His prayer.

22. Solomon stood before the altar – This position was in the court of the people, on a brazen scaffold erected for the occasion (2Ch 6:13), fronting the altar of burnt offering, and surrounded by a mighty concourse of people. Assuming the attitude of a suppliant, kneeling (1Ki 8:54; compare 2Ch 6:24) and with uplifted hands, he performed the solemn act of consecration – an act remarkable, among other circumstances, for this, that it was done, not by the high priest or any member of the Aaronic family, but by the king in person, who might minister *about,* though not in, holy things. This sublime prayer [1Ki 8:22–35], which breathes sentiments of the loftiest piety blended with the deepest humility, naturally bore a reference to the national blessing and curse contained in the law – and the burden of it – after an ascription of praise to the Lord for the bestowment of the former, was an earnest supplication for deliverance from the latter. He specifies seven cases in which the merciful interposition of God would be required; and he earnestly bespeaks it on the condition of people praying towards that holy place. The blessing addressed to the people at the close is substantially a brief recapitulation of the preceding prayer [1Ki 8:56–61].

1Ki 8:62–64. His sacrifice of peace offering.

62. the king, and all Israel – offered sacrifice before the Lord – This was a burnt offering with its accompaniments, and being the first laid on the altar of the temple, was, as in the analogous case of the tabernacle, consumed by miraculous fire from heaven (see 2Ch 7:1). On remarkable occasions, the heathens sacrificed hecatombs (a hundred animals), and even chiliombs (a thousand animals), but the public sacrifices offered by Solomon on this occasion surpassed all the other oblations on record, without taking into account those presented by private individuals, which, doubtless, amounted to a large additional number. The large proportion of the sacrifices were peace offerings, which afforded the people an opportunity of festive enjoyment.

63. So the king and all the children of Israel dedicated the house of the Lord – The dedication was not a ceremony ordained by the law, but it was done in accordance with the sentiments of reverence naturally associated with edifices appropriated to divine worship.

64. The same day did the king hallow the middle of the court – that is, the whole extent of the priests' court – the altar of burnt offerings, though large (2Ch 4:1), being totally inadequate for the vast number of sacrifices that distinguished this occasion. It was only a temporary erection to meet the demands of an extraordinary season, in aid of the established altar, and removed at the conclusion of the sacred festival.

1Ki 8:65. The people joyful.

65. from the entering in of Hamath unto the river of Egypt – that is, from one extremity of the kingdom to the other. The people flocked from all quarters.

seven days and seven days, even fourteen days – The first seven were occupied with the dedication, and the other seven devoted to the feast of tabernacles (2Ch 7:9). The particular form of expression indicates that the fourteen days were not continuous. Some interval occurred in consequence of the great day of atonement falling on the tenth of the seventh month (1Ki 8:2), and the last day of the feast of tabernacles was on the twenty-third (2Ch 7:10), when the people returned to their homes with feelings of the greatest joy and gratitude 'for all the goodness that the Lord had done for David his servant, and for Israel his people.'

Chapter 9

1Ki 9:1–9. God's covenant in a second vision with Solomon.

1. And it came to pass, when Solomon had finished the building of the house – This first verse is connected with 1Ki 9:11, all that is contained between 1Ki 9:2-10 being parenthetical.

2. That – rather, 'For.'

the Lord appeared – This appearance was, like the former one at Gibeon, most probably made in a supernatural vision, and on the night immediately following the dedication of the temple (2Ch 7:12). The strain of it corresponds to this view, for it consists of direct answers to his solemn inaugural prayer (1Ki 9:3 is in answer to 1Ki 8:29 9:4,5 is in answer to 1Ki 8:25,26 9:6–9 to 1Ki 8:33–46; see also De 29:22–24).

8, 9. this house, which is high – 'high,' either in point of situation, for it was built on a hill, and therefore conspicuous to every beholder; or 'high' in respect to privilege, honour, and renown; or this 'house of the Most High,' notwithstanding all its beauty and magnificence, shall be destroyed, and remain in such a state of ruin and degradation as to be a striking monument of the just judgment of God. The record of this second vision, in which were rehearsed the conditions of God's covenant with Solomon and the consequences of breaking them, is inserted here as a proper introduction to the narrative about to be given of this king's commercial enterprises and ambitious desire for worldly glory; for this king, by encouraging an influx of foreign people and a taste for foreign luxuries, rapidly corrupted his own mind and that of this subjects, so that they turned from following God, they and their children (1Ki 9:6).

1Ki 9:10–23. The mutual presents of Solomon and Hiram.

10. at the end of twenty years – Seven and a half years were spent in building the temple, and twelve and a half or thirteen in the erection of his palace (1Ki 7:1 2Ch 8:1). This verse is only a recapitulation of 1Ki 9:1, necessary to recover the thread of connection in the narrative.

11. Solomon gave Hiram twenty cities in the land of Galilee – According to JOSEPHUS, they were situated on the northwest of it, adjacent to Tyre. Though lying within the boundaries of the promised land (Ge 15:18 Jos 1:4), they had never been conquered till then, and were inhabited by Canaanite heathens (Jud 4:2-13 2Ki 15:29). They were probably given to Hiram, whose dominions were small, as a remuneration for his important services in furnishing workmen, materials, and an immense quantity of *wrought* gold (1Ki 9:14) for the temple and other buildings [MICHAELIS]. The gold, however, as others think, may have been the amount of forfeits paid to Solomon by Hiram for not being able to answer the riddles and apothegms, with which, according to JOSEPHUS, in their private correspondence, the two sovereigns amused themselves. Hiram having refused these cities, probably on account of their inland situation making them unsuitable to his maritime and commercial people, Solomon satisfied his ally in some other way; and, taking these cities into his own hands, he first repaired their shattered walls, then filled them with a colony of Hebrews (2Ch 8:2).

15-24. this is the reason of the levy – A levy refers both to men and money, and the necessity for Solomon making it arose from the many gigantic works he undertook to erect.

Millo – part of the fort of Jerusalem on Mount Zion (2Sa 5:9 1Ch 11:8), or a row of stone bastions around Mount Zion, Millo being the great corner tower of that fortified wall (1Ki 11:27 2Ch 32:5).

the wall of Jerusalem – either repairing some breaches in it (1Ki 11:27), or extending it so as to enclose Mount Zion.

Hazor – fortified on account of its importance as a town in the northern boundary of the country.

Megiddo – (now Leijun) – Lying in the great caravan road between Egypt and Damascus, it was the key to the north of Palestine by the western lowlands, and therefore fortified.

Gezer – on the western confines of Ephraim, and, though a Levitical city, occupied by the Canaanites. Having fallen by right of conquest to the king of Egypt, who for some cause attacked it, it was given by him as a dowry to his daughter, and fortified by Solomon.

17. Beth-horon the nether – situated on the way from Joppa to Jerusalem and Gibeon; it required, from so public a road, to be strongly garrisoned.

18. Baalath – Baal-bek.

Tadmor – Palmyra, between Damascus and the Euphrates, was rebuilt and fortified as a security against invasion from northern Asia. In accomplishing these and various other works which were carried on throughout the kingdom, especially in the north, where Rezon of Damascus, his enemy, might prove dangerous, he employed vast numbers of the Canaanites as galley slaves (2Ch 2:18), treating them as prisoners of war, who were compelled to do the drudgery and hard labour, while the Israelites were only engaged in honourable employment.

23. These were the chief of the officers – (See on 2Ch 8:10).

1Ki 9:24–28. Solomon's yearly sacrifices.

24, 25. three times in a year – namely, at the Passover, Pentecost, and feast of tabernacles (2Ch 8:13 31:3). The circumstances mentioned in these two verses form a proper conclusion to the record of his buildings and show that his design in erecting those at Jerusalem was to remedy defects existing at the commencement of his reign (see 1Ki 3:1-4).

26. Ezion-geber, which is beside Eloth – These were neighbouring ports at the head of the eastern or Elanitic branch of the Red Sea. Tyrian ship carpenters and sailors were sent there for Solomon's vessels (see on 2Ch 8:17,18).

Ezion-geber – that is, 'the giant's backbone'; so called from a reef of rocks at the entrance of the harbor.

Eloth – Elim or Elath; that is, 'the trees'; a grove of terebinths still exists at the head of the gulf.

28. Ophir – a general name, like the East or West Indies with us, for all the southern regions lying on the African, Arabian, or Indian seas, in so far as at that time known [HEEREN].

Chapter 10

1 Ki 10:1–13. The Queen of Sheba admires the wisdom of Solomon.

1. the queen of Sheba – Some think her country was the Sabean kingdom of Yemen, of which the capital was Saba, in Arabia-Felix; others, that it was in African Ethiopia, that is, Abyssinia, towards the south of the Red Sea. The opinions preponderate in favour of the former. This view harmonizes with the language of our Lord, as Yemen means 'South'; and this country, extending to the shores of the Indian ocean, might in ancient times be considered 'the uttermost parts of the earth.'

heard of the fame of Solomon – doubtless by the Ophir fleet.

concerning the name of the Lord – meaning either his great knowledge of God, or the extraordinary things which God had done for him.

hard questions – enigmas or riddles. The Orientals delight in this species of intellectual exercise and test wisdom by the power and readiness to solve them.

2. she came to Jerusalem with a very great train, with camels – A long train of those beasts of burden forms the common way of travelling in Arabia; and the presents specified consist of the native produce of that country. Of course, a royal equipage would be larger and more imposing than an ordinary caravan.

6. It was a true report that I heard in mine own land of thy acts and of thy wisdom – The proofs she obtained of Solomon's wisdom – not from his conversation only, but also from his works; the splendour of his palace; the economy of his kitchen and table; the order of his court; the gradations and gorgeous costume of his servants; above all, the arched viaduct that led from his palace to the temple (2 Ki 16:18), and the remains of which have been recently discovered [ROBINSON] – overwhelmed her with astonishment.

9. Blessed be the Lord thy God – (See on 1 Ki 5:7). It is quite possible, as Jewish writers say, that this queen was converted, through Solomon's influence, to the worship of the true God. But there is no record of her making any gift or offering in the temple.

11. almug trees – Parenthetically, along with the valuable presents of the queen of Sheba, is mentioned a foreign wood, which was brought in the Ophir ships. It is thought by some to be the sandalwood; by others, to be the deodar – a species of fragrant fir, much used in India for sacred and important works. Solomon used it for stairs in his temple and palace (2 Ch 9:11), but chiefly for musical instruments.

13. King Solomon gave unto the queen of Sheba all her desire, whatsoever she asked, beside – that is, Solomon not only gave his illustrious guest all the insight and information she wanted; but, according to the Oriental fashion, he gave her ample remuneration for the presents she had brought.

1 Ki 10:14–29. His riches.

14, 15. Now the weight of gold that came to Solomon in one year – The sources whence this was derived are not mentioned; nor was it the full amount of his revenue; for this was 'Beside that he had of the merchantmen, and of the traffic of the spice merchants, and of all the kings of Arabia, and of the governors of the country.' The great encouragement he gave to commerce was the means of enriching his royal treasury. By the fortifications which he erected in various parts of his kingdom, (particularly at such places as Thapsacus, one of the passages of Euphrates, and at Tadmot, in the Syrian desert), he gave complete security to the caravan trade from the depredations of the Arab marauders; and it was reasonable that, in return for this protection, he should exact a certain toll or duty for the importation of foreign goods. A considerable revenue, too, would arise from the use of the store cities and khans he built; and it is not improbable that those cities were emporia, where the caravan merchants unloaded their bales of spices and other commodities and sold them to the king's factors, who, according to the modern practice in the East, retailed them in the Western markets at a profit. 'The revenue derived from the tributary kings and from the governors of the country' must have consisted in the tribute which all inferior magistrates periodically bring to their sovereigns in the East, in the shape of presents of the produce of their respective provinces.

16, 17. two hundred targets, six hundred shekels – These defensive arms were anciently made of wood and covered with leather; those were covered with fine gold. They were intended for the state armoury of the palace (see 1 Ki 14:26).

18–26. a great throne of ivory – It seems to have been made not of solid ivory, but veneered. It was in the form of an armchair, with a carved back. The ascent to it was by six steps, on each of which stood lions, in place of a railing – while a lion, probably of gilt metal, stood at each side, which, we may suppose from the analogy of other Oriental thrones, supported a canopy. A golden footstool is mentioned (2 Ch 9:18) as attached to this throne, whose magnificence is described as unrivalled.

22. a navy of Tharshish – Tartessus in Spain. There gold, and especially silver, was obtained, anciently, in so great abundance that it was nothing accounted of in the days of Solomon. But 'Tarshish' came to be a general term for the West (Jon 1:3).

at sea – on the Mediterranean.

once in three years – that is, every third year. Without the mariner's compass they had to coast along the shore. The ivory, apes, and peacocks might have been purchased, on the outward or homeward voyage, on the north coast of Africa, where the animals were to be found. They were particularized, probably as being the rarest articles on board.

Chapter 11

1Ki 11:1–8. Solomon's wives and concubines in his old age.

1, 2. But King Solomon loved many strange women – Solomon's extraordinary gift of wisdom was not sufficient to preserve him from falling into grievous and fatal errors. A fairer promise of true greatness, a more beautiful picture of juvenile piety, never was seen than that which he exhibited at the commencement of his reign. No sadder, more humiliating, or awful spectacle can be imagined than the besotted apostasy of his old age; and to him may be applied the words of Paul (Ga 3:3), of John (Re 3:17), and of Isaiah (Isa 14:21). A love of the world, a ceaseless round of pleasure, had insensibly corrupted his heart, and produced, for a while at least, a state of mental darkness. The grace of God deserted him; and the son of the pious David – the religiously trained child of Bath-sheba (Pr 31:1–3), and pupil of Nathan, instead of showing the stability of sound principle and mature experience became at last an old and foolish king (Ec 4:13). His fall is traced to his 'love of many strange women.' Polygamy was tolerated among the ancient Hebrews; and, although in most countries of the East, the generality of men, from convenience and economy, confine themselves to one woman, yet a number of wives is reckoned as an indication of wealth and importance, just as a numerous stud of horses and a grand equipage are among us. The sovereign, of course, wishes to have a more numerous harem than any of his subjects; and the female establishments of many Oriental princes have, both in ancient and modern times, equalled or exceeded that of Solomon's. It is probable, therefore, that, in conformity with Oriental notions, he resorted to it as a piece of state magnificence. But in him it was unpardonable, as it was a direct and outrageous violation of the divine law (De 17:17), and the very result which that statute was ordained to prevent was realized in him. His marriage with the daughter of Pharaoh is not censured either here or elsewhere (see on 1Ki 3:1). It was only his love for many strange women; for women, though in the East considered inferiors, exert often a silent but powerful seductive influence over their husbands in the harem, as elsewhere, and so it was exemplified in Solomon.

3. he had seven hundred wives, princesses – They were, probably, according to an existing custom, the daughters of tributary chiefs, given as hostages for good conduct of their fathers.

concubines – were legitimate, but lower or secondary wives. These the chief or first wife regards without the smallest jealousy or regret, as they look up to her with feelings of respectful submission. Solomon's wives became numerous, not all at once, but gradually. Even at an early period his taste for Oriental show seems to have led to the establishment of a considerable harem (So 6:8).

4. when Solomon was old – He could not have been more than fifty.

his wives turned away his heart after other gods – Some, considering the lapse of Solomon into idolatry as a thing incredible, regard him as merely humouring his wives in the practice of their superstition; and, in countenancing their respective rites by his presence, as giving only an outward homage – a sensible worship, in which neither his understanding nor his heart was engaged. The apology only makes matters worse, as it implies an adding of hypocrisy and contempt of God to an open breach of His law. There seems no possibility of explaining the language of the sacred historian, but as intimating that Solomon became an actual and open idolater, worshipping images of wood or stone in sight of the very temple which, in early life, he had erected to the true God. Hence that part of Olivet was called the high place of Tophet (Jer 7:30–34), and the hill is still known as the Mount of Offense, of the Mount of Corruption (2Ki 23:13).

5–7. Ashtoreth – Astarte,

Milcom – Molech,

and Chemosh – He built altars for these three; but, although he is described (1Ki 11:8) as doing the same for 'all his strange wives,' there is no evidence that they had idols distinct from these; and there is no trace whatever of Egyptian idolatry.

8. burnt incense and sacrificed unto their gods – The first was considered a higher act of homage, and is often used as synonymous with worship (2Ki 22:17 23:5).

1Ki 11:9–13. God threatens him.

9–12. the Lord was angry with Solomon – The divine appearance, first at Gibeon [1Ki 3:5], and then at Jerusalem [1Ki 9:2], after the dedication of the temple, with the warnings given him on both occasions [1Ki 3:11-14 9:3–9], had left Solomon inexcusable; and it was proper and necessary that on one who had been so signally favoured with the gifts of Heaven, but who had grossly abused them, a terrible judgment should fall. The divine sentence was announced to him probably by Ahijah; but there was mercy mingled with judgment, in the circumstance, that it should not be inflicted on Solomon personally. and that a remnant of the kingdom should be spared – 'for David's sake, and for Jerusalem's sake, which had been chosen' to put God's name there; not from a partial bias in favour of either, but that the divine promise might stand (2Sa 7:12–16).

13. I will give one tribe to thy son – There were left to Rehoboam the tribes of Judah, Benjamin, and Levi (2Ch 11:12,13); and multitudes of Israelites, who, after the schism of the kingdom, established their residence within the territory of Judah to enjoy the privileges of the true religion (1Ki 12:17). These are all reckoned as one tribe.

1Ki 11:14–40. Solomon's adversaries.

14–25. the Lord stirred up an adversary – that is, permitted him, through the impulse of his own ambition, or revenge, to attack Israel. During the war of extermination, which Joab carried on in Edom (2Sa 8:13), this Hadad, of the royal family, a mere boy when rescued from the sword of the ruthless conqueror, was carried into Egypt, hospitably entertained, and became allied with the house of the Egyptian king. In after years, the thought of his native land and his lost kingdom taking possession of his mind, he, on learning the death of David and Joab, renounced the ease, possessions, and glory of his Egyptian residence, to return to Edom and attempt the recovery of his ancestral throne. The movements of this prince seem to have given much annoyance to the Hebrew government; but as he was defeated by the numerous and strong garrisons planted throughout the Edomite territory, Hadad seems to have offered his services to Rezon, another of Solomon's adversaries (1Ki 11:23–25). This man, who had been general of Hadadezer and, on the defeat of that great king, had successfully withdrawn a large force, went into the wilderness, led a predatory life, like Jephthah, David, and others, on the borders of the Syrian and Arabian deserts. Then, having acquired great power, he at length became king in Damascus, threw off the yoke, and was 'the adversary of Israel all the days of Solomon.' He was succeeded by Hadad, whose successors took the official title of Ben-hadad from him, the illustrious founder of the powerful kingdom of Damascene-Syria. These hostile neighbours, who had been long kept in check by the traditional fame of David's victories, took courage; and breaking out towards the latter end of Solomon's reign, they must have not only disturbed his kingdom by their inroads, but greatly crippled his revenue by stopping his lucrative traffic with Tadmor and the Euphrates.

26–40. Jeroboam – This was an internal enemy of a still more formidable character. He was a young man of talent and energy, who, having been appointed by Solomon superintendent of the engineering works projected around Jerusalem, had risen into public notice, and on being informed by a very significant act of the prophet Ahijah of the royal destiny which, by divine appointment, awaited him, his mind took a new turn.

29. clad – rather, 'wrapped up.' The meaning is, 'Ahijah, the Shilonite, the prophet, went and took a fit station *in the way;* and, in order that he might not be known, *he wrapped himself up,* so as closely to conceal himself, in *a new garment,* a *surtout,* which he afterwards tore in twelve pieces.' Notwithstanding this privacy, the story, and the prediction connected with it [1Ki 11:30–39], probably reached the king's ears; and Jeroboam became a marked man [1Ki 11:40]. His aspiring ambition, impatient for the death of Solomon, led him to form plots and conspiracies, in consequence of which he was compelled to flee to Egypt. Though chosen of God, he would not wait the course of God's providence, and therefore incurred the penalty of death by his criminal rebellion. The heavy exactions and compulsory labour (1Ki 11:28) which Solomon latterly imposed upon his subjects, when his foreign resources began to fail, had prepared the greater part of the kingdom for a revolt under so popular a demagogue as Jeroboam.

40. Shishak – He harbored and encouraged the rebellious refugee, and was of a different dynasty from the father-in-law of Solomon.

Chapter 12

1Ki 12:1–5. Refusing the old men's counsel.

1. Rehoboam went to Shechem – He was the oldest, and perhaps the only son of Solomon, and had been, doubtless, designated by his father heir to the throne, as Solomon had been by David. The incident here related took place after the funeral obsequies of the late king and the period for public mourning had past. When all Israel came to make him king, it was not to exercise their old right of election (1Sa 10:19-21), for, after God's promise of the perpetual sovereignty to David's posterity, their duty was submission to the authority of the rightful heir; but their object was, when making him king, to renew the conditions and stipulations to which their constitutional kings were subject (1Sa 10:25). To the omission of such rehearsing which, under the peculiar circumstances in which Solomon was made king, they were disposed to ascribe the absolutism of his government.

Shechem – This ancient, venerable, and central town was the place of convocation; and it is evident, if not from the appointment of that place, at least from the tenor of their language, and the concerted presence of Jeroboam [1Ki 12:3], that the people were determined on revolt.

4. Thy father made our yoke grievous – The splendour of Solomon's court and the magnitude of his undertakings being such, that neither the tribute of dependent states, nor the presents of foreign princes, nor the profits of his commercial enterprises, were adequate to carry them on, he had been obliged, for obtaining the necessary revenue, to begin a system of heavy taxation. The people looked only to the burdens, not to the benefits they derived from Solomon's peaceful and prosperous reign – and the evils from which they demanded deliverance were civil oppressions, not idolatry, to which they appear to have been indifferent or approving.

5-8. he said … Depart yet for three days – It was prudent to take the people's demand into calm and deliberate consideration. Whether, had the advice of the sage and experienced counsellors been followed, any good result would have followed, it is impossible to say. It would at least have removed all pretext for the separation. But he preferred the counsel of his young companions (not in age, for they were all about forty-one, but inexperienced), who recommended prompt and decisive measures to quell the malcontents.

11. whips … scorpions – The latter [instruments], as contrasted with the former, are supposed to mean thongs thickly set with sharp iron points, used in the castigation of slaves.

15–18. the king hearkened not unto the people, for the cause was from the Lord – That was the overruling cause. Rehoboam's weakness (Ec 2:18,19) and inexperience in public affairs has given rise to the probable conjecture, that, like many other princes in the East, he had been kept secluded in the harem till the period of his accession (Ec 4:14), his father being either afraid of his aspiring to the sovereignty, like the two sons of David, or, which is more probable, afraid of prematurely exposing his imbecility. The king's haughty and violent answer to a people already filled with a spirit of discontent and exasperation, indicated so great an incapacity to appreciate the gravity of the crisis, so utter a want of common sense, as to create a belief that he was struck with judicial blindness. It was received with mingled scorn and derision. The revolt was accomplished, and yet so quietly, that Rehoboam remained in Shechem, fancying himself the sovereign of a united kingdom, until his chief tax gatherer, who had been most imprudently sent to treat with the people, had been stoned to death. This opened his eyes, and he fled for security to Jerusalem.

1Ki 12:20–33. Jeroboam made king over them.

20–24. when all Israel heard that Jeroboam was come again – This verse closes the parenthetical narrative begun at 1Ki 12:2, and 1Ki 12:21–24 resume the history from 1Ki 12:1. Rehoboam determined to assert his authority by leading a large force into the disaffected provinces. But the revolt of the ten tribes was completed when the prophet Shemaiah ordered, in the Lord's name, an abandonment of any hostile measures against the revolutionists. The army, overawed by the divine prohibition, dispersed, and the king was obliged to submit.

25. Jeroboam built Shechem – destroyed by Abimelech (Jud 9:1–49). It was rebuilt, and perhaps fortified, by Jeroboam, as a royal residence.

built Penuel – a ruined city with a tower (Jud 8:9), east of Jordan, on the north bank of the Jabbok. It was an object of importance to restore this fortress (as it lay on the caravan road from Gilead to Damascus and Palmyra) and to secure his frontier on that quarter.

26–32. Jeroboam said in his heart, Now shall the kingdom return to the house of David – Having received the kingdom from God, he should have relied on the divine protection. But he did not. With a view to withdraw the people from the temple and destroy the sacred associations connected with Jerusalem, he made serious and unwarranted innovations on the religious observances of the country, on pretext of saving the people the trouble and expense of a distant journey. First, he erected two golden calves – the young bulls, Apis and Mnevis, as symbols (in the Egyptian fashion) of the true God, and the nearest, according to his fancy, to the figures of the cherubim. The one was placed at Dan, in the northern part of his kingdom; the other at Beth-el, the southern extremity, in sight of Jerusalem, and in which place he probably thought God was as likely to manifest Himself as at Jerusalem (Ge 32:1–32 2Ki 2:2). The latter place was the most frequented – for the words (1Ki 12:30) should be rendered, 'the people even to Dan went to worship before the one' (Jer 48:13 Am 4:4,5 5:5 Ho 5:8 10:8). The innovation was a sin because it was setting up the worship of God by symbols and images and departing from the place where He had chosen to put His name. Secondly, he changed the feast of tabernacles from the fifteenth of the seventh to the fifteenth of the eighth month. The ostensible reason might be, that the ingathering or harvest was later in the northern parts of the kingdom; but the real reason was to eradicate the old association with this, the most welcome and joyous festival of the year.

31. made priests of the lowest of the people –

literally, 'out of all the people,' the Levites refusing to act. He himself assumed to himself the functions of the high priest, at least, at the great festival, probably from seeing the king of Egypt conjoin the royal and sacred offices, and deeming the office of the high priest too great to be vested in a subject.

Chapter 13

1Ki 13:1–22. Jeroboam's hand withers.

1. there came a man of God out of Judah – Who this prophet was cannot be ascertained, He came by divine authority. It could not be either Iddo or Ahijah, for both were alive after the events here related.

Jeroboam stood by the altar to burn incense – It was at one of the annual festivals. The king, to give interest to the new ritual, was himself the officiating priest. The altar and its accompaniments would, of course, exhibit all the splendour of a new and gorgeously decorated temple. But the prophet foretold its utter destruction [1Ki 13:3].

2–9. he cried against the altar – which is put for the whole system of worship organized in Israel.

Behold, a child shall be born … Josiah by name – This is one of the most remarkable prophecies recorded in the Scriptures; and, in its clearness, circumstantial minuteness, and exact prediction of an event that took place three hundred sixty years later, it stands in striking contrast to the obscure and ambiguous oracles of the heathen. Being publicly uttered, it must have been well known to the people; and every Jew who lived at the accomplishment of the event must have been convinced of the truth of a religion connected with such a prophecy as this. A present sign was given of the remote event predicted, in a visible fissure being miraculously made on the altar. Incensed at the man's license of speech, Jeroboam stretched out his hand and ordered his attendants to seize the bold intruder. That moment the king's arm became stiff and motionless, and the altar split asunder, so that the fire and ashes fell on the floor. Overawed by the effects of his impiety, Jeroboam besought the prophet's prayer. His request was acceded to, and the hand was restored to its healthy state. Jeroboam was artful, and invited the prophet to the royal table, not to do him honour or show his gratitude for the restoration of his hand, but to win, by his courtesy and liberal hospitality, a person whom he could not crush by his power. But the prophet informed him of a divine injunction expressly prohibiting him from all social intercourse with any in the place, as well as from returning the same way. The prohibition not to eat or drink in Beth-el was because all the people had become apostates from the true religion, and the reason he was not allowed to return the same way was lest he should be recognized by any whom he had seen in going.

11. Now there dwelt an old prophet in Beth-el – If this were a true prophet, he was a bad man.

18. an angel spake unto me by the word of the Lord – This circuitous mode of speaking, instead of simply saying, 'the LORD spake to me,' was adopted to hide an equivocation, to conceal a double meaning – an inferior sense given to the word 'angel' – to offer a *seemingly superior* authority to persuade the prophet, while really the authority was secretly known to the speaker to be *inferior*. The 'angel,' that is, 'messenger,' was his own sons, who were worshippers, perhaps priests, at Beth-el. As this man was governed by self-interest, and wished to curry favour with the king (whose purpose to adhere to his religious polity, he feared, might be shaken by the portents that had occurred), his hastening after the prophet of Judah, the deception he practised, and the urgent invitation by which, on the ground of a falsehood, he prevailed on the too facile man of God to accompany him back to his house in Beth-el, were to create an impression in the king's mind that he was an impostor, who acted in opposition to his own statement.

21. he cried unto the man of God that came from Judah – rather, 'it cried,' that is, the word of the Lord.

1Ki 13:23–32. The disobedient prophet slain by a lion.

24. a lion met him by the way, and slew him – There was a wood near Beth-el infested with lions (2Ki 2:24). This sad catastrophe was a severe but necessary judgment of God, to attest the truth of the message with which the prophet had been charged. All the circumstances of this tragic occurrence (the undevoured carcass, the untouched ass, the passengers unmolested by the lion, though standing there) were calculated to produce an irresistible impression that the hand of God was in it.

31. bury me in the sepulchre wherein the man of God is buried – His motive in making this request was either that his remains might not be disturbed when the predicted events took place (see 2Ki 23:18), or he had some superstitious hope of being benefited at the resurrection by being in the same cave with a man of God.

Chapter 14

1Ki 14:1–20. Ahijah denounces God's judgments against Jeroboam.

1. At that time – a phrase used often loosely and indefinitely in sacred history. This domestic incident in the family of Jeroboam probably occurred towards the end of his reign; his son Abijah was of age and considered by the people the heir to the throne.

2. Jeroboam said to his wife, Arise, I pray thee, and disguise thyself – His natural and intense anxiety as a parent is here seen, blended with the deep and artful policy of an apostate king. The reason of this extreme caution was an unwillingness to acknowledge that he looked for information as to the future, not to his idols, but to the true God; and a fear that this step, if publicly known, might endanger the stability of his whole political system; and a strong impression that Ahijah, who was greatly offended with him, would, if consulted openly by his queen, either insult or refuse to receive her. For these reasons he selected his wife, as, in every view, the most proper for such a secret and confidential errand, but recommended her to assume the garb and manner of a peasant woman. Strange infatuation, to suppose that the God who could reveal futurity could not penetrate a flimsy disguise!

3–11. And take with thee ten loaves, and cracknels, and a cruse of honey, and go to him – This was a present in unison with the peasant character she assumed. Cracknels are a kind of sweet seed-cake. The prophet was blind, but having received divine premonition of the pretended countrywoman's coming, he addressed her as the queen the moment she appeared, apprised her of the calamities which, in consequence of the ingratitude of Jeroboam, his apostasy, and outrageous misgovernment of Israel, impended over their house, as well as over the nation which too readily followed his idolatrous innovations.

8. thou hast not been as my servant David – David, though he fell into grievous sins, repented and always maintained the pure worship of God as enjoined by the law.

10, 11. I will bring evil upon the house of Jeroboam – Strong expressions are here used to indicate the utter extirpation of his house;

him that is shut up and left in Israel – means those who were concealed with the greatest privacy, as the heirs of royalty often are where polygamy prevails; the other phrase, from the loose garments of the East having led to a different practice from what prevails in the West, cannot refer to men; it must signify either a very young boy, or rather, perhaps, a dog, so entire would be the destruction of Jeroboam's house that none, not even a dog, belonging to it should escape. This peculiar phrase occurs only in regard to the threatened extermination of a family (1Sa 25:22–34). See the manner of extermination (1Ki 16:4 21:24).

12. the child shall die – The death and general lamentation felt through the country at the loss of the prince were also predicted. The reason for the profound regret shown at his death

arose, according to Jewish writers, from his being decidedly opposed to the erection of the golden calves, and using his influence with his father to allow his subjects the free privilege of going to worship in Jerusalem.

13. all Israel shall mourn for him, and bury him – the only one of Jeroboam's family who should receive the rites of sepulture.

14. the Lord shall raise him up a king ... but what? even now – namely, Baasha (1Ki 15:27); he was already raised – he was in being, though not in power.

17. Tirzah – a place of pre-eminent beauty (So 6:4), three hours' travelling east of Samaria, chosen when Israel became a separate kingdom, by the first monarch, and used during three short reigns as a residence of the royal house. The fertile plains and wooded hills in that part of the territory of Ephraim gave an opening to the formation of parks and pleasure-grounds similar to those which were the 'paradises' of Assyrian and Persian monarchs [STANLEY]. Its site is occupied by the large village of Taltise [ROBINSON]. As soon as the queen reached the gate of the palace, she received the intelligence that her son was dying, according to the prophet's prediction [1Ki 14:12].

19. the rest of the acts of Jeroboam – None of the threatenings denounced against this family produced any change in his policy or government.

1Ki 14:21–24. Rehoboam's wicked reign.

21. he reigned ... in Jerusalem – Its particular designation as 'the city which the Lord did choose out of all the tribes of Israel, to put his name there,' seems given here, both as a reflection on the apostasy of the ten tribes, and as a proof of the aggravated wickedness of introducing idolatry and its attendant vices there.

his mother's name was Naamah an Ammonitess – Her heathen extraction and her influence as queen mother are stated to account for Rehoboam's tendency to depart from the true religion. Led by the warning of the prophet (1Ki 12:23), as well as by the large immigration of Israelites into his kingdom (1Ki 12:17 2Ch 11:16), he continued for the first three years of his reign a faithful patron of true religion (2Ch 11:17). But afterwards he began and encouraged a general apostasy; idolatry became the prevailing form of worship, and the religious state of the kingdom in his reign is described by the high places, the idolatrous statues, the groves and impure rites that with unchecked license were observed in them. The description is suited to the character of the Canaanitish worship.

1Ki 14:25–31. Shishak spoils Jerusalem.

25, 26. Shishak king of Egypt came up – He was the instrument in the hand of Providence for punishing the national defection. Even though this king had been Solomon's father-in-law, he was no relation of Rehoboam's; but there is a strong probability that he belonged to another dynasty (see on 2Ch 12:2). He was the Sheshonk of the Egyptian monuments, who is depicted on a bas-relief at Karnak, as dragging captives, who, from their peculiar physiognomy, are universally admitted to be Jews.

29. Now the rest of the acts of Rehoboam … are they not written in the book of the chronicles? – not the book so called and comprehended in the sacred canon, but the national archives of Judah.

30. there was war between Rehoboam and Jeroboam – The former was prohibited from entering on an aggressive war; but as the two kingdoms kept up a jealous rivalry, he might be forced into vigilant measures of defence, and frequent skirmishes would take place on the borders.

Chapter 15

1Ki 15:1–8. Abijam's wicked reign over Judah.

1. Abijam – His name was at first Abijah (2Ch 12:16); 'Jah,' the name of God, according to an ancient fashion, being conjoined with it. But afterwards, when he was found 'walking in all the sins of his father' [1Ki 15:3], that honourable addition was withdrawn, and his name in sacred history changed into Abijam [LIGHTFOOT].

2. Three years reigned he – (compare 1Ki 15:1 with 1Ki 15:9). Parts of years are often counted in Scripture as whole years. The reign began in Jeroboam's eighteenth year, continued till the nineteenth, and ended in the course of the twentieth.

his mother's name was Maachah – or Michaiah (2Ch 13:2), probably altered from the one to the other on her becoming queen, as was very common under a change of circumstances. She is called the daughter of Abishalom, or Absalom (2Ch 11:21), of Uriel (2Ch 13:2). Hence, it has been thought probable that Tamar, the daughter of Absalom (2Sa 14:27 18:18), had been married to Uriel, and that Maachah was their daughter.

3. his heart was not perfect with the Lord … as the heart of David his father – (Compare 1Ki 11:4 14:22). He was not positively bad at first, for it appears that he had done something to restore the pillaged treasures of the temple (1Ki 15:15). This phrase contains a comparative reference to David's heart. His doing that which was right in the eyes of the Lord (1Ki 15:5) is frequently used in speaking of the kings of Judah, and means only that they did or did not do that which, in the general course and tendency of their government, was acceptable to God. It furnishes no evidence as to the lawfulness or piety of one specific act.

4. for David's sake did the Lord his God give him a lamp – 'A lamp' in one's house is an Oriental phrase for continuance of family name and prosperity. Abijam was not rejected only in consequence of the divine promise to David (see on 1Ki 11:13–36).

1Ki 15:9–24. Asa's good reign.

10–13. his mother's name was Maachah – She was properly his grandmother, and she is here called 'the king's mother,' from the post of dignity which at the beginning of his reign she possessed. Asa, as a constitutional monarch, acted like the pious David, labouring to abolish the traces and polluting practices of idolatry, and in pursuance of his impartial conduct, he did not spare delinquents even of the highest rank.

13. also Maachah his mother, even her he removed from being queen – The sultana, or queen dowager, was not necessarily the king's natural mother (see 1Ki 2:19), nor was Maachah. Her title, and the privileges connected with that honour and dignity which gave her precedency among the ladies of the royal family, and great influence in the kingdom, were taken away. She was degraded for her idolatry.

because she had made an idol in a grove – A very obscene figure, and the grove was devoted to the grossest licentiousness. His plans of religious reformation, however, were not completely carried through, 'the high places were not removed' (see 1Ki 3:2). The suppression of this private worship on natural or artificial hills, though a forbidden service after the temple had been declared the exclusive place of worship, the most pious king's laws were not able to accomplish.

15. he brought in the things which his father had dedicated – Probably the spoils which Abijam had taken from the vanquished army of Jeroboam (see 2Ch 13:16).

and the things which himself had dedicated – after his own victory over the Cushites (2Ch 14:12).

16, 17. there was war between Asa and Baasha king of Israel all their days – Asa enjoyed a ten years' peace after Jeroboam's defeat by Abijam, and this interval was wisely and energetically spent in making internal reforms, as well as increasing the means of national defence (2Ch 14:1–7). In the fifteenth year of his reign, however, the king of Israel commenced hostilities against him, and, invading his kingdom, erected a strong fortress at Ramah, which was near Gibeah, and only six Roman miles from Jerusalem. Afraid lest his subjects might quit his kingdom and return to the worship of their fathers, he wished to cut off all intercourse between the two nations. Ramah stood on an eminence overhanging a narrow ravine which separated Israel from Judah, and therefore he took up a hostile position in that place.

18–20. Then Asa took all the silver and the gold that were left in the ... house of the Lord – Asa's religious character is now seen to decline. He trusted not in the Lord (2Ch 16:7). In this emergency Asa solicited the powerful aid of the king of Damascene-Syria; and to bribe him to break off his alliance with Baasha, he transmitted to him the treasure lying in the temple and palace. The Syrian mercenaries were gained. Instances are to be found, both in the ancient and modern history of the East, of the violation of treaties equally sudden and unscrupulous, through the presentation of some tempting bribe. Ben-hadad poured an army into the northern provinces of Israel, and having captured some cities in Galilee, on the borders of Syria, compelled Baasha to withdraw from Ramah back within his own territories.

Ben-hadad – (See on 1Ki 11:14).

22. Then king Asa made a proclamation – The fortifications which Baasha had erected at Ramah were demolished, and with the materials were built other defences, where Asa thought they were needed – at Geba (now Jeba) and Mizpeh (now Neby Samuil), about two hours' travelling north of Jerusalem.

1Ki 15:25–34. Nadab's wicked reign.

25. Nadab the son of Jeroboam began to reign – No record is given of him, except his close adherence to the bad policy of his father.

27. Baasha smote him at Gibbethon – This town, within the tribe of Dan, was given to the Levites (Jos 19:44). It lay on the Philistine borders, and having been seized by that people, Nadab laid siege to recover it.

29. when he reigned, he smote all the house of Jeroboam – It was according to a barbarous practice too common in the East, for a usurper to extirpate all rival candidates for the throne; but it was an accomplishment of Ahijah's prophecy concerning Jeroboam (1Ki 14:10,11).

Chapter 16

1Ki 16:1–8. Jehu's prophecy against Baasha.

1. Then the word of the Lord came to Jehu – This is the only incident recorded in the life of this prophet. His father was also a prophet (2Ch 16:7).

2. Forasmuch as I exalted thee – The doom he pronounced on Baasha was exactly the same as denounced against Jeroboam and his posterity. Though he had waded through slaughter to his throne, he owed his elevation to the appointment or permission of Him 'by whom kings reign.'

over my people Israel – With all their errors and lapses into idolatry, they were not wholly abandoned by God. He still showed His interest in them by sending prophets and working miracles in their favour, and possessed a multitude of faithful worshippers in the kingdom of Israel.

7. also by the hand of the prophet Jehu – This is not another prophecy, but merely an addition by the sacred historian, explanatory of the death of Baasha and the extinction of his family. The doom pronounced against Jeroboam (1Ki 14:9), did not entitle him to take the execution of the sentence into his own hands; but from his following the same calf-worship, he had evidently plotted the conspiracy and murder of that king in furtherance of his own ambitious designs; and hence, in his own assassination, he met the just reward of his deeds. The similitude to Jeroboam extends to their deaths as well as their lives – the reign of their sons, and the ruin of their families.

8. began Elah the son of Baasha to reign – (compare 1Ki 15:33). From this it will appear that Baasha died in the twenty-third year of his reign (see on 1Ki 15:2), and Elah, who was a prince of dissolute habits, reigned not fully two years.

1Ki 16:9–22. Zimri's conspiracy.

9–12. Zimri ... conspired against him – 'Arza which was over his house.' During a carousal in the house of his chamberlain, Zimri slew him, and having seized the sovereignty, endeavoured to consolidate his throne by the massacre of all the royal race.

15–18. did Zimri reign seven days – The news of his conspiracy soon spread, and the army having proclaimed their general, Omri, king, that officer immediately raised the siege at Gibbethon and marched directly against the capital in which the usurper had established himself. Zimri soon saw that he was not in circumstances to hold out against all the forces of the kingdom; so, shutting himself up in the palace, he set it on fire, and, like Sardanapalus, chose to perish himself and reduce all to ruin, rather than that the palace and royal treasures should fall into the hands of his successful rival. The seven days' reign may refer either to the brief duration of his royal authority, or the period in which he enjoyed unmolested tranquillity in the palace.

19. For his sins which he sinned – This violent end was a just retribution for his crimes. 'His walking in the ways of Jeroboam' might have been manifested either by the previous course of his life, or by his decrees published on his ascension, when he made a strong effort to gain popularity by announcing his continued support of the calf worship.

21, 22. Then were the people of Israel divided into two parts – The factions that ensued occasioned a four years' duration (compare 1Ki 16:15 with 1Ki 16:23), of anarchy or civil war.

Whatever might be the public opinion of Omri's merits a large body of the people disapproved of the mode of his election, and declared for Tibni. The army, however, as usual in such circumstances (and they had the will of Providence favouring them), prevailed over all opposition, and Omri became undisputed possessor of the throne.

1Ki 16:23–28. Omri builds Samaria.

23. In the thirty and first year of Asa ... began Omri to reign – The twelve years of his reign are computed from the beginning of his reign, which was in the twenty-seventh year of Asa's reign. He held a contested reign for four years with Tibni; and then, at the date stated in this verse, entered on a sole and peaceful reign of eight years.

24. he bought the hill Samaria of Shemer – The palace of Tirzah being in ruins, Omri, in selecting the site of his royal residence, was naturally influenced by considerations both of pleasure and advantage. In the centre of a wide amphitheatre of mountains, about six miles from Shechem, rises an oblong hill with steep, yet accessible sides, and a long flat top extending east and west, and rising five hundred or six hundred feet above the valley. What Omri in all probability built as a mere palatial residence, became the capital of the kingdom instead of Shechem. It was as though Versailles had taken the place of Paris, or Windsor of London. The choice of Omri was admirable, in selecting a position which combined in a union not elsewhere found in Palestine: strength, beauty, and fertility [STANLEY].

two talents of silver – Shemer had probably made it a condition of the sale, that the name should be retained. But as city and palace were built there by Omri, it was in accordance with Eastern custom to call it after the founder. The Assyrians did so, and on a tablet dug out of the ruins of Nineveh, an inscription was found relating to Samaria, which is called Beth-khumri – the house of Omri [LAYARD]. (See 2Ki 17:5).

25-27. But Omri wrought evil – The character of Omri's reign and his death are described in the stereotyped form used towards all the successors of Jeroboam in respect both to policy as well as time.

29-33. Ahab the son of Omri did evil in the sight of the Lord above all that were before him – The worship of God by symbols had hitherto been the offensive form of apostasy in Israel, but now gross idolatry is openly patronized by the court. This was done through the influence of Jezebel, Ahab's queen. She was 'the daughter of Eth-baal, king of the Zidonians.' He was priest of Ashtaroth or Astarte, who, having murdered Philetes, king of Tyre, ascended the throne of that kingdom, being the eighth king since

Hiram. Jezebel was the wicked daughter of this regicide and idol priest – and, on her marriage with Ahab, never rested till she had got all the forms of her native Tyrian worship introduced into her adopted country.

32. reared up an altar for Baal – that is, the sun, worshipped under various images. Ahab set up one (2Ki 3:2), probably as the Tyrian Hercules, in the temple in Samaria. No human sacrifices were offered – the fire was kept constantly burning – the priests officiated barefoot. Dancing and kissing the image (1Ki 19:18) were among the principal rites.

1Ki 16:34. Joshua's curse fulfilled upon Hiel the builder of Jericho.

34. In his days did Hiel the Beth-elite build Jericho – The curse took effect on the family of this reckless man but whether his oldest son died at the time of laying the foundation, and the youngest at the completion of the work, or whether he lost all his sons in rapid succession, till, at the end of the undertaking, he found himself childless, the poetical form of the ban does not enable us to determine. Some modern commentators think there is no reference either to the natural or violent deaths of Hiel's sons; but that he began in presence of his oldest son, but some unexpected difficulties, losses, or obstacles, delayed the completion till his old age, when the gates were set up in the presence of his youngest son. But the curse *was* fulfilled more than five hundred years after it was uttered; and from Jericho being inhabited after Joshua's time (Jud 3:13 2Sa 10:5), it has been supposed that the act against which the curse was directed, was an attempt at the restoration of the walls – the very walls which had been miraculously cast down. It seems to have been within the territory of Israel; and the unopposed act of Hiel affords a painful evidence how far the people of Israel had lost all knowledge of, or respect for, the word of God.

Chapter 17

1Ki 17:1–7. Elijah, prophesying against Ahab, is sent to Cherith.

1. Elijah the Tishbite – This prophet is introduced as abruptly as Melchisedek – his birth, parents, and call to the prophetic office being alike unrecorded. He is supposed to be called the Tishbite from Tisbeh, a place east of Jordan.

who was of the inhabitants of Gilead – or residents of Gilead, implying that he was not an Israelite, but an Ishmaelite, as MICHAELIS conjectures, for there were many of that race on the confines of Gilead. The employment of a Gentile as an extraordinary minister might be to rebuke and shame the apostate people of Israel.

said unto Ahab – The prophet appears to have been warning this apostate king how fatal both to himself and people would be the reckless course he was pursuing. The failure of Elijah's efforts to make an impression on the obstinate heart of Ahab is shown by the penal prediction uttered at parting.

before whom I stand – that is, whom I serve (De 18:5).

there shall not be dew nor rain these years – not absolutely; but the dew and the rain would not fall in the usual and necessary quantities. Such a suspension of moisture was sufficient to answer the corrective purposes of God, while an absolute drought would have converted the whole country into an uninhabitable waste.

but according to my word – not uttered in spite, vengeance, or caprice, but as the minister of God. The impending calamity was in answer to his earnest prayer, and a chastisement intended for the spiritual revival of Israel. Drought was the threatened punishment of national idolatry (De 11:16,17 28:23).

2, 3. the word of the Lord came unto him, saying, Get thee hence, and turn thee eastward, – At first the king may have spurned the prediction as the utterance of a vain enthusiast; but when he found the drought did last and increase in severity, he sought Elijah, who, as it was necessary that he should be far removed from either the violence or the importunities of the king, was divinely directed to repair to a place of retreat, perhaps a cave on 'the brook Cherith, that is, before [east of] Jordan.' Tradition points it out in a small winter torrent, a little below the ford at Beth-shan.

6. the ravens brought him bread – The idea of such unclean and voracious birds being employed to feed the prophet has appeared to many so strange that they have laboured to make out the *Orebim,* which in our version has been rendered 'ravens,' to be as the word is used (in Eze 27:27) 'merchants'; or Arabians (2Ch 21:16 Ne 4:7); or, the citizens of Arabah, near Beth-shan (Jos 15:6 18:18). But the common rendering is, in our opinion, preferable to these conjectures. And, if Elijah was miraculously fed by ravens, it is idle to inquire where they found the bread and the flesh, for God would direct them. After the lapse of a year, the brook dried up, and this was a new trial to Elijah's faith.

1Ki 17:8–16. He is sent to a widow of Zarephath.

8–16. the word of the Lord came to him – Zarephath, Sarepta, now Surafend, whither he was directed to go, was far away on the western coast of Palestine, about nine miles south of Sidon, and within the dominions of Jezebel's impious father, where the famine also prevailed. Meeting, at his entrance into the town, the very woman who was appointed by divine providence to support him, his faith was severely tested by learning from her that her supplies were exhausted and that she was preparing her last meal for herself and son. The Spirit of God having prompted him to ask, and her to grant, some necessary succour, she received a prophet's reward (Mt 10:41,42), and for the one meal afforded to him, God, by a miraculous increase of the little stock, afforded many to her.

1Ki 17:17–24. He raises her son to life.

17–24. the son of the woman, the mistress of the house, fell sick – A severe domestic calamity seems to have led her to think that, as God had shut up heaven upon a sinful land in consequence of the prophet, she was suffering on a similar account. Without answering her bitter upbraiding, the prophet takes the child, lays it on his bed, and after a very earnest prayer, had the happiness of seeing its restoration, and along with it, gladness to the widow's heart and home. The prophet was sent to this widow, not merely for his own security, but on account of her faith, to strengthen and promote which he was directed to go to her rather than to many widows in Israel, who would have eagerly received him on the same privileged terms of exception from the grinding famine. The relief of her bodily necessities became the preparatory means of supplying her spiritual wants, and bringing her and her son, through the teachings of the prophet, to a clear knowledge of God, and a firm faith in His word (Lu 4:25).

Chapter 18

1Ki 18:1–16. Elijah meets Obadiah.

1. the third year – In the New Testament, it is said there was no rain 'for the space of three years and six months' [Jas 5:17]. The early rain fell in our March, the latter rain in our October. Though Ahab might have at first ridiculed Elijah's announcement, yet when neither of these rains fell in their season, he was incensed against the prophet as the cause of the national judgment, and compelled him, with God's direction, to consult his safety in flight. This was six months after the king was told there would be neither dew nor rain, and from this period the three years in this passage are computed.

Go, show thyself unto Ahab – The king had remained obdurate and impenitent. Another opportunity was to be given him of repentance, and Elijah was sent in order to declare to him the cause of the national judgment, and to promise him, on condition of his removing it, the immediate blessing of rain.

2. Elijah went – a marvellous proof of the nat-ural intrepidity of this prophet, of his moral courage, and his unfaltering confidence in the protecting care of God, that he ventured to approach the presence of the raging lion.

there was a sore famine in Samaria – Elijah found that the famine was pressing with intense severity in the capital. Corn must have been obtained for the people from Egypt or the adjoining countries, else life could not have been sustained for three years; but Ahab, with the chamberlain of his royal household, is represented as giving a personal search for pasture to his cattle. On the banks of the rivulets, grass, tender shoots of grass, might naturally be expected; but the water being dried up, the verdure would disappear. In the pastoral districts of the East it would be reckoned a most suitable occupation still for a king or chief to go at the head of such an expedition. Ranging over a large tract of country, Ahab had gone through one district, Obadiah through another.

3. Obadiah feared the Lord greatly – Although he did not follow the course taken by the Levites and the majority of pious Israelites at that time of emigration into Judah (2Ch 11:13–16), he was a secret and sincere worshipper. He probably considered the violent character of the government, and his power of doing some good to the persecuted people of God as a sufficient excuse for his not going to worship in Jerusalem.

4. an hundred prophets – not men endowed with the extraordinary gifts of the prophetic office, but who were devoted to the service of God, preaching, praying, praising, (1Sa 10:10–12).

fed them with bread and water – These articles are often used to include sustenance of any kind. As this succour must have been given them at the hazard, not only of his place, but his life, it was a strong proof of his attachment to the true religion.

7-16. Obadiah was in the way ... Elijah met him – Deeming it imprudent to rush without previous intimation into Ahab's presence, the prophet solicited Obadiah to announce his return to Ahab. The commission, with a delicate allusion to the perils he had already encountered in securing others of God's servants, was, in very touching terms, declined, as unkind and peculiarly hazardous. But Elijah having dispelled all the apprehensions entertained about the Spirit's carrying him away, Obadiah undertook to convey the prophet's message to Ahab and solicit an interview. But Ahab, bent on revenge, or impatient for the appearance of rain, went himself to meet Elijah.

17, 18. Art thou he that troubleth Israel – A violent altercation took place. Ahab thought to awe him into submission, but the prophet boldly and undisguisedly told the king that the national calamity was traceable chiefly to his own and his family's patronage and practice of idolatry. But, while rebuking the sins, Elijah paid all due respect to the high rank of the offender. He urged the king to convene, by virtue of his royal mandate, a public assembly, in whose presence it might be solemnly decided which was the troubler of Israel. The appeal could not well be resisted, and Ahab, from whatever motives, consented to the proposal. God directed and overruled the issue.

19. gather . . . the prophets of Baal ... the prophets of the groves – From the sequel it appears that the former only came. The latter, anticipating some evil, evaded the king's command.

which eat at Jezebel's table – that is, not at the royal table where she herself dined, but they were maintained from her kitchen establishment (see on 1Sa 20:25 and 1Ki 4:22). They were the priests of Astarte, the Zidonian goddess.

20. mount Carmel – is a bold, bluff promontory, which extends from the western coast of Palestine, at the bay of Acre, for many miles eastward, to the central hills of Samaria. It is a long range, presenting many summits, and intersected by a number of small ravines. The spot where the contest took place is situated at the eastern extremity, which is also the highest point of the whole ridge. It is called El-Mohhraka, 'the Burning,' or 'the Burnt Place.' No spot could have been better adapted for the thousands of Israel to have stood drawn up on those gentle slopes. The rock shoots up in an almost perpendicular wall of more than two hundred feet in height, on the side of the vale of Esdraelon. This wall made it visible over the whole plain, and from all the surrounding heights, where gazing multitudes would be stationed.

21-40. Elijah said unto all the people, How long halt ye? – They had long been attempting to conjoin the service of God with that of Baal. It was an impracticable union and the people were so struck with a sense of their own folly, or dread of the king's displeasure, that they 'answered not a word.' Elijah proposed to decide for them the controversy between God and Baal by an appeal, not to the authority of the law, for that would have no weight, but by a visible token from Heaven. As fire was the element over which Baal was supposed to preside, Elijah proposed that two bullocks should be slain and placed on separate altars of wood, the one for Baal, and the other for God. On whichever the fire should descend to consume it, the event should determine the true God, whom it was their duty to serve. The proposal, appearing every way reasonable, was received by the people with unanimous approval. The priests of Baal commenced the ceremony by calling on their god. In vain did they continue invoking their senseless deity from morning till noon, and from noon till evening, uttering the most piercing cries, using the most frantic gesticulations, and mingling their blood with the sacrifice. No response was heard. No fire descended. Elijah exposed their folly and imposture with the severest irony and, as the day was far advanced, commenced his operations. Inviting the people to approach and see the entire proceeding, he first repaired an old altar of God, which Jezebel had demolished. Then, having arranged the cut pieces of the bullock, he caused four barrels or jars of water to be dashed all over the altar and round in the trench. Once, twice, a third time this precaution was taken, and then, when he had offered an earnest prayer, the miraculous fire descended (Le 9:24 Jud 6:21 13:20 1Ch 21:26 2Ch 7:1), and consumed not only the sacrifice, but the very stones of the altar. The impression on the minds of the people was that of admiration mingled with awe; and with one voice they acknowledged the supremacy of Jehovah as the true God. Taking advantage of their excited feelings, Elijah called on them to seize the priestly impostors, and by their blood fill the channel of the river (Kishon), which, in consequence of their idolatries, the drought had dried up – a direction, which, severe and relentless as it seems, it was his duty as God's minister to give (De 15:5 18:20). The natural features of the mount exactly correspond with the details of this narrative. The conspicuous summit, 1635 feet above the sea, on which the altars were placed, presents an esplanade spacious enough for the king and the priests of Baal to stand on the one side, and Elijah on the other. It is a rocky soil, on which there is abundance of loose stones, to furnish the twelve stones of which the altar was built – a bed of thick earth, in which a trench could be dug; and yet the earth not so loose that the water poured into it would be absorbed; two hundred fifty feet beneath the altar plateau, there is a perennial fountain, which, being close to the altar of the Lord, might not have been accessible to the people; and whence, therefore, even in that season of severe drought, Elijah could procure those copious supplies of water which he poured over the altar. The distance between this spring and the site of the altar is so short, as to make it perfectly possible to go thrice thither and back again, whereas it would have been impossible *once* in an afternoon to fetch water from the sea [VAN DE VELDE]. The summit is one thousand feet above the Kishon, which nowhere runs from the sea so close to the base of the mount as just beneath El-Mohhraka; so that the priests of Baal could, in a few minutes, be taken down to the brook (torrent), and slain there.

1Ki 18:41-46. Elijah, by prayer, obtains rain.

42. Ahab went up to eat and to drink – Ahab, kept in painful excitement by the agonizing scene, had eaten nothing all the day. He was recommended to refresh himself without a moment's delay; and, while the king was thus occupied, the prophet, far from taking rest, was absorbed in prayer for the fulfilment of the promise (1Ki 18:1).

put his face between his knees – a posture of earnest supplication still used.

43. Go up now, look toward the sea – From the place of worship there is a *small eminence,* which, on the west and northwest side, intercepts the view of the sea [STANLEY, VAN DE VELDE]. It can be ascended in a few minutes, and presents a wide prospect of the Mediterranean. Six times the servant went up, but the sky was clear – the sea tranquil. On the seventh he described the sign of approaching rain [1Ki 18:44].

44. Behold, there ariseth a little cloud out of the sea, like a man's hand – The clearness of the sky renders the smallest speck distinctly visible; and this is in Palestine the uniform precursor of rain. It rises higher and higher, and becomes larger and larger with astonishing celerity, till the whole heaven is black, and the cloud bursts in a deluge of rain.

Prepare thy chariot, and get thee down, that the rain stop thee not – either by the river Kishon being suddenly so swollen as to be impassable, or from the deep layer of dust in the arid plain being turned into thick mud, so as to impede the wheels.

45. Ahab rode, and went to Jezreel – now Zerin, a distance of about ten miles. This race was performed in the midst of a tempest of rain. But all rejoiced at it, as diffusing a sudden refreshment over all the land of Jezreel.

46. Elijah … girded up his loins, and ran before Ahab – It was anciently, and still is in some countries of the East, customary for kings and nobles to have runners before their chariots, who are tightly girt for the purpose. The prophet, like the Bedouins of his native Gilead, had been trained to run; and, as the Lord was with him, he continued with unabated agility and strength. It was, in the circumstances, a most proper service for Elijah to render. It tended to strengthen the favourable impression made on the heart of Ahab and furnished an answer to the cavils of Jezebel for it showed that he who was so zealous in the service of God, was, at the same time, devotedly loyal to his king. The result of this solemn and decisive contest was a heavy blow and great discouragement to the cause of idolatry. But subsequent events seem to prove that the impressions, though deep, were but partial and temporary.

Chapter 19

1Ki 19:1–3. Elijah flees to Beer-sheba.

3. he arose, and went for his life – He entered Jezreel full of hope. But a message from the incensed and hard-hearted queen, vowing speedy vengeance for her slaughtered priests, dispelled all his bright visions of the future. It is probable, however, that in the present temper of the people, even she would not have dared to lay violent hands on the Lord's servant, and purposely threatened him because she could do no more. The threat produced the intended effect, for his faith suddenly failed him. He fled out of the kingdom into the southernmost part of the territories in Judah; nor did he deem himself safe even there, but, dismissing his servant, he resolved to seek refuge among the mountain recesses of Sinai, and there longed for death (Jas 5:17). This sudden and extraordinary depression of mind arose from too great confidence inspired by the miracles wrought at Carmel, and by the disposition the people evinced there. Had he remained steadfast and immovable, the impression on the mind of Ahab and the people generally might have been followed by good results. But he had been exalted above measure (2Co 12:7–9), and being left to himself, the great prophet, instead of showing the indomitable spirit of a martyr, fled from his post of duty.

1Ki 19:4–18. He is comforted by an angel.

4–18. went a day's journey into the wilderness – on the way from Beer-sheba to Horeb – a wide expanse of sand hills, covered with the retem (not juniper, but broom shrubs), whose tall and spreading branches, with their white leaves, afford a very cheering and refreshing shade. His gracious God did not lose sight of His fugitive servant, but watched over him, and, miraculously ministering to his wants, enabled him, in a better but not wholly right frame of mind, by virtue of that supernatural supply, to complete his contemplated journey. In the solitude of Sinai, God appeared to instruct him. 'What doest thou here, Elijah?' was a searching question addressed to one who had been called to so arduous and urgent a mission as his. By an awful exhibition of divine power, he was made aware of the divine speaker who addressed him; his attention was arrested, his petulance was silenced, his heart was touched, and he was bid without delay return to the land of Israel, and prosecute the Lord's work there. To convince him that an idolatrous nation will not be unpunished, He commissions him to anoint three persons who were destined in Providence to avenge God's controversy with the people of Israel. Anointing is used synonymously with appointment (Jud 9:8), and is applied to all named, although Jehu alone had the consecrated

oil poured over his head. They were all three destined to be eminent instruments in achieving the destruction of idolaters, though in different ways. But of the three commissions, Elijah personally executed only one; namely, the call of Elisha to be his assistant and successor [1Ki 19:19], and by him the other two were accomplished (2Ki 8:7–13 9:1–10). Having thus satisfied the fiery zeal of the erring but sincere and pious prophet, the Lord proceeded to correct the erroneous impression under which Elijah had been labouring, of his being the sole adherent of the true religion in the land; for God, who seeth in secret, and knew all that were His, knew that there were seven thousand persons who had not done homage (literally, 'kissed the hand') to Baal.

16. Abel-meholah – that is, 'the meadow of dancing,' in the valley of the Jordan.

1Ki 19:19–21. Elisha follows Elijah.

19. Elisha the son of Shaphat – Most probably he belonged to a family distinguished for piety, and for their opposition to the prevailing calf-worship.

ploughing with twelve yoke of oxen – indicating that he was a man of substance.

Elijah … cast his mantle upon him – This was an investiture with the prophetic office. It is in this way that the Brahmins, the Persian Sufis, and other priestly or sacred characters in the East are appointed – a mantle being, by some eminent priest, thrown across their shoulders. Elisha had probably been educated in the schools of the prophets.

20. what have I done to thee? – that is, Go, but keep in mind the solemn ceremony I have just performed on thee. It is not I, but God, who calls thee. Do not allow any earthly affection to detain you from obeying His call.

21. took a yoke of oxen – Having hastily prepared (2Sa 24:22) a farewell entertainment to his family and friends, he left his native place and attached himself to Elijah as his minister.

Chapter 20

1Ki 20:1–12. Ben-hadad besieges Samaria.

1. Ben-hadad the king of Syria – This monarch was the son of that Ben-hadad who, in the reign of Baasha, made a raid on the northern towns of Galilee (1Ki 15:20). The thirty-two kings that were confederate with him were probably tributary princes. The ancient kings of Syria and Phoenicia ruled only over a single city, and were independent of each other, except when one great city, as Damascus, acquired the ascendency, and even then they were allied only in time of war. The Syrian army encamped at the gates and besieged the town of Samaria.

2–12. Thus said Ben-hadad, Thy silver and thy gold is mine – To this message sent him during the siege, Ahab returned a tame and submissive answer, probably thinking it meant no more than an exaction of tribute. But the demand was repeated with greater insolence; and yet, from the abject character of Ahab, there is reason to believe he would have yielded to this arrogant claim also, had not the voice of his subjects been raised against it. Ben-hadad's object in these and other boastful menaces was to intimidate Ahab. But the weak sovereign began to show a little more spirit, as appears in his abandoning 'my lord the king' for the single 'tell him,' and giving him a dry but sarcastic hint to glory no more till the victory is won. Kindling into a rage at the cool defiance, Ben-hadad gave orders for the immediate sack of the city.

12. as he was drinking, he and the kings in the pavilions – booths made of branches of trees and brushwood; which were reared for kings in the camp, as they still are for Turkish pashas or agas in their expeditions [KEIL].

1Ki 20:13–21. The Syrians are slain.

13–21. behold, there came a prophet unto Ahab – Though the king and people of Israel had highly offended Him, God had not utterly cast them off. He still cherished designs of mercy towards them, and here, though unasked, gave them a signal proof of His interest in them, by a prophet's animating announcement that the Lord would that day deliver the mighty hosts of the enemy into his hand by means of a small, feeble, inadequate band. Conformably to the prophet's instructions, two hundred thirty-two young men went boldly out towards the camp of the enemy, while seven thousand more, apparently volunteers, followed at some little distance, or posted themselves at the gate, to be ready to reinforce these in front if occasion required it. Ben-hadad and his vassals and princes were already, at that early hour – scarcely midday – deep in their cups; and though informed of this advancing company, yet confiding in his numbers, or it may be, excited with wine, he ordered with indifference the proud intruders to be taken alive, whether they came with peaceful or hostile intentions. It was more easily said than done; the young men smote right and left, making terrible havoc among their intended captors; and their attack, together with the sight of the seven thousand, who soon rushed forward to mingle in the fray, created a panic in the Syrian army, who immediately took up flight. Ben-hadad himself escaped the pursuit of the victors on a fleet horse, surrounded by a squadron of horse guards. This glorious victory, won so easily, and with such a paltry force opposed to overwhelming numbers, was granted that Ahab and his people might know that God is the Lord. But we do not read of this acknowledgment being made, or of any sacrifices being offered in token of their national gratitude.

22-26. the prophet came to the king of Israel, and said – The same prophet who had predicted the victory shortly reappeared, admonishing the king to take every precaution against a renewal of hostilities in the following campaign.

at the return of the year – that is, in spring, when, on the cessation of the rainy season, military campaigns (2Sa 11:1), were anciently begun. It happened as the prophet had forewarned. Brooding over their late disastrous defeat, the attendants of Ben-hadad ascribed the misfortune to two causes – the one arose from the principles of heathenism which led them to consider the gods of Israel as 'gods of the hills'; whereas their power to aid the Israelites would be gone if the battle was maintained on the plains. The other cause to which the Syrian courtiers traced their defeat at Samaria, was the presence of the tributary kings, who had probably been the first to take flight; and they recommended 'captains to be put in their rooms.' Approving of these recommendations, Ben-hadad renewed his invasion of Israel the next spring by the siege of Aphek in the valley of Jezreel (compare 1Sa 29:1, with 1Sa 28:4), not far from En-dor.

27-31. like two little flocks of kids – Goats are never seen in large flocks, or scattered, like sheep; and hence the two small but compact divisions of the Israelite force are compared to goats, not sheep. Humanly speaking, that little handful of men would have been overpowered by numbers. But a prophet was sent to the small Israelite army to announce the victory, in order to convince the Syrians that the God of Israel was omnipotent everywhere, in the valley as well as on the hills. And, accordingly, after the two armies had pitched opposite each other for seven days, they came to an open battle. One hundred thousand Syrians lay dead on the field, while the fugitives took refuge in Aphek, and there, crowding on the city walls, they endeavoured to make a stand against their pursuers; but the old walls giving way under the incumbent weight, fell and buried twenty-seven thousand in the ruins. Ben-hadad succeeded in extricating himself, and, with his attendants, sought concealment in the city, fleeing from chamber to chamber; or, as some think it, an inner chamber, that is, a harem; but seeing no ultimate means of escape, he was advised to throw himself on the tender mercies of the Israeli monarch.

32-34. put ropes on their heads – Captives were dragged by ropes round their necks in companies, as is depicted on the monuments of Egypt. Their voluntary attitude and language of submission flattered the pride of Ahab, who, little concerned about the dishonour done to the God of Israel by the Syrian king, and thinking of nothing but victory, paraded his clemency, called the vanquished king 'his brother,' invited him to sit in the royal chariot, and dismissed him with a covenant of peace.

34. streets for thee in Damascus – implying that a quarter of that city was to be assigned to Jews, with the free exercise of their religion and laws, under a judge of their own. This misplaced kindness to a proud and impious idolater, so unbecoming a theocratic monarch, exposed Ahab to the same censure and fate as Saul (1Sa 15:9,). It was in opposition to God's purpose in giving him the victory.

1Ki 20:35–42. A prophet reproves him.

35–38. Smite me – This prophet is supposed (1Ki 20:8) to have been Micaiah. The refusal of his neighbours to smite the prophet was manifestly wrong, as it was a withholding of necessary aid to a prophet in the discharge of a duty to which he had been called by God, and it was severely punished (1Ki 20:36), as a beacon to warn others (see on 1Ki 13:2–24). The prophet found a willing assistant, and then, waiting for Ahab, leads the king unconsciously, in the parabolic manner of Nathan (2Sa 12:1–4), to pronounce his own doom; and this consequent punishment was forthwith announced by a prophet (see on 1Ki 21:17).

Chapter 21

1Ki 21:1–4. Naboth refuses Ahab his vineyard.

1–3. Naboth the Jezreelite had a vineyard, which was in Jezreel – Ahab was desirous, from its contiguity to the palace, to possess it for a vegetable garden. He proposed to Naboth to give him a better in exchange, or to obtain it by purchase; but the owner declined to part with it. In persisting in his refusal, Naboth was not actuated by any feelings of disloyalty or disrespect to the king, but solely from a conscientious regard to the divine law, which, for important reasons, had prohibited the sale of a paternal inheritance [Le 25:23 Nu 36:7]; or if, through extreme poverty or debt, an assignation of it to another was unavoidable, the conveyance was made on the condition of its being redeemable at any time [Le 25:25–27]; at all events, of its reverting at the jubilee to the owner [Le 25:28]. In short, it could not be alienated from the family, and it was on this ground that Naboth (1Ki 21:3) refused to comply with the king's demand. It was not, therefore, any rudeness or disrespect that made Ahab heavy and displeased, but his sulky and pettish demeanor betrays a spirit of selfishness that could not

brook to be disappointed of a favourite object, and that would have pushed him into lawless tyranny had he possessed any natural force of character.

4. turned away his face – either to conceal from his attendants the vexation of spirit he felt, or, by the affectation of great sorrow, rouse them to devise some means of gratifying his wishes.

1Ki 21:5–16. Jezebel causes Naboth to be stoned.

7. Dost thou now govern the kingdom of Israel? – This is not so much a question as an exclamation – a sarcastic taunt; 'A pretty king thou art! Canst thou not use thy power and take what thy heart is set upon?'

arise, and eat bread, and let thine heart be merry: I will give thee the vineyard – After upbraiding Ahab for his pusillanimity and bidding him act as a king, Jezebel tells him to trouble himself no more about such a trifle; she would guarantee the possession of the vineyard.

8. So she wrote letters in Ahab's name, and sealed them with his seal – The seal-ring contained the name of the king and gave validity to the documents to which it was affixed (Es 8:8 Da 6:17). By allowing her the use of his signet-ring, Ahab passively consented to Jezebel's proceeding. Being written in the king's name, it had the character of a royal mandate.

sent the letters unto the elders and to the nobles that were in his city – They were the civic authorities of Jezreel, and would, in all likelihood, be the creatures and fit tools of Jezebel. It is evident that, though Ahab had recently been in Jezreel, when he made the offer to Naboth, both he and Jezebel were now in Samaria (1Ki 20:43).

9. Proclaim a fast, – Those obsequious and unprincipled magistrates did according to orders. Pretending that a heavy guilt lay on one, or some unknown party, who was charged with blaspheming God and the king and that Ahab was threatening vengeance on the whole city unless the culprit were discovered and punished, they assembled the people to observe a solemn fast. Fasts were commanded on extraordinary occasions affecting the public interests of the state (2Ch 20:3 Ezr 8:21 Joe 1:14 2:15 Jon 3:5). The wicked authorities of Jezreel, by proclaiming the fast, wished to give an external appearance of justice to their proceedings and convey an impression among the people that Naboth's crime amounted to treason against the king's life.

set Naboth on high – During a trial the panel, or accused person, was placed on a high seat, in the presence of all the court; but as the guilty person was supposed to be unknown, the setting of Naboth on high among the people must have been owing to his being among the distinguished men of the place.

13. there came in two men – worthless fellows who had been bribed to swear a falsehood. The law required two witnesses in capital offenses (De 17:6 19:15 Nu 35:30 Mt 26:60). Cursing God and cursing the king are mentioned in the law (Ex 22:28) as offenses closely connected, the king of Israel being the earthly representative of God in His kingdom.

they carried him forth out of the city, and stoned him – The law, which forbade cursing the rulers of the people, does not specify the penalty for this offense but either usage had sanctioned or the authorities of Jezreel had originated stoning as the proper punishment. It was always inflicted out of the city (Ac 7:58).

14–16. Jezebel said to Ahab, Arise, take possession – Naboth's execution having been announced, and his family being involved in the same fatal sentence (2Ki 9:26), his property became forfeited to the crown, not by law, but traditionary usage (see 2Sa 16:4).

16. Ahab rose up to go down – from Samaria to Jezreel.

1Ki 21:17–29. Elijah denounces judgments against Ahab and Jezebel.

17–19. Hast thou killed, and also taken possession? – While Ahab was in the act of surveying his ill-gotten possession, Elijah, by divine commission, stood before him. The appearance of the prophet, at such a time, was ominous of evil, but his language was much more so (compare Eze 45:8 46:16-18). Instead of shrinking with horror from the atrocious crime, Ahab eagerly hastened to his newly acquired property.

19. In the place where dogs licked– a righteous retribution of Providence. The prediction was accomplished, not in Jezreel, but in Samaria; and not on Ahab personally, in consequence of his repentance (1Ki 21:29), but on his son (2Ki 9:25). The words 'in the place where' might be rendered 'in like manner as'.

20. thou hast sold thyself to work evil – that is, allowed sin to acquire the unchecked and habitual mastery over thee (2Ki 17:17 Ro 7:11).

21, 22. will make thine house, – (see on 1Ki 15:29 and 1Ki 16:3–12). Jezebel, though included among the members of Ahab's house, has her ignominious fate expressly foretold (see 2Ki 9:30).

27–29. Ahab … rent his clothes, and put sackcloth upon his flesh, and fasted, and lay in sackcloth, and went softly – He was not obdurate, like Jezebel. This terrible announcement made a deep impression on the king's heart, and led, for a while, to sincere repentance. Going softly, that is, barefoot, and with a pensive manner, within doors. He manifested all the external signs, conventional and natural, of the deepest

sorrow. He was wretched, and so great is the mercy of God, that, in consequence of his humiliation, the threatened punishment was deferred.

Chapter 22

1Ki 22:1–36. Ahab slain at Ramoth-gilead.

1. continued three years without war between Syria and Israel – The disastrous defeat of Ben-hadad had so destroyed his army and exhausted the resources of his country, that, however eager, he was unable to recommence active hostilities against Israel. But that his hereditary enmity remained unsubdued, was manifest by his breach of faith concerning the treaty by which he had engaged to restore all the cities which his father had seized (1Ki 20:34).

2. Jehoshaphat the king of Judah came down to the king of Israel – It was singular that a friendly league between the sovereigns of Israel and Judah should, for the first time, have been formed by princes of such opposite characters – the one pious, the other wicked. Neither this league nor the matrimonial alliance by which the union of the royal families was more closely cemented, met the Lord's approval (2Ch 19:2). It led, however, to a visit by Jehoshaphat, whose reception in Samaria was distinguished by the most lavish hospitality (2Ch 18:2). The opportunity of this visit was taken advantage of, to push an object on which Ahab's heart was much set.

3–8. Know ye that Ramoth in Gilead is ours – a Levitical and free town on the north border of Gad (De 4:43 Jos 21:38), on the site of the present Salt Lake, in the province of Belka. It lay within the territories of the Israeli monarch, and was unjustly alienated; but whether it was one of the cities usurped by the first Ben-hadad, which his son had promised to restore, or was retained for some other reasons, the sacred historian has not mentioned. In the expedition which Ahab meditated for the recovery of this town, the aid of Jehoshaphat was asked and promised (see 2Ch 18:3). Previous to declaring hostilities, it was customary to consult the prophets (see on 1Sa 28:8); and Jehoshaphat having expressed a strong desire to know the Lord's will concerning this war, Ahab assembled four hundred of his prophets. These could not be either the prophets of Baal or of Ashteroth (1Ki 18:19), but seem (1Ki 22:12) to have been false prophets, who conformed to the symbolic calf-worship of Jehovah. Being the creatures of Ahab, they unanimously predicted a prosperous issue to the war. But dissatisfied with them, Jehoshaphat inquired if there was any true prophet of the Lord. Ahab agreed, with great reluctance, to allow Micaiah to be summoned. He was the only true prophet then to be found residing in Samaria, and he had to be brought out of prison (1Ki 22:26), into which, according to JOSEPHUS, he had been cast on account of his rebuke to Ahab for sparing the king of Syria.

10. a void place – literally, 'a threshing-floor,' formed at the gate of Samaria.

11. Zedekiah the son of Chenaanah made him horns of iron – Small projections, of the size and form of our candle extinguishers (worn in many parts of the East as military ornaments), were worn by the Syrians of that time, and probably by the Israelite warriors also. Zedekiah, by assuming two horns, personated two heroes, and, pretending to be a prophet, wished in this manner to represent the kings of Israel and Judah in a military triumph. It was a symbolic action, to impart greater force to his language (see De 33:17); but it was little more than a flourish with a *spontoon* [CALMET, *Fragments*].

14–17. what the Lord saith unto me, that will I speak – On the way the messenger who conducted [Micaiah] to the royal presence informed him of the tenor of the prophecies already given and recommended him to agree with the rest, no doubt from the kindly motive of seeing him released from imprisonment. But Micaiah, inflexibly faithful to his divine mission as a prophet, announced his purpose to proclaim honestly whatever God should bid him. On being asked by the king, 'Shall I go against Ramoth-gilead, or shall I forbear?' the prophet gave precisely the same answer as the previous oracles that had been consulted; but it must have been given in a sarcastic tone and in ironical mockery of their way of speaking. Being solemnly urged to give a serious and truthful answer, Micaiah then declared the visionary scene the Spirit had revealed to him; –

17. I saw all Israel scattered upon the hills, as sheep that have not a shepherd – The purport of this was that the army of Israel would be defeated and dispersed; that Ahab would fall in the battle, and the people return without either being pursued or destroyed by the enemy.

18–23. Did I not tell thee that he would prophesy no good concerning me, but evil? – Since Ahab was disposed to trace this unwelcome truth to personal enmity, Micaiah proceeded fearlessly to tell the incensed monarch in full detail what had been revealed to him. The Hebrew prophets, borrowing their symbolic pictures from earthly scenes, described God in heaven as a king in His kingdom. And as earthly princes do nothing of importance without asking the advice of their counsellors, God is represented as consulting about the fate of Ahab. This prophetic language must not be interpreted literally, and the command must be viewed as only a permission to the lying spirit (Ro 11:34) [CALMET].

24, 25. Zedekiah the son of Chenaanah went near, and smote Micaiah on the cheek – The insolence of this man, the leader of the false prophets, seems to have been provoked by jealousy at Micaiah's assumed monopoly of the spirit of inspiration. This mode of smiting, usually with a shoe, is both severe and ignominious. The calm reply of the Lord's prophet consisted in announcing the fate of the false prophets who suffered as the advisers of the disastrous expedition.

26–28. Take Micaiah, ... Put this fellow in prison – Ahab, under the impulse of vehement resentment, remands the prophet until his return.

27, 28. bread of affliction, water of affliction – that is, the poorest prison fare. Micaiah submitted, but reiterated aloud, in the presence of all, that the issue of the war would be fatal to Ahab.

29–38. went up to Ramoth-gilead – The king of Israel, bent on this expedition, marched, accompanied by his ally, with all his forces to the siege; but on approaching the scene of action, his courage failed, and, hoping to evade the force of Micaiah's prophecy by a secret stratagem, he assumed the uniform of a subaltern, while he advised Jehoshaphat to fight in his royal attire. The Syrian king, with a view either to put the speediest end to the war, or perhaps to wipe out the stain of his own humiliation (1Ki 20:31), had given special instructions to his generals to single out Ahab, and to take or kill him, as the author of the war. The officers at first directed their assault on Jehoshaphat, but, becoming aware of their mistake, desisted. Ahab was wounded by a random arrow, which, being probably poisoned, and the state of the weather increasing the virulence of the poison, he died at sunset. The corpse was conveyed to Samaria; and, as the chariot which brought it was being washed, in a pool near the city, from the blood that had profusely oozed from the wound, the dogs, in conformity with Elijah's prophecy, came and licked it [1Ki 21:19]. Ahab was succeeded by his son Ahaziah.

2 KINGS

Robert Jamieson

Introduction

See 1 Kings Introduction

Chapter 1

2Ki 1:1. Moab rebels.

1. Then Moab rebelled – Subdued by David (2Sa 8:2), they had, in the partition of Israel and Judah, fallen to the share of the former kingdom. But they took advantage of the death of Ahab to shake off the yoke (see on 2Ki 3:6). The casualty that befell Ahaziah [2Ki 1:2] prevented his taking active measures for suppressing this revolt, which was accomplished as a providential judgment on the house of Ahab for all these crimes.

2Ki 1:2–8. Ahaziah's judgment by Elijah.

2–8. Ahaziah fell down through a lattice in his upper chamber – This lattice was either a *part* of the wooden parapet, or fence, which surrounds the flat roofs of houses, and over which the king was carelessly leaning when it gave way; or it might be an opening like a skylight in the roof itself, done over with lattice – work, which, being slender or rotten, the king stepped on and slipped through. This latter supposition is most probably the true one, as Ahaziah did not fall either into the street or the court, but 'in his upper chamber.'
inquire of Baalzebub – Anxious to learn whether he should recover from the effects of this severe fall, he sent to consult Baalzebub, that is, the god of flies, who was considered the patron deity of medicine. A temple to that idol was erected at Ekron, which was resorted to far and wide, though it afterwards led to the destruction of the place (Zec 9:5 Am 1:8 Zep 2:4). 'After visiting Ekron, 'the god of flies' is a name that gives me no surprise. The flies there

swarmed, in fact so innumerably, that I could hardly get any food without these troublesome insects getting into it' [VAN DE VELDE].
3. the angel of the Lord – not *an* angel, but *the* angel, who carried on all communications between the invisible God and His chosen people [HENGSTENBERG]. This angel commissioned Elijah to meet the king's messengers, to stop them peremptorily on the idolatrous errand, and convey by them to the king information of his approaching death. This consultation of an idol, being a breach of the fundamental law of the kingdom (Ex 20:3 De 5:7), was a daring and deliberate rejection of the national religion. The Lord, in making this announcement of his death, designed that he should see in that event a judgment for his idolatry.
4. Thou shalt not come down from that bed – On being taken up, he had probably been laid on the divan – a raised frame, about three feet broad, extended along the sides of a room, covered with cushions and mattresses – serving, in short, as a sofa by day and a bed by night, and ascended by steps. **Elijah departed** – to his ordinary abode, which was then at Mount Carmel (2Ki 2:25 1Ki 18:42).
5. the messengers turned back – They did not know the stranger; but his authoritative tone, commanding attitude, and affecting message determined them at once to return.
8. an hairy man – This was the description not of his person, as in the case of Esau, but of his dress, which consisted either of unwrought sheep or goatskins (Heb 11:37), or of camel's haircloth – the coarser manufacture of this material like our rough haircloth. The Dervishes and Bedouins are attired in this wild, uncouth

manner, while their hair flows loose on the head, their shaggy cloak is thrown over their shoulders and tied in front on the breast, naked, except at the waist, round which is a skin girdle – a broad, rough leathern belt. Similar to this was the girdle of the prophets, as in keeping with their coarse garments and their stern, uncompromising office.

2Ki 1:9–16. Elijah brings fire from heaven on Ahaziah's messengers.

9. Then the king sent unto him a captain of fifty – Any appearance of cruelty that there is in the fate of the two captains and their men will be removed, on a full consideration of the circumstances. God being the King of Israel, Ahaziah was bound to govern the kingdom according to the divine law; to apprehend the Lord's prophet, for discharging a commanded duty, was that of an impious and notorious rebel. The captains abetted the king in his rebellion; and they exceeded their military duty by contemptuous insults.

man of God – In using this term, they either spoke derisively, believing him to be no true prophet; or, if they regarded him as a true prophet, the summons to him to surrender himself bound to the king was a still more flagrant insult; the language of the second captain being worse than that of the first.

10. let fire come down – rather, 'fire shall come down.' Not to avenge a personal insult of Elijah, but an insult upon God in the person of His prophet; and the punishment was inflicted, not by the prophet, but by the direct hand of God.

15, 16. he arose, and went down with him – a marvellous instance of faith and obedience. Though he well knew how obnoxious his presence was to the king, yet, on receiving God's command, he goes unhesitatingly, and repeats, with his own lips, the unwelcome tidings conveyed by the messengers.

2Ki 1:17, 18. Ahaziah dies, and is succeeded by Jehoram.

17. Jehoram – The brother of Ahaziah (see on 2Ki 3:1).

Chapter 2

2Ki 2:1–10. Elijah divines Jordan.

1–7. when the Lord would take up Elijah – A revelation of this event had been made to the prophet; but, unknown to him, it had also been revealed to his disciples, and to Elisha in particular, who kept constantly beside him.

Gilgal – This Gilgal (Jiljil) was near Ebal and Gerizim; a school of the prophets was established there. At Beth-el there was also a school of the prophets, which Elijah had founded, notwithstanding that place was the headquarters

of the calf-worship; and at Jericho there was another (2Ki 2:4). In travelling to these places, which he had done through the impulse of the Spirit (2Ki 2:2,4–6), Elijah wished to pay a farewell visit to these several institutions, which lay on his way to the place of ascension and, at the same time, from a feeling of humility and modesty, to be in solitude, where there would be no eye-witnesses of his glorification. All his efforts, however, to prevail on his attendant to remain behind, were fruitless. Elisha knew that the time was at hand, and at every place the sons of the prophets spoke to him of the approaching removal of his master. Their last stage was at the Jordan. They were followed at a distance by fifty scholars of the prophets, from Jericho, who were desirous, in honour of the great occasion, to witness the miraculous translation of the prophet. The revelation of this striking event to so many was a necessary part of the dispensation; for it was designed to be under the law, like that of Enoch in the patriarchal age, a visible proof of another state, and a type of the resurrection of Christ.

3. take away thy master from thy head – an allusion to the custom of scholars sitting at the feet of their master, the latter being over their heads (Ac 22:3).

8. Elijah took his mantle, and wrapped it together, and smote the waters – Like the rod of Moses, it had the divinely operating power of the Spirit.

9. Elijah said unto Elisha, Ask what I shall do for thee – trusting either that it would be in his power to bequeath it, or that God, at his entreaty, would grant it.

let a double portion of thy spirit be upon me – This request was not, as is commonly supposed, for the power of working miracles exceeding the magnitude and number of his master's, nor does it mean a higher endowment of the prophetic spirit; for Elisha was neither superior to, nor perhaps equally great with, his predecessor. But the phrase, 'a double portion,' was applied to the first-born [De 21:17], and therefore Elisha's request was, simply, to be heir to the prophetic office and gifts of his master.

10. Thou hast asked a hard thing – an extraordinary blessing which *I* cannot, and God only, can give. Nevertheless he, doubtless by the secret directions of the Spirit, proposed to Elisha a sign, the observation of which would keep him in the attitude of an anxious waiter, as well as suppliant for the favour.

2Ki 2:11–18. He is taken up to heaven in a chariot of fire.

11. behold, there appeared a chariot of fire, and horses of fire – some bright effulgence, which, in the eyes of the spectators, resembled those objects.

went up by a whirlwind – a tempest or storm wind accompanied with vivid flashes of fire, figuratively used for the divine judgments (Isa 29:6).

12. Elisha saw it, and he cried, My father – that is, spiritual father, as the pupils of the prophets are called their sons.

the chariot of Israel, and the horseman thereof – that is, that as earthly kingdoms are dependent for their defence and glory upon warlike preparations, there a single prophet had done more for the preservation and prosperity of Israel than all her chariots and horsemen.

took hold of his own clothes and rent them – in token of his grief for his loss.

13. He took up also the mantle of Elijah – The transference of this prophetic cloak was, to himself, a pledge of his being appointed successor, and it was an outward token to others of the spirit of Elijah resting upon him.

14–18. smote the waters – The waving of the mantle on the river, and the miraculous division of the waters consequent upon it, was an evidence that the Lord God of Elijah was with him, and as this miracle was witnessed by the scholars of the prophets from Jericho, they forthwith recognized the pre-eminence of Elisha, as now the prophet of Israel.

16–18. fifty strong men, let them go, we pray thee, and seek thy master – Though the young prophets from Jericho had seen Elijah's miraculous passage of the Jordan, they had not witnessed the ascension. They imagined that he might have been cast by the whirlwind on some mountain or valley; or, if he had actually been admitted into heaven, they expected that his body would still be remaining somewhere on earth. In compliance with their importunity, he gave them permission, but told them what the result would be.

2Ki 2:19–25. Elisha heals the waters.

20. Bring me a new cruse, and put salt therein – The noxious qualities of the water could not be corrected by the infusion of salt – for, supposing the salt was possessed of such a property, a whole spring could not be purified by a dishful for a day, much less in all future time. The pouring in of the salt was a symbolic act with which Elisha accompanied the word of the Lord, by which the spring was healed [KEIL].

23, 24. there came forth little children out of the city – that is, the idolatrous, or infidel young men of the place, who affecting to disbelieve the report of his master's translation, sarcastically urged him to follow in the glorious career.

bald head – an epithet of contempt in the East, applied to a person even with a bushy head of hair. The appalling judgment that befell them was God's interference to uphold his newly invested prophet.

Chapter 3

2Ki 3:1–3. Jehoram's evil reign over Israel.

1, 2. Jehoram the son of Ahab began to reign over Israel in Samaria the eighteenth year of Jehoshaphat – (compare 1Ki 22:51). To reconcile the statements in the two passages, we must suppose that Ahaziah, having reigned during the seventeenth and the greater part of the eighteenth year of Jehoshaphat, was succeeded by his brother Joram or Jehoram, in the end of that eighteenth year, or else that Ahaziah, having reigned two years in conjunction with his father, died at the end of that period when Jehoram ascended the throne. His policy was as hostile as that of his predecessors to the true religion; but he made some changes. Whatever was his motive for this alteration – whether dread of the many alarming judgments the patronage of idolatry had brought upon his father; or whether it was made as a small concession to the feelings of Jehoshaphat, his ally, he abolished idolatry in its gross form and restored the symbolic worship of God, which the kings of Israel, from the time of Jeroboam, had set up as a partition wall between their subjects and those of Judah.

2Ki 3:4, 5. Mesha, king of Moab, rebels.

4–6. Mesha king of Moab, – As his dominions embraced an extensive pasture country, he paid, as annual tribute, the wool of a hundred thousand lambs and a hundred thousand rams. It is still common in the East to pay custom and taxes in the fruits or natural produce of the land.

5. king of Moab rebelled – This is a repetition of 2Ki 1:1, in order to introduce an account of the confederate expedition for crushing this revolt, which had been allowed to continue unchecked during the short reign of Ahaziah.

2Ki 3:6–24. Elisha promises water and victory over Moab.

6. King Jehoram ... numbered Israel – made a levy from his own subjects, and at the same time sought an alliance with Jehoshaphat, which, as on the former occasion with Ahab, was readily promised (1Ki 22:4).

8-12. Which way shall we go up? And he answered, The way through the wilderness of Edom – This was a long and circuitous route, by the southern bend of the Dead Sea. Jehoshaphat, however, preferred it, partly because the part of the Moabite territory at which they would arrive, was the most defenceless; and partly because he would thereby enlist, in the expedition, the forces of the king of Edom. But, in penetrating this deep, rocky valley, which forms the boundary between Edom and Moab, the confederate army was reduced, both man and beast, to the greatest extremities for want of water. They were disappointed by finding the wady of this valley, the brook Zered (De 2:13–18) [ROBINSON], dry. Jehoram was in despair. But the pious mind of Jehoshaphat inquired for a prophet of the Lord; and, on being informed that Elisha was at hand, the three kings 'went down to him'; that is, to his tent, which was either in the camp, or close by it. He had been directed thither by the Spirit of God for this special purpose. They went to him, not only as a mark of respect, but to supplicate for his assistance.

11. which poured water on the hands of Elijah – that is, was his servant – this being one of the common offices of a servant. The phrase is used here as synonymous with 'a true and eminent prophet,' who will reveal God's will to us.

13, 14. What have I to do with thee? – Wishing to produce a deep spirit of humility and contrition, Elisha gave a stern repulse to the king of Israel, accompanied by a sarcastic sneer, in bidding him go and consult Baal and his soothsayers. But the distressed condition, especially the imploring language, of the royal suppliants, who acknowledged the hand of the Lord in this distress, drew from the prophet the solemn assurance, that solely out of respect to Jehoshaphat, the Lord's true servant, did he take any interest in Jehoram.

15. bring me a minstrel – The effect of music in soothing the mind is much regarded in the East; and it appears that the ancient prophets, before entering their work, commonly resorted to it, as a preparative, by praise and prayer, to their receiving the prophetic afflatus.

the hand of the Lord – a phrase significantly implying that the gift of prophecy was not a natural or inherent gift, but conferred by the power and grace of God.

16. Make this valley full of ditches – capable of holding water.

17. Ye shall not see wind – It is common in the East to speak of *seeing* wind, from the clouds of straw, dust, or sand, that are often whirled into the air, after a long drought.

20–24. when the meat offering was offered – that is, at the time of the morning sacrifice, accompanied, doubtless, with solemn prayers; and these led, it may be, by Elisha on this occasion, as on a similar one by Elijah (1Ki 18:36).

behold, there came water by the way of Edom – Far from the Israeli camp, in the eastern mountains of Edom, a great fall of rain, a kind of cloudburst, took place, by which the wady was at once filled, but they saw neither the wind nor the rains. The divine interposition was shown by introducing the laws of nature to the determined end in the predetermined way [KEIL]. It brought not only aid to the Israeli army in their distress, by a plentiful supply of water, but destruction on the Moabites, who, perceiving the water, under the refulgent rays of the morning sun, red like blood, concluded the confederate kings had quarrelled and deluged the field with their mutual slaughter; so that, rushing to their camp in full expectation of great spoil, they were met by the Israelites, who, prepared for battle, fought and pursued them. Their country was laid waste in the way, which has always been considered the greatest desolation in the East.

25. Kir-haraseth – (now Kerak) – Castle of Moab – then, probably, the only fortress in the land.

27. took his eldest son that should have reigned in his stead, and offered him for a burnt offering, – By this deed of horror, to which the allied army drove the king of Moab, a divine judgment came upon Israel; that is, the besiegers feared the anger of God, which they had incurred by giving occasion to the human sacrifice forbidden in the law (Le 18:21 20:3), and hastily raised the siege.

Chapter 4

2Ki 4:1–7. Elisha augments the widow's oil.

1. there cried a certain woman of the wives of the sons of the prophets – They were allowed to marry as well as the priests and Levites. Her husband, not enjoying the lucrative profits of business, had nothing but a professional income, which, in that irreligious age, would be precarious and very scanty, so that he was not in a condition to provide for his family.

the creditor is come to take unto him my two sons to be bondmen – By the enactment of the law, a creditor was entitled to claim the person and children of the insolvent debtor, and compel them to serve him as bondmen till the year of jubilee should set them free.

2–4. a pot – or cruet of oil. This comprising her whole stock of domestic utensils, he directs her to borrow empty vessels not a few; then, secluding herself with her children, [the widow] was to pour oil from her cruse into the borrowed vessels, and, selling the oil, discharge the debt, and then maintain herself and family with the remainder.

6. the oil stayed – that is, ceased to multiply; the benevolent object for which the miracle had been wrought having been accomplished.

2Ki 4:8-17. Promises a son to the Shunammite.

8. Elisha passed to Shunem – now Sulam, in the plain of Esdraelon, at the southwestern base of Little Hermon. The prophet, in his journey, was often entertained here by one of its pious and opulent inhabitants.

10. Let us make a little chamber – not build, but prepare it. She meant a room in the *oleah*, the porch, or gateway (2Sa 18:33 1Ki 17:19), attached to the front of the house, leading into the court and inner apartments. The front of the house, excepting the door, is a dead wall, and hence this room is called a chamber in the wall. It is usually appropriated to the use of strangers, or lodgers for a night, and, from its seclusion, convenient for study or retirement.

13–16. what is to be done for thee? – Wishing to testify his gratitude for the hospitable attentions of this family, he announced to her the birth of a son 'about this time next year.' The interest and importance of such an intelligence can only be estimated by considering that Oriental women, and Jewish in particular, connect ideas of disgrace with barrenness, and cherish a more ardent desire for children than women in any other part of the world (Ge 18:10–15).

2Ki 4:18–37. Raises her dead son.

19. My head, my head! – The cries of the boy, the part affected, and the season of the year, make it probable that he had been overtaken by a stroke of the sun. Pain, stupor, and inflammatory fever are the symptoms of the disease, which is often fatal.

22. she called unto her husband – Her heroic concealment of the death from her husband is not the least interesting feature of the story.

24. Drive, and go forward – It is usual for women to ride on asses, accompanied by a servant, who walks behind and drives the beast with his stick, goading the animal at the speed required by his mistress. The Shunammite had to ride a journey of five or six hours to the top of Carmel.

26–28. And she answered, It is well – Her answer was purposely brief and vague to Gehazi, for she reserved a full disclosure of her loss for the ear of the prophet himself. She had met Gehazi at the foot of the hill, and she stopped not in her ascent till she had disburdened her heavy-laden spirit at Elisha's feet. The violent paroxysm of grief into which she fell on approaching him, appeared to Gehazi an act of disrespect to his master; he was preparing to remove her when the prophet's observant eye perceived that she was overwhelmed with some unknown cause of distress. How great is a mother's love! how wondrous are the works of Providence! The Shunammite had not sought a son from the prophet – her child was, in every respect, the free gift of God. Was she then allowed to rejoice in the possession for a little, only to be pierced with sorrow by seeing the corpse of the cherished boy? Perish, doubt and unbelief! This event happened that 'the works of God should be made manifest' in this prophet, 'and for the glory of God.'

29–31. take my staff … and lay … upon the face of the child – The staff was probably an official rod of a certain form and size. Necromancers used to send their staff with orders to the messengers to let it come in contact with nothing by the way that might dissipate or destroy the virtue imparted to it. Some have thought that Elisha himself entertained similar ideas, and was under an impression that the actual application of his staff would serve as well as the touch of his hand. But this is an imputation dishonourable to the character of the prophet. He wished to teach the Shunammite, who obviously placed too great dependence upon him, a memorable lesson to look to God. By sending his servant forward to lay his staff on the child, he raised [the Shunammite's] expectations, but, at the same time, taught her that his own help was unavailing – 'there was neither voice, nor hearing.' The command, to salute no man by the way, showed the urgency of the mission, not simply as requiring the avoidance of the tedious and unnecessary greetings so common in the East (Lu 10:1), but the exercise of faith and prayer. The act of Gehazi was allowed to fail, in order to free the Shunammite, and the people of Israel at large, of the superstitious notion of supposing a miraculous virtue resided in any *person,* or in any *rod,* and to prove that it was only through earnest prayer and faith in the power of God and for His glory that this and every miracle was to be performed.

34. lay upon the child, – (see 1Ki 17:21 Ac 20:10). Although this contact with a dead body would communicate ceremonial uncleanness, yet, in performing the great moral duties of piety and benevolence, positive laws were sometimes dispensed with, particularly by the prophets.

35. the child sneezed seven times, and the child opened his eyes – These were the first acts of restored respiration, and they are described as successive steps. Miracles were for the most part performed instantaneously; but sometimes, also, they were advanced progressively towards completion (1Ki 18:44,45 Mr 8:24,25).

2Ki 4:38–41. Purifies deadly pottage.

38. there was a dearth in the land – (see on 2Ki 8:1). **the sons of the prophets were sitting before him** – When receiving instruction, the scholars sat under their masters. This refers to their being domiciled under the same roof (compare 2Ki 6:1). **Set on the great pot** – As it is most likely that the Jewish would resemble the Egyptian 'great pot,' it is seen by the monumental paintings to have been a large goblet, with two long legs, which stood over the fire on the floor. The seethed pottage consisted of meat cut into small pieces, mixed with rice or meal and vegetables.

39. went out into the field to gather herbs – Wild herbs are very extensively used by the people in the East, even by those who possess their own vegetable gardens. The fields are daily searched for mallow, asparagus, and other wild plants.

wild vine – literally, 'the vine of the field,' supposed to be the *colocynth*, a cucumber, which, in its leaves, tendrils, and fruit, bears a strong resemblance to the wild vine. The 'gourds,' or fruit, are of the colour and size of an orange bitter to the taste, causing colic, and exciting the nerves, eaten freely they would occasion such a derangement of the stomach and bowels as to be followed by death. The meal which Elisha poured into the pot was a symbolic sign that the noxious quality of the herbs was removed.

lap full – The hyke, or large cloak, is thrown loosely over the left shoulder and fastened under the right arm, so as to form a lap or apron.

2Ki 4:42–44. Satisfies a hundred men with twenty loaves.

43. They shall eat, and shall leave thereof – This was not a miracle of Elisha, but only a prediction of one by the word of the Lord. Thus it differed widely from those of Christ (Mt 15:37 Mr 8:8 Lu 9:17 Joh 6:12).

Chapter 5

2Ki 5:1–7. Naaman's leprosy.

1. Naaman, captain of the host of the king of Syria, was a great man with his master – highly esteemed for his military character and success. **and honourable** – rather, 'very rich.'

but he was a leper – This leprosy, which, in Israel, would have excluded him from society, did not affect his free intercourse in the court of Syria.

2–5. a little maid – who had been captured in one of the many predatory incursions which were then made by the Syrians on the northern border of Israel (see 1Sa 30:8 2Ki 13:21 2Ki 24:2). By this young Hebrew slave of his wife, Naaman's attention was directed to the prophet of Israel, as the person who would remove his leprosy. Naaman, on communicating the matter to his royal master, was immediately furnished with a letter to the king of Israel, and set out for Samaria, carrying with him, as an indispensable preliminary in the East, very costly presents.

5. ten changes of raiment – splendid dresses, for festive occasions – the honour being thought to consist not only in the beauty and fineness of the material, but on having a variety to put on one after another, in the same night.

7. when the king of Israel had read the letter, that he rent his clothes – According to an ancient practice among the Eastern people, the main object only was stated in the letter that was carried by the party concerned, while other circumstances were left to be explained at the interview. This explains Jehoram's burst of emotion – not horror at supposed blasphemy, but alarm and suspicion that this was merely made an occasion for a quarrel. Such a prince as he was would not readily think of Elisha, or, perhaps, have heard of his miraculous deeds.

2Ki 5:8–15. Elisha sends him to Jordan, and he is healed.

8–12. when Elisha the man of God had heard that the king of Israel had rent his clothes, that he sent to the king, saying, … let him come now to me – This was the grand and ultimate object to which, in the providence of God, the journey of Naaman was subservient. When the Syrian general, with his imposing retinue, arrived at the prophet's house, Elisha sent him a message to 'go and wash in Jordan seven times.' This apparently rude reception to a foreigner of so high dignity incensed Naaman to such a degree that he resolved to depart, scornfully boasting that the rivers of Damascus were better than all the waters of Israel.

11. strike his hand over the place – that is, wave it over the diseased parts of his body. It was anciently, and still continues to be, a very prevalent superstition in the East that the hand of a king, or person of great reputed sanctity, touching, or waved over a sore, will heal it.

12. Abana and Pharpar – the Barrady and one of its five tributaries – uncertain which. The waters of Damascus are still highly extolled by their inhabitants for their purity and coldness.

14. Then went he down, and dipped himself seven times in Jordan – Persuaded by his calmer and more reflecting attendants to try a method so simple and easy, he followed their instructions, and was cured. The cure was performed on the basis of God's covenant with Israel, by which the land, and all pertaining to it, was blessed. Seven was the symbol of the covenant [Keil].

2Ki 5:15–19. Elisha refuses Naaman's gifts.

15, 16. he returned to the man of God – After the miraculous cure, Naaman returned to Elisha, to whom he acknowledged his full belief in the sole supremacy of the God of Israel and offered him a liberal reward. But to show that he was not actuated by the mercenary motives of the heathen priests and prophets, Elisha, though he accepted presents on other occasions (2Ki 4:42), respectfully but firmly declined them on this, being desirous that the Syrians should see the piety of God's servants, and their superiority to all worldly and selfish motives in promoting the honour of God and the interests of true religion.

17. **two mules' burden of earth** – with which to make an altar (Ex 20:24) to the God of Israel. What his motive or his purpose was in this proposal – whether he thought that God could be acceptably worshipped only on his own soil; or whether he wished, when far away from the Jordan, to have the *earth* of Palestine to rub himself with, which the Orientals use as a substitute for water; or whether, by making such a request of Elisha, he thought the prophet's grant of it would impart some virtue; or whether, like the modern Jews and Mohammedans, he resolved to have a portion of this *holy earth* for his nightly pillow – it is not easy to say. It is not strange to find such notions in so newly a converted heathen.

18. **goeth into the house of Rimmon** – a Syrian deity; probably the sun, or the planetary system, of which a pomegranate (*Hebrew, Rimmon*) was the symbol.

leaneth on my hand – that is, meaning the service which Naaman rendered as the attendant of his sovereign. Elisha's prophetic commission not extending to any but the conversion of Israel from idolatry, he makes no remark, either approving or disapproving, on the declared course of Naaman, but simply gives the parting benediction (2Ki 5:19).

2Ki 5:20–27. Gehazi, by a lie, obtains a present, but is smitten with leprosy.

20–25. **I will run after him, and take somewhat of him** – The respectful courtesy to Elisha, shown in the person of his servant, and the open-handed liberality of his gifts, attest the fulness of Naaman's gratitude; while the lie – the artful management is dismissing the bearers of the treasure, and the deceitful appearance before his master, as if he had not left the house – give a most unfavorable impression of Gehazi's character.

23. **in two bags** – People in the East, when travelling, have their money, in certain sums, put up in bags.

27. **leper as white as snow** – This heavy infliction was not too severe for the crime of Gehazi. For it was not the covetousness alone that was punished; but, at the same time, it was the ill use made of the prophet's name to gain an object prompted by a mean covetousness, and the attempt to conceal it by lying [KEIL].

Chapter 6

2Ki 6:1–7. Elisha causes iron to swim.

1. **the place where we dwell with thee** – *Margin*, 'sit before thee.' The one points to a common residence – the other to a common place of meeting. The tenor of the narrative shows the humble condition of Elisha's pupils. The place was either Beth-el or Jericho, probably the latter. The ministry and miracles of Elisha brought great accessions to his schools.

2. **Let us go, we pray thee, unto Jordan** – whose wooded banks would furnish plenty of timber.

5. **it was borrowed** – literally, 'begged.' The scholar's distress arose from the consideration that it had been presented to him; and that, owing to his poverty, he could not procure another.

6. **cut down a stick, and cast it in thither** – Although this means was used, it had no natural adaptation to make the iron swim. Besides, the Jordan is at Jericho so deep and rapid that there were one thousand chances to one against the stick falling into the hole of the axe-head. All attempts to account for the recovery of the lost implement on such a theory must be rejected.

the iron did swim – only by the miraculous exertion of Elisha's power.

2Ki 6:8–17. Discloses the king of Syria's counsel.

8–12. **the king of Syria warred against Israel** – This seems to have been a sort of guerrilla warfare, carried on by predatory inroads on different parts of the country. Elisha apprised King Jehoram of the secret purpose of the enemy; so, by adopting precautionary measures, he was always enabled to anticipate and defeat their attacks. The frequency of his disappointments having led the Syrian king to suspect some of his servants of carrying on a treacherous correspondence with the enemy, he was informed about Elisha, whose apprehension he forthwith determined to effect. This resolution was, of course, grounded on the belief that however great the knowledge of Elisha might be, if seized and kept a prisoner, he could no longer give information to the king of Israel.

13. **Dothan** – or, 'Dothaim,' a little north of Samaria.

15. **his servant said unto him, Alas, my master! how shall we do?** – When the Syrian detachment surrounded the place by night, for the apprehension of the prophet, his servant was paralysed with fear. This was a new servant, who had only been with him since Gehazi's dismissal and consequently had little or no experience of his master's powers. His faith was easily shaken by so unexpected an alarm.

17. **Elisha prayed, and said, Lord, I pray thee, open his eyes, that he may see** – The invisible guard of angels that encompass and defend us (Ps 34:7). The opening of the eyes, which Elisha prayed for, were those of the Spirit, not of the body – the eye of faith sees the reality of the divine presence and protection where all is vacancy or darkness to the ordinary eye. The horses and chariots were symbols of the divine power (see on 2Ki 2:12); and their fiery nature

denoted their supernatural origin; for fire, the most ethereal of earthly elements, is the most appropriate symbol of the Godhead [KEIL].

2Ki 6:18–23. His army smitten with blindness.

18. Smite this people, I pray thee, with blindness – not a total and material blindness, for then they could not have followed him, but a mental hallucination (see Ge 19:11) so that they did not perceive or recognize him to be the object of their search.

19–23. This is not the way, neither is this the city – This statement is so far true that, as he had now left the place of his residence, they would not have got him by that road. But the ambiguity of his language was purposely framed to deceive them; and yet the deception must be viewed in the light of a stratagem, which has always been deemed lawful in war.

he led them to Samaria – When they were arrived in the midst of the capital, their eyes, at Elisha's request, were opened, and they then became aware of their defenceless condition, for Jehoram had received private premonition of their arrival. The king, so far from being allowed to slay the enemies who were thus unconsciously put in his power, was recommended to entertain them with liberal hospitality and then dismiss them to their own country. This was humane advice; it was contrary to the usage of war to put war captives to death in cold blood, even when taken by the point of the sword, much more those whom the miraculous power and providence of God had unexpectedly placed at his disposal. In such circumstances, kind and hospitable treatment was every way more becoming in itself, and would be productive of the best effects. It would redound to the credit of the true religion, which inspired such an excellent spirit into its professors; and it would not only prevent the future opposition of the Syrians but make them stand in awe of a people who, they had seen, were so remarkably protected by a prophet of the Lord. The latter clause of 2Ki 6:23 shows that these salutary effects were fully realized. A moral conquest had been gained over the Syrians.

2Ki 6:24–33. Ben-hadad besieges Samaria.

24. Ben-hadad … besieged Samaria – This was the predicted accomplishment of the result of Ahab's foolish and misplaced kindness (1Ki 20:42).

25. an ass's head was sold for fourscore pieces of silver – Though the ass was deemed unclean food, necessity might warrant their violation of a positive law when mothers, in their extremity, were found violating the law of nature. The head was the worst part of the animal.

the fourth part of a cab – A cab was the smallest dry measure.

dove's dung – is thought by BOCHART to be a kind of pulse or pea, common in Judea, and still kept in the storehouses of Cairo and Damascus, and other places, for the use of it by pilgrim-caravans; and other botanists, it is said to be the root or white bulb of the plant *Ornithogalum umbellatum*, Star of Beth-lehem. The sacred historian does not say that the articles here named were regularly sold at the rates described, but only that instances were known of such high prices being given.

26. as the king was passing – to look at the defences, or to give some necessary orders for manning the walls.

30. had sackcloth within upon his flesh – The horrid recital of this domestic tragedy led the king soon after to rend his garment, in consequence of which it was discovered that he wore a penitential shirt of haircloth. It is more than doubtful, however, if he was truly humbled on account of his own and the nation's sins; otherwise he would not have vowed vengeance on the prophet's life. The true explanation seems to be, that Elisha having counselled him not to surrender, with the promise, on condition of deep humiliation, of being delivered, and he having assumed the signs of contrition without receiving the expected relief, regarded Elisha who had proved false and faithless as the cause of all the protracted distress.

32. But Elisha sat in his house, and the elders sat with him – The latter clause of 2Ki 6:33, which contains the king's impatient exclamation, enables us to account for the impetuous order he issued for the beheading of Elisha. Though Jehoram was a wicked king and most of his courtiers would resemble their master, many had been won over, through the prophet's influence, to the true religion. A meeting, probably a prayer-meeting, of those was held in the house where he lodged, for he had none of his own (1Ki 19:20,21); and them he not only apprised of the king's design against himself, but disclosed to them the proof of a premeditated deliverance.

Chapter 7

2Ki 7:1–16. Elisha prophesies incredible plenty in Samaria.

1. Hear ye the word of the Lord – This prediction, though uttered first to the assembled elders, was intimated to the king's messengers, who reported it to Jehoram (2Ki 7:18).

To-morrow about this time shall a measure of fine flour be sold for a shekel, – This may be estimated at a peck of fine flour for a dollar, and two pecks of barley at the same price.

in the gate of Samaria – Vegetables, cattle, all sorts of country produce, are still sold every morning at the gates of towns in the East.

2. a lord on whose hand the king leaned – When an Eastern king walks or stands abroad in the open air, he always supports himself on the arm of the *highest* courtier present.

if the Lord would make windows in heaven – The scoffing infidelity of this remark, which was a sneer against not the prophet only, but the God he served, was justly and signally punished (see 2Ki 7:20).

3. there were four leprous men – The account of the sudden raising of the siege and the unexpected supply given to the famishing inhabitants of Samaria, is introduced by a narrative of the visit and discovery, by these poor creatures, of the extraordinary flight of the Syrians.

leprous men at the entering in of the gate – living, perhaps, in some lazar house there (Le 13:4-6 Nu 5:3).

5. they rose up in the twilight – that is, the evening twilight (2Ki 7:12).

the uttermost part of the camp of Syria – that is, the extremity nearest the city.

6, 7. the Lord had made the host of the Syrians to hear a noise of chariots – This illusion of the sense of hearing, whereby the besiegers imagined the tramp of two armies from opposite quarters, was a great miracle which God wrought directly for the deliverance of His people.

8–11. these lepers … did eat and drink – After they had appeased their hunger and secreted as many valuables as they could carry, their consciences smote them for concealing the discovery and they hastened to publish it in the city.

10. horses tied, and asses tied, and the tents as they were – The uniform arrangement of encampments in the East is to place the tents in the centre, while the cattle are picketed all around, as an outer wall of defence; and hence the lepers describe the cattle as the first objects they saw.

12–15. the king . . . said unto his servants, I will now show you what the Syrians have done – Similar stratagems have been so often resorted to in the ancient and modern wars of the East that there is no wonder Jehoram's suspicions were awakened. But the scouts, whom he despatched, soon found unmistakable signs of the panic that had struck the enemy and led to a most precipitate flight.

2Ki 7:17–20. The unbelieving lord trodden to death.

17. the king appointed the lord on whose hand he leaned – The news spread like lightning

through the city, and was followed, as was natural, by a popular rush to the Syrian camp. To keep order at the gate, the king ordered his minister to keep guard; but the impetuosity of the famishing people could not be resisted. The lord was trodden to death, and Elisha's prophecy in all respects accomplished.

Chapter 8

2Ki 8:1–6. The Shunammite's land restored.

1. Then spake Elisha unto the woman – rather 'had spoken.' The repetition of Elisha's direction to the Shunammite is merely given as an introduction to the following narrative; and it probably took place before the events recorded in the chapters 5 and 6.

the Lord hath called for a famine – All such calamities are chastisements inflicted by the hand of God; and this famine was to be of double duration to that one which happened in the time of Elijah (Jas 5:17) – a just increase of severity, since the Israelites still continued obdurate and incorrigible under the ministry and miracles of Elisha (Le 26:21,24,28).

2. she … sojourned in the land of the Philistines seven years – Their territory was recommended to her from its contiguity to her usual residence; and now that this state had been so greatly reduced, there was less risk than formerly from the seductions of idolatry; and many of the Jews and Israelites were residing there. Besides, an emigration thither was less offensive to the king of Israel than going to sojourn in Judah.

3. she went forth to cry unto the king for her house and for her land – In consequence of her long-continued absence from the country, her possessions were occupied by her kindred, or had been confiscated by the crown. No statute in the law of Moses ordained that alienation. But the innovation seems to have been adopted in Israel.

4–6. the king talked with Gehazi – Ceremonial pollution being conveyed by contact alone, there was nothing to prevent a conference being held with this leper at a distance; and although he was excluded from the *town* of Samaria, this reported conversation may have taken place at the gate or in one of the royal gardens. The providence of God so ordained that King Jehoram had been led to inquire, with great interest, into the miraculous deeds of Elisha, and that the prophet's servant was in the act of relating the marvellous incident of the restoration of the Shunammite's son when she made her appearance to prefer her request. The king was pleased to grant it; and a state officer was charged to afford her every facility in the recovery of her family possession out of the hands of the occupier.

2Ki 8:7–15. Hazael kills his master, and succeeds him.

7, 8. Elisha came to Damascus – He was directed thither by the Spirit of God, in pursuance of the mission formerly given to his master in Horeb (1Ki 19:15), to anoint Hazael king of Syria. On the arrival of the prophet being known, Ben-hadad, who was sick, sent to inquire the issue of his disease, and, according to the practice of the heathens in consulting their soothsayers, ordered a liberal present in remuneration for the service.

9. forty camels' burden – The present, consisting of the rarest and most valuable produce of the land, would be liberal and magnificent. But it must not be supposed it was actually so large as to require forty camels to carry it. The Orientals are fond of display, and would, ostentatiously, lay upon forty beasts what might very easily have been borne by four.

Thy son Ben-hadad – so called from the established usage of designating the prophet 'father.' This was the same Syrian monarch who had formerly persecuted him (see 2Ki 6:13,14).

10. Go, say … Thou mayest certainly recover – There was no contradiction in this message. This part was properly the answer to Ben-hadad's inquiry [2Ki 8:9]. The second part was intended for Hazael, who, like an artful and ambitious courtier, reported only as much of the prophet's statement as suited his own views (compare 2Ki 8:14).

11. he settled his countenance steadfastly until he was ashamed – that is, Hazael. The steadfast, penetrating look of the prophet seemed to have convinced Hazael that his secret designs were known. The deep emotions of Elisha were justified by the horrible atrocities which, too common in ancient warfare, that successful usurper committed in Israel (2Ki 10:32 13:3,4,22).

15. took a thick cloth, – a coverlet. In the East, this article of bedding is generally a thick quilt of wool or cotton, so that, with its great weight, when steeped in water, it would be a fit instrument for accomplishing the murderous purpose, without leaving any marks of violence. It has been supposed by many that Hazael purposely murdered the king. But it is common for Eastern people to sleep with their faces covered with a mosquito net; and, in some cases of fever, they dampen the bedclothes. Hazael, aware of those chilling remedies being usually resorted to, might have, with an honest intention, spread a refreshing cover over him. The rapid occurrence of the king's death and immediate burial were favourable to his instant elevation to the throne.

2Ki 8:16–23. Jehoram's wicked reign.

16. Jehoram the son of Jehoshaphat …began to reign – (See on 2Ki 3:1). His father resigned the throne to him two years before his death.

18. daughter of Ahab – Athaliah, through whose influence Jehoram introduced the worship of Baal and many other evils into the kingdom of Judah (see 2Ch 21:2-20). This apostasy would have led to the total extinction of the royal family in that kingdom, had it not been for the divine promise to David (2Sa 7:16). A national chastisement, however, was inflicted on Judah by the revolt of Edom, which, being hitherto governed by a tributary ruler (2Ki 3:9 1Ki 22:47), erected the standard of independence (2Ch 21:9).

Chapter 9

2Ki 9:1–26. Jehu is anointed.

1. Ramoth-gilead – a city of great importance to the Hebrew people, east of Jordan, as a fortress of defence against the Syrians. Jehoram had regained it (2Ki 8:29). But the Israeli army was still encamped there, under the command of Jehu.

Elisha … called one of the children of the prophets – This errand referred to the last commission given to Elijah in Horeb (1Ki 19:16).

box of oil – (See 1Sa 10:1).

2. carry him to an inner chamber – both to ensure the safety of the messenger and to prevent all obstruction in the execution of the business.

3. I have anointed thee king over Israel – This was only a part of the message; the full announcement of which is given (2Ki 9:7–10).

flee, and tarry not – for fear of being surprised and overtaken by the spies or servants of the court.

4–6. So the young man … went to Ramoth-gilead – His ready undertaking of this delicate and hazardous mission was an eminent proof of his piety and obedience. The act of anointing being done through a commissioned prophet, was a divine intimation of his investiture with the sovereign power. But it was sometimes done long prior to the actual possession of the throne (1Sa 16:13); and, in like manner, the commission had, in this instance, been given also a long time before to Elijah (1Ki 19:16), who, for good reasons, left it in charge to Elisha; and he awaited God's time and command for executing it [Poole].

10. in the portion of Jezreel – that is, that had formerly been the vineyard of Naboth.

11. Is all well? – Jehu's attendants knew that the stranger belonged to the order of the prophets by his garb, gestures, and form of address; and soldiers such as they very readily concluded such persons to be crackbrained, not only from the sordid negligence of their personal appearance and their open contempt of the world, but from the religious pursuits in which their whole lives were spent, and the grotesque actions which they frequently performed (compare Jer 29:26).

13. they hasted, and took every man his garment – the upper cloak which they spread on the ground, as a token of their homage to their distinguished commander (Mt 21:7).

top of the stairs – from the room where the prophet had privately anointed Jehu. That general returned to join his brother officers in the public apartment, who, immediately on learning his destined elevation, conducted him to the top of the stairs leading to the roof. This was the most conspicuous place of an Oriental structure that could be chosen, being at the very top of the gate building, and fully in view of the people and military in the open ground in front of the building [KITTO]. The popularity of Jehu with the army thus favoured the designs of Providence in procuring his immediate and enthusiastic proclamation as king, and the top of the stairs was taken as a most convenient substitute for a throne.

14, 15. Joram had kept Ramoth-gilead – rather, 'was keeping,' guarding, or besieging it, with the greater part of the military force of Israel. The king's wounds had compelled his retirement from the scene of action, and so the troops were left in command of Jehu.

16. So Jehu rode in a chariot, and went to Jezreel – Full of ambitious designs, he immediately proceeded to cross the Jordan to execute his commission on the house of Ahab.

17–24. there stood a watchman on the tower of Jezreel – The Hebrew palaces, besides being situated on hills had usually towers attached to them, not only for the pleasure of a fine prospect, but as posts of useful observation. The ancient watchtower of Jezreel must have commanded a view of the whole region eastward, nearly down to the Jordan. Beth-shan stands on a rising ground about six or seven miles below it, in a narrow part of the plain; and when Jehu and his retinue reached that point between Gilboa and Beth-shan, they could be fully descried by the watchman on the tower. A report was made to Joram in his palace below. A messenger on horseback was quickly despatched down into the plain to meet the ambiguous host and to question the object of their approach. 'Is it peace?' We may safely assume that this messenger would meet Jehu at the distance of three miles or more. On the report made of his being detained and turned into the rear of the still advancing troops, a second messenger was in like manner despatched, who would naturally meet Jehu at the distance of a mile or a mile and a half down on the plain. He also being turned into the rear, the watchman now distinctly perceived 'the driving to be like the driving of Jehu, the son of Nimshi; for he driveth furiously.' The alarmed monarch, awakened to a sense of his impending danger, quickly summoned his forces to meet the crisis. Accompanied by Ahaziah, king of Judah, the two sovereigns ascended their chariots to make a feeble resistance to the impetuous onset of Jehu, who quickly from the plain ascended the steep northern sides of the site on which Jezreel stood, and the conflicting parties met 'in the portion of Naboth the Jezreelite,' where Joram was quickly despatched by an arrow from the strong arm of Jehu. We were impressed with the obvious accuracy of the sacred historian; the *localities* and *distances* being such as seem naturally to be required by the incidents related, affording just time for the transactions to have occurred in the order in which they are recorded [HOWE].

25. cast him in the portion of the field of Naboth the Jezreelite – according to the doom pronounced by divine authority on Ahab (1Ki 21:19), but which on his repentance was deferred to be executed on his son.

26. the blood of Naboth, and the blood of his sons, saith the Lord – Although their death is not expressly mentioned, it is plainly implied in the confiscation of his property (see 1Ki 21:16).

2Ki 9:27–35. Ahaziah is slain.

27. Ahaziah – was grandnephew to King Joram, and great-grandson to King Ahab. **Ibleam** – near Megiddo, in the tribe of Issachar (Jos 17:11 Jud 1:27); and Gur was an adjoining hill.

30. Jezebel painted her face – literally, 'her eyes,' according to a custom universal in the East among women, of staining the eyelids with a black powder made of pulverized antimony, or lead ore mixed with oil, and applied with a small brush on the border, so that by this dark ligament on the edge, the largeness as well as the luster of the eye itself was thought to be increased. Her object was, by her royal attire, not to captivate, but to overawe Jehu.

35. found no more of her than the skull, and the palms of her hands – The dog has a rooted aversion to prey on the human hands and feet.

2Ki 9:36, 37. Jezebel eaten by dogs.

36. This is the word of the Lord – (See 1Ki 21:23). Jehu's statement, however, was not a literal but a paraphrased quotation of Elijah's prophecy.

Chapter 10

2Ki 10:1–17. Jehu causes seventy of Ahab's children to be beheaded.

1–4. Ahab had seventy sons in Samaria – As it appears (2Ki 10:13) that grandsons are included it is probable that this number comprehended the whole posterity of Ahab. Their being all assembled in that capital might arise from their being left there on the king's departure for Ramoth-gilead, or from their taking refuge in some of the strongholds of that city on the news of Jehu's conspiracy. It may be inferred from the tenor of Jehu's letters that their first intention was to select the fittest of the royal family and set him up as king. Perhaps this challenge of Jehu was designed as a stroke of policy on his part to elicit their views, and to find out whether they were inclined to be pacific or hostile. The bold character of the man, and the rapid success of his conspiracy, terrified the civic authorities of Samaria and Jezreel into submission.

5. he that was over the house – the governor or chamberlain of the palace.

the bringers-up of the children – Anciently, and still also in many Eastern countries, the principal grandees were charged with the support and education of the royal princes. This involved a heavy expense which they were forced to bear, but for which they endeavoured to find some compensation in the advantages of their connection with the court.

6. take ye the heads of the men, your master's sons – The barbarous practice of a successful usurper slaughtering all who may have claims to the throne, has been frequently exemplified in the ancient and modern histories of the East.

8. Lay ye them in two heaps at the entering in of the gate – The exhibition of the heads of enemies is always considered a glorious trophy. Sometimes a pile of heads is erected at the gate of the palace; and a head of peculiarly striking appearance selected to grace the summit of the pyramid.

9–11. said to all the people, Ye be righteous – A great concourse was assembled to gaze on this novel and ghastly spectacle. The speech which Jehu addressed to the spectators was artfully framed to impress their minds with the idea that so wholesale a massacre was the result of the divine judgments denounced on the house of Ahab; and the effect of it was to prepare the public mind for hearing, without horror, of a similar revolting tragedy which was soon after perpetrated, namely, the extinction of all the influential friends and supporters of the dynasty of Ahab, including those of the royal house of Judah.

13, 14. We are the brethren of Ahaziah – that is, not full, but step-brothers, sons of Jehoram by various concubines. Ignorant of the revolution that had taken place, they were travelling to Samaria on a visit to their royal relatives of Israel, when they were seized and put to death, because of the apprehension that they might probably stimulate and strengthen the party that still remained faithful in their allegiance to Ahab's dynasty.

children of the queen – that is, of the queen mother, or regent, Jezebel.

15-18. Jehonadab the son of Rechab – (See 1Ch 2:55). A person who, from his piety and simple primitive manner of life (Jer 35:1-19), was highly esteemed, and possessed great influence in the country. Jehu saw in a moment the advantage that his cause would gain from the friendship and countenance of this venerable man in the eyes of the people, and accordingly paid him the distinguished attention of inviting him to a seat in his chariot.

give me thine hand – not simply to aid him in getting up, but for a far more significant and important purpose – the giving, or rather joining hands, being the recognized mode of striking a league or covenant, as well as of testifying fealty to a new sovereign; accordingly, it is said, 'he [Jehonadab] gave him [Jehu] his hand.'

2Ki 10:18–29. He destroys the worshippers of Baal.

19. call unto me all the prophets of Baal – The votaries of Baal are here classified under the several titles of prophets, priests, and servants, or worshippers generally. They might be easily convened into one spacious temple, as their number had been greatly diminished both by the influential ministrations of Elijah and Elisha, and also from the late King Joram's neglect and discontinuance of the worship. Jehu's appointment of a solemn sacrifice in honour of Baal, and a summons to all his worshippers to join in its celebration, was a deep-laid plot, which he had resolved upon for their extinction, a measure in perfect harmony with the Mosaic law, and worthy of a constitutional king of Israel. It was done, however, not from religious, but purely political motives, because be believed that the existence and interests of the Baalites were inseparably bound up with the dynasty of Ahab and because he hoped that by their extermination he would secure the attachment of the far larger and more influential party who worshipped God in Israel. Jehonadab's concurrence must have been given in the belief of his being actuated solely by the highest principles of piety and zeal.

22. Bring forth vestments for all the worshippers of Baal – The priests of Baal were clad, probably, in robes of white byssus while they were engaged in the functions of their office, and these were kept under the care of an officer in a particular wardrobe of Baal's temple. This treacherous massacre, and the means taken to accomplish it, are parallelled by the slaughter of the Janissaries and other terrible tragedies in the modern history of the East.

29. Howbeit from the sins of Jeroboam ... Jehu departed not from after them – Jehu had no intention of carrying his zeal for the Lord beyond a certain point, and as he considered it impolitic to encourage his subjects to travel to Jerusalem, he re-established the symbolic worship of the calves.

Chapter 11

2Ki 11:1–3. Jehoash saved from Athaliah's massacre.

1. Athaliah – (See on 2Ch 22:2). She had possessed great influence over her son, who, by her counsels, had ruled in the spirit of the house of Ahab.

destroyed all the seed royal – all connected with the royal family who might have urged a claim to the throne, and who had escaped the murderous hands of Jehu (2Ch 21:2–4 22:1 2Ki 10:13,14). This massacre she was incited to perpetrate – partly from a determination not to let David's family outlive hers; partly as a measure of self-defence to secure herself against the violence of Jehu, who was bent on destroying the whole of Ahab's posterity to which she belonged (2Ki 8:18–26); but chiefly from personal ambition to rule, and a desire to establish the worship of Baal. Such was the sad fruit of the unequal alliance between the son of the pious Jehoshaphat and a daughter of the idolatrous and wicked house of Ahab.

2. Jehosheba – or Jehoshabeath (2Ch 22:11). **daughter of King Joram** – not by Athaliah, but by a secondary wife.

stole him from among the king's sons which were slain – either from among the corpses, he being considered dead, or out of the palace nursery.

hid him ... in the bedchamber – for the use of the priests, which was in some part of the temple (2Ki 11:3), and of which Jehoiada and his wife had the sole charge. What is called, however, the bedchamber in the East is not the kind of apartment that we understand by the name, but a small closet, into which are flung during the day the mattresses and other bedding materials spread on the floors or divans of the sitting-rooms by day. Such a slumber-room was well suited to be a convenient place for the recovery of his wounds, and a hiding-place for the royal infant and his nurse.

2Ki 11:4–12. He is made king.

4. the seventh year – namely, of the reign of Athaliah, and the rescue of Jehoash.

Jehoiada sent and fetched the rulers, – He could scarcely have obtained such a general convocation except at the time, or on pretext, of a public and solemn festival. Having revealed to them the secret of the young king's preservation and entered into a covenant with them for the overthrow of the tyrant, he then arranged with them the plan and time of carrying their plot

into execution (see on 2Ch 22:10–23:21). The conduct of Jehoiada, who acted the leading and chief part in this conspiracy, admits of an easy and full justification; for, while Athaliah was a usurper, and belonged to a race destined by divine denunciation to destruction, even his own wife had a better and stronger claim to the throne; the sovereignty of Judah had been divinely appropriated to the family of David, and therefore the young prince on whom it was proposed to confer the crown, possessed an inherent right to it, of which a usurper could not deprive him. Moreover, Jehoiada was most probably the high priest, whose official duty it was to watch over the due execution of God's laws, and who in his present movement, was encouraged and aided by the countenance and support of the chief authorities, both civil and ecclesiastical, in the country. In addition to all these considerations, he seems to have been directed by an impulse of the Divine Spirit, through the counsels and exhortations of the prophets of the time.

2Ki 11:13–16. Athaliah slain.

13. Athaliah heard the noise of the guard and of the people – The profound secrecy with which the conspiracy had been conducted rendered the unusual acclamations of the vast assembled crowd the more startling and roused the suspicions of the tyrant.

she came . . . into the temple of the Lord – that is, the courts, which she was permitted to enter by Jehoiada's directions   [2Ki 11:8] in order that she might be secured.

14. the king stood by a pillar – or on a platform, erected for that purpose (see on 2Ch 6:13).

15. without the ranges – that is, fences, that the sacred place might not be stained with human blood.

2Ki 11:17–20. Jehoiada restores God's worship.

17, 18. a covenant between the Lord and the king and the people – The covenant with the Lord was a renewal of the national covenant with Israel (Ex 19:1–24:18; 'to be unto him a people of inheritance,' De 4:6 27:9). The covenant between the king and the people was the consequence of this, and by it the king bound himself to rule according to the divine law, while the people engaged to submit, to give him allegiance as the Lord's anointed. The immediate fruit of this renewal of the covenant was the destruction of the temple and the slaughter of the priests of Baal (see 2Ki 10:27); the restoration of the pure worship of God in all its ancient integrity; and the establishment of the young king on the hereditary throne of Judah (2Ki 11:19).

Chapter 12

2Ki 12:1–18. Jehoash reigns well while Jehoiada lived.

2. **Jehoash did that which was right in the sight of the Lord** – so far as related to his outward actions and the policy of his government. But it is evident from the sequel of his history that the rectitude of his administration was owing more to the salutary influence of his preserver and tutor, Jehoiada, than to the honest and sincere dictates of his own mind.

3. **But the high places were not taken away** – The popular fondness for the private and disorderly rites performed in the groves and recesses of hills was so inveterate that even the most powerful monarchs had been unable to accomplish their suppression; no wonder that in the early reign of a young king, and after the gross irregularities that had been allowed during the maladministration of Athaliah, the difficulty of putting an end to the superstitions associated with 'the high places' was greatly increased.

4. **Jehoash said to the priests,** – There is here given an account of the measures which the young king took for repairing the temple by the levying of taxes: 1. 'The money of every one that passeth the account,' namely, half a shekel, as 'an offering to the Lord' (Ex 30:13). 2. 'The money that every man is set at,' that is, the redemption price of every one who had devoted himself or any thing belonging to him to the Lord, and the amount of which was estimated according to certain rules (Le 27:1-8). 3. Free will or voluntary offerings made to the sanctuary. The first two were paid annually (see 2Ch 24:5).

7–10. **Why repair ye not the breaches of the house?** – This mode of collection not proving so productive as was expected (the dilatoriness of the priests was the chief cause of the failure), a new arrangement was proposed. A chest was placed by the high priest at the entrance into the temple, into which the money given by the people for the repairs of the temple was to be put by the Levites who kept the door. The object of this chest was to make a separation between the money to be raised for the building from the other moneys destined for the general use of the priests, in the hope that the people would be more liberal in their contributions when it was known that their offerings would be devoted to the special purpose of making the necessary repairs. The duty of attending to this work was no longer to devolve on the priests, but to be undertaken by the king.

11, 12. **they gave the money, being told, into the hands of them that did the work** – The king sent his secretary along with an agent of the high priest to count the money in the chest from time to time (2Ch 24:11), and deliver the amount to the overseers of the building, who paid the workmen and purchased all necessary materials. The custom of putting sums of certain amount in bags, which are labelled and sealed by a proper officer, is a common way of using the currency in Turkey and other Eastern countries.

13–16. **Howbeit there were not made … bowls** – When the repairs of the temple had been completed, the surplus was appropriated to the purchase of the temple furniture. The integrity of the overseers of the work being undoubted, no account was exacted of the way in which they applied the money given to them, while other moneys levied at the temple were left to the disposal of the priests as the law directed (Le 5:16 Nu 5:8).

17, 18. **Then Hazael … fought against Gath** – (See on 2Ch 24:23).

2Ki 12:19–21. He is slain.

20. **his servants arose … and slew Joash in the house of Millo** – (See on 2Ch 24:25).

Chapter 13

2Ki 13:1–7. Jehoahaz's wicked reign over Israel.

1–3. **Jehoahaz … reigned seventeen years** – Under his government, which pursued the policy of his predecessors regarding the support of the calf-worship, Israel's apostasy from the true God became greater and more confirmed than in the time of his father Jehu. The national chastisement, when it came, was consequently the more severe and the instruments employed by the Lord in scourging the revolted nation were Hazael and his son and general Ben-hadad, in resisting whose successive invasions the Israeli army was sadly reduced and weakened. In the extremity of his distress, Jehoahaz besought the Lord, and was heard, not on his own account (Ps 66:18 Pr 1:28 15:8), but that of the ancient covenant with the patriarchs (2Ki 13:23).

4. **he saw the oppression of Israel** – that is, commiserated the fallen condition of His chosen people. The divine honour and the interests of true religion required that deliverance should be granted them to check the triumph of the idolatrous enemy and put an end to their blasphemous taunts that God had forsaken Israel (De 32:27 Ps 12:4).

5. **a saviour** – This refers neither to some patriotic defender nor some signal victory, but to the deliverance obtained for Israel by the two successors of Jehoahaz, namely, Joash, who regained all the cities which the Syrians had taken from his father (2Ki 13:25); and Jeroboam, who restored the former boundaries of Israel (2Ki 14:25).

6. **there remained the grove** – Asherah – the idol set up by Ahab (1Ki 16:33), which ought to have been demolished (De 7:5).

7. made them like the dust in threshing – Threshing in the East is performed in the open air upon a level plot of ground, daubed over with a covering to prevent, as much as possible, the earth, sand, or gravel from rising; a great quantity of them all, notwithstanding this precaution, must unavoidably be taken up with the grain; at the same time the straw is shattered to pieces. Hence it is a most significant figure, frequently employed by Orientals to describe a state of national suffering, little short of extermination (Isa 21:10 Mic 4:12 Jer 51:33). The figure originated in a barbarous war custom, which Hazael literally followed (Am 1:3,4; compare 2Sam 18:31 Jud 8:7).

2Ki 13:8–25. Joash succeeds him.

8. his might – This is particularly noticed in order to show that the grievous oppression from foreign enemies, by which the Israelites were ground down, was not owing to the cowardice or imbecility of their king, but solely to the righteous and terrible judgment of God for their foul apostasy.

12, 13. his might wherewith he fought against Amaziah – (See on 2Ki 14:8–14). The usual summary of his life and reign occurs rather early, and is again repeated in the account given of the reign of the king of Judah (2Ki 14:15).

14–19. Elisha was fallen sick of his sickness whereof he died – Every man's death is occasioned by some disease, and so was Elisha's. But in intimating it, there seems a contrast tacitly made between him and his prophetic predecessor, who did not die.

Joash the king of Israel came down unto him, and wept over his face – He visited him where he was lying ill of this mortal sickness, and expressed deep sorrow, not from the personal respect he bore for the prophet, but for the incalculable loss his death would occasion to the kingdom.

my father, my father! – (See on 2Ki 2:12). These words seem to have been a complimentary phrase applied to one who was thought an eminent guardian and deliverer of his country. The particular application of them to Elisha, who, by his counsels and prayer, had obtained many glorious victories for Israel, shows that the king possessed some measure of faith and trust, which, though weak, was accepted, and called forth the prophet's dying benediction.

15–18. Take bow and arrows – Hostilities were usually proclaimed by a herald, sometimes by a king or general making a public and formal discharge of an arrow into the enemy's country. Elisha directed Joash to do this, as a symbolical act, designed to intimate more fully and significantly the victories promised to the king of Israel over the Syrians. His laying his hands upon the king's hands was to represent the power imparted to the bow shot as coming from the Lord through the medium of the prophet. His shooting the first arrow eastward – to that part of his kingdom which the Syrians had taken and which was east of Samaria – was a declaration of war against them for the invasion. His shooting the other arrows into the ground was in token of the number of victories he was taken to gain; but his stopping at the third betrayed the weakness of his faith; for, as the discharged arrow signified a victory over the Syrians, it is evident that the more arrows he shot the more victories he would gain. As he stopped so soon, his conquests would be incomplete.

20, 21. Elisha died – He had enjoyed a happier life than Elijah, as he possessed a milder character, and bore a less hard commission. His rough garment was honoured even at the court.

coming in of the year – that is, the spring, the usual season of beginning campaigns in ancient times. Predatory bands from Moab generally made incursions at that time on the lands of Israel. The bearers of a corpse, alarmed by the appearance of one of these bands, hastily deposited, as they passed that way, their load in Elisha's sepulchre, which might be easily done by removing the stone at the mouth of the cave. According to the Jewish and Eastern custom, his body, as well as that of the man who was miraculously restored, was not laid in a coffin, but only swathed; so that the bodies could be brought into contact, and the object of the miracle was to stimulate the king's and people of Israel's faith in the still unaccomplished predictions of Elisha respecting the war with the Syrians. Accordingly the historian forthwith records the historical fulfilment of the prediction (2Ki 13:22-25), in the defeat of the enemy, in the recovery of the cities that had been taken, and their restoration to the kingdom of Israel.

Chapter 14

2Ki 14:1–6. Amaziah's good reign over Judah.

3–6. He did that which was right in the sight of the Lord, yet not like David his father – The beginning of his reign was excellent, for he acted the part of a constitutional king, according to the law of God, yet not with perfect sincerity of heart (compare 2Ch 25:2). As in the case of his father Joash, the early promise was belied by the devious course he personally followed in later life (see 2Ch 20:14), as well as by the public irregularities he tolerated in the kingdom.

5. as soon as the kingdom was confirmed in his hand – It was an act of justice no less than of filial piety to avenge the murder of his father. But it is evident that the two assassins must have possessed considerable weight and influence, as the king was obliged to retain them in his service, and durst not, for fear of their friends and supporters, institute proceedings against them until his power had been fully consolidated.

6. But the children of the murderers he slew not – This moderation, inspired by the Mosaic law (De 24:16), displays the good character of this prince; for the course thus pursued toward the families of the regicides was directly contrary to the prevailing customs of antiquity, according to which all connected with the criminals were doomed to unsparing destruction.

2Ki 14:7. He smites Edom.

7. He slew of Edom in the valley of salt ten thousand – In the reign of Joram the Edomites had revolted (2Ki 8:20). But Amaziah, determined to reduce them to their former subjection, formed a hostile expedition against them, in which he routed their army and made himself master of their capital.

the valley of salt – that part of the Ghor which comprises the salt and sandy plain to the south of the Dead Sea.

Selah – literally, 'the rock'; generally thought to be Petra.

Joktheel – that is, 'given' or 'conquered by God.' See the history of this conquest more fully detailed (2Ch 25:6–16).

2Ki 14:8–16. Joash defeats him.

8. Amaziah sent messengers to Jehoash, the son of Jehoahaz, son of Jehu, king of Israel – This bold and haughty challenge, which was most probably stimulated by a desire of satisfaction for the outrages perpetrated by the discharged auxiliaries of Israel (2Ch 25:13) on the towns that lay in their way home, as well as by revenge for the massacre of his ancestors by Jehu (2Ki 9:1–37) sprang, there is little doubt, from pride and self-confidence, inspired by his victory over the Edomites.

9. Jehoash the king of Israel sent to Amaziah – People in the East very often express their sentiments in a parabolic form, especially when they intend to convey unwelcome truths or a contemptuous sneer. This was the design of the admonitory fable related by Joash in his reply. The thistle, a low shrub, might be chosen to represent Amaziah, a petty prince; the cedar, the powerful sovereign of Israel, and the wild beast that trampled down the thistle the overwhelming army with which Israel could desolate Judah. But, perhaps, without making so minute an application, the parable may be explained generally, as describing in a striking manner the effects of pride and ambition, towering far beyond their natural sphere, and sure to fall with a sudden and ruinous crash. The moral of the fable is contained in 2Ki 14:10.

11–14. But Amaziah would not hear – The sarcastic tenor of this reply incited the king of Judah the more; for, being in a state of judicial blindness and infatuation (2Ch 25:20), he was immovably determined on war. But the superior energy of Joash surprised him ere he had completed his military preparations. Pouring a large army into the territory of Judah, he encountered Amaziah in a pitched battle, routed his army, and took him prisoner. Then having marched to Jerusalem (2Ki 14:13), he not only demolished part of the city walls, but plundered the treasures of the palace and temple. Taking hostages to prevent any further molestation from Judah, he terminated the war. Without leaving a garrison in Jerusalem, he returned to his capital with all convenient speed, his presence and all his forces being required to repel the troublesome incursions of the Syrians.

2Ki 14:17–20. He is slain by a conspiracy.

19, 20. they made a conspiracy against him in Jerusalem – Amaziah's apostasy (2Ch 25:27) was followed by a general maladministration, especially the disastrous issue of the war with Israel. The ruinous condition of Jerusalem, the plunder of the temple, and the loss of their children who were taken as hostages [2Ki 14:13,14], lost him the respect and attachment not of the grandees only, but of his subjects generally, who were in rebellion. The king fled in terror to Lachish, a frontier town of the Philistines, where, however, he was traced and murdered. His friends had his corpse brought without any pomp or ceremony, in a chariot to Jerusalem, where he was interred among his royal ancestors.

2Ki 14:21, 22. Azariah succeeds him.

21. all the people of Judah took Azariah – or Uzziah (2Ki 15:30 2Ch 26:1). The popular opposition had been personally directed against Amaziah as the author of their calamities, but it was not extended to his family or heir.

22. He built Elath – fortified that seaport. It had revolted with the rest of Edom, but was now recovered by Uzziah. His father, who did not complete the conquest of Edom, had left him that work to do.

2Ki 14:23–29. Jeroboam's wicked reign over Israel.

23. Jeroboam, the son of Joash king of Israel – This was Jeroboam II who, on regaining the lost territory, raised the kingdom to great political power (2Ki 14:25), but adhered to the favourite religious policy of the Israeli sovereigns (2Ki 14:24). While God granted him so great a measure of national prosperity and eminence, the reason is expressly stated (2Ki 14:26,27) to be that the purposes of the divine covenant forbade as yet the overthrow of the kingdom of the ten tribes (see 2Ki 13:23).

Chapter 15

2Ki 15:1–7. Azariah's reign over Judah.

1–7. In the twenty and seventh year of Jeroboam – It is thought that the throne of Judah continued vacant eleven or twelve years, between the death of Amaziah and the inauguration of his son Azariah. Being a child only four years old when his father was murdered, a regency was appointed during Azariah's minority.

began Azariah ... to reign – The character of his reign is described by the brief formula employed by the inspired historian, in recording the religious policy of the later kings. But his reign was a very active as well as eventful one, and is fully related (2Ch 26:1–23). Elated by the possession of great power, and presumptuously arrogating to himself, as did the heathen kings, the functions both of the real and sacerdotal offices, he was punished with leprosy, which, as the offense was capital (Nu 8:7), was equivalent to death, for this disease excluded him from all society. While Jotham, his son, as his viceroy, administered the affairs of the kingdom – being about fifteen years of age (compare 2Ki 15:33) – he had to dwell in a place apart by himself (see on 2Ki 7:3). After a long reign he died, and was buried in the royal burying-field, though not in the royal cemetery of 'the city of David' (2Ch 26:23).

2Ki 15:8–16. Zechariah's reign over Israel.

8–10. In the thirty and eighth year of Azariah king of Judah did Zechariah the son of Jeroboam reign over Israel – There was an interregnum from some unknown cause between the reign of Jeroboam and the accession of his son, which lasted, according to some, for ten or twelve years, according to others, for twenty-two years, or more. This prince pursued the religious policy of the calf-worship, and his reign was short, being abruptly terminated by the hand of violence. In his fate was fulfilled the prophecy addressed to Jehu (2Ki 10:30; also Ho 1:4), that his family would possess the throne of Israel for four generations; and accordingly Jehoahaz, Joash, Jehoram, and Zechariah were his successors – but there his dynasty terminated; and perhaps it was the public knowledge of this prediction that prompted the murderous design of Shallum.

13. Shallum. He was opposed and slain by Menahem, who, according to JOSEPHUS, was commander of the forces, which, on the report of the king's murder, were besieging Tirzah, a town twelve miles east of Samaria, and formerly a seat of the kings of Israel. Raising the siege, he marched directly against the usurper, slew him, and reigned in his stead.

16. Menahem ... smote Tiphsah – Thapsacus, on the Euphrates, the border city of Solomon's kingdom (1Ki 4:24). The inhabitants refusing to open their gates to him, Menahem took it by storm. Then having spoiled it, he committed the most barbarous excesses, without regard either to age or sex.

2Ki 15:17–21. Menahem's reign.

17. reigned ten years in Samaria – His government was conducted on the religious policy of his predecessors.

19. Pul the king of Assyria – This is the first Assyrian king after Nimrod who is mentioned in biblical history. His name has been recently identified with that of Phalluka on the monuments of Nineveh, and that of Menahem discovered also.

came against the land – Elsewhere it is said 'Ephraim [Israel] went to the Assyrian' [Ho 5:13]. The two statements may be reconciled thus: 'Pul, of his own motion, induced, perhaps, by the expedition of Menahem against Thapsacus, advanced against the kingdom of Israel; then Menahem sent him a thousand talents in order not only to divert him from his plans of conquest, but at the same time to purchase his friendship and aid for the establishment of his own precarious sovereignty. So Menahem did not properly invite the Assyrian into the land, but only changed the enemy when marching against the country, by this tribute, into a confederate for the security of his usurped dominion. Thus the prophet Hosea, less concerned about the historical fact than the disposition betrayed therein, might very well censure as a going of Ephraim to the Assyrians (Ho 5:13 7:1 8:9), and a covenant-making with Asshur' (2Ki 12:1) [KEIL].

a thousand talents of silver – This tribute, which Menahem raised by a tax on the grandees of Israel, bribed Pul to return to his own country (see on 1Ch 5:26).

2Ki 15:22–26. Pekahiah's reign.

23. Pekahiah ... son of Menahem began to reign – On comparing the date given with Azariah's reign, it seems that several months had intervened between the death of Menahem and the accession of Pekahiah, probably owing to a contest about the throne.

25. with Argob and Arieh – Many commentators view these as the captain's accomplices. But it is more probable that they were influential friends of the king, who were murdered along with him.

2Ki 15:27–31. Pekah's reign.

29. in the days of Pekah king of Israel came Tiglath-pileser – This monarch, who succeeded Pul on the throne of Assyria, is the only one of all the kings who does not give his genealogy, and is therefore supposed to have been an usurper. His annals have been discovered in the Nimroud mound, describing this expedition into Syria. The places taken are here mentioned as they occurred and were conquered in the progress of an invasion.

30. Hoshea the son of Elah made a conspiracy ... and slew him – He did not, however, obtain possession of the kingdom till about nine or ten years after the perpetration of this crime [HALES].

in the twentieth year of Jotham – Jotham's reign lasted only sixteen years, but the meaning is that the reign of Hoshea began in the twentieth after the beginning of Jotham's reign. The sacred historian, having not yet introduced the name of Ahaz, reckoned the date by Jotham, whom he had already mentioned (see 2Ch 27:8).

2Ki 15:32–38. Jotham's reign over Judah.

33. Five and twenty years was he when he began to reign – that is, alone – for he had ruled as his father's viceroy (2Ki 15:5).

35. the higher gate of the house of the Lord – not the temple itself, but one of its courts; probably that which led into the palace (2Ch 23:20).

37. the Lord began to send against Judah Rezin the king of Syria – This is the first intimation of the hostile feelings of the kings of Israel and Syria, to Judah, which led them to form an alliance and make joint preparations for war. However, war was not actually waged till the reign of Ahaz.

Chapter 16

2Ki 16:1–16. Ahaz' wicked reign over Judah.

1–4. Ahaz ... did not that which was right in the sight of the Lord – The character of this king's reign, the voluptuousness and religious degeneracy of all classes of the people, are graphically portrayed in the writings of Isaiah, who prophesied at that period. The great increase of worldly wealth and luxury in the reigns of Azariah and Jotham had introduced a host of corruptions, which, during his reign, and by the influence of Ahaz, bore fruit in the idolatrous practices of every kind which prevailed in all parts of the kingdom (see 2Ch 28:24).

3. walked in the way of the kings of Israel – This is descriptive of the early part of his ,reign, when, like the kings of Israel, he patronized the symbolic worship of God by images but he gradually went farther into gross idolatry (2Ch 28:2).

made his son to pass through the fire – (2Ki 23:10). The hands of the idol Moloch being red hot, the children were passed through between them, which was considered a form of lustration. There is reason to believe that, in certain circumstances, the children were burnt to death (Ps 106:37). This was strongly prohibited in the law (Le 18:21 20:2–5 De 18:10), although there is no evidence that it was practised in Israel till the time of Ahaz.

5. Then Rezin king of Syria and Pekah son of Remaliah king of Israel came up to Jerusalem – Notwithstanding their great efforts and military preparations, they failed to take it and, being disappointed, raised the siege and returned home (compare Isa 7:1).

6. Rezin ... recovered Elath – which Azariah had got into his possession (2Ki 14:22).

the Syrians came to Elath, and dwelt there unto this day – The *Septuagint* version has 'the Edomites,' which the most judicious commentators and travellers [ROBINSON] prefer.

7-9. So Ahaz sent messengers to Tiglath-pileser – In spite of the assurance given him by Isaiah by two signs, the one immediate, the other remote (Isa 7:14 8:4), that the confederate kings would not prevail against him, Ahaz sought aid from the Assyrian monarch, to purchase which he sent the treasures of the palace and temple. Tiglath-pileser marched against Damascus, slew Rezin the king, and carried the people of Damascus into captivity to Kir, which is thought to have been the city Karine (now Kerend), in Media.

10–16. And king Ahaz went to Damascus to meet Tiglath-pileser – This was a visit of respect, and perhaps of gratitude. During his stay in that heathen city, Ahaz saw an altar with which he was greatly captivated. Forthwith a sketch of it was transmitted to Jerusalem, with orders to Urijah the priest to get one constructed according to the Damascus model, and let this new altar supersede the old one in the temple. Urijah, with culpable complaisance, acted according to his instructions (2Ki 16:16). The sin in this affair consisted in meddling with, and improving according to human taste and fancy, the altars of the temple, the patterns of which had been furnished by divine authority (Ex 25:40 26:30 27:1 1Ch 28:19). Urijah was one of the witnesses taken by Isaiah to bear his prediction against Syria and Israel (Isa 8:2).

2Ki 16:17–19. He spoils the temple.

17. cut off the borders of the bases – It is thought that he did this to use the elaborate sculpture in adorning his palace.

18. the covert for the Sabbath – the portico through which the priests entered the temple on the Sabbath.

the king's entry without – a private external entrance for the king into the temple. The change made by Ahaz consisted in removing both of these into the temple from fear of the king of Assyria, that, in case of a siege, he might secure the entrance of the temple from him.

Chapter 17

2Ki 17:1–6. Hoshea's wicked reign.

1. In the twelfth year of Ahaz king of Judah, began Hoshea ... to reign – The statement in 2Ki 15:30 may be reconciled with the present passage in the following manner: Hoshea conspired against Pekah in the twentieth year of the latter, which was the eighteenth of Jotham's reign. It was two years before Hoshea was acknowledged king of Israel, that is, in the fourth of Ahaz, and twentieth of Jotham. In the twelfth year of Ahaz his reign began to be tranquil and prosperous [CALMET].

2. he did evil ... but not as the kings of Israel – Unlike his predecessors from the time of Jeroboam, he neither established the rites of Baal, nor compelled the people to adhere to the symbolic worship of the calves. In these respects, Hoshea acted as became a constitutional king of Israel. Yet, through the influence of the nineteen princes who had swayed the sceptre before him (all of whom had been zealous patrons of idolatry, and many of whom had been also infamous for personal crimes), the whole nation had become so completely demoralized that the righteous judgment of an angry Providence impended over it.

3. Against him came up Shalmaneser – or Shalman (Ho 10:14), the same as the Sargon of Isaiah [Isa 20:1]. Very recently the name of this Assyrian king has been traced on the Ninevite monuments, as concerned in an expedition against a king of Samaria, whose name, though mutilated, [COLONEL RAWLINSON] reads as Hoshea.

4. found conspiracy in Hoshea – After having paid tribute for several years, Hoshea, determined on throwing off the Assyrian yoke, withheld the stipulated tribute. Shalmaneser, incensed at this rebellion, proclaimed war against Israel. This was in the sixth year of Hoshea's reign.

he had sent messengers to So, king of Egypt – the Saba co of the classic historians, a famous Ethiopian who, for fifty years, occupied the Egyptian throne, and through whose aid Hoshea hoped to resist the threatened attack of the Assyrian conqueror. But Shalmaneser, marching against [Hoshea], scoured the whole country of Israel, besieged the capital Samaria, and carried the principal inhabitants into captivity in his own land, having taken the king himself, and imprisoned him for life. This ancient policy of transplanting a conquered people into a foreign land, was founded on the idea that, among a mixed multitude, differing in language and religion, they would be kept in better subjection, and have less opportunity of combining together to recover their independence.

6. carried Israel away – that is, the remaining tribes (see on 2Ki 15:29).

Halvah – the same as Calash (Ge 10:11,12), in the region of the Laces or Sab. river, about a day's journey from the ruins of Nineveh.

Chador – is a river, and it is remarkable that there is a river rising in the central highlands of Assyria which retains this name Chubbier unchanged to the present day.

Golan – ('pasture') or Zozan, are the highlands of Assyria, which afford pasturage. The region in which the Chador and the Sab. rise, and through which they flow, is peculiarly of this character. The Nestorians repair to it with their numerous flocks, spending the summer on the banks or in the highlands of the Chador or the Sab. Considering the high authority we possess for regarding Golan and Zozan as one name, there can be no doubt that this is the Golan referred to in this passage.

cities of the Medes – 'villages,' according to the *Syriac* and *Vulgate* versions, or 'mountains,' according to the *Septuagint*. The Medish inhabitants of Golan, having revolted, had been destroyed by the kings of Assyria, and nothing was more natural than that they should wish to place in it an industrious people, like the captive Israelites, while it was well suited to their pastoral life [GRANT, *Nestorians*].

2Ki 17:7–41. Samaria taken, and israel for their sins carried captive.

7. For so it was, that the children of Israel had sinned – There is here given a very full and impressive vindication of the divine procedure in punishing His highly privileged, but rebellious and apostate, people. No wonder that amid so gross a perversion of the worship of the true God, and the national propensity to do reverence to idols, the divine patience was exhausted; and that the God whom they had forsaken permitted them to go into captivity, that they might learn the difference between His service and that of their despotic conquerors.

24–28. the king of Assyria brought men from Babylon – This was not Shalmaneser, but Esar-haddon (Eze 4:2). The places vacated by the captive Israelites he ordered to be occupied by several colonies of his own subjects from Babylon and other provinces.

from Cuthah – the Chaldee form of Cush or Susiana, now Khusistan. **Ava** – supposed to be Ahivaz, situated on the river Karuns, which empties into the head of the Persian Gulf.

Hamath – on the Orontes.

Sepharvaim – Siphara, a city on the Euphrates above Babylon.

placed them in the cities of Samaria, – It must not be supposed that the Israelites were universally removed to a man. A remnant was left, chiefly however of the poor and lower classes, with whom these foreign colonists mingled; so that the prevailing character of society about Samaria was heathen, not Israelite. For the Assyrian colonists became masters of the land; and, forming partial intermarriages with the remnant Jews, the inhabitants became a mongrel race, no longer a people of Ephraim (Isa 7:6). These people, imperfectly instructed in the creed of the Jews, acquired also a mongrel doctrine. Being too few to replenish the land, lions, by which the land had been infested (Jud 14:5 1Sa 17:34 1Ki 13:24 20:36 So 4:8), multiplied and committed frequent ravages upon them. Recognizing in these attacks a judgment from the God of the land, whom they had not worshipped, they petitioned the Assyrian court to send them some Jewish priests who might instruct them in the right way of serving Him. The king, in compliance with their request, sent them one of the exiled priests of Israel (2Ki 17:27), who established his headquarters at Beth-el, and taught them how they should fear the Lord. It is not said that he took a copy of the Pentateuch with him, out of which he might teach them. *Oral teaching* was much better fitted for the superstitious people than instruction out of a written book. He could teach them more effectually by word of mouth. Believing that he would adopt the best and simplest method for them, it is unlikely that he took the written law with him, and so gave origin to the Samaritan copy of the Pentateuch [DAVIDSON, *Criticism*]. Besides, it is evident from his being one of the exiled priests, and from his settlement at Beth-el, that he was not a Levite, but one of the calf-worshipping priests. Consequently his instructions would be neither sound nor efficient.

29. Howbeit every nation made gods of their own – These Assyrian colonists, however, though instructed in the worship, and acknowledging the being of the God of Israel, did not suppose Him to be the only God. Like other heathens, they combined His worship with that of their own gods; and as they formed a promiscuous society from different nations or provinces, a variety of idols was acknowledged among them.

30. Succoth-benoth – that is, the 'tents' or 'booths of the daughters,' similar to those in which the Babylonian damsels celebrated impure rites (Am 2:8).

Nergal – The Jewish writers say this idol was in the form of a cock, and it is certain that a cock is often associated with a priest on the Assyrian monuments [LAYARD]. But modern critics, looking to the astrological character of Assyrian idolatry, generally consider Nergal as the planet Mars, the god of war. The name of this idol formed part of the appellation of two of the king of Babylon's princes (Jer 39:3).

Ashima – an idol under the form of an entirely bald he-goat.

31. Nibhaz – under that of a dog – that Egyptian form of animal-worship having prevailed in ancient Syria, as is evident from the image of a large dog at the mouth of the Nahr-el-Kelb, or Dog river.

Tartak – According to the rabbis, it was in the form of an ass, but others understand it as a planet of ill-omen, probably Saturn.

Adrammelech – supposed by some to be the same as Molech, and in Assyrian mythology to stand for the sun. It was worshipped in the form of a mule – others maintain in that of a peacock.

Anammelech – worshipped in the form of a hare; others say in that of a goat.

34. Unto this day – the time of the Babylonian exile, when this book was composed. Their religion was a strange medley or compound of the service of God and the service of idols. Such was the first settlement of the people, afterwards called Samaritans, who were sent from Assyria to colonize the land, when the kingdom of Israel, after having continued three hundred fifty-six years, was overthrown.

Chapter 18

2Ki 18:1–3. Hezekiah's good reign.

1, 2. Hezekiah … began to reign. Twenty and five years old – According to this statement (compare 2Ki 16:2), he must have been born when his father Ahaz was no more than eleven years old. Paternity at an age so early is not unprecedented in the warm climates of the south, where the human frame is matured sooner than in our northern regions. But the case admits of solution in a different way. It was customary for the later kings of Israel to assume their son and heir into partnership in the government during their lives; and as Hezekiah began to reign in the third year of Hoshea (2Ki 18:1), and Hoshea in the twelfth year of Ahaz (2Ki 17:1), it is evident that Hezekiah began to reign in the fourteenth year of Ahaz his father, and so reigned two or three years before his father's death. So that, at the beginning of his reign in conjunction with his father, he might be only twenty-two or twenty-three, and Ahaz a few years older than the common calculation makes him. Or the case may be solved thus: As the ancient writers, in the computation of time, take notice of the year they mention, whether finished or newly begun, so Ahaz might be near twenty-one years old at the beginning of his reign, and near seventeen years older at his death; while, on the other hand, Hezekiah, when he began to reign, might be just entering into his twenty-fifth year, and so Ahaz would be near fourteen years old when his son Hezekiah was born – no uncommon age for a young man to become a father in southern latitudes [PATRICK].

2Ki 18:4–37. He destroys idolatry.

4. He removed the high places and brake the images, – The methods adopted by this good king for extirpating idolatry, and accomplishing a thorough reformation in religion, are fully detailed (2Ch 20:3 31:19). But they are indicated very briefly, and in a sort of passing allusion.

brake in pieces the brazen serpent – The preservation of this remarkable relic of antiquity (Nu 21:5–10) might, like the pot of manna and Aaron's rod, have remained an interesting and instructive monument of the divine goodness and mercy to the Israelites in the wilderness: and it must have required the exercise of no small courage and resolution to destroy it. But in the progress of degeneracy it had become an object of idolatrous worship and as the interests of true religion rendered its demolition necessary, Hezekiah, by taking this bold step, consulted both the glory of God and the good of his country.

unto those days the children of Israel did burn incense to it – It is not to be supposed that this superstitious reverence had been paid to it ever since the time of Moses, for such idolatry would not have been tolerated either by David or by Solomon in the early part of his reign, by Asa or Jehoshaphat had they been aware of such a folly. But the probability is, that the introduction of this superstition does not date earlier than the time when the family of Ahab, by their alliance with the throne of Judah, exercised a pernicious influence in paving the way for all kinds of idolatry. It is possible, however, as some think, that its origin may have arisen out of a misapprehension of Moses' language (Nu 21:8). Serpent-worship, how revolting so ever it may appear, was an extensively diffused form of idolatry; and it would obtain an easier reception in Israel because many of the neighbouring nations, such as the Egyptians and Phoenicians, adored idol gods in the form of serpents as the emblems of health and immortality.

5, 6. He trusted in the Lord God of Israel – without invoking the aid or purchasing the succour of foreign auxiliaries like Asa (1Ki 15:18,19) and Ahaz (2Ki 16:17 Isa 7:1–25).

so that after him was none like him among all the kings of Judah – Of course David and Solomon are excepted, they having had the sovereignty of the whole country. In the petty kingdom of Judah, Josiah alone had a similar testimony borne to him (2Ki 23:25). But even he was surpassed by Hezekiah, who set about a national reformation at the beginning of his reign, which Josiah did not. The pious character and the excellent course of Hezekiah was prompted, among other secondary influences, by a sense of the calamities his father's wicked career had brought on the country, as well as by the counsels of Isaiah.

7, 8. he rebelled against the king of Assyria – that is, the yearly tribute his father had stipulated to pay, he, with imprudent haste, withdrew. Pursuing the policy of a truly theocratic sovereign, he was, through the divine blessing which rested on his government, raised to a position of great public and national strength. Shalmaneser had withdrawn from Palestine, being engaged perhaps in a war with Tyre, or probably he was dead. Assuming, consequently, that full independent sovereignty which God had settled on the house of David, he both shook off the Assyrian yoke, and, by an energetic movement against the Philistines, recovered from that people the territory which they had taken from his father Ahaz (2Ch 28:18).

13. Sennacherib – the son and successor of Shalmaneser.

all the fenced cities of Judah – not absolutely all of them; for, besides the capital, some strong fortresses held out against the invader (2Ki 18:17 2Ki 19:8). The following account of Sennacherib's invasion of Judah and the remarkable destruction of his army, is repeated almost verbatim in 2Ch 32:1–33 and Isa 36:1-37:38. The expedition seems to have been directed against Egypt, the conquest of which was long a leading object of ambition with the Assyrian monarchs. But the invasion of Judah necessarily preceded, that country being the key to Egypt, the highway through which the conquerors from Upper Asia had to pass. Judah had also at this time formed a league of mutual defence with Egypt (2Ki 18:24). Moreover, it was now laid completely open by the transplantation of Israel to Assyria. Overrunning Palestine, Sennacherib laid siege to the fortress of Lachish, which lay seven Roman miles from Eleutheropolis, and therefore southwest of Jerusalem on the way to Egypt [ROBINSON]. Among the interesting illustrations of sacred history furnished by the recent Assyrian excavations, is a series of bas-reliefs, representing the siege of a town, which the inscription on the sculpture shows to be Lachish, and the figure of a king, whose name is given, on the same inscription, as Sennacherib. The legend, sculptured over the head of the king, runs thus: 'Sennacherib, the mighty king, king of the country of Assyria, sitting on the throne of judgment before the city of Lachish [Lakhisha], I give permission for its slaughter' [*Nineveh and Babylon*]. This minute confirmation of the truth of the Bible narrative is given not only by the name Lachish, which is contained in the inscription, but from the physiognomy of the captives brought before the king, which is unmistakably Jewish.

14–16. Hezekiah … sent to Lachish, saying, … that which thou puttest on me will I bear – Disappointed in his expectations of aid from

Egypt, and feeling himself unable to resist so mighty a conqueror who was menacing Jerusalem itself, Hezekiah made his submission. The payment of three hundred talents of silver, and thirty talents of gold, brought a temporary respite; but, in raising the imposed tribute, he was obliged not only to drain all the treasures of the palace and the temple, but even to strip the doors and pillars of the sacred edifice of the gold that adorned them.

2Ki 18:17. Sennacherib besieges Jerusalem.

17. king of Assyria sent Tartan – general (Isa 20:1).

Rab-saris – chief of the eunuchs.

Rab-shakeh – chief cupbearer. These were the great officers employed in delivering Sennacherib's insulting message to Hezekiah. On the walls of the palace of Sennacherib, at Khorsabad, certain figures have been identified with the officers of that sovereign mentioned in Scripture. In particular, the figures, Rab-shakeh, Rab-saris, and Tartan, appear as full-length portraits of the persons holding those offices in the reign of Sennacherib. Probably they represent the very individuals sent on this embassy.

with a great host to Jerusalem – Engaged in a campaign of three years in Egypt, Sennacherib was forced by the king of Ethiopia to retreat, and discharging his rage against Jerusalem, he sent an immense army to summon it to surrender. (See on 2Ch 32:30).

the conduit of the upper pool – the conduit which went from the reservoir of the Upper Gihon (Birket et Mamilla) to the lower pool, the Birket es Sultan.

the highway of the fuller's field – the public road which passed by that district, which had been assigned them for carrying on their business without the city, on account of the unpleasant smell [KEIL].

18. when they had called to the king – Hezekiah did not make a personal appearance, but commissioned his three principal ministers to meet the Assyrian deputies at a conference outside the city walls.

Eliakim – lately promoted to be master of the royal household (Isa 22:20).

Shebna – removed for his pride and presumption (Isa 22:15) from that office, though still royal secretary.

Joah … the recorder – that is, the keeper of the chronicles, an important office in Eastern countries.

19. Rab-shakeh said – The insolent tone he assumed appears surprising. But this boasting (2Ki 18:19-25), both as to matter and manner, his highly coloured picture of his master's powers and resources, and the impossibility of Hezekiah making any effective resistance, heightened by all the arguments and figures which an Oriental

imagination could suggest, has been paralleled in all, except the blasphemy, by other messages of defiance sent on similar occasions in the history of the East.

27. that they may eat – This was designed to show the dreadful extremities to which, in the threatened siege, the people of Jerusalem would be reduced.

Chapter 19

2Ki 19:1-5. Hezekiah in deep affliction.

1-3. when king Hezekiah heard it, he rent his clothes – The rending of his clothes was a mode of expressing horror at the daring blasphemy – the assumption of sackcloth a sign of his mental distress – his entrance into the temple to pray the refuge of a pious man in affliction – and the forwarding an account of the Assyrian's speech to Isaiah was to obtain the prophet's counsel and comfort. The expression in which the message was conveyed described, by a strong figure, the desperate condition of the kingdom, together with their own inability to help themselves; and it intimated also a hope, that the blasphemous defiance of Jehovah's power by the impious Assyrian might lead to some direct interposition for the vindication of His honour and supremacy to all heathen gods.

4. the living God – 'The living God' is a most significant expression taken in connection with the senseless deities that Rab-shakeh boasted were unable to resist his master's victorious arms.

2Ki 19:6,7. Comforted by Isaiah.

6. Isaiah said … Be not afraid – The prophet's answer was most cheering, as it held out the prospect of a speedy deliverance from the invader. The blast, the rumour, the fall by the sword, contained a brief prediction that was soon fulfilled in all the three particulars – namely, the alarm that hastened his retreat, the destruction that overtook his army, and the violent death that suddenly ended his career.

2Ki 19:8-13. Sennacherib sends a blasphemous letter to Hezekiah.

8. So Rab-shakeh … found the king of Assyria warring against Libnah – Whether Lachish had fallen or not, is not said. But Sennacherib had transferred his battering-rams against the apparently neighbouring fortress of Libnah (Jos 10:29; compare Jos 10:31 15:42), where the chief-cup-bearer reported the execution of his mission.

9-13. when he heard say of Tirhakah … Behold, he is come out to fight against thee – This was the 'rumour' to which Isaiah referred [2Ki 19:7]. Tirhakah reigned in Upper Egypt, while So (or Saba co) ruled in Lower Egypt. He was a powerful monarch, another Sesostris, and both he and Saba co have left many monuments of their greatness. The name and figure of Tirhakah receiving war captives, are still seen in the Egyptian temple of Medinet Abou. This was the expected succour which was sneered at by Rab-shakeh as 'a bruised reed' (2Ki 18:21). Rage against Hezekiah for allying himself with Egypt, or the hope of being better able to meet this attack from the south, induced him, after hearing the rumour of Tirhakah's advance, to send a menacing letter to Hezekiah, in order that he might force the king of Judah to an immediate surrender of his capital. This letter, couched in the same vaunting and imperious style as the speech of Rab-shakeh, exceeded it in blasphemy, and contained a larger enumeration of conquered places, with the view of terrifying Hezekiah and showing him the utter hopelessness of all attempts at resistance.

2Ki 19:14-34. Hezekiah's prayer.

14–19. Hezekiah received the letter … and went up into the house of the Lord – Hezekiah, after reading it, hastened into the temple, spread it in the childlike confidence of faith before the Lord, as containing taunts deeply affecting the divine honour, and implored deliverance from this proud defier of God and man. The devout spirit of this prayer, the recognition of the Divine Being in the plenitude of His majesty – so strikingly contrasted with the fancy of the Assyrians as to His merely local power; his acknowledgment of the conquests obtained over other lands; and of the destruction of their wooden idols which, according to the Assyrian practice, were committed to the flames – because their tutelary deities were no gods; and the object for which he supplicated the divine interposition – that all the kingdoms of the earth might know that the Lord was the only God – this was an attitude worthy to be assumed by a pious theocratic king of the chosen people.

20. Then Isaiah … sent – A revelation having been made to Isaiah, the prophet announced to the king that his prayer was heard. The prophetic message consisted of three different portions: – *First,* Sennacherib is apostrophized (2Ki 19:21–28) in a highly poetical strain, admirably descriptive of the turgid vanity, haughty pretensions, and presumptuous impiety of the Assyrian despot. *Secondly,* Hezekiah is addressed (2Ki 19:29–31), and a sign is given him of the promised deliverance – namely, that for two years the presence of the enemy would interrupt the peaceful pursuits of husbandry, but in the third year the people would be in circumstances to till their fields and vineyards and reap the fruits as formerly. *Thirdly,* the issue

of Sennacherib's invasion is announced (2Ki 19:32–34).

33. shall not come into this city – nor approach near enough to shoot an arrow, not even from the most powerful engine which throws missiles to the greatest distance, nor shall he occupy any part of the ground before the city by a fence, a mantelet, or covering for men employed in a siege, nor cast (raise) a bank (mound) of earth, overtopping the city walls, whence he may see and command the interior of the city. None of these, which were the principal modes of attack followed in ancient military art, should Sennacherib be permitted to adopt. Though the army under Rab-shakeh marched towards Jerusalem and encamped at a little distance with a view to blockade it, they delayed laying siege to it, probably waiting till the king, having taken Lachish and Libnah, should bring up his detachment, that with all the combined forces of Assyria they might invest the capital. So determined was this invader to conquer Judah and the neighbouring countries (Isa 10:7), that nothing but a divine interposition could have saved Jerusalem. It might be supposed that the powerful monarch who overran Palestine and carried away the tribes of Israel, would leave memorials of his deeds on sculptured slabs, or votive bulls. A long and minute account of this expedition is contained in the Annals of Sennacherib, a translation of which has recently been made into English, and, in his remarks upon it, COLONEL RAWLINSON says the Assyrian version confirms the most important features of the Scripture account. The Jewish and Assyrian narratives of the campaign are, indeed, on the whole, strikingly illustrative of each other [*Outlines of Assyrian History*].

2Ki 19:35, 36. An angel destroys the Assyrians.

35. in the morning … they were all dead corpses – It was the miraculous interposition of the Almighty that defended Jerusalem. As to the secondary agent employed in the destruction of the Assyrian army, it is most probable that it was effected by a hot south wind, the simoon, such as to this day often envelops and destroys whole caravans. This conjecture is supported by 2Ki 19:7, and Jer 51:1. The destruction was during the night; the officers and soldiers, being in full security, were negligent; their discipline was relaxed; the camp guards were not alert, or perhaps they themselves were the first taken off, and those who slept, *not wrapped up,* imbibed the poison plentifully. If this had been an evening of dissolute mirth (no uncommon thing in a camp), their joy (perhaps for a victory), or 'the first night of their attacking the city,' says

JOSEPHUS, became, by its effects, one means of their destruction [CALMET, *Fragments*].

36. So Sennacherib king of Assyria ... went and returned – the same way as he came (2Ki 19:33). The route is described (Isa 10:28-32). The early chariot track near Bayreuth is on the rocky edge of Lebanon, which is skirted by the ancient Locus (Nahr-el Kelb). On the perpendicular face of the limestone rock, at different heights, are seen slabs with Assyrian inscriptions, which having been deciphered, are found to contain the name of Sennacherib. Thus, by the preservation of these tablets, the wrath of the Assyrian invaders is made to praise the Lord.

dwelt at Nineveh – This statement implies a considerable period of time, and his Annals carry on his history at least five years after his disastrous campaign at Jerusalem. No record of his catastrophe can be found, as the Assyrian practice was to record victories alone. The sculptures give only the sunny side of the picture.

2Ki 19:37. Sennacherib slain.

37. as he was worshipping in the house of Nisroch – Assaræ, or Asshur, the head of the Assyrian Pantheon, represented not as a vulture-headed figure (that is now ascertained to be a priest), but as a winged figure in a circle, which was the guardian deity of Assyria. The king is represented on the monuments standing or kneeling beneath this figure, his hand raised in sign of prayer or adoration.

his sons smote him with the sword – Sennacherib's temper, exasperated probably by his reverses, displayed itself in the most savage cruelty and intolerable tyranny over his subjects and slaves, till at length he was assassinated by his two sons, whom, it is said, he intended to sacrifice to pacify the gods and dispose them to grant him a return of prosperity. The parricides taking flight into Armenia, a third son, Esar-haddon, ascended the throne.

Chapter 20

2Ki 20:1-7. Hezekiah's life lengthened.

1. In those days was Hezekiah sick – As his reign lasted twenty-nine years (2Ki 18:2), and his kingdom was invaded in the fourteenth (2Ki 18:13), it is evident that this sudden and severe illness must have occurred in the very year of the Syrian invasion. Between the threatened attack and the actual appearance of the enemy, this incident in Hezekiah's history must have taken place. But according to the usage of the sacred historian, the story of Sennacherib is completed before entering on what was personal to the king of Judah (see also Isa 37:36–38:1).

Set thine house in order – Isaiah, being of the blood royal, might have access to the king's private house. But since the prophet was commissioned to make this announcement, the message must be considered as referring to matters of higher importance than the settlement of the king's domestic and private affairs. It must have related chiefly to the state of his kingdom, he having not as yet any son (compare 2Ki 20:6 with 2Ki 21:1).

for thou shall die, and not live – The disease was of a malignant character and would be mortal in its effects, unless the healing power of God should miraculously interpose.

2. he turned his face to the wall – not like Ahab (1Ki 21:4), in fretful discontent, but in order to secure a better opportunity for prayer.

3. remember now how I have walked before thee – The course of Hezekiah's thoughts was evidently directed to the promise made to David and his successors on the throne (1Ki 8:25). He had kept the conditions as faithfully as human infirmity admitted; and as he had been all along free from any of those great crimes by which, through the judgment of God, human life was often suddenly cut short, his great grief might arise partly from the love of life, partly from the obscurity of the Mosaic dispensation, where life and immortality had not been fully brought to light, and partly from his plans for the reformation of his kingdom being frustrated by his death. He pleaded the fulfilment of the promise.

4. afore Isaiah was gone out into the middle court – of the royal castle.

5. Thus saith ... the God of David thy father – An immediate answer was given to his prayer, containing an assurance that the Lord was mindful of His promise to David and would accomplish it in Hezekiah's experience, both by the prolongation of his life, and his deliverance from the Assyrians.

on the third day – The perfect recovery from a dangerous sickness, within so short a time, shows the miraculous character of the cure (see his thanksgiving song, Isa 38:9). The disease cannot be ascertained; but the text gives no hint that the plague was raging then in Jerusalem; and although Arab physicians apply a cataplasm of figs to plague-boils, they also do so in other cases, as figs are considered useful in ripening and soothing inflammatory ulcers.

2Ki 20:8–20. The sun goes ten degrees backward.

8-11. Hezekiah said unto Isaiah, What will be the sign that the Lord shall heal me – His recovery in the course of nature was so unlooked for, that the king asked for some token to justify his reliance on the truth of the prophet's communication; and the sign he specified was granted to him. The shadow of the sun went back upon the dial of Ahaz the ten degrees it had gone down. Various conjectures have been formed as to this dial. The word in the original is 'degrees,' or 'steps,' and hence many commentators have supposed that it was a stair, so artfully contrived, that the shadows on the steps indicated the hours and course of the sun. But it is more probable that it was a proper instrument, and, from the Hebrews having no term to designate it, that it was one of the foreign novelties imported from Babylon by Ahaz. It seems to have been of such magnitude, and so placed in the court, that Isaiah could point to it, and the king see it, from his chamber. The retrogression of the sun's shadow on the dial was miraculously accomplished by the omnipotent power of God; but the phenomenon was temporary, local, confined to the notice, and intended for the satisfaction, only of Hezekiah and his court.

12. Berodach-baladan – (Isa 39:1), the first king of Babylon mentioned in sacred history; formerly its rulers were viceroys of the Assyrian monarchs. This individual threw off the yoke, and asserting his independence, made with varying success, a long and obstinate resistance [RAWLINSON, *Outlines*]. The message of congratulation to Hezekiah, was, in all likelihood, accompanied with proposals for a defensive alliance against their common Assyrian enemy. The king of Judah, flattered with this honour, showed the ambassadors all his treasures, his armoury and warlike stores; and his motive for this was evidently that the Babylonian deputies might be the more induced to prize his friendship.

13, 14. the silver, and the gold – He paid so much tribute to Sennacherib as exhausted his treasury (compare 2Ki 18:16). But, after the destruction of Sennacherib, presents were brought him from various quarters, out of respect to a king who, by his faith and prayer, saved his country; and besides, it is by no means improbable that from the corpses in the Assyrian camp, all the gold and silver he had paid might be recovered. The vain display, however, was offensive to his divine liege lord, who sent Isaiah to reprove him. The answer he gave the prophet shows how he was elated by the compliment of their visit; but it was wrong, as presenting a bait for the cupidity of these rapacious foreigners, who, at no distant period, would return and pillage his country, and transfer all the possessions he ostentatiously displayed to Babylon, as well as his posterity to be court attendants in that country – (see on 2Ch 32:31).

19. Good is the word of the Lord which thou hast spoken – indicating a humble and pious resignation to the divine will. The concluding part of his reply was uttered after a pause and was probably an ejaculation to himself, expressing his thankfulness, that, though great afflictions should befall his descendants, the execution of the divine judgment was to be suspended during his own lifetime.

Chapter 21

2Ki 21:1–18. Manasseh's wicked reign, and great idolatry.

1–3. Manasseh was twelve years old when he began to reign – He must have been born three years after his father's recovery; and his minority, spent under the influence of guardians who were hostile to the religious principles and reforming policy of his father, may account in part for the anti-theocratic principles of his reign. The work of religious reformation which Hezekiah had zealously carried on was but partially accomplished. There was little appearance of its influence on the heart and manners of the people at large. On the contrary, the true fear of God had vanished from the mass of the people; corruption and vice increased, and were openly practised (Isa 28:7,) by the degenerate leaders, who, having got the young prince Manasseh into their power, directed his education, trained him up in their views, and seduced him into the open patronage of idolatry. Hence, when he became sovereign, he introduced the worship of idols, the restoration of high places, and the erection of altars or pillars to Baal, and the placing, in the temple of God itself, a graven image of Asherah, the sacred or symbolic tree, which represented 'all the host of heaven.' This was not idolatry, but pure star-worship, of Chaldaic and Assyrian origin [KEIL]. The sun, as among the Persians, had chariots and horses consecrated to it (2Ki 23:11); and incense was offered to the stars on the housetops (2Ki 23:12 2Ch 33:5 Jer 19:13 Zep 1:5), and in the temple area with the face turned toward the sunrise (Eze 8:16).

5. the two courts of the house of the Lord – the court of the priests, and the large court of the people.

6. made his son pass through the fire – (See on 2Ki 16:3).

observed times – from an observation of the clouds.

used enchantments – jugglery and spells.

dealt with familiar spirits – *Septuagint*, 'ventriloquists,' who pretended to ask counsel of a familiar spirit and gave the response received from him to others.

and wizards – wise or knowing ones, who pretended to reveal secrets, to recover things lost and hidden treasure, and to interpret dreams. A great influx of these impostors had, at various times, poured from Chaldea into the land of Israel to pursue their gainful occupations, especially during the reigns of the latter kings; and Manasseh was not only their liberal patron, but zealous to appear himself an adept in the arts. He raised them to be an influential class at his court, as they were in that of Assyria and Babylon, where nothing was done till they had ascertained the lucky hour and were promised a happy issue.

7. And he set a graven image – The placing of the Asherah within the precincts of the temple, which was dedicated to the worship of the true God, is dwelt upon as the most aggravated outrage of the royal idolater.

8. Neither will I make the feet of Israel move ... out of the land which I gave their fathers – alluding to the promise (2Sa 7:10).

only if they will observe – This condition was expressed from the first plantation of Israel in Canaan. But that people not only did not keep it, but through the pernicious influence of Manasseh, were seduced into greater excesses of idolatrous corruption than even the original Canaanites.

10–17. And the Lord spake by his servants the prophets – These were Hosea, Joel, Nahum, Habakkuk, and Isaiah. Their counsels, admonitions, and prophetic warnings, were put on record in the national chronicles (2Ch 33:18) and now form part of the sacred canon.

12. whosoever heareth of it, both his ears shall tingle – a strong metaphorical form of announcing an extraordinary and appalling event (see 1Sa 3:11 Jer 19:3; also Hab 1:5).

13. the line of Samaria, and the plummet of the house of Ahab – Captives doomed to destruction were sometimes grouped together and marked off by means of a measuring-line and plummet (2Sa 8:2 Isa 34:11 Am 7:7); so that the line of Samaria means the line drawn for the destruction of Samaria; the plummet of the house of Ahab, for exterminating his apostate family; and the import of the threatening declaration here is that Judah would be utterly destroyed, as Samaria and the dynasty of Ahab had been.

I will wipe Jerusalem, – The same doom is denounced more strongly in a figure unmistakably significant.

14. I will forsake the remnant of mine inheritance – The people of Judah, who of all the chosen people alone remained. The consequence of the Lord's forsaking them would be their fall into the power of their enemies.

16. Moreover Manasseh shed innocent blood – Not content with the patronage and the practice of idolatrous abomination, he was a cruel persecutor of all who did not conform. The land was deluged with the blood of good men; among whom it is traditionally said Isaiah suffered a horrid death, by being sawn asunder.

2Ki 21:19–26. Amon's wicked reign.

19–24. Amon was twenty and two years old when he began to reign – This prince continued the idolatrous policy of his father; and, after an inglorious reign of two years, he was massacred by some of his own domestics. The people slew the regicide conspirators and placed his son Josiah on the throne.

Chapter 22

2Ki 22:1, 2. Josiah's good reign.

1, 2. Josiah was eight years old when he began to reign – Happier than his grandfather Manasseh, he seems to have fallen during his minority under the care of better guardians, who trained him in the principles and practice of piety; and so strongly had his young affections been enlisted on the side of true and undefiled religion, that he continued to adhere all his life, with undeviating perseverance, to the cause of God and righteousness.

2Ki 22:3–7. He provides for the repair of the temple.

3, 4. in the eighteenth year of king Josiah – Previous to this period, he had commenced the work of national reformation. The preliminary steps had been already taken; not only the builders were employed, but money had been brought by all the people and received by the Levites at the door, and various other preparations had been made. But the course of this narrative turns on one interesting incident which happened in the eighteenth year of Josiah's reign, and hence that date is specified. In fact the whole land was thoroughly purified from every object and all traces of idolatry. The king now addressed himself to the repair and embellishment of the temple and gave directions to Hilkiah the high priest to take a general survey, in order to ascertain what was necessary to be done (see on 2Ch 34:8–15).

2Ki 22:8–15. Hilkiah finds the book of the law.

8–11. Hilkiah said ... I have found the book of the law in the house of the Lord – that is, the law of Moses, the Pentateuch. It was the temple copy which had been laid (De 31:25,26) beside the ark in the most holy place. During the ungodly reigns of Manasseh and Amon – or perhaps under Ahaz, when the temple itself had been profaned by idols, and the ark also (2Ch 35:3) removed from its site; it was somehow lost, and was now found again during the repair of the temple [KEIL]. Delivered by Hilkiah the discoverer to Shaphan the scribe (2Ki 22:8), it was by the latter shown and read to the king. It is thought, with great probability, that the passage read to the king, and by which the royal mind was so greatly excited, was a portion of Deuteronomy, the twenty-eighth, twenty-ninth, and thirtieth chapters, in which is recorded a renewal of the national covenant, and an enumeration of the terrible threats and curses denounced against all who violated the law, whether prince or people. The impressions of grief and terror which the reading produced on the mind of Josiah have seemed to many unaccountable. But, as it is certain from the extensive and familiar knowledge displayed by the prophets, that there were numbers of other copies in popular circulation, the king must have known its sacred contents in some degree. But he might have been a stranger to the passage read him, or the reading of it might, in the peculiar circumstances, have found a way to his heart in a manner that he never felt before. His strong faith in the divine word, and his painful consciousness that the woeful and long-continued apostasies of the nation had exposed them to the infliction of the judgments denounced, must have come with overwhelming force on the heart of so pious a prince.

12–15. the king commanded … Go, inquire of the Lord for me – The agitated feelings of the king prompted him to ask immediate counsel how to avert those curses under which his kingdom lay; and forthwith a deputation of his principal officers was sent to one endowed with the prophetic spirit. **Ahikam** – a friend of Jeremiah (Jer 26:24).

14. Achbor – or Abdon (2Ch 34:20), a man of influence at court (Jer 26:22). The occasion was urgent, and therefore they were sent – not to Zephaniah (Zep 1:1), who was perhaps young – nor to Jeremiah, who was probably absent at his house in Anathoth, but to one who was at hand and known for her prophetic gifts – to Huldah, who was probably at this time a widow. Her husband Shallum was grandson of one Harhas, 'keeper of the wardrobe.' If this means the priestly wardrobe, [Harhas] must have been a Levite. But it probably refers to the royal wardrobe.

she dwelt … in the college – rather, 'in *the Misnah*,' taking the original word as a proper name, not a school or college, but a particular suburb of Jerusalem. She was held in such veneration that Jewish writers say she and Jehoiada the priest were the only persons not of the house of David (2Ch 24:15,16) who were ever buried in Jerusalem.

15–20. she said unto them, Thus saith the Lord God of Israel, Tell the man that sent you to me – On being consulted, she delivered an oracular response in which judgment was blended with mercy; for it announced the impending calamities that at no distant period were to overtake the city and its inhabitants. But at the same time the king was consoled with an assurance that this season of punishment and sorrow should not be during his lifetime, on account of the faith, penitence, and pious zeal

for the divine glory and worship which, in his public capacity and with his royal influence, he had displayed.

Chapter 23

2Ki 23:1–3. Josiah causes the law to be read.

1–3. the king sent, and they gathered unto him all the elders – This pious and patriotic king, not content with the promise of his own security, felt, after Huldah's response, an increased desire to avert the threatened calamities from his kingdom and people. Knowing the richness of the divine clemency and grace to the penitent, he convened the elders of the people, and placing himself at their head, accompanied by the collective body of the inhabitants, went in solemn procession to the temple, where ordered the book of the law to be read to the assembled audience, and covenanted, with the unanimous concurrence of his subjects, to adhere steadfastly to all the commandments of the Lord. It was an occasion of solemn interest, closely connected with a great national crisis, and the beautiful example of piety in the highest quarter would exert a salutary influence over all classes of the people in animating their devotions and encouraging their return to the faith of their fathers.

2. he read in their ears – that is, 'caused to be read.'

3. all the people stood to the covenant – that is, they agreed to the proposals made; they assented to what was required of them.

2Ki 23:4–28. He destroys idolatry.

4. the king commanded Hilkiah – that is, the high priest and other priests, for there was not a variety of official gradations in the temple.

all the vessels, – the whole apparatus of idol-worship.

burned them without Jerusalem – The law required them to be consigned to the flames (De 7:25).

in the fields of Kidron – most probably that part of the valley of Kidron, where lies Jerusalem and the Mount of Olives. It is a level, spacious basin, abounding at present with plantations [ROBINSON]. The brook winds along the east and south of the city, the channel of which is throughout a large portion of the year almost or wholly dry, except after heavy rains, when it suddenly swells and overflows. There were emptied all the impurities of the temple (2Ch 29:15,16) and the city. His reforming predecessors had ordered the mutilated relics of idolatry to be thrown into that receptacle of filth (1Ki 15:13 2Ch 15:16 30:14); but Josiah, while he imitated their piety, far outstripped them in zeal; for he caused the ashes of the burnt wood and the fragments of the broken metal to be collected and conveyed to Beth-el, in order thenceforth to associate ideas of horror and aversion with that place, as odious for the worst pollutions.

5. put down the idolatrous priests – Hebrew, chemarim, 'scorched,' that is, Guebres, or fire-worshippers, distinguished by a girdle (Eze 23:14-17) or belt of wool and camel's hair, twisted round the body twice and tied with four knots, which had a symbolic meaning, and made it a supposed defence against evil.

them also that burned incense unto Baal, to the sun, and to the moon, – or Baal-shemesh, for Baal was sometimes considered the sun. This form of false worship was not by images, but pure star-worship, borrowed from the old Assyrians.

and – rather, 'even to all the host of heaven.'

6. brought out the grove – that is, Asherah, the mystic tree, placed by Manasseh in the temple [2Ki 21:5 2Ch 33:5], removed by him after his conversion [2Ch 33:15], but replaced in the sanctuary by his wicked son Amon [2Ki 21:20,21]. Josiah had it taken to Kidron, burnt the wood, ground the metal about it to powder, and strewed the ashes 'on the graves of the children of the people.' The poor were buried in a common on part of the valley of Kidron. But reference is here made to the graves 'of those that had sacrificed' (2Ch 34:4).

7. brake down the houses of the sodomites – not solid houses, but tents, called elsewhere [2Ki 17:30] Succoth-benoth, 'the booths of the young women,' who were devoted to the service of Asherah, for which they made embroidered hangings, and in which they gave themselves to unbridled revelry and lust. Or the hangings might be for Asherah itself, as it is a popular superstition in the East to hang pieces of cloth on trees.

8, 9. he brought all the priests out of the cities of Judah, and defiled the high places – Many of the Levitical order, finding in the reigns of Manasseh and Amon the temple-worship abolished and the tithes and other offerings alienated, had been betrayed into the folly of officiating on high places, and presenting such sacrifices as were brought to them. These irregularities, even though the object of that worship was the true God, were prohibited in the law (De 12:11). Those who had been guilty of this sin, Josiah brought to Jerusalem. Regarding them as defiled, he debarred them from the service of the temple, but gave them an allowance out of the temple revenues, like the lame and disabled members of the priesthood (Le 21:21,22).

from Geba to Beer-sheba – the most northern and the most southern places in Judah – meaning all parts of the kingdom.

the high places ... which were in the entering in of the gate of Joshua – The governor's house

and gate were on the left of the city gate, and close by the entrance of that civic mansion house were public altars, dedicated, it might be, to the true God, but contrary to His own ordinance of worship (Isa 57:8).

10. Topheth – so called from Toph – a 'drum.' It is the prevailing opinion among Jewish writers that the cries of the terrified children made to pass through the fire in that place of idolatrous horror were drowned by the sound of that instrument.

11. took away the horses that the kings of Judah had given to the sun – Among the people who anciently worshipped the sun, horses were usually dedicated to that divinity, from the supposed idea that the sun himself was drawn in a chariot by horses. In some cases these horses were sacrificed; but more commonly they were employed either in the sacred processions to carry the images of the sun, or for the worshippers to ride in every morning to welcome his rise. It seems that the idolatrous kings, Ahaz, Manasseh, and Amon, or their great officers, proceeded on these horses early on each day from the east gate of the temple to salute and worship the sun at his appearing above the horizon.

12. the altars that were on the top of the upper chamber of Ahaz – Altars were reared on the flat roofs of houses, where the worshippers of 'the host of heaven' burnt incense (Zep 1:5 Jer 19:13). Ahaz had reared altars for this purpose on the oleah, or upper chamber of his palace, and Manasseh on some portion of the roof of the temple. Josiah demolished both of these structures.

13, 14. the high places ... which Solomon ... had builded – (See on 1Ki 11:5).

the right hand of the mount of corruption – The Mount of Olives is a hilly range on the east of Jerusalem. This range has three summits, of which the central one is the Mount of Corruption, so called from the idol temples built there, and of course the hill on the right hand denotes the southernmost peak. Josiah is said not to have destroyed, but only defiled, 'the high places on the hill of corruption.' It is most probable that Hezekiah had long before demolished the idolatrous temples erected there by Solomon but, as the superstitious people continued to regard the spot as consecrated ground, Josiah defiled it.

14. filled their places with the bones of men – Every monument of idolatry in his dominion he in like manner destroyed, and the places where they stood he defiled by strewing them with dead men's bones. The presence of a dead carcass rendered both persons and places unclean in the eyes both of Jews and heathens.

15–20. Moreover the altar that was at Beth-el – Not satisfied with the removal of every vestige of idolatry from his own dominion, this zealous iconoclast made a tour of inspection through the cities of Samaria and all the territory formerly occupied by the ten tribes, destroying the altars and temples of the high places, consigning the Asherim to the flames, putting to death the priests of the high places, and showing his horror at idolatry by ransacking the sepultures of idolatrous priests, and strewing the burnt ashes of their bones upon the altars before he demolished them.

16. according to the word of the Lord which the man of God proclaimed – In carrying on these proceedings, Josiah was prompted by his own intense hatred of idolatry. But it is remarkable that this act was predicted three hundred twenty-six years before his birth, and his name also was expressly mentioned, as well as the very place where it should be done (1Ki 13:2). This is one of the most remarkable prophecies in the Bible.

17. What title is that that I see? – The king's attention probably, had been arrested by a tombstone more conspicuous than the rest around it, bearing on an inscription the name of him that lay beneath; and this prompted his curiosity to make the inquiry.

the men of the city – not the Assyrian colonists – for they could know nothing about the ancient transactions of the place – but some of the old people who had been allowed to remain, and perhaps the tomb itself might not then have been discoverable, through the effects of time and neglect, had not some 'Old Mortality' garnished the sepulchre of the righteous.

21–23. the king commanded all the people, saying, Keep the Passover unto the Lord your God – It was observed with great solemnity and was attended not only by his own subjects, but by the remnant people from Israel (see on 2Ch 35:1–19). Many of the Israelites who were at Jerusalem might have *heard of*, if they did *not hear*, the law read by Josiah. It is probable that they might even have procured a copy of the law, stimulated as they were to the better observance of Jehovah's worship by the unusual and solemn transactions at Jerusalem.

26. Notwithstanding, the Lord turned not from the fierceness of his wrath – The national reformation which Josiah carried on was acquiesced in by the people from submission to the royal will; but they entertained a secret and strong hankering after the suppressed idolatries. Though outwardly purified, their hearts were not right towards God, as appears from many passages of the prophetic writings; their thorough reform was hopeless; and God, who saw no sign of genuine repentance, allowed His decree (2Ki 21:12–15) for the subversion of the kingdom to take fatal effect.

Chapter 24

2Ki 24:1–7. Jehoiakim procures his own ruin.

1, 2. Nebuchadnezzar – the son of Nabopolassar, the founder of the Chaldee monarchy. This invasion took place in the fourth year of Jehoiakim's, and the first of Nebuchadnezzar's reign (Jer 25:1; compare Jer 46:2). The young king of Assyria being probably detained at home on account of his father's demise, despatched, along with the Chaldean troops on his border, an army composed of the tributary nations which were contiguous to Judea, to chastise Jehoiakim's revolt from his yoke. But this hostile band was only an instrument in executing the divine judgment (2Ki 24:2) denounced by the prophets against Judah for the sins of the people; and hence, though marching by the orders of the Assyrian monarch, they are described as sent by the Lord (2Ki 24:3).

4. the Lord would not pardon – (see on 2Ki 23:26).

6. Jehoiakim slept with his fathers – This phraseology can mean nothing more than that he died; for he was not buried with his royal ancestors; and whether he fell in battle, or his body was subjected to posthumous insults, he was, according to the prediction (Jer 22:19), not honoured with the rites of sepulture (Jer 36:30).

Jehoiachin his son reigned in his stead – The very brief reign of this prince, which lasted only three months, during which he was a humble vassal of the Assyrians, is scarcely deserving to be taken into account, and therefore is in no way contradictory to the prophetic menace denounced against his father (Jer 36:30).

7. the king of Egypt – that is, Pharaohnechoh.

2Ki 24:8, 9. Jehoiachin succeeds him.

8. Jehoiachin – that is, 'God-appointed,' contracted into *Jeconiah* and *Coniah* (Jer 22:24).

eighteen years old when he began to reign – At the age of eight his father took him into partnership in the government (2Ch 36:9). He began to reign alone at eighteen.

9. he did that which was evil in the sight of the Lord – Untaught by experience, and deaf to the prophetic warnings, he pursued the evil courses which had brought so many disasters upon the royal family as well as the people of Judah. This bad character is figuratively but strongly depicted (Eze 19:5–7).

2Ki 24:10–16. Jerusalem taken.

10–13. At that time – within three months after his accession to the throne. It was the spring of the year (2Ch 36:10); so early did he indicate a feeling hostile to the interests of his Assyrian liege lord, by forming a league with Egypt. Nebuchadnezzar sent his generals to besiege Jerusalem, as Jeremiah had foretold (Jer 22:18 24:30), and soon after he followed in person. Convinced of the hopelessness of making any effectual resistance, Jehoiachin, going to the camp of the besiegers, surrendered (2Ki 24:12), in the expectation, probably, of being allowed to retain his throne as a vassal of the Assyrian empire. But Nebuchadnezzar's clemency towards the kings of Judah was now exhausted, so that Jehoiachin was sent as a captive to Babylon, according to Jeremiah's prediction (Jer 22:24), accompanied by the queen mother (the same who had held that dignity under Jehoahaz) (2Ki 23:31), his generals, and officers. This happened in the eighth year of Nebuchadnezzar's reign, computing from the time when he was associated with his father in the government. Those that were left consisted chiefly of the poorer sort of people and the unskilled workmen. The palace and the temple were ransacked. The smaller golden vessels had been taken on the first capture of Jerusalem and placed by Nebuchadnezzar in the temple of his god as tokens of victory. They were used by Belshazzar at his impious feast [Da 5:2], for the purpose of rewarding his army with these trophies, among which were probably the golden candlesticks, the ark, (compare 2Ch 36:7 Da 1:2). Now the gold plating was torn off all the larger temple furniture.

13-16. as the Lord had said – (compare 2Ki 20:17 Isa 39:6 Jer 15:13 17:3). The elite of the nation for rank, usefulness, and moral worth, all who might be useful in Babylon or dangerous in Palestine, were carried off to Babylon, to the number of ten thousand (2Ki 24:14). These are specified (2Ki 24:15,16), warriors, seven thousand; craftsmen and smiths, one thousand; king's wives, officers, and princes, also priests and prophets (Jer 29:1 Eze 1:1), two thousand; equal to ten thousand captives in all.

2Ki 24:17–20. Zedekiah's evil reign.

17–19. the king of Babylon made Mattaniah, his father's brother, king in his stead – Adhering to his former policy of maintaining a show of monarchy, Nebuchadnezzar appointed the third and youngest son of Josiah (1Ch 3:15), full brother of Jehoahaz, and uncle of the captive Jehoiachin. But, according to the custom of conquerors, who changed the names of the great men they took captives in war, in token of their supremacy, he gave him the new name of

Zedekiah – that is, 'The righteous of God.' This being a purely Hebrew name, it seems that he allowed the puppet king to choose his own name, which was confirmed. His heart towards God was the same as that of Jehoiakim, impenitent and heedless of God's word.

20. through the anger of the Lord … he cast them out from his presence – that is, in the course of God's righteous providence, his policy as king would prove ruinous to his country.

Zedekiah rebelled against the king of Babylon – instigated by ambassadors from the neighbouring states who came to congratulate him on his ascension to the throne (compare Jer 17:3, with Jer 28:1), and at the same time get him to join them in a common league to throw off the Assyrian yoke. Though warned by Jeremiah against this step, the infatuated and perjured (Eze 17:13) Zedekiah persisted in his revolt.

Chapter 25

2Ki 25:1–3. Jerusalem again besieged.

1. Nebuchadnezzar … came … against Jerusalem – Incensed by the revolt of Zedekiah, the Assyrian despot determined to put an end to the perfidious and inconstant monarchy of Judea. This chapter narrates his third and last invasion, which he conducted in person at the head of an immense army, levied out of all the tributary nations under his sway. Having overrun the northern parts of the country and taken almost all the fenced cities (Jer 34:7), he marched direct to Jerusalem to invest it. The date of the beginning as well as the end of the siege is here carefully marked (compare Eze 24:1 Jer 39:1 52:4–6); from which it appears, that, with a brief interruption caused by Nebuchadnezzar's marching to oppose the Egyptians who were coming to its relief but who retreated without fighting, the siege lasted a year and a half. So long a resistance was owing, not to the superior skill and valour of the Jewish soldiers, but to the strength of the city fortifications, on which the king too confidently relied (compare Jer 21:1–14 37:1–38:28).

pitched against it, and … built forts – rather, perhaps, drew lines of circumvolution, with a ditch to prevent any going out of the city. On this rampart were erected his military engines for throwing missiles into the city.

3. on the ninth day of the fourth month the famine prevailed – In consequence of the close and protracted blockade, the inhabitants were reduced to dreadful extremities; and under the maddening influence of hunger, the most inhuman atrocities were perpetrated (La 2:20,22 4:9,10 ESE 5:10). This was a fulfilment of the prophetic denunciations threatened on the apostasy of the chosen people (Le 26:29 De 28:53–57 Jer 15:2 27:13 ESE 4:16).

2Ki 25:4–30. Zedekiah taken.

4. the city was broken up – that is, a breach was effected, as we are elsewhere informed, in a part of the wall belonging to the lower city (Ch 32:5 33:14).

the men of war fled by night by the way of the gate between two walls, which is by the king's garden – The king's garden was (Ne 3:15) at the pool of Psyllium, that is, at the mouth of the Terrapene. A trace of the outermost of these walls appears to be still extant in the rude pathway which crosses the mouth of the Terrapene, on a mound hard by the old mulberry tree, which marks the traditional spot of Isaiah's martyrdom [ROBINSON]. It is probable that the besiegers had overlooked this pass.

the king went … toward the plain – that is, the Hor., or valley of Jordan, estimated at five hours' distance from Jerusalem. The plain near Jericho is about eleven or twelve miles broad.

6, 7. they took the king, and brought him … to Riblah – Nebuchadnezzar, having gone from the siege to oppose the auxiliary forces of Pharaoh-hophra, left his generals to carry on the blockade, he himself not returning to the scene of action, but taking up his station at Riblah in the land of Hamath (2Ki 23:33).

they gave judgment upon him – They, that is, the council (Jer 39:3,13 Da 6:7,8,12), regarding him as a seditious and rebellious vassal, condemned him for violating his oath and neglecting the announcement of the divine will as made known to him by Jeremiah (compare Jer 32:5 34:2 38:17). His sons and the nobles who had joined in his flight were slain before his eyes (Jer 39:6 52:10). In conformity with Eastern ideas, which consider a blind man incapable of ruling, his eyes were put out, and being put in chains, he was carried to perpetual imprisonment in Babylon (Jer 52:11), which, though he came to it, as Ezekiel had foretold, he did not see (Jer 32:5 ESE 12:13 17:16).

8–18. on the seventh day of the month … came Nebuzar-adan – (compare Jer 52:12). In attempting to reconcile these two passages, it must be supposed either that, though he had set out on the seventh, he did not arrive in Jerusalem till the tenth, or that he did not put his orders in execution till that day. His office as captain of the guard (Ge 37:36 39:1) called him to execute the awards of justice on criminals; and hence, although not engaged in the siege of Jerusalem (Jer 39:13), Nebuzar-adan was despatched to rase the city, to plunder the temple, to lay both in ruins, demolish the fortifications, and transport the inhabitants to Babylon. The most eminent of these were taken to the king at Riblah (2Ki 25:27) and executed, as instigators and abettors of the rebellion, or otherwise obnoxious to the Assyrian government. In their number were Seraiah, the high priest, grandfather of Ezra (Ezr 7:1), his sagan or deputy, a priest of the second order (Jer 21:2 29:25,29 37:3).

18. the three keepers of the door – not mere porters, but officers of high trust among the Levites (2Ki 22:4 1Ch 9:26).

19. five men of them that were in the king's presence – that is, who belonged to the royal retinue. It is probable that there were five at first, and that the other two were found afterwards (Jer 52:25).

22–26. Nebuchadnezzar … Gedaliah … ruler – The people permitted to remain were, besides the king's daughters, a few court attendants and others (Jer 40:7) too insignificant to be removed, only the peasantry who could till the land and dress the vineyards. Gedaliah was Jeremiah's friend (Jer 26:24), and having, by the prophet's counsel, probably fled from the city as abandoned of God, he surrendered himself to the conqueror (Jer 38:2,17), and being promoted to the government of Judea, fixed his provincial court at Mizpeh. He was well qualified to surmount the difficulties of ruling at such a crisis. Many of the fugitive Jews, as well as the soldiers of Zedekiah who had accompanied the king in his flight to the plains of Jericho, left their retreats (Jer 40:11,12) and flocked around the governor; who having counselled them to submit, promised them on complying with this condition, security on oath that they would retain their possessions and enjoy the produce of their land (Jer 40:9).

25. Ishmael … of the seed royal, came, and ten men with him, and smote Gedaliah – He had found refuge with Baalis, king of the Ammonites, and he returned with a bad design, being either instigated by envy of a governor not descended from the house of David, or bribed by Baalis to murder Gedaliah. The generous governor, though apprised of his intentions, refused to credit the report, much less to sanction the proposal made by an attached friend to cut off Ishmael. The consequence was that he was murdered by this same Ishmael when entertaining him in his own house (Jer 41:1).

26. and all the people … came to Egypt – In spite of Jeremiah's dissuasions (Jer 43:7,8) they settled in various cities of that country (Jer 44:1).

27. seven and thirtieth year of the captivity of Jehoiachin – corresponding with the year of Nebuchadnezzar's death, and his son Evilmerodach's ascension to the throne.

Evil-merodach … did lift up the head of Jehoiachin … and spake kindly – gave him liberty upon parole. This kindly feeling is said to have originated in a familiar acquaintance formed in prison, in which Evil-merodach had lain till his father's death, on account of some malversation while acting as regent during Nebuchadnezzar's seven years' illness (Da 4:32,33). But doubtless the improvement in Zedekiah's condition is to be traced to the overruling providence and grace of Him who still cherished purposes of love to the house of David (2Sa 7:14,15).

29. Jehoiachin ... did eat ... continually before him – According to an ancient usage in Eastern courts, had a seat at the royal table on great days, and had a stated provision granted him for the maintenance of his exiled court.

1 CHRONICLES

Robert Jamieson

Introduction

The first and second books of Chronicles were also considered as one by the ancient Jews, who called them 'words of days,' that is, diaries or journals, being probably compiled from those registers that were kept by the king's historiographers of passing occurrences. In the *Septuagint* the title given them is *Paraleipomenon*, 'of things omitted,' that is, the books are supplementary because many things unnoticed in the former books are here recorded; and not only the omissions are supplied, but some narratives extended while others are added. The authorship is commonly ascribed to Ezra, whose leading object seems to have been to show the division of families, possessions, before the captivity, with a view to the exact restoration of the same order after the return from Babylon. Although many things are restated and others are exact repetitions of what is contained in Kings, there is so much new and important information that, as JEROME has well said, the Chronicles furnish the means of comprehending parts of the New Testament, which must have been unintelligible without them. They are frequently referred to by Christ and the Apostles as forming part of 'the Word of God' (see the genealogies in Mt 1:1-16 Lu 3:23-38; compare 2Ch 19:7 with 1Pe 1:17; 2Ch 24:19-21 with Mt 23:32-35).

Chapter 1

1Ch 1:1–23. Adam's line to Noah.

1. Adam – 'Begat' must be understood. Only that one member of the family is mentioned, who came in the direct order of succession.

4–23. Noah, Shem, Ham, and Japheth – The three sons of this patriarch are enumerated, partly because they were the founders of the new world, and partly because the fulfilment of Noah's prophecy (Ge 9:25-27) could not otherwise appear to have been verified.

12. Casluhim (of whom came the Philistines), and Caphtorim – a better rendering is, 'and Casluhim, of whom came the Philistim and Caphtorim.' They were brethren, the sons of Casluhim, and at first dwelt together, whence their names are used interchangeably. The Caphtorim are described as inhabiting Azzah, or Gaza, the seat of the Philistines.

14–17. the Jebusite – At 1Ch 1:14-17 the names are not those of individuals, but of people who all sprang from Canaan; and as several of them became extinct or were amalgamated with their brethren, their national appellations are given instead of the personal names of their ancestors.

17. Uz, and Hul, and Gether, and Meshech – or, 'Mash'; these were the children of Aram, and *grandsons* of Shem (Ge 10:23).

18. Arphaxad begat Shelah – Cainan, the father's name, is omitted here. (See Lu 3:36).

19. Peleg – (See on Ge 10:25).

22. Ebal – or, 'Obal' (Ge 10:28).

1Ch 1:24–28. Shem's line to Abraham.

24–27. Shem – This comprises a list of ten, inclusive of Abraham.

1Ch 1:29–31. Sons of Ishmael.

29. These are their generations – the heads of his twelve tribes. The great northern desert of Arabia, including the entire neck, was colonized by these tribes; and if we can recover, in the modern geography of this part of the country, Arab tribes bearing the names of those patriarchs, that is, names corresponding with those preserved in the original catalogue of Scripture, we obtain at once so many evidences, not of mere similarity, but of absolute identification [Forster].

Nebaioth – gave rise to the Nabathæans of the classic, and the *Beni Nabat* of Oriental writers. **Kedar** – the Arab tribe, El Khedeyre, on the coast of Hedgar.

Abdeel – Abdilla, the name of a tribe in Yemen.

30. Dumah – Dumah and Tema, the great Arab tribes of Beni Teman. Thus this writer [*Historical Geography of Arabia*] traces the names of all the heads of the twelve tribes of Ishmael as perpetuated in the clans or tribes of the Arabs in the present day.

1Ch 1:32, 33. Sons of Keturah.

32. sons of Keturah – These became founders of nomadic tribes in the north of Arabia and Syria, as Midian of the Midianites (Ge 36:35 Jud 6:2).

and Shuah – from whom Bildad sprang (Job 2:11).

1Ch 1:34–42. Posterity of Abraham by Esau.

36. sons of Eliphaz – the tribe Adites, in the centre country of the Saracens, so called from his mother, Adah (Ge 36:10).

Teman – gave rise to the land of Teman, near the head of the Red Sea.

Omar – the tribe Beni-Amma, settled at the northern point of Djebel Shera (Mount Seir).

Zephi – the tribe Dzaf.

Gatam – Katam, inhabited by the tribe Al Saruat, or 'people of Sarah.'

Kenaz – the tribe Aenezes, a tribe whose settlement lies in the neighbourhood of Syria.

Amalek – the Beni Malak of Zohran, and the Beni Maledj of the Shat el Arab.

37. Reuel – a powerful branch of the great Aeneze tribe, the *Rowalla* Arabs.

Shammah – the great tribe Beni Shammar. In the same way, the names of the other kings and dukes are traced in the modern tribes of Arabia. But it is unnecessary to mention any more of these obscure nomads, except to notice that Jobab (1Ch 1:44), one of the kings of Edom, considered to be Job, and that his seat was in the royal city of Dinahab (Ge 36:32 1Ch 1:43), identified with O'Daeb, a well-known town in the centre of Al Dahna, a great northern desert in the direction of Chaldea and the Euphrates [Forster].

Chapter 2

1Ch 2:1, 2. Sons of Israel.

1Ch 2:3–12. Posterity of Judah.

3. The sons of Judah – His descendants are enumerated first, because the right and privileges of the primogeniture had been transferred to him (Ge 49:8), and because from his tribe the Messiah was to spring.

6. Zimri, and Ethan, and Heman, and Calcol, and Dara – These five are here stated to be the sons of Zerah, that is, of Ezra, whence they were called Ezrahites (1Ki 4:31). In that passage they are called 'the sons of Mahol,' which, however, is to be taken not as a proper name, but appellatively for 'sons of music, dancing.' The traditional fame of their great sagacity and acquirements had descended to the time of Solomon and formed a standard of comparison for showing the superior wisdom of that monarch. Jewish writers say that they were looked up to as prophets by their countrymen during the abode in Egypt.

7. the sons of Carli – He was the son of Zimri, or Zabdi, as he is called (Jos 7:1).

Achar – or Achan (Jos 7:1). This variety in the form of the name is with great propriety used here, since Achar means 'troubler.'

1Ch 2:13–17. Children of Jesse.

15. David the seventh – As it appears (1Sa 16:10 17:12) that Jesse had eight sons, the presumption is from David being mentioned here as the seventh son of his father, that one of them had died at an early age, without leaving issue.

17. Jether the Ishmaelite – (compare 2Sa 17:25). In that passage he is called Ithra an Israelite; and there seems no reason why, in the early days of David, anyone should be specially distinguished as an Israelite. The presumption is in favour of the reading followed by the *Septuagint,* which calls him 'Jetra the Jezreelite.' The circumstance of his settling in another tribe, or of a woman marrying out of her own tribe, was sufficiently rare and singular to call for the statement that Abigail was married to a man of Jezreel.

1Ch 2:18–55. Posterity of Caleb.

18. Caleb the son of Hezron – The notices concerning this person appear confused in our version. In 1Ch 2:19 he is said to be the father of Hur, whereas in 1Ch 2:50 he is called 'the son of Hur.' The words in this latter passage have been transposed in the copying, and should be read thus, 'Hur the son of Caleb.'

begat children of Azubah his wife, and of Jerioth – The former was his spouse, while Jerioth seems to have been a secondary wife, and the mother of the children whose names are here given. On the death of his principal wife, he married Ephrath, and by her had Hur [1Ch 2:19].

21. Hezron … daughter of Machir the father of Gilead – that is, chief of that town, which with the lands adjacent was no doubt the property of Machir, who was so desirous of a male heir. He was grandson of Joseph. The wife of Machir was of the tribe of Manasseh (Nu 26:29).

22. Jair, who had three and twenty cities in the land of Gilead – As the son of Segub and the grandson of Hezron, he was of the tribe of Judah; but from his maternal descent he is called (Nu 32:41 De 3:14) 'the son of Manasseh.' This designation implies that his inheritance lay in that tribe in right of his grandmother; in other words, his *maternal* and *adopting* great-grandfather was Machir the son of Manasseh. Jair, inheriting his property, was his lineal representative; and accordingly this is expressly stated to be the case; for the village group of 'Havoth-Jair' was awarded to him in that tribe, in consequence of his valiant and patriotic exploits. This arrangement, however, took place previous to the law (Nu 36:1–13), by which it was enacted that heiresses were to marry in their own tribe. But this instance of Jair shows that in the case of a man obtaining an inheritance in another tribe it required him to become thoroughly incorporated with it as a representative of the family through which the inheritance was received. He had been adopted into Manasseh, and it would never have been imagined that he was other than 'a son of Manasseh' naturally, had not this passage given information supplementary to that of the passage in Numbers.

23. he took – rather 'he had taken.' This statement is accounting for his acquisition of so large a territory; he got it by right of conquest from the former possessors.

Kenath – This place, along with its group of surrounding villages, was gained by Nobah, one of Jair's officers sent by him to capture it (Nu 32:1,2).

All these belonged to the sons of Machir – In their number Jair is included as having completely identified himself by his marriage and residence in Gilead with the tribe of Manasseh.

24. Caleb-ephratah – so called from uniting the names of husband and wife (1Ch 2:19), and supposed to be the same as was afterwards called Beth-lehem-ephratah.

Ashur, the father of Tekoa – (2Sa 14:2–4). He is called the father, either from his being the first founder, or perhaps the ruler, of the city.

34. Sheshan had no sons, but daughters – either he had no sons alive at his death, or his family consisted wholly of daughters, of whom Ahlai (1Ch 2:31) was one, she being specially mentioned on account of the domestic relations about to be noted.

35. Sheshan gave his daughter to Jarha his servant to wife – The adoption and marriage of a foreign slave in the family where he is serving, is far from being a rare or extraordinary occurrence in Eastern countries. It is thought, however, by some to have been a connection not sanctioned by the law of Moses [MICHAELIS]. But this is not a well-founded objection, as the history of the Jews furnishes not a few examples of foreign proselytes in the same manner obtaining an inheritance in Israel; and doubtless Jarha had previously embraced the Jewish faith in place of the grovelling idolatries of his native Egypt. In such a case, therefore, there could be no legal difficulty. Being a foreign slave, he had no inheritance in a different tribe to injure by this connection; while his marriage with Sheshan's daughter led to his adoption into the tribe of Judah, as well as his becoming heir of the family property.

42. the sons of Caleb – (compare 1Ch 2:18,25). The sons here noticed were the fruit of his union with a third wife.

55. the families of the scribes – either civil or ecclesiastical officers of the Kenite origin, who are here classed with the tribe of Judah, not as being descended from it, but as dwelling within its territory, and in a measure incorporated with its people.

Jabez – a place in Judah (1Ch 4:9).

Kenites that came of Hemath – who settled in Judah, and were thus distinguished from another division of the Kenite clan which dwelt in Manasseh (Jud 4:11).

Chapter 3

1Ch 3:1–9. Sons of David.

1–3. Now these were the sons of David, which were born unto him in Hebron – It is of consequence for the proper understanding of events in the domestic history of David, to bear in mind the place and time of his sons' birth. The oldest son, born *after* his father's *accession* to the sovereign authority, is according to Eastern notions, the proper heir to the throne. And hence the natural aspirations of ambition in Ammon, who was long unaware of the alienation of the crown, and could not be easily reconciled to the claims of a younger brother being placed above his own (see on 2Sa 3:1–5).

3. Eglah his wife – supposed to be another name of Michal, who, though she had no son after her mockery of David for dancing before the ark [2Sa 6:16,20], might have had one previous to that time. She has the title of wife appended to her name because she was his proper wife; and the mention of her name last probably arose from the circumstance that, having been withdrawn from David and married to another husband but afterwards restored, she had in reality become the last of his wives.

5. four, of Bath-shua the daughter of Ammiel – or, 'Bath-sheba' (2Sa 11:3), and there her father is called 'Eliam.' Of course Solomon was not her 'only son,' but he is called so (Pr 4:3) from the distinguished affection of which he was the object; and though the oldest, he is named the last of Bath-sheba's children.

6. Elishama and Eliphelet – Two sons of the same name are twice mentioned (1Ch 3:8). They were the children of different mothers, and had probably some title or epithet appended by which the one was distinguished from the other. Or, it might be, that the former two were dead, and their names had been given to sons afterwards born to preserve their memories.

8. nine – The number of David's sons born after his removal to Jerusalem, was eleven (2Sa 5:14), but only nine are mentioned here: two of them being omitted, either in consequence of their early deaths or because they left no issue.

1Ch 3:10–16. His line to Zedekiah.

10. Solomon's son was Rehoboam – David's line is here drawn down to the captivity, through a succession of good and bad, but still influential and celebrated, monarchs. It has rarely happened that a crown has been transmitted from father to son, in lineal descent, for seventeen reigns. But this was the promised reward of David's piety. There is, indeed, observable some vacillation towards the close of this period – the crown passing from one brother to another, and even from uncle to nephew – a sure sign of disorderly times and a disjointed government.

15. Zedekiah – called the son of Josiah (compare Jer 1:3 37:1), but in 2Ch 36:19 he is described as the brother of Jehoiachin, who was the son of Jehoiakim, and consequently the *grandson* of Josiah. Words expressive of affinity or relationship are used with great latitude in the Hebrew.

Shallum – No king of this name is mentioned in the history of Josiah's sons (2Ki 14:1–29 23:1–37), but there is a notice of Shallum the son of Josiah (Jer 22:11), who reigned in the stead of his father, and who is generally supposed to be Jehoahaz, a younger son, here called the fourth, of Josiah.

1Ch 3:17–24. Successors of Jeconiah.

17. the sons of Jeconiah; Assir – rather, 'Jeconiah the prisoner,' or 'captive.' This record of his condition was added to show that Salathiel was born during the captivity in Babylon (compare Mt 1:12). Jeconiah was written childless (Jer 22:30), a prediction which (as the words that follow explain) meant that this unfortunate monarch should have no son succeeding him on the throne.

Chapter 4

1Ch 4:1–8. Posterity of Judah by Caleb the son of Hur.

1. the sons of Judah – that is, 'the descendants,' for with the exception of Pharez, none of those here mentioned were his immediate sons. Indeed, the others are mentioned solely to introduce the name of Shobal, whose genealogy the historian intended to trace (1Ch 2:52).

1Ch 4:9–20. Of Jabez, and his prayer.

9, 10. Jabez – was, as many think, the son of Coz, or Kenaz, and is here eulogized for his sincere and fervent piety, as well, perhaps, as for some public and patriotic works which he performed. The Jewish writers affirm that he was an eminent doctor in the law, whose reputation drew so many scribes around him that a town was called by his name (1Ch 2:55); and to the piety of his character this passage bears ample testimony. The memory of the critical circumstances which marked his birth was perpetuated in his name (compare Ge 35:15); and yet, in the development of his high talents or distinguished worth in later life, his mother must have found a satisfaction and delight that amply compensated for all her early trials. His prayer which is here recorded, and which, like Jacob's, is in the form of a vow (Ge 28:20), seems to have been uttered when he was entering on an important or critical service, for the successful execution of which he placed confidence neither on his own nor his people's prowess, but looked anxiously for the aid and blessing of God. The enterprise was in all probability the expulsion of the Canaanites from the territory he occupied; and as this was a war of extermination, which God Himself had commanded, His blessing could be the more reasonably asked and expected in preserving them from all the evils to which the undertaking might expose him. In these words, 'that it may not grieve me,' and which might be more literally rendered, 'that I may have no more sorrow,' there is an allusion to the meaning of his name, Jabez, signifying 'grief'; and the import of this petition is, Let me not experience the grief which my name implies, and which my sins may well produce.

10. God granted him that which he requested – Whatever was the kind of undertaking which roused his anxieties, Jabez enjoyed a remarkable degree of prosperity, and God, in this instance, proved that He was not only the hearer, but the answerer of prayer.

13. the sons of Kenaz – the grandfather of Caleb, who from that relationship is called a Kenezite (Nu 32:12).

14. Joab, the father of the valley – literally, 'the father of the inhabitants of the valley' – 'the valley of craftsmen,' as the word denotes. They dwelt together, according to a custom which, independently of any law, extensively prevails in Eastern countries for persons of the same trade to inhabit the same street or the same quarter, and to follow the same occupation from father to son, through many generations. Their occupation was probably that of carpenters, and the valley where they lived seems to have been in the neighbourhood of Jerusalem (Ne 11:35).

17, 18. she bare Miriam – It is difficult, as the verses stand at present, to see who is meant. The following readjustment of the text clears away the obscurity: 'These are the sons of Bithiah the daughter of Pharaoh, which Mered took, and she bare Miriam, and his wife Jehudijah bare Jezreel.'

18. Jehudijah – 'the Jewess,' to distinguish her from his other wife, who was an Egyptian. This passage records a very interesting fact – the marriage of an Egyptian princess to a descendant of Caleb. The marriage must have taken place in the wilderness. The barriers of a different national language and national religion kept the Hebrews separate from the Egyptians; but they did not wholly prevent intimacies, and even occasional intermarriages between private individuals of the two nations. Before such unions, however, could be sanctioned, the Egyptian party must have renounced idolatry, and this daughter of Pharaoh, as appears from her name, had become a convert to the worship of the God of Israel.

1Ch 4:21–23. Posterity of Shelah.

21. Laadah … the father … of the house of them that wrought fine linen – Here, again, is another incidental evidence that in very early times certain trades were followed by particular families among the Hebrews, apparently in hereditary succession. Their knowledge of the art of linen manufacture had been, most probably, acquired in Egypt, where the duty of bringing up families to the occupations of their forefathers was a compulsory obligation, whereas in Israel, as in many parts of Asia to this day, it was optional, though common.

22, 23. had the dominion in Moab, and Jashubi-lehem – 'And these are ancient things' seems a strange rendering of a proper name; and, besides, it conveys a meaning that has no bearing on the record. The following improved translation has been suggested: 'Sojourned in Moab, but returned to Beth-lehem and Adaberim-athekim. These and the inhabitants of Netaim and Gedera were potters employed

by the king in his own work.' Gedera or Gederoth, and Netaim, belonged to the tribe of Judah, and lay on the southeast border of the Philistines' territory (Jos 15–36 2Ch 28:18).

1Ch 4:24–43. Of Simeon.

24. The sons of Simeon – They are classed along with those of Judah, as their possession was partly taken out of the extensive territory of the latter (Jos 19:1). The difference in several particulars of the genealogy given here from that given in other passages is occasioned by some of the persons mentioned having more than one name [compare Ge 46:10 Ex 6:15 Nu 26:12].

27. his brethren had not many children – (see Nu 1:22 26:14).

31-43. These were their cities unto the reign of David – In consequence of the sloth or cowardice of the Simeonites, some of the cities within their allotted territory were only nominally theirs. They were never taken from the Philistines until David's time, when, the Simeonites having forfeited all claim to them, he assigned them to his own tribe of Judah (1Sa 27:6).

38, 39. increased greatly, and they went to the entrance of Gedor – Simeon having only a part of the land of Judah, they were forced to seek accommodation elsewhere; but their establishment in the new and fertile pastures of Gederah was soon broken up; for, being attacked by a band of nomad plunderers, they were driven from place to place till some of them effected by force a settlement on Mount Seir.

Chapter 5

1Ch 5:1–10. The line of Reuben.

1. Now the sons of Reuben – In proceeding to give this genealogy, the sacred historian states, in a parenthesis (1Ch 5:1,2), the reason why it was not placed first, as Reuben was the oldest son of Jacob. The birthright, which by a foul crime he had forfeited, implied not only dominion, but a double portion (De 21:17); and both of these were transferred to Joseph, whose two sons having been adopted as the children of Jacob (Ge 48:5), received each an allotted portion, as forming two distinct tribes in Israel. Joseph then was entitled to the precedency; and yet, as his posterity was not mentioned first, the sacred historian judged it necessary to explain that 'the genealogy was not to be reckoned after the birthright,' but with a reference to a superior honour and privilege that had been conferred on Judah – not the man, but the tribe, whereby it was invested with the pre-eminence over all the other tribes, and out of it was to spring David with his royal lineage, and especially the great Messiah (Heb 7:14). These were the two reasons why, in the order of enumeration, the genealogy of Judah is introduced before that of Reuben.

9. Eastward he inhabited unto the entering in of the wilderness from the river Euphrates – The settlement was on the east of Jordan, and the history of this tribe, which never took any part in the public affairs or movements of the nation, is comprised in 'the multiplication of their cattle in the land of Gilead,' in their wars with the Bedouin sons of Hagar, and in the simple labours of pastoral life. They had the right of pasture over an extensive mountain range – the great wilderness of Kedemoth (De 2:26) and the Euphrates being a security against their enemies.

1Ch 5:11–26. The line of Gad.

11–15. the children of Gad dwelt over against them – The genealogy of the Gadites and the half-tribe of Manasseh (1Ch 5:24) is given along with that of the Reubenites, as these three were associated in a separate colony.

16. Sharon – The term 'Sharon' was applied as descriptive of any place of extraordinary beauty and productiveness. There were three places in Palestine so called. This Sharon lay east of the Jordan.

upon their borders – that is, of Gilead and Bashan: Gilead proper, or at least the largest part, belonged to the Reubenites; and Bashan, the greatest portion of it, belonged to the Manassites. The Gadites occupied an intermediate settlement on the land which lay upon their borders.

17. All these were reckoned ... in the days of Jotham – His long reign and freedom from foreign wars as well as intestine troubles were favourable for taking a census of the people.

and in the days of Jeroboam – the second of that name.

18–22. Hagarites – or, 'Hagarenes,' originally synonymous with 'Ishmaelites,' but afterwards applied to a particular tribe of the Arabs (compare Ps 83:6).

Jetur – His descendants were called Itureans, and the country Auranitis, from Hauran, its chief city. These, who were skilled in archery, were invaded in the time of Joshua by a confederate army of the tribes of Reuben, Gad, and half Manasseh, who, probably incensed by the frequent raids of those marauding neighbours, took reprisals in men and cattle, dispossessed almost all of the original inhabitants, and colonized the district themselves.

26. the God of Israel stirred up the spirit of Pul – the Phalluka of the Ninevite monuments (see on 2Ki 15:19).

and the spirit of Tilgath-pilneser – the son of the former. By them the trans-jordanic tribes, including the other half of Manasseh, settled in Galilee, were removed to Upper Media. This was the *first* captivity (2Ki 15:29).

Chapter 6

1Ch 6:1–48. Line of the priests.

5. Uzzi – It is supposed that, in his days, the high priesthood was, for unrecorded reasons, transferred from Eleazar's family to Ithamar's, in which it continued for several generations.

10. he it is that executed the priest's office in the temple that Solomon built in Jerusalem – It is doubtful whether the person in favour of whom this testimony is borne be Johanan or Azariah. If the former, he is the same as Jehoiada, who rendered important public services (2Ki 11); if the latter, it refers to the worthy and independent part he acted in resisting the unwarrantable encroachments of Uzziah (2Ch 26:17).

in the temple that Solomon built in Jerusalem – described in this particular manner to distinguish it from the second temple, which was in existence at the time when this history was written.

14. Azariah begat Seraiah – He filled the supreme pontifical office at the destruction of Jerusalem, and, along with his deputy and others, he was executed by Nebuchadnezzar's orders at Riblah (2Ki 25:18,21). The line of high priests, under the first temple, which from Zadok amounted to twelve, terminated with him.

16–48. The sons of Levi; Gershom – This repetition (see 1Ch 6:1) is made, as the historian here begins to trace the genealogy of the Levitical families who were not priests. The list is a long one, comprising the chiefs or heads of their several families until David's reign, who made a new and different classification of them by courses.

20. Zimmah his son – his grandson (1Ch 6:42).

24. Uriel – or Zephaniah (1Ch 6:36).

27. Elkanah – the father of the prophet Samuel (1Sa 1:1).

28. the sons of Samuel – The sons of Samuel are here named Vashni and Abiah. The first-born is called Joel (1Sa 8:2); and this name is given to him in 1Ch 6:33. It is now generally thought by the best critics that, through an error of the copyists, an omission has been made of the oldest son's name, and that Vashni, which is not the name of a person, merely signifies 'and the second.' This critical emendation of the text makes all clear, as well as consistent with other passages relating to the family of Samuel.

32. before the dwelling-place – that is, in the tent which David had erected for receiving the ark after it was removed from the house of Obed-edom [2Sa 6:17]. This was a considerable time before the temple was built.

they waited on their office according to their order – which David, doubtless by the direction of the Holy Spirit, had instituted for the better regulation of divine worship.

33. Shemuel – that is, Samuel. This is the exact representation of the Hebrew name.

39. his brother Asaph – They were brothers naturally, both being descended from Levi, as well as officially, both being of the Levitical order.

42. Ethan – or Jeduthun (1Ch 9:16 2Ch 35:15).

48. Their brethren also the Levites were appointed unto all manner of service – Those of them who were endowed with musical tastes and talents were employed in various other departments of the temple service.

1Ch 6:49–81. Office of Aaron and his sons.

49. But Aaron and his sons offered – The office and duties of the high priests having been already described, the names of those who successively filled that important office are recorded.

60. thirteen cities – No more than eleven are named here; but two additional ones are mentioned (Jos 21:16,17), which makes up the thirteen.

61. unto the sons of Kohath, which were left – that is, in addition to the priests belonging to the same family and tribe of Levi.

by lot, ten cities – (Jos 21:26). The sacred historian gives an explanation (1Ch 6:66). Eight of these are mentioned, but only two of them are taken out of the haft tribe of Manasseh (1Ch 6:70). The names of the other two are given (Jos 21:21), where full and detailed notices of these arrangements may be found.

62. to the sons of Gershom – Supply 'the children of Israel gave.'

67–81. they gave unto them of the cities of refuge – The names of the cities given here are considerably different from those applied to them (Jos 21:13–19). In the lapse of centuries, and from the revolutions of society, changes might have been expected to take place in the form or dialectic pronunciation of the names of those cities; and this will sufficiently account for the variations that are found in the lists as enumerated here and in an earlier book. As to these cities themselves that were assigned to the Levites, they were widely remote and separated – partly in fulfilment of Jacob's prophecy (Ge 49:7), and partly that the various districts of the country might obtain a competent supply of teachers who might instruct the people in the knowledge, and animate them to the observance, of a law which had so important a bearing on the promotion both of their private happiness and their national prosperity.

Chapter 7

1Ch 7:1–5. Sons of Issachar.

1. Jashub – or Job (Ge 46:13).

2. whose number was in the days of David two and twenty thousand and six hundred – Although a census was taken in the reign of David by order of that monarch, it is not certain that the sacred historian had it in mind, since we find here the tribe of Benjamin enumerated [1Ch 7:6-12], which was not taken in David's time; and there are other points of dissimilarity.

3. five: all of them chief men – Four only are mentioned; so that as they are stated to be five, in this number the father, Izrahiah, must be considered as included; otherwise one of the names must have dropped out of the text. They were each at the head of a numerous and influential division of their tribe.

5. fourscore and seven thousand – exclusive of the 58,600 men which the Tola branch had produced (1Ch 7:24), so that in the days of David the tribe would have contained a population of 45,600. This large increase was owing to the practice of polygamy, as well as the fruitfulness of the women. A plurality of wives, though tolerated among the Hebrews, was confined chiefly to the great and wealthy; but it seems to have been generally esteemed a privilege by the tribe of Issachar, 'for they had many wives and sons' [1Ch 7:4].

1Ch 7:6–12. Of Benjamin.

6. The sons of Benjamin – Ten are named in Ge 46:21, but only five later (1Ch 8:1 Nu 26:38). Perhaps five of them were distinguished as chiefs of illustrious families, but two having fallen in the bloody wars waged against Benjamin (Jud 20:46), there remained only three branches of this tribe, and these only are enumerated.

7. the sons of Bela – Each of them was chief or leader of the family to which he belonged. In an earlier period seven great families of Benjamin are mentioned (Nu 26:38), five of them being headed by these five sons of Benjamin, and two descended from Bela. Here five families of Bela are specified, whence we are led to conclude that time or the ravages of war had greatly changed the condition of Benjamin, or that the five families of Bela were subordinate to the other great divisions that sprang directly from the five sons of the patriarch.

12. Shuppim also, and Huppim – They are called Muppim and Huppim (Ge 46:21) and Hupham and Shupham (Nu 26:39). They were the children of Ir, or Iri (1Ch 7:7).

and Hushim, the sons – 'son.'

of Aher – 'Aher' signifies 'another,' and some eminent critics, taking 'Aher' as a common noun, render the passage thus, 'and Hushim, another son.' Shuppim, Muppim, and Hushim are plural words, and therefore denote not individuals, but the heads of their respective families; and as they were not comprised in the above enumeration (1Ch 7:7,9) they are inserted here in the form of an appendix. Some render the passage, 'Hushim, the son of another,' that is, tribe or family. The name occurs among the sons of Dan (Ge 46:23), and it is a presumption in favour of this being the true rendering, that after having recorded the genealogy of Naphtali (1Ch 7:13) the sacred historian adds, 'the sons of Bilhah, the handmaid, who was the mother of Dan and Naphtali.' We naturally expect, therefore, that these two will be noticed together, but Dan is not mentioned at all, if not in this passage.

1Ch 7:13. Of Naphtali.

13. Shallum – or Shillem (Ge 46:24).

sons of Bilhah – As Dan and Naphtali were her sons, Hushim, as well as these enumerated in 1Ch 7:13, were her grandsons.

1Ch 7:14–40. Of Manasseh.

14,15. The sons of Manasseh – or descendants; for Ashriel was a grandson, and Zelophehad was a generation farther removed in descent (Nu 26:33). The text, as it stands, is so confused and complicated that it is exceedingly difficult to trace the genealogical thread, and a great variety of conjectures have been made with a view to clear away the obscurity. The passage (1Ch 7:14,15) should probably be rendered thus: 'The sons of Manasseh were Ashriel, whom his Syrian concubine bare to him, and Machir, the father of Gilead (whom his wife bare to him). Machir took for a wife Maachah, sister to Huppim and Shuppim.'

21. whom the men of Gath … slew – This interesting little episode gives us a glimpse of the state of Hebrew society in Egypt; for the occurrence narrated seems to have taken place before the Israelites left that country. The patriarch Ephraim was then alive, though he must have arrived at a very advanced age; and the Hebrew people, at all events those of them who were his descendants, still retained their pastoral character. It was in perfect consistency with the ideas and habits of Oriental shepherds that they should have made a raid on the neighbouring tribe of the Philistines for the purpose of plundering their flocks. For nothing is more common among them than hostile incursions on the inhabitants of towns, or on other nomad tribes with whom they have no league of amity. But a different view of the incident is brought out, if, instead of 'because,' we render the Hebrew particle 'when' they came down to take their cattle, for the tenor of the context leads rather to the conclusion that 'the men of Gath' were the aggressors, who, making a sudden

foray on the Ephraimite flocks, killed the shepherds including several of the sons of Ephraim. The calamity spread a deep gloom around the tent of their aged father, and was the occasion of his receiving visits of condolence from his distant relatives, according to the custom of the East, which is remarkably exemplified in the history of Job (Job 2:11; compare Joh 11:19).

Chapter 8
1Ch 8:1–32. Sons and chief men of Benjamin.

1. Now Benjamin begat – This chapter contains some supplementary particulars in addition to what has been already said regarding the tribe of Benjamin (see on 1Ch 7:6). The names of many of the persons mentioned are different from those given by Moses – a diversity which may be accounted for in part on grounds formerly stated, namely, either that the persons had more than one name, or that the word 'sons' is used in a loose sense for grandsons or descendants. But there are other circumstances to be taken into account in considering the details of this chapter; namely, first, that the genealogies of the Benjamites were disordered or destroyed by the almost total extermination of this tribe (Jud 20:11–48); secondly, that a great number of Benjamites, born in Assyria, are mentioned here, who returned from the long captivity in Babylon, and established themselves – some in Jerusalem, others in different parts of Judea. There were more returned from Babylon of the families belonging to this tribe than to any other except Judah; and hence many strange names are here introduced; some of which will be found in the list of the restored exiles (compare Ezr 2:1–70).

6. these are the sons of Ehud – most probably the judge of Israel (Jud 3:15). His descendants, who had at first been established in Geba in Benjamin, emigrated in a body under the direction of Gera (1Ch 8:7) to Manahath, where their increased numbers would find more ample accommodation. Manahath was within the territory of Judah.

8. Shaharaim begat children in the country of Moab – He had probably been driven to take refuge in that foreign land on the same calamitous occasion that forced Elimelech to emigrate thither (Ru 1:1). But, destitute of natural affection, he forsook or divorced his two wives, and in the land of his sojourn married a third, by whom he had several sons. But there is another explanation given of the conduct of this Benjamite polygamist. His children by Hushim are mentioned (1Ch 8:11), while his other wife is unnoticed. Hence it has been thought probable that it is Baara who is mentioned under the name of Hodesh, so called because her husband, after long desertion, returned and cohabited with her as before.

28. These dwelt in Jerusalem – The ordinary and stated inhabitants of Jerusalem were Judahites, Benjamites, and Levites. But at the time referred to here, the chiefs or heads of the principal families who are enumerated (1Ch 8:14-27) established themselves in the city after their return from the captivity.

1Ch 8:33–40. Stock of Saul and Jonathan.

33. Ner begat Kish – The father of Ner, though not mentioned here, is stated (1Ch 9:35) to have been Jehiel. Moreover, the father of Kish is said (1Sa 9:1) to have been Abiel, the son of Zeror, whence it would seem that Abiel and Ner were names of the same person.

Abinadab – the same as Ishui (1Sa 14:49).

Esh-baal – that is, Ish-bosheth.

34. Merib-baal – that is, Mephibosheth.

36. Jehoadah – or, Jara (1Ch 9:42).

40. mighty men of valour, archers – Great strength as well as skill was requisite in ancient archery, as the bow, which was of steel, was bent by treading with the feet, and pulling the string with both hands.

Chapter 9

1Ch 9:1–26. Original registers of Israel and Judah's genealogies.

1. all Israel were reckoned by genealogies – From the beginning of the Hebrew nation, public records were kept, containing a registration of the name of every individual, as well as the tribe and family to which he belonged. 'The book of the kings of Israel and Judah' does not refer to the two canonical books that are known in Scripture by that name, but to authenticated copies of those registers, placed under the official care of the sovereigns; and as a great number of the Israelites (1Ch 9:3) took refuge in Judah during the invasion of Shalmaneser, they carried the public records along with them. The genealogies given in the preceding chapters were drawn from the public records in the archives both of Israel and Judah; and those given in this chapter relate to the period subsequent to the restoration; whence it appears (compare 1Ch 3:17-24) that the genealogical registers were kept during the captivity in Babylon. These genealogical tables, then, are of the highest authority for truth and correctness, the earlier portion being extracted from the authenticated records of the nation; and as to those which belong to the time of the captivity, they were drawn up by a contemporary writer, who, besides enjoying the best sources of information, and being of the strictest integrity, was guided and preserved from all error by divine inspiration.

2. the first inhabitants that dwelt in their possessions – This chapter relates wholly to the first returned exiles. Almost all the names recur in Nehemiah (Ne 11:1–36), although there are differences which will be explained there. The same division of the people into four classes was continued after, as before the captivity; namely, the priests, Levites, natives, who now were called by the common name of Israelites, and the Nethinims (Jos 9:27 Ezr 2:43 8:20). When the historian speaks of 'the first inhabitants that dwelt in their possessions,' he implies that there were others who afterwards returned and settled in possessions not occupied by the first. Accordingly, we read of a great number returning successively under Ezra, Nehemiah, and at a later period. And some of those who returned to the ancient inheritance of their fathers, had lived before the time of the captivity (Ezr 3:12 Hag 2:4,10).

18. the king's gate – The king had a gate from his palace into the temple (2Ki 16:18), which doubtless was kept constantly closed except for the monarch's use; and although there was no king in Israel on the return from the captivity, yet the old ceremonial was kept up, probably in the hope that the sceptre would, ere long, be restored to the house of David. It is an honour by which Eastern kings are distinguished, to have a gate exclusively devoted to their own special use, and which is kept constantly closed, except when he goes out or returns (Eze 44:2). There being no king then in Israel, this gate would be always shut.

Chapter 10

1Ch 10:1–7. Saul's overthrow and death.

1. Now the Philistines fought against Israel – The details of this chapter have no relation to the preceding genealogies and seem to be inserted solely to introduce the narrative of David's elevation to the throne of the whole kingdom. The parallel between the books of Samuel and Chronicles commences with this chapter, which relates the issue of the fatal battle of Gilboa almost in the very same words as 1Sa 31:1-13.

3. the battle went sore against Saul; and the archers hit him, and he was wounded – The *Hebrew* words may be thus rendered: 'The archers found (attacked) him, and he feared the archers.' He was not wounded, at least not dangerously, when he resolved on committing suicide. The deed was the effect of sudden terror and overwhelming depression of spirits [CALMET].

4. his armour-bearer would not; for he was sore afraid – He was, of course, placed in the same perilous condition as Saul. But it is probable that the feelings that restrained him from complying with Saul's wish were a profound respect for royalty, mingled with apprehension of the shock which such a catastrophe would give to the national feelings and interests.

6. Saul died, and his three sons, and all his house – his sons and courtiers who were there engaged in the battle. But it appears that Ish-bosheth and Mephibosheth were kept at Gibeah on account of their youth.

1Ch 10:8–14. The Philistines triumph over him.

10. put his armour in the house of their gods – It was common among the heathen to vow to a national or favourite deity, that, in the event of a victory, the armour of the enemy's king, or of some eminent leader, should be dedicated to him as an offering of gratitude. Such trophies were usually suspended on the pillars of the temple.

fastened his head in the temple of Dagon – while the trunk or headless corpse was affixed to the wall of Beth-shan (1Sa 31:10).

13. Saul died for his transgression which he committed against the Lord – in having spared the king of the Amalekites and taken the flocks of the people as spoils [1Sa 15:9], as well as in having consulted a pythoness [1Sa 28:7]. Both of these acts were great sins – the first as a violation of God's express and positive command [1Sa 15:3], and the second as contrary to a well-known statute of the kingdom (Le 19:31).

14. And inquired not of the Lord – He had done so in form (1Sa 28:6), but not in the spirit of a humble penitent, nor with the believing confidence of a sincere worshipper. His enquiry was, in fact, a mere mockery, and his total want of all right religious impressions was manifested by his rushing from God to a wretched impostor in the service of the devil [1Sa 28:7].

Chapter 11

1Ch 11:1–3. David made king.

1. Then all Israel gathered themselves to David unto Hebron – This event happened on the death of Ish-bosheth (see on 2Sa 5:1). The convention of the estates of the kingdom, the public and solemn homage of the representatives of the people, and the repeated anointing of the new king in their presence and by their direction, seem to have been necessary to the general acknowledgment of the sovereign on the part of the nation (compare 1Sa 11:15).

1Ch 11:4–9. He wins the castle of Zion from the Jebusites by Joab's valour.

4. David and all Israel went to … Jebus – (See on 2Sa 5:6).

8. Joab repaired the rest of the city – David built a new town to the north of the old one on Mount Zion; but Joab was charged with a commission to restore the part that had been occupied by the ancient Jebus, to repair the breaches made during the siege, to rebuild the houses which had been demolished or burned in the sacking of the town, and to preserve all that had escaped the violence of the soldiery. This work of reconstruction is not noticed elsewhere [CALMET].

1Ch 11:10–47. A catalogue of his worthies.

10. These … are the chief of the mighty men – (See on 2Sa 23:8). They are here described as those who held strongly with him (*Margin*) to make him king. In these words the sacred historian assigns a reason for introducing the list of their names, immediately after his account of the election of David as king, and the conquest of Jerusalem; namely, that they assisted in making David king. In the original form of the list, and the connection in which it occurs in Samuel, there is no reference to the choice of a king; and even in this passage it is only in the clause introduced into the superscription that such a reference occurs [KEIL].

11–13. Jashobeam, an Hachmonite – or, 'son of Hachmoni.' He is called also son of Zabdiel (1Ch 27:2), so that, strictly speaking, he was the grandson of Hachmoni (compare 1Ch 27:32).

lifted up his spear against three hundred slain by him at one time – The feat is said (2Sa 23:8) to have been a slaughter of eight hundred in one day. Some endeavour to reconcile the statements in that passage and in this by supposing that he slew eight hundred on one occasion and three hundred on another; while others conjecture that he attacked a body of eight hundred, and, having slain three hundred of them, the rest fled [LIGHTFOOT].

12. the three mighties – Only two are mentioned; namely, Jashobeam and Eleazar – the third, Shammah (2Sa 23:11), is not named in this passage.

13. He was with David at Pas-dammim – It was at the time when he was a fugitive in the wilderness, and, parched with thirst under the burning heat of noonday, he wistfully thought of the cool fountain of his native village [2Sa 23:15 1Ch 11:17]. This is a notice of the achievement, to which Eleazar owed his fame, but the details are found only in 2Sa 23:9–11, where it is further said that he was aided by the valour of Shammah, a fact corroborated in the passage before us (1Ch 11:14), where it is recorded of the heroes, that 'they set themselves in the midst of that parcel.' As the singular number is used in speaking of Shammah (2Sa 23:12), the true view seems to be that when Eleazar had given up from exhaustion, Shammah succeeded, and by his fresh and extraordinary prowess preserved the field. **barley** – or lentils (2Sa 23:11). Ephes-dammim was situated between Shocoh and Azekah, in the west of the Judahite territory. These feats were performed when David acted as Saul's general against the Philistines.

15–19. David longed, and said, Oh that one would give me drink ... of the well of Beth-lehem – (See on 2Sa 23:15). This chivalrous act evinces the enthusiastic devotion of David's men, that they were ready to gratify his smallest wish at the risk of their lives. It is probable that, when uttering the wish, David had no recollection of the military posted at Beth-lehem. It is generally taken for granted that those who fought a way to the well of Beth-lehem were the three champions just mentioned [see on 1Ch 11:13]. But this is far from being clear. On the contrary, it would seem that three different heroes are referred to, for Abishai (1Ch 11:20) was one of them. The camp of the Philistines was in the valley of Rephaim (1Ch 11:15), which lay on the west of Jerusalem, but an outpost was stationed at Beth-lehem (1Ch 11:16), and through this garrison they had to force a passage.

21. howbeit he attained not to the first three – (See on 2Sa 23:19).

22. Benaiah ... of Kabzeel – a town in the south of Judah (Jos 15:21 Ne 11:25). It is said that 'he had done many acts,' though three only are mentioned as specimens of his daring energy and fearless courage.

slew two lionlike men of Moab – literally, 'lions of God,' that is, great lions or champions. This gallant feat was probably achieved in David's hostile invasion of Moab (2Sa 8:2).

also he went down and slew a lion in a pit in a snowy day – probably a cave into which Benaiah had taken refuge from the snowstorm, and in which he encountered a savage lion which had its lair there. In a spacious cave the achievement would be far greater than if the monster had been previously snared or cabined in a pit.

23. he went down – the ordinary phraseology for expressing an engagement in battle. The encounter of Benaiah with this gigantic Egyptian reminds us, in some respects, of David's combat with Goliath. At least, the height of this giant, which was about eight feet, and his armour, resembled his of Gath.

with a staff – that is, having no other weapon in his hand than his walking stick.

25. David set him over his guard – the Cherethites and Pelethites that composed the small bodyguard in immediate attendance on the king.

26. Also the valiant men of the armies – This was the third degree of military rank, and Asahel was their chief; the names of few of those mentioned are historically known.

30. Maharai – chief of the detachment of the guards who attended on the king in the tenth month, January (1Ch 27:13 2Sa 23:28).

39. Naharai – armourbearer to Joab (2Sa 23:37). The non-occurrence of Joab's name in any of the three catalogues is most probably to be accounted for by the circumstance that his office as commander-in-chief raised him to a position superior to all these orders of military knighthood.

41. Uriah the Hittite – The enrolment of this name in such a list, attesting, as it does, his distinguished merits as a brave and devoted officer, aggravates the criminality of David's outrage on his life and honour. The number of the names at 1Ch 11:26-41 (exclusive of Asahel and Uriah, who were dead) is thirty, and at 1Ch 11:41–47 is sixteen – making together forty-eight (see on 1Ch 27:1–34). Of those mentioned (1Ch 11:26–41), the greater part belonged to the tribes of Judah and Benjamin; the sixteen names (1Ch 11:41–47) are all associated with places unknown, or with cities and districts on the east of the Jordan. The northern tribes do not appear to have furnished any leaders [BERTHEAU].

Chapter 12

1Ch 12:1–22. The companies that came to David at Ziklag.

1–7. Now these are they that came to David to Ziklag – There are three lists given in this chapter, arranged, apparently, according to the order of time when the parties joined the standard of David.

while he yet kept himself close because of Saul – that is, when the king's jealousy had driven him into exile from the court and the country.

Ziklag – (See on 1Sa 27:6). It was during his retirement in that Philistine town that he was joined in rapid succession by the heroes who afterwards contributed so much to the glory of his reign.

2. of Saul's brethren of Benjamin – that is, of the tribe of Benjamin (compare 1Ch 12:29), but some of them might be relatives of the king. This movement to which the parties were led, doubtless by the secret impulse of the Spirit, was of vast importance to the cause of David, as it must have been founded on their observation of the evident withdrawal of God's blessing from Saul, and His favouring presence with David, to whom it was universally known the Divine King of Israel had given the crown in reversion. The accession of the Benjamites who came first and their resolution to share his fortunes must have been particularly grateful to David. It was a public and emphatic testimony by those who had enjoyed the best means of information to the unblemished excellence of his character, as well as a decided protest against the grievous wrong inflicted by causelessly outlawing a man who had rendered such eminent services to his country.

4. Ismaiah the Gibeonite – It appears that not only the Canaanites who were admitted into the congregation (Jos 9:1-27), but people of the tribe of Benjamin, were among the inhabitants of Gibeon. The mention of 'the Gederathite,' probably from Gederah (Jos 15:36), in the lowlands of Judah; of the Korhites (1Ch 12:6), from Korah (1Ch 2:43), and of Gedor (1Ch 12:7), a town in Judah, to the southwest of Beth-lehem (compare 1Ch 4:4), shows that this first list contains men of Judah as well as Benjamin [BERTHEAU].

8–13. of the Gadites there separated themselves unto David – that is, from the service of Saul and from the rest of the Gadites who remained steadfast adherents of his cause.

into the hold – or fortress, that is, of Ziklag, which was in the wilderness of Judah.

whose faces were like the faces of lions – A fierce, lion-like countenance (2Sa 1:23), and great agility in pursuit (2Sa 2:18), were qualities of the highest estimation in ancient warfare.

14. one of the least was over an hundred, and the greatest over a thousand – David, while at Ziklag, had not so large an amount of forces as to give to each of these the command of so many men. Another meaning, therefore, must obviously be sought, and excluding was, which is a supplement by our translators, the import of the passage is, that one of the least could discomfit a hundred, and the greatest was worth a thousand ordinary men; a strong hyperbole to express their uncommon valour.

15. These are they that went over Jordan in the first month – that is, in spring, when the swollen river generally fills up the banks of its channel.

they put to flight all them of the valleys – This was probably done at the time of their separating themselves and their purpose being discovered, they had to cut their passage through the opposing adherents of Saul, both on the eastern and western banks. The impossibility of taking the fords at such a time, and the violent rapidity of the current, make this crossing of the Jordan – in whatever way these Gadites accomplished it – a remarkable feat.

16. the children of Benjamin and Judah – It is probable that the Benjamites invited the Judahites to accompany them, in order to prevent David being suspicious of them. Their anticipations, as the result showed, were well founded. He did suspect them, but the doubts of David as to their object in repairing to him, were promptly dispelled by Amasai or Amasa, who, by the secret impulse of the Spirit, assured him of their strong attachment and their zealous service from a unanimous conviction that his cause was owned and blessed of God (1Sa 18:12–14).

19–22. there fell some of Manasseh – The period of their accession is fixed as the time when David came with the Philistines against Saul to battle.

but they helped them not – (See on 1Sa 29:4).

20. As he went to Ziklag – If those Manassites joined him on his return to Ziklag, after his dismissal from the Philistine army, then their arrival took place before the battle of Gilboa could have been fought (compare 1Sa 29:11). Convinced of the desperate state of Saul's affairs, they abandoned him, and resolved to transfer their allegiance to David. But some learned men think that they came as fugitives from that disastrous field [CALMET and EWALD].

captains of the thousands ... of Manasseh – Those seven were commanders of the large military divisions of their tribe.

21, 22. they helped David against the band – that is, the Amalekites who had pillaged Ziklag in David's absence. This military expedition was made by all his men (1Sa 30:9), who, as David's early helpers, are specially distinguished from those who are mentioned in the latter portion of the chapter.

22. the host of God – that is, a great and powerful army.

1Ch 12:23–40. The armies that came to him at Hebron.

23. these are the numbers of the bands ... that came to David to Hebron – after the death of Ish-bosheth (see on 2Sa 5:1).

to turn the kingdom of Saul to him, according to the word of the Lord – (1Ch 10:14 11:3,10). The account commences with the southern tribes, Levi being associated with Judah and Simeon, as the great majority of the leading men in this tribe resided in Judah; and, after recounting the representatives of the northern tribes, it concludes with those on the east of Jordan.

27. Jehoiada, the leader of the Aaronites – not the high priest, for that was Abiathar (1Sa 23:9), but the leader of the Aaronite warriors, supposed to be the father of Benaiah (1Ch 11:22).

29. Benjamin ... three thousand – This small number shows the unpopularity of the movement in this tribe; and, indeed, it is expressly stated that the mass of the population had, even after Ish-bosheth's death, anxiously endeavoured to secure the crown in the family of Saul.

32. children of Issachar, ... that had understanding of the times – Jewish writers say that the people of this tribe were eminent for their acquirements in astronomical and physical science; and the object of the remark was probably to show that the intelligent and learned classes were united with the military, and had declared for David.

33. Zebulun … could keep rank – that is, were more disciplined soldiers than the rest.

not of double heart – Though their numbers were large, all were in a high degree well affected to David.

38. all the rest also of Israel were of one heart to make David king – that is, entertained a unanimous desire for his elevation.

39, 40. there they were with David three days, eating and drinking – According to the statements made in the preceding verses, the number of armed warriors assembled in Hebron on this occasion amounted to three hundred thousand. Supplies of provisions were abundantly furnished, not only by the people of the neighbourhood, but from distant parts of the country, for all wished the festivities to be on a scale of liberality and magnificence suitable to the auspicious occasion.

Chapter 13

1Ch 13:1–8. David fetches the ark from Kirjath-jearim.

1–3. David consulted … And let us bring again the ark of our God – Gratitude for the high and splendid dignity to which he had been elevated would naturally, at this period, impart a fresh animation and impulse to the habitually fervent piety of David; but, at the same time, he was animated by other motives. He fully understood his position as ruler under the theocracy, and, entering on his duties, he was resolved to fulfil his mission as a constitutional king of Israel. Accordingly, his first act as a sovereign related to the interests of religion. The ark being then the grand instrument and ornament of it, he takes the opportunity of the official representatives of the nation being with him, to consult them about the propriety of establishing it in a more public and accessible locality. The assembly at which he spoke of this consisted of the Sheloshim, princes of thousands (2Sa 6:1). During the reign of the late king, the ark had been left in culpable neglect. Consequently the people had, to a great extent, been careless about the ordinances of divine worship, or had contented themselves with offering sacrifices at Gibeon, without any thought of the ark, though it was the chief and most vital part of the tabernacle. The duty and advantages of this religious movement suggested by the king were apparent, and the proposal met with universal approval.

2. If it seem good unto you, and … it be of the Lord – that is, I shall conclude that this favourite measure of mine is agreeable to the mind of God, if it receive your hearty concurrence.

Let us send abroad to our brethren everywhere – He wished to make it known throughout the country, in order that there might be a general assembly of the nation, and that preparations might be made on a scale and of a kind suitable to the inauguration of the August ceremonial.

with them also to the priests and Levites … in their cities and suburbs – The original terms, 'Let us send,' imply immediate execution; and, doubtless, the publication of the royal edict would have been followed by the appointment of an early day for the contemplated solemnity, had it not been retarded by a sudden invasion of the Philistines, who were twice repulsed with great loss (2Sa 5:17), by the capture of Jerusalem, and the transference of the seat of government to that city. Finding, however, soon after, peace restored and his throne established, he resumed his preparations for removing the ark to the metropolis.

5. from Shihor of Egypt – (Jos 15:4,47 Nu 34:5 1Ki 8:65 2Ki 24:7 2Ch 7:8); a small brook flowing into the Mediterranean, near the modern El-arish, which forms the southern boundary of Palestine.

unto the entering of Hemath – the defile between the mountain ranges of Syria and the extreme limit of Palestine on the north.

6–14. David went up, and all Israel, to Baalah – (See on 2Sa 6:1–11). **whose name is called on it** – rather, 'who is worshipped there' (2Sa 6:2).

Chapter 14

1Ch 14:1, 2. Hiram's kindness to David; David's felicity.

1. Now Hiram king of Tyre – [See on 2Sa 5:11]. The alliance with this neighbouring king, and the important advantages derived from it, were among the most fortunate circumstances in David's reign. The providence of God appeared concurrent with His promise in smoothing the early course of his reign. Having conquered the Jebusites and made Zion the royal residence, he had now, along with internal prosperity, established an advantageous treaty with a neighbouring prince; and hence, in immediate connection with the mention of this friendly league, it is said, 'David perceived that the Lord had confirmed him king over Israel.'

2. his kingdom was lifted up on high, because of his people Israel – This is an important truth, that sovereigns are invested with royal honour and authority, not for their own sakes so much as for that of their people. But while it is true of all kings, it was especially applicable to the monarchs of Israel, and even David was made to know that all his glory and greatness were given only to fit him, as the minister of God, to execute the divine purposes towards the chosen people.

1Ch 14:3–7. His wives.

3. David took more wives at Jerusalem – (See on 2Sa 3:5). His concubines are mentioned (1Ch 3:9), where also is given a list of his children (1Ch 14:5–8), and those born in Jerusalem (2Sa 5:14–16). In that, however, the names of Eliphalet and Nogah do not occur, and Beeliada appears to be the same as Eliada.

1Ch 14:8–17. His victories over the Philistines.

8. all the Philistines went up to seek David – in the hope of accomplishing his ruin (for so the phrase is used, 1Sa 23:15 24:2,3) before his throne was consolidated. Their hostility arose, both from a belief that his patriotism would lead him, erelong, to wipe out the national dishonour at Gilboa, and by fear, that in any invasion of their country, his thorough knowledge of their weak points would give him superior advantages. They resolved, therefore, to surprise and crush him before he was fairly seated on his throne.

11. they came up to Baal-perazim; and David smote them there – In an engagement fought at Mount Perazim (Isa 28:21), in the valley of Rephaim, a few miles west of Jerusalem, the Philistines were defeated and put to flight.

12. when they had left their gods – (See on 2Sa 5:21).

13. the Philistines yet again spread themselves – They renewed the campaign the next season, taking the same route. David, according to divine directions, did not confront them.

14. Go not up after them – The text in 2Sa 5:23, more correctly has, 'Go not up.'

turn away from them – that is, by stealing round a baca-grove, come upon their rear.

15. for God is gone forth before thee – that is, the rustling of the leaves by a strong breeze suddenly rising, was the sign by which David was divinely apprised of the precise moment for the attack. The impetuosity of his onset was like the gush of a pent-up torrent, which sweeps away all in its course; and in allusion to this incident the place got its name.

16. from Gibeon … to Gazer – Geba or Gibea (2Sa 5:25), now Yefa, in the province of Judah. The line from this to Gazer was intersected by the roads which led from Judah to the cities of the Philistines. To recover possession of it, therefore, as was effected by this decisive battle, was equivalent to setting free the whole mountain region of Judah as far as their most westerly slope [BERTHEAU].

Chapter 15

1Ch 15:1–29. David brings the ark from Obed-edom.

1. David made him houses in the city of David – Through the liberality of his Tyrian ally (1Ch 14:1), David was enabled to erect not only a palace for himself, but to furnish suitable accommodation for his numerous family. Where polygamy prevails, each wife has a separate house or suite of apartments for herself and children.

prepared a place for the ark of God, and pitched for it a tent – that is, made an entirely new one upon the model of the former. The old tabernacle, which Moses had constructed in the wilderness and which had hitherto served the purpose of a sacred covering, was to be left at Gibeon, either because of the unwillingness of the inhabitants to part with such a venerable relic, or because there was no use for it in Jerusalem, where a more solid and sumptuous edifice was contemplated. If it appear surprising that David 'made him houses' before he prepared this new tabernacle, it should be remembered that he had received no divine intimation respecting such a work.

2. Then David said, None ought to carry the ark of God but the Levites – After the lapse of three months (1Ch 13:14) the purpose of transporting the ark to Jerusalem was resumed. Time and reflection had led to a discovery of the cause of the painful catastrophe that marred the first attempt. In preparing for the solemn procession that was now to usher the sacred symbol into its resting-place, David took special care that the carriage should be regulated in strict conformity to the law (Nu 4:5,15 7:9 10:17).

3. David gathered all Israel together – Some are of opinion that this was done on one of the three great festivals, but at whatever time the ceremonial took place, it was of great importance to summon a general convocation of the people, many of whom, from the long-continued disorders of the kingdom, might have had little or no opportunity of knowing anything of the ark, which had been allowed to remain so long in obscurity and neglect.

4. David assembled the children of Aaron, and the Levites – The children of Aaron were the two priests (1Ch 15:11), Zadok and Abiathar, heads of the two priestly houses of Eleazar and Ithamar, and colleagues in the high priesthood (2Sa 20:25). The Levites were the chiefs of their father's house (1Ch 15:12); four belonging to the Kohathite branch, on whose shoulders the ark was to be borne; namely, Uriel, Shemaiah – descended from Elizaphan or Elzaphan – (Ex 6:22), Hebron (Ex 6:18 1Ch

6:2), and Amminadab from Uzziel (Ex 6:22).

12. sanctify yourselves – This special sanctification, which was required on all grave and important occasions, consisted in observing the strictest abstinence, as well as cleanliness, both in person and dress; and in the neglect of these rules no step could have been taken (2Ch 30:3).

16–24. David spake to the chief of the Levites to appoint … the singers with instruments – These eminent Levites were instructed to train the musicians and singers who were under them, for the solemn procession. The performers were ranged in three choirs or bands, and the names of the principal leaders are given (1Ch 15:17,18,21), with the instruments respectively used by each. 'Ben' (1Ch 15:18) is omitted. Either it was used merely as a common noun, to intimate that Zechariah was the son of Jaaziel or Aziel, or Ben is the same as Azaziah.

22. Chenaniah, chief of the Levites – He was not of the six heads of the Levitical families, but a chief in consequence of his office, which required learning, without regard to birth or family.

instructed about the song – He directed all these bands as to the proper time when each was to strike in or change their notes; or, as some render the passage, 'He led the burdens, for he was skilled,' that is, in the custom which it was necessary to observe in the carriage of the holy things [BERTHEAU].

23. Berechiah and Elkanah were doorkeepers – who marched immediately in front, while Obed-edom and Jeiel went in the rear, of the ark.

25. So David, and the elders … and captains … went – The pious design of David in ordering all his principal ministers and officers to take part in this solemn work and imparting so much pomp and imposing ceremony to the procession, was evidently to inspire the popular mind with a profound veneration for the ark and to give the young especially salutary impressions of religion, which would be renewed by the remembrance that they had been witnesses of the August solemnity in which the king and the highest aristocracy of the land participated, vying with all other classes to do honour to the God of Israel.

26. it came to pass – (See on 2Sa 6:13–23). **they offered seven bullocks and seven rams** – The Levites seem to have entered on this duty with fear and trembling; and finding that they might advance without any such indications of divine wrath as Uzza had experienced (1Ch 13:10), they offered an ox and a fatted sheep immediately after starting (2Sa 6:13), and seven bullocks and seven rams – a perfect sacrifice, at the close of the procession (1Ch 16:1). It is probable that preparations had been made for the offering of similar sacrifices at regular intervals along the way.

27. an ephod – a shoulder-garment, a cincture or cape over his dress. It was worn by the priests, but was not so peculiar to them as to be forbidden others (1Sa 2:18 22:18).

29. Michal … saw … David dancing and playing – His movements would be slow and solemn, suitable to the grave and solemn character of the music. Though his royal robes were laid aside, he was attired like the other officials, showing a becoming humility in the immediate presence of God. The feelings manifested by Michal were only an ebullition of spleen from a proud and passionate woman.

Chapter 16

1Ch 16:1–6. David's festival sacrifice and liberality to the people.

2. he blessed the people in the name of the Lord – The king commended their zeal, supplicated the divine blessing upon them, and ordered the remains of the thank offerings which had been profusely sacrificed during the procession, to be distributed in certain proportions to every individual, that the ceremonial might terminate with appropriate festivities (De 12:7).

3. flagon of wine – The two latter words are a supplement by our translators, and the former is, in other versions, rendered not a 'flagon,' but a 'cake,' a confection, as the *Septuagint* renders it, made of flour and honey.

4–6. he appointed certain of the Levites to minister before the ark of the Lord – No sooner was the ark deposited in its tent than the Levites, who were to officiate in the choirs before it, entered upon their duties. A select number of the musicians were chosen for the service from the list (1Ch 15:19–21) of those who had taken a prominent part in the recent procession. The same arrangement was to be observed in their duties, now that the ark again was stationary; Asaph, with his associates, composing the first or principal company, played with cymbals; Zechariah and his colleagues, with whom were conjoined Jeiel and Obed-edom, forming the second company, used harps and similar instruments.

5. Jeiel – the same as Aziel (1Ch 15:20).

6. Benaiah also and Jahaziel – The name of the former is mentioned among the priests (1Ch 15:24), but not the latter. The office assigned to them was that of blowing trumpets at regular intervals before the ark and in the tabernacle.

1Ch 16:7–43. His psalm of thanksgiving.

7. Then on that day David delivered first this psalm – Among the other preparations for this solemn inauguration, the royal bard had composed a special hymn for the occasion. Doubtless it had been previously in the hands of Asaph and his assistants, but it was now publicly committed to them as they entered for the first time on the performance of their sacred duties. It occupies the greater part of this chapter (1Ch 16:8–36), and seems to have been compiled from other psalms of David, previously known to the Israelites, as the whole of it will be found, with very slight variations, in Ps 96:1–13 105:1–15 106:47,48. In the form, however, in which it is given by the sacred historian, it seems to have been the first psalm given for use in the tabernacle service. Abounding, as it does, with the liveliest ascriptions of praise to God for the revelation of His glorious character and the display of His marvellous works and containing, as it does, so many pointed allusions to the origin, privileges, and peculiar destiny of the chosen people, it was admirably calculated to animate the devotions and call forth the gratitude of the assembled multitude.

36. all the people said, Amen – (Compare Ps 72:19,20 106:48). In the former, the author of the doxology utters the 'amen' himself, while in the latter the people are exhorted to say 'amen.' This may arise from the fact that the latter psalm originally concluded with the injunction to say 'amen.' But in this historical account of the festival, it was necessary to relate that the people obeyed this injunction on the occasion referred to, and therefore the words 'let them praise,' were altered into 'and they praised' [BERTHEAU].

37–42. So he left there before the ark of the covenant of the Lord Asaph and his brethren – The sequel of the chapter describes the appointment of the sacred musicians and their respective duties.

38. Obed-edom with their brethren – Hosah, mentioned at the close of the verse, and a great number besides (see on 1Ch 26:1).

to be porters – doorkeepers.

39, 40. And Zadok ... before the tabernacle ... at Gibeon – While the above-mentioned officers under the superintendence of Abiathar, were appointed to officiate in Jerusalem, whither the ark had been brought, Zadok and the priests subordinate to him were stationed at Gibeon to perform the sacred service before the ancient tabernacle which still remained there.

40. continually morning and evening – as the law enjoined (Ex 29:38 Nu 28:3,6).

and do according to all that is written in the law – (See Nu 28:1–31). Thus, in the time of David, the worship was performed at two places, where the sacred things that had been transmitted from the age of Moses were preserved. Before the Ark in Jerusalem, Asaph and

his brethren officiated as singers, Obed-edom and Hosah served as doorkeepers, and Benaiah and Jahaziel blew the trumpets. While at the tabernacle and burnt offering in Gibeon, Heman and Jeduthun presided over the sacred music, the sons of Jeduthun were door keepers, and Zadok, with his suite of attendant priests, offered the sacrifices.

Chapter 17

1Ch 17:1–16. David forbidden to build God a house.

1. as David sat in his house – The details of this chapter were given in nearly similar terms (2Sa 7:1–29). The date was towards the latter end of David's reign, for it is expressly said in the former book to have been at the cessation of all his wars. But as to narrate the preparations for the removal of the ark and the erection of the temple was the principal object of the historian, the exact chronology is not followed.

5. I ... have gone from tent to tent, and from one tabernacle to another – The literal rendering is, 'I was walking in a tent and in a dwelling.' The evident intention (as we may see from 1Ch 17:6) was to lay stress upon the fact that God was a *Mithhatlek* (a travelling God) and went from one place to another with His *tent* and His entire *dwelling* (the dwelling included not merely the tent, but the fore-courts with the altar of burnt offerings) [BERTHEAU].

6. spake I a word to any of the judges – In 2Sa 7:7 it is 'any of the tribes' of Israel. Both are included. But the judges 'who were commanded to feed the people,' form the more suitable antithesis to David.

Why have ye not built me an house of cedars? – that is, a solid and magnificent temple.

7. Thus saith the Lord of hosts, I took thee from the sheepcote – a round tower of rude construction, high walled, but open at the top, in which sheep are often enclosed at night to protect them from wild beasts. The meaning is, I elevated you to the throne from a humble condition solely by an act of divine grace, and not from any antecedent merits of your own (see on 1Sa 16:11), and I enabled you to acquire renown, equal or superior to any other monarch. Your reign will ever be afterwards regarded as the best and brightest era in the history of Israel, for it will secure to the nation a settled inheritance of prosperity and peace, without any of the oppressions or disorders that afflicted them in early times.

9, 10. at the beginning, and since the time that I commanded judges – that is, including the whole period from Joshua to Saul.

I tell thee that the Lord will build thee an

house – This was the language of Nathan himself, who was specially directed to assure David, not only of personal blessing and prosperity, but of a continuous line of royal descendants.

13. I will not take my mercy away from him, as I took it from him that was before thee – My procedure in dealing with him will be different from My disposal of Saul. Should his misconduct call for personal chastisement, I shall spare his family. If I see it necessary to withdraw My favour and help for a time, it will be a corrective discipline only to reform and restore, not to destroy.

14. I will settle him in my house – over My people Israel.

and in my kingdom for ever – God here asserts His right of supreme sovereignty in Israel. David and Solomon, with their successors, were only the vicegerents whom He nominated, or, in His providence, permitted.

his throne shall be established for evermore – The posterity of David inherited the throne in a long succession – but not always. In such a connection as this, the phrase 'for evermore' is employed in a restricted sense. We naturally expect the prophet to revert to David before concluding, after having spoken (1Ch 17:12) of the building of Solomon's temple. The promise that his house should be blessed was intended as a compensation for the disappointment of his wish to build the temple, and hence this assurance is appropriately repeated at the conclusion of the prophet's address [BERTHEAU].

15. According to all … this vision – The revelation of the divine will was made to the prophet in a dream.

16. David the king … sat before the Lord, and said – (See on 2Sa 7:18).

Chapter 18

1Ch 18:1, 2. David subdues the Philistines and Moabites.

1. David … took Gath and her towns – The full extent of David's conquests in the Philistine territory is here distinctly stated, whereas in the parallel passage (2Sa 8:1) it was only described in a general way. Gath was the 'Metheg-ammah,' or 'arm-bridle,' as it is there called – either from its supremacy as the capital over the other Philistine towns, or, because, in the capture of that important place and its dependencies, he obtained the complete control of his restless neighbours.

2. he smote Moab – The terrible severities by which David's conquest of that people was marked, and the probable reason of their being subjected to such a dreadful retribution, are narrated (2Sa 8:2).

the Moabites … brought gifts – that is, became tributary to Israel.

1Ch 18:3–17. David smites Hadadezer and the Syrians.

3. Hadarezer – or, 'Hadadezer' (2Sa 8:3), which was probably the original form of the name, was derived from Hadad, a Syrian deity. It seems to have become the official and hereditary title of the rulers of that kingdom.

Zobah – Its situation is determined by the words 'unto' or 'towards Hamath,' a little to the northeast of Damascus, and is supposed by some to be the same place as in earlier times was called Hobah (Ge 14:15). Previous to the rise of Damascus, Zobah was the capital of the kingdom which held supremacy among the petty states of Syria.

as he went to stablish his dominion by the river Euphrates – Some refer this to David, who was seeking to extend his possessions in one direction towards a point bordering on the Euphrates, in accordance with the promise (Ge 15:18 Nu 24:17). But others are of opinion that, as David's name is mentioned (1Ch 18:4), this reference is most applicable to Hadadezer.

4–8. And David took from him a thousand chariots – (See on 2Sa 8:3-14). In 2Sa 8:4 David is said to have taken seven hundred horsemen, whereas here it is said that he took seven thousand. This great discrepancy in the text of the two narratives seems to have originated with a transcriber in confounding the two Hebrew letters which indicate the numbers, and in neglecting to mark or obscure the points over one of them. We have no means of ascertaining whether seven hundred or seven thousand be the more correct. Probably the former should be adopted [DAVIDSON'S HERMENUTICS].

but reserved of them an hundred chariots – probably to grace a triumphal procession on his return to Jerusalem, and after using them in that way, destroy them like the rest.

8. from Tibhath and from Chun – These places are called Betah and Berothai (2Sa 8:8). Perhaps the one might be the Jewish, the other the Syrian, name of these towns. Neither their situation nor the connection between them is known. The Arabic version makes them to be Emesa (now Hems) and Baal-bek, both of which agree very well with the relative position of Zobah.

9–13. Tou – or Toi – whose dominions border on those of Hadadezer. (See on 2Sa 8:9-12; 1Ki 11:15).

17. the Cherethites and the Pelethites – who formed the royal bodyguard. The Cherethites were, most probably, those brave men who all along accompanied David while among the Philistines, and from that people derived their name (1Sa 30:14 Eze 25:16 Zep 2:5) as well as their skill in archery – while the Pelethites were those who joined him at Ziklag, took their name from Pelet, the chief man in the company (1Ch

12:3), and, being Benjamites, were expert in the use of the sling.

Chapter 19

1Ch 19:1–5. David's messengers, sent to comfort Hanun, are disgracefully treated.

1. after this – This phrase seems to indicate that the incident now to be related took place immediately, or soon after the wars described in the preceding chapter. But the chronological order is loosely observed, and the only just inference that can be drawn from the use of this phrase is, that some farther account is to be given of the wars against the Syrians.

Nahash the king of the children of Ammon died – There had subsisted a very friendly relation between David and him, begun during the exile of the former, and cemented, doubtless, by their common hostility to Saul.

3. are not his servants come unto thee for to search? – that is, thy capital, Rabbah (2Sa 10:3).

4, 5. shaved them – not completely, but only the half of their face. This disrespect to the beard, and indecent exposure of their persons by their clothes being cut off from the girdle downwards, was the grossest indignity to which Jews, in common with all Orientals, could be subjected. No wonder that the men were ashamed to appear in public – that the king recommended them to remain in seclusion on the border till the mark of their disgrace had disappeared – and then they might, with propriety, return to the court.

1Ch 19:6–15. Joab and Abishai overcome the Ammonites.

6. when the children of Ammon saw that they had made themselves odious to David – One universal feeling of indignation was roused throughout Israel, and all classes supported the king in his determination to avenge this unprovoked insult on the Hebrew nation.

Hanun … sent a thousand talents of silver – to procure the services of foreign mercenaries.

chariots and horsemen out of Mesopotamia … Syria-maachah, and … Zobah – The Mesopotamian troops did not arrive during this campaign (1Ch 19:16). Syria-maachah lay on the north of the possessions of the transjordanic Israelites, near Gilead.

Zobah – (see on 1Ch 18:3).

7. So they hired thirty and two thousand chariots – *Hebrew*, 'riders,' or 'cavalry,' accustomed to fight either on horseback or in chariots, and occasionally on foot. Accepting this as the true rendering, the number of hired auxiliaries mentioned in this passage agrees exactly with the statement in 2Sa 10:6: twenty thousand (from Syria), twelve thousand (from Tob), equal

to thirty-two thousand, and one thousand with the king of Maachah.

8. David … sent Joab, and all the host of the mighty men – All the forces of Israel, including the great military orders, were engaged in this war.

9–15. children of Ammon … put the battle in array before the gate of the city – that is, outside the walls of Medeba, a frontier town on the Arnon.

the kings that were come were by themselves in the field – The Israelitish army being thus beset by the Ammonites in front, and by the Syrian auxiliaries behind, Joab resolved to attack the latter (the more numerous and formidable host), while he directed his brother Abishai, with a suitable detachment, to attack the Ammonites. Joab's address before the engagement displays the faith and piety that became a commander of the Hebrew people. The mercenaries being defeated, the courage of the Ammonites failed; so that, taking flight, they entrenched themselves within the fortified walls.

1Ch 19:16–19. Shophach slain by David.

16. And when the Syrians saw that they were put to the worse before Israel – (See on 2Sa 10:15–19).

18. David slew of the Syrians seven thousand men – (Compare 2Sa 10:18, which has seven hundred chariots. Either the text in one of the books is corrupt [KEIL, DAVIDSON], or the accounts must be combined, giving this result – seven thousand horsemen, seven thousand chariots, and forty thousand footmen [KENNICOTT, HOUBIGANT, CALMET].

Chapter 20

1Ch 20:1–3. Rabbah besieged by Joab, spoiled by David, and the people tortured.

1. at the time when kings go out to battle – in spring, the usual season in ancient times for entering on a *campaign;* that is, a year subsequent to the Syrian war.

Joab led forth the power of the army, and wasted the country … of Ammon – The former campaign had been disastrous, owing chiefly to the hired auxiliaries of the Ammonites; and as it was necessary, as well as just, that they should be severely chastised for their wanton outrage on the Hebrew ambassadors, Joab ravaged their country and invested their capital, Rabbah. After a protracted siege, Joab took one part of it, the lower town or 'city of waters,' insulated by the winding course of the Jabbok. Knowing that the fort called 'the royal city' would soon fall, he invited the king to come in person, and have the honour of storming it. The knowledge of this fact (mentioned in 2Sa 12:26) enables us to reconcile the two statements – 'David tarried at Jerusalem' (1Ch 20:1), and 'David and all the people returned to Jerusalem' (1Ch 20:3).

2. David took the crown of their king ... a talent of gold – equal to one hundred twenty-five pounds. Some think that *Malcom,* rendered in our version 'their king,' should be taken as a proper name, Milcom or Molech, the Ammonite idol, which, of course, might bear a heavy weight. But, like many other state crowns of Eastern kings, the crown got at Rabbah was not worn on the head, but suspended by chains of gold above the throne.

precious stones – *Hebrew,* a 'stone,' or cluster of precious stones, which was set on David's head.

3. cut them with saws – The *Hebrew* word, 'cut them,' is, with the difference of the final letter, the same as that rendered 'put them,' in the parallel passage of Samuel [2Sa 12:31]; and many consider that putting them to saws, axes, and so forth, means nothing more than that David condemned the inhabitants of Rabbah to hard and penal servitude.

1Ch 20:4–8. Three overthrows of the Philistines and three giants slain.

4. war at Gezer – or Gob (see 2Sa 21:18–22).

Chapter 21

1Ch 21:1–17. David sins in numbering the people.

1. Satan stood up against Israel – God, by withdrawing His grace at this time from David (see on 2Sa 24:1), permitted the tempter to prevail over him. As the result of this successful temptation was the entail of a heavy calamity as a punishment from God upon the people, it might be said that 'Satan stood up against Israel.'

number Israel – In the act of taking the census of a people, there is not only no evil, but much utility. But numbering Israel – that people who were to become as the stars for multitude, implying a distrust of the divine promise, was a sin; and though it had been done with impunity in the time of Moses, at that enumeration each of the people had contributed 'half a shekel towards the building of the tabernacle,' that there might be no plague among them when he numbered them (Ex 30:12). Hence the numbering of that people was in itself regarded as an undertaking by which the anger of God could be easily aroused; but when the arrangements were made by Moses for the taking of the census, God was not angry because the people were numbered for the express purpose of the tax for

the sanctuary, and the money which was thus collected ('the atonement money,' Ex 30:16) appeased Him. Everything depended, therefore, upon the design of the census [BERTHEAU]. The sin of David numbering the people consisted in its being either to gratify his pride to ascertain the number of warriors he could muster for some meditated plan of conquest; or, perhaps, more likely still, to institute a regular and permanent system of taxation, which he deemed necessary to provide an adequate establishment for the monarchy, but which was regarded as a tyrannical and oppressive exaction – an innovation on the liberty of the people – a departure from ancient usage unbecoming a king of Israel.

3. why will he be a cause of trespass to Israel? – or bring an occasion of punishment on Israel. In *Hebrew,* the word 'sin' is often used synonymously with the punishment of sin. In the course of Providence, the people frequently suffer for the misconduct of their rulers.

5. Joab gave the sum of the number of the children of Israel – It amounted to one million one hundred thousand men in Israel, capable of bearing arms, inclusive of the three hundred thousand military (1Ch 27:1–9), which, being already enlisted in the royal service, were not reckoned (2Sa 24:9), and to four hundred seventy thousand men in Judah, omitting thirty thousand which formed an army of observation stationed on the Philistine frontier (2Sa 6:1). So large a population at this early period, considering the limited extent of the country and comparing it with the earlier census (Nu 26:1-65), is a striking proof of the fulfilment of the promise (Ge 15:5).

6. Levi and Benjamin counted he not – If this census was ordered with a view to the imposition of taxes, this alone would account for Levi, who were not warriors (1Ch 21:5), not being numbered. The population of Benjamin had been taken (see on 1Ch 7:6–11), and the register preserved in the archives of that tribe. This, however, was taken on another occasion, and by other agency than that of Joab. The non-numbering of these two tribes might have originated in the special and gracious providence of God, partly because Levi was devoted to His service, and Benjamin had become the least of all the tribes (Jud 21:1–25); and partly because God foresaw that they would remain faithful to the house of David in the division of the tribes, and therefore He would not have them diminished [POOLE]. From the course followed in this survey (see on 2Sa 24:4–8), it would appear that Judah and Benjamin were the last tribes that were to be visited; and that, after the census in Judah had been finished, Joab, before entering on that of Benjamin, had to return to Jerusalem, where the king, now sensible of his great error, gave orders to stop all further proceedings in the business. Not only the remonstrance of Joab at the first, but his slow progress in the survey (2Sa 24:8) showed the strong repugnance and even horror of the old general at this unconstitutional measure.

9. the Lord spake unto Gad, David's seer – Although David was himself endowed with a prophetic gift, yet, in matters relating to himself or his kingdom, he was in the habit of consulting the Lord through the medium of the priests; and when he failed to do so, a prophet was sent on extraordinary occasions to admonish or chastise him. Gad, a private friend, was occasionally employed as the bearer of these prophetic messages.

11, 12. Choose thee – To the *three* evils these correspond in beautiful agreement: *three* years, *three* months, *three* days [BERTHEAU]. (See on 2Sa 24:13).

13. let me fall now into the hand of the Lord ... let me not fall into the hand of man – Experience had taught him that human passion and vengeance had no bounds, whereas our wise and gracious Father in heaven knows the kind, and regulates the extent, of chastisement which every one needs.

14, 15. So the Lord ... sent an angel unto Jerusalem to destroy it – The infliction only of the pestilence is here noticed, without any account of its duration or its ravages, while a minute description is given of the visible appearance and menacing attitude of the destroying angel.

15. stood by the threshing-floor of Ornan the Jebusite – Ornan was probably his Hebrew or Jewish, Araunah his Jebusite or Canaanitish, name. Whether he was the old king of Jebus, as that title is given to him (2Sa 24:23), or not, he had been converted to the worship of the true God, and was possessed both of property and influence.

16. David and the elders ... clothed in sackcloth, fell upon their faces – They appeared in the garb and assumed the attitude of humble penitents, confessing their sins, and deprecating the wrath of God.

1Ch 21:18–30. He builds an altar.

18. the angel of the Lord commanded Gad to say – The order about the erection of an altar, as well as the indication of its site, is described (2Sa 24:18) as brought directly by Gad. Here we are informed of the quarter whence the prophet got his commission. It is only in the later stages of Israel's history that we find angels employed in communicating the divine will to the prophets.

20, 21. Ornan was threshing wheat – If the census was entered upon in autumn, the beginning of the civil year, the nine and a half months

it occupied would end at wheat harvest. The common way of threshing corn is by spreading it out on a high level area, and driving backwards and forwards upon it two oxen harnessed to a clumsy sledge with three rollers and some sharp spikes. The driver sits on his knees on the box, while another person is employed in drawing back the straw and separating it from the grain underneath. By this operation the chaff is very much chopped, and the grain threshed out.

23. I give thee ... the threshing instruments for wood – that is, to burn the sacrifice of the oxen. Very little real import – the *haste* and the *value* of the present offered – can be understood in this country. The offering was made for *instant* use. Ornan, hereby hoping to terminate the pestilence without a moment's delay, 'gave all,' oxen, the large threshing machine, and the wheat.

25. David gave ... for the place six hundred shekels of gold – At first he bought only the cattle and the threshing instruments, for which he paid fifty shekels of silver (2Sa 24:24); afterwards he purchased the whole property, Mount Moriah, on which the future temple stood. High in the centre of the mountain platform rises a remarkable rock, now covered by the dome of 'the Sakrah.' It is irregular in its form, and measures about sixty feet in one direction and fifty feet in the other. It is the natural surface of Mount Moriah and is thought by many to be the rock of the threshing-floor of Araunah, selected by David, and continued by Solomon and Zerubbabel as 'the unhewn stone' on which to build the altar [BARTLETT, *Walks about Jerusalem*; STANLEY].

26. David built there an altar – He went in procession with his leading men from the royal palace, down Mount Zion, and through the intervening city. Although he had plenty of space on his own property, he was commanded, under peremptory *direction*, to go a considerable distance from his home, up Mount Moriah, to erect an altar on premises which he had to buy. It was on or close to the spot where Abraham had offered up Isaac.

answered him by fire from heaven – (See Le 9:24 1Ki 18:21–23 2Ki 1:12 2Ch 7:1).

28. when David saw that the Lord had answered him ... he sacrificed there – or, 'he continued to sacrifice there.' Perceiving his sacrifice was acceptable, he proceeded to make additional offerings there, and seek favour by prayer and expiatory rites; for the dread of the menacing angel destroying Jerusalem while he was absent in the centre of worship at Gibeon, especially reverence for the Divine Being, led him to continue his adorations in that place which God (2Ch 3:1) had hallowed by the tokens of His presence and gracious acceptance.

Chapter 22

1Ch 22:1–5. David prepares for building the temple.

1. David said, This is the home of the Lord God – By the miraculous sign of fire from heaven, and perhaps other intimations, David understood it to be the will of God that the national place of worship should be fixed there, and he forthwith proceeded to make preparations for the erection of the temple on that spot.

2. David commanded to gather together the strangers – partly the descendants of the old Canaanites (2Ch 8:7–10), from whom was exacted a tribute of bond service, and partly war captives (2Ch 2:7), reserved for the great work he contemplated.

1Ch 22:6–19. He instructs Solomon.

6. Then he called for Solomon … and charged him – The earnestness and solemnity of this address creates an impression that it was given a little before the old king's decease. He unfolded his great and long cherished plan, enjoined the building of God's house as a sacred duty on him as his son and successor, and described the resources that were at command for carrying on the work. The vast amount of personal property he had accumulated in the precious metals [1Ch 22:14] must have been spoil taken from the people he had conquered, and the cities he had sacked.

Chapter 23

Ch 23:1. David makes Solomon king.

1. when David was old … he made Solomon … king – This brief statement, which comprises the substance of 1Ki 1:32-48, is made here solely to introduce an account of the preparations carried on by David during the latter years of his life for providing a national place of worship.

1Ch 23:2–6. Number and distribution of the Levites.

2. he gathered together all the princes of Israel – All important measures relating to the public interest were submitted for consideration to a general assembly of the representatives of the tribes (1Ch 13:1 15:25 22:17 26:1–32).

3. the Levites were numbered … thirty and eight thousand – Four times their number at the early census taken by Moses (see on Nu 4:1–49; 26:1–51). It was, in all likelihood, this vast increase that suggested and rendered expedient that classification, made in the Fast year of David's reign, which the present and three subsequent chapters describe.

by their polls, man by man – Women and children were not included.

4. twenty and four thousand were to set forward the work of the house of the Lord – They were not to preside over all the services of the temple. The Levites were subject to the priests, and they were superior to the Nethinim and other servants, who were not of the race of Levi. But they had certain departments of duty assigned, some of which are here specified.

5. praised the Lord with the instruments which I made – David seems to have been an inventor of many of the musical instruments used in the temple (Am 6:5).

6. David divided them into courses among the sons of Levi – These are enumerated according to their fathers' houses, but no more of these are mentioned here than the twenty-four thousand who were engaged in the work connected with the Lord's house. The fathers' houses of those Levites corresponded with the classes into which they [JOSEPHUS, *Antiquities*] as well as the priests were divided (see on 1Ch 24:20–31; 1Ch 26:20–28).

1Ch 23:7–11. Sons of Gershon.

7–11. the Gershonites – They had nine fathers' houses, six descended from Laadan, and three from Shimei.

1Ch 23:12–20. Of Kohath.

12. The sons of Kohath – He was the founder of nine Levitical fathers' houses.

13. Aaron was separated – as high priest (see on 1Ch 25:1–19).

14. concerning Moses – His sons were ranked with the Levites generally, but not introduced into the distinctive portion of the descendants of Levi, who were appointed to the special functions of the priesthood.

1Ch 23:21–23. Of Merari.

21–23. The sons of Merari – They comprised six fathers' houses. Summing them together, Gershon founded nine fathers houses, Kohath nine, and Merari six: total, twenty-four.

1Ch 23:24–32. Office of the Levites.

24–27. These were the sons of Levi … that did the work … from the age of twenty years and upward – The enumeration of the Levites was made by David (1Ch 23:3) on the same rule as that followed by Moses (Nu 4:3), namely, from thirty years. But he saw afterwards that this rule might be beneficially relaxed, and that the enrolment of Levites for their proper duties might be made from twenty years of age. The ark and tabernacle being now stationary at Jerusalem, the labour of the Levites was greatly diminished, as they were no longer obliged to transport its heavy furniture from place to place. The number of thirty-eight thousand Levites, exclusive of priests, was doubtless more than sufficient for the ordinary service of the tabernacle. But this pious king thought that it would contribute to the glory of the Lord to employ as many officers in his divine service as possible. These first rules, however, which David instituted, were temporary, as very different arrangements were made after the ark had been deposited in the tabernacle of Zion.

Chapter 24

1Ch 24:1–19. Division of the sons of Aaron into four and twenty orders.

1. Now these are the divisions of the sons of Aaron – (See on 1Ch 23:6).

2. Nadab and Abihu died before their father – that is, not in his presence, but during his lifetime (see Nu 3:4 26:61).

therefore Eleazar and Ithamar executed the priest's office – In consequence of the death of his two oldest sons without issue, the descendants of Aaron were comprised in the families of Eleazar and Ithamar. Both of these sons discharged the priestly functions as assistants to their father. Eleazar succeeded him, and in his line the high priesthood continued until it was transferred to the family of Ithamar, in the person of Eli.

3. Zadok … and Ahimelech of the sons of Ithamar – This statement, taken in connection with 1Ch 24:6, is not a little perplexing, since (2Sa 15:24,35 20:25) Abiathar is mentioned as the person conjoined in David's time with Zadok, in the collegiate exercise of the high priesthood. Some think that the words have been transposed, reading Abiathar, the son of Ahimelech. But there is no ground for regarding the text as faulty. The high priests of the line of Ithamar were the following: Ahiah or Ahimelech, his son Abiathar, his son Ahimelech. We frequently find the grandfather and grandson called by the same name (see list of high priests of the line of Eleazar, 1Ch 6:30–41). Hence the author of the Chronicles was acquainted with Ahimelech, son of Abiathar, who, for some reason, discharged the duties of high priest in David's reign, and during the lifetime of his father (for Abiathar was living in the time of Solomon, 1Ki 2:27) [KEIL].

4. there were more chief men found – The *Hebrew* may be translated, 'There were more men as to heads of the sons of Eleazar.' It is true, in point of fact, that by the census the number of individuals belonging to the family of Eleazar was found greater than in that of Ithamar. And this, of necessity, led to there being more fathers' houses, and consequently more chiefs or presidents in the former.

5. Thus were they divided by lot – This method of allocation was adopted manifestly to remove all cause of jealousy as to precedence and the right of performing particular duties.

6. one principal household – The marginal reading is preferable, 'one house of the father.' The lot was cast in a deliberate and solemn manner in presence of the king, the princes, the two high priests, and the chiefs of the priestly and Levitical families. The heads of families belonging to Eleazar and Ithamar were alternately brought forward to draw, and the name of each individual, as called, registered by an attendant secretary. To accommodate the casting of the lots to the inequality of the number, there being sixteen fathers' houses of Eleazar, and only eight of Ithamar, it was arranged that every house of Ithamar should be followed by two of Eleazar, or, what is the same thing, that every two houses of Eleazar should be followed by one of Ithamar. If, then, we suppose a commencement to have been made by Eleazar, the order would be as follows: one and two, Eleazar; three, Ithamar; four and five, Eleazar; six, Ithamar; seven and eight, Eleazar; nine, Ithamar; and so forth [BERTHEAU]. The lot determined also the order of the priests' service. That of the Levites was afterwards distributed by the same arrangement (1Ch 24:31).

Chapter 25

1Ch 25:1–7. Number and office of the singers.

1. David and the captains of the host – that is, the princes (1Ch 23:2 24:6). It is probable that the king was attended on the occasion of arranging the singers by the same parties that are mentioned as having assisted him in regulating the order of the priests and Levites.

2. according to the order of the king – *Hebrew*, 'by the hands of the king,' that is, 'according to the king's order,' under the personal superintendence of Asaph and his colleagues.

which prophesied – that is, in this connection, played with instruments. This metaphorical application of the term 'prophecy' most probably originated in the practice of the prophets, who endeavoured to rouse their prophetic spirit by the animating influence of music (see on 2Ki 3:15). It is said that Asaph did this 'according to David's order,' because by royal appointment he officiated in the tabernacle on Zion (1Ch 16:37-41), while other leaders of the sacred music were stationed at Gibeon.

5. Heman the king's seer – The title of 'seer' or 'prophet of David' is also given to Gad (1Ch 21:9), and to Jeduthun (2Ch 29:14,15), in the words (*Margin*, 'matters') of God.

to lift up the horn – that is, to blow loudly in the worship of God; or perhaps it means nothing more than that he presided over the wind instruments, as Jeduthun over the harp. Heman had been appointed at first to serve at Gibeon

(1Ch 16:41). But his destination seems to have been changed at a subsequent period.

God gave to Heman fourteen sons and three daughters – The daughters are mentioned, solely because from their musical taste and talents they formed part of the choir (Ps 68:25).

6, 7. All these were under the hands of their father – Asaph had four sons, Jeduthun six, and Heman fourteen, equal to twenty-four; making the musicians with their brethren the singers, an amount of two hundred eighty-eight. For, like the priests and Levites, they were divided into twenty-four courses of twelve men each, equal to two hundred eighty-eight, who served a week in rotation; and these, half of whom officiated every week with a proportionate number of assistants, were skilful and experienced musicians, capable of leading and instructing the general musical corps, which comprised no less than four thousand (1Ch 23:5).

1Ch 25:8–31. Their division by lot into four and twenty orders.

8. they cast lots, ward against ward – 'Ward' is an old English word for 'division' or 'company.' The lot was cast to determine the precedence of the classes or divisions over which the musical leaders presided; and, in order to secure an impartial arrangement of their order, the master and his assistants, the teacher and his scholars, in each class or company took part in this solemn casting of lots. In the first catalogue given in this chapter the courses are classed according to their employment as musicians. In the second, they are arranged in the order of their service.

Chapter 26

1Ch 26:1–12. Divisions of the porters.

1, 2. Concerning the divisions of the porters – There were four thousand (1Ch 23:6), all taken from the families of the Kohathites and Merarites (1Ch 26:14), divided into twenty-four courses – as the priests and musicians.

Meshelemiah the son of Kore, of the sons of Asaph – Seven sons of Meshelemiah are mentioned (1Ch 26:2), whereas eighteen are given (1Ch 26:9), but in this latter number his relatives are included.

5. God blessed him – that is, Obed-edom. The occasion of the blessing was his faithful custody of the ark (2Sa 6:11,12). The nature of the blessing (Ps 127:5) consisted in the great increase of progeny by which his house was distinguished; seventy-two descendants are reckoned.

6. mighty men of valour – The circumstance of physical strength is prominently noticed in this chapter, as the office of the porters required

them not only to act as sentinels of the sacred edifice and its precious furniture against attacks of plunderers or popular insurrection – to be, in fact, a military guard – but, after the temple was built, to open and shut the gates, which were extraordinarily large and ponderous.

10. Simri the chief … though … not the first-born – probably because the family entitled to the right of primogeniture had died out, or because there were none of the existing families which could claim that right.

12. Among these were the divisions of the porters, even among the chief men – These were charged with the duty of superintending the watches, being heads of the twenty-four courses of porters.

1Ch 26:13–19. The gates assigned by lot.

13. they cast lots – Their departments of duty, such as the gates they should attend to, were allotted in the same manner as those of the other Levitical bodies, and the names of the chiefs or captains are given, with the respective gates assigned them.

15. the house of Asuppim – or, 'collections,' probably a storehouse, where were kept the grain, wine, and other offerings for the sustenance of the priests.

16. the gate Shallecheth – probably the rubbish gate, through which all the accumulated filth and sweepings of the temple and its courts were poured out.

by the causeway of the going up – probably the ascending road which was cast up or raised from the deep valley between Mount Zion and Moriah, for the royal egress to the place of worship (2Ch 9:4). **ward against ward** – Some refer these words to Shuppim and Hosah, whose duty it was to watch both the western gate and the gate Shallecheth, which was opposite, while others take it as a general statement applicable to all the guards, and intended to intimate that they were posted at regular distances from each other, or that they all mounted and relieved guard at the same time in uniform order.

17–19. Eastward were six Levites – because the gate there was the most frequented. There were four at the north gate; four at the south, at the storehouse which was adjoining the south, and which had two entrance gates, one leading in a southwesterly direction to the city, and the other direct west, two porters each. At the Parbar towards the west, there were six men posted – four at the causeway or ascent (1Ch 26:16), and two at Parbar, amounting to twenty-four in all, who were kept daily on guard.

18. Parbar – is, perhaps, the same as Parvar ('suburbs,' 2Ki 23:11), and if so, this gate might be so called as leading to the suburbs [CALMET].

1Ch 26:20–28. Levites that had charge of the treasures.

20. of the Levites, Ahijah – The heading of this section is altogether strange as it stands, for it looks as if the sacred historian were going to commence a new subject different from the preceding. Besides, 'Ahijah, whose name occurs after' the Levites, is not mentioned in the previous lists. It is totally unknown and is introduced abruptly without further information; and lastly, Ahijah must have united in his own person those very offices of which the occupants are named in the verses that follow. The reading is incorrect. The *Septuagint* has this very suitable heading, 'And their Levitical brethren over the treasures.' [BERTHEAU]. The names of those who had charge of the treasure chambers at their respective wards are given, with a general description of the precious things committed to their trust. Those treasures were immense, consisting of the accumulated spoils of Israelitish victories, as well as of voluntary contributions made by David and the representatives of the people.

1Ch 26:29–32. Officers and judges.

29. officers and judges – The word rendered 'officers' is the term which signifies scribes or secretaries, so that the Levitical class here described were magistrates, who, attended by their clerks, exercised judicial functions; there were six thousand of them (1Ch 23:4), who probably acted like their brethren on the principle of rotation, and these were divided into three classes – one (1Ch 26:29) for the outward business over Israel; one (1Ch 26:30), consisting of seventeen hundred, for the west of Jordan 'in all business of the Lord, and in the service of the king'; and the third (1Ch 26:31,32), consisting of twenty-seven hundred, 'rulers for every matter pertaining to God, and affairs of the king.'

Chapter 27

1Ch 27:1–15. Twelve captains for every month.

1. came in and went out month by month – Here is an account of the standing military force of Israel. A militia formed, it would seem, at the beginning of David's reign (see 1Ch 27:7) was raised in the following order: Twelve legions, corresponding to the number of tribes, were enlisted in the king's service. Each legion comprised a body of twenty-four thousand men, whose term of service was a month in rotation, and who were stationed either at Jerusalem or in any other place where they might be required. There was thus always a force sufficient for the ordinary purposes of state, as well as for resisting sudden attacks or popular tumults; and when extraordinary emergencies demanded a larger force, the whole standing army could easily be called to arms, amounting to two hundred eighty-eight thousand, or to three hundred thousand, including the twelve thousand officers that naturally attended on the twelve princes (1Ch 27:16–24). Such a military establishment would be burdensome neither to the country nor to the royal treasury; for attendance on this duty being a mark of honour and distinction, the expense of maintenance would be borne probably by the militiaman himself, or furnished out of the common fund of his tribe. Nor would the brief period of actual service produce any derangement of the usual course of affairs; for, on the expiry of the term, every soldier returned to the pursuits and duties of private life during the other eleven months of the year. Whether the same individuals were always enrolled, cannot be determined. The probability is, that provided the requisite number was furnished, no stricter scrutiny would be made. A change of men might, to a certain degree, be encouraged, as it was a part of David's policy to train all his subjects to skill in arms; and to have made the enlistment fall always on the same individuals would have defeated that purpose. To have confined each month's levy rigidly within the limits of one tribe might have fallen hard upon those tribes which were weak and small. The rotation system being established, each division knew its own month, as well as the name of the commander under whom it was to serve. These commanders are styled, 'the chief fathers,' that is, the hereditary heads of tribes, who, like chieftains of clans, possessed great power and influence.

captains of thousands and hundreds – The legions of twenty-four thousand were divided into regiments of one thousand, and these again into companies of a hundred men, under the direction of their respective subalterns, there being, of course, twenty-four captains of thousands, and two hundred forty centurions.

and their officers – the Shoterim, who in the army performed the duty of the commissariat, keeping the muster-roll.

2, 3. Jashobeam the son of Zabdiel – (See on 1Ch 11:11 and 2Sa 23:8). Hachmoni was his father, Zabdiel probably one of his ancestors; or there might be different names of the same individual. In the rotation of the military courses, the dignity of precedence, not of authority, was given to the hero.

4. second month was Dodai – or, 'Dodo.' Here the text seems to require the supplement of 'Eleazar the son of Dodo' (2Sa 23:9).

7. Asahel – This officer having been slain at the very beginning of David's reign [2Sa 2:23], his name was probably given to this division in honour of his memory, and his son was invested with the command.

1Ch 27:16–34. Princes of the twelve tribes.

16. over the tribes of Israel: the ruler – This is a list of the hereditary chiefs or rulers of tribes at the time of David's numbering the people. Gad and Asher are not included; for what reason is unknown. The tribe of Levi had a prince (1Ch 27:17), as well as the other tribes; and although it was ecclesiastically subject to the high priest, yet in all civil matters it had a chief or head, possessed of the same authority and power as in the other tribes, only his jurisdiction did not extend to the priests.

18. Elihu – probably the same as Eliab (1Sa 16:6).

23. But David took not the number of them from twenty years old and under – The census which David ordered did not extend to all the Israelites; for to contemplate such an enumeration would have been to attempt an impossibility (Ge 28:14), and besides would have been a daring offense to God. The limitation to a certain age was what had probably quieted David's conscience as to the *lawfulness* of the measure, while its *expediency* was strongly pressed upon his mind by the army arrangements he had in view.

24. neither was the number put in the account of the chronicles of King David – either because the undertaking was not completed, Levi and Benjamin not having been numbered (1Ch 21:6), or the full details in the hands of the enumerating officers were not reported to David, and, consequently, not registered in the public archives.

the chronicles – were the daily records or annals of the king's reign. No notice was taken of this census in the historical register, as from the public calamity with which it was associated it would have stood as a painful record of the divine judgment against the king and the nation.

25. over the king's treasures – Those treasures consisted of gold, silver, precious stones, cedar-wood; those which he had *in* Jerusalem as distinguished from others *without* the city.

the storehouses in the fields – Grain covered over with layers of straw is frequently preserved in the fields under little earthen mounds, like our potato pits.

27. the vineyards – These seem to have been in the vine growing districts of Judah, and were committed to two men of that quarter.

wine-cellars – The wine is deposited in jars sunk in the court of the house.

28. olive trees and the sycamore trees … in the low plains – that is, the Shephela, the rich, low-lying ground between the Mediterranean and the mountains of Judah.

29. herds that fed in Sharon – a fertile plain between Cæsarea and Joppa.

30. camels – These were probably in the countries east of the Jordan, and hence an Ishmaelite and Nazarite were appointed to take charge of them.

31. rulers of the substance that was king David's – How and when the king acquired these demesnes and this variety of property – whether it was partly by conquests, or partly by confiscation, or by his own active cultivation of waste lands – is not said. It was probably in all these ways. The management of the king's private possessions was divided into twelve parts, like his public affairs and the revenue derived from all these sources mentioned must have been very large.

Chapter 28

1Ch 28:1–8. David exhorts the people to fear God.

1. David assembled all the princes of Israel – that is, the representatives of the people, the leading men of the kingdom, who are enumerated in this verse according to their respective rank or degree of authority.

princes of the tribes – (1Ch 27:16–22). Those patriarchal chiefs are mentioned first as being the highest in rank – a sort of hereditary noblesse.

the captains of the companies – the twelve generals mentioned (1Ch 27:1–15).

the stewards – (1Ch 27:25–31).

the officers – *Hebrew*, 'eunuchs,' or attendants on the court (1Sa 8:15 1Ki 22:9 2Ki 22:18); and besides Joab, the commander-in-chief of the army, the heroes who had no particular office (1Ch 11:10–12:40 2Sa 23:8–39). This assembly, a very mixed and general one, as appears from the parties invited, was more numerous and entirely different from that mentioned (1Ch 23:2).

2. Hear me, my brethren, and my people – This was the style of address becoming a constitutional king of Israel (De 17:20 1Sa 30:23 2Sa 5:1).

I had in mine heart – I proposed, or designed.

to build an house of rest – a solid and permanent temple.

for the footstool of our God – God seated between the cherubim, at the two extremities of the ark, might be said to be enthroned in His glory, and the coverlet of the ark to be His footstool.

and had made ready for the building – The immense treasures which David had amassed and the elaborate preparations he had made, would have been amply sufficient for the erection of the temple of which he presented the model to Solomon.

3. thou hast been a man of war, and hast shed blood – The church or spiritual state of the world, of which the temple at Jerusalem was to be a type, would be presided over by One who was to be pre-eminently the Prince of Peace, and therefore would be represented not so fitly by David, whose mission had been a preparatory one of battle and conquest, as by his son, who should reign in unbroken peace.

4, 5. he hath chosen Solomon – The spirit of David's statement is this: – It was not my ambition, my valour, or my merit that led to the enthronement of myself and family; it was the grace of God which chose the tribe, the family, the person – myself in the first instance, and now Solomon, to whom, as the Lord's anointed, you are all bound to submit. Like that of Christ, of whom he was a type, the appointment of Solomon to the kingdom above all his brethren was frequently pre-intimated (1Ch 17:12 22:9 2Sa 7:12–14 12:24,25 1Ki 1:13).

7. I will establish his kingdom for ever, if he be constant to do my commandments – The same condition is set before Solomon by God (1Ki 3:14 9:4).

8. Now ... in the sight of all Israel, ... keep and seek for all the commandments of the Lord – This solemn and earnest exhortation to those present, and to all Israel through their representatives, to continue faithful in observing the divine law as essential to their national prosperity and permanence, is similar to that of Moses (De 30:15–20).

1Ch 28:9–21. He encourages Solomon to build the temple.

9, 10. And thou, Solomon my son – The royal speaker now turns to Solomon, and in a most impressive manner presses upon him the importance of sincere and practical piety.

know thou – He did not mean head knowledge, for Solomon possessed that already, but that experimental acquaintance with God which is only to be obtained by loving and serving Him.

11. Then David gave to Solomon ... the pattern – He now put into the hands of his son and successor the plan or model of the temple, with the elevations, measurements, apartments, and chief articles of furniture, all of which were designed according to the pattern given him by divine revelation (1Ch 28:19).

12. the pattern of all that he had by the spirit – rather, 'with him in spirit'; that is, was floating in his mind.

15, 16. the candlesticks of silver – Solomon made them all of gold – in this and a few minor particulars departing from the letter of his father's instructions, where he had the means of executing them in a more splendid style. There

was only one candlestick and one table in the tabernacle, but ten in the temple.

18, 19. the chariot of the cherubim – The expanded wings of the cherubim formed what was figuratively styled the throne of God, and as they were emblematical of rapid motion, the throne or seat was spoken of as a chariot (Ps 18:10 99:1). It is quite clear that in all these directions David was not guided by his own taste, or by a desire for taking any existing model of architecture, but solely by a regard to the express revelation of the divine will. In a vision, or trance, the whole edifice, with its appurtenances, had been placed before his eyes so vividly and permanently, that he had been able to take a sketch of them in the models delivered to Solomon.

20. Be strong and of good courage – The address begun in 1Ch 28:9 is resumed and concluded in the same strain.

21. behold, the courses of the priests and Levites – They were, most probably, represented in this assembly though they are not named.

also the princes and all the people – that is, as well the skilful, expert, and zealous artisan, as the workman who needs to be directed in all his labours.

Chapter 29

1Ch 29:1–9. David causes the princes and people to offer for the house of God.

1, 2. Solomon ... is yet young and tender – Though Solomon was very young when he was raised to the sovereign power, his kingdom escaped the woe pronounced (Ec 10:16). Mere childhood in a prince is not always a misfortune to a nation, as there are instances of the government being wisely administered during a minority. Solomon himself is a most illustrious proof that a young prince may prove a great blessing; for when he was but a mere child, with respect to his age, no nation was happier. His father, however, made this address before Solomon was endowed with the divine gift of wisdom, and David's reference to his son's extreme youth, in connection with the great national undertaking he had been divinely appointed to execute, was to apologize to this assembly of the estates – or, rather, to assign the reason of his elaborate preparations for the work.

3, 4. Moreover ... I have of mine own proper good – In addition to the immense amount of gold and silver treasure which David had already bequeathed for various uses in the service of the temple, he now made an additional contribution destined to a specific purpose – that of overlaying the walls of the house. This voluntary gift was from the private fortune of the royal donor, and had been selected with the greatest care. The gold was 'the gold of Ophir,' then esteemed the purest and finest in the world (Job 22:24 28:16 Isa 13:12). The amount was three thousand talents of gold and seven thousand talents of refined silver.

5. who then is willing to consecrate his service – Hebrew, 'fill his hand'; that is, make an offering (Ex 32:29 Le 8:33 1Ki 13:33). The meaning is, that whoever would contribute voluntarily, as he had done, would be offering a freewill offering to the Lord. It was a sacrifice which every one of them could make, and in presenting which the offerer himself would be the priest. David, in asking freewill offerings for the temple, imitated the conduct of Moses in reference to the tabernacle (Ex 25:1–8).

6–8. Then the chief of the fathers – or heads of the fathers (1Ch 24:31 27:1).

princes of the tribes – (1Ch 27:16–22).

rulers of the king's work – those who had charge of the royal demesnes and other possessions (1Ch 27:25–31).

offered willingly – Influenced by the persuasive address and example of the king, they acted according to their several abilities, and their united contributions amounted to the gross sum.

7. drams – rather, 'darics,' a Persian coin, with which the Jews from the time of the captivity became familiar, and which was afterwards extensively circulated in the countries of Western Asia.

of brass eighteen thousand talents, and one hundred thousand talents of iron – In Scripture, iron is always referred to as an article of comparatively low value, and of greater abundance and cheaper than bronze [Napier].

8. and they with whom precious stones were found – rather, 'whatever was found along with it of precious stones they gave' [Bertheau]. These gifts were deposited in the hands of Jehiel, whose family was charged with the treasures of the house of the Lord (1Ch 26:21).

1Ch 29:10–25. His thanksgiving.

10–19. Wherefore David blessed the Lord – This beautiful thanksgiving prayer was the effusion overflowing with gratitude and delight at seeing the warm and widespread interest that was now taken in forwarding the favourite project of his life. Its piety is displayed in the fervour of devotional feeling – in the ascription of all worldly wealth and greatness to God as the giver, in tracing the general readiness in contributing to the influence of His grace, in praying for the continuance of this happy dis-

position among the people, and in solemnly and earnestly commending the young king and his kingdom to the care and blessing of God.

16. all this store that we have prepared – It may be useful to exhibit a tabular view of the treasure laid up and contributions stated by the historian as already made towards the erection of the proposed temple. Though it has been the common practice of Eastern monarchs to hoard vast sums for the accomplishment of any contemplated project, this amount so far exceeds not only every Oriental collection on record, but even the bounds of probability, that it is very generally allowed that either there is a corruption of the text in 1Ch 22:14, or that the reckoning of the historian was by the Babylonian, which was only a half, or the Syrian, which was only a fifth part, of the Hebrew talent. This would bring the Scripture account more into accordance with the statements of Josephus, as well as within the range of credibility.

20. all the congregation … worshipped the Lord, and the king – Though the external attitude might be the same, the sentiments of which it was expressive were very different in the two cases – of divine worship in the one, of civil homage in the other.

21, 22. they sacrificed … And did eat and drink – After the business of the assembly was over, the people, under the exciting influence of the occasion, still remained, and next day engaged in the performance of solemn rites, and afterwards feasted on the remainder of the sacrifices.

22. before the Lord – either in the immediate vicinity of the ark, or, perhaps, rather in a religious and devout spirit, as partaking of a sacrificial meal.

made Solomon … king the second time – in reference to the first time, which was done precipitately on Adonijah's conspiracy (1Ki 1:35).

they … anointed … Zadok – The statement implies that his appointment met the popular approval. His elevation as sole high priest was on the disgrace of Abiathar, one of Adonijah's accomplices.

23. Solomon sat on the throne of the Lord – As king of Israel, he was the Lord's vicegerent.

24. submitted themselves – Hebrew, 'put their hands under Solomon,' according to the custom still practised in the East of putting a hand under the king's extended hand and kissing the back of it (2Ki 10:15).

1Ch 29:26–30. His reign and death.

26. Thus David … reigned – (See 1Ki 2:11)

2 CHRONICLES

Robert Jamieson

Introduction

See 1 Chronicles Introduction

Chapter 1

2Ch 1:1–6. Solemn offering of Solomon at Gibeon.

2–5. Then Solomon spake unto all Israel – The heads, or leading officers, who are afterwards specified, were summoned to attend their sovereign in a solemn religious procession. The date of this occurrence was the second year of Solomon's reign, and the high place at Gibeon was chosen for the performance of the sacred rites, because the tabernacle and all the ancient furniture connected with the national worship were deposited there. Zadok was the officiating high priest (1Ch 16:39). It is true that the ark had been removed and placed in a new tent which David had made for it at Jerusalem (2Ch 1:4). But the brazen altar, 'before the tabernacle of the Lord,' on which the burnt offerings were appointed by the law to be made, was at Gibeon. And although David had been led by extraordinary events and tokens of the divine presence to sacrifice on the threshing-floor of Araunah, Solomon considered it his duty to present his offerings on the legally appointed spot 'before the tabernacle,' and on the time-honoured altar prepared by the skill of Bezaleel in the wilderness (Ex 38:1).

6. offered a thousand burnt offerings – This holocaust he offered, of course, by the hands of the priests. The magnitude of the oblation became the rank of the offerer on this occasion of national solemnity.

2Ch 1:7–13. His choice of wisdom is blessed by God.

7. In that night did God appear unto Solomon – (See on 1Ki 3:5).

2Ch 1:14–17. His strength and wealth.

14. Solomon gathered chariots and horsemen – His passion for horses was greater than that of any Israelitish monarch before or after him. His stud comprised fourteen hundred chariots and twelve thousand horses. This was a prohibited indulgence, whether as an instrument of luxury or power. But it was not merely for his own use that he imported the horses of Egypt. The immense equestrian establishment he erected was not for show merely, but also for profit. The Egyptian breed of horses was highly valued; and being as fine as the Arabian, but larger and more powerful, they were well fitted for being yoked in chariots. These were light but compact and solid vehicles, without springs. From the price stated [2Ch 1:17] as given for a chariot and a horse, it appears that the chariot cost four times the value of a horse. A horse brought a hundred fifty shekels, while a chariot brought six hundred shekels. As the Syrians, who were fond of the Egyptian breed of horses, could import them into their own country only through Judea, Solomon early perceived the commercial advantages to be derived from this trade, and established a monopoly. His factors or agents purchased them in the markets or fairs of Egypt and brought them to the 'chariot cities,' the depots and stables he had erected on the frontiers of his kingdom, such as Bethmarcaboth, 'the house of chariots,' and Hazarsusah, 'the village of horses' (Jos 19:5 1Ki 10:28).

17. brought … for all the kings of the Hittites – A branch of this powerful tribe, when expelled from Palestine, had settled north of Lebanon, where they acquired large possessions contiguous to the Syrians.

Chapter 2

2Ch 2:1, 2. Solomon's labourers for building the temple.

1. Solomon determined to build – The temple is the grand subject of this narrative, while the palace – here and in other parts of this book – is only incidentally noticed. The duty of building the temple was reserved for Solomon before his birth. As soon as he became king, he addressed himself to the work, and the historian, in proceeding to give an account of the edifice, begins with relating the preliminary arrangements.

2Ch 2:3–10. Message to Huram for skilful artificers.

3–6. Solomon sent to Huram – The correspondence was probably conducted on both sides in writing (2Ch 2:11; also see on 1Ki 5:8). **As thou didst deal with David my father** – This would seem decisive of the question whether the Huram then reigning in Tyre was David's friend (see on 1Ki 5:1–6). In opening the business, Solomon grounded his request for Tyrian aid on two reasons: 1. The temple he proposed to build must be a solid and permanent building because the worship was to be continued in perpetuity; and therefore the building materials must be of the most durable quality. 2. It must be a magnificent structure because it was to be dedicated to the God who was greater than all gods; and, therefore, as it might seem a presumptuous idea to erect an edifice for a Being 'whom the heaven and the heaven of heavens do not contain,' it was explained that Solomon's object was not to build a house for Him to dwell in, but a temple in which His worshippers might offer sacrifices to His honour. No language could be more humble and appropriate than this. The pious strain of sentiment was such as became a king of Israel.

7. Send me now therefore a man cunning to work – Masons and carpenters were not asked for. Those whom David had obtained (1Ch 14:1) were probably still remaining in Jerusalem, and had instructed others. But he required a master of works; a person capable, like Bezaleel (Ex 35:31), of superintending and directing every department; for, as the division of labour was at that time little known or

observed, an overseer had to be possessed of very versatile talents and experience. The things specified, in which he was to be skilled, relate not to the building, but the furniture of the temple. Iron, which could not be obtained in the wilderness when the tabernacle was built, was now, through intercourse with the coast, plentiful and much used. The cloths intended for curtains were, from the crimson or scarlet-red and hyacinth colours named, evidently those stuffs, for the manufacture and dyeing of which the Tyrians were so famous. 'The graving,' probably, included embroidery of figures like cherubim in needlework, as well as wood carving of pomegranates and other ornaments.

8. Send me … cedar trees – The cedar and cypress were valued as being both rare and durable; the algum or almug trees (likewise a foreign wood), though not found on Lebanon, are mentioned as being procured through Huram (see on 1Ki 10:11).

10. behold, I will give to thy servants … beaten wheat – Wheat, stripped of the husk, boiled, and saturated with butter, forms a frequent meal with the labouring people in the East (compare 1Ki 5:11). There is no discrepancy between that passage and this. The yearly supplies of wine and oil, mentioned in the former, were intended for Huram's court in return for the cedars sent him; while the articles of meat and drink specified here were for the workmen on Lebanon.

2Ch 2:11–18. Huram's kind answer.

11. Because the Lord hath loved his people – This pious language creates a presumption that Huram might have attained some knowledge of the true religion from his long familiar intercourse with David. But the presumption, however pleasing, may be delusive (see on 1Ki 5:7).

13, 14. I have sent a cunning man – (See on 1Ki 7:13–51).

17, 18. Solomon numbered all the strangers – (See on 1Ki 5:13; 1Ki 5:18).

Chapter 3

2Ch 3:1, 2. Place and time of building the temple.

1. Mount Moriah, where the Lord appeared unto David – These words seem to intimate that the region where the temple was built was *previously* known by the name of Moriah (Ge 22:2), and do not afford sufficient evidence for affirming, as has been done [STANLEY], that the name was *first* given to the mount, in *consequence* of the vision seen by David. Mount Moriah was one summit of a range of hills which went under the general name of Zion. The platform of the temple is now, and has long been, occupied by the haram, or sacred enclosure, within which stand the three mosques of Omar (the smallest), of El Aksa, which in early times was a Christian church, and of Kubbet el Sakhara, 'The dome of the rock,' so called from a huge block of limestone rock in the centre of the floor, which, it is supposed, formed the elevated threshing-floor of Araunah, and on which the great brazen altar stood. The site of the temple, then, is so far established for an almost universal belief is entertained in the authenticity of the tradition regarding the rock El Sakhara; and it has also been conclusively proved that the area of the temple was identical on its western, eastern, and southern sides with the present enclosure of the haram [ROBINSON]. 'That the temple was situated *somewhere* within the oblong enclosure on Mount Moriah, all topographers are agreed, although there is not the slightest vestige of the sacred fane now remaining; and the greatest diversity of sentiment prevails as to its exact position within that large area, whether in the centre of the haram, or in its southwest corner' [BARCLAY]. Moreover, the full extent of the temple area is a problem that remains to be solved, for the platform of Mount Moriah being too narrow for the extensive buildings and courts attached to the sacred edifice, Solomon resorted to artificial means of enlarging and levelling it, by erecting vaults, which, as JOSEPHUS states, rested on immense earthen mounds raised from the slope of the hill. It should be borne in mind at the outset that the grandeur of the temple did not consist in its colossal structure so much as in its internal splendour, and the vast courts and buildings attached to it. It was not intended for the reception of a worshipping assembly, for the people always stood in the outer courts of the sanctuary.

2Ch 3:3–7. Measures and ornaments of the house.

3. these are the things wherein Solomon was instructed for the building of the house of God – by the written plan and specifications given him by his father. The measurements are reckoned by cubits, 'after the first measure,' that is, the old Mosaic standard. But there is great difference of opinion about this, some making the cubit eighteen, others twenty-one inches. The temple, which embodied in more solid and durable materials the ground-form of the tabernacle (only being twice as large), was a rectangular building, seventy cubits long from east to west, and twenty cubits wide from north to south.
4. the porch – The breadth of the house, whose length ran from east to west, is here given as the measure of the length of the piazza. The portico

would thus be from thirty to thirty-five feet long, and from fifteen to seventeen and a half feet broad.
the height was an hundred and twenty cubits – This, taking the cubit at eighteen inches, would be one hundred eighty feet; at twenty-one inches, two hundred ten feet; so that the porch would rise in the form of a tower, or two pyramidal towers, whose united height was one hundred twenty cubits, and each of them about ninety or one hundred five feet high [STIEGLITZ]. This porch would thus be like the propylæum or gateway of the palace of Khorsabad [LAYARD], or at the temple of Edfou.
5. the greater house – that is, the holy places, the front or outer chamber (see 1Ki 6:17).
6. he garnished the house with precious stones for beauty – better, he paved the house with precious and beautiful marble [KITTO]. It may be, after all, that these were stones with veins of different colours for decorating the walls. This was an ancient and thoroughly Oriental kind of embellishment. There was an under pavement of marble, which was covered with planks of fir. The whole interior was lined with boards, richly decorated with carved work, clusters of foliage and flowers, among which the pomegranate and lotus (or water-lily) were conspicuous; and overlaid, excepting the floor, with gold, either by gilding or in plates (1Ki 6:1–38).

2Ch 3:8–13. Dimensions, &c., Of the most holy house.

8. the most holy house – It was a perfect cube (compare 1Ki 6:20).
10–13. two cherubims – These figures in the tabernacle were of pure gold (Ex 25:1-40) and overshadowed the mercy seat. The two placed in the temple were made of olive wood, overlaid with gold. They were of colossal size, like the Assyrian sculptures; for each, with expanded wings, covered a space of ten cubits in height and length – two wings touched each other, while the other two reached the opposite walls; their faces were inward, that is, towards the most holy house, conformably to their use, which was to veil the ark.
2Ch 3:14–17. Veil and pillars (see 1Ki 6:21). The united height is here given; and though the exact dimensions would be thirty-six cubits, each column was only seventeen cubits and a half, a half cubit being taken up by the capital or the base. They were probably described as they were lying together in the mould before they were set up [POOLE]. They would be from eighteen to twenty-one feet in circumference, and stand forty feet in height. These pillars, or obelisks, as some call them, were highly ornamented, and formed an entrance in keeping with the splendid interior of the temple.

Chapter 4

2Ch 4:1. Altar of brass.

1. **he made an altar of brass** – Steps must have been necessary for ascending so elevated an altar, but the use of these could be no longer forbidden (Ex 20:26) after the introduction of an official costume for the priests (Ex 28:42). It measured thirty-five feet by thirty-five, and in height seventeen and a half feet. The thickness of the metal used for this altar is nowhere given; but supposing it to have been three inches, the whole weight of the metal would not be under two hundred tons [Napier].

2Ch 4:2–5. Molten sea.

2. **he made a molten sea** – (See on 1Ki 7:23), as in that passage 'knops' occur instead of 'oxen.' It is generally supposed that the rows of ornamental knops were in the form of ox heads.

3. **Two rows of oxen were cast, when it was cast** – The meaning is, that the circular basin and the brazen oxen which supported it were all of one piece, being cast in one and the same mould.

2Ch 4:6–18. The ten lavers, candlesticks, and tables.

6. **ten lavers** – (See on 1Ki 7:27). The laver of the tabernacle had probably been destroyed. The ten new ones were placed between the porch and the altar, and while the molten sea was for the priests to cleanse their hands and feet, these were intended for washing the sacrifices.

7. **ten candlesticks** – (See on 1Ki 7:49). The increased number was not only in conformity with the characteristic splendour of the edifice, but also a standing emblem to the Hebrews, that the growing light of the word was necessary to counteract the growing darkness in the world [Lightfoot].

11. **Huram made** – (See on 1Ki 7:40).

9. **there it is unto this day** – that is, at the time when this history was composed; for after the Babylonian captivity there is no trace of either ark or staves.

11. **all the priests that were present … did not then wait by course** – The rotation system of weekly service introduced by David was intended for the ordinary duties of the priesthood; on extraordinary occasions, or when more than wonted solemnity attached to them, the priests attended in a body.

12. **the Levites which were the singers** – On great and solemn occasions, such as this, a full choir was required, and their station was taken with scrupulous regard to their official parts: the family of Heman occupied the central place, the family of Asaph stood on his right, and that of Jeduthun on his left; the place allotted to the vocal department was a space between the court of Israel and the altar in the east end of the priests' court.

with them an hundred and twenty priests sounding with trumpets – The trumpet was always used by the priests, and in the divine service it was specially employed in calling the people together during the holy solemnities, and in drawing attention to new and successive parts of the ritual. The number of trumpets used in the divine service could not be less than two (Nu 10:2), and their greatest number never exceeded the precedent set at the dedication of the temple. The station where the priests were sounding with trumpets was apart from that of the other musicians; for while the Levite singers occupied an orchestra east of the altar, the priests stood at the marble table on the southwest of the altar. There both of them stood with their faces to the altar. The manner of blowing the trumpets was, first, by a long plain blast, then by one with breakings and quaverings, and then by a long plain blast again [Brown, *Jewish Antiquities*].

13. **the house was filled with a cloud** – (See on 1Ki 8:10).

Chapter 5

2Ch 5:1. The dedicated treasures.

1. **Solomon brought in all the things that David his father had dedicated** – the immense sums and the store of valuable articles which his father and other generals had reserved and appropriated for the temple (1Ch 22:14 26:26).

2Ch 5:2-13. Bringing up of the ark of the covenant.

2, 3. **Then Solomon assembled … in the feast which was in the seventh month** – The feast of the dedication of the temple was on the eighth day of that month. This is related, word for word, the same as in 1Ki 8:1–10.

Chapter 6

2Ch 6:1–41. Solomon blesses the people and praises God.

1. **The Lord hath said that he would dwell in the thick darkness** – This introduction to Solomon's address was evidently suggested by the remarkable incident recorded at the close of the last chapter: the phenomenon of a densely opaque and uniformly shaped cloud, descending in a slow and majestic manner and filling the whole area of the temple. He regarded it himself, and directed the people also to regard it, as an undoubted sign and welcome pledge of the divine presence and acceptance of the building

reared to His honour and worship. He referred not to any particular declaration of God, but to the cloud having been all along in the national history of Israel the recognized symbol of the divine presence (Ex 16:10 24:16 40:34 Nu 9:15 1Ki 8:10,11).

13. Solomon had made a brazen scaffold – a sort of platform. But the *Hebrew* term rendered 'scaffold,' being the same as that used to designate the basin, suggests the idea that this throne might bear some resemblance, in form or structure, to those lavers in the temple, being a sort of round and elevated pulpit, placed in the middle of the court, and in front of the altar of burnt offering.

upon it he stood, and kneeled down upon his knees – After ascending the brazen scaffold, he assumed those two attitudes in succession, and with different objects in view. He stood while he addressed and blessed the surrounding multitude (2Ch 6:3–11). Afterwards he knelt down and stretched out his hands towards heaven, with his face probably turned towards the altar, while he gave utterance to the beautiful and impressive prayer which is recorded in the remainder of this chapter. It is deserving of notice that there was no seat in this pulpit – for the king either stood or knelt all the time he was in it. It is not improbable that it was surmounted by a canopy, or covered by a veil, to screen the royal speaker from the rays of the sun.

18–21. how much less this house which I have built! Have respect therefore to the prayer of thy servant – No person who entertains just and exalted views of the spiritual nature of the Divine Being will suppose that he can raise a temple for the habitation of Deity, as a man builds a house for himself. Nearly as improper and inadmissible is the idea that a temple can contribute to enhance the glory of God, as a monument may be raised in honour of a great man. Solomon described the true and proper use of the temple, when he entreated that the Lord would 'hearken unto the supplications of His servant and His people Israel, which they should make towards this place.' In short, the grand purpose for which the temple was erected was precisely the same as that contemplated by churches – to afford the opportunity and means of public and social worship, according to the ritual of the Mosaic dispensation – to supplicate the divine mercy and favour – to render thanks for past instances of goodness, and offer petitions for future blessings (see on 1Ki 8:22). This religious design of the temple – the ONE temple in the world – is in fact its standpoint of absorbing interest.

22. If a man sin against his neighbour, and an oath be laid upon him to make him swear, and the oath come before thine altar in this house – In cases where the testimony of witnesses could not be obtained and there was no way of settling a difference or dispute between two people but by accepting the oath of the accused, the practice had gradually crept in, for the party to be brought before the altar, where his oath was taken with all due solemnity, together with the imprecation of a curse to fall upon himself if his disavowal should be found untrue. There is an allusion to such a practice in this passage.

38. If they return to thee … in the land of their captivity … and pray toward their land, which thou gavest unto their fathers – These words gave rise to the favourite usage of the ancient as well as modern Jews, of turning in prayer toward Jerusalem, in whatever quarter of the world they might be, and of directing their faces toward the temple when in Jerusalem itself or in any part of the holy land (1Ki 8:44).

41. arise, O Lord God into thy resting-place – These words are not found in the record of this prayer in the First Book of Kings; but they occur in Ps 132:8, which is generally believed to have been composed by David, or rather by Solomon, in reference to this occasion. 'Arise' is a very suitable expression to be used when the ark was to be removed from the tabernacle in Zion to the temple on Mount Moriah.

into thy resting-place – the temple so called (Isa 66:1), because it was a fixed and permanent mansion (Ps 132:14).

the ark of thy strength – the abode by which Thy glorious presence is symbolized, and whence Thou dost issue Thine authoritative oracles, and manifest Thy power on behalf of Thy people when they desire and need it. It might well be designated the ark of God's strength, because it was through means of it the mighty miracles were wrought and the brilliant victories were won, that distinguish the early annals of the Hebrew nation. The sight of it inspired the greatest animation in the breasts of His people, while it diffused terror and dismay through the ranks of their enemies (compare Ps 78:61).

let thy priests … be clothed with salvation – or with righteousness (Ps 132:9), that is, be equipped not only with the pure white linen garments Thou hast appointed for their robe of office, but also adorned with the moral beauties of true holiness, that their person and services may be accepted, both for themselves and all the people. Thus they would be 'clothed with salvation,' for that is the effect and consequence of a sanctified character.

42. turn not away the face of thine anointed – that is, of me, who by Thy promise and appointment have been installed as king and ruler of Israel. The words are equivalent in meaning to this: Do not reject my present petitions; do not send me from Thy throne of grace dejected in countenance and disappointed in heart.

remember the mercies of David thy servant – that is, the mercies promised to David, and in consideration of that promise, hear and answer my prayer (compare Ps 132:10).

Chapter 7

2Ch 7:1–3. God gives testimony to Solomon's prayer; the people worship.

1. the fire came down from heaven, and consumed the burnt offering – Every act of worship was accompanied by a sacrifice. The preternatural stream of fire kindled the mass of flesh, and was a token of the divine acceptance of Solomon's prayer.

the glory of the Lord filled the house – The cloud, which was the symbol of God's presence and majesty, filled the interior of the temple (Ex 40:35).

2. the priests could not enter – Both from awe of the miraculous fire that was burning on the altar and from the dense cloud that enveloped the sanctuary, they were unable for some time to perform their usual functions (see on 1Ki 8:10). But afterwards, their courage and confidence being revived, they approached the altar and busied themselves in the offering of an immense number of sacrifices.

3. all the children of Israel … bowed themselves with their faces to the ground upon the pavement – This form of prostration (that of lying on one's knees with the forehead touching the earth), is the manner in which the Hebrews, and Orientals in general, express the most profound sentiments of reverence and humility. The courts of the temple were densely crowded on the occasion, and the immense multitude threw themselves on the ground. What led the Israelites suddenly to assume that prostrate attitude on the occasion referred to, was the spectacle of the symbolical cloud slowly and majestically descending upon the temple, and then entering it.

2Ch 7:4–11. Solomon's sacrifices.

4. Then the king and all the people offered sacrifices – Whether the individual worshippers slaughtered their own cattle, or a certain portion of the vast number of the Levitical order in attendance performed that work, as they sometimes did, in either case the offerings were made through the priests, who presented the blood and the fat upon the altar (see on 1Ki 8:62).

5, 6. so the king and all the people dedicated the house of God – The ceremonial of dedication consisted principally in the introduction of the ark into the temple, and in the sacrificial offerings that were made on a scale of magnitude suitable to the extraordinary occasion. All

present, the king, the people, and the priests, took part according to their respective stations in the performance of the solemn service. The duty, of course, devolved chiefly on the priests, and hence in proceeding to describe their several departments of work, the historian says, generally, 'the priests waited on their offices.' While great numbers would be occupied with the preparation and offering of the victims, others sounded with their trumpets, and the different bands of the Levites praised the Lord with vocal and instrumental music, by Ps 136:1–26, the hundred thirty-sixth Psalm, the oft-recurring chorus of which is, 'for His mercy endureth for ever.'

7. Solomon hallowed the middle of the court – On this extraordinary occasion, when a larger number of animals were offered than one altar and the usual place of rings to which the animals were bound would admit, the whole space was taken in that was between the place of rings and the west end of the court to be used as a temporary place for additional altars. On that part of the spacious court holocausts were burning all round.

8. Solomon kept the feast seven days – The time chosen for the dedication of the temple was immediately previous to the feast of tabernacles (see on 1Ki 8:1–12). That season, which came after the harvest, corresponding to our September and October, lasted seven days, and during so prolonged a festival there was time afforded for the offering of the immense sacrifices enumerated. A large proportion of these were peace offerings, which afforded to the people the means of festive enjoyment.

all Israel … from the entering in of Hamath – that is, the defile at Lebanon.

unto the river of Egypt – that is, Rhinocorura, now El-Arish, the south boundary of Palestine.

10. on the three and twentieth day of the seventh month – This was the last day of the feast of tabernacles.

2Ch 7:12–22. God appears to him.

12. the Lord appeared to Solomon by night – (See on 1Ki 9:1-9). The dedication of the temple must have been an occasion of intense national interest to Solomon and his subjects. Nor was the interest merely temporary or local. The record of it is read and thought of with an interest that is undiminished by the lapse of time. The fact that this was the only temple of all nations in which the *true God* was worshipped imparts a moral grandeur to the scene and prepares the mind for the sublime prayer that was offered at the dedication. The pure theism of that prayer – its acknowledgment of the unity of God as well as of His moral perfections in providence and grace, came from the same divine source as the miraculous fire. They indicated sentiments and feelings of exalted and spiritual devotion, which sprang not from the unaided mind of man, but from the fountain of revelation. The reality of the divine presence was attested by the miracle, and that miracle stamped the seal of truth upon the theology of the temple-worship.

Chapter 8

2Ch 8:1–6. Solomon's buildings.

2. cities which Huram had restored ... Solomon built them – These cities lay in the northwest of Galilee. Though included within the limits of the promised land, they had never been conquered. The right of occupying them Solomon granted to Huram, who, after consideration, refused them as unsuitable to the commercial habits of his subjects (see on 1Ki 9:11). Solomon, having wrested them from the possession of the Canaanite inhabitants, repaired them and filled them with a colony of Hebrews.

3–6. And Solomon went to Hamath-zobah – Hamath was on the Orontes, in Coele-Syria. Its king, Toi, had been the ally of David; but from the combination, Hamath and Zobah, it would appear that some revolution had taken place which led to the union of these two petty kingdoms of Syria into one. For what cause the resentment of Solomon was provoked against it, we are not informed, but he sent an armed force which reduced it. He made himself master also of Tadmor, the famous Palmyra in the same region. Various other cities along the frontiers of his extended dominions he repaired and fitted up, either to serve as store-places for the furtherance of his commercial enterprises, or to secure his kingdom from foreign invasion (see on 2Ch 1:14; 1Ki 9:15).

2Ch 8:7–11. The Canaanites made tributaries.

7. all the people that were left – The descendants of the Canaanites who remained in the country were treated as war prisoners, being obliged to 'pay tribute or to serve as galley slaves' (2Ch 2:18), while the Israelites were employed in no works but such as were of an honourable character.

10. two hundred and fifty that bare rule – (Compare 1Ki 9:23). It is generally agreed that the text of one of these passages is corrupt.

11. Solomon brought up the daughter of Pharaoh out of the city of David unto the house that he had built for her – On his marriage with the Egyptian princess at the beginning of his reign, he assigned her a temporary abode in the city of David, that is, Jerusalem, until a suitable palace for his wife had been erected. While that palace was in progress, he himself lodged in the palace of David, but he did not allow her to occupy it, because he felt that she being a heathen proselyte, and having brought from her own country an establishment of heathen maid-servants, there would have been an impropriety in her being domiciled in a mansion which was or had been hallowed by the reception of the ark. It seems she was received on her arrival into his mother's abode (So 3:4 8:2).

2Ch 8:15–18. Solomon's festival sacrifices.

15. they departed not from the commandment of the king – that is, David, in any of his ordinances, which by divine authority he established.

unto the priests and Levites concerning any matter, or concerning the treasures – either in regulating the courses of the priests and Levites, or in the destination of his accumulated treasures to the construction and adornment of the temple.

17. Then went Solomon to Ezion-geber, and to Eloth – These two maritime ports were situated at the eastern gulf of the Red Sea, now called the Gulf of Akaba. Eloth is seen in the modern Akaba, Ezion-geber in El Gudyan [ROBINSON]. Solomon, determined to cultivate the arts of peace, was sagacious enough to perceive that his kingdom could become great and glorious only by encouraging a spirit of commercial enterprise among his subjects; and, accordingly, with that in mind he made a contract with Huram for ships and seamen to instruct his people in navigation.

18. Huram sent him ... ships – either sent him ship-*men*, able seamen, overland; or, taking the word 'sent' in a looser sense, *supplied* him, that is, *built* him ships – namely, in docks at Eloth (compare 1Ki 9:26,27). This navy of Solomon was manned by Tyrians, for Solomon had no seamen capable of performing distant expeditions. The Hebrew fishermen, whose boats plied on the Sea of Tiberias or coasted the shores of the Mediterranean, were not equal to the conducting of large vessels laden with valuable cargoes on long voyages and through the wide and unfrequented ocean.

four hundred and fifty talents of gold – (Compare 1Ki 9:28). The text in one of these passages is corrupt.

Chapter 9

2Ch 9:1–12. The Queen of Sheba visits Solomon; she admires his wisdom and magnificence.

1–4. when the queen of Sheba heard of the fame of Solomon – (See on 1Ki 10:1–13). It is said that among the things in Jerusalem which drew forth the admiration of Solomon's royal visitor was 'his ascent by which he went up into the house of the Lord.' This was the arched viaduct that crossed the valley from Mount Zion to the opposite hill. In the commentary on the passage quoted above, allusion was made to the recent discovery of its remains. Here we give a full account of what, for boldness of conceptions for structure and magnificence, was one of the greatest wonders in Jerusalem. 'During our first visit to the southwest corner of the area of the mosque, we observed several of the large stones jutting out from the western wall, which at first seemed to be the effect of a bursting of the wall from some mighty shock or earthquake. We paid little regard to this at the moment; but on mentioning the fact not long after to a circle of our friends, the remark was incidentally dropped that the stones had the appearance of having once belonged to a large arch. At this remark, a train of thought flashed across my mind, which I hardly dared to follow out until I had again repaired to the spot, in order to satisfy myself with my own eyes as to the truth or falsehood of the suggestion. I found it even so. The courses of these immense stones occupy their original position; their external surface is hewn to a regular curve; and, being fitted one upon another, they form the commencement or foot of an immense arch which once sprung out from this western wall in a direction towards Mount Zion, across the Tyropoeon valley. This arch could only have belonged to the bridge, which, according to Josephus, led from this part of the temple to the Xystus (covered colonnade) on Zion; and it proves incontestably the antiquity of that portion from which it springs' [Robinson]. The distance from this point to the steep rock of Zion Robinson calculates to be about three hundred and fifty feet, the probable length of this ancient viaduct. Another writer adds, that 'the arch of this bridge, if its curve be calculated with an approximation to the truth, would measure *sixty* feet, and must have been one of five sustaining the viaduct (allowing for the abutments on either side), and that the piers supporting the centre arch of this bridge must have been of great altitude – not less, perhaps, than one hundred and thirty feet. The whole structure, when seen from the southern extremity of the Tyropoeon, must have had an aspect of grandeur, especially as connected with the lofty and sumptuous edifices of the temple, and of Zion to the right and to the left' [Isaac Taylor's Edition of Traill's Josephus].

2Ch 9:13–28. His riches.

13. Now the weight of gold that came to Solomon in one year – (See on 1Ki 10:14-29).
21. the king's ships went to Tarshish – rather, 'the king's ships of Tarshish went' with the servants of Huram.

ships of Tarshish – that is, in burden and construction like the large vessels built for or used at Tarshish [Calmet, *Fragments*].

25. Solomon had four thousand stalls – It has been conjectured [Gesenius, *Hebrew Lexicon*] that the original term may signify not only stall or stable, but a number of horses occupying the same number of stalls. Supposing that ten were put together in one part, this would make forty thousand. According to this theory of explanation, the historian in Kings refers to horses [see 1Ki 10:26]; while the historian in Chronicles speaks of the stalls in which they were kept. But more recent critics reject this mode of solving the difficulty, and, regarding the four thousand stalls as in keeping with the general magnificence of Solomon's establishments, are agreed in considering the text in Kings as corrupt, through the error of some copyist.

28. they brought unto Solomon horses out of Egypt – (See on 2Ch 1:14). Solomon undoubtedly carried the Hebrew kingdom to its highest pitch of worldly glory. His completion of the grand work, the centralizing of the national worship at Jerusalem, whither the natives went up three times a year, has given his name a prominent place in the history of the ancient church. But his reign had a disastrous influence upon 'the peculiar people,' and the example of his deplorable idolatries, the connections he formed with foreign princes, the commercial speculations he entered into, and the luxuries introduced into the land, seem in a great measure to have altered and deteriorated the Jewish character.

Chapter 10

2Ch 10:1–15. Rehoboam refusing the old men's good counsel.

1. Rehoboam went to Shechem – (See on 1Ki 12:1). This chapter is, with a few verbal alterations, the same as in 1Ki 12:1–19.

7. If thou be kind to this people, and please them, and speak good words to them – In the Book of Kings [1Ki 12:7], the words are, 'If thou wilt be a servant unto this – people, and wilt serve them.' The meaning in both is the same, namely, If thou wilt make some reasonable concessions, redress their grievances, and restore their abridged liberties, thou wilt secure their strong and lasting attachment to thy person and government.

15–17. the king hearkened not unto the people, for the cause was of God – Rehoboam, in following an evil counsel, and the Hebrew people, in making a revolutionary movement, each acted as free agents, obeying their own will and passions. But God, who permitted the revolt of the northern tribes, intended it as a punishment of the house of David for Solomon's apostasy. That event demonstrates the immediate superintendence of His providence over the revolutions of kingdoms; and thus it affords an instance, similar to many other striking instances that are found in Scripture, of divine predictions, uttered long before, being accomplished by the operation of human passions, and in the natural course of events.

Chapter 11

2Ch 11:1–17. Rehoboam, raising an army to subdue Israel, is forbidden by Shemaiah.

1–4. Rehoboam … gathered of the house of Judah and Benjamin … to fight against Israel – (See 1Ki 12:21-24).

5–11. built cities for defence in Judah – This is evidently used as the name of the southern kingdom. Rehoboam, having now a bitter enemy in Israel, deemed it prudent to lose no time in fortifying several cities that lay along the frontier of his kingdom. Jeroboam, on his side, took a similar precaution (1Ki 12:25). Of the fifteen cities named, Aijalon and Zorah lay within the province of Benjamin. Gath, though a Philistine city, had been subject to Solomon. And Etham, which was on the border of Simeon, now incorporated with the kingdom of Israel, was fortified to repel danger from that quarter. These fortresses Rehoboam placed under able commanders and stocked them with provisions and military stores, sufficient, if necessary, to stand a siege. In the crippled state of his kingdom, he seems to have been afraid lest it might be made the prey of some powerful neighbours

13–17. the priests and the Levites … resorted to him out of all their coasts – This was an accession of moral power, for the maintenance of the true religion is the best support and safeguard of any nation; and as it was peculiarly the grand source of the strength and prosperity of the Hebrew monarchy, the great numbers of good and pious people who sought an asylum within the territories of Judah contributed greatly to consolidate the throne of Rehoboam. The cause of so extensive an emigration from the kingdom of Israel was the deep and daring policy of Jeroboam, who set himself to break the national unity by entirely abolishing, within his dominions, the religious institutions of Judaism. He dreaded an eventual reunion of the tribes if the people continued to repair thrice a year to worship in Jerusalem as they were obliged by law to do. Accordingly, on pretense that the distance of that city was too great for multitudes of his subjects, he fixed upon two more convenient places, where he established a new mode of worshipping God under gross and

prohibited symbols [1Ki 12:26–33]. The priests and Levites, refusing to take part in the idolatrous ceremonies, were ejected from their living (2Ch 11:13,14). Along with them a large body of the people who faithfully adhered to the instituted worship of God, offended and shocked by the impious innovations, departed from the kingdom.

15. he ordained him priests – The persons he appointed to the priesthood were low and worthless creatures (1Ki 12:31 13:33); any were consecrated who brought a bullock and seven rams (2Ch 13:9 Ex 29:37).

for the high places – Those favorite places of religious worship were encouraged throughout the country.

for the devils – a term sometimes used for idols in general (Le 17:7). But here it is applied distinctively to the goat deities, which were probably worshipped chiefly in the northern parts of his kingdom, where the heathen Canaanites still abounded.

for the calves which he had made – figures of the ox gods Apis and Mnevis, with which Jeroboam's residence in Egypt had familiarized him. (See on 1Ki 12:26).

17. they strengthened the kingdom of Judah – The innovating measures of Jeroboam were not introduced all at once. But as they were developed, the secession of the most excellent of his subjects began, and continuing to increase for three years, lowered the tone of religion in his kingdom, while it proportionally quickened its life and extended its influence in that of Judah.

2Ch 11:18–23. His wives and children.

18. Rehoboam took Mahalath – The names of her father and mother are given. Jerimoth, the father, must have been the son of one of David's concubines (1Ch 3:9). Abihail was, of course, his cousin, previous to their marriage.

20. after her he took Maachah … daughter – that is, granddaughter (2Sa 14:27) of Absalom, Tamar being, according to JOSEPHUS, her mother. (Compare 2Sa 18:18).

21. he took eighteen wives, and threescore concubines – This royal harem, though far smaller than his father's, was equally in violation of the law, which forbade a king to 'multiply wives unto himself' [De 17:17].

22. made Abijah … chief … ruler among his brethren – This preference seems to have been given to Abijah solely from the king's doting fondness for his mother and through her influence over him. It is plainly implied that Abijah was not the oldest of the family. In destining a younger son for the kingdom, without a divine warrant, as in Solomon's case, Rehoboam acted in violation of the law (De 21:15).

23. he dealt wisely – that is, with deep and calculating policy (Ex 1:10).

and dispersed of all his children … unto every fenced city – The circumstance of twenty-eight sons of the king being made governors of fortresses would, in our quarter of the world, produce jealousy and dissatisfaction. But Eastern monarchs ensure peace and tranquillity to their kingdom by bestowing government offices on their sons and grandsons. They obtain an independent provision, and being kept apart, are not likely to cabal in their father's lifetime. Rehoboam acted thus, and his sagacity will appear still greater if the wives he desired for them belonged to the cities where each son was located. These connections would bind them more closely to their respective places. In the modern countries of the East, particularly Persia and Turkey, younger princes were, till very lately, shut up in the harem during their father's lifetime; and, to prevent competition, they were blinded or killed when their brother ascended the throne. In the former country the old practice of dispersing them through the country as Rehoboam did, has been again revived.

Chapter 12

2Ch 12:1–12. Rehoboam, forsaking God, is punished by Shishak.

1. when Rehoboam had established the kingdom, and had strengthened himself – (See on 2Ch 11:17). During the first three years of his reign his royal influence was exerted in the encouragement of the true religion. Security and ease led to religious decline, which, in the fourth year, ended in open apostasy. The example of the court was speedily followed by his subjects, for 'all Israel was with him,' that is, the people in his own kingdom. The very next year, the fifth of his reign, punishment was inflicted by the invasion of Shishak.

2. Shishak king of Egypt came up against Jerusalem – He was the first king of the twenty-second or Bubastic Dynasty. What was the immediate cause of this invasion? Whether it was in resentment for some provocation from the king of Judah, or in pursuance of ambitious views of conquest, is not said. But the invading army was a vast horde, for Shishak brought along with his native Egyptians an immense number of foreign auxiliaries.

3–5. the Lubims – the Libyans of north-eastern Africa.

the Sukkiims – Some think these were the Kenite Arabs, dwellers in tents, but others maintain more justly that these were Arab troglodytes, who inhabited the caverns of a mountain range on the western coast of the Red Sea.

and the Ethiopians – from the regions south of Egypt. By the overwhelming force of numbers, they took the fortresses of Judah which had been recently put in a state of defense, and marched to lay siege to the capital. While Shishak and his army was before Jerusalem, the prophet Shemaiah addressed Rehoboam and the princes, tracing this calamity to the national apostasy and threatening them with utter destruction in consequence of having forsaken God (2Ch 12:6).

6. the princes of Israel – (compare 2Ch 12:5, 'the princes of Judah').

7, 8. when the Lord saw that they humbled themselves – Their repentance and contrition was followed by the best effects; for Shemaiah was commissioned to announce that the phial of divine judgment would not be fully poured out on them – that the entire overthrow of the kingdom of Judah would not take place at that time, nor through the agency of Shishak; and yet, although it should enjoy a respite from total subversion, [Judah] should become a tributary province of Egypt in order that the people might learn how much lighter and better is the service of God than that of idolatrous foreign despots.

9. So Shishak … came up against Jerusalem – After the parenthetical clause (2Ch 12:5–8) describing the feelings and state of the beleaguered court, the historian resumes his narrative of the attack upon Jerusalem, and the consequent pillage both of the temple and the palace.

he took all – that is, everything valuable he found.

the shields of gold – made by Solomon, were kept in the house of the forest of Lebanon (2Ch 9:16). They seem to have been borne, like maces, by the guards of the palace, when they attended the king to the temple or on other public processions. Those splendid insignia having been plundered by the Egyptian conqueror, others were made of inferior metal and kept in the guard room of the palace, to be ready for use; as, notwithstanding the tarnished glory of the court, the old state etiquette was kept up on public and solemn occasions. An account of this conquest of Judah, with the name of 'king of Judah' in the cartouche of the principal captive, according to the interpreters, is carved and written in hieroglyphics on the walls of the great palace of Karnak, where it may be seen at the present day. This sculpture is about twenty-seven hundred years old, and is of peculiar interest as a striking testimony from Egypt to the truth of Scripture history.

12. when he humbled himself, the wrath of the Lord turned from him – The promise (2Ch 12:7) was verified. Divine providence preserved the kingdom in existence, a reformation was

made in the court, while true religion and piety were diffused throughout the land.

2Ch 12:13–16. His reign and death.

13, 14. Rehoboam strengthened … and reigned – The Egyptian invasion had been a mere predatory expedition, not extending beyond the limits of Judah, and probably, ere-long, repelled by the invaded. Rehoboam's government acquired new life and vigor by the general revival of true religion, and his reign continued many years after the departure of Shishak. But

he prepared not his heart to seek the Lord – that is, he did not adhere firmly to the good course of reformation he had begun, 'and he did evil,' for through the unhappy influence of his mother, a heathen foreigner, he had no doubt received in his youth a strong bias towards idolatry (see on 1Ki 14:21).

Chapter 13

2Ch 13:1–20. Abijah, succeeding, makes war against Jeroboam, and overcomes him.

2. His mother's name also was Michaiah, the daughter of Uriel – the same as Maachah (see on 1Ki 15:2). She was 'the daughter,' that is, granddaughter of Absalom (1Ki 15:2; compare 2Sa 14:1–33), mother of Abijah, 'mother,' that is, grandmother (1Ki 15:10, *Margin*) of Asa.

of Gibeah – probably implies that Uriel was connected with the house of Saul.

there was war between Abijah and Jeroboam – The occasion of this war is not recorded (see 1Ki 15:6,7), but it may be inferred from the tenor of Abijah's address that it arose from his youthful ambition to recover the full hereditary dominion of his ancestors. No prophet now forbade a war with Israel (2Ch 11:23) for Jeroboam had forfeited all claim to protection.

3. Abijah set the battle in array – that is, took the field and opened the campaign.

with … four hundred thousand chosen men … Jeroboam with eight hundred thousand – These are, doubtless, large numbers, considering the smallness of the two kingdoms. It must be borne in mind, however, that Oriental armies are mere mobs – vast numbers accompanying the camp in hope of plunder, so that the gross numbers described as going upon an Asiatic expedition are often far from denoting the exact number of fighting men. But in accounting for the large number of soldiers enlisted in the respective armies of Abijah and Jeroboam, there is no need of resorting to this mode of explanation; for we know by the census of David the immense number of the population that was capable of bearing arms (1Ch 21:5; compare 2Ch 14:8 17:14).

4–12. Abijah stood up upon Mount Zemaraim – He had entered the enemy's territory and was encamped on an eminence near Beth-el (Jos 18:22). Jeroboam's army lay at the foot of the hill, and as a pitched battle was expected, Abijah, according to the singular usage of ancient times, harangued the enemy. The speakers in such circumstances, while always extolling their own merits, poured out torrents of invective and virulent abuse upon the adversary. So did Abijah. He dwelt on the divine right of the house of David to the throne; and sinking all reference to the heaven-condemned offenses of Solomon and the divine appointment of Jeroboam, as well as the divine sanction of the separation, he upbraided Jeroboam as a usurper, and his subjects as rebels, who took advantage of the youth and inexperience of Rehoboam. Then contrasting the religious state of the two kingdoms, he drew a black picture of the impious innovations and gross idolatry introduced by Jeroboam, with his expulsion and impoverishment (2Ch 11:14) of the Levites. He dwelt with reasonable pride on the pure and regular observance of the ancient institutions of Moses in his own dominion (2Ch 13:11) and concluded with this emphatic appeal: 'O children of Israel, fight ye not against Jehovah, the God of your fathers, for ye shall not prosper.'

13–17. But Jeroboam caused an ambushment to come about behind them – The oration of Abijah, however animating an effect it might have produced on his own troops, was unheeded by the party to whom it was addressed; for while he was wasting time in useless words, Jeroboam had ordered a detachment of his men to move quietly round the base of the hill, so that when Abijah stopped speaking, he and his followers found themselves surprised in the rear, while the main body of the Israelitish forces remained in front. A panic might have ensued, had not the leaders 'cried unto the Lord,' and the priests 'sounded with the trumpets' – the pledge of victory (Nu 10:9 31:6). Reassured by the well-known signal, the men of Judah responded with a war shout, which, echoed by the whole army, was followed by an impetuous rush against the foe. The shock was resistless. The ranks of the Israelites were broken, for 'God smote Jeroboam and all Israel.' They took to flight, and the merciless slaughter that ensued can be accounted for only by tracing it to the rancorous passions enkindled by a civil war.

19. Abijah pursued after Jeroboam, and took cities from him – This sanguinary action widened the breach between the people of the two kingdoms. Abijah abandoned his original design of attempting the subjugation of the ten tribes, contenting himself with the recovery of a few border towns, which, though lying within Judah or Benjamin, had been alienated to the new or northern kingdom. Among these was Beth-el, which, with its sacred associations, he might be strongly desirous to wrest from profanation.

20. Neither did Jeroboam recover strength again in the days of Abijah – The disastrous action at Zemaraim, which caused the loss of the flower and chivalry of his army, broke his spirits and crippled his power.

the Lord struck him, and he died – that is, Jeroboam. He lived, indeed, two years after the death of Abijah (1Ki 14:20 15:9). But he had been threatened with great calamities upon himself and his house, and it is apparently to the execution of these threatenings, which issued in his death, that an anticipatory reference is here made.

Chapter 14

2Ch 14:1–5. Asa destroys idolatry.

1. In his days the land was quiet ten years – This long interval of peace was the continued effect of the great battle of Zemaraim (compare 1Ki 15:11–14).

2. Asa did that which was good and right – (compare 1Ki 15:14). Still his character and life were not free from faults (2Ch 16:7,10,12).

3. brake down the images – of Baal (see on 2Ch 34:4; Le 26:30).

cut down the groves – rather, 'Asherim.'

5. he took away ... the high places – that is, those devoted to idolatrous rites.

took away out of all the cities of Judah the high places and the images – All public objects and relics of idolatry in Jerusalem and other cities through his kingdom were destroyed; but those high places where God was worshipped under the figure of an ox, as at Beth-el, were allowed to remain (1Ki 15:14); so far the reformation was incomplete.

2Ch 14:6–8. Having peace, he strengthens his kingdom with forts and armies.

6. he built fenced cities in Judah – (See on 1Ki 15:22).

7. while the land is yet before us – that is, while we have free and undisputed progress everywhere; no foe is near; but, as this happy time of peace may not last always and the kingdom is but small and weak, let us prepare suitable defences in case of need. He had also an army of five hundred eighty thousand men. Judah furnished the heavily armed soldiers, and Benjamin the archers. This large number does not mean a body of professional soldiers, but all capable of bearing arms and liable to be called into service.

2Ch 14:9–15. He overcomes Zerah, and spoils the Ethiopians.

9. there came out against them Zerah the Ethiopian – This could not have been from Ethiopia south of the cataracts of the Nile, for in the reign of Osorkon I, successor of Shishak, no foreign army would have been allowed a free passage through Egypt. Zerah must, therefore, have been chief of the Cushites, or Ethiopians of Arabia, as they were evidently a nomad horde who had a settlement of tents and cattle in the neighbourhood of Gerar.

a thousand thousand, and three hundred chariots – 'Twenty camels employed to carry couriers upon them might have procured that number of men to meet in a short time. As Zerah was the aggressor, he had time to choose when he would summon these men and attack the enemy. Every one of these Cushite shepherds, carrying with them their own provisions of flour and water, as is their invariable custom, might have fought with Asa without eating a loaf of Zerah's bread or drinking a pint of his water' [BRUCE, *Travels*].

10. Then Asa went out against him, and they set the battle in array ... at Mareshah – one of the towns which Rehoboam fortified (2Ch 11:8), near a great southern pass in the low country of Judah (Jos 15:44). The engagement between the armies took place in a plain near the town, called 'the valley of Zephathah,' supposed to be the broad way coming down Beit Jibrin towards Tell Es-Safren [ROBINSON].

11–13. Asa cried unto the Lord his God – Strong in the confidence that the power of God was able to give the victory equally with few as with many, the pious king marched with a comparatively small force to encounter the formidable host of marauders at his southern frontier. Committing his cause to God, he engaged in the conflict – completely routed the enemy, and succeeded in obtaining, as the reward of his victory, a rich booty in treasure and cattle from the tents of this pastoral horde.

Chapter 15

2Ch 15:1–15. Judah makes a solemn covenant with God.

1. Azariah the son of Oded – This prophet, who is mentioned nowhere else, appears at this stage of the sacred story in the discharge of an interesting mission. He went to meet Asa, as he was returning from his victorious pursuit of the Ethiopians, and the congratulatory address here recorded was publicly made to the king in presence of his army.

2. The Lord is with you, while ye be with him – You have had, in your recent signal success, a remarkable proof that God's blessing is upon you; your victory has been the reward of your faith and piety. If you steadfastly adhere to the cause of God, you may expect a continuance of His favor; but if you abandon it, you will soon reap the bitter fruits of apostasy.

3–6. Now for a long season Israel hath been without the true God – Some think that Azariah was referring to the sad and disastrous condition to which superstition and idolatry had brought the neighbouring kingdom of Israel. His words should rather be taken in a wider sense, for it seems manifest that the prophet had his eye upon many periods in the national history, when the people were in the state described – a state of spiritual destitution and ignorance – and exhibited its natural result as widespread anarchy, mutual dissension among the tribes, and general suffering (Jud 9:23 12:4 20:21 2Ch 13:17). These calamities God permitted to befall them as the punishment of their apostasy. Azariah's object in these remarks was to establish the truth of his counsel (2Ch 15:2), threatening, in case of neglecting it by describing the uniform course of the divine procedure towards Israel, as shown in all periods of their history. Then after this appeal to national experience, he concluded with an earnest exhortation to the king to prosecute the work of reformation so well begun (2Ch 15:7).

7. Be ye strong – Great resolution and indomitable energy would be required to persevere in the face of the opposition your reforming measures will encounter.

your work shall be rewarded – What you do in the cause and for the glory of God will assuredly be followed by the happiest results both to yourself and your subjects.

8. when Asa heard … the prophecy of Oded the prophet – The insertion of these words, 'of Oded the prophet,' is generally regarded as a corruption of the text. 'The sole remedy is to erase them. They are, probably, the remains of a note, which crept in from the margin into the text' [Bertheau].

he took courage – Animated by the seasonable and pious address of Azariah, Asa became a more zealous reformer than ever, employing all his royal authority and influence to extirpate every vestige of idolatry from the land.

and out of the cities which he had taken from mount Ephraim – He may have acquired cities of Ephraim, the conquest of which is not recorded (2Ch 17:2); but it has been commonly supposed that the reference is to cities which his father Abijah had taken in that quarter (2Ch 13:19).

renewed the altar of the Lord … before the porch – that is, the altar of burnt offering. As this was done on or about the fifteenth year of the reign of this pious king, the renewal must have consisted in some splendid repairs or embellishments, which made it look like a new dedication, or in a reconstruction of a temporary altar, like that of Solomon (2Ch 7:7), for extraordinary sacrifices to be offered on an approaching occasion.

9–15. he gathered all Judah and Benjamin – Not satisfied with these minor measures of purification and improvement, Asa meditated a grand scheme which was to pledge his whole kingdom to complete the work of reformation, and with this in view he waited for a general assembly of the people.

and the strangers with them out of Ephraim and Manasseh – The population of Asa's kingdom had been vastly increased by the continued influx of strangers, who, prompted by motives either of interest or of piety, sought in his dominions that security and freedom which they could not enjoy amid the complicated troubles which distracted Israel.

and out of Simeon – Although a portion of that tribe, located within the territory of Judah, were already subjects of the southern kingdom, the general body of the Simeonites had joined in forming the northern kingdom of Israel. But many of them now returned of their own accord.

10–14. the third month – when was held the feast of pentecost. On this occasion, it was celebrated at Jerusalem by an extraordinary sacrifice of seven hundred oxen and seven thousand sheep, the spoil of the Ethiopians being offered. The assembled worshippers entered with great and holy enthusiasm into a national covenant; and, at the same time, to execute with rigor the laws which made idolatry punishable with death (2Ch 15:13 De 17:2–5 Heb 10:2,8). The people testified unbounded satisfaction with this important religious movement, and its moral influence was seen in the promotion of piety, order, and tranquillity throughout the land.

18. the things that his father had dedicated – probably part of the booty obtained by his signal victory over Jeroboam, but which, though dedicated, had hitherto been unrepresented.

and that he himself had dedicated – of the booty taken from the Ethiopians. Both of these were now deposited in the temple as votive offerings to Him whose right hand and holy arm had given them the victory.

Chapter 16

2Ch 16:1–14. Asa, by a league with the Syrians, diverts Baasha from building Ramah.

1–6. In the six and thirtieth year of the reign of Asa, Baasha … came up against Judah – Baasha had died several years before this date (1Ki 15:33), and the best biblical critics are agreed in considering this date to be calculated from the separation of the kingdoms, and coincident with the sixteenth year of Asa's reign. This mode of reckoning was, in all likelihood, generally followed in the book of the kings of Judah and Israel, the public annals of the time (2Ch 16:11), the source from which the inspired historian drew his account.

Baasha ... built Ramah – that is, fortified it. The blessing of God which manifestly rested at this time on the kingdom of Judah, the signal victory of Asa, the freedom and purity of religious worship, and the fame of the late national covenant, were regarded with great interest throughout Israel, and attracted a constantly increasing number of emigrants to Judah. Baasha, alarmed at this movement, determined to stem the tide; and as the high road to and from Jerusalem passed by Ramah, he made that frontier town, about six miles north of Asa's capital, a military station, where the vigilance of his sentinels would effectually prevent all passage across the boundary of the kingdom (see on 1Ki 15:16–22).

4. Ben-hadad ... sent the captains of his armies ... and they smote ... Abelmaim – 'The meadow of waters,' supposed to have been situated on the marshy plain near the uppermost lake of the Jordan. The other two towns were also in the northern district of Palestine. These unexpected hostilities of his Syrian ally interrupted Baasha's fortifications at Ramah, and his death, happening soon after, prevented his resuming them.

7–10. Hanani the seer came to Asa ... and said – His object was to show the king his error in forming his recent league with Ben-hadad. The prophet represented the appropriation of the temple treasures to purchase the services of the Syrian mercenaries, as indicating a distrust in God most blameable with the king's experience. He added, that in consequence of this want of faith, Asa had lost the opportunity of gaining a victory over the united forces of Baasha and Ben-hadad, more splendid than that obtained over the Ethiopians. Such a victory, by destroying their armies, would have deprived them of all power to molest him in the future; whereas by his foolish and worldly policy, so unworthy of God's vicegerent, to misapply the temple treasures and corrupt the fidelity of an ally of the king of Israel, he had tempted the cupidity of the one, and increased the hostility of the other, and rendered himself liable to renewed troubles (1Ki 15:32). This rebuke was pungent and, from its truth and justness, ought to have penetrated and afflicted the heart of such a man as Asa. But his pride was offended at the freedom taken by the honest reprover of royalty, and in a burst of passionate resentment, he ordered Hanani to be thrown into prison.

10. Asa oppressed some of the people the same time – The form or degree of this oppression is not recorded. The cause of his oppressing them was probably due to the same offense as that of Hanani – a strong expression of their dissatisfaction with his conduct in leaguing with Ben-hadad, or it may have been his maltreatment of the Lord's servant.

12. Asa ... was diseased in his feet – probably the gout.

yet his disease was exceeding great – better, 'moved upwards' in his body, which proves the violent and dangerous type of the malady.

yet in his disease he sought not to the Lord, but to the physicians – most probably Egyptian physicians, who were anciently in high repute at foreign courts, and who pretended to expel diseases by charms, incantations, and mystic arts. Asa's fault consisted in his trusting to such physicians, while he neglected to supplicate the aid and blessing of God. The best and holiest men have been betrayed for a time into sins, but through repentance have risen again; and as Asa is pronounced a good man (2Ch 15:17), it may be presumed that he also was restored to a better state of mind.

14. they buried him in his own sepulchres – The tombs in the neighbourhood of Jerusalem were excavated in the side of a rock. One cave contained several tombs or sepulchres.

laid him in the bed ... filled with sweet odours and divers kinds of spices – It is evident that a sumptuous public funeral was given him as a tribute of respect and gratitude for his pious character and patriotic government. But whether 'the bed' means a state couch on which he lay exposed to public view, the odoriferous perfumes being designed to neutralize the offensive smell of the corpse, or whether it refers to an embalmment, in which aromatic spices were always used in great profusion, it is impossible to say.

they made a very great burning for him – according to some, for consuming the spices. According to others, it was a magnificent pile for the cremation of the corpse – a usage which was at that time, and long after, prevalent among the Hebrews, and the omission of which in the case of royal personages was reckoned a great indignity (2Ch 21:19 1Sa 31:12 Jer 34:5 Am 6:10).

Chapter 17

2Ch 17:1–6. Jehoshaphat reigns well and prospers.

1. Jehoshaphat ... strengthened himself against Israel – The temper and proceedings of the kings of Israel rendered it necessary for him to prepare vigorous measures of defense on the northern frontier of his kingdom. These consisted in filling all the fortresses with their full complement of troops and establishing military stations in various parts of the country, as well as in the cities of Mount Ephraim, which belonged to Jehoshaphat (2Ch 15:8).

3–5. he walked in the first ways of his father David – He imitated the piety of his great ancestor in the early part of his reign before he made those unhappy lapses which dishonored his character.

and sought not unto Baalim – a term used for idols generally in contradistinction to the Lord God of his father.

4. and not after the doings of Israel – He observed with scrupulous fidelity, and employed his royal influence to support the divine institutions as enacted by Moses, abhorring that spurious and unlawful calf-worship that now formed the established religion in Israel. Being thus far removed, alike from gross idolatry and Israelitish apostasy, and adhering zealously to the requirements of the divine law, the blessing of God rested on his government. Ruling in the fear of God, and for the good of his subjects, 'the Lord established the kingdom in his hand.'

5. all Judah brought ... presents – This was customary with the people generally at the beginning of a reign (1Sa 10:27), and with the nobles and high functionaries yearly afterwards. They were given in the form of voluntary offerings, to avoid the odious idea of a tax or tribute.

6. his heart was lifted up in the ways of the Lord – Full of faith and piety, he possessed zeal and courage to undertake the reformation of manners, to suppress all the works and objects of idolatry (see on 2Ch 20:33), and he held out public encouragement to the pure worship of God.

2Ch 17:7–11. He sends Levites to teach in Judah.

7–11. Also in the third year of his reign he sent to his princes, ... to teach in the cities of Judah – The ordinary work of teaching devolved on the priests. But extraordinary commissioners were appointed, probably to ascertain whether the work had been done or neglected. This deputation of five princes, assisted by two priests and nine Levites, was to make a circuit of the towns in Judah. It is the first practical measure we read of as being adopted by any of the kings for the religious instruction of the people. Time and unbroken opportunities were afforded for carrying out fully this excellent plan of home education, for the kingdom enjoyed internal tranquillity as well as freedom for foreign wars. It is conformable to the pious style of the sacred historian to trace this profound peace to the 'fear of the Lord having fallen on all kingdoms of the

lands that were round about Judah.'

9. the book of the law – that is, either the whole Pentateuch or only the book of Deuteronomy, which contains an abridgment of it.

11. Also some of the Philistines brought Jehoshaphat presents, and tribute silver – either they had been his tributaries, or they were desirous of securing his valuable friendship, and now made a voluntary offer of tribute. Perhaps they were the Philistines who had submitted to the yoke of David (2Sa 8:1 Ps 60:8).

the Arabians – the nomad tribes on the south of the Dead Sea, who, seeking the protection of Jehoshaphat after his conquest of Edom, paid their tribute in the way most suitable to their pastoral habits – the present of so many head of cattle.

2Ch 17:12–19. His greatness, captains, and armies.

14. these are the numbers – The warriors were arranged in the army according to their fathers houses. The army of Jehoshaphat, commanded by five great generals and consisting of five unequal divisions, comprised one million one hundred and sixty thousand men, without including those who garrisoned the fortresses. No monarch, since the time of Solomon, equalled Jehoshaphat in the extent of his revenue, in the strength of his fortifications, and in the number of his troops.

Chapter 18
2Ch 18:1–34. Jehoshaphat and Ahab go against Ramoth-gilead.

2. after certain years he went down to Ahab to Samaria – This is word for word, the same as 1Ki 22:1–53.

Chapter 19
2Ch 19:1–4. Jehoshaphat visits his kingdom.

1–4. Jehoshaphat ... returned to his house in peace – (See 2Ch 18:16). Not long after he had resumed the ordinary functions of royalty in Jerusalem, he was one day disturbed by an unexpected and ominous visit from a prophet of the Lord (2Ch 19:2). This was Jehu, of whose father we read in 2Ch 16:7. He himself had been called to discharge the prophetic office in Israel. But probably for his bold rebuke to Baasha (1Ki 16:1), he had been driven by that arbitrary monarch within the territory of Judah, where we now find him with the privileged license of his order, taking the same religious supervision of Jehoshaphat's proceedings as he had formerly done of Baasha's. At the interview here described, he condemned, in the strongest terms, the king of Judah's imprudent and incongruous league with Ahab – God's open enemy (1Ki 22:2) – as an unholy alliance that would be conducive neither to the honor and comfort of his house nor to the best interests of his kingdom. He apprised Jehoshaphat that, on account of that grave offense, 'wrath was upon him from before the Lord,' a judgment that was inflicted soon after (see 2Ch 20:1). The prophet's rebuke, however, was administered in a mingled strain of severity and mildness; for he interposed 'a nevertheless' (2Ch 19:3), which implied that the threatened storm would be averted, in token of the divine approval of his public efforts for the promotion of the true religion, as well as of the sincere piety of his personal character and life.

4. he went out again through the people – This means his reappointing the commissioners of public instruction (2Ch 17:7–9), perhaps with new powers and a larger staff of assistants to overtake every part of the land. The complement of teachers required for that purpose would be easily obtained because the whole tribe of Levites was now concentrated within the kingdom of Judah.

2Ch 19:5–7. His instructions to the judges.

5–7. he set judges in the land – There had been judicial courts established at an early period. But Jehoshaphat was the first king who modified these institutions according to the circumstances of the now fragmentary kingdom of Judah. He fixed local courts in each of the fortified cities, these being the provincial capitals of every district.

2Ch 19:8–11. To the priests and Levites.

8. set of the Levites … priests, and of the chief of the fathers of Israel – A certain number of these three classes constituted a supreme court, which sat in Jerusalem to review appellate cases from the inferior courts. It consisted of two divisions: the first of which had jurisdiction in ecclesiastical matters; the second, in civil, fiscal, and criminal cases. According to others, the two divisions of the supreme court adjudicated: the one according to the law contained in the sacred books; the other according to the law of custom and equity. As in Eastern countries at the present day, the written and unwritten law are objects of separate jurisdiction.

Chapter 20

2Ch 20:1–21. Jehoshaphat, invaded by the Moabites, proclaims a fast.

1. the children of Moab … Ammon, and with them other beside the Ammonites – supposed to be rather the name of a certain people called Mohammonim or Mehunim (2Ch 26:7), who dwelt in Mount Seir – either a branch of the old Edomite race or a separate tribe who were settled there.

2. from beyond the sea on this side Syria – Instead of 'Syria,' some versions read 'Edom,' and many able critics prefer this reading, both because the nomad tribes here mentioned were far from Syria, and because express mention is made of Mount Seir, that is, Edom. The meaning then is: this confederate horde was composed of the different tribes that inhabited the far distant regions bordering on the northern and eastern coasts of the Red Sea. Their progress was apparently by the southern point of the Dead Sea, as far as En-gedi, which, more anciently, was called Hazezon-tamar (Ge 14:7). This is the uniform route taken by the Arabs in their marauding expeditions at the present day; and in coming round the southern end of the Dead Sea, they can penetrate along the low-lying Ghor far north, without letting their movements be known to the tribes and villages west of the mountain chain [ROBINSON]. Thus, anciently, the invading horde in Jehoshaphat's time had marched as far north as En-gedi, before intelligence of their advance was conveyed to the court. En-gedi is recognized in the modern Ainjidy and is situated at a point of the western shore, nearly equidistant from both extremities of the lake [ROBINSON].

3, 4. Jehoshaphat … proclaimed a fast throughout all Judah – Alarmed by the intelligence and conscious of his total inability to repel this host of invaders, Jehoshaphat felt his only refuge was at the horns of the altar. He resolved to employ the aid of his God, and, in conformity with this resolution, he summoned all his subjects to observe a solemn fast at the sanctuary. It was customary with the Hebrew kings to proclaim fasts in perilous circumstances, either in a city, a district, or throughout the entire kingdom, according to the greatness of the emergency. On this occasion, it was a universal fast, which extended to infants (2Ch 20:13; see also Joe 2:15,16 Jon 3:7).

5–13. Jehoshaphat stood … in the house of the Lord, before the new court – that is, the great or outer court (2Ch 4:9) called the new court, probably from having been at that time enlarged or beautified.

6–12. And said, O Lord God of our fathers – This earnest and impressive prayer embraces every topic and argument which, as king and representative of the chosen people, he could urge. Then it concludes with an earnest appeal to the justice of God to protect those who, without provocation, were attacked and who were unable to defend themselves against overwhelming numbers.

14–18. Then upon Jahaziel ... came the Spirit of the Lord – This prophet is not elsewhere mentioned, but his claim to the inspiration of a prophetic spirit was verified by the calm and distinct announcement he gave, both of the manner and the completeness of the deliverance he predicted.

16. they come up by the cliff of Ziz – This seems to have been nothing else than the present pass which leads northwards, by an ascent from En-gedi to Jerusalem, issuing a little below Tekoa. The wilderness of Jeruel was probably the large flat district adjoining the desert of Tekoa, called El-Husasah, from a wady on its northern side [ROBINSON].

18. Jehoshaphat bowed his head ... and all Judah – This attitude was expressive of reverence to God and His Word, of confidence in His promise, and thankfulness for so extraordinary a favor.

19. the Levites ... stood up to praise the Lord – doubtless by the king's command. Their anthem was sung with such a joyful acclaim as showed that they universally regarded the victory as already obtained.

20, 21. as they went forth, Jehoshaphat stood ... Hear me, O Judah, and ye inhabitants of Jerusalem – probably in the gate of Jerusalem, the place of general rendezvous; and as the people were on the eve of setting out, he exhorted them to repose implicit trust in the Lord and His prophet, not to be timid or desponding at sight of the enemy, but to remain firm in the confident assurance of a miraculous deliverance, without their striking a single stroke.

21. he appointed singers ... that they should praise ... as they went out before the army – Having arranged the line of procession, he gave the signal to move forwards. The Levites led the van with their musical instruments; and singing the 136th Psalm, the people went on, not as an army marching against an enemy, but returning in joyful triumph after a victory.

2Ch 20:22–30. The overthrow of his enemies.

22. when they began to sing and to praise the Lord set ambushments against the children of Ammon, Moab, and Mount Seir – Some think that this was done by angels in human form, whose sudden appearance diffused an uncontrollable panic. Others entertain the more probable opinion that, in the camp of this vast horde, composed of different tribes, jealousies and animosities had sprung up, which led to widespread dissensions and fierce feuds, in which they drew the sword against each other. The consequence was, that as the mutual strife commenced when the Hebrew procession set out from Jerusalem, the work of destruction was completed before Jehoshaphat and his people arrived at the battlefield. Thus easy is it for God to make the wrath of man to praise Him, to confound the counsels of His enemies and employ their own passions in defeating the machinations they have devised for the overthrow of His Church and people.

24–26. when Judah came toward the watchtower in the wilderness – Most probably the conical hill, Jebel Fereidis, or Frank Mountain, from the summit of which they obtained the first view of the scene of slaughter. Jehoshaphat and his people found the field strewed with dead bodies, so that they had not to fight at all, but rather to take possession of an immense booty, the collection of which occupied three days. On the fourth they set out on their return to Jerusalem in the same order and joyful mood as they came. The place where they mustered previous to departure was, from their public thanksgiving service, called, 'The Valley of Berachah' ('benediction'), now Wady Bereikut.

2Ch 20:31–37. His reign.

31. Jehoshaphat reigned over Judah – (See 2Ch 24:1).

32. walked in the way of Asa his father, and departed not from it – He was more steadfast and consistently religious (compare 2Ch 15:18).

33. the high places were not taken away – Those on which idolatry was practised were entirely destroyed (2Ch 17:6); but those where the people, notwithstanding the erection of the temple, continued to worship the true God, prudence required to be slowly and gradually abolished, in deference to popular prejudice.

35–37. after this did Jehoshaphat ... join himself with Ahaziah ... to make ships – A combined fleet was built at Ezion-geber, the destination of which was to voyage to Tartessus, but it was wrecked. Jehoshaphat's motive for entering into this partnership was to secure a free passage through Israel, for the vessels were to be conveyed across the Isthmus of Suez, and to sail to the west of Europe from one of the ports of Palestine on the Mediterranean. Eliezer, a prophet, denounced this unholy alliance, and foretold, as divine judgment, the total wreck of the whole fleet. The consequence was, that although Jehoshaphat broke off – in obedience to the divine will – his league with Ahaziah, he formed a new scheme of a merchant fleet, and Ahaziah wished to be admitted a partner [1Ki 22:48]. The proposal of the Israelitish king was respectfully declined [1Ki 22:49]. The destination of this new fleet was to Ophir, because the Israelitish seaports were not accessible to him for the Tartessus trade; but the ships, when just off the docks, were wrecked in the rocky creek of Ezion-geber.

Chapter 21

2Ch 21:1–4. Jehoram succeeds Jehoshaphat.

1–4. Jehoshaphat slept with his fathers ... Jehoram ... reigned – The late king left seven sons; two of them are in our version named Azariah; but in the Hebrew they appear considerably different, the one being spelt 'Azariah,' and the other 'Azariahu.' Though Jehoshaphat had made his family arrangements with prudent precaution, and while he divided the functions of royalty in his lifetime (compare 2Ki 8:16), as well as fixed the succession to the throne in his oldest son, he appointed each of the others to the government of a fenced city, thus providing them with an honorable independence. But this good intentions were frustrated; for no sooner did Jehoram find himself in the sole possession of sovereign power than, from jealousy, or on account of their connections, he murdered all his brothers, together with some leading influential persons who, he suspected, were attached to their interest, or would avenge their deaths. Similar tragedies have been sadly frequent in Eastern courts, where the heir of the crown looks upon his brothers as his most formidable enemies, and is therefore tempted to secure his power by their death.

2Ch 21:5–7. His wicked reign.

6, 7. he walked ... as did the house of Ahab, for he had the daughter of Ahab to wife – The precepts and examples of his excellent father were soon obliterated by his matrimonial alliance with a daughter of the royal house of Israel. Through the influence of Athaliah he abolished the worship of the Lord, and encouraged an introduction of all the corruptions prevalent in the sister kingdom. The divine vengeance was denounced against him, and would have utterly destroyed him and his house, had it not been for a tender regard to the promise made to David (2Sa 7:29 2Ki 8:19).

2Ch 21:8–17. Edom and Libnah revolt.

8–10. the Edomites revolted – That nation had been made dependent by David, and down to the time of Jehoshaphat was governed by a tributary ruler (1Ki 22:47 2Ki 3:9). But that king having been slain in an insurrection at home, his successor thought to ingratiate himself with his new subjects by raising the flag of independence [JOSEPHUS]. The attempt was defeated in the first instance by Jehoram, who possessed all the military establishments of his father; but being renewed unexpectedly, the Edomites succeeded in completely emancipating their country from the yoke of Judah (Ge 27:40). Libnah, which lay on the southern frontier and towards Edom, followed the example of that country.

12–15. there came a writing to him from Elijah the prophet – That prophet's translation having taken place in the reign of Jehoshaphat [2Ki 2:11,12], we must conclude that the name of Elijah has, by the error of a transcriber, been put for that of Elisha.

13–19. hast made Judah and the inhabitants of Jerusalem ... like to the whoredoms of the house of Ahab – that is, introduced the superstitions and vices of Phoenician idolatry. On this account, as well as for his unnatural cruelties, divine vengeance was denounced against him, which was soon after executed exactly as the prophet had foretold. A series of overwhelming calamities befell this wicked king; for in addition to the revolts already mentioned, two neighbouring tribes (see 2Ch 17:11) made hostile incursions on the southern and western portions of his kingdom. His country was ravaged, his capital taken, his palace plundered, his wives carried off, and all his children slain except the youngest. He himself was seized with an incurable dysentery, which, after subjecting him to the most painful suffering for the unusual period of two years, carried him off, a monument of the divine judgment. To complete his degradation, his death was unlamented, his burial unhonored by his subjects. This custom, similar to what obtained in Egypt, seems to have crept in among the Hebrews, of giving funeral honors to their kings, or withholding them, according to the good or bad characters of their reign.

Chapter 22

2Ch 22:1–9. Ahaziah succeeding Jehoram, reigns wickedly.

1. the inhabitants of Jerusalem made Ahaziah ... king – or Jehoahaz (2Ch 21:17). All his older brothers having been slaughtered by the Arab marauders, the throne of Judah rightfully belonged to him as the only legitimate heir.

2. Forty and two years old was Ahaziah when he began to reign – (Compare 2Ki 8:26). According to that passage, the commencement of his reign is dated in the twenty-second year of his age, and, according to this, in the forty-second year of the kingdom of his mother's family [LIGHTFOOT]. 'If Ahaziah ascended the throne in the twenty-second year of his life, he must have been born in his father's nineteenth year. Hence, it may seem strange that he had older brothers; but in the East they marry early, and royal princes had, besides the wife of the first rank, usually concubines, as Jehoram had (2Ch 21:17); he might, therefore, in the nineteenth year of his age, very well have several sons' [KEIL] (compare 2Ch 21:20 2Ki 8:17).

Athaliah the daughter of Omri – more properly, 'granddaughter.' The expression is used loosely, as the statement was made simply for the purpose of intimating that she belonged to that idolatrous race.

3, 4. his mother was his counsellor … they were his counsellors – The facile king surrendered himself wholly to the influence of his mother and her relatives. Athaliah and her son introduced a universal corruption of morals and made idolatry the religion of the court and the nation. By them he was induced not only to conform to the religion of the northern kingdom, but to join a new expedition against Ramoth-gilead (see 2Ki 9:10).

5. went … to war against Hazael, king of Syria – It may be mentioned as a very minute and therefore important confirmation of this part of the sacred history that the names of Jehu and Hazael, his contemporary, have both been found on Assyrian sculptures; and there is also a notice of Ithbaal, king of Sidon, who was the father of Jezebel.

6. Azariah went down – that is, from Ramoth-gilead, to visit the king of Israel, who was lying ill of his wounds at Jezreel, and who had fled there on the alarm of Jehu's rebellion.

9. he sought Ahaziah, and they caught him (for he was hid in Samaria) – (compare 2Ki 9:27–29). The two accounts are easily reconciled. 'Ahaziah fled first to the garden house and escaped to Samaria; but was here, where he had hid himself, taken by Jehu's men who pursued him, brought to Jehu, who was still near or in Jezreel, and at his command slain at the hill Gur, beside Ibleam, in his chariot; that is, mortally wounded with an arrow, so that he, again fleeing, expired at Megiddo' [KEIL]. Jehu left the corpse at the disposal of the king of Judah's attendants, who conveyed it to Jerusalem, and out of respect to his grandfather Jehoshaphat's memory, gave him an honorable interment in the tombs of the kings. **So the house of Ahaziah had no power to keep still the kingdom** – His children were too young to assume the reins of government, and all the other royal princes had been massacred by Jehu (2Ch 22:8).

2Ch 22:10–12. Athaliah, destroying the seed royal save Joash, usurps the kingdom.

10. Athaliah … arose and destroyed all the seed royal – (See on 2Ki 11:1–3). Maddened by the massacre of the royal family of Ahab, she resolved that the royal house of David should have the same fate. Knowing the commission which Jehu had received to extirpate the whole of Ahab's posterity, she expected that he would extend his sword to her. Anticipating his movements, she resolved, as her only defense and security, to usurp the throne and destroy 'the seed royal,' both because they were hostile to the Phoenician worship of Baal, which she was determined to uphold, and because, if one of

the young princes became king, his mother would supersede Athaliah in the dignity of queen mother.

12. he was with them hid in the house of God – Certain persons connected with the priesthood had a right to occupy the buildings in the outer wall, and all within the outer wall was often called the temple. Jehoiada and his family resided in one of these apartments.

Chapter 23

2Ch 23:1–11. Jehoiada makes Joash king.

1. in the seventh year Jehoiada … took the captains of hundreds – (See on 2Ki 11:4; 2Ki 11:17). The five officers mentioned here had been probably of the royal guard, and were known to be – Strongly disaffected to the government of Athaliah.

2. chief of all the fathers of Israel – This name is frequently used in Chronicles for Judah and Benjamin, now all that remained of Israel. Having cautiously entrusted the secret of the young prince's preservation to all the leading men in the kingdom, he enlisted their interest in the royal cause and got their pledge to support it by a secret oath of fidelity.

they came to Jerusalem – The time chosen for the grand discovery was, probably, one of the annual festivals, when there was a general concourse of the nation at the capital.

4–9. This is the thing that ye shall do – The arrangements made for defense are here described. The people were divided into three bodies; one attended as guards to the king, while the other two were posted at all the doors and gates, and the captains and military officers who entered the temple unarmed to lull suspicion, were furnished with weapons out of the sacred armory, where David had deposited his trophies of victory and which was reopened on this occasion.

8. Jehoiada … dismissed not the courses – As it was necessary to have as large a disposable force as he could command on such a crisis, the high priest detained those who, in other circumstances, would have returned home on the expiry of their week of service.

11. Then they brought out the king's son, and put upon him the crown, and gave him the testimony – Some think that the original word rendered 'testimony,' as its derivation warrants, may signify here the regalia, especially the bracelet (2Sa 1:10); and this view they support on the ground that 'gave him' being supplemented, the text properly runs thus, 'put upon him the crown and testimony.' At the same time, it seems equally pertinent to take 'the testimony' in the usual acceptation of that term; and, accordingly, many are of opinion that a roll containing a copy of the law (De 17:18) was placed in the king's hands, which he held as a scepter or truncheon. Others, referring to a custom of Oriental people, who when receiving a letter or document from a highly respected quarter, lift it up to their heads before opening it, consider that Joash, besides the crown, had the book of the law laid upon his head (see Job 31:35,36). **God save the king** – literally, 'Long live the king.'

2Ch 23:12–15. Athaliah slain.

12. Athaliah heard the noise of the people – The unusual commotion, indicated by the blast of the trumpets and the vehement acclamations of the people, drew her attention, or excited her fears. She might have flattered herself that, having slain all the royal family, she was in perfect security; but it is just as likely that, finding on reflection, one had escaped her murderous hands, she might not deem it expedient to institute any enquiries; but the very idea would keep her constantly in a state of jealous suspicion and irritation. In that state of mind, the wicked usurper, hearing across the Tyropoeon the outburst of popular joy, rushed across the bridge to the temple grounds, and, penetrating from a single glance the meaning of the whole scene, raised a shriek of 'Treason!'

13. behold, the king stood at his pillar at the entering in – The king's pillar was in the people's court, opposite that of the priests'. The young king, arrayed in the royal insignia, had been brought out of the inner, to stand forth in the outer court, to the public view. Some think that he stood on the brazen scaffold of Solomon, erected beside the pillar [see on 2Ch 6:13].

14, 15. Slay her not in the house of the Lord … and when she was come to the entering of the horse gate by the king's house, they slew her there – The high priest ordered her immediately to be taken out of the temple grounds and put to death. 'And they laid hands on her; and she went by the way by the which horses came into the king's house: and there was she slain' (2Ki 11:16). 'Now, we are not to suppose that horses came into [the king's house] of residence, but into the king's (horses') house or hippodrome (the gate of the king's mules) [JOSEPHUS], he had built for them on the southeast of the temple, in the immediate vicinity of the horse gate in the valley of Kedron – a valley which was at that time a kind of desecrated place by the destruction of idols and their appurtenances' (2Ki 23:2,6,12) [BARCLAY, *City of the Great King*].

2Ch 23:16. Jehoiada restores the worship of God, and settles the king.

16. Jehoiada made a covenant – (See on 2Ki 11:17).

Chapter 24

2Ch 24:1–14. Joash reigns well all the days of Jehoiada.

1–3. Joash … began to reign – (See on 2Ki 12:1–3).

3. Jehoiada took for him two wives – As Jehoiada was now too old to contract such new alliances, the generality of interpreters apply this statement to the young king.

4–14. Joash was minded to repair the house of the Lord – (See on 2Ki 12:4–16).

2Ch 24:15, 16. Jehoiada being dead.

15, 16. Jehoiada waxed old … and died – His life, protracted to unusual longevity and spent in the service of his country, deserved some tribute of public gratitude, and this was rendered in the posthumous honors that were bestowed on him. Among the Hebrews, intramural interment was prohibited in every city but Jerusalem, and there the exception was made only to the royal family and persons of eminent merit, on whom the distinction was conferred of being buried in the city of David, among the kings, as in the case of Jehoiada.

2Ch 24:17–22. Joash falls into idolatry.

17–22. Now came the princes of Judah, and make obeisance to the king – Hitherto, while Joash occupied the throne, his uncle had held the reins of sovereign power, and by his excellent counsels had directed the young king to such measures as were calculated to promote both the civil and religious interests of the country. The fervent piety, practical wisdom, and inflexible firmness of that sage counsellor exerted immense influence over all classes. But now that the helm of the state-ship was no longer steered by the sound head and firm hand of the venerable high priest, the real merits of Joash's administration appear; and for want of good and enlightened principle, as well as, perhaps, of natural energy of character, he allowed himself to be borne onward in a course which soon wrecked the vessel upon hidden rocks.

the king hearkened unto them – They were secretly attached to idolatry, and their elevated rank affords sad proof how extensively and deeply the nation had become corrupted during the reigns of Jehoram, Ahaziah, and Athaliah. With strong professions of allegiance they humbly requested that they might not be subjected to the continued necessity of frequent and expensive journeys to Jerusalem, but allowed the privilege their fathers had enjoyed of worshipping God in high places at home. They framed their petition in this plausible and least offensive manner, well knowing that, if excused attendance at the temple, they might –

without risk of discovery or disturbance – indulge their tastes in the observance of any private rites they pleased. The weak-minded king granted their petition; and the consequence was, that when they left the house of the Lord God of their fathers, they soon 'served groves and idols.'

18. wrath came upon Judah and Jerusalem – The particular mention of Jerusalem as involved in the sin implies that the neglect of the temple and the consequent idolatry received not only the king's toleration, but his sanction; and it naturally occurs to ask how, at his mature age, such a total abandonment of a place with which all his early recollections were associated can be accounted for. It has been suggested that what he had witnessed of the conduct of many of the priests in the careless performance of the worship, and especially their unwillingness to collect the money, as well as apply a portion of their revenues for the repairs of the temple, had alienated and disgusted him [LE CLERC].

19. Yet he sent prophets – Elisha, Micah, Jehu son of Hanani, Jahaziel son of Zechariah (2Ch 20:14), Eliezer son of Dodavah (2Ch 20:37), lived and taught at that time. But all their prophetic warnings and denunciations were unheeded.

20, 21. the Spirit of God came upon Zechariah the son of Jehoiada – probably a younger son, for his name does not occur in the list of Aaron's successors (1Ch 6:4–47).

stood above the people – Being of the priestly order, he spoke from the inner court, which was considerably higher than that of the people.

and said unto them, Thus saith God, Why transgress ye the commandments of the Lord, that ye cannot prosper – His near relationship to the king might have created a feeling of delicacy and reluctance to interfere; but at length he, too, was prompted by an irresistible impulse to protest against the prevailing impiety. The bold freedom and energy of [Zechariah's] remonstrance, as well as his denunciation of the national calamities that would certainly follow, were most unpalatable to the king; while they so roused the fierce passions of the multitude that a band of miscreants, at the secret instigation of Joash, stoned him to death. This deed of violence involved complicated criminality on the part of the king. It was a horrid outrage on a prophet of the Lord – base ingratitude to a family who had preserved his life – atrocious treatment of a true Hebrew patriot – an illegal and unrighteous exercise of his power and authority as a king.

22. when he died, he said, The Lord look upon it and require it – These dying words, if they implied a vindictive imprecation, exhibit a striking contrast to the spirit of the first Christian martyr (Ac 7:60). But, instead of being the expression of a personal wish, they might be the utterance of a prophetic doom.

2Ch 24:23–27. He is slain by his servants.

23. at the end of the year the host of Syria came up – This invasion took place under the personal conduct of Hazael, whom Joash, to save the miseries of a siege, prevailed on to withdraw his forces by a large present of gold (2Ki 12:18). Most probably, also, he promised the payment of an annual tribute, on the neglect or refusal of which the Syrians returned the following year, and with a mere handful of men inflicted a total and humiliating defeat on the collected force of the Hebrews.

25. they left him in great diseases – The close of his life was embittered by a painful malady, which long confined him to bed.

his own servants conspired against him – These two conspirators (whose fathers were Jews, but their mothers aliens) were probably courtiers, who, having constant access to the bedchamber, could the more easily execute their design.

for the blood of the sons – read 'the son' of Jehoiada. Public opinion seems to have ascribed the disasters of his life and reign to that foul crime. And as the king had long lost the esteem and respect of his subjects, neither horror nor sorrow was expressed for his miserable end!

Chapter 25

2Ch 25:1–4. Amaziah begins to reign well.

1. Amaziah was twenty and five years old – (See 2Ki 14:1–6).

2Ch 25:5–10. Having hired an army of Israelites against the Edomites, at the word of a prophet he loses a hundred talents and dismisses them.

5. Amaziah … made captains – As all who were capable of bearing arms were liable to serve, it was quite natural in making up the muster-roll to class them according to their respective families and to appoint the officers of each corps from the same quarter; so that all the soldiers who formed a regiment were brothers, relatives, friends. Thus the Hebrew troops were closely linked together, and had strong inducements to keep steady in their ranks.

found them three hundred thousand choice men – This was only a fourth part of Jehoshaphat's army (2Ch 17:14–19), showing how sadly the kingdom of Judah had, in the space of eighty-two years, been reduced in population by foreign wars, no less than by internal corruptions. But the full amount of Amaziah's troops may not be here stated.

6. He hired also an hundred thousand mighty men of valour ... for an hundred talents of silver – This sum was paid into the treasury of Jehoahaz – not given as bounty to the mercenaries who were obliged to serve at the sovereign's call; their remuneration consisting only in the booty they might obtain. It was a very paltry pay, compared with the bounty given for a soldier in this country. But it must be remembered that in ancient times campaigns were short and the hazards of the service comparatively small.

7, 8. there came a man of God – sent to dissuade Amaziah from the course he was following, on the ground that 'the Lord is not with Israel.' This statement was perfectly intelligible to the king. But the historian, writing long after, thought it might require explanation, and therefore added the comment, 'with all the children of Ephraim.' Idolatry had long been the prevailing religion in that kingdom, and Ephraim its headquarters. As to the other part of the prophet's advice (2Ch 25:8), considerable obscurity hangs over it, as the text stands; and hence some able critics have suggested the insertion of 'not' in the middle clause, so that the verse will be thus: 'But if thou wilt go [alone], do, be strong for the battle; God shall *not* make thee fall before the enemy.'

10. separated them ... the army ... out of Ephraim ... their anger was greatly kindled against Judah – Amaziah, who knew his position as the Lord's viceroy, complied with the prophet's counsel, and, consenting to forfeit the purchase money of the Israelitish soldiers, discharged them. Exasperated at this treatment, they resolved to indemnify themselves for the loss of their expected booty, and so on their return home they plundered all the towns in their way, committing great havoc both of life and property without any stoppage, as the king of Judah and his army had set out on their expedition (2Ki 14:7).

11. valley of salt – This ravine lies to the south of the Dead Sea. The arms of Amaziah, in reward for his obedience to the divine will, were crowned with victory – ten thousand of the Edomites were slain on the field, and as many taken prisoners, who were put to death by precipitation 'from the top of the rock' [2Ch 25:12]. This rock might be situated in the neighbourhood of the battlefield, but more probably it formed one of the high craggy cliffs of Selah (Petra), the capital of the Edomites, whither Amaziah marched directly from the Valley of Salt, and which he captured (2Ki 14:7). The savage cruelty dealt out to them was either in retaliation for similar barbarities inflicted on the Hebrews, or to strike terror into so rebellious a people for the future. The mode of execution, by dashing against stones (Ps 137:9), was common among many ancient nations.

14–16. Amaziah ... brought the gods of the children of Seir – The Edomites worshipped the sun under different forms and with various rites. But burning incense upon altars was a principal act of worship, and this was the very thing Amaziah is described as having with strange infatuation performed. Whether he had been captivated with the beauty of the images, or hoped by honoring the gods to disarm their spite at him for his conquest and harsh treatment of their votaries, his conduct in establishing these objects of religious homage in Jerusalem was foolish, ignorant, and highly offensive to God, who commissioned a prophet to rebuke him for his apostasy, and threaten him with the calamity that soon after befell him.

16. as he talked with him – Those who were invested with the prophetic character were entitled to counsel kings. Amaziah, had he not been offended by unwelcome truths, would have admitted the claim of this prophet, who was probably the same that had given him counsel previous to the war with Edom. But victory had elated and blinded him.

2Ch 25:17. He provokes Joash to his overthrow.

17. Then Amaziah ... sent to Joash ... Come, let us see one another in the face – (See on 2Ki 14:8–20).

Chapter 26

2Ch 26:1–8. Uzziah succeeds Amaziah and reigns well in the days of Zechariah.

1. Then all the people of Judah took Uzziah – (See on 2Ki 14:21; 2Ki 15:1).

2. He built Eloth – or, 'He it was who built Eloth.' The account of the fortifications of this port on the Red Sea, which Uzziah restored to the kingdom of Judah (2Ch 33:13), is placed before the chronological notices (2Ch 26:3), either on account of the importance attached to the conquest of Eloth, or from the desire of the historian to introduce Uzziah as the king, who was known as the conqueror of Eloth. Besides, it indicates that the conquest occurred in the early part of his reign, that it was important as a port, and that Hebrew merchants maintained the old trade between it and the countries of the East [BERTHEAU].

5. he sought God in the days of Zechariah – a wise and pious counsellor, who was skilled in understanding the meaning and lessons of the ancient prophecies, and who wielded a salutary influence over Uzziah.

6, 7. he went forth and warred against the Philistines – He overcame them in many engagements – dismantled their towns, and erected fortified cities in various parts of the country, to keep them in subjection.

Jabneh – the same as Jabneel (Jos 15:11).

7. Gur-baal – thought by some to be Gerar, and by others Gebal.

8. the Ammonites gave gifts – The countries east of the Jordan became tributary to him, and by the rapid succession and extent of his victories, his kingdom was extended to the Egyptian frontier.

2Ch 26:9, 10. His buildings.

9. Uzziah built towers in Jerusalem – whence resistance could be made, or missiles discharged against assailants. The sites of the principal of these towers were: at the corner gate (2Ch 25:23), the northwest corner of the city; at the valley gate on the west, where the Joppa gate now is; at the 'turning' – a curve in the city wall on the eastern side of Zion. The town, at this point, commanded the horse gate which defended Zion and the temple hill on the southeast [BERTHEAU].

10. Also he built towers in the desert – for the threefold purpose of defense, of observation, and of shelter to his cattle. He dug also a great many wells, for he loved and encouraged all branches of agriculture. Some of these 'were in the desert,' that is, in the district to the southeast of Jerusalem, on the west of the Dead Sea, an extensive grazing district 'in the low country' lying between the mountains of Judah and the Mediterranean; 'and in the plains,' east of the Jordan, within the territory of Reuben (De 4:43 Jos 20:8).

in Carmel – This mountain, being within the boundary of Israel, did not belong to Uzziah; and as it is here placed in opposition to the vine-bearing mountains, it is probably used, not as a proper name, but to signify, as the word denotes, 'fruitful fields' (*Margin*).

2Ch 26:11–15. His host, and engines of war.

11–15. an host of fighting men, that went out to war by bands – He raised a strong body of militia, divided into companies or regiments of uniform size, which served in rotation. The enumeration was performed by two functionaries expert in the drawing up of military muster-rolls, under the superintendence of Hananiah, one of the high officers of the crown. The army consisted of 307,500 picked men, under the command of two thousand gallant officers, chiefs or heads of fathers' houses, so that each fathers house formed a distinct band. They were fully equipped with every kind of military accoutrements, from brazen helmets, a habergeon or coat of mail, to a sling for stones.

15. he made ... engines, invented by cunning men ... to shoot arrows and great stones – This is the first notice that occurs in history of the use of machines for throwing projectiles. The invention is apparently ascribed to the reign of Uzziah, and PLINY expressly says they originated in Syria.

he was marvellously helped till he was strong – He conducted himself as became the viceroy of the Divine King, and prospered.

2Ch 26:16–21. He invades the priest's office, and is smitten with leprosy.

16–21. he transgressed against the Lord – (See on 2Ki 15:5). This daring and wicked act is in both records traced to the intoxicating influence of overweening pride and vanity. But here the additional circumstances are stated, that his entrance was opposed, and strong remonstrances made (1Ch 6:10) by the high priest, who was accompanied by eighty inferior priests. Rage and threats were the only answers he deigned to return, but God took care to vindicate the sacredness of the priestly office. At the moment the king lifted the censer, He struck him with leprosy. The earthquake mentioned (Am 1:1) is said to have been felt at the moment [JOSEPHUS].

21. dwelt in a several house – in an infirmary [BERTHEAU].

23. they buried him ... in the field of the burial which belonged to the kings – He was interred not in, but near, the sepulcher of the kings, as the corpse of a leper would have polluted it.

Chapter 27

2Ch 27:1–4. Jotham, reigning well, prospers.

1. Jotham was twenty and five years old – (See on 2Ki 15:32–35).

His mother's name ... Jerushah, the daughter of Zadok – or descendant of the famous priest of that name [2Sa 8:17].

2. he did that which was right – The general rectitude of his government is described by representing it as conducted on the excellent principles which had guided the early part of his father's reign.

the people did yet corruptly – (See 2Ki 15:35); but the description here is more emphatic, that though Jotham did much to promote the good of his kingdom and aimed at a thorough reformation in religion, the widespread and inveterate wickedness of the people frustrated all his laudable efforts.

3. He built the high gate of the house of the Lord – situated on the north – that portion of the temple hill which was high compared with the southern part – hence 'the higher,' or upper gate (see on 2Ki 15:35). **and on the wall of Ophel** – *Hebrew*, 'the Ophel,' that is, the mound, or eminence on the southeastern slope of the temple mount, a ridge lying between the valleys Kedron and Tyropoeon, called 'the lower city' [JOSEPHUS]. He

built much – having the same desire as his father to secure the defense of Jerusalem in every direction.

4. in the mountains of Judah, and in the forests he built castles and towers – that is, in the elevated and wooded spots where fortified cities could not be placed, he erected castles and towers.

2Ch 27:5. He subdues the Ammonites.

5. He fought also with the king of the Ammonites – This invasion he not only repelled, but, pursuing the Ammonites into their own territory, he imposed on them a yearly tribute, which, for two years, they paid. But when Rezin, king of Syria, and Pekah, king of Israel, combined to attack the kingdom of Judah, they took the opportunity of revolting, and Jotham was too distracted by other matters to attempt the reconquest (see on 2Ki 15:37).

Chapter 28

2Ch 28:1–21. Ahaz, reigning wickedly, is afflicted by the Syrians.

1–4. Ahaz was twenty years old – (See on 2Ki 16:1–4). This prince, discarding the principles and example of his excellent father, early betrayed a strong bias to idolatry. He ruled with an arbitrary and absolute authority, and not as a theocratic sovereign: he not only forsook the temple of God, but embraced first the symbolic worship established in the sister kingdom, and afterwards the gross idolatry practised by the Canaanites.

5–7. the Lord ... delivered him into the hand of the king of Syria ... he was also delivered into the hand of the King of Israel – These verses, without alluding to the formation of a confederacy between the Syrian and Israelitish kings to invade the kingdom of Judah, or relating the commencement of the war in the close of Jotham's reign (2Ki 15:37), give the issue only of some battles that were fought in the early part of the campaign.

delivered him ... smote him ... he was also delivered – that is, his army, for Ahaz was not personally included in the number either of the slain or the captives. The slaughter of one hundred twenty thousand in one day was a terrible calamity, which, it is expressly said, was inflicted as a judgment on Judah, 'because they had forsaken the Lord God of their fathers.' Among the slain were some persons of distinction:

7. Maaseiah the king's son – the sons of Ahaz being too young to take part in a battle, this individual must have been a younger son of the late King Jotham;

Azrikam the governor of the house – that is, 'the palace'; and

Elkanah that was next to the king – that is, the vizier or prime minister (Ge 41:40 Es 10:3). These were all cut down on the field by Zichri, an Israelitish warrior, or as some think, ordered to be put to death after the battle. A vast number of captives also fell into the power of the conquerors; and an equal division of war prisoners being made between the allies, they were sent off under a military escort to the respective capitals of Syria and Israel (2Ch 28:8).

8–14. the children of Israel carried away captive of their brethren two hundred thousand – These captives included a great number of women, boys, and girls, a circumstance which creates a presumption that the Hebrews, like other Orientals, were accompanied in the war by multitudes of non-combatants (see on Jud 4:8). The report of these 'brethren,' being brought as captives to Samaria, excited general indignation among the better-disposed inhabitants; and Oded, a prophet, accompanied by the princes (2Ch 28:12, compared with 2Ch 28:14), went out, as the escort was approaching, to prevent the disgraceful outrage of introducing such prisoners into the city. The officers of the squadron were, of course, not to blame; they were simply doing their military duty in conducting those prisoners of war to their destination. But Oded clearly showed that the Israelitish army had gained the victory – not by the superiority of their arms, but in consequence of the divine judgment against Judah. He forcibly exposed the enormity of the offense of keeping 'their brethren' as slaves got in war. He protested earnestly against adding this great offense of unnatural and sinful cruelty (Le 25:43,44 Mic 2:8,9) to the already overwhelming amount of their own national sins. Such was the effect of his spirited remonstrance and the opposing tide of popular feeling, that 'the armed men left the captives and the spoil before the princes and all the congregation.'

15. the men which were expressed by name rose up – These were either the 'heads of the children of Ephraim' (mentioned 2Ch 28:12), or some other leading individuals chosen for the benevolent office. Under their kindly superintendence, the prisoners were not only released, but out of the spoils were comfortably relieved with food and clothing, and conveyed as far as Jericho on their way back to their own homes. This is a beautiful incident, and full of interest, as showing that even at this period of national decline, there were not a few who steadfastly adhered to the law of God.

16. At that time did king Ahaz send unto the kings of Assyria – 'kings,' the plural for the singular, which is found in many ancient versions. 'At that time,' refers to the period of Ahaz's great distress, when, after a succession of defeats, he retreated within the walls of Jerusalem. Either in the same or a subsequent campaign, the Syrian and Israelitish allies marched there to besiege him (see on 2Ki 16:7). Though delivered from this danger, other enemies infested his dominions both on the south and the west.

17. again the Edomites had come and smitten Judah – This invasion must have been after Rezin (at the beginning of the recent Syro-Israelitish war), had released that people from the yoke of Judah (2Ch 15:11; compare 2Ki 16:6).

18. Gederoth – on the Philistine frontier (Jos 15:41).

Shocho – or Socoh (Jos 15:35), now Shuweikeh, a town in the Valley of Judah (see on 1Sa 17:1). **Gimzo** – now Jimza, a little east of Ludd (Lydda) [ROBINSON]. All these disasters, by which the 'Lord brought Judah low,' were because of Ahaz, king of Israel (Judah), see 2Ch 21:2 24:16 28:27, who made Judah naked, and transgressed sore against the Lord.

20. Tilgath-pilneser … distressed him, but strengthened him not – that is, notwithstanding the temporary relief which Tilgath-pilneser afforded him by the conquest of Damascus and the slaughter of Rezin (2Ki 16:9), little advantage resulted from it, for Tilgath-pilneser spent the winter in voluptuous revelry at Damascus; and the connection formed with the Assyrian king was eventually a source of new and greater calamities and humiliation to the kingdom of Judah (2Ch 28:2,3).

2Ch 28:22–27. His idolatry in his distress.

22. in the time of his distress did he trespass yet more against the Lord – This infatuated king surrendered himself to the influence of idolatry and exerted his royal authority to extend it, with the intensity of a passion – with the ignorance and servile fear of a heathen (2Ch 28:23) and a ruthless defiance of God (see on 2Ki 16:10–20).

Chapter 29

2Ch 29:1, 2. Hezekiah's good reign.

1. Hezekiah began to reign – (see on 2Ki 18:1). His mother's name, which, in 2Ki 18:2, appears in an abridged form, is here given in full.

2Ch 29:3-11. He restores religion.

3. in the first year of his reign, in the first month – not the first month after his accession to the throne, but in Nisan, the first month of the sacred year, the season appointed for the celebration of the passover.

he opened the doors of the house of the Lord – which had been closed up by his father (2Ch

28:24). **and repaired them** – or embellished them (compare 2Ki 18:16).

4, 5. the east street – the court of the priests, which fronted the eastern gate of the temple. Assembling the priests and Levites there, he enjoined them to set about the immediate purification of the temple. It does not appear that the order referred to the removal of idols, for objects of idolatrous homage could scarcely have been put there, seeing the doors had been shut up (2Ch 29:3); but in its forsaken and desolate state the temple and its courts had been polluted by every kind of impurity.

6, 7. our fathers have trespassed – Ahaz and the generation contemporary with him were specially meant, for they 'turned away their faces from the habitation of the Lord,' and whether or not they turned east to the rising sun, they abandoned the worship of God. They 'shut up the doors of the porch,' so that the sacred ritual was entirely discontinued.

8, 9. Wherefore the wrath of the Lord was upon Judah and Jerusalem – This pious king had the discernment to ascribe all the national calamities that had befallen the kingdom to the true cause, namely, apostasy from God. The country had been laid waste by successive wars of invasion, and its resources drained. Many families mourned members of their household still suffering the miseries of foreign captivity; all their former prosperity and glory had fled; and to what was this painful and humiliating state of affairs to be traced, but to the manifest judgment of God upon the kingdom for its sins?

10, 11. Now it is in mine heart to make a covenant with the Lord God – Convinced of the sin and bitter fruits of idolatry, Hezekiah intended to reverse the policy of his father, and to restore, in all its ancient purity and glory, the worship of the true God. His commencement of this resolution at the beginning of his reign attests his sincere piety. It also proves the strength of his conviction that righteousness exalteth a nation; for, instead of waiting till his throne was consolidated, he devised measures of national reformation at the beginning of his reign and vigorously faced all the difficulties which, in such a course, he had to encounter, after the people's habits had so long been moulded to idolatry. His intentions were first disclosed to this meeting of the priests and Levites – for the agency of these officials was to be employed in carrying them into effect.

2Ch 29:12-36. The house of God cleansed.

12-19. Then the Levites arose – Fourteen chiefs undertook the duty of collecting and preparing their brethren for the important work of cleansing the Lord's house. Beginning with the outer courts – that of the priests and that of the people – the cleansing of these occupied eight days, after which they set themselves to purify the interior; but as the Levites were not allowed to enter within the walls of the temple, the priest brought all the sweepings out to the porch, where they were received by the Levites and thrown into the brook Kedron. This took eight days more. At the end of this period they repaired to the palace and announced that not only had the whole of the sacred edifice, within and without, undergone a thorough purification, but all the vessels which the late king had taken away and applied to a common use in his palace, had been restored, 'and sanctified'.

20–30. Then Hezekiah the king rose early, and gathered the rulers of the city – His anxiety to enter upon the expiatory service with all possible despatch, now that the temple had been properly prepared for it, prevented his summoning all the representatives of Israel. The requisite number of victims having been provided, and the officers of the temple having sanctified themselves according to the directions of the law, the priests were appointed to offer sacrifices of atonement successively, for 'the kingdom,' that is, for the sins of the king and his predecessors; for 'the sanctuary,' that is, for the sins of the priests themselves and for the desecration of the temple; 'and for Judah,' that is, for the people who, by their voluntary consent, were involved in the guilt of the national apostasy. Animals of the kinds used in sacrifice were offered by sevens, that number indicating completeness. The Levites were ordered to praise God with musical instruments, which, although not originally used in the tabernacle, had been enlisted in the service of divine worship by David on the advice of the prophets Gad and Nathan, as well as calculated to animate the devotions of the people. At the close of the special services of the occasion, namely, the offering of atonement sacrifices, the king and all civic rulers who were present joined in the worship. A grand anthem was sung (2Ch 29:30) by the choir, consisting of some of the psalms of David and Asaph, and a great number of thank offerings, praise offerings, and freewill burnt offerings were presented at the invitation of the king.

31. Hezekiah … said, Now ye have consecrated yourselves unto the Lord, come near – This address was made to the priests as being now, by the sacrifice of the expiation offerings, anew consecrated to the service of God and qualified to resume the functions of their sacred office (Ex 28:41 29:32).

the congregation brought in – that is, the body of civic rulers present.

34–36. the priests were too few, … wherefore their brethren the Levites did help them – The skins of beasts intended as peace offerings might be taken off by the officers, because, in such cases, the carcass was not wholly laid upon the altar; but animals meant for burnt offerings which were wholly consumed by fire could be flayed by the priests alone, not even the Levites being allowed to touch them, except in cases of unavoidable necessity (2Ch 35:11). The duty being assigned by the law to the priests (Le 1:6), was construed by consuetudinary practice as an exclusion of all others not connected with the Aaronic family.

for the Levites were more upright in heart to sanctify themselves than the priests – that is, displayed greater alacrity than the priests. This service was hastened by the irrepressible solicitude of the king. Whether it was that many of the priests, being absent in the country, had not arrived in time – whether from the long interruption of the public duties, some of them had relaxed in their wonted attentions to personal cleanliness, and had many preparations to make – or whether from some having participated in the idolatrous services introduced by Ahaz, they were backward in repairing to the temple – a reflection does seem to be cast upon their order as dilatory and not universally ready for duty (compare 2Ch 30:15). Thus was the newly consecrated temple reopened to the no small joy of the pious king and all the people.

Chapter 30

2Ch 30:1–12. Hezekiah proclaims a passover.

1–5. Hezekiah sent to all … Judah … to come to … Jerusalem, to keep the passover – This great religious festival had not been regularly observed by the Hebrews in their national capacity for a long time because of the division of the kingdom and the many disorders that had followed that unhappy event. Hezekiah longed extremely to see its observance revived; and the expression of his wishes having received a hearty response from the princes and chief men of his own kingdom, the preparatory steps were taken for a renewed celebration of the national solemnity.

letters also to Ephraim and Manasseh – The names of these leading tribes are used for the whole kingdom of Israel. It was judged impossible, however, that the temple, the priests, and people could be all duly sanctified at the usual time appointed for the anniversary, namely, the fourteenth day of the first month (Nisan). Therefore it was resolved, instead of postponing the feast till another year, to observe it on the fourteenth day of the second month; a liberty which, being in certain circumstances (Nu 9:6–13) granted to individuals, might, it was believed, be allowed to all the people. Hezekiah's proclamation was, of course, authoritative in his own kingdom, but it could not have been made and circulated in all the towns and villages of the neighbouring kingdom without the concurrence, or at least the permission, of the Israelitish sovereign. Hoshea, the reigning king, is described as, though evil in some respects, yet more favorably disposed to religious liberty than any of his predecessors since the separation of the kingdom. This is thought to be the meaning of the mitigating clause in his character (2Ki 17:2).

6. the posts – that is, runners, or royal messengers, who were taken from the king's bodyguard (2Ch 23:1,2). Each, well mounted, had a certain number of miles to traverse. Having performed his course, he was relieved by another, who had to scour an equal extent of ground; so that, as the government messengers were despatched in all directions, public edicts were speedily diffused throughout the country. The proclamation of Hezekiah was followed by a verbal address from himself, piously urging the duty, and setting forth the advantages, of a return to the pure faith and institutions which God had delivered to their ancestors through Moses.

the remnant of you, that are escaped out of the hand of the kings of Assyria – This implies that several expeditions against Israel had already been made by Assyrian invaders – by Pul (2Ki 15:19), but none of the people were then removed; at a later period by Tiglath-pileser, when it appears that numbers among the tribes east of Jordan (1Ch 5:26), and afterwards in the northern parts of Israel (2Ki 15:20), were carried into foreign exile. The invasion of Shalmaneser cannot be alluded to, as it did not take place till the sixth year of Hezekiah's reign (2Ki 17:6 18:9–12).

10–12. the posts passed from city to city – It is not surprising that after so long a discontinuance of the sacred festival, this attempt to revive it should, in some quarters, have excited ridicule and opposition. Accordingly, among the tribes of Ephraim, Manasseh, and Zebulun, Hezekiah's messengers met with open insults and ill usage. Many, however, in these very districts, as well as throughout the kingdom of the ten tribes, generally complied with the invitation; while, in the kingdom of Judah, there was one unanimous feeling of high expectation and pious delight. The concourse that repaired to Jerusalem on the occasion was very great, and the occasion was ever after regarded as one of the greatest passovers that had ever been celebrated.

2Ch 30:13–27. The assembly destroys the altars of idolatry.

14. they arose and took away the altars that were in Jerusalem – As a necessary preparation for the right observance of the approaching solemnity, the removal of the altars, which Ahaz

had erected in the city, was resolved upon (2Ch 28:24); for, as the people of God, the Hebrews were bound to extirpate all traces of idolatry; and it was a happy sign and pledge of the influence of the Spirit pervading the minds of the people when they voluntarily undertook this important preliminary work.

15. the priests and the Levites were ashamed – Though the Levites are associated in this statement, the priests were principally referred to; those of them who had been dilatory or negligent in sanctifying themselves (2Ch 29:34) were put to the blush and stimulated to their duty by the greater alacrity and zeal of the people.

16–18. the priests sprinkled the blood, which they received of the hand of the Levites – This was a deviation from the established rules and practices in presenting the offerings of the temple. The reason was, that many present on the occasion having not sanctified themselves, the Levites slaughtered the paschal victims (see on 2Ch 35:5) for everyone that was unclean. At other times the heads of families killed the lambs themselves, the priests receiving the blood from their hands and presenting it on the altar. Multitudes of the Israelites, especially from certain tribes (2Ch 30:18), were in this unsanctified state, and yet they ate the passover – an exceptional feature and one opposed to the law (Nu 9:6); but this exception was allowed in answer to Hezekiah's prayer (2Ch 30:18–20).

20. the Lord … healed the people – We imagine the whole affair to have been the following: In consequence of their transgressions they had cause to fear disease and even death (Le 15:31). Hezekiah prayed for the nation, which was on the point of being diseased, and might therefore be regarded as sick already [BERTHEAU].

21–24. the children of Israel … kept the feast – The time appointed by the law for the continuance of the feast was seven days [Ex 12:15 13:6 Le 23:6]; but in consequence of its having been allowed to fall so long into desuetude, they doubled the period of celebration and kept it fourteen days with unabated satisfaction and joy. Materials for the additional sacrificial meals were supplied by the munificence of the king and the princes.

24. and a great number of priests sanctified themselves – so that there would be a sufficient number of hands for the additional services.

Chapter 31

2Ch 31:1–10. The people forward in destroying idolatry.

1. all Israel … present went out to the cities of Judah – The solemnities of this paschal season left a deep and salutary impression on the minds of the assembled worshippers; attachment to the ancient institutions of their country was extensively revived; ardor in the service of God animated every bosom; and under the impulse of the devout feelings inspired by the occasion, they took measures at the close of the passover for extirpating idolatrous statues and altars out of every city, as at the beginning of the festival they had done in Jerusalem.

Judah and Benjamin – denote the southern kingdom.

Ephraim also and Manasseh – refer to the northern kingdom. This unsparing demolition of the monuments of idolatry would receive all encouragement from the king and public authorities of the former; and the force of the popular movement was sufficient to effect the same results among the tribes of Israel, whatever opposition the power of Hoshea or the invectives of some profane brethren might have made. Thus the reign of idolatry being completely overthrown and the pure worship of God re-established throughout the land, the people returned every one to his own home, in the confident expectation that, through the divine blessing, they would enjoy a happy future of national peace and prosperity.

2–5. Hezekiah appointed the courses of the priests – The king now turned his attention to provide for the orderly performance of the temple-worship – arranging the priests and Levites in their courses, assigning to every one his proper place and functions – and issuing edicts for the regular payment of those dues from which the revenues of the sanctuary were derived. To set a proper example to his subjects, his own proportion was announced in the first instance, for to the king it belonged, out of his privy purse, to defray the expenses of the altar, both stated and occasional (Nu 28:3,4,9,11,19); and in making this contribution from his own means, Hezekiah followed the course which David and Solomon had taken before him (see 2Ch 8:14 1Ki 9:25). Afterwards he reappointed the people's dues to the temple; and from its being necessary to issue a royal mandate in reference to this matter, it appears that the sacred tribute had been either totally neglected, or (as the idolatrous princes were known to appropriate it for their own purposes) the people had in many cases refused or evaded the duty. But with the improved state of public feeling, Hezekiah's commandment was readily obeyed, and contributions of first-fruits and tithes were poured in with great liberality from all parts of Judah, as well as from Israel. The first-fruits, even of some articles of produce that were unfit for sacrifice (Le 2:11), such as honey (*Margin*, 'dates'), were appropriated to the priests (Nu 18:12,13 De 18:4). The tithes (Le 27:31) were intended for the support of the whole Levitical tribe (Nu 18:8,20,24).

6, 7. and laid them by heaps – The contributions began to be sent in shortly after the cele-

bration of the passover, which had taken place in the middle of the second month. Some time would elapse before the king's order reached all parts of the kingdom. The wheat harvest occurred in the third month, so that the sheaves of that grain, being presented before any other, formed 'the foundation,' an under-layer in the corn stores of the temple. The first-fruits of their land produce which were successively sent in all the summer till the close of the fruit and vintage season, that is, the seventh month, continued to raise heap upon heap.

9. Hezekiah questioned with the priests and the Levites concerning the heaps – The object of his enquiries was to ascertain whether the supplies afforded the prospect of a sufficient maintenance for the members of the sacred order.

10. Azariah … answered … we have had enough – This is probably the person mentioned (2Ch 26:17), and his reply was to the following purport: There has been an abundant harvest, and a corresponding plenty in the incoming of first-fruits and tithes; the people have testified their gratitude to Him who has crowned the year with His goodness by their liberality towards His servants.

2Ch 31:11–19. Hezekiah appoints officers to dispose of the tithes.

11–18. Hezekiah commanded to prepare chambers in the house of the Lord – storehouses, granaries, or cellars; either the old ones, which had been allowed through neglect to fall into decay, were to be repaired, or additional ones built. Private individuals brought their own first-fruits to the temple; but the tithes were levied by the Levites, who kept a faithful account of them in their several places of abode and transmitted the allotted proportion to the priests. Officers were appointed to distribute equal rations to all in the cities of the priests who, from age or other reasons, could not repair to the temple. With the exception of children under three years of age – an exception made probably from their being considered too young to receive solid food – lists were kept of the number and age of every male; of priests according to their fathers' house, and Levites from twenty years (see Nu 4:3 28:24 1Ch 23:24). But, besides, provision was also made for their wives, daughters, and servants.

18. for in their set office they sanctified themselves – This is the reason assigned for providing for the wives and children out of the revenues of the sanctuary, that priests, withdrawing from those secular pursuits by which they might have maintained their households, devoted themselves entirely to the functions of the ministry.

2Ch 31:20, 21. His sincerity of heart.

20. Hezekiah ... wrought that which was good and right – He displayed the qualities of a constitutional king, in restoring and upholding the ancient institutions of the kingdom; while his zealous and persevering efforts to promote the cause of true religion and the best interests of his subjects entitled him to be ranked with the most illustrious of his predecessors (2Ki 18:15).

Chapter 32

2Ch 32:1–20. Sennacherib invades Judah.

1. After these things, and the establishment thereof – that is, the restoration of the temple-worship. The precise date is given, 2Ki 18:13. Determined to recover the independence of his country, Hezekiah had decided to refuse to pay the tribute which his father had bound himself to pay to Assyria.

Sennacherib ... entered into Judah, and encamped against the fenced cities – The whole land was ravaged; the strong fortresses of Ashdod (Isa 20:1) and Lachish had fallen; the siege of Libnah had commenced, when the king of Judah, doubting his ability to resist, sent to acknowledge his fault, and offer terms of submission by paying the tribute. The commencement of this Assyrian war was disastrous to Hezekiah (2Ki 18:13). But the misfortunes of the early period of the war are here passed over, as the historian hastens to relate the remarkable deliverance which God wrought for His kingdom of Judah.

2–8. when Hezekiah saw that Sennacherib ... was purposed to fight against Jerusalem – An account of the means taken to fortify Jerusalem against the threatened siege is given only in this passage. The polluting or filling up of wells, and the altering of the course of rivers, is an old practice that still obtains in the wars of the East. Hezekiah's plan was to cover the fountain heads, so that they might not be discovered by the enemy, and to carry the water by subterranean channels or pipes into the city – a plan which, while it would secure a constant supply to the inhabitants, would distress the besiegers, as the country all around Jerusalem was very destitute of water.

4. So there was gathered much people ... who stopped all the fountains, and the brook that ran through the midst of the land – 'Where these various fountains were, we have now no positive means of ascertaining; though En-rogel, and the spring now called the Virgin's Fount, may well be numbered among them. Josephus mentions the existence of various fountains without the city, but does not mention any of them in this connection but Siloam.

'The brook,' however, is located with sufficient precision to enable us to trace it very definitely. We are told that it 'ran through the midst of a land.' Now a stream running through either the Kedron or Hinnom Valley, could, in no proper sense, be said to run through the midst of the land, but one flowing through the true Gihon valley, and separating Akra and Zion from Bezetha, Moriah, and Ophel, as a stream once, doubtless, did, could, with peculiar propriety, be said to run through the midst of the land on which the [Holy] City was built. And that this is the correct meaning of the phrase is not only apparent from the force of circumstances, but is positively so declared in the Septuagint, where, moreover, it is called a 'river,' which, at least, implies a much larger stream than the Kedron, and comports well with the marginal reading, where it is said to overflow through the midst of the land. Previous to the interference of man, there was, no doubt, a very copious stream that gushed forth in the upper portion of that shallow, basin-like concavity north of Damascus Gate, which is unquestionably the upper extremity of the Gihon valley, and pursuing its meandering course through this valley, entered the Tyropoeon at its great southern curve, down which it flowed into the valley of the Kedron' [Barclay, City of the Great King].

5, 6. he strengthened himself – He made a careful inspection of the city defenses for the purpose of repairing breaches in the wall here, renewing the masonry there, raising projecting machines to the towers, and especially fortifying the lower portion of Zion, that is, Millo, '(in) the original city of David.' 'In' is a supplement of our translators, and the text reads better without it, for it was not the whole city that was repaired, but only the lower portion of Zion, or the original 'city of David'.

6. he ... gathered them together ... in the street – that is, the large open space at the gate of Eastern cities. Having equipped his soldiers with a full suit of military accoutrements, he addressed them in an animated strain, dwelling on the motives they had to inspire courage and confidence of success, especially on their consciousness of the favor and helping power of God.

9–20. (See on 2Ki 18:17–35; also 2Ki 19:8–34).

18. they cried with a loud voice ... unto the people of Jerusalem ... on the wall – It appears that the wall on the west side of the city reached as far to the side of the uppermost pool of Gihon at that time as it does now, if not farther; and the wall was so close to that pool that those sent to negotiate with the Assyrian general answered him in their own tongue (see on 2Ki 18:27).

2Ch 32:21–23. An angel destroys the Assyrians.

21. an angel … cut off all the mighty men – (See on 2Ki 19:35–37).

2Ch 32:24–26. Hezekiah's sickness and recovery.

24. In those days Hezekiah was sick to the death – (See on 2Ki 20:1–11).

2Ch 32:27–33. His riches and works.

27–29. he had exceeding much riches and honour – (compare 2Ki 20:13 Isa 39:2). A great portion of his personal wealth, like that of David and Uzziah, consisted in immense possessions of agricultural and pastoral produce. Besides, he had accumulated large treasures in gold, silver, and precious things, which he had taken as spoils from the Philistines, and which he had received as presents from neighbouring states, among which he was held in great honor as a king under the special protection of Heaven. Much of his great wealth he expended in improving his capital, erecting forts, and promoting the internal benefit of his kingdom.

30. stopped the … watercourse of Gihon, and brought it … to the west side of the city – (Compare 2Ki 20:20). Particular notice is here taken of the aqueduct, as among the greatest of Hezekiah's works. 'In exploring the subterranean channel conveying the water from Virgin's Fount to Siloam, I discovered a similar channel entering from the north, a few yards from its commencement; and on tracing it up near the Mugrabin gate, where it became so choked with rubbish that it could be traversed no farther, I there found it turn to the *west* in the direction of the south end of the cleft, or saddle, of Zion, and if this channel was not constructed for the purpose of conveying the waters of Hezekiah's aqueduct, I am unable to suggest any purpose to which it could have been applied. Perhaps the reason why it was not brought down on the Zion side, was that Zion was already well-watered in its lower portion by the Great Pool, "the lower pool of Gihon." And accordingly WILLIAMS [*Holy City*] renders this passage, "He stopped the upper outflow of the waters of Gihon, and led them down westward to the city" ' [BARCLAY, *City of the Great King*]. The construction of this aqueduct required not only masonic but engineering skill; for the passage was bored through a continuous mass of rock. Hezekiah's pool or reservoir made to receive the water within the northwest part of the city still remains. It is an oblong quadrangular tank, two hundred forty feet in length, from one hundred forty-four to one hundred fifty in breadth, but, from recent excavations, appears to have extended somewhat further towards the north.

31. in the business of the ambassadors who sent … to inquire of the wonder that was done in the land – They brought a present (2Ch 32:23; see on 2Ki 20:12,13), and a letter of congratulation on his recovery, in which particular enquiries were made about the miracle of the sun's retrocession – a natural phenomenon that could not fail to excite great interest and curiosity at Babylon, where astronomy was so much studied. At the same time, there is reason to believe that they proposed a defensive league against the Assyrians.

God left him, to try him – Hezekiah's offense was not so much in the display of his military stores and treasures, as in not giving to God the glory both of the miracle and of his recovery, and thus leading those heathen ambassadors to know Him.

Chapter 33

2Ch 33:1–10. Manasseh's wicked reign.

1, 2. Manasseh … did that which was evil in the sight of the Lord – (See on 2Ki 21:1–16).

2Ch 33:11–19. He is carried unto Babylon, where he humbles himself before God, and is restored to his kingdom.

11. the captains of the host of the king of Assyria – This king was Esar-haddon. After having devoted the first years of his reign to the consolidation of his government at home, he turned his attention to repair the loss of the tributary provinces west of the Euphrates, which, on the disaster and death of Sennacherib, had taken the opportunity of shaking off the Assyrian yoke. Having overrun Palestine and removed the remnant that were left in the kingdom of Israel, he despatched his generals, the chief of whom was Tartan (Isa 20:1), with a portion of his army for the reduction of Judah also. In a successful attack upon Jerusalem, they took multitudes of captives, and got a great prize, including the king himself, among the prisoners.

took Manasseh among the thorns – This may mean, as is commonly supposed, that he had hid himself among a thicket of briers and brambles. We know that the Hebrews sometimes took refuge from their enemies in thickets (1Sa 13:6). But, instead of the *Hebrew, Bacochim*, 'among the thorns', some versions read *Bechayim*, 'among the living', and so the passage would be 'took him alive.'

bound him with fetters, and carried him to Babylon – The *Hebrew* word rendered 'fetters' denotes properly two chains of brass. The humiliating state in which Manasseh appeared before the Assyrian monarch may be judged of by a picture on a tablet in the Khorsabad palace, representing prisoners led bound into the king's presence. 'The captives represented appear to be inhabitants of Palestine. Behind the prisoners stand four persons with inscriptions on the lower part of their tunics; the first two are bearded, and seem to be accusers; the remaining two are nearly defaced; but behind the last appears the eunuch, whose office it seems to be to usher into the presence of the king those who are permitted to appear before him. He is followed by another person of the same race as those under punishment; his hands are manacled, and on his ankles are strong rings fastened together by a heavy bar' [*Nineveh and Its Palaces*]. No name is given, and, therefore, no conclusion can be drawn that the figure represents Manasseh. But the people appear to be Hebrews, and this pictorial scene will enable us to imagine the manner in which the royal captive from Judah was received in the court of Babylon. Esar-haddon had established his residence there; for though from the many revolts that followed the death of his father, he succeeded at first only to the throne of Assyria, yet having some time previous to his conquest of Judah, recovered possession of Babylon, this enterprising king had united under his sway the two empires of Babylon and Chaldea and transferred the seat of his government to Babylon.

12, 13. when he was in affliction, he besought the Lord his God – In the solitude of exile or imprisonment, Manasseh had leisure for reflection. The calamities forced upon him a review of his past life, under a conviction that the miseries of his dethronement and captive condition were owing to his awful and unprecedented apostasy (2Ch 33:7) from the God of his fathers. He humbled himself, repented, and prayed for an opportunity of bringing forth the fruits of repentance. His prayer was heard; for his conqueror not only released him, but, after two years' exile, restored him, with honor and the full exercise of royal power, to a tributary and dependent kingdom. Some political motive, doubtless, prompted the Assyrian king to restore Manasseh, and that was most probably to have the kingdom of Judah as a barrier between Egypt and his Assyrian dominions. But God overruled this measure for higher purposes. Manasseh now showed himself, by the influence of sanctified affliction, a new and better man. He made a complete reversal of his former policy, by not only destroying all the idolatrous statues and altars he had formerly erected in Jerusalem, but displaying the most ardent zeal in restoring and encouraging the worship of God.

14. he built a wall without the city ... on the west side of Gihon ... even to the entering in at the fish gate – 'The well-ascertained position of the fish gate, shows that the valley of Gihon could be no other than that leading northwest of Damascus gate, and gently descending southward, uniting with the Tyropoeon at the northeast corner of Mount Zion, where the latter turns at right angles and runs towards Siloam. The wall thus built by Manasseh on the west side of the valley of Gihon, would extend from the vicinity of the northeast corner of the wall of Zion in a northerly direction, until it crossed over the valley to form a junction with the outer wall at the trench of Antonia, precisely in the quarter where the temple would be most easily assailed' [BARCLAY].

17. the people did sacrifice still in the high places, yet unto the Lord their God only – Here it appears that the worship on high places, though it originated in a great measure from the practice of heathenism, and too often led to it, did not necessarily imply idolatry.

2Ch 33:20–25. He dies and Amon succeeds him.

20, 21. Manasseh slept with his fathers ... Amon began to reign – (See on 2Ki 21:19).

Chapter 34

2Ch 34:1, 2. Josiah's good reign.

1. Josiah was eight years old – (See on 2Ki 22:1). The testimony borne to the undeviating steadfastness of his adherence to the cause of true religion places his character and reign in honorable contrast with those of many of his royal predecessors.

2Ch 34:3–7. He destroys idolatry.

3. in the eighth year of his reign – This was the sixteenth year of his age, and, as the kings of Judah were considered minors till they had completed their thirteenth year, it was three years after he had attained majority. He had very early manifested the piety and excellent dispositions of his character. In the twelfth year of his reign, but the twentieth of his age, he began to take a lively interest in the purgation of his kingdom from all the monuments of idolatry which, in his father's short reign, had been erected. At a later period, his increasing zeal for securing the purity of divine worship led him to superintend the work of demolition in various parts of his dominion. The course of the narrative in this passage is somewhat different from that followed in the Book of Kings. For the historian, having made allusion to the early manifestation of Josiah's zeal, goes on with a full detail of all the measures this good king adopted for the extirpation of idolatry; whereas the author of the Book of Kings sets out with the cleansing of the temple, immediately previous to the celebration of the passover, and embraces that occasion to give a general description of Josiah's policy for freeing the land from idolatrous pollution. The exact chronological order is not followed either in Kings or Chronicles. But it is clearly recorded in both that the abolition of idolatry began in the twelfth and was completed in the eighteenth year of Josiah's reign. Notwithstanding Josiah's undoubted sincerity and zeal and the people's apparent compliance with the king's orders, he could not extinguish a strongly rooted attachment to idolatries introduced in the early part of Manasseh's reign. This latent predilection appears unmistakably developed in the subsequent reigns, and the divine decree for the removal of Judah, as well as Israel, into captivity was irrevocably passed.

4. the graves of them that had sacrificed unto them – He treated the graves themselves as guilty of the crimes of those who were lying in them [BERTHEAU].

5. he burnt the bones of the priests upon their altars – A greater brand of infamy could not have been put on idolatrous priests than the disinterment of their bones, and a greater defilement could not have been done to the altars of idolatry than the burning upon them the bones of those who had there officiated in their lifetime.

6. with their mattocks – or, 'in their deserts' – so that the verse will stand thus: 'And so did [namely, break the altars and burn the bones of priests] he in the cities of Manasseh, and Ephraim, and Simeon, even unto Naphtali, in their deserted suburbs.' The reader is apt to be surprised on finding that Josiah, whose hereditary possessions were confined to the kingdom of Judah, exercised as much authority among the tribes of Ephraim, Manasseh, Simeon, and others as far as Naphtali, as he did within his own dominion. Therefore, it is necessary to observe that, after the destruction of Samaria by Shalmaneser, the remnant that continued on the mountains of Israel maintained a close intercourse with Judah, and looked to the sovereigns of that kingdom as their natural protectors. Those kings acquired great influence over them, which Josiah exercised in removing every vestige of idolatry from the land. He could not have done this without the acquiescence of the people in the propriety of this proceeding, conscious that this was conformable to their ancient laws and institutions. The Assyrian kings, who were now masters of the country, might have been displeased at the liberties Josiah took beyond his own territories. But either they were not informed of his doings, or they did not trouble themselves about his religious proceedings, relating, as they would think, to the god of the land, especially as he did not attempt to seize upon any place or to disturb the allegiance of the people [CALMET].

2Ch 34:8–18. He repairs the temple.

8. in the eighteenth year of his reign … he sent Shaphan – (See on 2Ki 22:3–9).

2Ch 34:19–33. And, causing the law to be read, renews the covenant between God and the people.

19. when the king had heard the words of the law – (See on 2Ki 22:11-20 23:1–3).

Chapter 35

2Ch 35:1–19. Josiah keeps a solemn passover.

1–3. Moreover Josiah kept a passover – (See on 2Ki 23:21). The first nine verses give an account of the preparations made for the celebration of the solemn feast (2Ch 35:1–9). The day appointed by the law was kept on this occasion (compare 2Ch 30:2,13). The priests were ranged in their courses and exhorted to be ready for their duties in the manner that legal purity required (compare 2Ch 29:5). The Levites, the ministers or instructors of the people in all matters pertaining to the divine worship, were commanded (2Ch 35:3) to 'put the holy ark in the house which Solomon did build.' Their duty was to transport the ark from place to place according to circumstances. Some think that it had been ignominiously put away from the sanctuary by order of some idolatrous king, probably Manasseh, who set a carved image in the house of God (2Ch 33:7), or Amon; while others are of opinion that it had been temporarily removed by Josiah himself into some adjoining chamber, during the repairs on the temple. In replacing it, the Levites had evidently carried it upon their shoulders, deeming that still to be the duty which the law imposed on them. But Josiah reminded them of the change of circumstances. As the service of God was now performed in a fixed and permanent temple, they were not required to be bearers of the ark any longer; and, being released from the service, they should address themselves with the greater alacrity to the discharge of other functions.

4. prepare yourselves by the houses of your fathers, after your courses – Each course or division was to be composed of those who belonged to the same fathers' house.

according to the writing of David and … Solomon – Their injunctions are recorded (2Ch 8:14 1Ch 23:1–26:32).

5. stand in the holy place – in the court of the priests, the place where the victims were killed. The people were admitted according to their families in groups or companies of several households at a time. When the first company entered the court (which consisted commonly of as many as it could well hold), the gates were shut and the offering was made. The Levites stood in rows from the slaughtering places to the altar, and handed the blood and fat from one to another of the officiating priests (2Ch 30:16–18).

6. **So kill the passover** – The design of the minute directions given here was to facilitate the distribution of the paschal lambs. These were to be eaten by the respective families according to their numbers (Ex 12:3). But multitudes of the people, especially those from Israel, having been reduced to poverty through the Assyrian devastations, were to be provided with the means of commemorating the passover. Therefore, the king enjoined the Levites that when the paschal lambs were brought to them to be killed (2Ch 35:7–9) they should take care to have everything put in so orderly a train, that the lambs, after due presentation, might be easily delivered to the various families to be roasted and eaten by themselves apart.

7. **Josiah gave to the people … lambs and kids** – These were in all probability destined for the poor; a lamb or a kid might be used at convenience (Ex 12:5).

and … bullocks – which were offered after the lambs on each of the successive days of the feast.

8, 9. **his princes** – These gave to the priests and Levites; as those of Hezekiah's princes (2Ch 30:24). They were ecclesiastical princes; namely, Hilkiah the high priest (2Ch 34:9). Zechariah, probably the second priest of the Eleazar (2Ki 16:18), and Jehiel, of the Ithamar line. And as the Levitical tribes were not yet sufficiently provided (2Ch 35:9), some of their eminent brethren who had been distinguished in Hezekiah's time (2Ch 31:12–15), gave a large additional contribution for the use of the Levites exclusively.

10, 11. **So the service was prepared** – All the necessary preparations having been completed, and the appointed time having arrived for the passover, the solemnity was celebrated. One remarkable feature in the account is the prominent part that was taken by the Levites in the preparation of the sacrifices; namely, the killing and stripping of the skins, which were properly the peculiar duties of the priests; but as those functionaries were not able to overtake the extraordinary amount of work and the Levites had been duly sanctified for the service, they were enlisted for the time in this priestly employment. At the passover in Hezekiah's time, the Levites officiated in the same departments of duty, the reason assigned for that deviation from the established rule being the unprepared state of many of the people (2Ch 30:17). But on this occasion the whole people had been duly sanctified, and therefore the exceptional enlistment of the Levites' services

must have been rendered unavoidably necessary from the multitudes engaged in celebrating the passover.

12. **they removed the burnt offerings** – Some of the small cattle being designed for burnt offerings were put apart by themselves, that they might not be intermingled with the paschal lambs, which were carefully selected according to certain rules, and intended to be sacramentally eaten; and the manner in which those burnt offerings were presented seems to have been the following: 'All the subdivisions of the different fathers' houses came one after another to the altar in solemn procession to bring to the priests the portions which had been cut off, and the priests laid these pieces upon the fire of the altar of burnt offering.'

13. **they roasted the passover with fire according to the ordinance** – (See Ex 12:7–9). This mode of preparation was prescribed by the law exclusively for the paschal lamb; the other offerings and thank offerings were cooked in pots, kettles, and pans (1Sa 2:14).

divided them speedily among the people – The haste was either owing to the multiplicity of the priests' business, or because the heat and flavor of the viands would have been otherwise diminished. Hence it appears that the meal consisted not of the paschal lambs alone, but of the meat of the thank offerings – for part of the flesh fell to the portion of the offerer, who, being in this instance, the king and the princes, were by them made over to the people, who were recommended to eat them the day they were offered, though not absolutely forbidden to do so on the next (Le 7:15–18).

14. **afterwards they made ready for themselves, and for the priests** – The Levites rendered this aid to the priests solely because they were so engrossed the entire day that they had no leisure to provide any refreshments for themselves.

15. **And the singers … were in their place** – While the priests and people were so much engaged, the choir was not idle. They had to sing certain Psalms, namely, the hundred thirteenth to the hundred eighteenth inclusive, once, twice, and even a third time, during the continuance of each company of offerers. As they could not leave their posts, for the singing was resumed as every fresh company entered, the Levites prepared for them also; for the various bands relieved each other in turn, and while the general choir was doing duty, a portion of the tuneful brethren, relieved for a time, partook of the viands that were brought them.

18. **there was no passover like to that kept in Israel from the days of Samuel** – One feature by which this passover was distinguished was the liberality of Josiah. But what distinguished it above all preceding solemnities was, not the

imposing grandeur of the ceremonies, nor the immensity of the assembled concourse of worshippers; for these, with the exception of a few from the kingdom of Israel, were confined to two tribes; but it was the ardent devotion of the king and people, the disregard of purely traditional customs, and the unusually strict adherence, even in the smallest minutiæ, to the forms of observance prescribed in the book of the law, the discovery of an original copy of which had produced so great a sensation. Instead of 'from the days of Samuel,' the author of the Book of Kings says, 'from the days of the judges who judged Israel' [2Ki 23:22]. The meaning is the same in both passages, for Samuel concluded the era of the judges.

all Judah and Israel that were present – The great majority of the people of the northern kingdom were in exile, but some of the remaining inhabitants performed the journey to Jerusalem on this occasion. 37,600 paschal lambs and kids were used, which (2Ch 35:7), at ten to a company, would make 376,000 persons attending the feast.

19. In the eighteenth year of the reign Josiah was this passover kept – 'It is said (2Ki 22:3) that Josiah sent Shaphan to Hilkiah in the eighth month of that year.' If this statement rests upon an historical basis, all the events narrated here (at 2Ch 34:8–35:19) must have happened in about the space of five months and a half. We should then have a proof that the eighteenth year of Josiah's reign was reckoned from the autumn (compare 2Ch 29:3). 'The eighth month' of the sacred year in the eighteenth year of his reign would be the second month of his eighteenth year, and the first month of the new year would be the seventh month [BERTHEAU].

2Ch 35:20–27. Josiah's death.

20. After all this, when Josiah had prepared the temple – He most probably calculated that the restoration of the divine worship, with the revival of vital religion in the land, would lead, according to God's promise and the uniform experience of the Hebrew people, to a period of settled peace and increased prosperity. His hopes were disappointed. The bright interval of tranquillity that followed his re-establishment of the true religion was brief. But it must be observed that this interruption did not proceed from any unfaithfulness in the divine promise, but from the state into which the kingdom of Judah had brought itself by the national apostasy, which was drawing down upon it the long threatened but long deferred judgments of God.

Necho king of Egypt came up to fight against Carchemish by Euphrates – Necho, son of Psammetichus, succeeded to the throne of Egypt in the twentieth year of Josiah. He was a bold and enterprising king, who entered with all his heart into the struggle which the two great powers of Egypt and Assyria had long carried on for the political ascendency. Each, jealous of the aggressive movements of its rival, was desirous to maintain Palestine as a frontier barrier. After the overthrow of Israel, the kingdom of Judah became in that respect doubly important. Although the king and people had a strong bias for alliance with Egypt, yet from the time of Manasseh it had become a vassal of Assyria. Josiah, true to his political no less than his religious engagements, thought himself bound to support the interests of his Assyrian liege lord. Hence, when 'Necho king of Egypt came up to fight Carchemish, Josiah went out against him.' Carchemish, on the eastern side of the Euphrates, was the key of Assyria on the west, and in going thither the king of Egypt would transport his troops by sea along the coast of Palestine, northwards. Josiah, as a faithful vassal, resolved to oppose Necho's march across the northern parts of that country. They met in the 'valley of Megiddo,' that is, the valley or plain of Esdraelon. The Egyptian king had come either by water or through the plains of Philistia, keeping constantly along the coast, round the north-west corner of Carmel, and so to the great plain of Megiddo. This was not only his direct way to the Euphrates, but the only route fit for his chariots, while thereby also he left Judah and Jerusalem quite to his right. In this valley, however, the Egyptian army had necessarily to strike across the country, and it was on that occasion that Josiah could most conveniently intercept his passage. To avoid the difficulty of passing the river Kishon, Necho kept to the south of it, and must, therefore, have come past Megiddo. Josiah, in following with his chariots and horsemen from Jerusalem, had to march northwards along the highway through Samaria by Kefr-Kud (the ancient Caper-Cotia) to Megiddo [VAN DE VELDE].

21, 22. But he sent ambassadors … What have I to do with thee, thou king of Judah? – Not wishing to spend time, or strength in vain, Necho informed the king of Judah that he had no intention of molesting the Jews; that his expedition was directed solely against his old Assyrian enemy; and that he had undertaken it by an express commission from God. Commentators are not agreed whether it was really a divine commission given him through Jeremiah, or whether he merely used the name of God as an authority that Josiah would not refuse to obey. As he could not know the truth of Necho's declaration, Josiah did not sin in opposing him; or, if he sinned at all, it was a sin of ignorance. The engagement took place. Josiah was mortally wounded (2Ch 35:23).

24. took him out of that chariot, and put him in the second chariot – the carriage he had for ordinary use, and which would be more comfortable for the royal sufferer than the war chariot. The death of this good king was the subject of universal and lasting regret.

25. Jeremiah lamented for Josiah – The elegy of the prophet has not reached us; but it seems to have been long preserved among his countrymen and chanted on certain public occasions by the professional singers, who probably got the dirges they sang from a collection of funeral odes composed on the death of good and great men of the nation. The spot in the valley of Megiddo where the battle was fought was near the town of Hadad-rimmon; hence the lamentation for the death of Josiah was called 'the lamentation of Hadad-rimmon in the valley of Megiddo,' which was so great and so long continued, that the lamentation of Hadad passed afterwards into a proverbial phrase to express any great and extraordinary sorrow (Zec 12:11).

Chapter 36

2Ch 36:1–4. Jehoahaz, succeeding, is deposed by Pharaoh.

1. the people of the land took Jehoahaz – Immediately after Josiah's overthrow and death, the people raised to the throne Shallum (1Ch 3:15), afterwards called Jehoahaz, in preference to his older brother Eliakim, from whom they expected little good. Jehoahaz is said (2Ki 23:30) to have received at Jerusalem the royal anointing – a ceremony not usually deemed necessary, in circumstances of regular and undisputed succession. But, in the case of Jehoahaz, it seems to have been resorted to in order to impart greater validity to the act of popular election; and, it may be, to render it less likely to be disturbed by Necho, who, like all Egyptians, would associate the idea of sanctity with the regal anointing. He was the youngest son of Josiah, but the popular favorite, probably on account of his martial spirit (Eze 19:3) and determined opposition to the aggressive views of Egypt. At his accession the land was free from idolatry; but this prince, instead of following the footsteps of his excellent father, adopted the criminal policy of his apostatizing predecessors. Through his influence, directly or indirectly used, idolatry rapidly increased (see 2Ki 23:32).

2. he reigned three months in Jerusalem – His possession of sovereign power was of but very brief duration; for Necho determined to follow up the advantage he had gained in Judah; and, deeming it expedient to have a king of his own nomination on the throne of that country, he deposed the popularly elected monarch and placed his brother Eliakim or Jehoiakim on the throne, whom he anticipated to be a mere obsequious vassal. The course of events seems to have been this: on receiving intelligence after the battle of the accession of Jehoahaz to the throne, and perhaps also in consequence of the complaint which Eliakim brought before him in regard to this matter, Necho set out with a part of his forces to Jerusalem, while the remainder of his troops pursued their way at leisure towards Riblah, laid a tribute on the country, raised Eliakim (Jehoiakim) as his vassal to the throne, and on his departure brought Jehoahaz captive with him to Riblah. The old expositors mostly assumed that Necho, after the battle of Megiddo, marched directly against Carchemish, and then on his return came to Jerusalem. The improbability, indeed the impossibility, of his doing so appears from this: Carchemish was from four hundred to five hundred miles from Megiddo, so that within 'three months' an army could not possibly make its way thither, conquer the fenced city of Carchemish, and then march back a still greater distance to Jerusalem, and take that city [KEIL].

4. carried him – Jehoahaz.

to Egypt – There he died (Jer 22:10–12).

2Ch 36:5–10. Jehoiakim, reigning ill, is carried into Babylon.

5. Jehoiakim … did that which was evil in the sight of the Lord – He followed the course of his idolatrous predecessors; and the people, to a great extent, disinclined to the reforming policy of his father, eagerly availed themselves of the vicious license which his lax administration restored. His character is portrayed with a masterly hand in the prophecy of Jeremiah (Jer 22:13–19). As the deputy of the king of Egypt, he departed further than his predecessor from the principles of Josiah's government; and, in trying to meet the insatiable cupidity of his master by grinding exactions from his subjects, he recklessly plunged into all evil.

6. Against him came up Nebuchadnezzar king of Babylon – This refers to the first expedition of Nebuchadnezzar against Palestine, in the lifetime of his father Nabopolassar, who, being old and infirm, adopted his son as joint sovereign and despatched him, with the command of his army, against the Egyptian invaders of his empire. Nebuchadnezzar defeated them at Carchemish, drove them out of Asia, and reduced all the provinces west of the Euphrates to obedience – among the rest the kingdom of Jehoiakim, who became a vassal of the Assyrian empire (2Ki 24:1). Jehoiakim at the end of three years threw off the yoke, being probably instigated to revolt by the solicitations of the king of Egypt, who planned a new expedition against Carchemish. But he was completely vanquished by the Babylonian king, who stripped him of all his possessions between the Euphrates and the Nile (2Ki 24:7). Then marching against the Egyptian's ally in Judah, he took Jerusalem, carried away a portion of the sacred vessels of the temple, perhaps in lieu of the unpaid tribute, and deposited them in the temple of his god, Belus, at Babylon (Da 1:2 5:2). Though Jehoiakim had been taken prisoner (and it was designed at first to transport him in chains to Babylon), he was allowed to remain in his tributary kingdom. But having given not long after some new offense, Jerusalem was besieged by a host of Assyrian dependents. In a sally against them Jehoiakim was killed (see on 2Ki 24:2–7).

9, 10. Jehoiachin was eight years old – called also Jeconiah or Coniah (Jer 22:24) – 'eight' should have been 'eighteen,' as appears from 2Ki 24:8, and also from the full development of his ungodly principles and habits (see Eze 19:5–7). His reign being of so short duration cannot be considered at variance with the prophetic denunciation against his father (Jer 36:30). But his appointment by the people gave umbrage to Nebuchadnezzar, who, 'when the year was expired' (2Ch 36:10) – that is, in the spring when campaigns usually began – came in person against Jerusalem, captured the city, and sent Jehoiachin in chains to Babylon, removing at the same time all the nobles and most skilful artisans, and pillaging all the remaining treasures both of the temple and palace (see on 2Ki 24:8–17).

2Ch 36:11–21. Zedekiah's reign.

11. Zedekiah – Nebuchadnezzar appointed him. His name, originally Mattaniah, was, according to the custom of Oriental conquerors, changed into Zedekiah. Though the son of Josiah (1Ch 3:15 Jer 1:2,3 37:1), he is called the brother of Jehoiachin (2Ch 36:10), that is, according to the latitude of Hebrew style in words expressing affinity, his relative or kinsman (see 2Ki 24:18 25:1–21).

13. who had made him swear by God – Zedekiah received his crown on the express condition of taking a solemn oath of fealty to the king of Babylon (Eze 17:13); so that his revolt by joining in a league with Pharaoh-hophra, king of Egypt, involved the crime of perjury. His own pride and obdurate impiety, the incurable idolatry of the nation, and their reckless disregard of prophetic warnings, brought down on his already sadly reduced kingdom the long threatened judgments of God. Nebuchadnezzar, the executioner of the divine vengeance, commenced a third siege of Jerusalem, which, after holding out for a year and a half, was taken in the eleventh year of the reign of Zedekiah. It resulted in the burning of the temple, with, most probably, the ark, and in the overthrow of the kingdom of Judah (see on 2Ki 25:1–7).

21. until the land had enjoyed her sabbaths – The return of every seventh was to be held as a sabbatic year, a season of rest to all classes, even to the land itself, which was to be fallow. This divine institution, however, was neglected – how soon and how long, appears from the prophecy of Moses, and of Jeremiah in this passage (see Jer 25:9–12), which told that for divine retribution it was now to remain desolate seventy years. As the Assyrian conquerors usually colonized their conquered provinces, so remarkable a deviation in Palestine from their customary policy must be ascribed to the overruling providence of God.

2Ch 36:22, 23. Cyrus' proclamation.

22. the Lord stirred up the spirit of Cyrus – (See Ezr 1:1–3)

EZRA

John Wesley

Introduction

The history of this book is the accomplishment of Jeremiah's prophecy, concerning the return of the Jews out of Babylon, at the end of seventy years, and a type of the accomplishment of the prophecies in the Revelation, touching the deliverance of the Gospel Church from Spiritual Babylon. Ezra preserved the records of that great revolution, and transmitted them to the church in this book. It gives us an account of the Jews return from their captivity, chap. 1, 2. Of the building of the temple, notwithstanding the opposition it met with, chap. 3-6. Of Ezra's coming to Jerusalem, chap. 7, 8. Of his obliging those that had married strange wives to put them away, chap. 9, 10.

Chapter 1

The proclamation of Cyrus, for the release of the Jews, and building of the temple (1–4)

The return of many of them (5, 6)

Orders given for restoring the vessels of the temple (7–11)

The proclamation of Cyrus, for the release of the Jews, and building of the temple (1–4)

1. Fulfilled – Nebuchadnezzar carried many of the Jews into captivity in the first year of his reign (the fourth of Jehoiakim). He reigned forty-five years, his son Evil-merodach twenty-three, and his grandson Belshazzar, three years, which make up the seventy years foretold by Jeremiah. **First year** – Of his reign in Babylon: for he had been king of Persia for many years.

2. All – In those parts of the world; all that vast empire formerly under the Assyrians and Babylonians. The gift of which he ascribes to the great God; by that express prophecy of Isaiah concerning him, Isa 44:28 45:1,13, so long

before he was born; which prophecy the Jews had doubtlessly showed him, which also carried a great evidence with it, especially to him who was so highly encouraged by it: or by a special illumination which God vouchsafed to him, as he did to Nebuchadnezzar and Darius, and some other Heathen princes.

The return of many of them (5, 6)

5. Then rose up – These being a new generation, went out like their father Abraham, from this land of the Chaldees, not knowing whither they went.

6. Strengthened their hands – God can, when he pleases, incline the hearts of strangers to be kind to his people; yea, make those strengthen their hands, who formerly weakened them.

Orders given for restoring the vessels of the temple (7–11)

8. Sheshbazzar – Zerubbabel; the Chaldeans called him Sheshbazzar, that is, Joy in tribulation, but among his own people he was called Zerubbabel, a stranger in Babylon. So he looked upon himself, though (Josephus says) he was captain of the life-guard.

Chapter 2

The leaders that returned (1, 2)

The people (3–35)

The priests, Levites and retainers to the temple (36–63)

The sum total and their substance (64–67)

Their offerings (68–70)

The leaders that returned (1, 2)

---

1. The province – Of Judah, called a province, chap.5:8. And he calls it thus emphatically to mind himself and his brethren of that sad change which their sins had made among them, that from an illustrious, independent, and formidable kingdom, were fallen to be an obscure, servile, and contemptible province, first under the Chaldeans, and now under the Persians.

2. Who came – This catalogue, differs in some names and numbers from that Neh 7:6–64, which might be because several names were given to the same persons; and because of the many changes which might happen in the same families between the time of the first making of this catalogue by Ezra, and the making it anew so many years after.

The people (3–35)

3. The children – The posterity, as that word is constantly taken in this catalogue. **Of Parosh** – That descend either from Parosh, or from that family whereof Parosh was the chief. And so for the rest.

5. Seven hundred – In Neh 7:10, they were only six hundred and fifty two, it seems seven hundred and seventy five marched out of Babylon, but some of them died, others were hindered by sickness, or other casualties, and so there came only six hundred and fifty two to Jerusalem. And the like is to be said in the like differences: which it suffices to hint once for all.

21. Beth-lehem – And so these were the remainders of the inhabitants of that city. (And the like may be said of the two following names, Netophah and Anathoth, or others of the like nature.) So little was Beth-lehem among the thousands of Judah! Yet thence must the Messiah arise.

The priests, Levites and retainers to the temple (36–63)

39. Harim – The head of one of the twenty four courses which David appointed, 1Chron 24:8, of all which courses, some observe here are not above four or five that returned. There is

another Harim mentioned above, ver.32, but that was no priest, as this was ver.36.

43. Nethinims – Persons devoted to the inferior services of the priests and Levites. Commonly supposed to be the Gibeonites, given (so their name signifies) by Joshua first, and again by David, when Saul had expelled them, to the priests and Levites, for those services.

55. Servants – Who had lived in Solomon's family, and after his death, called themselves and their families by that name, esteeming it a great honour that they had been servants to so great a prince.

62. Genealogy – The Jews were generally very exact in their genealogies from their own choice and interest, that they might preserve the distinctions of the several tribes and families, which was necessary both to make out their titles to offices or inheritances, and to govern themselves thereby in the matter of marriages, and from the special providence of God, that so it might be certainly known of what tribe and family the Messiah was born.

63. Tirshatha – The governor, Zerubbabel. **With Urim** – That this point which could not be found out by human skill, might be determined by Divine direction. Hereby it appears that the Urim and Thummim were lost in the destruction of the city and temple, although the Jews fed themselves with hopes of recovering them, but in vain. And by the want of that oracle, they were taught to expect the great oracle, the Messiah.

The sum total and their substance (64–67)

64. The whole – The particular sums here recited, come only to twenty and nine thousand eight hundred and eighteen. Unto whom are added in this total sum twelve thousand five hundred and forty two. Which, either were of the other tribes beside Judah and Benjamin: or were such as were supposed to be Israelites, but could not prove their pedigree by their genealogies.

65. Women – For women as well as men were employed in this exercise in the temple-service.

Their offerings (68–70)

68. The house – That is, to the ruins of the house; or to the place where it stood.

69. Sixty one thousand drams – Sixty one thousand drams of gold amount to something more than so many pounds of our money. So bishop Cumberland, who likewise supposes five thousand pounds of silver, to be about thirty seven thousand pounds sterling.

70. And all Israel in their cities – And they dwelt in peace, in perfect harmony, a blessed presage of their settlement, as their discord in the latter times of that state, was of their ruin.

Chapter 3

They set up the altar, offer sacrifices thereon, and keep the feasts (1–6)

They contribute, and lay the foundation of the temple (7–13)

They set up the altar, offer sacrifices thereon, and keep the feasts (1–6)

1. **Seventh month** – This was a sacred kind of month wherein there were divers festivals, for which the people had been preparing themselves, and now came to Jerusalem to the celebration of them.

2. **Altar** – Which was of more present necessity than the temple, both to make atonement to God for all their sins, and to obtain God's assistance for the building of the temple, and to strengthen their own hearts and hands in that great work.

3. **For fear** – So they made the more haste, lest they should be hindered. Apprehension of dangers should quicken us in our duty. Have we many enemies? We have the more need to have God for our friend and to keep up our correspondence with him.

4. **Tabernacles** – This seems to be mentioned for all the solemnities of this month, whereof this was the most eminent, otherwise it is not probable, that they would neglect the day of atonement which was so severely enjoined, Lev 23:27–29, and was so exceeding suitable to their present condition.

5. **Offering** – The morning and evening sacrifice. The law required much; but they offered more; for although they had little wealth, they had much zeal. Happy they that bring with them out of the furnace of affliction, such a holy heat as this!

6. **Burnt-offerings** – And the other sacrifices which were to be offered with them upon that day, being the feast of trumpets. Burnt-offerings are often put for all sacrifices.

They contribute, and lay the foundation of the temple (7–13)

9. **Joshua** – Not the high-priest so called, but a Levite, of whom see chap.2:40. **To set forward** – To encourage them to a vigorous prosecution of the work.

11. **Sung** – That everlasting hymn, which will never be out of date, and to which our tongue should never be out of tune, the burden of Psalm 136:1–26. Whatever our condition is, let it be owned, that God is good, and whatever fails, that his mercy fails not.

12. **Had seen** – Which divers of them might well do; because it was destroyed not sixty years ago. **Wept** – Because of the poor preparations

made for this, in comparison of what was made for the other temple: because this was destitute of those things which were the principal glory of the former temple, namely, the ark, and the Urim and Thummim; because these foundation-stones were far inferior to the former, both for quantity and price, 1Kings 7:9,10, and because these foundations were of a far narrower compass than the former: for although the foundations of this house of the Lord, strictly so called, were of equal largeness with those of the former, yet the foundations of the whole building belonging to the first temple, were far larger than these.

13. **Could not discern** – The mixture of sorrow and joy here, is a representation of this world. In heaven all are singing and none sighing; in hell all are wailing, and none rejoicing: but here on earth we can scarce discern the shouts of joy from the noise of the weeping, let us learn to rejoice with them that rejoice, and weep with them that weep. Meantime let us ourselves rejoice as though we rejoiced not, and weep as though we wept not.

Chapter 4

The adversaries, not being allowed to build with them, endeavour to hinder the work (1–5)

They falsely accuse them to Artaxerxes (6–16)

Who thereupon orders the work to be stopt (17–24)

The adversaries, not being allowed to build with them, endeavour to hinder the work (1–5)

1. **The adversaries** – The Samaritans. The relics of the ten tribes, and the foreigners who had joined with them.

2. **With you** – This they spake not sincerely, but that by this conjunction with them, they might pry into their counsels, and thereby find some matter of accusation against them. **We seek** – For so they did, though in a mongrel way, 2Kings 17:26. **Esarhaddon** – Son of Sennacherib, and after him king of Assyria, who brought or sent these persons hither, either,

1. in the day's of Salmanasar, who reigned in Assyria but eight years before Esarhaddon; and so Esarhaddon might be one of his commanders, and the man by whom that colony was sent.

Or, 2. in the reign of Esarhaddon, who sent this second colony to strengthen the first.

3. **With us** – As being of another nation and religion, and therefore not concerned in Cyrus's grant, which was confined to the Israelites. Take

heed, whom you go partners with, and on whose hand you lean. While we trust God with an absolute confidence, we must trust men with a prudent caution.

5. **Cyrus** – For though Cyrus still favoured the Jews, yet he was then diverted by his wars, and his son Cambyses was left his vice-roy, who was a wicked prince, and an enemy to the Jews. **Until** – Heb. and until not only in the reign of Cyrus but also of Cambyses, and of the magician, after whom was Darius.

They falsely accuse them to Artaxerxes (6–16)

6. **Ahasuerus** – A common name to divers kings of Persia. Cambyses the son and successor of Cyrus, was known to be no friend to the Jewish nation.

7. **Artaxerxes** – Cambyses, called by his Chaldee name, Ahashuerus, ver.6, and here by his Persian name, Artaxerxes: by which he is here called in the inscription of this letter, because so he was called by himself, and others in the letters written either by him; or to him. **Interpreted** – It was written in the Chaldee or Syrian language, and in the Syrian character: for sometimes the Chaldee or Syrian words are written in the Hebrew character.

10. **A snapper** – Either Esarhaddon, or some other eminent person, who was captain of this colony, and conducted them hither. **The river** – Euphrates. **Time** – The date of the epistle was particularly expressed therein, but here it was sufficient to note it in general.

12. **Be it known** – This is a mere fiction, which being confidently affirmed, they thought would easily find belief with a king whose heart and ears they possessed by their hired counsellors.

Who thereupon orders the work to be stopt (17–24)

23. **To cease** – As they abused the king by their misinformations, in the obtaining of this order, so they abused him in the execution of it; for the order was only to prevent the walling of the city. But having power in their hands, they, on this pretence, stopt the building of the temple. See what need we have to pray, not only for kings, but for all in authority under them: because the quietness of our lives depends much on the integrity and wisdom of inferior magistrates as well as the supreme.

24. **Darius** – Darius the son of Hystaspes, successor of Cambyses.

Chapter 5

Zerubbabel encouraged by Haggai and Zechariah, sets the work forward again (1, 2)

Their adversaries oppose them again (3–5)

Write to Darius (6–17)

Zerubbabel encouraged by Haggai and Zechariah, sets the work forward again (1, 2)

1. **The son** – His grand-child; for he was the son of Baraciah. **Prophesied** – Commanding them from God to return to building the temple, with a promise of his favour and assistance.

2. **Helping** – Encouraging the people to work by their presence, and assurance of success. It is supposed, the work had stopt about fifteen years. The first chapter of Haggai is the best comment on these two verses.

Their adversaries oppose them again (3–5)

3. **Shethar-boznai** – Not Rehum and Shimshai who were either dead, or removed from their office by Darius.

4. **We** – Jews. **Accordingly** – According to what they asked. **That made this building** – That were the undertakers and encouragers of it.

Write to Darius (6–17)

8. **Great God** – And indeed, thus far the greater part of the Samaritans agreed with them.

17. **Now therefore** – If the case had been so fairly stated to Artaxerxes, he would hardly have hindered the work. The people of God could not be persecuted, if they were not belied.

Chapter 6

Darius's answer (1–7)

His decree (8–12)

The temple is finished and dedicated (13–18)

The passover kept (19–22)

Darius's answer (1–7)

1. **A decree** – To search the rolls in Babylon, where search was first made; but not finding the edict there, they searched in Achmetha, or Ecbatana, and found it.

2. **Achmetha** – The royal city of the Medes and Persians.

3. **Cubits** – Those proportions differ from those of Solomon's temple, which was but thirty cubits high, only the porch was a hundred and twenty cubits high, and but twenty cubits in breadth. Either therefore Solomon's cubits were sacred cubits, which were larger than the other, and these but common cubits. Or, the sixty cubits of height are meant only for the porch. And

the word rendered breadth, may be rendered the extension or the length of it; it being improbable that the king should give orders about the breadth, and none about the length of it.

His decree (8–12)

12. **Destroy** – Although this temple was at length most justly destroyed by the righteous hand of God, yet perhaps the Romans, who were the instruments of that destruction, felt the effects of this curse. For that empire sensibly declined ever after, 'till it was wholly destroyed.

The temple is finished and dedicated (13–18)

14. **Through** the prophesying – This is a seasonable intimation that this great and unexpected success was not to be ascribed to chance, or to the kindness or good humour of Darius, but unto God only, who by his prophets had required and encouraged them to proceed in the work, and by his mighty power disposed Darius's heart to such kind and noble purposes.

The Passover kept (19–22)

21. **Children** of Israel – Probably some out of each of the twelve tribes.

22. **Joyful** – He had given them both cause to rejoice, and hearts to rejoice. God is the fountain whence all the streams of true joy flow. **Of Assyria** – Of the king of Persia, who was now king of Assyria also, here so called emphatically, to note the great power and goodness of God in turning the hearts of these great monarchs, whose predecessors had been the chief persecutors and oppressors of God's people.

Chapter 7

An account of Ezra and his expedition to Jerusalem (1–10)

The commission which Artaxerxes gave him (11–26)

His thankfulness to God for it (27, 28)

An account of Ezra and his expedition to Jerusalem (1–10)

1. **Artaxerxes** – The same of whom he speaks, chap.6:14. **The son** – His grand-son. Here are divers persons omitted for brevity sake, which may be supplied out of 1Chron 6:1–11:47. Ezra was not himself the high priest; but he was nearly related to him.

6. **Went** – With the king's consent and com-

mission. **Scribe** – A learned and expert doctor. The Jews say, he collected and collated all the copies of the law, and published an accurate edition of it, with all the books that were given by Divine inspiration, and so made up the canon of the Old Testament. Moses in Egypt, and Ezra in Babylon, were wonderfully fitted for eminent service to the church. **According** – By the favour of God so disposing the heart of the king.

10. **To teach** – The order of things in this verse is very observable; first he endeavours to understand God's law and word, and that not for curiosity or ostentation, but in order to practise: next he consciously practises what he did understand, which made his doctrine much more effectual: and then he earnestly desires and labours to instruct others, that they also might know and do it.

The commission which Artaxerxes gave him (11–26)

11. **Words** – The phrase seems emphatic, noting that he explained both the words and the things: for the Jews in the land of their captivity had in a great measure lost both the language, and the knowledge of God's commands, and therefore Ezra and his companions instructed them in both.

14. **According** – To make inquiry into all abuses and deviations from your law, and to redress them. **Which** – Which is now and always in thine hand, being the matter of thy daily study.

16. **Find** – Procure, as that word is used, Gen 6:8 26:12 Psal 84:3. Whatsoever thou canst get of my subjects by way of free gift. **The people** – Of Israel.

25. **The wisdom** – Which God hath put into thy heart, and which appears in the works of thy hand. All that professed the Jewish religion, were to be under the jurisdiction of these judges.

26. **Let judgment** – What could David himself, as king, have done more, for the honour of God, and the furtherance of religion?

His thankfulness to God for it (27, 28)

27. **Blessed** – Ezra cannot proceed in his story, without inserting this thankful acknowledgment of God's goodness to him and the people.

28. **As the hand** – If God gives us his hand, we are bold and cheerful: if he withdraws it, we are weak as water. Whatever service we are enabled to do for God and our generation, God must have all the glory of it.

Chapter 8

The company that went up with Ezra (1–15)

He sends for the Levites (16–20)

Proclaims a fast (21–23)

Delivers the treasure he brought to the priests and Levites; goes on to Jerusalem (24–34)

The people offer and the king's commissions delivered to his lieutenants (35–36)

The company that went up with Ezra (1–15)

3. Males – Though the males only be expressed yet doubtless they carried the women along with them, as they did the little ones.

13. Whose names are – It seems the rest came before; so that now all the sons of that family returned.

15. Of Levi – None who were simple Levites, and not the priests. And therefore the Levites mentioned, chap.7:7, by anticipation were not yet come to him.

He sends for the Levites (16–20)

18. By the good hand – If where ministers have been wanting, the vacancies are well supplied, let us ascribe it to the good hand of God, qualifying them for the service, inclining them to it, and opening a door for them.

Proclaims a fast (21–23)

21. A fast – For public mercies. Public prayers must be made, that all who are to share in the comfort, may share in the requests for it. **Afflict ourselves** – For our sins; and so be qualified for the pardon of them. When we are entering on any new condition of life, our care should be to bring into it none of the guilt of the sins of our former condition. When we are in any imminent danger, let us make our peace with God, and then nothing can hurt us. **Right way** – A safe and prosperous journey; such a way and course as might be best for us.

23. Intreated – He gave us an assurance of his gracious answer to our request.

Delivers the treasure he brought to the priests and Levites; goes on to Jerusalem (24–34)

The people offer and the king's commissions delivered to his lieutenants (35–36)

35. Sin offering – For it is the atonement that secures every mercy to us, which will not be truly comfortable, unless iniquity be taken away, and our peace made with God. They offer twelve bullocks, twelve he-goats, and ninety six rams, (eight times twelve) signifying the union of the two kingdoms. They did not any longer go two tribes one way, and ten tribes another; but all the twelve met by their representatives at the same altar.

Chapter 9

Ezra is troubled at the marriages with strange women (1–4)

His solemn confession to God (5–15)

Ezra is troubled at the marriages with strange women (1–4)

3. I rent – Both mine inner and my upper garment.

4. Evening sacrifice – When the people used to assemble together. All good people ought to own those that appear and act for God against vice and profaneness. Every one that fears God, ought to stand by them, and do what he can to strengthen their hands.

His solemn confession to God (5–15)

5. Heaviness – From that mournful posture, and put myself into the posture of a petitioner. He did this at the time of the evening sacrifice, because then devout people used to come into the courts of the temple, that hearing his confession, they likewise might be made sensible of the sins of the people. And he had an eye to that great propitiation, of which that sacrifice was a peculiar type.

6. Our – He includes himself in the number of the transgressors, because he himself was guilty of many sins; and because the princes and priests, and so many of the people having done this, the guilt was now become national.

7. Have we been – We are not purged from the guilt of our fathers sins, but we are still feeling the sad effects of them; yea, and are repeating the same sins.

8. A little space – It is but a little while since God hath delivered us, and yet we are already returned to our sin. **A remnant** – The far greatest part of the Israeli nation were yet in captivity. **A nail** – Some kind of settlement; whereas before we were tossed and removed from place to place as our masters pleased. It is a metaphor from tents, which are fastened by cords and nails, or pins. **Holy place** – In Jerusalem, called the holy city, Neh 11:1,18 Dan 9:24, which is peculiarly mentioned, because of the temple, which was the nail that fastened their tents and gave them some hopes of continuing in their land. **To lighten** – That he might revive and comfort our hearts. For as darkness is often put for a state of sorrow and affliction, so light is put for joy and comfort. **In bondage** – For we are not quite delivered, being even here in subjection to our former lords.

9. A wall – The favour of the kings of Persia whose edicts were their security against all those enemies wherewith they were encompassed: and the gracious providence of God, which had planted them in their own land, and watched over them from time to time.

11. It is unclean – This land is as corrupt as any of the rest of the heathen nations.

12. Strong – Although you may fancy making leagues and marriages with them, as the only way to establish you, yet I assure you, it will weaken and ruin you, and the contrary course will make you strong.

15. We are – We are here in thy presence, and so are all our sins; we are arraigning ourselves before thy tribunal, acknowledging thee to be just, if thou destroy us. **Before thee** – In judgment, as that word is often used, we must needs fall and perish at thy presence.

Chapter 10

The people mourn (1)

Shechaniah encourages Ezra to put away the strange wives (2–4)

All Israel swear to do it (5)

Ezra, mourning assembles the people (6–9)

They all, on his exhortation, agree to the reformation (10–14)

They perform it (15–17)

The names of them that had married strange wives (18–44)

The people mourn (1)

1. There assembled – The account of his grief, and public expressions thereof in the court before the temple, being in an instant dispersed over all the city, brought a great company together. See what an happy influence the example of great ones may have upon their inferiors!

Shechaniah encourages Ezra to put away the strange wives (2–4)

2. We – He saith, we, in the name of the people, and their several families, and his own amongst the rest. For this man's name is not in the following catalogue, but there we have his father, Jehiel, and his father's brethren, five other sons of his grandfather, Elam, ver.26. It was therefore an evidence of his great courage, and good conscience, that he durst so freely discharge his duty, whereby he showed, that he honoured God more than his nearest and dearest relations. **Hope** – In case of our repentance, and reformation.

3. Such as are born – These children were only cast out of the common-wealth of Israel, but were not utterly forsaken; probably care was taken by authority, that they should have provision made for them.

All Israel swear to do it (5)

Ezra, mourning assembles the people (6–9)

6. Went – That with the princes and elders, he might consult about the execution of their resolution. **Thither** – 'Till he saw something done.

9. Of Judah – Not only of these two tribes, as appears from the following catalogue, where there are priests and Levites; but all the Israelites, ver.25, who are thus described, because the greatest part of them were of these tribes, though others were mixed with them: and because they all now dwelt in that land, which formerly was appropriated to those tribes. **The street** – In that street of the city, which was next the temple, and within the view of it, that so they might be as in God's presence, whereby they might be awed to a more faithful and vigorous prosecution of their work. And this place they might choose rather than the court of the people, because they thought it might be polluted by the delinquents, who were all to come thither. **Great rain** – Which they took for a token of God's displeasure against them.

They all, on his exhortation, agree to the reformation (10–14)

14. Our rulers – Let the great council, called the Sanhedrim, be settled, and meet to determine of all particular causes. **Judges** – Who are best able to inform the great council of the quality of the persons, and all matters of fact and circumstances. **Until** – Until the thing be done, and God's wrath thereby removed.

They perform it (15–17)

15. Employed – To take care that the business should be executed in the manner proposed, that the officers and delinquents of every city should come successively in convenient time and order, as these should appoint, to keep an exact account of the whole transaction, and of the names of the cities and persons whose causes were dispatched, to give notice to others to come in their turns, and to prepare the business for the hearing of the judges. These two were priests, as their helpers were Levites; that so they might inform the persons concerned, in any matter of doubt.

16. Separated – Sequestered themselves from all other business, and gave themselves wholly to this.

The names of them that had married
strange wives (18–44)

25. Of Israel – Of the people of Israel, distinguished from the priests and Levites hitherto named.

44. Had children – This implies that most of their wives were barren. Which came to pass by God's special providence, to manifest his displeasure against such matches, and that the putting them away might not be encumbered with too many difficulties. One would think this grievance altogether removed. Yet we meet with it again, Neh 13:22. Such corruptions are easily and insensibly brought in, although not easily purged out. The best reformers can but do their endeavour. It is only the Redeemer himself, who when he cometh to Sion, will effectually turn away ungodliness from Jacob.

NEHEMIAH

John Wesley

Introduction

This book continues the history of the children of the captivity, the Jews lately returned out of Babylon. We have a full account of Nehemiah's labours for them, in these his commentaries: wherein he records not only the works of his hands, but the very workings of his heart, inserting many devout reflections and ejaculations, which are peculiar to his writing. Twelve years he was the tirshatha, or governor of Judea, under the same Artaxerxes that gave Ezra his commission. This book relates his concern for Jerusalem and commission to go thither, chap. 1, 2. His building the wall of Jerusalem, notwithstanding much opposition, chap. 3, 4. His redressing the grievances of the people, chap. 5. His finishing the wall, chap. 6. The account he took of the people, chap. 7. His calling the people to read the law, fast and pray, and renew their covenant, chap. 8-10. He peoples Jerusalem and settles the tribe of Levi, chap. 11, 12. He reforms divers abuses, chap. 13. This was the last historical book that was written, as Malachi, the last prophetical book of the old testament.

Chapter 1

Nehemiah is informed of the deplorable state of the Jews at Jerusalem (1–3)

He fasts and prays (4–11)

Nehemiah is informed of the deplorable state of the Jews at Jerusalem (1–3)

1. The words – Or rather, the acts, as the word often signifies. **Chisleu** – Which is the ninth month, containing part of November, and part of December. **Year** – Of Artaxerxes. **Shushan** – The royal city of Persia.

3. The province – In Judea, now a province under the Persian monarchs. **The wall** – The walls and gates continue as Nebuchadnezzar left them; the Jews not being in a condition to rebuild them, nor having commission from the kings of Persia to do so.

He fasts and prays (4-11)

4. The God of heaven – Who seeth in secret; having no opportunity of doing it openly.

6. Which I pray – He refers to all the prayers, which he had for some time been putting up.

11. To fear thy name – Those who truly desire to fear his name, shall be graciously accepted of God. **This man** – The king: who is but a man and therefore his heart is wholly at thy disposal. Favour with men is then comfortable, when we see it springing from the mercy of God. **Cup-bearer** – Whereby I had opportunity to speak to him, and some favour with him.

Chapter 2

Artaxerxes sends Nehemiah to Jerusalem, with a commission to build the wall (1–8)

He comes thither, to the grief of his enemies (9–11)

He secretly views the ruins of it (12–16)

He informs the rulers of his commission (17, 18)

Answers them that derided him (19, 20)

Artaxerxes sends Nehemiah to Jerusalem, with a commission to build the wall (1–8)

1. Nisan – Four months after he had heard those sad tidings. The reason of this long delay might be either that his turn of attending upon the king did not come 'till that time: or that 'till then he wanted a fit opportunity to move it to him.

2. Sad – His fasting joined with inward grief had made a sensible change in his countenance. **Afraid** – It was an unusual and ungrateful thing to come into the king of Persia's presence with any token of sorrow. And he feared a disappointment, because his request was great and invidious, and odious to most of the Persian courtiers.

3. Why should – All the grievances of the church, but especially its desolations, ought to be matter of grief to all good people, to all that have a concern for God's honour, and are of a public spirit.

4. Let – My sadness comes not from any disaffection to the king, for whom my hearty prayers are that he may live for ever; but from another cause. **Sepulchres** – Which by all nations are esteemed sacred and inviolable. He saith not a word of the temple as he spake before a Heathen king who cared for none of these things. **I prayed** – To direct my thoughts and words, and to incline the king's heart to grant my request.

6. The queen – Which is here noted, as an unusual thing; for commonly the kings of Persia dined alone, and perhaps because the queen expressed some kindness to him, and promoted his request. **How long** – This question showed the king's affection to him, and that he was not willing to want his attendance longer than was necessary. **A time** – He built the walls in fifty two days, chap.6:15, and probably not long after returned to the king, by whom he was sent a second time with a more ample commission.

8. King's forest – Of the forest of Lebanon, famous for choice trees. **Palace** – Of the king's palace, which was adjoining to the house of God. **Enter** – That I shall build to dwell in while I am there.

He comes thither, to the grief of his enemies (9–11)

10. Horonite – So called either, from the place of his birth or rule, which is supposed to be Horonaim, an eminent city of Moab. **The servant** – So called probably from the condition from which he was advanced to his present power and dignity: which also may be mentioned as one reason why he now carried himself so insolently, it being usual for persons suddenly raised from a low state, so to demean themselves.

He secretly views the ruins of it (12–16)

12. Night – Concealing both his intentions as long as he could, knowing that the life of his business lay in secrecy and expedition. **Beast** – To prevent noise.

13. I went – The footmen who accompanied him directing and leading him in the way. His design was to go round the city, to observe the compass and condition of the walls and gates, that he might make sufficient provisions for the work.

14. No place – The way being obstructed with heaps of rubbish.

16. That did – Or, were to do, whom he intended to employ in it.

He informs the rulers of his commission (17, 18)

18. Rise up – Let us do it with vigour, and diligence, and resolution, as those that are determined to go through with it. **Their hands** – Their own and one anothers.

Answers them that derided him (19, 20)

20. No portion – You have no authority over us, nor interest in our church and state, but are aliens from the common-wealth of Israel. **Memorial** – No testimony, or monument, either of your relation to us by birth or religion, or of your kindness to us, or to this place.

Chapter 3

The names of those who presided over the builders, and the parts which each company built (1–32)

1. Eliashib – Grand-child of Joshua, the first high-priest after their return from Babylon. **Rose** – Began the work. Ministers should be foremost in every good work, animating others by their example as well as doctrine. **Sheep-gate** – Which was next to the temple; so called, because the sheep were brought through it to be sacrificed. **Sanctified** – Or, they prepared or repaired it: for so the word sometimes signifies. But our translation seems best, both because that use of the word is most common, and because this is spoken only of this gate, which being built by the priests, and nighest to the temple, and with a special eye to the service of the temple, for which both men and things were most commonly brought in this way, and being also the first part of the building, might be in a peculiar manner sanctified by solemn prayer and sacrifice, whereby it was dedicated to God's service.

5. Their nobles – Did not submit to it, would not further it, either through sloth or covetousness, or secret compliance with the enemies of the Jews. **Of their Lord** – Of God, whom they owned for their Lord, whose work this was, because it had proceeded thus far by his singular providence: and because it was done for the defence of the city, and people, and temple of God. And therefore they are branded to all posterity. Let not nobles think any thing beneath them, by which they may benefit their country. What is their nobility good for, but that it places them in an higher and larger sphere of usefulness?

7. The throne – Unto the place where the governor of the country on this side Euphrates, under the Persian kings, sometimes had a palace or throne.

8. Fortified – It is not said, they repaired, but they fortified it, either because this part of the wall was less demolished than the other, and therefore they needed not to repair it, but only to make it stronger: or, to note their extraordinary care and diligence, that they would not only repair it, but make it stronger than ever.

9. Half part – As Rome was anciently divided into several quarters or regions, so was Jerusalem; and especially into two parts, whereof one was in the tribe of Benjamin, and nearest the temple, the other in the tribe of Judah, these accordingly had two several rulers, this man and the other, ver.12, but both under the chief governor of the city.

12. His daughters – Who were either heiresses or rich widows, and caused part to be done at their charges.

14. Beth-haccerem – A town or territory, the government whereof was divided between two persons.

16. Made – By Hezekiah, 2 Kings 20:20. Whereby it is distinguished from that pool which was natural. **Mighty** – Or, of the valiant: which possibly was formerly appointed for the receipt of those chief captains that should attend upon the king in their courses.

20. Earnestly – Did his work with eminent diligence and fervency: which is here noted to his commendation. And it is probable, this good man's zeal provoked many, to take the more pains, and make the more haste.

21. The door – Therefore the door was not in the middle of the house, as now they commonly are, but at one end of it.

27. Tektite – The same spoken of before, who having dispatched their first share sooner than their brethren, freely offered to supply the defects of others, who, as it seems, neglected that part of the work which had been committed to them. And this their double diligence is noted both for the greater shame of their nobles, who would not do any part of it, and for their own honour, who were so far from being corrupted by that bad example, that they were quickened to greater zeal and industry in this pious work.

30. The sixth son of Zalaph – It seems, his five elder brethren, laid not their hands to the work. But in doing that which is good, we need not stay to see our betters go before us.

Chapter 4

The enemies scoff, but Nehemiah prays, and continues the work (1–6)

To frustrate their design, he prays and sets a guard (7–13)

He encourages the workmen, and directs them how to proceed (14–18)

His further directions (19–23)

The enemies scoff, but Nehemiah prays, and continues the work (1–6)

2. In a day – Do they intend to begin, and finish the work, all in one day? For if they spend any long time about it, they cannot think that we will suffer them to do it. **The stones** – Will they pick up their broken stones out of the ruins, and patch them together. **Burnt** – Which stones were burnt, and broken, by the Chaldeans when they took the city.

4. A prey – Give them for a prey to their enemies, and let these carry them into the land of captivity.

5. Cover not – Let their wickedness be in thy sight, so as to bring down judgments upon them, that either they may be reformed, or others may be warned by their example. God is said to cover or hide sin when he forbears to punish it. **Provoked thee** – They have not only provoked us builders, but thee also.

6. The half – Unto half its height.

To frustrate their design, he prays and sets a guard (7–13)

10. Judah – The Jews now dwelling in Judah, some of them being partly terrified by their enemies, and partly wearied with continual labour. **Rubbish** – More than we are able suddenly to remove. **Not able** – Being forced to spend our time in removing the rubbish, and therefore we must desist for a season.

12. By them – Or, among them: whereby they came to the knowledge of their counsels. Although these had not zeal enough to help in the work, yet they had some concern for their brethren. **Ten tribes** – Very often, a certain number for an uncertain. **Be upon you** – They will invade you every way, by which we can come to you, or you to us; therefore keep watches on every side.

13. Behind – Within the walls where they were not yet raised to their due height, and therefore most liable to the enemies assault. **Higher** – Upon the tops of the walls where they were finished, and the towers which were built here and there upon the wall; whence they might shoot arrows, or throw stones.

He encourages the workmen, and directs them how to proceed (14–18)

14. Looked – He looked up, engaged God for him, and put himself and his cause under the Divine protection. That was his way, and should be ours: all his cares, all his griefs, all his fears he spread before God. **Great and terrible** – You think your enemies are great and terrible. But what are they in comparison of God? Especially in opposition to him?

16. From that time forth – Lest our enemies should repeat their enterprise. **My servants** – Of my domestic servants, and of my guards. **Held** – All their weapons: they stood in their arms prepared for battle. **Were behind** – To encourage them in their work, sometimes to assist with their own hands: and to direct and command them in case of an assault. **Judah** – The Jews who were upon the wall.

17. A Weapon – This is to be taken figuratively; being a proverbial speech, as when they say of a man pretending kindness, he carries bread in one hand, and a stone in another. Thus must we work out our salvation, with the weapons of our warfare in our hands. For in every duty we must expect opposition from our spiritual enemies.

18. Sounded – To call the people together, when, and where it was necessary.

His further directions (19–23)

23. Washing – When they were to wash and cleanse themselves from some impurity, which might befall them or their garments.

Chapter 5

The poor complain of being oppressed by the rich (1–5)

Nehemiah removes the oppression (6–13)

He sets an example of compassion on the poor (14–19)

The poor complain of being oppressed by the rich (1–5)

2. Many – Which is in itself a blessing, but to us is turned into a curse. **Take up** – We are forced to take up corn, upon unreasonable terms.

3. The dearth – Which might happen, both from the multitude of the people in and near Jerusalem, from their work, which wholly took them up, and kept them from taking care of their families, and from the expectation of their enemies invasion, which hindered them from going abroad to fetch provision, and the people round about from bringing it to them.

5. Our flesh – We are of the same nature, and religion with them, though they treat us as if we were beasts or Heathens. **Bondage** – We are compelled to sell them for our subsistence. **Daughters** – Which was an evidence of their great necessity, because their daughters were more tender, and weak, and unfit for bond-service, and more exposed to injuries than their sons. **Redeem** – Which we are allowed to do, Exod 21:7-11, but have not wherewith to do it.

Nehemiah removes the oppression (6–13)

7. Exact – Which was against the plain and positive law of God, Deut 23:19,20, especially in this time of public calamity. **I set** – I called a public congregation, both of the rulers and people, the greatest part whereof were free from this guilt, and therefore more impartial judges of the matter, and represented it to them, that the offenders might be convinced, and reformed; if not for fear of God, or love of their brethren, yet at least for the public shame and the cries of the poor. Ezra, and Nehemiah were both good and useful men; but of how different tempers? Ezra was a man of a mild tender spirit, and when told of the sin of the rulers, rent his clothes and wept: Nehemiah forced them to reform, being of a warm and eager spirit. So God's work may be done, and yet different methods taken in doing it; which is a good reason why we should not arraign the management of others, nor make our own standard.

8. We – I, and my brethren, and predecessors, have used our utmost interest and power, both with the kings of Persia, that our brethren might be redeemed from bondage, and with particular persons in Babylon, and Persia, whose bond-slaves the Jews were, and who would not part with them without a price. **Be sold** – Do you expect that we should pay you a price for them, as we did to the Babylonians? Or, must we use as much importunity to solicit you for their redemption, as we did to their enemies?

9. Reproach – Who are round about you, and observe all your actions, and will reproach both you for such barbarous usage of your brethren, and religion for your sakes.

10. Brethren – In office; these who are employed with me in the government of this people. **Servants** – In my name, and for my use. **Exact** – As a just recompense for our pains and care for the public good, to which we wholly devote ourselves, even to the neglect of all our private concerns. But I freely remit my own right, and therefore you also ought to do so, seeing I lay no burden upon you, but what I am willing to bear a part of upon my own shoulders.

11. Also – Also require not: which is to be supplied out of the next verse, where it is expressed in their grant of this desire. **Hundredth part** – Which they required every month for the use of their monies or goods, according to the custom then used.

12. Require – For the hundredth part. **Priests** – As witnesses; that the oath being taken before the priests, who acted in God's name, the oath might make the more deep and durable impression upon their consciences.

13. My lap – The extreme parts of my garment, which I first folded together, and then shook it and scattered it asunder. This was a form of swearing then in use.

He sets an example of compassion on the poor (14–19)

14. Twelve years – Not that he continued so long together at Jerusalem, but he so long governed Jerusalem by himself when present, and in his absence, by a deputy. **The bread** – That allowance which by the laws of God and nations, and of the king of Persia, the governors might require.

15. The former – Not Ezra, who was no governor, nor Zerubbabel, but others between him and Nehemiah, whom he forbears to name. **Beside** – Which they required of the people every day to defray their other expenses. **Their servants** – Ruled them with rigour and cruelty; which fault of the servants is charged upon their masters, because they did not restrain them. He had an awe of God's mercy, and a fear of offending him. Those that truly fear God, will not dare to do any thing cruel or unjust. And this is not only a powerful, but an acceptable principle both of justice and charity.

16. I continued – Overseeing, directing, and encouraging the workmen, which was my whole business; and this at my own cost. **Bought** – Of our poor brethren, whose necessities gave abundant opportunity of enriching myself with good bargains.

17. Rulers – Not only Jews of the inferior sort, for whom meaner provisions might suffice, but also their rulers, for whom better provision was fit; who resorted to him upon all occasions, to give him notice of the enemies designs; or to receive his orders.

18. Required not – But bore it out of my own estate: which was very considerable, his office in the Persian court being a place of great profit.

19. According – As I have done thy people good for thy sake, so do me good for thine own sake; for thou art pleased, and hast promised graciously to reward us according to our works, and to mete to men the same measure which they mete to others.

Chapter 6

Nehemiah's answer to his enemies, courting him to an interview (1–4)

To their charge of rebellion (5–9)

To Shemaiah's false prophecy (10–14)

Notwithstanding the treachery of some of the nobles, the work is finished (15–19)

Nehemiah's answer to his enemies, courting him to an interview (1–4)

1. The doors – Not all of them.

2. Meet – To consult about the common service of our master the king of Persia, or to make a friendly accommodation.

4. Four times – We must never be overcome by the greatest importunity, to do anything ill or imprudent: but when we are attacked with the same temptation, still resist it with the same reason and resolution.

To their charge of rebellion (5–9)

5. Open letter – As speaking of a thing commonly known.

7. A king – We have now a king of our nation. **Counsel** – That we may impartially examine the matter, that thy innocency may be cleared.

9. Strengthen my hands – A good prayer, when we are entering on any particular services or conflicts in our Christian warfare.

To Shemaiah's false prophecy (10–14)

10. Shut up – In his chamber adjoining to the temple, upon pretence of singular devotion, and communion with God, and withal upon pretence of certain knowledge, by the Spirit of God concerning their approaching danger, from which they could be safe nowhere but in the temple. For if Nehemiah had done this, the people would have left their work, and every one have shifted for his own safety.

11. As I – I the chief governor, upon whose presence, the very life of the whole city and nation in a great measure depends: I who have professed such resolution, and courage, and confidence in God. I, who have had such eminent experience of God's assistance, of his calling me to this employment, and carrying me

407

through it when our danger was greater than now it is. Shall I now dishonour God and religion, and betray the people and city of God by my cowardice? **Go in** – Although his life depended upon it.

13. And sin – By going into a place forbidden to me, and that in such a manner, which would have been both sinful and shameful. **Reproach** – As a coward, and conscious of my own guilt, that they might make me contemptible and odious both to my own people, and to the king of Persia.

14. My God – This prayer we are not to imitate.

Notwithstanding the treachery of some of the nobles, the work is finished (15–19)

15. Elul – Answering part to our August, and part to September.

Chapter 7

Nehemiah appoints persons to keep the city (1–4)

Reviews the people (5–7)

Nehemiah appoints persons to keep the city (1–4)

3. Hot – 'Till it be clear and broad day; when the people will be ready in case of an assault. **They** – The watches appointed to that end. **Watches** – Nehemiah was now about to return to the court, and left the charge of the city to these in his absence.

Reviews the people (5–7)

5. God put it into mine heart – Whatever good motion is in our minds, we must acknowledge it to come from God. What is done by human prudence is to be ascribed to the direction of Divine Providence.

7. Tirshatha – Nehemiah. So it is no wonder that the number of the monies, and other things here contributed, differ from that Ezra 2:68,69, because this is another collection.

Chapter 8

The solemn reading and expounding of the law (1–8)

The joy of the people (9–12)

The keeping of the feast of tabernacles (13–18)

The solemn reading and expounding of the law (1–8)

2. First day – This was the feast of trumpets, which is called a Sabbath, and on which they

were to have an holy convocation, Lev 23:24. And it was on this day, the altar was set up, after their return from captivity; in remembrance of which they had probably kept it ever since, with more than ordinary solemnity.

7. Understand – As well the words, which being Hebrew, now needed to be translated into the Chaldee or Syriac language, now, the common language of that people, who together with their religion, had also in a great part lost their language; as also the meaning of them: they expounded the mind and will of God in what they read, and applied it to the peoples present condition. **Place** – That is, In their several places and stations into which the company seems to have been distributed for convenience of hearing; it not being likely that so vast a congregation could distinctly hear one man's voice. Or, by their stations, that is, by the several stations of the Levites, and persons last named; who seem to have had several scaffolds, by comparing this with chap.9:4, upon which they stood, as Ezra did upon his pulpit, ver.8:4.

8. They – Ezra and his companions successively. **Sense** – The meaning of the Hebrew words, which they expounded in the common language. **And gave** – So they gave them both a translation of the Hebrew words into the Chaldee, and an exposition of the things contained in them.

The joy of the people (9–12)

9. Wept – Out of a sense of their guilt and danger by reason of it.

10. Eat – Feast before the Lord. **Send** – For the relief of your poor brethren. **Holy** – Being the feast of trumpets, and the beginning of this joyful month, wherein so many days of thanksgiving were to be observed. **Strength** – Rejoicing in God in serving him with cheerfulness, and thankfulness, which is your duty always, but now especially, will give you that strength both of mind and body, which you greatly need, both to perform all the duties required of you, and to oppose all the designs of your enemies.

The keeping of the feast of tabernacles (13–18)

13. Levites – Choosing rather to confess their ignorance than vainly to pretend to more knowledge than they had: wherein they shew both humility, and serious godliness, that they were more careful to learn their duty than to preserve their reputation.

15. Mount – The mount of Olives, which was next Jerusalem, and stored with olive-branches, and probably with the rest: for these trees seem to have been planted hereabouts principally, for the use of the city in this very feast, which, though, long neglected, should have been celebrated every year. And this place seems to be here designed as the most eminent place, being put for any place near to the several cities of Judah, where these branches were to be procured.

17. **Done so** – So, as to the manner and circumstances. They never kept this feast so joyfully, having not only the same causes of rejoicing which they formerly had, but special causes to increase their joy; they never kept it so solemnly and religiously: for whereas at other times, only the first and last day of that feast were celebrated with an holy convocation, now there was an holy convocation, and the people assembled, and attended upon the reading of the law, every day of this feast.

Chapter 9

The people keep a solemn fast (1–3)

The Levites bless God for his goodness to them and their fathers (4–8)

In Egypt and in their journey out of it, and on mount Sinai (9–14)

And their journey toward Canaan, and in the wilderness (15–21)

In driving out the Canaanites (22–26)

In hearing their prayer when in trouble (27–31)

They confess their sin (32–37)

And seal a covenant with God (38)

The people keep a solemn fast (1–3)

1. **Now** – The next day, but one after the feast of tabernacles, which begun on the fourteenth day, and ended on the twenty second, for their consciences having been fully awakened and their hearts filled with grief for their sins, which they were not allowed to express in that time of public joy; now they resume their former thoughts, and recalling their sins to mind, set apart a day for solemn fasting and humiliation.

2. **Separated** – From all unnecessary society with the Heathens, and particularly from those strange women whom some of them had married. For though Ezra had done this formerly, yet, it seems, there were some criminals, without his knowledge, or, these were some new delinquents, that since that time had fallen into the same error, and showed the truth of their repentance by forsaking their beloved sins, and dearest relations.

3. **Book of the law** – As they did before, giving them the sense of what they read. **Fourth part** – For three hours; there were twelve hours in their day, probably they began after the morning sacrifice, and continued their work till the evening sacrifice. The work of a fast-day is good work. We should endeavour to make a day's work, a good day's work of it.

The Levites bless God for his goodness to them and their fathers (4–8)

4. **Stairs** – Upon such stairs, or pulpits, as the Levites used to stand upon, when they taught the people. But they stood upon several pulpits, each of them teaching that part of the congregation which was allotted him, or praying, or blessing God with them. **Loud voice** – Thereby testifying their deep sense of their sins and miseries, and their servant, and importunate desire of God's mercy.

In Egypt and in their journey out of it, and on mount Sinai (9–14)

13. **Good statutes** – The moral and judicial precepts were all founded on natural equity. And even the ceremonial were tokens of God's goodness, being types of gospel-grace.

And their journey toward Canaan, and in the wilderness (15–21)

17. **Made** – Designed, and resolved to do so, Numb 14:4, and therefore they are said to do so, as Abraham is said to have offered up Isaac, Heb 11:17, because he intended to do it.

In driving out the Canaanites (22–26)

22. **Divide** – The Heathen nations, whom God in a great measure destroyed, and the remainders of them he dispersed into corners; that whereas before the Israelites came, they had large habitations, now they were cooped up, some in one town, and some in another, in the several corners of their land, while the Israelites dwelt in a large place, and had the possession of their whole land, some few and small parcels excepted.

In hearing their prayer when in trouble (27–31)

They confess their sin (32–37)

32. **Mercy** – He adds mercy, because the covenant in itself was not a sufficient ground of hope, because they had so basely broken it. God was discharged from keeping it, and therefore they fly to God's free and rich mercy for relief.

33. **Thou art just** – It becomes us, when we are under the rebukes of providence, be they ever so sharp, or ever so long continued, still to justify God, and to own we are punished less than our iniquities deserve.

37. **Yieldeth much** – We plow, and sow, and labour, and thou givest thy blessing to our endeavours; and yet in a great measure this is not for ourselves, as formerly it was, but for our kings, to whom we pay heavy tributes. **Dominion** – Pressing or forcing both us and our beasts to go and to do what they please.

And seal a covenant with God (38)

38. Sure covenant – It was sealed and left upon record, that it might be a witness against them, if they dealt deceitfully.

Chapter 10

The names of those who set their seal to the covenant (1–27)

An account of those who consented thereto (28–31)

They engage to adhere to the temple service (32–39)

The names of those who set their seal to the covenant (1–27)

1. Sealed – Both in their own names, and in the name of all the rest. It may seem strange that Ezra doth not appear among them. But that might be because he was prevented, by some sickness, or other extraordinary impediment. It is true, we meet with Ezra after this, at the dedication of the wall of Jerusalem, chap.12:36, and therefore he was then freed from this impediment, whatsoever it was.

An account of those who consented thereto (28–31)

29. Their nobles – The commonality agreed with the nobles in this good work, great men never look so great, as when they encourage religion and are examples of it: and they would by that, as much as any thing, make an interest in the most valuable of their inferiors, who would cleave to them closer than they can imagine. Observe their nobles are called their brethren; for in the things of God, rich and poor, high and low meet together. **They cleave** – They ratified what the others had done in their names, declaring their assent to it.

31. People of the land – The Heathens. **On the Sabbath** – They that covenant to keep all the commandments of God, must particularly covenant to keep the Sabbath holy. For the profanation of this is a sure inlet to all manner of profaneness.

They engage to adhere to the temple service (32–39)

Chapter 11

The rulers and men drawn by lot dwell at Jerusalem (1, 2)

Their names, numbers and families (3–19)

The cities and villages that were peopled by the rest (20–36)

The rulers and men drawn by lot dwell at Jerusalem (1, 2)

1. To dwell – That the buildings of the city might be completed, and the safety of it better provided for.

2. Blessed – Because they denied themselves, and their own safety and profit for the public good; for this city was the butt of all the malicious plots of their enemies; and for the present it was rather chargeable than beneficial to its inhabitants.

Their names, numbers and families (3–19)

3. Province – Of Judea, which was now made a province. **Israel** – The generality of the people of Israel, whether of Judah, or Benjamin, or any other tribe. These he calls Israel rather than Judah, because there were many of the other tribes now incorporated with them; and because none of the tribes of Israel, except Judah and Benjamin, dwelt in Jerusalem.

9. Overseer – The captain of their thousand.

16. Outward – For those things belonging to the temple and its service, which were to be done without it, or abroad in the country, as the gathering in of the voluntary contributions, or other necessary provision out of the several parts of the land.

17. To begin – In the public and solemn prayers and praises, which were constantly joined with the morning and evening sacrifice, at which the singers were present, and praised God with a psalm or hymn which, this man began.

The cities and villages that were peopled by the rest (20–36)

21. The Nethinims dwelt in Ophel – Which was upon the wall of Jerusalem, because they were to do the servile work of the temple: therefore they were to be posted near it, that they might be ready to attend.

24. Was – Or, on the king's part, to determine civil causes and controversies between man and man, by the laws of that kingdom; between the king and people; as in matters of tribute, or grievances.

36. Divisions – Or, for the Levites (those who were not settled in Jerusalem) there were divisions, places appointed for them, and distributed among them. Thus were they settled free and easy, although few and poor. And they might have been happy, but for that general lukewarmness, with which they are charged by the prophet Malachi, who prophesied about this time and in whom prophecy ceased for some ages, 'till it revived in the great prophet.

Chapter 12

The chief of the priests and Levites that
came up with Zerubbabel (1–9)

The succession of the chief-priests (10–21)

The eminent Levites (22–26)

The wall dedicated (27–43)

The offices of the priests and Levites settled
(44–47)

The chief of the priests and Levites that came up with Zerubbabel (1–9)

1. Priests – The chief of the priests, the heads of those twenty four courses which David appointed by divine direction, 1Chron 24:1–19. And whereas there were twenty four, and here but twenty-two, and ver.12 only twenty, the reason of this difference may be, because two of the twenty four courses were extinct in Babylon, and two of the persons here named, ver.2,5, Hattush, and Maadiah, may be omitted in the account of the posterity of these, ver.12 because they had no posterity. **Ezra** – Either this was another Ezra, or if it were the same mentioned Ezra 7:1, he lived to a great age; which may well be supposed, considering his great sobriety, and his great piety to which God promised long life, and withal the special providence of God continuing him so long in such a season, wherein the church of God did greatly need his help and counsel.

8. Moreover – He was to see, that the psalms of thanksgiving were continually sung in the temple, in due time and manner.

The succession of the chief-priests (10–21)

10. Jeshua – Here follows a catalogue of the Jewish high-priests; which was the more necessary, because their times were now to be measured, not by the years of their kings as formerly, but by their high-priests.

12. Priests – As their fathers were priests in the days of Joshua, so in the days of Joiakim the son of Joshua, the sons of those persons executed the priesthood in their father's steads, some of their fathers probably being yet living, and many of them dead.

The eminent Levites (22–26)

22. Darius – Darius Noehus; and so this Jaddua might be father to him who was in the days of Darius Codomanus, and of Alexander the Great.

The wall dedicated (27–43)

27. The wall – Of the city itself, which is here dedicated to God, and to his honour and service, not only upon a general account, by which we ought to devote ourselves, and all that is ours, to God; but upon a more special ground, because this was a place which God himself had chosen, and sanctified by his temple and gracious presence, and therefore did of right belong to him; whence it is often called the holy city. And they restored it to God by this dedication, withal imploring the presence, and favour, and blessing of to this city by solemn prayers, and praises, and sacrifices, wherewith this dedication was accompanied. **Places** – To which they were now retired after that great and general assembly, chap. 8-10. Ne 8:1.

30. Purified themselves – They that would be instrumental to sanctify others, must sanctify themselves, and set themselves apart for God, with purity of mind and sincerity of intention.

31. Princes – And half of the people with them. **The wall** – For the wall was broad and strong, and so ordered that men might conveniently walk upon it. **Right hand** – Towards the south and east.

39. Stood still – Waiting, as also their brethren did, that they might go together in due order into God's house, there to perfect the solemnity.

43. The children rejoiced – And their hosanna's were not despised, but are recorded to their praise. All that share in public mercies, ought to join in public thanksgivings.

The offices of the priests and Levites settled (44–47)

44. Rejoiced – For the eminent gifts and graces which they observed in many of them: for the great benefit which they had now received by their ministry: and for the competent provision which hereby was made for them, that so they might wholly wait upon their office. The sure way for ministers to gain an interest, in the affections of their people, is to wait on their ministry, to spend their whole time, and thought, and strength therein.

45. The ward – That ward, or charge, which God had prescribed to them. And in particular the charge of purification, of taking care that no unclean person or thing should enter into the house or courts of the Lord.

47. Sanctified – They set apart the first-fruits and tithes from their own share, and devoted them to the use of the Levites. And so did the Levites by the tithe of the tithes. Thus they all conscientiously paid their dues, and did not profane those things which God had sanctified, nor take them into their own common use. When what is contributed for the support of religion, is given with an eye to God, is sanctified, and will cause the blessing to rest upon the house, and all that is therein.

Chapter 13

The Israelites are separated from the mixt multitude (1–3)

Nehemiah cleansed the chambers of the temple (4–9)

He recovers and secures the portion of the priests and Levites (10–14)

Contends with the nobles concerning the Sabbath, and takes care for the due observance of it (15–22)

Restrains them from marrying strange wives (23–31)

The Israelites are separated from the mixt multitude (1–3)

1. That day – Not presently after the dedication of the wall and city, but upon a certain day, when Nehemiah was returned from the Persian court to Jerusalem, from which he had been absent for some considerable time, in which some errors and abuses had crept in. **Not come** – Not be incorporated into the common-wealth of Israel, nor be joined with any Israelite in marriage.

3. Multitude – All the heathenish people with whom they had contracted alliance.

Nehemiah cleansed the chambers of the temple (4–9)

4. Eliashib – The high-priest. **Chamber** – Of the chambers, the high-priest having the chief power over the house of God, and all the chambers belonging to it. **Tobiah** – The Ammonite, and a violent enemy to God's people.

5. Prepared – By removing the things out of it, uniting divers small chambers into one, and furnishing it for the use of Tobiah when he came to Jerusalem: whom he seems to have lodged there, that he might have more free communication with him.

6. But – Eliashib took the occasion of my absence to do these things. **Came I** – From Jerusalem; where he had been once and again.

8. Grieved me – That so sacred a place should be polluted by one who in many respects ought not to come there, being no priest, a stranger, an Ammonite, and one of the worst of that people; and that all this should be done by the permission and order of the high-priest.

He recovers and secures the portion of the priests and Levites (10–14)

10. Not given – Which might be either,

1. from this corrupt high-priest Eliashib, who took their portions, as he did the sacred chambers, to his own use, or employed them for the entertainment of Tobiah, and his other great allies.

Or, 2. from the people, who either out of covetousness reserved them to themselves, contrary to their own solemn agreement, or were so offended at Eliashib's horrid abuse of sacred things, that they abhorred the offering and service of God, and therefore neglected to bring in their tithes, which they knew would be perverted to bad uses.

Fled – To his possession in the country, being forced to do so for a livelihood.

11. Contended – I sharply reproved those priests to whom the management of those things was committed, for neglect of their duty, and breach of their late solemn promise. **Why** – You have not only injured men in with-holding their dues, but you have occasioned the neglect of God's house and service. **Gathered** – To Jerusalem from their several country possessions. **Set** – Restored them to the exercise of their office.

12. Bought – Out of the respect which they had to Nehemiah, and because they saw they would now be applied to their proper uses.

13. Faithful – By the consent of those who knew them. Such he now sought out the more diligently, because he had experience of the perfidiousness of the former trustees.

Contends with the nobles concerning the Sabbath, and takes care for the due observance of it (15–22)

16. Jerusalem – The holy city, where God's house was; and where the great judicatories of the nation were. So this is added as an aggravation of their sin, that it was done with manifest contempt of God and man.

17. Nobles – Their chief men and rulers; whom he charges with this sin, because though others did it, it was by their countenance or connivance: probably too by their example. If the nobles allowed themselves in recreations, in idle visits and idle talk on the Sabbath day, the men of business would profane it by their worldly employments, as the more justifiable of the two.

19. At the gates – Out of a diffidence in those, to whom the keeping of the gates was committed.

22. Cleanse – Because the work they now were set upon, though common in its nature, yet was holy in design of it, and had respect unto the Sabbath: and, because the day in which they were to do this was the Sabbath-day, for the observation whereof they were obliged to purify themselves. **Gates** – The gates of the city; not daring to trust the common porters, he commits the charge of them upon the Sabbath-days, to the Levites, to whom the care of sanctifying the Sabbath did properly belong. **Mercy** –

Whereby he intimates, that though he mentioned his good-works, as things wherewith God was well-pleased, and which he had promised to reward, yet he neither did, nor durst trust to their merit, or his own worthiness, but, when he had done all, he judged himself an unprofitable servant, and one that needed God's infinite mercy to pardon all his sins, and particularly those infirmities and corruptions which adhered to his good deeds.

Restrains them from marrying strange wives (23–31)

25. Cursed – Caused them to be excommunica-ted and cast out of the society of God's people. This and the following punishments were justly inflicted upon them, because this transgression was contrary both to a plain law of God, and to their own late solemn covenants. **Smote** – I caused to be beaten with stripes, according to the law, Deut 25:2, such whose faults were most aggravated; to whom he added this punishment over and above the former. **Plucked off** – Or, shaved them. The hair was an ensign of liberty among the eastern nations; and baldness was a disgrace, and token of slavery and sorrow.

28. And one – Said by Josephus to be that Manasses, who by Sanballat's interest procured liberty to build the Samaritan temple in mount Gerizim; to which those priests who had married strange wives, or been otherwise criminal, betook themselves, and with, or after them, others of the people in the same or like circumstances. **Chased** – From my presence and court, from the city and temple, and from the congregation and church of Israel.

31. For good – This may well be the summary of our petitions. We need no more to make us happy but this.

ESTHER

John Wesley

Introduction

Both Jews and Christians have generally supposed Mordecai to be the writer of this book, which shows the care of God even over those Israelites, who were still scattered among the Heathens. It is the narrative of a plot to cut off all the Jews, disappointed by a wonderful concurrence of providences. The name of God is not found in this book: but the, finger of God is, directing so many minute events for the deliverance of his people. The particulars are very encouraging to God's people, in the most difficult and dangerous times. Here we are told how Esther came to be queen, and Mordecai to be great at court, chap. 1, 2. How Haman obtained an order for the destruction of the Jews, chap. 3. The distress of the Jews thereupon, chap. 4. The defeating of Haman's plot against Mordecai, chap. 5–7. The defeating of his plot against the Jews, chap. 8. The care taken to perpetuate the memory of this, chap. 9, 10.

Chapter 1

Ahasuerus feasts his great men (1–9)

Sends for his queen, who refuses to come (10, 11)

He divorces her (12–22)

Ahasuerus feasts his great men (1–9)

1. Ahasuerus – Many suppose this to be Darius Hystapas, for his kingdom was thus vast, and he subdued India, as Herodotus reports: and one of his wives was called Atossa, differing little from Hadassah, which is Esther's other name, Esth 2:7. **Provinces** – So seven new provinces were added to those hundred and twenty mentioned, Dan 6:1.

2. Sat – Was settled in the peaceable possession of it. **Shushan** – The chief or royal city. Shushan might be the proper name of the palace, which thence was given to the whole city.

Here the kings of Persia used to keep their courts in winter, as at Exbatana in summer.

4. Many days – Making every day a magnificent feast, either for all his princes, or for some of them, who might come to the feast successively, as the king ordered them to do. The Persian feasts are much celebrated in authors, for their length and luxury.

6. Beds – For in those eastern countries, they did not then sit at tables as we do, but rested or leaned upon beds or couches.

8. The law – According to this law which the king had now made, that none should compel another to drink more than he pleased. How does this Heathen prince shame many, that are called Christians, who think they do not make their friends welcome, unless they make them drunk, and under pretence of sending the health round, send the sin round, and death with it!

9. Women – While the king entertained the men. For this was the common custom of the Persians, that men and women did not feast together.

Sends for his queen, who refuses to come (10, 11)

He divorces her (12–22)

12. Refused – Being favoured in this refusal by the law of Persia, which was to keep mens wives, and especially queens, from the view of other men.

13. The times – The histories of former times, what princes have done in such cases as this was.

14. Saw – Who had constant freedom of access to the king, and familiar converse with him: which is thus expressed, because the Persian kings were very seldom seen by their subjects. **Sat** – Who were his chief counsellors and officers.

18. Contempt – Contempt in the wives, and thereupon wrath in the husbands; and consequently strife in families.

Chapter 2

The virgins of the kingdom are gathered together (1–4)

And Esther with the rest (5–8)

She finds favour with the king's chamberlain (9–11)

The manner of preparing the virgins, and bringing them to the king (12–14)

Esther pleases him, who makes her queen (15–20)

Mordecai discovers a conspiracy against the king (21–23)

The virgins of the kingdom are gathered together (1–4)

3. Keeper – Of all the women, both virgins and concubines: only the virgins he himself took care of, as requiring more care and caution, and the concubines he committed to Shaashgaz, ver.14, his deputy. **Purification** – That is, to cleanse them from all impurities, to perfume, and adorn, and every way prepare them for the king: for the legal purification of the Jews he never regarded.

And Esther with the rest (5–8)

7. Esther – Hadassah was her Hebrew name before her marriage; and she was called Esther by the king after it.

She finds favour with the king's chamberlain (9–11)

9. Pleased – Because she was very beautiful, therefore he supposed she would be acceptable to the king; and by the Divine power, which

moveth the hearts of men which way he pleaseth.

10. Shew it – Lest the knowledge hereof should either make her contemptible, or bring some inconvenience to the whole nation; but there was also an hand of God in causing this to be concealed, for the better accomplishment of that which he designed, though Mordecai was ignorant of it.

The manner of preparing the virgins, and bringing them to the king (12–14)

13. Desired – For ornament, or by way of attendance. And it should be observed, that every one whom the king took to his bed, was his wife of a lower rank, as Hagar was Abraham's, so that it would have been no sin or dishonour to Esther, though she had not been made queen.

Esther pleases him, who makes her queen (15–20)

19. Sat – By office, as one of the king's guards or ministers; being advanced to this place by Esther's favour.

Mordecai discovers a conspiracy against the king (21–23)

Chapter 3

Haman offended at Mordecai, resolves to destroy all the Jews (1–6)

He obtains an order from the king, to have them all slain on one day (7–11)

This order is sent throughout the kingdom (12–15)

Haman offended at Mordecai, resolves to destroy all the Jews (1–6)

1. Agagite – An Amalekite of the royal seed of that nation, whose kings were successively called Agag. **All the princes** – Gave him the first place and seat, which was next to the king.

2. But – Probably the worship required was not only civil, but Divine: which as the kings of Persia arrogated to themselves, so they did sometimes impart this honour to some of their chief favourites, that they should be adored in like manner. And that it was so here, seems more than probable, because it was superfluous, to give an express command to all the kings servants, to pay a civil respect to so great a prince, which of course they used, and therefore a Divine honour must be here intended. And that a Jew should deny this honour, is not strange, seeing the wise Grecians did positively refuse to give this honour to the kings of Persia themselves, even when they were to make their addresses to them: and one Timocrates was put to death by the Athenians for worshipping Darius in that manner.

4. To see – What the event of it would be. **For** – And therefore did not deny this reverence out of pride, but merely out of conscience.

6. Scorn – He thought that vengeance was unsuitable to his quality. **Destroy** – Which he attempted, from that implacable hatred which, as an Amalekite, he had against them; from his rage against Mordecai; and from Mordecai's reason of this contempt, because he was a Jew, which as he truly judged, extended itself to all the Jews, and would equally engage them all in the same neglect. And doubtless Haman included those who were returned to their own land: for that was now a province of his kingdom.

He obtains an order from the king, to have them all slain on one day (7–11)

7. They cast – The diviners cast lots, according to the custom of those people, what day, and what month would be most lucky, not for his success with the king (of which he made no doubt) but for the most effectual extirpation of the Jews. Wherein appears likewise both his implacable malice, and unwearied diligence in seeking vengeance of them with so much trouble to himself; and God's singular providence in disposing the lot to that time, that the Jews might have space to get the decree reversed.

11. The silver – Keep it to thy own use; I accept the offer for the deed.

This order is sent throughout the kingdom (12–15)

15. The city – Not only the Jews, but a great number of the citizens, either because they were related to them, or engaged with them in worldly concerns; or out of humanity and compassion toward so vast a number of innocent people, appointed as sheep for the slaughter.

Chapter 4

The Jews fast and mourn (1–3)

Esther is informed of the design (4–9)

Mordecai presses her to intercede with the king (10–14)

She desires all the Jews to keep a solemn fast (15–19)

The Jews fast and mourn (1–3)

1. Cry – To express his deep sense of the mischief coming upon his people. It was bravely done, thus publically to espouse a just cause though it seemed to be a desperate one.

2. Sackcloth – Lest it should give the king any occasion of grief and trouble. But what availed, to keep out the badges of sorrow unless they could have kept out the causes of sorrow too? To forbid sackcloth to enter unless they could likewise forbid sickness, and trouble, and death?

Esther is informed of the design (4–9)

4. To clothe – That so he might be capable of returning to his former place, if not of coming to her to acquaint her with the cause of his sorrow.

Mordecai presses her to intercede with the king (10–14)

11. Inner court – Within which, the king's residence and throne was. **Not called** – This was decreed, to maintain both the majesty, and the safety of the king's person; and by the contrivance of the greater officers of state, that few or none might have access to the king but themselves and their friends. **I have not been called** – Which gives me just cause to fear that the king's affections are alienated from me, and that neither my person nor petition will be acceptable to him.

14. From another place – This was the language of strong faith, against hope believing in hope. **Who knoweth** – It is probable God hath raised thee to this honour for this very season. We should every one of us consider, for what end God has put us in the place where we are? And when an opportunity offers of serving God and our generation, we must take care not to let it slip.

She desires all the Jews to keep a solemn fast (15–19)

16. Fast – And pray; so as you use to do, leave off your common dinners by day, and suppers at night, and eat and drink no more than mere necessity requires; that so you may give yourselves to constant and fervent prayers. **Maidens** – Which she had chosen to attend upon her person, and were doubtless either of the Jewish nation, or Proselytes. **Which is not** – Which may belong, either:

1. to the thing only, that as they did fast, so she would.

Or, rather, 2. to the time of three days and three nights; for so she might do, though she went to the king on the third day.

For the fast began at evening, and so she might continue her fast three whole nights, and two whole days, and the greatest part of the third; a part of a day being reputed a day in the account of scripture, and other authors: of which see on Matt 12:40. Yea, she might fast all that day too: for it is probable she went not to the king 'till he had dined; when she supposed she might find him in the most mild and pleasant humour, and then returned to her apartment, where she fasted 'till the evening.

Chapter 5

Esther finding favour with the king, invites him and Haman to a banquet (1–5)

She invites them to a second (6–8)

Haman makes a gallows for Mordecai (9––14)

Esther finding favour with the king, invites him and Haman to a banquet (1–5)

2. Held out – In testimony that he pardoned her presumption, and was ready to grant her petition. **Touched** – In token of her thankful acceptance of the king's favour, and of her reverence and submission.

3. It shall be given – God in his providence often prevents the fears and outdoes the hopes of his servants. **To the half of the kingdom** – A proverbial expression: that is, nothing in reason shall be denied.

4. Haman – Whom she invited, that by showing such respect to the king's great favourite, she might insinuate herself the more into the king's affection; and, that if she saw fit, she might then present her request to the king.

She invites them to a second (6–8)

6. Of wine – So called, because it consisted not of meats, which probably the king had plentifully eaten before, but of fruits and wines; which banquets were very frequent among the Persians.

8. Tomorrow – I will acquaint thee with my humble request. She did not present her petition at this time, but delayed it 'till the next meeting; either because she was a little daunted with the king's presence, or, because she would farther engage the king's affection to her, and would also intimate to him that her petition was of a more than ordinary nature: but principally by direction of Divine providence, which took away her courage of utterance for this time, that she might have a better opportunity for it the next time, by that great accident which happened before it.

Haman makes a gallows for Mordecai (9–14)

9. Nor moved – To shew how little he feared him, and that he had a firm confidence in his God, that he would deliver him and his people in this great exigency.

10. Refrained – From taking present vengeance upon Mordecai, which he might easily have effected, either by his own, or any of his servants hands, without any fear of inconveniency

to himself. But herein God's wise and powerful providence appeared, in disposing Haman's heart, contrary to his own inclination, and making him, as it were, to put fetters upon his own hands.

12. Am I – Thus he makes that matter of glorying which was the occasion of his utter ruin. So ignorant are the wisest men, and subject to fatal mistakes, rejoicing when they have most cause of fear, and sorrowing for those things which tend to joy and comfort.

13. Availeth – Gives me no content. Such torment did his envy and malice bring upon him. **Sitting** – Enjoying that honour and privilege without disturbance, and denying me the worship due to me by the king's command. Thus tho' proud men have much to their mind, if they have not all to their mind, it is nothing. The thousandth part of what Haman had, would give a modest, humble man, as much happiness as he expects to receive from anything under the sun. And Haman as passionately complains, as if he was in the lowest depth of poverty!

14. Fifty cubits – That it may be more conspicuous to all, and thereby be more disgraceful to Mordecai, and strike all Haman's enemies with a greater dread of despising or opposing him.

Chapter 6

Providence recommends Mordecai to the king's favour (1–3)

Haman is constrained publically to honour him through the city (4–11)

His friends foretell his doom (12, 13)

He goes to the banquet (14)

Providence recommends Mordecai to the king's favour (1–3)

1. Sleep – How vain are all the contrivances of foolish man against the wise and omnipotent God, who hath the hearts and hands of kings and all men perfectly at his disposal, and can by such trivial accidents (as they are accounted) change their minds, and produce such terrible effects. **Were read** – His mind being troubled he knew not how, nor why, he chooses this for a diversion, God putting this thought into him, for otherwise he might have diverted himself, as he used to do, with his wives or concubines, or voices and instruments of music, which were far more agreeable to his temper.

3. Nothing – He hath had no recompense for this great and good service. Which might either happen through the king's forgetfulness; or through the envy of the courtiers; or because he was a Jew, and therefore odious and contemptible.

Haman is constrained publically to honour him through the city (4–11)

4. Haman – Early in the morning, because his malice would not suffer him to sleep; and he was impatient 'till he had executed his revenge; and was resolved to watch for the very first opportunity of speaking to the king, before he was engaged in other matters. **Outward court** – Where he waited; because it was dangerous to come into the inner court without special license, chap.4:11.

6. Man – He names none, because he would have the more impartial answer. And probably knew nothing of the difference between Haman and Mordecai. **Thought** – As he had great reason to do, because of the favour which the king had showed to him above all others.

8. Royal apparel – His outward garment, which was made of purple, interwoven with gold, as Justin and Cartius relate.

His friends foretell his doom (12, 13)

12. Gate – To his former place; shewing that as he was not overwhelmed by Haman's threats, so he was not puffed up with this honour. **Covered** – In token of his shame and grief for his unexpected disappointment, and for the great honour done to his abhorred adversary, by his own hands, and with his own public disgrace.

13. Wise men – The magicians, whom after the Persian manner he had called together to consult upon this strange emergency.

He goes to the banquet (14)

14. To bring – Who was now slack to go thither, by reason of the great dejection of his own mind.

Chapter 7

Esther petitions for her life, and the lives of her people (1–4)

She tells the king that Haman is the man who designed her ruin (5, 6)

By the king's order, he is hanged on the gallows he had prepared for Mordecai (7–10)

Esther petitions for her life, and the lives of her people (1–4)

3. My life – It is my only request, that thou wouldst not give me up to the malice of that man who designs to take away my life. Even a stranger, a criminal, shall be permitted to petition for his life. But that a friend, a wife, a queen, should have occasion to make such a petition, was very affecting.

4. Sold – By the cruelty of that man who offered a great sum to purchase our destruction. **Countervail** – His ten thousand talents would not repair the king's loss, in the customs and tributes which the king receives from the Jews, within his dominions.

She tells the king that Haman is the man who designed her ruin (5, 6)

5. Who – The expressions are short and doubled, as proceeding from a discomposed and enraged mind. **Durst** – That is, to circumvent me, and procure a decree, whereby not only my estate should be so much impaired, and so many of my innocent subjects destroyed, but my queen also involved in the same destruction. We sometimes startle at that evil, which we ourselves are chargeable with. Ahasuerus is amazed at that wickedness, which he himself was guilty of. For he consented to the bloody edict. So that Esther might have said, Thou art the man!

6. Afraid – And it was time for him to fear, when the queen was his prosecutor, the king his judge, his own conscience a witness against him. And the surprising turns of providence that very morning, could not but increase his fear.

By the king's order, he is hanged on the gallows he had prepared for Mordecai (7–10)

7. Went – As disdaining the company and sight of so audacious a person: to cool and allay his troubled and inflamed spirits, and to consider what punishment was fit to be inflicted upon him. **He saw** – By the violent commotion of the king's mind.

8. Bed – On which the queen sat at meat. **Force** – Will he attempt my queen's chastity, as he hath already attempted her life! He speaks not this out of real jealousy, but from an exasperated mind, which takes all occasions to vent itself against the person who gave the provocation. **They** – The king's and queen's chamberlains attending upon them. **Covered** – That the king might not be offended or grieved with the sight of a person whom he now loathed: and because they looked upon him as a condemned person; for the faces of such used to be covered.

Chapter 8

The estate of Haman is given to Esther (1, 2)

Esther petitions the king, to reverse the edict against the Jews (3–6)

They are authorized to defend themselves (7–14)

The Jews and their friends rejoice (15–17)

The estate of Haman is given to Esther (1, 2)

1. The house – With all his goods and estate, which being justly forfeited to the king, he no less justly bestows it upon the queen, to compensate the danger to which Haman had exposed her. **Came** – Was by the queen's desire admitted into the king's presence, and family, and, as it seems, made one of the seven princes. **Had told** – How nearly he was related to her: which 'till this time she had wisely concealed.

2. Ring – That ring which he had formerly given to Haman he now gives to Mordecai, and with it that power whereof this ring was a sign, making him, as Haman had been, the keeper of his signet. **Set** – As her steward, to manage that great estate for her as he thought fittest.

Esther petitions the king, to reverse the edict against the Jews (3–6)

3. To put – To repeal that cruel decree.

5. If – She uses various expressions, that she might confirm the king's favour, by such a full submission to his good pleasure. **Haman** – She prudently takes off the hatefulness of the action from the king, and lay's it upon Haman, who had for his own ends contrived the whole business, and circumvented the king in it.

They are authorized to defend themselves (7–14)

8. Reverse – For this reason he could not recall the former letters, because they were irrevocable by the law of the Medes and Persians. How much more prudent is our constitution, that no law whatever can be established as to be unrepealable? It is God's prerogative, not to repent, and to say what can never be altered.

9. Then – Which was above two months after the former decree. All which time God suffered the Jews to lie under the error of this dreadful day, that they might be more throughly humbled for, and purged from those many and great sins under which they lay; that they might be convinced of their great sin and folly in the many offers they had of returning to their native country, by which means being dispersed in the several parts of this vast dominion, they were like to be a very easy prey to their enemies, whereas their brethren in Judea were in a better capacity to preserve themselves: and for the greater illustration of God's glorious power, and wisdom, and goodness, in giving his people such a admirable and unexpected deliverance.

10. Riders – Which were not employed in sending the former letter: but this coming later required more care and speed, that the Jews might be eased from their present fears, and have time to provide for their own defence.

11. To stand – To fight for the defence of their lives against all that should seek to destroy them. **The power** – Either governors or governed, without any exception either of age, dignity, or sex. **Both little ones and women** – Which is here added, to strike the greater terror into their enemies; and according to the laws and customs of this kingdom; whereby children were punished for their parents offences: yet we read nothing in the execution of this decree of the slaughter of women or children, nor is it probable, they would kill their innocent children, who were so indulgent to their families, as not to meddle with the spoil.

The Jews and their friends rejoice (15–17)

15. Great crown – Which the chief of the Persian princes were permitted to wear but with sufficient distinction from the king's crown. **The city** – Not only Jews, but the greatest number of the citizens, who by the law of nature abhorred bloody counsels, and had a complacency in acts of mercy.

16. Joy – This explains the former metaphor by two words expressing the same thing, to denote the greatness of the joy. **Honour** – Instead of that contempt under which they had lain.

Chapter 9

The Jews slay their enemies (1–11)

A second day is granted them (12–19)

A yearly feast is instituted, in memory of this great deliverance (20–32)

The Jews slay their enemies (1–11)

2. No man – Their enemies, though they did take up arms against them, yet were easily conquered and destroyed by them.

6. Shushan – In the city so called. **Slew** – Whom they knew to be such as would watch all opportunities to destroy them; which also they might possibly now attempt to do.

10. But – Because they would leave it to their children, that it might appear what they did was not done out of malice, or covetousness, but out of mere necessity, and by that great law of self-preservation.

A second day is granted them (12–19)

12. What – In which doubtless many more were slain. So that I have fully granted thy petition. And yet, if thou hast any thing farther to ask, I am ready to grant it.

13. Let it – To kill their implacable enemies. For it is not improbable that the greatest and worst of them had hidden themselves for that day; after which, the commission granted to the

Jews being expired, they confidently returned to their homes. **Hanged** – They were slain before; now let their bodies be hanged on their father's gallows, for their greater infamy, and the terror of all others who shall presume to abuse the king in like manner, or to persuade him to execute such cruelties upon his subjects.

A yearly feast is instituted, in memory of this great deliverance (20–32)

26. Pur – This Persian word signifies a lot, because Haman had by lot determined this time to be the time of the Jews destruction.

27. As joined – Gentile Proselytes; who were obliged to submit to other of the Jewish laws, and therefore to this also; the rather because they enjoyed the benefit of this day's deliverance; without which the Jewish nation and religion had been in a great measure, if not wholly, extinct. **According** – According to that writing which was drawn up by Mordecai, and afterwards confirmed by the consent of the Jews.

29. Wrote – The former letter, ver.20, did only recommend but this enjoins the observation of this solemnity: because this was not only Mordecai's act, but the act of all the Jews, binding themselves and posterity.

30. Peace – With peace, friendship and kindness to his brethren, and truth, sincerity.

31. Cry – For those great calamities which were decreed to all the Jews, and for the removing of which, not only Esther, and the Jews in Shushan, but all other Jews in all places, did doubtless fly to God by fasting, and strong cries.

32. Either – Who had received authority from the king. **The book** – In the records which the Jews kept of their most memorable passages.

Chapter 10

The greatness of Ahasuerus, and of Mordecai (1–3)

2. Chronicles – These are lost long since, and buried in oblivion, while the sacred writings remain throughout the world. When the kingdoms of men, monarchs and their monarchies are destroyed, and their memorial is perished with them, the kingdom of God among men, and the records of that kingdom, shall remain as the days of heaven.

INTRODUCTION TO THE POETIC BOOKS OF THE OLD TESTAMENT

A.R. Faussett

Hebrew poetry is unique in its kind; in essence, the most sublime; in form, marked by a simplicity and ease which flow from its sublimity. 'The Spirit of the LORD spake by me [the Hebrew poet], and his word was in my tongue' (2Sa 23:2). Even the music was put under the charge of spiritually gifted men; and one of the chief musicians, Heman, is called 'the king's seer in the words of God' (1Ch 25:1,5). King David is stated to have invented instruments of music (Am 6:5). There is not in Hebrew poetry the artistic rhythm of form which appears in the classical poetry of Greece and Rome, but it amply makes up for this by its fresh and graceful naturalness.

Early specimens of Hebrew poetry occur; for example, Lamech's sceptical parody of Enoch's prophecy, or, as others think, lamentation for a homicide committed in those lawless times in self-defence (Ge 4:23; compare Jude 1:14 Ex 32:18 Nu 21:14,15,17,18,27 Nu 23:7,8,18 24:3,15). The poetical element appears much more in the Old than in the New Testament. The poetical books are exclusively those of the Old Testament; and in the Old Testament itself, the portions that are the most fundamental (for example, the Pentateuch of Moses, the lawgiver, in its main body) are those which have in them least of the poetical element in form. Elijah, the father of the prophets, is quite free of poetical art. The succeeding prophets were not strictly poets, except in so far as the ecstatic state in inspiration lifted them to poetic modes of thought and expression. The prophet was more of an inspired teacher than a poet. It is when the sacred writer acts as the representative of the personal experiences of the children of God and of the Church, that poetry finds its proper sphere.

The use of poetry

The use of poetry in Scripture was particularly to supply the want not provided for by the law, namely, of devotional forms to express in private, and in public joint worship, the feelings of pious Israelites. The schools of the prophets fostered and diffused a religious spirit among the people; and we find them using lyric instruments to accompany their prophesies (1Sa 10:5). However, it was David, who specially matured the lyric effusions of devotion into a perfection which they had not before attained.

Another purpose which Psalmody, through David's inspired productions, served, was to draw forth from under the typical forms of legal services their hidden essence and spirit, adapting them to the various spiritual exigencies of individual and congregational life. Nature, too, is in them shown to speak the glory and goodness of the invisible, yet ever present God. A handbook of devotion was furnished to the Israelite whereby he could enter into the true spirit of the services of the sanctuary, and so feel the need of that coming Messiah, of whom especially the Book of Psalms testifies throughout. We also, in our Christian dispensation, need its help in our devotions. Obliged as we are, notwithstanding our higher privileges in most respects, to walk by faith rather than by sight in a greater degree than they, we find the Psalms, with their realizing expression of the felt nearness of God, the best repertory whence to draw divinely sanctioned language, wherewith to express our prayers and thanksgivings to God, and our breathings after holy communion with our fellow saints.

As to the objection raised against the spirit of revenge which breathes in some psalms, the answer is: a wide distinction is to be drawn between personal vindictiveness and the desire for God's honour being vindicated. Personal revenge, not only in the other parts of Scripture, but also in the Psalms, in theory and in practice, is alike reprobated (Ex 23:4–5 Le 19:18 Job 31:29–30 Ps 7:4,5,8,11,12 Pr 25:21–22), which corresponds to David's practice in the case of his unrelenting enemy (1Sa 24:5–6 26:8–10). On the other hand, the people of God have always desired that whatever mars the cause of God, as for instance the prosperity of the enemies of God and His Church, should be brought to an end (Ps 10:12 35:27 40:16 79:6,10). It is well for us, too, in our dispensation of love, to be reminded by these psalms of the danger of lax views as to God's hatred of sin; and of the need there is that we should altogether enter into the mind of God on such points at the same time that we seek to convert all men to God (compare 1Sa 16:1 Ps 139:21 Isa 66:24 Re 14:10).

Composition

Some psalms are composed of twenty-two parallel sentences or strophes of verses, beginning with words of which the initial letters correspond with the Hebrew letters (twenty-two) in their order (compare Ps 37:1–40 and Ps 119:1–176). So also Lamentations. This arrangement was designed as a help to the memory and is found only in such compositions as do not handle a distinct and progressive subject, but a series of pious reflections, in the case of which the precise order was of less moment. The Psalmist in adopting it does not slavishly follow it; but, as in Psalm 25, he deviates from it, so as to make the form, when needful, bend to the sense. Of these poems there are twelve in all in the Hebrew Bible (Ps 25:1–22 34:1–22 37:1–40 111:1–10 112:1–10 119:1–176 145:1–21 Pr 31:10–31 La 1:1–4:22). The great excellence of the Hebrew principle of versification, namely, parallelism, or 'thought rhythm' [EWALD], is that, while the poetry of every other language, whose versification depends on the regular recurrences of certain sounds, suffers considerably by translation, Hebrew poetry, whose rhythm depends on the parallel correspondence of similar thoughts, loses almost nothing in being translated – the Holy Spirit having thus presciently provided for its ultimate translation into every language, without loss to the sense. Thus in our English Version, Job and Psalms, though but translations, are eminently poetical. On parallelism, see my Introduction to Job. Thus also a clue is given to the meaning in many passages, the sense of the word in one clause being more fully set forth by the corresponding word in the succeeding parallel clause.

In the Masoretic punctuation of the Hebrew, the metrical arrangement is marked by the distinctive accents. It accords with the divine inspiration of Scripture poetry, that the thought is more prominent than the form, the kernel than the shell. The Hebrew poetic rhythm resembled our blank verse, without, however, metrical feet. There is a verbal rhythm above that of prose; but as the true Hebrew pronunciation is lost, the rhythm is but imperfectly recognized.

The peculiarity of the Hebrew poetical age is that it was always historic and true, not mythical, as the early poetical ages of all other nations. Again, its poetry is distinguished from prose by the use of terms decidedly poetic. David's lament over Jonathan furnishes a beautiful specimen of another feature found in Hebrew poetry, the strophe: three strophes being marked by the recurrence three times of the dirge sung by the chorus; the first dirge sung by the whole body of singers, representing Israel; the second, by a chorus of damsels; the third, by a chorus of youths (2Sa 1:17–27).

Lyrical poetry

The lyrical poetry, which is the predominant style in the Bible and is especially terse and sententious, seems to have come from an earlier kind resembling the more modern Book of Proverbs (compare Ge 4:23,24). The Oriental mind tends to embody thought in pithy gnomes, maxims, and proverbs. 'The poetry of the Easterns is a string of pearls. Every word has life. Every proposition is condensed wisdom. Every thought is striking and epigrammatical' (KITTO, Biblical Cyclopaedia). We are led to the same inference from the term Maschal, a 'proverb' or 'similitude,' being used to designate poetry in general. 'Hebrew poetry, in its origin, was a painting to the eye, a parable or teaching by likenesses discovered by the popular mind, expressed by the popular tongue, and adopted and polished by the national poet.' Solomon, under inspiration, may have embodied in his Proverbs such of the pre-existing popular wise sayings as were sanctioned by the Spirit of God.

The Hebrew title for the Psalms, Tehilim, means 'hymns,' that is, joyous praises (sometimes accompanied with dancing, Ex 15:1–20 Jud 5:1–31), not exactly answering to the Septuagint title, Psalms, that is, 'lyrical odes,' or songs accompanied by an instrument. The title, Tehilim, 'hymns,' was probably adopted on account of the use made of the Psalms in divine service, though only a part can be strictly called songs of praise, others being dirges, and very many prayers (whence in Ps 72:20, David styles all his previous compositions, the prayers of David). Sixty-five bear the title, 'lyrical odes' (Mizmorim), while only one is styled Tehilah or 'Hymn.' From the title being Psalms in the Septuagint and New Testament, and also in the Peshito, it is probable that Psalms (Mizmorim) or 'lyrical odes,' was the old title before Tehilim.

Epic and dramatic poetry

Epic poetry, as having its proper sphere in a mythical heroic age, has no place among the Hebrews of the Old Testament Scripture age. For in their earliest ages, namely, the patriarchal, not fable as in Greece, Rome, Egypt, and all heathen nations, but truth and historic reality reigned; so much so, that the poetic element, which is the offspring of the imagination, is found less in those earlier, than in the later, ages. The Pentateuch is almost throughout historic prose. In the subsequent uninspired age, in Tobit we have some approach to the Epos.

Drama, also, in the full modern sense, is not found in Hebrew literature. This was due, not to any want of intellectual culture, as is fully shown by the high excellence of their lyric and didactic poetry, but to their earnest character, and to the solemnity of the subjects of their literature. The dramatic element appears in Job, more than in any other book in the Bible; there are the dramatis personae, a plot, and the 'denouement' prepared for by Elihu, the fourth friend's speech, and brought about by the interposition of Jehovah Himself. Still it is not a strict drama, but rather an inspired debate on a difficult problem of the divine government exemplified in Job's case, with historic narrative, prologue, and epilogue. The Song of Solomon, too, has much of the dramatic cast. See my Introductions to Job and Song of Solomon. The style of many psalms is very dramatic, transitions often occurring from one to another person, without introduction, and especially from speaking indirectly of God to addresses to God; thus in Ps 32:1–2, David makes a general introduction, 'Blessed is the man whose iniquity is forgiven'; then in Ps 32:3–7, he passes to addressing God directly; then in Ps 32:8, without preface God is introduced, directly speaking, in answer to the previous prayer; then in Ps 32:10,11, again he resumes indirect speaking of God, and addresses himself in conclusion to the righteous. These quick changes of person do not startle us, but give us a stronger sense of his habitual converse with God than any assertions could do. Compare also in Ps 132:8–10, the prayer, 'Arise, O Lord, into thy rest; thou, and the ark of thy strength. Let thy priests be clothed with righteousness; and let thy saints shout for joy. For thy servant David's sake turn not away the face of thine anointed,' with God's direct answer, which follows in almost the words of the prayer, 'The Lord hath sworn unto David,' &c. [Ps 132:11–18]. 'This is my rest for ever [Ps 132:14]. I will clothe her priests with salvation: and her saints shall shout aloud for joy.' Thus also in the second Psalm, various personages are introduced, dramatically acting and speaking – the confederate nations [Ps 2:1–3], Jehovah [Ps 2:4–6], the Messiah [Ps 2:7–9], and the Psalmist [Ps 2:10–12].

A frequent feature is the alternate succession of parts, adapting the several psalms to alternate recitation by two semi-choruses in the temple-worship, followed by a full chorus between the parts or at the end. (So Ps 107:15,21,31). De Burgh, in his valuable commentary on the Psalms, remarks, 'Our cathedral service exemplifies the form of chanting the Psalms, except that the semi-chorus is alternately a whole verse, instead of alternating, as of old, the half verse; while the full chorus is the "gloria" at the end of each Psalm.'

Conclusion

In conclusion, besides its unique point of excellence, its divine inspiration, Hebrew poetry is characterized as being essentially national, yet eminently catholic, speaking to the heart and spiritual sensibilities of universal humanity. Simple and unconstrained, it is distinguished by a natural freshness which is the result of its genuine truthfulness. The Hebrew poet sought not self or his own fame, as did heathen poets, but he was inspired by the Spirit of God to meet a pressing want which his own and his nation's spiritual aspirations after God made to be at once a necessity and a delight. Compare 2Sa 23:1,2, 'The sweet Psalmist of Israel said, The Spirit of the LORD spake by me,' &c.

Ewald rightly remarks that several odes of the highest poetic excellence are not included (for example, the songs of Moses, Ex 15:1–19 and De 32:1–43; of Deborah, Jud 5:1–31; of Hannah, 1Sa 2:1–10; of Hezekiah, Isa 38:9–20; of Habakkuk, Hab 3:1–19; and even David's dirge over Saul and Jonathan, 2Sa 1:17–18). The selection of the Psalms collected in one book was made not so much with reference to the beauty of the pieces, as to their adaptation for public worship. Still one overruling Spirit ordered the selection and arrangement of the contents of the book, as one pervading tone and subject appear throughout, Christ in His own inner life as the God-man, and in His past, present, and future relations to the

Church and the world. Isaac Taylor well calls the Psalms, 'The Liturgy of the spiritual life'; and Luther, 'A Bible in miniature.'

The principle of the order in which the Psalms are given to us, though not always discoverable, is in some cases clear, and shows the arrangement to be unmistakably the work of the Spirit, not merely that of the collector. Thus Psalm 22 plainly portrays the dying agonies of Messiah; Psalm 23, His peaceful rest in Paradise after His death on the cross; and Psalm 24, His glorious ascension into heaven.

JOB

Matthew Henry

Introduction

This book is so called from Job, whose prosperity, afflictions, and restoration, are here recorded. He lived soon after Abraham, or perhaps before that patriarch. Most likely it was written by Job himself, and it is the most ancient book in existence. The instructions to be learned from the patience of Job, and from his trials, are as useful now, and as much needed as ever. We live under the same Providence, we have the same chastening Father, and there is the same need for correction unto righteousness. The fortitude and patience of Job, though not small, gave way in his severe troubles; but his faith was fixed upon the coming of his Redeemer, and this gave him steadfastness and constancy, though every other dependence, particularly the pride and boast of a self-righteous spirit, was tried and consumed. Another great doctrine of the faith, particularly set forth in the book of Job, is that of Providence. It is plain, from this history, that the Lord watched over his servant Job with the affection of a wise and loving father.

Chapter 1

The piety and prosperity of Job (1–5)

Satan obtains leave to try Job (6–12)

The loss of Job's property, and the death of his children (13–19)

Job's patience and piety (20–22)

The piety and prosperity of Job (1–5)

Job was prosperous, and yet pious. Though it is hard and rare, it is not impossible for a rich man to enter into the kingdom of heaven. By God's grace the temptations of worldly wealth may be overcome. The account of Job's piety and prosperity comes before the history of his great afflictions, showing that neither will secure from troubles. While Job beheld the harmony and comforts of his sons with satisfaction, his knowledge of the human heart made him fearful for them. He sent and sanctified them, reminding them to examine themselves, to confess their sins, to seek forgiveness; and as one who hoped for acceptance with God through the promised Saviour, he offered a burnt-offering for each. We perceive his care for their souls, his knowledge of the sinful state of man, his entire dependence on God's mercy in the way he had appointed.

Satan obtains leave to try Job (6–12)

Job's afflictions began from the malice of Satan, by the Lord's permission, for wise and holy purposes. There is an evil spirit, the enemy of God, and of all righteousness, who is continually seeking to distress, to lead astray, and, if possible, to destroy those who love God. How far his influence may extend, we cannot say; but probably much unsteadiness and unhappiness in Christians may be ascribed to him. While we are on this earth we are within his reach. Hence the teaching in 1 Peter. This is the common way of slanderers, to suggest that which they have no reason to think is true. But as there is nothing we should dread more than really being hypocrites, so there is nothing we need dread less than being called and counted so without cause. It is not wrong to look at the eternal recompense in our obedience; but it is wrong to aim at worldly advantages in our religion. God's people are taken under his special protection; they, and all that belong to them. The blessing of the Lord makes rich; Satan himself owns it. God suffered Job to be tried, as he suffered Peter to be sifted. It is our comfort that God has the devil in a chain, Revelation 20:1. He has no power to lead men to sin, but what they give him themselves; nor any power to afflict men, but what is given him from above. All this is here described to us after the manner of men. The Scripture speaks thus to teach us that God directs the affairs of the world.

The loss of Job's property, and the death of his children (13–19)

Satan brought Job's troubles upon him on the day that his children began their course of feasting. The troubles all came upon Job at once; while one messenger of evil tidings was speaking, another followed. His dearest and most valuable possessions were his ten children; news is brought him that they are killed. They were taken away when he had most need of them to comfort him under other losses. In God only have we a help present at all times.

Job's patience and piety (20–22)

Job humbled himself under the hand of God. He reasons from the common state of human life, which he describes. We brought nothing of this world's goods into the world, but have them from others; and it is certain we can carry nothing out, but must leave them to others. Job, under all his losses, is but reduced to his first state. He is but where he must have been at last, and is only unclothed, or unloaded rather, a little sooner than he expected. If we put off our clothes before we go to bed, it is some inconvenience, but it may be the better borne when it is near bed-time. The same who gave hath taken away. See how Job looks above instruments, and keeps his eye upon the First Cause. Afflictions must not divert us from, but quicken us to, religion. If in all our troubles we look to the Lord, he will support us. The Lord is righteous. All we have is from his gift; we have forfeited it by sin, and ought not to complain if he takes any part from us. Discontent and impatience charge God with folly. Against these Job carefully watched; and so must we, acknowledging that as God has done right, but we have done wickedly, so God has done wisely, but we have done very foolishly. And may the malice and power of Satan render that Saviour more precious to our souls, who came to destroy the works of the devil; who, for our salvation, suffered from that enemy far more than Job suffered, or we can think.

Chapter 2

Satan obtains leave to try Job (1–6)
Job's sufferings (7–10)
His friends come to comfort him (11–13)

Satan obtains leave to try Job (1–6)

How well is it for us, that neither men nor devils are to be our judges! but all our judgment comes from the Lord, who never errs. Job holds fast his integrity still, as his weapon. God speaks with pleasure of the power of his own grace. Self-love and self-preservation are powerful in the hearts of men. But Satan accuses Job, representing him as wholly selfish, and minding nothing but his own ease and safety. Thus are the ways and people of God often falsely blamed by the devil and his agents. Permission is granted to Satan to make trial, but with a limit. If God did not chain up the roaring lion, how soon would he devour us! Job, thus slandered by Satan, was a type of Christ, the first prophecy of whom was, that Satan should bruise his heel, and be foiled.

Job's sufferings (7–10)

The devil tempts his own children, and draws them to sin, and afterwards torments, when he has brought them to ruin; but this child of God he tormented with affliction, and then tempted to make a bad use of his affliction. He provoked Job to curse God. The disease was very grievous. If at any time we are tried with sore and grievous distempers, let us not think ourselves dealt with otherwise than as God sometimes deals with the best of his saints and servants. Job humbled himself under the mighty hand of God, and brought his mind to his condition. His wife was spared to him, to be a troubler and tempter to him. Satan still endeavours to draw men from God, as he did our first parents, by suggesting hard thoughts of Him, than which nothing is more false. But Job resisted and overcame the temptation. Shall we, guilty, polluted, worthless creatures, receive so many unmerited blessings from a just and holy God, and shall we refuse to accept the punishment of our sins, when we suffer so much less than we deserve? Let murmuring, as well as boasting, be for ever done away. Thus far Job stood the trial, and appeared brightest in the furnace of affliction. There might be risings of corruption in his heart, but grace had the upper hand.

His friends come to comfort him (11–13)

The friends of Job seem noted for their rank, as well as for wisdom and piety. Much of the comfort of this life lies in friendship with the prudent and virtuous. Coming to mourn with him, they vented grief which they really felt. Coming to comfort him, they sat down with him. It would appear that they suspected his unexampled troubles were judgments for some crimes, which he had vailed under his professions of godliness. Many look upon it only as a compliment to visit their friends in sorrow; we must bring life. And if the example of Job's friends is not enough to lead us to pity the afflicted, let us seek the mind that was in Christ.

Chapter 3

Job complains that he was born (1–10)

Job complaining (11–19)

He complains of his life (20–26)

Job complains that he was born (1–10)

For seven days Job's friends sat by him in silence, without offering consolation: at the same time Satan assaulted his mind to shake his confidence, and to fill him with hard thoughts of God. The permission seems to have extended to this, as well as to torturing the body. Job was an especial type of Christ, whose inward sufferings, both in the garden and on the cross, were the most dreadful; and arose in a great degree from the assaults of Satan in that hour of darkness. These inward trials show the reason of the change that took place in Job's conduct, from entire submission to the will of God, to the impatience which appears here, and in other parts of the book. The believer, who knows that a few drops of this bitter cup are more dreadful than the sharpest outward afflictions, while he is favoured with a sweet sense of the love and presence of God, will not be surprised to find that Job proved a man of like passions with others; but will rejoice that Satan was disappointed, and could not prove him a hypocrite; for though he cursed the day of his birth, he did not curse his God. Job doubtless was afterwards ashamed of these wishes, and we may suppose what must be his judgment of them now he is in everlasting happiness.

Job complaining (11–19)

Job complained of those present at his birth, for their tender attention to him. No creature comes into the world so helpless as man. God's power and providence upheld our frail lives, and his pity and patience spared our forfeited lives. Natural affection is put into parents' hearts by God. To desire to die that we may be with Christ, that we may be free from sin, is the effect and evidence of grace; but to desire to die, only that we may be delivered from the troubles of this life, savours of corruption. It is our wisdom and duty to make the best of that which is, be it living or dying; and so to live to the Lord, and die to the Lord, as in both to be his, Romans

14:8. Observe how Job describes the repose of the grave. There the wicked cease from troubling. When persecutors die, they can no longer persecute. There the weary are at rest: in the grave they rest from all their labours. And a rest from sin, temptation, conflict, sorrows, and labours, remains in the presence and enjoyment of God. There believers rest in Jesus, nay, as far as we trust in the Lord Jesus and obey him, we here find rest to our souls, though in the world we have tribulation.

He complains of his life (20–26)

Job was like a man who had lost his way, and had no prospect of escape, or hope of better times. But surely he was in an ill frame for death when so unwilling to live. Let it be our constant care to get ready for another world, and then leave it to God to order our removal as he thinks fit. Grace teaches us in the midst of life's greatest comforts, to be willing to die, and in the midst of its greatest crosses, to be willing to live. Job's way was hid; he knew not wherefore God contended with him. The afflicted and tempted Christian knows something of this heaviness; when he has been looking too much at the things that are seen, some chastisement of his heavenly Father will give him a taste of this disgust of life, and a glance at these dark regions of despair. Nor is there any help until God shall restore to him the joys of his salvation. Blessed be God, the earth is full of his goodness, though full of man's wickedness. This life may be made tolerable if we attend to our duty. We look for eternal mercy, if willing to receive Christ as our Saviour.

Chapter 4

Eliphaz reproves Job (1–6)

And maintains that God's judgments are for the wicked (7–11)

The vision of Eliphaz (12–21)

Eliphaz reproves Job (1–6)

Satan undertook to prove Job a hypocrite by afflicting him; and his friends concluded him to be one because he was so afflicted, and showed impatience. This we must keep in mind if we would understand what passed. Eliphaz speaks of Job, and his afflicted condition, with tenderness; but charges him with weakness and faint-heartedness. Men make few allowances for those who have taught others. Even pious friends will count that only a touch which we feel as a wound. Learn from hence to draw off the mind of a sufferer from brooding over the affliction, to look at the God of mercies in the affliction. And how can this be done so well as by looking to Christ Jesus, in whose unequalled sorrows every child of God soonest learns to forget his own?

And maintains that God's judgments are for the wicked (7–11)

Eliphaz argues, 1. That good men were never thus ruined. But there is one event both to the righteous and to the wicked, Ecclesiastes 9:2, both in life and death; the great and certain difference is after death. Our worst mistakes are occasioned by drawing wrong views from undeniable truths. 2. That wicked men were often thus ruined: for the proof of this, Eliphaz vouches his own observation. We may see the same every day.

The vision of Eliphaz (12–21)

Eliphaz relates a vision. When we are communing with our own hearts, and are still, Psalms 4:4, then is a time for the Holy Spirit to commune with us. This vision put him into very great fear. Ever since man sinned, it has been terrible to him to receive communications from Heaven, conscious that he can expect no good tidings thence. Sinful man! shall he pretend to be more just, more pure, than God, who being his Maker, is his Lord and Owner? How dreadful, then, the pride and presumption of man! How great the patience of God!

Look upon man in his life. The very foundation of that cottage of clay in which man dwells, is in the dust, and it will sink with its own weight. We stand but upon the dust. Some have a higher heap of dust to stand upon than others but still it is the earth that stays us up, and will shortly swallow us up. Man is soon crushed; or if some lingering distemper, which consumes like a moth, be sent to destroy him, he cannot resist it. Shall such a creature pretend to blame the appointments of God? Look upon man in his death. Life is short, and in a little time men are cut off. Beauty, strength, learning, not only cannot secure them from death, but these things die with them; nor shall their pomp, their wealth, or power, continue after them. Shall a weak, sinful, dying creature, pretend to be more just than God, and more pure than his Maker? No: instead of quarrelling with his afflictions, let him wonder that he is out of hell. Can a man be cleansed without his Maker? Will God justify sinful mortals, and clear them from guilt? Or will he do so without their having an interest in the righteousness and gracious help of their promised Redeemer, when angels, once ministering spirits before his throne, receive the just recompense of their sins? Notwithstanding the seeming impunity of men for a short time, though living without God in the world, their doom is as certain as that of the fallen angels, and is continually overtaking them. Yet careless sinners note it so little that they expect not the change, nor are wise to consider their latter end.

Chapter 5

Eliphaz urges that the sin of sinners in their ruin (1–5)

God is to be regarded in affliction (6–16)

The happy end of God's correction (17–27)

Eliphaz urges that the sin of sinners in their ruin (1–5)

Eliphaz here calls upon Job to answer his arguments. Were any of the saints or servants of God visited with such Divine judgments as Job, or did they ever behave like him under their sufferings? The term, 'saints,' holy, or more strictly, consecrated ones, seems in all ages to have been applied to the people of God, through the Sacrifice slain in the covenant of their reconciliation. Eliphaz doubts not that the sin of sinners directly tends to their ruin. They kill themselves by some lust or other; therefore, no doubt, Job has done some foolish thing, by which he has brought himself into this condition. The allusion was plain to Job's former prosperity; but there was no evidence of Job's wickedness, and the application to him was unfair and severe.

God is to be regarded in affliction (6–16)

Eliphaz reminds Job, that no affliction comes by chance, nor is to be placed to second causes. The difference between prosperity and adversity is not so exactly observed, as that between day and night, summer and winter; but it is according to the will and counsel of God. We must not attribute our afflictions to fortune, for they are from God; nor our sins to fate, for they are from ourselves. Man is born in sin, and therefore born to trouble. There is nothing in this world we are born to, and can truly call our own, but sin and trouble. Actual transgressions are sparks that fly out of the furnace of original corruption. Such is the frailty of our bodies, and the vanity of all our enjoyments, that our troubles arise thence as the sparks fly upward; so many are they, and so fast does one follow another. Eliphaz reproves Job for not seeking God, instead of quarrelling with him. Is any afflicted? let him pray. It is heart's ease, a salve for every sore. Eliphaz speaks of rain, which we are apt to look upon as a little thing; but if we consider how it is produced, and what is produced by it, we shall see it to be a great work of power and goodness. Too often the great Author of all our comforts, and the manner in which they are conveyed to us, are not noticed, because they are received as things of course. In the ways of Providence, the experiences of some are encouragements to others, to hope the best in the worst of times; for it is the glory of God to send help to the helpless, and hope to the hopeless. And daring sinners are confounded, and forced to acknowledge the justice of God's proceedings.

The happy end of God's correction (17–27)

Eliphaz gives to Job a word of caution and exhortation: Despise not thou the chastening of the Almighty. Call it a chastening, which comes from the Father's love, and is for the child's good; and notice it as a messenger from Heaven. Eliphaz also encourages Job to submit to his condition. A good man is happy though he be afflicted, for he has not lost his enjoyment of God, nor his title to heaven; nay, he is happy because he is afflicted. Correction mortifies his corruptions, weans his heart from the world, draws him nearer to God, brings him to his Bible, brings him to his knees. Though God wounds, yet he supports his people under afflictions, and in due time delivers them. Making a wound is sometimes part of a cure. Eliphaz gives Job precious promises of what God would do for him, if he humbled himself. Whatever troubles good men may be in, they shall do them no real harm. Being kept from sin, they are kept from the evil of trouble. And if the servants of Christ are not delivered from outward troubles, they are delivered by them, and while overcome by one trouble, they conquer all. Whatever is maliciously said against them shall not hurt them. They shall have wisdom and grace to manage their concerns. The greatest blessing, both in our employments and in our enjoyments, is to be kept from sin. They shall finish their course with joy and honour. That man lives long enough who has done his work, and is fit for another world. It is a mercy to die seasonably, as the corn is cut and housed when fully ripe; not till then, but then not suffered to stand any longer. Our times are in God's hands; it is well they are so. Believers are not to expect great wealth, long life, or to be free from trials. But all will be ordered for the best. And remark from Job's history, that steadiness of mind and heart under trial, is one of the highest attainments of faith. There is little exercise for faith when all things go well. But if God raises a storm, permits the enemy to send wave after wave, and seemingly stands aloof from our prayers, then, still to hang on and trust God, when we cannot trace him, this is the patience of the saints. Blessed Saviour! how sweet it is to look unto thee, the Author and Finisher of faith, in such moments!

Chapter 6

Job justifies his complaints (1–7)
He wishes for death (8–13)
Job reproves his friends as unkind (14–30)

Job justifies his complaints (1–7)

Job still justifies himself in his complaints. In addition to outward troubles, the inward sense of God's wrath took away all his courage and resolution. The feeling sense of the wrath of God is harder to bear than any outward afflictions. What then did the Saviour endure in the garden and on the cross, when he bare our sins, and his soul was made a sacrifice to Divine justice for us! Whatever burden of affliction, in body or estate, God is pleased to lay upon us, we may well submit to it as long as he continues to us the use of our reason, and the peace of our conscience; but if either of these is disturbed, our case is very pitiable. Job reflects upon his friends for their censures. He complains he had nothing offered for his relief, but what was in itself tasteless, loathsome, and burdensome.

He wishes for death (8–13)

Job had desired death as the happy end of his miseries. For this, Eliphaz had reproved him, but he asks for it again with more vehemence than before. It was very rash to speak thus of God destroying him. Who, for one hour, could endure the wrath of the Almighty, if he let loose his hand against him? Let us rather say with David, O spare me a little. Job grounds his comfort upon the testimony of his conscience, that he had been, in some degree, serviceable to the glory of God. Those who have grace in them, who have the evidence of it, and have it in exercise, have wisdom in them, which will be their help in the worst of times.

Job reproves his friends as unkind (14–30)

In his prosperity Job formed great expectations from his friends, but now was disappointed. This he compares to the failing of brooks in summer. Those who rest their expectations on the creature, will find it fail when it should help them; whereas those who make God their confidence, have help in the time of need, Hebrews 4:16. Those who make gold their hope, sooner or later will be ashamed of it, and of their confidence in it. It is our wisdom to cease from man. Let us put all our confidence in the Rock of ages, not in broken reeds; in the Fountain of life, not in broken cisterns. The application is very close; 'for now ye are nothing.' It were well for us, if we had always such convictions of the vanity of the creature, as we have had, or shall have, on a sick-bed, a death-bed, or in trouble of conscience. Job upbraids his friends with their hard usage. Though in want, he desired no more from them than a good look and a good word. It often happens that, even when we expect little from man, we have less; but from God, even when we expect much, we have more. Though Job differed from them, yet he was ready to yield as soon as it was made to appear that he was in error. Though Job had been in fault, yet they ought not to have given him such hard usage. His righteousness he holds fast, and will not let it go. He felt that there had not been such iniquity in him as they supposed. But it is best to commit our characters to Him who keeps our souls; in the great day every upright believer shall have praise of God.

Chapter 7

Job's troubles (1–6)
Job expostulates with God (7–16)
He begs release (17–21)

Job's troubles (1–6)

Job here excuses what he could not justify, his desire of death. Observe man's present place: he is upon earth. He is yet on earth, not in hell. Is there not a time appointed for his abode here? yes, certainly, and the appointment is made by Him who made us and sent us here. During that, man's life is a warfare, and as day-labourers, who have the work of the day to do in its day, and must make up their account at night. Job had as much reason, he thought, to wish for death, as a poor servant that is tired with his work, has to wish for the shadows of the evening, when he shall go to rest. The sleep of the labouring man is sweet; nor can any rich man take so much satisfaction in his wealth, as the hireling in his day's wages. The comparison is plain; hear his complaint: His days were useless, and had long been so; but when we are not able to work for God, if we sit still quietly for him, we shall be accepted. His nights were restless. Whatever is grievous, it is good to see it appointed for us, and as designed for some holy end. When we have comfortable nights, we must see them also appointed to us, and be thankful for them. His body was noisome. See what vile bodies we have. His life was hastening apace. While we are living, every day, like the shuttle, leaves a thread behind: many weave the spider's web, which will fail, ch. 8:14. But if, while we live, we live unto the Lord, in works of faith and labours of love, we shall have the benefit, for every man shall reap as he sowed, and wear as he wove.

Job expostulates with God (7–16)

Plain truths as to the shortness and vanity of man's life, and the certainty of death, do us good, when we think and speak of them with application to ourselves. Dying is done but once, and therefore it had need be well done. An error here is past retrieve. Other clouds arise, but the same cloud never returns: so a new generation of men is raised up, but the former generation vanishes away. Glorified saints shall return no more to the cares and sorrows of their houses; nor condemned sinners to the gaieties and pleasures of their houses. It concerns us to secure a better place when we die. From these reasons Job might have drawn a better conclusion than this, I will complain. When we have but a few breaths to draw, we should spend them in the holy, gracious breathings of faith and prayer; not in the noisome, noxious breathings of sin and corruption. We have much reason to pray, that He who keeps Israel, and neither slumbers nor sleeps, may keep us when we slumber and sleep. Job covets to rest in his grave. Doubtless, this was his infirmity; for though a good man would choose death rather than sin, yet he should be content to live as long as God pleases, because life is our opportunity of glorifying him, and preparing for heaven.

He begs release (17–21)

Job reasons with God concerning his dealings with man. But in the midst of this discourse, Job seems to have lifted up his thoughts to God with some faith and hope. Observe the concern he is in about his sins. The best men have to complain of sin; and the better they are, the more they will complain of it. God is the Preserver of our lives, and the Saviour of the souls of all that believe; but probably Job meant the Observer of men, whose eyes are upon the ways and hearts of all men. We can hide nothing from Him; let us plead guilty before his throne of grace, that we may not be condemned at his judgment-seat. Job maintained, against his friends, that he was not a hypocrite, not a wicked man, yet he owns to his God, that he had sinned. The best must so acknowledge, before the Lord. He seriously inquires how he might be at peace with God, and earnestly begs forgiveness of his sins. He means more than the removing of his outward trouble, and is earnest for the return of God's favour. Wherever the Lord removes the guilt of sin, he breaks the power of sin. To strengthen his prayer for pardon, Job pleads the prospect he had of dying quickly. If my sins be not pardoned while I live, I am lost and undone for ever. How wretched is sinful man without a knowledge of the Saviour!

Chapter 8

Bildad reproves Job (1–7)
Hypocrites will be destroyed (8–19)
Bildad applies God's just dealing to Job (20–22)

Bildad reproves Job (1–7)

Job spake much to the purpose; but Bildad, like an eager, angry disputant, turns it all off with this, How long wilt thou speak these things? Men's meaning is not taken aright, and then they are rebuked, as if they were evil-doers. Even in disputes on religion, it is too common to treat others with sharpness, and their arguments with contempt. Bildad's discourse shows that he had not a favourable opinion of Job's character. Job owned that God did not pervert judgment; yet it did not therefore follow that his children were cast-aways, or that they did for some great transgression. Extraordinary afflictions are not always the punishment of extraordinary sins, sometimes they are the trials of extraordinary graces: in judging of another's case, we ought to take the favourable side. Bildad puts Job in hope, that if he were indeed upright, he should yet see a good end of his present troubles. This is God's way of enriching the souls of his people with graces and comforts. The beginning is small, but the progress is to perfection. Dawning light grows to noon-day.

Hypocrites will be destroyed (8–19)

Bildad discourses well of hypocrites and evil-doers, and the fatal end of all their hopes and joys. He proves this truth of the destruction of the hopes and joys of hypocrites, by an appeal to former times. Bildad refers to the testimony of the ancients. Those teach best that utter words out of their heart, that speak from an experience of spiritual and divine things. A rush growing, and looking very green, but withering in dry weather, represents the hypocrite's profession, which is maintained only in times of prosperity. The spider's web, spun with great skill, but easily swept away, represents a man's pretensions to religion when without the grace of God in his heart. A formal professor flatters himself in his own eyes, doubts not of his salvation, is secure, and cheats the world with his vain confidences. The flourishing of the tree, planted in the garden, striking root to the rock, yet after a time cut down and thrown aside, represents wicked men, when most firmly established, suddenly thrown down and forgotten. This doctrine of the vanity of a hypocrite's confidence, or the prosperity of a wicked man, is sound; but it was not applicable to the case of Job, if confined to the present world.

Bildad applies God's just dealing to Job (20–22)

Bildad here assures Job, that as he was so he should fare; therefore they concluded that as he fared so he was. God will not cast away an upright man; he may be cast down for a time, but he shall not be cast away for ever. Sin brings ruin on persons and families. Yet to argue that Job was an ungodly, wicked man, was unjust and uncharitable. The mistake in these reasonings arose from Job's friends not distinguishing between the present state of trial and discipline, and the future state of final judgment. May we choose the portion, possess the confidence, bear the cross, and die the death of the righteous; and, in the mean time, be careful neither to wound others by rash judgments, nor to distress ourselves needlessly about the opinions of our fellow-creatures.

Chapter 9

Job acknowledges God's justice (1–13)

He is not able to contend with God (14–21)

Men not to be judged by outward condition (22–24)

Job complains of troubles (25–35)

Job acknowledges God's justice (1–13)

In this answer Job declared that he did not doubt the justice of God, when he denied himself to be a hypocrite; for how should man be just with God? Before him he pleaded guilty of sins more than could be counted; and if God should contend with him in judgment, he could not justify one out of a thousand, of all the thoughts, words, and actions of his life; therefore he deserved worse than all his present sufferings. When Job mentions the wisdom and power of God, he forgets his complaints. We are unfit to judge of God's proceedings, because we know not what he does, or what he designs. God acts with power which no creature can resist. Those who think they have strength enough to help others, will not be able to help themselves against it.

He is not able to contend with God (14–21)

Job is still righteous in his own eyes, ch. 32:1, and this answer, though it sets forth the power and majesty of God, implies that the question between the afflicted and the Lord of providence, is a question of might, and not of right; and we begin to discover the evil fruits of pride and of a self-righteous spirit. Job begins to manifest a disposition to condemn God, that he may justify himself, for which he is afterwards reproved. Still Job knew so much of himself, that he durst not stand a trial. If we say, We have no sin, we not only deceive ourselves, but we affront God; for we sin in saying so, and give the lie to the Scripture. But Job reflected on God's goodness and justice in saying his affliction was without cause.

Men not to be judged by outward condition (22–24)

Job touches briefly upon the main point now in dispute. His friends maintained that those who are righteous and good, always prosper in this world, and that none but the wicked are in misery and distress: he said, on the contrary, that it is a common thing for the wicked to prosper, and the righteous to be greatly afflicted. Yet there is too much passion in what Job here says, for God doth not afflict willingly. When the spirit is heated with dispute or with discontent, we have need to set a watch before our lips.

Job complains of troubles (25–35)

What little need have we of pastimes, and what great need to redeem time, when it runs on so fast towards eternity! How vain the enjoyments of time, which we may quite lose while yet time continues! The remembrance of having done our duty will be pleasing afterwards; so will not the remembrance of having got worldly wealth, when it is all lost and gone. Job's complaint of God, as one that could not be appeased and would not relent, was the language of his corruption. There is a Mediator, a Daysman, or Umpire, for us, even God's own beloved Son, who has purchased peace for us with the blood of his cross, who is able to save to the uttermost all who come unto God through him. If we trust in his name, our sins will be buried in the depths of the sea, we shall be washed from all our filthiness, and made whiter than snow, so that none can lay any thing to our charge. We shall be clothed with the robes of righteousness and salvation, adorned with the graces of the Holy Spirit, and presented faultless before the presence of his glory with exceeding joy. May we learn the difference between justifying ourselves, and being thus justified by God himself. Let the tempest-tossed soul consider Job, and notice that others have passed this dreadful gulf; and though they found it hard to believe that God would hear or deliver them, yet he rebuked the storm, and brought them to the desired haven. Resist the devil; give not place to hard thoughts of God, or desperate conclusions about thyself. Come to Him who invites the weary and heavy laden; who promises in nowise to cast them out.

Chapter 10

Job complains of his hardships (1–7)

He pleads with God as his Maker (8–13)

He complains of God's severity (14–22)

Job complains of his hardships (1–7)

Job, being weary of his life, resolves to complain, but he will not charge God with unrighteousness. Here is a prayer that he might be delivered from the sting of his afflictions, which is sin. When God afflicts us, he contends with us; when he contends with us, there is always a reason; and it is desirable to know the reason, that we may repent of and forsake the sin for which God has a controversy with us. But when, like Job, we speak in the bitterness of our souls, we

increase guilt and vexation. Let us harbour no hard thoughts of God; we shall hereafter see there was no cause for them. Job is sure that God does not discover things, nor judge of them, as men do; therefore he thinks it strange that God continues him under affliction, as if he must take time to inquire into his sin.

He pleads with God as his Maker (8–13)

Job seems to argue with God, as if he only formed and preserved him for misery. God made us, not we ourselves. How sad that those bodies should be instruments of unrighteousness, which are capable of being temples of the Holy Ghost! But the soul is the life, the soul is the man, and this is the gift of God. If we plead with ourselves as an inducement to duty, God made me and maintains me, we may plead as an argument for mercy, Thou hast made me, do thou new-make me; I am thine, save me.

He complains of God's severity (14–22)

Job did not deny that as a sinner he deserved his sufferings; but he thought that justice was executed upon him with peculiar rigour. His gloom, unbelief, and hard thoughts of God, were as much to be ascribed to Satan's inward temptations, and his anguish of soul, under the sense of God's displeasure, as to his outward trials, and remaining depravity. Our Creator, become in Christ our Redeemer also, will not destroy the work of his hands in any humble believer; but will renew him unto holiness, that he may enjoy eternal life. If anguish on earth renders the grave a desirable refuge, what will be their condition who are condemned to the blackness of darkness for ever? Let every sinner seek deliverance from that dreadful state, and every believer be thankful to Jesus, who delivereth from the wrath to come.

Chapter 11

Zophar reproves Job (1–6)

God's perfections and almighty power (7–12)

Zophar assures Job of blessings if he repented (13–20)

Zophar reproves Job (1–6)

Zophar attacked Job with great vehemence. He represented him as a man that loved to hear himself speak, though he could say nothing to the purpose, and as a man that maintained falsehoods. He desired God would show Job that less punishment was exacted than he deserved. We are ready, with much assurance, to call God to act in our quarrels, and to think that if he would but speak, he would take our part.

We ought to leave all disputes to the judgment of God, which we are sure is according to truth; but those are not always right who are most forward to appeal to the Divine judgment.

God's perfections and almighty power (7–12)

Zophar speaks well concerning God and his greatness and glory, concerning man and his vanity and folly. See here what man is; and let him be humbled. God sees this concerning vain man, that he would be wise, would be thought so, though he is born like a wild ass's colt, so unteachable and untameable. Man is a vain creature; empty, so the word is. Yet he is a proud creature, and self-conceited. He would be wise, would be thought so, though he will not submit to the laws of wisdom. He would be wise, he reaches after forbidden wisdom, and, like his first parents, aiming to be wise above what is written, loses the tree of life for the tree of knowledge. Is such a creature as this fit to contend with God?

Zophar assures Job of blessings if he repented (13–20)

Zophar exhorts Job to repentance, and gives him encouragement, yet mixed with hard thoughts of him. He thought that worldly prosperity was always the lot of the righteous, and that Job was to be deemed a hypocrite unless his prosperity was restored. Then shalt thou lift up thy face without spot; that is, thou mayst come boldly to the throne of grace, and not with the terror and amazement expressed in ch. 9:34. If we are looked upon in the face of the Anointed, our faces that were cast down may be lifted up; though polluted, being now washed with the blood of Christ, they may be lifted up without spot. We may draw near in full assurance of faith, when we are sprinkled from an evil conscience, Hebrews 10:22.

Chapter 12

Job reproves his friends (1–5)

The wicked often prosper (6–11)

Job speaks of the wisdom and power of God (12–25)

Job reproves his friends (1–5)

Job upbraids his friends with the good opinion they had of their own wisdom compared with his. We are apt to call reproofs reproaches, and to think ourselves mocked when advised and admonished; this is our folly; yet here was colour for this charge. He suspected the true cause of their conduct to be, that they despised him who was fallen into poverty. It is the way of the world. Even the just, upright man, if he comes under a cloud, is looked upon with contempt.

The wicked often prosper (6–11)

Job appeals to facts. The most audacious robbers, oppressors, and impious wretches, often prosper. Yet this is not by fortune or chance; the Lord orders these things. Worldly prosperity is of small value in his sight: he has better things for his children. Job resolves all into the absolute proprietorship which God has in all the creatures. He demands from his friends liberty to judge of what they had said; he appeals to any fair judgment.

Job speaks of the wisdom and power of God (12–25)

This is a noble discourse of Job concerning the wisdom, power, and sovereignty of God, in ordering all the affairs of the children of men, according to the counsel of His own will, which none can resist. It were well if wise and good men, who differ about lesser things, would see how it is for their honour and comfort, and the good of others, to dwell most upon the great things in which they agree. Here are no complaints, or reflections. He gives many instances of God's powerful management of the children of men, overruling all their counsels, and overcoming all their oppositions. Having all strength and wisdom, God knows how to make use, even of those who are foolish and bad; otherwise there is so little wisdom and so little honesty in the world, that all had been in confusion and ruin long ago. These important truths were suited to convince the disputants that they were out of their depth in attempting to assign the Lord's reasons for afflicting Job; his ways are unsearchable, and his judgments past finding out. Let us remark what beautiful illustrations there are in the word of God, confirming his sovereignty, and wisdom in that sovereignty: but the highest and infinitely the most important is, that the Lord Jesus was crucified by the malice of the Jews; and who but the Lord could have known that this one event was the salvation of the world?

Chapter 13

Job reproves his friends (1–12)

He professes his confidence in God (13–22)

Job entreats to know his sins (23–28)

Job reproves his friends (1–12)

With self-preference, Job declared that he needed not to be taught by them. Those who dispute are tempted to magnify themselves, and lower their brethren, more than is fit. When dismayed or distressed with the fear of wrath, the force of temptation, or the weight of affliction, we should apply to the Physician of our souls, who never rejects any, never prescribes amiss, and never leaves any case uncured. To Him we may speak at all times. To broken hearts and wounded consciences, all creatures, without Christ, are physicians of no value. Job evidently speaks with a very angry spirit against his friends. They had advanced some truths which nearly concerned Job, but the heart unhumbled before God, never meekly receives the reproofs of men.

He professes his confidence in God (13–22)

Job resolved to cleave to the testimony his own conscience gave of his uprightness. He depended upon God for justification and salvation, the two great things we hope for through Christ. Temporal salvation he little expected, but of his eternal salvation he was very confident; that God would not only be his Saviour to make him happy, but his salvation, in the sight and enjoyment of whom he should be happy. He knew himself not to be a hypocrite, and concluded that he should not be rejected. We should be well pleased with God as a Friend, even when he seems against us as an enemy. We must believe that all shall work for good to us, even when all seems to make against us. We must cleave to God, yea, though we cannot for the present find comfort in him. In a dying hour, we must derive from him living comforts; and this is to trust in him, though he slay us.

Job entreats to know his sins (23–28)

Job begs to have his sins discovered to him. A true penitent is willing to know the worst of himself; and we should all desire to know what our transgressions are, that we may confess them, and guard against them for the future. Job complains sorrowfully of God's severe dealings with him. Time does not wear out the guilt of sin. When God writes bitter things against us, his design is to make us bring forgotten sins to mind, and so to bring us to repent of them, as to break us off from them. Let young persons beware of indulging in sin. Even in this world they may so possess the sins of their youth, as to have months of sorrow for moments of pleasure. Their wisdom is to remember their Creator in their early days, that they may have assured hope, and sweet peace of conscience, as the solace of their declining years. Job also complains that his present mistakes are strictly noticed. So far from this, God deals not with us according to our deserts. This was the language of Job's melancholy views. If God marks our steps, and narrowly examines our paths, in judgment, both body and soul feel

his righteous vengeance. This will be the awful case of unbelievers, yet there is salvation devised, provided, and made known in Christ.

Chapter 14

Job speaks of man's life (1–6)
Of man's death (7–15)
By sin man is subject to corruption (16–22)

Job speaks of man's life (1–6)

Job enlarges upon the condition of man, addressing himself also to God. Every man of Adam's fallen race is short-lived. All his show of beauty, happiness, and splendour falls before the stroke of sickness or death, as the flower before the scythe; or passes away like the shadow. How is it possible for a man's conduct to be sinless, when his heart is by nature unclean? Here is a clear proof that Job understood and believed the doctrine of original sin. He seems to have intended it as a plea, why the Lord should not deal with him according to his own works, but according to His mercy and grace. It is determined, in the counsel and decree of God, how long we shall live. Our times are in his hands, the powers of nature act under him; in him we live and move. And it is very useful to reflect seriously on the shortness and uncertainty of human life, and the fading nature of all earthly enjoyments. But it is still more important to look at the cause, and remedy of these evils. Until we are born of the Spirit, no spiritually good thing dwells in us, or can proceed from us. Even the little good in the regenerate is defiled with sin. We should therefore humble ourselves before God, and cast ourselves wholly on the mercy of God, through our Divine Surety. We should daily seek the renewing of the Holy Ghost, and look to heaven as the only place of perfect holiness and happiness.

Of man's death (7–15)

Though a tree is cut down, yet, in a moist situation, shoots come forth, and grow up as a newly planted tree. But when man is cut off by death, he is for ever removed from his place in this world. The life of man may fitly be compared to the waters of a land flood, which spread far, but soon dry up. All Job's expressions here show his belief in the great doctrine of the resurrection. Job's friends proving miserable comforters, he pleases himself with the expectation of a change. If our sins are forgiven, and our hearts renewed to holiness, heaven will be the rest of our souls, while our bodies are hidden in the grave from the malice of our enemies, feeling no more pain from our corruptions, or our corrections.

By sin man is subject to corruption (16–22)

Job's faith and hope spake, and grace appeared to revive; but depravity again prevailed. He represents God as carrying matters to extremity against him. The Lord must prevail against all who contend with him. God may send disease and pain, we may lose all comfort in those near and dear to us, every hope of earthly happiness may be destroyed, but God will receive the believer into realms of eternal happiness. But what a change awaits the prosperous unbeliever! How will he answer when God shall call him to his tribunal? The Lord is yet upon a mercy-seat, ready to be gracious. Oh that sinners would be wise, that they would consider their latter end! While man's flesh is upon him, that is, the body he is so loth to lay down, it shall have pain; and while his soul is within him, that is, the spirit he is so loth to resign, it shall mourn. Dying work is hard work; dying pangs often are sore pangs. It is folly for men to defer repentance to a death-bed, and to have that to do which is the one thing needful, when unfit to do anything.

Chapter 15

Eliphaz reproves Job (1–16)

The unquietness of wicked men (17–35)

Eliphaz reproves Job (1–16)

Eliphaz begins a second attack upon Job, instead of being softened by his complaints. He unjustly charges Job with casting off the fear of God, and all regard to him, and restraining prayer. See in what religion is summed up, fearing God, and praying to him; the former the most needful principle, the latter the most needful practice. Eliphaz charges Job with self-conceit. He charges him with contempt of the counsels and comforts given him by his friends. We are apt to think that which we ourselves say is important, when others, with reason, think little of it. He charges him with opposition to God. Eliphaz ought not to have put harsh constructions upon the words of one well known for piety, and now in temptation. It is plain that these disputants were deeply convinced of the doctrine of original sin, and the total depravity of human nature. Shall we not admire the patience of God in bearing with us? and still more his love to us in the redemption of Christ Jesus his beloved Son?

The unquietness of wicked men (17–35)

Eliphaz maintains that the wicked are certainly miserable: whence he would infer, that the miserable are certainly wicked, and therefore Job was so. But because many of God's people have prospered in this world, it does not therefore follow that those who are crossed and made poor, as Job, are not God's people. Eliphaz shows also that wicked people, particularly oppressors, are subject to continual terror, live very uncomfortably, and perish very miserably. Will the prosperity of presumptuous sinners end miserably as here described? Then let the mischiefs which befall others be our warnings. Though no chastening for the present seemeth to be joyous, but grievous, nevertheless, afterward it yieldeth the peaceable fruits of righteousness to them that are exercised thereby. No calamity, no trouble, however heavy, however severe, can rob a follower of the Lord of his favour. What shall separate him from the love of Christ?

Chapter 16

Job reproves his friends (1–5)

He represents his case as deplorable (6–16)

Job maintains his innocency (17–22)

Job reproves his friends (1–5)

Eliphaz had represented Job's discourses as unprofitable, and nothing to the purpose; Job here gives his the same character. Those who pass censures, must expect to have them retorted; it is easy, it is endless, but what good does it do? Angry answers stir up men's passions, but never convince their judgments, nor set truth in a clear light. What Job says of his friends is true of all creatures, in comparison with God; one time or other we shall be made to see and own that miserable comforters are they all. When under convictions of sin, terrors of conscience, or the arrests of death, only the blessed Spirit can comfort effectually; all others, without him, do it miserably, and to no purpose. Whatever our brethren's sorrows are, we ought by sympathy to make them our own; they may soon be so.

He represents his case as deplorable (6–16)

Here is a doleful representation of Job's grievances. What reason we have to bless God, that we are not making such complaints! Even good men, when in great troubles, have much ado not to entertain hard thoughts of God. Eliphaz had represented Job as unhumbled under his affliction: No, says Job, I know better things; the dust is now the fittest place for me. In this he reminds us of Christ, who was a man of sorrows, and pronounced those blessed that mourn, for they shall be comforted.

Job maintains his innocency (17–22)

Job's condition was very deplorable; but he had the testimony of his conscience for him, that he never allowed himself in any gross sin. No one was ever more ready to acknowledge sins of infirmity. Eliphaz had charged him with hypocrisy in religion, but he specifies prayer, the great act of religion, and professes that in this he was pure, though not from all infirmity. He had a God to go to, who he doubted not took full notice of all his sorrows. Those who pour out tears before God, though they cannot plead for themselves, by reason of their defects, have a Friend to plead for them, even the Son of man, and on him we must ground all our hopes of acceptance with God. To die, is to go the way whence we shall not return. We must all of us, very certainly, and very shortly, go this journey. Should not then the Saviour be precious to our souls? And ought we not to be ready to obey and to suffer for his sake? If our consciences are sprinkled with his atoning blood, and testify that we are not living in sin or hypocrisy, when we go the way whence we shall not return, it will be a release from prison, and an entrance into everlasting happiness.

Chapter 17

Job appeals from man to God (1–9)
His hope is not in life, but in death (10–16)

Job appeals from man to God (1–9)

Job reflects upon the harsh censures his friends had passed upon him, and, looking on himself as a dying man, he appeals to God. Our time is ending. It concerns us carefully to redeem the days of time, and to spend them in getting ready for eternity. We see the good use the righteous should make of Job's afflictions from God, from enemies, and from friends. Instead of being discouraged in the service of God, by the hard usage this faithful servant of God met with, they should be made bold to proceed and persevere therein. Those who keep their eye upon heaven as their end, will keep their feet in the paths of religion as their way, whatever difficulties and discouragements they may meet with.

His hope is not in life, but in death (10–16)

Job's friends had pretended to comfort him with the hope of his return to a prosperous estate; he here shows that those do not go wisely about the work of comforting the afflicted, who fetch their comforts from the possibility of recovery in this world. It is our wisdom to comfort ourselves, and others, in distress, with that which will not fail; the promise of God, his love and grace, and a well-grounded hope of eternal life. See how Job reconciles himself to the grave. Let this make believers willing to die; it is but going to bed; they are weary, and it is time that they were in their beds. Why should not they go willingly when their Father calls them? Let us remember our bodies are allied to corruption, the worm and the dust; and let us seek for that lively hope

which shall be fulfilled, when the hope of the wicked shall be put out in darkness; that when our bodies are in the grave, our souls may enjoy the rest reserved for the people of God.

Chapter 18

Bildad reproves Job (1–4)
Ruin attends the wicked (5–10)
The ruin of the wicked (11–21)

Bildad reproves Job (1–4)

Bildad had before given Job good advice and encouragement; here he used nothing but rebukes, and declared his ruin. And he concluded that Job shut out the providence of God from the management of human affairs, because he would not admit himself to be wicked.

Ruin attends the wicked (5–10)

Bildad describes the miserable condition of a wicked man; in which there is much certain truth, if we consider that a sinful condition is a sad condition, and that sin will be men's ruin, if they do not repent. Though Bildad thought the application of it to Job was easy, yet it was not safe nor just. It is common for angry disputants to rank their opponents among God's enemies, and to draw wrong conclusions from important truths. The destruction of the wicked is foretold. That destruction is represented under the similitude of a beast or bird caught in a snare, or a malefactor taken into custody. Satan, as he was a murderer, so he was a robber, from the beginning. He, the tempter, lays snares for sinners wherever they go. If he makes them sinful like himself, he will make them miserable like himself. Satan hunts for the precious life. In the transgression of an evil man there is a snare for himself, and God is preparing for his destruction. See here how the sinner runs himself into the snare.

The ruin of the wicked (11–21)

Bildad describes the destruction wicked people are kept for, in the other world, and which in some degree, often seizes them in this world. The way of sin is the way of fear, and leads to everlasting confusion, of which the present terrors of an impure conscience are earnests, as in Cain and Judas. Miserable indeed is a wicked man's death, how secure soever his life was. See him dying; all that he trusts to for his support shall be taken from him. How happy are the saints, and how indebted to the lord Jesus, by whom death is so far done away and changed, that this king of terrors is become a friend and a servant! See the wicked man's family sunk and cut off. His children shall perish, either with him or after him. Those who consult the true honour of their family, and its welfare, will be afraid of withering all by sin. The judgments of God follow the wicked man after death in this world, as a proof of the misery his soul is in after death, and as an earnest of that everlasting shame and contempt to which he shall rise in the great day. The memory of the just is blessed, but the name of the wicked shall rot, Pr 10:7. It would be well if this report of wicked men would cause any to flee from the wrath to come, from which their power, policy, and riches cannot deliver them. But Jesus ever liveth to deliver all who trust in him. Bear up then, suffering believers. Ye shall for a little time have sorrow, but your Beloved, your Saviour, will see you again; your hearts shall rejoice, and your joy no man taketh away.

Chapter 19

Job complains of unkind usage (1–7)

God was the Author of his afflictions (8–22)

Job's belief in the resurrection (23–29)

Job complains of unkind usage (1–7)

Job's friends blamed him as a wicked man, because he was so afflicted; here he describes their unkindness, showing that what they condemned was capable of excuse. Harsh language from friends, greatly adds to the weight of afflictions: yet it is best not to lay it to heart, lest we harbour resentment. Rather let us look to Him who endured the contradiction of sinners against himself, and was treated with far more cruelty than Job was, or we can be.

God was the Author of his afflictions (8–22)

How doleful are Job's complaints! What is the fire of hell but the wrath of God! Seared consciences will feel it hereafter, but do not fear it now: enlightened consciences fear it now, but shall not feel it hereafter. It is a very common mistake to think that those whom God afflicts he treats as his enemies. Every creature is that to us which God makes it to be; yet this does not excuse Job's relations and friends. How uncertain is the friendship of men! but if God be our Friend, he will not fail us in time of need. What little reason we have to indulge the body, which, after all our care, is consumed by diseases it has in itself. Job recommends himself to the compassion of his friends, and justly blames their harshness. It is very distressing to one who loves God, to be bereaved at once of outward comfort and of inward consolation; yet if this, and more, come upon a believer, it does not weaken the proof of his being a child of God and heir of glory.

Job's belief in the resurrection (23–29)

The Spirit of God, at this time, seems to have powerfully wrought on the mind of Job. Here he witnessed a good confession; declared the soundness of his faith, and the assurance of his hope. Here is much of Christ and heaven; and he that said such things are these, declared plainly that he sought the better country, that is, the heavenly. Job was taught of God to believe in a living Redeemer; to look for the resurrection of the dead, and the life of the world to come; he comforted himself with the expectation of these. Job was assured, that this Redeemer of sinners from the yoke of Satan and the condemnation of sin, was his Redeemer, and expected salvation through him; and that he was a living Redeemer, though not yet come in the flesh; and that at the last day he would appear as the Judge of the world, to raise the dead, and complete the redemption of his people. With what pleasure holy Job enlarges upon this! May these faithful sayings be engraved by the Holy Spirit upon our hearts. We are all concerned to see that the root of the matter be in us. A living, quickening, commanding principle of grace in the heart, is the root of the matter; as necessary to our religion as the root of the tree, to which it owes both its fixedness and its fruitfulness. Job and his friends differed concerning the methods of Providence, but they agreed in the root of the matter, the belief of another world.

Chapter 20

Zophar speaks of the short joy of the wicked (1–9)

The ruin of the wicked (10–22)

The portion of the wicked (23–29)

Zophar speaks of the short joy of the wicked (1–9)

Zophar's discourse is upon the certain misery of the wicked. The triumph of the wicked and the joy of the hypocrite are fleeting. The pleasures and gains of sin bring disease and pain; they end in remorse, anguish, and ruin. Dissembled piety is double iniquity, and the ruin that attends it will be accordingly.

The ruin of the wicked (10–22)

The miserable condition of the wicked man in this world is fully set forth. The lusts of the flesh are here called the sins of his youth. His hiding it and keeping it under his tongue, denotes concealment of his beloved lust, and delight therein. But He who knows what is in the heart, knows what is under the tongue, and will discover it. The love of the world, and of the wealth of it, also is wickedness, and man sets his heart upon these. Also violence and injustice, these sins bring God's judgments upon nations and families. Observe the punishment of the wicked man for these things. Sin is turned into gall, than which nothing is more bitter; it will prove to him poison; so will all unlawful gains be. In his fulness he shall be in straits, through the anxieties of his own mind. To be led by the sanctifying grace of God to restore what was unjustly gotten, as Zaccheus was, is a great mercy. But to be forced to restore by the horrors of a despairing conscience, as Judas was, has no benefit and comfort attending it.

The portion of the wicked (23–29)

Zophar, having described the vexations which attend wicked practices, shows their ruin from God's wrath. There is no fence against this, but in Christ, who is the only Covert from the storm and tempest, Isaiah 32:2. Zophar concludes, 'This is the portion of a wicked man from God;' it is allotted him. Never was any doctrine better explained, or worse applied, than this by Zophar, who intended to prove Job a hypocrite. Let us receive the good explanation, and make a better application, for warning to ourselves, to stand in awe and sin not. One view of Jesus, directed by the Holy Spirit, and by him suitably impressed upon our souls, will quell a thousand carnal reasonings about the suffering of the faithful.

Chapter 21

Job entreats attention (1–6)

The prosperity of the wicked (7--16)

The dealings of God's providence (17–26)

The judgment of the wicked is in the world to come (27–34)

Job entreats attention (1–6)

Job comes closer to the question in dispute. This was, Whether outward prosperity is a mark of the true church, and the true members of it, so that ruin of a man's prosperity proves him a hypocrite? This they asserted, but Job denied. If they looked upon him, they might see misery enough to demand compassion, and their bold interpretations of this mysterious providence should be turned into silent wonder.

The prosperity of the wicked (7–16)

Job says, Remarkable judgments are sometimes brought upon notorious sinners, but not always. Wherefore is it so? This is the day of God's patience; and, in some way or other, he

makes use of the prosperity of the wicked to serve his own counsels, while it ripens them for ruin; but the chief reason is, because he will make it appear there is another world. These prospering sinners make light of God and religion, as if because they have so much of this world, they had no need to look after another. But religion is not a vain thing. If it be so to us, we may thank ourselves for resting on the outside of it. Job shows their folly.

The dealings of God's providence (17–26)

Job had described the prosperity of wicked people; in these he opposes this to what his friends had maintained about their certain ruin in this life. He reconciles this to the holiness and justice of God. Even while they prosper thus, they are light and worthless, of no account with God, or with wise men. In the height of their pomp and power, there is but a step between them and ruin. Job refers the difference Providence makes between one wicked man and another, into the wisdom of God. He is Judge of all the earth, and he will do right. So vast is the disproportion between time and eternity, that if hell be the lot of every sinner at last, it makes little difference if one goes singing thither, and another sighing. If one wicked man die in a palace, and another in a dungeon, the worm that dies not, and the fire that is not quenched, will be the same to them. Thus differences in this world are not worth perplexing ourselves about.

The judgment of the wicked is in the world to come (27–34)

Job opposes the opinion of his friends, That the wicked are sure to fall into visible and remarkable ruin, and none but the wicked; upon which principle they condemned Job as wicked. Turn to whom you will, you will find that the punishment of sinners is designed more for the other world than for this, Jude 1:14,15. The sinner is here supposed to live in a great deal of power. The sinner shall have a splendid funeral: a poor thing for any man to be proud of the prospect of. He shall have a stately monument. And a valley with springs of water to keep the turf green, was accounted an honourable burial place among eastern people; but such things are vain distinctions. Death closes his prosperity. It is but a poor encouragement to die, that others have died before us. That which makes a man die with true courage, is, with faith to remember that Jesus Christ died and was laid in the grave, not only before us, but for us. That He hath gone before us, and died for us, who is alive and liveth for us, is true consolation in the hour of death.

Chapter 22

Eliphaz shows that a man's goodness profits not God (1–4)

Job accused of oppression (5–14)

The world before the flood (15–20)

Eliphaz exhorts Job to repentance (21–30)

Eliphaz shows that a man's goodness profits not God (1–4)

Eliphaz considers that, because Job complained so much of his afflictions, he thought God was unjust in afflicting him; but Job was far from thinking so. What Eliphaz says, is unjustly applied to Job, but it is very true, that when God does us good it is not because he is indebted to us. Man's piety is no profit to God, no gain. The gains of religion to men are infinitely greater than the losses of it. God is a Sovereign, who gives no account of his conduct; but he is perfectly wise, just, faithful, good, and merciful. He approves the likeness of his own holiness, and delights in the fruits of his Spirit; he accepts the thankful services of the humble believer, while he rejects the proud claim of the self-confident.

Job accused of oppression (5–14)

Eliphaz brought heavy charges against Job, without reason for his accusations, except that Job was visited as he supposed God always visited every wicked man. He charges him with oppression, and that he did harm with his wealth and power in the time of his prosperity.

The world before the flood (15–20)

Eliphaz would have Job mark the old way that wicked men have trodden, and see what the end of their way was. It is good for us to mark it, that we may not walk therein. But if others are consumed, and we are not, instead of blaming them, and lifting up ourselves, as Eliphaz does here, we ought to be thankful to God, and take it for a warning.

Eliphaz exhorts Job to repentance (21–30)

The answer of Eliphaz wrongly implied that Job had hitherto not known God, and that prosperity in this life would follow his sincere conversion. The counsel Eliphaz here gives is good, though, as to Job, it was built upon a false supposition that he was a stranger and enemy to God. Let us beware of slandering our brethren; and if it be our lot to suffer in this manner, let us remember how Job was treated; yea, how Jesus was reviled, that we may be patient. Let us examine whether there may not be some colour for the slander, and walk watchfully, so as to be clear of all appearances of evil.

Chapter 23

Job complains that God has withdrawn (1–7)

He asserts his own integrity (8–12)

The Divine terrors (13–17)

Job complains that God has withdrawn (1–7)

Job appeals from his friends to the just judgment of God. He wants to have his cause tried quickly. Blessed be God, we may know where to find him. He is in Christ, reconciling the world unto himself; and upon a mercy-seat, waiting to be gracious. Thither the sinner may go; and there the believer may order his cause before Him, with arguments taken from his promises, his covenant, and his glory. A patient waiting for death and judgment is our wisdom and duty, and it cannot be without a holy fear and trembling. A passionate wishing for death or judgment is our sin and folly, and ill becomes us, as it did Job.

He asserts his own integrity (8–12)

Job knew that the Lord was every where present; but his mind was in such confusion, that he could get no fixed view of God's merciful presence, so as to find comfort by spreading his case before him. His views were all gloomy. God seemed to stand at a distance, and frown upon him. Yet Job expressed his assurance that he should be brought forth, tried, and approved, for he had obeyed the precepts of God. He had relished and delighted in the truths and commandments of God. Here we should notice that Job justified himself rather than, or in opposition to him, ch. 32:2. Job might feel that he was clear from the charges of his friends, but boldly to assert that, though visited by the hand of God, it was not a chastisement of sin, was his error. And he is guilty of a second, when he denies that there are dealings of Providence with men in this present life, wherein the injured find redress, and the evil are visited for their sins.

The Divine terrors (13–17)

As Job does not once question but that his trials are from the hand of God, and that there is no such thing as chance, how does he account for them? The principle on which he views them is, that the hope and reward of the faithful servants of God are only laid up in another life; and he maintains that it is plain to all, that the wicked are not treated according to their deserts in this life, but often directly the reverse. But though the obtaining of mercy, the first-fruits of the Spirit of grace, pledges a God, who will certainly finish the work which he has begun; yet the afflicted believer is not to conclude that all prayer and entreaty will be in vain, and that he should sink into despair, and faint when he is reproved of Him. He cannot tell but the intention of God in afflicting him may be to produce penitence and prayer in his heart. May we learn to obey and trust the Lord, even in tribulation; to live or die as he pleases: we know not for what good ends our lives may be shortened or prolonged.

Chapter 24

Wickedness often unpunished (1–12)
The wicked shun the light (13–17)
Judgments for the wicked (18–25)

Wickedness often unpunished (1–12)

Job discourses further about the prosperity of the wicked. That many live at ease who are ungodly and profane, he had showed, ch. 21. Here he shows that many who live in open defiance of all the laws of justice, succeed in wicked practices; and we do not see them reckoned with in this world. He notices those that do wrong under pretence of law and authority; and robbers, those that do wrong by force. He says, 'God layeth not folly to them;' that is, he does not at once send his judgments, nor make them examples, and so manifest their folly to all the world. But he that gets riches, and not by right, at his end shall be a fool, Jeremiah 17:11.

The wicked shun the light (13–17)

See what care and pains wicked men take to compass their wicked designs; let it shame our negligence and slothfulness in doing good. See what pains those take, who make provision for the flesh to fulfil the lusts of it: pains to compass, and then to hide that which will end in death and hell at last. Less pains would mortify and crucify the flesh, and be life and heaven at last. Shame came in with sin, and everlasting shame is at the end of it. See the misery of sinners; they are exposed to continual frights: yet see their folly; they are afraid of coming under the eye of men, but have no dread of God's eye, which is always upon them: they are not afraid of doing things which they are afraid of being known to do.

Judgments for the wicked (18–25)

Sometimes how gradual is the decay, how quiet the departure of a wicked person, how is he honoured, and how soon are all his cruelties and oppressions forgotten! They are taken off with other men, as the harvestman gathers the ears of corn as they come to hand. There will often appear much to resemble the wrong view

of Providence Job takes in this chapter. But we are taught by the word of inspiration, that these notions are formed in ignorance, from partial views. The providence of God, in the affairs of men, is in every thing a just and wise providence. Let us apply this whenever the Lord may try us. He cannot do wrong. The unequalled sorrows of the Son of God when on earth, unless looked at in this view, perplex the mind. But when we behold him, as the sinner's Surety, bearing the curse, we can explain why he should endure that wrath which was due to sin, that Divine justice might be satisfied, and his people saved.

Chapter 25

Bildad shows that man cannot be justified before God (1–6)

Bildad drops the question concerning the prosperity of wicked men; but shows the infinite distance there is between God and man. He represents to Job some truths he had too much overlooked. Man's righteousness and holiness, at the best, are nothing in comparison with God's, Psalms 89:6. As God is so great and glorious, how can man, who is guilty and impure, appear before him? We need to be born again of water and of the Holy Ghost, and to be bathed again and again in the blood of Christ, that Fountain opened, Zechariah 13:1. We should be humbled as mean, guilty, polluted creatures, and renounce self-dependence. But our vileness will commend Christ's condescension and love; the riches of his mercy and the power of his grace will be magnified to all eternity by every sinner he redeems.

Chapter 26

Job reproves Bildad (1–4)
Job acknowledges the power of God (5–14)

Job reproves Bildad (1–4)

Job derided Bildad's answer; his words were a mixture of peevishness and self-preference. Bildad ought to have laid before Job the consolations, rather than the terrors of the Almighty. Christ knows how to speak what is proper for the weary, Isaiah 50:4; and his ministers should not grieve those whom God would not have made sad. We are often disappointed in our expectations from our friends who should comfort us; but the Comforter, the Holy Ghost, never mistakes, nor fails of his end.

Job acknowledges the power of God (5–14)

Many striking instances are here given of the wisdom and power of God, in the creation and preservation of the world. If we look about us, to the earth and waters here below, we see his almighty power. If we consider hell beneath, though out of our sight, yet we may conceive the discoveries of God's power there. If we look up to heaven above, we see displays of God's almighty power. By his Spirit, the eternal Spirit that moved upon the face of the waters, the breath of his mouth, Psalms 33:6, he has not only made the heavens, but beautified them. By redemption, all the other wonderful works of the Lord are eclipsed; and we may draw near, and taste his grace, learn to love him, and walk with delight in his ways. The ground of the controversy between Job and the other disputants was, that they unjustly thought from his afflictions that he must have been guilty of heinous crimes. They appear not to have duly considered the evil and just desert of original sin; nor did they take into account the gracious designs of God in purifying his people. Job also darkened counsel by words without knowledge. But his views were more distinct. He does not appear to have alleged his personal righteousness as the ground of his hope towards God. Yet what he admitted in a general view of his case, he in effect denied, while he complained of his sufferings as unmerited and severe; that very complaint proving the necessity for their being sent, in order to his being further humbled in the sight of God.

Chapter 27

Job protests his sincerity (1–6)
The hypocrite is without hope (7–10)
The miserable end of the wicked (11–23)

Job protests his sincerity (1–6)

Job's friends now suffered him to speak, and he proceeded in a grave and useful manner. Job had confidence in the goodness both of his cause and of his God; and cheerfully committed his cause to him. But Job had not due reverence when he spake of God as taking away his judgment, and vexing his soul. To resolve that our hearts shall not reproach us, while we hold fast our integrity, baffles the designs of the evil spirit.

The hypocrite is without hope (7–10)

Job looked upon the condition of a hypocrite and a wicked man, to be most miserable. If they gained through life by their profession, and kept up their presumptuous hope till death, what would that avail when God required their souls? The more comfort we find in our religion, the more closely we shall cleave to it. Those who have no delight in God, are easily drawn away by the pleasures, and easily overcome by the crosses of this life.

The miserable end of the wicked (11–23)

Job's friends, on the same subject, spoke of the misery of wicked men before death as proportioned to their crimes; Job considered that if it were not so, still the consequences of their death would be dreadful. Job undertook to set this matter in a true light. Death to a godly man, is like a fair gale of wind to convey him to the heavenly country; but, to a wicked man, it is like a storm, that hurries him away to destruction. While he lived, he had the benefit of sparing mercy; but now the day of God's patience is over, and he will pour out upon him his wrath. When God casts down a man, there is no flying from, nor bearing up under his anger. Those who will not now flee to the arms of Divine grace, which are stretched out to receive them, will not be able to flee from the arms of Divine wrath, which will shortly be stretched out to destroy them. And what is a man profited if he gain the whole world, and thus lose his own soul?

Chapter 28

Concerning worldly wealth (1–11)
Wisdom is of inestimable value (12–19)
Wisdom is the gift of God (20–28)

Concerning worldly wealth (1–11)

Job maintained that the dispensations of Providence were regulated by the highest wisdom. To confirm this, he showed of what a great deal of knowledge and wealth men may make themselves masters. The caverns of the earth may be discovered, but not the counsels of Heaven. Go to the miners, thou sluggard in religion, consider their ways, and be wise. Let their courage and diligence in seeking the wealth that perishes, shame us out of slothfulness and faint-heartedness in labouring for the true riches. How much better is it to get wisdom than gold! How much easier, and safer! Yet gold is sought for, but grace neglected. Will the hopes of precious things out of the earth, so men call them, though really they are paltry and perishing, be such a spur to industry, and shall not the certain prospect of truly precious things in heaven be much more so?

Wisdom is of inestimable value (12–19)

Job here speaks of wisdom and understanding, the knowing and enjoying of God and ourselves. Its worth is infinitely more than all the riches in this world. It is a gift of the Holy Ghost which cannot be bought with money. Let that which is most precious in God's account, be so in ours. Job asks after it as one that truly desired to find it, and despaired of finding it any where but in God; any way but by Divine revelation.

Wisdom is the gift of God (20–28)

There is a two-fold wisdom; one hid in God, which is secret, and belongs not to us; the other made known by him, and revealed to man. One day's events, and one man's affairs, have such reference to, and so hang one upon another, that He only, to whom all is open, and who sees the whole at one view, can rightly judge of every part. But the knowledge of God's revealed will is within our reach, and will do us good. Let man look upon this as his wisdom, To fear the Lord, and to depart from evil. Let him learn that, and he is learned enough. Where is this wisdom to be found? The treasures of it are hid in Christ, revealed by the word, received by faith, through the Holy Ghost. It will not feed pride or vanity, or amuse our vain curiosity. It teaches and encourages sinners to fear the Lord, and to depart from evil, in the exercise of repentance and faith, without desiring to solve all difficulties about the events of this life.

Chapter 29

Job's former comforts (1–6)

The honour paid to Job, his usefulness (7–17)

His prospect of prosperity (18–25)

Job's former comforts (1–6)

Job proceeds to contrast his former prosperity with his present misery, through God's withdrawing from him. A gracious soul delights in God's smiles, not in the smiles of this world. Four things were then very pleasant to holy Job. 1. The confidence he had in the Divine protection. 2. The enjoyment he had of the Divine favour. 3. The communion he had with the Divine word. 4. The assurance he had of the Divine presence. God's presence with a man in his house, though it be but a cottage, makes it a castle and a palace. Then also he had comfort in his family. Riches and flourishing families, like a candle, may be soon extinguished. But when the mind is enlightened by the Holy Spirit, when a man walks in the light of God's countenance, every outward comfort is doubled, every trouble is diminished, and he may pass cheerfully by this light through life and through death. Yet the sensible comfort of this state is often withdrawn for a season; and commonly this arises from sinful neglect, and grieving the Holy Spirit: sometimes it may be a trial of a man's faith and grace. But it is needful to examine ourselves, to seek for the cause of such a change by fervent prayer, and to increase our watchfulness.

The honour paid to Job, his usefulness (7–17)

All sorts of people paid respect to Job, not only for the dignity of his rank, but for his personal merit, his prudence, integrity, and good management. Happy the men who are blessed with such gifts as these! They have great opportunities of honouring God and doing good, but have great need to watch against pride. Happy the people who are blessed with such men! it is a token for good to them. Here we see what Job valued himself by, in the day of his prosperity. It was by his usefulness. He valued himself by the check he gave to the violence of proud and evil men. Good magistrates must thus be a restraint to evil-doers, and protect the innocent; in order to this, they should arm themselves with zeal and resolution. Such men are public blessings, and resemble Him who rescues poor sinners from Satan. How many who were ready to perish, now are blessing Him! But who can show forth His praises? May we trust in His mercy, and seek to imitate His truth, justice, and love.

His prospect of prosperity (18–25)

Being thus honoured and useful, Job had hoped to die in peace and honour, in a good old age. If such an expectation arise from lively faith in the providence and promise of God, it is well; but if from conceit of our own wisdom, and dependence on changeable, earthly things, it is ill grounded, and turns to sin. Every one that has the spirit of wisdom, has not the spirit of government; but Job had both. Yet he had the tenderness of a comforter. This he thought upon with pleasure, when he was himself a mourner. Our Lord Jesus is a King who hates iniquity, and upon whom the blessing of a world ready to perish comes. To Him let us give ear.

Chapter 30

Job's honour is turned into contempt (1–14)

Job a burden to himself (15–31)

Job's honour is turned into contempt (1–14)

Job contrasts his present condition with his former honour and authority. What little cause have men to be ambitious or proud of that which may be so easily lost, and what little confidence is to be put in it! We should not be cast down if we are despised, reviled, and hated by wicked men. We should look to Jesus, who endured the contradiction of sinners.

Job a burden to himself (15–31)

Job complains a great deal. Harbouring hard thoughts of God was the sin which did, at this time, most easily beset Job. When inward temptations join with outward calamities, the soul is hurried as in a tempest, and is filled with confusion. But woe be to those who really have God for an enemy! Compared with the awful state of ungodly men, what are all outward, or even inward temporal afflictions? There is something with which Job comforts himself, yet it is but a little. He foresees that death will be the end of all his troubles. God's wrath might bring him to death; but his soul would be safe and happy in the world of spirits. If none pity us, yet our God, who corrects, pities us, even as a father pitieth his own children. And let us look more to the things of eternity: then the believer will cease from mourning, and joyfully praise redeeming love.

Chapter 31

Job declares his uprightness (1–8)

His integrity (9–15)

Job merciful (16–23)

Job not guilty of covetousness or idolatry (24–32)

Job not guilty of hypocrisy and violence (33–40)

Job declares his uprightness (1–8)

Job did not speak the things here recorded by way of boasting, but in answer to the charge of hypocrisy. He understood the spiritual nature of God's commandments, as reaching to the thoughts and intents of the heart. It is best to let our actions speak for us; but in some cases we owe it to ourselves and to the cause of God, solemnly to protest our innocence of the crimes of which we are falsely accused. The lusts of the flesh, and the love of the world, are two fatal rocks on which multitudes split; against these Job protests he was always careful to stand upon his guard. And God takes more exact notice of us than we do of ourselves; let us therefore walk circumspectly. He carefully avoided all sinful means of getting wealth. He dreaded all forbidden profit as much as all forbidden pleasure. What we have in the world may be used with comfort, or lost with comfort, if honestly gotten. Without strict honesty and faithfulness in all our dealings, we can have no good evidence of true godliness. Yet how many professors are unable to abide this touchstone!

His integrity (9–15)

All the defilements of the life come from a deceived heart. Lust is a fire in the soul: those that indulge it, are said to burn. It consumes all that is good there, and lays the conscience waste. It kindles the fire of God's wrath, which, if not quenched by the blood of Christ, will consume even to eternal destruction. It consumes the body; it consumes the substance. Burning lusts bring burning judgments. Job had a numerous household, and he managed it well. He considered that he had a Master in heaven; and as we are undone if God should be severe with us, we ought to be mild and gentle towards all with whom we have to do.

Job merciful (16–23)

Job's conscience gave testimony concerning his just and charitable behaviour toward the poor. He is most large upon this head, because in this matter he was particularly accused. He was tender of all, and hurtful to none. Notice the principles by which Job was restrained from being uncharitable and unmerciful. He stood in awe of the Lord, as certainly against him, if he should wrong the poor. Regard to worldly interests may restrain a man from actual crimes; but the grace of God alone can make him hate, dread, and shun sinful thoughts and desires.

Job not guilty of covetousness or idolatry (24–32)

Job protests:
1. That he never set his heart upon the wealth of this world. How few prosperous professors can appeal to the Lord, that they have not rejoiced because their gains were great! Through the determination to be rich, numbers ruin their souls, or pierce themselves with many sorrows. 2. He never was guilty of idolatry. The source of idolatry is in the heart, and it corrupts men, and provokes God to send judgments upon a nation. 3. He neither desired nor delighted in the hurt of the worst enemy he had. If others bear malice to us, that will not justify us in bearing malice to them.

Job not guilty of hypocrisy and violence (33–40)

Job clears himself from the charge of hypocrisy. We are loth to confess our faults, willing to excuse them, and to lay the blame upon others. But he that thus covers his sins, shall not prosper, Proverbs 28:13. He speaks of his courage in what is good, as an evidence of his sincerity in it. When men get estates unjustly, they are justly deprived of comfort from them; it was sown wheat, but shall come up thistles. What men do not come honestly by, will never do them any good. The words of Job are ended. They end with a bold assertion, that, with respect to accusation against his moral and religious character as the cause for his sufferings, he could appeal to

God. But, however confident Job was, we shall see he was mistaken, chap. 40:4,5; 1Jo 1:8. Let us all judge ourselves; wherein we are guilty, let us seek forgiveness in that blood which cleanseth from all sin; and may the Lord have mercy upon us, and write his laws in our hearts!

Chapter 32

Elihu is displeased at the dispute between Job and his friends (1–5)

He reproves them (6–14)

He speaks without partiality (15–22)

Elihu is displeased at the dispute between Job and his friends (1–5)

Job's friends were silenced, but not convinced. Others had been present. Elihu was justly displeased with Job, as more anxious to clear his own character than the justice and goodness of God. Elihu was displeased with Job's friends because they had not been candid to Job. Seldom is a quarrel begun, more seldom is a quarrel carried on, in which there are not faults on both sides. Those that seek for truth, must not reject what is true and good on either side, nor approve or defend what is wrong.

He reproves them (6–14)

Elihu professes to speak by the inspiration of the Holy Spirit, and corrects both parties. He allowed that those who had the longest experience should speak first. But God gives wisdom as he pleases; this encouraged him to state his opinion. By attention to the word of God, and dependence upon the Holy Spirit, young men may become wiser than the aged; but this wisdom will render them swift to hear, slow to speak, and disposed to give others a patient hearing.

He speaks without partiality (15–22)

If we are sure that the Spirit of God suggested what we are about to say, still we ought to refrain, till it comes to our turn to speak. God is the God of order, not of confusion. It is great refreshment to a good man, to speak for the glory of the Lord, and to edify others. And the more we consider the majesty of God, as our Maker, and the more we dread his wrath and justice, the less shall we sinfully fear or flatter men. Could we set the wrath Lord always before us, in his mercies and his terrors, we should not be moved from doing our duty in whatever we are called to do.

Chapter 33

Elihu offers to reason with Job (1–7)

Elihu blames Job for reflecting upon God (8–13)

God calls men to repentance (14–18)

God sends afflictions for good (19–28)

Elihu entreats Job's attention (29–33)

Elihu offers to reason with Job (1–7)

Job had desired a judge to decide his appeal. Elihu was one according to his wish, a man like himself. If we would rightly convince men, it must be by reason, not by terror; by fair argument, not by a heavy hand.

Elihu blames Job for reflecting upon God (8–13)

Elihu charges Job with reflecting upon the justice and goodness of God. When we hear any thing said to God's dishonour, we ought to bear our testimony against it. Job had represented God as severe in marking what he did amiss. Elihu urges that he had spoken wrong, and that he ought to humble himself before God, and by repentance to unsay it. God is not accountable to us. It is unreasonable for weak, sinful creatures, to strive with a God of infinite wisdom, power, and goodness. He acts with perfect justice, wisdom, and goodness, where we cannot perceive it.

God calls men to repentance (14–18)

God speaks to us by conscience, by providences, and by ministers; of all these Elihu discourses. There was not then, that we know of, any Divine revelation in writing, though now it is our principal guide. When God designs men's good, by the convictions and dictates of their own consciences, he opens the heart, as Lydia's, and opens the ears, so that conviction finds or forces its way in. The end and design of these admonitions are to keep men from sin, particularly the sin of pride. While sinners are pursuing evil purposes, and indulging their pride, their souls are hastening to destruction. That which turns men from sin, saves them from hell. What a mercy it is to be under the restraints of an awakened conscience!

God sends afflictions for good (19–28)

Job complained of his diseases, and judged by them that God was angry with him; his friends did so too: but Elihu shows that God often afflicts the body for good to the soul. This thought will be of great use for our getting good from sickness, in and by which God speaks to men. Pain is the fruit of sin; yet, by the grace of

God, the pain of the body is often made a means of good to the soul. When afflictions have done their work, they shall be removed. A ransom or propitiation is found. Jesus Christ is the Messenger and the Ransom, so Elihu calls him, as Job had called him his Redeemer, for he is both the Purchaser and the Price, the Priest and the sacrifice. So high was the value of souls, that nothing less would redeem them; and so great the hurt done by sin, that nothing less would atone for it, than the blood of the Son of God, who gave his life a ransom for many. A blessed change follows. Recovery from sickness is a mercy indeed, when it proceeds from the remission of sin. All that truly repent of their sins, shall find mercy with God. The works of darkness are unfruitful works; all the gains of sin will come far short of the damage. We must, with a broken heart confess the fact of sin, 1 John; and not try to justify or excuse ourselves. We must confess the fault of sin; I have perverted that which was right. We must confess the folly of sin; So foolish have I been and ignorant. Is there not good reason why we should make such a confession?

Elihu entreats Job's attention (29–33)

Elihu shows that God's great and gracious design toward the children of men, is to save them from being for ever miserable, and to bring them to be for ever happy. By whatever means we are kept back from them we shall bless the Lord for them at least, and should bless him for them though they be painful and distressing. Those that perish for ever are without excuse, for they would not be healed.

Chapter 34

Elihu accuses Job of charging God with injustice (1–9)

God cannot be unjust (10–15)

God's power and providence (16–30)

Elihu reproves Job (31–37)

Elihu accuses Job of charging God with injustice (1–9)

Elihu calls upon those present to decide with him upon Job's words. The plainest Christian, whose mind is enlightened, whose heart is sanctified by the Spirit of God, and who is versed in the Scriptures, can say how far matters, words, or actions, agree with true religion, better than any that lean to their own understandings. Job had spoken as if he meant wholly to justify himself. He that say, I have cleansed my hands in vain, does not only offend against God's children, Ps 73:13-15, but gratifies his enemies, and says as they say.

God cannot be unjust (10–15)

Elihu had showed Job, that God meant him no hurt by afflicting him, but intended his spiritual benefit. Here he shows, that God did him no wrong by afflicting him. If the former did not satisfy him, this ought to silence him. God cannot do wickedness, nor the Almighty commit wrong. If services now go unrewarded, and sins now go unpunished, yet there is a day coming, when God will fully render to every man according to his works. Further, though the believer's final condemnation is done away through the Saviour's ransom, yet he has merited worse than any outward afflictions; so that no wrong is done to him, however he may be tried.

God's power and providence (16–30)

Elihu appeals directly to Job himself. Could he suppose that God was like those earthly princes, who hate right, who are unfit to rule, and prove the scourges of mankind? It is daring presumption to condemn God's proceedings, as Job had done by his discontents. Elihu suggests divers considerations to Job, to produce in him high thoughts of God, and so to persuade him to submit. Job had often wished to plead his cause before God. Elihu asks, To what purpose? All is well that God does, and will be found so. What can make those uneasy, whose souls dwell at ease in God? The smiles of all the world cannot quiet those on whom God frowns.

Elihu reproves Job (31–37)

When we reprove for what is amiss, we must direct to what is good. Job's friends would have had him own himself a wicked man. That will only oblige him to own that he spoke unadvisedly with his lips. Let us, in giving reproof, not make a matter worse than it is. Elihu directs Job to humble himself before God for his sins, and to accept the punishment. Also to pray to God to discover his sins to him. A good man is willing to know the worst of himself; particularly, under affliction, he desires to be told wherefore God contends with him. It is not enough to be sorry for our sins, but we must go and sin no more. And if we are affectionate children, we shall love to speak with our Father, and to tell him all our mind. Elihu reasons with Job concerning his discontent under affliction. We are ready to think every thing that concerns us should be just as we would have it; but it is not reasonable to expect this. Elihu asks whether there was not sin and folly in what Job said. God is righteous in all his ways, and holy in all his works, Ps 145:17. The believer saith, Let my Saviour, my wise and loving Lord, choose every thing for me. I am sure that will be wisest, and the best for his glory and my good.

Chapter 35

Elihu speaks of man's conduct (1–8)

Why those who cry out under afflictions are not regarded (9–13)

Elihu reproves Job's impatience (14–26)

Elihu speaks of man's conduct (1–8)

Elihu reproves Job for justifying himself more than God, and called his attention to the heavens. They are far above us, and God is far above them; how much then is he out of the reach, either of our sins or of our services! We have no reason to complain if we have not what we expect, but should be thankful that we have better than we deserve.

Why those who cry out under afflictions are not regarded (9–13)

Job complained that God did not regard the cries of the oppressed against their oppressors. This he knew not how to reconcile the justice of God and his government. Elihu solves the difficulty. Men do not notice the mercies they enjoy in and under their afflictions, nor are thankful for them, therefore they cannot expect that God should deliver them out of affliction. He gives songs in the night; when our condition is dark and melancholy, there is that in God's providence and promise, which is sufficient to support us, and to enable us even to rejoice in tribulation. When we only pore upon our afflictions, and neglect the consolations of God which are treasured up for us, it is just in God to reject our prayers. Even the things that will kill the body, cannot hurt the soul. If we cry to God for the removal of an affliction, and it is not removed, the reason is, not because the Lord's hand is shortened, or his ear heavy; but because we are not sufficiently humbled.

Elihu reproves Job's impatience (14–26)

As in prosperity we are ready to think our mountain will never be brought low; so when in adversity, we are ready to think our valley will never be filled up. But to conclude that tomorrow must be as this day, is as absurd as to think that the weather, when either fair or foul, will be always so. When Job looked up to God, he had no reason to speak despairingly. There is a day of judgment, when all that seems amiss will be found to be right, and all that seems dark and difficult will be cleared up and set straight. And if there is Divine wrath in our troubles, it is because we quarrel with God, are fretful, and distrust Divine Providence. This was Job's case. Elihu was directed by God to humble Job, for as to some things he had both opened his mouth in vain, and had multiplied words without knowledge. Let us be admonished, in our afflictions, not so much to set forth the greatness of our suffering, as the greatness of the mercy of God.

Chapter 36

Elihu desires Job's attention (1–4)

The methods in which God deals with men (5–14)

Elihu counsels Job (15–23)

The wonders in the works of creation (24–33)

Elihu desires Job's attention (1–4)

Elihu only maintained that the affliction was sent for his trial; and lengthened because Job was not yet thoroughly humbled under it. He sought to ascribe righteousness to his Maker; to clear this truth, that God is righteous in all his ways. Such knowledge must be learned from the word and Spirit of God, for naturally we are estranged from it. The fitness of Elihu's discourse to the dispute between Job and his friends is plain. It pointed out to Job the true reason of those trials with which he had been visited. It taught that God had acted in mercy towards him, and the spiritual benefit he was to derive from them. It corrected the mistake of his friends, and showed that Job's calamities were for good.

The methods in which God deals with men (5–14)

Elihu here shows that God acts as righteous Governor. He is always ready to defend those that are injured. If our eye is ever toward God in duty, his eye will be ever upon us in mercy, and, when we are at the lowest, will not overlook us. God intends, when he afflicts us, to discover past sins to us, and to bring them to our remembrance. Also, to dispose our hearts to be taught: affliction makes people willing to learn, through the grace of God working with and by it. And further, to deter us from sinning for the future. It is a command, to have no more to do with sin. If we faithfully serve God, we have the promise of the life that now is, and the comforts of it, as far as is for God's glory and our good: and who would desire them any further? We have the possession of inward pleasures, the great peace which those have that love God's law. If the affliction fail in its work, let men expect the furnace to be heated till they are consumed. Those that die without knowledge, die without grace, and are undone for ever. See the nature of hypocrisy; it lies in the heart: that is for the world and the flesh, while perhaps the outside seems to be for God and religion. Whether sinners die in youth, or live long to heap up wrath, their case is dreadful. The souls of the wicked live after death, but it is in everlasting misery.

Elihu counsels Job (15–23)

Elihu shows that Job caused the continuance of his own trouble. He cautions him not to persist in frowardness. Even good men need to be kept to their duty by the fear of God's wrath; the wisest and best have enough in them to deserve his stroke. Let not Job continue his unjust quarrel with God and his providence. And let us never dare to think favourably of sin, never indulge it, nor allow ourselves in it. Elihu thinks Job needed this caution, he having chosen rather to gratify his pride and humour by contending with God, than to mortify them by submitting, and accepting the punishment. It is absurd for us to think to teach Him who is himself the Fountain of light, truth, knowledge, and instruction. He teaches by the Bible, and that is the best book; teaches by his Son, and he is the best Master. He is just in all proceedings.

The wonders in the works of creation (24–33)

Elihu endeavours to fill Job with high thought of God, and so to persuade him into cheerful submission to his providence. Man may see God's works, and is capable of discerning his hand in them, which the beasts are not, therefore they ought to give him the glory. But while the worker of iniquity ought to tremble, the true believer should rejoice. Children should hear with pleasure their Father's voice, even when he speaks in terror to his enemies. There is no light but there may be a cloud to intercept it. The light of the favour of God, the light of his countenance, the most blessed light of all, even that light has many a cloud. The clouds of our sins cause a barrier between us and the Lord's face and hinder the light of his loving-kindness from shining on our souls.

Chapter 37

Elihu observes the power of God (1–13)

Job required to explain the works of nature (14–20)

God is great, and is to be feared (21–24)

Elihu observes the power of God (1–13)

The changes of the weather are the subject of a great deal of our thoughts and common talk; but how seldom do we think and speak of these things, as Elihu, with a regard to God, the director of them! We must notice the glory of God, not only in the thunder and lightning, but in the more common and less awful changes of the

weather; as the snow and rain. Nature directs all creatures to shelter themselves from a storm; and shall man only be unprovided with a refuge? Oh that men would listen to the voice of God, who in many ways warns them to flee from the wrath to come; and invites them to accept his salvation, and to be happy. The ill opinion which men entertain of the Divine direction, peculiarly appears in their murmurs about the weather, though the whole result of the year proves the folly of their complaints. Believers should avoid this; no days are bad as God makes them, though we make many bad by our sins.

Job required to explain the works of nature (14–20)

Due thoughts of the works of God will help to reconcile us to all his providences. As God has a powerful, freezing north wind, so he has a thawing, composing south wind: the Spirit is compared to both, because he both convinces and comforts, So 4:16. The best of men are much in the dark concerning the glorious perfections of the Divine nature and the Divine government. Those who, through grace, know much of God, know nothing, in comparison with what is to be known, and of what will be known, when that which is perfect is come.

God is great, and is to be feared (21–24)

Elihu concludes his discourse with some great sayings concerning the glory of God. Light always is, but is not always to be seen. When clouds come between, the sun is darkened in the clear day. The light of God's favour shines ever towards his faithful servants, though it be not always seen. Sins are clouds, and often hinder us from seeing that bright light which is in the face of God. Also, as to those thick clouds of sorrow which often darken our minds, the Lord hath a wind which passes and clears them away. What is that wind? It is his Holy Spirit. As the wind dispels and sweeps away the clouds which are gathered in the air, so the Spirit of God clears our souls from the clouds and fogs of ignorance and unbelief, of sin and lust. From all these clouds the Holy Spirit of God frees us in the work of regeneration. And from all the clouds which trouble our consciences, the Holy Spirit sets us free in the work of consolation. Now that God is about to speak, Elihu delivers a few words, as the sum of all his discourse. With God is terrible majesty. Sooner or later all men shall fear him.

Chapter 38

God calls upon Job to answer (1–3)

God questions Job (4–11)
Concerning the light and darkness (12–24)
Concerning other mighty works (25–41)

God calls upon Job to answer (1–3)

Job had silenced, but had not convinced his friends. Elihu had silenced Job, but had not brought him to admit his guilt before God. It pleased the Lord to interpose. The Lord, in this discourse, humbles Job, and brings him to repent of his passionate expressions concerning God's providential dealings with him; and this he does, by calling upon Job to compare God's being from everlasting to everlasting, with his own time; God's knowledge of all things, with his own ignorance; and God's almighty power, with his own weakness. Our darkening the counsels of God's wisdom with our folly, is a great provocation to God. Humble faith and sincere obedience see farthest and best into the will of the Lord.

God questions Job (4–11)

For the humbling of Job, God here shows him his ignorance, even concerning the earth and the sea. As we cannot find fault with God's work, so we need not fear concerning it. The works of his providence, as well as the work of creation, never can be broken; and the work of redemption is no less firm, of which Christ himself is both the Foundation and the Corner-stone. The church stands as firm as the earth.

Concerning the light and darkness (12–24)

The Lord questions Job, to convince him of his ignorance, and shame him for his folly in questioning God. If we thus try ourselves, we shall soon be brought to own that what we know is nothing in comparison with what we know not. By the tender mercy of our God, the Day-spring from on high has visited us, to give light to those that sit in darkness, whose hearts are controlled by the world is said to be in the sea; this means, that it is hid from us. Let us make sure that the gates of heaven shall be opened to us on the other side of death, and then we need not fear the opening of the gates of death. It is presumptuous for us, who perceive not the breadth of the earth, to dive into the depth of God's counsels. We should neither in the brightest noon count upon perpetual day, nor in the darkest midnight despair of the return of the morning; and this applies to our inward as well as to our outward condition. What folly it is to strive against God! How much is it our interest to seek peace with him, and to keep in his love!

Concerning other mighty works (25–41)

Hitherto God had put questions to Job to show him his ignorance; now God shows his weakness. As it is but little that he knows, he ought not to arraign the Divine counsels; it is but little he can do, therefore he ought not to oppose the ways of Providence. See the all-sufficiency of the Divine Providence; it has wherewithal to satisfy the desire of every living thing. And he that takes care of the young ravens, certainly will not be wanting to his people. This being but one instance of the Divine compassion out of many, gives us occasion to think how much good our God does, every day, beyond what we are aware of. Every view we take of his infinite perfections, should remind us of his right to our love, the evil of sinning against him, and our need of his mercy and salvation.

Chapter 39

God inquires of Job concerning several animals (1–30)

In these questions the Lord continued to humble Job. In this chapter several animals are spoken of, whose nature or situation particularly show the power, wisdom, and manifold works of God. The wild ass. It is better to labour and be good for something, than to ramble and be good for nothing. From the untameableness of this and other creatures, we may see, how unfit we are to give law to Providence, who cannot give law even to a wild ass's colt. The unicorn, a strong, stately, proud creature. He is able to serve, but not willing; and God challenges Job to force him to it. It is a great mercy if, where God gives strength for service, he gives a heart; it is what we should pray for, and reason ourselves into, which the brutes cannot do. Those gifts are not always the most valuable that make the finest show. Who would not rather have the voice of the nightingale, than the tail of the peacock; the eye of the eagle and her soaring wing, and the natural affection of the stork, than the beautiful feathers of the ostrich, which can never rise above the earth, and is without natural affection? The description of the war-horse helps to explain the character of presumptuous sinners. Every one turneth to his course, as the horse rushes into the battle. When a man's heart is fully set in him to do evil, and he is carried on in a wicked way, by the violence of his appetites and passions, there is no making him fear the wrath of God, and the fatal consequences of sin. Secure sinners think themselves as safe in their sins as the eagle in her nest on high, in the clefts of the rocks; but I will bring thee down from thence, saith the Lord, Jeremiah 49:16. All these beautiful references to the works of nature, should teach us a right view of the riches of the wisdom of Him who made and sustains all things. The want of right views concerning the wisdom of God, which is ever present in all things, led Job to think and speak unworthily of Providence.

Chapter 40

Job humbles himself to God (1–5)

The Lord reasons with Job to show his righteousness, power, and wisdom (6–14)

God's power shown in Behemoth (15–24)

Job humbles himself to God (1–5)

Communion with the Lord effectually convinces and humbles a saint, and makes him glad to part with his most beloved sins. There is need to be thoroughly convinced and humbled, to prepare us for remarkable deliverances. After God had shown Job, by his manifest ignorance of the works of nature, how unable he was to judge of the methods and designs of Providence, he puts a convincing question to him: Shall he that contendeth with the Almighty instruct him? Now Job began to melt into godly sorrow: when his friends reasoned with him, he did not yield; but the voice of the Lord is powerful. When the Spirit of truth is come, he shall convince. Job yields himself to the grace of God. He owns himself an offender, and has nothing to say to justify himself. He is now sensible that he has sinned; and therefore he calls himself vile. Repentance changes men's opinion of themselves. Job is now convinced of his error. Those who are truly sensible of their own sinfulness and vileness, dare not justify themselves before God. He perceived that he was a poor, mean, foolish, and sinful creature, who ought not to have uttered one word against the Divine conduct. One glimpse of God's holy nature would appal the stoutest rebel. How, then, will the wicked bear the sight of his glory at the day of judgment? But when we see this glory revealed in Jesus Christ, we shall be humbled without being terrified; self-abasement agrees with filial love.

The Lord reasons with Job to show his righteousness, power, and wisdom (6–14)

Those who profit by what they have heard from God, shall hear more from him. And those who are truly convinced of sin, yet need to be more thoroughly convinced and more humbled. No doubt God, and he only, has power to humble and bring down proud men; he has wisdom to know when and how to do it, and it is not for us to teach him how to govern the world. Our own hands cannot save us by recommending us to God's grace, much less rescuing us from his

justice; and therefore into his hand we must commit ourselves. The renewal of a believer proceeds in the same way of conviction, humbling, and watchfulness against remaining sin, as his first conversion. When convinced of many evils in our conduct, we still need convincing of many more.

God's power shown in Behemoth (15–24)

God, for the further proving of his own power, describes two vast animals, far exceeding man in bulk and strength. Behemoth signifies beasts. Most understand it of an animal well known in Egypt, called the river-horse, or hippopotamus. This vast animal is noticed as an argument to humble ourselves before the great God; for he created this vast animal, which is so fearfully and wonderfully made. Whatever strength this or any other creature has, it is derived from God. He that made the soul of man, knows all the ways to it, and can make the sword of justice, his wrath, to approach and touch it. Every godly man has spiritual weapons, the whole armour of God, to resist, yea, to overcome the tempter, that his never-dying soul may be safe, whatever becomes of his frail flesh and mortal body.

Chapter 41

Concerning Leviathan (1–34)

The description of the Leviathan, is yet further to convince Job of his own weakness, and of God's almighty power. Whether this Leviathan be a whale or a crocodile, is disputed. The Lord, having showed Job how unable he was to deal with the Leviathan, sets forth his own power in that mighty creature. If such language describes the terrible force of Leviathan, what words can express the power of God's wrath? Under a humbling sense of our own vileness, let us revere the Divine Majesty; take and fill our allotted place, cease from our own wisdom, and give all glory to our gracious God and Saviour. Remembering from whom every good gift cometh, and for what end it was given, let us walk humbly with the Lord.

Chapter 42

Job humbly submits unto God (1–6)

Job intercedes for his friends (7–9)

His renewed prosperity (10–17)

Job humbly submits unto God (1–6)

Job was now sensible of his guilt; he would no longer speak in his own excuse; he abhorred himself as a sinner in heart and life, especially for murmuring against God, and took shame to himself. When the understanding is enlightened by the Spirit of grace, our knowledge of Divine things as far exceeds what we had before, as the sight of the eyes excels report and common fame. By the teachings of men, God reveals his Son to us; but by the teachings of his Spirit he reveals his Son in us, Galatians 1:16, and we are deeply humbled by the sins of which we are convinced. Self-loathing is ever the companion of true repentance. The Lord will bring those whom he loveth, to adore him in self-abasement; while true grace will always lead them to confess their sins without self-justifying.

Job intercedes for his friends (7–9)

After the Lord had convinced and humbled Job, and brought him to repentance, he owned him, comforted him, and put honour upon him. The devil had undertaken to prove Job a hypocrite, and his three friends had condemned him as a wicked man; but if God say, Well done, thou good and faithful servant, it is of little consequence who says otherwise. Job's friends had wronged God, by making prosperity a mark of the true church, and affliction a certain proof of God's wrath. Job had referred things to the future judgment and the future state, more than his friends, therefore he spake of God that which was right, better than his friends had done. And as Job prayed and offered sacrifice for those that had grieved and wounded his spirit, so Christ prayed for his persecutors, and ever lives, making intercession for the transgressors. Job's friends were good men, and belonged to God, and He would not let them be in their mistake any more than Job; but having humbled him by a discourse out of the whirlwind, he takes another way to humble them. They are not to argue the matter again, but they must agree in a sacrifice and a prayer, and that must reconcile them, Those who differ in judgment about lesser things, yet are one in Christ the great Sacrifice, and ought therefore to love and bear with one another. When God was angry with Job's friends, he put them in a way to make peace with him. Our quarrels with God always begin on our part, but the making peace begins on his. Peace with God is to be had only in his own way, and upon his own terms. These will never seem hard to those who know how to value this blessing: they will be glad of it, like Job's friends, upon any terms, though ever so humbling. Job did not insult over his friends, but God being graciously reconciled to him, he was easily reconciled to them. In all our prayers and services we should aim to be accepted of the Lord; not to have praise of men, but to please God.

His renewed prosperity (10–17)

In the beginning of this book we had Job's patience under his troubles, for an example; here, for our encouragement to follow that example, we have his happy end. His troubles began in Satan's malice, which God restrained; his restoration began in God's mercy, which Satan could not oppose. Mercy did not return when Job was disputing with his friends, but when he was praying for them. God is served and pleased with our warm devotions, not with our warm disputes. God doubled Job's possessions. We may lose much for the Lord, but we shall not lose any thing by him. Whether the Lord gives us health and temporal blessings or not, if we patiently suffer according to his will, in the end we shall be happy. Job's estate increased. The blessing of the Lord makes rich; it is he that gives us power to get wealth, and gives success in honest endeavours. The last days of a good man sometimes prove his best, his last works his best works, his last comforts his best comforts; for his path, like that of the morning light, shines more and more unto the perfect day.

PSALMS

Matthew Henry

Introduction

David was the penman of most of the psalms, but some evidently were composed by other writers, and the writers of some are doubtful. But all were written by the inspiration of the Holy Ghost; and no part of the Old Testament is more frequently quoted or referred to in the New. Every psalm either points directly to Christ, in his person, his character, and offices; or may lead the believer's thoughts to Him. And the psalms are the language of the believer's heart, whether mourning for sin, thirsting after God, or rejoicing in Him. Whether burdened with affliction, struggling with temptation, or triumphing in the hope or enjoyment of deliverance; whether admiring the Divine perfections, thanking God for his mercies, mediating on his truths, or delighting in his service; they form a Divinely appointed standard of experience, by which we may judge ourselves. Their value, in this view, is very great, and the use of them will increase with the growth of the power of true religion in the heart. By the psalmist's expressions, the Spirit helps us to pray. If we make the psalms familiar to us, whatever we have to ask at the throne of grace, by way of confession, petition, or thanksgiving, we may be assisted from thence. Whatever devout affection is working in us, holy desire or hope, sorrow or joy, we may here find words to clothe it; sound speech which cannot be condemned. In the language of this Divine book, the prayers and praises of the church have been offered up to the throne of grace from age to age.

Psalm 1

The holiness and happiness of a godly man (1–3)

The sinfulness and misery of a wicked man; the ground and reason of both (4–6)

The holiness and happiness of a godly man (1–3)

To meditate in God's word, is to discourse with ourselves concerning the great things contained in it, with close application of mind and fixedness of thought. We must have constant regard to the word of God, as the rule of our actions, and the spring of our comforts; and have it in our thoughts night and day. For this purpose no time is amiss.

The sinfulness and misery of a wicked man; the ground and reason of both (4–6)

The ungodly are the reverse of the righteous, both in character and condition. The ungodly are not so, ver. 4; they are led by the counsel of the wicked, in the way of sinners, to the seat of the scornful; they have no delight in the law of God; they bring forth no fruit but what is evil. The righteous are like useful, fruitful trees: the ungodly are like the chaff which the wind drives away: the dust which the owner of the floor desires to have driven away, as not being of any use. They are of no worth in God's account, how highly soever they may value themselves. They are easily driven to and fro by every wind of temptation. The chaff may be, for a while, among the wheat, but He is coming, whose fan is in his hand, and who will thoroughly purge his floor. Those that, by their own sin and folly, make themselves as chaff, will be found so before the whirlwind and fire of Divine wrath. The doom of the ungodly is fixed, but whenever the sinner becomes sensible of this guilt and misery, he may be admitted into the company of the righteous by Christ the living way, and become in Christ a new creature. He has new desires, new pleasures, hopes, fears, sorrows, companions, and employments. His thoughts, words, and actions are changed. He enters on a new state, and bears a new character. Behold, all things are become new by Divine grace, which changes his soul into the image of the Redeemer. How different the character and end of the ungodly!

Psalm 2

Threatenings against the enemies of Christ's kingdom (1–6)

Promise to Christ as the Head of this kingdom (7–9)

Counsel to all, to espouse its interests (10–12)

Threatenings against the enemies of Christ's kingdom (1–6)

We are here told who would appear as adversaries to Christ. As this world is the kingdom of Satan, unconverted men, of every rank, party, and character, are stirred up by him to oppose the cause of God. But the rulers of the earth generally have been most active. The truths and precepts of Christianity are against ambitious projects and worldly lusts. We are told what they aim at in this opposition. They would break asunder the bands of conscience, and the cords of God's commandments; they will not receive, but cast them away as far as they can. These enemies can show no good cause for opposing so just and holy a government, which, if received by all, would bring a heaven upon earth. They can hope for no success in opposing so powerful a kingdom. The Lord Jesus has all power both in heaven and in earth, and is Head over all things to the church, notwithstanding the restless endeavours of his enemies. Christ's throne is set up in his church, that is, in the hearts of all believers.

Promise to Christ as the Head of this kingdom (7–9)

The kingdom of the Messiah is founded upon an eternal decree of God the Father. This our Lord Jesus often referred to, as what he governed himself by. God hath said unto him, Thou art my Son, and it becomes each of us to say to him, Thou art my Lord, my Sovereign. The Son, in asking the heathen for his inheritance, desires their happiness in him; so that he pleads for them, ever lives to do so, and is able to save to the uttermost, and he shall have multitudes of willing, loyal subjects, among them. Christians are the possession of the Lord Jesus; they are to him for a name and a praise. God the Father gives them to him, when, by his Spirit and grace, he works upon them to submit to the Lord Jesus.

Counsel to all, to espouse its interests (10–12)

Whatever we rejoice in, in this world, it must always be with trembling, because of the uncertainty of all things in it. To welcome Jesus Christ, and to submit to him, is our wisdom and interest. Let him be very dear and precious; love him above all, love him in sincerity, love him much, as she did, to whom much was forgiven, and, in token of it, kissed his feet, Luke 7:38. And with a kiss of loyalty take this yoke upon you, and give up yourselves to be governed by his laws, disposed of by his providence, and entirely devoted to his cause. Unbelief is a sin against the remedy. It will be utter destruction to yourselves; lest ye perish in the way of your sins, and from the way of your vain hopes; lest your way perish, lest you prove to have missed the way of happiness. Christ is the way; take heed lest ye be cut off from Him as your way to God. They thought themselves in the way; but neglecting Christ, they perish from it. Blessed will those be in the day of wrath, who, by trusting in Christ, have made him their Refuge.

Psalm 3

David complains to God of his enemies, and confides in God (1–3)

He triumphs over his fears, and gives God the glory, and takes to himself the comfort (4–8)

David complains to God of his enemies, and confides in God (1–3)

An active believer, the more he is beaten off from God, either by the rebukes of providence, or the reproaches of enemies, the faster hold he will take, and the closer will he cleave to him. A child of God startles at the very thought of despairing of help in God. See what God is to his people, what he will be, what they have found him, what David found in him. 1. Safety; a shield for me; which denotes the advantage of that protection. 2. Honour; those whom God owns for his, have true honour put upon them. 3. Joy and deliverance. If, in the worst of times, God's people can lift up their heads with joy, knowing that all shall work for good to them, they will own God as giving them both cause and hearts to rejoice.

He triumphs over his fears, and gives God the glory, and takes to himself the comfort (4–8)

Care and grief do us good, when they engage us to pray to God, as in earnest. David had always found God ready to answer his prayers. Nothing can fix a gulf between the communications of God's grace towards us, and the working of his grace in us; between his favour and our faith. He had always been very safe under the Divine protection. This is applicable to the common mercies of every night, for which we ought to give thanks every morning. Many lie down, and cannot sleep, through pain of body, or anguish of mind, or the continual alarms of fear in the night. But it seems here rather to be meant of the calmness of David's spirit, in the midst of his dangers. The Lord, by his grace and the consolations of his Spirit, made him easy. It is a great mercy, when we are in trouble, to have our minds stayed upon God. Behold the Son of David composing himself to his rest upon the cross, that bed of sorrows; commending his Spirit into the Father's hands in full confidence of a joyful resurrection. Behold this, O Christian: let faith teach thee how to sleep, and how to die; while it assures thee that as sleep is a short death, so death is only a longer sleep; the same God watches over thee, in thy bed and in thy grave. David's faith became triumphant. He began the psalm with complaints of the strength and malice of his enemies; but concludes with rejoicing in the power and grace of his God, and now sees more with him than against him. Salvation belongeth unto the Lord; he has power to save, be the danger ever so great. All that have the Lord for their God, are sure of salvation; for he who is their God, is the God of Salvation.

Psalm 4

The children of men proved, and the happiness of godly people (1–5)
God's favour is happiness (6–8)

The children of men proved, and the happiness of godly people (1–5)

Hear me for thy mercysake, is our best plea. He who will not ask such blessings as pardon, and justifying righteousness, and eternal life, must perish for the want of them. Alas! that so many should make so fearful a choice. The psalmist warns against sin. Keep up holy reverence of the glory and majesty of God. You have a great deal to say to your hearts, they may be spoken with, let it not be unsaid. Examine them by serious self-reflection; let your thoughts fasten upon that which is good, and keep close to it. Consider your ways, and before you turn to sleep at night, examine your consciences with respect to what you have done in the day; particularly what you have done amiss, that you may repent of it. When you awake in the night, meditate upon God, and the things that belong to your peace. Upon a sick-bed, particularly, we should consider our ways. Be still. When you have asked conscience a question, be serious, be silent, wait for an answer. Open not the mouth to excuse sin. All confidence must be silenced. Open not the mouth to excuse sin. All confidence only: therefore, after commanding the sacrifices of righteousness, the psalmist says, Put your trust in the Lord.

God's favour is happiness (6–8)

Worldly people inquire for good, not for the chief good; all they want is outward good, present good, partial good, good meat, good drink, a good trade, and a good estate; but what are all these worth? Any good will serve the turn of most men, but a gracious soul will not be put off so. Lord, let us have thy favour, and let us know that we have it, we desire no more; let us be satisfied of thy loving-kindness, and will be satisfied with it. Many inquire after happiness, but David had found it. When God puts grace in the heart, he puts gladness in the heart. Thus comforted, he pitied, but neither envied nor feared the most prosperous sinner. He commits all his affairs to God, and is prepared to welcome his holy will. But salvation is in Christ alone; where will those appear who despise him as their Mediator, and revile him in his disciples? May they stand in awe, and no longer sin against the only remedy.

Psalm 5

God will certainly hear prayer: David gives to God the glory, and takes to himself the comfort (1–6)

He prayed for himself, that God would guide him, and for all the Lord's people, that God would give them joy, and keep them safe (7–12)

God will certainly hear prayer: David gives to God the glory, and takes to himself the comfort (1–6)

God is a prayer-hearing God. Such he has always been, and he is still as ready to hear prayer as ever. The most encouraging principle of prayer, and the most powerful plea in prayer, is, to look upon him as our King and our God. David also prays to a sin-hating God. Sin is folly, and sinners are the greatest of all fools; fools of their own making. Wicked people hate God; justly are they hated of him, and this will be their endless misery and ruin. Let us learn the importance of truth and sincerity, in all the affairs of life. Liars and murderers resemble the devil, and are his children, therefore it may well be expected that God should abhor them. These were the characters of David's enemies; and such as these are still the enemies of Christ and his people.

He prayed for himself, that God would guide him, and for all the Lord's people, that God would give them joy, and keep them safe (7–12)

David prayed often alone, yet was very constant in attendance on public worship. The mercy of God should ever be the foundation both of our hope and of our joy, in every thing wherein we have to do with him. Let us learn to pray, not for ourselves only, but for others; grace be with all that love Christ in sincerity. The Divine blessing comes down upon us through Jesus Christ, the righteous or just One, as of old it did upon Israel through David, whom God protected, and placed upon the throne. Thou, O Christ, art the righteous Saviour, thou art the King of Israel, thou art the Fountain of blessing to all believers; thy favour is the defence and protection of thy church.

Psalm 6

The psalmist deprecates God's wrath, and begs for the return of his favour (1–7)

He assures himself of an answer of peace (8–10)

The psalmist deprecates God's wrath, and begs for the return of his favour (1–7)

These speak the language of a heart truly humbled, of a broken and contrite spirit under great afflictions, sent to awaken conscience and mortify corruption. Sickness brought sin to his remembrance, and he looked upon it as a token of God's displeasure against him. The affliction of his body will be tolerable, if he has comfort in his soul. Christ's sorest complaint, in his sufferings, was of the trouble of his soul, and the want of his Father's smiles. Every page of Scripture proclaims the fact that salvation is only of the Lord. Man is a sinner, his case can only be reached by mercy; and never is mercy more illustrious than in restoring backsliders. With good reason we may pray, that if it be the will of God, and he has any further work for us or our friends to do in this world, he will yet spare us or them to serve him. To depart and be with Christ is happiest for the saints; but for them to abide in the flesh is more profitable for the church.

He assures himself of an answer of peace (8–10)

What a sudden change is here! Having made his request known to God, the psalmist is confident that his sorrow will be turned into joy. By the workings of God's grace upon his heart, he knew his prayer was accepted, and did not doubt but it would, in due time, be answered. His prayers will be accepted, coming up out of the hands of Christ the Mediator. The word signifies prayer made to God, the righteous Judge, as the God of his righteousness, who would plead his cause, and right his wrongs. A believer, through the blood and righteousness of Christ, can go to God as a righteous God, and plead with him for pardon and cleansing, who is just and faithful to grant both. He prays for the conversion of his enemies, or foretells their ruin.

Psalm 7

The psalmist prays to God to plead his cause, and judge for him (1–9)

He expresses confidence in God, and will

**give him the glory of his deliverance
(10–17)**

The psalmist prays to God to plead his cause, and judge for him (1–9)

David flees to God for succour. But Christ alone could call on Heaven to attest his uprightness in all things. All His works were wrought in righteousness; and the prince of this world found nothing whereof justly to accuse him. Yet for our sakes, submitting to be charged as guilty, he suffered all evils, but, being innocent, he triumphed over them all. The plea is, 'For the righteous God trieth the hearts and the reins.' He knows the secret wickedness of the wicked, and how to bring it to an end; he is witness to the secret sincerity of the just, and has ways of establishing it. When a man has made peace with God about all his sins, upon the terms of grace and mercy, through the sacrifice of the Mediator, he may, in comparison with his enemies, appeal to God's justice to decide.

He expresses confidence in God, and will give him the glory of his deliverance (10–17)

David is confident that he shall find God his powerful Saviour. The destruction of sinners may be prevented by their conversion; for it is threatened, If he turn not from his evil way, let him expect it will be his ruin. But amidst the threatenings of wrath, we have a gracious offer of mercy. God gives sinners warning of their danger, and space to repent, and prevent it. He is slow to punish, and long-suffering to us-ward, not willing that any should perish. The sinner is described, ver. 14–16, as taking more pains to ruin his soul than, if directed aright, would save it. This is true, in a sense, of all sinners. Let us look to the Saviour under all our trials. Blessed Lord, give us grace to look to thee in the path of tribulation, going before thy church and people, and marking the way by thine own spotless example. Under all the persecutions which in our lesser trials mark our way, let the looking to Jesus animate our minds and comfort our hearts.

The psalmist seeks to give unto God the glory due to his name. How bright this glory shines even in this lower world! He is ours, for he made us, protects us, and takes special care of us. The birth, life, preaching, miracles, suffering, death, resurrection, and ascension of Jesus are known through the world. No name is so universal, no power and influence so generally felt, as those of the Saviour of mankind. But how much brighter it shines in the upper world! We, on this earth, only hear God's excellent name, and praise that; the angels and blessed spirits above, see his glory, and praise that; yet he is exalted far above even their blessing and praise. Sometimes the grace of God appears wonderfully in young children. Sometimes the power of God brings to pass great things in his church, by very weak and unlikely instruments, that the excellency of the power might the more evidently appear to be of God, and not of man. This he does, because of his enemies, that he may put them to silence.

And for making even the heavenly bodies useful to man, thereby placing him but little lower than the angels (3–9)

We are to consider the heavens, that man thus may be directed to set his affections on things above. What is man, so mean a creature, that he should be thus honoured! So sinful a creature, that he should be thus favoured! Man has sovereign dominion over the inferior creatures, under God, and is appointed their lord. This refers to Christ. In Hebrews 2:68, the apostle, to prove the sovereign dominion of Christ, shows he is that Man, that Son of man, here spoken of, whom God has made to have dominion over the works of his hands. The greatest favour ever showed to the human race, and the greatest honour ever put upon human nature, were exemplified in the Lord Jesus. With good reason does the psalmist conclude as he began, Lord, how excellent is thy name in all the earth, which has been honoured with the presence of the Redeemer, and is still enlightened by his gospel, and governed by his wisdom and power! What words can reach his praises, who has a right to our obedience as our Redeemer?

Psalm 8

God is to be glorified, for making known himself to us (1, 2)

And for making even the heavenly bodies useful to man, thereby placing him but little lower than the angels (3–9)

God is to be glorified, for making known himself to us (1, 2)

Psalm 9

David praises God for protecting his people (1–10)

And for cause to praise him (11–20)

David praises God for protecting his people (1–10)

If we would praise God acceptably, we must praise him in sincerity, with our whole heart.

When we give thanks for some one particular mercy, we should remember former mercies. Our joy must not be in the gift, so much as in the Giver. The triumphs of the Redeemer ought to be the triumphs of the redeemed. The almighty power of God is that which the strongest and stoutest of his enemies are no way able to stand before. We are sure that the judgment of God is according to truth, and that with him there is no unrighteousness. His people may, by faith, flee to him as their Refuge, and may depend on his power and promise for their safety, so that no real hurt shall be done to them. Those who know him to be a God of truth and faithfulness, will rejoice in his word of promise, and rest upon that. Those who know him to be an everlasting Father, will trust him with their souls as their main care, and trust in him at all times, even to the end; and by constant care seek to approve themselves to him in the whole course of their lives. Who is there that would not seek him, who never hath forsaken those that seek Him?

And for cause to praise him (11–20)

Those who believe that God is greatly to be praised, not only desire to praise him better themselves, but desire that others may join with them. There is a day coming, when it will appear that he has not forgotten the cry of the humble; neither the cry of their blood, or the cry of their prayers. We are never brought so low, so near to death, but God can raise us up. If he has saved us from spiritual and eternal death, we may thence hope, that in all our distresses he will be a very present help to us. The overruling providence of God frequently so orders it, that persecutors and oppressors are brought to ruin by the projects they formed to destroy the people of God. Drunkards kill themselves; prodigals beggar themselves; the contentious bring mischief upon themselves: thus men's sins may be read in their punishment, and it becomes plain to all, that the destruction of sinners is of themselves. All wickedness came originally with the wicked one from hell; and those who continue in sin, must go to that place of torment. The true state, both of nations and of individuals, may be correctly estimated by this one rule, whether in their doings they remember or forget God. David encourages the people of God to wait for his salvation, though it should be long deferred. God will make it appear that he never did forget them: it is not possible he should. Strange that man, although he is made of dust should yet need some sharp affliction, some severe visitation from God, to bring him to the knowledge of himself, and make him feel who and what he is.

Psalm 10

The psalmist complains of the wickedness of the wicked (1–11)

He prays to God to appear for the relief of his people (12–18)

The psalmist complains of the wickedness of the wicked (1–11)

God's withdrawings are very grievous to his people, especially in times of trouble. We stand afar off from God by our unbelief, and then complain that God stands afar off from us. Passionate words against bad men do more hurt than good; if we speak of their badness, let it be to the Lord in prayer; he can make them better. The sinner proudly glories in his power and success. Wicked people will not seek after God, that is, will not call upon him. They live without prayer, and that is living without God. They have many thoughts, many objects and devices, but think not of the Lord in any of them; they have no submission to his will, nor aim for his glory. The cause of this is pride. Men think it below them to be religious. They could not break all the laws of justice and goodness toward man, if they had not first shaken off all sense of religion.

He prays to God to appear for the relief of his people (12–18)

The psalmist speaks with astonishment, at the wickedness of the wicked, and at the patience and forbearance of God. God prepares the heart for prayer, by kindling holy desires, and strengthening our most holy faith, fixing the thoughts, and raising the affections, and then he graciously accepts the prayer. The preparation of the heart is from the Lord, and we must seek unto him for it. Let the poor, afflicted, persecuted, or tempted believer recollect, that Satan is the prince of this world, and that he is the father of all the ungodly. The children of God cannot expect kindness, truth, or justice from such persons as crucified the Lord of glory. But this once suffering Jesus, now reigns as King over all the earth, and of his dominion there shall be no end. Let us commit ourselves unto him, humbly trusting in his mercy. He will rescue the believer from every temptation, and break the arm of every wicked oppressor, and bruise Satan under our feet shortly. But in heaven alone will all sin and temptation be shut out, though in this life the believer has a foretaste of deliverance.

Psalm 11

David's struggle with, and triumph over a strong temptation to distrust God, and betake himself to indirect means for his own safety, in a time of danger (1–7)

Those that truly fear God and serve him, are welcome to put their trust in him. The psalmist, before he gives an account of his temptation to distrust God, records his resolution to trust in Him, as that by which he was resolved to live and die. The believer, though not terrified by his enemies, may be tempted, by the fears of his friends, to desert his post, or neglect his work. They perceive his danger, but not his security; they give him counsel that savours of worldly policy, rather than of heavenly wisdom. The principles of religion are the foundations on which the faith and hope of the righteous are built. We are concerned to hold these fast against all temptations to unbelief; for believers would be undone, if they had not God to go to, God to trust in, and future bliss to hope for.

The prosperity of wicked people in their wicked, evil ways, and the straits and distresses which the best men are sometimes brought into, tried David's faith. We need not say, Who shall go up to heaven, to fetch us thence a God to trust in? The word is nigh us, and God in the word; his Spirit is in his saints, those living temples, and the Lord is that Spirit. This God governs the world. We may know what men seem to be, but God knows what they are, as the refiner knows the value of gold when he has tried it. God is said to try with his eyes, because he cannot err, or be imposed upon. If he afflicts good people, it is for their trial, therefore for their good. However persecutors and oppressors may prosper awhile, they will for ever perish. God is a holy God, and therefore hates them. He is a righteous Judge, and will therefore punish them. In what a horrible tempest are the wicked hurried away at death! Every man has the portion of his cup assigned him. Impenitent sinner, mark your doom! The last call to repentance is about to be addressed to you, judgement is at hand; through the gloomy shade of death you pass into the region of eternal wrath. Hasten then, O sinner, to the cross of Christ. How stands the case between God and our souls? Is Christ our hope, our consolation, our security? Then, not otherwise, will the soul be carried through all its difficulties and conflicts.

Psalm 12

The psalmist begs help of God, because there were none among men whom he durst trust (1–8)

This psalm furnishes good thoughts for bad times; a man may comfort himself with such meditations and prayers. Let us see what makes the times bad, and when they may be said to be so. Ask the children of this world, What makes the times bad? they will tell you, Scarcity of money, decay of trade, and the desolations of war, make the times bad: but the Scripture lays the badness of the times on causes of another nature, 2 Ti 3:1, &c.: perilous times shall come, for sin shall abound; and of this David complains. When piety decays times really are bad. He who made man's mouth will call him to an account for his proud, profane, dissembling, or even useless words. When the poor and needy are oppressed, then the times are very bad. God himself takes notice of the oppression of the poor, and the sighing of the needy. When wickedness abounds, and is countenanced by those in authority, then the times are very bad. See with what good things we are here furnished for such bad times; and we cannot tell what times we may be reserved for:

1. We have a God to go to, from whom we may ask and expect the redress of all our grievances.

2. God will certainly punish and restrain false and proud men.

3. God will work deliverance for his oppressed people. His help is given in the fittest time. Though men are false, God is faithful; though they are not to be trusted, God is. The preciousness of God's word is compared to silver refined to the highest degree. How many proofs have been given of its power and truth! God will secure his chosen remnant, however bad the times are. As long as the world stands, there will be a generation of proud and wicked men. But all God's people are put into the hands of Christ our Saviour; there they are in safety, for none can pluck them thence; being built on Him, the Rock, they are safe, notwithstanding temptation or persecution come with ever so much force upon them.

Psalm 13

The psalmist complains that God had long withdrawn. He earnestly prays for comfort. He assures himself of an answer of peace (1–6)

God sometimes hides his face, and leaves his own children in the dark concerning their interest in him: and this they lay to heart more than any outward trouble whatever. But anxious cares are heavy burdens with which believers often load themselves more than they need. The bread of sorrows is sometimes the saint's daily bread; our Master himself was a man of sorrows. It is a common temptation, when trouble lasts long, to think that it will last always. Those who have long been without joy, begin to be without hope. We should never allow ourselves to make any complaints but what drive us to our knees. Nothing is more killing to a soul than the want of God's favour; nothing more reviving than the return of it. The sudden, delightful changes in the book of Psalms, are often very remarkable. We pass from depth of despondency to the height of religious confidence and joy. It is thus, ver. 5. All is gloomy dejection in ver. 4; but here the mind of the despondent worshipper rises above all its distressing fears, and throws itself, without reserve, on the mercy and care of its Divine Redeemer. See the power of faith, and how good it is to draw near to God. If we bring our cares and griefs to the throne of grace, and leave them there, we may go away like Hannah, and our countenances will be no more sad, 1 Samuel. As I put my trust in this, I am comforted, though I have no merit of my own. His faith in God's mercy filled his heart with joy in his salvation; for joy and peace come by believing. He has dealt bountifully with me. By faith he was as confident of salvation, as if it had been completed already. In this way believers pour out their prayers, renouncing all hopes but in the mercy of God through the Saviour's blood: and sometimes suddenly, at others gradually, they will find their burdens removed, and their comforts restored; they then allow that their fears and complaints were unnecessary, and acknowledge that the Lord hath dealt bountifully with them.

them. They are gone aside from the right way of their duty, the way that leads to happiness, and are turned into the paths of the destroyer. Let us lament the corruption of our nature, and see what need we have of the grace of God: let us not marvel that we are told we must be born again. And we must not rest in any thing short of union with Christ, and a new creation to holiness by his Spirit. The psalmist endeavours to convince sinners of the evil and danger of their way, while they think themselves very wise, and good, and safe. Their wickedness is described. Those that care not for God's people, for God's poor, care not for God himself. People run into all manner of wickedness, because they do not call upon God for his grace. What good can be expected from those that live without prayer? But those that will not fear God, may be made to fear at the shaking of a leaf. All our knowledge of the depravity of human nature should endear to us salvation out of Zion. But in heaven alone shall the whole company of the redeemed rejoice fully, and for evermore. The world is bad; oh that the Messiah would come and change its character! There is universal corruption; oh for the times of reformation! The triumphs of Zion's King will be the joys of Zion's children. The second coming of Christ, finally to do away the dominion of sin and Satan, will be the completing of this salvation, which is the hope, and will be the joy of every Israelite indeed. With this assurance we should comfort ourselves and one another, under the sins of sinners and sufferings of saints.

Psalm 14

A description of the depravity of human nature, and the deplorable corruption of a great part of mankind (1–7)

The fool hath said in his heart, There is no God. The sinner here described is an atheist, one that saith there is no Judge or Governor of the world, no Providence ruling over the affairs of men. He says this in his heart. He cannot satisfy himself that there is none, but wishes there were none, and pleases himself that it is possible there may be none; he is willing to think there is none. This sinner is a fool; he is simple and unwise, and this is evidence of it: he is wicked and profane, and this is the cause. The word of God is a discerner of these thoughts. No man will say, There is no God, till he is so hardened in sin, that it is become his interest that there should be none to call him to an account. The disease of sin has infected the whole race of mankind. They are all gone aside, there is none that doeth good, no, not one. Whatever good is in any of the children of men, or is done by them, it is not of themselves, it is God's work in

Psalm 15

The way to heaven, if we would be happy, we must be holy. We are encouraged to walk in that way (1–5)

Here is a very serious question concerning the character of a citizen of Zion. It is the happiness of glorified saints, that they dwell in the holy hill; they are at home there, they shall be for ever there. It concerns us to make it sure to ourselves that we have a place among them. A very plain and particular answer is here given. Those who desire to know their duty, will find the Scripture a very faithful director, and conscience a faithful monitor. A citizen of Zion is sincere in his religion. He is really what he professes to be, and endeavours to stand complete in all the will of God. He is just both to God and man; and, in speaking to both, speaks the truth in his heart. He scorns and abhors wrong and fraud; he cannot reckon that a good bargain, nor a saving one, which is made with a lie; and knows that he who wrongs his neighbour will prove, in the end, to have most injured himself. He is very careful to do hurt to no man. He speaks evil of no man, makes not others' faults the matter of his common talk; he makes the best of every body, and the worst of nobody.

If an ill-natured story be told him, he will disprove it if he can; if not, it goes no further. He values men by their virtue and piety. Wicked people are vile people, worthless, and good for nothing; so the word signifies. He thinks the worse of no man's piety for his poverty and mean condition. He reckons that serious piety puts honour upon a man, more than wealth, or a great name. He honours such, desires their conversation and an interest in their prayers, is glad to show them respect, or do them a kindness. By this we may judge of ourselves in some measure. Even wise and good men may swear to their own hurt: but see how strong the obligation is, a man must rather suffer loss to himself and his family, than wrong his neighbour. He will not increase his estate by extortion, or by bribery. He will not, for any gain, or hope of it to himself, do anything to hurt a righteous cause. Every true living member of the church, like the church itself, is built upon a Rock. He that doeth these things shall not be moved for ever. The grace of God shall always be sufficient for him. The union of these tempers and this conduct, can only spring from repentance for sin, faith in the Saviour, and love to him. In these respects let us examine and prove our own selves.

Psalm 16

This psalm begins with expressions of devotion, which may be applied to Christ; but ends with such confidence of a resurrection, as must be applied to Christ, and to him only (1–11)

David flees to God's protection, with cheerful, believing confidence. Those who have avowed that the Lord is their Lord, should often put themselves in mind of what they have done, take the comfort of it, and live up to it. He devotes himself to the honour of God, in the service of the saints. Saints on earth we must be, or we shall never be saints in heaven. Those renewed by the grace of God, and devoted to the glory of God, are saints on earth. The saints in the earth are excellent ones, yet some of them so poor, that they needed to have David's goodness extended to them. David declares his resolution to have no fellowship with the works of darkness; he repeats the solemn choice he had made of God for his portion and happiness, takes to himself the comfort of the choice, and gives God the glory of it. This is the language of a devout and pious soul.

Most take the world for their chief good, and place their happiness in the enjoyments of it; but how poor soever my condition is in this world, let me have the love and favour of God, and be accepted of him; let me have a title by promise to life and happiness in the future state; and I have enough. Heaven is an inheritance; we must take that for our home, our rest, our everlasting good, and look upon this world to be no more ours, than the country through which is our road to our Father's house. Those that have God for their portion, have a goodly heritage. Return unto thy rest, O my soul, and look no further. Gracious persons, though they still covet more of God, never covet more than God; but, being satisfied of his loving-kindness, are abundantly satisfied with it: they envy not any their carnal mirth and delights. But so ignorant and foolish are we, that if left to ourselves, we shall forsake our own mercies for lying vanities. God having given David counsel by his word and Spirit, his own thoughts taught him in the night season, and engaged him by faith to live to God. 8–11, are quoted by St. Peter in his first sermon, after the pouring out of the Spirit on the day of Pentecost, Ac 2:25–31; he declared that David in them speaks concerning Christ, and particularly of his resurrection. And Christ being the Head of the body, the church, these may be applied to all Christians, guided and animated by the Spirit of Christ; and we may hence learn, that it is our wisdom and duty to set the Lord always before us. And if our eyes are ever toward God, our hearts and tongues may ever rejoice in him. Death destroys the hope of man, but not the hope of a real Christian. Christ's resurrection is an earnest of the believer's resurrection. In this world sorrow is our lot, but in heaven there is joy, a fulness of joy; our pleasures here are for a moment, but those at God's right hand are pleasures for evermore. Through this thy beloved Son, and our dear Saviour, thou wilt show us, O Lord, the path of life; thou wilt justify our souls now, and raise our bodies by thy power at the last day; when earthly sorrow shall end in heavenly joy, pain in everlasting happiness.

Psalm 17

David's integrity (1–7)

The character of his enemies. His hope of happiness (8–15)

David's integrity (1–7)

This psalm is a prayer. Feigned prayers are fruitless; but if our hearts lead our prayers, God will meet them with his favour. The psalmist had been used to pray, so that it was not his distress and danger that now first brought him to his duty. And he was encouraged by his faith to expect God would notice his prayers. Constant resolution and watchfulness against sins of the tongue, will be a good evidence of our integrity. Aware of man's propensity to wicked works, and of his own peculiar temptations, David had made God's word his preservative from the paths of Satan, which lead to destruction. If we carefully avoid the paths of sin, we will avoid destruction. If we carefully avoid the paths of sin, it will be very comfortable in the reflection, when we are in trouble. Those that are, through grace, going in God's paths, should pray that their goings may be held up in those paths. David prays, Lord, still hold me up. Those who would proceed and persevere in the ways of God, must, by faith prayer, get daily fresh supplies of grace and strength from him. Show thy marvellous loving-kindness, distinguishing favours, not common mercies, but be gracious to me; do as thou usest to do to those who love thy name.

The character of his enemies. His hope of happiness (8–15)

Being compassed with enemies, David prays to God to keep him in safety. This prayer is a prediction that Christ would be preserved, through all the hardships and difficulties of his humiliation, to the glories and joys of his exalted state, and is a pattern to Christians to commit the keeping of their souls to God, trusting him to preserve them to his heavenly kingdom. Those are our worst enemies, that are enemies to our souls. They are God's sword, which cannot move without him, and which he will sheathe when he has done his work with it. They are his hand, by which he chastises his people. There is no fleeing from God's hand, but by fleeing to it. It is very comfortable, when we are in fear of the power of man, to see it dependent upon, and in subjection to the power of God. Most men look on the things of this world as the best things; and they look no further, nor show any care to provide for another life. The things of this world are called treasures, they are so accounted; but to the soul, and when compared with eternal blessings, they are trash. The most afflicted Christian need not envy the most prosperous men of the world, who have their portion in this life. Clothed with Christ's righteousness, having through his grace a good heart and a good life, may we by faith behold God's face, and set him always before us. When we awake every morning, may we be satisfied with his likeness set before us in his word, and with his likeness stamped upon us by his renewing grace. Happiness in the other world is prepared only for those that are justified and sanctified: they

shall be put in possession of it when the soul awakes, at death, out of its slumber in the body, and when the body awakes, at the resurrection, out of its slumber in the grave. There is no satisfaction for a soul but in God, and in his good will towards us, and his good work in us; yet that satisfaction will not be perfect till we come to heaven.

Psalm 18

David rejoices in the deliverances God wrought for him (1–19)

He takes the comfort of his integrity, which God had cleared up (20–28)

He gives to God the glory of all his mighty deeds (29–50)

David rejoices in the deliverances God wrought for him (1–19)

The first words, 'I will love thee, O Lord, my strength,' are the scope and contents of the psalm. Those that truly love God, may triumph in him as their Rock and Refuge, and may with confidence call upon him. It is good for us to observe all the circumstances of a mercy which magnify the power of God and his goodness to us in it. David was a praying man, and God was found a prayer-hearing God. If we pray as he did, we shall speed as he did. God's manifestation of his presence is very fully described, ver. 7–15. Little appeared of man, but much of God, in these deliverances. It is not possible to apply to the history of the son of Jesse those awful, majestic, and stupendous words which are used through this description of the Divine manifestation. Every part of so solemn a scene of terrors tells us, a greater than David is here. God will not only deliver his people out of their troubles in due time, but he will bear them up under their troubles in the mean time. Can we meditate on ver. 18, without directing one thought to Gethsemane and Calvary? Can we forget that it was in the hour of Christ's deepest calamity, when Judas betrayed, when his friends forsook, when the multitude derided him, and the smiles of his Father's love were withheld, that the powers of darkness prevented him? The sorrows of death surrounded him, in his distress he prayed, Hebrews 5:7. God made the earth to shake and tremble, and the rocks to cleave, and brought him out, in his resurrection, because he delighted in him and in his undertaking.

He takes the comfort of his integrity, which God had cleared up (20–28)

Those that forsake the ways of the Lord, depart from their God. But though conscious to ourselves of many a false step, let there not be a wicked departure from our God. David kept his eye upon the rule of God's commands. Constant care to keep from that sin, whatever it be, which most easily besets us, proves that we are upright before God. Those who show mercy to others, even they need mercy. Those who are faithful to God, shall find him all that to them which he has promised to be. The words of the Lord are pure words, very sure to be depended on, and very sweet to be delighted in. Those who resist God, and walk contrary to him, shall find that he will walk contrary to them, Leviticus 26:21–24. The gracious recompense of which David spoke, may generally be expected by those who act from right motives. Hence he speaks comfort to the humble, and terror to the proud; 'Thou wilt bring down high looks.' And he speaks encouragement to himself: 'Thou wilt light my candle;' thou wilt revive and comfort my sorrowful spirit; thou wilt guide my way, that I may avoid the snares laid for me. Thou wilt light my candle to work by, and give me an opportunity of serving thee. Let those that walk in darkness, and labour under discouragements, take courage; God himself will be a Light to them.

He gives to God the glory of all his mighty deeds (29–50)

When we praise for one mercy, we must observe the many more, with which we have been compassed all our days. Many things had contributed to David's advancement, and he owns the hand of God in them all, to teach us to do likewise. In verse 32, and the following verses, are the gifts of God to the spiritual warrior, whereby he is prepared for the contest, after the example of his victorious Leader. Learn that we must seek release through Christ and so not be defeated. In David the type, we escape from trouble through Christ. If we pray without being reconciled to Jesus our Redeemer, conflicting with enemies, compassed with sorrows and with floods of ungodly men, enduring not only the pains of death, then the wrath of God will be on us; yet calling upon the Father with strong cries and tears; rescued from the grave; proceeding to reconcile, or to put under his feet all other enemies, till death, the last enemy, shall be destroyed. We should love the Lord, our Strength, and our Salvation; we should call on him in every trouble, and praise him for every deliverance; we should aim to walk with him in all righteousness and true holiness, keeping from sin. If we belong to him, he conquers and reigns for us, and we shall conquer and reign through him, and partake of the mercy of our anointed King, which is promised to all his seed for evermore. Amen.

Psalm 19

The glory of God's works (1–6)

His holiness and grace as shown in his word (7–10)

Prayer for the benefit of them (11–14)

The glory of God's works (1–6)

The heavens so declare the glory of God, and proclaim his wisdom, power, and goodness, that all ungodly men are left without excuse. They speak themselves to be works of God's hands; for they must have a Creator who is eternal, infinitely wise, powerful, and good. The counter-changing of day and night is a great proof of the power of God, and calls us to observe, that, as in the kingdom of nature, so in that of providence, he forms the light, and creates the darkness, Isaiah 45:7, and sets the one against the other. The sun in the firmament is an emblem of the Sun of righteousness, the Bridegroom of the church, and the Light of the world, diffusing Divine light and salvation by his gospel to the nations of the earth. He delights to bless his church, which he has espoused to himself; and his course will be unwearied as that of the sun, till the whole earth is filled with his light and salvation. Let us pray for the time when he shall enlighten, cheer, and make fruitful every nation on earth, with the blessed salvation. They have no speech or language, so some read it, and yet their voice is heard. All people may hear these preachers speak in their own tongue the wonderful works of God. Let us give God the glory of all the comfort and benefit we have by the lights of heaven, still looking above and beyond them to the Sun of righteousness.

His holiness and grace as shown in his word (7–10)

The Holy Scripture is of much greater benefit to us than day or night, than the air we breathe, or the light of the sun. To recover man out of his fallen state, there is need of the word of God. The word translated 'law,' may be rendered doctrine, and be understood as meaning all that teaches us true religion. The whole is perfect; its tendency is to convert or turn the soul from sin and the world, to God and holiness. It shows our sinfulness and misery in departing from God, and the necessity of our return to him. This testimony is sure, to be fully depended on: the ignorant and unlearned believing what God saith, become wise unto salvation. It is a sure direction in the way of duty. It is a sure fountain of living comforts, and a sure foundation of lasting hopes. The statues of the Lord are right, just as they should be; and, because they are right, they rejoice the heart. The commandments of the Lord are pure, holy, just, and good. By them we discover our need of a Saviour; and then learn how to adorn his gospel. They are the means which the Holy Spirit uses in enlightening the eyes; they bring us to a sight and sense of our sin and misery, and direct us in the way of duty. The fear of the Lord, that is, true religion and godliness, is clean, it will cleanse our way; and it endureth for ever. The ceremonial law is long since done away, but the law concerning the fear of God is ever the same. The judgments of the Lord, his precepts, are true; they are righteous, and they are so altogether; there is no unrighteousness in any of them. Gold is only for the body, and the concerns of time; but grace is for the soul, and the concerns of eternity. The word of God, received by faith, is more precious than gold; it is sweet to the soul, sweeter than honey. The pleasures of sense soon surfeit, yet never satisfy; but those of religion are substantial and satisfying; there is no danger of excess.

Prayer for the benefit of them (11–14)

God's word warns the wicked not to go on in his wicked way, and warns the righteous not to turn from his good way. There is a reward, not only after keeping, but in keeping God's commandments. Religion makes our comforts sweet, and our crosses easy, life truly valuable, and death itself truly desirable. David not only desired to be pardoned and cleansed from the sins he had discovered and confessed, but from those he had forgotten or overlooked. All discoveries of sin made to us by the law, should drive us to the throne of grace, there to pray. His dependence was the same with that of every Christian who says, Surely in the Lord Jesus have I righteousness and strength. No prayer can be acceptable before God which is not offered in the strength of our Redeemer or Divine Kinsman, through Him who took our nature upon him, that he might redeem us unto God, and restore the long-lost inheritance. May our hearts be much affected with the excellence of the word of God; and much affected with the evil of sin, and the danger we are in of it, and the danger we are in by it.

Psalm 20

This psalm is a prayer for the kings of Israel, but with relation to Christ (1–9)

Even the greatest of men may be much in trouble. Neither the crown on the king's head, nor the grace in his heart, would make him free from trouble. Even the greatest of men must be much in prayer. Let none expect benefit by the prayers of the church, or their friends, who are capable of praying for themselves, yet neglect it. Pray that God would protect his person, and preserve his life. That God would enable him to go on in his undertakings for the public good. We may know that God accepts our spiritual sacrifices, if by his Spirit he kindles in our souls a holy fire of piety and love to God. Also, that the Lord would crown his enterprises with success. Our first step to victory in spiritual warfare is to trust only in the mercy and grace of God; all who trust in themselves will soon be cast down. Believers triumph in God, and his revelation of himself to them, by which they distinguish themselves from those that live without God in the world. Those who make God and his name their praise, may make God and his name their trust.

This was the case when the pride and power of Jewish unbelief, and pagan idolatry, fell before the sermons and lives of the humble believers in Jesus. This is the case in every conflict with our spiritual enemies, when we engage them in the name, the spirit, and the power of Christ; and this will be the case at the last day, when the world, with the prince of it, shall be brought down and fall; but believers, risen from the dead, through the resurrection of the Lord, shall stand, and sing his praises in heaven. In Christ's salvation let us rejoice; and set up our banners in the name of the Lord our God, assured that by the saving strength of his right hand we shall be conquerors over every enemy.

Psalm 21

Thanksgiving for victory (1–6)
Confidence of further success (7–13)

Thanksgiving for victory (1–6)

Happy the people whose king makes God's strength his confidence, and God's salvation his joy; who is pleased with all the advancements of God kingdom, and trusts God to support him in all he does for the service of it. All our blessings are blessings of goodness, and are owing, not to any merit of ours, but only to God's goodness. But when God's blessings come sooner, and prove richer than we imagine; when they are given before we prayed for them, before we were ready for them, nay, when we feared the contrary; then it may be truly said that he prevented, or went before us, with them. Nothing indeed prevented, or went before Christ, but to mankind never was any favour more preventing than our redemption by Christ. Thou hast made him to be a universal, everlasting blessing to the world, in whom the families of the earth are, and shall be blessed; and so thou hast made him exceeding glad with the countenance thou hast given to his undertaking, and to him in the prosecution of it. The Spirit of prophecy rises from what related to the king, to that which is peculiar to Christ; none other is blessed for ever, much less a blessing for ever.

Confidence of further success (7–13)

The psalmist teaches to look forward with faith, and hope, and prayer upon what God would further do. The success with which God blessed David, was a type of the total overthrow of all Christ's enemies. Those who might have had Christ to rule and save them, but rejected him and fought against him, shall find the remembrance of it a worm that dies not. God makes sinners willing by his grace, receives them to his favour, and delivers them from the wrath to come. May he exalt himself, by his all-powerful grace, in our hearts, destroying all the strongholds of sin and Satan. How great should be our joy and praise to behold our Brother and Friend upon the throne, and for all the blessings we may expect from him! Yet he delights in his exalted state, as enabling him to confer happiness and glory on poor sinners, who are taught to love and trust in him.

Psalm 22

Complaints of discouragement (1–10)

With prayer for deliverance (11–21)

Praises for mercies and redemption (22–31)

Complaints of discouragement (1–10)

The Spirit of Christ, which was in the prophets, testifies in this psalm, clearly and fully, the sufferings of Christ, and the glory that should follow. We have a sorrowful complaint of God's withdrawings. This may be applied to any child of God, pressed down, overwhelmed with grief and terror. Spiritual desertions are the saints' sorest afflictions; but even their complaint of these burdens is a sign of spiritual life, and spiritual senses exercised. To cry out, My God, why am I sick? why am I poor? savours of discontent and worldliness. But, 'Why hast thou forsaken me?' is the language of a heart binding up its happiness in God's favour. This must be applied to Christ. In the first words of this complaint, he poured out his soul before God when he was upon the cross, Matthew 27:46. Being truly man, Christ felt a natural unwillingness to pass through such great sorrows, yet his zeal and love prevailed. Christ declared the holiness of God, his heavenly Father, in his sharpest sufferings; nay, declared them to be a proof of it, for which he would be continually praised by his Israel, more than for all other deliverances they received. Never any that hoped in thee, were made ashamed of their hope; never any that sought thee, sought thee in vain. Here is a complaint of the contempt and reproach of men. The Saviour here spoke of the abject state to

which he was reduced. The history of Christ's sufferings, and of his birth, explains this prophecy.

With prayer for deliverance (11–21)

In these we have Christ suffering, and Christ praying; by which we are directed to look for crosses, and to look up to God under them. The very manner of Christ's death is described, though not in use among the Jews. They pierced his hands and his feet, which were nailed to the accursed tree, and his whole body was left so to hang as to suffer the most severe pain and torture. His natural force failed, being wasted by the fire of Divine wrath preying upon his spirits. Who then can stand before God's anger? or who knows the power of it? The life of the sinner was forfeited, and the life of the Sacrifice must be the ransom for it. Our Lord Jesus was stripped, when he was crucified, that he might clothe us with the robe of his righteousness. Thus it was written, therefore thus it behoved Christ to suffer. Let all this confirm our faith in him as the true Messiah, and excite our love to him as the best of friends, who loved us, and suffered all this for us. Christ in his agony prayed, prayed earnestly, prayed that the cup might pass from him. When we cannot rejoice in God as our song, yet let us stay ourselves upon him as our strength; and take the comfort of spiritual supports, when we cannot have spiritual delights. He prays to be delivered from the Divine wrath. He that has delivered, doth deliver, and will do so. We should think upon the sufferings and resurrection of Christ, till we feel in our souls the power of his resurrection, and the fellowship of his sufferings.

Praises for mercies and redemption (22–31)

The Saviour now speaks as risen from the dead. The first words of the complaint were used by Christ himself upon the cross; the first words of the triumph are expressly applied to him, Hebrews 2:12. All our praises must refer to the work of redemption. The suffering of the Redeemer was graciously accepted as a full satisfaction for sin. Though it was offered for sinful men, the Father did not despise or abhor it for our sakes. This ought to be the matter of our thanksgiving. All humble, gracious souls should have a full satisfaction and happiness in him. Those that hunger and thirst after righteousness in Christ, shall not labour for that which satisfies not. Those that are much in praying, will be much in thanksgiving. Those that turn to God, will make conscience of worshipping before him. Let every tongue confess that he is Lord. High and low, rich and poor, bond and free, meet in Christ. Seeing we cannot keep alive our own souls, it is our wisdom, by obedient faith, to commit our souls to Christ, who is able to save and keep them alive for ever. A seed shall serve him. God will have a church in the world to the end of time. They shall be accounted to him for a generation; he will be the same to them that he was to those who went before them. His righteousness, and not any of their own, they shall declare to be the foundation of all their hopes, and the fountain of all their joys. Redemption by Christ is the Lord's own doing. Here we see the free love and compassion of God the Father, and of our Lord Jesus Christ, for us wretched sinners, as the source of all grace and consolation; the example we are to follow, the treatment as Christians we are to expect, and the conduct under it we are to adopt. Every lesson may here be learned that can profit the humbled soul. Let those who go about to establish their own righteousness inquire, why the beloved Son of God should thus suffer, if their own doings could atone for sin? Let the ungodly professor consider whether the Saviour thus honoured the Divine law, to purchase him the privilege of despising it. Let the careless take warning to flee from the wrath to come, and the trembling rest their hopes upon this merciful Redeemer. Let the tempted and distressed believer cheerfully expect a happy end of every trial.

Psalm 23

Confidence in God's grace and care (1–6)

'The Lord is my shepherd.' In these words, the believer is taught to express his satisfaction in the care of the great Pastor of the universe, the Redeemer and Preserver of men. With joy he reflects that he has a shepherd, and that shepherd is Jehovah. A flock of sheep, gentle and harmless, feeding in verdant pastures, under the care of a skilful, watchful, and tender shepherd, forms an emblem of believers brought back to the Shepherd of their souls. The greatest abundance is but a dry pasture to a wicked man, who relishes in it only what pleases the senses; but to a godly man, who by faith tastes the goodness of God in all his enjoyments, though he has but little of the world, it is a green pasture. The Lord gives quiet and contentment in the mind, whatever the lot is. Are we blessed with the green pastures of the ordinances, let us not think it enough to pass through them, but let us abide in them. The consolations of the Holy Spirit are the still waters by which the saints are led; the streams which flow from the Fountain of living waters. Those only are led by the still waters of comfort, who walk in the paths of righteousness. The way of duty is the truly pleasant way. The work of righteousness is peace. In these paths we cannot walk, unless God lead us into them, and lead us on in them. Discontent and distrust proceed from unbelief; an unsteady

walk is the consequence: let us then simply trust our Shepherd's care, and hearken to his voice. The valley of the shadow of death may denote the most severe and terrible affliction, or dark dispensation of providence, that the psalmist ever could come under. Between the part of the flock on earth and that which is gone to heaven, death lies like a dark valley that must be passed in going from one to the other. But even in this there are words which lessen the terror. It is but the shadow of death: the shadow of a serpent will not sting, nor the shadow of a sword kill. It is a valley, deep indeed, and dark, and miry; but valleys are often fruitful, and so is death itself fruitful of comforts to God's people. It is a walk through it: they shall not be lost in this valley, but get safe to the mountain on the other side. Death is a king of terrors, but not to the sheep of Christ. When they come to die, God will rebuke the enemy; he will guide them with his rod, and sustain them with his staff. There is enough in the gospel to comfort the saints when dying, and underneath them are the everlasting arms. The Lord's people feast at his table, upon the provisions of his love. Satan and wicked men are not able to destroy their comforts, while they are anointed with the Holy Spirit, and drink of the cup of salvation which is ever full. Past experience teaches believers to trust that the goodness and mercy of God will follow them all the days of their lives, and it is their desire and determination, to seek their happiness in the service of God here, and they hope to enjoy his love for ever in heaven. While here, the Lord can make any situation pleasant, by the anointing of his Spirit and the joys of his salvation. But those that would be satisfied with the blessings of his house, must keep close to the duties of it.

Psalm 24

Concerning the kingdom of Christ, and the subjects of that kingdom (1–6)

Concerning the King of that kingdom (7–10)

Concerning the kingdom of Christ, and the subjects of that kingdom (1–6)

We ourselves are not our own; our bodies, our souls, are not. Even those of the children of men are God's, who know him not, nor own their relation to him. A soul that knows and considers its own nature, and that it must live for ever, when it has viewed the earth and the fulness thereof, will sit down unsatisfied. It will think of ascending toward God, and will ask, What shall I do, that I may abide in that happy, holy place, where he makes his people holy and happy? We make nothing of religion, if we do not make heartwork of it. We can only be cleansed from our sins, and renewed unto holiness, by the blood of Christ and the washing of the Holy Ghost. Thus we become his people; thus we receive blessing from the Lord, and righteousness from the God of our salvation. God's peculiar people shall be made truly and for ever happy. Where God gives righteousness, he designs salvation. Those that are made meet for heaven, shall be brought safe to heaven, and will find what they have been seeking.

Concerning the King of that kingdom (7–10)

The splendid entry here described, refers to the solemn bringing in of the ark into the tent David pitched for it, or the temple Solomon built for it. We may also apply it to the ascension of Christ into heaven, and the welcome given to him there. Our Redeemer found the gates of heaven shut, but having by his blood made atonement for sin, as one having authority, he demanded entrance. The angels were to worship him, Hebrews 1:6: they ask with wonder, Who is he? It is answered, that he is strong and mighty; mighty in battle to save his people, and to subdue his and their enemies. We may apply it to Christ's entrance into the souls of men by his word and Spirit, that they may be his temples. Behold, he stands at the door, and knocks, 3:20. The gates and doors of the heart are to be opened to him, as possession is delivered to the rightful owner. We may apply it to his second coming with glorious power. Lord, open the everlasting door of our souls by thy grace, that we may now receive thee, and be wholly thine; and that, at length, we may be numbered with thy saints in glory.

Psalm 25

Confidence in prayer (1–7)
Prayer for remission of sins (8–14)
For help in affliction (15–22)

Confidence in prayer (1–7)

In worshipping God, we must lift up our souls to him. It is certain that none who, by a believing attendance, wait on God, and, by a believing hope, wait for him, shall be ashamed of it. The most advanced believer both needs and desires to be taught of God. If we sincerely desire to know our duty, with resolution to do it, we may be sure that God will direct us in it. The psalmist is earnest for the pardon of his sins. When God pardons sin, he is said to remember it no more, which denotes full remission. It is God's goodness, and not ours, his mercy, and not our merit, that must be our plea for the pardon of sin, and all the good we need. This plea we must rely upon, feeling our own unworthiness, and satisfied of the riches of God's mercy and grace. How boundless is that mercy which covers for ever the sins and follies of a youth spent without God and without hope! Blessed be the Lord, the blood of the great Sacrifice can wash away every stain.

Prayer for remission of sins (8–14)

We are all sinners; and Christ came into the world to save sinners, to teach sinners, to call sinners to repentance. We value a promise by the character of him that makes it; we therefore depend upon God's promises. All the paths of the Lord, that is, all his promises and all his providences, are mercy and truth. In all God's dealings his people may see his mercy displayed, and his word fulfilled, whatever afflictions they are now exercised with. All the paths of the Lord are mercy and truth; and so it will appear when they come to their journey's end. Those that are humble, that distrust themselves, and desire to be taught and to follow Divine guidance, these he will guide in judgment, that is, by the rule of the written word, to find rest for their souls in the Saviour. Even when the body is sick, and in pain, the soul may be at ease in God.

For help in affliction (15–22)

The psalmist concludes, as he began, with expressing dependence upon God, and desire toward him. It is good thus to hope, and quietly to wait for the salvation of the Lord. And if God turns to us, no matter who turns from us. He pleads his own integrity. Though guilty before God, yet, as to his enemies, he had the testimony of conscience that he had done them no wrong. God would, at length, give Israel rest from all their enemies round about. In heaven, God's Israel will be perfectly redeemed from all troubles. Blessed Saviour, thou hast graciously taught us that without thee we can do nothing. Do thou teach us how to pray, how to appear before thee in the way which thou shalt choose, and how to lift up our whole hearts and desires after thee, for thou art the Lord our righteousness.

Psalm 26

David, in this psalm, appeals to God touching his integrity (1-12)

David here, by the Spirit of prophecy, speaks of himself as a type of Christ, of whom what he here says of his spotless innocence was fully and eminently true, and of Christ only, and to Him we may apply it. We are complete in him. The man that walks in his integrity, yet trusting wholly in the grace of God, is in a state of acceptance, according to the covenant of which Jesus was the Mediator, in virtue of his spotless obedience even unto death. This man desires to have his inmost soul searched and proved by the Lord. He is aware of the deceitfulness of his own heart; he desires to detect and mortify every sin; and he longs to be satisfied of his being a true believer, and to practise the holy commands of God. Great care to avoid bad company, is both a good evidence of our integrity, and a good means to keep us in it. Hypocrites and dissemblers may be found attending on God's ordinances; but it is a good sign of sincerity, if we attend upon them, as the psalmist here tells us he did, in the exercise of repentance and conscientious obedience. He feels his ground firm under him; and, as he delights in blessing the Lord with his congregations on earth, he trusts that shortly he shall join the great assembly in heaven, in singing praises to God and to the Lamb for evermore.

Psalm 27

The psalmist's faith (1–6)

His desire toward God, and expectation from him (7–14)

The psalmist's faith (1–6)

The Lord, who is the believer's light, is the strength of his life; not only by whom, but in whom he lives and moves. In God let us strengthen ourselves. The gracious presence of God, his power, his promise, his readiness to hear prayer, the witness of his Spirit in the hearts of his people; these are the secret of his tabernacle, and in these the saints find cause for that holy security and peace of mind in which they dwell at ease. The psalmist prays for constant communion with God in holy ordinances. All God's children desire to dwell in their Father's house. Not to sojourn there as a wayfaring man, to tarry but for a night; or to dwell there for a time only, as the servant that abides not in the house for ever; but to dwell there all the days of their life, as children with a father. Do we hope that the praising of God will be the blessedness of our eternity? Surely then we ought to make it the business of our time. This he had at heart more than any thing. Whatever the Christian is as to this life, he considers the favour and service of God as the one thing needful. This he desires, prays for and seeks after, and in it he rejoices.

His desire toward God, and expectation from him (7–14)

Wherever the believer is, he can find a way to the throne of grace by prayer. God calls us by his Spirit, by his word, by his worship, and by special providences, merciful and afflicting. When we are foolishly making court to lying vanities, God is, in love to us, calling us to seek our own mercies in him. The call is general, 'Seek ye my face;' but we must apply it to ourselves, 'I will seek it.' The word does us no good, when we do not ourselves accept the exhortation: a gracious heart readily answers to the call of a gracious God, being made willing in the day of his power. The psalmist requests the favour of the Lord; the continuance of his presence with him; the benefit of Divine guidance, and the benefit of Divine protection. God's time to help those that trust in him, is, when all other helpers fail. He is a surer and better Friend than earthly parents are, or can be. What was the belief which supported the psalmist? That he should see the goodness of the Lord. There is nothing like the believing hope of eternal life, the foresights of that glory, and foretastes of those pleasures, to keep us from fainting under all calamities. In the mean time he should be strengthened to bear up under his burdens. Let us look unto the suffering Saviour, and pray in faith, not to be delivered into the hands of our enemies. Let us encourage each other to wait on the Lord, with patient expectation, and fervent prayer.

Psalm 28

A prayer in distress (1–5)

Thanksgiving for deliverance (6–9)

A prayer in distress (1–5)

David is very earnest in prayer. Observe his faith in prayer; God is my rock, on whom I build my hope. Believers should not rest till they have received some token that their prayers are heard. He prays that he may not be numbered with the wicked. Save me from being entangled in the snares they have laid for me. Save me from being infected with their sins, and from doing as they do. Lord, never leave me to use such arts of deceit and treachery for my safety, as they use for my ruin. Believers dread the way of sinners; the best are sensible of the danger they are in of being drawn aside: we should all pray earnestly to God for his grace to keep us. Those who are careful not to partake with sinners in their sins, have reason to hope that they shall not receive their plagues. He speaks of the just judgments of the Lord on the workers of iniquity, ver. 4. This is not the language of passion or revenge. It is a prophecy that there will certainly come a day, when God will punish every man who persists in his evil deeds. Sinners shall be reckoned with, not only for the mischief they have done, but for the mischief they designed, and did what they could to effect. Disregard of the works of the Lord, is the cause of the sin of sinners, and becomes the cause of their ruin.

Thanksgiving for deliverance (6–9)

Has God heard our supplications? Let us then bless his name. The Lord is my strength, to support me, and carry me on through all my services and sufferings. The heart that truly believes, shall in due time greatly rejoice: we are to expect joy and peace in believing. God shall have the praise of it: thus must we express our gratitude. The saints rejoice in others' comfort as well as their own: we have the less benefit from the light of the sun, nor from the light of God's countenance, for others' sharing therein. The psalmist concludes with a short, but comprehensive prayer. God's people are his inheritance, and precious in his eyes. He prays that God would save them; that he would bless them with all good, especially the plenty of his ordinances, which are food to the soul. And direct their actions and overrule their affairs for good. Also, lift them up for ever; not only those of that age, but his people in every age to come; lift them up as high as heaven. There, and there only, will saints be lifted up for ever, never more to sink, or be depressed. Save us, Lord Jesus, from our sins; bless us, thou Son of Abraham, with the blessing of righteousness; feed us, thou good Shepherd of the sheep, and lift us up for ever from the dust, O thou, who art the Resurrection and the Life.

Psalm 29

Exhortation to give glory to God (1–11)

The mighty and honourable of the earth are especially bound to honour and worship him; but, alas, few attempt to worship him in the beauty of holiness. When we come before him as the Redeemer of sinners, in repentance faith, and love, he will accept our defective services, pardon the sin that cleaves to them, and approve of that measure of holiness which the Holy Spirit enables us to exercise. We have here the nature of religious worship; it is giving to the Lord the glory due to his name. We must be holy in all our religious services, devoted to God, and to his will and glory. There is a beauty in holiness, and that puts beauty upon all acts of worship. The psalmist here sets forth God's dominion in the kingdom of nature. In the thunder, and lightning, and storm, we may see and hear his glory. Let our hearts be thereby filled with great, and high, and honourable thoughts of God, in the holy adoring of whom, the power of godliness so much consists. O Lord our God, thou art very great! The power of the lightning equals the terror of the thunder. The fear caused by these effects of the Divine power, should remind us of the mighty power of God, of man's weakness, and of the defenceless and desperate condition of the wicked in the day of judgment. But the effects of the Divine word upon the souls of men, under the power of the Holy Spirit, are far greater than those of thunder storms in the nature world. Thereby the stoutest are made to tremble, the proudest are cast down, the secrets of the heart are brought to light, sinners are converted, the savage, sensual, and unclean, become harmless, gentle, and pure. If we have heard God's voice, and have fled for refuge to the hope set before us, let us remember that children need not fear their Father's voice, when he speaks in anger to his enemies. While those tremble who are without shelter, let those who abide in his appointed refuge bless him for their security, looking forward to the day of judgment without dismay, safe as Noah in the ark.

Psalm 30

Praise to God for deliverance (1–5)
Others encouraged by his example (6–12)

Praise to God for deliverance (1–5)

The great things the Lord has done for us, both by his providence and by his grace, bind us in gratitude to do all we can to advance his kingdom among men, though the most we can do is but little. God's saints in heaven sing to him; why should not those on earth do the same? Not one of all God's perfections carries in it more terror to the wicked, or more comfort to the godly, than his holiness. It is a good sign that we are in some measure partakers of his holiness, if we can heartily rejoice at the remembrance of it. Our happiness is bound up in the Divine favour; if we have that, we have enough, whatever else we want; but as long as God's anger continues, so long the saints' weeping continues.

Others encouraged by his example (6–12)

When things are well with us, we are very apt to think that they will always be so. When we see our mistake, it becomes us to think with shame upon our carnal security as our folly. If God hide his face, a good man is troubled, though no other calamity befall him. But if God, in wisdom and justice, turn from us, it will be the greatest folly if we turn from him. No; let us learn to pray in the dark. The sanctified spirit, which returns to God, shall praise him, shall be still praising him; but the services of God's house cannot be performed by the dust; it cannot praise him; there is none of that device or working in the grave, for it is the land of silence. We ask aright for life, when we do so that we may live to praise him. In due time God delivered the psalmist out of his troubles. Our tongue is our glory, and never more so than when employed in praising God. He would persevere to the end in praise, hoping that he should shortly be where this would be the everlasting work. But let all beware of carnal security. Neither outward prosperity, nor inward peace, here, are sure and lasting. The Lord, in his favour, has fixed the believer's safety firm as the deep-rooted mountains, but he must expect to meet with temptations and afflictions. When we grow careless, we fall into sin, the Lord hides his face, our comforts droop, and troubles assail us.

Psalm 31

Confidence in God (1–8)

Prayer in trouble (9–18)

Praise for God's goodness (19–24)

Confidence in God (1–8)

Faith and prayer must go together, for the prayer of faith is the prevailing prayer. David gave up his soul in a special manner to God. And with the words, ver. 5, our Lord Jesus yielded up his last breath on the cross, and made his soul a free-will offering for sin, laying down his life as a ransom. But David is here as a man in distress and trouble. And his great care is about his soul, his spirit, his better part. Many think that while perplexed about their worldly affairs, and their cares multiply, they may be excused if they neglect their souls; but we are the more concerned to look to our souls, that, though the outward man perish, the inward man may suffer no damage. The redemption of the soul is so precious, that it must have ceased for ever, if Christ had not undertaken it. Having relied on God's mercy, he will be glad and rejoice in it. God looks upon our souls, when we are in trouble, to see whether they are humbled for sin, and made better by the affliction. Every believer will meet with such dangers and deliverances, until he is delivered from death, his last enemy.

Prayer in trouble (9–18)

David's troubles made him a man of sorrows. Herein he was a type of Christ, who was acquainted with grief. David acknowledged that his afflictions were merited by his own sins, but Christ suffered for ours. David's friends durst not give him any assistance. Let us not think it strange if thus deserted, but make sure of a Friend in heaven who will not fail. God will be sure to order and dispose all for the best, to all those who commit their spirits also into his hand. The time of life is in God's hands, to lengthen or shorten, make bitter or sweet, according to the counsel of his will. The way of man is not in himself, nor in our friend's hands, nor in our enemies' hands, but in God's. In this faith and confidence he prays that the Lord would save him for his mercies's sake, and not

for any merit of his own. He prophesies the silencing of those that reproach and speak evil of the people of God. There is a day coming, when the Lord will execute judgment upon them. In the mean time, we should engage ourselves by well-doing, if possible, to silence the ignorance of foolish men.

Praise for God's goodness (19–24)

Instead of yielding to impatience or despondency under our troubles, we should turn our thoughts to the goodness of the Lord towards those who fear and trust in Him. All comes to sinners through the wondrous gift of the only-begotten Son of God, to be the atonement for their sins. Let not any yield to unbelief, or think, under discouraging circumstances, that they are cut off from before the eyes of the Lord, and left to the pride of men. Lord, pardon our complaints and fears; increase our faith, patience, love, and gratitude; teach us to rejoice in tribulation and in hope. The deliverance of Christ, with the destruction of his enemies, ought to strengthen and comfort the hearts of believers under all their afflictions here below, that having suffered courageously with their Master, they may triumphantly enter into his joy and glory.

Psalm 32

The happiness of a pardoned sinner (1, 2)

The misery that went before, and the comfort that followed the confession of sins (3–7)

Sinners instructed, believers encouraged (8–11)

The happiness of a pardoned sinner (1, 2)

Sin is the cause of our misery; but the true believer's transgressions of the Divine law are all forgiven, being covered with the atonement. Christ bare his sins, therefore they are not imputed to him. The righteousness of Christ being reckoned to us, and we being made the righteousness of God in him, our iniquity is not imputed, God having laid upon him the iniquity of us all, and made him a sin-offering for us. Not to impute sin, is God's act, for he is the Judge. It is God that justifies. Notice the character of him whose sins are pardoned; he is sincere, and seeks sanctification by the power of the Holy Ghost. He does not profess to repent, with an intention to indulge in sin, because the Lord is ready to forgive. He will not abuse the doctrine of free grace. And to the man whose iniquity is forgiven, all manner of blessings are promised.

The misery that went before, and the comfort that followed the confession of sins (3–7)

It is very difficult to bring sinful man humbly to accept free mercy, with a full confession of his sins and self-condemnation. But the true and only way to peace of conscience, is to confess our sins, that they may be forgiven; to declare them that we may be justified. Although repentance and confession do not merit the pardon of transgression, they are needful to the real enjoyment of forgiving mercy. And what tongue can tell the happiness of that hour, when the soul, oppressed by sin, is enabled freely to pour forth its sorrows before God, and to take hold of his covenanted mercy in Christ Jesus! Those that would speed in prayer, must seek the Lord, when, by his providence, he calls them to seek him, and, by his Spirit, stirs them up to seek him. In a time of finding, when the heart is softened with grief, and burdened with guilt; when all human refuge fails; when no rest can be found to the troubled mind, then it is that God applies the healing balm by his Spirit.

Sinners instructed, believers encouraged (8–11)

God teaches by his word, and guides with the secret intimations of his will. David gives a word of caution to sinners. The reason for this caution is that the way of sin will certainly end in sorrow. Here is a word of comfort to saints. They may see that a life of communion with God is far the most pleasant and comfortable. Let us rejoice, O Lord Jesus, in thee, and in thy salvation; so shall we rejoice indeed.

Psalm 33

God to be praised (1–11)

His people encouraged by his power (12–22)

God to be praised (1–11)

Holy joy is the heart and soul of praise, and that is here pressed upon the righteous. Thankful praise is the breath and language of holy joy. Religious songs are proper expressions of thankful praise. Every endowment we possess, should be employed with all our skill and earnestness in God's service. His promises are all wise and good. His word is right, and therefore we are only in the right when we agree with it. His works are all done in truth. He is the righteous Lord, therefore loveth righteousness. What a pity it is that this earth, which is so full of the proofs and instances of God's goodness, should be so empty of his praises; and that of the multitudes who live upon his bounty, there

are so few who live to his glory! What the Lord does, he does to purpose; it stands fast. He overrules all the counsels of men, and makes them serve his counsels; even that is fulfilled, which to us is most surprising, the eternal counsel of God, nor can any thing prevent its coming to pass.

His people encouraged by his power (12–22)

All the motions and operations of the souls of men, which no mortals know but themselves, God knows better than they do. Their hearts, as well as their times, are all in his hand; he formed the spirit of each man within him. All the powers of the creature depend upon him, and are of no account, of no avail at all, without him. If we make God's favour sure towards us, then we need not fear whatever is against us. We are to give to him the glory of his special grace. All human devices for the salvation of our souls are vain; but the Lord's watchful eye is over those whose conscientious fear of his name proceeds from a believing hope in his mercy. In difficulties they shall be helped; in dangers they shall not receive any real damage. Those that fear God and his wrath, must hope in God and his mercy; for there is no flying from him, but by flying to him. Let thy mercy, O Lord, be upon us; let us always have the comfort and benefit, not according to our merits, but according to the promise which thou hast in thy word given to us, and according to the faith thou hast by thy Spirit and grace wrought in us.

Psalm 34

David praises God, and encourages to trust him (1–10)

He exhorts to fear (11–22)

David praises God, and encourages to trust him (1–10)

If we hope to spend eternity in praising God, it is fit that we should spend much of our time here in this work. He never said to any one, Seek ye me in vain. David's prayers helped to silence his fears; many besides him have looked unto the Lord by faith and prayer, and it has wonderfully revived and comforted them. When we look to the world, we are perplexed, and at a loss. But on looking to Christ depends our whole salvation, and all things needful thereunto do so also. This poor man, whom no man looked upon with any respect, or looked after with any concern, was yet welcome to the throne of grace; the Lord heard him, and saved him out of all his troubles. The holy angels minister to the saints, and stand for them against the powers of darkness. All the glory be to the Lord of the angels. By taste and sight we both make discoveries, and have enjoyment; Taste and see God's goodness; take notice of it, and take the comfort of it. He makes all truly blessed that trust in him. As to the things of the other world, they shall have grace sufficient for the support of spiritual life. And as to this life, they shall have what is necessary from the hand of God. Paul had all, and abounded, because he was content, Philippians 4:11–18. Those who trust to themselves, and think their own efforts sufficient for them, shall want; but they shall be fed who trust in the Lord. Those shall not want, who with quietness work, and mind their own business.

He exhorts to fear (11–22)

Let young persons set out in life with learning the fear of the Lord, if they desire true comfort here, and eternal happiness hereafter. Those will be most happy who begin the soonest to serve so good a Master. All aim to be happy. Surely this must look further than the present world; for man's life on earth consists but of few days, and those full of trouble. What man is he that would see the good of that where all bliss is perfect? Alas! few have this good in their thoughts. That religion promises best which creates watchfulness over the heart and over the tongue. It is not enough not to do hurt, we must study to be useful, and to live to some purpose; we must seek peace and pursue it; be willing to deny ourselves a great deal for peace' sake. It is the constant practice of real believers, when in distress, to cry unto God, and it is their constant comfort that he hears them.

The righteous are humbled for sin, and are low in their own eyes. Nothing is more needful to true godliness than a contrite heart, broken off from every self-confidence. In this soil every grace will flourish, and nothing can encourage such a one but the free, rich grace of the gospel of Jesus Christ. The righteous are taken under the special protection of the Lord, yet they have their share of crosses in this world, and there are those that hate them. Both from the mercy of Heaven, and the malice of hell, the afflictions of the righteous must be many. But whatever troubles befall them, shall not hurt their souls, for God keeps them from sinning in troubles. No man is desolate, but he whom God has forsaken.

Psalm 35

David prays for safety (1–10)

He complains of his enemies (11–16)

And calls upon God to support him (17–28)

David prays for safety (1–10)

It is no new thing for the most righteous men, and the most righteous cause, to meet with enemies. This is a fruit of the old enmity in the seed of the serpent against the Seed of the woman. David in his afflictions, Christ in his sufferings, the church under persecution, and the Christian in the hour of temptation, all beseech the Almighty to appear in their behalf, and to vindicate their cause. We are apt to justify uneasiness at the injuries men do us, by our never having given them cause to use us so ill; but this should make us easy, for then we may the more expect that God will plead our cause. David prayed to God to manifest himself in his trial. Let me have inward comfort under all outward troubles, to support my soul. If God, by his Spirit, witness to our spirits that he is our salvation, we need desire no more to make us happy. If God is our Friend, no matter who is our enemy. By the Spirit of prophecy, David foretells the just judgments of God that would come upon his enemies for their great wickedness. These are predictions, they look forward, and show the doom of the enemies of Christ and his kingdom. We must not desire or pray for the ruin of any enemies, except our lusts and the evil spirits that would compass our destruction. A traveller benighted in a bad road, is an expressive emblem of a sinner walking in the slippery and dangerous ways of temptation. But David having committed his cause to God, did not doubt of his own deliverance. The bones are the strongest parts of the body. The psalmist here proposes to serve and glorify God with all his strength. If such language may be applied to outward salvation, how much more will it apply to heavenly things in Christ Jesus!

He complains of his enemies (11–16)

Call a man ungrateful, and you can call him no worse: this was the character of David's enemies. Herein he was a type of Christ. David shows how tenderly he had behaved towards them in afflictions. We ought to mourn for the sins of those who do not mourn for themselves. We shall not lose by the good offices we do to any, how ungrateful soever they may be. Let us learn to possess our souls in patience and meekness like David, or rather after Christ's example.

And calls upon God to support him (17–28)

Though the people of God are, and study to be, quiet, yet it has been common for their enemies to devise deceitful matters against them. David prays, My soul is in danger, Lord, rescue it; it belongs to thee the Father of spirits, therefore claim thine own; it is thine, save it! Lord, be not far from me, as if I were a stranger. He who exalted the once suffering Redeemer, will appear for all his people: the roaring lion shall not destroy their souls, any more than he could that of Christ, their Surety. They trust their souls in his hands, they are one with him by faith, are precious in his sight, and shall be rescued from destruction, that they may give thanks in heaven.

Psalm 36
The bad state of the wicked (1–4)
The goodness of God (5–12)

The bad state of the wicked (1–4)

From this psalm our hearts should be duly affected with hatred of sin, and seek satisfaction in God's loving-kindness. Here is the root of bitterness, from which all the wickedness of wicked men comes. It takes rise from contempt of God, and the want of due regard to him. Also from the deceit they put upon their own souls. Let us daily beg of God to preserve us from self-flattery. Sin is very hurtful to the sinner himself, and therefore ought to be hateful; but it is not so. It is no marvel, if those that deceive themselves, seek to deceive all mankind; to whom will they be true, who are false to their own souls? It is bad to do mischief, but worse to devise it, to do it with plot and management. If we willingly banish holy meditations in our solitary hours, Satan will soon occupy our minds with sinful imaginations. Hardened sinners stand to what they have done, as though they could justify it before God himself.

The goodness of God (5–12)

Men may shut up their compassion, yet, with God we shall find mercy. This is great comfort to all believers, plainly to be seen, and not to be taken away. God does all wisely and well; but what he does we know not now, it is time enough to know hereafter. God's loving-kindness is precious to the saints. They put themselves under his protection, and then are safe and easy. Gracious souls, though still desiring more of God, never desire more than God. The gifts of Providence so far satisfy them, that they are content with such things as they have. The benefit of holy ordinances is sweet to a sanctified soul, and strengthening to the spiritual and Divine life. But full satisfaction is reserved for the future state. Their joys shall be constant. God not only works in them a gracious desire for these pleasures, but by his Spirit fills their souls with joy and peace in believing. He quickens whom he will; and whoever will, may come, and take from him of the waters of life freely. May we know, and love, and uprightly serve the Lord; then no proud enemy, on earth or from hell, shall separate us from his love. Faith calleth things that are not, as though they were. It carries us forward to the end of time; it shows us

the Lord, on his throne of judgment; the empire of sin fallen to rise no more.

Psalm 37
The recompense of the wicked and the reward of the righteous (1–6)
David persuades to patience and confidence in God, by the state of the godly and of the wicked (7–20)
What the Lord requires (21–33)
Judgment and salvation are contrasted (34–40)

The recompense of the wicked and the reward of the righteous (1–6)

When we look abroad we see the world full of evil-doers, that flourish and live in ease. So it was seen of old, therefore let us not marvel at the matter. We are tempted to fret at this, to think them the only happy people, and so we are prone to do like them: but this we are warned against. Outward prosperity is fading. When we look forward, with an eye of faith, we shall see no reason to envy the wicked. Their weeping and wailing will be everlasting. The life of religion is a believing trust in the Lord, and diligent care to serve him according to his will. It is not trusting God, but tempting him, if we do not make conscience of our duty to him. A man's life consists not in abundance, but, Thou shalt have food convenient for thee. This is more than we deserve, and it is enough for one that is going to heaven. To delight in God is as much a privilege as a duty. He has not promised to gratify the appetites of the body, and the humours of the fancy, but the desires of the renewed, sanctified soul. What is the desire of the heart of a good man? It is this, to know, and love, and serve God. Commit thy way unto the Lord; roll thy way upon the Lord, so the margin reads it. Cast thy burden upon the Lord, the burden of thy care. We must roll it off ourselves, not afflict and perplex ourselves with thoughts about future events, but refer them to God. By prayer spread thy case and all thy cares before the Lord, and trust in him. We must do our duty, and then leave the event with God. The promise is very sweet: He shall bring that to pass, whatever it is, which thou has committed to him.

David persuades to patience and confidence in God, by the state of the godly and of the wicked (7–20)

Let us be satisfied that God will make all to work for good to us. Let us not discompose ourselves at what we see in this world. A fretful, discontented spirit is open to many temptations.

For, in all respects, the little which is allotted to the righteous, is more comfortable and more profitable than the ill-gotten and abused riches of ungodly men. It comes from a hand of special love. God provides plentifully and well, not only for his working servants, but for his waiting servants. They have that which is better than wealth, peace of mind, peace with God, and then peace in God; that peace which the world cannot give, and which the world cannot have. God knows the believer's days. Not one day's work shall go unrewarded. Their time on earth is reckoned by days, which will soon be numbered; but heavenly happiness shall be for ever. This will be a real support to believers in evil times. Those that rest on the Rock of ages, have no reason to envy the wicked the support of their broken reeds.

What the Lord requires (21–33)

The Lord our God requires that we do justly, and render to all their due. It is a great sin for those that are able, to deny the payment of just debts; it is a great misery not to be able to pay them. He that is truly merciful, will be ever merciful. We must leave our sins; learn to do well, and cleave to it. This is true religion. The blessing of God is the spring, sweetness, and security of all earthly enjoyments. And if we are sure of this, we are sure not to want any thing good for us in this world. By his grace and Holy Spirit, he directs the thoughts, affections, and designs of good men. By his providence he overrules events, so as to make their way plain. He does not always show them his way for a distance, but leads them step by step, as children are led. God will keep them from being ruined by their falls, either into sin or into trouble, though such as fall into sin will be sorely hurt. Few, if any, have known the consistent believer, or his children, reduced to abject, friendless want. God forsakes not his saints in affliction; and in heaven only the righteous shall dwell for ever; that will be their everlasting habitation. A good man may fall into the hands of a messenger of Satan, and be sorely buffeted, but God will not leave him in his enemy's hands.

Judgment and salvation are contrasted (34–40)

Duty is ours, and we must mind it; but events are God's, we must refer the disposal of them to him. How striking it is that God remarkably blights the projects of the prosperous wicked, especially persecutors. None are perfect in themselves, but believers are so in Christ Jesus. If all the saint's days continue dark and cloudy, his dying day may prove comfortable, and his sun set bright; or, if it should set under a cloud, yet his future state will be everlasting peace. The salvation of the righteous will be the Lord's

doing. He will help them to do their duties, to bear their burdens; help them to bear their troubles well, and get good by them, and, in due time, will deliver them out of their troubles. Let sinners then depart from evil, and do good; repent of and forsake sin, and trust in the mercy of God through Jesus Christ. Let them take his yoke upon them, and learn of him, that they may dwell for evermore in heaven. Let us mark the closing scenes of different characters, and always depend on God's mercy.

Psalm 38

God's displeasure at sin (1–11)
The psalmist's sufferings and prayers (12–22)

God's displeasure at sin (1–11)

Nothing will disquiet the heart of a good man so much as the sense of God's anger. The way to keep the heart quiet, is to keep ourselves in the love of God. But a sense of guilt is too heavy to bear; and would sink men into despair and ruin, unless removed by the pardoning mercy of God. If there were not sin in our souls, there would be no pain in our bones, no illness in our bodies. The guilt of sin is a burden to the whole creation, which groans under it. It will be a burden to the sinners themselves, when they are heavy-laden under it, or a burden of ruin, when it sinks them to hell. When we perceive our true condition, the Good Physician will be valued, sought, and obeyed. Yet many let their wounds rankle, because they delay to go to their merciful Friend. When, at any time, we are distempered in our bodies, we ought to remember how God has been dishonoured in and by our bodies. The groanings which cannot be uttered, are not hid from Him that searches the heart, and knows the mind of the Spirit. David, in his troubles, was a type of Christ in his agonies, of Christ on his cross, suffering and deserted.

The psalmist's sufferings and prayers (12–22)

Wicked men hate goodness, even when they benefit by it. David, in the complaints he makes of his enemies, seems to refer to Christ. But our enemies do us real mischief only when they drive us from God and our duty. The true believer's trouble will be made useful; he will learn to wait for his God, and will not seek relief from the world or himself. The less we notice the unkindness and injuries that are done us, the more we consult the quiet of our own minds. David's troubles were the chastisement and the consequence of his transgressions, whilst Christ suffered for our sins and ours only. What right can a sinner have to yield to impatience or anger, when mercifully corrected for his sins? David was very sensible of the present workings of corruption in him. Good men, by setting their sorrow continually before them, have been ready to fall; but by setting God always before them, they have kept their standing. If we are truly penitent for sin, that will make us patient under affliction. Nothing goes nearer to the heart of a believer when in affliction, than to be under the apprehension of God's deserting him; nor does any thing come more feelingly from his heart than this prayer, 'Be not far from me.' The Lord will hasten to help those who trust in him as their salvation.

Psalm 39

David meditates on man's frailty (1–6)

He applies for pardon and deliverance (7–13)

David meditates on man's frailty (1–6)

If an evil thought should arise in the mind, suppress it. Watchfulness in the habit, is the bridle upon the head; watchfulness in acts, is the hand upon the bridle. When not able to separate from wicked men, we should remember they will watch our words, and turn them, if they can, to our disadvantage. Sometimes it may be necessary to keep silence, even from good words; but in general we are wrong when backward to engage in edifying discourse. Impatience is a sin that has its cause within ourselves, and that is, musing; and its ill effects upon ourselves, and that is no less than burning. In our greatest health and prosperity, every man is altogether vanity, he cannot live long; he may die soon. This is an undoubted truth, but we are very unwilling to believe it. Therefore let us pray that God would enlighten our minds by his Holy Spirit, and fill our hearts with his grace, that we may be ready for death every day and hour.

He applies for pardon and deliverance (7–13)

There is no solid satisfaction to be had in the creature; but it is to be found in the Lord, and in communion with him; to him we should be driven by our disappointments. If the world be nothing but vanity, may God deliver us from having or seeking our portion in it. When creature-confidences fail, it is our comfort that we have a God to go to, a God to trust in. We may see a good God doing all, and ordering all events concerning us; and a good man, for that reason, says nothing against it. He desires the pardoning of his sin, and the preventing of his shame. We must both watch and pray against sin. When under the correcting hand of the Lord, we must look to God himself for relief,

not to any other. Our ways and our doings bring us into trouble, and we are beaten with a rod of our own making. What a poor thing is beauty! and what fools are those that are proud of it, when it will certainly, and may quickly, be consumed! The body of man is as a garment to the soul. In this garment sin has lodged a moth, which wears away, first the beauty, then the strength, and finally the substance of its parts. Whoever has watched the progress of a lingering distemper, or the work of time alone, in the human frame, will feel at once the force of this comparison, and that, surely every man is vanity. Afflictions are sent to stir up prayer. If they have that effect, we may hope that God will hear our prayer. The believer expects weariness and ill treatment on his way to heaven; but he shall not stay here long: walking with God by faith, he goes forward on his journey, not diverted from his course, nor cast down by the difficulties he meets. How blessed it is to sit loose from things here below, that while going home to our Father's house, we may use the world as not abusing it! May we always look for that city, whose Builder and Maker is God.

Psalm 40

Confidence for deliverance (1–5)

Christ's work of redemption (6–10)

Prayer for mercy and grace (11–17)

Confidence for deliverance (1–5)

Doubts and fears about the eternal state, are a horrible pit and miry clay, and have been so to many a dear child of God. There is power enough in God to help the weakest, and grace enough to help the unworthiest of all that trust in him. The psalmist waited patiently; he continued believing, hoping, and praying. This is applicable to Christ. His agony, in the garden and on the cross, was a horrible pit and miry clay. But those that wait patiently for God do not wait in vain. Those that have been under religious melancholy, and by the grace of God have been relieved, may apply ver. 2 very feelingly to themselves; they are brought up out of a horrible pit. Christ is the Rock on which a poor soul can alone stand fast. Where God has given steadfast hope, he expects there should be a steady, regular walk and conduct. God filled the psalmist with joy, as well as peace in believing. Multitudes, by faith beholding the sufferings and glory of Christ, have learned to fear the justice and trust in the mercy of God through Him. Many are the benefits with which we are daily loaded, both by the providence and by the grace of God.

Christ's work of redemption (6–10)

The psalmist foretells that work of wonder, redemption by our Lord Jesus Christ. The Substance must come, which is Christ, who must bring that glory to God, and that grace to man, which it was impossible the sacrifices should ever do. Observe the setting apart of our Lord Jesus to the work and office of Mediator. In the volume, or roll, of the book it was written of him. In the close rolls of the Divine decrees and counsel, the covenant of redemption was recorded. Also, in all the volumes of the Old Testament something was written of him, John 19:28. Now the purchase of our salvation is made, the proclamation is sent forth, calling us to come and accept it. It was preached freely and openly. Whoever undertook to preach the gospel of Christ, would be under great temptation to conceal it; but Christ, and those he calls to that work, are carried on in it. May we believe his testimony, trust his promise, and submit to his authority.

Prayer for mercy and grace (11–17)

The best saints see themselves undone, unless continually preserved by the grace of God. But see the frightful view the psalmist had of sin. This made the discovery of a Redeemer so welcome. In all his reflections upon each step of his life, he discovered something amiss. The sight and sense of our sins in their own colours, must distract us, if we have not at the same time some sight of a Saviour. If Christ has triumphed over our spiritual enemies, then we, through him, shall be more than conquerors. This may encourage all that seek God and love his salvation, to rejoice in him, and to praise him. No griefs nor poverty can render those miserable who fear the Lord. Their God, and all that he has or does, is the ground of their joy. The prayer of faith can unlock his fulness, which is adapted to all their wants. The promises are sure, the moment of fulfilment hastens forward. He who once came in great humility, shall come again in glorious majesty.

Psalm 41

God's care for his people (1–4)
The treachery of David's enemies (5–13)

God's care for his people (1–4)

The people of God are not free from poverty, sickness, or outward affliction, but the Lord will consider their case, and send due supplies. From his Lord's example the believer learns to consider his poor and afflicted brethren. This branch of godliness is usually recompensed with temporal blessings. But nothing is so dis-

tressing to the contrite believer, as a fear or sense of the Divine displeasure, or of sin in his heart. Sin is the sickness of the soul; pardoning mercy heals it, renewing grace heals it, and for this spiritual healing we should be more earnest than for bodily health.

The treachery of David's enemies (5–13)

We complain, and justly, of the want of sincerity, and that there is scarcely any true friendship to be found among men; but the former days were no better. One particularly, in whom David had reposed great confidence, took part with his enemies. And let us not think it strange, if we receive evil from those we suppose to be friends. Have not we ourselves thus broken our words toward God? We eat of his bread daily, yet lift up the heel against him. But though we may not take pleasure in the fall of our enemies, we may take pleasure in the making vain designs. When we can discern the Lord's favour in any mercy, personal or public, that doubles it. If the grace of God did not take constant care of us, we should not be upheld. But let us, while on earth, give heartfelt assent to those praises which the redeemed on earth and in heaven render to their God and Saviour.

Psalm 42

Thirsting for God (1–5)
The conflict in the soul of a believer (6–11)

Thirsting for God (1-5)

The psalmist looked to the Lord as his chief good, and set his heart upon him accordingly; casting anchor thus at first, he rides out the storm. A gracious soul can take little satisfaction in God's courts, if it do not meet with God himself there. Living souls never can take up their rest any where short of a living God. To appear before the Lord is the desire of the upright, as it is the dread of the hypocrite. Nothing is more grievous to a gracious soul, than what is intended to shake its confidence in the Lord. It was not the remembrance of the pleasures of his court that afflicted David; but the remembrance of the free access he formerly had to God's house, and his pleasure in attending there. Those that commune much with their own hearts, will often have to chide them. See the cure of sorrow. When the soul rests on itself, it sinks; if it catches hold on the power and promise of God, the head is kept above the billows. And what is our support under present woes but this, that we shall have comfort in him. We have great cause to mourn for sin; but being cast down springs from unbelief and a rebellious will; we should therefore strive and pray against it.

The conflict in the soul of a believer (6–11)

The way to forget our miseries, is to remember the God of our mercies. David saw troubles coming from God's wrath, and that discouraged him. But if one trouble follow hard after another, if all seem to combine for our ruin, let us remember they are all appointed and over-ruled by the Lord. David regards the Divine favour as the fountain of all the good he looked for. In the Saviour's name let us hope and pray. One word from him will calm every storm, and turn midnight darkness into the light of noon, the bitterest complaints into joyful praises. Our believing expectation of mercy must quicken our prayers for it. At length, his faith came off conqueror, by encouraging him to trust in the name of the Lord, and to stay himself upon his God. He adds, And my God; this thought enabled him to triumph over all his griefs and fears. Let us never think that the God of our life, and the Rock of our salvation, has forgotten us, if we have made his mercy, truth, and power, our refuge. Thus the psalmist strove against his despondency: at last his faith and hope obtained the victory. Let us learn to check all unbelieving doubts and fears. Apply the promise first to ourselves, and then plead it to God.

Psalm 43

David endeavours to still his spirit, with hope and confidence in God (1–5)

As to the quarrel God had with David for sin, he prays, Enter not into judgment with me, if Thou doest so I shall be condemned; but as to the quarrel his enemies had with him, he prays, Lord, judge me, and in thy providence appear on my behalf. If we cannot comfort ourselves in God, we may stay ourselves upon him, and may have spiritual supports, when we want spiritual delights. He never cast off any that trusted in him, whatever fears they may have had of their own state. We need desire no more to make us happy, than the good that flows from God's favour, and is included in his promise. Those whom God leads, he leads to his holy hill; those, therefore, who pretend to be led by the Spirit, and yet turn their backs upon ordinance, deceive themselves. We are still to pray for the Spirit of light and truth, who supplies the want of Christ's bodily presence, to guide us in the way to heaven. Whatever we rejoice or triumph in, the Lord must be the joy of it. David applies to God as his never-failing hope. Let us pray earnestly, that the Lord would send forth the truth of his word, and the light of his Spirit, to guide us into the way of holiness, peace, and salvation. The desire of the Christian, like that of the prophet in distress, is to be saved from sin as well as sorrow; to be taught in the way of righteousness by the light of

heavenly wisdom, shining in Jesus Christ, and to be led by this light and truth to the New Jerusalem.

Psalm 44

Past faith and present calamities (1–8)

Enemies are powerless in God's sight (9–16)

A petition for succour and relief (17–26)

Past faith and present calamities (1–8)

Former experiences of God's power and good-ness are strong supports to faith, and powerful pleas in prayer under present calamities. The many victories Israel obtained, were not by their own strength or merit, but by God's favour and free grace. The less praise this allows us, the more comfort it affords, that we may see all as coming from the favour of God. He fought for Israel, else they had fought in vain. This is applicable to the planting of the Christian church in the world, which was not by any human policy or power. Christ, by his Spirit, went forth conquering and to conquer; and he that planted a church for himself in the world, will support it by the same power and goodness. They trusted and triumphed in and through him. Let him that glories, glory in the Lord. But if they have the comfort of his name, let them give unto him the glory due unto it.

Enemies are powerless in God's sight (9–16)

The believer must have times of temptation, affliction, and discouragement; the church must have seasons of persecution. At such times the people of God will be ready to fear that he has cast them off, and that his name and truth will be dishonoured. But they should look above the instruments of their trouble, to God, well know-ing that their worst enemies have no power against them, but what is permitted from above.

A petition for succour and relief (17–26)

In afflictions, we must not seek relief by any sin-ful compliance; but should continually meditate on the truth, purity, and knowledge of our heart-searching God. Hearts sins and secret sins are known to God, and must be reckoned for. He knows the secret of the heart, therefore judges of the words and actions. While our troubles do not drive us from our duty to God, we should not suffer them to drive us from our comfort in God. Let us take care that prosperity and ease do not render us careless and luke-warm. The church of God cannot be prevailed on by persecution to forget God; the believer's heart does not turn back from God. The Spirit of prophecy had reference to those who suffered unto death, for the testimony of Christ. Observe but the poor sinner's pleas. None that belong to Christ shall be cast off, but every one of them shall be saved, and that for ever. The mercy of God, purchased, promised, and constantly flowing forth, and offered to believers, does away every doubt arising from our sins; while we pray in faith, Redeem us for thy mercies' sake.

Psalm 45

The King and his kingdom (1–5)

God is the Mediator (6--9)

Turning from idols to God (10–17)

The King and his kingdom (1–5)

This psalm is a prophecy of Messiah the Prince, and points to him as a Bridegroom espousing the church to himself, and as a King ruling in it, and for it. The psalmist's tongue was guided by the Spirit of God, as the pen is by the hand of a ready writer. This psalm is touching the King Jesus, his kingdom and government. It is a shame that this good matter is not more the subject of our discourse. There is more in Christ to engage our love, than there is or can be in any creature. This world and its charms are ready to draw away our hearts from Christ; therefore we are concerned to understand how much more worthy he is of our love. By his word, his promise, his gospel, the good will of God is made known to us, and the good work of God is begun and carried on in us. The psalmist, ver. 35, joyfully foretells the progress and success of the Messiah. The arrows of conviction are very terrible in the hearts of sinners, till they are humbled and reconciled; but the arrows of vengeance will be more so to his enemies who refuse to submit. All who have seen his glory and tasted his grace, rejoice to see him, by his word and Spirit, bring enemies and strangers under his dominion.

God is the Mediator (6–9)

The throne of this almighty King is established for ever. While the Holy Spirit leads Christ's people to look to his cross, he teaches them to see the evil of sin and the beauty of holiness; so that none of them can feel encouragement to continue in sin. The Mediator is God, else he had been neither able to do the Mediator's work, nor fit to wear the Mediator's crown. God the Father, as his God in respect to his human nature and mediatorial offices, has given to him the Holy Spirit without measure. Thus anointed to be a Prophet, Priest, and King, Christ has preeminence in the gladdening gifts and graces of the spirit, and from his fulness communicates them to his brethren in human nature. The Spirit is called the oil of gladness, because of the delight wherewith Christ was filled, in carrying on his undertakings. The salvation of sinners is the joy of angels, much more of the Son. And in proportion as we are conformed to his holy image, we may expect the gladdening gifts of the Comforter. The excellences of the Messiah, the suitableness of his offices, and the sufficiency of his grace, seem to be intended by the fragrance of his garments. The church formed of true believers, is here compared to the queen, whom, by an everlasting covenant, the Lord Jesus has betrothed to himself. This is the bride, the Lamb's wife, whose graces are compared to fine linen, for their purity; to gold, for their costliness: for as we owe our redemption, so we owe our adorning, to the precious blood of the Son of God.

Turning from idols to God (10–17)

If we desire to share these blessings, we must hearken to Christ's word. We must forget our carnal and sinful attachments and pursuits. He must be our Lord as well as our Saviour; all idols must be thrown away, that we may give him our whole heart. And here is good encouragement, thus to break off from former alliances. The beauty of holiness, both on the church and on particular believers, is, in the sight of Christ, of great price, and very amiable. The work of grace is the workmanship of the Spirit, it is the image of Christ upon the soul, a partaking of the Divine nature. It is clear of all sin, there is none in it, nor any comes from it. There is nothing glorious in the old man or corrupt nature; but in the new man, or work of grace upon the soul, every thing is glorious. The robe of Christ's righteousness, which he has wrought out for his church, the Father imputes unto her, and bestows upon her. None are brought to Christ, but those whom the Father brings. This notes the conversion of souls to him. The robe of righteousness, and garments of salvation, the change of raiment Christ has put upon her. Such as strictly cleave to Christ, loving him in singleness of heart, are companions of the bride, who partake of the very same grace, enjoy the same privileges, and share in one common salvation. These, every one, shall be brought to the King; not one lost or left behind. Instead of the Old Testament church, there shall be a New Testament church, a Gentile church. In the believing hope of our everlasting happiness in the other world, let us always keep up the remembrance of Christ, as our only way thither; and transmit the remembrance of him to succeeding generations, that his name may endure for ever.

Psalm 46

Confidence in God (1–5)

An exhortation to behold it (6–11)

Confidence in God (1–5)

This psalm encourages to hope and trust in God; in his power and providence, and his gracious presence with his church in the worst of times. We may apply it to spiritual enemies, and the encouragement we have that, through Christ, we shall be conquerors over them. He is a Help, a present Help, a Help found, one whom we have found to be so; a Help at hand, one that is always near; we cannot desire a better, nor shall we ever find the like in any creature. Let those be troubled at the troubling of the waters, who build their confidence on a floating foundation; but let not those be alarmed who are led to the Rock, and there find firm footing. Here is joy to the church, even in sorrowful times. The river alludes to the graces and consolations of the Holy Spirit, which flow through every part of the church, and through God's sacred ordinances, gladdening the heart of every believer. It is promised that the church shall not be moved. If God be in our hearts, by his word dwelling richly in us, we shall be established, we shall be helped; let us trust and not be afraid.

An exhortation to behold it (6–11)

Come and see the effects of desolating judgments, and stand in awe of God. This shows the perfect security of the church, and is an assurance of lasting peace. Let us pray for the speedy approach of these glorious days, and in silent submission let us worship and trust in our almighty Sovereign. Let all believers triumph in this, that the Lord of hosts, the God of Jacob, has been, is, and will be with us; and will be our Refuge. Mark this, take the comfort, and say, If God be for us, who can be against us? With this, through life and in death, let us answer every fear.

Psalm 47

God is King of all the earth (1–4)

The people exhorted to praise God (5–9)

God is King of all the earth (1–4)

The God with whom we have to do, is a God of awful majesty. The universal and absolute sovereignty of a holy God would be too terrible for us even to think of, were it not exercised by his Son from a mercy-seat; but now it is only terrible to the workers of iniquity. While his people express confidence and joy, and animate each other in serving him, let sinners submit to his authority, and accept his salvation. Jesus Christ shall subdue the Gentiles; he shall bring them as sheep into the fold, not for slaughter, but for preservation. He shall subdue their affections, and make them a willing people in the day of his power. Also it speaks of his giving them rest and settlement. Apply this spiritually; the Lord himself has undertaken to be the inheritance of his people. It shows the faith and submission of the saints. This is the language of every gracious soul, The Lord shall choose my inheritance for me; he knows what is good for me better than I do.

The people exhorted to praise God (5–9)

Praise is a duty in which we ought to be frequent and abundant. But here is a needful rule; Sing ye praises with understanding. As those that understand why and for what reasons they praise God, and what is the meaning of the service. It is not an acceptable service, if it is not a reasonable service. We are never to forget the end of Messiah's exaltation, so continually do the prophets dwell upon the conversion of the nations to the gospel of Christ. Why do we vainly fancy that we belong to him, unless the Spirit reign in our hearts by faith? Lord, is it not thy glory and delight to give repentance to Israel and remission of sins, now that thou art exalted as a Prince and a Saviour? Set up thy kingdom in our hearts. Bring into captivity every thought to the obedience of Christ. And so sweetly constrain all the powers and faculties of the souls of thy redeemed, into holy love, fear, and delight in thee, that praise with the understanding may rise from every heart, both here and for ever, to Thee, our God.

Psalm 48

The glories of the church of Christ (1–7)

The God of Zion (8–14)

The glories of the church of Christ (1–7)

Jerusalem is the city of our God: none on earth render him due honour except the citizens of the spiritual Jerusalem. Happy the kingdom, the city, the family, the heart, in which God is great, in which he is all. There God is known. The clearer discoveries are made to us of the Lord and his greatness, the more it is expected that we should abound in his praises. The earth is, by sin, covered with deformity, therefore justly might that spot of ground, which was beautified with holiness, be called the joy of the whole earth; that which the whole earth has reason to rejoice in, that God would thus in very deed dwell with man upon the earth. The kings of the earth were afraid of it. Nothing in nature can more fitly represent the overthrow of heathenism by the Spirit of the gospel, than the wreck of a fleet in a storm. Both are by the mighty power of the Lord.

The God of Zion (8–14)

We have here the improvement which the people of God are to make of his glorious and gracious appearances for them. Let our faith in the word of God be hereby confirmed. Let our hope of the stability of the church be encouraged. Let our minds be filled with good thoughts of God. All the streams of mercy that flow down to us, must be traced to the fountain of His lovingkindness. Let us give to God the glory of the great things he has done for us. Let all the members of the church take comfort from what the Lord does for his church. Let us observe the beauty, strength, and safety of the church. Consider its strength; see it founded on Christ the Rock, fortified by the Divine power, guarded by him who neither slumbers nor sleeps. See what precious ordinances are its palaces, what precious promises are its bulwarks, that you may be encouraged to join yourselves to it: and tell this to others. This God, who has now done such great things for us, is unchangeable in his love to us, and his care for us. If he is our God, he will lead and keep us even to the last. He will so guide us, as to set us above the reach of death, so that it shall not do us any real hurt. He will lead us to a life in which there shall be no more death.

Psalm 49

A call for attention (1–5)
Folly of worldlings (6–14)
Against fear of death (15–20)

A call for attention (1–5)

We seldom meet with a more solemn introduction: there is no truth of greater importance. Let all hear this with application to ourselves. The poor are in danger from undue desire toward the wealth of the world, as rich people from undue delight in it. The psalmist begins with applying it to himself, and that is the right method in which to treat of Divine things. Before he sets down the folly of carnal security, he lays down, from his own experience, the benefit and comfort of a holy, gracious security, which they enjoy who trust in God, and not in their worldly wealth. In the day of judgment, the iniquity of our heels, or of our steps, our past sins, will compass us. In those days, worldly, wicked people will be afraid; but wherefore should a man fear death who has God with him?

Folly of worldlings (6–14)

Here is a description of the spirit and way of worldly people. A man may have wealth, and may have his heart enlarged in love, thankfulness, and obedience, and may do good with it. Therefore it is not men's having riches that proves them to be worldly, but their setting their hearts upon them as the best things. Worldly men have only some floating thoughts of the things of God, while their fixed thoughts, their inward thoughts, are about the world; that lies nearest the heart. But with all their wealth they cannot save the life of the dearest friend they have. This looks further, to the eternal redemption to be wrought out by the Messiah. The redemption of the soul shall cost very dear; but, being once wrought, it shall never need to be repeated. And he, the Redeemer, shall rise again before he sees corruption, and then shall live for evermore, Re 1:18. This likewise shows the folly of worldly people, who sell their souls for that which will never buy them. With all their wealth they cannot secure themselves from the stroke of death. Yet one generation after another applaud their maxims; and the character of a fool, as drawn by heavenly Wisdom itself, Lu 12:16–21, continues to be followed even among professed Christians. Death will ask the proud sinner, Where is thy wealth, thy pomp? And in the morning of the resurrection, when all that sleep in the dust shall awake, the upright shall be advanced to the highest honour, when the wicked shall be filled with everlasting shame and contempt, Daniel 12:2. Let us now judge of things as they will appear in that day. The beauty of holiness is that alone which the grave cannot touch, or damage.

Against fear of death (15–20)

Believers should not fear death. The distinction of men's outward conditions, how great soever in life, makes none at death; but the difference of men's spiritual states, though in this life it may seem of small account, yet at and after death is very great. The soul is often put for the life. The God of life, who was its Creator at first, can and will be its Redeemer at last. It includes the salvation of the soul from eternal ruin. Believers will be under strong temptation to envy the prosperity of sinners. Men will praise thee, and cry thee up, as having done well for thyself in raising an estate and family. But what will it avail to be approved of men, if God condemn us? Those that are rich in the graces and comforts of the Spirit, have something of which death cannot strip them, nay, which death will improve; but as for worldly possessions, as we brought nothing into the world, so it is certain that we shall carry nothing out; we must leave all to others. The sum of the whole matter is, that it can profit a man nothing to gain the whole world, to become possessed of all its wealth and all its power, if he lose his own soul, and is cast away for want of that holy and heavenly wisdom which distinguishes man from the brutes, in his life and at his death. And are there men who can prefer the lot of the rich sinner to that of poor Lazarus, in life and death, and to eternity? Assuredly there are. What need then we have of the teaching of the Holy Ghost; when, with all our boasted powers, we are prone to such folly in the most important of all concerns!

Psalm 50

The glory of God (1–6)

Sacrifices to be changed for prayers (7–15)

Sincere obedience required (16–23)

The glory of God (1–6)

This psalm is a psalm of instruction. It tells of the coming of Christ and the day of judgment, in which God will call men to account; and the Holy Ghost is the Spirit of judgment. All the children of men are concerned to know the right way of worshipping the Lord, in spirit and in truth. In the great day, our God shall come, and make those hear his judgment who would not hearken to his law. Happy are those who come into the covenant of grace, by faith in the Redeemer's atoning sacrifice, and show the sincerity of their love by fruits of righteousness. When God rejects the services of those who rest in outside performances, he will graciously accept those who seek him aright. It is only by sacrifice, by Christ, the great Sacrifice, from whom the sacrifices of the law derived what value they had, that we can be accepted of God. True and righteous are his judgments; even sinners' own consciences will be forced to acknowledge the righteousness of God.

Sacrifices to be changed for prayers (7–15)

To obey is better than sacrifice, and to love God and our neighbour better than all burnt-offerings. We are here warned not to rest in these performances. And let us beware of resting in any form. God demands the heart, and how can human inventions please him, when repentance, faith, and holiness are neglected? In the day of distress we must apply to the Lord by fervent prayer. Our troubles, though we see them coming from God's hand, must drive us to him, not drive us from him. We must acknowledge him in all our ways, depend upon his wisdom, power, and goodness, and refer ourselves wholly to him, and so give him glory. Thus must we keep up communion with God; meeting him with prayers under trials, and with praises in deliverances. A believing supplicant shall not only be graciously answered as to his petition, and so have cause for praising God, but shall also have grace to praise him.

Sincere obedience required (16–23)

Hypocrisy is wickedness, which God will judge. And it is too common, for those who declare the Lord's statutes to others, to live in disobedience to them themselves. This delusion arises from the abuse of God's long-suffering, and a wilful mistake of his character and the intention of his gospel. The sins of sinners will be fully proved on them in the judgment of the great day. The day is coming when God will set their sins in order, sins of childhood and youth, of riper age and old age, to their everlasting shame and terror. Let those hitherto forgetful of God, given up to wickedness, or in any way negligent of salvation, consider their urgent danger. The patience of the Lord is very great. It is the more wonderful, because sinners make such ill use of it; but if they turn not, they shall be made to see their error when it is too late. Those that forget God, forget themselves; and it will never be right with them till they consider. Man's chief end is to glorify God: whoso offers praise, glorifies him, and his spiritual sacrifices shall be accepted. We must praise God, sacrifice praise, put it into the hands of the Priest, our Lord Jesus, who is also the altar: we must be fervent in spirit, praising the Lord. Let us thankfully accept God's mercy, and endeavour to glorify him in word and deed.

Psalm 51

The psalmist prays for mercy, humbly confessing and lamenting his sins (1–6)

He pleads for pardon, that he may promote the glory of God and the conversion of sinners (7–15)

God is pleased with a contrite heart, A prayer for the prosperity of Zion (16–19)

The psalmist prays for mercy, humbly confessing and lamenting his sins (1–6)

David, being convinced of his sin, poured out his soul to God in prayer for mercy and grace. Whither should backsliding children return, but to the Lord their God, who alone can heal them? he drew up, by Divine teaching, an account of the workings of his heart toward God. Those that truly repent of their sins, will not be ashamed to own their repentance. Also, he instructs others what to do, and what to say. David had not only done much, but suffered much in the cause of God; yet he flees to God's infinite mercy, and depends upon that alone for pardon and peace. He begs the pardon of sin. The blood of Christ, sprinkled upon the conscience, blots out the transgression, and, having reconciled us to God, reconciles us to ourselves. The believer longs to have the whole debt of his sins blotted out, and every stain cleansed; he would be thoroughly washed from all his sins; but the hypocrite always has some secret reserve, and would have some favourite lust spared. David had such a deep sense of his sin, that he was continually thinking of it, with sorrow and shame. His sin was committed against God, whose truth we deny by wilful sin; with him we deal deceitfully. And the truly penitent will ever trace back the streams of actual sin to the fountain of original depravity. He confesses his original corruption. This is that foolishness which is bound in the heart of a child, that proneness to evil, and that backwardness to good, which is the burden of the regenerate, and the ruin of the unregenerate. He is encouraged, in his repentance, to hope that God would graciously accept him. Thou desirest truth in the inward part; to this God looks, in a returning sinner. Where there is truth, God will give wisdom. Those who sincerely endeavour to do their duty shall be taught their duty; but they will expect good only from Divine grace overcoming their corrupt nature.

He pleads for pardon, that he may promote the glory of God and the conversion of sinners (7–15)

Purge me with hyssop, with the blood of Christ applied to my soul by a lively faith, as the water of purification was sprinkled with a bunch of hyssop. The blood of Christ is called the blood of sprinkling, Hebrews 12:24. If this blood of Christ, which cleanses from all sin, cleanse us from our sin, then we shall be clean indeed, Hebrews 10:2. He asks not to be comforted, till he is first cleansed; if sin, the bitter root of sorrow, be taken away, he can pray in faith, Let me have a well-grounded peace, of thy creating, so that the bones broken by convictions may rejoice, may be comforted. Hide thy face from my sins; blot out all mine iniquities out of thy book; blot them out, as a cloud is blotted out and dispelled by the beams of the sun. And the believer desires renewal to holiness as much as the joy of salvation. David now saw, more than ever, what an unclean heart he had, and sadly laments it; but he sees it is not in his own power to amend it, and therefore begs God would create in him a clean heart. When the sinner feels this change is necessary, and reads the promise of God to that purpose, he begins to ask it. He knew he had by his sin grieved the Holy Spirit, and provoked him to withdraw. This he dreads more than anything. He prays that Divine comforts may be restored to him. When we give ourselves cause to doubt our interest in salvation, how can we expect the joy of it? This had made

him weak; he prays, I am ready to fall, either into sin or into despair, therefore uphold me with thy Spirit. Thy Spirit is a free Spirit, a free Agent himself, working freely. And the more cheerful we are in our duty, the more constant we shall be to it. What is this but the liberty wherewith Christ makes his people free, which is contrasted with the yoke of bondage? Galatians 5:1. It is the Spirit of adoption spoken to the heart. Those to whom God is the God of salvation, he will deliver from guilt; for the salvation he is the God of, is salvation from sin. We may therefore plead with him, Lord, thou art the God of my salvation, therefore deliver me from the dominion of sin. And when the lips are opened, what should they speak but the praises of God for his forgiving mercy?

God is pleased with a contrite heart, A prayer for the prosperity of Zion (16–19)

Those who are thoroughly convinced of their misery and danger by sin, would spare no cost to obtain the remission of it. But as they cannot make satisfaction for sin, so God cannot take any satisfaction in them, otherwise than as expressing love and duty to him. The good work wrought in every true penitent, is a broken spirit, a broken and a contrite heart, and sorrow for sin. It is a heart that is tender, and pliable to God's word. Oh that there were such a heart in every one of us! God is graciously pleased to accept this; it is instead of all burnt-offering and sacrifice. The broken heart is acceptable to God only through Jesus Christ; there is no true repentance without faith in him. Men despise that which is broken, but God will not. He will not overlook it, he will not refuse or reject it; though it makes God no satisfaction for the wrong done to him by sin. Those who have been in spiritual troubles, know how to pity and pray for others afflicted in like manner. David was afraid lest his sin should bring judgements upon the city and kingdom. No personal fears or troubles of conscience can make the soul, which has received grace, careless about the interests of the church of God. And let this be the continued joy of all the redeemed, that they have redemption through the blood of Christ, the forgiveness of sins according to the riches of his grace.

Psalm 52

The enemies of the truth and the church described, Their destruction (1–5)
The righteous rejoice (6–9)

The enemies of the truth and the church described, Their destruction (1–5)

Those that glory in sin, glory in their shame. The patience and forbearance of God are abused by sinners, to the hardening of their hearts in their wicked ways. But the enemies in vain boast in their mischief, while we have God's mercy to trust in. It will not save us from the guilt of lying, to be able to say, there was some truth in what we said, if we make it appear otherwise than it was. The more there is of craft and contrivance in any wickedness, the more there is of Satan in it. When good men die, they are transplanted from the land of the living on earth, to heaven, the garden of the Lord, where they shall take root for ever; but when wicked men die, they are rooted out, to perish for ever. The believer sees that God will destroy those who make not him their strength.

The righteous rejoice (6–9)

Those wretchedly deceive themselves, who think to support themselves in power and wealth without God. The wicked man trusted in the abundance of his riches; he thought his wickedness would help him to keep his wealth. Right or wrong, he would get what he could, and keep what he had, and ruin any one that stood in his way; this he thought would strengthen him; but see what it comes to! Those who by faith and love dwell in the house of God, shall be like green olive-trees there. And that we may be as green olive-trees, we must live a life of faith and holy confidence in God and his grace. It adds much to the beauty of our profession, and to fruitfulness in every grace, to be much in praising God; and we never can want matter for praise. His name alone can be our refuge and strong tower. It is very good for us to wait on that saving name; there is nothing better to calm and quiet our spirits, when disturbed, and to keep us in the way of duty, when tempted to use any crooked courses for our relief, than to hope, and quietly wait for the salvation of the Lord. None ever followed his guidance but it ended well.

Psalm 53

The corruption of man by nature (1-6)

This psalm is almost the same as the 14th. The scope of it is to convince us of our sins. God, by the psalmist, here shows us how bad we are, and proves this by his own certain knowledge. He speaks terror to persecutors, the worst of sinners. He speaks encouragement to God's persecuted people. How comes it that men are so bad? Because there is no fear of God before their eyes. Men's bad practices flow from their bad principles; if they profess to know God, yet in works, because in thoughts, they deny him. See the folly of sin; he is a fool, in the account of God, whose judgment we are sure is right, that harbours such corrupt thoughts. And see the

fruit of sin; to what it brings men, when their hearts are hardened through the deceitfulness of sin. See also the faith of the saints, and their hope and power as to the cure of this great evil. There will come a Saviour, a great salvation, a salvation from sin. God will save his church from its enemies. He will save all believers from their own sins, that they may not be led captive by them, which will be everlasting joy to them. From this work the Redeemer had his name JESUS, for he shall save his people from their sins, Mt 1:21.

Psalm 54

David complains of the malice of his enemies (1–3)

Assurance of the Divine favour and protection (4–7)

David complains of the malice of his enemies (1–3)

God is faithful, though men are not to be trusted, and it is well for us it is so. David has no other plea to depend upon than God's name, no other power to depend upon than God's strength, and these he makes his refuge and confidence. This would be the effectual answer to his prayers. Looking unto David, betrayed by the men of Judah, and to Jesus, betrayed by one of his apostles, what can we expect from any who have not set God before them, save ingratitude, treachery, malice, and cruelty? What bonds of nature, or friendship, or gratitude, or covenant, will hold those that have broken through the fear of God? Selah; Mark this. Let us set God before us at all times; for if we do not, we are in danger of despair.

Assurance of the Divine favour and protection (4–7)

Behold, God is mine Helper. If we are for him, he is for us; and if he is for us, we need not fear. Every creature is that to us, and no more, which God makes it to be. The Lord will in due time save his people, and in the mean time he sustains them, and bears them up, so that the spirit he has made shall not fail. There is truth in God's threatenings, as well as in his promises; sinners that repent not, will find it so to their cost. David's present deliverance was an earnest of further deliverance. He speaks of the completion of his deliverance as a thing done, though he had as yet many troubles before him; because, having God's promise for it, he was as sure of it as if it was done already. The Lord would deliver him out of all his troubles. May he help us to bear our cross without repining, and at length bring us to share his victories and glory. Christians never should suffer the voice of praise and thanksgiving to cease in the church of the redeemed.

Psalm 55

Prayer to God to manifest his favour (1–8)

The great wickedness and treachery of his enemies (9–15)

He is sure that God would in due time appear for him (16–23)

Prayer to God to manifest his favour (1–8)

In these we have, 1. David praying. Prayer is a salve for every sore, and a relief to the spirit under every burden. 2. David weeping. Griefs are thus, in some measure, lessened, while those increase that have no vent given them. David in great alarm. We may well suppose him to be so, upon the breaking out of Absalom's conspiracy, and the falling away of the people. Horror overwhelmed him. Probably the remembrance of his sin in the matter of Uriah added much to the terror. When under a guilty conscience we must mourn in our complaint, and even strong believers have for a time been filled with horror. But none ever was so overwhelmed as the holy Jesus, when it pleased the Lord to put him to grief, and to make his soul an offering for our sins. In his agony he prayed more earnestly, and was heard and delivered; trusting in him, and following him, we shall be supported under, and carried through all trials. See how David was weary of the treachery and ingratitude of men, and the cares and disappointments of his high station: he longed to hide himself in some desert from the fury and fickleness of his people. He aimed not at victory, but rest; a barren wilderness, so that he might be quiet. The wisest and best of men most earnestly covet peace and quietness, and the more when vexed and wearied with noise and clamour. This makes death desirable to a child of God, that it is a final escape from all the storms and tempests of this world, to perfect and everlasting rest.

The great wickedness and treachery of his enemies (9–15)

No wickedness so distresses the believer, as that which he witnesses in those who profess to be of the church of God. Let us not be surprised at the corruptions and disorders of the church on earth, but long to see the New Jerusalem. He complains of one that had been very industrious against him. God often destroys the enemies of the church by dividing them. And an interest divided against itself cannot long stand. The true Christian must expect trials from professed friends, from those with whom he has been united; this will be very painful; but by looking unto Jesus we shall be enabled to bear it. Christ was betrayed by a companion, a disciple, an apostle, who resembled Ahithophel in his crimes and doom. Both were speedily overtaken by Divine vengeance. And this prayer is a prophecy of the utter, the everlasting ruin, of all who oppose and rebel against the Messiah.

He is sure that God would in due time appear for him (16–23)

In every trial let us call upon the Lord, and he will save us. He shall hear us, and not blame us for coming too often; the oftener the more welcome. David had thought all were against him; but now he sees there were many with him, more than he supposed; and the glory of this he gives to God, for it is he that raises us up friends, and makes them faithful to us. There are more true Christians, and believers have more real friends, than in their gloomy hours they suppose. His enemies should be reckoned with, and brought down; they could not ease themselves of their fears, as David could, by faith in God. Mortal men, though ever so high and strong, will easily be crushed by an eternal God. Those who are not reclaimed by the rod of affliction, will certainly be brought down to the pit of destruction. The burden of afflictions is very heavy, especially when attended with the temptations of Satan; there is also the burden of sin and corruption. The only relief under it is, to look to Christ, who bore it. Whatever it is that thou desirest God should give thee, leave it to him to give it in his own way and time. Care is a burden, it makes the heart stoop. We must commit our ways and works to the Lord; let him do as seemeth him good, and let us be satisfied. To cast our burden upon God, is to rest upon his providence and promise. And if we do so, he will carry us in the arms of his power, as a nurse carries a child; and will strengthen our spirits by his Spirit, so that they shall sustain the trial. He will never suffer the righteous to be moved; to be so shaken by any troubles, as to quit their duty to God, or their comfort in him. He will not suffer them to be utterly cast down. He, who bore the burden of our sorrows, desires us to leave to him to bear the burden of our cares, that, as he knows what is best for us, he may provide it accordingly. Why do not we trust Christ to govern the world which he redeemed?

Psalm 56

David seeks mercy from God, amidst the malice of his enemies (1–7)

He rests his faith on God's promises, and declares his obligation to praise him for mercies (8–13)

David seeks mercy from God, amidst the malice of his enemies (1–7)

Be merciful unto me, O God. This petition includes all the good for which we come to the throne of grace. If we obtain mercy there, we need no more to make us happy. It implies likewise our best plea, not our merit, but God's mercy, his free, rich mercy. We may flee to, and trust the mercy of God, when surrounded on all sides by difficulties and dangers. His enemies were too hard for him, if God did not help him. He resolves to make God's promises the matter of his praises, and so we have reason to make them. As we must not trust an arm of flesh when engaged for us, so we must not be afraid of an arm of flesh when stretched out against us. The sin of sinners will never be their security. Who knows the power of God's anger; how high it can reach, how forcibly it can strike?

He rests his faith on God's promises, and declares his obligation to praise him for mercies (8–13)

The heavy and continued trials through which many of the Lord's people have passed, should teach us to be silent and patient under lighter crosses. Yet we are often tempted to repine and despond under small sorrows. For this we should check ourselves. David comforts himself, in his distress and fear, that God noticed all his grievances and all his griefs. God has a bottle and a book for his people's tears, both the tears for their sins, and those for their afflictions. He observes them with tender concern. Every true believer may boldly say, The Lord is my helper, and then I will not fear what man shall do unto me; for man has no power but what is given him from above. Thy vows are upon me, O Lord; not as a burden, but as that by which I am known to be thy servant; as a bridle that restrains me from what would be hurtful, and directs me in the way of my duty. And vows of thankfulness properly accompany prayers for mercy. If God deliver us from sin, either from doing it, or by his pardoning mercy, he has delivered our souls from death, which is the wages of sin. Where the Lord has begun a good work he will carry it on and perfect it. David hopes that God would keep him even from the appearance of sin. We should aim in all our desires and expectations of deliverance, both from sin and trouble, that we

may do the better service to the Lord; that we may serve him without fear. If his grace has delivered our souls from the death of sin, he will bring us to heaven, to walk before him for ever in light.

Psalm 57

David begins with prayer and complaint (1–6)

He concludes with joy and praise (7–11)

David begins with prayer and complaint (1–6)

All David's dependence is upon God. The most eminent believers need often repeat the publican's prayer, 'God be merciful to me a sinner.' But if our souls trust in the Lord, this may assure us, in our utmost dangers, that our calamities will at length be overpast, and in the mean time, by faith and prayer, we must make him our refuge. Though God be most high, yet he condescends so low, as to take care that all things are made to work for good to his people. This is a good reason why we should pray earnestly. Look which way we will on this earth, refuge fails, no help appears; but we may look for it from heaven. If we have fled from the wrath to come, unto Jesus Christ, he that performed all things needful to purchase the salvation of his people, will do for us and in us all things needful for our enjoyment of it. It made David droop to think there should be those that bore him so much ill-will. But the mischief they designed against him, returned on themselves. And when David was in the greatest distress and disgrace, he did not pray, Lord, exalt me, but, Lord, exalt thine own name. Our best encouragement in prayer, is taken from the glory of God, and to that, more than to our own comfort, we should have regard in all our petitions for mercy.

He concludes with joy and praise (7–11)

By lively faith, David's prayers and complaints are at once turned into praises. His heart is fixed; it is prepared for every event, being stayed upon God. If by the grace of God we are brought into this even, composed frame of mind, we have great reason to be thankful. Nothing is done to purpose, in religion, unless it is done with the heart. The heart must be fixed for the duty, put in frame for it; fixed in the duty by close attention. Our tongue is our glory, and never more so than when praising God; dull and sleepy devotions will never be acceptable to God. Let us awake early in the morning, to begin the day with God; early in the beginning of a mercy. When God comes toward us with his favours, let us go forth to meet him with our praises. David desired to bring others to join in praising God; and in his psalms, he is still praising God among the people, singing to him among the nations. Let us seek to have our hearts fixed to praise his boundless mercy and unfailing faithfulness; and to glorify him with body, soul, and spirit, which are his. Let us earnestly pray that the blessings of the gospel may be sent through every land.

Psalm 58

Wicked judges described and reproved (1–5)

A prayer that they may be disabled, and their ruin predicted (6–11)

Wicked judges described and reproved (1–5)

When wrong is done under the form of law, it is worse than any other; especially it is grievous to behold those who profess to be children of God, joining together against any of his people. We should thank the Lord for merciful restraints; we should be more earnest in seeking renewing grace, more watchful over ourselves, and more patient under the effects of fallen nature in others. The corruption of their nature was the root of bitterness. We may see in children the wickedness of the world beginning. They go astray from God and their duty as soon as possibly they can. And how soon will little children tell lies! It is our duty to take pains to teach them, and above all, earnestly to pray for converting grace, to make our children new creatures. Though the poison be within, much of it may be kept from breaking forth to injure others. When the Saviour's words are duly regarded, the serpent becomes harmless. But those who refuse to hear heavenly wisdom, must perish miserably, for ever.

A prayer that they may be disabled, and their ruin predicted (6–11)

David prayed that the enemies of God's church and people might be disabled to do further mischief. We may, in faith, pray against the designs of the enemies of the church. He foretells their ruin. And who knows the power of God's anger? The victories of the Just One, in his own person and that of his servants, over the enemies of man's salvation, produce a joy which springs not from revenge, but from a view of the Divine mercy, justice, and truth, shown in the redemption of the elect, the punishment of the ungodly, and the fulfilment of the promises. Whoever duly considers these things, will diligently seek the reward of righteousness, and adore the Providence which orders all things aright in heaven and in earth.

Psalm 59

David prays for deliverance from his enemies (1–7)

He foresees their destruction (8–17)

David prays for deliverance from his enemies (1–7)

In these words we hear the voice of David when a prisoner in his own house; the voice of Christ when surrounded by his merciless enemies; the voice of the church when under bondage in the world; and the voice of the Christian when under temptation, affliction, and persecution. And thus earnestly should we pray daily, to be defended and delivered from our spiritual enemies, the temptations of Satan, and the corruptions of our own hearts. We should fear suffering as evil-doers, but not be ashamed of the hatred of workers of iniquity. It is not strange, if those regard not what they themselves say, who have made themselves believe that God regards not what they say. And where there is no fear of God, there is nothing to secure proper regard to man.

He foresees their destruction (8–17)

It is our wisdom and duty, in times of danger and difficulty, to wait upon God; for he is our defence, in whom we shall be safe. It is very comfortable to us, in prayer, to look to God as the God of our mercy, the Author of all good in us, and the Giver of all good to us. The wicked can never be satisfied, which is the greatest misery in a poor condition. A contented man, if he has not what he would have, yet he does not quarrel with Providence, nor fret within himself. It is not poverty, but discontent that makes a man unhappy. David would praise God because he had many times, and all along, found him his refuge in the day of trouble. He that is all this to us, is certainly worthy of our best affections, praises, and services. The trials of his people will end in joy and praise. When the night of affliction is over, they will sing of the Lord's power and mercy in the morning. Let believers now, in assured faith and hope, praise him for those mercies, for which they will rejoice and praise him for ever.

Psalm 60

David prays for the deliverance of Israel from their enemies (1–5)

He entreats God to carry on and complete their victories (6–12)

David prays for the deliverance of Israel from their enemies (1–5)

David owns God's displeasure to be the cause of all the hardships he had undergone. And when God is turning his hand in our favour, it is good to remember our former troubles. In God's displeasure their troubles began, therefore in his favour their prosperity must begin. Those breaches and divisions which the folly and corruption of man make, nothing but the wisdom and grace of God can repair, by pouring out a spirit of love and peace, by which only a kingdom is saved from ruin. The anger of God against sin, is the only cause of all misery, private or public, that has been, is, or shall be. In all these cases there is no remedy, but by returning to the Lord with repentance, faith, and prayer; beseeching him to return to us. Christ, the Son of David, is given for a banner to those that fear God; in him they are gathered together in one, and take courage. In his name and strength they wage war with the powers of darkness.

He entreats God to carry on and complete their victories (6–12)

If Christ be ours, all things, one way or another, shall be for our eternal good. The man who is a new creature in Christ, may rejoice in all the precious promises God has spoken in his holiness. His present privileges, and the sanctifying influences of the Spirit, are sure earnests of heavenly glory. David rejoices in conquering the neighbouring nations, which had been enemies to Israel. The Israel of God are through Christ more than conquerors. Though sometimes they think that the Lord has cast them off, yet he will bring them into the strong city at last. Faith in the promise will assure us that it is our Father's good pleasure to give us the kingdom: But we are not yet made complete conquerors, and no true believer will abuse these truths to indulge sloth, or vain confidence. Hope in God is the best principle of true courage, for what need those fear who have God on their side? All our victories are from him, and while those who willingly submit to our anointed King shall share his glories, all his foes shall be put under his feet.

Psalm 61

David seeks God upon former experience (1–4)

He vows to serve God (5–8)

David seeks God upon former experience (1–4)

David begins with prayers and tears, but ends with praise. Thus the soul, being lifted up to God, returns to the enjoyment of itself. Wherever we are, we have liberty to draw near to God, and may find a way open to the throne of grace. And that which separates us from other comforts, should drive us nearer to God, the fountain of all comfort. Though the heart is overwhelmed, yet it may be lifted up to God in prayer. Nay, I will cry unto thee, for by that means it will be supported and relieved. Weeping must quicken praying, and not deaden it. God's power and promise are a rock that is higher than we are. This rock is Christ. On the Divine mercy, as on a rock, David desired to rest his soul; but he was like a ship-wrecked sailor, exposed to the billows at the bottom of a rock too high for him to climb without help. David found that he could not be fixed on the Rock of salvation, unless the Lord placed him upon it. As there is safety in him, and none in ourselves, let us pray to be led to and fixed upon Christ our Rock. The service of God shall be his constant work and business: all must make it so who expect to find God their shelter and strong tower. The grace of God shall be his constant comfort.

He vows to serve God (5–8)

There is a people in the world that fear God's name. There is a heritage peculiar to that people; present comforts in the soul, earnests of future bliss. Those that fear God have enough in him, and must not complain. We need desire no better heritage than that of those who fear God. Those abide to good purpose in this world, who abide before God, serve him, and walk in his fear; those who do so, shall abide before him for ever. And these words are to be applied to him of whom the angel said, the Lord shall give unto him the throne of his father David, and of his kingdom there shall be no end, Luke 1:32. God's promises, and our faith in them, are not to do away, but to encourage prayer. We need not desire to be better secured than under the protection of God's mercy and truth. And if we partake of that grace and truth which came by Jesus Christ, we may praise him, whatever be our outward circumstances. But renewed experience of God's mercy and truth towards his people in Christ, is the main matter of our joy in him, and our praise unto him.

Psalm 62

David's confidence in God (1–7)

No trust to be put in worldly things (8–12)

David's confidence in God (1–7)

We are in the way both of duty and comfort, when our souls wait upon God; when we cheerfully give up ourselves, and all our affairs, to his will and wisdom; when we leave ourselves to all the ways of his providence, and patiently expect the event, with full satisfaction in his goodness.

See the ground and reason of this dependence. By his grace he has supported me, and by his providence delivered me. He only can be my Rock and my salvation; creatures are nothing without him, therefore I will look above them to him. Trusting in God, the heart is fixed. If God be for us, we need not fear what man can do against us. David having put his confidence in God, foresees the overthrow of his enemies. We have found it good to wait upon the Lord, and should charge our souls to have such constant dependence upon him, as may make us always easy. If God will save my soul, I may well leave every thing else to his disposal, knowing all shall turn to my salvation. And as David's faith in God advances to an unshaken steadfastness, so his joy in God improves into a holy triumph. Meditation and prayer are blessed means of strengthening faith and hope.

No trust to be put in worldly things (8–12)

Those who have found the comfort of the ways of God themselves, will invite others into those ways; we shall never have the less for others sharing with us. The good counsel given is, to trust wholly in God. We must so trust in him at all times, as not at any time to put that trust in ourselves, or in any creature, which is to be put in him only. Trust in him to guide us when in doubt, to protect us when in danger, to supply us when in want, to strengthen us for every good word and work. We must lay our wants and our wishes before him, and then patiently submit our wills to his: this is pouring out our hearts. God is a refuge for all, even for as many as will take shelter in him. The psalmist warns against trusting in men. The multitude, those of low degree, are changeable as the wind. The rich and noble seem to have much in their power, and lavish promises; but those that depend on them, are disappointed. Weighed in the balance of Scripture, all that man can do to make us happy is lighter than vanity itself. It is hard to have riches, and not to trust in them if they increase, though by lawful and honest means; but we must take heed, lest we set our affections unduly upon them. A smiling world is the most likely to draw the heart from God, on whom alone it should be set. The consistent believer receives all from God as a trust; and he seeks to use it to his glory, as a steward who must render an account. God hath spoken as it were once for all, that power belongs to him alone. He can punish and destroy. Mercy also belongs to him; and his recompensing the imperfect services of those that believe in him, blotting out their transgressions for the Redeemer's sake, is a proof of abundant mercy, and encourages us to trust in him. Let us trust in his mercy and grace, and abound in his work, expecting mercies from him alone.

Psalm 63

David's desire toward God (1, 2)

His satisfaction in God (3–6)

His dependence upon God, and assurance of safety (7–11)

David's desire toward God (1, 2)

Early will I seek thee. The true Christian devotes to God the morning hour. He opens the eyes of his understanding with those of his body, and awakes each morning to righteousness. He arises with a thirst after those comforts which the world cannot give, and has immediate recourse by prayer to the Fountain of the water of life. The true believer is convinced, that nothing in this sinful world can satisfy the wants and desires of his immortal soul; he expects his happiness from God, as his portion. When faith and hope are most in exercise, the world appears a weary desert, and the believer longs for the joys of heaven, of which he has some foretastes in the ordinances of God upon earth.

His satisfaction in God (3–6)

Even in affliction we need not want matter for praise. When this is the regular frame of a believer's mind, he values the loving-kindness of God more than life. God's loving-kindness is our spiritual life, and that is better than temporal life. We must praise God with joyful lips; we must address ourselves to the duties of religion with cheerfulness, and speak forth the praises of God from a principle of holy joy. Praising lips must be joyful lips. David was in continual danger; care and fear held his eyes waking, and gave him wearisome nights; but he comforted himself with thoughts of God. The mercies of God, when called to mind in the night watches, support the soul, making darkness cheerful. How happy will be that last morning, when the believer, awaking up after the Divine likeness, shall be satisfied with all the fulness of God, and praise him with joyful lips, where there is no night, and where sorrow and sighing flee away!

His dependence upon God, and assurance of safety (7–11)

True Christians can, in some measure, and at some times, make use of the strong language of David, but too commonly our souls cleave to the dust. Having committed ourselves to God, we must be easy and pleased, and quiet from the fear of evil. Those that follow hard after God, would soon fail, if God's right hand did not uphold them. It is he that strengthens us and comforts us. The psalmist doubts not but that though now sowing in tears, he should reap in joy. Messiah the Prince shall rejoice in God; he is already entered into the joy set before him, and his glory will be completed at his second coming. Blessed Lord, let our desire towards thee increase every hour; let our love be always upon thee; let all our enjoyment be in thee, and all our satisfaction from thee. Be thou all in all to us while we remain in the present wilderness state, and bring us home to the everlasting enjoyment of thee for ever.

Psalm 64

Prayer for deliverance (1–6)

The destruction of the wicked, encouragement to the righteous (7–10)

Prayer for deliverance (1–6)

The psalmist earnestly begs of God to preserve him from disquieting fear. The tongue is a little member, but it boasts great things. The upright man is the mark at which the wicked aim, they cannot speak peaceably either of him or to him. There is no guard against a false tongue. It is bad to do wrong, but worse to encourage ourselves and one another in it. It is a sign that the heart is hardened to the greatest degree, when it is thus fully set to do evil. A practical disbelief of God's knowledge of all things, is at the bottom of every wickedness. The benefit of a good cause and a good conscience, appears most when nothing can help a man against his enemies, save God alone, who is always a present help.

The destruction of the wicked, encouragement to the righteous (7–10)

When God brings upon men the mischiefs they have desired on others, it is weight enough to sink a man to the lowest hell. Those who love cursing, it shall come upon them. Those who behold this shall understand, and observe God's hand in all; unless we do so, we are not likely to profit by the dispensations of Providence. The righteous shall be glad in the Lord; not glad of the misery and ruin of their fellow-creatures, but glad that God is glorified, and his word fulfilled, and the cause of injured innocence pleaded effectually. They rejoice not in men, nor in themselves, nor in any creature, or creature enjoyments, nor in their wisdom, strength, riches, or righteousness; but in Christ, in whom all the seed of Israel are justified and glory, and in what he is to them, and has done for them.

Psalm 65

God is to be praised in the kingdom of grace (1–5)

In the kingdom of providence (6–13)

God is to be praised in the kingdom of grace (1–5)

All the praise the Lord receives from this earth is from Zion, being the fruit of the Spirit of Christ, and acceptable through him. Praise is silent unto thee, as wanting words to express the great goodness of God. He reveals himself upon a mercy-seat, ready to hear and answer the prayers of all who come unto him by faith in Jesus Christ. Our sins prevail against us; we cannot pretend to balance them with any righteousness of our own: yet, as for our transgressions, of thine own free mercy, and for the sake of a righteousness of thine own providing, we shall not come into condemnation for them. Observe what it is to come into communion with God in order to blessedness. It is to converse with him as one we love and value; it is to apply ourselves closely to religion as to the business of our dwelling-place. Observe how we come into communion with God; only by God's free choice. There is abundance of goodness in God's house, and what is satisfying to the soul; there is enough for all, enough for each: it is always ready; and all without money and without price. By faith and prayer we may keep up communion with God, and bring in comfort from him, wherever we are. But it is only through that blessed One, who approaches the Father as our Advocate and Surety, that sinners may expect or can find this happiness.

In the kingdom of providence (6–13)

That Almighty strength which sets fast the mountains, upholds the believer. That word which stills the stormy ocean, and speaks it into a calm, can silence our enemies. How contrary soever light and darkness are to each other, it is hard to say which is most welcome. Does the watchman wait for the morning? so does the labourer earnestly desire the shades of evening. Some understand it of the morning and evening sacrifices. We are to look upon daily worship, both alone and with our families, to be the most needful of our daily occupations, the most delightful of our daily comforts. How much the fruitfulness of this lower part of the creation depends upon the influence of the upper, is easy to observe; every good and perfect gift is from above. He who enriches the earth, which is filled with man's sins, by his abundant and varied bounty, can neither want power nor will to feed the souls of his people. Temporal mercies to us unworthy creatures, shadow forth more important blessings. The rising of the Sun of righteousness, and the pouring forth of the influences of the Holy Spirit, that river of God, full of the waters of life and salvation, render the hard, barren, worthless hearts of sinners fruitful in every good work, and change the face of nations more than the sun and rain change the face of nature. Wherever the Lord passes, by his preached gospel, attended by his Holy Spirit, his paths drop fatness, and numbers are taught to rejoice in and praise him. They will descend upon the pastures of the wilderness, all the earth shall hear and embrace the gospel, and bring forth abundantly the fruits of righteousness which are, through Jesus Christ, to the glory of the Father. Manifold and marvellous, O Lord, are thy works, whether of nature or of grace; surely in loving-kindness hast thou made them all.

Psalm 66

Praise for God's sovereign power in the creation (1–7)

For his favour to his church (8–12)

And the psalmist's praise for his experience of God's goodness (13–20)

Praise for God's sovereign power in the creation (1–7)

The holy church throughout all the world lifts up her voice, to laud that Name which is above every name, to make the praise of Jesus glorious, both by word and deed; that others may be led to glorify him also. But nothing can bring men to do this aright, unless his effectual grace create their hearts anew unto holiness; and in the redemption by the death of Christ, and the glorious deliverances it effects, are more wondrous works than Israel's deliverance from Egyptian bondage.

For his favour to his church (8–12)

The Lord not only preserves our temporal life, but maintains the spiritual life which he has given to believers. By afflictions we are proved, as silver in the fire. The troubles of the church will certainly end well. Through various conflicts and troubles, the slave of Satan escapes from his yoke, and obtains joy and peace in believing: through much tribulation the believer must enter into the kingdom of God.

And the psalmist's praise for his experience of God's goodness (13–20)

We should declare unto those that fear God, what he has done for our souls, and how he has heard and answered our prayers, inviting them to join us in prayer and praise; this will turn to our mutual comfort, and to the glory of God. We cannot share these spiritual privileges, if we retain the love of sin in our hearts, though we refrain from the gross practice, Sin, regarded in the heart, will spoil the comfort and success of prayer; for the sacrifice of the wicked is an abomination of the

Lord. But if the feeling of sin in the heart causes desires to be rid of it; if it be the presence of one urging a demand we know we must not, cannot comply with, this is an argument of sincerity. And when we pray in simplicity and godly sincerity, our prayers will be answered. This will excite gratitude to Him who hath not turned away our prayer nor his mercy from us. It was not prayer that fetched the deliverance, but his mercy that sent it. That is the foundation of our hopes, the fountain of our comforts; and ought to be the matter of our praises.

Psalm 67

A prayer for the enlargement of Christ's kingdom (1–7)

All our happiness comes from God's mercy; therefore the first thing prayed for is, God be merciful to us, to us sinners, and pardon our sins. Pardon is conveyed by God's blessing, and secured in that. If we, by faith, walk with God, we may hope that his face will shine on us. The psalmist passes on to a prayer for the conversion of the Gentiles, which shows that the Old Testament saints desired that their advantages might also be enjoyed by others. And many Scripture prophecies and promises are wrapped up in prayers: the answer to the prayer of the church is as sure as the performance of God's promises. The joy wished to the nations, is holy joy. Let them be glad that by his providence the Lord will overrule the affairs of kingdoms; that even the kingdoms of this world shall became the kingdom of the Lord, and of his Christ. Then is declared a joyful prospect of all good when God shall do this. The success of the gospel brings outward mercies with it; righteousness exalts a nation. The blessing of the Lord sweetens all our creature-comforts to us, and makes them comforts indeed. All the world shall be brought to worship him. When the gospel begins to spread, it shall go forward more and more, till it reaches to the ends of the earth. It is good to cast in our lot with those that are the blessed of the Lord. If nothing had been spoken in Scripture respecting the conversion of the heathen, we might think it vain to attempt so hopeless a work. But when we see with what confidence it is declared in the Scriptures, we may engage in missionary labours, assured that God will fulfil his own word. And shall we be backward to make known to the heathen the knowledge with which we are favoured, and the salvation we profess to glory in? They cannot learn unless they are taught. Then let us go forward in the strength of the Lord, and look to him to accompany the words of the Holy Ghost; then Satan's kingdom shall be destroyed, and the kingdom of our Redeemer established.

Psalm 68

A prayer – The greatness and goodness of God (1–6)

The wonderful works God wrought for his people (7–14)

The presence of God in his church (15–21)

The victories of Christ (22–28)

Enlargement of the church (29–31)

The glory and grace of God (32–35)

A prayer – The greatness and goodness of God (1–6)

None ever hardened his heart against God, and prospered. God is the joy of his people, then let them rejoice when they come before him. He who derives his being from none, but gives being to all, is engaged by promise and covenant to bless his people. He is to be praised as a God of mercy and tender compassion. He ever careth for the afflicted and oppressed: repenting sinners, who are helpless and exposed more than any fatherless children, are admitted into his family, and share all their blessings.

The wonderful works God wrought for his people (7–14)

Fresh mercies should put us in mind of former mercies. If God bring his people into a wilderness, he will be sure to go before them in it, and to bring them out of it. He provided for them, both in the wilderness and in Canaan. The daily manna seems here meant. And it looks to the spiritual provision for God's Israel. The Spirit of grace and the gospel of grace are the plentiful rain, with which God confirms his inheritance, and from which their fruit is found. Christ shall come as showers that water the earth. The account of Israel's victories is to be applied to the victories over death and hell, by the exalted Redeemer, for those that are his. Israel in Egypt among the kilns appeared wretched, but possessed of Canaan, during the reigns of David and Solomon, appeared glorious. Thus the slaves of Satan, when converted to Christ, when justified and sanctified by him, look honourable. When they reach heaven, all remains of their sinful state disappear, they shall be as the wings of the dove, covered with silver, and her feathers as gold. Full salvation will render those white as snow, who were vile and loathsome through the guilt and defilement of sin.

The presence of God in his church (15–21)

The ascension of Christ must here be meant, and thereto it is applied, Ephesians 4:8. He received as the purchase of his death, the gifts needful for the conversion of sinners, and the salvation of believers. These he continually bestows, even on rebellious men, that the Lord God might dwell among them, as their Friend and Father. He gave gifts to men. Having received power to give eternal life, the Lord Jesus bestows it on as many as were given him, John 17:2. Christ came to a rebellious world, not to condemn it, but that through him it might be saved. The glory of Zion's King is, that he is a Saviour and Benefactor to all his willing people, and a consuming fire to all that persist in rebellion against him. So many, so weighty are the gifts of God's bounty, that he may be truly said to load us with them. He will not put us off with present things for a portion, but will be the God of our salvation. The Lord Jesus has authority and power to rescue his people from the dominion of death, by taking away the sting of it from them when they die, and giving them complete victory over it when they rise again. The crown of the head, the chief pride and glory of the enemy, shall be smitten; Christ shall crush the head of the serpent.

The victories of Christ (22–28)

The victories with which God blessed David over the enemies of Israel, are types of Christ's victory, for himself and for all believers. Those who take him for theirs, may see him acting as their God, as their King, for their good, and in answer to their prayers; especially in and by his word and ordinances. The kingdom of the Messiah shall be submitted to by all the rulers and learned in the world. The people seem to address the king, ver. 28. But the words are applicable to the Redeemer, to his church, and every true believer. We pray, that thou, O God the Son, wilt complete thine undertaking for us, by finishing thy good work in us.

Enlargement of the church (29–31)

A powerful invitation is given to those that are without, to join the church. Some shall submit from fear; overcome by their consciences, and the checks of Providence, they are brought to make peace with the church. Others will submit service of God, and in the gospel of Christ which went forth from Jerusalem, which is enough to invite sinners out of all nations.

The glory and grace of God (32–35)

God is to be admired and adored with reverence and godly fear, by all that attend in his holy places. The God of Israel gives strength and power unto his people. Through Christ strengthening us we can do all things, not otherwise; therefore he must have the glory of all we do, with our humble thanks for enabling us to do it, and for accepting the work of his hands in us.

Psalm 69

David complains of great distress (1–12)

And begs for succour (13–21)

He declares the judgments of God (22–29)

He concludes with joy and praise (30–36)

David complains of great distress (1–12)

We should frequently consider the person of the Sufferer here spoken of, and ask why, as well as what he suffered, that, meditating thereon, we may be more humbled for sin, and more convinced of our danger, so that we may feel more gratitude and love, constraining us to live to His glory who died for our salvation. Hence we learn, when in affliction, to commit the keeping of our souls to God, that we may not be soured with discontent, or sink into despair. David was hated wrongfully, but the words far more fully apply to Christ. In a world where unrighteousness reigns so much, we must not wonder if we meet with those that are our enemies wrongfully. Let us take care that we never do wrong; then if we receive wrong, we may the better bear it. By the satisfaction Christ made to God for our sin by his blood, he restored that which he took not away, he paid our debt, suffered for our offences. Even when we can plead Not Guilty, as to men's unjust accusations, yet before God we must acknowledge ourselves to deserve all that is brought upon us. All our sins take rise from our foolishness. They are all done in God's sight. David complains of the unkindness of friends and relations. This was fulfilled in Christ, whose brethren did not believe on him, and who was forsaken by his disciples. Christ made satisfaction for us, not only by putting off the honours due to God, but by submitting to the greatest dishonours that could be done to any man. We need not be discouraged if our zeal for the truths, precepts, and worship of God, should provoke some, and cause others to mock our godly sorrow and deadness to the world.

And begs for succour (13–21)

Whatever deep waters of affliction or temptation we sink into, whatever floods of trouble or ungodly men seem ready to overwhelm us, let us persevere in prayer to our Lord to save us. The tokens of God's favour to us are enough to keep our spirits from sinking in the deepest outward troubles. If we think well of God, and continue to do so under the greatest hardships, we need not fear but he will do well for us. And if at any time we are called on to suffer reproach and shame, for Christ's sake, this may be our comfort, that he knows it. It bears hard on one that knows the worth of a good name, to be oppressed with a bad one; but when we consider what a favour it is to be accounted worthy to suffer shame for the name of Jesus, we shall see that there is no reason why it should be heartbreaking to us. The sufferings of Christ were here particularly foretold, which proves the Scripture to be the word of God; and how exactly these predictions were fulfilled in Jesus Christ, which proves him to be the true Messiah. The vinegar and the gall given to him, were a faint emblem of that bitter cup which he drank up, that we might drink the cup of salvation. We cannot expect too little from men, miserable comforters are they all; nor can we expect too much from the God of all comfort and consolation.

He declares the judgments of God (22–29)

These are prophecies of the destruction of Christ's upon the unbelieving Jews, in Romans 11:9,10. When the supports of life and delights of sense, through the corruption of our nature, are made the food and fuel of sin, then our table is a snare. Their sin was, that they would not see, but shut their eyes against the light, loving darkness rather; their punishment was, that they should not see, but should be given up to their own hearts' lusts which hardened them. Those who reject God's great salvation proffered to them, may justly fear that his indignation will be poured out upon them. If men will sin, the Lord will reckon for it. But those that have multiplied to sin, may yet find mercy, through the righteousness of the Mediator. God shuts not out any from that righteousness; the gospel excludes none who do not, by unbelief, shut themselves out. But those who are proud and self-willed, so that they will not come in to God's righteousness, shall have their doom accordingly; they themselves decide it. Let those not expect any benefit thereby, who are not glad to be beholden to it. It is better to be poor and sorrowful, with the blessing of the Lord, than rich and jovial, and under his curse. This may be applied to Christ. He was, when on earth, a man of sorrows that had not where to lay his head; but God exalted him. Let us call upon the Lord, and though poor and sorrowful, guilty and defiled, his salvation will set us up on high.

He concludes with joy and praise (30–36)

The psalmist concludes the psalm with holy joy and praise, which he began with complaints of his grief. It is a great comfort to us, that humble and thankful praises are more pleasing to God than the most costly, pompous sacrifices. The humble shall look to him, and be glad; those that seek him through Christ shall live and be comforted. God will do great things for the gospel church, in which let all who wish well to it rejoice. A seed shall serve him on earth, and his servants shall inherit his heavenly kingdom. Those that love his name shall dwell before him for ever. He that spared not his own Son, but delivered him up for us all, how shall he not with him also freely give us all things? Arise, thou great Restorer of the ancient places to dwell in, and turn away ungodliness from thy people.

Psalm 70

The speedy destruction of the wicked, and the preservation of the godly (1–5)

This psalm is almost the same as the last five of Ps 40. While here we behold Jesus Christ set forth in poverty and distress, we also see him denouncing just and fearful punishment on his Jewish, heathen, and antichristian enemies; and pleading for the joy and happiness of his friends, to his Father's honour. Let us apply these things to our own troubled circumstances, and in a believing manner bring them, and the sinful causes thereof, to our remembrance. Urgent trials should always awake fervent prayers.

Psalm 71

Prayers that God would deliver and save (1–13)
Believing praises (14–24)

Prayers that God would deliver and save (1–13)

David prays that he might never be made ashamed of dependence upon God. With this petition every true believer may come boldly to the throne of grace. The gracious care of Divine providence in our birth and infancy, should engage us to early piety. He that was our Help from our birth, ought to be our Hope from our youth. Let none expect ease or comfort from the world. Those who love the Lord, often are hated and persecuted; men wondered at for their principles and conduct; but the Lord has been their strong refuge. The faithful servants of God may be assured that he will not cast them off in old age, nor forsake them when their strength fails.

Believing praises (14–24)

The psalmist declares that the righteousness of Christ, and the great salvation obtained thereby, shall be the chosen subject of his discourse. Not on a Sabbath only, but on every day of the week,

of the year, of his life. Not merely at stated returns of solemn devotion, but on every occasion, all the day long. Why will he always dwell on this? Because he knew not the numbers thereof. It is impossible to measure the value or the fulness of these blessings. The righteousness is unspeakable, the salvation everlasting. God will not cast off his grey-headed servants when no longer capable of labouring as they have done. The Lord often strengthens his people in their souls, when nature is sinking into decay. And it is a debt which the old disciples of Christ owe to succeeding generations, to leave behind them a solemn testimony to the advantage of religion, and the truth of God's promises; and especially to the everlasting righteousness of the Redeemer. Assured of deliverance and victory, let us spend our days, while waiting the approach of death, in praising the Holy One of Israel with all our powers. And while speaking of his righteousness, and singing his praises, we shall rise above fears and infirmities, and have earnests of the joys of heaven. The work of redemption ought, above all God's works, to be spoken of by us in our praises. The Lamb that was slain, and has redeemed us to God, is worthy of all blessing and praise.

Psalm 72

David begins with a prayer for Solomon (1)
He passes into a prophecy of the glories of his reign, and of Christ's kingdom (2–17)
Praise to God (18–20)

David begins with a prayer for Solomon (1)

This psalm belongs to Solomon in part, but to Christ more fully and clearly. Solomon was both the king and the king's son, and his pious father desired that the wisdom of God might be in him, that his reign might be a remembrance of the kingdom of the Messiah. It is the prayer of a father for his child; a dying blessing. The best we can ask of God for our children is, that God would give them wisdom and grace to know and to do their duty.

He passes into a prophecy of the glories of his reign, and of Christ's kingdom (2–17)

This is a prophecy of the kingdom of Christ; many passages in it cannot be applied to the reign of Solomon. There were righteousness and peace at first in the administration of his government; but, before the end of his reign, there were troubles and unrighteousness. The kingdom here spoken of is to last as long as the sun, but Solomon's was soon at an end. Even the Jewish expositors understood it of the kingdom of the Messiah. Observe many great and precious promises here made, which were to have full accomplishment only in the kingdom of Christ. As far as his kingdom is set up, discord and contentions cease, in families, churches, and nations. The law of Christ, written in the heart, disposes men to be honest and just, and to render to all their due; it likewise disposes men to live in love, and so produces abundance of peace. Holiness and love shall be lasting in Christ's kingdom. Through all the changes of the world, and all the changes of life, Christ's kingdom will support itself. And he shall, by the graces and comforts of his Spirit, come down like rain upon the mown grass; not on that cut down, but that which is left growing, that it may spring again. His gospel has been, or shall be, preached to all nations. Though he needs not the services of any, yet he must be served with the best. Those that have the wealth of this world, must serve Christ with it, do good with it. Prayer shall be made through him, or for his sake; whatever we ask of the Father, should be in his name. Praises shall be offered to him: we are under the highest obligations to him. Christ only shall be feared throughout all generations. To the end of time, and to eternity, his name shall be praised. All nations shall call HIM blessed.

Praise to God (18–20)

We are taught to bless God in Christ, for all he has done for us by him. David is earnest in prayer for the fulfilment of this prophecy and promise. It is sad to think how empty the earth is of the glory of God, how little service and honour he has from a world to which he is so bountiful. May we, like David, submit to Christ's authority, and partake of his righteousness and peace. May we bless him for the wonders of redeeming love. May we spend our days, and end our lives, praying for the spread of his gospel.

Psalm 73

The psalmist's temptation (1–14)

How he gained a victory over it (15–20)

How he profited by it (21–28)

The psalmist's temptation (1–14)

The psalmist was strongly tempted to envy the prosperity of the wicked; a common temptation, which has tried the graces of many saints. But he lays down the great principle by which he resolved to abide. It is the goodness of God. This is a truth which cannot be shaken. Good thoughts of God will fortify against Satan's temptations. The faith even of strong believers may be sorely shaken, and ready to fail. There are storms that will try the firmest anchors. Foolish and wicked people have sometimes a great share of outward prosperity. They seem to have the least share of the troubles of this life; and they seem to have the greatest share of its comforts. They live without the fear of God, yet they prosper, and get on in the world. Wicked men often spend their lives without much sickness, and end them without great pain; while many godly persons scarcely know what health is, and die with great sufferings. Often the wicked are not frightened, either by the remembrance of their sins, or the prospect of their misery, but they die without terror. We cannot judge men's state beyond death, by what passes at their death. He looked abroad, and saw many of God's people greatly at a loss. Because the wicked are so very daring, therefore his people return hither; they know not what to say to it, and the rather, because they drink deep of the bitter cup of affliction. He spoke feelingly when he spoke of his own troubles; there is no disputing against sense, except by faith. From all this arose a strong temptation to cast off religion. But let us learn that the true course of sanctification consists in cleansing a man from all pollution both of soul and body. The heart is cleansed by the blood of Christ laid hold upon by faith; and by the begun works of the Lord's Spirit, manifested in the hearty resolution, purpose, and study of holiness, and a blameless course of life and actions, the hands are cleansed. It is not in vain to serve God and keep his ordinances.

How he gained a victory over it (15–20)

The psalmist having shown the progress of his temptation, shows how faith and grace prevailed. He kept up respect for God's people, and with that he restrained himself from speaking what he had thought amiss. It is a sign that we repent of the evil thoughts of the heart, if we suppress them. Nothing gives more offence to God's children, than to say it is vain to serve God; for there is nothing more contrary to their universal experience. He prayed to God to make this matter plain to him; and he understood the wretched end of wicked people; even in the height of their prosperity they were but ripening for ruin. The sanctuary must be the resort of a tempted soul. The righteous man's afflictions end in peace, therefore he is happy; the wicked man's enjoyments end in destruction, therefore he is miserable. The prosperity of the wicked is short and uncertain, slippery places. See what their prosperity is; it is but a vain show, it is only a corrupt imagination, not substance, but a mere shadow; it is as a dream, which may please us a little while we are slumbering, yet even then it disturbs our repose.

How he profited by it (21–28)

God would not suffer his people to be tempted, if his grace were not sufficient, not only to save them from harm, but to make them gainers by it. This temptation, the working of envy and discontent, is very painful. In reflecting upon it, the psalmist owns it was his folly and ignorance thus to vex himself. If good men, at any time, through the surprise and strength of temptation, think, or speak, or act amiss, they will reflect upon it with sorrow and shame. We must ascribe our safety in temptation, and our victory, not to our own wisdom, but to the gracious presence of God with us, and Christ's intercession for us. All who commit themselves to God, shall be guided with the counsel both of his word and of his Spirit, the best counsellors here, and shall be received to his glory in another world; the believing hopes and prospects of which will reconcile us to all dark providences. And the psalmist was hereby quickened to cleave the closer to God. Heaven itself could not make us happy without the presence and love of our God. The world and all its glory vanishes. The body will fail by sickness, age, and death; when the flesh fails, the conduct, courage, and comfort fail. But Christ Jesus, our Lord, offers to be all in all to every poor sinner, who renounces all other portions and confidences. By sin we are all far from God. And a profession of Christ, if we go on in sin, will increase our condemnation. May we draw near, and keep near, to our God, by faith and prayer, and find it good to do so. Those that with an upright heart put their trust in God, shall never want matter for thanksgiving to him. Blessed Lord, who hast so graciously promised to become our portion in the next world, prevent us from choosing any other in this.

Psalm 74

The desolations of the sanctuary (1–11)
Pleas for encouraging faith (12–17)
Petitions for deliverances (18–23)

The desolations of the sanctuary (1–11)

This psalm appears to describe the destruction of Jerusalem and the temple by the Chaldeans. The deplorable case of the people of God, at the time, is spread before the Lord, and left with him. They plead the great things God had done for them. If the deliverance of Israel out of Egypt was encouragement to hope that he would not cast them off, much more reason have we to believe, that God will not cast off any whom Christ has redeemed with his own blood. Infidels and persecutors may silence faithful ministers, and shut up places of worship, and say they will destroy the people of God and their religion together. For a long time they may prosper in these attempts, and God's oppressed servants may see no prospect of deliverance; but there is a remnant of believers, the seed of a future harvest, and the despised church has survived those who once triumphed over her. When the power of enemies is most threatening, it is comfortable to flee to the power of God by earnest prayer.

Pleas for encouraging faith (12–17)

The church silences her own complaints. What God had done for his people, as their King of old, encouraged them to depend on him. It was the Lord's doing, none besides could do it. This providence was food to faith and hope, to support and encourage in difficulties. The God of Israel is the God of nature. He that is faithful to his covenant about the day and the night, will never cast off those whom he has chosen. We have as much reason to expect affliction, as to expect night and winter. But we have no more reason to despair of the return of comfort, than to despair of day and summer. And in the world above we shall have no more changes.

Petitions for deliverances (18–23)

The psalmist begs that God would appear for the church against their enemies. The folly of such as revile his gospel and his servants will be plain to all. Let us call upon our God to enlighten the dark nations of the earth; and to rescue his people, that the poor and needy may praise his name. Blessed Saviour, thou art the same yesterday, today, and for ever. Make thy people more than conquerors. Be thou, Lord, all in all to them in every situation and circumstances; for then thy poor and needy people will praise thy name.

Psalm 75

The psalmist declares his resolution of executing judgment (1–5)
He rebukes the wicked, and concludes with resolutions to praise God (6–10)

The psalmist declares his resolution of executing judgment (1–5)

We often pray for mercy, when in pursuit of it; and shall we only once or twice give thanks, when we obtain it? God shows that he is nigh to us in what we call upon him for. Public trusts are to be managed uprightly. This may well be applied to Christ and his government. Man's sin threatened to destroy the whole creation; but

Christ saved the world from utter ruin. He who is made of God to us wisdom, bids us be wise. To the proud, daring sinners he says, Boast not of your power, persist not in contempt. All the present hopes and future happiness of the human race spring from the Son of God.

He rebukes the wicked, and concludes with resolutions to praise God (6–10)

No second causes will raise men to preferment without the First Cause. It comes neither from the east, nor from the west, nor from the south. He mentions not the north; the same word that signifies the north, signifies the secret place; and from the secret of God's counsel it does come. From God alone all must receive their doom. There are mixtures of mercy and grace in the cup of affliction, when it is put into the hands of God's people; mixtures of the curse, when it is put into the hands of the wicked. God's people have their share in common calamities, but the dregs of the cup are for the wicked. The exaltation of the Son of David will be the subject of the saints' everlasting praises. Then let sinners submit to the King of righteousness, and let believers rejoice in and obey him.

Psalm 76

The psalmist speaks of God's power (1–6)

All have to fear and to trust in him (7–12)

The psalmist speaks of God's power (1–6)

Happy people are those who have their land filled with the knowledge of God! happy persons that have their hearts filled with that knowledge! It is the glory and happiness of a people to have God among them by his ordinances. Wherein the enemies of the church deal proudly, it will appear that God is above them. See the power of God's rebukes. With pleasure may Christians apply this to the advantages bestowed by the Redeemer.

All have to fear and to trust in him (7–12)

God's people are the meek of the earth, the quiet in the land, that suffer wrong, but do none. The righteous God seems to keep silence long, yet, sooner or later, he will make judgment to be heard. We live in an angry, provoking world; we often feel much, and are apt to fear more, from the wrath of man. What will not turn to his praise, shall not be suffered to break out. He can set bounds to the wrath of man, as he does to the raging sea; hitherto it shall come, and no further. Let all submit to God. Our prayers and praises, and especially our hearts, are the presents we should bring to the Lord. His name is glorious, and he is the proper object

of our fear. He shall cut off the spirit of princes; he shall slip it off easily, as we slip off a flower from the stalk, or a bunch of grapes from the vine; so the word signifies. He can dispirit the most daring: since there is no contending with God, it is our wisdom, as it is our duty, to submit to him. Let us seek his favour as our portion, and commit all our concerns to him.

Psalm 77

The psalmist's troubles and temptation (1–10)

He encourages himself by the remembrance of God's help of his people (11–20)

The psalmist's troubles and temptation (1–10)

Days of trouble must be days of prayer; when God seems to have withdrawn from us, we must seek him till we find him. In the day of his trouble the psalmist did not seek for the diversion of business or amusement, but he sought God, and his favour and grace. Those that are under trouble of mind, must pray it away. He pored upon the trouble; the methods that should have relieved him did but increase his grief. When he remembered God, it was only the Divine justice and wrath. His spirit was overwhelmed, and sank under the load. But let not the remembrance of the comforts we have lost, make us unthankful for those that are left. Particularly he called to remembrance the comforts with which he supported himself in former sorrows. Here is the language of a sorrowful, deserted soul, walking in darkness; a common case even among those that fear the Lord, Isaiah 50:10. Nothing wounds and pierces like the thought of God's being angry. God's own people, in a cloudy and dark day, may be tempted to make wrong conclusions about their spiritual state, and that of God's kingdom in the world. But we must not give way to such fears. Let faith answer them from the Scripture. The troubled fountain will work itself clear again; and the recollection of former times of joyful experience often raises a hope, tending to relief. Doubts and fears proceed from the want and weakness of faith. Despondency and distrust under affliction, are too often the infirmities of believers, and, as such, are to be thought upon by us with sorrow and shame. When unbelief is working in us, we must thus suppress its risings.

He encourages himself by the remembrance of God's help of his people (11–20)

The remembrance of the works of God, will be a powerful remedy against distrust of his promise and goodness; for he is God, and changes not. God's way is in the sanctuary. We are sure that God is holy in all his works. God's ways are like the deep waters, which cannot be fathomed; like the way of a ship, which cannot be tracked. God brought Israel out of Egypt. This was typical of the great redemption to be wrought out in the fulness of time, both by price and power. If we have harboured doubtful thoughts, we should, without delay, turn our minds to meditate on that God, who spared not his own Son, but delivered him up for us all, that with him, he might freely give us all things.

Psalm 78

Attention called for (1–8)

The history of Israel (9–39)

Their settlement in Canaan (40–55)

The mercies of God to Israel contrasted with their ingratitude (56–72)

Attention called for (1–8)

These are called dark and deep sayings, because they are carefully to be looked into. The law of God was given with a particular charge to teach it diligently to their children, that the church may abide for ever. Also, that the providences of God, both in mercy and in judgment, might encourage them to conform to the will of God. The works of God much strengthen our resolution to keep his commandments. Hypocrisy is the high road to apostacy; those that do not set their hearts right, will not be steadfast with God. Many parents, by negligence and wickedness, become murderers of their children. But young persons, though they are bound to submit in all things lawful, must not obey sinful orders, or copy sinful examples.

The history of Israel (9–39)

Sin dispirits men, and takes away the heart. Forgetfulness of God's works is the cause of disobedience to his laws. This narrative relates a struggle between God's goodness and man's badness. The Lord hears all our murmurings and distrusts, and is much displeased. Those that will not believe the power of God's mercy, shall feel the fire of his indignation. Those cannot be said to trust in God's salvation as their happiness at last, who can not trust his providence in the way to it. To all that by faith and prayer, ask, seek, and knock, these doors of heaven shall at any time be opened; and our distrust of God is a great aggravation of our sins. He expressed his resentment of their provocation; not in denying what they sinfully lusted after, but in granting it to them. Lust is contented with nothing. Those

that indulge their lust, will never be estranged from it. Those hearts are hard indeed, that will neither be melted by the mercies of the Lord, nor broken by his judgments. Those that sin still, must expect to be in trouble still. And the reason why we live with so little comfort, and to so little purpose, is, because we do not live by faith. Under these rebukes they professed repentance, but they were not sincere, for they were not constant. In Israel's history we have a picture of our own hearts and lives. God's patience, and warnings, and mercies, embolden them to harden their hearts against his word. And the history of kingdoms is much the same. Judgments and mercies have been little attended to, until the measure of their sins has been full. And higher advantages have not kept churches from declining from the commandments of God. Even true believers recollect, that for many a year they abused the kindness of Providence. When they come to heaven, how will they admire the Lord's patience and mercy in bringing them to his kingdom!

Their settlement in Canaan (40–55)

Let not those that receive mercy from God, be thereby made bold to sin, for the mercies they receive will hasten its punishment; yet let not those who are under Divine rebukes for sin, be discouraged from repentance. The Holy One of Israel will do what is most for his own glory, and what is most for their good. Their forgetting former favours, led them to limit God for the future. God made his own people to go forth like sheep; and guided them in the wilderness, as a shepherd his flock, with all care and tenderness. Thus the true Joshua, even Jesus, brings his church out of the wilderness; but no earthly Canaan, no worldly advantages, should make us forget that the church is in the wilderness while in this world, and that there remaineth a far more glorious rest for the people of God.

The mercies of God to Israel contrasted with their ingratitude (56–72)

After the Israelites were settled in Canaan, the children were like their fathers. God gave them his testimonies, but they turned back. Presumptuous sins render even Israelites hateful to God's holiness, and exposed to his justice. Those whom the Lord forsakes become an easy prey to the destroyer. And sooner or later, God will disgrace his enemies. He set a good government over his people; a monarch after his own heart. With good reason does the psalmist make this finishing, crowning instance of God's favour to Israel; for David was a type of Christ, the great and good Shepherd, who was humbled first, and then exalted; and of whom it was foretold, that he should be filled with the Spirit of wisdom and understanding. On the uprightness of his heart, and the skilfulness of his hands, all his subjects may rely; and of the increase of his government and peace there shall be no end. Every trial of human nature hitherto, confirms the testimony of Scripture, that the heart is deceitful above all things, and desperately wicked, and nothing but being created anew by the Holy Ghost can cure the ungodliness of any.

Psalm 79

The deplorable condition of the people of God (1–5)

A petition for relief (6–13)

The deplorable condition of the people of God (1–5)

God is complained to: whither should children go but to a Father able and willing to help them? See what a change sin made in the holy city, when the heathen were suffered to pour in upon them. God's own people defiled it by their sins, therefore he suffered their enemies to defile it by their insolence. They desired that God would be reconciled. Those who desire God's favour as better than life, cannot but dread his wrath as worse than death. In every affliction we should first beseech the Lord to cleanse away the guilt of our sins; then he will visit us with his tender mercies.

A petition for relief (6–13)

Those who persist in ignorance of God, and neglect of prayer, are the ungodly. How unrighteous soever men were, the Lord was righteous in permitting them to do what they did. Deliverances from trouble are mercies indeed, when grounded upon the pardon of sin; we should therefore be more earnest in prayer for the removal of our sins than for the removal of afflictions. They had no hopes but from God's mercies, his tender mercies. They plead no merit, they pretend to none, but, Help us for the glory of thy name; pardon us for thy name's sake. The Christian forgets not that he is often bound in the chain of his sins. The world to him is a prison; sentence of death is passed upon him, and he knows not how soon it may be executed. How fervently should he at all times pray, O let the sighing of a prisoner come before thee, according to the greatness of thy power preserve thou those that are appointed to die! How glorious will the day be, when, triumphant over sin and sorrow, the church beholds the adversary disarmed for ever! while that church shall, from age to age, sing the praises of her great Shepherd and Bishop, her King and her God.

Psalm 80

The psalmist complains of the miseries of the church (1–7)

Its former prosperity and present desolation (8–16)

A prayer for mercy (17–19)

The psalmist complains of the miseries of the church (1–7)

He that dwelleth upon the mercy-seat, is the good Shepherd of his people. But we can neither expect the comfort of his love, nor the protection of his arm, unless we partake of his converting grace. If he is really angry at the prayers of his people, it is because, although they pray, their ends are not right, or there is some secret sin indulged in them, or he will try their patience and perseverance in prayer. When God is displeased with his people, we must expect to see them in tears, and their enemies in triumph. There is no salvation but from God's favour; there is no conversion to God but by his own grace.

Its former prosperity and present desolation (8–16)

The church is represented as a vine and a vineyard. The root of this vine is Christ, the branches are believers. The church is like a vine, needing support, but spreading and fruitful. If a vine do not bring forth fruit, no tree is so worthless. And are not we planted as in a well-cultivated garden, with every means of being fruitful in works of righteousness? But the useless leaves of profession, and the empty boughs of notions and forms, abound far more than real piety. It was wasted and ruined. There was a good reason for this change in God's way toward them. And it is well or ill with us, according as we are under God's smiles or frowns. When we consider the state of the purest part of the visible church, we cannot wonder that it is visited with sharp corrections. They request that God would help the vine. Lord, it is formed by thyself, and for thyself, therefore it may, with humble confidence, be committed to thyself.

A prayer for mercy (17–19)

The Messiah, the Protector and Saviour of the church, is the Man of God's right hand; he is the Arm of the Lord, for all power is given to him. In him is our strength, by which we are enabled to persevere to the end. The vine, therefore, cannot be ruined, nor can any fruitful branch perish; but the unfruitful will be cut off and cast into the fire. The end of our redemption is, that we should serve Him who hath redeemed us, and not go back to our old sins.

Psalm 81

God is praised for what he has done for his people (1–7)

Their obligations to him (8–16)

God is praised for what he has done for his people (1–7)

All the worship we can render to the Lord is beneath his excellences, and our obligations to him, especially in our redemption from sin and wrath. What God had done on Israel's behalf, was kept in remembrance by public solemnities. To make a deliverance appear more gracious, more glorious, it is good to observe all that makes the trouble we are delivered from appear more grievous. We ought never to forget the base and ruinous drudgery to which Satan, our oppressor, brought us. But when, in distress of conscience, we are led to cry for deliverance, the Lord answers our prayers, and sets us at liberty. Convictions of sin, and trials by affliction, prove his regard to his people. If the Jews, on their solemn feast-days, were thus to call to mind their redemption out of Egypt, much more ought we, on the Christian Sabbath, to call to mind a more glorious redemption, wrought out for us by our Lord Jesus Christ, from worse bondage.

Their obligations to him (8–16)

We cannot look for too little from the creature, nor too much from the Creator. We may have enough from God, if we pray for it in faith. All the wickedness of the world is owing to man's wilfulness. People are not religious, because they will not be so. God is not the Author of their sin, he leaves them to the lusts of their own hearts, and the counsels of their own heads; if they do not well, the blame must be upon themselves. The Lord is unwilling that any should perish. What enemies sinners are to themselves! It is sin that makes our troubles long, and our salvation slow. Upon the same conditions of faith and obedience, do Christians hold those spiritual and eternal good things, which the pleasant fields and fertile hills of Canaan showed forth. Christ is the Bread of life; he is the Rock of salvation, and his promises are as honey to pious minds. But those who reject him as their Lord and Master, must also lose him as their Saviour and their reward.

Psalm 82

An exhortation to judges (1–5)

The doom of evil rulers (6–8)

An exhortation to judges (1–5)

Magistrates are the mighty in authority for the public good. Magistrates are the ministers of God's providence, for keeping up order and peace, and particularly in punishing evil-doers, and protecting those that do well. Good princes and good judges, who mean well, are under Divine direction; and bad ones, who mean ill, are under Divine restraint. The authority of God is to be submitted to, in those governors whom his providence places over us. But when justice is turned from what is right, no good can be expected. The evil actions of public persons are public mischiefs.

The doom of evil rulers (6–8)

It is hard for men to have honour put upon them, and not to be proud of it. But all the rulers of the earth shall die, and all their honour shall be laid in the dust. God governs the world. There is a righteous God to whom we may go, and on whom we may depend. This also has respect to the kingdom of the Messiah. Considering the state of affairs in the world, we have need to pray that the Lord Jesus would speedily rule over all nations, in truth, righteousness, and peace.

Psalm 83

The designs of the enemies of Israel (1–8)

Earnest prayer for their defeat (9–18)

The designs of the enemies of Israel (1–8)

Sometimes God seems not to be concerned at the unjust treatment of his people. But then we may call upon him, as the psalmist here. All wicked people are God's enemies, especially wicked persecutors. The Lord's people are his hidden one; the world knows them not. He takes them under his special protection. Do the enemies of the church act with one consent to destroy it, and shall not the friends of the church be united? Wicked men wish that there might be no religion among mankind. They would gladly see all its restraints shaken off, and all that preach, profess, or practise it, cut off. This they would bring to pass if it were in their power. The enemies of God's church have always been many: this magnifies the power of the Lord in preserving to himself a church in the world.

Earnest prayer for their defeat (9–18)

All who oppose the kingdom of Christ may here read their doom. God is the same still that ever he was; the same to his people, and the same against his and their enemies. God would make their enemies like a wheel; unsettled in all their counsels and resolves. Not only let them be driven away as stubble, but burnt as stubble. And this will be the end of wicked men. Let them be made to fear thy name, and perhaps that will bring them to seek thy name. We should desire no confusion to our enemies and persecutors but what may forward their conversion. The stormy tempest of Divine vengeance will overtake them, unless they repent and seek the pardoning mercy of their offended Lord. God's triumphs over his enemies, clearly prove that he is, according to his name JEHOVAH, an almighty Being, who has all power and perfection in himself. May we fear his wrath, and yield ourselves to be his willing servants. And let us seek deliverance by the destruction of our fleshly lusts, which war against the soul.

Psalm 84

The psalmist expresses his affection to the ordinances of God (1–7)

His desire towards the God of the ordinances (8–12)

The psalmist expresses his affection to the ordinances of God (1–7)

The ordinances of God are the believer's solace in this evil world; in them he enjoys the presence of the living God: this causes him to regret his absence from them. They are to his soul as the nest to the bird. Yet they are only an earnest of the happiness of heaven; but how can men desire to enter that holy habitation, who complain of Divine ordinances as wearisome? Those are truly happy, who go forth, and go on in the exercise of religion, in the strength of the grace of Jesus Christ, from whom all our sufficiency is. The pilgrims to the heavenly city may have to pass through many a valley of weeping, and many a thirsty desert; but wells of salvation shall be opened for them, and consolations sent for their support. Those that press forward in their Christian course, shall find God add grace to their graces. And those who grow in grace, shall be perfect in glory.

His desire towards the God of the ordinances (8–12)

In all our addresses to God, we must desire that he would look on Christ, his Anointed One, and accept us for his sake: we must look to him with faith, and then God will with favour look upon the face of the Anointed: we, without him, dare not show our faces. The psalmist pleads love to God's ordinances. Let us account one day in God's courts better than a thousand spent elsewhere; and deem the meanest place in his service preferable to the highest earthly preferment. We are here in darkness, but if God be our God, he will be to us a Sun, to enlighten and enliven us, to guide and direct us. We are here in danger, but he will be to us a Shield, to secure us from the fiery darts that fly thick about us. Though he has not promised to give riches and dignities, he has promised to give grace and glory to all that seek them in his appointed way. And what is grace, but heaven begun below, in the knowledge, love, and service of God? What is glory, but the completion of this happiness, in being made like to him, and in fully enjoying him for ever? Let it be our care to walk uprightly, and then let us trust God to give us every thing that is good for us. If we cannot go to the house of the Lord, we may go by faith to the Lord of the house; in him we shall be happy, and may be easy. That man is really happy, whatever his outward circumstances may be, who trusts in the Lord of hosts, the God of Jacob.

Psalm 85

Prayers for the continuance of former mercies (17)

Trust in God's goodness (813)

Prayers for the continuance of former mercies (17)

The sense of present afflictions should not do away the remembrance of former mercies. The favour of God is the fountain of happiness to nations, as well as to particular persons. When God forgives sin, he covers it; and when he covers the sin of his people, he covers it all. See what the pardon of sin is. In compassion to us, when Christ our Intercessor has stood before thee, thou hast turned away thine anger. When we are reconciled to God, then, and not till then, we may expect the comfort of his being reconciled to us. He shows mercy to those to whom he grants salvation; for salvation is of mere mercy. The Lord's people may expect sharp and tedious afflictions when they commit sin; but when they return to him with humble prayer, he will make them again to rejoice in him.

Trust in God's goodness (8–13)

Sooner or later, God will speak peace to his people. If he do not command outward peace, yet he will suggest inward peace; speaking to their hearts by his Spirit. Peace is spoken only to those who turn from sin. All sin is folly, especially backsliding; it is the greatest folly to return to sin. Surely God's salvation is nigh, whatever our difficulties and distresses are. Also, his honour is secured, that glory may dwell in our land. And the truth of the promises is shown by the Divine mercy in sending the Redeemer. The Divine justice is now satisfied by the great atonement. Christ, the way, truth, and life, sprang out of the earth when he took our nature upon him, and Divine justice looked upon him well pleased and satisfied. For his sake all good things, especially his Holy Spirit, are given to those who ask him. Through Christ, the pardoned sinner becomes fruitful in good works, and by looking to and trusting in the Saviour's righteousness, finds his feet set in the way of his steps. Righteousness is a sure guide, both in meeting God, and in following him.

Psalm 86

The psalmist pleads his earnestness, and the mercy of God, as reasons why his prayer should be heard (1–7)

He renews his requests for help and comfort (8–17)

The psalmist pleads his earnestness, and the mercy of God, as reasons why his prayer should be heard (1–7)

Our poverty and wretchedness, when felt, powerfully plead in our behalf at the throne of grace. The best self-preservation is to commit ourselves to God's keeping. I am one whom thou favoured, hast set apart for thyself, and made partaker of sanctifying grace. It is a great encouragement to prayer, to feel that we have received the converting grace of God, have learned to trust in him, and to be his servants. We may expect comfort from God, when we keep up our communion with God. God's goodness appears in two things, in giving and forgiving. Whatever others do, let us call upon God, and commit our case to him; we shall not seek in vain.

He renews his requests for help and comfort (8–17)

Our God alone possesses almighty power and infinite love. Christ is the way and the truth. And the believing soul will be more desirous to be taught the way and the truth. And the believing soul will be more desirous to be taught the way and the truth of God, in order to walk therein, than to be delivered out of earthly distress. Those who set not the Lord before them, seek after believers' souls; but the compassion, mercy, and truth of God, will be their refuge and consolation. And those whose parents were the servants of the Lord, may urge this as a plea why he should hear and help them. In considering David's experience, and that of the believer, we must not lose sight of Him, who though he was rich, for our sakes became poor, that we through his poverty might be rich.

Psalm 87

The glory of the church (1–3)

It is filled with the Divine blessing (4–7)

The glory of the church (1–3)

Christ himself is the Foundation of the church, which God has laid. Holiness is the strength and firmness of the church. Let us not be ashamed of the church of Christ in its meanest condition, nor of those that belong to it, since such glorious things are spoken of it. Other foundation can no man lay than that is laid, even Jesus Christ. The glorious things spoken of Zion by the Spirit, were all typical of Christ, and his work and offices; of the gospel church, its privileges and members; of heaven, its glory and perfect happiness.

It is filled with the Divine blessing (4–7)

The church of Christ is more glorious and excellent than the nations of the earth. In the records of heaven, the meanest of those who are born again stand registered. When God renders to every man according to his works, he shall observe who enjoyed the privileges of his sanctuary. To them much was given, and of them much will be required. Let those that dwell in Zion, mark this, and live up to their profession. Zion's songs shall be sung with joy and triumph. The springs of the joy of a carnal worldling are in wealth and pleasure; but of a gracious soul, in the word of God and prayer. All grace and consolation are derived from Christ, through his ordinances, to the souls of believers.

Psalm 88

The psalmist pours out his soul to God in lamentation (1–9)

He wrestles by faith, in his prayer to God for comfort (10–18)

The psalmist pours out his soul to God in lamentation (1–9)

The first words of the psalmist are the only words of comfort and support in this psalm. Thus greatly may good men be afflicted, and such dismal thoughts may they have about their afflictions, and such dark conclusion may they make about their end, through the power of melancholy and the weakness of faith. He complained most of God's displeasure. Even the children of God's love may sometimes think themselves children of wrath and no outward trouble can be so hard upon them as that. Probably the psalmist described his own case, yet he leads to Christ. Thus are we called to look unto Jesus, wounded and bruised for our iniquities. But the wrath of

God poured the greatest bitterness into his cup. This weighed him down into darkness and the deep.

He wrestles by faith, in his prayer to God for comfort (10–18)

Departed souls may declare God's faithfulness, justice, and loving-kindness; but deceased bodies can neither receive God's favours in comfort, nor return them in praise. The psalmist resolved to continue in prayer, and the more so, because deliverance did not come speedily. Though our prayers are not soon answered, yet we must not give over praying. The greater our troubles, the more earnest and serious we should be in prayer. Nothing grieves a child of God so much as losing sight of him; nor is there any thing he so much dreads as God's casting off his soul. If the sun be clouded, that darkens the earth; but if the sun should leave the earth, what a dungeon would it be! Even those designed for God's favours, may for a time suffer his terrors. See how deep those terrors wounded the psalmist. If friends are put far from us by providences, or death, we have reason to look upon it as affliction. Such was the calamitous state of a good man. But the pleas here used were peculiarly suited to Christ. And we are not to think that the holy Jesus suffered for us only at Gethsemane and on Calvary. His whole life was labour and sorrow; he was afflicted as never man was, from his youth up. He was prepared for that death of which he tasted through life. No man could share in the sufferings by which other men were to be redeemed. All forsook him, and fled. Oftentimes, blessed Jesus, do we forsake thee; but do not forsake us, O take not thy Holy Spirit from us.

Psalm 89

God's mercy and truth, and his covenant (1–4)

The glory and perfection of God (5–14)

The happiness of those in communion with him (15–18)

God's covenant with David, as a type of Christ (19–37)

A calamitous state lamented, Prayer for redress (38–52)

God's mercy and truth, and his covenant (1–4)

Though our expectations may be disappointed, yet God's promises are established in the heavens, in his eternal counsels; they are out of the reach of opposers in hell and earth. And faith in the boundless mercy and everlasting truth of God, may bring comfort even in the deepest trials.

The glory and perfection of God (5–14)

The more God's works are known, the more they are admired. And to praise the Lord, is to acknowledge him to be such a one that there is none like him. Surely then we should feel and express reverence when we worship God. But how little of this appears in our congregations, and how much cause have we to humble ourselves on this account! That almighty power which smote Egypt, will scatter the enemies of the church, while all who trust in God's mercy will rejoice in his name; for mercy and truth direct all he does. His counsels from eternity, and their consequences to eternity, are all justice and judgment.

The happiness of those in communion with him (15–18)

Happy are those who so know the joyful sound of the gospel as to obey it; who experience its power upon their hearts, and bring forth the fruit of it in their lives. Though believers are nothing in themselves, yet having all in Christ Jesus, they may rejoice in his name. May the Lord enable us to do so. The joy of the Lord is the strength of his people; whereas unbelief dispirits ourselves and discourages others. Though it steals upon us under a semblance of humility, yet it is the very essence of pride. Christ is the Holy One of Israel; and in him was that peculiar people more blessed than in any other blessing.

God's covenant with David, as a type of Christ (19–37)

The Lord anointed David with the holy oil, not only as an emblem of the graces and gifts he received, but as a type of Christ, the King Priest, and Prophet, anointed with the Holy Ghost without measure. David after his anointing, was persecuted, but none could gain advantage against him. Yet all this was a faint shadow of the Redeemer's sufferings, deliverance, glory, and authority, in whom alone these predictions and promises are fully brought to pass. He is the mighty God. This is the Redeemer appointed for us, who alone is able to complete the work of our salvation. Let us seek an interest in these blessings, by the witness of the Holy Spirit in our hearts. As the Lord corrected the posterity of David for their transgressions, so his people shall be corrected for their sins. Yet it is but a rod, not a sword; it is to correct, not to destroy. It is a rod in the hand of God, who is wise, and knows what he does; gracious, and will do what is best. It is a rod which they shall never feel, but when there is need. As the sun and moon remain in heaven, whatever changes there seem to be in them, and again appear in due season; so the covenant of grace made in Christ, whatever alteration seems to come to it, should not be questioned.

A calamitous state lamented, Prayer for redress (38–52)

Sometimes it is not easy to reconcile God's providences with his promises, yet we are sure that God's works fulfil his word. When the great Anointed One, Christ himself, was upon the cross, God seemed to have cast him off, yet did not make void his covenant, for that was established for ever. The honour of the house of David was lost. Thrones and crowns are often laid in the dust; but there is a crown of glory reserved for Christ's spiritual seed, which fadeth not away. From all this complaint learn what work sin makes with families, noble families, with families in which religion has appeared. They plead with God for mercy. God's unchangeableness and faithfulness assure us that He will not cast off those whom he has chosen and covenanted with. They were reproached for serving him. The scoffers of the latter days, in like manner, reproach the footsteps of the Messiah when 2 Peter records of the Lord's dealings with the family of David, show us his dealings with his church, and with believers. Their afflictions and distresses may be grievous, but he will not finally cast them off. Self-deceivers abuse this doctrine, and others by a careless walk bring themselves into darkness and distress; yet let the true believer rely on it for encouragement in the path of duty, and in bearing the cross. The psalm ends with praise, even after this sad complaint. Those who give God thanks for what he has done, may give him thanks for what he will do. God will follow those with his mercies, who follow him with praises.

Psalm 90

The eternity of God, the frailty of man (1–6)

Submission to Divine chastisements (7–11)

Prayer for mercy and grace (12–17)

The eternity of God, the frailty of man (1–6)

It is supposed that this psalm refers to the sentence passed on Israel in the wilderness, Numbers 14. The favour and protection of God are the only sure rest and comfort of the soul in this evil world. Christ Jesus is the refuge and dwelling-place to which we may repair. We are dying creatures, all our comforts in the world are dying comforts, but God is an everliving God, and believers find him so. When God, by sickness, or other afflictions, turns men to destruction, he thereby calls men to return unto him to repent of their sins, and live a new life. A thousand years are nothing to God's eternity: between a minute and a million of years there is some proportion; between time and eternity there is none. All the events of a thousand years, whether past or to come, are more present to the Eternal Mind, than what was done in the last hour is to us. And in the resurrection, the body and soul shall both return and be united again. Time passes unobserved by us, as with men asleep; and when it is past, it is as nothing. It is a short and quickly-passing life, as the waters of a flood. Man does but flourish as the grass, which, when the winter of old age comes, will wither; but he may be mown down by disease or disaster.

Submission to Divine chastisements (7–11)

The afflictions of the saints often come from God's love; but the rebukes of sinners, and of believers for their sins, must be seen coming from the displeasure of God. Secret sins are known to God, and shall be reckoned for. See the folly of those who go about to cover their sins, for they cannot do so. Our years, when gone, can no more be recalled than the words that we have spoken. Our whole life is toilsome and troublesome; and perhaps, in the midst of the years we count upon, it is cut off. We are taught by all this to stand in awe. The angels that sinned know the power of God's anger; sinners in hell know it; but which of us can fully describe it? Few seriously consider it as they ought. Those who make a mock at sin, and make light of Christ, surely do not know the power of God's anger. Who among us can dwell with that devouring fire?

Prayer for mercy and grace (12–17)

Those who would learn true wisdom, must pray for Divine instruction, must beg to be taught by the Holy Spirit; and for comfort and joy in the returns of God's favour. They pray for the mercy of God, for they pretend not to plead any merit of their own. His favour would be a full fountain of future joys. It would be a sufficient balance to former griefs. Let the grace of God in us produce the light of good works. And let Divine consolations put gladness into our hearts, and a lustre upon our countenances. The work of our hands, establish thou it; and, in order to that, establish us in it. Instead of wasting our precious, fleeting days in pursuing fancies, which leave the possessors for ever poor, let us seek the forgiveness of sins, and an inheritance in heaven. Let us pray that the work of the Holy Spirit may appear in converting our hearts, and that the beauty of holiness may be seen in our conduct.

Psalm 91

The safety of those who have God for their refuge (1–8)

Their favour with Him (9–16)

The safety of those who have God for their refuge (1–8)

He that by faith chooses God for his protector, shall find all in him that he needs or can desire. And those who have found the comfort of making the Lord their refuge, cannot but desire that others may do so. The spiritual life is protected by Divine grace from the temptations of Satan, which are as the snares of the fowler, and from the contagion of sin, which is a noisome pestilence. Great security is promised to believers in the midst of danger. Wisdom shall keep them from being afraid without cause, and faith shall keep them from being unduly afraid. Whatever is done, our heavenly Father's will is done; and we have no reason to fear. God's people shall see, not only God's promises fulfilled, but his threatenings. Then let sinners come unto the Lord upon his mercy-seat, through the Redeemer's name; and encourage others to trust in him also.

Their favour with Him (9–16)

Whatever happens, nothing shall hurt the believer; though trouble and affliction befall, it shall come, not for his hurt, but for good, though for the present it be not joyous but grievous. Those who rightly know God, will set their love upon him. They by prayer constantly call upon him. His promise is, that he will in due time deliver the believer out of trouble, and in the mean time be with him in trouble. The Lord will manage all his worldly concerns, and preserve his life on earth, so long as it shall be good for him. For encouragement in this he looks unto Jesus. He shall live long enough; till he has done the work he was sent into this world for, and is ready for heaven. Who would wish to live a day longer than God has some work to do, either by him or upon him? A man may die young, yet be satisfied with living. But a wicked man is not satisfied even with long life. At length the believer's conflict ends; he has done for ever with trouble, sin, and temptation.

Psalm 92

Praise is the business of the Sabbath (1–6)

The wicked shall perish, but God's people shall be exalted (7–15)

Praise is the business of the Sabbath (1–6)

It is a privilege that we are admitted to praise the Lord, and hope to be accepted in the morning, and every night; not only on Sabbath days, but every day; not only in public, but in private, and in our families. Let us give thanks every morning for the mercies of the night, and every night for the mercies of the day; going out, and coming in, let us bless God. As He makes us glad, through the works of his providence for us, and of his grace in us, and both through the great work of redemption, let us hence be encouraged. As there are many who know not the designs of Providence, nor care to know them, those who through grace do so, have the more reason to be thankful. And if distant views of the great Deliverer so animated believers of old, how should we abound in love and praise!

The wicked shall perish, but God's people shall be exalted (7–15)

God sometimes grants prosperity to wicked men in displeasure; yet they flourish but for a moment. Let us seek for ourselves the salvation and grace of the gospel, that being daily anointed by the Holy Spirit, we may behold and share the Redeemer's glory. It is from his grace, by his word and Spirit, that believers receive all the virtue that keeps them alive, and makes them fruitful. Other trees, when old, leave off bearing, but in God's trees the strength of grace does not fail with the strength of nature. The last days of the saints are sometimes their best days, and their last work their best work: perseverance is sure evidence of sincerity. And may every Sabbath, while it shows forth the Divine faithfulness, find our souls resting more and more upon the Lord our righteousness.

Psalm 93

The majesty, power, and holiness of Christ's kingdom (1–5)

The Lord might have displayed only his justice, holiness, and awful power, in his dealings with fallen men; but he has been pleased to display the riches of his mercy, and the power of his renewing grace. In this great work, the Father has given all power to his Son, the Lord from heaven, who has made atonement for our sins. He not only can pardon, but deliver and protect all who trust in him. His word is past, and all the saints may rely upon it. Whatever was foretold concerning the kingdom of the Messiah, must be fulfilled in due time. All his people ought to be very strictly pure. God's church is his house; it is a holy house, cleansed from sin, and employed in his service. Where there is purity, there shall be peace. Let all carefully look if this kingdom is set up in their hearts.

Psalm 94
The danger and folly of persecutors (1–11)
Comfort and peace to the persecuted (12–23)

The danger and folly of persecutors (1–11)

We may with boldness appeal to God; for he is the almighty Judge by whom every man is judged. Let this encourage those who suffer wrong, to bear it with silence, committing themselves to Him who judges righteously. These prayers are prophecies, which speak terror to the sons of violence. There will come a day of reckoning for all the hard speeches which ungodly sinners have spoken against God, his truths, and ways, and people. It would hardly be believed, if we did not witness it, that millions of rational creatures should live, move, speak, hear, understand, and do what they purpose, yet act as if they believed that God would not punish the abuse of his gifts. As all knowledge is from God, no doubt he knows all the thoughts of the children of men, and knows that the imaginations of the thoughts of men's hearts are only evil, and that continually. Even in good thoughts there is a want of being fixed, which may be called vanity. It concerns us to keep a strict watch over our thoughts, because God takes particular notice of them. Thoughts are words to God.

Comfort and peace to the persecuted (12–23)

That man is blessed, who, under the chastening of the Lord, is taught his will and his truths, from his holy word, and by the Holy Spirit. He should see mercy through his sufferings. There is a rest remaining for the people of God after the days of their adversity, which shall not last always. He that sends the trouble, will send the rest. The psalmist found succour and relief only in the Lord, when all earthly friends failed. We are beholden, not only to God's power, but to his pity, for spiritual supports; and if we have been kept from falling into sin, or shrinking from our duty, we should give him the glory, and encourage our brethren. The psalmist had many troubled thoughts concerning the case he was in, concerning the course he should take, and what was likely to be the end of it. The indulgence of such contrivances and fears, adds to care and distrust, and renders our views more gloomy and confused. Good men sometimes have perplexed and distressed thoughts concerning God. But let them look to the great and precious promises of the gospel. The world's comforts give little delight to the soul, when hurried with melancholy thoughts; but God's comforts bring that peace and pleasure which the smiles of the world cannot give, and which the frowns of the world cannot take away. God is his people's Refuge, to whom they may flee, in whom they are safe, and may be secure. And he will reckon with the wicked. A man cannot be more miserable than his own wickedness will make him, if the Lord visit it upon him.

Psalm 95
An exhortation to praise God (1–7)
A warning not to tempt Him (7–11)

An exhortation to praise God (1–7)

Whenever we come into God's presence, we must come with thanksgiving. The Lord is to be praised; we do not want matter, it were well if we did not want a heart. How great is that God, whose the whole earth is, and the fulness thereof; who directs and disposes of all!, The Lord Jesus, whom we are here taught to praise, is a great God; the mighty God is one of his titles, and God over all, blessed for evermore. To him all power is given, both in heaven and earth. He is our God, and we should praise him. He is our Saviour, and the Author of our blessedness. The gospel church is his flock, Christ is the great and good Shepherd of believers; he sought them when lost, and brought them to his fold.

A warning not to tempt Him (7–11)

Christ calls upon his people to hear his voice. You call him Master, or Lord; then be his willing, obedient people. Hear the voice of his doctrine, of his law, and in both, of his Spirit: hear and heed; hear and yield. Christ's voice must be heard to-day. This day of opportunity will not last always; improve it while it is called to-day. Hearing the voice of Christ is the same with believing. Hardness of heart is at the bottom of all distrust of the Lord. The sins of others ought to be warnings to us not to tread in their steps. The murmurings of Israel were written for our admonition. God is not subject to such passions as we are; but he is very angry at sin and sinners. That certainly is evil, which deserves such a recompense; and his threatenings are as sure as his promises. Let us be aware of the evils of our hearts, which lead us to wander from the Lord. There is a rest ordained for believers, the rest of everlasting refreshment, begun in this life, and perfected in the life to come. This is the rest which God calls his rest.

Psalm 96
A call to all people to praise God (1–9)
God's government and judgment (10–13)

A call to all people to praise God (1–9)

When Christ finished his work on earth, and was received into his glory in heaven, the church began to sing a new song unto him, and to bless his name. His apostles and evangelists showed forth his salvation among the heathen, his wonders among all people. All the earth is here summoned to worship the Lord. We must worship him in the beauty of holiness, as God in Christ, reconciling the world unto himself. Glorious things are said of him, both as motives to praise and matter of praise.

God's government and judgment (10–13)

We are to hope and pray for that time, when Christ shall reign in righteousness over all nations. He shall rule in the hearts of men, by the power of truth, and the Spirit of righteousness. His coming draws nigh; this King, this Judge standeth before the door, but he is not yet come. The Lord will accept the praises of all who seek to promote the kingdom of Christ. The sea can but roar, and how the trees of the wood can show that they rejoice we know not; but He that searches the heart knows what is the mind of the Spirit, and understands the words, the broken language of the weakest. Christ will come to judge the earth, to execute just vengeance on his enemies, and to fulfil his largest promises to his people. What then are we? Would that day be welcome to us? If this be not our case, let us now begin to prepare to meet our God, by seeking the pardon of our sins, and the renewal of our souls to holiness.

Psalm 97

The Lord Jesus reigns in power that cannot be resisted (1–7)

His care of his people, and his provision for them (8–12)

The Lord Jesus reigns in power that cannot be resisted (1–7)

Though many have been made happy in Christ, still there is room. And all have reason to rejoice in Christ's government. There is a depth in his counsels, which we must not pretend to fathom; but still righteousness and judgment are the habitation of his throne. Christ's government, though it might be matter of joy to all, will yet be matter of terror to some; but it is their own fault that it is so. The most resolute and daring opposition will be baffled at the presence of the Lord. And the Lord Jesus will ere long come, and put an end to idol worship of every kind.

His care of his people, and his provision for them (8–12)

The faithful servants of God may well rejoice and be glad, because he is glorified; and whatever tends to his honour, is his people's pleasure. Care is taken for their safety. But something more is meant than their lives. The Lord will preserve the souls of his saints from sin, from apostacy, and despair, under their greatest trials. He will deliver them out of the hands of the wicked one, and preserve them safe to his heavenly kingdom. And those that rejoice in Christ Jesus, and in his exaltation, have fountains of joy prepared for them. Those that sow in tears, shall reap in joy. Gladness is sure to the upright in heart; the joy of the hypocrite is but for a moment. Sinners tremble, but saints rejoice at God's holiness. As he hates sin, yet freely loves the person of the repentant sinner who believes in Christ, he will make a final separation between the person he loves and the sin he hates, and sanctify his people wholly, body, soul, and spirit.

Psalm 98

The glory of the Redeemer (1–3)
The joy of the Redeemer (4–9)

The glory of the Redeemer (1–3)

A song of praise for redeeming love is a new song, a mystery hidden from ages and generations. Converts sing a new song, very different from what they had sung. If the grace of God put a new heart into our breasts, it will put a new song into our mouths. Let this new song be sung to the praise of God, in consideration of the wonders he has wrought. The Redeemer has overcome all difficulties in the way of our redemption, and was not discouraged by the services or sufferings appointed him. Let us praise him for the discoveries made to the world of the work of redemption; his salvation and his righteousness fulfilling the prophecies and promises of the Old Testament. In pursuance of this design, God raised up his Son Jesus to be not only a Light to lighten the Gentiles, but the glory of his people Israel. Surely it behoves us to inquire whether his holy arm hath gotten the victory in our hearts, over the power of Satan, unbelief, and sin? If this be our happy case, we shall exchange all light songs of vanity for songs of joy and thanksgiving; our lives will celebrate the Redeemer's praise.

The joy of the Redeemer (4–9)

Let all the children of men rejoice in the setting up of the kingdom of Christ, for all may benefit by it. The different orders of rational creatures in the universe, seem to be described in figurative language in the reign of the great Messiah. The kingdom of Christ will be a blessing to the whole creation. We expect his second coming to begin his glorious reign. Then shall heaven and earth rejoice, and the joy of the redeemed shall be full. But sin and its dreadful effects will not be utterly done away, till the Lord come to judge the world in righteousness. Seeing then that we look for such things, let us give diligence that we may be found of him in peace, without spot, and blameless.

Psalm 99

The happy government God's people are under (1–5)

Its happy administration (6–9)

The happy government God's people are under (1–5)

God governs the world by his providence, governs the church by his grace, and both by his Son. The inhabitants of the earth have cause to tremble, but the Redeemer still waits to be gracious. Let all who hear, take warning, and seek his mercy. The more we humble ourselves before God, the more we exalt him; and let us be thus reverent, for he is holy.

Its happy administration (6–9)

The happiness of Israel is made out by referring to the most useful governors of that people. They in every thing made God's word and law their rule, knowing that they could not else expect that their prayers should be answered. They all wonderfully prevailed with God in prayer; miracles were wrought at their request. They pleaded for the people, and obtained answers of peace. Our Prophet and High Priest, of infinitely greater dignity than Moses, Aaron, or Samuel, has received and declared to us the will of the Father. Let us not only exalt the Lord with our lips, but give him the throne in our heart; and while we worship him upon his mercy-seat, let us never forget that he is holy.

Psalm 100

An exhortation to praise God, and rejoice in him (1–5)

This song of praise should be considered as a prophecy, and even used as a prayer, for the coming of that time when all people shall know that the Lord he is God, and shall become his worshippers, and the sheep of his pasture. Great encouragement is given us, in worshipping God, to do it cheerfully. If, when we strayed like wandering sheep, he has brought us again to his fold, we have indeed abundant cause to bless his name. The matter of praise, and the motives to it, are very important. Know ye what God is in himself, and what he is to you. Know it; consider and apply it, then you will be more close and constant, more inward and serious, in his worship. The covenant of grace set down in the Scriptures of the Old and New Testament, with so many rich promises, to strengthen the faith of every weak believer, makes the matter of God's praise and of his people's joys so sure, that how sad soever our spirits may be when we look to ourselves, yet we shall have reason to praise the Lord when we look to his goodness and mercy, and to what he has said in his word for our comfort.

Psalm 101

David's vow and profession of godliness (1–8)

In this psalm we have David declaring how he intended to regulate his household, and to govern his kingdom, that he might stop wickedness, and encourage godliness. It is also applicable to private families, and is the householder's psalm. It teaches all that have any power, whether more or less, to use it so as to be a terror to evil-doers, and a praise to them that do well. The chosen subject of the psalm is God's mercy and judgment. The Lord's providences concerning his people are commonly mixed: mercy and judgment. God has set the one over against the other, both to do good, like showers and sunshine. When, in his providence, he exercises us with the mixture of mercy and judgment, we must make suitable acknowledgments to him for both. Family mercies and family afflictions are both calls to family religion. Those who are in public stations are not thereby excused from care in governing their families; they are the more concerned to set a good example of ruling their own houses well. Whenever a man has a house of his own, let him seek to have God to dwell with him; and those may expect his presence, who walk with a perfect heart, in a perfect way. David resolves to practise no evil himself. He further resolves not to keep bad servants, nor to employ those about him that are wicked. He will not admit them into his family, lest they spread the infection of sin. A froward heart, one that delights to be cross and perverse, is not fit for society, the bond of which is Christian love. Nor will he countenance slanderers, those who take pleasure in wounding their neighbour's reputation. Also, God resists the proud, and false, deceitful people, who scruple not to tell lies, or commit frauds. Let every one be zealous and diligent to reform his own heart and ways, and to do this early; ever mindful of that future, most awful morning, when the King of righteousness shall cut off all wicked doers from the heavenly Jerusalem.

Psalm 102

A sorrowful complaint of great afflictions (1–11)

Encouragement by expecting the performances of God's promises to his church (12–22)

The unchangeableness of God (23–28)

A sorrowful complaint of great afflictions (1–11)

The whole word of God is of use to direct us in prayer; but here, as often elsewhere, the Holy Ghost has put words into our mouths. Here is a prayer put into the hands of the afflicted; let them present it to God. Even good men may be almost overwhelmed with afflictions. It is our duty and interest to pray; and it is comfort to an afflicted spirit to unburden itself, by a humble representation of its griefs. We must say, Blessed be the name of the Lord, who both gives and takes away. The psalmist looked upon himself as a dying man; My days are like a shadow.

Encouragement by expecting the performances of God's promises to his church (12–22)

We are dying creatures, but God is an everlasting God, the protector of his church; we may be confident that it will not be neglected. When we consider our own vileness, our darkness and deadness, and the manifold defects in our prayers, we have cause to fear that they will not be received in heaven; but we are here assured of the contrary, for we have an Advocate with the Father, and are under grace, not under the law. Redemption is the subject of praise in the Christian church; and that great work is described by the temporal deliverance and restoration of Israel. Look down upon us, Lord Jesus; and bring us into the glorious liberty of thy children, that we may bless and praise thy name.

The unchangeableness of God (23–28)

Bodily distempers soon weaken our strength, then what can we expect but that our months should be cut off in the midst; and what should we do but provide accordingly? We must own God's hand in it; and must reconcile this to his love, for often those that have used their strength well, have it weakened; and those who, as we think, can very ill be spared, have their days shortened. It is very comfortable, in reference to all the changes and dangers of the church, to remember that Jesus Christ is the same yesterday, today, and for ever. And in reference to the death of our bodies, and the removal of friends, to remember that God is an everlasting God. Do not let us overlook the assurance this psalm contains of a happy end to all the believer's trials. Though all things are changing, dying, perishing, like a vesture folding up and hastening to decay, yet Jesus lives, and thus all is secure, for he hath said, Because I live ye shall live also.

Psalm 103

An exhortation to bless God for his mercy (1–5)

And to the church and to all men (6–14)

For the constancy of his mercy (15–18)

For the government of the world (19–22)

An exhortation to bless God for his mercy (1–5)

By the pardon of sin, that is taken away which kept good things from us, and we are restored to the favour of God, who bestows good things on us. Think of the provocation; it was sin, and yet pardoned: how many the provocations, yet all pardoned! God is still forgiving, as we are still sinning and repenting. The body finds the melancholy consequences of Adam's offence, it is subject to many infirmities, and the soul also. Christ alone forgives all our sins; it is he alone who heals all our infirmities. And the person who finds his sin cured, has a well-grounded assurance that it is forgiven. When God, by the graces and comforts of his Spirit, recovers his people from their decays, and fills them with new life and joy, which is to them an earnest of eternal life and joy, they may then be said to return to the days of their youth, Job 33:25.

And to the church and to all men (6–14)

Truly God is good to all: he is in a special manner good to Israel. He has revealed himself and his grace to them. By his ways we may understand his precepts, the ways he requires us to walk in; and his promises and purposes. He always has been full of compassion. How unlike are those to God, who take every occasion to chide, and never know when to cease! What would become of us, if God should deal so with us? The Scripture says a great deal of the mercy of God, and we all have experienced it. The father pities his children that are weak in knowledge, and teaches them; pities them when they are froward, and bears with them; pities them when they are sick, and comforts them; pities them when they are fallen, and helps them to rise; pities them when they have offended, and, upon their submission, forgives them; pities them when wronged, and rights them: thus the Lord pities those that fear him. See why he pities. He considers the frailty of our bodies, and the folly of our souls, how little we can do, how little we can bear; in all which his compassion appears.

For the constancy of his mercy (15–18)

How short is man's life, and uncertain! The flower of the garden is commonly more choice, and will last the longer, for being sheltered by the garden-wall, and the gardener's care; but the flower of the field, to which life is here compared, is not only withering in itself, but exposed to the cold blasts, and liable to be cropped and trod on by the beasts of the field. Such is man. God considers this, and pities him; let him consider it himself. God's mercy is better than life, for it will outlive it. His righteousness, the truth of his promise, shall be unto children's children, who tread in the footsteps of their forefathers' piety. Then shall mercy be preserved to them.

For the government of the world (19–22)

He who made all, rules all, and both by a word of power. He disposes all persons and things to his own glory. There is a world of holy angels who are ever praising him. Let all his works praise him. Such would have been our constant delight, if we had not been fallen creatures. Such it will in a measure become, if we are born of God. Such it will be for ever in heaven; nor can we be perfectly happy till we can take unwearied pleasure in perfect obedience to the will of our God. And let the feeling of each redeemed heart be, Bless the Lord, O my soul.

Psalm 104

God's majesty in the heavens, The creation of the sea, and the dry land (1–9)

His provision for all creatures (10–18)

The regular course of day and night, and God's sovereign power over all the creatures (19–30)

A resolution to continue praising God (31–35)

God's majesty in the heavens, The creation of the sea, and the dry land (1–9)

Every object we behold calls on us to bless and praise the Lord, who is great. His eternal power and Godhead are clearly shown by the things which he hath made. God is light, and in him is no darkness at all. The Lord Jesus, the Son of his love, is the Light of the world.

His provision for all creatures (10–18)

When we reflect upon the provision made for all creatures, we should also notice the natural

worship they render to God. Yet man, forgetful ungrateful man, enjoys the largest measure of his Creator's kindness: the earth, varying in different lands. Nor let us forget spiritual blessings; the fruitfulness of the church through grace, the bread of everlasting life, the cup of salvation, and the oil of gladness. Does God provide for the inferior creatures, and will he not be a refuge to his people?

The regular course of day and night, and God's sovereign power over all the creatures (19–30)

We are to praise and magnify God for the constant succession of day and night. And see how those are like to the wild beasts, who wait for the twilight, and have fellowship with the unfruitful works of darkness. Does God listen to the language of mere nature, even in ravenous creatures, and shall he not much more interpret favourably the language of grace in his own people, though weak and broken groanings which cannot be uttered? There is the work of every day, which is to be done in its day, which man must apply to every morning, and which he must continue in till evening; it will be time enough to rest when the night comes, in which no man can work. The psalmist wonders at the works of God. The works of art, the more closely they are looked upon, the more rough they appear; the works of nature appear more fine and exact. They are all made in wisdom, for they all answer the end they were designed to serve. Every spring is an emblem of the resurrection, when a new world rises, as it were, out of the ruins of the old one. But man alone lives beyond death. When the Lord takes away his breath, his soul enters on another state, and his body will be raised, either to glory or to misery. May the Lord send forth his Spirit, and new-create our souls to holiness.

A resolution to continue praising God (31–35)

Man's glory is fading; God's glory is everlasting: creatures change, but with the Creator there is no variableness. And if meditation on the glories of creation be so sweet to the soul, what greater glory appears to the enlightened mind, when contemplating the great work of redemption! There alone can a sinner perceive ground of confidence and joy in God. While he with pleasure upholds all, governs all, and rejoices in all his works, let our souls, touched by his grace, meditate on and praise him.

Psalm 105

A solemn call to praise and serve the Lord (1–7)

His gracious dealings with Israel (8–23)

Their deliverance from Egypt, and their settlement in Canaan (24–45)

A solemn call to praise and serve the Lord (1–7)

Our devotion is here stirred up, that we may stir up ourselves to praise God. Seek his strength; that is, his grace; the strength of his Spirit to work in us that which is good, which we cannot do but by strength derived from him, for which he will be sought. Seek to have his favour to eternity, therefore continue seeking it while living in this world; for he will not only be found, but he will reward those that diligently seek him.

His gracious dealings with Israel (8–23)

Let us remember the Redeemer's marvellous works, his wonders, and the judgments of his mouth. Though true Christians are few in number, strangers and pilgrims upon earth, yet a far better inheritance than Canaan is made sure to them by the covenant of God; and if we have the anointing of the Holy Spirit, none can do us any harm. Afflictions are among our mercies. They prove our faith and love, they humble our pride, they wean us from the world, and quicken our prayers. Bread is the staff which supports life; when that staff is broken, the body fails and sinks to the earth. The word of God is the staff of spiritual life, the food and support of the soul: the sorest judgment is a famine of hearing the word of the Lord. Such a famine was sore in all lands when Christ appeared in the flesh; whose coming, and the blessed effect of it, are shadowed forth in the history of Joseph. At the appointed time Christ was exalted as Mediator; all the treasures of grace and salvation are at his disposal, perishing sinners come to him, and are relieved by him.

Their deliverance from Egypt, and their settlement in Canaan (24–45)

As the believer commonly thrives best in his soul when under the cross; so the church also flourishes most in true holiness, and increases in number, while under persecution. Yet instruments shall be raised up for their deliverance, and plagues may be expected by persecutors. And see the special care God took of his people in the wilderness. All the benefits bestowed on Israel as a nation, were shadows of spiritual blessings with which we are blessed in Christ Jesus. Having redeemed us with his blood, restored our souls to holiness, and set us at liberty from Satan's bondage, he guides and guards us all the way. He satisfies our souls with the bread of heaven, and the water of life from the Rock of salvation, and will bring us safely to heaven. He redeems his servants from all iniquity, and purifies them unto himself, to be a peculiar people, zealous of good works.

Psalm 106

The happiness of God's people (1–5)

Israel's sins (6–12)

Their provocations (13–33)

Their rebellions in Canaan and a prayer for more complete deliverance (34–48)

The happiness of God's people (1–5)

None of our sins or sufferings should prevent our ascribing glory and praise to the Lord. The more unworthy we are, the more is his kindness to be admired. And those who depend on the Redeemer's righteousness will endeavour to copy his example, and by word and deed to show forth his praise. God's people have reason to be cheerful people; and need not envy the children of men their pleasure or pride.

Israel's sins (6–12)

Here begins a confession of sin; for we must acknowledge that the Lord has done right, and we have done wickedly. We are encouraged to hope that though justly corrected, yet we shall not be utterly forsaken. God's afflicted people own themselves guilty before him. God is distrusted because his favours are not remembered. If he did not save us for his own name's sake, and to the praise of his power and grace, we should all perish.

Their provocations (13–33)

Those that will not wait for God's counsel, shall justly be given up to their own hearts' lusts, to walk in their own counsels. An undue desire, even for lawful things, becomes sinful. God showed his displeasure for this. He filled them with uneasiness of mind, terror of conscience, and self-reproach. Many that fare deliciously every day, and whose bodies are healthful, have leanness in their souls: no love to God, no thankfulness, no appetite for the Bread of life, and then the soul must be lean. Those wretchedly forget themselves, that feast their bodies and starve their souls. Even the true believer will see abundant cause to say, It is of the Lord's mercies that I am not consumed. Often have we set up idols in our hearts, cleaved to some forbidden object; so that if a greater than Moses had not stood to turn away the anger of the Lord, we should have been destroyed. If God dealt severely with Moses for unadvised words, what do those deserve who speak many proud and wicked words? It is just in God to remove those relations that are blessings to us, when we are peevish and provoking to them, and grieve their spirits.

Their rebellions in Canaan and a prayer for more complete deliverance (34–48)

The conduct of the Israelites in Canaan, and God's dealings with them, show that the way of sin is down-hill; omissions make way for commissions: when they neglected to destroy the heathen, they learned their works. One sin led to many more, and brought the judgments of God on them. Their sin was, in part, their own punishment. Sinners often see themselves ruined by those who led them into evil. Satan, who is a tempter, will be a tormentor. At length, God showed pity to his people for his covenant's sake. The unchangeableness of God's merciful nature and love to his people, makes him change the course of justice into mercy; and no other change is meant by God's repentance. Our case is awful when the outward church is considered. When nations professing Christianity, are so guilty as we are, no wonder if the Lord brings them low for their sins. Unless there is general and deep repentance, there can be no prospect but of increasing calamities. The psalm concludes with prayer for completing the deliverance of God's people, and praise for the beginning and progress of it. May all the people of the earth, ere long, add their Amen.

Psalm 107

God's providential care of the children of men in distresses, in banishment, and dispersion (1–9)

In captivity (10–16)

In sickness (17–22)

Danger at sea (23–32)

God's hand is to be seen by his own people (33–43)

God's providential care of the children of men in distresses, in banishment, and dispersion (1–9)

In these there is reference to the deliverance from Egypt, and perhaps that from Babylon: but the circumstances of travellers in those countries are also noted. It is scarcely possible to conceive the horrors suffered by the hapless traveller, when crossing the trackless sands, exposed to the burning rays of the sun. The words describe their case whom the Lord has redeemed from the bondage of Satan; who pass through the world as a dangerous and dreary wilderness, often ready to faint through troubles, fears, and temptations. Those who hunger and thirst after righteousness, after God, and communion with him, shall be filled with the goodness of his house, both in grace and glory.

In captivity (10–16)

This description of prisoners and captives intimates that they are desolate and sorrowful. In the eastern prisons the captives were and are treated with much severity. Afflicting providences must be improved as humbling providences; and we lose the benefit, if our hearts are unhumbled and unbroken under them. This is a shadow of the sinner's deliverance from a far worse confinement. The awakened sinner discovers his guilt and misery. Having struggled in vain for deliverance, he finds there is no help for him but in the mercy and grace of God. His sin is forgiven by a merciful God, and his pardon is accompanied by deliverance from the power of sin and Satan, and by the sanctifying and comforting influences of God the Holy Spirit.

In sickness (17–22)

If we knew no sin, we should know no sickness. Sinners are fools. They hurt their bodily health by intemperance, and endanger their lives by indulging their appetites. This their way is their folly. The weakness of the body is the effect of sickness. It is by the power and mercy of God that we are recovered from sickness, and it is our duty to be thankful. All Christ's miraculous cures were emblems of his healing diseases of the soul. It is also to be applied to the spiritual cures which the Spirit of grace works. He sends his word, and heals souls; convinces, converts them, makes them holy, and all by the word. Even in common cases of recovery from sickness, God in his providence speaks, and it is done; by his word and Spirit the soul is restored to health and holiness.

Danger at sea (23–32)

Let those who go to sea, consider and adore the Lord. Mariners have their business upon the tempestuous ocean, and there witness deliverances of which others cannot form an idea. How seasonable it is at such a time to pray! This may remind us of the terrors and distress of conscience many experience, and of those deep scenes of trouble which many pass through, in their Christian course. Yet, in answer to their cries, the Lord turns their storm into a calm, and causes their trials to end in gladness.

God's hand is to be seen by his own people (33–43)

What surprising changes are often made in the affairs of men! Let the present desolate state of Judea, and of other countries, explain this. If we look abroad in the world, we see many greatly increase, whose beginning was small. We see many who have thus suddenly risen, as suddenly brought to nothing. Worldly wealth is uncertain; often those who are filled with it, ere they are aware, lose it again. God has many ways of making men poor. The righteous shall rejoice. It shall fully convince all those who deny the Divine Providence. When sinners see how justly God takes away the gifts they have abused, they will not have a word to say. It is of great use to us to be fully assured of God's goodness, and duly affected with it. It is our wisdom to mind our duty, and to refer our comfort to him. A truly wise person will treasure in his heart this delightful psalm. From it, he will fully understand the weakness and wretchedness of man, and the power and loving-kindness of God, not for our merit, but for his mercy's sake.

Psalm 108

Old, yet always new (1–13)

We may usefully select passages from different psalms, as here, 60, to help our devotions, and enliven our gratitude. When the heart is firm in faith and love, the tongue, being employed in grateful praises, is our glory. Every gift of the Lord honours and profits the possessor, as it is employed in God's service and to his glory. Believers may pray with assured faith and hope, for all the blessings of salvation; which are secured to them by the faithful promise and covenant of God. Then let them expect from him help in every trouble, and victory in every conflict. Whatever we do, whatever we gain, God must have all the glory. Lord, visit all our souls with this salvation, with this favour which thou bearest to thy chosen people.

Psalm 109

David complains of his enemies (1–5)

He prophesies their destruction (6–20)

Prayers and praises (21–31)

David complains of his enemies (1–5)

It is the unspeakable comfort of all believers, that whoever is against them, God is for them; and to him they may apply as to one pleased to concern himself for them. David's enemies laughed at him for his devotion, but they could not laugh him out of it.

He prophesies their destruction (6–20)

The Lord Jesus may speak here as a Judge, denouncing sentence on some of his enemies, to warn others. When men reject the salvation of Christ, even their prayers are numbered among their sins. See what hurries some to shameful deaths, and brings the families and estates of others to ruin; makes them and theirs despicable and hateful, and brings poverty, shame, and misery upon their posterity: it is sin, that mischievous, destructive thing. And what will be the effect of the sentence, 'Go, ye cursed,' upon the bodies and souls of the wicked! How it will affect the senses of the body, and the powers of the soul, with pain, anguish, horror, and despair! Think on these things, sinners, tremble and repent.

Prayers and praises (21–31)

The psalmist takes God's comforts to himself, but in a very humble manner. He was troubled in mind. His body was wasted, and almost worn away. But it is better to have leanness in the body, while the soul prospers and is in health, than to have leanness in the soul, while the body is feasted. He was ridiculed and reproached by his enemies. But if God bless us, we need not care who curses us; for how can they curse whom God has not cursed; nay, whom he has blessed? He pleads God's glory, and the honour of his name. Save me, not according to my merit, for I pretend to none, but according to thy mercy. He concludes with the joy of faith, in assurance that his present conflicts would end in triumphs. Let all that suffer according to the will of God, commit the keeping of their souls to him. Jesus, unjustly put to death, and now risen again, is an Advocate and Intercessor for his people, ever ready to appear on their behalf against a corrupt world, and the great accuser.

Psalm 110

Christ's kingdom (1–7)

Glorious things are here spoken of Christ. Not only he should be superior to all the kings of the earth, but he then existed in glory as the eternal Son of God. Sitting is a resting posture: after services and sufferings, to give law, to give judgment. It is a remaining posture: he sits like a king for ever. All his enemies are now in a chain, but not yet made his footstool. And his kingdom, being set up, shall be kept up in the world, in despite of all the powers of darkness. Christ's people are a willing people. The power of the Spirit, going with the power of the world, to the people of Christ, is effectual to make them willing. They shall attend him in the beautiful attire of holiness; which becomes his house for ever. And he shall have many devoted to him. The dew of our youth, even in the morning of our days, ought to be consecrated to our Lord Jesus. Christ shall not only be a King, but a Priest. He is God's Minister to us, and our Advocate with the Father, and so is the Mediator between God and man. He is a Priest of the order of Melchizedek, which was before that of Aaron, and on many accounts superior to it, and a more lively representation of Christ's priesthood. Christ's sitting at the right hand of God, speaks as much terror to his enemies as happiness to his people. The effect of this victory shall be the utter ruin of his enemies. We have here the Redeemer saving his friends, and comforting them. He shall be humbled; he shall drink of the brook in the way. The wrath of God, running in the curse of the law, may be considered as the brook in the way of his undertaking. Christ drank of the waters of affliction in his way to the throne of glory. But he shall be exalted. What then are we? Has the gospel of Christ been to us the power of God unto salvation? Has his kingdom been set up in our hearts? Are we his willing subjects? Once we knew not our need of his salvation, and we were not willing that he should reign over us. Are we willing to give up every sin, to turn from a wicked, insnaring world, and rely only on his merits and mercy, to have him for our Prophet, Priest, and King? and do we desire to be holy? To those who are thus changed, the Saviour's sacrifice, intercession, and blessing belong.

Psalm 111

The Lord is to be praised for his works (1–10)

The psalmist resolves to praise God himself. Our exhortations and our examples should agree together. He recommends the works of the Lord, as the proper subject, when we are praising him; and the dealings of his providence toward the world, the church, and particular persons. All the works of the Lord are spoken of as one, it is his work; so admirably do all the dispensations of his providence centre in one design. The works of God, humbly and diligently sought into, shall all be found just and holy. God's pardoning sin is the most wonderful of all his works, and ought to be remembered to his glory. He will ever be mindful of his covenant; he has ever been so, and he ever will be so. His works of providence were done according to the truth of the Divine promises and prophecies, and so were verity, or truth; and by him who has a right to dispose of the earth as he pleases, and so are judgment, or righteous: and this holds good God's commandments are sure; all have been fulfilled by Christ, and remain with him for a rule for us to walk by. He sent redemption unto his people, out of Egypt at first, and often afterwards; and these were typical of the great

redemption, which in the fulness of time was to be wrought out by the Lord Jesus. Here his everlasting righteousness shines forth in union with his boundless mercy. No man is wise who does not fear the Lord; no man acts wisely except as influenced by that fear. This fear will lead to repentance, to faith in Christ, to watchfulness and obedience. Such persons are of a good understanding, however poor, unlearned, or despised.

Psalm 112

The blessedness of the righteous (1–10)

We have to praise the Lord that there are a people in the world, who fear him and serve him, and that they are a happy people; which is owing entirely to his grace. Their fear is not that which love casts out, but that which love brings in. It follows and flows from love. It is a fear to offend. This is both fear and trust. The heart touched by the Spirit of God, as the needle touched with the loadstone, turns direct and speedily to God, yet still with trembling, being filled with this holy fear. Blessings are laid up for the faithful and their children's children; and true riches are bestowed on them, with as much of this world's possessions as is profitable for them. In the darkest hours of affliction and trial, the light of hope and peace will spring up within them, and seasonable relief shall turn mourning into joy. From their Lord's example they learn to be kind and full of compassion, as well as just in all their dealings; they use discretion, that they may be liberal in that manner which appears most likely to do good. Envy and slander may for a time hide their true characters here, but they shall be had in everlasting remembrance. They need not fear evil tidings. A good man shall have a settled spirit. And it is the endeavour of true believers to keep their minds stayed upon God, and so to keep them calm and undisturbed; and God has promised them both cause to do so, and grace to do so. Trusting in the Lord is the best and surest way of establishing the heart. The heart of man cannot fix any where with satisfaction, but in the truth of God, and there it finds firm footing. And those whose hearts are established by faith, will patiently wait till they gain their point. Compare all this with the vexation of sinners. The happiness of the saints is the envy of the wicked. The desire of the wicked shall perish; their desire was wholly to the world and the flesh, therefore when these perish, their joy is gone. But the blessings of the gospel are spiritual and eternal, and are conferred upon the members of the Christian church, through Christ their Head, who is the Pattern of all righteousness, and the Giver of all grace.

Psalm 113

An exhortation to praise God (1–9)

God has praise from his own people. They have most reason to praise him; for those who attend him as his servants, know him best, and receive most of his favours, and it is easy, pleasant work to speak well of their Master. God's name ought to be praised in every place, from east to west. Within this wide space the Lord's name is to be praised; it ought to be so, though it is not. Ere long it will be, when all nations shall come and worship before him. God is exalted above all blessing and praise. We must therefore say, with holy admiration, Who is like unto the Lord our God? How condescending in him to behold the things in the earth! And what amazing condescension was it for the Son of God to come from heaven to earth, and take our nature upon him, that he might seek and save those that were lost! How vast his love in taking upon him the nature of man, to ransom guilty souls! God sometimes makes glorious his own wisdom and power, when, having some great work to do, he employs those least likely, and least thought of for it by themselves or others. The apostles were sent from fishing to be fishers of men. And this is God's constant method in his kingdom of grace. He takes men, by nature beggars, and even traitors, to be his favourites, his children, kings and priests unto him; and numbers them with the princes of his chosen people. He gives us all our comforts, which are generally the more welcome when long delayed, and no longer expected. Let us pray that those lands which are yet barren, may speedily become fruitful, and produce many converts to join in praising the Lord.

Psalm 114

An exhortation to fear God (1–8)

Let us acknowledge God's power and goodness in what he did for Israel, applying it to that much greater work of wonder, our redemption by Christ; and encourage ourselves and others to trust in God in the greatest straits. When Christ comes for the salvation of his people, he redeems them from the power of sin and Satan, separates them from an ungodly world, forms them to be his people, and becomes their King. There is no sea, no Jordan, so deep, so broad, but, when God's time is come, it shall be divided and driven back. Apply this to the planting of the Christian church in the world. What ailed Satan and his idolatries, that they trembled as they did? But especially apply it to the work of grace in the heart. What turns the stream in a regenerate soul? What affects the lusts and corruptions, that they fly back; that prejudices are

removed, and the whole man becomes new? It is at the presence of God's Spirit. At the presence of the Lord, not only mountains, but the earth itself may well tremble, since it has lain under a curse for man's sin. As the Israelites were protected, so they were provided for by miracles; such was that fountain of waters into which the flinty rock was turned, and that rock was Christ. The Son of God, the Rock of ages, gave himself to death, to open a fountain to wash away sins, and to supply believers with waters of life and consolation; and they need not fear that any blessing is too great to expect from his love. But let sinners fear before their just and holy Judge. Let us now prepare to meet our God, that we may have boldness before him at his coming.

Psalm 115

Glory to be ascribed to God (1–8)
Trusting in God and praising him (9–18)

Glory to be ascribed to God (1–8)

Let no opinion of our own merits have any place in our prayers or in our praises. All the good we do, is done by the power of his grace; and all the good we have, is the gift of his mere mercy, and he must have all the praise. Are we in pursuit of any mercy, and wrestling with God for it, we must take encouragement in prayer from God only. Lord, do so for us; not that we may have the credit and comfort of it, but that thy mercy and truth may have the glory of it. The heathen gods are senseless things. They are the works of men's hands: the painter, the carver, the statuary, can put no life into them, therefore no sense. The psalmist hence shows the folly of the worshippers of idols.

Trusting in God and praising him (9–18)

It is folly to trust in dead images, but it is wisdom to trust in the living God, for he is a help and a shield to those that trust in him. Wherever there is right fear of God, there may be cheerful faith in him; those who reverence his word, may rely upon it. He is ever found faithful. The greatest need his blessing, and it shall not be denied to the meanest that fear him. God's blessing gives an increase, especially in spiritual blessings. And the Lord is to be praised: his goodness is large, for he has given the earth to the children of men for their use. The souls of the faithful, after they are delivered from the burdens of the flesh, are still praising him; but the dead body cannot praise God: death puts an end to our glorifying him in this world of trial and conflict. Others are dead, and an end is thereby put to their service, therefore we will seek to do the more for God. We will not only do it ourselves, but will engage others to do it; to praise him when we are gone. Lord, thou art the only object for faith and love. Help us to praise thee while living and when dying, that thy name may be the first and last upon our lips: and let the sweet savour of thy name refresh our souls for ever.

Psalm 116

The psalmist declares his love to the Lord (1–9)

His desire to be thankful (10–19)

The psalmist declares his love to the Lord (1–9)

We have many reasons for loving the Lord, but are most affected by his loving-kindness when relieved out of deep distress. When a poor sinner is awakened to a sense of his state, and fears that he must soon sink under the just wrath of God, then he finds trouble and sorrow. But let all such call upon the Lord to deliver their souls, and they will find him gracious and true to his promise. Neither ignorance nor guilt will hinder their salvation, when they put their trust in the Lord. Let us all speak of God as we have found him; and have we ever found him otherwise than just and good? It is of his mercies that we are not consumed. Let those who labour and are heavy laden come to him, that they may find rest to their souls; and if at all drawn from their rest, let them haste to return, remembering how bountifully the Lord has dealt with them. We should deem ourselves bound to walk as in his presence. It is a great mercy to be kept from being swallowed up with overmuch sorrow. It is a great mercy for God to hold us by the right hand, so that we are not overcome and overthrown by a temptation. But when we enter the heavenly rest, deliverance from sin and sorrow will be complete; we shall behold the glory of the Lord, and walk in his presence with delight we cannot now conceive.

His desire to be thankful (10–19)

When troubled, we do best to hold our peace, for we are apt to speak unadvisedly. Yet there may be true faith where there are workings of unbelief; but then faith will prevail, and being humbled for our distrust of God's word, we shall experience his faithfulness to it. What can the pardoned sinner, or what can those who have been delivered from trouble or distress, render to the Lord for his benefits? We cannot in any way profit him. Our best is unworthy of his acceptance; yet we ought to devote ourselves and all we have to his service. I will take the cup of salvation; I will offer the drink-offerings appointed by the law, in token of thankfulness

to God, and rejoice in God's goodness to me. I will receive the cup of affliction; that cup, that bitter cup, which is sanctified to the saints, so that to them it is a cup of salvation; it is a means of spiritual health. The cup of consolation; I will receive the benefits God bestows upon me, as from his hand, and taste his love in them, as the portion not only of mine inheritance in the other world, but of my cup in this. Let others serve what masters they will, truly I am thy servant. Two ways men came to be servants. By birth. Lord, I was born in thy house; I am the son of thine handmaid, and therefore thine. It is a great mercy to be children of godly parents. By redemption, Lord, thou hast loosed my bonds, thou hast discharged me from them, therefore I am thy servant. The bonds thou hast loosed shall tie me faster unto thee. Doing good is sacrifice, with which God is well pleased; and this must accompany giving thanks to his name. Why should we offer that to the Lord which cost us nothing? The psalmist will pay his vows now; he will not delay the payment: publicly, not to make a boast, but to show he is not ashamed of God's service, and to invite others to join him. Such are true saints of God, in whose lives and deaths he will be glorified.

Psalm 117

All people called upon to praise God (1–2)

Here is a solemn call to all nations to praise the Lord, and proper matter for that praise is suggested. We are soon weary of well-doing, if we keep not up the pious and devout affections with which the spiritual sacrifice of praise ought to be kindled and kept burning. This is a gospel psalm. The apostle, Ro 15:11, quotes it as a proof that the gospel was to be preached to the Gentile nations, and that it would be entertained by them. For many ages, in Judah only was God known, and his name praised; this call was not then given to any Gentiles. But the gospel of Christ is ordered to be preached to all nations, and by him those that were afar off are made nigh. We are among the persons to whom the Holy Spirit here speaks, whom he calls upon to join his ancient people in praising the Lord. Grace has thus abounded to millions of perishing sinners. Let us then listen to the offers of the grace of God, and pray for that time when all nations of the earth shall show forth his praises. And let us bless God for the unsearchable riches of gospel grace.

Psalm 118

It is good to trust in the Lord (1–18)

The coming of Christ in his kingdom (19–29)

It is good to trust in the Lord (1–18)

The account the psalmist here gives of his troubles is very applicable to Christ: many hated him without a cause; nay, the Lord himself chastened him sorely, bruised him, and put him to grief, that by his stripes we might be healed. God is sometimes the strength of his people, when he is not their song; they have spiritual supports, though they want spiritual delights. Whether the believer traces back his comfort to the everlasting goodness and mercy of God, or whether he looks forward to the blessing secured to him, he will find abundant cause for joy and praise. Every answer to our prayers is an evidence that the Lord is on our side; and then we need not fear what man can do unto us; we should conscientiously do our duty to all, and trust in him alone to accept and bless us. Let us seek to live to declare the works of God, and to encourage others to serve him and trust in him. Such were the triumphs of the Son of David, in the assurance that the good pleasure of the Lord should prosper in his hand.

The coming of Christ in his kingdom (19–29)

Those who saw Christ's day at so great a distance, saw cause to praise God for the prospect. The prophecy, ver. 22, refers to Christ. 1. His humiliation; he is the Stone which the builders refused: they would go on in their building without him. This proved the ruin of those who thus made light of him. Rejecters of Christ are rejected of God. 2. His exaltation; he is the chief Cornerstone in the foundation. He is the chief Top-stone, in whom the building is completed, who must, in all things, have the pre-eminence. Christ's name is Wonderful; and the redemption he wrought out is the most amazing of all God's wondrous works. We will rejoice and be glad in the Lord's day; not only that such a day is appointed, but in the occasion of it, Christ's becoming the Head. Sabbath days ought to be rejoicing days, then they are to us as the days of heaven. Let this Saviour be my Saviour, my Ruler. Let my soul prosper and be in health, in that peace and righteousness which his government brings. Let me have victory over the lusts that war against my soul; and let Divine grace subdue my heart. The duty which the Lord has made, brings light with it, true light. The duty this privilege calls for, is here set forth; the sacrifices we are to offer to God in gratitude for redeeming love, are ourselves; not to be slain upon the altar, but living sacrifices, to be bound to the altar; spiritual sacrifices of prayer and praise, in which our hearts must be engaged. The psalmist praises God, and calls upon all about him to give thanks to God for the glad tidings of great joy to all people, that there is a Redeemer, even Christ the Lord. In him the covenant of grace is made sure and everlasting.

Psalm 119

The general scope and design of this psalm is to magnify the Divine law, and make it honourable. There are ten words by which Divine revelation is called in this psalm, and each expresses what God expects from us, and what we may expect from him.

1. God's law; this is enacted by him as our Sovereign.

2. His way; this is the rule of his providence.

3. His testimonies; they are solemnly declared to the world.

4. His commandments; given with authority.

5. His precepts; not left as indifferent matters to us.

6. His word, or saying; it is the declaration of his mind.

7. His judgments; framed in infinite wisdom.

8. His righteousness; it is the rule and standard of what is right.

9. His statutes; they are always binding.

10. His truth or faithfulness; it is eternal truth, it shall endure for ever.

(1–8)

This psalm may be considered as the statement of a believer's experience. As far as our views, desires, and affections agree with what is here expressed, they come from the influences of the Holy Spirit, and no further. The pardoning mercy of God in Christ, is the only source of a sinner's happiness. And those are most happy, who are preserved most free from the defilement of sin, who simply believe God's testimonies, and depend on his promises. If the heart be divided between him and the world, it is evil. But the saints carefully avoid all sin; they are conscious of much evil that clogs them in the ways of God, but not of that wickedness which draws them out of those ways. The tempter would make men think they are at them out of those ways. The tempter would make men think they are at liberty to follow the word of God or not, as they please. But the desire and prayer of a good man agree with the will and command of God. If a man expects by obedience in one thing to purchase indulgence for disobedience in others, his hypocrisy will be detected; if he is not ashamed in this world, everlasting shame will be his portion. The psalmist coveted to learn the laws of God, to give God the glory. And believers see that if God forsakes them, the temper will be too hard for them.

(9–16)

To original corruption all have added actual sin. The ruin of the young is either living by no rule at all, or choosing false rules: let them walk by Scripture rules. To doubt of our own wisdom and strength, and to depend upon God, proves the purpose of holiness is sincere. God's word is treasure worth laying up, and there is no laying it up safe but in our hearts, that we may oppose God's precepts to the dominion of sin, his promises to its allurements, and his threatenings to its violence. Let this be our plea with Him to teach us his statutes, that, being partakers of his holiness, we may also partake of his blessedness. And those whose hearts are fed with the bread of life, should with their lips feed many. In the way of God's commandments there is the unsearchable riches of Christ. But we do not meditate on God's precepts to good purpose, unless our good thoughts produce good works. I will not only think of thy statutes, but do them with delight. And it will be well to try the sincerity of our obedience by tracing the spring of it; the reality of our love by cheerfulness in appointed duties.

(17–24)

If God deals in strict justice with us, we all perish. We ought to spend our lives in his service; we shall find true life in keeping his word. Those that would see the wondrous things of God's law and gospel, must beg him to give them understanding, by the light of his Spirit. Believers feel themselves strangers on earth; they fear missing their way, and losing comfort by erring from God's commandments. Every sanctified soul hungers after the word of God, as food which there is no living without. There is something of pride at the bottom of every wilful sin. God can silence lying lips; reproach and contempt may humble and do us good, and then they shall be removed. Do we find the weight of the cross is above that we are able to bear? He that bore it for us will enable us to bear it; upheld by him we cannot sink. It is sad when those who should protect the innocent, are their betrayers. The psalmist went on in duty, and he found comfort in the word of God. The comforts of the word of God are most pleasant to a gracious soul, when other comforts are made bitter; and those that would have God's testimonies to be their delight, must be advised by them. May the Lord direct us in exercising repentance of sin, and faith in Christ.

(25–32)

While the souls of the children of this world cleave to the earth as their portion, the children of light are greatly burdened, because of the remains of carnal affections in their hearts. It is unspeakable comfort to a gracious soul, to think with what tenderness all its complaints are received by a gracious God. We can talk of the wonders of redeeming love, when we understand the way of God's precepts, and walk in that way. The penitent melts in sorrow for sin: even the patient spirit may melt in the sense of affliction, it is then its interest to pour out its soul before God. The way of lying means all false ways by which men deceive themselves and others, or are deceived by Satan and his instruments. Those who know and love the law of the Lord, desire to know it more, and love it better. The way of serious godliness is the way of truth; the only true way to happiness: we must always have actual regard to it. Those who stick to the word of God, may in faith expect and pray for acceptance with God. Lord, never leave me to do that by which I shall shame myself, and do not thou reject my services. Those that are going to heaven, should still press forward. God, by his Spirit, enlarges the hearts of his people when he gives them wisdom. The believer prays to be set free from sin.

(33–40)

Teach me thy statutes, not the mere words, but the way of applying them to myself. God, by his Spirit, gives a right understanding. But the Spirit of revelation in the word will not suffice, unless we have the Spirit of wisdom in the heart. God puts his Spirit within us, causing us to walk in his statutes. The sin here prayed against is covetousness. Those that would have the love of God rooted in them, must get the love of the world rooted out; for the friendship of the world is enmity with God. Quicken me in thy way; to redeem time, and to do every duty with liveliness of spirit. Beholding vanity deadens us, and slackens our pace; a traveller must not stand gazing upon every object that presents itself to his view. The promises of God's word greatly relate to the preservation of the true believer. When Satan has drawn a child of God into worldly compliances, he will reproach him with the falls into which he led him. Victory must come from the cross of Christ. When we enjoy the sweetness of God's precepts, it will make us long for more acquaintance with them. And where God has wrought to will, he will work to do.

(41–48)

Lord, I have by faith thy mercies in view; let me by prayer prevail to obtain them. And when the salvation of the saints is completed, it will plainly appear that it was not in vain to trust in God's word. We need to pray that we may never be afraid or ashamed to own God's truths and ways before men. And the psalmist resolves to keep

God's law, in a constant course of obedience, without backsliding. The service of sin is slavery; the service of God is liberty. There is no full happiness, or perfect liberty, but in keeping God's law. We must never be ashamed or afraid to own our religion. The more delight we take in the service of God, the nearer we come to perfection. Not only consent to his law as good, but take pleasure in it as good for us. Let me put forth all the strength I have, to do it. Something of this mind of Christ is in every true disciple.

(49–56)

Those that make God's promises their portion, may with humble boldness make them their plea. He that by his Spirit works faith in us, will work for us. The word of God speaks comfort in affliction. If, through grace, it makes us holy, there is enough in it to make us easy, in all conditions. Let us be certain we have the Divine law for what we believe, and then let not scoffers prevail upon us to decline from it. God's judgments of old comfort and encourage us, for he is still the same. Sin is horrible in the eyes of all that are sanctified. Ere long the believer will be absent from the body, and present with the Lord. In the mean time, the statutes of the Lord supply subjects for grateful praise. In the season of affliction, and in the silent hours of the night, he remembers the name of the Lord, and is stirred up to keep the law. All who have made religion the first thing, will own that they have been unspeakable gainers by it.

(57–64)

True believers take the Lord for the portion of their inheritance, and nothing less will satisfy them. The psalmist prayed with his whole heart, knowing how to value the blessing he prayed for: he desired the mercy promised, and depended on the promise for it. He turned from bypaths, and returned to God's testimonies. He delayed not. It behoves sinners to hasten to escape; and the believer will be equally in haste to glorify God. No care or grief should take away God's word out of our minds, or hinder the comfort it bestows. There is no situation on earth in which a believer has not cause to be thankful. Let us feel ashamed that others are more willing to keep from sleep to spend the time in sinful pleasures, than we are to praise God. And we should be more earnest in prayer, that our hearts may be filled with his mercy, grace, and peace.

(65–72)

However God has dealt with us, he has dealt with us better than we deserve; and all in love, and for our good. Many have knowledge, but little judgment; those who have both, are fortified against the snares of Satan, and furnished for the service of God. We are most apt to wander from God, when we are easy in the world. We should leave our concerns to the disposal of God, seeing we know not what is good for us. Lord, thou art our bountiful Benefactor; incline our hearts to faith and obedience. The psalmist will go on in his duty with constancy and resolution. The proud are full of the world, and its wealth and pleasures; these make them senseless, secure, and stupid. God visits his people with affliction, that they may learn his statutes. Not only God's promises, but even his law, his precepts, though hard to ungodly men, are desirable, and profitable, because they lead us with safety and delight unto eternal life.

(73–80)

God made us to serve him, and enjoy him; but by sin we have made ourselves unfit to serve him, and to enjoy him. We ought, therefore, continually to beseech him, by his Holy Spirit, to give us understanding. The comforts some have in God, should be matter of joy to others. But it is easy to own, that God's judgments are right, until it comes to be our own case. All supports under affliction must come from mercy and compassion. The mercies of God are tender mercies; the mercies of a father, the compassion of a mother to her son. They come to us when we are not able to go to them. Causeless reproach does not hurt, and should not move us. The psalmist could go on in the way of his duty, and find comfort in it. He valued the good will of saints, and was desirous to keep up his communion with them. Soundness of heart signifies sincerity in dependence on God, and devotedness to him.

(81–88)

The psalmist sought deliverance from his sins, his foes, and his fears. Hope deferred made him faint; his eyes failed by looking out for this expected salvation. But when the eyes fail, yet faith must not. His affliction was great. He was become like a leathern bottle, which, if hung up in the smoke, is dried and shrivelled up. We must ever be mindful of God's statutes. The days of the believer's mourning shall be ended; they are but for a moment, compared with eternal happiness. His enemies used craft as well as power for his ruin, in contempt of the law of God. The commandments of God are true and faithful guides in the path of peace and safety. We may best expect help from God when, like our Master, we do well and suffer for it. Wicked men may almost consume the believer upon earth, but he would sooner forsake all than forsake the word of the Lord. We should depend upon the grace of God for strength to do every good work. The surest token of God's good-will toward us, is his good work in us.

(89–96)

The settling of God's word in heaven, is opposed to the changes and revolutions of the earth. And the engagements of God's covenant are established more firmly than the earth itself. All the creatures answer the ends of their creation: shall man, who alone is endued with reason, be the only unprofitable burden of the earth? We may make the Bible a pleasant companion at any time. But the word, without the grace of God, would not quicken us. See the best help for bad memories, namely, good affections; and though the exact words be lost, if the meaning remain, that is well. I am thine, not my own, not the world's; save me from sin, save me from ruin. The Lord will keep the man in peace, whose mind is stayed on him. It is poor perfection which one sees an end of. Such are all things in this world, which pass for perfections. The glory of man is but as the flower of the grass. The psalmist had seen the fulness of the word of God, and its sufficiency. The word of the Lord reaches to all cases, to all times. It will take us from all confidence in man, or in our own wisdom, strength, and righteousness. Thus shall we seek comfort and happiness from Christ alone.

(97–104)

What we love, we love to think of. All true wisdom is from God. A good man carries his Bible with him, if not in his hands, yet in his head and in his heart. By meditation on God's testimonies we understand more than our teachers, when we understand our own hearts. The written word is a more sure guide to heaven, than all the fathers, the teachers, and ancients of the church. We cannot, with any comfort or boldness, attend God in holy duties, while under guilt, or in any by-way. It was Divine grace in his heart, that enabled the psalmist to receive these instructions. The soul has its tastes as well as the body. Our relish for the word of God will be greatest, when that for the world and the flesh is least. The way of sin is a wrong way; and the more understanding we get by the precepts of God, the more rooted will be our hatred of sin; and the more ready we are in the Scriptures, the better furnished we are with answers to temptation.

(105–112)

The word of God directs us in our work and way, and a dark place indeed the world would be without it. The commandment is a lamp kept burning with the oil of the Spirit, as a light to direct us in the choice of our way, and the steps we take in that way. The keeping of God's com-

mands here meant, was that of a sinner under a dispensation of mercy, of a believer having part in the covenant of grace. The psalmist is often afflicted; but with longing desires to become more holy, offers up daily prayers for quickening grace. We cannot offer any thing to God, that he will accept but what he is pleased to teach us to do. To have our soul or life continually in our hands, implies constant danger of life; yet he did not forget God's promises nor his precepts. Numberless are the snares laid by the wicked; and happy is that servant of God, whom they have not caused to err from his Master's precepts. Heavenly treasures are a heritage for ever; all the saints accept them as such, therefore they can be content with little of this world. We must look for comfort only in the way of duty, and that duty must be done. A good man, by the grace of God, brings his heart to his work, then it is done well.

(113–120)

Here is a dread of the risings of sin, and the first beginnings of it. The more we love the law of God, the more watchful we shall be, lest vain thoughts draw us from what we love. Would we make progress in keeping God's commands, we must be separate from evil-doers. The believer could not live without the grace of God; but, supported by his hand, his spiritual life shall be maintained. Our holy security is grounded on Divine supports. All departure from God's statutes is error, and will prove fatal. Their cunning is falsehood. There is a day coming which will put the wicked into everlasting fire, the fit place for the dross. See what comes of sin. Surely we who fall so low in devout affections, should fear, lest a promise being left us of entering into heavenly rest, any of us should be found to come short of it, Hebrews 4:1.

(121–128)

Happy is the man, who, acting upon gospel principles, does justice to all around. Christ our Surety, having paid our debt and ransom, secures all the blessings of salvation to every true believer. The psalmist expects the word of God's righteousness, and no other salvation than what is secured by that word, which cannot fall to the ground. We deserve no favour from God; we are most easy when we cast ourselves upon God's mercy, and refer ourselves to it. If any man resolve to do God's will as his servant, he shall be made to know his testimonies. We must do what we can for the support of religion, and, after all, must beg of God to take the work into his own hands. It is hypocrisy to say we love God's commandments more than our worldly interests. The way of sin is a false way, being directly contrary to God's precepts, which are right: those that love and esteem God's law, hate sin, and will not be reconciled to it.

(129–136)

The wonders of redeeming love will fix the heart in adoration of them. The Scriptures show us what we were, what we are, and what we shall be. They show us the mercy and the justice of the Lord, the joys of heaven, and the pains of hell. Thus they give to the simple, in a few days, understanding of those matters, which philosophers for ages sought in vain. The believer, wearied with the cares of life and his conflicts with sin, pants for the consolations conveyed to him by means of the sacred word. And every one may pray, Look thou upon me, and be merciful unto me as thou usest to do unto those that love thy name. We must beg that the Holy Spirit would order our steps. The dominion of sin is to be dreaded and prayed against by every one. The oppression of men is often more than flesh and blood can bear; and He who knoweth our frame, will not refuse to remove it in answer to the prayers of his people. Whatever obscurity may appear as to the faith of the Old Testament believers, their confidence at the throne of grace can only be explained by their having obtained more distinct views of gospel privileges, through the sacrifices and services of their law, than is generally imagined. Go to the same place, plead the name and merits of Jesus, and you will not, you cannot plead in vain. Commonly, where there is a gracious heart, there is a weeping eye. Accept, O Lord, the tears our blessed Redeemer shed in the days of his flesh, for us who should weep for our brethren or ourselves.

(137–144)

God never did, and never can do wrong to any. The promises are faithfully performed by Him that made them. Zeal against sin should constrain us to do what we can against it, at least to do more in religion ourselves. Our love to the word of God is evidence of our love to God, because it is designed to make us partake his holiness. Men's real excellency always makes them low in their own eyes. When we are small and despised, we have the more need to remember God's precepts, that we may have them to support us. The law of God is the truth, the standard of holiness, the rule of happiness; but the obedience of Christ alone justifies the believer. Sorrows are often the lot of saints in this vale of tears; they are in heaviness through manifold temptations. There are delights in the word of God, which the saints often most sweetly enjoy when in trouble and anguish. This is life eternal, to know God and Jesus Christ whom he has sent, John 17:3. May we live the life of faith

and grace here, and be removed to the life of glory hereafter.

(145–152)

Supplications with the whole heart are presented only by those who desire God's salvation, and who love his commandments. Whither should the child go but to his father? Save me from my sins, my corruptions, my temptations, all the hinderances in my way, that I may keep thy testimonies. Christians who enjoy health, should not suffer the early hours of the morning to glide away unimproved. Hope in God's word encourages us to continue in prayer. It is better to take time from sleep, than not to find time for prayer. We have access to God at all hours; and if our first thoughts in the morning are of God, they will help to keep us in his fear all the day long. Make me lively and cheerful. God knows what we need and what is good for us, and will quicken us. If we are employed in God's service, we need not fear those who try to set themselves as far as they can out of the reach of the convictions and commands of his law. When trouble is near, God is near. He is never far to seek. All his commandments are truth. And God's promises will be performed. All that ever trusted in God have found him faithful.

(153–160)

The closer we cleave to the word of God, both as our rule and as our stay, the more assurance we have of deliverance. Christ is the Advocate of his people, their Redeemer. Those who were quickened by his Spirit and grace, when they were dead in trespasses and sins, often need to have the work of grace revived in them, according to the word of promise. The wicked not only do not God's statutes, but they do not even seek them. They flatter themselves that they are going to heaven; but the longer they persist in sin, the further it is from them. God's mercies are tender; they are a fountain that can never be exhausted. The psalmist begs for God's reviving, quickening grace. A man, steady in the way of his duty, though he may have many enemies, needs to fear none. Those that hate sin truly, hate it as sin, as a transgression of the law of God, and a breaking of his word. Our obedience is only pleasing to God, and pleasant to ourselves, when it comes from a principle of love. All, in every age, who receive God's word in faith and love, find every saying in it faithful.

(161–168)

Those whose hearts stand in awe of God's word, will rather endure the wrath of man, than break the law of God. By the word of God we are unspeakable gainers. Every man hates to have a lie told him, but we should more hate telling a lie; by the latter we give an affront to God. The more we see the beauty of truth, the more we shall see the hateful deformity of a lie. We are to praise God even for afflictions; through grace we get good from them. Those that love the world have great vexation, for it does not answer what they expect; those that love God's word have great peace, for it outdoes what they expect. Those in whom this holy love reigns, will not perplex themselves with needless scruples, or take offence at their brethren. A good hope of salvation will engage the heart in doing the commandments. And our love to the word of God must subdue our lusts, and root out carnal affections: we must make heart work of it, or we make nothing of it. We must keep the commandments of God by obedience to them, and his promises by reliance on them. God's eye is on us at all times; this should make us very careful to keep his commandments.

(169–176)

The psalmist desired grace and strength to lift up his prayers, and that the Lord would receive and notice them. He desired to know more of God in Christ; to know more of the doctrines of the word, and the duties of religion. He had a deep sense of unworthiness, and holy fear that his prayer should not come before God; Lord, what I pray for is, what thou hast promised. We have learned nothing to purpose, if we have not learned to praise God. We should always make the word of God the rule of our discourse, so as never to transgress it by sinful speaking, or sinful silence. His own hands are not sufficient, nor can any creature lend him help; therefore he looks up to God, that the hand that had made him may help him. He had made religion his deliberate choice. There is an eternal salvation all the saints long for, and therefore they pray that God would help their way to it. Let thy judgments help me; let all ordinances and all providences, (both are God's judgments,) further me in glorifying God; let them help me for that work. He often looks back with shame and gratitude to his lost estate. He still prays for the tender care of Him who purchased his flock with his own blood, that he may receive from him the gift of eternal life. Seek me, that is, Find me; for God never seeks in vain. Turn me, and I shall be turned. Let this psalm be a touchstone by which to try our hearts, and our lives. Do our hearts, cleansed in Christ's blood, make these prayers, resolutions and confessions our own? Is God's word the standard of our faith, and the law of our practice? Do we use it as pleas with Christ for what we need? Happy those who live in such delightful exercises.

Psalm 120

The psalmist prays to God to deliver him from false and malicious tongues (1–4)
He complains of wicked neighbours (5–7)

The psalmist prays to God to deliver him from false and malicious tongues (1–4)

The psalmist was brought into great distress by a deceitful tongue. May every good man be delivered from lying lips. They forged false charges against him. In this distress, he sought God by fervent prayer. God can bridle their tongues. He obtained a gracious answer to this prayer. Surely sinners durst not act as they do, if they knew, and would be persuaded to think, what will be in the end thereof. The terrors of the Lord are his arrows; and his wrath is compared to burning coals of juniper, which have a fierce heat, and keep fire very long. This is the portion of the false tongue; for all that love and make a lie, shall have their portion in the lake that burns eternally.

He complains of wicked neighbours (5–7)

It is very grievous to a good man, to be cast into, and kept in the company of the wicked, from whom he hopes to be for ever separated. See here the character of a good man; he is for living peaceably with all men. And let us follow David as he prefigured Christ; in our distress let us cry unto the Lord, and he will hear us. Let us follow after peace and holiness, striving to overcome evil with good.

Psalm 121

The safety of the godly (1–8)

We must not rely upon men and means, instruments and second causes. Shall I depend upon the strength of the hills? upon princes and great men? No; my confidence is in God only. Or, we must lift up our eyes above the hills; we must look to God who makes all earthly things to us what they are. We must see all our help in God; from him we must expect it, in his own way and time. This psalm teaches us to comfort ourselves in the Lord, when difficulties and dangers are greatest. It is almighty wisdom that contrives, and almighty power that works the safety of those that put themselves under God's protection. He is a wakeful, watchful Keeper; he is never weary; he not only does not sleep, but he does not so much as slumber. Under this shade they may sit with delight and assurance. He is always near his people for their protection and refreshment. The right hand is the working hand; let them but turn to their duty, and they shall find

God ready to give them success. He will take care that his people shall not fall. Thou shalt not be hurt, neither by the open assaults, nor by the secret attempts of thine enemies. The Lord shall prevent the evil thou fearest, and sanctify, remove, or lighten the evil thou feelest. He will preserve the soul, that it be not defiled by sin, and disturbed by affliction; he will preserve it from perishing eternally. He will keep thee in life and death; going out to thy labour in the morning of thy days, and coming home to thy rest when the evening of old age calls thee in. It is a protection for life. The Spirit, who is their Preserver and Comforter, shall abide with them for ever. Let us be found in our work, assured that the blessings promised in this psalm are ours.

Psalm 122

Esteem for Jerusalem (1–5)

Concern for its welfare (6–9)

Esteem for Jerusalem (1–5)

The pleasure and profit from means of grace, should make us disregard trouble and fatigue in going to them; and we should quicken one another to what is good. We should desire our Christian friends, when they have any good work in hand, to call for us, and take us with them. With what readiness should we think of the heavenly Jerusalem! How cheerfully should we bear the cross and welcome death, in hopes of a crown of glory! Jerusalem is called the beautiful city. It was a type of the gospel church, which is compact together in holy love and Christian communion, so that it is all as one city. If all the disciples of Christ were of one mind, and kept the unity of the Spirit in the bond of peace, their enemies would be deprived of their chief advantages against them. But Satan's maxim always has been, to divide that he may conquer; and few Christians are sufficiently aware of his designs.

Concern for its welfare (6–9)

Those who can do nothing else for the peace of Jerusalem, may pray for it. Let us consider all who seek the glory of the Redeemer, as our brethren and fellow-travellers, without regarding differences which do not affect our eternal welfare. Blessed Spirit of peace and love, who didst dwell in the soul of the holy Jesus, descend into his church, and fill those who compose it with his heavenly tempers; cause bitter contentions to cease, and make us to be of one mind. Love of the brethren and love to God, ought to stir us up to seek to be like the Lord Jesus in fervent prayer and unwearied labour, for the salvation of men, and the Divine glory.

Psalm 123

Confidence in God under contempt (1–4)

Our Lord Jesus has taught us to look unto God in prayer as our Father in heaven. In every prayer a good man lifts up his soul to God; especially when in trouble. We desire mercy from him; we hope he will show us mercy, and we will continue waiting on him till it come. The eyes of a servant are to his master's directing hand, expecting that he will appoint him his work. And also to his supplying hand. Servants look to their master or their mistress for their portion of meat in due season. And to God we must look for daily bread, for grace sufficient; from him we must receive it thankfully. Where can we look for help but to our Master? And, further, to his protecting hand. If the servant is wronged and injured in his work, who should right him, but his master? And to his correcting hand. Whither should sinners turn but to him that smote them? They humble themselves under God's mighty hand. And lastly, to his rewarding hand. Hypocrites look to the world's hand, thence they have their reward; but true Christians look to God as their Master and their Rewarder. God's people find little mercy with men; but this is their comfort, that with the Lord there is mercy. Scorning and contempt have been, are, and are likely to be, the lot of God's people in this world. It is hard to bear; but the servants of God should not complain if they are treated as his beloved Son was. Let us then, when ready to faint under trials, look unto Jesus, and by faith and prayer cast ourselves upon the mercy of God.

Psalm 124

The deliverance of the church (1–5)

Thankfulness for the deliverance (6–8)

The deliverance of the church (1–5)

God suffers the enemies of his people sometimes to prevail very far against them, that his power may be seen the more in their deliverance. Happy the people whose God is Jehovah, a God all-sufficient. Besides applying this to any particular deliverance wrought in our days and the ancient times, we should have in our thoughts the great work of redemption by Jesus Christ, by which believers were rescued from Satan.

Thankfulness for the deliverance (6–8)

God is the Author of all our deliverances, and he must have the glory. The enemies lay snares for God's people, to bring them into sin and trouble, and to hold them there. Sometimes they seem to prevail; but in the Lord let us put our trust, and we shall not be put to confusion. The believer will ascribe all the honour of his salvation, to the power, mercy, and truth of God, and look back with wonder and thanksgiving on the way in which the Lord has led him. Let us rejoice that our help for the time to come is in him who made heaven and earth.

Psalm 125

The security of the righteous (1–3)

Prayer for them, The ruin of the wicked (4, 5)

The security of the righteous (1–3)

All those minds shall be truly stayed, that are stayed on God. They shall be as Mount Zion, firm as it is; a mountain supported by providence, much more as a holy mountain supported by promise. They cannot be removed from confidence in God. They abide for ever in that grace which is the earnest of their everlasting continuance in glory. Committing themselves to God, they shall be safe from their enemies. Even mountains may moulder and come to nothing, and rocks be removed, but God's covenant with his people cannot be broken, nor his care of them cease. Their troubles shall last no longer than their strength will bear them up under them. The rod of the wicked may come, may fall upon the righteous, upon their persons, their estates, their liberties, their families names, on any thing that falls to their lot; only it cannot reach their souls. And though it may come upon their lot, it shall not rest thereon. The Lord will make all work together for their good. The wicked shall only prove a correcting rod, not a destroying sword; even this rod shall not remain upon them, lest they distrust the promise, thinking God has cast them off.

Prayer for them, The ruin of the wicked (4, 5)

God's promises should quicken our prayers. The way of holiness is straight; there are no windings or shiftings in it. But the ways of sinners are crooked. They shift from one purpose to another, and turn hither and thither to deceive; but disappointment and misery shall befall them. Those who cleave to the ways of God, though they may have trouble in their way, their end shall be peace. The pleading of their Saviour for them, secures to them the upholding power and preserving grace of their God. Lord, number us with them, in time, and to eternity.

Psalm 126

Those returned out of captivity are to be thankful (1–3)

Those yet in captivity are encouraged (4–6)

Those returned out of captivity are to be thankful (1–3)

It is good to observe how God's deliverances of the church are for us, that we may rejoice in them. And how ought redemption from the wrath to come, from the power of sin and of Satan, to be valued! The sinner convinced of his guilt and danger, when by looking to a crucified Saviour he receives peace to his conscience, and power to break off his sins, often can scarcely believe that the prospect which opens to him is a reality.

Those yet in captivity are encouraged (4–6)

The beginnings of mercies encourage us to pray for the completion of them. And while we are in this world there will be matter for prayer, even when we are most furnished with matter for praise. Suffering saints are often in tears; they share the calamities of human life, and commonly have a greater share than others. But they sow in tears; they do the duty of an afflicted state. Weeping must not hinder sowing; we must get good from times of affliction. And they that sow, in the tears of godly sorrow, to the Spirit, shall of the Spirit reap life everlasting; and that will be a joyful harvest indeed. Blessed are those that mourn, for they shall be for ever comforted. When we mourn for our sins, or suffer for Christ's sake, we are sowing in tears, to reap in joy. And remember that God is not mocked; for whatever a man soweth that shall he reap, Ga 6:7–9. Here, O disciple of Jesus, behold an emblem of thy present labour and future reward; the day is coming when thou shalt reap in joy, plentiful shall be thy harvest, and great shall be thy joy in the Lord.

Psalm 127

The value of the Divine blessing (1–5)

Let us always look to God's providence. In all the affairs and business of a family we must depend upon his blessing. 1. For raising a family. If God be not acknowledged, we have no reason to expect his blessing; and the best-laid plans fail, unless he crowns them with success. 2. For the safety of a family or a city. Except the Lord keep the city, the watchmen, though they neither slumber nor sleep, wake but in vain; mischief may break out, which even early discoveries may not be able to prevent. 3. For enriching a family. Some are so eager upon the world, that they are continually full of care, which makes their comforts bitter, and their lives a burden. All this is to get money; but all in vain, except God prosper them: while those who love the Lord, using due diligence in their lawful callings, and casting all their care upon him, have needful success, without uneasiness or vexation. Our care must be to keep ourselves in the love of God; then we may be easy, whether we have little or much of this world. But we must use the proper means very diligently. Children are God's gifts, a heritage, and a reward; and are to be accounted blessings, and not burdens: he who sends mouths, will send meat, if we trust in him. They are a great support and defence to a family. Children who are young, may be directed aright to the mark, God's glory, and the service of their generation; but when they are gone into the world, they are arrows out of the hand, it is too late to direct them then. But these arrows in the hand too often prove arrows in the heart, a grief to godly parents. Yet, if trained according to God's word, they generally prove the best defence in declining years, remembering their obligations to their parents, and taking care of them in old age. All earthly comforts are uncertain, but the Lord will assuredly comfort and bless those who serve him; and those who seek the conversion of sinners, will find that their spiritual children are their joy and crown in the day of Jesus Christ.

Psalm 128
The blessings of those who fear God (1–6)

Only those who are truly holy, are truly happy. In vain do we pretend to be of those that fear God, if we do not make conscience of keeping steadfastly to his ways. Blessed is every one that fears the Lord; whether he be high or low, rich or poor in the world. If thou fear him and walk in his ways, all shall be well with thee while thou livest, better when thou diest, best of all in eternity. By the blessing of God, the godly shall get an honest livelihood. Here is a double promise; they shall have something to do, for an idle life is a miserable, uncomfortable life, and shall have health and strength, and power of mind to do it. They shall not be forced to live upon the labours of other people. It is as much a mercy as a duty, with quietness to work and eat our own bread. They and theirs shall enjoy what they get. Such as fear the Lord and walk in his ways, are the only happy persons, whatever their station in life may be. They shall have abundant comfort in their family relations. And they shall have all the good things God has promised, and which they pray for. A good man can have little comfort in seeing his children's children, unless he sees peace upon Israel. Every true believer rejoices in the prosperity of the church.

Hereafter we shall see greater things, with the everlasting peace and rest that remain for the Israel of God.

Psalm 129
Thankfulness for former deliverances (1–4)
A believing prospect of the destruction of the enemies of Zion (5–8)

Thankfulness for former deliverances (1–4)

The enemies of God's people have very barbarously endeavoured to wear out the saints of the Most High. But the church has been always graciously delivered. Christ has built his church upon a rock. And the Lord has many ways of disabling wicked men from doing the mischief they design against his church. The Lord is righteous in not suffering Israel to be ruined; he has promised to preserve a people to himself.

A believing prospect of the destruction of the enemies of Zion (5–8)

While God's people shall flourish as the loaded palm-tree, or the green and fruitful olive, their enemies shall wither as the grass upon the house-tops, which in eastern countries are flat, and what grows there never ripens; so it is with the designs of God's enemies. No wise man will pray the Lord to bless these mowers or reapers. And when we remember how Jesus arose and reigns; how his people have been supported, like the burning but unconsumed bush, we shall not fear.

Psalm 130
The psalmist's hope in prayer (1–4)
His patience in hope (5–8)

The psalmist's hope in prayer (1–4)

The only way of relief for a sin-entangled soul, is by applying to God alone. Many things present themselves as diversions, many things offer themselves as remedies, but the soul finds that the Lord alone can heal. And until men are sensible of the guilt of sin, and quit all to come at once to God, it is in vain for them to expect any relief. The Holy Ghost gives to such poor souls a fresh sense of their deep necessity, to stir them up in earnest applications, by the prayer of faith, by crying to God. And as they love their souls, as they are concerned for the glory of the Lord, they are not to be wanting in this duty. Why is it that these matters are so long uncertain with them? Is it not from sloth and despondency that they content themselves with common and customary applications to God? Then let us up and be doing; it must be done, and it is attended with safety. We are to humble ourselves before God, as guilty in his sight. Let us acknowledge our sinfulness; we cannot justify ourselves, or plead not guilty. It is our unspeakable comfort that there is forgiveness with him, for that is what we need. Jesus Christ is the great Ransom; he is ever an Advocate for us, and through him we hope to obtain forgiveness. There is forgiveness with thee, not that thou mayest be presumed upon, but that thou mayest be feared. The fear of God often is put for the whole worship of God. The only motive and encouragement for sinners is this, that there is forgiveness with the Lord.

His patience in hope (5–8)

It is for the Lord that my soul waits, for the gifts of his grace, and the working of his power. We must hope for that only which he has promised in his word. Like those who wish to see the dawn, being very desirous that light would come long before day; but still more earnestly does a good man long for the tokens of God's favour, and the visits of his grace. Let all that devote themselves to the Lord, cheerfully stay themselves on him. This redemption is redemption from all sin. Jesus Christ saves his people from their sins, both from the condemning and from the commanding power of sin. It is plenteous redemption; there is an all-sufficient fulness in the Redeemer, enough for all, enough for each; therefore enough for me, says the believer. Redemption from sin includes redemption from all other evils, therefore it is a plenteous redemption, through the atoning blood of Jesus, who shall redeem his people from all their sins. All that wait on God for mercy and grace, are sure to have peace.

Psalm 131

The psalmist's humility. Believers encouraged to trust in God (1–3)

The psalmist aimed at nothing high or great, but to be content in every condition God allotted. Humble saints cannot think so well of themselves as others think of them. The love of God reigning in the heart, will subdue self-love. Where there is a proud heart, there is commonly a proud look. To know God and our duty, is learning sufficiently high for us. It is our wisdom not to meddle with that which does not belong to us. He was well reconciled to every condition the Lord placed him in. He had been as humble as a little child about the age of weaning, and as far from aiming at high things; as entirely at God's disposal, as the child at the disposal of the mother or nurse. We must become as little children, Matthew 18:3. Our hearts are desirous of worldly things, cry for them, and are

fond of them; but, by the grace of God, a soul that is made holy, is weaned from these things. The child is cross and fretful while in the weaning; but in a day or two it cares no longer for milk, and it can bear stronger food. Thus does a converted soul quiet itself under the loss of what it loved, and disappointments in what it hoped for, and is easy whatever happens. When our condition is not to our mind, we must bring our mind to our condition; then we are easy to ourselves and all about us; then our souls are as a weaned child. And thus the psalmist recommends confidence in God, to all the Israel of God, from his own experience. It is good to hope, and quietly to wait for the salvation of the Lord under every trial.

Psalm 132

David's care for the ark (1–10)
The promises of God (11–18)

David's care for the ark (1–10)

David bound himself to find a place for the Lord, for the ark, the token of God's presence. When work is to be done for the Lord, it is good to tie ourselves to a time. It is good in the morning to fix upon work for the day, with submission to Providence, for we know not what a day may bring forth. And we should first, and without delay, seek to have our own hearts made a habitation of God through the Spirit. He prays that God would take up his dwelling in the habitation he had built; that he would give grace to the ministers of the sanctuary to do their duty. David pleads that he was the anointed of the Lord, and this he pleads as a type of Christ, the great Anointed. We have no merit of our own to plead; but, for His sake, in whom there is a fulness of merit, let us find favour. And every true believer in Christ, is an anointed one, and has received from the Holy One the oil of true grace. The request is, that God would not turn away, but hear and answer their petitions for his Son's sake.

The promises of God (11–18)

The Lord never turns from us when we plead the covenant with his anointed Prophet, Priest, and King. How vast is the love of God to man, that he should speak thus concerning his church! It is his desire to dwell with us; yet how little do we desire to dwell with him! He abode in Zion till the sins of Israel caused him to give them up to the spoilers. Forsake us not, O God, and deliver us not in like manner, sinful though we are. God's people have a special blessing on common enjoyments, and that blessing puts peculiar sweetness into them. Zion's poor have reason to be content with a little of this world, because they have better things prepared for them. God will abundantly bless the nourishment of the new man, and satisfy the poor in spirit with the bread of life. He gives more than we ask, and when he gives salvation, he will give abundant joy. God would bring to nothing every design formed to destroy the house of David, until King Messiah should arise out of it, to sit upon the throne of his Father. In him all the promises centre. His enemies, who will not have him to reign over them, shall at the last day be clothed with shame and confusion for ever.

Psalm 133

The excellency of brotherly love (1–3)

We cannot say too much, it were well if enough could be said, to persuade people to live together in peace. It is good for us, for our honour and comfort; and brings constant delight to those who live in unity. The pleasantness of this is likened to the holy anointing oil. This is the fruit of the Spirit, the proof of our union with Christ, and adorns his gospel. It is profitable as well as pleasing; it brings blessings numerous as the drops of dew. It cools the scorching heat of men's passions, as the dews cool the air and refresh the earth. It moistens the heart, and makes it fit to receive the good seed of the word, and to make it fruitful. See the proof of the excellency of brotherly love: where brethren dwell together in unity, the Lord commands the blessing. God commands the blessing; man can but beg a blessing. Believers that live in love and peace, shall have the God of love and peace with them now, and they shall shortly be with him for ever, in the world of endless love and peace. May all who love the Lord forbear and forgive one another, as God, for Christ's sake, hath forgiven them.

Psalm 134

An exhortation to bless the Lord (1–3)

We must stir up ourselves to give glory to God, and encourage ourselves to hope for mercy and grace from him. It is an excellent plan to fill up all our spare minutes with pious meditations, and prayers and praises. No time would then be a burden, nor should we murder our hours by trifling conversation and vain amusements, or by carnal indulgences. We need desire no more to make us happy, than to be blessed of the Lord. We ought to beg spiritual blessings, not only for ourselves, but for others; not only, The Lord bless me, but, The Lord bless thee; thus testifying our belief that there is enough for others as well as for us, and showing our good will to others.

Psalm 135

God to be praised for his mercy (1–4)
For his power and judgments (5–14)
The vanity of idols (15–21)

God to be praised for his mercy (1–4)

The subject-matter of praise, is the blessings of grace flowing from the everlasting love of God. The name of God as a covenant God and Father in Christ, blessing us with all spiritual blessings in him, is to be loved and praised. The Lord chose a people to himself, that they might be unto him for a name and a praise. If they do not praise him for this distinguishing favour, they are the most unworthy and ungrateful of all people.

For his power and judgments (5–14)

God is, and will be always, the same to his church, a gracious, faithful, wonder-working God. And his church is, and will be, the same to him, a thankful, praising people: thus his name endures for ever. He will return in ways of mercy to them, and will delight to do them good.

The vanity of idols (15–21)

These arm believers against idolatry and all false worship, by showing what sort of gods the heathen worshipped. And the more deplorable the condition of the Gentile nations that worship idols, the more are we to be thankful that we know better. Let us pity, and pray for, and seek to benefit benighted heathens and deluded sinners. Let us endeavour to glorify his name, and recommend his truth, not only with our lips, but by holy lives, copying the example of Christ's goodness and truth.

Psalm 136

God to be praised as the Creator of the world (1–9)
As Israel's God and Saviour (10–22)
For his blessings to all (23–26)

God to be praised as the Creator of the world (1–9)

Forgetful as we are, things must be often repeated to us. By 'mercy' we understand the Lord's disposition to save those whom sin has rendered miserable and vile, and all the provision he has made for the redemption of sinners by Jesus Christ. The counsels of this mercy have been from everlasting, and the effects of it will endure for ever, to all who are interested in it. The Lord continues equally ready to show mercy to all who seek for it, and this is the source of all our hope and comfort.

As Israel's God and Saviour (10–22)

The great things God did for Israel, when he brought them out of Egypt, were mercies which endured long to them; and our redemption by Christ, which was typified thereby, endures for ever. It is good to enter into the history of God's favours, and in each to observe, and own, that his mercy endureth for ever. He put them in possession of a good land; it was a figure of the mercy of our Lord Jesus Christ.

For his blessings to all (23–26)

God's everlasting mercy is here praised for the redemption of his church; in all his glories, and all his gifts. Blessed be God, who has provided and made known to us salvation through his Son. May we know and feel his redeeming power, that we may serve him in righteousness all our days. May He who giveth food to all flesh, feed our souls unto eternal life, and enliven our affections by his grace, that we may give thanks and praise to his holy name, for his mercy endureth for ever. Let us trace up all the favours we receive to this true source, and offer praise continually.

Psalm 137

The Jews bewail their captivity (1–4)

Their affection for Jerusalem (5–9)

The Jews bewail their captivity (1–4)

Their enemies had carried the Jews captive from their own land. To complete their woes, they insulted over them; they required of them mirth and a song. This was very barbarous; also profane, for no songs would serve but the songs of Zion. Scoffers are not to be complied with. They do not say, How shall we sing, when we are so much in sorrow? but, It is the Lord's song, therefore we dare not sing it among idolaters.

Their affection for Jerusalem (5–9)

What we love, we love to think of. Those that rejoice in God, for his sake make Jerusalem their joy. They steadfastly resolved to keep up this affection. When suffering, we should recollect with godly sorrow our forfeited mercies, and our sins by which we lost them. If temporal advantages ever render a profession, the worst calamity has befallen him. Far be it from us to avenge ourselves; we will leave it to Him who has said, Vengeance is mine. Those that are glad at calamities, especially at the calamities of Jerusalem, shall not go unpunished. We cannot pray for promised success to the church of God without looking to, though we do not utter a prayer for, the ruin of her enemies. But let us call to mind to whose grace and finished salvation alone it is, that we have any hopes of being brought home to the heavenly Jerusalem.

Psalm 138

The psalmist praises God for answering prayer (1–5)

The Lord's dealing with the humble and the proud (6–8)

The psalmist praises God for answering prayer (1–5)

When we can praise God with our whole heart, we need not be unwilling for the whole world to witness our gratitude and joy in him. Those who rely on his loving-kindness and truth through Jesus Christ, will ever find him faithful to his word. If he spared not his own Son, how shall he not with him freely give us all things? If God gives us strength in our souls, to bear the burdens, resist the temptations, and to do the duties of an afflicted state, if he strengthens us to keep hold of himself by faith, and to wait with patience for the event, we are bound to be thankful.

The Lord's dealing with the humble and the proud (6–8)

Though the Lord is high, yet he has respect to every lowly, humbled sinner; but the proud and unbelieving will be banished far from his blissful presence. Divine consolations have enough in them to revive us, even when we walk in the midst of troubles. And God will save his own people that they may be revived by the Holy Spirit, the Giver of life and holiness. If we give to God the glory of his mercy, we may take to ourselves the comfort. This confidence will not do away, but quicken prayer. Whatever good there is in us, it is God works in us both to will and to do. The Lord will perfect the salvation of every true believer, and he will never forsake those whom he has created anew in Christ Jesus unto good works.

Psalm 139

God knows all things (1–6)

He is every where present (7–16)

The psalmist's hatred to sin, and desire to be led aright (17–24)

God knows all things (1–6)

God has perfect knowledge of us, and all our thoughts and actions are open before him. It is more profitable to meditate on Divine truths, applying them to our own cases, and with hearts lifted to God in prayer, than with a curious or disputing frame of mind. That God knows all things, is omniscient; that he is every where, is omnipresent; are truths acknowledged by all, yet they are seldom rightly believed in by mankind. God takes strict notice of every step we take, every right step and every by step. He knows what rule we walk by, what end we walk toward, what company we walk with. When I am withdrawn from all company, thou knowest what I have in my heart. There is not a vain word, not a good word, but thou knowest from what thought it came, and with what design it was uttered. Wherever we are, we are under the eye and hand of God. We cannot by searching find how God searches us out; nor do we know how we are known. Such thoughts should restrain us from sin.

He is every where present (7–16)

We cannot see God, but he can see us. The psalmist did not desire to go from the Lord. Whither can I go? In the most distant corners of the world, in heaven, or in hell, I cannot go out of thy reach. No veil can hide us from God; not the thickest darkness. No disguise can save any person or action from being seen in the true light by him. Secret haunts of sin are as open before God as the most open villanies. On the other hand, the believer cannot be removed from the supporting, comforting presence of his Almighty Friend. Should the persecutor take his life, his soul will the sooner ascend to heaven. The grave cannot separate his body from the love of his Saviour, who will raise it a glorious body. No outward circumstances can separate him from his Lord. While in the path of duty, he may be happy in any situation, by the exercise of faith, hope, and prayer.

The psalmist's hatred to sin, and desire to be led aright (17–24)

God's counsels concerning us and our welfare are deep, such as cannot be known. We cannot think how many mercies we have received from him. It would help to keep us in the fear of the Lord all the day long, if, when we wake in the morning, our first thoughts were of him: and how shall we admire and bless our God for his precious salvation, when we awake in the world of glory! Surely we ought not to use our members and senses, which are so curiously fashioned, as instruments of unrighteousness unto sin. But our immortal and rational souls are a still more noble work and gift of God. Yet if it were not for his precious thoughts of love to us, our reason and our living for ever would, through our sins, prove the occasion of our eternal misery. How should we then delight to meditate on God's love to sinners in Jesus Christ, the sum of which exceeds all reckoning! Sin is hated, and sinners lamented, by all who fear the Lord. Yet while we shun them we should pray for them; with God their conversion and salvation are possible. As the Lord knows us thoroughly, and we are strangers to ourselves, we should

earnestly desire and pray to be searched and proved by his word and Spirit. if there be any wicked way in me, let me see it; and do thou root it out of me. The way of godliness is pleasing to God, and profitable to us; and will end in everlasting life. It is the good old way. All the saints desire to be kept and led in this way, that they may not miss it, turn out of it, or tire in it.

Psalm 140

David encourages himself in God (1–7)

He prays for, and prophesies the destruction of, his persecutors (8–13)

David encourages himself in God (1–7)

The more danger appears, the more earnest we should be in prayer to God. All are safe whom the Lord protects. If he be for us, who can be against us? We should especially watch and pray, that the Lord would hold up our goings in his ways, that our footsteps slip not. God is as able to keep his people from secret fraud as from open force; and the experience we have had of his power and care, in dangers of one kind, may encourage us to depend upon him in other dangers.

He prays for, and prophesies the destruction of, his persecutors (8–13)

Believers may pray that God would not grant the desires of the wicked, nor further their evil devices. False accusers will bring mischief upon themselves, even the burning coals of Divine vengeance. And surely the righteous shall dwell in God's presence, and give him thanks for evermore. This is true thanksgiving, even thanksliving: this use we should make of all our deliverances, we should serve God the more closely and cheerfully. Those who, though evil spoken of and ill-used by men, are righteous in the sight of God, being justified by the righteousness of Christ, which is imputed to them, and received by faith, as the effect of which, they live soberly and righteously; these give thanks to the Lord, for the righteousness whereby they are made righteous, and for every blessing of grace, and mercy of life.

Psalm 141

David prays for God's acceptance and assistance (1–4)

That God would appear for his rescue (5–10)

David prays for God's acceptance and assistance (1–4)

Make haste unto me. Those that know how to value God's gracious presence, will be the more fervent in their prayers. When presented through the sacrifice and intercession of the Saviour, they will be as acceptable to God as the daily sacrifices and burnings of incense were of old. Prayer is a spiritual sacrifice, it is the offering up the soul and its best affections. Good men know the evil of tongue sins. When enemies are provoking, we are in danger of speaking unadvisedly. While we live in an evil world, and have such evil hearts, we have need to pray that we may neither be drawn nor driven to do any thing sinful. Sinners pretend to find dainties in sin; but those that consider how soon sin will turn into bitterness, will dread such dainties, and pray to God to take them out of their sight, and by his grace to turn their hearts against them. Good men pray against the sweets of sin.

That God would appear for his rescue (5–10)

We should be ready to welcome the rebuke of our heavenly Father, and also the reproof of our brethren. It shall not break my head, if it may but help to break my heart: we must show that we take it kindly. Those who slighted the word of God before, will be glad of it when in affliction, for that opens the ear to instruction. When the world is bitter, the word is sweet. Let us lift our prayer unto God. Let us entreat him to rescue us from the snares of Satan, and of all the workers of iniquity. In language like this psalm, O Lord, would we entreat that our poor prayers should set forth our only hope, our only dependence on thee. Grant us thy grace, that we may be prepared for this employment, being clothed with thy righteousness, and having all the gifts of thy Spirit planted in our hearts.

Psalm 142

David's comfort in prayer (1–7)

There can be no situation so distressing or dangerous, in which faith will not get comfort from God by prayer. We are apt to show our troubles too much to ourselves, poring upon them, which does us no service; whereas, by showing them to God, we might cast the cares upon him who careth for us, and thereby ease ourselves. Nor should we allow any complaint to ourselves or others, which we cannot make to God. When our spirits are overwhelmed by distress, and filled with discouragement; when we see snares laid for us on every side, while we walk in his way, we may reflect with comfort that the Lord knoweth our path. Those who in sincerity take the Lord for their God, find him all-sufficient, as a Refuge, and as a Portion: every thing else is a refuge of lies, and a portion of no value. In this situation David prayed earnestly to God. We may apply it spiritually; the souls of believers are often straitened by doubts and fears. And it

is then their duty and interest to beg of God to set them at liberty, that they may run the way of his commandments. Thus the Lord delivered David from his powerful persecutors, and dealt bountifully with him. Thus he raised the crucified Redeemer to the throne of glory, and made him Head over all things for his church. Thus the convinced sinner cries for help, and is brought to praise the Lord in the company of his redeemed people; and thus all believers will at length be delivered from this evil world, from sin and death, and praise their Saviour for ever.

Psalm 143

David complains of his enemies and distresses (1–6)

He prays for comfort, guidance, and deliverance (7–12)

David complains of his enemies and distresses (1–6)

We have no righteousness of our own to plead, therefore must plead God's righteousness, and the word of promise which he has freely given us, and caused us to hope in. David, before he prays for the removal of his trouble, prays for the pardon of his sin, and depends upon mercy alone for it. He bemoans the weight upon his mind from outward troubles. But he looks back, and remembers God's former appearance for his afflicted people, and for him in particular. He looks round, and notices the works of God. The more we consider the power of God, the less we shall fear the face or force of man. He looks up with earnest desires towards God and his favour. This is the best course we can take, when our spirits are overwhelmed. The believer will not forget, that in his best actions he is a sinner. Meditation and prayer will recover us from distresses; and then the mourning soul strives to return to the Lord as the infant stretches out its hands to the indulgent mother, and thirsts for his consolations as the parched ground for refreshing rain.

He prays for comfort, guidance, and deliverance (7–12)

David prays that God would be well pleased with him, and let him know that he was so. He pleads the wretchedness of his case, if God withdrew from him. But the night of distress and discouragement shall end in a morning of consolation and praise. He prays that he might be enlightened with the knowledge of God's will; and this is the first work of the Spirit. A good man does not ask the way in which is the most pleasant walking, but what is the right way. Not only show me what thy will is, but teach me how to do it. Those who have the Lord for their God, have his Spirit for their Guide; they are led by the Spirit. He prays that he might be enlivened to do God's will. But we should especially seek the destruction of our sins, our worst enemies, that we may be devotedly God's servants.

Psalm 144

David acknowledges the great goodness of God, and prays for help (1–8)

He prays for the prosperity of his kingdom (9–15)

David acknowledges the great goodness of God, and prays for help (1–8)

When men become eminent for things as to which they have had few advantages, they should be more deeply sensible that God has been their Teacher. Happy those to whom the Lord gives that noblest victory, conquest and dominion over their own spirits. A prayer for further mercy is fitly begun with a thanksgiving for former mercy. There was a special power of God, inclining the people of Israel to be subject to David; it was typical of the bringing souls into subjection to the Lord Jesus. Man's days have little substance, considering how many thoughts and cares of a never-dying soul are employed about a poor dying body. Man's life is as a shadow that passes away. In their highest earthly exaltation, believers will recollect how mean, sinful, and vile they are in themselves; thus they will be preserved from self-importance and presumption. God's time to help his people is, when they are sinking, and all other helps fail.

He prays for the prosperity of his kingdom (9–15)

Fresh favours call for fresh returns of thanks; we must praise God for the mercies we hope for by his promise, as well as those we have received by his providence. To be saved from the hurtful sword, or from wasting sickness, without deliverance from the dominion of sin and the wrath to come, is but a small advantage. The public prosperity David desired for his people, is stated. It adds much to the comfort and happiness of parents in this world, to see their children likely to do well. To see them as plants, not as weeds, not as thorns; to see them as plants growing, not withered and blasted; to see them likely to bring forth fruit unto God in their day; to see them in their youth growing strong in the Spirit. Plenty is to be desired, that we may be thankful to God, generous to our friends, and charitable to the poor; otherwise, what profit is it to have our garners full? Also, uninterrupted

peace. War brings abundance of mischiefs, whether it be to attack others or to defend ourselves. And in proportion as we do not adhere to the worship and service of God, we cease to be a happy people. The subjects of the Saviour, the Son of David, share the blessings of his authority and victories, and are happy because they have the Lord for their God.

Psalm 145

David extols the power, goodness, and mercy of the Lord (1–9)

The glory of God's kingdom, and his care of those that love him (10–21)

David extols the power, goodness, and mercy of the Lord (1–9)

Those who, under troubles and temptations, abound in fervent prayer, shall in due season abound in grateful praise, which is the true language of holy joy. Especially we should speak of God's wondrous work of redemption, while we declare his greatness. For no deliverance of the Israelites, nor the punishment of sinners, so clearly proclaims the justice of God, as the cross of Christ exhibits it to the enlightened mind. It may be truly said of our Lord Jesus Christ, that his words are words of goodness and grace; his works are works of goodness and grace. He is full of compassion; hence he came into the world to save sinners. When on earth, he showed his compassion both to the bodies and souls of men, by healing the one, and making wise the other. He is of great mercy, a merciful High Priest, through whom God is merciful to sinners.

The glory of God's kingdom, and his care of those that love him (10–21)

All God's works show forth his praises. He satisfies the desire of every living thing, except the unreasonable children of men, who are satisfied with nothing. He does good to all the children of men; his own people in a special manner. Many children of God, who have been ready to fall into sin, to fall into despair, have tasted his goodness in preventing their falls, or recovering them speedily by his graces and comforts. And with respect to all that are heavy laden under the burden of sin, if they come to Christ by faith, he will ease them, he will raise them. He is very ready to hear and answer the prayers of his people. He is present every where; but in a special way he is nigh to them, as he is not to others. He is in their hearts, and dwells there by faith, and they dwell in him. He is nigh to those that call upon him, to help them in all times of need. He will be nigh to them, that they may have what they ask, and find what they seek, if they call upon him in truth and sincerity. And having taught men to love his name and holy ways, he will save them from the destruction of the wicked. May we then love his name, and walk in his ways, while we desire that all flesh should bless his holy name for ever and ever.

Psalm 146

Why we should not trust in men (1–4)
Why we should trust in God (5–10)

Why we should not trust in men (1–4)

If it is our delight to praise the Lord while we live, we shall certainly praise him to all eternity. With this glorious prospect before us, how low do worldly pursuits seem! There is a Son of man in whom there is help, even him who is also the Son of God, who will not fail those that trust in him. But all other sons of men are like the man from whom they sprung, who, being in honour, did not abide. God has given the earth to the children of men, but there is great striving about it. Yet, after a while, no part of the earth will be their own, except that in which their dead bodies are laid. And when man returns to his earth, in that very day all his plans and designs vanish and are gone: what then comes of expectations from him?

Why we should trust in God (5–10)

The psalmist encourages us to put confidence in God. We must hope in the providence of God for all we need as to this life, and in the grace of God for that which is to come. The God of heaven became a man that he might become our salvation. Though he died on the cross for our sins, and was laid in the grave, yet his thoughts of love to us did not perish; he rose again to fulfil them. When on earth, his miracles were examples of what he is still doing every day. He grants deliverance to captives bound in the chains of sin and Satan. He opens the eyes of the understanding. He feeds with the bread of life those who hunger for salvation; and he is the constant Friend of the poor in spirit, the helpless: with him poor sinners, that are as fatherless, find mercy; and his kingdom shall continue for ever. Then let sinners flee to him, and believers rejoice in him. And as the Lord shall reign for ever, let us stir up each other to praise his holy name.

Psalm 147

The people of God are exhorted to praise him for his mercies and care (1–11)
For the salvation and prosperity of the church (12–20)

The people of God are exhorted to praise him for his mercies and care (1–11)

Praising God is work that is its own wages. It is comely; it becomes us as reasonable creatures, much more as people in covenant with God. He gathers outcast sinners by his grace, and will bring them into his holy habitation. To those whom God heals with the consolations of his Spirit, he speaks peace, assures them their sins are pardoned. And for this, let others praise him also. Man's knowledge is soon ended; but God's knowledge is a depth that can never be fathomed. And while he telleth the number of the stars, he condescends to hear the broken-hearted sinner. While he feeds the young ravens, he will not leave his praying people destitute. Clouds look dull and melancholy, yet without them we could have no rain, therefore no fruit. Thus afflictions look black and unpleasant; but from clouds of affliction come showers that make the soul to yield the peaceable fruits of righteousness. The psalmist delights not in things wherein sinners trust and glory; but a serious and suitable regard to God is, in his sight, of very great price. We are not to be in doubt between hope and fear, but to act under the gracious influences of hope and fear united.

For the salvation and prosperity of the church (12–20)

The church, like Jerusalem of old, built up and preserved by the wisdom, power, and goodness of God, is exhorted to praise him for all the benefits and blessings vouchsafed to her; and these are represented by his favours in the course of nature. The thawing word may represent the gospel of Christ, and the thawing wind the Spirit of Christ; for the Spirit is compared to the wind, John 3:8. Converting grace softens the heart that was hard frozen, and melts it into tears of repentance, and makes good reflections to flow, which before were chilled and stopped up. The change which the thaw makes is very evident, yet how it is done no one can say. Such is the change wrought in the conversion of a soul, when God's word and Spirit are sent to melt it and restore it to itself.

Psalm 148

The creatures placed in the upper world called on to praise the Lord (1–6)

Also the creatures of this lower world, especially his own people (7–14)

The creatures placed in the upper world called on to praise the Lord (1–6)

We, in this dark and sinful world, know little of the heavenly world of light. But we know that there is above us a world of blessed angels. They are always praising God, therefore the psalmist shows his desire that God may be praised in the best manner; also we show that we have communion with spirits above, who are still praising him. The heavens, with all contained in them, declare the glory of God. They call on us, that both by word and deed, we glorify with them the Creator and Redeemer of the universe.

Also the creatures of this lower world, especially his own people (7–14)

Even in this world, dark and bad as it is, God is praised. The powers of nature, be they ever so strong, so stormy, do what God appoints them, and no more. Those that rebel against God's word, show themselves to be more violent than even the stormy winds, yet they fulfil it. View the surface of the earth, mountains and all hills; from the barren tops of some, and the fruitful tops of others, we may fetch matter for praise. And assuredly creatures which have the powers of reason, ought to employ themselves in praising God. Let all manner of persons praise God. Those of every rank, high and low. Let us show that we are his saints by praising his name continually. He is not only our Creator, but our Redeemer; who made us a people near unto him. We may by 'the Horn of his people' understand Christ, whom God has exalted to be a Prince and a Saviour, who is indeed the defence and the praise of all his saints, and will be so for ever. In redemption, that unspeakable glory is displayed, which forms the source of all our hopes and joys. May the Lord pardon us, and teach our hearts to love him more and praise him better.

Psalm 149

Joy to all the people of God (1–5)

Terror to their enemies (6–9)

Joy to all the people of God (1–5)

New mercies continually demand new songs of praise, upon earth and in heaven. And the children of Zion have not only to bless the God who made them, but to rejoice in him, as having created them in Christ Jesus unto good works, and formed them saints as well as men. The Lord takes pleasure in his people; they should rejoice in Him. When the Lord has made sinners feel their wants and unworthiness, he will adorn them with the graces of his Spirit, and cause them to bear his image, and rejoice in his happiness for ever. Let his saints employ their waking hours upon their beds in songs of praise. Let them rejoice, even upon the bed of death, assured that they are going to eternal rest and glory.

Terror to their enemies (6–9)

Some of God's servants of old were appointed to execute vengeance according to his word. They did not do it from personal revenge or earthly politics, but in obedience to God's command. And the honour intended for all the saints of God, consists in their triumphs over the enemies of their salvation. Christ never intended his gospel should be spread by fire and sword, or his righteousness by the wrath of man. But let the high praises of God be in our mouths, while we wield the sword of the word of God, with the shield of faith, in warfare with the world, the flesh, and the devil. The saints shall be more than conquerors over the enemies of their souls, through the blood of the Lamb and the word of his testimony. The completing of this will be in the judgment of the great day. Then shall the judgment be executed. Behold Jesus, and his gospel church, chiefly in her millennial state. He and his people rejoice in each other; by their prayers and efforts they work with him, while he goes forth in the chariots of salvation, conquering sinners by grace, or in chariots of vengeance, to destroy his enemies.

Psalm 150

A psalm of praise (1–6)

We are here stirred up to praise God. Praise God for his sanctuary, and the privileges we enjoy by having it among us; praise him because of his power and glory in the firmament. Those who praise the Lord in heaven, behold displays of his power and glory which we cannot now conceive. But the greatest of all his mighty acts is known in his earthly sanctuary. The holiness and the love of our God are more displayed in man's redemption, than in all his other works. Let us praise our God and Saviour for it. We need not care to know what instruments of music are mentioned. Hereby is meant that in serving God we should spare no cost or pains. Praise God with strong faith; praise him with holy love and delight; praise him with entire confidence in Christ; praise him with believing triumph over the powers of darkness; praise him by universal respect to all his commands; praise him by cheerful submission to all his disposals; praise him by rejoicing in his love, and comforting ourselves in his goodness; praise him by promoting the interests of the kingdom of his grace; praise him by lively hope and expectation of the kingdom of his glory. Since we must shortly breathe our last, while we have breath let us praise the Lord; then we shall breathe our last with comfort. Let every thing that hath breath praise the Lord. Praise ye the Lord. Such is the very suitable end of a book inspired by the Spirit of God, written for the work of praise; a book which has supplied the songs of the church for more than three thousand years; a book which is quoted more frequently than any other by Christ and his apostles; a book which presents the loftiest ideas of God and his government, which is fitted to every state of human life, which sets forth every state of religious experience, and which bears simple and clear marks of its Divine origin.

PROVERBS

Matthew Henry

Introduction

The subject of this book may be thus stated by an enlargement on the opening verses.

1. The Proverbs of Solomon, the son of David, king of Israel.

2. Which treat of the knowledge of wisdom, of piety towards God, of instruction and moral discipline, of the understanding wise and prudent counsels.

3. Which treat of the attainment of instruction in wisdom, which wisdom is to be shown in the conduct of life, and consists in righteousness with regard to our fellow-creatures.

4. Which treat of the giving to the simple sagacity to discover what is right, by supplying them with just principles, and correct views of virtue and vice; and to the young man knowledge, so that he need not err through ignorance; and discretion, so that by pondering well these precepts, he may not err through obstinacy. Take the proverbs of other nations, and we shall find great numbers founded upon selfishness, cunning, pride, injustice, national contempt, and animosities. The principles of the Proverbs of Solomon are piety, charity, justice, benevolence, and true prudence. Their universal purity proves that they are the word of God.

Chapter 1

The use of the Proverbs (1–6)

Exhortations to fear God and obey parents (7–9)

To avoid the enticings of sinners (10–19)

The address of Wisdom to sinners (20–33)

The use of the Proverbs (1–6)

The lessons here given are plain, and likely to benefit those who feel their own ignorance, and their need to be taught. If young people take heed to their ways, according to Solomon's Proverbs, they will gain knowledge and discretion. Solomon speaks of the most important points of truth, and a greater than Solomon is here. Christ speaks by his word and by his Spirit. Christ is the Word and the Wisdom of God, and he is made to us wisdom.

Exhortations to fear God and obey parents (7–9)

Fools are persons who have no true wisdom, who follow their own devices, without regard to reason, or reverence for God. Children are reasonable creatures, and when we tell them what they must do, we must tell them why. But they are corrupt and wilful, therefore with the instruction there is need of a law. Let Divine truths and commands be to us most honourable; let us value them, and then they shall be so to us.

To avoid the enticings of sinners (10–19)

Wicked people are zealous in seducing others into the paths of the destroyer: sinners love company in sin. But they have so much the more to answer for. How cautious young people should be! 'Consent thou not.' Do not say as they say, nor do as they do, or would have thee to do; have no fellowship with them. Who could think that it should be a pleasure to one man to destroy another! See their idea of worldly wealth; but it is neither substance, nor precious. It is the ruinous mistake of thousands, that they overvalue the wealth of this world. Men promise themselves in vain that sin will turn to their advantage. The way of sin is downhill; men cannot stop themselves. Would young people shun temporal and eternal ruin, let them refuse to take one step in these destructive paths. Men's greediness of gain hurries them upon practices which will not suffer them or others to live out half their days. What is a man profited, though he gain the world, if he lose his life? Much less if he lose his soul?

The address of Wisdom to sinners (20–33)

Solomon, having showed how dangerous it is to hearken to the temptations of Satan, here declares how dangerous it is not to hearken to the calls of God. Christ himself is Wisdom, is Wisdoms. Three sorts of persons are here called by Him: 1. Simple ones. Sinners are fond of their simple notions of good and evil, their simple prejudices against the ways of God, and flatter themselves in their wickedness. 2. Scorners. Proud, jovial people, that make a jest of every thing. Scoffers at religion, that run down every thing sacred and serious. 3. Fools. Those are the worst of fools that hate to be taught, and have a rooted dislike to serious godliness. The precept is plain; Turn you at my reproof. We do not make a right use of reproofs, if we do not turn from evil to that which is good. The promises are very encouraging. Men cannot turn by any power of their own; but God answers, Behold, I will pour out my Spirit unto you. Special grace is needful to sincere conversion. But that grace shall never be denied to any who seek it. The love of Christ, and the promises mingled with his reproofs, surely should have the attention of every one. It may well be asked, how long men mean to proceed in such a perilous path, when the uncertainty of life and the consequences of dying without Christ are considered? Now sinners live at ease, and set sorrow at defiance; but their calamity will come. Now God is ready to hear their prayers; but then they shall cry in vain. Are we yet despisers of wisdom? Let us hearken diligently, and obey the Lord Jesus, that we may enjoy peace of conscience and confidence in God; be free from evil, in life, in death, and for ever.

Chapter 2

Promises to those who seek wisdom (1–9)
The advantages of wisdom (10–22)

Promises to those who seek wisdom (1–9)

Those who earnestly seek heavenly wisdom, will never complain that they have lost their labour; and the freeness of the gift does not do away the necessity of our diligence, Joh 6:27. Let them seek, and they shall find it; let them ask, and it shall be given them. Observe who are thus favoured. They are the righteous, on whom the image of God is renewed, which consists in righteousness. If we depend upon God, and seek to him for wisdom, he will enable us to keep the paths of judgment.

The advantages of wisdom (10–22)

If we are truly wise, we shall be careful to avoid all evil company and evil practices. When wisdom has dominion over us, then it not only fills the head, but enters into the heart, and will preserve, both against corruptions within and temptations without. The ways of sin are ways of darkness, uncomfortable and unsafe: what fools are those who leave the plain, pleasant, lightsome paths of uprightness, to walk in such ways! They take pleasure in sin; both in committing it, and in seeing others commit it. Every wise man will shun such company. True wisdom will also preserve from those who lead to fleshly lusts, which defile the body, that living temple, and war against the soul. These are evils which excite the sorrow of every serious mind, and cause every reflecting parent to look upon his children with anxiety, lest they should be entangled in such fatal snares. Let the sufferings of others be our warnings. Our Lord Jesus deters from sinful pleasures, by the everlasting torments which follow them. It is very rare that any who are caught in this snare of the devil, recover themselves; so much is the heart hardened, and the mind blinded, by the deceitfulness of this sin. Many think that this caution, besides the literal sense, is to be understood as a caution against idolatry, and subjecting the soul to the body, by seeking any forbidden object. The righteous must leave the earth as well as the wicked; but the earth is a very different thing to them. To the wicked it is all the heaven they ever shall have; to the righteous it is the place of preparation for heaven. And is it all one to us, whether we share with the wicked in the miseries of their latter end, or share those everlasting joys that shall crown believers?

Chapter 3

Exhortations to obedience and faith (1–6)

To piety, and to improve afflictions (7–12)

To gain wisdom (13–20)

Guidance of Wisdom (21–26)

The wicked and the upright (27–35)

Exhortations to obedience and faith (1–6)

In the way of believing obedience to God's commandments health and peace may commonly be enjoyed; and though our days may not be long upon earth, we shall live for ever in heaven. Let not mercy and truth forsake thee; God's mercy in promising, and his truth in performing: live up to them, keep up thine interest in them, and take the comfort of them. We must trust in the Lord with all our hearts, believing he is able and wise to do what is best. Those who know themselves, find their own understandings a broken reed, which, if they lean upon, will fail. Do not design any thing but what is lawful, and beg God to direct thee in every case, though it may seem quite plain. In all our ways that prove pleasant, in which we gain our point, we must acknowledge God with thankfulness. In all our ways that prove uncomfortable, and that are hedged up with thorns, we must acknowledge him with submission. It is promised, He shall direct thy paths; so that thy way shall be safe and good, and happy at last.

To piety, and to improve afflictions (7–12)

There is not a greater enemy to the fear of the Lord in the heart, than self-conceit of our own wisdom. The prudence and sobriety which religion teaches, tend not only to the health of the soul, but to the health of the body. Worldly wealth is but poor substance, yet, such as it is, we must honour God with it; and those that do good with what they have, shall have more to do more good with. Should the Lord visit us with trials and sickness, let us not forget that the exhortation speaks to us as to children, for our good. We must not faint under an affliction, be it ever so heavy and long, not be driven to despair, or use wrong means for relief. The father corrects the son whom he loves, because he loves him, and desires that he may be wise and good. Afflictions are so far from doing God's children any hurt, that, by the grace of God, they promote their holiness.

To gain wisdom (13–20)

No precious jewels or earthly treasures are worthy to be compared with true wisdom, whether the concerns of time or eternity be considered. We must make wisdom our business; we must venture all in it, and be willing to part with all for it. This Wisdom is the Lord Jesus Christ and his salvation, sought and obtained by faith and prayer. Were it not for unbelief, remaining sinfulness, and carelessness, we should find all our ways pleasantness, and our paths peace, for his are so; but we too often step aside from them, to our own hurt and grief. Christ is that Wisdom, by whom the worlds were made, and still are in being; happy are those to whom he is made of God wisdom. He has wherewithal to make good all his promises.

Guidance of Wisdom (21–26)

Let us not suffer Christ's words to depart from us, but keep sound wisdom and discretion; then shall we walk safely in his ways. The natural life, and all that belongs to it, shall be under the protection of God's providence; the spiritual life, and all its interests, under the protection of his grace, so that we shall be kept from falling into sin or trouble.

The wicked and the upright (27–35)

Our business is to observe the precepts of Christ, and to copy his example; to do justice, to love mercy, and to beware of covetousness; to be ready for every good work, avoiding needless strife, and bearing evils, if possible, rather than seeking redress by law. It will be found there is little got by striving. Let us not envy prosperous oppressors; far be it from the disciples of Christ to choose any of their ways. These truths may be despised by the covetous and luxurious, but everlasting contempt will be the portion of such scorners, while Divine favour is shown to the humble believer.

Chapter 4

Exhortation to the study of wisdom (1–13)

Cautions against bad company, exhortation to faith and holiness (14–27)

Exhortation to the study of wisdom (1–13)

We must look upon our teachers as our fathers: though instruction carry in it reproof and correction, bid it welcome. Solomon's parents loved him, therefore taught him. Wise and godly men, in every age of the world, and rank in society, agree that true wisdom consists in obedience, and is united to happiness. Get wisdom, take pains for it. Get the rule over thy corruptions; take more pains to get this than the wealth of this world. An interest in Christ's salvation is necessary. This wisdom is the one thing needful. A soul without true wisdom and grace is a dead soul. How poor, contemptible, and wretched are those, who, with all their wealth and power, die without getting understanding, without Christ, without hope, and without God! Let us give heed to the sayings of Him who has the words of eternal life. Thus our path will be plain before us: by taking, and keeping fast hold of instruction, we shall avoid being straitened or stumbling.

Cautions against bad company, exhortation to faith and holiness (14–27)

The way of evil men may seem pleasant, and the nearest way to compass some end; but it is an evil way, and will end ill; if thou love thy God and thy soul, avoid it. It is not said, Keep at a due distance, but at a great distance; never think you can get far enough from it. The way of the righteous is light; Christ is their Way, and he is the Light. The saints will not be perfect till they reach heaven, but there they shall shine as the sun in his strength. The way of sin is as darkness. The way of the wicked is dark, therefore dangerous; they fall into sin, but know not how to avoid it. They fall into trouble, but never seek to know wherefore God contends with them, nor what will be in the end of it. This is the way we are bid to shun. Attentive hearing the word of God, is a good sign of a work of grace begun in the heart, and a good means of carrying it on. There is in the word of God a proper remedy for all diseases of the soul. Keep thy heart with all diligence. We must set a strict guard upon our souls; keep our hearts from doing hurt, and getting hurt. A good reason is given; because out of it are the issues of life. Above all, we should seek from the Lord Jesus that living water, the sanctifying Spirit, issuing forth unto everlasting life. Thus we shall be enabled to put away a froward mouth and perverse lips; our eyes will be turned from beholding vanity, looking straight forward, and walking by the rule of God's word, treading in the steps of our Lord and Master. Lord, forgive the past, and enable us to follow thee more closely for the time to come.

Chapter 5

Exhortations to wisdom. The evils of licentiousness (1–14)

Remedies against licentiousness. The miserable end of the wicked (15–23)

Exhortations to wisdom. The evils of licentiousness (1–14)

Solomon cautions all young men, as his children, to abstain from fleshly lusts. Some, by the adulterous woman, here understand idolatry, false doctrine, which tends to lead astray men's minds and manners; but the direct view is to warn against seventh-commandment sins. Often these have been, and still are, Satan's method of drawing men from the worship of God into false

religion. Consider how fatal the consequences; how bitter the fruit! Take it any way, it wounds. It leads to the torments of hell. The direct tendency of this sin is to the destruction of body and soul. We must carefully avoid every thing which may be a step towards it. Those who would be kept from harm, must keep out of harm's way. If we thrust ourselves into temptation we mock God when we pray, Lead us not into temptation. How many mischiefs attend this sin! It blasts the reputation; it wastes time; it ruins the estate; it is destructive to health; it will fill the mind with horror. Though thou art merry now, yet sooner or later it will bring sorrow. The convinced sinner reproaches himself, and makes no excuse for his folly. By the frequent acts of sin, the habits of it become rooted and confirmed. By a miracle of mercy true repentance may prevent the dreadful consequences of such sins; but this is not often; far more die as they have lived. What can express the case of the self-ruined sinner in the eternal world, enduring the remorse of his conscience!

Remedies against licentiousness. The miserable end of the wicked (15–23)

Lawful marriage is a means God has appointed to keep from these destructive vices. But we are not properly united, except as we attend to God's word, seeking his direction and blessing, and acting with affection. Ever remember, that though secret sins may escape the eyes of our fellow-creatures, yet a man's ways are before the eyes of the Lord, who not only sees, but ponders all his goings. Those who are so foolish as to choose the way of sin, are justly left of God to themselves, to go on in the way to destruction.

Chapter 6

Cautions against giving a rash surety (1–5)

A rebuke to slothfulness (6–11)

Seven things hateful to God (12–19)

Exhortations to walk according to God's commandments (20–35)

Cautions against giving a rash surety (1–5)

If we live as directed by the word of God, we shall find it profitable even in this present world. We are stewards of our worldly substance, and have to answer to the Lord for our disposal of it; to waste it in rash schemes, or such plans as may entangle us in difficulties and temptations, is wrong. A man ought never to be surety for more than he is able and willing to pay, and can afford to pay, without wronging his family; he ought to look upon every sum he is engaged for, as his own debt. If we must take all this care to get our debts to men forgiven, much more to obtain forgiveness with God. Humble thyself to him, make sure of Christ as thy Friend, to plead for thee; pray earnestly that thy sins may be pardoned, and that thou mayest be kept from going down to the pit.

A rebuke to slothfulness (6–11)

Diligence in business is every man's wisdom and duty; not so much that he may attain worldly wealth, as that he may not be a burden to others, or a scandal to the church. The ants are more diligent than slothful men. We may learn wisdom from the meanest insects, and be shamed by them. Habits of indolence and indulgence grow upon people. Thus life runs to waste; and poverty, though at first at a distance, gradually draws near, like a traveller; and when it arrives, is like an armed man, too strong to be resisted. All this may be applied to the concerns of our souls. How many love their sleep of sin, and their dreams of worldly happiness! Shall we not seek to awaken such? Shall we not give diligence to secure our own salvation?

Seven things hateful to God (12–19)

If the slothful are to be condemned, who do nothing, much more those that do all the ill they can. Observe how such a man is described. He says and does every thing artfully, and with design. His ruin shall come without warning, and without relief. Here is a list of things hateful to God. Those sins are in a special manner provoking to God, which are hurtful to the comfort of human life. These things which God hates, we must hate in ourselves; it is nothing to hate them in others. Let us shun all such practices, and watch and pray against them; and avoid, with marked disapproval, all who are guilty of them, whatever may be their rank.

Exhortations to walk according to God's commandments (20–35)

The word of God has something to say to us upon all occasions. Let not faithful reproofs ever make us uneasy. When we consider how much this sin abounds, how heinous adultery is in its own nature, of what evil consequence it is, and how certainly it destroys the spiritual life in the soul, we shall not wonder that the cautions against it are so often repeated. Let us notice the subjects of this chapter. Let us remember Him who willingly became our Surety, when we were strangers and enemies. And shall Christians, who have such prospects, motives, and examples, be slothful and careless? Shall we neglect what is pleasing to God, and what he will graciously reward? May we closely watch every sense by which poison can enter our minds or affections.

Chapter 7

Invitations to learn wisdom (1–5)
The arts of seducers, with warnings against them (6–27)

Invitations to learn wisdom (1–5)

We must lay up God's commandments safely. Not only, Keep them, and you shall live; but, Keep them as those that cannot live without them. Those that blame strict and careful walking as needless and too precise, consider not that the law is to be kept as the apple of the eye; indeed the law in the heart is the eye of the soul. Let the word of God dwell in us, and so be written where it will be always at hand to be read. Thus we shall be kept from the fatal effects of our own passions, and the snares of Satan. Let God's word confirm our dread of sin, and resolutions against it.

The arts of seducers, with warnings against them (6–27)

Here is an affecting example of the danger of youthful lusts. It is a history or a parable of the most instructive kind. Will any one dare to venture on temptations that lead to impurity, after Solomon has set before his eyes in so lively and plain a manner, the danger of even going near them? Then is he as the man who would dance on the edge of a lofty rock, when he has just seen another fall headlong from the same place. The misery of self-ruined sinners began in disregard to God's blessed commands. We ought daily to pray that we may be kept from running into temptation, else we invite the enemies of our souls to spread snares for us. Ever avoid the neighbourhood of vice. Beware of sins which are said to be pleasant sins. They are the more dangerous, because they most easily gain the heart, and close it against repentance. Do nothing till thou hast well considered the end of it. Were a man to live as long as Methuselah, and to spend all his days in the highest delights sin can offer, one hour of the anguish and tribulation that must follow, would far outweigh them.

Chapter 8

Christ, as Wisdom, calls to the sons of men (1–11)
The nature and riches of Wisdom (12–21)
Christ one with the Father, in the creation of the world, and rejoicing in his work for the salvation of man (22–31)
Exhortations to hear Christ's word (32–36)

537

Christ, as Wisdom, calls to the sons of men (1–11)

The will of God is made known by the works of creation, and by the consciences of men, but more clearly by Moses and the prophets. The chief difficulty is to get men to attend to instruction. Yet attention to the words of Christ, will guide the most ignorant into saving knowledge of the truth. Where there is an understanding heart, and willingness to receive the truth in love, wisdom is valued above silver and gold.

The nature and riches of Wisdom (12–21)

Wisdom, here is Christ, in whom are all the treasures of wisdom and knowledge; it is Christ in the word, and Christ in the heart; not only Christ revealed to us, but Christ revealed in us. All prudence and skill are from the Lord. Through the redemption of Christ's precious blood, the riches of his grace abound in all wisdom and prudence. Man found out many inventions for ruin; God found one for our recovery. He hates pride and arrogance, evil ways and froward conversation; these render men unwilling to hear his humbling, awakening, holy instructions. True religion gives men the best counsel in all difficult cases, and helps to make their way plain. His wisdom makes all truly happy who receive it in the love of Christ Jesus. Seek him early, seek him earnestly, seek him before any thing else. Christ never said, Seek in vain. Those who love Christ, are such as have seen his loveliness, and have had his love shed abroad in their hearts; therefore they are happy. They shall be happy in this world, or in that which is beyond compare better. Wealth gotten by vanity will soon be diminished, but that which is well got, will wear well; and that which is well spent upon works of piety and charity, will be lasting. If they have not riches and honour in this world, they shall have that which is infinitely better. They shall be happy in the grace of God. Christ, by his Spirit, guides believers into all truth, and so leads them in the way of righteousness; and they walk after the Spirit. Also, they shall be happy in the glory of God hereafter. In Wisdom's promises, believers have goods laid up, not for days and years, but for eternity; her fruit therefore is better than gold.

Christ one with the Father, in the creation of the world, and rejoicing in his work for the salvation of man (22–31)

The Son of God declares himself to have been engaged in the creation of the world. How able, how fit is the Son of God to be the Saviour of the world, who was the Creator of it! The Son of God was ordained, before the world, to that great work. Does he delight in saving wretched sinners, and shall not we delight in his salvation?

Exhortations to hear Christ's word (32–36)

Surely we should hearken to Christ's voice with the readiness of children. Let us all be wise, and not refuse such mercy. Blessed are those who hear the Saviour's voice, and wait on him with daily reading, meditation, and prayer. The children of the world find time for vain amusements, without neglecting what they deem the one thing needful. Does it not show contempt of Wisdom's instructions, when people professing godliness, seek excuses for neglecting the means of grace? Christ is Wisdom, and he is Life to all believers; nor can we obtain God's favour, unless we find Christ, and are found in him. Those who offend Christ deceive themselves; sin is a wrong to the soul. Sinners die because they will die, which justifies God when he judges.

Chapter 9

The invitations of Wisdom (1–12)
The invitations of folly (13–18)

The invitations of Wisdom (1–12)

Christ has prepared ordinances to which his people are admitted, and by which nourishment is given here to those that believe in him, as well as mansions in heaven hereafter. The ministers of the gospel go forth to invite the guests. The call is general, and shuts out none that do not shut out themselves. Our Saviour came, not to call the righteous, but sinners; not the wise in their own eyes, who say they see. We must keep from the company and foolish pleasures of the ungodly, or we never can enjoy the pleasures of a holy life. It is vain to seek the company of wicked men in the hope of doing them good; we are far more likely to be corrupted by them. It is not enough to forsake the foolish, we must join those that walk in wisdom. There is no true wisdom but in the way of religion, no true life but in the end of that way. Here is the happiness of those that embrace it. A man cannot be profitable to God; it is for our own good. Observe the shame and ruin of those who slight it. God is not the Author of sin: and Satan can only tempt, he cannot force. Thou shalt bear the loss of that which thou scornest: it will add to thy condemnation.

The invitations of folly (13–18)

How diligent the tempter is, to seduce unwary souls into sin! Carnal, sensual pleasure, stupifies conscience, and puts out the sparks of conviction. This tempter has no solid reason to offer; and where she gets dominion in a soul, all knowledge of holy things is lost and forgotten. She is very violent and pressing. We need to seek and pray for true wisdom, for Satan has many ways to withdraw our souls from Christ. Not only worldly lusts and abandoned seducers prove fatal to the souls of men; but false teachers, with doctrines that flatter pride and give liberty to lusts, destroy thousands. They especially draw off such as have received only partial serious impressions. The depths of Satan are depths of hell; and sin, without remorse, is ruin, ruin without remedy. Solomon shows the hook; those that believe him, will not meddle with the bait. Behold the wretched, empty, unsatisfying, deceitful, and stolen pleasure sin proposes; and may our souls be so desirous of the everlasting enjoyment of Christ, that on earth we may live to him, daily, by faith, and ere long be with him in glory.

Chapter 10

Through the whole of the Proverbs, we are to look for somewhat beyond the first sense the passage may imply, and this we shall find to be Christ. He is the Wisdom so often spoken of in this book.

1. The comfort of parents much depends on their children; and the righteous may be poor, the Lord will not suffer him to want what is needful for spiritual life.

4. Those who are fervent in spirit, serving the Lord, are likely to be rich in faith, and rich in good works.

5. Here is just blame of those who trifle away opportunities, both for here and for hereafter.

6. Abundance of blessings shall abide on good men; real blessings.

7. Both the just and the wicked must die; but between their souls there is a vast difference.

8. The wise in heart puts his knowledge in practice.

9. Dissemblers, after all their shuffling, will be exposed.

10. Trick and artifice will be no excuse for iniquity.

11. The good man's mouth is always open to teach, comfort, and correct others.

12. Where there is hatred, every thing stirs up strife. By bearing with each other, peace and harmony are preserved.

13. Those that foolishly go on in wicked ways, prepare rods for themselves.

14. Whatever knowledge may be useful, we must lay it up, that it may not be to seek when we want it. The wise gain this wisdom by reading, by hearing the word, by meditation, by prayer, by faith in Christ, who is made of God unto us wisdom.

15. This refers to the common mistakes both of rich and poor, as to their outward condition.

Rich people's wealth exposes them to many dangers; while a poor man may live comfortably, if he is content, keeps a good conscience, and lives by faith.

16. Perhaps a righteous man has no more than what he works hard for, but that labour tends to life.

17. The traveller that has missed his way, and cannot bear to be told of it, and to be shown the right way, must err still.

18. He is especially a fool who thinks to hide anything from God; and malice is no better.

19. Those that speak much, speak much amiss. He that checks himself is wise and sincere, freed from the dross of guile and evil design. Pious discourse is spiritual food to the needy. Fools die for want of a heart, so the word is; for want of thought.

22. That wealth which is truly desirable, has no vexation of spirit in the enjoyment; no grief for the loss; no guilt by the abuse of it. What comes from the love of God, has the grace of God for its companion.

23. Only foolish and wicked men divert themselves with doing harm to others, or tempting to sin.

24. The largest desire of eternal blessings the righteous can form, will be granted.

25. The course of prosperous sinners is like a whirlwind, which soon spends itself, and is gone.

26. As vinegar sets the teeth on edge, and as the smoke causes the eyes, so is he that loves life. Let him fear God, and that will secure to him life enough in this world, and eternal life in the other.

29. The believer grows stronger in faith, and obeys with increased delight.

30. The wicked would be glad to have this earth their home for ever, but it cannot be so. They must die wisely for the benefit of others. But it is the sin, and will be the ruin of a wicked man, that he speaks what is displeasing to God. The righteous is kept by the power of God; and nothing shall be able to separate him from the love of God which is in Christ Jesus.

Chapter 11

1. However men may make light of giving short weight or measure, and however common such crimes may be, they are an abomination to the Lord.

2. Considering how safe, and quiet, and easy the humble are, we see that with the lowly is wisdom.

3. An honest man's principles are fixed, therefore his way is plain.

4. The ways of wickedness are dangerous. And sin will be its own punishment.

6. When a godly man dies, all his fears vanish; but when a wicked man dies, his hopes vanish.

8. The righteous are often wonderfully kept from going into dangerous situations, and the ungodly go in their stead.

9. Hypocrites delude men into error and sin by artful objections against the truth.

12. A man of understanding does not judge of others by their success.

13. A faithful man will not disclose what he is trusted with, unless the honour of God and the real good of society require it.

14. We shall often find it to our advantage to advise with others.

15. The welfare of our families, our own peace, and our ability to pay just debts, must not be brought into danger. But here especially let us consider the grace of our Lord Jesus Christ in becoming Surety even for enemies.

16. A pious and discreet woman will keep esteem and respect, as strong men keep possession of wealth.

17. A cruel, froward, ill-natured man, is vexatious to those that are, and should be to him as his own flesh, and punishes himself.

18. He that makes it his business to do good, shall have a reward, as sure to him as eternal truth can make it.

19. True holiness is true happiness. The more violent a man is in sinful pursuits, the more he hastens his own destruction.

20. Nothing is more hateful to God, than hypocrisy and double dealing, which are here signified. God delights in such as aim and act with uprightness.

21. Joining together in sin shall not protect the sinners.

22. Beauty is abused by those who have not discretion or modesty with it. This is true of all bodily endowments.

23. The wicked desire mischief to others, but it shall return upon themselves.

24. A man may grow poor by not paying just debts, not relieving the poor, not allowing needful expenses. Let men be ever so saving of what they have, if God appoints, it comes to nothing.

25. Both in temporal and spiritual things, God commonly deals with his people according to the measure by which they deal with their brethren.

26. We must not hoard up the gifts of God's bounty, merely for our own advantage.

27. Seeking mischief is here set against seeking good; for those that are not doing good are doing hurt, even to themselves.

28. The true believer is a branch of the living Vine. When those that take root in the world wither, those who are grafted into Christ shall be fruitful.

29. He that brings trouble upon himself and his family, by carelessness, or by wickedness, shall be unable to keep and enjoy what he gets,

as a man is unable to hold the wind, or to satisfy himself with it.

30. The righteous are as trees of life; and their influence upon earth, like the fruits of that tree, support and nourish the spiritual life in many.

31. Even the righteous, when they offend on earth, shall meet with sharp corrections; much more will the wicked meet the due reward of their sins. Let us then seek those blessings which our Surety purchased by his sufferings and death; let us seek to copy his example, and to keep his commandments.

Chapter 12

1. Those who have grace, will delight in the instructions given them. Those that stifle their convictions, are like brutes.

2. The man who covers selfish and vicious designs under a profession of religion or friendship, will be condemned.

3. Though men may advance themselves by sinful arts, they cannot settle and secure themselves. But those who by faith are rooted in Christ, are firmly fixed.

4. A wife who is pious, prudent, and looks well to the ways of her household, who makes conscience of her duty, and can bear crosses; such a one is an honour and comfort to her husband. She that is the reverse of this, preys upon him, and consumes him.

5. Thoughts are not free; they are under the Divine knowledge, therefore under the Divine command. It is a man's shame to act with deceit, with trick and design.

6. Wicked people speak mischief to their neighbours. A man may sometimes do a good work with one good word.

7. God's blessing is often continued to the families of godly men, while the wicked are overthrown.

8. The apostles showed wisdom by glorying in shame for the name of Christ.

9. He that lives in a humble state, who has no one to wait upon him, but gets bread by his own labour, is happier than he that glories in high birth or gay attire, and wants necessaries.

10. A godly man would not put even an animal to needless pain. But the wicked often speak of others as well used, when they would not endure like treatment for a single day.

11. It is men's wisdom to mind their business, and follow an honest calling. But it is folly to neglect business; and the grace of God teaches men to disdain nothing but sin.

12. When the ungodly see others prosper by sin, they wish they could act in the same way. But the root of Divine grace, in the heart of the righteous, produces other desires and purposes.

13. Many a man has paid dear in this world for the transgression of his lips.

14. When men use their tongues aright, to teach and comfort others, they enjoy acceptance through Christ Jesus; and the testimony of their conscience, that they in some measure answer the end of their being.

15. A fool, in the sense of Scripture, means a wicked man, one who acts contrary to the wisdom that is from above. His rule is, to do what is right in his own eyes.

16. A foolish man is soon angry, and is hasty in expressing it; he is ever in trouble and running into mischief. It is kindness to ourselves to make light of injuries and affronts, instead of making the worst of them.

17. It is good for all to dread and detest the sin of lying, and to be governed by honesty.

18. Whisperings and evil surmises, like a sword, separate those that have been dear to each other. The tongue of the wise is health, making all whole.

19. If truth be spoken, it will hold good; whoever may be disobliged, still it will keep its ground.

20. Deceit and falsehood bring terrors and perplexities. But those who consult the peace and happiness of others have joy in their own minds.

21. If men are sincerely righteous, the righteous God has engaged that no evil shall happen to them. But they that delight in mischief shall have enough of it.

22. Make conscience of truth, not only in words, but in actions.

23. Foolish men proclaim to all the folly and emptiness of their minds.

24. Those who will not take pains in an honest calling, living by tricks and dishonesty, are paltry and beggarly.

25. Care, fear, and sorrow, upon the spirits, deprive men of vigour in what is to be done, or courage in what is to be borne. A good word from God, applied by faith, makes the heart glad.

26. The righteous is abundant; though not in this world's goods, yet in the graces and comforts of the Spirit, which are the true riches. Evil men vainly flatter themselves that their ways are not wrong.

27. The slothful man makes no good use of the advantages Providence puts in his way, and has no comfort in them. The substance of a diligent man, though not great, does good to him and his family. He sees that God gives it to him in answer to prayer.

28. The way of religion is a straight, plain way; it is the way of righteousness. There is not only life at the end, but life in the way; all true comfort.

Chapter 13

1. There is great hope of those that reverence their parents. There is little hope of any who will not hear those that deal faithfully with them.

2. By our words we must be justified or condemned.

3. He that thinks before he speaks, that suppresses evil if he have thought it, keeps his soul from a great deal both of guilt and grief. Many a one is ruined by an ungoverned tongue.

4. The slothful desire the gains the diligent get, but hate the pains the diligent take; therefore they have nothing. This is especially true as to the soul.

5. Where sin reigns, the man is loathsome. If his conscience were awake, he would abhor himself, and repent in dust and ashes.

6. An honest desire to do right, preserves a man from fatal mistakes, better than a thousand fine-drawn distinctions.

7. Some who are really poor, trade and spend as if they were rich: this is sin, and will be shame, and it will end accordingly. Some that are really rich, would be thought to be poor: in this there is want of gratitude to God, want of justice and charity to others. There are many hypocrites, empty of grace, who will not be convinced of their poverty. There are many fearing Christians, who are spiritually rich, yet think themselves poor; by their doubts, and complaints, and griefs, they make themselves poor.

8. Great riches often tempt to violence against those that possess them; but the poor are free from such perils.

9. The light of the righteous is as that of the sun, which may be eclipsed and clouded, but will continue: the Spirit is their Light, he gives a fulness of joy: that of the wicked is as a lamp of their own kindling, easily put out.

10. All contentions, whether between private persons, families, churches, or nations, are begun and carried forward by pride. Disputes would be easily prevented or ended, if it were not for pride.

11. Wealth gotten by dishonesty or vice, has a secret curse, which will speedily waste it.

12. The delay of what is anxiously hoped for, is very painful to the mind; obtaining it is very pleasant. But spiritual blessings are chiefly intended.

13. He that stands in awe of God, and reverences his word, shall escape destruction, and be rewarded for his godly fear.

14. The rule by which the wise regulate their conduct, is a fountain yielding life and happiness.

15. The way of sinners is hard upon others, and hard to the sinner himself. The service of sin is slavery; the road to hell is strewed with the thorns and thistles that followed the curse.

16. It is folly to talk of things of which we know nothing, and to undertake what we are no way fit for.

17. Those that are wicked, and false to Christ and to the souls of men, do mischief, and fall into mischief; but those that are faithful, find sound words healing to others and to themselves.

18. He that scorns to be taught, will certainly be brought down.

19. There are in man strong desires after happiness; but never let those expect any thing truly sweet to their souls, who will not be persuaded to leave their sins.

20. Multitudes are brought to ruin by bad company. And all that make themselves wicked will be destroyed.

21. When God pursues sinners he is sure to overtake them; and he will reward the righteous.

22. The servant of God who is not anxious about riches, takes the best method of providing for his children.

23. The poor, yet industrious, thrive, though in a homely manner, while those who have great riches are often brought to poverty for want of judgment.

24. He acts as if he hated his child, who, by false indulgence, permits sinful habits to gather strength, which will bring sorrow here, and misery hereafter.

25. It is the misery of the wicked, that even their sensual appetites are always craving. The righteous feeds on the word and ordinances, to the satisfying of his soul with the promises of the gospel, and the Lord Jesus Christ, who is the Bread of life.

Chapter 14

1. A woman who has no fear of God, who is wilful and wasteful, and indulges her ease, will as certainly ruin her family, as if she plucked her house down.

2. Here are grace and sin in their true colours. Those that despise God's precepts and promises, despise God and all his power and mercy.

3. Pride grows from that root of bitterness which is in the heart. The root must be plucked up, or we cannot conquer this branch. The prudent words of wise men get them out of difficulties.

4. There can be no advantage without something which, though of little moment, will affright the indolent.

5. A conscientious witness will not dare to represent anything otherwise than according to his knowledge.

6. A scorner treats Divine things with contempt. He that feels his ignorance and unworthiness will search the Scriptures in a humble spirit.

7. We discover a wicked man if there is no savour of piety in his discourse.

8. We are travellers, whose concern is, not to spy out wonders, but to get to their journey's end; to understand the rules we are to walk by, also the ends we are to walk toward. The bad man cheats himself, and goes on in his mistake.

9. Foolish and profane men consider sin a mere trifle, to be made light of rather than mourned over. Fools mock at the sin-offering; but those that make light of sin, make light of Christ.

10. We do not know what stings of conscience, or consuming passions, torment the prosperous sinner. Nor does the world know the peace of mind a serious Christian enjoys, even in poverty and sickness.

11. Sin ruins many great families; whilst righteousness often raises and strengthens even mean families.

12. The ways of carelessness, of worldliness, and of sensuality, seem right to those that walk in them; but self-deceivers prove self-destroyers. See the vanity of carnal mirth.

14. Of all sinners backsliders will have the most terror when they reflect on their own ways.

15. Eager readiness to believe what others say, has ever proved mischievous. The whole world was thus ruined at first. The man who is spiritually wise, depends on the Saviour alone for acceptance. He is watchful against the enemies of his salvation, by taking heed to God's word.

16. Holy fear guards against every thing unholy.

17. An angry man is to be pitied as well as blamed; but the revengeful is more hateful.

18. Sin is the shame of sinners; but wisdom is the honour of the wise.

19. Even bad men acknowledge the excellency of God's people.

20. Friendship in the world is governed by self-interest. It is good to have God our Friend; he will not desert us.

21. To despise a man for his employment or appearance is a sin.

22. How wisely those consult their own interest, who not only do good, but devise it!

23. Labour of the head, or of the hand, will turn to some good account. But if men's religion runs all out in talk and noise, they will come to nothing.

24. The riches of men of wisdom and piety enlarge their usefulness.

25. An upright man will realise that those who fear the Lord so as to obey and serve him, have a strong ground of confidence, and will be preserved. Let us seek to this Fountain of life, that we may escape the snares of death.

28. Let all that wish well to the kingdom of Christ, do what they can, that many may be added to his church.

29. A mild, patient man is one that learns of Christ, who is Wisdom itself. Unbridled passion is folly made known.

30. An upright, contented, and benevolent mind, tends to health.

31. To oppress the poor is to reproach our Creator.

32. The wicked man has his soul forced from him; he dies in his sins, under the guilt and power of them. But godly men, though they have pain and some dread of death, have the blessed hope, which God, who cannot lie, has given them.

33. Wisdom possesses the heart, and thus regulates the affections and tempers.

34. Piety and holiness always promote industry, sobriety, and honesty.

35. The great King who reigns over heaven and earth, will reward faithful servants who honour his gospel by the proper discharge of the duties of their stations: he despises not the services of the lowest.

Chapter 15

1. A right cause will be better pleaded with meekness than with passion. Nothing stirs up anger like grievous words.

2. He that has knowledge, is to use it aright, for the good of others.

3. Secret sins, services, and sorrows, are under God's eye. This speaks comfort to saints, and terror to sinners.

4. A good tongue is healing to wounded consciences, by comforting them; to sin-sick souls, by convincing them; and it reconciles parties at variance.

5. If instruction is despised, reprove men rather than suffer them to go on undisturbed in the way to ruin.

6. The wealth of worldly men increases their fears and suspicions, adds strength to their passions, and renders the fear of death more distressing.

7. We use knowledge aright when we disperse it; but the heart of the foolish has nothing to stead of Christ's atonement, or in the place of holy obedience. Praying graces are his gift, and the work of his Spirit, with which he is well pleased.

10. He that hates reproof shall perish in his sins, since he would not be parted from them.

11. There is nothing that can be hid from the eyes of God, not even man's thoughts.

12. A scorner cannot bear to reflect seriously within his own heart.

13. A gloomy, impatient, unthankful spirit, springing from pride and undue attachment to worldly objects, renders a man uneasy to himself and others.

14. A wise man seeks to gain more wisdom, growing in grace and in the knowledge of Christ. But a carnal mind rests contented, flattering itself.

15. Some are much in affliction, and of a sorrowful spirit. Such are to be pitied, prayed for, and comforted. And others serve God with gladness of heart, and it prompts their obedience, yet they should rejoice a little with trembling. The Lord is with them, without the cares, troubles, and temptations which are with the wealth of the wicked.

18. He that is slow to anger, not only prevents strife, but appeases it, if kindled.

19. Those who have no heart to their work, pretend that they cannot do their work without hardship and danger. And thus many live always in doubt about their state, because always in neglect of some duty.

20. Those who treat an aged mother or a father with contempt or neglect, show their own folly.

21. Such as are truly wise, study that their thoughts, words, and actions should be regular, sincere, and holy.

22. If men will not take time and pains to deliberate, they are not likely to bring any thing to pass.

23. Wisdom is needed to suit our discourse to the occasions.

24. A good man sets his affections on things above; his way leads directly thither.

25. Pride is the ruin of multitudes. But those who are in affliction God will support.

26. The thoughts of wicked men offend Him who knows the heart.

27. The covetous man lets none of his family have rest or enjoyment. And greediness of gain often tempts to projects that bring ruin.

28. A good man is proved to be a wise man by this; he governs his tongue well.

29. God sets himself at a distance from those who set him at defiance.

30. How delightful to the humbled soul to hear the good report of salvation by the Lord Jesus Christ!

31. Faithful, friendly reproofs help spiritual life, and lead to eternal life.

32. Sinners undervalue their own souls; therefore they prefer the body before the soul, and wrong the soul to please the body.

33. The fear of the Lord will dispose us to search the Scriptures with reverence; and it will cause us to follow the leadings of the Holy Spirit. While we humbly place all our dependence on the grace of God, we are exalted in the righteousness of Christ.

Chapter 16

1. The renewing grace of God alone prepares the heart for every good work. This teaches us that we are not sufficient of ourselves to think or speak any thing wise and good.

2. Ignorance, pride, and self-flattery render us partial judges respecting our own conduct.

3. Roll the burden of thy care upon God, and leave it with him, by faith and dependence on him.

4. God makes use of the wicked to execute righteous vengeance on each other; and he will be glorified by their destruction at last.

5. Though sinners strengthen themselves and one another, they shall not escape God's judgments.

6. By the mercy and truth of God in Christ Jesus, the sins of believers are taken away, and the power of sin is broken.

7. He that has all hearts in his hand, can make a man's enemies to be at peace with him.

8. A small estate, honestly come by, will turn to better account than a great estate ill-gotten.

9. If men make God's glory their end, and his will their rule, he will direct their steps by his Spirit and grace.

10. Let kings and judges of the earth be just, and rule in the fear of God.

11. To observe justice in dealings between man and man is God's appointment.

12. The ruler that uses his power aright, will find that to be his best security.

13. Put those in power who know how to win the favour of an earthly prince, and they will throw themselves out of God's favour.

16. There is joy and satisfaction of spirit, only in getting wisdom.

17. A sincerely religious man keeps at a distance from every appearance of evil. Happy is the man that walks in Christ, and is led by the Spirit of Christ.

18. When men defy God's judgments, and think themselves far from them, it is a sign they are at the door. Let us not fear the pride of others, but fear pride in ourselves.

19. Humility, though it exposes to contempt in the world, is much better than high-spiritedness, which makes God an enemy. He that understands God's word shall find good.

21. The man whose wisdom dwells in his heart, will be found more truly prudent than many who possess shining talents.

22. As waters to a thirsty land, so is a wise man to his friends and neighbours.

23. The wise man's self-knowledge, always suggests something proper to be spoken to others.

24. The word of God cures the diseases that weaken our souls.

25. This is caution to all, to take heed of deceiving themselves as to their souls.

26. We must labour for the meat which endureth to everlasting life, or we must perish. Be needful to do good. The whisperer separates friends: what a mischief they can do by force and violence, and are blind to the result.

31. Old people especially should be found in the way of religion and godliness.

32. To overcome our own passions, requires more steady management, than obtaining victory over an enemy.

33. All the disposal of Providence concerning our affairs, we must look upon to be the determining what we referred to God; and we must be reconciled to them accordingly. Blessed are those that give themselves up to the will of God; for he knows what is good for them.

Chapter 17

1. These words recommend family love and peace, as needful for the comfort of human life.

2. The wise servant is more deserving, and more likely to appear one of the family, than a profligate son.

3. God tries the heart by affliction. He thus has often shown the sin remaining in the heart of the believer.

4. Flatterers, especially false teachers, are welcome to those that live in sin.

5. Those that laugh at poverty, treat God's providence and precepts with contempt.

6. It is an honour to children to have wise and godly parents continued to them, even after they are grown up and settled in the world.

7. A fool, in Solomon's Proverbs, signifies a wicked man, whom excellent speech does not become, because his conversation contradicts it.

8. Those who set their hearts upon money, will do any thing for it. What influence should the gifts of God have on our hearts!

9. The way to preserve peace is to make the best of every thing; not to notice what has been said or done against ourselves.

10. A gentle reproof will enter, not only into the head, but into the heart of a wise man.

11. Satan, and the messengers of Satan, shall be let loose upon an evil man.

12. Let us watch over our own passions, and avoid the company of furious men.

13. To render evil for good is devilish. He that does so, brings a curse upon his family.

14. What danger there is in the beginning of strife! Resist its earliest display; and leave it off, if it were possible, before you begin.

15. It is an offence to God to acquit the guilty, or to condemn those who are not guilty.

16. Man's neglect of God's favour and his own interest is very absurd.

17. No change of outward circumstances should abate our affection for our friends or relatives. But no friend, except Christ, deserves unlimited confidence. In Him this text did receive, and still receives its most glorious fulfilment.

18. Let not any wrong their families. Yet

Christ's becoming Surety for men, was a glorious display of Divine wisdom; for he was able to discharge the bond.

19. If we would keep a clear conscience and a quiet mind, we must shun all excitements to anger. And a man who affects a style of living above his means, goes the way to ruin.

20. There is nothing got by ill designs. And many have paid dear for an unbridled tongue.

21. This speaks very plainly what many wise and good men feel very strongly, how grievous it is to have a foolish, wicked child.

22. It is great mercy that God gives us leave to be cheerful, and cause to be cheerful, if by his grace he gives us hearts to be cheerful.

23. The wicked are ready to part with their money, though loved, that they may not suffer for their crimes.

24. The prudent man keeps the word of God continually in view. But the foolish man cannot fix his thoughts, nor pursue any purpose with steadiness.

25. Wicked children despise the authority of their father, and the tenderness of their mother.

26. It is very wrong to find fault wise man, by the good temper of his mind, and by the good government of his tongue. He is careful when he does speak, to speak to the purpose. God knows his heart, and the folly that is bound there; therefore he cannot be deceived in his judgment as men may be.

Chapter 18

1. If we would get knowledge and grace, we must try all methods of improving ourselves.

2. Those make nothing to purpose, of learning or religion, whose only design is to have something to make a show with.

3. As soon as sin entered, shame followed.

4. The well-spring of wisdom in the heart of a believer, continually supplies words of wisdom.

5. The merits of a cause do to themselves by their ungoverned tongues!

8. How base are those that sow contention! And what fatal effects may be expected from small beginnings of jealousy!

9. Omissions of duty, and in duty, are fatal to the soul, as well as commissions Lord Jesus Christ, forms a strong tower for the believer, who relies on the Lord. How deceitful the defence of the rich man, who has his portion and treasure in this world! It is a strong city and a high wall only in his own conceit; for it will fail when most in need. They will be exposed to the just wrath of that Judge whom they despised as a Saviour.

12. After the heart has been lifted up with pride, a fall comes. But honour shall be the reward of humility.

13. Eagerness, with self-conceit, will expose to shame.

14. Firmness of mind supports under many pains and trials. But when the conscience is tortured with remorse, no human fortitude can bear the misery; what then will hell be?

15. We must get knowledge, not only into our heads, but into our hearts.

16. Blessed be the Lord, who makes us welcome to come to his throne, without money and without price. May his gifts make room for him in our souls.

17. It is well to listen to our enemies, that we may form a better judgment of ourselves.

18. It was customary sometimes to refer matters to God, by casting lots, with solemn prayer. The profaning the lot, by using it in matters of diversion, or coveting what belongs to others, forms an objection to this now.

19. Great care must be taken to prevent quarrels among relations and those under obligations to each other. Wisdom and grace make it easy to forgive; but corruption makes it difficult.

20. The belly is here put for the heart, as elsewhere; and what that is filled with, our satisfaction will be accordingly, and our inward peace.

21. Many a one has caused his own death, or the death of others, by a false or injurious tongue.

22. A good wife is a great blessing to a man, and it is a token of Divine favour.

23. Poverty tells men they must not order or demand. And at the throne of God's grace we are all poor, and must use entreaties.

24. Christ Jesus never will forsake those who trust in and love him. May we be such friends to others, for our Master's sake. Having loved his own, which were in the world, he loved them unto the end; and we are his friends if we do whatever he commands us, John 15:14.

Chapter 19

1. A poor man who fears God, is more honourable and happy, than a man without wisdom and grace, however rich or advanced in rank.

2. What good can the soul do, if without knowledge? And he sins who will not take time to ponder the path of his feet.

3. Men run into troubles by their own folly, and then fret at the appointments of God.

4. Here we may see how strong is men's love of money.

5. Those that tell lies in discourse, are in a fair way to be guilty of bearing false-witness.

6. We are without excuse if we do not love God with all our hearts. His gifts to us are past number, and all the gifts of men to us are fruits of his bounty.

7. Christ was left by all his disciples; but the Father was with him. It encourages our faith that he had so large an experience of the sorrows of poverty.

8. Those only love their souls aright that get true wisdom.

9. Lying is a damning, destroying sin.

10. A man that has not wisdom and grace, has no right or title to true joy. It is very unseemly for one who is a servant to sin, to oppress God's free-men.

11. He attains the most true glory who endeavours most steadily to overcome evil with good.

12. Christ is a King, whose wrath against his enemies will be as the roaring of a lion, and his favour to his people as the refreshing dew.

13. It shows the vanity of the world, that we are liable to the greatest griefs where we promise ourselves the greatest comfort.

14. A discreet and virtuous wife is more valuable than house and riches.

15. A sluggish, slothful disposition makes men poor; it brings them to want. And this applies both to the present life and that which is to come.

16. If we keep God's word, God's word will keep us from every thing really hurtful. We abuse the doctrine of free grace, if we think that it does away the necessity and advantage of obedience. Those that live at random must die. This truth is clearly taught in words enough to alarm the stoutest sinner.

17. God has chosen the poor of this world, to be rich in faith, and heirs of his kingdom.

18. When parents keep under foolish tenderness, they do their best to render children a comfort to them, and happy in themselves.

19. The spared and spoiled child is likely to become a man of great wrath.

20. Those that would be wise in their latter end, must be taught and ruled when young.

21. What should we desire, but that all our purposes may agree with God's holy will?

22. It is far better to have a heart to do good, and want ability for it, than to have ability for it, and want a heart to it.

23. Those that live in the fear of God, shall get safety, satisfaction, and true and complete happiness.

24. Indolence, when indulged, so grows upon people, that they have no heart to do the most needful things for themselves.

25. A gentle rebuke goes farthest with a man of understanding.

26. The young man who wastes his father's substance, or makes his aged mother destitute, is hateful, and will come to disgrace.

27. It is the wisdom of young men to dread hearing such talk as puts loose and evil principles into the mind.

28. Those are the worst of sinners, who are glad of an opportunity to sin.

29. The unbelief of man shall not make God's threatenings of no effect. Christ himself, when bearing sins not his own, was not spared. Justice and judgment took hold of our blessed Surety; and will God spare obstinate sinners?

Chapter 20

1. It seems hard to believe that men of the greatest abilities, as well as the ignorant, should render themselves fools and madmen, merely for the taste or excitement produced by strong liquors.

2. How formidable kings are to those who provoke them! How much more foolish then is it to provoke the King of kings!

3. To engage in quarrels is the greatest folly that can be. Yield, and even give up just demands, for peace' sake.

4. He who labours and endures hardship in his seed-time for eternity, will be properly diligent as to his earthly business.

5. Though many capable of giving wise counsel are silent, yet something may be drawn from them, which will reward those who obtain it.

6. It is hard to find those that have done, and will do more good than they speak, or care to hear spoken of.

7. A good man is not liable to uneasiness in contriving what he shall do, or in reflecting on what he has done, as those who walk in deceit. And his family fare better for his sake.

8. If great men are good men, they may do much good, and prevent very much evil.

9. Some can say, Through grace, we are cleaner than we have been; but it was the work of the Holy Spirit.

10. See the various deceits men use, of which the love of money is the root. The Lord will not bless what is thus gotten.

11. Parents should observe their children, that they may manage them accordingly.

12. All our powers and faculties are from God, and are to be employed for him.

13. Those that indulge themselves, may expect to want necessaries, which should have been gotten by honest labour.

14. Men use arts to get a good bargain, and to buy cheap; whereas a man ought to be ashamed of a fraud and a lie.

15. He that prefers true knowledge to riches, follows the ways of religion and happiness. If we really believed this truth, the word of God would be valued as it deserves, and the world would lose its tempting influence.

16. Those ruin themselves who entangle themselves in giving a surety rashly. Also those who are in league with abandoned women. Place no confidence in either.

17. Wealth gotten by fraud may be sweet, for the carnal mind takes pleasure in the success of wicked devices; but it will be bitter in the reflection.

18. Especially we need advice in spiritual warfare. The word and Spirit of God are the best counsellors in every point.

19. Those dearly buy their own praise, who put confidence in a man because he speaks fairly.

20. An undutiful child will become very miserable. Never let him expect any peace or comfort.

21. An estate suddenly raised, is often as suddenly ruined.

22. Wait on the Lord, attend his pleasure, and he will protect thee.

23. A bargain made by fraud will prove a losing bargain in the end.

24. How can we form plans, and conduct business, independently of the Lord?

25. The evasions men often use with their own consciences show how false and deceitful man is.

26. Justice should crush the wicked, and separate them from the virtuous.

27. The rational soul and conscience are as a lamp within us, which should be used in examining our dispositions and motives with the revealed will of God.

28. Mercy and truth are the glories of God's throne.

29. Both young and old have their advantages; and let neither despise or envy the other.

30. Severe rebukes sometimes do a great deal of good. But such is the corruption of nature, that men are loth to be rebuked for their sins. If God uses severe afflictions, to purify our hearts and fit us for his service, we have cause to be very thankful.

Chapter 21

1. The believer, perceiving that the Lord rules every heart as he sees fit, like the husbandman who turns the water through his grounds as he pleases, seeks to have his own heart, and the hearts of others, directed in his faith, fear, and love.

2. We are partial in judging ourselves and our actions.

3. Many deceive themselves with a conceit that outward devotions will excuse unrighteousness.

4. Sin is the pride, the ambition, the glory, the joy, and the business of wicked men.

5. The really diligent employ foresight as well as labour.

6. While men seek wealth by unlawful practices, they seek death.

7. Injustice will return upon the sinner, and will destroy him here and for ever.

8. The way of mankind by nature is froward and strange.

9. It is best to shun bitter contention by pouring out the heart before God. For by prudence and patience, with constant prayer, the cross may be removed.

10. The evil desires of a wicked man's heart, lead to baseness in his conduct.

11. The simple may be made wise by punishments on the wicked, and by instructions to those who are willing to be taught.

12. Good men envy not the prosperity of evil-doers; they see there is a curse on them.

13. Such as oppress the poor by beating down wages, such as will not relieve according to their ability those in distress, and those in authority who neglect to do justice, stop their ears at the cry of the poor. But doubtless care is to be used in the exercise of charity.

14. If money can conquer the fury of the passions, shall reason, the fear of God, and the command of Christ, be too weak to bridle them?

15. There is true pleasure only in the practice of religion.

16. Of all wanderers in the ways of sin, those are in the most dangerous condition who turn aside into the ways of darkness. Yet there is hope even for them in the all-sufficient Saviour; but let them flee to him without delay.

17. A life of worldly pleasure brings ruin on men.

18. The righteous is often delivered out of trouble, and the wicked comes in his stead, and so seems as a ransom for him.

19. Unbridled passions spoil the comfort of all relations.

20. The plenty obtained by prudence, industry, and frugality, is desirable. But the foolish misspend what they have upon their lusts.

21. True repentance and faith will lead him that relies on the mercy of God in Christ, to follow after righteousness and mercy in his own conduct.

22. Those that have wisdom, often do great things, even against those confident of their strength.

23. It is our great concern to keep our souls from being entangled and disquieted.

24. Pride and haughtiness make men passionate; such continually deal in wrath, misery of the slothful; their hands refuse to labour in an honest calling, by which they might get an honest livelihood; yet their hearts cease not to covet riches, pleasures, and honours, which cannot be obtained without labour. But the righteous and industrious have their desires satisfied.

27. When holiness is pretended, but wickedness intended, that especially is an abomination.

28. The doom of a false witness is certain.

29. A wicked man bids defiance to the terrors

of the law and the rebukes of Providence. But a good man asks, What after all, our safety and salvation are only of the Lord. In our spiritual warfare we must arm ourselves with the whole armour of God; but our strength must be in the Lord, and in the power of his might.

Chapter 22

1. We should be more careful to do that by which we may get and keep a good name, than to raise or add unto a great estate.

2. Divine Providence has so ordered it, that some are rich, and others poor, but all are guilty before God; and at the throne of God's grace the poor are as welcome as the rich.

3. Faith foresees the evil coming upon sinners, and looks to Jesus Christ as the sure refuge from the storm.

4. Where the fear of God is, there will be humility. And much is to be enjoyed by it; spiritual riches, and eternal life at last.

5. The way of sin is vexatious and dangerous. But the way of duty is safe and easy.

6. Train children, not in the way they would go, that of their corrupt hearts, but in the way they should go; in which, if you love them, you would have them go. As soon as possible every child should be led to the knowledge of the Saviour.

7. This shows how important it is for every man to keep out of debt. As to the things of this life, there is a difference between the rich and the poor; but let the poor remember, it is the Lord that made the difference.

8. The power which many abuse, will soon fail them.

9. He that seeks to relieve the wants and miseries of others shall be blessed.

10. Profane scoffers and revilers disturb the peace.

11. God will be the Friend of a man in whose spirit there is no guile; this honour have all the saints.

12. God turns the counsels and designs of treacherous men to their own confusion.

13. The slothful man talks of a lion without, but considers not his real danger from the devil, that roaring lion within, and from his own slothfulness, which kills him.

14. The vile sin of licentiousness commonly besots the mind beyond recovery.

15. Sin is foolishness, it is in the heart, there is an inward inclination to sin: children bring it into the world with them; and it cleaves close to the soul. We all need to be corrected by our heavenly Father.

16. We are but stewards, and must distribute what God intrusts to our care, according to his will.

17–21. To these words, to this knowledge, the

ear must be bowed down, and the heart applied by faith and love. To live a life of delight in God and dependence on him, is the foundation of all practical religion. He that robs and oppresses the poor, does so at his peril. And if hearts have so much tinder in them, that it is dangerous to have to do with those that throw about the sparks of their passion. those are not so, who, by folly or other carelessness, waste what they have.

28. We are taught not to trespass on another man's right. And it is hard to find a truly industrious man. Such a man will rise. Seest thou a man diligent in the business of religion? He is likely to excel. Let us then be diligent in God's work.

Chapter 23

1–3. God's restraints of the appetite only say, Deny yourself in this world, for it brings no happiness to the soul. Those that hold them ever so fast, cannot hold them always, cannot hold them long.

6–8. Do not make thyself burdensome to any, especially those not sincere. When we are called by God to his feast, and to let our souls delight themselves, Isa 25:6; 55:2, we may safely partake of the Bread of life.

9. It is our duty to take all fit occasions to speak of Divine things; but if what a wise man says will not be heard, let him hold his protection. He is their Redeemer, who will take their part; and he is mighty, almighty.

12–16. Here is a parent instructing his child to give his mind to the Scriptures. Here is a parent correcting his child: accompanied with prayer, and blessed of God, it may prove a means of preventing his destruction. Here is a parent encouraging his child, telling him what would be for his good. And what a comfort it would be, if the child responded to correction; the end of his trials, and of the sinner's prosperity, is at hand.

19–28. The gracious Saviour who purchased pardon and peace for his people, with all the affection of a tender parent, counsels us to hear and be wise, and is ready to guide our hearts in his way. Here we have an earnest call to young people, to attend to the advice of their godly parents. If the heart be guided, the steps will be guided. Buy the truth, and sell it not; be willing to part with any thing for it. Do not part with it for pleasures, honours, riches, or any thing in this world. The heart is what the great God requires. We must not think to divide the heart between God and the world; he will have all or none. Look to the rule of God's word, the conduct of his providence, and the good examples of his people. Particular cautions are given against sins most destructive to wisdom and grace in the soul. It is really a shame to make a god of the belly. Drunkenness stupifies men, and then all goes to ruin. Licentiousness takes away the heart that should be given to God. Take heed of any approaches toward this sin, it is very hard to retreat from it. It bewitches men to their ruin.

29–35. Solomon warns against drunkenness. Those that would be kept from sin, must keep from all the beginnings of it, and fear coming within reach of its allurements. Foresee the punishment, what it will at last end in, if repentance prevent not. It makes men quarrel. Drunkards wilfully make woe and sorrow for themselves. It makes men impure and insolent. The tongue grows unruly; the heart utters things contrary to reason, religion, and common civility. It stupifies and besots men. They are in danger of death, of damnation; as much exposed as if they slept upon the top of a mast, yet feel secure. They fear no peril when the terrors of the Lord are before them; they feel no pain when the judgments of God are actually upon them. So lost is a drunkard to virtue and honour, so wretchedly is his conscience seared, that he is not ashamed to say, I will seek it again. With good reason we were bid to stop before the beginning. Who that has common sense would contract a habit, or sell himself to a sin, which tends to such guilt and misery, and exposes a man every day to the danger of dying insensible, and awaking in hell? Wisdom seems in these chapters to take up the discourse as at the beginning of the book. They must be considered as the words of Christ to the sinner.

Chapter 24

1–2. Envy not sinners. And let not a desire ever come into thy mind, Oh that I could shake off restraints!

3–6. Piety and prudence in outward affairs, both go together to complete a wise man. By knowledge the soul is filled with the graces and comforts of the spirit, those precious and pleasant riches. The spirit is strengthened for the spiritual work and the spiritual warfare, by true wisdom.

7–9. A weak man thinks wisdom is too high for him, therefore he will take no pains for it. It is bad to do evil, but worse to devise it. Even the first risings of sin in the heart are sin, and must be repented of. Those that strive to make others hateful, make themselves so.

10. Under troubles we are apt to despair of relief. But remember that if his neighbour is in danger by any unjust proceeding, he is bound to do all in his power to deliver him. And what is it to suffer immortal souls to perish, when our persuasions and quickened to the study of wisdom by considering both the pleasure and the profit of it. All men relish things that are sweet to the palate; but many have no relish for the

things that are sweet to the purified soul, and that make us wise unto do, by stumbling at some stone in his path; but gets up, and goes on his way with more care and speed. This is rather to be understood of falls into affliction, than falls into actual sin. The godly in the land, will be quiet in the land. There may be cause to change for the better, but have nothing to do with them that are given change.

23–26. The wisdom God giveth, renders a man fit for his station. Every one who finds the benefit of the right answer, will be attached to him that gave it.

27. We must prefer necessaries before conveniences, and not go in debt.

30–34. See what a blessing the husbandman's calling is, and what a wilderness this earth would be without it. See what great difference there is in the management even of worldly affairs. Sloth and self-indulgence are the bane of all good. When we see fields overgrown with thorns and thistles, and the fences broken down, we see an emblem of the far more deplorable state of many souls. Every vile affection grows in men's hearts; yet they compose themselves to sleep. Let us show wisdom by doubling our diligence in every good thing.

Chapter 25

1–3. God needs not search into any thing; nothing can be hid from him. But it is the honour of rulers to search out matters, to suppress vice, and reform his people, is the best way to self-denial. He who has seen the glory of the Lord in Christ Jesus, will feel his own unworthiness.

8–10. To be hasty in beginning strife, will bring into difficulties. War must at length end, and might better be prevented. It is so in private word of counsel, or reproof, rightly spoken, is especially beautiful, as fine fruit becomes still more beautiful in silver baskets.

13. See what ought to be the aim of him that is trusted with any business; to be faithful. A faithful minister, Christ's messenger, should be thus acceptable to us.

14. He who pretends to have received or given that which he never had, is like the morning cloud, that disappoints those who look for rain.

15. Be patient to bear a present hurt. Be mild to speak without passion; for persuasive language is the most effectual to prevail over the hardened mind.

16. God has given us leave to use grateful things, but we are cautioned against excess.

17. We cannot be upon good terms with our neighbours, without discretion as well as sincerity. How much better a Friend is God than any other friend! The oftener we come to him, the more welcome.

18. A false testimony is dangerous in every thing.

19. Confidence in an unfaithful man is painful and vexatious; when we put any stress on him, he not only fails, but makes us feel for it.

20. We take a wrong course if we think to relieve precept to love even our enemies is an Old Testament commandment. Our Saviour has shown his own great example in loving us when we were enemies.

23. Slanders would not be so readily spoken, if they were not readily heard. Sin, if it receives any check, becomes cowardly.

24. It is better to be alone, than to be joined to one who is a hindrance to the comfort of life.

25. Heaven is a country afar off; how refreshing is good news from thence, in the everlasting gospel, which signifies glad tidings, and in the witness of the Spirit with our spirits that we are God's children!

26. When the righteous are led into sin, it is as hurtful as if the public fountains were poisoned.

27. We must be, through grace, dead to the pleasures of sense, and also to the praises of men.

28. The man who has no command over his anger, is easily robbed of peace. Let us give up ourselves to the Lord, and pray him to put his Spirit within us, and cause us to walk in his statutes.

Chapter 26

1. Honour is out of season to those unworthy and unfit for it.

2. He that is cursed without cause, the curse shall do him no more harm than the bird that flies over his head.

3. Every creature must be dealt with according to its nature, but careless and profligate sinners never will be ruled by reason and persuasion. Man indeed is born like the wild ass's colt; but remarks to the man, and address them to his conscience, so as may best end the debate.

6–9. Fools are not fit to be trusted, nor to have any honour. Wise sayings, as a foolish man delivers and applies them, lose their usefulness.

10. This verse may either declare how the Lord, the Creator of all men, will deal with sinners according to their guilt, or, how the powerful among men should disgrace and punish the wicked.

11. The dog is a loathsome emblem of those sinners who return to their vices.

12. We see many a one who has some little sense, but is proud of it. This describes those who think their spiritual state to be good, when really it is very bad.

13. The slothful man hates every thing that requires care and labour. But it is foolish to frighten ourselves from real duties by fancied difficulties. This may be applied to a man slothful in the duties of religion.

14. Having seen the slothful man in fear of his work, here we find him in love with his ease. Bodily ease is the sad occasion of many spiritual diseases. He does not care to get forward with his business. Slothful professors turn thus. The world and the flesh are hinges on which they are hung; and though they move in a course of outward services, yet they are not the nearer to heaven.

15. The sluggard is now out of his bed, but he might have lain there, for any thing he is likely to bring to pass in his work. It is common for men who will not do their duty, to pretend they cannot. Those that are slothful in religion, will not be at the pains to feed their souls with the bread of life, nor to fetch in promised blessings by prayer.

16. He that takes pains in religion, knows he is working for a good Master, and that his labour shall not be in vain.

17. To make ourselves busy in other men's matters, is to must repent in earnest, or his sin will be his ruin.

20–22. Contention heats the spirit, and puts families and societies into a flame. And that fire is commonly kindled and kept burning by whisperers and backbiters.

23. A wicked heart disguising itself, is like a potsherd covered with the dross of silver.

24–26. Always distrust when a man speaks fair unless you know him well. Satan, in his temptations, speaks fair, as he did to Eve; but it is madness to give credit to him.

27. What pains men take to do mischief to others! But it is digging a pit, it is rolling a stone, hard work; and they prepare mischief to themselves.

28. There are two sorts of lies equally detestable. A slandering lie, the mischief of this every body sees. A flattering lie, which secretly works ruin. A wise man will be more afraid of a flatterer than of a slanderer.

Chapter 27

1. We know not what a day may bring forth. This does not forbid preparing for to-morrow, but presuming upon to-morrow. We must not put off the great work of conversion, that one thing needful.

2. There may be occasion for us to justify ourselves, rebukes are better, not only than secret hatred, but than love which compliments in sin, to the hurt of the soul.

6. The poor have a better relish of their enjoyments, and are often more thankful for them, than the rich. In like manner the proud and self-sufficient disdain the gospel; but those who hunger and thirst after righteousness, find comfort from the meanest book or sermon that testifies of Christ Jesus.

8. Every man has his proper place in society, where he may be safe and comfortable. kindred's sake; apply to those who are at hand, and will help in need. But there is a Friend that sticketh closer than a brother, and let us place entire confidence in him.

11. An affectionate parent urges his son to prudent conduct that should gladden his heart. The good conduct of Christians is the best answer to all who find fault with the gospel.

12. Where there is temptation, if we thrust ourselves into it, there will be sin, and punishment will follow.

13. An honest man may be made a beggar, but he is not honest that makes himself one.

14. It is folly to be fond of being praised; it is a temptation to pride. A shower is troublesome for a time; the contentions of a wife are like constant rain.

17. We are cautioned to take heed whom we converse with. And directed to have in view, in conversation, to make one another wiser and better.

18. Though a calling be labourious and despised, yet those who keep to it, will find there is something to be got by it. God is a Master who has engaged to honour those who serve him faithfully.

19. One corrupt heart is like another; so are sanctified hearts: the former bear the same image of the earthly, the latter the same image of the heavenly. Let us carefully watch our own hearts, comparing them with the word of God.

20. Two things are here said to be never satisfied, death and sin. The appetites of the carnal mind for profit or pleasure are always desiring more. Those whose eyes are ever toward the Lord, are satisfied in him, and shall for ever be so.

21. Silver and gold are tried by putting them into the furnace and fining-pot; so is a man tried by praising him.

22. Some are so bad, that even severe methods do not answer the end; what remains but that they should be rejected? The new-creating power of God's grace alone is able to make a change.

23–27. We ought to have some business to do in this world, and not to live in idleness, and not to meddle with what we do not understand. We must be diligent and take pains. Let us do what we can, still the world cannot be secured to us, therefore we must choose a more lasting portion; but by the blessing of God upon our honest labours, we may expect to enjoy as much of earthly blessings as is good for us.

Chapter 28

1. Sin makes men cowards. Whatever difficulties the righteous meet in the way of duty, they are not daunted.

2. National sins disturb the public repose.

3. If needy persons get opportunities of oppressing, their extortion will be more severe than that of the more wealthy.

4. Wicked people strengthen one another in wicked ways.

5. If a man seeks the Lord, it is a good sign that he understands much, and it is a good means of understanding more.

6. An honest, godly, poor man, is better than a wicked, ungodly, rich man; has more comfort in himself, and is a greater blessing to the world.

7. Companions of riotous men not only grieve their parents, but shame them.

8. That which is ill got, though it may increase much, will not last long. Thus the poor are repaid, and God is glorified.

9. The sinner at whose prayers God is angry, is one who obstinately refuses to obey God's commands.

10. The success of ungodly men is their own misery.

11. Rich men are so flattered, that they think themselves superior to others.

12. There is glory in the land when the righteous have liberty.

13. It is folly to indulge sin, and excuse it. He who covers his sins, shall not have any true peace. He who humbly confesses his sins, with true repentance and faith, shall find mercy from God. The Son of God is our great atonement. Under a deep sense of our guilt and danger, we may claim salvation from that mercy which reigns through righteousness unto eternal life, by Jesus Christ our Lord.

14. There is a fear which causes happiness. Faith and love will deliver from the fear of eternal misery; but we should always fear offending God, and fear sinning against him.

15. A wicked ruler, whatever we may call him, this scripture calls a roaring lion, and a ranging bear.

16. Oppressors want understanding; they do not consult their own honour, ease, and safety.

17. The murderer shall be haunted with terrors. None shall desire to save him from deserved punishment, nor pity him.

18. Uprightness will give men holy security in the worst times; but the false and dishonest are never safe.

19. Those who are diligent, take the way to live comfortably.

20. The true way to be happy, is to be holy and honest; not to raise an estate suddenly, without regard to right or wrong.

21. Judgment is perverted, when any thing but pure right is considered.

22. He that hastens to be rich, never seriously thinks how quickly God may take his wealth from him, and leave him in poverty.

23. Upon reflection, most will have a better opinion of a faithful reprover than of a soothing flatterer.

24. Here is the wickedness of those who think it no sin to rob their parents, by wheedling them or threatening them, or by wasting what they have, and running into debt.

25. Those make themselves always easy, that live in continual dependence upon God and his grace, and live by faith.

26. A fool trusts to his own strength, merit, and righteousness. And trusts to his own heart, which is not only deceitful above all things, but which has often deceived him.

27. A selfish man not only will not look out for objects of compassion, but will look off from those that call for his attention.

28. When power is put into the hands of the wicked, wise men decline public business. If the reader will go diligently over this and the other chapters, in many places where at first he may suppose there is least of Christ, still he will find what will lead to him.

Chapter 29

1. If God wounds, who can heal? The word of God warns all to flee from the wrath to come, to the hope set before us in Jesus Christ.

2. The people have cause to rejoice or mourn, as their rulers are righteous or wicked.

3. Divine wisdom best keeps us from ruinous lusts.

4. The Lord Jesus is the King who will minister true judgment to the people.

5. Flatterers put men off their guard, which betrays them into foolish conduct.

6. Transgressions always end in vexations. Righteous men walk at liberty, and walk in safety.

7. This verse is applicable to compassion for the distress of the poor, and the unfeeling disregard shown by the wicked.

8. The scornful mock at things sacred and serious. Men who promote religion, which is true wisdom, turn away the wrath of God.

9. If a wise man dispute with a conceited wrangler, he will be treated with anger or ridicule; and no good is done.

10. Christ told his disciples that they should be hated of all men. The just, whom the bloodthirsty hate, gladly do any thing for their salvation.

11. He is a fool who tells every thing he knows, and can keep no counsel.

12. One who loves flatterers, and hearkens to slanderers, causes his servants to become liars and false accusers.

13. Some are poor, others have a great deal of deceitful riches. They meet in the business of this world; the Lord gives to both the comforts of this life. To some of both sorts he gives his grace.

14. The rich will look to themselves, but the poor and needy the prince must defend and plead for.

15. Parents must consider the benefit of due correction, and the mischief of undue indulgence.

16. Let not the righteous have their faith and hope shocked by the increase of sin and sinners, but let them wait with patience.

17. Children must not be suffered to go without rebuke when they do amiss.

18. How bare does a place look without Bibles and ministers! And what an easy prey is it to the enemy of souls! That gospel is an open vision, which holds forth Christ, which humbles the sinner and exalts the Saviour, which promotes holiness in the life and conversation: and these are precious truths to keep the soul alive, and prevent it from perishing.

19. Here is an unprofitable, slothful, wicked servant; one that serves not from conscience, or love, but from fear.

20. When a man is self-conceited, rash, and given to wrangling, there is more hope of the ignorant and profligate.

21. Good usage to a servant does not mean indulgence, which would ruin even a child. The body is a servant to the soul; those that humour it, and are over-tender of it, will find it forget its place.

22. An angry, passionate disposition makes men provoking to one another, and provoking to God.

23. Only those who humble themselves shall be exalted and established.

24. The receiver is as bad as the thief.

25. Many are ashamed to own Christ now; and he will not own them in the day of judgment. But he that trusts in the Lord will be saved from this snare.

26. The wisest course is, to look to God, and seek the favour of the Ruler of rulers; for every creature is that to us which God makes it to be.

27. The just man abhors the sins of the wicked, and shuns their company. Christ exposed the wickedness of men, yet prayed for the wicked when they were crucifying him. Hatred to sin in ourselves and others, is a needful branch of the Christian temper. But all that are unholy, have rooted hatred to godliness.

Chapter 30

1–6. Agur speaks of himself as wanting a righteousness, and having done very foolishly.

And it becomes us all to have low thoughts of ourselves. He speaks of himself as wanting revelation to guide him in the ways of truth and wisdom. The more enlightened people are, the more they lament their ignorance; the more they pray for clearer, still clearer discoveries of God, and his rich grace in Christ Jesus. In ver. 4, there is a prophetic notice of Him who came down from heaven to be our Instructor and Saviour, and then ascended into heaven to be our Advocate. The Messiah is here spoken of as a Person distinct from the Father, but his name as yet secret. The great Redeemer, in the glories of his providence and grace, cannot be found out to perfection. Had it not been for Christ, the foundations of the earth had sunk under the load of the curse upon the ground, for man's sin. Who, and what is the mighty One that doeth all this? There is not the least ground to suspect anything wanting in the word of God; adding to his words opens the way to errors and corruptions.

7–9. Agur wisely prayed for a middle state, that he might be kept at a distance from temptations; he asked daily bread suited to his station, his family, and his real good. There is a remarkable similarity between this prayer and several clauses of the Lord's prayer. If we are removed from vanity and lies; if we are interested in the pardoning love of Christ, and have him for our portion; if we walk with God, then we shall have all we can ask or think, as to spiritual things. When we consider how those who have abundance are prone to abuse the gift, and what it is to suffer want, Agur's prayer will ever be found a wise one, though seldom offered. Food convenient; what is so for one, may not be so for another; but we may be sure that our heavenly Father will supply all our need, and not suffer us to want anything good for us; and why should we wish for more?

10. Slander not a servant to his master, accuse him not in small matters, to make mischief.

11–14. In every age there are monsters of ingratitude who ill-treat their parents. Many persuade themselves they are holy persons, whose hearts are full of sin, and who practise secret wickedness. There are others whose lofty pride is manifest. There have also been cruel monsters in every age.

15–17. Cruelty and covetousness are two daughters of the horseleech, that still cry, 'Give, give,' and they are continually uneasy to themselves. Four things never are satisfied, to which these devourers are compared. Those are never rich that are always coveting. And many who have come to a bad end, have owned that their wicked courses began by despising their parents' authority.

18–20. Four things cannot be fully known. The kingdom of nature is full of marvels. The fourth is a mystery of iniquity; the cursed arts by which a vile seducer gains the affections of a female; and the arts which a vile woman uses to conceal her wickedness.

21–23. Four sorts of persons are very troublesome. Men of low origin and base spirit, who, getting authority, become tyrants. Foolish and violent men indulging in excesses. A woman of a contentious spirit and vicious habits. A servant who has obtained undue influence. Let those whom Providence has advanced from low beginnings, carefully watch against that sin which most easily besets them.

24–28. Four things that are little, are yet to be admired. There are those who are poor in the world, and of small account, yet wise for their souls and another world.

29–33. We may learn from animals to go well; also to keep our temper under all provocations. We must keep the evil thought in our minds from breaking out into evil speeches. We must not stir up the passions of others. Let nothing be said or done with violence, but every thing with softness and calmness. Alas, how often have we done foolishly in rising up against the Lord our King! Let us humble ourselves before him. And having found peace with Him, let us follow peace with all men.

Chapter 31

An exhortation to king Lemuel to take heed of sin, and to do duties (1–9)

The description of a virtuous woman (10–31)

An exhortation to king Lemuel to take heed of sin, and to do duties (1–9)

When children are under the mother's eye, she has an opportunity of fashioning their minds aright. Those who are grown up, should often call to mind the good teaching they received when children. The many awful instances of promising characters who have been ruined by vile women, and love of wine, should warn every one to avoid these evils. Wine is to be used for want or medicine. Every creature of God is good, and wine, though abused, has its use. By the same rule, due praise and consolation should be used as cordials to the dejected and tempted, not administered to the confident and self-sufficient. All in authority should be more carefully temperate even than other men; and should be protectors of those who are unable or afraid to plead their own cause. Our blessed Lord did not decline the bitterest dregs of the cup of sorrow put into his hands; but he puts the cup of consolation into the hands of his people, and causes those to rejoice who are in the deepest distress.

The description of a virtuous woman (10–31)

This is the description of a virtuous woman of those days, but the general outlines equally suit every age and nation. She is very careful to recommend herself to her husband's esteem and affection, to know his mind, and is willing that he rule over her.

1. She can be trusted, and he will leave such a wife to manage for him. He is happy in her. And she makes it her constant business to do him good.

2. She is one that takes pains in her duties, and takes pleasure in them. She is careful to fill up time, that none be lost. She rises early. She applies herself to the business proper for her, to women's business. She does what she does, with all her power, and trifles not.

3. She makes what she does turn to good account by prudent management. Many undo themselves by buying, without considering whether they can afford it. She provides well for her house. She lays up for hereafter.

4. She looks well to the ways of her household, that she may oblige all to do their duty to God and one another, as well as to her.

5. She is intent upon giving as upon getting, and does it freely and cheerfully.

6. She is discreet and obliging; every word she says, shows she governs herself by the rules of wisdom. She not only takes prudent measures herself, but gives prudent advice to others. The law of love and kindness is written in the heart, and shows itself in the tongue. Her heart is full of another world, even when her hands are most busy about this world.

7. Above all, she fears the Lord. Beauty recommends none to God, nor is it any proof of wisdom and goodness, but it has deceived many a man who made his choice of a wife by it. But the fear of God reigning in the heart, is the beauty of the soul; it lasts for ever.

8. She has firmness to bear up under crosses and disappointments. She shall reflect with comfort when she comes to be old, that she was not idle or useless when young. She shall rejoice in a world to come. She is a great blessing to her relations. If the fruit be good, the tree must have our good word. But she leaves it to her own works to praise her. Every one ought to desire this honour that cometh from God; and according to this standard we all ought to regulate our judgments. This description let all women daily study, who desire to be truly beloved and respected, useful and honourable. This passage is to be applied to individuals, but may it not also be applied to the church of God, which is described as a virtuous spouse? God by his grace has formed from among sinful men a church of true believers, to possess all the excellences here described.

ECCLESIASTES

Matthew Henry

Introduction

The name of this book signifies 'The Preacher'. The wisdom of God here preaches to us, speaking by Solomon, who it is evident was the author. At the close of his life, being made sensible of his sin and folly, he recorded here his experience for the benefit of others, as the book of his repentance; and he pronounced all earthly good to be 'vanity and vexation of spirit.' It convinces us of the vanity of the world, and that it cannot make us happy; of the vileness of sin, and its certain tendency to make us miserable. It shows that no created good can satisfy the soul, and that happiness is to be found in God alone; and this doctrine must, under the blessed Spirit's teaching, lead the heart to Christ Jesus.

Chapter 1

Solomon shows that all human things are vain (1–3)

Man's toil and want of satisfaction (4–8)

There is nothing new (9–11)

The vexation in pursuit of knowledge (12–18)

Solomon shows that all human things are vain (1–3)

Much is to be learned by comparing one part of Scripture with another. We here behold Solomon returning from the broken and empty cisterns of the world, to the Fountain of living water; recording his own folly and shame, the bitterness of his disappointment, and the lessons he had learned. Those that have taken warning to turn and live, should warn others not to go on and die. He does not merely say all things are vain, but that they are vanity. VANITY OF VANITIES, ALL IS VANITY. This is the text of the preacher's sermon, of which in this book he never loses sight. If this world, in its present state, were all, it would not be worth living for; and the wealth and pleasure of this world, if we had ever so much, are not enough to make us happy. What profit has a man of all his labour? All he gets by it will not supply the wants of the soul, nor satisfy its desires; will not atone for the sins of the soul, nor hinder the loss of it: what profit will the wealth of the world be to the soul in death, in judgment, or in the everlasting state?

Man's toil and want of satisfaction (4–8)

All things change, and never rest. Man, after all his labour, is no nearer finding rest than the sun, the wind, or the current of the river. His soul will find no rest, if he has it not from God. The senses are soon tired, yet still craving what is untried.

There is nothing new (9–11)

Men's hearts and their corruptions are the same now as in former times; their desires, and pursuits, and complaints, still the same. This should take us from expecting happiness in the creature, and quicken us to seek eternal blessings. How many things and persons in Solomon's day were thought very great, yet there is no remembrance of them now!

The vexation in pursuit of knowledge (12–18)

Solomon tried all things, and found them vanity. He found his searches after knowledge weariness, not only to the flesh, but to the mind. The more he saw of the works done under the sun, the more he saw their vanity; and the sight often vexed his spirit. He could neither gain that satisfaction to himself, nor do that good to others, which he expected. Even the pursuit of knowledge and wisdom discovered man's wickedness and misery; so that the more he knew, the more he saw cause to lament and mourn. Let us learn to hate and fear sin, the cause of all this vanity and misery; to value Christ; to seek rest in the knowledge, love, and service of the Saviour.

Chapter 2

The vanity and vexation of mirth, sensual pleasure, riches, and pomp (1–11)

Human wisdom insufficient (12–17)

This world to be used according to the will of God (18–26)

The vanity and vexation of mirth, sensual pleasure, riches, and pomp (1–11)

Solomon soon found mirth and pleasure to be vanity. What does noisy, flashy mirth towards making a man happy? The manifold devices of men's hearts, to get satisfaction from the world, and their changing from one thing to another, are like the restlessness of a man in a fever. Perceiving it was folly to give himself to wine, he next tried the costly amusements of princes. The poor, when they read such a description, are ready to feel discontent. But the remedy against all such feelings is in the estimate of it all by the owner himself. All was vanity and vexation of spirit: and the same things would yield the same result to us, as to Solomon. Having food and raiment, let us therewith be content. His wisdom remained with him; a strong understanding, with great human knowledge. But every earthly pleasure, when unconnected with better blessings, leaves the mind as eager and unsatisfied as before. Happiness arises not from the situation in which we are placed. It is only through Jesus Christ that final blessedness can be attained.

Human wisdom insufficient (12–17)

Solomon found that knowledge and prudence were preferable to ignorance and folly, though human wisdom and knowledge will not make a man happy. The most learned of men, who dies a stranger to Christ Jesus, will perish equally with the most ignorant; and what good can commendations on earth do to the body in the grave, or the soul in hell? And the spirits of just men made perfect cannot want them. So that if this were all, we might be led to hate our life, as it is all vanity and vexation of spirit.

This world to be used according to the will of God (18–26)

Our hearts are very loth to quit their expectations of great things from the creature; but Solomon came to this at length. The world is a vale of tears, even to those that have much of it. See what fools they are, who make themselves drudges to the world, which affords a man nothing better than subsistence for the body. And the utmost he can attain in this respect is to allow himself a sober, cheerful use thereof, according to his rank and condition. But we must enjoy good in our labour; we must use those things to make us diligent and cheerful in worldly business. And this is the gift of God. Riches are a blessing or a curse to a man, according as he has, or has not, a heart to make a good use of them. To those that are accepted of the Lord, he gives joy and satisfaction in the knowledge and love of him. But to the sinner he allots labour, sorrow, vanity, and vexation, in seeking a worldly portion, which yet afterwards comes into better hands. Let the sinner seriously consider his latter end. To seek a lasting portion in the love of Christ and the blessings it bestows, is the only way to true and satisfying enjoyment even of this present world.

Chapter 3

The changes of human affairs (1–10)

The Divine counsels unchangeable (11–15)

The vanity of worldly power (16–22)

The changes of human affairs (1–10)

To expect unchanging happiness in a changing world, must end in disappointment. To bring ourselves to our state in life, is our duty and wisdom in this world. God's whole plan for the government of the world will be found altogether wise, just, and good. Then let us seize the favourable opportunity for every good purpose and work. The time to die is fast approaching. Thus labour and sorrow fill the world. This is given us, that we may always have something to do; none were sent into the world to be idle.

The Divine counsels unchangeable (11–15)

Every thing is as God made it; not as it appears to us. We have the world so much in our hearts, are so taken up with thoughts and cares of worldly things, that we have neither time nor spirit to see God's hand in them. The world has not only gained possession of the heart, but has formed thoughts against the beauty of God's works. We mistake if we think we were born for ourselves; no, it is our business to do good in this life, which is short and uncertain; we have but little time to be doing good, therefore we should redeem time. Satisfaction with Divine Providence, is having faith that all things work together for good to them that love him. God doeth all, that men should fear before him. The world, as it has been, is, and will be. There has no change befallen us, nor has any temptation by it taken us, but such as is common to men.

The vanity of worldly power (16–22)

Without the fear of the Lord, man is but vanity; set that aside, and judges will not use their power well. And there is another Judge that stands before the door. With God there is a time for the redressing of grievances, though as yet we see it not. Solomon seems to express his wish that men might perceive, that by choosing this world as their portion, they brought themselves to a level with the beasts, without being free, as they are, from present vexations and a future account. Both return to the dust from whence they were taken. What little reason have we to be proud of our bodies, or bodily accomplishments! But as none can fully comprehend, so few consider properly, the difference between the rational soul of man, and the spirit or life of the beast. The spirit of man goes upward, to be judged, and is then fixed in an unchangeable state of happiness or misery. It is as certain that the spirit of the beast goes downward to the earth; it perishes at death. Surely their case is lamentable, the height of whose hopes and wishes is, that they may die like beasts. Let our inquiry be, how an eternity of existence may be to us an eternity of enjoyment? To answer this, is the grand design of revelation. Jesus is revealed as the Son of God, and the Hope of sinners.

Chapter 4

Miseries from oppression (1–3)

Troubles from envy (4–6)

The folly of covetousness (7, 8)

The advantages of mutual assistance (9–12)

The changes of royalty (13–16)

Miseries from oppression (1–3)

It grieved Solomon to see might prevail against right. Wherever we turn, we see melancholy proofs of the wickedness and misery of mankind, who try to create trouble to themselves and to each other. Being thus hardly used, men are tempted to hate and despise life. But a good man, though badly off while in this world, cannot have cause to wish he had never been

born, since he is glorifying the Lord, even in the fires, and will be happy at last, for ever happy. Ungodly men have most cause to wish the continuance of life with all its vexations, as a far more miserable condition awaits them if they die in their sins. If human and worldly things were our chief good, not to exist would be preferable to life, considering the various oppressions here below.

Troubles from envy (4–6)

Solomon notices the sources of trouble peculiar to well-doers, and includes all who labour with diligence, and whose efforts are crowned with success. They often become great and prosperous, but this excites envy and opposition. Others, seeing the vexations of an active course, foolishly expect more satisfaction in sloth and idleness. But idleness is a sin that is its own punishment. Let us by honest industry lay hold on the handful, that we may not want necessaries, but not grasp at both hands full, which would only create vexation of spirit. Moderate pains and gains do best.

The folly of covetousness (7, 8)

Frequently, the more men have, the more they would have; and on this they are so intent, that they get no enjoyment from what they have. Selfishness is the cause of this evil. A selfish man cares for nobody; there is none to take care of but himself, yet he will scarcely allow necessary rest to himself, and the people he employs. He never thinks he has enough. He has enough for his calling, for his family, but he has not enough for his eyes. Many are so set upon the world, that in pursuit of it they bereave themselves, not only of the favour of God and eternal life, but of the pleasures of this life. The distant relations or strangers who inherit such a man's wealth, never thank him. Covetousness gathers strength by time and habit; men tottering on the brink of the grave, grow more grasping and griping. Alas, and how often do we see men professing to be followers of Him, who, 'though he was rich, for our sakes became poor,' anxiously scraping money together and holding it fast, excusing themselves by common-place talking about the necessity of care, and the danger of extravagance!

The advantages of mutual assistance (9–12)

Surely he has more satisfaction in life, who labours hard to maintain those he loves, than the miser has in his toil. In all things union tends to success and safety, but above all, the union of Christians. They assist each other by encouragement, or friendly reproof. They warm each other's hearts while they converse together of the love of Christ, or join in singing his praises. Then let us improve our opportunities of

Christian fellowship. In these things all is not vanity, though there will be some alloy as long as we are under the sun. Where two are closely joined in holy love and fellowship, Christ will by his Spirit come to them; then there is a threefold cord.

The changes of royalty (13–16)

People are never long easy and satisfied; they are fond of changes. This is no new thing. Princes see themselves slighted by those they have studied to oblige; this is vanity and vexation of spirit. But the willing servants of the Lord Jesus, our King, rejoice in him alone, and they will love Him more and more to all eternity.

Chapter 5

What renders devotion vain (1–3)

Of vows, and oppression (4–8)

The vanity of riches shown (9–17)

The right use of riches (18–20)

What renders devotion vain (1–3)

Address thyself to the worship of God, and take time to compose thyself for it. Keep thy thoughts from roving and wandering: keep thy affections from running out toward wrong objects. We should avoid vain repetitions; copious prayers are not here condemned, but those that are unmeaning. How often our wandering thoughts render attendance on Divine ordinances little better than the sacrifice of fools! Many words and hasty ones, used in prayer, show folly in the heart, low thoughts of God, and careless thoughts of our own souls.

Of vows, and oppression (4–8)

When a person made engagements rashly, he suffered his mouth to cause his flesh to sin. The case supposes a man coming to the priest, and pretending that his vow was made rashly, and that it would be wrong to fulfil it. Such mockery of God would bring the Divine displeasure, which might blast what was thus unduly kept. We are to keep down the fear of man. Set God before thee; then, if thou seest the oppression of the poor, thou wilt not find fault with Divine Providence; nor think the worse of the institution of magistracy, when thou seest the ends of it thus perverted; nor of religion, when thou seest it will not secure men from suffering wrong. But though oppressors may be secure, God will reckon for all.

The vanity of riches shown (9–17)

The goodness of Providence is more equally distributed than appears to a careless observer. The king needs the common things of life, and the poor share them; they relish their morsel better than he does his luxuries. There are bodily desires which silver itself will not satisfy, much less will worldly abundance satisfy spiritual desires. The more men have, the better house they must keep, the more servants they must employ, the more guests they must entertain, and the more they will have hanging on them. The sleep of the labourer is sweet, not only because he is tired, but because he has little care to break his sleep. The sleep of the diligent Christian, and his long sleep, are sweet; having spent himself and his time in the service of God, he can cheerfully repose in God as his Rest. But those who have every thing else, often fail to secure a good night's sleep; their abundance breaks their rest. Riches do hurt, and draw away the heart from God and duty. Men do hurt with their riches, not only gratifying their own lusts, but oppressing others, and dealing hardly with them. They will see that they have laboured for the wind, when, at death, they find the profit of their labour is all gone like the wind, they know not whither. How ill the covetous worldling bears the calamities of human life! He does not sorrow to repentance, but is angry at the providence of God, angry at all about him; which doubles his affliction.

The right use of riches (18–20)

Life is God's gift. We must not view our calling as a drudgery, but take pleasure in the calling where God puts us. A cheerful spirit is a great blessing; it makes employments easy, and afflictions light. Having made a proper use of riches, a man will remember the days of his past life with pleasure. The manner in which Solomon refers to God as the Giver, both of life and its enjoyments, shows they ought to be received and to be used, consistently with his will, and to his glory. Let this passage recommend to all the kind words of the merciful Redeemer, 'Labour not for the meat that perisheth, but for that meat which endureth unto everlasting life.' Christ is the Bread of life, the only food of the soul. All are invited to partake of this heavenly provision.

Chapter 6

The vanity of riches. Also of long life and flourishing families (1–6)

The little advantage any one has in outward things (7–12)

The vanity of riches. Also of long life and flourishing families (1–6)

A man often has all he needs for outward enjoyment; yet the Lord leaves him so to covetousness or evil dispositions, that he makes no good or comfortable use of what he has. By one means or other his possessions come to strangers; this is vanity, and an evil disease. A numerous family was a matter of fond desire and of high honour among the Hebrews; and long life is the desire of mankind in general. Even with these additions a man may not be able to enjoy his riches, family, and life. Such a man, in his passage through life, seems to have been born for no end or use. And he who has entered on life only for one moment, to quit it the next, has a preferable lot to him who has lived long, but only to suffer.

The little advantage any one has in outward things (7–12)

A little will serve to sustain us comfortably, and a great deal can do no more. The desires of the soul find nothing in the wealth of the world to give satisfaction. The poor man has comfort as well as the richest, and is under no real disadvantage. We cannot say, Better is the sight of the eyes than the resting of the soul in God; for it is better to live by faith in things to come, than to live by sense, which dwells only upon present things. Our lot is appointed. We have what pleases God, and let that please us. The greatest possessions and honours cannot set us above the common events of human life. Seeing that the things men pursue on earth increase vanities, what is man the better for his worldly devices? Our life upon earth is to be reckoned by days. It is fleeting and uncertain, and with little in it to be fond of, or to be depended on. Let us return to God, trust in his mercy through Jesus Christ, and submit to his will. Then soon shall we glide through this vexatious world, and find ourselves in that happy place, where there is fulness of joy and pleasures for evermore.

Chapter 7

The benefit of a good name; of death above life; of sorrow above vain mirth (1–6)

Concerning oppression, anger, and discontent (7–10)

Advantages of wisdom (11–22)

Experience of the evil of sin (23–29)

The benefit of a good name; of death above life; of sorrow above vain mirth (1–6)

Reputation for piety and honesty is more desirable than all the wealth and pleasure in this world. It will do more good to go to a funeral than to a feast. We may lawfully go to both, as there is occasion; our Saviour both feasted at the wedding of his friend in Cana, and wept at the grave of his friend in Bethany. But, considering how apt we are to be vain and indulge the flesh, it is best to go to the house of mourning, to learn the end of man as to this world. Seriousness is better than mirth and jollity. That is best for us which is best for our souls, though it be unpleasing to sense. It is better to have our corruptions mortified by the rebuke of the wise, than to have them gratified by the song of fools. The laughter of a fool is soon gone, the end of his mirth is heaviness.

Concerning oppression, anger, and discontent (7–10)

The event of our trials and difficulties is often better than at first we thought. Surely it is better to be patient in spirit, than to be proud and hasty. Be not soon angry, nor quick in resenting an affront. Be not long angry; though anger may come into the bosom of a wise man, it passes through it as a way-faring man; it dwells only in the bosom of fools. It is folly to cry out upon the badness of our times, when we have more reason to cry out for the badness of our own hearts; and even in these times we enjoy many mercies. It is folly to cry up the goodness of former times; as if former ages had not the like things to complain of that we have: this arises from discontent, and aptness to quarrel with God himself.

Advantages of wisdom (11–22)

Wisdom is as good as an inheritance, yea better. It shelters from the storms and scorching heat of trouble. Wealth will not lengthen out the natural life; but true wisdom will give spiritual life, and strengthen men for services under their sufferings. Let us look upon the disposal of our condition as the work of God, and at last all will appear to have been for the best. In acts of righteousness, be not carried into heats or passions, no, not by a zeal for God. Be not conceited of thine own abilities; nor find fault with every thing, nor busy thyself in other men's matters. Many who will not be wrought upon by the fear of God, and the dread of hell, will avoid sins which ruin their health and estate, and expose to public justice. But those that truly fear God, have but one end to serve, therefore act steadily. If we say we have not sinned, we deceive ourselves. Every true believer is ready to say, God be merciful to me a sinner. Forget not at the same time, that personal righteousness, walking in newness of life, is the only real evidence of an interest by faith in the righteousness of the Redeemer. Wisdom teaches us not to be quick in resenting affronts. Be not desirous to know what people say; if they speak well of thee, it will feed thy pride, if ill, it will stir up thy passion. See that thou approve thyself to God and thine own conscience, and then heed not what men say of thee; it is easier to pass by twenty affronts than to avenge one. When any harm is done to us, examine whether we have not done as bad to others.

Experience of the evil of sin (23–29)

Solomon, in his search into the nature and reason of things, had been miserably deluded. But he here speaks with godly sorrow. He alone who constantly aims to please God, can expect to escape; the careless sinner probably will fall to rise no more. He now discovered more than ever the evil of the great sin of which he had been guilty, the loving many strange women, found in 1 Kings. How was he likely to find such a one among those he had collected? If any of them had been well disposed, their situation would tend to render them all nearly of the same character. He here warns others against the sins into which he had been betrayed. Many a godly man can with thankfulness acknowledge that he has found a prudent, virtuous woman in the wife of his bosom; but those men who have gone in Solomon's track, cannot expect to find one. He traces up all the streams of actual transgression to the fountain. It is clear that man is corrupted and revolted, and not as he was made. It is lamentable that man, whom God made upright, has found out so many ways to render himself wicked and miserable. Let us bless Him for Jesus Christ, and seek his grace, that we may be numbered with his chosen people.

Chapter 8

Commendations of wisdom (1–5)

To prepare for sudden evils and death (6–8)

It shall be well with the righteous, and ill with the wicked (9–13)

Mysteries of Providence (14–17)

Commendations of wisdom (1–5)

None of the rich, the powerful, the honourable, or the accomplished of the sons of men, are so excellent, useful, or happy, as the wise man. Who else can interpret the words of God, or teach aright from his truths and dispensations? What madness must it be for weak and dependent creatures to rebel against the Almighty! What numbers form wrong judgments, and bring misery on themselves, in this life and that to come!

To prepare for sudden evils and death (6–8)

God has, in wisdom, kept away from us the knowledge of future events, that we may be always ready for changes. We must all die, no flight or hiding-place can save us, nor are there any weapons of effectual resistance. Ninety thousand die every day, upwards of sixty every minute, and one every moment. How solemn the thought! Oh that men were wise, that they understood these things, that they would consider their latter end! The believer alone is prepared to meet the solemn summons. Wickedness, by which men often escape human justice, cannot secure from death.

It shall be well with the righteous, and ill with the wicked (9–13)

Solomon observed, that many a time one man rules over another to his hurt, and that prosperity hardens them in their wickedness. Sinners herein deceive themselves. Vengeance comes slowly, but it comes surely. A good man's days have some substance; he lives to a good purpose: a wicked man's days are all as a shadow, empty and worthless. Let us pray that we may view eternal things as near, real, and all-important.

Mysteries of Providence (14–17)

Faith alone can establish the heart in this mixed scene, where the righteous often suffer, and the wicked prosper. Solomon commended joy, and holy security of mind, arising from confidence in God, because a man has no better thing under the sun, though a good man has much better things above the sun, than soberly and thankfully to use the things of this life according to his rank. He would not have us try to give a reason for what God does. But, leaving the Lord to clear up all difficulties in his own time, we may cheerfully enjoy the comforts, and bear up under the trials of life; while peace of conscience and joy in the Holy Ghost will abide in us through all outward changes, and when flesh and heart shall fail.

Chapter 9

Good and bad men fare alike as to this world (1–3)

All men must die, Their portion as to this life (4–10)

Disappointments common (11, 12)

Benefits of wisdom (13–18)

Good and bad men fare alike as to this world (1–3)

We are not to think our searching into the word or works of God useless, because we cannot explain all difficulties. We may learn many things good for ourselves and useful to others. But man cannot always decide who are objects of God's special love, or under his wrath; and God will certainly put a difference between the precious and the vile, in the other world. The difference as to present happiness, arises from the inward supports and consolations the righteous enjoy, and the benefit they derive from varied trials and mercies. As far as the sons of men are left to themselves, their hearts are full of evil; and prosperity in sin, causes them even to set God at defiance by daring wickedness. Though, on this side death, the righteous and the wicked may often seem to fare alike, on the other side there will be a vast difference between them.

All men must die, Their portion as to this life (4–10)

The most despicable living man's state, is preferable to that of the most noble who have died impenitent. Solomon exhorts the wise and pious to cheerful confidence in God, whatever their condition in life. The meanest morsel, coming from their Father's love, in answer to prayer, will have a peculiar relish. Not that we may set our hearts upon the delights of sense, but what God has given us we may use with wisdom. The joy here described, is the gladness of heart that springs from a sense of the Divine favour. This is the world of service, that to come is the world of recompense. All in their stations, may find some work to do. And above all, sinners have the salvation of their souls to seek after, believers have to prove their faith, adorn the gospel, glorify God, and serve their generation.

Disappointments common (11, 12)

Men's success seldom equals their expectations. We must use means, but not trust to them: if we succeed, we must give God the praise; if crossed, we must submit to his will. Those who put off the great concerns of their souls, are caught in Satan's net, which he baits with some worldly object, for which they reject or neglect the gospel, and go on in sin till they suddenly fall into destruction.

Benefits of wisdom (13–18)

A man may, by his wisdom, bring to pass that which he could never do by his strength. If God be for us, who can be against us, or stand before us? Solomon observes the power of wisdom, though it may labour under outward disadvantages. How forcible are right words! But wise and good men must often content themselves with the satisfaction of having done good, or, at least, endeavoured to do it, when they cannot do the good they would, nor have the praise they should. How many of the good gifts, both of nature and Providence, does one sinner destroy and make waste! He who destroys his own soul destroys much good. One sinner may draw many into his destroying ways. See who are the friends and enemies of a kingdom or a family, if one saint does much good, and one sinner destroys much good.

Chapter 10

To preserve a character for wisdom (1–3)

Respecting subjects and rulers (4–10)

Of foolish talk (11–15)

Duties of rulers and subjects (16–20)

To preserve a character for wisdom (1–3)

Those especially who make a profession of religion, should keep from all appearances of evil. A wise man has great advantage over a fool, who is always at a loss when he has anything to do. Sin is the reproach of sinners, wherever they go, and shows their folly.

Respecting subjects and rulers (4–10)

Solomon appears to caution men not to seek redress in a hasty manner, nor to yield to pride and revenge. Do not, in a passion, quit thy post of duty; wait awhile, and thou wilt find that yielding pacifies great offences. Men are not preferred according to their merit. And those are often most forward to offer help, who are least aware of the difficulties, or the consequences. The same remark is applied to the church, or the body of Christ, that all the members should have the same care one for another.

Of foolish talk (11–15)

There is a practice in the East, of charming serpents by music. The babbler's tongue is an unruly evil, full of deadly poison; and contradiction only makes it the more violent. We must find the way to keep him gentle. But by rash, unprincipled, or slanderous talk, he brings open or secret vengeance upon himself. Would we duly consider our own ignorance as to future events, it would cut off many idle words which we foolishly multiply. Fools toil a great deal to no purpose. They do not understand the plainest things, such as the entrance into a great city. But it is the excellency of the way to the heavenly city, that it is a highway, in which the simplest wayfaring men shall not err, Isaiah 25:8. But sinful folly makes men miss that only way to happiness.

Duties of rulers and subjects (16–20)

The happiness of a land depends on the character of its rulers. The people cannot be happy when their princes are childish, and lovers of pleasure. Slothfulness is of ill consequence both to private and public affairs. Money, of itself, will neither feed nor clothe, though it answers the occasions of this present life, as what is to be had, may generally be had for money. But the soul, as it is not redeemed, so it is not maintained with corruptible things, as silver and gold. God sees what men do, and hears what they say in secret; and, when he pleases, brings it to light by strange and unsuspected ways. If there be hazard in secret thoughts and whispers against earthly rulers, what must be the peril from every deed, word, or thought of rebellion against the King of kings, and Lord of lords! He seeth in secret. His ear is ever open. Sinner! curse not THIS KING in thy inmost thought. Your curses cannot affect Him; but his curse, coming down upon you, will sink you to the lowest hell.

Chapter 11

Exhortation to liberality (1–6)

An admonition to prepare for death, and to young persons to be religious (7–10)

Exhortation to liberality (1–6)

Solomon presses the rich to do good to others. Give freely, though it may seem thrown away and lost. Give to many. Excuse not thyself with the good thou hast done, from the good thou hast further to do. It is not lost, but well laid out. We have reason to expect evil, for we are born to trouble; it is wisdom to do good in the day of prosperity. Riches cannot profit us, if we do not benefit others. Every man must labour to be a blessing to that place where the providence of God casts him. Wherever we are, we may find good work to do, if we have but hearts to do it. If we magnify every little difficulty, start objections, and fancy hardships, we shall never go on, much less go through with our work. Winds and clouds of tribulation are, in God's hands, designed to try us. God's work shall agree with his word, whether we see it or not. And we may well trust God to provide for us, without our anxious, disquieting cares. Be not weary in well-doing, for in due season, in God's time, you shall reap, Galatians 6:9.

An admonition to prepare for death, and to young persons to be religious (7–10)

Life is sweet to bad men, because they have their portion in this life; it is sweet to good men, because it is the time of preparation for a better; it is sweet to all. Here is a caution to think of death, even when life is most sweet. Solomon makes an effecting address to young persons. They would desire opportunity to pursue every pleasure. Then follow your desires, but be assured that God will call you into judgment. How many give loose to every appetite, and rush into every vicious pleasure! But God registers every one of their sinful thoughts and desires, their idle words and wicked words. If they would avoid remorse and terror, if they would have hope and comfort on a dying bed, if they would escape misery here and hereafter, let

them remember the vanity of youthful pleasures. That Solomon means to condemn the pleasures of sin is evident. His object is to draw the young to purer and more lasting joys. This is not the language of one grudging youthful pleasures, because he can no longer partake of them; but of one who has, by a miracle of mercy, been brought back in safety. He would persuade the young from trying a course whence so few return. If the young would live a life of true happiness, if they would secure happiness hereafter, let them remember their Creator in the days of their youth.

Chapter 12

A description of the infirmities of age (1–7)

All is vanity: also a warning of the judgment to come (8–14)

A description of the infirmities of age (1–7)

We should remember our sins against our Creator, repent, and seek forgiveness. We should remember our duties, and set about them, looking to him for grace and strength. This should be done early, while the body is strong, and the spirits active. When a man has the pain of reviewing a misspent life, his not having given up sin and worldly vanities till he is forced to say, I have no pleasure in them, renders his sincerity very questionable. Then follows a figurative description of old age and its infirmities, which has some difficulties; but the meaning is plain, to show how uncomfortable, generally, the days of old age are. As the four verses, 2–5, are a figurative description of the infirmities that usually accompany old age, ver. 6 notices the circumstances which take place in the hour of death. If sin had not entered into the world, these infirmities would not have been known. Surely then the aged should reflect on the evil of sin.

All is vanity: also a warning of the judgment to come (8–14)

Solomon repeats his text, VANITY OF VANITIES, ALL IS VANITY. These are the words of one that could speak by dear-bought experience of the vanity of the world, which can do nothing to ease men of the burden of sin. As he considered the worth of souls, he gave good heed to what he spake and wrote; words of truth will always be acceptable words. The truths of God are as goads to such as are dull and draw back, and nails to such as are wandering and draw aside; means to establish the heart, that we may never sit loose to our duty, nor be taken from it. The Shepherd of Israel is the Giver of inspired wisdom. Teachers and guides all receive their communications from him. The title is applied in Scripture to the Lord Jesus Christ, the Son of God. The prophets sought diligently, what, or what manner of time, the Spirit of Christ in them did signify, when it testified beforehand the sufferings of Christ, and the glory that should follow. To write many books was not suited to the shortness of human life, and would be weariness to the writer, and to the reader; and then was much more so to both than it is now. All things would be vanity and vexation, except they led to this conclusion, That to fear God, and keep his commandments, is the whole of man. The fear of God includes in it all the affections of the soul towards him, which are produced by the Holy Spirit. There may be ter-ror where there is no love, nay, where there is hatred. But this is different from the gracious fear of God, as the feelings of an affectionate child. The fear of God, is often put for the whole of true religion in the heart, and includes its practical results in the life. Let us attend to the one thing needful, and now come to him as a merciful Saviour, who will soon come as an almighty Judge, when he will bring to light the things of darkness, and manifest the counsels of all hearts. Why does God record in his word, that ALL IS VANITY, but to keep us from deceiving ourselves to our ruin? He makes our duty to be our interest. May it be graven in all our hearts. Fear God, and keep his commandments, for this is all that concerns man.

THE SONG OF
SOLOMON

A.R. Faussett

Introduction

The Song of Solomon, called in the *Vulgate* and *Septuagint*, 'The Song of Songs,' from the opening words. This *title* denotes its *superior excellence*, according to the Hebrew idiom; *so holy of holies*, equivalent to 'most holy' (Ex 29:37); *the heaven of heavens*, equivalent to the highest heavens (De 10:14).

ORIGEN and JEROME tell us that the Jews forbade it to be read by any until he was thirty years old. It certainly needs a degree of spiritual maturity to enter aright into the holy mystery of love which it allegorically sets forth. To such as have attained this maturity, of whatever age they be, the Song of Songs is one of the most edifying of the sacred writings. Understood allegorically, the Song is cleared of all difficulty. 'Shulamith' (So 6:13), the bride, is thus an appropriate name, *Daughter of Peace* being the feminine of Solomon, equivalent to the *Prince of Peace*. She by turns is a vinedresser, shepherdess, midnight inquirer, and prince's consort and daughter, and He a suppliant drenched with night dews, and a king in His palace, in harmony with the various relations of the Church and Christ. As Ecclesiastes sets forth the vanity of love of the creature, Canticles sets forth the fullness of the love which joins believers and the Saviour. God is love, and Christ is the embodiment of the love of God. As the other books of Scripture present severally their own aspects of divine truth, so Canticles furnishes the believer with language of holy love, wherewith his heart can commune with his Lord; and it portrays the intensity of Christ's love to him; the affection of love was created in man to be a transcript of the divine love, and the Song clothes the latter in words; were it not for this, we should be at a loss for language, having the divine warrant, wherewith to express, without presumption, the fervour of the love between Christ and us. The image of a bride, a bridegroom, and a marriage, to represent this spiritual union, has the sanction of Scripture throughout; nay, the spiritual union was *the original fact in the mind of God*, of which marriage is the transcript (Isa 54:5 62:5 Jer 3:1 Eze 16:1–63 23:1–49 Mt 9:15 22:2 25:1; Joh 3:29 2Co 11:2 Eph 5:23–32).

We have: (1) In the individual soul the longing for the manifestation of Christ to it, and the various alternations in its experience (So 1:2,4 2:8 3:1,4,6,7) of His manifestation;

(2) The abundant enjoyment of His sensible consolations, which is soon withdrawn through the bride's carelessness (So 5:1–3), and her longings after Him, and reconciliation (So 5:8–16 6:3 So 7:1);

(3) Effects of Christ's manifestation on the believer; namely, assurance, labours of love, anxiety for the salvation of the impenitent, eagerness for the Lord's second coming (So 7:10,12 8:8–10,14).

Chapter 1

So 1:1–17. Canticle I. – (So 1:2–2:7) – The bride searching for and finding the king.

1. The song of songs – The most excellent of all songs, *Hebrew* idiom (Ex 29:37 De 10:14). A foretaste on earth of the 'new song' to be sung in glory (Re 5:9 14:3 15:2–4).

Solomon's – 'King of Israel,' or 'Jerusalem,' is not added, as in the opening of Proverbs and Ecclesiastes, because his personality is hid under that of Christ, the true Solomon (equivalent to *Prince of Peace*). The earthly Solomon is not introduced, which would break the consistency of the allegory. Though the bride bears the chief part, the Song throughout is not hers, but that of her 'Solomon.' He animates her. Aaron prefigured Him as priest; Moses, as prophet; David, as a suffering king; Solomon, as the triumphant prince of peace. The camp in the wilderness represents the Church in the world; the peaceful reign of Solomon, after all enemies had been subdued, represents the Church in heaven, of which joy the Song gives a foretaste.

2. him – abruptly. She names him not, as is natural to one whose heart is full of some much desired friend: so Mary Magdalene at the sepulchre (Joh 20:15), as if everyone must know whom she means, the *one* chief object of her desire (Ps 73:25 Mt 13:44–46 Php 3:7,8).

kiss – the token of *peace* from the Prince of Peace (Lu 15:20); 'our Peace' (Ps 85:10 Col 1:21 Eph 2:14).

of his mouth – marking the tenderest affection. For a king to permit his hands, or even garment, to be kissed, was counted a great honour; but that he should himself kiss another *with his mouth* is the greatest honour.

thy love – *Hebrew*, 'loves,' namely, tokens of love, loving blandishments.

wine – which makes glad 'the heavy heart' of one ready to perish, so that he 'remembers his misery no more' (Pr 31:6,7). So, in a 'better' sense, Christ's love (Hab 3:17,18). The spiritual wine is His blood and His spirit.

3. thy name – Christ's *character and office* as the 'Anointed' (Isa 9:6 61:1), as 'the savour of ointments' are the graces that surround His *person* (Ps 45:7,8). Ec 7:1, in its fullest sense, applies to Him. The holy anointing oil of the high priest, which it was death for anyone else to make (so Ac 4:12), implies the exclusive preciousness of Messiah's name (Ex 30:23–28,31–38).

poured – (Isa 53:12 Ro 5:5).

therefore – because of the manifestation of God's character in Christ (1Jo 4:9,19). So the penitent woman (Lu 7:37,38,47).

virgins – the pure in heart (2Co 11:2 Re 14:4).

4. (1) The cry of ancient Israel for Messiah, for example, Simeon, Anna.

(2) The cry of an awakened soul for the drawing of the Spirit, after it has got a glimpse of Christ's loveliness and its own helplessness.

Draw me – The Father draws (Joh 6:44). The Son draws (Jer 31:3 Ho 11:4 Joh 12:32). 'Draw' here, and 'Tell' (So 1:7), reverently qualify the word 'kiss' (So 1:2).

me, we – No believer desires to go to heaven alone. We are converted as *individuals*; we follow Christ as joined in a *communion* of saints (Joh 1:41,45). Individuality and community meet in the bride.

run – Her earnestness kindles as she prays (Isa 40:31 Ps 119:32,60).

chambers – Her prayer is answered even beyond her desires. Not only is she permitted to *run* after Him, but is brought into the inmost pavilion, where Eastern kings admitted none but the most intimate friends (Es 4:11 5:2 Ps 27:5). The erection of the temple of Solomon was the first bringing of the bride into permanent, instead of migratory, chambers of the King.

be glad and rejoice – *inward* and *outward* rejoicing.

in thee – (Isa 61:10 Php 4:1,4). Not in our spiritual frames (Ps 30:6,7).

remember – rather, 'commemorate with praises' (Isa 63:7). The mere *remembrance* of spiritual joys is better than the *present enjoyment* of carnal ones (Ps 4:6,7).

upright – rather, 'uprightly,' 'sincerely' (Ps 58:1 Ro 12:9); so Nathanael (Joh 1:47); Peter (Joh 21:17).

5. black – namely, 'as the tents of Kedar,' equivalent to *blackness* (Ps 120:5). She draws the image from the black goatskins with which the Scenite Arabs cover their tents. To feel this blackness, and yet also feel one's self in Jesus Christ, marks the believer (Ro 7:18 Ro 8:1); 1Ti 1:15, 'I *am* chief'; so she says not merely, 'I was,' but 'I am'; *still* black in herself, but comely through *His* comeliness put upon her (Eze 16:14).

curtains – first, the hangings and veil in the temple of Solomon (Eze 16:10); then, also, the 'fine linen which is the righteousness of saints' (Re 19:8), the white wedding garment provided by Jesus Christ (Isa 61:10 Mt 22:11 1Co 1:30 Col 1:28 2:10 Re 7:14). *Historically*, the dark tents of Kedar represent the Gentile Church (Isa 60:3–7).

daughters of Jerusalem – professors, not the bride, or 'the virgins,' yet not enemies; invited to gospel blessings (So 3:10,11); so near to Jesus Christ as not to be unlikely to find Him (So 5:8); desirous to seek Him with her (So 6:1; compare So 6:13 7:1,5,8).

mother's children – (Mt 10:36). She is to forget 'her own people and her father's house,' that is, the worldly connections of her unregenerate state (Ps 45:10); they had maltreated her (Lu 15:15,16).

7. my soul loveth – more intense than 'the virgins' and 'the upright love thee' (So 1:3,4 Mt 22:37). To carry out the design of the allegory, the royal encampment is here represented as moving from place to place, in search of green pastures, under the *Shepherd King* (Ps 23:1–6). The bride, having first enjoyed communion with him in the pavilion, is willing to follow Him into labours and dangers; arising from all absorbing love (Lu 14:26); this distinguishes her from the formalist (Joh 10:27 Re 14:4).

feedest – tendest thy flock (Isa 40:11 Heb 13:20 1Pe 2:25 5:4 Re 7:17). No *single* type expresses *all* the office of Jesus Christ; hence arises the variety of *diverse* images used to portray the manifold aspects of Him: these would be quite incongruous, if the Song referred to the earthly Solomon.

makest ... to rest – distinct from 'feedest'; periods of rest are vouchsafed after labour (Isa 4:6 49:10 Eze 34:13–15). Communion in private must go along with public following of Him.

8. If – she ought to have *known* (Joh 14:8,9).

shepherds' tents – ministers in the sanctuary (Ps 84:1).

9. horses in Pharaoh's chariots – celebrated for *beauty, swiftness,* and *ardor,* at the Red Sea (Ex 14:15). These qualities, which *seem* to belong to the ungodly, *really* belong to the saints.

As Jesus Christ is both Shepherd and Conqueror, so believers are not only His *sheep,* but also, as a Church *militant* now, His *chariots and horses* (So 6:4).

10. rows of jewels – (Eze 16:11–13). Persian ladies wear two or three rows of pearls round the head, beginning on the forehead and descending down to the cheeks and under the chin, so that their faces seem to be set in pearls (Eze 16:11) implies the vital energy of the bride; this verse, her superadded graces (Pr 1:9 4:9 1Ti 2:9 2Pe 1:5).

11. We – the Trinity implied by the Holy Ghost, whether it was so by the writer of the Song or not (Ge 1:26 Pr 8:30 30:4).

12. While – It is the presence of the Sun of Righteousness that draws out the believer's odours of grace. It was the sight of Him at table that caused the two women to bring forth their ointments for Him (Lu 7:37,38 Joh 12:3 2Co 2:15).

my spikenard – not boasting, but *owning* the Lord's grace to and in her. The spikenard is a lowly herb, the emblem of humility. She rejoices that *He* is well pleased with her graces, His own work (Php 4:18).

13. bundle of myrrh – abundant *preciousness* (*Greek*), (1Pe 2:7). Even a *little* myrrh was costly; much more a *bundle* (Col 2:9).

all night – an undivided heart (Eph 3:17; contrast Jer 4:14 Eze 16:15,30).

14. cluster – Jesus Christ is one, yet *manifold* in His graces.

camphire – or, 'cypress.' The 'hennah' is meant, whose odorous flowers grow in clusters, of a color white and yellow softly blended; its bark is dark, the foliage light green. Women deck their persons with them. The loveliness of Jesus Christ.

vineyards – appropriate in respect to Him who is 'the vine.' The spikenard was for the banquet (So 1:12); the myrrh was in her bosom continually (So 1:13); the camphire is in the midst of natural beauties, which, though lovely, are eclipsed by the one cluster, Jesus Christ, pre-eminent above them all.

En-gedi – in South Palestine, near the Dead Sea (Jos 15:62 Eze 47:10), famed for aromatic shrubs.

15. fair – He discerns beauty in her, who had said, 'I am black' (So 1:5), because of the everlasting covenant (Ps 45:11 Isa 62:5 Eph 1:4,5).

doves' eyes – large and beautiful in the doves of Syria. The prominent features of her beauty (Mt 10:16), gentleness, innocence, and constant love, emblem of the Holy Ghost, who changes us to *His own* likeness (Ge 8:10,11 Mt 3:16).

16. *Reply of the Bride.* She presumes to call Him beloved, because He called her so first. Thou callest me 'fair'; if I am so, it is not in myself; it is all from Thee (Ps 90:17); but *Thou* art fair in Thyself (Ps 45:2).

pleasant – (Pr 3:17) towards Thy friends (2Sa 1:26).

bed ... green – the couch of green grass on which the King and His bride sit to 'rest at noon.' Thus her prayer in So 1:7 is here granted; a green oasis in the desert, always found near waters in the East (Ps 23:2 Isa 41:17–19). The scene is a summer house.

Chapter 2

So 2:1–17.

1. rose – if applied to Jesus Christ, it, with the white lily (lowly, 2Co 8:9), answers to 'white and ruddy' (So 5:10). But it is rather the *meadow-saffron:* the *Hebrew* means radically a plant with a *pungent bulb,* inapplicable to the *rose.* The bride thus speaks of herself as lowly though lovely, in contrast with the lordly 'apple' or citron tree, the bridegroom (So 2:3); so the 'lily' is applied to her (So 2:2),

Sharon – (Isa 35:1,2). In North Palestine, between Mount Tabor and Lake Tiberias (1Ch 5:16). Beauty, delicacy, and lowliness, are to be in her, as they were in Him (Mt 11:29).

2. *Jesus Christ to the Bride* (Mt 10:16 Joh 15:19 1Jo 5:19).

Thorns, equivalent to the wicked (2Sa 23:6 Ps 57:4).

daughters – of men, not of God; not 'the

virgins.' 'If thou art the lily of Jesus Christ, take heed lest by impatience, rash judgments, and pride, thou thyself become a thorn' [LUTHER].

3. *Her reply.*

apple – generic including the golden citron, pomegranate, and orange apple (Pr 25:11). He combines the *shadow* and fragrance of the citron with the *sweetness* of the orange and pomegranate fruit.

among the sons – parallel to 'among the daughters' (So 2:2). He alone is ever fruitful among the fruitless wild trees (Ps 89:6 Heb 1:9).

I sat … with … delight – literally, 'I eagerly desired and sat' (Ps 94:19 Mr 6:31 Eph 2:6 1Pe 1:8). **shadow** – (Ps 121:5 Isa 4:6 25:4 32:2). Jesus Christ interposes the shadow of His cross between the blazing rays of justice and us sinners.

fruit – Faith plucks it (Pr 3:18). Man lost the tree of life (Ge 3:22,23). Jesus Christ regained it for him; he eats it partly now (Ps 119:103 Joh 6:55,57 1Pe 2:3); fully hereafter (Re 2:7 22:2,14); not earned by the sweat of his brow, or by his righteousness (Ro 10:1–21). Contrast the worldling's fruit (De 32:32 Lu 15:16).

4. Historically fulfilled in the joy of Simeon and Anna in the temple, over the infant Saviour (Lu 2:25–38), and that of Mary, too (compare Lu 1:53); typified (Ex 24:9–11).

his banner … love – After having rescued us from the enemy, our victorious captain (Heb 2:10) seats us at the banquet under a banner inscribed with *His name,* 'love' (1Jo 4:8). His love conquered us to Himself; this banner rallies round us the forces of Omnipotence, as our protection; it marks to what country we belong, heaven, the abode of love, and in what we most glory, the cross of Jesus Christ, through which we triumph (Ro 8:37 1Co 15:57 Re 3:21). Compare with *'over me,' 'underneath* are the everlasting arms' (De 33:27).

5. apples – from the tree (So 2:3), so sweet to her, the promises of God.

sick of love – the highest degree of sensible enjoyment that can be attained here. It may be at an early or late stage of experience. Paul (2Co 12:7).

6. The 'stay' she prayed for (So 2:5) is granted (De 33:12,27 Ps 37:24 Isa 41:16). None can pluck from that *embrace* (Joh 10:28–30). His hand keeps us from falling (Mt 14:30,31); to it we may commit ourselves (Ps 31:5).

left hand – the left is the inferior hand, by which the Lord less signally manifests His love, than by the right; the secret hand of ordinary providence, as distinguished from that of manifested grace (the 'right'). They really go together, though sometimes they seem divided; here both are felt at once.

7. by the roes – not an oath but a solemn charge, to act as cautiously as the hunter would

with the wild roes, which are proverbially timorous; he must advance with breathless circumspection, if he is to take them; so he who would not lose Jesus Christ and His Spirit, which is easily grieved and withdrawn, must be tender of conscience and watchful (Eze 16:43 Eph 4:30 5:15 1Th 5:19).

my love – The *lovingness* and *pleasantness* of the hind and roe (Pr 5:19) is included in this image of Jesus Christ.

Canticle II. – (So 2:8–3:5) – John The Baptist's ministry.

8. voice – an exclamation of joyful surprise, evidently after a long silence.

leaping – hounding, as the roe does, over the roughest obstacles (2Sa 2:18 1Ch 12:8); as the father of the prodigal 'had compassion and *ran*' (Lu 15:20).

upon the hills – as the sunbeams glancing from hill to hill. So *Margin,* title of Jesus Christ (Ps 22:1), 'Hind of the *morning*' (type of His resurrection). Historically, the coming of the kingdom of heaven (the gospel dispensation), announced by John Baptist, is meant; it primarily is the garden or vineyard; the bride is called so in a secondary sense. 'The voice' of Jesus Christ is indirect, through 'the friend of the bridegroom' (Joh 3:29), John the Baptist.

9. he standeth – after having bounded over the intervening space like a roe. He often stands near when our unbelief hides Him from us (Ge 28:16 Re 3:14–20). His usual way; long promised and expected; sudden at last: so, in visiting the second temple (Mal 3:1); so at Pentecost (Ac 2:1,2); so in visiting an individual soul, Zaccheus (Lu 19:5,6 Joh 3:8); and so, at the second coming (Mt 24:48,50 2Pe 3:4,10). So it shall be at His second coming (1Th 5:2,3).

10, 11. Loving reassurance given by Jesus Christ to the bride, lest she should think that He had ceased to love her, on account of her unfaithfulness, which had occasioned His temporary withdrawal. He allures her to brighter than worldly joys (Mic 2:10). Not only does the saint wish to depart to be with Him, but He still more desires to have the saint with Him above (Joh 17:24). Historically, the vineyard or garden of the King, here first introduced, is 'the kingdom of heaven preached' by John the Baptist, before whom 'the law and the prophets were' (Lu 16:16).

11. the winter – the law of the covenant of works (Mt 4:16).

12. flowers – tokens of anger past, and of grace come.

13. vines with the tender grape – The vine flowers were so sweet that they were often put, when dried, into new wine to give it flavour. Applicable to the first manifestations of Jesus

Christ, 'the true Vine,' both to the Church and to individuals; as to Nathanael under *the fig tree* (Joh 1:48).

Arise – His call, described by the bride, ends as it began (So 2:10); it is a consistent whole; 'love' from first to last (Isa 52:1,2 2Co 6:17, 18).

14. dove – here expressing endearment (Ps 74:19). Doves are noted for *constant attachment; gregarious*, flocking together to the kingdom of Jesus Christ (Isa 60:8); *harmless simplicity* (Mt 10:16).

clefts – the refuge of doves from storm and heat (Jer 48:28; see Jer 49:16).

stairs – (Eze 38:20, *Margin*), a steep rock, broken into stairs or terraces. It is in 'secret places' and rugged scenes that Jesus Christ woos the soul from the world to Himself (Mic 2:10 7:14).

15. Transition to the vineyard, often formed in 'stairs' (So 2:14), or terraces, in which, amidst the vine leaves, foxes hid.

foxes – generic term, including jackals. They eat only grapes, not the vine flowers; but they need to be driven out *in time* before the grape is ripe. She had failed in watchfulness before (So 1:6); now when converted, she is the more jealous of *subtle* sins (Ps 139:23).

16. mine … his – rather, 'is *for me … for Him*' (Ho 3:3), where, as here, there is the assurance of indissoluble union, in spite of temporary absence.

I am his – by creation (Ps 100:3), by redemption (Joh 17:10 Ro 14:8 1Co 6:19).

feedeth – as a 'roe,' or gazelle (So 2:17); instinct is sure to lead him back to his feeding ground, where the lilies abound. So Jesus Christ, though now withdrawn, the bride feels sure will return to His favourite resting-place (So 7:10 Ps 132:14).

17. Night – is the image of the present world (Ro 13:12).

break – rather, 'breathe'; referring to the refreshing breeze of dawn in the East.

Bether – Mountains of Bithron, separated from the rest of Israel by the Jordan (2Sa 2:29), not far from Bethabara, where John baptized and Jesus was first manifested. Historically, in the ministry of John the Baptist, Christ's call to the bride was not, as later (So 4:8), 'Come *with* me,' but 'Come away,' namely, to meet Me (So 2:2,10,13). Sitting in darkness (Mt 4:16), she 'waited' and 'looked' eagerly for Him, the 'great light' (Lu 1:79 2:25,38); at His rising, the shadows of the law (Col 2:16,17 Heb 10:1) were to 'flee away.' So we wait for the second coming, when means of grace, so precious now, shall be superseded by the Sun of righteousness (1Co 13:10,12 Re 21:22,23). The Word is our light until then (2Pe 1:19).

Chapter 3
So 3:1–11.

1. By night – literally, 'By nights.' Continuation of the longing for the dawn of the Messiah (So 2:17 Ps 130:6 Mal 4:2).

loveth – no want of sincerity, but of diligence, which she now makes up for by leaving her bed to seek Him (Ps 22:2 63:8 Isa 26:9 Joh 20:17). Four times (So 3:1–4) she calls Jesus Christ, 'Him whom my soul loveth,' designating Him as *absent;* language of desire: 'He loved me,' would be language of *present* fruition (Re 1:5). In questioning the watchmen (So 3:3), she does not even name Him, so full is her heart of Him. Having found Him at dawn (for throughout *He* is the *morning*), she charges the daughters not to abridge by intrusion the period of His stay. Compare as to the thoughtful seeking for Jesus Christ in the time of John the Baptist, in vain at first, but presently after successful (Lu 3:15–22 Joh 1:19–34).

found him not – Oh, for such honest dealings with ourselves (Pr 25:14 Jude 1:12)!

2. Wholly awake for God (Lu 14:18–20 Eph 5:14).

the city – Jerusalem, literally (Mt 3:5 Joh 1:19), and spiritually the *Church* here (Heb 12:22), in glory (Re 21:2).

broad ways – open spaces at the gates of Eastern cities, where the public assembled for business.

found him not – Nothing short of Jesus Christ can satisfy her (Job 23:8–10 Ps 63:1,2).

3. watchmen – ministers (Isa 62:6 Jer 6:17 Eze 3:17 Heb 13:17), fit persons to consult (Isa 21:11 Mal 2:7).

found me – the general ministry of the Word 'finds' individually souls in quest of Jesus Christ (Ge 24:27, end of verse Ac 16:14); whereas formalists remain unaffected.

4. Jesus Christ is generally 'found' near the watchmen and means of grace; but they are not Himself.

held him – willing to be held; not willing, if not held (Ge 32:26 Mt 28:9 Lu 24:28,29 Re 3:11).

5. So 2:7; but *there* it was for the non-interruption of her own fellowship with Jesus Christ that she was anxious; *here* it is for the not grieving of the Holy Ghost, on the part of the daughters of Jerusalem. Jealously avoid levity, heedlessness, and offenses which would mar the gracious work begun in others (Mt 18:7 Ac 2:42,43 Eph 4:30).

Canticle III. – (So 3:6–5:1) – The bridegroom with the bride.

Historically, the ministry of Jesus Christ on earth.

6. New scene (So 3:6–11). The friends of the Bridegroom see a cortege approach. His palanquin and guard.

pillars of smoke – from the perfumes burned around Him and His bride. Image from Israel and the tabernacle (answering to 'bed,' So 3:7) marching through the desert with the pillar of smoke by day and fire by night (Ex 14:20), and the pillars of smoke ascending from the altars of incense and of atonement; so Jesus Christ's righteousness, atonement, and ever-living intercession.

7. In So 3:6 the *wilderness* character of the Church is portrayed; in So 3:7,8, its *militant* aspect. In So 3:9,10, Jesus Christ is seen dwelling in believers, who are His 'chariot' and 'body.' In So 3:11, the consummation in glory.

bed – palanquin. His body, literally, guarded by a definite number of angels, *threescore*, or sixty (Mt 26:53), from the wilderness (Mt 4:1,11), and continually (Lu 2:13 22:43 Ac 1:10,11); just as six hundred thousand of Israel guarded the Lord's tabernacle (Nu 2:17–32), one for every ten thousand. In contrast to the 'bed of sloth' (So 3:1).

valiant – (Jos 5:13,14). Angels guarding His *tomb* used like words (Mr 16:6).

of Israel – true subjects, not mercenaries.

8. hold – not actually grasping them, but having them girt on the thigh ready for use, like their Lord (Ps 45:3). So believers too are guarded by angels (Ps 91:11 Heb 1:14), and they themselves need 'every man' (Ne 4:18) to be armed (Ps 144:1,2 2Co 10:4 Eph 6:12,17 1Ti 6:12), and 'expert' (2Co 2:11).

because of fear in the night – Arab marauders often turn a wedding into mourning by a night attack. So the bridal procession of saints in the night of this wilderness is the chief object of Satan's assault.

10. pillars – supporting the canopy at the four corners; curtains at the side protect the person within from the sun. Pillars with silver sockets supported the veil that enclosed the holy of holies; emblem of Jesus Christ's *strength* (1Ki 7:21).

covering – rather, 'seat,' as in Le 15:9. Hereafter the saints shall share His *seat* (Re 3:21).

purple – the veil of the holiest, partly purple, and the *purple* robe put on Jesus Christ. 'Purple' (including scarlet and crimson) is the emblem of *royalty*, and of *His blood*.

paved – translated, like mosaic pavement, with the various acts and promises of love of Father, Son, and Holy Ghost (Zep 3:17 1Jo 4:8,16), in contrast with the tables of stone in the 'midst' of the ark, covered with writings of stern command (compare Joh 19:13); *this* is all grace and love to believers, who answer to 'the daughters of Jerusalem' (Joh 1:17).

11. Go forth – (Mt 25:6).

daughters of Zion – spirits of saints, and angels (Isa 61:10 Zec 9:9).

crown – nuptial (Eze 16:8–12); the Hebrews wore costly crowns or chaplets at weddings (Ps 2:6 Re 19:12).

day of his espousals – chiefly final marriage, when the number of the elect is complete (Re 6:11). **gladness** – (Ps 45:15 Isa 62:5 Re 19:7).

Chapter 4
So 4:1–16.

1. Contrast with the bride's state by nature (Isa 1:6) *her state by grace* (So 4:1–7), 'perfect through His comeliness put upon her' (Eze 16:14 Joh 15:3). The praise of Jesus Christ, unlike that of the world, hurts not, but edifies; as His, not ours, is the glory (Joh 5:44 Re 4:10,11). Seven features of beauty are specified (So 4:1–5) ('lips' and 'speech' are but one feature, So 4:3), the number for *perfection*. To each of these is attached a comparison from nature: the resemblances consist not so much in outward likeness, as in the combined sensations of delight produced by contemplating these natural objects.

doves – the large melting eye of the Syrian dove appears especially beautiful amid the foliage of its native groves: so the bride's 'eyes within her locks' (Lu 7:44).

eyes – (Mt 6:22 Eph 1:18; contrast Mt 5:28 Eph 4:18 1Jo 2:16). Chaste and guileless ('harmless,' Mt 10:16, *Margin*; Joh 1:47). John the Baptist, historically, was the 'turtledove' (So 2:12), with eye directed to the coming Bridegroom: his Nazarite unshorn hair answers to 'locks' (Joh 1:29,36).

hair … goats – The hair of goats in the East is fine like silk. As long hair is her glory, and marks her subjection to man (1Co 11:6–15), so the Nazarite's hair marked his subjection and separation unto God. (Compare Jud 16:17, with 2Co 6:17 Tit 2:14 1Pe 2:9.) Jesus Christ cares for the minutest concerns of His saints (Mt 10:30).

appear from – literally, 'that lie down from'; lying along the hillside, they seem to *hang from* it: a picture of the bride's hanging tresses.

Gilead – beyond Jordan: there stood 'the heap of witness' (Ge 31:48).

2. even shorn – is translated (1Ki 6:25), 'of one size'; so the point of comparison to *teeth* is their *symmetry* of form; as in 'came up from the washing,' the *spotless whiteness;* and in 'twins,' the *exact correspondence of the upper and lower teeth:* and in 'none barren,' *none wanting*, none without its fellow. Faith is the tooth with which we eat the living bread (Joh 6:35,54). Contrast the teeth of sinners (Ps 57:4 Pr 30:14); also their end (Ps 3:7 Mt 25:30). Faith leads the flock to the washing (Zec 13:1 1Co 6:11 Tit 3:5).

none … barren – (2Pe 1:8). He who is begotten of God begets instrumentally other sons of God.

3. thread – like a delicate fillet. Not thick and white as the leper's lips (type of sin), which were therefore to be 'covered,' as 'unclean' (Le 13:45).

scarlet – The blood of Jesus Christ (Isa 6:5–9) cleanses the leprosy, and unseals the lips (Isa 57:19 Ho 14:2 Heb 13:15). Rahab's scarlet thread was a type of it (Jos 2:18).

speech – not a separate feature from the *lips* (Zep 3:9 Col 4:6). Contrast 'uncircumcised lips' (Ex 6:12).

temples – rather, *the upper part of the cheek* next the temples: the seat of shamefacedness; so, 'within thy locks,' no display (1Co 11:5,6,15). Mark of true penitence (Ezr 9:6 Eze 16:63). Contrast Jer 3:3 Eze 3:7.

pomegranate – When cut, it displays in rows seeds pellucid, like crystal, tinged with red. Her modesty is not on the surface, but within, which Jesus Christ can see into.

4. neck – stately: in beautiful contrast to the blushing temples (So 4:3); not 'stiff' (Isa 48:4 Ac 7:51), as that of unbroken nature; nor 'stretched forth' wantonly (Isa 3:16); nor burdened with the legal yoke (La 1:14 Ac 15:10); but erect in gospel freedom (Isa 52:2).

tower of David – probably on Zion. He was a man of war, preparatory to the reign of Solomon, the king of peace. So warfare in the case of Jesus Christ and His saints precedes the coming rest. Each soul won from Satan by Him is a trophy gracing the bride (Lu 11:22); (each hangs on Him, Isa 22:23,24); also each victory of her faith. As shields adorn a temple's walls (Eze 27:11), so necklaces hang on the bride's neck (Jud 5:30 1Ki 10:16).

5. breasts – The bust is left open in Eastern dress. The breastplate of the high priest was made of 'two' pieces, folded one on the other, in which were the Urim and Thummim (*lights* and *perfection*). 'Faith and love' are the double breastplate (1Th 5:8), answering to 'hearing the word' and 'keeping it,' in a similar connection with breasts (Lu 12:27,28).

roes – He reciprocates her praise (So 2:9). Emblem of *love* and *satisfaction* (Pr 5:19).

feed – (Ps 23:2).

among the lilies – shrinking from thorns of strife, worldliness, and ungodliness (2Sa 23:6 Mt 13:7). Roes feed *among,* not *on* the lilies: where these grow, there is moisture producing green pasturage. The lilies represent her white dress (Ps 45:14 Re 19:8).

6. Historically, *the hill of frankincense* is Calvary, where, 'through the eternal Spirit He offered Himself'; the mountain of myrrh is His embalmment (Joh 19:39) till the resurrection 'daybreak.' The third Canticle occupies the one cloudless day of His presence on earth, beginning from the night (So 2:17) and ending with the night of His departure (So 4:6). His promise is almost exactly in the words of her prayer (So

2:17), (the same Holy Ghost breathing in Jesus Christ and His praying people), with the difference that she then looked for His visible coming. He now tells her that when He shall have gone from sight, He still is to be met with spiritually in prayer (Ps 68:16 Mt 28:20), until the everlasting day break, when we shall see face to face (1Co 13:10,12).

7. Assurance that He is going from her in love, not in displeasure (Joh 16:6,7).

all fair – still stronger than So 1:15 So 4:1.

no spot – our privilege (Eph 5:27 Col 2:10); our duty (2Co 6:17 Jude 1:23 Jas 1:27).

8. Invitation to her to leave the border mountains (the highest worldly elevation) between the hostile lands north of Palestine and the Promised Land (Ps 45:10 Php 3:13).

Amana – south of Anti-Libanus; the river Abana, or Amana, was near Damascus (2Ki 5:12).

Shenir – The whole mountain was called *Hermon;* the part held by the Sidonians was called *Sirion;* the part held by the Amorites, *Shenir* (De 3:9). Infested by the devouring lion and the stealthy and swift leopard (Ps 76:4 Eph 6:11 1Pe 5:8). Contrasted with the mountain of myrrh (So 4:6 Isa 2:2); the good land (Isa 35:9).

with me – twice repeated emphatically. The presence of Jesus Christ makes up for the absence of all besides (Lu 18:29,30 2Co 6:10). Moses was permitted to see Canaan from Pisgah; Peter, James, and John had a foretaste of glory on the mount of transfiguration.

9. sister … spouse – This title is here first used, as He is soon about to institute the Supper, the pledge of the nuptial union. By the term 'sister,' carnal ideas are excluded; the ardor of a spouse's love is combined with the purity of a sister's (Isa 54:5; compare Mr 3:35).

one – Even *one* look is enough to secure His love (Zec 12:10 Lu 23:40-43). Not merely the Church collectively, but each *one* member of it (Mt 18:10,14 Lu 15:7,24,32).

chain – necklace (Isa 62:3 Mal 3:17), answering to the 'shields' hanging in the tower of David (So 4:4). Compare the 'ornament' (1Pe 3:4); 'chains' (Pr 1:9 3:22).

10. love – *Hebrew,* 'loves'; manifold tokens of thy love.

much better – answering to her 'better' (So 1:2), but with *increased* force. An Amoebean pastoral character pervades the Song, like the classic Amoebean idylls and eclogues.

wine – The love of His saints is a more reviving cordial to Him than wine; for example, at the feast in Simon's house (Lu 7:36,47 Joh 4:32; compare Zec 10:7).

smell of … ointments than all spices – answering to her praise (So 1:3) with increased force. Fragrant, as being fruits of *His* Spirit in us (Ga 5:22).

11. drop – always ready to fall, being full of honey, though not always (Pr 10:19) actually *dropping* (So 5:13 De 32:2 Mt 12:34).

honeycomb – (Pr 5:3 16:24).

under thy tongue – not always *on*, but *under*, the tongue, ready to fall (Ps 55:21). Contrast her former state (Ps 140:3 Ro 3:13). 'Honey and milk' were the glory of the good land. The change is illustrated in the penitent thief. Contrast Mt 27:44 with Lu 23:39. It was literally with 'one' eye, a sidelong glance of love 'better than wine,' that he refreshed Jesus Christ (So 4:9,10). 'To-day shalt thou be *with Me* (compare So 4:8) in Paradise' (So 4:12), is the only joyous sentence of His seven utterances on the cross.

smell of ... garments – which are often perfumed in the East (Ps 45:8). The perfume comes from Him on us (Ps 133:2). We draw nigh to God in the perfumed garment of our elder brother (Ge 27:27; see Jude 1:23).

Lebanon – abounding in odoriferous trees (Ho 14:5–7).

12. The *Hebrew* has no 'is.' Here she is distinct from the garden (So 5:1), yet identified with it (So 4:16) as being one with Him in His sufferings. Historically the Paradise, into which the soul of Jesus Christ entered at death; and the tomb of Joseph, in which His body was laid amid 'myrrh,' (So 4:6), situated in *a nicely kept* garden (compare 'gardener,' Joh 20:15); 'sealed' with a stone (Mt 27:66); in which it resembles 'wells' in the East (Ge 29:3,8). It was in a garden of light Adam fell; in a garden of darkness, Gethsemane, and chiefly that of the tomb, the second Adam retrieved us. Spiritually the garden is the gospel kingdom of heaven. Here all is ripe; previously (So 2:13) it was 'the *tender* grape.' The garden is His, though He calls the plants hers (So 4:13) by His gift (Isa 61:3, end).

spring ... fountain – Jesus Christ (Joh 4:10) sealed, while He was in the sealed tomb: it poured forth its full tide on Pentecost (Joh 7:37–39). Still He is a sealed fountain until the Holy Ghost opens it to one (1Co 12:3). The Church also is 'a garden enclosed' (Ps 4:3 Isa 5:1). Contrast Ps 80:9–12. So 'a spring' (Isa 27:3 58:11); 'sealed' (Eph 4:30 2Ti 2:19). As wives in the East are secluded from public gaze, so believers (Ps 83:3 Col 3:3). Contrast the open streams which 'pass away' (Job 6:15–18 2Pe 2:17).

13. orchard – Hebrew, 'a paradise,' that is, a pleasure-ground and orchard. Not only flowers, but fruit trees (Joh 15:8 Php 1:11).

14. calamus – 'sweet cane' (Ex 30:23 Jer 6:20).

myrrh and aloes – Ointments are associated with His death, as well as with feasts (Joh 12:7). The bride's ministry of 'myrrh and aloes' is recorded (Joh 19:39).

15. of – This pleasure-ground is not dependent on mere reservoirs; it has a fountain *sufficient to water* many 'gardens' (*plural*).

living – (Jer 17:8 Joh 4:13,14 7:38,39).

from Lebanon – Though the fountain is lowly, the source is lofty; fed by the perpetual snows of Lebanon, refreshingly cool (Jer 18:14), fertilizing the gardens of Damascus. It springs upon earth; its source is heaven. It is now not 'sealed,' but open 'streams' (Re 22:17).

16. Awake – literally, 'arise.' All besides is ready; one thing alone is wanted – the breath of God. This follows rightly after His death (So 6:12 Ac 2:1–4). It is His call to the Spirit to come (Joh 14:16); in Joh 3:8, compared to 'the wind'; quickening (Joh 6:63 Eze 27:9). Saints offer the same prayer (Ps 85:6 Hab 3:2). The north wind 'awakes,' or *arises* strongly, namely, the Holy Ghost as a reprover (Joh 16:8–11); the south wind '*comes*' gently, namely, the Holy Ghost as the comforter (Joh 14:16). The west wind brings rain from the sea (1Ki 18:44,45 Lu 12:54). The east wind is tempestuous (Job 27:21 Isa 27:8) and withering (Ge 41:23). These, therefore, are not wanted; but first the north wind clearing the air (Job 37:22 Pr 25:23), and then the warm south wind (Job 37:17); so the Holy Ghost first clearing away mists of gloom, error, unbelief, sin, which intercept the light of Jesus Christ, then infusing spiritual warmth (2Co 4:6), causing the graces to exhale their odour.

Let my beloved – *the bride's reply.* The fruit was now at length ripe; the last Passover, which He had so desired, is come (Lu 22:7,15,16,18), the only occasion in which He took charge of the preparations.

his – answering to Jesus Christ's 'My.' She owns that the garden is His, and the fruits in her, which she does not in false humility deny (Ps 66:16 Ac 21:19 1Co 15:10) are His (Joh 15:8 Php 1:11).

Chapter 5
So 5:1–16.

1. Answer to her prayer (Isa 65:24 Re 3:20).

am come – already (So 4:16); 'come' (Ge 28:16).

sister ... spouse – As Adam's was created of his flesh, out of his opened side, there being none on earth on a level with him, so the bride out of the pierced Saviour (Eph 5:30–32).

have gathered ... myrrh – His course was already complete; the myrrh (Mt 2:11 26:7–12 Joh 19:39), emblems of the indwelling of the anointing Holy Ghost, were already gathered.

spice – literally, 'balsam.'

have eaten – answering to her 'eat' (So 4:16).

honeycomb – distinguished here from liquid 'honey' dropping from trees. The last supper, here set forth, is one of *espousal*, a pledge of the future *marriage* (So 8:14 Re 19:9). Feasts often took place in gardens. In the absence of sugar, then unknown, honey was more widely used than with us. His eating honey with milk indicates His true, yet spotless, human nature from infancy (Isa 7:15); and after His resurrection (Lu 24:42).

my wine – (Joh 18:11) – a cup of wrath to Him, of mercy to us, whereby God's Word and promises become to us 'milk' (Ps 19:10 1Pe 2:2). 'My' answers to 'His' (So 4:16). The myrrh (emblem, by its bitterness, of *repentance*), honey, milk (*incipient faith*), wine (*strong faith*), in reference to believers, imply that He accepts all their graces, however various in degree.

eat – He desires to make us partakers in His joy (Isa 55:1,2 Joh 6:53–57 1Jo 1:3).

drink abundantly – so as to be filled (Eph 5:18; as Hag 1:6).

friends – (Joh 15:15).

Canticle IV. – (So 5:2–8:4) – from the agony of Gethsemane to the conversion of Samaria.

2. Sudden change of scene from evening to midnight, from a betrothal feast to cold repulse. He has gone from the feast alone; night is come; He knocks at the door of His espoused; she hears, but in sloth does not shake off half-conscious drowsiness; namely, the disciples' torpor (Mt 26:40–43), 'the spirit willing, the flesh weak' (compare Ro 7:18–25 Ga 5:16,17,24). Not *total* sleep. The lamp was burning beside the *slumbering* wise virgin, but wanted trimming (Mt 25:5–7). It is *His* voice that rouses her (Jon 1:6 Eph 5:14 Re 3:20). Instead of bitter reproaches, He addresses her by the most endearing titles, 'my sister, my love'. Compare His thought of *Peter* after the denial (Mr 16:7).

dew – which falls heavily in summer nights in the East (see Lu 9:58).

drops of the night – (Ps 22:2 Lu 22:44). His death is not *expressed*, as unsuitable to the allegory, a song of love and joy; So 5:4 refers to the scene in the judgment hall of Caiaphas, when Jesus Christ employed the cock-crowing and look of love to awaken Peter's sleeping conscience, so that his 'bowels were moved' (Lu 22:61,62); So 5:5,6, the disciples with 'myrrh,'. (Lu 24:1,5), seeking Jesus Christ in the tomb, but finding Him not, for He has 'withdrawn Himself' (Joh 7:34 13:33); So 5:7, the trials by watchmen extend through the whole night of His withdrawal from Gethsemane to the resurrection; they took off the 'veil' of Peter's disguise; also, literally the linen cloth from the young man (Mr 14:51); So 5:8, the sympathy of friends (Lu 23:27).

undefiled – not polluted by spiritual adultery (Re 14:4 Jas 4:4).

3. Trivial excuses (Lu 14:18).

coat – rather, the inmost vest, next the skin, taken off before going to bed.

washed ... feet – before going to rest, for they had been soiled, from the Eastern custom of wearing sandals, not shoes. Sloth (Lu 11:7) and despondency (De 7:17–19).

4. A key in the East is usually a piece of wood with pegs in it corresponding to small holes in a wooden bolt within, and is put through a hole in the door, and thus draws the bolt. So Jesus Christ 'puts forth His hand (namely, His Spirit, Eze 3:14), by (*Hebrew*, 'from,' so in So 2:9) the hole'; in 'chastening' (Ps 38:2 Re 3:14–22, singularly similar to this passage), and other unexpected ways letting Himself in (Lu 22:61,62).

bowels ... moved for him – It is His which are first troubled for us, and which cause ours to be troubled for Him (Jer 31:20 Ho 11:8).

5. dropped with myrrh – The best proof a bride could give her lover of welcome was to anoint herself (the back of the hands especially, as being the coolest part of the body) *profusely* with the *best* perfumes (Ex 30:23 Es 2:12 Pr 7:17); 'sweet-smelling' is in the *Hebrew* rather, 'spontaneously exuding' from the tree, and therefore the *best*. She designed also to anoint Him, whose 'head was filled with the drops of night' (Lu 24:1). The myrrh typifies *bitter* repentance, the fruit of the Spirit's unction (2Co 1:21,22).

handles of the lock – sins which closed the heart against Him.

6. withdrawn – He *knocked* when she was sleeping; for to have left her then would have ended in the death sleep; He *withdraws* now that she is roused, as she needs correction (Jer 2:17,19), and can appreciate and safely bear it now, which she could not then. 'The strong He'll strongly try' (1Co 10:13).

when he spake – rather, 'because of His speaking'; at the remembrance of His tender words (Job 29:2,3 Ps 27:13 142:7), or *till He should speak*. no answer – (Job 23:3–9 30:20 34:29 La 3:44). Weak faith receives immediate comfort (Lu 8:44,47,48); strong faith is tried with delay (Mt 15:22,23).

7. watchmen – historically, the Jewish priests (see on So 5:2); spiritually, ministers (Isa 62:6 Heb 13:17), faithful in 'smiting' (Ps 141:5) too harsh; or, perhaps, unfaithful; disliking her zeal wherewith she sought Jesus Christ, first, with spiritual prayer, 'opening' her heart to Him, and then in charitable works 'about the city'; miscalling it fanaticism (Isa 66:5), and taking away her veil (the greatest indignity to an Eastern lady), as though she were positively immodest. She had before sought Him by night in the streets, under strong affection (So 3:2–4), and so without rebuff from 'the watchmen,' found Him immediately; but now after sinful neglect, she encounters pain and delay. God forgives believers, but it is a serious thing to draw on His forgiveness; so the *growing reserve* of God towards Israel observable in Judges, as His people repeat their demands on His grace.

8. She turns from the unsympathizing watchmen to humbler persons, not yet themselves knowing Him, but in the way towards it. Historically, His secret friends in the night of His withdrawal (Lu 23:27,28). Inquirers *may* find ('*if* ye find') Jesus Christ before she who has grieved His Spirit finds Him again.

tell – in prayer (Jas 5:16).

sick of love – from an opposite cause (So 2:5) than through excess of delight at His *presence*; now excess of pain at His *absence*.

9. Her own beauty (Eze 16:14), and lovesickness for Him, elicit now their enquiry (Mt 5:16); heretofore 'other lords besides Him had dominion over them'; thus they had seen 'no beauty in Him' (Isa 26:13 53:2).

10. (1Pe 3:15).

white and ruddy – health and beauty. So David (equivalent to *beloved*), His forefather after the flesh, and type (1Sa 17:42). 'The Lamb' is at once His nuptial and sacrificial name (1Pe 1:19 Re 19:7), characterized by white and red; *white,* His spotless manhood (Re 1:14). The *Hebrew* for *white* is properly 'illuminated by the sun,' white as the light' (compare Mt 17:2); *red,* in His blood-dyed garment as slain (Isa 63:1-3 Re 5:6 19:13). Angels are white, not red; the blood of martyrs does not enter heaven; His alone is seen there.

chiefest – literally, 'a standard bearer'; that is, as conspicuous above all others, as a standard bearer is among hosts (Ps 45:7 89:6 Isa 11:10 55:4 Heb 2:10; compare 2Sa 18:3 Job 33:23 Php 2:9–11 Re 1:5). The chief of sinners needs the 'chiefest' of Saviours.

11. head … gold – *the Godhead* of Jesus Christ, as distinguished from His *heel,* that is, His manhood, which was 'bruised' by Satan; both together being one Christ (1Co 11:3). Also His sovereignty, as Nebuchadnezzar, the supreme king was 'the head of gold' (Da 2:32–38 Col 1:18), the highest creature, compared with Him, is brass, iron, and clay. 'Preciousness' (*Greek,* 1Pe 2:7).

bushy – *curled,* token of Headship. In contrast with her *flowing* locks (So 4:1), the token of her subjection to Him (Ps 8:4–8 1Co 11:3,6–15). The *Hebrew* is (pendulous as) the *branches of a palm,* which, when in leaf, resemble waving plumes of feathers.

black – implying youth; no 'gray hairs' (Ps 102:27 110:3,4 Ho 7:9). Jesus Christ was crucified in the prime of vigour and manliness. In heaven, on the other hand, His hair is 'white,' He being the Ancient of days (Da 7:9). These contrasts often concur in Him (So 5:10), 'white and ruddy'; here the 'raven' (So 5:12), the 'dove,' as both with Noah in the ark (Ge 8:11); emblems of judgment and mercy.

12. as the eyes of doves – rather, 'as doves' (Ps 68:13); bathing in 'the rivers'; so combining in their 'silver' feathers the *whiteness* of milk with the *sparkling brightness* of the water trickling over them (Mt 3:16). The 'milk' may allude to the white around the pupil of the eye. The 'waters' refer to the eye as the fountain of *tears of sympathy* (Eze 16:5,6 Lu 19:41). Vivacity, purity, and love, are the three features typified.

fitly set – as a gem in a ring; as the precious stones in the high priest's breastplate. Rather, translate as *Vulgate* (the doves), *sitting at the fulness* of the stream; by the full stream.

13. cheeks – the seat of beauty, according to the *Hebrew* meaning. Yet men smote and spat on them (Isa 50:6).

bed – full, like the raised surface of the garden bed; fragrant with ointments, as beds with aromatic plants (literally, 'balsam').

sweet flowers – rather, 'terraces of aromatic herbs' – 'high-raised' parterres of sweet plants,' in parallelism to 'bed,' which comes from a *Hebrew* root, meaning 'elevation.'

lips – (Ps 45:2 Joh 7:46).

lilies – red lilies. Soft and gentle (1Pe 2:22,23). How different lips were man's (Ps 22:7)!

dropping … myrrh – namely, His lips, just as the sweet dewdrops which hang in the calyx of the lily.

14. rings set with … beryl – *Hebrew, Tarshish,* so called from the city. The ancient chrysolite, gold in Collor (*Septuagint*), our topaz, one of the stones on the high priest's breastplate, also in the foundation of New Jerusalem (Re 21:19,20; also Da 10:6). A ring is the token of sonship (Lu 15:22). A slave was not allowed to wear a *gold* ring. He imparts His sonship and freedom to us (Ga 4:7); also of authority (Ge 41:42; compare Joh 6:27). He seals us in the name of God with His signet (Re 7:2–4), compare below, So 8:6, where she desires to be herself *a signet-ring* on His arms; so 'graven on the palms,' that is, on the signet-ring in His hand (Isa 49:16; contrast Hag 2:23, with Jer 22:24).

bright – literally, 'elaborately wrought so as to shine,' so His 'prepared' body (Heb 10:5); the 'ivory palace' of the king (Ps 45:8); spotless, pure, so the bride's 'neck is as to tower of *ivory*' (So 7:4).

sapphires – spangling in the girdle around Him (Da 10:5). 'To the pure all things are pure.' As in statuary to the artist the partly undraped figure is suggestive only of beauty, free from indelicacy, so to the saint the personal excellencies of Jesus Christ, typified under the ideal of the noblest human form. As, however, the bride and bridegroom are in public, the usual robes on the person, richly ornamented, are presupposed (Isa 11:5). Sapphires indicate His *heavenly* nature (so Joh 3:13, '*is* in heaven'), even in His humiliation, *overlaying* or cast 'over' His ivory human body (Ex 24:10). Sky-blue in Collor, the *height* and *depth* of the love of Jesus Christ (Eph 3:18).

15. pillars – strength and steadfastness. Contrast man's 'legs' (Ec 12:3). Allusion to the temple (1Ki 5:8,9 7:21), the 'cedars' of 'Lebanon' (Ps 147:10). Jesus Christ's 'legs' were not broken on the cross, though the thieves' were; on them rests the weight of our salvation (Ps 75:3).

sockets of fine gold – His sandals, answering to the bases of the pillars; 'set up from everlasting' (Pr 8:22,23) to the feet, 'of fine gold.' He was tried in the fire and found without alloy.

countenance – rather, 'His aspect,' including both *mien* and *stature* (compare 2Sa 23:21, *Margin;* with 1Ch 11:23). From the several *parts,* she proceeds to the general effect of the *whole* person of Jesus Christ.

Lebanon – so called from its *white* limestone rocks.

excellent – literally, 'choice,' that is, fair and tall as the cedars on Lebanon (Eze 31:3). Majesty is the prominent thought (Ps 21:5). Also the cedars' *duration* (Heb 1:11); *greenness* (Lu 23:31), and refuge afforded by it (Eze 17:22,23).

16. Literally, 'His *palate* is *sweetness,* yea, all over loveliness,' that is, He is the *essence* of these qualities.

mouth – So 1:2, not the same as 'lips' (So 5:13), His breath (Isa 11:4 Joh 20:22). 'All over,' all the beauties scattered among creatures are transcendently concentrated in Him (Col 1:19 2:9).

my beloved – for I love Him.

my friend – for He loves me (Pr 18:24). Holy boasting (Ps 34:2 1Co 1:31).

Chapter 6
So 6:1–13.

1. Historically, at Jesus Christ's crucifixion and burial, Joseph of Arimathea, and Nicodemus, and others, joined with His professed disciples. By speaking of Jesus Christ, the bride does good not only to her own soul, but to others (see on So 1:4). Compare the hypocritical use of similar words (Mt 2:8).

2. gone down – Jerusalem was on a hill (answering to its *moral* elevation), and the gardens were at a little distance in the valleys below.

beds of spices – (balsam) which He Himself calls the 'mountain of myrrh,' (So 4:6), and again (So 8:14), the resting-place of His body amidst spices, and of His soul in paradise, and now in heaven, where He stands as High Priest for ever. Nowhere else in the Song is there mention of mountains of spices.

feed in … gardens – that is, in the churches, though He may have withdrawn for a time from the individual believer: she implies an invitation

to the daughters of Jerusalem to enter His spiritual Church, and become lilies, made white by His blood. He is gathering some lilies now to plant on earth, others to transplant into heaven (So 5:1 Ge 5:24 Mr 4:28,29 Ac 7:60).

3. In speaking of Jesus Christ to others, she regains her own assurance. Literally, 'I am *for* my beloved … *for* me.' Reverse order from So 2:16. She *now,* after the season of darkness, grounds her convictions on His love towards her, more than on hers towards Him (De 33:3). *There,* it was the young believer concluding that she was His, from the sensible assurance that He was hers.

4. Tirzah – meaning 'pleasant' (Heb 13:21); 'well-pleasing' (Mt 5:14); the royal city of one of the old Canaanite kings (Jos 12:24); and after the revolt of Israel, the royal city of its kings, before Omri founded Samaria (1Ki 16:8,15). No ground for assigning a later date than the time of Solomon to the Song, as Tirzah was even in his time the capital of the north (Israel), as Jerusalem was of the south (Judah).

Jerusalem – residence of the kings of *Judah,* as Tirzah, of *Israel* (Ps 48:1; Ps 122:1–3 125:1,2). Loveliness, security, unity, and loyalty; also the union of Israel and Judah in the Church (Isa 11:13 Jer 3:18 Eze 37:16,17,22; compare Heb 12:22 Re 21:2,12).

terrible – awe-inspiring. Not only armed as a city on the defensive, but as an army on the offensive. **banners** – (See on So 5:10); Jehovahnissi (2Co 10:4).

5. (So 4:9 Ge 32:28 Ex 32:9–14 Ho 12:4). This is the way 'the army' (So 6:4) 'overcomes' not only enemies, but Jesus Christ Himself, with eyes fixed on Him (Ps 25:15 Mt 11:12). Historically. So 6:3–5 represent the restoration of Jesus Christ to His Church at the resurrection; His sending her forth as an army, with new powers (Mr 16:15–18,20); His rehearsing the *same* instructions (see on So 6:6) as when with them (Lu 24:44).

overcome – literally, 'have taken me by storm.'

6. Not vain repetition of So 4:1,2. The use of the same words shows His love unchanged after her temporary unfaithfulness (Mal 3:6).

8. threescore – indefinite number, as in So 3:7. Not queens, *of Solomon,* but witnesses of the espousals, rulers of the earth contrasted with the saints, who, though many, are but 'one' bride (Isa 52:15 Lu 22:25,26 Joh 17:21 1Co 10:17). The one Bride is contrasted with the many wives whom Eastern kings had in violation of the marriage law (1Ki 11:1–3).

9. Hollow professors, like half wives, have no part in the one bride.

only one of her mother – namely, 'Jerusalem above' (Ga 4:26). The 'little sister' (So 8:8) is not inconsistent with her being 'the only one'; for that sister is one with herself (Joh 10:16).

choice – (Eph 1:4 2Th 2:13). As she exalted Him above all others (So 5:10), so He now her. **daughters … blessed her** – (Isa 8:18 61:9 Eze 16:14 2Th 1:10). So at her appearance after Pentecost (Ac 4:13 6:15 24:25 26:28).

10. The words expressing the admiration of the daughters. Historically (Ac 5:24–39).

as the morning – As yet she is not come to the fulness of her light (Pr 4:18).

moon – shining in the night, by light borrowed from the sun; so the bride, in the darkness of this world, reflects the light of the Sun of righteousness (2Co 3:18).

sun – Her light of justification is perfect, for it is His (2Co 5:21 1Jo 4:17). The moon has less light, and has only one half illuminated; so the bride's sanctification is as yet imperfect. Her future glory (Mt 13:43).

army – (So 6:4). The climax requires this to be applied to the starry and angelic hosts, from which God is called Lord of Sabaoth. Her final glory (Ge 15:5 Da 12:3 Re 12:1). The Church Patriarchal, 'the morning'; Levitical, 'the moon'; Evangelical, 'the sun'; Triumphant, 'the bannered army' (Re 19:14).

11. The bride's words; for she everywhere is the narrator, and often soliloquizes, which He never does. The first garden (So 2:11–13) was that of spring, full of flowers and grapes not yet ripe; the second, autumn, with spices (which are always connected with the person of Jesus Christ), and nothing unripe (So 4:13). The third here, of 'nuts,' from the previous autumn; the end of winter, and verge of spring; the Church in the upper room (Ac 1:13), when one dispensation was just closed, the other not yet begun; the hard shell of the old needing to be broken, and its inner sweet kernel extracted (Lu 24:27,32); waiting for the Holy Ghost to usher in spiritual spring. The *walnut* is meant, with a bitter outer husk, a hard shell, and sweet kernel. So the Word is distasteful to the careless; when awakened, the sinner finds the letter hard, until the Holy Ghost reveals the sweet inner spirit.

12. Sudden outpourings of the Spirit on Pentecost (Ac 2:1–13), while the Church was using the means (answering to 'the garden,' So 6:11 Joh 3:8).

Ammi-nadib – supposed to me one proverbial for swift driving. Similarly (So 1:9). Rather, 'my willing people' (Ps 110:3). A willing chariot bore a 'willing people'; or Nadib is *the Prince*, Jesus Christ (Ps 68:17). She is borne in a moment into His presence (Eph 2:6).

13. Entreaty of the daughters of Jerusalem to her, in her chariot-like flight from them (compare 2Ki 2:12 2Sa 19:14).

Shulamite – new name applied to her now for the first time. *Feminine* of Solomon, Prince of Peace; His bride, daughter of peace, accepting and proclaiming it (Isa 52:7 Joh 14:27 Ro 5:1

Eph 2:17). Historically, this name answers to the time when, not without a divine design in it, the young Church met in *Solomon's* porch (Ac 3:11 5:12). The entreaty, 'Return, O Shulamite,' answers to the people's desire to keep Peter and John, after the lame man was healed, when they were about to enter the temple. Their reply attributing the glory not to themselves, but to Jesus Christ, answers to the bride's reply here, 'What will ye see' in me? 'As it were'. She accepts the name Shulamite, as truly describing her. But adds, that though 'one' (So 6:9), she is nevertheless 'two.' Her glories are her Lord's, beaming through her (Eph 5:31,32). The two armies are the family of Jesus Christ in heaven, and that on earth, joined and one with Him; the one militant, the other triumphant. Or Jesus Christ and His ministering angels are one army, the Church the other, both being one (Joh 17:21,22). Allusion is made to Mahanaim (meaning *two hosts*), the scene of Jacob's victorious conflict by prayer (Ge 32:2,9,22–30). Though she is peace, yet she has warfare here, between flesh and spirit within and foes without; her strength, as Jacob's at Mahanaim, is Jesus Christ and His host enlisted on her side by prayer; whence she obtains those graces which raise the admiration of the daughters of Jerusalem.

Chapter 7

So 7:1–13.

1. thy feet – rather, 'thy goings' (Ps 17:5). Evident allusion to Isa 52:7: '*How beautiful … are the feet of him … that publisheth peace*' (Shulamite, So 6:13).

shoes – Sandals are richly jewelled in the East (Lu 15:22 Eph 6:15). She is evidently 'on the mountains,' whither she was wafted (So 6:12), *above* the daughters of Jerusalem, who therefore portray her *feet* first.

daughter – of God the Father, with whom Jesus Christ is one (Mt 5:9), 'children of (the) God' (of *peace*), equivalent to Shulamite (Ps 45:10–15 2Co 6:18), as well as bride of Jesus Christ.

prince's – therefore princely herself, freely giving the word of life to others, not sparing her 'feet,' as in So 5:3 Ex 12:11. To act on the offensive is defensive to ourselves.

joints – rather, 'the rounding'; the full graceful curve of the hips in the female figure; like the *rounding of a necklace* (as the *Hebrew* for 'jewels' means). Compare with Eph 4:13–16 Col 2:19. Or, applying it to the girdle binding together the robes round the hips (Eph 6:14).

cunning workman – (Ps 139:14–16 Eph 2:10,22:5:29,30,32).

2. navel – rather, 'girdle-clasp,' called from the part of the person underneath. The 'shoes' (So 7:1) prove that *dress* is throughout presupposed on all parts where it is usually worn. She is 'a bride adorned for her husband'; the 'uncomely parts,' being most adorned (1Co 12:23). The girdle-clasp was adorned with red rubies resembling the 'round goblet' of spice – mixed wine. The wine of the 'New Testament in His blood' (Lu 22:20). The spiritual exhilaration by it was mistaken for that caused by new wine (Ac 2:13–17 Eph 5:18).

belly – that is, *the vesture* on it. As in Ps 45:13,14, gold and needlework compose the bride's attire, so golden-coloured 'wheat' and white 'lilies' here. The ripe grain, in token of harvest joy, used to be decorated with lilies; so the accumulated spiritual food (Joh 6:35 12:24), free from chaff, not fenced with thorns, but made attractive by lilies ('believers,' So 2:2 Ac 2:46,47 5:13,14, in common partaking of it). Associated with the exhilarating wine cup (Zec 9:17), as here.

3. The daughters of Jerusalem describe her in the same terms as Jesus Christ in So 4:5. The testimonies of heaven and earth coincide.

twins – faith and love.

4. tower of ivory – In So 4:4, Jesus Christ saith, 'a tower of David builded for an armoury.' Strength and conquest are the main thought in His description; here, beauty and polished whiteness; contrast So 1:1–17.

fishpools – clear (Re 22:1), deep, quiet, and full (1Co 2:10,15).

Heshbon – east of Jordan, residence of the Amorite king, Sihon (Nu 21:25), afterwards held by Gad.

Bath-rabbim – 'daughter of a multitude'; a crowded thoroughfare. Her eyes (So 4:1) are called by Jesus Christ, 'doves eyes,' waiting on Him. But here, looked on by the daughters of Jerusalem, they are compared to a placid lake. She is calm even amidst the crowd (Pr 8:2 Joh 16:33).

nose – or, face.

tower of Lebanon – a border-fortress, watching the hostile Damascus. Towards Jesus Christ her face was full of holy shame (see on So 4:1; So 4:3); towards spiritual foes, like a watchtower (Hab 2:1 Mr 13:37 Ac 4:13), elevated, so that she looks not up from earth to heaven, but down from heaven to earth. If we retain 'nose,' discernment of spiritual fragrance is meant.

5. upon thee – the headdress 'upon' her.

Carmel – signifying a well-cultivated field (Isa 35:2). In So 5:15 He is compared to *majestic* Lebanon; she hero, to *fruitful* Carmel. Her headdress, or crown (2Ti 4:8 1Pe 5:4). Also the souls won by her (1Th 2:19,20), a token of her fruitfulness.

purple – royalty (Re 1:6). As applied to hair, it expresses the glossy splendour of black hair (literally, 'pendulous hair') so much admired in the East (So 4:1). While the King compares her hair to the flowering hair of goats (the token of

her *subjection*), the daughters of Jerusalem compare it to *royal* purple.

6. Nearer advance of the daughters to the Church (Ac 2:47 5:13ff.). Love to her is the first token of love to Him (1Jo 5:1, end).

delights – fascinating charms to them and to the King (So 7:5 Isa 62:4, Hephzi-bah). Hereafter, too (Zep 3:17 Mal 3:12 Re 21:9).

7. palm tree – (Ps 92:12). The sure sign of *water near* (Ex 15:27 Joh 7:38).

clusters – The parallelism (So 7:8), 'clusters of the vine,' shows it is here clusters of grapes. Vines were often trained (termed 'wedded') on other trees.

8. The daughters are no longer content to admire, but resolve to lay hold of her fruits, high though these be. The palm stem is bare for a great height, and has its crown of fruit-laden boughs at the summit. It is the symbol of triumphant joy (Joh 12:13); so hereafter (Re 7:9).

breasts – (Isa 66:11).

the vine – Jesus Christ (Ho 14:7, end; Joh 15:1).

nose – that is, breath; the Holy Ghost breathed into her *nostrils* by Him, whose 'mouth is most sweet' (So 5:16).

apples – citrons, off the tree to which He is likened (So 2:3).

9. roof of thy mouth – thy voice (Pr 15:23).

best wine – the *new* wine of the gospel kingdom (Mr 14:25), poured out at Pentecost (Ac 2:4,13,17). **for my beloved** – (So 4:10). Here first the daughters call Him theirs, and become one with the bride. The steps successively are (So 1:5) where they misjudge her (So 3:11); So 5:8, where the possibility of their finding Him, before she regained Him, is expressed; So 5:9 (So 6:1 7:6,9 Joh 4:42).

causing ... asleep to speak – (Isa 35:6 Mr 5:19,20 Ac 2:47 Eph 5:14). Jesus Christ's first miracle turned water into 'good wine kept until now' (Joh 2:10); just as the Gospel revives those asleep and dying under the law (Pr 31:6 Ro 7:9,10,24,25 8:1).

10. Words of the daughters of Jerusalem and the bride, now united into one (Ac 4:32). They are mentioned again distinctly (So 8:4), as fresh converts were being added from among enquirers, and these needed to be charged not to grieve the Spirit.

his desire is toward me – strong assurance. He so desires us, as to give us sense of His desire toward us (Ps 139:17,18 Lu 22:15 Ga 2:20 1Jo 4:16).

11. field – the country.

lodge – forsaking *home* for Jesus Christ's sake (Mt 19:29).

12. (Mr 1:35 Joh 9:4 Ga 6:10). Assurance fosters diligence, not indolence.

13. mandrakes – *Hebrew, audaim,* from a root meaning 'to love'; love apples, supposed to exhilarate the spirits and excite love. Only here and Ge 30:14–16.

gates – the entrance to the summer house. Love 'lays up' the best of everything for the person beloved (1Co 10:31 Php 3:8 1Pe 4:11), thereby really, though unconsciously, laying up for itself (1Ti 6:18,19).

Chapter 8
So 8:1–14.

1. He had been a brother already. Why, then, this prayer here? It refers to the time after His resurrection, when the previous *outward* intimacy with Him was no longer allowed, but it was implied it should be renewed at the second coming (Joh 20:17). For this the Church here prays; meanwhile she enjoys *inward* spiritual communion with Him. The last who ever 'kissed' Jesus Christ on earth was the traitor Judas. The bride's return with the King to her mother's house answers to Ac 8:25, after the mission to Samaria. The rest spoken of (So 8:4) answers to Ac 9:31.

that sucked ... mother – a brother born of the same mother; the closest tie.

2. Her desire to bring Him into her home circle (Joh 1:41).

who would instruct me – rather, 'thou wouldest instruct me,' namely, how I might best please thee (Isa 11:2,3 50:4 Lu 12:12 Joh 14:26 16:13).

spiced wine – seasoned with aromatic perfumes. Jesus Christ ought to have our choicest gifts. Spices are never introduced in the song in His absence; therefore the time of His return from 'the mountain of spices' (So 8:14) is contemplated. The cup of betrothal was given by Him at the last supper; the cup or marriage shall be presented by her at His return (Mt 26:29). Till then the believer often cannot feel towards, or speak of, Him as he would wish.

3, 4. The 'left and right hand,' occurred only once actually (So 2:6), and here optatively. Only at His first manifestation did the Church palpably embrace Him; at His second coming there shall be again sensible communion with Him. The rest in So 8:4, which is a *spiritual* realization of the wish in So 8:3 (1Pe 1:8), and the charge not to disturb it, close the first, second, and fourth canticles; not the third, as the bridegroom there takes charge Himself; nor the fifth, as, if *repose* formed its close, we might mistake the present state for our rest. The broken, longing close, like that of the whole Bible (Re 22:20), reminds us we are to be waiting for a Saviour to come. On 'daughters of Jerusalem,' see on So 7:10.

Canticle V. – (So 8:5–14) – from the call of the Gentiles to the close of Revelation.

5. *Who is this* – Words of the daughters of Jerusalem, that is, the churches of Judea; referring to Paul, on his return from Arabia ('the wilderness'), whither he had gone after conversion (Ga 1:15–24).

I raised thee ... she ... bare thee – (Ac 26:14-16). The first words of Jesus Christ to the bride since her going to the garden of nuts (So 6:9,10); so His appearance to Paul is the only one since His ascension, So 8:13 is not an address of Him as *visible:* her reply implies He is not visible (1Co 15:8). Spiritually, she was found in the moral wilderness (Eze 16:5 Ho 13:5); but now she is 'coming up from' it (Jer 2:2 Ho 2:14), especially in the last stage of her journey, her conscious weakness casting itself the more wholly on Jesus Christ (2Co 12:9). 'Raised' (Eph 2:1–7). Found ruined under the forbidden tree (Ge 3:22–24); restored under the shadow of Jesus Christ crucified, 'the green tree' (Lu 23:31), fruit-'bearing' by the cross (Isa 53:11 Joh 12:24). 'Born again by the Holy Ghost' 'there' (Eze 16:3-6). In this verse, *her dependence,* in the similar verse, So 3:6, *His omnipotence to support her,* are brought out (De 33:26).

6. Implying approaching absence of the Bridegroom.

seal – having her name and likeness engraven on it. His Holy Priesthood also in heaven (Ex 28:6–12,15–30 Heb 4:14); 'his heart' there answering to 'thine heart' here, and 'two shoulders' to 'arm.' (Compare Jer 22:24, with Hag 2:23.) But the Holy Ghost (Eph 1:13,14). As in So 8:5, she was 'leaning' on Him, that is, her arm on His *arm,* her head on His *bosom;* so she prays now that before they part, her impression may be engraven both on His *heart* and His *arm,* answering to His *love* and His *power* (Ps 77:15; see Ge 38:18 Isa 62:3).

love is strong as death – (Ac 21:13 Ro 8:35–39 Re 12:11). This their love unto death flows from His (Joh 10:15 15:13).

jealousy ... the grave – *Zealous love,* jealous of all that would come between the soul and Jesus Christ (1Ki 19:10 Ps 106:30,31 Lu 9:60 14:26 1Co 16:22).

cruel – rather, 'unyielding' hard, as the grave will not let go those whom it once holds (Joh 10:28).

a most vehement flame – literally, 'the fire-flame of Jehovah' (Ps 80:16 Isa 6:6). Nowhere else is *God's* name found in the Song. The zeal that burnt in Jesus Christ (Ps 69:9 Lu 12:49,50) kindled in His followers (Ac 2:3 Ro 15:30 Php 2:17).

7. waters – in contrast with the 'coals of fire' (So 8:6 1Ki 18:33–38). Persecutions (Ac 8:1) cannot quench love (Heb 10:34 Re 12:15,16). Our many provocations have not quenched His love (Ro 8:33–39).

if ... give all the substance ... contemned – Nothing short of Jesus Christ Himself, not even heaven without Him, can satisfy the saint (Php 3:8). Satan offers the world, as to Jesus Christ (Mt 4:8), so to the saint, in vain (1Jo 2:15–17 5:4). Nothing but our love in turn can satisfy Him (1Co 13:1–3).

8. The Gentile Church (Eze 16:48). 'We,' that is, the Hebrew Church, which heretofore admitted Gentiles to communion, only by becoming *Judaic proselytes.* Now first *idolatrous* Gentiles are admitted *directly* (Ac 11:17–26). Generally, the saint's anxiety for other souls (Mr 5:19 Joh 4:28,29).

no breasts – neither faith nor love as yet (see on So 4:5), which 'come by hearing' of Him who first loved us. Not yet fit to be His bride, and mother of a spiritual offspring.

what shall we do – the chief question in the early Church at the first council (Ac 15:23–29). How shall 'the elder brother' treat the 'younger,' already received by the Father (Lu 15:25–32)? Generally (2Sa 15:15 Joh 9:4 Ac 9:6 Ga 6:10).

In the day ... spoken for – that is, when she shall be *sought in marriage* (Jud 14:7), namely, by Jesus Christ, the heavenly bridegroom.

9. wall ... door – the very terms employed as to the Gentile question (Ac 14:27 Eph 2:14). If she be a wall in Zion, founded on Jesus Christ (1Co 3:11), we will not 'withstand God' (Ac 11:17 15:8–11). But if so, we must not 'build' (Ac 15:14–17) on her 'wood, hay, stubble' (1Co 3:12), that is, Jewish rites, but 'a palace of silver,' that is, all the highest privileges of church communion (Ga 2:11–18 Eph 2:11–22). Image from the splendid turrets 'built' on the 'walls' of Jerusalem, and flanking the 'door,' or gateway. The Gentile Church is the 'door,' the type of catholic accessibleness (1Co 16:9); but it must be not a mere thoroughfare but furnished with a wooden framework, so as not merely to admit, but also to safely enclose: cedar is fragrant, beautiful, and enduring.

10. The Gentile Church's joy at its free admission to gospel privileges (Ac 15:30,31). She is one wall in the spiritual temple of the Holy Ghost, the Hebrew Church is the other; Jesus Christ, the common foundation, joins them (Eph 2:11–22).

breasts ... towers – alluding to the silver palace, which the bridal virgins proposed to build on her (So 8:9). 'Breasts' of consolation (Isa 66:11); faith and love (1Th 5:8); opposed to her previous state, 'no breasts' (So 8:8 2Th 1:3). Thus Eze 16:46,61 was fulfilled, both Samaria and the Gentiles being joined to the Jewish gospel Church.

favour – rather, 'peace.' The Gentile Church too is become the Shulamite (So 6:13), or

peace-enjoying bride of Solomon, that is, Jesus Christ, the Prince of Peace (Ro 5:1 Eph 2:14). Reject not those whom God accepts (Nu 11:28 Lu 9:49 Ac 15:8,9).

11. The joint Church speaks of Jesus Christ's vineyard. Transference of it from the Jews, who rendered not the fruits, as is implied by the silence respecting any, to the Gentiles (Mt 21:33–43).

Baal-hamon – equivalent to *the owner of a multitude;* so Israel in Solomon's day (1Ki 4:20); so Isa 5:1, '*a very fruitful hill*' abounding in *privileges,* as in *numbers.* **Thousand pieces** – namely, silverlings, or shekels. The vineyard had a thousand vines probably; a vine at a silverling (Isa 7:23), referring to this passage.

12. 'mine' by grant of the true Solomon. Not merely 'let out to keepers,' as in the Jewish dispensation of *works,* but 'mine' by grace.

13. Jesus Christ's address to her; now no longer visibly present. Once she 'had not kept' her vineyard (So 1:6); now she 'dwells' in it, not as its owner, but its superintendent under Jesus Christ, with vinedressers ('companions'), for example, Paul (Ac 15:25,26), under her (So 8:11,12); these ought to obey her when she obeys Jesus Christ. Her voice in prayer and praise is to be heard continually by Jesus Christ, if her voice before men is to be effective (So 2:14, end; Ac 6:4 13:2,3).

14. (See on So 2:17). As she began with longing for His first coming (So 1:2), so she ends with praying for His second coming (Ps 130:6 Php 3:20,21 Re 22:20).As there are four gardens, so four mountains, which form not mere images, as Gilead, Carmel, but part of the structure of the Song:

(1) Bether, or *division* (So 2:17), God's justice *dividing* us from God.

(2) Those 'of leopards' (So 4:8), sin, the world, and Satan.

(3) That 'of myrrh and aloes' (So 4:6,14), the sepulchre of Calvary.

(4) Those 'of spices,' here answering to 'the hill of frankincense' (So 4:6), where His *soul* was for the three days of His death, and heaven, where He is a High Priest now, offering incense for us on the fragrant mountain of His own finished work (Heb 4:14, 7:25 Re 8:3,4); thus He surmounts the other three mountains, God's justice, our sin, death. The mountain of spices is as much greater than our sins, as heaven is higher than earth (Ps 103:11). The abrupt, unsatisfied close with the yearning prayer for His *visible* coming shows that the marriage is future, and that to wait eagerly for it is our true attitude (1Co 1:7 1Th 1:10 Tit 2:13 2Pe 3:12).

INTRODUCTION TO THE PROPHETS OF THE RESTORATION

A.R. Faussett

The prophetic gift existed long before the prophetic office was instituted. Thus Enoch had the former (Jude 1:14); so Abraham is called a prophet (Ge 20:7) as are also the patriarchs (Ps 105:15). The office was first instituted under the Mosaic economy; but even then the gift was not always connected with the office; for example, Daniel was endowed largely with the gift, but was never called to the office, as living in a heathen court where he could not have exercised it. So David (Mt 13:35 27:35). Hence the writings of both are classed with the Hagiographa, not with the prophets. Moreover, though the office ceased with the close of the Old Testament dispensation, the gift continued, and was among the leading charisms of the New Testament Church. 'Prophet' (in Hebrew, from a root, 'to gush out like a fountain') meant one acting as spokesman for another (Ex 7:1); so, one speaking authoritatively for God as interpreter of His will. 'Seer' was the more ancient term (1Sa 9:9), implying that he spake by a divine communication presented either to his senses or his mind: as 'prophet' indicated his authority as speaking for God.

The three dispensations

Christ was the only fountain of prophecy (1Pe 1:11 Re 19:10; also Ac 16:7, the oldest reading, 'the Spirit of Jesus'), and declared God's will to men by His Holy Spirit acting on the minds of the prophets. Thus the history of the Church is the history of God's revelations of Himself in His Son to man. The three divisions of this history, the Patriarchal, the Mosaic, and the Christian dispensations, are characterized each by a distinct mode of God's manifestations – that is, by a distinct form of the prophetic gift.

(1) The theophanic mode characterizes the Patriarchal dispensation: God revealing Himself in visible appearances, or theophanies.

(2) The theopneustic mode, the Mosaic: God revealing Himself through God-inspired men.

(3) The theologic mode, the Christian: God revealing Himself, not merely at intervals as before, but permanently by inspired writings ('the oracles of God,' 1Pe 4:11).

In the first or patriarchal age, men work no miracles, unlike all other primeval histories, which abound in miracles wrought by men: a proof of genuineness. All the miracles are wrought by God without man's intervention; and the divine communications are usually by direct utterance, whence the prophetic gift is rare, as God in this dispensation only exceptionally employs the prophetic agency of men in it: only in Ge 20:7, is the term 'prophet' found. In the second or Mosaic dispensation, God withdraws Himself more from direct communication with man and manifests Himself through human instruments. Instead of working miracles directly, Moses, Joshua, &c., are His agents. So in His communications He speaks not directly, but through Moses and his successors. The theocracy needed a new form of prophetic gift: God-inspired (theopneustic) men must speak and act for God, the Head of the theocracy, as His administrators; the prophetic gift is therefore now connected with the prophetic office. These prophets accordingly are acting, not writing, prophets. The latter did not arise till the later ages of this second dispensation. Moses acted as a legislator; Joshua, the Judges, and Samuel as executive prophets; David and Solomon as devotional prophets. Even in the case of the writing prophets of the latter half of the Mosaic dispensation, their primary duty was to speak and act. Their writing had reference more to the use of the New Testament dispensation than to their own (1Pe 1:12). So that even in their case the characteristic of the Mosaic dispensation was theopneustic, rather than theologic. The third, or Christian dispensation, is theologic, that is, a revelation of God by inspired writings. Compare 1Pe 4:11 2Pe 1:16–21, where he contrasts 'the old time' when 'holy men spake by the Holy Ghost' with our time when we have the 'sure word of prophecy'; or, as it may be translated, 'the word of prophecy confirmed [to us].' Thus God now reveals His will, not by direct theophanies, as in the first dispensation; not by inspired men, as in the second; but by the written word which liveth and abideth for ever (as opposed to the desultory manifestations of God, and the noncontinuance in life of the prophets, under the two former dispensations respectively, 1Pe 1:23 2Pe 3:2,16). The next form shall be the return of the theophanic manifestations on earth, in a more perfect and abiding form than in the first age (Re 21:3).

The Mosaic dispensation

The history of the prophetic office under the Mosaic dispensation falls into three divisions.

(1) The first ends with the age of Samuel and has no regular succession of prophets, these not being needed while God Himself ruled the people without an hereditary executive.

(2) The second period extends from Samuel to Uzziah, 800 B.C., and is the age of prophets of action. Samuel combined in himself the three elements of the theocracy, being a judge, a priest, and a prophet. The creation of a human king rendered the formal office of prophet more necessary as a counterpoise to it. Hence the age of the kings is the age of the prophets. But at this stage they were prophets of action, rather than of writing. Towards the close of this second period, the devotional and Messianic prophecies of David and Solomon prepared the way for the third period (from 800 B.C. to 400 B.C.), which began under Uzziah, and which was the age of written prophecy.

(3) In this third period the prophets turn from the present to the future, and so the Messianic element grows more distinct. Thus in these three shorter periods the grand characteristics of the three great dispensations reappear. The first is theophanic; the second, theopneustic; and the third, theologic. Just as the great organic laws of the world reappear in smaller departments, the law of the tree developing itself in miniature forms in the struc-

ture of the leaf, and the curve of the planet's orbit reappearing in the line traced by the projected cannon ball [MOORE].

Samuel probably enacted rules giving a permanent form to the prophetic order; at least in his time the first mention occurs of 'schools of the prophets.' These were all near each other, and in Benjamin, namely, in Beth-el, Gilgal, Ramah, and Jericho. Had the prophet been a mere foreteller of events, such schools would have been useless. But he was also God's representative to ensure the due execution of the Mosaic ritual in its purity; hence arose the need of schools wherein to study that divinely ordained institution. God mostly chose His prophets from those thus educated, though not exclusively, as the cases of Amos (Am 7:14) and Elisha (1Ki 19:19) prove. The fact that the humblest might be called to the prophetic office acted as a check to the hereditary kingly power and a stimulus to seeking the qualifications needed for so exalted an office. The Messianic Psalms towards the close of this second period form the transition between the prophets of action and the prophets of word, the men who were busy only with the present, and the men who looked out from the present into the glorious future.

The third period

The third period, that from Uzziah to Malachi, includes three classes of prophets: (1) Those of the ten tribes; (2) Those of the Gentiles; (3) Those of Judah. In the first class were Hosea and Amos. Few of the writing prophets belonged to Israel. They naturally gathered about the seat of the theocracy in Judah. Hence those of the ten tribes were mostly prophets of action. Under the second class fall Jonah, Nahum, and Obadiah, who were witnesses for God's authority over the Gentile world, as others witnessed for the same in the theocracy. The third class, those of Judah, have a wider scope and a more hopeful, joyous tone. They fall into five divisions: (1) Those dwelling in Judah at the highest point of its greatness during its separate state; namely, the century between Uzziah and Hezekiah, 800–700 B.C., Isaiah, Joel, and Micah. (2) The declining period of Judah, from Manasseh to Zedekiah, for example, Zephaniah and Habakkuk. (3) The captivity: Jeremiah. (4) The exile, when the future was all that the eye could rest on with hope; for example, Ezekiel and Daniel, who are chiefly prophets of the future. (5) The restoration: to which period belong the three last writing prophets of the Old Testament, Haggai, Zechariah, and Malachi. John the Baptist long subsequently belonged to the same dispensation, but he wrote nothing (Mt 11:9–11); like Elijah, he was a prophet of action and preaching, preparing the way for the prophets of word, as John did for the Incarnate Word.

To understand the spirit of each prophet's teaching, his historical position and the circumstances of the time must be considered. The captivity was designed to eradicate the Jews' tendency to idolatry and to restore the theocratic spirit which recognized God as the only ruler, and the Mosaic institutions as His established law, for a time until Messiah should come. Hence the prophets of the restoration are best illustrated by comparison with the histories of Ezra and Nehemiah, contemporaries of Malachi.

The three prophets

Of the three prophets of the restoration, two, Haggai and Zechariah, are at the beginning of the period, and the remaining one, Malachi, is at the close. The exile was not one complete deportation of the people, but a series of deportations extending over a century and a half. So the restoration was not accomplished at once, but in successive returns extending over a century. Hence arises the different tone of Haggai and Zechariah at its beginning, and of Malachi at its close. The first return took place in the first year of Cyrus, 536 B.C.; 42,360 persons returned under Shesh-bazzar or Zerubbabel and Joshua (Ezr 2:64). They built an altar and laid the foundations of the temple. They were interrupted by the misrepresentations of the Samaritans, and the work was suspended for fourteen years. The death of Smerdis gave an opportunity of renewing the work, seventy years after the destruction of the first temple. This was the time when Haggai and Zechariah arose, the former to incite to the immediate rebuilding of the temple and restoration of the Mosaic ritual, the latter to aid in the work and to unfold the grand future of the theocracy as an incentive to present labour. The impossibility of observing the Mosaic ritual in the exile generated an anti-theocratic indifference to it in the young who were strangers to the Jerusalem worship, from which the nation had been debarred for upwards of half a century. Moreover, the gorgeous pomp of Babylon tended to make them undervalue the humble rites of Jehovah's worship at that time. Hence there was need of a Haggai and a Zechariah to correct these feelings by unfolding the true glory of the theocratic institutions.

The next great epoch was the return of Ezra, 458 B.C., eighty years after the first expedition under Zerubbabel. Thirteen years later, 445 B.C., Nehemiah came to aid Ezra in the good work. It was now that Malachi arose to second these works, three-fourths of a century after Haggai and Zechariah. As their work was that of restorers, his was that of a reformer. The estates of many had become mortgaged, and depression of circumstances had led many into a sceptical spirit as to the service of God. They not only neglected the temple of worship, but took heathen wives, to the wrong of their Jewish wives and the dishonour of God. Therefore, besides the reformation of civil abuses and the rebuilding of the wall, effected through Nehemiah's exertions, a religious reformer was needed such as was Ezra, who reformed the ecclesiastical abuses, established synagogues, where regular instruction in the law could be received, restored the Sabbath, and the Passover, and the dignity of the priesthood, and generated a reverence for the written law, which afterwards became a superstition. Malachi aided in this good work by giving it his prophetical authority. How thoroughly the work was effected is proved by the utter change in the national character. Once always prone to idolatry, ever since the captivity they have abhorred it. Once loving kingly rule, now contrary to the ordinary course of history, they became submissive to priestly rule. Once negligent of the written Word, now they regarded it with reverence sometimes bordering on superstition. Once fond of foreign alliances, henceforth they shrank with abhorrence from all foreigners. Once fond of agriculture, now they became a trading people. From being pliable before, they now became intensely bigoted and nationally intolerant. Thus the restoration from Babylon moulded the national character more than any event since the exodus from Egypt.

The twelve tribes

Now the distinction between Judah and the ten tribes of Israel disappears. So in the New Testament the twelve tribes are mentioned (Ac 26:7 Jas 1:1). The theocratic feeling generated at the restoration drew all of the elect nation round the seat of the theocracy, the metropolis of the true religion, Jerusalem. Malachi tended to promote this feeling; thus his prophecy, though addressed to the people of Jerusalem, is called 'the word of the Lord to Israel' (Mal 1:1).

The long silence of prophets from Malachi to the times of Messiah was calculated to awaken in the Jewish mind the more earnest desire for Him who was to exceed infinitely in word and deed all the prophets, His forerunners. The three prophets of the restoration being the last of the Old Testament, are especially distinct in pointing to Him who, as the great subject of the New Testament, was to fulfil all the Old Testament.

ISAIAH

John Wesley

Introduction

The holy prophets, whose writings are contained in the sacred scripture, are sixteen. Of these, Isaiah is first in place, and, as may seem probable, in time also. But undoubtedly he was cotemporary with Hosea. Compare Isa 1:1, with Hos 1:1. The Jews tell us that he was of the blood royal of Judah. But undoubtedly he was the prince of all the prophets, whether we consider the great extent and variety of his prophecies, the excellency and sublimity of those mysteries which were revealed to him and by him, the majesty and elegancy of his style, or the incomparable liveliness and power of his sermons. He so evidently and fully describes the person, and offices, and sufferings, and kingdom of Christ, that some of the ancients called him the fifth Evangelist. And it is observed, that there are more quotations in the New Testament taken out of Isaiah, than out of all the other prophets.

Chapter 1

Judah's sins (1–4)

Her judgments (5–9)

Her worship is rejected (10–15)

Exhortations to repentance, promises of grace and mercy, threatenings of sore judgments, and complaints by reason of their backsliding (16–31)

Judah's sins (1–4)

1. **Vision** – Or, the visions; the word being here collectively used: the sense is, this is the book of the visions or prophecies. As prophets were called Seers, 1Sam 9:9, so prophecies are called visions, because they were as clearly and certainly represented to the prophets minds, as bodily objects are to mens eyes. **Saw** – Foresaw and foretold. But he speaks, after the manner of the prophets, of things to come, as if they were either past or present. **Judah** – Principally, but not exclusively. For he prophesies also concerning Egypt and Babylon, and divers other countries; yet with respect to Judah. **The days** – In the time of their reign. Whence it may be gathered, that Isaiah exercised his prophetical office above fifty years altogether.

2. **Hear** – He directs his speech to those senseless creatures, that he might awaken the Israelites, whom he hereby proclaims to be so dull and stupid that they were past hearing, and therefore calls in the whole creation of God to bear witness against them. **The Lord** – This is his plea against them, of the equity whereof he is willing that all the creatures should be judges.

3. **Know** – Me their owner and master. Knowing is here taken practically, as it is usually in scripture, and includes reverence and obedience.

4. **A seed** – The children of wicked parents, whose guilt they inherit, and whose evil example they follow. **Corrupters** – Heb. that corrupt themselves, or others by their counsel and example. **Backward** – Instead of proceeding forward and growing in grace.

Her judgments (5–9)

5. **Head** – The very head and heart of the body politick, from whence the plague is derived to all the other members.

7. **In your presence** – Which your eye shall see to torment you, when there is no power in your hands to deliver you. **As** – Heb. as the overthrow of strangers, that is, which strangers bring upon a land which is not likely to continue in their hands, and therefore they spare no persons, and spoil and destroy all things, which is not usually done in wars between persons of the same, or of a neighbouring nation.

8. **Is left** – Is left solitary, all the neighbouring villages and country round about it being laid waste.

Her worship is rejected (10–15)

10. **Of Sodom** – So called for their resemblance of them in wickedness. **The law** – The message which I am now to deliver to you from God, your great lawgiver.

11. **To me** – Who am a spirit, and therefore cannot be satisfied with such carnal oblations, but expect to have your hearts and lives, as well as your bodies and sacrifices, presented unto me. **Blood** – He mentions the fat and blood, because these were in a peculiar manner reserved for God, to intimate that even the best of their sacrifices were rejected by him.

12. **To appear** – Upon the three solemn feasts, or upon other occasions. **Who required** – The thing I commanded, was not only, nor chiefly, that you should offer external sacrifices, but that you should do it with true repentance, with faith in my promises, and sincere resolutions of devoting yourselves to my service.

13. **The solemn meeting** – The most solemn day of each of the three feasts, which was the last day.

15. **Blood** – You are guilty of murder, and oppression.

Exhortations to repentance, promises of grace and mercy, threatenings of sore judgments, and complaints by reason of their backsliding (16–31)

16. **Wash** – Cleanse your hearts and hands.

17. **Learn** – Begin to live soberly, righteously, and godly. **Judgment** – Shew your religion to God, by practising justice to men. **Judge** – Defend and deliver them.

19. **If** – If you are fully resolved to obey all my commands. **Shall eat** – Together with pardon, you shall receive temporal and worldly blessings.

21. **The city** – Jerusalem, which in the reign of former kings was faithful to God. **An harlot** – Is filled with idolatry. **Murderers** – Under that one gross kind, he comprehends all sorts of unrighteous men and practices.

23. **Rebellious** – Against me their sovereign Lord. **Companions of thieves** – Partly by giving them connivance and countenance, and partly by practising the same violence, and cruelty, and injustice that thieves used to do. **Gifts** – That is, bribes given to pervert justice.

25. **And purge** – I will purge out of thee, those wicked men that are incorrigible, and for those of you that are curable, I will by my word, and by the furnace of affliction, purge out all that corruption that yet remains in you.

26. **Thy counsellors** – Thy princes shall hearken to wise and faithful counsellors. **Called faithful** – Thou shalt be such.

27. **Redeemed** – Shall be delivered from all their enemies and calamities. **With** – Or, by judgment, that is, by God's righteous judgment, purging out those wicked and incorrigible Jews, and destroying their unmerciful enemies. **Converts** – Heb. her returners, those of them who shall come out of captivity into their own land. **Righteousness** – Or, by righteousness, either by my faithfulness, in keeping my promise, or by my goodness.

29. **The oaks** – Which, after the manner of the Heathen, you have consecrated to idolatrous uses. **Gardens** – In which, as well is in the groves, they committed idolatry.

31. **The strong** – Your idols, which you think to be strong and able to defend you. **As tow** – Shall be as suddenly and easily, consumed by my judgments, as tow is by fire. **The maker** – Of the idol, who can neither save himself nor his workmanship.

Chapter 2

A prophecy of Christ's kingdom, and the calling of the Gentiles (1–5)

And rejection of the Jews for their idolatry and pride (6–9)

The great majesty and power of God, and his terrors on the wicked; with an exhortation to fear God, and not to trust in man (10–22)

A prophecy of Christ's kingdom, and the calling of the Gentiles (1–5)

1. **The word** – Or, the matter or thing, as this Hebrew word commonly signifies; the prophecy or vision.

2. **In the last days** – In the times of the Messiah. For Christ's institutions were to continue to the end of the world. **The mountain** – The temple of the Lord which is upon mount Moriah; which yet is not to be understood literally of that material temple, but mystically of the church of God; as appears from the flowing of all

nations to it, which was not to that temple, nor indeed was fulfilled 'till that temple was destroyed. **Exalted** – Shall be placed and settled in a most conspicuous and glorious manner, being advanced above all other churches and kingdoms.

3. The law – The new law, the doctrine of the gospel, which is frequently called a law, because it hath the nature and power of a law, obliging us no less to the belief and practice of it, than the old law did.

4. He – Christ shall set up his authority among all nations, not only giving laws to them, but doing what no other can do, convincing their consciences, changing their hearts, and ordering their lives. **Rebuke** – By his word and Spirit, convincing the world of sin; and by his judgments upon his implacable enemies, which obstruct the propagation of the gospel.

5. The light – Take heed that you do not reject that light which is so clear that even the blind Gentiles will discern it.

And rejection of the Jews for their idolatry and pride (6–9)

6. Therefore – For the following reasons. **Thou** – Wilt certainly forsake and reject. **Thy people** – The body of that nation. **Because** – Their land is full of the idolatrous manners of the eastern nations, the Syrians and Chaldeans. **Philistines** – Who were infamous for those practices. **They please** – They delight in their company, and conversation, making leagues, and friendships, and marriages with them.

7. Treasures – They have heaped up riches, and still are greedily pursuing after more.

9. The great man – Men of all ranks fall down and worship idols.

The great majesty and power of God, and his terrors on the wicked; with an exhortation to fear God, and not to trust in man (10–22)

10. Enter – Such calamities are coming upon you, that you will be ready to hide yourselves in rocks and caves of the earth, for fear of the glorious and terrible judgments of God.

12. The day – The time of God's taking vengeance upon sinners.

13. The cedars – The cedars and oaks on the mountains shall be either thrown down by furious winds or earthquakes, or torn in pieces by thunder and lightning; and the stately houses built with cedars and oaks, shall be destroyed.

14. Hills – To which men used to betake themselves in times of danger.

15. Wall – To which you trusted for your defence.

16. Tarshish – The ships of the sea, as that

word is used, Psal 48:7, whereby you fetched riches from the remote parts of the world.

19. They – The idolatrous Israelites.

20. Shall cast – Into the meanest and darkest places, in which moles and bats have their abode.

22. Cease ye – Never admire or place your trust in man. **Breath** – Whose breath is quickly stopped and taken away. **Wherein** – What excellency is in him, considered in himself, and without dependence on God?

Chapter 3

Great confusion on both people and rulers for their sin and impudence in it (1–9)

Peace to the righteous, and misery to the wicked (10, 11)

The oppression and covetousness of the rulers (12–15)

The pride of women, and its judgments (16–26)

Great confusion on both people and rulers for their sin and impudence in it (1–9)

2. The judge – The civil magistrates. **The ancient** – Whose wisdom was increased by long experience.

5. Oppressed – By thy command or permission of such childish rulers.

6. Thou hast – We are utterly undone, and have neither food nor raiment; but thou hast something left to support the dignity which we offer to thee. **Under thine hand** – To heal it.

7. An healer – A repairer of the ruins of the state.

9. The shew – Their pride, and wantonness, and impiety manifestly shows itself in their very looks. **They declare** – They act it publically, casting off all fear of God and reverence to men. **Rewarded** – Procured a fit recompense for their wickedness, even utter ruin.

Peace to the righteous, and misery to the wicked (10, 11)

10. Say ye – O ye priests and Levites, that God will be their safeguard and portion.

12. Women – Weak and effeminate rulers. **They** – Thy rulers civil and ecclesiastical.

The oppression and covetousness of the rulers (12–15)

13. Standeth – He will shortly and certainly stand up as a judge, to enquire into the cause, and to give sentence. **To judge** – To defend and deliver them.

14. Ancients – The princes or rulers; such were commonly chosen out of those who were in ripe years. **Eaten** – Destroyed instead of preserving the church and commonwealth of Israel. **Spoil** – The goods which you have violently taken away from the poor.

16. **The daughters** – The women; (hitherto he reproved the men). **A tinkling** – By some ornaments which they wore upon their shoes.

The pride of women, and its judgments (16–26)

17. **Secret paths** – By giving her into the power of those enemies that shall strip her of all her raiment.

18. **Cauls** – It is agreed by all, that this and several words that follow, were ornaments used in those times. And it is of no concern, exactly to understand the nature and differences of them. **The moon** – There were in ancient times, and at this day there are some ornaments worn, which carry a manifest resemblance to the moon or half moon.

20. **Tablets** – He seems to mean boxes of perfumes.

21. **Nose-jewels** – Which were fastened to the head, and hung down upon the forehead to the beginning of the nose.

22. **Pins** – Of silver or gold, either used to curl the hair, or fastened and worn in the hair.

23. **Glasses** – The looking-glasses, as we call them, tho' in truth they were not made of glass, but of bright and burnished brass.

24. **Girdle** – Which were fine and costly, and useful to gird their garments about them. **A rent** – Torn and tattered garments. **Burning** – By the heat of the sun, to which they are now commonly exposed, from which they used formerly to guard themselves with the utmost care.

26. **Gates** – The gates of Zion or Jerusalem, which, by a figure, are said to lament, to imply the great desolation of the place; that there would be no people to go out and come in by the gates, as they used to do. **Shall sit** – Like a mournful woman bewailing the loss of her husband and children.

Chapter 4

In the extremity of evils, Christ's glorious kingdom should appear to those who are left alive (1, 2)

They shall be holy (3)

Purged (4)

A glory and a defence upon them (5)

A sanctuary from evils (6)

In the extremity of evils, Christ's glorious kingdom should appear to those who are left alive (1, 2)

1. **In that day** – In that calamitous time. **Seven** – Many. A certain number for an uncertain. **One man** – Because few men shall survive that dreadful stroke. **Only** – Own us for thy wives. **Our reproach** – Virginity was esteemed a reproach; children, the usual fruit of marriage, being both an honour to their parents, and a blessing of God, especially to that people, from some of whose loins the Messiah was to spring.

2. **In that day** – About that time: when the Lord shall have washed away the filth of Zion, by those dreadful judgments now described. **The branch** – The Messiah. **The earth** – The land which for the sins of the people was made barren, upon their return to Christ shall recover its fertility. Under this one mercy he includes all temporal blessings, together with spiritual and eternal. **For them** – That shall survive all the aforementioned calamities.

They shall be holy (3)

3. **Holy** – Shall be really holy. **Jerusalem** – Of the people living in or belonging to Jerusalem.

Purged (4)

4. **When** – This shall be accomplished when God hath throughly cleansed the Jewish nation from their sins. **The blood** – The blood-guiltiness, and especially that of killing the Lord of life. **Burning** – This is opposed to the former legal way of purification, which was by water. The Holy Spirit of old accompanied the preaching of the gospel, and did this work in part, and will do it fully. This spirit may well be called a spirit of judgment, because it executes judgment in the church, and in the consciences of men, separating the precious from the vile, convincing men of sin, and righteousness, and judgment. And the same spirit may be fitly called the spirit of burning, because he doth burn up and consume the dross which is in the church, and in the hearts of men, and inflames the souls of believers with love to God, and zeal for his glory.

A glory and a defence upon them (5)

5. **Create** – Will in a marvellous manner produce, as it were by a new creation. **A cloud** – A pillar of cloud and fire, like that wherewith he directed the Israelites, when they came out of Egypt: whereby he implies, that God would be their protector, and their glory. **The glory** – Upon all that church and people, which God will make so glorious; upon all holy assemblies of sincere Christians.

A sanctuary from evils (6)

6. **And there** – Or, he, the Lord, shall be a tabernacle, to defend them from the heat of the sun, and other injuries of the weather.

Chapter 5

Israel, God's vineyard, his mercies, and their faithfulness, should be laid waste (1–7)

Judgments upon covetousness (8–10)

Upon drunkards, and the lascivious (11, 12)

The great misery of the Jews (13–17)

Judgments on impiety, scoffers at God's threatnings, those who corrupt the notions of good and ill, strong-drinkers, and unjust judges (18–23)

God's anger, and the Chaldeans army against them (24–30)

Israel, God's vineyard, his mercies, and their faithfulness, should be laid waste (1–7)

1. **Now** – I will record it to be a witness for God, and against you, as Moses did his song, Deut 31:19 32:1. **To** – To the Lord of the vineyard. **Of my beloved** – Not devised by me, but inspired by God. **Vineyard** – His church. **Hill** – Hills being places most commodious for vines.

2. **He gathered** – He removed all hindrances, and gave them all the means of fruitfulness. A **tower** – For the residence of the keepers.

6. **Nor digged** – Vine-dressers use to dig up and open the earth about the roots of the vines. The meaning is, I will remove my ministers, who used great care and diligence to make you fruitful. **Thorns** – I will give you up to your own lusts. **No rain** – I will deprive you of all my blessings.

7. **Pleasant** – In whom God formerly delighted. **A cry** – From the oppressed, crying to men for help, and to God for vengeance.

8. **Alone** – That they alone may be the lords and owners, and all others only their tenants and servants.

Judgments upon covetousness (8–10)

9. **In mine ears** – I heard God speak what I am about to utter.

10. **One bath** – Of wine. The bath contained about eight gallons. Thus an acre did not yield one gallon. **An ephah** – Which was of the same quantity with the bath, only the bath was the measure of liquid things, the ephah of dry things; and a ephah was the tenth part of an homer. So instead of the increase which that fruitful land commonly yielded, they should loose nine parts of their seed.

Upon drunkards, and the lascivious (11, 12)

12. **The harp** – They give up themselves wholly to luxury. **The work** – What God hath lately done, and is yet doing, and about to do among them; his grievous judgments, partly inflicted, and partly threatened, which required another course of life.

The great misery of the Jews (13–17)

13. **No knowledge** – No serious consideration of God's works, and of their own duty and danger. **Honourable men** – Who thought themselves quite out of the reach of famine.

14. **And he** – That spends all his days in mirth and jollity.

15. **The mighty** – All of them, both high and low, shall be brought to destruction.

16. **Exalted** – By the execution of this just judgment. **Sanctified** – Shall appear to be an holy God, by his righteous judgments.

17. **Then** – When God shall have finished that work of judgment. **The lambs** – The poor and harmless people, who shall be left in the land when the rich are carried into captivity. **Manner** – Or, by their fold, as this word is manifestly used, Mic 2:12, the only place of scripture, except this, in which this word is found. **Waste places** – The lands left by their owners. **Fat ones** – Of the rich and great men. **Strangers** – The poor Israelites, who were left to be vine-dressers and husbandmen, 2Kings 25:12, who are called strangers, because they were so, in reference to that hand, not being the proper owners of it.

Judgments on impiety, scoffers at God's threatnings, those who corrupt the notions of good and ill, strong-drinkers, and unjust judges (18–23)

18. **That draw** – That are not only drawn to sin by the allurements of the world; but are active and illustrious in drawing sin to themselves. **Cords** – Or, with cords of lying, as the last word frequently signifies, with vain and deceitful arguments and pretences, whereby sinners generally draw themselves to sin. **A rope** – With all their might, as beasts commonly do that draw carts with ropes.

19. **Let him** – God, in whose name thou and other prophets are always threatening us. This was the plain language of their actions; they lived as if they were of this opinion. **The Holy One** – They scornfully repeated the title usually given by the prophets to God.

20. **To them** – That take away the difference between good and evil; that justify wicked men and things, and condemn piety, or righteous persons.

22. **To mingle** – To drink: the antecedent

being put for the consequent: for they mingled it in order to drinking.

23. **Take away** – Pronounce sentence against him.

God's anger, and the Chaldeans army against them (24–30)

24. **Rottenness** – They shall be like a tree which not only withers in its branches, but dies and rots at the roots, therefore is past recovery. **Dust** – Shall be resolved into dust, and yield no fruit.

26. **An ensign** – To call them together for his service. **From far** – To the Chaldeans; for even Babylon is called a far country, chap.39:3. And he saith **nations**, because the Chaldean army was made up of several nations. **Will hiss** – Or, will whistle unto, or for them: will gather them together by his word. as shepherds gather their sheep. He intimates how easily and speedily God can do this work. **From the ends** – Which is not to be understood strictly, but with a latitude, from very remote places.

27. **Nor sleep** – They shall all be watchful and diligent to take all opportunities of executing my judgments. **Nor latchet** – I will take all impediments out of their way.

28. **Bent** – Who are every way furnished and ready for my work, waiting only for my command. **Flint** – Because they shall not be broken or battered by the length or stoniness and ruggedness of the way. **Whirlwind** – For the swiftness of their march, and for the force and violence of their chariots in battle.

29. **Roar** – Which signifies both their cruelty, and their eagerness to devour the prey.

30. **Sorrow** – Darkness; that is, sorrow; the latter word explains the former. **The heavens** – When they look up to the heavens, as men in distress usually do, they see no light there.

Chapter 6

The glory of the Lord (1–4)

Isaiah is terrified (5)

Is confirmed for his message (6–8)

The people's obstinacy unto desolation (9–12)

A remnant shall be saved (13)

The glory of the Lord (1–4)

1. **I saw** – In a vision. **The Lord** – The Divine Majesty as he subsisteth in three persons. **His train** – His royal and judicial robe; for he is represented as a judge.

2. **Stood** – As ministers attending upon their Lord. **Seraphim** – An order of holy angels, thus called from fire and burning, which this word properly signifies; to represent either their nature, which is bright and glorious, subtle, and pure; or their property, of fervent zeal for God's service and glory. **Covered** – Out of profound reverence.

3. **Cried** – Singing in consort. **Holy** – This is repeated thrice, to intimate the Trinity of persons united in the Divine essence. **Glory** – Of the effects and demonstrations of his glorious holiness, as well as of his power, wisdom, and goodness.

4. **The posts** – Together with the door itself. Such violent motions were commonly tokens of God's anger. **Smoke** – Which elsewhere is a token of God's presence and acceptance, but here of his anger.

Isaiah is terrified (5)

5. **I am** – I am a great sinner, as many other ways, so particularly by my lips. I am an unclean branch of an unclean tree; besides my own uncleanness, I have both by my omissions and commissions involved myself in the guilt of their sins. **Have seen** – The sight of this glorious and holy God gives me cause to fear that he is come to judgment against me.

Is confirmed for his message (6–8)

6. **Flew** – By God's command. **A coal** – Both a token and an instrument of purification. **The altar** – Of burnt-offering.

7. **Laid it** – So as only to touch my lips, and not to burn them; which God could easily effect. **Lo** – This is a sign that I have pardoned and purged the uncleanness of thy lips.

8. **Who** – To deliver the following message. The change of the number, I and us, is very remarkable; and both being meant of one and the same Lord, do sufficiently intimate a plurality of persons in the Godhead.

The people's obstinacy unto desolation (9–12)

9. **Perceive not** – The Hebrew words are imperative; yet they are not to be taken as a command what the people ought to do, but only as a prediction what they would do. The sense is, because you have so long heard my words, and seen my works, to no purpose, and have hardened your hearts, and will not learn nor reform, I will punish you in your own kind, your sin shall be your punishment. I will still continue my word and works to you, but will withdraw my Spirit, so that you shall be as unable, as now you are unwilling, to understand.

10. **Fat** – Stupid and senseless. This making of their hearts fat, is here ascribed to the prophet, as it is ascribed to God in the repetition of this

prophecy, John 12:40, because God inflicted this judgment upon them by the ministry of the prophet, partly by way of prediction, foretelling that this would be the effect of his preaching; and partly by withdrawing the light and help of his Spirit. **Heavy** – Make them dull of hearing. **Lest** – That they may not be able, as before they were not willing to see. **Convert** – Turn to God.

11. **Lord** – An abrupt speech, arising from the prophet's great passion and astonishment: how long shall this dreadful judgment last? **Until** – Until this land be totally destroyed, first by the Babylonians, and afterward by the Romans.

12. **Removed** – Hath caused this people to be carried away captive into far countries. **A forsaking** – 'Till houses and lands be generally forsaken of their owners.

A remnant shall be saved (13)

13. **A tenth** – A small remnant reserved, that number being put indefinitely. **Return** – Out of the Babylonian captivity, into their own land. **Eaten** – That remnant shall be devoured a second time, by the kings of Syria, and afterwards by the Romans. **Yet** – Yet there shall be another remnant, not such an one as that which came out of Babylon, but an holy seed, who shall afterwards look upon him whom they have pierced, and mourn over him. **When** – Who when their leaves are cast in winter, have a substance within themselves, a vital principle, which preserves life in the root of the tree, and in due time sends it forth into all the branches. **The support** – Of the land or people, which, were it not for the sake of these, should be finally rooted out.

Chapter 7

Ahaz afraid of Rezin and Pekah, is comforted by Isaiah (1–9)

Refusing to choose a sign, Christ is promised for one (10–16)

His judgment should come by Assyria (17–25)

Ahaz afraid of Rezin and Pekah, is comforted by Isaiah (1–9)

1. **Ahaz** – A most wicked king: yet no prophecies are more comfortable than those which were delivered in his time; God so ordering it for the encouragement of the faithful that lived under his impious reign.

2. **David** – Ahaz, and his relations. He calls them the house of David, to intimate that the following comfortable message was sent to Ahaz, not for his own sake, but for the sake of his worthy progenitor David. **Ephraim** – The kingdom of the ten tribes, commonly called

Ephraim, because that was the most numerous of all. **Moved** – With fear, arising from a consciousness of their own guilt, and their enemies strength.

3. **Thy son** – Whose very name carried in it a sign and pledge of the promised deliverance, signifying, The remnant shall return. **Fuller's field** – Whither he probably went to take care about the waters which thence were brought into the city, to secure them to himself, or keep them from the enemy, as Hezekiah afterward did, 2Chron 32:3,4.

4. **Be quiet** – Settle thy mind by the belief of that joyful message which I am now to deliver thee from the Lord. **Fire-brands** – They are not whole fire-brands, but small pieces or ends of them, taken out of the fire, in which there is more smoke than fire. They have more of shew and terror, than of strength. Pekah, king of Israel, he calls only the son of Remaliah, to intimate, that he was unworthy the name of king, as having got that title by usurpation, and the murder of his master, 2Kings 15:25.

6. **Let us** – Break their power and kingdom and subdue it to ourselves.

7. **It** – Their evil counsel.

8. **Damascus** – Damascus shall still continue the capital of the kingdom of Syria; and therefore Jerusalem shall not become a part of Rezin's dominion: but he shall keep within his own bounds, and be king of Damascus only.

9. **Samaria** – Samaria shall continue to be the chief city if the kingdom of Israel, and Pekah shall not conquer Jerusalem. **If** – If you do not believe this, but seek to the Assyrians for succour, ye shall be consumed thereby.

Refusing to choose a sign, Christ is promised for one (10–16)

12. **I will not** – By asking a sign, as if I questioned the truth of his word: but this was deep hypocrisy.

13. **David** – He reproves them all, because they were the king's counsellors. **Is it a small thing** – Is it not wickedness enough. **My God** – To vex God's prophets and people, with your oppressions and horrid impieties. And by your ingratitude and unbelief, and disobedience of his commands.

14. **Therefore** – Because you despise me, and the sign which I now offer to you, God of his own free grace will send you a more honourable messenger, and give you a nobler sign. **A sign** – Of your deliverance. But how was this birth, which was not to happen 'till many ages after, a sign of their deliverance from present danger? This promised birth supposed the preservation of that city, and nation and tribe, in and of which the Messiah was to be born; and therefore there was no cause to fear that ruin which their enemies now threatened. **Immanuel** – God with

us; God dwelling among us, in our nature, John 1:14. God and man meeting in one person, and being a mediator between God and men. For the design of these words is not so much to relate the name by which Christ should commonly he called, as to describe his nature and office.

15. Butter – The common food of children in that country. **He** – The virgin's son. **Know** – To discern between things good and evil.

16. Yea – Not only this land shall be preserved until the virgin's son shall be born, but thine enemies land shall be sorely scourged, and these two kings destroyed within a very little time. **This child** – Shear-Jashub, whom in all probability the prophet pointed at, and who was brought hither by God's special command, ver.3. for this very use. **The land** – The lands of Syria and Israel. **Forsaken** – So far shall Pekah and Rezin be from conquering thy land, that they shall lose their own lands, and their lives too; which they did within two years after this time, being both slain by the king of Assyria.

His judgment should come by Assyria (17–25)

17. Shall bring – But although God will deliver you at this time, yet he will requite all your wickedness. **Thee** – For part of this Assyrian storm fell in Ahaz's reign. **And** – Upon thy sons and successors, the kings of Judah. **Days** – Calamities. **Departed** – When ten tribes revolted from thy father's house. **The king** – Who may well be called their plague or calamity, as he is called the rod of God's anger, chap.10:5.

18. The fly – The flies. So he calls these enemies, to imply their great numbers. **In** – In their extremity, where they go out into the sea. **Rivers** – Of the river Nile, which may be called rivers, either for its greatness, or because towards the end of it, it is divided into seven streams. When the Chaldeans had in good measure subdued the Egyptians, it is probable great numbers of the Egyptian soldiers listed themselves in the Chaldean army, and with them invaded the land of Judah. **The bee** – The Assyrian army, compared to bees, as for their numerous forces and orderly march, so for their fierce attempts and mischievous effects. **Assyria** – In the empire of Assyria, or Babylon; for these two were united into one empire, and therefore in scripture are promiscuously called sometimes by one title, and sometimes by the other.

19. Valleys – Such as they found fruitful, but made desolate. **Rocks** – To which possibly the Israelites fled for refuge. **Bushes** – Which he mentions because flies and bees use frequently to rest there; and to intimate, that no place should escape their fury.

20. Shave – Utterly spoil, as shaving takes away the hair. **Hired** – By Ahaz, who did hire them, 2Kings 16:7,8. And so the prophet notes the just judgment of God, in scourging them with a rod of their own making. **By** – By the successive kings of the Assyrian empire, Sennacherib, Esarhaddon, and especially by Nebuchadnezzar. **The head** – By these metaphorical expressions he signifies the total destruction of their state, from head to foot, from the highest to the lowest.

21. Sheep – They who formerly used to keep great herds of cattle, and many flocks of sheep, shall esteem it a happiness if they can keep but one cow and two sheep.

22. Abundance – Because they shall have large pastures, by reason of the great scarcity of cattle. **Butter** – Which the poorer sort had formerly used to sell, to procure them cheaper food for themselves: but now the land should be so destitute of people, that there were none to whom they could sell them.

23. Of silver – Each of the thousand vineyards might have been sold or let for a thousand shekels, which was the yearly rent of some excellent vineyards.

24. With arrows – Either to hunt, or to defend themselves from wild beasts, which commonly abide in desolate grounds.

25. Digged – That used to be digged and dressed for the planting of vines, and other choice fruit-trees. **The fear** – That they might be freed from briars and thorns. **Cattle** – All sorts of cattle may enter, and feed there, the fences being broken down, and the owners slain, or carried into captivity.

Chapter 8

Syria and Israel should be subdued by Assyria (1–4)

Judah also should be afflicted (5–8)

God's judgments irresistible, and to be feared (9–13)

The Lord is a sanctuary to the godly, a stone of stumbling to the wicked (14, 15)

The prophecy sure, God to be waited on, necromancers not to be consulted, but the prophecy, their misery (16–22)

Syria and Israel should be subdued by Assyria (1–4)

1. A roll – Or, a great volume, because the prophecy to be written in it was large, and God would have it written in large and legible characters. **Pen** – With such a pen as writers use. **Concerning** – Concerning that thing which is signified by the name of the child, which is here mentioned by way of anticipation.

3. Prophetess – To his own wife, so called, because the wife of a prophet.

4. To cry – To speak and to know his parents; which is within the space of two years. And his agrees with the other prophecy, chap.7:16. Before the child shall know to refuse the evil and choose the good, which requires a longer time than to distinguish his parents, and suits well to Shear-Jashub, who, being born some years before, was capable of that farther degree of knowledge, as soon as this was capable of the lower degree. **Before** – In his presence, and by himself and his forces.

Judah also should be afflicted (5–8)

6. This people – The people of Israel, of whom he last spake, who rejoiced not only in their own king, but also in the assistance of so powerful an ally as Rezin. **Shiloah** – That small brook which ran by Jerusalem. Hereby he understands the munitions and strength of the Jews, which their enemies derided.

7. The river – Of Euphrates, called the river, for its eminent greatness; whereby he understands the Assyrian forces. **Glory** – His numerous and puissant army. **He** – This great river shall overflow its own proper channels. That is, this great monarch shall enlarge his dominions, and add the lands of Syria and Israel to them.

8. Reach – So that they shall be in great danger of being desired. He persists in the metaphor of a river swelling so high as to reach to a man's neck, and be ready to overwhelm him. Such was the danger of Judah's land, when Sennacherib took all the fenced cities of Judah, 2Kings 18:13, and sent his army against Jerusalem. **Wings** – Of his forces, or of the wings of his army, as they still are called. **My land** – Of the land of Judah, so called because the Messiah, who is called Immanuel, should be born there. And this is added emphatically for the consolation of God's people, to assure them, that notwithstanding this dreadful scourge, yet God would make a difference between Israel and Judah, and whereas Israel should not be a people, Judah should be restored, for the sake of the Messiah, to be the place of his birth and ministry.

God's judgments irresistible, and to be feared (9–13)

9. Ye people – Syrians and Israelites. **All ye** – Whosoever you be, who conspire against Immanuel's land. **Gird** – Prepare yourselves for war. **Broken** – This is repeated for the greater assurance of the thing, and the comfort of God's people.

11. Spake – With a vehement and more than ordinary inspiration. **In the way** – Of the

generality of the people of Judah; whose eminent danger and calamity he foretells.

12. Say not – Thou Isaiah, and my children, do not consent to this confederacy with the king of Assyria. **Their fear** – That thing which they fear, that, if they do not call in the Assyrian succours, they shall be destroyed by those two potent kings.

13. Sanctify – Give him the glory of his power, and goodness, and faithfulness, by trusting to his promises. **Let him** – Let God, and not the kings of Syria and Israel be the object of your fear.

The Lord is a sanctuary to the godly, a stone of stumbling to the wicked (14, 15)

14. Sanctuary – A sure refuge to all that truly fear him, and rely upon him. **A stone** – An occasion of sin and ruin, at whom they will take offence and stumble, so as to fall and be broken. **To both** – To the two kingdoms, that of the ten tribes, and that of the two tribes. **Jerusalem** – Which are distinctly mentioned, as a wonderful thing, because Jerusalem was the seat of the temple, and of God's solemn worship, where all the means of knowledge and grace were in greatest plenty, where the thrones of civil and ecclesiastical judicature were established, where the most wise and learned doctors had their constant abode. And that such a place and people should reject Immanuel when he should appear, was so strange an occurrence, that the prediction of it was highly necessary, lest otherwise, when it came to pass, it should shake the faith of all who did believe on him; whereas now the accomplishment hereof was a notable confirmation of their faith.

15. Many – Not all; for there shall be a remnant, as was foretold, chap.4:2 6:13. **Stumble** – At that stone or rock, mentioned, ver.8:14. This was accomplished at the coming of the Messiah, whom the Jews rejected to their own destruction.

The prophecy sure, God to be waited on, necromancers not to be consulted, but the prophecy, their misery (16–22)

16. The testimony – By the testimony and the law or doctrine, he understands one and the same thing, as he doth also, ver.20, the word of God, and especially that which is the main scope thereof, the doctrine of the Messiah, which, though now professed by all the Israelites, shall be disowned by the generality of them, when the Messiah shall come. Bind up and seal are to be understood prophetically, declare and prophesy, that it shall be bound up and sealed. Moreover, bind up and seal, design the same thing. Security and secrecy, signifying, that it should certainly be fulfilled, yet withal kept secret from the unbelieving Jews. By the disciples he means those who were taught of God.

17. Yet – Yet, notwithstanding this dreadful prophecy concerning the rejection of Israel. **Wait** – I will cast my care upon him, and expect the accomplishment of his promise, in sending the Messiah, and in conferring upon me and all believing Israelites all his mercies and blessings. **Hideth** – That now withdraws his favour and blessings, from the people of Israel.

18. Behold – These words are literally spoken by Isaiah concerning himself, but mystically concerning Christ; and therefore they are fitly ascribed to Christ, Heb 2:13. **The children** – His spiritual children, whom he had either begotten or brought up by his ministry. **Wonders** – Are a gazing flock, for our folly in believing God's promises. **From the Lord** – Which comes to pass by the wise providence of God. **Zion** – Where the temple now was, and where the Messiah was to set up his kingdom.

19. And when they – The Israelites, who are fallen from God, into superstition and idolatry. **You** – My children, whom the prophet arms against the common temptation. **Mutter** – That speak with a low voice, as these two words signify, which they affected to do, speaking rather inwardly in their bellies, than audibly with their mouths. **Should not** – This answer the prophet puts into their mouths, doth not every nation, in cases of difficulty, seek to their gods? Much more should we do so, that have the only true God for our God. **For the living** – That is, for living men to enquire of the living God, is proper and reasonable; but it is highly absurd for them to forsake him, and to seek dead idols, either to the images, or to the spirits of dead men, which are supposed to speak in them.

20. To the law – Let this dispute between you and them be determined by God's word, which is here and in many other places called the law, to signify their obligation to believe and obey it; and the testimony, because it is a witness between God and man, of God's will, and of man's duty. **They** – Your antagonists. **No light** – This proceeds from the darkness of their minds, they are blind, and cannot see.

21. It – Their own land. **Hungry** – Sorely distressed, and destitute of food, and all necessaries. **Their king** – Either because he doth not relieve them; or because by his foolish counsels, he brought them into these miseries. **God** – Their idol, to whom they trusted, and whom they now find unable to help them. **Look** – To heaven for help.

22. Earth – Finding no help from heaven, they turn their eyes downward, looking hither and thither for comfort.

Chapter 9

Joy in the midst of affliction (1–5)

The birth, person, office, and kingdom of Christ (6, 7)

Judgments for their pride (8–12)

For their impenitency and hypocrisy (13–21)

Joy in the midst of affliction (1–5)

1. Nevertheless – The calamity of this land and its inhabitants shall be great, yet not such as that which was brought upon it by the king of Assyria, who at first indeed dealt more gently with them, but afterwards rooted them out. **He** – God. **Zebulun** – These parts are particularly mentioned, because this storm fell most heavily upon them; but under them the other parts of the land are understood. **Afterward** – By Shalmaneser, who took Samaria, and carried Israel into captivity, 2Kings 17:5,6. Of which calamity, though yet to come, he speaks as if it were past, as the manner of the prophet is. **The sea** – In that part of the land which borders upon the sea, the lake Genesareth, upon which the portions of Zebulun and Naphtali bordered. **Galilee** – Or, Galilee of the Gentiles, namely, the upper Galilee, so called because it bordered upon the Gentiles.

2. The people – Israel and Judah. **Darkness** – The expression is general and so may well comprehend both calamity and ignorance, idolatry and profaneness, in which those parts were eminently involved. **Have seen** – Shall see at the coming of the Messiah.

3. Thou hast – Thou hast made good thy promise to Abraham concerning the multiplication of his seed, by gathering in the Gentiles to the Jews. **Before thee** – In thy presence, and in the place of thy worship.

4. The yoke – His burdensome yoke. **The staff** – The staff or staves by which he was forced to carry burdens upon his shoulders. **The rod** – Wherewith he beat him. **Oppressor** – Of all his oppressors, but especially of sin and the devil. **As** – When God destroyed the Midianites in so admirable a manner by three hundred men.

5. Noise – With the triumphant exclamations of the conqueror, and the bitter lamentations of the conquered, and the different cries of the same persons, sometimes conquering, and sometimes conquered. **Blood** – With great difficulty and slaughter. **But** – But this victory which God's people shall have over all their enemies, shall be more terrible to their adversaries, whom God will utterly consume, as it were by fire.

The birth, person, office, and kingdom of Christ (6, 7)

6. For – Having spoken of the glorious light, and joy, and victory of God's people, he now proceeds to shew the ground of it. **Us** – Unto us Jews, of whom Christ was born, and to whom he was primarily sent. **A child** – The Messiah by the consent of interpreters, not only Christian, but Jewish: for so the ancient Hebrew doctors understood the place, and particularly the Chaldee paraphrast; although the latter Jews, out of opposition to Christ, wrest it to Hezekiah. Which extravagant conceit, as it hath no foundation in this or any other text of scripture, so it is fully confuted by the following titles, which are such as cannot without blasphemy and nonsense be ascribed to Hezekiah, nor indeed to any mere mortal man, as we shall see. **Is born** – Or, shall be born, as the prophets generally speak. **The government** – Of God's people, to whom he is given. **Shoulders** – Upon him, or in his hands. He mentions shoulders, because great burdens are commonly laid upon men's shoulders. **His name** – This is not to be taken for a description of his name, but of his glorious nature and qualities. **Wonderful counsellor** – And so Christ is, because he hath been the counsellor of his church in all ages, and the author and giver of all those excellent counsels delivered not only by the apostles, but also by the prophets, and hath gathered and enlarged, and preserved his church, by admirable counsels and methods of his providence, and, in a word, hath in him all the treasures of wisdom and knowledge, Col 2:3. **Mighty God** – This title can agree to no man but Christ, who was God as well as man, to whom the title of God or Jehovah is given, both in the Old and New Testament. And it is a true observation, that this Hebrew word El is never used in the singular number, of any creature, but only of the almighty God. **The father** – The father of eternity. Who, though as man he was then unborn, yet was and is from everlasting to everlasting.

7. No end – His peaceable and happy government shall be extended to all the ends of the earth. **The throne** – Which was promised to David, and to his seed for ever. **For ever** – From the beginning of it to all eternity. **The zeal** – This great work shall be brought to pass by almighty God, out of that fervent affection which he hath to his own glory, to the honour of his son, and to his people.

Judgments for their pride (8–12)

8. The Lord – The prophet, having inserted some consolatory passages for God's faithful people, returns to his former attack against the rebellious Israelites. **And** – Heb. it fell, that is, it shall fall, in the prophetical style. It shall certainly be accomplished.

9. Know – They shall know whether my word be true or false. **Even** – The people of the ten tribes, and particularly Ephraim, the proudest of them all. **Samaria** – The strongest place, and the seat of the king and court.

10. Stones – We have received some damage; but, we doubt not we shall quickly repair it with advantage.

11. Therefore – To chastise your pride, and defeat your hopes. **Set up** – The Assyrians, who, presently after this prophecy, prevailed against him, 2Kings 16:7. He mentions Rezin, because he was confederate with Ephraim. **Join** – So that they shall invade him from several quarters. **His** – Not Rezin's, but Ephraim.

12. Syrians – For though Rezin, king of Syria was destroyed, yet the body of the nation survived, and submitted themselves to the king of Assyria, and upon his command invaded Israel afterwards. **Before** – Heb. on the east: for Syria stood eastward from Israel. **Behind** – On the western side of the land of Israel. **Devour** – Like wild beasts.

For their impenitency and hypocrisy (13–21)

13. Him – To God.

14. Head – High and low. **Branch** – The goodly branches of tall trees, the mighty and noble. **Rush** – The bulrush, the weakest and meanest persons. **One day** – All together, one as well as another.

15. The prophet – Whose destruction he mentions, not as if it were a punishment to them to be deprived of such persons, but partly to shew the extent of the calamity, that it should reach all sorts of persons; and partly to beat down their vain presumptions of peace and prosperity, by showing that those false prophets, which had fed their vain hopes, should perish, and their false prophecies with them. **Tail** – The basest part of the whole people.

16. The leaders – Their false prophets. **Cause** – By false doctrines and evil counsels and persuasions. **Destroyed** – Shall certainly perish.

17. No joy – Shall not rejoice over them to do them good. **Fatherless** – Who are the special objects of his care and pity, and much less upon others. **Every one** – Not precisely; for there were seven thousand elect persons among them, when they seemed to Elijah to be universally corrupt, but the body of the people. **Hypocrite** – For though they professed to worship God, yet indeed they had forsaken him. **Folly** – Wickedness.

18. Burneth – Shall burn you, as it follows, shall devour. **Thorns** – The low and mean persons; for these are opposed to the thickets of the forest, in the next clause. **Forest** – In the wood, where the trees are tall, and stand thick, having their bows entangled together, which makes them more ready both to catch and to spread the fire. **Smoke** – Sending up smoke like a vast furnace.

21. Manasseh – Though more near and dear to one another than any other tribe, being both sons of Joseph.

Chapter 10

The woe of unjust oppressors (1–4)

Of Assyria for their pride and ambition, his folly in it (5–19)

A remnant of Israel shall be saved, and that speedily (20–27)

Sennacherib marching toward Jerusalem (28–31)

His judgment (32–34)

The woe of unjust oppressors (1–4)

1. Woe – Unto those magistrates who make unjust laws, and give unjust sentences. **Grievousness** – Grievous things, such unjust decrees as cause grief and vexation to their subjects.

2. Judgment – From obtaining a just sentence.

3. From far – From the Assyrians. This he adds, because the Israelites, having weakened the Jews and being in amity with the Assyrians their next neighbours, were secure. **Leave** – To be kept safe for your use. **Glory** – Your wealth.

4. Without me – Without my favour and help, which you have forfeited. **Shall bow down** – Notwithstanding all your succours.

Of Assyria for their pride and ambition, his folly in it (5–19)

5. O Assyrian – This is God's invitation to him to take the charge, and set upon the work. **The rod** – The instrument of mine anger, wherewith I shall chastise my people. **Anger** – Mine anger against my people puts the weapons of war into their hand.

6. Send him – By my providence, giving him both occasion and inclination to this expedition.

7. Howbeit – He doth not design the execution of my will, but only to enlarge his own empire. Which is seasonably added, to justify God in his judgments threatened to the Assyrian. **To cut off** – To sacrifice multitudes of people to his own ambition and covetousness.

8. Kings – Equal for power and wealth, and glory, to the kings of other nations.

9. Is not – Have not I conquered one place as well as another, the stronger as well as the weaker? **Samaria** – Or, shall not Samaria be as Damascus? Shall I not take that, as I have done this city?

10. The kingdoms – Which worshipped their own idols, and vainly imagined that they could protect them from my power. He calls the gods of the nations, not excepting Jerusalem, idols, by way of contempt, because none of them could deliver their people out of his hands, and because he judged them to be but petty gods, far inferior to the sun, which was the god of the Assyrians.

12. Wherefore – Because of this impudent blasphemy. **His work** – Of chastising his people so long as he sees fit. **Looks** – His insolent words and carriage.

13. Removed – I have invaded their lands, and added them to my own dominions, Prov 22:28. **Put down** – Deprived of their former glory and power.

14. Eggs – Which the dam left in her nest. **Gathered** – All the riches of the earth. An hyperbole not unusual in the mouths of such persons. **Peeped** – As birds do, which, when they see the robbing of their nest, express their grief and anger, by hovering about them, and by mournful cries.

15. The ax – How absurd is it, for thee, who art but an instrument in God's hand, to blaspheme thy Lord and master, who has as great power over thee, as a man hath over the ax wherewith he heweth?

16. The Lord – The sovereign Lord of thine and all other armies, shall strip him and all his princes, of their wealth, and might, and glory; and destroy his numerous army, as the fire doth those combustible things which are cast into it.

17. The light – That God who is and will be a comfortable light to his people. **A fire** – To the Assyrians. **Thorns** – His vast army, which is no more able to resist God, than dry thorns and briars are to oppose the fire.

18. The glory – Of his great army, which may not unfitly be compared to a forest, for the numbers of men, who stood as thick as trees do in a forest. **Field** – Of his soldiers, who stood as thick as ears of corn in a fruitful field. **Soul and body** – Totally, both inwardly and outwardly. **They shall be** – Like that of an army when their standard-bearer is slain or flees away, which strikes a panic into the whole army.

19. The rest – The remainder of that mighty host.

A remnant of Israel shall be saved, and that speedily (20–27)

20. And such – Such Jews as shall be preserved from that sweeping Assyrian scourge. **Stay** – Shall no more trust to the Assyrians for help.

22. A remnant – Or, a remnant only. **The consumption** – The destruction of Israel was already decreed by the fixed counsel of God, and therefore must needs be executed, and like a deluge overflow them. **Righteousness** – With justice, and yet with clemency, inasmuch as he has spared a considerable remnant of them, when he might have destroyed them utterly.

23. In the midst – In all the parts of the land, not excepting Jerusalem, which was to be preserved in the Assyrian invasion.

24. Therefore – This is an inference, not from the words immediately foregoing, but from the whole prophecy. Seeing the Assyrian shall be destroyed. **Smite** – He shall afflict, but not destroy thee. **Egypt** – As the Egyptians formerly did.

25. Indignation – Mine anger towards the Assyrian. **Cease** – As anger commonly does when vengeance is fully executed.

26. Stir up – Shall send a destroying angel. **Midian** – Whom God slew suddenly and unexpectedly, in the night. **Oreb** – Upon which one of their chief princes was slain, and nigh unto which the Midianites were destroyed. **The sea** – To divide it, and make way for thy deliverance, and for the destruction of the Egyptians.

27. Burden – The burden of the Assyrian. **The anointing** – Possibly this may be understood of David, who is often mentioned in scripture by the name of God's anointed; and for whose sake, God gave many deliverances to the succeeding kings and ages, as is expressly affirmed, 1Kings 11:32,34. God declares that he would give this very deliverance from the Assyrian, for David's sake, 2Kings 19:34 20:6. But the Messiah is principally intended, of whom David was but a type; and who was in a particular manner anointed above his fellows, as is said, Psal 45:7. For he is the foundation of all the promises, 2Cor 1:20, and of all the deliverances and mercies granted to God's people in all ages.

Sennacherib marching toward Jerusalem (28–31)

28. He – Here the prophet returns to the Assyrian invasion; which he describes, after the manner of the prophets, as a thing present, and sets down the several stages by which he marched towards Jerusalem. He, Sennacherib, king of Assyria, is come, in his way to Jerusalem. **Laid up** – Leaving such things there as were less necessary, that so he might march with more expedition.

29. Fled – The people fled to Jerusalem for fear of the Assyrian.

30. Daughter – Jerusalem was the mother city, and lesser towns are commonly called her daughters.

His judgment (32–34)

32. Shake – By way of commination.
33. The bough – The top-bough, Sennacherib, with a most terrible stroke.

34. Iron – Or, as with iron, as the trees of the forest are cut down with instruments of iron. **Lebanon** – Or, his Lebanon, the Assyrian army, which being before compared to a forest, and being called his Carmel in the Hebrew text, ver.18, may very fitly upon the same ground, be called his Lebanon here.

Chapter 11

Christ, a branch cut of the root of Jesse, endued with the spirit of the Lord, should set up a kingdom by the preaching of his word (1–5)

The members of his church should live in peace and unity (6–9)

And be victorious over their enemies: and to him should the Gentiles seek (10–16)

Christ, a branch cut of the root of Jesse, endued with the spirit of the Lord, should set up a kingdom by the preaching of his word (1–5)

1. And – And having said that the Assyrian yoke should be destroyed because of the anointing, he now explains who that anointed person was. **The stem** – Or, stump: for the word signifies properly a trunk cut off from the root. By which he clearly implies, that the Messiah should be born of the royal house of David, at that time when it was in a most forlorn condition, like a tree cut down, and whereof nothing is left but a stump or root under ground. **Of Jesse** – He doth not say of David, but of Jesse, who was a private and mean person, to intimate, that at the time of Christ's birth the royal family should be reduced to its primitive obscurity.

2. Wisdom – It is not needful, exactly to distinguish these two gifts; it is sufficient that they are necessary qualifications for a governor, and a teacher, and it is evident they signify perfect knowledge of all things necessary for his own and peoples good, and a sound judgment, to distinguish between things that differ. **Counsel** – Of prudence, to give good counsel; and of might and courage, to execute it. **Knowledge** – Of the perfect knowledge of the whole will and counsel of God, as also of all secret things, yea of the hearts of men. **Fear** – A fear of reverence, a care to please him, and loathing to offend him.

3. In the fear – He shall not judge rashly and partially, but considerately and justly, as the fear of God obliges all judges to do. **Judge** – Of persons or causes. **After the sight** – According to outward appearance, as men do, because they cannot search mens hearts. **Reprove** – Condemn or pass sentence against a person. **His ears** – By uncertain rumours or suggestions.

4. **Judge** – Defend and deliver them. **Reprove** – Or condemn their malicious enemies. **Thy rod** – With his word, which is his sceptre, and the rod of his power, Psal 110:2, which is sharper than a sword, Heb 4:12, by the preaching whereof he subdued the world to himself, and will destroy his enemies, 2Thes 2:8. This he adds farther, to declare the nature of Christ's kingdom, that it is not of this world.

5. **The girdle** – It shall adorn him, and be the glory of his government, as a girdle was used for an ornament, Isa 3:24, and as an ensign of power, Job 12:18, and it shall constantly cleave to him in all his administrations, as a girdle clings to a man's loins.

The members of his church should live in peace and unity (6–9)

6. **The wolf** – The creatures shall be restored to that state of innocency in which they were before the fall of man. Men of fierce, and cruel dispositions, shall be so transformed by the grace of Christ, that they shall become gentle, and tractable. **A child** – They will submit their rebellious wills to the conduct of the meanest persons that speak to them in Christ's name.

7. **Feed** – Together, without any danger or fear. **Straw** – The grass of the earth, as they did at first, and shall not devour other living creatures.

9. **My holy mountain** – In Zion, in my church. **The sea** – The channel of the sea.

And be victorious over their enemies: and to him should the Gentiles seek (10–16)

10. **A root** – A branch growing upon the root. **Ensign** – Shall grow up into a great tree, shall become an eminent ensign. **The people** – Which not only the Jews, but all nations, may discern, and to which they shall resort. **Rest** – His resting-place, his temple or church, the place of his presence and abode. **Glorious** – Shall be filled with greater glory than the Jewish tabernacle and temple were; only this glory shall be spiritual, consisting in the plentiful effusions of the gifts, and graces, of the Holy Spirit.

11. **The second** – The first time, to which this word second relates, seems to be the deliverance out of Babylon: and then this second deliverance must be in the days of the Messiah. **To recover** – From all places far and near, into which either the ten tribes or the two tribes were carried captives. Pathros was a province in Egypt.

12. **Nations** – All nations, Jews and Gentiles. **Out-casts** – That were driven out of their own land, into foreign parts. **Israel** – Of the ten tribes.

13. **Ephraim** – Of the ten tribes, frequently called by the name of Ephraim. Of enemies they shall be made friends. **The adversaries** – Not the body of Ephraim, for they are supposed to be reconciled, and they shall not be cut off, but live in love with Judah, as we see by the next clause; but those few of them who continue in their enmity together with all the rest of their adversaries.

14. **Fly** – It is a metaphor from birds and beasts of prey. **Spoil** – They shall subdue them, which is to be understood of the spiritual victory which the Messiah shall obtain by his apostles and ministers over all nations.

15. **Destroy** – Shall not only divide it, as of old, but dry it up, that it may be an high-way. **The sea** – The Red Sea, which may well be called the Egyptian sea, both because it borders upon Egypt, and because the Egyptians were drowned in it, which is called a tongue in the Hebrew text, Jos 15:2,5, as having some resemblance with a tongue: for which reason the name of tongue hath been given by geographers to promontories of land which shoot forth into the sea, as this sea did shoot out of the main ocean into the land. **Rivers** – Nile. **Seven streams** – For which it is famous in all authors.

16. **As it was** – As there was another high-way from Egypt. All impediments shall be removed, and a way made for the return of God's Israel from all parts of the world. He mentions Assyria, because thither the ten tribes were carried, whose case seemed to be most desperate.

Chapter 12
A thanksgiving of the faithful for their redemption (1–6)

1. **In that day** – When this great work of the reduction of Israel, and conversion of the Gentiles is fulfilled.

2. **God** – My salvation hath not been brought to pass by man, but by the almighty power of God.

3. **With joy** – Your thirsty souls shall be filled with Divine graces and comforts, which you may draw from God, in the use of gospel-ordinances.

Chapter 13
God's armies (1–5)

The destruction of Babylon by the Persians and Medes, their great distress, anguish, and utter desolation (6–22)

God's armies (1–5)

1. **The burden** – This title is commonly given to sad prophecies, which indeed are grievous burdens to them on whom they are laid. **Babylon** – Of the city and empire of Babylon by Cyrus.

2. A banner – To gather soldiers together. **Mountain** – Whence it may be discerned at a considerable distance. Withal he seems to intimate, that their enemies should come from the mountainous country of Media. **Them** – To the Medes. **Shake** – Beckon to them with your hand, that they may come to this service, that they may go and fight against Babylon, and take it, and so enter in to the palaces of the king, and his princes.

3. Sanctified ones – The Medes and Persians, so called, because they were set apart by God, for this holy work of executing his just vengeance. **Mighty ones** – Those whom I have made mighty for this work. **Highness** – Or, as others render it, in my glory, in the doing of that work which tends to the advancement of my glory. Tho' the Medes had no regard to God, but only to their own ends.

4. Nations – The Medes and Persians and other nations, which served under them in this war.

5. Thy come – From the ends of the earth under heaven, which is not to be understood strictly. **The weapons** – The Medes and Persians, who were but a rod in God's hand, and the instruments of his anger. **Land** – Of Babylon.

The destruction of Babylon by the Persians and Medes, their great distress, anguish, and utter desolation (6–22)

7. Amazed – To see so impregnable a city as Babylon, so easily and unexpectedly taken. **Flames** – Heb. faces of flame, inflamed with rage and torment.

9. Behold – Divers words are heaped together, to signify the extremity of his anger.

10. Constellations – Which consist of many stars, and therefore give a greater sight. **Darkened** – All things shall look darkly and dismally; men shall have no comfort or hope. **Going forth** – As soon as he rises. As soon as they have any appearance or hope of amendment, they shall be instantly disappointed.

11. The world – The Babylonian empire, which is called the world, as the Roman empire afterwards was, because it was extended to a great part of the world.

12. More precious – The city and nation shall be so depopulated.

13. Therefore – A poetical and prophetical description of great horrors and confusions, as if heaven and earth were about to meet together.

14. It – Babylon. **A roe** – Fearful in itself, especially when it is pursued by the hunter. **A sheep** – In a most forlorn condition. **Every man** – Those soldiers of other nations, whom she had hired to assist her.

15. Found – In Babylon, at the taking of it.

17. Medes – Under whom he comprehends the Persians. **Not delight** – Which is to be

understood comparatively. They shall more eagerly pursue the destruction of the people, than the getting of spoil.

18. Bows – Under which are comprehended, other weapons of war. **Dash** – Or, shalt pierce the young men through, as the Chaldee, renders it.

19. Glory – Which once was the most noble of all the kingdoms. **Beauty** – The beautiful seat of the Chaldean monarchy shall be totally and irrecoverably destroyed.

20. Inhabited – After the destruction threatened shall be fully accomplished. **Arabian** – Who dwelt in tents, and wandered from place to place, where they could find pasture.

21. Satyrs – The learned agree, that these are frightful and solitary creatures.

22. Prolonged – Beyond the time appointed by God.

Chapter 14

Israel shall be delivered from the Babylonian captivity, their triumph over Babylon (1–13)

God's purpose against Assyria (14–27)

Palestina threatened (28–32)

Israel shall be delivered from the Babylonian captivity, their triumph over Babylon (1–13)

1. Choose – Will renew his choice of them; for he had rejected them.

2. Rule – Which they literally did, after their return into their own land. But this was more eminently verified in a spiritual sense, in the days of the gospel.

4. Golden city – As they used to call themselves; which therefore he expresses here in a word of their own language.

6. Anger – With rigour and not with clemency. **None** – Neither the Babylonians themselves, nor their confederates.

7. The earth – The subjects of that vast empire, who groaned under their cruel bondage.

8. The trees – Which were felled for the service of her pride and luxury, but now are suffered to stand.

9. Thrones – From their graves, which he seems to call their thrones by way of irony: the only thrones now left to them. Thrones both paved and covered with worms, instead of their former thrones, adorned with gold and precious stones.

11. Thy pomp – All thy glory is buried with thee. **Viols** – All thy musical instruments, which were much used in Babylon, and were doubtless used in Belshazzar's solemn feasts, Dan 5:1, at which time the city was taken; to which possibly the prophet here alludes. **The worm** – Instead of those stately carpets upon which thou didst frequently tread.

12. Fallen – From the height of thy glory. **Lucifer** – Which properly is a bright star, that ushers in the morning; but is here metaphorically taken for the mighty king of Babylon. **Son** – The title of son is given in scripture not only to a person or thing begotten or produced by another, but also to any thing which is related, to it, in which sense we read of the son of a night, Jonah 4:10, a son of perdition, John 17:12, and, which is more agreeable, to the present case, the sons of Arcturus, Job 38:32.

13. I – I will advance myself above the state of a weak man. **Above** – Above all other kings and potentates; or, above the most eminent persons of God's church. **North** – This is added as a more exact description of the place of the temple; it stood upon mount Moriah, which was northward from the hill of Zion strictly so called.

God's purpose against Assyria (14–27)

14. Like – In the uncontrollableness of my power, and the universal extent of my dominion.

17. Cried not – Whereby he signifies both his irresistible power, and his continued cruelty.

18. All – That is, other things most commonly do. **Lie** – Are buried in their own sepulchres, having stately monuments erected to their memory.

19. Cast out – Or, cast from thy grave or burying-place. Which very probably happened to Belshazzar, when his people had neither opportunity nor heart to bestow an honourable interment upon him, and the conquerors would not suffer them to do it. **Like** – Like a rotten twig of a tree, which he that prunes the trees, casts away. **Raiment** – Which, being mangled, and besmeared with mire, and blood, was cast away with contempt. **Go down** – Who being slain, are cast into some pit. He saith, to the stones of the pit, because when dead bodies are cast in thither, men use to throw an heap of stones upon them. **Trodden** – Neglected, like such a carcase. And this might literally happen to Belshazzar's dead body.

20. Joined – Not buried as they are. **Slain** – Thou hast exercised great tyranny and cruelty, not only to thine enemies, but even to thine own subjects. **The seed** – Such as Belshazzar was, being descended from that Nebuchadnezzar who had made such horrid slaughters and devastations in the world, merely to gratify his own insatiable lusts, and who had been so impious towards God and his temple, and so bloody towards his church and people.

Renowned – Or, shall not be renowned for ever: although I have long borne with thee and thy family.

21. Children – Cut off all the branches of the royal family. **Rise** – Not recover their former power.

22. Remnant – The remembrance of those that are dead, and the persons of those who yet survive.

23. Bittern – A great water fowl, which delights in solitary places, as also in watery grounds. Such as those were about Babylon. **Pools** – The ground about Babylon was of itself very moist, because of the great river Euphrates, running by it, which was kept from overflowing the country with charge and labour; this being neglected, when the city was destroyed, it was easily turned into pools of water.

24. Saying – This verse does not only concern Babylon's destruction, but also the overthrow of Sennacherib and the Assyrian host, which was a pledge of the destruction of the city and empire of Babylon.

25. My land – In Judea, which is my land in a peculiar manner. **Mountains** – In my mountainous country, for such Judea was, especially about Jerusalem.

26. The earth – Upon this vast empire, now in the hands of the Assyrians, and shortly to come into the hands of the Babylonians. **The hand** – The providence of God executing his purpose.

Palestina threatened (28–32)

28. This burden – This following burdensome prophecy concerning the Philistines, who in Ahaz's time, made an inroad into Judah, and took divers of their cities.

29. Of him – Most understand this of Uzziah, who did then much mischief, 2Chron 26:3,6. But he was dead thirty-two years before this time, and therefore their joy for his death was long since past. Others understand it of Ahaz: but he was so far from smiting them, that he was smitten by them. We may understand this of the royal race of Judah, who had been a terrible scourge to them, whose rod might be said to be broken, because that sceptre was come into the hands of slothful princes. **A serpent** – From the root of David shall come Hezekiah, who, like a serpent, shall sting thee to death, as he did, 2Kings 18:8.

30. The poor – The people of the Jews, who are brought to extreme poverty. **The title of first-born** is given to persons or things which are most eminent in their kinds, as to the people of Israel, Exod 4:22, to David, Psal 89:27 Job 18:13, and here to persons eminently poor. **Feed** – Shall have plenty of provisions. **Kill** – I will utterly destroy thee both root and branch.

31. Gate – The gate is put for the city. **City** – City is here put collectively for their cities. **The**

north – From Chaldea. **A smoke** – A grievous judgment and calamity. **Times** – When God's appointed time shall come, not one of all that numerous army shall desert his colours, or lag behind the rest.

32. What – What shall a Jew say to the people of other nations, who shall enquire concerning the state of Zion, when not only the Philistines, but even the Jews themselves, shall fall by the hands of the same enemy? **That** – They shall give them this answer, That although Zion at present be in a very distressed condition, yet she stands upon a firm foundation, and God who first founded her, will restore her, and his poor despised people shall resort to her, as to a strong refuge.

Chapter 15

The Destruction of Moab (1–9)

1. The burden – A prophecy of the destruction of the Moabites, the inveterate enemies of the Jews, begun by the Assyrian, and finished by the Babylonian emperors. **In a night** – Suddenly and unexpectedly. **Ar** – The chief city of Moab. **Kir** – Another eminent city of Moab.

2. Bajith – Which signifies an house. It is supposed to be some eminent house or temple of their idols. **Dibon** – Another city of Moab. **To weep** – To offer their supplications with tears to their idols for help. **Medeba** – Two considerable cities, anciently belonging to the Moabites. **Beard** – The hair of their heads and beards was shaved, as was usual in great mournings.

3. On the tops – Which were made flat, to which men used to go up, to cry to God in heaven, or to men for help.

4. Heshbon – Two other Moabitish cities. **Jahaz** – Another city in the utmost borders of Moab. **Soldiers** – Who use to be the most courageous.

5. Moab – Tho' they are a most vile nation. **Zoar** – Zoar was a town bordering upon Moab. **Of destruction** – Such a cry as men send forth when they are just falling into the pit of destruction.

6. Waters – Watery grounds being very fruitful, are commonly most inhabited; but now they also, much more the dry and barren grounds, shall be desolate and without inhabitant.

7. They – Their enemies. **Brook** – Possibly he means some such river which ran into Euphrates, and so gave them opportunity of carrying their spoils by water unto Babylon.

8. The cry – Their cry fills all the parts of the country.

9. More – More than hath been already mentioned. **Lions** – God shall send lions to find out those that escape the fury of men.

Chapter 16

The Moabites exhorted to entertain kindly the banished Jews (1–5)

They are threatened for their pride and arrogance (6–8)

The prophet bewaileth them (9–11)

Their judgment (12–14)

The Moabites exhorted to entertain kindly the banished Jews (1–5)

1. Send – The prophet continues his prophecy against Moab, and gives them counsel what to do, to prevent, if possible, the desolation. Make your peace with God, by sacrifice, for all your injuries done to him, and to his people. **Sela** – An eminent city of Moab, seated upon a rock. **Unto the mount** – Unto the temple upon mount Zion.

2. Cast out – Which knows not whither to go. **Arnon** – Which was the border of the land of Moab, where they were, with design to flee out of their land, tho' they knew not whither.

3. Take counsel – Consider seriously what course to take. **Shadow** – Or, as the shadow of the night, large and dark, as the shadow of the earth is in the night-season. Conceal and protect my people in the time of their distress. **The outcasts** – Those of my people who are driven out of their land. **Wandereth** – Unto their enemies.

4. Mine out-casts – Whom tho' I have sorely chastened, yet I own for my people. **At an end** – Shall shortly be destroyed, and then thou wilt not lose the fruit of thy kindness. The present tense is put for the future.

5. In mercy – By my mercy. I am now punishing their sins, yet I will deliver them for my own mercy's sake. **The throne** – The kingdom of Judah. **He** – Their king. **In truth** – That is, firmly and constantly; for truth is often put for the stability and certainty of a thing, as 2Chron 32:1 Prov 11:18. **Tabernacle** – In the house, or palace, which is called a tent, or tabernacle, with respect to the unsettledness of David's house, which now indeed was more like a tabernacle than a strong palace. **Seeking** – Searching out the truth of things with care and diligence. **Hasting** – Neither denying, nor yet delaying justice.

6. We – The prophet having spoken to the Moabites, now turns his speech to God's people. The sense is, I do not expect that my counsels will have any good effect upon Moab; they will still carry themselves insolently and outrageously. **His lies** – His vain imaginations, and false and crafty counsels, shall not take effect.

Chapter 17

They are threatened for their pride and arrogance (6–8)

7. Moab – One Moabite shall howl or lament to or for another. **Kirhareseth** – An ancient and eminent city of Moab, which was preserved when their other cities were ruined, and therefore the destruction of it was more lamented. **Stricken** – Or, broken, overthrown or destroyed.

8. The lords – The Assyrians or Chaldeans, the great rulers of the eastern nations. **Plants** – The choicest vines. Under which one particular he seems to understand, not only all other fruits and goods, but even their choicest people. **They** – The lords of the heathen are come as far as Jazer, which is the utmost border of Moab. **Wandered** – The Moabites fled for their lives, and wandered hither and thither in the wilderness of Moab. **Branches** – Her people, called plants before. **Stretched** – Driven from their own homes, and dispersed into several countries. **The sea** – Over the Dead-sea, which was the border of Moab. They were forced to flee out of their own country to save their lives.

The prophet bewaileth them (9–11)

9. Sibmah – I will bewail Sibmah, as I did bewail Jazer, which was destroyed before Sibmah. **Fallen** – Those joyful shouts which were customary in the time of harvest and vintage, shall cease.

10. Treaders – In those times they used to squeeze out the juice of their grapes by treading them with their feet.

11. My bowels – Through compassion. In excessive grief, the bowels are sometimes rolled together, so as to make an audible noise.

Their judgment (12–14)

12. When – When it shall appear that all their other devotions are vain. **His sanctuary** – To the temple of his great god Chemosh. **But** – His god can neither hear nor help him.

13. Since – Since the beginning of God's revelation to me concerning Moab, hitherto.

14. The Lord – Hath made this farther discovery of his mind to me. **Three years** – This may well be understood of some great blow given to the Moabites, either by Sennacherib, or his son Esarhaddon, from which notwithstanding they recovered and flourished again 'till Nebuchadnezzar competed their destruction. **Hireling** – Within three years precisely counted; for hirelings are very punctual in observing the time for which they are hired. **The glory** – Their strength, and wealth, and other things in which they glory, shall be made contemptible to those who formerly admired them. **With** – With the great numbers of their people, of which they boasted.

Chapter 17

Damascus, Samaria, Israel, and their cities, to be ruined by the Assyrians (1–5)

1. Damascus – Both of that city and kingdom. **A heap** – This was fulfilled by Tiglath-pilneser, 2Kings 16:9, although afterwards it was re-edified.

2. Aroer – Of that part of Syria, called Aroer, from a great city of that name. These cities were possessed by the Reubenites and Gadites, whom Tiglath-pilneser carried into captivity, 1Chron 5:26. These he mentions here, as he doth Ephraim in the next verse, because they were confederate with Syria against Judah. **Afraid** – Because the land shall be desolate, and destitute of men who might disturb them.

3. The fortress – All their fortresses; the singular number being put for the plural. **Remnant** – The remainders of Damascus and Syria shall be an headless body, a people without a king. **Of Israel** – Syria shall have as much glory as Israel; that is, neither of them shall have any at all.

5. Gathereth – Taking care, as far as may be, that all may be gathered in, and nothing left. So shall the whole body of the ten tribes be carried away captive, some few gleanings only being left. **Rephaim** – A very fruitful place near Jerusalem.

A remnant shall consider and repent (6–8)

6. Yet – Some few Israelites were left after their captivity, who joined themselves to Judah, and were carried captive to Babylon with them, from whence also they returned with them.

7. A man – Those few men that are left. **Look** – They shall sincerely respect, and trust, and worship God, and God only.

8. Not look – Not trust to them, or to worship offered to idols upon them. **The work** – Their own inventions. **Groves** – Which were devised by men, as fit places for the worship of their gods. **Images** – Worshipped in their groves.

The rest plagued for their impiety (9–11)

9. In – The day of Jacob's trouble, of which he spake ver.4. **Uppermost branch** – Which he that prunes the tree neglects, because he esteems it useless and inconsiderable. **Left** – Which the Canaanites forsook for fear of the children of Israel. And this was a fit example, to awaken the Israelites to a serious belief of this threatening, because God had inflicted the same judgment upon the Canaanites, for the same sins of which they were guilty.

10. Thou – O Israel. **The rock** – That God who was thy only sure defence. **Plants** – Excellent flowers and fruit-trees. **Strange** – Fetched from far countries, and therefore highly esteemed.

11. In the day – Thou shalt from day to day, beginning early in the morning, use all diligence that what thou hast planted may thrive. **But** – When this grievous calamity shall come, all your harvest shall be but one heap.

The woe of Israel's enemies (12–14)

12. Woe – This is a new prophecy, added for the comfort of God's people. **Many** – Combined together against Judah. **Seas** – Who invade my land and people with great force, as the sea does when it enters into the land by a breach.

14. Behold – At even there is great terror among God's people, for fear of their enemies; and before the morning comes, their enemies are cut off.

Chapter 18

God in defence of his church and punishing her enemies, will destroy the Ethiopians (1–6)

An access thereby shall be to the church (7)

God in defence of his church and punishing her enemies, will destroy the Ethiopians (1–6)

1. The land – Either Ethiopia beyond Egypt; or of Egypt. **Wings** – The title of wings is given, in scripture, to divers things which have some kind of resemblance to wings, as to the battlements of an house or temple, to an army, and to the sails of a ship, as this word is here commonly understood. And shadowing with wings is nothing else but overspread or filled with them. Which title may be given either to Ethiopia or Egypt, in regard of the great numbers either of their armies, or of their ships or vessels sailing upon the sea or rivers. **Besides** – Situated on both sides of the Nile. **Rivers** – Called rivers, in the plural number, either for its greatness, or for the many rivulets that run into it, or for the various streams into which it is divided.

2. Sendeth – That at this time are sending ambassadors, to strengthen themselves with alliances. **Bulrushes** – Both the Egyptians and Ethiopians, used boats of rushes or reeds, which were more convenient for them than those of wood, because they were both cheaper and swifter, and lighter for carriage from place to place. These seem to be the words of the prophet, who having pronounced a woe against

the land hitherto described, here continues his speech, and gives a commission from God to these messengers, to go to this nation scattered. Then he calls to all nations to be witnesses of the message sent, ver.3, and then the message follows in the succeeding verses. **Messengers** – Whom I have appointed for this work, and tell them what I am about to do with them. **Scattered** – Not by banishment but in their habitations. Which agrees well to the Ethiopians, for the manner of their habitation, which is more scattered than that of other people. **Peeled** – Having their hair plucked off. This is metaphorically used in scripture, for some great calamity, whereby men are stripped of all their comforts. And this title may be given to them prophetically, to signify their approaching destruction. **Terrible** – Such were the Egyptians, and Ethiopians, as appears both from sacred and profane histories. **Meted** – Meted out as it were with lines to destruction. **Trodden** – By Divine sentence, and to be trodden down by their enemies. **The rivers** – Which may be understood of the Assyrians or Babylonians breaking in upon them like a river, and destroying their land and people.

3. When – When God shall gather together the nations, as it were by the lifting up of an ensign, or by the sound of a trumpet, to execute his judgments upon this people.

4. Rest – I will not bestir myself, to help this people. God is said in scripture to rest, or sit still, when he doth not work on the behalf of a person or people. **Dwelling-place** – In heaven, the place where God dwells. **Harvest** – The sense is, that God would look upon them with as uncomfortable an influence as the sun with a clear heat upon the herbs, which are scorched and killed by it; and as a cloud of the dew, which brings dew or rain, in the heat of harvest, when it is unwelcome and hurtful.

5. For – Before they receive the end of their hopes. **When** – When the bud or flower is turned into a grape, which gives hopes of good vintage. **He** – The Lord. **The branches** – Instead of gathering the grapes, shall cut down the tree, and throw it into the fire.

6. Thy – The branches being cut down and thrown upon the ground, with the unripe grapes upon them. **Left** – They shall lie upon the earth, so that either birds or beasts may shelter themselves with them, or feed on them, both summer and winter.

An access thereby shall be to the church (7)

7. In that time – At or after that time, when the judgment shall be completely executed. **A people** – The people of whom I am speaking shall present themselves, and their sacrifices, to the true God.

Chapter 19

The confusion of Egypt, their intestine dissension, their idols deceive them, cruel lords over them, waters fail them, their trade dead, their princes and counsellors made foolish, their terror before the Lord (1–17)

The calling of Egypt to the church (18–22)

The covenant of Egypt, Assyria and Israel (23–25)

The confusion of Egypt, their intestine dissension, their idols deceive them, cruel lords over them, waters fail them, their trade dead, their princes and counsellors made foolish, their terror before the Lord (1–17)

1. Rideth – As a general in the head of his army. **A swift cloud** – This phrase shews that the judgment should come speedily, unexpectedly, and unavoidably. **Shall be moved** – So far shall they be from helping the Egyptians, that they shall tremble for themselves.

2. I will set – Egypt was now one kingdom, but not many years after this time it was divided into twelve kingdoms, between whom there were many and cruel wars.

3. The spirit – Their courage.

4. A fierce king – Psammetichus, who being at first one of those twelve kings, waged war with the rest, and subdued them, and conquered all the land of Egypt and ruled it with rigour.

5. The waters – Which may be understood either:

1. Metaphorically, of the taking away of their dominion or commerce, or rather, 2. Properly, as may be gathered from the following words. For as the river Nile, when it had a full stream, and free course, did pour forth a vast quantity of waters by its seven famous mouths into the sea, so when that was dried up, which is expressed in the next clause, those waters did truly and properly fail from the sea.

So there is no need of understanding by sea either the river Nile, or the great lake of Maeris, which, after the manner of the Hebrews, might be so called. **The river** – Nile: upon whose fulness and overflow both the safety and the wealth of the land depended; and therefore this was a very terrible judgment. **Dried up** – Not totally, but in a very great measure.

6. Rivers – The rivers shall be turned far away, as they must needs be, when the river which fed them was dried up. **Brooks** – The several branches of the river Nile, which were a great defence to Egypt. **Reeds** – Which were useful to them for making their boats. **Whither** – As they commonly do for want of water.

7. Paper reeds – These by a needle, or other fit instrument, were divided into thin and broad leaves, which being dried and fitted, were used at that time for writing; and consequently was a very good commodity. **By brooks** – And much more what was sown in more dry and unfruitful places.

8. Mourn – Because they could catch no fish; which was a great loss to the people, whose common diet this was.

9. They – That make fine linen, which was one of their best commodities.

10. Thereof – Of Egypt, or of the Egyptians. They shall lose their hopes; for the fishes in them shall die for want of water.

11. Zoan – The chief city, in which the king and court frequently resided. **How** – Why do you put such foolish words into Pharaoh's mouth? **I am the son** – Wisdom is heredity and natural to me.

13. Noph – Another chief city, and one of the kings seats, called also Moph, and by latter authors, Memphis. **The stay** – Their chief counsellors. **Tribes** – Of the provinces, which he calls by a title borrowed from the Hebrews, in whose language he spake and wrote this prophecy.

14. Mingled – Or, hath poured out or given them to drink. **To err** – In all their designs and undertakings. **Staggereth** – When he is so drunk, that he reels to and fro, and vomits up his drink.

15. Head – All people, both high and low, shall be at their wits end.

16. Women – Feeble and fearful. **Because** – Because they shall perceive that they do not fight with men only, but with the Lord of hosts, who now lifts up his hand against them, as he did against their forefathers.

17. A terror – Because of their manifold injuries against Judah, for which they now apprehend God is calling them to account. **Determined** – Because God is now about to execute his appointed judgments. **It** – Against Egypt.

The calling of Egypt to the church (18–22)

18. In that day – After that time. In the times of the gospel. **Five** – A considerable number of their chief cities: a certain number being put for an uncertain. **Speak** – Profess the Jewish religion, agree with them in the same mind; which is fitly signified by speaking the same language. **Swear** – This implies the dedication, and yielding up of a person or thing to the Lord, by a solemn vow, or covenant. **One** – Not one of the five, but another city, the sixth city. As divers cities shall be converted and saved, so some other cities shall continue in their impenitency, and be destroyed.

19. An altar – The altar is put for the worship of God, as it is in many places both of the Old and New Testament. And nothing is more common in the prophets than to speak of gospel-worship in the phrases of the law. **Pillar** – A monument of the true religion. Here also he alludes to the ancient custom of erecting pillars to God. **The border** – As before, in the midst of it. The meaning is, There shall be evidences of their piety in all places.

20. It – The altar or pillar last mentioned.

A witness – To testify that they own the Lord for their God. **Cry** – Being sorely distressed, they shall turn unto the true God. **A great one** – A great or mighty Saviour, even Christ.

21. Shall sacrifice – Shall worship God spiritually; which yet is signified by typical phrases.

22. Smite – God will afflict them and by those afflictions will convert and save them.

The covenant of Egypt, Assyria and Israel (23–25)

23. Assyria – They who were implacable enemies one to another, and both to the church of God, shall now be reconciled and united together in the service of God, and love to his church. **Serve** – The Lord.

24. The third – The third party, in that sacred league, whereby all of them oblige themselves to serve God. **Egypt** – These are named, because they were the most obstinate enemies to God's church, but they are here put for all the Gentiles. **A blessing** – This is peculiar to Israel, who is not only a third party, but is the most eminent of the three, as being the fountain, by which the blessing is conveyed to the other two; because Christ was to be born of them, and the gospel-church and ordinances were first established among them, and from them derived to the Gentiles. **The land** – Or, of those lands, Egypt and Assyria, between which Israel lay.

25. Whom – That is, which people, Israel, Egypt, and Assyria; of whom he speaks as of one people, because they are all united into one church. **My people** – This title, and those which follow, that were peculiar to the people of Israel, shall now be given to these and all other nations.

Chapter 20

The captivity of Egypt and Ethiopia represented, to take off the Jews from seeking to them for help (1–6)

1. Saigon – Sennacherib, who, before he came to Jerusalem, came up against and took all the walled cities of Judah, of which Ashdod might be reckoned one, as being in the tribe of Judah.

2. Sackcloth – Which he wore in token of his grief for the calamities that were already come

upon Israel, and were coming upon Judah. **Naked** – Not wholly naked, but without his upper garment, as slaves and prisoners used to do, whose posture he was to represent. **Bare-foot** – After the manner of mourners and captives.

3. Three years – Not constantly, but when he went abroad among the people, to whom this was appointed for a sign. **A sign** – When this judgment should come, namely, three years after this prophecy.

4. Uncovered – Having their garments cut off by the middle.

5. They – All that shall trust to them. But under this general expression the Israelites, seem to be principally intended.

6. Of the country – Of this land, in which the prophet was, and to whose inhabitants, these words were uttered. **Such** – So vain is our hope placed upon such a people as are unable to deliver themselves.

Chapter 21

The prophet's fear and trouble at his vision of Babylon's ruin, the Medes and Persians (1–4)

He mocketh Babel (5–9)

Edom scorning the prophet is called to repentance (11, 12)

The time of Arab's calamity set (13–17)

The prophet's fear and trouble at his vision of Babylon's ruin, the Medes and Persians (1–4)

1. The plain – Of Babylon, which lay in a very plain country. And the title of the sea might well be given to the waters of Babylon, because of the great plenty and multitude of them. **South** – In those parts which lay southward from Judea, where there were many and great deserts. **Pass through** – As meeting with no opposition. **It** – The burden or judgment. **Desert** – From Media and Persia; a great desert lay between them and Chaldea. **A terrible land** – From the Medes, a warlike and formidable people.

2. A vision – A vision or prophecy, containing dreadful calamities which were to fall upon Babylon. **The spoiler** – The Medes and Persians used treachery as well as force against Babylon. **Elam** – Persia, so called, because Elam was an eminent province of Persia, bordering upon the Medes. **Besiege** – Namely, Babylon, ver.9. **The sighing** – The sighing and groaning of God's people, and other nations under the oppressions of that cruel empire.

3. My loins – Which he mentions with respect to the following similitude of child-bearing. **Pangs** – Sharp and grievous pains.

4. The night – In which I used to have sweet repose. He seems to have had this vision in a night. But withal this signified that horror and destruction, which should befal the Babylonians in a night of feasting and jollity. **He** – God, who shewed him that vision.

5. Prepare – Furnish it with meats and drinks. The prophet foretells what the Babylonians would be doing when their enemies were at their doors. **Watch** – To give us notice of any approaching danger, that in the meantime we may more securely indulge ourselves. **Princes** – Of Babylon: arise from the table and run to your arms. **Shield** – Prepare yourselves and your arms for the approaching battle. The shield is put for all their weapons of offence and defence. They used to anoint their shields with oil, to preserve and polish them, and to make them slippery.

He mocketh Babel (5–9)

6. Go set – This was now done only in a vision, but it signified what should be done really afterwards.

7. A chariot – Hereby he signifies the variety and abundance of warlike provisions which the Medes and Persians should have for their expedition, and particularly of chariots, whereof some were for the carriage of necessary things, and others for the battle.

8. A lion – The watchmen cried out, I see also a lion marching before the horsemen and chariots: which they suppose to represent Cyrus or Darius marching in the head of their armies. **My lord** – The watchman speaks to the prophet, who had set him in this station. **Whole nights** – According to thy command I have stood, and do yet stand continually, both day and night, upon my watch-tower.

9. Men – Not fitted with goods, but provided with men to fight. **He** – The prophet, who here gives an explication of the vision. **He** – God, by the hands of Cyrus.

Edom scorning the prophet is called to repentance (11, 12)

10. Threshing – Threshing is put for the corn threshed; and the corn threshed for people sorely afflicted. This is probably spoken of Babylon. **The corn** – Which I will cause to be threshed upon the floor. **You** – Unto you my people; for all the prophecies, even concerning other nations, were published to them, and for their use and comfort.

11. Dumah – Of Edom or Idumea. **He** – The people of Dumah, one of them in the name and by the appointment of the rest. **Me** – To the watchman: the prophet delivers his prophecy in the form of a dialogue between the people and the watchman.

12. The night – The night is past without any mischief, and the light of the morning is approaching; but tho' the morning is coming, it will be gone, and the night will return, and your fears with it. **Come** – If you will enquire, enquire: I perceive your danger is not past, and there will be occasion for farther enquiries. Therefore **return, come** – Come to me the next morning, and so from morning to morning.

The time of Arab's calamity set (13–17)

13. Forest – Not as you used to do, in the houses or tents of the Arabians: whereby he implies, that that populous country should be a wilderness. **Companies** – In those parts travellers then did, and still do, go together in companies. **Dedanim** – These were merchants, who used to trade with Tyre, and their way lay through Arabia.

14. Tema – A part of Arabia. **Fled** – Whereby he implies, that those other Arabians, against whom this prophecy is principally directed, should be reduced to great scarcity, and forced to flee for their lives, from a bloody enemy.

16. A year – From the time of this prophecy: an exact year. **Glory** – Their power, and riches, and all things wherein they used to glory. This was executed by the Assyrians.

Chapter 22

The anguish of Judah, the prophet much grieved (1–5)

By the Persians, Medes, and Assyrians (6, 7)

He reproves their human wisdom (8–11)

And profane joy (12, 13)

Which God would certainly punish (14)

Shebnah's deprivation for his pride (15–19)

Eliakim put in his place, his glory (20–25)

The anguish of Judah, the prophet much grieved (1–5)

1. The valley – Of Judah; and especially of Jerusalem, called a valley, because great part of it flood in a valley; and the valley of vision, because of the many and clear visions or revelations of God's mind, in that place. **House-tops** – As they used to do in times of great consternation, that they might look, to and cry to heaven for help.

2. Noises – Of joyful shouts. **Tumultuous** – Through revelling and jollity. **Battle** – But either by famine or pestilence in the siege, or in their flight.

3. Rulers – Zedekiah and his chief commanders, whose flight he foretells. **Found** – That remain there with Zedekiah in the siege; for those who had fled to the Chaldeans saved their lives and liberties. **Bound** – In fetters, Jer 52:11. **Fled** – Who fled from Jerusalem, but were pursued and overtaken by their enemies, and bound, as others had been.

4. Look away – Take off your eyes and thoughts from me, and leave me alone.

5. Treading down – In which my people are trodden under foot by their enemies. **By the Lord** – Not only men, but God himself fought against them. **Walls** – Of the strong cities of Judah. **Mountains** – With such loud and dismal outcries as should reach to the neighbouring mountains.

By the Persians, Medes, and Assyrians (6, 7)

6. Elam – The Persians, who now, and for a long time after, were subject to the Assyrian and Chaldean emperors. **Quiver** – Being expert bowmen. **Horsemen** – As some fought on foot, so others fought from chariots and horses. **Kir** – The Medes, so called from Kir, an eminent city and region of Media. **Uncovered** – Prepared it and themselves for the battle.

7. Valleys – Valleys were the most proper places for the use of chariots. **Gate** – To assist the footmen while they made their assault, and to prevent those who endeavoured to escape.

He reproves their human wisdom (8–11)

8. He – The enemy. **Covering** – He took those fenced cities, which were a covering or safeguard both to the people of Judah, and to Jerusalem. **The armour** – Thy trust was placed in the arm of flesh. **The forest** – More fully called the house of the forest of Lebanon, 1Kings 7:2, not because it was built in Lebanon, for it was in Jerusalem; but because it was built of the trees of Lebanon.

9. Seen – That is, observed in order to the reparation of them. **The waters** – That you might both deprive the enemy of water, and supply the city with it.

10. Numbered – That they might exactly know their own strength. **The houses** – Which stood upon or without the walls, and so gave their enemies advantage, and hindered the fortifying the city.

11. Thereof – Of Jerusalem, expressed in the foregoing verse. **Him** – God, who made it a city, and the place of his special presence and worship. **Long ago** – Which may be added to aggravate their sin, in distrusting that God, who had now for a long time given proof of his care and kindness in defending this city.

And profane joy (12, 13)

12. Call – By his providence, and by his precepts requiring these things in such times. **Baldness** – By plucking or shaving off the hair of their heads, as was usual in great sorrows.

13. Let us – A most perverse and desperate conclusion.

Which God would certainly punish (14)

14. 'Till ye die – You shall feel the sad effects of this, as long as you live.

Shebnah's deprivation for his pride (15–19)

16. What – What right hast thou to this place and office? **Whom** – What kindred or relations? For the Jews say, he was a stranger by birth; which is the more probable, because his pedigree is not mentioned in any of those places of scripture where he is named. **On high** – In an high and eminent place. **An habitation** – He erected a stately house to live in, and a stately sepulchre to receive him when he died. And these two are fitly joined together, because their sepulchres were commonly built in or near their houses. **A rock** – A fit place both for strength and state.

17. Will carry – Will cause thee to be carried into captivity by a strong hand. **Cover** – This may be an allusion to the ancient custom of covering the faces of condemned persons.

18. Thy chariots – Thy glorious chariots where thou didst ride in great state at Jerusalem, shall be turned into shame to thyself, and to thy master.

19. He – The Lord; such sudden changes of persons being very usual in these writings.

Eliakim put in his place, his glory (20–25)

20. Call – By my powerful providence.

21. Girdle – There was a peculiar sort of robe and girdle which was the badge of his office. **A father** – He shall govern them with fatherly care and affection.

22. The key – The government, the power of opening and shutting, of letting men into it, or putting them out of it, whereof a key is a fit emblem. **Shoulder** – He mentions the shoulder rather than the hand, in which keys are commonly carried, from some ceremony then in use, of carrying a key upon the shoulder of the officer of state.

23. Fasten – I will establish the power in his hands. **Sure place** – In the strong walls, or solid timber, in the house. **He shall be** – By his prudent and righteous government he shall procure great glory, to all that have any relation to him.

24. The glory – Of his own kindred and family, who shall all depend upon him, and receive glory from him; of the house of David, which is called his father's house, because he was of the blood-royal. **The offspring** – Great and small, the children and grand-children of his father's house, the meanest of them shall receive a lustre from their relation to him. **All vessels** – All sorts of vessels, great or small, mean or precious, may be hanged upon him, without any fear of falling.

25. The nail – Shebna, who seemed to be so. **The burden** – All those wicked officers that were advanced and supported by his power.

Chapter 23

The destruction of Tyre, from God, for their pride (1–14)

The time of her rising again (15–17)

And conversion to God (18)

The destruction of Tyre, from God, for their pride (1–14)

1. Of Tyre – The prophecy of the heavy calamity and destruction of Tyre. Tyre was, according to this prophecy, destroyed; first by Nebuchadnezzar, and afterwards by Alexander the great. And tho' this prophecy seemed directly to respect the former destruction, yet it seems to have some reference to the latter also; only it is intimated, that after seventy years, Tyre should recover some former power and glory, before her second and final destruction. **Howl** – To which howling and lamenting is ascribed by a known figure. **No house** – So effectually wasted, that there is not an house left in it, nor any merchants or others that go into it, for traffick. **Chittim** – He mentions the land of Chittim, because this was an eminent place for shipping and trading, and therefore doubtless had great dealings with Tyre. It may here be put for all other countries which traded with her. It is not necessary to determine what Chittim is; it is sufficient to know, that it was a seafaring place in the Midland Sea.

2. Be still – Heb. be silent, boast no more of thy wealth and power. **The isle** – Of Tyre, which was an island, 'till Alexander joined it to the continent. The title of islands is often given by the Hebrews to places bordering upon the sea. **That pass** – That are a sea-faring people. **Replenished** – With manners, and commodities.

4. Zidon – Zidon was a great city near Tyre, strongly united to her by commerce and league, and called by some the mother of Tyre, which they say, was built and first inhabited by a colony of the Sidonians. **The sea** – That part of the sea in which Tyre was, and from which ships and men were sent into all countries. **The strength** – Tyre might be called the strength of the sea, because it defendeth that part of the sea from piracies and injuries. **I travel not** – I, who was so fruitful, that I sent forth colonies into other countries, am now barren and desolate.

5. Waters – By the sea, which is very fitly called the great waters, understand, cometh, or is brought to her. **The seed** – The corn of Egypt, wherewith Egypt abounded. Sihor is the same as the Nile. **The harvest** – The plentiful harvest of corn which comes from the inundation of the Nile; emphatically called the river. **The revenue** – Is as plentifully enjoyed by her, as if it grew in her own territories. **A mart** – A place to which all nations resort for traffic.

7. Antiquity – Being built before Joshua's time, Joshua 19:29. **Her feet** – Whereas before, like a delicate lady, she would not set her foot to the ground, but used to be carried in stately chariots. **To sojourn** – To seek for new habitations.

8. Who – This is the word of God, and not of man. **The crowning city** – Which was a royal city, and carried away the crown from all other cities. **Princes** – Equal to princes for wealth, and power, and reputation.

9. The Lord – This is the Lord's own doing. **To stain** – God's design is by this example to abase the pride of all the potentates of the earth.

10. Pass through – Tarry no longer in thy own territories, but flee through them, into other countries, for safety and relief. **As a river** – Swiftly, lest you be prevented. **Tarshish** – Tyre, which might well be called daughter of Tarshish, that is, of the sea, as that word is used, ver.1, and elsewhere, because it was an island, and therefore as it were, born of the sea, and nourished and brought up by it.

11. He – The Lord. **Shook** – Heb. he made the kingdoms to tremble; the neighbouring and confederate kingdoms, who might justly quake at her fall, for the dreadfulness and unexpectedness of the thing; and because Tyre was a bulwark, and a refuge to them. **A commandment** – Hath put this design into the hearts of her enemies, and given them courage to attempt, and strength to execute it.

12. Virgin – So he calls her, because she had hitherto never borne the yoke of a conquering enemy. **Zidon** – Tyre may be called the daughter of Zidon, because she was first built and possessed by a colony of the Zidonians. **No rest** – Thither thine enemies shall pursue thee, and there shall they overtake thee.

13. Behold – Thou Tyrians, cast your eyes upon the Chaldeans or Babylonians; who tho' now flourishing, grow far more glorious and potent, even the glory of kingdoms, yet shall certainly be brought to utter ruin. **This people** – The Chaldeans at first were not a people, not formed into any commonwealth or kingdom, 'till Nimrod, the head and founder of the Assyrian monarchy, built Babel, Gen 10:9,10, now the head of the Chaldean monarchy; which he built for those people, who then lived in tents, and were dispersed here and there in waste places. **He** – The Lord. **To ruin** – Will infallibly bring that great empire to ruin. He speaks of a future thing as if it were already past.

14. Your strength – The city of Tyre, where you found safety and wealth.

The time of her rising again (15–17)

15. Forgotten – Neglected and forsaken. **Seventy years** – During the time of the Jewish captivity in Babylon. Tyre was taken by Nebuchadnezzar, Jer 27:3,8 Ezek 26:7, a little after the taking of Jerusalem and was restored by the favour of the Persian monarchs after the return of the Jews. **One king** – One royal race of Nebuchadnezzar, including his son, and his son's son, in whom his family and kingdom were to expire. **Sing** – She shall by degrees return to her former traffic, whereby she shall easily entice the merchants of the world to trade with her, as harlots use to entice men by lascivious songs.

16. Go about – As harlots use to do. **Thou harlot** – So he calls Tyre, because she enticed the merchants to deal with her by various artifices, and even by dishonest practices, and because of the great and general uncleanness which was committed in it.

17. Visit – In mercy. **Her hire** – The Hebrew word properly signifies, the hire of an harlot. **Fornication** – Shall trade promiscuously with people of all nations, as harlots entertain all comers.

And conversion to God (18)

18. Holiness – This is a prophecy concerning the conversion of the Tyrians to the true religion. **Laid up** – Either out of covetousness, or for their pride and luxury, as they formerly did; but now they shall freely lay it out upon pious and charitable uses. **Shall be** – For the support and encouragement of the ministers of holy things, who shall teach the good knowledge of the Lord. Although this does not exclude, but rather imply their liberality in contributing to the necessities of all Christians.

Chapter 24

Judgments on Judah for their defilements and transgression (1–12)

A remnant shall praise God (13–15)

God, by his judgments on his people and their enemies, will advance his kingdom (16–23)

Judgments on Judah for their defilements and transgression (1–12)

1. The land – Of Canaan. **Waste** – He will shortly make it waste, first by the Assyrians, and then by the Chaldeans. **Turneth** – Brings it into great disorder and confusion.

2. It shall be – The approaching calamity shall be universal, without any distinction of persons or ranks; the priests themselves having been partakers of the peoples sins, shall also partake with them in their plagues. **The seller** – The purchaser of lands shall have no more left than he that hath sold all his patrimony; and all persons shall be made equal in beggary and slavery.

4. The world – The land of Judea. **The majesty** – Not only common people, but the high and lofty ones.

5. Defiled – By the wickedness of its people. **The laws** – The laws of God. **Ordinance** – God's ordinances concerning his worship and service; the singular being put for the plural. **Covenant** – The covenant made between God and Abraham, and all his posterity, which was everlasting, both on God's part, who, upon the conditions therein expressed, engaged himself to be a God to them and to their seed forever; and on Israel's part, who were obliged thereby to constant and perpetual obedience through all generations.

6. The curse – The curse of God threatened to transgressors. **Burned** – Are consumed by the wrath of God, which is commonly compared to fire.

7. Mourneth – Because there are none to drink it. Grief is ascribed to senseless creatures by a figure usual in all authors. **Languisheth** – Because there are no people left to dress it, or gather its grapes. **The merry-hearted** – That made their hearts merry with wine.

8. Tabrets – Which they used in their feasts. **The noise** – The word properly signifies a confused clamour, such as drunken men make.

9. Bitter – Because of the fears and miseries wherewith it is mixed.

10. The city – Jerusalem, and other cities; for the singular word may be here taken collectively. A city of confusion or disorder, breaking all the laws and orders which God had established among them. **Shut up** – Because the inhabitants are either dead, or gone into captivity.

11. A crying – Such was their gross sensuality and sottishness, that instead of crying for their sins, they did only howl for their corn, and wine, and oil, Hosea 7:14.

A remnant shall praise God (13–15)

God, by his judgments on his people and their enemies, will advance his kingdom (16–23)

13. When – When this judgment shall be executed, there shall be left a remnant; as there are some few olives or grapes left after the vintage is over.

14. They – The remnant shall sing for the glorious power and goodness of God, manifested in their deliverance. **The sea** – From the isles of the sea; from those parts beyond the sea into which, they were carried captive.

15. In distress – When you are in the furnace of affliction. **In the isles** – In remote countries, beyond the sea, which in scripture are commonly called isles.

God, by his judgments on his people and their enemies, will advance his kingdom (16–23)

16. From – From all the parts of the earth in which the Jews are or shall be. **Songs** – Of joy and praise. **Glory** – Or, glory be to the righteous. The Lord, the righteous one. **But** – In the midst of these joyful tidings, I discern something which gives me cause of lamentation. **My leanness** – I faint and pine away for grief, for the following reason. **Treacherously** – The Jews, who have been frequently guilty of great perfidiousness towards God, are now acting the same part. Even the Hebrew doctors expound this place of the perfidiousness of some Jews in the times of the Messiah. And it is not strange that so sad a sight made the prophet cry out, My leanness. He repeats it to shew the horridness of the crime.

17. The snare – Great and various judgments, some actually inflicted, and others justly feared.

18. Fleeth – Upon the report of some terrible evil. **The foundations** – Both heaven and earth conspire against him. He alludes to the deluge of waters which God poured down from heaven, and to the earthquakes which he often causes below.

19. The earth – This is repeated again, to shew the dreadfulness and, certainty of these judgments, and to awaken the stupid Israelites.

20. A tent – Which is easily and commonly carried from place to place.

22. Gathered – By God's special providence, in order to their punishment. And thus the unbelieving Jews were generally gathered together at Jerusalem, to their solemn feast, when Titus came and besieged, and destroyed them. **Shut up** – As malefactors, which are taken in several places, are usually brought to one common prison. **After** – After the apostate Jews shall have been shut up in unbelief, and in great tribulations for many ages together, they shall be convinced of their sin in crucifying the Messiah, and brought home to God and Christ by true repentance.

23. The sun – All earthly powers and glories shall be obscured with the far greater splendour of Christ, the king of kings, at whose feet even the kings of the earth shall fall down and worship. **The Lord** – The Messiah, who, tho' man, yet is also God, and the Lord of hosts. **Shall reign** – Shall come in the flesh, and set up his kingdom, first in Jerusalem, and afterward in all other nations. **Before** – Before his ministers, who are in some sort the courtiers of the King of Glory. But the ancients are here put for the whole church, in whose name and for whose service they act.

Chapter 25

God glorious in his judgments on Babel (1–5)

God glorious in his people's salvation (6–12)

God glorious in his judgments on Babel (1–5)

1. O Lord – The prophet reflecting upon those great and glorious prophecies which he had delivered, interrupts the course of his prophecies, and breaks forth into a solemn celebration of God's wonderful works. **Thy counsels** – From which all thy works proceed, and which thou hast from time to time revealed to thy prophets and people, which were of old, being conceived from all eternity, are true and firm, and shall certainly be accomplished.

2. A city – Which is put for cities: or of enemies of God and his people. And under the name cities he comprehends their countries and kingdoms. **Strangers** – The royal cities, in which were the palaces of strangers, of Gentiles. **No city** – Their cities and palaces have been or shall be utterly and irrecoverably destroyed.

3. Shall fear – Thy stoutest enemies observing thy wonderful works, shall be converted, or at least forced to tremble before thee.

4. For – For thou hast defended thy poor and helpless people. **As a storm** – Makes a great noise, but without any effect.

5. The noise – The tumultuous noise, as the word properly signifies; the rage and furious attempts of those Heathen nations that fought against God's people. **As the heat** – With as much ease as thou dost allay the heat of a dry place, by the shadow of thy clouds, or by the rain which falls from black and shadowy clouds. **The branch** – The arm or power, as a branch is the arm of a tree.

God glorious in his people's salvation (6–12)

6. And – In mount Zion, in God's church. **All people** – Both Jews and Gentiles. **A feast** – A feast made up of the most delicate provisions, which is manifestly meant of the ordinances, graces, and comforts given by God in his church. **Of wines** – Which have continued upon the lees a competent time, whereby they gain strength, and are afterwards drawn off, and refined.

7. The face – The covering of the face. **The veil** – The ignorance of God, and of the true religion, which then was upon the Gentiles, and now is upon the Jews.

8. He – Christ will by his death destroy the power of death, take away the sting of the first death, and prevent the second. **In victory** – Heb.

unto victory; so as to overcome it perfectly; which complete victory Christ hath already purchased for, and will in due time actually confer upon his people. **Rebuke** – The reproach and contempt cast upon his faithful people by the ungodly world.

9. **Our God** – Our Messiah, long since promised, and for whom we have waited long, is come into the world, bringing salvation with him.

10. **Rest** – The powerful and gracious presence, of God shall have its constant and settled abode. **Moab** – The Moabites are put for all the enemies of God's church.

11. **He** – The Lord, whose power they shall be no more able to resist, than the waters can resist a man that swims. **Spread** – To smite and destroy them. **The spoils** – With all their wealth which they have gained by rapine, and spoiling of God's people.

12. **And** – All thy fortifications, in which thou trustest.

Chapter 26

A song of praise and confidence in God, for the blessings of righteousness, judgments on their enemies, and favour to his people: their chastisement, repentance, and hope (1–21)

1. **In that day** – When God shall do such glorious works, as are described in the foregoing chapter. **Sung** – In the church of God. **A city** – Jerusalem, or the church, which is often compared to a city. **For walls** – God's immediate and saving protection shall be to his church instead of walls.

2. **The gates** – Of the city, mentioned ver.1. **The nation** – The whole body of righteous men, whether Jews or Gentiles. For he seems to speak here, as he apparently did in the foregoing chapter, of the times of the gospel. **Keepeth truth** – Which is sincere in the true religion.

4. **For ever** – In all times and conditions.

5. **On high** – He speaks not so much of height of place, as of dignity and power, in which sense also he mentions the lofty city in the next clause. **Lofty city** – Which may be understood either of proud Babylon, or of all the strong and stately cities of God's enemies.

6. **The needy** – God will bring it under the feet of his poor, and weak, and despised people.

7. **Thou** – O God, who art upright in all thy ways, and therefore a lover of uprightness, and of all upright men, dost weigh the path of the just, the course of his actions, and, which is implied, dost approve of them, and therefore direct them to an happy issue.

9. **In the night** – When others are sleeping, my thoughts and desires are working towards

God. **Early** – Betimes in the morning. **For** – And good reason it is that we should thus desire and seek thee in the way of thy judgments, because this is the very design of thy judgments, that men should thereby be awakened to learn and return to their duty; and this is a common effect, that those who have been careless in prosperity, are made wiser and better by afflictions.

10. **Will not learn** – This is the carriage of thy people; but the course of wicked men is directly contrary in all conditions: for if thou dost spare them, they will not accept of that gracious invitation to repentance. **In the land** – Even in God's church, and among his people, where righteousness is taught and practised. **Will not behold** – Tho' God gives such plain discoveries of his majesty and glory, not only in his word, but also in works, and especially in this glorious work of his patience and mercy to wicked men, yet they will not acknowledge it.

11. **Will not see** – And they are guilty of the same obstinate blindness when thou dost smite and punish them, which is commonly signified by lifting up the hand. **They shall see** – They shall know that by sad experience, which they would not learn by easier ways. **These** – Such fire or wrath as thou usest to pour forth upon thine implacable enemies.

12. **Our works** – All the good works done by us, are the effects of thy grace.

13. **Other lords** – Others besides thee, and besides those governors who have been set up by thee, even foreign and heathen lords. **By thee** – By thy favour and help. **Will we** – Celebrate thy praise.

14. **Rise** – Those tyrants are destroyed; they shall never live or rise again to molest us.

15. **The nation** – This nation seems to be the people of Israel. **Removed** – Thou hast removed thy people out of their own land, and suffered them to be carried captive to the ends of the earth.

16. **They** – Thy people. **Visited** – Come into thy presence, with their prayers and supplications.

17. **Like** – Such was our anguish and danger.

18. **We** – We have had the torment of a woman in child-bearing, but not the comfort of a living child, for we have brought forth nothing but wind; all our labours and hopes were unsuccessful. **The world** – The Assyrians, or our other enemies.

19. **Thy** – The prophet here turns his speech to God's people, and gives them a cordial in their distress. Thy dead men are not like those, ver.14, for they shall not live; but thine shall live. You shall be delivered from all your fears and dangers. **My dead body** – As I myself, who am one of these dead men, shall live again; you shall be delivered together with me. **Awake** – Out of your sleep, even the sleep of death, you that are

dead and buried in the dust. **Thy dew** – The favour and blessing of God upon thee. **The dew** – Which makes them grow and flourish.

20. Shut thy doors – Withdraw thyself from the world, and pour out thy prayers to God in thy closet. **Indignation** – The dreadful effects of God's anger, mentioned in the following verse.

21. Cometh – Cometh down from heaven. **To punish** – All the enemies of God, and of his people. **Her slain** – The innocent blood which hath been spilled upon the earth shall be brought to light, and severely revenged upon the murderers.

Chapter 27

God's care over his vineyard (1–6)

His chastisements on them (7–9)

His severe judgments against them (10, 11)

Their return (12, 13)

God's care over his vineyard (1–6)

1. Leviathan – By this leviathan, or serpent or dragon he understands some powerful enemy or enemies of God, and of his church or people, which may well be called by these names, partly for their great might, and partly for the great terror and destruction which they cause upon the earth. **The piercing** – Which by its sting pierces deeply into mens bodies. **Crooked serpent** – Winding and turning itself with great variety and dexterity. Whereby he seems to signify the craftiness and activity of this enemy, whose strength makes it more formidable.

2. In that day – When this enemy shall be destroyed. **A vineyard** – My church and people, of red wine, of the choicest and best wine, which in those parts was red.

3. I keep it – I will protect my church from all her enemies, and supply her with all necessary provisions.

5. Or – Or if at any time fury seem to be in me against my people. **Let him** – My people. **Take hold** – Which he may by humble prayer not only restrain from doing him hurt, but engage to do him good.

6. Take root – To be firmly settled in their possessions. **Fruit** – Their posterity shall seek habitations in other countries, and replenish them with people. But this seems to be understood of the spiritual seed of Jacob.

His chastisements on them (7–9)

7. Hath he – He hath not dealt so severely with his people, as he hath dealt with their enemies, whom he hath utterly destroyed. **Of them** – Of those who were slain by God on the behalf of Israel.

8. In measure – With moderation. **When** – When the vine shooteth forth its luxuriant branches, he cuts them off, but so as not to destroy the vine. **Contend** – God is said to contend with men, when he executes his judgments upon them, Amos 7:4. **Stayeth** – He mitigates the severity of the judgment. **In the day** – In the time when he sends forth his east-wind; which he mentions because that wind in those parts was most violent and most hurtful.

9. By this – By this manner of God's dealing with them. **When** – Which sin of Jacob's shall be purged, when he shall truly repent of all his sins, and especially of his idolatry. **Altar** – Their idolatrous altars. Possibly he may say the altar, with respect to that particular altar, which Ahaz had set upon the place of God's own altar; and this prophecy might be delivered in Ahaz's time, while that altar stood. **Chalkstones** – When he shall break all those goodly altars in pieces. **Not stand** – Shall be thrown down with contempt.

His severe judgments against them (10, 11)

10. Yet – Yet before this glorious promise be fulfilled, a dreadful and desolating judgment shall come. **The city** – Jerusalem and the rest of the defended cities in the land. **The habitation** – The most inhabited and populous places. **The calf** – This is put for all sorts of cattle, which may securely feed there, because there shall be no men left to disturb them.

11. Broken – That there may be no hopes of their recovery. **Women** – He mentions women, because the men would be destroyed. **Not understanding** – They know not the things which concerns their peace, but they blindly and wilfully go on in sin. **Therefore** – Thus he overthrows their conceit that God would never destroy the work of his own hands.

Their return (12, 13)

12. Beat out – It is a metaphor from grain which was beaten out with a rod or staff, and then carefully gathered and laid up. **From** – From Euphrates to the Nile, which were the two borders of the land of promise. All the Israelites who are left in the land. **One by one** – Which signifies, God's exact care of them.

13. Trumpet – God shall summon them altogether by sound of trumpet, by an eminent call of his providence. He alludes to the custom of calling the Israelites together with trumpets.

Chapter 28

The drunkenness of Ephraim bringeth destruction on them, a remnant shall be honourable (1–8)

Their unteachableness (9–13)

Their mock at God's threatening (14, 15)

Christ a sure foundation to believers (16)

And destruction to the mockers, who are exhorted to amend (17–22)

God's providence, its work and seasons towards the church, under the figure of a husbandman (23–29)

The drunkenness of Ephraim bringeth destruction on them, a remnant shall be honourable (1–8)

1. Pride – That proud and insolent kingdom. **Drunkards** – Having many and excellent vines among them, they were much exposed to this sin. **Ephraim** – Of the kingdom of the ten tribes. **Who are** – Who have their common abode. **The head** – Samaria, might well be called the head, as being seated upon a mountain, and the head of the kingdom, and the head of the fat valleys, because it was encompassed with many fat and rich valleys.

2. A strong one – The king of Assyria. **Shall cast down** – The crown of pride. **The hand** – By the hand of God, which shall strengthen him in this work.

3. Trodden – The expression is emphatic; the crown which was upon their own heads, shall be trodden under the feet of others; and they, whose drunkenness made them fall to the ground, shall be trodden down there.

4. He eateth – Which, as soon as a man sees he plucks it off, and devours it, as soon as he can get it into his hand. And so shall it be with Ephraim's glory, which his enemies shall devour greedily.

5. In that day – When the kingdom of Israel shall be destroyed. **A diadem** – God shall give eminent glory and beauty, to the kingdom of Judah.

6. To them – Who not only drive their enemies from their land, but pursue them into their own lands, and besiege them in their own cities.

7. But – Judah is guilty of the same sins with Israel, therefore they also must expect the same calamities; of which he speaks afterward. **The prophet** – The teachers, who should have been patterns of sobriety to the people. **They err** – The prophets miscarry in their sacred employment. **Stumble** – The priests mistake in pronouncing the sentence of the law, which was their duty.

Their unteachableness (9–13)

9. He – God. **Them** – Who is there among this people that are willing to be taught the knowledge of God? A minister may as soon teach an infant as these men.

10. For – They must be taught like little children, because of their great dullness. **Line** – One line of the book after another, as children are taught to read.

11. Another tongue – By people of a strange language, whom he shall bring among them, seeing they will not hear him speaking, by his prophets, in their own language.

12. This – This doctrine. **The rest** – The only way, in which you will find rest.

13. Here a little – As this method has been used and was altogether necessary for them; so it still is, and for the future shall be. As they were children in understanding, they shall still continue to be such; they shall be ever learning, and never come to the knowledge of the truth. **That** – This will be the event, or consequence of their sin: they will fall backward, which is the worst, and most dangerous way of falling; and so be broken to pieces.

Their mock at God's threatening (14, 15)

15. Said – In your hearts. **We** – We are as safe from death, and hell, or the grave, as if they had entered into covenant with us. **The scourge** – The judgment of God.

Christ a sure foundation to believers (16)

16. Therefore – Because your refuges are so vain, and deceitful; therefore I will direct you to a surer refuge, which God hath laid in Zion. But if you despise that refuge; then know, that I will lay judgment to the line. **I lay** – I have promised it, and will, in the fulness of time, perform it. **In Zion** – In my church. **A foundation** – Upon which I will build my church. **A stone** – The Messiah. **Tried** – Which I have tried, and approved as every way sufficient. **Corner-stone** – Uniting the several parts of the building together. **Sure** – Upon whom you may securely rest. **Believeth** – This promise. **Shall not** – Hastily catch at any way of escaping danger, but shall patiently wait upon God in his way, 'till he deliver him.

And destruction to the mockers, who are exhorted to amend (17–22)

17. Plummet – I will execute just judgment, as it were by a line and plummet annexed to it; that is, with exactness and care: I will severely punish, and utterly destroy all who reject that stone. For the line and plummet, or the plumb-line, was not only used in erecting buildings, but also in pulling them down; those parts of the building being thus marked out, which were to be demolished.

19. Pass over – It shall not only come to you, but it shall abide upon you; and when it hath passed over you, it shall return again to you, morning after morning; and shall follow you day and night, without giving you the least respite. **The report** – So dreadful shall the judgment be, that it shall strike you with horror, when you only hear the rumour of it.

20. For – For those lying refuges, to which you trust, will not be able to give you that protection, which you expect from them; no more than a man can stretch himself upon a bed that is too short for him.

21. Perazim – Where he fought against the Philistines, 2Sam 5:20. **Gibeon** – Where he fought against the Canaanites, Josh 10:10, and afterwards against the Philistines, 1Chron 14:16. **Strange work** – For this work of bringing total destruction upon Israel, was contrary to the benignity of his own nature, and to the usual way of dealing with his people.

22. Lest – Lest thereby you make the judgments of God sure and unavoidable. **For** – God hath assured me, that he will utterly destroy the people of Israel.

God's providence, its work and seasons towards the church, under the figure of a husbandman (23–29)

24. Doth – The plowman doth not spend all his time in plowing the ground; but he has several times for several works. And so God has his times and seasons for several works, and his providence is various at several times, and towards several people. Therefore those scoffing Israelites were guilty of great folly, in flattering themselves, because of God's long patience towards them; for God will certainly take a time to thresh, and break them with his judgments, as at present he plowed and harrowed them, and so prepared them for it by his threatenings. **Open** – Understand, all day. **Break** – Which they used to do with a kind of harrow.

25. Made plain – By breaking the clods. **The wheat** – The best which he chooses for seed. **Barley** – That proportion of barley which he appointed. **Place** – Heb. in his border; each seed in a several place.

27. A threshing instrument – This then was made like a sledge shod with iron, which was drawn by men or beasts, over the sheafs of corn, to bruise them, and tear the grain out of them. **A wheel** – A lower wheel than a cart wheel, but of the same form, upon which possibly the threshing instrument was drawn.

28. Bruised – With a threshing instrument. **Break it** – Understand, forever. **Horses** – This was another way of threshing out the corn, by driving horses, or other cattle, over the sheaves to tread it.

29. This also – This part of the husbandman's discretion. These words contain the application of the similitude. The husbandman manages his affairs with common discretion; but God governs the world, and his church, with wonderful wisdom: he is great and marvellous, both in the contrivance of things, and in the execution of them.

Chapter 29

The temple and city of Jerusalem destroyed (1–6)

Her enemies insatiable (7, 8)

Their senselessness (9–12)

And deep hypocrisy (13–17)

These scorner and oppressor being cut off, the rest shall be converted (18–24)

The temple and city of Jerusalem destroyed (1–6)

1. The city – The royal city, and seat of David and his posterity. **Set them** – Go on in killing sacrifices from time to time, one year after another, whereby you think to appease me, but all shall be in vain.

4. And thou – Thou who now speakest so loftily, shall be humbled, and with a low voice, beg the favour of thine enemies. **As one** – Who, that they might possess the people with a kind of reverence and horror, used to deliver their answers with a low voice, from some cave under the ground.

5. Strangers – Whom thou hast hired to assist thee, as indeed they did, when the Chaldeans came against them. **Terrible ones** – Thy great commanders, and stout soldiers. **It** – This destruction of thy strangers, and terrible ones shall come to pass.

6. Thou – Thou, O Jerusalem. **Fire** – With dreadful judgments, which are frequently expressed by these metaphors.

Her enemies insatiable (7, 8)

8. His soul – His appetite or desire is unsatisfied. **So** – No less unsatisfied and insatiable; they shall be always thirsting after more of your blood.

Their senselessness (9–12)

9. Wonder – At the stupidity of this people. **Cry** – Cry out again and again through astonishment. **They stagger** – With giddiness or stupidity, which makes them like drunken men, insensible of their danger.

10. Dead sleep – Hardness of heart, and insensibleness of your danger. **Seers** – Your magistrates and ministers. **Covered** – With the veil of ignorance and stupidity.

12. Of all – Of all, your prophets. **As a book** – In which no man can read, while it is sealed up, as books then sometimes were, being made in the form of rolls. **Delivered** – Unsealed and opened.

And deep hypocrisy (13–17)

13. Draw near – Namely, in acts of worship. **With lips** – With outward devotions. **But** – They do not pay me that love, and fear, and obedience, which I require. **And** – They worship me not in such a manner, as I have prescribed, but according to mens inventions, preferring the devices and traditions of their false prophets, before my institutions.

14. Hid – Shall disappear and vanish.

15. Seek deep – A metaphor from men, who use to dig deep into the earth, that they may hide any thing there. **To hide** – Vainly imagining, that they can deceive, not only men, but God, by their external professions. **Who** – Neither God nor man can discover us.

16. Surely – All your subtle devices, by which you turn yourselves into all shapes. **As clay** – It is no more to me, than the clay is to the potter, who can alter and dispose it as he sees fit.

17. As a forest – The forest of Lebanon, which was a barren mountain, shall by God's providence, become a fruitful and populous place; and these places which are now fruitful and populous, shall then become as barren and desolate, as that forest. This is a prophecy of the rejection of the Jews, and of the calling of the Gentiles.

These scorner and oppressor being cut off, the rest shall be converted (18–24)

18. Shall see – Being, by God's grace, brought out of gross, ignorance and wickedness, unto a clear and saving knowledge of the truth.

19. Meek – The humble and meek believers. **Poor** – Mean and despicable people, such as the Gentiles were in the opinion of the Jews, and such as the greatest part of the first Christians were.

20. That watch – That early and diligently apply themselves to the practice of wickedness.

21. That make a man – That condemn a man, as if he was a great criminal. **For him** – For God's faithful prophets and ministers. **The gate** – There the people used to assemble, both upon civil and sacred accounts, and there prophets used to deliver their prophecies. **Turn** – From his right. **The just** – The faithful ministers of God. **Nought** – Not for any great advantage, but for a trifle.

22. Redeemed – From manifold dangers, and especially from idolatry. **Jacob** – The Israelites or posterity of Jacob, who had great cause to be ashamed, for their continued infidelity, shall at last be brought back to the God of their fathers,

and to their Messiah. **Pale** – Through fear of their enemies.

23. He seeth – When the believing seed of Jacob shall see those children, whom they have begotten to God, by the gospel, even the Gentiles. **The work** – The children, not of the flesh, but of the promise, whom I, by my almighty grace, have regenerated. **In the midst** – Incorporated with the Jews, into one and the same body. **Shall sanctify** – They shall glorify God, with them and for them.

24. That erred – Those Gentiles who erred from God's truth. **Murmured** – They that murmured at God's faithful teachers, shall now receive God's truth in the love of it.

Chapter 30

The prophet threatens the people for their confidence in Egypt (1–7)

And contempt of God's word (8–11)

Wherefore they shall be destroyed (12–17)

God's mercies towards the church (18–26)

God's wrath and the peoples joy in the destruction of Assyria (27–33)

The prophet threatens the people for their confidence in Egypt (1–7)

1. The rebellious – The Jews. **Take counsel** – That consult together. **Cover** – That seek protection. **But not** – Not such as by my spirit, speaking in my word, I have required them to do. **That they may add** – That unto all their sins, they may add distrust of my power and mercy, and put confidence in an arm of flesh.

2. Asked – Either by the priests or prophets.

4. His princes – The princes of Judah. **Hanes** – An eminent city of Egypt.

5. They – Both the messengers, and they who sent them.

6. The burden – The treasures, which were carried upon asses or camels, into Egypt, which lay southward from Judea. **The land of trouble** – Egypt, so called prophetically. **From whence** – This may be understood properly, but withal, seems to design the craft and cruelty of that people. **They** – The Jews. **Their riches** – To procure their assistance. **Bunches** – Upon the backs.

7. To her – To Jerusalem or Judah. **Sit still** – It is safer and better for them to sit quietly at home, seeking to me for help.

And contempt of God's word (8–11)

8. Write – This warning. **Before** – In their presence. **Note it** – So this was to be written twice over, once in a table, to be hanged up in some public place, that all present might read it; and again, in a book, that it might be kept for the use of posterity. **The time to come** – As a witness for me and against them.

11. Cause – Do not trouble us with harsh messages from God.

Wherefore they shall be destroyed (12–17)

12. And trust – In the wealth which you have gotten by oppression, and in your perverse course of sending to Egypt for help.

13. This iniquity – Of trusting to Egypt, shall be like a wall which is high, but swelling forth in some parts, which, upon the least accident, falls down suddenly.

14. He – God.

15. In returning – To God. **Quietness** – In sitting still, and quieting your minds. **Confidence** – Placed upon me, and my promises.

17. 'Till – 'Till you be destroyed, and but a few of you left.

God's mercies towards the church (18–26)

18. Wait – Patiently expect your repentance. **Exalted** – He will work gloriously. **Judgment** – Or mercy. **That wait** – In his way, with faith and patience.

19. Shall dwell – After a set time, they shall return to Jerusalem, and have a fixed abode. This was in part accomplished upon their return from Babylon; but more fully in the times of the gospel, when many of them were, and the whole body of them shall be brought into Christ's church.

21. Shall hear – Thou shalt hear the voice of God's word and spirit. **Behind thee** – A metaphor borrowed from shepherds, who use to follow their sheep, and recall them when they go out of the way.

22. Defile – To shew your contempt of it. **Covering** – The leaves or plates wherewith their images were frequently covered. **Ornament** – It was a costly and glorious robe.

23. Bread – Which shall be the fruit of thy own land and labour: and excellent for quality, which is called, fat, Deut 32:14, and abundant for quantity.

24. Clean provender – There should be such plenty of corn, that the very beasts, instead of straw, should eat corn; and that not in the ear, or with the straw, but the pure grain.

25. Hill – Which is commonly dry and barren. **In the day** – When God shall destroy the enemies of his people. **The towers** – The mighty potentates, who fought against God's people.

26. Sevenfold – As if the light of seven days were combined together in one. **Healeth** – When God shall effectually cure the wounds of his people, making Israel and Judah to be one, and making Jew and Gentile to be one fold under one shepherd.

God's wrath and the peoples joy in the destruction of Assyria (27–33)

27. Behold – Here he gives them an earnest of those greater mercies in times to come, by assuring them of the approaching destruction of the Assyrian forces. **The name** – The Lord himself. **From far** – From a remote place: even from heaven. **Heavy** – He will inflict heavy judgments upon them. **Indignation** – He hath pronounced a severe sentence against them, and will give command for the execution of it.

28. His breath – God's anger. **A stream** – Coming from him as vehemently, as a mighty torrent of waters. **To sift** – To shake and scatter, as it were with a sieve. **The nations** – The Assyrian army, which was made up of several nations. **With** – Not with an ordinary sieve, which casteth away the chaff only, but with a sieve, which should shake them so long and so vehemently, as to cast away altogether. **A bridle** – God will over-rule them by his powerful providence. **To err** – Whereas other bridles guide into the right way, this shall turn them out of the way, by giving them up to their own foolish counsels, which shall bring them to certain ruin.

29. A song – You shall have songs of praise. **The night** – He seems to have a particular respect to the solemnity of the Passover, in which they spent some considerable part of the night in rejoicing, and singing psalms before the Lord. **As when** – Like the joy of one that is going up to the solemn feasts with music.

30. His voice – His thunder, metaphorically taken for some terrible judgment. **The lightning** – Upon the Assyrian. **With** – With great wrath; which is signified by heaping so many words of the same signification together.

32. The rod – Heb. the founded rod, the judgment of God, called a founded rod, because it was firmly established, by God's immutable purpose. **Him** – Upon the Assyrian. **With harps** – Their destruction shall be celebrated by God's people, with joy and music, and songs of praise. **Of shaking** – Or, shaking of the hand, of which kind of shaking this Hebrew word is constantly used. God will fight against them, and destroy them by his own hand. **With it** – With the army of the Assyrians.

33. Tophet – This was a place near Jerusalem, in which the idolatrous Israelites used to offer up their children to Moloch. It may be put, for any place of torment; and particularly it is put for hell. **For the king** – For the king of Assyria. **Fire** – He alludes to the ancient custom, of burning sacrifices, and particularly of burning children to Moloch. **The breath** – The immediate hand of God, or his word of anger. **Brimstone** – He seems to allude to that shower of fire and brimstone, Gen 19:24.

Chapter 31

The folly and punishment of trusting in Egypt (1–3)

God will fight for Jerusalem if they will turn unto him (4–7)

The fall of Assyria (8, 9)

The folly and punishment of trusting in Egypt (1–3)

1. Horses – For Egypt had many and choice horses.

2. He is safe – You think you are safe, in engaging the Egyptians; but God is not inferior to them in wisdom or strength, and therefore you have done foolishly, in preferring them before him, who will execute his judgments upon you, notwithstanding all the Egyptians can do. **The help** – The helpers, as it is explained in the next verse.

3. Flesh – Weak and frail.

God will fight for Jerusalem if they will return to him (4–7)

4. For – Although you have done evil in sending to Egypt for help, yet the Lord himself will, of his own grace, give you that help which you do not deserve.

5. As birds – Which come from above, and so cannot be kept off; which fly swiftly, and engage resolutely, when their young ones are in danger. **Passing over** – The destroying angel shall pass over Jerusalem.

The fall of Assyria (8, 9)

8. The sword – Not of any man, but of an angel. **Discomfited** – Heb. shall melt away, a great part of them being destroyed by the angel; and the hearts of the rest melting for fear.

9. He – Sennacherib shall flee away, from Jerusalem, to his strong city of Nineveh. **The ensign** – Of the Lord's ensign, which he hath lifted up against them. **Whose fire** – Who is, and will appear to be in Zion, like a fire to defend his people, and to consume their enemies.

Chapter 32

Christ's kingdom and its blessings (1–8)

Careless women, shall be troubled (9–11)

And the land laid waste (12–14)

Until a restoration (16–20)

Christ's kingdom and its blessings (1–8)

1. Behold – This seems to be a distinct prophecy from the former, and delivered before that which is related in the former chapters. The prophecies are not always set down in that order, in which the prophets delivered them. The foregoing prophecy was delivered, not in the time of Ahaz for he sent to the Assyrian, not the Egyptian, for help; it was Hezekiah, who rebelled against the king of Assyria, and was too prone to trust upon the staff of Egypt. But this seems to have been delivered in the time of Ahaz. **A king** – Hezekiah, a type of Christ, and Christ typified by him.

2. A man – Each of his princes. **A hiding place** – Unto the people under their government. **The wind** – From the rage and violence of evil men. **As rivers** – No less refreshing. **As the shadow** – In a dry and scorched country, which is called weary, because it makes travellers weary; as death is called pale in other authors, because it makes mens faces pale.

3. The eyes – The people, they shall not shut their eyes and ears against the good counsels and examples of their religious king and rulers, as they have done formerly: both princes and people shall be reformed.

4. The rash – Who were hasty in judging of things; which is an argument of ignorance and folly. **The tongue** – That used to speak of the things of God, darkly, and doubtfully; which though it was in part fulfilled in Hezekiah, yet was truly and fully accomplished only by Christ, who wrought this wonderful change in an innumerable company both of Jews and Gentiles.

5. The vile – Base and worthless men. **Liberal** – Shall no longer be reputed honourable, because of their high and honourable places, but wickedness shall be discovered where ever it is, and virtue manifested and rewarded. **The churl** – The sordid and covetous man; but under this one vice, all vices are understood, as under the opposite virtue of bountifulness; all virtues are comprehended.

6. Villainy – Men shall no longer be miscalled; for every one will discover what he is by his words and actions. **Will work** – He will, from time to time, be advising wickedness, that he may execute it when he hath opportunity. **To practise** – To do bad things, tho' with a pretence of religion and justice. **To utter** – To pass unjust sentence, directly contrary to the command of God. **Cause the drink** – Whereby they take away the bread and the drink of the poor.

7. Lying words – With false and unrighteous decrees. **Even** – When their cause is just and good.

Careless women, shall be troubled (9–11)

9. Ye – That indulge yourselves in idleness and luxury. **Careless** – Who are insensible of your sin and danger.

10. The vintage shall fail – During the time

of the Assyrian invasion. **The gathering** – Of the other fruits of the earth.

11. Strip – Put off your ornaments.

And the land laid waste (12–14)

12. The teats – For the pleasant and fruitful fields, which like teats yielded you plentiful and excellent nourishment.

13. Yea – Upon that ground, where now your houses stand, in which you take your fill of mirth and pleasure.

14. Forsaken – Of God, and given up into their enemies hands. **A joy** – Desolate places, in which wild asses delight to be.

Until a restoration (16–20)

15. Until – Until the time come, in which God will pour, or, as the Hebrew word properly signifies, reveal, evidently and plentifully pour out his spirit from heaven upon his people, which was fully accomplished in the days of the Messiah. **The fruitful field** – God's people who were desolate, shall be revived and flourish, and their flourishing enemies shall be brought to destruction.

16. Judgment – Just judgment. **Righteousness** – Justice shall be executed in all the parts of the land.

17. The work – The effect of this shall be prosperity. **Quietness** – Tranquillity, both of mind and outward estate. **Assurance** – Of God's mercy, and the fulfilling of his promises.

19. It shall hail – As my blessings shall be poured down upon my people, who, from a wilderness, are turned into a fruitful field, so my judgments shall fall upon them, who were a fruitful field, but are turned into a forest, upon the unbelieving and rebellious Jews. **The city** – Jerusalem, which, though now it was the seat of God's worship and people, yet he foresaw, would be the great enemy of the Messiah. **Low** – Heb. shall be humbled with humiliation: shall be greatly humbled, or brought very low.

20. Blessed – As the barren forest shall be destroyed, so the fruitful field shall be improved, and bring forth much fruit; which is signified by a declaration of the blessedness of them that sow in it. **Waters** – In all moist grounds, which are like to yield good fruit. But this also is to be understood of the times of the gospel, and of the great and happy success of the ministers of it. **The ox** – Which they employed in plowing and sowing the ground.

Chapter 33

The destruction of the enemies of the church, who are derided (1–14)

The safety and privileges of the godly (15–24)

The destruction of the enemies of the church, who are derided (1–14)

1. To thee – Sennacherib, who wasted the land of Judah.

2. O Lord – The prophet contemplating the judgment which was now coming upon God's people, directs his prayer to God for them. **Their arm** – Our arm or strength. The change of persons is frequent in prophetical writings. **Every morning** – When we offer the morning sacrifice, and call upon thee: which yet is not meant exclusively, as if he did not desire God's help at other times; but comprehensively, the morning being put for the whole day. The sense is, help us speedily and continually.

3. The noise – Which the angel shall make in destroying the army. **The people** – Those of the army, who escaped that stroke. **The nations** – The people of divers nations, which made up this army.

4. Your spoil – That treasure which you have raked together, by spoiling divers people. **Gathered** – By the Jews at Jerusalem, when you flee away. **Like the caterpillar** – As caterpillars gather and devour the fruits of the earth. **As locusts** – As locusts, especially when they are armed by commission from God, come with great force, and run hither and thither.

5. Exalted – By the destruction of so potent an army; and by the defence of this people.

6. Thy times – He turns his speech to Hezekiah. Thy throne shall be established upon the sure foundations of wisdom and justice. **And strength** – Thy strong salvation. **The fear** – Thy chief treasure is in promoting the fear and worship of God.

7. Behold – That the mercy promised might be duly magnified, he makes a lively representation of their great danger and distress. **The ambassadors** – Whom he shall send to beg peace of the Assyrian. **Shall weep** – Because they cannot obtain their desires.

8. The covenant – Sennacherib broke his faith, given to Hezekiah, of departing for a sum of money, 2Kings 18:14,17. **Cities** – The defended cities of Judah, which he contemned, and easily took.

9. Mourneth – Being desolate and neglected. **Hewn** – By the Assyrians. **Bashan** – Two places eminent for fertility, are spoiled of their fruits.

11. Stubble – Instead of solid corn. Your great hopes and designs, shall be utterly disappointed. **Your breath** – Your rage against my people shall bring ruin upon yourselves.

12. The people – Shall be burnt as easily and effectually as chalk is burned to lime.

14. The sinners – This is spoken of the Jews. The prophet having foretold the deliverance of God's people, and the destruction of their enemies, gives a lively representation of the unbelieving condition, in which the Jews were, before their deliverance came. **Who** – How shall we be able to endure, or avoid the wrath of that God, who is a consuming fire; who is now about to destroy us utterly by the Assyrians, and will afterwards burn us with unquenchable fire?

The safety and privileges of the godly (15–24)

15. He – Who is just in all his dealings. **From hearing** – Who will not hearken to any counsels, tending to shed innocent blood. **From seeing** – That abhors the very sight of sin committed by others, and guards his eyes from beholding occasions of sin.

16. On high – Out of the reach of danger. **His waters** – God will furnish him with all necessaries.

17. The king – First Hezekiah, and then Christ, triumphing over all enemies, and ruling his own people with righteousness. **Very far** – Thou shalt not be shut up in Jerusalem, but shalt have free liberty to go abroad with honour and safety.

18. Thine heart – This is a thankful acknowledgment of deliverance from their former terrors and miseries. **Where** – These words they spoke in the time of their distress. The scribe, whom we call muster-master, was to make and keep a list of the soldiers, and to call them together as occasion required: the receiver, received and laid out the money for the charges of the war; and he that counted the towers, surveyed all the parts of the city, and considered what towers or fortifications were to be made or repaired. And unto these several officers the people resorted, with great distraction and confusion.

19. A fierce – That fierce and warlike people, whom thou hast seen with terror, near the walls of Jerusalem, thou shalt see no more. **A people** – A foreign nation, whose language is unknown to thee.

20. Look upon – Contemplate Zion's glorious and peculiar privileges. **Solemnities** – This was the chief part of Zion's glory, that God was solemnly worshipped, and the solemn assemblies and feasts kept in her. **Quiet** – This was but imperfectly fulfilled in the literal Zion; but clearly and fully in the mystical Zion, the church of God, in the times of the gospel.

21. There – In and about Zion. **Rivers** – Tho' we have nothing but a small and contemptible brook to defend us; yet God will be as sure a defence to us, as if we were surrounded with great rivers. **No galley** – No ships of the enemies shall be able to come into this river to annoy them.

22. Is judge – To plead our cause against our enemies. **Lawgiver** – Our chief governor, to whom it belongs, to give laws, and to defend his people.

23. Tacklings – He directs his speech to the Assyrians; and having designed their army under the notion of a gallant ship, ver.21, he here represents their undone condition, by the metaphor of a ship, tossed in a tempestuous sea, having her cables broke, and all her tacklings loose, so that she could have no benefit of her masts and sails; and therefore is quickly swallowed up. **The lame** – They shall leave so many spoils behind them, that there shall be enough left for the lame, who come last to the spoil.

24. The inhabitant – Of Jerusalem. **Sick** – Shall have no cause to complain of any sickness or calamity. **Forgiven** – They shall not only receive from me a glorious temporal deliverance; but, which is infinitely better, the pardon of all their sins, and all those spiritual and everlasting blessings, which attend upon that mercy.

Chapter 34

God's fury and wrath against his church's enemies (1–10)

Their land utterly desolate (11–15)

The certainty hereof, and duration (16, 17)

God's fury and wrath against his church's enemies (1–10)

2. All nations – Not only upon the Assyrians, but on all enemies of my people.

3. Cast out – Into the fields.

4. Dissolved – The sun, moon, and stars. So great shall be the confusion and consternation of mankind, as if all the frame of the creation were broken into pieces. It is usual for prophetic writers, both in the Old and New Testament, to represent great and general calamities, in such words and phrases, as properly agree to the day of judgment; as on the contrary, the glorious deliverances of God's people, in such expressions, as properly agree to the resurrection from the dead.

5. Bathed – In the blood of these people. **Heaven** – Where God dwells; in which this is said to be done, because it was there decreed and appointed. **Idumea** – Upon the Edomites, who, tho' they were nearly related to the Israelites, yet were their implacable enemies. But these are named for all the enemies of God's church, of whom they were an eminent type. **The people** – Whom I have cursed, and devoted to utter destruction, as the word properly signifies.

6. The sword – The metaphor is taken from a great glutton, who is almost insatiable. **Rams** – By lambs, and goats, and rams, he means people of all ranks and conditions, high and low, rich and poor. **Bozrah** – A chief city of Edom, and a type of those cities which should be most opposite to God's people.

7. The unicorns – It is confessed, this was a beast of great strength and fierceness; and it is used in this place to signify their princes and potentates, who shall be humbled and cast down. **Them** – With the lambs, and goats, and rams. **Fatness** – With the fat of the slain sacrifices, mingled with it.

8. For – This is the time which God hath fixed, to avenge the cause of his persecuted people.

9. The land – Idumea shall be dealt with, as Sodom and Gomorrah were.

10. For ever – It shall remain as a spectacle of God's vengeance to all succeeding ages.

Their land utterly desolate (11–15)

11. Dwell – It shall be entirely possessed by those creatures which delight in deserts and waste places. **Stretch** – He shall use the line, or the stone or plummet joined to it, not to build them, but to mark them out to destruction, as workmen commonly use them to mark what they are to pull down.

12. None – They shall not find any willing to undertake the government. **Nothing** – Shall have no courage or strength left in them.

The certainty hereof, and duration (16, 17)

16. Seek – When this judgment is executed, if you pursue this prophecy, you will find, that all things exactly come to pass, as I have told you. **His** – My spirit, hath brought all these creatures together, as he formerly brought the creatures to Adam, and to Noah, by an instinct which he put into them.

17. Divided – He hath divided the land to them, as it were by lot and line, as Canaan was divided among the Israelites.

Chapter 35

The joyful flourishing of Christ's kingdom (1, 2)

The weak he strengthens and comforts (3, 4)

His miracles (5, 6)

The prosperity and peace of his people (7–10)

The joyful flourishing of Christ's kingdom (1, 2)

1. The solitary place – Emmanuel's land, or the seat of God's church and people, which for-

merly was despised like a wilderness, and which the rage of their enemies had brought to desolation, shall flourish exceedingly.

2. The excellency – The wilderness shall be as pleasant and fruitful as Lebanon, and Carmel, and Sharon. **They** – The inhabitants of the wilderness aforesaid. **The glory** – The glorious discoveries of God's power and goodness.

The weak he strengthens and comforts (3, 4)

3. Strengthen – Ye ministers of God, comfort and encourage God's people, who are now ready to faint.

4. Your God – Tho' he seems to be departed, he will come to you, and abide with you. He will shortly come in the flesh, to execute vengeance upon the enemies of God.

His miracles (5, 6)

5. Then – The poor Gentiles, who before were blind and deaf, shall now have the eyes and ears of their minds opened to see God's works, and to hear and receive his word.

The prosperity and peace of his people (7–10)

7. Streams – The most dry and barren places shall be made moist and fruitful; which is principally meant of the plentiful effusion of God's grace upon such persons and nations, as had been wholly destitute of it. **Rushes** – Those dry and parched deserts, in which dragons have their abode, shall yield abundance of grass, and reeds, and rushes, which grow only in moist ground.

8. A way – The high-way and the way are not to be taken for two different ways, but for one and the same way, even a causey, which is raised ground, and a way. **Holiness** – The people shall be all righteous. **For those** – But this way shall be appropriated to those persons abovementioned; the weak, and blind, and lame, whom God will lead and save. **Though fools** – The way shall be so plain and strait, that even the most foolish travellers cannot easily mistake it.

Chapter 36

Sennacherib invades Judah (1)

He sends Rabshakeh, who by his blasphemous persuasions tempts Hezekiah to despair, and the people to revolt (2–22)

The history related here, and in the three following chapters, is, almost in the same words contained 2Kings 18, 19, 20. It is inserted here, to explain and confirm some of the foregoing predictions. It may seem to have first been written by this prophet, and from him taken into the book of Kings, to complete that history.

Chapter 37

Hezekiah mourns and sends to Isaiah to pray for them (1–5)

He comforts them (6, 7)

Sennacherib called away against the king of Ethiopia, sends a blasphemous letter to Hezekiah (8–13)

His prayer (14–20)

Isaiah's prophecy (21–35)

An angel slays the Assyrians (36)

Sennacherib is slain at Nineveh by his own sons (37, 38)

Chapter 38

Hezekiah in his sickness receives from Isaiah a message of death (1)

By prayer (2, 3) hath his life lengthened; the sun goeth backward for a sign thereof (4–8)

His song of praise to God (9–20)

13. I reckon – When I could not rest all the night even 'till morning, my thoughts were presaging that God would instantly break me to pieces, and the like thoughts followed me from morning 'till evening.

16. By these – By thy promises, and thy performance of them; therefore it is not strange, that one word of God hath brought me back from the jaws of death.

18. Praise – The dead are not capable of glorifying thy name among men upon earth. They cannot expect nor receive the accomplishment of thy promised goodness in the land of the living.

20. Was ready – Was a present help.

Chapter 39

The king of Babylon sends ambassadors with letters and a present to Hezekiah, who shews them his treasures (1, 2)

Isaiah foretells the Babylonish captivity (4–7)

His resignation (8)

Chapter 40

The prophet having now foretold the Babylonian captivity, chap.39:6,7, does here arm his people against it by the consideration of

their certain deliverance out of it, and their blessed condition after it, as in other things so especially in the coming of the Messiah, and the great and glorious privileges conferred upon God's church and people in his days.

The preaching of the gospel by John the Baptist and the apostles (1–11)

The power and wisdom of God in governing the world (12–17)

The folly of idolatry (18–26)

God knows the state of his people, and both can and will protect them (27–31)

The preaching of the gospel by John the Baptist and the apostles (1–11)

1. Ye – Ye prophets and ministers.

2. Warfare – The time of her captivity, and misery. **Double** – Not twice as much as her sins deserved, but abundantly enough to answer God's design in this chastisement, which was to humble and reform them, and to warn others by their example.

3. The voice – An abrupt speech. Methinks I hear a voice. **Wilderness** – This immediately relates to the deliverance of the Jews out of Babylon, and smoothing their passage from thence to Judea, which lay through a great wilderness; but principally to their redemption by the Messiah, whose coming was ushered in by the cry of John the Baptist, in the wilderness. **Prepare ye the way** – You to whom this work belongs. He alludes to the custom of princes who send pioneers before them to prepare the way through which they are to pass. The meaning is, God shall by his spirit so dispose mens hearts, and by his providence so order the affairs of the world, as to make way for the accomplishment of his promise. This was eminently fulfilled, when Christ, who was, and is God, blessed for ever, came into the world in a visible manner.

6. Cry – God speaks unto his ministers. **He** – The prophet. **All flesh** – The prophet having foretold glorious things, confirms the certainty of them, by representing the vast difference between the nature, and word, and work of men and of God. All that men are or have, yea, their highest accomplishments, are but like the grass of the field, weak and vanishing, soon brought to nothing; but God's word is like himself, immutable and irresistible: and therefore as the mouth of the Lord, and not of man, hath spoken these things, so doubt not but they shall be fulfilled.

9. Zion – Zion or Jerusalem is the publisher, and the cities of Judah the hearers. **Get up** – That thy voice may be better heard. **Afraid** – Lest thou shouldest be found a false prophet.

Say – To all my people in the several places of their abode. **Behold** – Take notice of this wonderful work, and glorious appearance of your God.

10. **His arm** – He shall need no succours, for his own power shall be sufficient to govern his people, and to destroy his adversaries. **His reward** – He comes furnished with recommences as well of blessings for his friends, as of vengeance for his enemies. **His work** – He carries on his work effectually: for that is said in scripture to be before a man which is in his power.

The power and wisdom of God in governing the world (12–17)

12. **Who hath** – Who can do this but God? And this discourse of God's infinite power and wisdom, is added to give them the greater assurance, that God was able to do the wonderful things, he had promised.

13. **Who** – Who did God either need or take to advise him in any of his works, either of creation or the government of the world.

15. **Are counted** – By him, and in comparison of him. **The dust** – Which accidentally cleaves to the balance, but makes no alteration in the weight. **The isles** – Those numerous and vast countries, to which they went from Judea by sea, which are commonly called isles.

16. **Lebanon** – If men were to offer a sacrifice agreeable to his infinite excellency, the whole forest of Lebanon could not afford either a sufficient number of beasts to be sacrificed: or, a sufficient quantity of wood to consume the sacrifice.

The folly of idolatry (18–26)

18. **To whom** – This is a proper inference from the foregoing discourse of God's infinite greatness; from whence he takes occasion to shew both the folly of those that make mean and visible representations of God, and the utter inability of men or idols to give any opposition to God.

19. **Melteth** – He melts metal into a mould, which afterwards is graven or carved to make it more exact.

20. **He** – That can hardly procure money to buy a sacrifice. **Chooseth** – He is so mad upon his idols, that he will find money to procure the choicest materials, and the best artist to make his idol. **An image** – Which after all this cost, cannot stir one step out of its place to give you any help.

21. **Known** – God to be the only true God, the maker and governor of the world.

22. **Sitteth** – Far above this round earth, even in the highest heavens; from whence he looketh down upon the earth, where men appear to him like grasshoppers. As here we have the circle of the earth, so elsewhere we read of the circle of heaven, Job 22:14, and of the circle of the deep, or sea, Prov 8:27, because the form of the heaven, and earth and sea is circular. **Spreadeth** – For the benefit of the earth and of mankind, that all parts might partake of its comfortable influences.

24. **Sown** – They shall take no root, for planting and sowing are in order to taking root. They shall not continue and flourish, as they have vainly imagined, but shall be rooted up and perish.

26. **Bringeth** – That at first brought them out of nothing, and from day to day brings them forth, making them to rise and set in their appointed times. **Faileth** – Either to appear when he calls them; or to do the work to which he sends them.

God knows the state of his people, and both can and will protect them (27–31)

27. **What** – Why dost thou give way to such jealousies concerning thy God, of whose infinite power and wisdom, and goodness, there are such evident demonstrations. **Is hid** – He takes no notice of my prayers and tears, and sufferings, but suffers mine enemies to abuse me at their pleasure. This complaint is uttered in the name of the people, being prophetically supposed to be in captivity. **Judgment** – My cause. God has neglected to plead my cause, and to give judgment for me against mine enemies.

30. **The youths** – The youngest and strongest men, left to themselves.

31. **Wait** – That rely upon him. **Renew** – Shall grow stronger and stronger.

Chapter 41

God called Cyrus, and was with him, the nations idolatrous (1–8)

Israel encouraged by promises of safety and deliverance (9–20)

The vanity of idols (21–24)

Redemption by Christ (25–29)

God called Cyrus, and was with him, the nations idolatrous (1–8)

1. **Keep silence** – Attend diligently to my plea. **Islands** – By islands he means countries remote from Judea, inhabited by the idolatrous Gentiles. **Renew** – Strengthen themselves to maintain their cause against me; let them unite all their strength together. **Near** – Unto me that we may stand together, and plead our cause, and I will give them free liberty to say what they can on their own behalf.

2. **Who** – Was it not my work alone? **Raised** –

Into being and power, stirring up his spirit, and strengthening him to the work. **The man** – Cyrus. **The east** – Persia was directly eastward, both from Judea and from Babylon. He was raised up by God in an eminent manner. And although these things were yet to come; yet the prophet speaks of them as if they were already past. And by this instance he pleads his cause against the Gentiles; because this was an evident proof of God's almighty power, and of the vanity of idols, which eminently appeared in the destruction of the Babylonians, who were a people mad upon their idols. **Called him** – To march after him, and under God's banner against Babylon.

3. Pursued – Went on in the pursuit with ease and safety. **Even** – Through unknown paths.

4. Calling – Them out of nothing, giving them breath and being: disposing and employing them as he sees fit. **From the beginning** – All persons and generations of mankind from the beginning of the world. **I** – Who was before all things even from eternity, and shall be unto eternity.

5. The isles – Even remote countries. **Saw** – Discerned the mighty work of God in delivering his people, and overthrowing their enemies. **Feared** – Lest they should be involved in the same calamity. **Came** – They gathered themselves together.

7. Fastened it – To the wall or pillar.

Israel encouraged by promises of safety and deliverance (9–20)

9. Thou – Thou Israel, whom I took to myself, and brought hither in the loins of thy father Abraham, from a remote country. **Called thee** – From the midst of many great persons among whom he lived in Chaldea. **Chosen** – I have chosen thee and thy seed through all generations.

11. Confounded – Because the mischief which they contrived against thee shall fall upon themselves.

13. Will hold – Will enable thee to vanquish all thine enemies.

14. Thou worm – Who art weak in thyself, and trodden under foot by thy proud enemies.

15. An instrument – Such as were usual in those times and places. **The mountains** – The great and lofty potentates of the world.

16. Fan – When thou hast beaten them as small as chaff. **In the Holy One** – For to him, thou shalt ascribe thy victory.

18. In high places – Upon the mountains where by the course of nature there are no rivers. **The dry land** – Their people who are like a dry and barren wilderness. I will abundantly water with my blessings.

19. The box tree – Trees which are both useful and pleasant to the eye, and giving a good shadow to the traveller. But what particular trees these Hebrew words signify, is not certainly known.

The vanity of idols (21–24)

22. Them – The idols. **Former things** – Such things as should shortly come to pass. **The latter end** – Whether the events answer to their predictions.

23. Do good – Protect your worshippers whom I intend to destroy, and destroy my people whom I intend to save. **That** – That I and my people may be astonished, and forced to acknowledge your godhead.

24. Your work – Your operations are like your beings: there is no reality in your beings, nor efficacy in your actions.

Redemption by Christ (25–29)

25. Raised – Cyrus, might be said to come from the north, because he was a Mede by his mother, as he was a Persian by his father; or because a great part of his army was gathered out of Media, which was northward, in reference to Judea, and because Darius the Mede was joined with him in this expedition. **Proclaim** – This Cyrus did in express, emphatic terms, Ezra 1:1,2. **As on mortar** – Treading them down, as easily as a man treads down mortar.

26. Who – Which of your idols could foretell such things as these from the beginning of the world unto this day? **Before-time** – Before the things come to pass. **Righteous** – His cause is good: he is a God indeed. **Heareth** – Because you are dumb and cannot speak.

27. The first – I who am the first, do and will foretell to my people things to come. **Them** – I also represent future things as if they were present. By them he means things which are to come. **One** – Messengers, who shall foretell the good tidings of their deliverance from captivity.

28. For – I looked to see if I could find any man that could foretell future events. **No man** – Not any, of the idols; for the word man is sometimes used by the Hebrews of brute creatures, and even of lifeless things. **No counsellor** – Though these idols were often consulted, yet none of them were able to give any solid and certain advice concerning future things.

29. Behold – This is the conclusion of the dispute, but under these he comprehends all images whatsoever. **Wind** – Empty and unsatisfying things. **Confusion** – Confused and useless things, like that rude heap in the beginning of God's creation, of which this very word is used, Gen 1:2.

Chapter 42

The person and office of Christ appointed by the Father (1–9)

A new song to God for his gospel, among the Gentiles (10–16)

The idolatry of the Heathen, and obstinacy of the Jews (17–25)

The person and office of Christ appointed by the Father (1–9)

1. Behold – The prophet having given one eminent instance of God's certain fore-knowledge, in the deliverance of the Jews by Cyrus, now adds another more eminent example of it, by foretelling the coming of the Messiah. This place therefore is expressly interpreted of Christ, Matt 12:18. And to him, and to him only, all the particulars following, truly and evidently belong. **Whom** – Whom I will enable to do and suffer all those things which belong to his office. **Elect** – Chosen by me to this great work. **Delighteth** – Both for himself and for all his people, being fully satisfied with that sacrifice, which he shall offer up to me. **Bring forth** – Shall publish or shew, as this word is translated, Matt 12:18. **Judgment** – The law, and will, and counsel of God, concerning man's salvation. **Gentiles** – Not only to the Jews, but to the Heathen nations.

2. Cry – In a way of contention, or ostentation. **Lift** – His voice. **Heard** – As contentious and vain-glorious persons frequently do.

3. Break – Christ will not deal rigorously with those that come to him, but he will use all gentleness, cherishing the smallest beginnings of grace, comforting and healing wounded consciences. **Quench** – That wick of a candle which is almost extinct, he will not quench, but revive and kindle it again. **Judgment** – The law of God, or the doctrine of the gospel, which he will bring forth, unto, with, or according to truth, that is, truly and faithfully.

4. 'Till – 'Till he has established his law or doctrine, among the nations of the earth. **Isles** – The countries remote from Judea, shall gladly receive his doctrine.

5. He – This description of God's infinite power, is seasonably added, to give them assurance of the certain accomplishment of his promises.

6. Called thee – To declare my righteousness, or faithfulness. **With-hold** – Will give thee counsel and strength for the work. **Give thee** – To be the mediator in whom my covenant of grace is confirmed with mankind. **The people** – Of all people, not only of Jews but Gentiles. **A light** – To enlighten them with true and saving knowledge.

8. The Lord – Heb. Jehovah: who have all being in and of myself, and give being to all my creatures. The everlasting, and unchangeable, and omnipotent God, who therefore both can, and will fulfil all my promises.

9. I tell you – That when they come to pass, you may know that I am God, and that this is my work.

A new song to God for his gospel, among the Gentiles (10–16)

10. Sing – Upon this new and great occasion, the salvation of the world by Christ. **From the end** – All nations from one end of the earth to another. **Ye** – You that go by sea carry these glad tidings from Judea, where Christ was born, and lived, and died, and published the gospel, unto the remotest parts of the earth.

11. The wilderness – Those parts of the world which are now desolate and forsaken of God, and barren of all good fruits. **Kedar** – The Arabians: who were an Heathen and barbarous people, and are put for all nations. **Mountains** – Who are commonly more savage and ignorant than others.

12. The islands – In the remotest parts of the world, as well as in Arabia, which was near to them.

13. Go forth – To battle. **Stir up** – He shall stir up his strength, and anger against the obstinate enemies of his Son and gospel. **Roar** – As a lion doth upon his prey, and as soldiers do when they begin the battle.

14. Long – I have for many ages suffered the devil and his servants, to prevail in the world, but now I will bring forth and accomplish that glorious work which I have long conceived in my mind; yea, I will suddenly destroy the incorrigible enemies of my truth.

15. Hills – My most lofty and flourishing enemies. **Dry up** – I will remove all impediments out of the way.

16. The blind – The Gentiles. **By a way** – By the way of truth, which hitherto has been hidden from them, yea, I will take away all hindrances; I will direct then in the right way; I will enlighten their dark minds, and rectify their perverse wills and affections, until I have brought theirs to the end of their journey.

The idolatry of the Heathen, and obstinacy of the Jews (17–25)

18. Hear – O you, whosoever you are, who resist this clear light.

19. My servant – The Jews, who will not receive their Messiah. **Messenger** – My messengers, the singular number being put for the plural, namely the priests and other teachers whom I have appointed to instruct my people. **The Lord's servant** – As the most eminent teachers and rulers of the Jews, who were called and obliged to be the Lord's servants, in a special manner.

20. Heareth not – Thou dost not seriously consider the plain word, and the wonderful works of God.

21. Well pleased – Although God might justly destroy thee suddenly, yet he will patiently wait for thy repentance, that he may be gracious; and that not for thy sake, but for the glory of his own faithfulness, in fulfilling that covenant, which he made with thy pious progenitors. **Magnify** – He will maintain the honour of his law, and therefore is not forward to destroy you, who profess the true religion, lest his law should upon that occasion be exposed to contempt.

22. But – But not withstanding this respect which God hath to his people, he hath severely scourged you for your sins. **Hid** – They have been taken in snares made by their own hands, and by God's just judgment cast into dungeons and prisons. **None** – None afforded them help.

25. Fury – Most grievous judgments. **Yet** – They were secure and stupid under God's judgments.

Chapter 43

Promises to protect and enlarge the church (1–5)

God appeals to them as witnesses of his power and knowledge (6–13)

He foretells the destruction of Babylon, and a new deliverance of his people (14–21)

whose sins against God's mercies render them inexcusable (22–28)

Promises to protect and enlarge the church (1–5)

1. But – Notwithstanding thy gross insensibleness, I will deal mercifully with thee. **Created** – That made thee his people, and that in so miraculous a manner as if he had created thee a second time. **Redeemed** – From the Egyptians. **Called thee** – By the name of God's people, which was as proper and peculiar to them, as the name of Israel.

3. I gave Egypt – This was fulfilled when the king of Assyria, Esar-haddon, who designed to revenge his father's disgrace, upon the Jews, was diverted and directed by God to employ his forces against Egypt, and Ethiopia, and Seba. **Seba** – The Sabaeans were confederate with the Ethiopians.

4. Since – From the time that I chose thee for my people, I have had an affection for thee. **Men** – As I gave up the Egyptians, so I am ready to give up others to save thee, as occasion requires.

God appeals to them as witnesses of his power and knowledge (6–13)

7. For my glory – And therefore I will glorify my power and goodness, and faithfulness in delivering them. **Formed** – I have not only created them out of nothing, but I have also formed and made them my peculiar people.

8. Bring – O ye idolatrous Gentiles, bring forth your false gods, which have eyes but see not, and ears but hear not.

9. Assembled – To plead the cause of their idols with me. **This** – This wonderful work of mine in bringing my people out of captivity. **Former things** – Such things as shall happen long before the return from the captivity, which yet your blind idols cannot foresee. **Witnesses** – Who can testify the truth of any such predictions of theirs, that they may be owned for true gods; or if they can produce no evidence of any such thing, let them confess, that what I say is truth, that I only am the true God.

10. Ye – You my people are able to witness for me, that I have given you plain demonstrations of my certain knowledge of future events. **My servant** – Cyrus who is an eminent instance and proof of God's foreknowledge: or, the Messiah, who is the most eminent witness in this cause. **Understand** – That I am the true God. **Nor after me** – The gods of the Heathens neither had a being before me nor shall continue after me: whereas the Lord is God from everlasting to everlasting; but these pretenders are but of yesterday. And withal he calls them formed gods, in a way of contempt, and to shew the ridiculousness of their pretence.

12. I – I first foretold your deliverance, and then effected it. **When** – And this I did when you did not worship any idols.

13. Yea – Before all time; from all eternity, I am God.

He foretells the destruction of Babylon, and a new deliverance of his people (14–21)

14. Sent – I have sent Cyrus against Babylon, to this very end, that he might deliver you out of captivity. **Chaldeans** – The common people of Chaldea, who make fearful outcries, as they flee away from the Persians in ships.

17. The chariot – Pharaoh and his chariots and horses, and army. **Lay down** – In the bottom of the sea. They never rose again to molest the Israelites. **Quenched** – As the wick of a candle when it is put into the water, is extinguished.

18. Remember not – Tho' your former deliverance out of Egypt was glorious: yet in comparison of that inestimable mercy of sending the Messiah, all your former deliverances are scarce worthy of your remembrance and consideration.

19. **A new thing** – Such a work as was never yet done in the world. **Now** – The scripture often speaks of things at a great distance of time, as if they were now at hand; to make us sensible of the inconsiderableness of time, and all temporal things, in comparison of God, and eternal things; upon which account it is said, that a thousand years are in God's sight but as one day.

20. **The beast** – Shall have cause, if they had abilities, to praise me for their share in this mercy. **Dragons** – Which live in dry and barren deserts.

whose sins against God's mercies render them inexcusable (22–28)

22. **For** – God called to the Gentiles to be his people, because the Jews forsook him. **Weary** – Thou hast not esteemed my service to be a privilege, but a burden and bondage.

23. **Honoured** – Either thou didst neglect sacrificing to me; or didst perform it merely out of custom or didst dishonour me, and pollute thy sacrifices by thy wicked life. **Although** – Although God had not laid such heavy burdens upon them, nor required such costly offerings, as might give them cause to be weary, nor such as idolaters did freely perform in the service of their idols.

24. **Sweet cane** – This was used in the making of that precious ointment, Exod 30:34, and for the incense, Exod 30:7. Thou hast been niggardly in my service, when thou hast spared for no cost in the service of thine idols. **Nor filled me** – Thou hast not multiplied thy thank-offerings and free-will offerings, tho' I have given thee sufficient occasion to do so. **But** – Thou hast made me to bear the load and burden of thy sins.

25. **I** – I whom thou hast thus provoked. **Mine own sake** – Not for thy merits, but my own mere goodness.

26. **Put me** – I remember nothing by which thou hast deserved my favour.

27. **Thy father** – This may be put for their forefathers; and so he tells them, that as they were sinners, so also were their progenitors, yea even the best of them. **Teachers** – Thy priests and prophets; who were their intercessors with God: and if these were transgressors, the people had no reason to fancy themselves innocent.

28. **Therefore** – I have exposed them to contempt and destruction. **Princes** – The highest and best of your priests. **Curse** – To utter destruction, to which persons or things accursed were devoted.

Chapter 44

A farther promise of spiritual blessings (1–6)

The vanity of idols, and folly of idol-makers, and worshippers (7–20)

An exhortation to praise God our Redeemer and Maker for his wisdom, truth, power, and goodness (21–28)

A farther promise of spiritual blessings (1–6)

2. **Formed thee** – From the time that I first took thee to be my people, I have been forming and fashioning thee. **Jesurun** – Another name of Jacob or Israel, given to him, Deut 32:15.

3. **Water** – Upon him that is destitute of it.

5. **Israel** – The blessing of God upon the Jews shall be so remarkable, that the Gentiles shall join them, and accept the Lord for their God.

7. **Who** – Which of all the Heathen gods. **Declare** – Shall by his powerful word cause it to be, and by his fore-knowledge declare that it shall be. **Set in order** – Orderly relate all future events in the same manner as they shall happen. **Since** – Since I first made man upon earth. **The things** – Such things as are near at hand, and such as are to come hereafter.

The vanity of idols, and folly of idol-makers, and worshippers (7–20)

8. **Ye** – Thee, O Israel, whom he bids not to fear. **Told thee** – Even from the first ages of the world. **Declared** – Have published it to the world in my sacred records. **Witnesses** – Both of my predictions, and of the exact agreeableness of events to them.

9. **Delectable things** – Their idols, in which they take so much pleasure. **They** – They that make them, are witnesses against themselves, and against their idols, because they know they are the work of their own hands. **See not** – Have neither sense nor understanding, therefore they have just cause to be ashamed of their folly, in worshipping such senseless things.

11. **Men** – They are of mankind, and therefore cannot possibly make a god. **Together** – Tho' all combine together, they shall be filled with fear and confusion, when God shall plead his cause against them.

12. **Faint** – This is mentioned as an evidence of great zeal and industry in carrying on this work; so that they forget or neglect to eat and drink.

13. **According to** – In the same comely shape and proportions which are in a living man. **House** – In the dwelling-house of him that made it.

14. **Oak** – Which afford the best and most durable timber. **Strengtheneth** – He plants, and with care and diligence improves those trees, that he or his posterity may thence have materials for their images, and those things which belong to them.

15. Fallen down – Having related the practices of idolaters, he now discovers the folly of them, that he makes his fire and his god of the same materials, distinguished only by the art of man.

17. He eateth – He dresses flesh for his eating. **Seen** – I have felt the warmth of it.

18. Not known – This shows that they have not the understanding of a man. **For he** – God. Not as if God did make men wicked; he only permits them so to be, and orders, and overrules their wickedness to his own glorious ends.

20. Ashes – An unprofitable and pernicious food, and no less unsatisfying and mischievous is the worship of idols. **Deceived heart** – A mind corrupted and deceived by deep prejudice, gross error, and especially by his own lusts. **Turned** – From the way of truth. **Deliver** – From the snares and dangers of idolatry. **Is there not** – What is this idol which I set at my right-hand, as the true God is said in scripture to be at the right-hand of his people; which I highly honour, for the most honourable place was on the right-hand; to which I look for relief and assistance, which God in scripture is said to afford to his people, by being at and holding their right-hand. What, I say, is this idol? Is it not a lie, which tho' it pretends to be a god, yet, in truth is nothing but vanity and falsehood?

An exhortation to praise God our Redeemer and Maker for his wisdom, truth, power and goodness (21–28)

21. These – These things, the deep ignorance and stupidity of idolaters. **Forgotten** – I will not forget nor forsake thee; therefore thou shalt have no need of idols.

22. As a cloud – So that there is no remnant of it left.

23. Sing – By such invitations to the senseless creatures, he signifies the transcendent greatness of this mercy, sufficient to make even the stones, if it were possible, to break forth into God's praises.

25. Liars – Of the magicians, and astrologers, who were numerous, and greatly esteemed in Babylon, and who had foretold the long continuance and prosperity of the Chaldean empire. **Mad** – With grief for the disappointment of their predictions, and their disgrace which followed it. **Turneth** – Stopping their way, and blasting their designs.

27. That saith – That with a word can dry up the sea and rivers, and remove all impediments.

28. Cyrus – Whom God here mentions by his proper name, two hundred years before he was born, that this might be an undeniable evidence of the exactness of God's fore-knowledge, and a convincing argument to conclude this dispute between God and idols. **Shepherd** – Then will I set up to be the shepherd of my people, to rescue them from wolves or tyrants, to gather them together, to rule them gently, and to provide comfortably for them.

Chapter 45

Cyrus's work and strength foretold (1–4)

God hath all power (5–12)

Will assist Cyrus (13, 14)

The mystery of providence (15)

Idols and their worshippers shall be destroyed, and God alone exalted (16–21)

The Gentiles come in to Christ (22–25)

Cyrus's work and strength foretold (1–4)

1. His anointed – His king, whom God has designed, and separated, and fitted, in all respects, for this work. **Loose** – I will take away their girdle, which was about their loins; their power and authority, whereof that was an ensign. **Gates** – The great and magnificent gates of their cities and palaces, which shall be opened to him as conqueror.

2. Go – To remove all obstructions, to destroy all them that oppose thee, and carry thee through the greatest difficulties.

3. The treasures – Such as have been long kept in dark and secret places.

4. I have – I knew, and called thee by thy name, when thou didst neither know nor think of me; nay, when thou hadst no being.

God hath all power (5–12)

5. I girded – I made thee strong and active, and disposed thee for these great and warlike enterprises.

6. That – That all nations may know it by my foretelling these things so long before, and by the wonderful success that I shall give thee, and by my over-ruling thine heart and counsels, to the deliverance of my people.

7. Light – All mens comforts and calamities come from thy hand.

8. Drop – The righteous and gracious acts of God for his people, shall be so many, as if God rained showers of righteousness out of heaven. **Open** – Open itself to bring forth those fruits which may be expected from such showers. **Them** – The heavens and the earth conspiring together. **Together** – Together with salvation. **It** – This great work of salvation and righteousness; whereof, tho' Cyrus is the instrument, I am the author.

9. Woe – As God here makes many glorious promises to Cyrus, so he pronounces a curse upon them, who should endeavour to hinder him. **Contend** – Contend, if you please, with your fellow creatures, but not with your creator. **Or** – He turns his speech to the potter.

11. Thus saith – Will you not allow me that liberty which yourselves take, of disposing of my own children and works, as I see fit?

Will assist Cyrus (13, 14)

13. Him – Cyrus. **In righteousness** – Most justly, to punish the wicked Babylonians, to plead the cause of the oppressed ones, to manifest my righteousness, and truth, and goodness.

14. The labour – The wealth gotten by their labour. **Thee** – Jerusalem shall not only be rebuilt, but the wealth and glory of other countries shall be brought to it again. This was in part verified in Jerusalem; but it was much more fully accomplished in the church of the gospel, in the accession of the Gentiles to that church which began in Jerusalem, and from thence spread itself into all the parts of the world. **Come over** – They shall be taken captive by thee, and willingly submit themselves to thee.

The mystery of providence (15)

15. Verily – These are the words of the prophet, on contemplation of the various dispensations of God towards his church, and in the world. **Hidest** – Thy counsels are deep and incomprehensible, thy ways are past finding out.

Idols and their worshippers shall be destroyed, and God alone exalted (16–21)

19. In secret – The Heathen idols deliver oracles in obscure cells and caverns: but I have delivered my oracles to Israel publically and plainly. **In vain** – Serve and worship me for nought. As I appointed them work, so from time to time I have given them abundant recompense. **Right** – I require nothing of my people which is not highly just and good.

20. Draw near – To hear what I have said, and am now about to say. **Of the nations** – The remnant of the Gentiles, who survive the many destructions, which I am bringing upon the Heathen nations.

21. Take counsel – To maintain the cause of their idols. **This** – This great work, Babylon's destruction, and the redemption of God's people.

The Gentiles come in to Christ (22–25)

23. In righteousness – It is what I will faithfully perform. **Return** – Without effect. It is a metaphor from ambassadors, who sometimes return to their princes without any success in their business. **Every tongue** – Not only the Jews, but all nations.

24. In the Lord – By or from God alone, or the Messiah, who is the true Jehovah as well as man. **Righteousness** – To justify me from all

things which I could not be justified by the law of Moses. **Strength** – Support and assistance to bear all my burdens, overcome all my enemies, and perform all my duties. **Men** – The Gentiles shall come to Christ. **Ashamed** – But all his implacable enemies shall be brought to shame.

25. All – All Israelites indeed, whether Jews or Gentiles.

Chapter 46

The ruin of Babylon and her idols (1–2)

God's love and faithfulness to the Jews (3–4)

Idols not to be compared with God (5–8)

for power, knowledge, and sure salvation (9–13)

The ruin of Babylon and her idols (1–2)

1. Bel – The chief idol of the Babylonians, called by profane historians Jupiter Belus. **Boweth** – As the Babylonians used to bow down to him to worship, so now he bows down to the victorious Persians. **Nebo** – Another of the famous idols, which used to deliver oracles. **Their idols** – Were taken and broken, and the materials of them, gold, silver, and brass, were carried upon beasts into Persia. **Your carriages** – O ye Persians, to whom he turns his speech.

2. They – The Babylonians. **Together** – The Babylonians and their idols together, neither could help the other. **Deliver** – The Babylonians could not deliver their idols.

God's love and faithfulness to the Jews (3–4)

3. Carried – Whom I have nourished, ever since you were a people, and came out of Egypt; and that as tenderly, as parents bring up their own children.

Idols not to be compared with God (5–8)

7. Remove – He can stir neither hand nor foot to help his people.

8. Bring it – Think of this again and again, ye who have been guilty of this foolish sin.

for power, knowledge, and sure salvation (9–13)

10. Declaring – Foretelling from the beginning of the world, future events which should happen in succeeding ages, even to the end of the world.

11. A bird – Cyrus, called a bird for his swiftness, and ravenous for his fierceness, and victoriousness over his enemies.

13. I bring – Tho' you are unrighteous, I will

shew myself a righteous and faithful God, making good my promise of delivering you out of Babylon after seventy years. **It** – My work of saving you from the Babylonian captivity. **Will place** – I will bring my people to Zion, and save them from all their enemies. **My glory** – In whom I will once again glory as my people.

Chapter 47

God's judgments upon Babylon and Chaldea, for their cruelty towards God's people (1–6)

Their pride and other sins (7–10)

Their enchantments shall not deliver them (11–15)

God's judgments upon Babylon and Chaldea, for their cruelty towards God's people (1–6)

1. Down – From thy throne. **Virgin** – So, called, because she was tender and delicate. **No throne** – For thee. The empire is taken from thee, and translated to the Persians. **Called** – Be so.

2. Millstones – Thou shalt be brought to the basest slavery, which grinding at the mill was esteemed. For this work was not performed by horses, as now it is, but by the labour of slaves and captives. **Grind** – Grind bread-corn into meal for thy master's use. **Uncover** – Take off the ornaments wherewith such women as were of good quality, used to cover and dress their heads. These are predictions of what they should be forced to do or suffer. **Thigh** – Gird up thy garments close and short about thee, that thou mayest be fit for travelling on foot, and for passing over those rivers, through which thou wilt be constrained to wade, in the way to the land of thy captivity.

3. Uncovered – Either for want of raiment to cover it; or rather, by thine enemies in way of scorn and contumely. **As a man** – With moderation and gentleness, as those men who have not quite put off humanity use to do.

5. Silent – Through grief and shame, as mourners use to do. **The lady** – The chief and glory of all kingdoms.

6. Polluted – I cast them away as an unclean thing. **Into thine hand** – To punish them. **No mercy** – Thou hast exceeded the bounds of thy commission. **The ancient** – Who besides their common calamity were afflicted with the miseries of old age, and therefore did require both pity and reverence.

Their pride and other sins (7–10)

7. These things – Thy cruel usages of my people, and the heavy judgments which thou hadst reason to expect for them. **Nor remember** – Thou didst not consider what might and was likely to befall thee afterward.

8. I am – Independent, and self-sufficient. **None** – Which is not either subject to me, or far inferior to me in power and glory. **Shall not sit** – I shall never want either a king or people to defend me.

9. Perfection – In the highest degree.

10. Trusted – Confidently expecting to preserve thyself by these and other wicked arts. **None seeth** – My counsels are so deeply laid. **Perverted** – Hath misled thee into the way of perdition. **None seeth** – Which is repeated, to denote their intolerable self-confidence.

Their enchantments shall not deliver them (11–15)

11. Therefore – This agrees with the history. Babylon being surprised by Cyrus, when they were in deep security.

12. Stand – Persist in these practices. **Laboured** – From the beginning of thy kingdom. For the Chaldeans in all ages were famous for the practice of these arts.

13. Wearied – Thou hast spent thy time and strength in going from one to another, and all to no purpose.

15. Thus – Such comfortless and helpless creatures. **They** – Merchants who came from several countries to trade with Babylon. And the verse may be thus rendered; Thus shall they with whom thou hast laboured be unto thee: also thy merchants, or they with whom thou hast traded from thy youth, shall wander every one to his own quarter.

Chapter 48

God reproves their hypocrisy and obstinacy by his prophecies (1–8)

He spares them for his name's sake, and that they may learn to know him aright (9–11)

God's powerful salvation a motive to obedience (12–17)

God laments their backwardness (18, 19)

Deliverance out of Babylon (20, 21)

No peace to the wicked (22)

God reproves their hypocrisy and obstinacy by his prophecies (1–8)

1. Called – Who are Israelites in name, but not in truth. **Are come** – From the lineage of your progenitor, Judah, as waters flow from a fountain. **Swear** – Who profess the true religion; and call themselves by his name.

2. Though – They glory that they are citizens of Jerusalem, a city sanctified by God, to be the place of his true worship, and gracious presence. **And stay** – Not by a true faith, but a vain confidence.

4. I knew – Therefore I gave thee clearer demonstrations of my nature and providence, because I knew thou wast an unbelieving nation. **Thy neck** – Will not bow down to receive my yoke. **Thy brow** – Thou wast impudent.

6. See – As thou hast heard all these things, from time to time, seriously consider them. **Declare** – I call you to witness: must you not be forced to acknowledge the truth of what I say? **Shewed** – And I have now given thee new predictions of secret things, such as 'till this time were wholly unknown to thee, concerning thy deliverance out of Babylon by Cyrus.

7. Created – Revealed to thee by me; brought to light, as things are by creation. **Not** – Heb. not from thence, not from these ancient times when other things were revealed to thee. **Or** – Heb. and before this day. This day answers to now in the first clause: and seems to be added as an exposition of it. Before this time in which God hath revealed them to thee by my ministry. **I knew** – Either by thine own sagacity: or by the help of thine idols.

8. Yea – The same thing is repeated, because this was so illustrious a proof of the infinite power and providence of God. **Thine ear** – Thou didst not hear, I did not reveal these things unto thee: for so this phrase of opening the ear is understood, 1Sam 9:15. **I knew** – I knew all these cautions were necessary to cure thine infidelity. **Called** – Justly, thou wast indeed such.

He spares them for his name's sake, and that they may learn to know him aright (9–11)

9. For my sake – I will spare thee, and deliver thee out of captivity, not for thy sake, but merely for my own sake, and for the vindication of my name, that I may be praised for my power, faithfulness, and goodness.

10. Behold – Although I will not cut thee off, yet I will put thee into the furnace. **Silver** – Which is kept in the furnace so long 'till all the dross be purged away, I will not deal so rigorously with thee; for then I should wholly consume thee. **I will choose** – God had in a manner rejected Israel, and therefore it was necessary he should choose and try this people a second time.

11. It – This great work of delivering my people out of Babylon. **Name** – If I should not deliver my people, my name would be profaned and blasphemed. **Glory** – I will not give any colour to idolaters, to ascribe the divine nature and properties, to idols, as they would do if I did not rescue my people out of their hands in spite of their idols.

God's powerful salvation a motive to obedience (12–17)

12. O Israel – Whom I have called out of the world to be my peculiar people.

13. Stand up – They are still continually in readiness to execute my commands.

14. Which – Which of the gods whom any of you serve. **Him** – Cyrus.

16. In secret – I have openly revealed my mind to you. **The beginning** – Either from the first time that I began to prophecy until this time: or from the beginning of my taking you to be my people, and of revealing my mind unto you. **From the time** – From the time that I first spoke of it, I am or was there, to effect what I had foretold. **The Lord** – God by his Spirit. **Me** – The prophet Isaiah; who was a type of Christ, and so this may have a respect to him also.

17. Teacheth – Who from time to time have made known to thee, all necessary doctrines; which, if observed by thee, would have been infinitely profitable to thee, both for this life and that to come. So that it is not my fault, but thine own, if thou dost not profit. **Leadeth** – Who acquainteth thee with thy duty in all the concerns of thy life; so that thou canst not pretend ignorance.

God laments their backwardness (18, 19)

18. As the waves – Infinite and continual.

Deliverance out of Babylon (20, 21)

20. Singing – With joy and songs of praise. **Declare** – Publish God's wonderful works.

21. They thirsted not – They shall not thirst. He speaks of things to come, as if they were already past.

No peace to the wicked (22)

22. No peace – God having foretold that peace which he would give to his servant Jacob, adds an explication; and declares, that wicked men should not enjoy the benefit of this mercy.

Chapter 49

Christ, being sent to the Jews complains of them (1–4)

He is sent to the Gentiles with gracious promises (5–12)

God's love to his church perpetual (13–17)

The ample restoration of the church, and its enlargement (18–23)

Its powerful deliverance out of captivity (24–26)

Christ, being sent to the Jews complains of them (1–4)

1. Listen – God turns his speech to the Gentiles, and invites them to hearken to those counsels and doctrines which the Jews would reject. **Me** – Unto Christ: Isaiah speaks these words in the name of Christ.

2. A sword – As he made me the great teacher of his church, so he made my word, quick and powerful, and sharper than any two-edged sword. **Hath he hid** – He will protect me from all mine enemies. **Made me** – Like an arrow, whose point is bright and polished; which therefore pierceth deeper.

3. O Israel – As the name of David is sometimes given to his successors, so here the name of Israel may not unfitly be given to Christ, not only because he descended from his loins; but also because he was the true and the great Israel, who, in a more eminent manner, prevailed with God, as that name signifies, of whom Jacob, who was first called Israel, was but a type.

4. Then said I – Lord, thou sayest thou wilt be glorified by my ministry; but I find it otherwise. **In vain** – Without any considerable fruit of my word and works among the Israelites. **My judgment** – My right, the reward which by his promise, and my purchase, is my right.

He is sent to the Gentiles with gracious promises (5–12)

5. To bring – To convert the apostate Israelites to God. **Not gathered** – Not brought home to God by my ministry. **Yet** – God will not despise me for the unsuccessfulness of my labours, but will honour and glorify me. **My strength** – To support and strengthen me under this and all other discouragements.

6. He – The Lord. **It is** – This is but a small favour. **The tribes** – That remnant which shall survive all their calamities. **My salvation** – The great instrument and author of that eternal salvation which I will give to the Gentiles.

7. His Holy One – The Holy One of Israel. **To him** – To Christ, to whom, in the days of his flesh, this description fully agrees: for men, both Jews and Gentiles among whom he lived, did despise him from their hearts; and the nation, of which he was a member, abhorred both his person and his doctrine; and he was so far from being a temporal monarch, that he came in the form of a servant, and was a servant of rulers, professing subjection and paying tribute unto Caesar. **Kings** – Though for a time thou shalt be despised, yet after a while thou shalt be advanced to such glory, that kings shall look upon thee with reverence. **Arise** – From their seats to worship thee. **Faithful** – Because God shall make good his promises to thee. **Choose thee** – And although thou shalt be rejected by thine own people, yet God will manifest to the world, that thou, and thou only, art the person whom he hath chosen to be the Redeemer of mankind.

8. The Lord – God the Father unto Christ. **Heard thee** – Though not so as to deliver thee from death; yet so as to crown thee with glory and honour. **For a covenant** – To be the Mediator and surety of that covenant, which is made between me and them. **To establish** – To establish truth and righteousness upon earth, and subdue those lusts and passions, which are the great disturbers of human society. **Desolate heritages** – That desolate places may be repaired and repossessed. That Christ may possess the Heathen, who were in a spiritual sense in a most desolate condition.

9. Prisoners – To the Gentiles who are fast bound by the cords of their sins, and taken captive by the devil at his will. **Go forth** – Come forth to the light, receive divine illumination. **In high places** – They shall have abundant provision in all places, yea even in those which commonly are unfruitful, such are both common roads and high grounds.

11. A way – I will remove all hindrances, and prepare the way for them, by levelling high grounds, and raising low grounds.

12. These – My people shall be gathered from the most remote parts of the earth. He speaks here, and in many other places, of the conversion of the Gentiles, with allusion to that work of gathering, and bringing back the Jews from all parts where they were dispersed, into their own land. **Sinim** – Either of the Sinites as they are called, Gen 10:17, who dwelt about the wilderness. Or of Sin, a famous city of Egypt, which may be put for all Egypt, and that for all southern parts.

God's love to his church perpetual (13–17)

14. But – This is an objection. How can these things be true, when the condition of God's church is now so desperate?

16. Graven – He alludes to the common practice of men who put signs upon their hands or fingers of such things as they would remember.

The ample restoration of the church, and its enlargement (18–23)

18. These – Gentiles. Thy church shall not only be restored, but vastly enlarged and adorned by the accession of the Gentiles.

19. Thy waste places – Thy own land, whereof divers parts lie waste for want of people to possess them. **Land of destruction** – Which before was desolate and destroyed.

20. The children – Those Gentiles which shall be begotten by thee, when thou shalt be deprived of thine own natural children, when the generality of the Jews cut themselves off from God.

21. Who – Whence have I this numberless issue? **Seeing** – Seeing I was in a manner left childless. **Desolate** – Without an husband, being forsaken by God, who formerly owned himself for my husband.

22. Behold – I will call them to me. **Set my standard** – As generals do to gather their forces together. **Thy sons** – Those who shall be thine by adoption, that shall own God for their father, and Jerusalem for their mother. **Carried** – With great care and tenderness, as nurses carry young infants. **Carried** – As sick or infirm persons used to be carried.

23. Lick the dust – They shall highly reverence and honour thee. These expressions are borrowed from the practice of the eastern people, who bowed so low as to touch the ground. **Ashamed** – Their expectations shall not be disappointed.

Its powerful deliverance out of captivity (24–26)

24. Shall the prey – Here is a double impediment to their deliverance, the power of the enemy who kept them in bondage, and the justice of God which pleads against their deliverance.

25. For I – I the almighty God will undertake this work.

Chapter 50

The dereliction of the Jews is not of Christ; for he hath power to save (1–4)

And was obedient in that work, and God is present with him (5–9)

An exhortation not to trust in ourselves, but in God (10, 11)

The dereliction of the Jews is not of Christ; for he hath power to save (1–4)

1. Thus saith the Lord – The scope of this and the next chapter, is to vindicate God's justice and to convince the Jews that they were the causes of their own calamities. **Behold** – You can blame none but yourselves and your own sins, for all your captivities and miseries.

2. Wherefore – The general accusation delivered in the last words he now proves by particular instances. **When** – When I, first by my prophets, came to call them to repentance. **No man** – That complied with my call. **To answer** – To come at my call. **Is my hand** – What is the reason of this contempt? Is it because you think I am either unwilling or unable to save you? **A wilderness** – As dry and fit for travelling as a wilderness.

3. I clothe – When it is necessary to save my people, I cover them with thick and dark clouds black as sackcloth, Rev 6:12.

4. Given me – This and the following passages may be in some sort understood of the prophet Isaiah, but they are far more evidently and eminently verified in Christ, and indeed seem to be meant directly of him. **The tongue** – All ability of speaking plainly, and convincingly, and persuasively. **Weary** – Burdened with the sense of his, deplorable condition. **Wakeneth** – Me, from time to time, and continually. **To hear** – He by his Divine power assists me to the practice of all his commands and my duties, with all attention and diligence.

And was obedient in that work, and God is present with him (5–9)

6. I gave – I patiently yielded up myself to those who smote me.

8. Justifieth – God will clear up my righteousness, and shew by many and mighty signs and wonders, that I lived and died his faithful servant. **Let him come** – I am conscious of mine own innocency, and I know that God will give sentence for me.

9. They – Mine accusers and enemies. **The moth** – Shall be cut off and consumed by a secret curse.

An exhortation not to trust in ourselves, but in God (10, 11)

10. The voice – Of Christ, who is called God's servant, by way of eminency and to intimate that though he was God, yet he would take upon himself the form of a servant. **In darkness** – Not in sin, but in misery, that lives in a disconsolate and calamitous condition. **No light** – No comfort. **Trust** – Let him fix his faith and hope in the mercy, and faithfulness, of the Lord, declared in his word, and in his interest in God, who by the mediation of this servant is reconciled to him and made his God.

11. All ye – You that reject the light which God hath set up, and seek for comfort and safety, by your own inventions. **Walk** – Use your utmost endeavours to get comfort from these devices. **This** – This shall be the fruit of all, you shall receive nothing but vexation and misery.

Chapter 51

Abraham, our pattern to trust in Christ, in his promises, and righteous salvation: this is constant, but men are transitory (1–8)

A prayer of the Godly in affliction (9–11)

The Lord's answer (12–17)

He bewails Jerusalem (18–20)

The bitter cup taken from her, and given to her enemies (21–23)

Abraham, our pattern to trust in Christ, in his promises, and righteous salvation: this is constant, but men are transitory (1–8)

1. Look – Consider the state of Abraham and Sarah, from whom all of you sprang.

2. Him alone – To follow me to an unknown land: him only of all his kindred. **Increased** – Into a vast multitude, when his condition was desperate in the eye of reason. And therefore God can as easily raise his church when they are in the most forlorn condition.

3. Therefore – For the sake of Abraham, and of that covenant which I made with him. **Garden** – Flourishing as the garden of Eden.

4. My people – Ye Jews, whom I chose to be my peculiar people. **A law** – A new law, even the doctrine of the gospel. **Judgment** – Judgment is here the same thing with law, the word of God, or the evangelical doctrine, of which he saith that he will make it to rest, that is settle and establish it. **The people** – People of all nations.

5. My righteousness – My salvation, the redemption of all my people, Jews and Gentiles, which is the effect of his righteousness, his justice, faithfulness, or mercy. **Is gone** – Shall shortly go forth. **Judge** – Shall subdue the Gentiles to my authority, and rule them by my word and spirit. **Isles** – The remote countries shall expect this salvation from me, and from me only.

6. The heavens – The heavens and earth shall pass away, in regard of their present state, and properties, and use, as smoke is said to vanish, tho' the substance of it be not destroyed.

7. Know – That love and practise it.

8. Like wool – Like a woollen garment, which is sooner corrupted by moths or such creatures, than linen.

A prayer of the Godly in affliction (9–11)

9. Put on – Put forth thy strength. **Rahab** – Egypt, from its pride or strength. **The dragon** – Pharaoh so called, Psa 74:13.

11. Therefore – This verse contains an answer to the prophet's prayer. I did these great things, and I will do the like again. **Joy** – Like a crown of glory.

The Lord's answer (12–17)

13. Where is the fury – Is it not all gone? He speaks of the thing as if it were already done, because it should certainly and suddenly be done.

16. I have – These words are spoken by God to his church and people, to whom he speaks both in the foregoing and following verses. For God's word is frequently said to be put into the mouths, not only of the prophets, but of the people also. **Covered** – Have protected thee by my almighty power, that I may bring thee to that perfect and blessed estate which is reserved for the days of the Messiah, which in scripture phrase is called a making of new heavens, and a new earth, chap.65:17.

17. Awake – Heb. Rouse up thyself: come out of that forlorn condition in which thou hast so long been. **Stand up** – Upon thy feet, O thou who hast been thrown to the ground. **Drunk** – Who hast been sorely afflicted. **The cup** – Which strikes him that drinks it with deadly horror. **And wrung** – Drunk every drop of it.

He bewails Jerusalem (18–20)

18. None to guide – When thou wast drunk with this cup, and not able to go.

19. These things – Those which follow, which tho' expressed in four words, may fitly be reduced to two things, the desolation or devastation of the land, and the destruction of the people by famine and sword. So famine and sword are not named as new evils, but only as the particular ways of bringing the destruction. **By whom** – I cannot find any man who is able to comfort and relieve thee.

20. Fainted – They are so far from being able to comfort thee, that they themselves faint away. **They lie** – Dead by famine or the sword. **As a bull** – Those of them who are not slain are struggling for life.

The bitter cup taken from her, and given to her enemies (21–23)

21. Not with wine – But with the cup of God's fury.

22. That pleadeth – Who, tho' he has fought against thee, is now reconciled to thee, and will maintain thy cause against all thine adversaries.

23. Go over – That we may trample upon thee.

Chapter 52

The church redeemed and called upon to rejoice therein (1–6)

The universal preaching of the gospel glorious (7–10)

A call to free ourselves from bondage (11, 12)
Christ's kingdom shall be exalted (13–15)

The church redeemed and called upon to rejoice therein (1–6)

1. Awake – This is a prediction and promise what she should do, that she should awake or arise out of her low estate, and be strong and courageous. **Beautiful garments** – Thy sorrows shall be ended, and thou shalt be advanced into a glorious condition. **O Zion** – O my church. **Come** – Either to molest thee, or defile thee. **The uncircumcised** – Heathens or infidels. **Unclean** – Nor any others, who are unholy.

2. The dust – In which thou hast sat as a mourner. **The bands** – The yoke of thy captivity shall be taken off from thee.

3. Sold yourselves – By your sins, without any valuable consideration paid by them either to you, or to your Lord and owner. **Without money** – Without paying any ransom.

4. Egypt – Where they had protection and sustenance, and therefore owed subjection to the king of Egypt. And yet when he oppressed them, I punished him severely, and delivered them out of his hands. **The Assyrian** – The king of Babylon, who is called the king of Assyria, 2Kings 23:29, as also the Persian emperor is called, Ezra 6:22, because it was one and the same empire which was possessed, first by the Assyrians, then by the Babylonians, and afterwards by the Persians. **Without cause** – Without any such ground or colour, by mere force invading their land, and carrying them away into captivity.

5. What have I – Why do I sit still here, and not go to Babylon to punish the Babylonians, and to deliver my people? **For nought** – Without any provocation, or pretence of right. **Howl** – By their unmerciful usage. **Blasphemed** – The Babylonians blasphemed me as if I wanted either power or good will to save my people out of their hands.

6. Shall know – They shall experience my power and goodness in fighting for them. **In that day** – When I shall redeem my people: which work was begun by the return of the Jews from Babylon, and perfected by the coming of the Messiah. **Behold** – That all these promises are the words of the omnipotent, unchangeable God.

The universal preaching of the gospel glorious (7–10)

7. The mountains – Of Judea, to which these glad tidings were brought, and from which they were spread abroad into other countries. **Of him** – Or, of them; the singular number being put for the plural. **Returneth** – In the days of the Messiah, God did discover and exercise his dominion over the world far more eminently than ever he had done from the beginning of the world until that time.

8. Thy watchmen – Thy ministers, who descry the approach of this heavenly king. **Lift up thy voice** – To give notice to all people of these glad tidings; and by way of exultation, to sing forth the praises of God for this glorious day. **Eye** – Distinctly and familiarly, their eyes beholding the eyes of this king of glory. **They shall be eye and ear** – witnesses of the words and works of Christ, and therefore their testimony shall be more certain and valuable. **Bring again** – When God shall complete the work of bringing his church out of captivity.

A call to free ourselves from bondage (11, 12)

11. Depart – Out of Babylon. **Touch** – Carry not along with you any of their superstitions or idolatries. **Ye** – And especially your priests and Levites, who minister in holy things, and carry the holy vessels of the temple, keep yourselves from all pollution.

12. Not by flight – But securely, and in triumph, being conducted by your great captain the Lord of hosts. **Rereward** – So that none shall be able either to oppose you in your march, or to fall upon you in the rear.

Christ's kingdom shall be exalted (13–15)

13. Behold – This is the beginning of a new prophecy, which is continued from hence to the end of the next chapter. **My servant** – That it is Christ who is here spoken of, is so evident, that the Chaldee paraphrast, and other ancient, and some later Hebrew doctors, understand it directly of him, and that divers Jews have been convinced and converted to the Christian faith, by the evidence of this prophecy. **Prosper** – This is fitly put in the first place to prevent those scandals which otherwise might arise from the succeeding passages, which describe his state of humiliation. **Very high** – Here are three words signifying the same thing to express the height and glory of his exaltation.

14. Astonished – At his humiliation. **Thee** – At thee, O my servant. **His form** – Christ, in respect of his birth, breeding, and manner of life, was most obscure and contemptible. His countenance also was so marred with frequent watchings, and fastings, and troubles, that he was thought to be near fifty years old when he was but about thirty, John 8:57, and was farther spoiled with buffetings, and crowning with thorns, and other cruel and despiteful usages.

15. So – His exaltation shall be answerable to his humiliation. **Sprinkle** – With his word or doctrine; which being often compared to rain or water, may be said to be sprinkled, as it is said to be dropped, Deut 32:2 Ezek 20:46. **Kings** – Shall be silent before him out of profound humility, reverence, and admiration of his wisdom. **For** – They shall hear from his mouth many excellent doctrines, which will be new and strange to them. And particularly that comfortable doctrine of the salvation of the Gentiles, which was not only new to them, but strange and incredible to the Jews themselves.

Chapter 53

The incredulity of the Jews; the death of Christ, and the blessed effects thereof (1–10)

His exaltation and glory (11, 12)

The incredulity of the Jews; the death of Christ, and the blessed effects thereof (1–10)

1. **Who** – Who, not only of the Gentiles, but even of the Jews, will believe the truth of what I say? And this premonition was highly necessary, both to caution the Jews that they should not stumble at this stone, and to instruct the Gentiles that they should not be seduced with their example. **The arm** – The Messiah, called the arm or power of God, because the almighty power of God was seated in him. **Revealed** – Inwardly and with power.

2. **As a root** – And the reason why the Jews will generally reject their Messiah, is, because he shall not come into the world with secular pomp, but he shall grow up, before him, as a tender plant and as a root, or branch, grows out of a dry, barren ground. **No form** – His bodily presence shall be mean and contemptible. **No beauty** – This the prophet speaks in the person of the unbelieving Jews. **We** – Our people, the Jewish nation.

3. **We hid** – We scorned to look upon him.

4. **Yet** – Our people believed that he was thus punished by the just judgment of God.

5. **Wounded** – Which word comprehends all his pains and punishments. **For our iniquities** – For the guilt of their sins, which he had voluntarily taken upon himself, and for the expiation of their sins, which was hereby purchased. **The chastisement** – Those punishments by which our peace, our reconciliation to God, was to be purchased, were laid upon him by God's justice with his own consent. **Healed** – By his sufferings we are saved from our sins.

6. **We** – All mankind. **Astray** – From God. **Have turned** – In general, to the way of sin, which may well be called a man's own way, because sin is natural to us, inherent in us, born

with us; and in particular, to those several paths, which several men choose, according to their different opinions, and circumstances. **Hath laid** – Heb. hath made to meet, as all the rivers meet in the sea. **The iniquity** – Not properly, for he knew no sin; but the punishment of iniquity, as that word is frequently used. That which was due for all the sins of all mankind, which must needs be so heavy a load, that if he had not been God as well as man, he must have sunk under the burden.

7. **He opened not** – He neither murmured against God, nor reviled men.

8. **Taken away** – Out of this life. **By distress and judgment** – By oppression and violence. and a pretence of justice. **His generation** – His posterity. For his death shall not be unfruitful; when he is raised from the dead, he shall have a spiritual seed, a numberless multitude of those who shall believe in him. **Cut off** – By a violent death. And this may be added as a reason of the blessing of a numerous posterity conferred upon him, because he was willing to be cut off for the transgression of his people.

9. **With the wicked** – This was a farther degree of humiliation. He saith, he made his grave, because this was Christ's own act, and he willingly yielded up himself to death and burial. And that which follows, with the wicked, does not denote the sameness of place, as if he should be buried in the same grave with other malefactors, but the sameness of condition.

10. **He** – God was the principal cause of all his sufferings, tho' mens sins were the deserving cause. **When** – When thou, O God, shalt have made, thy son a sacrifice, by giving him up to death for the atonement of mens sins. His soul is here put for his life, or for himself. **Shall see** – He shall have a numerous issue of believers reconciled by God, and saved by his death. **Prolong** – He shall live and reign with God for ever. **The pleasure** – God's gracious decree for the salvation of mankind shall be effectually carried on by his ministry and mediation.

His exaltation and glory (11, 12)

11. **Shall see** – He shall enjoy. **The travel** – The blessed fruit of all his labours, and sufferings. **Satisfied** – He shall esteem his own and his father's glory, and the salvation of his people, an abundant recompense. **By his knowledge** – By the knowledge of him. **Justify** – Acquit them from the guilt of their sins, and all the dreadful consequences thereof. And Christ is said to justify sinners meritoriously, because he purchases and procures it for us. **Many** – An innumerable company of all nations. **For** – For he shall satisfy the justice of God, by bearing the punishment due to their sins.

12. **I** – God the father. **A portion** – Which is very commodiously supplied out of the next clause. **With the strong** – God will give him

happy success in his glorious undertaking: he shall conquer all his enemies, and set up his universal and everlasting kingdom in the world. **Because** – Because he willingly laid down his life. **Transgressors** – He prayed upon earth for all sinners, and particularly for those that crucified him, and in heaven he still intercedes for them, by a legal demand of those good things which he purchased; by the sacrifice of himself, which, though past, he continually represents to his father, as if it were present.

Chapter 54

The blessings and fulness of the gospel-church (1–4)

The Gentiles becoming Christ's spouse, to whom his love is everlasting (5–10)

Her glories (11, 12)

The gifts of the Holy Ghost (13)

Her sure preservation (14–17)

The blessings and fulness of the gospel-church (1-4)

1. Sing – The prophet having largely discoursed of the sufferings of Christ, and of the blessed fruits thereof, and here foreseeing that glorious state of the church, he breaks forth into this song of triumph. And as the foregoing chapter literally speaks of Christ, so doth this of the church of Christ. This church, consisting at first of the Jews, and afterwards of the Gentiles, had been barren, 'till the coming of Christ. **The desolate** – The church of the Gentiles, which in the times of the Old Testament was desolate, does now bring forth to God a more numerous posterity than that of the Jews.

2. Enlarge – That it may be capable of the Gentiles, who shall flock to thee in great numbers. **Strengthen** – That they may be able to support that great weight which the tents thus enlarged, shall be upon them.

3. For – Thou shalt bring forth a multitude of children; for this word is commonly used of any extraordinary propagation of living creatures. On the left – On every side, in all the parts of the world. Thy seed – Thy spiritual seed, the church of the New Testament, which is accounted Abraham's seed, or children.

4. Ashamed – For the barrenness and widowhood, which once was the matter of thy grief and shame. **Forget** – Thou shalt not be upbraided with thy former barrenness in thy youthful state.

The Gentiles becoming Christ's spouse, to whom his love is everlasting (5–10)

5. Thy maker – Will own thee for his spouse. **The Lord** – Who hath the sovereign command of all men and creatures, and therefore can subdue the Gentiles to thee, and can make thee to increase and multiply in so prodigious a measure, even in thine old age, notwithstanding thy barrenness in the days of thy youth, of which he speaks in the foregoing verse. **The God** – The God and father of all nations, whereas formerly he was called only the God of Israel.

6. Called thee – To return to him. **As forsaken** – When thou wast like a woman forsaken. **And grieved** – For the loss of her husband's favour. **Of youth** – As affectionately as an husband recalls his wife which he married in his youth.

7. For a moment – In comparison of God's everlasting kindness. **Gather thee** – From all the places where thou art dispersed, from all parts of the world.

8. With everlasting kindness – With kindness to thee and thy seed through all succeeding generations.

9. This – This covenant of grace and peace made with thee shall be as certain and perpetual as that which I made with Noah, that there should never be another flood to drown the world. **Wrath** – So as to forsake thee utterly.

10. The mountains – Shall sooner depart from their places than any kindness shall depart from thee. **The covenant** – That covenant whereby I have made peace and friendship with thee, and have promised to thee all manner of happiness. God will not cast off his Christian church, as he cast off the church of the Jews, the New covenant is established upon better and surer promises than the Old. **The Lord** – Who doth this not for thine own merits, but merely for his own grace and mercy.

Her glories (11, 12)

11. O thou – Who hast been, in a most afflicted and comfortless condition. **With sapphires** – I will make thee exceeding beautiful and glorious, by a plentiful effusion of excellent gifts, and graces.

12. Agates – The proper signification of the Hebrew names of precious stones is unknown to the Jews themselves. It may suffice us to know that this was some very clear and transparent, and precious stone. **Thy borders** – The utmost parts or walls.

The gifts of the Holy Ghost (13)

13. Taught – Not only outwardly by his word, but inwardly by his spirit. **The peace:**

1. Inward peace arising from the clear discoveries of God's love and reconciliation to us, and wrought by the spirit of adoption, which is more abundantly given to believers under the gospel, than under the law.

2. Outward peace, safety, and happiness.

Her sure preservation (14–17)

14. Established – Thine affairs shall be managed with righteousness, which is the glory of any society. **Oppression** – Either by thine own governors, or by foreign powers.

15. Behold – It is true some will combine and make an attempt against thee. **But** – Without any such commission from me, as Sennacherib and Nebuchadnezzar had.

16. The smith – Both the smith that makes warlike instruments, and the soldier that uses them, are my creatures, and totally at my command, and therefore they cannot hurt you without my leave. **The waster** – To destroy only whom and when I please.

17. Condemn – And I will deliver thee not only from the fury of war, but also from the strife of tongues. **This** – This blessed condition, is the portion allotted them by me. **Righteousness** – The reward of their righteousness. **Of me** – I give it, and I will continue it to them.

Chapter 55

An invitation to seek for spiritual blessings from Christ, whom the Father sends (1–5)

To come to him speedily and by repentance (6, 7)

His grace infinite (8, 9)

His word powerful (10, 11)

The joy of believers (12, 13)

An invitation to seek for spiritual blessings from Christ, whom the Father sends (1–5)

1. Thirsteth – For the grace of God and the blessings of the gospel. This thirst implies a vehement, and active, and restless desire after it. **No money** – Those who are most worthless and wicked, if they do but thirst may be welcome. **Buy** – Procure or receive that which is freely offered. **Wine and milk** – All gospel-blessings; in particular, that peace and joy in the Holy Ghost, which are better than wine, and that love of God which nourishes the soul, as milk does the body.

2. Money – All your time, and strength, and cost. **Not bread** – For those things which can never nourish or satisfy you, such as worldly goods, or pleasures. **Eat ye** – That which is truly and solidly, and everlastingly good. **In fatness** – In this pleasant food of gospel-enjoyments.

3. An everlasting covenant – That everlasting covenant of grace and peace which I made with Abraham, and his seed. **Of David** – Even that covenant which was made first with Abraham,

and then with David, concerning those glorious and sure blessings which God hath promised to his people, one and the chief of which was giving Christ to die for their sins. David here seems to be put for the son of David.

4. Behold – I have appointed, and will in due time actually give. **Him** – The David last mentioned, even Christ. **A witness** – To declare the will of God concerning the duty and salvation of men, to bear witness to truth, to confirm God's promises, and, among others, those which respect the calling of the Gentiles: to be a witness of both parties of that covenant made between God and men. **The people** – To all people.

5. Thou – Thou, O Messiah. **Call** – To the knowledge of thyself. **Knewest not** – With that special knowledge which implies approbation. **Because** – Because the Lord shall by many tokens, manifest himself to be thy God, and thee to be his son and faithful servant. **Glorify thee** – By confirming thy word with illustrious signs and miracles, and particularly by thy resurrection, and glorious ascension.

To come to him speedily and by repentance (6, 7)

6. Seek – Labour to get the knowledge of God's will, and to obtain his grace and favour. **While** – In this day of grace, while he offers mercy and reconciliation. **Near** – Ready and desirous to receive you to mercy.

7. Return – By sincere repentance, and faith.

His grace infinite (8, 9)

8. For – If any man injure you, especially if he do it greatly and frequently, you are slow and backward to forgive him. But I am ready to forgive all penitents, how many, and great, and numberless soever their sins be.

His word powerful (10, 11)

10. The snow – Which in its season contributes to the fruitfulness of the earth. **Returneth not** – Without effect. **And bread** – That it may bring forth store of bread-corn, both for mens present supplies, and for seed for the next year.

11. My word – My promises, concerning the pardon of the greatest sinners. **Void** – Without success.

The joy of believers (12, 13)

12. Therefore – Ye shall be released from your bondage. **Peace** – Safely and triumphantly. **Clap** – There shall be a general rejoicing, so that even the senseless creatures shall seem to rejoice with you.

13. Instead – Whereas your land was filled with thorns and briars, as was foretold, they shall be rooted out, and it shall be planted with fir-trees and myrtle-trees, and such other trees, as are useful either for fruit or for delight. The church shall be delivered from pernicious things, and replenished with all divine graces and blessings. **It** – This wonderful change shall bring much honour to God. **A sign** – For a monument, of God's infinite power, and faithfulness, and love to his people to all succeeding generations.

Chapter 56

The blessedness of the Godly without any respect of persons (1–8)

Blind watchmen shall be destroyed (9–12)

The blessedness of the Godly without any respect of persons (1–8)

1. **My salvation** – That eminent salvation by the Messiah, and in which, without this you shall have no share. **Is near** – So the scripture often speaks of things which are at a great distance, as if they were present or at hand, Hab 2:3 James 5:8,9 Rev 22:20. **My righteousness** – The same thing which he called salvation.

2. **The man** – Every man not only Jews but Gentiles, as it is explained in the following verses. **The sabbath** – The sabbath seems to be put here, as sacrifice is elsewhere, for the whole worship of God

3. **The stranger** – The stranger, the Gentile, who by birth is a stranger to God, that hath turned from dumb idols to the living God. **The eunuch** – Who is here joined with the stranger, because he was forbidden to enter into the congregation of the Lord, Deut 23:1. Under these two instances he understands all those, who either by birth, or by any ceremonial pollution, were excluded from church privileges, and so he throws open the door to all true believers. **A dry tree** – A fruitless tree, accursed by God with the curse of barrenness.

4. **Take hold** – That stedfastly keep the conditions of my covenant.

5. **In mine house** – In my temple. **Better** – A far greater blessing and honour than that of having posterity, even my favour, and my spirit, and eternal felicity.

7. **Mountain** – To my house, which stood upon mount Zion. **Joyful** – By accepting their services, and comforting their hearts with the sense of my love. **Accepted** – They shall have as free access to mine house and altar, as the Jews themselves, and their services shall be as acceptable to me. Evangelical worship is here described under such expressions as agreed to the worship of God which then was in use.

8. **The Lord** – Who will gather to himself, and bring into their own land, those that are cast out of their own land. **Yet** – I will make a far more comprehensive gathering of the Gentiles.

Blind watchmen shall be destroyed (9–12)

9. **Come** – This is a prediction of Israel's destruction by their cruel enemies. The prophet having largely discoursed concerning the Messiah, and his kingdom, and having encouraged the Gentiles with God's gracious promises made to them, now proceeds to terrify the unbelieving Jews, and to shew that as the Gentiles would believe, and be saved, so they would reject their Messiah, and be destroyed.

10. **His** – Israel's. **Watchmen** – Priests and teachers; he mentions only the teachers, because ignorance was most shameful in them, but hereby he supposes the gross ignorance of the people. **Bark** – They are also slothful and negligent in instructing the people, and do not faithfully reprove them for their sins.

11. **They look** – They regard neither God's glory, nor the peoples good, but only the satisfaction of their own base desires. **Quarter** – In their several stations.

12. **Say they** – Unto their brethren, fellow-priests, or other jolly companions. **Fill ourselves** – We will drink not only to delight, but even to drunkenness, as the word signifies, which shows their dreadful security and contempt of God, and their abandoning of all care of their own or peoples souls.

Chapter 57

The blessed death of the righteous, not duly lamented by the Jews, who also commit idolatry, and trust in man: they are threatened (1–12)

Evangelical promises to the penitent (13–19)

No peace to the wicked (20, 21)

The blessed death of the righteous, not duly lamented by the Jews, who also commit idolatry, and trust in man: they are threatened (1–12)

1. **The righteous** – Just and holy men. **No man** – Few or none. **Layeth it to heart** – Is duly affected with this sad sign of God's displeasure.

2. **He** – This just and merciful man shall enter into a state of rest, where he shall be out of the reach of the approaching miseries. **They** – just men. Here is a sudden change of the number, which is very frequent in the prophets. **Beds** – In their graves, which are not unfitly called their beds, as their death is commonly called sleep in scripture.

3. **Hither** – To God's tribunal, to receive your

sentence. **Sons** – Not by propagation, but by imitation. **And the whore** – Not the genuine children of Abraham, their dispositions were far more suitable to a bastardly brood, than to Abraham's seed.

4. **Against whom** – Consider whom it is that you mock and scoff, when you deride God's prophets. **A seed** – A generation of liars, whose practices contradict your professions, who deal deceitfully both with God and men.

5. **Enflaming** – Lusting after them, and mad upon them. **Slaying** – In way of sacrifice to their idols. **Valleys** – He seems to allude to the valley of Hinnom in which these cruelties were practised. **Clifts** – Which they choose either for shade, or for those dark vaults, in rocks, which were convenient for idolatrous uses.

6. **Portion** – Thou hast chosen for thy portion those idols, which were worshipped by the sides of brooks or rivers where such smooth stones commonly lie. **They** – Thou hast forsaken me and chosen idols. **Offered** – For the devil is God's ape, and idolaters used the same rites and offerings in the worship of idols which God had prescribed in his own. **Comfort** – Should I be pleased with such a people and such actions?

7. **Mountain** – In high places, which were much used for religious worship, both by Israelites and by Heathens. **Thy bed** – Thine altar, in which thou didst commit spiritual whoredom with idols.

8. **The posts** – Behind the posts of the doors of thine house: where the Heathens placed their tutelar gods to whose protection they committed their houses, that so they might have their eyes and minds upon them, whensoever they went out or came in. **Set up** – Those monuments which thou didst set up there as remembrances of those idol-gods whom they represented. **Discovered** – Thou hast uncovered thy nakedness; to others beside me thine husband. **Gone up** – Into the adulterous bed. **Enlarged** – That it might receive many adulterers together. Thou hast multiplied thine idols and altars. **A covenant** – Thou hast covenanted to serve them.

9. **The king** – The king of Assyria, called the king by way of eminency, to whom the Israelites in the days of Isaiah were very prone to trust, and send presents. And so the prophet passes from their idolatry to another sin, even their confidence in Heathen princes. **Increase** – Didst send great quantities. **Far off** – Into Assyria, which was far from Judea. **Debase** – Thou wast willing to submit to the basest terms to procure their aid.

10. **Wearied** – Thou hast not eased, but tired thyself with thy tedious journey. **Yet** – And yet thou didst not perceive that thy labour was lost. **Hast found** – Thou hast sometimes found success in these ways. **Not grieved** – Therefore thou didst not repent of thy sin herein.

11. **Feared** – And who are they, the fear of whom drives thee to these wicked courses? **Lied** – That thou hast dealt thus perfidiously with me. **Not remembered** – Hast thou forgotten all those great things which I have done for thee. **Held my peace** – Have not I forbore to punish thee from time to time, that by this goodness I might oblige thee to love me. **And thou** – Or, therefore thou dost not fear or regard me. Thou abusest my long-suffering.

Evangelical promises to the penitent (13–19)

13. **But** – But they shall be carried away suddenly and violently by the blast of mine anger. **Vanity** – A vapour which quickly vanishes away. **Inherit** – Shall enjoy my favour and presence in my temple.

14. **And he** – God will raise up a man who shall say with authority and efficacy. **Cast up** – Make causeways, where it is needful, for their safe and easy passage, and remove all things which may hinder them in their return.

16. **For** – I will not proceed to the utmost severity with sinful men.

17. **Covetousness** – Of which sin the Jews were eminently guilty. But this comprehends all those sins for which God contended with them. **He went** – Yet he was not reformed, but trespassed more and more.

18. **Mourners** – To those who are humbled under God's hand, that mourn in Zion for their own and others sins.

19. **I create** – I will by my almighty power produce. **Peace** – That peace which is not wrought by mens hands, but only by God's lips or word. The doubling of the word signifies the certainty and abundance this peace. **Far off** – To the Gentiles who are far from God, as well as to the Jews, who are called a people near unto God, Psal 148:14.

No peace to the wicked (20, 21)

20. **Cast up** – Their minds are restless, being perpetually hurried with their own lusts and passions, and with guilt, and the dread of the divine vengeance.

21. **No peace** – Though they may have a great share of prosperity, yet they have no share in this inward, and spiritual, and everlasting peace.

Chapter 58

The hypocrisy of the Jews, in their fasts (1–5)

A true fast described (6, 7)

Promises to Godliness (8–12)

To the keeping of the sabbath (13, 14)

The hypocrisy of the Jews, in their fasts (1–5)

2. Yet – They cover all their wickedness with a profession of religion. **Delight** – There are many men who take some pleasure in knowing God's will and word, and yet do not conform their lives to it. **As** – As if they were a righteous people. **Forsook** – As if they were not guilty of any apostasy from God, or disobedience to God's precepts. **Ask** – As if they resolved to observe them. **In approaching** – In coming to my temple to hear my word, and to offer sacrifices.

3. Afflicted – Defrauded our appetites with fasting, of which this phrase is used, Levit 16:29. **Ye find** – Either you indulge yourselves in sensuality, as they did, Isa 22:13. But this does not agree with that afflicting of their souls which they now professed, and which God acknowledges; or you pursue and satisfy your own desires: though you abstain from bodily food, you do not mortify your sinful inclinations. **Exact** – Your money, got by your labour, and lent to others, either for their need or your own advantage, which you require either with usury, or at least with rigour, when either the general law of charity, or God's particular law, commanded the release, or at least the forbearance of them.

4. Behold – Your fasting days, wherein you ought in a special manner to implore the mercy of God, and to shew compassion to men, you employ in injuring or quarrelling with your brethren, your servants or debtors, or in contriving mischief against them. **Heard** – In strife and debate. By way of ostentation.

5. Chosen – Approve of, accept, or delight in, by a metonymy, because we delight in what we freely choose. **For a day** – This may be understood, either for a man to take a certain time to afflict his soul in, and that either from even to even, Lev 23:32, or from morning to evening, or for a little time. **Wilt thou call** – Canst thou suppose it to be so? **A fast** – It being such an one as has nothing in it, but the dumb signs of a fast, nothing of deep humiliation appearing in it, or, real reformation proceeding from it. **Acceptable day** – A day that God will approve of.

A true fast described (6, 7)

6. The bands – The cruel obligations of usury and oppression.

7. Cast out – And thereby become wanderers, having no abiding place. **To thy house** – That thou be hospitable, and make thy house a shelter to them that have none of their own left. **Hide not** – That seek no occasion to excuse thyself. **Thy own flesh** – Some confine this to our own kindred; but we can look on no man, but there we contemplate our own flesh, and there-fore it is barbarous, not only to tear, but not to love and succour him. Therefore feed him as thou wouldest feed thyself, or be fed; shelter him as thou wouldest shelter thyself, or be sheltered; clothe him as thou wouldest clothe thyself, or be clothed; if in any of these respects thou wert in his circumstances.

Promises to Godliness (8–12)

8. Thy light – Happiness and prosperity. **Break forth** – It shall not only appear, but break forth, dart itself forth, notwithstanding all difficulties, as the sun breaks, and pierces through a cloud. **Thy health** – Another metaphor to express the same thing. **Righteousness** – The reward of thy righteousness. **Before thee** – As the morning-star goes before the sun. **The glory** – His glorious power and providence. **Thy rereward** – Thus the angel of his presence secured the Israelites when they came up out of Egypt.

9. Answer – He will give an effectual demonstration, that he hears thee. **Here I am** – A phrase that notes a person to be ready at hand to help. **Take away** – From among you. **The yoke** – All those pressures and grievances before mentioned. **Putting forth** – Done by way of scoff, or disdainful insulting. **Vanity** – Any kind of evil words.

10. Draw out – Or, open, as when we open a store, to satisfy the wants of the needy. **Thy soul** – Thy affection, thy pity and compassion. **Thy darkness** – In the very darkness of the affliction itself thou shalt have comfort.

11. Guide thee – Like a shepherd. And he adds continually to shew that his conduct and blessing shall not be momentary, or of a short continuance, but all along as it was to Israel in the wilderness. **Satisfy** – Thou shalt have plenty, when others are in scarcity. **Make fat** – This may be spoken in opposition to the sad effects of famine, whereby the flesh is consumed away, that it cannot be seen, and the bones that were not seen, stick out. **A garden** – If thou relieve the poor, thou shalt never be poor, but as a well-watered garden, always flourishing. **Fail not** – Heb. deceive not, a metaphor which farther notes also the continuance of this flourishing state, which will not be like a land-flood, or brooks, that will soon be dried up with drought. Thou shalt be fed with a spring of blessing, that will never fail.

12. They shall be of thee – Thy posterity. **Waste places** – Cities which have lain long waste; that shall continue for many generations to come. **The breach** – Breach is put for breaches, which was made by God's judgment breaking in upon them in suffering the walls of their towns and cities to be demolished. **Paths** – Those paths that led from city to city, which being now laid desolate, and uninhabited, were grown over with grass, and weeds. **To dwell in** – These accommodations being recovered, their ancient cities might be fit to be re-inhabited.

To the keeping of the sabbath (13, 14)

13. If – If thou take no unnecessary journeys, or do any servile works on the sabbath-day. **A delight** – Performing the duties of it with chearfulness, delighting in the ordinances of it. **Holy** – Dedicated to God, consecrated to his service.

14. In the Lord – In his goodness and faithfulness to thee, and in the assurance of his love and favour. **To ride** – Thou shalt be above the reach of danger. **Feed thee** – Thou shalt enjoy the good of the land of Canaan, which God promised as an heritage to Jacob, and his seed, Gen 35:12.

Chapter 59

Sin separates between God and us (1, 2)

Murder, theft, falsehood, injustice, cruelty (3–8)

Calamity for sin (9–15)

Salvation only of God (16–19)

The covenant of the redeemer (20, 21)

Sin separates between God and us (1, 2)

Murder, theft, falsehood, injustice, cruelty (3–8)

3. Perverseness – Perverse words are such as are contrary to God's word. Words every way contrary to God's will.

4. None – None seek to redress these wrongs, and violences; they commit all rapines, and frauds with impunity. **Bring forth** – These two words of conceiving, and bringing forth, denote their whole contrivance, and perfecting their wickedness.

5. Cockatrice eggs – One kind put for any venomous creature, a proverbial speech signifying by these eggs mischievous designs, and by hatching them, their putting them in practice. **Web** – Another proverbial speech whereby is taught, both how by their plots they weave nets, lay snares industriously with great pains and artifice. And also how their designs will come to nothing, as the spider's web is soon swept away.

6. Webs – Their contrivances shall not be able to cover or defend them.

7. Wasting – They meditate on little or nothing else. **Paths** – In what way or work soever they are engaged, it all tends to ruin and destruction.

8. The way of peace – They live in continual contentions, and discords. **Judgment** – No justice, equity, faith, or integrity.

Calamity for sin (9–15)

9. Justice – Judgment, and so justice is here taken for deliverance. God doth not defend our right, nor revenge our wrong, because of these outrages, and acts of violence, injustice, and oppression.

10. As dead men – He compares their captivity to men dead without hope of recovery.

11. Mourn – Their oppressing governors made the wicked roar like bears, and the good mourn like doves.

12. Transgressions – The word here signifies sins of an high nature, such as wherein there is much of man's will against light: rebellious sins. **Multiplied** – They admit of no excuse; for they are acted before thee, and multiplied against thee, whereby thou art justly provoked to deny us all help. **Testify** – As so many witnesses produced proves our guilt. **Are with us** – Are still unforgiven. **We know** – We are convinced of them.

13. Lying – Transgressing here, and lying, seem to be one and the same thing, inasmuch as in their transgressing the law of God, they broke their solemn engagement to God upon mount Sinai. **Departing** – Turning from God to idols. **Speaking** – As it were, talking of little else one among another, but how to oppress their neighbours, and apostatize from God. **Uttering** – That is, first contriving in their heart false accusations, false worship to the dishonour of God; laying the contrivances and uttering them. **From the heart** – And when they dealt with men in ways of fraud, it was from the heart, but when they spake with God it was but from the lip.

14. Judgment – He speaks here of the sentences in courts of judicature. **Truth** – Truth is cast to the ground, and justice trampled under foot, even in public. **Equity** – No such thing will be admitted in their courts.

15. Faileth – All things are amiss, neither judgment or justice, or truth, is to be found among us. **A prey** – Or, as some render it, is accounted mad, is laughed at. Josephus tells us, that immediately before the destruction of Jerusalem, it was matter of scorn to be religious. The translators reach the meaning of the word by prey: the wicked, like wild beasts, endeavouring to devour such as are not as bad as themselves: where wickedness rules, innocency is oppressed.

Salvation only of God (16–19)

16. No man – To appear in the behalf of equity. **His arm** – He would do his work without help from any other. **Righteousness** – His justice; seeing there could be no justice found among them, he would avenge the innocent himself.

17. For – God, resolving to appear as a man

of war, puts on his arms; he calls righteousness his breast-plate, to shew the justness of his cause, as also his faithfulness in making good his promises. **Vengeance** – Or garments made of vengeance: as God is said to put on the former for their sakes, whom he would preserve, so he puts on these for their sakes, whom he will destroy, namely, his peoples enemies. **Zeal** – For his own honour, and for his own people. The sum of all these expressions is, to describe both the cause and effect together; the cause was righteousness and zeal in God, the effect, salvation to his people, and vengeance on his enemies.

18. **Deeds** – Heb. recommences or deserts. That is, he will recompense his adversaries with those effects of his fury that they have deserved. **Islands** – To those remoter nations under the king of Babylon, that thought themselves secure.

19. **Fear** – Worship the Lord. **The west** – The western part of the world. **His glory** – The glorious God. **The rising of the sun** – The eastern parts. **When** – At what time soever the devil, or his instruments shall make violent irruptions upon the church. **A standard** – God shall make known himself to take their part and defend them, by his spirit alone.

The covenant of the redeemer (20, 21)

20. **The Redeemer** – Christ, of whom the apostle expounds it, Rom 11:26, the prophets usually concluding their promises of temporal deliverances with the promises of spiritual, especially such, of which the temporal were evident types.

21. **My covenant** – What I have promised, to them that turn from their iniquity. **My words** – Which thou hast uttered by virtue of my spirit. **Of thy seed** – A promise of the perpetual presence of his word and spirit with the prophets, apostles, and teachers of the church to all ages.

Chapter 60

The glory and blessing of the new church after a short affliction (1–22)

1. **Arise** – A word of encouragement accommodated to the Jewish, or Hebrew style, wherein, as by lying down, is described a servile and calamitous condition, chap.47:1, so by rising, and standing up, a recovery out of it, into a free, and prosperous one. Here under a type, of Jerusalem's restoration, is displayed the flourishing state of the Gentile-church, under the Messiah. **Thy light** – Thy flourishing and prosperous state.

2. **The darkness** – All kinds of errors. **The Lord** – Christ. **Shall be seen** – Shall be conspicuous;

as the Lord's arising, to the darkness covering the earth, so the glory being seen, answers to that gross darkness.

3. **The Gentiles** – A plain prophecy of the calling of the Gentiles.

5. **See** – With delight the multitudes of thy children running to thee. **Flow** – They shall flock together to behold such an amazing sight. **Fear** – Or stand amazed. **Enlarged** – Both with joy, and love. **The abundance** – The islands of the sea, the nations, shall turn to thee in religion, and affection. **The forces** – Or wealth.

6. **The multitude** – The treasure, that is brought upon camels. By these, and such like figurative expressions in several verses of this chapter is implied the coming in of all nations to Christ, and therefore they are brought in as presenting the chief commodities of their respective countries. **Dromedaries** – A smaller sort of camel. **Ephah** – The Midianites, and Ephahites dwelt beyond Arabia. **Sheba** – A country in Arabia Felix, whose queen it was, that came to visit Solomon, and her bringing gifts might be a type of this, Solomon being a type of Christ. **Gold** – The principal commodities with which this country abounded, by which we are to understand whatever is precious.

7. **Kedar** – Arabia Petrea. **Acceptance** – They shall not now, as heretofore, be rejected. **The house** – The temple, or my house: God shall become glorious by the multitude of sacrifices, that shall be offered, and accepted here. This is a type of how glorious his New Testament worship shall be.

8. **A cloud** – These metaphors import the number as well as speed, of those that should be begotten by the apostles doctrine.

9. **Ships** – To convey them to me. **Tarshish** – Those that traffic by sea. In naming this he implies all that had commerce with other nations. **From far** – From the remotest parts. **Glorified** – He will make thee honourable in the eyes of the world, especially in setting up the ministry of the gospel in the midst of thee.

10. **Minister** – Shall administer all necessaries to thee. **I had mercy** – As I afflicted thee in my anger, so out of my compassion I will abundantly bless thee.

11. **Therefore** – For that purpose; by reason of the conflux of people, that shall be continually flocking thither.

12. **Serve** – That will not submit to Christ's sceptre.

13. **The glory** – The box, the fir, the pine, and the cedar, on account whereof Lebanon was so famous; kings and great ones, the glory of the world, and also persons of a lower rank, shall be the materials, and members of Christ's church. **To beautify** – This is the reason and end why the glory of Lebanon is to be brought hither; by

these trees understand the beauty, and nobility of the church. **Sanctuary** – The temple wherein was the sanctuary. **The place of my feet** – The ark, so called, because, supposing God after the manner of men, to sit between the wings of the cherubim, his feet would rest upon the ark. All this is made good in the gospel-church.

14. The sons – Either their posterity, or themselves, for it is the manner of the Hebrews so to speak. **Bending** – Humbling themselves, as penitents. **Call thee** – They shall acknowledge her to be so.

15. Forsaken – Both of God and of her inhabitants. **No man went** – Thy streets were left desolate.

16. Shalt suck – That the church shall draw, or receive the wealth of nations, and the riches, and power of kings, and whatever is most excellent, and that it shall come freely, and affectionately, as milk flows from the breast of the mother.

17. For brass – An allusion to the days of Solomon, when gold was as brass. **Peace** – Loving, meek, and peaceable. **Righteousness** – Most righteous. Such even thy tax-gatherers shall be.

18. Salvation – They shall be safe, and able to defend thee; thou shalt be as safe, as salvation itself can make thee. **Thy gates** – Within and upon thy gates and walls, thou shalt sing praises. All this will be fulfilled during the thousand years wherein Christ shall reign upon earth.

19. The sun – These shall not be esteemed in comparison of the spiritual light of the church; but here laid down for the churches comfort as the former was for her safety, so that God will not only be a shield, but a sun. **The Lord** – Christ shall scatter all darkness and ignorance, and this light shall not wax, and wane, and suffer eclipses, and settings, as the sun and moon do, but shall be constant, without shadow of change. **The glory** – Always ministering matter of glorying in him.

21. The branch – Thy people being of my planting, the work of my hands.

22. In time – In due time, the time that I have appointed.

Chapter 61

Christ and his blessed office (1–3)

The church's repair and increase (4–6)

And joy (7–11)

Christ and his blessed office (1–3)

1. Upon me – Though the prophet may speak of himself, yet it is principally to be understood of Christ. **Anointed** – Set me apart, both capacitating him with gifts, and commissioning him

with authority; and yet more, as it is applied to Christ, a power to make all effectual, from whence he hath also the name of Messiah among the Hebrews, and of Christ among the Greeks; nay, Christ alone among the prophets hath obtained this name, Psal 45:7. The prophet describes first, who Christ is, and then what are his offices. **Liberty** – This appertains to Christ's kingly office, whereby he proclaims liberty from the dominion of sin, and from the fear of hell.

2. Vengeance – It being necessary, that where God will deliver his people, he should take vengeance on their enemies; principally on the enemies of his church, and the spiritual ones chiefly, Satan, sin, and death.

3. Ashes – By ashes understand whatever is proper for days of mourning, as by beauty whatever may become times of rejoicing. **Oil of joy** – He calls it oil of joy in allusion to those anointings they were wont to use in times of joy, gladness for heaviness; and it is called a garment in allusion to their festival ornaments, for they had garments appropriated to their conditions, some suitable to times of rejoicing, and some to times of mourning. **Called** – That they may be so. **Trees** – That they shall be firm, solid, and well rooted, being by faith engrafted into Christ, and bringing forth fruit suitable to the soil wherein they are planted.

The church's repair and increase (4–6)

5. Strangers – Gentiles, such as are not of the natural race of the Jews, but Gentile converts. Or, such as shall have no more than an outward profession. **Stand** – Ready to be at thy service. **Flocks** – The churches with the word of God. **Plow-men** – Shall manage the whole work of God's spiritual husbandry.

6. The priests – The whole body of them shall now be as near to God as the priests were formerly, and shall be a royal priesthood. This is most certainly true of all the faithful under the gospel.

And joy (7–11)

7. Double – Honour. **Portion** – Of honour, that God will give them.

8. Love judgment – I will do them right, for I love justice in myself, and in them that practise it. **Robbery** – All things gotten by injustice, though it be for sacrifice. **Direct** – I will lead them so, that they shall do all things in sincerity. **Everlasting covenant** – Though you have broken covenant with me, yet I will renew my ancient covenant made with your fathers, confirmed with the blood of Christ, and it shall be everlasting, never to be abrogated.

9. Shall be – That is, eminently a promise of the increase of the church; such shall be their prosperity, and multiplying, that they shall be known abroad by their great increase; or else, the meaning is, the church shall have a seed of the Gentiles, whereas the church has been confined to one corner of the world, now it shall remain in one nation alone no more, but shall fill all the nations of the earth. **Hath blessed** – There shall be such visible characters of God's love to them, and of God's grace in them.

10. **I will** – This is spoken in the person of the church. **Garments** – With salvation as with a garment, and with righteousness as with a robe.

11. **Righteousness** – His great work of salvation shall break out and appear. **Praise** – As the natural product, and fruit of it.

Chapter 62

A prayer of the watchmen for the church in confidence of God's gracious designs and promises to it (1–12)

1. **Zion's sake** – Zion and Jerusalem are both put for the church, Heb 12:22. **My peace** – These seem to be the words of the prophet strongly resolving, notwithstanding all difficulties, to solicit God for the church's happiness, and constantly excite to the belief of it by his preaching, though it were long before it came, for Isaiah lived near two hundred years before this was accomplished. **Righteousness** – With reference to the Babylonians, understand it of the righteousness of God, who hath promised his people deliverance, and he must be righteous, and so understand salvation before; or rather, the vindicating of his people's cause in the eyes of the nations by the ruin of the Babylonians; he will shew that his people have a righteous cause. **Lamp** – And to that purpose is set up where it may be seen continually, to signify how eminently conspicuous this prosperous estate of the church should be among the nations, and as it may particularly relate to revealing of Christ unto the world.

2. **A new name** – The church shall be more renowned than ever, both in respect of her condition, and so called Hephzi-bah, and of her relation, and so called Beulah, and this new name the Lord gives them accordingly, ver.4.

3. **Crown of glory** – An expression to set forth the dignity of her state. **In the hand** – Preserved and defended by God's hand. **Royal diadem** – The same thing with the former for substance. Or, the royal priesthood, whereof the apostle speaks, 1Pet 2:9.

4. **Forsaken** – As a woman forsaken by her husband. **Thy land** – The inhabitants of the land. **Hephzi-bah** – My delight is in her; a new name agreeing with her new condition. **Beulah** – Married; agreeing to her new relation. **Married** – Thou shalt see the increase of thy children again in the land, as the fruit of thy married condition, which by reason of thy being forsaken of thy husband, were in a manner wasted and decayed: and this refers to the great enlargement of the church in the gospel days.

6. **Day nor night** – There shall be a vigilant and industrious ministry. **Ye** – That is, are his servants. And here especially are meant his servants in ordinary, his remembrancers, such as put God in mind of his promise, and such as make the Lord to be remembered, putting his people in mind of him.

7. **A praise** – By sending the Messiah, and those labourers into his vineyard, whereby the church may be established, and settled on sure foundations, and so become a matter of praise to God. All the nations shall praise him for her.

9. **But** – Thou shalt not sow, and another reap, as formerly. **Courts** – In my courts: holiness being put for God himself.

10. **Go through** – It is doubled by way of emphasis. Go meet the Gentiles, whom God purposes to bring into the church. **Prepare** – Let them not have any obstructions in their way. **Stones** – That there be no stumbling-stone, or offence in their way. **Standard** – An allusion to soldiers, that set up their standard that the army may know where to repair from all quarters.

11. **Zion** – To Jerusalem, or the church. **Thy salvation** – Thy saviour. **Reward** – The reward due to the work.

Chapter 63

Christ's victory over his enemies (1–6)

and mercy towards his church: in judgment remembering mercy (7–14)

The church's prayer and complaint in faith (15–19)

Christ's victory over his enemies (1–6)

1. **Who** – The church makes enquiry, and that with admiration, who it is that appears in such a habit or posture? **Edom** – Idumea, where Esau dwelt. It is put for all the enemies of the church. **Bozrah** – The capital city of Idumea. Here is also an allusion to the garments of this conqueror, Edom signifying red, and Bozrah a vintage. **Glorious** – Such as generals march before their armies in. **Righteousness** – Here Christ gives an answer, wherein he both asserts his fidelity, that he will faithfully perform what he hath promised, and that he will truly execute justice. **Mighty** – I have power to accomplish salvation.

3. **Trodden** – I have destroyed the enemies of my people, I have crushed them as grapes are crushed, this being an usual metaphor to describe the utter destruction of a people.

4. Of vengeance – To take vengeance on the enemies of my church.

5. None to help – Not that he needed it, but to see what men would do, in regard his people needed it; therefore the standing, or not standing by his people, is the same thing with standing, or not standing by him. **Uphold** – A metaphor, taken from a staff, that is an help to one that leans on it.

6. Drunk – They go as it were to and fro, not knowing what to do with themselves. **Bring down** – Whatever it is wherein their strength lies, he will bring to the very dust, to nothing.

and mercy towards his church: in judgment remembering mercy (7–14)

7. Mention – Here begins a new matter, which contains the prophet's prayer, to the end of chap. 64, wherein he begins with mentioning the great kindnesses that God had shewn the Jews, and that emphatically, setting them forth with the greatest advantages.

8. He said – When he made a covenant with our fathers, and brought them out of Egypt. **Not lie** – That will keep my covenant. **So he** – Not Cyrus, Zerubbabel, or Nehemiah, but Christ himself.

9. The angel – The same that conducted them through the wilderness; the Lord Jesus Christ, who appeared to Moses in the bush. **Saved them** – From the house of bondage. **Carried** – He carried them in the arms of his power, and on the wings of his providence. And he is said to do it of old, To remember his ancient kindness for many generations past.

11. He remembered – This relates, either:

1. To the people, and then he is collectively taken, and so it looks like the language of the people in Babylon, and must be read, he shall remember.

Or, 2. It may look back to their condition in the wilderness, and thus they may properly say, Where is he? Or that God who delivered his people of old, to do the like for us now? There is a like phrase used by God, as it were recollecting himself, Where is he? Where am I with my former bowels, that moved me to help them of old? **His people** – What great things he had done for them by Moses. **The sea** – Here God speaks of himself, as in the former clause, that divided the sea for them. **Shepherds** – Moses and Aaron. **Holy Spirit** – Those abilities and gifts, wherewith God furnished Moses, as properly proceeding from the Spirit.

13. As an horse – With as much ease and tenderness, as an horse led by the bridle. **Not stumble** – That, tho' the sea were but newly divided, yet it was dried and smoothed by the wind, that God sent, as it were to prepare the way before them.

14. The valley – A laden beast goeth warily and gently down the hill. **Rest** – Led them easily, that they should not be over-travelled, or fall down, through weariness; thus Jeremiah expresses it, Jer 31:2, and thus God gave them rest from their enemies, drowning them in the sea, and in their safe conduct, that they could not annoy or disturb them, leading them 'till he found them a place for resting; the word for leading, and resting, being much of a like notion, Zech 10:6, pointing at their several rests by the way, Numb 10:33, or it may be read by way of interrogation, as all the foregoing words, and be the close of that enquiry, And where is the spirit, that caused then to rest? Or, he led them to Canaan the place of their rest.

The church's prayer and complaint in faith (15–19)

15. Look – Now the prophet begins to expostulate with God, and to argue both from the goodness of his nature, and from the greatness of his works. God sees every where, and every thing, but he is said to look down from heaven, because there is his throne whereon he sits in majesty. **Behold** – Not barely see, but behold with regard, and respect thy poor people. **Where** – What is become of that love, which of old would not let thee suffer thy people to be wronged? **Strength** – That power of thine manifested in those great acts? **The founding** – This is spoken of God after the manner of men.

16. Abraham – He who was our father after the flesh, though he be dead, and so ignorant of our condition. **Redeemer** – This is urged as another argument for pity; because their Father was their Redeemer. **From everlasting** – Thou hast been our Redeemer of old.

17. Made us – Suffered us to err. **Hardened** – Suffered it to be hardened. **Thy fear** – The fear of thee. **Servants sake** – For our sakes, that little remnant that are thy servants. **Inheritance** – The land of Canaan, which God gave them as an inheritance.

18. People – The people set apart for his servants. **A little while** – Comparatively to the promise, which was for ever. **Sanctuary** – The temple.

19. Thine – We continue so; we are in covenant, which they never were; and thus it is an argument they use with God to look upon them. **Never** – Not in that manner thou didst over us. **They** – Neither owned thee, nor were owned by thee.

Chapter 64

The church's prayer continued, for the illustration of God's glory (1–5)

With a confession of their sins, and complaint of their afflictions (6–12)

The church's prayer continued, for the illustration of God's glory (1–5)

1. Rent – A metaphor taken from men, that when they would resolutely help one in distress, break and fling open doors and whatever may hinder. **Flow down** – That all impediments might be removed out of the way: possibly an allusion to God's coming down upon mount Sinai, in those terrible flames of fire.

2. Fire – Come with such zeal for thy people, that the solid mountains may be no more before thy breath, than metal that runs, or water that boils by the force of a vehement fire. **Known** – That thine enemies may know thy power, and that thy name may be dreaded among them.

3. Terrible things – This may relate to what he did among the Egyptians, tho' it be not recorded, and afterward in the wilderness. **Looked not for** – Such things as we could never expect. **Mountains** – Kings, princes, and potentates, may metaphorically be understood by these mountains.

4. Besides thee – This is to be applied to all the wonderful works, that God at all times wrought for his people: and thus they are a plea with God, that they might well expect such things from him now, that had done such wonderful things for their fathers. **Waiteth** – This may be taken with reference both to the state of grace and glory, those incomprehensible things that are exhibited through Christ in the mysteries of the gospel.

5. Meetest – As the father the prodigal. **Worketh** – That rejoices to work righteousness. **Continuance** – To those that work righteousness. **Be saved** – In so doing, in working righteousness.

With a confession of their sins, and complaint of their afflictions (6–12)

6. Unclean – Formerly there were some that feared thee; but now we are all as one polluted mass, nothing of good left in us by reason of an universal degeneracy. **And all** – The very best of us all are no better than the uncleanest things. **Taken** – Carried away to Babylon, as leaves hurried away by a boisterous wind.

7. That calleth – That call upon thee as they ought. **Take hold** – Either to stay thee from departing from us, or to fetch thee back when departed.

8. Our father – Notwithstanding all this thou art our father both by creation, and by adoption, therefore pity us thy children.

9. Thy people – Thou hast no people in covenant but us, and wilt thou not leave thyself a people in the world?

11. Pleasant things – The king's palace, and the houses of the nobles, and other pieces of state and magnificence.

12. Wilt thou – Do none of these things move thee to take vengeance? **Thy peace** – Wilt thou be as one that regards not?

Chapter 65

The calling of the Gentiles: the Jews for their incredulity, idolatry, and hypocrisy, rejected (1–7)

A remnant shall be saved (8–10)

Judgments on the wicked, and blessings on the Godly (11–16)

The flourishing and peaceable state of the New Jerusalem (17–26)

The calling of the Gentiles: the Jews for their incredulity, idolatry, and hypocrisy, rejected (1–7)

1. I am – This in the primary sense of this text, is a prophecy of the conversion of the Gentiles, upon the rejection of the Jews; for their contempt and crucifying of Christ, cannot be doubted by any, who will not arrogate to themselves a greater ability to interpret the prophesies of the Old Testament, than St. Paul had, who, Rom 10:20, expressly so interprets it, and applies it, which shows the vanity of the Jews in their other interpretations of it. **Sought** – The word signifies properly a diligent enquiry in things relating to God. **Asked not** – That in times past made no enquiry after me; I am now found by them that formerly sought me not. **I said** – I invited whole nations by the preaching of my gospel to behold me, and that with importunity, doubling my words upon them, and this I did unto a nation not called by my name, with whom I was not in covenant.

2. I have spread – Applied to the Jews, Rom 10:21. I have stretched out my hands, I have used all means to reduce them, I have stretched out the hands of a passionate orator to persuade them, of a liberal benefactor to load them with my benefits; this I have done continually in the whole course of my providence with them.

3. To my face – With the utmost impudence, not taking notice of God's omnipresence, and omniscience. **In gardens** – Directly contrary to the divine rule.

4. Remain – They remained among the graves, there consulting with devils, who were thought to delight in such places; or to practice necromancy, all which were forbidden, Deut 18:11 Isa 8:19. **Monuments** – Some interpret it of idol temples, some of caves and dens, in which the Heathens used to worship their idols.

Broth of abominable things – Of such flesh as was to the Jews unclean by the law.

5. **Holier** – Thus they esteemed themselves holier than others, though all their holiness lay in rituals, and those too, such as God never commanded. Of these God saith, These are a smoke in my nostrils, a fire that burneth all the day; that is, a continual provocation to me: as smoke is an offence to our noses.

6. **Behold** – They may think I take no notice of these things; but I will as certainly remember them, as princes or great men that record things in writing which they would not forget.

7. **Together** – Yea, and when I reckon with them, I will punish them, not only for their personal sins, but for the sins of their parents, which they have made their own, by imitation. **Their former** – I will not only punish the late sins that they have committed, but the former sins of this kind, which those that went before did commit, and they have continued in.

A remnant shall be saved (8–10)

8. **Thus** – These word's may be conceived as a gracious answer from God to the prophet, pleading God's covenant with Abraham, Isaac, and Israel. To this God replies, that he intended no such severity. His threatening should be made good upon the generality of this people. **Blessing** – But yet, as in a vineyard, which is generally unfruitful, there may be some vine that brings forth fruit, and has the hopes of new wine in the cluster, and as to such, the gardener bids his servant destroy it not, for there is in them what speaks God's blessing. **So** – So will I do for my servants sake, that I may not destroy them all, for the sake of my servants, Abraham, Isaac, and Jacob.

9. **Judah** – God farther promises to bring out of Judah, an inheritor of his mountains which refers to the Jews return out of the captivity of Babylon to Jerusalem, to worship God in his temple, upon mount Zion. **Mine elect** – My chosen ones. The term signifies such as are dignified with some special favour. The whole nation of the Jews are called a chosen people.

10. **A fold** – Sharon was a place of great fruitfulness for pastures. It was become like a wilderness, God here promises that it should again be a place for the flocks.

Judgments on the wicked, and blessings on the Godly (11–16)

11. **Forget** – To forget God's holy mountains, signifies not to regard the true worship of God. God calls Zion his holy mountain. **That troop** – The idols of the ten tribes, and of the Assyrians, were a troop, where as the God of Israel was one God. By preparing a table, here seems to be meant, the feasts they made upon their sacrifices in imitation of what the true God had

commanded his people. **Furnish** – God had appointed drink offerings for his honour, but the people had paid their homage to idols. **Number** – The multitude of their idols.

12. **To the sword** – A great number of you shall perish by the sword; or possibly the term number may refer to all in the next phrase, so that none of them should escape. God saith he will number them, tell them out one by one to the sword. **Bow down** – As you have bowed down to idols. **I called** – By my prophets, you did not answer by doing the things which I enjoined. **Choose** – You sinned deliberately choosing sinful courses, the things which I hated.

15. **A curse** – They shall use your names as examples, of the eminent wrath of God upon sinners. **Another name** – He will not suffer his own people to be called by a name by which idolaters are known.

16. **God of truth** – Because they shall see what God promised is fulfilled. **Are hid** – That is, they are at an end.

The flourishing and peaceable state of the New Jerusalem (17–26)

17. **I create** – I am about wholly to change the state not only of my people, but to bring a new face upon the world, which shall abide until a new heavens and earth appear, in which shall dwell nothing but righteousness. **Not be remembered** – That state of things shall be so glorious, that the former state of my people shall not be remembered.

18. **You** – The church, as well under the gospel, as under the law.

20. **An infant** – Those that were now children, shall die at a great age. **But** – Yet none of these things shall be of any advantage to wicked men, but if any of them shall live to be an hundred years old, yet they shall die accursed.

23. **With them** – Is blessed with them.

24. **Before they call** – God promised, chap. 58:9, to answer them, when they called: here he promises to answer the words, as soon as they should be formed in their hearts before they could get them out of their lips. **While** – Yea, while they were speaking.

25. **The wolf** – God here promises to take off the fierceness of the spirits of his peoples enemies, so that they shall live quietly and peaceably together. **And dust** – God promises a time of tranquillity to his church under the metaphor of serpents eating the dust, their proper meat, Gen 3:14, instead of flying upon men: it signifies such a time, when wicked men shall no more eat up the people of God.

Chapter 66

God is served with the spirit, and not by ceremonies (1–5)

The wonderful birth and benefits of the gospel-church (6–14)

Severe judgments against the wicked (15–17)

The Gentiles shall be an holy church (18–23)

The eternal punishment of the wicked (24)

God is served with the spirit, and not by ceremonies (1–5)

1. The heaven – The highest heaven, is the place where I shew myself in my majesty. So Psal 11:4 Psal 103:19 Matt 5:34. Hence we are taught to pray; our father which art in heaven. **And the earth is my footstool** – Or a place wherein I set my feet, Matt 5:35. **The house** – Can there be an house built, that will contain me? **My rest** – Or where is the place wherein I can be said to rest in a proper sense?

2. Have been – They were not only made by God, but kept in being by him. **Look** – Yet God will look with a favourable eye to him that hath a broken and contrite spirit, whose heart is subdued to the will of God, and who is poor, and low in his own eyes. **Trembleth** – Who trembleth when he hears God's threatening words, and hears every revelation of his will with reverence.

3. He that – Solomon, Prov 15:8, gives a full commentary on the whole verse; The sacrifice of the wicked is an abomination to the Lord. **As if** – From hence it is plain, that the prophet is not here reflecting upon idolatrous worship, but formal worship: upon those who in a formality worshipped the true God, and by acts which he had appointed. God by the prophet declares, that these mens services were no more acceptable to him than murder, idolatry, or the most horrid profanation of his name. **Own ways** – They live as they lust. **Delight** – They take pleasure in their sins.

4. Choose – They have chosen to mock and delude me, I will choose to suffer them to delude themselves; they have chosen to work wickedness, I will choose the effect. **Their fears** – That is, the things which they feared. **Did not hear** – God accounts that those do not hear, who do not obey his will.

5. You – That truly fear God. **Your brethren** – By nation. **Cast you out** – That cast you out of their synagogues, cast you out of their city, and some of you out of the world. **For my names sake** – For my sake; for your adherence to my law. **Glorified** – Thinking they did God good service, John 16:2.

The wonderful birth and benefits of the gospel-church (6–14)

6. A voice – The expression of a prophetical ecstasy, as if he said, I hear a sad and affrighting noise; it comes not from the city only, but from the temple, wherein these formalists have so much gloried. There is a noise of soldiers slaying, and of the poor people shrieking or crying out. **Of the Lord** – A voice of the Lord, not in thunder, but that rendereth recompense to his enemies. Thus he seems to express the destruction of the Jews by the Roman armies, as a thing at that time doing.

7. Before – The whole verse is expressive of a great and sudden salvation, which God would work for his church, like the delivery of a woman, and that of a man-child, before her travail, and without pain. Doubtless it refers to the coming of Christ, and the sudden propagation of the gospel.

8. For – As soon as the voice of the gospel put the church of the Jews into her travail, in Christ's and the Apostles time, it presently brought forth.

9. Shall I – I, that in the ordinary course of my providence use to give a birth to women, to whom I have given a power to conceive, shall I not give a birth to my people, whom by my promises I have made to conceive such expectations? **And shut** – Nor shall Zion once only bring forth, but she shall go on, but her womb shall not be shut, she shall every day bring forth more and more children, and my presence shall be with my church, to the end of the world.

11. Consolations – The gospel doctrine was their breasts of consolation. **Her glory** – Christ was the glory of the people of Israel, though he was also a light to the Gentiles.

12. Like a river – It is plain this prophecy relates to a farther conversion of the Jews than hath been yet seen. **Ye** – Ye Jews also. **Her sides** – The Gentiles were borne upon the sides of Jerusalem and dandled upon her knees, as first hearing from the Apostles the glad tidings of salvation.

13. As one whom – That is, in the most tender, and compassionate way.

14. Rejoice – The peace of the church and the propagation of the kingdom of Christ, is always the cause of an heart rejoicing to such as fear God, so that they flourish like an herb in the spring. **The hand** – The power, protection, and influence of God.

Severe judgments against the wicked (15–17)

15. With fire – With terrible judgments, or with fire in a proper sense, understanding it of the fire with which enemies use to consume places brought under their power. **Whirlwind** – With a sudden sweeping judgment. **Fury** – That is, with fervour; for fury properly taken is not in

God. **Rebukes** – They had contemned the rebukes of the law, now God will rebuke them with fire, and sword.

16. Plead – God at first pleads with sinners by words, but if he cannot so prevail, he will plead with them in a way by which he will overcome; by fire, pestilence and blood. **All flesh** – Thus he threatens to do with all the wicked Jews. **The slain** – Those whom God should cause to be slain.

17. Gardens – In which they worshipped idols. **In the midst** – Behind one of the trees, or one by one behind the trees. **The abominations** – All those beasts forbidden the Jews for meat. God will not only destroy gross idolaters, but all those who make no conscience of yielding obedience to the law of God in such things as seemed to them of a minute nature, and such as they easily might have obeyed.

The Gentiles shall be an holy church (18–23)

18. Come – It shall come to pass that I will cast them off, and then I will gather all nations. **My glory** – My oracles, my ordinances, which hitherto have been locked up in the church of the Jews, and been their glory, shall be published to the Gentiles.

19. A sign – By this may be understood Christ, Luke 2:34, or the ministry of the word attended with miracles, these were set up among the Jews first, then among the Gentiles. **Afar off** – To all the quarters of the world. **They shall** – This was eminently made good after the destruction of Jerusalem, when the believers among the Jews, as well as the apostles went about publishing the gospel to all people, which was declaring the Lord's glory.

20. Your brethren – Those who are the children of Abraham, not considered as the father of the Jewish nation only, but considered as the father of many nations, and as the father of the faithful, and so are your brethren, shall be brought out of all nations for an offering to the Lord. **Holy mountain** – And they shall be brought into the church, which began at Jerusalem. **As** – And they shall come with as much joy and gladness, with as much sincerity and holiness, as the Godly Jews do when they bring their offerings in clean vessels.

21. For priests – God will find among the converted Gentiles those who though they are not of the tribe of Levi, yet shall do the true work of priests and Levites.

22. The new heavens – The new state of the church to be raised up under the Messiah. **Remain** – As I intend that shall abide, so there shall be a daily succession of true believers for the upholding of it.

23. And – In the gospel-church there shall be as constant and settled a course of worship as ever was in the Jewish church: Christians are not bound to keep the Jewish Sabbaths or new-moons. But New Testament worship is expressed by Old Testament phrases. The Jews were only obliged to appear three times in a year at Jerusalem, but the gospel-church shall worship God from one Sabbath to another.

The eternal punishment of the wicked (24)

JEREMIAH

Matthew Henry

Introduction

Jeremiah was a priest, a native of Anathoth, in the tribe of Benjamin. He was called to the prophetic office when very young, about seventy years after the death of Isaiah, and exercised it for about forty years with great faithfulness, till the sins of the Jewish nation came to their full measure and destruction followed. The prophecies of Jeremiah do not stand as they were delivered. Blayney has endeavoured to arrange them in more regular order, namely, ch. 1–20; 22; 23; 25; 26; 35; 36; 45; 24; 29; 30; 31; 27; 28; 21; 34; 37; 32; 33; 38; 39; (ver. 15–18, 1–14) 40–44; 46–52. The general subject of his prophecies is the idolatry and other sins of the Jews; the judgments by which they were threatened, with references to their future restoration and deliverance, and promises of the Messiah. They are remarkable for plain and faithful reproofs, affectionate expostulations, and awful warnings.

Chapter 1

**Jeremiah's call to the prophetic office
(1–10)**

**A vision of an almond-tree and of a
seething-pot, divine protection is promised
(11–19)**

Jeremiah's call to the prophetic office
(1–10)

Jeremiah's early call to the work and office of a prophet is stated. He was to be a prophet, not to the Jews only, but to the neighbouring nations. He is still a prophet to the whole world, and it would be well if they would attend to these warnings. The Lord who formed us, knows for what particular services and purposes he intended us. But unless he sanctifies us by his new-creating Spirit, we shall neither be fit for his holy service on earth, nor his holy happiness in heaven. It becomes us to have low thoughts of ourselves. Those who are young, should consider that they are so, and not venture beyond their powers. But though a sense of our own weakness and insufficiency should make us go humbly about our work, it should not make us draw back when God calls us. Those who have messages to deliver from God, must not fear the face of man. The Lord, by a sign, gave Jeremiah such a gift as was necessary. God's message should be delivered in his own words. Whatever worldly wise men or politicians may think, the safety of kingdoms is decided according to the purpose and word of God.

A vision of an almond-tree and of a
seething-pot, divine protection is promised
(11–19)

God gave Jeremiah a view of the destruction of Judah and Jerusalem by the Chadians. The almond-tree, which is more forward in the spring than any other, represented the speedy approach of judgments. God also showed whence the intended ruin should arise. Jeremiah saw a seething-pot boiling, representing Jerusalem and Judah in great commotion. The mouth or face of the furnace or hearth, was toward the north; from whence the fire and fuel were to come. The northern powers shall unite. The cause of these judgments was the sin of Judah. The whole counsel of God must be declared. The fear of God is the best remedy against the fear of man. Better to have all men our enemies than God our enemy; those who are sure they have God with them, need not, ought not to fear, whoever is against them. Let us pray that we may be willing to give up personal interests, and that nothing may move us from our duty.

Chapter 2

God expostulates with his people (1–8)

Their revolt beyond example (9–13)

Guilt the cause of sufferings (14–19)

The sins of Judah (20–28)

Their false confidence (29–37)

God expostulates with his people (1–8)

Those who begin well, but do not persevere, will justly be upbraided with their hopeful and promising beginnings. Those who desert religion, commonly oppose it more than those who never knew it. For this they could have no excuse. God's spiritual Israel must own their obligations to him for safe conduct through the wilderness of this world, so dangerous to the soul. Alas, that many, who once appeared devoted to the Lord, so live that their professions aggravate their crimes! Let us be careful that we do not lose in zeal and fervency, as we gain knowledge.

Their revolt beyond example (9–13)

Before God punishes sinners, he pleads with them, to bring them to repentance. He pleads with us, what we should plead with ourselves. Be afraid to think of the wrath and curse which will be the portion of those who throw themselves out of God's grace and favour. Grace in Christ is compared to water from a fountain, it being cooling and refreshing, cleansing and making fruitful: to living water, because it quickens dead sinners, revives drooping saints, supports and maintains spiritual life, and issues in eternal life, and is ever-flowing. To forsake this Fountain is the first evil; this is done when the people of God neglect his word and ordinances. They hewed them out broken cisterns, that could hold no water. Such are the world, and the things in it; such are the inventions of men when followed and depended on. Let us, with purpose of heart, cleave to the Lord only; whither else shall we go? How prone are we to forego the consolations of

the Holy Spirit, for the worthless joys of the enthusiast and hypocrite!

Guilt the cause of sufferings (14–19)

Is Israel a servant? No, they are the seed of Abraham. We may apply this spiritually: Is the soul of man a slave? No, it is not; but has sold its own liberty, and enslaved itself to divers lusts and passions. The Assyrian princes, like lions, prevailed against Israel. People from Egypt destroyed their glory and strength. They brought these calamities on themselves by departing from the Lord. The use and application of this is, Repent of thy sin, that thy correction may not be thy ruin. What has a Christian to do in the ways of forbidden pleasure or vain sinful mirth, or with the pursuits of covetousness and ambition?

The sins of Judah (20–28)

Notwithstanding all their advantages, Israel had become like the wild vine that bears poisonous fruit. Men are often as much under the power of their unbridled desires and their sinful lusts, as the brute beasts. But the Lord here warns them not to weary themselves in pursuits which could only bring distress and misery. As we must not despair of the mercy of God, but believe that to be sufficient for the pardon of our sins, so neither must we despair of the grace of God, but believe that it is able to subdue our corruptions, though ever so strong.

Their false confidence (29–37)

The nation had not been wrought upon by the judgements of God, but sought to justify themselves. The world is, to those who make it their home and their portion, a wilderness and a land of darkness; but those who dwell in God, have the lines fallen to them in pleasant places. Here is the language of presumptuous sinners. The Jews had long thrown off serious thoughts of God. How many days of our lives pass without suitable remembrance of him! The Lord was displeased with their confidences, and would not prosper them therein. Men employ all their ingenuity, but cannot find happiness in the way of sin, or excuse for it. They may shift from one sin to another, but none ever hardened himself against God, or turned from him, and prospered.

Chapter 3

Exhortations to repentance (1–5)

Judah more guilty than Israel (6–11)

But pardon is promised (12–20)

The children of Israel express their sorrow and repentance (21–25)

Exhortations to repentance (1–5)

In repentance, it is good to think upon the sins of which we have been guilty, and the places and companies where they have been committed. How gently the Lord had corrected them! In receiving penitents, he is God, and not man. Whatever thou hast said or done hitherto, wilt thou not from this time apply to me? Will not this grace of God overcome thee? Now pardon is proclaimed, wilt thou not take the benefit? They will hope to find in him the tender compassions of a Father towards a returning prodigal. They will come to him as the Guide of their youth: youth needs a guide. Repenting sinners may encourage themselves that God will not keep his anger to the end. All God's mercies, in every age, suggest encouragement; and what can be so desirable for the young, as to have the Lord for their Father, and the Guide of their youth? Let parents daily direct their children earnestly to seek this blessing.

Judah more guilty than Israel (6–11)

If we mark the crimes of those who break off from a religious profession, and the consequences, we see abundant reason to shun evil ways. It is dreadful to be proved more criminal than those who have actually perished in their sins; yet it will be small comfort in everlasting punishment, for them to know that others were viler than they.

But pardon is promised (12–20)

See God's readiness to pardon sin, and the blessings reserved for gospel times. These words were proclaimed toward the north; to Israel, the ten tribes, captive in Assyria. They are directed how to return. If we confess our sins, the Lord is faithful and just to forgive them. These promises are fully to come to pass in the bringing back the Jews in after-ages. God will graciously receive those that return to him; and by his grace, he takes them out from among the rest. The ark of the covenant was not found after the captivity. The whole of that dispensation was to be done away, which took place after the multitude of believers had been greatly increased by the conversion of the Gentiles, and of the Israelites scattered among them. A happy state of the church is foretold. He can teach all to call him Father; but without thorough change of heart and life, no man can be a child of God, and we have no security for not departing from Him.

The children of Israel express their sorrow and repentance (21–25)

Sin is turning aside to crooked ways. And forgetting the Lord our God is at the bottom of all sin. By sin we bring ourselves into trouble. The promise to those that return is, God will heal their backslidings, by his pardoning mercy, his quieting peace, and his renewing grace. They come devoting themselves to God. They come disclaiming all expectations of relief and succour from any but the Lord. Therefore they come depending upon him only. He is the Lord, and he only can save. It points out the great salvation from sin Jesus Christ wrought out for us. They come justifying God in their troubles, and judging themselves for their sins. True penitents learn to call sin shame, even the sin they have been most pleased with. True penitents learn to call sin death and ruin, and to charge upon it all they suffer. While men harden themselves in sin, contempt and misery are their portion: for he that covereth his sins shall not prosper, but he that confesseth and forsaketh them, shall find mercy.

Chapter 4

Exhortations and promises (1–2)
Judah exhorted to repentance (3–4)
Judgments denounced (5–18)
The approaching ruin of Judah (19–31)

Exhortations and promises (1–2)

The first two should be read with the last chapter. Sin must be put away out of the heart, else it is not put away out of God's sight, for the heart is open before him.

Judah exhorted to repentance (3–4)

An unhumbled heart is like ground untilled. It is ground which may be improved; it is our ground let out to us; but it is fallow; it is over-grown with thorns and weeds, the natural product of the corrupt heart. Let us entreat the Lord to create in us a clean heart, and to renew a right spirit within us; for except a man be born again, he cannot enter into the kingdom of heaven.

Judgments denounced (5–18)

The fierce conqueror of the neighbouring nations was to make Judah desolate. The prophet was afflicted to see the people lulled into security by false prophets. The approach of the enemy is described. Some attention was paid in Jerusalem to outward reformation; but it was necessary that their hearts should be washed, in the exercise of true repentance and faith, from the love and pollution of sin. When lesser calamities do not rouse sinners and reform nations, sentence will be given against them. The Lord's voice declares that misery is approaching, especially against wicked professors of the gospel; when it overtakes them, it will be plainly seen that the fruit of wickedness is bitter, and the end is fatal.

The approaching ruin of Judah (19–31)

The prophet had no pleasure in delivering messages of wrath. He is shown in a vision the whole land in confusion. Compared with what it was, every thing is out of order; but the ruin of the Jewish nation would not be final. Every end of our comforts is not a full end. Though the Lord may correct his people very severely, yet he will not cast them off. Ornaments and false colouring would be of no avail. No outward privileges or profession, no contrivances would prevent destruction. How wretched the state of those who are like foolish children in the concerns of their souls! Whatever we are ignorant of, may the Lord make of good understanding in the ways of godliness. As sin will find out the sinner, so sorrow will, sooner or later, find out the secure.

Chapter 5

The Jews' profession of religion was hypocritical (1–9)

The cruel proceedings of their enemies (10–18)

Their apostasy and idolatry (19–31)

The Jews' profession of religion was hypocritical (1–9)

None could be found who behaved as upright and godly men. But the Lord saw the true character of the people through all their disguises. The poor were ignorant, and therefore they were wicked. What can be expected but works of darkness, from people that know nothing of God and religion? There are God's poor, who, notwithstanding poverty, know the way of the Lord, walk in it, and do their duty; but these were willingly ignorant, and their ignorance would not be their excuse. The rich were insolent and haughty, and the abuse of God's favours made their sin worse.

The cruel proceedings of their enemies (10–18)

Multitudes are ruined by believing that God will not be so strict as his word says he will; by this artifice Satan undid mankind. Sinners are not willing to own any thing to be God's word, that tends to part them from, or to disquiet them in, their sins. Mocking and misusing the Lord's messengers, filled the measure of their iniquity. God can bring trouble upon us from places and causes very remote. He has mercy in store for his people, therefore will set bounds to this desolating judgment. Let us not overlook the 'nev-ertheless,' ver. 18. This is the Lord's covenant with Israel. He thereby proclaims his holiness, and his utter displeasure against sin while sparing the sinner, Psalms 89:30–35.

Their apostasy and idolatry (19–31)

Unhumbled hearts are ready to charge God with being unjust in their afflictions. But they may read their sin in their punishment. If men will inquire wherefore the Lord doeth hard things unto them, let them think of their sins. The restless waves obeyed the Divine decree, that they should not pass the sandy shores, which were as much a restraint as lofty mountains; but they burst all restraints of God's law, and were wholly gone into wickedness. Neither did they consider their interest. While the Lord, year after year, reserves to us the appointed weeks of harvest, men live on his bounty; yet they transgress against him. Sin deprives us of God's blessings; it makes the heaven as brass, and the earth as iron. Certainly the things of this world are not the best things; and we are not to think, that, because evil men prosper, God allows their practices. Though sentence against evil works is not executed speedily, it will be executed. Shall I not visit for these things? This speaks the certainty and the necessity of God's judgments. Let those who walk in bad ways consider that an end will come, and there will be bitterness in the latter end.

Chapter 6

The invasion of Judea (1–8)

The justice of God's proceedings (9–17)

All methods used to amend them had been without success (18–30)

The invasion of Judea (1–8)

Whatever methods are used, it is vain to contend with God's judgments. The more we indulge in the pleasures of this life, the more we unfit ourselves for the troubles of this life. The Chaldean army shall break in upon the land of Judah, and in a little time devour all. The day is coming, when those careless and secure in sinful ways will be visited. It is folly to trifle when we have eternal salvation to work out, and the enemies of that salvation to fight against. But they were thus eager, not that they might fulfil God's counsels, but that they might fill their own treasures; yet God thereby served his own purposes. The corrupt heart of man, in its natural state, casts out evil thoughts, just as a fountain casts out her waters. It is always flowing, yet always full. The God of mercy is loth to depart even from a provoking people, and is earnest with them, that by repentance and reformation, they may prevent things from coming to extremity.

The justice of God's proceedings (9–17)

When the Lord arises to take vengeance, no sinners of any age or rank, or of either sex escape. They were set upon the world, and wholly carried away by the love of it. If we judge of this sin by God's word, we find multitudes in every station and rank given up to it. Those are to be reckoned our worst and most dangerous enemies, who flatter us in a sinful way. Oh that men would be wise for their souls! Ask for the old paths; the way of godliness and righteousness has always been the way God has owned and blessed. Ask for the old paths set forth by the written word of God. When you have found the good way, go on in it, you will find abundant recompense at your journey's end. But if men will not obey the voice of God and flee to his appointed Refuge, it will plainly appear at the day of judgment, that they are ruined because they reject God's word.

All methods used to amend them had been without success (18–30)

God rejects their outward services, as worthless to atone for their sins. Sacrifice and incense were to direct them to a Mediator; but when offered to purchase a license to go on in sin, they provoke God. The sins of God's professing people make them an easy prey to their enemies. They dare not show themselves. Saints may rejoice in hope of God's mercies, though they see them only in the promise: sinners must mourn for fear of God's judgments, though they see them only in the threatenings. They are the worst of revolters, and are all corrupters. Sinners soon become tempters. They are compared to ore supposed to have good metal in it, but which proves all dross. Nothing will prevail to part between them and their sins. Reprobate silver shall they be called, useless and worthless. When warnings, corrections, rebukes, and all means of grace, leave men unrenewed, they will be left, as rejected of God, to everlasting misery. Let us pray, then, that we may be refined by the Lord, as silver is refined.

Chapter 7

Confidence in the temple is vain (1–16)

The provocation by persisting in idolatry (17–20)

God justifies his dealings with them (21–28)

And threatens vengeance (29–34)

Confidence in the temple is vain (1–16)

No observances, professions, or supposed revelations, will profit, if men do not amend their ways and their doings. None can claim an interest in free salvation, who allow themselves in the practice of known sin, or live in the neglect of known duty. They thought that the temple they profaned would be their protection. But all who continue in sin because grace has abounded, or that grace may abound, make Christ the minister of sin; and the cross of Christ, rightly understood, forms the most effectual remedy to such poisonous sentiments. The Son of God gave himself for our transgressions, to show the excellence of the Divine law, and the evil of sin. Never let us think we may do wickedness without suffering for it.

The provocation by persisting in idolatry (17–20)

The Jews took pride in showing zeal for their idols. Let us learn to be earnest in the service of our God, even from this bad example. Let us think it an honour to be employed in any work for God. Let us be as diligent ourselves, and as careful to teach our children the truths of God, as many are to teach the mysteries of iniquity. The direct tendency of this sin is malice against God, but it will hurt themselves. And they shall find there is no escaping. God's wrath is fire unquenchable.

God justifies his dealings with them (21–28)

God shows that obedience was required of them. That which God commanded was, Hearken diligently to the voice of the Lord thy God. The promise is very encouraging. Let God's will be your rule, and his favour shall be your happiness. God was displeased with disobedience. We understand the gospel as little as the Jews understood the law, if we think that even the sacrifice of Christ lessens our obligation to obey.

And threatens vengeance (29–34)

In token both of sorrow and of slavery, Jerusalem must be degraded, and separated from God, as she had been separated to him. The heart is the place in which God has chosen to put his name; but if sin has the innermost and uppermost place there, we pollute the temple of the Lord. The destruction of Jerusalem appears here very terrible. The slain shall be many; they having made it the place of their sin. Evil pursues sinners, even after death. Those who will not, by the grace of God, be cured of vain mirth, shall, by the justice of God, be deprived of all mirth. How many ruin their health and property without complaining, when engaged in Satan's service! May we learn to relish holy joys, and to sit loose to all others though lawful.

Chapter 8

The remains of the dead exposed (1–3)

The stupidity of the people, compared with the instinct of the brute creation (4–13)

The alarm of the invasion, and lamentation (14–22)

The remains of the dead exposed (1–3)

Though no real hurt can be done to a dead body, yet disgrace to the remains of wicked persons may alarm those yet alive; and this reminds us that the Divine justice and punishments extend beyond the grave. Whatever befalls us here, let us humble ourselves before God, and seek his mercy.

The stupidity of the people, compared with the instinct of the brute creation (4–13)

What brought this ruin? 1. The people would not attend to reason; they would not act in the affairs of their souls with common prudence. Sin is backsliding; it is going back from the way that leads to life, to that which leads to destruction. 2. They would not attend to the warning of conscience. They did not take the first step towards repentance: true repentance begins in serious inquiry as to what we have done, from conviction that we have done amiss. 3. They would not attend to the ways of providence, nor understand the voice of God in them, ver. 7. They know not how to improve the seasons of grace, which God affords. Many boast of their religious knowledge, yet, unless taught by the Spirit of God, the instinct of brutes is a more sure guide than their supposed wisdom. 4. They would not attend to the written word. Many enjoy abundance of the means of grace, have Bibles and ministers, but they have them in vain. They will soon be ashamed of their devices. The pretenders to wisdom were the priests and the false prophets. They flattered people in sin, and so flattered them into destruction, silencing their fears and complaints with, All is well. Selfish teachers may promise peace when there is no peace; and thus men encourage each other in committing evil; but in the day of visitation they will have no refuge to flee unto.

The alarm of the invasion, and lamentation (14–22)

At length they begin to see the hand of God lifted up. And when God appears against us, every thing that is against us appears formidable. As salvation only can be found in the Lord, so the present moment should be seized. Is there no medicine proper for a sick and dying kingdom? Is there no skilful, faithful hand to apply the medicine? Yes, God is able to help and to heal them. If sinners die of their wounds, their blood is upon their own heads. The blood of Christ is balm in Gilead, his Spirit is the Physician there, all-sufficient; so that the people may be healed, but will not. Thus men die unpardoned and unchanged, for they will not come to Christ to be saved.

Chapter 9

The people are corrected, Jerusalem is destroyed (1–11)

The captives suffer in a foreign land (12–22)

God's loving-kindness, He threatens the enemies of his people (23–26)

The people are corrected, Jerusalem is destroyed (1–11)

Jeremiah wept much, yet wished he could weep more, that he might rouse the people to a due sense of the hand of God. But even the desert, without communion with God, through Christ Jesus, and the influences of the Holy Spirit, must be a place for temptation and evil; while, with these blessings, we may live in holiness in crowded cities. The people accustomed their tongues to lies. So false were they, that a brother could not be trusted. In trading and bargaining they said any thing for their own advantage, though they knew it to be false. But God marked their sin. Where no knowledge of God is, what good can be expected? He has many ways of turning a fruitful land into barrenness for the wickedness of those that dwell therein.

The captives suffer in a foreign land (12–22)

In Zion the voice of joy and praise used to be heard, while the people kept close to God; but sin has altered the sound, it is now the voice of lamentation. Unhumbled hearts lament their calamity, but not their sin, which is the cause of it. Let the doors be shut ever so fast, death steals upon us. It enters the palaces of princes and great men, though stately, strongly built, and guarded. Nor are those more safe that are abroad; death cuts off even the children from without, and the young men from the streets. Hearken to the word of the Lord, and mourn with godly sorrow. This alone can bring true comfort; and it can turn the heaviest afflictions into precious mercies.

God's loving-kindness, He threatens the enemies of his people (23–26)

In this world of sin and sorrow, ending soon in death and judgement, how foolish for men to glory in their knowledge, health, strength, riches, or in any thing which leaves them under the dominion of sin and the wrath of God! and of which an account must hereafter be rendered; it will but increase their misery. Those are the true Israel who worship God in the Spirit, rejoice in Christ Jesus, and have no confidence in the flesh. Let us prize the distinction which comes from God, and will last for ever. Let us seek it diligently.

Chapter 10

The absurdity of idolatry (1–16)

Destruction denounced against Jerusalem (17–25)

The absurdity of idolatry (1–16)

The prophet shows the glory of Israel's God, and exposes the folly of idolaters. Charms and other attempts to obtain supernatural help, or to pry into futurity, are copied from the wicked customs of the heathen. Let us stand in awe, and not dare provoke God, by giving that glory to another which is due to him alone. He is ready to forgive, and save all who repent and believe in the name of his Son Jesus Christ. Faith learns these blessed truths from the word of God; but all knowledge not from that source, leads to doctrines of vanity.

Destruction denounced against Jerusalem (17–25)

The Jews who continued in their own land, felt secure. But, sooner or later, sinners will find all things as the word of God has declared, and that its threatenings are not empty terrors. Submission will support the believer under every grief allotted to him; but what can render the load of Divine vengeance easy to be borne by those who fall under it in sullen despair? Those cannot expect to prosper, who do not, by faith and prayer, take God with them in all their ways. The report of the enemy's approach was very dreadful. Yet the designs which men lay deep, and think well formed, are dashed to pieces in a moment. Events are often overruled, so as to be quite contrary to what we intended and expected. If the Lord has directed our steps into the ways of peace and righteousness, let us entreat him to enable us to walk therein. Say not, Lord, do not correct me; but, Lord, do not correct me in anger. We may bear the smart of God's rod, but we cannot bear the weight of his wrath. Those who restrain prayer, prove that they know not God; for those who know him will seek him, and seek his favour. If even severe corrections lead sinners to be convinced of wholesome truths, they will have abundant cause for gratitude. And they will then humble themselves before the Lord.

Chapter 11

The disobedient Jews reproved (1–10)

Their utter ruin (11–17)

The people would be destroyed who sought the prophet's life (18–23)

The disobedient Jews reproved (1–10)

God never promised to bestow blessings on his rational creatures, while they persist in wilful disobedience. Pardon and acceptance are promised freely to all believers; but no man can be saved who does not obey the command of God to repent, to believe in Christ, to separate from sin and the world, to choose self-denial and newness of life. In general, men will hearken to those who speak of doctrines, promises, and privileges; but when duties are mentioned, they will not bend their ear.

Their utter ruin (11–17)

Evil pursues sinners, and entangles them in snares, out of which they cannot free themselves. Now, in their distress, their many gods and many altars stand them in no stead. And those whose own prayers will not be heard, cannot expect benefit from the prayers of others. Their profession of religion shall prove of no use. When trouble came upon them, they made this their confidence, but God has rejected it. His altar shall yield them no satisfaction. The remembrance of God's former favours to them shall be no comfort under troubles; and his remembrance of them shall be no argument for their relief. Every sin against the Lord is a sin against ourselves, and so it will be found sooner or later.

The people would be destroyed who sought the prophet's life (18–23)

The prophet Jeremiah tells much concerning himself, the times he lived in being very troublesome. Those of his own city plotted how they might cause his death. They thought to end his days, but he outlived most of his enemies; they thought to blast his memory, but it lives to this day, and will be blessed while time lasts. God knows all the secret designs of his and his people's enemies, and can, when he pleases, make them known. God's justice is a terror to the wicked, but a comfort to the godly. When we are wronged, we have a God to commit our cause to, and it is our duty to commit it to him. We should also look well to our own spirits, that we are not overcome with evil, but that by patient continuance in praying for our enemies, and in kindness to them, we may overcome evil with good.

Chapter 12

Jeremiah complains of the prosperity of the wicked (1–6)

The heavy judgments to come upon the nation (7–13)

Divine mercy to them, and even to the nations around (14–17)

Jeremiah complains of the prosperity of the wicked (1–6)

When we are most in the dark concerning God's dispensations, we must keep up right thoughts of God, believing that he never did the least wrong to any of his creatures. When we find it hard to understand any of his dealings with us, or others, we must look to general truths as our first principles, and abide by them: the Lord is righteous. The God with whom we have to do, knows how our hearts are toward him. He knows both the guile of the hypocrite and the sincerity of the upright. Divine judgments would pull the wicked out of their pasture as sheep for the slaughter. This fruitful land was turned into barrenness for the wickedness of those that dwelt therein. The Lord reproved the prophet. The opposition of the men of Anathoth was not so formidable as what he must expect from the rulers of Judah. Our grief that there should be so much evil is often mixed with peevishness on account of the trials it occasions us. And in this our favoured day, and under our trifling difficulties, let us consider how we should behave, if called to sufferings like those of saints in former ages.

The heavy judgments to come upon the nation (7–13)

God's people had been the dearly-beloved of his soul, precious in his sight, but they acted so, that he gave them up to their enemies. Many professing churches become like speckled birds, presenting a mixture of religion and the world, with its vain fashions, pursuits, and pollutions. God's people are as men wondered at, as a speckled bird; but this people had by their own folly made themselves so; and the beasts and birds are called to prey upon them. The whole land would be made desolate. But until the judgments were actually inflicted, none of the people would lay the warning to heart. When God's hand is lifted up, and men will not see, they shall be made to feel. Silver and gold shall not profit in the day of the Lord's anger. And the efforts of sinners to escape misery, without repentance and works answerable thereto, will end in confusion.

Divine mercy to them, and even to the nations around (14–17)

The Lord would plead the cause of his people against their evil neighbours. Yet he would afterwards show mercy to those nations, when they should learn true religion. This seems to look forward to the times when the fulness of the Gentiles shall come in. Those who would have their lot with God's people, and a last end like theirs, must learn their ways, and walk in them.

Chapter 13

The glory of the Jews should be marred (1–11)

All ranks should suffer misery, An earnest exhortation to repentance (12–17)

An awful message to Jerusalem and its king (18–27)

The glory of the Jews should be marred (1–11)

It was usual with the prophets to teach by signs. And we have the explanation, ver. 9-11. The people of Israel had been to God as this girdle. He caused them to cleave to him by the law he gave them, the prophets he sent among them, and the favours he showed them. They had by their idolatries and sins buried themselves in foreign earth, mingled among the nations, and were so corrupted that they were good for nothing. If we are proud of learning, power, and outward privileges, it is just with God to wither them. The minds of men should be awakened to a sense of their guilt and danger; yet nothing will be effectual without the influences of the Spirit.

All ranks should suffer misery, An earnest exhortation to repentance (12–17)

As the bottle was fitted to hold the wine, so the sins of the people made them vessels of wrath, fitted for the judgments of God; with which they should be filled till they caused each other's destruction. The prophet exhorts them to give glory to God, by confessing their sins, humbling themselves in repentance, and returning to his service. Otherwise they would be carried into other countries in all the darkness of idolatry and wickedness. All misery, witnessed or foreseen, will affect a feeling mind, but the pious heart must mourn most over the afflictions of the Lord's flock.

An awful message to Jerusalem and its king (18–27)

Here is a message sent to king Jehoiakim, and his queen. Their sorrows would be great indeed.

Do they ask, Wherefore come these things upon us? Let them know, it is for their obstinacy in sin. We cannot alter the natural colour of the skin; and so is it morally impossible to reclaim and reform these people. Sin is the blackness of the soul; it is the discolouring of it; we were shaped in it, so that we cannot get clear of it by any power of our own. But Almighty grace is able to change the Ethiopian's skin. Neither natural depravity, nor strong habits of sin, form an obstacle to the working of God, the new-creating Spirit. The Lord asks of Jerusalem, whether she is determined not be made clean. If any poor slave of sin feels that he could as soon change his nature as master his headstrong lusts, let him not despair; for things impossible to men are possible with God. Let us then seek help from Him who is mighty to save.

Chapter 14

A drought upon the land of Judah, and a confession of sin in the name of the people (1–9)

The Divine purpose to punish is declared (10–16)

The people supplicate (17–22)

A drought upon the land of Judah, and a confession of sin in the name of the people (1–9)

The people were in tears. But it was rather the cry of their trouble, and of their sin, than of their prayer. Let us be thankful for the mercy of water, that we may not be taught to value it by feeling the want of it. See what dependence husbandmen have upon the Divine providence. They cannot plough nor sow in hope, unless God water their furrows. The case even of the wild beasts was very pitiable. The people are not forward to pray, but the prophet prays for them. Sin is humbly confessed. Our sins not only accuse us, but answer against us. Our best pleas in prayer are those fetched from the glory of God's own name. We should dread God's departure, more than the removal of our creature-comforts. He has given Israel his word to hope in. It becomes us in prayer to show ourselves more concerned for God's glory than for our own comfort. And if we now return to the Lord, he will save us to the glory of his grace.

The Divine purpose to punish is declared (10–16)

The Lord calls the Jews 'this people,' not 'his people.' They had forsaken his service, therefore he would punish them according to their sins. He forbade Jeremiah to plead for them. The false prophets were the most criminal. The Lord pronounces condemnation on them; but as the people loved to have it so, they were not to escape judgments. False teachers encourage men to expect peace and salvation, without repentance, faith, conversion, and holiness of life. But those who believe a lie must not plead if for an excuse. They shall feel what they say they will not fear.

The people supplicate (17–22)

Jeremiah acknowledged his own sins, and those of the people, but pleaded with the Lord to remember his covenant. In their distress none of the idols of the Gentiles could help them, nor could the heavens give rain of themselves. The Lord will always have a people to plead with him at his mercy-seat. He will heal every truly repenting sinner. Should he not see fit to hear our prayers on behalf of our guilty land, he will certainly bless with salvation all who confess their sins and seek his mercy.

Chapter 15

The destruction of the wicked described (1–9)

The prophet laments such messages, and is reproved (10–14)

He supplicates pardon, and is promised protection (15–21)

The destruction of the wicked described (1–9)

The Lord declares that even Moses and Samuel must have pleaded in vain. The putting of this as a case, though they should stand before him, shows that they do not, and that saints in heaven do not pray for saints on earth. The Jews were condemned to different kinds of misery by the righteous judgment of God, and the remnant would be driven away, like the chaff, into captivity. Then was the populous city made desolate. Bad examples and misused authority often produce fatal effects, even after men are dead, or have repented of their crimes: this should make all greatly dread being the occasion of sin in others.

The prophet laments such messages, and is reproved (10–14)

Jeremiah met with much contempt and reproach, when they ought to have blessed him, and God for him. It is a great and sufficient support to the people of God, that however troublesome their way may be, it shall be well with them in their latter end. God turns to the people. Shall the most hardy and vigorous of their efforts be able to contend with the counsel of God, or with the army of the Chadians? Let them hear their doom. The enemy will treat the prophet well. But the people who had great estates would be used hardly. All parts of the country had added to the national guilt; and let each take shame to itself.

He supplicates pardon, and is promised protection (15–21)

It is matter of comfort that we have a God, to whose knowledge of all things we may appeal. Jeremiah pleads with God for mercy and relief against his enemies, persecutors, and slanderers. It will be a comfort to God's ministers, when men despise them, if they have the testimony of their own consciences. But he complains, that he found little pleasure in his work. Some good people lose much of the pleasantness of religion by the fretfulness and uneasiness of their natural temper, which they indulge. The Lord called the prophet to cease from his distrust, and to return to his work. If he attended thereto, he might be assured the Lord would deliver him from his enemies. Those who are with God, and faithful to him, he will deliver from trouble or carry through it. Many things appear frightful, which do not at all hurt a real believer in Christ.

Chapter 16

Prohibitions given to the prophet (1–9)

The justice of God in these judgments (10–13)

Future restoration of the Jews, and the conversion of the Gentiles (14–21)

Prohibitions given to the prophet (1–9)

The prophet must conduct himself as one who expected to see his country ruined very shortly. In the prospect of sad times, he is to abstain from marriage, mourning for the dead, and pleasure. Those who would convince others of the truths of God, must make it appear by their self-denial, that they believe it themselves. Peace, inward and outward, family and public, is wholly the work of God, and from his loving-kindness and mercy. When He takes his peace from any people, distress must follow. There may be times when it is proper to avoid things otherwise our duty; and we should always sit loose to the pleasures and concerns of this life.

The justice of God in these judgments (10–13)

Here seems to be the language of those who quarrel at the word of God, and instead of

humbling and condemning themselves, justify themselves, as though God did them wrong. A plain and full answer is given. They were more obstinate in sin than their fathers, walking every one after the devices of his heart. Since they will not hearken, they shall be hurried away into a far country, a land they know not. If they had God's favour, that would make even the land of their captivity pleasant.

Future restoration of the Jews, and the conversion of the Gentiles (14–21)

The restoration from the Babylonian captivity would be remembered in place of the deliverance from Egypt; it also typified spiritual redemption, and the future deliverance of the church from antichristian oppression. But none of the sins of sinners can be hidden from God, or shall be overlooked by him. He will find out and raise up instruments of his wrath, that shall destroy the Jews, by fraud like fishers, by force like hunters. The prophet, rejoicing at the hope of mercy to come, addressed the Lord as his strength and refuge. The deliverance out of captivity shall be a figure of the great salvation to be wrought by the Messiah. The nations have often known the power of Jehovah in his wrath; but they shall know him as the strength of his people, and their refuge in time of trouble.

Chapter 17

The fatal consequences of the idolatry of the Jews (1–4)

The happiness of the man that trusts in God; the end of the opposite character (5–11)

The malice of the prophet's enemies (12–18)

The observance of the Sabbath (19–27)

The fatal consequences of the idolatry of the Jews (1–4)

The sins which men commit make little impression on their minds, yet every sin is marked in the book of God; they are all so graven upon the table of the heart, that they will all be remembered by the conscience. That which is graven in the heart will become plain in the life; men's actions show the desires and purposes of their hearts. What need we have to humble ourselves before God, who are so vile in his sight! How should we depend on his mercy and grace, begging of God to search and prove us; not to suffer us to be deceived by our own hearts, but to create in us a clean and holy nature by his Spirit!

The happiness of the man that trusts in God; the end of the opposite character (5–11)

He who puts confidence in man, shall be like the heath in a desert, a naked tree, a sorry shrub, the product of barren ground, useless and worthless. Those who trust to their own righteousness and strength, and think they can do without Christ, make flesh their arm, and their souls cannot prosper in graces or comforts. Those who make God their Hope, shall flourish like a tree always green, whose leaf does not wither. They shall be fixed in peace and satisfaction of mind; they shall not be anxious in a year of drought. Those who make God their Hope, have enough in him to make up the want of all creature-comforts. They shall not cease from yielding fruit in holiness and good works. The heart, the conscience of man, in his corrupt and fallen state, is deceitful above all things. It calls evil good, and good evil; and cries peace to those to whom it does not belong. Herein the heart is desperately wicked; it is deadly, it is desperate. The case is bad indeed, if the conscience, which should set right the errors of other faculties, is a leader in the delusion. We cannot know our own hearts, nor what they will do in an hour of temptation. Who can understand his errors? Much less can we know the hearts of others, or depend upon them. He that believes God's testimony in this matter, and learns to watch his own heart, will find this is a correct, though a sad picture, and learns many lessons to direct his conduct. But much in our own hearts and in the hearts of others, will remain unknown. Yet whatever wickedness there is in the heart, God sees it. Men may be imposed upon, but God cannot be deceived. He that gets riches, and not by right, though he may make them his hope, never shall have joy of them. This shows what vexation it is to a worldly man at death, that he must leave his riches behind; but though the wealth will not follow to another world, guilt will, and everlasting torment. The rich man takes pains to get an estate, and sits brooding upon it, but never has any satisfaction in it; by sinful courses it comes to nothing. Let us be wise in time; what we get, let us get it honestly; and what we have, use it charitably, that we may be wise for eternity.

The malice of the prophet's enemies (12–18)

The prophet acknowledges the favour of God in setting up religion. There is fulness of comfort in God, overflowing, ever-flowing fulness, like a fountain. It is always fresh and clear, like spring-water, while the pleasures of sin are puddle-waters. He prays to God for healing, saving mercy. He appeals to God concerning his faithful discharge of the office to which he was called. He humbly begs that God would own and protect him in the work to which he had plainly called him. Whatever wounds or diseases we find to be in our hearts and consciences, let us apply to the Lord to heal us, to save us, that our souls may praise his name. His hands can bind up the troubled conscience, and heal the broken heart; he can cure the worst diseases of our nature.

The observance of the Sabbath (19–27)

The prophet was to lay before the rulers and the people of Judah, the command to keep holy the Sabbath day. Let them strictly observe the fourth command. If they obeyed this word, their prosperity should be restored. It is a day of rest, and must not be made a day of labour, unless in cases of necessity. Take heed, against the profanation of the Sabbath. Let not the soul be burdened with the cares of this world on Sabbath days. The streams of religion run deep or shallow, according as the banks of the Sabbath are kept up or neglected. The degree of strictness with which this ordinance is observed, or the neglect shown towards it, is a good test to find the state of spiritual religion in any land. Let all, by their own example, by attention to their families, strive to check this evil, that national prosperity may be preserved, and, above all, that souls may be saved.

Chapter 18

God's power over his creatures is represented by the potter (1–10)

The Jews exhorted to repentance, and judgments foretold (11–17)

The prophet appeals to God (18–23)

God's power over his creatures is represented by the potter (1–10)

While Jeremiah looks upon the potter's work, God darts into his mind two great truths. God has authority, and power, to form and fashion kingdoms and nations as he pleases. He may dispose of us as he thinks fit; and it would be as absurd for us to dispute this, as for the clay to quarrel with the potter. But he always goes by fixed rules of justice and goodness. When God is coming against us in judgments, we may be sure it is for our sins; but sincere conversion from the evil of sin will prevent the evil of punishment, as to persons, and to families, and nations.

The Jews exhorted to repentance, and judgments foretold (11–17)

Sinners call it liberty to live at large; whereas for a man to be a slave to his lusts, is the very worst slavery. They forsook God for idols. When men are parched with heat, and meet with cooling, refreshing streams, they use them. In these things men will not leave a certainty for an uncertainty; but Israel left the ancient paths appointed by the Divine law. They walked not in the highway, in which they might travel safely, but in a way in which they must stumble: such was the way of idolatry, and such is the way of iniquity. This made their land desolate, and themselves miserable. Calamities may be borne, if God smile upon us when under them; but if he is displeased, and refuses his help, we are undone. Multitudes forget the Lord and his Christ, and wander from the ancient paths, to walk in ways of their own devising. But what will they do in the day of judgment!

The prophet appeals to God (18–23)

When the prophet called to repentance, instead of obeying the call, the people devised devices against him. Thus do sinners deal with the great Intercessor, crucifying him afresh, and speaking against him on earth, while his blood is speaking for them in heaven. But the prophet had done his duty to them; and the same will be our rejoicing in a day of evil.

Chapter 19

By the type of breaking an earthen vessel, Jeremiah is to predict the destruction of Judah.

1–9. The prophet must give notice of ruin coming upon Judah and Jerusalem. Both rulers and ruled must attend to it. That place which holiness made the joy of the whole earth, sin made the reproach and shame of the whole earth. There is no fleeing from God's justice, but by fleeing to his mercy.

10–15. The potter's vessel, after it is hardened, can never be pieced again when it is broken. And as the bottle was broken, so shall Judah and Jerusalem be broken by the Chadians. No human hand can repair it; but if they return to the Lord he will heal. As they filled Tophet with the slain sacrificed to their idols, so will God fill the whole city with the slain that shall fall as sacrifices to his justice. Whatever men may think, God will appear as terrible against sin and sinners as the Scriptures state; nor shall the unbelief of men make his promise or his threatenings of no effect. The obstinacy of sinners in sinful ways, is their own fault; if they are deaf to the word of God, it is because they have stopped their ears. We have need to pray that God, by his grace, would deliver us from hardness of heart, and contempt of his word and commandments.

Chapter 20

The doom of Pashur, who ill-treated the prophet (1–6)

Jeremiah complains of hard usage (7–13)

He regrets his ever having been born (14–18)

The doom of Pashur, who ill-treated the prophet (1–6)

Pashur smote Jeremiah, and put him in the stocks. Jeremiah was silent till God put a word into his mouth. To confirm this, Pashur has a name given him, 'Fear on every side.' It speaks a man not only in distress, but in despair; not only in danger, but in fear on every side. The wicked are in great fear where no fear is, for God can make the most daring sinner a terror to himself. And those who will not hear of their faults from God's prophets, shall be made to hear them from their consciences. Miserable is the man thus made a terror to himself. His friends shall fail him. God lets him live miserably, that he may be a monument of Divine justice.

Jeremiah complains of hard usage (7–13)

The prophet complains of the insult and injury he experienced. But ver. 7 may be read, Thou hast persuaded me, and I was persuaded. Thou wast stronger than I; and didst overpower me by the influence of thy Spirit upon me. So long as we see ourselves in the way of God, and of duty, it is weakness and folly, when we meet with difficulties and discouragements, to wish we had never set out in it. The prophet found the grace of God mighty in him to keep him to his business, notwithstanding the temptation he was in to throw it up. Whatever injuries are done to us, we must leave them to that God to whom vengeance belongs, and who has said, I will repay. So full was he of the comfort of God's presence, the Divine protection he was under, and the Divine promise he had to depend upon, that he stirred up himself and others to give God the glory. Let the people of God open their cause before Him, and he will enable them to see deliverance.

He regrets his ever having been born (14–18)

When grace has the victory, it is good to be ashamed of our folly, to admire the goodness of God, and be warned to guard our spirits another time. See how strong the temptation was, over which the prophet got the victory by Divine assistance! He is angry that his first breath was not his last. While we remember that these wishes are not recorded for us to utter the like, we may learn good lessons from them. See how much those who think they stand, ought to take heed lest they fall, and to pray daily, Lead us not into temptation. How frail, changeable, and sinful is man! How foolish and unnatural are the thoughts and wishes of our hearts, when we yield to discontent! Let us consider Him who endured the contradiction of sinners against himself, lest we should be at any time weary and faint in our minds under our lesser trials.

Chapter 21

The only way of deliverance is to be surrendering to the Babylonians (1–10)

The wickedness of the king and his household (11–14)

The only way of deliverance is to be surrendering to the Babylonians (1–10)

When the siege had begun, Zedekiah sent to ask of Jeremiah respecting the event. In times of distress and danger, men often seek those to counsel and pray for them, whom, at other times, they despise and oppose; but they only seek deliverance from punishment. When professors continue in disobedience, presuming upon outward privileges, let them be told that the Lord will prosper his open enemies against them. As the king and his princes would not surrender, the people are exhorted to do so. No sinner on earth is left without a Refuge, who really desires one; but the way of life is humbling, it requires self-denial, and exposes to difficulties.

The wickedness of the king and his household (11–14)

The wickedness of the king and his family was the worse because of their relation to David. They were urged to act with justice, at once, lest the Lord's anger should be unquenchable. If God be for us, who can be against us? But if he be against us, who can do any thing for us?

Chapter 22

Justice is recommended, and destruction threatened in case of disobedience (1–9)

The captivity of Jehoiakim, and the end of Jeconiah (10–19)

The doom of the royal family (20–30)

Justice is recommended, and destruction threatened in case of disobedience (1–9)

The king of Judah is spoken to, as sitting upon the throne of David, the man after God's own heart. Let him follow his example, that he may have the benefit of the promises made to him. The way to preserve a government, is to do the duty of it. But sin will be the ruin of the houses of princes, as well as of meaner men. And who can contend with destroyers of God's preparing? God destroys neither persons, cities, nor nations, except for sin; even in this world he often makes it plain for what crimes he sends punishment; and it will be clear at the day of judgement.

The captivity of Jehoiakim, and the end of Jeconiah (10–19)

Here is a sentence of death upon two kings, the wicked sons of a very pious father. Josiah was prevented from seeing the evil to come in this world, and removed to see the good to come in the other world; therefore, weep not for him, but for his son Shallum, who is likely to live and die a wretched captive. Dying saints may be justly envied, while living sinners are justly pitied. Here also is the doom of Jehoiakim. No doubt it is lawful for princes and great men to build, beautify, and furnish houses; but those who enlarge their houses, and make them sumptuous, need carefully to watch against the workings of vain-glory. He built his houses by unrighteousness, with money gotten unjustly. And he defrauded his workmen of their wages. God notices the wrong done by the greatest to poor servants and labourers, and will repay those in justice, who will not, in justice, pay those whom they employ. The greatest of men must look upon the meanest as their neighbours, and be just to them accordingly. Jehoiakim was unjust, and made no conscience of shedding innocent blood. Covetousness, which is the root of all evil, was at the bottom of all. The children who despise their parents' old fashions, commonly come short of their real excellences. Jehoiakim knew that his father found the way of duty to be the way of comfort, yet he would not tread in his steps. He shall die unlamented, hateful for oppression and cruelty.

The doom of the royal family (20–30)

The Jewish state is described under a threefold character. Very haughty in a day of peace and safety. Very fearful on alarm of trouble. Very much cast down under pressure of trouble. Many never are ashamed of their sins till brought by them to the last extremity. The king shall close his days in bondage. Those that think themselves as signets on God's right hand, must not be secure, but fear lest they should be plucked thence. The Jewish king and his family shall be carried to Babylon. We know where we were born, but where we shall die we know not; it is enough that our God knows. Let it be our care that we die in Christ, then it will be well with us wherever we die, thought it may be in a far country. The Jewish king shall be despised. Time was when he was delighted in; but all those in whom God has no pleasure, some time or other, will be so lowered, that men will have no pleasure in them. Whoever are childless, it is the Lord that writes them so; and those who take no care to do good in their days, cannot expect to prosper. How little is earthly grandeur to be depended upon, or flourishing families to be rejoiced in! But those who hear the voice of Christ, and follow him, have eternal life, and shall never perish, neither shall any enemy pluck them out of his almighty hands.

Chapter 23

The restoration of the Jews to their own land (1–8)

The wickedness of the priests and prophets of Judah, The people exhorted not to listen to false promises (9–22)

The pretenders to inspiration threatened (23–32)

Also the scoffers at true prophecy (33–40)

The restoration of the Jews to their own land (1–8)

Woe be to those who are set to feed God's people, but take no concern to do them good! Here is a word of comfort to the neglected sheep. Though only a remnant of God's flock is left, he will find them out, and they shall be brought to their former habitations. Christ is spoken of as a branch from David's family. He is righteous himself, and through him all his people are made righteous. Christ shall break the usurped power of Satan. All the spiritual seed of believing Abraham and praying Jacob shall be protected, and shall be saved from the guilt and dominion of sin. In the days of Christ's government in the soul, the soul dwells at ease. He is here spoken of as 'the Lord our Righteousness.' He is so our Righteousness as no creature could be. His obedience unto death is the justifying righteousness of believers, and their title to heavenly happiness. And their sanctification, as the source of all their personal obedience is the effect of their union with him, and of the supply of this Spirit. By this name every true believer shall call him, and call upon him. We have nothing to plead but this, Christ has died, yea, rather is risen again; and we have taken him for our Lord. This righteousness which he has wrought out to the satisfaction of law and justice, becomes ours; being a free gift given to us, through the Spirit of God, who puts it upon us, clothes us with it, enables us to lay hold upon it, and claim an interest in it. 'The Lord our Righteousness' is a sweet name to a convinced sinner; to one that has felt the guilt of sin in his conscience; seen his need of that righteousness, and the worth of it. This great salvation is far more glorious than all former deliverances of his church. May our souls be gathered to Him, and be found in him.

The wickedness of the priests and prophets of Judah, The people exhorted not to listen to false promises (9–22)

The false prophets of Samaria had deluded the Israelites into idolatries; yet the Lord considered the false prophets of Jerusalem as guilty of more horrible wickedness, by which the people were made bold in sin. These false teachers would be compelled to suffer the most bitter part of the Lord's indignation. They made themselves believe that there was no harm in sin, and practised accordingly; then they made others believe so. Those who are resolved to go on in evil ways, will justly be given up to believe strong delusions. But which of them had received any revelation of God, or understood any thing of his word? There was a time coming when they would reflect on their folly and unbelief with remorse. The teaching and example of the true prophets led men to repentance, faith, and righteousness. The false prophets led men to rest in forms and notions, and to be quiet in their sins. Let us take heed that we do not follow unrighteousness.

The pretenders to inspiration threatened (23–32)

Men cannot be hidden from God's all-seeing eye. Will they never see what judgments they prepare for themselves? Let them consider what a vast difference there is between these prophecies and those delivered by the true prophets of the Lord. Let them not call their foolish dreams Divine oracles. The promises of peace these prophets make are no more to be compared to God's promises than chaff to wheat. The unhumbled heart of man is like a rock; if not melted by the word of God as a fire, it will be broken to pieces by it as a hammer. How can they be long safe, or at all easy, who have a God of almighty power against them? The word of God is no smooth, lulling, deceitful message. And by its faithfulness it may certainly be distinguished from false doctrines.

Also the scoffers at true prophecy (33–40)

Those are miserable indeed who are forsaken and forgotten of God; and men's jesting at God's judgments will not baffle them. God had taken Israel to be a people near to him, but they shall now be cast out of his presence. It is a mark of great and daring impiety for men to jest with the words of God. Every idle and profane word will add to the sinner's burden in the day of judgment, when everlasting shame will be his portion.

Chapter 24

Good and bad figs represent the Jews in captivity, and those who remain in their own land.

The prophet saw two baskets of figs set before the temple, as offerings of first-fruits. The figs in one basket were very good, those in the other basket very bad. What creature viler than a wicked man? and what more valuable than a godly man? This vision was to raise the spirits of those gone into captivity, by assuring them of a happy return; and to humble and awaken the proud and secure spirits of those yet in Jerusalem, by assuring them of a miserable captivity. The good figs represents the pious captives. We cannot determine as to God's love or hatred by what is before us. Early suffering sometimes proves for the best. The sooner the child is corrected, the better effect the correction is likely to have. Even this captivity was for their good; and God's intentions never are in vain. By afflictions they were convinced of sin, humbled under the hand of God, weaned from the world, taught to pray, and turned from sins, particularly from idolatry. God promises that he will own them in captivity. The Lord will own those who are his, in all conditions. God assures them of his protection in trouble, and a glorious deliverance in due time. When our troubles are sanctified to us, we may be sure that they will end well. They shall return to him with their whole heart. Thus they should have liberty to own him for their God, to pray to him, and expect blessings from him. The bad figs were Zedekiah and those of his party yet in the land. These should be removed for their hurt, and forsaken of all mankind. God has many judgments, and those that escape one, may expect another, till they are brought to repent. Doubtless, this prophecy had its fulfilment in that age; but the Spirit of prophecy may here look forward to the dispersion of the unbelieving Jews, in all the nations of the earth. Let those who desire blessings from the Lord, beg that he will give them a heart to know him.

Chapter 25

The Jews rebuked for not obeying calls to repentance (1–7)

Their captivity during seventy years is expressly foretold (8–14)

Desolations upon the nations shown by the emblem of a cup of wrath (15–29)

The judgments again declared (30–38)

The Jews rebuked for not obeying calls to repentance (1–7)

The call to turn from evil ways to the worship and service of God, and for sinners to trust in Christ, and partake of his salvation, concerns all men. God keeps an account how long we possess the means of grace; and the longer we have them, the heavier will our account be if we have not improved them. Rising early, points out the earnest desire that this people should turn and live. Personal and particular reformation must be insisted on as necessary to a national deliverance; and every one must turn from his own evil way. Yet all was to no purpose. They would not take the right and only method to turn away the wrath of God.

Their captivity during seventy years is expressly foretold (8–14)

The fixing of the time during which the Jewish captivity should last, would not only confirm the prophecy, but also comfort the people of God, and encourage faith and prayer. The ruin of Babylon is foretold: the rod will be thrown into the fire when the correcting work is done. When the set time to favour Zion is come, Babylon shall be punished for their iniquity, as other nations have been punished for their sins. Every threatening of the Scripture will certainly be accomplished.

Desolations upon the nations shown by the emblem of a cup of wrath (15–29)

The evil and the good events of life are often represented in Scripture as cups. Under this figure is represented the desolation then coming upon that part of the world, of which Nebuchadnezzar, who had just began to reign and act, was to be the instrument; but this destroying sword would come from the hand of God. The desolations the sword should make in all these kingdoms, are represented by the consequences of excessive drinking. This may make us loathe the sin of drunkenness, that the consequences of it are used to set forth such a woeful condition. Drunkenness deprives men of the use of their reason, makes men as mad. It takes from them the valuable blessing, health; and is a sin which is its own punishment. This may also make us dread the judgments of war. It soon fills a nation with confusion. They will refuse to take the cup at thy hand. They will not believe Jeremiah; but he must tell them it is the word of the Lord of hosts, and it is in vain for them to struggle against Almighty power. And if God's judgments begin with backsliding professors, let not the wicked expect to escape.

The judgments again declared (30–38)

The Lord has just ground of controversy with every nation and every person; and he will execute judgment on all the wicked. Who can avoid trembling when God speaks in displeasure? The days are fully come; the time fixed in the Divine counsels, which will make the nations wholly desolate. The tender and delicate shall share the common calamity. Even those who used to live in peace, and did nothing to provoke, shall not escape. Blessed be God, there is a peaceable habitation above, for all the sons of peace. The Lord will preserve his church and all believers in all changes; for nothing can separate them from his love.

Chapter 26

The destruction of the temple and city foretold (1–6)

Jeremiah's life is threatened (7–15)

He is defended by the elders (16–24)

The destruction of the temple and city foretold (1–6)

God's ambassadors must not seek to please men, or to save themselves from harm. See how God waits to be gracious. If they persisted in disobedience, it would ruin their city and temple. Can any thing else be expected? Those who will not be subject to the commands of God, make themselves subject to the curse of God.

Jeremiah's life is threatened (7–15)

The priests and prophets charged Jeremiah as deserving death, and bore false witness against him. The elders of Israel came to inquire into this matter. Jeremiah declares that the Lord sent him to prophesy thus. As long as ministers keep close to the word they have from God, they need not fear. And those are very unjust who complain of ministers for preaching of hell and damnation; for it is from a desire to bring them to heaven and salvation. Jeremiah warns them of their danger if they go on against him. All men may know, that to hurt, or put to death, or to show hatred to their faithful reprovers, will hasten and increase their own punishment.

He is defended by the elders (16–24)

When secure sinners are threatened with taking away the Spirit of God, and the kingdom of God, it is what is warranted from the word of God. Hezekiah who protected Micah, prospered. Did Jehoiakim, who slew Urijah, prosper? The examples of bad men, and the bad consequences of their sins, should deter from what is evil. Urijah was faithful in delivering his message, but faulty in leaving his work. And the Lord was pleased to permit him to lose his life, while Jeremiah was protected in danger. Those are safest who most simply trust in the Lord, whatever their outward circumstances may be; and that He has all men's hearts in his hands, encourages us to trust him in the way of duty. He will honour and recompense those who show kindness to such as are persecuted for his sake.

Chapter 27

The neighbouring nations to be subdued (1–11)

Zedekiah is warned to yield (12–18)

The vessels of the temple to be carried to Babylon, but afterwards to be restored (19–22)

The neighbouring nations to be subdued (1–11)

Jeremiah is to prepare a sign that all the neighbouring countries would be made subject to the king of Babylon. God asserts his right to dispose of kingdoms as he pleases. Whatever any have of the good things of this world, it is what God sees fit to give; we should therefore be content. The things of this world are not the best things, for the Lord often gives the largest share to bad men. Dominion is not founded in grace. Those who will not serve the God who made them, shall justly be made to serve their enemies that seek to ruin them. Jeremiah urges them to prevent their destruction, by submission. A meek spirit, by quiet submission to the hardest turns of providence, makes the best of what is bad. Many persons may escape destroying providences, by submitting to humbling providences. It is better to take up a light cross in our way, than to pull a heavier on our own heads. The poor in spirit, the meek and humble, enjoy comfort, and avoid many miseries to which the high-spirited are exposed. It must, in all cases, be our interest to obey God's will.

Zedekiah is warned to yield (12–18)

Jeremiah persuades the king of Judah to surrender to the king of Babylon. Is it their wisdom to submit to the heavy iron yoke of a cruel tyrant, that they may secure their lives; and is it not much more our wisdom to submit to the pleasant and easy yoke of our Lord and Master, Jesus Christ, that we may secure our souls? It were well if sinners would be afraid of the destruction threatened against all who will not have Christ to reign over them. Why should they die the second death, infinitely worse than that by sword and famine, when they may submit and live? And those who encourage sinners to go on in sinful ways, will perish with them.

The vessels of the temple to be carried to Babylon, but afterwards to be restored (19–22)

Jeremiah assures them that the brazen vessels should go after the golden ones. All shall be carried to Babylon. But he concludes with a gracious promise, that the time would come when they should be brought back. Though the return of the prosperity of the church does not come in our time, we must not despair, for it will come in God's time.

Chapter 28

A false prophet opposes Jeremiah (1–9)
The false prophet warned of his approaching death (10–17)

A false prophet opposes Jeremiah (1–9)

Hananiah spoke a false prophecy. Here is not a word of good counsel urging the Jews to repent and return to God. He promises temporal mercies, in God's name, but makes no mention of the spiritual mercies which God always promised with earthly blessings. This was not the first time Jeremiah had prayed for the people, though he prophesied against them. He appeals to the event, to prove Hananiah's falsehood. The prophet who spake only of peace and prosperity, without adding that they must not by wilful sin stop God's favours, will be proved a false prophet. Those who do not declare the alarming as well as the encouraging parts of God's word, and call men to repentance, and faith, and holiness, tread in the steps of the false prophets. The gospel of Christ encourages men to do works meet for repentance, but gives no encouragement to continue in sin.

The false prophet warned of his approaching death (10–17)

Hananiah is sentenced to die, and Jeremiah, when he has received direction from God, boldly tells him so; but not before he received that commission. Those have much to answer for, who tell sinners that they shall have peace, though they harden their hearts in contempt of God's word. The servant of God must be gentle

to all men. He must give up even his right, and leave the Lord to plead his cause. Every attempt of ungodly men to make vain the purposes of God, will add to their miseries.

Chapter 29

Two letters to the captives in Babylon; In the first, they are recommended to be patient and composed (1–19)

In the second, judgments are denounced against the false prophets who deceived them (20–32)

Two letters to the captives in Babylon; In the first, they are recommended to be patient and composed (1–19)

The written word of God is as truly given by inspiration of God as his spoken word. The zealous servant of the Lord will use every means to profit those who are far off, as well as those who are near him. The art of writing is very profitable for this end; and by the art of printing it is rendered most beneficial for circulating the knowledge of the word of God. God's sending to the captives by this letter would show that he had not forsaken them, though he was displeased, and corrected them. If they live in the fear of God, they may live comfortably in Babylon. In all conditions of life, it is our wisdom and duty not to throw away the comfort of what we may have, because we have not all we would have. They are directed to seek the good of the country where they were captives. While the king of Babylon protected them, they must live quiet and peaceable lives under him, in all godliness and honesty; patiently leaving it to God to work deliverance for them in due time.

Let men beware how they call those prophets whom they choose after their own fancies, and how they consider their fancies and dreams to be revelations from God. False prophets flatter people in their sins, because they love to be flattered; and they speak smoothly to their prophets, that their prophets may speak smoothly to them. God's promises that they should return after seventy years were accomplished. By this it appears, that the seventy years of the captivity are not to be reckoned from the last captivity, but the first. It will be the bringing to pass of God's good word to them. This shall form God's purposes. We often do not know our own minds, but the Lord is never at an uncertainty. We are sometimes ready to fear that God's designs are all against us; but as to his own people, even that which seems evil, is for good. He will give them, not the expectations of their fears, or the expectations of their fancies, but the expectations of their faith; the end he has promised, which will be the best for them. When the Lord pours out an especial spirit of prayer, it is a good sign that he is coming toward us in mercy. Promises are given to quicken and encourage prayer. He never said, Seek ye me in vain. Those who remained at Jerusalem would be utterly destroyed, notwithstanding what the false prophets said to the contrary. The reason has often been given, and it justifies the eternal ruin of impenitent sinners; Because they have not hearkened to my words; I called, but they refused.

In the second, judgments are denounced against the false prophets who deceived them (20–32)

Jeremiah foretells judgments upon the false prophets, who deceived the Jews in Babylon. Lying was bad; lying to the people of the Lord, to delude them into a false hope, was worse; but pretending to rest their own lies upon the God of truth, was worst of all. They flattered others in their sins, because they could not reprove them without condemning themselves. The most secret sins are known to God; and there is a day coming when he will bring to light all the hidden works of darkness. Shemaiah urges the priests to persecute Jeremiah. Their hearts are wretchedly hardened who justify doing mischief by having power to do it. They were in a miserable thraldom for mocking the messengers of the Lord, and misusing his prophets; yet in their distress they trespass still more against the Lord. Afflictions will not of themselves cure men of their sins, unless the grace of God works with them. Those who slight the blessings, deserve to lose the benefit of God's word, like Shemaiah. The accusations against many active Christians in all ages, amount to no more than this, that they earnestly counsel men to attend to their true interest and duties, and to wait for the performance of God's promises in his appointed way.

Chapter 30

Troubles which shall be before the restoration of Israel (1–11)

Encouragement to trust Divine promises (12–17)

The blessings under Christ, and the wrath on the wicked (18–24)

Troubles which shall be before the restoration of Israel (1–11)

Jeremiah is to write what God had spoken to him. The very words are such as the Holy Ghost teaches. These are the words God ordered to be written; and promises written by his order, are truly his word. He must write a description of the trouble the people were now in, and were likely to be in. A happy end should be put to these calamities. Though the afflictions of the church may last long, they shall not last always. The Jews shall be restored again. They shall obey, or hearken to the Messiah, the Christ, the Son of David, their King. The deliverance of the Jews from Babylon, is pointed out in the prophecy, but the restoration and happy state of Israel and Judah, when converted to Christ their King, are foretold; also the miseries of the nations before the coming of Christ. All men must honour the Son as they honour the Father, and come into the service and worship of God by him. Our gracious Lord pardons the sins of the believer, and breaks off the yoke of sin and Satan, that he may serve God without fear, in righteousness and true holiness before him all the remainder of his days, as the redeemed subject of Christ our King.

Encouragement to trust Divine promises (12–17)

When God is against a people, who will be for them? Who can be for them, so as to do them any kindness? Incurable griefs are owing to incurable lusts. Yet, though the captives suffered justly, and could not help themselves, the Lord intended to appear for them, and to punish their oppressors; and he will still do so. But every effort to heal ourselves must prove fruitless, so long as we neglect the heavenly Advocate and sanctifying Spirit. The dealings of His grace with every true convert, and every returning backslider, are the same in effect as his proceedings to the Jews.

The blessings under Christ, and the wrath on the wicked (18–24)

We have here further intimations of the favour of God for them after the days of their calamity have expired. The proper work and office of Christ, as Mediator, is to draw near unto God, for us, as the High Priest of our profession. His own undertaking, in compliance with his Father's will, and in compassion to fallen man, engaged him. Jesus Christ was, in all this, truly wonderful. They shall be taken again into covenant with the Lord, according to the covenant made with their fathers. 'I will be your God': it is his good-will to us, which is the summary of that part of the covenant. The wrath of God against the wicked is very terrible, like a whirlwind. The purposes of his wrath, as well as the purposes of his love, will all be fulfilled. God will comfort all that turn to him; but those who approach him must have their hearts engaged to do it with reverence, devotion, and faith. How will they escape who neglect so great salvation?

Chapter 31

The restoration of Israel (1–9)

Promises of guidance and happiness; Rachel lamenting (10–17)

Ephraim laments his errors (18–20)

The promised Saviour (21–26)

God's care over the church (27–34)

Peace and prosperity in gospel time (35–40)

The restoration of Israel (1–9)

God assures his people that he will again take them into covenant relation to himself. When brought very low, and difficulties appear, it is good to remember that it has been so with the church formerly. But it is hard under present frowns to take comfort from former smiles; yet it is the happiness of those who, through grace, are interested in the love of God, that it is an everlasting love, from everlasting in the counsels, to everlasting in the continuance. Those whom God loves with this love, he will draw to himself, by the influences of his Spirit upon their souls. When praising God for what he has done, we must call upon him for the favours his church needs and expects. When the Lord calls, we must not plead that we cannot come; for he that calls us, will help us, will strengthen us. The goodness of God shall lead them to repentance. And they shall weep for sin with more bitterness, and more tenderness, when delivered out of their captivity, than when groaning under it. If we take God for our Father, and join the church of the first-born, we shall want nothing that is good for us. These predictions doubtless refer also to a future gathering of the Israelites from all quarters of the globe. And they figuratively describe the conversion of sinners to Christ, and the plain and safe way in which they are led.

Promises of guidance and happiness; Rachel lamenting (10–17)

He that scattered Israel, knows where to find them. It is comfortable to observe the goodness of the Lord in the gifts of providence. But our souls are never valuable as gardens, unless watered with the dews of God's Spirit and grace. A precious promise follows, which will not have full accomplishment except in the heavenly Zion. Let them be satisfied of God's loving-kindness, and they will be satisfied with it, and desire no more to make them happy. Rachel is represented as rising from her grave, and refusing to be comforted, supposing her offspring rooted out. The murder of the children at Bethlehem, by Herod, Matthew 2:16–18,

in some degree fulfilled this prediction, but could not be its full meaning. If we have hope in the end, concerning an eternal inheritance, for ourselves and those belonging to us, all temporal afflictions may be borne, and will be for our good.

Ephraim laments his errors (18–20)

Ephraim (the ten tribes) is weeping for sin. He is angry at himself for his sin, and folly, and frowardness. He finds he cannot, by his own power, keep himself close with God, much less bring himself back when he is revolted. Therefore he prays, Turn thou me, and I shall be turned. His will was bowed to the will of God. When the teaching of God's Spirit went with the corrections of his providence, then the work was done. This is our comfort in affliction, that the Lord thinks upon us. God has mercy in store, rich mercy, sure mercy, suitable mercy, for all who seek him in sincerity.

The promised Saviour (21–26)

The way from the bondage of sin to the liberty of God's children, is a high-way. It is plain, it is safe; yet none are likely to walk in it, unless they set their hearts towards it. They are encouraged by the promise of a new, unheard-of, extraordinary thing; a creation, a work of Almighty power; the human nature of Christ, formed and prepared by the power of the Holy Ghost: and this is here mentioned as an encouragement to the Jews to return to their own land. And a comfortable prospect is given them of a happy settlement there. Godliness and honesty God has joined: let no man think to put them asunder, or to make the one atone for the want of the other. In the love and favour of God the weary soul shall find rest, and the sorrowful shall find joy. And what can we see with more satisfaction than the good of Jerusalem, and peace upon Israel?

God's care over the church (27–34)

The people of God shall become numerous and prosperous. In Hebrews 8:8,9, this place is quoted as the sum of the covenant of grace made with believers in Jesus Christ. Not, I will give them a new law; for Christ came not to destroy the law, but to fulfil it; but the law shall be written in their hearts by the finger of the Spirit, as formerly written in the tables of stone. The Lord will, by his grace, make his people willing people in the day of his power. All shall know the Lord; all shall be welcome to the knowledge of God, and shall have the means of that knowledge. There shall be an outpouring of the Holy Spirit, at the time the gospel is published. No man shall finally perish, but for his own sins; none, who is willing to accept of Christ's salvation.

Peace and prosperity in gospel time (35–40)

As surely as the heavenly bodies will continue their settled course, according to the will of their Creator, to the end of time, and as the raging sea obeys him, so surely will the Jews be continued a separate people. Words can scarcely set forth more strongly the restoration of Israel. The rebuilding of Jerusalem, and its enlargement and establishment, shall be an earnest of the great things God will do for the gospel church. The personal happiness of every true believer, as well as the future restoration of Israel, is secured by promise, covenant, and oath. This Divine love passes knowledge; and to those who take hold upon it, every present mercy is an earnest of salvation.

Chapter 32

Jeremiah buys a field (1–15)

The prophet's prayer (16–25)

God declares that he will give up his people, but promises to restore them (26–44)

Jeremiah buys a field (1–15)

Jeremiah, being in prison for his prophecy, purchased a piece of ground. This was to signify, that though Jerusalem was besieged, and the whole country likely to be laid waste, yet the time would come, when houses, and fields, and vineyards, should be again possessed. It concerns ministers to make it appear that they believe what they preach to others. And it is good to manage even our worldly affairs in faith; to do common business with reference to the providence and promise of God.

The prophet's prayer (16–25)

Jeremiah adores the Lord and his infinite perfections. When at any time we are perplexed about the methods of Providence, it is good for us to look to first principles. Let us consider that God is the fountain of all being, power, and life; that with him no difficulty is such as cannot be overcome; that he is a God of boundless mercy; that he is a God of strict justice; and that he directs every thing for the best. Jeremiah owns that God was righteous in causing evil to come upon them. Whatever trouble we are in, personal or public, we may comfort ourselves that the Lord sees it, and knows how to remedy it. We must not dispute God's will, but we may seek to know what it means.

God declares that he will give up his people, but promises to restore them (26–44)

God's answer discovers the purposes of his wrath against that generation of the Jews, and the purposes of his grace concerning future generations. It is sin, and nothing else, that ruins them. The restoration of Judah and Jerusalem is promised. This people were now at length brought to despair. But God gives hope of mercy which he had in store for them hereafter. Doubtless the promises are sure to all believers. God will own them for his, and he will prove himself theirs. He will give them a heart to fear him. All true Christians shall have a disposition to mutual love. Though they may have different views about lesser things, they shall all be one in the great things of God; in their views of the evil of sin, and the low estate of fallen man, the way of salvation through the Saviour, the nature of true holiness, the vanity of the world, and the importance of eternal things. Whom God loves, he loves to the end. We have no reason to distrust God's faithfulness and constancy, but only our own hearts. He will settle them again in Canaan. These promises shall surely be performed. Jeremiah's purchase was the pledge of many a purchase that should be made after the captivity; and those inheritances are but faint resemblances of the possessions in the heavenly Canaan, which are kept for all who have God's fear in their hearts, and do not depart from him. Let us then bear up under our trials, assured we shall obtain all the good he has promised us.

Chapter 33

The restoration of the Jews (1–13)

The Messiah promised; happiness of his times (14–26)

The restoration of the Jews (1–13)

Those who expect to receive comforts from God, must call upon him. Promises are given, not to do away, but to quicken and encourage prayer. These promises lead us to the gospel of Christ; and in that God has revealed truth to direct us, and peace to make us easy. All who by sanctifying grace are cleansed from the filth of sin, by pardoning mercy are freed from the guilt. When sinners are thus justified, washed, and sanctified in the name of the Lord Jesus, and by the Holy Spirit, they are enabled to walk before God in peace and purity. Many are led to perceive the real difference between the people of God and the world around them, and to fear the Divine wrath. It is promised that the people who were long in sorrow, shall again be filled with joy. Where the Lord gives righteousness and peace, he will give all needful supplies for temporal wants; and all we have will be comforts, as sanctified by the word and by prayer.

The Messiah promised; happiness of his times (14–26)

To crown the blessings God has in store, here is a promise of the Messiah. He imparts righteousness to his church, for he is made of God to us righteousness; and believers are made the righteousness of God in him. Christ is our Lord God, our righteousness, our sanctification, and our redemption. His kingdom is an everlasting kingdom. But in this world prosperity and adversity succeed each other, as light and darkness, day and night. The covenant of priesthood shall be secured. And all true believers are a holy priesthood, a royal priesthood, they offer up spiritual sacrifices, acceptable to God; themselves, in the first place, as living sacrifices. The promises of that covenant shall have full accomplishment in the gospel Israel. In Ga 6:16, all that walk according to the gospel rule, are made to be the Israel of God, on whom shall be peace and mercy. Let us not despise the families which were of old the chosen people of God, though for a time they seem to be cast off.

Chapter 34

Zedekiah's death at Babylon foretold (1–7)

The Jews reproved for compelling their poor brethren to return to unlawful bondage (8–22)

Zedekiah's death at Babylon foretold (1–7)

Zedekiah is told that the city shall be taken, and that he shall die a captive, but he shall die a natural death. It is better to live and die penitent in a prison, than to live and die impenitent in a palace.

The Jews reproved for compelling their poor brethren to return to unlawful bondage (8–22)

A Jew should not be held in servitude above seven years. This law they and their fathers had broken. And when there was some hope that the siege was raised, they forced the servants they had released into their services again. Those who think to cheat God by dissembled repentance and partial reformation, put the greatest cheat upon their own souls. This shows that liberty to sin, is really only liberty to have the sorest judgments. It is just with God to disappoint expectations of mercy, when we disappoint the expectations of duty. And when reformation springs only from terror, it is seldom lasting. Solemn vows thus entered into, profane the ordinances of God; and the most forward to bind themselves by appeals to God, are commonly most ready to break them. Let us look to our hearts, that our repentance may be real, and take care that the law of God regulates our conduct.

Chapter 35

The obedience of the Rechabites (1–11)

The Jews' disobedience to the Lord (12–19)

The obedience of the Rechabites (1–11)

Jonadab was famous for wisdom and piety. He never drank wine while he lived. He also appointed them to dwell in tents, or movable dwelling: this would teach them not to think of settling any where in this world. To keep low, would be the way to continue long in the land where they were strangers. Humility and contentment are always the best policy, and men's surest protection. Also, that they might not run into unlawful pleasures, they were to deny themselves even lawful delights. The consideration that we are strangers and pilgrims should oblige us to abstain from all fleshly lusts. Let them have little to lose, and then losing times would be the less dreadful: let them sit loose to what they had, and then they might with less pain be stript of it. Those are in the best frame to meet sufferings who live a life of self-denial, and who despise the vanities of the world. Jonadab's posterity observed these rules strictly, only using proper means for their safety in a time of general suffering.

The Jews' disobedience to the Lord (12–19)

The trial of the Rechabites' constancy was for a sign; it made the disobedience of the Jews to God the more marked. The Rechabites were obedient to one who was but a man like themselves, and Jonadab never did for his seed what God has done for his people. Mercy is promised to the Rechabites. We are not told respecting the performance of this promise; but doubtless it was performed, and travellers say the Rechabites may be found a separate people to this day. Let us follow the counsels of our pious forefathers, and we shall find good in so doing.

Chapter 36

Baruch is to write the prophecies of Jeremiah (1–8)

The princes advise them to hide themselves (9–19)

The king having heard a part, burns the roll (20–32)

Baruch is to write the prophecies of Jeremiah (1–8)

The writing of the Scriptures was by Divine appointment. The Divine wisdom directed to this as a proper means; if it failed, the house of Judah would be the more without excuse. The

Lord declares to sinners the evil he purposes to do against them, that they may hear, and fear, and return from their evil ways; and whenever any one makes this use of God's warnings, in dependence on his promised mercy, he will find the Lord ready to forgive his sins. All others will be left without excuse; and the consideration that great is the anger God has pronounced against us for sin, should quicken both our prayers and our endeavours.

The princes advise them to hide themselves (9–19)

Shows of piety and devotion may be found even among those, who, though they keep up forms of godliness, are strangers and enemies to the power of it. The princes patiently attended the reading of the whole book. They were in great fear. But even those who are convinced to the truth and importance of what they hear, and are disposed to favour those who preach it, often have difficulties and reserves about their safety, interest, or preferment, so that they do not act according to their convictions, and try to get rid of what they find troublesome.

The king having heard a part, burns the roll (20–32)

Those who despise the word of God, will soon show, as this king did, that they hate it; and, like him, they would wish it destroyed. See what enmity there is against God in the carnal mind, and wonder at his patience. The princes showed some concern, till they saw how light the king made of it. Beware of making light of God's word!

Chapter 37

The Chaldean army will return (1–10)
Jeremiah is imprisoned (11–21)

The Chaldean army will return (1–10)

Numbers witness the fatal effects of other men's sins, yet heedlessly step into their places, and follow the same destructive course. When in distress, we ought to desire the prayers of ministers and Christian friends. And it is common for those to desire to be prayed for, who will not be advised; yet sinners are often hardened by a pause in judgments. But if God help us not, no creature can. Whatever instruments God has determined to use, they shall do the work, though they seem unlikely.

Jeremiah is imprisoned (11–21)

There are times when it is the wisdom of good men to retire, to enter into their chambers, and to shut the doors, Isaiah 26:20. Jeremiah was seized as a deserter, and committed to prison.

But it is no new thing for the best friends of the church to be belied, as in the interests of her worst enemies. When thus falsely accused, we may deny the charge, and commit our cause to Him who judges righteously. Jeremiah obtained mercy of the Lord to be faithful, and would not, to obtain mercy of man, be unfaithful to God or to his prince; he tells the king the whole truth. When Jeremiah delivered God's message, he spake with boldness; but when he made his own request, he spake submissively. A lion in God's cause must be a lamb in his own. And God gave Jeremiah favour in the eyes of the king. The Lord God can make even the cells of a prison become pastures to his people, and will raise up friends to provide for them, so that in the days of famine they shall be satisfied.

Chapter 38

Jeremiah is cast into a dungeon, from whence he is delivered by an Ethiopian (1–13)

He advises the king to surrender to the Chadians (14–28)

Jeremiah is cast into a dungeon, from whence he is delivered by an Ethiopian (1–13)

Jeremiah went on in his plain preaching. The princes went on in their malice. It is common for wicked people to look upon God's faithful ministers as enemies, because they show what enemies the wicked are to themselves while impenitent. Jeremiah was put into a dungeon. Many of God's faithful witnesses have been privately made away in prisons. Ebed-melech was an Ethiopian; yet he spoke to the king faithfully, These men have done ill in all they have done to Jeremiah. See how God can raise up friends for his people in distress. Orders were given for the prophet's release, and Ebed-melech saw him drawn up. Let this encourage us to appear boldly for God. Special notice is taken of his tenderness for Jeremiah. What do we behold in the different characters then, but the same we behold in the different characters now, that the Lord's children are conformed to his example, and the children of Satan to their master?

He advises the king to surrender to the Chadians (14–28)

Jeremiah was not forward to repeat the warnings, which seemed only to endanger his own life, and to add to the king's guilt, but asked whether he feared to do the will of God. The less men fear God, the more they fear men; often they dare not act according to their own judgments and consciences.

Chapter 39

The taking of Jerusalem (1–10)

Jeremiah used well (11–14)

Promises of safety to Ebed-melech (15–18)

The taking of Jerusalem (1–10)

Jerusalem was so strong, that the inhabitants believed the enemy could never enter it. But sin provoked God to withdraw his protection, and then it was as weak as other cities. Zedekiah had his eyes put out; so he was condemned to darkness who had shut his eyes against the clear light of God's word. Those who will not believe God's words, will be convinced by the event. Observe the wonderful changes of Providence, how uncertain are earthly possessions; and see the just dealings of Providence: but whether the Lord makes men poor or rich, nothing will profit them while they cleave to their sins.

Jeremiah used well (11–14)

The servants of God alone are prepared for all events; and they are delivered and comforted, while the wicked suffer. They often meet with more kindness from the profane, than from hypocritical professors of godliness. The Lord will raise them up friends, do them good, and perform all his promises.

Promises of safety to Ebed-melech (15–18)

Here is a message to assure Ebed-melech of a recompense for his great kindness to Jeremiah. Because thou hast put thy trust in me, saith the Lord. God recompenses men's services according to their principles. Those who trust God in the way of duty, as this good man did, will find that their hope shall not fail in times of the greatest danger.

Chapter 40

Jeremiah is directed to go to Gedaliah (1–6)

A conspiracy against Gedaliah (7–16)

Jeremiah is directed to go to Gedaliah (1–6)

The captain of the guard seems to glory that he had been God's instrument to fulfil, what Jeremiah had been God's messenger to foretell. Many can see God's justice and truth with regard to others, who are heedless and blind as to themselves and their own sins. But, sooner or later, all men shall be made sensible that their sin is the cause of all their miseries. Jeremiah has leave to dispose of himself; but is advised to go to Gedaliah, governor of the land under the king of Babylon. It is doubtful whether Jeremiah acted right in this decision. But those who desire the salvation of sinners, and the good of the church, are apt to expect better times from slight appearances, and they will prefer the hope of being useful, to the most secure situations without it.

A conspiracy against Gedaliah (7–16)

Jeremiah had never in his prophecies spoken of any good days for the Jews, to come immediately after the captivity; yet Providence seemed to encourage such an expectation. But how soon is this hopeful prospect blighted! When God begins a judgment, he will complete it. While pride, ambition, or revenge, bears rule in the heart, men will form new projects, and be restless in mischief, which commonly ends in their own ruin. Who would have thought, that after the destruction of Jerusalem, rebellion would so soon have sprung up? There can be no thorough change but what grace makes. And if the miserable, who are kept in everlasting chains for the judgment of the great day, were again permitted to come on earth, the sin and evil of their nature would be unchanged. Lord, give us new hearts, and that new mind in which the new birth consists, since thou hast said we cannot without it see thy heavenly kingdom.

Chapter 41

Ishmael murders Gedaliah (1–10)

Johanan recovers the captives, and purposes to retire to Egypt (11–18)

Ishmael murders Gedaliah (1–10)

Those who hate the worshippers of God, often put on the appearance of piety, that they may the easier hurt them. As death often meets men where they least expect it, we should continually search whether we are in such a state and frame of mind, as we would wish to be found in when called to appear before our Judge. Sometimes the ransom of a man's life is his riches. But those who think to bribe death, saying, Slay us not, for we have treasures in the field, will find themselves wretchedly deceived. This melancholy history warns us, never to be secure in this world. We never can be sure of peace on this side heaven.

Johanan recovers the captives, and purposes to retire to Egypt (11–18)

The success of villainy must be short, and none can prosper who harden their hearts against God. And those justly lose comfort in real fears, who excuse themselves in sin by pretended fears. The removal of a prudent and peaceable ruler, and the succession of another who is rash and ambitious, affects the welfare of many. Only those are happy and steady who fear the Lord and walk in his ways.

Chapter 42

Johanan desires Jeremiah to ask counsel of God (1–6)

They are assured of safety in Judea, but of destruction in Egypt (7–22)

Johanan desires Jeremiah to ask counsel of God (1–6)

To serve a turn, Jeremiah is sought out, and the captains ask for his assistance. In every difficult, doubtful case, we must look to God for direction; and we may still, in faith, pray to be guided by a spirit of wisdom in our hearts, and the leadings of Providence. We do not truly desire to know the mind of God, if we do not fully resolve to comply with it when we know it. Many promise to do what the Lord requires, while they hope to have their pride flattered, and their favourite lusts spared. Yet something betrays the state of their hearts.

They are assured of safety in Judea, but of destruction in Egypt (7–22)

If we would know the mind of the Lord in doubtful cases, we must wait as well as pray. God is ever ready to return in mercy to those he has afflicted; and he never rejects any who rely on his promises. He has declared enough to silence even the causeless fears of his people. Whatever loss or suffering we may fear from obedience, is provided against in God's word; and he will protect and deliver all who trust in him and serve him. It is folly to quit our place, especially to quit a holy land, because we meet with trouble in it. And the evils we think to escape by sin, we certainly bring upon ourselves. We may apply this to the common troubles of life; and those who think to avoid them by changing their place, will find that the grievances common to men will meet them wherever they go. Sinners who dissemble with God in solemn professions especially should be rebuked with sharpness; for their actions speak more plainly than words. We know not what is good for ourselves; and what we are most fond of, and have our hearts most set upon, often proves hurtful, and sometimes fatal.

Chapter 43

The leaders carry the people to Egypt (1–7)

Jeremiah foretells the conquest of Egypt (8–13)

The leaders carry the people to Egypt (1–7)

Only by pride comes contention, both with God and man. They preferred their own wisdom to the revealed will of God. Men deny the Scriptures to be the word of God, because they are resolved not to conform themselves to Scripture rules. When men will persist in sin, they charge the best actions to bad motives. These Jews deserted their own land, and threw themselves out of God's protection. It is the folly of men, that they often ruin themselves by wrong endeavours to mend their situation.

Jeremiah foretells the conquest of Egypt (8–13)

God can find his people wherever they are. The Spirit of prophecy was not confined to the land of Israel. It is foretold that Nebuchadnezzar should destroy and carry into captivity many of the Egyptians. Thus God makes one wicked man, or wicked nation, a scourge and plague to another. He will punish those who deceive his professing people, or tempt them to rebellion.

Chapter 44

The Jews in Egypt persist in idolatry (1–14)

They refuse to reform (15–19)

Jeremiah then denounces destruction upon them (20–30)

The Jews in Egypt persist in idolatry (1–14)

God reminds the Jews of the sins that brought desolations upon Judah. It becomes us to warn men of the danger of sin with all seriousness: Oh, do not do it! If you love God, do not, for it is provoking to him; if you love your own souls, do not, for it is destructive to them. Let conscience do this for us in the hour of temptation. The Jews whom God sent into the land of the Chadians, were there, by the power of God's grace, weaned from idolatry; but those who went by their own perverse will into the land of the Egyptians, were there more attached than ever to their idolatries. When we thrust ourselves without cause or call into places of temptation, it is just with God to leave us to ourselves. If we walk contrary to God, he will walk contrary to us. The most awful miseries to which men are exposed, are occasioned by the neglect of offered salvation.

They refuse to reform (15–19)

These daring sinners do not attempt excuses, but declare they will do that which is forbidden. Those who disobey God, commonly grow worse and worse, and the heart is more hardened by the deceitfulness of sin. Here is the real language of the rebellious heart. Even the afflictions which should have parted them from their sins, were taken so as to confirm them in their sins. It is sad when those who should quicken each other to what is good, and so help one another to heaven, harden each other in sin, and so ripen one another for hell. To mingle idolatry with Divine worship, and to reject the mediation of Christ, are provoking to God, and ruinous to men. All who worship images, or honour saints, and angels, and the queen of heaven, should recollect what came from the idolatrous practices of the Jews.

Jeremiah then denounces destruction upon them (20–30)

Whatever evil comes upon us, it is because we have sinned against the Lord; we should therefore stand in awe, and sin not. Since they were determined to persist in their idolatry, God would go on to punish them. What little remains of religion were among them, would be lost. The creature-comforts and confidences from which we promise ourselves most, may fail as soon as those from which we promise ourselves least; and all are what God makes them, not what we fancy them to be. Well-grounded hopes of our having a part in the Divine mercy, are always united with repentance and obedience.

Chapter 45

An encouragement sent to Baruch

Baruch was employed in writing Jeremiah's prophecies, and reading them, see ch. Jeremiah 36, and was threatened for it by the king. Young beginners in religion are apt to be discouraged with little difficulties, which they commonly meet with at first in the service of God. These complaints and fears came from his corruptions. Baruch had raised his expectations too high in this world, and that made the distress and trouble he was in harder to be borne. The frowns of the world would not disquiet us, if we did not foolishly flatter ourselves with the hopes of its smiles, and court and covet them. What a folly is it then to seek great things for ourselves here, where every thing is little, and nothing certain! The Lord knows the real cause of our fretfulness and despondency better than we do, and we should beg of him to examine our hearts, and to repress every wrong desire in us.

Chapter 46

The defeat of the Egyptians (1–12)
Their overthrow after the siege of Tyre (13–26)
A promise of comfort to the Jews (27, 28)

The defeat of the Egyptians (1–12)

The whole word of God is against those who obey not the gospel of Christ; but it is for those, even of the Gentiles, who turn to Him. The

prophecy begins with Egypt. Let them strengthen themselves with all the art and interest they have, yet it shall be all in vain. The wounds God inflicts on his enemies, cannot be healed by medicines. Power and prosperity soon pass from one to another in this changing world.

Their overthrow after the siege of Tyre (13–26)

Those who encroached on others, shall now be themselves encroached on. Egypt is now like a very fair heifer, not accustomed to the yoke of subjection; but destruction comes out of the north: the Chadians shall come. Comfort and peace are spoken to the Israel of God, designed to encourage them when the judgments of God were abroad among the nations. He will be with them, and only correct them in measure; and will not punish them with everlasting destruction from his presence.

A promise of comfort to the Jews (27, 28)

Chapter 47

The calamities of the Philistines

The Philistines had always been enemies to Israel; but the Chaldean army shall overflow their land like a deluge. Those whom God will spoil, must be spoiled. For when the Lord intends to destroy the wicked, he will cut off every helper. So deplorable are the desolations of war, that the blessings of peace are most desirable. But we must submit to His appointments who ordains all in perfect wisdom and justice.

Chapter 48

Prophecies against Moab for pride and security (1–13)
For carnal confidence and contempt of God (14–47)

Prophecies against Moab for pride and security (1–13)

The Chadians are to destroy the Moabites. We should be thankful that we are required to seek the salvation of men's lives, and the salvation of their souls, not to shed their blood; but we shall be the more without excuse if we do this pleasant work deceitfully. The cities shall be laid in ruins, and the country shall be wasted. There will be great sorrow. There will be great hurry. If any could give wings to sinners, still they could not fly out of the reach of Divine indignation. There are many who persist in unrepented iniquity, yet long enjoy outward prosperity. They had been long corrupt and unreformed, secure and sensual in prosperity. They have no changes of their peace and prosperity, therefore their hearts and lives are unchanged, Psalms 55:19.

For carnal confidence and contempt of God (14–47)

The destruction of Moab is further prophesied, to awaken them by national repentance and reformation to prevent the trouble; or by a personal repentance and reformation to prepare for it. In reading this long roll of threatenings, and mediating on the terror, it will be of more use to us to keep in view the power of God's anger and the terror of his judgments, and to have our hearts possessed with a holy awe of God and of his wrath, than to search into all the figures and expressions here used. Yet it is not perpetual destruction. The chapter ends with a promise of their return out of captivity in the latter days. Even with Moabites God will not contend for ever, nor be always wroth. The Jews refer it to the days of the Messiah; then the captives of the Gentiles, under the yoke of sin and Satan, shall be brought back by Divine grace, which shall make them free indeed.

Chapter 49

Prophecies relative to the Ammonites (1–6)

The Edomites (7–22)

The Syrians (23–27)

The Kedarenes (28–33)

The Elamites (34–39)

Prophecies relative to the Ammonites (1–6)

Might often prevails against right among men, yet that might shall be controlled by the Almighty, who judges aright; and those will find themselves mistaken, who, like the Ammonites, think every thing their own on which they can lay their hands. The Lord will call men to account for every instance of dishonesty, especially to the destitute.

The Edomites (7–22)

The Edomites were old enemies to the Israel of God. But their day is now at hand; it is foretold, not only to warn them, but for the sake of the Israel of God, whose afflictions were aggravated by them. Thus Divine judgments go round from nation to nation; the earth is full of commotion, and nothing can escape the ministers of Divine vengeance. The righteousness of God is to be observed amidst the violence of men.

The Syrians (23–27)

How easily God can dispirit those nations that have been most celebrated for valour! Damascus waxes feeble. It was a city of joy,

having all the delights of the sons of men. But those deceive themselves who place their happiness in carnal joys.

The Kedarenes (28–33)

Nebuchadnezzar would make desolation among the people of Kedar, who dwelt in the deserts of Arabia. He who conquered many strong cities, will not leave those unconquered that dwell in tents. He will do this to gratify his own covetousness and ambition; but God orders it for correcting an unthankful people, and for warning a careless world to expect trouble when they seem most safe. They shall flee, get far off, and dwell deep in the deserts; they shall be dispersed. But privacy and obscurity are not always protection and security.

The Elamites (34–39)

The Elamites were the Persians; they acted against God's Israel, and must be reckoned with. Evil pursues sinners. God will make them know that he reigns. Yet the destruction of Elam shall not be for ever. But this promise was to have its full accomplishment in the days of the Messiah. In reading the Divine assurance of the destruction of all the enemies of the church, the believer sees that the issue of the holy war is not doubtful. It is blessed to recollect, that He who is for us, is more than all against us. And he will subdue the enemies of our souls.

Chapter 50

The ruin of Babylon (1–3, 8–16, 21–32, 35–46)

The redemption of God's people (4–7, 17–20, 33, 34)

1–7. The king of Babylon was kind to Jeremiah, yet the prophet must foretell the ruin of that kingdom. If our friends are God's enemies, we dare not speak peace to them. The destruction of Babylon is spoken of as done thoroughly. Here is a word for the comfort of the Jews. They shall return to their God first, then to their own land; the promise of their conversion and reformation makes way for the other promises. Their tears flow not from the sorrow of the world, as when they went into captivity, but from godly sorrow. They shall seek after the Lord as their God, and have no more to do with idols. They shall think of returning to their own country. This represents the return of poor souls to God. In true converts there are sincere desires to attain the end, and constant cares to keep in the way. Their present case is lamented as very sad. The sins of professing Christians never will excuse those who rejoice in destroying them.

8–20. The desolation that shall be brought upon Babylon is set forth in a variety of expressions. The cause of this destruction is the wrath of the Lord. Babylon shall be wholly desolated; for she hath sinned against the Lord. Sin makes men a mark for the arrows of God's judgments. The mercy promised to the Israel of God, shall not only accompany, but arise from the destruction of Babylon. These sheep shall be gathered from the deserts, and put again into good pasture. All who return to God and their duty, shall find satisfaction of soul in so doing. Deliverances out of trouble are comforts indeed, when fruits of the forgiveness of sin.

21–32. The forces are mustered and empowered to destroy Babylon. Let them do what God demands, and they shall bring to pass what he threatens. The pride of men's hearts sets God against them, and ripens them apace for ruin. Babylon's pride must be her ruin; she has been proud against the Holy One of Israel; who can keep those up whom God will throw down?

33–46. It is Israel's comfort in distress, that, though they are weak, their Redeemer is strong. This may be applied to believers, who complain of the dominion of sin and corruption, and of their own weakness and manifold infirmities. Their Redeemer is able to keep what they commit to him; and sin shall not have dominion over them. He will give them that rest which remains for the people of God. Also here is Babylon's sin, and their punishment. The sins are, idolatry and persecution. He that will not save his people in their sins, never will countenance the wickedness of his open enemies. The judgments of God for these sins will lay them waste. In the judgments denounced against prosperous Babylon, and the mercies promised to afflicted Israel, we learn to choose to suffer affliction with the people of God, rather than to enjoy the pleasures of sin for a season.

Chapter 51

Babylon's doom; God's controversy with her; encouragements from thence to the Israel of God (1–58)

The confirming of this (59–64)

Babylon's doom; God's controversy with her; encouragements from thence to the Israel of God (1–58)

The particulars of this prophecy are dispersed and interwoven, and the same things left and returned to again. Babylon is abundant in treasures, yet neither her waters nor her wealth shall secure her. Destruction comes when they did not think of it. Wherever we are, in the greatest depths, at the greatest distances, we are to remember the Lord our God; and in the times of the greatest fears and hopes, it is most needful to remember the Lord. The feeling excited by Babylon's fall is the same with the New Testament Babylon, Revelation 18:9,19. The ruin of all who support idolatry, infidelity, and superstition, is needful for the revival of true godliness; and the threatening prophecies of Scripture yield comfort in this view. The great seat of antichristian tyranny, idolatry, and superstition, the persecutor of true Christians, is as certainly doomed to destruction as ancient Babylon. Then will vast multitudes mourn for sin, and seek the Lord. Then will the lost sheep of the house of Israel be brought back to the fold of the good Shepherd, and stray no more. And the exact fulfilment of these ancient prophecies encourages us to faith in all the promises and prophecies of the sacred Scriptures.

The confirming of this (59–64)

This prophecy is sent to Babylon, to the captives there, by Seraiah, who is to read it to his countrymen in captivity. Let them with faith see the end of these threatening powers, and comfort themselves herewith. When we see what this world is, how glittering its shows, and how flattering its proposals, let us read in the book of the Lord that it shall shortly be desolate. The book must be thrown into the river Euphrates. The fall of the New Testament Babylon is thus represented, Revelation 18:21. Those that sink under the weight of God's wrath and curse, sink for ever. Babylon, and every antichrist, will soon sink and rise no more for ever. Let us hope in God's word, and quietly wait for his salvation; then we shall see, but shall not share, the destruction of the wicked.

Chapter 52

The fate of Zedekiah (1–11)
The destruction of Jerusalem (12–23)
The captivities (24–30)
The advancement of Jehoiachin (31–34)

The fate of Zedekiah (1–11)

This fruit of sin we should pray against above any thing; Cast me not away from thy presence, Psalms 51:11. None are cast out of God's presence but those who by sin have first thrown themselves out. Zedekiah's flight was in vain, for there is no escaping the judgments of God; they come upon the sinner, and overtake him, let him flee where he will.

The destruction of Jerusalem (12–23)

The Chaldean army made woeful havoc. But nothing is so particularly related here, as the carrying away of the articles in the temple. The remembrance of their beauty and value shows us the more the evil of sin.

The captivities (24–30)

The leaders of the Jews caused them to err; but now they are, in particular, made monuments of Divine justice. Here is an account of two earlier captivities. This people often were wonders both of judgment and mercy.

The advancement of Jehoiachin (31–34)

Those under oppression will find it is not in vain for them to hope and quietly to wait for the salvation of the Lord. Our times are in God's hand, for the hearts of all we have to deal with are so. May we be enabled, more and more, to rest on the Rock of Ages, and to look forward with holy faith to that hour, when the Lord will bring again Zion, and overthrow all the enemies of the church.

LAMENTATIONS

Matthew Henry

Introduction

It is evident that Jeremiah was the author of the Lamentations which bear his name. The book was not written till after the destruction of Jerusalem by the Chadians. May we be led to consider sin as the cause of all our calamities, and under trials exercise submission, repentance, faith, and prayer, with the hope of promised deliverance through God's mercy.

Chapter 1

The miserable state of Jerusalem, the just consequences of its sins (1–11)

Jerusalem represented as a captive female, lamenting, and seeking the mercy of God (12–22)

The miserable state of Jerusalem, the just consequences of its sins (1–11)

The prophet sometimes speaks in his own person; at other times Jerusalem, as a distressed female, is the speaker, or some of the Jews. The description shows the miseries of the Jewish nation. Jerusalem became a captive and a slave, by reason of the greatness of her sins; and had no rest from suffering. If we allow sin, our greatest adversary, to have dominion over us, justly will other enemies also be suffered to have dominion. The people endured the extremities of famine and distress. In this sad condition Jerusalem acknowledged her sin, and entreated the Lord to look upon her case. This is the only way to make ourselves easy under our burdens; for it is the just anger of the Lord for man's transgressions, that has filled the earth with sorrows, lamentations, sickness, and death.

Jerusalem represented as a captive female, lamenting, and seeking the mercy of God (12–22)

Jerusalem, sitting dejected on the ground, calls on those that passed by, to consider whether her example did not concern them. Her outward sufferings were great, but her inward sufferings were harder to bear, through the sense of guilt. Sorrow for sin must be great sorrow, and must affect the soul. Here we see the evil of sin, and may take warning to flee from the wrath to come. Whatever may be learned from the sufferings of Jerusalem, far more may be learned from the sufferings of Christ. Does he not from the cross speak to every one of us? Does he not say, Is it nothing to you, all ye that pass by? Let all our sorrows lead us to the cross of Christ, lead us to mark his example, and cheerfully to follow him.

Chapter 2

Lamentation for the misery of Jerusalem

1–9. A sad representation is here made of the state of God's church, of Jacob and Israel; but the notice seems mostly to refer to the hand of the Lord in their calamities. Yet God is not an enemy to his people, when he is angry with them and corrects them. And gates and bars stand in no stead when God withdraws his protection. It is just with God to cast down those by judgments, who debase themselves by sin; and to deprive those of the benefit and comfort of Sabbaths and ordinances, who have not duly valued nor observed them. What should they do with Bibles, who make no improvement of them? Those who misuse God's prophets, justly lose them. It becomes necessary, though painful, to turn the thoughts of the afflicted to the hand of God lifted up against them, and to their sins as the source of their miseries.

10–22. Causes for lamentation are described. Multitudes perished by famine. Even little children were slain by their mother's hands, and eaten, according to the threatening, Deuteronomy 28:53. Multitudes fell by the sword. Their false prophets deceived them. And their neighbours laughed at them. It is a great sin to jest at others' miseries, and adds much affliction to the afflicted. Their enemies triumphed over them. The enemies of the church are apt to take its shocks for its ruins; but they will find themselves deceived. Calls to lamentation are given; and comforts for the cure of these lamentations are sought. Prayer is a salve for every sore, even the sorest; a remedy for every malady, even the most grievous. Our business in prayer is to refer our case to the Lord, and leave it with him. His will be done. Let us fear God, and walk humbly before him, and take heed lest we fall.

Chapter 3

The faithful lament their calamities, and hope in God's mercies

1–20. The prophet relates the more gloomy and discouraging part of his experience, and how he found support and relief. In the time of his trial the Lord had become terrible to him. It was an affliction that was misery itself; for sin makes the cup of affliction a bitter cup. The struggle between unbelief and faith is often very severe. But the weakest believer is wrong, if he thinks that his strength and hope are perished from the Lord.

21–36. Having stated his distress and temptation, the prophet shows how he was raised above it. Bad as things are, it is owing to the mercy of God that they are not worse. We should observe what makes for us, as well as what is against us. God's compassions fail not; of this we have fresh instances every morning. Portions on earth are perishing things, but God is a portion for ever. It is our duty, and will be our comfort and satisfaction, to hope and quietly to wait for the salvation of the Lord. Afflictions do and will work very much for good: many have found it good to bear this yoke in their youth; it has made many humble and serious, and has weaned them from the world, who otherwise would have been proud and unruly. If tribulation work patience, that patience will work experience, and that experience a hope that makes not ashamed. Due thoughts of the evil of sin, and of our own sinfulness, will convince us that it is of the Lord's mercies we are not consumed. If we cannot say with unwavering voice, The Lord is my portion;

may we not say, I desire to have Him for my portion and salvation, and in his word do I hope? Happy shall we be, if we learn to receive affliction as laid upon us by the hand of God.

37–41. While there is life there is hope; and instead of complaining that things are bad, we should encourage ourselves with the hope they will be better. We are sinful men, and what we complain of, is far less than our sins deserve. We should complain to God, and not of him. We are apt, in times of calamity, to reflect on other people's ways, and blame them; but our duty is to search and try our own ways, that we may turn from evil to God. Our hearts must go with our prayers. If inward impressions do not answer to outward expressions, we mock God, and deceive ourselves.

42–54. The more the prophet looked on the desolations, the more he was grieved. Here is one word of comfort. While they continued weeping, they continued waiting; and neither did nor would expect relief and succour from any but the Lord.

55–66. Faith comes off conqueror, for in these the prophet concludes with some comfort. Prayer is the breath of the new man, drawing in the air of mercy in petitions, and returning it in praises; it proves and maintains the spiritual life. He silenced their fears, and quieted their spirits. Thou saidst, Fear not. This was the language of God's grace, by the witness of his Spirit with their spirits. And what are all our sorrows, compared with those of the Redeemer? He will deliver his people from every trouble, and revive his church from every persecution. He will save believers with everlasting salvation, while his enemies perish with everlasting destruction.

Chapter 4

The deplorable state of the nation is contrasted with its ancient prosperity

1–12. What a change is here! Sin tarnishes the beauty of the most exalted powers and the most excellent gifts; but that gold, tried in the fire, which Christ bestows, never will be taken from us; its outward appearance may be dimmed, but its real value can never be changed. The horrors of the siege and destruction of Jerusalem are again described. Beholding the sad consequences of sin in the church of old, let us seriously consider to what the same causes may justly bring down the church now. But, Lord, though we have gone from thee in rebellion, yet turn to us, and turn our hearts to thee, that we may fear thy name. Come to us, bless us with awakening, converting, renewing, confirming grace.

13–20. Nothing ripens a people more for ruin, nor fills the measure faster, than the sins of priests and prophets. The king himself cannot escape, for Divine vengeance pursues him. Our anointed King alone is the life of our souls; we may safely live under his shadow, and rejoice in Him in the midst of our enemies, for He is the true God and eternal life.

21–22. Here it is foretold that an end should be put to Zion's troubles. Not the fulness of punishment deserved, but of what God has determined to inflict. An end shall be put to Edom's triumphs. All the troubles of the church and of the believer will soon be accomplished. And the doom of their enemies approaches. The Lord will bring their sins to light, and they shall lie down in eternal sorrow. Edom here represents all the enemies of the church. And the corruption, and sin of Israel, which the prophet has proved to be universal, justifies the judgments of the Lord. It shows the need of that grace in Christ Jesus, which the sin and corruption of all mankind make so necessary.

Chapter 5

The Jewish nation supplicating the Divine favour

1–16. Is any afflicted? Let him pray; and let him in prayer pour out his complaint to God. The people of God do so here; they complain not of evils feared, but of evils felt. If penitent and patient under what we suffer for the sins of our fathers, we may expect that He who punishes, will return in mercy to us. They acknowledge, Woe unto us that we have sinned! All our woes are owing to our own sin and folly.

Though our sins and God's just displeasure cause our sufferings, we may hope in his pardoning mercy, his sanctifying grace, and his kind providence. But the sins of a man's whole life will be punished with vengeance at last, unless he obtains an interest in Him who bare our sins in his own body on the tree.

17–22. The people of God express deep concern for the ruins of the temple, more than for any other of their calamities. But whatever changes there are on earth, God is still the same, and remains for ever wise and holy, just and good; with Him there is no variableness nor shadow of turning. They earnestly pray to God for mercy and grace; Turn us to thee, O Lord. God never leaves any till they first leave him; if he turns them to him in a way of duty, no doubt he will quickly return to them in a way of mercy. If God by his grace renew our days. Troubles may cause our hearts to be faint, and our eyes to be dim, but the way to the mercy-seat of our reconciled God is open. Let us, in all our trials, put our whole trust and confidence in his mercy; let us confess our sins, and pour out our hearts before him. Let us watch against repinings and despondency; for we surely know, that it shall be well in the end with all that trust in, fear, love, and serve the Lord. Are not the Lord's judgments in the earth the same as in Jeremiah's days? Let Zion then be remembered by us in our prayers, and her welfare be sought above every earthly joy. Spare, Lord, spare thy people, and give not thine heritage to reproach, for the heathen to rule over them.

EZEKIEL

John Wesley

Introduction

The name Ezekiel signifies, The strength of God. And God did indeed make his face strong against all opposition. It was the tradition of the Jews, that for his boldness and faithfulness in reproving them, he was put to death by the captives in Babylon.

The prophecies of this book were spoken and written in Babylon, to the Jews who were captives there. Ezekiel prophesied in the beginning of their captivity, to convince them when they were secure and unhumbled; Daniel, in the latter end of it, to comfort them, when they were dejected and discouraged.

There is much in this book which is very mysterious, especially in the beginning and latter end of it. But although the visions are intricate, the sermons are plain, and the design of them is, to shew God's people their transgressions. And although the reproofs and threatenings are very sharp, yet toward the close we have very comfortable promises, to be fulfilled in the kingdom of the Messiah, of whom indeed Ezekiel speaks less than almost any of the prophets.

The visions, which are his credentials, we have, chap. 1–3. The reproofs and threatenings, chap. 4–24. We have messages sent to the neighbouring nations, foretelling their destruction, chap. 25–35. To make way for the restoration of Israel, and the re-establishment of their city and temple, which are foretold, chap. 36–48.

Chapter 1

The time when this prophecy was delivered, the place where, and person by whom (1–3)

His vision of the glory of God, in his attendance, surrounded with angels, (here called living creatures) (4–14)

In his providences, represented by the wheels and their motions (15–25)

And in the face of Jesus Christ, sitting upon the throne (26–28)

The time when this prophecy was delivered, the place where, and person by whom (1–3)

1. Thirtieth year – From the finding the book of the law in the eighteenth year of Josiah, from which date to the fifth year of the captivity are thirty years. **Fifth day** – Probably it was the Sabbath-day, when the Jews were at leisure to hear the prophet. **River** – Perhaps retiring thither to lament their own sins, and Jerusalem's desolation. **Chebar** – A river now called Giulap, arising out of the mountain Masius, and falling into Euphrates, somewhat below a city called by the same name.

2. The month – Thamus, as ver.1, answering to our June and July. **Fifth year** – This account observed will guide us in computing the times referred to ver.1. These five of Jehoiachin, and the eleven of his predecessor, added to fourteen of Josiah's reign, after he found the law, make up thirty years, ver.1. **Jehoiachin** – Who is also called Jechoniah, and Coniah. It may be of use to keep an account, when and where God has manifested himself to us in a peculiar manner. Remember, O my soul, what thou didst receive at such a time, at such a place: tell others what God did for thee.

3. The word – What was visions, ver.1, is here the word, both as signifying and declaring the mind of God, what he would do, and as continuing his commands to Ezekiel and to the people. **Ezekiel** – He speaks of himself in a third person. **Priest** – He was of the priests originally; he was a prophet by an extraordinary call. **The hand** – He felt the power of God opening his eyes to see the visions, opening his ear to hear the voice, and his heart to receive both. When the hand of the Lord goes along with his word, then it becomes effectual.

His vision of the glory of God, in his attendance, surrounded with angels, (here called living creatures) (4–14)

4. Looked – I very diligently surveyed the things that were represented to me in the vision. **Whirlwind** –This denotes the indignation and judgments of God; a quick, impetuous and irresistible vengeance. **North** – From Babylon, which lay northward from Judea; and the prophet, although now in Babylon, speaks of the Jews, as if they were in Jerusalem. **A fire** – An orb or wheel of fire: God being his own cause, his own rule, and his own word. **Brightness** – Yet round about it was not smoke and darkness, but a clear light. **The midst** – Of the fire.

5. The likeness – Such a representation of the holy angels as God saw fit to make use of, came out of the midst of the fire: for angels derive their being and power from God: their glory is a ray of his.

6. Wings – With two they flew, denoting the speed of their obedience; and with two they covered their body, denoting their reverence.

7. Feet – Their thighs, legs and feet, were of a human shape. **Straight** – Not bowed to this or that part, which argues weakness. **The sole** – That which is properly the foot. **A calf's** – A divided hoof spake the cleanness of the creature. **They** – Their feet.

8. Under – Their power and manner of exerting it is secret and invisible. **Sides** – On each side of the chariot one of these living creatures stood, and so on each side hands were ready to act as they were moved. **They four** – It is doubled to confirm the truth and certainty of the thing.

9. Their wings – The wings of the two cherubim which went foremost, and the wings of the two hindermost, were joined together when they moved. **Went** – This explains the former words, assuring us, that every one of those living creatures are ready, and unwearied in doing the pleasure of their Creator.

10. A man – Each face is compared to what is most excellent in its kind, man excels in wisdom, lions in strength, the ox in patience and constancy of labour, the eagle in speed and high flight.

11. Divided – So each face appeared distinct above the shoulders, and there the wings divided from each other were united to the body of the living creature.

12. Straight – Which way soever they went, each living creature had one face looking straight forward. **The spirit** – The will, command, and breathing of the Spirit of God, both gave and guided their motions. **Was to go** – Going is attributed here to the Spirit of God, by allusion, for he who is in every place cannot properly be said to go from or to any place. **Turned not** – They looked not back, they turned not out of the way, they gave not over, until they had competed their course.

13. The fire – This fire stood not still, but as the Hebrew is, Made itself walk up and down. It moved itself, which is too much to ascribe to creatures: God only moved all these living creatures.

14. Ran – They ran into the lower world, to do what was to be done there: and when they had done, returned as a flash of lightning, to the upper world, to the vision of God. Thus we should be in the affairs of this world: though we run into them we must not repose in them, but our souls must presently return like lightning, to God, their rest and centre.

In his providences, represented by the wheels and their motions (15–25)

15. Living creatures – By each of the living creatures stood one wheel, so that they were four in number, according to the number of living creatures. **Four faces** – By this it appears, each wheel had its four faces. While he was contemplating the glory of the former vision, this other was presented to him: wherein the dispensations of providence are compared to the wheels of a machine, which all contribute to the regular motion of it. Providence orders, changes: sometimes one spoke of the wheel is uppermost, sometimes another. But the motion of the wheel on its own axle-tree, is still regular and steady. And the wheel is said to be by the living creatures, who attend to direct its motion. For all inferior creatures are, and move, and act, as the Creator, by the ministration of angels directs and influences them: visible effects are managed and governed by invisible causes.

16. Work – All that was wrought, whether engraved or otherwise was of one colour. **Beryl** – A sea green. **One likeness** – The same for dimensions, colour, frame, and motion. **In the**

middle – It is probable, the wheels were framed so as to be an exact sphere, which is easily rolled to any side.

17. They – The wheels. **Four sides** – The wheels being supposed round every way as a globe, by an exact framing of two wheels one in the other; the four semi-circles which are in two whole wheels, may be well taken for these four sides on which these wheels move, and such a wheel will readily be turned to all points of the compass. **Returned not** – They returned not until they came to their journey's end; nothing could divert them, or put them out of their course. So firm and sure are the methods, so unalterable and constant the purposes of God, and so invariable the obedience and observance of holy angels. So subject to the sovereign will of God are all second causes.

18. The rings – The circumference of the wheels. **Dreadful** – Their very height impressed a fear on the beholder. **Them four** – Every one of the four wheels. How fitly do the wheels, their motion, their height, and eyes, signify the height, unsearchableness, wisdom, and vigilance of the Divine Providence.

20. The spirit – The Spirit of God. These angels in their ministry punctually observed both his impulse and conduct. **They** – The wheels, inferior agents and second causes. **Their spirit** – The wheels concurred with the spirit of the living creatures, so that there was an hearty accord between those superior and inferior causes. **For** – An undiscerned, yet divine, mighty, wise, and ever-living power, spirit, and being, actuated all, and governed all.

21. For – The same wisdom, power, and holiness of God, the same will and counsel of his, that guides and governs the angels, does by them order and dispose all the motions of the creatures in this lower world.

22. Likeness – The appearance or resemblance. **As crystal** – For splendour, purity, and solidity, all that was above these creatures and wheels was beautiful and very majestic, and it is therefore called terrible, because it impressed a veneration upon the mind of the beholders.

23. Under – Below at a great distance, stood these living creatures. **Straight** – Stretched forth, ready for motion. **One** – Each of the four had two other wings with which they covered their bodies.

24. The voice – Thunder. **Speech** – The prophet heard the voice in an articulate manner. **An host** – A tumultuous voice of men. **Stood** – Having done their office they present themselves before God, waiting for the commands of their Lord.

And in the face of Jesus Christ, sitting upon the throne (26–28)

26. A man – Christ, God-man, who here appears as king and judge.

27. Amber – In this colour does Christ appear against the rebellious Jews; he that would have visited them clothed with the garments of salvation, now puts on the garments of vengeance, expressed by such metaphors. **Brightness** – Majesty, justice, and unstained holiness, shine round about him.

28. The bow – A like appearance of Christ in a surrounding brightness, as of the rainbow you have, Rev 4:3. Mercy, and truth, and both according to covenant are about the throne of Christ. **Glory** – It was not the full glory of God, but such as the prophet might bear. **I fell** – With deep humility and reverence.

Chapter 2

Ezekiel is commissioned to prophesy to the Jewish captives (1–5)

Is cautioned not to be afraid of them (6)

Has words put into his mouth, signified by the vision of a roll, which he is ordered to eat (7–10)

Ezekiel is commissioned to prophesy to the Jewish captives (1–5)

1. And – He that sat upon the throne, Jesus Christ. **Son of man** – A phrase which is ninety-five times, at least, used in this prophecy to keep him humble who had such great revelations. **Stand** – Arise, fear not. And with this command God sent forth a power enabling him to rise and stand.

2. The spirit – The same spirit which actuated the living creatures.

5. Shall know – They that obey shall know by the good I will do them, those that will not, by the evil which I will bring upon them.

Is cautioned not to be afraid of them (6)

6. Words – Accusations, threats, or whatever else a malicious heart can suggest to the tongue. **Briers** – Which usually run up among thorns, are a very fit emblem of the frowardness and keenness of sinners against God and his prophet. **Scorpions** – Malicious, revengeful men. They that will do any thing to purpose in the service of God, must not fear the faces of men.

Has words put into his mouth, signified by the vision of a roll, which he is ordered to eat (7–10)

8. Hear – Obey. **Open** – This was done only in a vision.

9. Roll – Their books were not like ours, but written in parchment and in the length of it, and so one piece fastened to another, until the whole would contain what was to be written, and then it was wrapped or rolled about a round piece of wood, fashioned for that purpose.

10. **And** – The person, who held out his hand. **Spread** – Unrolled it. **Within** – On both sides, on that side which was inward when rolled, and on that side also that was outward.

Chapter 3

His eating the roll (1–3)

Farther instructions and encouragements given him (4–11)

He is carried to the captive Jews (12–15)

An illustration of his office by that of a watchman (16–21)

The restraining and restoring of his liberty of speech (22–27)

His eating the roll (1–3)

1. **Eat** – This was done in a vision. **Findeth** – In the hand which was sent to him.

3. **Belly** – The mouth is the proper instrument of eating, but when meat is digested, the belly is said to eat. **Fill thy bowels** – This denotes the fulness of the measure wherewith we should read, meditate, and digest the word of God. **Honey** – It was sweet to receive things by revelation from God, and so to converse with God. And usually the first part of the ministerial work is pleasant.

Farther instructions and encouragements given him (4–11)

4. **Speak** – What things I shall shew thee, and in what words I shall declare them to thee.

6. **Many people** – Divers nations, that thou shouldest need divers tongues, to speak to them all in their own language.

7. **All** – The far greater part, although not every particular person.

8. **I have** – I have given thee, constancy, and manly carriage. The more impudent wicked people are in their opposition to religion, the more openly and resolutely should God's people appear in the practice and defence of it.

11. **Captivity** – Of the first captivity under Jeconiah's reign, who succeeded his father Jehoiakim, slain for his conspiracy with Egypt against Nebuchadnezzar.

He is carried to the captive Jews (12–15)

12. **A voice** – An articulate sound, of many angels, attended with the rushing of the wheels, added to the noise of their wings. **Blessed** – Praised be the gloriously holy and just God. **His place** – Coming down from heaven.

13. **Rushing** – The wheels of providence moved over against the angels, and in concert with them.

14. **Spirit** – Caught him up into the air. **Took** – Carried me to the place where the captive Jews were crowded together. **Bitterness** – Not at all pleased with my work. He went in the heat of his spirit; because of the discouragements he foresaw he should meet with. But the hand of the Lord was strong upon him, not only to compel him to the work, but to fit him for it.

15. **Tel-abib** – A part of Mesopotamia, which was shut up within Chebar westward, and Saocora eastward. **By** – On that part of the river Chebar, which runs west-ward of Tel-abib. **Where** – Where I found them sitting astonished, at the sight of their change from freedom and honour to servitude and shame. **Seven days** – Mourning no doubt all that while, and waiting until the spirit of prophecy should open his mouth.

An illustration of his office by that of a watchman (16–21)

20. **I Lay** – Permit it to be laid before him. **He shall** – Perish in his sin. **Remembered** – Shall not be profitable to him; 'he that apostatizes is the worst of men, because he falls from known ways of goodness and holiness.'

The restraining and restoring of his liberty of speech (22–27)

22. **There** – At Tel-abib. **Go forth** – Withdraw from the multitude.

23. **As the glory** – We are not now to expect such visions. But we have a favour done us nothing inferior, if we by faith behold the glory of the Lord, so as to be changed into the same image. And this honour have all his saints.

24. **Shut** – To foresignify the shutting up of the Jews in Jerusalem.

25. **Not go** – Thou shalt be straitly confined.

26. **I** – I will make thee as dumb as if thy tongue clave to the roof of thy mouth.

27. **But** – When ever I shall reveal any thing to thee. **Open** – I will give thee power to speak. **Let** – It is his duty and safety. **Forbear** – It is at his own peril.

Chapter 4

Two things are here represented to the prophet in vision

1. The fortifications that shall be shortly raised against the city, signified by his laying siege to the portrait of Jerusalem (1–3)

And lying first on one side, and then on the other side before it (4–8)

2. The famine that would rage therein, signified by his eating coarse fare, and little

of it, so long as this typical representation lasted (9–17)

The fortifications that shall be shortly raised against the city, signified by his laying siege to the portrait of Jerusalem (1–3)

1. **Portray** – Draw a map of Jerusalem.

2. **Lay siege** – Draw the figure of a siege about the city. **Build** – Raise a tower and bulwarks.

3. **A wall** – That it may resemble a wall of iron, for as impregnable as such a wall, shall the resolution and patience of the Chaldeans be.

And lying first on one side, and then on the other side before it (4–8)

4. **Lay** – Take upon thee the representation of their guilt and punishment. **House of Israel** – The ten tribes. **The number** – By this thou shalt intimate how long I have borne with their sins, and how long they shall bear their punishment.

5. **I have laid** – I have pointed out the number of years wherein apostate Israel sinned against me, and I did bear with them. **Years** – These years probably began at Solomon's falling to idolatry, in the twenty-seventh year of his reign, and ended in the fifth of Zedekiah's captivity.

6. **Accomplished** – That is, almost accomplished. **House of Judah** – Of the two tribes. **Forty days** – Probably from Josiah's renewing the covenant, until the destruction of the temple, during which time God deferred to punish, expecting whether they would keep their covenant, or retain their idolatries, which latter they did for thirteen years of Josiah's reign, for eleven of Jehoiakim's, and eleven of Zedekiah's reign, and five of his captivity, which amount to just forty years. But all this was done in a vision.

7. **Set** – While thou liest on thy side thou shalt fix thy countenance on the portrait of besieged Jerusalem. **Uncovered** – Naked and stretched out as being ready to strike.

8. **Bands** – An invisible restraint assuring him, that those could no more remove from the siege, than he from that side he lay on.

The famine that would rage therein, signified by his eating coarse fare, and little of it, so long as this typical representation lasted (9–17)

9. **Take** – Provide thee corn enough: for a grievous famine will accompany the siege. **Wheat** – All sorts of grain are to be provided, and all will be little enough. **One vessel** – Mix the worst with the best to lengthen out the provision.

10. **By weight** – Not as much as you will, but a small pittance delivered by weight to all.

Twenty shekels – Ten ounces: scarce enough to maintain life. **From time to time** – At set hours this was weighed out.

11. **The sixth part** – About six ounces.

12. **As barley cakes** – Because they never had enough to make a loaf with, they eat them as barley cakes. **With dung** – There was no wood left, nor yet dung of other creatures. This also was represented in a vision.

17. **May want** – So because they served not God with cheerfulness in the abundance of all things, He made them serve their enemies in the want of all things.

Chapter 5

The destruction of Jerusalem, represented by a sign, the cutting and burning and scattering of hair (1–4)

Sin, the cause of this destruction (5–7)

Wrath, misery and ruin threatened (8–15)

The destruction of Jerusalem, represented by a sign, the cutting and burning and scattering of hair (1–4)

1. **Take** – Thus foretell the mourning, reproach, and deformity that are coming, for all this is signified by shaving the head and beard.

2. **A third part** – Described on the tile, chap.4:1, a type of what should be done in Jerusalem. **The days** – When the three hundred and ninety days of thy lying against the portrayed city shall be ended. **With a knife** – To signify them that fall by the sword. **Scatter** – To typify them that fell to the Chaldeans, or fled to Egypt, or other countries.

3. **Take** – Of the last third. **Bind** – As men tied up in the skirt of their garment what they would not lose: to signify the small remnant.

4. **Of them** – Out of that little remnant. **In the fire** – For their sin against God, their discontents at their state, and conspiracies against their governor, another fire shall break out which shall devour the most, and be near consuming all the houses of Israel.

Sin, the cause of this destruction (5–7)

5. **This is Jerusalem** – This portrayed city, is typically Jerusalem. **The midst** – Jerusalem was set in the midst of the nations, to be as the heart in the body, to invigorate the dead world with a divine life, as well as to enlighten the dark world with a divine light.

6. **More** – More than the heathen.

7. **Multiplied** – In idols, superstitions, and wickedness. **Neither** – You have exceeded them in superstition and idolatry, and fallen short of them in moral virtues.

Wrath, misery and ruin threatened (8–15)

9. Not done – Though the old world perished by water, and Sodom by fire, yet neither one or other was so lingering a death.

10. Scatter – This was verified when they were fetched away, who were left at the departure of the besiegers, and when the very small remnant with Johanan fled into Egypt.

11. Sanctuary – My temple. **Detestable things** – Thy idols.

13. Comforted – In executing my vengeance. **In my zeal** – For my own glory.

15. Taunt – A very proverb among them. **Instruction** – Sinners shall learn by thy miseries, what they may expect from me.

17. Bereave thee – Of your children, friends, and your own life. **Pestilence and blood** – Thy land shall be the common road for pestilence and blood. Although this prophecy was to be accomplished presently, in the destruction of Jerusalem by the Chaldeans; yet it may well be supposed to look forward, to the final destruction of it by the Romans, when God made a full end of the Jewish nation, and caused his fury to rest upon them.

Chapter 6

A threatening of the destruction of Israel for their idolatry (1–7)

A promise of the gracious return of a remnant (8–10)

Directions to lament the sins and calamities of Israel (11–14)

A threatening of the destruction of Israel for their idolatry (1–7)

2. The mountains – The inhabitants of the mountains, who were secure in their fastnesses.

3. Rivers – To those who dwell by river sides, or in the valleys. **High places** – The places of your idolatrous worship.

4. Cast down – Before the altars of your idols, which you fly to for refuge.

5. And – Thus the idols were upbraided with their inability to help their worshippers, and the idolaters, with the folly of trusting in them.

6. Your works – All your costly work for your idols.

A promise of the gracious return of a remnant (8–10)

8. Remnant – It is the Lord that preserves a remnant, the enemies rage would destroy all.

9. Shall remember – So as to turn unto me. **Broken** – I am much grieved. **Whorish heart** – Idolatrous hearts depart from God, as an adulterous wife departs from her husband. **Loath**

– With a mixture of grief towards God, of indignation against themselves, and abhorrence of the offence.

10. In vain – Either without cause, the sufferers gave him just cause to pronounce that evil; or without effect. Their sins where the cause, and their destruction is the effect of their sufferings.

Directions to lament the sins and calamities of Israel (11–14)

11. Smite – To shew thy wonder, indignation, sorrow, and pity, for their sins and sufferings.

12. Far off – Either by flight, or captivity. **Shall fall** – Who dwell near to Jerusalem, or would retire to it, when the Babylonians approach.

14. Wilderness – The horrid wilderness of Moab. Therein the fiery serpents so much annoyed Israel. Accordingly the land of Canaan is at this day one of the most desolate countries in the world.

Chapter 7

In this chapter the prophet tells them, that a final ruin is coming (1–6)

A ruin just at the door (7–10)

An unavoidable ruin, because of their sins (11–15)

That their strength and wealth would be no fence against it (16–19)

That the temple, which they trusted in, should itself be ruined (20–22)

That it should be an universal ruin, the sin that brought it being universal (23–27)

In this chapter the prophet tells them, that a final ruin is coming (1–6)

1. An end – An end of God's patience, and of the peace and welfare of the people.

4. Recompense – The punishment of them.

5. An evil – An evil and sore affliction, a singular, uncommon one.

6. An end – When the end is come upon the wicked world, then an only evil comes upon it. The sorest of temporal judgments have their allays; but the torments of the damned are an evil, an only evil.

A ruin just at the door (7–10)

7. The morning – The fatal morning, the day of destruction. **Sounding** – Not a mere echo, not a fancy, but a real thing.

10. Is come – Of your wickedness; pride and violence in particular.

An unavoidable ruin, because of their sins (11–15)

11. None – They shall be utterly wasted for their sins. **Wailing** – The living shall not bewail their dead friends, because they shall judge the dead in a better case than the living.

12. Mourn – Men usually part with their estates grieving that they must transmit their right to others; but let them now think how little a while they could have kept them, and how little time they shall keep them who have bought them.

13. Yet alive – For if any should survive the captivity, yet the conqueror wasting and destroying all, would confound all ancient boundaries. **Touching** – The evils threatened are designed against all the multitude of Israel. **Strengthen** – Nor shall any one man of them all he able to secure himself, by any sinful contrivance.

14. They – The house of Israel have summoned in all fit for arms. **None** – There is not a man going to the war. **Wrath** – That displeasure which takes away their courage.

15. Without – In the countries. **Within** – The besieged city. **Field** – Whoever is in the field.

That their strength and wealth would be no fence against it (16–19)

16. Iniquity – Either for the punishment of their iniquity, or for their iniquity itself.

18. Baldness – Either by pulling off the hair amidst their sorrows, or cutting it off in token of mourning.

19. Cast – That they may be the lighter to fly. **Removed** – Carried away into Babylon. **Not satisfy** – They shall afford them no comfort. **Stumbling-block** – This silver and gold they coveted immeasurably, and abused to pride, luxury, idolatry and oppression; this that they stumbled at and fell into sin, now they stumble at and fall into the deepest misery.

That the temple, which they trusted in, should itself be ruined (20–22)

20. The beauty – The temple, and all that pertained to it, which was the beauty and glory of that nation. **He set** – God commanded it should be beautiful and magnificent. **Images** – Their idols. **Far from them** – I have sent them far from the temple.

21. It – My temple.

22. Turn – Either from the Jews, or from the Chaldeans, neither relieving the one nor restraining the other. **Secret place** – The temple, and the holy of holies. **Robbers** – The soldiers.

That it should be an universal ruin, the sin that brought it being universal (23–27)

23. A chain – To bind the captives.

24. The pomp – The magnificence and glory, wherein they boasted; or the temple that the Jews gloried in.

26. Seek – But in vain. **The priest** – He shall have no words either of counsel or comfort to say to them. **Ancients** – Nor shall their senators know what to advise.

27. The king – Zedekiah. **The prince** – Every magistrate. **Troubled** – Hang down, and melt away. What can men contrive or do for themselves, when God is departed from them? All must needs be in tears, all in trouble, when God comes to judge them according to their deserts, and so make them know, that he is the Lord, to whom vengeance belongeth.

Chapter 8

God in vision brings Ezekiel to Jerusalem (1–4)

There he sees the image of jealousy (5, 6)

The elders of Israel worshipping all manner of images (7–12)

The women weeping for Tammuz (13, 14)

The men worshipping the sun (15, 16)

Threatenings against them (17, 18)

God in vision brings Ezekiel to Jerusalem (1–4)

1. Sixth year – Of Jeconiah's captivity. **Sixth month** – Elul or our August. **The elders** – The chief of those that were now in captivity. They were come either to spend the Sabbath in religious exercises, or to enquire what would become of their brethren in Jerusalem. **The hand** – The spirit of prophecy.

2. A likeness – Of a man; the man whom he had seen upon the throne. **Fire** – This fire might denote the wrath of God against Jerusalem.

3. And – This, and all the passages to the end of the 16th verse, was done in vision only. **Inner gate** – To the door of the gate of the inner court. **The north** – The temple courts had four gates towards the four quarters, and this was the north gate, which opened into the great court where Ahaz had set up his Damascen altar, and where the idols were set up. **The image** – Baal, which Manasseh had set up, Josiah had destroyed, but succeeding kings had again set it up. **Jealousy** – Because it was so notorious an affront to God, who had married Israel to himself.

There he sees the image of jealousy (5, 6)

5. Northward – Ahaz had removed it from the middle of the court and set it near this north gate, to which it gave name. **Entry** – In the very passage to the temple, to affront the worship of God.

6. They – The generality of the Jews. **Great abominations** – The notorious idolatries. **Here** – In this court, in view of my temple. **Far off** – Not that they designed this, but no other could be expected.

The elders of Israel worshipping all manner of images (7–12)

7. The door – The second door, for there were two in the north side.

8. A door – A private door, by which the priests entered into the chamber of their imagery, to perform idolatrous worship to their images.

9. Are doing – Under the approach of judgments, in this very place, under the walls of my temple.

10. Every form – Of such creatures as the Egyptians, or any others with whom the Jews had acquaintance, worshipped.

11. Seventy – Heads of the tribes or families, who should have been examples of true religion, not ringleaders in idolatry. **Shaphan** – Mentioned 2Kings 22:9. Shaphan was forward in reforming under Josiah and his son is as forward in corrupting the worship of God.

12. Seeth not – They deny God's care of them and their affairs, and therefore they must choose some other god.

The women weeping for Tammuz (13, 14)

13. Greater – Either because added to all the rest: or, because some circumstances in these make them more abominable.

14. The door – Of the outer court, or court of the women, so called, because they were allowed to come into it. **Weeping** – Performing all the lewd and beastly rites of that idol, called by the Greeks, Adonis.

The men worshipping the sun (15, 16)

15. Greater – These later wickednesses may be accounted greater, because acted in a more sacred place.

16. Inner court – The innermost, that which was next the temple, called here the Lord's house. **At the door** – Before he saw abominations in the gates of the courts, now he is come to the very house itself. **The porch** – That stately porch, beautified with the curious and mighty brass pillars, Jachin and Boaz. **Altar** – The brazen altar for burnt-offerings, which was placed in the court before the front of the temple, and is here represented in its proper place. **Their backs** – In contempt of God, and his worship. **The sun** – In imitation of the Persians, Egyptians, and other eastern idolaters; these Jews turn their back on God who created the sun, and worship the creature in contempt of the Creator.

Threatenings against them (17, 18)

17. Violence – All injustice is here meant towards all sorts of men, whom they first despise and next destroy. **Returned** – From injustice against man they return to impiety against God. **The branch** – As the worshippers of Bacchus waved their Thyrsus, the stalk wreathed with ivy, and bowed their bodies and often kissed the branches, so did these idolatrous Jews.

18. Will not hear – The time was, when God was ready to have heard, even before they cried: but now they cry aloud, and yet cry in vain. It is the upright heart which God regards, and not the loud voice.

Chapter 9

Instruments prepared to destroy the city (1–2)

The glory removes to the threshold of the temple (3)

Orders given to mark a remnant (3, 4)

The execution of them who were not marked begun (5–7)

The prophet intercedes, but in vain (8–10)

The report of him that had marked the remnant (11)

Instruments prepared to destroy the city (1–2)

1. He – The man whom he had seen upon the throne. **Them** – Those whom God hath appointed to destroy the city: perhaps angels. **Every man** – Every one; it is an Hebrew idiom. Each of these had a weapon proper for that kind of destruction which he was to effect; and so, some to slay with the sword, another with the pestilence, another with famine. **In his hand** – Denoting both expedition in, and strength for the work.

2. And – As soon as the command was given, the ministers of God's displeasure appear. **Men** – In appearance and vision they were men, and the prophet calls them as he saw them. **The north** – Insinuating whence their destruction should come. **One man** – Not a companion, but as one of authority over them. **With linen** – A garment proper to the priesthood. **They** – All the seven.

The glory removes to the threshold of the temple (3)

3. **The glory** – The glorious brightness, such as sometimes appeared above the cherubim in the most holy place. **Gone up** – Departing from the place he had so long dwelt in. **He was** – Wont to sit and appear. **Threshold** – Of the temple, in token of his sudden departure from the Jews, because of their sins.

Orders given to mark a remnant (3, 4)

4. **That sigh** – Out of grief for other mens sins and sorrows. **Cry** – Who dare openly bewail the abominations of this wicked city, and so bear their testimony against it.

The execution of them who were not marked begun (5–7)

5. **The others** – The six slaughter-men.

6. **At my sanctuary** – There are the great sinners, and the abominable sins which have brought this on them.

7. **And slew** – The slaughter also was in vision.

The prophet intercedes, but in vain (8–10)

8. **Was left** – Left alone, now both the sealer, and the slayers were gone.

The report of him that had marked the remnant (11)

Chapter 10

The scattering the coals of fire upon the city (1–7)

The removal of the glory of God from the temple (8–22)

The scattering the coals of fire upon the city (1–7)

2. **He** – That sat on the throne. **Scatter** – That it may take fire in all parts, and none may escape.

3. **The right side** – The north-side, the side towards Babylon, from whence the fire came which consumed the city. **The man** – Christ, the Lord of angels, who now attend his coming and commands. **The cloud** – As the sign of God's presence. **The inner court** – The court of the priests, who were chief in the apostasy.

4. **The glory** – The visible token of the presence of the God of glory. **Went up** – In token of his departure from the temple. **And stood** – Showing his unwillingness to leave, and giving them time to return to him, he stands where he might he seen, both by priests and people, that both might be moved to repentance.

5. **Was heard** – As a mighty and terrible thunder.

6. **And stood** – Either as one that deferred execution, to try whether the city would repent, or as one who was to give some farther order to the angels, that were to be the ministers of his just displeasure.

7. **One Cherub** – One of the four. **And took** – As a servant that reaches what his master would have. **Went out** – Out of the temple.

The removal of the glory of God from the temple (8–22)

9. **Looked** – Attentively viewed. **Beryl stone** – Of sea-green.

10. **They** – The wheels. This intimates the references of providence to each other, and their dependences on each other: and the joint tendency of all to one common end, while their motions appear to us intricate and perplexed, yea, seemingly contrary.

11. **When** – The wheels moved by the cherubim, or that spirit of life, which moved the living creatures. **They went** – They were so framed, that they could move on all four sides without the difficulty and delay of turning. **Head** – Of the living creatures.

12. **And** – Now he describes both the cherubim and wheels as full of wisdom, and as governed by an excellent wisdom. **The wheels** – Which the four cherubim had to move, govern, and direct.

13. **The wheels** – As to their frame and motion. **It was cried** – Still there was one who guided, as by vocal direction. **Unto them** – To each of them.

14. **Every one** – Of the living creatures, chap.1:6.

17. **For** – There is a perfect harmony between second causes in their dependence on, and subjection to, the one infinite, wise, good, holy, and just God. The spirit of God directs all the creatures, upper and lower, so that they shall serve the divine purpose. Events are not determined by the wheel of fortune, which is blind, but by the wheels of providence, which are full of eyes.

18. **And stood** – On the right side of the house, where the cherubim were in the inner court.

19. **And every one** – The glory, the cherubim, the wheels, all stood, respiting execution, and giving opportunity of preventing the approaching misery. **The east gate** – The last court, the court of the people.

20. **I knew** – Either by special assurance as a prophet, or by comparing them with those which he had often seen in the temple.

Chapter 11

God's message of wrath to those who remained secure at Jerusalem (1–13)

A message of comfort to the dejected captives at Babylon (14–21)

The glory of God removes farther (22, 23)

The vision disappears, of which Ezekiel gives an account (24, 25)

God's message of wrath to those who remained secure at Jerusalem (1-13)

1. Jaazaniah – Not him that is mentioned chap.8:11. **Pelatiah** – Named here for that dreadful sudden death, whereby he became a warning to others.

2. He – The Lord sitting on the cherub.

3. It – The threatened danger and ruin by the Chaldeans. **The caldron** – This is an impious scoff, yet mixt with some fear of the prophet, Jer 1:13.

6. Ye – Many murders have you committed yourselves, and you are accountable to God for all those whom the Chaldeans have slain, seeing you persuaded them, thus obstinately to stand out.

7. Bring you forth – Not in mercy, but in wrath, by the conquering hand of Babylon.

9. Deliver you – Defeating all your projects for escape.

10. Will judge – My just judgments shall pursue you, whithersoever you fly.

11. Your caldron – The place of your sufferings; greater are reserved for you in a strange land. **Judge you** – I will do more against you at Riblah, where the captive king had his children, and others with them, first murdered before his eyes, and then his own eyes put out; Riblah is called the border of Israel: for Syria was adjoining to Israel on the north, and Riblah was on the frontiers of Syria.

13. Pelatiah – Mentioned ver.1, a principal man among the twenty-five princes, who made all the mischief in Jerusalem. It should seem this was done in vision now, but it was an assurance, that when this prophecy was published, it would be done in fact. And the death of Pelatiah was an earnest of the complete accomplishment of the prophecy. **A full end** – By slaying all, as this man is cut off.

A message of comfort to the dejected captives at Babylon (14–21)

15. Thy brethren – Thy nearest kindred, which it seems were left in Jerusalem. Their degeneracy is more noted in the repetition of the word brethren. **Gone far** – Ye are gone far from the Lord; as much as the Heathens accused the Christians of atheism.

16. Say – In vindication of them. **Although** – The obstinate Jews at Jerusalem will call them apostates; but I the Lord sent them thither, and will own them there. **Scattered** – Dispersed

them in many countries which are under the king of Babylon: yet they are dear to me. **A little sanctuary** – A little one in opposition to that great temple at Jerusalem. To him they shall flee, and in him they shall be safe, as he was that took hold on the horns of the altar. And they shall have such communion with God in the land of their captivity, as it was thought could be had no where but in the temple.

18. They – They who assemble upon Cyrus's proclamation first, and then upon Darius's proclamation, shall overcome all difficulties, dispatch the journey, and come safely to their own land. **Take away** – They shall abolish superstition and idolatry from the temple.

19. One heart – Cyrus shall give them leave, and I will give them a heart to return; and on their way shall be great utility; and, when come to Jerusalem, they shall own me, and my laws, and with one consent, build Jerusalem and the temple, and restore true religion. **The stony** – That hard, inflexible, undutiful, incorrigible disposition.

21. Heart – Soul and affections. **Walketh** – Either secretly adhere to, or provide for the service of idols, called here detestable things.

The glory of God removes farther (22, 23)

23. Went up – The glory of the Lord removes now out of the city, over which it had stood some time, waiting for their repentance. **The mountain** – Mount Olivet. He removed thither, to be as it were within call, and ready to return, if now at length in this their day, they would have understood the things that made for their peace.

The vision disappears, of which Ezekiel gives an account (24, 25)

24. The spirit – The same spirit which carried him to Jerusalem, now brings him back to Chaldea. **Went up** – Was at an end.

Chapter 12

The prophet by removing his stuff, and quitting his lodgings is a sign of Zedekiah's flight out of Jerusalem (1–16)

By eating his meat with trembling, he is a sign, to set forth the famine and consternation in the city (17–20)

An assurance that these things shall be fulfilled (21–28)

The prophet by removing his stuff, and quitting his lodgings is a sign of Zedekiah's flight out of Jerusalem (1–16)

2. **Eyes to see** – They have capacity, if they would, to understand, but they will not understand, what thou speakest.

3. **Stuff** – Vessels or instruments, wherein thou mayest put what is portable.

4. **In their sight** – Before it is quite night, that they, who should learn by this sign, may see and consider it.

5. **Dig** – Come not through the door, but as one who knows there is a guard upon the door, get to some back part of thy house, and dig there thyself, either to make the greater haste, or to keep all secret; for all will be little enough for them that must act what thou dost represent. **Carry out** – Through the hole thou hast dug.

6. **Bare it** – In testimony of the servitude they shall be reduced to, who then must do what servants or beasts were wont to be employed in. **Cover thy face** – As unwilling to be seen or known. **For** – I have set thee for a sign to them, and thou shalt tell them the meaning of these things in due time.

7. **I brought forth** – Here is a transposing of his actions, and rehearsal of that in the first place, which was acted in the second place.

10. **Say** – Though they enquire not, yet tell them what I mean hereby, that this prophecy is a burden which the kingdom shall groan under. **The prince** – Zedekiah.

11. **I am your sign** – My person is the emblem of yours, and my actions of that you shall do. And the like shall be done to you, O inhabitants of Jerusalem. We cannot say concerning our dwelling place, that it is our resting place. For how far we may be tossed from it before we die, we cannot foresee.

12. **The prince** – Zedekiah. **Shall bear** – Disguised, as a servant, in hope to conceal himself, chooses the twilight as the time that would best favour his design. **They shall dig** – This was fulfilled when they broke down the wall to fly, Jer 39:4. **Cover his face** – Zedekiah did by this aim at concealing himself.

13. **It** – Neither the land nor the city; for his eyes will be put out at Riblah.

16. **Declare** – By relating those sins, for which God was justly angry, and for which he punished them, though they were his own people. **They** – The Chaldeans. See how God brings good out of evil! The dispersion of sinners, who had done God much dishonour and disservice in their own country, proves the dispersion of penitents, who shall do him much honour and service in other countries!

By eating his meat with trembling, he is a sign, to set forth the famine and consternation in the city (17–20)

19. **The people** – Thy fellow captives. **And of the land** – Those that dwell in the countries round about Jerusalem. **Her land** – Jerusalem's land, so called because it was the head city thereof. **Desolate** – Because it shortly shall be laid waste, emptied of inhabitants, wealth and plenty. **Violence** – Injustice, oppression and tyranny of the Jews toward one another.

An assurance that these things shall be fulfilled (21–28)

22. **That proverb** – That short saying commonly used. **Days** – Of wrath and vengeance, are to come a great while hence. **Every vision** – Threatening vision, which Jeremiah and Ezekiel would fright us with, comes to nothing.

25. **I will speak** – There has been and shall be a succession of God's ministers, by whom he will speak, to the end of the world. Even in the worst times, God left not himself without witness, but raised up men that spoke for him, and spoke from him.

Chapter 13

The prophet shows the sin and punishment of the false prophets (1–16)

Of the false prophetesses (17–23)

The prophet shows the sin and punishment of the false prophets (1–16)

2. **That prophesy** – Out of their own deceiving hearts, not from God.

3. **Foolish prophets** – Foolish prophets are not of God's sending: for whom he sends, he either finds fit, or makes fit. Where he gives warrant, he gives wisdom. **Their own spirit** – Not the spirit of God. **Seen nothing** – God hath shewed them no vision.

4. **Thy prophets** – Thy prophets, not mine. **Like the foxes** – Hungry, and ravening, crafty, and guileful. **In the deserts** – Where want makes them more eager after their prey.

5. **Ye** – Vain prophets. **Gone up** – As in a besieged city, whose wall is broken down, a valiant soldier would run up into the breach to repel the enemy; so true prophets partly by prayer, and partly by doctrine, labour to preserve God's people. **Hedge** – The house of Israel is the Lord's vineyard, through the hedge whereof many breaches are made. **To stand** – Not with arms, but with fasting, prayer, and repentance.

6. **Vanity** – Things that have no foundation.

9. **Mine hand** – My power striking them. **In the assembly** – Have no seat among the rulers, nor voice among the counsellors. **Written** – Not registered among those that return, Ezra 2:1,2. **Enter** – They shall never come into the land of Israel. They shall not be written in the book of

eternal life, which is written for the just ones of the house of Israel, saith the Chaldea paraphrast.

10. Peace – They told sinners, no harm would happen to them. And those are the most dangerous seducers, who suggest to sinners that which tends to lessen their dread of sin, or their fear of God. These are compared to men who build a slight tottering wall, which others daub with untempered mortar; sorry stuff, that will not bind, nor hold the bricks together: doctrines not grounded on the word of God.

14. Ye shall know – Those that deceived others, will in the end be found to have deceived themselves. And no doom will be more fearful, than that of unfaithful ministers.

15. Accomplish – Fulfil what my prophets foretold.

Of the false prophetesses (17–23)

18. Sew pillows – A figurative speech, expressing the security, which they promised to every one that came to them. **Kerchiefs** – Triumphal caps, which were made by these prophetesses, and put upon the head of every who one consulted them, and by these they were to interpret, as a promise of victory over the Babylonians. **Stature** – That is, of every age, whether younger or elder, which usually is seen by their stature. **To hunt** – All this is really spreading a net, as hunters do, to catch the prey. **Will ye save** – Can you preserve them alive, whom you deceive by your promises?

19. Pollute me – Pretending my name for what I never spake. **My people** – My own people. **Handfuls of barley** – For a mean reward. **To slay** – You denounce evil to the best, whom God wilt keep alive. **To save** – Declaring safety, to the worst, whom God will destroy.

20. There – At Jerusalem. **Grow** – You promise a flourishing, growing, state to all enquirers; and this is the net with which you hunt souls. **Tear them** – With violence, and suddenness.

23. See no more vanity – They shall see all their predictions vanish, which shall so confound them, that they shall pretend no more to visions.

Chapter 14

The elders of Israel come to enquire of the prophet (1–5)

They are ordered to repent, or not to pretend to enquire of God (6–11)

Although Noah, Daniel and Job were to pray for the people, yet they would not prevail (12–21)

Yet a remnant shall escape (22, 23)

The elders of Israel come to enquire of the prophet (1–5)

1. Elders – Men of note, that were in office and power among the Jews, who were come from Jerusalem.

3. Set up – Are resolved idolaters. **The stumbling block** – Their idols which were both the object of their sin, and occasion of their ruin.

4. According – According to his desert, I will give answer, but in just judgment.

5. Take – That I may lay open what is in their heart, and discover their hypocrisy, and impiety. **Through their idols** – It is always through some idol or other, that the hearts of men are estranged from God: some creature has gained that place in the heart, which belongs to none but God.

They are ordered to repent, or not to pretend to enquire of God (6–11)

7. The stranger – Every proselyte. **I the Lord** – He shall find by the answer, 'twas not the prophet, but God that answered: so dreadful, searching, and astonishing shall my answer be.

8. A sign – Of divine vengeance.

9. The prophet – The false prophet, who speaks all serene, and quiet, in hope of reward. **Have deceived** – Permitted him to err, or justly left him in his blindness.

Although Noah, Daniel and Job were to pray for the people, yet they would not prevail (12–21)

13. When – At what time soever.

14. Noah – Who it is probable prevailed with God to spare the world for some years, and saved his near relations when the flood came. **Daniel** – Who prevailed for the life of the wise men of Chaldea. **Job** – Who daily offered sacrifice for his children, and at last reconciled God to those that had offended.

19. In blood – In death and destruction, not by the sword.

21. How much more – If they could not be able to keep off one of the four, how much less would they be able to keep off all four, when I commission them all to go at once.

Yet a remnant shall escape (22, 23)

22. Their way – Their sin and their punishment. **Comforted** – In this proof of the truth of God.

23. Comfort you – That is, you will be comforted, when you compare their case with your own: when they tell you how righteous God was, in bringing these judgments upon them. This will reconcile you to the justice of God, in thus punishing his own people, and to the goodness of God, who now appeared to have had kind intentions in all.

Chapter 15

God by the similitude of a vine, foreshows the utter destruction of Jerusalem (1–8)

2. The vine-tree – Israel is here compared to a vine, which, when fruitless, is utterly unprofitable. This the prophet minds them of to humble them, and awaken them to fruitfulness. **A branch** – One branch of a tree in the forest is of more use than the whole vine-tree is, except for its fruit.

3. A pin – Will it afford even a pin to drive into a wall or post, on which you may safely fasten any weight.

4. For fuel – When for its barrenness it is cut down, it is fit only to burn.

6. Given – Doomed for food to the fire.

8. Because – They have been so perpetually trespassing, that it seems a continued act.

Chapter 16

The mean beginning of the Jewish church and nation (1–5)

The many favours God bestowed upon them (6–14)

Their treacherous and ungrateful requital (15–34)

Terrible judgments threatened (35–43)

An aggravation of their sin and of their punishment (44–59)

A promise of mercy to a remnant (60–63)

The mean beginning of the Jewish church and nation (1–5)

3. Jerusalem – The whole race of the Jews. **Thy birth** – Thy root whence thou didst spring. **Thy father** – Abraham, before God called him, worshipped strange gods beyond the river, Josh 24:14. **An Amorite** – This comprehended all the rest of the cursed nations.

4. In the day – In the day I called Abraham to leave his idolatry. **Salted** – Salt was used to purge, dry, and strengthen the new-born child. **Nor swaddled** – So forlorn was the state of the Jews in their birth, without beauty, without strength, without friend.

5. To the loathing – In contempt of thee as unlovely and worthless; and in abhorrence of thee as loathsome to the beholder. This seems to have reference to the exposing of the male children of the Israelites in Egypt. And it is an apt illustration of the Natural State of all the children of men. In the day that we were born, we were shaped in iniquity: our understandings darkened, our minds alienated from the life of God: all polluted with sin, which rendered us loathsome in the eyes of God.

The many favours God bestowed upon them (6–14)

6. When I passed by – God here speaks after the manner of men. **Live** – This is such a command as sends forth a power to effect what is commanded; he gave that life: he spake, and it was done.

7. Thou art come – Thou wast adorned with the choicest blessings of Divine Providence. **Thy breasts** – Grown up and fashioned under God's own hand in order to be solemnly affianced to God.

8. When I passed – This second passing by, may be understood of God's visiting and calling them out of Egypt. **Thy time** – The time of thy misery was the time of love in me towards thee. **I spread my skirt** – Espoused thee, as Ruth 3:9. **Entered into a covenant** – This was done at mount Sinai, when the covenant between God and Israel was sealed and ratified. Those to whom God gives spiritual life, he takes into covenant with himself. By this covenant they become his, his subjects and servants; that speaks their duty: and at the same time his portion, his treasure; that speaks their privilege.

9. Washed – It was a very ancient custom among the eastern people, to purify virgins who were to be espoused. **And I anointed** – They were anointed that were to be married, as Ruth 3:3.

10. Broidered – Rich and beautiful needlework. **Badgers skin** – The eastern people had an art of curiously dressing and colouring the skins of those beasts, of which they made their neatest shoes, for the richest and greatest personages.

11. A chain – Of gold, in token of honour and authority.

14. My comeliness – 'That is, through the beauty of their holiness, as they were a people devoted to God. This was it that put a lustre upon all their other honours, and was indeed the perfection of their beauty. Sanctified souls are truly beautiful in God's sight, and they themselves may take the comfort of it. But God must have all the glory for whatever comeliness they have, it is that which God has put upon them.'

Their treacherous and ungrateful requital (15–34)

15. Playedst the harlot – Thou didst go a whoring after idols. **Thy renown** – Her renown abroad drew to her idolatrous strangers, who brought their idols with them. **Pouredst out** – Didst readily prostitute thyself to them; every stranger, who passed through thee, might find room for his idol, and idolatry. **He it was** – Thy person was at the command of every adulterer.

16. Thy garments – Those costly, royal robes, the very wedding clothes. **High places** – Where the idol was. **With divers colours** – With those beautiful clothes I put upon thee. **The like things** – As there was none before her that had done thus, so shall there be none to follow her in these things.

17. Images – Statues, molten and graven images. **Commit whoredom** – Idolatry, spiritual adultery. And possibly here is an allusion to the rites of Adonis, or the images of Priapus.

18. Coveredst – Didst clothe the images thou hadst made. **Set mine oil** – In lamps to burn before them.

19. For a sweet savour – To gain the favour of the idol. **Thus it was** – All which is undeniable.

20. And those – These very children of mine hast thou destroyed. **Sacrificed** – Not only consecrating them to be priests to dumb idols; but even burning them in sacrifice to Molech. **Devoured** – Consumed to ashes. **Is this** – Were thy whoredoms a small matter, that thou hast proceeded to this unnatural cruelty?

21. For them – For the idols.

24. In every street – Idol temples were in every street; both in Jerusalem and her cities.

25. At every head of the way – Not content with what was done in the city, she built her idol temples in the country, wherever it was likely passengers would come.

26. Great of flesh – Naturally big in size and men of great stature.

30. How weak – Unstable, like water. **An imperious woman** – A woman, that knows no superior, nor will be neither guided nor governed.

31. Not as an harlot – Common harlots make gain of their looseness, and live by that gain; thou dost worse, thou lavishest out thy credit, wealth, and all, to maintain thine adulterers.

34. Contrary – Here we may see, what the nature of men is, when God leaves them to themselves: yea, although they have the greatest advantage, to be better, and to do better.

Terrible judgments threatened (35–43)

38. Blood – Thou gavest the blood of thy children to idols in sacrifice; I will give thee thine own blood to drink.

42. My jealousy – The jealousy whereto you have provoked me, will never cease, until these judgments have utterly destroyed you, as the anger of an abused husband ceases in the public punishment of the adulteress. **No more angry** – I will no more concern myself about thee.

44. The mother – Old Jerusalem, when the seat of the Jebusites, or the land of Canaan, when full of the idolatrous, bloody, barbarous nations. **Her daughter** – Jerusalem, or the Jews

who are more like those accursed nations in sin, than near them in place of abode.

An aggravation of their sin and of their punishment (44–59)

45. Thou – The nation of the Jews. **Thy mother's daughter** – As much in thy inclinations, as for thy original. **Loatheth** – That was weary of the best husband.

46. Thine elder sister – The greater for power, riches, and numbers of people. **Her daughters** – The lesser cities of the kingdom of Israel. **Thy left hand** – Northward as you look toward the east. **Thy younger sister** – Which was smaller and less populous. **Thy right hand** – Southward from Jerusalem.

47. Not walked after their ways – For they, all things considered, were less sinners than thou. **Nor done** – Their doings were abominable, but thine have been worse.

49. This was – The fountain and occasion of all. **Fulness of bread** – Excess in eating and drinking. **Strengthen** – She refused to help strangers.

51. Hast justified – Not made them righteous, but declared them less unrighteous, than thou; of the two they are less faulty.

52. Hast judged – Condemned their apostasy, and hast judged their punishment just.

53. When – Sodom and Samaria never were restored to that state they had been in; nor were the two tribes ever made so rich, mighty, and renowned, though God brought some of them out of Babylon: the words confirm an irrecoverably low, and despised state, of the Jews in their temporals. **Then** – Then, not before.

54. A comfort – Encouraging sinners like those of Sodom and Samaria.

56. Not mentioned – The sins of Sodom, and her plagues, were not minded or mentioned by thee.

57. Before – The time of her pride was, when they were not yet afflicted, and despised by the Syrians. **And all** – The nations that were round about and combined in league against the house of David. **Her** – Syria, the chief whereof were the Philistines.

58. Thy lewdness – The punishment thereof.

59. In breaking the covenant – So will I break my covenant with thee.

A promise of mercy to a remnant (60–63)

60. Nevertheless – The Lord having denounced a perpetual punishment to the impenitent body of the Jewish nation, doth now promise to the remnant, that they shall be remembered, and obtain covenanted mercy. **My covenant** – In which I promised I would not utterly cut off the seed of Israel, nor fail to send the redeemer, who should turn away iniquity from Jacob. **With thee** – In the loins of Abraham, and solemnly renewed after their coming out of Egypt, which is the time, called the days of thy youth, Isa 44:2. **Establish** – Confirm and ratify. It shall be sure, and unfailing. **An everlasting covenant** – Of long continuance, as to their condition in the land of Canaan, and in what is spiritual, it shall be absolutely everlasting.

61. Then – When that new covenant shall take effect. **Receive** – Admit into church-communion, the Gentiles, now strangers, but then sisters. **Thine elder** – Those that are greater and mightier than thou; that by their power, wealth and honour are as much above thee as the elder children are above the younger. **Thy younger** – Thy lesser or meaner sister. **For daughters** – As daughters hearken to, and obey, so shall the Gentiles brought into the church, hearken to the word of God, which sounded out from Jerusalem. **But not** – Not by that old covenant which was violated; nor by external ceremonies, which were a great part of the first covenant, but by that covenant which writes the law in the heart, and puts the fear of God into the inward parts.

63. Open thy mouth – Neither to justify thyself, or to condemn others, or to quarrel with thy God. **Because of thy shame** – Such a confusion for thy sin will cover thee. Indeed the more we feel of God's love, the more ashamed we are that ever we offended him. And the more our shame for sin is increased, the more will our comfort in God be increased also.

Chapter 17

The parable of two eagles and a vine (1–10)

The application of it (11–21)

A promise to raise the house of David again (22–24)

The parable of two eagles and a vine (1–10)

2. A riddle – A dark saying. **The house of Israel** – The remainders of the house of Israel, whether of the ten, or of the two tribes.

3. A great eagle – Nebuchadnezzar king of Babylon is compared to a great eagle, the king of birds, swift, strong, rapacious. **Great wings** – Mighty provinces on each side of his kingdom. **Long winged** – His kingdom was widely extended. **Full of feathers** – And full of people. **Divers colours** – Who were of divert nations, languages and manners. **Lebanon** – Jerusalem the chief city of the country where this great, fruitful and pleasant hill was. **And took** – Took, captive and carried away with him the king of Judah, Jehoiachin. **The cedar** – The nation.

4. The top – Both the king of Judah, now eighteen years old, and the nobles and chief of the land. **Into a land** – Babylon, which was a city of mighty trade.

5. The seed – Mattaniah, whom he called Zedekiah. **Planted** – Settled him on the throne of Judah. **As a willow** – The prophet compares this new made king to a willow, which grows no where so well as near great waters.

6. Of low stature – They grew and flourish, while they owned their state tributary to Babylon. **Toward him** – Nebuchadnezzar as their protector, and sovereign lord. **The roots** – All the firmness, fruitfulness, and life of this state, was in subjection to him.

7. Another – The king of Egypt. **This vine** – Zedekiah, his nobles and people. **Did bend** – Sought his friendship. **Shot forth** – Sent ambassadors, and trusted to the power of Egypt. **Water it** – That they might add to their greatness, as trees grow by seasonable watering them. **By the furrows** – Alluding to the manner of watering used in Egypt, by furrows or trenches to convey the water from the river Nile.

8. Was planted – By Nebuchadnezzar, in a very hopeful condition, where it might have been fruitful, and flourished.

9. Say – Tell them what will be the issue of all this, and tell it to them in my name. **It prosper** – Shall Zedekiah and his people thrive by this? **Pull up** – Utterly overthrow this kingdom. **Cut Off** – Put to the sword the children of Zedekiah, and of the nobles. **The leaves** – All the promising hope they had shall vanish. **Without great power** – The king of Babylon shall do this easily, when it is God that sends him. For God needs not great power and many people, to effect his purposes. He can without any difficulty overturn a sinful king and kingdom, and make no more of it than we do of rooting up a tree that cumbers the ground.

10. Yea – Suppose this vine were planted by the help of Egypt. **The east wind** – When the king of Babylon, who like the blasting wind comes from the north-east, shall but touch it, it shall wither. **In the furrows** – Even amidst its greatest helps, to make it flourish.

The application of it (11–21)

15. He – Zedekiah. **Shall he break** – Can perjury be the way for deliverance?

18. Given his hand – Solemnly confirming the oath.

20. Plead – I will punish him.

21. All – Not strictly, but the greatest part.

A promise to raise the house of David again (22–24)

22. The highest branch – Of the royal seed; of the highest branch that is heir to the throne;

namely, the Messiah. **An high mountain** – Upon mount Zion. **Eminent** – Not for outward splendour, but for spiritual advantages.

23. In the mountain – In Jerusalem. **All fowl** – All nations. **In the shadow** – There they shall find peace and safety.

24. The trees – The great ones on earth. **The high tree** – The kingdom of Babylon, which was brought low indeed, when overthrown by Darius and Cyrus.

Chapter 18

God reproves a corrupt proverb (1–4)

It shall be well with the righteous (5–9)

but ill with the wicked man, although he had a good father (10–13)

It shall be well with a good man, although he had a wicked father (14–18)

Therefore God is righteous (19–20)

It shall be well with penitents, but ill with apostates (21–29)

An exhortation to repentance (30–32)

God reproves a corrupt proverb (1–4)

2. The land of Israel – The two tribes, not the ten. **The fathers** – Our fore-fathers. **Have eaten** – Have sinned. **The children's** – We their children, who were unborn, suffer for their sins.

4. Behold – There can be no colour of partial judgment in the proceedings of God, who is equally God to all. **All souls** – All persons. **The soul** – The person, whether father or son, shall die, shall bear his own punishment.

It shall be well with the righteous (5–9)

6. Hath not eaten – Hath not committed idolatry, offering sacrifice, and eating of the things sacrificed to idols; whose temples and altars were on mountains, chaps. 20, 28, and Hos 4:13.

8. Increase – Illegal interest. **Iniquity** – Injustice of every kind.

9. Shall live – Shall be delivered from famine, pestilence, and sword, and shall see good days.

but ill with the wicked man, although he had a good father (10–13)

13. His blood – Heb. It is plural, bloods; both the blood of the innocent which he murdered, and his own blood which thereby he forfeited; the blood of his own soul and life: that is the whole blame of his misery in time and eternity, shall lie upon himself.

It shall be well with a good man, although he had a wicked father (14–18)

17. Hath taken off – Withdrawn his hand from hurting or wronging the poor, although he had power to do it securely.

Therefore God is righteous (19–20)

20. Shall not bear – This is a most unquestionable truth; and although perhaps it may seem otherwise in some cases, yet could we see perfectly the connexion between persons and persons; could we see the connexion of sins and sins, and how easily, secretly, and undiscerned men become guilty of the same sins, we should see father and son, though perhaps one of them might not do the evil, both guilty, and neither punished for the sin farther than if it was his own: nor do the scriptures, Exod 20:5 Deut 28:18, doom persons to punishment for sins from which they are wholly free; but if children shall follow their fathers in sin, then if they die for those sins, it is because these are their own, not as they are their fathers. **The righteousness** – It shall be well with the righteous, for he shall eat the fruit of his doing, he shall be rewarded as a righteous one. **The wickedness** – The reward of wickedness. 'The son shall not die, not die eternally, for the iniquity of the father, if he do not tread in the steps of it: nor the father for the iniquity of the son, if he do all he can to prevent it.'

It shall be well with penitents, but ill with apostates (21–29)

22. Not mentioned – Not to him.

25. The way – His whole management of affairs. **Not equal** – Not right, or consistent with his own declaration, and law.

28. He shall surely live – 'That is, he shall be restored to the favour of God, which is the life of the soul.'

An exhortation to repentance (30–32)

31. Make you a new heart – Suffer me to do it in you.

32. I have no pleasure – Sinners displease God when they undo themselves; they please him when they return.

Chapter 19

The kingdom of Judah and house of David is compared to a lioness, and their princes to lions taken in nets (1–9)

The kingdom and house are compared to a vine, and these princes to branches, now broken off and burnt (10–14)

The kingdom of Judah and house of David is compared to a lioness, and their princes to lions taken in nets (1–9)

1. For the princes – Jehoahaz, Jehoiachim, Jehoiachin, and Zedekiah.

2. What – What resemblance shall I use to set out the nature, deportment, and state of the mother of these princes? **Thy** – One of whom was upon the throne at once, and therefore the prophet speaks to one at a time. **Mother** – The land of Judea, and Jerusalem, the chief city of it, the royal family of David. **Lioness** – Although chosen of God to execute justice; yet they soon degenerated into the fierce and ravening nature of the lioness. **Lay down** – Associated, and grew familiar with neighbour kings, called here lions; fierce and bloody. **Her whelps** – Her sons, successors to the crown. **Young lions** – Either foreign princes and kings, or some of the fierce, unjust, tyrannizing princes at home.

3. Brought up – Advanced, caused him to take the throne after the slaughter of Josiah. **One** – Jehoahaz the second son of Josiah. **Became** – Soon showed his fierce, cruel, and bloody disposition.

4. The nations – The Egyptians heard what he did.

5. Made him – King, and infused the lion-like maxims into him.

6. He – Jehoiachim. **Went up** – He continued eleven years on the throne; whereas Jehoahaz was taken as soon as he first ventured out. **The lions** – Heathen kings, with whom he entered into leagues. **He became** – Fierce, ravenous, unsatiable.

7. He knew – By taking them, he came to know their places, which are here called, what he made them, desolate. **Roaring** – By the perpetual violent threats of this cruel king.

8. The nations – Which were tributary to Nebuchadnezzar. **Set against** – By order of the king of Babylon. **The provinces** – Which belonged to the Babylonish kingdom.

The kingdom and house are compared to a vine, and these princes to branches, now broken off and burnt (10–14)

10. Thy mother – O thou prince of Israel. **By the waters** – In a very fruitful soil. **Full of branches** – Full of children; when Josiah died, he left four behind him, beside other branches of the royal line.

11. Strong rods – Many excellent persons endowed with qualifications befitting kings, that they might sway the sceptre. **Exalted** – Above the ordinary majesty of other kingdoms. **Thick branches** – This kingdom equalled, if not excelled, the greatest neighbour-kingdoms, and her kings exceeded all their neighbouring kings, in riches and power.

12. The east wind – God raised up the king of Babylon to pull up this sinful kingdom. **Dried up** – Blasted all her fruit, deposed her king,

captivated him, his family, and the whole kingdom. **Strong rods** – All the choice men.

13. She – A few of the branches of the last pruning. **In the wilderness** – Although Babylon was in a very fruitful place, yet the cruelty of the Babylonians, made it to the Jews as terrible as a wilderness.

14. Fire – The fire of rebellion, kindled by Zedekiah, who is of the blood-royal. **No strong rod** – The regal dignity is ceased.

Chapter 20

The prophet consulted by the elders, signifies God's displeasure against them (1–3)

Gives them a history of God's dealings with their fathers, and their treacherous dealings with God in Egypt (4–9)

In the wilderness (10–26)

In Canaan (27–32)

Judgments denounced against them (33–36)

Mercy promised to a remnant (37–44)

A word dropt toward Jerusalem (45-49)

The prophet consulted by the elders, signifies God's displeasure against them (1–3)

1. The seventh year – Of Zedekiah's reign, two years and five months before Nebuchadnezzar besieged Jerusalem. **Came** – Yet resolved before-hand what they would do.

3. Are ye come – Are ye in good earnest?

Gives them a history of God's dealings with their fathers, and their treacherous dealings with God in Egypt (4–9)

4. Wilt thou – Wilt thou not convince and reprove them? And denounce my judgments against them? **The abominations** – What their fathers have done, they approve, and have outdone; by that let them know what to expect.

5. When I chose – When I showed that I had chosen them. The history of the rebellions of the children of Israel, begins as early, as their beginning. So does the history of man's apostasy from his Maker. No sooner have we read the story of his creation, but we meet with that of his rebellion. So we see here, it was with Israel; a people designed to represent the body of mankind, both in their dealings with God, and in God's dealing with them. **Lifted up my hand** – Or stretched out and made bare my arm; that is, magnified my power for their deliverance.

When I lifted up mine hand – Showed my power in performing my oath, and assuring them of doing what was farther promised.

6. I had espied – God speaks after the manner of men. Milk and honey – Literally milk and honey in abundance were in the land of Canaan. Proverbially it speaks the plenty and abundance of all the blessings of life.

7. Of his eyes – To which you have looked for help.

8. To accomplish – To make an end of them.

9. For my name's sake – For the glory of my mercy and faithfulness. Polluted – Reproached and blasphemed.

In the wilderness (10–26)

12. A sign – Of their being peculiarly my people.

13. In the wilderness – Where they most needed my care and favour; where the preserving their life from destruction by the noxious creatures, and from famine by the barrenness of the wilderness, was a continued miracle.

15. I lifted up my hand – I sware. Them – So all the murmuring, disobedient, unbelieving generation was excluded, and their children were brought in.

18. Walk ye not – Live not as your fathers did.

20. Hallow – Remember to keep them holy.

22. I withdrew – God seems to take the posture of one that was just going to smite, yet draws back that he might spare.

23. I lifted – I sware.

25. Wherefore – Because they rejected my good laws and judgments. I gave them – Not by enjoining, but by permitting them to make such for themselves. Not good – That were pernicious to the users.

26. Polluted – I permitted them to pollute themselves. Might know – Be forced to own, that the Lord is a mighty king in punishing those that would not have him a gracious king in governing them.

In Canaan (27–32)

29. What – What mean you that you go to the high place? What do you find so inviting there, that you will leave God's altar, where he requires your attendance, to frequent such places as he has forbidden you to worship in? Bamah – That is, the high place.

31. Shall I be enquired of – Are you fit to ask counsel of me, whom you have so obstinately forsaken and reproached?

32. And that – God to convince them, tells them what they think and have purposed. Shall not be – Shall be quite frustrated. We will be – Will unite with them in marriages, commerce, and religion too; and then we shall be safe among them.

Judgments denounced against them (33–36)

34. The people – Sidonians, Ammonites, Moabites, or whoever they were, to whom the apostate Jews betook themselves, where they thought to lurk, God will bring them thence into Babylonish captivity.

35. Bring you – Drive you. The wilderness – Into the most horrid parts of the world; into the mountainous parts of Media, Hyrcania, Iberia, Caspia, Albania, and Scythia. Plead with you – Pass sentence, and execute it on you.

36. Your fathers – Who died there, and never entered Canaan.

Mercy promised to a remnant (37–44)

37. I will cause – I will bring you out by number, so that you shall either own my sceptre, or by a conquered subjection, yield to my sword and power. Under the rod – Referring to the manner of shepherds in that country, who did tell their sheep in, and out of the fold. Bring you – The voluntary and obedient into covenant with myself.

38. The rebels – The stubborn sinners.

39. But pollute – But while ye are such idolaters, forbear to take my name into your lips.

40. Mine holy mountain – Sion, God's holy hill, Psa 2:6. Holy by designation, and God's own appointing it for his temple and presence. Of the height – Sion, although lower than many other hills, yet was above them all for God's peculiar presence. In the land – Their own land. Your offerings – When I have brought you into the land, then I will require your offerings as formerly: you shall see my temple built, Jerusalem filled with inhabitants, and my worship restored.

41. Sanctified – Magnified and praised for the good I do to my people.

43. Remember – Review your former ways with sorrow: remember, and grieve.

A word dropt toward Jerusalem (45–49)

46. The south – Look toward Jerusalem, and the land of Canaan. Drop thy word – Let thy word distil, begin with softer words, before thou shower down with the vehemency of a storm. The forest – Jerusalem, which was become like a forest.

47. Every green tree – All that flourish, and all that are poor. All faces – All persons and orders of men, from one end of the land to the other.

49. Parables – So absolutely, that we cannot understand him.

Chapter 21

An explication of the prophecy in the close of the last chapter, with directions to the prophet upon it (1–7)

A prediction of the sword that was coming on the land (8–17)
A prospect given of the king of Babylon's coming to Jerusalem, to which he was determined by divination (18–24)
Sentence passed on Zedekiah (25–27)
The destruction of the Ammonites (28–32)

An explication of the prophecy in the close of the last chapter, with directions to the prophet upon it (1–7)

2. The holy places – The temple and all parts of it.

3. The righteous – It is no unusual thing, that in publick calamities, those who are indeed righteous should be involved with others.

4. All flesh – All the Jews that dwell in the land.

5. Shall not return – It shall not return into the scabbard until it hath done full execution.

6. Sigh therefore – Thereby express deep sorrow. **Breaking of thy loins** – Like a woman in travail.

7. Because – The saddest news you ever heard is coming.

A prediction of the sword that was coming on the land (8–17)

9. Furbished – Made clean and bright.

10. Of my son – To whom God saith, Thou shalt break them with a rod of iron, Psa 2:9. This sword is that rod of iron, which despiseth every tree, and will bear it down.

12. It – The devouring sword. **Upon thy thigh** – In token of thy sense of what they must suffer.

13. If – But if the king and kingdom of Judah despise this trial, both shall be destroyed and be no more.

14. And smite – In token of amazement and sorrow. **Of the slain** – Wherewith many shall be slain. **Privy chambers** – Where they were hidden in hope to escape.

15. All their gates – Both of cities, of palaces, and of private houses. **Wrapt up** – And hath been carefully kept in the scabbard, that it might not be blunted.

16. Go – O sword, take thy own course.

17. Smite my hands – In token of my approbation.

A prospect given of the king of Babylon's coming to Jerusalem, to which he was determined by divination (18–24)

19. Appoint – Paint, or describe them on a tile. **One land** – That is, Babylon. **Choose** – Pitch on some convenient place, where thou mayest place Nebuchadnezzar's army, consult-

ing where this one way divides into two, which was on the edge of the desert of Arabia. **At the head** – Where each way runs, toward either Rabbath, or Jerusalem; for there Nebuchadnezzar will cast lots.

20. To Judah – The Jews.

21. Stood – The prophet speaks of what shall be, as if it were already. **To use** – To consult with his gods, and to cast lots. **Arrows** – Writing on them the names of the cities, then putting them into a quiver, and thence drawing them out and concluding, according to the name which was drawn. **He consulted** – Perhaps by a divine permission, the devil gave them answers from those images. **In the liver** – They judged of future events, by the entrails, and more especially by the liver.

22. The divination – The divination which concerned Jerusalem, was managed on his right hand.

23. Them – The Jews. **That have sworn** – Zedekiah, his princes, and nobles, who swore allegiance to the king of Babylon, these perjured persons will contemn all predictions of the prophet. **He** – Nebuchadnezzar. **The iniquity** – The wickedness of their perjury and rebellion. **They** – Zedekiah, and the Jews with him.

24. Your transgressions – Against God, and against the king of Babylon. **Discovered** – To all in court, city, and country. **With the hand** – As birds, or beasts in the net, are taken with the hands, so shall you, and be carried into Babylon.

Sentence passed on Zedekiah (25–27)

25. And thou – Zedekiah. **Whose day** – The day of sorrows, and sufferings, and punishment is at hand. **Shall have an end** – Shall bring the ruin of king and kingdom, and with the overthrow of your state, the means of sinning shall end too.

26. The diadem – The royal attire of the head, which the king daily wore. **Shall not be the same** – The kingdom shall never be what it hath been. **Him that is low** – Jeconiah. The advance of this captive king, came to pass in the thirty-seventh year of his captivity.

27. Shall be no more – Never recover its former glory, until the sceptre be quite taken away from Judah, and way be made for the Messiah. He hath an incontestable right to the dominion both in the church and in the world. And in due time he shall have the possession of it, all adverse power being overturned.

The destruction of the Ammonites (28–32)

28. Their reproach – Wherewith they reproached Israel in the day of Israel's afflictions.

29. While – While thy astrologers, and soothsayers, deceive thee with fair, but false divinations. **To bring thee** – To bring thee under the sword of the Chaldeans, and destroy thee as the Jews; to make thee stumble and fall on their necks, as men that fall among a multitude of slain.

30. Shall I cause it – God will by no means suffer the sword to be sheathed. **Judge thee** – Condemn, and execute.

31. I will blow – As those who melt down metals blow upon the metal in the fire, that the fire may burn the fiercer.

Chapter 22

A catalogue of the sins of Jerusalem (1–12)

Punishment threatened (13–16)

They are condemned as dross to the fire (17–22)

All orders of men having contributed to the national guilt, must share in the punishment of it (23–31)

A catalogue of the sins of Jerusalem (1–12)

2. Judge – The question is doubled, to awaken the prophet more fully, and to quicken him to his work.

3. Her time – The time of ripeness in her sins, and of execution of judgments on her. **To defile** – For this does more defile them, and provoke God to wrath against them.

4. Thy days – The days of thy sorrows, and punishment. **Art come** – Thou art grown up to the eldest years in sin, beyond which thou art not to go.

5. Much vexed – Afflicted, impoverished, and ruined.

6. Every one – Not one to be found of a more merciful temper. **To their power** – According to their ability.

7. In thee – In Jerusalem.

8. Thou – O Jerusalem. **Mine holy things** – All mine institutions, temple, sacrifices, feasts.

9. Carry tales – Informers, or persons that for money, give in false witness against the innocent. **They eat** – Offer sacrifice on the mountains and feast there, in honour of their idols.

10. Discovered – Defiled their fathers bed.

Punishment threatened (13–16)

13. Smitten mine hand – In testimony of my abhorrence.

14. Endure – Withstand the evils that are coming, or bear them when come.

16. In thyself – Whereas I was thine inheritance so long as thou wert a holy, obedient people; now be an inheritance to thyself, if thou canst.

They are condemned as dross to the fire (17–22)

18. Dross – Utterly degenerate, and base metal. **The furnace** – The afflictions I have laid upon them have not bettered them. **The dross** – While they loved mercy, did justly, walked humbly with their God, they were as silver; now they are but dross.

19. Gather you – From all parts. I will, by a secret over-ruling providence, bring you into Jerusalem, as into a furnace, where you may be consumed.

All orders of men having contributed to the national guilt, must share in the punishment of it (23–31)

23. Her – The land of Israel. **Not cleansed** – Though God's judgments have been as violent floods; and as hottest fires. **Nor rained upon** – Yet neither thy filth hath been carried away, nor thy dross melted out of thee. Therefore thou shalt be deprived of the rain, that should cool thy thirsty land.

25. A conspiracy – A contrivance, to speak all alike, smooth words, and give out promises of peace and safety. **Thereof** – Of the land. **The treasure** – As a reward of their lies. **Made her** – By persuading Zedekiah to hold out the war, which filled Jerusalem with dead husbands, and forlorn widows.

26. My holy things – Sacrifices, and oblations. **Put no difference** – Neither have they in their practice, differenced holy and profane, nor in their teaching acquainted the people with the difference, nor in the exercise of their authority, separated the profane from the holy, either persons, or things. **Hid their eyes** – Despised, and would not see the holiness of the Sabbaths. Profaned – Contemned, dishonoured, disobeyed.

27. Destroy souls – Ruin families; cutting off the fathers, and impoverishing the widow, and fatherless.

28. Daubed them – Flattered them, in their ways of sin. **Untempered mortar** – With promises that like ill-tempered mortar, will deceive them, though all seems at present smooth and safe.

30. I sought – God speaks after the manner of men. **A man** – Any one, among princes, prophets, priests, or people, to repair the breach. **And stand** – Interpose between a sinful people, and their offended God, and entreat for mercy. **But** – All were corrupted.

Chapter 23

The apostasy of Israel and Samaria from God (1–8)

Their ruin (9, 10)

The apostasy of Judah and Jerusalem from God (11–21)

Their ruin (22–35)

The joint wickedness of them both (36–44)

And their joint ruin (45–49)

The apostasy of Israel and Samaria from God (1–8)

2. Two women – Judah, and Israel, two kingdoms.

3. Whoredoms – Idolatry.

4. Aholah – That is, his own tabernacle; for Israel falling off from the house of David, fell off from the tabernacle, or temple of God; so that all the temple they had was of their own making. **The elder** – Greater for number of tribes, and for power, wealth, and for multitudes of people. **Aholibah** – That is, my tabernacle in her: the two tribes had the temple of God with them. **Mine** – By solemn marriage-covenant. **Bare sons** – Were fruitful and brought forth children to me; they increased in numbers of people; and among these, some there were that were children of God by faith, love, and obedience.

5. Played the harlot – United in idolatry, with the Assyrians. **Mine** – When under my government, and protection.

6. Horsemen – Skilful in riding, and well furnished with choice horses.

7. With all – Other nations, with whom she had commerce.

Their ruin (9, 10)

10. Discovered – Stript her naked, and exposed her to shame. **Took her sons** – Captives. **Slew her** – The kingdom of Israel, under Hoshea, was by Salmanasar utterly destroyed. **They** – The Assyrians, had executed God's just displeasure upon her.

The apostasy of Judah and Jerusalem from God (11–21)

15. Girded – With soldiers belts, which includes the rest of the habit of soldiers. **In dyed attire** – Both rich, comely, large, and of divers colours. **Princes** – Of princely aspect and majesty.

17. Alienated – She grew weary of the Chaldeans.

18. Discovered – Made it appear to all, far and near.

19. By – Remembering her idolatries in Egypt, her alliance with it in days past, which she now resolved to act over again.

20. Paramours – The nations, that were confederate with the Egyptians.

Their ruin (22–35)

23. Pekod – Pekod is the province between Tigris, and Lycus; in this was old Nineveh. **Shoa** – Either Sia in Armenia, or the Sohia, among which were the Adiabeni, and this contained the middle part of the kingdom of Babylon. **Koa** – This bordered upon Media, the inhabitants were called Kohai, and dwelt about Arbela. **And all** – All subjects of the Assyrian monarchy.

24. And wheels – Lest in their march the carriage wheels should break, a store of these were provided. **An assembly** – A mighty confluence of people. **I will set** – Give them a power in right of conquest over their rebels, as well as mine, and I will give them a spirit of judgment to discern the greatness of this people's sins. **Judge** – Condemn, and execute sentence upon thee. **According** – To their will, power, wrath, and custom, against rebels; for these are their rules of judgment.

25. I will set my jealousy – As a jealous provoked husband, I will be as much against thee as they are. **Thy residue** – Either the people, who hid themselves in vaults and cellars, or what the Chaldeans cannot carry away, all this shall be devoured by fire.

29. Take away – Deprive thee of the comfortable use of all thy labour, which they will exact of thee in captivity.

32. It – Is large, and contains what will last many years, even until the seventy years be expired.

34. Thou – Shalt stagger with sorrows, that shall intoxicate, and astonish. **Suck it out** – The dregs shalt thou drink, and multiply thine own sorrows. **Break the sheards** – To suck out what remains. **And pluck** – Revenging thyself upon thyself.

35. Bear thou – The guilt, I will impute it, the punishment, I will not pardon it.

The joint wickedness of them both (36–44)

38. In the same day – When they had newly polluted themselves with idolatry and murder, they thrust into the temple.

39. My house – Nay, these things have been in my house.

40. Wash thyself – After the manner of harlots.

41. Sattest – Prepared to feast them. **A stately bed** – A magnificent bed, on which women sat to feast, when men leaned on their sides. **Incense** – Offered to their idols.

42. A voice – A shout for joy, that there was a treaty of peace between the Jews, and the Chaldeans.

And their joint ruin (45–49)

45. Righteous men – Men that keep the law of their God.

46. Upon them – Against the Jews, the children of this Aholibah.

47. The company – The Babylonian army.

48. Lewdness – Idolatry. And indeed we do not read of any after their return out of this captivity.

49. They – The Babylonians. **The sins** – The guilt of worshipping idols; and you shall bear the punishment of idolaters.

Chapter 24

By the sign of flesh boiling in a pot are showed, the miseries of Jerusalem during the siege (1–14)

By the sign of Ezekiel's not mourning for his wife is showed, that the approaching calamities would be too great to be lamented (15–27)

By the sign of flesh boiling in a pot are showed, the miseries of Jerusalem during the siege (1–14)

1. In the ninth year – Of Zedekiah's reign. **Came unto me** – The prophet was now in Babylon.

2. Set himself – Sat down to besiege.

4. Every good piece – All the chief of the inhabitants of the land, the wealthiest, who will fly from their country-houses to live in safety in Jerusalem: the most war-like, who will betake themselves to Jerusalem for its defence. **Fill it** – With those pieces that are biggest, fullest of marrow, and which are divided according to the bones; these are the principal members of the state, the king, princes, priests, magistrates, and the most wealthy citizens.

5. The bones – Not of the pieces to be boiled, but of the many innocents murdered in Jerusalem; for their blood crieth for vengeance, and their bones scattered on the face of the earth, will both make and maintain this fire.

6. The bloody city – Jerusalem. **Whose scum** – Her wickedness is still within her. **Piece by piece** – One piece after another until all be consumed. **No lot** – Lots are for saving some, but here shall be no sparing any.

7. The blood – Innocent blood which she hath shed. **The top of a rock** – Where it might be long seen. **To cover it** – These butchers of innocent ones leave their blood uncovered.

8. I have set – I will openly punish, and in such a manner as shall not be soon forgotten.

10. And spice it well – To express this justice, that is acceptable to God and men. **The bones** – The greatest, strongest, and firmest of the Jews shall perish in this fiery indignation.

11. The filthiness – A type of the unreformed sinfulness of the city. **Molten** – That their wickedness may be taken away with their persons, and city.

12. She – Jerusalem. **With lies** – Her allies, their promises, their forces, and their idols, all prove a lie to the house of Judah. **Her scum** – Her unrepented sins shall be punished in the fire that burns their city.

13. Lewdness – Or obstinacy and boldness. **Purged thee** – Used all means to purge thee.

By the sign of Ezekiel's not mourning for his wife is showed, that the approaching calamities would be too great to be lamented (15–27)

16. With a stroke – A sudden stroke, by my own immediate hand. We know not how soon the desire of our eyes may be removed from us. Death is a stroke, which the most pious, the most useful, the most amiable are not exempted from.

17. Bind the tire – Adorn thy head, as thou wast used to do; go not bare-headed as a mourner. **Thy shoes** – In great mournings the Jews went bare-footed. **Cover not thy lips** – It was a custom among them to cover the upper lip. **Eat not** – Of thy neighbours and friends, who were wont to visit their mourning friends, and send in choice provision to their houses.

18. I spake – Told them what I expected would be.

21. Profane – Cast off, and put into the hands of Heathens. **The excellency of your strength** – So it was while God's presence was there. **The desire** – As much your desire, as my wife was mine; most dear to you.

22. Ye shall do – When you are in captivity, where you may not use your own customs.

23. Pine away – You shall languish with secret sorrow, when you shall not dare to shew it openly.

25. Their strength – Their walls and fortifications. **The joy** – All their public and private joys and hopes shall be destroyed in the destruction of the kingdom, and their children.

26. To hear it – To give thee a narrative of all he had seen.

27. No more dumb – From this prophecy for eighteen months during the siege, he does not prophesy of Israel, but of other nations. **Thou shalt be a sign** – Until the event shall convince the Jews, thou shalt by sign, signify to them, what is coming.

Chapter 25

A prophesy against the Ammonites (1–7)

The Moabites (8–11)

The Edomites (12–14)

And the Philistines (15–17)

A prophesy against the Ammonites (1–7)

3. Aha – When thou shouldest have pitied, thou didst proudly insult over my people.

4. The men of the east – The Arabians, associates of Nebuchadnezzar, who recompensed their service, with giving them this country when it was conquered, as it was five years after the desolation of Jerusalem.

5. Rabbah – The royal city, called since Philadelphia from the king of Egypt who built it. **The Ammonites** – The land they dwelt in.

7. Know – Thus God will bring those that were strangers to him into an acquaintance with him, and it will be a blessed effect of their calamities. How much better is it, to be poor and know God, than to be rich, and ignorant of him?

The Moabites (8–11)

8. Seir – The seed of Esau, the Edomites. Seir was the mountain where they first planted themselves. **Is like** – Are no more a select people than others.

9. The side – That part of his country which was best fortified. **Bethjeshimoth** – An ancient city; it was a fortress toward the desert, which watched lest any should make an inroad on the country.

10. With the Ammonites – As I have given Ammon, so I will with them give Moab to the Chaldeans, who will give it to the Arabians.

The Edomites (12–14)

13. Teman – A country in the southern coast of Edom. **Dedan** – Adjoining to Edom.

And the Philistines (15–17)

15. It – Israel.

16. The Cherethim – The bowmen, the strength of Philistia. **The remnant** – Who had escaped the sword of Samuel, David, Hezekiah, and of Psammetichus king of Egypt.

Chapter 26

The sin of Tyre (1, 2)

The utter destruction of it
(3–14)

The astonishment of the neighbouring
nations (15–21)

The sin of Tyre (1, 2)

1. In the eleventh year – Of Jechoniah's captivity, the year wherein Jerusalem was taken. **The month** – That month which followed the taking of Jerusalem.

2. Because – Probably God revealed this to the prophet as soon as these insulting Tyrians

spoke it. **The gates** – The great mart of nations, people from all parts. **She is turned** – The trading interest will turn to me.

The utter destruction of it
(3–14)

4. Scrape – I will leave thee nothing; thou shalt be scraped, and swept, that not so much as dust shall remain in thee. **Like** – As bare as was the rock on which thy city is built.

6. Her daughters – The lesser cities. **In the field** – On the firm land.

11. Garrisons – Bastions, or forts, or triumphal arches.

12. Shall lay – It had been a quicker way, to have burnt all; but the greedy soldier might dream of treasures hid in walls, or under the timber, and therefore take the pains to pull all down, and throw it into the sea.

14. No more – Although there was a city of that name built, yet it was built on the continent; and in propriety of speech, was another city.

The astonishment of the neighbouring
nations (15–21)

15. The isles – Isles which are places freest from danger of invasions, will shake with fear, when they learn that Tyre is fallen.

16. The princes – Who were lords of the islands of that sea. **Come down** – In token of condolence. **Trembling** – They shall be afraid of their own concerns, and astonished in the midst of their fears.

18. In the sea – At a great distance, and farther from land. **Departure** – Leaving thy ancient dwelling, to go into captivity.

19. The deep – Nebuchadnezzar's army. **Great waters** – Great afflictions.

20. Bring thee down – When I shall slay thee, and throw thee into the grave. **With the people** – Who are long since dead, and gone to eternity. **The low parts** – Another description of the grave, from the situation and solitude of it. **Set glory** – Then I will restore the beauty, strength, and wealth of Israel, and bring them back to Jerusalem. **In the land** – In the land of Judea, called, land of the living, because a land, where God will bless, and give life by his word, ordinances, and spirit: thus different shall Tyre's captivity and Jerusalem's be.

21. A terror – To all that hear of thee.

Chapter 27

A large account of the wealth, splendour
and trade of Tyre (1–25)

Its utter ruin, and the consternation of its
neighbours (26–36)

A large account of the wealth, splendour and trade of Tyre (1–25)

2. A lamentation – We ought to mourn for the miseries of other nations, as well as of our own, out of an affection for mankind in general; yea, although they have brought them upon themselves.

3. At the entry – Heb. Entrances. She was about four furlongs, or half an English mile from the continent, as it were in the very door of the sea.

5. They – The shipwrights. **Shipboards** – The planks and benches, or transoms for their ships. **Fir-trees** – Of the best and finest fir-trees. **Lebanon** – Whose cedars excelled others.

6. With box – From the isles, and parts about the Ionian, Aegean, and other seas of the Mediterranean, where box-tree is a native, and of great growth and firmness, fit to saw into boards for benches; they were conveyed to Tyre, where their artists inlaid these box boards with ivory, and made them beautiful seats in their ships.

7. The isles of Elishah – Probably the sea-coast of Aeolis in the lesser Asia, the inhabitants whereof were excellent in the skill of dying wool. **Which covered** – He speaks of the coverings they used in their ships or galleys: their tilts, as our boat-men call them.

8. Zidon – An ancient town and haven of Phoenicia, not far from Tyre. **Arvad** – Or Aradus, an island belonging to Phoenicia, twenty furlongs from the continent. **Mariners** – Rowers in thy galleys; the rich Tyrians would not employ their own in such servile works, they hired strangers. **Wise men** – Thy learned men: for navigation was the great study of the Tyrians.

9. The ancients – Old experienced workmen. **Gebal** – A town of Phoenicia near the sea. **The wise men** – Skilful in their trades. **Were in thee** – Who dwelt in Tyre for gain. **All the ships** – Ships from all parts of the sea, full of mariners, not only to manage the ships at sea, but to offer their service to the Tyrians for bringing in, or carrying out their wares.

10. Lud – Lydians, not those Cresus was king over, but those that dwelt in Egypt about the lake Maraeolis. **Phut** – Lybians, a people of Africa; these were their hired soldiers. **Hanged the shield** – In time of peace. **They set forth** – These stout, expert, well armed guards, were an honour to thee.

11. With – Mixed with other hired soldiers. **The Gammadim** – Probably men of Gammade, a town of Phoenicia.

13. Javan – The Grecians, particularly the Ionians. **Tubal** – The Asiatic Iberians, and the Albanians toward the Caspian sea. **Meshech** – The Cappadocians. **They traded** – Brought men to sell for slaves.

14. Of the house – Of the country. **Togarmah** – Armenia the lesser, Phrygia, Galatia, or Cappadocia. **Horsemen** – It is likely they might sell grooms, as best able to manage, and keep those horses.

15. Isles – In the Indian seas, and in the Red-sea traded with thee. **Horns** – Elk's horns, or wild goats. **Ebony** – Is a very solid, heavy, shining, black wood, fit for many choice works.

16. The multitude – The abundance of the Tyrian manufactures.

17. Minnith – The name of an excellent wheat country. **Pannag** – Some obscure place, which now is forgotten.

19. Javan – In the isle of Meroe, in Egypt.

20. Dedan – The posterity of Abraham by Keturah, who dwelt in Arabia, and were sheep-masters. **Clothes** – With which they lined their chariots.

22. Sheba – A country in Arabia Felix. **Raamah** – Another people of the same Arabia.

23. Haran – In Mesopotamia, where Abraham dwelt. **Canneh** – This is supposed to be the same with Calneh, Gen 10:10, afterwards Ctesiphon, a pleasant city on Tigris. **Ashur** – Assyria. **Chilmad** – A country between Assyria and Parthia.

25. The ships – The ships from all parts of the sea. **Did sing** – Had their songs to commend thy state.

Its utter ruin, and the consternation of its neighbours (26–36)

26. Thy rowers – Thy governors and counsellors. **Great waters** – Dangers and difficulties. **The east wind** – The king of Babylon with his army. **Hath broken** – As surely will, as if he had already done it. **In the midst** – Where thou thoughtest thyself impregnable.

27. All thy company – All that are men fit for war, in the multitudes of people that are in thee. **Shall fall** – These all shall fall together.

28. The suburbs – The suburbs, which are nearest the sea, shall first hear the out-cries of pilots, and mariners.

29. Shall come down – In the allegory of a miserable shipwreck, the prophet sets forth the fall of Tyre; and in this verse he represents them all shifting out of the sinking ship, in great confusion.

30. Wallow themselves in ashes – As men use to do in their greatest mournings.

32. In the sea – Alas! what was once her safeguard, is now her grave.

33. Went forth – Were landed. **Thou filledst** – There was enough to supply to the full.

34. By the seas – The Babylonians, that like seas shall swell, roar, and break in upon thee.

35. Troubled – They shall not be able to conceal the discomposure of their mind, but will shew it in their countenance.

36. Shall hiss – Will mock at thy fall.

Chapter 28

A prediction of the ruin of the king of Tyre (1–10)

A lamentation for him (11–19)

A prediction of the destruction of Zidon (20–23)

The restoration of Israel (24–26)

A prediction of the ruin of the king of Tyre (1–10)

2. Hast said – In thy heart. **In the seat of God** – Safe and impregnable as heaven itself. **A man** – Subject to casualties, sorrows, and distresses. **Set thine heart** – Thou hast entertained thoughts, which become none but God.

3. Wiser – In thy own thoughts. **Daniel** – Who was then famous for his wisdom.

7. The beauty – Those beautiful things, in which thy wisdom appeared.

10. The deaths – Temporal and eternal. **Of the uncircumcised** – Of the wicked, an accursed death.

A lamentation for him (11–19)

12. Thou sealest up – Thou fanciest that fulness of wisdom, and perfection of beauty are in thee.

13. In Eden – In the midst of all delights. **The workmanship** – Now the prophet notes their joys, musick, and songs, both to loud, and to softer musick, as the lute, and tabret in the day of their kings coronation, and all this on instruments of most exquisite make, and of their own artists work; in this they exceeded as in the other. **Created** – King: in the day of thy coronation.

14. Cherub – For thy wisdom, power, and excellency, like a cherub, or angel; for the sacredness of thy person, and office, as the anointed of God; for the exercise of thy power, as a shield, as a protector of the weak. **And I** – I, whom thou forgetest have made thee so. **Thou wast** – Thou wast advanced to kingly dignity, a sacred office, and of divine institution. **In the midst** – Surrounded with stones, that sparkle like fire.

15. Thou wast perfect – Is not this an irony?

16. I will cast – Out thy kingly dignity.

17. Corrupted – Depraved, or lost thy wisdom. **Behold thee** – That thou mayst be a spectacle, and warning to them.

18. I will bring thee – Thou shalt be burnt to ashes, and trampled under feet.

19. All – All that have formerly known thy riches, power, allies, and wisdom.

A prediction of the destruction of Zidon (20–23)

22. Zidon – A city, north-west from Canaan, a king's seat of old, and from which Tyre descended. **I will be glorified** – When my judgments make my justice, power and truth appear, both you, and others shall confess my glory. **Sanctified** – Owned as holy, reverenced as just, obeyed as sovereign.

23. And blood – Bloody war by an enemy, that shall bring the war to the gates, nay into the streets of Zidon. **Judged** – Be punished in the midst of the city. **The sword** – By the sword of her enemies.

The restoration of Israel (24–26)

24. A pricking briar – By these two metaphors the prophet points out the troublesome neighbours of the Jews, such as Moab, Ammon, Edom, Tyre, and Zidon. This never had a full accomplishment yet. But it will, for the scripture cannot be broken.

25. Sanctified – I was dishonoured by the Jews in the sight of the heathen, and I will be honoured by the Jews in their sight.

Chapter 29

A prediction of the destruction of Pharaoh, for his treacherous dealing with Israel (1–7)

A prediction of the desolation of Egypt (8–12)

A promise of the restoration thereof in part (13–16)

A prediction of Nebuchadrezzar's passing it (17–20)

A promise of mercy to Israel (21)

A prediction of the destruction of Pharaoh, for his treacherous dealing with Israel (1–7)

1. The tenth year – Of Jeconiah's captivity.

3. The great dragon – The crocodile; our prophet, as well as Isaiah, compares the Egyptian king to that devouring serpent, or dragon. **That lieth** – Not only at rest, but waiting for prey. **My river** – My kingdom, power, riches, and forces, all the strength and glory of Egypt.

4. Put hooks – The Allegory is continued. **The fish** – The people of Egypt. **To stick** – To adhere to their king.

5. Leave thee – When thus brought out, I will leave thee. **The wilderness** – The deserts of Libya and Syene. **All the fish** – The whole army of the Egyptians. **The open fields** – There was this king and his army ruined. **Gathered** – These were not buried, but left in the wilderness, a prey to wild beasts, and birds.

7. Rent – Didst them much mischief instead of benefiting them, as thou hast promised, Jer 37:7.

A prediction of the desolation of Egypt (8–12)

10. Syene – Boundary between Ethiopia and Egypt; that is, all Egypt from north-east to south-west.

11. Forty years – These forty years began about the thirtieth year of Jeconiah's captivity, and end with the seventieth year of the captivity, which was the first of Cyrus.

A promise of the restoration thereof in part (13–16)

14. Pathros – The southern part of Egypt, in which was the famous city Thebae, known for its hundred gates. **Their habitation** – The ancient habitation of their fathers. **A base** – A low, tributary, dependent kingdom.

15. No more rule – Though in the times of the Ptolemeys, it was considerable, yet then, even then it did not rule the nations about her.

16. Which – Which sinful reliance on the arm of flesh provoked God to call to mind their other iniquities. **When** – When they forgot God, and respected Egypt. **They** – The house of Israel.

A prediction of Nebuchadrezzar's passing it (17–20)

17. In the seven and twentieth year – Of Jeconiah's captivity, the year after the conquest of Tyre.

18. Caused – The army, and commanders were weary of the siege, but the immovable resolution of the king kept them on. **A great service** – It was service to the justice of God. It was great service both for hardness of work, heaviness of burdens, and length of the siege, thirteen years together. **Made bald** – Through age, or sicknesses, or continued wearing of helmets. **Peeled** – Galled with carrying burdens. **No wages** – For though Tyre was very rich, when first besieged, much wealth was carried away during the siege, much spent and wasted in the siege, and what was left, preserved by articles of surrender.

19. Her multitude – Common people, who shall be made captives, and servants or slaves. **Her prey** – What she had before taken from others. **The wages** – God will be behind-hand with none, who do any service for him; one way or other he will recompence them. None shall kindle a fire at his altar for nought.

20. They – The Babylonians. **For me** – God's work was doing by them, although they thought nothing less.

A promise of mercy to Israel (21)

21. The horn – Jehoiakim, who was then advanced by Evil-Merodach. **The opening of the**

mouth – Thou shalt have liberty, to open thy mouth in comforting the good among them, and to give praise to God.

Chapter 30

The steps by which Nebuchadrezzar would destroy Egypt (1–19)

A repetition of a former prophecy against it (20–26)

The steps by which Nebuchadrezzar would destroy Egypt (1–19)

2. Ye – Inhabitants of Egypt.

3. A cloudy day – So times of trouble are called. **Of the heathen** – The time when God will reckon with the Heathens.

4. Ethiopia – The neighbour and ally to Egypt. **Take away** – Into miserable captivity. **Her foundations** – Their government, laws, and strong holds.

5. Lydia – Not the Asiatic, but the Africans placed between some part of Cyrene and Egypt. **The mingled people** – The hired soldiers from all parts, a confused mixture of nations. **And Chub** – The inhabitants of the inmost Libya; perhaps they may be the Nubians at this day. **The men** – All the allies of Egypt. **With them** – With the Egyptians.

6. Upheld – Those that favour and help her. **The pride** – The glory of all her strength.

7. They – All those before mentioned.

8. Destroyed – The fire that consumes nations is of God's kindling: and when he sets fire to a kingdom, all they that go about to quench the fire, shall be consumed by it.

9. Messengers – Such as having escaped the sword, shall tell the news. **From me** – By my permission and providence. **In ships** – Messengers by ships might carry the news to both the Ethiopian, Asian, and African, by the Red-sea. **As in the day** – During the mighty havoc made by the Chaldeans. **It** – A like storm.

11. His people – His own subjects, not hired soldiers.

12. The rivers dry – Probably the Chaldeans diverted them, and so their fortified towns wanted one great defence. **Sell** – Give it up entirely.

13. Noph – Memphis, now Grand Cairo, the chief city of the country. **A prince** – Either an Egyptian born, or independent, and over all Egypt. **A fear** – Consternation and cowardice.

14. In Zoan – Zoan shall be burnt down to ashes. **In No** – A great and populous city situate on one of the mouths of the Nile.

15. Sin – Pelusium, which was the key of Egypt, and therefore always well fortified, and strongly garrisoned.

16. Shall be rent – Her walls, and towers, and fortresses broken through by the violence of engines, and by the assaults of the soldiers.

17. Young men – It is probable these might be a body of valiant youths, collected out of these ten cities. **Aven** – Bethshemesh, or Heliopolis, an idolatrous city, in which was a stately temple of the sun: an hundred and fifty furlongs, that is six miles and three quarters in compass. Phibeseth-Bubastus, sometimes called Hoephestus, not far from Aven.

18. Tehaphnehes – A great and goodly city of Egypt; Tachapanes, Tachpanes, Tahapanes, Tahpanes, Chanes, and Hanes, are names given it, and this from a queen of Egypt of that name in Solomon's time. It stood not far from Sin, or Pelusium. **Darkened** – A night shall come upon it. **Break** – I shall break the kingdom of Egypt, that it no more oppress with yokes, that is, burdens. **Her daughters** – Her towns and villages.

A repetition of a former prophecy against it (20–26)

20. The eleventh year – Of Jeconiah's captivity, three months and two days before Jerusalem was taken, about the time that the Egyptians attempted to raise the siege of Jerusalem.

21. Have broken – Partly by the victory of the Chaldeans over Pharaoh-necho, partly by the victory of the Cyreneans over Pharaoh-hophra. **The sword** – None can heal the wounds that God gives but himself. They whom he disables, cannot again hold the sword.

22. His arms – Both his arms. **The strong** – That part of his kingdom which remains entire. **Broken** – That which was shattered before.

25. Will strengthen – As judges on the bench like Pilate, so generals in the field, like Nebuchadrezzar, have no power but what is given them from above.

Chapter 31

The greatness and power of the king of Assyria (1–9)

His security and destruction (10–17)

This applied to Pharaoh (18)

The greatness and power of the king of Assyria (1–9)

2. His multitude – His numerous subjects.

3. A cedar – Like the most goodly cedar for strength and beauty.

4. The waters – Cedars grow great by the water-courses. **The deep** – The sea sent out her waters, which gave being to the rivers, that watered him. **His plants** – The provinces of this mighty kingdom, that were like plants about a great tree. **All the trees** – To all his subjects.

5. All the fowls – All kind of men, nobles, merchants, husbandmen. **Made their nests** – Settled their habitations. **In his boughs** – In his kingdom, in the cities and towns of it. **All great nations** – No nation that was great at that time, but, sought the friendship of this kingdom.

8. The cedars – The greatest kings. **Garden of God** – In the most fruitful gardens. **Hide** – Could not ever top, and shade him. **The fir-trees** – Lesser kings, and kingdoms, were not equal to his boughs. **Nor any tree** – All summed up, none like him in all the kingdoms of the world.

His security and destruction (10–17)

11. Him – The proud king of Assyria, Sardanapalus. **The mighty one** – Arbaces, who first struck at the root of this Cedar, might well be styled the mighty one of the heathen, since he could bring together four hundred thousand of Medes, Persians, Babylonians, and Arabians.

12. Strangers – Foreigners.

14. To the end – All this is designed to be a warning to mortals. **All the trees** – The emperors, kings, or flourishing states. **By the waters** – Planted most commodiously, and furnished most abundantly with power and wealth. **The children of men** – As common men, of no quality or distinction.

15. He – The king of Assyria. **A mourning** – There was much lamentation. **Fainted** – Probably there were portentous signs in the sea, and great waters, and the rivers, and among the trees.

16. Shake – All that heard the noise of his fall, trembled at it. **Cast him down** – Brought the king and kingdom, as a dead man to the grave among them, that before were dead and buried. **All the trees** – All kings, and particularly the greatest. **All that drink water** – Enjoyed great power, riches, and glory. **Comforted** – He speaks to the dead with allusion to the manner of the living, who rejoice to see the proud brought low.

17. They also – His neighbouring kings. **Hell** – Perished with him, and went to those whom God had slain for their pride and wickedness. **They that were his arm** – His loyal and faithful subjects and friends, on whom he relied, and by whom he acted.

This applied to Pharaoh (18)

18. Yet – Thou shalt be like them in thy fall. **Thou shalt lie** – As unclean, despised, loathsome and under a curse. **This is** – This will be their end.

Chapter 32

The destruction of Egypt is represented under the similitude of killing a lion and a crocodile (1–16)

Under that of the funeral of a great general (17–32)

The destruction of Egypt is represented under the similitude of killing a lion and a crocodile (1–16)

1. Twelfth year – Of the captivity of Jeconiah.

2. Like a young lion – Spoiling all thou canst. **Crocodile** – The crocodiles lay in the rivers, though sometimes they went down the river to the sea. **With thy rivers** – Raisedst mighty armies, and didst lead them out against thy neighbours. **The waters** – The people, and kings near thee. **Thy feet** – With thy soldiers. **Fouledst** – Didst spoil all the conveniences of thy neighbours.

3. With a company – In the countries, where these creatures were hunted, they went in mighty companies.

4. Leave thee – This was literally fulfilled in the deserts of Lybia, where the slain of Hophra's army, were left to be devoured by fowls and beasts.

5. With thy height – With the carcasses of thy princes.

6. Even to the mountains – Blood shall be poured forth, as if it were to rise to the very mountains. **Full of thee** – O thy blood, and of thy carcasses cast into them.

7. Put thee out – As a torch is extinguished. **Cover the sun** – Probably some unusual darkness was seen in the heavens, and on the earth, about that time.

9. Thy destruction – The fame of it. **Not known** – Such as were strangers to Egypt, shall be troubled with apprehension of what mischief may come upon the world from so mighty a conqueror.

10. Shall tremble – Be greatly afraid, lest Nebuchadnezzar, who is God's sword, should smite them. **Every man** – Every one of the kings, whose kingdoms are near to Egypt.

13. All the beasts – The sheep, and oxen devoured, or driven away: the horses taken up to mount the horsemen, whose own horses were tired, or spoiled. **Great waters** – The pasture lying along the river side. **Trouble them** – There shall be so few men left in Egypt, that they shall not as formerly, disturb the waters by digging, swimming, or rowing on them. **Nor the hoofs** – So few horses or cows, that they shall not at watering-times, or in the heat of the day, foul the waters.

14. Like oil – A figurative expression, signifying, there shall be such an universal sadness and heaviness upon the whole nation, that the very rivers which used to flow briskly, shall grow deep, and slow, and heavy.

15. Of that – Men and women, cattle, wealth, and peace.

16. This is the lamentation – This mournful account, which the prophet has given of Egypt.

Under that of the funeral of a great general (17–32)

18. Wail – Prepare the funeral ceremonies at the burial of Egypt. **The daughters** – And celebrate the funerals of other cities and kingdoms that lie buried in their own ruins. **The nether parts of the earth** – A well known description of the state of the dead. **The pit** – The Egyptians affected to be buried in the Pyramids, and their kings, and great ones, would be laid by themselves; but Ezekiel provides them their grave among common people, being buried just where they fall.

19. Whom – Art thou better than others that thou shouldest not die, and be laid in the dust, as well as they. **Go** – Go down like others. **With the uncircumcised** – Among profane and loathed carcasses, such the uncircumcised were in the opinion of the circumcised, as were the Egyptians.

20. They – The Egyptians. **She** – The whole Egyptian kingdom. **Draw** – And throw them together into the pit.

21. Him – The king of Egypt. **The grave** – Where they lie without strength, as dead mortals, although while they lived, they bore themselves, as gods. **That help** – His helpers, dead before him, shall speak to him. **Gone down** – To the grave. **They lie** – Neglected, and forgotten.

22. Ashur – The famous, warlike, king of Assyria. **Is there** – In the state of the dead, in the land of darkness and oblivion. **Her company** – Princes, soldiers, subjects, and confederates. **Are about him** – They are about him, who were slain with him.

23. Whose graves – Here is supposed a spacious vault, in the midst whereof the king of Ashur lies, and round the vault, his familiar captains and commanders. **Her company** – The common subjects of the Assyrian empire, all buried undistinguished about her. **Her grave** – The ruins of an empire are its grave. **In the land** – While they were in the land of the living.

24. Elam – The Persians, and their famous kings, who lived in former days. **Their shame** – God, and man poured contempt upon them, and turned their glory into shame.

25. A bed – The Persians had their coffins, in which with balms and spices, the dead were kept, in the midst of places provided for them; in such is the king of Elam here placed with his slaughtered captains about him. All the honour he can now pretend to, is to be buried in the chief sepulchre.

26. Her multitude – With the Cappadocians and Albanians, the Scythians may be included, many of whom were next neighbors to them.

27. They – The leaders of these Scythians were not buried with a pomp like that of Ashur, or Elan, but surprised by Halyattes and Cyaxares, were cut off with all their multitude, and tumbled into pits with the rabble. **With their weapons** – A ceremony observed in pompous funerals of great captains, to have their weapons, and their armour carried before the hearse. **Laid their swords** – In their graves, as if they could sleep the sweeter there, when they laid their heads on such a pillow: These barbarous Scythians were not so buried. **Their iniquity** – The exemplary punishment of their iniquity shall be seen upon their bones unburied.

28. Thou – Chief of Mesech, and Tubal. **Shalt be broken** – Shalt be killed with the rest of thy wicked followers. **Shalt lie** – Without regard, hurled into the pit with common soldiers.

29. With the uncircumcised – The Edomites retained circumcision, being of the seed of Abraham. But that shall stand them in no stead: they shall lie with the uncircumcised.

30. Of the north – Tyrians, Assyrians, and Syrians, who lay northward from Judea, now swallowed up by the Babylonian. **Of their might** – When it appeared too weak to resist the enemy. **Uncircumcised** – Scorned, and cast out as profane and loathsome.

31. Comforted – Poor comfort! Yet all that he will find!

32. My terror – These tyrants were a terror to the world by their cruelty; and God hath made them a terror by his just punishments; and so, saith God, will I do with Pharaoh. Come and see the calamitous state of human life! See what a dying world this is! The strong die, the mighty die; Pharaoh and all his multitude! But here is likewise an allusion to the final and everlasting death of impenitent sinners. Those that are uncircumcised in heart, are slain by the sword of Divine Justice. Their iniquity is upon them, and they bear their shame for ever.

Chapter 33

The duty of a spiritual watchman (1–9)

A declaration of the safety of penitents, and the destruction of apostates (10–20)

A message to those who flattered themselves with hopes of safety, although they repented not (21–29)

A reproof of those who approved the word of God, but did not practise it (30–33)

The duty of a spiritual watchman (1–9)

6. Is taken away – Punished by the Lord for his sin.

A declaration of the safety of penitents, and the destruction of apostates (10–20)

10. Our sins – The unpardoned guilt, and the unsupportable punishment of our sins, in the wasting of our country, burning our city, abolishing the publick worship of God; we shall pine away, it is too late to hope. **How** – How can it be better with us?

A message to those who flattered themselves with hopes of safety, although they repented not (21–29)

21. Smitten – Taken and plundered.

22. Opened my mouth – Not that the prophet was utterly dumb before, for he had prophesied against many nations, only he was forbidden to say anything of the Jews, But now the spirit moved him to speak, and continued his motion, until the messenger came, and ever after.

24. They – Who were left behind, now come out of their holes, or returned from neighbouring countries, or permitted by the conqueror to stay and plant vineyards. **Wastes** – Places once fruitful and abounding with people, but now, made a desolate wilderness. **He inherited** – Our father had a right to all this land, when but one; we his children though diminished, are many, and the divine goodness will surely continue to us both right and possession. **Is given** – It was given by promise to us, the seed, as well as to our progenitor; nay more, it is given us in possession, whereas Abraham had not one foot of it.

26. Ye stand – You trust to your sword; you do all with violence. **Abominations** – Idolatry.

A reproof of those who approved the word of God, but did not practise it (30–33)

30. The children – Captives in Babylon.

31. They come – As if they were really the people of God. **They sit** – So we find the elders of Judah, chap.8:1, so the disciples of the rabbis sat at their feet.

Chapter 34

A charge against the shepherds of Israel (1–10)

A promise, that God would take care of his flock (11–16)

Another charge against the strong of the flock, for their injuring the weak (17–22)

A promise of the Messiah, the great and good shepherd (23–31)

A charge against the shepherds of Israel (1–10)

2. **The shepherds** – The rulers of the people kings, magistrates, and princes; as also priests, and prophets. **Of Israel** – The two tribes, and the few out of the ten that adhere to the house of David. **That feed** – Contrive their own ease, advantage, and honour.

3. **Ye kill** – You contrive methods, to take first the life, and next the estate of the well-fed, the rich and wealthy. **But** – You take care to lead, protect, provide for, and watch over them.

4. **The diseased** – The weak and languishing. **Bound up** – Oppressors in the state, or church, broke many then, but these shepherds bound them not up.

5. **No shepherd** – No vigilant, faithful shepherd. **Became meat** – Were made a prey of, and devoured by all their neighbours.

A promise, that God would take care of his flock (11–16)

12. **In the cloudy and dark day** – In the time of general distress.

16. **The fat** – The powerful and rich. **I will feed** – I will judge and punish them.

Another charge against the strong of the flock, for their injuring the weak (17–22)

17. **I judge** – Between men and men, between the smaller and weaker, and the greater and stronger, as their different state requires I will do. **The rams** – Rulers, who also shalt be dealt with according to their behaviour.

18. **But ye must tread down** – You great ones, eat the fat, and sweet; and what you cannot eat, you waste and spoil. **The deep waters** – Which are sufficient for all.

20. **I will judge** – I will vindicate the poor. **The fat cattle** – The rich. **The lean** – The poor.

A promise of the Messiah, the great and good shepherd (23–31)

23. **One shepherd** – Christ, the great good, chief, only shepherd, that laid down his life for his sheep. **My servant David** – The seed of David, the beloved one, who was typified by David, and is in other places called by his name, as Jer 30:9 Eze 37:24 Isa 37:35 Hos 3:5. **He shall feed** – Do all the office of a good and faithful shepherd, and that for ever.

24. **My servant** – Christ was in this great work his fathers servant, Isa 42:1.

25. **A covenant** – A covenant of promises, which contain, and shall bring peace, that is all good.

26. **Them** – My returned captives. **The places** – All the country. **My hill** – Jerusalem.

29. **A plant** – The Messiah. **The shame** – The reproach.

30. **Their God** – By covenant, from their forefathers. **Am with them** – Present with them, and reconciled to them.

Chapter 35

A prophecy against Edom for their hatred to Israel (1–13)

Their ruin shall be perpetual (14, 15)

A prophecy against Edom for their hatred to Israel (1–13)

2. **Mount Seir** – The Edomites, who inhabited it.

5. **Their iniquity** – When their iniquity was punished on them, which brought them to final ruin.

6. **And blood** – Thy guilt, and my just revenge of innocent blood. **Hast not hated** – Thou hast loved, rather than hated, blood-shed; therefore vengeance it follows thee.

7. **That passeth out** – All travellers that go to or from Edom.

9. **Return** – To their former glory.

10. **Though** – Though God was with Israel.

11. **Judged** – Punished thee.

Their ruin shall be perpetual (14, 15)

14. **The whole earth** – The inhabitants of all the countries round about thee. **Rejoiceth** – Is in peace and plenty.

Chapter 36

A promise of the restoration of Israel, from their present deplorable condition (1–15)

They are reminded of their former sins, and God's judgments (16–20)

A promise of pardon (21–24)

A promise of sanctification (25–38)

A promise of the restoration of Israel, from their present deplorable condition (1–15)

1. **The mountains** – The inhabitants being in captivity, speak to the mountains, that is, the land of Judah, and Israel, which was a country full of mountains.

2. **Because the enemy** – Many were the enemies of God's people; but they so conspired in one design, that the prophet speaks of them as one, and particularly of Edom.

3. **Swallowed** – Devoured you, as hungry beasts devour their prey. **Ye are taken up** – You are the subject of all their discourse. **An infamy** – Ever branding you as infamous.

7. **Lifted up mine hand** – Sworn in my wrath. **The heathen** – The Moabites, Ammonites, and Idumeans.

8. **At hand** – The time is near, when my people shall come out of Babylon to settle in their own land.

12. And thou – O land of Canaan. **Bereave** – Consume thine inhabitants.

13. They – The heathen round about.

14. Therefore – I will so bless thee, O land, that thou shalt bring forth and breed up many sons and daughters, and this reproach shall cease for ever.

They are reminded of their former sins, and God's judgments (16–20)

17. By their doings – By their carriage, and whole conversation. **As the uncleanness** – Or as one cut off from the congregation, because of some great sin.

20. Entered – When they were come into Babylon. **Profaned** – They sinned. **They** – Their heathen neighbours. **Them** – The profane Jews. **These** – These profane slaves, call themselves the people of the Lord and say, he gave them the land out of which they are driven.

A promise of pardon (21–24)

21. But I had pity – For these sins I had just cause to cut them off; but I had pity, for the glory of my name: had I destroyed them, the heathen would have concluded against my omnipotence, and my truth.

23. I will sanctify my great name – They gave the heathen occasion to think meanly of me, but I will shew I am as great as good. When God performs what he hath sworn by his holiness, then he sanctifies his name.

A promise of sanctification (25–38)

25. Sprinkle – This signifies both the blood of Christ sprinkled upon their conscience, to take away their guilt, as the water of purification was sprinkled, to take away their ceremonial uncleanness and the grace of the spirit sprinkled on the whole soul, to purify it from all corrupt inclinations and dispositions.

26. A new heart – A new frame of soul, a mind changed, from sinful to holy, from carnal to spiritual. A heart in which the law of God is written, Jer 31:33. A sanctified heart, in which the almighty grace of God is victorious, and turns it from all sin to God. **A new spirit** – A new, holy frame in the spirit of man; which is given to him, not wrought by his own power. **The stony** – The senseless unfeeling. **Out of your flesh** – Out of you. **Of flesh** – That is, quite of another temper, hearkening to God's law, trembling at his threats, moulded into a compliance with his whole will; to forbear, do, be, or suffer what God will, receiving the impress of God, as soft wax receives the impress of the seal.

27. My spirit – The holy spirit of God, which is given to, and dwelleth in all true believers. **And cause you** – Sweetly, powerfully, yet without compulsion; for our spirits, framed by God's spirit to a disposition suitable to his

holiness, readily concurs. **Ye shall keep** – Be willing; and able to keep the judgments, and to walk in the statutes of God, which is, to live in all holiness.

28. Ye shall dwell – Observe: then, and not before, are these promises to be fulfilled to the house of Israel. **And I will be your God** – This is the foundation of the top-stone of a believer's happiness.

29. I will also save you – I will continue to save you. **From all your uncleannesses** – Salvation from all uncleannessess, includes justification, entire sanctification, and meetness for glory. **The corn** – All necessaries comprised in one.

35. And they – Strangers, or foreigners.

37. Enquired of – Though I have repeated so often my promise to do this, yet it is their duty to intreat it, to wait on me, and then I will do it.

38. As the holy flock – Flocks designed to holy uses. **In her solemn feasts** – These flocks were for quality, the best of all; and for numbers, very great, on the solemn feasts. Thus shall men multiply, and fill the cities of replanted Judea. And the increase of the numbers of men is then honourable, when they are all dedicated to God as a holy flock, to be presented to him for living sacrifices. Crowds are a lovely sight in God's temple.

Chapter 37

The vision of the resurrection of the dry bones (1–10)

The explication of it (11–14)

A type of the happy coalition which would be between Israel and Judah (15–22)

A prediction of the kingdom of Christ, and of the glories and graces of that kingdom (23–28)

The vision of the resurrection of the dry bones (1–10)

1. And set me down – So it seemed to me in the vision. Which is a lively representation of a threefold resurrection:

1. Of the resurrection of souls, from the death of sin, to the life of righteousness:
2. The resurrection of the church from an afflicted state, to liberty and peace:
3. The resurrection of the body at the great day, especially the bodies of believers to life eternal.

3. And he – The Lord.

7. Prophesied – Declared these promises. **As I prophesied** – While I was prophesying. **A noise** – A rattling of the bones in their motion. **A shaking** – A trembling or commotion among the bones, enough to manifest a divine presence, working among them. **Came together** – Glided nearer and nearer, until each bone met the bone to which it was to be joined. Of all the bones of all those numerous slain, not one was missing, not one missed its way, not one missed its place, but each knew and found its fellow. Thus in the resurrection of the dead, the scattered atoms shall be arranged in their proper place and order, and every bone come to his bone, by the same wisdom and power by which they were first formed in the womb of her that is with child.

8. Came up – Gradually spreading itself.

9. Prophesy – Declare what my will is. **O breath** – The soul, whose emblem here is wind; which, as it gently blew upon these lifeless creatures, each was inspired with its own soul or spirit.

10. And the breath – The spirit of life, or the soul, Gen 2:7.

The explication of it (11–14)

11. The whole house – The emblem of the house of Israel. **Are dried** – Our state is as hopeless, as far from recovery, as dried bones are from life.

12. I will open – Though your captivity be as death, your persons close as the grave, yet I will open those graves.

A type of the happy coalition which would be between Israel and Judah (15–22)

16. One stick – A writing tablet or a tally, such as is fit to be written upon. **His companions** – Benjamin and part of Levi, who kept with the tribe of Judah. **Ephraim** – Ephraim was the most considerable tribe in the kingdom of Israel, when divided from the other two. **The house of Israel** – The other nine tribes, who continued with Ephraim.

19. In mine hand – Under my government, care, and blessing. God will make the two kingdoms one in his hand, as I make these two sticks one in my hand.

A prediction of the kingdom of Christ, and of the glories and graces of that kingdom (23–28)

22. One nation – They were one in David's time, who was a type of the Messiah, and continued so to the end of Solomon's time, whose name includes peace. So when the Beloved, the Peace-maker, the Messiah shall be king, they shall be one again. **And one king** – The Messiah.

23. I will save – I will bring them safe out of them. **And will cleanse** – Both justify and sanctify them.

24. David – The son of David. **One shepherd** – This king shall be their one chief shepherd, others that feed and rule the flock, are so by commission from him.

25. For ever – Until Christ's coming to judgment, the Jews converted to Christ, shall inherit Canaan.

26. My sanctuary – I will set up a spiritual glorious temple, and worship among you. **For evermore** – Never to be altered or abolished on earth, but to be consummated in heaven.

27. My tabernacle – The tabernacle wherein I will shew my presence among them. Their fathers had a tabernacle, but the Messiah shall bring with him a better, a spiritual, and an heavenly. **They shall be my people** – By my grace I will make them holy, as the people of a holy God; and I will make them happy, as the people of the ever blessed God.

Chapter 38

The attempt of Gog and Magog on the land of Israel (1–13)

The terror occasioned thereby (14–20)

Their defeat by the immediate hand of God (21–23)

The attempt of Gog and Magog on the land of Israel (1–13)

1. Saying – God now forewarns the Jews, what enemies and troubles would interpose, before he would fully deliver them.

2. Gog – This cannot be one single person, or prince, though perhaps it points out some one, by whom the troubles foretold were begun. Some believe the time is still to come, wherein this prophecy is to be fulfilled. And that it must intend those enemies of God's church who descended from the Scythians, and are now masters of Cappadocia, Iberia, Armenia, or are in confederacy with the Tartars, and those northern heathens. But others think, all the enemies of Israel in all quarters, both open and secret are here intended, and that the Antichristian forces and combination, are what the prophet foretells. **Magog** – Magog is, at least, part of Scythia, and comprehends Syria, in which was Hierapolis. taken by the Scythians, and called of them Scythopolis. It is that country, which now is in subjection to the Turks, and may be extended through Asia minor, the countries of Sarmatia, and many others, under more than one in succession of time. And in the last time under some one active and daring prince, all their power will be stirred up against Christians.

4. Handling swords – That is, very ready, expert and strong in using the sword.

6. Gomer – Inhabitants of Galatia. **Togarmah** – Paphlagonia, and Cappadocia. **The north quarters** – The more northern people, the numerous Tartars.

7. Be thou prepared – God and the church deride this mighty preparation.

8. After many days – In the latter days of the Messiah's kingdom among men. **In the later years** – These must be cotemporary with the many days already mentioned. **Thou** – Gog with all thy numbers. **The land** – The land of the Jews, a people recovered from captivity, into which the sword of their enemy had brought them. **Always waste** – It is already two thousand four hundred years since the ten tribes were carried away by Salmanezer. **But it** – The land of Canaan, that is, the people of it.

11. Unwalled – Weak, and without any considerable defences.

13. Sheba – This Sheba was southward, and contains all of that coast which assisted Gog. **Dedan** – By these are noted, the eastern nations that assisted. **Tarshish** – The inhabitants of the sea-coast westward, and Magog north. **The young lions** – Young men thirsty of blood, but more of spoil, resolve to join, if they may rob and spoil for themselves. **Art thou come** – This repeated enquiry seems to be an agreement to come to his assistance, on condition they might have, possess, and carry away what they seize.

The terror occasioned thereby (14–20)

14. Know it – Thou wilt be informed of it.

15. The north parts – From Scythia, from the Euxine and Caspian seas, and countries thereabouts.

16. I will bring – I will permit thee to come. **Sanctified** – Confessed to be a great God over all, a gracious and faithful God to his people, and a dreadful enemy and avenger against the wicked. **Before** – In the sight of all the heathen that are with Gog, and much more in the sight of God's own people.

17. Spoken – All these enterprises I have spoken of, and will as well defeat as I did foretell them.

19. For – For my own people, and for mine own glory. **Have I spoken** – Against mine enemies Gog, and all his herd. **A great shaking** – A great disturbance and tumult, like an earthquake.

Their defeat by the immediate hand of God (21–23)

21. Sword – Israel. **Throughout** – From all parts of the land, which was full of mountains. **Every man's sword** – As it was in Jehoshaphat's time; and these swords may be meant by the sword God will call for through all, for they ranged all over his mountains.

23. Magnify – Undeniably prove that I am the mighty, just, faithful, wise, holy, and merciful God. **Sanctify** – Declare I am holy, and true to my word.

Chapter 39

A prediction of the utter destruction of Gog and Magog (1–7)

An illustration of the vastness of that destruction (8–22)

God's mercy to his people (23–29)

A prediction of the utter destruction of Gog and Magog (1–7)

2. The sixth part – I will leave in thy country but one in six.

3. Thy bow – What is said of the bow rendered useless, is to be understood of all other weapons of war; this is one kind, the bow, being most in use with the Scythians, is mentioned for all the rest.

An illustration of the vastness of that destruction (8–22)

8. It is come – As sure as if already come. **The day** – That notable day of recompences against the last great enemies of the church.

9. The weapons – The warlike provision, instruments, engines, carriages and wagons. **Shall burn** – It may be wondered why they burn these weapons, which might be of use to them for defence; but it was done in testimony that God was their defence, on whom only they relied. **With fire** – In such a country where the need of fire is much less than with us, it will not seem incredible, that the warlike utensils of so numerous an army might be enough to furnish them with fuel for many years.

11. Gog – And to many of those with him; but many were given to the birds and beasts to be devoured. **Graves** – Gog came to take possession; and so he shall, but not as he purposed and hoped. He shall possess his house of darkness in that land which he invaded. **The valley of the passengers** – So called from the frequent travels of passengers through it from Egypt and Arabia Felix, into the more northern parts, and from these again into Egypt and Arabia. **The sea** – The Dead Sea. **Hamon Gog** – That is, the multitude of Gog.

13. Glorified – The day of my being glorified shall be a renown to Israel.

14. They – The rulers of Israel. **Sever** – Choose out men who shall make it their work. **Passing** – To go up and down over the whole land; for many of Gog's wounded, flying soldiers, died in thickets, and corners into which they crept. **The passengers** – Whose assistance they would desire of courtesy. **Remain** – Unburied by the public labour of the house of Israel during the seven months.

16. The city – That is, the multitude: the city which is next to this common tomb of Gog.

17. **I do sacrifice** – The punishment of these God calls a sacrifice, which he offers to his own justice. **Upon the mountains** – Where more thousands are offered at once, than ever were at any time offered; it is a sacrifice so great, that none ever was, or will be like it.

18. **Ye shall eat** – In these two and the following verses, God takes on him the person of one that makes a feast, invites his guests, and promises to satisfy them. Of the two former, the first is an enigmatical invitation, or an invitation in a riddle; the latter is the key to this character. **The mighty** – Who had great authority, great courage and strength, the giant-like ones, commanders of great note in the army. **Princes** – Many princes came with their country men and subjects to assist in this war. **Rams** – These are compared to rams which lead the flock. **Lambs** – Lambs are the more ordinary in the army. **Goats** – Goats signify the more lascivious, and impetuous among them. **Bullocks** – Bullocks, such as though more slow, were of great strength. **Fatlings** – Well fed. **Bashan** – A mountain of most rich, and sweet soil.

20. **At my table** – In the field where Gog, his princes, and army, are slain, compared to a table. **Horses** – Horsemen, not common foot soldiers. **Chariots** – The men that ride in them.

21. **All the heathen** – In the countries to which the news shall come.

God's mercy to his people (23–29)

26. **Their shame** – Reproach for their sins.

Chapter 40

In this and the following chapter, under the type of a temple and altar, priests and sacrifices, is fore showed, the spiritual worship which should be performed in Gospel times, and that perfected at last in the kingdom of glory: yea probably, in an happy and glorious state of the church on this side heaven: in this chapter we have:

A general account of the temple and city (1–4)

A particular account of the east-gate, north-gate and south-gate (5–31)

Of the inner court (32–38)

Of the tables (39–43)

Of the lodgings for the singers and the priests (44–47)

Of the porch (48, 49)

A general account of the temple and city (1–4)

1. **Of our captivity** – Of those that were carried away into captivity with Jeconiah eleven years before Jerusalem was burnt. And this falls in with the three thousand three hundred and seventy fourth year of the world, about five hundred and seventy four years before Christ's incarnation. **The beginning** – In the month Nisan. **The tenth day** – The day that the paschal lamb was to be taken up in order to the feast on the tenth day. **Brought me** – To Jerusalem, the place where it did stand.

2. **In the visions of God** – By this it appears it was not a corporeal transportation of the prophet. **The frame** – The portrait of a city. **On the south** – On the south of the mountain, where the prophet was set.

3. **A man** – The same no doubt that appeared to the prophet, chap.1:26, whose name is the branch, and who builds the temple, Zech 6:12,13, whose colour was like burnished brass; Rev 1:15, which speaks glory and strength. **A line** – A plumb-line, a mason's line to discover the rectitude of the building, or its defects. **In the gate** – In the north-gate, next toward the east.

A particular account of the east-gate, north-gate and south-gate (5–31)

5. **A wall** – This was that outmost wall, that compassed the whole mount Sion, upon whose top the temple stood. **The man's hand** – Christ, hath, and keeps the reed in his own hand, as the only fit person to take the measures of all. **A measuring reed** – Or cane, for this measuring rod was of those canes growing in that country, long, and light, which architects made use of. **Six cubits long** – Each cubit consisting of eighteen inches in our common account. **An hand breadth** – Added to each six cubits. **The breadth** – The thickness of the walls, which were one reed, and one hand's breadth, or three yards, and three inches thick. **Height** – And the height equal, taking the measure from the floor on the inside of the wall.

6. **The east** – Either of one of the inner walls, or of the temple itself. **Went up** – Until he was got up, he could not measure the threshold, which was at the top of the stairs, and these were ten, if the measurer be supposed in the gate of the house; or eight, if in the gate of the court of the priests; or seven, if in the court of Israel; and each stair was half a cubit in height, too high for him to take the measure of the threshold, if he did not go up the stairs. **The threshold** – It is probable he measured the lower threshold first, as next at hand. **The other threshold** – The upper threshold, or lintel of the gate, which was of equal dimensions with the lower, three yards and three inches broad, or thick.

7. **Chamber** – Along the wall of the porch were chambers, three on one side, and three on the other, each one reed square. **Five cubits** – A space of two yards and one half between each chamber, either filled with some neat posts or

pillars, or it may be quite void. **Within** – The inward and outward threshold, were of the same measures, and curiously arched over head from side to side, and end to end, which was from east to west.

8. The porch – The posts which were joined together at the top by an arch, and so made the portico.

9. The porch – Probably another porch, or another gate distinct from that. **The posts** – These were half columns, that from the floor to the height of the wall jetted out, as if one half of the column were in the wall, and the other without, and the protuberance of this half column, was one cubit.

10. Chambers – These chambers were for the priests and Levites to lodge in during their ministration.

11. Of the entry – It is meant of the whole length of the entry, or walk through the porch, to which they ascended by stairs of a semicircular form.

12. The space – The rails, which were set up at a cubit distance from the front of these little chambers, on the outside for convenient placing of benches for the priests to sit on. **The space** – Between the rails, and the chambers.

13. From the roof – From the extremity of one little chamber on the north side of the gate, to the extremity of the opposite chamber on the south side, and so one cubit and half for the back wall of one chamber, and as much for the back wall of the other chamber, with the length of the chambers, six cubits each, and ten for the breadth of the gate, amounts to twenty five cubits. **Door against door** – It seems the doors of the chambers were two in each chamber in the east and west parts, and so exactly set, that the doors being all open you had a clear prospect through all the chambers to the temple.

14. He made – Measured, and thereby shewed what kind of posts they should be. **Threescore cubits** – Probably this refers to the height of this gate built up two stories above the arch, and the posts in their height are only mentioned, but imply all the rest of the building over the east gate. **Unto the post** – These high columns, on the inner front of this gate were so disposed, that the last on each side was very near the first post, or pillar of the court on either side of the gate, and so the posts and buildings laid on those posts joined on each side of this gate.

15. And – This verse seems to sum up all the dimensions; this gate, its porch, and thickness of its walls, and so sum the cubits, six in the thickness of the outer wall, eighteen in the three chambers, twenty in the spaces between the chambers, and six cubits in the thickness in the inner wall of the porch.

16. Narrow windows – Windows narrowed inward to the middle. **Their posts** – The upper lintel of each door over which was a window. **To the arches** – Windows under the arches between post and post, to give light to the five cubits space between chamber and chamber. **Round about** – These were on both sides of the porch within the gate, exactly alike.

17. The outward court – So called in regard of the more inward court, between that where he was, and the temple itself; this court, was the second about the temple. **Chambers** – Not only lodging rooms for the priests, but also storehouses for tithes and offerings. **A pavement** – A beautiful floor laid with checker works. The whole floor of this court was thus paved. **Thirty chambers** – That is, fifteen on the south side of the gate, and fifteen on the north side, built over the pavement.

18. The pavement – That mentioned, ver.17. **By the side** – That part which lay on each side of the gate, and from thence spread itself toward the chambers, leaving a space of pavement of equal breadth with the porch, or gate in the middle. **The length** – The length was measured fifty cubits. **The inner pavement** – The side pavement was laid somewhat lower than this middle pavement, not only for state, but for the more convenient, keeping it clean; so the middle pavement rose with a little convex surface.

19. The breadth – Of the whole ground between the inner front of one gate and porch, to the outer front of the next gate more inward to the temple. **The lower gate** – Called so in respect to the next gate, which was on the higher ground. **The forefront** – To the outside front of the gate of the priests court, which was next to this gate now measured, that is from the west front of the lower to the east front of the upper gate. **The inner court** – This court from the west front of the lower gate, was one hundred cubits in length to the east front of the gate of the inner court. **East-ward and north-ward** – And so was the space from the south front of the court to the north front. So the court was exactly square. Divers courts are here spoken of, which may put us in mind, of the diversity of gifts, graces and offices in the church: as also of the several degrees of glory in the courts and mansions of heaven.

22. Before them – Within the steps or gate.

23. Toward the east – The east gate of the inner court was directly over against the east gate of the outer court, and equally distant from each other.

26. To it – The floor, or square court.

28. Brought me – From the south-gate of the outer court through the porch, and over the hundred cubit pavement, to the south-gate of the inner court.

Of the inner court (32–38)

32. The inner court – The court of the priests, which was next to the temple.

Of the tables (39–43)

43. Within – Within the porch, where these tables stood. **Hooks** – Hooks on which the slaughtered sacrifice might be hanged, while they prepared it farther. **Fastened** – To walls no doubt, near these tables.

Of the lodgings for the singers and the priests (44–47)

45. The keepers – While, according to their courses, they had the charge of the house of God, and attended on the service of it.

46. The keepers – To preserve the fire perpetually on the altar.

Of the porch (48, 49)

48. The breadth – The whole breadth was eleven cubits, but the breadth of each leaf of this folding-gate was three cubits, and they met, or shut on an upright post, set in the middle of the gate space, and this was one cubit broad. And each leaf hung on posts two cubits thick, which amount to eleven cubits.

Chapter 41

The dimensions of the house and various parts of it (1–13)

An account of another building, and the manner of the building of the house (14–17)

The ornaments of the house (18–20)

The altar of incense and the table (21, 22)

The doors between the temple and the oracle (23–26)

The dimensions of the house and various parts of it (1–13)

1. The breadth – These walls in their thickness took up as much space as the whole breadth of Moses's tabernacle, Exod 26:16,22.

3. Went he – From the porch through the body of the temple, to the partition between the body of the temple and the holy of holies. **Measured** – Either the thickness of that partition wall, or of the pilasters, which stood one on the one side, and the other on the other side of the door. **Of the door** – Or entrance out of the temple into the oracle. **And the door** – This door was six cubits broad, and an upright bar or post on which the leaves met, and which was of one cubit's breadth, make out seven cubits.

4. Thereof – Of the holy of holies, which was an exact square. **Before** – Parallel with the breadth of the temple.

5. After – Having left the holy of holies, now he is come to take the measures of the outer wall. **The house** – The temple. **Six cubits** – Three yards thick was this wall from the ground to the first story of the side-chambers. **Side-chamber** – Of the lowest floor; for there were three stories of these, and they differed in their breadth, as the wall of the temple, on which they rested, abated of its thickness; for the middle chambers were broader than the lowest by a cubit, and the highest as much broader than the middle. **Round about** – On the north, south, and west parts, on each side of every one of these three gates.

6. They might – That the beams of the chambers might have good and firm resting-hold. **Had not hold** – The ends of the beams were not thrust into the main body of the wall of the temple.

7. An enlarging – Of the side chambers, so much of breadth added to the chamber, as was taken from the thickness of the wall; that is, two cubits in the uppermost, and one cubit in the middle-most, more than in the lowest chambers. **A winding about** – Winding stairs, which enlarged as the rooms did, and these run up between each two chambers from the bottom to the top; so there were two doors at the head of each pair of stairs, one door opening into one chamber, and the other into the opposite chamber. **For the winding about** – These stairs, as they rose in height, enlarged themselves too. **Round about** – On all sides of the house where these chambers were. **The breadth** – Of each chamber. **Increased** – Grew broader by one cubit in every upper chamber. From five in the lowest to six in the middle, and to seven in the highest chamber.

8. The foundations – The lowest chamber had properly a foundation laid on the earth, but the floor of the middle, and highest story must be accounted here a foundation; so from the ground to the ceiling of the first room, was six great cubits; from the first to the second, six great cubits; and from the third floor to the roof of the chamber, a like number; to which add we one cubit for thickness of each of the three floors, you have twenty-one cubits for height, ten yards and a half high.

9. The place – The walk and wall.

11. The doors – The doors of the lowest row opened into this void paved space.

12. The building – This is a new building not yet mentioned, but now measured by itself.

13. The house – The whole temple, oracle, sanctuary and porch, with the walls. **The building** – On both the north and south-side of the temple.

An account of another building, and the manner of the building of the house (14–17)

14. The breadth – The whole front of the house eastward.

The ornaments of the house (18–20)

18. Cherubim – Generally taken for the portrait of angels, or young men with wings: yet is the description of them very different in different places; in Ezekiel's vision, Eze 1:5–14 10:14, Isaiah's vision, Isa 6:2, John's vision, Rev 4:6–8, and in Solomon's temple, 1Kin 6:23–26.

19. Through all the house – And thus it was through the whole house round about.

The altar of incense and the table (21, 22)

21. The face – The door or gate of the temple was square, not arched. **As the appearance** – As was the form of the gate of the temple in its larger, so was the form of the gate of the oracle in its lesser dimensions.

22. The altar – Of incense. **The corners** – The horns framed out of the four posts at each angle on the top of the altar. **The walls** – The sides. **Before the Lord** – In the temple, not in the holy of holies.

The doors between the temple and the oracle (23–26)

23. Two doors – Each had one.

25. Them – The doors of both temple and oracle. **The temple** – Including the holy of holies also.

Chapter 42

A description of the chambers that were about the courts (1–12)

The uses of them (13–14)

The whole compass of ground, which was taken up by the house and courts (15-–20)

A description of the chambers that were about the courts (1–12)

2. The length – The temple of one hundred cubits long, and of fifty broad, was on the south prospect of these chambers.

3. Against gallery – That is, a gallery on the south part toward the inner court, and a gallery toward the pavement north-ward, and between the backs of these galleries were chambers.

4. A way – Before the galleries probably, was a ledge of one cubit broad, running the whole length from east to west, called here a way, though not designed for any to walk on it.

5. Shorter – At first view it should seem to refer to the length, but indeed it refers to the

height of the chambers, of which the lowest chamber was highest, the second lower pitched than the first, yet of greater height than the uppermost between the floor and ceiling.

6. As the pillars – So thick and strong as those were.

7. The wall – A wall at a distance from them, perhaps some wall that might keep up a terrace-walk.

11. The way – The walk. **Was like** – Exactly uniform with the fabric on the north-side. **All their goings** – Every window and door. **Were** – Framed in the same manner. In all things exactly alike.

The uses of them (13–14)

13. Shall they lay – In some of these chambers the holy things that might be eat, were laid up as in a store-house; and those which were not for present use, were reserved, until they were to be used.

14. Which are – Which common people may meddle with.

The whole compass of ground, which was taken up by the house and courts (15–20)

20. Five hundred broad – Each reed was above three yards and an half, so that it was about eight miles round. Thus large were the suburbs of this mystical temple, signifying the great extent of the church in gospel times. It is in part fulfilled already, by the accession of the Gentiles to the church: and will be throughly accomplished, when the fulness of the Gentiles shall come in, and all Israel shall be saved. **A separation** – To distinguish, and accordingly to exclude, or admit persons, for all might not go in.

Chapter 43

In this chapter and the next, the temple-service is described, but under the type of the Old Testament service.

The glory of God first fills the temple (1–6)

A promise of God's continuing with his people, if they obey him (7–12)

A description of the altar of burnt offerings (13–17)

Directions for the consecration of that altar (18-–27)

The glory of God first fills the temple (1–6)

2. Came – When the glory departed, it went eastward, and now it returns, it comes from the east. **And his voice** – Though by the voice of God, thunder is sometimes meant, yet here it was an articulate voice.

3. And it – This glory of the God of Israel. **To destroy** – To declare, that their sins would ruin their city, chap.9:3,4. **I fell** – Overwhelmed, and as it were swallowed up.

4. Came – The sins of Israel caused the glory of the Lord to go out of his house, now the repentance of Israel is blest with the return of this glory.

6. The man – Christ. **Stood** – To encourage, and strengthen him.

A promise of God's continuing with his people, if they obey him (7–12)

7. He – The glorious God of Israel. **My throne** – The throne of his grace is in his temple; in the dispensations of grace, God manifests himself a king. **My feet** – Speaking after the manner of men, and expressing his abode and rest, in his temple, as the type, in his church, as the antitype. **In their high places** – Perhaps some kings were buried in the temples of their idols, near the idols they worshipped.

8. Their threshold – The kings of Judah and Israel, built temples and altars for their idols, and these are called their thresholds. They erected these in the courts, or near the courts of the temple. **Abominations** – Idolatries, and wickednesses not to be named.

9. Far from me – From my temple.

10. Son of man – Ezekiel, who is called thus above eighty times in this book. **Shew** – Describe it to them in all the parts. **To the house** – To the rulers, prophets, and priests especially, not excluding others. **Their iniquities** – When they shall blush to see what glory their iniquities had ruined.

12. The law – This is the first comprehensive rule: holiness becomes God's house; and this relative holiness referred to personal and real holiness. **The top** – The whole circuit of this mountain shall be holy, but the top of it on which the temple stands, shall be most holy.

A description of the altar of burnt offerings (13–17)

13. The altar – Of burnt-offerings. **And an hand-breath** – The sacred cubit, three inches longer than the common cubit. **The bottom** – The ledge or settle, fastened to the altar on all sides at the bottom, shall be a cubit in height. **The breadth** – From the edge of this bench on the outside to the edge where it joined the body of the altar, a cubit, and this the breadth, twenty-one inches, broad enough for the priests to walk on. **Border** – A ledge going round on all the squares. **The edge** – On the outer edge of this settle a span high. **The back** – As the back bears burdens, so this was to bear the weight of the whole altar.

14. From the bottom – From the first ledge, which was a cubit broad, and a cubit high from the ground. **To the lower** – To the top of that square settle, which is called lower, because another settle is raised upon it. **Two cubits** – In height. **The lesser** – From the highest edge of the uppermost settle, down to the cubit broad ledge about the lower settle. **The greater** – So called, because it exceeded the upper settle a cubit in breadth. **Four cubits** – In height.

15. Four cubits – In height. **From the altar** – From the top of the altar.

17. Stairs – Or steps, for such they needed, to carry them, up to the first and second settles.

Directions for the consecration of that altar (18–27)

19. Give – Direct, or command that it be given.

20. Shalt take – Appoint it to be taken.

21. He – The priest. **In the appointed place** – That is, in the court of the house, and on the altar appointed; this is the first day's sacrifice.

22. They – The priests in attendance.

23. Shalt offer – On the third day, and so on, through seven days.

24. Shalt offer – Direct them to offer. **Salt** – It may allude to the perpetuity of the covenant thus made by sacrifice.

26. They – The priests in course.

27. I will accept you – Those that give themselves to God, shall be accepted of God, their persons first, and then their performances, through the mediator.

Chapter 44

The appropriating the east-gate of the temple to the prince (1–3)

A reproof to Israel for their former profanations of the sanctuary, and a caution (4–9)

The degrading of one part of the Levites, and establishing of the family of Zadock in the priesthood (10–16)

Laws and ordinances concerning the priesthood (17–31)

The appropriating the east-gate of the temple to the prince (1–3)

2. Shall not be opened – Shall not ordinarily stand open. **No man** – None of the common people. **The Lord** – That glory which was the visible sign of his presence.

3. He – The king might sit before the Lord, others might not. **Bread** – That part of the sacrifice, which was allowed to the offerer.

A reproof to Israel for their former profanations of the sanctuary, and a caution (4–9)

4. He – Christ in the appearance of a man.

5. The entering – The persons who may, and who may not enter. **The sanctuary** – Taken here for the courts, rather than the house itself.

6. Let it suffice – Let the time you have spent on your sins suffice.

7. Bread – Either the meal-offering or first-fruits of corn and dough, and the shew-bread. **They** – The whole nation of the Jews.

8. Have not kept – You have not observed the laws I gave you for the keeping of my holy things, house, sacrifices, and worship. **Have set** – You have substituted others in your rooms.

The degrading of one part of the Levites, and establishing of the family of Zadock in the priesthood (10–16)

10. Are gone away – By their idolatry.

11. Ministers – Servants employed in the lowest work. **Sanctuary** – Not the temple itself, but about the courts of it. **Having charge** – They shall be porters to open and shut, and sweep, and go on errands. **To minister** – To wait on the priests.

12. Iniquity – The punishment of it.

13. Shall bear their shame – They shall be dealt with according to their abominations, and bear the punishment thereof.

15. That kept the charge – Were constant, zealous, and faithful in their priestly office.

16. Into my sanctuary – Both to the altar, to the temple, and the high-priest into the holy of holies. **Come near** – To set the shew-bread on, and to take it off. **To minister** – To offer sacrifice at the altar, and incense in the house. God will put marks of honour upon those who are faithful to him in trying times, and will, employ those in his service, who have kept close to it, when others drew back.

Laws and ordinances concerning the priesthood (17–31)

17. And within – In the temple.

19. Shall not sanctify – By the law, common things, touching holy things, became consecrated, and no more fit for common use.

20. To grow long – Priding themselves in it, as Absalom. **Shall only poll** – When the hair is grown, they shall cut the ends of their hair, and keep it in moderate size.

21. Drink wine – Or any other strong liquor, when they go either to trim the lamps or set the shew-bread in order, or to offer incense in the temple, or when they go to the altar to offer a sacrifice, which stood in the inner court.

24. Shall judge – Shall determine the controversy. **Assemblies** – Public congregations.

26. Cleansed – After for seven days he hath kept from the dead. **They** – The priests, who are about the house of God, shall appoint seven days more to this defiled person for his cleansing before he is admitted into the sanctuary.

28. It – The sin-offering: but under this one, all other offerings are couched. **For an inheritance** – Instead of lands and cities.

30. And the first – So soon as the first-fruits are ripe in the field, your vineyards, and olive yards. **Every oblation** – Whether free-will offering, or prescribed. **The first of your dough** – It is conceived this was of every mass of dough they made, and of the first of the dough, which every year they first made of the new corn, as by the custom of the Jews at this day appears. **That he** – The priest may bless, and pray for thee.

Chapter 45

The division of the holy land (1–8)

The ordinances that were given both to the prince and to the people (9–12)

The oblations to be offered, and the princes part therein (13–17)

Particularly, in the beginning of the year (18–20)

And in the Passover, and feast of tabernacles (21–25)

The division of the holy land (1–8)

2. Of this – Whole portion of twenty five thousand cubits long, or twelve miles and half, and ten thousand broad, or five miles and a little more. **For the sanctuary** – For a platform for the sanctuary, both house and court.

3. And in it – In the centre of this.

6. The possession – Land to be a possession to the citizens of Jerusalem, and to be the content of the city. **Broad** – About two miles and half broad, and twelve miles and half long. **Long** – This must run along parallel in length with the holy portion, though but half its breadth. **For the whole house** – As the capital city, to which the tribe's resort, it must be large enough to entertain them.

7. The prince – The king. **Our side** – One half of the prince's portion lay on the west side of those three already set out. **The other side** – The other half lay on the east-side thereof, so the portion of the city, Levites and priests, lay in the middle. **The holy portion** – Of priests, and Levites, and sanctuary. **Before** – It lay parallel as broad as these three were broad, and so run on both sides in its breadth from north to south, and had its length as the other, from east to west. **Over against** – What is called now over-against, or by the side, is called before three times together. So now you have an exact square of twenty-five thousand cubits laid out for God, the Levites and city, which appears thus in the breadth. 10,000 for the priests.10,000 for the Levites. 5000 for the city. And the length of each, twenty-five thousand, that is twelve miles and half square.

The ordinances that were given both to the prince and to the people (9–12)

9. Let it suffice – Be content, aim not at more.

11. Of one measure – One shall contain as much as the other, the ephah shall contain as many gallons of dry, as the bath of liquid things. **An homer** – Thirty bushels. So the ephah will be three bushels in dry things, and the bath eight gallons in liquid things.

12. Twenty gerahs – A gerah was one penny half-penny, the shekel then was two shillings and six-pence, twenty shekels was two pounds ten shillings, fifteen shekels was one pound seventeen shillings and six-pence, and twenty-five was three pound two shillings and six-pence. **Maneh** – It seems there was the small, the middle, and the great Maneh.

The oblations to be offered, and the princes part therein (13–17)

13. Offer – In the daily service, the morning and evening sacrifice.

14. Bath – Which contained about twenty-four gallons. **The cor** – Or homer; these were two names of the same measure.

16. With the prince – By a common purse of prince and people.

Particularly, in the beginning of the year (18–20)

18. Thou shalt take – Procure, this the prince must do.

20. For every one that erreth – For all the errors of all the house of Israel, through ignorance. **For him that is simple** – That is half-witted, or a fool. **Reconcile** – Cleanse, as ver.18, which legally was defiled by those errors done in the city, or courts of the house, whither these persons might come.

And in the Passover, and feast of tabernacles (21–25)

21. In the first month – Nisan, which is part of March, and part of April with us.

22. Upon that day – Upon the fourteenth day, on which the Passover was slain.

24. An hin – This was about one gallon and three quarters of a pint.

25. In the seventh month – According to their ecclesiastical account, which is Tisri, and answers to part of our August and September. **In the fifteenth day** – On that day the feast of tabernacles began, and continued seven days. **He** – The prince. **In the feast of the seven days** – Hence we also may learn the necessity of

frequently repeating the same religious exercises. Indeed the sacrifice of atonement was offered once for all. But the sacrifice of acknowledgement, that of a broken heart, that of a thankful heart, must be offered every day. And these spiritual sacrifices are always acceptable to God through Christ Jesus.

Chapter 46

Farther rules for the worship of the priests and the people (1–15)

A rule, for the prince's disposal of his inheritance (16–18)

A description of the places for the boiling and baking the offerings (19–24)

Farther rules for the worship of the priests and the people (1–15)

3. In the Sabbaths – Both weekly and other holy days, which are called Sabbaths.

9. Go forth over against it – Perhaps, only to prevent all jostling and confusion.

A rule, for the prince's disposal of his inheritance (16–18)

17. His inheritance – Whatever lands of the prince are given to servants, shall at the year of Jubilee revert to the sons of the prince. **For them** – And to theirs after them.

A description of the places for the boiling and baking the offerings (19–24)

20. The outer court – Where the people were.

21. A court – A smaller court made up on the outer sides with the walls of the greater square, and on the inside made with two walls, the one forty cubits long, the other thirty cubits broad.

23. A row of building – A range of building on the inside of the walls of the lesser courts. **Four** – Four courts in the four corners.

Chapter 47

The vision of the holy waters (1–12)

The borders of the land of Canaan (13–23)

The vision of the holy waters (1–12)

1. Eastward – The fountain lay to the west, the conduit pipes were laid to bring the water to the temple, and so must run eastward, and perhaps one main pipe might be laid under the east-gate of the temple. **The right side** – On the south-side of the temple.

2. Out – Of the inmost court. **The outer gate** – The outmost north-gate in the wall that compassed the whole mountain of the Lord's house.

3. He measured – By the line in his hand. **He**

brought me – Went before, and the prophet followed; all this was in vision.

8. The sea – The Dead-sea, or lake of Sodom. Shall be healed – The waters of the sea shall be healed, made wholesome. So where the grace of God from his temple and altar flows, it heals the corrupt nature of man, and renders barren terrible deserts, as a land of waters and gardens.

9. Shall live – Be preserved alive, and thrive, whereas no fish can live in the Dead-sea. For they – The poisonous waters of the Dead-sea shall be made wholesome for fish. Shall live – Thrive, and multiply in the virtue of the healing streams. Thus is the fruitfulness of the grace of God in the church set forth.

10. En-gedi – Which lay on the south-west of the lake of Sodom. En-eglaim – A city on the north-east of the Dead-sea. To spread forth nets – All along on the west-side of this sea to dry them.

12. Consumed – Never be consumed, never decay, there shall always be fruit, and enough. Their waters – Those that watered them. Issued out – And so carried a blessing with them.

The borders of the land of Canaan (13–23)

13. The border – The utmost bounds of the whole land. Shall inherit – That is, shall divide for inheritance to the tribes of Israel. Joseph – That is, the two sons of Joseph, Ephraim, and Manasseh.

15. The great sea – The Mediterranean, which was the greatest sea the Jews knew.

18. The east sea – The Dead-sea, which lay on the east of Jerusalem. Thus a line drawn from Damascus through Auranitis, Gilead, the land of Israel beyond Jordan to the east-sea, made the eastern frontier.

19. The river – Called the river of Egypt, lay directly in the way to Egypt from Jerusalem. The great sea – To the south-west part of the Mediterranean sea near Gaza.

22. Children – Who from their birth should be invested with this right of inheriting.

23. His inheritance – This certainly looks at gospel times, when the partition-wall between Jew and Gentile was taken down, and both put on a level before God, both made one in Christ Jesus.

Chapter 48

The portion of seven tribes (1–7)

The allotment of land for the sanctuary, priests and Levites (8–14)

For the city and prince (15–22)

For the other five tribes (23–29)

A plan of the city, its gates, and new name (30–35)

The portion of seven tribes (1–7)

The allotment of land for the sanctuary, priests and Levites (8–14)

For the city and prince (15–22)

15. A profane place – A common, not consecrated place.

16. The measures thereof – The extent and proportions of the city, a square of four thousand five hundred shall be taken out of the middle of the twenty five thousand or the ground-plan of the city. So it shall be an equilateral square, every side exactly the same, north, south, east, and west, four thousand five hundred apiece, by which measures the whole content is visible eighteen thousand cubits not reeds.

18. For food – For the maintenance of the city-officers.

20. The possession – The land assigned for the city.

For the other five tribes (23–29)

28. To the river – The river of Egypt.

A plan of the city, its gates, and new name (30–35)

35. Eighteen thousand cubits – About five miles in compass. From that day – From the day of the Lord's restoring this people, and rebuilding their city, and their thankful, holy, and pure worshipping of God there, from that day it shall be said of Jerusalem. The Lord is there – The Lord who as his name alone is Jehovah, so is the only true God, faithful to his promise, rich in mercy, glorious in majesty, righteous in his judgments, wise and holy in his government, whose presence makes us happy, whose withdrawing from us leaves us to misery. This God will by his favour and presence, bring the confluence of all good to persons, families, and cities; this God will be there to dwell, govern, defend, prosper, and crown. Such is to be the case of earthly Jerusalem, such shall be for ever the case of the heavenly Jerusalem. Such is the case of every true believer, who may, wherever he is, in his way of duty, still write Jehovah-Shammah, My God is here. And it is best to be where he is until he bring us within the gates of the glorious city, where inconceivable light and love from the immediate presence of God, give every one an eternal demonstration that God is here: to him be glory for ever.

DANIEL

John Wesley

Introduction

Daniel was of the tribe of Judah, and it is thought, of the royal family. Ezekiel, his cotemporary, but much his senior, speaks of him as wise to a proverb, when he upbraids the king of Tyre with his self-conceit, Thou art wiser than Daniel. He likewise names Noah, Daniel, and Job, as having the greatest interest in heaven of any. He lived a long and active life in the courts and councils of some of the greatest monarchs the world ever had. Yet none was more intimately acquainted with the mind of God than he that was a courtier, a statesman, and a man of business. It is generally supposed he lived to be very old, and died at Shushan in Persia.

The first chapter of this book, and the three first verses of the second are in Hebrew: and so are the four last chapters. The rest of the book is in the Chaldee: Daniel continues the holy story, from the first taking of Jerusalem by the Chaldean Babel, until the last destruction of it by Rome, the mystical Babel.

Chapter 1

Jehoiakim's first captivity (1, 2)

The choice made of Daniel and some other young men, to be brought up for Nebuchadnezzar's service (3–7)

Their preferring pulse before the king's meat (8–16)

Their wonderful improvement (17–21)

Jehoiakim's first captivity (1, 2)

2. With part of the vessels – In this expedition Nebuchadnezzar carried away some captives, among whom were Daniel and his friends. **His god** – Baal, or Bell, and Nebo, which words they put into the names of their kings and favourites.

The choice made of Daniel and some other young men, to be brought up for Nebuchadnezzar's service (3–7)

3. Of the eunuchs – These were chief among the king's servants; and they are called eunuchs, because many of them were such. **And of the princes** – Here was fulfilled what the prophet Isaiah had foretold, Isa 39:7.

4. The learning and the tongue – The Chaldeans were skilled above any other nation, in natural philosophy. Their tongue differed from the Hebrew in dialect and in pronunciation, which they learned that they might be the more acceptable to the king, and court.

5. The king's meat – Such as he had at his own table.

6. And Azariah – Probably all of the royal lineage of Judah.

7. Gave names – That is, other names, relating to the idol-gods. **Belteshazzar** – So Daniel had the name of Belteshazzar, from the great Babylonian idol Baal or Bell. This was by the king's command, and herein he put forth an act of his sovereignty.

Their preferring pulse before the king's meat (8–16)

8. But Daniel purposed – There may be several weighty reasons assigned why Daniel did this.
1. Because many of those meats provided for the king's table, were forbidden by the Jewish law.
2. Daniel knew these delicacies would too much gratify the flesh.
3. He did not dare to eat and drink things consecrated to idols.
4. He was sensible, how unsuitable delicate fare would be to the afflicted state of God's people. Therefore he was herein a rare pattern of avoiding all the occasions of evil.

15. Fairer and fatter – The blessing of God upon homely fare, affords often more health and strength, than more costly fare to them that eat the fat, and drink the sweet.

Their wonderful improvement (17–21)

19. Before – Both in the presence chamber, and in the council chamber, to try their proficiency; this shows the king's ability and judgment, how else could he discern their fitness, and their excellency above others.

20. The king enquired – This is a farther confirmation of the king's noble endowments, and of his great care whom he chose to be in offices of trust, namely persons excellently qualified to serve him in the great affairs of the kingdom. And thus did God pour contempt upon the pride of the Chaldeans, and put honour on the low estate of his people.

21. Continued – in the court of Babylon until Cyrus, and then he was in the Persian court, and he lived in honour and high employment all that time, yea, after Cyrus began to reign. For chap.10:1, he had visions and revelations in the third year of Cyrus.

Chapter 2

In this chapter we have:

The perplexity of Nebuchadnezzar through his dream which he had forgotten, and which the magicians could not tell him (1–11)

Orders given to destroy all the wise men of Babylon (12–15)

The dream discovered to Daniel, and his thanksgiving (16–23)

His discovery of the dream and the meaning of it to the king (24–45)

The honour put upon Daniel and his companions (46–49)

The perplexity of Nebuchadnezzar through his dream which he had forgotten, and which the magicians could not tell him (1–11)

1. In the second year – This was properly in the fifth year of that king's reign, but in the second year after Daniel had been brought before the king. **Dreams** – It was one dream, but of many parts.

2. The astrologers – Who pretended great skill in natural, and supernatural things. **The sorcerers** – Or necromancers, who used diabolical arts. **Chaldeans** – This name the magicians assumed as being national, and most noble.

3. To know – He remembered the fact in general, but could not repeat it perfectly. Yet it had left such an impression on him, as put him in great perplexity. The Lord hath ways to affright the greatest men in the world, in the midst of their security.

4. In Syriac – That is in the Chaldee tongue, for Syria or Aram is sometimes taken in a large sense, containing, Assyria, Babylon, Mesopotamia, Phoenicia, Palestine, 2Kings 18:26. From hence all is written in the Chaldee language, to the eighth chapter.

9. But one decree – I will not retract my sentence.

Orders given to destroy all the wise men of Babylon (12–15)

13. Daniel and his fellows – Daniel and his fellows were not called, because of their youth, which the Chaldeans despised. Here it is observable:
1. The magicians confessed, that knowledge and revelation must come from God, and therefore what Daniel did, was not of any human strength.
2. That the Lord held the governor's hands, so that he did not slay Daniel presently with the first.
3. That Daniel by his prudence and piety, saved all the magicians lives.

The dream discovered to Daniel, and his thanksgiving (16–23)

21. He changeth – God can make the sun go back or stand still, as in Ahaz and Joshua's time, it is the great part of God's power and prerogative to change times. Daniel here attributes that to God, which Heathens attributed to nature, or chance. God only, that made all by his power, doth rule, and over-rule all by his providence.

His discovery of the dream and the meaning of it to the king (24–45)

26. Belteshazzar – By this name of Belteshazzar he had given Daniel, he took courage as if he might expect some great thing from him: for the word signifies the keeper of secret treasure.

28. What shall be – Observe the prophet's wisdom, he does not fall abruptly upon the dream, but first prepares this lofty king for it, and by degrees labours to win him to the knowledge of the true God.

30. But – But that the interpretation may be manifest to the king, and that thou mayest be better instructed and satisfied in thy mind.

36. And we – By this word we appears Daniel's piety and modesty, or he declares by it, that he and his companions had begged this skill from God, and therefore he did not arrogate it to himself.

38. Made thee ruler – He hath given thee absolute dominion of all creatures, men and beasts within the bounds of thy vast kingdom. **Thou** – He was first in order, as the head is before the other parts, and the vision began in him, and descended downwards to the other three monarchies. He was the head of gold, because of the vast riches wherein this monarchy abounded, and because it stood longest, five hundred years, and was fortunate and flourishing to the last.

39. Another kingdom – This was that of the Medes and Persians, inferior in time for it lasted not half so long as the Assyrian in prosperity and tranquillity; yet, was this wonderful, rich and large for a time. **Third kingdom** – This was the Grecian monarchy under Alexander the great, called brass, because coarser than the other. **Over all the earth** – Alexander marched even to the Indies, and was said to conquer the world.

40. Fourth kingdom – This is the kingdom of the Romans, and was to last not only to Christ's first coming, but under antichrist, to his second coming. This did break in pieces all other kingdoms, being too strong for them, and brought all into subjection to it, until the stone fell upon it.

41. Divided – Partly strong, and partly weak; the Roman kingdom was divided, partly by their civil wars, partly when conquered provinces and kingdoms cast off the Roman yoke, and set up king's of their own, and so the empire was divided into ten kingdoms or toes.

42. Broken – This was plain in the civil wars of the Romans, and the falling off of some countries, especially towards the end of it.

43. Mingle themselves – By marriage, but they shall never knit well together, because ambition is stronger than affinity.

44. In the days of these kings – While the iron kingdom stood, for Christ was born in the reign of Augustus Caesar. And this kingdom is not bounded by any limits, as worldly empires are, but is truly universal. And it shall be for ever, never destroyed or given to others, as the rest were.

45. And the gold – This denotes the small beginning of Christ's visible kingdom, and the different rise of Christ from all other; his conception by the Holy Ghost, without father and mother, respectively as to his two natures. This stone, falling from the mountain, brake the image in pieces; for Christ is a stone that grinds to powder those it falls on: and he is a growing stone even to a mountain, and therefore will fill the earth.

The honour put upon Daniel and his companions (46–49)

46. That they should offer – This was strange, that so great a monarch should thus worship his vassal, which he did in consternation and admiration. But doubtless Daniel put a stop to it: though he could not hinder the king in his prostration, and in his word of command. And the king being instructed of Daniel, gives God all the glory in the next words.

47. God of gods – The supreme God of all the world, above Baal and all other gods. **Lord of kings** – The word in the Syriac signifies, high Lord, seeing he is the highest king of all the earth.

49. And he set – He substituted them as lieutenants for the king's service under Daniel, but Daniel sat in the king's gate to be ready for the king's chief business.

Chapter 3

Nebuchadnezzar erects a golden image, and requires all his subjects to worship it (1–7)

He is informed that the Jewish princes refuse to worship it (8–12)

They resolutely persist in their refusal (13–18)

They are cast into the fiery furnace (19–23)

Their preservation and the conviction of the king (24–27)

The honour which he gave to God, and the favour he showed to his servants (28–30)

Nebuchadnezzar erects a golden image, and requires all his subjects to worship it (1–7)

1. Made an image – Perhaps he did this, that he might seem no ways inclined to the Jews, or their religion, whereof the Chaldeans might be jealous, seeing he had owned their God to be greatest, and had preferred Daniel and his friends to great honours.

4. Nations and languages – Proclamation was made therefore in several languages.

He is informed that the Jewish princes refuse to worship it (8–12)

They resolutely persist in their refusal (13–18)

16. We are not careful – Heb. We care not: there is no need of any answer in this case for it is in vain for us to debate the matter; the king is resolved to have his will of us, and we are resolved on the contrary.

18. But if not – It was therefore all one to them, which way God would honour himself; they were resolved to suffer rather than sin, and leave the cause to God. Indeed if God be for us, we need not fear what man can do unto us. Let him do his worst. God will deliver us either from death, or in death.

They are cast into the fiery furnace (19–23)

20. To bind – What did he think these three men would have refused? Or that their God would defend them from his power, or that if he had, his mighty men could have prevailed? None of all this was the case; for God purposed to shew his power when the king did his worst, and in the thing wherein he dealt proudly, to be above him.

23. Fell down – All this is expressed with emphasis, to make the power of God more glorious in their preservation; for that shame that slew the executioners, might much more easily have killed them, even before they fell down.

Their preservation and the conviction of the king (24–27)

25. No hurt – See how the God of nature can when he pleases control the powers of nature! **The Son of God** – Probably he had heard David speak of him. Jesus Christ, the Angel of the covenant, did sometimes appear before his incarnation. Those who suffer for Christ, have his gracious presence with them in their sufferings, even in the fiery furnace, even in the valley of the shadow of death, and therefore need fear no evil.

26. And spake – With a milder tone than before, God having abated the fire of his fury. Now he could at once acknowledge the true God to be the most high above all gods, and the three worthies to be his faithful servants.

The honour which he gave to God, and the favour he showed to his servants (28–30)

Chapter 4

The writer of this chapter is Nebuchadnezzar himself. The story of him is given in his own words.

The preface (1–3)

His dream, which puzzled the magicians (4–18)

The interpretation of it by Daniel (19–27)

The accomplishment of it (28–33)

Nebuchadnezzar's recovery and adoration of God (34–37)

The preface (1–3)

1. Nebuchadnezzar the king – Daniel here sets down another strange relation in the words of the king's own proclamation, sent to all his vast kingdoms, and questionless put into the king's archives, and court-rolls. **Peace be multiplied** – All health and happiness; this was always the form of salutation among the eastern nations.

3. How great are his signs – Nothing less than a real change of heart could cause such a confession as this! Nebuchadnezzar was now old, had reigned above forty years, and seen as much of the world as most men ever did. And yet never until now, did he admire surprising events, as the signs and wonders of the high God!

His dream, which puzzled the magicians (4–18)

4. Was at rest – When my wars were over, I sat down quiet, enjoying the spoils of my enemies.

13. A watcher – A holy angel, the instrument of God, to execute God's judgments which the angels watch constantly to perform.

17. Of the holy ones – The decree was God's, and the demand was of the holy angels; if God enact it, the angels had the dispensation of it put into their hands, and they all consent to it as a just judgment of God to be executed by them according to the will of God. **The most high ruleth** – Nebuchadnezzar and his flatterers conceded he was a god in earth unaccountable to any. But the great God will make all men know he rules all in earth too, and sets up at his pleasure whom he will, and plucks them down again.

The interpretation of it by Daniel (19–27)

19. Troubled him – Because he fore-saw such troubles coming upon the king for whom he had a high reverence. **Let not the dream trouble thee** – Speak out, let the event be what it will. **Belteshazzar said** – What address and how excellent a spirit is shewn in this short preface.

22. Reacheth unto heaven – Thou art high and mighty in the majesty which God hath given thee. **To the end of the earth** – To the Caspian sea north, to the Euxine and Aegean sea west, to the Mediterranean south.

25. They shall drive thee – This was such a thundering peal, that it was wonderful the king could endure to hear it without fury boiling in his heart, yet the Lord with-held him. **Seven times** – Seven years. **Until thou know** – How hard is it for lofty princes to learn this lesson.

26. **The heavens do rule** – That God, who sits in heaven rules over all.

27. **If it may be** – Daniel was not certain of pardon for him, nor did he altogether despair of it. With what wisdom and tenderness does he speak: and yet with what plainness?

The accomplishment of it (28–33)

28. **King Nebuchadnezzar** – With how admirable propriety is the person changed here! These six verses speaking in the third person. But in the thirty fourth, Nebuchadnezzar having recovered his reason, speaks in the first person again.

33. **Was driven from men** – Being bereft of his understanding, as a man distracted he fled, and betook himself to the woods.

Nebuchadnezzar's recovery and adoration of God (34–37)

34. **Mine understanding returned** – God shined upon his soul, and gave him understanding to consider his sad state, and the causes of it. **And honoured him** – By prayer and praise, adoring the justice and mercy of God, giving God the glory of his sovereignty and unchangeableness.

35. **As nothing** – A due consideration of God's infinite greatness, makes the creature appear as nothing; creatures are nothing to help, nothing to hurt, nothing in duration, nothing solid and substantial, nothing without dependence, and influence, and support from God. **His will** – Being the Lord of hosts, and the only absolute and universal monarch of the world.

36. **Brightness** – I had again the majesty of a king in my countenance. **I was established** – In wonted power and place, owned and obeyed, by all. **Majesty was added** – He was the most August and magnificent prince on earth, much more so than before.

37. **Now I praise** – Thus can the Lord make the stoutest hearts to stoop, and do him homage. This doxology proceeds from his heart. **Are truth** – God is truth essentially: he is the rule and standard of truth, his words are truth, his ways are truth, and they are judgment: he is wise, and hath dealt justly with me for my pride, and in very faithfulness hath afflicted me, and in very tenderness hath restored me; I do, and ever shall adore him for it. **Able to abase** – As he hath declared upon me, in stupendous changes, which I proclaim to all the world. He had a just controversy with me, and I have no ground to quarrel with him, but to give him glory by this confession. What authority had any one to say,

That this man 'was no convert?' We can no more doubt of his salvation than of Solomon's.

Chapter 5

Belshazzar's profane feast (1–4)

The hand writing on the wall (5–9)

Interpreted and applied by Daniel (10–29)

The accomplishment of it (30, 31)

Belshazzar's profane feast (1–4)

1. **Belshazzar** – The grandson of Nebuchadnezzar. **Made a great feast** – After the manner of the eastern kings who showed their magnificence this way. But this is prodigious that he should carouse when the city was besieged, and ready to be taken by Darius the Mede.

2. **To bring the vessels** – Triumphing thereby over God and his people.

4. **And praised the gods of gold** – At the same time insulting the great God of heaven and earth.

The hand writing on the wall (5–9)

5. **Came forth fingers** – The likeness of a man's hand.

6. **His knees smote** – So soon can the terrors of God make the loftiest cedars, the tyrants of the earth.

Interpreted and applied by Daniel (10–29)

10. **The queen came** – The women in those courts had an apartment by themselves, and this being the queen-mother, and aged, did not mingle herself with the king's wives and concubines, yet she broke the rule in coming in now, upon this solemn occasion.

24. **From him** – From that God whom thou hast despised.

26. **MENE, MENE** – MENE, it is numbered, it is numbered; the words are doubled for the greater confirmation. It relates to the number of the seventy years for the overthrow of the Babylonian empire.

27. **Art found wanting** – There is no weight nor worth in thee; thou hast made light of God, and the Lord makes light of thee.

28. **PERES** – Separated, divided, broken. Peres signifies two things, broken off, and Persian; noting that, first, this kingdom was broken down from Belshazzar. Secondly, that it was given to the Persians.

The accomplishment of it (30, 31)

31. **Darius the Mede** – This was he that with Cyrus besieged and took Babylon.

Chapter 6

Daniel's preferment (1–3)

Envy against him, and the decree against prayer (4–9)

Daniel's continuance in prayer notwithstanding (10)

He is informed against and cast into the den of lions (11–17)

His preservation and deliverance (18–23)

The death of his accusers, and the decree of Darius, and prosperity of Daniel (24–28)

Daniel's preferment (1–3)

2. **Daniel was first** – Belshazzar's promise to Daniel was, that he should be the third ruler in the kingdom, chap.5:7,16,29. The first was general of the army, the second president of the palace, the third of the land and provinces.

Envy against him, and the decree against prayer (4–9)

4. **Concerning the kingdom** – And so to have made him guilty of treason, or other high misdemeanours, in the king's business.

Daniel's continuance in prayer notwithstanding (10)

10. **Toward Jerusalem** – The temple was the place where the Lord placed his name, and promised to appear, and accept his people, all being a type of Christ, through whom only sinners are accepted. **As he did aforetime** – He did not abate his prayers for the king's command, nor did he break the law purposely, because he did no more than he was wont to do in serving his God.

He is informed against and cast into the den of lions (11–17)

14. **Displeased with himself** – For having made that foolish decree. **To deliver him** – To find out some way of delivering him.

His preservation and deliverance (18–23)

20. **Able to deliver** – What he doubted of, we are sure of, that the servants of the living God, have a master who is able to deliver them and bear them out in his service.

22. **His angel** – The same that was with the three children in the fiery furnace, whose presence made even the lion's den a strong-hold, his palace, his paradise. See the power of God over the fiercest creatures! See the care God takes of his faithful servants, especially when they are called to suffer for him! See how ready the angels are to minister to the heirs of salvation!

The death of his accusers, and the decree of Darius, and prosperity of Daniel (24–28)

25. **In all the earth** – In all that great empire. It is usual with the Turk, Tartar, Chinese, to arrogate the same universality.

Chapter 7

We come now to the prophetical part of Daniel, in which are many things hard to be understood. In this chapter we have:

The vision of the four beasts (1–8)

The vision of God's throne of government and judgment (9–14)

The interpretation of those visions (15–28)

The vision of the four beasts (1–8)

1. **In the first year of Belshazzar** – This prophecy is written in Chaldee, to be a monument to him, of the reverence his father and grandfather showed towards God, who had done such mighty works for them. **Then he wrote** – These visions were recorded for the benefit of the church, to rectify their mistake: for they thought all things would succeed prosperously after they returned out of their captivity.

2. **The four winds** – Probably by the four winds of the great sea is signified commotions of contrary nations, striving together by wars, and producing these four beasts successively.

3. **Four great beasts** – That is, four great monarchies, great, in comparison of particular kingdoms; beasts for their tyrannical oppressions.

4. **The first** – This was the Chaldean, or Assyrian; whose seat was first at Babylon, afterwards at Nineveh, and then at Babylon again. **Eagle's wings** – They were swift, over-running many countries, and brought their monarchy to a prodigious height in a short time. **The wings were plucked** – Which was first done in stopping the career of their victories, and afterwards in casting them out of their kingdom. **A man's heart** – They lost their lion-like courage, and became faint and cowardly like other men.

5. **Another beast** – The Medes and Persians, a fierce, ravenous creature. **On one side** – The north side; for the Mede first arose and sent to Cyrus the Persian to come and assist him against the Assyrian. **Three ribs** – Several of the Babylonian subjects revolted, and all these made the three ribs.

6. **Like a leopard** – This leopard was the Grecian monarchy; a leopard is less than a lion, so was this monarchy at first, but yet durst fight with a lion; so did Alexander encounter Darius with an inferior force. A leopard also for his swiftness; therefore described with four wings on his back. **Four heads** – He was succeeded by

four of his chief commanders, who divided that empire into four parts.

7. A fourth beast – The Roman empire.

8. Another little horn – Probably either the Turk or the Romish antichrist.

The vision of God's throne of government and judgment (9–14)

9. The thrones – The kingdoms of this world were destroyed by God the king, and judge of all, called the Ancient of days, because of his eternal deity.

11. Destroyed – This cannot but be meant of the ruin and judgment of antichrist.

13. A son of man – That is, the Messiah, he came with the clouds of heaven, gloriously, swiftly and terribly. **And came** – This relates to his ascension, at which time, he received his royal investiture, for the protection of his church, and curbing of their enemies.

The interpretation of those visions (15–28)

16. Unto one – That is, to an angel, that ministered. **The truth** – The true meaning of this vision.

18. But the saints – Jesus Christ being their king, they shall reign with him, and possess the kingdom for ever.

24. And another – This seems to mean the Romish antichrist.

25. Until a time and times – The numbers of Daniel and John seem to agree. Daniel was certainly prophetical in these things, and his prophecy reacheth to the end of times, even of antichrist's reign.

28. Of the matter – Of the vision, and the angel's interpretation.

Chapter 8

This and the following chapters are not written in Chaldee, but in Hebrew, for the benefit of the Jews. Here is:

The vision of the ram, and the he-goat, and the little horn (1–14)

The interpretation of it (15–27)

The vision of the ram, and the he-goat, and the little horn (1–14)

1. After that – In the other vision he speaks of all the four monarchies; here only of the three first; this vision being a comment upon the first.

2. The river of Ulai – Which ran round the city.

3. Two horns – The kingdom of Media and Persia. **And the higher** – The kingdom of Persia which rose last, in Cyrus, became more eminent than that of the Medes.

4. West-ward – Toward Babylon, Syria,

Cappadocia, Asia the less, and Greece, all westward from Media and Persia. **North-ward** – Against the Armenians, Iberians, Lydians, Colchi Caspians. **South-ward** – Against Ethiopia, Arabia, Egypt.

5. An he-goat – The Grecian empire. **The whole earth** – The whole Persian empire. **Touched not the ground** – Went with incredible swiftness. **A horn** – This was Alexander the great.

6. The ram – The king of Media and Persia.

8. Was broken – When Alexander was greatest, then was he broken, and that to pieces, for he, his mother, son, brother, and all his kindred were destroyed. **The four winds:**
1. Antipater got Greece.
2. Asia was possessed by Antigonus.
3. Ptolemy got Egypt.
4. Seleucus had Babylon and Syria.
All these were variously situated; to the east, Babylon and Syria; to the south, Egypt; to the north, Asia the less; to the west, Greece.

9. A little horn – This little horn was Antiochus Epiphanes. **The south** – Egypt where he besieged and took many places. **The east** – In Syria, Babylon, Armenia. **The pleasant land** – Judea, so called because of the temple and people of God in it, and the fruitfulness of it.

10. The host of heaven – The church of God militant, who worship the God of heaven, who are citizens of heaven, whose names are written in heaven; and among these the priests, and champions, who were as stars shining above the rest; these he profaned and slew cruelly.

11. The prince – Not only against the highpriest, but against God himself. **Was cast down** – He took away the use of the temple as to the holy service and sacrifices.

12. By reason of transgression – Both the transgression of the priests, and of the people.

13. One saint – That is, one holy angel. **How long** – How long shall Antiochus continue his vexations against the people and prevent the worship of God? This is, the treading down of the sanctuary, and the host.

14. He – That angel. **Then** – Just so long it was, from the defection of the people, procured by Menelaus, the high-priest, to the cleansing of the sanctuary, and the re-establishment of religion among them.

The interpretation of it (15–27)

15. The meaning – A more clear discovery of those things. **The appearance of a man** – Probably Gabriel.

16. A man's voice – Of him before mentioned, namely, Christ.

17. He came near – That he might speak more familiarly to him, yet Daniel could not bear the glory of it. How much less can we bear the glory of God, and how graciously hath the

Lord dealt with us, to teach us by men, and not by angels? **O son of man** – He calls him son of man, to make him mind his frailty, and not to be lifted up with this great condescension of heaven. **At the time** – In God's appointed time, in the latter day, but not now in thy life-time.

18. Toward the ground – Being terrified with the splendour and grandeur both of the messenger and message. **Set me upright** – By one touch only. The power of spirits is incomparably greater than that of the strongest of men.

19. The indignation – God will raise up Antiochus to execute his wrath against the Jews for their sins, yet there shall be an end of that indignation.

23. In the latter time – When they were come to the height, and beginning to decline. **When the transgressors** – When the Jews were grown to an excess of wickedness, then God suffered Antiochus to persecute them. **Dark sentences** – Full of subtlety: such all histories declare Antiochus to be.

24. Not by his own power – Not by any heroic deeds, but by making use of the Jewish factions, through the divine commission to punish a backsliding nation; and by means of Eumenes and Attalus, by whose help he got up to this height. **Shall destroy** – He shall by force, craft, and cruelty, destroy many of God's people.

25. By peace – Under colour of kindness. **Against the prince of princes** – He fought against God, affronting God's laws, profaning God's worship, and temple, and setting up the image and worship of Jupiter there. **Without hand** – By a disease whereof he died, 1Macc 6:8.

26. Shut thou up – Lay it up in thy heart. **For many days** – Three hundred years after this; long after Daniel's days.

27. Was sick – Being overwhelmed by a sense of the calamity that should befall the people of God. **Did the king's business** – Having recovered strength, he minded his place, duty and trust, and concealed the whole, that they might not see it by his countenance.

Chapter 9

This is the clearest prophecy of the Messiah in all the Old Testament.

Daniel's prayer for the restoration of Israel (1–23)

The answer sent him by an angel (24–27)

Daniel's prayer for the restoration of Israel (1–23)

1. In the first year of Darius – That is, immediately after the overthrow of the kingdom of Babylon, which was the year of the Jews deliverance from captivity. **Of the Medes** – This Darius

was not Darius the Persian, under whom the temple was built, as some have asserted, to invalidate the credibility of this book; but Darius the Mede, who lived in the time of Daniel.

2. By books – By the sacred books.

12. Judged us – Whose duty it was to govern the people, and to judge their causes; wherein if there was a failure, it was a sin, and judgment upon the people, and upon the rulers and judges themselves also. **Upon Jerusalem** – A place privileged many ways above all others, and punished above all others.

14. The Lord watched – God's watching denotes the fit ways that he always takes to punish sinners.

17. For the Lord's sake – For the sake of the Messiah: to whom the title Lord is frequently given in the Old Testament.

21. About the time – The time of the evening sacrifice was a solemn and set time of devotion. Although the altar was in ruins, and there was no oblation offered upon it, yet the pious Jews were daily thoughtful of the time when it should have been offered, and hoped that their prayer would be set forth before God as incense, and the lifting up of their hands, as the evening sacrifice. This was peculiarly a type of that great sacrifice, which Christ was to offer: and it was in virtue of that sacrifice, that Daniel's prayer was accepted, when he prayed for the Lord's sake.

The answer sent him by an angel (24–27)

24. Seventy weeks – These weeks are weeks of days, and these days are so many years. **To finish the transgression** – The angel discovers first the disease in three several words, which contain all sorts of sin, which the Messiah should free us from by his full redemption. He shews the cure of this disease in three words.

1. To finish transgression.
2. To make an end of sin.
3. To make reconciliation:

all which words are very expressive in the original, and signify to pardon, to blot out, to destroy. **To bring in everlasting righteousness** – To bring in justification by the free grace of God in Christ, and sanctification by his spirit: called everlasting, because Christ is eternal, and so are the acceptance and holiness purchased for us. Christ brings this in:

1. By his merit.
2. By his gospel declaring it.
3. By faith applying, and sealing it by the Holy Ghost.

To seal up – To abrogate the former dispensation of the law, and to ratify the gospel covenant. **To anoint** – This alludes to his name Messiah and Christ, both which signify anointed. Christ was anointed at his first conception, and personal union, Luke 1:35. In his baptism,

Matt 3:17, to his three offices by the holy Ghost:
1. King, Matt 2:2.
2. Prophet, Isa 61:1.
3. Priest, Psal 110:4.

25. From the going forth – From the publication of the edict, whether of Cyrus or Darius, to restore and to build it.

26. And after – After the seven and the sixty two that followed them. **Not for himself** – But for our sakes, and for our salvation. **And the people** – The Romans under the conduct of Titus. **Determined** – God hath decreed to destroy that place and people, by the miseries and desolations of war.

27. He shall confirm – Christ confirmed the new covenant:
1. By the testimony of angels, of John baptist, of the wise men, of the saints then living, of Moses and Elias.
2. By his preaching.
3. By signs and wonders.
4. By his holy life.
5. By his resurrection and ascension.
6. By his death and blood shedding.

Shall cause the sacrifice to cease – All the Jewish rites, and Levitical worship. By his death he abrogated, and put an end to this laborious service, for ever. **And that determined** – That spirit of slumber, which God has determined to pour on the desolate nation, until the time draws near, when all Israel shall be saved.

Chapter 10

This chapter and the two next make one entire vision and prophecy, given Daniel about two years after the former. This chapter is introductory: the next has the prophecy itself, and the twelfth chapter, the conclusion of it. In this we have

Daniel's solemn humiliation (1–3)

A glorious appearance of the Son of God (4–9)

The encouragement given him to expect a full discovery of future events (10–25)

Daniel's solemn humiliation (1–3)

2. Was mourning – Because he foresaw the many calamities that would befall the Jews for their sins, especially for destroying the Messiah, and rejecting his gospel.

A glorious appearance of the Son of God (4–9)

4. The first month – Nisan, which is March. Hiddekel – Or Tigris.

5. A certain man – Very probably Christ, who appeared to Daniel in royal and priestly robes, and in so great brightness and majesty.

The encouragement given him to expect a full discovery of future events (10–25)

12. He – Not Christ, but Gabriel.

13. Withstood me – God suffered the wicked counsels of Cambyses to take place awhile; but Daniel by his prayers, and the angel by his power, overcame him at last: and this very thing laid a foundation of the ruin of the Persian monarchies. **Michael** – Michael here is commonly supposed to mean Christ. **I remained** – To counter-work their designs against the people of God.

15. I set my face – I prostrated myself upon the earth. **And I became dumb** – Through astonishment.

16. One like the sons of men – This likewise seems to have been Gabriel. **I have retained no strength** – Although he appeared to him, and spake to him as a man, yet Daniel could not bear his presence, without some dread.

20. To fight – To oppose his mischievous designs.

21. Michael – Christ alone is the protector of his church, when all the princes of the earth desert or oppose it.

Chapter 11

A prediction of the setting up of the Grecian monarchy (1–4)

Of the affairs of Egypt and Syria (5–20)

The rise and success of Antiochus Epiphanes (21–29)

The mischief he would do to the Jews (30–43)

His fall (44, 45)

A prediction of the setting up of the Grecian monarchy (1–4)

2. He – Xerxes was more potent than all the other three, because his father Darius had gathered an incredible mass for him, which he himself increased for six years together, before he made his expedition against Greece. There were more kings of Persia besides those four, but they had no concern with the people of God.

3. A mighty king – Alexander the great.

4. When he shall stand up – When he is come to his highest point. **Nor according to his dominion** – They did not reign as kings at first, but only as captains; and as to the extent of their dominion, it was far less than Alexander's, yea, all four fell short of his. **Even for others** – Some lesser commanders shared several parts of the empire.

Of the affairs of Egypt and Syria (5–20)

5. The king of the south – This king was Ptolemy, the first king of Egypt after Alexander who is brought in, because he took Jerusalem by treachery; for the angel minds only those persons and things which related to the Jews. **One of his princes** – Seleucus Nicanor, who overcame Demetrius, and added Asia to his empire.

6. They – The successors of those first kings of Egypt and Syria. **Make an agreement** – Bernice shall come from Egypt and marry with Antiochus Theus, who was the son of Antiochus Soter, and nephew to Seleucus Nicanor; for her father brought her to Pelusium with an infinite sum of gold and silver for her dowry. **She shall not retain** – She continued not in favour and authority. **Nor his arm** – His power.

7. Shall one stand up – Of Bernice shall come Ptolemaeus Euergetes, who shall revenge the wrong done to his sister. **Shall enter into the fortress** – For he invaded Syria, and took many strong-holds.

8. He shall continue more years – He continued forty-six years.

9. Return – So he did with a booty of forty thousand talents of silver.

10. But his sons – He means the sons of the king of the north, shall be incensed with the deeds of Ptolemaeus Euergetes, and his son Ptolemaeus Philopator. **One shall come** – Antiochus the great, shall pass through Syria and recover what the king of Egypt took from his father. **Even to his fortress** – To Raphia, which was a strong fortress at the entrance of Egypt.

11. His hand – Into the hand of Ptolemy.

12. His heart shall be lifted up – He might have recovered all, but he grew proud of his victory, and returned again to his luxury.

16. But he – Antiochus, that comes against Ptolemy. **The glorious land** – Judea. Antiochus held all Judea, and with the provision and product of it, maintained his army.

17. He shall also set his face – He shall use all the force he can to master Egypt, and engross it to himself. **Upright ones** – Many of the religious Jews joined with him: the rest of his army was a profane rabble of rude Heathens. **He shall give** – Antiochus shall give Cleopatra his daughter to young Ptolemy, called the daughter of women, for her beauty. **Corrupting her** – Persuading her to betray her husband: but she stuck to her husband's interest, and not her father's.

18. The isles – The isles and sea-coasts of the Mediterranean and Aegean sea. **But a prince** – The Roman ambassador Scipio beat Antiochus at his own weapons of power and policy, and turned the reproach upon his own head.

19. Then – Then he turned his face homeward, yet was he not in safety, but was quickly after killed.

20. A raiser of taxes – Seleucus Philopator, who peeled his subjects, and spared not to rob the temple. **Within few days** – For he lived not out the third part of his father's reign. **Not in battle** – Not by open force, but by poison.

The rise and success of Antiochus Epiphanes (21–29)

21. A vile person – Antiochus, called Epiphanes by his flatterers, but the people of God accounted him infamous, base, and treacherous. **They** – Neither peers nor people, nor was he the heir, but his nephew; but he crept in by flatteries.

22. Overflown – The Egyptian force near Pelusium, where they fell by the power of Antiochus, with a great slaughter, near the river Nile. **The prince** – The high-priest with his place and honour, for he put out Onias, and set up in his stead, Jason his brother.

23. After the league – For he made a league with Egypt, and came with a few, and took the passes, and put all in subjection to him.

24. He shall enter peaceably – He shall come in upon the Egyptians under pretence of peace, in a plentiful and delicious country, and among a mass of treasures which the kings successively had heaped up; the greatest part of which Antiochus distributed among his confidants, whereby he obliged them the faster to him. He did herein what his fathers had not done; for kings of Syria before him, could never attain to this success over Egypt. **Against the strong-holds** – Having succeeded thus far, he shall proceed to the places of greatest strength in that kingdom. **For a time** – That is until God put a stop to his career, for the Egyptians found means to deliver themselves from his yoke.

25. But he shall not stand – He might have prospered, if he had not been betrayed by Eulaius, Benaeus, and the rest of his nobles, corrupted by Antiochus.

26. Yea – His most familiar friends and confidants; for he shall be overthrown with a great slaughter, as when the Nile overflows the country.

27. At one table – They shall meet under pretence of peace. **But it shall not prosper** – For neither shall Antiochus gain Egypt by all his artifice, nor Ptolemy, Syria. **At the time appointed** – By the Lord, whose purpose and counsel shall stand.

28. Then shall he return – Antiochus shall depart with his booty gotten in Egypt. **Against the holy covenant** – Against the law of God, with the people that worshipped God according to his will.

29. Toward the south – Egypt, to fight against Ptolemy. **But** – This shall not be so prosperous as the two former expeditions, but shall fail both of his victory and booty.

The mischief he would do to the Jews (30–43)

30. The ships of Chittim – The Romans out of Italy, and the Archipelago. This made his heart boil with rancour, which he spit out against the Jews; especially being solicited to it by Jason first, and Menelaus after, who were apostates, and betrayers of their brethren.

31. And arms – Not only of his own army, but many Jews. **The sanctuary** – Even the holy of holies. **The abomination** – The statue of Jupiter placed in the temple.

36. The king – Antiochus was an eminent type of antichrist; to whom many things that follow may be applied by way of accommodation: although they principally refer to Antiochus, and had their primary accomplishment in him. **For that that is determined** – That which God hath decreed to be done by him shall be done; and that which God hath purposed to be done upon him.

38. But in his estate – In the room of his father's god. **The God of forces** – This seems to be Jupiter Olympius, never introduced among the Syrians, until Antiochus did it.

39. With a strange god – Using all art and authority to propagate his worship.

41. The children of Ammon – He will not hurt them; because they helped him against the Jews.

43. At his steps – He had them at his foot, at his beck.

His fall (44, 45)

45. None shall help him – God shall cut him off in the midst of his days. And when he destroys, who can help?

Chapter 12

A promise of deliverance, and of a joyful resurrection (1–4)

A conference concerning the time of these events (5–7)

An answer to Daniel's enquiry (8–13)

A promise of deliverance, and of a joyful resurrection (1–4)

1. For the children – The meaning seems to be, as after the death of Antiochus the Jews had some deliverance, so there will be yet a greater deliverance to the people of God, when Michael your prince, the Messiah shall appear for your salvation. **A time of trouble** – A the siege of Jerusalem, before the final judgment. The phrase at that time, probably includes all the time of Christ, from his first, to his last coming.

4. Seal the book – The book was command to be sealed, because it would be long before the words would be fulfilled, whereas those that were shortly to be fulfilled, were forbidden to be sealed. **Shall run** – Shall diligently search these prophecies; and they shall know the signs of the times, and wait upon God in the way of his judgments: he means chiefly in gospel-times.

A conference concerning the time of these events (5–7)

5. Other two – Two angels waiting on Christ.

6. To the man – To Christ, who seemed to stand in the air above the waters, or upon them.

7. He held up his right hand – He held up both hands to heaven, for the more sure and solemn confirmation of it; and to denote the unchangeableness of God's decrees both for good to the church, and for evil to her enemies. **By him** – By God the father, and by himself that liveth for ever, to shew the eternal God only knew that decreed it, and would bring it to pass. **And an half** – That is, a year, two years and half a year. We meet with this in the revelation, under the title, some times of three days and an half, put for three years and an half, sometimes, forty two months, sometimes, twelve hundred and sixty days. **Shall be finished** – Which reaches to the calling of the Jews upon the destruction of antichrist.

An answer to Daniel's enquiry (8–13)

8. What shall be the end – What is the meaning of all this?

9. And sealed – They shall not be clearly understood, until the event make them good.

10. And tried – The afflictions of the church are to prepare them, by taking away their filth, for the bridegroom, as gold and silver are tried and refined.

13. But go thou – I have revealed to thee these things, that thou and thy people, might be prepared for sufferings, and yet not without hope of a glorious deliverance. **For thou shalt rest** – In which hope thou shalt die, and rest from trouble, until the resurrection of the just. It ought to be the great concern of every one of us, to secure a happy lot in the end of the days, and then we may well be content with our present lot, welcoming the will of God.

HOSEA

A.R. Faussett

Introduction

The first of the twelve minor prophets in the order of the canon (called 'minor,' not as less in point of inspired authority, but simply in point of size). The twelve are first mentioned by Jesus, the son of Sirach (Ecclesiasticus 49:10). St. Stephen, in Ac 7:42 (in referring to Am 5:27), quotes them as forming one collective body of writings, 'the book of the prophets.' The prophets were not uninterruptedly engaged in prophesying. Considerable intervals elapsed, though their office as divinely commissioned public teachers was never wholly laid aside. The Book of Hosea which we have constitutes only that portion of his public teachings which the Holy Spirit saw fit to preserve for the benefit of the Church. His style is abrupt, sententious, and unrounded; the connecting particles are few; there are changes of person, and anomalies of gender, number, and construction. His name means *Salvation*.

Hosea (Ho 11:1) is quoted in Mt 2:15; also Ho 6:6 in Mt 9:13 12:7; compare Ro 9:25,26, quoting Ho 1:10 2:1,23; 1Co 15:55, quoting Ho 13:14; 1Pe 2:10, quoting Ho 1:9,10 2:23. Messianic references are not frequent; but the predictions of the future conversion of Israel to the Lord their God, and David their king, and of the fulfilment of the promise to Abraham that his spiritual seed should be as the sand of the sea (Ho 1:10 3:5), clearly refer to the New Testament dispensation.

The first and third chapters are in prose, the rest of the book is rhythmical.

Chapter 1

Ho 1:1-11. Inscription.

Spiritual whoredom of Israel set forth by symbolical acts; Gomer taken to wife at God's command: Jezreel, Lo-ruhamah, and Lo-Ammi, the children. Yet a promise of Judah and Israel's restoration.

1. Jeroboam – the second; who died in the fifteenth year of Uzziah's forty-one years' reign. From his time forth *all* Israel's kings worshipped false gods: Zachariah (2Ki 15:9), Menahem (2Ki 15:18), Pekahiah (2Ki 15:24), Pekah (2Ki 15:28), Hoshea (2Ki 17:2). As Israel was most flourishing externally under Jeroboam II, who recovered the possessions seized on by

Syria, Hosea's prophecy of its downfall at that time was the more striking as it could not have been foreseen by mere human sagacity. Jonah the prophet had promised success to Jeroboam II from God, not for the king's merit, but from God's mercy to Israel; so the coast of Israel was restored by Jeroboam II from the entering of Hamath to the sea of the plain (2Ki 14:23–27).

2. beginning – not of the prophet's predictions generally, but of those spoken by *Hosea*.

take ... wife of whoredoms – not externally acted, but internally and in vision, as a pictorial illustration of Israel's unfaithfulness [HENG-STENBERG]. Compare Eze 16:8,15. Besides the loathsomeness of such a marriage, if an external act, it would require years for the birth of three children, which would weaken the symbol (compare Eze 4:4). HENDERSON objects that there is no hint of the transaction being fictitious: Gomer fell into lewdness *after* her union with Hosea, not before; for thus only she was a fit symbol of Israel, who lapsed into spiritual whoredom *after* the marriage contract with God on Sinai, and made even before at the call of the patriarchs of Israel. Gomer is called 'a wife of whoredoms,' anticipatively.

children of whoredoms – The kingdom collectively is viewed as a *mother;* the individual subjects of it are spoken of as her *children.* 'Take' being applied to both implies that they refer to the same thing viewed under different aspects. The 'children' were not the prophet's own, but born of adultery, and presented to him as his [KITTO, *Biblical Cyclopædia*]. Rather, 'children of whoredoms' means that the children, like their mother, fell into spiritual fornication. Compare 'bare *him* a son' (see Ho 2:4,5). Being children of a spiritual whore, they naturally fell into her whorish ways.

3. Gomer ... daughter of Diblaim – symbolical names; literally, 'completion, daughter of grape cakes'; the dual expressing the double layers in which these dainties were baked. So, *one completely given up to sensuality.* MAURER explains 'Gomer' as literally, 'a burning coal.' Compare Pr 6:27,29, as to an adulteress; Job 31:9,12.

4. Jezreel – that is, 'God will scatter' (compare Zec 10:9). It was the royal city of Ahab and his successors, in the tribe of Issachar. Here Jehu exercised his greatest cruelties (2Ki 9:16,25,33 10:11,14,17). There is in the name an allusion to 'Israel' by a play of letters and sounds.

5. bow – the prowess (Jer 49:35; compare Ge 49:24).

valley of Jezreel – afterwards called Esdraelon, extending ten miles in breadth, and in length from Jordan to the Mediterranean near Mount Carmel, the great battlefield of Palestine (Jud 6:33 1Sa 29:1).

6. Lo-ruhamah – that is, 'not an object of mercy or gracious favour.'

take ... away – Israel, as a kingdom, was never restored from Assyria, as Judah was from Babylon after seventy years. MAURER translates according to the primary meaning, 'No more will I have mercy on the house of Israel, so as to *pardon* them.'

7. *Judah* is only incidentally mentioned to form a contrast to *Israel.*

by the Lord their God – more emphatic than 'by Myself'; by that Jehovah whom they worship as *their* God, whereas ye despise Him.

not ... by bow – on which ye Israelites rely (Ho 1:5, 'the bow of Israel'); Jeroboam II was famous as a warrior (2Ki 14:25). Yet it was not by their warlike power Jehovah would save

Judah (1Sa 17:47 Ps 20:7). The deliverance of Jerusalem from Sennacherib (2Ki 19:35), and the restoration from Babylon, are herein predicted.

8. weaned – said to complete the symbolical picture, not having any special signification as to Israel [HENDERSON]. Israel was bereft of all the privileges which were as needful to them as milk is to infants (compare Ps 131:2 1Pe 2:2) [VATABLUS]. Israel was *not suddenly,* but *gradually* cast off; God bore with them with long-suffering, until they were incurable [CALVIN]. But as it is not God, but *Gomer* who weans Lo-ruhamah, the weaning may imply the lust of Gomer, who was hardly weaned when she is again pregnant [MANGER].

9. Lo-Ammi – once 'My people,' but henceforth *not* so (Eze 16:8). The intervals between the marriage and the successive births of the three children, imply that three successive generations are intended. Jezreel, the first child, represents the dynasty of Jeroboam I and his successors, ending with Jehu's shedding the blood of Jeroboam's line in Jezreel; it was there that Jezebel was slain, in vengeance for Naboth's blood shed in the same Jezreel (1Ki 16:1 2Ki 9:21,30). The scenes of Jezreel were to be enacted over again on Jehu's degenerate race. At Jezreel Assyria routed Israel [JEROME]. The child's name associates past sins, intermediate punishments, and final overthrow. Lo-ruhamah ('not pitied'), the second child, is a *daughter,* representing the effeminate period which followed the overthrow of the first dynasty, when Israel was at once abject and impious. Lo-Ammi ('not my people'), the third child, a *son,* represents the vigorous dynasty (2Ki 14:25) of Jeroboam II; but, as prosperity did not bring with it revived piety, they were still *not God's people.*

10. Literally fulfilled *in part* at the return from Babylon, in which many Israelites joined with Judah. Spiritually, the believing seed of Jacob or Israel, Gentiles as well as Jews, numerous 'as the sand' (Ge 32:12); the Gentiles, once not God's people, becoming His 'sons' (Joh 1:12 Ro 9:25,26 1Pe 2:10 1Jo 3:1). To be fulfilled in its literal *fulness* hereafter in Israel's restoration (Ro 11:26).

the living God – opposed to their *dead* idols.

11. Judah ... Israel ... together – (Isa 11:12,13 Jer 3:18 Eze 34:23 37:16–24).

one head – Zerubbabel typically; Christ antitypically, under whom alone Israel and Judah are joined, the 'Head' of the Church (Eph 1:22 5:23), and of the hereafter united kingdom of Judah and Israel (Jer 34:5,6 Eze 34:23). Though 'appointed' by the Father (Ps 2:6), Christ is in another sense 'appointed' as their Head by His people, when they accept and embrace Him as such.

out of the land – of the Gentiles among whom they sojourn.

the day of Jezreel – 'The day of one' is the time of God's special visitation of him, either in wrath or in mercy. Here 'Jezreel' is in a different sense from that in Ho 1:4, 'God will sow,' not 'God will scatter'; they shall be *the seed of God*, planted by God again in their own land (Jer 24:6 31:28 32:41 Am 9:15).

Chapter 2

Ho 2:1–23. Application of the symbols in the first chapter.

Israel's spiritual fornication, and her threatened punishment: yet a promise of God's restored favour, when chastisements have produced their designed effect.

1. Say … unto … brethren, Ammi. – that is, When the prediction (Ho 1:11) shall be accomplished, then ye will call one another, as *brothers* and *sisters* in the family of God, Ammi and Ruhamah.

2. Plead – expostulate.

mother – that is the nation *collectively.* The address is to 'her children,' that is, to the *individual* citizens of the state (compare Isa 50:1).

for she is not my wife – She has deprived herself of her high privilege by spiritual adultery.

out of her sight – rather, 'from her face.' Her very countenance unblushingly betrayed her lust, as did also her exposed 'breasts.'

3. set her as in the day … born – (Eze 16:4 23:25,26,28,29). The day of her political 'birth' was when God delivered her from the bondage of Egypt, and set up the theocracy.

make her as a wilderness – (Jer 6:8 Zep 2:13). Translate, 'make her as the wilderness,' namely, that in which she passed forty years on her way to her goodly possession of Canaan. With this agrees the mention of 'thirst' (compare Jer 2:6).

4. her children – Not even her *individual* members shall escape the doom of the nation collectively, for they are individually guilty.

5. I will go after – The *Hebrew* expresses a *settled determination.*

lovers – the idols which Israel fancied to be the givers of all their goods, whereas God gave all these goods (Ho 2:8-13; compare Jer 44:17-19).

bread and … water – the *necessaries* of life in food.

wool … flax – clothing.

oil … drink – perfumed unguents and palatable drinks: the *luxuries* of Hebrew life.

6, 7. thorns … wall – (Job 19:8 La 3:7,9). The hindrances which the captivity interposed between Israel and her idols. As she attributes all her temporal blessings to idols, I will reduce her to straits in which, when she in vain has sought help from false gods, she will at last seek Me as

her only God and Husband, as at the first (Isa 54:5 Jer 3:14 Eze 16:8).

then – before Israel's apostasy, under Jeroboam. The way of duty is hedged *about* with thorns; it is the way of sin that is hedged *up* with thorns. Crosses in an evil course are God's hedges to turn us from it. Restraining grace and restraining providences (even sicknesses and trials) are great blessings when they stop us in a course of sin. Compare Lu 15:14-18, 'I will arise, and go to my father.' So here, 'I will go, and return,' etc; crosses in the both cases being sanctified to produce this effect.

8. she did not know that I – not the idols, as she thought: the 'lovers' alluded to in Ho 2:5.

which they prepared for Baal – that is, of which they made images of Baal, or at least the plate covering of them (Ho 8:4). Baal was the Phoenician sun-god: answering to the female Astarte, the moon-goddess.

9. my corn … my wool … my flax – in contrast to '*my* bread … *my* wool … *my* flax,' (Ho 2:5). Compare also Ho 2:21-23, on God as the great First Cause giving these through secondary instruments in nature. 'Return, and take away,' is equivalent to, 'I will take back again,' namely, by sending storms, locusts, Assyrian enemies. 'Therefore,' that is, because she did not acknowledge Me as the Giver.

in the time thereof – in the harvest-time.

10. lewdness – rather, 'the shame of her nakedness'; laying aside the figure, 'I will expose her in *her state, bereft of every necessary,* before her lovers,' that is, the idols (personified, as if they could see), who, nevertheless, can give her no help. 'Discover' is appropriate to stripping off the self-flatteries of her hypocrisy.

11. her feast days – of Jeroboam's appointment, distinct from the Mosaic (1Ki 12:32). However, most of the Mosaic feasts, 'new-moons' and 'Sabbaths' to Jehovah, remained, but to degenerate Israel worship was a weariness; they cared only for the carnal indulgence on them (Am 8:5).

12. my rewards – my hire as a harlot (Isa 23:17,18).

lovers – idols.

destroy … vines … make … forest – (Isa 5:6 7:23,24). Fulfilled in the overthrow of Israel by Assyria (Ho 9:4,5).

13. days of Baalim – the days consecrated to the Baals, or various images of Baal in different cities, whence the names *Baal-gad, Baal-hermon.*

decked herself with … earrings – rather, 'nose-rings' (Isa 3:21 Eze 16:12, *Margin*), with which harlots decked themselves to attract admirers: answering to the ornaments in which the Israelites decked themselves on the idols' feasts.

forgat me – worse than the nations which had never known God. Israel *wilfully apostatized* from Jehovah, whom she had known.

14. Therefore – rather, 'Nevertheless' [HENDERSON]. *English Version* gives a more lovely idea of God. That which would provoke all others to unappeasable wrath, Israel's perversity and consequent punishment, is made a reason why God should at last have mercy on her. As the 'therefore' (Ho 2:9) expresses Israel's punishment as the *consequence* of Israel's guilt, so 'therefore' here, as in Ho 2:6, expresses, that when that punishment has effected its designed end, the hedging up her way with thorns so that she returns to God, her first love, the *consequence* in God's wondrous grace is, He 'speaks comfortably' (literally, 'speaks to her heart'; compare Jud 19:8 Ru 2:13). So obstinate is she that God has to 'allure her,' that is, so to temper judgment with unlooked-for grace as to *win* her to His ways. For this purpose it was necessary to 'bring her into the wilderness' (that is, into temporal want and trials) first, to make her sin hateful to her by its bitter fruits, and God's subsequent grace the more precious to her by the contrast of the 'wilderness.' JEROME makes the 'bringing into the wilderness' to be rather a *deliverance from her enemies,* just as ancient Israel was brought into the wilderness from the bondage of Egypt; to this the phrase here alludes (compare Ho 2:15). The wilderness sojourn, however, is not literal, but moral: while still in the land of their enemies *locally,* by the discipline of the trial rendering the word of God sweet to them, they are to be brought *morally* into the wilderness state, that is, into a state of preparedness for returning to their temporal and spiritual privileges in their own land; just as the literal wilderness prepared their fathers for Canaan: thus the bringing of them into the *wilderness state is virtually* a deliverance from their enemies.

15. from thence – returning from the wilderness. God gives Israel a fresh grant of Canaan, which she had forfeited; so of her vineyards. (Ho 2:9,12).

Achor – that is 'trouble.' As formerly Israel, after their tedious journey through the wilderness, met with the *trouble* resulting from Achan's crime in this valley, on the very threshold of Canaan, and yet that *trouble* was presently turned into *joy* at the great victory at Ai, which threw all Canaan into their hands (Jos 7,8); so the very trouble of Israel's wilderness state will be the 'door of hope' opening to better days. The valley of Achor, near Jericho, was specially fruitful (Isa 65:10); so 'trouble' and 'hope' are rightly blended in connection with it.

sing ... as ... when she came ... out of ... Egypt – It shall be a second exodus song, such as Israel sang after the deliverance at the Red Sea (Ex 15:1-21; compare Isa 11:15,16); and 'the song of Moses' (Re 15:2,3) sung by those who through the Lamb overcome the beast, and so

stand on the sea of glass mingled with fire, emblems of fiery trial, such as that of Israel at the Red Sea.

16. Ishi ... no more Baali – 'my *Husband* ... no more my *Lord.' Affection* is the prominent idea in 'Husband'; *rule,* in 'Lord.' The chief reason for the substitution of *Husband* for *Lord* appears in Ho 2:17; namely, *Baali,* the *Hebrew* for *my Lord,* had been perverted to express the images of Baal, whose name ought not to be taken on their lips (Ex 23:13 Zec 13:2).

17. Baalim – *plural,* expressing the various images of Baal, which, according to the places of their erection, received various names, Baal-gad, Baal-ammon.

18. for them – for their benefit.

covenant ... with the beasts – not to hurt them (Job 5:23). They shall fulfil the original law of their creation by becoming subject to man, when man fulfils the law of his being by being subject to God. To be realized fully in millennial times (Isa 11:6-9).

break the bow ... out of the earth – rather, 'out of the *land*'; that is, I will break *and remove* war out of the earth (Ps 46:9); and 'out of the *land*' of Israel first (Isa 2:4 Eze 39:9,10 Zec 9:9,10).

lie down – A reclining posture is the usual one with Orientals when not in action.

safely – (Jer 23:6).

19, 20. 'Betroth' is *thrice* repeated, implying the intense love of God to His people; and perhaps, also, *the three Persons* of the *Triune God,* severally engaging to make good the betrothal. The marriage covenant will be as it were renewed from the beginning, on a different footing; not for a time only, as before, through the apostasy of the people, but 'forever' through the grace of God writing the law on their hearts by the Spirit of Messiah (Jer 31:31-37).

righteousness ... judgment – in rectitude and truth.

loving-kindness. – Hereby God assures Israel, who might doubt the possibility of their restoration to His favour; low, sunk, and unworthy as thou art. I will restore thee from a regard to My own 'loving-kindness,' not thy merits.

20. faithfulness – to My new covenant of grace with thee (1Th 5:24 Heb 10:23).

21. in that day – of grace to Israel.

heavens ... hear the earth – personification. However many be the intermediate instruments, God is the Great First Cause of all nature's phenomena. God had threatened (Ho 2:9) He would *take back His corn, His wine.* Here, on the contrary, God promises to *hearken to the skies,* as it were, supplicating Him to fill them with rain to pour on the earth; and that the skies again would hearken to the earth begging for a supply of the rain it requires; and again, that the earth would hearken to the corn, wine, and oil, begging it to bring them forth; and these again would hear Jezreel, that is, would fulfil Israel's prayers for a supply of them. Israel is now no longer 'Jezreel' in the sense, 'God will Scatter' (Ho 1:4), but in the sense, 'God will Plant' (Ho 1:11).

23. I will sow her – referring to the meaning of *Jezreel* (Ho 2:22).

Chapter 3

Ho 3:1–5. Israel's condition in their present dispersion, subsequent to their return from Babylon, symbolized.

The prophet is to take back his wife, though unfaithful, as foretold in Ho 1:2. He purchases her from her paramour, stipulating she should wait for a long period before she should be restored to her conjugal rights. So Israel is to live for a long period without her ancient rites of religion, and yet be free from idolatry; then at last she shall acknowledge Messiah, and know Jehovah's goodness restored to her.

1. Go yet – 'Go *again*,' referring to Ho 1:2 [Henderson].

a woman – purposely indefinite, for *thy wife*, to express the *separation* in which Hosea had lived from Gomer for her unfaithfulness.

beloved of her friend – used for 'her *husband*,' on account of the estrangement between them. She was still beloved of her husband, though an adulteress; just as God still loved Israel, though idolatrous (Jer 3:20). Hosea is told, not as in Ho 1:2, '*take a wife*,' but '*love*' her, that is, renew thy conjugal kindness to her.

who look to other gods – that is, have done so heretofore, but henceforth (from the return from Babylon) shall do so no more (Ho 3:4).
flagons of wine – rather, pressed cakes of dried grapes, such as were offered to idols (Jer 7:18) [Maurer].

2. I bought her – The price paid is too small to be a probable dowry wherewith to buy *a wife* from her parents; but it is just half the price of a female *slave*, in money, the rest of the price being made up in grain (Ex 21:32). Hosea pays this for the redemption of his wife, who has become the *slave of her paramour*. The price being *half grain* was because the latter was the allowance of food for the slave, and of the coarsest kind, not *wheat*, but *barley*. Israel, as *committing sin*, was the *slave of sin* (Joh 8:34 Ro 6:16-20 2Pe 2:19). The low price expresses Israel's *worthlessness*.

3. abide for me – separate from intercourse with any other man, and *remaining* for me who have redeemed thee (compare De 21:13).

so will I also be for thee – *remain for thee*, not taking any other consort. As Israel should long *remain* without serving other gods, yet separate

from Jehovah; so Jehovah on His part, in this long period of estrangement, would form no marriage covenant with any other people (compare Ho 3:4). He would not *immediately* receive her to marriage privileges, but would test her repentance and discipline her by the long probation; still the marriage covenant would hold good, she was to be kept separated for but a time, not divorced (Isa 50:1); in God's good time she shall be restored.

4. The long period here foretold was to be one in which Israel should have no civil polity, king, or prince, no sacrifice to Jehovah, and yet no idol, or false god, no ephod, or teraphim. Exactly describing their state for the last nineteen centuries, separate from idols, yet without any legal sacrifice to Jehovah, whom they profess to worship, and without being acknowledged by Him as His Church. So Kimchi, a Jew, explains it. The ephod was worn by the high priest above the tunic and robe. It consisted of two finely wrought pieces which hung down, the one in front over the breast, the other on the back, to the middle of the thigh; joined on the shoulders by golden clasps set in onyx stones with the names of the twelve tribes, and fastened round the waist by a girdle (Ex 28:6-12). The *common* ephod worn by the lower priests, Levites, and any person performing sacred rites, was of linen (2Sa 6:14 1Ch 15:27). In the breast were the Urim and Thummim by which God gave responses to the Hebrews. The latter was one of the five things which the second temple lacked, and which the first had. It, as representing the divinely constituted priesthood, is opposed to the idolatrous 'teraphim,' as 'sacrifice' (to Jehovah) is to 'an (idolatrous) image.' 'Abide' answers to 'thou shalt *abide* for me' (Ho 3:3). *Abide* in solitary isolation, as a separated wife. The teraphim were tutelary household gods, in the shape of human busts, cut off at the waist (as the root of the *Hebrew* word implies) [Maurer], (Ge 31:19,30–35). They were supposed to give responses to consulters (2Ki 23:24 Eze 21:21, *Margin*; Zec 10:2). Saul's daughter, Michal, putting one in a bed, as if it were David, proves the shape to have been that of a man.

5. Afterward – after the long period ('many days,' Ho 3:4) has elapsed.

return – from their idols to 'their God,' from whom they had wandered.

David their king – Israel had forsaken the worship of Jehovah at the same time that they forsook their allegiance to David's line. Their repentance towards God is therefore to be accompanied by their return to the latter. So Judah and Israel shall be one, and under 'one head,' as is also foretold (Ho 1:11). That representative and antitype of David is Messiah. 'David' means 'the beloved.' Compare as to

Messiah, Mt 3:17 Eph 1:6. Messiah is called David (Isa 55:3,4 Jer 30:9 Eze 34:23,24 37:24,25).

fear the Lord and his goodness – that is, tremblingly flee to the Lord, to escape from the wrath to come; and to His goodness, as manifested in Messiah, which attracts them to Him (Jer 31:12). The 'fear' is not that which 'hath torment' (1Jo 4:18), but *reverence* inspired by His goodness realized in the soul (Ps 130:4).

the latter days – those of Messiah [KIMCHI].

Chapter 4

Ho 4:1–19. Henceforth the prophet speaks plainly and without symbol, in terse, sententious propositions.

In this chapter he reproves the people and priests for their sins in the interregnum which followed Jeroboam's death; hence there is no mention of the king or his family; and in Ho 4:2 bloodshed and other evils usual in a civil war are specified.

1. **Israel** – the ten tribes.

controversy – judicial ground of complaint (Isa 1:18 Jer 25:31 Mic 6:2).

no ... knowledge of God – exhibited in practice (Jer 22:16).

2. **they break out** – bursting through every restraint.

blood toucheth blood – literally, 'bloods.' One act of bloodshed follows another without any interval between (see 2Ki 15:8–16,25 Mic 7:2).

3. **land ... languish** – (Isa 19:8 24:4 Joe 1:10,12).

sea – including all bodies of water, as pools and even rivers. A general drought, the greatest calamity in the East, is threatened.

4. **let no man ... reprove** – Great as is the sin of Israel, it is hopeless to reprove them; for their presumptuous guilt is as great as that of one who refuses to obey the priest when giving judgment in the name of Jehovah, and who therefore is to be put to death (De 17:12). They rush on to their own destruction as wilfully as such a one.

thy people – the ten tribes of Israel; distinct from Judah (Ho 4:1).

5. **fall in the day** – in broad *daylight*, a time when an attack would not be expected.

in ... night – No time, night or day, shall be free from the slaughter of individuals of the people, as well as of the false prophets.

thy mother – the Israeli state, of which the citizens are the children (Ho 2:2).

6. **lack of knowledge** – 'of God' (Ho 4:1), that is, lack of piety. Their ignorance was wilful, as the epithet, '*My* people,' implies; they *ought* to have known, having the opportunity, as the

people of God. **thou** – O priest, so-called. Not regularly constituted, but still bearing the name, while confounding the worship of Jehovah and of the calves in Beth-el (1Ki 12:29,31).

I will ... forget thy children – Not only those who then were alive should be deprived of the priesthood, but their children who, in the ordinary course would have succeeded them, should be set aside.

7. **As they were increased** – in numbers and power. Compare Ho 4:6, 'thy children,' to which their 'increase' in *numbers* refers.

will I change their glory into shame – that is, I will strip them of all they now *glory* in (their numbers and power), and give them *shame* instead. A just retribution: as they changed their glory into shame, by idolatry (Ps 106:20 Jer 2:11 Ro 1:23 Php 3:19).

8. **eat ... sin of my people** – that is, the sin offerings (Le 6:26 10:17). The priests greedily devoured them.

set their heart on their iniquity – literally 'lift up the animal soul to lust after,' or strongly desire. Compare De 24:15, *Margin*; Ps 24:4 Jer 22:27. The priests set *their own* hearts on the iniquity *of the people*, instead of trying to suppress it. For the more the people sinned, the more sacrificial victims in atonement for sin the priests gained.

9. **like people, like priest** – They are one in guilt; therefore they shall be one in punishment (Isa 24:2).

reward them their doings – in homely phrase, 'pay them back in their own coin' (Pr 1:31).

10. **eat, and not have enough** – just retribution on those who 'eat up (greedily) the sin of My people' (Ho 4:8 Mic 6:14 Hag 1:6).

whoredom, and ... not increase – literally 'break forth'; used of *giving birth to children* (Ge 28:14, *Margin*; compare Ge 38:29). Not only their wives, but their concubines, shall be barren. To be childless was considered a great calamity among the Jews.

11. A moral truth applicable to all times. The special reference here is to the licentious orgies connected with the Syrian worship, which lured Israel away from the pure worship of God (Isa 28:1,7 Am 4:1).

take away the heart – that is, the understanding; make men blind to their own true good (Ec 7:7).

12. Instances of their understanding ('heart') being 'taken away.'

stocks – wooden idols (Jer 2:27 Hab 2:19).

staff – alluding to divination by rods . The diviner, says ROSENMULLER, threw a rod from him, which was stripped of its bark on one side, not on the other: if the bare side turned uppermost, it was a good omen; if the side with the bark, it was a bad omen. The Arabs used two rods, the one marked *God bids,* the other, *God forbids;* whichever came out first, in drawing them out of a case, gave the omen for, or against, an undertaking.

declareth – that is, is consulted to inform them of future events.

spirit of whoredoms – a general *disposition* on the part of all *towards idolatry* (Ho 5:4).

err – go astray from the true God.

from under their God – They have gone away from God *under* whom they were, as a wife is under the dominion of her husband.

13. upon … mountains – High places were selected by idolaters on which to sacrifice, because of their greater nearness to the heavenly hosts which they worshipped (De 12:2).

shadow … good – screening the lascivious worshippers from the heat of the sun.

daughters … commit whoredom … spouses … adultery – in the polluted worship of Astarte, the Phoenician goddess of love.

14. I will not punish … daughters – I will visit with the heaviest punishments 'not' the unchaste 'daughters and spouses,' but the fathers and husbands; for it is these who 'themselves' have set the bad example, so that as compared with the punishment of the latter, that of the former shall seem as nothing [MUNSTER].

separated with whores – withdrawn from the assembly of worshippers to some receptacle of impurity for carnal connection with *whores.*

sacrifice with harlots – They commit lewdness with *women* who *devote their persons* to be violated in honour of Astarte. Compare Nu 25:1–3; and the prohibition, De 23:18.

not understand – (Isa 44:18 45:20).

shall fall – shall be cast down.

15. Though *Israel's* ten tribes indulge in spiritual harlotry, at least thou, *Judah,* who hast the legal priesthood, and the temple rites, and Jerusalem, do not follow her bad example.

Gilgal – situated between Jordan and Jericho on the confines of Samaria; once a holy place to Jehovah (Jos 5:10–15 1Sa 10:8 15:21); afterwards desecrated by idol-worship (Ho 9:15 12–11 Am 4:4 5:5; compare Jud 3:19, *Margin*).

Beth-aven – that is, 'house of vanity' or idols: a name substituted in contempt for *Beth-el,* 'the house of God'; once sacred to Jehovah (Ge 28:17,19 35:7), but made by Jeroboam the seat of the worship of the calves (1Ki 12:28–33 13:1 Jer 48:13 Am 3:14 7:13). 'Go up' refers to the fact that Beth-el was on a hill (Jos 16:1).

nor swear, The Lord liveth – This formula of oath was appointed by God Himself (De 6:13 10:20 Jer 4:2). It is therefore here forbidden not absolutely, but in conjunction with idolatry and falsehood (Isa 48:1 Eze 20:39 Zep 1:5).

16. backsliding – Translate, 'Israel is refractory, as a refractory heifer,' namely, one that throws the yoke off her neck. Israel had

represented God under the form of 'calves' (1Ki 12:28); but it is she herself who is one.

lamb in a large place – not in a good sense, as in Isa 30:23. Here there is irony: lambs like a large pasture; but it is not so safe for them as a small one, duly fenced from wild beasts. God will 'feed' them, but it shall be with the 'rod' (Mic 7:14). It shall be no longer in the narrow territory of Israel, but 'in a large place,' namely, they shall be scattered in exile over the wide realm of Assyria, a prey to their foes; as lambs, which are timid, gregarious, and not solitary, are a prey when scattered asunder to wild beasts.

17. Ephraim – the ten tribes. Judah was at this time not so given to idolatry as afterwards.

joined to – closely and voluntarily; identifying themselves with them as a whoremonger becomes one flesh with the harlot (Nu 25:3 1Co 6:16,17).

idols – The *Hebrew* means also 'sorrows,' 'pains,' implying the pain which idolatry brings on its votaries.

let him alone – Leave him to himself. Let him reap the fruits of his own perverse choice; his case is desperate; say nothing to him (compare Jer 7:16). Here Ho 4:15 shows the address is to *Judah,* to avoid the contagion of Israel's bad example. He is bent on his own ruin; leave him to his fate, lest, instead of saving him, thou fall thyself (Isa 48:20 Jer 50:8 51:6,45 2Co 6:17).

18. Their drink is sour – metaphor for *utter degeneracy* of principle (Isa 1:22). Or, *unbridled licentiousness;* not mere ordinary sin, but as abandoned as drunkards who vomit and smell sour with wine potations [CALVIN].

her rulers – Israel's; literally, 'shields' (compare Ps 47:9).

with shame … love, Give ye – (Pr 30:15). No remedy could be effectual against their corruptions since the very rulers sold justice for gifts [CALVIN].

19. Israel shall be swept away from her land (Ho 4:16) suddenly and violently as if by 'the wings of the wind' (Ps 18:10 104:3 Jer 4:11,12).

ashamed – of their sacrifices – disappointed to their shame in their hope of help through their sacrifices to idols.

Chapter 5

Ho 5:1–15. God's judgments on the priests, people, and princes of Israel for their sins.

Judah, too, being guilty shall be punished; nor shall Assyria, whose aid they both sought, save them; judgments shall at last lead them to repentance.

1. the king – probably Pekah; the contemporary of Ahaz, king of Judah, under whom idolatry was first carried so far in Judah as to call for the judgment of the joint Syrian and Israelite invasion, as also that of Assyria.

judgment is towards you – that is, threatens you from God.

ye have been a snare on Mizpah ... net ... upon Tabor – As hunters spread their net and snares on the hills, *Mizpah* and *Tabor*, so ye have snared the people into idolatry and made them your prey by injustice. As Mizpah and Tabor mean a 'watch tower,' and a 'lofty place,' a fit scene for hunters, playing on the words, the prophet implies, in the lofty place in which I have set you, whereas ye ought to have been the *watchers* of the people, guarding them from evil, ye have been as *hunters entrapping* them into it [Jerome]. These two places are specified, Mizpah in the east and Tabor in the west, to include the *high places* throughout the *whole* kingdom, in which Israel's rulers set up idolatrous altars.

2. revolters – apostates.

profound – *deeply* rooted [Calvin] and sunk to the lowest depths, *excessive* in their idolatry (Ho 9:9 Isa 31:6) [Henderson]. From the antithesis (Ho 5:3), 'not hid from me,' I prefer explaining, *profoundly cunning* in their idolatry. Jeroboam thought it a *profound* piece of policy to set up golden calves to represent God in Dan and Beth-el, in order to prevent Israel's heart from turning again to David's line by going up to Jerusalem to worship. So Israel's subsequent idolatry was grounded by their leaders on various pleas of state expediency (compare Isa 29:15).

to ... slaughter – He does not say 'to *sacrifice*,' for their so-called sacrifices were *butcheries* rather than sacrifices; there was nothing sacred about them, being to idols instead of to the holy God.

3. Ephraim – the tribe so called, as distinguished from 'Israel' here, the other nine tribes. It was always foremost of the tribes of the northern kingdom. For four hundred years in early history, it, with Manasseh and Benjamin, its two dependent tribes, held the pre-eminence in the whole nation. Ephraim is here addressed as foremost in idolatry.

I how ... not hid from me – notwithstanding their supposed *profound* cunning (Ho 5:2 Re 2:2,9,13,19).

now – 'though I have been a rebuker of all them' (Ho 5:2) who *commit* such spiritual *whoredoms*, thou art *now* continuing in them.

4. They – Turning from a direct address to Ephraim, he uses the third person *plural* to characterize the people in general.

5. the pride of Israel – wherewith they reject the warnings of God's prophets (Ho 5:2), and prefer their idols to God (Ho 7:10 Jer 13:17).

testify to his face – openly *to his face* he shall be convicted of the pride which is so palpable in him. Or, '*in* his face,' as in Isa 3:9.

Judah ... shall fall with them – This prophecy is later than Ho 4:15, when Judah had not gone so far in idolatry; now her imitation of Israel's bad example provokes the threat of her being doomed to share in Israel's punishment.

6. with ... flocks – to propitiate Jehovah (Isa 1:11–15).

seek ... not find – because it is slavish fear that leads them to seek Him; and because it then shall be too late (Pr 1:28 Joh 7:34).

7. treacherously – as to the marriage covenant (Jer 3:20).

strange children – alluding to 'children of whoredoms' (Ho 1:2 2:4). 'Strange' or *foreign* implies that their idolatry was imported from abroad [Henderson]. Or rather, 'regarded by God as strangers, not His,' as being reared in idolatry. The case is desperate, when not only the existing, but also the rising, generation is reared in apostasy.

a month – *a very brief space of time* shall elapse, and then punishment shall overtake them (Zec 11:8). The allusion seems to be to money loans, which were *by the month*, not as with us by the year. You cannot put it off; the time of your destruction is immediately and suddenly coming on you; just as the debtor must meet the creditor's demand at the expiration of the month. The prediction is of the invasion of Tiglath-pileser, who carried away Reuben, Gad, Naphtali, and the half tribe of Manasseh.

portions – that is, possessions. Their resources and garrisons will not avail to save them. Henderson explains from Isa 57:6, 'portions' as *their idols;* the context favours this, 'the Lord' the true '*portion* of His people' (De 32:9), being in antithesis to 'their portions,' the idols.

8. The arrival of the enemy is announced in the form of an injunction to *blow an alarm.*

cornet ... trumpet – The 'cornet' was made of the curved horn of animals and was used by shepherds. The 'trumpet' was of brass or silver, straight, and used in wars and on solemn occasions. The *Hebrew* is *hatzotzerah,* the sound imitating the trumpet note (Ho 8:1 Nu 10:2 Jer 4:5 Joe 2:1).

Gibeah ... Ramah – both in Benjamin (Isa 10:29).

Beth-aven – in Benjamin; not as in Ho 4:15; *Beth-el,* but a town east of it (Jos 7:2). 'Cry aloud,' namely, to raise the alarm. 'Benjamin' is put for the whole southern kingdom of Judah (compare Ho 5:5), being the first part of it which would meet the foe advancing from the north. 'After thee, O Benjamin,' implies the position of Beth-aven, *behind* Benjamin, at the borders of Ephraim. When the foe is at Beth-aven, he is at Benjamin's rear, close upon thee, O Benjamin (Jud 5:14).

9, 10. Israel is referred to in Ho 5:9, Judah in Ho 5:10.

the day of rebuke – the day when I shall chastise him.

among the tribes of Israel have I made known – proving that the scene of Hosea's labour was among the ten tribes.

that which shall surely be – namely, the coming judgment here foretold. It is no longer a conditional decree, leaving a hope of pardon on repentance; it is absolute, for Ephraim is hopelessly impenitent.

10. remove the bound – (De 19:14 27:17 Job 24:2 Pr 22:28 23:10). Proverbial for the rash setting aside of the ancestral laws by which men are kept to their duty. Ahaz and his courtiers ('the princes of Judah'), setting aside the ancient ordinances of God, removed the borders of the bases and the layer and the sea and introduced an idolatrous altar from Damascus (2Ki 16:10–18); also he burnt his children in the valley of Hinnom, after the abominations of the heathen (2Ch 28:3).

11. broken in judgment – namely, the 'judgment' of God on him (Ho 5:1).

walked after the commandment – Jeroboam's, to worship the calves (2Ki 10:28–33). Compare Mic 6:16, 'the statutes of Omri,' namely, idolatrous statutes. We ought to obey God rather than men (Ac 5:29).

12. as a moth – consuming a garment (Job 13:28 Ps 39:11 Isa 50:9).

Judah … rottenness – Ephraim, or the ten tribes, are as a garment eaten by the moth; Judah as the body itself consumed by rottenness (Pr 12:4). Perhaps alluding to the superiority of the latter in having the house of David, and the temple, the religious centre of the nation [GROTIUS]. As in Ho 5:13,14, the violence of the calamity is prefigured by the 'wound' which 'a lion' inflicts, so here its long protracted duration, and the certainty and completeness of the destruction from small unforeseen beginnings, by the images of a slowly but surely consuming moth and rottenness.

13. wound – literally, 'bandage'; hence a bandaged wound (Isa 1:6 Jer 30:12). 'Saw,' that is, felt its weakened state politically, and the dangers that threatened it. It aggravates their perversity, that, though aware of their unsound and calamitous state, they did not inquire into the cause or seek a right remedy.

went … to the Assyrian – First, Menahem (2Ki 15:19) applied to Pul; again, Hoshea to Shalmaneser (2Ki 17:3).

sent to King Jareb – Understand Judah as the nominative to 'sent.' Thus, as 'Ephraim saw his sickness' answers in the parallelism to 'Ephraim went to the Assyrian,' so 'Judah saw his wound' answers to (Judah) 'sent to King Jareb.' Jareb ought rather to be translated, 'their defender,' literally, 'avenger' [JEROME]. The Assyrian 'king,' ever ready, for his own aggrandizement, to mix himself up with the affairs of neighbouring states, professed to undertake Israel's and Judah's cause; in Jud 6:32, Jerub, in Jerub-baal is so used, namely, 'plead one's cause.' Judah, under Ahaz, applied to Tiglath-pileser for aid against Syria and Israel (2Ki 16:7,8 2Ch 28:16–21); the Assyrian 'distressed him, but strengthened him not,' fulfilling the prophecy here, 'he could not heal your, nor cure. you of your wound.

14. lion – The black lion and the young lion are emblems of strength and ferocity (Ps 91:13).

I, even I – emphatic; when I, even I, the irresistible God, tear in pieces (Ps 50:22), no Assyrian power can rescue.

go away – as a lion stalks leisurely back with his prey to his lair.

15. return to my place – that is, withdraw My favour.

seek my face – that is, seek My favour (Pr 29:26, Margin).

in … affliction … seek me early – that is, diligently; rising up before dawn to seek Me (Ps 119:147; compare Ps 78:34).

Chapter 6

Ho 6:1–11. The Israelites' exhortation to one another to seek the Lord.

At Ho 6:4 a new discourse, complaining of them, begins; for Ho 6:1–3 evidently belong to Ho 5:15, and form the happy termination of Israel's punishment: primarily, the return from Babylon; ultimately, the return from their present long dispersion. Ho 6:8 perhaps refers to the murder of Pekahiah; the discourse cannot be later than Pekah's reign, for it was under it that Gilead was carried into captivity (2Ki 15:29).

1. let us return – in order that God who has 'returned to His place' may return to us (Ho 5:15).

torn, and … heal – (De 32:39 Jer 30:17). They ascribe their punishment not to fortune, or man, but to God, and acknowledge that none (not the Assyrian, as they once vainly thought, Ho 5:13) but God can heal their wound. They are at the same time persuaded of the mercy of God, which persuasion is the starting-point of true repentance, and without which men would not seek, but hate and flee from God. Though our wound be severe, it is not past hope of recovery; there is room for grace, and a hope of pardon. He hath smitten us, but not so badly that He cannot heal us (Ps 130:4).

2. Primarily, in type, Israel's national revival, in a short period ('two or three' being used to denote a few days, Isa 17:6 Lu 13:32,33); antitypically the language is so framed as to refer in its full accuracy only to Messiah, the ideal Israel (Isa 49:3; compare Mt 2:15, with Ho 11:1), raised on the third day (Joh 2:19 1Co 15:4;

compare Isa 53:10). 'He shall *prolong* His *days.*' Compare the similar use of Israel's political resurrection as the type of the general resurrection of which 'Christ is the first-fruits' (Isa 26:19 Eze 37:1–14 Da 12:2).

live in his sight – enjoy His countenance shining on us, as of old; in contrast to Ho 5:6,15, 'Withdrawn Himself from them.'

3. know, if we follow on to know the Lord – The result of His recovered favour (Ho 6:2) will be onward growth in saving knowledge of God, as the result of perseverance in following after Him (Ps 63:8 Isa 54:13). 'Then' implies the consequence of the revival in Ho 6:2. The 'if' is not so much *conditional,* as expressive of the *means* which God's grace will sanctify to the full enlightenment of Israel in the knowledge of Him. As want of 'knowledge of God' has been the source of all evils (Ho 4:1 5:4), so the knowledge of Him will bring with it all blessings; yea, it is 'life' (Joh 17:3). This knowledge is practice, not mere theory (Jer 22:15,16). Theology is life, not science; realities, not words. This onward progress is illustrated by the light of 'morning' increasing more and more 'unto the perfect day' (Pr 4:18).

prepared – 'is sure,' literally, 'fixed,' ordered in His everlasting purposes of love to His covenant-people. Compare 'prepared of God' (Ge 41:32, *Margin;* Re 12:6). Jehovah shall surely come to the relief of His people after their dark night of calamity.

as the morning – (2Sa 23:4).

as the rain … latter … former – (Job 29:23 Joe 2:23). First, 'the rain' generally is mentioned; then the two rains (De 11:14) which caused the fertility of Palestine, and the absence of which was accounted the greatest calamity: 'the latter rain' which falls in the latter half of February, and during March and April, just before the harvest whence it takes its name, from a root meaning '*to gather*'; and 'the former rain,' literally, 'the darting rain,' from the middle of October to the middle of December. As the rain fertilizes the otherwise barren land, so God's favour will restore Israel long nationally lifeless.

4. what shall I do unto thee – to bring thee back to piety. What more could be done that I have not done, both in mercies and chastenings (Isa 5:4)? At this verse a new discourse begins, resuming the threats (Ho 5:14). See opening remarks on this chapter.

goodness – godliness.

morning cloud – soon dispersed by the sun (Ho 13:3). There is a tacit contrast here to the promise of God's grace to Israel hereafter, in Ho 6:3. *His* going forth is 'as the morning,' shining more and more unto the perfect day; *your* goodness is 'as a morning cloud,' soon vanishing. His coming to His people is 'as the (fertilizing) latter and former rains'; your coming to Him 'as the early dew goeth away.'

5. I hewed them by the prophets – that is, I *announced* by the prophets that they should be hewn asunder, like trees of the forest. God identifies His act with that of His prophets; the word being His instrument for executing His will (Jer 1:10 Eze 43:3).

by … words of my mouth – (Isa 11:4 Jer 23:29 Heb 4:12).

thy judgments – the judgments which I will inflict on thee, Ephraim and Judah (Ho 6:4). So '*thy* judgments,' that is, those inflicted *on thee* (Zep 3:15).

are as the light. – like the light, palpable to the eyes of all, as coming from God, the punisher of sin. HENDERSON translates, 'lightning' (compare Job 37:3, *Margin;* Job 35:15).

6. mercy – put for *piety* in general, of which *mercy* or *charity* is a branch.

not sacrifice – that is, '*rather than* sacrifice.' So 'not' is merely comparative (Ex 16:8 Joe 2:13 Joh 6:27 1Ti 2:14). As God Himself instituted sacrifices, it cannot mean that He desired them not absolutely, but that even in the Old Testament, He valued *moral obedience* as the only end for which *positive* ordinances, such as sacrifices, were instituted – as of more importance than a mere external ritual obedience (1Sa 15:22 Ps 50:8,9 51:16 Isa 1:11,12 Mic 6:6-8 Mt 9:13 12:7).

knowledge of God – experimental and practical, not merely theoretical (Ho 6:3 Jer 22:16 1Jo 2:3,4). 'Mercy' refers to the *second* table of the law, our duty to our fellow man; 'the knowledge of God' to the *first* table, our duty to God, including inward spiritual worship. The second table is put first, not as superior in dignity, for it is secondary, but in the order of our understanding.

7. like men – the common sort of men (Ps 82:7).

there – in the northern kingdom, Israel.

8. Gilead … city – probably Ramoth-gilead, metropolis of the hilly region beyond Jordan, south of the Jabbok, known as 'Gilead' (1Ki 4:13; compare Ge 31:21-25).

work iniquity – (Ho 12:11).

polluted with blood – 'marked with blood-traces' [MAURER]. Referring to Gilead's complicity in the regicidal conspiracy of Pekah against Pekahiah (2Ki 15:25). See on Ho 6:1. Many homicides were there, for there were beyond Jordan more cities of refuge, in proportion to the extent of territory, than on this side of Jordan (Nu 35:14 De 4:41–43 Jos 20:8). Ramoth-gilead was one.

9. company – 'association' or guild of priests.

murder by consent – literally, 'with one shoulder' (compare Zep 3:9, *Margin*). The image is from oxen putting their *shoulders together* to pull the same yoke [RIVETUS]. MAURER translates, 'in the way *towards*

Shechem.' It was a city of refuge between Ebal and Gerizim; on Mount Ephraim (Jos 20:7 21:21), long the civil capital of Ephraim, as Shiloh was the religious capital; now called Naploos; for a time the residence of Jeroboam (1Ki 12:25). The priests there became so corrupted that they waylaid and murdered persons fleeing to the asylum for refuge [HENDERSON]; the sanctity of the place enhanced the guilt of the priests who abused their priestly privileges, and the right of asylum to perpetrate murders themselves, or to screen those committed by others [MAURER].

commit lewdness – *deliberate* crime, presumptuous wickedness, from an *Arabic* root, 'to form a deliberate purpose.'

10. horrible thing – (Jer 5:30 18:13 23:14). **whoredom** – idolatry.

11. an harvest – namely, of judgments (as in Jer 51:33 Joe 3:13 Re 14:15). Called a 'harvest' because it is the fruit of the seed which Judah herself had sown (Ho 8:7 10:12 Job 4:8 Pr 22:8). Judah, under Ahaz, lost a hundred twenty thousand 'slain in one day (by Israel under Pekah), because they had forsaken the Lord God of their fathers.'

when I returned the captivity of my people – when I, by Oded My prophet, caused two hundred thousand women, sons, and daughters, of Judah to be restored from captivity by Israel (2Ch 28:6–15).

Chapter 7

Ho 7:1–16. Reproof of Israel.

Probably delivered in the interreign and civil war at Pekah's death; for Ho 7:7, 'all their kings . . . fallen,' refers to the murder of Zechariah, Shallum, Menahem, Pekahiah, and Pekah. In Ho 7:8 the reference seems to be to Menahem's payment of tribute to Pul, in order to secure himself in the usurped throne, also to Pekah's league with Rezin of Syria, and to Hoshea's connection with Assyria during the interregnum at Pekah's death [MAURER].

1. I would have healed Israel – Israel's restoration of the two hundred thousand Jewish captives at God's command (2Ch 28:8–15) gave hope of Israel's reformation [HENDERSON]. Political, as well as moral, healing is meant. When I would have healed Israel in its calamitous state, then their iniquity was discovered to be so great as to preclude hope of recovery. Then he enumerates their wickedness: 'The thief cometh in (indoors stealthily), and the troop of robbers spoileth without' (out-of-doors with open violence).

2. consider not in their hearts – literally 'say not to,' (Ps 14:1).

that I remember – and will punish.

their own doings have beset them about – as so many witnesses against them (Ps 9:16 Pr 5:22).

before my face – (Ps 90:8).

3. Their princes, instead of checking, 'have pleasure in them that do' such crimes (Ro 1:32).

4. who ceaseth from raising – rather, 'heating' it, from an *Arabic* root, 'to be hot.' So the *Septuagint*. Their adulterous and idolatrous lust is inflamed as the oven of a baker who has it at such a heat that he ceaseth from heating it only from the time that he hath kneaded the dough, until it be leavened; he only needs to omit feeding it during the short period of the fermentation of the bread. Compare 2Pe 2:14, 'that cannot cease from sin' [HENDERSON].

5. the day of our king – his birthday or day of inauguration.

with bottles of wine – drinking not merely glasses, but *bottles*.

he stretched out his hand with scorners – the gesture of revellers in holding out the cup and in drinking to one another's health. Scoffers were the king's boon companions.

6. they have made ready – rather, 'they make their heart approach,' namely, their king, in going to drink with him.

like an oven – following out the image in Ho 7:4. As it conceals the lighted fire all night while the baker sleeps but in the morning burns as a flaming fire, so they brood mischief in their hearts while conscience is lulled asleep, and their wicked designs wait only for a fair occasion to break forth [HORSLEY]. Their heart is the oven, their baker the ringleader of the plot. In Ho 7:7 their plots appear, namely, the intestine disturbances and murders of one king after another, after Jeroboam II.

7. all hot – All burn with eagerness to cause universal disturbance (2Ki 15:1–38).

devoured their judges – magistrates; as the fire of the oven devours the fuel.

all their kings ... fallen – See on Ho 7:1.

none ... calleth unto me – Such is their perversity that amid all these national calamities, none seeks help from Me (Isa 9:13 64:7).

8. mixed ... among the people – by leagues with idolaters, and the adoption of their idolatrous practices (Ho 7:9,11 Ps 106:35).

Ephraim ... cake not turned – a cake burnt on one side and unbaked on the other, and so uneatable; an image of the *worthlessness* of Ephraim. The Easterners bake their bread on the ground, covering it with embers (1Ki 19:6), and *turning* it every ten minutes, to bake it thoroughly without burning it.

9. Strangers – foreigners: the Syrians and Assyrians (2Ki 13:7 15:19,20 17:3–6).

gray hairs – that is, symptoms of approaching national dissolution.

are here and there upon – literally, 'are sprinkled on' him.

yet he knoweth not – Though old age ought to bring with it wisdom, he neither knows of his senile decay, nor has the true knowledge which leads to reformation.

10. Repetition of Ho 5:5.

not return to … Lord … for all this – notwithstanding all their calamities (Isa 9:13).

11. like a silly dove – a bird proverbial for simplicity: easily deceived.

without heart – that is, understanding.

call to Egypt – Israel lying between the two great rival empires Egypt and Assyria, sought each by turns to help her against the other. As this prophecy was written in the reign of Hoshea, the allusion is probably to the alliance with So or Sabacho II which ended in the overthrow of Hoshea and the deportation of Israel (2Ki 17:3–6). As the dove betrays its foolishness by fleeing in alarm from its nest only to fall into the net of the fowler, so Israel, though warned that foreign alliances would be their ruin, rushed into them.

12. When they shall go – to seek aid from this or that foreign state.

spread my net upon them – as on birds taken on the ground (Eze 12:13), as contrasted with *'bringing them down'* as the *'fowls of the heavens,'* namely, by the use of missiles.

as their congregation hath heard – namely, by My prophets through whom I threatened *'chastisement'* (Ho 5:9 2Ki 17:13-18).

13. fled – as birds from their nest (Pr 27:8 Isa 16:2).

me – who both could and would have healed them (Ho 7:1), had they applied to Me.

redeemed them – from Egypt and their other enemies (Mic 6:4).

lies – (Ps 78:36 Jer 3:10). Pretending to be My worshippers, when they all the while worshipped idols (Ho 7:14 Ho 12:1); also defrauding Me of the glory of their deliverance, and ascribing it and their other blessings to idols [CALVIN].

14. not cried unto me – but unto other gods [MAURER], (Job 35:9,10). Or, they did indeed cry unto Me, but not *'with their heart':* answering to *'lies,'* Ho 7:13 (see on Ho 7:13).

when they howled upon their beds – sleepless with anxiety; image of *deep affliction.* Their cry is termed *'howling,'* as it is the cry of anguish, not the cry of repentance and faith.

assemble … for corn. – namely in the temples of their idols, to obtain from them a good harvest and vintage, instead of coming to Me, the true Giver of these (Ho 2:5,8,12), proving that their cry to God was *'not with their heart.'*

rebel against me – literally, *'withdraw themselves against Me,'* that is, not only withdraw *from* Me, but also rebel *against* Me.

15. I … bound – when I saw their arms as it were relaxed with various disasters, I bound them so as to strengthen their sinews; image from surgery [CALVIN].

16. return, but not to the Most High – or, 'to one who is *not the Most High,'* one very different from Him, a stock or a stone.

deceitful bow – (Ps 78:57). A bow which, from its faulty construction, shoots wide of the mark. So Israel pretends to seek God, but turns aside to idols.

for the rage of their tongue – their boast of safety from Egyptian aid, and their 'lies' (Ho 7:13), whereby they pretended to serve God, while worshipping idols; also their perverse defence for their idolatries and blasphemies against God and His prophets (Ps 73:9 120:2,3).

their derision in … Egypt – Their 'fall' shall be the subject of 'derision' to Egypt, to whom they had applied for help (Ho 9:3,6 2Ki 17:4).

Chapter 8

Ho 8:1–14. Prophecy of the irruption of the Assyrians, in punishment for Israel's apostasy, idolatry, and setting up of kings without God's sanction.

In Ho 8:14, *Judah* is said to multiply fenced cities; and in Ho 8:7–9, Israel, to its great hurt, is said to have gone up to Assyria for help. This answers best to the reign of Menahem. For it was then that Uzziah of Judah, his contemporary, built fenced cities (2Ch 26:6,9,10). Then also Israel turned to Assyria and had to pay for their sinful folly a thousand talents of silver (2Ki 15:19) [MAURER].

1. Set the trumpet. – to give warning of the approach of the enemy: 'To thy *palate* (that is, "mouth," Job 31:30, *Margin*) the trumpet'; the abruptness of expression indicates the suddenness of the attack. So Ho 5:8.

as … eagle – the Assyrian (De 28:49 Jer 48:40 Hab 1:8).

against … house of … Lord – not the temple, but Israel viewed as *the family of God* (Ho 9:15 Nu 12:7 Zec 9:8 Heb 3:2 1Ti 3:15 1Pe 4:17).

2. My God, we know thee – the singular, 'My,' is used distributively, each one so addressing God. They, in their hour of need, plead their knowledge of God as the covenant-people, while in their *acts* they acknowledge Him not (compare Mt 7:21,22 Tit 1:16; also Isa 29:13 Jer 7:4).

3. Israel – God repeats the name in opposition to *their* use of it (Ho 8:2).

the enemy shall pursue him – in just retribution from God.

4. kings … not by me – not with My sanction (1Ki 11:31 12:20). Israel set up Jeroboam and his successors, whereas God had appointed the house of David as the rightful kings of the whole nation.

I knew it not – I *approved* it not (Ps 1:6).

of … gold … idols – (Ho 2:8 13:2).

that they may be cut off – that is, though warned of the consequences of idolatry, as it were with open eyes they rushed on their own destruction. So Jer 27:10,15 44:8.

6. from Israel was it – that is, the calf originated with them, not from Me. 'It also,' as well as their 'kings set up' by them, 'but not by Me' (Ho 8:4).

7. the bud – or, 'growth.'

strangers – foreigners (Ho 7:9).

8. vessel wherein is no pleasure – (Ps 41:12 Jer 22:28 48:38).

9. gone ... to Assyria – referring to Menahem's application for Pul's aid in establishing him on the throne (compare Ho 5:13 7:11). Menahem's name is read in the inscriptions in the southwest palace of Nimrod, as a tributary to the Assyrian king in his eighth year. The dynasty of Pul, or Phalluka, was supplanted at Nineveh by that of Tiglath-pileser, about 768 (or 760) B.C. Semiramis seems to have been Pul's wife, and to have withdrawn to Babylon in 768; and her son, Nabonassar, succeeding after a period of confusion, originated 'the era of Nabonassar,' 747 B.C. [G. V. Smith]. Usually foreigners coming to Israel's land were said to 'go up'; here it is the reverse, to intimate Israel's *sunken* state, and Assyria's superiority.

wild ass – a figure of Israel's headstrong perversity in following her own bent (Jer 2:24).

alone by himself – characteristic of Israel in all ages: 'lo, the people shall dwell alone' (Nu 23:9; compare Job 39:5–8).

hired lovers – reversing the ordinary way, namely, that lovers should hire her (Eze 16:33,34).

10. will I gather them – namely, the *nations* (Assyria) against Israel, instead of their assisting her as she had wished (Eze 16:37).

a little – rather, 'in a little': They shall sorrow 'a little' at the imposition of the tribute; God suspended yet the *great* judgment, namely, their deportation by Assyria.

the burden of the king of princes – the tribute imposed on Israel (under Menahem) by the Assyrian king Pul, (2Ki 15:19–22), who had many 'princes' under his sway (Isa 10:8).

11. God in righteous retribution gives them up to their own way; the sin becomes its own punishment (Pr 1:31).

many altars – in opposition to God's law (De 12:5,6,13,14).

to sin ... to sin – Their altars which were 'sin' (whatever religious intentions they might plead) should be treated as such, and be the source of their punishment (1Ki 12:30 13:34).

13. sacrifices of mine offerings – that is, which they offer to Me.

eat it – Their own carnal gratification is the object which they seek, not My honour.

now – that is, 'speedily.'

shall return to Egypt – (Ho 9:3,6 11:11). The same threat as in De 28:68. They fled thither to escape from the Assyrians (compare as to *Judah,* Jer 42:1–44:30), when these latter had overthrown their nation.

14. forgotten ... Maker – (De 32:18).

temples – to idols.

Judah ... fenced cities – Judah, though less idolatrous than Israel, betrayed lack of faith in Jehovah by trusting more to its fenced cities than to Him; instead of making peace with God, Judah multiplied human defences (Isa 22:8 Jer 5:17 Mic 5:10,11).

I will send ... fire upon ... cities – Sennacherib burned all Judah's fenced cities except Jerusalem (2Ki 18:13).

palaces thereof – namely, of the land. Compare as to Jerusalem, Jer 17:27.

Chapter 9

Ho 9:1–17. Warning against Israel's joy at partial relief from their troubles: their crops shall fail, and the people leave the Lord's land for Egypt and Assyria, where they cannot, if so inclined, serve God according to the ancient ritual: folly of their false prophets.

1. Rejoice not ... for joy – literally, 'to exultation.' Thy exultation at the league with Pul, by which peace seems secured, is out of place: since thy idolatry will bring ruin on thee.

as other people – the Assyrians for instance, who, unlike thee, are in the height of prosperity.

loved a reward upon every corn floor – Thou hast desired, in *reward* for thy homage to idols, abundance of corn on every threshing-floor (Ho 2:12).

2. (Ho 2:9,12).

fail – disappoint her expectation.

3. return to Egypt – (See on Ho 8:13). As in Ho 11:5 it is said, 'He shall *not return* into ... Egypt.'

eat unclean things in Assyria – reduced by necessity to eat meats pronounced unclean by the Mosaic law (Eze 4:13). See 2Ki 17:6.

4. offer wine offerings – literally, 'pour as a libation' (Ex 30:9 Le 23:13).

neither shall they be pleasing unto him – as being offered on a profane soil.

sacrifices ... as the bread of mourners – which was unclean (De 26:14 Jer 16:7 Eze 24:17).

their bread for their soul – their offering for the expiation of their soul [Calvin], (Le 17:11). Rather, 'their bread for their sustenance ("soul" being often used for *the animal life,* Ge 14:21, *Margin*) shall not come into the Lord's house'; it shall only subserve their own uses, not My worship.

5. (Ho 2:11).

6. **because of destruction** – to escape from the devastation of their country.

Egypt shall gather them up – that is, into its sepulchres (Jer 8:2 Eze 29:5). Instead of returning to Palestine, they should die in Egypt.

Memphis – famed as a necropolis.

the pleasant *places* **for their silver** – that is, their desired treasuries for their money. Or, 'whatever precious thing they have of silver' [MAURER].

nettles – the sign of desolation (Isa 34:13).

7. **visitation** – vengeance: punishment (Isa 10:3).

Israel shall know it – to her cost experimentally (Isa 9:9).

the prophet is a fool – The false prophet who foretold prosperity to the nation shall be convicted of folly by the event.

the spiritual man – the man pretending to inspiration (La 2:14 Eze 13:3 Mic 3:11 Zep 3:4).

for the multitude of thine iniquity. – Connect these words with, 'the days of visitation … are come'; 'the prophet … is mad,' being parenthetical.

8. **The watchman … was with my God** – The spiritual watchmen, the true prophets, formerly consulted my God (Jer 31:6 Hab 2:1); but their so-called *prophet* is a snare, entrapping Israel into idolatry.

hatred – rather, '(a cause of) apostasy' (see Ho 9:7) [MAURER].

house of his God – that is, the state of Ephraim, as in Ho 8:1 [MAURER]. Or, 'the house of his (false) god,' the calves [CALVIN]. Jehovah, '*my* God,' seems contrasted with '*his* God.' CALVIN's view is therefore preferable.

9. **as in the days of Gibeah** – as in the day of the perpetration of the atrocity of Gibeah, narrated in Jud 19:16-22.

10. As the traveller in a wilderness is delighted at finding grapes to quench his thirst, or the early fig (esteemed a great delicacy in the East, Isa 28:4 Jer 24:2 Mic 7:1); so it was My delight to choose your fathers as My peculiar people in Egypt (Ho 2:15).

at her first time – when the first-fruits of the tree become ripe.

went to Baal-peor – (Nu 25:3): the Moabite idol, in whose worship young women prostituted themselves; the very sin Israel latterly was guilty of.

separated themselves – consecrated themselves.

unto that shame – to that shameful or foul idol (Jer 11:13).

11. **their glory shall fly away** – fit retribution to those who 'separated themselves unto that *shame*' (Ho 9:10). Children were accounted the *glory* of parents; sterility, a reproach. 'Ephraim' means 'fruitfulness' (Ge 41:52); this its name shall cease to be its characteristic.

from the birth … womb … conception – Ephraim's children shall perish in a threefold gradation; (1) From the time of birth. (2) From the time of pregnancy. (3) From the time of their first conception.

12. Even though they should rear their children, yet will I bereave them (the Ephraimites) of them (Job 27:14).

woe … to them when I depart – Yet the ungodly in their madness desire God to depart from them (Job 21:14 22:17 Mt 8:34). At last they know to their cost how awful it is when God has departed (De 31:17 1Sa 28:15,16; compare Ho 9:11 1Sa 4:21).

13. **Ephraim, as I saw Tyrus … in a pleasant place** – that is, in looking towards Tyrus (on whose borders Ephraim lay) I saw Ephraim beautiful in situation like her (Eze 26:1–28:26).

is planted – as a *fruitful* tree; image suggested by the meaning of 'Ephraim' (Ho 9:11).

bring forth his children to the murderer – (Ho 9:16 Ho 13:16). With all his fruitfulness, his children shall only be brought up to be slain.

14. **what wilt thou give?** – As if overwhelmed by feeling, he deliberates with God what is most desirable.

give … a miscarrying womb – Of two evils he chooses the least. So great will be the calamity, that barrenness will be a blessing, though usually counted a great misfortune (Job 3:3 Jer 20:14 Lu 23:29).

15. **All their wickedness** – that is, their chief guilt.

Gilgal – This was the scene of their first contumacy in rejecting God and choosing a king (1Sa 11:14,15; compare 1Sa 8:7), and of their subsequent idolatry.

there I hated them – not with the human passion, but holy hatred of their sin, which required punishment to be inflicted on themselves (compare Mal 1:3).

out of mine house – as in Ho 8:1: out of the land holy unto ME. Or, as 'love' is mentioned immediately after, the reference may be to the Hebrew mode of divorce, the husband (God) putting the wife (Israel) out of the house.

princes … revolters – '*Sarim … Sorerim*' (*Hebrew*), a play on similar sounds.

16. The figures 'root,' 'fruit,' are suggested by the word 'Ephraim,' that is, *fruitful* (see on Ho 9:11,12). 'Smitten,' namely, with a blight (Ps 102:4).

17. **My God** – 'My,' in contrast to 'them,' that is, the people, whose God Jehovah no longer is. Also Hosea appeals to God as supporting his authority against the whole people.

wanderers among … nations – (2Ki 15:29 1Ch 5:26).

Chapter 10

Ho 10:1–15. Israel's idolatry, the source of perjuries and unlawful leagues, soon destined to be the ruin of the state, their king and their images being about to be carried off; a just chastisement, the reaping corresponding to the sowing.

The prophecy was uttered between Shalmaneser's first and second invasions of Israel. Compare Ho 10:14; also Ho 10:6, referring to Hoshea's calling So of Egypt to his aid; also Ho 10:4,13.

1. empty – stripped of its fruits [CALVIN], (Na 2:2); compelled to pay tribute to Pul (2Ki 15:20). MAURER translates, 'A *widespreading* vine'; so the *Septuagint.* Compare Ge 49:22 Ps 80:9–11 Eze 17:6.

bringeth forth fruit unto himself – not unto ME.

according to ... multitude of ... fruit ... increased ... altars – In proportion to the abundance of their prosperity, which called for fruit unto God (compare Ro 6:22), was the abundance of their idolatry (Ho 8:4,11).

2. heart ... divided – (1Ki 18:21 Mt 6:24 Jas 4:8).

now – that is soon.

he – Jehovah.

break down – 'cut off,' namely the heads of the victims. Those altars, which were the scene of *cutting off* the victims' heads, shall be themselves cut off.

3. now – Soon they, deprived of their king, shall be reduced to say, We have no king (Ho 10:7,15), for Jehovah deprived us of him, because of our not fearing God. What then (seeing God is against us) should a king be able to do for us, if we had one? As they rejected the heavenly King, they were deprived of their earthly king.

4. words – mere empty words.

swearing falsely in making a covenant – breaking their engagement to Shalmaneser (2Ki 17:4), and making a covenant with So, though covenants with foreigners were forbidden.

judgment ... as hemlock – that is, divine judgment shall spring up as rank, and as deadly, as hemlock in the furrows (De 29:18 Am 5:7 6:12). GESENIUS translates, 'poppy.' GROTIUS, 'darnel.'

5. fear because of the calves – that is, shall fear *for* them.

Beth-aven – substituted for Beth-el in contempt (Ho 4:15).

it – *singular,* the *one* in Beth-el; after the pattern of which the other 'calves' (*plural*) were made. 'Calves' in the *Hebrew* is *feminine,* to express contempt.

priests – The *Hebrew* is only used of *idolatrous priests* (2Ki 23:5 Zep 1:4), from a root meaning either 'the black garment' in which they were attired; or, 'to resound,' referring to their howling cries in their sacred rites [CALVIN].

that rejoiced on it – because it was a source of gain to them.

the glory thereof – the magnificence of its ornaments and its worship.

6. It ... also – The calf, so far from saving its worshippers from deportation, itself shall be carried off; hence 'Israel shall be ashamed' of it.

Jareb – (See on Ho 5:13). 'A present to the king (whom they looked to as) their *defender,*' or else *avenger,* whose wrath they wished to appease, namely, Shalmaneser. The minor states applied this title to the Great King, as the avenging Protector.

his own counsel – the calves, which Jeroboam set up as a stroke of policy to detach Israel from Judah. Their severance from Judah and Jehovah proved now to be not politic, but fatal to them.

7. (Ho 10:3,15).

foam – denoting short-lived existence and speedy dissolution. As the foam, though seeming to be eminent raised on the top of the water, yet has no solidity, such is the throne of Samaria.

8. Aven – that is, Beth-aven.

the sin – that is, the occasion of sin (De 9:21 1Ki 12:30).

they shall say to ... mountains, Cover us – So terrible shall be the calamity, that men shall prefer death to life (Lu 23:30 Re 6:16 9:6). Those very hills on which were their idolatrous altars (one source of their confidence, as their 'king,' Ho 10:7, was the other), so far from helping them, shall be called on by them to overwhelm them.

9. Gibeah – (Ho 9:9 Jud 19:1–20:48). They are singled out as a specimen of the whole nation.

there they stood – The Israelites have, as there and then, so ever since, *persisted* in their sin [CALVIN]. Or, better, 'they stood their ground,' that is, did not perish then [MAURER].

the battle ... did not overtake them – Though God spared you then, He will not do so now; nay, the battle whereby God punished the Gibeonite 'children of iniquity,' shall the more heavily visit you for your continued impenitence. Though 'they stood' then, it shall not be so now. The change from 'thou' to 'they' marks God's alienation from them; they are, by the use of the third person, put to a greater distance from God.

10. my desire ... chastise – expressing God's *strong inclination* to vindicate His justice against sin, as being the infinitely holy God (De 28:63).

the people – *Foreign invaders* 'shall be gathered against them.'

when they shall bind themselves in their two furrows – image from two oxen ploughing together side by side, in two contiguous furrows: so the Israelites shall join themselves, to unite their powers against all dangers, but it will not save them from My destroying them [CALVIN]. Their 'two furrows' may refer to their *two places of setting up the calves,* their ground of confidence, Dan and Beth-el; or, the two divisions of the nation, *Israel and Judah,* 'in their two furrows,' that is, in their respective two places of habitation; Ho 10:11, which specifies the two, favours this view.

11. taught – that is, accustomed.

loveth to tread out ... corn – a far easier and more self-indulgent work than ploughing. In treading corn, cattle were not bound together under a yoke, but either trod it singly with their feet, or drew a threshing sledge over it (Isa 28:27,28): they were free to eat some of the corn from time to time, as the law required they should be unmuzzled (De 25:4), so that they grew fat in this work. An image of Israel's freedom, prosperity, and self-indulgence heretofore. But now God will put the Assyrian yoke upon her, instead of freedom, putting her to servile work.

I passed over upon – I put the yoke upon.

make ... to ride – as in Job 30:22; that is, *hurry* Ephraim *away* to a distant region [CALVIN]. LYRA translates, 'I will make (the Assyrian) to ride upon Ephraim.' MAURER, 'I will make Ephraim to carry,' namely, a charioteer.

his clods – 'the clods before him.'

12. Continuation of the image in Ho 10:11 (Pr 11:18). Act righteously and ye shall reap the reward; a reward not of debt, but of grace.

in mercy – according to the measure of the divine 'mercy,' which over and above repays the *goodness* or 'mercy' which we show to our fellow man (Lu 6:38).

break ... fallow ground – Remove your superstitions and vices, and be renewed.

seek ... Lord, fill he come – Though not answered immediately, persevere unceasingly '*till* He come.'

rain – send down as a copious shower.

righteousness – the reward of righteousness, that is, *salvation,* temporal and spiritual (1Sa 26:23; compare Joe 2:23).

13. reaped iniquity – that is, the *fruit* of iniquity; as 'righteousness' (Ho 10:12) is 'the *fruit* of righteousness' (Job 4:8 Pr 22:8 Ga 6:7,8).

lies – false and spurious worship.

trust in thy way – thy perverse way (Isa 57:10 Jer 2:23), thy worship of false gods. This was their internal safeguard, as their external was 'the multitude of their mighty men.'

14. tumult – a tumultuous war.

among thy people – literally, 'peoples': the war shall extend to the whole people of Israel, through all the tribes, and the peoples allied to her.

Shalman spoiled Beth-arbel – that is, Shalmaneser, a compound name, in which the part common to it and the names of three other Assyrian kings, is omitted; Tiglath-pileser, Esar-haddon, Shar-ezer. So Jeconiah is abbreviated to Coniah. Arbel was situated in Naphtali in Galilee, on the border nearest Assyria. Against it Shalmaneser, at his first invasion of Israel (2Ki 17:3), vented his chief rage. God threatens Israel's fortresses with the same fate as Arbel suffered 'in the day (on the occasion) of the battle' then well-known, though not mentioned elsewhere (compare 2Ki 18:34). This event, close on the reign of Hezekiah, shows the inscription of Hosea (Ho 1:1) to be correct.

15. So shall Beth-el do unto you – Your idolatrous calf at Beth-el shall be the cause of a like calamity befalling you.

your great wickedness – literally, 'the wickedness of your wickedness.'

in a morning – speedily as quickly as the dawn is put to flight by the rising sun (Ho 6:4 13:3 Ps 30:5).

king – Hoshea.

Chapter 11

Ho 11:1–12. God's former benefits, and Israel's ingratitude resulting in punishment, yet Jehovah promises restoration at last.

Ho 11:5 shows this prophecy was uttered after the league made with Egypt (2Ki 17:4).

1. Israel ... called my son out of Egypt – BENGEL translates, '*From* the time that he (Israel) was *in* Egypt, I called him My son,' which the parallelism proves. So Ho 12:9 and Ho 13:4 use 'from ... Egypt,' for 'from the time that thou didst sojourn *in* Egypt.' Ex 4:22 also shows that Israel was called by God, 'My son,' from the time of his Egyptian sojourn (Isa 43:1). God is always said to have *led* or *brought forth,* not to have 'called,' Israel from Egypt. Mt 2:15, therefore, in quoting this prophecy, applies it to Jesus' sojourn *in* Egypt, not His return *from* it. Even from His infancy, partly spent in Egypt, God called Him His son. God included Messiah, and Israel for Messiah's sake, in one common love, and therefore in one common prophecy. Messiah's people and Himself are one, as the Head and the body. Isa 49:3 calls Him 'Israel.' The same general reason, danger of extinction, caused the infant Jesus, and Israel in its national infancy (compare Ge 42:1–43:34 45:18 46:3,4 Eze 16:4–6 Jer 31:20) to sojourn in Egypt. So He, and His spiritual Israel, are already called 'God's sons' while yet in the Egypt of the world.

2. As they called them – 'they,' namely, monitors sent by Me. 'Called,' in Ho 11:1, suggests the idea of the many subsequent calls by the prophets.

went from them – turned away in contempt (Jer 2:27).

Baalim – images of Baal, set up in various places.

3. taught ... to go – literally 'to use his feet.' Compare a similar image, De 1:31 8:2,5,15 32:10,11 Ne 9:21 Isa 63:9 Am 2:10. God bore them as a parent does an infant, unable to supply itself, so that it has no anxiety about food, raiment, and its going forth. Ac 13:18, which probably refers to this passage of Hosea; He took them by the arms, to guide them that they might not stray, and to hold them up that they might not stumble.

knew not that I healed them – that is, that My design was to restore them spiritually and temporally (Ex 15:26).

4. cords of a man – parallel to 'bands of love'; not such cords as oxen are led by, but *humane methods,* such as men employ when inducing others, as for instance, a father drawing his child, by leading-strings, teaching him to go (Ho 11:1).

I was ... as they that take off the yoke on their jaws ... I laid meat – as the humane husbandman occasionally loosens the straps under the jaws by which the yoke is bound on the neck of oxen and lays food before them to eat. An appropriate image of God's deliverance of Israel from the Egyptian yoke, and of His feeding them in the wilderness.

5. He shall not return into ... Egypt – namely, to seek help against Assyria (compare Ho 7:11), as Israel lately had done (2Ki 17:4), after having revolted from Assyria, to whom they had been tributary from the times of Menahem (2Ki 15:19). In a *figurative* sense, 'he *shall* return to Egypt' (Ho 9:3), that is, to Egypt-like bondage; also many Jewish fugitives were literally to *return* to Egypt, when the Holy Land was to be in Assyrian and Chaldean hands.

Assyrian shall be his king – instead of having kings of their own, and Egypt as their auxiliary.

because they refused to return – just retribution. They would not return (spiritually) to God, therefore they shall not return (corporally) to Egypt, the object of their desire.

6. abide – or, 'fall upon' [CALVIN].

branches – villages, which are the branches or dependencies of the cities [CALVIN]. GROTIUS translates, 'his bars' (so La 2:9), that is, the warriors who were the bulwarks of the state. Compare Ho 4:18, 'rulers' (*Margin*), 'shields' (Ps 47:9).

because of their own counsels – in worshipping idols, and relying on Egypt (compare Ho 10:6).

7. bent to backsliding – Not only do they *backslide,* and that too *from* ME, their 'chief

good,' but they are *bent upon it.* Though they (the prophets) called them (the Israelites) to the Most High (from their idols), 'none would exalt (that is, extol or honour) Him.' To exalt God, they must cease to be '*bent on* backsliding,' and *must* lift themselves upwards.

8. as Admah ... Zeboim – among the cities, including Sodom and Gomorrah, irretrievably overthrown (De 29:23).

heart is turned within me – with the deepest compassion, so as not to execute My threat (La 1:20; compare Ge 43:30 1Ki 3:26). So the phrase is used of a new turn given to the feeling (Ps 105:25).

repentings – God speaks according to *human* modes of thought (Nu 23:19). God's *seeming* change is in accordance with His secret everlasting purpose of love to His people, to magnify His grace after their desperate rebellion.

9. I will not return to destroy Ephraim – that is I will no more, as in past times, destroy Ephraim. The destruction primarily meant is probably that by Tiglath-pileser, who, as the Jewish king Ahaz' ally against Pekah of Israel and Rezin of Syria, deprived Israel of Gilead, Galilee, and Naphtali (2Ki 15:29). The ulterior reference is to the long dispersion hereafter, to be ended by God's covenant mercy restoring His people, not for their merits, but of His grace.

God, ... not man – not dealing as man would, with implacable wrath under awful provocation (Isa 55:7–9 Mal 3:6). I do not, like man, change when once I have made a covenant of everlasting love, as with Israel (Nu 23:19). We measure God by the human standard, and hence are slow to credit fully His promises; these, however, belong to the faithful remnant, not to the obstinately impenitent.

in the midst of thee – as peculiarly thy God (Ex 19:5,6).

not enter into the city – as an enemy: as I entered Admah, Zeboim, and Sodom, utterly destroying them, whereas I will not utterly destroy thee. Somewhat similarly JEROME: 'I am *not one such as human dwellers in a city,* who take cruel vengeance; I save those whom I correct.' Thus 'not man,' and 'in the midst of thee,' are parallel to 'into the city.' Though I am in the midst of thee, it is not as man entering a rebellious city to destroy utterly.

10. he shall roar like a lion – by awful judgments on their foes (Isa 31:4 Jer 25:26–30 Joe 3:16), calling His dispersed 'children' from the various lands of their dispersion.

shall tremble – shall flock in eager agitation of haste.

from the west – (Zec 8:7). Literally, 'the sea.' Probably the Mediterranean, including its 'isles of the sea,' and maritime coast. Thus as Ho 11:11 specifies regions of Africa and Asia, so here Europe. Isa 11:11–16, is parallel, referring to the very same regions. On 'children,' see Ho 1:10.

11. tremble – flutter in haste.

dove – no longer 'a silly dove' (Ho 7:11), but as 'doves flying to their windows' (Isa 60:8).

in their houses – (Eze 28:26). Literally, 'upon,' for the Orientals live almost as much *upon* their flat-roofed houses as *in* them.

12. ruleth with God – to serve God is to reign. Ephraim wished to rule *without God* (compare 1Co 4:8); nay, even, in order to rule, cast off God's worship [RIVETUS]. In Judah was the legitimate succession of kings and priests.

with the saints – the holy priests and Levites [RIVETUS]. With the fathers and prophets who handed down the pure worship of God. Israel's apostasy is the more culpable, as he had before him the good example of Judah, which he set at naught. The parallelism ('with GOD') favours *Margin*, 'With THE MOST HOLY ONE.'

Chapter 12

Ho 12:1–14. Reproof of Ephraim and Judah: their father Jacob ought to be a pattern to them.

This prophecy was delivered about the time of Israel's seeking the aid of the Egyptian king So, in violation of their covenant with Assyria (see Ho 12:1). He exhorts them to follow their father Jacob's persevering prayerfulness, which brought God's favour upon him. As God is unchangeable, He will show the same favour to Jacob's posterity as He did to Jacob, if, like him, they seek God.

1. feedeth on wind – (Pr 15:14 Isa 44:20). Followeth after vain objects, such as alliances with idolaters and their idols (compare Ho 8:7).

east wind – the simoon, blowing from the desert east of Palestine, which not only does not benefit, but does injury. Israel follows not only things vain, but things pernicious (compare Job 15:2). **increaseth lies** – accumulates lie upon lie, that is, impostures wherewith they deceive themselves, forsaking the truth of God.

desolation – *violent oppressions* practised by Israel [MAURER]. Acts which would prove the *cause* of Israel's own desolation [CALVIN].

covenant with ... Assyrians – (Ho 5:13 7:11).

oil ... into Egypt – as a present from Israel to secure Egypt's alliance (Isa 30:6 57:9; compare 2Ki 17:4). Palestine was famed for oil (Eze 27:17).

2. controversy with Judah – (Ho 4:1 Mic 6:2). Judah, under Ahaz, had fallen into idolatry (2Ki 16:3.).

Jacob – that is, the ten tribes. If Judah, the favoured portion of the nation, shall not be spared, much less degenerate Israel.

3. He – Jacob, contrasted with his degenerate

descendants, called by his name, Jacob (Ho 12:2; compare Mic 2:7). *He* took Esau by the heel in the womb in order to obtain, if possible, the privileges of the first-born (Ge 25:22–26), whence he took his name, Jacob, meaning 'supplanter'; and again, by his strength, prevailed in wrestling with God for a blessing (Ge 32:24–29); whereas ye disregard My promises, putting your confidence in idols and foreign alliances. *He* conquered God, *ye* are the slaves of idols. Only have Jehovah on your side, and ye are stronger than Edom, or even Assyria. So the spiritual Israel lays hold of the heel of Jesus, 'the First-born of many brethren,' being born again of the Holy Spirit. Having no right in themselves to the inheritance, they lay hold of the bruised heel, the humanity of Christ crucified, and let not go their hold of Him who is not, as Esau, a curse (Heb 12:16,17), but, by becoming a curse for us, is a blessing to us.

power with God – referring to his name, 'Israel,' *prince of God*, acquired on that occasion (compare Mt 11:12). As the promised Canaan had to be gained forcibly by Israel, so heaven by the faithful (Re 3:21; compare Lu 13:24). 'Strive,' literally, 'as in the agony of a contest.' So the Canaanitess (Mt 15:22).

his strength – which lay in his conscious weakness, whence, when his thigh was put out of joint by God, he *hung upon Him.* To seek strength was his object; to grant it, God's. Yet God's mode of procedure was strange. In human form He tries as it were to throw Jacob down. When simple wrestling was not enough, He does what seems to ensure Jacob's fall, dislocating his thigh joint, so that he could no longer stand. Yet it was then that Jacob prevailed. Thus God teaches us the irresistible might of conscious weakness. For when weak in ourselves, we are strong by His strength put in us (Job 23:6 Isa 27:5 2Co 12:9,10).

4. the angel – the uncreated Angel of the Covenant, as God the Son appears in the Old Testament (Mal 3:1).

made supplication – Ge 32:26; 'I will not let thee go, except thou bless me.'

he found him – The angel found Jacob, when he was fleeing from Esau into Syria: the Lord appearing to him 'in Beth-el' (Ge 28:11-19 35:1). What a sad contrast, that in this same Beth-el now Israel worships the golden calves!

there he spake with us – 'with *us*,' as being in the loins of our progenitor Jacob (compare Ps 66:6, 'They ... *we*;' Heb 7:9,10). What God there spoke to Jacob appertains to us. God's promises to him belong to all his posterity who follow in the steps of his prayerful faith.

5. Lord God – JEHOVAH, a name implying His *immutable constancy to His promises*. From the *Hebrew* root, meaning 'existence.' 'He that is, was, and is to be,' always the same (Heb 13:8

Re 1:4,8; compare Ex 3:14,15 6:3). As He was unchangeable in His favour to Jacob, so will He be to His believing posterity.

of hosts – which Israel foolishly worshipped. Jehovah has all the hosts (*saba*) or powers of heaven and earth at His command, so that He is as all-powerful, as He is faithful, to fulfil His promises (Ps 135:6 Am 5:27).

memorial – the name expressive of the character in which God was ever to be remembered (Ps 135:13).

6. thou – who dost wish to be a true descendant of Jacob.

to THY God – who is therefore bound by covenant to hear thy prayers.

keep mercy and judgment – (Mic 6:8). These two include the second-table commandments, duty towards one's neighbours, the most visible test of the sincerity on one's repentance.

wait on thy God – alone, not on thy idols. Including all the duties of the first table (Ps 37:3,5,7 40:1).

7. merchant – a play on the double sense of the *Hebrew,* 'Canaan,' that is, a Canaanite and a 'merchant' Eze 16:3: 'Thy birth is … of Canaan.' They who naturally were descendants of pious *Jacob* had become virtually *Canaanites,* who were proverbial as cheating *merchants* (compare Isa 23:11, *Margin*), the greatest reproach to Israel, who despised Canaan. The Phoenicians called themselves *Canaanites* or *merchants* (Isa 23:8).

oppress – *open* violence: as the 'balances of deceit' imply *fraud.*

8. And – that is, Notwithstanding.

Yet I am … rich – I regard not what the prophets say: I am content with my state, as I am rich (Re 3:17). Therefore, in just retribution, this is the very language of the enemy in being the instrument of Israel's punishment. Zec 11:5: 'They that sell them say … *I am rich.*' Far better is poverty with honesty, than riches gained by sin.

my labours – my gains by labour.

they shall find none – that is, none shall find any.

iniquity … that were sin – iniquity that would bring down the penalty of sin. Ephraim argues, My success in my labours proves that I am not a guilty sinner as the prophets assert. Thus sinners pervert God's long-suffering goodness (Mt 5:45) into a justification of their impenitence (compare Ec 8:11–13).

9. And – rather, 'And yet.' Though Israel deserves to be cast off for ever, yet I am still what I have been from the time of My delivering them out of Egypt, their covenant God; therefore, 'I will yet make thee to dwell in tabernacles,' that is, to keep the feast of tabernacles again in remembrance of a new deliverance out of bondage. Fulfilled primarily at the return

from Babylon (Ne 8:17). Fully and antitypically to be fulfilled at the final restoration from the present dispersion (Zec 14:16; compare Le 23:42,43).

10. by … the prophets – literally, 'upon,' that is, My spirit resting *on* them. I deposited *with them* My instructions which ought to have brought you to the right way. An aggravation of your guilt, that it was not through ignorance you erred, but in defiance of God and His prophets [CALVIN]. Ahijah the Shilonite, Shemaiah, Iddo, Azariah, Hanani, Jehu, Elijah, Elisha, Micaiah, Joel, and Amos were 'the prophets' before Hosea.

visions … similitudes – I adopted such modes of communication, adapted to man's capacities, as were calculated to arouse attention: I left no means untried to reform you. The first, second, and third chapters contain examples of 'similitudes.'

11. Is there iniquity in Gilead? – He asks the question, not as if the answer was doubtful, but to strengthen the affirmation: 'Surely they are vanity'; or as MAURER translates, 'They are *nothing but* iniquity.' *Iniquity,* especially idolatry, in Scripture is often termed 'vanity.' Pr 13:11: 'Wealth gotten by *vanity,*' that is, *iniquity.* Isa 41:29: 'They are all *vanity … images.*' 'Gilead' refers to Mizpah-gilead, a city representing the region beyond Jordan (Ho 6:8 Jud 11:29); as 'Gilgal,' the region on this side of Jordan (Ho 4:15). In all quarters alike they are utterly vile.

their altars are as heaps in the furrows – that is, as numerous as such heaps: namely, the heaps of stones cleared out of a stony field. An appropriate image, as at a distance they look like altars (compare Ho 10:1,4 8:11). As the third member in the parallelism answers to the first, 'Gilgal' to 'Gilead,' so the fourth to the second, 'altars' to 'vanity.' The word 'heaps' alludes to the name 'Gilgal,' meaning 'a heap of stones.' The very scene of the general circumcision of the people, and of the solemn Passover kept after crossing Jordan, is now the stronghold of Israel's idolatry.

12. Jacob fled … served – Though ye pride yourselves on the great name of 'Israel,' forget not that your progenitor was the same Jacob who was a fugitive, and who served for Rachel fourteen years. *He* forgot not ME who delivered him when fleeing from Esau, and when oppressed by Laban (Ge 28:5 29:20,28 De 26:5). *Ye,* though delivered from Egypt (Ho 12:13), and loaded with My favours, are yet unwilling to return to Me.

country of Syria – the champaign region of Syria, the portion lying between the Tigris and Euphrates, hence called Mesopotamia. Padan-aram means the same, that is, 'Low Syria,' as opposed to Aramea (meaning the 'high country') or Syria (Ge 48:7).

13. by a prophet – Moses (Nu 12:6–8 De 18:15,18).

preserved – Translate, 'kept'; there is an allusion to the same *Hebrew* word in Ho 12:12, '*kept sheep*'; Israel was *kept* by God as *His flock,* even as *Jacob kept sheep* (Ps 80:1 Isa 63:11).

14. provoked him – that is, God.

leave his blood upon him – not take away the guilt and penalty of the innocent blood shed by Ephraim in general, and to Moloch in particular.

his reproach shall his Lord return unto him – Ephraim's dishonour to God in worshipping idols, God will repay to him. That God is '*his* Lord' by right redemption and special revelation to Ephraim only aggravates his guilt, instead of giving him hope of escape. God does not give up His claim to them as *His,* however they set aside His dominion.

Chapter 13

Ho 13:1–16. Ephraim's sinful ingratitude to God, and its fatal consequence; God's promise at last.

This chapter and the fourteenth chapter probably belong to the troubled times that followed Pekah's murder by Hoshea (compare Ho 13:11 2Ki 15:30). The subject is the idolatry of Ephraim, notwithstanding God's past benefits, destined to be his ruin.

1. When Ephraim spake trembling – rather, 'When Ephraim (the tribe most powerful among the twelve in Israel's early history) spake (authoritatively) there was trembling'; all reverentially feared him [Jerome], (compare Job 29:8,9,21).

offended in Baal – that is, *in respect to* Baal, by worshipping him (1Ki 16:31), under Ahab; a more heinous offense than even the calves. Therefore it is at this climax of guilt that Ephraim 'died.' Sin has, in the sight of God, within itself the germ of death, though that death may not visibly take effect till long after. Compare Ro 7:9, 'Sin revived, and I *died.*' So Adam in the day of his sin was to die, though the sentence was not visibly executed till long after (Ge 2:17 5:5). Israel is similarly represented as politically dead in Eze 37:1–28.

2. according to their own understanding – that is, their arbitrary devising. Compare 'will-worship,' Col 2:23. Men are not to be 'wise above that which is written,' or to follow their own understanding, but God's command in worship.

kiss the calves – an act of adoration to the golden calves (compare 1Ki 19:18 Job 31:27 Ps 2:12).

3. they shall be as the morning cloud ... dew – (Ho 6:4). As their 'goodness' soon vanished

like the morning cloud and dew, so they shall perish like them.

the floor – the threshing-floor, generally an open area, on a height, exposed to the winds.

chimney – generally in the East an orifice in the wall, at once admitting the light, and giving egress to the smoke.

4. (Ho 12:9 Isa 43:11).

no saviour – temporal as well as spiritual.

besides me – (Isa 45:21).

5. I did know thee – did acknowledge thee as Mine, and so took care of thee (Ps 144:3 Am 3:2). As *I knew* thee as Mine, so *thou* shouldest *know* no God but Me (Ho 13:4).

in ... land of ... drought – (De 8:15).

6. Image from cattle, waxing wanton in abundant pasture (compare Ho 2:5,8 De 32:13–15). In proportion as I fed them to the full, they were so satiated that 'their heart was exalted'; a sad contrast to the time when, by God's blessing, Ephraim truly 'exalted himself in Israel' (Ho 13:1).

therefore have they forgotten me – the very reason why men should remember God (namely, prosperity, which comes from Him) is the cause often of their forgetting Him. God had warned them of this danger (De 6:11,12).

7. (Ho 5:14 La 3:10).

leopard – The *Hebrew* comes from a root meaning 'spotted' (compare Jer 13:23). Leopards lurk in thickets and thence spring on their victims.

observe – that is, *lie in wait* for them.

8. 'Writers on the natures of beasts say that none is more savage than a *she bear,* when *bereaved of her whelps*' [Jerome].

caul of ... heart – the membrane enclosing it: the pericardium.

there – 'by the way' (Ho 13:7).

9. thou ... in me – in contrast.

hast destroyed thyself – that is, thy destruction is of thyself (Pr 6:32 8:36).

in me is thine help – literally, 'in thine help' (compare De 33:26). Hadst thou rested thy hope *in Me,* I would have been always ready at hand *for thy help* [Grotius].

10. where ... Give me a king – Where now is the king whom ye substituted in My stead? Neither Saul, whom the whole nation begged for, not contented with Me their true king (1Sa 8:5,7,19,20 10:19), nor Jeroboam, whom subsequently the ten tribes chose instead of the line of David My anointed, can save thee now. They had expected from their kings what is the prerogative of God alone, namely, the power of saving them.

judges – including all civil authorities under the king (compare Am 2:3).

11. I gave ... king in ... anger ... took ... away in ... wrath – true both of Saul (1Sa 15:22,23 16:1) and of Jeroboam's line (2Ki 15:30). Pekah was taken away through Hoshea, as he himself took away Pekahiah; and as Hoshea was soon to be taken away by the Assyrian king.

12. bound up ... hid – Treasures, meant to be kept, are bound up and hidden; that is, do not flatter yourselves, because of the delay, that I have forgotten your sin. Nay (Ho 9:9), Ephraim's iniquity is kept as it were safely sealed up, until the due time comes for bringing it forth for punishment (De 32:34 Job 14:17 21:19; compare Ro 2:5). Opposed to 'blotting out the handwriting against' the sinner (Col 2:14).

13. sorrows of a travailing woman – calamities sudden and agonizing (Jer 30:6).

unwise – in not foreseeing the impending judgment, and averting it by penitence (Pr 22:3).

he should not stay long in the place of the breaking forth of children – When Israel might deliver himself from calamity by the pangs of penitence, he brings ruin on himself by so long deferring a new birth unto repentance, like a child whose mother has not strength to bring it forth, and which therefore remains so long in the passage from the womb as to run the risk of death (2Ki 19:3 Isa 37:3 66:9).

14. Applying primarily to God's restoration of Israel from Assyria partially, and, in times yet future, fully from all the lands of their present long-continued dispersion, and political *death* (compare Ho 6:2 Isa 25:8 26:19 Eze 37:12). God's power and grace are magnified in quickening what to the eye of flesh seems dead and hopeless (Ro 4:17,19). As Israel's history, past and future, has a representative character in relation to the Church, this verse is expressed in language alluding to Messiah's (who is the ideal Israel) grand victory over the grave and death, the first-fruits of His own resurrection, the full harvest to come at the general resurrection; hence the similarity between this verse and Paul's language as to the latter (1Co 15:55). The question is that of one triumphing over a foe, once a cruel tyrant, but now robbed of all power to hurt.

repentance shall be hid from mine eyes – that is, I will not change My purpose of fulfilling My promise by delivering Israel, on the condition of their return to Me (compare Ho 14:2–8 Nu 23:19 Ro 11:29).

15. fruitful – referring to the meaning of 'Ephraim,' from a *Hebrew* root, 'to be fruitful' (Ge 41:52). It was long the most numerous and flourishing of the tribes (Ge 48:19).

wind of the Lord – that is, sent by the Lord (compare Isa 40:7), who has His instruments of punishment always ready. The Assyrian, Shalmaneser., is meant (Jer 4:11 18:17 Eze 19:12).

from the wilderness – that is, the desert part of Syria (1Ki 19:15), the route from Assyria into Israel.

he – the Assyrian invader. Shalmaneser began the siege of Samaria in 723 B.C. Its close was in 721 B.C., the first year of Sargon, who seems to have usurped the throne of Assyria while Shalmaneser was at the siege of Samaria. Hence, while 2Ki 17:6 states, 'the *king of Assyria* took Samaria,' 2Ki 18:10 says, 'at the end of three years *they* took it.' In Sargon's magnificent palace at Khorsabad, inscriptions mention the number – 27,280 – of Israelites carried captive from Samaria and other places of Israel by the founder of the palace [G. V. SMITH].

16. This verse and Ho 13:15 foretell the calamities about to befall Israel before her restoration (Ho 13:14), owing to her impenitence.

her God – the greatest aggravation of her rebellion, that it was against *her* God (Ho 13:4).

infants ... dashed in pieces. – (2Ki 8:12 15:16 Am 1:13).

Chapter 14

Ho 14:1–9. God's promise of blessing, on their repentance: their abandonment of idolatry foretold: the conclusion of the whole, the just shall walk in God's ways, but the transgressor shall fall therein.

1. fallen by thine iniquity – (Ho 5:5 13:9).

2. Take with you words – instead of sacrifices, namely, the words of penitence here put in your mouths by God. 'Words,' in *Hebrew,* mean 'realities,' there being the same term for 'words' and 'things'; so God implies, He will not accept empty professions (Ps 78:36 Isa 29:13). He does not ask costly sacrifices, but *words* of heartfelt penitence.

receive us graciously – literally '(for) good.'

calves of our lips – that is, instead of sacrifices of *calves,* which we cannot offer to Thee in exile, we present the praises of our *lips.* Thus the exile, wherein the temple service ceased, prepared the way for the gospel time when the types of the animal sacrifices of the Old Testament being realized in Christ's perfect sacrifice once for all, 'the sacrifice of praise to God continually that is *the fruit of our lips*' (Heb 13:14) takes their place in the New Testament.

3. Three besetting sins of Israel are here renounced, trust in Assyria, application to Egypt for its cavalry (forbidden, De 17:16; compare Ho 7:11 11:5 12:1 2Ki 17:4 Ps 33:17 Isa 30:2,16 31:1), and idolatry.

fatherless – descriptive of the *destitute* state of Israel, when severed from God, their true Father. We shall henceforth trust in none but Thee, the only Father of the fatherless, and Helper of the destitute (Ps 10:14 68:5); our nation has experienced Thee such in our helpless state in Egypt, and now in a like state again our only hope is Thy goodness.

4. God's gracious reply to their self-condemning prayer.

backsliding – *apostasy:* not merely occasional backslidings. God can heal the most desperate sinfulness [CALVIN].

freely – with a gratuitous, unmerited, and abundant love (Eze 16:60–63). So as to the spiritual Israel (Joh 15:16 Ro 3:24 5:8 1Jo 4:10).

5. as the dew – which falls copiously in the East, taking the place of the more frequent rains in other regions. God will not be 'as the early dew that goeth away,' but constant (Ho 6:3,4 Job 29:19 Pr 19:12).

the lily – No plant is more productive than the lily, one root often producing fifty bulbs [PLINY, *Natural History*, 21.5]. The common lily is white, consisting of six leaves opening like bells. The royal lily grows to the height of three or four feet; Mt 6:29 alludes to the beauty of its flowers.

roots as Lebanon – that is, as the trees of Lebanon, which cast down their roots as deeply as is their height upwards; so that they are immovable [JEROME], (Isa 10:34). Spiritual growth consists most in the growth of the root which is out of sight.

6. branches – shoots, or suckers.

beauty … as the olive – which never loses its verdure. One plant is not enough to express the graces of God's elect people. The *lily* depicts its lovely growth; but as it wants duration and firmness, the deeply rooted cedars of Lebanon are added; these, however, are fruitless, therefore the fruitful, peace-bearing, fragrant, ever green olive is added.

smell as Lebanon – which exhaled from it the fragrance of odoriferous trees and flowers. So Israel's name shall be in good savour with all (Ge 27:27 So 4:11).

7. *They that* used to *dwell under* Israel's *shadow* (but who shall have been forced to leave it), shall *return*, that is, be restored (Eze 35:9). Others take 'His' shadow' to mean *Jehovah's* (compare Ps 17:8 91:1 Isa 4:6), which Ho 14:1,2 ('*return* unto *the Lord*,') favour. But the 'his' in Ho 14:6 refers to Israel, and therefore must refer to the same here.

revive as … corn – As the corn long buried in the earth springs up, with an abundant produce, so shall they revive from their calamities, with a great increase of offspring (compare Joh 12:24).

scent thereof – that is, Israel's *fame*. Compare Ho 14:6, 'His smell as Lebanon'; So 1:3: 'Thy *name* is as ointment poured forth.'

as the wine of Lebanon – which was most celebrated for its aroma, flavour, and medicinal restorative properties.

8. Ephraim *shall say* – being brought to penitence by God's goodness, and confessing and abhorring his past madness.

I have heard … and observed him – I Jehovah have *answered* and *regarded* him *with favour;* the opposite of God's 'hiding His face from' one (De 31:17). It is the experience of God's favour, in contrast to God's wrath heretofore, that leads Ephraim to abhor his past idolatry. Jehovah *heard* and answered: whereas the idols, as Ephraim now sees, could not *hear,* much less answer.

I am … a green fir – or cypress; ever green, winter and summer alike; the leaves not falling off in winter.

From me is thy fruit found – 'From Me,' as the root. Thou needest go no farther than Me for the supply of all thy wants; not merely the *protection* implied by the *shadow* of the cypress, but that which the cypress has not, namely, *fruit,* all spiritual and temporal blessings. It may be also implied, that whatever spiritual graces Ephraim seeks for or may have, are not of themselves, but of God (Ps 1:3 Joh 15:4,5,8 Jas 1:17). God's promises to us are more our security for mortifying sin than our promises to God (Isa 27:9).

9. EPILOGUE, summing up the whole previous teaching. Here alone Hosea uses the term 'righteous,' so rare were such characters in his day. There is enough of saving truth clear in God's Word to guide those humbly seeking salvation, and enough of difficulties to confound those who curiously seek them out, rather than practically seek salvation.

fall – stumble and are offended at difficulties opposed to their prejudices and lusts, or above their self-wise understanding (compare Pr 10:29 Mic 2:7 Mt 11:19 Lu 2:34 Joh 7:17 1Pe 2:7,8). Christ is the foundation-stone to some: a stone of stumbling and rock of offense to others. The same sun softens wax and hardens clay. But their fall is the most fatal who fall in the ways of God, split on the Rock of ages, and suck poison out of the Balm of Gilead.

JOEL

A.R. Faussett

Introduction

Joel (meaning 'one to whom Jehovah is God,' that is, worshipper of Jehovah) seems to have belonged to Judah, as no reference occurs to Israel; whereas he speaks of Jerusalem, the temple, the priests, and the ceremonies, as if he were intimately familiar with them (compare Joe 1:14 2:1,15,32 3:1,2,6,16,17,20,21). His predictions were probably delivered in the early days of Joash 870-865 B.C.; for no reference is made in them to the Babylonian, Assyrian, or even the Syrian invasion; and the only enemies mentioned are the Philistines, Phoenicians, Edomites, and Egyptians (Joe 3:4,19). Had he lived after Joash, he would doubtless have mentioned the Syrians among the enemies whom he enumerates since they took Jerusalem and carried off immense spoil to Damascus (2Ch 24:23,24). No idolatry is mentioned; and the temple services, the priesthood, and other institutions of the theocracy, are represented as flourishing. This all answers to the state of things under the high priesthood of Jehoiada, through whom Joash had been placed on the throne and who lived in the early years of Joash (2Ki 11:17,18 12:2–16 2Ch 24.4–14). He was the son of Pethuel.

The first chapter describes the desolation caused by an inroad of locusts – one of the instruments of divine judgment mentioned by Moses (De 28:38,39) and by Solomon (1Ki 8:37). The second chapter (Joe 2:1–11): the appearance of them, under images of a hostile army suggesting that the locusts were symbols and forerunners of a more terrible scourge, namely, foreign enemies who would consume all before them. (The absence of mention of *personal* injury to the inhabitants is not a just objection to the figurative interpretation; for the figure is consistent throughout in attributing to the locusts only injury to *vegetation*, thereby injuring indirectly man and beast). Joe 2:12–17: exhortation to repentance, the result of which will be: God will deliver His people, the former and latter rains shall return to fertilize their desolated lands, and these shall be the pledge of the spiritual outpouring of grace beginning with Judah, and thence extending to 'all flesh.' Joe 2:18–3:21: God's judgments on Judah's enemies, whereas Judah shall be established for ever.

Joel's style is pre-eminently pure. It is characterized by smoothness and fluency in the rhythms, roundness in the sentences, and regularity in the parallelisms. With the strength of Micah it combines the tenderness of Jeremiah, the vividness of Nahum, and the sublimity of Isaiah. As a specimen of his style take the second chapter wherein the terrible aspect of the locusts, their rapidity, irresistible progress, noisy din, and instinct-taught power of marshalling their forces for their career of devastation, are painted with graphic reality.

Chapter 1

Joe 1:1–20. The desolate aspect of the country through the plague of locusts; the people admonished to offer solemn prayers in the temple; for this calamity is the earnest of a still heavier one.

1. Joel – meaning, 'Jehovah is God.'
son of Pethuel – to distinguish Joel the prophet from others of the name. Persons of eminence also were noted by adding the father's name.
2, 3. A spirited introduction calling attention.
old men – the best judges in question concerning the past (De 32:7 Job 32:7).
Hath this been – that is, Hath any *so grievous* a calamity *as this* ever been before? No such plague of locusts had been since the ones *in Egypt*. Ex 10:14 is not at variance with this verse, which refers to *Judea*, in which Joel says there had been no such devastation before.
3. Tell ye your children – in order that they may be admonished by the severity of the punishment to fear God (Ps 78:6–8; compare Ex 13:8 Jos 4:7).
4. This verse states the subject on which he afterwards expands. Four species or stages of locusts, rather than four different insects, are meant (compare Le 11:22). Literally, (1) the *gnawing* locust; (2) the *swarming* locust; (3) the *licking* locust; (4) the *consuming* locust; forming a climax to the most destructive kind. The last is often three inches long, and the two antennæ, each an inch long. The two hinder of its six feet are larger than the rest, adapting it for leaping. The first 'kind' is that of the locust, having just emerged from the egg in spring, and without wings. The second is when at the end of spring, still in their first skin, the locusts put forth little ones without legs or wings. The third, when after their third casting of the old skin, they get small wings, which enable them to leap the better, but not to fly. Being unable to go away till their wings are matured, they devour all before them, grass, shrubs, and bark of trees: translated 'rough caterpillars' (Jer 51:27). The fourth kind, the matured winged locusts (see on Na 3:16). In Joe 2:25 they are enumerated in the reverse order, where the restoration of the devastations caused by them is promised. The Hebrews make the first species refer to Assyria and Babylon; the second species, to Medo-Persia; the third, to Greco-Macedonia and Antiochus Epiphanes; the fourth, to the Romans. Though the primary reference be to literal locusts, the Holy Spirit doubtless had in view the successive empires which assailed Judea, each worse than its predecessor, Rome being the climax.
5. Awake – out of your ordinary state of drunken stupor, to realize the cutting off from you of your favourite drink. Even the drunkards (from a *Hebrew* root, 'any strong drink') shall be forced to 'howl,' though usually laughing in the midst of the greatest national calamities, so palpably and universally shall the calamity affect all.
wine … new wine – 'New' or 'fresh wine,' in *Hebrew*, is the unfermented, and therefore unintoxicating, *sweet juice* extracted by pressure from grapes or other fruit, as *pomegranates* (So 8:2). 'Wine' is the produce of the grape alone, and is intoxicating (see on Joe 1:10).
6. nation – applied to the locusts, rather than 'people' (Pr 30:25,26), to mark not only their *numbers*, but also their *savage hostility;* and also to prepare the mind of the hearer for the transition to the figurative locusts in the second chapter, namely, the 'nation' or *Gentile* foe coming against Judea (compare Joe 2:2).
my land – that is, Jehovah's; which never would have been so devastated were *I* not pleased to inflict punishment (Joe 2:18 Isa 14:25 Jer 16:18 Eze 36:5 38:16).
strong – as irresistibly sweeping away before its compact body the fruits of man's industry.
without number – so Jud 6:5 7:12, 'like grasshoppers (or 'locusts') for multitude' (Jer 46:23 Na 3:15).
teeth … lion – that is, the locusts are as destructive as a lion; there is no vegetation that can resist their bite (compare Re 9:8). Pliny says 'they gnaw even the doors of houses.'
7. my vine … my fig tree – being in 'My land,' that is, Jehovah's (Joe 1:6). As to the vine-abounding nature of ancient Palestine, see Nu 13:23,24.
cast it away – down to the ground.
branches . . . white – both from the bark being stripped off (Ge 30:37), and from the branches drying up through the trunk, both bark and wood being eaten up below by the locusts.
8. Lament – O 'my land' (Joe 1:6 Isa 24:4).
virgin … for the husband – A virgin betrothed was regarded as married (De 22:23 Mt 1:19). The *Hebrew* for 'husband' is 'lord' or 'possessor,' the husband being considered the master of the wife in the East.
of her youth – when the affections are strongest and when sorrow at bereavement is consequently keenest. Suggesting the thought of what Zion's grief ought to be for her separation from Jehovah, the betrothed husband of her early days (Jer 2:2 Eze 16:8 Ho 2:7; compare Pr 2:17 Jer 3:4).
9. The greatest sorrow to the mind of a religious Jew, and what ought to impress the whole nation with a sense of God's displeasure, is the cessation of the usual temple-worship.
meat offering – *Hebrew, mincha;* 'meat' not in the English sense 'flesh,' but the unbloody offering made of flour, oil, and frankincense. As it

and the drink offering or libation *poured out* accompanied every sacrificial *flesh* offering, the latter is included, though not specified, as being also 'cut off,' owing to there being no food left for man or beast.

priests … mourn – not for their own loss of sacrificial perquisites (Nu 18:8–15), but because they can no longer offer the appointed offerings to Jehovah, to whom they minister.

10. field … land – differing in that 'field' means the open, unenclosed country; 'land,' the rich *red* soil (from a root 'to be red') fit for cultivation. Thus, 'a man of the field,' in *Hebrew*, is a 'hunter'; a 'man of the ground' or 'land,' an 'agriculturist' (Ge 25:27). 'Field' and 'land' are here personified.

new wine – from a *Hebrew* root implying that it *takes possession* of the brain, so that a man is not master of himself. So the *Arabic* term is from a root 'to hold captive.' It is already fermented, and so intoxicating, unlike the *sweet fresh wine*, in Joe 1:5, called also 'new wine,' though a different *Hebrew* word. It and 'the oil' stand for the vine and the olive tree, from which the 'wine' and 'oil' are obtained (Joe 1:12).

11. Be … ashamed – that is, Ye shall have the *shame* of disappointment on account of the failure of 'the wheat' and 'barley … harvest.'

12. pomegranate – a tree straight in the stem growing twenty feet high; the fruit is of the size of an orange, with blood-red coloured pulp.

palm tree – The dates of Palestine were famous. The palm is the symbol of Judea on coins under the Roman emperor Vespasian. It often grows a hundred feet high.

apple tree – The *Hebrew* is generic, including the orange, lemon, and pear tree.

joy is withered away – such as is felt in the harvest and the vintage seasons (Ps 4:7 Isa 9:3).

13. Gird yourselves – namely, with sackcloth; as in Isa 32:11, the ellipsis is supplied (compare Jer 4:8).

lament, ye priests – as it is your duty to set the example to others; also as the guilt was greater, and a greater scandal was occasioned, by your sin to the cause of God.

lie all night in sackcloth – so Ahab (1Ki 21:27).

ministers of my God – (1Co 9:13). Joel claims authority for his doctrine; it is *in God's name and by His mission* I speak to you.

14. Sanctify … a fast – Appoint a solemn fast.

solemn assembly – literally, a 'day of restraint' or cessation from work, so that all might give themselves to supplication (Joe 2:15,16 1Sa 7:5,6 2Ch 20:3–13).

elders – The contrast to 'children' (Joe 2:16) requires age to be intended, though probably elders in *office* are included. Being the people's leaders in guilt, they ought to be their leaders also in repentance.

15. day of the Lord – (Joe 2:1,11); that is, the day of His anger (Isa 13:9 Ob 1:15 Zep 1:7,15). It will be a foretaste of the coming day of the Lord as Judge of all men, whence it receives the same name. Here the transition begins from the plague of locusts to the worse calamities (Joe 2:1–11) from invading armies about to come on Judea, of which the locusts were the prelude.

16. Compare Joe 1:9, and latter part of Joe 1:12.

joy – which prevailed at the annual feasts, as also in the ordinary sacrificial offerings, of which the offerers ate before the Lord with gladness and thanksgivings (De 12:6,7,12 16:11,14,15).

17. is rotten – 'is dried up,' 'vanishes away,' from an *Arabic* root [MAURER]. 'Seed,' literally, 'grains.' The drought causes the seeds to lose all their vitality and moisture.

garners – granaries; generally underground, and divided into separate receptacles for the different kinds of grain.

18. cattle … perplexed – implying the restless gestures of the dumb beasts in their inability to find food. There is a tacit contrast between the sense of the brute creation and the insensibility of the people.

yea, the … sheep – *Even the sheep*, which are content with less rich pasturage, cannot find food.

are made desolate – literally, 'suffer *punishment*.' The innocent brute shares the 'punishment' of guilty man (Ex 12:29 Jon 3:7 4:11).

19. to thee will I cry – Joel here interposes, As this people is insensible to shame or fear and will not hear, I will leave them and address myself directly to Thee (compare Isa 15:5 Jer 23:9).

fire – that is, the parching heat.

pastures – 'grassy places'; from a *Hebrew* root 'to be pleasant.'

20. beasts … cry … unto thee – that is, look up to heaven with heads lifted up, as if their only expectation was from God (Job 38:41 Ps 104:21 145:15 147:9; compare Ps 42:1). They tacitly reprove the deadness of the Jews for not even now invoking God.

Chapter 2

Joe 2:1–32. The coming judgment a motive to repentance. Promise of blessings in the last days.

A more terrific judgment than that of the locusts is foretold, under imagery drawn from that of the calamity then engrossing the afflicted nation. He therefore exhorts to repentance, assuring the Jews of Jehovah's pity if they would repent. Promise of the Holy Spirit in the last days under Messiah, and the deliverance of all believers in Him.

1. Blow ... trumpet – to sound an alarm of coming war (Nu 10:1–10 Ho 5:8 Am 3:6); the office of the priests. Joe 1:15 is an anticipation of the fuller prophecy in this chapter.

2. darkness ... gloominess ... clouds ... thick darkness – accumulation of synonyms, to intensify the picture of *calamity* (Isa 8:22). Appropriate here, as the swarms of locusts intercepting the sunlight suggested *darkness* as a fit image of the coming visitation.

there hath not been ever the like – (Compare Joe 1:2 Ex 10:14).

3. before ... behind – that is, *on every side* (1Ch 19:10).

fire ... flame – destruction ... desolation (Isa 10:17).

as ... Eden ... wilderness – conversely (Isa 51:3 Eze 36:35).

4. appearance ... of horses – (Re 9:7). Not literal, but figurative locusts. The fifth trumpet, or first woe, in the parallel passage (Re 9:1–11), cannot be literal: for in Re 9:11 it is said, 'they had *a king* over them, the angel of the bottomless pit' – in the *Hebrew, Abaddon* ('destroyer'), but in the *Greek, Apollyon* – and (Re 9:7) 'on their heads were as it were *crowns* like gold, and their faces were as the faces of *men.*' Compare Joe 2:11, 'the day of the Lord ... great and very terrible'; implying their ultimate reference to be connected with Messiah's second coming in judgment. The locust's head is so like that of a horse that the Italians call it *cavalette.* Compare Job 39:20, 'the horse ... as the grasshopper,' or *locust.*

run – The locust *bounds,* not unlike the horse's gallop, raising and letting down together the two front feet.

5. Like the noise of chariots – referring to the loud sound caused by their wings in motion, or else the movement of their hind legs.

6. much pained – namely, with terror. The Arab proverb is, 'More terrible than the locusts.'

faces shall gather blackness – (Isa 13:8 Jer 30:6 Na 2:10).

7–9. Depicting the regular military order of their advance, 'One locust not turning a nail's breadth out of his own place in the march' [JEROME]. Compare Pr 30:27, 'The locusts have no king, yet go they forth all of them *by bands.*'

8. Neither shall one thrust another – that is, press upon so as to thrust his next neighbours out of his place, as usually occurs in a large multitude.

when they fall upon the sword – that is, among *missiles.*

not be wounded – because they are protected by defensive armour [GROTIUS].

9. run to and fro in the city – greedily seeking what they can devour.

the wall – surrounding each house in Eastern buildings.

enter in at the windows – though barred.

like a thief – (Joh 10:1; compare Jer 9:21).

10. earth ... quake before them – that is, the inhabitants of the earth quake with fear of them.

heavens ... tremble – that is, the powers of heaven (Mt 24:29); its illumining powers are disturbed by the locusts which intercept the sunlight with their dense flying swarms. These, however, are but the images of revolutions of states caused by such foes as were to invade Judea.

11. Lord ... his army – So among Mohammedans, 'Lord of the locusts' is a title of God.

his voice – His word of command to the locusts, and to the antitypical human foes of Judea, as 'His army.'

strong that executeth his word – (Re 18:8).

12. With such judgments impending over the Jews, Jehovah Himself urges them to repentance.

also now – *Even now,* what none could have hoped or believed possible, God still invites you to the hope of salvation.

fasting ... weeping ... mourning – Their sin being most heinous needs extraordinary humiliation. The outward marks of repentance are to signify the depth of their sorrow for sin.

13. Let there be the inward sorrow of heart, and not the mere outward manifestation of it by 'rending the garment' (Jos 7:6).

the evil – the calamity which He had threatened against the impenitent.

14. leave ... a meat offering and a drink offering – that is, give plentiful harvests, out of the first-fruits of which we may offer the meat and drink offering, now 'cut off' through the famine (Joe 1:9,13,16). 'Leave *behind Him*': as God in visiting His people now has left behind Him a curse, so He will, on returning to visit them, leave behind Him a blessing.

15. Blow the trumpet – to convene the people (Nu 10:3). Compare Joe 1:14. The nation was guilty, and therefore there must be a national humiliation. Compare Hezekiah's proceedings before Sennacherib's invasion (2Ch 30:1–27).

16. sanctify the congregation – namely, by expiatory rites and purification with water [CALVIN], (Ex 19:10,22).

elders ... children – No age was to be excepted (2Ch 20:13).

bridegroom – ordinarily exempted from public duties (De 24:5; compare 1Co 7:5,29).

closet – or, nuptial bed, from a *Hebrew* root 'to cover,' referring to the canopy over it.

17. between the porch and ... altar – the porch of Solomon's temple on the east (1Ki 6:3); the altar of burnt offerings in the court of the priests, before the porch (2Ch 8:12; compare Eze 8:16 Mt 23:35). The suppliants thus were to

stand with their backs to the altar on which they had nothing to offer, their faces towards the place of the Shekinah presence.

heathen should rule over them – This shows that not locusts, but human foes, are intended. The *Margin* translation, 'use a byword against them,' is not supported by the *Hebrew*.

wherefore should they say … Where is their God? – that is, do not for thine own honour's sake, let the heathen sneer at the God of Israel, as unable to save His people (Ps 79:10 115:2).

18. Then – when God sees His people penitent.

be jealous for his land – as a husband *jealous* of any dishonour done to the wife whom he loves, as if done to himself. The *Hebrew* comes from an *Arabic* root, 'to be flushed in face' through indignation.

19. corn … wine … oil – rather, as *Hebrew*, '*the* corn … *the* wine … *the* oil,' namely, which the locusts have destroyed [HENDERSON].

20. the northern *army* – The *Hebrew* expresses that the *north* in relation to Palestine is not merely the quarter whence the invader comes, but is his native land, 'the Northlander'; namely, the Assyrian or Babylonian (compare Jer 1:14,15 Zep 2:13). The locust's native country is not the *north*, but the *south*, the deserts of Arabia, Egypt, and Libya. Assyria and Babylon are the type and forerunner of all Israel's foes (Rome, and the final Antichrist), from whom God will at last deliver His people, as He did from Sennacherib (2Ki 19:35).

face … hinder part – more applicable to a human army's *van* and *rear*, than to locusts. The northern invaders are to be dispersed in every other direction but that from which they had come: 'a land barren and desolate,' that is, Arabia-Deserta: 'the eastern (or *front*) sea,' that is, the Dead Sea: 'the utmost (or *hinder*) sea,' that is, the Mediterranean. *In front* and *behind* mean east and west; as, in marking the quarters of the world, they *faced* the east, which was therefore 'in front'; the west was *behind* them; the south was on their *right*, and the north on their *left*.

stink – metaphor from *locusts*, which perish when blown by a storm into the sea or the desert, and emit from their putrefying bodies such a stench as often breeds a pestilence.

because he hath done great things – that is, because the invader hath *haughtily magnified himself in his doings.* Compare as to Sennacherib, 2Ki 19:11–13,22,28. This is quite inapplicable to the locusts, who merely seek food, not self-glorification, in invading a country.

21–23. In an ascending gradation, the *land* destroyed by the enemy, *the beasts of the field,* and the *children of Zion,* the land's inhabitants, are addressed, the former two by personification.

Lord will do great things – In contrast to the 'great things' done by the haughty foe (Joe 2:20)

to the hurt of Judah stand the 'great things' to be done by Jehovah for her benefit (compare Ps 126:2,3).

22. (Zec 8:12). As before (Joe 1:18,20) he represented the beasts as *groaning* and *crying* for want of food in the 'pastures,' so now he reassures them by the promise of *springing pastures.*

23. rejoice in the Lord – not merely *in the springing pastures,* as the brute 'beasts' which cannot raise their thoughts higher (Isa 61:10 Hab 3:18).

former rain … the rain … the former … the latter rain – The autumnal, or 'former rain,' from the middle of October to the middle of December, is put first, as Joel prophesies in summer when the locusts' invasion took place, and therefore looks to the time of early sowing in autumn, when the autumnal rain was indispensably required. Next, 'the rain,' *generically,* literally, 'the showering' or 'heavy rain.' Next, the two species of the latter, 'the former and the latter rain' (in March and April). The repetition of the 'former rain' implies that He will give it not merely for the exigence of that particular season when Joel spake, but also for the future in the regular course of nature, the autumn and the spring rain; the former being put first, in the order of nature, as being required for the sowing in autumn, as the latter is required in spring for maturing the young crop.

moderately – rather, 'in due measure,' as much as the land requires; literally, 'according to right'; neither too much nor too little, either of which extremes would hurt the crop (compare De 11:14 Pr 16:15 Jer 5:24; see on Ho 6:3). The phrase, 'in due measure,' in this clause is parallel to 'in the first month,' in the last clause (that is, '*in the month* when *first* it is needed,' each rain in its proper season). Heretofore the *just* or *right* order of nature has been interrupted through your sin; now God will restore it.

24. The effect of the seasonable rains shall be abundance of all articles of food.

25. locust … cankerworm … caterpillar … palmer worm – the reverse order from Joe 1:4, where God will restore not only what has been lost by the full-grown *consuming locust,* but also what has been lost by the less destructive *licking locust,* and *swarming locust,* and *gnawing locust.*

27. know that I am in the midst of Israel – As in the Old Testament dispensation God was present by the Shekinah, so in the New Testament first, for a brief time by the Word made flesh dwelling among us (Joh 1:14), and to the close of this dispensation by the Holy Spirit in the Church (Mt 28:20), and probably in a more perceptible manner with Israel when restored (Eze 37:26–28).

never be ashamed – not an unmeaning repetition from Joe 2:26. The twice-asserted truth enforces its unfailing certainty. As the 'shame' in

Joe 2:26 refers to temporal blessings, so in this verse it refers to the spiritual blessings flowing from the presence of God with His people (compare Jer 3:16,17 Re 21:3).

28. afterward – 'in the last days' (Isa 2:2) under Messiah *after* the invasion and deliverance of Israel from the *northern army*. Having heretofore stated the outward blessings, he now raises their minds to the expectation of extraordinary spiritual blessings, which constitute the true restoration of God's people (Isa 44:3). Fulfilled in earnest (Ac 2:17) on Pentecost; among the Jews and the subsequent election of a people among the Gentiles; hereafter more fully at the restoration of Israel (Isa 54:13 Jer 31:9,34 Eze 39:29 Zec 12:10) and the consequent conversion of the whole world (Isa 2:2 11:9 66:18–23 Mic 5:7 Ro 11:12,15). As the Jews have been the seedmen of the elect Church gathered out of Jews and Gentiles, the first Gospel preachers being Jews from Jerusalem, so they shall be the harvest men of the coming world-wide Church, to be set up at Messiah's appearing. That the promise is not *restricted* to the first Pentecost appears from Peter's own words: 'The promise is (not only) unto you and to your children, (but also) to *all that are afar off* (both in space and in time), even as many as the Lord our God shall call' (Ac 2:39). So here 'upon *all* flesh.'

I will *pour out* – under the new covenant: not merely, *let fall drops*, as under the Old Testament (Joh 7:39).

my spirit – the Spirit 'proceeding from the Father and the Son,' and at the same time one with the Father and the Son (compare Isa 11:2).

sons … daughters … old … young – not merely on a privileged few (Nu 11:29) as the prophets of the Old Testament, but men of all ages and ranks. See Ac 21:9 1Co 11:5, as to 'daughters,' that is, women, prophesying.

dreams … visions – (Ac 9:10 16:9). The 'dreams' are attributed to the 'old men,' as more in accordance with their years; 'visions' to the 'young men,' as adapted to their more lively minds. The three modes whereby God revealed His will under the Old Testament (Nu 12:6), 'prophecy, dreams, and visions,' are here made the symbol of the full manifestation of Himself to all His people, not only in miraculous gifts to some, but by His indwelling Spirit to all in the New Testament (Joh 14:21,23 15:15). In Ac 16:9 18:9, the term used is 'vision,' though in the night, not a *dream*. No other dream is mentioned in the New Testament save those given to Joseph in the very beginning of the New Testament, before the full Gospel had come; and to the wife of Pilate, a *Gentile* (Mt 1:20 2:13 27:19). 'Prophesying' in the New Testament is applied to all speaking under the enlightenment of the Holy Spirit, and not merely to foretelling events. All true Christians are 'priests' and 'ministers' of our God (Isa 61:6), and have the Spirit (Eze 36:26,27). Besides this, probably, a special gift of prophecy and miracle-working is to be given at or before Messiah's coming again.

29. And also – 'And even.' The very slaves by becoming the Lord's servants are His freemen (1Co 7:22 Ga 3:28 Col 3:11 Phm 1:16). Therefore, in Ac 2:18 it is quoted, '*My* servants' and '*My* handmaidens'; as it is only by becoming *the Lord's* servants they are spiritually free, and partake of the same spirit as the other members of the Church.

30, 31. As Messiah's manifestation is full of joy to believers, so it has an aspect of wrath to unbelievers, which is represented here. Thus when the Jews received Him not in His coming of grace, He came in judgment on Jerusalem. Physical prodigies, massacres, and conflagrations preceded its destruction [Josephus, *Wars of the Jews*]. To these the language here may allude; but the figures chiefly symbolize political revolutions and changes in the ruling powers of the world, prognosticated by previous disasters (Am 8:9 Mt 24:29 Lu 21:25–27), and convulsions such as preceded the overthrow of the Jewish polity. Such shall probably occur in a more appalling degree before the final destruction of the ungodly world ('the great and terrible day of Jehovah,' compare Mal 4:5), of which Jerusalem's overthrow is the type and earnest.

32. call on … name of … Lord – Hebrew, Jehovah. Applied to Jesus in Ro 10:13 (compare Ac 9:14 1Co 1:2). Therefore, Jesus is Jehovah; and the phrase means, 'Call on Messiah in His divine attributes.'

shall be delivered – as the Christians were, just before Jerusalem's destruction, by retiring to Pella, warned by the Saviour (Mt 24:16); a type of the spiritual deliverance of all believers, and of the last deliverance of the elect 'remnant' of Israel from the final assault of Antichrist. 'In Zion and Jerusalem' the Saviour first appeared; and there again shall He appear as the *Deliverer* (Zec 14:1–5).

as the Lord hath said – Joel herein refers, not to the other prophets, but to his own words preceding.

call – metaphor from an invitation to a feast, which is an act of gratuitous kindness (Lu 14:16). So the remnant called and saved is according to the election of grace, not for man's merits, power, or efforts (Ro 11:5).

Chapter 3

Joe 3:1–21. God's vengeance on Israel's foes in the valley of Jehoshaphat. His blessing on the Church.

1. bring again the captivity – that is, reverse it. The Jews restrict this to the return from

Babylon. Christians refer it to the coming of Christ. But the prophet comprises the whole redemption, beginning from the return out of Babylon, then continued from the first advent of Christ down to the last day, when God will restore His Church to perfect felicity [CALVIN].

2. Parallel to Zec 14:2,3,4, where the 'Mount of Olives' answers to the 'Valley of Jehoshaphat' here. The latter is called 'the valley of blessing' (*Berachah*) (2Ch 20:26). It lies between Jerusalem and the Mount of Olives and has the Kedron flowing through it. As Jehoshaphat overthrew the confederate foes of Judah, namely, Ammon, Moab. (Ps 83:6–8), in this valley, so God was to overthrow the Tyrians, Zidonians, Philistines, Edom, and Egypt, with a similar utter overthrow (Joe 3:4,19). This has been long ago fulfilled; but the ultimate event shadowed forth herein is still future, when God shall specially interpose to destroy Jerusalem's last foes, of whom Tyre, Zidon, Edom, Egypt, and Philistia are the types. As 'Jehoshaphat' means 'the judgment of Jehovah,' *the valley of Jehoshaphat* may be used as a *general* term for the theatre of God's final judgments on Israel's foes, with an allusion to the judgment inflicted on them by Jehoshaphat. The definite mention of the Mount of Olives in Zec 14:4, and the fact that this was the scene of the ascension, makes it likely the same shall be the scene of Christ's coming again: compare 'this same Jesus ... shall so come *in like manner* as ye have seen Him go into heaven' (Ac 1:11).

all nations – namely, which have maltreated Judah.

plead with them – (Isa 66:16 Eze 38:22).

my heritage Israel – (De 32:9 Jer 10:16). Implying that the source of Judah's redemption is God's free love, wherewith He chose Israel as *His peculiar heritage,* and at the same time assuring them, when desponding because of trials, that He would plead their cause as His own, and as if He were injured in their person.

3. cast lots for my people – that is, divided among themselves My people as their captives by lot. Compare as to the distribution of captives by lot (Ob 1:11 Na 3:10).

given a boy for ... harlot – Instead of paying a harlot for her prostitution in money, they gave her a Jewish captive boy as a slave.

girl for wine – So valueless did they regard a Jewish girl that they would sell her for a draught of wine.

4. what have ye to do with me – Ye have no connection with Me; I have given you no cause of quarrel, why then do ye trouble Me? (Compare the same phrase, Jos 22:24 Jud 11:12 2Sa 16:10 Mt 8:29).

Tyre ... Zidon ... Palestine – (Am 1:6,9).

if ye recompense me – If *ye injure Me, in revenge* for fancied wrongs (Eze 25:15–17), I will requite you in your own coin swiftly and speedily.

5. my silver ... my gold – that is, the gold and silver of My people. The Philistines and Arabians had carried off all the treasures of King Jehoram's house (2Ch 21:16,17). Compare also 1Ki 15:18 2Ki 12:18 14:14, for the spoiling of the treasures of the temple and the king's palace in Judah by Syria. It was customary among the heathen to hang up in the idol temples some of the spoils of war as presents to their gods.

6. Grecians – literally, 'Javanites,' that is, the Ionians, a Greek colony on the coast of Asia Minor who were the first Greeks known to the Jews. The Greeks themselves, however, in their *original descent* came from Javan (Ge 10:2,4). Probably the germ of Greek civilization in part came through the Jewish slaves imported into Greece from Phoenicia by traffickers. Eze 27:13 mentions *Javan* and Tyre as trading in the persons of men.

far from their border – far from Judea; so that the captive Jews were cut off from all hope of return.

7. raise them – that is, I will *rouse* them. Neither sea nor distance will prevent My bringing them back. Alexander, and his successors, restored to liberty many Jews in bondage in Greece [JOSEPHUS, *Antiquities,* 13.5; *Wars of the Jews,* 9,2].

8. sell them to ... Sabeans – The Persian Artaxerxes Mnemon and Darius Ochus, and chiefly the Greek Alexander, reduced the Phoenician and Philistine powers. Thirty thousand Tyrians after the capture of Tyre by the last conqueror, and multitudes of Philistines on the taking of Gaza, were sold as slaves. The Jews are here said to do that which the God of Judah does in vindication of their wrong, namely, sell the Phoenicians who sold them, to a people 'far off,' as was Greece, whither the Jews had been sold. The Sabeans at the most remote extremity of Arabia Felix are referred to (compare Jer 6:20 Mt 12:42).

9. The nations hostile to Israel are summoned by Jehovah to 'come up' (this phrase is used because Jerusalem was on a *hill*) against Jerusalem, not that they may destroy it, but to be destroyed by the Lord (Eze 38:7–23 Zec 12:2–9 14:2,3).

Prepare war – literally, *sanctify* war: because the heathen always began war with religious ceremonies. The very phrase used of Babylon's *preparations* against Jerusalem (Jer 6:4) is now used of the final foes of Jerusalem. As Babylon was then desired by God to advance against her for her destruction, so now all her foes, of whom Babylon was the type, are desired to advance against her for *their own* destruction.

10. Beat your ploughshares into swords – As the foes are desired to 'beat their *ploughshares* *into swords,* and *their pruning hooks into spears,'* that so they may perish in their unhallowed attack on Judah and Jerusalem, so these latter, and the nations converted to God by them, after the overthrow of the antichristian confederacy, shall, on the contrary, 'beat their *swords into ploughshares,* and their *spears into pruning hooks,'* when under Messiah's coming reign there shall be war no more (Isa 2:4 Ho 2:18 Mic 4:3).

let the weak say, I am strong – So universal shall be the rage of Israel's foes for invading her, that even the *weak* among them will fancy themselves *strong* enough to join the invading forces. Age and infirmity were ordinarily made valid excuses for exemption from service, but so mad shall be the fury of the world against God's people, that even the feeble will not desire to be exempted (compare Ps 2:1–3).

11. thither – to the valley of Jehoshaphat.

thy mighty ones – the warriors who fancy themselves 'mighty ones,' but who are on that very spot to be overthrown by Jehovah [MAURER]. Compare 'the mighty men' (Joe 3:9). Rather, Joel speaks of God's really 'mighty ones' in contrast to the self-styled 'mighty men' (Joe 3:9 Ps 103:20 Isa 13:3; compare Da 10:13). AUBERLEN remarks: One prophet supplements the other, for they all prophesied only 'in part.' What was obscure to one was revealed to the other; what is briefly described by one is more fully so by another. Daniel calls Antichrist a king, and dwells on his worldly conquests; John looks more to his spiritual tyranny, for which reason he adds a second beast, wearing the semblance of spirituality. Antichrist *himself* is described by Daniel. Isaiah (Isa 29:1–24), Joel (Joe 3:1-21) describe *his army* of heathen followers coming up against Jerusalem, but not Antichrist himself.

12. See Joe 3:2.

judge all the heathen round about – that is, all the nations from all parts of the earth which have maltreated Israel; not merely, as HENDERSON supposes, the nations *round about* Jerusalem (compare Ps 110:6 Isa 2:4 Mic 4:3,11–13 Zep 3:15–19 Zec 12:9 14:3–11 Mal 4:1–3).

13. Direction to the ministers of vengeance to execute God's wrath, as the enemy's wickedness is come to its full maturity, God does not cut off the wicked at once, but waits till their guilt is at its *full* (so as to the Amorites iniquity, Ge 15:16), to show forth His own long-suffering, and the justice of their doom who have so long abused it (Mt 13:27–30,38,40 Re 14:15–19). For the image of a harvest to be threshed, compare Jer 51:33; and a wine-press, Isa 63:3 and La 1:15.

14. The prophet in vision seeing the immense array of nations congregating, exclaims, 'Multitudes, multitudes!' a Hebraism for *immense multitudes.*

valley of decision – that is, the valley in which they are to meet their 'determined doom.' The same as 'the valley of Jehoshaphat,' that is, 'the valley *of judgment'* (see on Joe 3:2).

15. (See on Joe 2:10; Joe 2:30).

16. (Compare Eze 38:18–22). The victories of the Jews over their cruel foe Antiochus, under the Maccabees, may be a reference of this prophecy; but the ultimate reference is to the last Antichrist, of whom Antiochus was the type. Jerusalem being the central seat of the theocracy (Ps 132:13), it is from thence that Jehovah discomfits the foe.

roar – as a lion (Jer 25:30 Am 1:2 3:8). Compare as to Jehovah's voice thundering, Ps 18:13 Hab 3:10,11.

Lord ... the hope of his people – or, 'their refuge' (Ps 46:1).

17. shall ye know – experimentally by the proofs of favours which I shall vouchsafe to you. So 'know' (Isa 60:16 Ho 2:20).

dwelling in Zion – as peculiarly *your God.*

holy ... no strangers pass through – to attack, or to defile, the holy city (Isa 35:8 52:1 Zec 14:21). *Strangers,* or Gentiles, shall come to Jerusalem, but it shall be in order to worship Jehovah there (Zec 14:16).

18. mountains ... drop ... wine – figurative for *abundance of vines,* which were cultivated in terraces of earth between the rocks on the sides of the hills of Palestine (Am 9:13).

hills ... flow with milk – that is, they shall abound in flocks and herds yielding milk plentifully, through the richness of the pastures.

waters – the great desideratum for fertility in the parched East (Isa 30:25).

fountain ... of ... house of ... Lord ... water ... valley of Shittim – The blessings, temporal and spiritual, issuing from Jehovah's house at Jerusalem, shall extend even to Shittim, on the border between Moab and Israel, beyond Jordan (Nu 25:1 33:49 Jos 2:1 Mic 6:5). 'Shittim' means 'acacias,' which grow only in arid regions: implying that even *the arid desert* shall be fertilized by the blessing from Jerusalem. So Eze 47:1–12 describes the waters issuing from the threshold of the house as flowing into the Dead Sea, and purifying it. Also in Zec 14:8 the waters flow on one side into the Mediterranean, on the other side into the Dead Sea, near which latter Shittim was situated (compare Ps 46:4 Re 22:1).

19. Edom – It was subjugated by David, but revolted under Jehoram (2Ch 21:8–10); and at every subsequent opportunity tried to injure Judah. Egypt under Shishak spoiled Jerusalem under Rehoboam of the treasures of the temple and the king's house; subsequently to the captivity, it inflicted under the Ptolemies various injuries on Judea. Antiochus spoiled Egypt (Da 11:40–43). Edom was made 'desolate' under the Maccabees [JOSEPHUS, *Antiquities,* 12.11,12].

The low condition of the two countries for centuries proves the truth of the prediction (compare Isa 19:1. Jer 49:17 Ob 1:10). So shall fare all the foes of Israel, typified by these two (Isa 63:1.).

20. dwell for ever – (Am 9:15), that is, be established as a flourishing state.

21. cleanse ... blood ... not cleansed – I will purge away from Judah the extreme guilt (represented by 'blood,' the shedding of which was the climax of her sin, Isa 1:15) which was for long not purged away, but visited with judgments (Isa 4:4). Messiah saves from guilt, in order to save from punishment.

AMOS

A.R. Faussett

Introduction

AMOS (meaning in *Hebrew* 'a burden') was (Am 1:1) a shepherd of Tekoa, a small town of Judah, six miles southeast from Beth-lehem, and twelve from Jerusalem, on the borders of the great desert (2Ch 20:20; compare 2Ch 11:6). The region being sandy was more fit for pastoral than for agricultural purposes. Amos therefore owned and tended flocks, and collected sycamore figs; not that the former was a menial office, kings themselves, as Mesha of Moab (2Ki 3:4), exercising it. Amos, however (from Am 7:14,15), seems to have been of humble rank.

Though belonging to Judah, he was commissioned by God to exercise his prophetical function in Israel; as the latter kingdom abounded in impostors, and the prophets of God generally fled to Judah through fear of the kings of Israel, a true prophet from Judah was the more needed in it. His name is not to be confounded with that of Isaiah's father, Amoz.

The time of his prophesying was in the reigns of Uzziah king of Judea, and Jeroboam II, son of Joash, king of Israel (Am 1:1), that is, in part of the time in which the two kings were contemporary; probably in Jeroboam's latter years, after that monarch had recovered from Syria 'the coast of Israel from the entering of Hamath to the sea of the plain' (2Ki 14:25–27); for Amos foretells that these same coasts, 'from the entering in of Hamath unto the river of the wilderness,' should be the scene of Israel's being afflicted (Am 6:14); also his references to the state of luxurious security then existing (Am 6:1,4,13), and to the speedy termination of it by the Assyrian foe (Am 1:5 3:12,15 5:27 8:2), point to the latter part of Jeroboam's reign, which terminated in 784 B.C., the twenty-seventh year of Uzziah's reign, which continued down to 759 B.C. He was contemporary with Hosea, only that the latter continued to prophesy in reigns subsequent to Uzziah (Ho 1:1); whereas Amos ceased to prophesy in the reign of that monarch. The scene of his ministry was Beth-el, where the idol calves were set up (Am 7:10–13). There his prophecies roused Amaziah, the idol priest, to accuse him of conspiracy and to try to drive him back to Judah.

The first six chapters are without figure; the last three symbolical, but with the explanation subjoined. He first denounces the neighbouring peoples, then the Jews, then Israel (from the third chapter to the end), closing with the promise or restoration under Messiah (Am 9:11–15). His style is thought by JEROME to betray his humble origin; but though not sublime, it is regular, perspicuous, and energetic; his images are taken from the scenes in nature with which he was familiar; his rhythms are flowing, his parallelisms exact, and his descriptions minute and graphic. Some peculiar expressions occur: 'cleanness of teeth,' that is, *want of bread* (Am 4:6); 'the excellency of Jacob' (Am 6:8 8:7); 'the high places of Isaac' (Am 7:9); 'the house of Isaac' (Am 7:16); 'he that createth the wind' (Am 4:13).

Two quotations from Amos occur in the New Testament (compare Ac 7:42,43, with Am 5:25,26; and Ac 15:16,17, with Am 9:11).

Chapter 1

Am 1:1–15. God's judgments on Syria, Philistia, Tyre, Edom, and Ammon.

1. The words of Amos – that is, Amos' *oracular communications*. A heading found only in Jer 1:1.

among the herdmen – rather, 'shepherds'; both owning and tending sheep; from an *Arabic* root, 'to mark with pricks,' namely, to select the best among a species of sheep and goats *ill-shapen and short-footed*, but distinguished by their wool [MAURER]. God chooses 'the weak things of the world to confound the mighty,' and makes a humble shepherd reprove the arrogance of Israel and her king arising from prosperity (compare 1Sa 17:40).

which he saw – in supernatural *vision* (Isa 1:1).

two years before the earthquake – mentioned in Zec 14:5. The earthquake occurred in Uzziah's reign, at the time of his being stricken with leprosy for usurping the priest's functions [JOSEPHUS, *Antiquities*, 9:10.4]. This clause must have been inserted by Ezra and the compilers of the Jewish canon.

2. will roar – as a lion (Joe 3:16). Whereas Jehovah is there represented roaring in Israel's behalf, here He roars against her (compare Ps 18:13 Jer 25:30).

from Zion ... Jerusalem – the seat of the theocracy, from which ye have revolted; not from Dan and Beth-el, the seat of your idolatrous worship of the calves.

habitations ... mourn – poetical personification. Their *inhabitants* shall mourn, imparting a sadness to the very *habitations*.

Carmel – the mountain promontory north of Israel, in Asher, abounding in rich pastures, olives, and vines. The name is the symbol of *fertility*. When Carmel itself 'withers,' how utter the desolation! (So 7:5 Isa 33:9 35:2 Jer 50:19 Na 1:4).

3. Here begins a series of threatenings of vengeance against six other states, followed by one against Judah, and ending with one against Israel, with whom the rest of the prophecy is occupied. The eight predictions are in symmetrical stanzas, each prefaced by 'Thus saith the Lord.' Beginning with the sin of others, which Israel would be ready enough to recognize, he proceeds to bring home to Israel her own guilt. Israel must not think hereafter, because she sees others visited similarly to herself, that such judgments are matters of chance; nay, they are divinely foreseen and foreordained, and are confirmations of the truth that God will not clear the guilty. If God spares not the nations that know not the truth, how much less Israel that sins wilfully (Lu 12:47,48 Jas 4:17)!

for three transgressions ... and for four – If Damascus had only sinned once or twice, I would have spared them, but since, after having been so often pardoned, they still persevere *so continually*, I will no longer 'turn away' *their punishment*. The *Hebrew* is simply, 'I will not reverse *it*,' namely, the sentence of punishment which follows; the negative expression implies more than it expresses; that is, 'I will *most surely execute* it'; God's fulfilment of His threats being more awful than human language can express. 'Three and four' imply sin *multiplied on sin* (compare Ex 20:5 Pr 30:15,18,21; 'six and seven,' Job 5:19; 'once and twice,' Job 33:14). There may be also a reference to *seven*, the product of *three* and *four* added; *seven* expressing the *full completion* of the measure of their guilt (Le 26:18,21,24; compare Mt 23:32).

threshed – the very term used of the Syrian king Hazael's oppression of Israel under Jehu and Jehoahaz (2Ki 10:32,33 13:7). The victims were thrown before the threshing sledges, the teeth of which tore their bodies. So David to Ammon (2Sa 12:31; compare Isa 28:27).

4. Hazael ... Ben-hadad – A black marble obelisk found in the central palace of Nimroud, and now in the British Museum, is inscribed with the names of Hazael and Ben-hadad of Syria, as well as Jehu of Israel, mentioned as tributaries of 'Shalmanubar,' king of Assyria. The kind of tribute from Jehu is mentioned: gold, pearls, precious oil. [G. V. SMITH]. The Ben-hadad here is the son of Hazael (2Ki 13:3), not the Ben-hadad supplanted and slain by Hazael (2Ki 8:7,15). The phrase, 'I will send a fire,' that is, the flame of war (Ps 78:63), occurs also in Am 1:7,10,12,14, and Am 2:2,5 Jer 49:27 Ho 8:14.

5. bar of Damascus – that is, the bar of its gates (compare Jer 51:30).

the inhabitant – *singular* for *plural*, 'inhabitants.' HENDERSON, because of the parallel, 'him that holdeth the sceptre,' translates, 'the ruler.' But the parallelism is that of one clause complementing the other, 'the inhabitant' or *subject* here answering to 'him that holdeth the sceptre' or *ruler* there, both ruler and subject alike being cut off.

Aven – the same as *Oon* or *Un*, a delightful valley, four hours' journey from Damascus, towards the desert. It is termed by Amos 'the valley of Aven,' or 'vanity,' from the worship of idols in it.

Kir – a region subject to Assyria (Isa 22:6) in Iberia, the same as that called now in *Armenian Kur*, lying by the river Cyrus which empties itself into the Caspian Sea. Tiglath-pileser fulfilled this prophecy when Ahaz applied for help to him against Rezin king of Syria, and the Assyrian king took Damascus, slew Rezin, and carried away its people captive to Kir.

6. Gaza – the southernmost of the five capitals of the five divisions of Philistia, and the key to Palestine on the south: hence put for the whole Philistine nation. Uzziah commenced the fulfilment of this prophecy (see 2Ch 26:6).

because they carried away ... the whole captivity – that is, they left none. Compare with the phrase here, Jer 13:19, 'Judah ... carried captive *all* of it ... *wholly* carried away.' Under Jehoram already the Philistines had carried away all the substance of the king of Judah, and his wives and his sons, 'so that there was never a son left to him, save Jehoahaz'; and after Amos' time (if the reference includes the *future*, which to the prophet's eye is as if already done), under Ahaz (2Ch 28:18), they seized on all the cities and villages of the low country and south of Judah.

to deliver them up to Edom – Judah's bitterest foe; as slaves (Am 1:9; compare Joe 3:1,3,6). GROTIUS refers it to the fact (Isa 16:4) that on Sennacherib's invasion of Judah, many fled for refuge to neighbouring countries; the Philistines, instead of hospitably sheltering the refugees, sold them, as if captives in war, to their enemies, the Idumeans.

7. fire – that is, the flame of war (Nu 21:28 Isa 26:11). Hezekiah fulfilled the prophecy, smiting the Philistines unto Gaza (2Ki 18:8). Foretold also by Isa 14:29,31.

8. Ashdod. – Gath alone is not mentioned of the five chief Philistine cities. It had already been subdued by David; and it, as well as Ashdod, was taken by Uzziah (2Ch 26:6). Gath perhaps had lost its position as one of the five primary cities before Amos uttered this prophecy, whence arose his omission of it. So Zep 2:4,5. Compare Jer 47:4 Eze 25:16. Subsequently to the subjugation of the Philistines by Uzziah, and then by Hezekiah, they were reduced by Psammetichus of Egypt, Nebuchadnezzar, the Persians, Alexander, and lastly the Asmoneans.

9. Tyrus ... delivered up the ... captivity to Edom – the same charge as against the Philistines (Am 1:6).

remembered not the brotherly covenant – the league of Hiram of Tyre with David and Solomon, the former supplying cedars for the building of the temple and king's house in return for oil and corn (2Sa 5:11 1Ki 5:2–6 9:11–14,27 10–22 1Ch 14:1 2Ch 8:18 9:10).

10. fire – (Compare Am 1:4,7 Isa 23:1–18 Eze 26:1–28:26). Many parts of Tyre were burnt by fiery missiles of the Chaldeans under Nebuchadnezzar. Alexander of Macedon subsequently overthrew it.

11. Edom ... did pursue his brother – (Isa 34:5). The chief aggravation to Edom's violence against Israel was that they both came from the same parents, Isaac and Rebekah (compare Ge 25:24–26 De 23:7,8 Ob 1:10,12 Mal 1:2).

cast off all pity – literally, 'destroy compassions,' that is, did suppress all the natural feeling of pity for a brother in distress.

his wrath for ever – As Esau kept up his grudge against Jacob, for having twice supplanted him, namely, as to the birthright and the blessing (Ge 27:41), so Esau's posterity against Israel (Nu 20:14,21). Edom first showed his spite in not letting Israel pass through his borders when coming from the wilderness, but threatening to 'come out against him with the sword'; next, when the Syrians attacked Jerusalem under Ahaz (compare 2Ch 28:17, with 2Ki 16:5); next, when Nebuchadnezzar assailed Jerusalem (Ps 137:7,8). In each case Edom chose the day of Israel's calamity for venting his grudge. This is the point of Edom's guilt dwelt on in Ob 1:10–13. God punishes the children, not for the sin of their fathers, but for their own filling up the measure of their fathers' guilt, as children generally follow in the steps of, and even exceed, their fathers' guilt (compare Ex 20:5).

12. Teman – a city of Edom, called from a grandson of Esau (Ge 36:11,15 Ob 1:8,9); situated five miles from Petra; south of the present Wady Musa. Its people were famed for wisdom (Jer 49:7).

Bozrah – a city of Edom (Isa 63:1). Selah or Petra is not mentioned, as it had been overthrown by Amaziah (2Ki 14:7).

13. Ammon – The Ammonites under Nahash attacked Jabesh-gilead and refused to accept the offer of the latter to save them, unless the Jabesh-gileadites would put out all their right eyes (1Sa 11:1.). Saul rescued Jabesh-gilead. The Ammonites joined the Chaldeans in their invasion of Judea for the sake of plunder.

ripped up ... women with-child – as Hazael of Syria also did (2Ki 8:12; compare Ho 13:16). Ammon's object in this cruel act was to leave Israel without 'heir,' so as to seize on Israel's inheritance (Jer 49:1).

14. Rabbah – the capital of Ammon: meaning 'the Great.' Distinct from Rabbah of Moab. Called *Philadelphia*, afterwards, from Ptolemy Philadelphus.

tempest – that is, with an onset swift, sudden, and resistless as a *hurricane*.

day of the whirlwind – parallel to 'the day of battle'; therefore meaning 'the day of the foe's *tumultuous assault.*'

Chapter 2

Am 2:1–16. Charges against Moab, Judah, and lastly Israel, the chief subject of Amos' prophecies.

1. burned ... bones of ... king of Edom into lime – When Jehoram of Israel, Jehoshaphat of Judah, and the king of Edom, combined against Mesha king of Moab, the latter failing in battle to break through to the king of Edom, took the oldest son of the latter and offered him as a burnt offering on the wall (2Ki 3:27) [MICHAELIS]. Thus, 'king of Edom' is taken as *the heir to the throne of Edom*. But 'his son' is rather the *king of Moab's own son*, whom the father offered to Molech [JOSEPHUS, *Antiquities*, 9.3]. Thus the reference here in Amos is not to that fact, but to the revenge which probably the king of Moab took on the king of Edom, when the forces of Israel and Judah had retired after their successful campaign against Moab, leaving Edom without allies. The Hebrew tradition is that Moab in revenge tore from their grave and burned the bones of the king of Edom, the ally of Jehoram and Jehoshaphat, who was already buried. Probably the 'burning of the bones' means, 'he burned the king of Edom alive, reducing his very bones to lime' [MAURER].

2. Kirioth – the chief city of Moab, called also Kir-Moab (Isa 15:1). The form is *plural* here, as including both the acropolis and town itself (see Jer 48:24,41, *Margin*).

die with tumult – that is, amid the tumult of battle (Ho 10:14).

3. the judge – the chief magistrate, the supreme source of justice. 'King' not being used, it seems likely a change of government had before this time substituted for *kings*, supreme *judges*.

4. From foreign kingdoms he passes to Judah and Israel, lest it should be said, he was strenuous in denouncing sins abroad, but connived at those of his own nation. Judah's guilt differs from that of all the others, in that it was directly against God, not merely against man. Also because Judah's sin was wilful and wittingly against light and knowledge.

law – the Mosaic code in general.

commandments – or *statutes*, the ceremonies and civil laws.

their lies – their lying idols (Ps 40:4 Jer 16:19), from which they drew false hopes. The order is to be observed. The Jews first cast off the divine *law*, then fall into *lying errors;* God thus visiting them with a righteous retribution (Ro 1:25,26,28 2Th 2:11,12). The pretext of a *good intention* is hereby refuted: the 'lies' that mislead them are *'their* (own) lies' [CALVIN].

after ... which their fathers ... walked – We are not to follow the fathers in error, but must follow the word of God alone. It was an aggravation of the Jews' sin that it was not confined to preceding generations; the sins of the sons rivalled those of their fathers (Mt 23:32 Ac 7:51) [CALVIN].

5. a fire – Nebuchadnezzar.

6. Israel – the ten tribes, the main subject of Amos' prophecies.

sold the righteous – Israel's judges for a bribe are induced to condemn in judgment him who has a righteous cause; in violation of De 16:19.

the poor for a pair of shoes – literally, 'sandals' of wood, secured on the foot by leather straps; less valuable than shoes. Compare the same phrase, for 'the most paltry bribe,' Am 8:6 Eze 13:19 Joe 3:3. They were not driven by poverty to such a sin; beginning with suffering themselves to be tempted by a large bribe, they at last are so reckless of all shame as to prostitute justice for the merest trifle. Amos convicts them of injustice, incestuous unchastity, and oppression first, as these were so notorious that they could not deny them, before he proceeds to reprove their contempt of God, which they would have denied on the ground that they worshipped God in the form of the calves.

7. pant after ... dust of ... earth on ... head of ... poor – that is, eagerly thirst for this object, by their oppression to prostrate the poor so as to cast on their heads dust (compare 2Sa 1:2 Job 2:12 Eze 27:30).

turn aside ... way of ... meek – pervert their cause (Am 5:12 Job 24:4 [GROTIUS]; Isa 10:2).

a man and his father – a crime 'not so much as named among the Gentiles' (1Co 5:1). When God's people sin in the face of light, they often fall lower than even those who know not God.

go in unto the same maid – from Am 2:8 it seems likely 'the damsel' meant is one of the prostitutes attached to the idol Astarte's temple: prostitution being part of her filthy worship.

to profane my ... name – Israel in such abominations, as it were, *designedly* seeks to insult God.

8. lay themselves ... upon clothes laid to pledge – the *outer garment*, which Ex 22:25–27 ordered to be restored to the poor man before sunset, as being his only covering. It aggravated the crime that they lay on these clothes in an idol temple.

by every altar – They partook in a recumbent posture of their idolatrous feasts; the ancients being in the habit of reclining at full length in eating, the upper part of the body resting on the left elbow, not sitting as we do.

drink ... wine of the condemned – that is, wine bought with the money of those whom they unjustly fined.

9. Yet – My former benefits to you heighten your ingratitude.

the Amorite – the most powerful of all the Canaanite nations, and therefore put for them all (Ge 15:16 48:22 De 1:20 Jos 7:7).

height ... like ... cedars – (Nu 13:32,33).

destroyed his fruit ... above ... roots ... beneath – that is, destroyed him *utterly* (Job 18:16 Eze 17:9 Mal 4:1).

10. brought you up from ... Egypt – 'brought up' is the phrase, as Egypt was low and flat, and Canaan hilly.

to possess the land of the Amorite – The Amorites strictly occupied both sides of the

Jordan and the mountains afterward possessed by Judah; but they here, as in Am 2:9, stand for *all* the Canaanites. God kept Israel forty years in the wilderness, which tended to discipline them in His statutes, so as to be the better fitted for entering on the possession of Canaan.

11. Additional obligations under which Israel lay to God; the *prophets* and *Nazarites,* appointed by Him, to furnish religious instruction and examples of holy self-restraint.

of your young men – It was a specimen of Israel's highly favoured state, that, of the class most addicted to pleasures, God chose those who by a solemn vow bound themselves to abstinence from all produce of the vine, and from all ceremonial and moral defilement. The Nazarite was not to shave (Nu 6:2.). God left nothing undone to secure the purity of their worship and their faithfulness to it (La 4:7). The same comes from a *Hebrew* root, *nazar,* 'to set apart.' Samson, Samuel, and John the Baptist were Nazarites.

Is it not even thus – Will any of you dare to deny it is so?

12. Ye so despised these My favours, as to tempt the Nazarite to break his vow; and forbade the prophets prophesying (Isa 30:10). So Amaziah forbade Amos (Am 7:12,13,14).

13. I am pressed under you – so CALVIN (Compare Isa 1:14). The *Margin* translates actively, 'I will depress your place,' that is, 'I will make it narrow,' a metaphor for *afflicting* a people; the opposite of *enlarging,* that is, relieving (Ps 4:1 Pr 4:12).

14. flight shall perish from … swift – Even the swift shall not be able to escape.

strong shall not strengthen his force – that is, shall not be able to use his strength.

himself – literally, 'his life.'

16. flee … naked – If any escape, it must be with the loss of accoutrements, and all that would impede rapid flight. They must be content with saving their life alone.

Chapter 3

Am 3:1–15. God's extraordinary love, being repaid by Israel with ingratitude, of necessity calls for judgments, which the prophets announce, not at random, but by God's commission, which they cannot but fulfil. The oppression prevalent in Israel will bring down ruin on all save a small remnant.

1. children of Israel – not merely the ten tribes, but 'the *whole family* brought up from Egypt'; all the descendants of Jacob, including Judah and Benjamin. Compare Jer 8:3, and Mic 2:3, on 'family' for the nation. However, as the prophecy following refers to the ten tribes, *they*

must be chiefly, if not solely, meant: they were the majority of the nation; and so Amos concedes what they so often boasted, that they were the elect people of God [CALVIN], *but* implies that this only heightens their sins.

2. You only have I known – that is, acknowledged as My people, and treated with peculiar favour (Ex 19:5 De 4:20). Compare the use of 'know,' Ps 1:6 144:3 Joh 10:14 2Ti 2:19.

therefore I will punish – the greater the privileges, the heavier the punishment for the abuse of them; for to the other offences there is added, in this case, ingratitude. When God's people do not glorify Him, He glorifies Himself by punishing them.

3–6. Here follow several questions of a parable-like kind, to awaken conviction in the people.

Can two walk together, except they be agreed? – Can God's prophets be so unanimous in prophesying against you, if God's Spirit were not joined with them, or if their prophecies were false? The Israelites were 'at ease,' not believing that God was with the prophets in their denunciations of coming ruin to the nation (Am 6:1,3; compare 1Ki 22:18,24,27 Jer 43:2). This accords with Am 3:7,8. So 'I will be with thy mouth' (Ex 4:12 Jer 1:8 Mt 10:20). If the prophets and God were not agreed, the former could not predict the future as they do. In Am 2:12 He had said, the Israelites forbade the prophets prophesying; therefore, in Am 3:3,8, He asserts the agreement between the prophets and God who spake by them against Israel [ROSENMULLER]. Rather, 'I once walked with you' (Le 26:12) as a Father and Husband (Isa 54:5 Jer 3:14); but now your way and Mine are utterly diverse; there can therefore be no fellowship between us such as there was (Am 3:2); I will walk with you only to 'punish you'; as a 'lion' walks with his 'prey' (Am 3:4), as a bird-catcher with a bird [TARNOVIUS]. The prophets, and all servants of God, can have no fellowship with the ungodly (Ps 119:63 2Co 6:16,17 Eph 5:11 Jas 4:4).

4. The same idea as in Mt 24:28. Where a corrupt nation is, there God's instruments of punishment are sure also to be. The lion roars loudly only when he has prey in sight.

Will a young lion cry out … if he – the 'lion,' not the 'young lion.'

have taken nothing? – The young lion just weaned lies silent, until the old lion brings the prey near; then the scent rouses him. So, the prophet would not speak against Israel, if God did not reveal to him Israel's sins as requiring punishment.

5. When a bird trying to fly upwards is made to fall upon the earth snare, it is a plain proof that the snare is there; so, Israel, now that thou art falling, infer thence, that it is in the snare of the divine judgment that thou art entangled [Ludovicus De Dieu].

shall _one_ take up a snare from the earth, and have taken nothing – The bird-catcher does not remove his snare off the ground till he has caught some prey; so God will not withdraw the Assyrians, the instruments of punishment, until they have had the success against you which God gives them. The foe corresponds to the 'snare,' suddenly _springing_ from the ground and enclosing the bird on the latter touching it; the _Hebrew_ is literally, 'Shall the snare _spring_ from the earth?' Israel entangled in judgments answers to the bird 'taken.'

6. When the sound of alarm is trumpeted by the watchman in the city, the people are sure to _run to and fro in alarm_ (_Hebrew_, literally). Yet Israel is not alarmed, though God threatens judgments.

shall there be evil in a city, and the Lord hath not done it? – This is the explanation of the preceding similes: God is the Author of all the calamities which come upon you, and which are foretold by His prophets. The evil of sin is from ourselves; the evil of trouble is from God, whoever be the instruments.

7. his secret – namely, His purpose hidden from all, until it is revealed to His prophets (compare Ge 18:17). In a wider sense, God's will is revealed to all who love God, which it is not to the world (Ps 25:14 Joh 15:15 17:25,26).

unto his servants – who being _servants_ cannot but obey their Lord in setting forth His purpose (namely, that of judgment against Israel) (Jer 20:9 Eze 9:11). Therefore the fault which the ungodly find with them is groundless (1Ki 18:17). It aggravates Israel's sin, that God is not about to inflict judgment, without having fully warned the people, if haply they might repent.

8. As when 'the lion roars' (compare Am 1:2 Am 3:4), none can help but 'fear,' so when Jehovah communicates His awful message, the prophet cannot but prophesy. Find not fault with me for prophesying; I must obey God. In a wider sense true of all believers (Ac 4:20 5:29).

9. Publish in ... palaces – as being places of greatest resort (compare Mt 10:27); and also as it is the sin of _princes_ that he arraigns, he calls on princes (the occupants of the 'palaces') to be the witnesses.

Ashdod – put for all Philistia. Convene the Philistine and the Egyptian magnates, from whom I have on various occasions rescued Israel. (The opposite formula to 'Tell it not in Gath,' namely, lest the heathen should glory over Israel). Even these idolaters, in looking on your enormities, will condemn you; how much more will the holy God?

upon the mountains of Samaria – on the hills surrounding and commanding the view of Samaria, the metropolis of the ten tribes, which was on a lower hill (Am 4:1 1Ki 16:24). The mountains are to be the tribunal on which the Philistines and Egyptians are to sit aloft to have a view of your crimes, so as to testify to the justice of your punishment (Am 3:13).

tumults – caused by the violence of the princes of Israel in 'oppressions' of the poor (Job 35:9 Ec 4:1).

10. know not to do – Their moral corruption blinds their power of discernment so that they cannot do right (Jer 4:22). Not simple intellectual ignorance; the defect lay in the heart and will.

store up violence and robbery – that is, treasures obtained by 'violence and robbery' (Pr 10:2).

11. Translate, 'An adversary (the abruptness produces a startling effect)! _and that too,_ from every side of the land.' So in the fulfilment, 2Ki 17:5: 'The king of Assyria (Shalmaneser) came up _throughout all the land,_ and went up to Samaria, and besieged it three years.'

bring down thy strength from thee – that is, bring thee down from thy strength (the strength on which thou didst boast thyself): all thy resources (Pr 10:15).

palaces shall be spoiled – a just retribution in kind (Am 3:10). _The palaces_ in which spoils of _robbery_ were _stored up,_ 'shall be spoiled.'

12. shepherd – a pastoral image, appropriately used by Amos, a shepherd himself.

piece of ... ear – brought by the shepherd to the owner of the sheep, so as not to have to pay for the loss (Ge 31:39 Ex 22:13). So if aught of Israel escapes, it shall be a miracle of God's goodness. It shall be but a scanty remnant. There is a kind of goat in the East the ears of which are a foot long, and proportionally broad. Perhaps the reference is to this. Compare on the image 1Sa 17:34,35 2Ti 4:17.

that dwell in Samaria in the corner of a bed – that is, that live luxuriously in Samaria (compare Am 6:1,4). 'A bed' means here the Oriental divan, a raised part of the room covered with cushions.

in Damascus in a couch – Jeroboam II had lately restored Damascus to Israel (2Ki 14:25,28). So the Israelites are represented as not merely in 'the corner of a bed,' as in Samaria, but 'in a (whole) couch,' at Damascus, living in luxurious ease. Of these, now so luxurious, soon but a remnant shall be left by the foe. The destruction of Damascus and that of Samaria shall be conjoined; as here their luxurious lives, and subsequently under Pekah and Rezin their inroads on Judah, were combined (Isa 7:1–8 8:4,9 17:3). The parallelism of 'Samaria' to 'Damascus,' and the _Septuagint_ favour _English Version_ rather than Gesenius: 'on a _damask_ couch.' The _Hebrew_ pointing, though generally expressing _damask,_ may express the city 'Damascus'; and many manuscripts point it so. Compare for Israel's overthrow, 2Ki 17:5,6 18:9-12.

13. testify in the house. – that is, *against* the house of Jacob. God calls on the same persons as in Am 3:9, namely, the heathen Philistines and the Egyptians to witness with their own eyes Samaria's corruptions above described, so that none may be able to deny the justice of Samaria's punishment [MAURER].

God of hosts – having all the powers of heaven and earth at His command, and therefore One calculated to strike terror into the hearts of the guilty whom He threatens.

14. I will also visit … Beth-el – the golden calves which were the source of all 'the transgressions of Israel' (1Ki 12:32 13:2 2Ki 23:15,16), though Israel thought that by them their transgressions were atoned for and God's favour secured.

horns of the altar – which used to be sprinkled with the blood of victims. They were horn-like projecting points at the corners of ancient altars. The *singular*, 'altar,' refers to the great altar erected by Jeroboam to the calves. The 'altars,' *plural*, refer to the lesser ones made in imitation of the great one (2Ch 34:5, compare with 1Ki 13:2 Ho 8:11 10:1).

15. winter … summer house – (Jud 3:20 Jer 36:22). Winter houses of the great were in sheltered positions facing the south to get all possible sunshine, summer houses in forests and on hills, facing the east and north.

houses of ivory – having their walls, doors, and ceilings inlaid with ivory. So Ahab's house (1Ki 22:39 Ps 45:8).

Chapter 4

Am 4:1–13. Denunciation of Israel's nobles for oppression; and of the whole nation for idolatry; and for their being unreformed even by God's judgments: therefore they must prepare for the last and worst judgment of all.

1. kine of Bashan – fat and wanton cattle such as the rich pasture of Bashan (east of Jordan, between Hermon and Gilead) was famed for (De 32:14 Ps 22:12 Eze 39:18). Figurative for those luxurious nobles mentioned, Am 3:9,10,12,15. The feminine, *kine*, or *cows*, not *bulls*, expresses their effeminacy. This accounts for masculine forms in the *Hebrew* being intermixed with feminine; the latter being figurative, the former the real persons meant.

say to their masters – that is to *their king*, with whom the princes indulged in potations (Ho 7:5), and whom here they importune for more wine. 'Bring' is *singular*, in the *Hebrew* implying that *one* 'master' alone is meant.

2. The Lord – the same *Hebrew* as 'masters' (Am 4:1). Israel's nobles say to their master or lord, Bring us drink: but 'the Lord' of him and them 'hath sworn,.'

by his holiness – which binds Him to punish the guilty (Ps 89:35).

he will take you away – that is God by the instrumentality of the enemy.

with hooks – literally, 'thorns' (compare 2Ch 33:11). As fish are taken out of the water by hooks, so the Israelites are to be taken out of their cities by the enemy (Eze 29:4; compare Job 41:1,2 Jer 16:16 Hab 1:15). The image is the more appropriate, as anciently captives were led by their conquerors by a hook made to pass through the nose (2Ki 19:28), as is to be seen in the Assyrian remains.

3. go out at the breaches – namely, of the city walls broken by the enemy.

every *cow at that which is* before her – figurative for *the once luxurious nobles* (compare 'kine of Bashan,' Am 4:1) shall go out *each one right before her;* not through the gates, but *each at the breach before him,* not turning to the right or left, apart from one another.

ye shall cast *them* into the palace – 'them,' that is, 'your posterity,' from Am 4:2. You yourselves shall escape through the breaches, after having cast your little children into the palace, so as not to see their destruction, and to escape the more quickly. Rather, 'ye shall cast *yourselves* into the palace,' so as to escape from it out of the city [CALVIN]. The palace, the scene of the princes riots (Am 3:10,15 4:1), is to be the scene of their ignominious flight. Compare in the similar case of *Jerusalem's* capture, the king's escape by way of the palace, through a breach in the wall (Eze 12:5,12).

4. God gives them up to their self-willed idolatry, that they may see how unable their idols are to save them from their coming calamities. So Eze 20:39.

Beth-el – (Am 3:14).

Gilgal – (Ho 4:15 9:15 12:11).

sacrifices every morning – as commanded in the law (Nu 28:3,4). They imitated the letter, while violating by calf-worship the spirit, of the Jerusalem temple-worship.

after three years – every third year; literally, 'after three (years of) days' (that is, the fullest complement of days, or *a year*); 'after three full years.' Compare Le 25:20 Jud 17:10, and 'the days' for the *years*, Joe 1:2. So *a month of days* is used for *a full month*, wanting no day to complete it (Ge 29:14, *Margin*; Nu 11:20,21). The Israelites here also kept to the letter of the law in bringing in the tithes of their increase every third year (De 14:28 26:12).

5. offer – literally, 'burn incense'; that is, 'offer a sacrifice of thanksgiving with *burnt incense* and with leavened bread.' The frankincense was laid on the meat offering, and taken by the priest from it to burn on the altar (Le 2:1,2,8–11). Though *unleavened cakes* were to accompany the peace offering sacrifice of animals, *leavened bread* was also commanded (Le 7:12,13), but not as a 'meat offering' (Le 2:11).

this liketh you – that is, this is what ye like.

6–11. Jehovah details His several chastisements inflicted with a view to reclaiming them: but adds to each the same sad result, 'yet have ye not returned unto Me' (Isa 9:13 Jer 5:3 Ho 7:10); the monotonous repetition of the same burden marking their pitiable obstinacy.

cleanness of teeth – explained by the parallel, 'want of bread.' The famine alluded to is that mentioned in 2Ki 8:1 [GROTIUS]. Where there is no food to masticate, the teeth are free from uncleanness, but it is the cleanness of want. Compare Pr 14:4, 'Where no oxen are, the crib is clean.' So spiritually, where all is outwardly smooth and clean, it is often because there is no solid religion. Better fighting and fears with real piety, than peace and respectable decorum without spiritual life.

7. withholden … rain … three months to … harvest – the time when rain was most needed, and when usually 'the latter rain' fell, namely, in spring, the latter half of February, and the whole of March and April (Ho 6:3 Joe 2:23). The drought meant is that mentioned in 1Ki 17:1 [GROTIUS].

rain upon one city … not … upon another – My rain that fell was only partial.

8. three cities wandered – that is, *the inhabitants of* three cities (compare Jer 14:1–6). GROTIUS explains this verse and Am 4:7, 'The rain fell on neighbouring countries, but not on Israel, which marked the drought to be, not accidental, but the special judgment of God.' The Israelites were obliged to leave their cities and homes to seek water at a distance [CALVIN].

9. blasting – the blighting influence of the east wind on the corn (Ge 41:6).

when … gardens … increased – In vain ye multiplied your gardens, for I destroyed their produce.

palmer worm – A species of *locust* is here meant, hurtful to fruits of trees, not to herbage or corn. The same east wind which brought the drought, blasting, and mildew, brought also the locusts into Judea [BOCHART], (Ex 10:13).

10. pestilence after the manner of Egypt – such as I formerly sent on the Egyptians (Ex 9:3,8. Ex 12:29 De 28:27,60). Compare the same phrase, Isa 10:24.

have taken away your horses – literally, 'accompanied with the captivity of your horses'; I have given up your young men to be slain, and their horses to be taken by the foe (compare 2Ki 13:7).

stink of your camps – that is, of your slain men (compare Isa 34:3 Joe 2:20).

to come up unto your nostrils – The *Hebrew* is more emphatic, 'to come up, *and that* unto your nostrils.'

11. some of you – some parts of your territory.

as God overthrew Sodom – (De 29:23 Isa 13:19 Jer 49:18 50:40 2Pe 2:6 Jude 1:7). 'God' is often repeated in *Hebrew* instead of 'I.' The earthquake here apparently alluded to is not that in the reign of Uzziah, which occurred 'two years' later (Am 1:1). Traces of earthquakes and volcanic agency abound in Palestine. The allusion here is to some of the effects of these in previous times. Compare the prophecy, De 28:15–68, with Am 4:6–11 here.

as a firebrand plucked out of … burning – (Compare Isa 7:4 Zec 3:2). The phrase is proverbial for a narrow escape from utter extinction. Though Israel revived as a nation under Jeroboam II, it was but for a time, and that after an almost utter destruction previously (2Ki 14:26).

12. Therefore – as all chastisements have failed to make thee 'return unto Me.'

thus will I do unto thee – as I have threatened (Am 4:2,3).

prepare to meet thy God – God is about to inflict the last and worst judgment on thee, the extinction of thy nationality; consider then what preparation thou canst make for encountering Him as thy foe (Jer 46:14 Lu 14:31,32). But as that would be madness to think of (Isa 27:4 Eze 22:14 Heb 10:31), see what can be done towards mitigating the severity of the coming judgment, by penitence (Isa 27:5 1Co 11:31). This latter exhortation is followed up in Am 5:4,6,8,14,15.

13. The God whom Israel is to 'prepare to meet' (Am 4:12) is here described in sublime terms.

wind – not as the *Margin*, 'spirit.' The God with whom thou hast to do is the Omnipotent Maker of things *seen*, such as the stupendous mountains, and of things *too subtle* to be seen, though of powerful agency, as the 'wind.'

declareth unto man … his thought – (Ps 139:2). Ye think that your secret thoughts escape My cognizance, but I am the searcher of hearts.

maketh … morning darkness – (Am 5:8 8:9). Both literally turning the sunshine into darkness, and figuratively turning the prosperity of the ungodly into sudden adversity (Ps 73:12,18,19; compare Jer 13:16).

treadeth upon … high places – God treadeth down the proud of the earth. He subjects to Him all things however high they be (Mic 1:3). Compare De 32:13 33:29, where the same phrase is used of God's people, elevated by God above every other human height.

Chapter 5

Am 5:1–27. Elegy over the prostrate kingdom: renewed exhortations to repentance: God declares that the coming day of judgment shall be terrible to the scorners who despise it: ceremonial services are not acceptable to him where true piety exists not: Israel shall therefore be removed far eastward.

1. lamentation – an elegy for the destruction coming on you. Compare Eze 32:2, 'take up,' namely, as a mournful *burden* (Eze 19:1 27:2).

2. virgin of Israel – the Israelite state heretofore unsubdued by foreigners. Compare Isa 23:12 Jer 18:13 31:4,21 La 2:13; may be interpreted, Thou who wast once the 'virgin daughter of Zion.' Rather, 'virgin' as applied to a state implies its beauty, and the delights on which it prides itself, its luxuries, power, and wealth [CALVIN].

no more rise – in the existing order of things: in the Messianic dispensation it is to rise again, according to many prophecies. Compare 2Ki 6:23 24:7, for the restricted sense of 'no more.'

forsaken upon her land – or, 'prostrated upon,' (compare Eze 29:5 32:4) [MAURER].

3. went out by a thousand – that is, 'the city from which there used to go out a thousand' equipped for war. 'City' is put for 'the inhabitants of the city,' as in Am 4:8.

shall leave ... hundred – shall have only a hundred left, the rest being destroyed by sword and pestilence (De 28:62).

4. Seek ye me, and ye shall live – literally, 'Seek ... Me, and *live.*' The second imperative expresses the *certainty* of 'life' (escape from judgment) resulting from obedience to the precept in the first imperative. If they perish, it is their own fault; God would forgive, if they would repent (Isa 55:3,6).

5. seek not Beth-el – that is, the calves at Beth-el.

Gilgal – (See on Am 4:4).

Beer-sheba – in Judah on the southern frontier towards Edom. Once 'the well of the oath' by Jehovah, ratifying Abraham's covenant with Abimelech, and the scene of his calling on 'the Lord, the everlasting God' (Ge 21:31,33), now a stronghold of idolatry (Am 8:14).

Gilgal shall surely go into captivity – a play on similar sounds in the *Hebrew, Gilgal, galoh, yigleh:* 'Gilgal (the place of *rolling*) shall rolling be rolled away.'

Beth-el shall come to naught – Beth-el (that is, the 'house of God'), called because of its vain idols Beth-aven (that is, 'the house of vanity,' or 'naught,' Ho 4:15 10:5,8), shall indeed 'come to naught.'

6. break out like fire – bursting through everything in His way. God is 'a consuming fire' (De 4:24 Isa 10:17 La 2:3).

the house of Joseph – the kingdom of Israel, of which the tribe of Ephraim, Joseph's son, was the chief tribe (compare Eze 37:16).

none to quench it in Beth-el – that is, none in Beth-el to quench it; none of the Beth-el idols on which Israel so depended, able to remove the divine judgments.

7. turn judgment to wormwood – that is, pervert it to most bitter wrong. As justice is sweet, so injustice is bitter to the injured. 'Wormwood' is from a *Hebrew* root, to 'execrate,' on account of its noxious and bitter qualities.

8. the seven stars – literally, the *heap* or cluster of *seven* larger stars and others smaller (Job 9:9 38:31). The former whole passage seems to have been in Amos mind. He names the stars well known to shepherds (to which class Amos belonged), Orion as the precursor of the tempests which are here threatened, and the Pleiades as ushering in spring.

shadow of death – Hebraism for *the densest darkness.*

calleth for the waters of the sea – both to send *deluges* in judgment, and the ordinary *rain* in mercy (1Ki 18:44).

9. strengtheneth the spoiled – literally, 'spoil' or 'devastation': hence the 'person spoiled.'

the spoiled shall come – 'devastation.'

10. him that rebuketh in the gate – the *judge* who condemns their iniquity *in the place of judgment* (Isa 29:21).

abhor him that speaketh uprightly – the *prophet* telling them the unwelcome truth: answering in the parallelism to the *judge,* 'that rebuketh in the gate' (compare 1Ki 22:8 Pr 9:8 12:1 Jer 36:23).

11. burdens of wheat – *burdensome taxes* levied in kind from the *wheat* of the needy, to pamper the lusts of the great [HENDERSON]. Or wheat advanced in time of scarcity, and exacted again at a burdensome interest [RABBI SALOMON].

built houses ... but not dwell in them ... vineyards, ... but not drink wine of them – according to the original prophecy of Moses (De 28:30,38,39). The converse shall be true in restored Israel (Am 9:14 Isa 65:21,22).

12. they afflict ... they take – rather, '(ye) who afflict ... take.'

bribe – literally, a *price* with which one who has an unjust cause *ransoms* himself from your sentence (1Sa 12:3, *Margin;* Pr 6:35).

turn aside the poor in the gate – refuse them their right *in the place of justice* (Am 2:7 Isa 29:21).

13. the prudent – the spiritually wise.

shall keep silence – not mere silence of tongue, but the prudent shall keep himself quiet from taking part in any public or private affairs which he can avoid: as it is 'an evil time,' and one in which all law is set at naught. Eph 5:16 refers to this. Instead of impatiently agitating against irremediable evils, the godly wise will not cast pearls before swine, who would trample these, and rend the offerers (Mt 7:6), but will patiently wait for God's time of deliverance in silent submission (Ps 39:9).

14. and so – on condition of your 'seeking good.'

shall be with you, as ye have spoken – as ye have boasted; namely, that God is with you, and that you are His people (Mic 3:11).

15. Hate … evil … love … good – (Isa 1:16,17 Ro 12:9).

judgment in the gate – *justice* in the place where causes are tried.

it may be that the Lord … will be gracious – so, 'peradventure' (Ex 32:30). Not that men are to come to God with an *uncertainty* whether or no He will be gracious: the expression merely implies the difficulty in the way, because of the want of true repentance on man's part, so as to stimulate the zealous earnestness of believers in seeking God (compare Ge 16:2 Joe 2:14 Ac 8:22).

the remnant of Joseph – (see Am 5:6). Israel (represented by 'Ephraim,' the leading tribe, and descendant of Joseph) was, as compared to what it once was, now but a remnant, Hazael of Syria having smitten all the coasts from Jordan eastward, Gilead and Bashan, Gad, Reuben, and Manasseh (2Ki 10:32,33) [HENDERSON]. Rather, 'the remnant of Israel that shall have been left after the wicked have been destroyed' [MAURER].

16. Therefore – resumed from Am 5:13. God foresees they will not obey the exhortation (Am 5:14,15), but will persevere in the unrighteousness stigmatized (Am 5:7,10,12).

the Lord – JEHOVAH.

the God of hosts, the Lord – an accumulation of titles, of which His lordship over all things is the climax, to mark that from His judgment there is no appeal.

streets … highways – the *broad open spaces* and the *narrow streets* common in the East.

call the husbandman to mourning – The citizens shall call the inexperienced *husbandmen* to act the part usually performed by professional mourners, as there will not be enough of the latter for the universal mourning which prevails.

such as are skilful of lamentation – professional mourners hired to lead off the lamentations for the deceased; alluded to in Ec 12:5; generally women (Jer 9:17–19).

17. in all vineyards … wailing – where usually songs of joy were heard.

pass through thee – taking vengeance (Ex 12:12,23 Na 1:12). 'Pass *over*' and 'pass by,' on the contrary, are used of God's *forgiving* (Ex 12:23 Mic 7:18; compare Am 7:8).

18. Woe unto you who do not scruple to say in irony, 'We desire that the day of the Lord would come,' that is, 'Woe to you who treat it as if it were a mere dream of the prophets' (Isa 5:19 Jer 17:15 Eze 12:22).

to what end is it for you! – Amos taking their ironical words in earnest: for God often takes the blasphemer at his own word, in righteous retribution making the scoffer's jest a terrible reality against himself. Ye have but little reason to desire the day of the Lord; for it will be to you calamity, and not joy.

19. As if a man did flee … a lion, and a bear met him – Trying to escape one calamity, he falls into another. This perhaps implies that in Am 5:18 their ironical desire for the day of the Lord was as if it would be an escape from existing calamities. The coming of the day of the Lord would be good news to us, if true: for we have served God (that is, the golden calves). So do hypocrites flatter themselves as to death and judgment, as if these would be a relief from existing ills of life. The lion may from generosity spare the prostrate, but the *bear* spares none (compare Job 20:24 Isa 24:18).

leaned … on the wall – on the side wall of the house, to support himself from falling. Snakes often hid themselves in fissures in a wall. Those not reformed by God's judgments will be pursued by them: if they escape one, another is ready to seize them.

21. I hate, I despise – The two verbs joined without a conjunction express God's strong abhorrence.

your feast days – *yours*; not *Mine*; I do not acknowledge them: unlike those in Judah, yours are of human, not divine institution.

I will not smell – that is, I will take *no delight in* the sacrifices offered (Ge 8:21 Le 26:31).

in your solemn assemblies – literally, 'days of restraint.' Isa 1:10–15 is parallel. Isaiah is fuller; Amos, more condensed. Amos condemns Israel not only on the ground of their thinking to satisfy God by sacrifices without obedience (the charge brought by Isaiah against the Jews), but also because even their external ritual was a mere corruption, and unsanctioned by God.

22. meat offerings – flour. Unbloody offerings.

peace offerings – offerings for obtaining from God peace and prosperity. *Hebrew*, 'thank offerings.'

23. Take … away from me – literally, 'Take away, *from upon* Me'; the idea being that of a *burden* pressing *upon* the bearer. So Isa 1:14, 'They are a trouble unto Me (literally, "a burden *upon* Me"): I am weary to bear them.'

the noise of thy songs – The hymns and instrumental music on sacred occasions are to Me nothing but a disagreeable *noise*.

I will not hear – Isaiah substitutes 'prayers' (Isa 1:15) for the 'songs' and 'melody' here; but, like Amos, closes with 'I will not hear.'

24. judgment – justice, run down – literally, 'roll,' that is, flow abundantly (Isa 48:18). Without the desire to fulfil righteousness in the offerer, the sacrifice is hateful to God (1Sa 15:22 Ps 66:18 Ho 6:6 Mic 6:8).

25, 26. Have ye offered? – Yes: ye have. 'But (all the time with strange inconsistency) ye have borne (aloft in solemn pomp) the tabernacle (that is, the portable shrine, or model *tabernacle*: small enough not to be detected by Moses; compare Ac 19:24) of your Molech' (that idol is *'your'* god; I am not, though ye go through the form of presenting offerings to Me). The question, 'Have ye,' is not a denial (for they *did* offer in the wilderness to Jehovah sacrifices of the cattle which they took with them in their nomad life there, Ex 24:4 Nu 7:1–89 9:1.), but a strong affirmation (compare 1Sa 2:27,28 Jer 31:20 Eze 20:4). The sin of Israel in Amos' time is the very sin of their forefathers, mocking God with worship, while at the same time worshipping idols (compare Eze 20:39). It was clandestine in Moses' time, else he would have put it down; he was aware generally of their unfaithfulness, though not knowing the particulars (De 31:21,27).

Molech … Chiun – 'Molech' means 'king' answering to *Mars* [Bengel]; *the Sun* [Jablonski]; *Saturn*, the same as 'Chiun' [Maurer]. The *Septuagint* translates 'Chiun' into *Remphan*, as Stephen quotes it (Ac 7:42,43). The same god often had different names. *Molech* is the Ammonite name; *Chiun*, the Arabic and Persian name, written also *Chevan*. In an Arabic lexicon *Chiun* means 'austere'; so astrologers represented *Saturn* as a planet baleful in his influence. Hence the Phoenicians offered human sacrifices to him, children especially; so idolatrous Israel also. *Rimmon* was the Syrian name (2Ki 5:18); pronounced as *Remvan*, or 'Remphan,' just as *Chiun* was also *Chevan*. Molech had the form of a king; Chevan, or Chiun, of a star [Grotius]. Remphan was the Egyptian name for *Saturn*: hence the *Septuagint* translator of Amos gave the Egyptian name for the *Hebrew*, being an Egyptian. [Hodius II, *De Bibliorum Textibus Originalibus*. 4.115]. The same as the Nile, of which the Egyptians made the star *Saturn* the representative [Harenberg]. Bengel considers *Remphan* or *Rephan* akin to *Teraphim* and *Remphis*, the name of a king of Egypt. The Hebrews became infected with Sabeanism, the oldest form of idolatry, the worship of the *Saba* or starry hosts, in their stay in the Arabian desert, where Job notices its prevalence (Job 31:26); in opposition, in Am 5:27, Jehovah declares Himself 'the God of *hosts*.'

the star of your god – R. Isaac Caro says all the astrologers represented Saturn as *the star*

of Israel. Probably there was a figure of a star on the head of the image of the idol, to represent the planet Saturn; hence 'images' correspond to 'star' in the parallel clause. A star in hieroglyphics represents God (Nu 24:17). 'Images' are either a Hebraism for 'image,' or refer to the many images made to represent Chiun.

27. beyond Damascus – In Ac 7:43 it is 'beyond *Babylon*,' which includes *beyond Damascus*. In Amos time, Damascus was the object of Israel's fear because of the Syrian wars. Babylon was not yet named as the place of their captivity. Stephen supplies this name. Their place of exile was in fact, as he states, *'beyond* Babylon,' in Halah and Habor by the river Gozan, and in the cities of the Medes (2Ki 17:6; compare here Am 1:5 4:3 6:14). The road to Assyria lay through 'Damascus.' It is therefore specified, that not merely shall they be carried captives to Damascus, as they had been by Syrian kings (2Ki 10:32,33 13:7), but, beyond that, to a region whence a return was not so possible as from Damascus. They were led captive by Satan into idolatry, therefore God caused them to go captive among idolaters. Compare 2Ki 15:29 16:9 Isa 8:4, whence it appears Tiglath-pileser attacked Israel and Damascus at the same time at Ahaz' request (Am 3:1).

Chapter 6

Am 6:1–14. Denunciation of both the sister nations for wanton security – Zion, as well as Samaria: threat of the exile: ruin of their palaces and slaughter of the people: their perverse injustice.

1. named chief of the nations – that is, you nobles, so eminent in influence, that your names are celebrated among the chief nations [Ludovicus De Dieu]. *Hebrew*, 'Men designated by name among the first-fruits of the nations,' that is, men of note in Israel, the people chosen by God as first of the nations (Ex 19:5; compare Nu 24:20) [Piscator].

2. Calneh – on the east bank of the Tigris. Once powerful, but recently subjugated by Assyria (Isa 10:9; about 794 B.C.).

Hameth – subjugated by Jeroboam II (2Ki 14:25). Also by Assyria subsequently (2Ki 18:34). Compare Am 6:14.

Gath – subjugated by Uzziah (2Ch 26:6).

be they better – no. Their so recent subjugation renders it needless for Me to tell you they *are* not. And yet they *once were*; still they could not defend themselves against the enemy. How vain, then, *your* secure confidence in the strength of Mounts Zion and Samaria! He takes cities respectively east, north, south, and west of Israel (compare Na 3:8).

3. Ye persuade yourselves that 'the evil day' foretold by the prophets is 'far off,' though they declare it near (Eze 12:22,27). Ye in your imagination put it far off, and therefore bring near *violent oppression,* suffering it to *sit enthroned,* as it were, among you (Ps 94:20). The notion of judgment being far off has always been an incentive to the sinner's recklessness of living (Ec 8:12,13 Mt 24:48). Yet that very recklessness brings near the evil day which he puts far off. 'Ye bring on fever by your intemperance, and yet would put it far off' [CALVIN].

4. (See Am 2:8).

beds of ivory – that is, adorned, or inlaid, with ivory (Am 3:15).

stretch themselves – in luxurious self-indulgence.

lambs out of the flock – picked out as the choicest, for their owners selfish gratification.

5. **chant** – literally, 'mark distinct sounds and tones.'

viol – the lyre, or lute.

invent ... instruments ... like David – They fancy they equal David in musical skill (1Ch 23:5 Ne 12:36). They defend their luxurious passion for music by his example: forgetting that *he* pursued this study when at peace and free from danger, and that for the praise of God; but *they* pursue for their own self-gratification, and that when God is angry and ruin is imminent.

6. **drink ... in bowls** – in the *large vessels* or basins in which wine was mixed; not satisfied with the smaller *cups* from which it was ordinarily drunk, after having been poured from the large mixer.

chief ointments – that is, the most costly: not for health or cleanliness, but wanton luxury.

not grieved for the affliction of Joseph – literally, 'the breach,' that is, the national wound or calamity (Ps 60:2 Eze 34:4) of the house of *Joseph* (Am 5:6); resembling in this the heartlessness of their forefathers, the sons of Jacob, towards Joseph, 'eating bread' while their brother lay in the pit, and then selling him to Ishmaelites.

7. **Therefore ... shall they go captive with the first** – As they were first among the people in rank (Am 6:1), and anointed themselves 'with the chief ointments' (Am 6:6), so shall they be among the foremost in going into captivity.

banquet – literally, the 'merry-making shout of revellers'; from an *Arabic* root, 'to cry out.' In the *Hebrew, marzeach;* here, there is an allusion to *mizraqu,* 'bowls' (Am 6:6).

them that stretched themselves – on luxurious couches (Am 6:4).

8. **the excellency of Jacob** – (Ps 47:4). The *sanctuary* which was the great glory of the covenant-people [VATABLUS], (Eze 24:21). The priesthood, and kingdom, and dignity, conferred

on them by God. These, saith God, are of no account in My eyes towards averting punishment [CALVIN].

hate his palaces – as being the storehouses of 'robbery' (Am 3:10,15). How sad a change from God's *love* of Zion's gates (Ps 87:2) and palaces (Ps 48:3,13), owing to the people's sin!

the city – collectively: both Zion and Samaria (Am 6: 1).

all that is therein – literally, 'its fulness'; the *multitude* of men and of riches in it (compare Ps 24:1).

9. If as many as *ten* (Le 26:26 Zec 8:23) remain in a house (a rare case, and only in the scattered villages, as there will be scarcely a house in which the enemy will leave any), they shall all, to a man, die of the plague, a frequent concomitant of war in the East (Jer 24:10 44:13 Eze 6:11).

10. **a man's uncle** – The nearest relatives had the duty of burying the dead (Ge 25:9 35:29 Jud 16:31). No nearer relative was left of this man than an *uncle.*

and he that burneth him – the uncle, who is *also* at the same time the one that burneth him (one of the 'ten,' Am 6:9). Burial was the usual Hebrew mode of disposing of their dead. But in cases of necessity, as when the men of Jabesh-gilead took the bodies of Saul and his three sons from the walls of Beth-shan and burned them to save them from being insulted by the Philistines, burning was practised. So in this case, to prevent contagion.

the bones – that is, the dead *body* (Ge 50:25). Perhaps here there is an allusion in the phrase to the *emaciated* condition of the body, which was little else but skin and bones.

Hold thy tongue ... we may not ... mention ... the Lord – After receiving the reply, that none is left besides the one addressed, when the man outside fancies the man still surviving inside to be on the point, as was customary, of expressing devout gratitude to God who spared him, the man outside interrupts him, 'Hold thy tongue! for there is not now cause for mentioning with praise (Jos 23:7) the name of Jehovah'; for *thou* also must die; as all the ten are to die to the last man (Am 6:9; compare Am 8:3). Formerly ye boasted in the name of Jehovah, as if ye were His peculiar people; now ye shall be silent and shudder at His name, as hostile to you, and as one from whom ye wish to be hidden (Re 6:16), [CALVIN].

11. **commandeth, and he will smite** – His word of command, when once given, cannot but be fulfilled (Isa 55:11). His mere word is enough to smite with destruction.

great house ... little house – He will spare none, great or small (Am 3:15). JEROME interprets 'the great house' as Israel, and 'the small house' as Judah: the former being reduced to branches or ruins, literally, 'small drops'; the latter, though injured with 'clefts' or rents, which threaten its fall, yet still permitted to stand.

12. In turning 'judgment (justice) into gall (poison), and ... righteousness into hemlock' (or wormwood, bitter and noxious), ye act as perversely as if one were to make 'horses run upon the rock' or to 'plough with oxen there' [MAURER]. As horses and oxen are useless on a rock, so ye are incapable of fulfilling justice [GROTIUS]. Ye impede the course of God's benefits, because ye are as it were a hard rock on which His favour cannot run. 'Those that will not be tilled as fields, shall be abandoned as rocks' [CALVIN].

13. rejoice in a thing of naught – that is, in your vain and fleeting riches.

Have we not taken to us horns – that is, acquired power, so as to conquer our neighbours (2Ki 14:25). *Horns* are the Hebrew symbol of *power*, being the instrument of strength in many animals (Ps 75:10).

14. from the entering in of Hamath – the point of entrance for an invading army (as Assyria) into Israel from the north; specified here, as Hamath had been just before subjugated by Jeroboam II (Am 6:2). Do not glory in your recently acquired city, for it shall be the starting-point for the foe to afflict you. How sad the contrast to the feast of Solomon attended by a congregation *from* this same *Hamath,* the most northern boundary of Israel, *to* the Nile, the *river of Egypt,* the most southern boundary!

unto the river of the wilderness – that is, to Kedron, which empties itself into the north bay of the Dead Sea below Jericho (2Ch 28:15), the southern boundary of the ten tribes (2Ki 14:25, 'from the entering of Hamath unto the sea of the plain') [MAURER]. *To the river Nile,* which skirts the Arabian wilderness and separates Egypt from Canaan [GROTIUS]. If this verse includes Judah, as well as Israel (compare Am 6:1, 'Zion' and 'Samaria'), GROTIUS' view is correct; and it agrees with 1Ki 8:65.

Chapter 7

The seventh, eighth, and ninth chapters contain

Visions, with their explanations.

The seventh chapter consists of two parts.

First:

(1) A vision of *grasshoppers* or young locusts, which devour the grass, but are removed at Amos' entreaty;

(2) *Fire* drying up even the deep, and withering part of the land, but removed at Amos' entreaty;

(3) A *plumb-line* to mark the buildings for destruction.

Secondly

(Am 7:10–17): Narrative of Amaziah's interruption of Amos in consequence of the foregoing prophecies, and prediction of his doom.

(Am 7:1–9): Prophecies illustrated by three symbols.

1. showed ... me; and, behold – The same formula prefaces the three visions in this chapter, and the fourth in Am 8:1.

grasshoppers – rather, 'locusts' in the caterpillar state, from a *Hebrew* root, 'to creep forth.' In the autumn the eggs are deposited in the earth; in the spring the young come forth [MAURER].

the latter growth – namely, of grass, which comes up after the mowing. They do not in the East mow their grass and make hay of it, but cut it off the ground as they require it.

the king's mowings – the first-fruits of the mown grass, tyrannically exacted by the king from the people. The literal locusts, as in Joel, are probably symbols of human foes: thus the 'growth' of grass 'after the king's mowings' will mean the political revival of Israel under Jeroboam II (2Ki 14:25), after it had been mown down, as it were, by Hazael and Ben-hadad of Syria (2Ki 13:3), [GROTIUS].

2. by whom shall Jacob arise? – If Thou, O God, dost not spare, how can *Jacob maintain his ground,* reduced as he is by repeated attacks of the Assyrians, and ere long about to be invaded by the Assyrian Pul (2Ki 15:19,20)? Compare Isa 51:19. The mention of 'Jacob' is a plea that God should 'remember for them His covenant' with their forefather, the patriarch (Ps 106:45).

he is small – reduced in numbers and in strength.

3. repented for this – that is, of this. The change was not in the mind of God (Nu 2:19 Jas 1:17), but in the effect outwardly. God unchangeably does what is just; it is just that He should hear intercessory prayer (Jas 5:16-18), as it would have been just for Him to have let judgment take its course at once on the guilty nation, but for the prayer of one or two righteous men in it (compare Ge 18:23–33 1Sa 15:11 Jer 42:10). The repentance of the sinner, and God's regard to His own attributes of mercy and covenanted love, also cause God outwardly to deal with him as if He repented (Jon 3:10), whereas the change in outward dealing is in strictest harmony with God's own unchangeableness.

It shall not be – Israel's utter overthrow now. Pul was influenced by God to accept money and withdraw from Israel.

4. called to contend – that is with Israel judicially (Job 9:3 Isa 66:16 Eze 38:22). He ordered to come at His call the infliction of punishment by 'fire' on Israel, that is, drought (compare Am 4:6–11), [Maurer]. Rather, *war* (Nu 21:28), namely, Tiglath-pileser [Grotius]. **devoured the … deep** – that is a great part of Israel, whom he carried away. *Waters* are the symbol for *many people* (Re 17:15).

did eat up a part – namely, all the *land* (compare Am 4:7) of Israel east of Jordan (1Ch 5:26 Isa 9:1). This was a worse judgment than the previous one: the locusts ate up the grass: the fire not only affects the surface of the ground, but burns up the very roots and reaches even to the deep.

7. wall made by a plumb-line – namely, perpendicular.

8. plumb-line in … midst of … Israel – No longer are the symbols, as in the former two, stated generally; this one is expressly applied to Israel. God's long-suffering is worn out by Israel's perversity: so Amos ceases to intercede (compare Ge 18:33). The plummet line was used not only in building, but in destroying houses (2Ki 21:13 Isa 28:17 34:11 La 2:8). It denotes that God's judgments are measured out by the most exact rules of justice. Here it is placed 'in the midst' of Israel, that is, the judgment is not to be confined to an outer part of Israel, as by Tiglath-pileser; it is to reach the very centre. This was fulfilled when Shalmaneser, after a three years' siege of Samaria, took it and carried away Israel captive finally to Assyria (2Ki 17:3,5,6,23).

not … pass by … any more – not forgive them any more (Am 8:2 Pr 19:11 Mic 7:18).

9. high places – dedicated to idols.

of Isaac – They boasted of their following the example of their forefather Isaac, in erecting high places at Beer-sheba (Am 5:5; compare Ge 26:23,24 46:1); but he and Abraham erected them before the temple was appointed at Jerusalem – and to God; whereas they did so, after the temple had been fixed as the only place for sacrifices – and to idols. In the *Hebrew* here 'Isaac' is written with *s*, instead of the usual *ts*; both forms mean 'laughter'; the change of spelling perhaps expresses that their 'high places of Isaac' may be well so called, but not as they meant by the name; for they are only fit to be *laughed at* in scorn. Probably, however, the mention of 'Isaac' and 'Israel' simply expresses that these names, which their degenerate posterity boasted in as if ensuring their safety, will not save them and their idolatrous 'sanctuaries' on which they depended from ruin (compare Am 8:14).

house of Jeroboam with … sword – fulfilled in the extinction of Zachariah, son of Jeroboam II, the last of the descendants of Jeroboam I, who had originated the idolatry of the calves (2Ki 15:8–10).

Am 7:10–17. Amaziah's charge against Amos: his doom foretold.

10. priest of Beth-el – chief priest of the royal sanctuary to the calves at Beth-el. These being a device of state policy to keep Israel separate from Judah. Amaziah construes Amos words against them as treason. So in the case of Elijah and Jeremiah (1Ki 18:17 Jer 37:13,14). So the antitype Jesus was charged (Joh 19:12); political expediency being made in all ages the pretext for dishonouring God and persecuting His servants (Joh 11:48–50). So in the case of Paul (Ac 17:6,7 24:5).

in the midst of … Israel – probably alluding to Amos' own words, 'in the midst of … Israel' (Am 7:8), foretelling the state's overthrow *to the very centre*. Not secretly, or in a corner, but openly, in *the very centre of the state*, so as to upset the whole utterly.

land is not able to bear all his words – They are so many and so intolerable. A sedition will be the result. The mention of his being 'priest of Beth-el' implies that it was for his own priestly gain, not for the king or state, he was so keen.

11. Jeroboam shall die. – Amos had not said this: but that 'the *house* of Jeroboam' should fall 'with the sword' (Am 7:9). But Amaziah exaggerates the charge, to excite Jeroboam against him. The king, however, did not give ear to Amaziah, probably from religious awe of the prophet of Jehovah.

12. Also – Besides informing the king against Amos, lest that course should fail, as it did, Amaziah urges the troublesome prophet himself to go back to his own land Judah, pretending to advise him in friendliness.

seer – said contemptuously in reference to Amos' *visions* which precede.

there eat bread – You can earn a livelihood there, whereas remaining here you will be ruined. He judges of Amos by his own selfishness, as if regard to one's own safety and livelihood are the paramount considerations. So the false prophets (Eze 13:19) were ready to say whatever pleased their hearers, however false, for 'handfuls of barley and pieces of bread.'

13. prophesy not again – (Am 2:12).

at Beth-el – Amaziah wants to be let alone at least in his own residence.

the king's chapel – Beth-el was preferred by the king to Dan, the other seat of the calf-worship, as being nearer Samaria, the capital, and as hallowed by Jacob of old (Ge 28:16,19 35:6,7). He argues by implication against Amos' presumption, as a private man, in speaking against the worship sanctioned by the king, and that in the very place consecrated to it for the king's own devotions.

king's court – that is, residence: the seat of empire, where the king holds his court, and which thou oughtest to have reverenced. Samaria was the usual king's residence: but for the convenience of attending the calf-worship, a royal palace was at Beth-el also.

14. I *was* **no prophet** – in answer to Amaziah's insinuation (Am 7:12), that he discharged the prophetical office to earn his 'bread' (like Israel's mercenary prophets). So far from being rewarded, Jehovah's prophets had to expect imprisonment and even death as the result of their prophesying in Samaria or Israel: whereas the prophets of Baal were maintained at the king's expense (compare 1Ki 18:19). I was not, says Amos, of the order of prophets, or educated in their schools, and deriving a livelihood from exercising the public functions of a prophet. I am a *shepherd* (compare Am 7:15, 'flock'; the *Hebrew* for 'herdsman' includes the meaning, *shepherd*, compare Am 1:1) in humble position, who did not even think of prophesying among you, until a divine call impelled me to it.

prophet's son – that is, disciple. Schools of prophets are mentioned first in First Samuel; in these youths were educated to serve the theocracy as public instructors. Only in the kingdom of the ten tribes is the continuance of the schools of the prophets mentioned. They were missionary stations near the chief seats of superstition in Israel, and associations endowed with the Spirit of God; none were admitted but those to whom the Spirit had been previously imparted. Their spiritual fathers travelled about to visit the training schools, and cared for the members and even their widows (2Ki 4:1,2). The pupils had their common board in them, and after leaving them still continued members. The offerings which in Judah were given by the pious to the Levites, in Israel were to the schools of the prophets (2Ki 4:42). Prophecy (for example, Elijah and Elisha) in Israel was more connected with extraordinary events than in Judah, inasmuch as, in the absence of the legal hierarchy of the latter, it needed to have more palpable divine sanction.

sycamore – abounding in Palestine. The fruit was like the fig, but inferior; according to PLINY, a sort of compound, as the name expresses, of the fig and the mulberry. It was only eaten by the poorest (compare 1Ki 10:27).

gatherer – one occupied with their cultivation [MAURER]. To cultivate it, an incision was made in the fruit when of a certain size, and on the fourth day afterwards it ripened [PLINY, *Natural History*, 13.7,14].

15. took me as I followed the flock – So David was taken (2Sa 7:8 Ps 78:70,71). Messiah is the antitypical *Shepherd* (Ps 23:1–6 Joh 10:1–18).

unto my people – 'against' [MAURER]; so Am 7:16. Jehovah claims them still as *His* by right, though slighting His authority. God would recover them to His service by the prophet's ministry.

16. drop – distil as the refreshing drops of rain (De 32:2 Eze 21:2; compare Mic 2:6,11).

17. Thy wife shall be an harlot in the city – that is, shall be forced by the enemy, while thou art looking on, unable to prevent her dishonour (Isa 13:16 La 5:11). The words, 'saith the Lord,' are in striking opposition to '*Thou* sayest' (Am 7:16).

divided by line – among the foe.

a polluted land – Israel regarded every foreign land as that which really her own land was now, 'polluted' (Isa 24:5 Jer 2:7).

Chapter 8

Am 8:1–14. Vision of a basket of summer fruit symbolical of Israel's end. Resuming the series of symbols interrupted by Amaziah, Amos adds a fourth. The avarice of the oppressors of the poor: the overthrow of the nation: the wish for the means of religious counsel, when there shall be a famine of the word.

1. summer fruit – *Hebrew, kitz.* In Am 8:2 'end' is in *Hebrew, keetz.* The similarity of sounds implies that, as the *summer* is the *end* of the year and the time of the ripeness of fruits, so Israel is *ripe* for her *last* punishment, *ending* her national existence. As the fruit is plucked when ripe from the tree, so Israel from her land.

2. end – (Eze 7:2,6).

3. songs of ... temple – (Am 5:23). The joyous hymns in the temple of Judah (or rather, in the *Beth-el* 'royal temple,' Am 7:13; for the allusion is to *Israel*, not Judah, throughout this chapter) shall be changed into 'howlings.'

they shall cast them forth with silence – not as the *Margin*, 'be silent.' It is an adverb, 'silently.' There shall be such great slaughter as even to prevent the bodies being buried [CALVIN]. There shall be none of the usual professional mourners (Am 5:16), but the bodies will be cast out in silence. Perhaps also is meant that terror, both of God (compare Am 6:10) and of the foe, shall close their lips.

4. Hear – The nobles needed to be urged thus, as hating to *hear* reproof.

swallow up the needy – or, 'gape after,' that is, pant for their goods; so the word is used, Job 7:2, *Margin.*

to make the poor ... to fail – 'that they (themselves) may be placed alone in the midst of the earth' (Isa 5:8).

5. So greedy are they of unjust gain that they cannot spare a single day, however sacred, from pursuing it. They are strangers to God and enemies to themselves, who love market days better than Sabbath days; and they who have lost piety will not long keep honesty. The new moons (Nu 10:10) and Sabbaths were to be kept without working or trading (Ne 10:31).

set forth wheat – literally, 'open out' stores of wheat for sale.

ephah – containing three seahs, or above three pecks.

making ... small – making it below the just weight to purchasers.

shekel great – taking from purchasers a greater weight of money than was due. Shekels used to be *weighed out* in payments (Ge 23:16). Thus they committed a double fraud against the law (De 25:13,14).

6. buy ... poor for silver ... pair of shoes – that is, that we may compel the needy for money, or any other thing of however little worth, to sell themselves to us as bondmen, in defiance of Le 25:39; the very thing which brings down God's judgment (Am 2:6).

sell the refuse of ... wheat – which contains no nutriment, but which the poor eat at a low price, being unable to pay for flour.

7. Lord hath sworn by the excellency of Jacob – that is by Himself, in whom Jacob's seed glory [Maurer]. Rather, by the spiritual privileges of Israel, the adoption as His peculiar people [Calvin], the temple, and its Shekinah symbol of His presence. Compare Am 6:8, where it means Jehovah's *temple* (compare Am 4:2).

never forget – not *pass by* without punishing (Am 8:2 Ho 8:13 9:9).

8. the land ... rise up wholly as a flood – The land will, as it were, be wholly turned into a flooding river (a flood being the image of overwhelming calamity, Da 9:26).

cast out and drowned – swept away and overwhelmed, as the land adjoining the Nile is by it, when flooding (Am 9:5). The Nile rises generally twenty feet. The waters then 'cast out' mire and dirt (Isa 57:20).

9. 'Darkness' made to rise 'at noon' is the emblem of great calamities (Jer 15:9 Eze 32:7–10).

10. baldness – a sign of mourning (Isa 15:2 Jer 48:37 Eze 7:18).

I will make it as ... mourning of an only son – 'it,' that is, 'the earth' (Am 8:9). I will reduce the land to such a state that there shall be the same occasion for mourning as when parents mourn for an only son (Jer 6:26 Zec 12:10).

11. famine of ... hearing the words of the Lord – a just retribution on those who now will not hear the Lord's prophets, nay even try to drive them away, as Amaziah did (Am 7:12); they shall look in vain, in their distress, for divine counsel, such as the prophets such now offer (Eze 7:26 Mic 3:7). Compare as to the Jews' rejection of Messiah, and their consequent rejection by Him (Mt 21:43); and their desire for Messiah too late (Lu 17:22 Joh 7:34 8:21). So, the prodigal when he had sojourned awhile in the 'far-off country, began to be in want' in the 'mighty famine' which arose (Lu 15:14; compare 1Sa 3:1 7:2). It is remarkable that the Jews' religion is almost the only one that *could* be abolished *against the will of the people themselves,* on account of its being dependent on a particular *place,* namely, the temple. When that was destroyed, the Mosaic ritual, which could not exist without it, necessarily ceased. Providence designed it, that, as the law gave way to the Gospel, so all men should perceive it was so, in spite of the Jews' obstinate rejection of the Gospel.

12. they shall wander from sea to sea – that is, from the Dead Sea to the Mediterranean, from east to west.

from ... north ... to ... east – where we might expect 'from north to south.' But so alienated was Israel from Judah, that no Israelite even then would think of repairing *southward,* that is, to Jerusalem for religious information. The circuit is traced as in Nu 34:3, except that the south is omitted. Their 'seeking the word of the Lord' would not be from a sincere desire to obey God, but under the pressure of punishment.

13. faint for thirst – namely, thirst for hearing the words of the Lord, being destitute of all other comfort. If even the young and strong faint, how much more the infirm (Isa 40:30,31)!

14. swear by the sin of Samaria – namely, the calves (De 9:21 Ho 4:15). 'Swear by' means to *worship* (Ps 63:11).

The manner – that is, as 'the way' is used (Ps 139:24 Ac 9:2), *the mode of worship.*

Thy god, O Dan – the other golden calf at Dan (1Ki 22:26–30).

liveth ... liveth – rather, 'May thy god ... live ... may the manner ... live.' Or, 'As (surely as) thy god, O Dan, liveth.' This is their formula when they swear; not 'May Jehovah live!' or, 'As Jehovah liveth!'

Chapter 9

Am 9:1–15. Fifth and last vision.

None can escape the coming judgment in any hiding-place: for God is omnipresent and irresistible (Am 9:1–6). As a kingdom, Israel shall perish as if it never was in covenant with Him: but as individuals the house of Jacob shall not utterly perish, nay, not one of the least of the righteous shall fall, but only all the sinners (Am 9:7–10). Restoration of the Jews finally to their own land after the re-establishment of the fallen tabernacle of David; consequent conversion of all the heathen (Am 9:11–15).

1. Lord ... upon the altar – namely, in the idolatrous temple at Beth-el; the calves which were spoken of in Am 8:14. Hither they would flee for protection from the Assyrians, and would perish in the ruins, with the vain object of their trust [HENDERSON]. Jehovah stands here to direct the destruction of it, them, and the idolatrous nation. He demands many victims on the altar, but they are to be human victims. CALVIN and FAIRBAIRN, and others, make it in the *temple at Jerusalem*. Judgment was to descend both on Israel and Judah. As the services of both alike ought to have been offered on the Jerusalem temple-altar, it is there that Jehovah ideally stands, as if the whole people were assembled there, their abominations lying unpardoned there, and crying for vengeance, though in fact committed elsewhere (compare Eze 8:1–18). This view harmonizes with the similarity of the vision in Amos to that in Isa 6:1–13, *at Jerusalem*. Also with the end of this chapter (Am 9:11–15), which applies both to *Judah* and Israel: 'the tabernacle of David,' namely, at Jerusalem. His attitude, 'standing,' implies fixity of purpose.

lintel – rather, the sphere-like *capital* of the column [MAURER].

posts – rather, 'thresholds,' as in Isa 6:4, *Margin*. The temple is to be smitten below as well as above, to ensure utter destruction.

cut them in the head – namely, with the broken fragments of the capitals and columns (compare Ps 68:21 Hab 3:13).

slay the last of them – their posterity [HENDERSON]. The survivors [MAURER]. Jehovah's directions are addressed to His angels, ministers of judgment (compare Eze 9:1–11).

he that fleeth ... shall not flee away – He who fancies himself safe and out of reach of the enemy shall be taken (Am 2:14).

2. Though they dig into hell – though they hide ever so deeply in the earth (Ps 139:8).

though they climb up to heaven – though they ascend the greatest heights (Job 20:6,7 Jer 51:53 Ob 1:4).

3. Carmel – where the forests, and, on the west side, the caves, furnished hiding-places (Am 1:2 Jud 6:2 1Sa 13:6).

the sea – the Mediterranean, which flows at the foot of Mount Carmel; forming a strong antithesis to it.

command the serpent – the sea-serpent, a term used for any great water monster (Isa 27:1). The symbol of *cruel and oppressive kings* (Ps 74:13,14).

4. though they go into captivity – hoping to save their lives by voluntarily surrendering to the foe.

5. As Amos had threatened that nowhere should the Israelites be safe from the divine judgments, he here shows God's omnipotent ability to execute His threats. So in the case of the threat in Am 8:8, God is here stated to be the first cause of the mourning of 'all that dwell' in the land, and of its rising 'like a flood, and of its being 'drowned, as by the flood of Egypt.'

6. stories – literally, 'ascents,' that is, upper chambers, to which the ascent is by steps [MAURER]; evidently referring to the words in Ps 104:3,13. GROTIUS explains it, *God's royal throne*, expressed in language drawn from Solomon's throne, to which the ascent was by steps (compare 1Ki 10:18,19).

founded his troop – namely, all animate creatures, which are God's *troop*, or *host* (Ge 2:1), doing His will (Ps 103:20,21 Joe 2:11).

7. unto me – however great ye seem *to yourselves*. Do not rely on past privileges, or on My having delivered you from Egypt, as if therefore I never would remove you from Canaan. I make no more account of you than of 'the Ethiopian'. 'Have not I brought you out of Egypt,' done as much for other peoples?

8. eyes ... upon the sinful kingdom – that is, I am watching all its sinful course in order to punish it (compare Am 9:4 Ps 34:15,16).

not utterly destroy the house of Jacob – Though as a 'kingdom' the nation is now utterly to perish, a remnant is to be spared for 'Jacob,' their forefather's sake (compare Jer 30:11); to fulfil the covenant whereby 'the seed of Israel' is hereafter to be 'a nation for ever' (Jer 31:36).

9. sift – I will cause the Israelites to be tossed about through all nations as corn is shaken about in a sieve, in such a way, however, that while the chaff and dust, the wicked, fall through, perish, all the solid grains, the godly elect, remain, are preserved, (Ro 11:2; see on Jer 3:14). So spiritual Israel's final safety is ensured (Lu 22:32 Joh 10:28 6:39).

10. All the sinners – answering to the chaff in the image in Am 9:9, which falls on the earth, in opposition 'to the grain' that does not 'fall.'

11. In that day – quoted by James (Ac 15:16,17), 'After this,' that is, in the dispensation of Messiah (Ge 49:10 Ho 3:4,5 Joe 2:28 3:1).

tabernacle of David – not 'the *house* of David,' which is used of his affairs when prospering (2Sa 3:1), but the *tent* or *booth*, expressing the low condition to which his kingdom and family had fallen in Amos' time, and subsequently at the Babylonian captivity before the restoration; and secondarily, in the last days preceding Israel's restoration under Messiah, the antitype to David (Ps 102:13,14 Jer 30:9 Eze 34:24 37:24). The type is taken from architecture (Eph 2:20). The restoration under Zerubbabel can only be a partial, temporary fulfilment; for it did not include Israel, which nation is the main subject of Amos prophecies, but only Judah; also Zerubbabel's kingdom was not independent and settled; also all the prophets end their prophecies with Messiah, whose advent is the cure of all previous disorders. 'Tabernacle' is appropriate to Him, as His human nature is the tabernacle which He assumed in becoming Immanuel, 'God with us' (Joh 1:14). 'Dwelt,' literally, *tabernacled* 'among us' (compare Re 21:3). Some understand 'the tabernacle of David' as that which David pitched for the ark in Zion, after bringing it from Obed-edom's house. It remained there all his reign for thirty years, till the temple of Solomon was built, whereas the 'tabernacle of the congregation' remained at Gibeon (2Ch 1:3), where the priests ministered in sacrifices (1Ch 16:39). Song and praise was the service of David's attendants before the ark (Asaph.): a type of the gospel separation between the sacrificial service (*Messiah's* priesthood now *in heaven*) and the access of *believers on earth* to the presence of God, apart from the former (compare 2Sa 6:12–17 1Ch 16:37–39 2Ch 1:3).

breaches thereof – literally, 'of them,' that is, of the *whole* nation, Israel as well as Judah.

as in … days of old – as it was formerly in the days of David and Solomon, when the kingdom was in its full extent and undivided.

12. That they may possess … remnant of Edom, and of all the heathen – 'Edom,' the bitter foe, though the brother, of Israel; therefore to be punished (Am 1:11,12), Israel shall be lord of the 'remnant' of Edom left after the punishment of the latter. James quotes it, 'That *the residue of men* might *seek after the Lord, and all the Gentiles*,' For 'all the heathen' nations stand on the same footing as *Edom*: Edom is the representative of them all. The *residue* or *remnant* in both cases expresses those left after great antecedent calamities (Ro 9:27 Zec 14:16). Here the conversion of '*all* nations' (of which the earnest was given in James's time) is represented as only to be realized on the re-establishment of the theocracy under Messiah, the Heir of the throne of David (Am 9:11). The possession of

the heathen nations by Israel is to be spiritual, the latter being the ministers to the former for their conversion to Messiah, King of the Jews; just as the first conversions of pagans were through the ministry of the apostles, who were Jews. Compare Isa 54:3, 'thy seed shall *inherit the Gentiles*' (compare Isa 49:8 Ro 4:13). A remnant of Edom became Jews under John Hyrcanus, and the rest amalgamated with the Arabians, who became Christians subsequently.

which are called by my name – that is, who belong to Me, whom I claim as Mine (Ps 2:8); in the purposes of electing grace, God terms them already *called by His name*. Compare the title, 'the children,' applied by anticipation, Heb 2:14. Hence as an act of sovereign grace, fulfilling His promise, it is spoken of. Proclaim His title as sovereign, 'the Lord that doeth this' ('all these things,' Ac 15:17, namely, all these and such like acts of sovereign love).

13. the days come – at the future restoration of the Jews to their own land.

ploughman shall overtake … reaper … treader of grapes him that soweth – fulfilling Le 26:5. Such shall be the abundance that the harvest and vintage can hardly be gathered before the time for preparing for the next crop shall come. Instead of the greater part of the year being spent in war, the whole shall be spent in sowing and reaping the fruits of earth. Compare Isa 65:21–23, as to the same period.

soweth seed – literally, 'draweth it forth,' namely, from the sack in order to sow it.

mountains … drop sweet wine – an appropriate image, as the vines in Palestine were trained on *terraces at the sides of the hills.*

14. build the waste cities – (Isa 61:4 Eze 36:33-36).

15. plant them … no more be pulled up – (Jer 32:41).

thy God – Israel's; this is the ground of their restoration, God's original choice of them as His.

OBADIAH

A.R. Faussett

Introduction

This is the shortest book in the Old Testament. The name means 'servant of Jehovah.' Obadiah stands fourth among the minor prophets according to the Hebrew arrangement of the canon, the fifth according to the Greek. Some consider him to be the same as the Obadiah who superintended the restoration of the temple under Josiah, 627 B.C. (2Ch 34:12). But Ob 2:11–16,20 imply that Jerusalem was by this time overthrown by the Chaldeans, and that he refers to the cruelty of Edom towards the Jews on that occasion, which is referred to also in La 4:21,22 Eze 25:12–14 35:1–15 Ps 137:7. From comparing Ob 2:5 with Jer 49:9, Ob 2:6 with Jer 49:10, Ob 2:8 with Jer 49:7, it appears that Jeremiah embodied in his prophecies part of Obadiah's, as he had done in the case of other prophets also (compare Isa 15:1–16:14 with Jer 48:1–47). The reason for the present position of Obadiah before other of the minor prophets anterior in date is: Amos at the close of his prophecies foretells the subjugation of Edom hereafter by the Jews; the arranger of the minor prophets in one volume, therefore, placed Obadiah next, as being a fuller statement, and, as it were, a commentary on the foregoing briefer prophecy of Amos as to Edom [MAURER]. (Compare Am 1:11). The date of Obadiah's prophecies was probably immediately after the taking of Jerusalem by Nebuchadnezzar, 588 B.C. Five years afterwards (583 B.C.). Edom was conquered by Nebuchadnezzar. Jeremiah must have incorporated part of Obadiah's prophecies with his own immediately after they were uttered, thus stamping his canonicity.

JEROME makes him contemporary with Hosea, Joel, and Amos. It is an argument in favour of this view that Jeremiah would be more likely to insert in his prophecies a portion from a preceding prophet than from a contemporary. If so, the allusion in Ob 2:11–14 will be to one of the former captures of Jerusalem: by the Egyptians under Rehoboam (1Ki 14:25,26 2Ch 12:2), or that by the Philistines and Arabians in the reign of Joram (2Ch 21:16,17); or that by Joash, king of Israel, in the reign of Amaziah (2Ch 25:22,23); or that in the reign of Jehoiakim (2Ki 24:1.); or that in the reign of Jehoiachin (2Ki 24:8–16). On all occasions the Idumeans were hostile to the Jews; and the terms in which that enmity is characterized are not stronger in Obadiah than in Joe 3:19 (compare Ob 1:10 Am 1:11,12). The probable capture of Jerusalem alluded to by Obadiah is that by Joash and the Israelites in the reign of Amaziah. For as, a little before, in the reign of the same Amaziah, the Jews had treated harshly the Edomites after conquering them in battle (2Ch 25:11–23), it is probable that the Edomites, in revenge, joined the Israelites in the attack on Jerusalem [JAEGER].

This book may be divided into two parts: (1) Ob 1:1–6 set forth Edom's violence toward his brother Israel in the day of the latter's distress, and his coming destruction with the rest of the foes of Judah; (2) Ob 1:17–21, the coming re-establishment of the Jews in their own possessions, to which shall be added those of the neighbouring peoples, and especially those of Edom.

Chapter 1

Ob 1:1–21. Doom of Edom for cruelty to Judah, Edom's brother; restoration of the Jews.

1. Obadiah – that is, servant of Jehovah; same as *Abdeel* and *Arabic Abd-allah.*

We – I and my people.

heard – (Isa 21:10).

and an ambassador is sent – Yea, an ambassador is *already* sent, namely, an angel, to stir up the Assyrians (and afterwards the Chaldeans) against Edom. The result of the ambassador's message on the heathen is, they simultaneously exclaim, 'Arise ye, and let us (with united strength) rise'. Jer 49:14 quotes this.

2. I have made thee small – Thy reduction to insignificance is *as sure as if it were already accomplished;* therefore the past tense is used [MAURER]. Edom then extended from Dedan of Arabia to Bozrah in the north (Jer 49:8,13).

3. clefts of … rock – (So 2:14 Jer 48:28). The cities of Edom, and among them Petra (*Hebrew, sela,* meaning 'rock,' 2Ki 14:7, *Margin*), the capital, in the Wady Musa, consisted of houses mostly cut in the rocks.

4. exalt *thyself* – or supply from the second clause, 'thy nest' [MAURER] (Compare Job 20:6 Jer 49:16 Am 9:2).

set … nest among … stars – namely, on the loftiest hills which seem to reach the very stars. Edom is a type of Antichrist (Isa 14:13 Da 8:10 11:37).

thence will I bring thee down – in spite of thy boast (Ob 1:3), 'Who shall bring me down?'

5. The spoliation which thou shalt suffer shall not be such as that which thieves cause, bad as that is, for these when they have seized enough, or all they can get in a hurry, leave the rest – nor such as grape-gatherers cause in a vineyard, for they, when they have gathered most of the grapes, leave gleanings behind – but it shall be utter, so as to leave thee nothing. The exclamation, 'How art thou cut off!' bursting in amidst the words of the image, marks strongly excited feeling. The contrast between Edom where no gleanings shall be left, and Israel where at the worst a gleaning is left (Isa 17:6 24:13), is striking.

6. How are *the things of* **Esau searched out!** – by hostile soldiers seeking booty. Compare with Ob 1:5,6 here, Jer 49:9,10.

hidden things – or 'places.' Edom abounded in such hiding-places, as caves, clefts in the rock. None of these would be left unexplored by the foe.

7. Men of thy confederacy – that is, thy confederates.

brought thee … to the border – that is, when Idumean ambassadors shall go to confederate states seeking aid, these latter shall conduct them with due ceremony to their border, giving them empty compliments, but not the aid required [DRUSIUS]. This view agrees with the context, which speaks of false friends *deceiving* Edom: that is, failing to give help in need (compare Job 6:14,15). CALVIN translates, 'have *driven,*' that is, *shall drive thee;* shall help to drive thee *to thy border* on thy way into captivity in foreign lands.

the men that were at peace with thee – literally, 'the men of thy peace.' Compare Ps 41:9 Jer 38:22, *Margin,* where also the same formula occurs, 'prevailed against thee.'

they that eat thy bread – the poorer tribes of the desert who subsisted on the bounty of Edom. Compare again Ps 41:9, which seems to have been before Obadiah's mind, as his words were before Jeremiah's.

have laid a wound under thee – 'laid' implies that their intimacy was used as a SNARE laid with a view to wound; also, these guest friends of Edom, instead of the cushions ordinarily *laid* under guests at table, *laid* snares to wound, that is, had a secret understanding with Edom's foe for that purpose.

none understanding – none of the wisdom for which Edom was famed (see Ob 1:8) to extricate him from his perilous position.

in him – instead of 'in thee.' The change implies the alienation of God from Edom: Edom has so estranged himself from God, that He speaks now *of* him, not *to* him.

8. (Isa 49:7; compare Job 5:12,13 Isa 19:3 Jer 19:7).

in that day … even destroy – Heretofore Edom, through its intercourse with Babylon and Egypt, and from its means of information through the many caravans passing to and fro between Europe and India, has been famed for knowledge; but in that day at last ('even') I will destroy its wise men.

mount of Esau – that is, Idumea, which was a mountainous region.

10. against thy brother – This aggravates the sin of Esau, that it was against him who was his brother by birth and by circumcision. The posterity of Esau followed in the steps of their father's hatred to Jacob by violence against Jacob's seed (Ge 27:41).

Jacob – not merely his own brother, but his *twin* brother; hence the name *Jacob,* not Israel, is here put emphatically. Compare De 23:7 for the opposite feeling which Jacob's seed was commanded to entertain towards Edom's.

shame … cover thee – (Ps 35:26 69:7).

for ever – (Isa 34:10 Eze 35:9 Mal 1:4). Idumea, *as a nation,* should be 'cut off for ever,' though the land should be again inhabited.

11. thou stoodest on the other side – in an attitude of hostility, rather than the sympathy which became a brother, feasting thine eyes (see

Ob 1:12) with the misery of Jacob, and eagerly watching for his destruction. So Messiah, the antitype to Jerusalem, abandoned by His kinsmen (Ps 38:11).

strangers – the Philistines, Arabians in the reign of Jehoram. (2Ch 21:16); the Syrians in the reign of Joash of Judah (2Ch 24:24); the Chaldeans (2Ch 36:1–23).

carried … captive his forces – his 'host' (Ob 1:20) the multitude of Jerusalem's inhabitants.

cast lots upon Jerusalem – (Joe 3:3). So Messiah, Jerusalem's antitype, had lots cast for His only earthly possessions (Ps 22:18).

12. looked on – with malignant pleasure, and a brutal stare. So the antitypes, Messiah's foes (Ps 22:17).

the day of thy brother – his day of calamity.

became a stranger – that is, was banished as an alien from his own land. God sends heavy calamities on those who rejoice in the calamities of their enemies (Pr 17:5 24:17,18). Contrast the opposite conduct of David and of the divine Son of David in a like case (Ps 35:13–15).

spoken proudly – literally, 'made great the mouth'; proudly insulting the fallen (Eze 35:13, *Margin;* compare 1Sa 2:8 Re 13:6).

13. substance – translated 'forces' in Ob 1:11.

14. stood in the crossway, to cut off those of his – Judah's.

that did escape – The Jews naturally fled by the crossways.

15. For – resumptive in connection with Ob 1:10, wherein Edom was threatened with *cutting off for ever.*

the day of the Lord – the day in which He will manifest Himself as the Righteous Punisher of the ungodly peoples (Joe 3:14). The 'all' shows that the fulfilment is not exhausted in the punishment inflicted on the surrounding nations by the instrumentality of Nebuchadnezzar; but, as in Joe 3:14, and Zec 12:3, that the last judgment to come on the nations confederate against Jerusalem is referred to.

as thou hast done, it shall be done unto thee – the righteous principle of retribution in kind (Le 24:17 Mt 7:2; compare Jud 1:6,7 8:19 Es 7:10).

thy reward – the reward of thy deed (compare Isa 3:9–11).

16. ye … upon my holy mountain – a periphrasis for, 'ye Jews' [MAURER], whom Obadiah now by a sudden apostrophe addresses. The clause, 'upon My holy mountain,' expresses the reason of the vengeance to be taken on Judah's foes; namely, that Jerusalem is God's holy mountain, the seat of His temple, and Judah His covenant-people. Jer 49:12, which is copied from Obadiah, establishes this view (compare 1Pe 4:17).

as ye have drunk – namely, the cup of wrath, being dispossessed of your goods and places as a

nation, by Edom and all the heathen; so shall all the heathen (Edom included) drink the same cup (Ps 60:3 Isa 51:17,22 Jer 13:12,13 25:15–33 49:12 51:7; Lam 4:21, 22 Na 3:11 Hab 2:16).

continually – whereas Judah's calamity shall be temporary (Ob 1:17). The foes of Judah shall never regain their former position (Ob 1:18,19).

swallow down – so as not to leave anything in the cup of calamity; not merely 'drink' (Ps 75:8).

be as though they had not been – not a trace left of their national existence (Job 10:19 Ps 37:36 Eze 26:21).

17. upon … Zion … deliverance – both in the literal sense and spiritual sense (Joe 2:32 Isa 46:13 59:20 Ro 11:26).

there shall be holiness – that is, Zion shall be sacrosanct or inviolable: no more violated by foreign invaders (Isa 42:1 Joe 3:17).

18. fire – See the same figure, Nu 21:28 Isa 5:24 10:17.

house of Jacob … Joseph – that is, the two kingdoms, Judah and Ephraim or Israel [JEROME]. The two shall form one kingdom, their former feuds being laid aside (Isa 11:12,13 37:22–28 Jer 3:18 Ho 1:11). The Jews returned with some of the Israelites from Babylon; and, under John Hyrcanus, so subdued and, compelling them to be circumcised, incorporated the Idumeans with themselves that they formed part of the nation [JOSEPHUS, *Antiquities,* 13.17; 12.11]. This was but an earnest of the future union of Israel and Judah in the possession of the enlarged land as one kingdom (Eze 37:16.).

stubble – (Mal 4:1).

19. they of the south – The Jews who in the coming time are to occupy the south of Judea shall possess, in addition to their own territory, the adjoining *mountainous region of Edom.*

they of the plain – The Jews who shall occupy the low country along the Mediterranean, south and southwest of Palestine, shall possess, in addition to their own territory, the land of 'the Philistines,' which runs as a long strip between the hills and the sea.

and they shall possess the fields of Ephraim – that is, the rightful owners shall be restored, the Ephraimites to the fields of Ephraim.

Benjamin shall possess Gilead – that is, the region east of Jordan, occupied formerly by Reuben, Gad, and half Manasseh. Benjamin shall possess besides its own territory the adjoining territory eastward, while the two and a half tribes shall in the redistribution occupy the adjoining territory of Moab and Ammon.

20. the captivity of this host – that is, the captives of this multitude of Israelites.

even unto Zarephath – near Zidon; called Sarepta in Lu 4:26. The name implies it was a place for smelting metals. From this quarter came the 'woman of Canaan' (Mt 15:21,22).

Captives of the Jews had been carried into the coasts of Palestine or Canaan, about Tyre and Zidon (Joe 3:3,4 Am 1:9). The Jews when restored shall possess the territory of their ancient oppressors.

21. saviours – There will be in the kingdom yet to come no king, but a prince; the sabbatic period of the judges will return (compare the phrase so frequent in Judges, only once found in the times of the kings, 2Ch 14:1, 'the land had *rest*'), when there was no visible king, but God reigned in the theocracy. Israelites, not strangers, shall dispense justice to a God-fearing people (Isa 1:26 Eze 45:1–25). The judges were not such a burden to the people as the kings proved afterwards (1Sa 8:11–20). In their time the people more readily repented than under the kings (compare 2Ch 15:17), [Roos]. Judges were from time to time raised up as *saviours* or *deliverers* of Israel from the enemy. These, and the similar deliverers in the long subsequent age of Antiochus, the Maccabees, who conquered the *Idumeans* (as here foretold, compare II Maccabees 10:15,23), were types of the peaceful period yet to come to Israel.

to judge ... Esau – *to punish* (so 'judge,' 1Sa 3:13) ... Edom (compare Ob 1:1–9,15–19). Edom is the type of Israel's and God's last foes (Isa 63:1–4).

kingdom shall be the Lord's – under Messiah (Da 2:44 7:14,27 Zec 14:9 Lu 1:33 Re 11:15 19:6).

JONAH

A.R. Faussett

Introduction

Jonah was the son of Amittai, of Gath-hepher in Zebulun, so that he belonged to the kingdom of the ten tribes, not to Judah. His date is to be gathered from 2Ki 14:25–27, 'He (Jeroboam II) restored the coast of Israel from the entering of Hamath unto the sea of the plain, according to the word of the Lord God of Israel, which He spake by the hand of His servant Jonah, the son of Amittai, the prophet, which was of Gath-hepher. For the Lord saw the affliction of Israel, that it was very bitter: for there was not any shut up, nor any left, nor any helper for Israel. And the Lord said not that He would blot out the name of Israel from under heaven: but He saved them by the hand of Jeroboam the son of Joash.' Now as this prophecy of Jonah was given at a time when Israel was at the lowest point of depression, when 'there was not any shut up or left,' that is, confined or left at large, none to act as a helper for Israel, it cannot have been given in Jeroboam's reign, which was marked by prosperity, for in it Syria was worsted in fulfilment of the prophecy, and Israel raised to its former 'greatness.' It must have been, therefore, in the early part of the reign of Joash, Jeroboam's father, who had found Israel in subjection to Syria, but had raised it by victories which were followed up so successfully by Jeroboam. Thus Jonah was the earliest of the prophets, and close upon Elisha, who died in Joash's reign, having just before his death given en a token prophetical of the thrice defeat of Syria (2Ki 13:14–21). Hosea and Amos prophesied also in the reign of Jeroboam II, but towards the closing part of his forty-one years' reign. The transactions in the Book of Jonah probably occurred in the latter part of his life; if so, the book is not much older than part of the writings of Hosea and Amos. The use of the third person is no argument against Jonah himself being the writer: for the sacred writers in mentioning themselves do so in the third person (compare Joh 19:26). Nor is the use of the past tense (Jon 3:3, 'Now Nineveh *was* an exceeding great city') a proof that Nineveh's greatness was past when the Book of Jonah was being written; it is simply used to carry on the negative uniformly – 'the word of the Lord *came* to Jonah … so Jonah *arose* … now Nineveh *was*' (Jon 1:1 3:3). The mention of its *greatness* proves rather that the book was written at an early date, before the Israelites had that intimate knowledge of it which they must have had soon afterwards through frequent Assyrian inroads.

That the account of Jonah is history, and not parable (as rationalists represent), appears from our Lord's reference to it, in which the *personal existence, miraculous fate,* and *prophetical office* of Jonah are explicitly asserted: 'No sign shall be given but the *sign of the prophet* Jonas: for, as Jonas was three days and three nights in the whale's belly, so shall the Son of man be three days and three nights in the heart of the earth' (Mt 12:39,40). The Lord recognizes his being in the belly of the fish as a 'sign,' that is, a real miracle, typical of a similar event in His own history; and assumes the execution of the prophet's commission to

Nineveh, 'The men of Nineveh … repented at the preaching of Jonas; and behold, a greater than Jonas is here' (Mt 12:41).

It seemed strange to KIMCHI, a Jew himself, that the Book of Jonah is among the Scriptures, as the only prophecy in it concerns Nineveh, a heathen city, and makes no mention of Israel, which is referred to by every other prophet. The reason seems to be: a tacit reproof of Israel is intended; a heathen people were ready to repent at the first preaching of the prophet, a stranger to them; but Israel, who boasted of being God's elect, repented not, though warned by their own prophets at all seasons. This was an anticipatory streak of light before the dawn of the full 'light to lighten the Gentiles' (Lu 2:32). Jonah is himself a strange paradox: a prophet of God, and yet a runaway from God: a man drowned, and yet alive: a preacher of repentance, yet one that repines at repentance. Yet Jonah, saved from the jaws of death himself on repentance, was the fittest to give a hope to Nineveh, doomed though it was, of a merciful respite on its repentance. The patience and pity of God stand in striking contrast with the selfishness and hard-heartedness of man.

Nineveh in particular was chosen to teach Israel these lessons, on account of its being capital of the then world kingdom, and because it was now beginning to make its power felt by Israel. Our Lord (Mt 12:41) makes Nineveh's repentance a reproof of the Jews' impenitence in His day, just as Jonah provoked Israel to jealousy (De 32:21) by the same example. Jonah's mission to Nineveh implied that a heathen city afforded as legitimate a field for the prophet's labours as Israel, and with a more successful result (compare Am 9:7).

Chapter 1

Jon 1:1–17. Jonah's commission to Nineveh, flight, punishment, and preservation by miracle.

1. Jonah – meaning in *Hebrew*, 'dove.' Compare Ge 8:8,9, where the dove in vain seeks rest after flying from Noah and the ark: so Jonah. GROTIUS not so well explains it, 'one sprung from Greece' or Ionia, where there were prophets called *Amythaonidæ.*

Amittai – *Hebrew* for 'truth,' 'truth-telling'; appropriate to a prophet.

2. to Nineveh – east of the Tigris, opposite the modern Mosul. The only case of a prophet being sent to the heathen. Jonah, however, is sent to Nineveh, not solely for Nineveh's good, but also to shame *Israel*, by the fact of a heathen city repenting at the first preaching of a single stranger, Jonah, whereas God's people will not repent, though preached to by their many national prophets, late and early. Nineveh means 'the residence of Ninus,' that is, Nimrod. Ge 10:11, where the translation ought to be, 'He (Nimrod) went forth *into Assyria* and builded Nineveh.' Modern research into the cuneiform inscriptions confirms the Scripture account that Babylon was founded earlier than Nineveh, and that both cities were built by descendants of Ham, encroaching on the territory assigned to Shem (Ge 10:5,6,8,10,25).

great city – four hundred eighty stadia in circumference, one hundred fifty in length, and ninety in breadth [DIODORUS SICULUS, 2.3]. Taken by Arbaces the Mede, in the reign of Sardanapalus, about the seventh year of Uzziah; and a second time by Nabopolassar of Babylon and Cyaxares the Mede in 625 B.C. See on Jon 3:3.

cry – (Isa 40:6 58:1).

come up before me – (Ge 4:10 6:13 18:21 Ezr 9:6 Re 18:5); that is, their wickedness is so great as to require My open interposition for punishment.

3. flee – Jonah's motive for flight is hinted at in Jon 4:2: fear that after venturing on such a dangerous commission to so powerful a heathen city, his prophetical threats should be set aside by God's 'repenting of the evil,' just as God had so long spared Israel notwithstanding so many provocations, and so he should seem a false prophet. Besides, he may have felt it beneath him to discharge a commission to a foreign idolatrous nation, whose destruction he desired rather than their repentance. This is the only case of a prophet, charged with a prophetical message, concealing it.

from the presence of the Lord – (Compare Ge 4:16). Jonah thought in fleeing from the land of Israel, where Jehovah was peculiarly present, that he should escape from Jehovah's prophecy-inspiring influence. He probably knew the truth stated in Ps 139:7–10, but virtually ignored it (compare Ge 3:8-10 Jer 23:24).

went down – appropriate in going from land to the sea (Ps 107:23).

Joppa – now Jaffa, in the region of Dan; a harbor as early as Solomon's time (2Ch 2:16).

Tarshish – Tartessus in Spain; in the farthest west at the greatest distance from Nineveh in the east.

4. sent out – literally, *caused* a wind *to burst forth*. COVERDALE translates, 'hurled a greate wynde into the see.'

5. mariners were afraid – though used to storms; the danger therefore must have been extreme.

cried every man unto his god – The idols proved unable to save them, though each, according to Phoenician custom, called on his tutelary god. But Jehovah proved able: and the heathen sailors owned it in the end by sacrificing to Him (Jon 1:16).

into the sides – that is, the interior recesses (compare 1Sa 24:3 Isa 14:13,15). Those conscious of guilt shrink from the presence of their fellow man into concealment.

fast asleep – Sleep is no necessary proof of innocence; it may be the fruit of carnal security and a seared conscience. How different was Jesus' sleep on the Sea of Galilee! (Mr 4:37–39). Guilty Jonah's indifference to fear contrasts with the unoffending mariners' alarm. The original therefore is in the nominative absolute: 'But *as for Jonah*, he'. Compare spiritually, Eph 5:14.

6. call upon thy God – The ancient heathen in dangers called on foreign gods, besides their national ones (compare Ps 107:28).

think upon us – for good (compare Ge 8:1 Ex 2:25 3:7,9 Ps 40:17).

7. cast lots – God sometimes sanctioned this mode of deciding in difficult cases. Compare the similar instance of Achan, whose guilt involved Israel in suffering, until God revealed the offender, probably by the casting of lots (Pr 16:33 Ac 1:26). Primitive tradition and natural conscience led even the heathen to believe that one guilty man involves all his associates, though innocent, in punishment.

8. The guilty individual being discovered is interrogated so as to make full confession with his own mouth. So in Achan's case (Jos 7:19).

9. I am an Hebrew – He does not say 'an Israelite.' For this was the name used among themselves; 'Hebrew,' among foreigners (Ge 40:15 Ex 3:18).

I fear the Lord – in profession: his practice belied his profession: his profession aggravated his guilt.

God … which … made the sea – appropriately expressed, as accounting for the tempest sent on the *sea*. The heathen had distinct gods for the 'heaven,' the 'sea,' and the 'land.' Jehovah is the one and only true God of all alike. Jonah at last is awakened by the violent remedy from his lethargy. Jonah was but the reflection of Israel's backsliding from God, and so must bear the righteous punishment. The guilt of the minister is the result of that of the people, as in Moses' case (De 4:21). This is what makes Jonah a suitable type of Messiah, who bore the *imputed* sin of the people.

10. 'The men were exceedingly afraid,' when made aware of the wrath of so powerful a God at the flight of Jonah.

Why hast thou done this? – If professors of religion do wrong, they will hear of it from those who make no such profession.

11. What shall we do unto thee? – They ask this, as Jonah himself must best know how his God is to be appeased. 'We would gladly save thee, if we can do so, and yet be saved ourselves' (Jon 1:13,14).

12. cast me … into the sea – Herein Jonah is a type of Messiah, the one man who offered Himself to die, in order to allay the stormy flood of God's wrath (compare Ps 69:1,2, as to Messiah), which otherwise must have engulfed all other men. So Caiaphas by the Spirit declared it expedient that one man should die, and that the whole nation should not perish (Joh 11:50). Jonah also herein is a specimen of true repentance, which leads the penitent to 'accept the punishment of his iniquity' (Le 26:41,43), and to be more indignant at his sin than at his suffering.

13. they could not – (Pr 21:30). Wind and tide – God's displeasure and God's counsel were against them.

14. for this man's life – that is, for taking this man's life.

innocent blood – Do not punish us as Thou wouldst punish the shedders of innocent blood (compare De 21:8). In the case of the Antitype, Pontius Pilate washed his hands and confessed Christ's *innocence*, 'I am innocent of the blood of this *just* person.' But whereas Jonah the victim was guilty and the sailors innocent, Christ our sacrificial victim was innocent and Pontius Pilate and nil of us men were guilty. But by *imputation* of our guilt to Him and His righteousness to us, the spotless Antitype exactly corresponds to the guilty type.

thou … Lord, hast done as it pleased thee – That Jonah has embarked in this ship, that a tempest has arisen, that he has been detected by casting of lots, that he has passed sentence on himself, is all Thy doing. We reluctantly put him to death, but it is Thy pleasure it should be so.

15. sea ceased … raging – so at Jesus' word (Lu 8:24). God spares the prayerful penitent, a truth illustrated now in the case of the sailors, presently in that of Jonah, and thirdly, in that of Nineveh.

16. offered a sacrifice – They offered some sacrifice of thanksgiving at once, and vowed more when they should land. GLASSIUS thinks it means only, 'They *promised* to offer a sacrifice.'

17. prepared a great fish – not *created* specially for this purpose, but appointed in His providence, to which all creatures are subservient. The fish, through a mistranslation of Mt 12:40, was formerly supposed to be a whale; there, as here, the original means 'a great fish.' The whale's neck is too narrow to receive a man. A *miracle* in any view is needed, and we have no data to speculate further. A 'sign' or miracle it is expressly called by our Lord in Mt 12:39. Respiration in such a position could only be by miracle. The miraculous interposition was not without a sufficient reason; it was calculated to affect not only Jonah, but also Nineveh and Israel. The life of a prophet was often marked by experiences which made him, through sympathy, best suited for discharging the prophetical function to his hearers and his people. The infinite resources of God in mercy as well as judgment are prefigured in the devourer being transformed into Jonah's preserver. Jonah's condition under punishment, shut out from the outer world, was rendered as much as possible the emblem of death, a present type to Nineveh and Israel, of the death in sin, as his deliverance was of the spiritual resurrection on repentance; as also, a future type of Jesus' literal death for sin, and resurrection by the Spirit of God.

three days and three nights – probably, like the Antitype, Christ, Jonah was cast forth on the land on the *third* day (Mt 12:40); the Hebrew counting the first and third parts of days as whole twenty-four hour days.

Chapter 2

Jon 2:1–10. Jonah's prayer of faith and deliverance.

1. his God – 'his' still, though Jonah had fled from Him. Faith enables Jonah now to feel this; just as the returning prodigal says of the Father, from whom he had wandered, 'I will arise and go to my Father' (Lu 15:18).

out of the fish's belly – Every place may serve as an oratory. No place is amiss for prayer.

2. Jonah incorporates with his own language inspired utterances familiar to the Church long before in Jon 2:2, Ps 120:1; in Jon 2:3, Ps 42:7; in Jon 2:4, Ps 31:22; in Jon 2:5, Ps 69:1; in Jon 2:7, Ps 142:3 18:6; in Jon 2:8, Ps 31:6; in Jon 2:9, Ps 116:17,18,3:8. Jonah, an inspired man, thus attests both the antiquity and inspiration of the Psalms. It marks the spirit of faith, that Jonah identifies himself with the saints of old, appropriating their experiences as recorded in the Word of God (Ps 119:50). Affliction opens up the mine of Scripture, before seen only on the surface.

out of the belly of hell – *Sheol*, the unseen world, which the belly of the fish resembled.

3. thou hadst cast … thy billows … thy waves – Jonah recognizes the source whence his sufferings came. It was no mere chance, but *the hand of God* which sent them. Compare Job's similar recognition of God's hand in calamities, Job 1:21 2:10; and David's, 2Sa 16:5–11.

4. cast out from thy sight – that is, from Thy favourable regard. A just retribution on one who had fled '*from the presence* of the Lord' (Jon 1:3). Now that he has got his desire, he feels it to be his bitterest sorrow to be deprived of God's presence, which once he regarded as a burden, and from which he desired to escape. He had turned his back on God; so God turned His back on him, making his sin his punishment.

toward thy holy temple – In the confidence of faith he anticipates yet to see the temple at Jerusalem, the appointed place of worship (1Ki 8:38), and there to render thanksgiving [HENDERSON]. Rather, I think, 'Though cast out of Thy sight, I will still *with the eye of faith* once more *look in prayer* towards Thy temple at Jerusalem, whither, as Thy earthly throne, Thou hast desired Thy worshippers to direct their prayers.'

5. even to the soul – that is, threatening to extinguish the *animal life.*

weeds – He felt as if the seaweeds through which he was dragged were wrapped about his head.

6. bottoms of … mountains – their *extremities* where they *terminate* in the hidden depths of the sea. Compare Ps 18:7, 'the foundations of the hills' (Ps 18:15).

earth with her bars was about me – Earth, the land of the living, is (not 'was') shut against me.

for ever – so far as any effort of *mine* can deliver me.

yet hast thou brought up my life from corruption – rather, 'Thou *bringest* … from the pit' [MAURER]. As in the previous clauses he expresses the hopelessness of his state, so in this, his sure hope of deliverance through Jehovah's infinite resources. 'Against hope he believes in hope,' and speaks as if the deliverance were actually being accomplished. Hezekiah seems to have incorporated Jonah's very words in his prayer (Isa 38:17), just as Jonah appropriated the language of the Psalms.

7. soul fainted … I remembered the Lord – beautifully exemplifying the triumph of spirit over flesh, of faith over sense (Ps 73:26 42:6). For a time troubles shut out hope; but faith revived when Jonah 'remembered the Lord,' what a gracious God He is, and how now He still preserves his life and consciousness in his dark prison-house.

into thine holy temple – the temple at Jerusalem (Jon 2:4). As there he looks in believing prayer towards it, so here he regards his prayer as already heard.

8. observe lying vanities – regard or reverence idols, powerless to save (Ps 31:6).

mercy – Jehovah, the very idea of whom is identified now in Jonah's mind with mercy and loving-kindness. As the Psalmist (Ps 144:2) styles Him, 'my goodness'; God who is to me all beneficence. Compare Ps 59:17, 'the God of my mercy,' literally, 'my kindness-God.' Jonah had 'forsaken His own mercy,' God, to flee to heathen lands where 'lying vanities' (idols) were worshipped. But now, taught by his own preservation in conscious life in the fish's belly, and by the inability of the mariners idols to lull the storm (Jon 1:5), estrangement from God seems estrangement from his own happiness (Jer 2:13 17:13). Prayer has been restrained in Jonah's case, so that he was 'fast asleep' in the midst of danger, heretofore; but now prayer is the sure sign of his return to God.

9. I will sacrifice ... thanksgiving – In the believing anticipation of sure deliverance, he offers thanksgivings already. So Jehoshaphat (2Ch 20:21) appointed singers to *praise* the Lord in front of the army before the battle with Moab and Ammon, as if the victory was already gained. God honours such confidence in Him. There is also herein a mark of sanctified affliction, that he vows amendment and thankful obedience (Ps 119:67).

10. upon the dry land – probably on the coast of Palestine.

Chapter 3

Jon 3:1–10. Jonah's second commission to Nineveh: the Ninevites repent of their evil way: so God repents of the evil threatened.

2. preach ... the preaching – literally, 'proclaim the proclamation.' On the former occasion the specific object of his commission to Nineveh was declared; here it is indeterminate. This is to show how freely he yields himself, in the spirit of unconditional obedience, to speak whatever God may please.

3. arose and went – like the son who was at first disobedient to the father's command, 'Go work in my vineyard,' but who afterwards 'repented and went' (Mt 21:28,29). Jonah was thus the fittest instrument for proclaiming judgment, and yet hope of mercy on repentance to Nineveh, being himself a living exemplification of both – judgment in his entombment in the fish, mercy on repentance in his deliverance. Israel professing to obey, but not obeying, and so doomed to exile in the same Nineveh, answers to the son who said, 'I go, sir, and went not.' In Lu 11:30 it is said that Jonas was not only a sign to the men in Christ's time, but also

'unto the Ninevites.' On the latter occasion (Mt 16:1–4) when the Pharisees and Sadducees tempted Him, asking a sign *from heaven,* He answered, 'No sign shall be given, but the sign of the prophet Jonas,' Mt 12:39. Thus the sign had a *twofold* aspect, a direct bearing on the Ninevites, an indirect bearing on the Jews in Christ's time. To the Ninevites he was not merely a prophet, but himself a wonder in the earth, as one who had tasted of death, and yet had not seen corruption, but had now returned to witness among them for God. If the Ninevites had indulged in a captious spirit, they never would have inquired and so known Jonah's wonderful history; but being humbled by God's awful message, they learned from Jonah himself that it was the previous concealing in his bosom of the same message of their own doom that caused him to be entombed as an outcast from the living. Thus he was a 'sign' to them of wrath on the one hand, and, on the other, of mercy. Guilty Jonah saved from the jaws of death gives a ray of hope to guilty Nineveh. Thus God, who brings good from evil, made Jonah in his fall, punishment, and restoration, a sign (an *embodied lesson* or *living symbol*) through which the Ninevites were roused to hear and repent, as they would not have been likely to do, had he gone on the first commission before his living entombment and resurrection. To do evil that good may come, is a policy which can only come from Satan; but from evil already done to extract an instrument against the kingdom of darkness, is a triumphant display of the grace and wisdom of God. To the Pharisees in Christ's time, who, not content with the many signs exhibited by Him, still demanded a sign *from heaven,* He gave a sign in the opposite quarter, namely, Jonah, who came 'out of the belly of hell' (the unseen region). They looked for a Messiah gloriously coming in the clouds of *heaven;* the Messiah, on the contrary, is to pass through a like, though a deeper, humiliation than Jonah; He is to lie 'in the heart of *the earth.*' Jonah and his Antitype alike appeared low and friendless among their hearers; both victims to death for God's wrath against sin, both preaching repentance. Repentance derives all its efficacy from the death of Christ, just as Jonah's message derived its weight with the Ninevites from his entombment. The Jews stumbled at Christ's death, the very fact which ought to have led them to Him, as Jonah's entombment attracted the Ninevites to his message. As Jonah's restoration gave hope of God's placability to Nineveh, so Christ's resurrection assures us God is fully reconciled to man by Christ's death. But Jonah's entombment only had the effect of a *moral suasive;* Christ's resurrection assures us God is fully reconciliation between God and man [FAIRBAIRN].

Nineveh was an exceeding great city – literally, 'great to God,' that is, before God. All greatness was in the Hebrew mind associated with GOD; hence arose the idiom (compare 'great mountains,' *Margin,* 'mountains of God,' Ps 36:6; 'goodly cedars,' *Margin,* 'cedars of God,' Ps 80:10; 'a mighty hunter *before the Lord,*' Ge 10:9).

three days' journey – that is, about sixty miles, allowing about twenty miles for a day's journey.

4. a day's journey – not going straight forward without stopping: for the city was but eighteen miles in length; but stopping in his progress from time to time to announce his message to the crowds gathering about him.

Yet forty days, and Nineveh shall be overthrown – The commission, given indefinitely at his setting out, assumes now on his arrival a definite form, and that severer than before. It is no longer a cry against the sins of Nineveh, but an announcement of its ruin in forty days. This number is in Scripture associated often with humiliation. It was forty days that Moses, Elijah, and Christ fasted. Forty years elapsed from the beginning of Christ's ministry (the antitype of Jonah's) to the destruction of Jerusalem. The more definite form of the denunciation implies that Nineveh has now almost filled up the measure of her guilt. The change in the form which the Ninevites would hear from Jonah on anxious inquiry into his history, would alarm them the more, as implying the increasing nearness and certainty of their doom, and would at the same time reprove Jonah for his previous guilt in delaying to warn them. The very solitariness of the one message announced by the stranger thus suddenly appearing among them, would impress them with the more awe. Learning from him, that so far from lightly prophesying evil against them, he had shrunk from announcing a less severe denunciation, and therefore had been east into the deep and only saved by miracle, they felt how imminent was their peril, threatened as they now were by a prophet whose fortunes were so closely bound up with theirs. In Noah's days one hundred twenty years of warning were given to men, yet they repented not till the flood came, and it was too late. But in the case of Nineveh, God granted a double mercy: first, that its people should repent immediately after threatening; second, that pardon should immediately follow their repentance.

5. believed God – gave credit to Jonah's message from God; thus recognizing Jehovah as the true God.

fast … sackcloth – In the East outward actions are often used as symbolical expressions of inward feelings. So fasting and clothing in sackcloth were customary in humiliation. Compare in Ahab's case, parallel to that of

Nineveh, both receiving a *respite* on penitence (1Ki 21:27 20:31,32 Joe 1:13).

from the greatest … to the least – The penitence was not partial, but pervading all classes.

6. in ashes – emblem of the deepest humiliation (Job 2:8 Eze 27:30).

7. neither … beast … taste any thing – The brute creatures share in the evil effects of man's sin (Jon 4:11 Ro 8:20,22); so they here according to Eastern custom, are made to share in man's outward indications of humiliation. 'When the Persian general Masistias was slain, the horses and mules of the Persians were shorn, as well as themselves' [NEWCOME from PLUTARCH; also HERODOTUS, 9.24].

8. cry … turn – Prayer without reformation is a mockery of God (Ps 66:18 Isa 58:6). Prayer, on the other hand, must precede true reformation, as we cannot turn to God from our evil way unless God first turns us (Jer 31:18,19).

9. Who can tell – (Compare Joe 2:14). Their acting on a vague possibility of God's mercy, without any special ground of encouragement, is the more remarkable instance of faith, as they had to break through long-rooted prejudices in giving up idols to seek Jehovah at all. The only ground which their ready faith rested on, was the fact of God sending one to warn them, instead of destroying them at once; this suggested the thought of a possibility of pardon. Hence they are cited by Christ as about to condemn in the judgment those who, with much greater light and privileges, yet repent not (Mt 12:41).

10. God repented of the evil – When the message was sent to them, they were so ripe for judgment that a purpose of destruction to take effect in forty days was the only word God's righteous abhorrence of sin admitted of as to them. But when they repented, the position in which they stood towards God's righteousness was altered. So God's mode of dealing with them must alter accordingly, if God is not to be inconsistent with His own immutable character of dealing with men according to their works and state of heart, taking vengeance at last on the hardened impenitent, and delighting to show mercy on the penitent. Compare Abraham's reasoning, Ge 18:25 Eze 18:21–25 Jer 18:7–10. What was really a change *in them* and in God's corresponding dealings is, in condescension to human conceptions, represented as a change in God (compare Ex 32:14), who, in His essential righteousness and mercy, changeth not (Nu 23:19 1Sa 15:29 Mal 3:6 Jas 1:17). The reason why the announcement of destruction was made absolute, and not dependent on Nineveh's continued impenitence, was that this form was the only one calculated to rouse them; and at the same time it was a *truthful* representation of God's purpose towards Nineveh under its existing state, and of Nineveh's due. When that state ceased, a new relation of Nineveh to God, not contemplated in the message, came in, and room was made for the word to take effect, 'the curse causeless shall not come' [FAIRBAIRN]. Prophecy is not merely for the sake of proving God's omniscience by the verification of predictions of the future, but is mainly designed to vindicate God's justice and mercy in dealing with the impenitent and penitent respectively (Ro 11:22). The Bible ever assigns the first place to the eternal principles of righteousness, rooted in the character of God, subordinating to them all divine arrangements. God's sparing Nineveh, when in the jaws of destruction, on the first dawn of repentance encourages the timid penitent, and shows beforehand that Israel's doom, soon after accomplished, is to be ascribed, not to unwillingness to forgive on God's part, but to their own obstinate impenitence.

Chapter 4

Jon 4:1–11. Jonah frets at God's mercy to Nineveh: is reproved by the type of a gourd.

1. angry – literally, 'hot,' probably, with *grief* or *vexation,* rather than *anger* [FAIRBAIRN]. How sad the contrast between God's feeling on the repentance of Nineveh towards Him, and Jonah's feeling on the repentance of God towards Nineveh. Strange in one who was himself a monument of mercy on his repentance! We all, like him, need the lesson taught in the parable of the unforgiving, though forgiven, debtor (Mt 18:23–35). Jonah was grieved because Nineveh's preservation, after his denunciation, made him seem a false prophet [CALVIN]. But it would make Jonah a demon, not a man, to have preferred the destruction of six hundred thousand men rather than that his prophecy should be set aside through God's mercy triumphing over judgment. And God in that case would have severely chastised, whereas he only expostulates mildly with him, and by a mode of dealing, at once gentle and condescending, tries to show him his error. Moreover, Jonah himself, in apologizing for his vexation, does not mention *the failure of his prediction* as the cause: but solely the thought of God's *slowness to anger.* This was what led him to flee to Tarshish at his first commission; not the likelihood *then* of his prediction being falsified; for in fact his commission then was not to foretell Nineveh's downfall, but simply to 'cry against' Nineveh's 'wickedness' as having 'come up before God.' Jonah could hardly have been so vexed for the letter of his prediction failing, when the end of his commission had virtually been gained in leading Nineveh to repentance. This then cannot have been regarded by Jonah as the *ultimate* end of his commission. If Nineveh had been the prominent object with

him, he would have rejoiced at the result of his mission. But Israel was the prominent aim of Jonah, as a prophet of the elect people. Probably then he regarded the destruction of Nineveh as fitted to be an example of God's judgment at last suspending His long forbearance so as to startle Israel from its desperate degeneracy, heightened by its new prosperity under Jeroboam II at that very time, in a way that all other means had failed to do. Jonah, despairing of anything effectual being done for God in Israel, unless there were first given a striking example of severity, thought when he proclaimed the downfall of Nineveh in forty days, that now at last God is about to give such an example; so when this means of awakening Israel was set aside by God's mercy on Nineveh's repentance, he was bitterly disappointed, not from pride or mercilessness, but from hopelessness as to anything being possible for the reformation of Israel, now that his cherished hope is baffled. But GOD's plan was to teach Israel, by the example of Nineveh, how inexcusable is their own impenitence, and how inevitable their ruin if they persevere. Repenting Nineveh has proved herself more worthy of God's favour than apostate Israel; the children of the covenant have not only fallen down to, but actually below, the level of a heathen people; Israel, therefore, must go down, and the heathen rise above her. Jonah did not know the important lessons of hope to the penitent, and condemnation to those amidst outward privileges impenitent, which Nineveh's preservation on repentance was to have for aftertimes, and to all ages. He could not foresee that Messiah Himself was thus to apply that history. A lesson to us that if we *could* in any particular alter the plan of Providence, it would not be for the better, but for the worse [FAIRBAIRN].

2. my saying – my thought, or feeling.

fled before – *I anticipated by fleeing,* the disappointment of my design through Thy long-suffering mercy.

gracious … and merciful. – Jonah here has before his mind Ex 34:6; as Joel (Joe 2:13) in his turn quotes from Jonah.

3. Jonah's impatience of life under disappointed hopes of Israel's reformation through the destruction of Nineveh, is like that of Elijah at his plan for reforming Israel (1Ki 18:1–46) failing through Jezebel (1Ki 19:4).

4. Doest thou well to be angry? – or *grieved;* rather as the *Margin,* 'Art thou *much* angry,' or 'grieved?' [FAIRBAIRN with the *Septuagint* and *Syriac*]. But *English Version* suits the spirit of the passage, and is quite tenable in the *Hebrew* [GESENIUS].

5. made him a booth – that is, a temporary hut of branches and leaves, so slightly formed as to be open to the wind and sun's heat.

see what would become of the city – The term of forty days had not yet elapsed, and Jonah did not know that anything more than a suspension, or mitigation, of judgment had been granted to Nineveh. Therefore, not from sullennesss, but in order to watch the event from a neighbouring station, he lodged in the booth. As a stranger, he did not know the depth of Nineveh's repentance; besides, from the Old Testament standpoint he knew that chastening judgments often followed, as in David's case (2Sa 12:10–12,14), even where sin had been repented of. To show him what he knew not, the largeness and completeness of God's mercy to penitent Nineveh, and the reasonableness of it, God made his booth a school of discipline to give him more enlightened views.

6. gourd – Hebrew, *kikaion;* the Egyptian *kiki,* the 'ricinus' or castor-oil plant, commonly called 'palm-christ' (*palma-christi*). It grows from eight to ten feet high. Only one leaf grows on a branch, but that leaf being often more than a foot large, the collective leaves give good shelter from the heat. It grows rapidly, and fades as suddenly when injured.

to deliver him from his grief – It was therefore *grief,* not selfish anger, which Jonah felt (see on Jon 4:1). Some external comforts will often turn the mind away from its sorrowful bent.

7. a worm – of a particular kind, deadly to the ricinus. A small worm at the root destroys a large gourd. So it takes but little to make our creature comforts wither. It should silence discontent to remember, that when our gourd is gone, our God is not gone.

the next day – after Jonah was so 'exceeding glad' (compare Ps 80:7).

8. vehement – rather, 'scorching'; the *Margin,* 'silent,' expressing sultry *stillness,* not *vehemence.*

9. I do well to be angry, even unto death – 'I am very much grieved, even to death' [FAIRBAIRN]. So the Antitype (Mt 26:38).

10, 11. The main lesson of the book. If Jonah so pities a plant which cost him no toil to rear, and which is so short lived and valueless, much more must Jehovah pity those hundreds of thousands of immortal men and women in great Nineveh whom He has made with such a display of creative power, especially when many of them repent, and seeing that, if all in it were destroyed, 'more than six score thousand' of *unoffending* children, besides 'much cattle,' would be involved in the common destruction: Compare the same argument drawn from God's justice and mercy in Ge 18:23–33. A similar illustration from the insignificance of a plant, which 'to-day is and to-morrow is cast into the oven,' and which, nevertheless, is clothed by God with surpassing beauty, is given by Christ to prove that God will care for the infinitely more precious bodies and souls of men who are to live for ever (Mt 6:28–30). One soul is of more value than the whole world; surely, then, one soul is of more value than many gourds. The point of comparison spiritually is the *need* which Jonah, for the time being, had of the foliage of the gourd. However he might dispense with it at other times, now it was necessary for his comfort, and almost for his life. So now that Nineveh, as a city, fears God and turns to Him, God's cause needs it, and would suffer by its overthrow, just as Jonah's material well-being suffered by the withering of the gourd. If there were any hope of Israel's being awakened by Nineveh's destruction to fulfil her high destination of being a light to surrounding heathenism, then there would not have been the same need to God's cause of Nineveh's preservation. But as Israel, after judgments, now with returning prosperity turns back to apostasy, the means *needed* to vindicate God's cause, and provoke Israel, if possible, to jealousy, is the example of the great capital of heathendom suddenly repenting at the first warning, and consequently being spared. Thus Israel would see the kingdom of heaven transplanted from its ancient seat to another which would willingly yield its spiritual fruits. The tidings which Jonah brought back to his countrymen of Nineveh's repentance and rescue, would, if believingly understood, be far more fitted than the news of its overthrow to recall Israel to the service of God. Israel failed to learn the lesson, and so was cast out of her land. But even this was not an unmitigated evil. Jonah was a type, as of Christ, so also of Israel. Jonah, though an outcast, was highly honoured of God in Nineveh; so Israel's outcast condition would prove no impediment to her serving God's cause still, if only she was faithful to God. Ezekiel and Daniel were so at Babylon; and the Jews, scattered in all lands as witnesses for the one true God, pioneered the way for Christianity, so that it spread with a rapidity which otherwise was not likely to have attended it [FAIRBAIRN].

11. that cannot discern between their right hand and their left – children under three or four years old (De 1:39). *Six score thousand* of these, allowing them to be a fifth of the whole, would give a *total* population of six hundred thousand.

much cattle – God cares even for the brute creatures, of which man takes little account. These in wonderful powers and in utility are far above the shrub which Jonah is so concerned about. Yet Jonah is reckless as to their destruction and that of innocent children. The abruptness of the close of the book is more strikingly suggestive than if the thought had been followed out in detail.

MICAH

A.R. Faussett

Introduction

Micah was a native of Moresheth, not the same as Mareshah in Mic 1:15, but the town called Moresheth-gath (Mic 1:14), which lay near Eleutheropolis, west of Jerusalem, on the border of the Philistine country; so called to distinguish it from Moresheth of Judah. His full name is *Micaiah* (not the Micaiah mentioned 1Ki 22:8, the son of Imlah), signifying, *Who is like Jehovah?* The time of his prophesying is stated in the introduction to be in the reigns of Jotham. Ahaz, and Hezekiah, that is, between 757 and 699 B.C. Jeremiah (Jer 26:18) quotes Mic 3:12, as delivered in the reign of Hezekiah. He was thus a contemporary of Isaiah and Hosea. The idolatries practised in the reign of Ahaz accord with Micah's denunciations of such gross evils, and confirm the truth of the time assigned Mic 1:1. His prophecies are partly against Israel (Samaria), partly against Judah. As Samaria, Israel's metropolis, was taken first, and Jerusalem, the capital of Judah subsequently, in the introductory heading, Mic 1:1, *Samaria* is put first, then *Jerusalem*. He prophesies the capture of both; the Jews captivity and restoration; and the coming and reign of Messiah. His style is full, round, and perspicuous; his diction pure, and his parallelisms regular. His description of Jehovah (Mic 7:18,19) is not surpassed by any elsewhere in Scripture.

The book consists of two parts: (1) the first through fifth chapters; (2) the sixth and seventh chapters, a dialogue or contestation between Jehovah and His people, in which He reproaches them with their unnatural and ungrateful conduct, and threatens judgment for their corruptions, but consoles them with the promise of restoration from captivity.

Chapter 1

Mic 1:1–16. God's wrath against Samaria and Judah; the former is to be overthrown; such judgments in prospect call for mourning.

2. all that therein is – *Hebrew*, 'whatever fills it.' Micaiah, son of Imlah, begins his prophecy similarly, 'Hearken, O people, every one of you.' Micah designedly uses the same preface, implying that his ministrations are a continuation of his predecessor's of the same name. Both probably had before their mind Moses' similar attestation of heaven and earth in a like case (De 31:28 32:1; compare Isa 1:2).

God be witness against you – namely, that none of you can say, when the time of your punishment shall come, that you were not forewarned. The punishment denounced is stated in Mic 1:3.

from his holy temple – that is, heaven (1Ki 8:30 Ps 11:4 Jon 2:7; compare Ro 1:18).

3. tread upon the high places of the earth – He shall destroy the fortified heights (compare De 32:13 33:29) [Grotius].

4. Imagery from earthquakes and volcanic agency, to describe the terrors which attend

Jehovah's coming in judgment (compare Jud 5:5). Neither men of high degree, as the mountains, nor men of low degree, as the valleys, can secure themselves or their land from the judgments of God.

as wax – (Ps 97:5; compare Isa 64:1–3). The third clause, 'as wax,'; answers to the first in the parallelism, 'the mountains shall be molten'; the fourth, 'as the waters,'; to the second, 'the valleys shall be cleft.' As wax melts by fire, so the mountains before God, at His approach; and as waters poured down a steep cannot stand but are diffused abroad, so the valleys shall be cleft before Jehovah.

5. For the transgression of Jacob is all this – All these terrors attending Jehovah's coming are caused by the sins of Jacob or Israel, that is, the whole people.

What is the transgression of Jacob? – Taking up the question often in the mouths of the people when reproved, 'What is our transgression?' (compare Mal 1:6,7), He answers, Is it not Samaria? Is not that city (the seat of the calf-worship) the cause of Jacob's apostasy (1Ki 14:16 15:26,34 16:13,19,25,30)?

and what are the high places of Judah? – What city is the cause of the idolatries on the high places of Judah? Is it not Jerusalem (compare 2Ki 18:4)?

6. Samaria's punishment is mentioned first, as it was to fall before Jerusalem.

as an heap of the field – (Mic 3:12). Such a heap of stones and rubbish as is gathered out of fields, to clear them (Ho 12:11). Palestine is of a soil abounding in stones, which are gathered out before the vines are planted (Isa 5:2).

as plantings of a vineyard – as a place where vines are planted. Vineyards were cultivated on the sides of hills exposed to the sun. The hill on which Samaria was built by Omri, had been, doubtless, planted with vines originally; now it is to be reduced again to its original state (1Ki 16:24).

pour down – *dash down* the stones of the city into the valley beneath. A graphic picture of the present appearance of the ruins, which is as though 'the buildings of the ancient city had been thrown down from the brow of the hill' [*Scottish Mission of Inquiry*, pp. 293,294].

discover the foundations – destroy it so utterly as to lay bare its foundations (Eze 13:14). Samaria was destroyed by Shalmaneser.

7. all the hires – the wealth which Israel boasted of receiving from her idols as the 'rewards' or 'hire' for worshipping them (Ho 2:5,12).

idols … will I … desolate – that is, give them up to the foe to strip off the silver and gold with which they are overlaid.

she gathered it of the hire of an harlot, and they shall return to the hire of an harlot – Israel gathered (made for herself) her idols from the gold and silver received from false gods, as she thought, the 'hire' of her worshipping them; and they shall again become what they had been before, the hire of spiritual harlotry, that is, the prosperity of the foe, who also being worshippers of idols will ascribe the acquisition to their idols [MAURER]. GROTIUS explains it, *The offerings sent to Israel's temple by the Assyrians, whose idolatry Israel adopted, shall go back to the Assyrians,* her teachers in idolatry, as the hire or *fee for having taught it.* The image of a *harlot's hire* for the supposed temporal reward of spiritual fornication, is more common in Scripture (Ho 9:1).

8. Therefore I will wail – The prophet first shows how the coming judgment affects himself, in order that he might affect the minds of his countrymen similarly.

stripped – that is, *of shoes,* or *sandals,* as the *Septuagint* translates. Otherwise 'naked' would be a tautology.

naked – 'Naked' means *divested of the upper garment* (Isa 20:2). 'Naked and barefoot,' the sign of mourning (2Sa 15:30). The prophet's upper garment was usually rough and coarse-haired (2Ki 1:8 Zec 13:4).

like the dragons – so JEROME. Rather, 'the wild dogs,' jackals or wolves, which wail like an infant when in distress or alone [MAURER].

owls – rather, 'ostriches,' which give a shrill and long-drawn, sigh-like cry, especially at night.

9. wound … incurable – Her case, politically and morally, is desperate (Jer 8:22).

it is come – the wound, or impending calamity (compare Isa 10:28).

he is come … even to Jerusalem – The evil is no longer limited to Israel. The prophet foresees Sennacherib coming even 'to the gate' of the principal city. The use of 'it' and 'he' is appropriately distinct. 'It,' the calamity, 'came unto' Judah, many of the inhabitants of which suffered, but did not reach the citizens of Jerusalem, 'the gate' of which the foe ('he') 'came unto,' but did not enter (Isa 36:1;37:33–37).

10. Declare ye it not at Gath – on the borders of Judea, one of the five cities of the Philistines, who would exult at the calamity of the Hebrews (2Sa 1:20). Gratify not those who exult over the falls of the Israel of God.

weep ye not at all – Do not betray your inward sorrow by outward weeping, within the cognizance of the enemy, lest they should exult at it.

11. Pass ye away – that is, Thou shall go into captivity.

inhabitant of Saphir – a village amidst the hills of Judah, between Eleutheropolis and Ascalon, called so, from the *Hebrew* word for 'beauty.' Though thy name be 'beauty,' which heretofore was thy characteristic, thou shalt have thy 'shame' made 'naked.' This city shall be dismantled of its walls, which are the garments, as it were, of cities; its citizens also shall be hurried into captivity, with persons exposed (Isa 47:3 Eze 16:37 Ho 2:10).

the inhabitant of Zaanan came not forth – Its inhabitants did not come forth to console the people of Beth-ezel in their mourning, because the calamity was universal; none was exempt from it (compare Jer 6:25). 'Zaanan' is the same as Zenan, in Judah (Jos 15:37), meaning the 'place of flocks.' The form of the name used is made like the *Hebrew* for 'came forth.' Though in name seeming to imply that thou dost *come forth*, thou 'camest not forth.'

Beth-ezel – perhaps Azal (Zec 14:5), near Jerusalem. It means a 'house on the side,' or 'near.' Though *so near*, as its name implies, to Zaanan, Beth-ezel received no succour or sympathy from Zaanan.

12. Maroth – possibly the same as Maarath (Jos 15:59). Perhaps a different town, lying between the previously mentioned towns and the capital, and one of those plundered by Rab-shakeh on his way to it.

waited carefully for good – that is, for better fortune, but in vain [Calvin].

from the Lord – not from *chance*.

unto the gate of Jerusalem – after the other cities of Judah have been taken.

13. 'Bind the chariot to the swift *steed*,' in order by a hasty flight to escape the invading foe.

she is the beginning of the sin to ... Zion – Lachish was the first of the cities of Judah, according to this passage, to introduce the worship of false gods, imitating what Jeroboam had introduced in Israel. As lying near the border of the north kingdom, Lachish was first to be infected by its idolatry, which thence spread to Jerusalem.

14. shalt thou give presents to Moresheth-gath – that its inhabitants may send thee help.

Achzib – meaning 'lying.' Achzib, as its name implies, shall prove a 'lie to ... Israel,' that is, shall disappoint Israel's hopes of succour from her (compare Job 6:15–20 Jer 15:18). Achzib was in Judah between Keilah and Mareshah (Jos 15:44). Perhaps the same as Chezib (Ge 38:5).

15. Yet will I bring an heir unto thee – rather, '*the* heir.' As thou art now occupied by possessors who expelled the former inhabitants, so will I bring 'yet' again the new *possessor*, namely, the Assyrian foe. Other heirs will supplant us in every inheritance but that of heaven. There is a play upon the meaning of Mareshah, 'an inheritance': there shall come the new *heir* of the *inheritance*.

Adullam the glory of Israel – so called as being superior in situation; when it and the neighbouring cities fell, Israel's glory was gone.

16. Make thee bald. – a token of deep mourning (Ezr 9:3 Job 1:20). Mourn, O land, for thy darling children.

poll – shave off thy hair.

enlarge thy baldness – Mourn grievously. The land is compared to a mother weeping for her children.

as the eagle – the bald eagle, or the dark-winged vulture. In the moulting season all eagles are comparatively bald (compare Ps 103:5).

Chapter 2

Mic 2:1–13. Denunciation of the evils prevalent: the people's unwillingness to hear the truth: their expulsion from the land the fitting fruit of their sin: yet Judah and Israel are hereafter to be restored.

1. devise ... work ... practise – They do evil not merely on a sudden impulse, but with deliberate design. As in the former chapter sins against the first table are reproved, so in this chapter sins against the second table. A gradation: 'devise' is the *conception* of the evil purpose; 'work' (Ps 58:2), or 'fabricate,' the *maturing* of the scheme; 'practise,' or 'effect,' the *execution* of it.

because it is in the power of their hand – for the phrase see Ge 31:29 Pr 3:27. Might, not right, is what regulates their conduct. Where they can, they commit oppression; where they do not, it is because they cannot.

2. Parallelism, 'Take by violence,' answers to 'take away'; 'fields' and 'houses,' to 'house' and 'heritage' (that is, one's land).

3. against this family – against the nation, and especially against those reprobates in Mic 2:1,2.

I devise an evil – a happy antithesis between God's dealings and the Jews dealings (Mic 2:1). Ye 'devise evil' against your fellow countrymen; I devise evil against you. Ye devise it wrongfully, I by righteous retribution in kind.

from which ye shall not remove your necks – as ye have done from the law. The yoke I shall impose shall be one which ye cannot shake off. They who will not bend to God's 'easy yoke' (Mt 11:29,30), shall feel His iron yoke.

go haughtily – Ye shall not walk as now with neck haughtily uplifted, for the yoke shall press down your 'neck.'

this time is evil – rather, 'for *that* time shall be an evil time,' namely, the time of the carrying away into captivity (compare Am 5:13 Eph 5:16).

4. one take up a parable against you – that is, Some of your foes shall do so, taking in derision from your own mouth your 'lamentation,' namely, 'We be spoiled.'

lament with a doleful lamentation – literally, 'lament with a lamentation of lamentations.' *Hebrew, naha, nehi, nihyah,* the repetition representing the continuous and monotonous wail.

he hath changed the portion of my people – a charge of injustice against Jehovah. He transfers to other nations the sacred territory assigned as the rightful portion of our people (Mic 1:15).

turning away he hath divided our fields – Turning away from us to the enemy, He hath divided among them our fields. CALVIN, as the *Margin,* explains, '*Instead of restoring* our territory, He hath divided our fields among our enemies, each of whom henceforward will have an interest in keeping what he hath gotten: so that we are utterly shut out from hope of restoration.'

5. Therefore – resumed from Mic 2:3. On account of your crimes described in Mic 2:1,2.

thou – the ideal individual ('me,' Mic 2:4), representing the guilty people in whose name he spoke.

none that … cast a cord by lot – none who shall have any possession *measured out.*

in the congregation of the Lord – among the people consecrated to Jehovah. By covetousness and violence (Mic 2:2) they had forfeited 'the portion of Jehovah's people.' This is God's implied answer to their complaint of injustice (Mic 2:4).

6. Prophesy ye not, say they – namely, the Israelites say to the true prophets, when announcing unwelcome truths. Therefore God judicially abandons them to their own ways: 'The prophets, by whose ministry they might have been saved from *shame* (ignominious captivity), shall not (that is, no longer) prophesy to them' (Isa 30:10 Am 2:12 7:16).

7. O thou … named the house of Jacob – priding thyself on the *name,* though having naught of the spirit, of thy progenitor. Also, bearing the name which ought to remind thee of God's favours granted to thee because of His covenant with Jacob.

is the Spirit of the Lord straitened? – Is His *compassion* contracted within narrower limits now than formerly, so that He should delight in your destruction (compare Ps 77:7-9 Isa 59:1,2)?

are these his doings? – that is, Are such threatenings His delight? Ye dislike the prophets' threatenings (Mic 2:6): but who is to blame? Not God, for He delights in blessing, rather than threatening; but yourselves (Mic 2:8) who provoke His threatenings [GROTIUS]. CALVIN translates, 'Are your doings such as are prescribed by Him?' Ye boast of being God's peculiar people: Do ye then conform your lives to God's law?

do not my words do good to him that walketh uprightly – Are not My words good to the upright? If your ways were upright, My words would not be threatening (compare Ps 18:26 Mt 11:19 Joh 7:17).

8. Your ways are not such that I can deal with you as I would with the upright.

Even of late – literally, 'yesterday,' 'long ago.' So 'of old.' *Hebrew,* 'yesterday' (Isa 30:33); 'heretofore,' *Hebrew,* 'since yesterday' (Jos 3:4).

my people is risen up as an enemy – that is, has rebelled against My precepts; also has become *an enemy* to the unoffending passers-by.

robe with the garment – Not content with the outer 'garment,' ye greedily rob passers-by of the ornamental 'robe' fitting the body closely and flowing down to the feet [LUDOVICUS DE DIEU] (Mt 5:40).

as men averse from war – in antithesis to (*My people*) 'as an enemy.' Israel treats the innocent passers-by, though 'averse from war,' as an enemy' would treat captives in his power, stripping them of their habiliments as lawful spoils.

9. The women of my people – that is, the *widows* of the men slain by you (Mic 2:2) ye cast out from their homes which had been their delight, and seize on them for yourselves.

from their children – that is, from the orphans of the widows.

taken away my glory – namely, their substance and raiment, which, being the fruit of God's blessing on the young, reflected *God's glory.* Thus Israel's crime was not merely robbery, but sacrilege. Their sex did not save the women, nor their age the children from violence.

for ever – There was no repentance. They persevered in sin. The pledged garment was to be restored to the poor before sunset (Ex 22:26,27); but these *never* restored their unlawful booty.

10. Arise ye, and depart – not an exhortation to the children of God to depart out of an ungodly world, as it is often applied; though that sentiment is a scriptural one. This world is doubtless not our 'rest,' being 'polluted' with sin: it is our passage, not our portion; our aim, not our home (2Co 6:17 Heb 13:14). The imperatives express the *certainty* of the *future* event *predicted.* 'Since such are your doings (compare Mic 2:7,8), My sentence on you is irrevocable (Mic 2:4,5), however distasteful to you (Mic 2:6); ye who have *cast out* others from their homes and possessions (Mic 2:2,8,9) must *arise, depart,* and be cast out of your own (Mic 2:4,5): *for this is not your rest*' (Nu 10:33 De 12:9 Ps 95:11). Canaan was designed to be a *rest* to them after their wilderness fatigues. But it is to be so no longer. Thus God refutes the people's self-confidence, as if God were bound to them inseparably. The promise (Ps 132:14) is quite

consistent with temporary withdrawal of God from Israel for their sins.

it shall destroy you – *The land* shall spew you out, because of the defilements wherewith ye 'polluted' it (Le 18:25,28 Jer 3:2 Eze 36:12–14).

11. walking in the spirit – The *Hebrew* means also 'wind.' 'If a man professing to have the "spirit" of inspiration (Eze 13:3; so "man of the spirit," that is, one claiming inspiration, Ho 9:7), but really walking in "wind" (prophecy void of nutriment for the soul, and unsubstantial as the *wind*) and falsehood, do lie, saying (that which ye like to hear), I will prophesy', even such a one, however false his prophecies, since he flatters your wishes, shall be your prophet (compare Mic 2:6 Jer 5:31).

prophesy ... of wine – that is, of an abundant supply of wine.

12. A sudden transition from threats to the promise of a glorious restoration. Compare a similar transition in Ho 1:9,10. Jehovah, too, prophesies of good things to come, but not like the false prophets, 'of wine and strong drink' (Mic 2:11). After I have sent you into captivity as I have just threatened, I will thence assemble you again (compare Mic 4:6,7).

all of thee – The restoration from Babylon was partial. Therefore that here meant must be still future, when '*all* Israel shall be saved' (Ro 11:26). The restoration from 'Babylon' (specified (Mic 4:10) is the type of the future one.

Jacob ... Israel – the ten tribes' kingdom (Ho 12:2) and Judah (2Ch 19:8 21:2,4).

remnant – the elect remnant, which shall survive the previous calamities of Judah, and from which the nation is to spring into new life (Isa 6:13 10:20–22).

as the sheep of Bozrah – a region famed for its rich pastures (compare 2Ki 3:4). GESENIUS for Bozrah translates, 'sheepfold.' But thus there will be tautology unless the next clause be translated, 'in the midst of their *pasture*.'

13. The breaker – Jehovah-Messiah, who *breaks* through every obstacle in the way of their restoration: not as formerly *breaking forth* to destroy them for transgression (Ex 19:22 Jud 21:15), but breaking a way for them through their enemies.

they – the returning Israelites and Jews.

passed through the gate – that is, through the gate of the foe's city in which they had been captives. So the image of the resurrection (Ho 13:14) represents Israel's restoration.

their king – 'the Breaker,' peculiarly '*their* king' (Ho 3:5 Mt 27:37).

pass before them – as He did when they went up out of Egypt (Ex 13:21 De 1:30,33).

the Lord on the head of them – Jehovah at their head (Isa 52:12). Messiah, the second person, is meant (compare Ex 23:20 33:14 Isa 63:9).

Chapter 3

Mic 3:1–12. The sins of the princes, prophets, and priests: the consequent desolation of Zion.

1. princes – magistrates or judges.

Is it not for you? – Is it not your special function (Jer 5:4,5)?

judgment – justice. Ye sit in judgment on others; surely then ye ought to know the judgment for injustice which awaits yourselves (Ro 2:1).

2. pluck off their skin ... flesh – rob their fellow countrymen of all their substance (Ps 14:4 Pr 30:14).

3. pot ... flesh within ... caldron – manifold species of cruel oppressions. Compare Eze 24:3, containing, as to the coming punishment, the same figure as is here used of the sin: implying that the sin and punishment exactly correspond.

4. Then – at the time of judgment, which Micah takes for granted, so certain is it (compare Mic 2:3).

they cry ... but he will not hear – just as those oppressed by them had formerly cried, and they would not hear. Their prayer shall be rejected, because it is the mere cry of nature for deliverance from pain, not that of repentance for deliverance from sin.

ill in their doings – Men cannot expect to do ill and fare well.

5. Here he attacks the false prophets, as before he had attacked the 'princes.'

make my people err – knowingly mislead My people by not denouncing their sins as incurring judgment.

bite with ... teeth, and cry, Peace – that is, who, so long as they are supplied with food, promise *peace* and prosperity in their prophecies.

he that putteth not into their mouths, they ... prepare war against him – Whenever they are not supplied with food, they foretell war and calamity.

prepare war – literally, 'sanctify war,' that is, proclaim it as a *holy* judgment of God because they are not fed.

6. night ... dark – Calamities shall press on you so overwhelming as to compel you to cease pretending to *divine* (Zec 13:4). Darkness is often the image of calamity (Isa 8:22 Am 5:18 8:9).

7. cover their lips – The Orientals prided themselves on the moustache and beard ('upper lip,' *Margin*). To *cover* it, therefore, was a token of shame and sorrow (Le 13:45 Eze 24:17,22). 'They shall be so ashamed of themselves as *not to dare to open their mouths* or boast of the name of prophet' [CALVIN].

there is no answer of God – They shall no more profess to have responses from God, being struck dumb with calamities (Mic 3:6).

8. I – in contrast to the false prophets (Mic 3:5,7).

full of power – that which 'the Spirit of Jehovah' imparts for the discharge of the prophetical function (Lu 1:17 Ac 1:8).

judgment – a sense of *justice* [MAURER]; as opposed to the false prophets' speaking to please men, not from a regard to truth. Or, 'judgment' to discern between graver and lighter offences, and to denounce punishments accordingly [GROTIUS].

might – moral *intrepidity* in speaking the truth at all costs (2Ti 1:7).

to declare unto Jacob his ... sin – (Isa 58:1). Not to flatter the sinner as the false prophets do with promises of peace.

9. Hear – resumed from Mic 3:1. Here begins the leading subject of the prophecy: a demonstration of his assertion that he is 'full of power by the Spirit of Jehovah' (Mic 3:8).

10. They – change of person from 'ye' (Mic 3:9); the third person puts them to a greater distance as estranged from Him. It is, literally, '*Whosoever* builds,' *singular.*

build up Zion with blood – build on it stately mansions with wealth obtained by the condemnation and murder of the innocent (Jer 22:13 Eze 22:27 Hab 2:12).

11. heads thereof – the princes of Jerusalem.

judge for reward – take bribes as judges (Mic 7:3).

priests teach for hire – It was their duty to teach the law and to decide controversies gratuitously (Le 10:11 De 17:11 Mal 2:7; compare Jer 6:13 Jude 1:11).

prophets ... divine – that is, false prophets.

Is not the Lord among us? – namely in the temple (Isa 48:2 Jer 7:4,8–11).

12. Jer 26:18 quotes this verse. The Talmud records that at the destruction of Jerusalem by the Romans under Titus, Terentius Rufus, who was left in command of the army, with a ploughshare tore up the foundations of the temple.

mountain of the house – the height on which the temple stands.

as the high places of the forest – shall become as heights in a forest overrun with wild shrubs and brushwood.

Chapter 4

Mic 4:1–13. Transition to the glory, peace, kingdom, and victory of Zion.

1–3. Almost identical with Isa 2:2-4.

the mountain of the house of the Lord – which just before (Mic 3:12) had been doomed to be a wild forest height. Under Messiah, its elevation is to be not that of situation, but of moral dignity, as the seat of God's universal empire.

people shall flow into it – In Isaiah it is 'all nations': a more universal prophecy.

3. rebuke – convict of sin (Joh 16:8,9); and subdue with judgments (Ps 2:5,9 110:5,6 Re 2:27 12:5).

many people ... strong nations afar off – In Isa 2:4 it is 'the nations ... many people.'

4. sit every man under his vine. – that is, enjoy the most prosperous tranquillity (1Ki 4:25 Zec 3:10). The 'vine' and 'fig tree' are mentioned rather than a *house,* to signify, there will be no need of a covert; men will be safe even in the fields and open air.

Lord of hosts hath spoken it – Therefore it must come to pass, however unlikely now it may seem.

6. assemble her that halteth – feminine for neuter in *Hebrew* idiom, '*whatever halteth*': metaphor from sheep wearied out with a journey: all the suffering exiles of Israel (Eze 34:16 Zep 3:19).

her ... driven out – all Israel's outcasts. Called 'the Lord's flock' (Jer 13:17 Eze 34:13 37:21).

7. I will make her that halted a remnant – I will cause a remnant to remain which shall not perish.

Lord shall reign ... in ... Zion – David's kingdom shall be restored in the person of Messiah, who is the seed of David and at the same time Jehovah (Isa 24:23).

for ever – (Isa 9:6,7 Da 7:14,27 Lu 1:33 Re 11:15).

8. tower of the flock – following up the metaphor of *sheep.* Jerusalem is called the 'tower,' from which the King and Shepherd observes and guards His flock: both the spiritual Jerusalem, the Church whose tower-like elevation is that of doctrine and practice (So 4:4, 'Thy neck is like the *tower* of David'), and the literal hereafter (Jer 3:17). In large pastures it was usual to erect a high wooden tower, so as to oversee the flock.

stronghold – *Hebrew,* 'Ophel'; an impregnable height on Mount Zion (2Ch 27:3 33:14 Ne 3:26,27).

unto thee shall ... come ... the first dominion – namely, the dominion formerly exercised by thee shall come back to thee.

kingdom shall come to the daughter of Jerusalem – rather, 'the kingdom *of* the daughter of Jerusalem shall come'; such as it was under David, before its being weakened by the secession of the ten tribes.

9. Addressed to the daughter of Zion, in her consternation at the approach of the Chaldeans.

is there no king in thee? – asked tauntingly. There is a king in her; but it is the same as if there were none, so helpless to devise means of escape are he and his counsellors [MAURER]. Or, Zion's pains are because her king is taken away from her (Jer 52:9 La 4:20 Eze 12:13) [CALVIN]. The former is perhaps the preferable view (compare Jer 49:7). The latter, however, describes better Zion's kingless state during her present long dispersion (Ho 3:4,5).

10. Be in pain, and labour – carrying on the metaphor of a pregnant woman. Thou shalt be affected with bitter sorrows before thy deliverance shall come. I do not forbid thy grieving, but I bring thee consolation. Though God cares for His children, yet they must not expect to be exempt from trouble, but must prepare for it.

go forth out of the city – on its capture. So 'come out' is used 2Ki 24:12 Isa 36:16.

dwell in the field – namely, in the open country, defenceless, instead of their fortified *city*. Beside the Chebar (Ps 137:1 Eze 3:15).

Babylon – Like Isaiah, Micah looks beyond the existing Assyrian dynasty to the Babylonian, and to Judah's captivity under it, and restoration (Isa 39:7 43:14 48:20). Had they been, as rationalists represent, merely sagacious politicians, they would have restricted their prophecies to the sphere of the existing *Assyrian* dynasty. But their seeing into the far-off future of *Babylon's* subsequent supremacy, and Judah's connection with her, proves them to be inspired prophets.

there ... there – emphatic repetition. The very scene of thy calamities is to be the scene of thy deliverance. In the midst of enemies, where all hope seems cut off, *there* shall Cyrus, the deliverer, appear (compare Jud 14:14). Cyrus again being the type of the greater Deliverer, who shall finally restore Israel.

11. many nations – the subject peoples composing Babylon's armies: and also Edom, Ammon., who exulted in Judah's fall (La 2:16 Ob 1:11–13).

defiled – metaphor from a virgin. Let her be defiled (that is, outraged by violence and bloodshed), and let our eye gaze insultingly on her shame and sorrow (Mic 7:10). Her foes desired to feast their *eyes* on her calamities.

12. thoughts of the Lord – Their *unsearchable wisdom*, overruling seeming disaster to the final good of His people, is the very ground on which the restoration of Israel hereafter (of which the restoration from Babylon is a type) is based in Isa 55:8; compare with Mic 4:3,12,13, which prove that *Israel*, not merely the Christian Church, is the ultimate subject of the prophecy; also in Ro 11:13. God's counsel is to discipline His people for a time with the foe as a scourge; and then to destroy the foe by the hands of His people.

gather them as ... sheaves – them who 'gathered' themselves for Zion's destruction (Mic 4:11) the Lord 'shall gather' for destruction by Zion (Mic 4:13), like *sheaves gathered to be threshed* (compare Isa 21:10 Jer 51:33). The *Hebrew* is *singular*, 'sheaf.' However great the numbers of the foe, they are all but as *one sheaf* ready to be threshed [CALVIN]. Threshing was done by treading with the feet: hence the propriety of the image for treading under foot and breaking asunder the foe.

13. thresh – destroy thy foes 'gathered' by Jehovah as 'sheaves' (Isa 41:15,16).

thine horn – Zion being compared to an ox treading corn, and an ox's strength lying in the horns, her *strength* is implied by giving her a *horn of iron* (compare 1Ki 22:11).

beat in pieces many – (Da 2:44).

I will consecrate their gain unto the Lord – God subjects the nations to Zion, not for her own selfish aggrandizement, but for His glory (Isa 60:6,9 Zec 14:20, with which compare Isa 23:18) and for their ultimate good; therefore He is here called, not merely God of Israel, but 'Lord of the whole earth.'

Chapter 5

Mic 5:1–15. The calamities which precede Messiah's advent. His kingdom, conquest of Jacob's foes, and blessing upon his people.

1. gather thyself in troops – that is, thou shalt do so, to resist the enemy. Lest the faithful should fall into carnal security because of the previous promises, he reminds them of the calamities which are to precede the prosperity.

daughter of troops – Jerusalem is so called on account of her numerous *troops*.

he hath laid siege – *the enemy* hath.

they shall smite the judge of Israel with a rod upon the cheek – the greatest of insults to an Oriental. Zedekiah, the judge (or *king*, Am 2:3) of Israel, was loaded with insults by the Chaldeans; so also the other princes and judges (La 3:30). The smiting on the cheek of other judges of Israel was a type of the same indignity offered to Him who nevertheless is the Judge, not only of Israel, but also of the world, and who is 'from everlasting' (Mic 5:2 Isa 50:6 Mt 26:67 27:30).

2. Beth-lehem Ephratah – (Ge 48:7), or, Beth-lehem Judah; so called to distinguish it from Beth-lehem in Zebulun. It is a few miles southwest of Jerusalem. Beth-lehem means 'the house of bread'; *Ephratah* means 'fruitful': both names referring to the fertility of the region.

though thou be little among – *though thou be scarcely large enough to be reckoned among*. It was insignificant in size and population; so that in Jos 15:21., it is not enumerated among the cities of Judah; nor in the list in Ne 11:25. Under Rehoboam it became a city: 2Ch 11:6, 'He *built*

Beth-lehem.' Mt 2:6 seems to contradict Micah, 'thou art *not* the least,' But really he, by an independent testimony of the Spirit, confirms the prophet, Little in *worldly* importance, thou art not least (that is, far from least, yea, *the very greatest*) among the thousands, of princes of Judah, in the spiritual significance of being the birthplace of Messiah (Joh 7:42). God chooses the little things of the world to eclipse in glory its greatest things (Jud 6:15 Joh 1:46 1Co 1:27,28). The low state of David's line when Messiah was born is also implied here.

thousands – Each tribe was divided into *clans* or 'thousands' (each thousand containing a thousand families), which had their several heads or 'princes'; hence in Mt 2:6 it is quoted 'princes,' substantially the same as in Micah, and authoritatively explained in Matthew. It is not so much this thousand that is preferred to the other thousands of Judah, but the Governor or Chief Prince out of it, who is preferred to the governors of all the other thousands. It is called a 'town' (rather in the *Greek,* 'village'), Joh 7:42; though scarcely containing a thousand inhabitants, it is ranked among the 'thousands' or larger divisions of the tribe, because of its being the cradle of David's line, and of the Divine Son of David. Moses divided the people into thousands, hundreds, fifties, and tens, with their respective 'rulers' (Ex 18:25; compare 1Sa 10:19).

unto me – unto God the Father (Lu 1:32): to fulfil all the Father's will and purpose from eternity. So the Son declares (Ps 2:7 40:7,8 Joh 4:34); and the Father confirms it (Mt 3:17 12:18, compare with Isa 42:1). God's glory is hereby made the ultimate end of redemption.

ruler – the 'Shiloh,' 'Prince of peace,' 'on whose shoulders the government is laid' (Ge 49:10 Isa 9:6). In 2Sa 23:3, '*He that ruleth* over men must be just,' the same *Hebrew* word is employed; Messiah alone realizes David's ideal of a ruler. Also in Jer 30:21, '*their governor shall proceed from the midst of them*'; answering closely to 'out of thee shall come forth *the ruler,*' here (compare Isa 11:1–4).

goings forth ... from everlasting – The plain antithesis of this clause, to 'come forth out of thee' (*from Beth-lehem*), shows that the eternal generation of the Son is meant. The terms convey the strongest assertion of infinite duration of which the *Hebrew* language is capable (compare Ps 90:2 Pr 8:22,23 Joh 1:1). Messiah's generation as man coming forth unto God to do His will on earth is *from Beth-lehem*; but as Son of God, His goings forth are *from everlasting.* The promise of the Redeemer at first was vaguely general (Ge 3:15). Then the Shemitic division of mankind is declared as the quarter in which He was to be looked for (Ge 9:26,27); then it

grows clearer, defining the race and nation whence the Deliverer should come, namely, the seed of Abraham, the Jews (Ge 12:3); then the particular tribe, Judah (Ge 49:10); then the family, that of David (Ps 89:19,20); then the very town of His birth, here. And as His coming drew nigh, the very parentage (Mt 1:1–17 Lu 1:26–35 2:1–7); and then all the scattered rays of prophecy concentrate in Jesus, as their focus (Heb 1:1,2).

3. '*Therefore* (because of His settled plan) *will* God *give up* to their foes His people Israel, *until*.'

she which travaileth hath brought forth – namely, 'the virgin' mother, mentioned by Micah's contemporary, Isa 7:14. *Zion* 'in travail' (Mic 4:9,10) answers to the *virgin* in travail of Messiah. Israel's deliverance from her long travail-pains of sorrow will synchronize with the appearance of Messiah as her Redeemer (Ro 11:26) in the last days, as the Church's spiritual deliverance synchronized with the virgin's giving birth to Him at His first advent. The ancient *Church's* travail-like waiting for Messiah is represented by *the virgin's* travail. Hence, *both* may be meant. It cannot be *restricted* to the Virgin Mary: for Israel is still 'given up,' though Messiah has been 'brought forth' almost two thousand years ago. But the Church's throes are included, which are only to be ended when Christ, having been preached for a witness to all nations, shall at last appear as the Deliverer of Jacob, and when the times of the Gentiles shall be fulfilled, and Israel as a nation shall be born in a day (Isa 66:7–11 Lu 21:24 Re 12:1,2,4; compare Ro 8:22).

the remnant of his brethren shall return unto the children of Israel – (Compare Mic 4:7). The remainder of the Israelites dispersed in foreign lands shall return to join their countrymen in Canaan. The *Hebrew* for 'unto' is, literally, 'upon,' implying superaddition to those already gathered.

4. he shall stand – that is, persevere: implying the endurance of His kingdom [CALVIN]. Rather, His sedulous care and pastoral circumspection, as a shepherd *stands* erect to survey and guard His flock on every side (Isa 61:5) [MAURER].

feed – that is, rule: as the *Greek* word similarly in Mt 2:6, *Margin,* means both 'feed' and 'rule' (Isa 40:11 49:10 Eze 34:23; compare 2Sa 5:2 7:8).

in the majesty of the name of the Lord – possessing the majesty of all Jehovah's *revealed attributes* ('name') (Isa 11:2 Php 2:6,9 Heb 2:7–9).

his God – God is '*His* God' in a oneness of relation distinct from the sense in which God is *our* God (Joh 20:17).

they shall abide – the Israelites ('they,' namely,

the *returning remnant* and the 'children of Israel previously in Canaan) shall *dwell in permanent security and prosperity* (Mic 4:4 Isa 14:30).

unto the ends of the earth – (Mic 4:1 Ps 72:8 Zec 9:10).

5. this man – in *Hebrew* simply 'This.' The One just mentioned; He and He alone. Emphatic for Messiah (compare Ge 5:29).

the peace – the fountainhead of peace between God and man, between Israel and Israel's justly offended God (Ge 49:10 Isa 9:6 Eph 2:14,17 Col 1:20), and, as the consequence, the fountain of 'peace on earth,' where heretofore all is strife (Mic 4:3 Ho 2:18 Zec 9:10 Lu 2:14).

the Assyrian – Being Israel's most powerful foe at that time, Assyria is made the representative of all the foes of Israel in all ages, who shall receive their final destruction at Messiah's appearing (Eze 38:1-23).

seven shepherds, and eight – 'Seven' expresses perfection; 'seven and eight' is an idiom for *a full and sufficient number* (Job 5:19 Pr 6:16 Ec 11:2).

principal men – literally, 'anointed (humble) men' (Ps 62:9), such as the apostles were. Their anointing, or consecration and qualification to office, was by the Holy Spirit [CALVIN] (1Jo 2:20,27). 'Princes' also were anointed, and they are mentioned as under Messiah (Isa 32:1). *English Version* therefore gives the probable sense.

6. waste – literally, 'eat up': following up the metaphor of 'shepherds' (compare Nu 22:4 Jer 6:3).

land of Nimrod – Babylon (Mic 4:10 Ge 10:10); or, including Assyria also, to which he extended his borders (Ge 10:11).

in the entrances – the passes into Assyria (2Ki 3:21).

he ... he – *Messiah* shall deliver us, when the *Assyrian* shall come.

7. remnant of Jacob – already mentioned in Mic 5:3. It in comparative smallness stands in antithesis to the 'many people.' Though Israel be but a remnant amidst many nations after her restoration, yet she shall exercise the same blessed influence in quickening them spiritually that the small imperceptible dew exercises in refreshing the grass (De 32:2 Ps 72:6 110:3). The influence of the Jews restored from Babylon in making many Gentile proselytes is an earnest of a larger similar effect hereafter (Isa 66:19 Zec 8:13).

from the Lord – Israel's restoration and the consequent conversion of the Gentiles are solely of grace.

tarrieth not for man – entirely God's work, as

independent of human contrivance as the dew and rains that fertilize the soil.

8. as a lion – In Mic 5:7 Israel's benignant influence on the nations is described; but here her vengeance on the godless hosts who assail her (Isa 66:15,16,19,24 Zec 12:3,6,8,9 14:17,18). Judah will be 'as a lion,' not in respect to its cruelty, but in its power of striking terror into all opponents. Under the Maccabees, the Jews acquired Idumea, Samaria, and parts of the territory of Ammon and Moab [GROTIUS]. But this was only the earnest of their future glory on their coming restoration.

9. Thine hand shall be lifted up – In Isa 26:11 it is *Jehovah's* hand that is lifted up; here *Israel's* as Mic 5:8 implies just as 'Zion' is addressed and directed to 'beat in pieces many people' (Mic 4:13; compare Isa 54:15,17). For Israel's foes are Jehovah's foes. When her hand is said to be lifted up, it is Jehovah's hand that strikes the foe by her (compare Ex 13:9, with Ex 14:8).

10. cut off thy horses ... chariots – namely, those used for the purposes of war. Israel had been forbidden the use of cavalry, or to go to Egypt for horses (De 17:16), lest they should trust in worldly forces, rather than in God (Ps 20:7). Solomon had disregarded this command (1Ki 10:26,28). Hereafter, saith God, I will remove these impediments to the free course of My grace: horses, chariots, on which ye trust. The Church will never be safe, till she is stripped of all creature trusts, and rests on Jehovah alone [CALVIN]. The universal peace given by God shall cause warlike instruments to be needless. He will *cut* them *off* from Israel (Zec 9:10); as she will cut them off from Babylon, the representative of the nations (Jer 50:37 51:21).

11. cut off ... cities ... strongholds – such as are fortified for war. In that strong time of peace, men shall live in unwalled villages (Eze 38:11; compare Jer 23:6 49:31 Zec 2:8).

12. witchcrafts out of thine hand – that is, which thou now usest.

13. graven images ... cut off – (Compare Isa 2:8,18-21 30:22 Zec 13:2).

standing images – statues.

14. groves ... cities – The 'groves' are the idolatrous symbol of Astarte (De 16:21 2Ki 21:7). 'Cities' being parallel to 'groves,' must mean cities in or near which such idolatrous groves existed. Compare 'city of the house of Baal' (2Ki 10:25), that is, a portion of the city sacred to Baal.

15. vengeance ... such as they have not heard – or, as the *Hebrew order* favours, 'the *nations* that have not hearkened to My warnings.' So the *Septuagint* (Ps 149:7).

Chapter 6

Mic 6:1–16. Appeal before all creation to the Israelites to testify, if they can, if Jehovah ever did aught but acts of kindness to them from the earliest period: God requires of them not so much sacrifices, as real piety and justice: their impieties and coming punishment.

1. contend thou – Israel is called by Jehovah to plead with Him in controversy. Mic 5:11–13 suggested the transition from those happy times described in the fourth and fifth chapters, to the prophet's own degenerate times and people.

before the mountains – in their presence; personified as if witnesses (compare Mic 1:2 De 32:1 Isa 1:2). Not as the *Margin,* 'with'; as God's controversy is with Israel, not *with* them.

2. Lord's controversy – How great is Jehovah's condescension, who, though the supreme Lord of all, yet wishes to prove to worms of the earth the equity of His dealings (Isa 5:3 43:26).

3. my people – the greatest aggravation of their sin, that God always treated them, and still treats them, as *His people.*

what have I done unto thee? – save kindness, that thou revoltest from Me (Jer 2:5,31).

wherein have I wearied thee? – What commandments have I enjoined that should have wearied thee as irksome (1Jo 5:3)?

4. For – *On the contrary,* so far from doing anything harsh, I did thee every kindness from the earliest years of thy nationality.

Miriam – mentioned, as being the prophetess who led the female chorus who sang the song of Moses (Ex 15:20). God sent Moses to give the best laws; Aaron to pray for the people; Miriam as an example to the women of Israel.

5. what Balak … consulted – how Balak plotted to destroy thee by getting Balaam to curse thee (Nu 22:5).

what Balaam … answered – how the avaricious prophet was constrained against his own will, to bless Israel whom he had desired to curse for the sake of Balak's reward (Nu 24:9–11) [MAURER]. GROTIUS explains it, 'how Balaam *answered,* that the only way to injure thee was by tempting thee to idolatry and whoredom' (Nu 31:16). The mention of 'Shittim' agrees with this: as it was the scene of Israel's sin (Nu 25:1–5 2Pe 2:15 Re 2:14).

from Shittim unto Gilgal – not that Balaam accompanied Israel from Shittim *to Gilgal:* for he was slain in Midian (Nu 31:8). But the clause, 'from Shittim,' alone applies to Balaam. 'Remember' God's kindnesses 'from Shittim,' the scene of Balaam's wicked counsel taking effect in Israel's sin, whereby Israel merited utter

destruction but for God's sparing mercy, 'to Gilgal,' the place of Israel's first encampment in the promised land between Jericho and Jordan, where God renewed the covenant with Israel by circumcision (Jos 5:2–11).

know the righteousness – Recognize that, so far from God having treated thee harshly (Mic 6:3), His dealings have been kindness itself (so 'righteous acts' for *gracious,* Jud 5:11 Ps 24:5,112:9).

6. Wherewith shall I come before the Lord? – The people, convicted by the previous appeal of Jehovah to them, ask as if they knew not (compare Mic 6:8) what Jehovah requires of them to appease Him, adding that they are ready to offer an immense heap of sacrifices, and those the most costly, even to the fruit of their own body.

burnt offerings – (Le 1:1–17).

calves of a year old – which used to be offered for a priest (Le 9:2,3).

7. rivers of oil – used in sacrifices (Le 2:1,15). Will God be appeased by my offering so much oil that it shall flow in myriads of torrents?

my first-born – (2Ki 3:27). As the king of Moab did.

fruit of my body – *my children,* as an atonement (Ps 132:11). The Jews offered human sacrifices in the valley of Hinnom (Jer 19:5 32:35 Eze 23:27).

8. He – Jehovah.

hath showed thee – long ago, so that thou needest not ask the question as if thou hadst never heard (Mic 6:6; compare De 10:12 30:11–14).

what is good – 'the good things to come' under Messiah, of which 'the law had the shadow.' The Mosaic sacrifices were but suggestive foreshadowings of His *better* sacrifice (Heb 9:23 10:1). To have this 'good' first 'showed,' or *revealed* by the Spirit, is the only basis for the superstructure of the moral requirements which follow. Thus the way was prepared for the Gospel. The banishment of the Jews from Palestine is designed to preclude the possibility of their looking to the Mosaic rites for redemption, and shuts them up to Messiah.

justly … mercy – preferred by God to sacrifices. For the latter being *positive* ordinances, are only *means* designed with a view to the former, which being *moral* duties are the *ends,* and of everlasting obligation (1Sa 15:22 Ho 6:6 12:6 Am 5:22,24). Two duties towards *man* are specified – *justice,* or strict equity; and *mercy,* or a kindly abatement of what we might justly demand, and a hearty desire to do good to others.

to walk humbly with thy God – passive and active obedience towards God. The three moral duties here are summed up by our Lord (Mt 23:23), 'judgment, mercy, and faith' (in Lu

11:42, 'the love of God'). Compare Jas 1:27. *To walk with God* implies constant prayer and watchfulness, familiar yet 'humble' converse with God (Ge 5:24 17:1).

9. unto the city – Jerusalem.

the man of wisdom – As in Pr 13:6, *Hebrew*, 'sin' is used for '*a man of* sin,' and in Ps 109:4, 'prayer' for '*a man of* prayer'; so here 'wisdom' for '*the man of* wisdom.'

shall see thy name – shall regard Thee, in Thy revelations of Thyself. Compare the end of Mic 2:7. God's 'name' expresses the sum-total of His revealed attributes. Contrast with this Isa 26:10, 'will not behold the majesty of the Lord.' Another reading is adopted by the *Septuagint*, *Syriac*, and *Vulgate*, 'there is deliverance for those who *fear* Thy name.' *English Version* is better suited to the connection; and the rarity of the *Hebrew* expression, as compared with the frequency of that in the other reading, makes it less likely to be an interpolation.

hear … the rod – Hear what punishment (compare Mic 6:13. Isa 9:3 10:5,24) awaits you, and from whom. I am but a man, and so ye may disregard me; but remember my message is not mine, but God's. Hear the rod when it is come, and you feel its smart. Hear what counsels, what cautions it speaks.

appointed it – (Jer 47:7).

10. Are there yet – notwithstanding all My warnings. Is there to be no end of acquiring treasures by wickedness? Jehovah is speaking (Mic 6:9).

scant measure … abominable – (Pr 11:1 Am 8:5).

11. Shall I count them pure – literally, 'Shall I be pure with?'. *With the pure God shows Himself pure*; but *with the froward* God *shows Himself froward* (Ps 18:26). Men often are changeable in their judgments. But God, in the case of the impure who use 'wicked balances,' cannot be pure, that is, cannot deal with them as He would with the pure.

the bag – in which weights used to be carried, as well as money (De 25:13 Pr 16:11).

12. For – rather, 'Inasmuch as'; the conclusion 'therefore,' following in Mic 6:13.

thereof – of Jerusalem.

13. make *thee* sick in smiting – (Le 26:16, to which perhaps the allusion here is, as in Mic 6:14 Ps 107:17,18 Jer 13:13).

14. eat … not be satisfied – fulfilling the threat, Le 26:26.

thy casting down shall be in the midst of thee – Thou shalt be cast down, not merely on My borders, but in the midst of thee, thy metropolis and temple being overthrown [Tirinus]. Even though there should be no enemy, yet thou shalt be consumed with intestine evils [Calvin].

thou shalt take hold, but … not deliver –

Thou shalt take hold (with thine arms), in order to save [Calvin] thy wives, children and goods.

that which thou deliverest – If haply thou dost rescue aught, it will be for a time: I will give it up to the foe's sword.

15. sow … not reap – fulfilling the threat (Le 26:16 De 28:38–40 Am 5:11).

16. statutes of Omri – the founder of Samaria and of Ahab's wicked house; and a supporter of Jeroboam's superstitions (1Ki 16:16-28). This verse is a recapitulation of what was more fully stated before, Judah's sin and consequent punishment. Judah, though at variance with Israel on all things else, imitated her impiety.

works of … Ahab – (1Ki 21:25,26).

ye walk in their counsels – Though these superstitions were the fruit of their king's 'counsels' as a master stroke of state policy, yet these pretexts were no excuse for setting at naught the counsels and will of God.

that I should make thee a desolation – Thy conduct is framed so, as if it was thy set purpose 'that I should make thee a desolation.'

inhabitants thereof – namely, of Jerusalem.

hissing – (La 2:15).

the reproach of my people – The very thing ye boast of, namely, that ye are 'My people,' will only increase the severity of your punishment. The greater My grace to you, the greater shall be your punishment for having despised it, Your being God's people in name, while walking in His love, was an honour; but now the name, without the reality, is only a 'reproach' to you.

Chapter 7

Mic 7:1–20. The universality of the corruption; the chosen remnant, driven from every human confidence, turns to God; triumphs by faith over her enemies; is comforted by God's promises in answer to prayer, and by the confusion of her enemies, and so breaks forth into praises of God's character.

1. I am as when. – It is the same with me as with one seeking fruits after the harvest, grapes after the vintage. 'There is not a cluster' to be found: no 'first-ripe fruit' (or 'early fig') which 'my soul desireth' [Maurer]. So I look in vain for any good men left (Mic 7:2).

2. The *Hebrew* expresses 'one *merciful and good* in relation to man,' rather than to God.
is perished out of the earth – (Ps 12:1).

3. That they may do evil with both hands earnestly – literally, 'Their hands are for evil that they may do it well' (that is, cleverly and successfully).

the great man, he – emphatic repetition. *As for the great man*, he no sooner has expressed his bad desire (literally, the 'mischief or lust of his soul), than the venal judges are ready to wrest the decision of the case according to his wish.

so they wrap it up – The *Hebrew* is used of *intertwining cords together*. The 'threefold cord is not quickly broken' (Ec 4:12); here the 'prince,' the 'judge,' and the 'great man' are the three in guilty complicity. 'They wrap it up,' namely, they conspire to carry out the great man's desire at the sacrifice of justice.

4. as a brier – or *thorn*; pricking with injury all who come in contact with them (2Sa 23:6,7 Isa 55:13 Eze 2:6).

the day of thy watchmen – the day foretold by thy (true) prophets, as the time of 'thy visitation' in wrath [GROTIUS]. Or, 'the day of thy *false* prophets being punished'; they are specially threatened as being not only blind themselves, but leading others blindfold [CALVIN].

now – at the time foretold, 'at that time'; the prophet transporting himself into it.

perplexity – (Isa 22:5). They shall not know whither to turn.

5. Trust ye not in a friend – Faith is kept nowhere: all to a man are treacherous (Jer 9:2-6). When justice is perverted by the great, faith nowhere is safe. So, in gospel times of persecution, 'a man's foes are they of his own household' (Mt 10:35,36 Lu 12:53).

guide – a counsellor [CALVIN] able to help and advise (compare Ps 118:8,9 146:3). *The head of your family*, to whom all the members of the family would naturally repair in emergencies. Similarly the *Hebrew* is translated in Jos 22:14 and 'chief friends' in Pr 16:28 [GROTIUS].

her that lieth in thy bosom – thy wife (De 13:6).

6. son dishonoureth the father – The state of unnatural lawlessness in all relations of life is here described which is to characterize the last times, before Messiah comes to punish the ungodly and save Israel (compare Lu 21:16 2Ti 3:1–3).

7. Therefore I will look unto the Lord – as if no one else were before mine eyes. We must not only 'look *unto* the Lord,' but also 'wait *for* Him.' Having no hope from man (Mic 7:5,6), Micah speaks in the name of Israel, who herein, taught by chastisement (Mic 7:4) to feel her sin (Mic 7:9), casts herself on the Lord as her only hope,' in patient waiting (La 3:26). She did so under the Babylonian captivity; she shall do so again hereafter when the spirit of grace shall be poured on her (Zec 12:10–13).

8. Rejoice not – at my fall.

when I fall, I shall arise – (Ps 37:24 Pr 24:16).

when I sit in darkness, the Lord shall be a light – Israel reasons as her divine representative, Messiah, reasoned by faith in His hour of darkness and desertion (Isa 50:7,8,10). Israel addresses Babylon, her triumphant foe (or Edom), as a *female;* the type of her last and worst foes (Ps 137:7,8). 'Mine enemy,' in *Hebrew*, is feminine.

9. bear – patiently.

the indignation of the Lord – His punishment inflicted on me (La 3:39). The true penitent 'accepts the punishment of his iniquity' (Le 26:41,43); they who murmur against God, do not yet know their guilt (Job 40:4,5).

execute judgment for me – against my foe. God's people plead guilty before God; but, in respect to their human foes, they are innocent and undeserving of their foes' injuries.

bring me forth to the light – to the temporal and spiritual redemption.

I shall behold his righteousness – His gracious faithfulness to His promises (Ps 103:17).

10. shame shall cover her – in seeing how utterly mistaken she was in supposing that I was utterly ruined.

Where is … thy God – (Ps 42:3,10). If He be '*thy* God,' as thou sayest, let Him come now and deliver thee. So as to Israel's representative, Messiah (Mt 27:43).

mine eyes shall behold her – a just retribution in kind upon the foe who had said, 'Let our *eye look upon* Zion.' Zion shall behold her foe prostrate, not with the carnal joy of revenge, but with spiritual joy in God's vindicating His own righteousness (Isa 66:24 Re 16:5–7).

shall she be trodden down – herself, who had trodden me down.

11. thy walls … be built – under Cyrus, after the seventy years' captivity; and again, hereafter, when the Jews shall be restored (Am 9:11 Zec 12:6).

shall the decree be far removed – namely, thy tyrannical decree or rule of Babylon shall be put away from thee, 'the statutes that were not good' (Eze 20:25) [CALVIN]. Ps 102:13–16 Isa 9:4.

12. In that day also – rather, an answer to the supposed question of Zion, When shall my walls be built? 'The day (of thy walls being built) is the day when he (that is, many) shall come to thee from Assyria.' The Assyrians who spoiled thee shall come.

and *from* the fortified cities – rather, to suit the parallelism, 'from Assyria *even to* Egypt.' (*Matzor* may be so translated). So Assyria and Egypt are contrasted in Isa 19:23 [MAURER].

from the fortress even to the river – 'from *Egypt* even to the river' Euphrates (answering in parallelism to 'Assyria') [MAURER]. Compare Isa 11:15,16 19:23–25 27:13 Ho 11:11 Zec 10:10.

13. However glorious the prospect of restoration, the Jews are not to forget the visitation on their 'land' which is to intervene for the 'fruit of (evil caused by) their doings' (compare Pr 1:31 Isa 3:10,11 Jer 21:14).

14. Feed thy people – Prayer of the prophet, in the name of his people to God, which, as God fulfils believing prayer, is prophetical of what

God *would* do. When God is about to deliver His people, He stirs up their friends to pray for them.

Feed – including the idea of both pastoral *rule* and care over His people (Mic 5:4, *Margin*), regarded as a flock (Ps 80:1 100:3). Our calamity must be fatal to the nation, unless Thou of Thy unmerited grace, remembering Thy covenant with 'Thine heritage' (De 4:20 7:6 32:9), shalt restore us.

thy rod – the shepherd's rod, wherewith He directs the flock (Ps 23:4). No longer the rod of punishment (Mic 6:9).

which dwell solitarily in the wood, in …Carmel – Let Thy people who have been dwelling as it were in a solitude of woods (*in the world, but not of it), scattered among various nations, dwell in Carmel, that is, where there are fruit-bearing lands and vineyards [CALVIN]. Rather, 'which are about to dwell (that is, that they may dwell) separate in the wood, in …Carmel' [MAURER], which are to be no longer mingled with the heathen, but are to dwell as a distinct people in their own land. Micah has here Balaam's prophecy in view (compare Mic 6:5, where also Balaam is referred to). 'Lo, the people shall dwell *alone*' (Nu 23:9; compare De 33:28). To 'feed in the wood in Carmel,' is to feed in the rich pastures among its woods. To 'sleep in the woods,' is the image of *most perfect security* (Eze 34:25). So that the Jews' 'security,' as well as their *distinct nationality*, is here foretold. Also Jer 49:31.

Bashan – famed for its cattle (Ps 22:12 Am 4:1). Parallel to this passage is Jer 50:19. Bashan and Gilead, east of Jordan, were chosen by Reuben, Gad, and half Manasseh, as abounding in pastures suited for their many cattle (Nu 32:1–42 De 3:12–17).

15. thy … him – both referring to Israel. So in Mic 7:19 the person is changed from the first to the third, 'us … our … their.' Jehovah here answers Micah's prayer in Mic 7:14, assuring him, that as He delivered His people from Egypt by miraculous power, so He would again 'show' it in their behalf (Jer 16:14,15).

16. shall see – the 'marvellous things' (Mic 7:15 Isa 26:11).

confounded at all their might – having so suddenly proved unavailing: that might wherewith they had thought that there is nothing which they could not effect against God's people.

lay … hand upon … mouth – the gesture of silence (Job 21:5 40:4 Ps 107:42 Isa 52:15). They shall be struck dumb at Israel's marvellous deliverance, and no longer boast that God's people is destroyed.

ears … deaf – They shall stand astounded so as not to hear what shall be said [GROTIUS]. Once they had eagerly drunk in all rumours as so many messages of victories; but then they shall be afraid of hearing them, because they continually fear new disasters, when they see the God of Israel to be so powerful [CALVIN]. They shall close their ears so as not to be compelled to hear of Israel's successes.

17. lick the dust – in abject prostration as suppliants (Ps 72:9; compare Isa 49:23 65:25).

move out of their holes – As reptiles from their holes, they shall come forth from their hiding-places, or fortresses (Ps 18:45), to give themselves up to the conquerors. More literally, 'they shall tremble from,' that is, tremblingly come forth from their coverts.

like worms – reptiles or crawlers (De 32:24).

they shall be afraid of the Lord – or, they shall *in fear turn with haste* to the Lord. Thus the antithesis is brought out. They shall tremble forth *from* their holes: they shall in trepidation turn to the Lord for salvation (see on Ho 3:5).

fear because of thee – shall fear Thee, Jehovah (and so fear Israel as under Thy guardianship).

18. Grateful at such unlooked-for grace being promised to Israel, Micah breaks forth into praises of Jehovah.

passeth by the transgression – not conniving at it, but forgiving it; leaving it unpunished, as a traveller *passes by* what he chooses not to look into (Pr 19:11). Contrast Am 7:8, and '*mark* iniquities,' Ps 130:3.

the remnant – who shall be permitted to survive the previous judgment: the elect remnant of grace (Mic 4:7 5:3,7,8).

retaineth not … anger – (Ps 103:9).

delighteth in mercy – God's forgiving is founded on His nature, which delights in loving-kindness, and is averse from wrath.

19. turn again – to us, from having been turned away from us.

subdue our iniquities – literally, 'tread under foot,' as being hostile and deadly to us. Without subjugation of our bad propensities, even pardon could not give us peace. When God takes away the guilt of sin that it may not condemn us, He takes away also the power of sin that it may not rule us.

cast … into … depths of the sea – never to rise again to view, buried out of sight in eternal oblivion: not merely at the shore side, where they may rise again.

our … their – change of person. Micah in the first case identifying himself and his sins with his people and their sins; in the second, speaking *of* them and their sins.

20. perform the truth – the faithful promise.

to Jacob … Abraham – Thou shalt make good to their posterity the promise made to the patriarchs. God's promises are called 'mercy,' because they flow slowly from grace; 'truth,' because they will be surely performed (Lu 1:72,73 1Th 5:24).

sworn unto our fathers – (Ps 105:9,10). The promise to Abraham is in Ge 12:2; to Isaac, in Ge 26:24; to Jacob, in Ge 28:13. This unchange- able promise implied an engagement that the seed of the patriarchs should never perish, and should be restored to their inheritance as often as they turned wholly to God.

NAHUM

A.R. Faussett

Introduction

Nahum means 'consolation' and 'vengeance'; symbolizing the 'consolation' in the book for God's people, and the 'vengeance' coming on their enemies. In the first chapter the two themes alternate; but as the prophet advances, vengeance on the capital of the Assyrian foe is the predominant topic. He is called 'the Elkoshite' (Na 1:1), from *Elkosh*, or Elkesi, a village of Galilee. The name *Capernaum*, that is, 'village of Nahum,' seems to take its name from Nahum having resided in it, though born in Elkosh in the neighbourhood. There is another Elkosh east of the Tigris, and north of Mosul, believed by Jewish pilgrims to be the birthplace and burial place of the prophet. But the book of Nahum in its allusions shows a particularity of acquaintance with Palestine (Na 1:4), and only a more general knowledge as to Nineveh (Na 2:4–6 3:2,3).

His graphic description of Sennacherib and his army (Na 1:9–12) makes it not unlikely that he was in or near Jerusalem at the time: hence the number of phrases corresponding to those of Isaiah (compare Na 1:8,9, with Isa 8:8 10:23; Na 2:10, with Isa 24:1 21:3; Na 1:15, with Isa 52:7). The prophecy in Na 1:14 probably refers to the murder of Sennacherib twenty years after his return from Palestine (Isa 37:38). He plainly writes while the Assyrian power was yet unbroken (Na 1:12 2:11–13 Na 3:15–17). The correspondence between the sentiments of Nahum and those of Isaiah and Hezekiah, as recorded in Second Kings and Isaiah, proves the likelihood of Nahum's prophecies belonging to the time when Sennacherib was demanding the surrender of Jerusalem, and had not yet raised the siege (compare Na 1:2, with 2Ki 19:14,15; Na 1:7, with 2Ki 18:22 19:19,31 2Ch 32:7,8; Na 1:9,11, with 2Ki 19:22,27,28; Na 1:14, with 2Ki 19:6,7; Na 1:15 2:1,2, with 2Ki 19:32,33; Na 2:13, with 2Ki 19:22,23). The historical data in the book itself are the humiliation of Israel and Judah by Assyria (Na 2:2); the invasion of Judah (Na 1:9,11); and the conquest of No-ammon, or Thebes, in Upper Egypt (Na 3:8–10). Tiglath-pileser and Shalmaneser had carried away Israel. The Jews were harassed by the Syrians, and impoverished by Ahaz' payments to Tiglath-pileser (2Ch 28:1–27 Isa 7:9). Sargon, Shalmaneser's successor, after the reduction of Phoenicia by the latter, fearing lest Egypt should join Palestine against him, undertook an expedition to Africa (Isa 20:1–6), and took Thebes; the latter fact we know only from Nahum, but the success of the expedition in general is corroborated in Isa 20:1–6. Sennacherib, Sargon's successor, made the last Assyrian attempt against Judea, ending in the destruction of his army in the fourteenth year of Hezekiah (713–710 B.C.). As Nahum refers to this in part prophetically, in part as matter of history (Na 1:9–13 2:13), he must have lived about 720–714 B.C., that is, almost a hundred years before the event foretold, namely, the overthrow of Nineveh by the joint forces of Cyaxares and Nabopolassar in the reign of Chyniladanus, 625 or 603 B.C.

The prophecy is remarkable for its unity of aim. Nahum's object was to inspire his countrymen, the Jews, with the assurance that, however alarming their position might seem, exposed to the attacks of the mighty Assyrian, who had already carried away the ten tribes, yet that not only should the Assyrian (Sennacherib) fail in his attack on Jerusalem, but Nineveh, his own capital, be taken and his empire overthrown; and this, not by an arbitrary exercise of Jehovah's power, but for the iniquities of the city and its people.

Chapter 1

Na 1:1–15. Jehovah's attributes as a jealous judge of sin, yet merciful to his trusting people, should inspire them with confidence. He will not allow the Assyrians again to assail them, but will destroy the foe.

1. burden of Nineveh – the *prophetic doom* of Nineveh. Nahum prophesied against that city a hundred fifty years after Jonah.

2. jealous – In this there is sternness, yet tender affection. We are jealous only of those we love: a husband, of a wife; a king, of his subjects' loyalty. God is jealous of men because He loves them. God will not bear a rival in His claims on them. His burning jealousy for His own wounded honour and their love, as much as His justice, accounts for all His fearful judgments: the flood, the destruction of Jerusalem, that of Nineveh. His jealousy will not admit of His friends being oppressed, and their enemies flourishing (compare Ex 20:5 1Co 16:22 2Co 11:2). *Burning zeal* enters into the idea in 'jealous' here (compare Nu 25:11,13 1Ki 19:10).

the Lord revengeth … Lord revengeth – The repetition of the incommunicable name JEHOVAH, and of His *revenging,* gives an awful solemnity to the introduction.

furious – literally, 'a master of fury.' So *a master of the tongue,* that is, 'eloquent.' 'One who, if He pleases, can most readily give effect to His fury' [GROTIUS]. Nahum has in view the provocation to fury given to God by the Assyrians, after having carried away the ten tribes, now proceeding to invade Judea under Hezekiah.

reserveth wrath for his enemies – *reserves it* against His own appointed time (2Pe 2:9). After long waiting for their repentance in vain, at length punishing them. A wrong estimate of Jehovah is formed from His suspending punishment: it is not that He is insensible or dilatory, but He reserves wrath for His own fit time. In the case of the penitent, He does not *reserve* or retain His anger (Ps 103:9 Jer 3:5,12 Mic 7:18).

3. slow to anger, and great in power – that is, *but* great in power, so as to be able in a moment, if He pleases, to destroy the wicked. His long-suffering is not from want of power to punish (Ex 34:6,7).

not at all acquit – literally, 'will not acquitting acquit,' or treat as innocent.

Lord hath his way in the whirlwind – From this to Na 1:5, inclusive, is a description of His power exhibited in the phenomena of nature, especially when He is wroth. His vengeance shall sweep away the Assyrian foe like a whirlwind (Pr 10:25).

clouds are the dust of his feet – Large as they are, He treads on them, as a man would on the small dust; He is Lord of the clouds, and uses them as He pleases.

4. rebuketh the sea – as Jesus did (Mt 8:26), proving Himself God (compare Isa 50:2).

Bashan languisheth – through drought; ordinarily it was a region famed for its rich pasturage (compare Joe 1:10).

flower of Lebanon – its *bloom;* all that blooms so luxuriantly on Lebanon (Ho 14:7). As Bashan was famed for its pastures, Carmel for its corn fields and vineyards, so Lebanon for its forests (Isa 33:9). There is nothing in the world so blooming that God cannot change it when He is wroth.

6. fury is poured out like fire – like the liquid fire poured out of volcanoes in all directions (see Jer 7:20).

rocks are thrown down – or, 'are burnt asunder'; the usual effect of volcanic fire (Jer 51:25,56). As Hannibal burst asunder the Alpine rocks by fire to make a passage for his army, [GROTIUS].

7. Here Nahum enters on his special subject, for which the previous verses have prepared the way, namely, to assure his people of safety in Jehovah under the impending attack of Sennacherib (Na 1:7), and to announce the doom of Nineveh, the capital of the Assyrian foe (Na 1:8). The contrast of Na 1:7,8 heightens the force.

he knoweth – recognizes as His own (Ho 13:5 Am 3:2); and so, cares for and guards (Ps 1:6 2Ti 2:19).

8. with an overrunning flood – that is, with irresistible might which *overruns* every barrier like a flood. This image is often applied to overwhelming *armies* of invaders. Also of *calamity* in general (Ps 32:6 42:7 90:5). There is, perhaps, a special allusion to the mode of Nineveh's capture by the Medo-Babylonian army; namely, through a *flood* in the river which broke down the wall twenty furlongs (see on Na 2:6).

end of the place thereof – He shall so utterly destroy Nineveh that its place cannot be found; Na 3:17 confirms this (compare Ps 37:36 Da 2:35 Re 12:8 20:11).

darkness – the severest calamities.

9. **What do ye imagine against the Lord?** – abrupt address to the Assyrians. How mad is your attempt, O Assyrians, to resist so powerful a God! What can ye do against such an adversary, successful though ye have been against all other adversaries? Ye *imagine* ye have to *do* merely with mortals and with a weak people, and that so you will gain an easy victory; but you have to encounter God, the protector of His people. Parallel to Isa 37:23–29; compare Ps 1:1.

he will make an utter end – The utter overthrow of Sennacherib's host, soon about to take place, is an earnest of the 'utter end' of Nineveh itself.

affliction shall not rise up the second time – Judah's 'affliction' caused by the invasion shall never rise again. So Na 1:12. But CALVIN takes the 'affliction' to be that *of Assyria:* 'There will be no need of His inflicting on you a second blow: He will make an utter end of you once for all' (1Sa 3:12 26:8 2Sa 20:10). If so, this verse, in contrast to Na 1:12, will express, Affliction shall visit the Assyrian no more, in a sense very different from that in which God will afflict Judah no more. In the Assyrian's case, because the blow will be fatally final; the latter, because God will make lasting blessedness in Judah's case succeed temporary chastisement. But it seems simpler to refer 'affliction' here, as in Na 1:12, to Judah; indeed *destruction,* rather than *affliction,* applies to the Assyrian.

10. **while they are folden together as thorns** – literally, 'to the same degree as thorns' (compare 1Ch 4:27, *Margin*). As thorns, so folded together and entangled that they cannot be loosed asunder without trouble, are thrown by the husbandmen all in a mass into the fire, so the Assyrians shall all be given together to destruction. Compare 2Sa 23:6,7, where also 'thorns' are the image of the wicked. As this image represents the speediness of their destruction *in a mass,* so that of 'drunkards,' their rushing as it were *of their own accord* into it; for drunkards fall down without any one pushing them [KIMCHI]. CALVIN explains, *Although* ye be *dangerous to touch* as thorns (that is, full of rage and violence), yet the Lord can easily consume you. But 'although' will hardly apply to the next clause. *English Version* and KIMCHI, therefore,

are to be preferred. The comparison to drunkards is appropriate. For drunkards, though exulting and bold, are weak and easily thrown down by even a finger touching them. So the insolent self-confidence of the Assyrians shall precipitate their overthrow by God. The *Hebrew* is '*soaked,*' or 'drunken as with their own wine.' Their drunken revelries are perhaps *alluded to,* during which the foe broke into their city, and Sardanapalus *burned* his palace; though the main and ultimate destruction of Nineveh referred to by Nahum was long subsequent to that under Sardanapalus.

11. The cause of Nineveh's overthrow: Sennacherib's plots against Judah.

come out of thee – O Nineveh. From thyself shall arise the source of thy own ruin. Thou shalt have only thyself to blame for it.

imagineth evil – Sennacherib carried out the *imaginations* of his countrymen (Na 1:9) against the Lord and His people (2Ki 19:22,23).

a wicked counsellor – literally, 'a counsellor of Belial.' Belial means 'without profit,' worthless, and so bad (1Sa 25:25 2Co 6:15).

12–14. The same truths repeated as in Na 1:9–11, Jehovah here being the speaker. He addresses Judah, prophesying good to it, and evil to the Assyrian.

Though they be quiet – that is, without fear, and tranquilly secure. So *Chaldee* and CALVIN. Or, 'entire,' 'complete'; 'Though their power be *unbroken* [MAURER], and though they be *so many, yet even so* they shall be cut down' (literally, 'shorn'; as *hair shaved off closely by a razor,* Isa 7:20). As the Assyrian was a razor shaving others, so shall he be shaven himself. Retribution in kind. In the height of their pride and power, they shall be clean cut off. The same *Hebrew* stands for 'likewise' and 'yet thus.' So *many* as they are, so many shall they perish.

when he shall pass through – or, 'and he shall pass away,' namely, 'the wicked counsellor' (Na 1:11), Sennacherib.

Though I have afflicted thee – Judah, 'I will afflict thee no more' (Isa 40:1,2 52:1,2). The contrast is between 'they,' the Assyrians, and 'thee,' Judah. *Their* punishment is fatal and final. Judah's was temporary and corrective.

13. **will I break his yoke** – the Assyrian's yoke, namely, the tribute imposed by Sennacherib on Hezekiah (2Ki 18:14).

from off thee – O Judah (Isa 10:27).

14. **that no more of thy name be sown** – that no more of thy seed, bearing thy name, as kings of Nineveh, be propagated; that thy dynasty become extinct, namely, on the destruction of Nineveh here foretold; 'thee' means the *king of Assyria.*

will I cut off ... graven image – The Medes under Cyaxares, the joint destroyers of Nineveh with the Babylonians, hated idolatry, and would delight in destroying its idols. As the Assyrians had treated the gods of other nations, so their own should be treated (2Ki 19:18). The Assyrian palaces partook of a sacred character [LAYARD]; so that 'house of thy gods' *may* refer to the *palace*. At Khorsabad there is remaining a representation of a man cutting an idol to pieces.

I will make thy grave – rather, 'I will make it (namely, "the house of thy gods," that is, "Nisroch") thy grave' (2Ki 19:37 Isa 37:38). Thus, by Sennacherib's being slain in it, Nisroch's house should be defiled. Neither thy gods, nor thy temple, shall save thee; but the latter shall be thy sepulchre.

thou art vile – or, thou art lighter than due weight (Da 5:27; compare Job 31:6) [MAURER].

15. This verse is joined in the *Hebrew* text to the second chapter. It is nearly the same as Isa 52:7, referring to the similar deliverance from Babylon.

him that bringeth good tidings – announcing the overthrow of Sennacherib and deliverance of Jerusalem. The 'mountains' are those round Jerusalem, on which Sennacherib's host had so lately encamped, preventing Judah from keeping her 'feasts,' but on which messengers now speed to Jerusalem, publishing his overthrow with a loud voice where lately they durst not have opened their mouths. A type of the far more glorious spiritual deliverance of God's people from Satan by Messiah, heralded by ministers of the Gospel (Ro 10:15).

perform thy vows – which thou didst promise if God would deliver thee from the Assyrian.

the wicked – literally, 'Belial'; the same as the 'counsellor of Belial' (Na 1:11, *Margin*); namely, Sennacherib.

Chapter 2

Na 2:1–13. The advance of the destroying forces against Nineveh, after it was used as God's rod for a time to chastise his people: the capture of that lion's dwelling, according to the sure word of Jehovah.

1. He that dasheth in pieces – God's 'battle axe,' wherewith He 'breaks in pieces' His enemies. Jer 51:20 applies the same *Hebrew* term to Nebuchadnezzar (compare Pr 25:18 Jer 50:23, 'the hammer of the whole earth'). Here the Medo-Babylonian army under Cyaxares and Nabopolassar, that destroyed Nineveh, is prophetically meant.

before thy face – before Nineveh. *Openly,* so that the work of God may be manifest.

watch the way – by which the foe will attack, so as to be ready to meet him. Ironical advice; equivalent to a prophecy, Thou shalt have need to use all possible means of defence; but use

what thou wilt, all will be in vain.

make thy loins strong – The loins are the seat of strength; to gird them up is to prepare all one's strength for conflict (Job 40:7). Also gird on thy sword (2Sa 20:8 2Ki 4:29).

2. For the Lord hath turned away the excellency of Jacob – that is, the time for Nineveh's overthrow is ripe, because Jacob (Judah) and Israel (the ten tribes) have been sufficiently chastised. The Assyrian rod of chastisement, having done its work, is to be thrown into the fire. If God chastised Jacob and Israel with all their 'excellency' (Jerusalem and the temple, which was their pre-eminent excellency above all nations in God's eyes, Ps 47:4 87:2 Eze 24:21), how much more will He punish fatally Nineveh, an alien to Him, and idolatrous?

emptiers – the Assyrian spoilers.

have emptied them out – have spoiled the Israelites and Jews (Ho 10:1). Compare Ps 80:8–16, on 'vine branches,' as applied to Israel.

3. his mighty men – The Medo-Babylonian generals *mighty men* attacking Nineveh.

made red – The ancients dyed their bull's-hide shields *red*, partly to strike terror into the enemy, chiefly lest the blood from wounds which they might receive should be perceived and give confidence to the foe [CALVIN]. G. V. SMITH conjectures that the reference is to the red reflection of the sun's rays from shields of bronze or copper, such as are found among the Assyrian remains.

in scarlet – or *crimson* military tunics (compare Mt 27:28). XENOPHON mentions that the Medes were fond of this collor. The Lydians and Tyrians extracted the dye from a particular worm.

chariots … with flaming torches – that is, the chariots shall be like flaming torches, their wheels in lightning-like rapidity of rotation flashing light and striking sparks from the stones over which they pass (compare Isa 5:28). Iron scythes were fixed at right angles to the axles and turned down, or parallel to it, inserted into the felly of the wheel. The Medes, perhaps, had such chariots, though no traces of them are found in Assyrian remains. On account of the latter fact, it may be better to translate, 'the chariots (shall come) with the glitter of *steel weapons*' [MAURER and G. V. SMITH].

in the day of his preparation – JEHOVAH's (Isa 13:3). Or, 'Medo-Babylonian *commander's* day of preparation for the attack' (Na 2:1). 'He' confirms this, and 'his' in this verse.

the fir trees – their fir-tree lances.

terribly shaken – branded so as to strike terror.

4. rage – are driven in furious haste (Jer 46:9).

justle one against another – run to and fro [MAURER].

in the broad ways – (2Ch 32:6). Large open spaces in the suburbs of Nineveh.

run like the lightnings – with rapid violence (Mt 24:27 Lu 10:18).

5. The Assyrian king. The Assyrian preparations for defence.

shall recount his worthies – (Na 3:18). *Review*, or *count over in his mind*, his nobles, choosing out the bravest to hasten to the walls and repel the attack. But in vain; for

they shall stumble in their walk – 'they shall stumble in their *advance*' through fear and hurry.

the defence shall be prepared – rather, *the covering machine* used *by besiegers* to protect themselves in advancing to the wall. Such sudden transitions, as here from the besieged to the besiegers, are frequent (compare Eze 4:2), [MAURER]. Or, used *by the besieged Assyrians* [CALVIN].

6. The gates of the rivers ... opened – The river wall on the Tigris (the west defence of Nineveh) was 4,530 yards long. On the north, south, and east sides, there were large moats, capable of being easily filled with water from the Khosru. Traces of dams ('gates,' or sluices) for regulating the supply are still visible, so that the whole city could be surrounded with a water barrier (Na 2:8). Besides, on the east, the weakest side, it was further protected by a lofty double rampart with a moat two hundred feet wide between its two parts, cut in the rocky ground. The moats or canals, flooded by the Ninevites before the siege to repel the foe, were made a dry bed to march into the city, by the foe turning the waters into a different channel: as Cyrus did in the siege of Babylon [MAURER]. In the earlier capture of Nineveh by Arbaces the Mede, and Belesis the Babylonian, DIODORUS SICULUS, [1.2.80], states that there was an old prophecy that it should not be taken till the river became its enemy; so in the third year of the siege, the river by a flood broke down the walls twenty furlongs, and the king thereupon burnt himself and his palace and all his concubines and wealth together, and the enemy entered by the breach in the wall. Fire and water were doubtless the means of the second destruction here foretold, as of the first.

7. Huzzab – Nineveh personified as a queen. She who had long *stood* in the most supreme prosperity.

led away captive – The *Hebrew* requires rather, 'she *is laid bare*'; brought forth from the apartments where Eastern women remained secluded, and is stripped of her ornamental attire. Compare Isa 47:2,3, where the same image of a woman with face and legs exposed is used of a city captive and dismantled (compare Na 3:5), [MAURER].

brought up – Her people shall be *made to go*

up to Babylon. Compare the use of 'go up' for *moving from* a place in Jer 21:2.

her maids ... as ... doves – As Nineveh is compared to a queen dethroned and dishonoured, so she has here assigned to her in the image *handmaids attending her with dove-like plaints* (Isa 38:14 59:11. The image implies *helplessness and grief suppressed, but at times breaking out*). The minor cities and dependencies of Nineveh may be meant, or her captive women [JEROME].

tabering – *beating* on their breasts *as on a tambourine.*

8. of old – rather, 'from the days that she hath been'; from the earliest period of her existence. Alluding to Nineveh's antiquity (Ge 10:11). 'Though Nineveh has been of old defended by water surrounding her, yet her inhabitants shall flee away.' GROTIUS, less probably (compare Na 3:8–12), interprets, the 'waters' of her *numerous population* (Isa 8:7 Jer 51:13 Re 17:15).

Stand, stand, *shall they cry* – that is, the few patriotic citizens *shall cry* to their *fleeing* countrymen; 'but none looketh back,' much less stops in flight, so panic-stricken are they.

9. silver ... gold – The conquerors are summoned to plunder the city. Nineveh's riches arose from the annual tribute paid by so many subject states, as well as from its extensive merchandise (Na 3:16 Eze 27:23,24).

store – accumulated by the plunder of subject nations. It is remarkable, that while small articles of value (bronze inlaid with gold, gems, seals, and alabaster *vases*) are found in the ruins of Nineveh, there are is none of *gold* and *silver*. These, as here foretold, were 'taken for spoil' before the palaces were set on fire.

glory out of all the pleasant furniture – or, 'there is abundance of precious vessels of every kind' [MAURER].

10. Literally, 'emptiness, and emptiness, and devastation.' The accumulation of substantives without a verb (as in Na 3:2), the two first of the three being derivatives of the same root, and like in sound, and the number of syllables in them increasing in a kind of climax, intensify the gloomy effectiveness of the expression. *Hebrew, Bukah, Mebukah, Mebullakah* (compare Isa 24:1,3,4 Zep 1:15).

faces of all gather blackness – CALVIN translates, 'withdraw (literally, "gather up") their glow,' or flush, that is grow pale.

11. dwelling of ... lions – Nineveh, the seat of empire of the rapacious and destructive warriors of various ranks, typified by the 'lions,' 'young lions,' 'old lion' (or *lioness* [MAURER]), 'the lion's whelp.' The image is peculiarly appropriate, as lions of every form, winged, and sometimes with the head of a man, are frequent in the Assyrian sepulchres. It was as full of spoils of all nations as a lion's den is of remains of its

prey. The question, 'Where,' implies that Jehovah 'would make an utter end of *the place*,' so that its very site could not be found (Na 1:8). It is a question expressing wonder, so incredible did it then seem.

12. prey ... ravin – different kinds of prey. Compare Isa 3:1, 'the stay and the staff.'

13. burn ... in the smoke – or (so as to pass) '*into* smoke,' that is, 'entirely' [Maurer], (Ps 37:20 46:9).

cut off thy prey from the earth – Thou shalt no more carry off prey from the nations of the earth.

the voice of thy messengers ... no more ... heard – No more shall thy emissaries be heard throughout thy provinces conveying thy king's commands, and exacting tribute of subject nations.

Chapter 3

Na 3:1–19. Repetition of Nineveh's doom, with new features; the cause is her tyranny, rapine, and cruelty: No-ammon's fortifications did not save her; it is vain, therefore, for Nineveh to think her defences will secure her against god's sentence.

1. the bloody city! – literally, 'city of blood,' namely, shed by Nineveh; just so now her own blood is to be shed.

2. The reader is transported into the midst of the fight (compare Jer 47:3). The 'noise of the whips' urging on the horses (in the chariots) is heard, and of 'the rattling of the wheels' of war chariots, and the 'horses' are seen 'prancing,' and the 'chariots jumping'.

3. horseman – distinct from 'the horses' (in the chariots, Na 3:2).

lifteth up – denoting readiness for fight.

the bright sword and the glittering spear – literally, 'the glitter of the sword and the flash of the spear!' This, as well as the translation, 'the horseman advancing up,' more graphically presents the battle scene to the eye.

they stumble upon their corpses – The *Medo-Babylonian* enemy stumble upon the *Assyrian* corpses.

4. Because of the multitude of the whoredoms – This assigns the reason for Nineveh's destruction.

of the well-favoured harlot – As Assyria was not a worshipper of the true God, 'whoredoms' cannot mean, as in the case of Israel, apostasy to the worship of false gods; but, her *harlot-like artifices* whereby she allured neighbouring states so as to subject them to herself. As the unwary are allured by the 'well-favoured harlot's' looks, so Israel, Judah (for example, under Ahaz, who, calling to his aid Tiglath-pileser, was made

tributary by him, 2Ki 16:7–10), and other nations, were tempted by the plausible professions of Assyria, and by the lure of commerce (Re 18:2,3), to trust her.

witchcrafts – (Isa 47:9,12). Alluding to the love incantations whereby harlots tried to dement and ensnare youths; answering to the subtle machinations whereby Assyria attracted nations to her.

selleth – deprives of their liberty; as slaves used to be *sold*: and in other property also *sale* was a usual mode of transfer.

families – peoples.

5. I will discover thy skirts upon thy face – that is, discover thy nakedness by *throwing up thy skirts upon thy face* (the greatest possible insult), pulling them up as high as thy head (Jer 13:22 Eze 16:37–41). I will treat thee not as a matron, but as a harlot whose shame is exposed; her gaudy finery being lifted up off her (Isa 47:2,3). So Nineveh shall be stripped of all her glory and defences on which she prides herself.

6. cast abominable filth upon thee – as infamous harlots used to be treated.

gazing stock – exposed to public ignomy as a warning to others (Eze 28:17).

7. all ... that look upon thee – when thou hast been made 'a gazing stock' (Na 3:6).

shall flee from thee – as a thing horrible to look upon. Compare 'standing *afar off*,' Re 18:10.

whence shall I seek comforters for thee? – Compare Isa 51:19, which Nahum had before his mind.

8. populous No – rather, as *Hebrew*, 'No-ammon,' the Egyptian name for Thebes in Upper Egypt; meaning the *portion* or *possession of Ammon*, the Egyptian Jupiter (whence the Greeks called the city Diospolis), who was especially worshipped there. The Egyptian inscriptions call the god *Amon-re*, that is, *Amon the Sun*; he is represented as a human figure with a ram's head, seated on a chair (Jer 46:25 Eze 30:14–16). The blow inflicted on No-ammon, described in Na 3:10, was probably by the Assyrian Sargon. As Thebes, with all her resources, was overcome by Assyria, so Assyrian Nineveh, notwithstanding all her might, in her turn, shall be overcome by Babylon. *English Version*, 'populous,' if correct, implies that No's large population did not save her from destruction.

situate among the rivers – probably the *channels* into which the Nile here divides (compare Isa 19:6–8). Thebes lay on both sides of the river. It was famed in Homer's time for its hundred gates [*Iliad*, 9.381]. Its ruins still describe a circumference of twenty-seven miles. Of them the temples of Luxor and Karnak, east of the river, are most famous. The colonnade of the former, and the grand hall of the latter, are of stupendous dimensions. One wall still represents the expedition of Shishak against Jerusalem under Rehoboam (1Ki 14:25 2Ch 12:2–9).

whose ... wall was from the sea – that is, *rose up* 'from the sea.'

9. Ethiopia – *Hebrew, Cush.* Ethiopia is thought at this time to have been mistress of Upper Egypt.

Egypt – Lower Egypt.

her strength – her safeguard as an ally.

it was infinite – The resources of these, her allies, were endless.

Put – or Phut (Ge 10:6); descended from Ham (Eze 27:10). From a root meaning a *bow;* as they were famed as archers [GESENIUS]. Probably west of Lower Egypt. JOSEPHUS [*Antiquities*, 1:6.2] identifies it with Mauritania (compare Jer 46:9, *Margin;* Eze 38:5).

Lubim – the Libyans, whose capital was Cyrene; extending along the Mediterranean west of Egypt (2Ch 12:3 16:8 Ac 2:10). As, however, the *Lubim* are always connected with the Egyptians and Ethiopians, they are perhaps distinct from the *Libyans.* The Lubim were probably at first wandering tribes, who afterwards were settled under Carthage in the region of Cyrene, under the name Libyans.

thy – No's.

helpers – literally, 'in thy help,' that is, among thy auxiliaries.

10. Notwithstanding all her might, she was overcome.

cast lots for her honourable men – They divided them among themselves by lot, as slaves (Joe 3:3).

11. drunken – made to drink of the cup of Jehovah's wrath (Isa 51:17,21 Jer 25:15).

hid – covered out of sight: a prediction remarkably verified in the state in which the ruins of Nineveh have been found [G. V. SMITH]. But as 'hid' precedes 'seek strength', it rather refers to Nineveh's state when attacked by her foe: 'Thou who now so vauntest thyself, shalt be compelled to seek a hiding-place from the foe' [CALVIN]; or, shalt be neglected and slighted by all [MAURER].

seek strength because of the enemy – Thou too, like Thebes (Na 3:9), shalt have recourse to other nations for help against thy Medo-Babylonian enemy.

12. thy strongholds – on the borders of Assyria, protecting the approaches to Nineveh: 'the gates of thy land' (Na 3:13).

fig trees with the first ripe figs – expressing the rapidity and ease of the capture of Nineveh (compare Isa 28:4 Re 6:13).

13. thy people – thy soldiers.

women – unable to fight for thee (Isa 19:16 Jer 50:37 51:30).

gates on thy land – the fortified passes or entrances to the region of Nineveh (compare Jer 15:7). Northeast of Nineveh there were hills affording a natural barrier against an invader; the guarded passes through these are probably 'the gates of the land' meant.

fire shall devour thy bars – the 'bars' of the fortresses at the passes into Assyria. So in Assyrian remains the Assyrians themselves are represented as setting fire to the gates of a city [BONOMI, *Nineveh*, pp. 194, 197].

14. Ironical exhortation to Nineveh to defend herself.

Draw ... waters – so as not to be without water for drinking, in the event of being cut off by the besiegers from the fountains.

make strong the brick-kiln – or 'repair' so as to have a supply of bricks formed of kiln-burnt clay, to repair breaches in the ramparts, or to build new fortifications inside when the outer ones are taken by the foe.

15. There – in the very scene of thy great preparations for defence; and where thou now art so secure.

fire – even as at the former destruction; Sardanapalus (Pul?) perished with all his household in the conflagration of his palace, having in despair set it on fire, the traces of which are still remaining.

cankerworm – 'the licking locust' [Henderson].

make thyself many as the locusts – 'the swarming locusts' [HENDERSON]; that is, however 'many' be thy forces, like those of 'the swarming locusts,' or the 'licking locusts,' yet the foe shall consume thee as the 'licking locust' licks up all before it.

16. multiplied thy merchants – (Eze 27:23,24). Nineveh, by large canals, had easy access to Babylon; and it was one of the great routes for the people of the west and northwest to that city; lying on the Tigris it had access to the sea. The Phoenicians carried its wares everywhere. Hence its merchandise is so much spoken of.

the cankerworm spoileth, and fleeth away – that is, spoiled *thy merchants.* The 'cankerworm,' or licking locust, answers to the Medo-Babylonian invaders of Nineveh [G. V. SMITH]. CALVIN explains less probably, 'Thy merchants spoiled many regions; but the same shall befall them as befalls locusts; they in a moment shall be scattered and flee away.'

17. Thy crowned – Thy princes (Re 9:7). The king's nobles and officers wore the tiara, as well as the king; hence they are called here 'thy crowned ones.'

as the locusts – as many as *the swarming locusts.*

thy captains – Tiphsar, an *Assyrian* word; found also in Jer 51:27, meaning *satraps*

[MICHAELIS]; or rather, 'military leaders' [MAURER]. The last syllable, *sar* means a 'prince,' and is found in *Belshaz-zar, Nabopolas-sar, Nebuchadnez-zar.*

as the great grasshoppers – literally, 'as the locust of locusts,' that is, the largest locust. MAURER translates, 'as many as *locusts upon locusts,*' that is, swarms of locusts.

in the hedges in the cold – Cold deprives the locust of the power of flight; so they alight in cold weather and at night, but when warmed by the sun soon 'flee away.' So shall the Assyrian multitudes suddenly disappear, not leaving a trace behind (compare PLINY, *Natural History,* 11.29).

18. Thy shepherds – that is, Thy leaders.

shall dwell *in the dust* – (Ps 7:5 94:17).

thy people is scattered – the necessary consequence of their leaders being laid low (1Ki 22:17).

19. bruit – the report.

clap the hands – with joy at thy fall. The sole descendants of the ancient Assyrians and Babylonians in the whole country are the Nestorian Christians, who speak a Chaldean language [LAYARD].

upon whom hath not thy wickedness passed continually? – implying God's long forbearance, and the consequent enormity of Assyria's guilt, rendering her case one that admitted no hope of restoration.

HABAKKUK

A.R. Faussett

Introduction

Habakkuk, from a *Hebrew* root meaning to 'embrace,' denoting a 'favourite' (namely, of God) and a 'struggler' (for his country's good). Some ancient authors represent him as belonging to the tribe of Levi; others [PSEUDO EPIPHANIUS], to that of Simeon. The inscription to Bel and the dragon in the *Septuagint* asserts the former; and Hab 3:19 perhaps favours this. EUSEBIUS [*Ecclesiastical History,* 7.29] states that in his time Habakkuk's tomb was shown at Ceila in Palestine.

The time seems to have been about 610 B.C. For the Chaldeans attacked Jerusalem in the ninth month of the fifth year of Jehoiakim, 605 B.C. (2Ki 24:1 2Ch 36:6 Jer 46:2 36:9). And Habakkuk (Hab 1:5,6.) speaks of the Chaldeans as about to invade Judah, but not as having actually done so. In the second chapter he proceeds to comfort his people by foretelling the humiliation of their conquerors, and that the vision will soon have its fulfilment. In the third chapter the prophet in a sublime ode celebrates the deliverances wrought by Jehovah for His people in times past, as the ground of assurance, notwithstanding all their existing calamities, that He will deliver them again. Hab 3:16 shows that the invader is still coming, and not yet arrived; so that the whole refers to the invasion in Jehoiakim's times, not those under Jehoiachin and Zedekiah. The Apocryphal appendix to Daniel states that he lived to see the Babylonian exile (588 B.C.), which accords with his prophesying early in Jehoiakim's reign, about 610 B.C.

The position of the book immediately after Nahum is appropriate; as Nahum treated of the judgments of the Lord on Assyria, for its violence against Israel, so Habakkuk, those inflicted by, and on, the Chaldeans for the same reason.

The style is poetical and sublime. The parallelisms are generally regular. Borrowed ideas occur (compare Hab 3:19, with Ps 18:33; Hab 2:6, with Isa 14:4; Hab 2:14, with Isa 11:9). The ancient catalogues imply that his book is part of the canon of Scripture. In the New Testament, Ro 1:17 quotes Hab 2:4 (though not naming him); compare also Ga 3:11 Heb 10:38. Ac 13:40, 41 quotes Hab 1:5. One or two *Hebrew* words peculiar to Habakkuk occur (Hab 1:9 2:6,16).

Chapter 1

Hab 1:1–17. Habakkuk's expostulation with Jehovah on account of the prevalence of injustice: Jehovah summons attention to his purpose of sending the Chaldeans as the avengers. The prophet complains, that these are worse than those on whom vengeance was to be taken.

1. burden – the prophetic sentence.

2, 3. violence … Why dost thou show me iniquity? – Similar language is used of the Chaldeans (Hab 1:9,13), as here is used of the Jews: implying, that as the Jews sinned by *violence* and *injustice,* so they should be punished by *violence* and *injustice* (Pr 1:31). Jehoiakim's reign was marked by injustice, treachery, and bloodshed (Jer 22:3,13–17). Therefore the Chaldeans should be sent to deal with him and his nobles according to their dealings with others (Hab 1:6,10,11,17). Compare Jeremiah's expostulation with Jehovah, Jer 12:1 20:8; and Job 19:7,8.

4. Therefore – because Thou dost suffer such crimes to go unpunished.

law is slacked – is chilled. It has no authority and secures no respect.

judgment – justice.

wrong judgment proceedeth – Decisions are given contrary to right.

5. Behold … marvellously … a work – (Compare Isa 29:14). Quoted by Paul (Ac 13:41).

among the heathen – In Ac 13:41, 'ye despisers,' from the *Septuagint.* So the *Syriac* and *Arabic* versions; perhaps from a different *Hebrew* reading. In the *English Version* reading of Habakkuk, God, in reply to the prophet's expostulation, addresses the Jews as about to be punished, 'Behold ye *among the heathen* (with whom ye deserve to be classed, and by whom ye shall be punished, as despisers; the sense *implied,* which Paul *expresses*): learn from them what ye refused to learn from Me!' For 'wonder marvellously,' Paul, in Ac 13:41, has, 'wonder *and perish,*' which gives the *sense,* not the literal wording, of the *Hebrew,* 'Wonder, wonder,' that is, be overwhelmed in wonder. The despisers are to be given up to their own stupefaction, and so perish. The Israelite unbelievers would not credit the prophecy as to the fearfulness of the destruction to be wrought by the Chaldeans, nor afterwards the deliverance promised from that nation. So analogously, in Paul's day, the Jews would not credit the judgment coming on them by the Romans, nor the salvation proclaimed through Jesus. Thus the same Scripture applied to both.

ye will not believe, though it be told you – that is, ye will not believe *now that I foretell it.*

6. I raise up – not referring to God's having brought the Chaldeans from their original seats to Babylonia, for they had already been upwards of twenty years (since Nabopolassar's era) in political power there; but to His being about now to raise them up as the instruments of God's 'work' of judgment on the Jews (2Ch 36:6). The *Hebrew* is *future,* 'I will raise up.'

bitter – that is, cruel (Jer 50:42; compare Jud 18:25, *Margin;* 1Sa 17:8).

hasty – not *passionate,* but 'impetuous.'

7. their judgment and … dignity … proceed of themselves – that is, they recognize no *judge* save themselves, and they get for themselves and keep their own 'dignity' without needing others' help. It will be vain for the Jews to complain of their tyrannical *judgments;* for whatever the Chaldeans decree they will do according to their own will, they will not brook anyone attempting to interfere.

8. swifter than the leopards – OPPIAN [*Cynegeticks,* 3.76], says of the leopard, 'It runs most swiftly straight on: you would fancy it was flying through the air.'

more fierce – rather, 'more keen'; literally, 'sharp.'

evening wolves – wolves famished with fasting all day and so most keen in attacking the fold under covert of the approaching night (Jer 5:6 Zep 3:3; compare Ge 49:27). Hence 'twilight' is termed in *Arabic* and *Persian* 'the wolf's tail'; and in French, *entre chien et loup.*

spread themselves – proudly; as in Jer 50:11, and Mal 4:2, it implies *strength* and *vigour.*

their horsemen … come from far – and yet are not wearied by the long journey.

9. all for violence – The sole object of all is not to establish just rights, but to get all they can by violence.

their faces shall sup up as the east wind – that is, they shall, as it were, *swallow up* all before them; so the horse in Job 39:24 is said to 'swallow the ground with fierceness and rage.' MAURER takes it from an *Arabic* root, 'the *desire* of their faces,' that is, the eager desire expressed by their faces. HENDERSON, with SYMMACHUS and *Syriac,* translates, 'the aspect.'

as the east wind – the simoon, which spreads devastation wherever it passes (Isa 27:8). GESENIUS translates, '(is) forwards.' The rendering proposed, *eastward,* as if it referred to the Chaldeans' return home *eastward* from Judea, laden with spoils, is improbable. Their 'gathering the sand' accords with the simoon being meant, as it carries with it whirlwinds of sand collected in the desert.

10. scoff at … kings – as unable to resist them.

they shall heap dust, and take it – 'they shall heap' earth mounds outside, and so 'take every stronghold' (compare 2Sa 20:15 2Ki 19:32) [GROTIUS].

11. **Then** – when elated by his successes.

shall his mind change – He shall lose whatever of reason or moderation ever was in him, with pride.

he shall pass over – all bounds and restraints: his pride preparing the sure way for his destruction (Pr 16:18). The language is very similar to that describing Nebuchadnezzar's 'change' from man's heart (understanding) to that of a beast, because of pride. An undesigned coincidence between the two sacred books written independently.

imputing this his power unto his god – (Da 5:4). Sacrilegious arrogance, in ascribing to his idol Bel the glory that belongs to God [CALVIN]. GROTIUS explains, '(saying that) his power is his own as one who is a god to himself' (compare Hab 1:16, and Da 3:1–30). So MAURER, 'He shall offend as one to whom his power is his god' (Job 12:6; see on Mic 2:1).

12. In opposition to the impious deifying of the Chaldeans power as their god, the prophet, in an impassioned address to Jehovah, vindicates His being 'from everlasting,' as contrasted with the Chaldean so-called 'god.'

my God, mine Holy One – Habakkuk speaks in the name of his people. God was 'the Holy One of *Israel*,' against whom the Chaldean was setting up himself (Isa 37:23).

we shall not die – Thou, as being *our* God, wilt not permit the Chaldeans utterly to destroy us. This reading is one of the eighteen called by the Hebrews 'the appointment of the scribes'; the Rabbis think that Ezra and his colleagues corrected the old reading, '*Thou shalt not die.*'

thou hast ordained them for judgment – that is, to execute Thy judgments.

for correction – to chastise transgressors (Isa 10:5–7). But not that they may deify their own power (Hab 1:11, for their power is from Thee, and but for a time); nor that they may destroy utterly Thy people. The *Hebrew* for 'mighty God' is *Rock* (De 32:4). However the world is shaken, or man's faith wavers, God remains unshaken as the Rock of Ages (Isa 26:4, *Margin*).

13. **purer ... than to behold evil** – without being displeased at it.

canst not look on iniquity – unjust injuries done to Thy people. The prophet checks himself from being carried too far in his expostulatory complaint, by putting before himself honourable sentiments of God.

them that deal treacherously – the Chaldeans, once allies of the Jews, but now their violent oppressors. Compare 'treacherous dealers,' (Isa 21:2 24:16). Instead of speaking evil against God, he goes to God Himself for the remedy for his perplexity (Ps 73:11–17).

devoureth the man that is more righteous – The Chaldean oppresses the Jew, who with all his faults, is better than his oppressor (compare Eze 16:51,52).

14. **And** – that is, And *so*, by suffering oppressors to go unpunished, 'Thou makest men as the fishes ... that have no ruler'; that is, no defender. All may fish in the sea with impunity; so the Chaldeans with impunity afflict Thy people, as these have no longer the God of the theocracy, their King, to defend them. Thou reducest men to such a state of anarchy, by wrong going unpunished, as if there were no God. He compares the world to the *sea;* men to *fishes;* Nebuchadnezzar to a *fisherman* (Hab 1:15–17).

15. **they take up all of them** – all kinds of fishes, that is, *men,* as captives, and all other prey that comes in their way.

with the angle – that is, the hook. Some they take up as with the hook, one by one; others in shoals, as in a 'net' and 'drag' or enclosing net.

therefore – because of their successes.

they rejoice – They glory in their crimes because attended with success (compare Hab 1:11).

16. **sacrifice unto their net** – that is, their arms, power, and military skill, wherewith they gained their victories; instead of to God

by them – by their net and dragnet.

their portion – image from a banquet: the prey which they have gotten.

17. **Shall they ... empty their net?** – Shall they be allowed without interruption to enjoy the fruits of their violence?

therefore – seeing that they attribute all their successes to themselves, and not to Thee. The answer to the prophet's question, he by inspiration gives himself in the second chapter.

Chapter 2

Hab 2:1–20. The prophet, waiting earnestly for an answer to his complaints (first chapter), receives a revelation, which is to be fulfilled, not immediately, yet in due time, and is therefore to be waited for in faith: the Chaldeans shall be punished for their cruel rapacity, nor can their false gods avert the judgment of Jehovah, the only true God.

1. **stand upon ... watch** – that is, watch-post. The prophets often compare themselves, awaiting the revelations of Jehovah with earnest patience, to watchmen on an eminence watching with intent eye all that comes within their view (Isa 21:8,11 Jer 6:17 Eze 3:17 33:2,3; compare Ps 5:3 85:8). The 'watch-post' is the withdrawal of the whole soul from earthly, and fixing it on heavenly, things. The accumulation of synonyms, 'stand open ... watch ... set me upon ... tower ... watch to see' implies persevering fixity of attention.

what he will say unto me – in answer to my complaints (Hab 1:13). Literally, 'in me,' God speaking, not to the prophet's outward ear, but *inwardly*. When we have prayed to God, we must observe what answers God gives by His word, His Spirit, and His providences.

what I shall answer when I am reproved – what answer I am to make to the *reproof* which I anticipate from God on account of the liberty of my expostulation with Him.

2. Write the vision – which I am about to reveal to thee.

make it plain – (De 27:8). In large legible characters.

upon tables – boxwood tables covered with wax, on which national affairs were engraved with an iron pen, and then hung up in public, at the prophets own houses, or at the temple, that those who passed might read them. Compare Lu 1:63, 'writing table,' that is, tablet.

that he may run that readeth it – commonly explained, 'so intelligible as to be easily read by any one running past'; but then it would be, *that he that runneth may read it.* The true sense is, 'so legible that whoever readeth it, may run to tell all whom he can the good news of the foe's coming doom, and Judah's deliverance.' Compare Da 12:4, 'many shall *run* to and fro,' namely, with the explanation of the prophecy, then unsealed; also, Re 22:17, 'let him that heareth (the good news) say (to every one within his reach), Come.' 'Run' is equivalent to *announce the divine revelation* (Jer 23:21); as everyone who becomes informed of a divine message is bound to *run*, that is, use all despatch to make it known to others [HENDERSON]. GROTIUS, LUDOVICUS DE DIEU, and MAURER interpret it: 'Run' is not literal *running*, but 'that he who reads it may run through it,' that is, read it *at once without difficulty.*

3. for – assigning the cause why it ought to be *committed to writing: because* its fulfilment belongs to the future.

the vision is yet for an appointed time – (Da 10:14 11:27,35). Though the time appointed by God for the fulfilment be yet future, it should be enough for your faith that God hath spoken it (La 3:26).

though it tarry, wait for it – (Ge 49:18).

4. is not upright in him – that is, is not accounted upright in God's sight; in antithesis to 'shall live.' So Heb 10:38, which with inspired authority applies the general sense to the particular case which Paul had in view, 'If any man *draw back* (one result of being "lifted up" with overweening arrogancy), *my soul shall have no pleasure in him.'*

the just shall live by his faith – the *Jewish nation,* as opposed to the unbelieving Chaldean (compare Hab 2:5, Hab 1:6, Hab 1:13) [MAURER]. HENDERSON's view is that the

believing Jew is meant, as opposed to the unbelieving Jew (compare Ro 1:17 Ga 3:11). The believing Jew, though God's promise tarry, will wait for it; the unbelieving 'draws back,' as Heb 10:38 expresses it. The sense, in MAURER's view, which accords better with the context (Hab 2:5.). is: the Chaldean, though for a time seeming to prosper, yet being lifted up with haughty unbelief (Hab 1:11,16), is not upright; that is, has *no right* stability of soul resting on God, to ensure permanence of prosperity; hence, though for a time executing God's judgments, he at last becomes 'lifted up' so as to attribute to his own power what is the work of God, and in this sense 'draws back' (Heb 10:38), becoming thereby a type of all backsliders who thereby incur God's displeasure; as the believing Jew is of all who *wait* for God's promises with patient *faith,* and so 'live' (stand accepted) before God. The *Hebrew* accents induce BENGEL to translate, 'he who is just by his faith shall live.' Other manuscripts read the accents as *English Version,* which agrees better with *Hebrew* syntax.

5. Yea also, because – additional reason why the Jews may look for God punishing their Chaldean foe, namely, *because ... he is*

a proud man – rather, this clause continues the reason for the Jews expecting the punishment of the Chaldeans, 'because he transgresseth by wine (a besetting sin of Babylon, compare Da 5:1–31, and CURTIUS [5.1]), *being* a proud man.' Love of wine often begets a *proud* contempt of divine things, as in Belshazzar's case, which was the immediate cause of the fall of Babylon (Da 5:2–4,30; compare Pr 20:1 30:9 31:5).

enlargeth his desire as hell – the grave, or the unseen world, which is 'never full' (Pr 27:20 30:16 Isa 5:14). The Chaldeans under Nebuchadnezzar were filled with an insatiable desire of conquest. Another reason for their punishment.

6. Shall not all these – the 'nations' and 'peoples' (Hab 2:5) 'heaped unto him' by the Chaldean.

take up a parable – a derisive song. Habakkuk follows Isaiah (Isa 14:4) and Micah (Mic 2:4) in the phraseology.

against him – when dislodged from his former eminence.

Woe – The 'derisive song' here begins, and continues to the end of the chapter. It is a symmetrical whole, and consists of five stanzas, the first three consisting of three verses each, the fourth of four verses, and the last of two. Each stanza has its own subject, and all except the last begin with 'Woe'; and all have a closing verse introduced with 'for,' 'because,' or 'but.'

how long? – *how long* destined to retain his ill-gotten gains? But for a short time, as his fall now proves [MAURER]. 'Covetousness is the greatest bane to men. For they who invade others' goods, often lose even their own' [MENANDER]. CALVIN makes 'how long?' to be the cry of those groaning under the Chaldean oppression while it still lasted: How long shall such oppression be permitted to continue? But it is plainly part of the *derisive song,* after the Chaldean tyranny had passed away.

ladeth himself with thick clay – namely, gold and silver dug out of the 'clay,' of which they are a part. The covetous man in heaping them together is only lading himself with a clay burden, as he dares not enjoy them, and is always anxious about them. LEE and FULLER translate the *Hebrew* as a reduplicated single noun, and not two words, 'an accumulation of pledges' (De 24:10–13). The Chaldean is compared to a harsh usurer, and his ill-gotten treasures to heaps of pledges in the hands of a usurer.

7. suddenly – the answer to the question, 'How long?' (Hab 2:6).

bite – often used of *usury;* so favouring LEE's rendering (Hab 2:6). As the Chaldean, like a usurer, oppressed others, so other nations shall, like usurers, *take pledges of,* that is, spoil, him.

8. the remnant of the people – Those remaining of the peoples spoiled by thee, though but a remnant, will suffice to inflict vengeance on thee.

the violence of the land ... city – that is, on account of *thy violent oppression of the lands and cities* of the earth [GROTIUS] (compare Hab 2:5,6,12). The same phrase occurs in Hab 2:17, where the 'land' and 'city' are Judea and Jerusalem.

9. coveteth an evil covetousness – that is, a covetousness so surpassingly evil as to be fatal to himself.

to his house – greedily seizing enormous wealth, not merely for himself, but for his family, to which it is destined to be fatal. The very same 'evil covetousness' that was the cause of Jehoiakim's being given up to the Chaldean oppressor (Jer 22:13) shall be the cause of the Chaldean's own destruction.

set his nest on high – (Nu 24:21 Jer 49:16 Ob 1:4). The image is from an eagle (Job 39:27). The *royal citadel* is meant. The Chaldean built high towers, like the Babel founders, to 'be delivered from the power of evil' (Ge 11:4).

10. Thou hast consulted shame ... by cutting off many – MAURER, more literally, 'Thou hast consulted shame ... to destroy many,' that is, in consulting (determining) to cut off many, thou hast consulted shame to thy house.

sinned against thy soul – that is, against thyself; thou art the guilty cause of thine own ruin (Pr 8:36 20:2). They who wrong their neighbours, do much greater wrong to their own souls.

11. stone ... cry out – personification. The very stones of thy palace built by rapine shall testify against thee (Lu 19:40).

the beam out of the timber – the crossbeam or main rafter connecting the timbers in the walls.

shall answer it – namely, the stone. The stone shall begin and the crossbeam continue the cry against thy rapine.

12. buildeth a town with blood – namely, Babylon rebuilt and enlarged by blood-bought spoils (compare Da 4:30).

13. is it not of the Lord of hosts – JEHOVAH, who has at His command all the *hosts* of heaven and earth, is the righteous author of Babylon's destruction. 'Shall not God have His turn, when cruel rapacious men have triumphed so long, though He seem now to be still?' [CALVIN].

people ... labour in the ... fire ... weary themselves for ... vanity – The Chaldeans labour at what is to be food for the fire, namely, their city and fortresses which shall be burnt. Jer 51:58 adopts the same phraseology to express the vanity of the Chaldean's labour on Babylon, as doomed to the flames.

14. Adapted from Isa 11:9. Here the sense is, 'The Jews shall be restored and the temple rebuilt, so that God's glory in saving His people, and punishing their Chaldean foe, shall be manifested throughout the world,' of which the Babylonian empire formed the greatest part; a type of the ultimate full manifestation of His glory in the final salvation of Israel and His Church, and the destruction of all their foes.

waters cover the sea – namely, the bottom of the sea; the sea-bed.

15. giveth ... neighbour drink ... puttest ... bottle to him – literally, 'skin,' as the Easterns use 'bottles' of skin for wine.

that thou mayest look on their nakedness! – with light, like Ham of old (Ge 9:22).

16. art filled – now that thou art fallen. 'Thou art filled' indeed (though so insatiable), but it is 'with shame.'

shame for glory – instead of thy former glory (Ho 4:7).

drink thou also – The cup of sorrow is now in thy turn to pass to thee (Jer 25:15–17 La 4:21).

thy foreskin – expressing in Hebrew feeling the most utter contempt. So of Goliath (1Sa 17:36). It is not merely thy 'nakedness,' as in Hab 2:15, that shall be 'uncovered,' but the foreskin, the badge of thy being an uncircumcised alien from God. The same shall be done to thee, as thou didst to others, and worse.

cup ... shall be turned unto thee – literally, 'shall *turn itself,*' namely, from the nations whom thou hast made to drink it. 'Thou shalt drink it *all,* so that it may be *turned* as being drained' [GROTIUS].

shameful spewing – that is, vomiting; namely, that of the king of Babylon, compelled to disgorge the spoil he had swallowed. It expresses also the ignominious state of Babylon in its calamity (Jer 25:27). 'Be drunken, spew, and fall.' Less appropriately it is explained *of the foe* spewing in the face of the Babylonian king.

17. the violence of Lebanon – thy 'violence' against 'Lebanon,' that is, Jerusalem (Isa 37:24 Jer 22:23 Eze 17:3,12; for Lebanon's cedars were used in building the temple and houses of Jerusalem; and its beauty made it a fit type of the metropolis), shall fall on thine own head.

cover – that is, *completely* overwhelm.

the spoil of beasts, which made them afraid – MAURER explains, '*the spoiling* inflicted on *the beasts* of Lebanon (that is, on the people of Jerusalem, of which city "Lebanon" is the type), *which made them afraid* (shall cover thee).' But it seems inappropriate to compare the elect people to 'beasts.' I therefore prefer explaining, 'the spoiling of beasts,' that is, such as is inflicted on beasts caught in a net, and 'which makes them afraid (shall cover thee).' Thus the Babylonians are compared to wild beasts terrified at being caught suddenly in a net. In cruel rapacity they resembled wild beasts. The ancients read, 'the spoiling of wild beasts *shall make* THEE *afraid.*' Or else explain, 'the spoiling of beasts (the Medes and Persians) which (*inflicted by thee*) made them afraid (shall in turn cover thyself – revert on thyself from them).' This accords better with the parallel clause, 'the violence of Lebanon,' that is, inflicted by thee on Lebanon. As thou didst hunt men as wild beasts, so shalt thou be hunted thyself as a wild beast, which thou resemblest in cruelty.

because of men's blood – shed by thee; repeated from Hab 2:8. But here the 'land' and 'city' are used of *Judea* and *Jerusalem:* not of the *earth* and cities *generally,* as in Hab 2:8.

the violence of the land. – that is, inflicted *on the* land by thee.

18. The powerlessness of the idols to save Babylon from its doom is a fitting introduction to the last stanza (Hab 2:19), which, as the former four, begins with 'Woe.'

teacher of lies – its priests and prophets uttering lying oracles, as if from it.

make dumb idols – Though men can 'make' idols, they cannot *make them speak.*

19. Awake – Arise to my help.

it shall teach! – rather, An exclamation *of the prophet,* implying an ironical question to which a negative answer must be given. What! 'It teach?' Certainly not [MAURER].

Behold – The *Hebrew* is nominative, 'There it is' [HENDERSON].

it is laid over with gold … no breath … in the midst – Outside it has some splendour, within none.

20. But the Lord – JEHOVAH; in striking contrast with the idols.

in his holy temple – 'His place' (Isa 26:21); heaven (Ps 11:4 Jon 2:7 Mic 1:2). The temple at Jerusalem is a type of it, and there God is to be worshipped. He does not lie hid under gold and silver, as the idols of Babylon, but reigns in heaven and fills heaven, and thence succours His people.

keep silence – in token of reverent submission and subjection to His judgments (Job 40:4 Ps 76:8 Zep 1:7 Zec 2:13).

Chapter 3

Hab 3:1–19. Habakkuk's prayer to God: God's glorious revelation of himself at Sinai and at Gibeon, a pledge of his interposing again in behalf of Israel against Babylon, and all other foes; hence the prophet's confidence amid calamities.

This sublime ode begins with an exordium (Hab 3:1,2), then follows the main subject, then the peroration (Hab 3:16–19), a summary of the practical truth, which the whole is designed to teach. (De 33:2–5 Ps 77:13–20 are parallel odes). This was probably designed by the Spirit to be a fit formula of prayer for the people, first in their Babylonian exile, and now in their dispersion, especially towards the close of it, just before the great Deliverer is to interpose for them. It was used in public worship, as the musical term, 'Selah!' (Hab 3:3,9,13), implies.

1. prayer – the only strictly called prayers are in Hab 3:2. But all devotional addresses to God are called 'prayers' (Ps 72:20). The *Hebrew* is from a root 'to apply to a judge for a favourable decision.' *Prayers* in which *praises* to God for deliverance, anticipated in the sure confidence of faith, are especially calculated to enlist Jehovah on His people's side (2Ch 20:20–22,26).

upon Shigionoth – a musical phrase, 'after the manner of elegies,' or mournful odes, from an *Arabic* root [LEE]; the phrase is *singular* in Ps 7:1, title. More simply, from a *Hebrew* root to 'err,' 'on account of *sins of ignorance.*' Habakkuk thus teaches his countrymen to confess not only their more grievous sins, but also their *errors* and *negligences,* into which they were especially likely to fall when in exile away from the Holy Land [CALVIN]. So *Vulgate* and AQUILA, and SYMMACHUS. 'For voluntary transgressors' [JEROME]. Probably the subject would regulate the kind of music. DELITZSCH and HENDERSON translate, 'With triumphal music,' from the same root 'to err,' implying its enthusiastic irregularity.

2. I have heard thy speech – Thy revelation to me concerning the coming chastisement of the Jews [CALVIN], and the destruction of their oppressors. This is Habakkuk's reply to God's communication [Grotius].

and was afraid – reverential fear of God's judgments (Hab 3:16).

revive thy work – Perfect the *work* of delivering *Thy* people, and do not let Thy promise lie as if it were dead, but *give it new life* by performing it [Menochius]. Calvin explains 'thy work' to be *Israel;* called 'the work of My hands' (Isa 45:11). God's elect people are peculiarly His work (Isa 43:1), pre-eminently illustrating His power, wisdom, and goodness. 'Though we seem, as it were, dead nationally, *revive* us' (Ps 85:6). However (Ps 64:9), where 'the work of God' refers to *His judgment on their enemies,* favours the former view (Ps 90:16,17 Isa 51:9,10).

in the midst of the years – namely, of calamity in which we live. Now that our calamities are at their height; during our seventy years' captivity. Calvin more fancifully explains it, in the midst of the years of Thy people, extending from Abraham to Messiah; if they be cut off before His coming, they will be cut off as it were *in the midst of their years,* before attaining their maturity. So Bengel makes *the midst of the years* to be the middle point of the years of the world. There is a strikingly similar phrase (Da 9:27), *In the midst of the week.* The parallel clause, 'in wrath' (that is, *in the midst* of wrath), however, shows that 'in the midst of the years' means 'in the years of our present exile and calamity.'

make known – Made *it* (*Thy* work) known by experimental proof; show in very deed, that this is Thy work.

3. God – *singular* in the *Hebrew,* 'Eloah,' instead of 'Elohim,' *plural,* usually employed. The *singular* is not found in any other of the minor prophets, or Jeremiah, or Ezekiel; but it is in Isaiah, Daniel, Job, and Deuteronomy.

from Teman – the country south of Judea and near Edom, in which latter country Mount Paran was situated [Henderson]. 'Paran' is the desert region, extending from the south of Judah to Sinai. Seir, Sinai, and Paran are adjacent to one another, and are hence associated together, in respect to God's giving of the law (De 33:2). Teman is so identified with Seir or *Edom,* as here to be substituted for it. Habakkuk appeals to God's glorious manifestations to His people at Sinai, as the ground for praying that God will 'revive His work' (Hab 2:2) now. For He is the same God now as ever.

Selah – a musical sign, put at the close of sections and strophes, always at the end of a verse, except thrice; namely, here, and Hab 3:9, and Ps 55:19 57:3, where, however, it closes the hemistich. It implies a change of the modulation. It comes from a root to 'rest' or 'pause' [Gesenius]; implying a cessation of the chant, during an instrumental interlude. The solemn

pause here prepares the mind for contemplating the glorious description of Jehovah's manifestation which follows.

earth … full of his praise – that is, of His glories which were calculated to call forth universal *praise;* the parallelism to 'glory' proves this to be the sense.

4. as the light – namely, of the sun (Job 37:21 Pr 4:18).

horns – the emblem of *power* wielded by 'His hand' [Ludovicus de Dieu]. 'Rays' emanating from 'His hand,' compared by the Arabs to the horns of the gazelle (compare 'hind of the morning,' Ps 22:1, title, *Margin*). The *Hebrew* verb for to 'emit rays,' is from the root meaning 'horns' (Ex 34:29,30,35) [Grotius]. The rays are His *lightnings* (Ps 18:8), [Maurer].

there – *in that 'brightness.' In it,* notwithstanding its brilliancy, there was but the veil '(*the hiding*) of His power.' Even 'light,' God's 'garment,' covers, instead of revealing fully, His surpassing glory (Ps 104:2) [Henderson]. Or, *on Mount Sinai* [Drusius]. (Compare Ex 24:17). The *Septuagint* and *Syriac* versions read for 'there,' *He made* a hiding; He hid Himself with clouds. *English Version* is better, which Calvin explains, there is said to be 'a hiding of God's power,' because God did not reveal it indiscriminately to all, but specially to His people (Ps 31:20). The contrast seems to me to be between the 'horns' or *emanations* out of His power ('hand'), and that 'power' itself. The latter was *hidden,* whereas the 'horns' or *emanations* alone were manifested. If the mere scintillations were so awfully overwhelming, how much more so the hidden power itself! This was especially true of His manifestation at Sinai (Ps 18:11; compare Isa 45:15,17).

5. pestilence – to destroy His people's foes (1Sa 5:9,11). As Jehovah's advent is glorious to His people, so it is terrible to His foes.

burning coals – Ps 18:8 favours *English Version*. But the parallelism requires, as the *Margin* translates, 'burning disease' (compare De 32:24 Ps 91:6).

went … at his feet – that is, after Him, as His attendants (Jud 4:10).

6. He stood, and measured the earth – Jehovah, in His advance, is represented as stopping suddenly, and *measuring* the earth with His all-seeing glance, whereat there is universal consternation.

everlasting mountains – which have ever been remembered as retaining the same place and form from the foundation of the world.

did bow – as it were, in reverent submission.

his ways are everlasting – His marvellous ways of working for the salvation of His people mark His everlasting character: such as He was in His workings for them formerly, such shall He be now.

7. **the tents** – that is, the dwellers. **Cushan** – the same as *Cush;* made 'Cush-*an*' to harmonize with 'Midi-*an*' in the parallel clause. So *Lotan* is found in the *Hebrew* of Genesis for *Lot.* BOCHART therefore considers it equivalent to Midian, or a part of Arabia. So in Nu 12:1, Moses' Midianite wife is called an Ethiopian (*Hebrew, Cushite*).

in affliction – rather, '*under* affliction' (regarded) as a heavy burden. Literally, 'vanity' or 'iniquity,' hence the *punishment* of it (compare Nu 25:17,18).

curtains – the coverings of their tents; the shifting habitations of the nomad tribes, which resembled the modern Bedouins.

tremble – namely, at Jehovah's terrible interposition for Israel against them.

8. **Was the Lord displeased against the rivers?** – 'Was the cause of His dividing the Red Sea and Jordan His displeasure against these waters?' The answer to this is tacitly implied in 'Thy chariots *of salvation.*' 'Nay; it was not displeasure against the waters, but His pleasure in interposing for His people's *salvation*' (compare Hab 3:10).

thy chariots – in antithesis to Thy foe, *Pharaoh's* chariots,' which, notwithstanding their power and numbers, were engulfed in the waters of *destruction.* God can make the most unlikely means work for His people's salvation (Ex 14:7,9,23,25–28 15:3–8,19). Jehovah's chariots are His angels (Ps 68:17), or the cherubim, or the ark (Jos 3:13 4:7; compare So 1:9).

9. **bow ... made ... naked** – that is, was drawn forth from its cover, in which bows usually were cased when not in use. Compare Isa 22:6, 'Kir uncovered the shield.'

according **to the oaths of the tribes** *even thy* **word** – that is, Thy *oaths* of promise to *the tribes* of Israel (Ps 77:8 Lu 1:73,74). Habakkuk shows that God's miraculous interpositions for His people were not limited to one time, but that God's *oaths* to His people are sure ground for their always expecting them. The mention of the *tribes,* rather than *Abraham* or Moses, is in order that they may not doubt that to them belongs this grace of which Abraham was the depository [CALVIN and JEROME].

Thou didst cleave the earth with rivers – the result of the earthquake caused by God's approach [MAURER]. GROTIUS refers it to the bringing forth water from the rock (Ex 17:6 Nu 20:10,11 Ps 78:15,16 105:4). But the context implies not the giving of water to His people to drink, but the fearful physical phenomena attending Jehovah's attack on Israel's foes.

10. **The mountains** – repetition with increased emphasis of some of the tremendous phenomena mentioned in Hab 3:6.

overflowing of the water passed by – namely, of the Red Sea; and again, of the Jordan. God

marked His favour to His people in all the elements, causing every obstacle, whether mountains or waters, which impeded their progress, to 'pass away' [CALVIN].

lifted ... hands on high – namely, its billows *lifted on high* by the tempest. Personification. As men signify by voice or gesture of *hand* that they will do what they are commanded, so these parts of nature testified their obedience to God's will (Ex 14:22 Jos 3:16 Ps 77:17,18 114:4).

11. **sun ... moon stood still** – at Joshua's command (Jos 10:12,13).

light of thine arrows – hail mixed with lightnings (Jos 10:10,11).

they went – The *sun* and *moon* 'went,' not as always heretofore, but according to the light and direction of Jehovah's arrows, namely, His lightnings hurled in defence of His people; astonished at these they stood still [CALVIN].

12. **march** – implying Jehovah's majestic and irresistible progress before His people (Jud 5:4 Ps 68:7). Israel would not have dared to attack the nations, unless Jehovah had gone before.

thresh – (Mic 4:13).

13. **with thine anointed** – with Messiah; of whom Moses, Joshua, and David, God's anointed leaders of Israel, were the types (Ps 89:19,20,38). God from the beginning delivered His people in person, or by the hand of a Mediator (Isa 63:11). Thus Habakkuk confirms believers in the hope of their deliverance, as well because God is always the same, as also because the same anointed Mediator is ready now to fulfil God's will and interpose for Israel, as of old [CALVIN].

woundedst the head out of the house of the wicked – probably an allusion to Ps 68:21. Each *head person* sprung from and belonging to *the house of* Israel's *wicked* foes; such as Jabin, whose city Hazor was 'the head of all the kingdoms' of Canaan (Jos 11:10; compare Jud 4:2,3,13).

discovering the foundation – Thou destroyedst high and low. As 'the *head* of the house' means the prince, so the 'foundation' means the general *host* of the enemy.

unto the neck – image from a flood reaching *to the neck* (Isa 8:8 30:28). So God, by His wrath overflowing on the foe, caused their princes' *necks* to be trodden under foot by Israel's leaders (Jos 10:24 11:8,12).

14. **strike ... with his staves** – with the 'wicked' (Hab 3:13) foe's own sword (Jud 7:22).

head of his villages – Not only kings were overthrown by God's hand, but His vengeance passed through the foe's *villages* and dependencies. A just retribution, as the foe had made 'the inhabitants of Israel's villages to cease' (Jud 5:7). GROTIUS translates, 'of his warriors'; GESENIUS, 'the chief of his captains.'

to scatter me – *Israel,* with whom Habakkuk identifies himself (compare Hab 1:12).

rejoicing ... to devour the poor secretly – 'The poor' means the *Israelites*, for whom in their helpless state the foe lurks *in his lair,* like a wild beast, to pounce on and *devour* (Ps 10:9 17:12).

15. Thou didst walk through the sea with thine horses – (Hab 3:8). No obstacle could prevent Thy progress when leading Thy people in safety to their inheritance, whether the Red Sea, Jordan, or the figurative waves of foes raging against Israel (Ps 65:7 77:19).

16. When I heard ... trembled – namely, at the judgments which God had declared (Hab 1:1–17) were to be inflicted on Judea by the Chaldeans.

belly – The *bowels* were thought by the Hebrews to be the seat of yearning compassion (Jer 31:20).

at the voice – of the divine threatenings (Hab 1:6). The faithful tremble at the *voice* alone of God before He inflicts punishment. Habakkuk speaks in the person of all the faithful in Israel.

trembled in myself – that is, I trembled all over [Grotius].

that I might rest in the day of trouble – The true and only path to *rest* is through such fear. Whoever is securely torpid and hardened towards God, will be tumultuously agitated in the day of affliction, and so will bring on himself a worse destruction; but he who in time meets God's wrath and trembles at His threats, prepares the best *rest* for himself in the day of affliction [Calvin]. Henderson translates, 'Yet I shall have rest.' Habakkuk thus consoling his mind, Though trembling at the calamity coming, yet I shall have rest in God (Isa 26:3). But that sentiment does not seem to be directly asserted till Hab 3:17, as the words following at the close of this verse imply.

when he cometh up unto the people, he will invade – rather (as *English Version* is a mere truism), connected with the preceding clause, 'that I might rest ... when he (the Chaldean foe) cometh up unto the people (the Jews), *that he may cut them off* [Calvin]. The *Hebrew* for

'invade' means, *to rush upon, or to attack and cut off with congregated troops.*

17. Destroy the 'vines' and 'fig trees' of the carnal heart, and his mirth ceases. But those who when full enjoyed God in all, when emptied can enjoy all in God. They can sit down upon the heap of ruined creature comforts, and rejoice in Him as the 'God of their salvation.' Running in the way of His commandments, we outrun our troubles. Thus Habakkuk, beginning his prayer with trembling, ends it with a song of triumph (Job 13:15 Ps 4:7 43:3,5).

labour of the olive – that is, the *fruit* expected from the olive.

fail – literally, 'lie,' that is, disappoint the hope (Isa 58:11, *Margin*).

fields – from a *Hebrew* root meaning 'to be yellow'; as they look at harvest-time.

meat – food, grain.

cut off – that is, cease.

18. yet I will rejoice – The prophet speaks in the name of his people.

19. hinds' feet ... walk upon ... high places – Habakkuk has here before his mind Ps 18:33,34 De 32:13. 'Hinds' (gazelles') feet' imply the *swiftness* with which God enables him (the prophet and his people) to escape from his enemies, and return to his native land. The 'high places' are called 'mine,' to imply that Israel shall be restored to *his own* land, a land of hills which are places of safety and of eminence (compare Ge 19:17 Mt 24:16). Probably not only the *safety,* but the *moral elevation,* of Israel above all the lands of the earth is implied (De 33:29).

on my stringed instruments – *neginoth.* This is the prophet's direction to the *precentor* ('chief singer') as to how the preceding ode (Hab 3:1–19) is to be performed (compare Ps 4:1 6:1, titles). The prophet had in mind a certain form of stringed instrument adapted to certain numbers and measures. This formula at the end of the ode, directing the kind of instrument to be used, agrees with that in the beginning of it, which directs the kind of melody (compare Isa 38:20).

ZEPHANIAH

A.R. Faussett

Introduction

Zephaniah, ninth in order of the minor prophets, prophesied 'in the days of Josiah' (Zep 1:1), that is, between 642 and 611 B.C. The name means 'Jehovah hath guarded,' literally, 'hidden' (Ps 27:5 Ps 83:3). The specification in the introductory heading, of not only his father, but also his grandfather, and great-grandfather, and great-great-grandfather, implies that the latter were persons of note, or else the design was to distinguish him from another Zephaniah of note at the time of the captivity. The Jews' supposition, that persons recorded as a prophet's ancestors were themselves endowed with the prophetic spirit, seems groundless. There is no impossibility of the Hezekiah, who was Zephaniah's great-great-grandfather, being King Hezekiah as to the number of generations; for Hezekiah's reign of twenty-nine years, and his successor's reign of fifty-five years, admit of *four* generations interposing between. Yet the omission of the designation, 'king of Judah,' is fatal to the theory (compare Pr 25:1 Isa 38:9).

He must have flourished in the earlier part of Josiah's reign. In Zep 2:13–15 he foretells the doom of Nineveh, which happened in 625 B.C.; and in Zep 1:4 he denounces various forms of idolatry, and specially that of Baal. Now Josiah's reformation began in the twelfth and was completed in the eighteenth year of his reign. Zephaniah, therefore, in denouncing Baal worship, co-operated with that good king in his efforts, and so must have prophesied somewhere between the twelfth and eighteenth years of his reign. The silence of the historical books is no argument against this, as it would equally apply against Jeremiah's prophetical existence at the same time. Jewish tradition says that Zephaniah had for his colleagues Jeremiah, whose sphere of labour was the thoroughfares and market places, and Huldah the prophetess, who exercised her vocation in the college in Jerusalem. The prophecy begins with the nation's sin and the fearful retribution coming at the hands of the Chaldeans. These are not mentioned by name, as in Jeremiah; for the prophecies of the latter, being nearer the fulfilment, become more explicit than those of an earlier date. The second chapter dooms the persecuting states in the neighbourhood as well as Judea itself. The third chapter denounces Jerusalem, but concludes with the promise of her joyful re-establishment in the theocracy.

The style, though not generally sublime, is graphic and vivid in details (compare Zep 1:4–12). The language is pure, and free from Aramaisms. There are occasional coincidences with former prophets (compare Zep 2:14, with Isa 34:11; Zep 2:15, with Isa 47:8; Zep 3:10, with Isa 18:1; Zep 2:8, with Isa 16:6; also Zep 1:5, with Jer 8:2; Zep 1:12, with Jer 48:11). Such coincidences in part arise from the phraseology of *Hebrew* prophetic poetry being the common language of the inspired brotherhood. The New Testament, at Ro 15:6, seems to refer to Zep 3:9.

Chapter 1

Zep 1:1–18. God's severe judgment on Judah for its idolatry and neglect of him: the rapid approach of the judgment, and the impossibility of escape.

1. days of Josiah – Had their idolatries been under former kings, they might have said, Our kings have forced us to this and that. But under Josiah, who did all in his power to reform them, they have no such excuse.

son of Amon – the idolater, whose bad practices the Jews clung to, rather than the good example of Josiah, his son; so incorrigible were they in sin.

Judah – Israel's ten tribes had gone into captivity before this.

2. utterly consume – from a root to 'sweep away,' or 'scrape off utterly.' See Jer 8:13, *Margin*, and here.

from off the land – of Judah.

3. Enumeration in detail of the 'all things' (Zep 1:2; compare Jer 9:10 Ho 4:3).

the stumbling-blocks – idols which cause Judah to offend or stumble (Eze 14:3,4,7).

with the wicked – The idols and their worshippers shall be involved in a common destruction.

4. stretch out mine hand – indicating some remarkable and unusual work of vengeance (Isa 5:25 9:12,17,21).

Judah – including Benjamin. These two tribes are to suffer, which thought themselves perpetually secure, because they escaped the captivity in which the ten tribes were involved.

Jerusalem – the fountainhead of the evil. God begins with His sanctuary (Eze 9:6), and those who are nigh Him (Le 10:3).

the remnant of Baal – the remains of Baal worship, which as yet Josiah was unable utterly to eradicate in remote places. Baal was the Phoenician tutelary god. From the time of the Judges (Jud 2:13), Israel had fallen into this idolatry; and Manasseh lately had set up this idol within Jehovah's temple itself (2Ki 21:3,5,7). Josiah began his reformation in the twelfth year of his reign (2Ch 34:4,8), and in the eighteenth had as far as possible completed it.

Chemarims – idol priests, who had not reached the age of puberty; meaning 'ministers of the gods' [SERVIUS], the same name as the Tyrian *Camilli, r* and *l* being interchangeable (compare Ho 10:5, *Margin*). Josiah is expressly said (2Ki 23:5, *Margin*) to have 'put down the Chemarim.' The *Hebrew* root means 'black' (from the *black garments* which they wore or the *marks* which they branded on their foreheads); or 'zealous,' from their idolatrous fanaticism. The very 'name,' as well as themselves, shall be forgotten.

the priests – of Jehovah, of Aaronic descent, who ought to have used all their power to eradicate, but who secretly abetted, idolatry (compare Zep 3:4 Eze 8 22:26 44:10). From the *priests* Zephaniah passes to the *people*.

5. worship the host of heaven – *Saba*: whence, in contrast to Sabeanism, Jehovah is called *Lord of Sabaoth*.

upon the housetops – which were flat (2Ki 23:5,6,12 Jer 19:13 32:29).

swear by the Lord – rather, 'swear *to* JEHOVAH' (2Ch 15:14); solemnly dedicating themselves to Him (compare Isa 48:1 Ho 4:15).

and – '*and yet* (with strange inconsistency, 1Ki 18:21 Eze 20:39 Mt 6:24) swear by Malcham,' that is, '*their king*' [MAURER]: the same as Molech (see on Am 5:25), and 'Milcom the god of ... Ammon' (1Ki 11:33). If Satan have half the heart, he will have all; if the Lord have but half offered to Him, He will have none.

6. This verse describes more comprehensively those guilty of defection from Jehovah in any way (Jer 2:13,17).

7. Hold thy peace at the presence of the Lord – (Hab 2:20). Let the *earth* be silent at His approach [MAURER]. Or, 'Thou whosoever hast been wont to speak against God, as if He had no care about earthly affairs, cease thy murmurs and self-justifications; submit thyself to God, and repent in time' [CALVIN].

Lord ... prepared a sacrifice – namely, a slaughter of the guilty Jews, the victims due to His justice (Isa 34:6 Jer 46:10 Eze 39:17).

bid his guests – literally, 'sanctified His called ones' (compare Isa 13:3). It enhances the bitterness of the judgment that the heathen Chaldeans should be *sanctified*, or consecrated as it were, by God as His priests, and be *called* to eat the flesh of the elect people; as on feast days the priests used to feast among themselves on the remains of the sacrifices [CALVIN]. *English Version* takes it not of the *priests*, but the *guests* bidden, who also had to 'sanctify' or purify themselves before coming to the sacrificial feast (1Sa 9:13,22 16:5). Nebuchadnezzar was *bidden* to come to take vengeance on guilty Jerusalem (Jer 25:9).

8. the princes – who ought to have been an example of good to others, but were ringleaders in all evil.

the king's children – fulfilled on Zedekiah's children (Jer 39:6); and previously, on Jehoahaz and Eliakim, the sons of Josiah (2Ki 23:31,36 2Ch 36:6; compare also 2Ki 20:18 21:13). Huldah the prophetess (2Ki 22:20) intimated that which Zephaniah now more expressly foretells.

all such as are clothed with strange apparel – the *princes* or *courtiers* who attired themselves in costly garments, imported from abroad; partly for the sake of luxury, and partly to ingratiate themselves with foreign great nations whose costume as well as their idolatries they imitated, [Calvin]; whereas in costume, as in other respects, God would have them to be separate from the nations. Grotius refers the 'strange apparel' to garments forbidden by the law, for example, men's garments worn by women, and vice versa, a heathen usage in the worship of Mars and Venus (De 22:5).

9. those that leap on the threshold – the servants of the princes, who, after having gotten prey (like hounds) for their masters, leap exultingly on their masters' thresholds; or, on the thresholds of the houses which they break into [Calvin]. Jerome explains it of those *who walk up the steps into the sanctuary with haughtiness.* Rosenmuller translates, 'Leap *over* the threshold'; namely, in imitation of the Philistine custom of not treading on the threshold, which arose from the head and hands of Dragon being broken off on the threshold before the ark (1Sa 5:5). Compare Isa 2:6, 'thy people … are soothsayers *like the Philistines.*' Calvin's view agrees best with the latter clause of the verse.

fill … masters' houses with violence. – that is, with goods obtained *with violence.*

10. fish gate – (2Ch 33:14 Ne 3:3 12:39). Situated on the east of the lower city, north of the sheep gate [Maurer]: near the stronghold of David in Milo, between Zion and the lower city, towards the west [Jerome]. This verse describes the state of the city when it was besieged by Nebuchadnezzar. It was through the fish gate that he entered the city. It received its name from the fish market which was near it. Through it passed those who used to bring fish from the lake of Tiberias and Jordan. It answers to what is now called the Damascus gate [Henderson].

the second – namely, the gate which was *second* in dignity [Calvin]. Or, the *second* or lower part of the city. Appropriately, the fish gate, or extreme end of the lower part of the city, first resounds with the cries of the citizens as the foe approaches; then, as he advances further, that part of the city itself, namely, its inner part; lastly, when the foe is actually come and has burst in, the hills, the higher ones, especially Zion and Moriah, on which the upper city and temple were founded [Maurer]. The *second,* or lower city, answers to Akra, north of Zion, and separated from it by the valley of Tyropoeon running down to the pool of Siloam [Henderson]. The *Hebrew* is translated 'college,' 2Ki 22:14; so Vatablus would translate here.

hills – not here those outside, but those within the walls: Zion, Moriah, and Ophel.

11. Maktesh – rather, 'the mortar,' a name applied to the valley of Siloam from its hollow shape [Jerome]. The valley between Zion and Mount Olivet, at the eastern extremity of Mount Moriah, where the merchants dwelt. Zec 14:21, 'The Canaanite,' namely, merchant [*Chaldee Version*]. The Tyropoeon (that is, cheese-makers') valley below Mount Akra [Rosenmuller]. Better *Jerusalem itself,* so called as lying in the midst of hills (Isa 22:1 Jer 21:13) and as doomed to be the scene of its people being destroyed as corn or drugs are pounded in a *mortar* (Pr 27:22) [Maurer]. Compare the similar image of a 'pot' (Eze 24:3,6). The reason for the destruction is subjoined, namely, its *merchant people's* greediness of gain.

all the merchant people – literally, the 'Canaanite people': irony: all the merchant people of Jerusalem are very *Canaanites* in greed for gain and in idolatries (see on Ho 12:7).

all … that bear silver – loading themselves with that which will prove but a *burden* (Hab 2:6).

12. search … with candles – or lamps; so as to leave no dark corner in it wherein sin can escape the punishment, of which the Chaldeans are My instruments (compare Zep 1:13 Lu 15:8).

settled on their lees – 'hardened' or crusted; image from the crust formed at the bottom of wines long left undisturbed (Jer 48:11). The effect of *wealthy undisturbed ease* ('lees') on the ungodly is *hardening:* they become stupidly secure (compare Ps 55:19 Am 6:1).

Lord will not do good … evil – They deny that God regards human affairs, or renders good to the good; or evil to the evil, but that all things go haphazard (Ps 10:4 Mal 2:17).

13. Therefore their goods shall become a booty. – Fulfilling the prophecy in De 28:30,39 (compare Am 5:11).

14. voice of … day of … Lord – that is, Jehovah ushering in that day with a roar of vengeance against the guilty (Jer 25:30 Am 1:2). They who will not now heed (Zep 1:12) His voice by His prophets, must heed it when uttered by the avenging foe.

mighty … shall cry … bitterly – in hopeless despair; the might on which Jerusalem now prides itself, shall then fail utterly.

15. wasteness … desolation – The *Hebrew* terms by their similarity of sounds, *Shoah, Umeshoah,* express the dreary monotony of desolation (see on Na 2:10).

16. the trumpet – namely, of the besieging enemy (Am 2:2).

alarm – the war shout [Maurer].

towers – literally 'angles'; for city walls used not to be built in a direct line, but with sinuous curves and angles, so that besiegers advancing might be assailed not only in front, but on both sides, caught as it were in a cul-de-sac; towers were built especially at the angles. So Tacitus describes the walls of Jerusalem [*Histories,* 5.11.7].

17. **like blind men** – unable to see whither to turn themselves so as to find an escape from existing evils.

flesh – *Hebrew*, 'bread'; so the *Arabic* term for 'bread' is used for 'flesh' (Mt 26:26).

18. **Neither ... silver nor ... gold shall ... deliver them.** – (Pr 11:4).

fire of his jealousy – (Eze 38:19); His wrath jealous for His honour consuming the guilty like fire.

make even a speedy riddance of all – rather, a 'consummation' (complete destruction: 'full end,' Jer 46:28 Eze 11:13) 'altogether sudden' [MAURER]. 'A consumption, *and that* a sudden one' [CALVIN].

Chapter 2

Zep 2:1–15. Exhortation to repent before the Chaldean invaders come. Doom of Judah's foes, the Philistines, Moab, Ammon, with their idols, and Ethiopia and Assyria.

1. **Gather yourselves** – *to a religious assembly*, to avert the judgment by prayers (Joe 2:16) [GROTIUS]. Or, so as not to be dissipated 'as chaff' (Zep 2:2). The *Hebrew* is akin to a root meaning 'chaff.' Self-confidence and corrupt desires are the dissipation from which they are exhorted to *gather themselves* [CALVIN]. The foe otherwise, like the wind, will scatter you 'as the chaff.' Repentance is the *gathering of themselves* meant.

nation not desired – (Compare 2Ch 21:20), that is, not desirable; unworthy of the grace or favour of God; and yet God so magnifies that grace as to be still solicitous for their safety, though they had destroyed themselves and forfeited all claims on His grace [CALVIN]. The *Margin* from *Chaldee Version* has, 'not desirous,' namely of returning to God.

2. **Before the decree bring forth** – that is, Before God's decree against you announced by me (Zep 1:1–18) *have its fulfilment*. As the embryo lies hid in the womb, and then emerges to light in its own due time, so though God for a time hides His vengeance, yet He *brings* it *forth* at the proper season.

before the day pass as the chaff – that is, before *the day* for repentance *pass*, and with it you, the ungodly, pass away *as the chaff* (Job 21:18 Ps 1:4). MAURER puts it parenthetically, 'the day (that is, time) passes as the chaff (that is, most quickly).' CALVIN, 'before the decree bring forth' (the predicted vengeance), (then) the chaff (the Jews) shall pass in a day, that is, in a moment, though they thought that it would be long before they could be overthrown. *English Version* is best; the latter clause being explanatory of the former, and so the *before*

being understood, not expressed.

3. As in Zep 2:1 (compare *Note*, see on Zep 1:12) he had warned the hardened among the people to humble themselves, so now he admonishes 'the meek' to proceed in their right course, that so they may escape the general calamity (Ps 76:9). The *meek* bow themselves under God's chastisements to God's will, whereas the ungodly become only the more hardened by them.

Seek ye the Lord – in contrast to those that 'sought not the Lord' (Zep 1:6). The *meek* are not to regard what the multitudes do, but seek God at once.

his judgment – that is, law. The true way of 'seeking the Lord' is to 'work judgment,' not merely to be zealous about outward ordinances.

seek meekness – not perversely murmuring against God's dealings, but patiently submitting to them, and composedly waiting for deliverance.

it may be ye shall be hid – (Isa 26:20 Am 5:6). This phrase does not imply doubt of the deliverance of the godly, but expresses the difficulty of it, as well that the ungodly may see the certainty of their doom, as also that the faithful may value the more the grace of God in their case (1Pe 4:17–19) [CALVIN]. Compare 2Ki 25:12.

4. **For** – He makes the punishment awaiting the neighbouring states an argument why the ungodly should repent (Zep 2:1) and the godly persevere, namely, that so they may escape from the general calamity.

Gaza shall be forsaken – In the *Hebrew* there is a play of similar sounds, *Gaza Gazubah;* Gaza shall be forsaken, as its name implies. So the *Hebrew* of the next clause, *Ekron teeakeer.*

at the noonday – when on account of the heat Orientals usually sleep, and military operations are suspended (2Sa 4:5). Hence an attack *at noon* implies one sudden and unexpected (Jer 6:4,5 15:8).

Ekron – *Four* cities of the Philistines are mentioned, whereas *five* was the normal number of their leading cities. Gath is omitted, being at this time under the Jews' dominion. David had subjugated it (1Ch 18:1). Under Joram the Philistines almost regained it (2Ch 21:16), but Uzziah (2Ch 26:6) and Hezekiah (2Ki 18:8) having conquered them, it remained under the Jews. Am 1:6 Zec 9:5,6 Jer 25:20, similarly mention only *four* cities of the Philistines.

5. **inhabitants of the seacoast** – the Philistines dwelling on the strip of seacoast southwest of Canaan. Literally, the 'cord' or 'line' of sea (compare Jer 47:7 Eze 25:16).

the Cherethites – the Cretans, a name applied to the Philistines as sprung from Crete (De 2:23 Jer 47:4 Am 9:7). *Philistine* means 'an emigrant.'

Canaan ... land of the Philistines – They occupied the southwest of *Canaan* (Jos 13:2,3); a name which hints that they are doomed to the same destruction as the early occupants of the land.

6. dwellings *and* cottages for shepherds – rather, 'dwellings with cisterns' (that is, water-tanks *dug* in the earth) *for shepherds.* Instead of a thick population and tillage, the region shall become a pasturage for nomad shepherds' flocks. The *Hebrew* for 'dug cisterns,' *Ceroth,* seems a play on sounds, alluding to their name Cherethites (Zep 2:5): Their land shall become what their national name implies, a land of *cisterns.*

7. remnant of ... Judah – those of the Jews who shall be left after the coming calamity, and who shall return from exile.

feed thereupon – namely, in the pastures of that seacoast region (Zep 2:6).

visit – in mercy (Ex 4:31).

8. I have heard – A seasonable consolation to Judah when wantonly assailed by Moab and Ammon with impunity: God saith, 'I have heard it all, though I might seem to men not to have observed it because I did not immediately inflict punishment.'

magnified themselves – acted haughtily, invading the territory of Judah (Jer 48:29 49:1; compare Zep 2:10 Ps 35:26 Ob 1:12).

9. the breeding of nettles – or, *the overspreading* of nettles, that is, a place overrun with them.

salt pits – found at the south of the Dead Sea. The water overflows in the spring, and salt is left by the evaporation. Salt land is barren (Jud 9:45 Ps 107:34, *Margin*).

possess them – that is, their land; in retribution for their having occupied Judah's land.

10. (Compare Zep 2:8).

their pride – in antithesis to the *meek* (Zep 2:3).

11. famish – bring low by taking from the idols their former fame; as beasts are famished by their food being withheld. Also by destroying the kingdoms under the tutelage of idols (Ps 96:4 Isa 46:1).

gods of the earth – who have their existence only *on earth,* not in heaven as the true God.

every one from his place – each *in his own* Gentile *home,* taught by the Jews in the true religion: not in Jerusalem alone shall men worship God, but everywhere (Ps 68:29,30 Mal 1:11 Joh 4:21 1Co 1:2 1Ti 2:8). It does not mean, as in Isa 2:2 Mic 4:1,2 Zec 8:22 14:16 that they shall come *from* their several *places* to Jerusalem to worship [MAURER].

all ... isles of ... heathen – that is, all the maritime regions, especially the west, now being fulfilled in the gathering in of the Gentiles to Messiah.

12. Fulfilled when Nebuchadnezzar (God's

sword, Isa 10:5) conquered Egypt, with which Ethiopia was closely connected as its ally (Jer 46:2-9 Eze 30:5-9).

Ye – literally, 'They.' The third person expresses estrangement; while doomed before God's tribunal in the second person, they are spoken of in the third as aliens from God.

13. Here he passes suddenly to the north. Nineveh was destroyed by Cyaxares and Nabopolassar, 625 B.C. The Scythian hordes, by an inroad into Media and thence in the southwest of Asia (thought by many to be the forces described by Zephaniah, as the invaders of Judea, rather than the Chaldeans), for a while interrupted Cyaxares' operations; but he finally succeeded. Arbaces and Belesis previously subverted the Assyrian empire under Sardanapalus (that is, Pul?), 877 B.C.

14. flocks – of sheep; answering to 'beasts' in the parallel clause. Wide pastures for sheep and haunts for wild beasts shall be where once there was a teeming population (compare Zep 2:6).

beasts of the nations – that is, beasts of the earth (Ge 1:24).

cormorant – rather, the 'pelican' (so Ps 102:6 Isa 34:11, *Margin*).

upper lintels – rather, '*the capitals* of her columns,' namely, in her temples and palaces [MAURER]. Or, 'on the pomegranate-like knops at the tops of the houses' [GROTIUS].

their voice shall sing in the windows – The desert-frequenting birds' 'voice in the windows' implies desolation reigning in the upper parts of the palaces, answering to 'desolation ... in the thresholds,' that is, in the lower.

he shall uncover the cedar work – laying the cedar wainscoting on the walls, and beams of the ceiling, bare to wind and rain, the roof being torn off, and the windows and doors broken through. All this is designed as a consolation to the Jews that they may bear their calamities patiently, knowing that God will avenge them.

15. Nothing then seemed more improbable than that the capital of so vast an empire, a city sixty miles in compass, with walls one hundred feet high, and so thick that three chariots could go abreast on them, and with fifteen hundred towers, should be so totally destroyed that its site is with difficulty discovered. Yet so it is, as the prophet foretold.

there is none beside me – This peculiar phrase, expressing self-gratulation as if peerless, is plainly adopted from Isa 47:8. The later prophets, when the spirit of prophecy was on the verge of departing, leaned more on the predictions of their predecessors.

hiss – in astonishment at a desolation so great and sudden (1Ki 9:8); also in derision (Job 27:23 La 2:15 Eze 27:36).

Chapter 3

Zep 3:1–20. Resumption of the denunciation of Jerusalem, as being unreformed by the punishment of other nations: after her chastisement Jehovah will interpose for her against her foes; his worship shall flourish in all lands, beginning at Jerusalem, where he shall be in the midst of his people, and shall make them a praise in all the earth.

1. oppressing – namely, the poor, weak, widows, orphans and strangers (Jer 22:3).

2. received not correction – Jerusalem is incurable, obstinately rejecting salutary admonition, and refusing to be reformed by 'correction' (Jer 5:3).

trusted not in … Lord – Distrust in the Lord as if He were insufficient, is the parent of all superstitions and wickednesses [CALVIN].

drew not near to her God – Though God was specially near to her (De 4:7) as 'her God,' yet she drew not near to Him, but gratuitously estranged herself from Him.

3. roaring – for prey (Pr 28:15 Eze 22:27 Am 3:4 Mic 2:2).

evening wolves – which are most ravenous at evening after being foodless all day (Jer 5:6 Hab 1:8).

they gnaw not the bones till the morrow – rather, 'they put not off till to-morrow to gnaw the bones'; but devour all at once, bones and flesh, so ragingly ravenous are they [CALVIN].

4. light – in whose life and teaching there is no truth, gravity, or steadiness.

treacherous – false to Jehovah, whose prophets they profess to be (Jer 23:32 Eze 22:28).

polluted … sanctuary – by their profane deeds.

5–7. The Jews regard not God's justice manifested in the midst of them, nor His judgments on the guilty nations around.

The just Lord – Why then are ye so unjust?

every morning – literally, 'morning by morning.' The time in the sultry East for dispensing justice.

bring … to light – publicly and manifestly by the teaching of His prophets, which aggravates their guilt; also by samples of His judgments on the guilty.

he faileth not – He is continually setting before you samples of His justice, sparing no pains. Compare Isa 5:4 50:4, 'he wakeneth *morning by morning.*'

knoweth no shame – The unjust Jews are not shamed by His justice into repentance.

6. I had hoped that My people by My judgments on other nations would be led to amendment; but they are not, so blinded by sin are they.

towers – literally, 'angles' or 'corners'; hence the *towers* built at the angles of their city walls. Under Josiah's long and peaceful reign the Jews were undisturbed, while the great incursion of Scythians into Western Asia took place. The judgment on the ten tribes in a former reign also is here alluded to.

7. I said, Surely – God speaks after the manner of men in condescension to man's infirmity; not as though God was ignorant of the future contingency, but in their sense, *Surely one might have expected* ye would under such circumstances repent: but no!

thou – at least, O Jerusalem! Compare '*thou, even thou,* at least in this thy day' (Lu 19:42).

howsoever I punished them – Howsoever I might have punished them, I would not have *cut off their dwelling.* CALVIN, 'Howsoever I had marked them out for punishment' because of their provocations, still, if even then they had repented, taught by My corrections, I was ready to have pardoned them.

rose early, and corrupted. – Early morning is in the East the best time for transacting serious business, before the relaxing heat of midday comes on. Thus it means, With the greatest earnestness they set themselves to 'corrupt all their doings' (Ge 6:12 Isa 5:11 Jer 11:7 25:3).

8. wait ye upon me – Here Jehovah turns to the pious Jews. Amidst all these judgments on the Jewish nation, look forward to the glorious time of restoration to be ushered in by God's precious outpouring of wrath on all nations, Isa 30:18-33; where the same phrase, 'blessed are all they that *wait for* Him,' is used as to the same great event.

until the day – that is, waiting for the day (Hab 2:3).

rise up to the prey – like a savage beast rising from his lair, greedy for the prey (compare Mt 24:28). Or rather, as a warrior leading Israel to *certain victory,* which is expressed by 'the prey,' or *booty,* which is the reward of victory.

gather the nations – against Jerusalem (Zec 14:2), to pour out His indignation upon them there (Joe 3:2 Zec 12:2,3).

9. For – The blessed things promised in this and Zep 3:10 are the immediate results of the punishment inflicted on the nations, mentioned in Zep 3:8 (compare Zep 3:19).

turn to the people a pure language – that is, *changing* their impure language I will *give* to them again *a pure language* (literally, 'lip'). Compare for this *Hebrew* idiom, 1Sa 10:9, *Margin.* The confusion of languages was of the penalty sin, probably idolatry at Babel (Ge 11:1–6, *Margin,* where also 'lip' expresses *language,* and perhaps also *religion; Zep 3:4,* 'a tower whose top *may reach* unto heaven,' or rather, *points to heaven,* namely, dedicated to *the heavens* idolized, or Bel); certainly, of rebellion against God's will. An earnest of the removal of this penalty was the gift of tongues on Pentecost (Ac 2:6–13). The full restoration of the earth's unity of language and of worship is yet future, and is connected with the restoration of the Jews, to be followed by the conversion of the world. Compare Isa 19:18 Zec 14:9 Ro 15:6, 'with one mind and *one mouth* glorify God.' The Gentiles' *lips* have been rendered impure through being the instruments of calling on idols and dishonouring God (compare Ps 16:4 Ho 2:17). Whether *Hebrew* shall be the one universal language or not, the God of the Hebrews shall be the one only object of worship. Until the Holy Ghost purify the *lips*, we cannot rightly call upon God (Isa 6:5–7).

serve him with one consent – literally, 'shoulder' or 'back'; metaphor from a yoke, or burden, borne between two (Nu 13:23); helping one another with conjoint effort. If one of the two bearers of a burden, laid on both conjointly, give way, the burden must fall to the earth [CALVIN]. Christ's rule is called a *burden* (Mt 11:30 Ac 15:28 Re 2:24; compare 2Co 6:14 for the same image).

10. From beyond … Ethiopia my suppliants – literally, 'burners of incense' (compare Ps 141:2 Re 5:8 8:3,4). The Israelites are meant, called 'the daughter of My dispersed,' a *Hebrew* idiom for *My dispersed people.* 'The rivers of Ethiopia' are those which enclose it on the north. In the west of Abyssinia there has long existed a people called *Falashas,* or 'emigrants' (akin to the synonym 'Philistine'). These trace their origin to Palestine and profess the Jewish religion. In physical traits they resemble the Arabs. When Bruce was there, they had a Jewish king, Gideon, and his queen, Judith. Probably the Abyssinian Christians were originally in part converted Jews. They are here made the representatives of all Israel which is to be restored.

11. shalt thou not be ashamed – Thou shalt then have no cause to be ashamed; for I will then *take away out of the midst of thee* those who by their sins gave thee cause for shame (Zep 3:7).

them that rejoice in thy pride – those priding themselves *on that which thou boastest of,* thy temple ('My holy mountain'), thy election as God's people, in the Pharisaic spirit (Jer 7:4 Mic 3:11 Mt 3:9). Compare Jer 13:17, 'mine eyes shall weep for *your* pride.' The converted remnant shall be of a humble spirit (Zep 3:12 Isa 66:2,10).

12. afflicted … they shall trust in … Lord – the blessed effect of sanctified affliction on the Jewish remnant. Entire trust in the Lord cannot be, except where all cause for boasting is taken away (Isa 14:32 Zec 11:11).

13. nor speak lies – worshipping God in truth, and towards man having love without

dissimulation. The characteristic of the 144,000 *sealed of Israel.*

none shall make them afraid – either foreign foe, or unjust prince (Zep 3:3), prophet, or priest (Zep 3:4).

14. The prophet in mental vision sees the joyful day of Zion present, and bids her rejoice at it.

15. The cause for joy: 'The Lord hath taken away thy judgments,' namely, those sent by Him upon thee: After the taking away of sin (Zep 3:13) follows the taking away of trouble. When the cause is removed, the effect will cease. Happiness follows in the wake of holiness.

the Lord is in the midst of thee – Though He seemed to desert thee for a time, He is now present as thy safeguard (Zep 3:17).

not see evil any more – Thou shalt not *experience* it (Jer 5:12 44:17).

16. Let not thine hands be slack – (Heb 12:12). Do not faint in the work of the Lord.

17. he will rest in his love – content with it as His supreme delight (compare Lu 15:7,10) [CALVIN], (Isa 62:5 65:19). Or, *He shall be silent,* namely as to thy faults, not imputing them to thee [MAURER] (Ps 32:2 Eze 33:16). I prefer explaining it of that calm *silent* joy in the possession of the object of one's love, too great for words to express: just as God after the six days of creation *rested* with silent satisfaction in His work, for 'behold it was very good' (Ge 1:31 2:2). So the parallel clause by contrast expresses the joy, not kept silent as this, but uttered in 'singing.'

18. sorrowful for the solemn assembly – pining after the solemn assembly which they cannot celebrate in exile (La 1:4 2:6).

who are of thee – that is, of thy true citizens; and whom therefore I will restore.

to whom the reproach of it was a burden – that is, to whom *thy* reproach ('the reproach of My people,' Mic 6:16; their ignominious captivity) was a burden. 'Of it' is put *of thee,* as the person is often changed. Those who shared in the burden of reproach which fell on My people. Compare Isa 25:8, 'the rebuke of His people shall He take away from off all the earth.'

19. undo – MAURER translates, 'I will deal with,' that is, as they deserve. Compare Eze 23:25, where the *Hebrew* is similarly translated. The destruction of Israel's foes precedes Israel's restoration (Isa 66:15,16).

her that halteth – all that are helpless. Their weakness will be no barrier in the way of My restoring them. So in Ps 35:15, *Margin,* 'halting' is used for *adversity.* Also Eze 34:16 Mic 4:6,7.

I will get them praise. – literally, 'I will make them (to become) a praise and a name'.

shame – (Eze 34:29).

20. make you a name … praise – make you to become celebrated and praised.

turn back your captivity – bring back your captives [MAURER]. The *Hebrew* is *plural*, 'captivities'; to express the captivities of different ages of their history, as well as the diversity of places in which they were and are dispersed.

before your eyes – Incredible as the event may seem, *your own eyes* with delight shall see it. You will scarcely believe it for joy, but the testimony of your own eyes shall convince you of the delightful reality (compare Lu 24:41).

HAGGAI

A.R. Faussett

Introduction

The name *Haggai* means 'my feast'; given, according to Cocceius, in anticipation of the joyous return from exile. He probably was one of the Jewish exiles (of the tribes Judah, Benjamin, and Levi) who returned under Zerubbabel, the civil head of the people, and Joshua, the high priest, 536 B.C., when Cyrus (actuated by the striking prophecies as to himself, Isa 44:28 45:1) granted them their liberty, and furnished them with the necessaries for restoring the temple (2Ch 36:23 Ezr 1:1 2:2). The work of rebuilding went on under Cyrus and his successor Cambyses (called Ahasuerus in Ezr 4:6) in spite of opposition from the Samaritans, who, when their offers of help were declined, began to try to hinder it. These at last obtained an interdict from the usurper Smerdis the Magian (called Artaxerxes in Ezr 4:7–23), whose suspicions were easy to rouse. The Jews thereupon became so indifferent to the work that when Darius came to the throne (521 B.C.), virtually setting aside the prohibitions of the usurper, instead of recommencing their labours, they pretended that as the prophecy of *the seventy years* applied to the temple as well as to the captivity in Babylon (Hag 1:2), they were only in the sixty-eighth year of it [Henderson]; so that, the proper time not having yet arrived, they might devote themselves to building splendid mansions for themselves. Haggai and Zechariah were commissioned by Jehovah (Hag 1:1) in the second year of Darius (Hystaspes), 520 B.C., sixteen years after the return under Zerubbabel, to rouse them from their selfishness to resume the work which for fourteen years had been suspended. Haggai preceded Zechariah in the work by two months.

The dates of his four distinct prophecies are accurately given: (1) The first (Hag 1:1–15), on the first day of the sixth month of the second year of Darius, 520 B.C., reproved the people for their apathy in allowing the temple to lie in ruins and reminded them of their ill success in everything because of their not honouring God as to His house. The result was that twenty-four days afterwards they commenced building under Zerubbabel (Hag 1:12–15). (2) The second, on the twenty-first day of the seventh month (Hag 2:1–9), predicts that the glory of the new temple would be greater than that of Solomon's, so that the people need not be discouraged by the inferiority in outward splendour of the new, as compared with the old temple, which had so moved to tears the elders who had remembered the old (Ezr 3:12,13). Isaiah, Jeremiah, and Ezekiel had implied the same prediction, whence some had doubted whether they ought to proceed with a building so inferior to the former one; but Haggai shows wherein the superior glory was to consist, namely, in the presence of Him who is the 'desire of all nations' (Hag 2:7). (3) The third, on the twenty-fourth day of the ninth month (Hag 2:10–19), refers to a period when building materials had been collected, and the workmen had begun to put them together, from which time forth God promises His blessing; it begins with removing their past error as to the efficacy of mere outward observances to cleanse from the taint of disobedience as to the temple building. (4) The fourth (Hag 2:20-23), on the same day as the preceding, was addressed to Zerubbabel, as the representative of the theocratic people, and as having asked as to the national revolutions spoken of in the second prophecy (Hag 2:7). The prophecies are all so brief as to suggest the supposition that they are only a summary of the original discourses. The space occupied is but three months from the first to the last. The Jews' adversaries, on the resumption of the work under Zerubbabel, Haggai, and Zechariah, tried to set Darius against it; but that monarch confirmed Cyrus' decree and ordered all help to be given to the building of the temple (Ezr 5:3. Ezr 6:1,). So the temple was completed in the sixth year of Darius' reign 516-515 B.C. (Ezr 6:14).

The style of Haggai is consonant with his messages: pathetic in exhortation, vehement in reproofs, elevated in contemplating the glorious future. The repetition of the same phrases (for example, 'saith the Lord,' or 'the Lord of hosts,' Hag 1:2,5,7; and thrice in one verse, Hag 2:4; so 'the spirit,' thrice in one verse, Hag 1:14) gives a simple earnestness to his style, calculated to awaken the solemn attention of the people, and to awaken them from their apathy, to which also the interrogatory form, often adopted, especially tends. Chaldaisms occur (Hag 2:3 2:6 2:16), as might have been expected in a writer who was so long in Chaldea. Parts are purely prose history; the rest is somewhat rhythmical, and observant of poetic parallelism.

Haggai is referred to in Ezr 5:1 6:14; and in the New Testament (Heb 12:26; compare Hag 2:6,7,22).

Chapter 1

Hag 1:1–15. Haggai calls the people to consider their ways in neglecting to build God's house: the evil of this neglect to themselves: the honour to God of attending to it: the people's penitent obedience under Zerubbabel followed by God's gracious assurance.

1. **second year of Darius** – Hystaspes, the king of Medo-Persia, the second of the world empires, Babylon having been overthrown by the Persian Cyrus. The Jews having no king of their own, dated by the reign of the world kings to whom they were subject. Darius was a common name of the Persian kings, as Pharaoh of those of Egypt, and Cæsar of those of Rome.

sixth month – of the Hebrew year, not of Darius' reign (compare Zec 1:7 7:1,3 8:19). Two months later ('the eighth month,' Zec 1:1) Zechariah began to prophesy, seconding Haggai.

the Lord – Hebrew, Jᴇʜᴏᴠᴀʜ: God's covenant title, implying His unchangeableness, the guarantee of His faithfulness in keeping His promises to His people.

by Haggai – Hebrew, 'in the hand of Haggai'; God being the real speaker, His prophet but the instrument (compare Ac 7:35 Ga 3:19).

Zerubbabel – called also Shesh-bazzar in Ezr 1:8 5:14,16, where the same work is attributed to Shesh-bazzar that in Ezr 3:8 is attributed to Zerubbabel. Shesh-bazzar is probably his Chaldean name; as Belteshazzar was that of Daniel. Zerubbabel, his Hebrew name, means 'one born in Babylon.'

son of Shealtiel – or Salathiel. But 1Ch 3:17,19 makes Pedaiah his father. Probably he was adopted by his uncle Salathiel, or Shealtiel, at the death of his father (compare Mt 1:12 Lu 3:27).

governor of Judah – to which office Cyrus had appointed him. The Hebrew Pechah is akin to the original of the modern Turkish Pasha; one ruling a region of the Persian empire of less extent than that under a satrap.

Joshua – called Jeshua (Ezr 2:2); so the son of Nun in Ne 8:17.

Josedech – or Jehozadak (1Ch 6:15), one of those carried captive by Nebuchadnezzar. Haggai addresses the civil and the religious representatives of the people, so as to have them as his associates in giving God's commands; thus priest, prophet, and ruler jointly testify in God's name.

2. **the Lord of hosts** – Jehovah, Lord of the powers of heaven and earth, and therefore requiring implicit obedience.

This people – 'This' sluggish and selfish 'people.' He does not say, *My* people, since they had neglected the service of God.

The time – the proper time for building the temple. Two out of the seventy predicted years of captivity (dating from the destruction of the temple, 558 B.C., 2Ki 25:9) were yet unexpired; this they make their plea for delay [HENDERSON]. The seventy years of captivity were completed long ago in the first year of Cyrus, 536 B.C. (Jer 29:10); dating from 606 B.C., Jehoiakim's captivity (2Ch 36:6). The seventy years to the completion of the temple (Jer 25:12) were completed this very year, the second of Darius [VATABLUS]. Ingenious in excuses, they pretended that the interruption in the work caused by their enemies proved it was *not yet the proper time;* whereas their real motive was selfish dislike of the trouble, expense, and danger from enemies. 'God,' say they, 'hath interposed many difficulties to punish our rash haste' [CALVIN]. But the Jews were easily turned aside from the work. Spiritually, like the Jews, men do not say they will never be religious, but, It is not time yet. So the great work of life is left undone.

4. Is it time – It is not time (Hag 1:2), ye say, to build Jehovah's house; yet how is it that ye make it a fit time not only to *build,* but to 'dwell' at ease in your own houses?

you, O ye – rather, for 'you, you'; the repetition marking the shameful contrast between their concern for *themselves,* and their unconcern for God [MAURER]. Compare a similar repetition in 1Sa 25:24 Zec 7:5.

ceiled – rather, or 'panelled,' referring to the walls as well as the ceilings; furnished not only with comfort but luxury, in sad contrast to God's house not merely unadorned, but the very walls not raised above the foundations. How different David's feelings (2Sa 7:2)!

5. Consider your ways – literally, 'Set your heart' on your ways. The *plural* implies, Consider both what ye have done (actively, La 3:40) and what ye have suffered (passively) [JEROME]. Ponder earnestly whether ye have gained by seeking self at the sacrifice of God.

6. Nothing has prospered with you while you neglected your duty to God. The punishment corresponds to the sin. They thought to escape poverty by not building, but keeping their money to themselves; God brought it on them *for* not building (Pr 13:7 11:24 Mt 6:33). Instead of cheating God, they had been only cheating themselves.

ye clothe ... but ... none warm – through insufficiency of clothing; as ye are unable through poverty from failure of your crops to purchase sufficient clothing. The verbs are infinitive, implying a *continued state:* 'Ye have

sown, and *been bringing in* but little; ye have *been eating,* but not to *being satisfied;* ye have *been drinking,* but not to *being filled;* ye have been *putting* on clothes, but not to *being warmed'* [MOORE]. Careful consideration of God's dealings with us will indicate God's will regarding us. The events of life are the hieroglyphics in which God records His feelings towards us, the key to which is found in the Bible [MOORE].

wages ... put ... into a bag with holes – proverbial for labour and money spent profitlessly (Zec 8:10; compare Isa 55:2 Jer 2:13). Contrast, spiritually, the 'bags that wax not old, the treasure in heaven that faileth not' (Lu 12:33). Through the high cost of necessaries, those who wrought for a day's wages parted with them at once, as if they had put them into a bag with holes.

8. Go up to the mountain – Rather, generally, *the mountains* around, now covered with wood, the growth of the long period of the captivity. So Ne 8:15, 'Go forth unto *the mount,'* that is, the neighbouring hills [MAURER].

wood – Haggai specifies this as being the first necessary; not to the exclusion of other materials. *Stones* also were doubtless needed. That the old walls were not standing, as the Hebrew interpreters quoted by JEROME state, or the new walls partly built, appears from Hag 2:18, where express mention is made of *laying the foundations.*

I will take pleasure in it, and I will be glorified – I will be propitious to suppliants in it (1Ki 8:30), and shall receive the honour due to Me which has been withheld. In neglecting the temple, which is the mirror of My presence, ye dishonour Me [CALVIN]; in its being built, ye shall glorify Me.

9. Ye looked for much – literally 'looked' so as to turn your eyes 'to much.' The *Hebrew* infinitive here expresses *continued* looking. Ye hoped to have your store made 'much' by neglecting the temple. The greater was your greediness, the more bitter your disappointment in being poorer than ever.

when ye brought it home, I did blow upon it – even the little crop brought into your barns I *dissipated.* 'I did blow upon,' that is, I scattered and caused to perish with My mere breath, as scattered and blighted corn.

mine house ... his own house – in emphatic antithesis.

ye run – expressing the keenness of everyone of them in pursuing their own selfish interests. Compare 'run,' Ps 119:32 Pr 1:16, contrasted with their apathy about God's house.

10. heaven ... is stayed from dew – literally 'stays itself.' Thus heaven or the sky is personified;

implying that inanimate nature obeys Jehovah's will; and, shocked at His people's disobedience, withholds its goods from them (compare Jer 2:12,13).

11. I called – what the 'heaven' and 'earth,' the second causes, were said to do (Hag 1:10), being the *visible* instruments, Jehovah, in this verse, the invisible first cause, declares to be His doing. He 'calls for' famine, as instruments of His wrath (2Ki 8:1 Ps 105:16). The contrast is striking between the prompt obedience of these material agencies, and the slothful disobedience of living men, His people.

drought – Hebrew, *Choreb*, like in sound to *Chareeb*, 'waste' (Hag 1:4,9), said of God's house; implying the correspondence between the sin and its punishment. Ye have let My house be *waste*, and I will send on all that is yours a *wasting drought*. This would affect not merely the 'corn', but also 'men' and 'cattle,' who must perish in the absence of the 'corn', lost by the drought.

labour of the hands – all the fruits of lands, gardens, and vineyards, obtained by labour of the hands (De 28:33 Ps 78:46).

12. remnant of the people – all those who have returned from the exile (Zec 8:6).

13. the Lord's messenger – so the priests (Mal 2:7) are called (compare Ga 4:14 2Pe 1:21).

in the Lord's message – by the Lord's authority and commission: on the Lord's embassage.

I *am* **with you** – (Mt 28:20). On the people showing the mere disposition to obey, even before they actually set to work, God passes at once from the reproving tone to that of tenderness. He hastens as it were to forget their former unfaithfulness, and to assure them, when obedient, that He *both is and will be* with them: Hebrew, 'I with you!' God's presence is the best of blessings, for it includes all others. This is the sure guarantee of their success no matter how many their foes might be (Ro 8:31). Nothing more inspirits men and rouses them from torpor, than, when relying on the promises of divine aid, they have a sure hope of a successful issue [CALVIN].

14. Lord stirred up the spirit of. – God gave them alacrity and perseverance in the good work, though slothful in themselves. Every good impulse and revival of religion is the direct work of God by His Spirit.

came and did work – collected the wood and stones and other materials (compare Hag 1:8) for the work. Not actually built or 'laid the (secondary) foundations' of the temple, for this was not done till three months after, namely, the twenty-fourth day of the *ninth* month (Hag 2:18) [GROTIUS].

15. four and twentieth day – twenty-three days after the first message of Haggai (Hag 1:1).

Chapter 2

Hag 2:1–9. SECOND PROPHECY. The people, discouraged at the inferiority of this temple to Solomon's, are encouraged nevertheless to persevere, because God is with them, and this house by its connection with Messiah's kingdom shall have a glory far above that of gold and silver.

1. seventh month – of the Hebrew year; in the second year of Darius reign (Hag 1:1); not quite a month after they had begun the work (Hag 1:15). This prophecy was very shortly before that of Zechariah.

3. Who is left ... that saw ... first glory – Many elders present at the laying of the foundation of the second temple who had seen the first temple (Ezr 3:12,13) in all its glory, wept at the contrast presented by the rough and unpromising appearance of the former in its beginnings. From the destruction of the first temple to the second year of Darius Hystaspes, the date of Haggai's prophecy, was a space of seventy years (Zec 1:12); and to the first year of Cyrus, or the end of the captivity, fifty-two years; so that the elders might easily remember the first temple. The Jews note five points of inferiority: The absence from the second temple of (1) the sacred fire; (2) the Shekinah; (3) the ark and cherubim; (4) the Urim and Thummim; (5) the spirit of prophecy. The connection of it with Messiah more than counterbalanced all these; for He is the antitype to all the five (Hag 2:9).

how do ye see it now? – God's estimate of things is very different from man's (Zec 8:6; compare 1Sa 16:7). However low their estimate of the present temple ('it') from its outward inferiority, God holds it superior (Zec 4:10 1Co 1:27,28).

4. be strong ... for I am with you – The greatest *strength* is to have Jehovah with us as our strength. Not in man's 'might,' but in that of God's Spirit (Zec 4:6).

5. *According to* **the word that** – literally, '(I am with you) the word (or *thing*) which I covenanted'; that is, I am with you as I covenanted with you when ye came out of Egypt (Ex 19:5,6 34:10,11). The *covenant* promise of God to the elect people at Sinai is an additional motive for their persevering. The *Hebrew* for to 'covenant' is literally 'to cut,' alluding to the sacrificial victims *cut* in ratification of a covenant.

so – or, 'and.'

my Spirit remaineth among you – to strengthen you for the work (Hag 1:14 Zec 4:6). The inspiration of Haggai and Zechariah at this time was a specimen of the presence of God's *Spirit* remaining still *with* His people, as He had been with Moses and Israel of old (Ezr 5:1 Isa 63:11).

6. The *shaking of nations* implies judgments of wrath on the foes of God's people, to precede the reign of the Prince of peace (Isa 13:13). The kingdoms of the world are but the scaffolding for God's spiritual temple, to be thrown down when their purpose is accomplished. The transitoriness of all that is earthly should lead men to seek 'peace' in Messiah's everlasting kingdom (Hag 2:9 Heb 12:27,28) [Moore]. The Jews in Haggai's times hesitated about going forward with the work, through dread of the world power, Medo-Persia, influenced by the craft of Samaria. The prophet assures them this and all other world powers are to fall before Messiah, who is to be associated with this temple; therefore they need fear naught. So Heb 12:26, which quotes this passage; the apostle compares the heavier punishment which awaits the disobedient under the New Testament with that which met such under the Old Testament. At the establishment of the Sinaitic covenant, only the earth was shaken to introduce it, but now heaven and earth and all things are to be shaken, that is, along with prodigies in the world of nature, all kingdoms that stand in the way of Messiah's kingdom, 'which cannot be shaken,' are to be upturned (Da 2:35,44 Mt 21:44).

7. shake – not *convert;* but cause that agitation which is to precede Messiah's coming as the healer of the nations' agitations. The previous shaking shall cause the yearning *'desire'* for the Prince of peace. What is implied is not that the nations definitely desired *Him,* but that He was the only one to satisfy the yearning desires which all felt unconsciously for a Saviour, shown in their painful rites and bloody sacrifices. Moreover, while the Jews as a nation desired Him not, the Gentiles, who are plainly pointed out by 'all nations,' accepted Him; and so to them He was peculiarly desirable. The Jews, and those in the adjoining nations instructed by them, looked for *Shiloh to come unto whom the gathering of the people was to be,* from Jacob's prophecy (Ge 49:10). The early patriarchs, Job (Job 19:25–27 33:23–26) and Abraham (Joh 8:56), *desired Him.*

fill this house with glory – (Hag 2:9). As the first temple was filled with the cloud of glory, the symbol of God (1Ki 8:11 2Ch 5:14), so this second temple was filled with the 'glory' of God (Joh 1:14) *veiled* in the flesh (as it were in the cloud) at Christ's first coming, when He entered it and performed miracles there (Mt 21:12–14); but that 'glory' is to be *revealed* at His second coming, as this prophecy in its ulterior reference foretells (Mal 3:1). The Jews before the destruction of Jerusalem all expected Messiah would appear in the second temple.

Since that time they invent various forced and false interpretations of such plain Messianic prophecies.

8. The silver is mine – (Job 41:11 Ps 50:12). Ye are disappointed at the absence of these precious metals in the adorning of this temple, as compared with the first temple: If I pleased I could adorn this temple with them, but I will adorn it with a 'glory' (Hag 2:7,9) far more precious; namely, with the presence of My divine Son in His veiled glory first, and at His second coming with His revealed glory, accompanied with outward adornment of gold and silver, of which the golden covering within and without put on by Herod is the type. Then shall the nations bring offerings of those precious metals which ye now miss so much (Isa 2:3 60:3,6,7 Eze 43:2,4,5 44:4). The heavenly Jerusalem shall be similarly adorned, but shall need 'no temple' (Re 21:10–22). Compare 1Co 3:12, where *gold* and *silver* represent the most precious things (Zec 2:5). The inward glory of New Testament redemption far exceeds the outward glory of the Old Testament dispensation. So, in the case of the individual poor believer, God, if He pleased, could bestow gold and silver, but He bestows far better treasures, the possession of which might be endangered by that of the former (Jas 2:5).

9. The glory of this latter house … greater than of the former – namely, through the presence of Messiah, *in* (whose) *face is given the light of the knowledge of the glory of God* (2Co 4:6; compare Heb 1:2), and who said of Himself, 'in this place is one greater than the temple' (Mt 12:6), and who 'sat daily teaching in it' (Mt 26:55). Though Zerubbabel's temple was taken down to the foundations when Herod rebuilt the temple, the latter was considered, in a religious point of view, as not a *third* temple, but virtually the second temple.

in this place … peace – namely, at Jerusalem, the metropolis of the kingdom of God, whose seat was the temple: where Messiah 'made peace through the blood of His cross' (Col 1:20). Thus the 'glory' consists in this 'peace.' This peace begins by the removal of the difficulty in the way of the just God accepting the guilty (Ps 85:8,10 Isa 9:6,7 53:5 Zec 6:13 2Co 5:18,19); then it creates peace in the sinner's own heart (Isa 57:19 Ac 10:36 Ro 5:1 14:17 Eph 2:13–17 Php 4:7); then peace in the whole earth (Mic 5:5 Lu 2:14). First peace between God and man, then between man and God, then between man and man (Isa 2:4 Ho 2:18 Zec 9:10). As 'Shiloh' (Ge 49:10) means *peace,* this verse confirms the view that Hag 2:7, 'the desire of all nations,' refers to Shiloh or Messiah, foretold in Ge 49:10.

Hag 2:10–19. Third Prophecy. Sacrifices without obedience (in respect to God's command to build the temple) could not sanctify. Now that they are obedient, God will bless them, though no sign is seen of fertility as yet.

10. four and twenty day ... ninth month – three days more than two months from the second prophecy (Hag 2:1); in the month Chisleu, the lunar one about the time of our December. The Jews seem to have made considerable progress in the work in the interval (Hag 2:15–18).

11. Ask ... the priests – Propose this question to them on the law. The priests were the authorized expounders of the law (Le 10:11 De 33:10 Eze 44:23 Mal 2:7).

12. 'Holy flesh' (that is, the flesh of a sacrifice, Jer 11:15), indeed, makes holy the 'skirt' in which it is carried; but that 'skirt' cannot impart its sanctity to any thing beyond, as 'bread,' (Le 6:27). This is cited to illustrate the principle, that a sacrifice, holy, as enveloping divine things (just as the 'skirt' is 'holy' which envelops 'holy' flesh), cannot by its inherent efficacy make holy a person whose disobedience, as that of the Jew while neglecting God's house, made him unholy.

13. On the other hand, a legally 'unclean' person imparts his uncleanness to any thing, whereas a legally holy thing cannot confer its sanctity on an 'unclean' person (Nu 19:11,13,22). Legal sanctity is not so readily communicated as legal impurity. So the paths to sin are manifold: the paths to holiness one, and that one of difficult access [Grotius]. One drop of filth will defile a vase of water: many drops of water will not purify a vase of filth [Moore].

14. so is this people – heretofore not in such an obedient state of mind as to deserve to be called *My* people (Tit 1:15).

15. consider – literally, 'lay it to heart.' Ponder earnestly, retracing the past 'upward' (that is, backward), comparing what evils heretofore befell you before ye set about this work, with the present time when you have again commenced it, and when in consequence I now engage to 'bless you.' Hence ye may perceive the evils of disobedience and the blessing of obedience.

16. Since those *days* **were** – from the time that those days of your neglect of the temple work have been.

when *one* **came to an heap of twenty** *measures* – that is to a heap *which he had expected would be one* of twenty measures, there were but ten.

fifty *vessels* **out of the press** – As the *Septuagint* translates 'measure,' and *Vulgate* 'a flagon,' and as we should rather expect *vat* than *press.*

17. Appropriated from Am 4:9, whose canonicity is thus sealed by Haggai's inspired authority; in the last clause, '*turned*,' however, has to be supplied, its omission marking by the elliptical abruptness ('yet ye not to Me!') God's displeasure. Compare '(*let him come*) unto Me!' Moses in excitement omitting the bracketed words (Ex 32:26).

18. Resumed from Hag 2:15 after Hag 2:16,17, that the blessing in Hag 2:19 may stand in the more marked contrast with the curse in Hag 2:16,17. Affliction will harden the heart, if not referred to God as its author [Moore].

even **from the day that the foundation of ... temple was laid** – The first foundation beneath the earth had been long ago laid in the second year of Cyrus, 535 B.C. (Ezr 3:10,11); the foundation now laid was the secondary one, which, above the earth, was laid on the previous work [Tirinus].

19. Is the seed yet in the barn? – implying, It is *not*. It has been already sown this month, and there are no more signs of its bearing a good crop, much less of its being safely stored *in the barn*, than there were in the past season, when there was such a failure; yet I promise to you *from this day* (emphatically marking by the repetition the connection of the blessing with *the day* of their obedience) a *blessing* in an abundant harvest. So also the vine, which heretofore have borne little or nothing, shall be *blessed* with productiveness. Thus it will be made evident that the blessing is due to Me, not to nature. We may trust God's promise to bless us, though we see no visible sign of its fulfilment (Hab 2:3).

Hag 2:20–23. Fourth Prophecy. God's promise through Zerubbabel to Israel of safety in the coming commotions.

20. the month – the ninth in the second year of Darius. The same date as Prophecy III (Hag 2:10).

21. to Zerubbabel – Perhaps Zerubbabel had asked as to the convulsions foretold (Hag 2:6,7). This is the reply: The Jews had been led to fear that these convulsions would destroy their national existence. *Zerubbabel*, therefore, as their civil leader and representative is addressed, not Joshua, their religious leader. Messiah is the antitypical Zerubbabel, their national Representative and King, with whom God the Father makes the covenant wherein they, as identified with Him, are assured of safety in God's electing love (compare Hag 2:23, 'will make thee as a signet'; 'I have chosen thee').

shake ... heavens – (see on Hag 2:6,7); violent political convulsions accompanied with physical prodigies (Mt 24:7,29).

22. All other world kingdoms are to be overthrown to make way for Christ's universal kingdom (Da 2:44). War chariots are to give place to His reign of peace (Mic 5:10 Zec 9:10).

23. take thee – under My protection and to promote thee and thy people to honour (Ps 78:70).

a signet – (So 8:6 Jer 22:24). A ring with a seal on it; the legal representative of the owner; generally of precious stones and gold, and much valued. Being worn on the finger, it was an object of constant regard. In all which points of view the theocratic people, and their representative, Zerubbabel the type, and Messiah his descendant the Antitype, are regarded by God.

The safety of Israel to the end is guaranteed in Messiah, in whom God hath chosen them as His own (Isa 42:1 43:10 44:1 49:3). So the spiritual Israel is sealed in their covenant head by His Spirit (2Co 1:20,22 Eph 1:4,13,14). All is ascribed, not to the merits of Zerubbabel, but to God's gratuitous *choice*. Christ is the 'signet' on God's hand: always in the Father's presence, ever pleasing in his sight. The signet of an Eastern monarch was the sign of *delegated authority;* so Christ.

ZECHARIAH

A.R. Faussett

Introduction

The name *Zechariah* means *one whom Jehovah remembers:* a common name, four others of the same name occurring in the Old Testament. Like Jeremiah and Ezekiel, he was a priest as well as a prophet, which adapts him for the sacerdotal character of some of his prophecies (Zec 6:13). He is called 'the son of Berechiah the son of Iddo' (Zec 1:1); but simply 'the son of Iddo' in Ezr 5:1 6:14. Probably his father died when he was young; and hence, as sometimes occurs in Jewish genealogies, he is called 'the son of Iddo,' his grandfather. Iddo was one of the priests who returned to Zerubbabel and Joshua from Babylon (Ne 12:4).

Zechariah entered early on his prophetic functions (Zec 2:4); only two months later than Haggai, in the second year of Darius' reign, 520 B.C. The design of both prophets was to encourage the people and their religious and civil leaders, Joshua and Zerubbabel, in their work of rebuilding the temple, after the interruption caused by the Samaritans. Zechariah does so especially by unfolding in detail the glorious future in connection with the present depressed appearance of the theocracy, and its visible symbol, the temple. He must have been very young in leaving Babylonia, where he was born. The Zechariah, son of Barachias, mentioned by our Lord (Mt 23:35) as slain between the porch and the altar, must have been the one called the son of *Jehoiada* in 2Ch 24:21, who so perished: the same person often had two names; and our Lord, in referring to the *Hebrew* Bible, of which Second Chronicles is the last book, would naturally mention the last martyr in the *Hebrew* order of the canon, as He had instanced Abel as the first.

The prophecy consists of four parts: (1) Introductory, Zec 1:1–6. (2) Symbolical, Zec 1:7, to the end of the sixth chapter, containing nine visions; all these were vouchsafed in one night, and are of a symbolical character. (3) Didactic, the seventh and eighth chapters containing an answer to a query of the Beth-elites concerning a certain feast. And (4) Prophetic, the ninth chapter to the end. These six last chapters predict Alexander's expedition along the west coast of Palestine to Egypt; God's protection of the Jews, both at that time and under the Maccabees; the advent, sufferings, and reign of Messiah; the destruction of Jerusalem by Rome, and dissolution of the Jews' polity; their conversion and restoration; the overthrow of the wicked confederacy which assailed them in Canaan; and the Gentiles' joining in their holy worship [HENDERSON].

Chapter 1

Zec 1:1–17. INTRODUCTORY
EXHORTATION TO REPENTANCE. THE
VISION. The man among the myrtles:
Comforting explanation by the angel,
an encouragement to the Jews to build
the city and temple: The four horns and
four artificers.

2. God fulfilled His threats against your
fathers; beware, then, lest by disregarding His
voice by me, as they did in the case of former
prophets, *ye* suffer like them. The special object
Zechariah aims at is that they should awake
from their selfish negligence to obey God's command to rebuild His temple (Hag 1:4–8).

sore displeased – *Hebrew*, 'displeased with a
displeasure,' that is, vehemently, with no common displeasure, exhibited in the destruction of
the Jews' city and in their captivity.

3. saith the Lord of hosts – a phrase frequent
in Haggai and Zechariah, implying God's
boundless resources and universal power, so as
to inspire the Jews with confidence to work.

Turn ye unto me … and I will turn – that is,
and then, as the sure consequence, 'I will turn
unto you' (Mal 3:7 Jas 4:8; compare also Jer 3:12
Eze 18:30 Mic 7:19). Though God hath brought
you back from captivity, yet this state will not
last long unless ye are really converted. God has
heavier scourges ready, and has begun to give
symptoms of displeasure [CALVIN]. (Hag 1:6).

4. Be ye not as your fathers – The Jews boasted of their *fathers;* but he shows that their
fathers were refractory, and that ancient example and long usage will not justify disobedience
(2Ch 36:15,16).

the former prophets – those who lived before
the captivity. It aggravated their guilt that, not
only had they the law, but they had been often
called to repent by God's *prophets.*

5. Your fathers … and the prophets, do they
live for ever? – In contrast to '*My* words' (Zec
1:6), which 'endure for ever' (1Pe 1:25). 'Your
fathers have perished, as was foretold; and their
fate ought to warn you. But you may say, The
prophets too are dead. I grant it, but still My
words do not die: though dead, their prophetical words from Me, fulfilled against *your fathers,*
are not dead with them. Beware, then, lest ye
share their fate.'

6. statutes – My determined purposes to
punish for sin.

which I commanded my servants – namely,
to announce to your fathers.

did they not take hold – that is, overtake, as a
foe overtakes one fleeing.

they returned – *Turning* from their former
self-satisfaction, they recognized their punish-

ment as that which God's prophets had foretold.

thought to do – that is, decreed to do.
Compare with this verse La 2:17.

our ways – evil ways (Jer 4:18 17:10 23:2).

7. The general plan of the nine following
visions (Zec 1:8-6:15) is first to present the symbol; then, on a question being put, to subjoin
the interpretation. Though the visions are distinct, they form one grand whole, presented in
one night to the prophet's mind, two or three
months after the prophet's first commission
(Zec 1:1).

Sebat – the eleventh month of the Jewish
year, from the new moon in February to the new
moon in March. The term is *Chaldee,* meaning a
'shoot,' namely, the month when trees begin to
shoot or bud.

8. by night – The Jews begin their day with
sunset; therefore the night which preceded the
twenty-fourth day of the month is meant (Zec
1:7).

a man – Jehovah, the second person of the
Trinity, manifested in *man's* form, an earnest of
the incarnation; called the 'angel of Jehovah'
(Zec 1:11,12), 'Jehovah the angel of the cov-
enant' (Mal 3:1; compare Ge 16:7 with Zec 1:13;
Ge 22:11 with Zec 1:12; Ex 3:2 with Zec 1:4).
Being at once divine and human, He must be
God and man in one person.

riding – implying swiftness in executing
God's will in His providence; hastening to help
His people.

red horse – the Collor that represents *bloodshed:* implying vengeance to be inflicted on the
foes of Israel (compare 2Ki 3:22 Isa 63:1,2 Re
6:4); also *fiery zeal.*

among the myrtle trees – symbol of the
Jewish Church: not a stately cedar, but a lowly,
though fragrant, myrtle. It was its depressed
state that caused the Jews to despond; this vision
is designed to cheer them with better hopes. The
uncreated angel of Jehovah's presence *standing*
(as His abiding place, Ps 132:14) *among* them,
is a guarantee for her safety, lowly though she
now be.

in the bottom – in a low place or bottom
of a river; alluding to Babylon near the rivers
Euphrates and Tigris, the scene of Judah's captivity. The myrtle delights in low places and the
banks of waters [PEMBELLUS].

red horses – that is, *horsemen* mounted *on
red horses;* Zec 1:10,11, confirm this view.

speckled … white – The 'white' implies triumph and victory for Judah; 'speckled' (from a
root 'to intertwine'), a combination of the two
colours *white* and *red* (bay [MOORE]), implies a
state of things mixed, partly prosperous, partly
otherwise [HENDERSON]; or, the connection of
the wrath (answering to the 'red') about to fall
on the Jews' foes, and triumph (answering to
the 'white') to the Jews themselves in God's

arrangements for His people [MOORE]. Some angels ('the red horses') exercised offices of vengeance; others ('the white'), those of joy; others ('the speckled'), those of a mixed character (compare Zec 6:2,3). God has ministers of every kind for promoting the interests of His Church.

9. the angel that talked with me – not the 'man upon the red horse,' as is evident from Zec 1:10, where he (the Divine Angel) is distinguished from the 'angel that talked with me' (the phrase used of him, Zec 1:13,14 Zec 2:3 4:1,4,5 5:5,10 6:4), that is, the interpreting angel. The *Hebrew* for *'with me,'* or, *'in me'* (Nu 12:8), implies *internal, intimate* communication [JEROME].

show thee – reveal to thy mental vision.

10. answered – The 'angel of the covenant' here gives the reply instead of the interpreting angel, to imply that all communications through the interpreting angel come from Him as their source.

Lord hath sent to walk to and fro through the earth – If 'Satan walks to and fro in the earth' (implying *restless activity*) on errands of mischief to God's people (Job 1:7), the Lord *sends* other angels to 'walk to and fro' with unceasing activity everywhere to counterwork Satan's designs, and to defend His people (Ps 34:7 91:11 103:20,21 Heb 1:14).

11. The attendant angels report to the Lord of angels, 'the earth ... is at rest.' The flourishing state of the heathen 'earth,' while Judah was desolate and its temple not yet restored, is the powerful plea in the Divine Angel's intercession with God the Father in Zec 1:12. When Judah was depressed to the lowest point, and the heathen elated to the highest, it was time for Jehovah to work for His people.

sitteth still – dwells surely.

12. Not only does Messiah *stand among* His people (the 'myrtles,' Zec 1:8), but intercedes for them with the Father ('Lord,' or 'Jehovah of hosts') effectively (Zec 1:13 Heb 7:25). Compare Ps 102:13–20 Isa 62:6,7, as to Judah's restoration in answer to prayer.

answered and said – said *in continuation* of the discourse: *proceeded to say.*

how long – Messiah's people pray similarly to their Head. Re 6:10, 'How long'. Heretofore it was vain to pray, but now that the divinely appointed 'threescore and ten years' (Jer 25:11 29:10) are elapsed, it is time to pray to Thee for the fulfilment of Thy promise, seeing that Thy grace is not yet fully manifested, nor Thy promise fulfilled. God's promises are not to make us slothful, but to quicken our prayers.

13. the Lord – JEHOVAH, called 'the angel of the Lord (Jehovah)' (Zec 1:12).

good words *and* comfortable words – literally, 'words, consolations.' The subject of these consolatory words is stated in Zec 1:14.; the promise of full re-establishment, Jer 29:10,11 (compare Isa 57:18 Ho 11:8).

14. Cry – Proclaim so as to be heard clearly by all (Isa 40:6 58:1).

I am jealous for Jerusalem – As a husband jealous for his wife, wronged by others, so Jehovah is for Judah, who has been injured wantonly by the heathen (Zec 8:2 Nu 25:11,13 1Ki 19:10 Joe 2:18).

15. very sore displeased with the heathen – in contrast with 'I was *but a little* displeased' with My people. God's displeasure with His people is temporary and for their chastening; with the heathen oppressors, it is final and fatal (Jer 30:11). God's instruments for chastising His people, when He has done with them, He casts into the fire.

are at ease – carnally secure. A stronger phrase than 'is at rest' (Zec 1:11). They are 'at ease,' but as I am 'sore displeased' with them, their ease is accursed. Judah is in 'affliction,' but as I love her and am jealous for her, she has every reason to be encouraged in prosecuting the temple work.

helped forward the affliction – afflicted My people more than I desired. The heathen sought the utter extinction of Judah to gratify their own ambition and revenge (Isa 47:6 Eze 25:3,6 Ob 1:10–17).

16. I am returned – whereas in anger I had before withdrawn from her (Ho 5:15).

with mercies – not merely of one kind, nor once only, but repeated mercies.

my house shall be built – which at this time (the second year of Darius, Zec 1:1) had only its foundations laid (Hag 2:18). It was not completed till the sixth year of Darius (Ezr 6:15).

line – (Job 38:5). The measuring-line for building, not hastily, but with measured regularity. Not only the temple, but *Jerusalem* also was to be rebuilt (Ne 2:3.; compare Zec 2:1,2). Also, as to the future temple and city, Eze 41:3 42:1–44:31 45:6.

17. yet – though heretofore lying in abject prostration.

My cities – not only Jerusalem, but the subordinate *cities* of Judah. God claims them all as peculiarly *His,* and therefore will restore them.

through prosperity ... spread abroad – or *overflow;* metaphor from an overflowing vessel or fountain (compare Pr 5:16) [PEMBELLUS]. Abundance of fruits of the earth, corn and wine, and a large increase of citizens, are meant; also spiritual prosperity.

comfort Zion – (Isa 40:1,2 51:3).

choose – (Zec 2:12 3:2 Isa 14:1). Here meaning, *'show by acts of loving-kindness* that He has chosen.' His immutable *choice* from everlasting is the fountain whence flow all such particular acts of love.

Zec 1:18–21. Second Vision. The power of the Jews foes shall be dissipated.

18. four horns – To a pastoral people like the Jews the *horns* of the strongest in the herd naturally suggested a symbol of *power* and *pride* of conscious strength: hence *the ruling powers of the world* (Re 17:3,12). The number *four* in Zechariah's time referred to the four cardinal points of the horizon. Wherever God's people turned, there were foes to encounter (Ne 4:7); the Assyrian, Chaldean, and Samaritan on the north; Egypt and Arabia on the south; Philistia on the west; Ammon and Moab on the east. But the Spirit in the prophet looked farther; namely, to the *four* world powers, the only ones which were, or are, to rise till the kingdom of Messiah, the fifth, overthrows and absorbs all others in its universal dominion. Babylon and Medo-Persia alone had as yet risen, but soon Græco-Macedonia was to succeed (as Zec 9:13 foretells), and Rome the fourth and last, was to follow (Da 2:1–49 7:1–28). The fact that the repairing of the evils caused to Judah and Israel by *all four* kingdoms is spoken of here, proves that the exhaustive fulfilment is yet future, and only the earnest of it given in the overthrow of the two world powers which up to Zechariah's time had 'scattered' Judah (Jer 51:2 Eze 5:10,12). That only two of the four had as yet risen, is an argument having no weight with us, as we believe God's Spirit in the prophets regards the future as present; we therefore are not to be led by Rationalists who on such grounds deny the reference here and in Zec 6:1 to the four world kingdoms.

19. Judah, Israel – Though some of the ten tribes of *Israel* returned with *Judah* from Babylon, the full return of the former, as of the latter, is here foretold and must be yet future.

20. four carpenters – or 'artificers.' The several instrumentalities employed, or to be employed, in crushing the 'Gentile' powers which 'scattered' Judah, are hereby referred to. For every one of the *four horns* there was a cleaving 'artificer' to beat it down. For every enemy of God's people, God has provided a counteracting power adequate to destroy it.

21. These are the horns – rather, *Those*, namely, the horns being distinguished from the 'carpenters,' or destroying workmen ('skilful to destroy,' Ex 21:31), intended in the 'these' of the question.

no man ... lift up his head – so depressed were they with a heavy weight of evils (Job 10:15).

to fray – *to strike terror into* them (Eze 30:9).

lifted up ... horn – in the haughtiness of conscious strength (Ps 75:4,5) tyrannizing over Judah (Eze 34:21).

Chapter 2

Zec 2:1–13. Third Vision. The man with the measuring-line.

The city shall be fully restored and enlarged (Zec 2:2–5). Recall of the exiles (Zec 2:6,7). Jehovah will protect His people and make their foes a spoil unto them (Zec 2:8,9). The nations shall be converted to Jehovah, as the result of His dwelling manifestly amidst His people (Zec 2:10–13).

1. man with a measuring-line – the same image to represent the same future fact as in Eze 40:3 41,42. The 'man' is Messiah (see on Zec 1:8), who, by measuring Jerusalem, is denoted as the Author of its coming restoration. Thus the Jews are encouraged in Zechariah's time to proceed with the building. Still more so shall they be hereby encouraged in the future restoration.

2. To measure Jerusalem – (Compare Re 11:1 21:15,16).

to see what *is* the breadth ... what *is* the length – rather, 'what *is to be the due* breadth and length.'

3. angel that talked with me ... another angel – The interpreting angel is met by another angel sent by the measuring Divine Angel to 'run' to Zechariah (Zec 2:4). Those who perform God's will must not merely creep, nor walk, but *run* with alacrity.

went forth – namely, from me (Zechariah).

went out – from the measuring angel.

4. this young man – So Zechariah is called as being still a *youth* when prophetically inspired [Grotius]. Or, he is so called in respect to his *ministry* or *service* (compare Nu 11:27 Jos 1:1) [Vatablus]. Naturally the 'angel that talked with' Zechariah is desired to 'speak to' him the further communications to be made from the Divine Being.

towns without walls for the multitude ... Cattle – So many shall be its inhabitants that all could not be contained within the walls, but shall spread out in the open country around (Es 9:19); and so secure shall they be as not to need to shelter themselves and their cattle behind walls. So hereafter Judea is to be 'the land of unwalled villages' (Eze 38:11). Spiritually, now the Church has extended herself beyond the walls (Eph 2:14,15) of Mosaic ordinances and has spread from cities to country villages, whose inhabitants gave their Latin name (*pagani*) to *pagans*, as being the last in parting with heathenism.

5. I ... wall of fire round – Compare Zec 2:4. Yet as a city needs some wall, I JEHOVAH will act as one of fire which none durst approach (Zec 9:8 Isa 26:1).

glory in the midst – not only a defence from foes outside, but a *glory* within (Isa 60:19 Re 21:23). The same combination of 'glory and defence' is found in Isa 4:5, alluding to the pillar of cloud and fire which defended and enlightened Israel in the desert. Compare Elisha in Dothan (2Ki 6:17). As God is to be her 'glory,' so she shall be His 'glory' (Isa 62:3).

6. flee from the land of the north – that is, from Babylon: a type of the various Gentile lands, from which the Jews are to be recalled hereafter; hence 'the four winds of heaven' are specified, implying that they are to return from all quarters (De 28:64 Jer 16:15 Eze 17:21). The reason why they should flee from Babylon is: (1) because of the blessings promised to God's people in their own land; (2) because of the evils about to fall on their foe (Zec 2:7-9). Babylon was soon to fall before Darius, and its inhabitants to endure fearful calamities (Isa 48:20 Jer 50:8 51:6,45). Many of the Jews in Zechariah's time had not yet returned to Judea. Their tardiness was owing to (1) unbelief; (2) their land had long lain waste, and was surrounded with bitter foes; (3) they regarded suspiciously the liberty of return given by Cyrus and Darius, as if these monarchs designed suddenly to crush them; (4) their long stay in Babylon had obliterated the remembrance of their own land; (5) the wealth and security there contrasted with Judea, where their temple and city were in ruins. All this betrayed foul ingratitude and disregard of God's extraordinary favour, which is infinitely to be preferred to all the wealth of the world [CALVIN and PEMBELLUS].

for I have spread you abroad – The reasoning is: I who scattered you from your land to all quarters, can also gather you again to it.

7. O Zion … daughter of Babylon – Thou whose only sure dwelling is 'Zion,' inseparably connected with the temple, art altogether out of thy place in 'dwelling with the daughter of Babylon' (that is, Babylon and her people, Ps 137:8 Isa 1:8).

After the glory – *After* restoring the 'glory' (Zec 2:5 Isa 4:5 Ro 9:4) of Jehovah's presence to Jerusalem, He (God the Father) hath commissioned ME (God the Son, Isa 48:16, the Divine Angel: God thus being at once the Sender and the Sent) to visit in wrath 'the nations which spoiled you.' Messiah's twofold office from the Father is: (1) to glorify His Church; (2) to punish His foes (2Th 1:7–10). Both offices manifest His *glory* (Pr 16:4).

toucheth … the apple of his eye – namely, of Jehovah's eye (De 32:10 Ps 17:8 Pr 7:2). The pupil, or aperture, through which rays pass to the retina, is the tenderest part of the eye; the member which we most sedulously guard from hurt as being the dearest of our members; the one which feels most acutely the slightest injury, and the loss of which is irreparable.

9. shake … hand – A mere wave of God's hand can prostrate all foes (compare Ru 1:13 Job 31:21 Isa 11:15 19:16 Ac 13:11).

a spoil to their servants – to the Jews whom they had once as their slaves (compare Isa 14:2). As the Jews' state between the return from Babylon and Christ's coming was checkered with much adversity, this prophecy can only have its fulfilment under Christ.

sent me – (Isa 48:16 61:1 Joh 10:36).

10. I will dwell in … midst of thee – primarily at Messiah's first advent (Ps 40:7 Joh 1:14 Col 2:9 1Ti 3:16); more fully at His second advent (Isa 40:10). So Zec 9:9, where see on Zec 9:9 (Isa 12:6 Eze 37:27 Zep 3:14). Meanwhile God dwells spiritually in His people (2Co 6:16).

11. many nations … joined to the Lord in that day – The result of the Jews' exile in Babylon was that, at their subsequent return, through the diffusion of knowledge of their religion, many Gentiles became proselytes, worshipping in the court of the Gentiles (1Ki 8:41). Cyrus, Darius, Alexander, Ptolemy Philadelphus, Augustus, and Tiberius, paid respect to the temple by sending offerings [GROTIUS]. But all this is but a shadow of the future conversion of the Gentiles which shall result from Jehovah dwelling in Jerusalem (Ps 102:15,16 Php 2:10,11).

sent me unto thee – 'unto thee' is here added to the same formula (Zec 2:9). Zion first shall 'know (generally) that Jehovah of hosts hath sent' Messiah, by the judgments inflicted by Him on her foes. Subsequently, she shall know experimentally the particular *sending* of Messiah *unto her*. Jehovah here says, 'I will dwell,' and then that JEHOVAH of hosts sent Him; therefore Jehovah the Sender and Jehovah the Sent must be One.

12. Judah his portion in the holy land – Lest the joining of the Gentile 'nations to Jehovah' (Zec 2:11) should lead the Jews to fear that their peculiar relation to Him (De 4:20 9:29 32:9) as 'His inheritance' should cease, this verse is added to assure them of His making them so hereafter 'again.'

choose Jerusalem again – The course of God's grace was interrupted for a time, but His covenant was not set aside (Ro 11:28,29); the election was once for all, and therefore shall hold good for ever.

13. Be silent, O all flesh – (Hab 2:20). 'Let all in silent awe and reverence await the Lord's coming interposition in behalf of His people!' The address is both to the Gentile foes, who prided themselves on their power as if irresistible, and to the unbelieving Jews, who distrusted God's promises as incredible. Three reasons why they must be silent are implied: (1) they are but 'flesh,' weak and ignorant; (2) He is JEHOVAH, all-wise and all-powerful; (3) He is already 'raised up out of His place,' and who can stand before Him? [PEMBELLUS], (Ps 76:8,9).

he is raised up out of his holy habitation – that is, out of *heaven* (De 26:15 2Ch 30:27 Isa

843

63:15), to judge and avenge His people (Isa 26:21); or, 'out of His holy' *temple,* contemptible and incomplete as it looked then when Zechariah urged them to rebuild it [CALVIN]. But the call to all to 'be silent' is rather when God has come forth from heaven where so long He has dwelt unseen, and is about to inflict vengeance on the foe, *before* taking up His dwelling in Zion and the temple. However, Ps 50:1,2 ('Out of Zion'), Ps 50:3 (compare Hab 2:3), Ps 50:4, favours CALVIN's view. God is now 'silent' while the Gentile foe speaks arrogance against His people; but 'our God shall come and *no longer keep silence*'; then in turn must all flesh 'be silent' before Him.

Chapter 3

Zec 3:1–10. FOURTH VISION. Joshua the high priest before the angel of Jehovah; accused by Satan, but justified by Jehovah through Messiah the coming Branch.

1. Joshua as high priest (Hag 1:1) represents 'Jerusalem' (Zec 3:2), or the elect people, put on its trial, and 'plucked' narrowly 'out of the fire.' His attitude, 'standing before the Lord,' is that of a high priest ministering before the altar erected previously to the building of the temple (Ezr 3:2,3,6 Ps 135:2). Yet, in this position, by reason of his own and his people's sins, he is represented as on his and their trial (Nu 35:12).

he showed me – 'He' is *the interpreting angel.* Jerusalem's (Joshua's) 'filthy garments' (Zec 3:3) are its sins which had hitherto brought down God's judgments. The 'change of raiment' implies its restoration to God's favour. Satan suggested to the Jews that so consciously polluted a priesthood and people could offer no acceptable sacrifice to God, and therefore they might as well desist from the building of the temple. Zechariah encourages them by showing that their demerit does not disqualify them for the work, as they are accepted in the righteousness of another, their great High Priest, the Branch (Zec 3:8), a scion of their own royal line of David (Isa 11:1). The full accomplishment of Israel's justification and of Satan the accuser's being 'rebuked' finally, is yet future (Re 12:10). Compare Re 11:8, wherein 'Jerusalem,' as here, is shown to be meant primarily, though including the whole Church in general (compare Job 1:9).

Satan – the *Hebrew* term meaning 'adversary' in a law court: as *devil* is the *Greek* term, meaning *accuser.* Messiah, on the other hand, is 'advocate' for His people in the court of heaven's justice (1Jo 2:1).

standing at his right hand – the usual position of a *prosecutor* or *accuser* in court, as the left hand was the position of the defendant (Ps 109:6). The 'angel of the Lord' took the same position just

before another high priest was about to beget the forerunner of Messiah (Lu 1:11), who supplants Satan from his place as accuser. Some hence explain Jude 1:9 as referring to this passage: 'the body of Moses' being thus *the Jewish Church,* for which Satan contended as his by reason of its sins; just as the 'body of Christ' is *the Christian Church.* However, Jude 1:9 plainly speaks of the literal body of Moses, the resurrection of which at the transfiguration Satan seems to have opposed on the ground of Moses' error at Meribah; the same divine rebuke, 'the Lord rebuke thee,' checked Satan in contending for judgment against Moses' body, as checked him when demanding judgment against the Jewish Church, to which Moses' body corresponds.

2. the Lord – JEHOVAH, hereby identified with the 'angel of the Lord (Jehovah)' (Zec 3:1).

rebuke thee – twice repeated to express the certainty of Satan's accusations and machinations against Jerusalem being frustrated. Instead of lengthened argument, Jehovah *silences* Satan by the one plea, namely, God's *choice.*

chosen Jerusalem – (Ro 9:16 11:5). The conclusive answer. If the issue rested on Jerusalem's merit or demerit, condemnation must be the award; but Jehovah's 'choice' (Joh 15:16) rebuts Satan's charge against Jerusalem (Zec 1:17 2:12 Ro 8:33,34,37), represented by Joshua (compare in the great atonement, Le 16:6–20.), not that she may continue in sin, but to be freed from it (Zec 3:7).

brand plucked out of … fire – (Am 4:11 1Pe 4:18 Jude 1:23). Herein God implies that His acquittal of Jerusalem is not that He does not recognize her sin (Zec 3:3,4,9), but that having punished her people for it with a seventy years' captivity, He on the ground of His *electing* love has delivered her from the fiery ordeal; and when once He has begun a deliverance, as in this case, He will perfect it (Ps 89:30–35 Php 1:6).

3. filthy garments – symbol of sin (Pr 30:12; Isa 4:4 64:6); proving that it is not on the ground of His people's righteousness that He accepts them. Here primarily the 'filthy garments' represent the abject state temporally of the priesthood and people at the return from Babylon. Yet he 'stood before the angel.' Abject as he was, he was *before Jehovah's eye,* who graciously accepts His people's services, though mixed with sin and infirmity.

4. those that stood before him – the ministering angels (compare the phrase in 1Ki 10:8 Da 1:5).

Take away the filthy garments – In Zec 3:9 it is 'remove the iniquity of *that land*'; therefore Joshua represents the land.

from him – literally, 'from upon him'; pressing upon him as an overwhelming burden.

change of raiment – festal robes of the high priest, most costly and gorgeous; symbol of

Messiah's imputed righteousness (Mt 22:11). The restoration of the glory of the priesthood is implied: first, partially, at the completion of the second temple; fully realized in the great High Priest *Jesus,* whose name is identical with *Joshua* (Heb 4:8), the Representative of Israel, the 'kingdom of priests' (Ex 19:6); once clad in the filthy garments of our vileness, but being the chosen of the Father (Isa 42:1 44:1 49:1–3), He hath by death ceased from sin, and in garments of glory entered the heavenly holy place as our High Priest (Heb 8:1 9:24). Then, as the consequence (1Pe 2:5), realized in the Church generally (Lu 15:22 Re 19:8), and in Israel in particular (Isa 61:10; compare Isa 3:6 66:21).

5. And I said – Here the prophet, rejoicing at the change of raiment so far made, interposes to ask for the crowning assurance that the priesthood would be fully restored, namely, the putting *the mitre* or priestly turban on Joshua: its *fair* Collor symbolizing the official purity of the order restored.

angel of … Lord stood by – the Divine Angel had been sitting (the posture of a judge, Da 7:9); now He 'stands' to see that Zechariah's prayer be executed, and then to give the charge (Zec 3:6,7).

6. protested – proceeded *solemnly to declare.* A forensic term for an affirmation on oath (Heb 6:17,18). God thus solemnly states the end for which the priesthood is restored to the people, His own glory in their obedience and pure worship, and their consequent promotion to heavenly honour.

7. God's *choice* of Jerusalem (Zec 3:2) was unto its sanctification (Joh 15:16 Ro 8:29); hence the charge here which connects the promised blessing with obedience.

my charge – the ordinances, ritual and moral (Nu 3:28,31,32,38 Jos 1:7–9 1Ki 2:3 Eze 44:16).

judge my house – Thou shalt long preside over the temple ceremonial as high priest (Le 10:10 Eze 44:23 Mal 2:7) [Grotius]. Or, rule over My house, that is, My people [Maurer] (Nu 12:7 Ho 8:1). We know from De 17:9 that the priest judged cases. He was not only to obey the Mosaic institute himself, but to see that it was obeyed by others. God's people are similarly to exercise judgment hereafter, as the reward of their present faithfulness (Da 7:18,22 Lu 19:17 1Co 6:2); by virtue of their royal priesthood (Re 1:6).

keep my courts – guard My house from profanation.

places to walk – free ingress and egress (1Sa 18:16 1Ki 3:7 15:17), so that thou mayest go through these ministering angels who stand by Jehovah (Zec 4:14 6:5 1Ki 22:19) into His presence, discharging thy priestly function. In Eze 42:4 the same *Hebrew* word is used of a *walk* before the priests' chambers in the future temple.

Zechariah probably refers here to such a *walk* or *way;* Thou shalt not merely walk among priests like thyself, as in the old temple *walks,* but among the very angels as thine associates. Priests are called *angels* or 'messengers' (Mal 2:7); they are therefore thought worthy to be associated with heavenly angels. So these latter are present at the assemblies of true Christian worshippers (1Co 11:10; compare Ec 5:6 Eph 3:10 Re 22:9).

8. Hear – On account of the magnitude of what He is about to say, He at once demands solemn attention.

thy fellows that sit before thee – thy subordinate colleagues in the priesthood; not that they were actually then *sitting before him;* but their usual posture in consultations was on chairs or benches before him, while he sat on an elevated seat as their president.

they are – From speaking to Joshua He passes to speaking *of him and them,* in the third person, to the attendant angels (compare Zec 3:9).

men wondered at – *Hebrew,* 'men of wonder,' that is, having a typical character (Isa 8:18 20:3 Eze 12:11 24:24). Joshua the high priest typifies Messiah, as Joshua's 'fellows' typify believers whom Messiah admits to share His Priesthood (1Pe 2:5 Re 5:10). This, its typical character, then, is a pledge to assure the desponding Jews that the priesthood shall be preserved till the great Antitype comes. There may be also an indirect reproof of the unbelief of the multitude who 'wonder' at God's servants and even at God's Son incredulously (Ps 71:7 Isa 8:18 53:1.).

behold – marking the greatness of what follows.

my servant – the characteristic title of Messiah (Isa 42:1 49:3 50:10 52:13 53:11 Eze 34:23,24).

the Branch – Messiah, a tender branch from the almost extinct royal line of David (Zec 6:12 Isa 4:2 11:1 Jer 23:5 33:15). Lu 1:78, where for 'day spring,' 'branch' may be substituted.

9. For – expressing the ground for encouragement to the Jews in building the temple: I (Jehovah) have laid the (foundation) stone as the chief architect, before (in the presence of) Joshua, by 'the hand of Zerubbabel' (Zec 4:10 Ezr 3:8–13), so that your labour in building shall not be vain. Antitypically, the (foundation) stone alluded to is Christ, before called 'the Branch.' Lest any should think from that term that His kingdom is weak, He now calls it 'the stone,' because of its solidity and strength whereby it is to be the foundation of the Church, and shall crush all the world kingdoms (Ps 118:22; compare Isa 28:16 Da 2:45 Mt 21:42 1Co 3:11 1Pe 2:6,7). The angel pointing to the chief stone lying before Him, intimates that a deeper mystery than the material temple is symbolized. Moore thinks the 'stone' is *the Jewish Church,* which Jehovah engages watchfully to guard. *The* *temple,* rather, is that symbolically. But the anti-type of the foundation-*stone* is Messiah.

upon one stone shall be seven eyes – namely, the watchful 'eyes' of Jehovah's care ever fixed 'upon' it (Zec 4:10) [MAURER]. The eye is the symbol of *Providence:* 'seven,' of *perfection* (Re 5:6; compare 2Ch 16:9 Ps 32:8). Antitypically, 'the seven eyes upon the stone' are the eyes of all angels (1Ti 3:16), and of all saints (Joh 3:14,15 12:32), and of the patriarchs and prophets (Joh 8:56 1Pe 1:10,11), fixed on Christ; above all, the eyes of the Father ever rest with delight on Him. CALVIN (perhaps better) considers *the seven eyes* to be *carved on the stone,* that is, not the eyes of the Father and of angels and saints ever *fixed* on Him, but His *own* sevenfold (perfect) fullness of grace, and of gifts of the Spirit (Isa 11:2,3 Joh 1:16 3:34 Col 1:19 2:9), and *His* watchful providence now for the Jews in building the temple, and always for His Church, His spiritual temple. Thus the 'stone' is not as other stones senseless, but *living* and full of eyes of perfect intelligence (1Pe 2:4, 'a *living* stone'), who not only attracts the eyes (Joh 12:32) of His people, but emits illumination so as to direct them to Him.

engrave … graving – implying Messiah's exceeding beauty and preciousness; alluding to the polished stones of the temple: Christ excelled them, as much as God who 'prepared His body' (Heb 10:5; compare Joh 2:21) is superior to all human builders.

remove … iniquity of that land in one day – that is, the iniquity and its consequences, namely the punishment to which the Jews heretofore had been subjected (Hag 1:6,9–11). The remission of sin is the fountain of every other blessing. The 'one day' of its *removal* is primarily the day of national atonement celebrated after the completion of the temple (Le 23:27) on the tenth day of the seventh month. Antitypically, the atonement by Messiah for all men, *once for all* ('one day') offered, needing no repetition like the Mosaic sacrifices (Heb 10:10,12,14).

10. under … vine … fig tree – emblem of tranquil prosperity (1Ki 4:25). Type of spiritual *peace* with God through Christ (Ro 5:1); and of millennial blessedness (Mic 4:4).

Chapter 4

Zec 4:1–14. FIFTH VISION. The golden candlestick and the two olive trees. The temple shall be completed by the aid of God's Spirit.

1. waked me – The prophet was lying in a state of ecstatic slumber with astonishment at the previous vision. 'Came again, and waked me,' does not imply that the angel had departed and now returned, but is an idiom for 'waked me again.'

2. candlestick – symbolizing the Jewish theocracy; and ultimately, the Church of which the Jewish portion is to be the head: the *light-bearer* (so the original is of 'lights,' Mt 5:14,16 Php 2:15) to the world.

all … gold – all pure in doctrine and practice, precious and indestructible; such is the true ideal of the Church; such she shall be (Ps 45:13).

bowl upon the top – In the candlestick of the tabernacle the *plural* is used, *bowls* (Ex 25:1–31:18). The *Hebrew* implies that it was the *fountain* of supply of oil to the lamps. Christ at the head ('on the top') of the Church is the true fountain, *of* whose *fulness of the Spirit all we receive grace* (Joh 1:16).

his seven lamps – united in one stem; so in Ex 25:32. But in Re 1:12 the seven candlesticks are separate. The Gentile churches will not realize their unity till the Jewish Church as the stem unites all the lamps in one candlestick (Ro 11:16–24). The 'seven lamps,' in Re 4:5, are the 'seven Spirits of God.'

seven pipes – feeding tubes, seven apiece from the 'bowl' to each lamp (see *Margin*) [MAURER and CALVIN]; literally, 'seven and seven': forty-nine in all. The greater the number of oil-feeding pipes, the brighter the light of the lamps. The explanation in Zec 4:6 is, that man's power by itself can neither retard nor advance God's work, that the real motive-power is God's *Spirit.* The seven times seven imply the manifold modes by which the Spirit's grace is imparted to the Church in her manifold work of enlightening the world.

3. two olive trees – supplying oil to the bowl. The Holy Ghost, who fills with His fulness Messiah (the *anointed:* the 'bowl'), from whom flow supplies of grace to the Church.

by it – literally, 'upon it,' that is, growing so as somewhat to overtop it. For the explanation of the 'two' see Zec 4:12,14.

4. The prophet is instructed in the truths meant, that we may read them with the greater reverence and attention [CALVIN].

5. Knowest thou not. – Not a reproof of his ignorance, but a stimulus to reflection on the mystery.

No, my lord – ingenious confession of ignorance; as a little child he casts himself for instruction at the feet of the Lord.

6. Not by might … but by my Spirit – As the lamps burned continually, supplied with oil from a source (the living olive trees) which man did not make, so Zerubbabel need not be disheartened because of his weakness; for as the work is one to be effected by the living Spirit (compare Hag 2:5) of God, man's weakness is no obstacle, for God's might will perfect strength out of weakness (Ho 1:7 2Co 12:10 Heb 11:34). 'Might and power' express human strength of every description, physical, mental, moral. Or, 'might' is the strength *of many* (an 'army'); 'power,' that *of one man* [PEMBELLUS] God can save, 'whether with many, or with them that have no power' (2Ch 14:11; compare 1Sa 14:6). So in the conversion of sinners (1Co 3:6 2Co 10:4). 'Zerubbabel' is addressed as the chief civil authority in directing the work.

7. All *mountain*-like obstacles (Isa 40:4 49:11) in *Zerubbabel's* way shall be removed, so that the crowning top-stone shall be put on, and the completion of the work be acknowledged as wholly of 'grace.' Antitypically, the antichristian last foe of Israel, the obstacle preventing her establishment in Palestine, about to be crushed before Messiah, is probably meant (Jer 51:25 Da 2:34,44 Mt 21:44).

bring forth the headstone – Primarily, bring it forth from the place where it was chiselled and give it to the workmen to put on the top of the building. It was customary for chief magistrates to lay the foundation, and also the crowning top-stone (compare Ezr 3:10). Antitypically, the reference is to the time when the full number of the spiritual Church shall be completed, and also when 'all Israel shall be saved' (compare Ro 11:26 Heb 11:40 12:22,23 Re 7:4–9).

Grace, grace – The repetition expresses, *Grace* from first to last (Isa 26:3, *Margin*). Thus the Jews are urged to pray perseveringly and earnestly that the same grace which completed it may always preserve it. 'Shoutings' of acclamation accompanied the foundation of the literal temple (Ezr 3:11,13). So shoutings of 'Hosanna' greeted the Saviour in entering Jerusalem (Mt 21:9), when about to complete the purchase of salvation by His death: His Body being the second temple, or place of God's inhabitation (Joh 2:20,21). So when the full number of the saints and of Israel is complete, and God shall say, 'It is done,' then again shall 'a great voice of much people in heaven' attribute all to the 'grace' of God, saying, 'Alleluia! Salvation, and glory, and honour, and power, unto the Lord our God' (Re 19:1,6). Ps 118:22 regards Him as 'the headstone of the corner,' that is, the *foundation*-stone. Compare the angels acclamations at His birth, Lu 2:14. Here it is the *top-stone*. Messiah is not only the 'Author,' but also the Finisher (Heb 12:2). 'Grace' is ascribed 'unto it,' that is, the stone, Messiah. Hence the benediction begins, 'The *grace* of the Lord Jesus Christ' (2Co 13:14).

9. Zerubbabel ... shall ... finish it – (Ezr 6:15) in the sixth year of Darius' reign.

Lord ... sent me unto you – (Zec 2:9). The Divine Angel announces that in what He has just spoken, He has been commissioned by God the Father.

10. who ... despised ... small things – He reproves their ungrateful unbelief, which they felt because of the humble beginning, compared with the greatness of the undertaking; and encourages them with the assurance that their progress in the work, though small, was an earnest of great and final success, because Jehovah's eye is upon Zerubbabel and the work, to support Him with His favour. Contrast, 'great is *the day* of Jezreel' (Ho 1:11) with 'the day of *small* things' here.

they shall rejoice ... with those seven; they *are* the eyes of the Lord – rather, 'they, *even* those seven eyes of the Lord (compare Zec 3:9), which ... shall rejoice and see (that is, rejoicingly see) the plummet (literally, the "stone of tin") in the hand of Zerubbabel' [MOORE]; the plummet in his hand indicating that the work is going forward to its completion. The *Hebrew* punctuation, however, favours *English Version*, of which the sense is, They who incredulously 'despised' such 'small' beginnings of the work as are made now, shall rejoicingly see it going on to completion under Zerubbabel, 'with (*the aid of*) those seven,' namely, the 'seven eyes upon one stone' (Zec 3:9): which are explained, 'They are the eyes of the Lord which,' [PEMBELLUS]. So differently do men and Jehovah regard the 'small' beginnings of God's work (Ezr 3:12 Hag 2:3). Men 'despised' the work in its early stage: God rejoicingly regards it, and shall continue to do so.

run to and fro. – Nothing in the whole earth escapes the eye of Jehovah, so that He can ward off all danger from His people, come from what quarter it may, in prosecuting His work (Pr 15:3 1Co 16:9).

11, 12. Zechariah three times (Zec 4:4,11,12) asks as to the two olives before he gets an answer; the question becomes more minute each time. What he at first calls 'two olive trees,' he afterwards calls 'branches,' as on closer looking he observes that the 'branches' of the trees are the channels through which a continual flow of oil dropped into the bowl of the lamps (Zec 4:2), and that this is the purpose for which the two olive trees stand beside the candlestick. Primarily, the 'two' refer to Joshua and Zerubbabel. God, says AUBERLEN, at each of the transition periods of the world's history has sent great men to guide the Church. So the two witnesses shall appear before the destruction of Antichrist. Antitypically, 'the two anointed ones' (Zec 4:14) are the twofold supports of the Church, the civil power (answering to Zerubbabel) and the ecclesiastical (answering to Joshua, the high priest), which in the restored Jewish polity and temple shall 'stand by,' that is, minister to 'the Lord of the whole earth,' as He shall be called in the day that He sets up His throne in Jerusalem (Zec 14:9 Da 2:44 Re 11:15). Compare the description of the offices of the 'priests' and the 'prince' (Isa 49:23 Eze 44:1–46:24). As in Re 11:3,4, the 'two witnesses' are identified with the two olive trees and the two candlesticks. WORDSWORTH explains them to mean the Law and the Gospel: the two Testaments that *witness* in the Church for the truth of God. But this is at variance with the sense here, which requires Joshua and Zerubbabel to be primarily meant. So Moses (the prophet and lawgiver) and Aaron (the high priest) ministered to the Lord among the covenant-people at the exodus; Ezekiel (the priest) and Daniel (a ruler) in the Babylonian captivity; so it shall be in restored Israel. Some think Elijah will appear again (compare the transfiguration, Mt 17:3,11, with Mal 4:4,5 Joh 1:21) with Moses. Re 11:6, which mentions the very miracles performed by Elijah and Moses (shutting heaven so as not to rain, and turning water into blood), favours this (compare Ex 7:19 1Ki 17:1 Lu 4:25 Jas 5:16,17). The period is the same, 'three years and six months'; the scene also is in Israel (Re 11:8), 'where our Lord was crucified.' It is supposed that for the first three and a half years of the hebdomad (Da 9:20–27), God will be worshipped in the temple; in the latter three and a half years, Antichrist will break the covenant (Da 9:27), and set himself up in the temple to be worshipped as God (2Th 2:4). The witnesses prophesy the former three and a half years, while corruptions prevail and faith is rare (Lu 18:8); then they are slain and remain dead three and a half years. Probably, besides individual witnesses and literal years, there is a fulfilment in long periods and general witnesses, such as the Church and the Word, the civil and religious powers so far as they have witnessed for God. So 'the beast' in Revelation answers to the civil power of the apostasy; 'the false prophet' to the spiritual power. Man needs the *priest* to atone for guilt, and the *prophet-king* to teach holiness with kingly authority. These two typically united in Melchisedek were divided between two till they meet in Messiah, the Antitype. Zec 6:11–13 accords with this. The Holy Spirit in this His twofold power of applying to man the grace of the *atonement,* and that of *sanctification,* must in one point of view be meant by the two olive trees which supply the bowl at the top of the candlestick (that is, Messiah at the head of the Church); for it is He who filled Jesus with all the fulness of His unction (Joh 3:34). But this does not exclude the primary application to *Joshua and Zerubbabel,* 'anointed' (Zec 4:14) with grace to minister to the Jewish Church: and so applicable to the twofold supports of the Church which are anointed with the Spirit, the *prince* and the *priest,* or *minister.*

12. through – literally, 'by the hand of,' that is, by the agency of.

branches – literally, 'ears'; so the olive branches are called, because as ears are full of grain, so the olive branches are full of olives.

golden *oil* – literally, 'gold,' that is, gold-like liquor.

out of themselves – Ordinances and ministers are channels of grace, not the grace itself. The supply comes not from a dead reservoir of oil, but through living olive trees (Ps 52:8 Ro 12:1) fed by God.

13. Knowest thou not – God would awaken His people to zeal in learning His truth.

14. anointed ones – literally, 'sons of oil' (Isa 5:1, *Margin*). Joshua the high priest, and Zerubbabel the civil ruler, must first be anointed with grace themselves, so as to be the instruments of furnishing it to others (compare 1Jo 2:20,27).

Chapter 5

Zec 5:1–4. SIXTH VISION. THE FLYING ROLL. The fraudulent and perjuring transgressors of the law shall be extirpated from Judea.

1. flying roll – of papyrus, or dressed skins, used for writing on when paper was not known. It was inscribed with the words of the curse (De 27:15-26 28:15–68). Being written implied that its contents were beyond all escape or repeal (Eze 2:9). Its 'flying' shows that its curses were ready swiftly to visit the transgressors. It was unrolled, or else its dimensions could not have been seen (Zec 5:2). Being open to all, none could say in excuse he knew not the law and the curses of disobedience. As the previous visions intimated God's favour in restoring the Jewish state, so this vision announces judgment, intimating that God, notwithstanding His favour, did not approve of their sins. Being written on both sides, 'on this and on that side' (Zec 5:3), VATABLUS connects it with the two tables of the law (Ex 32:15), and implies its comprehensiveness. One side denounced 'him that sweareth falsely (Zec 5:4) by God's name,' according to the third commandment of *the first table,* duty to God; the other side denounced *theft,* according to the eighth commandment, which is in *the second table,* duty to one's neighbours.

2. length ... twenty cubits ... breadth ... ten cubits – thirty feet by fifteen, the dimensions of the temple porch (1Ki 6:3), where the law was usually read, showing that it was divinely authoritative in the theocracy. Its large size implies the great number of the curses contained. The *Hebrew* for 'roll' or 'volume' is used of the law (Ps 40:7).

3. curse ... earth – (Mal 4:6). The Gentiles are amenable to the curse of the law, as they have its substance, so far as they have not seared and corrupted conscience, written on their hearts (Ro 2:15).

cut off – literally, 'cleared away.'

as on this side … as on that side – both sides of the *roll* [Vatablus]. From this place … from this place (repeated twice, as 'the house' is repeated in Zec 5:4) [Moore]; so 'hence' is used, Ge 37:17 (or, 'on this and on that side,' that is, *on every side*) [Henderson]. None can escape, sin where he may: for God from one side to the other shall call all without exception to judgment [Calvin]. God will not spare even 'this place,' Jerusalem, when it sins [Pembellus].

according to it – according as it is written.

4. The 'theft' immediately meant is similar sacrilege to that complained of in Ne 13:10 Mal 3:8. They robbed God by neglecting to give Him His due in building His house, while they built their own houses, forswearing their obligations to Him; therefore, the 'houses' they build shall be 'consumed' with God's 'curse.' Probably literal theft and perjury accompanied their virtual theft and perjury as to the temple of God (Mal 3:5). Stealing and perjury go together; for the covetous and fraudulent perjure themselves by God's name without scruple (see Pr 30:9).

enter … the house – In vain they guard and shut themselves up who incur the curse; it will inevitably enter even when they think themselves most secure.

consume … timber … stones – not leaving a vestige of it. So the 'stones' and 'timber' of the house of a leper (type of the sinner) were to be utterly removed (Le 14:15; compare 1Ki 18:38).

Zec 5:5–11. Seventh Vision. The Woman in the Ephah. Wickedness and idolatry removed from the Holy Land to Babylon, there to mingle with their kindred elements.

The 'ephah' is the Hebrew dry measure containing about thirty-seven quarts. Alluding to the previous vision as to theft and perjury: the ephah which, by falsification of the measure, they made the instrument of defrauding, shall be made the instrument of their punishment [Grotius]. Compare 'this is their resemblance' (Zec 5:6), that is, this is a representation of what the Jews have done, and what they shall suffer. Their total dispersion ('the land of Shinar' being the emblem of the various Gentile lands of their present dispersion) is herein foretold, when the *measure* (to which the ephah alludes) of their sins should be full. The former vision denounces judgment on individuals; this one, on the whole state: but enigmatically, not to discourage their present building [Pembellus]. Rather, the vision is consolatory after the preceding one [Calvin]. Idolatry and its kindred sins, covetousness and fraud (denounced in the vision of the roll), shall be removed far out of the Holy Land to their own congenial soil, never

to return (so Zec 3:9 Isa 27:9 52:1 60:21 Jer 50:20 Zep 3:13). For more than two thousand years, ever since the Babylonian exile, the Jews have been free from *idolatry;* but the full accomplishment of the prophecy is yet future, when *all* sin shall be purged from Israel on their return to Palestine, and conversion to Christ.

5. **went forth** – The interpreting angel had withdrawn after the vision of the roll to receive a fresh revelation from the Divine Angel to communicate to the prophet.

6. **This is their resemblance** – literally, 'eye' (compare Eze 1:4,5,16).

This – Here used of what was *within* the ephah, not the ephah itself.

7. **lifted up** – The cover is lifted off the ephah to let the prophet see the female personification of 'wickedness' within, about to be removed from Judea. The cover being 'of lead,' implies that the 'woman' cannot escape from the ponderous load which presses her down.

talent – literally, 'a round piece': hence a talent, a weight of one hundred twenty-five pounds troy.

woman – for comparison of 'wickedness' to a *woman,* Pr 2:16 5:3,4. In personifying abstract terms, the feminine is used, as the idea of giving birth to life is associated with woman.

8. **wickedness** – literally, '*the* wickedness': implying wickedness in its peculiar development. Compare '*the* man of sin,' 2Th 2:3.

cast it – that is, her, Wickedness, who had moved more freely while the heavy lid was partially lifted off.

weight – literally, 'stone,' that is, round mass.

9. The agents to carry away the 'woman,' are, consistently with the image, 'women.' God makes the wicked themselves the agents of punishing and removing wickedness. 'Two' are employed, as one is not enough to carry such a load [Maurer]. Or, the Assyrians and Babylonians, who carried away idolatry in the persons, respectively, of Israel and Judah [Henderson]. As two 'anointed ones' (Zec 4:14) stand by the Lord as His ministers, so *two* winged women execute His purpose here in removing the embodiment of 'wickedness': answering to the 'mystery of iniquity' (the *Septuagint* here in Zechariah uses the same words as Paul and 'the man of sin,' whom the Lord shall destroy with the spirit of His mouth and the brightness of His coming, 2Th 2:3,7,8). Their 'wings' express velocity. The 'stork' has long and wide wings, for which reason it is specified; also it is a migratory bird. The 'wind' helps the rapid motion of the wings. The being 'lifted up between heaven and earth' implies open execution of the judgment before the eyes of all. As the 'woman' here is removed to Babylon as her own dwelling, so the woman in the Apocalypse of St. John is Babylon (Re 17:3–5).

11. To build … house in … Shinar – Babylonia (Ge 10:10), the capital of the God-opposed world kingdoms, and so representing in general the seat of irreligion. As the 'building of houses' in Babylon (Jer 29:5,28) by the Jews themselves expressed their long exile there, so the building of an house for 'wickedness' there implies its permanent stay.

set … upon her own base – fixed there as in its proper place. 'Wickedness' being cast out of Judah, shall for ever dwell with the antichristian apostates (of whom Babylon is the type), who shall reap the fruit of it, which they deserve.

Chapter 6

Zec 6:1–8. Eighth Vision. The Four Chariots.

1. four chariots – symbolizing the various dispensations of Providence towards the Gentile nations which had been more or less brought into contact with Judea; especially in punishing Babylon. Compare Zec 6:8 ('the north country,' that is, Babylon); Zec 1:15 2:6. The number 'four' is specified not merely in reference to the four quarters of the horizon (implying *universal* judgments), but in allusion to the *four* world kingdoms of Daniel.

from between two mountains – the valley of Jehoshaphat, between Moriah and Mount Olivet [Moore]; or the valley between Zion and Moriah, where the Lord is (Zec 2:10), and whence He sends forth His ministers of judgment on the heathen [Maurer]. The temple on Mount Moriah is the symbol of the theocracy; hence the nearest spot accessible to chariots in the valley below is the most suitable for a vision affecting Judah in relation to the Gentile world powers. The chariot is the symbol of war, and so of judgments.

of brass – the metal among the ancients representing hard solidity; so the immovable and resistless firmness of God's people (compare Jer 1:18). Calvin explains the 'two mountains' thus: The secret purpose of God from eternity does not come forth to view before the execution, but is hidden and kept back irresistibly till the fit time, as it were *between* lofty *mountains;* the *chariots* are the various changes wrought in nations, which, as swift heralds, announce to us what before we knew not. The 'two' may thus correspond to the number of the 'olive trees' (Zec 4:3); the *allusion* to the 'two mountains' near the temple is not necessarily excluded in this view. Henderson explains them to be the Medo-Persian kingdom, represented by the 'two horns' (Da 8:3,4), now employed to execute God's purpose in punishing the nations; but the prophecy reaches far beyond those times.

2. red – implying carnage.

black – representing sorrow; also famine (Re 6:5,6; compare Zec 1:8).

3. white – implying joy and victory [Calvin].

grizzled – piebald. Implying a *mixed* dispensation, partly prosperity, partly adversity. All four dispensations, though various in character to the Gentile nation, portended alike good to God's people.

4. The prophet humbly and teachably seeks instruction from God, and therefore seeks not in vain.

5. four spirits of the heavens – heavenly spirits who 'stand before Jehovah' to receive God's commands (Zec 4:14 1Ki 22:19 Job 2:1 Lu 1:19) in heaven (of which Zion is the counterpart on earth, see on Zec 6:1), and proceed with chariot speed (2Ki 6:17 Ps 68:17) to execute them on earth in its four various quarters (Ps 104:4 Heb 1:7,14) [Pembellus]. Or, the secret impulses of God which emanate from His counsel and providence; the prophet implies that all the revolutions in the world are from the Spirit of God and are as it were, His messengers or spirits [Calvin].

6. north country – Babylon. The north is the quarter specified in particular whence Judah and Israel are hereafter to return to their own land (Zec 2:6 Jer 3:18). 'The black horses' go to Babylon, primarily to represent the awful desolation with which Darius visited it in the fifth year of his reign (two years after this prophecy) for revolting [Henderson]. The 'white' go after the 'black' horses to the same country; *two* sets being sent to it because of its greater cruelty and guilt in respect to Judea. The white represent Darius triumphant subjugation of it [Moore]. Rather, I think, the white are sent to victoriously subdue Medo-Persia, the second world kingdom, lying in the same quarter as Babylon, namely, north.

grizzled … toward the south – that is, to Egypt, the other great foe of God's people. It, being a part of the Græco-Macedonian kingdom, stands for the whole of it, the third world kingdom.

7. bay – rather, the 'fleet' (or 'strong'). As the 'red' are not otherwise mentioned, the epithet 'fleet' (as the *Hebrew* for 'bay' ought to be translated) in Zec 6:3 seems to apply to all four, and here especially to the 'red.' Their office is to complete hereafter the work already in part executed by the previous three who have stilled Babylon, Medo-Persia, and Græco-Macedonia; namely, to punish finally the last great foe of Israel, the final form assumed by the fourth world kingdom, Rome, which is to continue down to the second advent of Christ. Hence they 'walk to and fro through the earth,' counterworking Satan's 'going to and fro in the earth' (Job 1:7 2Th 2:8,9 1Ti 4:1), in connection with

the last awful development of the fourth world kingdom. Their 'fleetness' is needed to counteract his restless activity; their red Collor implies the final great carnage (Eze 39:1-29 Re 19:17,18,21).

8. north ... quieted ... my spirit – that is, caused My *anger* to rest (Jud 8:3, *Margin;* Ec 10:4 Eze 5:13 16:42). Babylon alone of the four great world kingdoms had in Zechariah's time been finally punished; therefore, in its case alone does God now say His anger is satisfied; the others had as yet to expiate their sin; the fourth has still to do so.

Zec 6:9–15. Ninth Vision. The Crowning of Joshua.

The double crown is placed on Joshua's head, symbolizing that the true priesthood and the kingdom shall be conferred on the one Messiah. Compare Heb 6:20 7:1-21, on Melchisedek, who similarly combined the kingdom and priesthood as type of Messiah.

10. Take of *them of* **the captivity** – Take *silver and gold* (Zec 6:11) *from* them. The three named came from Babylon (where some of the exiled Jews still were left) to present gifts of silver and gold towards the building of the temple. But in Zec 6:11,14, 'crowns' are directed to be made of them, then to be set on Joshua's head, and to be deposited in the temple as a memorial of the donors, until Messiah shall appear.

Heldai – meaning 'robust.' Called *Helem* below.

Tobijah – that is, 'the goodness of God.'

Jedaiah – that is, 'God knows.'

the same day – No time was to be lost to mark the significance of their coming from afar to offer gifts to the temple, typifying, in the double crown made of their gifts and set on Joshua's head, the gathering in of Israel's outcasts to Messiah hereafter, who shall then be recognized as the true king and priest.

11. The high priest wore a crown above the mitre (Zec 3:5 Le 8:9). Messiah shall wear many *crowns,* one surmounting the other (Re 19:12). It was a thing before unknown in the Levitical priesthood that the same person should wear at once the crown of a king and that of a high priest (Ps 110:4 Heb 5:10). Messiah shall be revealed fully in this twofold dignity when He shall 'restore the kingdom to Israel' (Ac 1:6).

12. Behold, the man – namely, shall arise. Pilate unconsciously spake God's will concerning Him, '*Behold* the man' (Joh 19:5). The sense here is, 'Behold in Joshua a remarkable shadowing forth of Messiah.' It is not for his own sake that the crown is placed on him, but as type of Messiah about to be at once king and priest. Joshua could not personally be crowned king, not being of the royal line of David, but only in his *representative* character.

Branch – (See on Zec 3:8).

he shall grow up out of his place – retaining the image of a 'Branch'; 'He shall sprout up from His place,' that is, the place peculiar to Him: not merely from Beth-lehem or Nazareth, but by His own power, without man's aid, in His miraculous conception [Henderson]; a sense brought out in the original, 'from under Himself,' or 'from (of) Himself' [Calvin]. Moore makes it refer to His growing lowly *in His place* of obscurity, 'as a tender plant and a root out of a dry ground' (Isa 53:2), for thirty years unknown except as the son of a carpenter.

build the temple – The promise of the future true building of the spiritual temple by Messiah (Mt 16:18 1Co 3:17 2Co 6:16 Eph 2:20–22 Heb 3:3) is an earnest to assure the Jews, that the material temple will be built by Joshua and Zerubbabel, in spite of all seeming obstacles. It also raises their thoughts beyond the material to the spiritual temple, and also to the future glorious temple, to be reared in Israel under Messiah's superintendence (Eze 40:1–43:27). The repetition of the same clause (Zec 6:13) gives emphasis to the statement as to Messiah's work.

13. bear the glory – that is, wear the insignia of the kingly glory, 'the crowns' (Ps 21:5 102:16 Isa 52:13). He *himself* shall bear the glory, not thou, Joshua, though thou dost bear the crowns. The Church's dignity is in her head alone, Christ. So Eliakim, type of Messiah, was to have 'all the glory of his father's house hung upon him' (Isa 22:24).

sit – implying security and permanence.

priest ... throne – (Ge 14:18 Ps 110:4 Heb 5:6,10 6:20 7).

counsel of peace ... between ... both – Joshua and Zerubbabel, the religious and civil authorities co-operating in the temple, typify the *peace,* or harmonious union, *between both* the kingly and priestly offices. The kingly majesty shall not depress the priestly dignity, nor the priestly dignity the kingly majesty [Jerome]. The peace of the Church, formerly sought for in the mutual 'counsels' of the kings and the priests, who had been always distinct, shall be perfectly ensured by the concurrence of the two offices in the one Messiah, who by His mediatorial priesthood purchases it, and by His kingly rule maintains it. Vitringa takes '*His* throne' to be Jehovah the Father's. Thus it will be, 'there shall be ... peace between the Branch and Jehovah' [Ludovicus De Dieu]. The other view is better, namely, '*Messiah's* throne.' As Priest He expiates sin; as King, extirpates it. '*Counsel* of peace,' implies that it is the plan of infinite 'wisdom,' whence Messiah is called 'Counsellor' (Isa 9:6 Eph 1:8,11 Heb 6:17). Peace between the kingly and priestly attributes of Messiah implies the harmonizing of the conflicting claims of God's justice as a

King, and His love as a Father and Priest. Hence is produced peace to man (Lu 2:14 Ac 10:36 Eph 2:13–17). It is only by being pardoned through His atonement and ruled by His laws, that we can find 'peace.' The royal 'throne' was always connected with the 'temple,' as is the case in the Apocalypse (Re 7:15), because Christ is to be a king on His throne and a priest, and because the people, whose 'king' the Lord is, cannot approach Him except by a priestly mediation [Roos]. Jesus shall come to effect, by His presence (Isa 11:4 Da 7:17), that which in vain is looked for, in His absence, by other means. He shall exercise His power mediatorially as priest on His throne (Zec 6:13); therefore His reign is for a limited period, which it could not be if it were the final and everlasting state of glory. But being for a special purpose, to reconcile all things in this world, now disordered by sin, and so present it to God the Father that He may again for the first time since the fall come into direct connection with His creatures; therefore it is limited, forming the dispensation in the fulness of times (Eph 1:10), when God shall gather in one all things in Christ, the final end of which shall be, 'God all in all' (1Co 15:24–28).

14. the crowns shall be to Helem ... a memorial – deposited in the temple, to the honour of the donors; a memorial, too, of the coronation of Joshua, to remind all of Messiah, the promised antitypical king-priest, soon to come. Helem, the same as Heldai above. So Hen (that is, 'favour') is another name for Josiah (that is, 'God founds') above. The same person often had two names.

15. they ... far off shall ... build – The reason why the crowns were made of gold received from afar, namely, from the Jews of Babylon, was to typify the conversion of the Gentiles to Messiah, King of Israel. This, too, was included in the 'peace' spoken of in Zec 6:13 (Ac 2:39 Eph 2:12–17). Primarily, however, the return of the dispersed Israelites 'from afar' (Isa 60:9) to the king of the Jews at Jerusalem is intended, to be followed, secondly, by the conversion of the Gentiles from 'far off' (Zec 2:11 8:2–2,23 Isa 60:10 57:19).

build in the temple – Christ 'builds the temple' (Zec 6:12,13 Heb 3:3,4): His people 'build *in* the temple.' Compare Heb 3:2, 'Moses in His house.'

ye shall know – when the event corresponds to the prediction (Zec 2:9 4:9).

this shall come to pass, if ye ... obey – To the Jews of Zechariah's day a stimulus is given to *diligent* prosecution of the temple building, the work which it was meanwhile their duty to fulfil, relying on the hope of the Messiah afterwards to glorify it. The completion of the temple shall 'come to pass,' if ye diligently on your part 'obey the Lord.' It is not meant that their

unbelief could set aside God's gracious purpose as to Messiah's coming. But there is, secondarily, meant, that Messiah's glory as priest-king of Israel shall not be manifested to the Jews till they turn to Him with obedient penitence. They meanwhile are cast away 'branches' until they be grafted in again on the Branch and their own olive tree (Zec 3:8 12:10-12 Mt 23:39 Ro 11:16–24).

Chapter 7

Zec 7:1–14. II. Didactic part, seventh and eighth chapters. Obedience, rather than fasting, enjoined: its reward.

1. fourth year of ... Darius – two years after the previous prophecies (Zec 1:1.).

Chisleu – meaning 'torpidity,' the state in which nature is in November, answering to this month.

2. they ... sent unto ... house of God – *The Jews* of the country sent to the house of God or congregation at Jerusalem. The altar was long since reared (Ezr 3:3), though the temple was not completed till two years afterwards (Ezr 6:15). The priests' duty was to give decision on points of the law (De 17:9 Mt 2:4). *Beth-el* is here used instead of *Beth-Jehovah*, because the religious authorities, rather than the house itself (designated 'Beth-Jehovah' in Zec 7:3), are intended. The old Beth-el had long ceased to be the seat of idol-worship, so that the name had lost its opprobrious meaning. 'The house of the Lord' is used for the congregation of worshippers headed by their priests (Zec 3:7 Ho 8:1).

Sherezer – an Assyrian name meaning, 'Prefect of the treasury.'

Regemmelech – meaning, 'The king's official.' These names perhaps intimate the semi-heathen character of the inquirers, which may also be implied in the name 'Beth-el' (*Hebrew* for 'house of God'), so notorious once for its calf-worship. They sent to *Jehovah's house* as their forefathers sent to old *Beth-el*, not in the spirit of true obedience.

pray before the Lord – literally, 'to entreat the face of,' that is, to offer sacrifices, the accompaniment of prayers, to conciliate His favour (1Sa 13:12).

3. Should I weep in the fifth month – 'I' represents here the people of God (compare Zec 8:21).

to the prophets – Haggai and Zechariah especially. *The tenth day of the fifth month* was kept a fast, being the anniversary of the destruction of Jerusalem (Jer 52:12–14). They ask, Should the fast *be continued*, now that the temple and city are being restored?

separating myself – sanctifying myself by separation, not only from food, but from all defilements (compare Joe 2:16) as was usual in a solemn fast.

5. Speak unto all – The question had been asked in the name of the people in general by Sherezer and Regemmelech. The self-imposed fast they were tired of, not having observed it in the spirit of true religion.

seventh month – This fast was in memory of the murder of Gedaliah and those with him at Mizpah, issuing in the dispersion of the Jews (2Ki 25:25,26 Jer 41:1–3).

did ye … fast unto me? – No; it was to gratify yourselves in hypocritical will-worship. If it had been 'unto *Me*,' ye would have 'separated yourselves' not only from food, but from your sins (Isa 58:3-7). They falsely made the fast an end intrinsically meritorious in itself, not a means towards God's glory in their sanctification. The true principle of piety, *reference to God*, was wanting: hence the emphatic repetition of 'unto Me.' Before settling questions as to the outward forms of piety (however proper, as in this case), the great question was as to piety itself; that being once settled, all their outward observances become sanctified, being 'unto the Lord' (Ro 14:6).

6. did not ye eat *for yourselves?* – literally, 'Is it not *ye* who eat?' that is, it is not unto Me and My glory. It tends no more to My glory, your feasting than your fasting.

7. *Should ye* not *hear* the words – rather, 'Should *ye* not *do* the words,' as their question naturally was as to what they should do (Zec 7:3); 'hearing' is not mentioned till Zec 7:12. The sense is, It is not fasts that Jehovah requires of you, but that ye should keep His precepts given to you at the time when Jerusalem was in its integrity. Had ye done so then, ye would have had no occasion to institute fasts to commemorate its destruction, for it would never have been destroyed (Zec 7:9–14) [MAURER].

the plain – southwest of Jerusalem. They then inhabited securely the region most unguarded.

9. speaketh – implying that these precepts addressed to their ancestors were the requirements of Jehovah not merely then, but *now*. We must not only not hurt, but we must help our fellow men. God is pleased with such loving obedience, rather than with empty ceremonies.

10. imagine evil – that is, devise evil. The *Septuagint* takes it, Harbor not the desire of revenge (Le 19:18). 'Devise evil against one another' is simpler (Ps 36:4 Mic 2:1).

11. pulled away the shoulder – literally, 'presented a refractory shoulder'; an image from beasts refusing to bear the yoke (Ne 9:29, *Margin*).

stopped … ears – (Isa 6:10 Jer 7:26 Ac 7:57).

12. hearts … adamant – (Eze 3:9 11:19).

Lord … sent in Spirit by … prophets – that is, sent by the former prophets *inspired with His Spirit.*

therefore … great wrath – (2Ch 36:16). As they pushed from them the yoke of obedience, God laid on them the yoke of oppression. As they made their heart hard as adamant, God brake their hard hearts with judgments. Hard hearts must expect hard treatment. The harder the stone, the harder the blow of the hammer to break it.

13. he cried – by His prophets.

they cried – in their calamities.

I … not hear – retribution in kind (Pr 1:24-26 Isa 1:15 Mic 3:4).

14. whirlwind – of wrath (Na 1:3).

nations whom they knew not – foreign and barbarous.

desolate after them – after their expulsion and exile. It was ordered remarkably by God's providence, that no occupants took possession of it, but that during the Jews' absence it was reserved for them against their return after seventy years.

they laid … desolate – The Jews did so by their sins. The blame of their destruction lay with themselves, rather than with the Babylonians (2Ch 36:21).

pleasant land – Canaan. Literally, 'the land of desire' (Jer 3:19).

Chapter 8

Zec 8:1–23. Continuation of the subject in the seventh chapter. After urging them to obedience by the fate of their fathers, he urges them to it by promises of coming prosperity.

2. jealous for Zion – (Zec 1:14).

with great fury – against her oppressors.

3. I am returned – that is, I am determined to return. My decree to that effect is gone forth.

Jerusalem … city of truth – that is, faithful to her God, who is the God of truth (Isa 1:21,26 Joh 17:17). Never yet fully fulfilled, therefore still to be so.

the mountain of the Lord – (Isa 2:2,3).

holy mountain – (Jer 31:23).

4. So tranquil and prosperous shall the nation be that wars shall no longer prematurely cut off the people: men and women shall reach advanced ages. The promise of long life was esteemed one of the greatest blessings in the Jewish theocracy with its temporal rewards of obedience (Ex 20:12 De 4:40). Hence this is a leading feature in millennial blessedness (Isa 65:20,22).

for very age – literally, 'for multitude of days.'

5. boys and girls playing – implying security and a numerous progeny, accounted a leading blessing among the Jews. Contrast Jer 6:11 9:21.

6. However impossible these things just promised by Me seem to you, they are not so with God. The 'remnant' that had returned from the captivity, beholding the city desolate and the walls and houses in ruins, could hardly believe what God promised. The expression 'remnant' glances at their ingratitude in rating so low God's power, though they had experienced it so 'marvellously' displayed in their restoration. A great source of unbelief is, men 'limit' God's power by their own (Ps 78:19,20,41).

these days – 'of small things' (Zec 4:10), when such great things promised seemed incredible.

7. save my people from … east … west – that is, from every region (compare Ps 50:1; the 'West' is literally, 'the going down of the sun') to which they are scattered; they are now found especially in countries west of Jerusalem. The dispersion under Nebuchadnezzar was only to the east, namely, to Babylonia. The restoration, including a spiritual return to God (Zec 8:8), here foretold, must therefore be still future (Isa 11:11,12 43:5,6 Eze 37:21 Am 9:14,15; also Zec 13:9 Jer 30:22 31:1,33).

8. in truth – in good faith, both on their side and Mine: God being faithful to His everlasting covenant and enabling them by His Spirit to be faithful to Him.

9–13. All adversities formerly attended them when neglecting to build the temple: but now God promises all blessings, as an encouragement to energy in the work.

hands … strong – be of courageous mind (2Sa 16:21), not merely in building, but in general, as having such bright prospects (Zec 8:13.).

these days – the time that had elapsed between the prophet's having spoken 'these words' and the time (Zec 8:10; compare Hag 2:15-19) when they set about in earnest restoring the temple.

the prophets – Haggai and Zechariah himself (Ezr 5:1,2). The same prophets who promised prosperity at the foundation of the temple, now promised still greater blessings hereafter.

10. before these days – before the time in which ye again proceeded with the building of the temple (Zec 8:9), namely, at the time that the temple lay neglected.

no hire for man … beast – that is, no produce of the field to repay the labour of man and beast on it (Hag 1:6,9,10 2:16).

neither … peace to him that went out or came in – (2Ch 15:5). No one could in safety do his business at home or abroad, in the city or in the country, whether going or returning.

because of the affliction – so *sorely pressed* were they by the foe outside.

every one against … neighbour – There was internal discord, as well as foes from without.

11. 'But now that the temple has been built, I will not do as I had formerly done to those who returned from Babylon' [JEROME]. Henceforth I will bless you.

12. seed … prosperous – that is, shall not fair to yield abundantly (Ho 2:21,22 Hag 2:19). Contrast with this verse Hag 1:6,9–11 2:16.

dew – especially beneficial in hot countries where rain is rare.

13. a curse – As the heathen have made you another name for 'a curse,' wishing to their foes as bad a lot as yours (Jer 24:9 29:18); so your name shall be a formula of blessing, so that men shall say to their friend, May thy lot be as happy as that of Judah (Ge 48:20). Including also the idea of the Jews being a source of blessing to the Gentile nations (Mic 5:7 Zep 3:20). The distinct mention of 'Judah' and 'Israel' proves that the prophecy has not yet had its full accomplishment, as *Israel* (the ten tribes) has never yet been restored, though *individuals* of Israel returned with Judah.

14. I thought – I determined.

you – that is, your fathers, with whom ye are one; the Jewish Church of all ages being regarded as an organic whole (compare Hag 2:5 Mt 23:31,32).

repented not – I changed not My purpose, because they changed not their mind (2Ch 36:16). With the froward God shows Himself froward (Ps 18:26). If the threatened punishment has been so unchangeably inflicted, much more will God surely give the promised blessing, which is so much more consonant to His nature (Jer 31:28).

16, 17. The promised blessings are connected with obedience. God's covenanted grace will lead those truly blessed by it to holiness, not licentiousness.

truth to … neighbour – not that the truth should not be spoken to foreigners too; but He makes it an aggravation of their sin, that they spared not even their brethren. Besides, and above all outward ordinances (Zec 7:3), God requires truth and justice.

judgment of … peace – Equitable decisions tend to allay feuds and produce peace.

gates – the place where courts of judicature in the East were held.

17. all these … I hate – therefore ye too ought to hate them. Religion consists in conformity to God's nature, that we should love what God loves and hate what God hates.

18, 19. The prophet answers the query (Zec 7:3) as to the fast in the fifth month, by a reply applying to all their fasts: these are to be turned into days of rejoicing. So Jesus replied to His disciples when similarly consulting Him as to why fasting was not imposed by Him, as it was by John the Baptist. When the Sun of righteousness shines, tears are dried up (Mt 9:15). So hereafter (Isa 35:10).

19. fast of … fourth month – On the fourth

month of the eleventh year of Zedekiah's reign, on the ninth day, Jerusalem was taken (Jer 39:2 52:6,7). It was therefore made a fast day.

fifth … seventh – (See on Zec 7:3; Zec 7:5).

tenth – On the tenth month and tenth day, in the ninth year of Zedekiah, the siege began (Jer 52:4).

therefore love the truth – God's blessing covenanted to Israel is not made to depend on Israel's goodness: but Israel's goodness should follow as the consequence of God's gracious promises (Zec 8:16,17 Zec 7:9,10). God will bless, but not those who harden themselves in sin.

20. (Isa 2:3 Mic 4:2).

Thus saith the Lord of hosts – a preface needed to assure the Jews, now disheartened by the perils surrounding them, and by the humble aspect of the temple. 'Unlikely as what follows may seem to you, *Jehovah of hosts,* boundless in resources, *saith* it, therefore it shall be so.' Just before Christ's coming, a feeling grew up among the heathen of the unsatisfactoriness of their systems of religion and philosophy; this disposed them favourably towards the religion of the Jew, so that proselytes embraced the worship of Jehovah from various parts of Asia; these again were predisposed to embrace Christianity when it was preached to them (Ac 2:9–12,41). But the full accomplishment of the conversion of the Gentiles foretold here is reserved till 'Jerusalem' (Zec 8:22) becomes the centre of Christianized Jewry (Ro 11:12,15).

21. Let us … I – manifesting zeal and love: converted themselves, they seek the conversion of others (So 1:4). To exhortation in *general* ('Let us go'), they add *individual* example ('I will go'). Or, the change from *plural* to *singular* implies that the *general* consent in religious earnestness leads *each individual* to decide for God.

go speedily – literally, 'go, going'; implying intense earnestness.

pray – Hebrew, 'entreat the face' (Zec 7:2); entreat His favour and grace.

22. many … strong nations … in Jerusalem – In contrast to the few and weak Jews now building the temple and city, then such shall be their influence that *many and strong nations* shall come to worship Jehovah their God in Jerusalem (Isa 60:3 66:23).

23. ten – a definite number for an indefinite. So in Le 22:26 Nu 14:22.

of all languages of the nations – that is, of nations of all languages (compare Isa 66:18 Re 7:9).

take hold of the skirt – a gesture of suppliant entreaty as to a superior. Compare Isa 3:6 4:1, on a different occasion. The Gentiles shall eagerly seek to share the religious privileges of the Jew. The skirt with a fringe and blue ribbon upon it (Nu 15:38 De 22:12) was a distinguishing badge of a Jew.

God is with you – the effect produced on unbelievers in entering the assemblies of the Church (1Co 14:25). But primarily, that produced on the nations in witnessing the deliverance of the Jews by Cyrus. Finally, that to be produced on the nations by the future grand interposition of Messiah in behalf of His people.

Chapter 9

Zec 9:1-17. Ninth to fourteenth chapters are prophetical.

Alexander's conquests in Syria (Zec 9:1–8).

God's people safe because he cometh lowly, but a saviour (Zec 9:9–10).

The Maccabean deliverance a type thereof (Zec 9:11–17).

1. in … Hadrach – rather, *concerning* or *against* Hadrach (compare Isa 21:13). 'Burden' means a *prophecy* BURDENED *with wrath against the guilty.*

Hadrach – a part of Syria, near Damascus. As the name is not mentioned in ancient histories, it probably was the less-used name of a region having two names ('Hadrach' and 'Bikathaven,' Am 1:5, *Margin*); hence it passed into oblivion. The name means 'enclosed' in Syrian, that is, the west interior part of Syria, *enclosed* by hills.

Damascus … rest thereof – that is, the place on which the 'burden' of the Lord's wrath shall rest. It shall permanently settle on it until Syria is utterly prostrate. Fulfilled under Alexander the Great, who overcame Syria [CURTIUS, Books 3 and 4].

eyes of man, as of all … Israel … toward the Lord – The eyes of men in general, and of all Israel in particular, through consternation at the victorious progress of Alexander, shall be directed to Jehovah. The Jews, when threatened by him because of Jaddua the high priest's refusal to swear fealty to him, prayed earnestly to the Lord, and so were delivered (2Ch 20:12 Ps 23:2). Typical of the effect of God's judgments hereafter on all men, and especially on the Jews in turning them to Him.

2. Hamath – a Syrian kingdom with a capital of the same name, north of Damascus.

shall border thereby – shall be joined to Damascus in treatment, as it is in position; shall share in the burden of wrath of which Damascus is the resting-place.

Tyrus … Zidon – lying in the conqueror's way on his march along the Mediterranean to Egypt (compare Isa 23:1–18). Zidon, the older city, surrendered, and Abdolonymus was made its viceroy.

very wise – in her own eyes. Referring to Tyre: Zec 9:3 shows wherein her *wisdom* consisted, namely, *in building a stronghold,* and *heaping up gold and silver* (Eze 38:3,5,12,17). On Alexander's expressing his wish to sacrifice in Hercules' temple in New Tyre on the island, she showed her wisdom in sending a golden crown, and replying that the true and ancient temple of Hercules was at Old Tyre on the mainland. With all her wisdom she cannot avert her doom.

3. The heathen historian, DIODORUS SICULUS [17.40], confirms this. 'Tyre had the greatest confidence owing to her insular position and fortifications, and the abundant stores she had prepared.' New Tyre was on an island seven hundred paces from the shore. As Isaiah's and Ezekiel's (Eze 27:1–36) prophecies were directed against Old Tyre on the mainland and were fulfilled by Nebuchadnezzar, so Zechariah's are against New Tyre, which was made seemingly impregnable by a double wall one hundred fifty feet high, as well as the sea on all sides.

4. (Eze 26:4,12 27:27).

cast her out – Hebrew, 'dispossess her,' that is, will cast her inhabitants into exile [GROTIUS]. Alexander, though without a navy, by incredible labour constructed a mole of the ruins of Old Tyre (fulfilling Eze 26:4–12., by 'scraping her dust from her,' and 'laying her stones, timber, and dust in the midst of the water'), from the shore to the island, and, after a seven months' siege, took the city by storm, slew with the sword about eight thousand, enslaved thirteen thousand, crucified two thousand, and set the city on 'fire,' as here foretold [CURTIUS, Book 4].

smite her power in the sea – situated though she be *in the sea*, and so seeming impregnable (compare Eze 28:2, 'I sit in the seat of God, *in the midst of the sea*'). 'Her power' includes not only her fortifications, but her fleet, all of which Alexander sank *in the sea* before her very walls [CURTIUS, Book 4]. Eze 26:17 corresponds, 'How art thou destroyed which wast strong in the sea!'

5. Ashkelon. – Gath alone is omitted, perhaps as being somewhat inland, and so out of the route of the advancing conqueror.

Ekron ... expectation ... ashamed – Ekron, the farthest north of the Philistine cities, had *expected* Tyre would withstand Alexander, and so check his progress southward through Philistia to Egypt. This hope being confounded ('put to *shame*'), Ekron shall 'fear.'

king shall perish from Gaza – Its government shall be overthrown. In literal fulfilment of this prophecy, after a two month's siege, Gaza was taken by Alexander, ten thousand of its inhabitants slain, and the rest sold as slaves. Betis the satrap, or petty 'king,' was bound to a chariot by thongs thrust through the soles of his feet, and dragged round the city.

6. bastard – not the rightful heir; vile and low men, such as are bastards (De 23:2) [GROTIUS].

An alien; so the *Septuagint;* implying the desolation of the region wherein men shall not settle, but sojourn in only as aliens passing through [CALVIN].

7. take ... his blood out of ... mouth – *Blood* was forbidden as food (Ge 9:4 Le 7:26).

abominations – things sacrificed to idols and then partaken of by the worshippers (Nu 25:2 Ac 15:29). The sense is, 'I will cause the Philistines to cease from the worship of idols.'

even he *shall be* for our God – 'even he,' like Hamath, Damascus, Tyre, which, these words imply, shall also be converted to God (Isa 56:3, 'son of the stranger joined himself to the Lord') [ROSENMULLER].

he shall be as a governor in Judah – On the conversion of the Philistine prince, he shall have the same dignity 'in Judah as a governor'; there shall be no distinction [HENDERSON]. The Philistine princes with their respective states shall equally *belong to the Jews'* communion, as if they were among the 'governors' of states 'in Judah' [MAURER].

Ekron as a Jebusite – The Jebusites, the original inhabitants of Jerusalem, who, when subjugated by David, were incorporated with the Jews (2Sa 24:16.), and enjoyed their privileges: but in a subordinate position *civilly* (1Ki 9:20,21). The Jebusites' condition under Solomon being that of bond-servants and tributaries, CALVIN explains the verse differently: 'I will rescue the Jew *from the teeth* of the Philistine foe (image from wild beasts rending their prey with their *teeth*), who would have devoured him, as he would devour *blood* or flesh of his *abominable* sacrifices to idols: and *even he,* the seemingly ignoble remnant of the Jews, shall be sacred to *our* God (consecrated by His favour); and though so long bereft of dignity, I will make them to be *as governors* ruling others, and Ekron shall be a tributary bond-servant as the Jebusite? Thus the antithesis is between the Jew *that remaineth* (the elect remnant) and the Ekronite.

8. encamp about – (Ps 34:7).

mine house – namely, the Jewish people (Zec 3:7 Ho 8:1) [MAURER]. Or, *the temple:* reassuring the Jews engaged in building, who might otherwise fear their work would be undone by the conqueror [MOORE]. The Jews were, in agreement with this prophecy, uninjured by Alexander, though he punished the Samaritans. Typical of their final deliverance from every foe.

passeth by ... returneth – Alexander, when advancing against Jerusalem, was arrested by a dream, so that neither in 'passing by' to Egypt, nor in 'returning,' did he injure the Jews, but conferred on them great privileges.

no oppressor ... pass through ... any more – The prophet passes from the immediate future to the final deliverance to come (Isa 60:18 Eze 28:24).

seen with mine eyes – namely, how Jerusalem has been oppressed by her foes [ROSEN-MULLER] (Ex 3:7 2:25). God is said *now* to have *seen*, because He now begins to bring the foe to judgment, and manifests to the world His sense of His people's wrongs.

9. From the coming of the Grecian conqueror, Zechariah makes a sudden transition, by the prophetical law of suggestion, to the coming of King Messiah, a very different character.

daughter of Zion – The theocratic people is called to 'rejoice' at the coming of her King (Ps 2:11).

unto thee – He comes not for His own gain or pleasure, as earthly kings come, but for the sake of His Church: especially for the Jews' sake, at His second coming (Ro 11:26).

he is just – *righteous*: an attribute constantly given to Messiah (Isa 45:21 53:11 Jer 23:5,6) in connection with *salvation*. He does not merely pardon by conniving at sin, but He *justifies* by becoming the Lord our righteousness fulfiller, so that not merely mercy, but justice, requires the justification of the sinner who by faith becomes one with Christ. God's justice is not set aside by the sinner's salvation, but is magnified and made honourable by it (Isa 42:1,21). His future *reign* 'in righteousness,' also, is especially referred to (Isa 32:1).

having salvation – not passively, as some interpret it, 'saved,' which the context, referring to a 'king' coming to reign, forbids; also the old versions, the *Septuagint, Syriac,* and *Vulgate,* give *Saviour*. The *Hebrew* is reflexive in sense, 'showing Himself a Saviour; … having salvation in Himself' for us. Endowed with a salvation which He bestows as a king. Compare *Margin*, 'saving Himself.' Compare Mt 1:21, in the *Greek*, '*Himself* shall save His people'; that is, not by any other, but by Himself shall He save [PEARSON *On the Creed*]. His 'having salvation' for others manifested that He had in Himself that righteousness which was indispensable for the justification of the unrighteous (1Co 1:30 2Co 5:21 1Jo 2:1). This contrasts beautifully with the haughty Grecian conqueror who came to destroy, whereas Messiah came to save. Still, Messiah shall come to take 'just' vengeance on His foes, previous to His reign of peace (Mt 4:1,2).

lowly – mild, gentle: corresponding to His 'riding on an ass' (not a despised animal, as with us; nor a badge of humiliation, for princes in the East rode on asses, as well as low persons, Jud 5:10), that is, coming as 'Prince of *peace*' (Zec 9:10 Isa 9:6); the 'horse,' on the contrary is the emblem of *war,* and shall therefore be 'cut off.' Perhaps the *Hebrew* includes both the 'lowliness' of His *outward* state (which applies to His

first coming) and His 'meekness *of disposition,*' as Mt 21:5 quotes it (compare Mt 11:29), which applies to both His comings. Both adapt Him for loving sympathy with us men; and at the same time are the ground of His coming manifested exaltation (Joh 5:27 Php 2:7–9).

colt – untamed, 'whereon yet never man sat' (Lu 19:30). The symbol of a triumphant conqueror and judge (Jud 5:10 10:4 12:14).

foal of an ass – literally, 'asses': in *Hebrew* idiom, the indefinite *plural* for *singular* (so Ge 8:4, '*mountains* of Ararat,' for *one* of the mountains). The dam accompanied the colt (Mt 21:2). The entry of Jesus into Jerusalem at His first coming is a pledge of the full accomplishment of this prophecy at His second coming. It shall be 'the day of the Lord' (Ps 118:24), as that first Palm *Sunday* was. The Jews shall then *universally* (Ps 118:26) say, what *some* of them said then, 'Blessed is He that cometh in the name of the Lord' (compare Mt 21:9, with Mt 23:39); also 'Hosanna,' or 'Save now, I beseech thee.' 'Palms,' the emblem of triumph, shall then also be in the hands of His people (compare Joh 12:13, with Re 7:9,10). Then also, as on His former entry, shall be the feast of tabernacles (at which they used to draw water from Siloam, quoting Isa 12:3). Compare Ps 118:15, with Zec 14:16.

10. (Isa 2:4 Ho 2:18 Mic 5:10).

Ephraim … Jerusalem – the ten tribes, and Judah and Benjamin; both alike to be restored hereafter.

speak peace – command it authoritatively.

dominion … from sea … river … ends of … earth – fulfilling Ge 15:18 Ex 23:31; and Ps 72:8. 'Sea … sea,' are the Red Sea and Mediterranean. The 'river' is the Euphrates. Jerusalem and the Holy Land, extended to the limits promised to Abraham, are to be the centre of His future dominion; whence it will extend to the remotest parts of the earth.

11. As for thee also – that is, the daughter of Zion,' or 'Jerusalem' (Zec 9:9):the theocracy. The 'thee also,' in contradistinction to *Messiah* spoken of in Zec 9:10, implies that besides *cutting off the battle-bow* and extending MESSIAH's 'dominion to the ends of the earth,' God would *also* deliver *for her* her exiled people from their foreign captivity.

by the blood of thy covenant – that is, according to the covenant vouchsafed to thee on Sinai, and ratified by the blood of sacrifices (Ex 24:8 Heb 9:18–20).

pit wherein … no water – Dungeons were often pits without water, miry at the bottom, such as Jeremiah sank in when confined (Ge 37:24 Jer 38:6). An image of the misery of the Jewish exiles in Egypt, Greece, under the successors of Alexander, especially under Antiochus Epiphanes, who robbed and profaned the temple, slew thousands, and enslaved more. God delivered them by the Maccabees. A type of the future deliverance from their last great persecutor hereafter (Isa 51:14 60:1).

12. stronghold – in contrast to the 'pit' (Zec 9:11); literally, 'a place *cut off* from access.'

prisoners of hope – that is, who in spite of afflictions (Job 13:15 Ps 42:5,11) maintain hope in the covenant-keeping God; in contrast to unbelievers, who say, 'There is no hope' (Jer 2:25 18:12). Especially those *Jews* who believe God's word to Israel (Jer 31:17), 'there is hope in the end, that thy children shall come again to their own border,' and do not say, as in Eze 37:11, 'Our hope is lost.' Primarily, the Jews of Zechariah's time are encouraged not to be dispirited in building by their trials; secondarily, the Jews before the coming restoration are encouraged to look to Messiah for deliverance from their last oppressors.

even to-day – when your circumstances seem so unpromising; in contrast with the 'day of the Lord,' when Zion's King shall come to her deliverance (Zec 9:9).

I will render double – Great as has been thy adversity, thy prosperity shall be *doubly* greater (Isa 61:7).

13. bent Judah – made Judah as it were My bow, and 'filled' it 'with Ephraim,' as My arrow, wherewith to overcome the successor of the Grecian Alexander, Antiochus Epiphanes, the oppressor of Judah. Having spoken (Zec 9:1–8) of Alexander's victories, after the parenthesis (Zec 9:9,10) as to Messiah the infinitely greater King coming, he passes to the victories which God would enable Judah to gain over Alexander's successor, after his temporary oppression of them.

O Zion … O Greece – God on one hand addresses Zion, on the other Greece, showing that He rules all people.

14. Another image: 'Jehovah shall be seen (conspicuously manifesting His power) over them' (that is, in behalf of the Jews and against their foes), as formerly He appeared in a cloud over the Israelites against the Egyptians (Ex 14:19,24).

his arrow … as … lightning – flashing forth instantaneous destruction to the foe (Ps 18:14).

blow … trumpet – to summon and incite His people to battle for the destruction of their foe.

go with whirlwinds of the south – that is, go forth in the most furious storm, such as is one from the south (Isa 21:1). Alluding, perhaps, to Jehovah's ancient miracles at Sinai coming 'from Teman' ('*the south*,' in the *Margin*).

15. devour – the flesh of their foes.

drink – the blood of their foes; that is, utterly destroy them. Image (as Jer 46:10) from a sacrifice, wherein part of the flesh was eaten, and the blood poured in libation (compare Isa 63:1).

subdue with sling-stones – or, 'tread under foot the sling-stones' hurled by the foe at them; that is, will contemptuously trample on the hostile missiles which shall fall harmless under their feet (compare Job 41:28). Probably, too, it is implied that *their foes* are as impotent as the common *stones* used in *slinging* when they have fallen under foot: in contrast to the people of God (Zec 9:16), 'the (precious) stones of a crown' (compare 1Sa 25:29) [MAURER].

noise – the battle shout.

through wine – (Zec 10:7). The Spirit of God fills them with triumph (Eph 5:18).

filled – with blood.

like bowls – the bowls used to receive the blood of the sacrifices.

as … corners – or 'horns' of the altar, which used to be sprinkled with blood from the bowls (Ex 29:12 Le 4:18).

16. save them … as the flock of his people – as the flock of His people ought to be saved (Ps 77:20). Here the image of *war* and *bloodshed* (Zec 9:15) is exchanged for the *shepherd* and *flock*, as God will give not only victory, but afterwards safe and lasting peace. In contrast to the worthless *sling-stones* trodden under foot stand the (gems) 'stones of the crown (Isa 62:3 Mal 3:17), lifted up as an ensign,' that all may flock to the Jewish Church (Isa 11:10,12 62:10).

17. his goodness … his beauty – the goodness and beauty which Jehovah-Messiah bestows on His people.

make … cheerful – literally, 'make it grow.'

new wine the maids – supply, 'shall make … to grow.' *Corn* and *wine* abundant indicate peace and plenty. The new wine gladdening the maids is peculiar to this passage. It confutes those who interdict the use of wine as food. The Jews, heretofore straitened in provisions through pressure of the foe, shall now have abundance to cheer, not merely the old, but even the youths and maidens [CALVIN].

Chapter 10

Zec 10:1–12. Prayer and promise.

Call to prayer to Jehovah, as contrasted with the idol-worship which had brought judgments on the princes and people. Blessings promised in answer to prayer: (1) rulers of themselves; (2) conquest of their enemies; (3) restoration and establishment of both Israel and Judah in their own land in lasting peace and piety.

1. Ask … rain – on which the abundance of 'corn' promised by the Lord (Zec 9:17) depends. Jehovah alone can give it, and will give it on being asked (Jer 10:13 14:22).

rain in … time of … latter rain – that is, the latter rain in its due time, namely, in spring, about February or March (Job 29:23 Joe 2:23). The latter rain ripened the grain, as the former rain in October tended to fructify the seed. Including *all* temporal blessings; these again being types of spiritual ones. Though God has begun to bless us, we are not to relax our prayers. The former rain of conversion may have been given, but we must also ask for the latter rain of ripened sanctification. Though at Pentecost there was a former rain on the Jewish Church, a latter rain is still to be looked for, when the full harvest of the nation's conversion shall be gathered in to God. The spirit of prayer in the Church is an index at once of her piety, and of the spiritual blessings she may expect from God. When the Church is full of prayer, God pours out a full blessing.

bright clouds – rather, 'lightnings,' the precursors of rain [MAURER].

showers of rain – literally, 'rain of heavy rain.' In Job 37:6 the same words occur in inverted order [HENDERSON].

grass – a general term, including both *corn* for men and *grass* for cattle.

2. idols – literally, 'the teraphim,' the household gods, consulted in divination (see on Ho 3:4). Derived by GESENIUS from an *Arabic* root, 'comfort,' indicating them as the givers of comfort. Or an Ethiopian root, 'relics.' Herein Zechariah shows that the Jews by their own idolatry had stayed the grace of God heretofore, which otherwise would have given them all those blessings, temporal and spiritual, which they are now (Zec 10:1) urged to 'ask' for.

diviners – who gave responses to consulters of the teraphim: opposed to Jehovah and His true prophets.

seen a lie – pretending to see what they saw not in giving responses.

comfort in vain – literally, 'give *vapour* for comfort'; that is, give comforting promises to consulters which are sure to come to naught (Job 13:4 16:2 21:34).

therefore they went their way – that is, Israel and Judah were led away captive.

as a flock ... no shepherd – As sheep wander and are a prey to every injury when without a shepherd, so the Jews had been while they were without Jehovah, the true shepherd; for the false prophets whom they trusted were no shepherds (Eze 34:5). So now they are scattered, while they know not Messiah their shepherd; typified in the state of the disciples, when they had forsaken Jesus and fled (Mt 26:56; compare Zec 13:7).

3. against the shepherds – the civil rulers of Israel and Judah who abetted idolatry.

punished – literally, 'visited upon.' The same word 'visited,' without the *upon*, is presently after used in a good sense to heighten the contrast.

goats – he-goats. As 'shepherds' described what they *ought* to have been, so 'he-goats' describes what they *were*, the emblem of head-strong wantonness and offensive lust (Isa 14:9, *Margin;* Eze 34:17 Da 8:5 Mt 25:33). The he-goats head the flock. They who are first in crime will be first in punishment.

visited – in mercy (Lu 1:68).

as his goodly horse – In Zec 9:13 they were represented under the image of *bows and arrows*, here under that of their commander-in-chief, Jehovah's *battle horse* (So 1:9). God can make His people, timid though they be as sheep, courageous as the charger. The general rode on the most beautiful and richly caparisoned, and had his horse tended with the greatest care. Jehovah might cast off the Jews for their vileness, but He regards His election or adoption of them: whence He calls them here '*His* flock,' and therefore saves them.

4. Out of him – *Judah* is to be no more subject to foreigners, but *from itself* shall come its rulers.

the corner – stone, Messiah (Isa 28:16). 'Corners' simply express *governors* (1Sa 14:38, *Margin;* Isa 19:13, *Margin*). The Maccabees, Judah's governors and deliverers from Antiochus the oppressor, are primarily meant; but Messiah is the Antitype. Messiah supports and binds together the Church, Jews and Gentiles.

the nail – (Jud 4:21 Isa 22:23). The large peg inside an Oriental tent, on which is hung most of its valuable furniture. On Messiah hang all the glory and hope of His people.

bow – (Zec 9:13). Judah shall not need foreign soldiery. Messiah shall be her battle-bow (Ps 45:4,5 Re 6:2).

every oppressor – rather, in a good sense, *ruler,* as the kindred Ethiopic term means. So 'exactor,' in Isa 60:17, namely, one who exacts the tribute from the nations made tributary to Judah [LUDOVICUS DE DIEU].

5. riders on horses – namely, the enemy's horsemen. Though the Jews were forbidden by the law to multiply horses in battle (De 17:16), they are made Jehovah's war horse (Zec 10:3 Ps 20:7), and so tread down on foot the foe with all his cavalry (Eze 38:4 Da 11:40). Cavalry was the chief strength of the Syro-Grecian army (I Maccabees 3:39).

6. Judah ... Joseph – that is, the ten tribes. The distinct mention of both Judah and Israel shows that there is yet a more complete restoration than that from Babylon, when Judah alone and a few Israelites from the other tribes returned. The Maccabean deliverance is here connected with it, just as the painter groups on the same canvas objects in the foreground and hills far distant; or as the comparatively near planet and the remote fixed star are seen together in the same firmament. Prophecy ever hastens to the glorious final consummation under Messiah.

bring them again to place them – namely, securely in their own land.

7. like a mighty man – in the battle with the foe (Zec 10:3,5).

rejoice – at their victory over the foe.

children shall see it – who are not yet of age to serve. To teach patient waiting for God's promises. If ye do not at present see the fulfilment, your *children* shall, and their joy shall be complete.

rejoice in the Lord – the Giver of such a glorious victory.

8. hiss for them – Keepers of bees by a whistle call them together. So Jehovah by the mere word of His call shall gather back to Palestine His scattered people (Zec 10:10 Isa 5:26 Eze 36:11). The multitudes mentioned by JOSEPHUS [*Wars of the Jews*, 3:2], as peopling Galilee two hundred years after this time, were a pledge of the future more perfect fulfilment of the prophecy.

for I have redeemed them – namely, in My covenant purpose 'redeemed' both temporally and spiritually.

as they have increased – in former times.

9. sow them among ... people – Their dispersion was with a special design. Like seed sown far and wide, they shall, when quickened themselves, be the fittest instruments for quickening others (compare Mic 5:7). The slight hold they have on every soil where they now live, as also the commercial and therefore cosmopolitan character of their pursuits, making a change of residence easy to them, fit them peculiarly for missionary work [MOORE]. The wide dispersion of the Jews just before Christ's coming prepared the way similarly for the apostles' preaching in the various Jewish synagogues throughout the world; everywhere some of the Old Testament seed previously sown was ready to germinate when the New Testament light and heat were brought to bear on it by Gospel preachers. Thus the way was opened for entrance among the Gentiles. '*Will sow*' is the *Hebrew* future, said of that which has been done, is being done, and may be done afterwards [MAURER], (compare Ho 2:23).

shall remember me in far countries – (De 30:1 2Ch 6:37). Implying the Jews return to a right mind in 'all the nations' where they are scattered simultaneously. Compare Lu 15:17,18, with Ps 22:27, 'All the ends of the world *remembering* and turning unto the Lord,' preceded by the 'seed of Jacob ... Israel ... fearing and glorifying Him'; also Ps 102:13–15.

live – in political and spiritual life.

10. Egypt ... Assyria – the former the first, the latter among the last of Israel's oppressors (or *representing the four great world kingdoms*, of which it was the first): types of the present *universal* dispersion, Egypt being south, Assyria north, opposite ends of the compass.

Gilead ... Lebanon – The whole of the Holy Land is described by two of its boundaries, the eastern ('Gilead' beyond Jordan) and the northern ('Lebanon').

place shall not be found for them – that is, there shall not be room enough for them through their numbers (Isa 49:20 54:3).

11. pass ... sea with affliction – Personifying the 'sea'; He shall afflict the sea, that is, cause it to cease to be an obstacle to Israel's return to Palestine (Isa 11:15,16). As Jehovah smote the Red Sea to make a passage for His people (Ex 14:16,21), so hereafter shall He make a way through every obstacle which opposes Israel's restoration.

the river – the Nile (Am 8:8 9:5), or the Euphrates. Thus the Red Sea and the Euphrates in the former part of the verse answer to 'Assyria' and 'Egypt' in the latter.

sceptre of Egypt ... depart – (Eze 30:13).

12. I ... strengthen them in ... Lord – (Ho 1:7). I, the Father, will strengthen them in the name, that is, the manifested power, of the Lord, Messiah, the Son of God.

walk ... in his name – that is, live everywhere and continually under His protection, and according to His will (Ge 5:22 Ps 20:1,7 Mic 4:5).

Chapter 11

Zec 11:1–17. Destruction of the second temple and Jewish polity for the rejection of Messiah.

1. Open thy doors, O Lebanon – that is, the temple so called, as being constructed of cedars of Lebanon, or as being lofty and conspicuous like that mountain (compare Eze 17:3 Hab 2:17). Forty years before the destruction of the temple, the tract called 'Massecheth Joma' states, its doors of their own accord opened, and Rabbi Johanan in alarm said, I know that thy desolation is impending according to Zechariah's prophecy. CALVIN supposes Lebanon to refer to *Judea*, described by its north boundary: 'Lebanon,' the route by which the Romans, according to JOSEPHUS, gradually advanced towards Jerusalem. MOORE, from HENGSTENBERG, refers the passage to the civil war which caused the calling in of the Romans, who, like a storm sweeping through the land from Lebanon, deprived Judea of its independence. Thus the passage forms a fit introduction to the prediction as to Messiah born when Judea became a Roman province. But the weight of authority is for the former view.

2. fir tree ... cedar – if even the *cedars* (the highest in the state) are not spared, how much less *the fir trees* (the lowest)!

forest of ... vintage – As the vines are stripped of their grapes in the vintage (compare

Joe 3:13), so the forest of Lebanon 'is come down,' stripped of all its beauty. Rather, '*the fortified*' or '*inaccessible forest*' [MAURER]; that is, Jerusalem dense with houses as a thick forest is with trees, and 'fortified' with a wall around. Compare Mic 3:12, where its desolate state is described as a forest.

3. shepherds – the Jewish rulers.

their glory – *their* wealth and magnificence; or that *of the temple*, 'their glory' (Mr 13:1 Lu 21:5).

young lions – the princes, so described on account of their cruel rapacity.

pride of Jordan – its thickly wooded banks, the lair of 'lions' (Jer 12:5 49:19). Image for Judea 'spoiled' of the magnificence of its rulers ('the young lions'). The valley of the Jordan forms a deeper gash than any on the earth. The land at Lake Merom is on a level with the Mediterranean Sea; at the Sea of Tiberias it falls six hundred fifty feet below that level, and to double that depression at the Dead Sea, that is, in all, 1950 feet below the Mediterranean; in twenty miles' interval there is a fall of from three thousand to four thousand feet.

4. The prophet here proceeds to show the cause of the destruction just foretold, namely, the rejection of Messiah.

flock of … slaughter – (Ps 44:22). God's people doomed to slaughter by the Romans. Zechariah here represents typically Messiah, and performs in vision the actions enjoined: hence the language is in part appropriate to him, but mainly to the Antitype, Messiah. A million and a half perished in the Jewish war, and one million one hundred thousand at the fall of Jerusalem. 'Feed' implies that the Jews could not plead ignorance of God's will to execute their sin. Zechariah and the other prophets had by God's appointment 'fed' them (Ac 20:28) with the word of God, teaching and warning them to escape from coming wrath by repentance: the type of Messiah, the chief Shepherd, who receives the commission of the Father, with whom He is one (Zec 11:4); and Himself says (Zec 11:7), '*I* will feed the flock of slaughter.' Zechariah did not live to 'feed' literally the 'flock of slaughter'; Messiah alone 'fed' those who, because of their rejection of Him, were condemned to slaughter. Jehovah-Messiah is the speaker. It is He who threatens to inflict the punishments (Zec 11:6,8). The typical breaking of the staff, performed in vision by Zechariah (Zec 11:10), is fulfilled in His breaking the covenant with Judah. It is He who was sold for thirty pieces of silver (Zec 11:12,13).

5. possessors – The *buyers* [MAURER], their Roman oppressors, contrasted with 'they that sell men.' The instruments of God's righteous judgment, and therefore 'not holding themselves guilty' (Jer 50:7). It is meant that they

might use this plea, not that they actually used it. Judah's adversaries felt no compunction in destroying them; and God in righteous wrath against Judah allowed it.

they that sell them – (Compare Zec 11:12). The rulers of Judah, who by their avaricious rapacity and selfishness (Joh 11:48,50) virtually sold their country to Rome. Their covetousness brought on Judea God's visitation by Rome. The climax of this was the sale of the innocent Messiah for thirty pieces of silver. They thought that Jesus was thus sold and their selfish interest secured by the delivery of Him to the Romans for crucifixion; but it was themselves and their country that they thus sold to the Roman possessors.

I am rich – by selling the sheep (De 29:19 Ho 12:8). In short-sighted selfishness they thought they had gained their object, covetous self-aggrandizement (Lu 16:14), and hypocritically 'thanked' God for their wicked gain (compare Lu 18:11).

say … pity – In *Hebrew* it is *singular:* that is, *each* of those that sell them *saith:* Not *one* of their own shepherds *pitieth* them. An emphatic mode of expression by which each individual is represented as doing, or not doing, the action of the verb [HENDERSON]. HENGSTENBERG refers the *singular* verbs to JEHOVAH, the true actor; the wicked shepherds being His unconscious instruments. Compare Zec 11:6, For *I* will no more pity, with the *Hebrew* 'pitieth not' here.

6. Jehovah, in vengeance for their rejection of Messiah, gave them over to intestine feuds and Roman rule. The Zealots and other factious Jews expelled and slew one another by turns at the last invasion by Rome.

his king – Vespasian or Titus: they themselves (Joh 19:15) had said, unconsciously realizing Zechariah's words, identifying Rome's king with Judah's ('his') king, 'We have no king but Cæsar.' God took them at their word, and gave them the Roman king, who 'smote (literally, "dashed in pieces") their land,' breaking up their polity, when they rejected their true King who would have saved them.

7. And – rather, '*Accordingly*': implying the motive cause which led Messiah to assume the office, namely, the will of the Father (Zec 11:4,5), who pitied the sheep without any true shepherd.

I will feed – '*I* fed' [CALVIN], which comes to the same thing, as the past tense must in Zechariah's time have referred to the event of Messiah's advent then future: the prophets often speaking of the future in vision as already present. It was not My fault, Jehovah implies, that these sheep were not fed; the fault rests solely with you, because ye rejected the grace of God [CALVIN].

even you, O poor of the flock – rather, 'in order that (I might feed, that is, save) the poor (humble; compare Zec 11:11 Zep 3:12 Mt 5:3) of the flock'; literally, not *you*, but, '*therefore* (I will feed)' [MOORE]. See *Margin*, 'Verily the poor.' It is for the sake of the believing remnant that Messiah took charge of the flock, though He would have saved all, if they would have come to Him. They would not come; therefore, *as a nation*, they are 'the flock of (that is, doomed to) slaughter.'

I took ... two staves – that is, shepherds' staves or rods (Ps 23:4). Symbolizing His assumption of the pastor's office.

Beauty – The Jews' peculiar *excellency* above other nations (De 4:7), God's special manifestation to them (Ps 147:19,20), the glory of the temple ('the *beauty* of holiness,' Ps 29:2; compare Ps 27:4 90:17 2Ch 20:21), the 'pleasantness' of their land (Ge 49:15 Da 8:9 11:16), 'the glorious land.'

Bands – implying the *bond* of 'brotherhood' between Judah and Israel. 'Bands,' in Ps 119:61, *Margin*, is used for confederate *companies*: The Easterns in making a confederacy often tie a cord or band as a symbol of it, and untie it when they dissolve the confederacy [LUDOVICUS DE DIEU]. Messiah would have joined Judah and Israel in the *bonds* of a common faith and common laws (Zec 11:14), but they would not; therefore in just retribution He broke 'His covenant which He had made with all the people.' Alexander, Antiochus Epiphanes, and Pompey were all kept from marring utterly the distinctive 'beauty' and 'brotherhood' of Judah and Israel, which subsisted more or less so long as the temple stood. But when Jehovah brake the staves, not even Titus could save the temple from his own Roman soldiery, nor was Jurian able to restore it.

8. Three shepherds ... I cut off – literally, 'to cause to disappear,' to destroy so as not to leave a vestige of them. The three shepherds whom Messiah removes are John, Simon, and Eleazar, three leaders of factions in the Jewish war [DRUSIUS]. Or, as Messiah, the Antitype, was at once *prophet, priest, and king*, so He by the destruction of the Jewish polity destroyed these *three* orders for the unbelief of both the rulers and people [MOORE]. If they had accepted Messiah, they would have had all three combined in Him, and would have been themselves spiritually prophets, priests, and kings to God. Refusing Him, they lost all three, in every sense.

one month – a brief and fixed space of time (Ho 5:7). Probably alluding to the last period of the siege of Jerusalem, when all authority within the city was at an end [HENDERSON].

loathed them – literally, 'was straitened' as to them; instead of being *enlarged* towards them in love (2Co 6:11,12). The same *Hebrew* as in Nu 21:4, *Margin*. No room was left by them for the

grace of God, as His favours were rejected [CALVIN]. The mutual distaste that existed between the holy Messiah and the guilty Jews is implied.

9. Then said I – at last when all means of saving the nation had been used in vain (Joh 8:24).

I will not – that is, *no more* feed you. The last rejection of the Jews is foretold, of which the former under Nebuchadnezzar, similarly described, was the type (Jer 15:1–3 34:17 43:11 Eze 6:12). Perish those who are doomed to perish, since they reject Him who would have saved them! Let them rush on to their own ruin, since they will have it so.

eat ... flesh of another – Let them madly perish by mutual discords. JOSEPHUS attests the fulfilment of this prophecy of *threefold calamity*: pestilence and famine ('dieth ... die'), war ('cut off ... cut off'), intestine discord ('eat ... one ... another').

10. covenant which I made with all the people – The covenant made with the *whole nation* is to hold good no more except to the elect remnant.

11. poor ... knew – The humble, godly remnant knew by the event the truth of the prediction and of Messiah's mission. He had, thirty-seven years before the fall of Jerusalem, forewarned His disciples when they should see the city compassed with armies, to 'flee unto the mountains.' Accordingly, Cestius Gallus, when advancing on Jerusalem, unaccountably withdrew for a brief space, giving Christians the opportunity of obeying Christ's words by fleeing to Pella.

waited upon me – looked to the hand of God in all these calamities, not blindly shutting their eyes to the true cause of the visitation, as most of the nation still do, instead of referring it to their own rejection of Messiah. Isa 30:18-21 refers similarly to the Lord's return in mercy to the remnant that 'wait for Him' and 'cry' to Him (Zep 3:12,13).

12. I said – The prophet here represents the person of Jehovah-Messiah.

If ye think good – literally, 'If it be good in your eyes.' Glancing at their self-sufficient pride in not *deigning* to give Him that return which His great love in coming down to them from heaven merited, namely, their love and obedience. 'My price'; my reward for pastoral care, both during the whole of Israel's history from the Exodus, and especially the three and a half years of Messiah's ministry. He speaks as their 'servant,' which He was to them in order to fulfil the Father's will (Php 2:7).

if not, forbear – They withheld that which He sought as His only reward, their love; yet He will not force them, but leave His cause with God (Isa 49:4,5). Compare the type Jacob cheated of his wages by Laban, but leaving his cause in the hands of God (Ge 31:41,42).

So ... thirty pieces of silver – *thirty shekels*. They not only refused Him His due, but added insult to injury by giving for Him the price of a gored bond-servant (Ex 21:32 Mt 26:15). A freeman was rated at twice that sum.

13. Cast it unto the potter – proverbial: Throw it to the temple potter, the most suitable person to whom to cast the despicable sum, plying his trade as he did in the polluted valley (2Ki 23:10) of Hinnom, because it furnished him with the most suitable clay. This same valley, and the potter's shop, were made the scene of symbolic actions by Jeremiah (Jer 18:1–19:15) when prophesying of this very period of Jewish history.

in the house of the Lord – The thirty pieces are thrown down *in the temple*, as the house of Jehovah, the fit place for the money of Jehovah-Messiah being deposited, in the treasury, and the very place accordingly where Judas 'cast them down.' The thirty pieces were cast 'to the potter,' because it was to him they were 'appointed by the Lord' ultimately to go, as a worthless price (compare Mt 27:6,7,10). For 'I took,' 'I threw,' here Matthew has '*they* took,' '*they* gave them'; because their (the Jews' and Judas') act was all *His* '*appointment*' (which Matthew also expresses), and therefore is here attributed to Him (compare Ac 2:23 4:28).

14. The breaking of the bond of union between Judah and Israel's ten tribes under Rehoboam is here the image used to represent the *fratricidal discord of factions* which raged within Jerusalem on the eve of its fall, while the Romans were thundering at its gates without. See Josephus [*Wars of the Jews*]. Also the continued *severance of the tribes* till their coming reunion (Ro 11:15).

15. yet – 'take *again*'; as in Zec 11:7 previously he had taken other implements.

instruments – the accoutrements, namely, the shepherd's crook and staff, wallet. Assume the character of a bad ('foolish' in Scripture is synonymous with *wicked*, Ps 14:1) shepherd, as before thou assumedst that of a good shepherd. Since the Jews would not have Messiah, 'the Good Shepherd' (Joh 10:11), they were given up to Rome, heathen and papal, both alike their persecutor, especially the latter, and shall be again to Antichrist, the 'man of sin,' the instrument of judgment by Christ's permission. Antichrist will first make a covenant with them as their ruler, but then will break it, and they shall feel the iron yoke of his tyranny as the false Messiah, because they rejected the light yoke of the true Messiah (Da 11:35–38 12:1 9:27 2Th 2:3–12). But at last he is to perish utterly (Zec 11:17), and the elect remnant of Judah and

Israel is to be saved gloriously.

16. in the land – Antichrist will probably he a Jew, or at least one in Judea.

not visit ... neither ... seek ... heal ... broken, nor feed ... but ... eat ... flesh ... tear – Compare similar language as to the unfaithful shepherds of Israel in Eze 34:2–4. This implies, they shall be paid in kind. Such a shepherd in the worst type shall 'tear' them for a limited time.

those ... cut off – 'those perishing' [*Septuagint*], that is, those sick unto death, as if already cut off.

the young – The *Hebrew* is always used of human youths, who are really referred to under the image of the young of the flock.

broken – the wounded.

standeth still – with faintness lagging behind.

tear ... claws – expressing cruel voracity; tearing off the very hoofs (compare Ex 10:26), giving them excruciating pain, and disabling them from going in quest of pasture.

17. the idol – The *Hebrew* expresses both *vanity* and *an idol*. Compare Isa 14:13 Da 11:36 2Th 2:4 Re 13:5,6, as to the idolatrous and blasphemous claims of Antichrist. The 'idol shepherd *that leaveth the flock*' cannot apply to Rome, but to some ruler among the Jews themselves, at first cajoling, then 'leaving' them, nay, destroying them (Da 9:27 11:30-38). God's sword shall descend on his 'arm,' the instrument of his tyranny towards the sheep (2Th 2:8); and on his 'right eye,' wherewith he ought to have watched the sheep (Joh 10:12,13). However, Antichrist shall *destroy*, rather than 'leave the flock.' Perhaps, therefore, the reference is to the shepherds who *left the flock* to Antichrist's rapacity, and who, in just retribution, shall feel his 'sword' on their 'arm,' which ought to have protected the flock but did not, and on their 'eye,' which had failed duly to watch the sheep from hurt. The blinding of 'the *right eye*' has attached to it the notion of ignominy (1Sa 11:2).

Chapter 12

Zec 12:1–14. Jerusalem the instrument of judgment on her foes hereafter; her repentance and restoration.

1. burden – 'weighty prophecy'; fraught with destruction to Israel's foes; the expression may also refer to the distresses of Israel *implied* as about to precede the deliverance.

stretcheth forth – present; *now*, not merely '*hath* stretched forth,' as if God only created and then left the universe to itself (Joh 5:17). To remove all doubts of unbelief as to the possibility of Israel's deliverance, God prefaces the prediction by reminding us of His creative and sustaining power. Compare a similar preface in Isa 42:5 43:1 65:17,18.

formeth ... spirit of man – (Nu 16:22 Heb 12:9).

2. cup of trembling – a cup causing those who drink it to *reel* (from a *Hebrew* root 'to reel'). Jerusalem, who drank the 'cup of trembling' herself, shall be so to her foes (Isa 51:17,22 Jer 13:13).

both against Judah – The *Hebrew* order of words is literally, 'And also against Judah shall he (the foe) be in the siege against Jerusalem'; implying virtually that Judah, as it shares the invasion along with Jerusalem, so it shall, like the metropolis, prove a cup of trembling to the invaders.

3. (Compare Zec 14:4,6-9,13). JEROME states it was a custom in Palestine to test the strength of youths by their lifting up a massive stone; the phrase, 'burden themselves with it,' refers to this custom. Compare Mt 21:44: The Jews 'fell' on the rock of offense, Messiah, and were 'broken'; but the rock shall fall on Antichrist, who 'burdens himself with it' by his assault on the restored Jews, and 'grind him to powder.'

all ... people of ... earth – The Antichristian confederacy against the Jews shall be almost universal.

4. I will smite ... horse – The arm of attack especially formidable to Judah, who was unprovided with cavalry. So in the overthrow of Pharaoh (Ex 15:19,21).

open mine eyes upon ... Judah – to watch over Judah's safety. Heretofore Jehovah seemed to have shut His eyes, as having no regard for her.

blindness – so as to rush headlong on to their own ruin (compare Zec 14:12,13).

5. shall say – when they see the foe divinely smitten with 'madness.'

Judah ... Jerusalem – here distinguished as the country and the metropolis. Judah recognizes her 'strength' to be 'Jerusalem and its inhabitants' as the instrument, and 'Jehovah of hosts their God' (dwelling especially there) as the author of all power (Joe 3:16). My strength is the inhabitants of Jerusalem, who have the Lord their God as their help. The repulse of the foe by the metropolis shall assure the Jews of the country that the same divine aid shall save them.

6. On 'governors of Judah,' see on Zec 9:7.

hearth – or pan.

torch ... in a sheaf – Though small, it shall consume the many foes around. One prophet supplements the other. Thus Isa 29:1-24 Joe 3:1-21 Zec 12:1-14:21, describe more Antichrist's *army* than himself. Daniel represents him as a horn growing out of the fourth beast or fourth kingdom; St. John, as a separate beast having an individual existence. Daniel dwells on his worldly conquests as a king; St. John, more on his spiritual tyranny,

whence he adds a second beast, the false prophet coming in a semblance of spirituality. What is briefly described by one is more fully prophesied by the other [ROOS].

7. Judah is to be 'first saved,' because of her meek acknowledgment of dependence on Jerusalem, subordinate to Jehovah's aid.

tents – shifting and insecure, as contrasted with the solid fortifications of Judah. But God chooses the weak to confound the mighty, that all human glorying may be set aside.

8. Jerusalem, however, also shall be specially strengthened against the foe.

feeble ... shall be as David – to the Jew, the highest type of strength and glory on earth (2Sa 17:8 18:3 Joe 3:10).

angel of the Lord before them – the divine angel that went 'before them' through the desert, the highest type of strength and glory in heaven (Ex 23:20 32:34). 'The house of David' is the 'prince,' and his family sprung from David (Eze 45:7,9). David's house was then in a comparatively weak state.

9. I will seek to destroy – I will set Myself with determined earnestness to destroy (Hag 2:22).

10. Future conversion of the Jews is to flow from an extraordinary outpouring of the Holy Spirit (Jer 31:9,31-34 Eze 39:29).

spirit of grace ... supplications – 'spirit' is here not the spirit produced, but THE HOLY SPIRIT *producing* a 'gracious' disposition, and inclination for '*supplications.*' CALVIN explains 'spirit of grace' as *the grace of God* itself (whereby He 'pours' out His bowels of mercy), 'conjoined with the sense of it in man's heart.' The 'spirit of supplications' is the mercury whose rise or fall is an unerring test of the state of the Church [MOORE]. In *Hebrew*, 'grace' and 'supplications' are kindred terms; translate, therefore, 'gracious supplications.' The *plural* implies suppliant prayers 'without ceasing.' Herein not merely external help against the foe, as before, but internal grace is promised subsequently.

look upon me – with profoundly earnest regard, as the Messiah whom they so long denied.

pierced – implying Messiah's humanity: as 'I will pour ... spirit' implies His divinity.

look ... mourn – True repentance arises from the sight by faith of the crucified Saviour. It is the tear that drops from the eye of faith looking on Him. Terror only produces remorse. The true penitent weeps over his sins in love to Him who in love has suffered for them.

me ... him – The change of person is due to Jehovah-Messiah speaking *in His own person* first, then the prophet speaking *of Him*. The Jews, to avoid the conclusion that He whom they have 'pierced' is Jehovah-Messiah, who says, 'I will pour out ... spirit,' altered 'me' into 'him,' and represent the 'pierced' one to be Messiah Ben (son of) Joseph, who was to suffer in the battle with Cog, before Messiah Ben David should come to reign. But *Hebrew, Chaldee, Syriac,* and *Arabic* oppose this; and the ancient Jews interpreted it of Messiah. Ps 22:16 also refers to His being 'pierced.' So Joh 19:37 Re 1:7. The actual piercing of His side was the culminating point of all their insulting treatment of Him. The act of the Roman soldier who pierced Him was their act (Mt 27:25), and is so accounted here in Zechariah. The *Hebrew* word is always used of a literal piercing (so Zec 13:3).

as one mourneth for … son – (Jer 6:26 Am 8:10). A proverbial phrase peculiarly forcible among the Jews, who felt childlessness as a curse and dishonour. Applied with peculiar propriety to mourning for Messiah, 'the *first-born* among many brethren' (Ro 8:29).

11. As in Zec 12:10 the bitterness of their mourning is illustrated by a private case of mourning, so in this verse by a public one, the greatest recorded in Jewish history, that for the violent death in battle with Pharaoh-necho of the good King Josiah, whose reign had been the only gleam of brightness for the period from Hezekiah to the downfall of the state; lamentations were written by Jeremiah for the occasion (2Ki 23:29,30 2Ch 35:22–27).

Hadad-rimmon – a place or city in the great plain of Esdraelon, the battlefield of many a conflict, near Megiddo; called so from the Syrian idol Rimmon. the Syrians [MACROB, *Saturnalia,* 1.23]. *Hadad* also was the name of the sun, a chief god of universal and an individual mourning at once.

12–14. David … Nathan – representing the highest and lowest of the royal order. Nathan, not the prophet, but a younger son of David (2Sa 5:14 Lu 3:31).

apart – Retirement and seclusion are needful for deep personal religion.

wives apart – Jewish females worship separately from the males (Ex 15:1,20).

13. Levi … Shimei – the highest and lowest of the priestly order (Nu 3:18,21). Their example and that of the royal order would of course influence the rest.

14. All … that remain – after the fiery ordeal, in which two-thirds fall (Zec 13:8,9).

Chapter 13

Zec 13:1–9. Cleansing of the Jews from sin; abolition of idolatry; the shepherd smitten; the people of the land cut off, except a third part refined by trials.

1. Connected with the close of the twelfth chapter. The mourning penitents are here comforted.

fountain opened – It has been long opened, but then first it shall be so '*to the house of David,*' (representing all Israel) after their long and weary wanderings. Like Hagar in the wilderness they remain ignorant of the refreshment near them, until God '*opens* their eyes' (Ge 21:19) [MOORE]. It is not the fountain, but their eyes that need to be opened. It shall be a 'fountain' ever flowing; not a laver needing constantly to be replenished with water, such as stood between the tabernacle and altar (Ex 30:18).

for sin … uncleanness – that is, judicial guilt and moral impurity. Thus justification and sanctification are implied in this verse as both flowing from the blood of Christ, not from ceremonial sacrifices (1Co 1:30 Heb 9:13,14 1Jo 1:7; compare Eze 36:25). *Sin* in *Hebrew* is literally *a missing the mark* or *way.*

2. Consequences of pardon; not indolence, but the extirpation of sin.

names of … idols – Their very names were not to be mentioned; thus the Jews, instead of Mephibaal, said Mephibosheth (*Bosheth* meaning a contemptible thing) (Ex 23:13 De 12:3 Ps 16:4).

out of the land – Judea's two great sins, idolatry and false prophecy, have long since ceased. But these are types of all sin (for example, covetousness, Eph 5:5, a besetting sin of the Jews now). Idolatry, combined with the 'spirit' of 'Satan,' is again to be incarnated in 'the man of sin,' who is to arise in Judea (2Th 2:3–12), and is to be 'consumed with the Spirit of the Lord's mouth.' Compare as to Antichrist's papal precursor, 'seducing spirits … doctrines of devils', 1Ti 4:1–3 2Pe 2:1.

the unclean spirit – *Hebrew, spirit of uncleanness* (compare Re 16:13); opposed to 'the Spirit of holiness' (Ro 1:4), 'spirit of error' (1Jo 4:6). One assuming to be divinely inspired, but in league with Satan.

3. The form of phraseology here is drawn from De 13:6–10 18:20. The substantial truth expressed is that false prophecy shall be utterly abolished. If it were possible for it again to start up, the very parents of the false prophet would not let parental affection interfere, but would be the first to thrust him through. Love to Christ must be paramount to the tenderest of natural ties (Mt 10:37). Much as the godly love their children, they love God and His honour more.

4. prophets … ashamed – of the false prophecies which they have uttered in times past, and which the event has confuted.

rough garment – sackcloth. The badge of a prophet (2Ki 1:8 Isa 20:2), to mark their frugality alike in food and attire (Mt 3:4); also, to be consonant to the mournful warnings which they delivered. It is not the dress that is here condemned, but the purpose for which it was worn, namely, to conceal wolves under sheep's clothing [Calvin]. The monkish hair-shirt of Popery, worn to inspire the multitude with the impression of superior sanctity, shall be then cast aside.

5, 6. The detection of one of the false prophets dramatically represented. He is seized by some zealous vindicator of the law, and in fear cries out, 'I am no prophet.'

man – that is, one.

6. wounds in thine hand – The interrogator still suspects him: 'If so, if you have never pretended to be a prophet, whence come those wounds?' The *Hebrew* is literally, '*between* thine hands.' The hands were naturally held up to ward off the blows, and so were 'thrust through' (Zec 13:3) 'between' the bones of the hand. *Stoning* was the usual punishment; 'thrusting through' was also a fit retribution on one who tried to 'thrust Israel away' from the Lord (De 13:10); and perfects the type of Messiah, condemned as a false prophet, and pierced with 'wounds *between* His hands.' Thus the transition to the direct prophecy of Him (Zec 13:7) is natural, which it would not be if He were not indirectly and in type alluded to.

wounded in ... house of my friends – an implied admission that he had pretended to prophecy, and that his friends had wounded him for it in zeal for God (Zec 13:3). The Holy Spirit in Zechariah alludes indirectly to Messiah, the Antitype, wounded by those whom He came to befriend, who ought to have been His 'friends,' who were His kinsmen (compare Zec 13:3, as to the false prophet's friends, with Mr 3:21, 'His friends,' *Margin*, 'kinsmen'; Joh 7:5; 'His own,' Joh 1:11; *the Jews*, 'of whom as concerning the flesh He came,' Ro 9:5), but who wounded Him by the agency of the Romans (Zec 12:10).

7. Expounded by Christ as referring to Himself (Mt 26:31,32). Thus it is a resumption of the prophecy of His betrayal (Zec 11:4,10,13,14), and the subsequent punishment of the Jews. It explains the mystery why He, who came to be a blessing, was cut off while bestowing the blessing. God regards sin in such a fearful light that He spared not His own co-equal Son in the one Godhead, when that Son bore the sinner's guilt.

Awake – Compare a similar address to the sword of justice personified (Jer 46:6,7). For 'smite' (imperative), Mt 26:31 has 'I will smite.' The act of the sword, it is thus implied, is God's act. So the prophecy in Isa 6:9, 'Hear ye,' is imperative; the fulfilment as declared by Jesus is future (Mt 13:14), 'ye shall hear.'

sword – the symbol of judicial power, the highest exercise of which is to take away the life of the condemned (Ps 17:13 Ro 13:4). Not

merely a show, or expression, of justice (as Socinians think) is distinctly implied here, but an actual execution of it on Messiah the shepherd, the substitute for the sheep, by God as judge. Yet God in this shows His love as gloriously as His justice. For God calls Messiah '*My* shepherd,' that is, provided (Re 13:8) for sinners by My love to them, and ever the object of My love, though judicially smitten (Isa 53:4) for their sins (Isa 42:1 59:16).

man that is my fellow – literally, 'the man of my union.' The *Hebrew* for 'man' is 'a mighty man,' one peculiarly man in his noblest ideal. 'My nearest kinsman' [Hengstenberg], (Joh 10:30 14:10,11 Php 2:6).

sheep shall be scattered – The scattering of Christ's disciples on His apprehension was the partial fulfilment (Mt 26:31), a pledge of the dispersion of the Jewish nation (once the Lord's *sheep,* Ps 100:3) consequent on their crucifixion of Him. The Jews, though 'scattered,' are still the Lord's 'sheep,' awaiting their being 'gathered' by Him (Isa 40:9,11).

I will turn ... hand upon ... little ones – that is, I will interpose in favour of (compare the phrase in a good sense, Isa 1:25) 'the little ones,' namely, the humble followers of Christ from the Jewish Church, despised by the world: 'the poor of the flock' (Zec 11:7,11); comforted after His crucifixion at the resurrection (Joh 20:17–20); saved again by a special interposition from the destruction of Jerusalem, having retired to Pella when Cestius Gallus so unaccountably withdrew from Jerusalem. Ever since there has been a Jewish 'remnant' of 'the little ones ... according to the election of grace.' The hand of Jehovah was laid in wrath on the Shepherd that His *hand might be turned* in grace *upon the little ones.*

8, 9. Two-thirds of the Jewish nation were to perish in the Roman wars, and a third to survive. Probably from the context (Zec 14:2-9), which has never yet been fulfilled, the destruction of the two-thirds (literally, 'the proportion of two,' or 'portion of two') and the saving of the remnant, the one-third, are still future, and to be fulfilled under Antichrist.

9. through ... fire – of trial (Ps 66:10 Am 4:11 1Co 3:15 1Pe 1:6,7). It hence appears that the Jews' conversion is not to precede, but to follow, their external deliverance by the special interposition of Jehovah; which latter shall be the main cause of their conversion, combined with a preparatory inward shedding abroad in their hearts of the Holy Spirit (Zec 12:10–14); and here, 'they shall call on My name,' in their trouble, which brings Jehovah to their help (Ps 50:15).

my people – (Jer 30:18–22 Eze 11:19,20 Ho 2:23).

Chapter 14

Zec 14:1–21. Last struggle with the hostile world powers: Messiah-Jehovah saves Jerusalem and destroys the foe, of whom the remnant turns to the lord reigning at Jerusalem.

1. day of the Lord – in which He shall vindicate His justice by punishing the wicked and then saving His elect people (Joe 2:31 3:14 Mal 4:1,5).

thy spoil … divided in the midst of thee – by the foe; secure of victory, they shall not divide the spoil taken from thee in their camp outside, but 'in the midst' of the city itself.

2. gather all nations. – The prophecy seems literal (compare Joe 3:2). If Antichrist be the leader of the nations, it seems inconsistent with the statement that he will at this time be sitting in the temple as God at Jerusalem (2Th 2:4); thus Antichrist outside would be made to besiege Antichrist within the city. But difficulties do not set aside revelations: the event will clear up seeming difficulties. Compare the complicated movements, Da 11:1–45.

half … the residue – In Zec 13:8,9, it is 'two-thirds' that perish, and 'the *third*' escapes. There, however, it is 'in *all the land*'; here it is 'half *of the city*.' Two-thirds of the '*whole people*' perish, one-third survives. One-half of the *citizens* are led captive, the residue are not cut off. Perhaps, too, we ought to translate, 'a (not "the") residue.'

3. Then – In Jerusalem's extremity.

as … in … day of battle – as when Jehovah fought for Israel against the Egyptians at the Red Sea (Ex 14:14 15:3). As He then made a way through the divided sea, so will He now divide in two 'the Mount of Olives' (Zec 14:4).

4. The object of the cleaving of the mount in two by a fissure or valley (a prolongation of the valley of Jehoshaphat, and extending from Jerusalem on the west towards Jordan, eastward) is to open a way of escape to the besieged (compare Joe 3:12,14). Half the divided mount is thereby forced northward, half southward; the valley running between. The place of His departure at His ascension shall be the place of His return: and the 'manner' of His return also shall be similar (Ac 1:11). He shall probably 'come from the east' (Mt 24:27). He so made His triumphal entry into the city from the Mount of Olives from the east (Mt 21:1–10). This was the scene of His agony: so it shall be the scene of His glory. Compare Eze 11:23, with Eze 43:2, 'from the way of the east.

5. ye shall flee *to* the valley – rather '*through* the valley,' as in 2Sa 2:29.

of the mountains – rather, 'of *My* mountains,' namely, Zion and Moriah, peculiarly sacred to Jehovah [MOORE].

Azal – the name of a place *near* a gate east of the city. The *Hebrew* means 'adjoining' [HENDERSON]. Others give the meaning, 'departed,' 'ceased.' The valley reaches up to the city gates, so as to enable the fleeing citizens to betake themselves immediately to it on leaving the city.

Lord my God … with thee – The mention of the 'Lord my God' leads the prophet to pass suddenly to a direct address to Jehovah. It is as if 'lifting up his head' (Lu 21:28), he suddenly sees in vision the Lord coming, and joyfully exclaims, 'All the saints with Thee!' So Isa 25:9.

saints – *holy angels* escorting the returning King (Mt 24:30,31 Jude 1:14); and redeemed men (1Co 15:23 1Th 3:13 4:14). Compare the similar mention of the 'saints' and 'angels' at His coming on Sinai (De 32:2,3 Ac 7:53 Ga 3:19 Heb 2:2). Phillips thinks Azal is Ascalon on the Mediterranean. An earthquake beneath Messiah's tread will divide Syria, making from Jerusalem to Azal a valley which will admit the ocean waters from the west to the Dead Sea. The waters will rush down the valley of Arabah, the old bed of the Jordan, clear away the sand-drift of four thousand years, and cause the commerce of Petra and Tyre to centre in the holy city. The Dead Sea rising above its shores will overflow by the valley of Edom, completing the straits of Azal into the Red Sea. Thus will be formed the great pool of Jerusalem (compare Zec 14:8 Eze 47:1. Joe 3:18). Euphrates will be the north boundary, and the Red Sea the south. Twenty-five miles north and twenty-five miles south of Jerusalem will form one side of the fifty miles square of the Lord's Holy Oblation (Eze 48:1-35). There are seven spaces of fifty miles each from Jerusalem northward to the Euphrates, and five spaces of fifty miles each southward to the Red Sea. Thus there are thirteen equal distances on the breadth of the future promised land, one for the oblation and twelve for the tribes, according to Eze 48:1–35. That the Euphrates north, Mediterranean west, the Nile and Red Sea south, are to be the future boundaries of the holy land, which will include Syria and Arabia, is favoured by Ge 15:8 Ex 23:31 De 11:24 Jos 1:4 1Ki 4:21 2Ch 9:26 Isa 27:12; all which was partially realized in Solomon's reign, shall be antitypically so hereafter. The theory, if true, will clear away many difficulties in the way of the literal interpretation of this chapter and Eze 48:1-35.

6. light … not … clear … dark – JEROME, *Chaldee, Syriac,* and *Septuagint* translate, 'There shall not be light, but cold and ice'; that is, a day full of horror (Am 5:18). But the *Hebrew* for 'clear' does not mean 'cold,' but 'precious,' 'splendid' (compare Job 31:26). CALVIN translates, 'The light shall not be clear, *but* dark' (literally, 'condensation,' that is, thick mist); like a dark day in which you can hardly distinguish between day and night. *English Version* accords with Zec 14:7: 'There shall not be altogether light nor altogether darkness,' but an intermediate condition in which sorrows shall be mingled with joys.

7. one day – a day altogether *unique*, different from all others [MAURER]. Compare 'one,' that is, unique (So 6:9 Jer 30:7).

known to ... Lord – This truth restrains man's curiosity and teaches us to wait the Lord's own time (Mt 24:36).

not day, nor night – answering to 'not ... clear nor ... dark' (Zec 14:6); not altogether daylight, yet not the darkness of night.

at evening ... shall be light – Towards the close of this twilight-like time of calamity, 'light' shall spring up (Ps 97:11 112:4 Isa 30:26 60:19,20).

8. living waters – (Eze 47:1 Joe 3:18).

former sea – that is, the *front*, or east, which Orientalists face in taking the points of the compass; the Dead Sea.

hinder sea – the west or Mediterranean.

summer ... winter – neither dried up by heat, nor frozen by cold; ever flowing.

9. king over all ... earth – Isa 54:5 implies that this is to be the consequence of Israel being again recognized by God as His own people (Da 2:44 Re 11:15).

one Lord ... name one – Not that He is not so already, but He shall then be *recognized by all unanimously* as 'One.' Now there are 'gods many and lords many.' Then Jehovah alone shall be worshipped. The *manifestation* of the unity of the Godhead shall be simultaneous with that of the unity of the Church. Believers are one in spirit already, even as God is one (Eph 4:3–6). But externally there are sad divisions. Not until these disappear, shall God reveal fully His unity to the world (Joh 17:21,23). Then shall there be 'a pure language, that all may call upon the name of the Lord with one consent' (Zep 3:9). The Son too shall at last give up His mediatorial kingdom to the Father, when the purposes for which it was established shall have been accomplished, 'that God may be all in all' (1Co 15:24).

10. turned – or, 'changed round about': literally, 'to make a circuit.' The whole hilly land *round* Jerusalem, which would prevent the free passage of the living waters, shall be *changed* so as to be 'as a (or *the*) plain' (Isa 40:4).

from Geba to Rimmon – Geba (2Ki 23:8) in Benjamin, the north border of Judah. Rimmon, in Simeon (Jos 15:32), the south border of Judah; not the Rimmon northeast of Michmash. 'The plain from Geba to Rimmon' (that is, from one boundary to the other) is the Arabah or plain of the Jordan, extending from the Sea of Tiberias to the Elanitic Gulf of the Red Sea.

it shall be lifted up – namely, Jerusalem shall be exalted, the hills all round being lowered (Mic 4:1).

inhabited in her place – (Zec 12:6).

from Benjamin's gate – leading to the territory of Benjamin. The same as Ephraim's gate, the north boundary of the city (2Ki 14:13).

the first gate – west of the city [GROTIUS]. 'The place of,' implies that the gate itself was then not in existence. 'The old gate' (Ne 3:6).

the corner gate – east of the city [GROTIUS]. Or the 'corner' joining the north and west parts of the wall [VILLALPANDUS]. GROTIUS thinks 'corners' refers to the *towers* there built (compare Zep 3:6, *Margin*).

tower of Hananeel – south of the city, near the sheep gate (Ne 3:1 12:39 Jer 31:38) [GROTIUS].

king's wine-presses – (So 8:11). In the interior of the city, at Zion [GROTIUS].

11. no more utter destruction – (Jer 31:40). Literally, 'no more *curse*' (Re 22:3; compare Mal 4:6), for there will be no more sin. Temporal blessings and spiritual prosperity shall go together in the millennium: long life (Isa 65:20–22), peace (Isa 2:4), honour (Isa 60:14–16), righteous government (Isa 54:14 60:18). Judgment, as usual, begins at the house of God, but then falls fatally on Antichrist, whereon the Church obtains perfect liberty. The last day will end everything evil (Ro 8:21) [AUBERLEN].

12. Punishment on the foe, the last Antichristian confederacy (Isa 59:18 66:24 Eze 38,39 Re 19:17-21). A living death: the *corruption* (Ga 6:8) of death combined in ghastly union with the conscious sensibility of life. Sin will be felt by the sinner in all its loathsomeness, inseparably clinging to him as a festering, putrid body.

13. tumult – consternation (Zec 12:4 1Sa 14:15,20).

lay hold ... on ... hand of ... neighbour – instinctively grasping it, as if thereby to be safer, but in vain [MENOCHIUS]. Rather, in order to assail 'his neighbours' [CALVIN], (Eze 38:21). Sin is the cause of all quarrels on earth. It will cause endless quarrels in hell (Jas 3:15,16).

14. Judah ... fight at Jerusalem – namely, against the foe. As to the spoil gained from the foe, compare Eze 39:10,17.

15. The plague shall affect the very beasts belonging to the foe. A typical foretaste of all this befell Antiochus Epiphanes and his host at Jerusalem (I Maccabees 13:49; II Maccabees 9:5).

16. every one ... left – (Isa 66:19,23). God will conquer all the foes of the Church, Some He will destroy; others He will bring into willing subjection.

from year to year – literally, 'from the sufficiency of a year in a year.'

feast of tabernacles – The other two great yearly feasts, Passover and Pentecost, are not specified, because, their antitypes having come, the types are done away with. But the feast of tabernacles will be commemorative of the Jews' sojourn, not merely forty years in the wilderness, but for almost two thousand years of their dispersion. So it was kept on their return from the Babylonian dispersion (Ne 8:14–17). It was the feast on which Jesus made His triumphal entry into Jerusalem (Mt 21:8); a pledge of His return to His capital to reign (compare Le 23:34, 39,40,42 Re 7:9 21:3). A feast of peculiar joy (Ps 118:15 Ho 12:9). The feast on which Jesus gave the invitation to the living waters of salvation ('Hosanna,' *save us now*, was the cry, Mt 21:9; compare Ps 118:25,26) (Joh 7:2,37). To the Gentiles, too, it will be significant of perfected salvation after past wanderings in a moral wilderness, as it originally commemorated the ingathering of the harvest. The seedtime of tears shall then have issued in the harvest of joy [MOORE]. 'All the nations' could not possibly in person go up to the feast, but they may do so by representatives.

17. no rain – including every calamity which usually follows in the East from want of rain, namely, scarcity of provisions, famine, pestilence. Rain is the symbol also of God's favour (Ho 6:3). That there shall be unconverted men under the millennium appears from the outbreak of Gog and Magog at the end of it (Re 20:7-9); but they, like Satan their master, shall be restrained during the thousand years. Note, too, from this verse that the Gentiles shall come up to Jerusalem, rather than the Jews go as missionaries to the Gentiles (Isa 2:2 Mic 5:7). However, Isa 66:19 *may* imply the converse.

18. if ... Egypt go not up – specified as Israel's ancient foe. If Egypt go not up, and so there be no rain on them (a judgment which Egypt would condemn, as depending on the Nile's overflow, not on rain), there shall be the plague. Because the guilty are not affected by one judgment, let them not think to escape, for God has other judgments which shall plague them.

19. punishment – literally, 'sin'; that is, 'punishment for sin.'

20. shall there be upon the bells – namely, this inscription, 'Holiness to the Lord,' the same as was on the mitre of the high priest (Ex 28:36). This implies that all things, even the most common, shall be sacred to Jehovah, and not merely the things which under the law had peculiar sanctity attached to them. The 'bells' were metal plates hanging from the necks of horses and camels as ornaments, which *tinkled* (as the *Hebrew* root means) by striking against each other. Bells attached to horses are found represented on the walls of Sennacherib's palace at Koyunjik.

pots ... like ... bowls – the vessels used for boiling, for receiving ashes., shall be as holy as the bowls used for catching the blood of the sacrificial victims (see on Zec 9:15; 1Sa 2:14). The priesthood of Christ will be explained more fully both by the Mosaic types and by the New Testament in that temple of which Ezekiel speaks. Then the Song of Solomon, now obscure, will be understood, for the marriage feast of the Lamb will be celebrated in heaven (Re 19:1–21), and on earth it will be a Solomonic period, peaceful, glorious, and nuptial. There will be no king but a prince; the sabbatic period of the judges will return, but not with the Old Testament, but New Testament glory (Isa 1:26 Eze 45:1–25) [ROOS].

21. every pot – even in private houses, as in the temple, shall be deemed holy, so universal shall be the consecration of all things and persons to Jehovah.

take of them – as readily as they would take of the pots of the temple itself, whatever number they wanted for sacrifice.

no ... Canaanite – no unclean or ungodly person (Isa 35:8 52:1 Joe 3:17). Compare as to the final state subsequent to the millennium, Re 21:27 22:15.

MALACHI

A.R. Faussett

Introduction

Malachi forms the transition link between the two dispensations, the Old and the New, 'the skirt and boundary of Christianity' [TERTULLIAN], to which perhaps is due the abrupt earnestness which characterizes his prophecies. His very name is somewhat uncertain. Malachi is the name of an office, rather than a person, 'My messenger,' and as such is found in Mal 3:1. The *Septuagint* favours this view in Mal 1:1; translate, not 'by Malachi,' but 'by the hand of His messenger' (compare Hag 1:13). Malachi is the last inspired messenger of the Old Testament, announcing the advent of the Great Messenger of the New Testament.

As Haggai and Zechariah, the contemporary prophets, supported Joshua and Zerubbabel in the building of the temple, so Malachi at a subsequent period supported the priest Ezra and the governor Nehemiah. Like that ruler, he presupposes the temple to have been already built (Mal 1:10 3:1–10). Both alike censure the abuses still unreformed (Ne 13:5,15–22,23-30), the profane and mercenary character of the priests, the people's marriages contracted with foreigners, the non-payment of the tithes, and want of sympathy towards the poor on the part of the rich (Ne 6:7) implies that Nehemiah was supported by prophets in his work of reformation. The date thus will be about 420 B.C., or later. Both the periods after the captivity (that of Haggai and Zechariah, and that of Malachi) were marked by royal, priestly, and prophetic men at the head of God's people. The former period was that of the building of the temple; the latter, that of the restoration of the people and rebuilding of the city. It is characteristic of the people of God that the first period after the restoration was exclusively devoted to the rebuilding of the temple; the political restoration came secondarily. Only a colony of fifty thousand settled with Joshua and Zerubbabel in Palestine (Ezr 2:64). Even these became intermingled with the heathen around during the sixty years passed over by Ezra in silence (Ezr 9:6–15 Ne 1:3). Hence a second restoration was needed which should mould the national life into a Jewish form, re-establishing the holy law and the holy city – a work effected by Ezra and Nehemiah, with the aid of Malachi, in a period of about half a century, ending with the deaths of Malachi and Nehemiah in the last ten years of the fifth century B.C.

MOORE distinguishes six portions:

(1) Charge against Israel for insensibility to God's love, which so distinguished Israel above Edom (Mal 1:1–5).

(2) The priests are reproved for neglect and profanation (Mal 1:6–2:9).

(3) Mixed marriages, and the wrongs done to Jewish wives, are reproved (Mal 2:10–16).

(4) Coming of Messiah and His forerunners (Mal 2:17–3:6).

(5) Reproof for tithes withheld (Mal 3:7–12).

(6) Contrast between the godly and the ungodly at the present time, and in the future judgment; exhortation, therefore, to return to the law (Mal 3:13–4:6).

The style is animated, but less grand, and the rhythm less marked, than in some of the older prophets. The canonicity of the book is established by the references to it in the New Testament (Mt 11:10 17:12 Mr 1:2 9:11,12 Lu 1:17 Ro 9:13).

Chapter 1

Mal 1:1–14. God's love: Israel's ingratitude: the priests' mercenary spirit: a gentile spiritual priesthood shall supersede them.

1. burden – heavy sentence.

to Israel – represented now by the two tribes of Judah and Benjamin, with individuals of the ten tribes who had returned with the Jews from Babylon. So 'Israel' is used, Ezr 7:10. Compare 2Ch 21:2, 'Jehoshaphat king of *Israel*,' where Judah, rather than the ten tribes, is regarded as the truest representative of Israel (compare 2Ch 12:6 28:19).

Malachi – see *Introduction.* God sent no prophet after him till John the Baptist, the forerunner of Christ, in order to enflame His people with the more ardent desire for Him, the great antitype and fulfiller of prophecy.

2. I have loved you – above other men; nay, even above the other descendants of Abraham and Isaac. Such gratuitous love on My part called for love on yours. But the return ye make is sin and dishonour to Me. This which is to be supplied is left unexpressed, sorrow as it were breaking off the sentence [MENOCHIUS], (De 7:8 Ho 11:1).

Wherein hast thou loved us? – In painful contrast to the tearful tenderness of God's love stands their insolent challenge. The root of their sin was insensibility to God's *love,* and to their own wickedness. Having had prosperity taken from them, they imply they have no tokens of God's love; they look at what God had taken, not at what God had left. God's love is often least acknowledged where it is most manifested. We must not infer God does not love us because He afflicts us. Men, instead of referring their sufferings to their proper cause, their own sin, impiously accuse God of indifference to their welfare [MOORE]. Thus Mal 1:1–4 form a fit introduction to the whole prophecy.

Was not Esau Jacob's brother? – and so, as far as dignity went, as much entitled to God's favour as Jacob. My adoption of Jacob, therefore, was altogether of gratuitous favour (Ro 9:13). So God has passed by our elder brethren, the angels who kept not their first estate, and yet He has provided salvation for man. The perpetual rejection of the fallen angels, like the perpetual desolations of Edom, attests God's severity to the lost, and goodness to those gratuitously saved. The sovereign eternal purpose of God is the only ground on which He bestows on one favours withheld from another. There are difficulties in referring salvation to the election of God, there are greater in referring it to the election of man [MOORE]. Jehovah illustrates His condescension and patience in arguing the case with them.

3. hated – not positively, but relatively; that is, did not choose him out to be the object of gratuitous favour, as I did Jacob (compare Lu 14:26, with Mt 10:37 Ge 29:30,31 De 21:15,16).

laid his mountains … waste – that is, his territory which was generally mountainous. Israel was, it is true, punished by the Chaldeans, but Edom has been utterly destroyed; namely, either by Nebuchadnezzar [ROSENMULLER], or by the neighbouring peoples, Egypt, Ammon, and Moab [JOSEPHUS, *Antiquities,* 10.9,7; MAURER], (Jer 49:18).

dragons – jackals [MOORE] (compare Isa 34:13).

4. Whereas – '*But if* Edom say [MAURER]. Edom may strive as she may to recover herself, but it shall be in vain, for I doom her to perpetual desolation, whereas I restore Israel. This Jehovah states, to illustrate His gratuitous love to Israel, rather than to Edom.

border of wickedness – a region given over to the curse of reprobation [CALVIN]. For a time Judea seemed as desolate as Idumea; but though the latter was once the highway of Eastern commerce, now the lonely rock-houses of Petra attest the fulfilment of the prophecy. It is still 'the border of wickedness,' being the resort of the marauding tribes of the desert. Judea's restoration, though delayed, is yet certain.

the Lord hath indignation – 'the people of My curse' (Isa 34:5).

5. from the border of Israel – Ye, restored to your own 'borders' in Israel, 'from' them shall raise your voices to 'magnify the Lord,' acknowledging that Jehovah has shown to you a gratuitous favour not shown to Edom, and so ought to be especially 'magnified from the borders of Israel.'

6. Turning from the people to the priests, Jehovah asks, whereas His love to the people was so great, where was their love towards Him? If the priests, as they profess, regard Him as their Father (Isa 63:16) and Master, let them show the reality of their profession by *love and reverential fear* (Ex 20:12 Lu 6:46). He addresses the priests because they ought to be leaders in piety to the rest of the people, whereas they are foremost in 'despising His name.'

Wherein have we despised – The same captious spirit of self-satisfied insensibility as prompted their question (Mal 1:2), 'Wherein hast Thou loved us?' They are blind alike to God's love and their own guilt.

7. **ye offer** – God's answer to their challenge (Mal 1:6), 'Wherein have we despised?'

polluted bread – namely, blemished sacrifices (Mal 1:8,13,14 De 15:21). So 'the *bread* of thy God' is used for '*sacrifices* to God' (Le 21:8).

polluted thee – that is, offered to thee 'polluted bread.'

table of the Lord – that is, the altar (Eze 41:22) (not the table of showbread). Just as the sacrificial *flesh* is called 'bread.'

contemptible – (Mal 1:12,13). Ye sanction the niggardly and blemished offerings of the people on the altar, to gain favour with them. Darius, and probably his successors, had liberally supplied them with victims for sacrifice, yet they presented none but the worst. A cheap religion, costing little, is rejected by God, and so is worth nothing. It costs more than it is worth, for it is worth nothing, and so proves really dear. God despises not the widow's mite, but he does despise the miser's mite [MOORE].

8. Your earthly ruler would feel insulted, if offered by you the offering with which ye put off God (see Le 22:22,24).

9. **now … beseech God that he will be gracious** – Ironical. Think you that God will be persuaded by such polluted gifts to be gracious to you? Far from it.

this hath been by your means – literally, 'hand.' These contemptible offerings are your doing, as being the priests mediating between God and the people; and think you, will God pay any regard to you (compare Mal 1:8,10)? 'Accept thy person' ('face'), Mal 1:8, answers to 'regard your persons,' in this verse.

10. **Who … for naught** – Not one even of the least priestly functions (as shutting the doors, or kindling a fire on the altar) would ye exercise without pay, therefore ye ought to fulfil them faithfully (1Co 9:13).

11. **For** – Since ye Jewish priests and people 'despise My name' (Mal 1:6), I shall find others who will magnify it (Mt 3:9). Do not think I shall have no worshippers because I have not you; for from the east to the west My name shall be great among the Gentiles (Isa 66:19,20), those very peoples whom ye look down upon as abominable.

pure offering – not 'the blind, the lame, and

the sick,' such as ye offer (Mal 1:8). 'In every place,' implies the catholicity of the Christian Church (Joh 4:21,23 1Ti 2:8). The 'incense' is figurative of *prayers* (Ps 141:2 Re 8:3). 'Sacrifice' is used metaphorically (Ps 51:17 Heb 13:10, 15,16 1Pe 2:5,12). In this sense the reference to the Lord's Supper, maintained by many of the fathers, may be admitted; it, like prayer, is a spiritual offering, accepted through the literal offering of the 'Lamb without blemish,' once for all slain.

12. Renewal of the charge in Mal 1:7.

fruit … meat – the offerings of the people. The 'fruit' is the *produce* of the altar, on which the priests subsisted. They did not literally say, The Lord's table is contemptible; but their *acts* virtually said so. They did not act so as to lead the people to reverence, and to offer their best to the Lord on it. The people were poor, and put off God with the worst offerings. The priests let them do so, for fear of offending the people, and so losing all gains from them.

13. **what a weariness is it!** – Ye regard God's service as irksome, and therefore try to get it over by presenting the most worthless offerings. Compare Mic 6:3, where God challenges His people to show wherein is the 'weariness' or hardship of His service. Also Isa 43:22-24, wherein He shows that it is they who have 'wearied' Him, not He who has wearied them.

snuffed at – despised.

it – the table of the Lord, and the meat on it (Mal 1:12).

torn – namely, by beasts, which it was not lawful to eat, much less to offer (Ex 22:31).

thus … offering – Hebrew, *mincha;* the *unbloody offering* of flour. Though this may have been of ordinary ingredients, yet the *sacrifices* of blemished animals accompanying it rendered it unacceptable.

14. **deceiver** – hypocrite. Not poverty, but avarice was the cause of their mean offerings.

male – required by law (Le 1:3,10).

great King – (Ps 48:2 Mt 5:35).

my name … dreadful among … heathen – Even the heathen dread Me because of My judgments; what a reproach this is to you, My people, who fear Me not (Mal 1:6)! Also it may be translated, '*shall be* feared among,' agreeing with the prophecy of the call of the Gentiles (Mal 1:11).

Chapter 2

Mal 2:1–17. Reproof of the priests for violating the covenant; and the people also for mixed marriages and unfaithfulness.

1. **for you** – The priests in particular are reproved, as their part was to have led the people aright, and reproved sin, whereas they

encouraged and led them into sin. Ministers cannot sin or suffer alone. They drag down others with them if they fall [Moore].

2. lay … to heart – My commands.

send a curse – rather, as Hebrew, '*the* curse'; namely, that denounced in De 27:15–26 28:15–68.

curse your blessings – turn the blessings you enjoy into curses (Ps 106:15).

cursed them – Hebrew, *them severally;* that is, I have cursed each one of your blessings.

3. corrupt – literally, 'rebuke,' answering to the opposite prophecy of blessing (Mal 3:11), 'I will *rebuke* the devourer.' To rebuke the seed is to forbid its growing.

your – literally, '*for you*'; that is, to your hurt.

dung of … solemn feasts – The dung in the maw of the victims sacrificed on the feast days; the maw was the perquisite of the priests (De 18:3), which gives peculiar point to the threat here. You shall get the dung of the maw as your perquisite, instead of the maw.

one shall take you away with it – that is, ye shall be taken away with it; it shall cleave to you wherever ye go [Moore]. Dung shall be thrown on your faces, and ye shall be taken away as dung would be, dung-begrimed as ye shall be (1Ki 14:10; compare Jer 16:4 22:19).

4. ye shall know – by bitter experience of consequences, that it was with this design I admonished you, in order 'that My covenant with Levi might be' maintained; that is, that it was for your own good (which would be ensured by your maintaining the Levitical command) I admonished you, that ye should return to your duty [Maurer] (compare Mal 2:5,6). Malachi's function was that of a reformer, leading back the priests and people to the law (Mal 4:4).

5–9. He describes the promises, and also the conditions of the covenant; Levi's observance of the conditions and reward (compare Nu 25:11–13, Phinehas' zeal); and on the other hand the violation of the conditions, and consequent punishment of the present priests. 'Life' here includes the *perpetuity* implied in Nu 25:13, '*everlasting* priesthood.' 'Peace' is specified both here and there.

6. law of truth was in his mouth – He taught the people the truths of the law in all its fulness (De 33:10). The priest was the ordinary expounder of the law; the prophets were so only on special occasions.

iniquity … not found – no injustice in his judicial functions (De 17:8,9 19:17).

walked with me – by faith and obedience (Ge 5:22).

in peace – namely, the 'peace' which was the fruit of obeying the covenant (Mal 2:5). Peace with God, man, and one's own conscience, is the result of 'walking with God' (compare Job 22:21 Isa 27:5 Jas 3:18).

turn may … from iniquity – both by positive precept and by tacit example 'walking with God' (Jer 23:22 Da 12:3 Jas 5:20).

7. In doing so (Mal 2:6) he did his duty as a priest, 'for'.

knowledge – of the law, its doctrines, and positive and negative precepts (Le 10:10,11 De 24:8 Jer 18:18 Hag 2:11).

the law – that is, its true sense.

messenger of … Lord – the interpreter of His will; compare as to the prophets, Hag 1:13. So ministers are called 'ambassadors of Christ' (2Co 5:20); and the bishops of the seven churches in Revelation, 'angels' or messengers (Re 2:1,8,12,18 3:1,7,14; compare Ga 4:14).

8. out of the way – that is, from the covenant.

caused many to stumble – By scandalous example, the worse inasmuch as the people look up to you as ministers of religion (1Sa 2:17 Jer 18:15 Mt 18:6 Lu 17:1).

at the law – that is, in respect to the observances of the law.

corrupted … covenant – made it of none effect, by not fulfilling its conditions, and so forfeiting its promises (Zec 11:10 Ne 13:29).

9. Because ye do not keep the condition of the covenant, I will not fulfil the promise.

partial in the law – having respect to persons rather than to truth in the interpretation and administration of the law (Le 19:15).

10–16. Reproof of those who contracted marriages with foreigners and repudiated their Jewish wives.

Have we not all one father? – Why, seeing we all have one common origin, 'do we deal treacherously against *one another*' ('His brother' being a general expression implying that all are 'brethren' and sisters as children of the same Father above, 1Th 4:3–6 and so including the *wives* so injured)? namely, by putting away our Jewish wives, and taking foreign women to wife (compare Mal 2:14 and Mal 2:11 Ezr 9:1–9), and so violating 'the covenant' made by Jehovah with 'our fathers,' by which it was ordained that we should be a people separated from the other peoples of the world (Ex 19:5 Le 20:24,26 De 7:3). To intermarry with the heathen would defeat this purpose of Jehovah, who was the common Father of the Israelites in a peculiar sense in which He was not Father of the heathen. The 'one Father' is Jehovah (Job 31:15 1Co 8:6 Eph 4:6). 'Created us': not merely physical creation, but 'created us' to be His peculiar and chosen people (Ps 102:18 Isa 43:1 45:8 60:21 Eph 2:10), [Calvin]. How marked the contrast between the honour here done to the female sex, and the degradation to which Oriental women are generally subjected!

11. dealt treacherously – namely, in respect to the Jewish wives who were put away (Mal 2:14; also Mal 2:10,15,16).

profaned the holiness of ... Lord – by ill-treating the Israelites (namely, the wives), who were set apart as a people *holy unto the Lord:* 'the holy seed' (Ezr 9:2; compare Jer 2:3). Or, 'the holiness of the Lord' means His holy ordinance and covenant (De 7:3). But 'which He loved,' seems to refer to *the holy people,* Israel, whom God so gratuitously loved (Mal 1:2), without merit on their part (Ps 47:4).

married. – (Ezr 9:1,2 10:2 Ne 13:23.).

daughter of a strange god – women worshipping idols: as the worshipper in Scripture is regarded in the relation of a child to a father (Jer 2:27).

12. master and ... scholar – literally, 'him that watcheth and him that answereth.' So 'wakeneth' is used of *the teacher* or 'master' (Isa 50:4); masters are *watchful* in guarding their scholars. The reference is to the priests, who ought to have taught the people piety, but who led them into evil. 'Him that answereth' is the *scholar* who has to answer the questions of his teacher (Lu 2:47) [GROTIUS]. The Arabs have a proverb, 'None calling and none answering,' that is, there being *not one alive.* So GESENIUS explains it of the Levite watches in the temple (Ps 134:1), one *watchman* calling and another *answering.* But the scholar is rather the *people,* the pupils of the priests 'in doing this,' namely, forming unions with foreign wives. 'Out of the tabernacles of Jacob' proves it is not the priests alone. God will spare neither priests nor people who act so.

him that offereth – His offerings will not avail to shield him from the penalty of his sin in repudiating his Jewish wife and taking a foreign one.

13. done again – 'a second time': an aggravation of your offense (Ne 13:23–31), in that it is a relapse into the sin already checked once under Ezra (Ezr 9:10) [HENDERSON]. Or, 'the second time' means this: Your first sin was your blemished offerings to the Lord: now 'again' is added your sin towards your wives [CALVIN].

covering ... altar ... with tears – shed by your unoffending wives, repudiated by you that ye might take foreign wives. CALVIN makes the 'tears' to be those of all the people on perceiving their sacrifices to be sternly rejected by God.

14. Wherefore? – Why does God reject our offerings?

Lord ... witness between thee and ... wife – (so Ge 31:49,50).

of thy youth – The Jews still marry very young, the husband often being but thirteen years of age, the wife younger (Pr 5:18 Isa 54:6).

wife of thy covenant – not merely joined to thee by the marriage covenant generally, but by *the covenant between God and Israel,* the covenant-people, whereby a sin against a wife, a daughter of Israel, is a sin against God

[MOORE]. Marriage also is called 'the covenant of God' (Pr 2:17), and to it the reference may be (Ge 2:24 Mt 19:6 1Co 7:10).

15. MAURER and HENGSTENBERG explain the verse thus: The Jews had defended their conduct by the precedent of Abraham, who had taken Hagar to the injury of Sarah, his lawful wife; to this Malachi says now, 'No one (ever) did so in whom there was a residue of intelligence (discriminating between good and evil); and what did the one (Abraham, to whom you appeal for support) do, seeking a godly seed?' His object (namely, not to gratify passion, but to obtain the seed promised by God) makes the case wholly inapplicable to defend your position. MOORE (from FAIRBAIRN) better explains, in accordance with Mal 2:10, 'Did not He make (us Israelites) one? Yet He had the residue of the Spirit (that is, His isolating us from other nations was not because there was no residue of the Spirit left for the rest of the world). And wherefore (that is, *why then* did He thus isolate us as) the one (people; the *Hebrew* is "*the* one")? In order that He might seek a godly seed'; that is, that He might have 'a seed of God,' a nation the repository of the covenant, and the stock of the Messiah, and the witness for the one God amidst the surrounding polytheisms. Marriage with foreign women, and repudiation of the wives wedded in the Jewish covenant, utterly set aside this divine purpose. CALVIN thinks 'the one' to refer to the conjugal one body formed by the original pair (Ge 2:24). God might have joined many wives as one with the one husband, for He had no lack of spiritual being to impart to others besides Eve; the design of the restriction was to secure a pious offspring. One object of the marriage relation is to raise a seed for God and for eternity.

16. putting away – that is, divorce.

for one covereth violence with ... garment – MAURER translates, 'And (Jehovah hateth him who) covereth his garment (that is, his *wife,* in Arabic idiom; compare Ge 20:16, "He is to thee *a covering* of thy eyes"; the husband was so to the wife, and the wife to the husband; also De 22:30 Ru 3:9 Eze 16:8) with injury.' The *Hebrew* favours 'garment,' being accusative of the *thing covered.* Compare with *English Version,* Ps 73:6, 'violence covereth them as a garment.' Their 'violence' is the putting away of their wives; the 'garment' with which they try to cover it is the plea of Moses' permission (De 24:1; compare Mt 19:6–9).

17. wearied ... Lord – (Isa 43:24). This verse forms the transition to Mal 3:1. The Jewish sceptics of that day said virtually, God delighteth in evil-doers (inferring this from the prosperity of the surrounding heathen, while they, the Jews, were comparatively not prosperous: forgetting that their attendance to minor and external duties did not make up for their neglect of the weightier duties of the law; for example, the duty they owed their wives, just previously discussed); or (if not) Where (is the proof that He is) the God of judgment? To this the reply (Mal 3:1) is, 'The Lord whom ye seek, and whom as messenger of the covenant (that is, divine ratifier of God's covenant with Israel) ye delight in (thinking He will restore Israel to its proper place as first of the nations), shall suddenly come,' not as a Restorer of Israel temporally, but as a consuming *Judge* against Jerusalem (Am 5:18,19,20). The 'suddenly' implies the unpreparedness of the Jews, who, to the last of the siege, were expecting a temporal deliverer, whereas a destructive judgment was about to destroy them. So scepticism shall be rife before Christ's second coming. He shall suddenly and unexpectedly come then also as a consuming Judge to unbelievers (2Pe 3:3,4). Then, too, they shall affect to seek His coming, while really denying it (Isa 5:19 Jer 17:15 Eze 12:22,27).

Chapter 3

Mal 3:1–18. Messiah's coming, preceded by his forerunner, to punish the guilty for various sins, and to reward those who fear God.

1. Behold – Calling especial attention to the momentous truths which follow. Ye unbelievingly ask, Where is the God of judgment (Mal 2:7)? 'Behold,' therefore, 'I send,' Your unbelief will not prevent My keeping My covenant, and bringing to pass in due time that which ye say will never be fulfilled.

I will *send* **... he shall** *come* – The Father *sends* the Son: the Son *comes*. Proving the distinctness of personality between the Father and the Son.

my messenger – John the Baptist; as Mt 3:3 11:10 Mr 1:2,3 Lu 1:76 3:4 7:26,27 Joh 1:23, prove. This passage of Malachi evidently rests on that of Isaiah his predecessor (Isa 40:3–5). Perhaps also, as HENGSTENBERG thinks, 'messenger' includes *the long line of prophets* headed by *Elijah* (whence his name is put in Mal 4:5 as a representative name), and terminating in John, the last and greatest of the prophets (Mt 11:9–11). John as the representative prophet (the forerunner of Messiah the representative God-man) gathered in himself all the scattered lineaments of previous prophecy (hence Christ terms him 'much more than a prophet,' Lu 7:26), reproducing all its awful and yet inspiriting utterances: his coarse garb, like that of the old prophets, being a visible exhortation to repentance; the wilderness in which he preached symbolizing the lifeless, barren state of the Jews at that time, politically and spiritually;

his topics sin, repentance, and salvation, presenting for the last time the condensed epitome of all previous teachings of God by His prophets; so that he is called pre-eminently God's 'messenger.' Hence the oldest and true reading of Mr 1:2 is, 'as it is written in *Isaiah* the prophet'; the difficulty of which is, How can the prophecy of Malachi be referred to Isaiah? The explanation is: the passage in Malachi rests on that in Isa 40:3, and therefore the *original source* of the prophecy is referred to in order to mark this dependency and connection.

the Lord – *Ha-Adon* in *Hebrew*. The article marks that it is JEHOVAH (Ex 23:17 34:23; compare Jos 3:11,13). Compare Da 9:17, where the Divine Son is meant by 'for THE Lord's sake.' God the speaker makes 'the Lord,' the 'messenger of the covenant,' one with Himself. 'I will send ... before Me,' adding, 'THE LORD ... shall ... come'; so that '*the Lord*' must be one with the 'Me,' that is, He must be GOD, 'before' whom John was *sent*. As the divinity of the Son and His oneness with the Father are thus proved, so the distinctness of personality is proved by 'I send' and He 'shall come,' as distinguished from one another. He also comes to the temple as 'His temple': marking His divine lordship *over* it, and contrasted with all creatures, who are but 'servants *in*' it (Hag 2:7 Heb 3:2,5,6).

whom ye seek ... whom ye delight in – (see on Mal 2:17). At His first coming they 'sought' and 'delighted in' the hope of a *temporal* Saviour: not in what He then was. In the case of those whom Malachi in his time addresses, 'whom ye seek ... delight in,' is ironical. They unbelievingly asked, When will He come at last? Mal 2:17, 'Where is the God of judgment' (Isa 5:19 Am 5:18 2Pe 3:3,4)? In the case of the godly the desire for Messiah was sincere (Lu 2:25,28). He is called 'Angel of God's presence' (Isa 63:9), also Angel of Jehovah. Compare His appearances to Abraham (Ge 18:1,2,17,33), to Jacob (Ge 31:11 48:15,16), to Moses in the bush (Ex 3:2–6); He went before Israel as the Shekinah (Ex 14:19), and delivered the law at Sinai (Ac 7:38).

suddenly – This epithet marks the second coming, rather than the first; the earnest of that unexpected coming (Lu 12:38–46 Re 16:15) to judgment was given in the judicial expulsion of the money-changing profaners from the temple by Messiah (Mt 21:12,13), where also as here He calls the temple *His temple*. Also in the destruction of Jerusalem, most unexpected by the Jews, who to the last deceived themselves with the expectation that Messiah would suddenly appear as a temporal Saviour. Compare the use of 'suddenly' in Nu 12:4–10, where He appeared in wrath.

messenger of the covenant – namely, of the ancient covenant with Israel (Isa 63:9) and

Abraham, in which the promise to the Gentiles is ultimately included (Ga 4:16,17). The gospel at the first advent began with Israel, then embraced the Gentile world: so also it shall be at the second advent. All the manifestations of God in the Old Testament, the Shekinah and human appearances, were made in the person of the Divine Son (Ex 23:20,21 Heb 11:26 12:26). He was the messenger of the old covenant, as well as of the new.

2. (Mal 4:1 Re 6:16,17). The Messiah would come, not, as they expected, to flatter the theocratic nation's prejudices, but to subject their principles to the fiery test of His heart-searching truth (Mt 3:10–12), and to destroy Jerusalem and the theocracy after they had rejected Him. His mission is here regarded as a whole from the first to the second advent: the process of refining and separating the godly from the ungodly beginning during Christ's stay on earth, going on ever since, and about to continue till the final separation (Mt 25:31–46). The refining process, whereby a third of the Jews is refined as silver of its dross, while two-thirds perish, is described, Zec 13:8,9 (compare Isa 1:25).

3. sit – The purifier *sits* before the crucible, fixing his eye on the metal, and taking care that the fire be not too hot, and keeping the metal in, only until he knows the dross to be completely removed by his seeing his own image reflected (Ro 8:29) in the glowing mass. So the Lord in the case of His elect (Job 23:10 Ps 66:10 Pr 17:3 Isa 48:10 Heb 12:10 1Pe 1:7). He will *sit* down to the work, not perfunctorily, but with patient love and unflinching justice. The Angel of the Covenant, as in leading His people out of Egypt by the pillar of cloud and fire, has an aspect of terror to His foes, of love to His friends. The same separating process goes on in the world as in each Christian. When the godly are completely separated from the ungodly, the world will end. When the dross is taken from the gold of the Christian, he will be for ever delivered from the furnace of trial. The purer the gold, the hotter the fire now; the whiter the garment, the harder the washing [MOORE].

purify … sons of Levi – of the sins specified above. The very Levites, the ministers of God, then needed cleansing, so universal was the depravity.

that they may offer … in righteousness – as originally (Mal 2:6), not as latterly (Mal 1:7–14). So believers, the spiritual priesthood (1Pe 2:5).

4. as in the days of old – (Mal 1:11 2:5,6). The 'offering' (*Mincha, Hebrew*) is not expiatory, but prayer, thanksgiving, and self-dedication (Ro 12:1 Heb 13:15 1Pe 2:5).

5. I … come near … to judgment – *I* whom ye challenged, saying, 'Where is the God of judgment?' (Mal 2:17). I whom ye think far off, and

to be slow in judgment, am 'near,' and will come as a 'swift witness'; not only a judge, but also an eye-*witness* against sorcerers; for Mine eyes see every sin, though ye think I take no heed. Earthly judges need witnesses to enable them to decide aright: I alone need none (Ps 10:11 73:11 94:7.).

sorcerers – a sin into which the Jews were led in connection with their foreign idolatrous wives. The Jews of Christ's time also practised sorcery (Ac 8:9 13:6 Ga 5:20; JOSEPHUS [*Antiquities,* 20.6; *Wars of the Jews,* 2.12.23]). It shall be a characteristic of the last Antichristian confederacy, about to be consumed by the brightness of Christ's Coming (Mt 24:24 2Th 2:9 Re 13:13,14 16:13,14; also Re 9:21 18:23 21:8 22:15). Romanism has practised it; an order of *exorcists* exists in that Church.

adulterers – (Mal 2:15,16).

fear not me – the source of all sins.

6. the Lord – Jehovah: a name implying His immutable faithfulness in fulfilling His promises: the covenant name of God to the Jews (Ex 6:3), called here 'the sons of Jacob,' in reference to God's covenant with that patriarch.

I change not – Ye are mistaken in inferring that, because I have not yet executed judgment on the wicked, I am changed from what I once was, namely, a God of judgment.

therefore ye … are not consumed – Ye yourselves being 'not consumed,' as ye have long ago deserved, are a signal proof of My unchangeableness. Ro 11:29: compare the whole chapter, in which God's mercy in store for Israel is made wholly to flow from God's unchanging faithfulness to His own covenant of love. So here, as is implied by the phrase 'sons of *Jacob*' (Ge 28:13 35:12). They are spared because I am JEHOVAH, and they *sons of Jacob;* while I spare them, I will also punish them; and while I punish them, I will not wholly consume them. The unchangeableness of God is the sheet-anchor of the Church. The perseverance of the saints is guaranteed, not by their unchangeable love to God, but by His unchangeable love to them, and His eternal purpose and promise in Christ Jesus [MOORE]. He upbraids their ingratitude that they turn His very long-suffering (La 3:22) into a ground for sceptical denial of His coming as a Judge at all (Ps 50:1,3,4,21 Ec 8:11,12 Isa 57:11 Ro 2:4-10).

7–12. Reproof for the non-payment of tithes and offerings, which is the cause of their national calamities, and promise of prosperity on their paying them.

from … days of your fathers – Ye live as your fathers did when they brought on themselves the Babylonian captivity, and ye wish to follow in their steps. This shows that nothing but God's unchanging long-suffering had prevented their being long ago 'consumed' (Mal 3:6).

Return unto me – in penitence.

I will return unto you – in blessings.

Wherein. – (Mal 3:16). The same insensibility to their guilt continues: they speak in the tone of injured innocence, as if God calumniated them.

8. rob – literally, 'cover': hence, defraud. Do ye call defrauding God no sin to be 'returned' from (Mal 3:7)? Yet ye have done so to Me in respect to the tithes due to Me, namely, the tenth of all the remainder after the first-fruits were paid, which tenth was paid to the Levites for their support (Le 27:30–33): a tenth paid by the Levites to the priests (Nu 18:26–28): a second tenth paid by the people for the entertainment of the Levites, and their own families, at the tabernacle (De 12:18): another tithe every third year for the poor. (De 14:28,29).

offerings – the first-fruits, not less than one-sixtieth part of the corn, wine, and oil (De 18:4 Ne 13:10,12). The priests had this perquisite also, the tenth of the tithes which were the Levites perquisite. But they appropriated all the tithes, robbing the Levites of their due nine-tenths; as they did also, according to JOSEPHUS, before the destruction of Jerusalem by Titus. Thus doubly God was defrauded, the priests not discharging aright their sacrificial duties, and robbing God of the services of the Levites, who were driven away by destitution [GROTIUS].

9. cursed – (Mal 2:2). As ye despoil Me, so I despoil you, as I threatened I would, if ye continued to disregard Me. In trying to defraud God we only defraud ourselves. The eagle who robbed the altar set fire to her nest from the burning coal that adhered to the stolen flesh. So men who retain God's money in their treasuries will find it a losing possession. No man ever yet lost by serving God with a whole heart, nor gained by serving Him with a half one. We may compromise with conscience for half the price, but God will not endorse the compromise; and, like Ananias and Sapphira, we shall lose not only what we thought we had purchased so cheaply, but also the price we paid for it. If we would have God 'open' His treasury, we must open ours. One cause of the barrenness of the Church is the parsimony of its members [MOORE].

10. (Pr 3:9,10).

storehouse – (2Ch 31:11, *Margin;* compare 1Ch 26:20 Ne 10:38 13:5,12).

prove me ... herewith – with this; by doing so. Test Me whether I will keep My promise of blessing you, on condition of your doing your part (2Ch 31:10).

pour ... out – literally, 'empty out': image from a vessel completely emptied of its contents: no blessing being kept back.

windows of heaven – (2Ki 2:7).

that ... not ... room enough. – literally, 'even to not ... sufficiency,' that is, either, as *English Version.* Or, even so as that there should be '*not merely*' 'sufficiency' but *superabundance* [JEROME, MAURER]. GESENIUS not so well translates, 'Even to a failure of sufficiency,' which in the case of God could never arise, and therefore means *for ever, perpetually:* so Ps 72:5, 'as long as the sun and moon endure'; literally, 'until a failure of the sun and moon,' which is never to be; and therefore means, *for ever.*

12. Fulfilling the blessing (De 33:29 Zec 8:13).

delightsome land – (Da 8:9).

13–18. He notices the complaint of the Jews that it is of no profit to serve Jehovah, for that the ungodly proud are happy; and declares He will soon bring the day when it shall be known that He puts an everlasting distinction between the godly and the ungodly.

words ... stout – *Hebrew,* 'hard'; so 'the *hard* speeches which ungodly sinners have spoken against Him' (Jude 1:15) [HENDERSON].

have we spoken – The *Hebrew* expresses at once their *assiduity* and *habit* of speaking against God [VATABLUS]. The niphal form of the verb implies that these things were said, not directly *to* God, but *of* God, to one another (Eze 33:20) [MOORE].

14. what profit ... that we ... kept – (See on Mal 2:17). They here resume the same murmur against God. Job 21:14,15 22:17 describe a further stage of the same sceptical spirit, when the sceptic has actually ceased to keep God's service. Ps 73:1–14 describes the temptation to a like feeling in the saint when seeing the really godly suffer and the ungodly prosper in worldly goods now. The Jews here mistake utterly the nature of God's service, converting it into a mercenary bargain; they attended to outward observances, not from love to God, but in the hope of being well paid for in outward prosperity; when this was withheld, they charged God with being unjust, forgetting alike that God requires very different motives from theirs to accompany outward observances, and that God rewards even the true worshipper not so much in this life, as in the life to come.

his ordinance – literally, what He requires to be kept, 'His observances.'

walked mournfully – *in mournful garb,* sackcloth and ashes, the emblems of penitence; they forget Isa 58:3-8, where God, by showing what is true fasting, similarly rebukes those who then also said, Wherefore have we fasted and Thou seest not? They mistook the outward show for real humiliation.

15. And now – Since we who serve Jehovah are not prosperous and 'the proud' heathen flourish in prosperity, we must pronounce them the favourites of God (Mal 2:17 Ps 73:12).

set up – literally, 'built up': metaphor from architecture (Pr 24:3; compare Ge 16:2, *Margin*; Ge 30:3, *Margin.*)

tempt God – dare God to punish them, by breaking His laws (Ps 95:9).

16. 'Then,' when the ungodly utter such blasphemies against God, the godly hold mutual converse, defending God's righteous dealings against those blasphemers (Heb 3:13). The 'often' of *English Version* is not in the *Hebrew*. There has been always in the darkest times a remnant that feared God (1Ki 19:18 Ro 11:4).

feared the Lord – reverential and loving fear, not slavish terror. When the fire of religion burns low, true believers should draw the nearer together, to keep the holy flame alive. Coals separated soon go out.

book of remembrance … for them – for their advantage, against the day when those found faithful among the faithless shall receive their final reward. The kings of Persia kept a record of those who had rendered services to the king, that they might be suitably rewarded (Es 6:1,2; compare Es 2:23 Ezr 4:15 Ps 56:8 Isa 65:6 Da 7:10 Re 20:12). CALVIN makes the fearers of God to be those awakened from among the ungodly mass (before described) to true repentance; the *writing* of the book thus will imply that some were reclaimable among the blasphemers, and that the godly should be assured that, though no hope appeared, there would be a door of penitence opened for them *before* God. But there is nothing in the context to support this view.

17. jewels – (Isa 62:3). Literally, 'My peculiar treasure' (Ex 19:5 De 7:6 14:2 26:18 Ps 135:4 Tit 2:14 1Pe 2:9; compare Ec 2:8). CALVIN translates more in accordance with *Hebrew* idiom, 'They shall be My peculiar treasure *in the day in which I will do it*' (that is, fulfil My promise of gathering My completed Church; or, 'make' those things come to pass foretold in Mal 3:5 above [GROTIUS]); so in Mal 4:3 'do' is used absolutely, 'in the day that I shall do *this.*'

as … man spareth … son – (Ps 103:18).

18. Then shall ye … discern – Then shall ye see the falseness of your calumny against God's government (Mal 3:15), that the 'proud' and wicked prosper. Do not judge before the time till My work is complete. It is in part to test your disposition to trust in God in spite of perplexing appearances, and in order to make your service less mercenary, that the present blended state is allowed; but at last *all* ('ye,' both godly and ungodly) shall see the eternal difference there really is 'between him that serveth God and him that serveth Him not' (Ps 58:11).

return – Ye shall turn to a better state of mind on this point.

Chapter 4

Mal 4:1–6. God's coming judgment: triumph of the godly: return to the law the best preparation for Jehovah's coming: Elijah's preparatory mission of reformation.

1. the day cometh … burn – (Mal 3:2 2Pe 3:7). Primarily is meant the judgment coming on Jerusalem; but as this will not exhaust the meaning, without supposing what is inadmissible in Scripture – exaggeration – the final and full accomplishment, of which the former was the earnest, is the day of general judgment. This principle of interpretation is not double, but *successive fulfilment.* The language is abrupt, 'Behold, the day cometh! It burns like a furnace.' The abruptness imparts terrible reality to the picture, as if it suddenly burst on the prophet's view.

all the proud – in opposition to the cavil above (Mal 3:15), 'now we call the *proud* (haughty despisers of God) happy.'

stubble – (Ob 1:18 Mt 3:12). As Canaan, the inheritance of the Israelites, was prepared for their possession by purging out the heathen, so judgment on the apostates shall usher in the entrance of the saints upon the Lord's inheritance, of which Canaan is the type – not heaven, but earth to its utmost bounds (Ps 2:8) purged of all things that offend (Mt 13:41), which are to be 'gathered *out of His kingdom,*' the scene of the judgment being that also of the kingdom. The present dispensation is a spiritual kingdom, parenthetical between the Jews' literal kingdom and its antitype, the coming literal kingdom of the Lord Jesus.

neither root nor branch – proverbial for *utter* destruction (Am 2:9).

2. The effect of the judgment on the righteous, as contrasted with its effect on the wicked (Mal 4:1). To the wicked it shall be as an oven that consumes the stubble (Mt 6:30); to the righteous it shall be the advent of the gladdening Sun, not of condemnation, but 'of righteousness'; not destroying, but 'healing' (Jer 23:6).

you that fear my name – The same as those in Mal 3:16, who confessed God amidst abounding blasphemy (Isa 66:5 Mt 10:32). The spiritual blessings brought by Him are summed up in the two, 'righteousness' (1Co 1:30) and spiritual 'healing' (Ps 103:3 Isa 57:19). Those who walk in the dark now may take comfort in the certainty that they shall walk hereafter in eternal light (Isa 50:10).

in his wings – implying the *winged swiftness* with which He shall appear (compare 'suddenly,' Mal 3:1) for the relief of His people. The *beams* of the Sun are His 'wings.' Compare 'wings of the morning,' Ps 139:9. The 'Sun' gladdening the righteous is suggested by the previous 'day' of terror consuming the wicked. Compare as to Christ, 2Sa 23:4 Ps 84:11 Lu 1:78 Joh 1:9 8:12 Eph 5:14; and in His second coming, 2Pe 1:19. The Church is the *moon* reflecting His light (Re 12:1). The righteous shall by His righteousness 'shine as the Sun in the kingdom of the Father' (Mt 13:43).

ye shall go forth – from the straits in which you were, as it were, held captive. An earnest of this was given in the escape of the Christians to Pella before the destruction of Jerusalem.

grow up – rather, 'leap' as frisking calves [CALVIN]; literally, 'spread,' 'take a wide range.'

as calves of the stall – which when set free from the stall disport with joy (Ac 8:8 13:52 20:24 Ro 14:17 Ga 5:22 Php 1:4 1Pe 1:8). Especially the godly shall rejoice at their final deliverance at Christ's second coming (Isa 61:10).

3. Solving the difficulty (Mal 3:15) that the wicked often now prosper. Their prosperity and the adversity of the godly shall soon be reversed. Yea, the righteous shall be the army attending Christ in His final destruction of the ungodly (2Sa 22:43 Ps 49:14 47:3 Mic 7:10 Zec 10:5 1Co 6:2 Re 2:26,27 19:14,15).

ashes – after having been burnt with the fire of judgment (Mal 4:1).

4. Remember … law – 'The law and all the prophets' were to be in force until John (Mt 11:13), no prophet intervening after Malachi; therefore they are told, 'Remember the law,' for in the absence of living prophets, they were likely to forget it. The office of Christ's forerunner was to bring them back to the law, which they had too much forgotten, and so 'to make ready a people prepared for the Lord' at His coming (Lu 1:17). God withheld prophets for a time that men might seek after Christ with the greater desire [CALVIN]. The history of human advancement is marked by periods of rest, and again progress. So in Revelation: it is given for a time; then during its suspension men live on the memories of the past. After Malachi there was a silence of four hundred years; then a harbinger of light in the wilderness, ushering in the brightest of all the lights that had been manifested, but short-lived; then eighteen centuries during which we have been guided by the light which shone in that last manifestation. The silence has been longer than before, and will be succeeded by a more glorious and awful revelation than ever. John the Baptist was to 'restore' the defaced image of 'the law,' so that the original might be recognized when it appeared among men [HINDS]. Just as 'Moses' and 'Elias' are here connected with the Lord's coming, so at the transfiguration they converse with Him, implying that the law and prophets which had prepared His way were now fulfilled in Him.

statutes … judgments – *ceremonial* 'statutes': 'judgments' in civil questions at issue. 'The law' refers to *morals* and *religion*.

5. I send you Elijah – as a means towards your 'remembering the law' (Mal 4:4).

the prophet – emphatic; not 'the Tishbite'; for it is in his official, not his personal capacity, that his coming is here predicted. In this sense, John the Baptist was *an* Elijah in spirit (Lu 1:16,17), but not *the literal* Elijah; whence when asked, 'Art thou Elias?' (Joh 1:21), He answered, 'I am not.' 'Art thou that prophet?' 'No.' This implies that John, though knowing from the angel's announcement to his father that he was referred to by Mal 4:5 (Lu 1:17), whence he wore the costume of Elijah, yet knew by inspiration that he did not exhaustively fulfil *all* that is included in this prophecy: that there is a further fulfilment (compare *Note*, see on Mal 3:1). As Moses in Mal 4:4 represents the law, so Elijah represents the prophets. The Jews always understood it of the literal Elijah. Their saying is, 'Messiah must be anointed by Elijah.' As there is another consummating advent of Messiah Himself, so also of His forerunner Elijah; perhaps in person, as at the transfiguration (Mt 17:3; compare Mt 17:11). He in his appearance at the transfiguration in that body on which death had never passed is the forerunner of the saints who shall be found alive at the Lord's second coming. Re 11:3 may refer to the same witnesses as at the transfiguration, Moses and Elijah; Re 11:6 identifies the latter (compare 1Ki 17:1 Jas 5:17). Even after the transfiguration Jesus (Mt 17:11) speaks of Elijah's coming 'to restore all things' as still future, though He adds that Elijah (in the person of John the Baptist) is come already *in a sense* (compare Ac 3:21). However, the future forerunner of Messiah at His second coming may be a prophet or number of prophets clothed with Elijah's power, who, with zealous upholders of 'the law' clothed in the spirit of 'Moses,' may be the forerunning witnesses alluded to here and in Re 11:2–12. The words 'before the … *dreadful* day of the Lord,' show that John cannot be exclusively meant; for he came before the day of Christ's coming in grace, not before His coming in terror, of which last the destruction of Jerusalem was the earnest (Mal 4:1 Joe 2:31).

6. turn … heart of … fathers to … children. – Explained by some, that John's preaching should restore harmony in families. But Lu 1:16,17 substitutes for 'the heart of the children to the fathers,' 'the disobedient to the wisdom of the just,' implying that the reconciliation to be effected was that between the unbelieving disobedient children and the believing ancestors, Jacob, Levi, 'Moses,' and 'Elijah' (just mentioned) (compare Mal 1:2 2:4,6 3:3,4). The threat here is that, if this restoration were not effected, Messiah's coming would prove 'a curse' to the 'earth,' not a blessing. It proved so to guilty Jerusalem and the 'earth,' that is, the *land* of Judea when it rejected Messiah at His first advent, though He brought blessings (Ge 12:3) to those who accepted Him (Joh 1:11–13). Many were delivered from the common destruction of the nation through John's preaching (Ro 9:29 11:5). It will prove so to the disobedient at His second advent, though He comes to be glorified in His saints (2Th 1:6-10).

curse – *Hebrew, Cherem,* 'a ban'; the fearful term applied by the Jews to the extermination of the guilty Canaanites. Under this ban Judea has long lain. Similar is the awful curse on all of Gentile churches who love not the Lord Jesus now (1Co 16:22). For if God spare not the natural branches, the Jews, much less will He spare unbelieving professors of the Gentiles (Ro 11:20,21). It is deeply suggestive that the last utterance from heaven for four hundred years before Messiah was the awful word 'curse.' Messiah's first word on the mount was 'Blessed' (Mt 5:3). The law speaks wrath; the Gospel, blessing. Judea is now under the 'curse' because it rejects Messiah; when the spirit of Elijah, or a literal Elijah, shall bring the Jewish children back to the Hope of their 'fathers,' blessing shall be theirs, whereas the apostate 'earth' shall be 'smitten with the curse' previous to the coming restoration of all things (Zec 12:13,14).

May the writer of this Commentary and his readers have grace 'to take heed to the sure word of prophecy as unto a light shining in a dark place, until the day dawn!' To the triune Jehovah be all glory ascribed for ever!

THE NEW
TESTAMENT

OUTLINES OF THE NEW TESTAMENT BOOKS

John Wesley

Matthew

I. The birth of Christ, and what presently followed it:–
   a. His genealogy 1:1–17
   b. His birth 1:18–25
   c. The coming of the wise men. 2:1–12
   d. His flight into Egypt, and return 2:13–23

II. The introduction
   a. John the Baptist 3:1–12
   b. The baptism of Christ 3:13–17
   c. His temptation and victory. 4:1–11

III. The actions and words by which Jesus proved he was the Christ
   a. At Capernaum 4:12–16
      Where we may observe
      1. His preaching 4:17
      2. Calling Andrew and Peter, James and John. 4:18–22
      3. Preaching and healing, with a great concourse of people 4:23–25
      4. Sermon on the mount 5–7
      5. Healing the leper 8:1–4
      6. The centurion's servant. 8:5–13
      7. Peter's mother-in-law 8:14–15
      8. Many that were sick. 8:16–17
   b. In his journey over the sea
      Here we may observe
      1. His dominion over the winds and sea 8:18–27
      2. The devils passing from the men into the swine 8:28–34
   c. At Capernaum again . . . . Here,
      1. He cures the paralytic. 9:1–8
      2. Calls Matthew, and defends his conversing with
         publicans and sinners 9:9–13
      3. Answers concerning fasting 9:14–17

Mark

I. The beginning of the Gospel,

    a. John prepares the way 1:1–8

    b. Baptizes Jesus, who is proclaimed the Son of God 9–11

    c. Tempted of Satan, served by angels 12,13

II. The Gospel itself,

    A. In Galilee: where we may observe three periods,

        a. After John was cast into prison,

            In general,

            1. The place and matter of his preaching, ... 14,15

            2. The calling of several of the apostles. 16–20

            In particular,

            1. Actions not censured by his adversaries

                1. He teaches with authority 21,22

                2. Cures the demoniac. 23–28

                3. Heals many sick 29–34

                4. Prays. 35

                5. Teaches every where 36–39

                6 Cleanses the leper 40–45

            2. Actions censured by them,

               Here occur,

                1. The paralytic forgiven and healed 2:1–12

                2. The call of Levi, and eating with publicans and sinners. 13–17

                3. The question concerning fasting answered 18–22

                4. The ears of corn plucked. 23–28

                5. The withered hand restored: Snares laid 3:1–6

            3. Our Lord's retirement,

                1. At the sea. 7–12

                2. In the mountain, where the apostles are called 13–19

                3. In the house, where after refuting the blasphemy of the
                   Pharisees, he shows who are his mother and his brethren 20–35

                4. In the ship; various parables 3:1–34

                5. On the sea, and beyond it. 3:35–5:20

                6. On this side the sea: Again: Jairus, and the woman with
                   the flux of blood 5:21–43

                7. At Nazareth: His countrymen offended. 6:1–6

                8. The apostles sent forth 7–13

        b. After John was put to death,

            1. Herod's hearing of Jesus, and judgment of him 14–29

            2. Christ's retiring with his apostles, now returned. 30–32

Luke

John

Acts

Romans

I. The introduction,. 1:1–15

II. The proposition briefly proved,

    1. Concerning faith and justification,

    2. Concerning salvation,

    3. Concerning the equality of believers, Jews or gentiles, ... 16–17

    To these three parts, whereof

    The first is treated of,. 1:18 4:25

    The second,. . . . . chapters 5–8

    The third, ... chapters 9–11

    not only the treatise itself, but also the exhortation,

    answers in the same order.

III. The treatise,

    1. Concerning justification, which is,

    1. Not by works, for 1:18

    The gentiles,. 2:1–10

    The Jews, and 11–29

    Both together are under sin,. 3:1–20

    2. But by faith, ... 21–31

    as appears by the example of Abraham,

    and the testimony of David,. 4:1–25

    2. Concerning salvation, ... chapters 5–8

    3. Concerning the equal privileges of Jewish and gentile

    believers, ... chapters 9–11

IV. The exhortation,. 12:1–2

    1. Concerning faith and its fruits, love and practical holiness, ... 3–21

    13:1–10

    2. Concerning salvation,. 11–14

    3. Of the conjunction of Jews and gentiles,. 14:1–15:13

V. The conclusion,. 15:14–16:25

1 Corinthians

2 Corinthians

Galatians

I. The inscription, ... 1:1–5

II. The calling the Galatians back to the true gospel; wherein he,

   1. Reproves them for leaving it, ... 6–10

   2. Asserts the authority of the gospel he had preached, who,

      1. Of a persecutor was made an apostle, by an immediate call from heaven, ... 11–17

      2. Was no way inferior to Peter himself,. 1:18–2:21

      3. Defends justification by faith, and again reproves the Galatians, ... 3:1–4:11

      4. Explains the same thing by an allegory taken out of the law itself, ... 4:12–31

      5. Exhorts them to maintain their liberty, ... 5:1–12

      warns them not to abuse it, and admonishes them to walk not after the flesh, but after the Spirit, ... 5:13–6:10

III. The conclusion, ... 6:11–18

Ephesians

I. The inscription, ... 1:1,2

II. The doctrine pathetically explained, which contains,

   1. Praise to God for the whole gospel blessing, ... 3–14

   With thanksgiving and prayer for the saints, ... 1:15–2:10

   2. A more particular admonition concerning their once miserable, but now happy, condition, ... 2:11–12

   A prayer for their establishment, ... 3:1–19

   A doxology, ... 20,21

III. The exhortation,

   1. General: to walk worthy of their calling, agreeably to,

      1. The unity of the Spirit, and the diversity of his gifts, ... 4:1–16

      2. The difference between their former and their present state, . . . 17–24

   2. Particular: to avoid,

      1. Lying, ... 25

      2. Anger, ... 26,27

      3. Theft, ... 28

      4. Corrupt communication, ... 29,30

      5. Bitterness, ... 4:31–5:2

      6. Uncleanness, ... 5:3–14

      7. Drunkenness, ... 15–21

   With a commendation of the opposite virtues

Philippians

Colossians

1 Thessalonians

2 Thessalonians

1 Timothy

2 Timothy

Titus

Philemon

Hebrews

James

1 Peter

2 Peter

1 John

In the preface he shows the authority of his own preaching and writing, and expressly points out, verse 3, the design of his present writing. To the preface exactly answers the conclusion, more largely explaining the same design, and recapitulating those marks, by we know thrice repeated, v. 18–20. The tract itself has two parts, treating,

2 John

3 John

Jude

Revelation

THE PARABLES
OF CHRIST

Put into chronological order by David Brown

PARABLES	WHERE SPOKEN	WHERE RECORDED
The two debtors	[Capernaum]	Lu 7:40-43.
The strong man armed	Galilee	Mt 12:29 Mr 3:27 Lu 11:21,22.
The unclean spirit	Galilee	Mt 12:43-45 Lu 11:24-26.
The sower of Galilee	Seashore	Mt 13:3-9,18-23 Mr 4:3-9,14-20 Lu 8:5-8,11-15.
The tares and wheat	Seashore of Galilee	Mt 13:24-30,36-43.
The mustard seed	Seashore of Galilee	Mt 13:31,32 Mr 4:30-32 Lu 13:18,19.
The seed growing secretly	Seashore of Galilee	Mr 4:26-29.
The leaven	Seashore of Galilee	Mt 13:33 Lu 13:20,21.
The hid treasure	Seashore of Galilee	Mt 13:44.
The pearl of great price	Seashore of Galilee	Mt 13:45,46.
The draw net	Seashore of Galilee	Mt 13:47-50.
The unmerciful servant	Capernaum	Mt 18:21-35.
The good Samaritan	Near Jerusalem	Lu 10:29-37.
The friend at midnight	Near Jerusalem	Lu 11:5-8.
The rich fool	Galilee	Lu 12:16-21.
The barren fig tree	Galilee	Lu 13:6-9.
The great supper	Perea	Lu 14:15-24.
The lost sheep	Perea	Mt 18:12-14 Lu 15:3-7.
The lost piece of money	Perea	Lu 15:8-10.
The prodigal son	Perea	Lu 15:11-32.
The good shepherd	Jerusalem	Joh 10:1-18.
The unjust steward	Perea	Lu 16:1-8.
The rich man and Lazarus	Perea	Lu 16:19-31.
The profitable servants	Perea	Lu 17:7-10.
The importunate widow	Perea	Lu 18:1-8.

The Pharisee and publican	Perea	Lu 18:9-14.
The labourers in the vineyard	Perea	Mt 20:1-16.
The pounds	Jericho	Lu 19:11-27.
The two sons	Jerusalem	Mt 21:28-32.
The wicked husbandmen	Jerusalem	Mt 21:33-44 Mr 12:1-12 Lu 20:9-18.
The marriage of the king's son	Jerusalem	Mt 22:1-14.
The ten virgins	Mount of Olives	Mt 25:1-13.
The talents	Mount of Olives	Mt 25:14-30.

MATTHEW

John Wesley

Introduction

The Gospel means a book containing the good tidings of our salvation by Jesus Christ. St. Mark in his Gospel presupposes that of St. Matthew, and supplies what is omitted therein. St. Luke supplies what is omitted by both the former: St. John what is omitted by all the three. St. Matthew particularly points out the fulfilling of the prophecies for the conviction of the Jews. St. Mark wrote a short compendium, and yet added many remarkable circumstances omitted by St. Matthew, particularly with regard to the apostles, immediately after they were called. St. Luke treated principally of the office of Christ, and mostly in a historical manner. St. John refuted those who denied his Godhead: each choosing to treat more largely on those things, which most suited the time when, and the persons to whom, he wrote.

Contents

See *Outlines of the New Testament Books*, pp. 883–6.

Chapter 1

1. The book of the generation of Jesus Christ – That is, strictly speaking, the account of his birth and genealogy. This title therefore properly relates to the verses that immediately follow: but as it sometimes signifies the history of a person, in that sense it may belong to the whole book. If there were any difficulties in this genealogy, or that given by St. Luke, which could not easily be removed, they would rather affect the Jewish tables, than the credit of the evangelists: for they act only as historians setting down these genealogies, as they stood in those public and allowed records. Therefore they were to take them as they found them. Nor was it needful they should correct the mistakes, if there were any. For these accounts sufficiently answer the end for which they are recited. They unquestionably prove the grand point in view, that Jesus was of the family from which the promised seed was to come. And they had more weight with the Jews for this purpose, than if alterations had been made by inspiration itself. For such alterations would have occasioned endless disputes between them and the disciples of our Lord. **The son of David, the son of Abraham** – He is so called, because to these he was more peculiarly promised; and of these it was often foretold the Messiah should spring. Luke 3:31.

3. Of Thamar – St. Matthew adds the names of those women also, that were remarkable in the sacred history.

4. Naasson – Who was prince of the tribe of Judah, when the Israelites entered into Canaan.

5. Obed begat Jesse – The providence of God was peculiarly shown in this, that Salmon, Boaz, and Obed, must each of them have been near a hundred years old, at the birth of his son here recorded.

6. David the king – Particularly mentioned under this character, because his throne is given to the Messiah.

8. Jehoram begat Uzziah – Jehoahaz, Joash, and Amaziah coming between. So that he begat him mediately, as Christ is mediately the son of David and of Abraham. So the progeny of Hezekiah, after many generations, are called the sons that should issue from him, which he should beget, Isaiah 39:7.

11. Josiah begat Jeconiah – Mediately, Jehoiakim coming between. **And his brethren** – That is, his uncles. The Jews term all kinsmen brethren. **About the time they were carried away** – Which was a little after the birth of Jeconiah.

16. The husband of Mary – Jesus was generally believed to be the son of Joseph. It was needful for all who believed this, to know, that Joseph was sprung from David. Otherwise they would not allow Jesus to be the Christ. **Jesus, who is called Christ** – The name Jesus respects chiefly the promise of blessing made to Abraham: the name Christ, the promise of the Messiah's kingdom, which was made to David. It may be farther observed, that the word Christ in Greek, and Messiah in Hebrew, signify anointed, and imply the prophetic, priestly, and royal characters, which were to meet in the Messiah. Among the Jews, anointing was the ceremony whereby prophets, priests, and kings were initiated into those offices. And if we look into ourselves, we shall find a want of Christ in all these respects. We are by nature at a distance from God, alienated from him, and incapable of a free access to him. Hence we want a mediator, an intercessor, in a word, a Christ, in his priestly office. This regards our state with respect to God. And with respect to ourselves, we find a total darkness, blindness, ignorance of God, and the things of God. Now here we want Christ in his prophetic office, to enlighten our minds, and teach us the whole will of God. We find also within us a strange misrule of appetites and passions. For these we want Christ in his royal character, to reign in our hearts, and subdue all things to himself.

17. So all the generations – Observe, in order to complete the three fourteens, David ends the first fourteen, and begins the second and Jesus ends the third fourteen. When we survey such a series of generations, it is a natural and obvious reflection, how like the leaves of a tree one passeth away, and another cometh! Yet the earth still abideth. And with it the goodness of the Lord which runs from generation to generation, the common hope of parents and children. Of those who formerly lived upon earth, and perhaps made the most conspicuous figure, how many are there whose names are perished with them? How many, of whom only the names are

remaining? Thus are we likewise passing away! And thus shall we shortly be forgotten! Happy are we, if, while we are forgotten by men, we are remembered by God! If our names, lost on earth, are at length found written in the book of life!

19. A just man – A strict observer of the law: therefore not thinking it right to keep her.

21. Jesus – That is, a Saviour. It is the same name with Joshua which properly signifies, The Lord, Salvation. **His people** – Israel. And all the Israel of God.

23. They shall call his name Emmanuel – To be called, only means, according to the Hebrew manner of speaking, that the person spoken of shall really and effectually be what he is called, and actually fulfil that title. Thus, **Unto us a child is born** – and his name shall be called Wonderful, Counsellor, the Mighty God, the Prince of Peace – That is, he shall be all these, though not so much nominally, as really, and in effect. And thus was he called Emmanuel; which was no common name of Christ, but points out his nature and office; as he is God incarnate, and dwells by his Spirit in the hearts of his people.

25. He knew her not, till after she had brought forth – It cannot be inferred from hence, that he knew her afterward: no more than it can be inferred from that expression, 2Sam 6:23, Michal had no child till the day of her death, that she had children afterward. Nor do the words that follow, the first-born son, alter the case. For there are abundance of places, wherein the term first born is used, though there were no subsequent children. Luke 2:7.

Chapter 2

1. Bethlehem of Judea – There was another Bethlehem in the tribe of Zebulon. **In the days of Herod** – commonly called Herod the Great, born at Ascalon. The sceptre was now on the point of departing from Judah. Among his sons were Archelaus, mentioned Mt 2:22; Herod Antipas, mentioned Mt 14:1; &c., and Philip, mentioned Luke 3:19. Herod Agrippa, mentioned Acts 12:1; &c., was his grandson. **Wise men** – The first fruits of the Gentiles. Probably they were Gentile philosophers, who, through the Divine assistance, had improved their knowledge of nature, as a means of leading to the knowledge of the one true God. Nor is it unreasonable to suppose, that God had favoured them with some extraordinary revelations of himself, as he did Melchisedec, Job, and several others, who were not of the family of Abraham; to which he never intended absolutely to confine his favours. The title given them in the original was anciently given to all philosophers, or men of learning; those particularly who were curious in examining the works of nature, and observing the motions of the heavenly bodies. **From the east** – So Arabia is frequently called in Scripture. It lay to the east of Judea, and was famous for gold, frankincense, and myrrh. **We have seen his star** – Undoubtedly they had before heard Balaam's prophecy. And probably when they saw this unusual star, it was revealed to them that this prophecy was fulfilled. **In the east** – That is, while we were in the east.

2. To do him homage – To pay him that honour, by bowing to the earth before him, which the eastern nations used to pay to their monarchs.

4. The chief priests – That is, not only the high priest and his deputy, with those who formerly had borne that office: but also the chief man in each of those twenty-four courses, into which the body of priests were divided, 1Chron 24:6-19. The scribes were those whose peculiar business it was to explain the Scriptures to the people. They were the public preachers, or expounders of the law of Moses. Whence chief of them were called doctors of the law.

6. Thou art in nowise the least among the princes of Judah – That is, among the cities belonging to the princes or heads of thousands in Judah. When this and several other quotations from the Old Testament are compared with the original, it plainly appears, the apostles did not always think it necessary exactly to transcribe the passages they cited, but contented themselves with giving the general sense, though with some diversity of language. The words of Micah, which we render, Though thou be little, may be rendered, Art thou little? And then the difference which seems to be here between the prophet and the evangelist vanishes away. Micah 5:2.

8. And if ye find him, bring me word – Probably Herod did not believe he was born; otherwise would not so suspicious a prince have tried to make sure work at once?

10. Seeing the star – Standing over where the child was.

11. They presented to him gifts – It was customary to offer some present to any eminent person whom they visited. And so it is, as travellers observe, in the eastern countries to this day. **Gold, frankincense, and myrrh** – Probably these were the best things their country afforded; and the presents ordinarily made to great persons. This was a most seasonable, providential assistance for a long and expensive journey into Egypt, a country where they were entirely strangers, and were to stay for a considerable time.

15. That it might be fulfilled – That is, whereby was fulfilled. The original word frequently signifies, not the design of an action, but barely the consequence or event of it. **Which was spoken of the Lord by the prophet** – on another occasion: **Out of Egypt have I called my Son** – which was now fulfilled as it were anew;

Christ being in a far higher sense the Son of God than Israel, of whom the words were originally spoken. Hosea 11:1.

16. Then Herod, seeing that he was deluded by the wise men – So did his pride teach him to regard this action, as if it were intended to expose him to the derision of his subjects. **Sending forth** – a party of soldiers: **In all the confines thereof** – In all the neighbouring places, of which Rama was one.

17. Then was fulfilled – A passage of Scripture, whether prophetic, historical, or poetical, is in the language of the New Testament fulfilled, when an event happens to which it may with great propriety be accommodated.

18. Rachel weeping for her children – The Benjamites, who inhabited Rama, sprung from her. She was buried near this place; and is here beautifully represented risen, as it were out of her grave, and bewailing her lost children. **Because they are not** – that is, are dead. The preservation of Jesus from this destruction, may be considered as a figure of God's care over his children in their greatest danger. God does not often, as he easily could, cut off their persecutors at a stroke. But he provides a hiding place for his people, and by methods not less effectual, though less pompous, preserves them from being swept away, even when the enemy comes in like a flood. Jer 31:15.

22. He was afraid to go thither – into Judea; and so turned aside into the region of **Galilee** – a part of the land of Israel not under the jurisdiction of Archelaus.

23. He came and dwelt in Nazareth – a place contemptible to a proverb. So that hereby was fulfilled what has been spoken in effect by several of the prophets, **He shall be called a Nazarene** – that is, he shall be despised and rejected, shall be a mark of public contempt and reproach.

Chapter 3

1. In those days – that is, while Jesus dwelt there. **In the wilderness of Judea** – This was a wilderness properly so called, a wild, barren, desolate place as was that also where our Lord was tempted. But, generally speaking, a wilderness in the New Testament means only a common, or less cultivated place, in opposition to pasture and arable land. Mark 1:1; Luke 3:1.

2. The kingdom of heaven, and the kingdom of God, are but two phrases for the same thing. They mean, not barely a future happy state, in heaven, but a state to be enjoyed on earth: the proper disposition for the glory of heaven, rather than the possession of it. **Is at hand** – As if he had said, God is about to erect that kingdom, spoken of by Daniel Dan 2:44; 7:13,14; the kingdom of the God of heaven. It properly signifies here, the Gospel dispensation, in which subjects were to be gathered to God by his Son, and a society to be formed, which was to subsist first on earth, and afterward with God in glory. In some places of Scripture, the phrase more particularly denotes the state of it on earth: in others, it signifies only the state of glory: but it generally includes both. The Jews understood it of a temporal kingdom, the seat of which they supposed would be Jerusalem; and the expected sovereign of this kingdom they learned from Daniel to call the Son of man. Both John the Baptist and Christ took up that phrase, the kingdom of heaven, as they found it, and gradually taught the Jews to understand it right. The very demand of repentance, as previous to it, showed it was a spiritual kingdom, and that no wicked man, how politic, brave, or learned soever, could possibly be a subject of it.

3. The way of the Lord – Of Christ. **Make his paths straight** – By removing every thing which might prove a hinderance to his gracious appearance. Isaiah 40:3.

4. John had his raiment of camels' hair – Coarse and rough, suiting his character and doctrine. **A leathern girdle** – Like Elijah, in whose spirit and power he came. **His food was locusts and wild honey** – Locusts are ranked among clean meats, Lev 11:22. But these were not always to be had. So in default of those, he fed on wild honey.

6. Confessing their sins – Of their own accord; freely and openly. Such prodigious numbers could hardly be baptized by immerging their whole bodies under water: nor can we think they were provided with change of raiment for it, which was scarcely practicable for such vast multitudes. And yet they could not be immerged naked with modesty, nor in their wearing apparel with safety. It seems, therefore, that they stood in ranks on the edge of the river, and that John, passing along before them, cast water on their heads or faces, by which means he might baptize many thousands in a day. And this way most naturally signified Christ's baptizing them with the Holy Ghost and with fire, which John spoke of, as prefigured by his baptizing with water, and which was eminently fulfilled, when the Holy Ghost sat upon the disciples in the appearance of tongues, or flames of fire.

7. The Pharisees were a very ancient sect among the Jews. They took their name from a Hebrew word, which signifies to separate, because they separated themselves from all other men. They were outwardly strict observers of the law, fasted often, made long prayers, rigorously kept the Sabbath, and paid all tithes, even of mint, anise, and cummin. Hence they were in high esteem among the people. But inwardly, they were full of pride and hypocrisy. The

Sadducees were another sect among the Jews, only not so considerable as the Pharisees. They denied the existence of angels, and the immortality of the soul, and by consequence the resurrection of the dead. **Ye brood of vipers** – In like manner, the crafty Herod is styled a fox, and persons of insidious, ravenous, profane, or sensual dispositions, are named respectively by him who saw their hearts, serpents, dogs, wolves, and swine; terms which are not the random language of passion, but a judicious designation of the persons meant by them. For it was fitting such men should be marked out, either for a caution to others, or a warning to themselves.

8. Repentance is of two sorts; that which is termed legal, and that which is styled evangelical repentance. The former is a thorough conviction of sin. The latter is a change of heart from all sin to all holiness.

9. And say not confidently – The word in the original, vulgarly rendered, **Think not**, seems here, and in many places, not to diminish, but rather add to the force of the word with which it is joined. **We have Abraham to our father** – It is almost incredible, how great the presumption of the Jews was on this their relation to Abraham. One of their famous sayings was, 'Abraham sits near the gates of hell, and suffers no Israelite to go down into it.' **I say unto you** – This preface always denotes the importance of what follows. **Of these stones** – Probably pointing to those which lay before them.

10. But the axe also already lieth – That is, there is no room for such idle pretences. Speedy execution is determined against all that do not repent. The comparison seems to be taken from a woodman that has laid down his axe to put off his coat, and then immediately goes to work to cut down the tree. This refers to the wrath to come in verse 7, Mt 3:7. **Is hewn down** – Instantly, without farther delay.

11. He shall baptize you with the Holy Ghost, and with fire – He shall fill you with the Holy Ghost, inflaming your hearts with that fire of love, which many waters cannot quench. And this was done, even with a visible appearance as of fire, on the day of Pentecost.

12. Whose fan – That is, the word of the Gospel. **His floor** – That is, his Church, which is now covered with a mixture of wheat and chaff. **He will gather the wheat into the garner** – Will lay up those who are truly good in heaven.

13. Mark 1:9; Luke 3:21

15. It becometh us to fulfil all righteousness – It becometh every messenger of God to observe all his righteous ordinances. But the particular meaning of our Lord seems to be, that it becometh us to do in order to fulfil, that is, that I may fully perform every part of the righteous law of God, and the commission he hath given me.

16. And Jesus being baptized – Let our Lord's submitting to baptism teach us a holy exactness in the observance of those institutions which owe their obligation merely to a Divine command. Surely thus it becometh all his followers to fulfil all righteousness. Jesus had no sin to wash away. And yet he was baptized. And God owned his ordinance, so as to make it the season of pouring forth the Holy Spirit upon him. And where can we expect this sacred effusion, but in an humble attendance on Divine appointments?

Lo, the heavens were opened, and he saw the Spirit of God – St. Luke adds, in a bodily form – Probably in a glorious appearance of fire, perhaps in the shape of a dove, descending with a hovering motion, till it rested upon him. This was a visible token of those secret operations of the blessed Spirit, by which he was anointed in a peculiar manner; and abundantly fitted for his public work.

17. And lo, a voice – We have here a glorious manifestation of the ever-blessed Trinity: the Father speaking from heaven, the Son spoken to, the Holy Ghost descending upon him. **In whom I delight** – What an encomium is this! How poor to this are all other kinds of praise! To be the pleasure, the delight of God, this is praise indeed: this is true glory: this is the highest, the brightest light, that virtue can appear in.

Chapter 4

1. Then – After this glorious evidence of his Father's love, he was completely armed for the combat. Thus after the clearest light and the strongest consolation, let us expect the sharpest temptations. **By the Spirit** – Probably through a strong inward impulse. Mark 1:12; Luke 4:1.

2. Having fasted – Whereby doubtless he received more abundant spiritual strength from God. **Forty days and forty nights** – As did Moses, the giver of the law, and Elijah, the great restorer of it. **He was afterward hungry** – And so prepared for the first temptation.

3. Coming to him – In a visible form; probably in a human shape, as one that desired to inquire farther into the evidences of his being the Messiah.

4. It is written – Thus Christ answered, and thus we may answer all the suggestions of the devil. **By every word that proceedeth out of the mouth of God** – That is, by whatever God commands to sustain him. Therefore it is not needful I should work a miracle to procure bread, without any intimation of my Father's will. Deut 8:3.

5. The holy city – So Jerusalem was commonly called, being the place God had peculiarly chosen for himself. **On the battlement of the temple** – Probably over the king's gallery, which was of such a prodigious height, that no one could look down from the top of it without making himself giddy.

6. In their hands – That is, with great care. Psalm 91:11,12.

7. Thou shalt not tempt the Lord thy God – By requiring farther evidence of what he hath already made sufficiently plain. Deut 6:16.

8. Showeth him all the kingdoms of the world – In a kind of visionary representation.

9. If thou wilt fall down and worship me – Here Satan clearly shows who he was. Accordingly Christ answering this suggestion, calls him by his own name, which he had not done before.

10. Get thee hence, Satan – Not, get thee behind me, that is, into thy proper place; as he said on a quite different occasion to Peter, speaking what was not expedient. Deut 6:13.

11. Angels came and waited upon him – Both to supply him with food, and to congratulate his victory.

12. He retired into Galilee – This journey was not immediately after his temptation. He first went from Judea into Galilee, John 1:43; 2:1. Then into Judea again, and celebrated the Passover at Jerusalem, John 2:13. He baptized in Judea while John was baptizing at Enon, John 3:22,23. All this time John was at liberty, John 3:24. But the Pharisees being offended, John 4:1; and John put in prison, he then took this journey into Galilee. Mark 1:14.

13. Leaving Nazareth – Namely, when they had wholly rejected his word, and even attempted to kill him, Luke 4:29.

15. Galilee of the Gentiles – That part of Galilee which lay beyond Jordan was so called, because it was in a great measure inhabited by Gentiles, that is, heathens. Isaiah 9:1,2.

16. Here is a beautiful gradation, first, they walked, then they sat in darkness, and lastly, in the region of the shadow of death.

17. From that time Jesus began to preach – He had preached before, both to Jews and Samaritans, John 4:41,45. But from this time began his solemn stated preaching. **Repent, for the kingdom of heaven is at hand** – Although it is the peculiar business of Christ to establish the kingdom of heaven in the hearts of men, yet it is observable, he begins his preaching in the same words with John the Baptist: because the repentance which John taught still was, and ever will be, the necessary preparation for that inward kingdom. But that phrase is not only used with regard to individuals in whom it is to be established, but also with regard to the Christian Church, the whole body of believers. In the former sense it is opposed to repentance; in the latter the Mosaic dispensation.

18. Mark 1:16; Luke 5:1.

23. The Gospel of the kingdom – The Gospel, that is, the joyous message, is the proper name of our religion: as will be amply verified in all who earnestly and perseveringly embrace it.

24. Through all Syria – The whole province, of which the Jewish country was only a small part. **And demoniacs** – Men possessed with devils: and lunatics, and paralytics – Men ill of the palsy, whose cases were of all others most deplorable and most helpless.

25. Decapolis – A tract of land on the east side of the sea of Galilee, in which were ten cities near each other.

Chapter 5

1. And seeing the multitudes – At some distance, as they were coming to him from every quarter. **He went up into the mountain** – Which was near: where there was room for them all. **His disciples** – not only his twelve disciples, but all who desired to learn of him.

2. And he opened his mouth – A phrase which always denotes a set and solemn discourse; **and taught them** – To bless men; to make men happy, was the great business for which our Lord came into the world. And accordingly he here pronounces eight blessings together, annexing them to so many steps in Christianity. Knowing that happiness is our common aim, and that an innate instinct continually urges us to the pursuit of it, he in the kindest manner applies to that instinct, and directs it to its proper object. Though all men desire, yet few attain, happiness, because they seek it where it is not to be found. Our Lord therefore begins his Divine institution, which is the complete art of happiness, by laying down before all that have ears to hear, the true and only true method of acquiring it. Observe the benevolent condescension of our Lord. He seems, as it were, to lay aside his supreme authority as our legislator, that he may the better act the part of: our friend and Saviour. Instead of using the lofty style, in positive commands, he, in a more gentle and engaging way, insinuates his will and our duty, by pronouncing those happy who comply with it.

3. Happy are the poor – In the following discourse there is,

1. A sweet invitation to true holiness and happiness, ver. 3–12. Matt 5:3–12.

2. A persuasive to impart it to others, ver. 13–16. Matt 5:13-16.

3. A description of true Christian holiness, ver. 17; 7:12, Matt 5:17; Matt 7:12.

4. The conclusion: giving a sure mark of the true way, warning against false prophets, exhorting to follow after holiness.

The poor in spirit – They who are unfeignedly penitent, they who are truly convinced of sin; who see and feel the state they are in by nature, being deeply sensible of their sinfulness, guiltiness, helplessness. **For theirs is the kingdom of heaven** – The present inward kingdom: righteousness, and peace, and joy in the Holy Ghost, as well as the eternal kingdom, if they endure to the end. Luke 6:20.

4. They that mourn – Either for their own sins, or for other men's, and are steadily and habitually serious. **They shall be comforted** – More solidly and deeply even in this world, and eternally in heaven.

5. Happy are the meek – They that hold all their passions and affections evenly balanced. **They shall inherit the earth** – They shall have all things really necessary for life and godliness. They shall enjoy whatever portion God hath given them here, and shall hereafter possess the new earth, wherein dwelleth righteousness.

6. They that hunger and thirst after righteousness – After the holiness here described. They shall be satisfied with it.

7. The merciful – The tender-hearted: they who love all men as themselves: **They shall obtain mercy** – Whatever mercy therefore we desire from God, the same let us show to our brethren. He will repay us a thousand fold, the love we bear to any for his sake.

8. The pure in heart – The sanctified: they who love God with all their hearts. **They shall see God** – In all things here; hereafter in glory.

9. The peace makers – They that out of love to God and man do all possible good to all men. Peace in the Scripture sense implies all blessings temporal and eternal. **They shall be called the children of God** – Shall be acknowledged such by God and man. One would imagine a person of this amiable temper and behaviour would be the darling of mankind. But our Lord well knew it would not be so, as long as Satan was the prince of this world. He therefore warns them before of the treatment all were to expect, who were determined thus to tread in his steps, by immediately subjoining, Happy are they who are persecuted for righteousness' sake. Through this whole discourse we cannot but observe the most exact method which can possibly be conceived. Every paragraph, every sentence, is closely connected both with that which precedes, and that which follows it. And is not this the pattern for every Christian preacher? If any then are able to follow it without any premeditation, well: if not, let them not dare to preach without it. No rhapsody, no incoherency, whether the things spoken be true or false, comes of the Spirit of Christ.

10. For righteousness' sake – That is, because they have, or follow after, the righteousness here described. He that is truly a righteous man, he that mourns, and he that is pure in heart, yea, all that will live godly in Christ Jesus, shall suffer persecution, 2Tim 3:12. The world will always say, Away with such fellows from the earth. They are made to reprove our thoughts. They are grievous to us even to behold. Their lives are not like other men's; their ways are of another fashion.

11. Revile – When present: **say all evil** – When you are absent.

12. Your reward – Even over and above the happiness that naturally and directly results from holiness.

13. Ye – Not the apostles, not ministers only; but all ye who are thus holy, **are the salt of the earth** – Are to season others. Mark 9:50; Luke 14:34.

14. Ye are the light of the world – If ye are thus holy, you can no more be hid than the sun in the firmament: no more than **a city** on a mountain – Probably pointing to that on the brow of the opposite hill.

15. Nay, the very design of God in giving you this light was, that it might shine. Mark 4:21; Luke 8:16; 11:33.

16. That they may see – and **glorify** – That is, that seeing your good works, they may be moved to love and serve God likewise.

17. Think not – Do not imagine, fear, hope, **that I am come** – Like your teachers, **to destroy the law or the prophets. I am not come to destroy** – The moral law, **but to fulfil** – To establish, illustrate, and explain its highest meaning, both by my life and doctrine.

18. Till all things shall be effected – Which it either requires or foretells. For the law has its effect, when the rewards are given, and the punishments annexed to it inflicted, as well as when its precepts are obeyed. Luke 16:17; 21:33.

19. One of the least – So accounted by men; **and shall teach** – Either by word or example; **shall be the least** – That is, shall have no part therein.

20. The righteousness of the scribes and Pharisees – Described in the sequel of this discourse.

21. Ye have heard – From the scribes reciting the law; **Thou shalt do no murder** – And they interpreted this, as all the other commandments, barely of the outward act. **The judgement** – The Jews had in every city a court of twenty-three men, who could sentence a criminal to be strangled. But the Sanhedrim only could sentence to the more terrible death of stoning. That was called the judgment, this the council. Exod 20:13.

22. But I say unto you – Which of the prophets ever spake thus? Their language is, Thus saith the Lord. Who hath authority to use this language, but the one lawgiver, who is able to save and to destroy. **Whosoever is angry with his brother** – Some copies add, **without a cause** – But this is utterly foreign to the whole scope and tenor of our Lord's discourse. If he had only forbidden the being angry without a cause, there was no manner of need of that solemn declaration, I say unto you; for the scribes and Pharisees themselves said as much as this. Even they taught, men ought not to be angry without a cause. So that this righteousness does not exceed theirs. But Christ teaches, that we ought not, for any cause, to be so angry as to call any man **Raca**, or fool. We ought not, for any cause, to be angry at the person of the sinner, but at his sins only. Happy world, were this plain and necessary distinction thoroughly understood, remembered, practised! Raca means, a silly man, a trifler. **Whosoever shall say, Thou fool** – Shall revile, or seriously reproach any man. Our Lord specified three degrees of murder, each liable to a sorer punishment than the other: not indeed from men, but from God. **Hell fire** – In the valley of Hinnom the children were used to be burnt alive to Moloch. It was afterward made a receptacle for the filth of the city, where continual fires were kept to consume it. And it is probable, if any criminals were burnt alive, it was in this accursed and horrible place. Therefore both as to its former and latter state, it was a fit emblem of hell. It must here signify a degree of future punishment, as much more dreadful than those incurred in the two former cases, as burning alive is more dreadful than either strangling or stoning.

23. Thy brother hath aught against thee – On any of the preceding accounts: for any unkind thought or word: any that did not spring from love.

24. Leaving thy gift, go – For neither thy gift nor thy prayer will atone for thy want of love: but this will make them both an abomination before God.

25. Agree with thine adversary – With any against whom thou hast thus offended: **while thou art in the way** – Instantly, on the spot; before you part. **Lest the adversary deliver thee to the judge** – Lest he commit his cause to God. Luke 12:58.

26. Till thou hast paid the last farthing – That is, for ever, since thou canst never do this. What has been hitherto said refers to meekness: what follows, to purity of heart.

27. Thou shalt not commit adultery – And this, as well as the sixth commandment, the scribes and Pharisees interpreted barely of the outward act. Exod 20:14. Mt 5:21, 22, 27, 28, 29, 30. As if he had said, Part with any thing, however dear to you, or otherwise useful, if you cannot avoid sin while you keep it. Even cut off your right hand, if you are of so passionate a temper, that you cannot otherwise be restrained from hurting your brother. Pull out your eyes, if you can no otherwise be restrained from lusting after women. Matt 18:8; Mark 9:43.

31. Let him give her a writing of divorce – Which the scribes and Pharisees allowed men to do on any trifling occasion. Deut 24:1; Matt 19:7; Mark 10:2; Luke 16:18.

32. Causeth her to commit adultery – If she marry again.

33. Our Lord here refers to the promise made to the pure in heart of seeing God in all things, and points out a false doctrine of the scribes, which arose from their not thus seeing God. What he forbids is, the swearing at all:
1. by any creature,
2. in our ordinary conversation:
both of which the scribes and Pharisees taught to be perfectly innocent. Exod 20:7.

36. For thou canst not make one hair white or black – Whereby it appears, that this also is not thine but God's.

37. Let your conversation be yea, yea; nay, nay – That is, in your common discourse, barely affirm or deny.

38. Ye have heard – Our Lord proceeds to enforce such meekness and love on those who are persecuted for righteousness' sake as were utterly unknown to the scribes and Pharisees. It **hath been said** – In the law, as a direction to judges, in case of violent and barbarous assaults. **An eye for an eye, and a tooth for a tooth** – And this has been interpreted, as encouraging bitter and rigorous revenge. Deut 19:21.

39. But I say unto you, that ye resist not the evil man – Thus; the Greek word translated resist signifies standing in battle array, striving for victory. **If a man smite thee on the right cheek** – Return not evil for evil: yea, **turn to him the other** – Rather than revenge thyself.

40, 41. Where the damage is not great, choose rather to suffer it, though possibly it may on that account be repeated, than to demand an eye for an eye, to enter into a rigorous prosecution of the offender. The meaning of the whole passage seems to be, rather than return evil for evil, when the wrong is purely personal, submit to one bodily wrong after another, give up one part of your goods after another, submit to one instance of compulsion after another. That the words are not literally to be understood, appears from the behaviour of our Lord himself, John 18:22,23.

42. Thus much for your behaviour toward the violent. As for those who use milder methods, **Give to him that asketh thee** – Give and lend to any so far, as is consistent with thy engagements to thy creditors, thy family, and the household of faith. Luke 6:30.

43. Thou shalt love thy neighbour; And hate thy enemy – God spoke the former part; the scribes added the latter. Lev 19:18.

44. Bless them that curse you – Speak all the good you can to and of them, who speak all evil to and of you. Repay love in thought, word, and deed, to those who hate you, and show it both in word and deed. Luke 6:27,35.

45. That ye may be the children – That is, that ye may continue and appear such before men and angels. **For he maketh his sun to rise** – He gives them such blessings as they will receive at his hands. Spiritual blessings they will not receive.

46. The publicans – were officers of the revenue, farmers, or receivers of the public money: men employed by the Romans to gather the taxes and customs, which they exacted of the nations they had conquered. These were generally odious for their extortion and oppression, and were reckoned by the Jews as the very scum of the earth.

47. And if ye salute your friends only – Our Lord probably glances at those prejudices, which different sects had against each other, and intimates, that he would not have his followers imbibe that narrow spirit. Would to God this had been more attended to among the unhappy divisions and subdivisions, into which his Church has been crumbled! And that we might at least advance so far, as cordially to embrace our brethren in Christ, of whatever party or denomination they are!

48. Therefore ye shall be perfect; as your Father who is in heaven is perfect – So the original runs, referring to all that holiness which is described in the foregoing verses, which our Lord in the beginning of the chapter recommends as happiness, and in the close of it as perfection. And how wise and gracious is this, to sum up, and, as it were, seal all his commandments with a promise! Even the proper promise of the Gospel! That he will put those laws in our minds, and write them in our hearts! He well knew how ready our unbelief would be to cry out, this is impossible! And therefore stakes upon it all the power, truth, and faithfulness of him to whom all things are possible.

Chapter 6

In the foregoing chapter our Lord particularly described the nature of inward holiness. In this he describes that purity of intention without which none of our outward actions are holy. This chapter contains four parts:
1. The right intention and manner of giving alms, ver.1–4.
2. The right intention, manner, form, and prerequisites of prayer, ver.5–15.
3. The right intention, and manner of fasting, ver.16–18.
4. The necessity of a pure intention in all things, unmixed either with the desire of riches, or worldly care, and fear of want, ver.19–34.

1. This verse is a general caution against vain glory, in any of our good works: All these are here summed up together, in the comprehensive word righteousness. This general caution our

Lord applies in the sequel to the three principal branches of it, relating to our neighbour, ver.2–4: to God, ver.5, 6: and to ourselves, ver.16-18. **To be seen** – Barely the being seen, while we are doing any of these things, is a circumstance purely indifferent. But the doing them with this view, to be seen and admired, this is what our Lord condemns.

2. As the hypocrites do – Many of the scribes and Pharisees did this, under a pretence of calling the poor together. **They have their reward** – All they will have; for they shall have none from God.

3. Let not thy left hand know what thy right hand doth – A proverbial expression for doing a thing secretly. Do it as secretly as is consistent: 1. With the doing it at all. 2. With the doing it in the most effectual manner.

5. The synagogues – These were properly the places where the people assembled for public prayer, and hearing the Scriptures read and expounded. They were in every city from the time of the Babylonian captivity, and had service in them thrice a day on three days in the week. In every synagogue was a council of grave and wise persons, over whom was a president, called the ruler of the synagogue. But the word here, as well as in many other texts, signifies any place of public concourse.

6. Enter into thy closet – That is, do it with as much secrecy as thou canst.

7. Use not vain repetitions – To repeat any words without meaning them, is certainly a vain repetition. Therefore we should be extremely careful in all our prayers to mean what we say; and to say only what we mean from the bottom of our hearts. The vain and heathenish repetitions which we are here warned against, are most dangerous, and yet very common; which is a principal cause why so many, who still profess religion, are a disgrace to it. Indeed all the words in the world are not equivalent to one holy desire. And the very best prayers are but vain repetitions, if they are not the language of the heart.

8. Your Father knoweth what things ye have need of – We do not pray to inform God of our wants. Omniscient as he is, he cannot be informed of any thing which he knew not before: and he is always willing to relieve them. The chief thing wanting is, a fit disposition on our part to receive his grace and blessing. Consequently, one great office of prayer is, to produce such a disposition in us: to exercise our dependence on God; to increase our desire of the things we ask for; to us so sensible of our wants, that we may never cease wrestling till we have prevailed for the blessing.

9. Thus therefore pray ye – He who best knew what we ought to pray for, and how we ought to pray, what matter of desire, what manner of address would most please himself, would best become us, has here dictated to us a most perfect and universal form of prayer, comprehending all our real wants, expressing all our lawful desires; a complete directory and full exercise of all our devotions. **Thus** – For these things; sometimes in these words, at least in this manner, short, close, full. This prayer consists of three parts, the preface, the petitions, and the conclusion. The preface, **Our Father, which art in heaven,** lays a general foundation for prayer, comprising what we must first know of God, before we can pray in confidence of being heard. It likewise points out to us that our faith, humility, love, of God and man, with which we are to approach God in prayer. **Our Father** – Who art good and gracious to all, our Creator, our Preserver; the Father of our Lord, and of us in him, thy children by adoption and grace: not my Father only, who now cry unto thee, but the Father of the universe, of angels and men: **which art in heaven** – Beholding all things, both in heaven and earth; knowing every creature, and all the works of every creature, and every possible event from everlasting to everlasting: the almighty Lord and Ruler of all, superintending and disposing all things; **in heaven** – Eminently there, but not there alone, seeing thou fillest heaven and earth. **Hallowed be thy name** – Mayest thou, O Father, be truly known by all intelligent beings, and with affections suitable to that knowledge: mayest thou be duly honoured, loved, feared, by all in heaven and in earth, by all angels and all men.

10. Thy kingdom come – May thy kingdom of grace come quickly, and swallow up all the kingdoms of the earth: may all mankind, receiving thee, O Christ, for their king, truly believing in thy name, be filled with righteousness, and peace, and joy; with holiness and happiness, till they are removed hence into thy kingdom of glory, to reign with thee for ever and ever. **Thy will be done on earth, as it is in heaven** – May all the inhabitants of the earth do thy will as willingly as the holy angels: may these do it continually even as they, without any interruption of their willing service; yea, and perfectly as they: mayest thou, O Spirit of grace, through the blood of the everlasting covenant, make them perfect in every good work to do thy will, and work in them all that is well pleasing in thy sight.

11. Give us – O Father **this day** – **our daily bread** – All things needful for our souls and bodies: not only the meat that perisheth, but the sacramental bread, and thy grace, the food which endureth to everlasting life.

12. And forgive us our debts, as we also forgive our debtors – Give us, O Lord, redemption in thy blood, even the forgiveness of sins: as thou enablest us freely and fully to forgive every man, so do thou forgive all our trespasses.

13. And lead us not into temptation, but

deliver us from evil – Whenever we are tempted, O thou that helpest our infirmities, suffer us not to enter into temptation; to be overcome or suffer loss thereby; but make a way for us to escape, so that we may be more than conquerors, through thy love, over sin and all the consequences of it. Now the principal desire of a Christian's heart being the glory of God, Mt 6:9,10 and all he wants for himself or his brethren being the daily bread of soul and body, pardon of sin, and deliverance from the power of it and of the devil, Mt 6:11,12,13 there is nothing beside that a Christian can wish for; therefore this prayer comprehends all his desires. Eternal life is the certain consequence, or rather completion of holiness. **For thine is the kingdom** – The sovereign right of all things that are or ever were created: **The power** – the executive power, whereby thou governest all things in thy everlasting kingdom: **And the glory** – The praise due from every creature, for thy power, and all thy wondrous works, and the mightiness of thy kingdom, which endureth through all ages, even for ever and ever. It is observable, that though the doxology, as well as the petitions of this prayer, is threefold, and is directed to the Father, Son, and Holy Ghost distinctly, yet is the whole fully applicable both to every person, and to the ever-blessed and undivided trinity. Luke 11:2.

14. Mark 11:25.

16. When ye fast – Our Lord does not enjoin either fasting, alms-deeds, or prayer: all these being duties which were before fully established in the Church of God. **Disfigure** – By the dust and ashes which they put upon their heads, as was usual at the times of solemn humiliation.

17. Anoint thy head – So the Jews frequently did. Dress thyself as usual.

19. Lay not up for yourselves – Our Lord here makes a transition from religious to common actions, and warns us of another snare, the love of money, as inconsistent with purity of intention as the love of praise. **Where rust and moth consume** – Where all things are perishable and transient. He may likewise have a farther view in these words, even to guard us against making any thing on earth our treasure. For then a thing properly becomes our treasure, when we set our affections upon it. Luke 12:33.

21. Luke 11:34.

22. The eye is the lamp of the body – And what the eye is to the body, the intention is to the soul. We may observe with what exact propriety our Lord places purity of intention between worldly desires and worldly cares, either of which directly tend to destroy. **If thine eye be single** – Singly fixed on God and heaven, thy whole soul will be full of holiness and happiness. **If thine eye be evil** – Not single, aiming at any thing else.

24. Mammon – Riches, money; any thing loved or sought, without reference to God. Luke 16:13.

25. And if you serve God, you need be careful for nothing. **Therefore take not thought** – That is, be not anxiously careful. Beware of worldly cares; for these are as inconsistent with the true service of God as worldly desires. **Is not the life more than meat?** – And if God give the greater gift, will he deny the smaller? Luke 12:22.

27. And which of you – If you are ever so careful, can even add a moment to your own life thereby? This seems to be far the most easy and natural sense of the words.

29. Solomon in all his glory was not arrayed like one of these – Not in garments of so pure a white. The eastern monarchs were often clothed in white robes.

30. The grass of the field – is a general expression, including both herbs and flowers. **If God so clothe** – The word properly implies, the putting on a complete dress, that surrounds the body on all sides; and beautifully expresses that external membrane, which at once adorns the tender fabric of the vegetable, and guards it from the injuries of the weather. Every microscope in which a flower is viewed gives a lively comment on this text.

31. Therefore take not thought – How kind are these precepts! The substance of which is only this, Do thyself no harm! Let us not be so ungrateful to him, nor so injurious to ourselves, as to harass and oppress our minds with that burden of anxiety, which he has so graciously taken off. Every verse speaks at once to the understanding, and to the heart. We will not therefore indulge these unnecessary, these useless, these mischievous cares. We will not borrow the anxieties and distresses of the morrow, to aggravate those of the present day. Rather we will cheerfully repose ourselves on that heavenly Father, who knows we have need of these things; who has given us the life, which is more than meat, and the body, which is more than raiment. And thus instructed in the philosophy of our heavenly Master, we will learn a lesson of faith and cheerfulness from every bird of the air, and every flower of the field.

33. Seek the kingdom of God and his righteousness – Singly aim at this, that God, reigning in your heart, may fill it with the righteousness above described. And indeed whosoever seeks this first, will soon come to seek this only.

34. The morrow shall take thought for itself – That is, be careful for the morrow when it comes. **The evil thereof** – Speaking after the manner of men. But all trouble is, upon the whole, a real good. It is good physic which God dispenses daily to his children, according to the need and the strength of each.

Chapter 7

Our Lord now proceeds to warn us against the chief hinderances of holiness. And how wisely does he begin with judging? wherein all young converts are so apt to spend that zeal which is given them for better purposes.

1. Judge not – any man without full, clear, certain knowledge, without absolute necessity, without tender love. Luke 6:37.

2. With what measure ye mete, it shall be measured to you – Awful words! So we may, as it were, choose for ourselves, whether God shall be severe or merciful to us. God and man will favour the candid and benevolent: but they must expect judgment without mercy, who have showed no mercy.

3. In particular, why do you open your eyes to any fault of your brother, while you yourself are guilty of a much greater? **The mote** – The word properly signifies a splinter or shiver of wood. This and a beam, its opposite, were proverbially used by the Jews, to denote, the one, small infirmities, the other, gross, palpable faults. Luke 6:41.

4. How sayest thou – With what face?

5. Thou hypocrite – It is mere hypocrisy to pretend zeal for the amendment of others while we have none for our own. **Then** – When that which obstructed thy sight is removed.

6. Give not – **to dogs** – lest turning they rend you: **Cast not** – **to swine** – lest they trample them under foot. Yet even then, when the beam is cast out of thine own eye, **Give not** – That is, talk not of the deep things of God to those whom you know to be wallowing in sin, neither declare the great things God hath done for your soul to the profane, furious, persecuting wretches. Talk not of perfection, for instance, to the former; not of your experience to the latter. But our Lord does in nowise forbid us to reprove, as occasion is, both the one and the other.

7. But ask – Pray for them, as well as for yourselves: in this there can be no such danger. **Seek** – Add your own diligent endeavours to your asking: **and knock** – Persevere importunately in that diligence. Luke 11:9.

8. For every one that asketh receiveth – Provided he ask aright, and ask what is agreeable to God's will.

11. To them that ask him – But on this condition, that ye follow the example of his goodness, by doing to all as ye would they should do to you. **For this is the law and the prophets** – This is the sum of all, exactly answering Mt 5:17. The whole is comprised in one word, Imitate the God of love. Thus far proceeds the doctrinal part of the sermon. In the next verse begins the exhortation to practise it.

12. Luke 6:31.

13. The strait gate – The holiness described in the foregoing chapters. And this is the narrow way. **Wide is the gate, and many there are that go in through it** – They need not seek for this; they come to it of course. **Many go in through it, because strait is the other gate** – Therefore they do not care for it; they like a wider gate. Luke 13:24.

15. Beware of false prophets – Who in their preaching describe a broad way to heaven: it is their prophesying, their teaching the broad way, rather than their walking in it themselves, that is here chiefly spoken of. All those are false prophets, who teach any other way than that our Lord hath here marked out. **In sheep's clothing** – With outside religion and fair professions of love: **Wolves** – Not feeding, but destroying souls.

16. By their fruits ye shall know them – A short, plain, easy rule, whereby to know true from false prophets: and one that may be applied by people of the weakest capacity, who are not accustomed to deep reasoning. True prophets convert sinners to God, or at least confirm and strengthen those that are converted. False prophets do not. They also are false prophets, who though speaking the very truth, yet are not sent by the Spirit of God, but come in their own name, to declare it: their grand mark is, 'Not turning men from the power of Satan to God.' Luke 6:43,44.

18. A good tree cannot bring forth evil fruit, neither a corrupt tree good fruit – But it is certain, the goodness or badness here mentioned respects the doctrine, rather than the personal character. For a bad man preaching the good doctrine here delivered, is sometimes an instrument of converting sinners to God. Yet I do not aver, that all are true prophets who speak the truth, and thereby convert sinners. I only affirm, that none are such who do not.

19. Every tree that bringeth not forth good fruit is hewn down and cast into the fire – How dreadful then is the condition of that teacher who hath brought no sinners to God!

21. Not every one – That is, no one **that saith, Lord, Lord** – That makes a mere profession of me and my religion, **shall enter** – Whatever his false teachers may assure them to the contrary: **He that doth the will of my Father** – as I have now declared it. Observe: every thing short of this is only saying, Lord, Lord. Luke 6:46.

22. We have prophesied – We have declared the mysteries of thy kingdom, wrote books; preached excellent sermons: **In thy name done many wonderful works** – So that even the working of miracles is no proof that a man has saving faith.

23. I never knew you – There never was a time that I approved of you: so that as many souls as they had saved, they were themselves never saved from their sins. Lord, is it my case? Luke 13:27.

24. Luke 6:47.

29. **He taught them** – The multitudes, **as one having authority** – With a dignity and majesty peculiar to himself as the great Lawgiver, and with the demonstration and power of the Spirit: **and not as the scribes** – Who only expounded the law of another; and that in a lifeless, ineffectual manner.

Chapter 8

2. **A leper came** – Leprosy in those countries was seldom curable by natural means, any more than palsies or lunacy. Probably this leper, though he might not mix with the people, had heard our Lord at a distance. Mark 1:40; Luke 5:12.

4. **See thou tell no man** – Perhaps our Lord only meant here, Not till thou hast **showed thyself to the priest** – who was appointed to inquire into the case of leprosy. But many others he commanded, absolutely, to tell none of those miracles he had wrought upon them. And this he seems to have done, chiefly for one or more of these reasons:

1. To prevent the multitude from thronging him, in the manner related Mark 1:45.
2. To fulfil the prophecy, Isaiah 42:1, that he would not be vain or ostentatious. This reason St. Matthew assigns, Matt 12:17.
3. To avoid the being taken by force and made a king, John 6:15.

And, 4. That he might not enrage the chief priests, scribes, and Pharisees, who were the most bitter against him, any more than was unavoidable, Matt 16:20,21.

For a testimony – That I am the Messiah; **to them** – The priests, who otherwise might have pleaded want of evidence. Lev 14:2.

5. **There came to him a centurion** – A captain of a hundred Roman soldiers. Probably he came a little way toward him, and then went back. He thought himself not worthy to come in person, and therefore spoke the words that follow by his messengers. As it is not unusual in all languages, so in the Hebrew it is peculiarly frequent, to ascribe to a person himself the thing which is done, and the words which are spoken by his order. And accordingly St. Matthew relates as said by the centurion himself, what others said by order from him. An instance of the same kind we have in the case of Zebedee's children. From St. Matthew, Mt 20:20, we learn it was their mother that spoke those words, which, Mark 10:35,37, themselves are said to speak; because she was only their mouth. Yet from ver. 13, Mt 8:13, Go thy way home, it appears he at length came in person, probably on hearing that Jesus was nearer to his house than he apprehended when he sent the second message by his friends. Luke 7:1.

8. **The centurion answered** – By his second messengers.

9. **For I am a man under authority** – I am only an inferior officer: and what I command, is done even in my absence: how much more what thou commandest, who art Lord of all!

10. **I have not found so great faith, no, not in Israel** – For the centurion was not an Israelite.

11. Many from the farthest parts of the earth shall embrace the terms and enjoy the rewards of the Gospel covenant established with Abraham. But the Jews, who have the first title to them, shall be shut out from the feast; from grace here, and hereafter from glory. Luke 13:29.

12. **The outer darkness** – Our Lord here alludes to the custom the ancients had of making their feast in the night time. Probably while he was speaking this, the centurion came in person. Matt 13:42,50; 22:13; 24:51; 25:30.

14. **Peter's wife's mother** – St. Peter was then a young man, as were all the apostles. Mark 1:29; Luke 4:38.

16. Mark 1:32; Luke 4:40.

17. **Whereby was fulfilled what was spoken by the Prophet Isaiah** – He spoke it in a more exalted sense. The evangelist here only alludes to those words, as being capable of this lower meaning also. Such instances are frequent in the sacred writings, and are elegancies rather than imperfections. He fulfilled these words in the highest sense, by bearing our sins in his own body on the tree: in a lower sense, by sympathizing with us in our sorrows, and healing us of the diseases which were the fruit of sin. Isaiah 53:4.

18. **He commanded to go to the other side** – That both himself and the people might have a little rest.

19. Luke 9:57.

20. **The Son of man** – The expression is borrowed from Daniel 7:13, and is the appellation which Christ generally gives himself: which he seems to do out of humility, as having some relation to his mean appearance in this world. **Hath not where to lay his head** – Therefore do not follow me from any view of temporal advantage.

21. **Another said** – I will follow thee without any such view; but I must mind my business first. It is not certain that his father was already dead. Perhaps his son desired to stay with him, being very old, till his death.

22. **But Jesus said** – When God calls, leave the business of the world to them who are dead to God.

23. Mark 4:35; Luke 8:22.

24. **The ship was covered** – So man's extremity is God's opportunity.

26. **Why are ye fearful** – Then he **rebuked the winds** – First, he composed their spirits, and then the sea.

28. The country of the Gergesenes – Or of the Gadarenes – Gergesa and Gadara were towns near each other. Hence the country between them took its name, sometimes from the one, sometimes from the other. **There met him two demoniacs** – St. Mark and St. Luke mention only one, who was probably the fiercer of the two, and the person who spoke to our Lord first. But this is no way inconsistent with the account which St. Matthew gives. **The tombs** – Doubtless those malevolent spirits love such tokens of death and destruction. Tombs were usually in those days in desert places, at a distance from towns, and were often made in the sides of caves, in the rocks and mountains. **No one could pass** – Safely. Mark 5:1; Luke 8:26.

29. What have we to do with thee – This is a Hebrew phrase, which signifies. Why do you concern yourself about us? 2Sam 16:10. **Before the time** – The great day.

30. There was a herd of many swine – Which it was not lawful for the Jews to keep. Therefore our Lord both justly and mercifully permitted them to be destroyed.

31. He said, Go – A word of permission only, not command.

34. They besought him to depart out of their coasts – They loved their swine so much better than their souls! How many are of the same mind!

Chapter 9

1. His own city – Capernaum, Matt 4:13. Mark 5:18; Luke 8:37.

2. Seeing their faith – Both that of the paralytic, and of them that brought him. **Son** – A title of tenderness and condescension. Mark 2:3; Luke 5:18.

3. This man blasphemeth – Attributing to himself a power which belongs to God only.

5. Which is easier – Do not both of them argue a Divine power? Therefore if I can heal his disease, I can forgive his sins: especially as his disease is the consequence of his sins. Therefore these must be taken away, if that is.

6. On earth – Even in my state of humiliation.

8. So what was to the scribes an occasion of blaspheming, was to the people an incitement to praise God.

9. He saw a man named Matthew – Modestly so called by himself. The other evangelists call him by his more honourable name, Levi. **Sitting** – In the very height of his business, **at the receipt of custom** – The custom house, or place where the customs were received. Mark 2:14; Luke 5:27.

10. As Jesus sat at table in the house – Of Matthew, who having invited many of his old companions, made him a feast, Mark 2:15; and

that a great one, though he does not himself mention it. **The publicans**, or collectors of the taxes which the Jews paid the Romans, were infamous for their illegal exactions: **Sinners** – Open, notorious, sinners.

11. The Pharisees said to his disciples, Why eateth your Master? – Thus they commonly ask our Lord, Why do thy disciples this? And his disciples, Why doth your Master?

13. Go ye and learn – Ye that take upon you to teach others. **I will have mercy and not sacrifice** – That is, I will have mercy rather than sacrifice. I love acts of mercy better than sacrifice itself. Hosea 6:6.

14. Then – While he was at table. Mark 2:18; Luke 5:33.

15. The children of the bride chamber – The companions of the bridegroom. **Mourn** – Mourning and fasting usually go together. As if he had said, While I am with them, it is a festival time, a season of rejoicing, not mourning. But after I am gone, all my disciples likewise shall be in fastings often.

16. This is one reason, – It is not a proper time for them to fast. Another is, they are not ripe for it. **New cloth** – The words in the original properly signify cloth that hath not passed through the fuller's hands, and which is consequently much harsher than what has been washed and worn; and therefore yielding less than that, will tear away the edges to which it is sewed.

17. New – Fermenting wine will soon burst those bottles, the leather of which is almost worn out. The word properly means vessels made of goats' skins, wherein they formerly put wine, to convey it from place to place. **Put new wine into new bottles** – Give harsh doctrines to such as have strength to receive them.

18. Just dead – He had left her at the point of death, Mark 5:23. Probably a messenger had now informed him she was dead. Mark 5:22; Luke 8:41.

20. Coming behind – Out of bashfulness and humility.

22. Take courage – Probably she was struck with fear, when he turned and looked upon her, Mark 5:33; Luke 8:47; lest she should have offended him, by touching his garment privately; and the more so, because she was unclean according to the law, Lev 15:25.

23. The minstrels – The musicians. The original word means flute players. Musical instruments were used by the Jews as well as the heathens, in their lamentations for the dead, to soothe the melancholy of surviving friends, by soft and solemn notes. And there were persons who made it their business to perform this, while others sung to their music. Flutes were used especially on the death of children; louder instruments on the death of grown persons.

24. Withdraw – There is no need of you now; **for the maid is not dead** – Her life is not at an end; **but sleepeth** – This is only a temporary suspension of sense and motion, which should rather be termed sleep than death.

25. The maid arose – Christ raised three dead persons to life; this child, the widow's son, and Lazarus: one newly departed, another on the bier, the third smelling in the grave: to show us that no degree of death is so desperate as to be past his help.

32. Luke 11:14.

33. Even in Israel – Where so many wonders have been seen.

36. Because they were faint – In soul rather than in body. **As sheep having no shepherd** – And yet they had many teachers; they had scribes in every city. But they had none who cared for their souls, and none that were able, if they had been willing, to have wrought any deliverance. They had no pastors after God's own heart.

37. The harvest truly is great – When Christ came into the world, it was properly the time of harvest; till then it was the seed time only. **But the labourers are few** – Those whom God sends; who are holy, and convert sinners. Of others there are many. Luke 10:2.

38. The Lord of the harvest – Whose peculiar work and office it is, and who alone is able to do it: **that he would thrust forth** – for it is an employ not pleasing to flesh and blood; so full of reproach, labour, danger, temptation of every kind, that nature may well be averse to it. Those who never felt this, never yet knew what it is to be labourers in Christ's harvest. He sends them forth, when he calls them by his Spirit, furnishes them with grace and gifts for the work, and makes a way for them to be employed therein.

Chapter 10

1. His twelve disciples – Hence it appears that he had already chosen out of his disciples, those whom he afterward termed apostles. The number seems to have relation to the twelve patriarchs, and the twelve tribes of Israel. Mark 3:14; 6:7; Luke 6:13; 9:1.

2. The first, Simon – The first who was called to a constant attendance on Christ; although Andrew had seen him before Simon. Acts 1:13.

3. Lebbeus – Commonly called Judas, the brother of James.

4. Iscariot – So called from Iscarioth, a town of the tribe of Ephraim, near the city of Samaria.

5. These twelve Jesus sent forth – Herein exercising his supreme authority, as God over all. None but God can give men authority to preach his word. **Go not** – Their commission was thus confined now, because the calling of the Gentiles was deferred till after the more plentiful effusion of the Holy Ghost on the day of Pentecost. **Enter not** – Not to preach; but they might go to buy what they wanted, John 4:9.

8. Cast out devils – It is a great relief to the spirits of an infidel, sinking under a dread, that possibly the Gospel may be true, to find it observed by a learned brother, that the diseases therein ascribed to the operation of the devil have the very same symptoms with the natural diseases of lunacy, epilepsy, or convulsions; whence he readily and very willingly concludes, that the devil had no hand in them. But it were well to stop and consider a little. Suppose God should suffer an evil spirit to usurp the same power over a man's body, as the man himself has naturally; and suppose him actually to exercise that power; could we conclude the devil had no hand therein, because his body was bent in the very same manner wherein the man himself might have bent it naturally? And suppose God gives an evil spirit a greater power, to effect immediately the organ of the nerves in the brain, by irritating them to produce violent motions, or so relaxing them that they can produce little or no motion; still the symptoms will be those of over tense nerves, as in madness, epilepsies, convulsions; or of relaxed nerves, as in paralytic cases. But could we conclude thence that the devil had no hand in them? Will any man affirm that God cannot or will not, on any occasion whatever, give such a power to an evil spirit? Or that effects, the like of which may be produced by natural causes, cannot possibly be produced by preternatural? If this be possible, then he who affirms it was so, in any particular case, cannot be justly charged with falsehood, merely for affirming the reality of a possible thing. Yet in this manner are the evangelists treated by those unhappy men, who above all things dread the truth of the Gospel, because, if it is true, they are of all men the most miserable. **Freely ye have received** – All things; in particular the power of working miracles; **freely give** – Exert that power wherever you come. Mark 6:7; Luke 9:2.

9. Provide not – The stress seems to lie on this word: they might use what they had ready; but they might not stay a moment to provide any thing more, neither take any thought about it. Nor indeed were they to take any thing with them, more than was strictly necessary.

1. Lest it should retard them.

2. Because they were to learn hereby to trust to God in all future exigencies.

10. Neither scrip – That is, a wallet, or bag to hold provisions: **Nor yet a staff** – We read, Mark 6:8, **Take nothing, save a staff only.** He that had one might take it; they that had none, might not provide any. **For the workman is worthy of his maintenance** – The word includes all that is mentioned in the 9th and 10th verses; Mt 10:9,10 all that they were forbidden to provide for themselves, so far as it was needful for them. Luke 10:7.

11. **Inquire who is worthy** – That you should abide with him: who is disposed to receive the Gospel. **There abide** – In that house, till ye leave the town. Mark 6:10; Luke 9:4.

12. **Salute it** – In the usual Jewish form, 'Peace be to this house.'

13. **If the house be worthy** – of it, God shall give them the peace you wish them. If not, he shall give you what they refuse. The same will be the case, when we pray for them that are not worthy.

14. **Shake off the dust from your feet** – The Jews thought the land of Israel so peculiarly holy, that when they came home from any heathen country, they stopped at the borders and shook or wiped off the dust of it from their feet, that the holy land might not be polluted with it. Therefore the action here enjoined was a lively intimation, that those Jews who had rejected the Gospel were holy no longer, but were on a level with heathens and idolaters.

16. Luke 10:3.

17. But think not that all your innocence and all your wisdom will screen you from persecution. **They will scourge you in their synagogues** – In these the Jews held their courts of judicature, about both civil and ecclesiastical affairs. Matt 24:9.

19. **Take no thought** – Neither at this time, on any sudden call, need we be careful how or what to answer. Luke 12:11.

21. Luke 21:16.

22. **Of all men** – That know not God. Mt 24:13.

23. **Ye shall not have gone over the cities of Israel** – Make what haste ye will; **till the Son of man be come** – To destroy their temple and nation.

24. Luke 6:30; John 15:20.

25. **How much more** – This cannot refer to the quantity of reproach and persecution: but only to the certainty of it. Mt 12:24.

26. **Therefore fear them not** – For ye have only the same usage with your Lord. **There is nothing covered** – So that however they may slander you now, your innocence will at length appear. Mark 4:22; Luke 8:17; 12:2.

27. Even what I now tell you secretly is not to be kept secret long, but declared publicly. Therefore, **What ye hear in the ear, publish on the house-top** – Two customs of the Jews seem to be alluded to here. Their doctors used to whisper in the ear of their disciples what they were to pronounce aloud to others. And as their houses were low and flat roofed, they sometimes preached to the people from thence. Luke 12:3.

28. **And be not afraid** – of any thing which ye may suffer for proclaiming it. **Be afraid of him who is able to destroy both body and soul in hell** – It is remarkable, that our Lord commands those who love God, still to fear him, even on this account, under this notion.

29, 30. The particular providence of God is another reason for your not fearing man. For this extends to the very smallest things. And if he has such care over the most inconsiderable creatures, how much more will he take care of you, and that not only in this life, but in the other also?

32. **Whosoever shall confess me** – Publicly acknowledge me for the promised Messiah. But this confession implies the receiving his whole doctrine, Mark 8:38, and obeying all his commandments. Luke 9:26.

33, 34. **Whosoever shall deny me before men** – To which ye will be strongly tempted. For **Think not that I am come** – That is, think not that universal peace will be the immediate consequence of my coming. Just the contrary. Both public and private divisions will follow, wheresoever my Gospel comes with power. **Ye** – this is not the design, though it be the event of his coming, through the opposition of devils and men.

36. **And the foes of a man** – That loves and follows me. Micah 7:6.

37. **He that loveth father or mother more than me** – He that is not ready to give up all these, when they stand in competition with his duty.

38. **He that taketh not his cross** – That is, whatever pain or inconvenience cannot be avoided, but by doing some evil, or omitting some good. Mt 16:24; Luke 14:27.

39. **He that findeth his life shall lose it** – He that saves his life by denying me, shall lose it eternally; and he that loseth his life by confessing me, shall save it eternally. And as you shall be thus rewarded, so in proportion shall they who entertain you for my sake. Mt 16:25; John 12:25.

40. Mt 18:5; Luke 10:16; John 13:20.

41. **He that entertaineth a prophet** – That is, a preacher of the Gospel: **In the name of a prophet** – That is, because he is such, shall share in his reward.

42. **One of these little ones** – The very least Christian. Mark 9:41.

Chapter 11

1. **In their cities** – The other cities of Israel.

2. **He sent two of his disciples** – Not because he doubted himself; but to confirm their faith. Luke 7:18.

3. **He that is to come** – The Messiah.

4. **Go and tell John the things that ye hear and see** – Which are a stronger proof of my being the Messiah, than any bare assertion can be.

5. The poor have the Gospel preached to them – The greatest mercy of all. Isaiah 29:18; 35:5.

6. Happy is he who shall not be offended at me – Notwithstanding all these proofs that I am the Messiah.

7. As they departed, he said concerning John – Of whom probably he would not have said so much when they were present. A reed shaken by the wind? – No; nothing could ever shake John in the testimony he gave to the truth. The expression is proverbial.

8. A man clothed in soft, delicate raiment – An effeminate courtier, accustomed to fawning and flattery? You may expect to find persons of such a character in palaces; not in a wilderness.

9. More than a prophet – For the prophets only pointed me out afar off; but John was my immediate forerunner.

10. Mal 3:1.

11. But he that is least in the kingdom of heaven, is greater than he – Which an ancient author explains thus: – 'One perfect in the law, as John was, is inferior to one who is baptized into the death of Christ. For this is the kingdom of heaven, even to be buried with Christ, and to be raised up together with him. John was greater than all who had been then born of women, but he was cut off before the kingdom of heaven was given.' He seems to mean, that righteousness, peace, and joy, which constitute the present inward kingdom of heaven. 'He was blameless as to that righteousness which is by the law; but he fell short of those who are perfected by the spirit of life which is in Christ. Whosoever, therefore, is least in the kingdom of heaven, by Christian regeneration, is greater than any who has attained only the righteousness of the law, because the law maketh nothing perfect.' It may farther mean, the least true Christian believer has a more perfect knowledge of Jesus Christ, of his redemption and kingdom, than John the Baptist had, who died before the full manifestation of the Gospel.

12. And from the days of John – That is, from the time that John had fulfilled his ministry, men rush into my kingdom with a violence like that of those who are taking a city by storm.

13. For all the prophets and the law prophesied until John – For all that is written in the law and the prophets only foretold as distant what is now fulfilled. In John the old dispensation expired, and the new began. Luke 16:16.

14. Mal 4:5.

15. He that hath ears to hear, let him hear – A kind of proverbial expression; requiring the deepest attention to what is spoken.

16. This generation – That is, the men of this age. They are like those froward children of whom their fellows complain, that they will be pleased no way.

18. John came neither eating nor drinking – In a rigorous austere way, like Elijah. And they say, He hath a devil – Is melancholy, from the influence of an evil spirit.

19. The Son of man came eating and drinking – Conversing in a free, familiar way. Wisdom is justified by her children – That is, my wisdom herein is acknowledged by those who are truly wise.

20. Then began he to upbraid the cities – It is observable he had never upbraided them before. Indeed at first they received him with all gladness, Capernaum in particular.

21. Woe to thee, Chorazin – That is, miserable art thou. For these are not curses or imprecations, as has been commonly supposed; but a solemn, compassionate declaration of the misery they were bringing on themselves. Chorazin and Bethsaida were cities of Galilee, standing by the lake Gennesareth. Tyre and Sidon were cities of Phenicia, lying on the sea shore. The inhabitants of them were heathens. Luke 10:13.

22, 24. Moreover I say unto you – Beside the general denunciation of woe to those stubborn unbelievers, the degree of their misery will be greater than even that of Tyre and Sidon, yea, of Sodom.

23. Thou Capernaum, who hast been exalted to heaven – That is, highly honoured by my presence and miracles.

25. Jesus answering – This word does not always imply, that something had been spoken, to which an answer is now made. It often means no more than the speaking in reference to some action or circumstance preceding. The following words Christ speaks in reference to the case of the cities above mentioned: I thank thee – That is, I acknowledge and joyfully adore the justice and mercy of thy dispensations: Because thou hast hid – That is, because thou hast suffered these things to be hid from men, who are in other respects wise and prudent, while thou hast discovered them to those of the weakest understanding, to them who are only wise to Godward. Luke 10:21.

27. All things are delivered to me – Our Lord, here addressing himself to his disciples, shows why men, wise in other things, do not know this: namely, because none can know it by natural reason: none but those to whom he revealeth it.

28. Come to me – Here he shows to whom he is pleased to reveal these things, to the weary and heavy laden; ye that labour – After rest in God: and are heavy laden – With the guilt and power of sin: and I will give you rest – I alone will freely give you rest from the guilt of sin by justification, and from the power of sin by sanctification.

29. Take my yoke upon you – Believe in me: receive me as your prophet, priest, and king. For

I am meek and lowly in heart – Meek toward all men, lowly toward God: **and ye shall find rest** – Whoever therefore does not find rest of soul, is not meek and lowly. The fault is not in the yoke of Christ: but in thee, who hast not taken it upon thee. Nor is it possible for any one to be discontented, but through want of meekness or lowliness.

30. **For my yoke is easy** – Or rather gracious, sweet, benign, delightful: **and my burden** – Contrary to those of men, is ease, liberty, and honour.

Chapter 12

1. **His disciples plucked the ears of corn, and ate** – Just what sufficed for present necessity: dried corn was a common food among the Jews. Mark 2:23; Luke 6:1.

3. **Have ye not read what David did** – And necessity was a sufficient plea for his transgressing the law in a higher instance.

4. **He entered into the house of God** – Into the tabernacle. The temple was not yet built. **The show bread** – So they called the bread which the priest, who served that week, put every Sabbath day on the golden table that was in the holy place, before the Lord. The loaves were twelve in number, and represented the twelve tribes of Israel: when the new were brought, the stale were taken away, but were to be eaten by the priests only. 1Sam 21:6.

5. **The priests in the temple profane the Sabbath** – That is, do their ordinary work on this, as on a common day, cleansing all things, and preparing the sacrifices. **A greater than the temple** – If therefore the Sabbath must give way to the temple, much more must it give way to me.

7. **I will have mercy and not sacrifice** – That is, when they interfere with each other, I always prefer acts of mercy, before matters of positive institution: yea, before all ceremonial institutions whatever; because these being only means of religion, are suspended of course, if circumstances occur, wherein they clash with love, which is the end of it. Matt 9:13.

8. **For the Son of man** – Therefore they are guiltless, were it only on this account, that they act by my authority, and attend on me in my ministry, as the priests attended on God in the temple: **is Lord even of the Sabbath** – This certainly implies, that the Sabbath was an institution of great and distinguished importance; it may perhaps also refer to that signal act of authority which Christ afterward exerted over it, in changing it from the seventh to the first day of the week. If we suppose here is a transposition of the 7th and 8th verses, then the 8th verse is a proof of the 6th. Mt 12:7,8,6.

9. Mark 3:1; Luke 6:6.

12. **It is lawful to do good on the Sabbath day** – To save a beast, much more a man.

18. **He shall show judgment to the heathens** – That is, he shall publish the merciful Gospel to them also: the Hebrew word signifies either mercy or justice. Isa 42:1.

19. **He shall not strive, nor clamour; neither shall any man hear his voice in the streets** – That is, he shall not be contentious, noisy, or ostentatious: but gentle, quiet, and lowly. We may observe each word rises above the other, expressing a still higher degree of humility and gentleness.

20. **A bruised reed** – A convinced sinner: one that is bruised with the weight of sin: **smoking flax** – One that has the least good desire, the faintest spark of grace: **till he send forth judgment unto victory** – That is, till he make righteousness completely victorious over all its enemies.

21. **In his name** – That is, in him.

22. **A demoniac, blind and dumb** – Many undoubtedly supposed these defects to be merely natural. But the Spirit of God saw otherwise, and gives the true account both of the disorder and the cure. How many disorders, seemingly natural, may even now be owing to the same cause? Luke 11:14.

23. **Is not this the son of David** – That is, the Messiah.

24. Mark 3:22.

25. **Jesus knowing their thoughts** – It seems they had as yet only said it in their hearts.

26. **How shall his kingdom be established** – Does not that subtle spirit know this is not the way to establish his kingdom?

27. **By whom do your children** – That is, disciples, **cast them out** – It seems, some of them really did this; although the sons of Sceva could not. **Therefore shall they be your judge** – Ask them, if Satan will cast out Satan: let even them be judges in this matter. And they shall convict you of obstinacy and partiality, who impute that in me to Beelzebub, which in them you impute to God. Beside, how can I rob him of his subjects, till I have conquered him?

28. **The kingdom of God is come upon you** – Unawares; before you expected: so the word implies.

29. **How can one enter into the strong one's house, unless he first bind the strong one** – So Christ coming into the world, which was then eminently the strong one's, Satan's house, first bound him, and then took his spoils.

30. **He that is not with me is against me** – For there are no neuters in this war. Every one must be either with Christ or against him; either a loyal subject or a rebel. And there are none upon earth, who neither promote nor obstruct his kingdom. For he that does not gather souls to God, scatters them from him.

31. The blasphemy against the Spirit – How much stir has been made about this? How many sermons, yea, volumes, have been written concerning it? And yet there is nothing plainer in all the Bible. It is neither more nor less than the ascribing those miracles to the power of the devil, which Christ wrought by the power of the Holy Ghost. Mark 3:28; Luke 12:10.

32. Whosoever speaketh against the Son of man – In any other respects: **It shall be forgiven him** – Upon his true repentance: **But whosoever speaketh thus against the Holy Ghost, it shall not be forgiven, neither in this world nor in the world to come** – This was a proverbial expression among the Jews, for a thing that would never be done. It here means farther, He shall not escape the punishment of it, either in this world, or in the world to come. The judgment of God shall overtake him, both here and hereafter.

33. Either make the tree good and its fruit good: or make the tree corrupt and its fruit corrupt – That is, you must allow, they are both good, or both bad. – For if the fruit is good, so is the tree; if the fruit is evil, so is the tree also. **For the tree is known by its fruit** – As if he had said, Ye may therefore know me by my fruits. By my converting sinners to God, you may know that God hath sent me. Mt 7:16; Luke 6:43.

34. In another kind likewise, the tree is known by its fruit – Namely, the heart by the conversation.

36. Ye may perhaps think, God does not so much regard your words. But I say to you – That not for blasphemous and profane words only, but for every idle word which **men shall speak** – For want of seriousness or caution; for every discourse which is not conducive to the glory of God, they shall give account in the day of judgment.

37. For by thy words thou shalt then be either acquitted or condemned. Your words as well as actions shall he produced in evidence for or against you, to prove whether you were a true believer or not. And according to that evidence you will either be acquitted or condemned in the great day.

38. We would see a sign – Else we will not believe this. Matt 16:1; Luke 11:16,29.

39. An adulterous generation – Whose heart wanders from God, though they profess him to be their husband. Such adulterers are all those who love the world, and all who seek the friendship of it. **Seeketh a sign** – After all they have had already, which were abundantly sufficient to convince them, had not their hearts been estranged from God, and consequently averse to the truth. **The sign of Jonah** – Who was herein a type of Christ.

40. Three days and three nights – It was customary with the eastern nations to reckon any part of a natural day of twenty-four hours, for the whole day. Accordingly they used to say a thing was done after three or seven days, if it was done on the third or seventh day, from that which was last mentioned. Instances of this may be seen, 1Kings 20:29; and in many other places. And as the Hebrews had no word to express a natural day, they used night and day, or day and night for it. So that to say a thing happened after three days and three nights, was with them the very same, as to say, it happened after three days, or on the third day. See Esther 4:16; 5:1; Gen 7:4,12; Exod 24:18; 34:28. Jonah 2:1.

42. She came from the uttermost parts of the earth – That part of Arabia from which she came was the uttermost part of the earth that way, being bounded by the sea. 1Kings 10:1.

43. But how dreadful will be the consequence of their rejecting me? When the unclean spirit goeth out – Not willingly, but being compelled by one that is stronger than he. **He walketh** – Wanders up and down; **through dry places** – Barren, dreary, desolate; or places not yet watered with the Gospel: **Seeking rest, and findeth none** – How can he, while he carries with him his own hell? And is it not the case of his children too? Reader, is it thy case? Luke 11:24.

44. Whence he came out – He speaks as if he had come out of his own accord: See his pride! **He findeth it empty** – of God, of Christ, of his Spirit: **Swept** – from love, lowliness, meekness, and all the fruits of the Spirit: **And garnished** – With levity and security: so that there is nothing to keep him out, and much to invite him in.

45. Seven other spirits – That is, a great many; a certain number being put for an uncertain: **More wicked than himself** – Whence it appears, that there are degrees of wickedness among the devils themselves: **They enter in and dwell** – For ever in him who is forsaken of God. **So shall it be to this wicked generation** – Yea, and to apostates in all ages.

46. His brethren – His kinsmen: they were the sons of Mary, the wife of Cleopas, or Alpheus, his mother's sister; and came now seeking to take him, as one beside himself, Mark 3:21. Mark 3:31; Luke 8:19.

48. And he answering, said – Our Lord's knowing why they came, sufficiently justifies his seeming disregard of them.

49, 50. See the highest severity, and the highest goodness! Severity to his natural, goodness to his spiritual relations! In a manner disclaiming the former, who opposed the will of his heavenly Father, and owning the latter, who obeyed it.

Chapter 13

1. Mark 4:1; Luke 8:4.

2. He went into the vessel – Which constantly waited upon him, while he was on the sea coast.

3. In parables – The word is here taken in its proper sense, for apt similes or comparisons. This way of speaking, extremely common in the eastern countries, drew and fixed the attention of many, and occasioned the truths delivered to sink the deeper into humble and serious hearers. At the same time, by an awful mixture of justice and mercy, it hid them from the proud and careless. In this chapter our Lord delivers seven parables; directing the four former to all the people; the three latter to his disciples.

Behold the sower – How exquisitely proper is this parable to be an introduction to all the rest! In this our Lord answers a very obvious and a very important question. The same sower, Christ, and the same preachers sent by him, always sow the same seed: why has it not always the same effect? He that hath ears to hear, let him hear!

4. And while he sowed, some seeds fell by the highway side, and the birds came and devoured them – It is observable, that our Lord points out the grand hinderances of our bearing fruit, in the same order as they occur. The first danger is, that the birds will devour the seed. If it escape this, there is then another danger, namely, lest it be scorched, and wither away. It is long after this that the thorns spring up and choke the good seed. A vast majority of those who hear the word of God, receive the seed as by the highway side. Of those who do not lose it by the birds, yet many receive it as on stony places. Many of them who receive it in a better soil, yet suffer the thorns to grow up, and choke it: so that few even of these endure to the end, and bear fruit unto perfection: yet in all these cases, it is not the will of God that hinders, but their own voluntary perverseness.

8. Good ground – Soft, not like that by the highway side; deep, not like the stony ground; purged, not full of thorns.

11. To you, who have, it is given to know the mysteries of the kingdom of heaven – The deep things which flesh and blood cannot reveal, pertaining to the inward, present kingdom of heaven. **But to them who have not, it is not given** – Therefore speak I in parables, that ye may understand, while they do not understand.

12. Whosoever hath – That is, improves what he hath, uses the grace given according to the design of the giver; **to him shall be given** – More and more, in proportion to that improvement. **But whosoever hath not** – Improves it not, **from him shall be taken even what he hath** – Here is the grand rule of God's dealing with the children of men: a rule fixed as the pillars of heaven. This is the key to all his providential dispensations; as will appear to men and angels in that day. Mt 25:29; Mark 4:25; Luke 8:18; 19:26.

13. Therefore I speak to them in parables, because seeing, they see not – In pursuance of this general rule, I do not give more knowledge to this people, because they use not that which they have already: having all the means of seeing, hearing, and understanding, they use none of them: they do not effectually see, or hear, or understand any thing.

14. Hearing ye will hear, but in nowise understand – That is, Ye will surely hear. All possible means will be given you: yet they will profit you nothing; because your heart is sensual, stupid, and insensible; your spiritual senses are shut up; yea, you have closed your eyes against the light; as being unwilling to understand the things of God, and afraid, not desirous that he should heal you. Isaiah 6:9; John 12:40; Acts 28:26.

16. But blessed are your eyes – For you both see and understand. You know how to prize the light which is given you. Luke 10:23.

19. When any one heareth the word, and considereth it not – The first and most general cause of unfruitfulness. **The wicked one cometh** – Either inwardly; filling the mind with thoughts of other things; or by his agent. Such are all they that introduce other subjects, when men should be considering what they have heard.

20. The seed sown on stony places, therefore sprang up soon, because it did not sink deep, Mt 13:5. He receiveth it with joy – Perhaps with transport, with ecstasy: struck with the beauty of truth, and drawn by the preventing grace of God.

21. Yet hath he not root in himself – No deep work of grace: no change in the ground of his heart. Nay, he has no deep conviction; and without this, good desires soon wither away. **He is offended** – He finds a thousand plausible pretences for leaving so narrow and rugged a way.

22. He that received the seed among the thorns, is he that heareth the word and considereth it – In spite of Satan and his agents: yea, hath root in himself, is deeply convinced, and in a great measure inwardly changed; so that he will not draw back, even when tribulation or persecution ariseth. And yet even in him, together with the good seed, the thorns spring up, Mt 13:7, till they gradually choke it, destroy all its life and power, and it becometh unfruitful. Cares are thorns to the poor: wealth to the rich; the desire of other things to all. **The deceitfulness of riches** – Deceitful indeed! for they smile, and betray: kiss, and smite into hell. They put out the eyes, harden the heart, steal away all the life of God; fill the soul with pride, anger, love of the world; make men enemies to the whole cross of Christ! And all the while are eagerly desired, and vehemently pursued, even by those who believe there is a God!

23. Some an hundred fold, some sixty, some thirty – That is, in various proportions; some abundantly more than others.

24. He proposed another parable – in which he farther explains the case of unfruitful hearers. The kingdom of heaven sometimes signifies eternal glory: sometimes the way to it, inward religion; sometimes, as here, the Gospel dispensation: the phrase is likewise used for a person or thing relating to any one of those: so in this place it means, Christ preaching the Gospel, who is like **a man sowing good seed** – The expression, is like, both here and in several other places, only means, that the thing spoken of may be illustrated by the following similitude. Who **sowed good seed in his field** – God sowed nothing but good in his whole creation. Christ sowed only the good seed of truth in his Church.

25. But while men slept – They ought to have watched: the Lord of the field sleepeth not. **His enemy came and sowed darnel** – This is very like wheat, and commonly grows among wheat rather than among other grain: but tares or vetches are of the pulse kind, and bear no resemblance to wheat.

26. When the blade was sprung up, then appeared the darnel – It was not discerned before: it seldom appears, as soon as the good seed is sown: all at first appears to be peace, and love, and joy.

27. Didst not thou sow good seed in thy field? Whence then hath it darnel? – Not from the parent of good. Even the heathen could say, 'No evil can from thee proceed: it is only suffered, not decreed: As darkness is not from the sun, Nor mount the shades, till he is gone.'

28. He said, An enemy hath done this – A plain answer to the great question concerning the origin of evil. God made men intelligent creatures, and consequently free either to choose good or evil: but he implanted no evil in the human soul: An enemy hath done this. Darnel, in the Church, is properly outside Christians, such as have the form of godliness, without the power. Open sinners, such as have neither the form nor the power, are not so properly darnel, as thistles and brambles: these ought to be rooted up without delay, and not suffered in the Christian community. Whereas should fallible men attempt to gather up the darnel, they would often root up the wheat with them.

31. He proposed to them another parable – The former parables relate chiefly to unfruitful hearers; these that follow, to those who bear good fruit. **The kingdom of heaven** – Both the Gospel dispensation, and the inward kingdom. Mark 4:30; Luke 13:18.

32. The least – That is, one of the least: a way of speaking extremely common among the Jews. **It becometh a tree** – In those countries it grows exceeding large and high. So will the Christian doctrine spread in the world, and the life of Christ in the soul.

33. Three measures – This was the quantity which they usually baked at once: **till the whole was leavened** – Thus will the Gospel leaven the world and grace the Christian. Luke 13:20.

34. Without a parable spake he not unto them – That is, not at that time; at other times he did.

35. Psalm 78:2.

38. The good seed are the children of the kingdom – That is, the children of God, the righteous.

41. They shall gather all things that offend – Whatever had hindered or grieved the children of God; whatever things or persons had hindered the good seed which Christ had sown from taking root or bearing fruit. The Greek word is, All scandals.

44. The three following parables are proposed, not to the multitude, but peculiarly to the apostles: the two former of them relate to those who receive the Gospel; the third, both to those who receive, and those who preach it. **The kingdom of heaven is like treasure hid in a field** – The kingdom of God within us is a treasure indeed, but a treasure hid from the world, and from the most wise and prudent in it. He that finds this treasure, hides it deep in his heart, and gives up all other happiness for it.

45. The kingdom of heaven – That is, one who earnestly seeks for it: in verse Mt 13:47 it means, the Gospel preached, which is like a net gathering of every kind: just so the Gospel, wherever it is preached, gathers at first both good and bad, who are for a season full of approbation and warm with good desires. But Christian discipline, and strong, close exhortation, begin that separation in this world, which shall be accomplished by the angels of God in the world to come.

52. Every scribe instructed unto the kingdom of heaven – That is, every duly prepared preacher of the Gospel has a treasure of Divine knowledge, out of which he is able to bring forth all sorts of instructions. The word treasure signifies any collection of things whatsoever, and the places where such collections are kept.

53. He departed thence – He crossed the lake from Capernaum: and came once more into his own country – Nazareth: but with no better success than he had there before.

54. Whence hath HE – Many texts are not understood, for want of knowing the proper emphasis; and others are utterly misunderstood, by placing the emphasis wrong. To prevent this in some measure, the emphatic words are here printed in capital letters. Mark 6:1; Luke 4:16,22.

55. The carpenter's son – The Greek word means, one that works either in wood, iron, or stone. **His brethren** – Our kinsmen. They were the sons of Mary, sister to the virgin, and wife of

Cleophas or Alpheus. **James** – Styled by St. Paul also, the Lord's brother, Gal 1:19. **Simon** – Surnamed the Canaanite.

57. They were offended at him – They looked on him as a mean, ignoble man, not worthy to be regarded. John 4:44; Luke 7:23.

58. He wrought not many mighty works, because of their unbelief – And the reason why many mighty works are not wrought now, is not, that the faith is not every where planted; but, that unbelief every where prevails.

Chapter 14

1. At that time – When our Lord had spent about a year in his public ministry. **Tetrarch** – King of a fourth part of his father's dominions. Mark 6:14.

2. He is risen from the dead – Herod was a Sadducee: and the Sadducees denied the resurrection of the dead. But Sadduceeism staggers when conscience awakes.

3. His brother Philip's wife – Who was still alive. Mark 6:17.

4. It is not lawful for thee to have her – It was not lawful indeed for either of them to have her. For her father Aristobulus was their own brother. John's words were rough, like his raiment. He would not break the force of truth by using soft words, even to a king.

5. He would have put him to death – In his fit of passion; but he was then restrained by fear of the multitude; and afterward by the reverence he bore him.

6. The daughter of Herodias – Afterward infamous for a life suitable to this beginning.

8. Being before instructed by her mother – Both as to the matter and manner of her petition: **She said, Give me here** – Fearing if he had time to consider, he would not do it: **John the Baptist's head in a charger** – A large dish or bowl.

9. And the king was sorry – Knowing that John was a good man. **Yet for the oath's sake** – So he murdered an innocent man from mere tenderness of conscience.

10. And he sent and beheaded John in the prison, and his head was given to the damsel – How mysterious is the providence, which left the life of so holy a man in such infamous hands! which permitted it to be sacrificed to the malice of an abandoned harlot, the petulancy of a vain girl, and the rashness of a foolish, perhaps drunken prince, who made a prophet's head the reward of a dance! But we are sure the Almighty will repay his servants in another world for what ever they suffer in this.

13. Jesus withdrew into a desert place:
1. To avoid Herod.
2. Because of the multitude pressing upon him, Mark 6:32:

and 3. To talk with his disciples, newly returned from their progress, Luke 9:10.

Apart – From all but his disciples. John 6:1.

15. The time is now past – The usual meal time. Mark 6:35; Luke 9:12.

22. He constrained his disciples – Who were unwilling to leave him. Mark 6:45; John 6:15.

24. In the evening – Learned men say the Jews reckoned two evenings; the first beginning at three in the afternoon, the second, at sunset. If so, the latter is meant here.

25. The fourth watch – The Jews usually divided the night into four watches, of three hours each. The first watch began at six, the second at nine, the third at twelve, the fourth at three in the morning. **If it be thou** – It is the same as, Since it is thou. The particle if frequently bears this meaning, both in ours and in all languages. So it means, John 13:14,17. St. Peter was in no doubt, or he would not have quitted the ship.

30. He was afraid – Though he had been used to the sea, and was a skilful swimmer. But so it frequently is. When grace begins to act, the natural courage and strength are withdrawn.

33. Thou art the Son of God – They mean, the Messiah.

35. Mark 6:45.

Chapter 15

1. Mark 7:1.

2. The elders – The chief doctors or, teachers among the Jews.

3. They wash not their hands when they eat bread – Food in general is termed bread in Hebrew; so that to eat bread is the same as to make a meal.

4. Honour thy father and mother – Which implies all such relief as they stand in need of. Exod 20:12; 21:17.

5. It is a gift by whatsoever thou mightest have been profited by me – That is, I have given, or at least, purpose to give to the treasury of the temple, what you might otherwise have had from me.

7. Well did Isaiah prophesy of you, saying – That is, the description which Isaiah gave of your fathers, is exactly applicable to you. The words therefore which were a description of them, are a prophecy with regard to you.

8. Their heart is far from me – And without this all outward worship is mere mockery of God. Isaiah 29:13.

9. Teaching the commandments of men – As equal with, nay, superior to, those of God. What can be a more heinous sin?

13. Every plant – That is, every doctrine.

14. Let them alone – If they are indeed blind leaders of the blind; let them alone: concern not yourselves about them: a plain direction how to behave with regard to all such. Luke 6:39.

17. **Are ye also yet without understanding** – How fair and candid are the sacred historians? Never concealing or excusing their own blemishes.

19. **First evil thoughts** – then **murders** – and the rest. **Railings** – The Greek word includes all reviling, backbiting, and evil speaking.

21. Mark 7:24.

22. **A woman of Canaan** – Canaan was also called Syrophenicia, as lying between Syria properly so called, and Phenicia, by the sea side. **Cried to him** – From afar, **Thou Son of David** – So she had some knowledge of the promised Messiah.

23. **He answered her not a word** – He sometimes tries our faith in like manner.

24. **I am not sent** – Not primarily; not yet.

25. **Then came she** – Into the house where he now was.

28. **Thy faith** – Thy reliance on the power and goodness of God.

29. **The sea of Galilee** – The Jews gave the name of seas to all large lakes. This was a hundred furlongs long, and forty broad. It was called also, the sea of Tiberias. It lay on the borders of Galilee, and the city of Tiberias stood on its western shore. It was likewise styled the lake of Gennesareth: perhaps a corruption of Cinnereth, the name by which it was anciently called, Num 34:11. Mark 7:31.

32. **They continue with me now three days** – It was now the third day since they came. Mark 8:1.

36. **He gave thanks**, or blessed the food – That is, he praised God for it, and prayed for a blessing upon it.

Chapter 16

1. **A sign from heaven** – Such they imagined Satan could not counterfeit. Mark 8:11; Matt 12:38.

2. Luke 12:54.

3. **The signs of the times** – The signs which evidently show, that this is the time of the Messiah.

4. **A wicked and adulterous generation** – Ye would seek no farther sign, did not your wickedness, your love of the world, which is spiritual adultery, blind your understanding.

5. Mark 8:14.

6. **Beware of the leaven of the Pharisees** – That is, of their false doctrine: this is elegantly so called; for it spreads in the soul, or the Church, as leaven does in meal. Luke 12:1.

7. **They reasoned among themselves** – What must we do then for bread, since we have taken no bread with us?

8. **Why reason ye** – Why are you troubled about this? Am I not able, if need so require, to supply you by a word?

11. **How do ye not understand** – Beside, do you not understand, that I did not mean bread, by the leaven of the Pharisees and Sadducees?

13. **And Jesus coming** – There was a large interval of time between what has been related, and what follows. The passages that follow were but a short time before our Lord suffered. Mark 8:27; Luke 9:18.

14. **Jeremiah, or one of the prophets** – There was at that time a current tradition among the Jews, that either Jeremiah, or some other of the ancient prophets would rise again before the Messiah came.

16. **Peter** – Who was generally the most forward to speak.

17. **Flesh and blood** – That is, thy own reason, or any natural power whatsoever.

18. **On this rock** – Alluding to his name, which signifies a rock, namely, the faith which thou hast now professed; **I will build my Church** – But perhaps when our Lord uttered these words, he pointed to himself, in like manner as when he said, Destroy this temple, John 2:19; meaning the temple of his body. And it is certain, that as he is spoken of in Scripture, as the only foundation of the Church, so this is that which the apostles and evangelists laid in their preaching. It is in respect of laying this, that the names of the twelve apostles were equally inscribed on the twelve foundations of the city of God, Rev 21:14. **The gates of hell** – As gates and walls were the strength of cities, and as courts of judicature were held in their gates, this phrase properly signifies the power and policy of Satan and his instruments. **Shall not prevail against it** – Not against the Church universal, so as to destroy it. And they never did. There hath been a small remnant in all ages.

19. **I will give thee the keys of the kingdom of heaven** – Indeed not to him alone, but to him were first given the keys both of doctrine and discipline. He first, after our Lord's resurrection, exercised the apostleship, Acts 1:15. And he first by preaching opened the kingdom of heaven, both to the Jews, Acts 2:14, and to the Gentiles, Acts 10:34. Under the term of binding and loosing are contained all those acts of discipline which Peter and his brethren performed as apostles: and undoubtedly what they thus performed on earth, God confirmed in heaven. Matt 18:18.

20. **Then charged he his disciples to tell no one that he was the Christ** – Jesus himself had not said it expressly even to his apostles, but left them to infer it from his doctrine and miracles. Neither was it proper the apostles should say this openly, before that grand proof of it, his resurrection. If they had, they who believed them would the more earnestly have sought to take and make him a king: and they who did not believe them would the more vehemently have rejected and opposed such a Messiah.

21. From that time Jesus began to tell his disciples, that he must suffer many things – Perhaps this expression, began, always implied his entering on a set and solemn discourse. Hitherto he had mainly taught them only one point, That he was the Christ. From this time he taught them another, That Christ must through sufferings and death enter into his glory. **From the elders** – The most honourable and experienced men; **the chief priests** – Accounted the most religious; and **the scribes** – The most learned body of men in the nation. Would not one have expected, that these should have been the very first to receive him? But not many wise, not many noble were called. **Favour thyself** – The advice of the world, the flesh, and the devil, to every one of our Lord's followers. Mark 8:31; Luke 9:22.

23. Get thee behind me – Out of my sight. It is not improbable, Peter might step before him, to stop him. **Satan** – Our Lord is not recorded to have given so sharp a reproof to any other of his apostles on any occasion. He saw it was needful for the pride of Peter's heart, puffed up with the commendation lately given him. Perhaps the term Satan may not barely mean, Thou art my enemy, while thou fanciest thyself most my friend; but also, Thou art acting the very part of Satan, both by endeavouring to hinder the redemption of mankind, and by giving me the most deadly advice that can ever spring from the pit of hell. **Thou savourest not** – Dost not relish or desire. We may learn from hence

1. That whosoever says to us in such a case, Favour thyself, is acting the part of the devil:
2. That the proper answer to such an adviser is, Get thee behind me:
3. That otherwise he will be an offence to us, an occasion of our stumbling, if not falling:
4. That this advice always proceeds from the not relishing the things of God, but the things of men.

Yea, so far is this advice, favour thyself, from being fit for a Christian either to give or take, that if any man will come after Christ, his very first step is to deny, or renounce himself: in the room of his own will, to substitute the will of God, as his one principle of action.

24. If any man be willing to come after me – None is forced; but if any will be a Christian, it must be on these terms, **Let him deny himself, and take up his cross** – A rule that can never be too much observed: let him in all things deny his own will, however pleasing, and do the will of God, however painful. Should we not consider all crosses, all things grievous to flesh and blood, as what they really are, as opportunities of embracing God's will at the expense of our own? And consequently as so many steps by which we may advance toward perfection? We should make a swift progress in the spiritual life,

if we were faithful in this practice. Crosses are so frequent, that whoever makes advantage of them, will soon be a great gainer. Great crosses are occasions of great improvement: and the little ones, which come daily, and even hourly, make up in number what they want in weight. We may in these daily and hourly crosses make effectual oblations of our will to God; which oblations, so frequently repeated, will soon amount to a great sum. Let us remember then that God is the author of all events: that none is so small or inconsiderable, as to escape his notice and direction. Every event therefore declares to us the will of God, to which thus declared we should heartily submit. We should renounce our own to embrace it; we should approve and choose what his choice warrants as best for us. Herein should we exercise ourselves continually; this should be our practice all the day long. We should in humility accept the little crosses that are dispensed to us, as those that best suit our weakness. Let us bear these little things, at least for God's sake, and prefer his will to our own in matters of so small importance. And his goodness will accept these mean oblations; for he despiseth not the day of small things. Matt 10:38.

25. Whosoever will save his life – At the expense of his conscience: whosoever, in the very highest instance, that of life itself, will not renounce himself, shall be lost eternally. But can any man hope he should be able thus to renounce himself, if he cannot do it in the smallest instances? **And whosoever will lose his life shall find it** – What he loses on earth he shall find in heaven. Matt 10:39; Mark 8:35; Luke 9:24; 17:33; John 12:25.

27. For the Son of man shall come – For there is no way to escape the righteous judgment of God.

28. And as an emblem of this, there are some here who shall live to see the Messiah coming to set up his mediatorial kingdom, with great power and glory, by the increase of his Church, and the destruction of the temple, city, and polity of the Jews.

Chapter 17

1. A high mountain – Probably Mount Tabor. Mark 9:2; Luke 9:28.

2. And was transfigured – Or transformed. The indwelling Deity darted out its rays through the veil of the flesh; and that with such transcendent splendour, that he no longer bore the form of a servant. His face shone with Divine majesty, like the sun in its strength; and all his body was so irradiated by it, that his clothes could not conceal its glory, but became white and glittering as the very light, with which he covered himself as with a garment.

3. There appeared Moses and Elijah – Here for the full confirmation of their faith in Jesus, Moses, the giver of the law, Elijah, the most zealous of all the prophets, and God speaking from heaven, all bore witness to him.

4. Let us make three tents – The words of rapturous surprise. He says three, not six: because the apostles desired to be with their Master.

5. Hear ye him – As superior even to Moses and the prophets. See Deut 18:17.

7. Be not afraid – And doubtless the same moment he gave them courage and strength.

9. Tell the vision to no man – Not to the rest of the disciples, lest they should be grieved and discouraged because they were not admitted to the sight: nor to any other persons, lest it should enrage some the more, and his approaching sufferings shall make others disbelieve it; **till the Son of man be risen again** – Till the resurrection should make it credible, and confirm their testimony about it.

10. Why then say the scribes, that Elijah must come first – Before the Messiah? If no man is to know of his coming? Should we not rather tell every man, that he is come, and that we have seen him, witnessing to thee as the Messiah?

11. Regulate all things – In order to the coming of Christ.

12. Elijah is come already – And yet when the Jews asked John, Art thou Elijah? He said, I am not, John 1:21. His meaning was, I am not Elijah the Tishbite, come again into the world. But he was the person of whom Malachi prophesied under that name.

14. Mark 9:14; Luke 11:37.

15. He is lunatic – This word might with great propriety he used, though the case was mostly preternatural; as the evil spirit would undoubtedly take advantage of the influence which the changes of the moon have on the brain and nerves.

17. O unbelieving and perverse generation – Our Lord speaks principally this to his disciples. **How long shall I be with you?** – Before you steadfastly believe?

20. Because of your unbelief – Because in this particular they had not faith. **If ye have faith as a grain of mustard seed** – That is, the least measure of it. But it is certain, the faith which is here spoken of does not always imply saving faith. Many have had it who thereby cast out devils, and yet will at last have their portion with them. It is only a supernatural persuasion given a man, that God will work thus by him at that hour. Now, though I have all this faith so as to remove mountains, yet if I have not the faith which worketh by love, I am nothing. To remove mountains was a proverbial phrase among the Jews, and is still retained in their writings, to

express a thing which is very difficult, and to appearance impossible. Matt 21:21; Luke 17:6.

21. This kind of devil – goeth not out but by prayer and fasting – What a testimony is here of the efficacy of fasting, when added to fervent prayer! Some kinds of devils the apostles had cast out before this, without fasting.

22. Mark 9:30; Luke 9:44.

24. When they were come to Capernaum – Where our Lord now dwelt. This was the reason why they stayed till he came thither, to ask him for the tribute. **Doth not your Master pay tribute?** – This was a tribute or payment of a peculiar kind, being half a shekel, which every master of a family used to pay yearly to the service of the temple, to buy salt, and little things not otherwise provided for. It seems to have been a voluntary thing, which custom rather than any law had established.

25. Jesus prevented him – Just when St. Peter was going to ask him for it. **Of their own sons, or of strangers?** – That is, such as are not of their own family.

26. Then are the sons free – The sense is, This is paid for the use of the house of God. But I am the Son of God. Therefore I am free from any obligation of paying this to my own Father.

27. Yet that, we may not offend them – Even those unjust, unreasonable men, who claim what they have no manner of right to: do not contest it with them, but rather yield to their demand, than violate peace or love. O what would not one of a loving spirit do for peace! Any thing which is not expressly forbidden in the word of God. **A piece of money** – The original word is a stater, which was in value two shillings and sixpence: just the sum that was wanted. **Give for me and thee** – Peter had a family of his own: the other apostles were the family of Jesus. How illustrious a degree of knowledge and power did our Lord here discover! Knowledge, penetrating into this animal, though beneath the waters; and power, in directing this very fish to Peter's hook, though he himself was at a distance! How must this have encouraged both him and his brethren in a firm dependence on Divine Providence.

Chapter 18

1. Who is the greatest in the kingdom of heaven? – Which of us shall be thy prime minister? They still dreamed of a temporal kingdom.

2. And Jesus calling to him a little child – This is supposed to have been the great Ignatius, whom Trajan, the wise, the good Emperor Trajan, condemned to be cast to the wild beasts at Rome! Mark 9:36; Luke 9:47.

3. Except ye be converted – The first step toward entering into the kingdom of grace, is to become as little children: lowly in heart, knowing yourselves utterly ignorant and helpless, and hanging wholly on your Father who is in heaven, for a supply of all your wants. We may farther assert, except ye be turned from darkness to light, and from the power of Satan to God: except ye be entirely, inwardly changed, renewed in the image of God, ye cannot enter into the kingdom of glory. Thus must every man be converted in this life, or he can never enter into life eternal. **Ye shall in no wise enter** – So far from being great in it. Matt 19:14.

5, 6. And all who are in this sense little children are unspeakably dear to me. Therefore help them all you can, as if it were myself in person, and see that ye offend them not; that is, that ye turn them not out of the right way, neither hinder them in it. Matt 10:40; Luke 10:16; John 13:20.

7. Woe to the world because of offences – That is, unspeakable misery will be in the world through them; **for it must needs be that offences come** – Such is the nature of things, and such the weakness, folly, and wickedness of mankind, that it cannot be but they will come; **but woe to that man** – That is, miserable is that man, by whom the offence cometh. Offences are, all things whereby any one is turned out of, or hindered in the way of God.

8, 9. If thy hand, foot, eye, cause thee to offend – If the most dear enjoyment, the most beloved and useful person, turn thee out of, or hinder thee in the way. Is not this a hard saying? Yes; if thou take counsel with flesh and blood. Matt 5:29; Mark 9:43.

10. See that ye despise not one of these little ones – As if they were beneath your notice. Be careful to receive and not to offend, the very weakest believer in Christ: for as inconsiderable as some of these may appear to thee, the very angels of God have a peculiar charge over them: even those of the highest order, who continually appear at the throne of the Most High. To behold the face of God seems to signify the waiting near his throne; and to be an allusion to the office of chief ministers in earthly courts, who daily converse with their princes.

11. Another, and yet a stronger reason for your not despising them is, that I myself came into the world to save them. Luke 19:10.

12. Luke 15:4.

14. So it is not the will of your Father – Neither doth my Father despise the least of them. Observe the gradation. The angels, the Son, the Father.

15–17. But how can we avoid giving offence to some? or being offended at others! Especially suppose they are quite in the wrong? Suppose they commit a known sin? Our Lord here teaches us how: he lays down a sure method of avoiding all offences. Whosoever closely observes this threefold rule, will seldom offend others, and

never be offended himself. If any do any thing amiss, of which thou art an eye or ear witness, thus saith the Lord, **If thy brother** – Any who is a member of the same religious community: Sin against thee

1. Go and reprove him alone – If it may be in person; if that cannot so well be done, by thy messenger; or in writing. Observe, our Lord gives no liberty to omit this; or to exchange it for either of the following steps. If this do not succeed

2. Take with thee one or two more – Men whom he esteems or loves, who may then confirm and enforce what thou sayest; and afterward, if need require, bear witness of what was spoken. If even this does not succeed, then, and not before:

3. Tell it to the elders of the Church – Lay the whole matter open before those who watch over yours and his soul. If all this avail not, have no farther intercourse with him, only such as thou hast with heathens.

Can any thing be plainer? Christ does here as expressly command all Christians who see a brother do evil, to take this way, not another, and to take these steps, in this order, as he does to honour their father and mother. But if so, in what land do the Christians live? If we proceed from the private carriage of man to man, to proceedings of a more public nature, in what Christian nation are Church censures conformed to this rule? Is this the form in which ecclesiastical judgments appear, in the popish, or even the Protestant world? Are these the methods used even by those who boast the most loudly of the authority of Christ to confirm their sentences? Let us earnestly pray, that this dishonour to the Christian name may be wiped away, and that common humanity may not, with such solemn mockery, be destroyed in the name of the Lord! **Let him be to thee as the heathen** – To whom thou still owest earnest good will, and all the offices of humanity. Luke 17:3.

18. Whatsoever ye shall bind on earth – By excommunication, pronounced in the spirit and power of Christ. **Whatsoever ye shall loose** – By absolution from that sentence. In the primitive Church, absolution meant no more than a discharge from Church censure. **Again I say** – And not only your intercession for the penitent, but all your united prayers, shall be heard. How great then is the power of joint prayer! **If two of you** – Suppose a man and his wife. Matt 16:19.

20. Where two or three are gathered together in my name – That is, to worship me. **I am in the midst of them** – By my Spirit, to quicken their prayers, guide their counsels, and answer their petitions.

22. Till seventy times seven – That is, as often as there is occasion. A certain number is put for an uncertain.

23. **Therefore** – In this respect.

24. **One was brought who owed him ten thousand talents** – According to the usual computation, if these were talents of gold, this would amount to seventy-two million pounds sterling. If they were talents of silver, it must have been four millions, four hundred thousand pounds. Hereby our Lord intimates the vast number and weight of our offences against God, and our utter incapacity of making him any satisfaction.

25. **As he had not to pay, his lord commanded him to be sold** – Such was the power which creditors anciently had over their insolvent debtors in several countries.

30. Went with him before a magistrate, and cast him into prison, protesting he should lie there, till he should pay the whole debt.

34. **His lord delivered him to the tormentors** – Imprisonment is a much severer punishment in the eastern countries than in ours. State criminals, especially when condemned to it, are not only confined to a very mean and scanty allowance, but are frequently loaded with clogs or heavy yokes, so that they can neither lie nor sit at ease: and by frequent scourgings and sometimes rackings are brought to an untimely end. **Till he should pay all that was due to him** – That is, without all hope of release, for this he could never do. How observable is this whole account; as well as the great inference our Lord draws from it:

1. The debtor was freely and fully forgiven;
2. He wilfully and grievously offended;
3. His pardon was retracted, the whole debt required, and the offender delivered to the tormentors for ever.

And shall we still say, but when we are once freely and fully forgiven, our pardon can never be retracted? Verily, verily, I say unto you, **So likewise will my heavenly Father do to you, if ye from your hearts forgive not every one his brother their trespasses.**

Chapter 19

1. **He departed** – and from that time walked no more in Galilee. Mark 10:1.

2. **Multitudes followed him, and he healed them there** – That is, wheresoever they followed him.

3. **The Pharisees came tempting him** – Trying to make him contradict Moses. **For every cause** – That is, for any thing which he dislikes in her. This the scribes allowed.

4. **He said, Have ye not read** – So instead of contradicting him, our Lord confutes them by the very words of Moses. **He which made them, made them male and female from the beginning** – At least from the beginning of the Mosaic creation. And where do we read of any other?

Does it not follow, that God's making Eve was part of his original design, and not a consequence of Adam's beginning to fall? By making them one man and one woman, he condemned polygamy: by making them one flesh, he condemned divorce.

5. **And said** – By the mouth of Adam, who uttered the words. Gen 2:24.

7. **Why did Moses command** – Christ replies, Moses permitted it, **because of the hardness of your hearts** – Because neither your fathers nor you could bear the more excellent way. Deut 24:1 Matt 5:31; Mark 10:2; Luke 16:18.

9. **And I say to you** – I revoke that indulgence from this day, so that from henceforth, **Whosoever.**

11. **But he said to them** – This is not universally true; it does not hold, with regard to all men, but with regard to those only to whom is given this excellent gift of God. Now this is given to three sorts of persons: to some by natural constitution, without their choice: to others by violence, against their choice; and to others by grace with their choice: who steadily withstand their natural inclinations, that they may wait upon God without distraction.

12. **There are eunuchs who have made themselves eunuchs for the kingdom of heaven's sake** – Happy they! who have abstained from marriage that they might walk more closely with God! **He that is able to receive it, let him receive it** – This gracious command is not designed for all men: but only for those few who are able to receive it. O let these receive it joyfully!

13. **That he should lay his hands on them** – This was a rite which was very early used, in praying for a blessing on young persons. See Gen 48:14,20. **The disciples rebuked them** – That is, them that brought them: probably thinking such an employ beneath the dignity of their Master. Mark 10:13; Luke 18:15.

14. **Of such is the kingdom of heaven** – Little children, either in a natural or spiritual sense, have a right to enter into my kingdom. Mt 18:3.

16. **And behold one came** – Many of the poor had followed him from the beginning. One rich man came at last. Mark 10:17; Luke 18:18.

17. **Why callest thou me good** – Whom thou supposest to be only a man. **There is none good** – Supremely, originally, essentially, but God. **If thou wilt enter into life, keep the commandments** – From a principle of loving faith. Believe, and thence love and obey. And this undoubtedly is the way to eternal life. Our Lord therefore does not answer ironically, which had been utterly beneath his character, but gives a plain, direct, serious answer to a serious question.

19. Exod 20:12.

20. **The young man saith, All these have I kept from my childhood** – So he imagined; and

perhaps he had, as to the letter; but not as to the spirit, which our Lord immediately shows.

21. If thou desirest to be perfect – That is, to be a real Christian: **Sell what thou hast** – He who reads the heart saw his bosom sin was love of the world; and knew he could not be saved from this, but by literally renouncing it. To him therefore he gave this particular direction, which he never designed for a general rule. For him that was necessary to salvation: to us it is not. To sell all was an absolute duty to him; to many of us it would be an absolute sin. **The young man went away** – Not being willing to have salvation at so high a price.

24. It is easier for a camel to go through the eye of a needle, than for a rich man to go through the strait gate: that is, humanly speaking, it is an absolute impossibility. Rich man! tremble! feel this impossibility; else thou art lost for ever!

25. His disciples were amazed, saying, Who then can be saved? – If rich men, with all their advantages, cannot? Who? A poor man; a peasant; a beggar: ten thousand of them, sooner than one that is rich.

26. Jesus looking upon them – To compose their hurried spirits. O what a speaking look was there! **Said to them** – With the utmost sweetness: **With men this is impossible** – It is observable, he does not retract what he had said: no, nor soften it in the least degree, but rather strengthens it, by representing the salvation of a rich man as the utmost effort of Omnipotence.

28. In the renovation – In the final renovation of all things: **Ye shall sit** – In the beginning of the judgment they shall stand, 2Cor 5:10. Then being absolved, they shall sit with the Judge, 1Cor 6:2: On **twelve thrones** – So our Lord promised, without expressing any condition: yet as absolute as the words are, it is certain there is a condition implied, as in many scriptures, where none is expressed. In consequence of this, those twelve did not sit on those twelve thrones: for the throne of Judas another took, so that he never sat thereon.

29. And every one – In every age and country; not you my apostles only; **That hath forsaken houses, or brethren, or wife, or children** – Either by giving any of them up, when they could not be retained with a clear conscience or by willingly refraining from acquiring them: **Shall receive an hundred-fold** – In value, though not in kind, even in the present world.

30. But many first – Many of those who were first called, shall be last – Shall have the lowest reward: those who came after them being preferred before them: and yet possibly both the first and the last may be saved, though with different degrees of glory. Mt 20:16; Mark 10:31; Luke 13:30.

Chapter 20

1. That some of those who were first called may yet be last, our Lord confirms by the following parable: of which the primary scope is, to show, That many of the Jews would be rejected, and many of the Gentiles accepted; the secondary, That of the Gentiles, many who were first converted would be last and lowest in the kingdom of glory; and many of those who were last converted would be first, and highest therein. **The kingdom of heaven is like** – That is, the manner of God's proceeding in his kingdom resembles that of a householder. **In the morning** – At six, called by the Romans and Jews, the first hour. From thence reckoning on to the evening, they called nine, the third hour; twelve, the sixth; three in the afternoon, the ninth; and five, the eleventh. **To hire labourers into his vineyard** – All who profess to be Christians are in this sense labourers, and are supposed during their life to be working in God's vineyard.

2. The Roman penny was then the usual price of a day's labour.

6. About the eleventh hour – That is, very late; long after the rest were called.

8. In the evening – Of life; or of the world.

9. Who were hired about the eleventh hour – Either the Gentiles, who were called long after the Jews into the vineyard of the Church of Christ; or those in every age who did not hear, or at least understand the Gospel call, till their day of life was drawing to a period. Some circumstances of the parable seem best to suit the former, some the latter of these senses.

10. The first supposed they should have received more – Probably the first here may mean the Jews, who supposed they should always be preferred before the Gentiles.

12. Thou hast made them equal to us – So St. Peter expressly, Acts 15:9. God hath put no difference between us and them, purifying their hearts by faith. And those who were equally holy here, whenever they were called, will be equally happy hereafter.

14. It is my will to give to this last called among the heathens even as to the first called among the Jews: yea, and to the late converted publicans and sinners, even as to those who, were called long before.

15. Is it not lawful for me to do what I will with my own? – Yea, doubtless, to give either to Jew or Gentile a reward infinitely greater than he deserves. But can it be inferred from hence, that it is lawful, or possible, for the merciful Father of spirits to 'Consign an unborn soul to hell? Or damn him from his mother's womb?' **Is thine eye evil because I am good** – Art thou envious, because I am gracious? Here is an evident reference to that malignant aspect, which is generally the attendant of a selfish and envious temper.

16. So the last shall be first, and the first last – Not only with regard to the Jews and Gentiles, but in a thousand other instances. **For many are called** – All who hear the Gospel; **but few chosen** – Only those who obey it. Mt 19:30; 22:14.

17. Mark 10:32; Luke 18:31.

20. Then came to him the mother of Zebedee's children – Considering what he had been just speaking, was ever any thing more unreasonable? Perhaps Zebedee himself was dead, or was not a follower of Christ. Mark 10:35.

21. In thy kingdom – Still they expected a temporal kingdom.

22. Ye know not what is implied in being advanced in my kingdom, and necessarily prerequired thereto. All who share in my kingdom must first share in my sufferings. Are you able and willing to do this? Both these expressions, The cup, the baptism, are to be understood of his sufferings and death. The like expressions are common among the Jews.

23. But to sit on my right hand – Christ applies to the glories of heaven, what his disciples were so stupid as to understand of the glories of earth. But he does not deny that this is his to give. It is his to give in the strictest propriety, both as God, and as the Son of man. He only asserts, that he gives it to none but those for whom it is originally prepared; namely, those who endure to the end in the faith that worketh by love.

25. Ye know that the princes of the Gentiles lord it over them – And hence you imagine, the chief in my kingdom will do as they: but it will be quite otherwise.

26. Your minister – That is, your servant. Mt 23:11.

29. Mark 10:46; Luke 18:35.

30. Behold two blind men cried out – St. Mark and St. Luke mention only one of them, blind Bartimeus. He was far the more eminent of the two, and, as it seems, spoke for both.

31. The multitude charged them to hold their peace – And so they will all who begin to cry after the Son of David. But let those who feel their need of him cry the more; otherwise they will come short of a cure.

Chapter 21

1. Mark 11:1; Luke 19:29; John 12:12.

5. The daughter of Sion – That is, the inhabitants of Jerusalem: the first words of the passage are cited from Isa 62:11; the rest from Zech 9:9. The ancient Jewish doctors were wont to apply these prophecies to the Messiah. **On an ass** – The Prince of Peace did not take a horse, a warlike animal. But he will ride on that by and by, Rev 19:11. In the patriarchal ages, illustrious persons thought it no disgrace to make use of this animal: but it by no means appears, that

this opinion prevailed, or this custom continued, till the reign of Tiberias. Was it a mean attitude wherein our Lord then appeared? Mean even to contempt! I grant it: I glory in it: it is for the comfort of my soul, for the honour of his humility, and for the utter confusion of all worldly pomp and grandeur.

7. They set him thereon – That is, on the clothes.

8. A great multitude spread their garments in the way – A custom which was usual at the creation of a king, 2Kings 9:13.

9. The multitudes cried, saying – Probably from a Divine impulse; for certainly most of them understood not the words they uttered. **Hosanna** – was a solemn word in frequent use among the Jews. The meaning is, 'We sing hosanna to the Son of David. Blessed is he, the Messiah, of the Lord. Save us. Thou that art in the highest heavens.' Our Lord restrained all public tokens of honour from the people till now, lest the envy of his enemies should interrupt his preaching before the time. But this reason now ceasing, he suffered their acclamations, that they might be a public testimony against their wickedness, who in four or five days after cried out, Crucify him, crucify him. The expressions recorded by the other evangelists are somewhat different from these: but all of them were undoubtedly used by some or others of the multitude.

11. This is Jesus from Nazareth – What a stumbling block was this! if he was of Nazareth, he could not be the Messiah. But they who earnestly desired to know the truth would not stumble threat: for upon inquiry they would find, he was not of Nazareth, but Bethlehem.

12. He cast out all that sold and bought – Doves and oxen for sacrifice. He had cast them out three years before, John 2:14; bidding them not make that house a house of merchandise. Upon the repetition of the offence, he used sharper words. **In the temple** – That is, in the outer court of it, where the Gentiles used to worship. **The money changers** – The exchangers of foreign money into current coin, which those who came from distant parts might want to offer for the service of the temple. Mark 11:11,15; Luke 19:45.

13. A den of thieves – A proverbial expression, for a harbour of wicked men. Isa 56:7; Jer 7:11.

16. Psalm 8:2.

17. Mark 11:11,12.

20. The disciples seeing it – As they went by, the next day.

21. Jesus answering, said, If ye have faith – Whence we may learn, that one great end of our Lord in this miracle was to confirm and increase their faith: another was, to warn them against unfruitfulness. Mt 17:20.

23. When he was come into the temple, the chief priests came – Who thought he violated their right: **and the elders of the people** – Probably, members of the Sanhedrim, to whom that title most properly belonged: which is the more probable, as they were the persons under whose cognizance the late action of Christ, in purging the temple, would naturally fall. These, with the chief priests, seem purposely to have appeared in a considerable company, to give the more weight to what they said, and if need were, to bear a united testimony against him. **As he was teaching** – Which also they supposed he had no authority to do, being neither priest, nor Levite, nor scribe. Some of the priests and all the scribes were authorized teachers. **By what authority dost thou these things** – Publicly teach the people! And drive out those who had our commission to traffic in the outer court? Luke 20:1; Mark 11:27.

24. I will ask you one thing – Who have asked me many: **The baptism,** that is, the whole ministry of John, was it from heaven or from men? – By what authority did he act and teach? Did man or God give him that authority? Was it not God? But if so, the consequence was clear. For John testified that Jesus was the Christ.

25. Why did ye not believe him? – Testifying this.

27. Neither tell I you – Not again, in express terms: he had often told them before, and they would not believe him.

30. He answered, I go, sir: but went not – Just so did the scribes and Pharisees: they professed the greatest readiness and zeal in the service of God: but it was bare profession, contradicted by all their actions.

32. John came in a way of righteousness – Walking in it, as well as teaching it. **The publicans and harlots** – The most notorious sinners were reformed, though at first they said, I will not. And ye seeing the amazing change which was wrought in them, though at first ye said, I go, sir, **repented not afterward** – Were no more convinced than before. O how is this scripture fulfilled at this day!

33. A certain householder planted a vineyard – God planted the Church in Canaan; **and hedged it round about** – First with the law, then with his peculiar providence: **and digged a wine press** – Perhaps it may mean Jerusalem: **and built a tower** – The temple: **and went into a far country** – That is, left the keepers of his vineyard, in some measure, to behave as they should see good. Mark 12:1; Luke 20:9.

34. He sent his servants – His extraordinary messengers, the prophets: **to the husbandmen** – The ordinary preachers or ministers of the Jews.

41. They say – Perhaps some of the bystanders, not the chief priests or Pharisees; who, as St. Luke relates, said, God forbid, Luke 20:16.

42. The builders – The scribes and priests, whose office it was to build up the Church. **Is become the head of the corner** – Or the chief corner stone: he is become the foundation of the Church, on which the whole building rests, and is the principal corner stone, for uniting the Gentiles to it, as the chief corner stone of a house supports and links its two sides together. Psalm 118:22.

43. Therefore – Because ye reject this corner stone. **The kingdom of God** – That is, the Gospel.

44. Whosoever shall fall on this stone shall be broken – Stumblers at Christ shall even then receive much hurt. He is said to fall on this stone, who hears the Gospel and does not believe. **But on whomsoever it shall fall** – In vengeance, it will utterly destroy him. It will fall on every unbeliever, when Christ cometh in the clouds of heaven. Luke 20:18.

Chapter 22

1. Jesus answering, spake – That is, spake with reference to what had just past.

2. A king, who made a marriage feast for his son – So did God, when he brought his first-begotten into the world.

3. Them that were invited – Namely, the Jews.

4. Fatlings – Fatted beasts and fowls.

5. One to his farm, another to his merchandise – One must mind what he has; another, gain what he wants. How many perish by misusing lawful things!

7. The king sending forth his troops – The Roman armies employed of God for that purpose. **Destroyed those murderers** – Primarily the Jews.

8. Go into the highways – The word properly signifies, the by-ways, or turnings of the road.

10. They gathered all – By preaching every where.

11. The guests – The members of the visible Church.

12. A wedding garment – The righteousness of Christ, first imputed, then implanted. It may easily be observed, this has no relation to the Lord's Supper, but to God's proceeding at the last day.

14. Many are called; few chosen – Many hear; few believe. Yea, many are members of the visible, but few of the invisible Church. Mt 20:16.

15. Mark 12:13; Luke 20:20.

16. The Herodians were a set of men peculiarly attached to Herod, and consequently zealous for the interest of the Roman government, which was the main support of the dignity and royalty of his family. **Thou regardest not the person of men** – Thou favourest no man for his riches or greatness.

17. Is it lawful to give tribute to Caesar? – If he had said, Yes, the Pharisees would have accused him to the people, as a betrayer of the liberties of his country. If he had said, No, the Herodians would have accused him to the Roman governor.

18. Ye hypocrites – Pretending a scruple of conscience.

20. The tribute money – A Roman coin, stamped with the head of Cesar, which was usually paid in tribute.

21. They say to him, Caesar's – Plainly acknowledging, by their having received his coin, that they were under his government. And indeed this is a standing rule. The current coin of every nation shows who is the supreme governor of it. Render therefore, ye Pharisees, to Cesar the things which ye yourselves acknowledge to be Cesar's: and, ye Herodians, while ye are zealous for Cesar, see that ye render to God the things that are God's.

23. Mark 12:18.

24. Deut 25:5.

25. Now there were with us seven brethren – This story seems to have been a kind of common-place objection, which no doubt they brought upon all occasions.

29. Ye err, not knowing the Scriptures – Which plainly assert a resurrection. **Nor the power of God** – Which is well able to effect it. How many errors flow from the same source?

30. They are as the angels – Incorruptible and immortal. So is the power of God shown in them! So little need had they of marriage!

31. Have ye not read – The Saducees had a peculiar value for the books of Moses. Out of these therefore our Lord argues with them.

32. I am the God of Abraham – The argument runs thus: God is not the God of the dead, but of the living: but he is the God of Abraham, Isaac, and Jacob: therefore, Abraham, Isaac, and Jacob are not dead, but living. Therefore, the soul does not die with the body. So indeed the Sadducees supposed, and it was on this ground that they denied the resurrection. Exod 3:6.

33. At his doctrine – At the clearness and solidity of his answers.

34. Mark 12:28; Luke 10:25.

35. A scribe asking him a question, trying him – Not, as it seems, with any ill design: but barely to make a farther trial of that wisdom, which he had shown in silencing the Sadducees.

37. Deut 6:5.

39. Lev 19:18.

42. Luke 20:41.

43. How doth David then by the Spirit – By inspiration, call him Lord? If he be merely the son of David? If he be, as you suppose, a mere man, the son of a man?

44. The Lord said to my Lord – This his dominion, to which David himself was subject, shows both the heavenly majesty of the king, and the nature of his kingdom. **Sit thou on my right hand** – That is, remain in the highest authority and power. Psalm 110:1.

46. Neither durst any question him any more – Not by way of ensnaring or tempting him.

Chapter 23

1. Then – Leaving all converse with his adversaries, whom he now left to the hardness of their hearts.

2. The scribes sit in the chair of Moses – That is, read and expound the law of Moses, and are their appointed teachers.

3. All things therefore – Which they read out of the law, and enforce therefrom.

4. Luke 11:46.

5. Their phylacteries – The Jews, understanding those words literally, It shall be as a token upon thy hand, and as frontlets between thine eyes, Exod 13:16. And thou shalt bind these words for a sign upon thine hand, and they shall be as frontlets between thine eyes, Deut 6:8; used to wear little scrolls of paper or parchment, bound on their wrist and foreheads, on which several texts of Scripture were writ. These they supposed, as a kind of charm, would preserve them from danger. And hence they seem to have been called phylacteries, or preservatives. **The fringes of their garments** – Which God had enjoined them to wear, to remind them of doing all the commandments, Num 15:38. These, as well as their phylacteries, the Pharisees affected to wear broader and larger than other men. Mark 12:38.

8–10. The Jewish rabbis were also called father and master, by their several disciples, whom they required:

1. To believe implicitly what they affirmed, without asking any farther reason;

2. To obey implicitly what they enjoined, without seeking farther authority.

Our Lord, therefore, by forbidding us either to give or receive the title of rabbi, master, or father, forbids us either to receive any such reverence, or to pay any such to any but God.

11. Mt 20:26.

12. Whosoever shall exalt himself shall be humbled, and he that shall humble himself shall be exalted – It is observable that no one sentence of our Lord's is so often repeated as this: it occurs, with scarce any variation, at least ten times in the evangelists. Luke 14:11; 18:14.

13. Woe to you – Our Lord pronounced eight blessings upon the mount: he pronounces eight woes here; not as imprecations, but solemn, compassionate declarations of the misery, which these stubborn sinners were bringing upon themselves. **Ye go not in** – For ye are not poor in spirit; and ye hinder those that would be so.

14. Mark 12:40; Luke 20:47.

16. **Woe to you, ye blind guides** – Before he had styled them hypocrites, from their personal character: now he gives them another title, respecting their influence upon others. **The gold of the temple** – The treasure kept there. **He is bound** – To keep his oath.

18–20. **He that sweareth by the altar, sweareth by it, and by all things thereon** – Not only by the gift, but by the holy fire, and the sacrifice; and above all, by that God to whom they belong; inasmuch as every oath by a creature is an implicit appeal to God.

23. **Judgment** – That is, justice: **Faith** – The word here means fidelity.

24. **Ye blind guides,** who teach others to do as you do yourselves, **to strain out a gnat** – From the liquor they are going to drink! **and swallow a camel** – It is strange, that glaring false print, strain at a gnat, which quite alters the sense, should run through all the editions of our English Bibles.

25. **Full of rapine and intemperance** – The censure is double. These miserable men procured unjustly what they used intemperately. No wonder tables so furnished prove a snare, as many find by sad experience. Thus luxury punishes fraud while it feeds disease with the fruits of injustice. But intemperance in the full sense takes in not only all kinds of outward intemperance, particularly in eating and drinking, but all intemperate or immoderate desires, whether of honour, gain, or sensual pleasure.

29. **Ye build the tombs of the prophets** – And that is all, for ye neither observe their sayings, nor imitate their actions.

30. **We would not have been partakers** – So ye make fair professions, as did your fathers.

31. **Wherefore ye testify against yourselves** – By your smooth words as well as devilish actions: that ye are the genuine sons of them who killed the prophets of their own times, while they professed the utmost veneration for those of past ages.

From Mt 23:3 to Mt 23:30 is exposed every thing that commonly passes in the world for religion, whereby the pretenders to it keep both themselves and others from entering into the kingdom of God; from attaining, or even seeking after those tempers, in which alone true Christianity consists. As:

1. Punctuality in attending on public and private prayer, ver. 4–14. Mt 23:4–14
2. Zeal to make proselytes to our opinion or communion, though they have less of the spirit of religion than before, ver. 15. Mt 23:15
3. A superstitious reverence for consecrated places or things, without any for Him to whom they are consecrated, ver. 16–22. Mt 23:16–22
4. A scrupulous exactness in little observances, though with the neglect of justice, mercy, and faith, ver. 23, 24. Mt 23:23,24
5. A nice cautiousness to cleanse the outward behaviour, but without any regard to inward purity, ver. 25, 26. Mt 23:25,26
6. A specious face of virtue and piety, covering the deepest hypocrisy and villany, ver. 27, 28. Mt 23:27,28
7. A professed veneration for all good men, except those among whom they live.

32. **Fill ye up** – A word of permission, not of command: as if he had said, I contend with you no longer: I leave you to yourselves: you have conquered: now ye may follow the devices of your own hearts. **The measure of your fathers** – Wickedness: ye may now be as wicked as they.

33. **Ye serpents** – Our Lord having now lost all hope of reclaiming these, speaks so as to affright others from the like sins.

34. **Wherefore** – That it may appear you are the true children of those murderers, and have a right to have their iniquities visited on you: **Behold, I send** – Is not this speaking as one having authority? **Prophets** – Men with supernatural credentials: **Wise men** – Such as have both natural abilities and experience; and **scribes** – Men of learning: but all will not avail. Luke 11:49.

35. **That upon you may come** – The consequence of which will be, that upon you will come the vengeance of all the righteous **blood shed on the earth** – **Zechariah the son of Barachiah** – Termed Jehoiada, 2Chron 24:20, where the story is related: **Ye slew** – Ye make that murder also of your fathers your own, by imitating it: **Between the temple** – That is, the inner temple, **and the altar** – Which stood in the outer court. Our Lord seems to refer to this instance, rather than any other, because he was the last of the prophets on record that were slain by the Jews for reproving their wickedness: and because God's requiring this blood as well as that of Abel, is particularly taken notice of in Scripture.

37. Luke 13:34.

38. **Behold your house** – The temple, which is now your house, not God's: **Is left unto you** – Our Lord spake this as he was going out of it for the last time: **Desolate** – Forsaken of God and his Christ, and sentenced to utter destruction.

39. **Ye** – Jews in general; men of Jerusalem in particular: **shall not see me from this time** – Which includes the short space till his death, till, after a long interval of desolation and misery, ye say, **Blessed is he that cometh in the name of the Lord** – Ye receive me with joyful and thankful hearts. This also shall be accomplished in its season.

Chapter 24

Mark 13:1; Luke 21:5.

2. There shall not be left one stone upon another – This was most punctually fulfilled; for after the temple was burnt, Titus, the Roman general, ordered the very foundations of it to be dug up; after which the ground on which it stood was ploughed up by Turnus Rufus.

3. As he sat on the mount of Olives – Whence they had a full view of the temple. **When shall these things be? And what shall be the sign of thy coming, and of the end of the world?** – The disciples inquire confusedly:
1. Concerning the time of the destruction of the temple;
2. Concerning the signs of Christ's coming, and of the end of the world, as if they imagined these two were the same thing.

Our Lord answers distinctly concerning:
1. The destruction of the temple and city, with the signs preceding, ver. 4, 15. Mt 24:4,15.
2. His own coming, and the end of the world, with the signs thereof, ver. 29-31. Mt 24:29–31.
3. The time of the destruction of the temple, ver. 32. Mt 24:32.
4. The time of the end of the world, ver. 36. Mt 24:36.

4. Take heed that no man deceive you – The caution is more particularly designed for the succeeding Christians, whom the apostles then represented. The first sign of my coming is, the rise of false prophets. But it is highly probable, many of these things refer to more important events, which are yet to come.

5. Many shall come in my name – First, false Christs, next, false prophets, Mt 24:11. At length, both together, Mt 24:24. And indeed never did so many impostors appear in the world as a few years before the destruction of Jerusalem; undoubtedly because that was the time wherein the Jews in general expected the Messiah.

6. Wars – Near: **Rumours of wars** – At a distance. **All these things must come to pass** – As a foundation for lasting tranquillity. **But the end** – Concerning which ye inquire – So far from it, that this is but the beginning sorrows.

9. Then shall they deliver you up to affliction – As if ye were the cause of all these evils. **And ye shall he hated of all nations** – Even of those who tolerate all other sects and parties; but in no nation will the children of the devil tolerate the children of God. Matt 10:17.

10. Then shall many be offended – So as utterly to make shipwreck of faith and a pure conscience. But hold ye fast faith, Mt 24:11. In spite of false prophets: love, even when iniquity and offences abound, Mt 24:12. And hope, unto the end, Mt 24:13. He that does so, shall be snatched out of the burning.

12. The love of many will wax cold – The generality of those who love God will leave their first love.

13. Matt 10:22; Mark 13:13; Luke 21:17.

14. This Gospel shall be preached in all the world – Not universally: this is not done yet: but in general through the several parts of the world, and not only in Judea. And this was done by St. Paul and the other apostles, before Jerusalem was destroyed. **And then shall the end come** – Of the city and temple. Josephus's History of the Jewish War is the best commentary on this chapter. It is a wonderful instance of God's providence, that he, an eye witness, and one who lived and died a Jew, should, especially in so extraordinary a manner, be preserved, to transmit to us a collection of important facts, which so exactly illustrate this glorious prophecy, in almost every circumstance. Mark 13:10.

15. When ye see the abomination of desolation – Daniel's term is, The abomination that maketh desolate, Dan 11:31; that is, the standards of the desolating legions, on which they bear the abominable images of their idols: **Standing in the holy place** – Not only the temple and the mountain on which it stood, but the whole city of Jerusalem, and several furlongs of land round about it, were accounted holy; particularly the mount on which our Lord now sat, and on which the Romans afterward planted their ensigns. He that **readeth let him understand** – Whoever reads that prophecy of Daniel, let him deeply consider it. Mark 13:14; Luke 21:20; Dan 9:27.

16. Then let them who are in Judea flee to the mountains – So the Christians did, and were preserved. It is remarkable that after the Romans under Cestus Gallus made their first advances toward Jerusalem, they suddenly withdrew again, in a most unexpected and indeed impolitic manner. This the Christians took as a signal to retire, which they did, some to Pella, and others to Mount Libanus.

17. Let not him that is on the house top come down to take any thing out of his house – It may be remembered that their stairs used to be on the outside of their houses.

19. Woe to them that are with child, and to them that give suck – Because they cannot so readily make their escape.

20. Pray ye that your flight be not in the winter – They did so; and their flight was in the spring. **Neither on the Sabbath** – Being on many accounts inconvenient; beside that many would have scrupled to travel far on that day. For the Jews thought it unlawful to walk above two thousand paces on the Sabbath day.

21. Then shall be great tribulation – Have not many things spoken in the chapter, as well as in Mark 13:14, Luke 21:21 a farther and much more extensive meaning than has been yet fulfilled?

22. **And unless those days were shortened –** By the taking of Jerusalem sooner than could be expected: **No flesh would be saved –** The whole nation would be destroyed. **But for the elect's sake –** That is, for the sake of the Christians.

23. Mark 13:21; Luke 17:23.

24. **They would deceive, if possible, the very elect –** But it is not possible that God should suffer the body of Christians to be thus deceived.

27. **For as the lightning goeth forth –** For the next coming of Christ will be as quick as lightning; so that there will not be time for any such previous warning.

28. **For wheresoever the carcass is, there will the eagles be gathered together –** Our Lord gives this, as a farther reason, why they should not hearken to any pretended deliverer. As if he had said, Expect not any deliverer of the Jewish nation; for it is devoted to destruction. It is already before God a dead carcass, which the Roman eagles will soon devour. Luke 17:37.

29. **Immediately after the tribulation of those days –** Here our Lord begins to speak of his last coming. But he speaks not so much in the language of man as of God, with whom a thousand years are as one day, one moment. Many of the primitive Christians not observing this, thought he would come immediately, in the common sense of the word: a mistake which St. Paul labours to remove, in his Second Epistle to the Thessalonians. **The powers of the heavens –** Probably the influences of the heavenly bodies. Mark 13:24; Luke 21:25.

30. **Then shall appear the sign of the Son of man in heaven –** It seems a little before he himself descends. The sun, moon, and stars being extinguished, the sign of the Son of man will appear in the glory of the Lord.

31. **They shall gather together his elect –** That is, all that have endured to the end in the faith which worketh by love.

32. **Learn a parable –** Our Lord having spoke of the signs preceding the two grand events, concerning which the apostles had inquired, begins here to speak of the time of them. And to the question proposed, Mt 24:3, concerning the time of the destruction of Jerusalem, he answers Mt 24:34. Concerning the time of the end of the world, he answers Mt 24:36. Mark 13:28; Luke 21:29.

34. **This generation of men now living shall not pass till all these things be done –** The expression implies, that great part of that generation would be passed away, but not the whole. Just so it was. For the city and temple were destroyed thirty-nine or forty years after.

36. **But of that day –** The day of judgment; **Knoweth no man –** Not while our Lord was on earth. Yet it might be afterward revealed to St. John consistently with this.

37. Luke 17:26.

40. **One is taken –** Into God's immediate protection: **and one is left –** To share the common calamities. Our Lord speaks as having the whole transaction present before his eyes.

41. **Two women shall be grinding –** Which was then a common employment of women.

42. **Ye know not what hour your Lord cometh –** Either to require your soul of you, or to avenge himself of this nation. Mark 13:33; Luke 12:35; 21:34.

45. **Who then is the faithful and wise servant –** Which of you aspires after this character? **Wise –** Every moment retaining the clearest conviction, that all he now has is only intrusted to him as a steward: **Faithful –** Thinking, speaking, and acting continually, in a manner suitable to that conviction.

48. **But if that evil servant –** Now evil, having put away faith and a good conscience.

51. **And allot him his portion with the hypocrites –** The worst of sinners, as upright and sincere as he was once. If ministers are the persons here primarily intended, there is a peculiar propriety in the expression. For no hypocrisy can be baser, than to call ourselves ministers of Christ, while we are the slaves of avarice, ambition, or sensuality. Wherever such are found, may God reform them by his grace, or disarm them of that power and influence, which they continually abuse to his dishonour, and to their own aggravated damnation!

Chapter 25

This chapter contains the last public discourse which our Lord uttered before he was offered up. He had before frequently declared what would be the portion of all the workers of iniquity. But what will become of those who do no harm? Honest, inoffensive, good sort of people? We have here a clear and full answer to this important question.

1. **Then shall the kingdom of heaven –** That is, the candidates for it, be like **ten virgins –** The bridesmaid on the wedding night were wont to go to the house where the bride was, with burning lamps or torches in their hands, to wait for the bride groom's coming. When he drew near, they went to meet him with their lamps, and to conduct him to the bride.

3. **The foolish took no oil with them –** No more than kept them burning just for the present. None to supply their future want, to recruit their lamp's decay. The lamp is faith. A lamp and oil with it, is faith working by love.

4. **The wise took oil in their vessels –** Love in their hearts. And they daily sought a fresh supply of spiritual strength, till their faith was made perfect.

5. **While the bridegroom delayed –** That is, before they were called to attend him, **they all**

slumbered and slept – Were easy and quiet, the wise enjoying a true, the foolish a false peace.

6. At midnight – In an hour quite unthought of.

7. They trimmed their lamps – They examined themselves and prepared to meet their God.

8. Give us of your oil, for our lamps are gone out – Our faith is dead. What a time to discover this! Whether it mean the time of death, or of judgment. Unto which of the saints wilt thou then turn? Who can help thee at such a season?

9. But the wise answered, Lest there be not enough for us and you! – Beginning the sentence with a beautiful abruptness; such as showed their surprise at the state of those poor wretches, who had so long received them, as well as their own souls. **Lest there be not enough** – It is sure there is not; for no man has more than holiness enough for himself. **Go ye rather to them that sell** – Without money and without price: that is, to God, to Christ. **And buy** – If ye can. O no! The time is past and returns no more!

13. Watch therefore – He that watches has not only a burning lamp, but likewise oil in his vessel. And even when he sleepeth, his heart waketh. He is quiet; but not secure.

14. Our Lord proceeds by a parable still plainer to declare the final reward of a harmless man. May God give all such in this their day, ears to hear and hearts to understand it! **The kingdom of heaven** – That is, the King of heaven, Christ. Mark 13:34; Luke 19:12.

15. To one he gave five talents, to another two, and to another one – And who knows whether there be a greater disproportion than this, in the talents of those who have received the most, and those who have received the fewest? **According to his own ability** – The words may be translated more literally, according to his own mighty power. **And immediately took his journey** – To heaven.

18. He that had received one – Made his having fewer talents than others a pretence for not improving any. **Went and hid his master's money** – Reader, art thou doing the same? Art thou hiding the talent God hath lent thee?

24. I knew thou art a hard man – No. Thou knowest him not. He never knew God, who thinks him a hard master. **Reaping where thou hast not sown** – That is, requiring more of us than thou hast given us power to perform. So does every obstinate sinner, in one kind or other, lay the blame of his own sins on God.

25. And I was afraid – Lest if I had improved my talent, I should have had the more to answer for. So from this fear, one will not learn to read, another will not hear sermons!

26. Thou knewest – That I require impossibilities! This is not an allowing, but a strong denial of the charge.

27. Thou oughtest therefore – On that very account, on thy own supposition, to have improved my talent, as far as was possible.

29. To every one that hath shall he given – So close does God keep to this stated rule, from the beginning to the end of the world. Matt 13:12.

30. Cast ye the unprofitable servant into the outer darkness – For what? what had he done? It is true he had not done good. But neither is he charged with doing any harm. Why, for this reason, for barely doing no harm, he is consigned to outer darkness. He is pronounced a wicked, because he was a slothful, an unprofitable servant. So mere harmlessness, on which many build their hope of salvation, was the cause of his damnation! **There shall be the weeping** – Of the careless thoughtless sinner; **and the gnashing of teeth** – Of the proud and stubborn. The same great truth, that there is no such thing as negative goodness, is in this chapter shown three times:

1. In the parable of the virgins;

2. In the still plainer parable of the servants, who had received the talents;

and 3. In a direct unparabolical declaration of the manner wherein our Lord will proceed at the last day. The several parts of each of these exactly answers each other, only each rises above the preceding.

31. When the Son of man shall come in his glory, and all the holy angels with him – With what majesty and grandeur does our Lord here speak of himself. Giving us one of the noblest instances of the true sublime. Indeed not many descriptions in the sacred writings themselves seem to equal this. Methinks we can hardly read it without imagining ourselves before the awful tribunal it describes.

34. Inherit the kingdom – Purchased by my blood, for all who have believed in me with the faith which wrought by love. **Prepared for you** – On purpose for you. May it not be probably inferred from hence, that man was not created merely to fill up the places of the fallen angels?

35. I was hungry, and ye gave me meat; I was thirsty, and ye gave me drink – All these works of outward mercy suppose faith and love, and must needs be accompanied with works of spiritual mercy. But works of this kind the Judge could not mention in the same manner. He could not say, I was in error, and ye recalled me to the truth; I was in sin, and ye brought me to repentance. **In prison** – Prisoners need to be visited above all others, as they are commonly solitary and forsaken by the rest of the world.

37. Then shall the righteous answer – It cannot be, that either the righteous or the wicked should answer in these very words. What we learn here from is, that neither of them have the same estimation of their own works as the Judge hath.

40. **Inasmuch as ye did it to one of the least of these my brethren, ye did it to me** – What encouragement is here to assist the household of faith? But let us likewise remember to do good to all men.

41. **Depart into the everlasting fire, which was prepared for the devil and his angels** – Not originally for you: you are intruders into everlasting fire.

44. **Then will they answer** – So the endeavour to justify themselves, will remain with the wicked even to that day!

46. **And these shall go away into everlasting punishment, but the righteous into life everlasting** – Either therefore the punishment is strictly eternal, or the reward is not: the very same expression being applied to the former as to the latter. The Judge will speak first to the righteous, in the audience of the wicked. The wicked shall then go away into everlasting fire, in the view of the righteous. Thus the damned shall see nothing of the everlasting life; but the just will see the punishment of the ungodly. It is not only particularly observable here:
1. That the punishment lasts as long as the reward;
but, 2. That this punishment is so far from ceasing at the end of the world, that it does not begin till then.

Chapter 26

1. **When Jesus had finished all these discourses** – When he had spoken all he had to speak. Till then he would not enter upon his passion: then he would delay it no longer. Mark 14:1; Luke 22:1.

2. **After two days is the Passover** – The manner wherein this was celebrated gives much light to several circumstances that follow. The master of the family began the feast with a cup of wine, which having solemnly blessed, he divided among the guests, Luke 22:17. Then the supper began with the unleavened bread and bitter herbs; which when they had all tasted, one of the young persons present, according to Exod 12:26, asked the reason of the solemnity. This introduced the showing forth, or declaration of it: in allusion to which we read of showing forth the Lord's death, 1Cor 11:26. Then the master rose up and took another cup, before the lamb was tasted. After supper, he took a thin loaf or cake, which he broke and divided to all at the table, and likewise the cup, usually called the cup of thanksgiving, of which he drank first, and then all the guests. It was this bread and this cup which our Lord consecrated to be a standing memorial of his death.

3. **The chief priests and the scribes and the elders of the people** –These together constituted the Sanhedrim, or great council, which had the supreme authority, both in civil and ecclesiastical affairs.

5. **But they said, Not at the feast** – This was the result of human wisdom. But when Judas came they changed their purpose. So the counsel of God took place, and the true paschal Lamb was offered up on the great day of the paschal solemnity.

6. Mark 14:3.

8. **His disciples seeing it, had indignation, saying** – It seems several of them were angry, and spoke, though none so warmly as Judas Iscariot.

11. **Ye have the poor always with you** – Such is the wise and gracious providence of God, that we may have always opportunities of relieving their wants, and so laying up for ourselves treasures in heaven.

12. **She hath done it for my burial** – As it were for the embalming of my body. Indeed this was not her design: but our Lord puts this construction upon it, to confirm thereby what he had before said to his disciples, concerning his approaching death.

13. **This Gospel** – That is, this part of the Gospel history.

14. Mark 14:10; Luke 22:3.

15. **They bargained with him for thirty pieces of silver** – the price of a slave, Exod 21:32.

17. **On the first day of unleavened bread** – Being Thursday, the fourteenth day of the first month, Exod 12:6,15. Mr 14:12 Lu 22:7.

18. **The Master saith, My time is at hand** – That is, the time of my suffering.

20. Mark 14:17; Luke 22:14.

23. **He that dippeth his hand with me in the dish** – Which it seems Judas was doing at that very time. This dish was a vessel full of vinegar, wherein they dipped their bitter herbs.

24. **The Son of man goeth through sufferings to glory, as it is written of him** – Yet this is no excuse for him that betrayeth him: miserable will that man be: **it had been good for that man if he had not been born** – May not the same be said of every man that finally perishes? But who can reconcile this, if it were true of Judas alone, with the doctrine of universal salvation?

25. **Thou hast said** – That is, it is as thou hast said.

26. **Jesus took the bread** – the bread or cake, which the master of the family used to divide among them, after they had eaten the Passover. The custom our Lord now transferred to a nobler use. This bread is, that is, signifies or represents my body, according to the style of the sacred writers. Thus Gen 40:12, The three branches are three days. Thus Gal 4:24, St. Paul speaking of Sarah and Hagar, says, These are the two covenants. Thus in the grand type of our Lord, Exod 12:11, God says of the paschal lamb, This is the Lord's Passover. Now Christ substituting the

holy communion for the Passover, follows the style of the Old Testament, and uses the same expressions the Jews were wont to use in celebrating the Passover.

27. And he took the cup – Called by the Jews the cup of thanksgiving; which the master of the family used likewise to give to each after supper.

28. This is the sign of **my blood,** whereby **the new testament** or covenant is confirmed. **Which is shed for many** – As many as spring from Adam.

29. I will not drink henceforth of this fruit of the vine, till I drink it new with you in my Father's kingdom – That is, I shall taste no more wine, till I drink wine of quite another kind in the glorious kingdom of my Father. And of this you shall also partake with me.

30. And when they had sung the hymn – Which was constantly sung at the close of the Passover. It consisteth of six psalms, from the 113th to the 118th. Psa 113:1. **The mount of Olives** – Was over against the temple, about two miles from Jerusalem. Mark 14:26; Luke 22:39; John 18:1.

31. All ye will be offended at me – Something will happen to me, which will occasion your falling into sin by forsaking me. Zech 13:7.

32. But notwithstanding this, after I am risen I will go before you into Galilee. Though you forsake me, I will not for this forsake you.

34. Before cock crowing thou wilt deny me thrice – That is, before three in the morning, the usual time of cock crowing: although one cock was heard to crow once, after Peter's first denial of his Lord.

35. In like manner also said all the disciples – But such was the tenderness of our Lord, that he would not aggravate their sin by making any reply.

36. Then cometh Jesus to a place called Gethsemane – That is, the valley of fatness. The garden probably had its name from its soil and situation, laying in some little valley between two of those many hills, the range of which constitutes the mount of Olives. Mark 14:32; Luke 22:40.

37. And taking with him Peter and the two sons of Zebedee – To be witnesses of all; he **began to be sorrowful and in deep anguish** – Probably from feeling the arrows of the Almighty stick fast in his soul, while God laid on him the iniquities of us all. Who can tell what painful and dreadful sensations were then impressed on him by the immediate hand of God? The former word in the original properly signifies, to be penetrated with the most exquisite sorrow; the latter to be quite depressed, and almost overwhelmed with the load.

39. And going a little farther – About a stone's cast, Luke 22:41 – So that the apostles could both see and hear him still. **If it be possi-**ble, let this cup pass from me – And it did pass from him quickly. When he cried unto God with strong cries and tears, he was heard in that which he feared. God did take away the terror and severity of that inward conflict.

41. The spirit – Your spirit: ye yourselves. **The flesh** – Your nature. How gentle a rebuke was this, and how kind an apology! especially at a time when our Lord's own mind was so weighed down with sorrow.

45. Sleep on now, if you can, **and take your rest** – For any farther service you can be of to me.

47. Mark 14:43; Luke 22:47; John 18:2.

50. The heroic behaviour of the blessed Jesus, in the whole period of his sufferings, will be observed by every attentive eye, and felt by every pious heart: although the sacred historians, according to their usual but wonderful simplicity, make no encomiums upon it. With what composure does he go forth to meet the traitor! With what calmness receive that malignant kiss! With what dignity does he deliver himself into the hands of his enemies! Yet plainly showing his superiority over them, and even then leading as it were captivity captive!

51. And one of them striking the servant of the high priest – Probably the person that seized Jesus first; **Cut off his ear** – Aiming, it seems, to cleave his head, but that by a secret providence interposing, he declined the blow. Mark 14:47; Luke 22:49; John 18:10.

52. All they that take the sword – Without God's giving it them: without sufficient authority.

53. He will presently give me more than twelve legions of angels – The least of whom, it is probable, could overturn the earth and destroy all the inhabitants of it.

55. Mark 14:48; Luke 22:52.

57. They led him away to Caiaphas – From the house of Annas, the father-in-law of Caiaphas, to whom they had carried him first. Mark 14:53; Luke 22:54; John 18:12.

58. But Peter followed him afar off – Variously agitated by conflicting passions; love constrained him to follow his Master; fear made him follow afar off. And going in, **sat with the servants** – Unfit companions as the event showed.

60. Yet found they none – On whose evidence they could condemn him to die. **At last came two false witnesses** – Such they were, although part of what they said was true; because our Lord did not speak some of those words at all; nor any of them in this sense.

64. Hereafter shall ye see the Son of man – He speaks in the third person, modestly, and yet plainly; **Sitting on the right hand of power** – That is, the right hand of God: **And coming upon the clouds of heaven** – As he is represented by Daniel, Dan 7:13,14. Our Lord looked very unlike that person now! But nothing could be more awful, more majestic and becoming, than such an admonition in such circumstances!

65. Then the high priest rent his clothes – Though the high priest was forbidden to rend his clothes in some cases where others were allowed to do it, Lev 21:10; yet in case of blasphemy or any public calamity, it was thought allowable. Caiaphas hereby expressed, in the most artful manner, his horror at hearing such grievous blasphemy.

67. Then – After he had declared he was the Son of God, the Sanhedrim doubtless ordered him to be carried out, while they were consulting what to do. And then it was that the soldiers who kept him began these insults upon him.

72. He denied with an oath – To which possibly he was not unaccustomed, before our Lord called him.

73. Surely thou art also one of them, for thy speech discovereth thee – Malchus might have brought a stronger proof than this. But such is the overruling providence of God, that the world, in the height of their zeal, commonly catch hold of the very weakest of all arguments against the children of God.

74. Then began he to curse and to swear – Having now quite lost the reins, the government of himself.

Chapter 27

1. In the morning – As the Sanhedrim used to meet in one of the courts of the temple, which was never opened in the night, they were forced to stay till the morning before they could proceed regularly, in the resolution they had taken to put him to death. Mark 15:1; Luke 22:66; 23:1; John 18:28.

2. Having bound him – They had bound him when he was first apprehended. But they did it now afresh, to secure him from any danger of an escape, as he passed through the streets of Jerusalem.

3. Then Judas seeing that he was condemned – Which probably he thought Christ would have prevented by a miracle.

4. They said, what is that to us? – How easily could they digest innocent blood! And yet they had a conscience! It is not lawful to put it into the treasury – But very lawful to slay the innocent!

**5. In that part of the temple where the Sanhedrim met.

7. They bought with them the potter's field – Well known, it seems, by that name. This was a small price for a field so near Jerusalem. But the earth had probably been digged for potters' vessels, so that it was now neither fit for tillage nor pasture, and consequently of small value.

Foreigners – Heathens especially, of whom there were then great numbers in Jerusalem.

9. Then was fulfilled – What was figuratively represented of old, was now really accomplished. **What was spoken by the prophet** – The word Jeremy, which was added to the text in latter copies, and thence received into many translations, is evidently a mistake: for he who spoke what St. Matthew here cites was not Jeremy, but Zechariah. Zech 11:12.

10. As the Lord commanded me – To write, to record.

11. Art thou the king of the Jews? – Jesus before Caiaphas avows himself to be the Christ, before Pilate to be a king; clearly showing thereby, that his answering no more, was not owing to any fear.

15. At every feast – Every year, at the feast of the Passover. Mark 15:6; Luke 23:17; John 18:39.

18. He knew that for envy they had delivered him – As well as from malice and revenge; they envied him, because the people magnified him.

22. They all say, Let him be crucified – The punishment which Barabbas had deserved: and this probably made them think of it. But in their malice they forgot with how dangerous a precedent they furnished the Roman governor. And indeed within the compass of a few years it turned dreadfully upon themselves.

24. Then Pilate took water and washed his hands – This was a custom frequently used among the heathens as well as among the Jews, in token of innocency.

25. His blood be on us and on our children – As this imprecation was dreadfully answered in the ruin so quickly brought on the Jewish nation, and the calamities which have ever since pursued that wretched people, so it was peculiarly fulfilled by Titus the Roman general, on the Jews whom he took during the siege of Jerusalem. So many, after having been scourged in a terrible manner, were crucified all round the city, that in a while there was not room near the wall for the crosses to stand by each other. Probably this befell some of those who now joined in this cry, as it certainly did many of their children: the very finger of God thus pointing out their crime in crucifying his Son.

26. He delivered him to be crucified – The person crucified was nailed to the cross as it lay on the ground, through each hand extended to the utmost stretch, and through both the feet together. Then the cross was raised up, and the foot of it thrust with a violent shock into a hole in the ground prepared for it. This shock disjointed the body, whose whole weight hung upon the nails, till the persons expired through mere dint of pain. This kind of death was used only by the Romans, and by them inflicted only on slaves and the vilest criminals.

27. The whole troop – or cohort. This was a body of foot commanded by the governor, which was appointed to prevent disorders and tumults, especially on solemn occasions. Mark 15:16; John 19:2.

28. They put on him a scarlet robe – Such as kings and generals wore; probably an old tattered one.

32. Him they compelled to bear his cross – He bore it himself, till he sunk under it, John 19:17.

33. A place called Golgotha, that is, the place of a skull – Golgotha in Syriac signifies a skull or head: it was probably called so from this time; being an eminence upon Mount Calvary, not far from the king's gardens. Mark 15:22; Luke 23:33; John 19:17

34. They gave him vinegar mingled with gall – Out of derision: which, however nauseous, he received and tasted of. St. Mark mentions also a different mixture which was given him, Wine mingled with myrrh: such as it was customary to give to dying criminals, to make them less sensible of their sufferings: but this our Lord refused to taste, determining to bear the full force of his pains.

35. They parted his garments – This was the custom of the Romans. The soldiers performed the office of executioners, and divided among them the spoils of the criminals. **My vesture** – That is, my inner garment. Psalm 22:18.

38. Mark 15:27; Luke 23:32.

44. Mark 15:32; Luke 23:33.

45. From the sixth hour, there was darkness over all the earth unto the ninth hour – Insomuch, that even a heathen philosopher seeing it, and knowing it could not be a natural eclipse, because it was at the time of the full moon, and continued three hours together, cried out, 'Either the God of nature suffers, or the frame of the world is dissolved.' By this darkness God testified his abhorrence of the wickedness which was then committing. It likewise intimated Christ's sore conflicts with the Divine justice, and with all the powers of darkness.

46. About the ninth hour, Jesus cried with a loud voice – Our Lord's great agony probably continued these three whole hours, at the conclusion of which he thus cried out, while he suffered from God himself what was unutterable. **My God, my God, why hast thou forsaken me?** – Our Lord hereby at once expresses his trust in God, and a most distressing sense of his letting loose the powers of darkness upon him, withdrawing the comfortable discoveries of his presence, and filling his soul with a terrible sense of the wrath due to the sins which he was bearing. Psalm 22:1.

48. One taking a sponge, filled it with vinegar – Vinegar and water was the usual drink of the Roman soldiers. It does not appear, that this

was given him in derision, but rather with a friendly design, that he might not die before Elijah came. John 19:28.

50. After he had cried with a loud voice – To show that his life was still whole in him. **He dismissed his spirit** – So the original expression may be literally translated: an expression admirably suited to our Lord's words, John 10:18: No man taketh my life from me, but I lay it down of myself. He died by a voluntary act of his own, and in a way peculiar to himself. He alone of all men that ever were, could have continued alive even in the greatest tortures, as long as he pleased, or have retired from the body whenever he had thought fit. And how does it illustrate that love which he manifested in his death? Insomuch as he did not use his power to quit his body, as soon as it was fastened to the cross, leaving only an insensible corpse, to the cruelty of his murderers: but continued his abode in it, with a steady resolution, as long as it was proper. He then retired from it, with a majesty and dignity never known or to be known in any other death: dying, if one may so express it, like the Prince of life.

51. Immediately upon his death, while the sun was still darkened, the veil of the temple, which separated the holy of holies from the court of the priests, though made of the richest and strongest tapestry, was rent in two from the top to the bottom: so that while the priest was ministering at the golden altar the sacred oracle, by an invisible power was laid open to full view: God thereby signifying the speedy removal of the veil of the Jewish ceremonies by the casting down the partition wall, so that the Jews and Gentiles were now admitted to equal privileges, and the opening a way through the veil of his flesh for all believers into the most holy place. **And the earth was shaken** – There was a general earthquake through the whole globe, though chiefly near Jerusalem: God testifying thereby his wrath against the Jewish nation, for the horrid impiety they were committing.

52–53. Some of the tombs were shattered and laid open by the earthquake, and while they continued unclosed many bodies of holy men were raised. **And coming out of the tombs after his resurrection, went into the holy city and appeared to many** – Who had probably known them before: God hereby signifying, that Christ had conquered death, and would raise all his saints in due season.

54. The centurion – The officer who commanded the guard; and they that were with him feared, saying, **Truly this was the Son of God** – Referring to the words of the chief priests and scribes, Mt 27:43: He said, I am the Son of God.

56. James – The less: he was so called, to distinguish him from the other James, the brother of John; probably because he was less in stature.

57. When the evening was come – That is, after three o'clock; the time from three to six they termed the evening. Mark 15:42; Luke 23:50; John 19:38.

62. On the morrow, the day that followed the day of the preparation – The day of preparation was the day before the Sabbath, whereon they were to prepare for the celebration of it. The next day then was the Sabbath according to the Jews. But the evangelist seems to express it by this circumlocution, to show the Jewish Sabbath was then abolished.

63. That impostor said, while he was yet alive, After three days I will rise again – We do not find that he had ever said this to them, unless when he spoke of the temple of his body, John 2:19,21. And if they here refer to what he then said, how perverse and iniquitous was their construction on these words, when he was on his trial before the council? Mt 26:61. Then they seemed not to understand them!

65. Ye have a guard – Of your own, in the tower of Antonia, which was stationed there for the service of the temple.

66. They went and secured the sepulchre, sealing the stone, and setting a guard – They set Pilate's signet, or the public seal of the Sanhedrim upon a fastening which they had put on the stone. And all this uncommon caution was overruled by the providence of God, to give the strongest proofs of Christ's ensuing resurrection; since there could be no room for the least suspicion of deceit, when it should be found, that his body was raised out of a new tomb, where there was no other corpse, and this tomb hewn out of a rock, the mouth of which was secured by a great stone, under a seal, and a guard of soldiers.

Chapter 28

1. Mark 16:1; Luke 24:1; John 20:1.

2. An angel of the Lord had rolled away the stone and sat upon it – St. Luke and St. John speak of two angels that appeared: but it seems as if only one of them had appeared sitting on the stone without the sepulchre, and then going into it, was seen with another angel, sitting, one where the head, the other where the feet of the body had lain.

6. Come, see the place where the Lord lay – Probably in speaking he rose up, and going before the women into the sepulchre, said, Come, see the place. This clearly reconciles what St. John relates, John 20:12, this being one of the two angels there mentioned.

7. There shall ye see him – In his solemn appearance to them all together. But their gracious Lord would not be absent so long: he appeared to them several times before then. Lo, I have told you – A solemn confirmation of what he had said.

9. Hail – The word in its primary sense means, 'Rejoice:' in its secondary and more usual meaning, 'Happiness attend you.'

10. Go tell my brethren – I still own them as such, though they so lately disowned and forsook me.

13. Say, his disciples came by night, and stole him while we slept – Is it possible, that any man of sense should digest this poor, shallow inconsistency? If ye were awake, why did you let the disciples steal him? If asleep, how do you know they did?

16. To the mountain where Jesus had appointed them – This was probably Mount Tabor, where, he had been before transfigured. It seems to have been here also, that he appeared to above five hundred brethren at once.

18. All power is given to me – Even as man. As God, he had all power from eternity.

19. Teach all nations – Make them my disciples. This includes the whole design of Christ's commission. Baptizing and teaching are the two great branches of that general design. And these were to be determined by the circumstances of things; which made it necessary in baptizing adult Jews or heathens, to teach them before they were baptized; in teaching their children, to baptize them before they were taught; as the Jewish children in all ages were first circumcised, and after taught to do all God had commanded them. Mark 16:15.

MARK

David Brown

Introduction

That the Second Gospel was written by Mark is universally agreed, though by what Mark, not so. No tradition is more ancient, more uniform, and better sustained by internal evidence, than that Mark, in his Gospel, was but 'the interpreter of Peter,' who, at the close of his first Epistle speaks of him as 'Marcus my son' (1Pe 5:13), that is, without doubt, his son in the Gospel – converted to Christ through his instrumentality. And when we consider how little the Apostles Peter and Paul were together – how seldom they even met – how different were their tendencies, and how separate their spheres of labor, is there not, in the absence of all evidence of the fact, something approaching to violence in the supposition that the same Mark was the intimate associate of both? 'In brief,' adds CAMPBELL, 'the accounts given of Paul's attendant, and those of Peter's interpreter, concur in nothing but the name, Mark or Marcus; too slight a circumstance to conclude the sameness of the person from, especially when we consider how common the name was at Rome, and how customary it was for the Jews in that age to assume some Roman name when they went thither.'

Regarding the Evangelist Mark, then, as another person from Paul's companion in travel, all we know of his personal history is that he was a convert, as we have seen, of the Apostle Peter. But as to his Gospel, the tradition regarding Peter's hand in it is so ancient, so uniform, and so remarkably confirmed by internal evidence, that we must regard it as an established fact. 'Mark,' says PAPIAS (according to the testimony of EUSEBIUS, [*Ecclesiastical History*, 3.39]), 'becoming the interpreter of Peter, wrote accurately, though not in order, whatever he remembered of what was either said or done by Christ; for he was neither a hearer of the Lord nor a follower of Him, but afterwards, as I said, [he was a follower] of Peter, who arranged the discourses for use, but not according to the order in which they were uttered by the Lord.' To the same effect IRENAEUS [*Against Heresies*, 3,1]: 'Matthew published a Gospel while Peter and Paul were preaching and founding the Church at Rome; and after their departure (or decease), Mark, the disciple and interpreter of Peter, he also gave forth to us in writing the things which were preached by Peter.' And CLEMENT OF ALEXANDRIA is still more specific, in a passage preserved to us by EUSEBIUS [*Ecclesiastical History*, 6.14]: 'Peter having publicly preached the word at Rome, and spoken forth the Gospel by the Spirit, many of those present exhorted Mark, as having long been a follower of his, and remembering what he had said, to write what had been spoken; and that having prepared the Gospel, he delivered it to those who had asked him for it; which, when Peter came to the knowledge of, he neither decidedly forbade nor encouraged him.' EUSEBIUS' own testimony, however, from other accounts, is rather different: that Peter's hearers were so penetrated by his preaching that they gave Mark, as being a follower of Peter, no rest till he consented to write his Gospel, as a memorial of his oral teaching; and 'that the apostle, when he knew by the revelation of the Spirit what had been done, was delighted with the zeal of those men, and sanctioned the reading of the writing (that is, of this Gospel of Mark) in the churches' [*Ecclesiastical History*, 2.15]. And giving in another of his works a similar statement, he says that 'Peter, from excess of humility, did not think himself qualified to write the Gospel; but Mark, his acquaintance and pupil, is said to have recorded his relations of the actings of Jesus. And Peter testifies these things of himself; for all things that are recorded by Mark are said to be memoirs of Peter's discourses.' It is needless to go farther – to ORIGEN, who says Mark composed his Gospel 'as Peter guided' or 'directed him, who, in his Catholic Epistle, calls him his son,' &c.; and to JEROME, who but echoes EUSEBIUS.

This, certainly, is a remarkable chain of testimony; which, confirmed as it is by such striking internal evidence, may be regarded as establishing the fact that the Second Gospel was drawn up mostly from materials furnished by Peter. In DA COSTA'S Four Witnesses the reader will find this internal evidence detailed at length, though all the examples are not equally convincing. But if the reader will refer to our remarks on Mr 16:7, and Joh 18:27, he will have convincing evidence of a Petrine hand in this Gospel.

It remains only to advert, in a word or two, to the readers for whom this Gospel was, in the first instance, designed, and the date of it. That it was not for Jews but Gentiles, is evident from the great number of explanations of Jewish usages, opinions, and places, which to a Jew would at that time have been superfluous, but were highly needful to a Gentile. We can here but refer to Mr 2:18 7:3,4 12:18 13:3 14:12 15:42, for examples of these. Regarding the date of this Gospel – about which nothing certain is known – if the tradition reported by IRENAEUS can be relied on that it was written at Rome, 'after the departure of Peter and Paul,' and if by that word 'departure' we are to understand their death, we may date it somewhere between the years 64 and 68; but in all likelihood this is too late. It is probably nearer the truth to date it eight or ten years earlier.

Contents

See *Outlines of the New Testament Books*, pp.887–9.

Chapter 1

Mr 1:1-8.
The preaching and baptism of John.
(= Mt 3:1–12 Lu 3:1–18).

1. The beginning of the gospel of Jesus Christ, the Son of God – By the 'Gospel' of Jesus Christ here is evidently meant the blessed Story which our Evangelist is about to tell of His Life, Ministry, Death, Resurrection, and Glorification, and of the begun Gathering of Believers in His Name. The abruptness with which he announces his subject, and the energetic brevity with which, passing by all preceding events, he hastens over the ministry of John and records the Baptism and Temptation of

Jesus – as if impatient to come to the Public Life of the Lord of glory – have often been noticed as characteristic of this Gospel – a Gospel whose direct, practical, and singularly vivid setting imparts to it a preciousness peculiar to itself. What strikes every one is, that though briefest of all the Gospels, this is in some of the principal scenes of our Lord's history the fullest. But what is not so obvious is, that wherever the finer and subtler feelings of humanity, or the deeper and more peculiar hues of our Lord's character were brought out, these, though they should be lightly passed over by all the other Evangelists, are sure to be found here, and in touches of such quiet delicacy and power, that though scarce observed by the cursory reader, they leave indelible impressions upon all the thoughtful and furnish a key to much that is in the other Gospels. These few opening words of the Second Gospel are enough to show, that though it was the purpose of this Evangelist to record chiefly the outward and palpable facts of our Lord's public life, he recognized in Him, in common with the Fourth Evangelist, the glory of the Only-begotten of the Father.

2, 3. As it is written in the prophets, Behold, I send my messenger before thy face, which shall prepare thy way before thee – (Mal 3:1 Isa 40:3).

3. The voice of one crying in the wilderness, Prepare ye the way of the Lord, make his paths straight – The second of these quotations is given by Matthew and Luke in the same connection, but they reserve the former quotation till they have occasion to return to the Baptist, after his imprisonment (Mt 11:10 Lu 7:27). (Instead of the words, 'as it is written in the Prophets,' there is weighty evidence in favour of the following reading: 'As it is written in Isaiah the prophet.' This reading is adopted by all the latest critical editors. If it be the true one, it is to be explained thus – that of the two quotations, the one from Malachi is but a later development of the great primary one in Isaiah, from which the whole prophetical matter here quoted takes its name. But the received text is quoted by IRENAEUS, before the end of the second century, and the evidence in its favour is greater in amount, if not in weight. The chief objection to it is, that if this was the true reading, it is difficult to see how the other one could have got in at all; whereas, if it be not the true reading, it is very easy to see how it found its way into the text, as it removes the startling difficulty of a prophecy beginning with the words of Malachi being ascribed to Isaiah.)

Mr 1:9–11.
Baptism of Christ and descent of the spirit upon him immediately thereafter.
(= Mt 3:13–17 Lu 3:21,22).

Mr 1:12, 13.
Temptation of Christ.
(= Mt 4:1–11 Lu 4:1–13).
See on Mt 4:1–11.

Mr 1:14–20.
Christ begins his Galilean ministry – calling of Simon and Andrew, James and John.
See on Mt 4:12–22.

Mr 1:21–39.
Healing of a demoniac in the synagogue of Capernaum and thereafter of Simon's mother-in-law and many others – Jesus, next day, is found in a solitary place at
morning prayers, and is entreated to return, but declines, and goes forth on his first missionary circuit.
(= Lu 4:31–44 Mt 8:14–17 4:23–25).

21. and straightway on the Sabbath day he entered into the synagogue, and taught – This should have been rendered, 'straightway on the Sabbaths He entered into the synagogue and taught,' or 'continued to teach.' The meaning is, that as He began this practice on the very first Sabbath after coming to settle at Capernaum, so He continued it regularly thereafter.

22. And they were astonished at his doctrine – or 'teaching' – referring quite as much to the manner as the matter of it.

23. And there was in their synagogue a man with an unclean spirit – literally, 'in an unclean spirit' – that is, so entirely under demoniacal power that his personality was sunk for the time in that of the spirit. The frequency with which this character of 'impurity' is ascribed to evil spirits – some twenty times in the Gospels – is not to be overlooked.

and he cried out – as follows:

24. Saying, Let us alone – or rather, perhaps, 'ah!' expressive of mingled astonishment and terror.

what have we to do with thee – an expression of frequent occurrence in the Old Testament (1Ki 17:18 2Ki 3:13 2Ch 35:21). It denotes entire separation of interests: – that is, 'Thou and we have nothing in common; we want not Thee; what wouldst Thou with us?' For the analogous application of it by our Lord to His mother.

thou Jesus of Nazareth – 'Jesus, Nazarene!' an epithet originally given to express contempt, but soon adopted as the current designation by those who held our Lord in honour (Lu 18:37 Mr 16:6 Ac 2:22).

art thou come to destroy us? – In the case of the Gadarene demoniac the question was, 'Art Thou come hither to torment us before the time?' (Mt 8:29). Themselves tormentors and destroyers of their victims, they discern in Jesus their own destined tormentor and destroyer, anticipating and dreading what they know and feel to be awaiting them! Conscious, too, that their power was but permitted and temporary, and perceiving in Him, perhaps, the woman's Seed that was to bruise the head and destroy the works of the devil, they regard His approach to them on this occasion as a signal to let go their grasp of this miserable victim.

I know thee who thou art, the Holy One of God – This and other even more glorious testimonies to our Lord were given, as we know, with no good will, but in hope that, by the acceptance of them, He might appear to the people to be in league with evil spirits – a calumny which His enemies were ready enough to throw out against Him. But a Wiser than either was here, who invariably rejected and silenced the testimonies that came to Him from beneath, and thus was able to rebut the imputations of His enemies against Him (Mt 12:24–30). The expression, 'Holy One of God,' seems evidently taken from that Messianic Psalm (Ps 16:10), in which He is styled 'Thine Holy One.'

25. And Jesus rebuked him, saying, Hold thy peace, and come out of him – A glorious word of command. BENGEL remarks that it was only the testimony borne to Himself which our Lord meant to silence. That he should afterwards cry out for fear or rage (Mr 1:26) He would right willingly permit.

26. And when the unclean spirit had torn him – Luke (Lu 4:35) says, 'When he had thrown him in the midst.' Malignant cruelty – just showing what he would have done, if permitted to go farther: it was a last fling!

and cried with a loud voice – the voice of enforced submission and despair.

he came out of him – Luke (Lu 4:35) adds, 'and hurt him not.' Thus impotent were the malignity and rage of the impure spirit when under the restraint of 'the Stronger than the strong one armed' (Lu 11:21,22).

27. What thing is this? what new doctrine – teaching is this? – The audience, rightly apprehending that the miracle was wrought to illustrate the teaching and display the character and glory of the Teacher, begin by asking what novel kind of teaching this could be, which was so marvellously attested.

28. And immediately his fame spread abroad throughout all the region round about Galilee – rather, 'the whole region of Galilee'; though some, as MEYER and ELLICOTT, explain it of the country surrounding Galilee.

29. And forthwith, when they were come out of the synagogue – so also in Lu 4:38.

they entered into the house of Simon and Andrew, with James and John – The mention of these four – which is peculiar to Mark – is the first of those traces of Peter's hand in this Gospel, of which we shall find many more. The house being his, and the illness and cure so nearly affecting himself, it is interesting to observe this minute specification of the number and names of the witnesses; interesting also – as the first occasion on which the sacred triumvirate of Peter and James and John are selected from among the rest, to be a threefold cord of testimony to certain events in their Lord's life (see on Mr 5:37) – Andrew being present on this occasion, as the occurrence took place in his own house.

30. But Simon's wife's mother lay sick of a fever – Luke, as was natural in 'the beloved physician' (Col 4:14), describes it professionally; calling it a 'great fever,' and thus distinguishing it from that lighter kind which the Greek physicians were wont to call 'small fevers,' as GALEN, quoted by WETSTEIN, tells us.

and anon – immediately.

they tell him of her – naturally hoping that His compassion and power towards one of His own disciples would not be less signally displayed than towards the demonized stranger in the synagogue.

31. And he came and took her by the hand – rather, 'And advancing, He took her,' &c. The beloved physician again is very specific: 'And He stood over her.'

and lifted her up – This act of condescension, most felt doubtless by Peter, is recorded only by Mark.

and immediately the fever left her, and she ministered unto them – preparing their Sabbath-meal: in token both of the perfectness and immediateness of the cure, and of her gratitude to the glorious Healer.

32. And at even, when the sun did set – so Mt 8:16. Luke (Lu 4:40) says it was setting.

they brought unto him all that were diseased, and them that were possessed with devils – the demonized. From Lu 13:14 we see how unlawful they would have deemed it to bring their sick to Jesus for a cure during the Sabbath hours. They waited, therefore, till these were over, and then brought them in crowds. Our Lord afterwards took repeated occasion to teach the people by example, even at the risk of His own life, how superstitious a straining of the Sabbath rest this was.

33. And all the city was gathered together at the door – of Peter's house; that is, the sick and those who brought them, and the wondering spectators. This bespeaks the presence of an eye-witness, and is one of those lively examples of word-painting so frequent in this Gospel.

34. And he healed many that were sick of divers diseases, and cast out many devils – In Mt 8:16 it is said, 'He cast out the spirits with His word'; or rather, 'with a word' – a word of command.

and suffered not the devils to speak, because they knew him – Evidently they would have spoken, if permitted, proclaiming His Messiahship in such terms as in the synagogue; but once in one day, and that testimony immediately silenced, was enough. See on Mr 1:24. After this account of His miracles of healing, we have in Mt 8:17 this pregnant quotation, 'That it might be fulfilled which was spoken by Esaias the prophet, saying (Isa 53:4), Himself took our infirmities, and bare our sicknesses.'

35. And in the morning – that is, of the day after this remarkable Sabbath; or, on the first day of the week. His choosing this day to inaugurate a new and glorious stage of His public work, should be noted by the reader.

rising up a great while before day – 'while it was yet night,' or long before daybreak.

he went out – all unperceived from Peter's house, where He slept.

and departed into a solitary place, and there prayed – or, 'continued in prayer.' He was about to begin His first preaching and healing circuit; and as on similar solemn occasions (Lu 5:16 6:12 9:18,28,29 Mr 6:46), He spent some time in special prayer, doubtless with a view to it. What would one not give to have been, during the stillness of those grey morning hours, within hearing – not of His 'strong crying and tears,' for He had scarce arrived at the stage for that – but of His calm, exalted anticipations of the work which lay immediately before Him, and the outpourings of His soul about it into the bosom of Him that sent Him! He had doubtless enjoyed some uninterrupted hours of such communings with His heavenly Father ere His friends from Capernaum arrived in search of Him. As for them, they doubtless expected, after such a day of miracles, that the next day would witness similar manifestations. When morning came, Peter, loath to break in upon the repose of his glorious Guest, would await His appearance beyond the usual hour; but at length, wondering at the stillness, and gently coming to see where the Lord lay, he finds it – like the sepulchre afterwards – empty! Speedily a party is made up to go in search of Him, Peter naturally leading the way.

36. And Simon and they that were with him followed after him – rather, 'pressed after Him.' Luke (Lu 4:42) says, 'The multitudes sought after Him'; but this would be a party from the town. Mark, having his information from Peter himself, speaks only of what related directly to him. 'They that were with him' would probably be Andrew his brother, James and John, with a few other choice brethren.

37. And when they had found him – evidently after some search.

they said unto him, All men seek for thee – By this time, 'the multitudes' who, according to Luke (Lu 4:42), 'sought after Him' – and who, on going to Peter's house, and there learning that Peter and a few more were gone in search of Him, had set out on the same errand – would have arrived, and 'came unto Him and stayed Him, that He should not depart from them' (Lu 4:42); all now urging His return to their impatient townsmen.

38. And he said unto them, Let us go – or, according to another reading, 'Let us go elsewhere.'

into the next towns – rather, 'unto the neighbouring village-towns'; meaning those places intermediate between towns and villages, with

which the western side of the Sea of Galilee was studded.

that I may preach there also; for therefore came I forth – not from Capernaum, as DE WETTE miserably interprets, nor from His privacy in the desert place, as MEYER, no better; but from the Father. Compare Joh 16:28, 'I came forth from the Father, and am come into the world,' &c. – another proof, by the way, that the lofty phraseology of the Fourth Gospel was not unknown to the authors of the others, though their design and point of view are different. The language in which our Lord's reply is given by Luke (Lu 4:43) expresses the high necessity under which, in this as in every other step of His work, He acted – 'I must preach the kingdom of God to other cities also; for therefore' – or, 'to this end' – 'am I sent.' An act of self-denial it doubtless was, to resist such pleadings to return to Capernaum. But there were overmastering considerations on the other side.

Mr 1:40–45.
Healing of a leper.
(= Mt 8:1–4 Lu 5:12–16).

See on Mt 8:1–4.

Chapter 2
Mr 2:1–12.
Healing of a paralytic.
(= Mt 9:1–8 Lu 5:17–26).

This incident, as remarked on Mt 9:1, appears to follow next in order of time after the cure of the leper (Mr 1:40–45).

1. And again he entered into Capernaum – 'His own city' (Mt 9:1).

and it was noised that he was in the house – no doubt of Simon Peter (Mr 1:29).

2. And straightway many were gathered together, insomuch that there was no room to receive them, no, not so much as about the door – This is one of Mark's graphic touches. No doubt in this case, as the scene occurred at his informant's own door, these details are the vivid recollections of that honoured disciple.

and he preached the word unto them – that is, indoors; but in the hearing, doubtless, of the multitude that pressed around. Had He gone forth, as He naturally would, the paralytic's faith would have had no such opportunity to display itself. Luke (Lu 5:17) furnishes an additional and very important incident in the scene – as follows: 'And it came to pass on a certain day, as He was teaching, that there were Pharisees and doctors of the law sitting by, which were come out of every town,' or village, 'of Galilee, and Judea, and Jerusalem.' This was the highest testimony yet borne to our Lord's growing influence, and the necessity increasingly felt by the ecclesiastics throughout the country of coming to some definite judgment regarding Him. 'And the power of the Lord was [present] to heal them' – or, 'was [efficacious] to heal them,' that is, the sick that were brought before Him. So that the miracle that is now to be described was among the most glorious and worthy to be recorded of many then performed; and what made it so was doubtless the faith which was manifested in connection with it, and the proclamation of the forgiveness of the patient's sins that immediately preceded it.

3. And they come unto him – that is, towards the house where He was.

bringing one sick of the palsy – 'lying on a bed' (Mt 9:2).

which was borne of four – a graphic particular of Mark only.

4. And when they could not come nigh unto him for the press – or, as in Luke (Lu 5:19), 'when they could not find by what way they might bring him in because of the multitude,' they 'went upon the housetop' – the flat or terrace-roof, universal in Eastern houses.

they uncovered the roof where he was: and when they had broken it up, they let down the bed – or portable couch

wherein the sick of the palsy lay – Luke (Lu 5:19) says, they 'let him down through the tiling with his couch into the midst before Jesus.' Their whole object was to bring the patient into the presence of Jesus; and this not being possible in the ordinary way, because of the multitude that surrounded Him, they took the very unusual method here described of accomplishing their object, and succeeded. Several explanations have been given of the way in which this was done; but unless we knew the precise plan of the house, and the part of it from which Jesus taught – which may have been a quadrangle or open court, within the buildings of which Peter's house was one, or a gallery covered by a veranda – it is impossible to determine precisely how the thing is done. One thing, however, is clear, that we have both the accounts from an eye-witness.

5. When Jesus saw their faith – It is remarkable that all the three narratives call it 'their faith' which Jesus saw. That the patient himself had faith, we know from the proclamation of his forgiveness, which Jesus made before all; and we should have been apt to conclude that his four friends bore him to Jesus merely out of benevolent compliance with the urgent entreaties of the poor sufferer. But here we learn, not only that his bearers had the same faith with himself, but that Jesus marked it as a faith which was not to be defeated – a faith victorious over all difficulties. This was the faith for which He was ever on the watch, and which He never saw without marking, and, in those who needed anything from Him, richly rewarding.

he said unto the sick of the palsy, Son –

'be of good cheer' (Mt 9:2).

thy sins be forgiven thee – By the word 'be,' our translators perhaps meant 'are,' as in Luke (Lu 5:20). For it is not a command to his sins to depart, but an authoritative proclamation of the man's pardoned state as a believer. And yet, as the Pharisees understood our Lord to be dispensing pardon by this saying, and Jesus not only acknowledges that they were right, but founds His whole argument upon the correctness of it, we must regard the saying as a royal proclamation of the man's forgiveness by Him to whom it belonged to dispense it; nor could such a style of address be justified on any lower supposition.

6. But there were certain of the scribes – 'and the Pharisees' (Lu 5:21)

sitting there – those Jewish ecclesiastics who, as Luke told us (Lu 5:17), 'were come out of every village of Galilee, and Judea, and Jerusalem,' to make their observations upon this wonderful Person, in anything but a teachable spirit, though as yet their venomous and murderous feeling had not showed itself.

7. Why doth this man thus speak blasphemies? who can forgive sins but God only? – In this second question they expressed a great truth. (See Isa 43:25 Mic 7:18 Ex 34:6,7.) Nor was their first question altogether unnatural, though in our Lord's sole case it was unfounded. That a man, to all appearances like one of themselves, should claim authority and power to forgive sins, they could not, on the first blush of it, but regard as in the last degree startling; nor were they entitled even to weigh such a claim, as worthy of a hearing, save on supposition of resistless evidence afforded by Him in support of the claim. Accordingly, our Lord deals with them as men entitled to such evidence, and supplies it; at the same time chiding them for rashness, in drawing harsh conclusions regarding Himself.

8. Why reason ye these things in your hearts – or, as in Matthew, (Mt 9:4) 'Wherefore think ye evil in your hearts?'

9. Whether is it easier to say to the sick of the palsy, Thy sins be forgiven thee – or 'are forgiven thee';

or to say, Arise, and take up thy bed and walk? – 'Is it easier to command away disease than to bid away sin? If, then, I do the one which you can see, know thus that I have done the other, which you cannot see.'

10. But that ye may know that the Son of man hath power on earth to forgive sins – that forgiving power dwells in the Person of this Man, and is exercised by Him while on this earth and going out and in with you.

(he saith to the sick of the palsy),

11. I say unto thee, Arise, and take up thy bed, and go thy way into thine house – This taking up the portable couch, and walking home with it, was designed to prove the completeness of the cure.

12. And immediately he arose, took up the bed – 'Sweet saying!' says BENGEL: 'The bed had borne the man: now the man bore the bed.'

and went forth before them all – proclaiming by that act to the multitude, whose wondering eyes would follow him as he pressed through them, that He who could work such a glorious miracle of healing, must indeed 'have power on earth to forgive sins.'

We never saw it on this fashion – 'never saw it thus,' or, as we say, 'never saw the like.' In Luke (Lu 5:26) it is, 'We have seen strange [unexpected] things to-day' – referring both to the miracles wrought and the forgiveness of sins pronounced by Human Lips. In Matthew (Mt 9:8) it is, 'They marvelled, and glorified God, which had given such power unto men.' At forgiving power they wondered not, but that a man, to all appearance like one of themselves, should possess it!

Mr 2:13–17.
Levi's (or Matthew's) call and feast.
(= Mt 9:9–13 Lu 5:27–32).
See on Mt 9:9–13.

Mr 2:18–22.
Discourse on fasting.
(= Mt 9:14–17 Lu 5:33–39).
See on Lu 5:33–39.

Mr 2:23–28. Plucking corn-ears on the sabbath day.
(= Mt 12:1–8 Lu 6:1–5).
See on Mt 12:1–8.

Chapter 3

Mr 3:1–12.
The healing of a withered hand on the sabbath day, and retirement of Jesus to avoid danger.
(= Mt 12:9–21 Lu 6:6–11).
See on Mt 12:9–21.

Mr 3:13–19.
The twelve apostles chosen.
See on Lu 6:12–19.

Mr 3:20–30.
Jesus is charged with madness and demoniacal possession – his reply.
(= Mt 12:22–37 Lu 11:14–26).
See on Mt 12:22–37; Lu 11:21–26.

Mr 3:31–35.
His mother and brethren seek to speak with him and the reply.
(= Mt 12:46–50 Lu 8:19–21).
See on Mt 12:46–50.

Chapter 4

Mr 4:1–34.
Parable of the sower – reason for teaching in parables – parables of the seed growing we know not how, and of the mustard seed.
(= Mt 13:1–23,31,32 Lu 8:4–18).

1. And he began again to teach by the seaside: and there was gathered unto him a great multitude – or, according to another well-supported reading, 'a mighty' or 'immense multitude.'

so that he entered into a ship – rather, 'the ship,' meaning the one mentioned in Mr 3:9.

and sat in the sea; and the whole multitude was by the sea on the land – crowded on the seashore to listen to Him.

2. And he taught them many things by parables, and said unto them in his doctrine – or 'teaching.'

Parable of the sower.
(Mr 4:3–9,13–20).

Mr 4:3, 14. The sower, the seed, and the soil.

3. Hearken; Behold, there went out a sower to sow – What means this? See on Mr 4:14.

First case: THE WAYSIDE. (Mr 4:4, 15).

4. And it came to pass, as he sowed, some fell by the wayside – by the side of the hard path through the field, where the soil was not broken up.

and the fowls of the air came and devoured it up – Not only could the seed not get beneath the surface, but 'it was trodden down' (Lu 8:5), and afterwards picked up and devoured by the fowls. What means this? See on Mr 4:15.

Second case: THE STONY or *rather,* ROCKY GROUND. (Mr 4:5, 16).

5. And some fell on stony ground, where it had not much earth – 'the rocky ground'; in Matthew (Mt 13:5), 'the rocky places'; in Luke (Lu 8:6), 'the rock.' The thing intended is, not ground with stones in it which would not prevent the roots striking downward, but ground where a quite thin surface of earth covers a rock. What means this? See on Mr 4:16.

Third case: THE THORNY GROUND.
(Mr 4:7, 18, 19).

7. And some fell among thorns, and the thorns grew up, and choked it, and it yielded no fruit – This case is that of ground not thoroughly cleaned of the thistles; which, rising above the good seed, 'choke' or 'smother' it, excluding light and air, and drawing away the moisture and richness of the soil. Hence it 'becomes unfruitful' (Mt 13:22); it grows, but its growth is checked, and it never ripens. The evil here is neither a hard nor a shallow soil – there is softness enough, and depth enough; but it is the existence in it of what draws all the moisture and richness of the soil away to itself, and so starves the plant. What now are these 'thorns?' See on Mr 4:19.

Fourth case: THE GOOD GROUND. (Mr 4:8, 20).

8. And other fell on good ground, and did yield fruit – The goodness of this last soil consists in its qualities being precisely the reverse of the other three soils: from its softness and tenderness, receiving and cherishing the seed; from its depth, allowing it to take firm root, and not quickly losing its moisture; and from its cleanness, giving its whole vigour and sap to the plant. In such a soil the seed 'brings forth fruit,' in all different degrees of profusion, according to the measure in which the soil possesses those qualities. See on Mr 4:20.

After this parable is recorded the Evangelist says:

10. And when he was alone, they that were about him with the twelve – probably those who followed Him most closely and were firmest in discipleship, next to the Twelve.

asked of him the parable – The reply would seem to intimate that this parable of the sower was of that fundamental, comprehensive, and introductory character which we have assigned to it.

Reason for teaching in parables
(Mr 4:11, 12, 21–25).

13. Know ye not this parable? and how then will ye know all parables? – Probably this was said not so much in the spirit of rebuke, as to call their attention to the exposition of it which He was about to give, and so train them to the right apprehension of His future parables. As in the parables which we have endeavoured to explain in Mt 13:1–58, we shall take this parable and the Lord's own exposition of the different parts of it together.

14. The sower soweth the word – or, as in Luke (Lu 8:11), 'Now the parable is this: The seed is the word of God.' But who is 'the sower?' This is not expressed here because if 'the word

of God' be the seed, every scatterer of that precious seed must be regarded as a sower. It is true that in the parable of the tares it is said, 'He that soweth the good seed is the Son of man,' as 'He that soweth the tares is the devil' (Mt 13:37,38). But these are only the great unseen parties, struggling in this world for the possession of man. Each of these has his agents among men themselves; and Christ's agents in the sowing of the good seed are the preachers of the word. Thus, as in all the cases about to be described, the sower is the same, and the seed is the same; while the result is entirely different, the whole difference must lie in the soils, which mean the different states of the human heart. And so, the great general lesson held forth in this parable of the sower is, that however faithful the preacher, and how pure soever his message, the effect of the preaching of the word depends upon the state of the hearer's heart. Now follow the cases. See on Mr 4:4.

15. And these are they by the wayside, where the word is sown; but, when they have heard – or, more fully (Mt 13:19), 'When any one heareth the word of the kingdom, and understandeth it not, then cometh the wicked one, and catcheth away that which was sown in his heart.' The great truth here taught is, that hearts all unbroken and hard are no fit soil for saving truth. They apprehend it not (Mt 13:19) as God's means of restoring them to Himself; it penetrates not, makes no impression, but lies loosely on the surface of the heart, till the wicked one – afraid of losing a victim by his 'believing to salvation' (Lu 8:12) – finds some frivolous subject by whose greater attractions to draw off the attention, and straightway it is gone. Of how many hearers of the word is this the graphic but painful history!

16. And these are they likewise which are sown on stony ground – 'Immediately' the seed in such a case 'springs up' – all the quicker from the shallowness of the soil – 'because it has no depth of earth.' But the sun, beating on it, as quickly scorches and withers it up, 'because it has no root' (Mr 4:6), and 'lacks moisture' (Lu 8:6). The great truth here taught is that hearts superficially impressed are apt to receive the truth with readiness, and even with joy (Lu 8:13); but the heat of tribulation or persecution because of the word, or the trials which their new profession brings upon them quickly dries up their relish for the truth, and withers all the hasty promise of fruit which they showed. Such disappointing issues of a faithful and awakening ministry – alas, how frequent are they!

19. And the cares of this world, and the deceitfulness of riches, and the lusts of other things entering in – or 'the pleasures of this life' (Lu 8:14).

choke the word, and it becometh unfruitful – First, 'The cares of this world' – anxious, unrelaxing attention to the business of this present life; second, 'The deceitfulness of riches' – of those riches which are the fruit of this worldly 'care'; third, 'The pleasures of this life,' or 'the lusts of other things entering in' – the enjoyments in themselves may be innocent, which worldly prosperity enables one to indulge. These 'choke' or 'smother' the word; drawing off so much of one's attention, absorbing so much of one's interest, and using up so much of one's time, that only the dregs of these remain for spiritual things, and a ragged, hurried, and heartless formalism is at length all the religion of such persons. What a vivid picture is this of the mournful condition of many, especially in great commercial countries, who once promised much fruit! 'They bring no fruit to perfection' (Lu 8:14); indicating how much growth there may be, in the early stages of such a case, and promise of fruit – which after all never ripens.

20. **And these are they which are sown on good ground; such as hear the word, and receive it, and bring forth fruit, some thirtyfold, some sixty, and some an hundred** – A heart soft and tender, stirred to its depths on the great things of eternity, and jealously guarded from worldly engrossments, such only is the 'honest and good heart' (Lu 8:15), which 'keeps,' that is, 'retains' the seed of the word, and bears fruit just in proportion as it is such a heart. Such 'bring forth fruit with patience' (Mr 4:15), or continuance, 'enduring to the end'; in contrast with those in whom the word is 'choked' and brings no fruit to perfection. The 'thirtyfold' is designed to express the lowest degree of fruitfulness; the 'hundredfold' the highest; and the 'sixtyfold' the intermediate degrees of fruitfulness. As a 'hundredfold,' though not unexampled (Ge 26:12), is a rare return in the natural husbandry, so the highest degrees of spiritual fruitfulness are too seldom witnessed. The closing words of this introductory parable seem designed to call attention to the fundamental and universal character of it.

21. **And he said unto them, Is a candle** – or 'lamp'

brought to be put under a bushel, or under a bed? and not to be set on a candlestick? – 'that they which enter in may see the light' (Lu 8:16).

22. **For there is nothing hid which shall not be manifested** – Here the idea seems to be this – 'I have privately expounded to you these great truths, but only that ye may proclaim them publicly; and if ye will not, others will. For these are not designed for secrecy. They are imparted to be diffused abroad, and they shall be so; yea, a time is coming when the most hidden things shall be brought to light.'

23. **If any man have ears to hear, let him hear** – This for the second time on the same subject (see on Mr 4:9).

24. **And he saith unto them, Take heed what ye hear** – In Luke (Lu 8:18) it is, 'Take heed how ye hear.' The one implies the other, but both precepts are very weighty.

and unto you that hear – that is, thankfully, teachably, profitably.

25. **For he that hath, to him shall be given; and he that hath not, from him shall be taken even that which he hath** – or 'seemeth to have,' or 'thinketh he hath.' This 'having' and 'thinking he hath' are not different; for when it hangs loosely upon him, and is not appropriated to its proper ends and uses, it both is and is not his.

Parable of the seed growing we know not how (Mr 4:26–29)

This beautiful parable is peculiar to Mark. Its design is to teach the Imperceptible Growth of the word sown in the heart, from its earliest stage of development to the ripest fruits of practical righteousness.

26, 27. **So is the kingdom of God, as if a man should cast seed into the ground; and should sleep, and rise night and day** – go about his other ordinary occupations, leaving it to the well-known laws of vegetation under the genial influences of heaven. This is the sense of 'the earth bringing forth fruit of herself,' in Mr 4:27.

28. **For the earth bringeth forth fruit of herself; first the blade, then the ear, after that the full corn in the ear** – beautiful allusion to the succession of similar stages, though not definitely marked periods, in the Christian life, and generally in the kingdom of God.

29. **But when the fruit is brought forth** – to maturity

immediately he putteth in the sickle, because the harvest is come – This charmingly points to the transition from the earthly to the heavenly condition of the Christian and the Church.

Parable of the mustard seed (Mr 4:30–32)

33. **And with many such parables spake he the word unto them, as they were able to hear it** – Had this been said in the corresponding passage of Matthew, we should have concluded that what that Evangelist recorded was but a specimen of other parables spoken on the same occasion. But Matthew (Mt 13:34) says, 'All these things spake Jesus unto the multitude in parables'; and as Mark records only some of the parables which Matthew gives, we are warranted to infer that the 'many such parables' alluded to here mean no more than the full complement of them which we find in Matthew.

34. **and when they were alone, he expounded all things to his disciples** – See on Mr 4:22.

Mr 4:35–5:20.
Jesus crossing the Sea of Galilee, miraculously stills a tempest – he cures the demoniac of Gadara.
(= Mt 8:23–34 Lu 8:22–39).

The time of this section is very definitely marked by our Evangelist, and by him alone, in the opening words.

Jesus stills a tempest on the Sea of Galilee (Mr 4:35–41)

35. And the same day – on which He spoke the memorable parables of the preceding section, and of the thirteenth chapter.

when the even was come – (See on Mr 6:35). This must have been the earlier evening – what we should call the afternoon – since after all that passed on the other side, when He returned to the west side, the people were waiting for Him in great numbers (Mr 4:21 Lu 8:40).

he saith unto them, Let us pass over unto the other side – to the east side of the lake, to grapple with a desperate case of possession, and set the captive free, and to give the Gadarenes an opportunity of hearing the message of salvation, amid the wonder which that marvellous cure was fitted to awaken and the awe which the subsequent events could not but strike into them.

36. And when they had sent away the multitude, they took him even as he was in the ship – that is, without any preparation, and without so much as leaving the vessel, out of which He had been all day teaching.

And there were also with him other little ships – with passengers, probably, wishing to accompany Him.

37. And there arose a great storm of wind – 'a tempest of wind.' To such sudden squalls the Sea of Galilee is very liable from its position, in a deep basin, skirted on the east by lofty mountain ranges, while on the west the hills are intersected by narrow gorges through which the wind sweeps across the lake, and raises its waters with great rapidity into a storm.

and the waves beat into the ship – kept beating or pitching on the ship.

so that it was now full – rather, 'so that it was already filling.' In Matthew (Mt 8:24), 'insomuch that the ship was covered with the waves'; but this is too strong. It should be, 'so that the ship was getting covered by the waves.' So we must translate the word used in Luke (Lu 8:23) – not as in our version – 'And there came down a storm on the lake, and they were filled [with water]' – but 'they were getting filled,' that is, those who sailed; meaning, of course, that their ship was so.

38. And he was in the hinder part of the ship – or stern.

asleep on a pillow – either a place in the vessel made to receive the head, or a cushion for the head to rest on. It was evening; and after the fatigues of a busy day of teaching under the hot sun, having nothing to do while crossing the lake, He sinks into a deep sleep, which even this tempest raging around and tossing the little vessel did not disturb.

and they awake him, and say unto him, Master – or 'Teacher.' In Luke (Lu 8:24) this is doubled – in token of their life-and-death earnestness – 'Master, Master.'

carest thou not that we perish? – Unbelief and fear made them sadly forget their place, to speak so. Luke has it, 'Lord, save us, we perish.' When those accustomed to fish upon that deep thus spake, the danger must have been imminent. They say nothing of what would become of Him, if they perished; nor think, whether, if He could not perish, it was likely He would let this happen to them; but they hardly knew what they said.

39. And he arose, and rebuked the wind – 'and the raging of the water' (Lu 8:24).

and said unto the sea, Peace, be still – two sublime words of command, from a Master to His servants, the elements.

And the wind ceased, and there was a great calm – The sudden hushing of the wind would not at once have calmed the sea, whose commotion would have settled only after a considerable time. But the word of command was given to both elements at once.

40. And he said unto them, Why are ye so fearful? – There is a natural apprehension under danger; but there was unbelief in their fear. It is worthy of notice how considerately the Lord defers this rebuke till He had first removed the danger, in the midst of which they would not have been in a state to listen to anything.

how is it that ye have no faith? – next to none, or none in present exercise. In Matthew (Mt 8:26) it is, 'Why are ye fearful, O ye of little faith?' Faith they had, for they applied to Christ for relief: but little, for they were afraid, though Christ was in the ship. Faith dispels fear, but only in proportion to its strength.

41. And they feared exceedingly – were struck with deep awe.

and said one to another, What manner of man is this, that even the wind and the sea obey him? – 'What is this?' Israel has all along been singing of JEHOVAH, 'Thou rulest the raging of the sea: when the waves thereof arise, Thou stillest them!' 'The Lord on high is mightier than the noise of many waters, yea, than the mighty waves of the sea!' (Ps 89:9 93:4). But, lo, in this very boat of ours is One of our own flesh and blood, who with His word of command hath done the same! Exhausted with the fatigues of the day, He was but a moment ago in a deep sleep, undisturbed by the howling tempest, and we had to waken Him with the cry of our terror; but rising at our call, His majesty was felt by the raging elements, for they were instantly hushed – 'WHAT MANNER OF MAN IS THIS?'

Chapter 5

Glorious cure of the Gadarene demoniac
(Mr 5:1–20)

2. And when he was come out of the ship, immediately – (see Mr 5:6).

there met him a man with an unclean spirit – 'which had devils [demons] long time' (Lu 8:27). In Matthew (Mt 8:28), 'there met him two men possessed with devils.' Though there be no discrepancy between these two statements – more than between two witnesses, one of whom testifies to something done by one person, while the other affirms that there were two – it is difficult to see how the principal details here given could apply to more than one case.

3. Who had his dwelling among the tombs – Luke (Lu 8:27) says, 'He ware no clothes, neither abode in any house.' These tombs were hewn out of the rocky caves of the locality, and served for shelters and lurking places (Lu 8:26).

4. Because that he had been often bound with fetters and chains – Luke says (Lu 8:29) that 'oftentimes it [the unclean spirit] had caught him'; and after mentioning how they had vainly tried to bind him with chains and fetters, because, 'he brake the bands,' he adds, 'and was driven of the devil [demon] into the wilderness.' The dark tyrant-power by which he was held clothed him with superhuman strength and made him scorn restraint. Matthew (Mt 8:28) says he was 'exceeding fierce, so that no man might pass by that way.' He was the terror of the whole locality.

5. And always, night and day, he was in the mountains, and in the tombs, crying, and cutting himself with stones – Terrible as he was to others, he himself endured untold misery, which sought relief in tears and self-inflicted torture.

6. But when he saw Jesus afar off, he ran and worshipped him – not with the spontaneous alacrity which says to Jesus, 'Draw me, we will run after thee,' but inwardly compelled, with terrific rapidity, before the Judge, to receive sentence of expulsion.

7. What have I to do with thee, Jesus, Son of the most high God? I adjure thee by God, that thou torment me not – or, as in Mt 8:29, 'Art Thou come to torment us before the time?' (See on Mr 1:24). Behold the tormentor anticipating, dreading, and entreating exemption from torment! In Christ they discern their destined Tormentor; the time, they know, is fixed, and they feel as if it were come already! (Jas 2:19).

8. For he said unto him – that is, before the unclean spirit cried out.

Come out of the man, unclean spirit! – Ordinarily, obedience to a command of this nature was immediate. But here, a certain delay is permitted, the more signally to manifest the power of Christ and accomplish His purposes.

9. And he asked him, What is thy name? – The object of this question was to extort an acknowledgment of the virulence of demoniacal power by which this victim was enthralled.

And he answered, saying, My name is Legion: for we are many – or, as in Luke (Lu 8:30) 'because many devils [demons] were entered into him.' A legion, in the Roman army, amounted, at its full complement, to six thousand; but here the word is used, as such words with us, and even this one, for an indefinitely large number – large enough however to rush, as soon as permission was given, into two thousand swine and destroy them.

10. And he besought him much that he would not send them away out of the country – The entreaty, it will be observed, was made by one spirit, but in behalf of many – 'he besought Him not to send them' – just as in Mr 5:9, 'he answered we are many.' But what do they mean by entreating so earnestly not to be ordered out of the country? Their next petition (Mr 5:12) will make that clear enough.

11. Now there was there, nigh unto the mountains – rather, 'to the mountain,' according to what is clearly the true reading. In Mt 8:30, they are said to have been 'a good way off.' But these expressions, far from being inconsistent, only confirm, by their precision, the minute accuracy of the narrative.

a great herd of swine feeding – There can hardly be any doubt that the owners of these were Jews, since to them our Lord had now come to proffer His services. This will explain what follows.

12. And all the devils besought him, saying – 'if thou cast us out' (Mt 8:31).

Send us into the swine, that we may enter into them – Had they spoken out all their mind, perhaps this would have been it: 'If we must quit our hold of this man, suffer us to continue our work of mischief in another form, that by entering these swine, and thus destroying the people's property, we may steel their hearts against Thee!'

13. And forthwith Jesus gave them leave – In Matthew (Mt 8:32) this is given with majestic brevity – 'Go!' The owners, if Jews, drove an illegal trade; if heathens, they insulted the national religion: in either case the permission was just.

And the unclean spirits went out – of the man.

and entered into the swine: and the herd ran violently – rushed.

down a steep place – down the hanging cliff.

into the sea (they were about two thousand)

– The number of them is given by this graphic Evangelist alone.

and were choked in the sea – 'perished in the waters' (Mt 8:32).

14. And they that fed the swine fled, and told it – 'told everything, and what was befallen to the possessed of the devils' (Mt 8:33).

in the city, and in the country. And they went out to see what it was that was done – Thus had they the evidence, both of the herdsmen and of their own senses, to the reality of both miracles.

15. And they come to Jesus – Matthew (Mt 8:34) says, 'Behold, the whole city came out to meet Jesus.'

and see him that was possessed with the devil – the demonized person.

and had the legion, sitting – 'at the feet of Jesus,' adds Luke (Lu 8:35); in contrast with his former wild and wandering habits.

and clothed – As our Evangelist had not told us that he 'ware no clothes,' the meaning of this statement could only have been conjectured but for 'the beloved physician' (Lu 8:27), who supplies the missing piece of information here. This is a striking case of what are called Undesigned Coincidences amongst the different Evangelists; one of them taking a thing for granted, as familiarly known at the time, but which we should never have known but for one or more of the others, and without the knowledge of which some of their statements would be unintelligible. The clothing which the poor man would feel the want of the moment his consciousness returned to him, was doubtless supplied to him by some of the Twelve.

and in his right mind – but now, oh, in what a lofty sense! (Compare an analogous, though a different kind of case, Da 4:34–37).

and they were afraid – Had this been awe only, it had been natural enough; but other feelings, alas! of a darker kind, soon showed themselves.

16. And they that saw it told them how it befell to him that was possessed with the devil – ('the demonized person').

and also concerning the swine – Thus had they the double testimony of the herdsmen and their own senses.

17. And they began to pray him to depart out of their coasts – Was it the owners only of the valuable property now lost to them that did this? Alas, no! For Luke (Lu 8:37) says, 'Then the whole .multitude of the country of the Gadarenes round about besought Him to depart from them; for they were taken with great fear.' The evil spirits had thus, alas! their object. Irritated, the people could not suffer His presence; yet awe-struck, they dared not order Him off: so they entreat Him to withdraw, and – He takes them at their word.

18. he that had been possessed with the devil prayed him that he might be with him – the grateful heart, fresh from the hand of demons, clinging to its wondrous Benefactor. How exquisitely natural!

19. Howbeit, Jesus suffered him not – To be a missionary for Christ, in the region where he was so well known and so long dreaded, was a far nobler calling than to follow Him where nobody had ever heard of him, and where other trophies not less illustrious could be raised by the same power and grace.

20. And he departed, and began to publish – not only among his friends, to whom Jesus immediately sent him, but

in Decapolis – so called, as being a region of ten cities.

how great things Jesus had done for him: and all men did marvel – Throughout that considerable region did this monument of mercy proclaim his new-found Lord; and some, it is to be hoped, did more than 'marvel.'

Mr 5:21–43.
The daughter of Jairus raised to life – the woman with an issue of blood healed.
(= Mt 9:18–26 Lu 8:41–56).

The occasion of this scene will appear presently.

Jairus' daughter (Mr 5:21–24)

21. And when Jesus was passed over again by ship unto the other side – from the Gadarene side of the lake, where He had parted with the healed demoniac, to the west side, at Capernaum.

much people gathered unto him – who 'gladly received Him; for they were all waiting for Him' (Lu 8:40). The abundant teaching earlier that day (Mr 4:1, and Mt 13:1–58) had only whetted the people's appetite: and disappointed, as would seem, that He had left them in the evening to cross the lake, they remain hanging about the beach, having got a hint, probably through some of His disciples, that He would be back the same evening. Perhaps they witnessed at a distance the sudden calming of the tempest. The tide of our Lord's popularity was now fast rising.

22. And, behold, there cometh one of the rulers of the synagogue – of which class there were but few who believed in Jesus (Joh 7:48). One would suppose from this that the ruler had been with the multitude on the shore, anxiously awaiting the return of Jesus, and immediately on His arrival had accosted Him as here related. But Matthew (Mt 9:18) tells us that the ruler came to Him while He was in the act of speaking at His own table on the subject of fasting; and as we must suppose that this converted publican ought to know what took place on that memorable occasion when he made a feast to his Lord, we conclude that here the right order is indicated by the First Evangelist alone.

Jairus by name – or 'Jaeirus.' It is the same name as Jair, in the Old Testament (Nu 32:41 Jud 10:3 Es 2:5).

and when he saw him, he fell at his feet – in Matthew (Mt 9:18), 'worshipped Him.' The meaning is the same in both.

23. **And besought him greatly, saying, My little daughter** – Luke (Lu 8:42) says, 'He had one only daughter, about twelve years of age.' According to a well-known rabbin, quoted by LIGHTFOOT, a daughter, till she had completed her twelfth year, was called 'little,' or 'a little maid'; after that, 'a young woman.'

lieth at the point of death – Matthew (Mt 9:18) gives it thus: 'My daughter is even now dead' – 'has just expired.' The news of her death reached the father after the cure of the woman with the issue of blood: but Matthew's brief account gives only the result, as in the case of the centurion's servant (Mt 8:5).

come and lay thy hands on her, that she may be healed; and she shall live – or, 'that she may be healed and live,' according to a fully preferable reading. In one of the class to which this man belonged, so steeped in prejudice, such faith would imply more than in others.

The woman with an issue of blood healed (Mr 5:24–34)

24. **And Jesus went with him; and much people followed him, and thronged him** – The word in Luke (Lu 8:42) is stronger – 'choked,' 'stifled Him.'

26. **And had suffered many things of many physicians** – The expression perhaps does not necessarily refer to the suffering she endured under medical treatment, but to the much varied treatment which she underwent.

and had spent all that she had, and was nothing bettered, but rather grew worse – pitiable case, and affectingly aggravated; emblem of our natural state as fallen creatures (Eze 16:5,6), and illustrating the worse than vanity of all human remedies for spiritual maladies (Ho 5:13). The higher design of all our Lord's miracles of healing irresistibly suggests this way of viewing the present case, the propriety of which will still more appear as we proceed.

27. **When she had heard of Jesus, came** – This was the right experiment at last. What had she 'heard of Jesus?' No doubt it was His marvellous cures she had heard of; and the hearing of these, in connection with her bitter experience of the vanity of applying to any other, had been blessed to the kindling in her soul of a firm confidence that He who had so willingly wrought such cures on others was able and would not refuse to heal her also.

in the press behind – shrinking, yet seeking.

touched his garment – According to the ceremonial law, the touch of anyone having the disease which this woman had would have defiled the person touched. Some think that the recollection of this may account for her stealthily approaching Him in the crowd behind, and touching but the hem of His garment. But there was an instinct in the faith which brought her to Jesus, which taught her, that if that touch could set her free from the defiling disease itself, it was impossible to communicate defilement to Him, and that this wondrous Healer must be above such laws.

28. **For she said** – 'within herself' (Mt 9:21).

If I may touch but his clothes, I shall be whole – that is, if I may but come in contact with this glorious Healer at all. Remarkable faith this!

29. **And straightway the fountain of her blood was dried up** – Not only was her issue of blood stanched (Lu 8:44), but the cause of it was thoroughly removed, insomuch that by her bodily sensations she immediately knew herself perfectly cured.

30. **And Jesus immediately knowing in himself that virtue** – or 'efficacy.'

had gone out of him – He was conscious of the forthgoing of His healing power, which was not – as in prophets and apostles – something foreign to Himself and imparted merely, but what He had dwelling within Him as 'His own fulness.'

turned him about in the press – crowd.

and said, Who touched my clothes?

31. **And his disciples said unto him** – Luke says (Lu 8:45), 'When all denied, Peter and they that were with Him said, Master.'

Thou seest the multitude thronging thee, and sayest thou, Who touched me? – 'Askest thou, Lord, who touched Thee? Rather ask who touched Thee not in such a throng.' 'And Jesus said, Somebody hath touched Me' – 'a certain person has touched Me' – 'for I perceive that virtue is gone out of Me' (Lu 8:46). Yes, the multitude 'thronged and pressed Him' – they jostled against Him, but all involuntarily; they were merely carried along; but one, one only – 'a certain person – TOUCHED HIM,' with the conscious, voluntary, dependent touch of faith, reaching forth its hand expressly to have contact with Him. This and this only Jesus acknowledges and seeks out. Even so, as AUGUSTINE long ago said, multitudes still come similarly close to Christ in the means of grace, but all to no purpose, being only sucked into the crowd. The voluntary, living contact of faith is that electric conductor which alone draws virtue out of Him.

32. **And he looked round about to see her that had done this thing** – not for the purpose of summoning forth a culprit, but, as we shall presently see, to obtain from the healed one a testimony to what He had done for her.

33. **But the woman, fearing and trembling,**

knowing what was done in her – alarmed, as a humble, shrinking female would naturally be, at the necessity of so public an exposure of herself, yet conscious that she had a tale to tell which would speak for her.

came and fell down before him, and told him all the truth – In Luke (Lu 8:47) it is, 'When the woman saw that she was not hid, she came trembling, and falling down before Him, she declared unto Him before all the people for what cause she had touched Him, and how she was healed immediately.' This, though it tried the modesty of the believing woman, was just what Christ wanted in dragging her forth, her public testimony to the facts of her case – the disease, with her abortive efforts at a cure, and the instantaneous and perfect relief which her touching the Great Healer had brought her.

34. And he said unto her, Daughter – 'be of good comfort' (Lu 8:48).

thy faith hath made thee whole; go in peace, and be whole of thy plague – Though healed as soon as she believed, it seemed to her a stolen cure – she feared to acknowledge it. Jesus therefore sets His royal seal upon it. But what a glorious dismissal from the lips of Him who is 'our Peace' is that, 'Go in peace!'

Jairus' daughter raised to life (Mr 5:35–43)

35. Thy daughter is dead; why troublest thou the Master any further? – the Teacher.

36. he saith unto the ruler of the synagogue, Be not afraid, only believe – Jesus, knowing how the heart of the agonized father would sink at the tidings, and the reflections at the delay which would be apt to rise in his mind, hastens to reassure him, and in His accustomed style: 'Be not afraid, only believe' – words of unchanging preciousness and power! How vividly do such incidents bring out Christ's knowledge of the human heart and tender sympathy! (Heb 4:15).

38. And he cometh – rather, 'they come.'

to the house of the ruler of the synagogue, and seeth the tumult, and them that wept and wailed greatly – 'the minstrels and the people making a noise' (Mt 9:23) – lamenting for the dead. (See 2Ch 35:25 Jer 9:20 Am 5:16.)

39. And when he was come in, he saith unto them, Why make ye this ado, and weep? the damsel is not dead, but sleepeth – so brief her state of death as to be more like a short sleep.

40. And they laughed him to scorn – rather, simply, 'laughed at Him' – 'knowing that she was dead' (Lu 8:53); an important testimony this to the reality of her death.

But when he had put them all out – The word is strong – 'turned them all out'; meaning all those who were making this noise, and any others that may have been there from sympathy, that only those might be present who were most

nearly concerned, and those whom He had Himself brought as witnesses of the great act about to be done.

he taketh the father and the mother of the damsel, and them that were with him – Peter, and James, and John.

and entereth in where the damsel was lying.

41. And he took the damsel by the hand – as He did Peter's mother-in-law (Mr 1:31).

and said unto her, Talitha cumi – The words are Aramaic, or Syro-Chaldaic, the then language of Palestine. Mark loves to give such wonderful words just as they were spoken. See Mr 7:34 14:36.

42. And straightway the damsel – The word here is different from that in Mr 5:39–41, and signifies 'young maiden,' or 'little girl.'

arose, and walked – a vivid touch evidently from an eye-witness.

And they were astonished with a great astonishment – The language here is the strongest.

43. And he charged them straitly – strictly.

that no man should know it – The only reason we can assign for this is His desire not to let the public feeling regarding Him come too precipitately to a crisis.

and commanded that something should be given her to eat – in token of perfect restoration.

Chapter 6

Mr 6:1–6.

Christ rejected at Nazareth.

(= Mt 13:54–58 Lu 4:16–30).

See on Lu 4:16–30.

Mr 6:7–13.

Mission of the twelve apostles.

(= Mt 10:1,5–15 Lu 9:1–6).

See on Mt 10:1; Mt 10:5–15.

Mr 6:14–29.

Herod thinks Jesus a resurrection of the murdered Baptist – account of his death.

(= Mt 14:1–12 Lu 9:7–9).

Herod's view of Christ (Mr 6:14–16)

14. And King Herod – that is, Herod Antipas, one of the three sons of Herod the Great, and own brother of Archelaus (Mt 2:22), who ruled as ethnarch over Galilee and Perea.

heard of him; (for his name was spread abroad); and he said – 'unto his servants' (Mt 14:2), his councillors or court ministers.

That John the Baptist was risen from the dead – The murdered prophet haunted his guilty breast like a spectre, and seemed to him alive again and clothed with unearthly powers, in the person of Jesus.

16. But when Herod heard thereof, he said, It

is John, whom I beheaded; he is risen from the dead – 'himself has risen'; as if the innocence and sanctity of his faithful reprover had not suffered that he should lie long dead.

Account of the Baptist's imprisonment and death (Mr 6:17–29)

17. For Herod himself had sent forth, and laid hold upon John, and bound him in prison – in the castle of Machaerus, near the southern extremity of Herod's dominions, and adjoining the Dead Sea [JOSEPHUS, *Antiquities*, 18.5,2].

for Herodias' sake – She was the granddaughter of Herod the Great.

his brother Philip's wife – and therefore the niece of both brothers. This Philip, however, was not the tetrarch of that name mentioned in Lu 3:1, but one whose distinctive name was 'Herod Philip,' another son of Herod the Great – who was disinherited by his father. Herod Antipas' own wife was the daughter of Aretas, king of Arabia; but he prevailed on Herodias, his half-brother Philip's wife, to forsake her husband and live with him, on condition, says JOSEPHUS [*Antiquities*, 18.5,1], that he should put away his own wife. This involved him afterwards in war with Aretas, who totally defeated him and destroyed his army, from the effects of which he was never able to recover himself.

18. For John had said unto Herod, It is not lawful for thee to have thy brother's wife – Noble fidelity! It was not lawful because Herod's wife and Herodias, husband were both living; and further, because the parties were within the forbidden degrees of consanguinity (see Le 20:21); Herodias being the daughter of Aristobulus, the brother of both Herod and Philip [JOSEPHUS, *Antiquities*, 18.5,4].

19. Therefore Herodias had a quarrel against him – rather, as in the Margin, 'had a grudge against him.' Probably she was too proud to speak to him; still less would she quarrel with him.

20. For Herod feared John – but, as BENGEL notes, John feared not Herod.

knowing that he was a just man and an holy – Compare the case of Elijah with Ahab, after the murder of Naboth (1Ki 21:20).

and observed him – rather, as in the Margin, 'kept' or 'saved him'; that is, from the wicked designs of Herodias, who had been watching for some pretext to get Herod entangled and committed to despatch him.

and when he heard him, he did many things – many good things under the influence of the Baptist on his conscience.

and heard him gladly – a striking statement this, for which we are indebted to our graphic Evangelist alone, illustrating the working of contrary principles in the slaves of passion. But this only shows how far Herodias must have

wrought upon him, as Jezebel upon Ahab, that he should at length agree to what his awakened conscience kept him long from executing.

21. And when a convenient day – for the purposes of Herodias.

was come, that Herod – rather, 'A convenient day being come,' when Herod.

on his birthday, made a supper to his lords, high captains, and chief estates of Galilee – This graphic minuteness of detail adds much to the interest of the tragic narrative.

22. And when the daughter of the said Herodias – that is, – her daughter by her proper husband, Herod Philip: Her name was Salome [JOSEPHUS, *Antiquities*, 18.5,4].

came in and danced, and pleased Herod and them that sat with him, the king said unto the damsel – 'the girl' (See on Mr 5:42).

23. And he – the king, so called, but only by courtesy (see on Mr 6:14).

sware unto her, Whatsoever thou shalt ask of me, unto the half of my kingdom – Those in whom passion and luxury have destroyed self-command will in a capricious moment say and do what in their cool moments they bitterly regret.

24. And she said, The head of John the Baptist – Abandoned women are more shameless and heartless than men. The Baptist's fidelity marred the pleasures of Herodias, and this was too good an opportunity of getting rid of him to let slip.

25. I will that thou give me by and by – rather, 'at once.'

in a charger – large, flat trencher –

the head of John the Baptist.

26. And the king was exceeding sorry – With his feelings regarding John, and the truths which so told upon his conscience from that preacher's lips, and after so often and carefully saving him from his paramour's rage, it must have been very galling to find himself at length entrapped by his own rash folly.

yet for his oath's sake – See how men of no principle, but troublesome conscience, will stick at breaking a rash oath, while yielding to the commission of the worst crimes!

and for their sakes which sat with him – under the influence of that false shame, which could not brook being thought to be troubled with religious or moral scruples. To how many has this proved a fatal snare!

27. And immediately the king sent an executioner – one of the guards in attendance. The word is Roman, denoting one of the Imperial Guard.

and commanded his head to be brought: and he went and beheaded him in the prison – after, it would seem, more than twelve months' imprisonment. Blessed martyr! Dark and cheerless was the end reserved for thee: but now thou hast thy Master's benediction, 'Blessed is he whosoever shall not be offended in Me' (Mt 11:6), and hast found the life thou gavest away (Mt 10:39). But where are they in whose skirts is found thy blood?

28. And brought his head in a charger, and gave it to the damsel: and the damsel gave it to her mother – Herodias did not shed the blood of the stern reprover; she only got it done, and then gloated over it, as it streamed from the trunkless head.

29. And when his disciples heard of it – that is, the Baptist's own disciples.

they came and took up his corpse, and laid it in a tomb – 'and went and told Jesus' (Mt 14:12). If these disciples had, up to this time, stood apart from Him, as adherents of John (Mt 11:2), perhaps they now came to Jesus, not without some secret reflection on Him for His seeming neglect of their master; but perhaps, too, as orphans, to cast in their lot henceforth with the Lord's disciples. How Jesus felt, or what He said, on receiving this intelligence, is not recorded; but He of whom it was said, as He stood by the grave of His friend Lazarus, 'Jesus wept,' was not likely to receive such intelligence without deep emotion. And one reason why He might not be unwilling that a small body of John's disciples should cling to him to the last, might be to provide some attached friends who should do for his precious body, on a small scale, what was afterwards to be done for His own.

Mr 6:30–56.

The Twelve on their return, having reported the success of their mission, Jesus crosses the Sea of Galilee with them, teaches the people, and miraculously feeds them to the number of five thousand – he sends his disciples by ship again to the western side, while he himself returns afterwards walking on the sea – incidents on landing.

(= Mt 14:13–36 Lu 9:10–17 Joh 6:1–24).

Here, for the first time, all the four streams of sacred text run parallel. The occasion and all the circumstances of this grand section are thus brought before us with a vividness quite remarkable.

Five thousand miraculously fed (Mr 6:30–44)

30. And the apostles gathered themselves together – probably at Capernaum, on returning from their mission (Mr 6:7–13).

and told him all things, both what they had done, and what they had taught – Observe the various reasons He had for crossing to the other side. First, Matthew (Mt 14:13) says, that 'when Jesus heard' of the murder of His faithful fore-runner – from those attached disciples of his who had taken up his body and laid it in a sepulchre (see on Mr 6:29) – 'He departed by ship into a desert place apart'; either to avoid some apprehended consequences to Himself, arising from the Baptist's death (Mt 10:23), or more probably to be able to indulge in those feelings which that affecting event had doubtless awakened, and to which the bustle of the multitude around Him was very unfavourable. Next, since He must have heard the report of the Twelve with the deepest interest, and probably with something of the emotion which He experienced on the return of the Seventy, He sought privacy for undisturbed reflection on this begun preaching and progress of His kingdom. Once more, He was wearied with the multitude of 'comers and goers' – depriving Him even of leisure enough to take His food – and wanted rest: 'Come ye yourselves apart into a desert place, and rest a while,' &c. Under the combined influence of all these considerations, our Lord sought this change.

32. And they departed into a desert place by ship privately – 'over the Sea of Galilee, which is the Sea of Tiberias,' says John (Joh 6:1), the only one of the Evangelists who so fully describes it; the others having written when their readers were supposed to know something of it, while the last wrote for those at a greater distance of time and place. This 'desert place' is more definitely described by Luke (Lu 9:10) as 'belonging to the city called Bethsaida.' This must not be confounded with the town so called on the western side of the lake. This town lay on its northeastern side, near where the Jordan empties itself into it: in Gaulonitis, out of the dominions of Herod Antipas, and within the dominions of Philip the Tetrarch (Lu 3:1), who raised it from a village to a city, and called it Julias, in honour of Julia, the daughter of Augustus [JOSEPHUS, *Antiquities*, 18.2,1].

33. And the people – the multitudes.

saw them departing, and many knew him – The true reading would seem to be: 'And many saw them departing, and knew or recognized [them].'

and ran afoot – Here, perhaps, it should be rendered 'by land' – running round by the head of the lake, and taking one of the fords of the river, so as to meet Jesus, who was crossing with the Twelve by ship.

thither out of all cities, and outwent them – got before them.

and came together unto him – How exceedingly graphic is this! every touch of it betokening the presence of an eye-witness. John (Joh 6:3) says, that 'Jesus went up into a mountain' – somewhere in that hilly range, the green table-land which skirts the eastern side of the lake.

34. And Jesus, when he came out of the ship – having gone on shore.

saw much people – a great multitude.

and was moved with compassion toward them, because they were as sheep not having a shepherd – At the sight of the multitudes who had followed Him by land and even got before Him, He was so moved, as was His wont in such cases, with compassion, because they were like shepherdless sheep, as to forego both privacy and rest that He might minister to them. Here we have an important piece of information from the Fourth Evangelist (Joh 6:4), 'And the Passover, a feast of the Jews, was nigh' – rather, 'Now the Passover, the feast of the Jews, was nigh.' This accounts for the multitudes that now crowded around Him. They were on their way to keep that festival at Jerusalem. But Jesus did not go up to this festival, as John expressly tells us, (Joh 7:1) – remaining in Galilee, because the ruling Jews sought to kill Him.

35. And when the day was now far spent – 'began to wear away' or 'decline,' says Luke (Lu 9:12). Matthew (Mt 14:15) says, 'when it was evening'; and yet he mentions a later evening of the same day (Mr 6:23). This earlier evening began at three p.m.; the latter began at sunset.

36. Send them away, that they may go into the country round about, and into the villages, and buy themselves bread: for they have nothing to eat – John tells us (Joh 6:5,6) that 'Jesus said to Philip, Whence shall we buy bread, that these may eat? (And this He said to prove him: for He Himself knew what He would do).' The subject may have been introduced by some remark of the disciples; but the precise order and form of what was said by each can hardly be gathered with precision, nor is it of any importance.

37. He answered and said unto them – 'They need not depart' (Mt 14:10).

Give ye them to eat – doubtless said to prepare them for what was to follow.

And they say unto him, Shall we go and buy two hundred pennyworth of bread, and give them to eat? – 'Philip answered Him, Two hundred pennyworth of bread is not sufficient for them, that every one of them may take a little' (Joh 6:7).

38. He saith unto them, How many loaves have ye? go and see. And when they knew, they say, Five, and two fishes – John is more precise and full: 'One of His disciples, Andrew, Simon Peter's brother, saith unto Him, There is a lad here which hath five barley loaves and two small fishes: but what are they among so many?' (Joh 6:8,9). Probably this was the whole stock of provisions then at the command of the disciples – no more than enough for one meal to them – and entrusted for the time to this lad. 'He said, Bring them hither to me' (Mt 14:18).

39. And he commanded them to make all sit down by companies upon the green grass – or 'green hay'; the rank grass of those bushy wastes. For, as John (Joh 6:10) notes, 'there was much grass in the place.'

40. And they sat down in ranks, by hundreds, and by fifties – Doubtless this was to show at a glance the number fed, and to enable all to witness in an orderly manner this glorious miracle.

41. And when he had taken the five loaves and the two fishes, he looked up to heaven – Thus would the most distant of them see distinctly what He was doing.

and blessed – John (Joh 6:11) says, 'And when he had given thanks.' The sense is the same. This thanksgiving for the meal, and benediction of it as the food of thousands, was the crisis of the miracle.

and brake the loaves, and gave them to his disciples to set before them – thus virtually holding forth these men as His future ministers.

42. And they did all eat, and were filled – All the four Evangelists mention this: and John (Joh 6:11) adds, 'and likewise of the fishes, as much as they would' – to show that vast as was the multitude, and scanty the provisions, the meal to each and all of them was a plentiful one. 'When they were filled, He said unto His disciples, Gather up the fragments that remain, that nothing be lost' (Joh 6:12). This was designed to bring out the whole extent of the miracle.

43. And they took up twelve baskets full of the fragments, and of the fishes – 'Therefore (says Joh 6:13), they gathered them together, and filled twelve baskets with the fragments of the five barley loaves, which remained over and above unto them that had eaten.' The article here rendered 'baskets' in all the four narratives was part of the luggage taken by Jews on a journey – to carry, it is said, both their provisions and hay to sleep on, that they might not have to depend on Gentiles, and so run the risk of ceremonial pollution. In this we have a striking corroboration of the truth of the four narratives. Internal evidence renders it clear, we think, that the first three Evangelists wrote independently of each other, though the fourth must have seen all the others. But here, each of the first three Evangelists uses the same word to express the apparently insignificant circumstance that the baskets employed to gather up the fragments were of the kind which even the Roman satirist, JUVENAL, knew by the name of cophinus, while in both the narratives of the feeding of the Four Thousand the baskets used are expressly said to have been of the kind called spuris. (See Mr 8:19,20.)

44. And they that did eat of the loaves were about five thousand men – 'besides women and children' (Mt 14:21). Of these, however, there would probably not be many; as only the males were obliged to go to the approaching festival.

Jesus recrosses to the western side of the lake walking on the sea (Mr 6:45–52)

One very important particular given by John alone (Joh 6:15) introduces this portion: 'When Jesus therefore perceived that they would take Him by force, to make Him a king, He departed again into a mountain Himself alone.'

45. And straightway he constrained his disciples to get into the ship, and to go to the other side before – Him.

unto Bethsaida – Bethsaida of Galilee (Joh 12:21). John (Joh 6:17) says they 'went over the sea towards Capernaum' – the wind, probably, occasioning this slight deviation from the direction of Bethsaida.

while he sent away the people – 'the multitude.' His object in this was to put an end to the misdirected excitement in His favour (Joh 6:15), into which the disciples themselves may have been somewhat drawn. The word 'constrained' implies reluctance on their part, perhaps from unwillingness to part with their Master and embark at night, leaving Him alone on the mountain.

46. And when he had sent them away, he departed into a mountain to pray – thus at length getting that privacy and rest which He had vainly sought during the earlier part of the day; opportunity also to pour out His soul in connection with the extraordinary excitement in His favour that evening – which appears to have marked the zenith of His reputation, for it began to decline the very next day; and a place whence He might watch the disciples on the lake, pray for them in their extremity, and observe the right time for coming to them, in a new manifestation of His glory, on the sea.

47. And when even was come – the later evening (see on Mr 6:35). It had come even when the disciples embarked (Mt 14:23 Joh 6:16).

the ship was in the midst of the sea, and he alone on the land – John says (Joh 6:17), 'It was now dark, and Jesus was not come to them.' Perhaps they made no great effort to push across at first, having a lingering hope that their Master would yet join them, and so allowed the darkness to come on. 'And the sea arose' (adds the beloved disciple, Joh 6:18), 'by reason of a great wind that blew.'

48. And he saw them toiling in rowing; for the wind was contrary unto them – putting forth all their strength to buffet the waves and bear on against a head wind, but to little effect. He 'saw' this from His mountain top, and through the darkness of the night, for His heart was all with them: yet would He not go to their relief till His own time came.

and about the fourth watch of the night – The Jews, who used to divide the night into three watches, latterly adopted the Roman division into four watches, as here. So that, at the rate of three hours to each, the fourth watch, reckoning from six P.M., would be three o'clock in the morning. 'So when they had rowed about five and twenty or thirty furlongs' (Joh 6:19) – rather more than halfway across. The lake is about seven miles broad at its widest part. So that in eight or nine hours they had only made some three and a half miles. By this time, therefore, they must have been in a state of exhaustion and despondency bordering on despair; and now at length, having tried them long enough.

he cometh unto them, walking upon the sea – 'and draweth nigh unto the ship' (Joh 6:19).

and would have passed by them – but only in the sense of Lu 24:28 Ge 32:26; compare Ge 18:3,5 42:7.

49. But when they saw him walking upon the sea, they supposed it had been a spirit, and cried out – 'for fear' (Mt 14:26). He would appear to them at first like a dark moving speck upon the waters; then as a human figure; but in the dark tempestuous sky, and not dreaming that it could be their Lord, they take it for a spirit. Compare Lu 24:37.

50. For they all saw him, and were troubled. And immediately he talked with them, and saith unto them, Be of good cheer: It is I; be not afraid – There is something in these two little words – given by Matthew, Mark and John (Mt 14:27 Mr 6:50 Joh 6:20) – 'It is I,' which from the mouth that spake it and the circumstances in which it was uttered, passes the power of language to express. Here were they in the midst of a raging sea, their little bark the sport of the elements, and with just enough of light to descry an object on the waters which only aggravated their fears. But Jesus deems it enough to dispel all apprehension to let them know that He was there. From other lips that 'I am' would have merely meant that the person speaking was such a one and not another person. That, surely, would have done little to calm the fears of men expecting every minute, it may be, to go to the bottom. But spoken by One who at that moment was 'treading upon the waves of the sea,' and was about to hush the raging elements with His word, what was it but the Voice which cried of old in the ears of Israel, even from the days of Moses, 'I AM'; 'I, EVEN I, AM HE!' Compare Joh 18:5,6 8:58. Now, that Word is 'made flesh, and dwells among us,' uttering itself from beside us in dear familiar tones – 'It is the Voice of my Beloved!' How far was this apprehended by these frightened disciples? There was one, we know, in the boat who outstripped all the rest in susceptibility to such sublime appeals. It was not the deep-toned writer of the Fourth Gospel, who, though he lived to soar beyond all the apostles, was as yet too young for prominence, and all unripe. It was Simon

Barjonas. Here follows a very remarkable and instructive episode, recorded by Matthew alone:

51. And he went up unto them into the ship – John (Joh 6:21) says, 'Then they willingly received him into the ship' – or rather, 'Then were they willing to receive Him' (with reference to their previous terror); but implying also a glad welcome, their first fears now converted into wonder and delight. 'And immediately,' adds the beloved disciple, 'they were at the land whither they went,' or 'were bound.' This additional miracle, for as such it is manifestly related, is recorded by the fourth Evangelist alone. As the storm was suddenly calmed, so the little bark – propelled by the secret power of the Lord of nature now sailing in it – glided through the now unruffled waters, and, while they were wrapt in wonder at what had happened, not heeding their rapid motion, was found at port, to their still further surprise.

> 'Then are they glad, because at rest
> And quiet now they be;
> So to the haven He them brings
> Which they desired to see.'

Matthew (Mt 14:33) says, 'Then they that were in the ship came [that is, ere they got to land] and worshipped him, saying, Of a truth Thou art the Son of God.' But our Evangelist is wonderfully striking.

and the wind ceased and they were sore amazed in themselves beyond measure, and wondered – The Evangelist seems hardly to find language strong enough to express their astonishment.

52. For they considered not the miracle of the loaves; for their heart was hardened – What a singular statement! The meaning seems to be that if they had but 'considered [reflected upon] the miracle of the loaves,' wrought but a few hours before, they would have wondered at nothing which He might do within the whole circle of power and grace.

Incidents on Landing (Mr 6:53–56)

The details here are given with a rich vividness quite peculiar to this charming Gospel.

53. And when they had passed over, they came into the land of Gennesaret – from which the lake sometimes takes its name, stretching along its western shore. Capernaum was their landing-place (Joh 6:24,25).

and drew to the shore – a nautical phrase, nowhere else used in the New Testament.

54. And when they were come out of the ship, straightway they knew him – 'immediately they recognized Him'; that is, the people did.

55. and began to carry about in beds those that were sick, where they heard he was – At this period of our Lord's ministry the popular enthusiasm in His favour was at its height.

56. and besought him that they might touch if it were but the border of his garment – having heard, no doubt, of what the woman with the issue of blood experienced on doing so (Mr 5:25–29), and perhaps of other unrecorded cases of the same nature.

and as many as touched him – or 'it' – the border of His garment.

were made whole – All this they continued to do and to experience while our Lord was in that region. The time corresponds to that mentioned (Joh 7:1), when He 'walked in Galilee,' instead of appearing in Jerusalem at the Passover, 'because the Jews,' that is, the rulers, 'sought to kill Him' – while the people sought to enthrone Him!

Chapter 7

Mr 7:1–23.
Discourse on ceremonial pollution.
(= Mt 15:1–20).
See on Mt 15:1–20.

Mr 7:24–37.

The Syrophoenician woman and her daughter – a deaf and dumb man healed.
(= Mt 15:21–31).

The Syrophoenician woman and her daughter (Mr 7:24–30)

The first words of this narrative show that the incident followed, in point of time, immediately on what precedes it.

24. And from thence he arose, and went into the borders – or 'unto the borders.'

of Tyre and Sidon – the two great Phoenician seaports, but here denoting the territory generally, to the frontiers of which Jesus now came. But did Jesus actually enter this heathen territory? The whole narrative, we think, proceeds upon the supposition that He did. His immediate object seems to have been to avoid the wrath of the Pharisees at the withering exposure He had just made of their traditional religion.

and entered into an house, and would have no man know it – because He had not come there to minister to heathens. But though not 'sent but to the lost sheep of the house of Israel' (Mt 15:24), He hindered not the lost sheep of the vast Gentile world from coming to Him, nor put them away when they did come – as this incident was designed to show.

but he could not be hid – Christ's fame had early spread from Galilee to this very region (Mr 3:8 Lu 6:17).

25. For a certain woman, whose young daughter had an unclean spirit – or, as in Matthew (Mt 15:22), 'was badly demonized.'

heard of him – One wonders how; but distress is quick of hearing.

26. **The woman was a Greek** – that is, 'a Gentile,' as in the Margin.

a Syrophoenician by nation – so called as inhabiting the Phoenician tract of Syria. JUVENAL uses the same term, as was remarked by JUSTIN MARTYR and TERTULLIAN. Matthew (Mt 15:22) calls her 'a woman of Canaan' – a more intelligible description to his Jewish readers (compare Jud 1:30,32,33).

and she besought him that he would cast forth the devil out of her daughter – 'She cried unto Him, saying, Have mercy on me, O Lord, Son of David: my daughter is grievously vexed with a devil' (Mt 15:22). Thus, though no Israelite herself, she salutes Him as Israel's promised Messiah. Here we must go to Mt 15:23–25 for some important links in the dialogue omitted by our Evangelist.

27. **But Jesus said unto her, Let the children first be filled** – 'Is there hope for me here? Filled FIRST?' 'Then my turn, it seems, is coming! ' – but then, 'The CHILDREN first? Ah! when, on that rule, shall my turn ever come!' But ere she has time for these ponderings of His word, another word comes to supplement it.

for it is not meet to take the children's bread, and to cast it unto the dogs – Is this the death of her hopes? Nay, rather it is life from the dead. Out of the eater shall come forth meat (Jud 14:14). 'At evening-time, it shall be light' (Zec 14:7). 'Ah! I have it now. Had He kept silence, what could I have done but go unblest? but He hath spoken, and the victory is mine.'

28. **And she answered and said unto him, Yes, Lord** – or, as the same word is rendered in Mt 15:27. 'Truth, Lord.'

yet the dogs eat of the children's crumbs – which fall from their master's table' (Mt 15:27). 'I thank Thee, O blessed One, for that word! That's my whole case. Not of the children? True. A dog? True also: Yet the dogs under the table are allowed to eat of the children's crumbs – the droppings from their master's full table: Give me that, and I am content: One crumb of power and grace from Thy table shall cast the devil out of my daughter.' Oh, what lightning quickness, what reach of instinctive ingenuity, do we behold in this heathen woman!

29. **And he said unto her** – 'O woman, great is thy faith' (Mt 15:28). As BENGEL beautifully remarks, Jesus 'marvelled' only at two things – *faith* and *unbelief* (see Lu 7:9).

For this saying go thy way; the devil is gone out of thy daughter – That moment the deed was done.

30. **And when she was come to her house, she found the devil gone out, and her daughter laid upon the bed** – But Matthew (Mt 15:28) is more specific; 'And her daughter was made whole from that very hour.' The wonderfulness of this case in all its features has been felt in every age

of the Church, and the balm it has administered, and will yet administer, to millions will be known only in that day that shall reveal the secrets of all hearts.

Deaf and Dumb Man Healed (Mr 7:31–37)

31. **And again, departing from the coasts of Tyre and Sidon, he came unto the Sea of Galilee** – or, according to what has very strong claims to be regarded as the true text here, 'And again, departing from the coasts of Tyre, He came through Sidon to the Sea of Galilee.' The manuscripts in favour of this reading, though not the most numerous, are weighty, while the versions agreeing with it are among the most ancient; and all the best critical editors and commentators adopt it. In this case we must understand that our Lord, having once gone out of the Holy Land the length of Tyre, proceeded as far north as Sidon, though without ministering, so far as appears, in those parts, and then bent His steps in a southeasterly direction. There is certainly a difficulty in the supposition of so long a *detour* without any missionary object: and some may think this sufficient to cast the balance in favour of the received reading. Be this as it may, on returning from these coasts of Tyre, He passed

through the midst of the coasts – frontiers.

of Decapolis – crossing the Jordan, therefore, and approaching the lake on its east side. Here Matthew, who omits the details of the cure of this deaf and dumb man, introduces some particulars, from which we learn that it was only one of a great number. 'And Jesus,' says that Evangelist (Mt 15:29–31), 'departed from thence, and came nigh unto the Sea of Galilee, and went up into a mountain' – the mountain range bounding the lake on the northeast, in Decapolis: 'And great multitudes came unto Him, having with them lame, blind, dumb, maimed' – not 'mutilated,' which is but a secondary sense of the word, but 'deformed' – 'and many others, and cast them down at Jesus' feet; and He healed them: insomuch that the multitude [multitudes] wondered, when they saw the dumb to speak, the maimed to be whole, the lame to walk, and the blind to see; and they glorified the God of Israel' – who after so long and dreary an absence of visible manifestation, had returned to bless His people as of old (compare Lu 7:16). Beyond this it is not clear from the Evangelist's language that the people saw into the claims of Jesus. Well, of these cases Mark here singles out one, whose cure had something peculiar in it.

32. **And they bring unto him one that was deaf ... and they beseech him to put his hand upon him** – In their eagerness they appear to have been somewhat too officious. Though

usually doing as here suggested, He will deal with this case in His own way.

33. And he took him aside from the multitude – As in another case He 'took the blind man by the hand and led him out of the town' (Mr 8:23), probably to fix his undistracted attention on Himself, and, by means of certain actions He was about to do, to awaken and direct his attention to the proper source of relief. **and put his fingers into his ears** – As his indistinct articulation arose from his deafness, our Lord addresses Himself to this first. To the impotent man He said, 'Wilt thou be made whole?' to the blind men, 'What will ye that I shall do unto you?' and 'Believe ye that I am able to do this?' (Joh 5:6 Mt 20:32 9:28). But as this patient could *hear* nothing, our Lord substitutes symbolical actions upon each of the organs affected.

and he spit and touched his tongue – moistening the man's parched tongue with saliva from His own mouth, as if to lubricate the organ or facilitate its free motion; thus indicating the source of the healing virtue to be His own person. (For similar actions, see Mr 8:23 Joh 9:6.)

34. And looking up to heaven – ever acknowledging His Father, even while the healing was seen to flow from Himself (see on Joh 5:19).

he sighed – 'over the wreck,' says TRENCH, 'which sin had brought about, and the malice of the devil in deforming the fair features of God's original creation.' But, we take it, there was a yet more painful impression of that 'evil thing and bitter' whence all our ills have sprung, and which, when 'Himself took our infirmities and bare our sicknesses' (Mt 8:17), became mysteriously His own

> In thought of these his brows benign,
> Not even in healing, cloudless shine.
> KEBLE

and saith unto him, Ephphatha, that is, Be opened – Our Evangelist, as remarked on Mr 5:41, loves to give such wonderful words just as they were spoken.

35. And straightway his ears were opened – This is mentioned first as the source of the other derangement.

and the string of his tongue was loosed, and he spake plain – The cure was thus alike instantaneous and perfect.

36. And he charged them that they should tell no man – Into this very region He had sent the man out of whom had been cast the legion of devils, to proclaim 'what the Lord had done for him' (Mr 5:19). Now He will have them 'tell no man.' But in the former case there was no danger of obstructing His ministry by 'blazing the matter' (Mr 1:45), as He Himself had left the region; whereas now He was sojourning in it.

but the more he charged them, so much the more a great deal they published it – They could not be restrained; nay, the prohibition seemed only to whet their determination to publish His fame.

37. And were beyond measure astonished, saying, He hath done all things well – reminding us, says TRENCH, Of the words of the first creation (Ge 1:31, *Septuagint*), upon which we are thus not unsuitably thrown back, for Christ's work is in the truest sense 'a new creation,' **he maketh both the deaf to hear and the dumb to speak** – 'and they glorified the God of Israel' (Mt 15:31). See on Mr 7:31.

Chapter 8

Mr 8:1–26.

Four thousand miraculously fed – a sign from heaven sought and refused – the leaven of the Pharisees and Sadducees – a blind man at Bethsaida restored to sight. (= Mt 15:32–16:12).

This section of miscellaneous matter evidently follows the preceding one in point of time, as will be seen by observing how it is introduced by Matthew.

Feeding of the four thousand (Mr 8:1–9)

2. I have compassion on the multitude – an expression of that deep emotion in the Redeemer's heart which always preceded some remarkable interposition for relief. (See Mt 14:14 20:34 Mr 1:41 Lu 7:13; also Mt 9:36, before the mission of the Twelve; compare Jud 2:18 10:16.)

because they have now been with me – in constant attendance.

three days, and have nothing to eat:

3. And if I send them away fasting to their own houses, they will faint by the way – In their eagerness they seem not to have thought of the need of provisions for such a length of time; but the Lord thought of it. In Matthew (Mt 15:32) it is, 'I will not send them away fasting' – or rather, 'To send them away fasting I am unwilling.'

4. From whence can a man satisfy these men with bread here in the wilderness? – Though the question here is the same as when He fed the five thousand, they evidently *now* meant no more by it than that *they* had not the means of feeding the multitude; modestly leaving the Lord to decide what was to be done. And this will the more appear from His not now trying them, as before, by saying, 'They need not depart, give ye them to eat'; but simply asking what they had, and then giving His directions.

5. And he asked them, How many loaves have ye? And they said, Seven – It was important in this case, as in the former, that the precise number of the loaves should be brought out. Thus also does the distinctness of the two miracles appear.

9. And they that had eaten were about four thousand: and he sent them away – Had not our Lord distinctly referred, in this very chapter and in two successive sentences, to the feeding of the five thousand and of the four thousand as two distinct miracles, many critics would have insisted that they were but two different representations of one and the same miracle, as they do of the two expulsions of the buyers and sellers from the temple, at the beginning and end of our Lord's ministry. But even in spite of what our Lord says, it is painful to find such men as NEANDER endeavouring to identify the two miracles. The localities, though both on the eastern side of the lake, were different; the time was different; the preceding and following circumstances were different; the period during which the people continued fasting was different – in the one case not even one entire day, in the other three days; the number fed was different – five thousand in the one case, in the other four thousand; the number of the loaves was different – five in the one case, in the other seven; the number of the fishes in the one case is definitely stated by all the four Evangelists – two; in the other case both give them indefinitely – 'a few small fishes'; in the one case the multitude were commanded to sit down 'upon the green grass'; in the other 'on the ground'; in the one case the number of the baskets taken up filled with the fragments was twelve, in the other seven; but more than all, perhaps, because apparently quite incidental, in the one case the name given to the kind of baskets used is the same in all the four narratives – the *cophinus* (see on Mr 6:43); in the other case the name given to the kind of baskets used, while it is the same in both the narratives, is quite different – the *spuris,* a basket large enough to hold a man's body, for Paul was let down in one of these from the wall of Damascus (Ac 9:25). It might be added, that in the one case the people, in a frenzy of enthusiasm, would have taken Him by force to make Him a king; in the other case no such excitement is recorded. In view of these things, who could have believed that these were one and the same miracle, even if the Lord Himself had not expressly distinguished them?

Sign from heaven sought (Mr 8:10–13)

10. And straightway he entered into a ship – 'into the ship,' or 'embarked.'

with his disciples, and came into the parts of Dalmanutha – In Matthew (Mt 15:39) it is 'the coasts of Magdala.' Magdala and Dalmanutha were both on the western shore of the lake, and probably not far apart. From the former the surname 'Magdalene' was probably taken, to denote the residence of Mary Magdalene. Dalmanutha may have been a village, but it cannot now be identified with certainty.

11. seeking of him a sign from heaven, tempting him – not in the least desiring evidence for their conviction, but hoping to entrap Him. The first part of the answer is given in Matthew alone (Mt 16:2,3): 'He answered and said unto them, When it is evening, ye say, It will be fair weather; for the sky is red. And in the morning, It will be foul weather to-day: for the sky is red and lowering [sullen, gloomy]. Hypocrites! ye can discern the face of the sky; but can ye not discern the signs of the times?' The same simplicity of purpose and careful observation of the symptoms of approaching events which they showed in common things would enable them to 'discern the signs of the times' – or rather 'seasons,' to which the prophets pointed for the manifestation of Messiah. The sceptre had departed from Judah; Daniel's seventy weeks were expiring; and many other significant indications of the close of the old economy, and preparations for a freer and more comprehensive one, might have been discerned. But all was lost upon them.

12. And he sighed deeply in his spirit – The language is very strong. These glimpses into the interior of the Redeemer's heart, in which our Evangelist abounds, are more precious than rubies. The state of the Pharisaic heart, which prompted this desire for a fresh sign, went to His very soul.

and saith, Why doth this generation – 'this wicked and adulterous generation' (Mt 16:4).

seek after a sign? – when they have had such abundant evidence already.

There shall no sign be given unto this generation – literally, 'If there shall be given to this generation a sign'; a Jewish way of expressing a solemn and peremptory determination to the contrary (compare Heb 4:5 Ps 95:11, *Margin*). 'A generation incapable of appreciating such demonstrations shall not be gratified with them.' In Mt 16:4 He added, 'but the sign of the prophet Jonas.' (See on Mt 12:39,40.)

13. And he left them – no doubt with tokens of displeasure.

The leaven of the Pharisees and Sadducees (Mr 8:14–21)

14. Now the disciples had forgotten to take bread, neither had they in the ship with them more than one loaf – This is another example of that graphic circumstantiality which gives such a charm to this briefest of the four Gospels. The circumstance of the 'one loaf' only remaining, as WEBSTER and WILKINSON remark, was more suggestive of their Master's recent miracles than the entire absence of provisions.

15. And he charged them, saying, Take heed, beware of the leaven of the Pharisees – 'and of the Sadducees' (Mt 16:6).

and of the leaven of Herod – The teaching or 'doctrine' (Mt 16:12) of the Pharisees and of the Sadducees was quite different, but both were equally pernicious; and the Herodians, though rather a political party, were equally envenomed against our Lord's spiritual teaching. See on Mt 12:14. The *penetrating* and *diffusive* quality of leaven, for good or bad, is the ground of the comparison.

16. And they reasoned among themselves, saying, It is because we have no bread – But a little while ago He was tried with the obduracy of the Pharisees; now He is tried with the obtuseness of His own disciples. The *nine* questions following each other in rapid succession (Mr 8:17–21) show how deeply He was hurt at this want of spiritual apprehension, and worse still, their low thoughts of Him, as if He would utter so solemn a warning on so petty a subject. It will be seen, however, from the very form of their conjecture, 'It is because *we* have no bread,' and our Lord's astonishment that they should not by that time have known better with what He took up His attention – that He ever left *the whole care for His own temporal wants to the Twelve:* that He did this so entirely, that finding they were reduced to their last loaf they felt as if unworthy of such a trust, and could not think but that the same thought was in their Lord's mind which was pressing upon their own; but that in this they were so far wrong that it hurt His feelings – sharp just in proportion to His love – that such a thought of Him should have entered their minds! Who that, like angels, 'desire to look into these things' will not prize such glimpses above gold?

17. have ye your heart yet hardened? – How strong an expression to use of true-hearted disciples! See on Mr 6:52.

18. Having eyes, see ye not? and having ears, hear ye not? – See on Mt 13:13.

and do ye not remember?

19. When I brake the five loaves among five thousand – 'the five thousand.'

how many baskets full of fragments took ye up?

21. How is it that ye do not understand? – 'do not understand that the warning I gave you could not have been prompted by any such petty consideration as the want of loaves in your scrip.' Profuse as were our Lord's miracles, we see from this that they were not wrought at random, but that He carefully noted their minutest details, and desired that this should be done by those who witnessed, as doubtless by all who read the record of them. Even the different kind of baskets used at the two miraculous feedings,

so carefully noted in the two narratives, are here also referred to; the one smaller, of which there were twelve, the other much larger, of which there were seven.

Blind man at Bethsaida restored to sight (Mr 8:22–26)

22. And he cometh to Bethsaida – Bethsaida Julias, on the northeast side of the take, whence after this He proceeded to Cæsarea Philippi (Mr 8:27).

and they bring a blind man unto him, and besought him to touch him – See on Mr 7:32.

23. And he took the blind man by the hand, and led him out of the town – Of the deaf and dumb man it is merely said that 'He took him aside' (Mr 7:33); but this blind man He *led by the hand* out of the town, doing it Himself rather than employing another – great humility, exclaims Bengel – that He might gain his confidence and raise his expectation.

and when be had spit on his eyes – the organ affected – See on Mr 7:33.

and put his hands upon him, he asked him if he saw aught.

24. And he looked up, and said, I see men as trees, walking – This is one of the cases in which one edition of what is called the received text differs from another. That which is decidedly the best supported, and has also internal evidence on its side is this: 'I see men; for I see [them] as trees walking' – that is, he could distinguish them from trees only by their motion; a minute mark of truth in the narrative, as Alford observes, describing how human objects had appeared to him during that gradual failing of sight which had ended in blindness.

25. After that he put his hands again upon his eyes, and made him look up; and he was restored, and saw every man clearly – Perhaps the one operation perfectly restored the *eyes*, while the other imparted immediately the *faculty of using them.* It is the only recorded example of a *progressive* cure, and it certainly illustrates similar methods in the spiritual kingdom. Of the four recorded cases of sight restored, all the patients save one either *came* or *were brought* to the Physician. In the case of the man born blind, *the Physician* came to the patient. So some seek and find Christ; of others He is found who seek Him not.

26. Neither go into the town, nor tell it to any in the town – Besides the usual reasons against going about 'blazing the matter,' retirement in this case would be salutary to himself.

Mr 8:27–38.
Peter's noble confession of Christ – our Lord's first explicit announcement of his approaching sufferings, death, and

resurrection – his rebuke of Peter, and warning to all the Twelve.
(= Mt 16:13–27 Lu 9:18–26).
For the exposition, see on Mt 16:13–28.

Chapter 9

Mr 9:1–13.
Jesus is transfigured – conversation about Elias.
(= Mt 16:28–17:13 Lu 9:27–36).
See on Lu 9:27–36.

Mr 9:14–32.
Healing of a demoniac boy – second explicit announcement of his approaching death and resurrection.
(= Mt 17:14–23 Lu 9:37–45).

Healing of the demoniac boy (Mr 9:14–29)

14. And when he came to his disciples, he saw a great multitude about them, and the scribes questioning with them – This was 'on the next day, when they were come down from the hill' (Lu 9:37). The Transfiguration appears to have taken place at night. In the morning, as He came down from the hill on which it took place – with Peter, and James, and John – on approaching the other nine, He found them surrounded by a great multitude, and the scribes disputing or discussing with them. No doubt these cavillers were twitting the apostles of Jesus with their inability to cure the demoniac boy of whom we are presently to hear, and insinuating doubts even of their Master's ability to do it; while they, zealous for their Master's honour, would no doubt refer to His past miracles in proof of the contrary.

15. And straightway all the people – the multitude.

when they beheld him, were greatly amazed – were astounded.

and running to him saluted him – The singularly strong expression of surprise, the sudden arrest of the discussion, and the rush of the multitude towards Him, can be accounted for by nothing less than something amazing in His appearance. There can hardly be any doubt that *His countenance still retained traces of His transfiguration-glory.* (See Ex 34:29,30.) No wonder, if this was the case, that they not only ran to Him, but saluted Him. Our Lord, however, takes no notice of what had attracted them, and probably it gradually faded away as He drew near; but addressing Himself to the scribes, He demands the subject of their discussion, ready to meet them where they had pressed hard upon His half-instructed and as yet timid apostles.

16. And he asked the scribes, What question ye with them? – Ere they had time to reply, the father of the boy, whose case had occasioned the dispute, himself steps forward and answers the question; telling a piteous tale of deafness, and dumbness, and fits of epilepsy – ending with this, that the disciples, though entreated, could not perform the cure.

17. And one of the multitude answered, and said, Master, I have brought unto thee my son – 'mine only child' (Lu 9:38).

which hath a dumb spirit – a spirit whose operation had the effect of rendering his victim speechless, and deaf also (Mr 9:25). In Matthew's report of the speech (Mt 17:15), the father says 'he is lunatic'; this being another and most distressing effect of the possession.

18. And wheresoever he taketh him, he teareth him; and he foameth, and gnasheth with his teeth, and pineth away – rather, 'becomes withered,' 'dried up,' or 'paralyzed'; as the same word is everywhere else rendered in the New Testament. Some additional particulars are given by Luke, and by our Evangelist below. 'Lo,' says he in Lu 9:39, 'a spirit taketh him, and he suddenly crieth out; and it teareth him that he foameth again, and bruising him hardly [or with difficulty] departeth from him.'

and I spake to thy disciples that they should cast him out; and they could not – Our Lord replies to the father by a severe rebuke to the disciples. As if wounded at the exposure before such a multitude, of the weakness of His disciples' faith, which doubtless He felt as a reflection on Himself, He puts them to the blush before all, but in language fitted only to raise expectation of what He Himself would do.

19. He answereth him, and saith, O faithless generation – 'and perverse,' or 'perverted' (Mt 17:17 Lu 9:41).

how long shall I be with you? how long shall I suffer you? – language implying that it was a shame to them to want the faith necessary to perform this cure, and that it needed some patience to put up with them. It is to us surprising that some interpreters, as CHRYSOSTOM and CALVIN, should represent this rebuke as addressed, not to the disciples at all, but to the scribes who disputed with them. Nor does it much, if at all, mend the matter to view it as addressed to both, as most expositors seem to do. With BENGEL, DEWETTE, and MEYER, we regard it as addressed directly to the nine apostles who were unable to expel this evil spirit. And though, in ascribing this inability to their 'want of faith' and the 'perverted turn of mind' which they had drunk in with their early training, the rebuke would undoubtedly apply, with vastly greater force, to those who twitted the poor disciples with their inability, it would be to change the whole nature of the rebuke to suppose it addressed to those who had *no faith at all,* and were *wholly perverted.* It was because faith sufficient for curing this youth was to be expected of the disciples, and because they should by that time have got rid of the perversity in which they had been reared, that Jesus exposes them thus before the rest. And who does not see that this was fitted, more than anything else, to impress upon the by-standers the severe loftiness of the training He was giving to the Twelve, and the unsophisticated footing He was on with them?

Bring him unto me – The order to bring the patient to Him was instantly obeyed; when, lo! as if conscious of the presence of his Divine Tormentor, and expecting to be made to quit, the foul spirit rages and is furious, determined to die hard, doing all the mischief he can to this poor child while yet within his grasp.

20. And they brought him unto him: and when he saw him, straightway the spirit tare him – Just as the man with the legion of demons, 'when he *saw* Jesus, ran and worshipped Him' (Mr 5:6), so this demon, *when he saw Him,* immediately 'tare him.' The feeling of terror and rage was the same in both cases.

and he fell on the ground, and wallowed foaming – Still Jesus does nothing, but keeps conversing with the father about the case – partly to have its desperate features told out by him who knew them best, in the hearing of the spectators; partly to let its virulence have time to show itself; and partly to deepen the exercise of the father's soul, to draw out his faith, and thus to prepare both him and the by-standers for what He was to do.

21. And he asked his father, How long is it ago since this came unto him? And he said, Of a child – Having told briefly the affecting features of the case, the poor father, half dispirited by the failure of the disciples and the aggravated virulence of the malady itself in presence of their Master, yet encouraged too by what he had heard of Christ, by the severe rebuke He had given to His disciples for not having faith enough to cure the boy, and by the dignity with which He had ordered him to be brought to Him – in this mixed state of mind, he closes his description of the case with these touching words:

22. but if thou canst do anything, have compassion on us, and help us – 'us,' says the father; for it was a sore family affliction. Compare the language of the Syrophoenician woman regarding her daughter, 'Lord, help *me.*' Still nothing is done: the man is but *struggling into faith:* it must come a step farther. But he had to do with Him who breaks not the bruised reed, and who knew how to inspire what He demanded. The man had said to Him, '*If Thou canst do.*'

23. Jesus said unto him, If thou canst believe – The man had said, 'If Thou canst do anything.'

Jesus replies.

all things are possible to him that believeth – 'My doing all depends on thy believing.' To impress this still more, He redoubles upon believing: 'If thou canst believe, all things are possible to him that believeth.' Thus the Lord helps the birth of faith in that struggling soul; and now, though with pain and sore travail, it comes to the birth, as TRENCH, borrowing from OLSHAUSEN, expresses it. Seeing the case stood still, waiting not upon the Lord's power but his own faith, the man becomes immediately conscious of conflicting principles, and rises into one of the noblest utterances on record.

24. And straightway the father of the child cried out, and said with tears, Lord, I believe: help thou mine unbelief – that is, 'It is useless concealing from Thee, O Thou mysterious, mighty Healer, the unbelief that still struggles in this heart of mine; but that heart bears me witness that I do believe in Thee; and if distrust still remains, I disown it, I wrestle with it, I seek help from Thee against it.' Two things are very remarkable here: First, *The felt and owned presence of unbelief,* which only the strength of the man's faith could have so revealed to his own consciousness. Second, *His appeal to Christ for help against his felt unbelief* – a feature in the case quite unparalleled, and showing, more than all protestations could have done, the insight he had attained into the existence of *a power in Christ more glorious them any he had besought for his poor child.* The work was done; and as the commotion and confusion in the crowd was now increasing, Jesus at once, as Lord of spirits, gives the word of command to the dumb and deaf spirit to be gone, never again to return to his victim.

26. And the spirit cried, and rent him sore, and came out of him; and he was as one dead; insomuch that many said, He is dead – The malignant, cruel spirit, now conscious that his time was come, gathers up his whole strength, with intent by a last stroke to kill his victim, and had nearly succeeded. But the Lord of life was there; the Healer of all maladies, the Friend of sinners, the Seed of the woman, 'the Stronger than the strong man armed,' was there. The very faith which Christ declared to be enough for everything being now found, it was not possible that the serpent should prevail. Fearfully is he permitted to bruise the *heel,* as in this case; but his own *head* shall go for it – his works shall be destroyed (1Jo 3:8).

27. But Jesus took him by the hand, and lifted him up; and he arose.

28. Why could not we cast him out?

29. And he said unto them, This kind can come forth by nothing but by prayer and fasting – that is, as nearly all good interpreters are agreed, 'this kind of evil spirits cannot be expelled,' or 'so desperate a case of demoniacal possession cannot be cured, but by prayer and fasting.' But since the Lord Himself says that His disciples could not fast while He was with them, perhaps this was designed, as ALFORD hints, for their after-guidance – unless we take it as but a definite way of expressing the general truth, that great and difficult duties require special preparation and self-denial. But the answer to their question, as given in Mt 17:20,21 is fuller: 'And Jesus said unto them, Because of your unbelief. For verily I say unto you, If ye have faith as a grain of mustard seed, ye shall say unto this mountain, Remove hence to yonder place, and it shall remove; and nothing shall be impossible unto you' (Mt 17:20). See on Mr 11:23. 'Howbeit this kind goeth not out but by prayer and fasting' (Mt 17:21), that is, though nothing is impossible to faith, yet such a height of faith as is requisite for such triumphs is not to be reached either in a moment or without effort – either with God in prayer or with ourselves in self-denying exercises. Luke (Lu 9:43) adds, 'And they were all amazed at the mighty power of God' – 'at the majesty' or 'mightiness of God,' in this last miracle, in the Transfiguration; or, at the *divine grandeur* of Christ rising upon them daily.

Second explicit announcement of His approaching death and resurrection (Mr 9:30–32)

30. **And they departed thence, and passed** – were passing along.

through Galilee; and he would not that any man should know it – By comparing Mt 17:22,23 and Lu 9:43,44 with this, we gather, that as our Lord's reason for going through Galilee more privately than usual on this occasion was to reiterate to them the announcement which had so shocked them at the first mention of it, and thus familiarize them with it by little and little, so this was His reason for enjoining silence upon them as to their present movements.

31. **For he taught his disciples, and said unto them** – 'Let these sayings sink down into your ears' (Lu 9:44); not what had been passing between them as to His grandeur, but what He was now to utter.

The Son of man is delivered – The use of the present tense expresses how near at hand He would have them to consider it. As BENGEL says, steps were already in course of being taken to bring it about.

into the hands of men – This remarkable antithesis, 'the Son of *man* shall be delivered into the hands of *men*,' it is worthy of notice, is in all the three Evangelists.

and they shall kill him – that is, 'Be not carried off your feet by all that grandeur of Mine which ye have lately witnessed, but bear in mind what I have already told you and now distinctly repeat, that that Sun in whose beams ye now rejoice is soon to set in midnight gloom.'

and after he is killed, he shall rise the third day.

32. **But they understood not that saying** – 'and it was hid from them, [so] that they perceived it not' (Lu 9:45).

and were afraid to ask him – Their most cherished ideas were so completely dashed by such announcements, that they were afraid of laying themselves open to rebuke by asking Him any questions. But 'they were exceeding sorry' (Mt 17:23). While the other Evangelists, as WEBSTER and WILKINSON remark, notice their ignorance and their fear, Matthew, who was one of them, retains a vivid recollection of their sorrow.

Mr 9:33–50.
Strife among the Twelve who should be greatest in the Kingdom of Heaven, with relative teaching – incidental rebuke of John for exclusiveness.
(= Mt 18:1–9 Lu 9:46–50).

Strife among the Twelve, with relative teaching (Mr 9:33–37)

33. **What was it that ye disputed among yourselves by the way?** – From this we gather that after the painful communication He had made to them, the Redeemer had allowed them to travel so much of the way by themselves; partly, no doubt, that He might have privacy for Himself to dwell on what lay before Him, and partly that they might be induced to weigh together and prepare themselves for the terrible events which He had announced to them. But if so, how different was their occupation!

34. **But they held their peace: for by the way they had disputed among themselves, who should be the greatest** – From Mt 18:1 we should infer that the subject was introduced, not by our Lord, but by the disciples themselves, who came and asked Jesus who should be greatest. Perhaps one or two of them first referred the matter to Jesus, who put them off till they should all be assembled together at Capernaum. He had all the while 'perceived the thought of their heart' (Lu 9:47); but now that they were all together 'in the house,' He questions them about it, and they are put to the blush, conscious of the *temper* towards each other which it had kindled. This raised the whole question afresh, and at this point our Evangelist takes it up. The subject was suggested by the recent announcement of the Kingdom (Mt 16:19–28), the transfiguration of their Master, and especially the preference given to three of them at that scene.

35. **If any man desire to be first, the same shall be last of all, and servant of all** – that is, 'let him be' such: he must be prepared to take the last and lowest place. See on Mr 10:42–45.

36. **And he took a child** – 'a little child' (Mt 18:2); but the word is the same in both places, as also in Lu 9:47.

and set him in the midst of them: and when he had taken him in his arms – This beautiful trait is mentioned by our Evangelist alone.

he said unto them – Here we must go to Matthew (Mt 18:3,4) for the first of this answer: 'Verily I say unto you, except ye be converted, and become as little children, ye shall not enter into the kingdom of Heaven;' that is, 'Conversion must be thorough; not only must the heart be turned to God in general, and from earthly to heavenly things, but in particular, except ye be converted from that carnal ambition which still rankles within you, into that freedom from all such feelings which ye see in this child, ye have neither part nor lot in the kingdom at all; and he who in this feature has most of the child, is highest there.' Whosoever, therefore, shall 'humble himself as this little child, the same is greatest in the kingdom of heaven': 'for he that is [willing to be] least among you all, the same shall be great' (Lu 9:48).

37. **Whosoever shall receive one of such children** – so manifesting the spirit unconsciously displayed by this child.

in my name – from love to Me.

receiveth me; and whosoever shall receive me, receiveth not me, but Him that sent me – (See on Mt 10:40.)

Incidental rebuke of John for exclusiveness (Mr 9:38–41)

38. **And John answered him, saying, Master, we saw one casting out devils in thy name, and he followeth not us: and we forbade him, because he followeth not us** – The link of connection here with the foregoing context lies, we apprehend, in the emphatic words which our Lord had just uttered, 'in My name.' 'Oh,' interposes John – young, warm, but not sufficiently apprehending Christ's teaching in these matters – 'that reminds me of something that we have just done, and we should like to know if we did right. We saw one casting out devils 'in *Thy name*,' and we forbade him, because he followeth not us. Were we right, or were we wrong?' Answer – 'Ye were wrong.' 'But we did it because he followeth not us.' 'No matter.'

39. **But Jesus said, Forbid him not: for there is no man which shall do a miracle in my name, that can lightly speak evil of me** – soon, that is, readily 'speak evil of me.'

40. **For he that is not against us is on our part** – Two principles of immense importance are here laid down: 'First, No one will readily speak evil of Me who has the faith to do a miracle in My name; and second, If such a person cannot be supposed to be *against* us, ye are to consider him *for* us.' Let it be carefully observed that our Lord does not say this man should *not* have 'followed them,' nor yet that it was indifferent whether he did or not; but simply teaches how such a person was to be regarded, *although he did not* – namely, as a reverer of His name and a promoter of His cause.

41. **For whosoever shall give you a cup of water to drink in my name, because ye belong to Christ, verily I say unto you, he shall not lose his reward** – (See on Mt 10:42.)

Continuation of teaching suggested by the disciples' strife (Mr 9:42–50)

What follows appears to have no connection with the incidental reproof of John immediately preceding. As that had interrupted some important teaching, our Lord hastens back to it, as if no such interruption had occurred.

42. **For whosoever shall offend one of these little ones that believe in me** – or, shall cause them to stumble; referring probably to the effect which such unsavoury disputes as they had held would have upon the inquiring and hopeful who came in contact with them, leading to the belief that after all they were no better than others.

it is better for him that a millstone were hanged about his neck – The word here is simply 'millstone,' without expressing of which kind. But in Mt 18:6 it is the 'ass-turned' kind, far heavier than the small hand-mill turned by female slaves, as in Lu 17:35. It is of course the same which is meant here.

and he were cast into the sea – meaning, that if by such a death that stumbling were prevented, and so its eternal consequences averted, it would be a happy thing for them. Here follows a striking verse in Mt 18:7, 'Woe unto the world because of offences!' (There will be stumblings and falls and loss of souls enough from the world's treatment of disciples, without any addition from you: dreadful will be its doom in consequence; see that ye share not in it.) 'For it must needs be that offences come; but woe to that man by whom the offence cometh!' (The struggle between light and darkness will inevitably cause stumblings, but not less guilty is he who wilfully makes any to stumble.)

43. **And if thy hand offend thee, cut it off: it is better for thee to enter into life maimed, than having two hands to go into hell** – See Mt 5:29,30. The only difference between the words there and here is that there they refer to impure inclinations; here, to an ambitious disposition, an irascible or quarrelsome temper, and the like: and the injunction is to strike at the root of such dispositions and cut off the occasions of them.

47. And if thine eye offend thee, pluck it out: it is better for thee to enter into the kingdom of God with one eye, than having two eyes to be cast into hell-fire – On the words 'hell' and 'hell-fire,' or 'the hell of fire,' see on Mt 5:22.

48. Where their worm dieth not, and the fire is not quenched – See on Mt 5:30. The 'unquenchableness' of this fire has already been brought before us (see on Mt 3:12); and the awfully vivid idea of an undying worm, everlastingly consuming an unconsumable body, is taken from the closing words of the evangelical prophet (Isa 66:24), which seem to have furnished the later Jewish Church with its current phraseology on the subject of future punishment (see LIGHTFOOT).

49. For every one shall be salted with fire, and every sacrifice shall be salted with salt – A difficult verse, on which much has been written – some of it to little purpose. 'Every one' probably means 'Every follower of mine'; and the 'fire' with which he 'must be salted' probably means 'a fiery trial' to season him. (Compare Mal 3:2.) The reference to salting the sacrifice is of course to that maxim of the Levitical law, that every acceptable sacrifice must be sprinkled with salt, to express symbolically its soundness, sweetness, wholesomeness, acceptability. But as it had to be *roasted* first, we have here the further idea of a salting with fire. In this case, 'every sacrifice,' in the next clause, will mean, 'Every one who would be found an acceptable offering to God'; and thus the whole verse may perhaps be paraphrased as follows: 'Every disciple of Mine shall have a fiery trial to undergo, and everyone who would be found an odour of a sweet smell, a sacrifice acceptable and well-pleasing to God, must have such a *salting,* like the Levitical sacrifices.' Another, but, as it seems to us, farfetched as well as harsh, interpretation – suggested first, we believe, by MICHAELIS, and adopted by ALEXANDER – takes the 'every sacrifice which must be salted with fire' to mean those who are 'cast into hell,' and the *preservative* effect of this salting to refer to the preservation of the lost not only *in* but *by means of* the fire of hell. Their reason for this is that the other interpretation changes the meaning of the 'fire,' and the characters too, from the lost to the saved, in these verses. But as our Lord confessedly ends His discourse with the case of His own true disciples, the transition to them in Mr 9:48 is perfectly natural; whereas to apply the preservative salt of the sacrifice to the preserving quality of hell-fire, is equally contrary to the symbolical sense of salt and the Scripture representations of future torment. Our Lord has still in His eye the unseemly jarrings which had arisen among the Twelve, the peril to themselves of allowing any indulgence to such passions, and the severe self-sacrifice which salvation would cost them.

50. Salt is good; but if the salt have lost his saltness – its power to season what it is brought into contact with.

wherewith will ye season it? – How is this property to be restored? See on Mt 5:13.

Have salt in yourselves – See to it that ye retain in yourselves those precious qualities that will make you a blessing to one another, and to all around you.

and – with respect to the miserable strife out of which all this discourse has sprung, in one concluding word.

have peace one with another – This is repeated in 1Th 5:13.

Chapter 10

Mr 10:1–12.
Final departure from Galilee – divorce.
(= Mt 19:1–12 Lu 9:51).
See on Mt 19:1–12.

Mr 10:13–19.
Little children brought to Christ.
(= Mt 19:13–15 Lu 18:15–17).
See on Lu 18:15–17.

Mr 10:17–31.
The rich young ruler.
(= Mt 19:16–30 Lu 18:18–30).
See on Lu 18:18–30.

Mr 10:32–45.
Third explicit and still fuller announcement of his approaching sufferings, death, and resurrection – the ambitious request of James and John, and the reply.
(= Mt 20:17–28 Lu 18:31–34).

Third announcement of His approaching sufferings, death, and resurrection
(Mr 10:32–34)

32. And they were in the way – on the road.

going up to Jerusalem – in Perea, and probably somewhere between Ephraim and Jericho, on the farther side of the Jordan, and to the northeast of Jerusalem.

and Jesus went before them – as GROTIUS says, in the style of an intrepid Leader.

and they were amazed – or 'struck with astonishment' at His courage in advancing to certain death.

and as they followed, they were afraid – for their own safety. These artless, lifelike touches – not only from an eye–witness, but one whom the noble carriage of the Master struck with wonder and awe – are peculiar to Mark, and give the second Gospel a charm all its own; making us feel as if we ourselves were in the midst of the scenes it describes. Well might the poet exclaim:

'The Saviour, what a noble flame
Was kindled in His breast,
When, hasting to Jerusalem,
He march'd before the rest!'
COWPER

And he took again the twelve – referring to His previous announcements on this sad subject. **and began to tell them what things should happen unto him** – 'were going to befall Him.' The word expresses something already begun but not brought to a head, rather than something wholly future.

33. Saying, Behold, we go up to Jerusalem – for the last time, and – 'all things that are written by the prophets concerning the Son of man shall be accomplished' (Lu 18:31).

the Son of man shall be delivered unto the chief priests and unto the scribes; and they shall condemn him to death, and shall deliver him to the Gentiles – This is the first express statement that the Gentiles would combine with the Jews in His death; the two grand divisions of the human race for whom He died thus taking part in crucifying the Lord of Glory, as WEBSTER and WILKINSON observe.

34. And they shall mock him, and shall scourge him, and shall spit upon him, and shall kill him: and the third day he shall rise again – Singularly explicit as this announcement was, Luke (Lu 18:34) says 'they understood none of these things; and this saying was hid from them, neither knew they the things which were spoken.' The meaning of the words they could be at no loss to understand, but their import in relation to His Messianic kingdom they could not penetrate; the whole prediction being right in the teeth of their preconceived notions. That they should have clung so tenaciously to the popular notion of an '*un*suffering' Messiah, may surprise us; but it gives inexpressible weight to their after-testimony to a suffering and dying Saviour.

Ambitious request of James and John – the reply (Mr 10:35–45)

35. And James and John, the sons of Zebedee, come unto him, saying – Matthew (Mt 20:20) says their 'mother came to Him with her sons, worshipping Him and desiring,' (Compare Mt 27:56, with Mr 15:40). Salome was her name (Mr 16:1). We cannot be sure with which of the parties the movement originated; but as our Lord, even in Matthew's account, addresses Himself to James and John, taking no account of the mother, it is likely the mother was merely set on by them. The thought

was doubtless suggested to her sons by the recent promise to the Twelve of 'thrones to sit on, when the Son of man should sit on the throne of His glory' (Mt 19:28); but after the reproof so lately given them (Mr 9:33), they get their mother to speak for them.

Master, we would that thou shouldest do for us whatsoever we shall desire – thus cautiously approaching the subject.

36. And he said unto them, What would ye that I should do for you? – Though well aware what was in their mind and their mother's, our Lord will have the unseemly petition uttered before all.

37. Grant unto us that we may sit, one on thy right hand, and the other on thy left hand, in thy glory – that is, Assign to us the two places of highest honour in the coming kingdom. The semblance of a plea for so presumptuous a request might possibly have been drawn from the fact that one of them usually leaned on the breast of Jesus, or sat next Him at meals, while the other was one of the favoured three.

38. But Jesus said unto them, Ye know not what ye ask – How gentle the reply to such a request, preferred at such a time, after the sad announcement just made!

can ye drink of the cup that I drink of? – To 'drink of a cup' is in Scripture a figure for getting one's fill either of good (Ps 16:5 23:5 116:13 Jer 16:7) or of ill (Ps 75:8 Joh 18:11 Re 14:10). Here it is the cup of suffering.

and be baptized with the baptism that I am baptized with – (Compare for the language, Ps 42:7). The object of this question seems to have been to try how far those two men were *capable* of the dignity to which they aspired and this on the principle that he who is able to suffer most for His sake will be the nearest to Him in His kingdom.

39. And they said unto him, We can – Here we see them owning their mother's petition for them as their own; and doubtless they were perfectly sincere in professing their willingness to follow their Master to any suffering He might have to endure. As for James, he was the first of the apostles who was honoured, and showed himself able to be baptized with his Master's baptism of blood (Ac 12:1,2); while *John*, after going through all the persecutions to which the infant Church was exposed from the Jews, and sharing in the struggles and sufferings occasioned by the first triumphs of the Gospel among the Gentiles, lived to be the victim, after all the rest had got to glory, of a bitter persecution in the evening of his days, for the word of God and for the testimony of Jesus Christ. Yes, they were dear believers and blessed men, in spite of this unworthy ambition, and their Lord knew it; and perhaps the foresight of what they would have to pass through, and the courageous testimony He would yet receive from them, was the cause of that gentleness which we cannot but wonder at in His reproof.

And Jesus said unto them, Ye shall indeed drink of the cup that I drink of; and with the baptism that I am baptized withal shall ye be baptized – No doubt this prediction, when their sufferings at length came upon them, cheered them with the assurance, not that they would sit on His right and left hand – for of that thought they would be heartily ashamed – but that 'if they suffered with Him, they should be also glorified together.'

40. But to sit on my right hand and on my left hand is not mine to give; but it shall be given to them for whom it is prepared – 'of My Father' (Mt 20:23). The supplement which our translators have inserted is approved by some good interpreters, and the proper sense of the word rendered 'but' is certainly in favour of it. But besides that it makes the statement too elliptical – leaving too many words to be supplied – it seems to make our Lord repudiate the right to assign to each of His people his place in the kingdom of glory; a thing which He nowhere else does, but rather the contrary. It is true that He says their place is 'prepared for them by His Father.' But that is true of their admission to heaven at all; and yet from His great white throne Jesus will Himself adjudicate the kingdom, and authoritatively invite into it those on His right hand, calling them the 'blessed of His Father'; so little inconsistency is there between the eternal choice of them by His Father, and that public adjudication of them, not only to heaven in general, but each to his own position in it, which all Scripture assigns to Christ. The true rendering, then, of this clause, we take it, is this: 'But to sit on My right hand and on My left hand is not Mine to give, save to them for whom it is prepared.' When therefore He says, 'It is not Mine to give,' the meaning is, 'I cannot give it as a *favour* to whomsoever I *please,* or on a principle of *favouritism;* it belongs exclusively to those for whom it is prepared.' And if this be His meaning, it will be seen how far our Lord is from disclaiming the right to assign to each his proper place in His Kingdom; that on the contrary, He expressly asserts it, merely announcing that the principle of distribution is quite different from what these petitioners supposed. Our Lord, it will be observed, does not *deny* the petition of James and John, or say they shall *not* occupy the place in His kingdom which they now improperly sought: – for aught we know, *that may be their true place.* All we are sure of is, that their asking it was displeasing to Him 'to whom all judgment is committed,' and so was not fitted to gain their object, but just the reverse. (See what

is taught in Lu 14:8–11). One at least of these brethren, as ALFORD strikingly remarks, saw on the right and on the left hand of their Lord, as He hung upon the tree, the crucified thieves; and bitter indeed must have been the remembrance of this ambitious prayer at that moment.

41. And when the ten heard it, they began to be much displeased with James and John – or 'were moved with indignation,' as the same word is rendered in Mt 20:24. The expression '*began* to be,' which is of frequent occurrence in the Gospels, means that more passed than is expressed, and that we have but the result. And can we blame the ten for the indignation which they felt? Yet there was probably a spice of the old spirit of rivalry in it, which in spite of our Lord's recent lengthened, diversified, and most solemn warnings against it, had not ceased to stir in their breasts.

42. But Jesus called them to him, and saith unto them, Ye know that they which are accounted to rule – are recognized or acknowledged as rulers.

over the Gentiles exercise lordship over them: and their great ones exercise authority upon them – as superiors exercising an acknowledged authority over inferiors.

43. But so shall it not be among you: but whosoever will be great among you, shall be your minister – a subordinate servant.

44. And whosoever of you will be the chiefest – or 'first.'

shall be – that is, 'let him be, or 'shall be he who is prepared to be.'

servant of all – one in the lowest condition of service.

45. For even the Son of man came not to be ministered unto, but to minister, and to give his life a ransom for many – 'instead of many,' that is, 'In the kingdom about to be set up, this principle shall have no place. All My servants shall there be equal; and the only greatness known to it shall be the greatness of humility and devotedness to the service of others. He that goes down the deepest in these services of self-denying humility shall rise the highest and hold the chiefest place in that kingdom; even as the Son of man, whose abasement and self-sacrifice for others, transcending all, gives Him of right a place above all!' As 'the Word in the beginning with God,' He *was* ministered unto; and as the risen Redeemer in our nature He now *is* ministered unto, 'angels and authorities and powers being made subject unto Him' (1Pe 3:22); but not for this came He hither. The Served of all came to be the Servant of all; and His last act was the grandest Service ever beheld by the universe of God – 'HE GAVE HIS LIFE A RANSOM FOR MANY!' Many' is here to be taken, not in contrast with *few* or with *all,* but in opposition to *one* – the one Son of man for the many sinners.

Mr 10:46–52.
Blind Bartimaeus healed.
(= Mt 20:29–34 Lu 18:35–43).

See on Lu 18:35–43.

Chapter 11

Mr 11:1–11.
Christ's triumphal entry into Jerusalem, on the first day of the week.
(= Mt 21:1–9 Lu 19:29–40 Joh 12:12,19).

See on Lu 19:29–40.

Mr 11:11–26.
The barren fig tree cursed with lessons from it – second cleansing of the temple, on the second and third days of the week.
(= Mt 21:12–22 Lu 19:45–48).

11. And Jesus entered into Jerusalem, and into the temple: and when he had looked round about upon – surveyed.

all things, and now the eventide was come, he went out into Bethany with the twelve – Thus briefly does our Evangelist dispose of this His first day in Jerusalem, after the triumphal entry. Nor do the Third and Fourth Gospels give us more light. But from Matthew (Mt 21:10,11, 14–16) we learn some additional and precious particulars, for which see on Lu 19:45–48. It was not now safe for the Lord to sleep in the city, nor, from the day of His Triumphal Entry, did He pass one night in it, save the last fatal one.

The barren fig tree cursed (Mr 11:12–14)

12. And on the morrow – The Triumphal Entry being on the first day of the week, this following day was Monday.

when they were come from Bethany – 'in the morning' (Mt 21:18).

he was hungry – How was that? Had he stolen forth from that dear roof at Bethany to the 'mountain to pray, and continued all night in prayer to God?' (Lu 6:12); or, 'in the morning,' as on a former occasion, 'risen up a great while before day, and departed into a solitary place, and there prayed' (Mr 1:35); not breaking His fast thereafter, but bending His steps straight for the city, that He might 'work the works of Him that sent Him while it was day?' (Joh 9:4). We know not, though one lingers upon and loves to trace out the every movement of that life of wonders. One thing, however, we are sure of – it was *real bodily hunger* which He now sought to allay by the fruit of this fig tree, 'if haply He might find any thing thereon'; not a mere *scene* for the purpose of teaching a lesson, as some early heretics maintained, and some still seem virtually to hold.

13. And seeing a fig tree – (In Mt 21:19, it is 'one fig tree,' but the sense is the same as here, 'a certain fig tree,' as in Mt 8:19). Bethphage, which adjoined Bethany, derives his name from its being a *fig region* – 'House of figs.'

afar off having leaves – and therefore promising fruit, which in the case of figs come before the leaves.

he came, if haply he might find any thing thereon: and when he came to it, he found nothing but leaves; for the time of figs was not yet – What the precise import of this explanation is, interpreters are not agreed. Perhaps all that is meant is, that as the proper fig season had not arrived, no fruit would have been expected even of this tree but for the leaves which it had, which were in this case prematurely and unnaturally developed.

14. And Jesus answered and said unto it, No man eat fruit of thee hereafter for ever – That word did not *make* the tree barren, but sealed it up in its own barrenness. See on Mt 13:13–15.

And his disciples heard it – and marked the saying. This is introduced as a connecting link, to explain what was afterwards to be said on the subject, as the narrative has to proceed to the other transactions of this day.

Second cleansing of the temple
(Mr 11:15–18)

For the exposition of this portion, see on Lu 19:45–48.

Lessons from the cursing of the fig tree
(Mr 11:20–26)

20. And in the morning – of Tuesday, the third day of the week: He had slept, as during all this week, at Bethany.

as they passed by – going into Jerusalem again.

they saw the fig tree dried up from the roots – no partial blight, leaving life in the root; but it was now dead, root and branch. In Mt 21:19 it is said it withered away as soon as it was cursed. But the full blight had not appeared probably at once; and in the dusk perhaps, as they returned to Bethany, they had not observed it. The precision with which Mark distinguishes the days is not observed by Matthew, intent only on holding up the truths which the incident was designed to teach. In Matthew the whole is represented as taking place at once, just as the two stages of Jairus' daughter – dying and dead – are represented by him as one. The only difference is between a mere summary and a more detailed narrative, each of which only confirms the other.

21. And Peter calling to remembrance saith unto him – satisfied that a miracle so very peculiar – a miracle, not of *blessing,* as all His other miracles, but of *cursing* – could not have been wrought but with some higher reference, and fully expecting to hear something weighty on the subject.

Master, behold, the fig tree which thou cursedst is withered away – so connecting the two things as to show that he traced the death of the tree entirely to the curse of his Lord. Matthew (Mt 21:20) gives this simply as a general exclamation of surprise by the disciples 'how soon' the blight had taken effect.

22. And Jesus answering saith unto them, Have faith in God.

23. For verily I say unto you, That whosoever shall say unto this mountain, Be thou removed … he shall have whatsoever he saith – Here is the lesson now. From the nature of the case supposed – that they might wish a mountain removed and cast into the sea, a thing far removed from anything which they could be thought actually to desire – it is plain that not physical but moral obstacles to the progress of His kingdom were in the Redeemer's view, and that what He designed to teach was the great lesson, that *no obstacle should be able to stand before a confiding faith in God.*

24. Therefore I say unto you, What things soever ye desire, when ye pray, believe that ye receive them, and ye shall have them – This verse only *generalizes* the assurance of Mr 11:23; which seems to show that it was designed for the special encouragement of *evangelistic* and *missionary* efforts, while this is a directory for prevailing *prayer in general.*

25. And when ye stand praying, forgive, if ye have aught against any; that your Father also which is in heaven may forgive you your trespasses – This is repeated from the Sermon on the Mount (see on Mt 6:12); to remind them that if this was necessary to the acceptableness of all prayer, much more *when great things were to be asked and confidently expected.*

Mr 11:27–33.
The authority of Jesus questioned – his reply.
(= Mt 21:23–27 Lu 20:1–8).
See on Mt 21:23–27.

Chapter 12

Mr 12:1–12.
Parable of the wicked husbandmen.
(= Mt 21:33–46 Lu 20:9–18).
See on Mt 21:33–46.

Mr 12:13–40.
Entangling questions about tribute, the resurrection, and the great commandment, with the replies – Christ baffles the Pharisees by a question about David, and denounces the scribes.
(= Mt 22:15–46 Lu 20:20–47).

The time of this section appears to be still the third day (Tuesday) of Christ's last week. Matthew introduces the subject by saying (Mt 22:15), 'Then went the Pharisees and took counsel how they might entangle Him in His talk.'

13. And they send unto him certain of the Pharisees – 'their disciples,' says Matthew (Mt 22:16); probably young and zealous scholars in that hardening school.

and of the Herodians – (See on Mt 12:14). In Lu 20:20 these willing tools are called 'spies, which should feign themselves just [righteous] men, that they might take hold of His words, that so they might deliver Him unto the power and authority of the governor.' Their plan, then, was to entrap Him into some expression which might be construed into disaffection to the Roman government; the Pharisees themselves being notoriously discontented with the Roman yoke.

Tribute to Cæsar (Mr 12:14–17)

14. And when they were come, they say unto him, Master – Teacher.

we know that thou art true, and carest for no man; for thou regardest not the person of men, but teachest the way of God in truth – By such flattery – though they said only the truth – they hoped to throw Him off His guard.

Is it lawful to give tribute to Cæsar, or not? – It was the civil poll tax paid by all enrolled in the 'census.' See on Mt 17:25.

15. Shall we give, or shall we not give? But he, knowing their hypocrisy – 'their wickedness' (Mt 22:18); 'their craftiness' (Lu 20:23). The malignity of their hearts took the form of craft, pretending what they did not feel – an anxious desire to be guided aright in a matter which to a scrupulous few might seem a question of some difficulty. Seeing perfectly through this,

He said unto them, Why tempt ye me? – 'hypocrites!'

bring me a penny that I may see it – 'the tribute money' (Mt 22:19).

16. And they brought it. And he saith unto them, Whose is this image – stamped upon the coin.

and superscription? – the words encircling it on the obverse side.

And they said unto him, Cæsar's.

17. And Jesus answering said unto them, Render to Cæsar the things that are Cæsar's – Putting it in this general form, it was impossible for sedition itself to dispute it, and yet it dissolved the snare.

and to God the things that are God's – How much is there in this profound but to them startling addition to the maxim, and how incomparable is the whole for fulness, brevity, clearness, weight!

and they marvelled at him – 'at His answer, and held their peace' (Lu 20:26), 'and left Him, and went their way' (Mt 22:22).

The resurrection (Mr 12:18–27)

18. Then come unto him the Sadducees, which say there is no resurrection – 'neither angel nor spirit' (Ac 23:7). They were the materialists of the day. See on Ac 23:6.

and they asked him, saying – as follows:

19–22. Master, Moses wrote unto us – (De 25:5).

24. Do ye not therefore err, because ye know not the scriptures – regarding the future state.

neither the power of God? – before which a thousand such difficulties vanish.

25. For when they shall rise from the dead, they neither marry, nor are given in marriage – 'neither can they die any more' (Lu 20:36). Marriage is ordained to perpetuate the human family; but as there will be no breaches by death in the future state, this ordinance will cease.

but are as the angels which are in heaven – In Luke (Lu 20:36) it is 'equal unto the angels.' But as the subject is death and resurrection, we are not warranted to extend the equality here taught beyond the one point – the *immortality* of their nature. A beautiful clause is added in Luke (Lu 20:36) – 'and are the children of God' – not in respect of *character,* which is not here spoken of, but of *nature* – 'being the children of the resurrection,' as rising to an undecaying existence (Ro 8:21,23), and so being the children of their Father's immortality (1Ti 6:16).

26. And as touching the dead, that they rise: have ye not read in the book of Moses – 'even Moses' (Lu 20:37), whom they had just quoted for the purpose of entangling Him.

how in the bush God spake unto him – either 'at the bush,' as the same expression is rendered in Lu 20:37, that is, when he was there; or 'in the [section of his history regarding the] bush.' The structure of our verse suggests the latter sense, which is not unusual.

saying, I am the God of Abraham, and the God of Isaac, and the God of Jacob? – (Ex 3:6).

27. He is not the God of the dead, but the God of the living – not 'the God of dead but [the God] of living persons.' The word in brackets is almost certainly an addition to the genuine text, and critical editors exclude it. 'For all live unto Him' (Lu 20:38) – 'in His view,' or 'in His estimation.' This last statement – found only in Luke – though adding nothing to the argument, is an important additional illustration. It is true, indeed, that to God no human being is dead or ever will be, but all mankind sustain an abiding conscious relation to Him; but the 'all' here means 'those who shall be accounted worthy to obtain that world.' These sustain a gracious covenant relation to God which cannot be dissolved. (Compare Ro 6:10,11.) In this sense our Lord affirms that for Moses to call the Lord the 'GOD' of His patriarchal servants, if at that moment they had no existence, would be

unworthy of Him. He 'would be *ashamed* to be called their God, if He had not prepared for them a city' (Heb 11:16). It was concluded by some of the early Fathers, from our Lord's resting His proof of the Resurrection on such a passage as this, instead of quoting some much clearer testimonies of the Old Testament, that the Sadducees, to whom this was addressed, acknowledged the authority of no part of the Old Testament but the Pentateuch; and this opinion has held its ground even till now. But as there is no ground for it in the New Testament, so JOSEPHUS is silent upon it; merely saying that they rejected the Pharisaic traditions. It was because the Pentateuch was regarded by all classes as the fundamental source of the Hebrew religion, and all the succeeding books of the Old Testament but as developments of it, that our Lord would show that even there the doctrine of the Resurrection was taught. And all the rather does He select this passage, as being not a bare annunciation of the doctrine in question, but as expressive of that glorious truth *out of which the Resurrection springs.* 'And when the multitude heard this' (says Mt 22:23), 'they were astonished at His doctrine.' 'Then,' adds Lu 20:39,40, 'certain of the scribes answering said, Master, thou hast well said' – enjoying His victory over the Sadducees. 'And after that they durst not ask Him any [question at all]' – neither party could; both being for the time utterly foiled.

The great commandment (Mr 12:28–34)

'But when the Pharisees had heard that He had put the Sadducees to silence, they were gathered together' (Mt 22:34).

28. And one of the scribes – 'a lawyer,' says Matthew (Mt 22:35); that is, teacher of the law.

came, and having heard them reasoning together, and perceiving that he had answered them well, asked him – manifestly in no bad spirit. When Matthew (Mt 22:35) therefore says he came 'tempting,' or 'trying him,' as one of the Pharisaic party who seemed to enjoy the defeat He had given to the Sadducees, we may suppose that though somewhat priding himself upon his insight into the law, and not indisposed to measure his knowledge with One in whom he had not yet learned to believe, he was nevertheless an honest-hearted, fair disputant.

Which is the first commandment of all? – first in importance; the primary, leading commandment, the most fundamental one. This was a question which, with some others, divided the Jewish teachers into rival schools. Our Lord's answer is in a strain of respect very different from what He showed to cavillers – ever observing His own direction, 'Give not that which is holy to the dogs, neither cast ye your pearls before swine; lest they trample them under their feet, and turn again and rend you' (Mt 7:6).

29. And Jesus answered him, The first of all the commandments is – The readings here vary considerably. TISCHENDORF and TREGELLES read simply, 'the first is'; and they are followed by MEYER and ALFORD. But though the authority for the precise form of the received text is slender, a form almost identical with it seems to have most weight of authority. Our Lord here gives His explicit sanction to the distinction between commandments of a more *fundamental* and *primary* character, and commandments of a more *dependent* and *subordinate* nature; a distinction of which it is confidently asserted by a certain class of critics that the Jews knew nothing, that our Lord and His apostles nowhere lay down, and which has been invented by Christian divines. (Compare Mt 23:23.)

Hear, O Israel; the Lord our God is one Lord – This every devout Jew recited twice every day, and the Jews do it to this day; thus keeping up the great ancient national protest against the polytheisms and pantheisms of the heathen world: it is the great utterance of the national faith in One Living and Personal God – 'ONE JEHOVAH!'

30. And thou shalt – We have here the language of *law,* expressive of God's *claims.* What then are we here bound down to do? One word is made to express it. And what a word! Had the essence of the divine law consisted in *deeds,* it could not possibly have been expressed in a single word; for no one deed is comprehensive of all others embraced in the law. But as it consists in *an affection of the soul,* one word suffices to express it – but only one. *Fear,* though due to God and enjoined by Him, is *limited* in its sphere and *distant* in character. *Trust, hope,* and the like, though essential features of a right state of heart towards God, are called into action only by *personal necessity,* and so are – in a good sense, it is true, but still are properly – *selfish* affections; that is to say, they have respect to *our own well-being.* But LOVE is an *all-inclusive* affection, embracing not only every other affection proper to its object, but all that is proper to be *done* to its object; for as love spontaneously seeks to please its object, so, in the case of men to God, it is the native well spring of a voluntary obedience. It is, besides, the most *personal* of all affections. One may fear an *event,* one may hope for an *event,* one may rejoice in an *event;* but one can love only a *Person.* It is the *tenderest,* the most *unselfish,* the most *divine* of all affections. Such, then, is the affection in which the essence of the divine law is declared to consist.

Thou shalt love – We now come to the glorious Object of that demanded affection.

Thou shalt love the Lord, thy God – that is, Jehovah, the Self-Existent One, who has revealed Himself as the 'I AM,' and there is *none else;* who, though by His name JEHOVAH apparently at an unapproachable distance from His finite creatures, yet bears to *thee* a real and definite relationship, out of which arises *His claim* and *thy duty* – of LOVE. But with what are we to love Him? Four things are here specified. First, 'Thou shalt love the Lord thy God'

with thy heart – This sometimes means 'the whole inner man' (as Pr 4:23); but that cannot be meant here; for then the other three particulars would be superfluous. Very often it means 'our emotional nature' – the seat of *feeling* as distinguished from our intellectual nature or the seat of *thought,* commonly called the 'mind' (as in Php 4:7). But neither can this be the sense of it here; for here the heart is distinguished both from the 'mind' and the 'soul.' The 'heart,' then, must here mean the *sincerity* of both the thoughts and the feelings; in other words, *uprightness* or *true-heartedness,* as opposed to a *hypocritical* or *divided* affection. But next, 'Thou shalt love the Lord thy God'

with thy soul. This is designed to command our emotional nature: Thou shalt put *feeling* or *warmth* into thine affection. Further, 'Thou shalt love the Lord thy God'

with thy mind – This commands our intellectual nature: Thou shalt put *intelligence* into thine affection – in opposition to a blind devotion, or mere devoteeism. Lastly, 'Thou shalt love the Lord thy God'

with thy strength – This commands our energies: Thou shalt put *intensity* into thine affection – 'Do it with thy might' (Ec 9:10). Taking these four things together, the command of the Law is, 'Thou shalt love the Lord thy God *with all thy powers* – with a *sincere,* a *fervid,* an *intelligent,* an *energetic* love.' But this is not all that the Law demands. God will have all these qualities in their most perfect exercise. 'Thou shalt love the Lord thy God,' says the Law, 'with *all* thy heart,' or, with perfect sincerity; 'Thou shalt love the Lord thy God with *all* thy soul,' or, with the utmost fervor; 'Thou shalt love the Lord thy God with *all* thy mind,' or, in the fullest exercise of an enlightened reason; and 'Thou shalt love the Lord thy God with *all* thy strength,' or, with the whole energy of our being! So much for the First Commandment.

31. And the second is like – 'unto it' (Mt 22:39); as demanding the same affection, and only the extension of it, in its proper measure, to the creatures of Him whom we thus love – our *brethren* in the participation of the same nature, and *neighbors,* as connected with us by ties that render each dependent upon and necessary to the other.

Thou shalt love thy neighbour as thyself – Now, as we are not to love ourselves supremely, this is virtually a command, in the first place, *not* to love our neighbor with all our heart and soul and mind and strength. And thus it is a condemnation of the idolatry of the creature. Our supreme and uttermost affection is to be reserved for God. But as *sincerely* as ourselves we are to love all mankind, and with *the same readiness to do and suffer for them* as we should reasonably desire them to show to us. The golden rule (Mt 7:12) is here our best interpreter of the nature and extent of these claims.

There is none other commandment greater than these – or, as in Mt 22:40, 'On these two commandments hang all the law and the prophets' (see on Mt 5:17). It is as if He had said, 'This is all Scripture in a nutshell; the whole law of human duty in a portable, pocket form.' Indeed, it is so *simple* that a child may understand it, so *brief* that all may remember it, so *comprehensive* as to embrace all possible cases. And from its very nature it is *unchangeable*. It is inconceivable that God should require from his rational creatures anything *less*, or in substance anything *else*, under any *dispensation*, in any *world*, at any *period* throughout eternal duration. He cannot but claim this – all this – alike in *heaven*, in *earth*, and in *hell!* And this incomparable summary of the divine law belonged to the *Jewish religion!* As it shines in its own self-evidencing splendor, so it reveals its own true source. The religion from which the world has received it could be none other than a *God-given religion!*

32. And the scribe said unto him, Well, Master – Teacher.

thou hast said the truth: for there is one God; and there is none other but he – The genuine text here seems clearly to have been, 'There is one,' without the word 'God'; and so nearly all critical editors and expositors read.

33. And to love him with all the heart … and to love his neighbour as himself, is more than all whole burnt offerings and sacrifices – more, that is, than all positive institutions; thereby showing insight into the essential difference between what is *moral* and in its own nature *unchangeable*, and what is obligatory only *because enjoined*, and only *so long as enjoined*.

34. And when Jesus saw that he answered discreetly – rather, 'intelligently,' or 'sensibly'; not only in a good spirit, but with a promising measure of insight into spiritual things.

he said unto him, Thou art not far from the kingdom of God – for he had but *to follow out a little further* what he seemed sincerely to own, to find his way into the kingdom. He needed only the experience of another eminent scribe who at a later period said, 'We know that *the law is spiritual,* but *I am carnal,* sold under sin': who exclaimed, 'O wretched man that I am! Who shall deliver me?' but who added, 'I thank God through Jesus Christ!' (Ro 7:14,24,25). Perhaps among the 'great company of the priests' and other Jewish ecclesiastics who 'were obedient to the faith,' almost immediately after the day of Pentecost (Ac 6:7), this upright lawyer was one. But for all his nearness to the Kingdom of God, it may be he never entered it.

And no man after that durst ask any question – all feeling that they were no match for Him, and that it was vain to enter the lists with Him.

Christ baffles the Pharisees regarding David (Mr 12:35–37)

35. And Jesus answered and said, while he taught in the temple – and 'while the Pharisees were gathered together' (Mt 22:41). **How say the scribes that Christ is the son of David?** – How come they to give it out that Messiah is to be the son of David? In Matthew (Mt 22:42), Jesus asks them, 'What think ye of Christ?' or of the promised and expected Messiah? 'Whose son is He [to be]? They say unto Him, The son of David.' The sense is the same. 'He saith unto them, How then doth David in spirit call Him Lord?' (Mt 22:42,43).

36. For David himself said by the Holy Ghost, The Lord said to my Lord, Sit thou on my right hand, till I make thine enemies thy footstool – (Ps 110:1).

37. David therefore himself calleth him Lord; and whence is he then his son? – There is but one solution of this difficulty. Messiah is at once inferior to David as his son according to the flesh, and superior to him as the Lord of a kingdom of which David is himself a subject, not the sovereign. The human and divine natures of Christ, and the spirituality of His kingdom – of which the highest earthly sovereigns are honored if they be counted worthy to be its subjects – furnish the only key to this puzzle.

And the common people – the immense crowd.

heard him gladly – 'And no man was able to answer Him a word; neither durst any man from that day forth ask Him any more questions' (Mt 22:46).

The scribes denounced (Mr 12:38–40)

38. And he said unto them in his doctrine – rather, 'in His teaching'; implying that this was but a specimen of an extended discourse, which Matthew gives in full (Mt 23:1–39). Luke says (Lu 20:45) this was 'in the audience of all the people said unto His disciples.'

Beware of the scribes, which love – or like. **to go in long clothing** – (see on Mt 23:5).

and *love* **salutations in the market-places,**

39. And the chief seats in the synagogues, and the uppermost rooms – or positions.

at feasts – On this love of distinction, see on Lu 14:7; Mt 6:5.

40. Which devour widows' houses, and for a pretence make long prayers: these shall receive greater damnation – They took advantage of their helpless condition and confiding character to obtain possession of their property, while by their 'long prayers' they made them believe they were raised far above 'filthy lucre.' So much the 'greater damnation' awaited them. (Compare Mt 23:33.) A lifelike description this of the Romish clergy, the true successors of 'the scribes.'

Mr 12:41–44.
The widow's two mites.
(= Lu 21:1–4).See on Lu 21:1–4.

Chapter 13

Mr 13:1–37.
Christ's prophecy of the destruction of Jerusalem, and warnings suggested by it to prepare for his second coming.
(= Mt 24:1–51 Lu 21:5–36).

Jesus had uttered all His mind against the Jewish ecclesiastics, exposing their character with withering plainness, and denouncing, in language of awful severity, the judgments of God against them for that unfaithfulness to their trust which was bringing ruin upon the nation. He had closed this His last public discourse (Mt 23:1–39) by a passionate lamentation over Jerusalem, and a solemn farewell to the temple. 'And,' says Matthew (Mt 24:1), 'Jesus went out and departed from the temple' – never more to re-enter its precincts, or open His mouth in public teaching. *With this act ended His public ministry.* As He withdrew, says OLSHAUSEN, the gracious presence of God left the sanctuary; and the temple, with all its service, and the whole theocratic constitution, was given over to destruction. What immediately followed is, as usual, most minutely and graphically described by our Evangelist.

1. And as he went out of the temple, one of his disciples saith unto him – The other Evangelists are less definite. 'As some spake,' says Luke (Lu 21:5); 'His disciples came to Him,' says Matthew (Mt 24:2). Doubtless it was the speech of one, the mouthpiece, likely, of others.

Master – Teacher.

see what manner of stones and what buildings are here – wondering probably, how so massive a pile could be overthrown, as seemed implied in our Lord's last words regarding it. JOSEPHUS, who gives a minute account of the wonderful structure, speaks of stones forty cubits long [*Wars of the Jews*, 5.5.1], and says the pillars supporting the porches were twenty-five cubits high, all of one stone, and that of the whitest marble [*Wars of the Jews*, 5.5.2]. Six

days' battering at the walls, during the siege, made no impression upon them [*Wars of the Jews*, 6.4.1]. Some of the under-building, yet remaining, and other works, are probably as old as the first temple.

2. And Jesus answering said unto him, Seest thou these great buildings? – 'Ye call My attention to these things? I have seen them. Ye point to their massive and durable appearance: now listen to their fate.'

there shall not be left – 'left here' (Mt 24:2).

one stone upon another, that shall not be thrown down – Titus ordered the whole city and temple to be demolished [JOSEPHUS, *Wars of the Jews*, 7.1.1]; Eleazar wished they had all died before seeing that holy city destroyed by enemies' hands, and before the temple was so profanely *dug up* [*Wars of the Jews*, 7.8.7].

3. And as he sat upon the Mount of Olives, over against the temple – On their way from Jerusalem to Bethany they would cross Mount Olivet; on its summit He seats Himself, over against the temple, having the city all spread out under His eye. How graphically is this set before us by our Evangelist! **Peter and James and John and Andrew asked him privately** – The other Evangelists tell us merely that 'the disciples' did so. But Mark not only says that it was four of them, but names them; and they were the first *quaternion* of the Twelve.

4. Tell us, when shall these things be? and what shall be the sign when all these things shall be fulfilled? – 'and what shall be the sign of Thy coming, and of the end of the world?' They no doubt looked upon the date of all these things as one and the same, and their notions of the things themselves were as confused as of the times of them. Our Lord takes His own way of meeting their questions.

Prophecies of the destruction of Jerusalem (Mr 13:5–31)

6. For many shall come in my name, saying, I am Christ – (see Mt 24:5) – 'and the time draweth nigh' (Lu 21:8); that is, the time of the kingdom in its full splendor.

and shall deceive many – 'Go ye not therefore after them' (Lu 21:8). The reference here seems not to be to pretended Messiahs, deceiving those who rejected the claims of Jesus, of whom indeed there were plenty – for our Lord is addressing His own genuine disciples – but to persons pretending to be Jesus Himself, returned in glory to take possession of His kingdom. This gives peculiar force to the words, 'Go ye not therefore after them.'

7. And when ye shall hear of wars and rumours of wars, be ye not troubled – (See on Mr 13:13, and compare Isa 8:11–14).

for such things must needs be; but the end shall not be yet – In Luke (Lu 21:9), 'the end is not by and by,' or 'immediately.' Worse must come before all is over.

8. These are the beginnings of sorrows – 'of travail-pangs,' to which heavy calamities are compared. (See Jer 4:31). The annals of TACITUS tell us how the Roman world was convulsed, before the destruction of Jerusalem, by rival claimants of the imperial purple.

9. But take heed to yourselves: for – 'before all these things' (Lu 21:12); that is, before these public calamities come.

they shall deliver you up to councils; and in the synagogues ye shall be beaten – These refer to *ecclesiastical* proceedings against them.

and ye shall be brought before rulers and kings – before *civil* tribunals next.

for my sake, for a testimony against them – rather 'unto them' – to give you an opportunity of bearing testimony to Me before them. In the Acts of the Apostles we have the best commentary on this announcement. (Compare Mt 10:17,18.)

10. And the gospel must first be published among all nations – 'for a witness, and then shall the end come' (Mt 24:14). God never sends judgment without previous warning; and there can be no doubt that the Jews, already dispersed over most known countries, had nearly all heard the Gospel 'as a witness,' before the end of the Jewish state. The same principle was repeated and will repeat itself to '*the* end.'

11. But when they shall lead you, and deliver you up, take no thought beforehand – 'Be not anxious beforehand.'

what ye shall speak, neither do ye premeditate – 'Be not filled with apprehension, in the prospect of such public appearances for Me, lest ye should bring discredit upon My name, nor think it necessary to prepare beforehand what ye are to say.'

but whatsoever shall be given you in that hour, that speak ye: for it is not ye that speak, but the Holy Ghost – (See on Mt 10:19,20.)

13. And ye shall be hated of all men for my name's sake – Matthew (Mt 24:12) adds this important intimation: 'And because iniquity shall abound, the love of many' – 'of the many,' or 'of the most,' that is, of the generality of professed disciples – 'shall wax cold.' Sad illustrations of the effect of abounding iniquity in cooling the love even of faithful disciples we have in the *Epistle of James*, written about the period here referred to, and too frequently ever since.

but he that shall endure unto the end, the same shall be saved – See on Mt 10:21,22; and compare Heb 10:38,39, which is a manifest allusion to these words of Christ; also Re 2:10. Luke (Lu 21:18) adds these reassuring words: 'But there shall not an hair of your heads perish.' Our Lord had just said (Lu 21:16) that they should

be *put to death;* showing that this precious promise is far above immunity from mere bodily harm, and furnishing a key to the right interpretation of the ninety-first Psalm and such like.

14. But when ye shall see – 'Jerusalem compassed by armies' – by encamped armies; in other words, when ye shall see it *besieged,* and **the abomination of desolation, spoken of by Daniel the prophet, standing where it ought not** – that is, as explained in Matthew (Mt 24:15), 'standing in the holy place.'

(let him that readeth understand) – readeth that prophecy. That 'the abomination of desolation' here alluded to was intended to point to the Roman ensigns, as the symbols of an idolatrous, and so unclean pagan power, may be gathered by comparing what Luke says in the corresponding verse (Lu 21:20); and commentators are agreed on it. It is worthy of notice, as confirming this interpretation, that in I Maccabees 1:54 – which, though aprocryphal *Scripture,* is authentic *history* – the expression of Daniel (Da 11:31 12:11) is applied to the idolatrous profanation of the Jewish altar by Antiochus Epiphanes.

then let them that be in Judea flee to the mountains – The ecclesiastical historian, EUSEBIUS, early in the fourth century, tells us that the Christians fled to *Pella,* at the northern extremity of Perea, being 'prophetically directed' – perhaps by some prophetic intimation more explicit than this, which would be their chart – and that thus they escaped the predicted calamities by which the nation was overwhelmed.

15. And let him that is on the housetop not get down into the house, neither enter therein, to take any thing out of his house – that is, let him take the outside flight of steps from the roof to the ground; a graphic way of denoting the extreme urgency of the case, and the danger of being tempted, by the desire to save his property, to delay till escape should become impossible.

16. And let him that is in the field not turn back again for to take up his garment.

17. But woe to them – or, 'alas for them.' **that are with child, and to them that give suck in those days** – in consequence of the aggravated suffering which those conditions would involve.

18. And pray ye that your flight be not in the winter – making escape perilous, or tempting you to delay your flight. Matthew (Mt 24:20) adds, 'neither on the sabbath day,' when, from fear of a breach of its sacred rest, they might be induced to remain.

19. For in those days shall be affliction, such as was not from the beginning of the creation which God created unto this time, neither shall be – Such language is not unusual in the Old Testament with reference to tremendous calamities. But it is matter of literal fact that there was crowded into the period of the Jewish war an amount and complication of suffering perhaps unparalleled; as the narrative of JOSEPHUS, examined closely and arranged under different heads, would show.

20. And except that the Lord had shortened those days, no flesh – that is, no human life.

should be saved: but for the elect's sake, whom he hath chosen, he hath shortened the days – But for this merciful 'shortening,' brought about by a remarkable concurrence of causes, the whole nation would have perished, in which there yet remained a remnant to be afterwards gathered out. This portion of the prophecy closes, in Luke, with the following vivid and important glance at the subsequent fortunes of the chosen people: 'And they shall fall by the sword, and shall be led away captive into all nations: and Jerusalem shall be trodden down of the Gentiles, until the times of the Gentiles be fulfilled' (Lu 21:24). The language as well as the idea of this remarkable statement is taken from Da 8:10,13. What, then, is its import here? It implies, first, that a time is coming when Jerusalem shall cease to be 'trodden down of the Gentiles'; which it was then by pagan, and since and till now is by Mohammedan unbelievers: and next, it implies that the period when this treading down of Jerusalem by the Gentiles is to cease will be when 'the times of the Gentiles are fulfilled' or 'completed.' But what does this mean? We may gather the meaning of it from Ro 11:1–36 in which the divine purposes and procedure towards the chosen people from first to last are treated in detail. In Ro 11:25 these words of our Lord are thus reproduced: 'For I would not, brethren, that ye should be ignorant of this mystery, lest ye should be wise in your own conceits; that blindness in part is happened to Israel, until the fulness of the Gentiles be come in.' See the exposition of that verse, from which it will appear that 'till the fulness of the Gentiles be come in' – or, in our Lord's phraseology, 'till the times of the Gentiles be fulfilled' – does not mean 'till the general conversion of the world to Christ,' but 'till the Gentiles have had their *full time* of that place in the Church which the Jews had before them.' After that period of *Gentilism*, as before of *Judaism*, 'Jerusalem' and Israel, no longer 'trodden down by the Gentiles,' but 'grafted into their own olive tree,' shall constitute, with the believing Gentiles, one Church of God, and fill the whole earth. What a bright vista does this open up!

21. And then, if any man shall say to you, Lo, here is Christ; or, lo he is there; believe him not – So Lu 17:23. No one can read JOSEPHUS' account of what took place before the destruction of Jerusalem without seeing how strikingly this was fulfilled.

to seduce, if it were possible, even the elect – implying that this, though all *but* done, will prove impossible. What a precious assurance! (Compare 2Th 2:9–12.)

23. But take ye heed; behold, I have foretold you all things – He had just told them that the seduction of the elect would prove impossible; but since this would be all but accomplished, He bids them be on their guard, as the proper means of averting that catastrophe. In Matthew (Mt 24:26–28) we have some additional particulars: 'Wherefore, if they shall say unto you, Behold, He is in the desert; go not forth: behold, He is in the secret chambers; believe it not. For as the lightning cometh out of the east, and shineth even unto the west; so shall also the coming of the Son of man be.' See on Lu 17:23,24. 'For wheresoever the carcass is, there will the eagles be gathered together.' See on Lu 17:37.

24. But in those days, after that tribulation – 'Immediately after the tribulation of those days' (Mt 24:29).

the sun shall be darkened, and the moon shall not give her light.

25. And the stars of heaven shall fall – 'and upon the earth distress of nations, with perplexity; the sea and the waves roaring; men's hearts failing them for fear, and for looking after those things which are coming on the earth' (Lu 21:25,26).

and the powers that are in heaven shall be shaken – Though the grandeur of this language carries the mind over the head of all periods but that of Christ's Second Coming, nearly every expression will be found used of the Lord's coming in terrible national judgments: as of Babylon (Isa 13:9–13); of Idumea (Isa 34:1,2,4,8–10); of Egypt (Eze 32:7,8); compare also Ps 18:7–15 Isa 24:1,17–19 Joe 2:10,11. We cannot therefore consider the mere strength of this language a proof that it refers exclusively or primarily to the precursors of the final day, though of course in '*that day*' it will have its most awful fulfilment.

26. And then shall they see the Son of man coming in the clouds with great power and glory – In Mt 24:30, this is given most fully: 'And then shall appear the sign of the Son of man in heaven; and then shall all the tribes of the earth mourn, and they shall see the Son of man.' That this language finds its highest interpretation in the Second Personal Coming of Christ, is most certain. But the question is, whether that be the primary sense of it as it stands here? Now if the reader will turn to Da 7:13,14, and connect with it the preceding verses, he will find, we think, the true key to our Lord's meaning here. There the powers that oppressed the Church – symbolized by rapacious wild beasts – are summoned to the bar of the Great God, who as the Ancient of days seats

Himself, with His assessors, on a burning Throne: thousand thousands ministering to Him, and ten thousand times ten thousand standing before Him. 'The judgment is set, and the books are opened.' Who that is guided by the *mere words* would doubt that this is a description of the Final Judgment? And yet nothing is clearer than that it is *not*, but a description of a vast *temporal* judgment, upon organized bodies of men, for their incurable hostility to the kingdom of God upon earth. Well, after the doom of these has been pronounced and executed, and room thus prepared for the unobstructed development of the kingdom of God over the earth, what follows? 'I saw in the night visions, and behold, one like THE SON OF MAN came with the clouds of heaven, and came to the Ancient of days, and they [the angelic attendants] brought Him near before Him.' For what purpose? To receive investiture in the kingdom, which, as Messiah, of right belonged to Him. Accordingly, it is added, 'And there was given Him dominion, and glory, and a kingdom, that all peoples, nations, and languages should serve Him: His dominion is an everlasting dominion, which shall not pass away, and His kingdom that which shall not be destroyed.' Comparing this with our Lord's words, He seems to us, by 'the Son of man [on which phrase, see on Joh 1:51] coming in the clouds with great power and glory,' to mean, that when judicial vengeance shall once have been executed upon Jerusalem, and the ground thus cleared for the unobstructed establishment of His own kingdom, His true regal claims and rights would be visibly and gloriously asserted and manifested. See on Lu 9:28 (with its parallels in Mt 17:1 Mr 9:2), in which nearly the same language is employed, and where it can hardly be understood of anything else than *the full and free establishment of the kingdom of Christ on the destruction of Jerusalem.* But what is that 'sign of the Son of man in heaven?' Interpreters are not agreed. But as before Christ came to destroy Jerusalem some appalling portents were seen in the air, so before His Personal appearing it is likely that something *analogous* will be witnessed, though of what nature it would be vain to conjecture.

27. And then shall he send his angels – 'with a great sound of a trumpet' (Mt 24:31).

and shall gather together his elect – As the tribes of Israel were anciently gathered together by sound of trumpet (Ex 19:13,16,19 Le 23:24 Ps 81:3–5), so any mighty gathering of God's people, by divine command, is represented as collected by sound of trumpet (Isa 27:13; compare Re 11:15); and the ministry of angels, employed in all the great operations of Providence, is here held forth as the agency by which the present assembling of the elect is to

be accomplished. LIGHTFOOT thus explains it: 'When Jerusalem shall be reduced to ashes, and that wicked nation cut off and rejected, then shall the Son of man send His ministers with the trumpet of the Gospel, and they shall gather His elect of the several nations, from the four corners of heaven: so that God shall not want a Church, although that ancient people of His be rejected and cast off: but that ancient Jewish Church being destroyed, a new Church shall be called out of the Gentiles.' But though something like this appears to be the primary sense of the verse, in relation to the destruction of Jerusalem, no one can fail to see that the language swells beyond any gathering of a human family into a Church upon earth, and forces the thoughts onward to that gathering of the Church 'at the last trump,' to meet the Lord in the air, which is to wind up the present scene. Still, this is not, in our judgment, the *direct* subject of the prediction; for Mr 13:28 limits the whole prediction to the generation then existing.

28. Now learn a parable of the fig tree – 'Now from the fig tree learn the parable,' or the high lesson which this teaches.

When her branch is yet tender, and putteth forth leaves – 'its leaves.'

29. So ye, in like manner, when ye shall see these things come to pass – rather, 'coming to pass.'

know that it – 'the kingdom of God' (Lu 21:31).

is nigh, even at the doors – that is, the full manifestation of it; for till then it admitted of no full development. In Luke (Lu 21:28) the following words precede these: 'And when these things begin to come to pass, then look up, and lift up your heads; for your redemption draweth nigh' – their redemption, in the first instance certainly, from Jewish oppression (1Th 2:14–16 Lu 11:52): but in the highest sense of these words, redemption from all the oppressions and miseries of the present state at the second appearing of the Lord Jesus.

30. Verily I say unto you, that this generation shall not pass till all these things be done – or 'fulfilled' (Mt 24:34 Lu 21:32). Whether we take this to mean that the whole would be fulfilled within the limits of the generation then current, or, according to a usual way of speaking, that the generation then existing would not pass away without seeing a *begun* fulfilment of this prediction, the facts entirely correspond. For either the whole was fulfilled in the destruction accomplished by Titus, as many think; or, if we stretch it out, according to others, till the thorough dispersion of the Jews a little later, under Adrian, every requirement of our Lord's words seems to be met.

31. Heaven and earth shall pass away; but my words shall not pass away – the strongest possible expression of the divine authority by which He spake; not as Moses or Paul might have said of their own inspiration, for such language would be unsuitable in any merely human mouth.

Warnings to prepare for the coming of Christ suggested by the foregoing prophecy (Mr 13:32–37)

It will be observed that, in the foregoing prophecy, as our Lord approaches the crisis of the day of vengeance on Jerusalem and redemption for the Church – at which stage the analogy between that and the day of final vengeance and redemption waxes more striking – His language rises and swells beyond all temporal and partial vengeance, beyond all earthly deliverances and enlargements, and ushers us resistlessly into the scenes of the final day. Accordingly, in these six concluding verses it is manifest that preparation for 'THAT DAY' is what our Lord designs to inculcate.

32. But of that day and that hour – that is, the precise time.

knoweth no man – literally, no one.

no, not the angels which are in heaven, neither the Son, but the Father – This very remarkable statement regarding 'the Son' is peculiar to Mark. Whether it means that the Son was *not at that time in possession of the knowledge* referred to, or simply that it was not *among the things which He had received to communicate* – has been matter of much controversy even among the firmest believers in the proper Divinity of Christ. In the latter sense it was taken by some of the most eminent of the ancient Fathers, and by LUTHER, MELANCTHON, and most of the older Lutherans; and it is so taken by BENGEL, LANGE, WEBSTER and WILKINSON. CHRYSOSTOM and others understood it to mean that *as man* our Lord was ignorant of this. It is taken literally by CALVIN, GROTIUS, DEWETTE, MEYER, FRITZSCHE, STIER, ALFORD, and ALEXANDER.

33. Take ye heed, watch and pray; for ye know not when the time is.

34. For the Son of man is as a man taking a far journey – The idea thus far is similar to that in the opening part of the parable of the talents (Mt 25:14,15).

and commanded the porter – the gatekeeper.

to watch – pointing to the official duty of the ministers of religion to give warning of approaching danger to the people.

35. Watch ye therefore; for ye know not when the master of the house cometh, at even, or at midnight, or at the cock-crowing, or in the morning – an allusion to the four Roman watches of the night.

36. Lest, coming suddenly, he find you sleeping – See on Lu 12:35–40; Lu 12:42–46.

37. And what I say unto you – this discourse, it will be remembered, was delivered in private.

I say unto all, Watch – anticipating and requiring the diffusion of His teaching by them among all His disciples, and its perpetuation through all time.

Chapter 14

Mr 14:1–11.
The conspiracy of the Jewish authorities to put Jesus to death – the supper and the anointing at Bethany – Judas agrees with the chief priests to betray his Lord.
(= Mt 26:1–16 Lu 22:1–6 Joh 12:1–11).

The events of this section appeared to have occurred on the fourth day (*Wednesday*) of the Redeemer's Last Week.

Conspiracy of the Jewish authorities to put Jesus to death (Mr 14:1, 2)

1. After two days was the feast of the passover, and of unleavened bread – The meaning is, that two days after what is about to be mentioned the passover would arrive; in other words, what follows occurred two days *before* the feast.

and the chief priests and the scribes sought how they might take him by craft, and put him to death – From Matthew's fuller account (Mt 26:1–75) we learn that our Lord announced this to the Twelve as follows, being the first announcement to them of the precise time: 'And it came to pass, when Jesus had finished all these sayings' (Mt 26:1) – referring to the contents of Mt 24:1—25:46, which He delivered to His disciples; His public ministry being now closed: from His *prophetical* He is now passing into His *priestly* office, although all along He Himself took our infirmities and bare our sicknesses – 'He said unto His disciples, Ye know that after two days is [the feast of] the passover, and the Son of man is betrayed to be crucified.' The *first* and the *last* steps of His final sufferings are brought together in this brief announcement of all that was to take place. The *passover* was the first and the chief of the three great annual festivals, commemorative of the redemption of God's people from Egypt, through the sprinkling of the blood of a lamb divinely appointed to be slain for that end; the destroying angel, 'when he saw the blood, *passing over*' the Israelitish houses, on which that blood was seen, when he came to destroy all the first-born in the land of Egypt (Ex 12:12,13) – bright typical foreshadowing of the great Sacrifice, and the Redemption effected thereby. Accordingly, 'by the determinate counsel and foreknowledge of God, who is wonderful in counsel and excellent in working,' it was so ordered that precisely at the passover season, 'Christ our Passover should be sacrificed for us.' On the day following the passover commenced 'the feast of unleavened bread,' so called because for seven days only unleavened bread was to be eaten (Ex 12:18–20). See on 1Co 5:6–8. We are further told by Matthew (Mt 26:3) that the consultation was held in the palace of Caiaphas the high priest, between the chief priests, [the scribes], and the elders of the people, how 'they might take Jesus by subtlety and kill Him.'

2. **But they said, Not on the feast day** – rather, not during the feast; not until the seven days of unleavened bread should be over.

lest there be an uproar of the people – In consequence of the vast influx of strangers, embracing all the male population of the land who had reached a certain age, there were within the walls of Jerusalem at this festival some two million people; and in their excited state, the danger of tumult and bloodshed among 'the people,' who for the most part took Jesus for a prophet, was extreme. See JOSEPHUS [*Antiquities*, 20.5.3]. What plan, if any, these ecclesiastics fixed upon for seizing our Lord, does not appear. But the proposal of Judas being at once and eagerly gone into, it is probable they were till then at some loss for a plan sufficiently quiet and yet effectual. So, just at the feast time shall it be done; the unexpected offer of Judas relieving them of their fears. Thus, as BENGEL remarks, did the divine counsel take effect.

The supper and the anointing at Bethany six days before the passover (Mr 14:3–11)

The time of this part of the narrative is *four days before* what has just been related. Had it been part of the regular train of events which our Evangelist designed to record, he would probably have inserted it in its proper place, before the conspiracy of the Jewish authorities. But having come to the treason of Judas, he seems to have gone back upon this scene as what probably gave immediate occasion to the awful deed.

3. **And being in Bethany, in the house of Simon the leper, as he sat at meat, there came a woman** – It was 'Mary,' as we learn from Joh 12:3.

having an alabaster box of ointment of spikenard – pure *nard*, a celebrated aromatic – (See So 1:12).

very precious – 'very costly' (Joh 12:3).

and she brake the box, and poured it on his head – 'and anointed,' adds John (Joh 12:3), 'the feet of Jesus, and wiped His feet with her hair: and the house was filled with the odor of the ointment.' The only use of this was to refresh and exhilarate – a grateful compliment in the East, amid the closeness of a heated atmosphere,

with many guests at a feast. Such was the form in which Mary's love to Christ, at so much cost to herself, poured itself out.

4. **And there were some that had indignation within themselves and said** – Matthew says (Mt 26:8), 'But when His disciples saw it, they had indignation, saying.' The spokesman, however, was none of the true-hearted Eleven – as we learn from John (Joh 12:4): 'Then saith one of His disciples, Judas Iscariot, Simon's son, which should betray Him.' Doubtless the thought stirred first in his breast, and issued from his base lips; and some of the rest, ignorant of his true character and feelings, and carried away by his plausible speech, might for the moment feel some chagrin at the apparent waste.

5. **and have been given to the poor. And they murmured against her** – 'This he said,' remarks John (Joh 12:6), and the remark is of exceeding importance, 'not that he cared for the poor but because he was a thief, and had the bag' – the scrip or treasure chest – 'and bare what was put therein' – not 'bare it off' by theft, as some understand it. It is true that he did this; but the expression means simply that he had charge of it and its contents, or was treasurer to Jesus and the Twelve. What a remarkable arrangement was this, by which an avaricious and dishonest person was not only taken into the number of the Twelve, but entrusted with the custody of their little property! The purposes which this served are obvious enough; but it is further noticeable, that the remotest hint was never given to the Eleven of his true character, nor did the disciples most favored with the intimacy of Jesus ever suspect him, till a few minutes before he voluntarily separated himself from their company – for ever!

6. **And Jesus said, Let her alone; why trouble ye her? she hath wrought a good work on me** – It was good in itself, and so was acceptable to Christ; it was eminently seasonable, and so more acceptable still; and it was 'what she could,' and so most acceptable of all.

7. **For ye have the poor with you always** – referring to De 15:11.

and whensoever ye will ye may do them good: but me ye have not always – a gentle hint of His approaching departure, by One who knew the worth of His own presence.

8. **She hath done what she could** – a noble testimony, embodying a principle of immense importance.

she is come aforehand to anoint my body to the burying – or, as in John (Joh 12:7), 'Against the day of my burying hath she kept this.' Not that she, dear heart, thought of His burial, much less reserved any of her nard to anoint her dead Lord. But as the time was so near at hand when that office would have to be performed, *and she was* not to have that privilege even after the spices were brought for the purpose (Mr 16:1), He lovingly regards it as done now. 'In the act of love done to Him,' says OLSHAUSEN beautifully, 'she has erected to herself an eternal monument, as lasting as the Gospel, the eternal Word of God. From generation to generation this remarkable prophecy of the Lord has been fulfilled; and even we, in explaining this saying of the Redeemer, of necessity contribute to its accomplishment.' 'Who but Himself,' asks STIER, 'had the power to ensure to any work of man, even if resounding in His own time through the whole earth, an imperishable remembrance in the stream of history? Behold once more here the majesty of His royal judicial supremacy in the government of the world, in this, "Verily I say unto you."'

10. And Judas Iscariot, one of the twelve, went unto the chief priests, to betray him unto them – that is, to make his proposals, and to bargain with them, as appears from Matthew's fuller statement (Mt 26:14,15) which says, he 'went unto the chief priests, and said, What will ye give me, and I will deliver Him unto you? And they covenanted with him for thirty pieces of silver.' The thirty pieces of silver were thirty shekels, the fine paid for man- or maid-servant accidentally killed (Ex 21:32) – 'a *goodly* price that I was prized at of them!' (Zec 11:13).

11. And when they heard it, they were glad, and promised to give him money – Matthew alone records the precise sum, because a remarkable and complicated prophecy, which he was afterwards to refer to, was fulfilled by it.

And he sought how he might conveniently betray him – or, as more fully given in Luke (Lu 22:6), 'And he promised, and sought opportunity to betray Him unto them in the absence of the multitude.' That he should avoid an 'uproar' or 'riot' among the people, which probably was made an essential condition by the Jewish authorities, was thus assented to by the traitor; into whom, says Luke (Lu 22:3), 'Satan entered,' to put him upon this hellish deed.

Mr 14:12–26.
Preparation for, and last celebration of, the passover – announcement of the traitor – institution of the supper.
(= Mt 26:17–30 Lu 22:7–23,39 Joh 13:21–30).
See on Lu 22:7–23; Lu 22:39; and see on
Joh 13:10,11; Joh 13:18,19;
Joh 13:21–30.

Mr 14:27–31.
The desertion of Jesus by his disciples and the fall of Peter, foretold.
(= Mt 26:31–35 Lu 22:31–38 Joh 13:36–38).
See on Lu 22:31–46.

Mr 14:32–42.
The agony in the garden.
(= Mt 26:36–46 Lu 22:39–46).
See on Lu 22:39–46.

Mr 14:43–52.
Betrayal and apprehension of Jesus – flight of his disciples.
(= Mt 26:47–56 Lu 22:47–53 Joh 18:1–12).
See on Joh 18:1–12.

Mr 14:53–72.
Jesus arraigned before the Sanhedrim, condemned to die, and shamefully entreated – the fall of Peter.
(= Mt 26:57–75 Lu 22:54–7
1 Joh 18:13–18,24–27).

Had we only the first three Gospels, we should have concluded that our Lord was led immediately to Caiaphas, and had before the Council. But as the Sanhedrim could hardly have been brought together at the dead hour of night – by which time our Lord was in the hands of the officers sent to take Him – and as it was only 'as soon as it was day' that the Council met (Lu 22:66), we should have had some difficulty in knowing what was done with Him during those intervening hours. In the Fourth Gospel, however, all this is cleared up, and a very important addition to our information is made (Joh 18:13,14,19–24).

53. And they led Jesus away to the high priest: and with him were assembled – or rather, 'there gathered together unto him.'

all the chief priests and the elders and the scribes – it was then a full and formal meeting of the Sanhedrim. Now, as the first three Evangelists place all Peter's denials of his Lord after this, we should naturally conclude that they took place *while our Lord stood before the Sanhedrim*. But besides that the natural impression is that the scene around the fire took place *overnight*, the *second crowing of the cock*, if we are to credit ancient writers, would occur about the beginning of the fourth watch, or between three and four in the morning. By that time, however, the Council had probably convened, being warned, perhaps, that they were to prepare for being called at any hour of the morning, should the Prisoner be successfully secured. If this be correct, it is fairly certain that only the *last* of Peter's three denials would take place while our Lord was under trial before the Sanhedrim. One thing more may require explanation. If our Lord had to be transferred from the residence of Annas to that of Caiaphas, one is apt to wonder that there is no mention of His being marched from the one to the other. But the building, in all likelihood, was one and the same; in which case He would merely have to be taken perhaps across the court, from one chamber to another.

54. And Peter followed him afar off, even into – or 'from afar, even to the interior of.' **the palace of the high priest** – 'An oriental house,' says ROBINSON, 'is usually built around a quadrangular interior court; into which there is a passage (sometimes arched) through the front part of the house, closed next the street by a heavy folding gate, with a smaller wicket for single persons, kept by a porter. The interior court, often paved or flagged, and open to the sky, is the *hall*, which our translators have rendered "palace," where the attendants made a fire; and the passage beneath the front of the house, from the street to this court, is the *porch.*' The place where Jesus stood before the high priest may have been an open room, or place of audience on the ground floor, in the rear or on one side of the court; such rooms, open in front, being customary. It was close upon the court, for Jesus heard all that was going on around the fire, and turned and looked upon Peter (Lu 22:61).

and he sat with the servants, and warmed himself at the fire – The graphic details, here omitted, are supplied in the other Gospels. See Joh 18:18–23; Mt 26:58.

The judicial trial and condemnation of the Lord Jesus by the Sanhedrim
(Mr 14:55–64)

But let the reader observe, that though this is introduced by the Evangelist before any of the denials of Peter are recorded, we have given reasons for concluding that probably the *first two denials* took place while our Lord was with Annas, and the last only during the trial before the Sanhedrim.

55. And the chief priests and all the council sought for witness against Jesus to put him to death – Matthew (Mt 26:59) says they 'sought *false* witness.' They knew they could find nothing valid; but having their Prisoner to bring before Pilate, they behooved to *make a case.*

and found none – none that would suit their purpose, or make a decent ground of charge before Pilate.

56. For many bare false witness against him – From their debasing themselves to '*seek*' them, we are led to infer that they were *bribed* to bear false witness; though there are never wanting sycophants enough, ready to sell themselves for naught, if they may but get a smile from those above them: see a similar scene in Ac 6:11–14. How is one reminded here of that complaint, 'False witnesses did rise up: they laid to my charge things that I knew not' (Ps 31:11)!

but their witness agreed not together – If even *two* of them had been agreed, it would have been greedily enough laid hold of, as all that the law insisted upon even in capital cases (De 17:6). But even in this they failed. One cannot but admire the providence which secured this result; since, on the one hand, it seems astonishing that those unscrupulous prosecutors and their ready tools should so bungle a business in which they felt their whole interests bound up; and, on the other hand, if they *had* succeeded in making even a plausible case, the effect on the progress of the Gospel might for a time have been injurious. But at the very time when His enemies were saying, 'God hath forsaken Him; persecute and take Him; for there is none to deliver Him' (Ps 71:11), He whose Witness He was and whose work He was doing was keeping Him as the apple of His eye, and while He was making the wrath of man to praise Him, was restraining the remainder of that wrath (Ps 76:10).

57. And there arose certain, and bare false witness against him – Matthew (Mt 26:60) is more precise here: '*At the last* came two false witnesses.' As no two had before agreed in anything, they felt it necessary to secure a duplicate testimony to something, but they were long of succeeding. And what was it, when at length it was brought forward?

saying – as follows:

58. We heard him say, I will destroy this temple that is made with hands, and within three days I will build another made without hands – On this charge, observe, first, that eager as His enemies were to find criminal matter against our Lord, they had to go back to the outset of His ministry, His first visit to Jerusalem, more than three years before this. In all that He said and did after that, though ever increasing in boldness, they could find nothing. Next, that even then, they fix only on one speech, of two or three words, which they dared to adduce against Him. Further, they most manifestly pervert the speech of our Lord. We say not this because in Mark's form of it, it differs from the report of the words given by the Fourth Evangelist (Joh 2:18–22) – the only one of the Evangelists who reports it all, or mentions even any visit paid by our Lord to Jerusalem before His last – but because the one report bears truth, and the other falsehood, on its face. When our Lord said on that occasion, 'Destroy this temple, and in three days I will raise it up,' they *might,* for a moment, have understood Him to refer to the temple out of whose courts He had swept the buyers and sellers. But *after* they had expressed their astonishment at His words, in that sense of them, and reasoned upon the time it had taken to rear the temple as it then stood, since *no answer* to this appears to have been given by our Lord, it is hardly conceivable that they should continue in the persuasion that this was really His meaning. But finally, even if the more ignorant among them had done so, it is next to certain that *the ecclesiastics*, who were *the prosecutors* in this case, *did not believe that this was His meaning*. For in less than three days after this they went to Pilate, saying, 'Sir, we remember that that deceiver said, while he was yet alive, *after three days I will rise again*' (Mt 27:63). Now what utterance of Christ known to His enemies, *could this refer to*, if not to this very saying about destroying and rearing up the temple? And if so, it puts it beyond a doubt that by this time, at least, they were perfectly aware that our Lord's words referred to *His death by their hands and His resurrection by His own*. But this is confirmed by Mr 14:59.

59. But neither so did their witness agree together – that is, not even as to so brief a speech, consisting of but a few words, was there such a concurrence in their mode of reporting it as to make out a decent case. In such a charge *everything depended on the very terms alleged to have been used*. For every one must see that a very slight turn, either way, given to such words, would make them either something like *indictable matter*, or else a *ridiculous ground for a criminal charge* – would either give them a tolerable pretext for the charge of impiety which they were bent on making out, or else make the whole saying appear, on the worst view that could be taken of it, as merely some mystical or empty boast.

60. Answerest thou nothing? what is it which these witness against thee? – Clearly, they felt that *their case had failed*, and by this artful question the high priest hoped to get *from His own mouth* what they had in vain tried to obtain from their false and contradictory witnesses. But in this, too, they failed.

61. But he held his peace, and answered nothing – This must have nonplussed them. But they were not to be easily baulked of their object.

Again the high priest – arose (Mt 26:62), matters having now come to a crisis.

asked him, and said unto him, Art thou the Christ, the Son of the Blessed? – Why our Lord should have answered this question, when He was silent as to the former, we might not have quite seen, but for Matthew, who says (Mt 26:63) that the high priest *put Him upon solemn oath*, saying, 'I adjure Thee by the living God, that Thou tell us whether Thou be the Christ, the Son of God.' Such an adjuration was understood to render an answer legally necessary (Le 5:1). (Also see on Joh 18:28.)

62. And Jesus said, I am – or, as in Matthew (Mt 26:64), 'Thou hast said [it].' In Luke, however (Lu 22:70), the answer, 'Ye say that I am,' should be rendered – as DeWette, Meyer, Ellicott, and the best critics agree that the preposition requires – 'Ye say [it], for I am [so].' Some words, however, were spoken by our Lord before giving His answer to this solemn question. These are recorded by Luke alone (Lu 22:67,68): 'Art Thou the Christ [they asked]? tell us. And He said unto them, If I tell you, ye will not believe: and if I also ask [interrogate] 'you, ye will not answer Me, nor let Me go.' This seems to have been uttered before giving His direct answer, as a calm remonstrance and dignified protest against the prejudgment of His case and the unfairness of their mode of procedure. But now let us hear the rest of the answer, in which the conscious majesty of Jesus breaks forth from behind the dark cloud which overhung Him as He stood before the Council. (Also see on Joh 18:28.)

and – in that character.

ye shall see the Son of man sitting on the right hand of power, and coming in the clouds of heaven – In Matthew (Mt 26:64) a slightly different but interesting turn is given to it by one word: 'Thou hast said [it]: nevertheless' – We prefer this sense of the word to 'besides,' which some recent critics decide for – 'I say unto you, Hereafter shall ye see the Son of man sit on the right hand of power, and coming in the clouds of heaven.' The word rendered 'hereafter' means, not 'at some future time' (as to-day 'hereafter' commonly does), but what the English word originally signified, 'after here,' 'after now,' or 'from this time.' Accordingly, in Lu 22:69, the words used mean 'from now.' So that though the reference we have given it to the day of His glorious Second Appearing is too obvious to admit of doubt, He would, by using the expression, 'From this time,' convey the important thought which He had before expressed, immediately after the traitor left the supper table to do his dark work, 'Now is the Son of man glorified' (Joh 13:31). At this moment, and by this speech, did He 'witness *the good confession*' emphatically and properly, as the apostle says in 1Ti 6:13. Our translators render the words there, 'Who *before* Pontius Pilate witnessed'; referring it to the admission of His being a *King*, in the presence of Cæsar's own chief representative. But it should be rendered, as Luther renders it, and as the best interpreters now understand it, 'Who *under* Pontius Pilate witnessed'. In this view of it, the apostle is referring not to what our Lord confessed *before* Pilate – which, though noble, was not of such primary importance – but to that sublime confession which, under Pilate's administration, He witnessed before the only competent tribunal on such occasions, the Supreme Ecclesiastical Council of God's chosen nation, that He was the Messiah, and the Son of the Blessed

ONE; in the former word owning His Supreme *Official,* in the latter His Supreme *Personal,* Dignity.

63. Then the high priest rent his clothes – On this expression of *horror of blasphemy,* see 2Ki 18:37.

and saith, What need we any further witnesses? (Also see on Joh 18:28.)

64. Ye have heard the blasphemy – (See Joh 10:33.) In Luke (Lu 22:71), 'For we ourselves have heard of His own mouth' – an affectation of religious horror. (Also see on Joh 18:28.)

what think ye? – 'Say what the verdict is to be.'

they all condemned him to be guilty of death – or of a capital crime, which *blasphemy* against God was according to the Jewish law (Le 24:16). Yet *not absolutely all;* for *Joseph* of Arimathea, 'a good man and a just,' was one of that Council, and '*he was not a consenting party* to the counsel and deed of them,' for that is the strict sense of the words of Lu 23:50,51. Probably he absented himself, and *Nicodemus* also, from this meeting of the Council, the temper of which they would know too well to expect their voice to be listened to; and in that case, the words of our Evangelist are to be taken strictly, that, without one dissentient voice, 'all [present] condemned him to be guilty of death.'

The Blessed One is now shamefully entreated (Mr 14:65)

Every word here must be carefully observed, and the several accounts put together, that we may lose none of the awful indignities about to be described.

65. some began to spit on him – or, as in Mt 26:67, 'to spit in [into] His face.' Luke (Lu 22:63) says in addition, 'And the men that held Jesus mocked him' – or cast their jeers at Him. (Also see on Joh 18:28.)

to cover his face – or 'to blindfold him' (as in Lu 22:64).

to buffet him – Luke's word, which is rendered 'smote Him' (Lu 22:63), is a stronger one, conveying an idea for which we have an exact equivalent in English, but one too colloquial to be inserted here.

began to say unto him, Prophesy – In Matthew (Mt 26:68) this is given more fully: 'Prophesy unto us, thou Christ, Who is he that smote Thee?' The sarcastic fling at Him as '*the Christ,*' and the demand of Him in this character to name the unseen perpetrator of the blows inflicted on Him, was in them as infamous as to Him it must have been, and was intended to be, stinging.

and the servants did strike him with the palms of their hands – or 'struck Him on the face' (Lu 22:64). Ah! Well did He say prophetically, in that Messianic prediction which we have often referred to, 'I gave My back to the smiters, and My cheeks to them that plucked off the hair: I hid not My face from shame and spitting!' (Isa 50:6). 'And many other things blasphemously spake they against Him' (Lu 22:65). This general statement is important, as showing that virulent and varied as were the *recorded* affronts put upon Him, they are but a *small specimen* of what He endured on that dark occasion.

Peter's FIRST DENIAL of his Lord (Mr 14:66–68)

66. And as Peter was beneath in the palace – This little word '*beneath*' – one of our Evangelist's graphic touches – is most important for the right understanding of what we may call the topography of the scene. We must take it in connection with Matthew's word (Mt 26:69): 'Now Peter sat *without* in the palace' – or quadrangular court, in the center of which the fire would be burning; and crowding around and buzzing about it would be the menials and others who had been admitted within the court. At the upper end of this court, probably, would be the memorable chamber in which the trial was held – *open to the court,* likely, and *not far from the fire* (as we gather from Lu 22:61), but *on a higher level;* for (as our verse says) the court, with Peter in it, was 'beneath' it. The ascent to the Council chamber was perhaps by a short flight of steps. If the reader will bear this explanation in mind, he will find the intensely interesting details which follow more intelligible.

there cometh one of the maids of the high priest – 'the damsel that kept the door' (Joh 18:17). The Jews seem to have employed women as porters of their doors (Ac 12:13).

67. And when she saw Peter warming himself, she looked upon him – Luke (Lu 22:56) is here more graphic; 'But a certain maid beheld him as he sat by the fire' – literally, 'by the *light,*' which, shining full upon him, revealed him to the girl – 'and earnestly looked upon him' – or, 'fixed her gaze upon him.' 'His demeanor and timidity, which must have attracted notice, as so generally happens, leading,' says OLSHAUSEN, 'to the recognition of him.'

and said, And thou also wast with Jesus of Nazareth – 'with Jesus the Nazarene,' or, 'with Jesus of Galilee' (Mt 26:69). The sense of this is given in John's report of it (Joh 18:17), 'Art not thou also one of this man's disciples?' that is, thou as well as 'that other disciple,' whom she knew to be one, but did not challenge, perceiving that he was a privileged person. In Luke (Lu 22:56) it is given as a remark made by the maid to one of the by-standers – 'this man was also with Him.' If so expressed in Peter's hearing – drawing upon him the eyes of every one that heard it (as we know it did, Mt 26:70), and compelling him to answer to it – that would explain the different forms of the report naturally enough. But in such a case this is of no real importance.

68. But he denied – 'before all' (Mt 26:70).

saying, I know not, neither understand I what thou sayest – in Luke (Lu 22:57), 'I know Him not.'

And he went out into the porch – the vestibule leading to the street – no doubt finding the fire-place too *hot* for him; possibly also with the hope of escaping – but that was not to be, and perhaps he dreaded that, too. Doubtless by this time his mind would be getting into a sea of commotion, and would fluctuate every moment in its resolves.

And the cock crew – (See on Lu 22:34.) This, then, was the First Denial.

Peter's SECOND DENIAL of His Lord
(Mr 14:69, 70)

There is here a verbal difference among the Evangelists, which without some information which has been withheld, cannot be quite extricated.

69. And a maid saw him again – or, 'a girl.' It might be rendered 'the girl'; but this would not necessarily mean the same one as before, but might, and probably does, mean just the female who had charge of the door or gate near which Peter now was. Accordingly, in Mt 26:71, she is expressly called 'another [maid].' But in Luke (Lu 22:58) it is a *male* servant: 'And after a little while [from the time of the first denial] another' – that is, as the word signifies, 'another male' servant. But there is no real difficulty, as the challenge, probably, after being made by one was reiterated by another. Accordingly, in John (Joh 18:25), it is, '*They* said therefore unto him' – as if more than one challenged him at once.

and began to say to them that stood by, This is one of them – or, as in Mt 26:71 – 'This [fellow] was also with Jesus the Nazarene.'

70. And he denied it again – In Luke (Lu 22:58), 'Man, I am not.' But worst of all in Matthew – 'And again he denied with an oath, I do not know the man' (Mt 26:72). This was the Second Denial, more vehement, alas! than the first.

Peter's THIRD DENIAL of His Lord
(Mr 14:70–72)

70. And a little after – 'about the space of one hour after' (Lu 22:59).

they that stood by said again to Peter, Surely thou art one of them: for thou art a Galilean, and thy speech agreeth thereto – 'bewrayeth [or "discovereth"] thee' (Mt 26:73). In Luke (Lu 22:59) it is, 'Another confidently affirmed, saying, Of a truth this [fellow] also was with him: for he is a Galilean.' The Galilean dialect had a more *Syrian* cast than that of Judea. *If Peter had*

held his peace, this peculiarity had not been observed; but hoping, probably, to put them off the scent by joining in the *fireside talk,* he was thus discovered. The Fourth Gospel is particularly interesting here: 'One of the servants of the high priest, being his kinsman [or kinsman to him] whose ear Peter cut off, saith, Did not I see thee in the garden with Him?' (Joh 18:26). No doubt his relationship to Malchus drew his attention to the man who had smitten him, and this enabled him to identify Peter. 'Sad reprisals!' exclaims BENGEL. Poor Peter! Thou art caught in thine own toils; but like a wild bull in a net, thou wilt toss and rage, filling up the measure of thy terrible declension by one more denial of thy Lord, and that the foulest of all.

71. But he began to curse – 'anathematize,' or wish himself accursed if what he was now to say was not true.

and to swear – or to take a solemn oath.

saying, I know not this man of whom ye speak.

72. And the second time the cock crew – The other three Evangelists, who mention but one crowing of the cock – and that not the first, but the second and last one of Mark – all say the cock crew 'immediately,' but Luke (Lu 22:60) says, 'Immediately, while he yet spake, the cock crew.' Alas! – But now comes the wonderful sequel. See Lu 22:61,62.

And Peter called to mind the word that Jesus said unto him, Before the cock crow twice, thou shalt deny me thrice. And when he thought thereon, he wept – To the same effect is the statement of the First Evangelist (Mt 26:75), save that like 'the beloved physician,' he notices the 'bitterness' of the weeping (Lu 22:62). The most precious link, however, in the whole chain of circumstances in this scene is beyond doubt that 'look' of deepest, tenderest import reported by Luke alone (Lu 22:61). Who can tell what lightning flashes of wounded love and piercing reproach shot from that 'look' through the eye of Peter into his heart! See Lu 22:62.

Chapter 15

Mr 15:1–20.

Jesus is brought before Pilate – at a second hearing, Pilate, after seeking to release him, delivers him up – after being cruelly entreated, he is led away to be crucified.
(= Mt 26:1,2,11–31 Lu 23:1–6,13–25
Joh 18:28—19:16).
See on Joh 18:28—19:16.

Mr 15:21–37.

Crucifixion and death of the Lord Jesus.
(= Mt 27:32–50 Lu 23:26–46 Joh 19:17–30).
See on Joh 19:17–30.

Mr 15:38–47.

Signs and circumstances following the death of the Lord Jesus – he is taken down from the cross and buried – the sepulchre is guarded.

(= Mt 27:51–66 Lu 23:45,47–56 Joh 19:31–42).
See on Mt 27:51–56; and Joh 19:31–42.

Chapter 16

Mr 16:1–20.

Angelic announcement to the women on the first day of the week, that Christ is risen – his appearances after his resurrection – his ascension – triumphant proclamation of his gospel.

(= Mt 28:1–10,16–20 Lu 24:1–51
Joh 20:1,2,11–29).

The resurrection announced to the women (Mr 16:1–8)

1. when the sabbath was past – that is, at sunset of our Saturday.

Mary Magdalene – (See on Lu 8:2.)

Mary the mother of James – James the Less (see Mr 15:40).

and Salome – the mother of Zebedee's sons (compare Mr 15:40 with Mt 27:56).

had bought sweet spices, that they might come and anoint him – The word is simply 'bought.' But our translators are perhaps right in rendering it here 'had bought,' since it would appear, from Lu 23:56, that they had purchased them immediately after the Crucifixion, on the *Friday* evening, during the short interval that remained to them before sunset, when the sabbath rest began; and that they had only deferred using them to anoint the body till the sabbath rest should be over. On this 'anointing,' see on Joh 19:40.

2. very early in the morning – (See on Mt 28:1.)

the first day of the week, they came unto the sepulchre at the rising of the sun – not quite literally, but 'at earliest dawn'; according to a way of speaking not uncommon, and occurring sometimes in the Old Testament. Thus our Lord rose on the third day; having lain in the grave part of Friday, the whole of Saturday, and part of the following First day.

3. they said among themselves – as they were approaching the sacred spot.

Who shall roll us away the stone from the door of the sepulchre? ... for it was very great – On reaching it they find their difficulty gone – the stone already rolled away by an unseen hand. *And are there no others who, when advancing to duty in the face of appalling difficulties, find their stone also rolled away?*

5. entering into the sepulchre, they saw a young man – In Mt 28:2 he is called 'the angel of the Lord'; but here he is described as he appeared to the eye, in the bloom of a life that knows no decay. In Matthew he is represented as sitting on the stone *outside* the sepulchre; but since even there he says, '*Come*, see the place where the Lord lay' (Mt 28:6), he seems, as ALFORD says, to have gone in with them from without; only awaiting their arrival to accompany them into the hallowed spot, and instruct them about it.

sitting on the right side – having respect to the position in which His Lord had lain there. This trait is peculiar to Mark; but compare Lu 1:11.

clothed in a long white garment – On its *length*, see on Isa 6:1; and on its *whiteness*, see on Mt 28:3.

and they were affrighted.

6. he saith unto them, Be not affrighted – a stronger word than 'Fear not' in Matthew (Mt 28:5).

Ye seek Jesus of Nazareth, which was crucified! – 'the Nazarene, the Crucified,'

he is risen; he is not here – (See on Lu 24:5,6.)

behold the place where they laid him – (See on Mt 28:6.)

7. But go your way, tell his disciples and Peter – This Second Gospel, being drawn up – as all the earliest tradition states – *under the eye of Peter*, or from materials chiefly furnished by him, there is something deeply affecting in the preservation of this little phrase by Mark alone.

that he goeth before you into Galilee; there shall ye see him, as he said unto you – (See on Mt 28:7.)

8. And they went out quickly, and fled from the sepulchre: for they trembled and were amazed – 'for tremor and amazement seized them.'

neither said they anything to any man; for they were afraid – How intensely natural and simple is this!

Appearances of Jesus after His resurrection (Mr 16:9–18)

9. Now when Jesus was risen early the first day of the week, he appeared first to Mary Magdalene, out of whom he had cast seven devils – There is some difficulty here, and different ways of removing it have been adopted. She had gone with the other women to the sepulchre (Mr 16:1), parting from them, perhaps, before their interview with the angel, and on finding Peter and John she had come with them back to the spot; and it was at this second visit, it would seem, that Jesus appeared to this Mary, as detailed in Joh 20:11–18. *To a woman was this honour given to be the first that saw the* *risen Redeemer, and that woman was* NOT *his virgin-mother.*

11. they, when they had heard that he was alive, and had been seen of her, believed not – This, which is once and again repeated of them all, is most important in its bearing on their subsequent testimony to His resurrection at the risk of life itself.

12. After that he appeared in another form – (compare Lu 24:16.)

unto two of them as they walked, and went into the country – The reference here, of course, is to His manifestation to the two disciples going to Emmaus, so exquisitely told by the Third Evangelist (see on Lu 24:13).

15. he said unto them, Go ye into all the world, and preach the Gospel to every creature – See on Joh 20:19–23 and Lu 24:36–49.

16. He that believeth and is baptized – Baptism is here put for the external signature of the inner faith of the heart, just as 'confessing with the mouth' is in Ro 10:10; and there also as here this *outward* manifestation, once mentioned as the proper fruit of faith, is not repeated in what follows (Ro 10:11).

shall be saved; but he that believeth not shall be damned – These awful issues of the reception or rejection of the Gospel, though often recorded in other connections, are given in this connection only by Mark.

17, 18. these signs shall follow them that believe ... They shall take up serpents – These two verses also are peculiar to Mark.

The ascension and triumphant proclamation of the Gospel thereafter (Mr 16:19, 20)

19. So then after the Lord – an epithet applied to Jesus by this Evangelist only in Mr 16:19,20, when He comes to His glorious Ascension and its subsequent fruits. It is most frequent in Luke.

had spoken unto them, he was received up into heaven – See on Lu 24:50,51.

and sat on the right hand of God – This great truth is here only related as a fact in the Gospel history. In that exalted attitude He appeared to Stephen (Ac 7:55,56); and it is thereafter perpetually referred to as His proper condition in glory.

20. they went forth, and preached everywhere, the Lord working with them, and confirming the word with signs following. Amen – We have in this closing verse a most important link of connection with the Acts of the Apostles, where He who directed all the movements of the infant Church is perpetually styled 'THE LORD'; thus illustrating His own promise for the rounding and building up of the Church, 'Lo, I AM WITH YOU alway!'

THE MIRACLES
OF CHRIST

Put into chronological order by David Brown

On the order of some of our Lord's Miracles and Parables, the data being scanty, considerable difference obtains.

MIRACLES	WHERE PERFORMED	WHERE RECORDED
Water made wine	Cana	Joh 2:1–11.
Traders cast out of the temple	Jerusalem	Joh 2:13–17.
Nobleman's son healed	Cana	Joh 4:46–54.
First miraculous draught of fishes	Sea of Galilee	Lu 5:1–11.
Leper healed	Capernaum	Mt 8:2–4 Mark 1:40–45 Lu 5:12–15.
Centurion's servant healed	Capernaum	Mt 8:5–13 Lu 7:1–10.
Widow's son raised to life	Nain	Lu 7:11–17.
Demoniac healed	Capernaum	Mr 1:21–28 Lu 4:31–37.
Peter's mother-in-law healed	Capernaum	Mt 8:14,15 Mr 1:29–31 Lu 4:38,39.
Paralytic healed	Capernaum	Mt 9:2–8 Mr 2:1–12 Lu 5:17–26.
Impotent man healed	Jerusalem	Joh 5:1–16.
Man with withered hand healed	Galilee	Mt 12:10–14 Mr 3:1–6 Lu 6:6–11.
Blind and dumb demoniac healed	Galilee	Mt 12:22–24 Lu 11:14.
Tempest stilled	Sea of Galilee	Mt 8:23–27 Mr 4:35–41 Lu 8:22–25.
Demoniacs dispossessed	Gadara	Mt 8:28–34 Mr 5:1–20.
Jairus' daughter raised to life	Capernaum	Mt 9:18–26 Mr 5:22–24 Lu 8:41–56.
Issue of blood healed	Near Capernaum	Mt 9:18–26 Mr 5:22–24 Lu 8:41–56.
Two blind men restored to sight	Capernaum	Mt 9:27–31.
Dumb demoniac healed	Capernaum	Mt 9:32–34.

Five thousand miraculously fed	Decapolis	Mt 14:13–21 Mr 6:31–44 Lu 9:10–17 Joh 6:5–14.
Jesus walks on the sea	Sea of Galilee	Mt 14:22–33 Mr 6:45–52 Joh 6:15–21.
Syrophoenician daughter healed	Coasts of Tyre and Sidon	Mt 15:21–28 Mr 7:24–30.
Deaf and dumb man healed	Decapolis	Mr 7:31–37.
Four thousand fed	Decapolis	Mt 15:32–39 Mr 8:1–9.
Blind man restored to sight	Bethsaida	Mr 8:22–26.
Demoniac and lunatic boy healed	Near Cæsarea Philippi	Mt 17:14–21 Mr 9:14–29 Lu 9:37–43.
Miraculous provision of tribute	Capernaum	Mt 17:24–27.
The eyes of one born blind opened	Jerusalem	Joh 9:1–41.
Woman, of eighteen years' infirmity, cured	[Perea]	Lu 13:10–17.
Dropsical man healed	[Perea]	Lu 14:1–6.
Ten lepers cleansed	Borders of Samaria	Lu 17:11–19.
Lazarus raised to life	Bethany	Joh 11:1–46.
Two blind beggars restored to sight	Jericho	Mt 20:29–34 Mr 10:46–52 Lu 18:35–43.
Barren fig tree blighted	Bethany	Mt 21:12,13,18,19 Mr 11:12–24.
Buyers and sellers again cast out	Jerusalem	Lu 19:45,46.
Malchus' ear healed	Gethsemane	Mt 26:51–54 Mr 14:47–49 Lu 22:50,51 Joh 18:10,11.
Second draught of fishes	Sea of Galilee	Joh 21:1–14.

LUKE

J.C. Ryle

Introduction

I have steadily adhered to the threefold object which I proposed to myself when I first began. I have endeavoured to produce something which may meet the needs of families conducting family prayers – of district visitors in reading to the sick and unlearned – and of private students of the Bible who have neither large libraries nor much leisure. These three classes I have constantly kept in view. Their needs have been constantly in my mind. Whatever would be unsuitable for them I have diligently tried to avoid.

In one important respect the present volume will be found to differ from the two which have preceded it. I allude to the explanatory notes which I have appended to each portion of Scripture expounded. A few words on the nature of these notes may not be out of place.

1. My first object has been to throw light on difficulties. I can say with a good conscience that I have endeavoured to examine every difficult passage, and have never turned aside from any perplexing expression or text. I have striven to gather together all the information I could obtain on each difficulty, and to present it to the reader in a compact and lucid form. I do not pretend for a moment to say that I have explained everything. I am deeply conscious that I have left many a hard thing in St. Luke where I found it. But I can honestly say that I have never shrunk from the discussion of difficulties. I have resolved that it should never be said that I commented upon easy things and left hard things untouched.

2. My second object has been to assist those readers who do not understand the Greek language. I have tried to point out the literal meaning of words in the original Greek which, for various reasons, our English translators have rendered less literally than they might have done.

3. My third aim has been to quote passages from approved writers which throw light on subjects under discussion, and to name writers who may be referred to on special points, by those who have libraries and leisure.

4. My last aim in these notes has been to combat the existing false teachings and heresies, on every occasion; and to point out the answers to them which the text of Scripture supplies. I have unhesitatingly avowed that I hold the plenary inspiration of every word of Holy Scripture, and that I thoroughly adhere to those views which are commonly called Protestant and Evangelical.

On one point only I have carefully abstained from offering any opinion. I refer to the vexed questions of the comparative claims of various readings, of the authority of manuscripts, and of the best Greek text of the New Testament.

It only remains for me to say that in the preparation of these notes, as well as of the Expository Thoughts, I have made a diligent use of all the commentators within my reach, both ancient and modern. I add a list of them, which may prove interesting to some readers, and useful to those who want to know the names of writers who have commented on St. Luke. In giving this list, I trust my motives will not be misunderstood. My simple desire is to show that I have not written on St. Luke's gospel in ignorance of other people's labours, and that when I disagree with them, it is not because I do not know what they have to say. The names of those writers whom I have consulted are as follows:

1. Fathers: Ambrose, Theophylact, Euthymius, Augustine's Sermons on the New Testament, and the Catena of Corderius.

2. Foreign Protestant commentators: Calvin, Brentius, Bucer, Bullinger, Beza, Pellican, Gualter, Chemnitius, Flavius, Illyricus, Piscator, Cocceius, De Dieu, Calovius, Aretius, Schottgen, Bengel, Heinsius, Olshausen, Stier.

3. Foreign Roman Catholic commentators: Jansenius, Barradius, Maldonatus, Cornelius a Lapide, Quesnel, Stella, Clarius, Novarinus.

4. English commentators: Trapp, Mayer, Cartwright, Lightfoot, Baxter, Ness, Leigh, Hammond, Poole's Synopsis and Annotations, Henry, Whitby, Burkitt, Gill, Pearce, Scott, A. Clarke, Barnes, Davidson, Alford, Wordsworth, Ford, Watson, Burgon, Major.

In reading these commentators I have often been surprised to find light where I expected darkness, and darkness where I expected light. I have also discovered that some of the best commentaries on Scripture are comparatively little known.

I now send forth this volume with an earnest prayer that the Holy Spirit may bless it, and that God may be pleased to use it for his own glory and the benefit of many souls. My chief aim in this, and in all my writings, is to exalt the Lord Jesus Christ and make him beautiful and glorious in the eyes of men, and to promote the increase of repentance, faith, and holiness on earth. If this is the result of this volume the labour that it has cost me will be more than repaid.

I have a strong conviction that we want more reverent, deep-searching study of the Scripture in the present day. Most Christians see nothing beyond the surface of the Bible when they read it. We want a more clear knowledge of Christ, as a living Person, a living Priest, a living Physician, a living Friend, a living Advocate at the right hand of God, and a living Saviour soon about to come again. Most Christians know little about Christianity but its skeleton of doctrines. I desire never to forget two things. If I can do anything to make Christ and the Bible more honourable in these latter days, I shall be truly thankful and content.

J.C. RYLE *August 1858, Christ Church Oxford*

Contents

See also, *Outlines of the New Testament Books*, pp. 890–3, for John Wesley's outline of contents.

The Virgin Mary's song of praise (1:46–56)
The birth of John the Baptist (1:57–66)
Zacharias's prophecy and song of praise (1:67–80)

St. Luke's general introduction to his Gospel (1:1–4)

St. Luke's Gospel contains many precious things which are not recorded in the other three Gospels. For example, the histories of Zechariah and Elizabeth, the angel's announcement to the Virgin Mary, and, in general terms, the first two chapters of his Gospel. Only St. Luke records the conversions of Zacchaeus and the penitent thief, the walk to Emmaus, and the famous parables of the Pharisee and the Tax Collector, the Rich Man and Lazarus, and the Lost Son. These are parts of Scripture for which every well-instructed Christian feels peculiarly thankful. And for these we are indebted to the Gospel of St. Luke.

The short preface (1–4) is a peculiar feature of St. Luke's Gospel.

1. A sketch of the nature of a Gospel

In the first place, St. Luke gives us a short, but valuable sketch of the nature of a Gospel. He calls it **an orderly account of the events that have been fulfilled among us** (verse 1). It is a narrative of facts about Jesus Christ.

Christianity is a religion built on facts. Let us never lose sight of this. It came before mankind at first in this shape. The first preachers did not go up and down the world proclaiming an elaborate, artificial system of abstruse doctrines and deep principles. They made it their first business to tell people great plain facts. They went about telling a sin-laden world that the Son of God had come down to earth, and lived for us, and died for us, and rose again for us. The Gospel, as it was first proclaimed, was far more simple than many make it now. It was neither more nor less than the history of Christ.

Let us aim at greater simplicity in our own personal religion. Let Christ be the Sun of our system, and let the main desire of our souls be to live the life of faith in him, and daily know him better. This was St. Paul's Christianity (see Philippians 1:21).

2. The true position of the apostles in the early church

In the second place, St. Luke draws a beautiful picture of the true position of the apostles in the early church. He calls them **eyewitnesses and servants of the word** (verse 2). There is an instructive humility in this expression. There is an utter absence of that man-exalting tone which has so often crept into the church. St.

Luke gives the apostles no flattering titles. He affords not the slightest excuse to those who speak of them with idolatrous veneration because of their office and nearness to our Lord.

He describes them as **eyewitnesses**. They told people what they had seen with their own eyes, and heard with their own ears (1 John 1:1). He describes them as **servants of the word**. They were servants of the Word of the Gospel. They were men who counted it their highest privilege to carry about, as messengers, the tidings of God's love to a sinful world, and to tell the story of the cross.

Well would it have been for the church and the world if Christian ministers had never laid claim to higher dignity and honour than the apostles claimed for themselves. It is a sad fact that ordained men have constantly exalted themselves and their office to a most unscriptural position. It is no less sad that people have constantly helped on this evil, by a lazy acquiescence in the demands of priestcraft, and by contenting themselves with a mere vicarious religion. There have been faults on both sides. Let us remember this, and be on our guard.

3. St. Luke's qualifications for writing a Gospel

In the third place, St. Luke describes his own qualifications for the work of writing a Gospel. He says that **after investigating everything carefully from the very first** (verse 3), he decided to write an orderly account.

It would be mere waste of time to inquire from what source St. Luke obtained the information which he has given us in his Gospel. We have no good reason for supposing that he saw our Lord work miracles, or heard him teach. To say that he obtained his information from the Virgin Mary, or any of the apostles, is mere conjecture and speculation. Enough for us to know that St. Luke wrote by God's inspiration. Unquestionably he did not neglect the ordinary means of obtaining knowledge. But the Holy Spirit guided him, no less than all other writers of the Bible, in his choice of matter. The Holy Spirit supplied him with thoughts, arrangements, sentences, and even words; and the result is that what St. Luke wrote is not to be read 'as a human word' but as 'God's word' (1 Thessalonians 2:13).

Let us take care to hold on to this great doctrine of the plenary inspiration of every word of the Bible. Let us never allow that any writer of the Old or New Testament could make even the slightest verbal mistake or error, when writing, since he was 'moved by the Holy Spirit' (2 Peter 1:21). Let it be a settled principle with us in reading the Bible, that when we cannot understand a passage, or reconcile it with some other passage, the fault is not in the Bible, but in ourselves. The adoption of this principle will place our feet on a rock. To give it up is to stand on quicksand, and to fill our minds with endless uncertainties and doubts.

4. St. Luke's main purpose in writing his Gospel

Finally, St. Luke informs us of one main purpose he had in mind in writing his Gospel. It was that Theophilus **may know the truth concerning the things about which** he had **been instructed** (verse 4). There is no encouragement here for those who place confidence in unwritten traditions, and the voice of the church. St. Luke knew well the weakness of human memory, and the readiness with which a history alters its shape both by additions and alterations, when it depends only on word of mouth and report. What therefore does he do? He takes care **to write** (verse 3).

There is no encouragement here for those who are opposed to the spread of religious knowledge, and talk of ignorance as the 'mother of devotion.' St. Luke does not wish his friend to remain in doubt on any matter of his faith. He tells him that he wants him to **know the truth concerning the things** he had **been taught** (verse 4).

Let us close the passage with thankfulness for the Bible. Let us bless God daily that we are not left dependent on human traditions, and need not be led astray by ministers' mistakes. We have a written volume, which is 'able to instruct you for salvation through faith in Christ Jesus' (2 Timothy 3:15).

Let us begin St. Luke's Gospel with an earnest desire to know more for ourselves the truth as it is in Jesus, and with a hearty determination to do as much as we can to spread the knowledge of that truth throughout the world.

Notes on Luke 1:1–4

Luke. Our information about St. Luke is scanty. What we have no reason to doubt is that he was the companion of St. Paul on his travels, and that he was a 'physician' (Colossians 4:14). It is generally agreed that his Gospel was written with a special reference to Gentile converts, rather than Jews.

1. Many have undertaken. Who these **many** were we do not know. St. Luke's meaning appears to be simply this, that they wrote without any divine call or inspiration.

2. The word. Some think that this means the Lord Jesus Christ, the 'Word,' who 'became flesh' (John 1:14). It seems, however, more probable that we are to take it as the written word, or word of the Gospel.

3. Orderly account. We must carefully observe that this expression does not imply that Luke followed the chronological order of the chief events in our Lord's life more than the other evangelists. It rather means that he grouped together, and classified in an orderly way the principal facts which he was inspired to record.

Theophilus. We know nothing certain about this person. The prevailing opinion is that he was some Christian Gentile, in a high position, to whom St. Luke, for wise reasons unknown to us, was directed to address himself in writing his Gospel. The expression **most excellent** seems to indicate that he was no common person. It is the same expression which St. Paul used in addressing Felix and Festus (Acts 24:3; 26:25).

Zechariah and Elizabeth, and Zechariah's vision (1:5–12)

The first event recorded in St. Luke's Gospel is the sudden appearance of an angel to a Jewish priest, named Zechariah. The angel announces to him that a son is to be born to him, by a miraculous interposition, and that this son is to be the forerunner of the long-promised Messiah. The word of God had plainly foretold that when the Messiah came, someone would go before him to prepare his way (Malachi 3:1). The wisdom of God provided that when this forerunner appeared, he would be born in the family of a priest.

It is hard for us to imagine the immense importance of the angel's announcement. To a pious Jew it must have been glad tidings of great joy. It was the first communication from God to Israel since the days of Malachi. It broke the long silence of four hundred years. It told the believing Israelites that the prophetic weeks of Daniel were at last fulfilled (Daniel 9:25), that God's choicest promise was at last going to be accomplished, and that 'the seed' was about to appear in whom all the nations of the earth would be blessed (Genesis 22:18). We must place ourselves in imagination in Zechariah's position if we are to give these verses their true weight.

The character of Zechariah and Elizabeth

Let us note, first, in this passage, the high testimony which is given about the character of Zechariah and Elizabeth. We are told that they were both **righteous before God, living blamelessly according to all the commandments and regulations of the Lord** (verse 6).

It matters little whether we interpret **righteous** as that which is imputed to all believers for their justification, or that which is wrought inwardly in believers by the work of the Holy Spirit, for their sanctification. The two sorts of righteousness are never separated. No one is justified who is not sanctified, and no one is sanctified who is not justified. It is enough for us to know that Zechariah and Elizabeth had grace when grace was very rare, and kept all the burdensome observances of the ceremonial law with devout conscientiousness, when few Israelites cared for them, except in name and form.

The main thing that concerns us all is the example that this holy pair hold up to Christians. Let us all strive to serve God faithfully, and live fully up to our light, just as they did. Let us not forget the plain words of Scripture, 'Everyone who does what is right is righteous' (1 John 3:7). Happy are those Christian families where both husband and wife are 'righteous,' and 'have a clear conscience towards God and all people' (Acts 24:16).

Notes on Luke 1:5–12

5. **The priestly order of Abijah.** There were twenty-four divisions of the sons of Aaron, among whom the temple service was divided. Abijah was the eighth at the original institution (1 Chronicles 24:10).

A descendant of Aaron. 'Yet Elizabeth was cousin to Mary, who was from the tribe of Judah. This indicates the marriage of some predecessor into the other tribe. The priests were allowed to marry into any of the tribes of Israel.' WATSON.

10. **The whole assembly of the people was praying outside.** 'When the priest came into the holy place to offer incense, notice was given to all, by the sound of a little bell, that the time of prayers was now.' LIGHTFOOT.

11. **An angel.** 'The presence of angels is no novelty, but their apparition. They are always with us, but rarely seen, that we may awfully respect their message when they are seen.' BISHOP HALL.

The angel announces John the Baptist's birth and describes his ministry (1:13–17)

We have, in these verses, the words of the angel who appeared to Zechariah. They are words full of deep spiritual instruction.

1. Long delay does not mean prayers are rejected

We learn here, first, that prayers are not necessarily rejected because the answer is long delayed. Zechariah, no doubt, had often prayed for the blessing of children, and, to all appearances, he prayed in vain. At his advanced age he had probably stopped mentioning the subject before God long ago, and given up all hope of being a father. Yet the very first words of the angel show clearly that the prayers of long ago of Zechariah had not been forgotten: **Your prayer has been heard** (verse 13).

2. The character of a really great and successful minister of God

We learn, lastly, from these verses, about the character of a really great and successful minister of God. The angel's description of John the Baptist sets a striking picture before us. He is one who will **turn … hearts** (verse 17) – turn them from ignorance to knowledge, from carelessness to thoughtfulness, from sin to God. He is one who will **go before him** (verse 17) – he will delight in nothing so much as being the messenger and herald of Jesus Christ. He is one who will **make ready a people prepared for the Lord** (verse 17). He will strive to collect from the world a company of believers, who will be ready to meet the Lord on the day he appears.

For such ministers let us pray night and day. They are the true pillars of a church, the true salt of the earth, the true light of the world. Happy is that church, and happy is that nation, which has many such men. Without such men, learning, titles, endowments, and splendid buildings, will keep no church alive. Souls will not be saved, good will not be done, Christ will not be glorified, except by men full of the Holy Spirit.

Notes on Luke 1:13–17

13. **You will name him John.** The word *John* means 'the grace, gift, or mercy of the Lord.' CRUDEN.

15. **He must never drink wine.** From this it would appear that John the Baptist was a Nazarite, or person separated by special vow to the Lord (see Numbers 4:3).

17. **To turn the hearts of parents to their children.** This is a difficult expression. De Dieu's is the most likely explanation. He says it means, 'the fathers upon, or together with the children' – that is, all ages and all sorts of people – parents and children together.

Zechariah's unbelief and punishment (1:18–25)

We see in this passage the power of unbelief in a good man. Righteous and holy as Zechariah was, the angel's announcement appears incredible to him. He thinks that it is impossible for an old man like him to have a son, (verse 18).

Let us learn from Zechariah's fault. It is a fault to which God's people in every age have been sadly liable. The stories of Abraham, and Isaac, and Moses, and Hezekiah, and Jehoshaphat, will all show us that a true believer may sometimes be overtaken by unbelief. It is one of the first corruptions which came into man's heart when he fell, when Eve believed the devil rather than God. It is one of the most deep-rooted sins which plague saints, and from which they are never entirely free until they die. Let us pray daily, 'Lord, increase my faith.' Let us not doubt then when God says a thing, that thing will be fulfilled.

Note on Luke 1:18–25

18. 'How will I know that this is so?' There is a big difference between Zechariah's question here and the Virgin Mary's in verse 34. Zechariah's question implies doubt about the angel's whole announcement, but Mary's question implies no doubt about the event, and is only asking about how it will be accomplished.

The angel's announcement to the Virgin Mary (1:26–33)

We have in these verses the announcement of the most marvellous event that ever happened in this world – the incarnation and birth of our Lord Jesus Christ. It is a passage which we should always read with mingled wonder, love, and praise.

We should notice the lowly and unassuming manner in which the Saviour of mankind came among us. The angel who announced his coming, was sent to an obscure town in Galilee, Nazareth. The woman who was honoured to be our Lord's mother evidently held a humble position in life.

We need not hesitate to conclude that there was a wise providence in all this arrangement. The almighty counsel, who gives orders for everything on earth and in heaven, could just as easily have appointed Jerusalem to be the place of Mary's residence as Nazareth, or could as easily have chosen the daughter of some rich scribe to be our Lord's mother, as a poor woman. But it seemed good that it should not be so. The first coming of the Messiah was to be a humble coming. This humility started from his conception and birth. (See 2 Corinthians 8:9.)

Let us wonder at the amazing condescension of the Son of God. The heir of all things not only took our nature on himself, but took it in the most humble way. It would have been great condescension to come to earth as a king and reign. It was a miracle of mercy beyond our understanding to come to earth as a poor man, to be despised, and suffer, and die. Let his love make us live not for ourselves, but for him. Let his example daily bring home to our conscience the precept of Scripture: 'Do not be haughty, but associate with the lowly' (Romans 12:16).

Notes on Luke 1:26–33

27. Engaged to a man. Let us note the wise providence through which the mother of our Lord, though a virgin, was a virgin **engaged to a man.** It screened her reputation from unseemly remarks. It provided a helper and protector for her in her time of weakness and need.

28. 'Favoured one!' 'The angel greets the virgin; he does not pray to her. He greets her, as a saint; he does not pray to her as a goddess.' BISHOP HALL.

29. Perplexed. The Greek word here is very strong and intense, and is used nowhere else in the New Testament.

The Virgin Mary's question to the angel, and his answer (1:34–38)

1. The reverent way Gabriel speaks about Christ's incarnation

Let us note, in these verses, the reverent manner in which the angel Gabriel speaks of the great mystery of Christ's incarnation. Replying to the Virgin Mary's question, **How will this be?** he says the remarkable words of verse 35.

We do well to follow the example of the angel in all our reflections on this deep subject. Let us always regard it with holy reverence, and abstain from unprofitable speculations about it. It is enough for us to know that the Word became flesh and that when the Son of God came into the world, a real body was prepared for him and that he was born of a woman (John 1:14; Hebrews 10:5; 2:14; Galatians 4:4). Here we must stop. The way in which all this was brought about is wisely hidden from us. In a religion which really comes down from heaven there will always be mysteries. Of such mysteries in Christianity, the incarnation is one.

2. The prominent position given to the Holy Spirit in the incarnation

Let us note, secondly, the prominent position given to the Holy Spirit in the great mystery of the incarnation. We find it written, **The Holy Spirit will come upon you** (verse 35).

An intelligent reader of the Bible will probably not fail to remember that the honour here given to the Spirit is in precise harmony with the teaching of Scripture in other places. In every step of the great work of mankind's redemption we find special mention made of the work of the Holy Spirit. Did Jesus die to make atonement for our sins? (See Hebrews 9:14.) Did he rise again for our justification? (See 1 Peter 3:18). Does he comfort his disciples between his first and second coming? (See John 14:17.)

3. The Virgin Mary's readiness to follow God's will for her

Let us note, lastly, the meek and ready acquiescence of the Virgin Mary to God's revealed will concerning her. She says to the angel, **Let it be with me according to your word** (verse 38).

There is greater grace here than at first meets the eye. It was no light matter to become the mother of our Lord in the unheard of and mysterious way. It brought with it, later on, great honour; but for the present it put Mary's reputation at stake and was a great test of Mary's faith. All this danger and trial the holy Virgin

Mary was willing to risk. She asks no additional questions. She raises no further objections. She accepts the honour placed on her. She says, **Here am I, the servant of the Lord** (verse 38).

Note on Luke 1:34–38

36. Your relative Elizabeth. The angel helps the Virgin Mary's faith by telling her about something that will assist her to receive his message. This is how God deals with us. He knows our weakness.

The Virgin Mary's visit to Elizabeth (1:39–45)

1. The benefit of fellowship among believers

We should observe, from this passage, the benefit of fellowship and communion among believers. We read about a visit made by the Virgin Mary to her cousin Elizabeth. We are told how the hearts of both these holy women were encouraged. If this visit had not taken place Elizabeth might not have been filled with the Holy Spirit as she was, and Mary may never have uttered her song of praise which is now known throughout Christ's church. The words of an old divine are deep and true: 'Happiness communicated doubles itself. Grief grows greater by concealing: joy by expression.'

The Virgin Mary's song of praise (1:46–56)

These verses contain the Virgin Mary's famous hymn of praise at the prospect of becoming the mother of the Lord. After the Lord's Prayer, perhaps, few passages of Scripture are better known than this. No words express more aptly the praise for redeeming mercy.

1. It shows deep knowledge of Scripture

Let us note the full acquaintance with Scripture which this hymn shows. We are reminded, as we read it, of many expressions from the Psalms. Above all, we recall the song of Hannah (1 Samuel 2:2ff.). Clearly, the Virgin Mary's mind was full of Scripture. So, when out of the fullness of her heart she spoke, she uttered scriptural language. Moved by the Holy Spirit to break into praise, she chose words which the Holy Spirit had already consecrated and used. Let us strive, every year we live, to become more deeply acquainted with Scripture. Let us study it, search into it, dig into it, meditate on it, until it dwells in us richly (Colossians 2:16).

2. The Virgin Mary's deep humility

Let us note, secondly, the Virgin Mary's deep humility. She who was chosen by God to the great honour of being the Messiah's mother, speaks about her **low estate** (verse 48) and acknowledges her need of a **Saviour** (verse 47). She does not say one word to indicate that she is

a sinless 'immaculate' person. On the contrary, she uses the language of someone who has been taught by the God's grace to feel her own sins, and so far from being able to save others, requires a Saviour for her own soul.

Let us copy this holy humility of our Lord's mother, while we steadfastly refuse to regard her as a mediator, or to pray to her. Like her, let us be lowly in our own eyes, and think little of ourselves. Humility is the highest grace that can adorn the Christian character. It is a true saying of an old divine, that 'a man has just so much Christianity as he has humility.' It is the grace which of all graces is the most becoming to human nature. Above all, it is the grace which is within the reach of every converted person. All are not rich. All are not learned. All are not highly gifted. All are not preachers. But all of God's children may be clothed with humility.

Notes on Luke 1:46–56

47. My Saviour. Let us notice the Virgin Mary's expressions of need of salvation. It would be difficult to find a more complete answer to the Roman Catholic teaching about her, and especially the doctrine of the immaculate conception, than her language in this hymn.

51. His arm. 'God's great power is represented by his finger, his greater power by his hand, his greatest power by his arm. The production of lice was by God's finger (Exodus 8:19). His other miracles in Egypt were performed by his hand (Exodus 3:20). The destruction of Pharaoh and army in the Red Sea, by God's arm (Exodus 15:6).' WHITBY.

The birth of John the Baptist (1:57–66)

This passage records the birth of a burning and shining light in the church, the forerunner of Christ himself, John the Baptist.

1. An example of the kindness we owe to each other

We see in the behaviour of Elizabeth's neighbours and cousins a striking example of the kindness we owe to each other. It is written that **they rejoiced with her** (verse 58). There would be a great deal more joy in this evil world if more people behaved like Elizabeth's relations. Sympathy over one another's joys and sorrows costs little, and yet it is a very powerful grace. The heart that is warmed by good news, or chilled by affliction, is particularly open and such a heart welcomes sympathy more than precious gold. (See Romans 12:15; John 2:1ff.; John 11:1ff.)

2. An example of the benefit affliction can bring

We see in Zechariah's behaviour in this passage a striking example of the beneficial result of affliction. Zechariah resists the wishes of his relations who want to call the new baby after him. Zechariah shows that his nine months dumbness had not been inflicted on him in vain. He is no longer faithless, but believing. Zechariah now believes every word that Gabriel told him, and he obeys every word of this message.

The sorrow that humbles us, and drives us closer to God, is a blessing, and a positive gain. No case is more hopeless than that of the person who, in times of affliction, turns his back on God. One of the kings of Judah, Ahaz made this terrible mistake (see 2 Chronicles 27:22).

Notes on Luke 1:57–66

59. On the eighth day. This is in line with Leviticus 12:3. If a child died uncircumcised before the eighth day, we find nothing in Scripture to say that it was not saved. Using the same argument, we may rightly conclude that baptism is not absolutely necessary for the salvation of infants under the Christian dispensation. It is not the lack of ordinances, but the contempt for them that destroys souls. A little child cannot be guilty of such contempt.

62. Began motioning. It is probable that Zechariah was deaf as well as dumb.

Zechariah's prophecy and song of praise (1:67–80)

Another hymn of praise demands our attention in these verses. We have read the thanksgiving of Mary, the mother of our Lord. Let us now read the thanksgiving of Zechariah, the father of John the Baptist. We have heard what praises the first coming of Christ drew from the Virgin of the house of David. Let us now hear what praise it draws from an elderly priest.

Notes on Luke 1:67–80

69. A mighty saviour. 'The horn of an animal [see AV] is its weapon for defence and vengeance, its ornament and beauty too. It is used therefore in the prophetic style, to denote the power of the strongest empires. This is how we are to understand it here. By this image the exceeding greatness of the Redeemer's strength, and the never-ceasing exertion of it on behalf of his church are signified.' HENRY VENN.

70. As he spoke through the mouth of his holy prophets. Let us note that he specifically said that God spoke through the prophets. When we read their words we read the words of God. 'They neither spake nor wrote any word of their own, but uttered syllable by syllable as the Spirit put it into their mouths; as a harp or lute gives a sound according to the discretion of the musician.' HOOKER.

Chapter 2

Christ's birth at Bethlehem (2:1–7)

The angel's announcement about Christ's birth to the shepherds (2:8–20)

The circumcision and presentation of Christ in the temple (2:21–24)

Simeon's praise and prophecy (2:25–35)

Anna the prophetess (2:36–40)

Christ found sitting among the teachers (2:41–52)

Christ's birth at Bethlehem (2:1–7)

We have, in these verses, the story of a birth – the birth of the incarnate Son of God, the Lord Jesus Christ. Every birth of a living child is a marvellous event. It brings into being a soul that will never die. But never since the world began was a birth so marvellous as Christ's birth. In itself it was a miracle: God was manifest in the flesh (see 1 Timothy 3:16). The blessings it brought into the world were unimaginable. It opened to men and women the door of everlasting life.

1. The time when Christ was born

In reading these verses, let us first notice the time when Christ was born. It was in the days when **Augustus,** the first Roman emperor, issued **a decree … that all the world should be registered** (verse 1).

God's wisdom is seen in this simple fact. The Jews were coming under the dominion and taxation of a foreign power. Strangers were beginning to rule over them. Augustus taxes the world, and at once Christ is born. It was a moment which was particularly suitable for the introduction of Christ's gospel. The whole civilized earth was at last governed by one ruler. There was nothing to stop the preacher of a new faith from going from city to city, and country to country. It was indeed 'the right time' (Romans 5:6) for God to interpose from heaven and for Christ to be born.

Let us always rest our souls on the thought, that times are in God's hands (Psalm 31:15). He knows the best time to send help to his church, and new light to the world. Let us beware of giving in to over anxiety about the events around us, as if we knew better than the King of kings when relief should come.

2. The place where Christ was born

Let us notice, secondly, the place where Christ was born. It was not at Nazareth in Galilee, where his mother, the Virgin Mary, lived. The prophet Micah had foretold that the event was to take place at Bethlehem (Micah 5:2). And so it came about. At Bethlehem Christ was born.

The overruling providence of God appears in this simple fact. He orders things in heaven and earth. He turns the hearts of kings to do his will. He overruled the time when Augustus decreed the taxation. He directed the enforcement of the decree in such a way that Mary had to be in Bethlehem when **the time came for her to deliver her child** (verse 6). Little did the haughty Roman Emperor, and his officer Quirinius, think that they were only instruments in the hand of the God of Israel, and were only carrying out the eternal purposes of the King of kings. Little did they think that they were helping to lay the foundation of a kingdom, before which the empires of this world would all fall down one day, and Roman idolatry pass away.

The heart of a believer should take comfort in recalling God's providential rule of the world. A true Christian should never be greatly upset by the conduct of the rulers of the earth. He should see with the eye of faith a hand overruling all that they do, to the praise and glory of God.

3. The way in which Christ was born

Let us notice, lastly, the way in which Christ was born. He was not born under the roof of his mother's house, but in a strange place. When born, he was not laid in a carefully prepared cradle. She **laid him in a manger, because there was no place for them in the inn** (verse 7).

We see here the grace and humility of Christ. Had he come to save mankind with royal majesty, surrounded by his Father's angels, it would have been an act of undeserved mercy. But to become poor as the very poorest of mankind, and lowly as the lowliest, this is a love which passes understanding. Never let us forget that through this humiliation Jesus has bought for us a title to glory, and through his poverty we are made rich (see 2 Corinthians 8:9).

Notes on Luke 2:1–7

1. Emperor Augustus. This is that Octavius who, after the defeat of Anthony and Cleopatra at Actium, took the government of the Roman Empire into his own hands, and was the first Caesar, or Roman Emperor.

3. All went to their own towns to be registered. Quesnel remarks, 'Augustus imagines that he is busy advancing the glory of his name, and the lustre of his reign. And yet his orders, by means of others more powerful and absolute than his, become subservient to the accomplishment of prophecies, of which he is altogether ignorant – about the birth of a King whom he will never know, and about the establishment of a monarchy, which will subject his and all others to itself. This is what happens in all ages, and people take no notice of it.'

7. Wrapped him in bands of cloth. On this expression the Fathers and most Roman Catholic writers have built the idea that our Lord's birth was a childbirth without labour or pain. Such an idea is, to say the least, an unprofitable conjecture. There is nothing mentioned here which a mother, in Mary's position, in an eastern climate, might not have done for herself without help. There is no need to imagine or invent miraculous circumstances in our Lord's incarnation, beside those which are fully revealed.

The angel's announcement about Christ's birth to the shepherds (2:8–20)

We read in these verses how the birth of the Lord Jesus was first announced to people. The birth of a king's son is normally the occasion for public celebration. The announcement of the birth of the Prince of Peace was made privately, at midnight, and without anything of worldly pomp and ostentation.

1. Who first heard about Christ's birth

Let us note who first heard about Christ's birth. They were **shepherds** (verse 8). This news was given to shepherds – not to priests and rulers, but to shepherds – not to scribes and Pharisees.

One of James's sayings should come to mind: see James 2:5. No one is debarred from spiritual privileges by lack of money. The things of God's kingdom are often hidden from the great and noble, and revealed to the poor. Let us resist Satan's suggestion that religion is not for the working man. The weak of the world are often called before the mighty. The last are often first, and the first last.

2. The language used by the angel to announce Christ's birth to the shepherds

Let us, secondly, note the language which the angel used to announce Christ's birth to the shepherds. He said, **I am bringing you good news of great joy for all the people** (verse 10).

We need not wonder at these words. The spiritual darkness which had covered the earth for four thousand years was about to be rolled away. The way of pardon and peace with God was about to be thrown open to all mankind. The knowledge of God was no longer confined to the Jews, but was on offer to the whole Gentile world. The first stone of God's kingdom was about to be set up. If this was not '**good news**' there never were tidings that deserved the name.

3. Who first praised God, when Christ was born

Let us note, thirdly, who first praised God, when Christ was born. They were angels, and not men; angels who had never sinned, and required no Saviour; angels who had not fallen, and needed no Redeemer, and no atoning blood. The first hymn to the honour of God manifest in the flesh was sung by **a multitude of the heavenly host** (verse 13).

Let us take note of this fact. It is full of deep spiritual lessons. It shows us what good servants the angels are. All that their heavenly Master does pleases and interests them. It shows us what clear knowledge they have. They know what misery sin has brought into creation. They know the blessedness of heaven, and the privilege of an open door into it. Above all, it shows us the deep love and compassion which the angels feel towards poor lost man. They rejoice at the glorious prospect of many souls being saved, and many brands plucked from the burning fire.

Note on Luke 2:8–20

8. Shepherds living in the fields. It has been argued from these words that our Lord could not have been born on Christmas day, because it was not the custom of the Jews to keep flocks in the field in winter. It may be doubted whether the argument is quite conclusive (see Genesis 31:40 where Jacob complains about the cold nights). However, it is an undeniable fact that the precise month or day of our Lord's nativity is not known. Every month in the year has found its advocates, in the conjectures made on the subject. There is no certainty about it. Had it been good for us to know the day God would have told us. For keeping Christmas we have no authority but that of the church.

The circumcision and presentation of Christ in the temple (2:21–24)

1. Our Lord's obedience to the Jewish law, as an infant

The first point which demands attention in this passage is the obedience which our Lord gave, as an infant, to the Jewish law. We read about him being circumcised on the eighth day. It is the first fact recorded about his life.

It is a waste of time to speculate about the reason why our Lord submitted to circumcision. We know that he had no sin in him (1 John 3:5) either original or actual. His circumcision was not at all meant to acknowledge that there was any tendency to corruption in his heart.

Let it suffice for us to remember that our Lord's circumcision was a public testimony to Israel, that according to the flesh he was a Jew, a Jewish woman gave birth to him, and that he was born under the law (Galatians 4:4). Without this he could not have fulfilled the law's requirements. Without it he could not have been recognized as the son of David, and the seed of Abraham. Let us remember, furthermore, that circumcision was absolutely necessary before our Lord could be heard as a teacher in Israel. Without it he would have had no place in any lawful Jewish assembly, and no right to any

Jewish ordinance. Without circumcision he would have been regarded by all Jews as nothing better than an uncircumcised Gentile, and an apostate from the faith of the fathers.

Let our Lord's submission to an ordinance which he did not need for himself, be a lesson to us in our daily life. Let us endure much, rather than increase the offence of the gospel, or in any way hinder God's work. Ponder St. Paul's words from 1 Corinthians 9:19–22. The man who wrote these words walked very closely in the footsteps of his crucified Master.

2. The name given to our Lord

The second point which demands our attention in this passage is the name our Lord was given, by God's special command. **He was called Jesus** (verse 21).

The word Jesus means simply Saviour. It is the same word as Joshua in the Old Testament. The choice of this name is very striking and instructive. The Son of God came down from heaven not just to be Saviour, but the King, the Lawgiver, the Prophet, the Priest, the Judge of fallen man. Had he chosen any one of these titles he would only have chosen that which was his own. But he passed them all by. He selects a name which speaks of mercy, grace, help, and deliverance for a lost world. It is as a Deliverer and Redeemer that he desires principally to be known.

Let us ask ourselves what our hearts know about the Son of God? Is he our Jesus, our Saviour? This is the question on which our salvation turns. Let us not be content to know Christ as One who performed mighty miracles, and spoke as no other man ever spoke. Let us see that we know him experimentally, as our Deliverer from the guilt and power of sin, and our Redeemer from Satan's bondage.

Notes on Luke 2:21–24

21. To circumcise the child. 'He who was above the law, would come under the law, to free us from the law.' BISHOP HALL.

The name given … before he was conceived. 'We read of four people in the Old Testament to whom God gave names before they were born: Isaac (Genesis 17:19); Josiah (1 Kings 13:2); Ishmael (Genesis 16:11); Cyrus (Isaiah 44:28); and in the New Testament we read of two: John the Baptist and Jesus Christ. This tells us how certain God was about future contingencies.' POOLE.

24. Two young pigeons. 'The offering of the poor, which if a rich man offered he did not do his duty.' LIGHTFOOT.

Simeon's praise and prophecy (2:25–35)

We have in these verses the account of one whose name is nowhere else mentioned in the New Testament, a **righteous and devout** (verse 25) man named Simeon. We know nothing about his life before or after the time of Christ's birth. We are only told that he came through the Spirit into the temple, when the child Jesus was brought there by his mother, and that he **took him in his arms and praised God** (verse 28), words which are known throughout the world.

1. God has believing people, even in the darkest days

We see, in the case of Simeon, how God has a believing people even in the worst places, and in the darkest times. Religion was at a very low ebb in Israel when Christ was born. Yet even then we find in the middle of Jerusalem a man who **was righteous and devout** (verse 25), and a man on whom **the Holy Spirit rested** (verse 25).

It is an encouraging thought that God never leaves himself entirely without a witness. Small as his believing church may sometimes be, the gates of hell will never completely prevail against it. True Christians, in every age, should remember this, and take comfort. It is a truth which they are apt to forget, and in consequence to give way to despondency (see 1 Kings 19:14,19). There are more Simeons in the world than we suppose.

2. We see how completely a believer can be delivered from the fear of death

We see in the song of Simeon how completely a believer can be delivered from the fear of death; **Master, now you are dismissing your servant in peace** (verse 29). Simeon speaks like a person for whom the grave has lost its terrors, and the world its charms. He speaks as one who knows where he is going when he departs this life and cares not how soon he goes.

What delivers us from that fear of death which enslaves so many people? There is only one answer to this question. Nothing except strong faith can do it. Faith laying firm hold on an unseen Saviour – faith resting on the promises of an unseen God – faith, and faith only, can enable a man to look death in the face, and say, 'I depart in peace.'

Notes on Luke 2:25–35

25. The consolation of Israel. This was a name given by the Jews to the Messiah. LIGHTFOOT says, 'the whole nation waited for the consolation of Israel; in that there was nothing more common with them than to swear by the desire which they had of seeing it.'

The Holy Spirit rested on him. Note that this was before the death and ascension of Christ, and the outpouring of the Spirit on the day of Pentecost. We must never forget that the Old Testament saints were taught by the Holy Spirit as much as believers after the Gospel was set up, though not in such full measure.

30. Salvation. The word so translated is only used here and in three other places (Luke 3:6; Acts 28:28: Ephesians 6:17). It is a more abstract, energetic word than the one commonly translated by this word.

35. A sword will pierce your own soul. The simplest explanation of these words is that Simeon foretells sorrow coming on the Virgin Mary, as cutting and heart-piercing as a sword. This was specially fulfilled when she stood by the cross, and saw her son dying there.

Anna the prophetess (2:36–40)

These verses introduce us to one of God's servants who is mentioned nowhere else in the New Testament. The story of Anna, like that of Simeon, is related only by St. Luke. The wisdom of God ordained that a woman as well as a man should testify to the fact that the Messiah was born. In the mouth of two witnesses it was established that Malachi's prophecy was fulfilled, and the messenger of the covenant had suddenly come to the temple (Malachi 3:1).

1. The character of a holy woman

Let us observe in these verses the character of a holy woman before Christ's gospel was established. The facts recorded about Anna are few and simple, but we shall find them very instructive.

Anna was a woman of irreproachable character. After a married life of only eleven years, she had spent eighty-four years as a lone widow. The trials, desolation, and temptation of such a condition were probably very great. But Anna, by grace, overcame them all.

Anna was a woman who loved God's house. **She never left the temple** (verse 37). She regarded it as the place where God especially dwelt, and toward which every pious Jew in foreign lands, like Daniel, loved to direct his prayers. Anna could enter into David's words, 'My soul longs, indeed it faints, for the courts of the LORD' (Psalm 84:2).

Anna was a woman of great self-denial. She **worshipped there with fasting and prayer night and day** (verse 37). She was continually crucifying the flesh and keeping it in subjection by voluntary abstemiousness. Anna was a woman of much prayer. She was continually communing with him, as her best Friend, about the things that concerned her own peace. Anna was a woman to spoke to other saints. As soon as she had seen Jesus, she began **to speak about the child** (verse 38) to others she knew in Jerusalem. And Anna received a rich reward for all her diligence in God's service, before she left the world. She was allowed to see him who had been so long promised, and for whose coming she had so often prayed. When we read of Anna's consistency, and holiness, and prayerfulness, and self-denial, we cannot but wish that many daughters of the Christian church would strive to be like her.

Notes on Luke 2:36–40

36. A prophet. 'Prophetess.' This is a remarkable expression, and only used on one other occasion in the New Testament (Revelation 2:20). If the word is to be taken in its fullest sense, it seems to show that the spirit of prophecy, which had been withheld for nearly four hundred years since Malachi's time, was being restored to Israel when Christ was born.

38. Began to … speak about the child to all who were looking for the redemption of Jerusalem. This presentation of our Lord in the temple appears to have been the primary fulfilment of the prophecy of Malachi 3:1, 'the Lord … will suddenly come to his temple.' It was indeed a sudden unostentatious coming. The only witnesses, apparently, were an old man and an old woman – and the only attendants a poor woman and her equally poor husband, – and the form in which the Lord appeared was as a little infant in arms! How little we would have expected this.

Christ found sitting among the teachers (2:41–52)

These verses should always be deeply interesting to a reader of the Bible. They record the only fact which we know about our Lord Jesus during the first thirty years of his life on earth, after his infancy. How many things a Christian would like to know about the events of those thirty years. We need not doubt that there is wisdom in the silence of Scripture on the subject. If it had been good for us to know more, more would have been revealed.

An example for all true Christians

Let us, lastly, draw from this passage, an example for all true Christians. We have it in the solemn words which our Lord addressed to his mother Mary, when she asked him, 'Child, why have you treated us like this? Look, your father and I have been searching for you in great anxiety' (verse 48); Jesus replied, 'Did you not know that I must be in my Father's house?' (verse 49). It was a solemn reminder that, as God, he had a Father in heaven, and that this heavenly Father's work demanded his first attention.

This incident should bring us to life when we are slothful. It should check us when we are inclined to return to the world. Are we about our Father's business? Are we walking in the steps of Jesus Christ? Such questions will often prove very humbling, and make us ashamed of ourselves. But such questions are eminently useful to our souls. Never is a church in so healthy a condition as when its believing members aim high, and strive in all things to be like Christ.

Notes on Luke 2:41–52

42. Twelve years old. This age appears to have been thought of by the Jews as a kind of turning point from out of the state of childhood. Lightfoot quotes a saying from one of the rabbinical writers: 'Let a man deal gently with his son, till he comes to be twelve years old; but from that time let him descend with him into his way of living – that is, let him diligently keep him close to that way, rule, and act, by which he may get his living.'

51. Was obedient. The words imply a continual habit during his stay at Nazareth, and not a single isolated act.

52. Increased in … divine and human favour. A sentence from Poole's Annotations on this subject is worth reading: 'If any ask how he who was the eternal wisdom of the Father, who is the only one God, increased in wisdom, they must know that all things in Scripture which are spoken of Christ, are not spoken with respect to his entire person, but with respect to the one or other nature united in that Person. He increased in wisdom, as he did in age or stature, with respect to his human, not his divine nature. And as God daily magnified his grace and favour towards him, so God gave him favour with the unrighteous and the people of Galilee.'

Chapter 3

The beginning of our Lord's earthly ministry; John the Baptist's preaching (3:1–6)

John the Baptist; how he spoke to those who came to listen to him (3:7–14)

The effect of John the Baptist's ministry; his testimony to Christ; his imprisonment (3:15–20)

Christ's baptism; the Virgin Mary's genealogy traced back to Adam (3:21–38)

The beginning of our Lord's earthly ministry: John the Baptist's preaching (3:1–6)

These verses describe the beginning of the gospel of Christ. It began with the preaching of John the Baptist. The Jews could never say that when the Messiah came he came without notice or preparation. He graciously sent a mighty forerunner before his face, by whose ministry the attention of the whole nation was awakened.

The wickedness of the times when Christ's gospel came into the world

Let us notice in this passage, the wickedness of the times when Christ's Gospel came into the world. The opening verses of the chapter tell us the names of some of the rulers and governors when John the Baptist's ministry began. It is a melancholy list and full of instruction. There is hardly a name in it which is not infamous for wickedness. Tiberius, Pontius Pilate, Herod and his brother Philip, and Annas and Caiaphas, were men of whom we know little or nothing but evil. When such were the rulers, what must the people have been like? Such was the state of things when Christ's forerunner was commissioned to begin preaching. We may truly say that God's ways are not our ways.

Let us learn never to despair about the cause of God's truth, however unfavourable its prospects appear. Let us beware of slacking our hands from any of God's work on account of the wickedness of the times, or the number and power of our adversaries (see Ecclesiastes 11:4). In a moment Christ can turn his church's midnight into the blaze of noon-day.

Notes on Luke 3:1–6

5. **Every valley shall be filled** … These and similar expressions in this verse are figurative. The prophecy does not refer to literal levelling of mountains and filling up of valleys, but that difficulties and obstacles as great as mountains and valleys in the way of a king's march, will go down before the progress of Christ's gospel.

6. **'All flesh shall see the salvation of God.'** This is a prophecy which has yet to be completely fulfilled. It will be completed when Christ's kingdom is fully set up at his second coming, when everyone will know him, from the least to the greatest. It is one among many examples that the prophets of the Old Testament often spoke about both comings in the same moment, and foretold the complete victories of the second appearing of Jesus, in the same breath with the partial victories of his first appearing. Some began to **see the salvation of God** as soon as the gospel was first preached. A little flock was taken out at once. All will eventually see God's salvation, from the least to the greatest.

John the Baptist: how he spoke to those who came to listen to him (3:7–14)

We have in these verses an example of John the Baptist's ministry. The immense effect which John had on the Jews, however temporary, is evident, in the Gospels. What then was the character of John's ministry? This is the question which this chapter answers.

1. John's boldness

We should first note the holy boldness John has in speaking to the crowds who came to him for baptism. He tells them that they are a **brood of vipers!** (verse 7). He saw the rottenness and hypocrisy of the profession of the surrounding crowd, and uses appropriate language to describe them. John the Baptist's head was not turned by popularity. He did not care if he offended people. There is no charity in flattering unconverted people, but not mentioning their vices, or in handing out smooth epithets to damnable sins. There are two texts which are often forgotten by Christian preachers, (see Luke 6:26 and Galatians 1:10).

2. John speaks about hell

We should note, secondly, how plainly John speaks to his hearers about hell and danger. He tells them that there is **the wrath to come** (verse 7). He speaks of **the axe** (verse 9) of God's judgments, and of unfruitful trees being **thrown into the fire** (verse 9).

Hell is always an offensive subject to human nature. People love to hear 'smooth things' (Isaiah 30:10) and to be told about peace, but not about danger. But the subject is one which should be spoken about, if we wish to do good to souls. It is one that our Lord Jesus Christ often spoke about in his public teaching. That loving Saviour, who spoke so graciously about the way to heaven, also used the plainest language about the way to hell.

Let us beware of being more wise that what is written, and more charitable than Scripture itself. Let the language of John the Baptist be deeply engraved on our hearts. The religion in which there is no mention of hell, is not the religion of John the Baptist, and of our Lord Jesus and his apostles.

Notes on Luke 3:7–14

8. **'Bear fruits worthy of repentance.'** The word translated **bear fruits** is the same one as that used by John when he speaks about breaking the law and being righteous (1 John 3:4, 7). Both in John and here a continued habit is implied, and not a single act.

'We have Abraham as our ancestor.' A passage in Stella, the Spanish commentator on Luke's Gospel, is worth quoting: 'There are many monks who imitate these Jews, saying, we have Benedict, Augustine, Jerome, Francis, or Dominic for our father, just as they said, We have Abraham for our father. They relate to others the marvellous doings of the founders of their order, and cry up their praises with wonderful commendation. They say, our order has so many holy men enrolled in the catalogue of saints, so many popes, so many cardinals, so many bishops, so many teachers. In them they rejoice and boast, while they themselves have degenerated from the true excellencies of their founders, by iniquity and laxity of morals. To all these we may deservedly say what Christ said to the Jews, "If you are Abraham's children, do the deeds of Abraham."'

'God is able from these stones to raise up children to Abraham.' These words mean: 'Think not that God will not have a people to praise him if he cuts you off and does not save you. Even if you were all thrown out, he could raise up a family for himself of true believers from these stones.' The calling of the Gentiles was evidently implied.

14. Let it be carefully noted that John the Baptist does not say a word to show that the work of tax collectors or soldiers is unlawful in God's sight.

The effect of John the Baptist's ministry; his testimony to Christ; his imprisonment (3:15–20)

One result of a faithful ministry is to set people thinking

We learn from these verses, that one result of a faithful ministry is to set people thinking. About John the Baptist's hearers we read, **The people were filled with expectation, and were all questioning in their hearts concerning John, whether he might be the Messiah** (verse 15).

The cause of true religion makes great strides when people are made to think. Thoughtlessness about spiritual things is one great feature of unconverted people. The truth about Christ has nothing to fear from sober examination. Thinking is not faith and repentance. But it is always a hopeful sign.

Note on Luke 3:15–20

16. Baptize … with … fire. The meaning of these words is doubtful and has never been fully known. Some restrict their meaning to the coming down of the Holy Spirit on the day of Pentecost, when 'tongues, as of fire' rested on each person (Acts 2:3). Others apply these words exclusively to the converting work of the Holy Spirit, purifying and refining the heart as fire purifies gold. Both views are probably included.

Christ's baptism; the Virgin Mary's genealogy traced back to Adam (3:21–38)

The high honour the Lord Jesus has put on baptism

We see in this passage the high honour the Lord Jesus has placed on baptism. We discover that among other people who came to John the Baptist, the Saviour of the world came, and was **baptized** (verse 21) too.

An ordinance which the Son of God was pleased to use, and later appointed to be used by his whole church, should always be held in special reverence by his people. Baptism cannot be of marginal importance if Christ himself was baptized. Baptism was intended by our Lord to assist his church, and be a means of grace, so when it is correctly used, we may confidently look to it for a blessing from God. But let us never forget that the grace of God is not tied to any sacrament, and that we may be baptized with water without being baptized with the Holy Spirit.

Notes on Luke 3:21–38

23. About thirty years old. This was the age, it will be recalled, when the Levites were first allowed to work in the tabernacle (Numbers 4:3).

Joseph son of Heli … Every careful reader of the Bible knows well that there is a great difficulty connected with our Lord's genealogy. The difficulty lies in the complete difference between the part of the genealogy between David and Joseph, as recorded by St. Luke, and the same part as recorded by St. Matthew. Between Abraham and David the two genealogies agree. Between David and Joseph they almost entirely differ. How can this difference be reconciled?

The most probable explanation is to view St. Luke's genealogy as the genealogy of Mary, and not of Joseph. Heli was the father of Mary, and the father-in-law, by his marriage, of Joseph. It does not say that Heli 'begat' Joseph; and that the Greek does not necessarily mean Joseph was 'his son' is clear from the expressions used about Mary and Jude, see Mark 16:1; Acts 1:15. It is Mary's family, therefore, and not Joseph's, that St. Luke describes, and Joseph's family, and not Mary's, that is described by St. Matthew.

Chapter 4

Christ's temptation in the desert (4:1–13)

Christ preaching in the synagogue of Nazareth (4:14–21)

The unbelief and wickedness of the people of Nazareth (4:22–32)

A devil cast out in the synagogue of Capernaum; Simon's mother-in-law healed, etc. (4:33–44)

Christ's temptation in the desert (4:1–13)

The first event recorded in our Lord's ministry after his baptism is his temptation by the devil. From a time of honour and glory he passed straight on to a time of conflict and suffering. First came the testimony of God the Father, 'You are my Son, my Beloved; with you I am well pleased' (Luke 3:22). Then came the sneering suggestion from Satan, '**If you are the Son of God**' (verse 3). For Christ, as well as for his followers, there is often but one step from great privilege to great trial.

1. The power and malice of the devil

Let us first note in this passage the power and untiring malice of the devil.

That old serpent who tempted Adam to sin in paradise was not afraid to assault the second Adam, the Son of God. The prince of the world would not give way to the Prince of peace without a mighty struggle. He had overcome the first Adam in the garden of Eden; why should he not overcome the second Adam in the desert?

Let it never surprise us if we are tempted by the devil. Let us rather expect it, as a matter of course, if we are living members of Christ. The Master's lot will be the lot of his disciples. Let us put on the whole armour of God and resist the devil, who will then flee from us (James 4:7).

2. The great subtlety of the devil

Let us note the exceeding subtlety of our great spiritual enemy, the devil. Three times we see him assaulting our Lord, and trying to draw him into sin. Each assault showed the hand of a master in the art of temptation.

Satan's first scheme was to persuade our Lord to distrust his Father's providential care. Satan comes to him, weak and exhausted with forty days hunger, and suggests that he performs a miracle, in order to gratify a human appetite. Why should he wait any longer? Why should the Son of God sit still and starve? Why not 'command this stone to become a loaf of bread' (verse 3)?

Satan's second scheme was to persuade our Lord to grasp at worldly power by unlawful means. He takes him to the top of a mountain and shows him all the kingdoms of the world (verse 5). All these he promises to give him if he will but worship (verse 7) him. The concession was small. The promise was large. Why not by a little momentary act obtain an enormous gain?

Satan's last device was to persuade our Lord to an act of presumption. He takes him to the pinnacle of the temple and suggests, throw yourself down from here (verse 9). In doing this Jesus would give public evidence that he was the One sent by God. In so doing he might even depend on being kept from harm. Was there not a text of Scripture which specially applied to the Son of God, in such a position? Was it not written that 'his angels ... protect you, ... On their hands they will bear you up, so that you will not dash your foot against a stone' (verses 10–11)?

We see in these three temptations the three favourite weapons of the devil. Unbelief, worldliness, and presumption are three enticements which Satan uses to make us run into sin. Let us remember this and be on our guard. The deeds which Satan suggests we do often appear to be trifling and unimportant; but the principle involved in each of these little deeds, we may be sure, is nothing short of rebellion against God. Let us not be ignorant of Satan's devices.

Notes on Luke 4:1–13

1. **Led by the Spirit.** The word translated **led** is the same one that we find in Romans 8:14, Galatians 5:18, applied to the influence of the Holy Spirit on the hearts of believers. Our Lord did not seek conflict with the devil, but was **led** to it.

4. **'It is written.'** This text, as well as the two others quoted by our Lord in reply to the devil, were taken from the Pentateuch (Deuteronomy 8:3; 6:13).

5. **In an instant.** LIGHTFOOT quotes a Rabbinical definition of a moment. The Rabbis consider it to be 'the 58,888th part of an hour.'

9. **The pinnacle of the temple.** This is supposed to have been a turret overhanging a deep valley. Josephus describes the place, and says, that 'if any looked down, his eyes would grow dizzy, and being able to reach to so vast a depth.'

10. **It is written.** Let it be carefully noted that the devil can quote Scripture when it suits him. There is no good thing which may not be abused.

13. **He departed from him.** This is evidence of the personality of Satan. If the devil was not a person, judging from the whole passage, there is no meaning in words. He 'speaks,' 'leads,' 'shows,' he offers to 'give' etc. These expressions can only be used about a person.

Christ preaching in the synagogue of Nazareth (4:14–22)

These verses relate events which are only recorded in St. Luke's gospel. They describe the first visit which our Lord paid, after starting his public ministry, to the city of Nazareth, where he had been brought up. Taken together with the two verses which immediately follow, they furnish striking proof that 'the flesh is hostile to God' (Romans 8:7).

How our Lord honoured public means of grace

We should observe from these verses what notable honour our Lord Jesus Christ gave to public means of grace. We are told that he went to the synagogue on the sabbath day, as was his custom. He stood up to read (verse 16) Scriptures. In our Lord's day the scribes and Pharisees were the chief teachers of the Jews. We can hardly imagine that a Jewish synagogue enjoyed much of the Holy Spirit's presence and blessing under such teaching. Yet even then we find our Lord visiting a synagogue, and reading and preaching in it. It was the place where his Father's day and Word were publicly recognized, and as such he thought it good to do it honour.

Note on Luke 4:14–21

21. **Then he began to say.** It is clear that the full exposition of the passage in Isaiah which

our Lord gave has been withheld from us. The words which are recorded in this verse are probably the beginning of what our Lord said, and from the keynote of his sermon. The sermon itself is not recorded.

The unbelief and wickedness of the people of Nazareth (4:22–32)

There are three great lessons which stand out from the passage. Each deserves the close attention of everyone who desires spiritual wisdom.

People despise the highest privileges

We learn, for one thing, how prone people are to despise the highest privileges, when they are familiar with them. We see it in the behaviour of the men of Nazareth when they had heard the Lord Jesus preach. They could find no fault in his sermon. They could point to no inconsistency in his past life and conversation. But because the preacher had lived among them for thirty years, and his face, and voice, and appearance were familiar to them, they would not accept his teaching. They said to each other, 'Is not this Joseph's son?' (verse 22). Is it possible that one so well-known as this man can be the Christ? They drew from our Lord's lips the solemn reply, 'no prophet is accepted in the prophet's home town' (verse 24).

We would do well to remember this lesson in connection with the means of grace. We are always in danger of undervaluing them when we have them in abundance. We tend to think lightly about the privilege of an open Bible, a preached gospel and the freedom to meet together to worship. Let us take heed to our own spirit as we use these sacred things.

Notes on Luke 4:22–32

22. 'Joseph's son?' These words show us in what light our Lord was regarded at Nazareth, and how little the miraculous circumstances of his conception and birth were generally known.

25. 'In the time of Elijah.' Let us not fail to note that our Lord speaks of the times of Elijah, and the events which happened in them, as realities. His language is one among many arguments to prove that the historical books of the Old Testament are authentic, and not mere collections of instructive fables, as some have dared to assert.

30. He passed through the midst of them. Clearly, this was a miracle. How it happened we are not told. It is enough for us to know that his enemies could not lay hands on him against his will, and that when finally he was handed over to be crucified, it was only because he was willing to allow himself to be slain.

A devil cast out in the synagogue of Capernaum; Simon's mother-in-law healed, etc. (4:33–44)

The devil has clear religious understanding

We should notice, in this passage, the clear religious understanding that the devil and his agents possess. Twice in these verses we have evidence of this. 'I know who you are, the Holy One of God' (verse 34) were the words of the evil spirit in one case. 'You are the Son of God!' (verse 41) were the words of many devils in the other case. Yet this knowledge was a knowledge unaccompanied by faith, or hope, or charity. Those who possessed it were miserable fallen beings, full of bitter hatred both against God and man.

Let us beware of an unsanctified knowledge of Christianity. It is a dangerous possession, but a fearfully common one in these latter days. Let us never be content to know religion with our heads only.

Notes on Luke 4:33–44

35. 'Be silent.' Literally, 'Be muzzled.' See 1 Corinthians 9:9; 1 Timothy 5:18. It is the same word our Lord uses to address the stormy sea (Mark 4:39), where it is translated, 'Peace! Be still!'

38. Simon's mother-in-law. Clearly, the apostle Simon Peter is married. The Roman Catholic doctrine of the celibacy of the clergy finds no countenance in the Bible.

39. Immediately she got up and began to serve them. The completeness of our Lord's cures is shown here. It is well known that fevers leave people too weak for any exertion, even when they begin to recover and are out of danger.

Chapter 5

Christ's readiness for every good deed; the miraculous catch of fish (5:1–11)

A leper healed; Christ's diligence about private prayer (5:12–16)

A paralytic healed (5:17–26)

The calling of Levi (5:27–32)

Christ the Bridegroom (5:33–39)

Christ's readiness for every good deed: the miraculous catch of fish (5:1–11)

We have, in these verses, the account of what is commonly called the miraculous draught of fishes. It is a remarkable miracle for two reasons. For one thing it shows us our Lord's complete dominion over the animal creation. The fish of the sea are as obedient to his will as the frogs and flies and locusts in the plagues of Egypt. All are his servants, and all obey his commands. For another thing, there is a striking similarity between this miracle, performed at the beginning of our Lord's ministry, and another which we find him performing after his resurrection, at the end of his ministry (John 21:1ff.). In both we read of a miraculous draught of fishes. In both the apostle Peter has a prominent place in the story. And in both there is, probably, a deep spiritual lesson, below the surface.

Our Lord's tireless readiness for every good deed

We should observe, in this passage, our Lord Jesus Christ's unwearied readiness for every good work. Once more we find him preaching to a people who were the crowd ... pressing in on him to hear the word of God (verse 1). And where does he preach? Not in any consecrated building, or place set apart for public worship, but in the open air; not in a pulpit built for a preacher's use, but in a fisherman's boat. Souls were waiting to be fed. Personal inconvenience was allowed no place in his thoughts. God's work must not stand still.

Christ's servants should not wait until every little difficulty is removed before we go and sow the seed of the Word. It is the slothful heart that is always looking at the thorny hedge and the lion on the path (Proverbs 15:19; 22:13). Where we are and as we are, in season and out of season, by one means or by another, by tongue or by pen, let us strive to be always working for God.

Notes on Luke 5:1–11

10. 'You will be catching people.' It has often been remarked, and with much justice, that the Greek word translated 'catching' means literally 'take alive.' It is only used here and in one other place, 2 Timothy 2:26: a passage which is often misinterpreted, but rightly understood is a remarkable parallel to our Lord's words in this place.

Let us not forget, in reading this miracle, that holy and good men in every age have seen in it a remarkable type and emblem of the history of Christ's church in the world. They have seen the ships as emblems of the churches; the fishermen as ministers; the net as the Gospel; the sea as the world; the shore as eternity and the miraculous catch of fish as the success attending work done in strict compliance with Christ's word. There may be truth in all this. But it needs to be cautiously and delicately used. The habit of allegorizing and seeing hidden meanings in the plain language of Scripture has often done great harm.

A leper healed: Christ's diligence about private prayer (5:12–16)

Our Lord's power over incurable disease

We see in this passage our Lord's power over incurable disease. A man covered with leprosy (verse 12) comes to Jesus for help and is healed. This was a mighty miracle. Of all ills which can afflict the body, leprosy appears to be the most severe. It affects every part of the constitution at once. It brings sores and decay on the skin, corruption into the blood, and rottenness into the bones. It is a living death, which no medicine can check or stay. Yet here we read of a leper being made well in a moment. It is but one touch from the hand of the Son of God, and the cure is effected. Immediately the leprosy left him (verse 13).

We have in this wonderful event a living emblem of Christ's power to heal our souls. What are we all but lepers spiritually in God's sight? Sin is the deadly sickness by which we are all affected. It is eaten into our constitution. It has infected all our faculties. Heart, conscience, mind, and will, all are diseased by sin. From the sole of our foot to the crown of our head, there is no soundness about us, but wounds, and bruises, and putrefying sores, (Isaiah 1:6). Such is the state in which we are born. Such is the state in which we naturally live. We are in one sense dead long before we are laid in the grave. Our bodies may be healthy and active, but our souls are by nature dead in trespasses and sins. But there is no spiritual leprosy too hard for Christ.

Notes on Luke 5:12–16

16. And pray. This frequent mention of our Lord's praying is peculiar to Luke. Wordsworth remarks, 'a similar instance is seen in his narrative of our Lord's baptism, and of the transfiguration (Luke 3:21; 9:28,29). The Gentiles, for whom St Luke's Gospel was especially designed, needed instruction in the duty and benefits of prayer. Accordingly this subject occupies a prominent place in his Gospel. It is eminently the Gospel of prayer.' (See Luke 6;12; 9:18, 28; 11:1; 18:41, 46.)

A paralytic healed (5:17–26)

A threefold miracle demands our attention in these verses. At one and the same time, we see our Lord forgiving sins, reading men's thoughts, and healing a paralysis. He who could do such things, and do them perfectly easily and with authority, must indeed be very God. Power like this was never possessed by man.

What lengths people will go to when they are in earnest

Let us notice in this passage, what lengths people will go to when they are in earnest. The friends of the sick man, a paralytic, wanted to bring him to Jesus so that he might be cured. At first they were unable to do this, because of the crowd which surrounded our Lord. So what did they do? They **went up on the roof and let him down with his bed through the tiles into the middle of the crowd in front of Jesus** (verse 19). At once they achieved their objective. Our Lord's attention was drawn to their sick friend, and he was healed. By hard work, effort, and perseverance, his friends succeeded in gaining for him the mighty blessing of a complete cure.

The importance of effort and diligence is a truth all around us. Bankers and merchants have as one of their favourite maxims, 'no gains without pains.' If the children of this world take such great pains about a corruptible crown, we ought to take far more pains about one that is incorruptible. Happy are those people who count everything as loss if only they may win Christ and be found in him.

Notes on Luke 5:17–26

19. Let him down with his bed through the tiles. In order to understand this we must remember the construction of houses in the countries where our Lord preached. It was, and is now, a common practice to construct them with a flat roof, and a small square or courtyard in the middle of the building. Access was obtained to the roof by an outside staircase, so a person could go up to the roof without entering the house.

Our Lord appears to have been preaching and teaching in the courtyard, under cover of the tiling projecting from one of the sides. The friends of the paralytic man were unable to make their way into the courtyard because of the crowd, so they carried him up the staircase outside the building, and so reached the flat roof of the house. Then they removed that part of the tiling which was above our Lord, and let down their friend in his bed, by ropes, into the courtyard below.

26. Amazement seized all of them. Literally, 'Amazement took them all.' The word used for amazement is the same that is translated in three places as 'a trance' (Acts 10:10; 11:5; 22:17). It is a word used concerning 'the highest sort of admiration or wonder.'

'We have seen strange things today.' This is the only place in the New Testament where this word **'strange'** is used. It is literally 'paradoxes' – things contrary to all common opinion and ordinary experiences.

The calling of Levi (5:27–32)

These verses should be deeply interesting to every one who knows the value of an immortal soul, and desires salvation. They describe the conversion and experience of one of Christ's earliest disciples. We, too, are all by nature born in sin, and need conversion. Let us see what we know of the mighty change. Let us compare our own experience with that of the man whose case is described here, and by comparison learn wisdom.

The power of Christ's calling grace

We read that our Lord called a tax collector called Levi to become one of his disciples. This man belonged to a group of people who were a byword for wickedness among the Jews. Yet even to him our Lord says, **'Follow me'** (verse 27). Then we read that this had such an effect on Levi that he **got up, left everything, and followed him** (verse 28) and became Christ's disciple. We must never despair of anyone's salvation, so long as he lives, after reading a case like this. Let us remember that he who called Levi never changes.

Notes on Luke 5:27–32

27. A tax-collector named Levi. The person called Levi here is called Matthew in St. Matthew's Gospel, and Levi in St. Mark's. It is almost universally agreed that it is one and the same person – Matthew the apostle. Like some others in the Bible, he had two names.

29. A great banquet. The word translated **banquet** is only used here and in Luke 14:13. It means a kind of large reception banquet, such as only wealthy people could give, and at which the guests were numerous. The worldly sacrifice which Levi made in becoming Christ's disciple was probably greater than that made by any of the apostles.

32. 'Call . . . to repentance.' Let it be carefully noted here, as well as elsewhere, that our Lord's call to sinners is not a bare call to become his disciples, but a call **'to repentance.'**

Stella, the Spanish annotator, remarks on this verse, 'You must not understand from this that Christ found some who were righteous. For the sentence of Paul is true: "All have sinned." Christ calls these scribes and Pharisees righteous, not because they were really so, but only according to the common estimation and appearance of them.'

Christ the Bridegroom (5:33–39)

People may disagree on the minor points about religion but agree over the weightier matters

We should observe in these verses that people may disagree on the minor points about religion but agree over the weightier matters. We have this brought out in the supposed difference between the disciples of John the Baptist, and Christ's disciples. The observation was put to our Lord, 'John's disciples, like the disciples of the Pharisees, frequently fast and pray, but your disciples eat and drink' (verse 33).

We cannot suppose that there was any essential difference between the teachings of these two groups of disciples. The teaching of John the Baptist was doubtless clear and explicit on all the main points essential for salvation. The man who could say of Jesus, 'Here is the Lamb of God who takes away the sin of the world!' (John 1:29), was not likely to teach his followers anything contrary to the Gospel. His teaching, of course, lacked the fullness and perfection of his divine Master's teaching, but it is absurd to suppose that it contradicted it. Nevertheless, there were points of practice on which his disciples differed from those of Christ. Agreeing, as they doubtless did, about the necessity of repentance, and faith, and holiness, they disagreed about such matters as fasting, eating, drinking, and the devotions held in public. One in heart, hope, and aim as they were about the weightier matter of inner religion, they were not entirely of one mind about outer matters.

We must make up our minds to see differences of this kind among Christians so long as the world stands. We may regret them much, because of the handle they give to an ignorant and prejudiced world. But they will exist, and are one of the many evidences of our fallen condition. About church government, about the way to conduct public worship, about fasts and feasts, and saints' days, and ceremonials, Christians have never been entirely of one mind, even from the days of the apostles. On all these points the holiest and ablest of God's servants have arrived at different conclusions. Argument, reasoning, persuasion, persecution, have all alike proved unable to produce unity.

Let us, however, bless God that there are many points on which all true servants of God are thoroughly agreed. About sin and salvation, about repentance, and faith, and holiness there is a much unity among all believers, from all over the world. Let us make much of these points in our own personal religion. These, after all, are the principal things which we shall think of in the hour of death, and the day of judgment. On other matters we must agree to differ. It will not matter much on the last day what we thought about fasting, eating, drinking and ceremonies. Did we repent, and bring forth fruit worthy of repentance? Did we behold the Lamb of God by faith, and receive him as our Saviour?

Notes on Luke 5:33–39

35. 'They will fast in those days.' The complete absence of any direct command to keep

fasts in the church of Christ either in the Acts of the Apostles or in the letters of the New Testament, and especially in the letters to Timothy and Titus, makes it clear that the matter is one which should be handled with caution, and on which everyone must be 'persuaded in his own mind.'

Chapter 6

The disciples picking grain on the Sabbath; Christ is Lord of the Sabbath (6:1–5)

The man with shrivelled hand cured; doing good on the Sabbath defended (6:6–11)

Christ's prayer before choosing the apostles; names of the apostles (6:12–19)

Those whom Christ called blessed and those to whom he said 'Woe to you' (6:20–26)

The nature and extent of Christian charity (6:27–38)

Warning against false teachers (6:39–45)

The two builders and the two foundations (6:46–49)

The disciples picking corn on the Sabbath: Christ is Lord of the Sabbath (6:1–5)

The excessive importance hypocrites attach to trifles

We should notice in this passage what excessive importance hypocrites attach to trifles. We are told that on a certain Sabbath day our Lord was passing **through the cornfields** (verse 1). His disciples, as they followed him, **plucked some heads of grain, rubbed them in their hands, and eat them** (verse 1). At once the hypocritical Pharisees found fault, and accused them of committing a sin. They said, '**Why are you doing what is not lawful on the sabbath?**' (verse 2). The mere act of picking the heads of grain they did not find fault with. This was an action sanctioned by the Mosaic law (Deuteronomy 23:25). The supposed fault they were accused of was breaking the fourth commandment. They had done work on the Sabbath, by taking and eating a handful of food.

This exaggerated zeal of the Pharisees about the Sabbath, we must remember, did not extend to other clear commands of God. It is obvious from many instances in the Gospels that these same people, who pretended such strictness on one little point, were more than lax and indifferent about other points of infinitely greater importance. While they stretched the commandment about the Sabbath beyond its true meaning they openly trampled on the tenth commandment, and were notorious for being covetous (Luke 16:14). But this is precisely the character of the hypocrite. To use our Lord's illustration, in some things he makes a great fuss about straining out a gnat from his cup, while in other matters he can swallow a camel (Matthew 23:24).

It is a bad symptom of anyone's state of soul when they begin to put secondary things in religion in the first place, and the first things in the second place; or when they put the things ordained by men above those things ordained by God.

Notes on Luke 6:1–5

5. 'The Son of Man is lord of the sabbath.' The 'Son of Man' means what it always means in the New Testament, the Lord Jesus Christ himself. The words 'lord of the sabbath' were not meant to imply that our Lord, by virtue of his divine authority, would alter, abrogate, or water down the law of the fourth commandment. They mean that Jesus is 'lord of the sabbath' to deliver it from Jewish traditions, to protect it from superstitious views of its observance, and to show the true spirit and manner in which it was always intended to be kept.

The man with shrivelled hand cured: doing good on the Sabbath defended (6:6–11)

These verses contain another example of our Lord Jesus Christ's teaching about the Sabbath. Once more we find him coming into collision with the vain traditions of the Pharisees about the observances of the fourth commandment. Once more we find him clearing the day of God from the rubbish of human traditions, and placing its requirements on the right foundation.

Doing acts of mercy on the Sabbath is lawful

We are taught in these verses that doing acts of mercy on the Sabbath is lawful. We read that in front of all the teachers of the law and Pharisees our Lord healed a man with a shrivelled hand. He knew that these enemies of righteousness were watching to see whether he would do it, in order that they might have **an accusation against him** (verse 7). He boldly asserts the right of doing such deeds of mercy, even on the day when it said that you should not do any work. He openly challenges them to show that such a work was contrary to the law. 'I ask you, is it lawful to do good or to do harm on the sabbath, to save life or to destroy it?' (verse 9). To this question his enemies were unable to find an answer.

The principle laid down here has a wide application. The fourth commandment was never meant to be interpreted so that it could inflict injury on anyone's body. It was not meant to forbid showing kindness on the Sabbath to the afflicted, or attending to the needs of the sick. We may drive a carriage to minister comfort to the dying. We may do any deed of mercy and still keep the Sabbath holy. This is not breaking God's law.

Christ's prayer before choosing the apostles: names of the apostles (6:12–19)

Our Lord appointed his first apostles after much prayer

Let us observe in these verses, that when our Lord appointed his first apostles he did so after much prayer. We read that he **went out to the mountain to pray; and spent the night in prayer to God. And when day came, he called his disciples and chose twelve of them, whom he also named apostles** (verses 12–13).

We need not doubt that there is deep significance in this special mention of our Lord's praying on this occasion. It was intended to be a perpetual lesson to Christ's church. Do we desire to help forward the cause of pure and undefiled religion in the world? Then let us never forget to pray for ministers.

Notes on Luke 6:12–19

12. Spent the night in prayer to God. Isidore Clarius, in his orations on St. Luke, published in Venice in 1565, has some striking remarks on the disgraceful contrast between the way in which the apostles were called to their office after a night spent in prayer, and the way in which ecclesiastical offices were filled in Italy in his own day. He exposes the system of jobbing, nepotism, corruption, and covetousness, which universally prevailed on such occasions, and enters a faithful protest against it.

16. Judas Iscariot. One reason our Lord chose a traitor to be an apostle was that the choice finally supplied a powerful indirect evidence of the purity, blamelessness, and faultlessness of our Lord's behaviour and ministry. When our Lord was accused before the High Priest and Pontius Pilate, if anything could be proved against him the traitor Judas Iscariot was exactly the witness who could have proved it. The mere fact that Judas never came forward to give evidence against our Lord is a convincing evidence that nothing could be proved against him.

Those whom Christ called blessed and those to whom he said 'Woe to you' (6:20–26)

Who are blessed by our Lord

Let us first notice in these verses who are blessed by our Lord Jesus. The list is a remarkable and startling one. It singles out those who are '**poor**' (verse 20), those who '**are hungry**' (verse 21), those who '**weep**' (verse 21), and those whom men 'hate' (verse 22). These are the people to whom the great Head of the church says, 'Blessed are you.'

We must take great care that we do not misunderstand our Lord's meaning when we read these words. We must not for a moment suppose that the mere fact of being poor, and hungry, and sorrowful, and hated by men, will entitle anyone to lay claim to being blessed by Christ. The poverty spoken about here is a poverty accompanied by grace. The afflictions are the afflictions of the gospel. Such poverty and persecution were the inevitable consequences of faith in Christ at the beginning of Christianity. Thousands had to give up everything in this world because of their religion. Jesus desired to give these people, and all who suffer like them for the Gospel's sake, special comfort and consolation.

Notes on Luke 6:20–26

22. 'Exclude you.' This Greek word, according to Suicer, is especially applied to ecclesiastical excommunication.

26. 'Woe to you when all speak well of you.' Let these words be carefully noted. Few of our Lord's sayings are more flatly contradictory to the common opinion of the church and the world than this. What is more common in the world than the love of every one's praise? To be universally popular is a most unsatisfactory symptom, and one of which a minister of Christ should always be afraid. It may well make him doubt whether he is faithfully doing his duty, and honestly declaring all the counsel of God.

The nature and extent of Christian love (6:27–38)

The teaching of our Lord Jesus Christ in these verses is confined to one great subject. The subject is Christian love. Love, which is the grand characteristic of the Gospel – love, which is the height of perfection – love, without which a person is nothing in God's sight – love is here fully expounded and strongly recommended. It would have been well for Christ's church if its Master's precepts in this passage had been more carefully studied and more diligently observed.

The nature and extent of Christian love

In the first place, our Lord explains the nature and extent of Christian love. The disciples might ask, Whom are we to love? He tells them to love their enemies, to do good to those who hate them, to bless those who curse them, and to pray for those who ill-treat them. Their love was to be like his own towards sinners: unselfish, disinterested, and uninfluenced by any hope of return. The disciples might ask how this kind of love was to express itself. It was to be self-sacrificing and self-denying: 'If anyone

strikes you on the cheek, offer the other also; and from anyone who takes away your coat do not withhold your shirt' (verse 28). They were to give up much, and endure more, for the sake of showing kindness and avoiding strife. They were to forgo even their rights, and submit to wrong, rather than awaken any angry passions and create quarrels. In this they were to be like their Master, long-suffering, meek, and lowly of heart.

Notes on Luke 6:27–38

28. **Pray for those who ill-treat you.** The behaviour recommended here is beautifully exemplified in the case of our Lord praying for those who crucified him, and Stephen praying for those who stoned him (Luke 23:34; Acts 7:60).

29–30. **'If someone strikes you on the one cheek. . . .'** The precepts of these two verses must be interpreted with scriptural qualifications. They are strong proverbial forms of expressing a great principle. If we were to press an extreme literal interpretation on them, we would be encouraging theft, burglary, violence, and murder. The earth would be given into the hands of the wicked.

On the one hand, our Lord did not mean to forbid the repression of crime, or to declare the office of magistrate and policeman unlawful. Nor did he mean to pronounce all war unlawful, or to prohibit the punishment of evildoers, and disturbers of the peace and order of society.

On the other hand, it is evident that our Lord condemns everything like a revengeful, pugnacious, litigious, or quarrelsome spirit. He forbids everything like duelling, or fighting, between individuals, for the settlement of private wrongs. He commends forbearance, patience, and long-suffering under injuries and insults. He would have us concede much, submit to much, and put up with much, rather than cause strife. (See Romans 12:18–21.) To return blow for blow and to repay anger with anger is the behaviour of a dog or a heathen, but not of a Christian.

33. **'Even "sinners" do the same.'** Quesnel remarks on this verse, 'A person ought to tremble with fear if beside the external part of his religion he finds nothing in his life but what may be found in a Turk or a heathen.'

Warning against false teachers (6:39–45)

The great danger of listening to false teachers

We learn from these verses, the great danger of listening to false teachers in religion. Our Lord compares such teachers and their hearers to the blind leading the blind, and asks the reasonable question, 'Will not both fall into a pit?' (verse 39). He goes on to confirm the importance of his warning by declaring that 'A disciple is not above his teacher' (verse 40). If a person will hear unsound instruction we cannot expect him to become otherwise than unsound in the faith himself.

The subject which our Lord brings before us here deserves far more attention than it generally receives. The amount of evil which unsound religious teaching has brought on the church in every age is incalculable. The loss of souls which it has occasioned is fearful to contemplate. A teacher who does not know the way to heaven himself is not likely to lead his hearers to heaven. The person who hears such a teacher runs the fearful risk himself of being lost eternally. 'Can a blind person guide a blind person? Will not both fall into a pit?' (verse 39).

If we escape the danger our Lord is warning us about, we must not neglect to test all the teaching we hear with the holy Scriptures. We must not believe things merely because ministers say them. We must not suppose, as a matter of course, that ministers make no mistakes. We must call to mind our Lord's words on another occasion: 'Beware of false prophets' (Matthew 7:15). We must remember St. Paul's advice, 'Test everything' (1 Thessalonians 5:21), and St. John's advice, 'test the spirits to see whether they are from God' (1 John 4:1). With the Bible in our hands, and the promise of the Holy Spirit to everyone who seeks him, we will have no excuse if we are led astray. The blindness of ministers is no excuse for the darkness of the people. If people will trust blind guides, they must not be surprised if they are led into the pit.

Notes on Luke 6:39–45

39. 'Can a blind person guide a blind person?' This is a warning against following unsound religious teachers.

40. 'A disciple is not above his teacher.' This verse is often taken to be a description of all believers in this world, and is paralleled with such sayings as 'If they persecuted me, they will persecute you.' 'If they kept my saying they would have kept your saying.' But I feel unable to interpret the verse in this way. It is good divinity, but not the sense of this passage. The true meaning, I believe, must be sought in connection with the preceding verse. There our Lord uses a parable to issue a warning about false teachers. He had been comparing them with blind guides, and shows that if the blind lead the blind both fall into a pit. He then seems to foresee the common objection that it does not follow because our teachers go astray that we, too, should go astray. 'Beware of that delusion,' he seems to say: 'disciples must not be expected to see more clearly than their teachers. The pupil will become as perfect as his master, but not more so. He will certainly copy his errors, and reproduce his faults. If you choose to

follow blind guides, do not wonder if you never get beyond them, and if you share in their final ruin.'

The two builders and the two foundations (6:46–49)

It has been said, with much truth, that no sermon should conclude without some personal application to the consciences of the listeners. The passage before us is an example of this rule, and a confirmation of its correctness. It is a solemn and heart-searching conclusion to a most solemn discourse.

Profession without practice is a common sin

Let us note, in these verses, what a common sin it is to profess something and to fail to practise it. It is written that our Lord said, 'Why do you call me, "Lord, Lord," and do not do what I tell you?' (verse 46). The Son of God himself had many followers, who pretended to honour him by calling him Lord, but never obeyed his commands.

The evil which our Lord exposes here has always existed in God's church (see Ezekiel 33:31; James 1:22). It is a disease which has never failed to prevail all over Christendom. Open sin, and avowed unbelief, no doubt slay their thousands. But profession without practice slays its tens of thousands.

Notes on Luke 6:46–49

48. 'That one is like a man building a house.' The object of the parable is not to teach the doctrine of justification, but the folly of Christian profession unaccompanied by Christian practice, and the certain ruin to which such profession must lead if persisted in. That Christ is the true Rock on which we must build our hopes, and that there is no other rock on which we can stand, is abundantly taught elsewhere. But it is not the lesson of the passage before us. The passage is a warning against antinomianism. Let us not forget that.

49. 'But the one who hears and does not act.' The clear words of John Bunyan, when he describes Talkative in *The Pilgrim's Progress*, are an admirable commentary on this verse. 'The soul of religion is the practical part. "Religion that is pure and undefiled before God, the Father, is this: to care for the orphans and widows in their distress, and to keep oneself unspotted by the world" (James 1:27). This Talkative is not aware of. He thinks that hearing and saying will make a good Christian, and thus he deceives his own soul. Hearing is but the sowing of the seed. Talking is not sufficient proof that fruit is indeed in the heart and life. Let us assure ourselves, that at the day of doom men shall be judged according to their fruits. It will not then be said, Did you believe? but, Were

you a doer, or talker only? And accordingly they shall be judged. The end of the world is compared to our harvest; and you know men at harvest regard nothing but fruit.'

Chapter 7

The centurion's servant healed at Capernaum (7:1–10)

The widow's son restored to life at Nain (7:11–17)

John the Baptist's message to Christ, and Christ's reply (7:18–23)

Christ's high testimony to John the Baptist (7:24–30)

Christ's description of the people of his generation, and their childish folly exposed (7:31–35)

The sinful woman who anointed Christ's feet in Simon the Pharisee's house (7:36–50)

The centurion's servant healed at Capernaum (7:1–10)

These verses describe the miraculous cure of a sick man. A centurion, or officer in the Roman army, speaks to our Lord on behalf of his servant, and obtains his request. A greater miracle of healing than this is nowhere recorded in the Gospels. Without even seeing the sufferer, without touch of hand or look of eye, our Lord restores health to a dying man by a single word. He speaks and the sick man is cured. He commands and the disease departs. We read of no prophet or apostle who performed miracles like this. We see here the finger of God.

The kindness of the centurion

We should notice in these verses the kindness of the centurion. His character is revealed in three ways. We see him as he treats his servant. He cares for him tenderly when he is sick and takes pains to have him restored to health. We note his disposition towards the Jewish people. He did not despise them as other Gentiles usually did. The elders of the Jews bore strong witness to this: 'he loves our people' (verse 5). We also see the centurion's character in his liberal support of the Jewish place of worship in Capernaum. He did not love Israel in word but not in deed. The messengers he sent to our Lord supported their petition by saying, he 'built our synagogue for us' (verse 5).

Now where did the centurion learn this kind-

ness? How can we account for one who was a heathen by birth, and a soldier by profession, showing such a spirit as this? Habits of mind like these were not likely to be gleaned from heathen teaching, or promoted by the society of a Roman camp. Greek and Latin philosophy would not recommend them. Tribunes, consuls, prefects, and emperors would not encourage them. There is only one way to account for the centurion's character. The centurion was what he was by the grace of God. The Spirit had opened the eyes of his understanding, and put a new heart within him. His knowledge of divine things no doubt was very dim. His religious views were probably built on a very imperfect acquaintance with the Old Testament Scriptures. But whatever light he had from above, it influenced his life, and resulted in the kindness described in this passage.

Notes on Luke 7:1–10

2. A centurion there had a slave. The centurion here must have been a Gentile. We learn this from our Lord's words, 'I tell you, not even in Israel have I found such faith' (verse 9).

3. He sent some Jewish elders. Bishop Hall notes, 'He is unworthy to be well served that will not sometimes wait on his followers.'

7. 'Only speak the word.' The Portuguese commentator, Barradius, has some striking remarks on these words spoken by the centurion. He says, 'This is a peculiar attribute of God's, to be able to do all things by a word and a command. "He commanded and they were created" (Psalm 148:5). Read the book of Genesis. You will see the world created by the Word of God: "God said, 'Let there be light'; and there was light."' He then shows from a quotation from Augustine how all the created beings in existence, whether kings, or angels, or seraphim, cannot create so much as an ant. But when God says, 'Let the world be made,' at once it is made through a word. And he concludes, 'Well therefore does the centurion say, "But only speak the word, and let my servant be healed."'

9. Jesus ... was amazed at him. There are two occasions where it is recorded that our Lord Jesus Christ was amazed, once here, and once in Mark 6:6. It is remarkable that in one case he is described as marvelling at faith, and in the other as marvelling at 'unbelief.' Bishop Hall, and Burkitt after him, both observe, 'What can be more wonderful than to see Christ wonder? Let it teach us to place our admiration where Christ placed his. Let us be more affected with the least measure of grace in a good man than with all the gaieties and glories of a great man.' Our Lord did not wonder at the gorgeous and beautiful buildings of the Jewish temple. But he did marvel at faith.

The widow's son restored to life at Nain (7:11–17)

The wonderful event described in these verses is only recorded in St. Luke's Gospel. It is one of the three great instances of our Lord restoring a dead person to life, and, like the raising of Lazarus and the ruler's daughter, is rightly regarded as one of the greatest miracles which he wrought on earth. In all three cases, we see divine power displayed. In each we see evidence that the Prince of Peace is stronger than the king of terrors, and that though death, the last enemy, is mighty, he is not so mighty as the sinner's Friend.

Notes on Luke 7:11–17

13. **When the Lord saw her, he had compassion for her.** Poole's remarks on these words are worth reading. 'None moved our Lord on behalf of the widow, neither do we read that she herself spoke to him. But our Saviour's compassion was moved at the sight of her sorrows, and consideration of her loss. It is observable that our Saviour performed his healing miracles: firstly, sometimes in response to a request from the person wishing to be healed; secondly, sometimes in response to a request from a friend of the sick person; and, thirdly, sometimes from his own initiative.' The leper was healed (Luke 5:12) in response to his own personal request; the centurion's servant (Luke 7:1) in response to the pleading of his master; and the widow's son was raised without anyone asking on his behalf.

15. **Began to speak.** This fact is mentioned in order to place it beyond doubt that the young man was really restored to life. Where there is speech, there must be life.

Let it be observed that we have no record about anything that was ever said, or thought, by those who were miraculously raised from the dead. Their experience and knowledge are wisely withheld from us.

17. **This word about him spread.** Poole remarks, 'The people here saw his divine power manifestly exerted; for the keys of the clouds, the womb, and the grave, are those keys which their teachers had taught them were kept in God's hand alone.'

John the Baptist's message to Christ, and Christ's reply (7:18–23)

The message which John the Baptist sent to our Lord, in these verses, is most instructive when we consider the circumstances under which it was sent. John the Baptist was now a prisoner in the hands of Herod. 'When John heard in prison what the Messiah was doing' (Matthew 11:2). His life was drawing to a close. His opportunities of active usefulness were ended. A long imprisonment or a violent death were the only prospects before him. Yet even in these dark days we see this holy man maintaining his old ground, as a witness to Christ. He is the same man that he was when he cried, 'Behold the Lamb of God.' To testify to Christ was his continual work as a preacher at liberty. To send men to Christ was one of his last deeds as a prisoner in chains.

Our Lord's solemn warning to John the Baptist's disciples

We should notice in these verses, the solemn warning which our Lord gave to John the Baptist's disciples. He knew the danger they were in. He knew that they were disposed to question his claim to be the Messiah, because of his humble appearance. They saw no signs of a king about him, no riches, nor royal clothes, no courtiers, and no crown. They only saw a man, to all appearances poor as they were, surrounded by a few fishermen and tax collectors. Their pride rebelled at the idea that such a person should be the Christ. It seemed incredible. There must be some mistake. Such thoughts as these, in all probability, passed through their minds. Our Lord read their hearts, and dismissed them with a searching caution. '**Blessed is anyone who takes no offence at me**' (verse 23).

Notes on Luke 7:18–23

21. **Diseases, plagues, and evil spirits.** Let it be noted that evil spirits are mentioned here as an affliction distinct from any bodily ailments. Bishop Pearce remarks, 'We may conclude that evil spirits are thought of by St. Luke (who speaks of illnesses with more accuracy than the other evangelists), as things different from any disorders of the body included in the two former words.'

22. **'The poor have good news brought to them.'** That this was a sign of the Messiah's appearing is seen in Isaiah's words, 'The meek shall obtain fresh joy in the LORD, and the neediest people shall exult in the Holy One of Israel' (Isaiah 29:19). Contempt for the poor, as ignorant and despicable, appears to have been very common in the times of the Gospel (see John 7:49; 9:34; and James 2:24). Concern and tender interest about the souls of the poor, as souls which would live as long as the souls of rich men, was a distinguishing feature of our Lord's ministry, and of that of his apostles. It is always an evil sign of the state of the church when the spiritual needs of poor people are neglected, and the rich man's way to heaven is made smoother than the way of the poor.

Christ's high testimony to John the Baptist (7:24–30)

Jesus' tender care for the reputation of John the Baptist

The first point that demands our notice in this passage is the tender care that our Lord has for the reputation of John the Baptist. As soon as his messengers have left Jesus defends John the Baptist's reputation. He saw that the people around him were likely to write John the Baptist off, partly because he was in prison, and partly because of the questions his messengers had brought. He pleads the cause of his absent friend in warm and strong language. He tells his hearers to throw out of their minds any suspicions they had about John the Baptist. He tells them that John was no wavering and unstable character, a mere reed shaken by the wind. He tells them that John was no mere courtier and hanger on around king's palaces, though circumstances at the end of his ministry had brought him into contact with king Herod. He declares that John was '**more than a prophet**' (verse 26), for he was a prophet who had been the subject of prophecy himself. And he winds up his testimony with the remarkable saying, that '**among those born of women no one is greater than John**' (verse 28).

There is something deeply touching about these sayings of our Lord on behalf of his absent servant. The position which John now occupied as Herod's prisoner was so different from that which he occupied at the beginning of his ministry. At one time he was the best-known and most popular preacher of his day. There was a time when 'the people of Jerusalem and all Judea were going out to him, and all the region along the Jordan' (Matthew 3:5). Now he was a solitary prisoner in Herod's hands, deserted, friendless, and with nothing before him but death. But the last of man's favour is no proof that God is displeased. John the Baptist had one Friend who never failed him and never forsook him – a Friend whose kindness did not ebb and flow like John's popularity, but was always the same. That Friend was our Lord Jesus Christ.

Christ's description of the people of his generation, and their childish folly exposed (7:31–35)

Unconverted hearts are desperately perverse as well as wicked

We learn from these verses, that unconverted hearts are desperately perverse as well as wicked.

Our Lord brings this lesson home in a remarkable comparison, describing the generation of people among whom he lived while he was on earth. He compares them to children. He says that children at play were no more perverse and hard to please than the Jews of his day. Nothing would satisfy them. They were always finding fault. Whatever ministry God used among them, they took exception to it. Whatever messenger God sent among them, they were not pleased. First came John the Baptist, living an ascetic and self-denying life. The Jews accused him of having a demon. After him came the Son of Man, eating and drinking, like ordinary people. The Jews accused him of being '**a glutton and a drunkard**' (verse 34). In short, it became evident that the Jews were determined to receive no message from God at all. Their fake objections were only a cloak to cover over their hatred of God's truth. What they really disliked was, not so much God's ministers, as God himself.

The plain truth is that the natural heart of man hates God. The earthly mind is at war with God. It dislikes his law, his Gospel, and his people. It will always find some excuse for not believing and obeying. The doctrine of repentance is too strict for it. The doctrine of faith and grace is too easy for it. John the Baptist goes too much out of the world. Jesus Christ goes too much into the world. And so the heart of man excuses himself for sitting still in his sins. All this must not surprise us. We must make up our minds to find unconverted people as perverse, unreasonable, and hard to please as the Jews of our Lord's time.

Notes on Luke 7:31–35

35. '**Wisdom is vindicated by all her children.**' I believe the right interpretation is to think of the **children** as the truly wise, the elect, the believers, the people who are really taught by God. By them 'the wisdom of God's ways is always justified, whatever others may like to think about it. They assent to them, approve of them, and regard them as being entirely right.'

The sinful woman who anointed Christ's feet in Simon the Pharisee's house (7:36–50)

The deeply interesting narrative in these verses is only found in St. Luke's Gospel. To see the full beauty of the story, we should read, in connection with it, Matthew chapter 1. We will then discover the striking fact that the woman whose actions are recorded here most probably owed her conversion to those well-known words, 'Come to me, all you that labour and are carrying heavy burdens, and I will give you rest' (Matthew 11:28). That wonderful invitation, in all probability, saved her soul, and gave her that sense of peace which we see she is so grateful for. A full offer of free pardon is generally God's chosen instrument for bringing the chief of sinners to repentance.

People may show outward respect for Christ,
but remain unconverted

We see in this passage that people may show outward respect for Christ, but remain unconverted. The Pharisee before us is a case in point. He showed our Lord Jesus Christ more respect than many did. He even **asked Jesus to eat with him** (verse 36). Yet all this time he was profoundly ignorant about the nature of Christ's Gospel. His proud heart secretly rebelled against the sight of a poor contrite sinner being allowed to wash our Lord's feet. And even the hospitality he showed appears to have been cold and niggardly. Our Lord himself says, '**You gave me no water for my feet … You gave me no kiss … You did not anoint my head with oil.**' (verses 44–46). In short, in all that the Pharisees did there was one great defect. There was outward civility, but there was no love from the heart.

We will do well to remember this Pharisee. It is quite possible to have a decent form of religion, and yet to know nothing about Christ's gospel, to treat Christianity with respect, and yet to be utterly blind about its cardinal doctrines, to behave with great correctness and propriety at church, and yet to hate justification by faith, and salvation by grace, with a deadly hatred. We need to take care to see that we are better than Simon the Pharisee, otherwise, our Lord might say to us, '**Simon, I have something to say to you**' (verse 40).

Notes on Luke 7:36–50

36. One of the Pharisees. We know nothing about this Pharisee, except his name, Simon.

38. Stood behind him at his feet. To understand this we must remember that in the country where our Lord ministered, people did not sit down to meals, as we do, but reclined, or lay at full length on couches, with their feet stretched out behind them. In this way it would be easy for this woman to do what she did to our Lord's feet. **Anointing them with the ointment.** Ointments and oils were used in eastern countries to an extent we can hardly understand. The excessive heat of the climate made it an almost necessity, to preserve the skin from cracking (see Psalm 104:15).

48. 'Your sins are forgiven.' We are not, of course, to suppose that these words mean that the woman's sins were now forgiven for the first time. Such an interpretation would be totally contradictory to the story of the two debtors. The woman was actually forgiven before she came to Christ during that meal. But she now received a public and authoritative declaration of it before many witnesses, as a reward for her open expression of love and gratitude. Before, she had hope through grace. Now, she received the assurance of hope.

50. 'Your faith has saved you.' Let it be observed that it is not said, 'Your love has saved you.' Here, as in every other part of the New Testament, faith is put forward as the key to salvation. By faith, the woman received our Lord's invitation. 'Come to me … and I will give you rest' Matthew 11:28. By faith, she embraced that invitation, and embracing it, threw off her sins under which she had been so long labouring and heavy laden. By faith, she boldly came to the Pharisee's house, and confessed by her behaviour that she had found rest in Christ. Her faith worked by love, and bore precious fruit. But it was not love but faith that saved her soul.

Chapter 8

The holy women who accompanied our Lord and his twelve apostles (8:1–3)

The parable of the sower (8:4–15)

Spiritual privileges to be used diligently; who were Christ's mother and brothers? (8:16–21)

The storm on the lake, and the miraculous calm (8:22–25)

The healing of the demon-possessed man from the region of the Gerasenes (8:26–36)

Christ rejected by the Gerasenes; Christ's command to the healed man from that region (8:37–40)

The woman who had been subject to bleeding for twelve years touches the edge of Christ's cloak (8:41–48)

The daughter of Jairus restored to life (8:49–56)

The holy women who accompanied our Lord and his twelve apostles (8:1–3)

God's grace and Christ's love

Let us notice from these verses, the power of God's grace, and the constraining influence of Christ's love. We read that among those who followed our Lord on his travels were **some women who had been cured of evil spirits and infirmities** (verse 2).

We can imagine that the difficulties these holy women had to face in becoming Christ's disciples were neither few nor small. They had their full share of the contempt and scorn which was poured on all followers of Jesus by the scribes and Pharisees. But they were unmoved. They were prepared to endure a great deal for the Lord's sake because they were so grateful to have received mercy from his hands. They were enabled to stay with Jesus and not to give up because of the inner power of the Holy Spirit. And how wonderfully they stayed with Jesus to the end. It was not a woman who sold our Lord for thirty silver coins. It was not a woman who fled from the Lord in the Garden of Gethsemane. It was not a woman who denied him three times in the high priest's house. But they were women who wailed and lamented when Jesus was led out to be crucified. They were women who stood by the cross to the end. And they were women who first visited the grave where the Lord had been laid. Great indeed is the power of the grace of God.

Notes on Luke 8:1–3

3. Joanna the wife of … Cuza. Cuza was a person holding high and responsible office.

Susanna. This is the only place in which we find this woman mentioned. Of her past or subsequent life we know nothing.

Who provided for them out of their own resources. Maldonatus in commenting on this quotes an enlightening passage from Jerome: 'It was a Jewish custom, and from the ancient habit of the nation it was thought a blameless custom, for women to supply to their instructors food and clothing from their substance.'

Spiritual privileges to be used diligently (Luke 8:4–15)

The parable of the sower contained in these verses is related more frequently than any parable in the Bible. It is a parable of universal application. The things it relates are continually going on in every congregation wherever the Gospel is preached. The four kinds of hearts which it describes are to be found in every assembly which hears the Word. These factors should make us read the parable very carefully. We should say to ourselves, as we read it: This concerns me. My heart is seen in this parable. I, too, am here.

The passage itself requires little explanation. In fact, the meaning of the whole picture is so fully explained by our Lord Jesus Christ that no human exposition can throw much additional light on it. The parable is preeminently a parable of caution, and caution about a most important subject – the way of hearing the Word of God. It was meant to be a warning to the apostles not to expect too much from hearers. It was meant to be a warning to all ministers of the Gospel not to look for too great results from sermons. It was meant, not least of all, to be a warning to hearers to take heed how they hear. Preaching is an ordinance of which the value can never be overrated in Christ's church. But it should never be forgotten that there must not only be good preaching, but good hearing.

Beware of the devil when we hear the Word

The first caution that we learn from the parable of the sower is to beware of the devil when we hear the Word. Our Lord tells us that the hearts of some hearers are like 'the path' (verse 5). The seed of the Gospel is snatched away from them by the devil almost as soon as it is sown. It does not sink down into their consciences. It does not make the least impression on their minds.

The devil, not doubt, is everywhere. That malicious spirit is unwearied in his efforts to do us harm. He is always watching for our halting, and seeking occasion to destroy our souls. But nowhere perhaps is the devil so active as in the congregation of Gospel-hearers. Nowhere does he work so hard to stop the progress of what is good, and to prevent men and women from being saved. From him come wandering thoughts, sleepy eyes and fidgety nerves, weary ears and distracted attention. In all these things Satan has a great hand. People wonder where they come from, and marvel how it is that they find sermons so dull, and hardly remember them. They forget the parable of the sower. They forget the devil. Let us take heed that we are not wayside hearers. Let us beware of the devil.

Notes on Luke 8:4–15

5. A farmer went out to sow his seed. It is highly probable that in this parable our Lord describes something which was actually going on in the sight of everybody. Many of our Lord's parables, we must remember, were spoken in the open air, and the images, in many cases, were borrowed from things that everyone could see. Hence our Lord's lessons could be seen as well as heard.

10. 'Looking they may not perceive.' This is a quotation from Isaiah 6:9. It is noteworthy that hardly any passage in the Old Testament is so frequently quoted in the New Testament as this. It is found six times, in Matthew 13:14–15; Mark 4:2; John 12:40; Acts 28:26; Romans 11:8; and here. On each occasion it refers to the same subject – the hardened and unbelieving state of mind in which the Jews were.

11. 'The seed is the word of God.' Let us observe here that the word is means 'signifies,' or 'represents,' according to the Hebrew way of speaking. It is important to remember this, because it throws light on the well-known words used by our Lord at the appointment of the Lord's supper, 'This is my body. This is my blood.'

13. 'Fall away.' The Greek word here is the one we derive our word 'apostasy' from.

Christ's mother and brothers (8:16–21)

These verses form a practical application of the famous parable of the sower. They are intended to hammer home to our minds the parable's important lesson.

Spiritual knowledge should be used

We learn from these verses, that spiritual knowledge ought to be used diligently. Our Lord tells us that it is like a lighted candle, utterly useless when it is put under a bed, and only of any use if put on a candlestick, and placed where it can be helpful to people's needs.

When we hear this lesson, let us first think about ourselves. The Gospel which we possess was not given to us just to be admired and talked about, but to be practised. It was not meant to live in our intellect, or in our tongues, but to be seen in our lives. Christianity is a talent committed to our charge, and one which brings with it great responsibility. We are not in darkness like the heathen. A glorious light is put before us. Let us take care that we use it. While we have the light let us walk in the light (John 12:35).

But let us not only think about ourselves. Let us also think of others. There are millions in the world who have no spiritual light at all. They are without God, without Christ, and without hope (Ephesians 2:12). Can we do nothing for them? There are thousands around us, in our own land, who are unconverted and dead in sins, seeing nothing and knowing nothing that is right. Can we do nothing for them? These are questions to which every true Christian ought to find an answer. We should strive, in every way, to spread our religion. The highest form of selfishness is that of the man who is content to go to heaven alone. The truest charity is to endeavour to share with others every spark of religious light we possess ourselves, and so to hold our own candle that it might give light to everyone around us. Happy is that soul, which, as soon as it receives light from heaven, begins to think of others as well as itself. No candle which God lights was ever meant to burn alone.

The storm on the lake, and the miraculous calm (8:22–25)

The event in our Lord's life described in these verses is related three times in the Gospels. Matthew, Mark, and Luke were all inspired to record it. This should teach us that it is a very important lesson which we must heed.

Our Lord Jesus Christ was really man as well as God

We see in these verses, that our Lord Jesus Christ was really man as well as God. We read that as he sailed over the Lake of Gennesaret in a boat with his disciples, **he fell asleep** (verse 23). Sleep, we must be all aware, is one of the conditions of our nature, as human beings. Angels and spirits require neither food nor refreshment. But flesh and blood, to keep up a healthy existence, must eat, and drink, and sleep. If the Lord Jesus could be weary, and needed to rest, he must have had two natures in one person – a human nature as well as a divine.

This truth is full of deep consolation to all true Christians. The one Mediator, in whom we are told to trust, has been himself a partaker of flesh and blood. The mighty High Priest, who is living for us at God's right hand, has had personal experience of all the sinless infirmities of the body. He has himself been hungry, thirsty and suffered pain. He has himself endured weariness, and sought rest in sleep. Let us pour out our hearts before him with freedom, and tell him our least troubles without reserve. He who made atonement for us on the cross is one who is able to sympathize with our weaknesses (Hebrews 4:15). To be weary of working for God is sinful, but to be wearied and worn in doing God's work is no sin at all. Jesus himself was weary, and Jesus slept.

Note on Luke 8:22–25

23. A gale swept down on the lake. Lake Gennesaret is prone to such storms. It lies very low, and is surrounded, on almost all sides, by high hills. Sudden gusts of wind are consequently very common.

The healing of the demon-possessed man from the region of the Gerasenes (8:26–36)

The well-known narrative before us is carefully recorded by all the three first Gospel-writers. It is a striking instance of our Lord's complete dominion over the prince of this world. We see the great enemy of our souls for once completely vanquished, the 'strong man' foiled by One stronger than he, and the lion spoiled of his prey.

Notes on Luke 8:26–36

27. A man ... who had demons. Let it suffice to believe implicitly that demon possession of the entire person, body, mind and spirit, was an undeniable fact during our Lord's earthly ministry, and all attempts to explain away the instances of this in the Gospels by calling them epilepsy, lunacy, and the like, are utterly unsatisfactory. For the rest, what we cannot completely understand we must be content to believe.

That there is such a thing as Satanic possession now, though comparatively a rare thing, is held by many able doctors who are specialists in this field. Disease of the mind, or madness, is always a very mysterious subject. It is highly probable that Satan has far more to do with it than we think.

30. 'Legion.' This is a well-known name for a division of troops in the Roman army, consisting of 5,000 or 6,000 men. The word is used here to convey a great number.

Christ rejected by the Gerasenes: Christ's command to the healed man from that region (8:37–40)

We see in this passage two requests made to our Lord Jesus Christ. They were very different from each other, and were asked for by two very different people. We see, moreover, how these requests were received by our Lord Jesus Christ. In both cases the request received a most remarkable reply. The whole passage is singularly instructive.

1. The people asked our Lord to leave them, and he granted their request

Let us observe, in the first place that the people of the region of the Gerasenes asked our Lord to leave them, and he granted their request. We read these painfully solemn words: **So he got into the boat and returned** (verse 37).

Now why did these unhappy people desire the Son of God to leave them? Why, after the amazing miracle of mercy which had just been performed among them, did they not want to know him better? Why, in a word, did they become their own enemies, and shut the door against the Gospel? There is only one answer to these questions. These people loved the world, and the things of the world, and were determined not to give them up. They felt convinced, in their own consciences, that they could not receive Christ among them and keep their sins, and their sins they were determined to keep. They saw, at a glance, that there was something about Jesus which their lifestyle did not match up to. They had to choose between their old ways and Jesus' new ways and they chose their own old ways.

Why did Jesus grant them their request and leave them? He did it in judgment, to highlight their great sin. He did it so his church in every age could learn how wicked it is to deliberately reject the truth. It seems an eternal law of his rule, that those who obstinately refuse to walk in the light will have that light taken from them. They said to Christ, 'Leave us,' and he took them at their word. Let us beware that coldness, inattention, worldliness do not drive Jesus from our doors and compel him to forsake us completely.

2. Legion asked to stay with our Lord, but the request was denied

Let us observe, secondly, that Legion's request to stay with our Lord was denied. We read that Jesus sent him away, saying, **Return home and tell how much God has done for you** (verse 39).

We can readily appreciate Legion's request. He felt deep gratitude for the amazing deliverance he had just received. He was full of love for

the One who had so wonderfully and graciously cured him. He felt that he could not see too much of him, be too much in his company or be close enough to him. These feelings overtook him. He wanted nothing, but to be with our Lord Jesus Christ.

So why did our Lord Jesus Christ refuse Legion's request? Why, at a time when he had few disciples, did he send this man away? Why, instead of allowing him to join up with Peter and James and John, did he tell him to return to his own home? Our Lord did what he did in infinite wisdom. He did it for the benefit of the man's own soul. He saw that it was better for him to witness about the Gospel at home than to be a disciple abroad. He did it for the sake of those who lived in that region. He did it, above all, for the continuous instruction of his whole church. Christ wants us to know that there are different ways of glorifying him. He may be honoured in private as well as in public, and that the first place we should witness for Christ is our own home.

Notes on Luke 8:37–40

37. Asked Jesus to leave them. They saw the loss of their pigs with deep concern. They cared more about this than about saving a soul. There are thousands like them. Tell them about the success of missionaries, and the conversion of souls at home or abroad, and they hear it with indifference, if not with a sneer. But if you tell them about the loss of property, or change in the exchange rate, they become animated. Truly the generation of the Gadarenes is not yet extinct!

39. 'Return to your home.' Let us note here that a literal following of Christ, and literal forsaking of relations, friends, and homes, are evidently not essential for salvation. It may be necessary for some people, and on some occasions, under certain circumstances. But it is clear from what happened to Legion that it is not necessary for everyone.

The woman who had been subject to bleeding for twelve years touches the edge of Christ's cloak (8:41–48)

How much misery and trouble sin has brought into the world! This passage offers melancholy proof of this. First we see a distressed father in bitter anxiety about a dying daughter. Then we see a suffering woman, who has been afflicted for twelve years with an incurable disease. And these are things which sin has spread throughout the world. These are the evils which God did not create at the beginning, but man has brought on himself by the fall. There would have been no sorrow and no sickness among Adam's children if there had been no sin.

A striking picture of the condition of many souls

Let us see in the description of this woman a striking picture of the condition of many souls. We are told that she had been afflicted with a debilitating disease for **twelve years** (verse 43). And though she **had spent all she had on physicians, no one could cure her** (verse 43). The state of many a sinner's heart is set before us in this description, as in mirror. Perhaps it describes ourselves.

There are people in most congregations who have felt their sins deeply and have been deeply troubled that they are not forgiven and not fit to die. They seek consolation but do not know where to look. They have tried many false remedies and only find themselves getting worse. They have tired themselves out with every conceivable man-made device for obtaining spiritual health. But all has been in vain. In short, like this woman, they are ready to say, 'There is no hope for me. I shall never be saved.'

Let all such people take comfort from the miracle we are now considering. There is one door on which they have never knocked in all their attempts to find relief. There is one Doctor who they have never visited, who never fails to heal. When all other means had failed this woman went to Jesus for help. Let them go and do likewise.

Notes on Luke 8:41–48

42. Was dying. 'At the point of death.'

43. Suffering from haemorrhages. In order to appreciate this woman's condition and the greatness of the miracle recorded here we should read Leviticus 15:19. This shows that the woman was ceremonially unclean, and would want to avoid all publicity.

45. 'Master.' Only St. Luke uses this word in the New Testament. Literally it means, 'one who is set over anything to care for it.' It is a title of respect, and an acknowledgment of authority.

The daughter of Jairus restored to life (8:49–56)

These verses contain one of the three great instances which the Holy Spirit has thought fit to record of our Lord bringing a dead person back to life. The other two instances are those of Lazarus and the widow's son at Nain. There seems no reason to doubt that our Lord raised other people as well. But these three instances are described as patterns of his almighty power. One was a young girl who had just breathed her last. One was a young man who was being carried to his burial. One was a man who had been dead in the grave for four days. In all three cases we see life restored at once at Christ's command.

Our Lord's power over death

Let us notice, finally, from these verses, the mighty power which our Lord Jesus Christ possesses even over death. We are told that he came to Jairus' house and turned the mourning into joy. He took the hand of the breathless body of the synagogue ruler's daughter and said, '**Child, get up!**' (verse 54). At once, by that all-powerful voice, life was restored. **Her spirit returned, and she got up at once** (verse 55).

Let us take comfort that there is a limit to death's power. The king of terrors is very strong. Patriarchs and kings and prophets and apostles, have all yielded to him. They have all died. But, thanks be to God, there is One stronger than death. That One is the Friend of sinners, Christ Jesus our Lord. He demonstrated his power frequently when he came to earth the first time – in the house of Jairus, by the tomb of Bethany, in the gate of Nain. He will prove it to all the world when he comes again. (See 1 Corinthians 15:26.)

Notes on Luke 8:49–56

51. Peter, John, and James. These three apostles were three times singled out from the rest of the twelve and allowed to be with our Lord on special occasions. They were with him during his transfiguration, in the Garden of Gethsemane, and during this miracle. None of the apostles had such a clear revelation of our Lord's divinity, our Lord's humanity, and our Lord's power and compassion towards the sorrowful and sinful.

55. Give her something to eat. This would be proof positive that her body really was alive again, and that her parents saw no vision, but real flesh and blood. It is the same evidence which our Lord gave his disciples after his own rising from the dead (see Luke 24:41–43).

Chapter 9

Christ's first commission to the twelve disciples when he sent them to preach (9:1–6)

Herod perplexed by Christ's words: the importance of occasional withdrawal: Christ's readiness to receive (9:7–11)

Five thousand men fed with five loaves and two fishes (9:12–17)

Different opinions about Christ; Peter's clear confession; Christ predicts his own death (9:18–22)

Necessity of self-denial and carrying the cross; value to the soul; danger of being ashamed of Christ (9:23–27)

The transfiguration of Christ (9:28–36)

The evil spirit cast out of a young man the disciples could not cure (9:37–45)

Christ rebukes the pride of his disciples; bigotry and meanness rebuked (9:46–50)

Christ's steady adherence to his great work; unholy zeal of James and John reproved (9:51–56)

Christ's followers must submit to hardships; must let the dead bury their dead; must not look back (9:57–62)

Christ's first commission to the twelve disciples when he sent them to preach (9:1–6)

These verses contain our Lord's instructions to the twelve apostles when he sent them out for the first time to preach the Gospel. The passage throws much light on the work of Christian ministers in every age. No doubt the miraculous powers which the apostles possessed, made their position very unlike that of any other group of people in the church. No doubt, in many respects, they stood alone, and had no successors. Yet our Lord's words here must not be restricted to just the apostles. They contain deep wisdom for Christian teachers and preachers, for all time.

The apostles' commission had special reference to the devil and physical sickness

Let us observe that the apostles' commission had special reference to the devil and physical sickness. We read that Jesus gave them **power and authority over all demons and to cure diseases** (verse 1).

There are two principal parts of the Christian minister's work here. We must not expect him to cast out evil spirits, but we may reasonably expect him to resist the devil and all his works and to constantly wage war against the prince of this world. We must not expect him to work miraculous cures, but we may expect him to take a special interest in all sick people, to visit them, sympathize with them, and help them as much as he can. The minister who neglects the sick members of his flock is no true pastor.

Notes on Luke 9:1–6

1. The twelve. Note that Judas Iscariot, the false apostle and traitor, was one of those twelve whom our Lord sent out to preach and heal the sick. We should not be surprised to see unconverted men preaching and being ministers of the Gospel. Our Lord allowed one such person to be among his apostles to show that we must expect to see the evil and good mixed together

in this world. The highest ecclesiastical office and dignity afford no proof that a man has the grace of God.

3. 'Bag.' This was a small bag to carry provisions in.

Herod perplexed by Christ's words: the importance of occasional withdrawal: Christ's readiness to receive (9:7–11)

The power of a bad conscience

Let us note, in this passage, the power of a bad conscience. We are told that when Herod the tetrarch heard about all that was going on … **he was perplexed** (verse 7). He said, 'John I beheaded; but who is this about whom I hear such things?' (verse 9). Great and powerful as he was, news of our Lord's ministry brought his sins to mind, and disturbed him even in his royal palace. Surrounded as he was by everything which is considered to make life enjoyable, the news of another preacher of righteousness filled him with alarm. The recollection of his own wickedness in killing John the Baptist flashed into his mind. He knew that he had done wrong. He felt guilty, and self-condemned, (see Proverbs 13:15). Herod's sin found him out.

Conscience is a most powerful part of our natural constitution. It cannot save our souls. It never leads a person to Christ. It is often blind, and ignorant, and misdirected. Yet conscience often testifies against sin in the sinner's heart and makes him realize that it is wrong to reject God. Happy are those who have found the only cure for a bad conscience. Nothing will ever heal it except the blood of Christ.

Notes on Luke 9:7–11

7. Raised from the dead. Resurrection from the dead was believed by the Jews. The idea that the Jews, before Christ, knew nothing of a resurrection or another life, is utterly untenable.

10. Withdrew privately. Cecil says, 'I do not know how some Christians can make so little of recollection and retirement. I am obliged to withdraw myself regularly, and to say to my heart, What are you doing? Where are you going?'

Five thousand men fed with five loaves and two fishes (9:12–17)

This miracle is recorded more frequently than any other miracle performed by our Lord. Its repetition draws attention to its great importance.

Our Lord's divine power

We see, for one thing, from these verses, a striking example of our Lord Jesus Christ's divine power. He feeds a crowd of five thousand men with five loaves and two fish. He makes a handful of food, barely enough to feed himself and his disciples for a single day, sufficient to feed a crowd the size of a Roman legion. There could be no mistake about the reality and greatness of this miracle. It was done publicly, before many witnesses. The same power which at the beginning made the world out of nothing enabled food to exist which had not previously existed. The circumstances of the whole event made deception impossible. Five thousand hungry men would not have agreed that they were all filled, if they had not received real food. Twelve baskets of leftovers would never have been collected up, if real loaves and fish had not been miraculously multiplied. Nothing, in short, can explain the whole event, except the finger of God. The same hand which sent manna from heaven in the wilderness to feed Israel, was the hand which made five loaves and two fish supply the needs of five thousand men.

Notes on Luke 9:12–17

17. What was left over was gathered up, twelve baskets of broken pieces. Our Lord disapproves of waste. If 'the great Housekeeper of the world,' Burkitt says, 'is so particular about saving fragments, what account will they give on the day of judgment who think nothing of wasting time, money, health, and strength, in the service of sin and the world?'

Brentius' words are worth noting: 'the whole of John chapter six is the true explanation of the use of this miracle. Christ is the bread of life, and he who eats of him will live forever.'

Different opinions about Christ: Peter's clear confession: Christ predicts his own death (9:18–22)

1. Variety of opinions about our Lord

Let us notice in this passage, the variety of opinions about our Lord Jesus Christ, which prevailed during his earthly ministry. We are told that some said that he was John the Baptist; some that he was Elijah; and some that he was one of the old prophets risen again. These opinions all agreed about thing. Our Lord's teaching was not like that of the teachers of the law and Pharisees. All saw in him a bold witness against the evil that was in the world. We must never be surprised to find the same variety of opinions about Christ and his Gospel in our own day.

2. Peter's knowledge and faith

Let us notice, secondly, in this passage, the singular knowledge and faith displayed by the apostle Peter. We read that when our Lord said to his disciples, '**Who do the crowds say that I am?**' (verse 18), Peter

answered, '**The Messiah of God**' (verse 20).

This was a noble confession, which we find it hard to appreciate today. To fully appreciate it we must put ourselves in the shoes of one of Christ's disciples. We should remember that the great, the wise, and learned of their own nation, saw nothing to admire in their Master, and would not receive him as their Messiah. We should recollect that they saw no royal dignity about our Lord, no crown, no army, no earthly power. They only saw a man who often had nowhere to sleep at night. And yet it was at this time and under these circumstances that Peter boldly declares his belief that Jesus it the Christ of God. Truly, this was a great faith. It was mingled, no doubt, with ignorance and imperfection. But, such as it was, it was a faith that stood alone. The person who possessed this faith was a remarkable man, far ahead of the age in which he lived.

Notes on Luke 9:18–22

21. He sternly ordered and commanded them not to tell anyone. There is a time to be silent as well as to speak. Our Lord knew that the public proclamation of him being Messiah would make him to be captured before his time.

The necessity of self-denial and carrying the cross: value to the soul: danger of being ashamed of Christ (9:23–27)

These words of our Lord contain three great lessons for all Christians. They apply to everyone without exception. They are meant for every age and every part of the visible church.

Daily self-denial

We learn, for one thing, the absolute necessity of daily self-denial. We should every day crucify the flesh, overcome the world and resist the devil. We should keep our bodies under and bring them into subjection. We should be on our guard, like soldiers in enemy country. We should fight a daily battle and engage in warfare every day. Our Master's command is clear and plain: **If anyone would come after me, he must deny himself and take up his cross daily and follow me** (verse 23).

Now what do we know of all this? Where is our self-denial? A crucified Saviour will never be content with self-indulgent people. No self-denial – no real grace! No cross – no crown. (See Galatians 5:24.) The Lord Jesus says, '**those who want to save their life will lose it, and those who want to lose their life for my sake will save it**' (verse 24).

Notes on Luke 9:23–27

23. 'Take up their cross.' Campbell remarks, 'Everyone condemned by the Romans to crucifixion was compelled to carry the cross on which he was to be suspended, to the place of execution. In this manner our Lord was treated.'

26. 'When he comes.' Three kinds of glory are mentioned here, which accompany the second coming of Christ: his own, the Father's and the glory of the angels.

27. 'Not taste death before they see the kingdom of God.' The correct interpretation of this verse is the one which links it to the transfiguration. It views the glorious vision of the kingdom, which the transfiguration supplied, as the fulfilment of the promise of this verse.

The transfiguration of Christ (9:28–36)

The event described in these verses, commonly called the transfiguration, is one of the most remarkable in the story of our Lord's earthly ministry. It is one of those passages which we should always read with special gratitude. It lifts a corner of the veil which hangs over the world to come, and throws light on some of the deepest truths of our religion.

The safety of all true believers

This passage shows us the safety of all true believers who have been removed from the world. We are told that when our Lord appeared in glory, Moses and Elijah were seen with him, standing and speaking with him. Moses had been dead nearly fifteen hundred years. Elijah had been taken by a whirlwind from the earth more than nine hundred years previously. Yet here these holy men were seen once more alive, and not only alive, but in glory.

Let us take comfort from the blessed thought that there is a resurrection and a life to come. There is another world beyond the grave. There is much about this future world that we are ignorant of. Where do people live? What knowledge do they have about the things on earth? These are questions we cannot answer. But it is enough to know that Jesus is taking care of them, and that he will bring them with him on the last day. He showed Moses and Elijah to his disciples on the Mount of Transfiguration, and he will show us all who have fallen asleep with him, at his second coming. Our brothers and sisters in Christ are in good keeping. They are not lost, but have gone ahead.

Notes on Luke 9:28–36

29. While he was praying. We are told that it was as our Lord was praying at his baptism that the Holy Spirit came down and the Father's voice was heard. So, also, prayer ushers in the great vision of glory here.

Bishop Hall remarks: 'Behold how Christ entered on all his great works, with prayers in his mouth. When he was about to start his great work of his humiliation in his passion, he went

into the garden to pray. When he is to start his great work of exaltation in his transfiguration, he went up the mountain to pray. He was taken up from his knees to both. O noble example of piety and devotion to us.'

30. Moses and Elijah. Moses represents the law, and Elijah the prophets. Both unite in acknowledging and recognizing Christ, about whom the law and the prophets testify.

It is also highly probable that they were meant to be types and emblems of the saints who will appear with Christ in glory at his second coming. Moses is the type of those who are dead, and will be raised at the Lord's coming. Elijah is the type of those who are alive, and are caught up and meet the Lord in the air (1 Thessalonians 4:17).

31. His departure. This expression is remarkable. Literally, it means his 'exodus.' It is used for 'death' by St. Peter, speaking about his own death (2 Peter 1:15). It is also remarkable that in Acts 13:24 we have a Greek word used for our Lord's 'coming' to take the office of a Saviour, which might be translated literally his 'entrance.' Both expressions are singularly applicable to him who came into the world and was made flesh, and after doing the work he came to do, left the world and went to the Father. The beginning of his ministry, was a coming or an entrance; his death, an exodus or departure.

32. Were weighed down with sleep. The same disciples who slept during a vision of glory, were also found sleeping during the agony in the garden of Gethsemane. Flesh and blood does indeed need to be changed before it can enter heaven.

33. 'It is good for us to be here.' Archbishop Usher remarks, 'When Peter saw Moses and Elijah with Christ in his transfiguration, though he had but a glimpse of glory, yet he says, "It is good for us to be here." But, oh, how infinitely good will it be for us to be in heaven. How shall we then be wrapt up with glory, when we will be forever with the Lord!'

35. 'Listen to him!' Calvin writes, 'We are placed under his tuition alone, and commanded from him alone to seek the doctrine of salvation, to depend on and listen to One – to adhere to One – in a word, as the terms import, to hearken to One only.'

The evil spirit cast out of a young man the disciples could not cure (9:37–45)

The events described in these verses took place immediately after the transfiguration. The Lord Jesus did not stay on the Mount of Transfiguration. His communion with Moses and Elijah was very short. He soon returned to his accustomed work of doing good to a sin-stricken world. In his life on earth, to receive honour and have visions of glory was the exception. To minister to others, to heal all who were oppressed by the devil, to do acts of mercy to sinners, was the rule. Happy are those Christians who have learned to live for others more than for themselves, and who understand that it is 'more blessed to give than to receive' (Acts 20:35).

Note on Luke 9:37–45

38. My only child. Let us remember that the daughter of Jairus, whom our Saviour raised from the dead, was an only daughter, and the widow's son at Nain an only son. These things are worth noticing. St. Luke is the only Gospel writer who specially mentions them.

Christ rebukes the pride of his disciples: bigotry and meanness rebuked (9:46–50)

These verses contain two important warnings. They are directed against two of the most common evils which exist in Christ's church. He who gave them knew what was in the human heart. Christ's church would have done well to have paid greater attention to these words.

A warning against pride and self-conceit

In the first place, the Lord Jesus gives us a warning against pride and self-conceit. We are told that **an argument arose among them as to which of them was the greatest** (verse 46). Amazing as it may seem, this little group of fishermen and tax collectors was not beyond the plague of a self-seeking and ambitious spirit. Filled with the incorrect idea that our Lord's kingdom was about to appear, they were ready to wrangle over who should have the top place in it. Each person thought that they had the best claim to this dominant position. This all happened in Christ's presence despite all his teaching. Such is the heart of man!

There is something very instructive in this fact. Of all the sins there is none which we need to watch and pray about more than pride. No sin is so specious and deceitful. It can wear the clothes of humility itself. It can lurk in the hearts of the ignorant, the ungifted, and the poor, as well as in the minds of the great, the learned, and the rich. It is a quaint and homely saying, but only too true, that no Pope has ever received such honour as Pope 'Self.'

Let a prayer for humility, and the spirit of a little child, form part of our daily supplications. Of all creatures none has so little right to be proud as man, and of all men none should be so humble as the Christian. In lowliness of mind, let us esteem others better than ourselves. Let us be ready, on all occasions, to take the lowest place. And let the words of our Saviour ring in our ears continually, **'for the least among all of you is the greatest'** (verse 48).

Christ's steady adherence to his great work: unholy zeal of James and John reproved (9:51–56)

Our Lord's view about his own crucifixion and death

Let us notice in these verses, the steady determination with which our Lord Jesus Christ viewed his own crucifixion and death. We read that, **When the days drew near for him to be taken up, he set his face towards Jerusalem** (verse 51). He knew full well what was before him. The betrayal, the unjust trial, the mockery, the scourging, the crown of thorns, the spitting, the nails, the spear, the agony on the cross – all, all were doubtless spread before his mind's eye, like a picture. But he never flinched for a moment from the work that he had undertaken. His heart was set on paying the price for our redemption. (Compare Hebrews 12:2.)

Notes on Luke 9:51–56

54. James and John. There is something very remarkable about the spirit exhibited by these two disciples on this occasion. It shows that it was not without good reason that our Lord called them Boanerges (which means Sons of Thunder: Mark 3:17), when he first appointed them. It shows us also the gradual transforming power of the grace of God in John's character. Three times we have sins against love recorded in the Gospels as committed by John. Once we find him and his brother asking to sit at Christ's right and left hand in his kingdom, and to be preferred before all the other apostles. Once we find him forbidding a man to drive out devils, because he did not follow the apostles. Here, we find him showing a fierce and cruel spirit against the Samaritan villagers for not receiving our Lord. Yet this was the apostle who proved at last most remarkable for preaching love and charity. No change is too great for the Lord to work.

54. 'Command fire to come down from heaven.' Bengel remarks that we should compare the behaviour of these two disciples with 'the fact that when Jesus prayed on the cross, using words from Psalms 22 and 31, he did not pray against his enemies, but for them.'

Christ's followers must submit to hardships: must let the dead bury their dead: must not look back (9:57–62)

This is a very remarkable passage of Scripture. It contains three short sayings of special solemnity, spoken by our Lord to three different people. We do not know any of their names. We do not know what effect our Lord's words had on them. We can be sure that they were all spoken to exactly fit the hearer's needs and that the passage is intended to help us examine ourselves.

Notes on Luke 9:57–62

60. 'Let the dead bury their own dead.' The first 'dead' here means spiritually dead, and the second 'dead' means naturally dead. The meaning is clear. Funerals may be safely left to those who, being without spiritual life themselves, attach importance to all ceremonies and customs belonging to this life, and are sure to go to them.

62. 'Fit for the kingdom of God.' 'Fit' means, literally, 'well-placed,' or, 'well-disposed.' It implies that a person wanting to go home to take leave of his friends is not rightly disposed for Gospel work, any more than a person looking back behind him is rightly placed for plowing.

Looking at the whole passage, note that both the second and third people have the great fault of desiring to do something **first** (verses 59,61), before doing Christ's work.

Chapter 10

Christ's appointment of the seventy disciples, and the instructions he gave them (10:1–7)

More of Christ's instructions to the seventy disciples (10:8–16)

The seventy return, elated with success; Christ's solemn warning to them (10:17–20)

Christ rejoices; the sovereignty of God in saving sinners; the privileges of those who have the Gospel (10:21–24)

The expert in the law's question to Christ; the rule of faith; the summary of duty (10:25–28)

The parable of the Good Samaritan (10:29–37)

Christ at Martha and Mary's house; over-carefulness reproved; the one necessary thing (10:38–42)

Christ's appointment of the seventy disciples, and the instructions he gave them (10:1–7)

Only St. Luke records this event. Our Lord appoints seventy disciples to go ahead of him, in addition to the twelve apostles. We do not know the names of any of them. Their subsequent lives have not been revealed to us. But the instructions they were given as they were sent out are very interesting, and deserve our close attention.

The importance of prayer and intercession

The first point in our Lord's charge to the seventy disciples is the importance of prayer and intercession. This is the leading thought with which our Lord opens his address. Before he tells his ambassadors what to do, he first tells them to pray: **'Therefore, ask the Lord of the harvest to send out labourers into his harvest field'** (verse 2).

Prayer is one of the best and most powerful ways to help Christ's cause in the world. It is within the reach of all who have the Spirit of adoption. Not all believers have money to give to missions. Very few have great intellectual gifts, or extensive influence among people. But all believers can pray for the success of the Gospel – and they should pray for this daily. Many wonderful answers to prayer are recorded in the Bible for our learning. Also see James 5:16; Acts 6:4; Ephesians 6:17–18.

Notes on Luke 10:1–7

2. 'Send out.' The Greek word here literally means 'to throw out,' or 'send out with a degree of force.' It implies that nothing but God's powerful and constraining call will ever move men to become labourers in the Gospel harvest.

5. 'Peace to this house!' This is probably a common Jewish greeting; see 1 Samuel 25:6; Psalm 122:7–8.

7. 'The labourer deserves to be paid.' This is a proverb. It is remarkable for being the only expression in the Gospels which is quoted in the letters of the New Testament (see 1 Timothy 5:18).

More of Christ's instructions to the seventy disciples (10:8–16)

These verses comprise the second part of our Lord Jesus Christ's charge to the seventy disciples. Its lessons, like those of the first part, have a special reference to ministers and teachers of the Gospel. But they contain truths which deserve the serious attention of all members of the church of Christ.

The simple message

We should notice in these verses the simplicity of the message which our Lord tells them to proclaim. We read that they were commissioned to say, **'The kingdom of God has come near you'** (verse 9).

These words should probably be thought of as the summary of all that the seventy disciples said. We are hardly meant to think that they said nothing else, except for this single sentence. The words, no doubt, implied far more to a Jewish hearer then than they do to us today. To a well-taught Israelite, they would sound like the announcement that the times of the Messiah had arrived, that the long-promised Saviour was about to be revealed, and that the desire of the nations was about to appear (Haggai 2:7).

Note on Luke 10:8–16

16. 'Whoever listens to you listens to me.' There is probably no stronger language than this in the New Testament about the dignity of a faithful minister's office, and the guilt incurred by those who refuse to hear his message.

The seventy return, elated with success: Christ's solemn warning to them (10:17–20)

Christians are all too liable to be puffed up by success

We learn, from this passage, how Christians are all too liable to be puffed up by success. It is written that the seventy returned from their first mission with joy, saying, '**Lord, in your name even the demons submit to us!**' (verse 17). There was much false fire in that joy. There was evidently self-satisfaction in that report about their achievements. The whole tenor of the passage leads us to this conclusion. The remarkable words our Lord says about Satan falling like lightning from heaven was most probably meant to caution them. He read the hearts of the young and inexperienced soldiers before him. He saw how much they were lifted up by their first victory. He wisely checks them in their undue exultation. He warns them against pride.

The lesson is one which everyone who works for Christ should note and remember. Never forget that a time of success is a time of danger to the Christian soul. The same hearts which are depressed when all things seem against them are often unduly exalted in the day of prosperity. No wonder St. Paul says of an overseer that he ought not to be 'a recent convert, or he may be puffed up with conceit and fall into the condemnation of the devil' (1 Timothy 3:6). Most of Christ's workers probably have as much success as their souls can bear.

Let us pray much for humility, and especially for humility in our days of peace and success. When everything around us seems to prosper, and all our plans work well, when family trials and sicknesses are kept from us, and our days are running smoothly, then, then is the time when our souls are in danger! The warning in this passage must never be forgotten. In the middle of our triumphs, let us cry earnestly, 'Lord, clothe us with humility.'

Notes on Luke 10:21–24

18. 'I watched Satan fall.' Cyprian, Jerome, Gregory, Bede, Erasmus, and Pellican, consider that our Lord's intention was to warn the disciples against vain glory: 'Be not puffed up because the devils are subject to you. Remember that Satan fell through pride, as I myself saw.'

20. 'Your names are written in heaven.' This means that 'you are registered in heaven as citizens of God's kingdom, and people who are chosen to salvation through Christ, pardoned, accepted, and saved.' It is the same as St. Paul's saying, 'whose names are in the book of life' (Philippians 4:3). See also Daniel 12:1; Revelation 13:8; 20:12. We find the opposite expression in Jeremiah 17:13, 'those who turn away from you shall be recorded in the underworld.'

Christ rejoices; the sovereignty of God in saving sinners; the privileges of those who have the Gospel (10:21–24)

The only record of our Lord rejoicing

We should observe, in the first place, that this is the only place where it is recorded that our Lord Jesus Christ rejoiced. We read that **At that same hour Jesus rejoiced in the Holy Spirit ...** (verse 21). Three times we are told in the Gospels that our Lord Jesus Christ wept. Only once are we told that he rejoiced.

And what was the cause of our Lord's joy? It was the conversion of souls. It was the reception of the Gospel by the weak and lowly among the Jews, when '**the wise and the intelligent**' (verse 21) on every side were rejecting it. Our blessed Lord, no doubt, saw much in this world to make him grieve. He saw the obstinate blindness and unbelief of the vast majority of those among whom he ministered. But when he saw a few poor men and women receiving the good news about salvation, even his heart was refreshed. He saw it and was glad.

Notes on Luke 10:21–24

21. 'Infants.' These were the fishermen, and tax collectors, and other poor and uneducated Jews, who became our Lord's disciples, and followed him, when the majority of the nation would not believe.

22. 'All things have been handed over to me. ...' All things, that is, all power both in heaven and earth (Matthew 28:18), all judgment (John 1:27), and power over all flesh to give eternal life (John 17:2). Now this includes power to raise the dead, and to pass judgment on people according to their deeds and secret thoughts, and so a power and wisdom which is plainly divine, and consequently the divine nature from which these attributes are inseparable. This is an argument for the divinity of Christ.

The expert in the law's question to Christ: the rule of faith: the summary of duty (10:25–28)

The solemn question which our Lord was asked

We should notice, in this passage, the solemn question which was addressed to our Lord Jesus Christ. We are told that an expert in the law asked Jesus, 'Teacher, … what must I do to inherit eternal life?' (verse 25). The man's motives were clearly not good. He **stood up to test Jesus** (verse 25). He wanted to provoke Jesus into saying something which his enemies could latch on to and use against him. Yet this question was an important one.

It is a question which deserves everyone's closest attention. We are all sinners, dying sinners, and sinners who are going to be judged after death. 'How are our sins going to be pardoned? How can we come before God? How can we escape damnation and hell? What must we do to be saved?' These questions are vital ones and we should not rest until we find answers to them.

Notes on Luke 10:25–28

26. 'What is written in the law?' Let the following quotation from Quesnel, the Roman Catholic writer, be observed. 'Jesus Christ himself refers us to God's law, though he was truth itself, and could give souls holy instruction. In vain do we seek after other lights and ways besides those which we find there. It is the Spirit of God who dictated the law and made it the rule of our life. It is injurious to God for us either not to study it, or to prefer the thoughts of man before it. The first question which will be put to a Christian at God's tribunal will be to this effect: "What is written in the law? What have you read in the Gospel? What use have you made thereof?" What answer can that person return who has not so much as read it, though he has sufficient ability and opportunity to do it?'

The parable of the Good Samaritan (10:29–37)

These words contain the well-known parable of the Good Samaritan. To understand the drift of this parable we must recall the occasion on which it was delivered. It was spoken in reply to the question from an expert in the law, 'And who is my neighbour?' (verse 29). Our Lord Jesus Christ answers that question by telling the parable of the good samaritan and concludes with an appeal to the teacher of the law's conscience. This must not be forgotten. The parable aims to show the nature of true charity and brotherly love. To lose sight of this aim, and discover profound allegories in the parable, is to

trifle with Scripture, and deprive our souls of most valuable lessons.

Who we are to show neighbourly love to

We are taught in this parable who we should show kindness to and whom we should love as neighbours. We are told that the only person who helped the wounded traveller was a Samaritan. This man was from a nation whom Jews 'do not share things in common with Samaritans' (John 4:9). He might have excused himself by saying that the road from Jerusalem to Jericho was through Jewish territory, and that Jews should care for any injured people. But he does nothing of the sort. He sees a man stripped of his clothes, and lying half dead. He asks no questions, but at once has compassion on him. He makes no problems, but at once gives aid. And our Lord says to us, 'Go and do likewise' (verse 37).

Now, if these words mean anything, a Christian ought to be ready to show kindness and brotherly love to every one who is in need. Our kindness must not merely extend to our families and friends and relatives. We must love all people, and be kind to everyone, whenever the opportunity arises. We must beware of excessive strictness in scrutinizing the past lives of those who need our help. Are they in real trouble? Are they in real distress? Do they really want help? Then, according to the teaching of this parable, we ought to be ready to help them. We should think of the whole world as our parish, and all of mankind as our neighbours. We should seek to be the friend of everyone who is oppressed, or neglected, or afflicted, or sick, or in prison, or poor, or an orphan, or a pagan, or a slave, or mentally ill, or starving, or dying. We should show such worldwide fellowship, doubtless, wisely, so that we should never need to be ashamed. The ungodly may sneer at this and call it extravagant or fanatical. But we need not mind that. To be friendly to everyone in this way, is to show something of the mind that was in Christ.

Notes on Luke 10:29–37

29. But wanting to justify himself. This detail reveals the true character of the teacher of the law. He was a self-righteous man, and flattered himself that he could deserve the eternal life he had inquired about, by his own efforts.

30. 'From Jerusalem to Jericho.' The road between these two places passed through a wild and rocky country, and was notorious for being infested by robbers. On this account, Jerome says, it was called, 'the bloody way.'

31. 'A priest.' Jericho was a city specially appointed for the residence of priests and Levites. No less than 12,000 of them, according to Lightfoot, lived there. They had to attend the temple in Jerusalem on monthly rotas.

Christ at Martha and Mary's house; over-carefulness reproved; the one necessary thing (10:38–42)

The little story which these verses contain is only recorded by St. Luke. So long as the world stands the story of Mary and Martha will furnish the church with lessons of wisdom which should never be forgotten. Taken with John 11 it throws much light on the inner life of the family Jesus loved.

Note on Luke 10:38–42

42. 'The better part.' This is a general expression, and should be interpreted in the light of Mary's behaviour, when her sister accused her. Mary chose what was for the benefit of her soul. She was seeking more grace. She was striving after closer communion with God and his Christ. This was the portion which she preferred to everything else, and to which she was willing for a time to postpone all earthly care. Those who seek such a portion will never be disappointed. Their treasure will never be taken from them.

Chapter 11

The Lord's Prayer (11:1–4)

The friend at midnight; encouragements to prayer (11:5–13)

The mute demon; the evil of divisions (11:14–20)

The strong man armed; the unclean spirit returning (11:21–26)

The blessedness of hearing the Word; the generation who wanted a sign (11:27–32)

The use of light; the good eye (11:33–36)

The Pharisees exposed and rebuked (11:37–44)

The teachers of the law exposed and rebuked (11:45–54)

The Lord's Prayer (11:1–4)

These verses contain the prayer commonly called the Lord's Prayer. Few passages of Scripture perhaps are so well known. The importance of the Lord's Prayer appears in the simple fact that our Lord Jesus Christ delivered it twice with very slight variations. The occasion of the Lord's Prayer being delivered a second time, in the verses before us, is full of interest. It appears that one of his disciples said, 'Lord, teach us to pray' (verse 1). The substance of the Lord's Prayer is a mine of spiritual treasure. We will note its leading divisions which will help us in our private meditation.

Notes on Luke 11:1–4

1. He was praying in a certain place. We see here another instance of our Lord's diligence in private prayer.

'Father.' Chrysostom and Augustine both remark that to address God as 'Father,' is peculiar to the New Testament dispensation, and that the Old Testament saints never use the expression. The remark is undoubtedly true, but requires fencing with cautions. We must be careful not to suppose that the Old Testament saints were destitute of the Holy Spirit, as some say, and were not born again. To say that God was in no sense the Father of Old Testament believers would be going much too far. He is the Father of all who are saved by Christ, and without Christ no one was ever saved.

'Our' [Margin]. The word 'Our' at the beginning of the Lord's Prayer should not be overlooked. It teaches believers that in all their prayers they should think of others as well as themselves. They should remember all of the members of Christ's mystical body as their brethren and sisters in the Lord.

'Your name.' To appreciate the meaning of this word we should note the many places that it comes in the Psalms (Psalm 22:21; 9:22; 52:9; 115:1; 140:13). In all these cases, and in many others, the idea is evidently that of God's revealed character and attributes.

'Your will be done, on earth as it is in heaven.' [Margin]. To see the full beauty of this prayer we should read the description of angels in Psalm 103:20–2. Heaven is the only place now where God's will is done perfectly, constantly, unhesitatingly, cheerfully, immediately, and without asking any questions.

3. 'Give us each day our daily bread.' The literal meaning appears to be: 'Give us for the day, or day by day, the bread which is sufficient for our substance.' Some think that the words should be translated, 'our supersubstantial bread,' thinking that it refers to the bread in the Lord's Supper. This is a most unlikely and improbable sense.

4. 'Forgive us our sins.' This expression answers those who say that the believer should never ask for pardon of sins. One text like this is worth a hundred arguments. The Lord Jesus bids us do it, and therefore it ought to be done.

The friend at midnight: encouragements to prayer (11:5–13)

[C] The importance of perseverance in prayer. The lesson is conveyed to us in the simple parable, commonly called the 'Friend at Midnight.' We are reminded what man can obtain from man by dint of importunity: selfish and indolent as we naturally are, we are capable of being roused to exertion by continuous asking. The man who would not give three loaves at midnight for friendship's sake, eventually gave them to save himself the trouble of being further entreated. The application of the parable is obvious. If importunity succeeds so well between man and man, how much more may we expect it to obtain mercies when used in prayer to God. The lesson is one which we do well to remember. It is much easier to start a habit of prayer than to keep it up. Myriads of professing Christians are regularly taught to pray when they are young, and then gradually leave off the practice as they grow up.

Let us resist this feeling whenever we feel it rising within us. Let us resolve by God's grace, that however poor and feeble our prayers may seem to be, we will pray on. It is not for nothing that the Bible tells us so frequently to 'watch and pray,' to 'pray without ceasing,' to 'continue in prayer,' and 'to pray always and not to faint.' These expressions all look one way: they are all meant to remind us of a danger and to quicken us to a duty. The time and way in which our prayers will be answered are matters which we must leave entirely to God; but that every petition which we offer in faith will certainly be answered, we need not doubt. Let us lay our matters before God again and again, day after day, week after week, month after month, year after year.

Notes on Luke 11:5–13

6. 'A friend of mine has arrived.' To understand the arrival of a friend at midnight we must remember that in hot countries people often travel by night and rest during the day.

7. 'My children are with me in bed.' The family of a poor man in eastern climates often all sleep in one common sleeping chamber. The meaning here is: 'We have all retired to our sleeping chamber. We are all in bed.'

8. 'Persistence' [KJV 'importunity']. This is the only place in the New Testament that this word is used. It could be translated 'shamelessness.' It signifies a constant asking and entreating, in spite of rebuffs, like the asking of an impudent beggar.

12. 'Egg … scorpion.' Large kinds of scorpion, when coiled and rolled up, had a white body not unlike an egg.

13. 'You … who are evil.' Let this expression be noted. It is one of those which show the natural wickedness of man. He is by nature evil (Genesis 6:5).

I cannot leave this passage without expressing my own dissent from the allegorical significance which the Fathers and other commentators have given to many of the words here. I cannot agree with Augustine that the three loaves represent the Trinity, man's food and life, or faith, hope, and charity; nor yet that the 'fish' represents faith, or the 'egg' hope.

Most parables are intended to convey one great lesson. Even those in which almost every part has a meaning, such as the Ten Virgins and the Prodigal Son, require to be handled with great caution. In the parable of the Friend at midnight I an unable to see any warrant for searching out farfetched allegorical meanings. We have no right to inquire what the words of Scripture can be twisted, and strained, and wrested into meaning.

The mute demon; the evil of divisions (11:14–20)

The link between these verses and the preceding ones is striking and instructive. In the preceding verses our Lord Jesus Christ had been showing the power and importance of prayer. In the verses in front of us he delivers a man from a demon that was mute. The miracle is evidently intended to throw fresh light on the lesson. The same Saviour who encourages us to pray is the Saviour who destroys Satan's power over our members, and restores our tongues to their proper use.

Notes on Luke 11:14–20

15. 'Beelzebub.' The meaning of this name is said to be the 'Lord of flies.' Beelzebub is mentioned as 'the god of Ekron' in 2 Kings 1:3. For what reason so peculiar a name was given to the chief of the demons is a question which has never been fully settled.

19. 'They will be your judges.' This means, 'They will condemn your supposition that I cast out devils by Beelzebub, as unreasonable and absurd. They will be witnesses that demons are not cast out by demons, but by the power of God.'

20. 'Then the kingdom of God has come to you.' The argument here appears to be this: 'If these miracles which I work are really worked by the finger of God, and I am clearly proved by them to be one sent from God, then, whether you will allow it or not, the times of the Messiah have evidently arrived. The kingdom of God has come down on you unawares, and these miracles are signs that it is so.' This gave our Lord's enemies a dilemma. Either they must deny that our Lord cast out demons, which they could not do; or else they must admit that their own sons cast out demons by the power of Beelzebub, which they would not do.

The strong man armed; the unclean spirit returning (11:21–26)

The subject of these words of Christ is mysterious, but deeply important. They were spoken about Satan and his work. They throw light on the power of Satan, and the nature of deeds. They deserve the close attention of all who wish to fight the Christian war successfully. Next to his friends and allies, a soldier ought to be well acquainted with his enemies. We should not be ignorant of Satan's devices.

Satan's power

Let us observe in these verses what a fearful picture our Lord draws of Satan's power. There are four points in his description which are especially instructive.

Christ speaks about Satan as a **strong man** (verse 21). Satan's strength has been only too well shown by his victories over the souls of men. He who tempted Adam and Eve to rebel against God, and brought sin into the world, he who has led captive the vast majority of mankind, and robbed them of heaven; that evil one is indeed a mighty foe. He who is called the Prince of this world is not an enemy to be despised. The devil is very strong.

Christ speaks about Satan as '**a strong man, fully armed**' (verse 21). Satan is well supplied with defensive armour. He cannot be defeated by any feeble attack. The person who wants to defeat him must use all his strength. Satan also has offensive weapons. He is never at a loss for a way to harm the soul of man. He knows about every kind of person and at what point they are most vulnerable. The devil is well armed.

Christ talks about man's heart being Satan's **property** (verse 21). The natural heart is the favourite living place for the evil one, and all its faculties and powers are his servants and do his will. He sits on the throne which God should occupy, and governs the inner man. The devil is the 'spirit that is now at work among those who are disobedient' (Ephesians 2:2).

Christ says that Satan's '**property is safe**' (verse 21). So long as a person is dead in trespasses and sin, his heart is untroubled about spiritual things. He has no fear about the future. He has no anxiety about his soul. Thoughtless, stolid, reckless insensibility about eternal things is one of the worst symptoms of the devil reigning over a man's soul.

Let us never think lightly about the devil. That common practice of idle jesting about Satan which we may often see in the world is a great evil. A prisoner must be very hardened if he can joke about the executioner and the gallows. The heart must be in a very bad state when a man can talk with levity about hell and the devil.

Let us thank God that there is One who is stronger even than Satan. That one is the Friend of sinners, Jesus the Son of God. Mighty as the devil is, he was overcome by Jesus on the cross, when he triumphed over him openly.

Notes on Luke 11:21–26

22. '**One stronger.**' This refers to our Lord, the great conqueror of Satan. There is a probable reference to Isaiah 53:12. John the Baptist calls our Lord 'one who is more powerful than I' in Mark 1:7 and Luke 3:16. In both these places the Greek is the same as it is here.

22. '**Divides his plunder.**' Ford quotes Bishop Reynolds: 'God makes use of that art, wealth, power, learning, wisdom, intellect, which Satan used against Christ's kingdom, as instruments and ornaments for the Gospel; as, when a magazine is taken in war, the general makes use of those arms which were ranged against him, for his own service.'

23. '**Whoever is not with me is against me.**' Our Lord is exposing the awful danger of many of his Jewish hearers, who had been a little roused by John the Baptist, and seemed likely to receive Christ when he appeared. And yet, when he did appear, they hung back and pretended to be troubled with doubts, and so continued neutral and undecided.

24. '**Looking for a resting place.**' What an awful expression! It shows the restless untiring craving to do mischief, and inflict harm on God's creatures, which seems at present a special attribute of the devil, during the period that he is allowed to do evil.

Then it says, '**I will return to my house.**' This is another awful expression! How many men and women are being daily watched by the devil, who is plotting mischief against them, while they, in their folly, never dream about what Satan is doing.

26. '**Seven other spirits.**' The number seven is often used in Scripture proverbially, to indicate a great increase in number, or size, or intensity. Thus Psalm 119:164; Proverbs 24:16; Matthew 18:21; Daniel 3:19.

'**The last state of that person is worse than the first.**' Ford quotes a striking sentence from Cowper's *Letters* on this subject: 'I have observed that when a man who once seemed a Christian has put off that character, and resumed his old one, he loses, together with the grace which he seemed to possess, the most amiable parts of the character that he resumes. The best features of his natural face seem to be struck out, that after having worn religion only as a mask, he may make a more disgusting appearance than he did before he assumed it.'

The story of the evil spirit admits of a threefold application. Firstly, it describes the history of the Jewish nation before Christ came on earth. Secondly, it describes the Gentile churches since the time Christ was on this earth. Thirdly, above all, the passage describes the state of individuals who are content with reformation without conversion. This is a sense which should never be lost sight of. Historical and prophetical interpretations are useful, but they must not be allowed to overlay and bury the lessons that concern each one of ourselves.

The blessedness in hearing the Word; the generation who wanted a sign (11:27–32)

A woman is brought before us in this passage of Scripture of whose name and background we know nothing. We read that, as our Lord spoke, **A woman in the crowd raised her voice, 'Blessed is the womb that bore you and the breasts that nursed you'** (verse 27). At once our Lord uses her remark to teach an important lesson. His perfect wisdom turned every incident within his reach to good.

Notes on Luke 11:27–32

30. **'Jonah became a sign.'** The three days and nights during which Jonah was in the fish's belly, and his coming out alive, are undoubtedly the main point here. They were a type of our Lord being in the grave, and rising again on the third day. The mighty fact of the resurrection is unquestionably the main point in the type.

31. **'The queen of the South.'** In this, as well as in other passages, we should not fail to remark that our Lord speaks of the story of Jonah as a true story, and of Jonah himself and the Queen of Sheba as real people. The modern theory which says that the events of the Old Testament are nothing better than amusing fables finds no countenance in the New Testament.

The use of light; the good eye (11:33–36)

Notes on Luke 11:33–36

33. **'No one after lighting a lamp puts it in a cellar.'** This verse is a rebuke to the unbelieving Jews, who had the light but would not use it; and a warning to our Lord's disciples, who believed in the light, that they should not keep it hidden away.

35. **'Therefore consider whether the light in you is not darkness.'** The meaning of this verse appears to be, 'Take care that the faculty in you which should be the eye of the soul, does not become dimmed and obscured by sin, sloth, or unbelief, so that it becomes useless as if it were in complete darkness. Take care, in case by hardening your heart against the light of my Gospel, you become utterly callous, and are given over to a reprobate mind.'

It must be remembered that the expression is parabolic and figurative. It must not be so strained that it is made to say that man naturally has inner light which can save his soul.

The Pharisees exposed and rebuked (11:37–44)

The great inconsistency of hypocrites

Let us notice in this passage, the great inconsistency which is often demonstrated by hypocrites in their religion. We read that our Lord says to the Pharisees, **'you tithe mint and rue and herbs of all kinds'** (verse 42). They carried to an extreme their zeal in giving tithes to the temple, and yet they neglected the most obvious duties towards God and their neighbours. They were scrupulous to an extreme about small matters of ceremonial law; and yet they were utterly dismissive about the first principles of justice to man and love towards God. In the secondary things of their religion they were great enthusiasts, but they were no better than pagans in many of the primary things.

Let us watch and pray that we may observe a scriptural balance in our religion. Let us beware of replacing the primary matters with secondary ones.

Notes on Luke 11:37–44

41. **'Give for alms those things that are within.'** Literally the Greek says: 'But rather give the things that are inside.' So the sense is: 'Give first the offering of the inner man. Give your heart, your affections, and your will to God, as your primary concern, and then all your other actions will flow from a right heart and your sacrifices and offerings will be acceptable to God. (Compare Romans 12:1; Psalm 51:7; 2 Corinthians 8:5.)

42. **'Woe to you.'** Here, as in other places, our Lord's stern and severe language should be noted. Nothing seems so odious in his eyes as hypocrisy.

The teachers of the law exposed and rebuked (11:45–54)

This passage is an example of our Lord Jesus Christ's faithful dealing with the souls of men. We see him without fear or favour rebuking the sins of the Jewish expounders of God's law.

Notes on Luke 11:45–54

45. **One of the lawyers.** These people studied God's law. We generally find them with the teachers of the law and Pharisees in the Gospels.

46. **'For you load people with burdens.'** These burdens included many trifling rules laid down by these teachers of the law, which they said needed to be kept if people were to be saved. Chemnitius notes the similarity between these Jewish teachers and the Roman Catholic priests, who lined the way to heaven with a long list of things to be observed – penances, pilgrimages, fastings, flagellations, confessions, and the like.

50. **'This generation.'** Both here and in the following verse, it seems probable that the word **generation** means nation or people as in Matthew 24:34. It is certain that most people who were alive when our Lord said these things must have died, when the great inquisition for blood took place, at the destruction of Jerusalem, forty years later.

52. 'You have taken away the key of knowledge.' Baxter remarks on this verse, 'This is just the description of a wicked clergyman.'

Chapter 12

Warnings against hypocrisy; encouragements against the fear of man (12:1–7)

Bold confession of Christ recommended (12:8–12)

Warning against covetousness (12:13–21)

Warning against over-anxiety about this world (12:22–31)

Believer's comfort; heavenly treasure: a waiting frame of mind ordered (12:32–40)

The active Christian praised; the indolent misuser of privileges warned (12:41–48)

Christ's zeal to do his work; division caused by the Gospel (12:49–53)

The duty of noticing the signs of the times; reconciliation by the way recommended (12:54–59)

Warnings against hypocrisy; encouragements not to fear men (12:1–7)

The opening words of this chapter are very striking when we consider its contents. We are told that **the crowd gathered in thousands, so that they trampled on one another** (verse 1). And what does our Lord do? In the hearing of this huge crowd he delivers warnings against false teachers, and denounces the sins of the times, unsparingly. This was true charity. This was the work of a physician. This was the pattern which all his ministers were intended to follow.

Christ's encouragement to persecuted believers

In these verses our attention is drawn to Christ's encouragement to persecuted believers. Our Lord reminds them of God's providential care over the least of his creation: 'not one of them [sparrows] is forgotten in God's sight' (verse 6). He goes on to assure them that the same Fatherly care is looking after them. '**The hairs of your head are all counted**' (verse 7). Nothing, large or small, can happen to a believer without God's permission.

God's providential rule over everything in this world is a truth that the Greek and Roman philosophers did not know about. It is a truth which is especially revealed to us in the Word of God. There is no such thing as 'chance,' 'luck,' or 'accident' in the Christian's journey through this world. Everything is arranged and appointed by

God: and 'all things work together for good for those who love God' (Romans 8:28).

Let us seek to have an abiding sense of God's hand in everything that happens to us, if we profess to be believers in Jesus Christ. We should say to ourselves, 'God could keep away from me these things if he thought fit. But he does not do so, and therefore they must be for my benefit. I will stay still, and bear them patiently. I have "an everlasting covenant, ordered in all things and secure" (2 Samuel 23:5). What pleases God will please me.'

Notes on Luke 12:1–7

1. He began to speak. Note that the following discourse contains many sayings which were spoken on other occasions. It is clear that our Lord repeated the same words in different places, and taught the same lessons on different occasions. All teachers repeat their lessons over and over again, to fix the lesson in their hearers' minds. It is absurd to suppose that our Lord Jesus Christ did not do so.

Be on your guard against the yeast of the Pharisees. This warning reminds the church to be on guard against formalism and hypocrisy. Few warnings have been so much needed and so often overlooked.

4. 'Those who kill the body. ...' The distinction between body and soul, and the separate existence of the soul after the body is dead, are clearly brought out in this passage. The use which martyrs have often made of this verse as they were killed is a striking and remarkable fact in church history.

5. 'Fear him who ... has authority ... into hell.' The reality and fearfulness of hell stand out awfully on the face of this verse. There is a hell after death. The state of the wicked person after this life is not annihilation. There is a hell which ought to be feared. There is a just God who will firmly throw into hell the obstinately impenitent and unbelieving.

6. 'Not one of them is forgotten in God's sight.' God's providential care over all his creatures is taught in this verse and the next one. Nothing was too little for God to create. Nothing is too little for God to preserve. Nothing that concerns God's people is too little for him to manage, or for them to bring before him in prayer.

Boldly confess Christ (12:8–12)

The unpardonable sin

We are taught in these verses, that there is such a thing as an unpardonable sin. Our Lord Jesus Christ declares, that '**whoever blasphemes against the Holy Spirit will not be forgiven**' (verse 10).

The sin to which our Lord refers in this passage appears to be the sin of deliberately rejecting God's truth with the heart, while the truth is clearly known with the head. It is a combination of light in the understanding, and determined wickedness in the will. It is the sin into which many of the scribes and Pharisees appear to have fallen, when they rejected the ministry of the Spirit after the day of Pentecost, and refused to believe the preaching of the apostles. It is a sin into which, it may be feared, many people who listen to the Gospel today fall into, as they are determined to cling on to the world. And, worst of all, it is a sin which is often accompanied by utter deadness, hardness. The person whose sins will not be forgiven is precisely the person who will never seek to have them forgiven. This is the root of his awful disease. He could be pardoned, but he will not seek to be pardoned. He is Gospel-hardened and twice dead. His conscience is 'seared with a hot iron' (1 Timothy 4:2).

Let us pray that we may be delivered from a cold, speculative, unsanctified head-knowledge of Christianity. No heart becomes so hard as that on which the light shines, but finds no admission. The same fire which melts the wax hardens the clay. Whatever light we have, let us use it: whatever knowledge we possess, let us live fully up to it.

Notes on Luke 12:8–12

10. 'Everyone who speaks a word against the Son of Man …' This verse is deep and mysterious. The distinction between speaking 'a word against the Son of Man' and blaspheming 'against the Holy Spirit' should not be overlooked. The explanation is probably something of this kind. The sin against the Son of Man was committed by those who did not know Christ to be the Messiah, and did not receive him, or obey him, but rejected him and crucified him. Doubtless many of those who sinned in this way were pardoned, as, for example, on the day of Pentecost, after Peter preached. The sin against the Holy Spirit was committed by those, who, after the day of Pentecost, and the outpouring of the Spirit, and the full proclamation of the Gospel, persisted in unbelief and obstinate impenitence, and were given over to a reprobate mind. These especially grieved the Spirit, and resisted the work of the Holy Spirit. That this was the state of many of the Jews appears from several places in the Acts, and especially Acts 28:25–28. See also 1 Thessalonians 2:15–16.

Warning against covetousness (12:13–21)

This passage tells us that somebody listening to Jesus asked him to help him with his temporal affairs. 'Teacher,' he said, 'tell my brother to divide the family inheritance with me' (verse 13). He asks our Lord's help about his earthly inheritance.

How many people who hear the Gospel are just like this. They plan and scheme about things of this world at the same time as they listen to things about eternity. The natural heart of man is always the same. Even Christ's own preaching did not arrest the attention of all his hearers. We must not be surprised to find worldliness and inattention in the middle of church congregations. The servant must not expect his sermons to be valued more highly that his Master's.

Notes on Luke 12:13–21

15. 'Be on your guard against all kinds of greed.' Latimer's sermon on this text starts by repeating the words three times, and then he says, 'And what if I should say nothing else?'

18. 'My barns.' Note that the rich man says my barns, my grain, my goods, with all the self-sufficiency and petty importance of one who knows only his own will, and has not master other than his own selfishness.

19. 'I will say to my soul.' Basil remarks, 'If this man had only had the sense of a hog, what other thing could have been said?'

20. 'And the things you have prepared, whose will they be?' The argument here seems to be similar to that found in Ecclesiastes 5:15 and Psalm 39:6. A person cannot possess his property a moment after he is dead. Grace is the only lasting possession.

21. 'Not rich towards God.' Many millionaires are paupers before God. They are not rich either in grace, or faith, or good works.

Warning against over-anxiety about this world (12:22–31)

A collection of arguments against over-anxiety

We have in these verses a collection of striking arguments against over-anxiety about the things of this world. At first sight they may seem to be rather common-place. But the more they are pondered, the more weighty the appear. An abiding recollection of them would save many Christians an immense amount of trouble.

Christ tells us to consider the 'ravens.' 'They neither sow nor reap, they have neither storehouse nor barn, and yet God feeds them' (verse 24). Now if the Maker of all things provides for the needs of birds, and supplies their daily food, we should not fear that he will let his spiritual children starve.

Christ tells us to consider the 'lilies.' 'They neither toil nor spin; yet I tell you, even Solomon in all his glory was not clothed like one of these' (verse 27). Now if God every year provides these flowers with a fresh supply of living leaves and blossoms, we should not doubt his power and willingness to give his believing servants all needful clothing.

Christ reminds us that a Christian should be ashamed of being as anxious as a pagan. The nations of the world may well be worried about food, and clothes, and the like, as they know nothing of the real nature of God; but for the person who says that 'God is my Father,' and of Christ, 'He is my Saviour,' should be beyond such anxieties. A clear faith should produce a light heart.

Finally, Christ tells us to reflect on the perfect knowledge of God: '**Your Father knows you need them**' (verse 30). That thought alone should make us content. All our needs are fully known to the Lord of heaven and earth. He can relieve those needs whenever he sees fit. He will relieve them whenever it is good for our souls.

Let these four arguments sink deep into our hearts, and bear fruit in our lives. Nothing is more common that an anxious and troubled spirit and nothing mars a believer's usefulness and attacks his inner peace so much. The person who can say boldly, 'The LORD is my shepherd,' is the person who will also be able to add, 'I shall not want' (Psalm 23:1).

Note on Luke 12:22–31

24. '**Ravens.**' Ravens are especially mentioned in Psalm 147:9 and Job 38:41, as objects of God's care. In the story of Elijah the Holy Spirit shows us the ravens providing for others, as well as providing for themselves (1 Kings 17:6).

The believer's comfort; heavenly treasure; watchfulness commanded (12:32–40)

A word of comfort for all believers

Let us note what a gracious word of comfort this passage has for all true believers. He knew that they were surrounded by fears of every kind – fears because they were so few, fears because of the power of their enemies, and fears because of their own weakness and unworthiness. Our Lord answers these many fears with a single golden sentence: '**Do not be afraid, little flock, for it is your Father's pleasure to give you the kingdom**' (verse 32).

Believers are a '**little flock.**' They always have been, ever since the world began. Professing servants of God have sometimes been numerous; baptized people today are a great company; but true Christians are very few. It is foolish to be surprised at this. It is vain to expect that it will be different from this until the Lord comes again. 'For the gate is narrow and the road that leads to life, and there are few who find it' (Matthew 7:14).

Believers have a glorious '**kingdom**' (verse 32) waiting for them. Here on earth they are often mocked, and ridiculed, and persecuted, and, like their Master, despised and rejected by men. But this will be reversed when Christ comes again (see Romans 8:18; Colossians 3:4).

Believers are loved by God the Father. The Father's '**good pleasure**' (verse 32) is to give them a kingdom. He does not receive them grudgingly, unwillingly, and coldly: he rejoices over them, and thinks of them as his dear children in Christ. Even now, when he looks down on them from heaven in the middle of their infirmities, he is well pleased; and hereafter when presented to him in his glory, he will welcome them with great joy (Jude 24).

Notes on Luke 12:32–40

32. '**Your Father's good pleasure.**' Our Lord lays special stress in this passage on the fatherly relationship of God to all believers, as an antidote to too much anxiety.

33. '**Sell your possessions.**' This expression, if not confined to the apostles, but applied generally to all believers, must evidently be interpreted with some scriptural limitation. There is nothing in the Acts of the Apostles or in the New Testament letters which shows that believers in the early church were expected to sell all their property as soon as they were converted. On the contrary, St. Peter's words to Ananias seem to show that it was quite optional with converts to sell their property or keep it (Acts 5:4; see also 1 Timothy 5:8).

35. '**Have your lamps lit.**' Marriages often took place in the evening. It was the duty of the servants to meet the wedding party with lighted torches. This verse exhorts us to be always ready to meet the Bridegroom, Jesus Christ, at his second coming.

37. '**He will come and serve …**' This is perhaps one of the most wonderful promises made to believers in the New Testament. It must probably be interpreted figuratively. It means that there is no limit to the honour and glory which the Lord Jesus will bestow on those who are ready to meet him at his second coming.

39. '**What hour the thief was coming.**' This teaches that the day of the Lord will come like a thief in the night (1 Thessalonians 5:2); and that there is no safety for Christians, except constant readiness for it.

The active Christian praised (12:41–48)

Notes on Luke 12:41–48

42. '**Prudent manager.**' Paul uses this word (1 Corinthians 4:1) to describe the office of a minister. It would seem to show that ministers are primarily pointed at in our Lord's teaching in this parable.

48. '**To whom much has been entrusted …**' Our Lord lays down here a great principle in his kingdom as an appropriate conclusion to his parable. Baxter remarks on this verse: 'Great gifts are to be used with great diligence; and great trusts, and powers, and charges, are rather

to be feared than sought. Little do the conquerors of the world, or those who strive for church preferments, believe and consider what duty, or what deep damnation, they labour for.'

Christ's zeal to do his work; divisions caused (12:49–53)

Our Lord's sayings in these five verses are especially weighty and suggestive. They reveal truths which every Christian would do well to note and digest. They explain things in the church, and in the world, which at first sight, are hard to understand.

Christ was set on finishing his work

We learn from these verses, how completely Christ's heart was set on finishing the work which he came into the world to do. He says, 'I have a baptism with which to be baptized' (verse 50), a baptism of suffering, of wounds, of agony, of blood, and of death. Yet none of these things moved him. He adds, 'and what a stress I am under until it is completed!' (verse 50). The prospect of coming trouble did not deter him for a moment. He was ready and willing to endure all things in order to provide eternal redemption for his people. Zeal for the cause which he had taken in hand was like a burning fire within him. To advance his Father's glory, to open the door of life to a lost world, to provide a fountain for all sin and uncleanness by the sacrifice of himself, were continually the uppermost thoughts of his mind. He was pressed in spirit until this mighty work was finished.

For ever let us bear in mind that all Christ's sufferings on our behalf were endured willingly, voluntarily, and of his own free choice. They were not submitted to patiently merely because he could not avoid them. They were not borne without a murmur merely because he could not escape them. He lived a humble life for thirty-three years because he loved to do so. He died an agonizing death with a willing and ready mind. Both in life and death he was carrying out the eternal counsel whereby God was to be glorified and sinners were to be saved. He carried it out with all his heart, mighty as the struggle was which it entailed on his flesh and blood. He was distressed until it was completed.

Notes on Luke 12:49–53

49. 'I came to bring fire.' I think this refers to persecutions, afflictions, dissensions, and strifes which were to accompany the introduction of the Gospel into the world. Fire is often used as a sign of trouble and affliction in Scripture. See Psalm 66:12; Isaiah 43:2. 'To bring fire' was often used in the Old Testament to express the idea of sending trouble and affliction. See Lamentations 1:13; Ezekiel 39:6; Hosea 8:14; Amos 2:2,5.

50. 'A baptism.' This baptism, clearly, is not of water or of the Holy Spirit, but of suffering. It is the same baptism which our Lord said to James and John: 'The cup that I drink you will drink; and with the baptism with which I am baptized, you will be baptized' (Mark 10:39).

The duty to notice the signs of the times (12:54–59)

The Jews in our Lord's day neglected the duty of noticing the signs of the times. They refused to see that prophecies were being fulfilled around them which were bound up with the coming of the Messiah, and that the Messiah himself must be among them. John the Baptist's ministry had aroused attention throughout the land. Christ's miracles were great, well-known and undeniable. But the Pharisees were blind to all this as they obstinately refused to believe that Jesus was the Christ. So they drew this question from our Lord: 'Why do you not know how to interpret the present time?' (verse 56).

Let us remember these words and not fall into error like the Jews. Let us not be blind, and deaf, and insensible to all that God is doing, both in the church and in the world. May we not sleep, as many do, but watch and discern our time. There is a solemn saying in the book of Revelation: 'If you do not wake up, I will come like a thief, and you will not know at what hour I will come to you' (Revelation 3:3).

Notes on Luke 12:54–59

56. 'You know how to interpret the appearance of the earth and sky.' Our Lord's argument appears to be that the signs of his coming as the true Messiah were so clearly visible that it required no more discernment to see them than it did to forecast heat or rain from looking at the sky and winds. If the Jews would honestly and impartially consider the signs of their times, they could not avoid the conclusion that Christ was the Messiah. The truth was that they were not honest in their inquiries, but prejudiced and unbelieving. He therefore calls them '**hypocrites.**'

59. '**You will not get out until.**' This means, 'you will never get out at all.'

Chapter 13

The absolute necessity of repentance (13:1–5)

The parable of the unfruitful fig tree (13:6–9)

Healing of the woman who had been ill for eighteen years (13:10–17)

Parable of the mustard seed, and the yeast (13:18–21)

Number of the saved; the narrow door (13:22–30)
Times in God's hands; Christ's compassionate words about Jerusalem (13:31–35)

The absolute necessity of repentance (13:1–5)

The murder of the Galileans (verse 1) is an event we know nothing about for certain. We are left to conjecture the motives of those who told our Lord about this event. But it did give him an opportunity to speak to them about their own souls, which he took full advantage of. He seized the moment, as was his custom, and made good use of it. He told his informants to look within themselves and to think about their own standing before God. Our Lord seems to say, 'What if these Galileans did die a sudden death? What is that to you? Consider your own ways. Unless you repent, you will perish in the same way.'

Notes on Luke 13:1–5

2. '**Worse sinners.**' Clearly, our Lord's informants believed that these sudden deaths were special judgments, and that if someone died suddenly he must have committed some special sin. Our Lord corrects this false view. It is not right to believe that God is angry with a man because he removes him suddenly from the world.

4. '**The tower in Siloam fell.**' We know nothing about the details of this event.

5. '**Unless you repent.**' The repetition of this sentence shows the general importance of repentance, and the great need in which the Jews in particular stood of it. Ford quotes a saying of Philip Henry's which is worth reading: 'Some people do not like to hear much about repentance. But I think it is so necessary, that if I should die in the pulpit, I would wish to die preaching about repentance; and if I should die out of the pulpit, I would wish to die practising it.'

The parable of the unfruitful fig tree (13:6–9)

This parable is particularly humbling and heart-searching. The Christian who listens to it without feeling sorrow and shame as he looks at the state of Christendom, must have a very unwell soul.

Spiritual privileges require returns

We learn from this passage, that where God gives spiritual privileges he expects proportionate returns.

Our Lord teaches this lesson by comparing the Jewish church of his day to 'a fig tree, planted in his vineyard' (verse 6). This was exactly the position of Israel in the world. They were separated from other nations by the Mosaic laws and ordinances, no less than by the position of their land. They enjoyed favoured relationships with God, which no other people had. Things were done for them which were never done for Egypt, Nineveh, Babylon, Greece, or Rome. It was only just and right that they should bear fruit to God's praise. It might be reasonably expected that there would be more faith, and penitence, and holiness, and godliness in Israel than among the pagans. This is what God looked for. The owner of the fig tree '**came looking for fruit**' (verse 6) on his fig tree.

But we must look beyond the Jewish church if we are to see the full meaning of this parable. We must look to the Christian churches. They have light, and truth, and doctrines, and precepts, which the ungodly have never heard of. How great is their responsibility. Is it not just and right that God should expect '**fruit**' from them? We must look to our own hearts. We live in a land of Bibles, and liberty, and Gospel preaching: how vast are the advantages we enjoy compared with Chinese and Hindus. Never let us forget that God expects '**fruit**' from us.

Note on Luke 13:6–9

8. '**Sir, let it alone.**' Euthymius and Theophylact consider that the interceding vineyard-dresser is an emblem of Christ himself. Matthew Henry says correctly that 'had it not been for Christ's intercession, the whole world would have been cut down.'

Healing of the woman who had been ill for eighteen years (13:10–17)

An example of the diligent use of the means of grace

We see in these verses a striking example of diligence in the use of the means of grace. We are told of a **woman with a spirit that had crippled her for eighteen years. She was bent over and quite unable to stand up straight** (verse 11). We do not know who the woman was. Our Lord called her '**a daughter of Abraham**' (verse 16) which leads us to think that she was a true believer. All we know is that when Jesus was **teaching in one of the synagogues** (verse 10) this woman was there. Sickness was not used as an excuse for not worshipping in God's house. In spite of her suffering she found her way to where the day and the Word of God were honoured, and where God's people met together. She was truly blessed by her action. She came sorrowing, but went home rejoicing.

Let us never forget that our feelings about Sunday are a sure test of the state of our souls.

The person who can find no pleasure in giving God one day in the week, is clearly unfit for heaven. Heaven itself is nothing other than an eternal Sabbath. If we cannot enjoy a few hours in God's service once a week in this world, it is obvious that we could not enjoy an eternity in his service in the world to come.

Notes on Luke 13:10–17

11. A spirit that had crippled her. The nature of this woman's disease we are left to conjecture. It seems to have been some illness mysteriously connected with possession by an unclean spirit, and caused by it. There is no other instance precisely like it in the New Testament.

12. He called her over. Our Lord performed this miracle without being asked. The widow at Nain is another example of this. In both instances the person to whom kindness was shown was a woman.

If our Lord does so much for a person when unsolicited, how much more will he do for those who call upon him in prayer.

14. 'Six days on which work ought to be done.' The bitterness and sarcasm of this unhappy speech are very remarkable. This is often the case with unconverted people. The nearer the kingdom of God comes to them, the more bitter and angry they become.

16. 'A daughter of Abraham.' This expression certainly appears to me to make it highly probable that this woman whom our Lord healed was a true believer. When Zacchaeus was converted our Lord said, the man 'is a son of Abraham' (Luke 19:9). To think of this expression as only meaning a 'daughter of Abraham according to natural descent – a Jewess,' seems to me a tame and unsatisfactory interpretation.

Whom Satan has kept bound. This is a remarkable expression. It appears that Satan has a permissive power to inflict bodily illness and disease. See Job 1–2 and 1 Corinthians 5:5.

Parable of the mustard seed, and the yeast (13:18–21)

We find these two parables delivered by our Lord, at two distinct periods in his ministry. This fact alone should make us give them special heed. They will be found rich both in prophetical and experimental truths.

1. The parable of the mustard seed

The parable of the mustard seed is intended to show the progress of the Gospel in the world.

The beginnings of the Gospel are exceedingly small. It was like 'a mustard seed which someone took and sowed in the garden' (verse 19). It was a religion which seemed at first so feeble, and helpless, and powerless, that it could not live. Its founder was a poor man who ended his life by dying a criminal's death on the cross. Its first adherents were a small group of people who probably numbered less than a thousand when our Lord left the world. Its first preachers were a few fishermen and tax collectors, who were, for the most part, uneducated and ignorant men. Its first starting-point was a despised corner of the earth called Judea, a petty province in the vast Roman empire. Its first doctrines were calculated to provoke enmity from the natural heart: Christ crucified was stumbling-block to the Jews and foolishness to the Greeks (1 Corinthians 1:23). Its first followers were persecuted on all sides: Pharisees and Sadducees, Jews and Gentiles, ignorant idolaters and self-conceited philosophers, all united in hated and opposing Christianity. This sect was spoken against everywhere. These are not empty assertions: they are the simple historical facts, which no one can deny. If ever there was a religion which was a little grain of seed at its beginning, that religion was the Gospel.

But the progress of the Gospel, after the seed had been planted in the earth, was great, steady, and continuous. The grain of mustard seed 'grew and became a tree' (verse 19). In spite of persecution, opposition, and violence, Christianity gradually spread and increased. Year after year its adherents became more numerous; year after year idolatry withered away before it. City after city, and country after country, received the new faith. Church after church was formed in almost every part of the known world. Preacher after preacher rose up, and missionary after missionary came forward to fill the place of those who died. Roman Emperors and heathen philosophers, sometimes by force and sometimes by argument, tried in vain to check the progress of Christianity. They may as well have tried to stop the tide from rising, or the sun from rising. In a few hundred years, the religion of the despised Nazarene – the religion which began in the upper room at Jerusalem – had spread out throughout the civilized world. The grain of mustard seed 'grew and became a tree, and the birds of the air made nests in its branches' (verse 19). The Lord Jesus said it would be so. And so it came to pass.

2. The parable of the yeast

The parable of the yeast shows the progress of the Gospel in the heart of a believer.

The start of the work of grace in a sinner is usually exceedingly small. It is like adding yeast to a lump of dough. A single sentence, or a single verse of Holy Scripture, a word of rebuke from a friend, or a casual religious remark overheard, a tract given by a stranger, or a trifling act of kindness received from a Christian – any one of these things can be the starting point for the life of a soul. The first signs of spiritual life are indeed often small in the extreme – so small, that for a long time they are not known about except to the person in whom they are taking place, and even he hardly understands what is going on. A few serious thoughts and a conscience pricked, a desire to pray really and not formally, a determination to begin to read the Bible in private, a gradual drawing towards the means of grace, a growing distaste for evil habits and bad companions – these, or some of them, are often the first signs of grace beginning to move the heart of man. They are symptoms which worldly people do not perceive, and ignorant believers may despise, and even old Christians may mistake; yet they are often the first steps in the mighty business of conversion. They are often the 'yeast' of grace working in a heart.

The work of grace once begun in the soul will never stand still. It will gradually work until 'all of it was leavened' (verse 21). Like yeast once introduced, it can never be separated from what it has been mixed into. Little by little, it will influence the conscience, the affections, the mind, and the will, until the whole person is affected by its power, and a thorough conversion to God takes place. In some people the process is far quicker than in others; in some people the result is far more clearly seen than in others. But wherever a real work of the Holy Spirit begins in the heart, the whole character is sooner or later leavened and changed. The tastes of the person are altered: the whole bias of his mind becomes different (2 Corinthians 5:17). The Lord Jesus said that it would be so, and all experience shows that it is so.

Let us learn from this parable never to despise the day of small things (Zechariah 4:10). The soul must creep before it can walk, and walk before it can run. If we see any sign of grace beginning in a brother, however feeble, let us thank God, and be hopeful. The leaven of grace once planted in his heart, will yet leaven the whole lump, see Philippians 1:6.

Note on Luke 13:18–21

Commentators have found many allegories in this parable: the mustard seed as Christ himself; the birds of the air as the corruption that came into Christ's church; and yeast as false teaching. I am quite unable to see the correctness in any of this. These two parables are meant to convey one great truth: the small beginning of grace in a heart, and the influence which it gradually acquires over the whole character. To this view let us adhere.

Number of the saved; the narrow door (13:22–30)

A remarkable question asked

We see in these verses a remarkable question asked. We are told that someone asked our Lord,

'Lord, will only a few be saved?' (verse 23).

If we want to know how many people will be saved we need only turn to the Bible to have this question answered. In the Sermon on the Mount we read, 'the gate is narrow and the road is hard that leads to life, and there are few who find it' (Matthew 7:14). Just by looking around we conclude that the saved are few. Christ is willing to receive sinners; but sinners are not willing to come to Christ. And hence few are saved.

Notes on Luke 13:22–30

24–25. 'Try to enter.' The Greek word gives us our English word 'agonize.' It implies great exertion and conflict. See Colossians 4:12; 1 Timothy 6:12.

Many will try to enter and not be able to. The time when people will 'try to enter,' and 'not be able to,' seems to me, most plainly, to be on the last day, when the door of mercy is shut forever. The whole context shows this, and the language used is parallel to that in the parable of the wise and foolish virgins (Matthew 25:11).

27. 'Go away from me, all you evildoers!' The similarity between this expression and Matthew 25:41 appears to show clearly that the time described is the second coming of Christ, and the judgment day.

30. 'Some are last who will be first, and some are first who will be last.' This is a proverb which was literally fulfilled when the Gospel was first preached, and has often been fulfilled since, both in churches and individuals. The Jews who were first became last, and the Gentiles who were last became first.

Times in God's hands; Christ's compassionate words about Jerusalem (13:31–35)

Notes on Luke 13:31–35

32. 'Today and tomorrow, and on the third day.' I think this probably signifies a short space of time: 'I am yet a little time with you, and during that time I shall continue my work, notwithstanding Herod's threats; and at the end of that time, and not before, I shall be perfected, or finish my course by death.' A similar way of speaking occurs in Hosea 6:2.

'I finish my work' [KJV: I shall be perfected]. This is a remarkable expression. In the Greek it is in the present tense. The meaning seems to be, 'I shall be perfected by my death: I shall finish the work which I came to do.' The same word is applied to our Lord in Hebrews 2:10; and Hebrews 5:9.

33. 'I must be on my way.' This seems to mean: 'I must continue in the course I have begun: I must go on, as I have hitherto.'

34. 'Jerusalem ...' This remarkable passage is found in St. Matthew's Gospel (Matthew 23:37),

at the very end of our Lord's ministry, in almost the same words. I cannot see any satisfactory explanation for this, except that our Lord must have used the same words twice about Jerusalem in the course of his ministry.

'I have desired … and you were not willing.' The Greek word in both these phrases is derived from the same word and is stronger than our English translation 'wish'. It is literally, 'I willed, and ye willed not!'

Few passages in the Bible throw the responsibility of the loss of the soul so distinctly on those who are lost: 'I would:' 'ye would not!' Two wills are expressly mentioned: the will of Christ to do good, and the will of man to refuse good when offered.

35. 'You will not see me until.' I strongly support the view of the commentators who think that our Lord's words here are not yet fulfilled, and that they refer to the last times, when the Jews after their last tribulation will look on him whom they pierced, and believe, at the time of his second coming in glory.

The triumphant entry into Jerusalem was a faint type, no doubt, of the honour which Christ will one day see in Jerusalem. But the Jewish nation, as a nation, never saw our Lord and honoured him as the Messiah, during the whole time of his first coming. But 'Look, he is coming with the clouds; every eye will see him, even those who pierced him' (Revelation 1:7).

Chapter 14

Christ at a Pharisee's house; the true teaching about Sabbath observance (14:1–6)

Humility recommended; who should be our guests (14:7–14)

The parable of the great banquet (14:15–24)

Self-denial; counting the cost; salt which has lost its saltiness (14:25–35)

Christ at a Pharisee's house: the true teaching about Sabbath observance (14:1–6)

Merciful deeds performed on the Sabbath

Let us notice in this passage, how our Lord asserts the lawfulness of doing deeds of mercy on the Sabbath day. We read that he healed a man who had dropsy on the Sabbath day, and

then said to the Pharisees and experts in the law, 'Is it lawful to cure people on the sabbath, or not?' (verse 3). They were unable to answer our Lord. **They were silent** (verse 4).

The qualification which our Lord here puts on the requirements of the fourth commandment is evidently based on Scripture, reason, and common sense. The Sabbath was made for man, for his benefit, not for his harm – for his advantage, not for his disadvantage. Interpreting God's law about the Sabbath was never meant to impinge on charity, kindness and the real needs of human nature. Our Lord shows that deeds of necessity and mercy do not break the observance of the Sabbath.

Humility recommended; who should be our guests (14:7–14)

The value of humility

Let us learn, from these verses, the value of humility. This is a lesson which our Lord teaches in two ways. Firstly, he advises those who are invited to a wedding to 'take the lowest place' (verse 9). Secondly, he backs up his advice by declaring the great principle, which he often said, 'all who exalt themselves will be humbled, and those who humble themselves will be exalted' (verse 11).

Humility may well be called the queen of the Christian graces. To know our own sinfulness and weakness, and to feel our need of Christ, is the start of saving religion. It is a grace which has always been a distinguishing feature in the character of the holiest saints in every age. Abraham, and Moses, and Job, and David, and Daniel, and Paul, were all eminently humble men. Above all, it is a grace within the reach of every true Christian. All converted people should work to adorn the doctrine they profess by humility. If they can do nothing else, they can strive to be humble.

Do you want to know the root and spring of humility? One word describes it. The root of humility is right knowledge. The person who really knows himself and his own heart, who knows God and his infinite majesty and holiness, who knows Christ, and the price at which he was redeemed, that person will never be a proud person. He will count himself, like Jacob, unworthy of the least of all God's mercies; he will say of himself, like Job, 'I am unworthy'; he will cry, like Paul, 'I am the worst [of sinners]' (see Genesis 32:10; Job 40:4; 1 Timothy 1:15). He will consider others better than himself (Philippians 2:3). Ignorance, nothing but sheer ignorance, ignorance of self, of God, and of Christ, is the real secret of pride. From that miserable self-ignorance may we daily pray to be delivered. The wise person knows himself, and will find nothing within to make him proud.

Notes on Luke 14:7–14

11. 'All who exalt themselves.' There is hardly any saying of our Lord's which is said more frequently as this sentence about humility.

14. 'You will be repaid.' These words deserve special attention. They confirm the doctrine of a reward according to deeds, though not on account of deeds, on the judgment day.

Our Lord is probably speaking here about the general judgment and the importance of deeds as an evidence of faith is the truth which he seeks to impress on our minds.

'The resurrection of the righteous.' This is a remarkable expression. I cannot think our Lord uses it in deference to a commonly held belief among the Jews, that the resurrection was the special privilege of the righteous. It seems to me far more probable that our Lord refers to the first resurrection, spoken about in Revelation 20. There is a resurrection which only the righteous will take part in – a resurrection which will be the special privilege of the righteous, and will precede that of the wicked.

The parable of the great banquet (14:15–24)

These verses contain one of our Lord's most instructive parables. It was spoken in response to a remark made by a person sitting next to Jesus in the Pharisee's house. Blessed is the man who will eat at the feast in the kingdom of God (verse 15). We are left to conjecture about the purpose of this remark. It is possible that the person who made it was the sort of person who wanted to go to heaven, liked to hear good things spoken about, but never got any further. Our Lord takes this opportunity to remind him, and those eating at the table, through the parable of the great banquet, that people may have the kingdom of God offered to them, but if they deliberately neglect the offer, will be lost forever.

Notes on Luke 14:15–24

18. 'Began to make excuses.' The various excuses which those who were invited made are types of the various worldly reasons with which men excuse themselves from accepting the offer of Christ's Gospel. Note that everything mentioned is in itself innocent and lawful.

21. 'The poor, the crippled, the blind, and the lame.' These words primarily describe the Gentiles, who were just in this miserable condition when compared with the Jews. Secondly, they describe all sinners to whom the Gospel is offered, who feel their sins, and acknowledge their own spiritual need and poverty.

22. 'There is still room.' This seems to show that there is a greater willingness on God's part to save sinners than there is on the part of sinners to be saved, and more grace is given than there are hearts willing to receive it.

Self-denial; counting the cost; salt which has lost its saltiness (14:25–35)

Christians must be prepared to give up everything for Christ

We learn from this passage, that true Christians must be ready, if necessary, to give up everything for Christ's sake. Our Lord says, 'Whoever comes to me and does not hate father and mother, wife and children, brothers and sisters, yes, even life itself, cannot be my disciple' (verses 26-27).

We must never explain any verses of Scripture in such a way that they contradict other verses of Scripture. Our Lord is not telling us here to hate our relatives. This would be against the fifth commandment. He only meant that those who follow him must love him with a deeper love than their nearest and dearest, or their own lives. He must be prepared to offend his family, rather than offend Christ. Thousands of Christians will bless God on the last day that they had relatives and friends who chose to displease them rather than Christ. That very decision was the first thing that made them think seriously, and led finally to the conversion of their souls.

Notes on Luke 14:25–35

26. 'Comes to me and does not hate.' The word 'hate' in this verse, must clearly be taken comparatively. The following quotation from Pearce deserves reading. 'Besides the proof from Matthew 10:37, that the word "hate" here means "love less," it may be added that in Matthew 6:24 the word "hate" is used in the same way. Also, when we read in Romans 9:13, "Jacob have I loved, but Esau have I hated," the meaning is that I have loved Jacob more than Esau. That this is no arbitrary interpretation of the word "hate," but one agreeable to the Hebrew idiom, appears from what is said in Genesis 29:30–31, where Leah being "hated" is explained by Rachel being loved more than Leah. See also Deuteronomy 21:15–17.'

34. 'If salt has lost its taste.' This striking and solemn saying about the salt that loses its saltiness is found on three occasions in the Gospels (see Matthew 5:13; Mark 9:50). The sinfulness of sins against light and knowledge, and the possibility of being given over to a reprobate mind, are fearful points to ponder. People seem to forget that there is such a thing as an unpardonable sin – and that if salt has once lost its saltiness it cannot be seasoned again.

The Bible teaches that no sinner is so unlikely to be saved as the person who after making a strong spiritual profession of faith falls away and returns to the world. There is no heart so unlikely to be changed as the heart which once professed to love the Gospel, but later becomes cold and indifferent.

Chapter 15

The parable of the lost sheep, and the lost piece of silver (15:1–10)

The parable of the prodigal son (15:11–24)

The elder brother (15:25–32)

The parable of the lost sheep, and the lost piece of silver (15:1–10)

This is one of the best-known chapters in the Bible. Few chapters have done more good to human souls.

How our Lord describes his own love for sinners

We should observe in these verses, the remarkable illustrations which our Lord uses to describe his own love for sinners. We read that in answer to the taunting remark of his enemies he delivered three parables: the parables of the lost sheep, the lost coin and the prodigal son. All three parables throw strong light on Christ's willingness to save sinners.

Christ's love is an active, working love. Just as the shepherd did not sit still bewailing his lost sheep, and the woman did not sit still bewailing her lost money, so our blessed Lord did not sit still in heaven pitying sinners. He left the glory which he had with the Father, and humbled himself to be made in the likeness of man. He came down into the world to seek and save those who were lost. He never rested until he had made atonement for our transgressions, brought in everlasting righteousness, provided eternal redemption, and opened a door of life to all who are willing to be saved.

Christ's love is a self-denying love. The shepherd brought his lost sheep home on his own shoulders rather than leave it in the wilderness. The woman lights a candle, sweeps the house, and searches carefully, sparing no pains, until she finds her money. In the same way Christ did not spare himself when he saved sinners (see John 15:13; Hebrews 12:2.)

Christ's love is a deep and mighty love. Just as the shepherd rejoiced to find his sheep, and the woman to find her money, so the Lord Jesus rejoices to save sinners. It is a real pleasure for him to pluck people out of the burning fire (see Jude 23). It is still his delight to show mercy. He is far more willing to save sinners than sinners are to be saved.

Notes on Luke 15:1–10

1. **Tax-collectors and sinners.** No Gospel writer gives so many instances of our Lord's mercy to sinners as St. Luke. It is correctly thought that this was done to encourage Gentile converts, for whom his Gospel was specially written. Observe, in addition to this chapter, Luke 18:10; 23:34–35. These passages are all unique to St. Luke.

2. **'This fellow welcomes sinners.'** These words are the key to the whole chapter. A constant recollection of them throws light on the interpretation of all three parables which follow. The Pharisees found fault with our Lord for welcoming sinners. Our Lord replies, in effect, that the thing which they found fault with was the very thing he came on earth to do, and a thing that he was not ashamed of. He came to do for sinners what the shepherd did for his lost sheep, the woman did for her lost money, and the father did for the prodigal son. As for his grumbling enemies, they were like the elder brother of the prodigal son.

I am sure that keeping this verse in mind will help us to make a correct interpretation of the whole chapter and save us from the many strange explanations which have been given to it. All three parables have a common message. They all exhibit the love and mercy of Christ towards sinners. I agree with Bengel that the lost sheep represents the stupid, foolish sinner; the lost piece of money the sinner completely ignorant about himself; and the younger son the willful sinner. But I also think that the love which goes after the sheep, seeks the money, and runs to meet the prodigal, is intended to show the love of Christ.

4. **'Which one of you?'** The main point of this parable is the deep self-sacrificing love of Christ towards sinners, and the delight he takes in saving them. The beautiful and appropriate images chosen in the parable are very striking. Our Lord speaks of himself in John 10 as the good Shepherd. Isaiah says, 'All we like sheep have gone astray' (Isaiah 53:6).

7. **'One sinner.'** Those who are depressed in their preaching and teaching by apparent lack of success should often think about this phrase, and the parallel one in verse 10. The value of one soul is not thought about enough.

'**Ninety-nine righteous people.'** I think this means people who think themselves righteous and just, like the Pharisees, and fancy they need no repentance. This is confirmed by Luke 5:32; 16:15; 18:9; Matthew 9:13; Mark 2:17.

The parable of the prodigal son (15:11–24)

This parable is known as the parable of the prodigal son. It is a forceful spiritual picture. Unlike some of our Lord's parables, it does not convey one great lesson only, but many.

The penitent freely pardoned

We see in this parable, how the penitent is readily received, pardoned freely, and completely accepted by God. Our Lord shows us this, in this part of the younger son's story, in a most touching way. We read that 'while he was still far off, his father saw him and was filled with compassion; he ran and put his arms around him and kissed him' (verse 20; see also verses 21–24).

More deeply moving words than these have, perhaps, never been written. To comment on them seems almost unnecessary. It is like gilding the lily. They show us in great bold letters the infinite love of the Lord Jesus Christ towards sinners. They teach us how infinitely willing he is to receive all who come to him, and how complete, and full, and immediate his pardon is (see Acts 13:39; Psalm 86:5).

Notes on Luke 15:11–24

11. 'There was a man who had two sons.' I believe that the younger son is a type of all unconverted sinners, and that his return to his father's house was a sign of true repentance. I believe that the father's kind reception of his son represents the Lord Jesus Christ's kindness and love to sinners who come to him, and the free and full pardon which he bestows on them. I believe that the elder son was meant to be a type of all narrow-minded self-righteous people in every age of the church, and especially of the scribes and Pharisees, who grumbled at our Lord receiving sinners. These are what I believe are the general lessons of the parable. I can go no further than this in interpreting it.

15. 'To feed the pigs.' Our Lord was speaking to Jews, who regarded pigs, because of the law of Moses, as unclean animals. This detail would probably indicate to Jews how degraded the younger son had become.

16. 'The pods that the pigs were eating.' These pods were, most probably, fruit from the carob tree, which were often used to feed pigs with, but were very unsuitable for human consumption.

17. 'He came to himself.' It has often been said about this phrase that a person must come to himself before he comes to God.

18. 'Against heaven and before you.' This is a confession of sin against God and man. It is one of the places in Scripture where **heaven**, the place where God dwells, is used for God himself. (See Daniel 4:26; Matthew 21:25.)

20. 'Far off ... ran ... kissed.' These three expressions are deeply touching. They bring out, in strong relief, the difficulty with which a sinner turns to Christ, and the readiness and willingness of Christ to receive him.

22. 'A ring.' This was a mark of honour, and confidence, and distinction. (See Genesis 41:42; Esther 3:10; James 2:2.)

23. 'The fatted calf.' This was kept for a special occasion, such as a sacrifice or a feast.

24. 'Was dead and is alive again.' Although this is part of the parable, our Lord's words here also describe the life of the prodigal son before his repentance, and the change when he repented. The one state was death: the other was life.

The elder brother (15:25–32)

These verses conclude the parable of the prodigal son. They are far less well known than the preceding verses. But they were spoken by the same lips which wanted the younger son's return to his father's house. Like everything which those lips said, they are profoundly profitable.

Notes on Luke 15:25–32

25. 'The elder son.' The older son represents the Pharisees. The unkindness, moroseness, and self-sufficiency of the older son are the exact type of the spirit shown by those who find fault with our Lord for showing kindness to tax collectors and sinners.

28. 'Became angry.' Anyone who thinks that the older son was a good man should note these words, as well as verse 20. It is just the counterpart of the grumbling of the teachers of the law and Pharisees at the beginning of the chapter. 'Plead with him.' The father's kindness is revealed again here. He might have rebuked his ill-natured son. He only pleads with him.

30. 'Prostitutes.' This is the first time we learn of this aspect of the younger son's profligacy. It may possibly have been true, but it is evidently brought out here in an uncharitable way and in a contemptuous manner.

32. 'We had to celebrate.' Whatever the older son might say, he could not deny these two great facts. His brother, who a short time ago had been as good as dead, was alive again. He was lost: he is now found. In the light of these facts all envious thoughts should have disappeared. It was right to celebrate and be glad.

Chapter 16

The parable of the unjust steward (16:1–12)

Neutrality impossible; the dignity of the law (16:13–18)

The parable of the rich man and Lazarus (16:19–31)

The parable of the unjust steward (16:1–12)

This is a difficult passage. There are knots in it which perhaps will never be untied until the Lord comes again. We might reasonably expect that because the Bible was written through inspiration, it would have some things in it that are hard to understand. The fault is not in the book, but in our own feeble understanding. If we learn nothing else from the passage before us, let us learn humility.

Do not draw lessons which are not taught

Let us beware not to draw lessons from this passage which it was never meant to teach.

The manager whom our Lord describes is not a pattern of morality. He is called a dishonest (verse 8) manager. The Lord Jesus never meant to sanction dishonesty. The manager cheated his master and broke the eighth commandment. His master commended him for acting shrewdly (verse 8), but there is no evidence that his master was pleased with his behaviour. Above all, there is not a word to show that the man was praised by Christ. In short, in his treatment of his master the manager is a beacon to be avoided and not a pattern to be followed.

Notes on Luke 16:1–12

1. **Said to his disciples.** In interpreting this parable, we should carefully observe to whom it was addressed. It was not spoken to the teachers of the law and Pharisees, like the previous three parables, but to his **disciples.** They had heard a lesson for the proud and self-righteous; now they hear a lesson for themselves.

The rich man and the manager and the master's debtors do not appear to me to be allegorical people. I view them as actors in the story which our Lord is telling, as I do not think that they were intended to represent any particular people.

8. **'The children of this age.'** This means worldly people, the opposite to people of light, who are godly people. These are the people who follow the light, and walk in the light (see John 12:36; Ephesians 5:8; compare Luke 7:35).

9. **'Friends.'** 'Use your money with an eye to the future, as the manager did his. Spend your money in such a way that your expenditure will be a friend to you, and not a witness against you in another world.'

I leave this verse with two words of caution. Firstly, do not suppose that through using money we can purchase God's favour and pardon for our sins. Heaven is not to be bought. Secondly, we must not close our eyes against the teaching of this verse. The verse plainly teaches that a right use of our money in the world, from the right motives, will be for our benefit in the world to come. It will not justify us; it will not save us from God's judgment, any more than good deeds can do this. But it does provide evidence about our grace which will befriend our souls. There is such a thing as laying up treasure in heaven (Matthew 6:20), and laying up treasure for ourselves as a firm foundation for the coming age (1 Timothy 6:19).

Neutrality impossible; the dignity of the law (16:13–18)

A divided heart

These verses teach us about the uselessness of trying to serve God with a divided heart. Our Lord Jesus Christ says, 'No slave can serve two masters; for a slave will either hate the one and love the other, or be devoted to the one and despise the other. You cannot serve both God and wealth' (verse 13).

The truth our Lord propounds here seems, at first sight, to be so obvious that there is nothing to discuss here. And yet thousands of people are constantly trying to do the things which Christ says are impossible. They try to be friends of the world and friends of God at the same time. Their consciences are enlightened to the extent that they want to have some religion, but their affections are chained down to earthly things, so that they never show that they are true Christians. This results in them living in a state of unhappiness. They have too much religion to be happy in this world, and they have too much of the world in their hearts to be happy with their religion. In short, they waste their time trying to do what cannot be done. They are striving to serve 'God and wealth.'

Notes on Luke 16:13–18

13. **'Devoted to the one and despise the other.'** This probably means that the person will love one more than the other.

16. **'The law and the prophets were in effect until John came.'** This verse probably means something like this: 'You make your boast about the law and the prophets, you Pharisees, and you do well to honour them. But you forget that the dispensation of the law and prophets was only intended to pave the way for the better dispensation of the kingdom of God which was to be ushered in by John the Baptist. That dispensation has come. John the Baptist has appeared. The kingdom of God is among you. While you are ignorantly deriding me and my teaching, multitudes of tax collectors and sinners are forcing their way into the kingdom. Your boasting is not good. With all your professed zeal for the law and the prophets, you are utterly blind to that kingdom into which the law and the prophets were meant to guide you.'

17. The chain of thought here is probably this: 'Think not because I say that the law and the prophets have introduced a better dispensation, the kingdom of God, that I count the law and the prophets of no value. On the contrary, I tell you that they are of eternal dignity and obligation. They have paved the way for a clearer revelation, but they have not been set aside.'

18. We must take care not to misinterpret the words about divorce and remarriage in this verse. It is perfectly clear from another passage that our Lord allowed divorce in cases of adultery (Matthew 5:33). The act of adultery dissolves the marriage tie, and makes those who were one become two again. Neither here nor elsewhere can I see that our Lord regards the remarriage of someone who has been divorced because of fornication, as adultery. It is divorce for frivolous reasons which he denounces, and marriage after such frivolous divorce which he pronounces to be adultery.

The parable of the rich man and Lazarus (16:19–31)

In one respect, this parable stands alone in the Bible. It is the only passage of Scripture which describes the feelings of the unconverted after death. For this reason, as well as for many others, the parable deserves special attention.

A person's standing in the world is no test of his standing in God's sight

We learn from this parable, that a person's standing in the world is no test of his standing in God's sight. The Lord Jesus describes two people, one was very rich, and the other very poor. One **lived in luxury every day** (verse 19), the other was a mere **beggar** (verse 19) who possessed nothing. And yet, of these two, the poor man had grace, and the rich man did not have grace. The poor man lived by faith, and walked in the steps of Abraham while the rich man was a selfish man, dead in his trespasses and sins.

Let us never give in to the popular notion that men are valued according to their income, and that the person who has the most money is to be most esteemed. There is no authority for this idea in the Bible. The general teaching of the Bible is opposed to it. See 1 Corinthians 1:26; Jeremiah 9:24. Wealth is not a sign of God's favour: poverty is not a sign of God's displeasure. God rarely justifies and glorifies those who are rich in this world. To see men as God sees them we must value them according to their grace.

Notes on Luke 16:19–31

19. I believe the parable was specially intended by our Lord for the benefit of the Pharisees, to whom he was speaking when he delivered it. I believe that our Lord's main aim was to rebuke the selfishness, worldliness, lack of charity, and general forgetfulness of their responsibilities, of which the Pharisees were guilty, and to expose the fearful end to which their unbelief and neglect of their own Scriptures were rapidly bringing them.

'Dressed in purple.' Purple was a particularly rich and expensive dye, and clothes dyed with it were only worn by the rich and noble. Lydia was a 'dealer in purple cloth' (Acts 6:15).

21. 'The dogs would come and lick his sores.' Some have thought that this increased Lazarus' misery, and the dogs made his suffering worse. I cannot see this. To me it implies that the dogs cared more for Lazarus than man did. It was an act of kindness.

22. 'To be with Abraham' [KJV **bosom**]. This is most probably a proverbial expression. It signifies the place of rest and safety to which all believing Jews were carried after death. Abraham was the father of the faithful, and the head of the whole Jewish family, and to be with him after death implied happiness. See Matthew 8:11.

23. 'In Hades, where he was being tormented.' In interpreting this verse, and several of the following verses, we must take care to remember that we are reading a parabolic narrative.

26. 'A great chasm has been fixed.' This verse clearly teaches, if words mean anything, that there is no hope of deliverance from hell for those who die in sin. Once in hell, men are in hell for ever. The doctrines of purgatory, or of a limited duration of punishment, cannot be reconciled with this text.

31. 'If someone rises from the dead.' Let the striking fact be noted that a man called Lazarus did rise from the dead, and yet the Jews stayed unbelieving. Above all, remember that Christ himself rose from the dead, and yet the Jewish nation would not believe.

Chapter 17

The sinfulness of causing offense; the duty of forgiveness (17:1–4)

The importance of faith (17:5–10)

The ten lepers (17:11–19)

The kingdom of God (17:20–25)

The days of Noah and Lot (17:26–37)

The sinfulness of causing offense; the duty of forgiveness (17:1–4)

1. The sinfulness of putting a stumbling-block in anyone's way

We are taught in these verses, about the great sinfulness of putting a stumbling-block in anyone's way. The Lord Jesus says, 'Occasions for stumbling are bound to come, but woe to anyone by whom they come. It would be better for you if a millstone were hung around your neck and you were thrown into the sea than for you to cause one of these little ones to stumble' (verses 1–2).

This sin which our Lord warns us against was David's sin. When he had broken the seventh commandment, and taken Uriah's wife to be his wife, Nathan the prophet said to him, 'by this deed you have utterly scorned the Lord' (2 Samuel 12:14). It was the sin which St. Paul accuses the Jews of (Romans 2:24), and a sin which he often warns Christians to guard against (1 Corinthians 10:32).

2. The importance of a forgiving spirit

We are taught, secondly, in these verses, the great importance of a forgiving spirit. The Lord Jesus says, 'If another disciple sins, you must rebuke the offender, and if there is repentance, you must forgive. And if the same person sins against you seven times a day, and turns back to you seven times and says, "I repent", you must forgive' (verses 3–4).

There are few Christian duties which the New Testament dwells on so frequently as for-giving other people. It has a prominent place in the Lord's Prayer. The only thing we do in the whole prayer is to forgive those who have sinned against us. It is a test for being forgiven our-selves. The person who cannot forgive his neighbour the few trifling offenses he may have committed against him, can know nothing about the free and full pardon which Christ offers us. (See Matthew 18:35; Ephesians 4:32.) Forgiving other people is also a leading charac-teristic of the indwelling Holy Spirit. The pres-ence of the Spirit in the heart is known by fruits born in the person's life. The fruits are both active and passive. The person who has not learned to bear and forebear, to put up with much, is not born of the Spirit (1 John 3:14; Matthew 5:44-45).

Notes on Luke 17:1–4

1. **Jesus said to his disciples.** A great teacher like our Lord has an undoubted right to open up entirely new subjects at his discretion. Perhaps this is the case here.

2. **'A millstone were hung around your neck.'** This is a proverbial expression. Anything is bet-ter than to give offense to believers and make them stumble.

'**These little ones.**' These are believers. They are God's children, and are tenderly cared for by the Father, as little infants in a man's family. See Mark 10:42. It is probable that our Lord pointed to some of the weak and unestablished followers who accompanied him and the twelve apostles. There are always many who are 'infants in Christ' (1 Corinthians 3:1).

4. **'Seven times a day.'** Here, as in other places, seven must be taken indefinitely. It means 'very frequently,' 'very often.' See also 1 Samuel 2:5; Ruth 4:15; Isaiah 4:1; Psalm 12:6; Micah 5:5.

The importance of faith (17:5–10)

Notes on Luke 17:5–10

6. **'A mustard seed.'** This is a proverbial expression for something very small and insignificant in size.

'**Say to this mulberry tree, "Be uprooted"'.** This is a proverbial expression, apparently com-mon among the Jews for doing great deeds and overcoming apparently insuperable difficulties. See 1 Corinthians 13:2. Major remarks, 'When the Jews intended to extol any of their doctors, they said of him that he plucked up mountains by the roots.'

8. **'Put on your apron.'** [KJV gird thyself]. The clothes people wore in the East were gener-ally loose and flowing. Before doing anything that required physical exertion, they first of all had to 'gird up the loins,' or tie the garments tightly round the waist, after gathering them up.

10. **'Worthless slaves.'** The contrast between what we must say about ourselves ('We are unworthy servants') and what Christ will be graciously pleased to say on the last day (Matthew 25:21; 25:34–40) is very striking.

The ten lepers (17:11–19)

Gratitude is rare

Let us note, lastly, in these verses, how rare grati-tude is. Only one out of the ten lepers turned back to give Christ thanks, after they were healed. Our Lord asks this solemn question: '**Were not ten made clean? But the other nine, where are they?**' (verse 17).

Here is a humbling and heart-searching les-son. The best of us are far too like the nine lep-ers. We are more ready to pray than praise, and more disposed to ask God for what we do not have than thank him for what we do have. The widespread thanklessness of Christians is a scan-dal. It reveals our lack of humility. So we must pray for a deeper sense of our own sinfulness, admit how unworthy we are. This, after all, is the true secret for a grateful heart. It is the person who daily feels his debt to grace, and daily remembers that in reality he deserves nothing but hell – this is the person who will be blessing and praising God every day. Thankfulness only blossoms from a root of deep humility.

Notes on Luke 17:11–19

12. **Keeping their distance.** Lepers were thought of as outcasts and were not allowed to live with other people. See Leviticus 13:46.

14. **'Go and show yourselves to the priests.'** Leviticus chapters 13—14 explain this. The priests were appointed by God to judge all lep-rous cases, and to decide whether the leper was clean or unclean, cured or uncured. See also Deuteronomy 24:8.

A Jewish leper would see from the command of our Lord's a hint that he would hear good news when he showed himself to the priests.

15. **One of them . . . turned back, praising God.** Burgeon has the following apt quotation: 'The nine were already healed, and going off to the priests so that they could be restored to society: but the first thoughts of the Samaritan are turned to his deliverer. He had forgotten all, in the sense of God's mercy and of his own unworthiness.'

The kingdom of God (17:20–25)

Two personal comings of Christ are revealed in the Scriptures

We are taught in this passage, that there are two personal comings of Christ revealed to us in Scripture. He was appointed to come the first time in weakness and humiliation, to suffer and to die. He was appointed to come a second time in power and glory to put down all enemies under his feet, and to reign. At his first coming he was to be made sin for us and to bear our sins on the cross. At the second coming he was to appear without sin, for the complete salvation of his people (2 Corinthians 5:21; Hebrews 9:28). In these verses our Lord speaks about both of these comings. He speaks about the first when he says that the Son of Man 'must endure much suffering and be rejected by this generation' (verse 25). He speaks about the second coming when he says that the Son of Man will return as 'the lightning flashes and lights up the sky from one side to the other' (verse 24).

It is very important to see these two comings of Christ separately, if we are to understand Scripture aright. The disciples, and all the Jews in our Lord's day, appear to have seen only one personal coming. They expected a Messiah who would reign, but not one who would come and suffer. In the same way, the majority of Christians appear to see only one personal coming. They believe that Christ came the first time to suffer; but they seem unable to understand that Christ is coming a second time to reign. Both parties have got hold of the truth, but neither, unhappily, has embraced the whole truth. Both are more or less in error, and the Christian's error is only second in importance to that of the Jew. Jesus coming in person the first time to suffer, and Jesus coming in person the second time to reign, are two landmarks of which we should never lose sight. We stand between the two. Let us believe that both are real and true.

Notes on Luke 17:20–25

20. The kingdom which our Lord speaks about here evidently includes both his present spiritual kingdom and his future glorious kingdom.

24. **'The lightning.'** Our Lord declares that his second coming, when it does take place, will be so sudden, so clearly-marked, and so unmistakable, that true believers will immediately recognize it as the coming of their King. It will not be a slow, gradual event. It will come on us in a moment.

25. **'Rejected by this generation.'** I am strongly disposed to think, that both here and in Luke 21:32, Mark 13:30, and Matthew 24:34, the word translated **generation** means this nation or people of the Jews, and not merely the people who were living when our Lord spoke.

The days of Noah and Lot (17:26–37)

The theme of these verses is particularly solemn. It is the second coming of our Lord Jesus Christ. That great event, and the things immediately connected with it, are described here by our Lord himself.

Notes on Luke 17:26–37

26. **'As it was in the days of Noah.'** The whole passage applies exclusively to the second personal coming of Christ, when he will come to set up his glorious kingdom. To apply the conclusion of this chapter, as many do, to the destruction of Jerusalem by the Romans, appears to me an unwarrantable and violent straining of Scripture.

31. **'Anyone on the housetop.'** Our Lord teaches his disciples that his own second coming in glory would not be a time of carnal ease for everybody, as the Jews thought, but a time of trial of people's religion, and of sifting and separation of the visible church. It would be ushered in by a time of such tribulation and suffering, that none but those who were sitting loose to the world, and ready to give up everything for Christ's sake, would come out of it unscathed.

37. **'The vultures will gather.'** This is a dark and mysterious saying, and has greatly perplexed the commentators. That it refers to the well-known power of the vulture to discern carcasses, whether by eye or by smell, is allowed by all. But when we come to the precise application of the saying, we find great variety of opinions. My opinion is that, looking at the context, the eagles are more likely to be signs of the angels who will be used at our Lord's second coming, than anything else. Verse 36 speaks about the separation between the just and the unjust which will take place at our Lord's appearing. In that separation we are specifically told that angels will be used (Matthew 13:49). Is it too much then to conjecture that our Lord's simple meaning is that wherever his body is, his professing church, there the angels will gather together at the last day, and separate the wicked from the just, in order to give to each his appointed place?

Chapter 18

The parable of the widow and the judge (18:1–8)

The parable of the Pharisee and the tax collector (18:9–14)

Christ's mind about children (18:15–17)

The rich ruler (18:18–27)

Encouragement to leave everything for Christ's sake; crucifixion predicted (18:28–34)

The blind beggar of Jericho healed (18:35–43)

The parable of the widow and the judge (18:1–8)

The meaning of this parable is explained by our Lord himself. To use the words of an old divine, 'The key hangs at the door.' **Jesus told them a parable about their need to pray always and not lose heart** (verse 1). These words are closely linked to the solemn words about the second coming at the end of the last chapter. It is prayer without fainting, during the long weary interval between the first and second comings, which Jesus is urging his disciples to keep up. We ourselves are standing in that interval. So this subject should be of special interest to us.

Notes on Luke 18:1–8

1. Their need to pray always. This does not mean that a person should be constantly performing the act of prayer. It means that a person should constantly keep up the habit of prayer, and endeavour to be always in a prayerful frame of mind.

2. 'In a certain city.' My own impression is that the parable was meant simply to describe the duty of individual believers during the whole period of the present dispensation, and to encourage them to persevering prayer, by holding out the hope that God will at length plead their cause, when things seem at the worst.

3. 'A widow.' The helpless and friendless condition of a widow in the East in Bible times should be remembered. See Exodus 22:22; Deuteronomy 10:18; Job 29:13; 1 Kings 17:9,12.

7. 'Who cry to him day and night.' This is doubtless a proverbial expression, signifying a habit of continual prayer.

8. 'He will quickly grant justice to them.' This sentence points to the second coming of Christ. To us it seems long delayed. But a thousand years in God's sight are but as one day (2 Peter 3:8).

There is doubtless an implied lesson here, that persevering prayer is the secret of keeping up faith. Augustine says, 'When faith fails, prayer dies. In order to pray, then, we must have faith; and that our faith fail not, we must pray. Faith pours forth prayer; and the pouring forth of the heart in prayer gives steadfastness to faith.'

The parable of the Pharisee and the tax collector (18:9–14)

This parable is linked to the previous one. The parable of the persevering widow teaches the value of importunity in prayer; the parable of the Pharisee and the tax collector teaches the spirit which should pervade our prayers. The first parable encourages us to pray and not to faint; the second parable reminds us how and in what matter we should pray.

Notes on Luke 18:9–14

11. 'Standing by himself, was praying.' It is wrong to think that there was anything wrong in standing to pray. Standing was as common a position for prayer as kneeling, among the Jews, see Matthew 6:5; Mark 11:25; 2 Chronicles 6:12.

12. 'I fast twice a week; I give a tenth of all my income.' A more miserable and defective righteousness than this Pharisee's it is hard to conceive. His negative goodness consisted in not being as bad as some people! His positive goodness consisted in fasting and paying tithes with excessive scrupulosity. We do not hear a word about heart-holiness.

13. 'A sinner!' Literally, 'the sinner.' That is, 'the great sinner.'

14. 'Went down to his home justified.' We must not think that this means that the Pharisee was a little justified, and the tax collector was greatly justified, and that the difference between them was only one of degree. There are no degrees in justification. The words mean that the Pharisee was not justified at all, or accepted with God, and that the tax collector went home pardoned, forgiven, and counted righteous before God.

'All who exalt themselves.' The truth of this great principle is illustrated throughout the Bible. Pharaoh, Goliath, Haman, Sennacherib, Nebuchadnezzar, Herod, are all cases in point.

Christ's mind about children (18:15–17)

People are ignorant about children's souls

Let us observe in this passage, how ignorant people are about children's souls. We read that there were some who were **bringing even infants to him that he might touch them; and when the disciples saw it, they sternly ordered them not to do it.** (verse 15). They most probably thought that it was a waste of their Master's time, and that infants could derive no benefit from being brought to Christ. They drew from our Lord a solemn rebuke. We read that **Jesus** called for them and said, 'Let the little children come to me, and do not stop them; for it is to such as these that the kingdom of God belongs' (verse 16).

The disciples are not the only people who are ignorant about this. There are few subjects about which we find such strange opinions held in churches, as on the subject of the souls of children. Some people think that children ought to be baptized, as a matter of course, and that if they die unbaptized they cannot be saved; others think that children should not be baptized. Some think that all children are regenerate by virtue of their baptism; others seem to think that children are incapable of receiving any grace, and that they should not join the visible church until they are grown up. Some think that children are naturally innocent, and would do no wickedness unless they learned it from others; others think that it is no use to expect them to be converted when young, and that they must be treated as unbelievers until they come to years of discretion. All these opinions are erroneous, one way or the other. All are to be deprecated, for all lead to many painful mistakes.

We would do well to get hold of some settled scriptural principles about the spiritual condition of children. To do so may save us much perplexity, and preserve us from grave false doctrine.

The souls of young children are evidently precious in God's sight. Both here and elsewhere there is clear evidence that Christ cares for them as much as he does for grown-ups. The souls of young children are capable of receiving grace: they are born in sin, and without grace cannot be saved. There is nothing, either in the Bible or experience, to make us think that they cannot receive the Holy Spirit, and be justified, even as infants.

Notes on Luke 18:15–17

15. Infants. It is children of the youngest and tenderest age. It is the same word used in Luke 1:41, 44; 2:12, 16; 1 Peter 2:2. It is impossible to interpret the word to mean young people who have come to years of discretion.

16. 'To such as these that the kingdom of God belongs.' Bearing in mind the preceding verses, and the subsequent verses, it seems probable that the principal idea in our Lord's mind was to set before us the beauty of a humble and child-like spirit, and to commend such a spirit to his disciples for imitation.

The rich ruler (18:18–27)

This story is repeated three times in the Gospels. Matthew, Mark, and Luke were all moved by the Holy Spirit to record the story of the rich man who came to Christ. This fact should be noted. It shows us that there are lessons for us here

which require special attention. When God wanted to impress on Peter the great importance about taking the gospel to the Gentiles he sent him a vision, which he repeated three times (Acts 10:16).

Notes on Luke 18:18–27

22. 'Sell all that you own and distribute the money to the poor.' Our Lord prescribed according to the disease before him. It was a case of desperate and idolatrous love of money. There was only one remedy: 'Sell all, and distribute.' Like St. Paul and his companions on board ship, he must throw overboard the ship's cargo if he was to save his life (see Acts 27:18).

25. 'It is easier for a camel …' This proverb was probably familiar to our Lord's hearers. The camel was the largest animal the Jews were used to, and a 'camel going through the eye of a needle,' according to some rabbinical writings, signified a thing absolutely impossible. Michaelis says that a similar proverb, about an elephant passing through a needle's eye, is used in India.

27. 'What is impossible for mortals …' This is a proverb, but its application is clear. The salvation of a rich man is possible with God's grace.

Encouragement to leave everything for Christ's sake: crucifixion predicted (18:28–34)

Our Lord's promise to all who make sacrifices for his sake

Let us observe in these verses, what a glorious and satisfying promise our Lord offers to all believers who make sacrifices for his sake. He says, 'there is no one who has left house or wife or brothers or parents or children, for the sake of the kingdom of God, who will not get back very much more in this age, and in the age to come eternal life' (verses 29–30).

This is a very particular promise. It does not refer to the believer's reward in another world, and the crown of glory which never fades; it refers to this life, to the here and now.

The 'very much more' in this promise must be taken in a spiritual sense. It means that the believer will find that whatever he has to give up will be more than compensated for in his fellowship with Christ. He will find such peace, and hope, and joy, and comfort and rest, in communion with the Father and the Son, that his losses will be more than counterbalanced by his gains. In short, the Lord Jesus Christ will be more to him than property, or relatives, or friends.

The complete fulfilment of this wonderful promise has often been experienced by God's saints. Hundreds, from every era of the Christian church, could testify that when they had to give up everything for the kingdom of

God they received such grace that they were kept in perfect peace (Isaiah 26:3). They were enabled to rejoice in their sufferings and delight in their weaknesses (Romans 5:3; 2 Corinthians 12:10). In their darkest hours they were enabled to rejoice and to count it an honour to suffer for their Master's name (1 Peter 1:8; Acts 5:41). The last day will show that in poverty and in exile, in prisons and before judgment seats, in the fire and under the sword, these words of Christ have proved true. Friends have often proved faithless; royal promises have often been broken; riches have flown away; but Christ's promises have never been known to fail.

Notes on Luke 18:28–34

28. 'We have left our homes.' It has often been noted that Peter and his fellow disciples had left little or nothing for Christ's sake. A few boats and fishing nets were probably all their worldly goods amounted to. Yet it must never be forgotten that a poor man's **all** is as dear to him, in a certain sense, as the rich man's palace. He knows nothing higher or better. In giving up everything for Christ's sake, he makes the greatest sacrifice in his power.

32–33. 'He will be handed over to the Gentiles …' The following passage from Doddridge is worth reading: 'This prediction is a strong instance of the spirit of prophecy exerted by our Lord. It was more probable that he would be privately killed, or stoned to death by a crowd. And when he was delivered back to the Jews by Pilate, with permission to judge him according to their law, it is amazing that he was not stoned. But all was done that the Scriptures might be fulfilled.'

The blind beggar of Jericho healed (18:35–43)

The importance of the diligent use of the means of grace

We see in this passage, the importance of the diligent use of the means of grace. We are told of **a blind man** who **was sitting by the roadside begging** (verse 35). He found the place where his pitiful condition was most likely to attract attention. He did not sit idly at home, and wait for help to come to him. He put himself by the roadside, so that travellers might see him and help him. This story shows the wisdom of such behaviour. Sitting by the roadside he heard that Jesus was approaching. So he called out for mercy and for his sight to be restored. This should be noted carefully. If the blind man had not sat down by the roadside on that day he may have stayed blind all his life.

The person who seeks salvation should remember the example of this blind man. He must seek out diligently every means of grace; he must be found regularly in those places where the Lord Jesus is especially present; he must sit by the roadside, wherever the Word is read and the Gospel preached, and God's people meet together.

Notes on Luke 18:35–43

35. **As he approached Jericho.** Matthew speaks of two blind men. Mark and Luke only mention one. There were doubtless two blind people healed. Mark and Luke, however, only mention one person, as he was probably the man best known in Jericho. Mark tells us that his name was Bartimaeus.

38. 'Son of David.' This expression is remarkable, because the previous verse informs us that the blind man was told that **Jesus of Nazareth** was passing by. To call our Lord the **Son of David** was a sign of faith, and showed that the blind man had some idea that Jesus was the Messiah. When the Pharisees were asked whose Son Christ would be, they replied at once, 'The Son of David' (Matthew 22:42). Our Lord's fame as a mighty worker of miracles had probably reached the blind man's ears, and made him believe that the person who could do such great miracles must be the one sent from God.

41. 'Let me see again.' Both here, and in the next two verses, the Greek word literally means, 'look up,' or 'see again.'

Chapter 19

Zacchaeus called (19:1–10)

The parable of the ten minas (19:11–27)

The triumphant entry into Jerusalem (19:28–40)

Christ weeps over Jerusalem; the temple is cleansed (19:41–48)

Zacchaeus called (19:1–10)

These verses describe the conversion of a soul. Like the stories of Nicodemus and the Samaritan woman, the story of Zacchaeus should be frequently studied by Christians. The Lord Jesus never changes. What he did for this man, he is able and willing to do for anyone else.

No one is too bad to be saved

We learn from these verses, that no one is too bad to be saved, or beyond the power of Christ's grace. We are told about a wealthy tax collector becoming a disciple of Christ: a more unlikely event we cannot imagine! We see the camel passing through the eye of a needle, and a rich man entering into God's kingdom. We have proof that all things are possible with God. We see a covetous tax collector transformed into a generous Christian.

The door of hope which the Gospel reveals to sinners is open very wide. Let us leave it open, as we find it: let us not attempt, in narrowminded ignorance, to shut it. We should never be afraid to maintain that Christ is able to save completely (Hebrews 7:25), and that the vilest sinners may be freely forgiven if they will only come to him. We should offer the Gospel boldly to the worst and wickedest, and say, 'Though your sins are like scarlet, they shall be like snow; though they are red crimson, they shall become like wool' (Isaiah 1:18).

Notes on Luke 19:1–10

2. The link between the story of Zacchaeus and the preceding chapter should not be overlooked. The difficulty of a rich man's salvation had been strongly set out there: the Holy Spirit now proceeds to show us, by the example of Zacchaeus, that nothing is impossible with God.

4. **Climbed a sycamore tree.** The ridicule that such an action would bring on Zacchaeus should be remembered. A wealthy tax collector climbing up a tree, after running along a road, to see a religious teacher, would doubtless call forth mockery from all who saw him. Yet this detail, trifling as it seems, throws light on Zacchaeus's character. He was someone who did not care about man's opinion. He wanted to see Christ, and he would not be stopped.

5. **'I must stay at your house today.'** It should be noted that this is the only place in the Gospels where our Lord goes to be a guest, uninvited. This is a very important point. Christ sometimes comes to those who do not seek him (Isaiah 65:1).

Our Lord's complete knowledge is clearly shown here. Not only did he know the name of the man in the tree, but the state of his heart (John 1:48).

6. **He hurried down and was happy to welcome him.** It is precisely at this point that the conversion of Zacchaeus seems to have taken place. The unexpected condescension of such a famous teacher of religion in offering to be a tax collector's guest, was made the means by which the Spirit changed his heart. Nothing is so frequently found to turn the hearts of great sinners as the unexpected and undeserved news that Christ loves them and cares for their souls. These tidings have often broken and melted hearts of stone.

7. **Began to grumble.** The Greek word here is only used in one other place in the New Testament (Luke 15:2). It is there used in precisely the same connection, to describe the feeling shown by self-righteous Pharisees on seeing sinners received by Christ.

The parable of the ten minas (19:11–27)

The occasion on which our Lord spoke this parable is clear. It was intended to correct the false expectations of the disciples about Christ's kingdom.

The reckoning which awaits all professing Christians

We see in this parable the certain reckoning which awaits all professing Christians. We are told that when the Master returned, 'he ordered these slaves, to whom he had given the money, to be summoned so that he might find out what they had gained by trading' (verse 15).

There is a day coming when the Lord Jesus Christ will judge his people. The course of this world will not always go on as it does now. Disorder, confusion, false profession, and unpunished sin, will not always cover the face of the earth. The great white throne will be set up; and the Judge of all will sit on it; the dead will be raised from their graves; the living will all be summoned to appear before Christ; the books will be opened. High and low, rich and poor, gentle and simple, all will have to given account to God, and all will receive an eternal sentence.

Notes on Luke 19:11–27

11. **A parable.** There is a great similarity between this parable and that of the talents in Matthew. Yet they are not the same. They were evidently spoken at different times, and differ in one important respect, namely, the sums of money given to the servants. In Matthew the servants receive different sums. In Luke all receive the same.

14. **'We do not want this man to rule over us.'** Theophylact remarks about the striking resemblance between this part of the parable and the cry of the Jews when Christ was before Pilate. They were asked, 'Shall I crucify your King?' They answered, 'We have no king but Caesar.' They said, 'Away with him! Crucify him!'

15. **'Having received royal power.'** This part of the parable describes the second coming of Jesus Christ. The kingdom for which we pray in the Lord's Prayer is not yet come.

16. **'Your pound.'** The humility of a true Christian is seen here. The servant does not say, 'By my skill I have earned,' but, '**your pound has made.**' We have nothing to boast of. All that we have we have received.

17. **'Take charge of ten cities.'** The servant who had turned one mina into ten was put in charge of ten cities, and the servant who had turned one into five was put in charge of five cities: each was rewarded according to his diligence. The doctrine of reward according to deeds seems to stand out here as well as in other

places in Scripture. Our title to heaven is all of grace. Our degree of glory in heaven will be in proportion to our deeds. Every person will receive his own reward according to his own labour.

Henry remarks, 'There are degrees of glory in heaven. Every vessel will be alike full, but not alike large. And the degree of glory there will be according to the degrees of usefulness here.' (See 1 Corinthians 3:8.)

21. 'You are a harsh man.' Unkind thoughts about God are a common mark of all unconverted people. They start by misrepresenting him, and then try to excuse themselves for not loving and serving him.

27. In leaving the parable let us not forget that it shows us three kinds of people.

Firstly, there are open opposers of Christ and the Gospel. Such were the Jews who refused to receive our Lord. Such are all pagans today.

Secondly, there are faithful Christians. Such are all who made good use of the Gospel, for their own good and for God's glory.

Thirdly, there are the unfaithful, formal Christians, who have Christianity, but make no real use of it. Of these it should be always noted that the parable does not charge them with being open enemies of Christ, or open breakers of God's commandments. But they keep it 'wrapped up in a piece of cloth.' They have a great gift from God, and make no use of it. This will prove at last their eternal ruin.

The triumphant entry into Jerusalem (19:28–40)

Our Lord's perfect knowledge

Let us note in these verses, the perfect knowledge of our Lord Jesus Christ. We see him sending two of his disciples into a village, and tell them that as they enter the village they will find 'tied there a colt that has never been ridden' (verse 30). We see our Lord describing what they would see and hear, with as much confidence as if the whole transaction had been previously arranged. In short, he speaks like one to whom all things were open, like one whose eyes are everywhere, like one who knew unseen things as well as visible things.

An attentive reader will observe the same thing in other parts of the Gospel (Matthew 12:25; John 2:25; John 6:64). Knowledge such as this is the special attribute of God. Such passages are meant to remind us that the man Jesus Christ is not only man, he is also God (Romans 9:5).

The thought of Christ's perfect knowledge should alarm sinners and wake them up to repentance. The great Head of the church knows them and all their doings; the Judge of all sees them all the time, and notes their ways. There is no darkness where the workers of iniquity can hide themselves.

The thought of Christ's perfect knowledge should comfort all truehearted Christians, and quicken them to increased diligence in good works. The Master's eye is always on them. He knows where they live, and their daily trials, and who their friends are. Jesus knows their every thought and word. Let them take courage when they are slandered, misunderstood, and misrepresented by the world: it does not matter so long as they can say, 'Lord, you know everything; you know that I love you' (John 21:17).

Notes on Luke 19:28–40

30. 'A colt tied there. ...' Note that the public entry into Jerusalem which we read about here is one of the few events in our Lord's life which all four Gospel writers relate. There is evidently an importance about it as a step in our Lord's earthly ministry, which we should not overlook.

40. 'The stones would shout out.' This is a proverb. If men did not rejoice at Christ's coming, even inanimate nature would cry shame.

Christ weeps over Jerusalem; the temple is cleansed (19:41–48)

Christ's compassion for sinners

We learn from these verses, about our Lord's tender compassion for sinners. We are told that when he came near Jerusalem for the last time, he wept over it (verse 41). He knew the character of its inhabitants well. Their cruelty, their self-righteousness, their stubbornness, their obstinate prejudice against the truth, their proud heart was not hidden from him. He knew only too well what they were going to do to him in the next few days. His unfair trial, his handing over to the Gentiles, his sufferings, his crucifixion, were all spread out clearly in his mind's eye. And yet, knowing all this, our Lord pitied Jerusalem! As he approached Jerusalem and saw the city, he wept over it (verse 41).

We make a big mistake if we think that Christ cares only for those who believe in him. He cares for everyone. His heart is wide enough to take an interest in all mankind; his compassion extends to every man, woman and child on earth. Hardened sinners are fond of making excuses for their behaviour; but they will never be able to say that Christ was not merciful, and was not ready to save.

We know too little of true Christianity if we do not feel a deep concern about the souls of unconverted people, Psalm 119:136; Romans 9:2. If Christ felt tenderly about wicked people, his disciples should feel the same way.

Notes on Luke 19:41–48

41. He wept over it. Wordsworth remarks, 'Christ here proves his twofold nature, by shed-

ding tears as man for what he foretold as God.'

43. 'The days will come. ....' The predictions of this and the next verse were fulfilled literally at the siege of Jerusalem under Titus. Not one word failed.

44. 'The time of your visitation from God.' Poole remarks: 'God's visitations are either for wrath, or mercy: for wrath, Exodus 32:34; for mercy, Jeremiah 29:10. It is plain that our Saviour uses the term here in its latter, not its former sense; and that by God's visitation is meant his visiting them by the prophets, John the Baptist, and himself.'

45. Then he entered the temple. Jerome considers our Lord's cleansing of the temple to be his greatest miracle.

46. 'It is written.' All reformation of abuses in churches should be built on God's Word.

47. Every day he was teaching in the temple. The link between this verse and the previous verse should not be overlooked. Our Lord had just called the temple 'a house of prayer.' Yet he proceeds to show, by his own example, that it is to be the house of **teaching** as well as praying.

Chapter 20

Christ's authority questioned; Christ's reply (20:1–8)

The parable of the wicked farmers (20:9–19)

The question about paying taxes to Caesar (20:20–26)

The Sadducees' question about the resurrection (20:27–40)

Christ's question about David's saying in the Psalms (20:41–47)

Christ's authority questioned; Christ's reply (20:1–8)

The chief priests' question

Let us notice in this passage, the question which the chief priests and teachers of the law ask our Lord. **'Tell us, by what authority you are doing these things? Who is it who gave you this authority?'** (verse 2).

They asked this question because they hated Christ and envied him. They saw his influence increasing, while theirs was waning. They resolved, if possible, to halt the progress of this new teacher, so they attacked his authority. They should have looked into his miracles and compared his teaching with their own Scriptures. Instead they called in question Christ's commission.

Every true-hearted Christian who tries to do good in the world must be prepared to be treated like his Master. He must never be surprised to find that self-righteous and worldly-minded people dislike his actions. The lawfulness of his behaviour will be constantly called into question. He will be thought of as meddling in other people's affairs and as being self-conceited, and a troubler in Israel (Acts 24:5; 1 Kings 18:17).

Notes on Luke 20:1–8

4. 'From heaven.' This means 'from God.' See Daniel 4:26; Luke 15:18,21.

6. 'All the people will stone us.' Grotius remarks, 'They had themselves accustomed the people to this violence. When they could not legally convict their enemies, they incited the people to stone them. It was called the judgment of zeal.' See John 10:31; Acts 14:19.

The parable of the wicked farmers (20:9–19)

This is one of the very few parables which is recorded more than once by the Gospel writers. Matthew, Mark and Luke, all give it in its entirety. This triple repetition is alone sufficient to underline its importance. Doubtless the parable was especially meant for the Jews to whom it was addressed. But we must not confine its application to them. It contains lessons which should be remembered in all Christian fellowships for as long as the world stands.

The deep corruption of human nature

The parable shows us the deep corruption of human nature. The behaviour of the wicked farmers is a vivid portrayal of man's dealings with God. It is a faithful picture of the history of the Jewish church. In spite of privileges which no other nation had, in the face of warnings which no other people ever received, the Jews rebelled against God's lawful authority, refused to give him his rightful dues, rejected the counsel of his prophets, and, at length, crucified his only Son. The Gentile churches were just as unfaithful. They were called out of pagan darkness through infinite mercy, but they did nothing worthy of their vocation; on the contrary, they allowed false teachings and evil behaviour to spring up among them, and have crucified Christ again. It is a sad fact that in hardness, unbelief, superstition, and self-righteousness, the Christian churches, as a whole, are little better than the Jewish church of our Lord's time. Both are described with painful accuracy in the story of the wicked farmers. In both we may point to countless privileges misused, and countless warnings despised.

Notes on Luke 20:9–19

9. He began to tell the people this parable. The parable itself is a remarkable combination of figure, history, and prophecy. Cyril calls it 'the history of Israel in a compendium.' The parable of the sower, the parable of the mustard seed, and the parable of the wicked farmers, are the only parables which are three times recorded in the Gospels.

'A vineyard.' The vineyard is used parabolically in Isaiah: 'The vineyard of the Lord of hosts is the house of Israel' (Isaiah 5:7). Here it seems to mean the land of Judea, and the special privileges of the Jewish nation.

13. 'My beloved son.' This part of the parable can be interpreted only in one way. The Lord Jesus speaks about himself and the treatment which he was on the point of receiving at the hands of the priests and elders. He knew that as he spoke they were already plotting his death, and saying, 'Let us kill him.'

16. 'He will come and destroy.' Here the parable passes into prophecy. Our Lord predicts the destruction of Jerusalem, the scattering of the Jews, and the calling of the Gentiles to enjoy their privileges.

17. 'The stone.' This means Christ. Though rejected by those who called themselves leaders and builders in the Jewish church, it was prophesied that he would become the capstone. And as it was foretold, so it would be. See Psalm 118:22.

The question about paying taxes to Caesar (20:20–26)

Notes on Luke 20:20–26

22. 'Is it lawful for us to pay taxes to the emperor, or not?' The question our Lord's enemies posed was done so cleverly that it seemed that he had to reply to an impossible dilemma. Whatever answer he gave, it seemed that he would offend one of the two parties; he must either offend the friends of the Roman supremacy or offend the zealots among the Jews.

23. Their craftiness. This Greek word is found only five times in the New Testament. It is the same word used to describe Satan's 'cunning' in tempting Eve (2 Corinthians 11:3).

25. 'Give to the emperor the things that are the emperor's. ...' Our Lord had probably in view two parties among his hearers. One party was the Jewish zealots. To them he said, 'Give to the emperor the things that are the emperor's.' The other party were the worldly Herodians. To them he said, '[give] to God the things that are God's.'

The Sadducees' question about the resurrection (20:27–40)

Unbelief is very ancient

We see in these verses what an old thing unbelief is. We are told that **Some Sadducees, those who say there is no resurrection, came to him and asked him a question** (verse 27). Even in the

Jewish church, the church of Abraham, and Isaac, and Jacob, – the church of Moses, and Samuel, and David, and the prophets – we find that there were bold, unblushing sceptics. If unfaithfulness like this existed among God's special people, the Jews, what must the state of the pagans have been like?

We must not be surprised when we hear about pagans, deists, heretics and free-thinkers rising up in the church, and drawing disciples after them. We must not think that it is some rare event. It is only one of many evidences that man is a fallen and corrupt being. It is not in reality a thing to wonder at that there should rise up so many who call in question the truths of the Bible; the marvel is rather, that in a fallen world the sect of the Sadducees should be so small. Bold pagans, like Porphyry, and Julian, and Hobbes, and Hume, and Voltaire, and Payne, arise from time to time and make a stir in the world; but they produce no lasting impression. They pass away like the Sadducees. The great evidences of Christianity remain, like the pyramids, unshaken and unmoved. The 'gates of Hades' (Matthew 16:18) will never prevail against Christ's truth.

Notes on Luke 20:27–40

28. 'The man shall marry the widow.' The law of Moses referred to here (Deuteronomy 25:5) ought to be carefully studied, and compared with Leviticus 18:16.

34. 'Those who belong to this age.' This does not refer to unconverted people, but simply to people who are living on earth.

Christ's question about David's saying in the Psalms (20:41–47)

The Psalms witness to Christ's divinity

Let us observe, in this passage, what a striking witness the book of Psalms gives to Christ's divinity. We read that after patiently replying to his enemies' attacks, our Lord in turn asks them a question. He asks them to explain an expression in Psalm 110:1, where David speaks of the Messiah as his Lord. The teachers of the law were unable to answer this question. They did not see the great truth that the Messiah was to be God as well as man, and that while as a man he was David's son, as God he was to be David's Lord. Their ignorance of Scripture was exposed for everyone to see. Professing themselves to be teachers, who possessed the key of knowledge, they were shown up as people who could not explain their own Scriptures. We may well believe that out of all the defects which our Lord's malicious enemies had, none was as galling as this one. Nothing so kills man's pride as to have his ignorance of the subject he considers himself to be an expert on shown up in public.

We probably have little idea how much deep truth the book of Psalms contains. No part of the Bible is better known in the letter, and so little understood in the spirit. We err greatly if we suppose that it is nothing but a record of David's feelings, or David's experience, David's praises, and David's prayers. The hand that held the pen was generally David's, but the subject matter was often something far deeper and higher than the history of the Son of Jesse. The Psalms, in a word, is a book full of Christ: Christ suffering, Christ in humiliation, Christ dying, Christ rising again, Christ coming the second time, Christ reigning over everyone. Both the advents are here: the coming in suffering, to bear the cross – the coming in power, to wear the crown. Both the kingdoms are here: the kingdom of grace, during which the elect are gathered – the kingdom of glory, when every tongue will confess that Jesus is Lord. Let us always read the Psalms with a special reverence.

Notes on Luke 20:41–47

41. 'How can they say that the Messiah is David's son?' Note that Christ was called 'Son of David' by sick people as they called out to our Lord to cure them. They meant more than appears at first sight. The expression was tantamount to a confession that our Lord was the Messiah.

46. 'Love to be greeted.' This expression is explained in Matthew 23:7–10. The teachers of the law loved to be called by honorable titles, such as, 'Rabbi,' 'Father,' 'Master,' and 'Teacher,' in public. Men often profess a desire to magnify their office, when in truth they want to magnify themselves.

47. 'They devour widows' houses.' This probably means that the teachers of the law, under the pretence of charity, took charge of the property of widows, and pretended to manage it for them. But instead of managing it honestly and faithfully, they embezzled it, and privately used it for their own interests.

Chapter 21

The widow's offering (21:1–4)

The temple's destruction predicted (21:5–9)

National troubles predicted; persecution foretold (21:10–19)

The destruction of Jerusalem, and tribulation of Israel (21:20–24)

The second coming, and the signs preceding it (21:25–33)

Watch, because of the second coming (21:34–38)

The widow's offering (21:1–4)

Our Lord notices what happens on earth

We learn from these verses, how keenly our Lord Jesus Christ observes what is done on earth. We read that **He looked up and saw rich people putting their gifts into the treasury; he also saw a poor widow put in two small copper coins** (verses 1–2). We might have supposed that our Lord's mind at this time would have been wholly preoccupied with what was going to happen to him. His betrayal, his unjust trial, his cross, his passion, his death, were all close at hand, and he knew it. The approaching destruction of the temple, the scattering of the Jews, the long period of time before his second coming, were all things which were spread before his mind like a picture. Yet we find him taking time to take notice of what was happening around him. He does not consider it beneath him to observe the actions of a poor widow.

Let poor believers take comfort from this great truth. Let them remember daily that their Master in heaven notices everything that is done on earth, and that the lives of cottagers are noticed by him as much as the lives of kings. The acts of a poor believer have as much dignity about them as the acts of a prince. The tiny contributions to the cause of Christianity made by a labourer out of his meagre wages are valued in God's sight as a ten thousand pound note from a peer. To know this thoroughly is one great secret of contentment. To feel that Christ looks at what a man is, and not what a man has, will help to stop us from being envious. Happy is the person who has learned to say with David, 'As for me, I am poor and needy, but the Lord takes thought of me' (Psalm 40:17).

Notes on Luke 21:1–4

1. **Rich people putting their gifts into the treasury.** Major says, 'In the second court of the temple, in the court of the women, were fixed thirteen chests, with inscriptions, directing to what use the offerings in each were allotted. Into one of these the widow put her two very small copper coins. This court was therefore called "the treasury" (John 8:20). These offerings were made at the three great feasts, as tithes and dues, and to fulfill the precept, "no man should appear before the Lord empty-handed"' (Deuteronomy 16:16: see also Exodus 23:15; 2 Kings 12:9).

4. 'Put in all she had to live on.' A person so poor as the widow would, from necessity, have to live from hand to mouth, and own no property or capital except what she received on a daily basis.

The temple's destruction predicted (21:5–9)

Our Lord's words about the temple at Jerusalem

Let us notice, in this passage, our Lord Jesus Christ's words about the temple at Jerusalem. We read that some people said that it was adorned with beautiful stones and gifts dedicated to God (verse 5). They praised it for its outward beauty. They admired its size, its architectural grandeur, and its expensive decorations. But this met no response from our Lord. We read that he said, 'As for these things that you see, the days will come when not one stone will be left upon another; all will be thrown down' (verse 6).

These words were a striking prophecy. They must have startled every Jewish ear that heard them. They were spoken about a building which every Israelite regarded with almost idolatrous veneration. They were spoken of a building which contained an ark, the holy of holies, and the symbolical furniture made to a God-given plan. They were spoken of a building associated with most of the principal names in Jewish history: with David, Solomon, Hezekiah, Josiah, Isaiah, Jeremiah, Ezra, and Nehemiah. They were spoken of a building towards which every devout Jew turned, wherever he was in the world, when he offered up his daily prayers. (See 1 Kings 8:44; Jonah 2:4; Daniel 6:10.) But they were words spoken advisedly. They were spoken to teach us the great truth that the true glory of a place of worship does not consist in outer ornaments. 'The LORD does not see as mortals see' (1 Samuel 16:7). Man looks on the outer appearance of a building, while the Lord looks for spiritual worship, and the presence of the Holy Spirit. In the temple at Jerusalem these things were completely lacking, and therefore Jesus Christ could take no pleasure in it.

Professing Christians should remember our Lord's words. It is right, beyond doubt, that buildings set apart for Christian worship should be worthy for the purpose for which they are used. Whatever is done for Christ should be well done. The house in which the Gospel is preached, and the Word of God read, and prayer offered up, should not lack anything which makes it comely and substantial. But it should never be forgotten that the material part of a Christian church is by far the least important part of it. The most beautiful use of marble, stone, wood, stained glass, are worthless in God's sight, unless there is truth in the pulpit and grace in the congregation. The dens and caves in which the early Christians used to meet were probably far more beautiful in Christ's sight than the noblest cathedral ever erected by man. The temple in which the Lord Jesus

delights most, is a broken and contrite heart, renewed by the Holy Spirit.

Notes on Luke 21:5–9

5. Beautiful stones. The enormous size of the stones which Herod used to build the temple at its last restoration is especially mentioned by Josephus. He says that 'many of them were about twenty-five cubits in length, eight in height, and twelve in breadth.' A cubit was about twenty-two inches.

Gifts. Tacitus, the Roman historian, and Josephus, the Jewish writer, both mention the enormous riches contained in the temple, consisting chiefly of offerings given by pious people, or by rulers who wanted to pay respect to the building. In particular there was a golden vine given by Herod, with clusters of grapes as tall as a man. Many of these offerings were suspended in the portico of the temple, so that everyone could see them.

6. 'Not one stone will be left upon another.' These words were literally fulfilled when Titus took Jerusalem.

National troubles predicted; persecution foretold (21:10–19)

Christ's predictions about the nations of the world

We should note in this passage, Christ's prediction about the nations of the world. He says, 'Nation will rise against nation, and kingdom against kingdom; there will be great earthquakes, and in various places famines and plagues; and there will be dreadful portents and great signs from heaven' (verses 10–11).

Doubtless, these words were partially fulfilled when the Romans took Jerusalem and the Jews were taken into captivity. It was a time of unparalleled desolation for Judea, and the countries around Judea. The last days of the Jewish dispensation were wound up by a struggle which, for bloodshed, misery, and tribulation, has never been equalled since the world began.

But these words also have a further fulfilment. They describe the time which will immediately precede Jesus Christ's second coming. The time of the end will be a time of war, and not of universal peace. The Christian dispensation will pass away like the Jewish one, with wars, tumults, and desolation, as empires and kingdoms crash, as never before. The last days of the earth will be its worst days. The last war will be the most terrible war that ever desolated the earth.

Notes on Luke 21:10–19

11. 'Great earthquakes, … famines and plagues.' These visitations from God were said to be especially frequent and severe in the last days of the Jewish dispensation. In particular, thousands died from famine and pestilence in Jerusalem during the siege, before the city was taken.

Fearful events and great signs from heaven. The following note of Bishop Pearce, deserves reading. 'Josephus has given us a very particular account of the prodigies of this kind which preceded the destruction of Jerusalem. He speaks of a flaming sword seen over the city, and of a comet which appeared there for twelve months. He mentions a light, which for half an hour, shone so bright in the night between the temple and the altar, that it seemed as if it was midday. He takes notice also, of what eye-witnesses told him, that chariots and armed troops were seen fighting in the sky on certain days. He adds, that on the day of Pentecost, when the priests entered into the inner temple, they heard a great noise and voice like a multitude, crying out, "Let us leave here." The substance of this account is also given by Tacitus, the Roman historian.'

There seems no reason to doubt the correctness of Josephus' report. As an unconverted Jew he had no motive for confirming statements contained in the Gospels.

13. **'This will give you an opportunity to testify.'** This seems to mean, 'sufferings of the Christians will prove evidence about the truth of Christianity.'

14. This was not intended to encourage ministers to neglect sermon preparation. It was spoken for the comfort of persecuted Christians. It was fulfilled in the Acts of the Apostles, as well as in the trials of many martyrs in modern times.

17. **'You will be hated by all because of my name.'** This shows that universal popularity is not a thing that Christians should covet, or greatly value, should it come to them. The Christian about whom everyone speaks well can hardly be a faithful person.

The destruction of Jerusalem, and tribulation of Israel (21:20–24)

The subject before us is the taking of Jerusalem by the Romans. It was appropriate that this great event, which ended the Old Testament dispensation, should be especially described by our Lord. It was fitting that the last days of that holy city, which had been the seat of God's presence for so many centuries, should receive a special mention in the greatest prophecy which was ever delivered to the church.

Notes on Luke 21:20–24

20. **'When you see Jerusalem surrounded by armies.'** The following facts of history are well worth noting. They show in a remarkable way how the words of our Lord in this verse came about. It appears that three years before the siege

of Jerusalem by Titus, the Roman army under Cestius unaccountably and without any apparent reason withdrew again, although the city might have been easily taken. This made a large number of the inhabitants of Jerusalem take fright, and flee the city, as soon as the Roman army withdrew. In the words of Josephus, 'they swam away, as from a ship about to sink.' Among those who escaped were the Christians, some of them going to Pella, and some to Mount Libanus. The result of this was, that when the last great war, under Vespasian and Titus, broke out shortly afterwards, the Christians almost entirely escaped its desolation.

21. **'Flee to the mountains.'** Major remarks, 'These were the mountains to the north-east of Jerusalem, towards the source of the Jordan, the territories of Agrippa. He continued faithful to the Romans, and so the Christians avoided the destruction which overtook Judea.'

24. **'They will fall by the edge of the sword.'** Josephus records that 110,000 Jews died by sword or famine during the siege of Jerusalem.

Taken as prisoners to all the nations. Josephus records that 97,000 Jews were taken away as prisoners. Most of them were sent as slaves into Egypt, or dispersed over the provinces of the Roman Empire, to be thrown to the wild beasts in the amphitheatres.

The second coming, and the signs preceding it (21:25–33)

The theme of this part of our Lord's great prophecy is his own second coming to judge the world. The strong wording in the passage appears inappropriate to any event less important than this. To confine these words to the capture of Jerusalem by the Romans, is to unnaturally strain the language of Scripture.

Watching out for the signs of our Lord's second coming

We see in the passage the necessity of watching out for the signs of the times which are linked to our Lord's second coming. Our Lord teaches this lesson with a parable: 'Look at the fig tree and all the trees; as soon as they sprout leaves you can see for yourselves and know that summer is near. So also, when you see these things taking place, you know that the kingdom of God is near' (verses 29–31). In their ignorance, the disciples supposed that the Messiah's kingdom would be ushered in by universal peace. In contrast to this, our Lord tells them that the signs immediately preceding his return would be war, and distress.

The general lesson from these verses is that we should observe carefully the public events of the times in which we live. We are not to be absorbed in politics, but we are to observe political events. We are not to turn into prophets ourselves but we are to study diligently the signs of the times. If we do this, the day of Christ's second coming will not catch us entirely unawares.

Notes on Luke 21:25–33

26. 'People will faint from fear.' Schleusner says this signifies, 'to become not dead, but as if dead.'

27. 'The Son of Man coming.' I think these words can only be interpreted in one way. They describe a literal personal coming of the Lord Jesus Christ, who ascended up in a cloud before the eyes of the disciples from Mount Olivet (Acts 1:9–12).

28. 'Your redemption.' The word redemption is used here in the same sense that it is used in Romans 8:23; Ephesians 1:14; 4:30. It signifies that full and complete redemption of the believer which will be accomplished when his body is raised again, and soul and body once more united. From the guilt and power of sin believers are redeemed already; but from all the humbling consequences of sin they will not be completely redeemed until Jesus comes again, and calls them from their graves at the last day.

32. 'This generation will not pass away until all things have taken place.' I think that the best way to interpret this is to say that 'this generation' means the Jewish nation. They had been spoken of by our Lord in this prophecy: their captivity and scattering had been plainly predicted. The disciples might naturally wonder how such a prediction could be reconciled with the many promises of glory to Israel in the Old Testament prophets. Our Lord answers their thoughts by declaring that this nation, the 'Jewish people' as a separate people, will not pass away. Though cast down, they would not be destroyed. Though scattered, they would one day be gathered together again before everything was fulfilled.

Of course the correctness of this view turns entirely on the question, whether the Greek word translated generation will honestly bear the sense of 'nation,' or 'people.' My own belief is that it will bear the sense, and that it does really bear it in many places in the New Testament, such as Matthew 11:16; 12:39; 23:36; Luke 11:50,51; Acts 2:40; Philippians 2:15.

Watch, because of the second coming (21:34–38)

These verses form the practical conclusion to our Lord Jesus Christ's great prophetic discourse. They supply a striking answer to those who condemn the study of unfulfilled prophecy as speculative and unprofitable. It would be hard to find a passage more practical, direct, plain, and heart-searching than this one.

Chapter 22

Judas Iscariot's plot with the chief priests; preparation for the Passover (22:1–13)

Institution of the Lord's Supper (22:14–23)

Love of preeminence reproved; true greatness explained; rewards promised (22:24–30)

Peter warned; the purse and sword recommended (22:31–38)

Agony in the garden (22:39–46)

Christ taken prisoner (22:47–53)

Peter's denial of Christ (22:54–62)

Christ insulted, and condemned by chief priests (22:63–71)

Judas Iscariot's plot with the chief priests; preparation for the Passover (22:1–13)

The opening of this chapter begins St. Luke's account of our Lord's suffering and death. No part of the Gospels is so important as this. The death of Christ was the life of the world. No part of our Lord's ministry is so fully given by all the Gospel writers as this: only two of them describe Christ's birth, all four dwell in minute detail on Christ's death. And of the four, no one gives us such a full and detailed account as St. Luke.

Religious leaders can sin

We see in these verses, that high offices in the church do not stop the holders of them from great blindness and sin. We read that the chief priests and the teachers of the law were looking for some way to get rid of Jesus (verse 2).

The first step in putting Christ to death was taken by the religious teachers of the Jewish nation. The very men who ought to have welcomed the Messiah were the men who conspired to kill him; the very pastors who ought to have rejoiced at the appearing of the Lamb of God had the main part in killing him. They sat in Moses' seat: they claimed to be guides of the blind and lights to those who were in darkness (Romans 2:19). They belonged to the tribe of Levi. Most of them were in direct succession and descent from Aaron, yet they were the very men who crucified the Lord of glory! With all their professed knowledge, they were far more ignorant than the few Galilean fishermen who followed Christ.

Let us beware of attaching an excessive importance to ministers of religion because of their office. Orders and ranks confer no exemption from error. We must try all teachers by the unerring rule of the Word of God. It matters little who says a thing in religion; but it matters greatly what it is that is said. Is it scriptural? Is it true? This is the only question. See Isaiah 8:20.

Notes on Luke 22:1–13

3. Then Satan entered into Judas. Calvin remarks on these words: 'Though Satan drives us every day to crime, and reigns in us when he hurries us into a course of extraordinary wickedness, yet he is said to enter into the reprobate when he takes possession of all their senses, overthrows the fear of God, extinguishes the light of reason, and destroys every feeling of shame.'

10. 'A man carrying a jar of water will meet you.' Here, as in other places, we should note our Lord's perfect knowledge. He mentions a number of circumstances in this and the following verses, with as much minuteness and precision as if the whole transaction had been previously arranged. And yet the disciples found things exactly as he had said they would.

Institution of the Lord's Supper (22:14–23)

These verses contain St. Luke's account of the institution of the Lord's Supper. It is a passage which every true Christian will always read with deep interest. How sad it seems that an ordinance, so beautifully simple at its first appointment, should have been obscured and made into a mystery by human inventions. What an example this is of human corruption, that some of the bitterest controversies which have disturbed the church have been about the Lord's table. Great indeed is people's ingenuity in perverting God's gifts. The ordinance which should have been for their benefit is too often made an occasion of their falling.

The Lord's Supper reminds us of Christ's death

We should notice in these verses, that the principal object of the Lord's supper was to remind Christians of Christ's death for sinners. In appointing the Lord's supper, Jesus distinctly tells his disciples that they were to do what they did 'in remembrance' of him (verse 19). In one word the Lord's supper is not a sacrifice, it is a commemorative ordinance.

The bread that believers eat at the Lord's table is intended to remind them of Christ's body given to die on the cross of their sins. The wine they drink is intended to remind them about Christ's blood shed to make atonement for their transgressions. The whole ordinance was meant to keep fresh in their memory the sacrifice of Christ on the cross, and the satisfaction which that sacrifice made for the sin of the world. The two elements of bread and wine were intended to preach Christ crucified as our substitute, under obvious emblems. They were to be a visible sermon, appealing to the believer's senses, and teaching the foundation truth of the Gospel, that Christ's death on the cross is the life of man's soul.

The less mystery and obscurity we attach to the Lord's supper, the better will it be for our souls. We should reject with abhorrence the unscriptural notion that there is any oblation or sacrifice in it, that the substance of the bread and wine is at all changed, or that the mere formal act of receiving the sacrament can do any good to the soul. We should cling firmly to the great principle laid down at its institution that it is eminently a commemorative ordinance, and that reception of it without faith and thankful remembrance of Christ's death can do us no good. The words of the Church of England Catechism are wise and true: 'It was ordained for the continual remembrance of the sacrifice of the death of Christ.' The declaration of the Thirty-Nine Articles is clear: 'The means whereby the body of Christ is received and taken in the supper is faith.' The exhortation of the Prayer Book points out the only way in which we can feed on Christ: 'Feed on him in your hearts by faith with thanksgiving.' Last, but not least, the caution of the Book of Homilies is most instructive: 'Let us take heed lest of the memory it be made a sacrifice.'

Notes on Luke 22:14–23

15. 'Before I suffer.' Alford remarks that this is the only place in the Gospels where this absolute use of the word 'suffer' is found.

16.2 'Until it is fulfilled.' This means that our Lord 'would never eat this Passover again.' Macknight observes, 'The particle "until," both here and in verse 18, does not imply that after the accomplishment of the salvation of men our Lord was to eat the Passover. It is a Hebrew expression, signifying that the thing mentioned was no more to be done forever. So it is said in Samuel, "Samuel did not see Saul again until the day of his death" (1 Samuel 15:35). That is, he saw him no more at all.'

19. 'This is my body.' It is almost needless to remark that the Protestant view of these words is the only satisfactory one: 'This represents and is an emblem of my body.' To a Jewish ear the expression would be simple and intelligible. There is no word in the Syriac or Hebrew which expresses 'to signify or represent.' (See Genesis 40:12; Daniel 7:24; Revelation 1:20; John 15:1–5).

'**Do this.**' The Roman Catholics struggle hard to make out that these words mean 'Offer up this sacrifice,' and that the words were especially intended to be confined to priests consecrating the bread and wine, and offering it up as a sacrifice in the mass. The idea will not bear calm examination. The natural meaning of the words is a command addressed to all disciples: 'Practise this,' 'Do what I have just showed you,' 'Keep up the ordinance I have just appointed,' 'Break, take, eat this bread in all ages, in remembrance of me.'

20. 'This cup … is the new covenant.' It is clear that a 'cup' is not literally a covenant or testament. The Roman Catholic who contends that in the former verse, where our Lord says, 'This is my body,' he meant 'This is my literal body, really and truly,' will find it hard to explain our Lord's meaning here. The Protestant view, that in both cases our Lord meant 'this bread represents my body,' and 'this cup represents the new covenant which is ratified by my blood,' is the only rational and satisfactory view.

If our Lord had really meant that what he gave his disciples was literally his 'blood,' it seems impossible to understand the calmness with which they received this announcement. They were all Jews, and as Jews they had all been taught from infancy that to eat blood was a great sin. They evidently understood the words as Protestants do now. (See Leviticus 3:17; 7:26.)

21. 'The one who betrays me is with me.' Clearly Judas Iscariot was at the first Lord's supper. Burkitt remarks, 'Nothing is more ordinary than for unholy people to press into the holy ordinances of God what they have no right to. Yet their presence pollutes the ordinance only to themselves.'

22. 'Woe to that one by whom he is betrayed!' Augustine remarks, 'God is said to will things, in the way of permission, which he does not will in the way of approbation.'

Bishop Hall says, 'It is the greatest praise of God's wisdom that he can turn the sins of man to his own glory.'

Love of preeminence reproved; true greatness explained; rewards promised (22:24–30)

Notes on Luke 22:24–30

30. 'Sit on thrones judging.' This 'judging' probably means that the apostles will have a preeminent place in the government of Israel, after Christ has come again and the Jews have been restored to their own land. It is clear that the word 'judge' in many places in the Bible means nothing more than 'ruling or governing,' and has no reference to passing a judicial sentence.

'The twelve tribes of Israel.' The twelve tribes are mentioned four times in the New Testament, here, and in Matthew 19:28; Acts 26:7; and James 1:1. It is clear that although the ten tribes never came back from captivity, they were regarded in the New Testament time as still existing, distinct and separate, and not lost and mingled with other nations. We should not

doubt that they still exist today and will one day be seen again by the world.

Peter warned; the purse and sword recommended (22:31–38)

The secret behind the believer's perseverance

We learn in these verses, one great secret of a believer's perseverance in the faith. We read that our Lord said to Peter, 'I have prayed for you that your own faith may not fail' (verse 32). Peter did not completely fall away because of our Lord's intercession.

The continued existence of grace in a believer's heart is a great and constant miracle. His enemies are so mighty, and his strength is so small; the world is so full of traps, and his heart is so weak, that it seems, at first sight, impossible for him to reach heaven. This passage explains how he is kept safe. He has a mighty Friend at the right hand of God, who always lives to intercede for him. He has a watchful Advocate, who is daily pleading for him, seeing all his daily necessities, and obtaining daily supplies of mercy and grace for his soul. His grace never totally dies, because Christ lives to intercede (Hebrews 7:25).

Notes on Luke 22:31–38

32. 'I have prayed for you.' This is an example of our Lord's office as intercessor for his people. What he did for Peter, when Peter knew nothing of his danger, he is daily and hourly doing for all who believe in his name.

'That your own faith may not fail.' Note that faith is the root of the whole Christian character, and the part which Satan especially works to overthrow. In the temptation of Eve, of Peter, and of our Lord himself, the assault was in each case directed against the same point, and the object sought was to produce unbelief.

'When once you have turned back.' Burkitt remarks, 'This conversion was not from a state of sin: Peter was so converted before; but it was from an act of sin into which he should lapse and relapse.'

'Strengthen your brothers.' Alford says that the Greek word for strengthen here is twice used by Peter in his two letters, and the word 'steadfastness,' which is also used, is directly derived from it. (1 Peter 5:10; 2 Peter 1:12; 2 Peter 3:17.)

37. 'This scripture must be fulfilled in me.' When our Lord refers to his impending crucifixion, he does not merely speak of it as his 'death.' He especially describes it as him being numbered with the transgressors. This reminds us that the main purpose of his death was not to be an example of self-denial, but to be a substitute for us, a sacrifice for us, to become sin for us, and be made a curse for us.

38. 'Here are two swords.' 'It is enough.' The disciples did not understand our Lord here. Our Lord, seeing their dullness of understanding, dismisses the subject. The disciples took his words about the swords literally, but he was talking figuratively. If they could not see his meaning now, they would later. At present he had said **enough**, and for wise reasons would say no more.

Agony in the garden (22:39–46)

These verses contain St. Luke's account of our Lord's agony in the garden. It is a passage of Scripture which we should always approach with special reverence. The event it records is one of the deep things of God. While we read it, the words of Exodus should come to our minds, 'Take off your sandals, for the place where you are standing is holy ground' (Exodus 3:5).

What to do in times of trouble

We see in this passage, an example of what believers ought to do in times of trouble. The great Head of the church himself supplies the pattern. We are told that when he came to the Mount of Olives, the night before he was crucified, he ... **knelt down, and prayed** (verse 41).

It is a striking fact that both the Old and New Testaments give the same prescription about coping with trouble. What do the Psalms say? 'Call on me in the day of trouble; I will deliver you' (Psalm 50:15). What does the apostle James say? 'Are any among you suffering? They should pray' (James 5:13). Prayer is the prescription which Jacob used when he was frightened by his brother Esau; prayer is the prescription which Hezekiah used when Sennacherib's threatening letter arrived, and prayer is the prescription which the Son of God himself was not ashamed to use in the days of his flesh. In the hour of his mysterious agony he prayed.

Let us take care that we use our Master's remedy, if we want comfort in affliction. Whatever other means of relief we use, let us pray. The first Friend we should turn to should be God. The first message we should send should be to the throne of grace. Beware of the temptation to brood sullenly over wounds. If we can say nothing else, we can say, 'O Lord, I am oppressed; be my security!' (Isaiah 38:14).

Notes on Luke 22:39–46

39. As was his custom. There was one particular place on the Mount of Olives to which our Lord was in the habit of going, which was well known to his disciples, including Judas Iscariot. So Judas, although it was night, could lead our Lord's enemies to the exact place where his Master was.

40. 'Pray that you may not come into the time of trial.' To be assaulted by temptation is one thing, but to enter into it quite another. We cannot avoid the attack, but we not obliged to give way to it. We cannot prevent temptation coming to us, but it is our own fault if we **enter into temptation**.

42. 'This cup.' Doddridge says about this word, 'It was customary among the ancients to assign to each guest at a feast a particular cup, as well as a dish, and by the kind and quantity of the liquor contained in it, the respect of the entertained was expressed. Hence the word "cup" came in general to signify a portion assigned, whether of pleasure or sorrow.' (See Psalm 11:6; 73:10: 75:8; Isaiah 51:17; Jeremiah 25:15; Matthew 20:23.)

'Not my will, but yours be done.' At no period in our Lord's earthly ministry does the reality of his manhood come out so clearly as in his agony in the garden, and his death on the cross. As man, he endured temptation for us, and overcame Satan; as man he showed the intensity of his sufferings by bloody sweat, strong crying and tears; as man he was thirsty on the cross and said, 'My God, why have you forsaken me?' The infinite merit of his passion unquestionably arose from the inseparable union of his Godhead and his manhood. But the nature which is most prominently brought before us in his passion is his nature as man.

43. An angel from heaven appeared. This verse gives additional proof that our Lord was really man. As man, he was for a little time 'made a little lower than the angels' (Hebrews 2:9). As man, he condescended to receive comfort from angelic ministry. As man, he was willing to receive an expression of sympathy from angels, which the weakness of his disciples prevented them from giving.

44. In his anguish. Hundreds of martyrs have suffered the most painful deaths without any such demonstrations of mental and bodily agony as are here recorded in the case of our Lord. How are we to account for this? How are we to explain the remarkable circumstance that our Lord appears to have felt more distressed than many a martyr had done at the prospect of being burned alive, or even when at the stake?

The only satisfactory explanation of Christ's intense agony is the old doctrine of imputed sin. He had engaged to die for our sins. His death was a vicarious death. As our substitute, he was about to bear our iniquities, to suffer for us, and to pay our debts to God with his own blood. He was about to be counted a sinner, and be punished, that we might be counted righteous, and be delivered from punishment. This sin of the world began to be laid on him in a special way in the garden. He was being 'made a curse' for us, by bearing our sins. This was the principal reason for his agony and bloody sweat. The words of Isaiah were being fulfilled (see Isaiah 53:6,10).

The following quotations on this most important subject are worth reading.

Baxter says, 'This agony was not from the fear of death, but from the deep sense of God's wrath against sin, which he as our sacrifice was to bear, in greater pain than mere dying, which his servants often bear with peace.'

Sir Matthew Hale, quoted by Ford, says, 'Christ stood under the imputation of all our sins; and though he was personally innocent, yet judicially and by way of imputation, he was the greatest offender that ever was. As our Lord was pleased to be our representative in bearing our sins, and to stand in our stead, so all these affections and motions of his soul did bear the same conformity as if acted by us. As he put on the person of the sinner, so he put on the same sorrow, the same shame, the same trembling, under the apprehension of the wrath of his Father, that we must have done. And as an imputed sin drew with it the obligation to punishment, so it did by necessary consequences raise all those storms and compassions in the soul of Christ as it would have done in the person of a sinner, sin only excepted.'

Christ taken prisoner (22:47–53)

Note on Luke 22:47–53

51. He touched his ear and healed him. There are several remarkable things about this miracle. It is the only instance in the Gospels of our Lord healing a fresh wound caused by external violence. It is a striking instance of a miracle worked on an enemy, unasked for, without faith in the person healed, and without any apparent thankfulness for the cure. It is an extraordinary proof of the wickedness and hardness of our Lord's enemies, that so wonderful a miracle as this could be wrought without any effect being produced on them. Some think that in the darkness the miracle was not seen by anyone except those immediately around Malchus.

Peter's denial of Christ (22:54–62)

These verses describe the fall of the apostle Peter. It is a passage which is deeply humbling to man's pride, and singularly instructive to true Christians. The fall of Peter has been a beacon to the church, and has probably preserved countless thousands of souls from destruction. It is a passage which supplies strong proof that the Bible is inspired, and Christianity is from God. If the Christian religion had been the invention of uninspired men, its first historians would never have told us that one of its leading apostles denied his Master three times.

Small steps lead to great sins

The story of Peter's fall teaches us how small and gradual are the steps by which people may go down into great sins.

The various steps in Peter's fall are clearly marked out by the Gospel writers. They should always be noted when reading this part of the apostle's life.

The first step was proud self-confidence. Though everyone denied Christ, Peter insisted he never would. He was ready to go with Christ both to prison and to death.

The second step was indolent neglect of prayer. When his Master told him to pray, so that he would not enter into temptation, he gave way to drowsiness, and was found asleep.

The third step was vacillating indecision. When Christ's enemies came up to him, Peter first of all fought, then ran away, then turned again, and finally followed at a distance.

The fourth step was mingling with bad company. He went into the high priest's house and sat among the servants by the fire, trying to conceal his religion, and hearing and seeing all kinds of evil.

The fifth and last step was the natural result of the first four steps. He was overwhelmed with fear when suddenly asked if he was a disciple of Christ's. The rope was around his neck. He could not escape. He plunged deeper into error than ever. He denied his blessed Master three times. The reasons for this, it must be remembered, had been sown before this. The denial was only the disease coming to a head.

Let us beware of the beginnings of backslidings, however small. We never know what we may come to, if we once leave the king's highway. The professing Christian who begins to say about any sin or evil habit, 'It's only a small one,' is in imminent danger. He is sowing seeds in his heart which will one day spring up and bear bitter fruit. A homely saying states that 'if you take care of the pence the pounds will take care of themselves.' We may borrow a good spiritual lesson from the saying: the Christian who keeps his heart diligently in little things will be kept from great falls.

Christ insulted, and condemned by chief priests (22:63–71)

Notes on Luke 22:63–71

69. 'The Son of Man will be seated at the right hand …' This is a reference to Daniel 7:9,14, and that famous prophecy. Our Lord implies that he is the person spoken about in that prophecy, and that, although condemned by the Jews, he would soon be exalted to the highest position of dignity in heaven. The Jews saw this at once, and proceeded to put the question in the next verse. There, it should be noted, is the last occasion on which our Lord ever called himself the 'Son of Man.'

70. 'Are you, then, the Son of God?' In the previous verse our Lord had called himself the

'Son of Man.' His enemies in their question, ask him if he is the 'Son of God.' They did so because his solemn saying about sitting at God's right hand showed them that he claimed to be the Messiah and very God.

Chapter 23

Christ before Pilate; Herod and Pilate reconciled (23:1–12)

Christ declared innocent by Pilate, and yet delivered to be crucified (23:13–25)

Women of Jerusalem warned; Christ's prayer for his murderers (23:26–38)

The penitent thief (23:39–43)

Signs accompanying Christ's death; the centurion's testimony (23:44–49)

Christ's burial by Joseph of Arimathea (23:50–56)

Christ before Pilate: Herod and Pilate reconciled (23:1–12)

Notes on Luke 23:1–12

1. Brought Jesus before Pilate. Pilate was the Roman Governor of Judea. Without him the Jews had no power to put our Lord to death. The mere fact that they were obliged to apply publicly to a foreign ruler to carry out their murderous plan was a striking proof that the 'sceptre had departed from Judah' (Genesis 49:10) when the Messiah came.

2. 'Forbidding us to pay taxes.' The duplicity and dishonesty of this charge are evident. When the enemies of our Lord wanted to bring him into disfavour with the Jews, they had asked him 'Is it lawful for us to pay taxes to the emperor or not?' (Luke 20:22). But now when they want to make him out to be an offender before the Roman Governor, they accuse him of forbidding paying taxes to Caesar the Roman Emperor. This false charge is as striking as it is dishonest.

3. 'You say so.' St. Paul refers to this saying when he tells Timothy that our Lord 'in his testimony before Pontius Pilate made the good confession' (1 Timothy 6:13).

5. They are insistent. The Greek word here, literally, means, 'they grew more strong, more violent, more urgent: they persisted in their accusation.'

7. He sent him off to Herod. This Herod was Herod Antipas the same Herod who killed John the Baptist. He was son of Herod the Great, who had all the children of two years and younger to be killed in Bethlehem. He was uncle of Herod Agrippa who killed the apostle James with the sword, and would have killed Peter if he had not been miraculously rescued from prison.

The family of the Herods was Idumaean. They were all descended from Esau, the father of Edom. The detail is worth noting, when we see their constant opposition against Christ and his followers. The seed of Esau seems to carry on the old enmity against the seed of Jacob.

11. Sent him back to Pilate. We are told that neither the ruler of Galilee nor the ruler of Judea could find any fault in our Lord. In Galilee most of his miracles had been performed, and he had spent much of his time there. Yet the ruler of Galilee accused him of nothing. He was to be crucified as 'a lamb without blemish or spot.'

12. Herod and Pilate became friends. Theophylact remarks on this verse that 'It is matter of shame to Christians, that while the devil can persuade wicked men to lay aside their enmities in order to do harm, Christians cannot even keep up friendship in order to do good.'

Christ declared innocent by Pilate, and yet delivered to be crucified (23:13–25)

Our Lord's innocence

We should observe in this passage, what striking testimony was borne to our Lord Jesus Christ's perfect innocence by his judges.

We are told that Pilate said to the Jews, '**You brought me this man as one who is perverting the people; and here I have examined him in your presence and have not found this man guilty of any charges against him. Neither has Herod …**' (verse 14). The Roman and the Galilean Governors were both of one mind. Both agreed in pronouncing our Lord not guilty of the things laid to his charge.

There was a special appropriateness in this public declaration of Christ's innocence. Our Lord was about to be offered up as a sacrifice for our sins. It was fitting that those who examined him should formally pronounce him guiltless and blameless. It was right that the Lamb of God should be found by those who slew him 'a lamb without defect or blemish' (1 Peter 1:19). God's providential hand so ordered the events of his trial that even when his enemies were judges they could not find any fault with him or prove anything against him.

Notes on Luke 23:13–25

14. 'Have not found this man guilty of any charges against him.' Burgon remarks here that we ought to notice 'how many and what various people bear testimony to the innocence of the Holy One: Pilate, Herod, Pilate's wife, Judas Iscariot, the thief on the cross, and the centurion' who supervised the crucifixion. We cannot doubt that this was specially overruled by God's providence.

21. 'Crucify, crucify him!' Crucifixion was not only the most painful, but the most ignominious and disgraceful death, to which a person could be sentenced. Bishop Pearson remarks, 'By the ignominy of this punishment we are taught how far our Saviour descended for us, that while we were slaves, and in the bondage of sin, he might redeem us by a servile death.'

25. As they wished. This means 'the will of the Jews.' Here, and throughout St. Luke's account of our Lord's passion, much less is made of the role of the Roman soldiers than in the other Gospels. The reason is simple. St. Luke wrote especially for Gentile Christians. He wanted to emphasize that although our Lord was crucified under Pontius Pilate, the people most to blame for his death were not Gentiles, but Jews.

Women of Jerusalem warned; Christ's prayer for his murderers (23:26–38)

Notes on Luke 23:26–38

26. They seized a man, Simon of Cyrene. It would appear that our Lord carried his cross himself until he was exhausted, and that after this Simon was pressed into carrying it, by the soldiers.

Nothing certain is known about this Simon, although his sons Alexander and Rufus are mentioned in Mark 15:2. This would lead us to suppose that Simon was a disciple of Christ when Mark wrote his Gospel, whatever he was at the time of the crucifixion.

27. A great number of people followed him, and among them were women. Burgon quotes a remark, 'That no woman is mentioned as speaking against our Lord in his life, or having a share in his death. On the contrary, he was anointed by a woman for his burial, women were the last at his grave and the first at his resurrection, to a woman he first appeared when he rose again, women ministered to his needs, women bewailed and lamented for him, a pagan woman pleaded with her husband, Pilate, for his life, and, above all, of a woman he was born.'

31. 'When the wood is green … it is dry.' Our Lord contrasts himself and the Jewish nation. 'If the Romans practise such cruelties on me, who am I a green tree, and the very source of life, what will they do one day to your nation, which is like a barren, withered trunk, dead in trespasses and sins?'

32. With the criminals. This is in literal fulfilment of Isaiah's prophecy that the Messiah would be 'numbered with the transgressors' (Isaiah 53:12).

33. They came to the place that is called The Skull. The commonly held opinion that Calvary was a mount or hill is destitute of any foundation in Scripture. All four Gospel writers speak of it as 'a place.' None of them calls it a 'mount.'

34. 'Father, forgive them.' These words were probably spoken while our Lord was being nailed to the cross, or as soon as the cross was set up on end. It is worth noting that as soon as the blood of the Great Sacrifice began to flow the Great High Priest began to intercede.

During the six hours that our Lord was on the cross he showed that he possessed full power as the Son of God, and that, although he suffered, his sufferings were undertaken voluntarily. As King and Prophet he opened the gates of life to the penitent thief, and foretold his entry into paradise. As Priest, he intercedes, in this prayer, for those who crucified him.

They cast lots to divide up his clothing. Our Lord evidently was crucified naked. The shame of such a posture in death must doubtless have added much to the misery of the punishment of crucifixion.

38. 'This is the King of the Jews.' Observe that our Lord was crucified, in the end, as a King. He came to set up a spiritual kingdom, and as a King he died.

The penitent thief (23:39–43)

These verses should be printed in letters of gold. They have probably been the salvation of countless thousands of souls. Multitudes will thank God for all eternity that the Bible contains the story of the penitent thief.

God's sovereignty

We see in the story before us, the sovereignty of God in saving sinners. We are told that two criminals were crucified along with our Lord, one on his right hand and the other on his left. Both were equally close to Christ. Both saw and heard all that happened, during the six hours that he hung on the cross. Both were dying men, and suffering acute pain. Both were equally sinners, and needed forgiveness. Yet one died in his sins, as he had lived, hardened, impenitent and unbelieving; the other repented, believed, cried to Jesus for mercy, and was saved.

A fact like this should teach us humility. We cannot account for it. We can only say, 'Yes, Father, for such was your gracious will' (Matthew 11:26). How is it that under precisely the same circumstances one man is converted and another remains dead in sins? Why is it that the same sermon which is heard by one person with complete indifference sends another person home to pray and seek Christ? Why is the Gospel hidden from one person and revealed to another person? We have no answer to these questions. We only know that it is so, and that it is useless to deny it.

Our own duty is plain. We are to make a diligent use of all the means which God has appointed for the good of souls. 'In all our doings,' says the seventeenth of the Thirty-Nine

Articles, 'that will of God is to be followed, which we have expressly declared to us in the Word of God. God's sovereignty was never meant to destroy man's responsibility. 'One thief was saved that no sinner might despair; but only one, that no sinner might presume.'

Notes on Luke 23:39–43

42. 'Jesus, remember me.' The remarks of Ness on this wonderful prayer are worth reading.

This short prayer contained a very large and long creed, the articles whereof are these.
1. He believed that the soul died not with the body of man.
2. That there is a world to come for rewarding the pious and penitent, and for punishing the impious and impenitent.
3. That Christ though now under crucifying and killing tortures, yet had a right to a kingdom.
4. That this kingdom was in a better world than the present evil world.
5. That Christ would not keep this kingdom all to himself.
6. That he would bestow a part and portion thereof on those that be truly penitent.
7. That the key of this kingdom did hang at Christ's girdle, though he now hung dying on the cross.
8. That he does roll his whole soul for eternal salvation upon a dying Saviour.

43. 'Today you will be with me in Paradise.' This sentence deserves close attention. It is a distinct answer to the Roman Catholic doctrine of purgatory. It shows clearly that no purification of any kind after death is needed for the person that dies a penitent believer. If the thief needed no purgatory, the whole doctrine of purgatory falls to the ground.

It is an instructive intimation about the state of believers after death. The moment they die they are 'with Christ.' Their condition, of course, is one we cannot pretend to explain. We cannot comprehend that state of a soul separate from the body. It is enough for us to know that a dead believer is immediately with Christ.

It is clear proof of the separate existence of the soul when the body is dead. We shall live and have a being even when our earthly tabernacle is mouldering in the grave. The thief's body was that day to be broken and mangled by the Roman soldiers. But the thief himself was to be with Christ.

'In paradise.' Heinsius remarks that Christ never performed a more illustrious miracle than he did in saving the penitent thief.

The Church of England Homily of Good Works quotes Chrysostom saying: 'I can show a man that by faith without deeds lived and came

to heaven: but without faith never man had life. The thief, who was hanged when Christ suffered, did believe only, and the most merciful God justified him. And because no man shall say, that he lacked time to do good deeds, for else he would have done them, truth it is, I will not contend therein. But this I will surely affirm, that faith only saved him.'

Luther says, 'This is a comfortable symbol and example for all Christians, how that God will never let faith in Christ and a confession of his name go down. If the disciples as a body, and those otherwise related to Christ, confess not and lose their faith, deny him in fear, are offended and forsake him, this malefactor and murderer must come forward and confess him, to preach him to others, and teach all men who he is and what consolation all may find in him.'

Signs accompanying Christ's death; the centurion's testimony (23:44–49)

Miraculous signs accompany our Lord's death

Let us observe, in these verses, the miraculous signs which accompanied our Lord's death on the cross. We are told that **darkness came over the whole land** (verse 44). **The sun's light failed; and the curtain of the temple was torn in two** (verse 45).

It was right that everyone in Jerusalem should focus on the great sacrifice for sin which was being offered and on the Son of God who was dying. There were signs and wonders wrought for all the Israelites to see when the law was given at Sinai. Similarly, there were signs and wonders when the atoning blood of Christ was shed on Calvary. There was a sign for an unbelieving world. The darkness at midday was a miracle which would force people to think. There was a sign for the professing church and the ministers of the temple. The tearing of the veil which hung between the holy place and the Most Holy Place was a miracle which would strike awe into the heart of every priest and Levite in Jewry.

Signs like these, on special occasions, are part of God's way of communicating with men and women. God knows how stupid and unbelieving mankind is. It is necessary for him to arouse our attention with miraculous deeds, as he ushers in a new dispensation. See Hebrews 12:26; Isaiah 24:23.

Notes on Luke 23:44–49

44. **It was now about noon.** Our Lord was crucified at 9 a.m. (the Jewish third hour). The darkness started at the 12 noon or 'sixth hour'. So this supernatural darkness existed during the brightest part of the day, from 12 noon to 3 p.m. Jesus hung on the cross for six hours before he gave up his spirit.

Darkness came over the whole land. This was a miraculous darkness. It could not have been an eclipse of the sun, because our Lord's crucifixion took place at the Passover, and the Passover was always kept at the full moon, when an eclipse of the sun is impossible.

45. The curtain of the temple was torn in two. This miracle must have been as striking and terrible to the priests who ministered in the temple, as the darkness was to the inhabitants of Palestine. It signified the opening of the way into the holiest by Christ's death – the passing away of the Jewish dispensation, and the revelation of the Gospel way of salvation to all mankind.

47. 'Certainly this man was innocent.' Alford translates the Greek here, 'truly this man was innocent, or just.'

Christ's burial by Joseph of Arimathea (23:50–56)

Christ has some little-known disciples

We see, from these verses, that Christ has some disciples about whom little is known. We are told of one Joseph, a good and righteous man (verse 50), a man who had not agreed to their plan and action. He was waiting expectantly for the kingdom of God (verse 51). This man went boldly to Pilate after the crucifixion, asked for Jesus' body, took it down from the cross, and laid it in a rock-hewn tomb (verse 53).

We know nothing about Joseph apart from what we are told here. He is not mentioned in the letters of the New Testament or in the Acts of the Apostles, and he does not feature in our Lord's ministry anywhere. We do not know why he did not openly join the disciples before. But here, at the eleventh hour, this man is not afraid to show himself as one of our Lord's friends. When the apostles had forsaken Jesus, Joseph is not ashamed to show his love and respect. Others had confessed him while he was living and doing miracles, but it was reserved for Joseph to confess him when he was dead.

Let us learn from Joseph of Arimathea to be charitable and hopeful in all our judgments. All is not barren in this world, when our eyes perhaps see nothing. There may be some latent sparks of light when all appears to be dark. Little plants of spiritual life may be existing in some remote Roman Catholic, or Greek Orthodox, or Armenian congregation. Grains of true faith may be lying hidden in some neglected English parish, which have been placed there by God. There were seven thousand true worshippers in Israel of whom Elijah knew nothing. The day of judgment will bring forward people who seemed last, and place them among the first (1 Kings 19:18).

Notes on Luke 23:50–56

51. Waiting expectantly for the kingdom of God. This expression reminds us about the words spoken of Simeon and Anna. Joseph expected the Messiah's spiritual kingdom to be set up, and believed that Jesus was the Messiah.

53. He took it down, wrapped it in a linen cloth. This deserves special note. It is absurd to suppose that the nails could have been withdrawn from our Lord's hands and feet, and the body prepared for burial by wrapping it in linen, without some signs of life being perceived, if life had remained in him. To see the vastness of the miracle of Christ's resurrection, it is essential to be thoroughly convinced that Christ really died.

Where no one had ever been laid. This detail is specially mentioned to show that no other body but our Lord's was in the tomb, and that the person who rose was Jesus Christ, and no one else.

56. Prepared spices and ointments. This shows that the women were fully satisfied that our Lord was dead, and had no expectation that he would rise again.

Chapter 24

The women's visit to the tomb; unbelief of the apostles (24:1–12)

The walk to Emmaus (24:13–31)

Christ's appearance to the eleven (24:36–43)

Christ's last instructions to the eleven (24:44–49)

The ascension (24:50–53)

The women's visit to the tomb; the unbelief of the first apostles (24:1–12)

The resurrection of Christ is one of the great foundation stones of the Christian religion: in practical importance it is second only to the crucifixion. The chapter sets out the evidence of the resurrection. It contains unanswerable proof that Jesus not only died, but rose again.

The reality of Christ's resurrection

We see, in these verses the reality of Christ's resurrection. We read that on the first day of the week certain women came to the tomb where Jesus' body had been laid, to anoint him (verse 1). But when they came to the place, they found the stone rolled away from the tomb, but when they went in, they did not find the body (verses 2–3).

This simple fact is the starting point in the history of the resurrection of Christ. On Friday evening his body was safe in the tomb; on

Sunday morning the body was gone. Who had taken it away? Surely not the priests and teachers of the law and other enemies of Christ. If they had taken Christ's body to discredit his resurrection they would have gladly produced it and shown it to everyone. The apostles and other disciples of the Lord were far too frightened and dispirited to attempt such a thing, especially as they had nothing to gain by it. One explanation, and one only, can meet the circumstance of the case. That explanation is the one supplied by the angels: 'he ... has risen' (verse 5). To seek him in the tomb was seeking 'the living among the dead' (verse 5). He had risen again, and was soon seen alive and talking by many credible witnesses.

The fact of our Lord's resurrection rests on evidence which no pagan can ever explain away. It is confirmed by testimony of every kind and description. The plain unvarnished story which the Gospel writers tell about it is one that cannot be overthrown; the more the account they give is examined, the more inexplicable the event seems, unless we accept it as true. If we choose to deny the truth of their account we may deny everything in the world. It is not so certain that Julius Caesar once lived, as it is that Christ rose again.

Let us cling firmly to the resurrection of Christ, as one of the pillars of the Gospel. It ought to produce in our minds a settled conviction of the truth of Christianity: our faith does not depend merely on a set of texts and doctrines; it is founded on a mighty fact which the skeptic has never been able to overturn. It should assure us of the certainty of the resurrection of our own bodies after death. If our Master has risen from the grave, we need not doubt that his disciples will rise again at the last day. Above all, it should fill our hearts with a joyful sense of the fullness of Gospel salvation. Who is to condemn us? Our great Surety has not only died for us but risen again (Romans 8:24). He has gone to prison for us, and come out triumphantly after atoning for our sins. The payment he made for us has been accepted: the work of satisfaction has been perfectly accomplished. No wonder St. Peter exclaims, 'Blessed be the God and Father of our Lord Jesus Christ! By his great mercy he has given us a new birth into a living hope through the resurrection of Jesus Christ from the dead' (1 Peter 1:3).

Notes on Luke 24:1–12

1. The first day of the week. This was our Sunday. The Jewish Sabbath was our Saturday.

2. The stone rolled away. This according to Matthew 28:1 had been the first great sign accompanying the resurrection. At the sight of the angels who rolled away the stone the Roman guard was first terrified and then fled: after this

the women came, and found the grave empty.

3. The body [of the Lord Jesus]. Bishop Browning remarks that this is the first time in the New Testament that our Saviour is called by this name. The Lord; Christ; Jesus; are names he frequently had. Here, after his resurrection as a conqueror, St. Luke calls him 'The Lord Jesus.'

4. They were perplexed. They could not tell what to make of the facts in front of them – the empty tomb – the linen clothes lying by themselves – the body gone.

Two men. Here, as in Acts 1:18, we are, of course, to understand angels in the likeness of men. The frequency with which St. Luke mentions angels is a peculiar feature in his Gospel. An angel appears to Zechariah, an angel appears to the Virgin Mary, angels appear to the shepherds when our Lord is born – all mentioned only by St. Luke.

8. They remembered. Ford quotes a good remark of Cecil's on this: 'It is not sufficiently considered how much more we need recollection than information.'

9. Told all this. Augustine remarks that these women were 'the first preachers of the resurrection of Christ.'

12. The linen cloths by themselves. All writers on the resurrection of Christ call attention, with much justice, to this fact. If the body of our Lord had been stolen from the grave by his friends, it is most improbable that those who stole it would have taken the trouble to remove the linen clothes and wrap them together in an orderly way.

The walk to Emmaus (24:13–35)

The events in these verses are not found in any of the other Gospels. Out of the eleven appearances of Christ after his resurrection, none perhaps is so interesting as the one described in this passage.

The Old Testament is full of Christ

Let us note in these verses, how full the Old Testament is of Christ. We are told that our Lord began **with Moses and all the prophets,** as **he interpreted to them the things about himself in all the Scripture** (verse 27).

How do we explain these words? In what way did our Lord explain things **about himself** in every part of the Old Testament? The answer is simple. Christ was the substance of every Old Testament sacrifice ordained in the law of Moses; Christ was the true Deliverer and King, of whom all the judges and deliverers in Jewish history were types; Christ was the coming Prophet greater than Moses, whose glorious coming filled the pages of the prophets; Christ was the true seed of the woman who was to bruise the serpent's head, the true Shiloh to whom the people were to be gathered, the true scapegoat, the true bronze serpent, the true lamb to which every daily offering pointed, the true High Priest of whom every descendant of Aaron was a figure. These things, or something like them, we need not doubt, were some of the things which our Lord expounded on the way to Emmaus.

Let it be a settled principle in our minds, in reading the Bible, that Christ is the central sun of all its books: so long as we keep him in view, we will never greatly err in our search for spiritual knowledge; once we lose sight of Christ, we will find the whole Bible dark and full of difficulty. The key to understanding the Bible is Jesus Christ.

Notes on Luke 24:13–35

16. Their eyes were kept from recognizing him. St. Mark says 'he appeared in another form' (Mark 16:12). This would account for the disciples not recognizing him. At the same time it is clear that in some miraculous way the eyes of the disciples were kept from seeing clearly (see 2 Kings 6:17–20).

18. The whole verse is important evidence about how well-known our Lord Jesus Christ's crucifixion was.

25. 'Slow of heart to believe all that the prophets have declared!' This should be noted carefully. The disciples believed many things which the prophets had spoken; but they did not believe everything. They believed the predictions of the Messiah's glory, but not the Messiah's sufferings. Christians today too often make similar mistakes, though in a totally different direction. They believe all that the prophets say about Christ's sufferings, but not all that they say about Christ coming the second time in glory.

27. Beginning with Moses. Alford remarks, 'Observe the testimony which this verse gives to the divine authority, and Christian interpretation of the Old Testament Scriptures. The denial of reference to Christ's death and glory in the Old Testament, is a denial of Christ's own teaching.'

29. 'Stay with us.' There are several other instances of similar expressions like this in Scripture used on similar occasions (see Genesis 32:26; Judges 6:18; 13:15). All show that God loves to be entreated by his people, and that those who wish to have much must ask much, and even do so with holy violence.

30. He took bread … blessed it and broke it … gave it. I think this refers to a well-known gesture of our Lord in the act of breaking bread, with which all his disciples were familiar. I think it even possible that there is a reference to our Lord's demeanor at the miracle of feeding the multitude with a few loaves and fishes.

Alford suggests that the marks of the nails of our Lord's hands may have been first noticed as he was breaking bread.

31. Their eyes were opened, and they recognized him. We cannot explain this sudden revelation of Christ. The whole transaction is so miraculous that we can only take the words as we find them, and must not waste time in attempting to define what is beyond our comprehension.

He vanished from their sight. This and other expressions concerning our Lord's risen body show plainly that it was a body in some wonderful way different from the common body of man. It was a real material body, and true flesh and blood; but it was a body capable of moving, appearing, and disappearing after a manner that we cannot explain.

33. They found the Eleven. This deserves close attention. Was Thomas with them or not? If he was, he must have gone out immediately after the two disciples came in; otherwise it would be difficult to reconcile the verses which immediately follow, describing our Lord's appearing when Thomas was not present. If Thomas was not present on this occasion, how can we explain St. Luke speaking of 'the Eleven'? Doddridge must supply the answer: 'As Paul calls the company of apostles "the twelve" (1 Corinthians 15:5), though Judas the twelfth person was dead: so Luke here calls them the "eleven," though Thomas the eleventh person was absent, as appears from John 20:24.' See Mark 16:14.

34. 'Appeared to Simon!' This appearance to Simon Peter alone is only mentioned here and in 1 Corinthians 15:2. The circumstances of the appearance we do not know.

It may be well to mention here the eleven separate appearances of our Lord after his resurrection.

1. To Mary Magdalene alone (Mark 16:1; John 20:14).
2. To the women returning from the tomb (Matthew 28:9–10).
3. To Simon Peter alone (Luke 24:34).
4. To the two disciples going to Emmaus (Luke 26:13)
5. To the apostles at Jerusalem, except for Thomas, who was absent (John 20:19).
6. To the apostles at Jerusalem, a second time, when Thomas was present (John 20:26,29).
7. At the sea of Tiberias, when seven disciples were fishing (John 21:1).
8. To the eleven disciples, on a mountain in Galilee (Matthew 28:16).
9. To more than 500 brethren at once (1 Corinthians 15:6).
10. To James on his own (1 Corinthians 15:7).
11. To all the apostles on Mount Olivet, at his ascension (Luke 24:51).

35. Made known to them in the breaking of the bread. To apply this to the Lord's Supper is mere accommodation of Scripture words, and not justified by the context.

Christ's appearance to the eleven (24:36–43)

How our Lord speaks to his disciples after his resurrection

We should observe, in this passage, the gracious words which our Lord uses to introduce himself to his disciples after his resurrection. We read that he suddenly stood in the middle of them and said, 'Peace be with you' (verse 36).

This was a wonderful saying, when we consider the men to whom it was addressed. It was spoken to eleven disciples, who three days before had shamefully forsaken their Master and fled. They had broken their promises; they had forgotten their profession to die for their faith. All of them had proved to be backsliders and cowards. But our Lord does not say one word of rebuke. Calmly and quietly he appears in the middle of them and starts talking about peace: 'Peace be with you' (verse 36).

Where is the sinner, however great his sins, who needs to be afraid of going to a Saviour such as this? In the hand of Jesus there is mercy enough and to spare. (See Psalm 130:4.) In the same way the professing Christian should use forgiving words to his brethren (see Colossians 3:13).

Notes on Luke 24:36–43

36. 'Peace be with you.' This greeting implied that the great battle was fought and the great victory won over the prince of this world, and peace with God was won for man. It implied that our Lord came to his disciples with peaceful, gracious and forgiving feelings, and with no resentment for them having forsaken him. 'Peace' was the last word in Zechariah's prophetic hymn; 'peace on earth' was part of the good news proclaimed by the angels when Christ was born; 'peace' was the proclamation which the seventy disciples were ordered to make in every house which they visited; 'peace' was the legacy which our Lord left and gave to the apostles on the night before he was crucified, and 'peace' was the first word which he spoke when he appeared among them again after his resurrection (Luke 1:79; 2:14; 10:5; John 14:27).

Peace, in short, is one main ingredient of the Gospel. All of St. Paul's letters begin with a gracious wish of 'peace' to those to whom they are addressed.

Christ's last injunctions to the eleven (24:44–49)

Our Lord's parting gift

Let us observe in these verses, the gift which our Lord bestowed on his disciples immediately before he left the world. We read that he **opened their minds to understand the scriptures** (verse 45).

We all need a similar enlightenment of our understandings (1 Corinthians 2:14). Anyone who wants to read the Bible profitably must first ask the Lord Jesus to open the eyes of his understanding through the Holy Spirit. Human commentaries have their place, as the help of good and learned men should not be despised, but no commentary compares with the teaching of Christ. A humble and prayerful spirit will find a thousand things in the Bible which the proud, self-conceited student will utterly fail to discern.

Notes on Luke 24:44–49

45. He opened their minds to understand the scriptures. Poole remarks, 'He did not open their understanding without the Scripture: he sends them there. He knows that Scripture would not give them a sufficient knowledge of the things of God without the influence and illumination of his Spirit. They are truly taught by God who are taught by his Spirit to understand the Scriptures. Christ gives great honour to the Scriptures. The devil cheats those whom he persuades to drive away from the Scriptures in expectation of a teaching by the Spirit. The Spirit teaches by, not without, not contrary to, the holy Scriptures.'

47. Beginning from Jerusalem. This teaches that the apostles and first preachers of the Gospel should not shrink from offering salvation to the worst and greatest sinners. The other lesson here is that the first offer of salvation should always be made to the Jews: hardened, unbelieving as they were, they were still 'loved on account of the patriarchs' (Romans 11:28), and were not to be despised.

49. 'I am sending you what my Father promised.' This refers to the Holy Spirit, whom the Father had promised in the Old Testament, and who came down on the day of Pentecost (see Isaiah 44:3; Joel 2:28; Jeremiah 31:33; Ezekiel 36:27).

'Clothed.' This word is frequently used in the New Testament, and implies a putting on something which we do not naturally possess. (See Romans 13:14; 1 Corinthians 15:53; Galatians 3:27; Colossians 3:9-10.)

The ascension (24:50–53)

These verses conclude St. Luke's account of our Lord's ministry. They are a fitting ending of the

Gospel, which in touching tenderness and a full demonstration of Christ's grace, stands first among the four records of the things which Jesus did and taught (Acts 1:1).

Notes on Luke 24:50–53

51. Was carried up into heaven. Where our Lord's body went to after it was taken up in this way is unprofitable speculation. It is enough for us to know that he went into the presence of God for us, and that he will come again exactly in the way that he went (Acts 1:11).

53. They were continually in the temple blessing God. Maldonatus remarks that 'it is a striking fact that St. Luke's Gospel begins by describing a scene in the temple when Zechariah had a vision, and also leaves us in the temple when it concludes.'

Burgon says, 'They repaired to the temple, and so the temple service became henceforth filled with new meaning. The song of Moses has become for them the song of the Lamb; for them the Psalms speak henceforth another language, for they speak to them only of Christ. Well may they have been henceforth "continually in the temple blessing God."'

JOHN

David Brown

Introduction

The author of the Fourth Gospel was the younger of the two sons of Zebedee, a fisherman on the Sea of Galilee, who resided at Bethsaida, where were born Peter and Andrew his brother, and Philip also. His mother's name was Salome, who, though not without her imperfections (Mt 20:20–28), was one of those dear and honoured women who accompanied the Lord on one of His preaching circuits through Galilee, ministering to His bodily wants; who followed Him to the cross, and bought sweet spices to anoint Him after His burial, but, on bringing them to the grave, on the morning of the First Day of the week, found their loving services gloriously superseded by His resurrection ere they arrived. His father, Zebedee, appears to have been in good circumstances, owning a vessel of his own and having hired servants (Mr 1:20).

Our Evangelist, whose occupation was that of a fisherman with his father, was beyond doubt a disciple of the Baptist, and one of the two who had the first interview with Jesus. He was called while engaged at his secular occupation (Mt 4:21,22), and again on a memorable occasion (Lu 5:1–11), and finally chosen as one of the Twelve Apostles (Mt 10:2). He was the youngest of the Twelve – the 'Benjamin,' as DaCosta calls him – and he and James his brother were named in the native tongue by Him who knew the heart, 'Boanerges,' which the Evangelist Mark (Mr 3:17) explains to mean 'Sons of thunder'; no doubt from their natural *vehemence* of *character*. They and Peter constituted that select triumvirate. But the highest honour bestowed on this disciple was his being admitted to the bosom place with his Lord at the table, as 'the disciple whom Jesus loved' (Joh 13:23 20:2 21:7, 20, 24), and to have committed to him by the dying Redeemer the care of His mother (Joh 19:26,27). There can be no reasonable doubt that this distinction was due to a sympathy with His own spirit and mind on the part of John which the all-penetrating Eye of their common Master beheld in none of the rest; and although this was probably never seen either in his life or in his ministry by his fellow apostles, it is brought out wonderfully in his writings, which, in Christ-like spirituality, heavenliness, and love, surpass, we may freely say, all the other inspired writings.

After the effusion of the Spirit on the day of Pentecost, we find him in constant but silent company with Peter, the great spokesman and actor in the infant Church until the accession of Paul. While his love to the Lord Jesus drew him spontaneously to the side of His eminent servant, and his chastened vehemence made him ready to stand courageously by him, and suffer with him, in all that his testimony to Jesus might cost him, his modest humility, as the youngest of all the apostles, made him an admiring listener and faithful supporter of his brother apostle rather than a speaker or separate actor. Ecclesiastical history is uniform in testifying that John went to Asia Minor; but it is next to certain that this could not have been till after the death both of Peter and Paul; that he resided at Ephesus, whence, as from a centre, he superintended the churches of that region, paying them occasional visits; and that he long survived the other apostles. Whether the mother of Jesus died before this, or went with John to Ephesus, where she died and was buried, is not agreed. One or two anecdotes of his later days have been handed down by tradition, one at least bearing marks of reasonable probability. But it is not necessary to give them here. In the reign of Domitian (A.D. 81–96) he was banished to 'the isle that is called Patmos' (a small rocky and then almost uninhabited island in the Aegean Sea), 'for the word of God and for the testimony of Jesus Christ' (Re 1:9). IRENAEUS and EUSEBIUS say that this took place about the end of Domitian's reign. That he was thrown into a cauldron of boiling oil, and miraculously delivered, is one of those legends which, though reported by TERTULLIAN and JEROME, is entitled to no credit. His return from exile took place during the brief but tolerant reign of Nerva; he died at Ephesus in the reign of Trajan [EUSEBIUS, *Ecclesiastical History,* 3.23], at an age above ninety, according to some; according to others, one hundred; and even one hundred twenty, according to others still. The intermediate number is generally regarded as probably the nearest to the truth.

As to the *date* of this Gospel, the arguments for its having been composed before the destruction of Jerusalem (though relied on by some superior critics) are of the slenderest nature; such as the expression in Joh 5:2, 'there *is* at Jerusalem, by the sheep-gate, a pool'; there being no allusion to Peter's martyrdom as having occurred according to the prediction in Joh 21:18 – a thing too well known to require mention. That it was composed long after the destruction of Jerusalem, and after the decease of all the other apostles, is next to certain, though the precise time cannot be determined. Probably it was before his banishment, however; and if we date it between the years 90 and 94, we shall probably be close to the truth.

As to the *readers* for whom it was more immediately designed, that they were Gentiles we might naturally presume from the lateness of the date; but the multitude of explanations of things familiar to every Jew puts this beyond all question.

No doubt was ever thrown upon the genuineness and authenticity of this Gospel till about the close of the eighteenth century; nor were these embodied in any formal attack upon it till BRETSCHNEIDER, in 1820, issued his famous treatise [*Probabilia*], the conclusions of which he afterwards was candid enough to admit had been satisfactorily disproved. To advert to these would be as painful as unnecessary; consisting as they mostly do of assertions regarding the Discourses of our Lord recorded in this Gospel which are revolting to every spiritual mind. The Tubingen school did their best, on their peculiar mode of reasoning, to galvanize into fresh life this theory of the post-Joannean date of the Fourth Gospel; and some Unitarian critics still cling to it. But to use the striking language of VANOOSTERZEE regarding similar speculations on the Third Gospel, 'Behold, the feet of them that shall carry it out dead are already at the door' (Ac 5:9). Is there one mind of the least elevation of spiritual discernment that does not see in this Gospel marks of historical truth and a surpassing glory such as none of the other Gospels possess, brightly as they too attest their own verity; and who will not be ready to say that if not historically true, and true *just as it stands,* it never could have been by mortal man composed or conceived?

Of the peculiarities of this Gospel, we note here only two. The one is its *reflective* character. While the others are purely *narrative,* the Fourth Evangelist, 'pauses, as it were, at every turn,' as DACOSTA says [*Four Witnesses,* p. 234], 'at one time to give a reason, at another to fix the attention, to deduce consequences, or make applications, or to give utterance to the language of praise.' See Joh 2:20,21,23–25 4:1,2 7:37–39 11:12,13,49–52 21:18,19,22,23. The other peculiarity of this Gospel is its *supplementary* character. By this, in the present instance, we mean something more than the studiousness with which he omits many most important particulars in our Lord's history, for no conceivable reason but that they were already familiar as household words to all his readers, through the three preceding Gospels, and his substituting in place of these an immense quantity of the richest matter not found in the other Gospels. We refer here more particularly to the *nature* of the additions which distinguish this Gospel; particularly the notices of the different Passovers which occurred during our Lord's public ministry, and the record of His teaching at Jerusalem, without which it is not too much to say that we could have had but a most imperfect conception either of the duration of His ministry or of the plan of it. But another feature of these additions is quite as noticeable and not less important. 'We find,' to use again the words of DaCosta [*Four Witnesses*, pp. 238, 239], slightly abridged, 'only six of our Lord's miracles recorded in this Gospel, but these are all of the most remarkable kind, and surpass the rest in depth, specialty of application, and fulness of meaning. Of these six we find only one in the other three Gospels – the multiplication of the loaves. That miracle chiefly, it would seem, on account of the important instructions of which it furnished the occasion (Joh 6:1–71), is here recorded anew. The five other tokens of divine power are distinguished from among the many recorded in the three other Gospels by their furnishing a still higher display of power and command over the ordinary laws and course of nature. Thus we find recorded here the first of all the miracles that Jesus wrought – the changing of water into wine (Joh 2:1–11), the cure of the nobleman's son *at a distance* (Joh 4:43–54); of the numerous cures of the lame and the paralytic by the word of Jesus, only one – of the man impotent for *thirty and eight years* (Joh 5:1–9); of the many cures of the blind, one only – of the man *born blind* (Joh 9:1–12); the restoration of Lazarus, not from a deathbed, like Jairus' daughter, nor from a bier, like the widow of Nain's son, but *from the grave*, and after lying there four days, and there sinking into corruption (Joh 11:1–44); and lastly, after His resurrection, the miraculous draught of fishes on the Sea of Tiberias (Joh 21:5–11). But these are all recorded chiefly to give occasion for the record of those astonishing discourses and conversations, alike with friends and with foes, with His disciples and with the multitude which they drew forth.'

Contents

See *Outlines of the New Testament Books*, pp. 893–5.

Chapter 1

Joh 1:1–14.

The word made flesh.

1. **In the beginning** – of all time and created existence, for this Word gave it being (Joh 1:3,10); therefore, 'before the world was' (Joh 17:5,24); or, from all eternity.

was the Word – He *who is to God what man's word is to himself, the manifestation or expression of himself to those without him.* (See on Joh 1:18.) On the *origin* of this most lofty and now for ever consecrated title of Christ, this is not the place to speak. It occurs only in the writings of this seraphic apostle.

was with God – having a conscious personal existence *distinct from God* (as one is from the person he is 'with'), but *inseparable from Him* and *associated with Him* (Joh 1:18 Joh 17:5 1Jo 1:2), where 'THE FATHER' is used in the same sense as 'GOD' here.

was God – in substance and essence GOD; or was possessed of essential or proper divinity. Thus, each of these brief but pregnant statements is the complement of the other, correcting any misapprehensions which the others might occasion. Was the Word *eternal?* It was *not* the eternity of *'the Father,'* but of a conscious personal existence *distinct from Him and associated with Him.* Was the Word thus 'with God?' It was not the distinctness and the fellowship of *another being,* as if there were *more Gods than one,* but of One who was *Himself God* – in such sense that the *absolute unity* of the God head, the great principle of all religion, is only transferred from the region of shadowy abstraction to the region of essential life and love. But why all this definition? Not to give us any *abstract information* about certain mysterious distinctions in the Godhead, but solely to let the reader know *who it was that* in the fulness of time '*was made flesh.*' After each verse, then, the reader must say, 'It was He who is thus, and thus, and thus described, who was made flesh.'

2. The same – See what property of the Word the stress is laid upon – His *eternal distinctness,* in unity, from God – the Father (Joh 1:2).

3. All things – all things *absolutely* (as is evident from Joh 1:10 1Co 8:6 Col 1:16,17; but put beyond question by what follows).

without Him was not any thing – *not one thing*

made – brought into being.

that was made – This is a denial of the *eternity* and *non-creation* of matter, which was held by the whole thinking world *outside of Judaism and Christianity:* or rather, its proper *creation* was never so much as dreamt of save by the children of *revealed religion.*

4. In Him was life – *essentially* and *originally,* as the previous verses show to be the meaning. Thus He is *the Living Word,* or, as He is called in 1Jo 1:1,2, 'the Word of Life.'

the life … the light of men – All that in men which is *true light* – knowledge, integrity, intelligent, willing subjection to God, love to Him and to their fellow creatures, wisdom, purity, holy joy, rational happiness – all this 'light of men' has its fountain in the essential original 'life' of 'the Word' (1Jo 1:5–7 Ps 36:9).

5. shineth in darkness – in this dark, fallen world, or in mankind 'sitting in darkness and the shadow of death,' *with no ability to find the way either of truth or of holiness.* In this thick darkness, and consequent intellectual and moral obliquity, 'the light of the Word' shineth – *by all the rays whether of natural or revealed teaching which men* (apart from the Incarnation of the Word) *are favoured with.*

the darkness comprehended it not – *did not take it in,* a brief summary of the effect of all the strivings of this *unincarnate* Word throughout this wide world from the beginning, and a hint of the necessity of His putting on *flesh,* if any recovery of men was to be effected (1Co 1:21).

6–9. The Evangelist here *approaches* his grand thesis, so paving his way for the full statement of it in Joh 1:14, that we may be able to bear the bright light of it, and take in its length and breadth and depth and height.

7. through him – John.

8. not that Light – (See on Joh 5:35.) What a testimony to John to have to explain that 'he was *not* that Light!' Yet was he but a foil to set it off, his night-taper dwindling before the Dayspring from on high (Joh 3:30).

9. lighteth every man – rather, 'which, coming into the world, enlighteneth every man'; or, is 'the Light of the world' (Joh 9:5). 'Coming into the world' is a superfluous and quite unusual description of 'every man'; but it is of all descriptions of Christ amongst the most familiar, especially in the writings of this Evangelist (Joh 12:46 16:28 18:37 1Jo 4:9 1Ti 1:15).

10–13. He was in the world – The language here is nearly as wonderful as the thought. Observe its compact simplicity, its sonorousness – 'the world' resounding in each of its three members – and the enigmatic form in which it is couched, startling the reader and setting his ingenuity a-working to solve the stupendous enigma of *Christ ignored in His own world.* 'The world,' in the first two clauses, plainly means the *created* world, *into* which He came, says Joh 1:9; '*in* it He was,' says this verse. By His Incarnation, He became *an inhabitant of it,* and bound up with it. Yet 'was made by Him' (Joh 1:3–5). Here, then, it is merely alluded to, in contrast partly with His being *in* it, but still more with the reception He met with from it. 'The world that knew Him not' (1Jo 3:1) is of course the intelligent world of mankind. (See on Joh 1:11,12.) Taking the first two clauses as one statement, we try to apprehend it by thinking of the infant Christ conceived in the womb and born in the arms of His own creature, and of the Man Christ Jesus breathing His own air, treading His own ground, supported by substances to which He Himself gave being, and the Creator of the very men whom He came to save. But the most vivid commentary on this entire verse will be got by tracing (in His matchless history) Him of whom it speaks walking amidst all the elements of nature, the diseases of men and death itself, the secrets of the human heart, and 'the rulers of the darkness of this world' in all their number, subtlety, and malignity, not only with absolute ease, as their conscious Lord, but, as we might say, with full consciousness on their part of the presence of their Maker, whose will to one and all of them was law. And this is He of whom it is added, 'the world knew Him not'!

11. his own – 'His own' (property or possession), for the word is in the *neuter* gender. It means His own land, city, temple, Messianic rights and possessions.

and his own – 'His own (people)'; for now the word is *masculine*. It means the Jews, as the 'peculiar people.' Both *they* and their *land*, with all that this included, were 'HIS OWN,' not so much as part of 'the world which was made by Him,' but as 'THE HEIR' of the inheritance (Lu 20:14; see also on Mt 22:1).

received him not – *nationally*, as God's chosen witnesses.

12. But as many – *individuals*, of the 'disobedient and gainsaying people.'

gave he power – The word signifies both *authority* and *ability*, and both are certainly meant here.

to become – Mark these words: Jesus is the Son of God; He is never said to have become such.

the sons – or more simply, 'sons of God,' in *name* and in *nature*.

believe on his name – *a phrase never used in Scripture of any mere creature*, to express the credit given to human testimony, even of prophets or apostles, inasmuch it carries with it the idea of *trust* proper only towards GOD. In this sense of *supreme faith*, as due to Him who 'gives those that *believe in Himself* power to become sons of God,' it is manifestly used here.

13. Which were born – a sonship therefore not of mere title and privilege, but of *nature*, the soul being made conscious of the vital capacities, perceptions, and emotions of *a child of God*, before unknown.

not of blood – not of superior human descent, not of human generation at all, not of man in any manner of way. By this elaborate threefold denial of the *human* source of this sonship, immense force is given to what follows,

but of God – Right royal gift, and He who confers must be absolutely divine. For who would not worship Him who can bring him into the family, and evoke within him the very life, of the sons of God?

14. And the Word – *To raise the reader to the altitude of this climax were the thirteen foregoing verses written.*

was made flesh – BECAME MAN, in man's present frail, mortal condition, denoted by the word 'flesh' (Isa 40:6 1Pe 1:24). It is directed probably against the *Docetæ*, who held that Christ was not really but only *apparently* man; against whom this gentle spirit is vehement in his Epistles (1Jo 4:3 2Jo 1:7:10,11), [LUCKE]. Nor could He be too much so, for with the verity of the Incarnation all substantial Christianity vanishes. But now, married to our nature, henceforth He is as *personally conscious of all that is strictly human as of all that is properly divine*; and our nature is in His Person redeemed and quickened, ennobled and transfigured.

and dwelt – tabernacled or pitched his tent; a word peculiar to John, who uses it four times, all in the sense of *a permanent stay* (Re 7:15 12:12

13:6 21:3). For ever wedded to our *'flesh,'* He has entered this tabernacle to 'go no more out.' The allusion is to that tabernacle where dwelt the Shekinah, or manifested 'GLORY OF THE LORD,' and with reference to God's *permanent dwelling among His people* (Le 26:11 Ps 68:18 132:13,14 Eze 37:27). This is put almost beyond doubt by what immediately follows, 'And we beheld his glory' [LUCKE, MEYER, DEWETTE which last critic, rising higher than usual, says that thus were perfected all former partial manifestations of God in an *essentially Personal and historically Human* manifestation].

full of grace and truth – So it should read: 'He dwelt among us full of grace and truth'; or, in Old Testament phrase, 'Mercy and truth,' denoting the whole fruit of God's purposes of love towards sinners of mankind, which until now existed only in *promise*, and the *fulfilment* at length of that promise in Christ; in one great word, '*the* SURE MERCIES *of David*' (Isa 55:3 Ac 13:34; compare 2Sa 23:5). In His Person all that Grace and Truth which had been floating so long in shadowy forms, and darting into the souls of the poor and needy its broken beams, took everlasting possession of human flesh and filled it full. By this Incarnation of Grace and Truth, the teaching of thousands of years was at once transcended and beggared, and the family of God sprang into Manhood.

and we beheld his glory – not by the eye of *sense*, which saw in Him only 'the carpenter.' His glory was 'spiritually discerned' (1Co 2:7–15 2Co 3:18 4:4,6 5:16) – the glory of surpassing grace, love, tenderness, wisdom, purity, spirituality; majesty and meekness, richness and poverty, power and weakness, meeting together in unique contrast; ever attracting and at times ravishing the 'babes' that followed and forsook all for Him.

the glory as of the only begotten of the Father – not *like*, but 'such as (belongs to),' such as *became* or was *befitting* the only begotten of the Father [Chrysostom in LUCKE, CALVIN], according to a well-known use of the word 'as.'

Joh 1:15.
A saying of the Baptist confirmatory of this.

15. after me – in *official manifestation*.

before me – in *rank and dignity*.

for he was before me – in *existence;* 'His goings forth being from of old, from everlasting' (Mic 5:2). (Anything lower than this His words cannot mean); that is, 'My Successor is my Superior, for He was my Predecessor.' This enigmatic play upon the different senses of the words 'before' and 'after' was doubtless employed by the Baptist to arrest attention, and rivet the thought; and the Evangelist introduces it just to clinch his own statements.

Joh 1:16–18.
Same subject continued.

16. of his fulness – of 'grace and truth,' resuming the thread of Joh 1:14.

grace for grace – that is, grace upon grace (so all the best interpreters), in successive communications and larger measures, as each was able to take it in. Observe, the word 'truth' is here dropped. 'Grace' being the chosen New Testament word for the whole fulness of the new covenant, all that dwells in Christ for men.

17. For – The Law elicits the consciousness of sin and the need of redemption; it only typifies the reality. The Gospel, on the contrary, actually communicates reality and power from above (compare Ro 6:14). Hence Paul terms the Old Testament 'shadow,' while he calls the New Testament 'substance' (Col 2:17) [OLSHAUSEN].

18. No man – 'No one,' in the widest sense.

hath seen God – by immediate gaze, or direct intuition.

in the bosom of the Father – A remarkable expression, used only here, presupposing *the Son's conscious existence distinct from the Father, and expressing His immediate and most endeared access to, and absolute acquaintance with, Him.*

he – emphatic; As if he should say, 'He and He only hath declared Him,' because He only *can.*

Joh 1:19–36.
The Baptist's testimony to Christ.

19. record – testimony.

the Jews – that is, the heads of the nation, the members of the Sanhedrim. *In this peculiar sense our Evangelist seems always to use the term.*

20. confessed – that is, While many were ready to hail him as the Christ, he neither gave the slightest ground for such views, nor the least entertainment to them.

21. Elias – in His own proper person.

that prophet – announced in De 18:15, about whom they seem not to have been agreed whether he were the same with the Messiah or no.

25. Why baptizest thou, if not – Thinking he disclaimed any special connection with Messiah's kingdom, they demand his right to gather disciples by baptism.

26. there standeth – This must have been spoken after the baptism of Christ, and possibly just after His temptation (see on Joh 1:29).

28. Bethabara – Rather, 'Bethany' (according to nearly all the best and most ancient manuscripts); not the Bethany of Lazarus, but another of the same name, and distinguished from it as lying 'beyond Jordan,' on the east.

29. seeth Jesus – fresh, probably, from the scene of the temptation.

coming unto him – as to congenial company (Ac 4:23), and to receive from him His first greeting.

and saith – catching a sublime inspiration at the sight of Him approaching.

the Lamb of God – the one God-ordained, God-gifted sacrificial offering.

that taketh away – *taketh up* and *taketh away.* The word signifies both, as does the corresponding *Hebrew* word. Applied to sin, it means to *be chargeable with the guilt of it* (Ex 28:38 Le 5:1 Eze 18:20), and to *bear it away* (as often). In the Levitical victims both ideas met, as they do in Christ, the people's guilt being viewed as *transferred* to them, *avenged* in their death, and so *borne away* by them (Le 4:15 16:15,21,22; and compare Isa 53:6–12 2Co 5:21).

the sin – The *singular* number being used to mark the *collective burden* and *all-embracing efficacy.*

of the world – not of Israel only, for whom typical victims were exclusively offered. Wherever there shall live a sinner throughout the wide world, sinking under that burden too heavy for him to bear, he shall find in this 'Lamb of God,' shoulder equal to the weight. The right note was struck at the first – balm, doubtless, to Christ's own spirit; nor was ever after, or ever will be, a more glorious utterance.

31–34. knew him not – Living mostly apart, the one at Nazareth, the other in the Judean desert – to prevent all appearance of collusion, John only knew that at a definite time after his own call, his Master would show Himself. As He drew near for baptism one day, the last of all the crowd, the spirit of the Baptist heaving under a divine presentiment that the moment had at length arrived, and an air of unwonted serenity and dignity, not without traits, probably, of the family features, appearing in this Stranger, the Spirit said to him as to Samuel of his youthful type, 'Arise, anoint Him, for this is He!' (1Sa 16:12). But *the* sign which he was told to expect was the visible descent of the Spirit upon Him as He emerged out of the baptismal water. *Then,* catching up the voice from heaven, 'he saw and bare record that this is the Son of God.'

35. John stood – 'was standing,' at his accustomed place.

36. looking – having fixed his eyes, with significant gaze, on Jesus.

as he walked – but not now *to him.* To have done this once (see on Joh 1:29) was humility enough [BENGEL].

Behold – The repetition of that wonderful proclamation, in identical terms and without another word, could only have been meant as a gentle hint to go after Him – as they did.

Joh 1:37–51.
First gathering of disciples – John, Andrew, Simon, Philip, Nathanael.

38. What seek ye – gentle, winning question, remarkable as the Redeemer's *first public utterance.*

where dwellest thou – that is, 'That is a question we cannot answer in a moment; but had we Thy company for a calm hour in private, gladly should we open our burden.'

39. Come and see – His *second utterance*, more winning still.

tenth hour – not ten A.M. (as some), according to *Roman*, but four P.M., according to *Jewish* reckoning, which John follows. The hour is mentioned to show why they stayed out the day with him – because little of it remained.

40. One ... was Andrew – The other was doubtless our Evangelist himself. His great sensitiveness is touchingly shown in his representation of this first contact with the Lord; the circumstances are present to him in the minutest details; he still remembers the very hour. But 'he reports no particulars of those discourses of the Lord by which he was bound to Him for the whole of His life; he allows everything personal to retire' [OLSHAUSEN].

Peter's brother – and the elder of the two.

41. have found the Messias – The previous preparation of their simple hearts under the Baptist's ministry, made quick work of this blessed conviction, while others hesitated till doubt settled into obduracy. *So it is still.*

42. brought him to Jesus – Happy brothers that thus do to each other!

beheld him – fixed his eyes on him, with significant gaze (as Joh 1:36).

Cephas ... stone – (See Mt 16:18).

43. would go ... into Galilee – for from His baptism He had sojourned in *Judea* (showing that the calling at the Sea of Galilee [Mt 4:18] was a *subsequent* one, See Lu 5:1).

Follow me – the first express call given, the former three having come to Him spontaneously.

44. the city of Andrew and Peter – of their *birth* probably, for they seem to have *lived* at Capernaum (Mr 1:29).

45. Nathanael – (See Mt 10:3.)

Moses – (See Joh 5:46.)

son of Joseph – the current way of speaking. (See Lu 3:23.)

46. any good out of Nazareth – remembering Bethlehem, perhaps, as Messiah's predicted birthplace, and Nazareth having no *express* prophetic place at all, besides being in no repute. The question sprang from mere dread of mistake in a matter so vital.

Come and see – Noble remedy against preconceived opinions [BENGEL]. Philip, though he could not perhaps solve his difficulty, could show him how to get rid of it. (See on Joh 6:68.)

47. an Israelite indeed ... no guile – not only no hypocrite, but with a guileless simplicity not always found even in God's own people, ready to follow wherever truth might lead him, saying, Samuel-like, 'Speak, Lord, for Thy servant heareth' (1Sa 3:10).

48. Whence knowest thou me – conscious that his very heart had been read, and at this critical moment more than ever before.

Before Philip called thee – showing He knew all that passed between Philip and him at a distance.

when ... under the fig tree – where retirement for meditation and prayer was not uncommon [LIGHTFOOT]. Thither, probably – hearing that his master's Master had at length appeared, and heaving with mingled eagerness to behold Him and dread of deception – he had retired to pour out his guileless heart for light and guidance, ending with such a prayer as this, 'Show me a token for good!' Now he has it, 'Thou guileless one, that fig tree scene, with all its heaving anxieties, deep pleadings and tremulous hopes – I saw it all.' The first words of Jesus had astonished, but this quite overpowered and won him.

49. Son of God ... King of Israel – the one denoting His person, the other His office. How much loftier this than anything Philip had said to him! But just as the earth's vital powers, the longer they are frost-bound, take the greater spring when at length set free, so souls, like Nathanael and Thomas (see on Joh 20:28), the outgoings of whose faith are hindered for a time, take the start of their more easy-going brethren when loosed and let go.

50, 51. Because I said – 'So quickly convinced, and on this evidence only?' – an expression of admiration.

51. Hereafter – The key to this great saying is Jacob's vision (Ge 28:12–22), to which the allusion plainly is. To show the patriarch that though alone and friendless on earth his interests were busying all heaven, he was made to see 'heaven opened and the angels of God ascending and descending upon a' mystic '*ladder* reaching from heaven to earth.' 'By and by,' says Jesus here, 'ye shall see this communication between heaven and earth thrown wide open, and the *Son of man the real Ladder of this fellowship.*'

Chapter 2

Joh 2:1–12.

First miracle, water made wine – brief visit to Capernaum.

1. third day – He would take two days to reach Galilee, and this was the third.

mother there – it being probably some relative's marriage. *John never names her* [BENGEL].

3. no wine – evidently expecting some display of His glory, and hinting that now was His time.

4, 5. Woman – no term of disrespect in the language of that day (Joh 19:26).

what ... to do with thee – that is, 'In my

Father's business I have to do with Him only.' It was a gentle rebuke for *officious interference*, entering a region from which all creatures were excluded (compare Ac 4:19,20).

mine hour – hinting that He *would* do something, but at His own time; and so she understood it (Joh 2:5).

6. firkins – about seven and a half gallons in Jewish, or nine in Attic measure; each of these huge water jars, therefore, holding some twenty or more gallons, for washings at such feasts (Mr 7:4).

7, 8. Fill … draw … bear – directing all, but Himself touching nothing, to prevent all appearance of collusion.

9, 10. well drunk – 'drunk abundantly' (as So 5:1), speaking of the general practice.

10. the good wine … until now – thus testifying, while ignorant of the source of supply, not only that it was real wine, but better than any at the feast.

11. manifested forth his glory – Nothing in the least like this is said of the miracles of prophet or apostle, nor could without manifest blasphemy be said of any mere creature. Observe, (1) At a marriage Christ made His first public appearance in any company, and at a marriage He wrought His first miracle – the noblest sanction that could be given to that God-given institution. (2) As the miracle did not make *bad good*, but *good better*, so Christianity only redeems, sanctifies, and ennobles the beneficent but abused institution of marriage; and Christ's whole work only turns the water of earth into the wine of heaven. Thus 'this beginning of miracles' exhibited the character and 'manifested forth the glory' of His entire Mission. (3) As Christ countenanced our seasons of *festivity*, so also that greater *fulness* which befits such; so far was He from encouraging that *asceticism* which has since been so often put for all religion. (4) The character and authority ascribed by Romanists to the Virgin is directly in the teeth of this and other scriptures.

12. Capernaum – on the Sea of Galilee.

his mother and his brethren – (See Lu 2:51, and Mt 13:54–56.)

Joh 2:13–25.
Christ's first passover – first cleansing of the temple.

14–17. in the temple – not the temple itself, as Joh 2:19–21, but the *temple-court*.

sold oxen – for the convenience of those who had to offer them in sacrifice.

changers of money – of Roman into Jewish money, in which the temple dues had to be paid.

15. small cords – likely some of the rushes spread for bedding, and when twisted used to tie up the cattle there collected. 'Not by this

slender whip but by divine majesty was the ejection accomplished, the whip being but a sign of the scourge of divine anger' [Grotius].

poured out … overthrew – thus expressing the mingled indignation and authority of the impulse.

16. my Father's house – How close the resemblance of these remarkable words to Lu 2:49; the same *consciousness of intrinsic relation to the temple* – as the seat of His Father's most August worship, and so the symbol of all that is due to Him on earth – dictating both speeches. Only, when but a youth, *with no authority*, He was simply 'a SON IN His own house'; now He was 'a SON OVER His own house' (Heb 3:6), the proper Representative, and in flesh 'the Heir,' of his Father's rights.

house of merchandise – There was nothing wrong in the merchandise; but to bring it, for their own and others' convenience, into that most sacred place, was a high-handed profanation which the eye of Jesus could not endure.

17. eaten me up – a glorious feature in the predicted character of the suffering Messiah (Ps 69:9), and rising high even in some not worthy to loose the latchet of His shoes. (Ex 32:19.)

18–22. What sign showest thou unto us, seeing that thou doest these things? – Though the *act* and the *words* of Christ, taken together, were sign enough, they were unconvinced: yet they were *awed*, and though at His very next appearance at Jerusalem they 'sought to kill Him' for speaking of 'His Father' just as He did now (Joh 5:18), they, at this early stage, only ask a sign.

19. Destroy this temple – (See Mr 14:58,59.)

20. Forty and six years – From the eighteenth year of Herod till then was just forty-six years [Josephus, *Antiquities*, 15.11.1].

21. temple of his body – in which was enshrined the glory of the eternal Word. (See on Joh 1:14.) By its resurrection the true Temple of God upon earth was reared up, of which the stone one was but a shadow; so that the allusion is not *quite* exclusively to Himself, but takes in that Temple of which He is the foundation, and all believers are the 'lively stones.' (1Pe 2:4,5.)

22. believed the scripture – on this subject; that is, what was meant, which was hid from them till then. Mark (1) *The act by which Christ signalized His first public appearance in the Temple.* Taking 'His fan in His hand, He purges His floor,' not thoroughly indeed, but enough to *foreshadow His last act* towards that faithless people – *to sweep them out of God's house.* (2) The sign of His authority to do this is the announcement, at this first outset of His ministry, of that coming death by their hands, and resurrection by His own, which were to pave the way for their judicial ejection.

23–25. in the feast day – the foregoing things occurring probably before the feast began.

many believed – superficially, struck merely by 'the miracles He did.' Of these we have no record.

24. did not commit – 'entrust,' or let Himself down familiarly to them, as to His genuine disciples.

25. knew what was in man – It is impossible for language more clearly to assert of Christ what in Jer 17:9,10, and elsewhere, is denied of all mere creatures.

Chapter 3

Joh 3:1–21.
Night interview of Nicodemus with Jesus.

1, 2. Nicodemus – In this member of the Sanhedrim sincerity and timidity are seen struggling together.

2. came to Jesus by night – One of those superficial 'believers' mentioned in Joh 2:23,24, yet inwardly craving further satisfaction, Nicodemus comes to Jesus in quest of it, but comes 'by night' (see Joh 19:38,39 12:42); he avows his conviction that He was

come from God – *an expression never applied to a merely human messenger,* and probably meaning more here – but only as 'a *teacher,*' and in His miracles he sees a proof merely that 'God is with Him.' Thus, while unable to repress his convictions, he is afraid of committing himself too far.

3. Except – This blunt and curt reply was plainly meant to shake the whole edifice of the man's religion, in order to lay a deeper and more enduring foundation. Nicodemus probably thought he had gone a long way, and expected, perhaps, to be complimented on his candor. Instead of this, he is virtually told that he has raised a question which he is not in a capacity to solve, and that before approaching it, *his spiritual vision required to be rectified by an entire revolution in his inner man.* Had the man been less sincere, this would certainly have repelled him; but with persons in his mixed state of mind – to which Jesus was no stranger (Joh 2:25) – such methods speed better than more honeyed words and gradual approaches.

a man – not *a Jew* merely; the necessity is a universal one.

be born again – or, as it were, *begin life anew* in relation to God; his manner of thinking, feeling, and acting, with reference to spiritual things, undergoing *a fundamental and permanent revolution.*

cannot see – can have no part in (just as one is said to 'see life,' 'see death.').

the kingdom of God – whether in its beginnings here (Lu 16:16), or its consummation hereafter (Mt 25:34 Eph 5:5).

4. How – The figure of the new birth, if it had been meant only of *Gentile proselytes* to the

Jewish religion, would have been intelligible enough to Nicodemus, being quite in keeping with the language of that day; but that *Jews themselves* should need a new birth was to him incomprehensible.

5. of water and of the Spirit – A twofold explanation of the 'new birth,' so startling to Nicodemus. To a Jewish ecclesiastic, so familiar with the symbolical application of water, in every variety of way and form of expression, this language was fitted to show that the thing intended was no other than a *thorough spiritual purification by the operation of the Holy Ghost.* Indeed, element of *water* and operation of *the Spirit* are brought together in a glorious evangelical prediction of Ezekiel (Eze 36:25–27), which Nicodemus might have been reminded of had such spiritualities not been almost lost in the reigning formalism. Already had the symbol of water been embodied in an initiatory ordinance, in the baptism of the Jewish expectants of Messiah by the Baptist, not to speak of the baptism of Gentile proselytes before that; and in the Christian Church it was soon to become the great visible door of entrance into 'the kingdom of God,' *the reality being the sole work of the Holy Ghost* (Tit 3:5).

6–8. That which is born – A great universal proposition; 'That which is begotten carries within itself the nature of that which begat it' [OLSHAUSEN].

flesh – Not the mere material body, but all that comes into the world by birth, *the entire man;* yet not humanity simply, but in its corrupted, depraved condition, *in complete subjection to the law of the fall* (Ro 8:1–9). So that though a man 'could enter a second time into his mother's womb and be born,' he would be no nearer this 'new birth' than before (Job 14:4 Ps 51:5).

is spirit – 'partakes of and possesses His spiritual nature.'

7. Marvel not – If a spiritual nature only can see and enter the kingdom of God; if all we bring into the world with us be the reverse of spiritual; and if this spirituality be solely of the Holy Ghost, no wonder a new birth is indispensable.

Ye must – 'Ye, says Jesus, not *we*' [BENGEL]. After those universal propositions, about what 'a man' must be, to 'enter the kingdom of God' (Joh 3:5) – this is remarkable, showing that our Lord meant to hold Himself forth as 'separate from sinners.'

8. The wind – *Breath* and *spirit* (one word both in *Hebrew* and *Greek*) are constantly brought together in Scripture as analogous (Job 27:3 33:4 Eze 37:9–14).

canst not tell – The laws which govern the motion of the *winds* are even yet but partially discovered; but the risings, failings, and change in direction many times in a day, of those *gentle breezes* here referred to, will probably ever be a mystery to us: So of the operation of the Holy Ghost in the new birth.

9, 10. How – Though the subject still confounds Nicodemus, the necessity and possibility of the new birth is no longer the point with him, but the nature of it and how it is brought about [LUTHARDT]. 'From this moment Nicodemus *says nothing more*, but has sunk unto a disciple who has found his true teacher. *Therefore* the Saviour now graciously advances in His communications of truth, and once more solemnly brings to the mind of this teacher in Israel, now become a learner, his own not guiltless *ignorance*, that He may then proceed to utter, out of the fulness of His divine knowledge, such farther testimonies both of earthly and heavenly things as his docile scholar may to his own profit receive' [STIER].

10. master – 'teacher.' The question clearly implies that *the doctrine of regeneration is so far disclosed in the Old Testament that Nicodemus was culpable in being ignorant of it.* Nor is it merely as something that should be experienced *under the Gospel* that the Old Testament holds it forth – as many distinguished critics allege, denying that there was any such thing as regeneration before Christ. For our Lord's proposition is universal, that no fallen man is or can be spiritual without a regenerating operation of the Holy Ghost, and the necessity of a *spiritual obedience* under whatever name, in opposition to mere mechanical services, is proclaimed throughout all the Old Testament.

11–13. We speak that we know, and ... have seen – that is, by *absolute* knowledge and *immediate* vision of God, which 'the only-begotten Son in the bosom of the Father' claims as exclusively His own (Joh 1:18). The 'we' and 'our' are here used, though Himself only is intended, in emphatic contrast, probably, with the opening words of Nicodemus, 'Rabbi, *we know.*'

ye receive not – referring to the *class* to which Nicodemus belonged, but from which he was beginning to be separated in spirit.

12. earthly things – such as *regeneration,* the gate of entrance to the kingdom of God *on earth,* and which Nicodemus should have understood better, as a truth even of that more *earthly* economy to which he belonged.

heavenly things – the things of the new and more heavenly evangelical economy, only to be fully understood after the effusion of the Spirit from heaven through the exalted Saviour.

13. no man hath ascended – There is something paradoxical in this language – 'No one has gone up but He that came down, even He who is at once both up and down.' Doubtless it was intended to startle and constrain His auditor to think that there must be mysterious elements in

His Person. The old Socinians, to subvert the doctrine of the pre-existence of Christ, seized upon this passage as teaching that the man Jesus was secretly caught up to heaven to receive His instructions, and then 'came down from heaven' to deliver them. But the sense manifestly is this: 'The perfect knowledge of God is not obtained by any man's going up from earth to heaven to receive it – no man hath so ascended – but He whose *proper habitation,* in His essential and eternal nature, is heaven, hath, by taking human flesh, descended as the Son of man to disclose the Father, whom He knows by immediate gaze alike in the flesh as before He assumed it, being essentially and unchangeably "in the bosom of the Father"' (Joh 1:18).

14–16. And as Moses – Here now we have the 'heavenly things,' as before the 'earthly,' but under a veil, for the reason mentioned in Joh 3:12. The crucifixion of Messiah is twice after this veiled under the same lively term – '*uplifting,*' Joh 8:28 12:32,33. Here it is still further veiled – though to us who know what it means, rendered vastly more instructive – by reference to the brazen serpent. The venom of the fiery serpents, shooting through the veins of the rebellious Israelites, was spreading death through the camp – lively emblem of the perishing condition of men by reason of sin. In both cases the remedy was divinely provided. In both the way of cure strikingly resembled that of the disease. Stung by serpents, by a serpent they are healed. By 'fiery serpents' bitten – serpents, probably, with skin spotted fiery red [KURTZ] – the instrument of cure is a serpent of brass or copper, having at a distance *the same appearance.* So in redemption, as by man came death, by Man also comes life – Man, too, 'in the *likeness of sinful flesh*' (Ro 8:3), differing in nothing *outward* and *apparent* from those who, pervaded by the poison of the serpent, were ready to perish. But as the uplifted serpent had none of the venom of which the serpent-bitten people were dying, so while the whole human family were perishing of the deadly wound inflicted on it by the old serpent, 'the Second Man,' who arose over humanity with healing in His wings, was without spot or wrinkle, or any such thing. In both cases the remedy is *conspicuously displayed;* in the one case on a pole, in the other on the cross, to 'draw all men unto Him' (Joh 12:32). In both cases it is by *directing the eye to the uplifted Remedy* that the cure is effected; in the one case the bodily eye, in the other the gaze of the soul by 'believing in Him,' as in that glorious ancient proclamation – '*Look* unto me and be ye saved, all the ends of the earth.' (Isa 45:22). Both methods are stumbling to human reason. What, to any thinking Israelite, could seem more unlikely than that a deadly poison should be dried up in his body by simply looking on a reptile of brass? Such a stumbling-block to the Jews and to the Greeks foolishness was faith in the crucified Nazarene as a way of deliverance from eternal perdition. Yet was the warrant in both cases to expect a cure equally rational and well grounded. As the serpent was *God's ordinance* for the cure of every bitten Israelite, so is Christ for the salvation of every perishing sinner – the one however a purely *arbitrary* ordinance, the other divinely *adapted* to man's complicated maladies. In both cases the efficacy is the same. As one simple look at the serpent, however distant and however weak, brought an instantaneous cure, even so, real faith in the Lord Jesus, however tremulous, however distant – be it but *real* faith – brings certain and instant healing to the perishing soul. In a word, the consequences of disobedience are the same in both. Doubtless many bitten Israelites, galling as their case was, would *reason* rather than *obey*, would *speculate* on the absurdity of expecting the bite of a living serpent to be cured by looking at a piece of dead metal in the shape of one – speculate thus *till they died.* Alas! is not salvation by a crucified Redeemer subjected to like treatment? Has the 'offense of the cross' yet ceased? (Compare 2Ki 5:12.)

16. For God so loved – What proclamation of the Gospel has been so oft on the lips of missionaries and preachers in every age since it was first uttered? What has sent such thrilling sensations through millions of mankind? What has been honoured to bring such multitudes to the feet of Christ? What to kindle in the cold and selfish breasts of mortals the fires of self-sacrificing love to mankind, as these words of transparent simplicity, yet overpowering majesty? The picture embraces several distinct compartments: 'THE WORLD' – in its widest sense – ready 'to perish'; the immense 'LOVE OF GOD' to *that perishing* world, measurable only, and conceivable only, by the gift which it drew forth from Him; THE GIFT itself – 'He *so* loved the world that He gave His only begotten Son,' or, in the language of Paul, '*spared not* His own Son' (Ro 8:32), or in that addressed to Abraham when ready to offer Isaac on the altar, '*withheld not* His Son, His only Son, whom He loved' (Ge 22:16); the FRUIT of this stupendous gift – not only *deliverance from* impending '*perdition,*' but the bestowal of everlasting life; the MODE in which all takes effect – by '*believing*' on the Son. How would Nicodemus' narrow Judaism become invisible in the blaze of this Sun of righteousness seen rising on 'the world' with healing in His wings! (Mal 4:2).

17–21. not to condemn – A statement of vast importance. Though 'condemnation' is to many the *issue* of Christ's mission (Joh 3:19), it is not the *object* of His mission, which is purely a *saving* one.

18. is not condemned – Having, immediately on his believing, 'passed from death unto life' (Joh 5:24).

condemned already – Rejecting the one way of deliverance from that 'condemnation' which God gave His Son to *remove,* and so wilfully *remaining* condemned.

19. this is the condemnation – emphatically so, *revealing* the condemnation already existing, and *sealing up* under it those who will not be delivered from it.

light is come into the world – in the Person of Him to whom Nicodemus was listening.

loved darkness – This can only be known by the deliberate rejection of Christ, but that *does* fearfully reveal it.

20. reproved – by detection.

21. doeth truth – whose only object in life is to be and do what will bear the light. Therefore he loves and 'comes to the light,' that all he is and does, being thus thoroughly tested, may be seen to have nothing in it but what is divinely wrought and divinely approved. This is the 'Israelite, indeed, in whom is no guile.'

Joh 3:22–36.
Jesus in the neighborhood of the Baptist – his noble testimony to his master.

22–24. land of Judea – the rural parts of that province, the foregoing conversation being held in the capital.

baptized – in the sense explained in Joh 4:2.

23. Aenon … Salim – on the west of Jordan. (Compare Joh 3:26 with Joh 1:28.)

24. John not yet cast into prison – Hence it is plain that our Lord's ministry did not *commence* with the imprisonment of John, though, but for this, we should have drawn that inference from Mt 4:12 and Mark's (Mr 1:14) express statement.

25, 26. between some of – rather, 'on the part of.'

and the Jews – rather (according to the best manuscripts), 'and a Jew,'

about purifying – that is, baptizing, the symbolical meaning of washing with water being put (as in Joh 2:6) for the act itself. As John and Jesus were the only teachers who baptized Jews, discussions might easily arise between the Baptist's disciples and such Jews as declined to submit to that rite.

26. Rabbi – 'Master, this man tells us that He to whom thou barest such generous witness beyond Jordan is requiting thy generosity by drawing all the people away to Himself. At this rate, thou shalt soon have no disciples at all.' The reply to this is one of the noblest and most affecting utterances that ever came from the lips of man.

27–30. A man – 'I do my heaven-prescribed work, and that is enough for me. Would you have me mount into my Master's place? Said I not unto you, I am not the Christ? The Bride is not mine, why should the people stay with me? Mine it is to point the burdened to the Lamb of God that taketh away the sin of the world, to tell them there is Balm in Gilead, and a Physician there. And shall I grudge to see them, in obedience to the call, flying as a cloud, and as doves to their windows? Whose is the Bride but the Bridegroom's? Enough for me to be the Bridegroom's *friend*, sent by Him to negotiate the match, privileged to bring together the Saviour and those He is come to seek and to save, and rejoicing with joy unspeakable if I may but "stand and hear the Bridegroom's voice," witnessing the blessed espousals. Say ye, then, they go from me to Him? Ye bring me glad tidings of great joy. He must increase, but I must decrease; this, my joy, therefore is fulfilled.'

A man can receive – assume nothing, that is, lawfully and with any success; that is, Every man has his work and sphere appointed him from above. Even Christ Himself came under this law (Heb 5:4).

31–34. He that – Here is the reason why He must increase while all human teachers must decrease. The Master 'cometh from above' – descending from *His proper element,* the region of those 'heavenly things' which He came to reveal, and so, although mingling with men and things on the earth, is not 'of the earth,' either in Person or Word. The servants, on the contrary, springing of earth, are of the earth, and their testimony, even though divine in authority, partakes necessarily of their own earthiness. (So strongly did the Baptist feel this contrast that the last clause just repeats the first.) It is impossible for a sharper line of distinction to be drawn between Christ and all human teachers, even when divinely commissioned and speaking by the power of the Holy Ghost. And who does not perceive it? The words of prophets and apostles are undeniable and most precious truth; but in the words of Christ we hear a voice as from the excellent Glory, the Eternal Word making Himself heard in our own flesh.

32. what he hath seen and heard – (See on Joh 3:11 and Joh 1:18.)

and no man receiveth – John's disciples had said, '*All* come to Him' (Joh 3:26). The Baptist here virtually says, Would it were so, but alas! they are next to '*none*' [BENGEL]. They were far readier to receive himself, and obliged him to say, I am not the Christ, and he seems pained at this.

33. hath set to His seal – gives glory to God whose words Christ speaks, not as prophets and apostles by a partial communication of the Spirit to them.

34. for God giveth not the Spirit by measure – Here, again, the sharpest conceivable line of distinction is drawn between Christ and all human-inspired teachers: 'They have the Spirit in a *limited* degree; but God giveth not [to Him] the Spirit by *measure.*' It means the entire fulness of divine life and divine power. The present tense '*giveth,*' very aptly points out the permanent communication of the Spirit by the Father to the Son, so that a constant flow and reflow of living power is to be understood (Compare Joh 1:15) [OLSHAUSEN].

35, 36. The Father loveth – See Mt 11:27, where we have the '*delivering over* of all things into the hands of the Son,' while here we have the deep spring of that august act in the Father's ineffable '*love of the Son.*'

36. hath everlasting life – already has it. (See on Joh 3:18 and Joh 5:24.)

shall not see life – The contrast here is striking: The one has already a life that will endure for ever – the other not only has it not now, but shall never have it – never see it.

abideth on him – It was on Him before, and not being *removed* in the only possible way, by 'believing on the Son,' it necessarily *remaineth* on him! *Note.* – How flatly does this contradict the teaching of many in our day, that there neither was, nor is, anything *in God* against sinners which needed to be removed by Christ, but only *in men* against God!

Chapter 4

Joh 4:1–42. Christ and the woman of Samaria – the Samaritans of Sychar

1–4. the Lord knew – not by report, but in the sense of Joh 2:25, for which reason He is here styled 'the Lord.'

2. Jesus baptized not – John being a servant baptized with his own hand; Christ as the Master, 'baptizing with the Holy Ghost,' administered the outward symbol only through His disciples.

3. left Judea – to avoid persecution, which at that early stage would have marred His work.

departed into Galilee – by which time John had been cast into prison (Mr 1:14).

4. must needs go through Samaria – for a geographical reason, no doubt, as it lay straight in His way, but certainly not without a higher design.

5. cometh … to – that is, as far as: for He remained at some distance from it.

Sychar – the 'Shechem' of the Old Testament, about thirty-four miles from Jerusalem, afterwards called 'Neapolis,' and now 'Nablous.'

6–8. wearied … sat thus – that is, 'as you might fancy a weary man would'; an instance of the graphic style of St. John [WEBSTER and WILKINSON]. In fact, this is perhaps the most *human* of all the scenes of our Lord's earthly history. We seem to be beside Him, overhearing all that is here recorded, nor could any painting of the scene on canvas, however perfect, do other than lower the conception which this exquisite narrative conveys to the devout and intelligent reader. But with all that is *human*, how much also of the *divine* have we here, both blended in one glorious manifestation of the majesty, grace, pity, patience with which 'the Lord' imparts light and life to this unlikeliest of strangers, standing midway between Jews and heathens.

the sixth hour – *noonday*, reckoning from six A.M. From So 1:7 we know, as from other sources, that the very flocks 'rested at noon.' But Jesus, whose maxim was, 'I must work the works of Him that sent Me while it is day' (Joh 9:4), seems to have denied Himself that repose, at least on this occasion, probably that He might reach this well when He knew the woman would be there. Once there, however, He accepts ... the grateful ease of a seat on the patriarchal stone. But what music is that which I hear from His lips, 'Come unto Me, all ye that labor and are heavy laden, and I will give you rest' (Mt 11:28).

7. Give me to drink – for the heat of a noonday sun had parched His lips. But 'in the last, that great day of the feast,' Jesus stood and cried, saying, 'If any man thirst let him come unto Me and *drink*' (Joh 7:37).

9–12. How is it that thou – not altogether refusing, yet wondering at so unusual a request from a Jew, as His dress and dialect would at once discover Him to be, to a Samaritan.

for – It is this national antipathy that gives point to the parable of the good Samaritan (Lu 10:30–37), and the thankfulness of the Samaritan leper (Lu 17:16,18).

10. If thou knewest – that is, 'In Me thou seest only a petitioner to thee but if thou knewest who that Petitioner is, and the Gift that God is giving to men, thou wouldst change places with Him, gladly suing of Him living water – nor shouldst thou have sued in vain' (gently reflecting on her for not immediately meeting His request).

12. Art thou greater – already perceiving in this Stranger a claim to some mysterious greatness.

our father Jacob – for when it went well with the Jews, they claimed kindred with them, as being descended from Joseph; but when misfortunes befell the Jews, they disowned all connection with them [JOSEPHUS, *Antiquities*, 9.14,3].

13, 14. thirst again ... never thirst – The contrast here is fundamental and all comprehensive. 'This water' plainly means 'this natural water and *all satisfactions of a like earthly and perishable nature.*' Coming to us *from without*, and reaching only the *superficial* parts of our nature, they are soon spent, and need to be anew supplied as much as if we had never expe-

rienced them before, while the deeper wants of our being are not reached by them at all; whereas the 'water' that Christ gives – *spiritual life* – is struck out of the very depths of our being, making the soul not a *cistern*, for holding water *poured into* it *from without*, but a *fountain* (the word had been better so rendered, to distinguish it from the word rendered 'well' in Joh 4:11), springing, gushing, bubbling up and flowing forth *within* us, ever fresh, ever living. *The indwelling of the Holy Ghost as the Spirit of Christ* is the secret of this life with all its enduring energies and satisfactions, as is expressly said (Joh 7:37–39). 'Never thirsting,' then, means simply that such souls have the supplies *at home.*

into everlasting life – carrying the thoughts up from the eternal freshness and vitality of these waters to the great ocean in which they have their confluence. 'Thither may I arrive!' [BENGEL].

15–18. give me this water – This is not obtuseness – that is giving way – it expresses a wondering desire after she scarce knew what from this mysterious Stranger.

16. call thy husband – now proceeding to arouse her slumbering conscience by laying bare the guilty life she was leading, and by the minute details which that life furnished, not only bringing her sin vividly up before her, but preparing her to receive in His true character that wonderful Stranger to whom her whole life, in its minutest particulars, evidently lay open.

19, 20. Sir, I perceive – Seeing herself all revealed, does she now break down and ask what hopes there might be for one so guilty? Nay, her convictions have not reached that point yet. She ingeniously shifts the subject from a personal to a public question. It is not, 'Alas, what a wicked life am I leading!' but 'Lo, what a wonderful prophet I got into conversation with! He will be able to settle that interminable dispute between us and the Jews. Sir, you must know all about such matters – our fathers hold to this mountain here,' pointing to *Gerizim* in Samaria, 'as the divinely consecrated place of worship, but ye Jews say that *Jerusalem* is the proper place – which of us is right?' How slowly does the human heart submit to *thorough* humiliation! (Compare the *prodigal*; See Lu 15:15). Doubtless our Lord saw through the fetch; but does He say, 'That question is not the point just now, but have you been living in the way described, yea or nay? Till this is disposed of I cannot be drawn into theological controversies.' The Prince of preachers takes another method: He humors the poor woman, letting her take her own way, allowing her to lead while He follows – but thus only the more effectually gaining His object. He answers her question, pours light into her mind on the *spirituality* of all true worship, as of its glorious Object, and so brings her insensibly to the point at which He could disclose to her wondering mind whom she was all the while speaking to.

21–24. Woman – Here are three weighty pieces of information: (1) The point raised will very soon cease to be of any moment, for a total change of dispensation is about to come over the Church. (2) The Samaritans are wrong, not only as to the *place,* but the whole *grounds* and *nature* of their worship, while in all these respects the truth lies with the Jews. (3) As God is a *Spirit,* so He both *invites* and *demands* a *spiritual worship,* and already all is in preparation for a *spiritual economy,* more in harmony with the true nature of acceptable service than the ceremonial worship by consecrated *persons, place,* and *times,* which God for a time has seen meet to keep up till fulness of the time should come.

neither in this mountain nor yet at Jerusalem – that is, *exclusively* (Mal 1:11 1Ti 2:8).

worship the Father – She had talked simply of 'worship'; our Lord brings up before her the great OBJECT of all acceptable worship – 'THE FATHER.'

22. Ye worship ye know not what – without any *revealed authority,* and so very much in the dark. In this sense, the Jews *knew what they were about.* But the most glorious thing here is the reason assigned,

for salvation is of the Jews – intimating to her that *Salvation* was not a thing left to be reached by any one who might vaguely desire it of a God of mercy, but something that had been *revealed, prepared, deposited with a particular people,* and must be sought *in connection with, and as issuing from them;* and that people, 'the Jews.'

23. hour cometh, and now is – evidently meaning her to understand that this new economy was in some sense being set up while He was talking to her, a sense which would in a few minutes so far appear, when He told her plainly He was *the Christ.*

25, 26. I know Messias cometh … when He is come – If we take our Lord's immediate disclosure of Himself, in answer to this, as the proper key to its meaning to *His ear,* we can hardly doubt that the woman was already *all but prepared for even this startling announcement,* which indeed she seems (from Joh 4:29) to have already begun to suspect by His revealing her to herself. Thus quickly, under so matchless a Teacher, was she brought up from her sunken condition to a frame of mind and heart capable of the noblest revelations.

tell us all things – an expectation founded probably on De 18:15.

26. I that speak … am he – He scarce ever said anything like this to His own people, the Jews. He had magnified them to the woman, and yet to themselves He is to the last far more reserved than to her – *proving* rather than plainly *telling* them He was the Christ. But what would not have been *safe* among them was safe enough with her, whose *simplicity* at this stage of the conversation appears from the sequel to have become perfect. What now will the woman say? We listen, the scene has changed, a new party arrives, the disciples have been to Sychar, at some distance, to buy bread, and on their return are astonished at the company their Lord has been holding in their absence.

27. marvelled that he talked with the woman – It never probably occurred to them to marvel that He talked with *themselves;* yet in His eye, as the sequel shows, He was quite as nobly employed. How poor, if not false, are many of our most plausible estimates!

no man said … What? … Why? – awed by the spectacle, and thinking there must be something under it.

28–30. left her water-pot – How exquisitely natural! The presence of strangers made her feel that it was time for her to withdraw, and He who knew what was in her heart, and what she was going to the city to do, let her go without exchanging a word with her in the hearing of others. Their interview was too sacred, and the effect on the woman too overpowering (not to speak of His own deep emotion) to allow of its being continued. But this one artless touch – that she 'left her water-pot' – speaks volumes. The living water was already beginning to spring up within her; she found that man doth not live by bread nor by water only, and that there was a water of wondrous virtue that raised people above meat and drink, and the vessels that held them, and all human things. In short, she was transported, forgot everything but One, and her heart running over with the tale she had to tell, she hastens home and pours it out.

29. is not this the Christ – The *form* of the question (in the *Greek*) is a distant, modest way of only half *insinuating* what it seemed hardly fitting for her to *affirm;* nor does she refer to what He said of Himself, but solely to His disclosure to her of the particulars of her own life.

30. Then they went out – How different from the Jews! and richly was their openness to conviction rewarded.

31–38. meantime – that is, while the woman was away.

Master, eat – *Fatigue* and *thirst* we saw He felt; here is revealed another of our common infirmities to which the Lord was subject – *hunger.*

32. meat ye know not of – What spirituality of mind! 'I *have* been eating all the while, and such food as ye dream not of.' What can that be? they ask each other; have any supplies been brought Him in our absence? He knows what they are saying though He hears it not.

34. My meat is – 'A Servant here to fulfil a prescribed work, to *do* and to *finish,* that is "meat" to Me; and of this, while you were away, I have had My fill.' And of what does He speak thus? Of the condescension, pity, patience, wisdom He had been laying out upon *one soul* – a very humble woman, and in some respects repulsive too! But He had gained her, and through her was going to gain more, and lay perhaps the foundations of a great work in the country of Samaria; and this filled His whole soul and raised Him above the sense of natural hunger (Mt 4:4).

35. yet four months, and then harvest – that is, 'In current speech, ye say thus at this season; but lift up your eyes and look upon those fields in the light of *another* husbandry, for lo! *in that sense,* they are even now white to harvest, ready for the sickle.' The simple beauty of this language is only surpassed by the glow of holy emotion in the Redeemer's own soul which it expresses. It refers to the *ripeness* of these Sycharites for accession to Him, and the joy of this great Lord of the reapers over the anticipated ingathering. Oh, could we but *so,* 'lift up our eyes and look' upon many fields abroad and at home, which to dull sense appear unpromising, as *He* beheld those of Samaria, what movements, as yet scarce in embryo, and accessions to Christ, as yet seemingly far distant, might we not discern as quite near at hand, and thus, amidst difficulties and discouragements too much for nature to sustain, be cheered – *as our Lord Himself was* in circumstances far more overwhelming – with 'songs in the night!'

36. he that reapeth – As our Lord could not mean that the reaper only, and not the sower, received 'wages,' in the sense of *personal reward* for his work, the 'wages' here can be no other than the joy of having such a harvest to gather in – the joy of 'gathering fruit unto life eternal.'

rejoice together – The blessed issue of the whole ingathering is the interest alike of the sower as of the reaper; it is no more the fruit of the last operation than of the first; and just as there can be no reaping without previous sowing, so have those servants of Christ, to whom is assigned the pleasant task of merely reaping the spiritual harvest, no work to do, and no joy to taste, that has not been prepared to their hand by the toilsome and often thankless work of their predecessors in the field. *The joy, therefore, of the great harvest festivity will be the common joy of all who have taken any part in the work from the first operation to the last.* (See De 16:11,14 Ps 126:6 Isa 9:3.) What encouragement is here for those 'fishers of men' who 'have toiled all the night' of their official life, and, to human appearance, 'have taken nothing!'

38. I sent you – The *I* is emphatic – I, the Lord of the whole harvest: 'sent you,' points to their *past* appointment to the apostleship, though it has reference only to their *future* discharge of it, for they had nothing to do with the present ingathering of the Sycharites.

ye bestowed no labour – meaning that much of their future success would arise from *preparation already made* for them. (See on Joh 4:42).

others laboured – Referring to the Old Testament labourers, the Baptist, and *by implication* Himself, though He studiously keeps this in the background, *that the line of distinction between Himself and all His servants might not be lost sight of.* 'Christ represents Himself as the Husbandman [rather the Lord of the labourers], who has the direction both of the sowing and of the harvest, who commissions *all* the agents – those of the Old Testament as well as of the New – and therefore does not stand on a level with either the sowers or the reapers' [OLSHAUSEN].

39–42. many … believed – The truth of Joh 4:35 begins to appear. These Samaritans were the foundation of the Church afterwards built up there. No miracle appears to have been wrought there (but unparalleled supernatural knowledge displayed): '*we have heard Him ourselves*' (Joh 4:42) sufficed to raise their faith to a point never attained by the Jews, and hardly as yet by the disciples – that He was 'the Saviour of *the world*' [ALFORD]. 'This incident is further remarkable as a rare instance of the Lord's ministry producing *an awakening on a large scale*' [OLSHAUSEN].

40. abode two days – Two precious days, surely, to the Redeemer Himself! Unsought, He had come to His own, yet His own received Him not: now those who were not His own had come to Him, been won by Him, and invited Him to their town that others might share with them in the benefit of His wonderful ministry. Here, then, would He solace His already wounded spirit and have in this outfield village triumph of His grace, a sublime foretaste of the inbringing of the whole Gentile world into the Church.

Joh 4:43–54.
Second Galilean miracle – healing of the courtier's son.

43, 44. after two days – literally, the two days of His stay at Sychar.

44. For Jesus testified – This verse had occasioned much discussion. For it seems strange, if 'His own country' here means *Nazareth,* which was in Galilee, that it should be said He came to Galilee *because* in one of its towns He expected no good reception. But all will be simple and natural if we fill up the statement thus: 'He went into the region of Galilee, but not, as might have been expected, to that part of it called "His own country," Nazareth (see Mr 6:4 Lu 4:24), *for* He acted on the maxim which He oft repeated, that "a prophet."

45. received – welcomed Him.

having seen ... at the feast – proud, perhaps, of their Countryman's wonderful works at Jerusalem, and possibly won by this circumstance to regard His claims as at least worthy of respectful investigation. Even this our Lord did not despise, for saving conversion often begins in less than this (so Zaccheus, Lu 19:3–10).

for they also went – that is, it was their practice to go up to the feast.

46, 47. nobleman – courtier, king's servant, or one connected with a royal household; such as Chuza (Lu 8:3), or Manaen (Ac 13:1).

heard that Jesus was come out of Judea – 'where he had doubtless seen or heard what things Jesus had done at Jerusalem' (Joh 4:45), [BENGEL].

come down – for Capernaum was down on the northwest shore of the Sea of Galilee.

48–54. Except ye see signs – He *did* believe, both as his coming and his urgent entreaty show; but how imperfectly we shall see; and our Lord would deepen his faith by such a blunt and seemingly rough answer as He made to Nicodemus.

49. come down ere my child die – 'While we talk, the case is at its crisis, and if Thou come not instantly, all is over.' This was faith, but partial, and our Lord would perfect it. The man cannot believe the cure could be wrought without the Physician coming to the patient – the thought of such a thing evidently never occurred to him. But Jesus will in a moment bring him up to this.

50. Go thy way; thy son liveth – Both effects instantaneously followed: – 'The man believed the word,' and the cure, shooting quicker than lightning from Cana to Capernaum, was felt by the dying youth. In token of faith, the father takes his leave of Christ – in the circumstances this evidenced full faith. The servants hasten to convey the joyful tidings to the anxious parent, whose faith now only wants one confirmation. '*When* began he to amend? ... Yesterday, at the seventh hour, the fever left him' – the very hour in which was uttered that great word, 'Thy son liveth!' So 'himself believed and his whole house.' He *had* believed before this, first very imperfectly; then with assured confidence of Christ's word; but now with a faith crowned by 'sight.' And the wave rolled from the head to the members of his household. 'To-day is salvation come to this *house*' (Lu 19:9); and no mean house this!

second miracle Jesus did – that is, in Cana; done 'after He came out of Judea,' as the former before.

Chapter 5

Joh 5:1–47.

The impotent man healed – discourse occasioned by the persecution arising there upon.

1. a feast of the Jews – *What feast?* No question has more divided the Harmonists of the Gospels, and the duration of our Lord's ministry may be said to hinge on it. For if, as the majority have thought (until of late years) it was a *Passover*, His ministry lasted three and a half years; if not, probably a year less. Those who are dissatisfied with the Passover-view all differ among themselves what other feast it was, and some of the most acute think there are no grounds for deciding. In our judgment the evidence is in favor of its being a *Passover*, but the reasons cannot be stated here.

2, 3. sheep *market* – The supplement should be (as in *Margin*) 'sheep [gate],' mentioned in Ne 3:1,32.

Bethesda – that is, 'house (place) of mercy,' from the cures wrought there.

five porches – for shelter to the patients.

3. impotent – infirm.

4. an angel – This miracle differed in two points from all other miracles recorded in Scripture: (1) It was not one, but a succession of miracles periodically wrought: (2) As it was only wrought 'when the waters were troubled,' so only upon one patient at a time, and that the patient 'who first stepped in after the troubling of the waters.' But this only the more undeniably fixed its miraculous character. We have heard of many waters having a medicinal virtue; but what water was ever known to cure *instantaneously* a single disease? And who ever heard of any water curing all, even the most diverse diseases – 'blind, halt, withered' – alike? Above all, who ever heard of such a thing being done 'only at a certain season,' and most singularly of all, doing it only to the first person who stepped in after the moving of the waters? Any of these peculiarities – much more all taken together – must have proclaimed the supernatural character of the cures wrought.

5–9. thirty and eight years – but not all that time at the pool. This was probably the most pitiable of all the cases, and *therefore selected*.

6. saw him lie, and knew – As He doubtless visited the spot just to perform this cure, so He knows where to find His patient, and the whole previous history of his case (Joh 2:25).

Wilt thou be made whole? – Could anyone doubt that a sick man would like to be made whole, or that the patients came thither, and this man had returned again and again, just in hope of a cure? But our Lord asked the question. (1) To fasten attention upon Himself; (2) By making him detail his case to deepen in him the feeling of entire helplessness; (3) By so singular a question to beget in his desponding heart the hope of a cure. (Compare Mr 10:51.)

7. Sir, I have no man – Instead of *saying* he wished to be cured, he just tells with piteous simplicity how fruitless had been all his efforts to obtain it, and how *helpless* and all but *hopeless* he was. Yet not quite. For here he is at the pool, waiting on. It seemed of no use; nay, only tantalizing,

while I am coming, another steppeth down before me – the fruit was snatched from his lips. Yet he will not go away. He may get nothing by staying, he may drop into his grave ere he get into the pool; but by going from the appointed, divine way of healing, he can get nothing. Wait therefore he will, wait he does, and when Christ comes to heal him, lo! he is waiting his turn. *What an attitude for a sinner* at Mercy's gate! The man's hopes seemed low enough ere Christ came to him. He might have said, just before 'Jesus passed by that way,' 'This is no use; I shall never get in; let me die at home.' Then all had been lost. But he *held on*, and his perseverance was rewarded with a glorious cure. Probably some rays of hope darted into his heart as he told his tale before those Eyes whose glance measured his whole case. But the word of command consummates his preparation to receive the cure, and instantaneously works it.

8. Rise, take up thy bed – 'Immediately' he did so. 'He *spake* and it was *done.*' The slinging of his portable couch over his shoulders was designed to show the perfection of the cure.

9. the same day was the sabbath – Beyond all doubt this was intentional, as in so many other healings, in order that when opposition arose on this account men might be compelled to listen to His claims and His teaching.

10–16. The Jews – that is, *those in authority.* (See on Joh 1:19.)

it is not lawful to carry thy bed – a glorious testimony to the cure, as *instantaneous* and *complete,* from the lips of the most prejudiced! (And what a contrast does it, as all our Lord's miracles, present to the bungling miracles of the Church of Rome!) In *ordinary* circumstances, the rulers had the law on their side (Ne 13:15 Jer 17:21). But when the man referred them to 'Him that had made him whole' (Joh 5:11) as his authority, the argument was resistless. Yet they ingeniously parried the thrust, asking him, not who had 'made him whole' – that would have condemned themselves and defeated their purpose – but who had bidden him 'take up his bed and walk,' in other words, who had dared to order a breach of the sabbath? It is time we were looking after Him – thus hoping to shake the man's faith in his Healer.

13. he that was healed wist not – That some one, with unparalleled generosity, tenderness

and power, had done it, the man knew well enough: but as he had never heard of Him before, so he disappeared too quickly for any inquiries.

conveyed himself away – slipped out of the crowd that had gathered, to avoid both hasty popularity and precipitate hatred (Mt 12:14–19).

14. findeth him in the temple – saying, perhaps, 'I will go into Thy house with burnt offerings, I will pay my vows which my lips have uttered and my mouth hath spoken when I was in trouble' (Ps 66:13,14). Jesus, there Himself for His own ends, 'findeth him there' – *not all accidentally*, be assured.

sin no more – a glimpse this of the reckless life he had probably led *before* his thirty-eight years' infirmity had come upon him, and which not improbably had brought on, in the just judgment of God, his chronic complaint. Fearful illustration this of 'the severity of God,' but glorious manifestation of our Lord's insight into 'what was in man.'

15. The man departed, and told – little thinking how unwelcome his grateful and eager testimony would be. 'The darkness received not the light which was pouring its rays upon it' (Joh 1:5,11) [OLSHAUSEN].

16. because he had done these things on the sabbath day – What to these hypocritical religionists was the doing of the most glorious and beneficent miracles, compared with the atrocity of doing them on the sabbath day! Having given them this handle, on purpose to raise the first public controversy with them, and thus open a fitting opportunity of laying His claims before them, He rises at once to the whole height of them, in a statement which for grandeur and terseness exceeds almost anything that ever afterwards fell from Him, at least to His enemies.

17, 18. My Father worketh hitherto and I work – The 'I' is emphatic; 'The creative and conservative activity of My Father has known no sabbath-cessation from the beginning until now, *and that is the law of My working.*'

18. God was his Father – literally, 'His own [or peculiar] Father,' (as in Ro 8:32). The addition is their own, but a very proper one.

making himself equal with God – rightly gathering this to be His meaning, not from the mere words 'My Father,' but from His claim of right to act as His Father did in the like high sphere, and by the same law of ceaseless activity in that sphere. And as, instead of instantly disclaiming any such meaning – as He must have done if it was false – He positively sets His seal to it in the following verses, merely explaining how consistent such claim was with the prerogatives of His Father, it is beyond all doubt that we have here an assumption of *peculiar personal Sonship,* or participation in the Father's essential nature.

19, 20. the Son can do nothing of himself – that is, *apart from* and *in rivalry of* the Father, as they supposed. The meaning is, 'The Son can have no separate *interest* or *action* from the Father.'

for what things – On the contrary, 'whatever the Father doeth that same doeth the Son,'

likewise – 'in the like manner.' What claim to absolute equality with the Father could exceed this: not only to do 'the same things,' but to do them *as the Father does them?*

20. Father loveth … and showeth him all – As love has no concealments, so it results from the perfect fellowship and mutual endearment of the Father and the Son (see on Joh 1:1; Joh 1:18), whose interests are one, even as their nature, that the Father communicates to the Son all His counsels, and what has been thus shown to the Son is by Him executed in His mediatorial character. 'With the Father, *doing* is *willing;* it is only the Son who *acts in Time*' [ALFORD]. Three things here are clear: (1) The *personal distinctions* in the Godhead. (2) Unity of *action* among the Persons results from unity of *nature.* (3) Their oneness of interest is no unconscious or involuntary thing, but a thing of glorious *consciousness, will,* and *love,* of which the Persons themselves are the proper Objects.

show him greater things – referring to what He goes on to mention (Joh 5:21–31), comprised in two great words, LIFE and JUDGMENT, which STIER beautifully calls God's *Regalia.* Yet these, Christ says, the Father and He do in common.

21–23. raiseth the dead and quickeneth *them* – one act in two stages. This is His absolute prerogative as God.

so the Son quickeneth them – that is, raiseth up and quickeneth.

whom he will – not only *doing the same divine act,* but doing it *as the result of His own will,* even as the Father does it. This statement is of immense importance in relation to the miracles of Christ, distinguishing them from similar miracles of prophets and apostles, who as *human instruments* were employed to perform super-natural actions, while Christ did all as the Father's *commissioned Servant* indeed, but *in the exercise of His own absolute right of action.*

22. For the Father judgeth no man – rather, 'For neither doth the Father judge any man,' implying that the same 'thing was meant in the former verse of the quickening of the dead' – both acts being done, not by the Father *and* the Son, as though twice done, but by the Father *through* the Son as His voluntary Agent.

all judgment – judgment in its most comprehensive sense, or as we should say, all *administration.*

23. honour the Son as … the Father – As he who believes that Christ in the foregoing verses has given a true account of His relation to the Father must of necessity hold Him entitled to the same *honor* as the Father, so He here adds that it was the Father's express intention in making over all judgment to the Son, that men *should* thus honor Him.

honoureth not the Father – does not do it in fact, whatever he may imagine, and will be held as not doing it by the Father Himself, who will accept no homage which is not accorded to His own Son.

24. believeth on him that sent me – that is, believeth in Him as having sent Me. I have spoken of the Son's right not only to heal the sick but to raise from the dead, and quicken whom He will: And now I say unto you, *That life-giving operation has already passed upon all who receive My words as the Sent of the Father* on the great errand of mercy.

hath everlasting life – immediately on his believing (compare Joh 3:18 1Jo 5:12,13).

is passed – 'hath passed over'

from death unto life – What a transition! (Compare 1Jo 3:14.)

25–29. The hour cometh – in its whole fulness, at Pentecost.

and now is – in its beginnings.

the dead – the *spiritually* dead, as is clear from Joh 5:28. Here He rises from the calmer phrase 'hearing *his word*' (Joh 5:24), to the grander expression, 'hearing *the voice of the Son of God,*' to signify that as it finds men in a *dead* condition, so it carries with it a *resurrection-power.*

shall live – in the sense of Joh 5:24.

26. given to the Son – Does this refer to the essential life of the Son before all time (Joh 1:4) (as most of the Fathers, and OLSHAUSEN, STIER, ALFORD, among the moderns), or to the purpose of God that this essential life should reside in the Person of the Incarnate Son, and be manifested thus to the world? [CALVIN, LUCKE, LUTHARDT] The question is as difficult as the subject is high. But as all that Christ says of His *essential* relation to the Father is intended to explain and exalt His *mediatorial* functions, so the one seems in our Lord's own mind and language mainly the starting-point of the other.

27. because he is the Son of man – This seems to confirm the last remark, that what Christ had properly in view was the indwelling of the Son's essential life in *humanity* as the great *theater* and *medium* of divine display, in both the great departments of His work – *life-giving and judgment.* The appointment of a Judge in our *own nature* is one of the most beautiful arrangements of divine wisdom in redemption.

28. Marvel not at this – this committal of all judgment to *the Son of man.*

for the hour is coming – He adds not in this case (as in Joh 5:25), 'and now is,' because this was not to be till the close of the whole dispensation of mercy.

29. resurrection of life – that is, to life everlasting (Mt 25:46).

of damnation – It would have been harsh to say 'the resurrection of death,' though that is meant, for sinners rise *from death to death* [BENGEL]. The resurrection of both classes is an exercise of *sovereign authority;* but in the one case it is an act of *grace,* in the other of *justice.* (Compare Da 12:2, from which the language is taken.) How awfully grand are these unfoldings of His dignity and authority from the mouth of Christ Himself! And they are all in the *third person;* in what follows He resumes the *first person.*

30–32. of mine own self do nothing – that is, apart from the Father, or in any interest than My own. (See on Joh 5:19.)

as I hear – that is, 'My judgments are all *anticipated* in the bosom of My Father, to which I have immediate access, and by Me only *responded to* and *reflected.* They cannot therefore err, as I live for one end only, to carry into effect the will of Him that sent Me.'

31. If I … witness of myself – standing alone, and setting up any separate interest.

32. There is another – that is, *the Father,* as is plain from the connection. How brightly the distinction of the Persons shines out here!

and I know that the witness – 'This is the Son's testimony to the Father's truth (see Joh 7:28 8:26,55). It testifies to the full consciousness on the part of the Son, even in the days of His humiliation, of the righteousness of the Father' [ALFORD]. And thus He cheered His spirit under the cloud of human opposition which was already gathering over His head.

33–35. Ye sent unto John – (See Joh 1:19.)

receive not testimony … from man – that is, depend not on human testimony.

but … that ye might be saved – 'I refer to him merely to aid your salvation.'

35. He was a burning and a shining light – literally, '*the* burning and shining lamp' (or torch): – that is, 'the great light of his day.' Christ is never called by the humble word here applied to John – a *light-bearer* – studiously used to distinguish him from his Master, but ever *the Light* in the most absolute sense. (See on Joh 1:6.)

willing for a season – that is, till they saw that it pointed whither they were not prepared to go.

to rejoice in his light – There is a play of irony here, referring to the hollow delight with which his testimony tickled them.

36–38. I have greater witness – rather, 'The witness which I have is greater.'

the works … bear witness of me – not simply as *miracles* nor even as a miracle of *mercy,* but these miracles, *as He did them,* with a *will* and a

power, a *majesty* and a *grace* manifestly *His own.*

37. the Father himself … hath borne witness of me – not referring, probably, to the voice of His baptism, but (as seems from what follows) to the testimony of the Old Testament Scripture [CALVIN, LUCKE, MEYER, LUTHARDT].

neither heard his voice – never recognized Him in this character. The words are 'designedly mysterious, like many others which our Lord uttered' [STIER].

38. not his word abiding in you – passing now from the *Witness* to the *testimony* borne by Him in 'the lively oracles' (Ac 7:38): both were alike strangers to their breasts, as was evidenced by their rejecting Him to whom all that witness was borne.

39–42. Search the scriptures – 'In the Scriptures ye find your charter of eternal life; go search them then, and you will find that I am the Great Burden of their testimony; yet ye will not come to Me for that life eternal which you profess to find there, and of which they tell you I am the appointed Dispenser.' (Compare Ac 17:11,12.) How touching and gracious are these last words! Observe here (1) The honour which Christ gives to the Scriptures, as a record which all *have a right* and *are bound* to search – the reverse of which the Church of Rome teaches; (2) The opposite extreme is, resting in the mere *Book* without *the living Christ,* to direct the soul to whom is its main use and chiefest glory.

41. I receive not honour from men – contrasting His own end with theirs, which was to obtain *human applause.*

42. not the love of God in you – which would inspire you with a single desire to know His mind and will, and yield yourselves to it, in spite of prejudice and regardless of consequences.

43–47. if another shall come – How strikingly has this been verified in the history of the Jews! 'From the time of the true Christ to our time, sixty-four false Christs have been reckoned by whom they have been deceived' [BENGEL].

44. How can ye believe – (See on Joh 5:40,41.) The '*will not*' of Joh 5:40, and '*cannot*' here are just different features of the same awful state of the human heart.

45. Do not think I will accuse you to the Father – 'My errand hither is not to collect evidence to condemn you at God's bar.'

one that accuseth you, *even* Moses – 'Alas! that will be too well done by another, and him the object of all your religious boastings – Moses,' here put for 'the Law,' the basis of the Old Testament Scriptures.

46. he wrote of me – 'an important testimony to the subject of the whole Pentateuch – "of Me"' [ALFORD].

47. If ye believe not – (See Lu 16:31.)

his writings ... my words – a remarkable contrast, not *absolutely* exalting Old Testament Scripture above His own words, but pointing to the office of those venerable documents to *prepare* Christ's way, to the necessity universally felt for *documentary* testimony in revealed religion, and perhaps (as STIER adds) to the relation which the comparative *'letter'* of the Old Testament holds to the more flowing 'words' of 'spirit and life' which characterize the New Testament.

Chapter 6

Joh 6:1–13.
Five thousand miraculously fed.

(See Mr 6:31–44).

3. a mountain – somewhere in that hilly range which skirts the east side of the lake.

4. passover ... was nigh – but for the reason mentioned (Joh 7:1), Jesus kept away from it, remaining in Galilee.

Joh 6:14–21.
Jesus walks on the sea.

14, 15. that prophet – (See on Joh 1:21.)

15. departed ... to a mountain himself alone – (1) to *rest,* which He came to this 'desert place' on purpose to do before the miracle of the loaves, but could not for the multitude that followed Him (see Mr 6:31); and (2) *'to pray'* (Mt 14:23 Mr 6:46). But from His mountain-top He kept watching the ship (see on Joh 6:18), and doubtless prayed both for them, and with a view to the new manifestation which He was to give them of His glory.

16, 17. when even was come – (See Mr 6:35.) **entered into a ship** – *'constrained'* to do so by their Master (Mt 14:22 Mr 6:45), in order to put an end to the misdirected excitement in His favour (Joh 6:15), into which the disciples themselves may have been somewhat drawn. The word 'constrained' implies reluctance on their part, perhaps from unwillingness to part with their Master and embark at night, leaving Him alone on the mountain.

went – rather, 'were proceeding.'

toward Capernaum – Mark says (Mr 6:45), 'unto Bethsaida,' meaning 'Bethsaida of Galilee' (Joh 12:21), on the west side of the lake. The place they left was of the same name (see Mr 6:32).

Jesus was not come to them – They probably lingered in hopes of His still joining them, and so let the darkness come on.

18, 19. sea arose – and they were 'now in the midst of it' (Mt 14:24). Mark adds the graphic and touching particular, 'He saw them toiling in rowing' (Mr 6:48), putting forth all their strength to buffet the waves and bear on against a head wind, but to little effect. He *saw* this from

His mountain-top, and through the darkness of the night, for His heart was all with them; yet would He not go to their relief till His own time came.

19. they see Jesus – 'about the fourth watch of the night' (Mt 14:25 Mr 6:48), or between three and six in the morning.

walking on the sea – What Job (Job 9:8) celebrates as the distinguishing prerogative of GOD, 'WHO ALONE spreadeth out the heavens, and TREADETH UPON THE WAVES OF THE SEA' – What AGUR challenges as GOD's unapproachable prerogative, to 'GATHER THE WIND IN HIS FISTS, and BIND THE WATERS IN A GARMENT' (Pr 30:4) – lo! this is here done *in flesh,* by 'THE SON OF MAN.'

drawing nigh to the ship – yet as though He *'would have passed by them,'* Mr 6:48 (compare Lu 24:28 Ge 18:3,5 32:24–26).

they were afraid – 'cried out for fear' (Mt 14:26), 'supposing it had been a spirit' (Mr 6:49). He would appear to them at first like a dark moving speck upon the waters; then as a human figure, but – in the dark tempestuous sky, and not dreaming that it could be their Lord – they take it for a spirit. (How often thus we miscall our chiefest mercies – not only thinking them distant when they are near, but thinking the best the worst!)

20. It is I; be not afraid – Matthew (Mt 14:27) and Mark (Mr 6:50) give before these exhilarating words, that to them so well-known one, 'Be of good cheer!'

21. willingly received him into the ship – their first fears being now converted into wonder and delight.

and immediately the ship was at the land – This additional miracle, for as such it is manifestly related, is recorded here alone. Yet all that is meant seems to be that as the storm was suddenly calmed, so the little bark – propelled by the secret power of the Lord of Nature now sailing in it – glided through the now unruffled waters, and while they were wrapt in wonder at what had happened, not heeding their rapid motion, *was found* at port, to their still further surprise.

Joh 6:22–71.
Jesus followed by the multitudes to Capernaum, discourses to them in the synagogue of the bread of life – effect of this on two classes of the disciples

22–24. These verses are a little involved, from the Evangelist's desire to mention every circumstance, however minute, that might call up the scene as vividly to the reader as it stood before his own view.

The day following – the miracle of the loaves, and the stormy night; the day on which they landed at Capernaum.

the people which stood on the other side of the sea – not the whole multitude that had been fed, but only such of them as remained over night about the shore, that is, on the *east* side of the lake; for we are supposed to have come, with Jesus and His disciples in the ship, to the *west* side, to Capernaum.

saw that there was none other boat there – The meaning is, the people had observed that there had been only one boat on the east side where they were; namely, the one in which the disciples had crossed at night to the other, the west side, and they had also observed that Jesus had not gone on board that boat, but His disciples had put off without Him:

23. Howbeit – 'Howbeit,' adds the Evangelist, in a lively parenthesis, 'there came other boats from Tiberias' (which lay near the southwest coast of the lake), whose passengers were part of the multitude that had followed Jesus to the east side, and been miraculously fed; these boats were fastened somewhere (says the Evangelist) nigh unto the place where they did eat bread, after that the Lord had given thanks – thus he refers to the glorious 'miracle of the loaves' – and now they were put in requisition to convey the people back again to the west side. For when 'the people saw that Jesus was not there, neither His disciples, they also took shipping [in these boats] and came to Capernaum, seeking for Jesus.'

25. when they had found him on the other side – at Capernaum.

they said – astonished at His *being* there, and wondering *how* He could have accomplished it, whether by land or water, and *when* He came; for being quite unaware of His having walked upon the sea and landed with the disciples in the ship, they could not see how, unless He had travelled all night round the head of the lake alone, He could have reached Capernaum, and even then, how He could have arrived before themselves.

26. Ye seek me – Jesus does not put them through their difficulty, says nothing of His treading on the waves of the sea, nor even notices their question, but takes advantage of the favourable moment for pointing out to them how forward, flippant, and superficial were their views, and how low their desires. 'Ye seek Me not because ye saw the miracles' – literally, 'the *signs*,' that is, supernatural tokens of a higher presence, and a divine commission, 'but because ye did eat of the loaves and were filled.' From this He proceeds at once to that *other Bread,* just as, with the woman of Samaria, to that *other Water* (Joh 4:9–15). We should have supposed all that follows to have been delivered by the wayside, or wherever they happened first to meet. But from Joh 6:59 we gather that they had probably met about the door of the synagogue – 'for that was the day in which they assembled in their synagogues' [LIGHTFOOT] – and that on being asked, at the close of the service, if He had any word of exhortation to the people, He had taken the two breads, the *perishing* and the *living* bread, for the subject of His profound and extraordinary discourse.

27. which the Son of man – taking that title of Himself which denoted His incarnate life.

shall give unto you – in the sense of Joh 6:51.

him hath God the Father sealed – marked out and authenticated for that transcendent office, to impart to the world the bread of an everlasting life, and this in the character of 'the Son of *man*.'

28–31. What shall we do … the works of God – such works as God will approve. Different answers may be given to such a question, according to the *spirit* which prompts the inquiry. (See Ho 6:6–8 Lu 3:12–14.) Here our Lord, knowing whom He had to deal with, shapes His reply accordingly.

29. This is the work of God – That lies at the threshold of all acceptable obedience, being not only the prerequisite to it, but the proper spring of it – in that sense, the work of works, emphatically 'the work of God.'

30. What sign showest thou – But how could they ask 'a sign,' when many of them scarce a day before had witnessed such a 'sign' as had never till then been vouchsafed to men; when after witnessing it, they could hardly be restrained from making Him a king; when they followed Him from the one side of the lake to the other; and when, in the opening words of this very discourse, He had chided them for seeking Him, 'not because they *saw the signs,*' but for the loaves? The truth seems to be that they were confounded by the *novel claims* which our Lord had just advanced. In proposing to make Him a king, it was for far other purposes than dispensing to the world the bread of an everlasting life; and when He seemed to raise His claims even higher still, by representing it as the grand 'work of God,' that they should believe *on Himself* as His Sent One, they saw very clearly that He was making a demand upon them beyond anything they were prepared to accord to Him, and beyond all that man had ever before made. Hence their question, 'What dost Thou *work?*'

31. Our fathers did eat manna – insinuating the inferiority of Christ's miracle of the loaves to those of Moses: 'When Moses claimed the confidence of the fathers, "he gave them bread from heaven to eat" – not for a few thousands, but for millions, and not once only, but daily throughout their wilderness journey.'

32, 33. Moses gave you not – 'It was not Moses that gave you the manna, and even it was but from the lower heavens; "but *My Father* giveth you *the true bread,*" and that *"from heaven.*"'

33. For the bread of God is he – This verse is perhaps best left in its own transparent grandeur – holding up the Bread Itself as *divine, spiritual,* and *eternal;* its ordained Fountain and essential Substance, '*Him who came down from heaven to give it*' (that Eternal Life which was with the Father and was manifested unto us, 1Jo 1:2); and its designed objects, '*the world.*'

34. Lord, evermore give us this bread – speaking now with a certain reverence (as at Joh 6:25), the perpetuity of the manna floating perhaps in their minds, and much like the Samaritan woman, when her eyes were but half opened, 'Sir, give Me this water,' (Joh 4:15).

35. I am the bread of life – Henceforth the discourse is all *in the first person,* 'I,' 'Me,' which occur in one form or other, as STIER reckons, thirty-five times.

he that cometh to me – to obtain what the soul craves, and as the only all-sufficient and ordained source of supply.

hunger … thirst – shall have conscious and abiding satisfaction.

36. But … ye have seen me, and believe not – seen Him not in His mere bodily presence, but in all the majesty of His life, His teaching, His works.

37–40. All that – This comprehensive and very grand passage is expressed with a peculiar artistic precision. The opening general statement (Joh 6:37) consists of two members: (1) 'ALL THAT THE FATHER GIVETH ME SHALL COME TO ME' – that is, 'Though ye, as I told you, have no faith in Me, My errand into the world shall in no wise be defeated; for all that the Father giveth Me shall infallibly come to Me.' Observe, what is *given* Him by the Father is expressed in the *singular* number and *neuter* gender – literally, 'everything'; while those who *come to* Him are put in the *masculine* gender and *singular* number – 'every one.' The *whole mass,* so to speak, is gifted by the Father to the Son as a *unity,* which the Son evolves, one by one, in the execution of His trust. So Joh 17:2, 'that He should give eternal life to *all that which* Thou hast given Him' [BENGEL]. This '*shall*' expresses the glorious *certainty* of it, the Father being pledged to see to it that the gift be no empty mockery. (2) 'AND HIM THAT COMETH TO ME I WILL IN NO WISE CAST OUT.' As the former was the *divine,* this is just the *human* side of the same thing. True, the 'coming' ones of the second clause are just the 'given' ones of the first. But had our Lord merely said, '*When those* that have been given Me of My Father shall come to Me, I will receive them' – besides being very flat, the impression conveyed would have been quite different, sounding as if there were *no other laws in operation,* in the movement of

sinners to Christ, but such as are wholly divine and *inscrutable* to us; whereas, though He does speak of it as a sublime certainty which men's *refusals* cannot frustrate, He speaks of that certainty as taking effect only by men's *voluntary advances* to Him and acceptance of Him – 'Him that cometh to Me,' 'whosoever will,' throwing the door wide open. Only it is not the simply *willing,* but the actually *coming,* whom He will not cast out; for the word here employed usually denotes *arrival,* as distinguished from the ordinary word, which rather expresses the *act of coming* (see Joh 8:42, *Greek*), [WEBSTER and WILKINSON]. 'In no wise' is an emphatic negative, to meet the fears of the timid (as in Re 21:27, to meet the presumption of the hardened). These, then, being the two members of the general opening statement, what follows is meant to take in both,

38. For I came down from heaven not to do Mine own will – to play an independent part.

but – in respect to both the foregoing things, the *divine* and the *human* side of salvation.

the will of Him that sent Me – What this twofold will of Him that sent Him is, we are next sublimely told (Joh 6:39,40):

39. And this – in the *first* place.

is the will of Him that sent me, that of all – everything.

which He hath given Me – (taking up the identical words of Joh 6:37).

I should lose nothing, but should raise it up at the last day – The meaning is not, of course, that He is charged to keep the objects entrusted to Him *as He received them,* so as they should merely suffer nothing in His hands. For as they were just 'perishing' *sinners* of Adam's family, to let 'nothing' of such 'be lost,' but 'raise them up at the last day,' must involve, *first,* giving His flesh for them (Joh 6:51), that they 'might not perish, but have everlasting life'; and *then,* after 'keeping them from falling,' raising their sleeping dust in incorruption and glory, and presenting them, body and soul, perfect and entire, wanting nothing, to Him who gave them to Him, saying, 'Behold I and the children which God hath given Me.' So much for the *first* will of Him that sent Him, the *divine* side of man's salvation, whose every stage and movement is inscrutable to us, but infallibly certain.

40. And this – in the *second* place.

is the will of Him that sent Me, that every one which seeth the Son and believeth on Him – seeing the Son believeth on Him.

may have everlasting life, and I will raise him up at the last day – This is the *human* side of the same thing as in the foregoing verse, and answering to '*Him that cometh unto Me I will in no wise cast out*'; that is, I have it expressly in charge that everyone that so 'beholdeth' (so vieweth) the Son as to believe on Him shall have everlasting life; and, that *none* of Him be lost, 'I will raise him up at the last day.' (See on Joh 6:54.)

41–46. Jews murmured – muttered, not in our Lord's hearing, but He knew it (Joh 6:43 Joh 2:25).

he said, I am the bread – Missing the sense and glory of this, and having no relish for such sublimities, they harp upon the 'Bread from heaven.' 'What can this mean? Do we not know all about Him – where, when, and of whom He was born? And yet He says He came down from heaven!'

43, 44. Murmur not ... No man – that is, Be not either startled or stumbled at these sayings; for it needs divine teaching to understand them, divine drawing to submit to them.

44. can come to me – in the sense of Joh 6:35.

except the Father which hath sent me – that is, the Father *as the Sender of Me* and *to carry out the design of My mission.*

draw him – by an *internal* and *efficacious* operation; though by all the means of rational conviction, and in a way altogether consonant to their moral nature (So 1:4 Jer 31:3 Ho 11:3,4).

raise him up – (See on Joh 6:54.)

45. written in the prophets – in Isa 54:13 Jer 31:33,34; other similar passages may also have been in view. Our Lord thus falls back upon Scripture authority for this seemingly hard saying.

all taught of God – not by *external* revelation merely, but by *internal illumination,* corresponding to the 'drawing' of Joh 6:44.

Every man therefore – that is, who hath been thus efficaciously taught of Him.

cometh unto me – *with absolute certainty,* yet in the sense above given of 'drawing'; that is, 'As none can come to Me but as divinely drawn, so none thus drawn shall fail to come.'

46. Not that any man hath seen – Lest they should confound that 'hearing and learning of the Father,' to which believers are admitted by divine *teaching,* with His own immediate access to Him, He here throws in a parenthetical explanation; stating, as explicitly as words could do it, how totally different the two cases were, and that only He who is 'from God' hath this naked, immediate access to the Father. (See Joh 1:18.)

47–51. He that believeth – (See on Joh 3:36; Joh 5:24.)

48. I am the bread of life – 'As he that believeth in Me hath everlasting life, so I am Myself the everlasting *Sustenance* of that life.' (Repeated from Joh 6:35.)

49. Your fathers – of whom ye spake (Joh 6:31); not 'ours,' by which He would hint that *He* had a higher descent, of which they dreamt not [BENGEL].

did eat manna ... and are dead – recurring to their own point about the manna, as one of the noblest of the *ordained* preparatory illustrations of His own office: 'Your fathers, ye say, ate manna in the wilderness; and ye say well, for so they did, *but they are dead* – even they whose carcasses fell in the wilderness did eat of that bread; the Bread whereof I speak cometh down from heaven, which the manna never did, that men, eating of it, may *live for ever.*'

51. I am – Understand, it is of MYSELF I now speak as the Bread from heaven; of ME if a man eat he shall live for ever; and 'THE BREAD WHICH I WILL GIVE IS MY FLESH, WHICH I WILL GIVE FOR THE LIFE OF THE WORLD.' Here, for the first time in this high discourse, our Lord explicitly introduces His sacrificial *death* – for only rationalists can doubt this not only as that which constitutes Him the Bread of life to men, but as THAT very element IN HIM WHICH POSSESSES THE LIFE-GIVING VIRTUE. – 'From this time we hear no more (in this discourse) of 'Bread'; this figure is dropped, and the reality takes its place' [STIER]. The words 'I will *give*' may be compared with the words of institution at the Supper, 'This is My body which is *given* for you' (Lu 22:19), or in Paul's report of it, '*broken* for you' (1Co 11:24).

52. Jews strove among themselves – arguing the point together.

How can – that is, Give us His flesh to eat? Absurd.

53–58. Except ye eat the flesh ... and drink the blood ... no life – The harshest word He had yet uttered in their ears. They asked how it was *possible* to eat His flesh. He answers, with great solemnity, 'It is *indispensable.*' Yet even here a thoughtful hearer might find something to temper the harshness. He says they must not only 'eat His *flesh*' but 'drink His *blood,*' which could not but suggest the idea of His *death* – implied in the separation of one's flesh from his blood. And as He had already hinted that it was to be something very different from a *natural* death, saying, 'My flesh I will give for the life of the world' (Joh 6:51), it must have been pretty plain to candid hearers that He meant something above the gross idea which the bare terms expressed. And farther, when He added that they 'had no *life* in them unless they thus ate and drank,' it was impossible they should think He meant that the *temporal* life they were then living was dependent on their eating and drinking, in this gross sense, His flesh and blood. Yet the whole statement was certainly confounding, and beyond doubt was meant to be so. Our Lord had told them that in spite of all they had 'seen' in Him, they 'did not believe' (Joh 6:36). For *their* conviction therefore he does not here lay Himself out; but having the ear not only of them but of the more *candid and thoughtful* in the crowded synagogue, and the miracle of the loaves having led up to the most exalted of all views of His Person and Office, He takes advantage of their very difficulties and objections to announce, for all time, those most profound truths which are here expressed, regardless of the disgust of the unteachable, and the prejudices even of the most sincere, which His language would seem only designed to deepen. The *truth* really conveyed here is no other than that expressed in Joh 6:51, though in more emphatic terms – that He Himself, in the virtue of His sacrificial death, is the spiritual and eternal life of men; and that unless men voluntarily appropriate to themselves this death, in its sacrificial virtue, so as to become the very life and nourishment of their inner man, they have no spiritual and eternal life at all. Not as if His death were the *only* thing of value, but it is what gives all else in Christ's Incarnate Person, Life, and Office, their whole value *to us sinners.*

54. Whoso eateth ... hath – The former verse said that *unless* they partook of Him they had no life; this adds, that *whoever* does so 'hath eternal life.'

and I will raise him up at the last day – For the *fourth* time this is repeated (see Joh 6:39,40,44) – showing most clearly that the 'eternal life' which such a man '*hath*' cannot be the same with the *future* resurrection life from which it is carefully distinguished each time, but a life communicated *here below* immediately on believing (Joh 3:36 5:24,25); and giving to *the resurrection of the body* as that which consummates the redemption *of the entire man,* a prominence which in the current theology, it is to be feared, it has seldom had. (See Ro 8:23 1Co 15:1–58, throughout.)

56. He that eateth ... dwelleth in me and I in him – As our food becomes incorporated with ourselves, so Christ and those who eat His flesh and drink His blood become spiritually *one life,* though *personally* distinct.

57. As the living Father hath sent me – to communicate His own life.

and I live by the Father – literally, 'because of the Father'; My life and His being one, but Mine that of a *Son,* whose it is to be '*of the Father.*' (See Joh 1:18 5:26.)

he that eateth me, ... shall live by me – literally, 'because of Me.' So that though *one spiritual life* with Him, 'the Head of every man is Christ, as the head of Christ is God' (1Co 11:3 3:23).

58. This is that bread – a sort of summing up of the whole discourse, on which let this one further remark suffice – that as our Lord, instead of softening down His figurative sublimities, or even putting them in naked phraseology, leaves the great truths of His Person and Office, and our participation of Him and it, enshrined for all time in those glorious forms of speech, so when

we attempt to strip the truth of these figures, figures though they be, it goes away from us, like water when the vessel is broken, and our wisdom lies in raising our own spirit, and attuning our own ear, to our Lord's chosen modes of expression. (It should be added that although this discourse has nothing to do with the Sacrament of the Supper, the Sacrament has everything to do with it, as *the visible embodiment* of these figures, and, to the believing partaker, a *real,* yea, and the most lively and affecting participation of His flesh and blood, and nourishment thereby of the spiritual and eternal life, here below.)

59. These things said he in the synagogue – which seems to imply that what follows took place after the congregation had broken up.

60–65. Many ... of his disciples – His pretty constant followers, though an outer circle of them.

hard saying – not merely harsh, but insufferable, as the word often means in the Old Testament.

who can hear – submit to listen to it.

61, 62. Doth this offend ... What and if – that is, 'If ye are stumbled at what I have said, how will ye bear what I *now* say?' Not that His ascension itself would stumble them more than His death, but that after recoiling from the *mention* of the one, they would not be in a state of mind to take in the other.

63. the flesh profiteth nothing – Much of His discourse was *about* 'flesh'; but flesh as such, mere flesh, could profit nothing, much less impart that *life* which the Holy Spirit alone communicates to the soul.

the words that I speak ... are spirit and ... life – The whole burden of the discourse is '*spirit,*' not mere flesh, and '*life*' in its highest, not its lowest sense, and the words I have employed are to be interpreted solely in that sense.

64. But there are some – that is, 'But it matters little to some of you in what sense I speak, for ye believe not.' This was said, adds the Evangelist, not merely of the outer but of the inner circle of His disciples; for He knew the traitor, though it was not yet time to expose him.

65. Therefore said I – that is, 'That was why I spoke to you of the necessity of divine teaching which some of you are strangers to.'

except it were given him – plainly showing that by the Father's 'drawing' (Joh 6:44) was meant an *internal* and *efficacious* operation, for in recalling the statement here He says, it must be '*given*' to a man to come' to Christ.

66–71. From that *time* – or, in consequence of this. Those last words of our Lord seemed to have given them the finishing stroke – they could not stand it any longer.

walked no more – Many a journey, it may be, they had taken with Him, but now they gave Him up finally!

67. the twelve – the first time they are thus mentioned in this Gospel.

Will ye also go away? – Affecting appeal! Evidently Christ *felt* the desertion of Him even by those miserable men who could not abide His statements; and seeing a disturbance even of the *wheat* by the violence of the wind which blew away the *chaff* (not yet visibly showing itself, but open to His eyes of fire), He would *nip it in the bud* by this home question.

68. Then Simon Peter – whose forwardness in this case was noble, and to the wounded spirit of His Lord doubtless very grateful.

Lord, to whom – that is, 'We cannot deny that *we* have been staggered as well as they, and seeing so many go away who, as we thought, might have been retained by teaching a little less hard to take in, our own endurance has been severely tried, nor have we been able to stop short of the question, Shall *we* follow the rest, and give it up? But when it came to this, our light returned, and our hearts were reassured. For as soon as we thought of going away, there arose upon us that awful question, "To WHOM shall we go?" To the lifeless formalism and wretched traditions of the elders? to the gods many and lords many of the heathen around us? or to blank unbelief? Nay, Lord, we are shut up. *They* have none of that "ETERNAL LIFE" to offer us whereof Thou hast been discoursing, in words rich and ravishing as well as in words staggering to human wisdom. That life we cannot want; that life we have learnt to crave as a necessity of the deeper nature which Thou hast awakened: "*the words* of that eternal life" (the authority to *reveal* it and the power to confer it). Thou hast: Therefore will we stay with Thee – we *must*.'

69. And we believe, – (See on Mt 16:16.) Peter seems to have added this not merely – probably not so much – as an assurance *to his Lord* of his heart's belief in Him, as for the purpose of fortifying *himself* and his faithful brethren against that *recoil* from his Lord's harsh statements which he was probably struggling against with difficulty at that moment. *Note.* – There are seasons when one's faith is tried to the utmost, particularly by speculative difficulties; the spiritual eye then swims, and all truth seems ready to depart from us. At such seasons, a clear perception that to abandon the faith of Christ is *to face black desolation, ruin and death;* and on recoiling from this, to be able to fall back, not merely on *first principles and immovable foundations,* but on *personal experience of a Living Lord in whom all truth is wrapt up and made flesh for our very benefit* – this is a relief unspeakable. Under that blessed Wing taking shelter, until we are again fit to grapple with the questions that have staggered us, we at length either find our way through them, or attain to a calm satisfaction in the discovery that they lie beyond the limits of present apprehension.

70. Have not I chosen … and one of you is a devil: – 'Well said, Simon-Barjonas, but that "we" embraces not so wide a circle as in the simplicity of thine heart thou thinkest; for though I have chosen you but twelve, one even of these is a "devil"' (the temple, the tool of that wicked one).

Chapter 7

Joh 7:1–53.
Christ at the feast of tabernacles.

1, 2. After these things – that is, *all that is recorded after* Joh 5:18.

walked in Galilee – continuing His labors there, instead of going to Judea, as might have been expected.

sought to kill him – referring back to Joh 5:18. *Hence it appears that our Lord did not attend the Passover mentioned in* Joh 6:4 – being the *third* since His ministry began, if the feast mentioned in Joh 5:1 was a Passover.

2. feast of tabernacles … at hand – This was the last of the three annual festivals, celebrated on the fifteenth of the seventh month (September). (See Le 23:33 De 16:13 Ne 8:14–18.)

3–5. His brethren said – (See Mt 13:54-56.) **Depart … into Judea** – In Joh 7:5 this speech is ascribed to their *unbelief.* But as they were in the 'upper room' among the one hundred and twenty disciples who waited for the descent of the Spirit after the Lord's ascension (Ac 1:14), they seem to have had their prejudices removed, perhaps after His resurrection. Indeed here their language is more that of strong prejudice and suspicion (*such as near relatives, even the best, too frequently show in such cases*), than from unbelief. There was also, probably, a tincture of *vanity* in it. 'Thou hast many disciples in Judea; here in Galilee they are fast dropping off; it is not like one who advances the claims Thou dost to linger so long here, away from the city of our solemnities, where surely "the kingdom of our father David" is to be set up: "seeking," as Thou dost, "to be known openly," those miracles of Thine ought not to be confined to this distant corner, but submitted at headquarters to the inspection of "the world."' (See Ps 69:8, 'I am become a stranger to my brethren, an alien unto *my mother's children!*')

6–10. My time is not yet come – that is, for showing Himself to the world.

your time is always ready – that is 'It matters little when we go up, for ye have no great plans in life, and nothing hangs upon your movements. With Me it is otherwise; on every movement of Mine there hangs what ye know not. The world has no quarrel with you, for ye bear no testimony against it, and so draw down upon yourselves none of its wrath; but I am here to lift up My voice against its hypocrisy, and denounce its abominations; therefore it cannot endure Me, and one false step might precipitate its fury on its Victim's head before the time. Away, therefore, to the feast as soon as it suits you; I follow at the fitting moment, but "My time is not yet full come.'"

10. then went he … not openly – not 'in the (caravan) company' [MEYER]. See Lu 2:44.

as it were in secret – rather, 'in a manner secretly'; perhaps by some other route, and in a way not to attract notice.

11–13. Jews – the rulers.

sought him – for no good end.

Where is He? – He had not been at Jerusalem for probably *a year and a half.*

12. much murmuring – buzzing.

among the people – the multitudes; the natural expression of a Jewish writer, indicating without design the crowded state of Jerusalem at this festival [WEBSTER and WILKINSON].

a good man … Nay … deceiveth the people – the two opposite views of His claims, that they were *honest,* and that they were an *imposture.*

13. none spake openly of him – that is, in His favor, 'for fear of the [*ruling*] Jews.'

14, 15. about the midst of the feast – the fourth or fifth day of the eight, during which it lasted.

went up into the temple and taught – The word denotes *formal* and *continuous teaching,* as *distinguished* from mere casual sayings. This was probably *the first time* that He did so thus openly in Jerusalem. He had kept back till the feast was half through, to let the stir about Him subside, and entering the city unexpectedly, had begun His 'teaching' at the temple, and created a certain awe, before the wrath of the rulers had time to break it.

15. How knoweth … letters – learning (Ac 26:24).

having never learned – at any rabbinical school, as Paul under Gamaliel. These rulers knew well enough that He had not *studied* under any human teacher – an important admission against ancient and modern attempts to trace our Lord's wisdom to human sources [MEYER]. Probably His teaching on this occasion was *expository,* manifesting that unrivalled faculty and depth which in the Sermon on the Mount had excited the astonishment of all.

16–18. doctrine … not mine – that is, from Myself unauthorized; I am here by commission.

17. If any man will do his will – 'is willing,' or 'wishes to do.'

whether … of God, or … of myself – from above or from beneath; is divine or an imposture of Mine. A principle of immense importance, showing, on the one hand, that *singleness of desire to please God is the grand inlet to light on* all questions vitally affecting one's eternal interests, and on the other, that *the want of this,* whether perceived or not, *is the chief cause of infidelity amidst the light of revealed religion.*

18. seeketh his own glory – (See on Joh 5:41–44.)

19, 20. Did not Moses – that is, In opposing Me ye pretend zeal for Moses, but to the spirit and end of that law which he gave ye are total strangers, and in 'going about to kill Me' ye are its greatest enemies.

20. The people answered, Thou hast a devil: who goeth about to kill thee? – This was said by *the multitude,* who as yet had no bad feeling to Jesus, and were not in the secret of the plot hatching, as our Lord knew, against Him.

21–24. I have done one work – Taking no notice of the popular appeal, as there were those there who knew well enough what He meant, He recalls His cure of the impotent man, and the murderous rage it had kindled (Joh 5:9,16,18). It may seem strange that He should refer to an event a year and a half old, as if but newly done. But their present attempt 'to kill Him' brought up the past scene vividly, not only to Him, but without doubt to them, too, if indeed they had ever forgotten it; and by this fearless reference to it, exposing their hypocrisy and dark designs, He gave His position great moral strength.

22. Moses … gave unto you circumcision – Though servile work was forbidden on the sabbath, the circumcision of males on that day (which certainly was a servile work) was counted no infringement of the Law. How much less ought fault to be found with One who had made a man 'every whit whole' – or rather, 'a man's entire body whole' – on the sabbath-day? What a testimony to the reality of the miracle, none daring to meet the bold appeal.

24. Judge not – that is, Rise above the *letter* into the *spirit* of the law.

25–27. some of them of Jerusalem – the citizens, who, knowing the long-formed purpose of the rulers to put Jesus to death, wondered that they were now letting Him teach openly.

26. Do the rulers know – Have they got some new light in favor of His claims?

27. Howbeit we know this man – This seems to refer to some current opinion that Messiah's origin would be mysterious (not *altogether* wrong), from which they concluded that Jesus could not be He, since they knew all about His family at Nazareth.

28, 29. cried Jesus – in a louder tone, and more solemn, witnessing style than usual.

Ye both – that is, 'Yes, ye know both Myself and My local parentage, and (yet) I am not come of Myself.'

but he that sent me is true – Probably the meaning is, 'He that sent Me is the only *real* Sender of any one.'

30–32. **sought to take … none laid hands** – their *impotence* being equal to their *malignity.*

31. **When Christ cometh, will he** – that is, If this be not the Christ, what can the Christ do, when He does come, which has not been anticipated and eclipsed by this man? This was evidently the language of friendly persons, overborne by their spiteful superiors, but unable to keep quite silent.

32. **heard that the people murmured** – that mutterings to this effect were going about, and thought it high time to stop Him if He was not to be allowed to carry away the people.

33, 34. **Yet a little while** – that is, 'Your desire to be rid of Me will be for you all too soon fulfilled. Yet a little while and we part company – for ever; for I go whither ye cannot come: nor, even when ye at length seek Him whom ye now despise, shall ye be able to find Him' – referring not to any penitential, but to purely selfish cries in their time of desperation.

35, 36. **Whither will he go** – They cannot comprehend Him, but seem awed by the solemn grandeur of His warning. He takes no notice, however, of their questions.

37–39. **the last day, that great day of the feast** – the eighth (Le 23:39). It was a sabbath, the last feast day of the year, and distinguished by very remarkable ceremonies. The generally joyous character of this feast broke out on this day into loud jubilation, particularly at the solemn moment when the priest, as was done on every day of this festival, brought forth, in golden vessels, water from the stream of Siloah, which flowed under the temple-mountain, and solemnly poured it upon the altar. Then the words of Isa 12:3 were sung, *With joy shall ye draw water out of the wells of Salvation,* and thus the symbolical reference of this act, intimated in Joh 7:39, was expressed' [OLSHAUSEN]. So ecstatic was the joy with which this ceremony was performed – accompanied with sound of trumpets – that it used to be said, 'Whoever had not witnessed it had never seen rejoicing at all' [LIGHTFOOT].

Jesus stood – On this high occasion, then, He who had already drawn all eyes upon Him by His supernatural power and unrivalled teaching – 'JESUS stood,' probably in some elevated position.

and cried – as if making proclamation in the audience of all the people.

If any man thirst, let him come unto me, and drink! – What an offer! The deepest cravings of the human spirit are here, as in the Old Testament, expressed by the figure of '*thirst,*' and the eternal satisfaction of them by '*drinking.*' To the woman of Samaria He had said almost the same thing, and in the same terms (Joh 4:13,14). But what to her was simply affirmed as a *fact*, is here turned into a

world-wide *proclamation;* and whereas there, the *gift* by Him of the living water is the most prominent idea – in contrast with her hesitation to give Him the perishable water of Jacob's well – here, the prominence is given to *Himself* as the Well spring of all satisfaction. He had in Galilee invited all the WEARY AND HEAVY-LADEN of the human family to come under His wing and they should find REST (Mt 11:28), which is just the same deep want, and the same profound relief of it, under another and equally grateful figure. He had in the synagogue of Capernaum (Joh 6:36) announced Himself, in every variety of form, as 'the BREAD of Life,' and as both able and authorized to appease the 'HUNGER,' and quench the 'THIRST,' of all that apply to Him. There is, and there can be, nothing beyond that here. But what was on all those occasions uttered in private, or addressed to a provincial audience, is here sounded forth in the streets of the great religious metropolis, and in language of surpassing majesty, simplicity, and grace. *It is just Jehovah's ancient proclamation now sounding forth through human flesh,* 'HO, EVERY ONE THAT THIRSTETH, COME YE TO THE WATERS, AND HE THAT HATH NO MONEY!' &c. (Isa 55:1). In this light we have but two alternatives; either to say with Caiaphas of Him that uttered such words, '*He is guilty of death,*' or falling down before Him to exclaim with Thomas, 'MY LORD AND MY GOD!'

38. **as the scripture hath said** – These words belong to what follows, 'Out of his belly, as the scripture hath said, shall flow,' referring not to any particular passage, but to such as Isa 58:11 Joe 3:18 Zec 14:8 Eze 47:1–12; in most of which the idea is that of waters issuing from beneath the temple, to which our Lord compares Himself and those who believe in Him.

out of his belly – that is, his inner man, his soul, as in Pr 20:27.

rivers of living water – (See on Joh 4:13.) It refers primarily to the *copiousness,* but indirectly also to the *diffusiveness,* of this living water to the good of others.

39. **this spake he of the Spirit** – who, by His direct personal agency, opens up this spring of living waters in the human spirit (Joh 3:6), and by His indwelling in the renewed soul ensures their *unfailing flow.*

they that believe – As the Holy Ghost is, in the redemption of man, entirely *at the service of Christ,* as His Agent, so it is *only in believing connection with Christ* that any one 'receives' the Spirit.

for the Holy Ghost was not yet *given* – Beyond all doubt the word 'given,' or some similar word, is the right supplement. In Joh 16:7 the Holy Ghost is represented not only as the *gift of Christ,* but a gift the communication of which was *dependent upon His own departure to the*

Father. Now as Christ was *not yet gone,* so the Holy Ghost *was not yet given.*

Jesus not yet glorified – The word *'glorified'* is here used advisedly, to teach the reader not only that the *departure* of Christ to the Father was *indispensable* to the giving of the Spirit, but that this illustrious Gift, direct from the hands of the ascended Saviour, was God's intimation to the world that He whom it had cast out, crucified, and slain, was 'His Elect, in whom His soul delighted,' and that it was through the smiting of that Rock that the waters of the Spirit – for which the Church was waiting, and with pomp at the feast of tabernacles proclaiming its expectation – had gushed forth upon a thirsty world.

40–43. Many … when they heard this … said, Of a truth – The only wonder is they did not all say it. 'But their minds were blinded.'

41. Others said, This is the Christ – (See on Joh 1:21.)

Shall Christ come out of Galilee?

42. scripture said … of the seed of David, and out of … Bethlehem – We accept this spontaneous testimony to our David-descended, Bethlehem-born Saviour. Had those who gave it made the inquiry which the case demanded, they would have found that Jesus 'came out of Galilee' (Joh 7:41) and 'out of Bethlehem' both, alike in fulfilment of prophecy as in point of fact. (Mt 2:23 4:13–16.)

44–49. would have taken him; but – (See on Joh 7:30.)

45. Then came the officers – 'sent to take him' (Joh 7:32).

Why … not brought him? – already thirsting for their Victim, and thinking it an easy matter to seize and bring Him.

46. Never man spake like this man – Noble testimony of unsophisticated men! Doubtless they were strangers to the profound intent of Christ's teaching, but there was that in it which by its mysterious grandeur and transparent purity and grace, held them spellbound. No doubt it was of God that they should so feel, that their arm might be paralyzed, as Christ's hour was not yet come; but even in human teaching there has sometimes been felt such a divine power, that men who came to kill them (for example, ROLAND HISS) have confessed to all that they were unmanned.

47. ye also deceived – In their own servants this seemed intolerable.

48. any of the rulers or … Pharisees believed – 'Many of them' did, including Nicodemus and Joseph, but not one of these had openly 'confessed Him' (Joh 12:42), and this appeal must have stung such of them as heard it to the quick.

49. But this people – literally, 'multitude,' meaning the *ignorant rabble.* (Pity these important distinctions, so marked in the original of this Gospel, should be not also in our version.)

knoweth not the law – that is, by school learning, which only subverted it by human traditions.

are cursed – a cursed set (a kind of swearing at them, out of mingled rage and scorn).

50–53. Nicodemus – reappearing to us after nearly three years' absence from the history, as a member of the council, probably then sitting.

51. Doth our law – a very proper, but all too tame rejoinder, and evidently more from pressure of conscience than any design to pronounce *positively* in the case. 'The feebleness of his defense of Jesus has a strong contrast in the fierceness of the rejoinders of the Pharisees' [WEBSTER and WILKINSON].

52. thou of Galilee – in this taunt expressing their scorn of the party. Even a word of caution, or the gentlest proposal to inquire before condemning, was with them equivalent to an espousal of the hated One.

Search … out of Galilee … no prophet – Strange! For had not *Jonah* (of Gath-hepher) and even Elijah (of Thisbe) arisen out of Galilee? And there it may be more, of whom we have no record. But rage is blind, and deep prejudice distorts all facts. Yet it looks as if they were afraid of losing Nicodemus, when they take the trouble to reason the point at all. It was just *because* he had 'searched,' as they advised him, that he went the length even that he did.

53. every man went unto his own home – *finding their plot could not at that time be carried into effect.* Is your rage thus impotent, ye chief priests?

Chapter 8

Joh 8:1–11.
The woman taken in adultery.

1, 2. Jesus went unto the Mount of Olives – This should have formed the last verse of the foregoing chapter. 'The return of the people to the inert quiet and security of their *dwellings* (Joh 7:53), at the close of the feast, is designedly contrasted with our Lord's *homeless* way, so to speak, of spending the short night, who is early in the morning on the scene again. One cannot well see why what is recorded in Lu 21:37,38 may not even thus early have taken place; it might have been the Lord's ordinary custom from the beginning to leave the brilliant misery of the city every night, that so He might compose His sorrowful and interceding heart, and collect His energies for new labors of love; preferring for His resting-place Bethany, and the *Mount of Olives,* the scene thus consecrated by many preparatory prayers for His final humiliation and exaltation' [STIER].

3-6. scribes and Pharisees – foiled in their yesterday's attempt, and hoping to succeed better in this.

4, 5. woman … in adultery … Moses … commanded … should be stoned – simply put to death (De 22:22), but in aggravated cases, at least in later times, this was probably by stoning (Eze 16:40).

but what sayest thou – hoping, whatever He might answer, to put Him in the wrong: – if He said, Stone her, that would seem a stepping out of His province; if He forbade it, that would hold Him up as a relaxer of the public morals. But these cunning hypocrites were overmatched.

6. stooped down – It will be observed He was *sitting* when they came to Him.

with his finger wrote on the ground – The words of our translators in italics ('as though He heard them not') have hardly improved the sense, for it is scarcely probable He could wish that to be thought. Rather He wished to show them His aversion to enter on the subject. But as this did not suit them, they 'continue asking Him,' pressing for an answer. At last, raising Himself He said.

7. He that is without sin – not meaning sinless altogether; nor yet, guiltless of a literal breach of the Seventh Commandment; but probably, he whose conscience acquits him of *any such* sin.

cast a stone – '*the* stone,' meaning the first one (De 17:7).

8. again he stooped down and wrote – The design of this second stooping and writing on the ground was evidently to give her accusers an opportunity to slink away unobserved *by Him*, and so avoid an exposure to His eye which they could ill have stood. Accordingly it is added.

9. they … convicted … went out one by one … Jesus was left alone – that is, without one of her accusers remaining; for it is added.

the woman in the midst – that is, of the remaining audience. While the trap failed to catch Him for whom it was laid, it caught those who laid it. Stunned by the unexpected home thrust, they immediately made off – which makes the impudence of those impure hypocrites in dragging such a case before the public eye the more disgusting.

10. Woman – What inimitable tenderness and grace! Conscious of her own guilt, and till now in the hands of men who had talked of stoning her, wondering at the *skill* with which her accusers had been dispersed, and the *grace* of the few words addressed to herself, she would be disposed to listen, with a reverence and teachableness before unknown, to our Lord's admonition. 'And Jesus said unto her, Neither do I condemn thee, go and sin no more.' He pronounces no pardon upon the woman (such as, 'Thy sins are forgiven thee' [compare Lu 5:28 7:48] – 'Go in peace' [compare Mr 5:34 Lu 7:50 8:48]), much less does He say that she had done

nothing condemnable; He simply leaves the matter where it was. He meddles not with the magistrate's office, nor acts the *Judge* in any sense (Joh 12:47). But in saying, 'Go and sin no more,' which had been before said to one who undoubtedly believed (Joh 5:14), more is probably implied than expressed. If brought suddenly to conviction of sin, admiration of her Deliverer, and a willingness to be admonished and guided by Him, this call to begin a new life may have carried with it what would ensure and naturally bring about a permanent change. (This whole narrative is wanting in some of the earliest and most valuable manuscripts, and those which have it vary to some extent. The internal evidence in its favor is almost overpowering. It is easy to account for its *omission*, though genuine; but if not so, it is next to impossible to account for its *insertion*.)

Joh 8:12–59.
Further discourses of Jesus – attempt to stone him.

12. I am the light of the world – As the former references to *water* (Joh 4:13,14 7:37–39) and to *bread* (Joh 6:35) were occasioned by outward occurrences, so this one to *light*. In 'the treasury' where it was spoken (see on Joh 8:20) stood two colossal golden lamp-stands, on which hung a multitude of lamps, lighted after the evening sacrifice (probably every evening during the feast of tabernacles), diffusing their brilliancy, it is said, over all the city. Around these the people danced with great rejoicing. Now, as amidst the festivities of the *water* from Siloam Jesus cried, saying, 'If any man thirst, let him come unto me and drink,' so now amidst the blaze and the joyousness of this illumination, He proclaims, 'I AM THE LIGHT OF THE WORLD' – plainly in the most *absolute* sense. For though He gives His disciples the same title, they are only 'light *in the Lord*' (Eph 5:8); and though He calls the Baptist 'the burning and shining light' (or '*lamp*' of his day, Joh 5:35), yet 'he was *not that Light,* but was sent to bear witness of that Light: that was THE TRUE LIGHT which, coming into the world, *lighteth every man*' (Joh 1:8,9). Under this magnificent title Messiah was promised of old (Isa 42:6 Mal 4:2).

he that followeth me – as one does a light going before him, and as the Israelites did the pillar of bright cloud in the wilderness.

but shall have the light of life – the light, as of a new world, a newly awakened spiritual and eternal life.

13–19. bearest record of thyself; thy record is not true – How does He meet this specious cavil? Not by disputing the wholesome human maxim that 'self-praise is no praise,' but by affirming that He was *an exception to the rule,* or rather, that *it had no application to Him.*

14. for I know whence I came, and whither I go – (See on Joh 7:28.)

15. Ye judge after the flesh – with no spiritual apprehension.

I judge no man.

16. And yet if I judge, my judgment is true – Ye not only *form* your carnal and warped judgments of Me, but are bent on carrying them into effect; I, though I form and utter My judgment of you, am not here to carry this into execution – that is reserved to a future day; yet the judgment I now pronounce and the witness I now bear is not Mine only as ye suppose, but His also that sent Me. (See on Joh 5:31,32.) And these are the two witnesses to any fact which your law requires.

20. These words spake Jesus in the treasury – a division, so called, of the fore court of the temple, part of the court of the women [JOSEPHUS, *Antiquities*, 19.6.2], which may confirm the genuineness of Joh 8:2–11, as the place where the woman was brought.

no man laid hands on him – (See on Joh 7:30.) In the dialogue that follows, the conflict waxes sharper on both sides, till rising to its climax, they take up stones to stone him.

21–25. Then said Jesus again unto them, I go my way – (See on Joh 7:33.)

22. Then said the Jews, Will he kill himself? – seeing something more in His words than before (Joh 7:35), but their question more malignant and scornful.

23. Ye are from beneath; I am from above – contrasting Himself, not as in Joh 3:31, simply with *earthborn messengers of God*, but *with men sprung from and breathing an opposite element* from His, which rendered it impossible that He and they should have any present fellowship, or dwell eternally together. (Again see on Joh 7:33; also see on Joh 8:44.)

24. if ye believe not that I am he, ye shall die in your sins – They knew well enough what He meant (Mr 13:6, *Greek;* compare Mt 24:5). But He would not, by speaking it out, give them the materials for a charge for which they were watching. At the same time, one is irresistibly reminded by such language, so far transcending what is becoming in *men*, of those ancient declarations of the God of Israel, 'I AM HE' (De 32:39 Isa 43:10,13 46:4 48:12). See on Joh 6:20.

25. Who art thou? – hoping thus to extort an explicit answer; but they are disappointed.

26, 27. I have many things to say and to judge of you; but he that sent me is true – that is, I could, and at the fitting time, will say and judge many things of you (referring perhaps to the work of the Spirit which is for *judgment* as well as *salvation*, Joh 16:8), but what I do say is just the message My Father hath given Me to deliver.

28–30. When ye have lifted up the Son of man – The plainest intimation He had yet given

in *public* of *the manner and the authors* of His death.

then shall ye know that I am *he* – that is, *find out*, or have sufficient evidence, how true was all He said, though they would be far from owning it.

29. the Father hath not left me alone; for I do always those things that please him – that is, To you, who gnash upon Me with your teeth, and frown down all open appearance for Me, I seem to stand uncountenanced and alone; but I have a sympathy and support transcending all human applause; I came hither to do My Father's will, and in the doing of it have not ceased to please Him; therefore is He ever by Me with His approving smile, His cheering words, His supporting arm.

30. As he spake these words, many believed on him – Instead of wondering at this, the wonder would be if words of such unearthly, surpassing grandeur *could* be uttered without captivating *some* that heard them. And just as 'all that sat in the council' to try Stephen '*saw his face*' – though expecting nothing but death – '*as it had been the face of an angel*' (Ac 6:15), so may we suppose that, full of the sweet supporting sense of His Father's presence, amidst the rage and scorn of the rulers, a divine benignity beamed from His countenance, irradiated the words that fell from Him, and won over the candid 'many' of His audience.

31–33. Then said Jesus to those Jews who believed, If ye continue in my word, then are ye my disciples indeed – The impression produced by the last words of our Lord may have become visible by some decisive movement, and here He takes advantage of it to press on them '*continuance*' in the faith, since then only were they His real disciples (compare Joh 15:3–8), and then should they *experimentally* 'know the truth,' and 'by the truth be made (*spiritually*) free.'

33. They answered him, We be Abraham's seed, and were never in bondage to any man – Who said this? Not surely the very class just spoken of as won over by His divine words, and exhorted to continue in them. Most interpreters seem to think so; but it is hard to ascribe such a petulant speech to the newly gained disciples, even in the lowest sense, much less persons *so* gained as were they. It came, probably, from persons mixed up with them in the same part of the crowd, but of a very different spirit. The *pride* of the Jewish nation, even now after centuries of humiliation, is the most striking feature of their character. 'Talk of freedom to *us*? Pray when or to whom were we ever in bondage?' This bluster sounds almost ludicrous from such a nation. Had they forgotten their long and bitter bondage in Egypt? their dreary captivity in Babylon? their present bondage to the Roman yoke, and their restless eagerness to

throw it off? But probably they saw that our Lord pointed to something else – freedom, perhaps, from the leaders of sects or parties – and were not willing to allow their subjection even to these. Our Lord, therefore, though He knew what slaves they were in this sense, drives the ploughshare somewhat deeper than this, to a bondage they little dreamt of.

34, 35. Whosoever committeth sin – that is, *liveth in the commission* of it – (Compare 1Jo 3:8 Mt 7:23).

is the servant of sin – that is, the *bond-servant*, or *slave* of it; for the question is not about free service, but who are in *bondage*. (Compare 2Pe 2:19 Re 6:16). The great truth here expressed was not unknown to heathen moralists; but it was applied only to vice, for they were total strangers to what in revealed religion is called *sin*. The thought of *slaves* and *freemen* in the house suggests to our Lord a wider idea.

35. And the servant abideth not in the house for ever, but the Son abideth ever – that is, 'And if your connection with the family of God be that of BOND-SERVANTS, ye have no *natural tie* to the house; your tie is essentially *uncertain and precarious*. But the SON's relationship to the FATHER is a *natural and essential* one; it is an indefeasible tie; His abode in it is *perpetual* and *of right*: That is My relationship, My tie: If, then, ye would have your connection with God's family made *real, rightful, permanent,* ye must by the Son be *manumitted* and *adopted* as sons and daughters of the Lord Almighty.' In this sublime statement there is no doubt a *subordinate* allusion to Ge 21:10, '*Cast out* this *bondwoman and her son, for the son of this bond-woman shall not be heir with my son,*' with Isaac.' (Compare Ga 4:22–30).

37–41. ye seek to kill me – He had said this to their face before: He now repeats it, and they do not deny it; yet are they held back, as by some marvellous spell – it was the awe which His combined dignity, courage, and benignity struck into them.

because my word hath no place in you – When did ever *human prophet* so speak of His words? They tell us of 'the word of the Lord' coming to them. But here is One who holds up 'His word' as that which ought to find entrance and abiding room for itself in the souls of all who hear it.

38. my Father ... your father – (See on Joh 8:23.)

39. If ye were Abraham's children, ye would do the works of Abraham – He had just said He 'knew they were Abraham's children,' that is, according to the *flesh*; but the children of his *faith and holiness* they were not, but the reverse.

40. this did not Abraham – In so doing ye act in direct opposition to him.

41. We be not born of fornication ... we have one Father, God – meaning, as is generally allowed, that they were not an illegitimate race in point of *religion,* pretending only to be God's people, but were descended from His own chosen Abraham.

42, 43. If God were your Father, ye would love me – 'If ye had anything of His moral image, as children have their father's likeness, ye would love Me, for I am immediately of Him and directly from Him.' But 'My speech' (meaning His peculiar style of expressing Himself on these subjects) is unintelligible to you because ye cannot take in the truth which it conveys.

44. Ye are of your father the devil – 'This is one of the most decisive testimonies to the *objective* (outward) *personality* of the devil. It is quite impossible to suppose an accommodation to Jewish views, or a metaphorical form of speech, in so solemn an assertion as this' [ALFORD].

the lusts of your father – his impure, malignant, ungodly propensities, inclinations, desires.

ye will do – are willing to do; not of any *blind necessity of nature,* but of *pure natural inclination.*

He was a murderer from the beginning – The reference is not to *Cain* (as LOCKE, DEWETTE, ALFORD), but to *Adam* [GROTIUS, CALVIN, MEYER, LUTHARDT]. The death of the human race, in its widest sense, is ascribed to the murderous seducer of our race.

and abode not in the truth – As, strictly speaking, the word means 'abideth,' it has been denied that the *fall* of Satan from a former holy state is here expressed [LOCKE], and some superior interpreters think it only *implied* [OLSHAUSEN]. But though the *form* of the thought is present – not past – this is to express the important idea, that his whole character and activity are just *a continual aberration from his own original truth or rectitude;* and thus his fall is not only the *implied basis* of the thought, but *part of the statement itself,* properly interpreted and brought out.

no truth in him – void of all that holy, transparent rectitude which, as His creature, he originally possessed.

When he speaketh a lie, he speaketh of his own – perhaps his own resources, treasures (Mt 12:35) [ALFORD]. (The word is *plural*). It means that he has no temptation to it *from without;* it is purely *self-begotten,* springing from a nature which is nothing but obliquity.

the father of it – that is, of lying: all the falsehood in the world owes its existence to him. What a verse is this! It holds up the devil (1) as the murderer of the human race; but as this is meant here in the more profound sense of *spiritual* death, it holds him up, (2) as the spiritual parent of this fallen human family, communicating to his offspring his own evil passions and universal obliquity, and stimulating these into active exercise. But as there is 'a stronger than he,' who comes upon him and overcomes him (Lu 11:21,22), it is only such as 'love the darkness,' who are addressed as children of the devil (Mt 13:38 1Jo 3:8–10).

45–47. And because I tell you the truth, ye believe me not – not *although,* but just *because* He did so, for the reason given in the former verse. Had He been *less* true they would have hailed Him more readily.

46. Which of you convinceth me of sin – 'Convicteth,' bringeth home a charge of sin. Glorious dilemma! 'Convict Me of sin, and reject Me: If not, why stand ye out against My claims?' Of course, they could only be supposed to impeach His *life;* but in One who had already passed through unparalleled complications, and had continually to deal with friends and foes of every sort and degree, such a challenge thrown wide among His bitterest enemies, can amount to nothing short of a claim to *absolute sinlessness.*

48–51. Say we not well that thou art a Samaritan, and hast a devil? – What intense and virulent scorn! (See Heb 12:3.) The 'say we not well' refers to Joh 7:20. 'A Samaritan' means more than 'no Israelite at all'; it means one who *pretended, but had no manner of claim* to the title – retorting perhaps, this denial of their *true* descent from Abraham.

49. Jesus answered, I have not a devil – What calm dignity is here! Verily, 'when reviled, He reviled not again' (1Pe 2:23). Compare Paul (Ac 26:25), 'I am not mad.' He adds not, 'Nor am I a Samaritan,' that He might not even seem to partake of their contempt for a race that had already welcomed Him as the Christ, and began to be blessed by Him.

I honour my Father, and ye do dishonour me – the language of *wounded feeling.* But the *interior* of His soul at such moments is only to be seen in such prophetic utterances as these, 'For thy sake I have borne reproach; shame hath covered my face; I am become a *stranger* unto my brethren, an alien unto my mother's children. For the zeal of thine house hath eaten me up, and *the reproaches of them that* reproached thee are fallen upon me' (Ps 69:7-9).

50. I seek not mine own glory: there is one that seeketh – that is, evidently, '*that seeketh My glory*'; *requiring* 'all men to honor the Son even as they honor the Father'; judicially *treating* him 'who honoreth not the Son as honoring not the Father that hath sent Him' (Joh 5:23; and compare Mt 17:5); but giving to Him (Joh 6:37) such as will yet cast their crowns before His throne, in whom He 'shall see of the travail of his soul, and be satisfied' (Isa 53:11).

51. If a man keep my saying, he shall never see death – Partly thus vindicating His lofty claims as Lord of the kingdom of life everlasting, and, at the same time, holding out even to His revilers the scepter of grace. The word '*keep*' is in harmony with Joh 8:31, 'If ye *continue* in My word,' expressing the permanency, as a living and paramount principle, of that faith to which He referred: '*never see death,*' though virtually uttered before (Joh 5:24 6:40,47,51), is the strongest and most naked statement of a very glorious truth yet given. (In Joh 11:26 it is repeated in nearly identical terms.)

52, 53. Then said the Jews unto him, Now we know that thou hast a devil – 'Thou art now self-convicted; only a demoniac could speak so; the most illustrious of our fathers are dead, and Thou promisest exemption from death to any-one who will keep *Thy saying!* pray, who art Thou?'

54–56. If I honour myself, my honour is nothing – (See on Joh 5:31.)

55. I shall be a liar like unto you – now rising to the summit of holy, naked severity, thereby to draw this long dialogue to a head.

56. Abraham rejoiced to see my day – exulted, or exceedingly rejoiced that he should see, he exulted to see it, that is, by *anticipation.* Nay, **he saw it, and was glad** – he *actually* beheld it, to his joy. If this mean no more than that he had a prophetic foresight of the gospel-day – the second clause just repeating the first – how could the Jews understand our Lord to mean that He 'had seen Abraham?' And if it mean that Abraham was *then beholding,* in his disembodied spirit, the incarnate Messiah [STIER, ALFORD], the words seem very unsuitable to express it. It expresses something past – 'he *saw* My day, and *was glad,*' that is, surely *while he lived.* He seems to refer to the familiar intercourse which Abraham had with *God,* who is once and again in the history called '*the Angel of the Lord,*' and whom Christ here identifies with Himself. On those occasions, Abraham 'saw ME' (OLSHAUSEN, though he thinks the reference is to some unrecorded scene). If this be the meaning, all that follows is quite natural.

57–59. Then said the Jews unto him, Thou art not yet fifty years old – 'No inference can be drawn from this as to the age of our Lord as time as man. Fifty years was with the Jews the completion of manhood' [ALFORD].

and hast thou seen Abraham? – He had said Abraham saw *Him,* as being his peculiar privilege. They give the opposite turn to it – 'Hast Thou seen *Abraham?*' as an honor too great for Him to pretend to.

58. Before Abraham was, I am – The words rendered 'was' and 'am' are quite different. The one clause means, 'Abraham was *brought into being*'; the other, '*I exist.*' The statement therefore is not that *Christ came into existence before*

Abraham did (as Arians affirm is the meaning), but that He never *came* into being at all, but *existed* before Abraham had a being; in other words, existed before *creation*, or *eternally* (as Joh 1:1). *In that sense the Jews plainly understood Him,* since 'then took they up stones to cast at Him,' *just as they had before done when they saw that He made Himself equal with God* (Joh 5:18). **hid himself** – (See Lu 4:30.)

Chapter 9

Joh 9:1–41.

The opening of the eyes of one born blind, and what followed on it.

1–5. as Jesus passed by, he saw a man which was blind from birth – and who 'sat begging' (Joh 9:8).

2. who did sin, this man or his parents, that he was born blind – not in a former state of existence, in which, as respects the wicked, the Jews did not believe; but, perhaps, expressing loosely that sin *somewhere* had surely been the cause of this calamity.

3. Neither … this man – The cause was neither in himself nor his parents, but, in order to the manifestation of 'the works of God,' in his cure.

4. I must work the works of him that sent me – a most interesting statement from the mouth of Christ; intimating, (1) that He had a precise work to do upon earth, with every particular of it arranged and laid out to Him; (2) that all He did upon earth was just 'the works of God' – particularly 'going about *doing good,'* though not exclusively by miracles; (3) that each work had its precise *time* and *place* in His programme of instructions, so to speak; hence, (4) that as His period for work had definite termination, so by letting any one service pass by its allotted time, the whole would be disarranged, marred, and driven beyond its destined period for completion; (5) that He acted ever under the impulse of these considerations, as man – 'the night cometh when no man (or no one) can work.' What lessons are here for others, and what encouragement from such Example!

5. As long as I am in the world, I am the light of the world – not as if He would cease, after that, to be so; but that He must make full proof of His fidelity while His earthly career lasted by displaying His glory. 'As before the raising of Lazarus (Joh 11:25), He announces Himself as *the Resurrection and the Life,* so now He sets Himself forth as the source of the archetypal spiritual light, of which the natural, now about to be conferred, is only a derivation and symbol' [ALFORD].

6, 7. he spat on the ground, and made clay …

and he anointed the eyes of the blind man – These operations were not so incongruous in their nature as might appear, though it were absurd to imagine that they contributed in the least degree to the effect which followed. (See Mr 6:13 and see on Joh 7:33.)

7. Go, wash in the pool of Siloam, … Sent – (See 2Ki 5:10,14). As the prescribed action was purely symbolical in its design, so in connection with it the Evangelist notices the symbolical name of the pool as in this case bearing testimony to him who was *sent* to do what it only *symbolized.* (See Isa 8:6, where this same pool is used figuratively to denote 'the streams that make glad the city of God,' and which, humble though they be, betoken *a present God of Israel.*)

8–15. The neighbours therefore … said, Is not this he that sat and begged – Here are a number of details to identify the newly seeing with the long-known blind beggar.

13. They brought to the Pharisees – sitting probably in council, and chiefly of that sect (Joh 7:47,48).

16, 17. This man is not of God – (See on Joh 5:9; Joh 5:16.)

Others said – such as Nicodemus and Joseph.

17. the blind man … said, He is a prophet – rightly viewing the miracle as but a 'sign' of His prophetic commission.

18–23. the Jews did not believe … he had been born blind … till they called the parents of him that had received his sight – Foiled by the testimony of the young man himself, they hope to throw doubt on the fact by close questioning his parents, who, perceiving the snare laid for them, ingeniously escape it by testifying simply to the identity of their son, and his birth-blindness, leaving it to himself, as a competent witness, to speak as to the cure. They prevaricated, however, in saying they 'knew not who had opened his eyes,' for 'they feared the Jews,' who had come to an understanding (probably after what is recorded, Joh 7:50 but by this time well known), that whoever owned Him as the Christ would be put out of the synagogue – that is, not simply *excluded,* but *excommunicated.*

24–34. Give God the praise; we know that this man is a sinner – not wishing to own, even to the praise of God, that a miracle had been wrought upon him, but to show more regard to the honor of God than ascribe any such act to one who was a sinner.

25. He answered and said, Whether he be a sinner *or no* – Not that the man meant to insinuate any doubt in his own mind on the point of His being 'a sinner,' but as his *opinion* on such a point would be of no consequence to others, he would speak only to what he *knew* as *fact* in his *own case.*

26. **Then said they … again, What did he to thee? &c.** – hoping by repeated questions to ensnare him, but the youth is more than a match for them.

27. **I have told you already … will ye also be his disciples?** – In a vein of keen irony he treats their questions as those of anxious inquirers, almost ready for discipleship! Stung by this, they retort upon *him* as the disciple (and here they plainly were not wrong); for themselves, they fall back upon Moses; about *him* there could be no doubt; but who knew about this upstart?

30. **The man answered, Herein is a marvellous thing, that ye know not from whence he is, and yet he hath opened mine eyes** – He had no need to say another word; but waxing bolder in defense of his Benefactor, and his views brightening by the very courage which it demanded, he puts it to them how they could pretend inability to tell whether one who opened the eyes of a man born blind was 'of God' or 'a sinner' – from above or from beneath – and proceeds to argue the case with remarkable power. So irresistible was his argument that their rage burst forth in a speech of intense Pharisaism, 'Thou wast altogether born in sins, and dost thou teach us?' – *thou*, a base-born, uneducated, impudent youth, teach *us*, the trained, constituted, recognized guides of the people in the things of God! Out upon thee!

31. **they cast him out** – judicially, no doubt, as well in fact. The allusion to his being 'born in sins' seems a tacit admission of his being blind from birth – the very thing they had been so unwilling to own. But rage and enmity to truth are seldom consistent in their outbreaks. The friends of this excommunicated youth, crowding around him with their sympathy, would probably express surprise that One who could work such a cure should be unable to protect his patient from the persecution it had raised against him, or should possess the power without using it. Nor would it be strange if such thoughts should arise in the youth's own mind. But if they did, it is certain, from what follows, that they made no lodgment there, conscious as he was that 'whereas he was blind, now he saw,' and satisfied that if his Benefactor 'were not of God, He could do nothing' (Joh 9:33). There was a word for him too, which, if whispered in his ear from the oracles of God, would seem expressly designed to describe his case, and prepare him for the coming interview with his gracious Friend. 'Hear the word of the Lord, ye that tremble at His word. *Your brethren that hated you, that cast you out for My name's sake, said, Let the Lord be glorified;* BUT HE SHALL APPEAR TO YOUR JOY, *and they shall be ashamed*' (Isa 66:5). But how was He engaged to whom such

noble testimony had been given, and for whom such persecution had been borne? Uttering, perhaps, in secret, 'with strong crying and tears,' the words of the prophetic psalm, 'Let not them that wait on Thee, O Lord God of hosts, be ashamed for my sake; let none that seek Thee be confounded for my sake, O God of Israel; because for Thy sake I have borne reproach … and the reproaches of them that reproached Thee are fallen upon me' (Ps 69:6,7,9).

35–38. **Jesus heard** – that is, by intelligence brought Him.

that they had cast him out; and when he had found him – by accident? Not very likely. Sympathy in that breast could not long keep aloof from its object.

he said unto him, Dost thou believe on the Son of God? – A question stretching purposely beyond his present attainments, in order the more quickly to lead him – in his present teachable frame – into the highest truth.

36. **He answered and said, Who is he, Lord, that I may believe on him?** – 'His reply is affirmative, and believing by anticipation, promising faith as soon as Jesus shall say who He is' [STIER].

37. **Jesus said unto him, Thou hast both seen him** – the new sense of sight having at that moment its highest exercise, in gazing upon 'the Light of the world.'

38. **he said, Lord, I believe: and he worshipped him** – a *faith* and a *worship*, beyond doubt, meant to express far more than he would think proper to any human 'prophet' (Joh 9:17) – the unstudied, resistless expression, probably of SUPREME faith and adoration, though without the full understanding of what that implied.

39–41. **Jesus said** – perhaps at the same time, but after a crowd, including some of the skeptical and scornful rulers, had, on seeing Jesus talking with the healed youth, hastened to the spot.

that they which see not might see – rising to that *sight* of which the natural vision communicated to the youth was but the symbol. (See on Joh 9:5, and compare Lu 4:18.)

that they which see might be made blind – judicially incapable of apprehending and receiving the truth, to which they have wilfully shut their eyes.

40. **Are we blind also?** – We, the constituted, recognized guides of the people in spiritual things? pride and rage prompting the question.

41. **If ye were blind** – wanted light to discern My claims, and only waited to receive it.

ye should have no sin – none of the guilt of shutting out the light.

ye say, We see; therefore your sin remaineth – Your claim to possess light, while rejecting Me, is that which seals you up in the guilt of unbelief.

Chapter 10

Joh 10:1–21.

The good shepherd.

This discourse seems plainly to be a continuation of the closing verses of the ninth chapter. The figure was familiar to the Jewish ear (from Jer 23:1–40 Eze 34:1–31 Zec 11:1–17). 'This simple creature [the sheep] has this special note among all animals, that it quickly hears the voice of the shepherd, follows no one else, depends entirely on him, and seeks help from him alone – cannot help itself, but is shut up to another's aid' [LUTHER in STIER].

1, 2. He that entereth not by the door – the legitimate way (without saying what that was, as yet).

into the sheepfold – the sacred enclosure of God's true people.

climbeth up some other way – not referring to the assumption of ecclesiastical office without an external call, for those Jewish rulers, specially aimed at, had this (Mt 23:2), but to the want of a true spiritual commission, the seal of heaven going along with the outward authority; it is the assumption of the spiritual guidance of the people *without this* that is meant.

2. he that entereth in by the door is the shepherd of the sheep – a true, divinely recognized shepherd.

3. To him the porter openeth – that is, *right of free access* is given, by order of Him to whom the sheep belong; for it is better not to give the allusion a more specific interpretation [CALVIN, MEYER, LUTHARDT].

and the sheep hear his voice – This and all that follows, though it admits of important *application* to every faithful shepherd of God's flock, is in its direct and highest sense true only of 'the great Shepherd of the sheep,' who in the first five verses seems plainly, under the simple character of a true shepherd, to be drawing His own portrait [LAMPE, STIER].

7–14. I am the door of the sheep – that is, *the way in* to the fold, with all blessed privileges, both for shepherds and sheep (compare Joh 14:6 Eph 2:18).

8. All that ever came before me – the false prophets; not as claiming the prerogatives of Messiah, but as perverters of the people from the way of life, all pointing to Him [OLSHAUSEN].

the sheep did not hear them – the instinct of their divinely taught hearts preserving them from seducers, and attaching them to the heaven-sent prophets, of whom it is said that 'the Spirit of Christ was in them' (1Pe 1:11).

9. by me if any man enter in – whether shepherd or sheep.

shall be saved – the great object of the pastoral office, as of all the divine arrangements towards mankind.

and shall go in and out and find pasture – *in,* as to a place of *safety* and *repose; out,* as to 'green pastures and still waters' (Ps 23:2) for nourishment and refreshing, and all this only transferred to another clime, and enjoyed in another manner, at the close of this earthly scene (Re 7:17).

10. I am come that they might have life, and ... more abundantly – not merely to *preserve* but *impart* LIFE, and communicate it in rich and unfailing exuberance. What a claim! Yet it is only an echo of all His teaching; and He who uttered these and like words must be either a blasphemer, all worthy of the death He died, or 'God with us' – there can be no middle course.

11. I am the good shepherd – emphatically, and, in the sense intended, exclusively so (Isa 40:11 Eze 34:23 37:24 Zec 13:7).

the good shepherd giveth his life for the sheep – Though this may be said of literal shepherds, who, even for their brute flock, have, like David, encountered 'the lion and the bear' at the risk of their own lives, and still more of faithful pastors who, like the early bishops of Rome, have been the foremost to brave the fury of their enemies against the flock committed to their care; yet here, beyond doubt, it points to the struggle which was to issue in the willing surrender of the Redeemer's own life, to save His sheep from destruction.

12. an hireling ... whose own the sheep are not – who has no *property,* in them. By this He points to His own peculiar relation to the sheep, the same as His Father's, the great Proprietor and Lord of the flock, who styles Him 'My Shepherd, *the Man that is My Fellow*' (Zec 13:7), and though faithful under-shepherds are so in their Master's interest, that they feel a measure of His own concern for their charge, the language is strictly applicable only to 'the Son over His own house' (Heb 3:6).

seeth the wolf coming – not *the devil* distinctively, as some take it [STIER, ALFORD], but generally whoever comes upon the flock with hostile intent, in whatever form: though the wicked one, no doubt, is *at the bottom* of such movements [LUTHARDT].

14. I am the good shepherd, and know my sheep – in the peculiar sense of 2Ti 2:19.

am known of mine – the soul's response to the voice that has inwardly and efficaciously called it; for of this mutual loving acquaintance ours is the *effect* of His. 'The Redeemer's knowledge of us is the *active* element, penetrating us with His power and life; that of believers is the *passive* principle, the reception of His life and light. In this reception, however, an assimilation of the soul to the sublime object of its knowledge and love takes place; and thus an activity, though a derived one, is unfolded, which shows itself in obedience to His commands'

[OLSHAUSEN]. From this mutual knowledge Jesus rises to another and loftier reciprocity of knowledge.

15–18. As the Father knoweth me, even so know I the Father – What claim to absolute equality with the Father could exceed this? (See on Mt 11:27.)

and I lay down my life for the sheep – How sublime this, immediately following the lofty claim of the preceding clause! It is the riches and the poverty of 'the Word made flesh' – one glorious Person reaching at once up to the Throne and down even to the dust of death, 'that we might live through Him.' A candid interpretation of the words, '*for the sheep,*' ought to go far to establish the special relation of the vicarious death of Christ to the Church.

16. other sheep I have … not of this fold: them also I must bring – He means the perishing Gentiles, *already* His '*sheep*' in the love of His heart and the purpose of His grace to '*bring them*' in due time.

they shall hear my voice – *This is not the language of mere foresight that they would believe, but the expression of a purpose to draw them to Himself by an inward and efficacious call, which would infallibly issue in their spontaneous accession to Him.*

and there shall be one fold – rather 'one flock' (for the word for 'fold,' as in the foregoing verses, is quite different).

17. Therefore doth my Father love me, because I lay down my life – As the highest act of the Son's love to the Father was the laying down of His life for the sheep at His 'commandment,' so the Father's love to Him as His *incarnate* Son reaches its consummation, and finds its highest justification, in that sublimest and most affecting of all acts.

that I might take it again – His resurrection-life being indispensable to the accomplishment of the fruit of His death.

18. No man taketh it from me, but I lay it down myself: I have power to lay it down, and I have power to take it again – It is impossible for language more plainly and emphatically to express the *absolute voluntariness* of Christ's death, such a voluntariness as it would be manifest presumption in any mere *creature* to affirm of his own death. It is beyond all doubt the language of One who was conscious that *His life was His own* (which no creature's is), and therefore His to surrender or retain *at will*. Here lay the glory of His sacrifice, that it was *purely* voluntary. The claim of 'power to take it again' is no less important, as showing that His resurrection, though ascribed to the Father, in the sense we shall presently see, was nevertheless *His own assertion of His own right to life* as soon as the purposes of His voluntary death were accomplished.

This commandment – to 'lay down His life, that He might take it again.'

have I received of my Father – So that Christ died at once by 'command' of His Father, and by such a voluntary obedience to that command as has made Him (so to speak) infinitely dear to the Father. The *necessity* of Christ's death, in the light of these profound sayings, must be manifest to all but the superficial student.

19–21. There was a division … again among the Jews for these sayings – the light and the darkness revealing themselves with increasing clearness in the separation of the teachable from the obstinately prejudiced. The one saw in Him only 'a devil and a madman'; the other revolted at the thought that *such words* could come from one possessed, and sight be given to the blind by a demoniac; showing clearly that a deeper impression had been made upon them than their words expressed.

Joh 10:22–42.
Discourse at the feast of dedication – from the fury of his enemies Jesus escapes beyond Jordan, where many believe on him.

22, 23. it was … the feast of the dedication – celebrated rather more than *two months* after the feast of tabernacles, during which intermediate period our Lord seems to have remained in the neighborhood of Jerusalem. It was instituted by Jude Maccabeus, to commemorate the purification of the temple from the profanations to which it had been subjected by Antiochus Epiphanes 165 B.C., and kept for eight days, from the twenty-fifth Chisleu (December), the day on which Judas began the first joyous celebration of it (I Maccabees 4:52,56,59; and JOSEPHUS, *Antiquities,* 7.7.7).

it was winter – implying some *inclemency.* Therefore,

23. Jesus walked … in Solomon's porch – for shelter. This portico was on the east side of the temple, and JOSEPHUS says it was part of the original structure of Solomon [*Antiquities,* 20.9.7].

24. Then came the Jews – *the rulers.* (See on Joh 1:19.)

How long dost thou make us to doubt? – 'hold us in suspense' (*Margin*).

If thou be the Christ, tell us plainly – But when the plainest *evidence* of it was resisted, what weight could a mere *assertion* of it have?

25, 26. Jesus answered them, I told you – that is, in substance, what I am (for example Joh 7:37,38 8:12,35,36,58).

26. ye believe not, because ye are not of my sheep, as I said – referring to the whole strain of the Parable of the Sheep, (Joh 10:1).

27–30. My sheep hear my voice – (See on Joh 10:8.)

28. I give unto them eternal life – not 'will give them'; for it is a present gift. (See on Joh 3:36; Joh 5:24.) It is a very grand utterance, couched in the language of majestic authority.

29. My Father, which gave them me – (See on Joh 6:37–39.)

is greater than all – with whom no adverse power can contend. It is a general expression of an admitted truth, and what follows shows for what purpose it was uttered, 'and none is able to pluck them out of My Father's hand.' The impossibility of true believers being lost, in the midst of all the temptations which they may encounter, does not consist in their fidelity and decision, but is founded upon the *power of God.* Here the doctrine of predestination is presented in its sublime and sacred aspect; there is a predestination of the holy, which is taught from one end of the Scriptures to the other; not, indeed, of such a nature that an 'irresistible grace' *compels* the opposing will of man (of course not), but so that that will of man which receives and loves the commands of God is *produced* only by God's grace (OLSHAUSEN – a testimony all the more valuable, being given in spite of *Lutheran* prejudice).

30. I and my Father are one – Our language admits not of the precision of the original in this great saying. '*Are*' is in the *masculine* gender – 'we (two persons) are'; while '*one*' is *neuter* – '*one thing.*' Perhaps '*one interest*' expresses, as nearly as may be, the purport of the saying. There seemed to be some contradiction between His saying they had been given by His Father into *His own* hands, out of which they could not be plucked, and then saying that none could pluck them out of His *Father's* hands, as if they had not been given out of them. '*Neither have they,*' says He; 'though He has given them to Me, they are as much in His own almighty hands as ever – they *cannot be,* and when given to Me they are not, given away from Himself; for HE AND I HAVE ALL IN COMMON.' Thus it will be seen, that, though *oneness of essence* is not the precise thing here affirmed, that truth is *the basis of what is affirmed,* without which it would not be true. And AUGUSTINE was right in saying the '*We are*' condemns the *Sabellians* (who denied the *distinction of Persons* in the Godhead), while the '*one*' (as explained) condemns the *Arians* (who denied the unity of their essence).

31. Then the Jews took up stones again to stone Him – and for precisely the same thing as before (Joh 8:58,59).

32. Many good works have I showed you – that is, works of pure benevolence (as in Ac 10:38, 'Who went about doing good'; see Mr 7:37).

from my Father – not so much by His power, but as directly *commissioned by Him to do them.*

This He says to meet the imputation of unwarrantable assumption of the divine prerogatives [LUTHARDT].

for which of those works do ye stone me? – 'are ye stoning (that is, going to stone) me?'

33. for a blasphemy – whose legal punishment was stoning (Le 24:11–16).

thou, being a man – that is, a man only.

makest thyself God – Twice before they understood Him to advance the same claim, and both times they prepared themselves to avenge what they took to be the insulted honor of God, as here, in the way directed by their law (Joh 5:18 8:59).

34–36. Is it not written in your law – in Ps 82:6, respecting judges or magistrates.

Ye are gods – being the *official representatives* and *commissioned agents* of God.

35, 36. If he called them gods unto whom the word of God came … Say ye of him whom the Father hath sanctified and sent into the world, Thou blasphemest – The whole force of this reasoning, which has been but in part seized by the commentators, lies in what is said of the two parties compared. The *comparison* of Himself with mere men, divinely commissioned, is intended to show (as NEANDER well expresses it) that the idea of a communication of the Divine Majesty to human nature was by no means foreign to the revelations of the Old Testament; but there is also a *contrast* between Himself and all merely human representatives of God – the one '*sanctified by the Father and sent into the world*'; the other, '*to whom the word of God (merely) came,*' which is expressly designed to prevent His being massed up with them as only one of many human officials of God. *It is never said of Christ* that 'the word of the Lord came to Him'; whereas this is the well-known formula by which the divine commission, even to the highest of *mere men,* is expressed, as John the Baptist (Lu 3:2). The reason is that given by the Baptist himself (see on Joh 3:31). The contrast is between those 'to whom the word of God came' – men of the earth, earthy, who were merely privileged to get a divine *message* to utter (if prophets), or a divine *office* to discharge (if judges) – and '*Him* whom (not being of the earth at all) *the Father* sanctified (or set apart), and *sent into the world,*' an expression *never used of any merely human messenger of God,* and *used only of Himself.*

because, I said, I am the Son of God – It is worthy of special notice that our Lord *had not* said, in so many words, that He was the Son of God, on this occasion. But He had said what beyond doubt amounted to it – namely, that He gave His sheep eternal life, and none could pluck them out of His hand; that He had got them from His Father, in whose hands, though given to Him, they still remained, and out of whose hand none could pluck them; and that they were *the indefeasible property of both,* inasmuch as 'He and His Father were one.' Our Lord considers all this as just saying of Himself, 'I am the Son of God' – *one nature* with Him, yet mysteriously *of Him.* The parenthesis (Joh 10:35), 'and the Scripture cannot be broken,' referring to the terms used of magistrates in the eighty-second Psalm, has an important bearing on the *authority* of the living oracles. 'The Scripture, as the expressed will of the unchangeable God, is itself unchangeable and indissoluble' [OLSHAUSEN]. (Compare Mt 5:17.)

37–39. though ye believe not me, believe the works – There was in Christ's words, independently of any miracles, a self-evidencing truth, majesty and grace, which those who had any spiritual susceptibility were unable to resist (Joh 7:46 8:30). But, for those who wanted this, 'the works' were a mighty help. When these failed, the case was desperate indeed.

that ye may know and believe that the Father is in me, and I in him – thus reiterating His claim to essential *oneness with the Father,* which He had only *seemed* to soften down, that He might calm their rage and get their ear again for a moment.

39. Therefore they sought again to take him – true to their original understanding of His words, for they saw perfectly well that He *meant* to 'make Himself God' throughout all this dialogue.

he escaped out of their hand – (See Lu 4:30; Joh 8:59.)

40–42. went away again beyond Jordan … the place where John at first baptized – (See on Joh 1:28.)

41. many resorted to him – on whom the ministry of the Baptist had left permanent impressions.

John did no miracle, but all things John spake of this man were true – what they now heard and saw in Jesus only confirming in their minds the divinity of His forerunner's mission, though unaccompanied by any of His Master's miracles. And thus, 'many believed on Him there.'

Chapter 11

Joh 11:1–46.

Lazarus raised from the dead – the consequences of this.

1. of Bethany – at the east side of Mount Olivet.

the town of Mary and her sister Martha – thus distinguishing it from the other Bethany, 'beyond Jordan.' (See on Joh 1:28; Joh 10:40.)

2. It was that Mary who anointed the Lord with ointment – This, though not recorded by our Evangelist till Joh 12:3, was so well known in the teaching of all the churches, according to our Lord's prediction (Mt 26:13), that it is here alluded to by anticipation, as the most natural way of identifying her; and she is first named, though the younger, as the more distinguished of the two. She 'anointed THE LORD,' says the Evangelist – led doubtless to the use of this term here, as he was about to exhibit Him illustriously as the *Lord of Life.*

3–5. his sisters sent unto him, saying, Lord, he whom thou lovest is sick – a most womanly appeal, yet how reverential, to the known affection of her Lord for the patient. (See Joh 11:5,11.) 'Those whom Christ loves are no more exempt than others from their share of earthly trouble and anguish: rather are they bound over to it more surely' [TRENCH].

4. When Jesus heard that, he said, This sickness is not unto death – to *result* in death.

but for the glory of God, that the Son of God may be glorified thereby – that is, by this glory of God. (See *Greek.*) Remarkable language this, which from creature lips would have been intolerable. It means that the glory of GOD manifested in the resurrection of dead Lazarus would be shown to be the glory, *personally* and immediately, of THE SON.

5. Jesus loved Martha and her sister and Lazarus – what a picture! – one that in every age has attracted the admiration of the whole Christian Church. No wonder that those miserable skeptics who have carped at the ethical system of the Gospel, as not embracing private friendships in the list of its virtues, have been referred to the Saviour's peculiar regard for this family as a triumphant refutation, if such were needed.

6. When he heard he was sick, he abode two days still … where he was – at least twenty-five miles off. Beyond all doubt this was just to let things come to their worst, in order to display His glory. But how trying, meantime, to the faith of his friends, and how unlike the way in which love to a dying friend usually shows itself, on which it is plain that Mary reckoned. But the ways of *divine* are not as the ways of *human* love. Often they are the reverse. When His people are sick, in body or spirit; when their case is waxing more and more desperate every day; when all hope of recovery is about to expire – just then and therefore it is that '*He abides two days still in the same place where He is.*' Can they still hope against hope? Often they do not; but 'this is their infirmity.' For it is His chosen style of acting. We have been well taught it, and should not *now* have the lesson to learn. From the days of Moses was it given sublimely forth as the character of His grandest interpositions, that 'the Lord will judge His people and repent Himself for His servants' – *when He seeth that their power is gone* (De 32:36).

7–10. Let us go into Judea again – He was now in Perea, 'beyond Jordan.'

8. His disciples say unto him, Master, the Jews of late sought – literally, 'were (just) now seeking' 'to stone thee' (Joh 10:31).

goest thou thither again? – *to certain death,* as Joh 11:16 shows they thought.

9. Jesus answered, Are there not twelve hours in the day? – (See on Joh 9:4.) Our Lord's day had now reached its eleventh hour, and having till now 'walked in the day,' He would not *mistime* the remaining and more critical part of His work, which would be as fatal, He says, as omitting it altogether; for 'if *a man* (so He speaks, putting Himself under the same great law of duty as all other men – if a man) walk in the night, he stumbleth, because there is no light in him.'

11–16. Our friend Lazarus sleepeth; but I go that I may wake him out of sleep – Illustrious title! 'Our friend Lazarus.' To *Abraham only* is it accorded in the Old Testament, and not till *after his death,* (2Ch 20:7 Isa 41:8), to which our attention is called in the New Testament (Jas 2:23). When Jesus came in the flesh, His forerunner applied this name, in a certain sense, to himself (Joh 3:29); and into the same fellowship the Lord's chosen disciples are declared to have come (Joh 15:13-15). 'The phrase here employed, "our friend Lazarus," means more than "he whom *Thou* lovest" in Joh 11:3, for it implies that Christ's affection is *reciprocated* by Lazarus' [LAMPE]. Our Lord had been told only that Lazarus was 'sick.' But the change which his two days' delay had produced is here tenderly alluded to. Doubtless, His spirit was all the while with His dying, and now dead 'friend.' The symbol of 'sleep' for *death* is common to all languages, and familiar to us in the Old Testament. In the New Testament, however, a higher meaning is put into it, in relation to believers in Jesus (see 1Th 4:14), a sense hinted at, and clearly, in Ps 17:15 [LUTHARDT]; and the 'awaking out of sleep' acquires a corresponding sense far transcending bare resuscitation.

12. if he sleep, he shall do well – literally, 'be preserved'; that is, recover. 'Why then go to Judea?'

14. Then said Jesus unto them plainly, Lazarus is dead – Says BENGEL beautifully, 'Sleep is the death of the saints, in the language of heaven; but this language the disciples here understood not; incomparable is the generosity of the divine manner of discoursing, but such is the slowness of men's apprehension that Scripture often has to descend to the more miserable style of human discourse; compare Mt 16:11.'

15. I am glad for your sakes I was not there – This certainly implies that if He had been present, Lazarus would not have died; not because

He could not have resisted the importunities of the sisters, but because, in presence of the personal Life, death could not have reached His friend [LUTHARDT]. 'It is beautifully congruous to the divine decorum that in presence of the Prince of Life no one is ever said to have died' [BENGEL].

that ye may believe – This is added to explain His 'gladness' at not having been present. His friend's death, as such, could not have been to Him 'joyous'; the sequel shows it was 'grievous'; but *for them* it was safe (Php 3:1).

16. Thomas, ... called Didymus – or 'the twin.'

Let us also go, that we may die with him – lovely spirit, though tinged with some sadness, such as reappears at Joh 14:5, showing the tendency of this disciple to take the *dark* view of things. On a memorable occasion this tendency opened the door to downright, though but momentary, unbelief (Joh 20:25). Here, however, though alleged by many interpreters there is nothing of the sort. He perceives clearly how this journey to Judea will end, as respects his Master, and not only sees in it peril to themselves, as they all did, but feels as if he could not and cared not to survive his Master's sacrifice to the fury of His enemies. It was that kind of affection which, living only in the light of its Object, cannot contemplate, or has no heart for life, without it.

17–19. when Jesus came, he found that he had lain in the grave four days – If he died on the day the tidings came of his illness – and was, according to the Jewish custom, buried the same day (see JAHN's *Archæology,* and Joh 11:39 Ac 5:5,6,10) – and if Jesus, after two days' further stay in Perea, set out on the day following for Bethany, some ten hours' journey, that would make out the four days; the first and last being incomplete [MEYER].

18. Bethany was nigh Jerusalem, about fifteen furlongs – rather less than two miles; mentioned to explain the visits of sympathy noticed in the following words, which the proximity of the two places facilitated.

19. many of the Jews came to Martha and Mary to comfort them – Thus were provided, in a most natural way, so many witnesses of the glorious miracle that was to follow, as to put the fact beyond possible question.

20–22. Martha, as soon as she heard that Jesus was coming, went and met him – true to the *energy* and *activity* of her character, as seen in Lu 10:38–42. (See Lu 10:38–42.)

but Mary sat ... in the house – equally true to her *placid* character. These undesigned touches not only charmingly illustrate the minute *historic fidelity* of both narratives, but their *inner harmony.*

21. Then said Martha ... Lord, if thou hadst been here, my brother had not died – As Mary afterwards said the same thing (Joh 11:32), it is plain they had made this very natural remark to each other, perhaps many times during these four sad days, and not without having their confidence in His love at times overclouded. Such trials of faith, however, are not peculiar to them.

22. But I know that even now – Energetic characters are usually sanguine, the rainbow of hope peering through the drenching cloud.

whatsoever thou wilt ask of God, God will give it thee – that is 'even to the restoration of my dead brother to life,' for that plainly is her meaning, as the sequel shows.

23–27. Jesus saith unto her, Thy brother shall rise again – purposely expressing Himself in general terms, to draw her out.

24. Martha said, ... I know that he shall rise again ... at the last day – 'But are we never to see him in life till then?'

25. Jesus said, I am the resurrection and the life – '*The whole power to restore, impart, and maintain* life, resides in Me.' (See on Joh 1:4; Joh 5:21.) What higher claim to supreme divinity than this grand saying can be conceived?

he that believeth in me, though ... dead ... shall he live – that is, The believer's death shall be swallowed up in life, and his life shall never sink into death. As death comes by sin, it is His to dissolve it; and as life flows through His righteousness, it is His to communicate and eternally maintain it (Ro 5:21). The temporary separation of soul and body is here regarded as not even interrupting, much less impairing, the new and everlasting life imparted by Jesus to His believing people.

Believest thou this? – Canst thou take this in?

27. Yea, ... I believe that thou art the Christ, the Son of God – that is, And having *such* faith in Thee, I can believe all which that comprehends. While she had a glimmering perception that Resurrection, in every sense of the word, belonged to the Messianic office and Sonship of Jesus, she means, by this way of expressing herself, to cover much that she felt her ignorance of – as no doubt belonging to Him.

28–32. The Master is come and calleth for thee – The narrative does not give us this interesting detail, but Martha's words do.

29. As soon as she heard that, she arose quickly – affection for her Lord, assurance of His sympathy, and His hope of interposition, putting a spring into her distressed spirit.

31. The Jews ... followed her ... to the grave – Thus *casually* were provided witnesses of the glorious miracle that followed, *not prejudiced*, certainly, *in favour* of Him who wrought it.

to weep there – according to Jewish practice, for some days after burial.

fell at his feet – more impassioned than her sister, though her words were fewer. (See on Joh 11:21.)

33–38. When Jesus ... saw her weeping, and the Jews ... weeping ... he groaned in the spirit – the tears of Mary and her friends acting sympathetically upon Jesus, and drawing forth His emotions. What a vivid and beautiful outcoming of His 'real' humanity! The word here rendered 'groaned' does not mean 'sighed' or 'grieved,' but rather 'powerfully checked his emotion' – made a visible effort to restrain those tears which were ready to gush from His eyes.

and was troubled – rather, 'troubled himself' (*Margin*); referring probably to this visible difficulty of repressing His emotions.

34. Where have ye laid him? ... Lord, come and see – Perhaps it was to retain composure enough to ask this question, and on receiving the answer to proceed with them to the spot, that He checked Himself.

35. Jesus wept – This beautifully conveys the sublime brevity of the two original words; else '*shed tears*' might have better conveyed the difference between the word here used and that twice employed in Joh 11:33, and there properly rendered 'weeping,' denoting the loud wail for the dead, while that of Jesus consisted of *silent tears*. Is it for nothing that the Evangelist, some *sixty years* after it occurred, holds up to all ages with such touching brevity the sublime spectacle of *the Son of God in tears?* What a seal of His perfect oneness with us in the most redeeming feature of our stricken humanity! But was there nothing in those tears beyond sorrow for human suffering and death? Could these *effects* move Him without suggesting the *cause?* Who can doubt that in His ear every feature of the scene proclaimed that stern law of the Kingdom, '*The wages of sin is death*' (Ro 6:23), and that this element in His visible emotion underlay all the rest?

36. Then said the Jews, Behold how he loved him! – We thank you, O ye visitors from Jerusalem, for this spontaneous testimony to the *human* tenderness of the Son of God.

37. And – rather, 'But.'

some ... said, Could not this man, which opened the eyes of the blind, have caused that this man should not have died? – The former exclamation came from the better-feeling portion of the spectators; this betokens a measure of suspicion. It hardly goes the length of attesting the miracle on the blind man; but 'if (as everybody says) He did that, why could He not also have kept Lazarus alive?' As to the restoration of the dead man to life, they never so much as thought of it. But *this disposition to dictate to divine power, and almost to peril our confidence in it upon its doing our bidding, is not confined to men of no faith.*

38. Jesus again groaning in himself – that is, as at Joh 11:33, checked or repressed His rising feelings, in the former instance, of sorrow, here of righteous indignation at their unreasonable unbelief; (compare Mr 3:5) [WEBSTER and WILKINSON]. But here, too, struggling emotion was deeper, now that His eye was about to rest on the spot where lay, in the still horrors of death, His 'friend.'

a cave – the cavity, natural or artificial, of a rock. This, with the number of condoling visitors from Jerusalem, and the costly ointment with which Mary afterwards anointed Jesus at Bethany, all go to show that the family was in good circumstances.

39–44. Jesus said, Take ye away the stone – spoken to the attendants of Martha and Mary; for it was a work of no little labour [GROTIUS]. According to the Talmudists, it was forbidden to open a grave after the stone was placed upon it. Besides other dangers, they were apprehensive of legal impurity by contact with the dead. Hence they avoided coming nearer a grave than four cubits [MAIMONIDES in LAMPE]. But He who touched the leper, and the bier of the widow of Nain's son, rises here also above these Judaic memorials of evils, every one of which He had come to roll away. *Observe here what our Lord did Himself, and what He made others do.* As Elijah himself repaired the altar on Carmel, arranged the wood, cut the victim, and placed the pieces on the fuel, but made the by-standers fill the surrounding trench with water, that no suspicion might arise of fire having been secretly applied to the pile (1Ki 18:30–35); so our Lord would let the most sceptical see that, without laying a hand on the stone that covered His friend, He could recall him to life. But what could be done by human hand He orders to be done, reserving only to Himself what transcended the ability of all creatures.

Martha, the sister of … the dead – and as such the proper guardian of the precious remains; the relationship being *here* mentioned to account for her venturing gently to remonstrate against their exposure, in a state of decomposition, to eyes that had loved him so tenderly in life.

Lord, by this time he stinketh, for he hath been dead four days – (See on Joh 11:17.) It is wrong to suppose from this (as LAMPE and others do) that, like the by-standers, she had not thought of his restoration to life. But the glimmerings of hope which she cherished from the first (Joh 11:22), and which had been brightened by what Jesus said to her (Joh 11:23–27), had suffered a momentary eclipse on the proposal to expose the now sightless corpse. *To such fluctuations all real faith is subject in dark hours.* (See, for example, the case of Job.)

40. Jesus saith unto her, Said I not unto thee, that if thou wouldest believe, thou shouldest see the glory of God? – He had not said those very words, but this was the scope of all that He had uttered to her about His life-giving power (Joh 11:23,25,26); a gentle yet emphatic and most instructive rebuke: 'Why doth the restoration of life, even to a decomposing corpse, seem hopeless in the presence of the Resurrection and the Life? Hast thou yet to learn that "if thou canst believe, all things are possible to him that believeth?"' (Mr 9:23).

41. Jesus lifted up his eyes – an expression marking His calm solemnity. (Compare Joh 17:1.)

Father, I thank thee that thou hast heard me – rather, 'heardest Me,' referring to a specific prayer offered by Him, probably on intelligence of the case reaching Him (Joh 11:3,4); for His living and loving oneness with the Father was maintained and manifested in the flesh, not merely by the spontaneous and uninterrupted outgoing of Each to Each in spirit, but by specific actings of faith and exercises of prayer about each successive case as it emerged. He prayed (says LUTHARDT well) not for what He wanted, but for the manifestation of what He had; and having the bright consciousness of the answer in the felt liberty to ask it, and the assurance that it was at hand, He gives thanks for this with a grand simplicity before performing the act.

42. And – rather, 'Yet.'

I knew that thou hearest me always, but because of the people that stand by I said it, that they might believe that thou hast sent me – Instead of praying now, He simply gives thanks for answer to prayer offered ere He left Perea, and adds that His doing even this, in the audience of the people, was not from any doubt of the prevalency of His prayers in any case, but to show the people that *He did nothing without His Father, but all by direct communication with Him.*

43, 44. and when he had thus spoken, he cried with a loud voice – On one other occasion only did He this – on the *cross.* His last utterance was a 'loud cry' (Mt 27:50). 'He shall not cry,' said the prophet, nor, in His ministry, did He. What a sublime contrast is this 'loud cry' to the magical 'whisperings' and 'mutterings' of which we read in Isa 8:19 29:4 (as GROTIUS remarks)! It is second only to the grandeur of that voice which shall raise all the dead (Joh 5:28,29 1Th 4:16).

44. Jesus saith unto them, Loose him and let him go – Jesus will no more do this Himself than roll away the stone. The one was the necessary *preparation* for resurrection, the other the necessary *sequel* to it. THE LIFE-GIVING ACT ALONE HE RESERVES TO HIMSELF. So *in the quickening of the dead to spiritual life, human instrumentality is employed first to prepare the way, and then to turn it to account.*

45, 46. many … which … had seen … believed … But some … went … to the

Pharisees and told them what Jesus had done – the two classes which continually reappear in the Gospel history; nor is there ever any great work of God which does not produce both. 'It is remarkable that on each of the three occasions on which our Lord raised the dead, a large number of persons was assembled. In two instances, the resurrection of the widow's son and of Lazarus, these were all witnesses of the miracle; in the third (of Jairus' daughter) they were necessarily cognizant of it. Yet this important circumstance is in each case only incidentally noticed by the historians, not put forward or appealed to as a proof of their veracity. In regard to this miracle, we observe a greater degree of preparation, both in the provident arrangement of events, and in our Lord's actions and words than in any other. The preceding miracle (cure of the man born blind) is distinguished from all others by the open and formal investigation of its facts. And both these miracles, the most public and best attested of all, are related by John, who wrote long after the other Evangelists' [WEBSTER and WILKINSON].

Joh 11:47–57.
The Pharisees plan to kill Christ.

47–54. What do we? for this man doeth many miracles – 'While we trifle, "this man," by His "many miracles," will carry all before Him; the popular enthusiasm will bring on a revolution, which will precipitate the Romans upon us, and our all will go down in one common ruin.' What a testimony to the reality of our Lord's miracles, and their resistless effect, from His bitterest enemies!

51. Caiaphas … prophesied that Jesus should die for that nation – He meant nothing more than that the way to prevent the apprehended ruin of the nation was to make a sacrifice of the Disturber of their peace. But in giving utterance to this suggestion of political expediency, he was so guided as to give forth a divine prediction of deep significance; and God so ordered it that it should come from the lips of the high priest for that memorable year, the recognized head of God's visible people, whose ancient office, symbolized by the Urim and Thummim, was to decide in the last resort, all vital questions as the oracle of the divine will.

52. and not for that nation only – These are the Evangelist's words, not Caiaphas'.

53. they took council together to put him to death – Caiaphas but expressed what the party was secretly wishing, but afraid to propose.

Jesus … walked no more openly among the Jews – How could He, unless He had wished to die before His time?

near to the wilderness – of Judea.

a city called Ephraim – between Jerusalem and Jericho.

55–57. passover … at hand … many went … up … before the passover, to purify themselves – from any legal uncleanness which would have disqualified them from keeping the feast. This is mentioned to introduce the graphic statement which follows.

56. sought they for Jesus, and spake among themselves, as they stood in the temple – giving forth the various conjectures and speculations about the probability of His coming to the feast.

that he will not come – The form of this question implies the opinion that He *would* come.

57. chief priests and the Pharisees had given a commandment that if any knew where he were, he should show it, that they might take him – This is mentioned to account for the conjectures whether He would come, in spite of this determination to seize Him.

Chapter 12
Joh 12:1–11.
The anointing at Bethany.
(See Mt 26:6–13).

1–8. six days before the passover – that is, on the sixth day before it; probably after sunset on *Friday* evening, or the commencement of the Jewish *Sabbath* preceding the Passover.

2. Martha served – This, with what is afterwards said of Mary's way of honouring her Lord, is so true to the character in which those two women appear in Lu 10:38–42, as to constitute one of the strongest and most delightful confirmations of the truth of both narratives. (See also on Joh 11:20.)

Lazarus … sat at the table – '*Between the raised Lazarus and the healed leper* (Simon, Mr 14:3), *the Lord probably sits as between two trophies of His glory*' [STIER].

3. spikenard – or pure *nard*, a celebrated aromatic (So 1:12).

anointed the feet of Jesus – and 'poured it on His head' (Mt 26:7 Mr 14:3). The only use of this was to refresh and exhilarate – a grateful compliment in the East, amidst the closeness of a heated atmosphere, with many guests at a feast. Such was the form in which Mary's love to Christ, at so much cost to herself, poured itself out.

4. Judas … who should betray him – For the reason why this is here mentioned, see Mr 14:11.

6. had the bag – the purse.

bare what was put therein – not, bare it off by theft, though that he did; but simply, had charge of its contents, was treasurer to Jesus and the Twelve. How worthy of notice is this arrangement, by which an avaricious and dishonest person was not only taken into the number of the Twelve, but entrusted with the custody of their little property! The purposes which this served are obvious enough; but it is further noticeable, that the remotest hint was never given to the eleven of His true character, nor did the disciples most favoured with the intimacy of Jesus ever suspect him, till a few minutes before he voluntarily separated himself from their company – for ever!

7. said Jesus, Let her alone, against the day of my burying hath she done this – not that she thought of His burial, much less reserved any of her nard to anoint her dead Lord. But as the time was so near at hand when that office would have to be performed, *and she was not to have that privilege even after the spices were brought for the purpose* (Mr 16:1), He lovingly *regards it as done now.*

8. the poor always ... with you – referring to De 15:11.

but me ... not always – a gentle hint of His approaching departure. He adds (Mr 14:8), '*She hath done what she could,*' a noble testimony, embodying a principle of immense importance. 'Verily, I say unto you, Wheresoever this Gospel shall be preached in the whole world, there shall also this, that this woman hath done, be told for a memorial of her' (Mt 26:13 Mr 14:9). 'In the act of love done to Him she had erected to herself an eternal monument, as lasting as the Gospel, the eternal word of God. From generation to generation this remarkable prophecy of the Lord has been fulfilled; and even we, in explaining this saying of the Redeemer, of necessity contribute to its accomplishment' [OLSHAUSEN]. 'Who but Himself had the power to ensure to any work of man, even if resounding in his own time through the whole earth, an imperishable remembrance in the stream of history? Behold once more here, the majesty of His royal judicial supremacy in the government of the world, in this, Verily I say unto you' [STIER]. Beautiful are the lessons here: (1) *Love to Christ transfigures the humblest services.* All, indeed, who have themselves a heart value its least outgoings beyond the most costly mechanical performances; but how does it endear the Saviour to us to find Him endorsing the principle as His own standard in judging of character and deeds!

> What though in poor and humble guise
>   Thou here didst sojourn, cottage-born,
> Yet from Thy glory in the skies
>   Our earthly gold Thou didst not scorn.
> For Love delights to bring her best,
> And where Love is, that offering evermore is blest.
> Love on the Saviour's dying head
>   Her spikenard drops unblam'd may pour,
> May mount His cross, and wrap Him dead
>   In spices from the golden shore.
>   KEBLE.

(2) Works of *utility* should never be set in opposition to the promptings of self-sacrificing *love,* and the sincerity of those who do so is to be suspected. Under the mask of concern for the poor at home, how many excuse themselves from all care of the perishing heathen abroad. (3) Amidst conflicting duties, that which our 'hand (*presently*) findeth to do' is to be preferred, and even a less duty *only to be done now* to a greater *that can be done at any time.* (4) 'If there be first a willing mind, it is accepted according to that a man hath, and not according to that he hath not' (2Co 8:12). – 'She hath done what she could' (Mr 14:8). (5) As Jesus beheld in spirit the universal diffusion of His Gospel, while His lowest depth of humiliation was only approaching, so He regards *the facts of His earthly history* as constituting *the substance of this Gospel,* and the relation of them as just the 'preaching of this Gospel.' Not that preachers are to confine themselves to a bare narration of these facts, but that they are to make their whole preaching turn upon them as its grand centre, and derive from them its proper vitality; all that goes before this in the Bible being but the *preparation* for them, and all that follows but the *sequel.*

9–11. Crowds of the Jerusalem Jews hastened to Bethany, not so much to see Jesus, whom they knew to be there, as to see dead Lazarus alive; and this, issuing in their accession to Christ, led to a plot against the life of Lazarus also, as the only means of arresting the triumphs of Jesus (see Joh 12:19) – to such a pitch had these chief priests come of diabolical determination to shut out the light from themselves, and quench it from the earth!

Joh 12:12–19.
Christ's triumphal entry into Jerusalem.
(See Mt 21:1–9; and Lu 19:29–36).

12. On the next day – the Lord's day, or Sunday (see on Joh 12:1); the tenth day of the Jewish month Nisan, on which the paschal lamb was set apart to be 'kept up until the fourteenth day of the same month, when the whole assembly of the congregation of Israel were to kill it in the evening' (Ex 12:3,6). Even so, from the day of this solemn entry into Jerusalem, 'Christ our Passover' was virtually set apart to be 'sacrificed for us' (1Co 5:7).

16. when Jesus was glorified, then remembered they that these things were written of him – The Spirit, descending on them from the glorified Saviour at Pentecost, opened their eyes suddenly to the true sense of the Old Testament, brought vividly to their recollection this and other Messianic predictions, and to their unspeakable astonishment showed them that they, and all the actors in these scenes, had been unconsciously fulfilling those predictions.

Joh 12:20–50. Some Greeks desire to see Jesus – the discourse and scene thereupon.

20–22. Greeks – Not Grecian Jews, but Greek proselytes to the Jewish faith, who were wont to attend the annual festivals, particularly this primary one, the Passover.

The same came therefore to Philip … of Bethsaida – possibly as being from the same quarter.

saying, Sir, we would see Jesus – certainly in a far better sense than Zaccheus (Lu 19:3). Perhaps He was then in that part of the temple court to which Gentile proselytes had no access. 'These men from the *west* represent, at the end of Christ's life, what the wise men from the *east* represented at its beginning; but those come to the cross of the King, even as these to His manger' [STIER].

22. Philip … telleth Andrew – As fellow townsmen of Bethsaida (Joh 1:44), these two seem to have drawn to each other.

Andrew and Philip tell Jesus – The minuteness of these details, while they add to the graphic force of the narrative, serves to prepare us for something important to come out of this introduction.

23–26. Jesus answered them, The hour is come that the Son of man should be glorified – that is, They would see Jesus, would they? Yet a little moment, and they shall see Him so as now they dream not of. The middle wall of partition that keeps them out from the commonwealth of Israel is on the eve of breaking down, 'and I, if I be lifted up from the earth, shall draw all men unto Me'; I see them 'flying as a cloud, and as doves to their cotes' – a glorious event that will be for the Son of man, by which this is to be brought about. It is His *death* He thus sublimely and delicately alludes to. Lost in the scenes of triumph which this desire of the Greeks to see Him called up before His view, He gives no direct answer to their petition for an interview, but sees the cross which was to bring them gilded with glory.

24. Except a corn of wheat fall into the ground and die, it abideth alone; but if it die, it bringeth forth much fruit – The *necessity* of His death is here brightly expressed, and its proper operation and fruit – *life springing forth out of death* – imaged forth by a beautiful and deeply significant law of the vegetable kingdom. For a double reason, no doubt, this was uttered – to explain what he had said of His death, as the hour of His own glorification, and to sustain His own Spirit under the agitation which was mysteriously coming over it in the view of that death.

25. He that loveth his life shall lose it; and he that hateth his life in this world shall keep it unto life eternal – (See Lu 9:24.) Did our Lord mean to exclude Himself from the operation of the great principle here expressed – *self-renunciation, the law of self-preservation;* and its converse, *self-preservation, the law of self-destruction?* On the contrary, as He became Man to exemplify this fundamental law of the Kingdom of God in its most sublime form, so the very utterance of it on this occasion served to sustain His own Spirit in the double prospect to which He had just alluded.

26. If any man serve me, let him follow me; and where I am, there shall also my servant be: If any man serve me, him will my Father honour – *Jesus here claims the same absolute subjection to Himself, as the law of men's exaltation to honour, as He yielded to the Father.*

27, 28. Now is my soul troubled – He means at the prospect of His death, just alluded to. Strange view of the Cross this, immediately after representing it as the hour of His glory! (Joh 12:23). But the two views naturally meet, and blend into one. It was the Greeks, one might say, that troubled Him. Ah! they shall see Jesus, but *to Him* it shall be a costly sight.

and what shall I say? – He is in a strait betwixt two. The death of the cross was, and could not but be, appalling to His spirit. But to shrink from absolute subjection to the Father, was worse still. In asking Himself, 'What shall I say?' He seems as if thinking aloud, feeling His way between two dread alternatives, looking both of them sternly in the face, measuring, weighing them, in order that the choice actually made might be seen, *and even by himself the more vividly felt,* to be a profound, deliberate, spontaneous election.

Father, save me from this hour – To take this as a question – 'Shall I say, Father, save me,' – as some eminent editors and interpreters do, is unnatural and jejune. It is a real petition, like that in Gethsemane, 'Let this cup pass from Me'; only whereas *there* He prefaces the prayer with an 'If it be possible,' *here* He follows it up with what is tantamount to that – 'Nevertheless for this cause came I unto this hour.' The sentiment conveyed, then, by the prayer, in both cases, is twofold: (1) that only one thing could reconcile Him to the death of the cross – its being His Father's will He should endure it – and (2) that in this view of it He yielded Himself freely to it. *What He recoils from is not subjection to His Father's will: but to show how tremendous a self-sacrifice that obedience involved,* He first asks the Father to save Him from it, and then signifies how perfectly He knows that He is there for the very purpose of enduring it. Only by letting these mysterious words speak their full meaning do they become intelligible and consistent. As for those who see *no bitter elements in the death of Christ* – nothing beyond mere dying – what can they make of such a scene? and when they place it over against the feelings with which thousands of His adoring followers have welcomed death for His sake, how can they hold Him up to the admiration of men?

28. Father, glorify thy name – by a present testimony.

I have both glorified it – referring specially to the voice from heaven at His *baptism*, and again at His *transfiguration*.

and will glorify it again – that is, in the yet future scenes of His still deeper necessity; although this promise was a present and sublime testimony, which would irradiate the clouded spirit of the Son of man.

29–33. The people therefore that stood by, said, It thundered; others, An angel spake to him – some hearing only a sound, others an articulate, but to them unintelligible voice.

30. Jesus ... said, This voice came not because of me, but for your sakes – that is, probably, to correct the unfavourable impressions which His momentary agitation and mysterious prayer for deliverance may have produced on the by-standers.

31. Now is the judgment of this world – the world that 'crucified the Lord of glory' (1Co 2:8), considered as a vast and complicated kingdom of Satan, breathing his spirit, doing his work, and involved in his doom, which Christ's death by its hands irrevocably sealed.

now shall the prince of this world be cast out – How differently is that fast-approaching 'hour' regarded in the kingdoms of darkness and of light! 'The hour of relief; from the dread Troubler of our peace – how near it is! Yet a little moment, and the day is ours!' So it was calculated and felt in the one region. 'Now shall the prince of this world be cast out,' is a somewhat different view of the same event. We know who was right. Though yet under a veil, He sees the triumphs of the Cross in unclouded and transporting light.

32. And I, if I be lifted up from the earth, will draw all men unto me – The 'I' here is emphatic – I, taking the place of the world's ejected prince. 'If lifted up,' means not only *after that I have been lifted up*, but, *through the virtue of that uplifting.* And truly, the death of the Cross, in all its significance, revealed in the light, and borne in upon the heart, by the power of the Holy Ghost, possesses an attraction over the wide world – to civilized and savage, learned and illiterate, alike – which breaks down all opposition, assimilates all to itself, and forms out of the most heterogeneous and discordant materials a kingdom of surpassing glory, whose uniting principle is adoring subjection 'to Him that loved them.' 'Will draw all men "UNTO ME,"' says He. What lips could venture to utter such a word but His, which 'dropt as an honeycomb,' whose manner of speaking was evermore in the same spirit of conscious equality with the Father?

33. This he said, signifying what death he should die – that is, 'by being lifted up from the earth' on 'the accursed tree' (Joh 3:14 8:28).

34. We have heard out of the law – the scriptures of the Old Testament (referring to such places as Ps 89:28,29 110:4 Da 2:44 7:13,14).

that Christ – the Christ 'endureth for ever.'

and how sayest thou, The Son of Man must be lifted up – How can that consist with this 'uplifting?' They saw very well both that He was holding Himself up as *the Christ* and *a Christ to die a violent death;* and as that ran counter to all their ideas of the Messianic prophecies, they were glad to get this seeming advantage to justify their unyielding attitude.

35, 36. Yet a little while is the light with you. Walk while ye have the light – Instead of answering their question, He warns them, with mingled majesty and tenderness, against trifling with their last brief opportunity, and entreats them to let in the Light while they have it in the midst of them, that they themselves might be 'light in the Lord.' In this case, all the clouds which hung around His Person and Mission would speedily be dispelled, while if they continued to hate the light, bootless were all His answers to their merely speculative or captious questions. (See Lu 13:23.)

36. These things spake Jesus, and departed, and did hide himself from them – He who spake as never man spake, and immediately after words fraught with unspeakable dignity and love, had to 'hide Himself' from His auditors! What then must *they* have been? He retired, probably to Bethany. (The parallels are: Mt 21:17 Lu 21:37.)

37–41. It is the manner of this Evangelist alone to record his own reflections on the scenes he describes; but here, having arrived at what was virtually the close of our Lord's public ministry, he casts an affecting glance over the fruitlessness of His whole ministry on the bulk of the now doomed people.

though he had done so many miracles – The word used suggests their *nature* as well as *number.*

38. That the saying of Esaias ... might be fulfilled – This unbelief did not at all set aside the purposes of God, but, on the contrary, fulfilled them.

39–40. Therefore they could not believe, because Esaias said again, He hath blinded their eyes, that they should not see – That this expresses *a positive divine act,* by which those who wilfully close their eyes and harden their hearts against the truth are judicially *shut up* in their unbelief and impenitence, is admitted by all candid critics [as OLSHAUSEN], though many of them think it necessary to contend that this is in no way inconsistent with the liberty of the human will, which of course it is not.

41. These things said Esaias, when he saw his glory, and spake of him – a key of immense importance to the opening of Isaiah's vision (Isa 6:1–13), and all similar Old Testament representations. 'THE SON is the King Jehovah who rules in the Old Testament and appears to the elect, as in the New Testament THE SPIRIT, the invisible Minister of the Son, is the Director of the Church and the Revealer in the sanctuary of the heart' [OLSHAUSEN].

42, 43. among the chief rulers also – rather, 'even of the rulers'; such as Nicodemus and Joseph.

because of the Pharisees – that is, the *leaders* of the sects; for they were of it themselves.

put out of the synagogue – See Joh 9:22,34.

43. they loved the praise of men more than the praise of God – 'a severe remark, considering that several at least of these persons afterwards boldly confessed Christ. It indicates the displeasure with which God regarded their conduct at this time, and with which He continues to regard similar conduct' [WEBSTER and WILKINSON].

44–50. Jesus cried – in a loud tone, and with peculiar solemnity. (Compare Joh 7:37.)

and said, He that believeth on me – This seems to be a supplementary record of some weighty proclamations, for which there had been found no natural place before, and introduced here as a sort of *summary and winding up* of His whole testimony.

Chapter 13

Joh 13:1–20.

At the last supper Jesus washes the disciples' feet – the discourse arising thereupon.

1. when Jesus knew that his hour was come that he should depart out of this world unto the Father – On these beautiful euphemisms, see Lu 9:31; Lu 9:51.

having loved his own which were in the world, he loved them unto the end – The meaning is, that on the very edge of His last sufferings, when it might have been supposed that He would be absorbed in His own awful prospects, He was so far from forgetting 'His own,' who were to be left struggling 'in the world' after He had 'departed out of it to the Father' (Joh 17:11), that in His care for them He seemed scarce to think of Himself save in connection with them: 'Herein is love,' not only 'enduring to the end,' but most affectingly manifested when, judging by a human standard, least to be expected.

2. supper being ended – rather, 'being prepared,' 'being served,' or, 'going on'; for that it was not 'ended' is plain from Joh 13:26.

the devil having now – or, 'already.' **put into the heart of Judas … to betray him** – referring to the agreement he had *already* made with the chief priests (Lu 22:3–6).

3. Jesus knowing that the Father had given all things into his hands – This verse is very sublime, and as a preface to what follows, were we not familiar with it, would fill us with inexpressible surprise. An unclouded perception of His relation to the Father, the commission He held from Him, and His approaching return to Him, possessed His soul.

4, 5. He riseth from supper, and laid aside his garments – outer garments which would have impeded the operation of washing.

and took a towel and girded himself – assuming a servant's dress.

5. began to wash – proceeded to wash. *Beyond all doubt the feet of Judas were washed*, as of all the rest.

6–11. Peter saith … Lord, dost thou wash my feet? – Our language cannot bring out the intensely vivid contrast between the '*Thou*' and the '*my*,' which, by bringing them together, the original expresses, for it is not good English to say, 'Lord, *Thou my* feet dost wash?' But *every word* of this question is emphatic. Thus far, and in the question itself, there was nothing but the most profound and beautiful astonishment at a condescension to him quite incomprehensible. Accordingly, though there can be no doubt that already Peter's heart rebelled against it as a thing not to be tolerated, Jesus ministers no rebuke as yet, but only bids him wait a little, and he should understand it all.

7. Jesus answered and said … What I do thou knowest not now – that is, Such condescension *does* need explanation; it *is* fitted to astonish.

but thou shalt know hereafter – afterwards, meaning *presently*; though viewed as a general maxim, applicable to all dark sayings in God's Word, and dark doings in God's providence, these words are full of consolation.

8. Peter saith unto him, Thou shalt never wash – more emphatically, 'Never shalt Thou wash my feet': that is, 'That is an incongruity to which I can never submit.' How like the man!

If I wash thee not, thou hast no part with me – What Peter could not submit to was, that the Master should serve His servant. But *the whole saving work of Christ was one continued series of such services, ending with and consummated by the most self-sacrificing and transcendent of all services:* THE SON OF MAN CAME *not to be ministered unto, but* TO MINISTER, AND TO GIVE HIS LIFE A RANSOM FOR MANY. (See Mr 10:45.) If Peter then could not submit to let his Master go down so low as to wash his feet, *how should he suffer himself to be served by Him at all?* This is couched under the one pregnant word 'wash,' which though applicable to the *lower* operation which Peter resisted, is the familiar scriptural symbol of that *higher* cleansing, which Peter little thought he was at the same time virtually putting from him. *It is not humility to refuse what the Lord deigns to do for us, or to deny what He has done,* but it is self-willed presumption – *not rare, however, in those inner circles of lofty religious profession and traditional spirituality, which are found wherever Christian truth has enjoyed long and undisturbed possession.* The truest humility is to receive reverentially, and thankfully to own, the gifts of grace.

9. Lord, not my feet only, but also my hands and my head – that is, 'To be severed from Thee, Lord, is death to me: If that be the meaning of my speech, I tread upon it; and if to be washed of Thee have such significance, then not my feet only, but hands, head, and all, be washed!' This artless expression of clinging, life-and-death attachment to Jesus, and felt dependence upon Him for his whole spiritual well-being, compared with the similar saying in Joh 6:68,69 (see Joh 6:68,69), furnishes such evidence of *historic verity* such as no thoroughly honest mind can resist.

10. He that is washed – in this *thorough* sense, to express which the word is carefully changed to one meaning to wash *as in a bath.*

needeth not – to be so washed any more.

save to wash his feet – needeth to do no more than wash his feet (and here the former word is resumed, meaning to wash *the hands or feet*).

but is clean every whit – as a whole. This sentence is singularly instructive. Of the *two cleansings,* the one points to that which takes place at the *commencement* of the Christian life, embracing *complete absolution from sin as a guilty state,* and *entire deliverance from it as a polluted life* (Re 1:5 1Co 6:11) – or, in the language of theology, *Justification* and *Regeneration.* This cleansing is effected *once for all,* and is never repeated. The other cleansing, described as that of 'the feet,' is *such as one walking from a bath quite cleansed still needs, in consequence of his contact with the earth.* (Compare Ex 30:18,19.) It is the *daily* cleansing which we are taught to seek, when in the spirit of adoption we say, 'Our Father which art in heaven … forgive us our debts' (Mt 6:9,12); and, when burdened with the sense of manifold shortcomings – as what tender spirit of a Christian is not? – is it not a relief to be permitted thus to wash our feet after a day's contact with the earth? This is not to call in question the completeness of our past justification. Our Lord, while graciously insisting on washing Peter's feet, refuses to extend the cleansing farther, that the symbolical instruction intended to be conveyed might not be marred.

and ye are clean – in the first and *whole* sense. but not all-important, as showing that

Judas, instead of being as true-hearted a disciple as the rest at first, and merely *falling away* afterwards – as many represent it – *never experienced that cleansing at all which made the others what they were.*

12–15. Know ye what I have done? – that is, its intent. The question, however, was put merely to summon their attention to His own answer.

13. Ye call me Master – Teacher.

and Lord – *learning* of Him in the one capacity, *obeying* Him in the other.

and ye say well, for so I am – The conscious dignity with which this claim is made is remarkable, following immediately on His laying aside the towel of service. Yet what is this whole history but a succession of such astonishing contrast from first to last?

14. If I then – the Lord.

have washed your feet – the servants'.

ye – but fellow servants.

ought to wash one another's feet – not in the narrow sense of a literal washing, profanely caricatured by popes and emperors, but by the very humblest *real* services one to another.

16, 17. The servant is not greater than his lord – an oft-repeated saying (Mt 10:24).

If ye know these things, happy are ye if ye do them – a hint that even among real Christians the *doing* of such things would come lamentably short of the *knowing.*

18, 19. I speak not of you all – the 'happy *are* ye,' of Joh 13:17, being on no supposition applicable to Judas.

I know whom I have chosen – in the *higher* sense.

But that the scripture may be fulfilled – that is, one has been added to your number, by no accident or mistake, who is none of Mine, but just that he might fulfil his predicted destiny.

He that eateth bread with me – 'did eat of *my bread*' (Ps 41:9), as one of My family; admitted to the nearest familiarity of discipleship and of social life.

hath lifted up his heel against me – turned upon Me, adding *insult* to injury. (Compare Heb 10:29.) In the Psalm the immediate reference is to Ahithophel's treachery against David (2Sa 17:1–23), one of those scenes in which the parallel of his story with that of His great Antitype is exceedingly striking. 'The eating bread derives a fearful meaning from the participation in the sacramental supper, a meaning which must be applied for ever to all unworthy communicants, as well as to all betrayers of Christ who eat the bread of His Church' (STIER, with whom, and others, we agree in thinking that Judas partook of the Lord's Supper).

19. I tell you before … that when it comes to pass, ye may believe – and it came to pass when they deeply needed such confirmation.

20. He that receiveth whomsoever I send, receiveth me – (See Mt 10:40.) The connection here seems to be that despite the dishonour done to Him by Judas, and similar treatment awaiting themselves, they were to be cheered by the assurance that their office, even as His own, was divine.

Joh 13:21–30.
The traitor indicated – he leaves the supper room.

21. When Jesus had thus said, he was troubled in spirit, and testified, and said, Verily, verily, I say unto you, One of you shall betray me – The announcement of Joh 13:18 seems not to have been plain enough to be quite apprehended, save by the traitor himself. He will therefore speak it out in terms not to be misunderstood. But how much it cost Him to do this, appears from the 'trouble' that came over His 'spirit' – visible emotion, no doubt – before He got it uttered. What wounded susceptibility does this disclose, and what exquisite delicacy in His social intercourse with the Twelve, to whom He cannot, without an effort, break the subject!

22. the disciples looked one on another, doubting of whom he spake – Further intensely interesting particulars are given in the other Gospels: (1) 'They were exceeding sorrowful' (Mt 26:22). (2) 'They began to inquire among themselves which of them it was that should do this thing' (Lu 22:23). (3) 'They began to say unto Him one by one, Is it I, and another, Is it I?' (Mr 14:19). Generous, simple hearts! They abhorred the thought, but, instead of putting it on others, each was only anxious to purge *himself* and know if *he* could be the wretch. Their putting it at once to Jesus Himself, as knowing doubtless who was to do it, was the best, as it certainly was the most spontaneous and artless evidence of their innocence. (4) Jesus, apparently while this questioning was going on, added, 'The Son of man goeth as it is written of Him, but woe unto that man by whom the Son of man is betrayed! It had been good for that man if he had not been born' (Mt 26:24). (5) 'Judas,' *last of all*, 'answered and said, *Lord, is it I?*' evidently feeling that when all were saying this, if he held his peace, that of itself would draw suspicion upon him. To prevent this the question was wrung out of him, but perhaps, amidst the stir and excitement at the table, in a half-suppressed tone as we are inclined to think the answer also was – 'Thou hast said' (Mt 26:25), or possibly by little more than a sign; for from Joh 13:28 it is evident that till the moment when he went out, he was not openly discovered.

23–26. there was leaning on Jesus' bosom one of his disciples, whom Jesus loved – Thus modestly does our Evangelist denote himself, as reclining next to Jesus at the table.

Peter … beckoned to him to ask who it should be of whom he spake – reclining probably at the corresponding place on the other side of Jesus.

25. He then lying – rather leaning over on Jesus' bosom.

saith – *in a whisper,* 'Lord, who is it?'

26. Jesus answered – *also inaudibly,* the answer being communicated to Peter perhaps from behind.

He … to whom I shall give a sop when I have dipped it – a piece of the bread soaked in the wine or the sauce of the dish; one of the ancient ways of testifying peculiar regard; compare Joh 13:18, '*he that eateth bread with Me.*'

And when he had dipped … he gave it to Judas – Thus the sign of Judas' treachery was an affecting expression, and the last, of the Saviour's wounded love!

27–30. after the sop Satan entered into him – Very solemn are these brief hints of the successive steps by which Judas reached the climax of his guilt. 'The devil had already put it into his heart to betray his Lord.' Yet who can tell what struggles he went through ere he brought himself to carry that suggestion into effect? Even after this, however, his compunctions were not at an end. With the thirty pieces of silver already in his possession, he seems still to have quailed – and can we wonder? When Jesus stooped to wash his feet, it may be the last struggle was reaching its crisis. But that word of the Psalm, about 'one that ate of his bread who would lift up his heel against Him' (Ps 41:9) probably all but turned the dread scale, and the still more explicit announcement, that one of those sitting with Him at the table should betray Him, would beget the thought, 'I am detected; it is now too late to draw back.' At that moment the sop is given; offer of friendship is once more made – and how affectingly! But already 'Satan has *entered into him,*' and though the Saviour's act might seem enough to recall him even yet, hell is now in his bosom, and he says within himself, 'The die is cast; now let me go through with it; fear, begone!' (See Mt 12:43).

Then said Jesus unto him, That thou doest, do quickly – that is, Why linger here? Thy presence is a restraint, and thy work stands still; thou hast the wages of iniquity, go work for it!

28, 29. no man … knew for what intent he spake this unto him … some thought … Jesus … said … But what we need … or, … give … to the poor – a very important statement, as showing how carefully Jesus had kept the secret, and Judas his hypocrisy, to the last.

30. He then, having received the sop, went immediately out – severing himself *for ever* from that holy society with which he never had any spiritual sympathy.

and it was night – but far blacker night in the soul of Judas than in the sky over his head.

Joh 13:31–38.

Discourse after the traitor's departure – Peter's self-confidence – his fall predicted.

31. when he was gone out, Jesus said, Now is the Son of man glorified – These remarkable words plainly imply that up to this moment our Lord had spoken *under a painful restraint,* the presence of a traitor within the little circle of His holiest fellowship on earth preventing the free and full outpouring of His heart; as is evident, indeed, from those oft-recurring clauses, 'Ye are not all clean,' 'I speak not of you all.' 'Now' the restraint is removed, and the embankment which kept in the mighty volume of living waters having broken down, they burst forth in a torrent which only ceases on His leaving the supper room and entering on the next stage of His great work – the scene in the Garden. But with what words is the silence first broken on the departure of Judas? By no reflections on the traitor, and, what is still more wonderful, by no reference to the dread character of His own approaching sufferings. He does not even name them, save by announcing, as with a burst of triumph, that the hour of His *glory* has arrived! And what is very remarkable, in five brief clauses He repeats this word 'glorify' *five times,* as if to His view a coruscation of glories played at that moment about the Cross. (See on Joh 12:23.)

God is glorified in him – the glory of Each reaching its zenith in the Death of the Cross! **32. If God be glorified in him, God shall also** – in return and reward of this highest of all services ever rendered to Him, or capable of being rendered.

glorify him in himself, and ... straightway glorify him – referring now to the Resurrection and Exaltation of Christ *after* this service was over, including all the honour and glory then put upon Him, and that will for ever encircle Him as Head of the new creation.

33–35. Little children – From the height of His own glory He now descends, with sweet pity, to His 'little children,' *all now His own.* This term of endearment, nowhere else used in the Gospels, and once only employed by Paul (Ga 4:19), is appropriated by the beloved disciple himself, who no fewer than seven times employs it in his first Epistle.

Ye shall seek me – feel the want of Me.

as I said to the Jews – (Joh 7:34 8:21). But oh in what a different sense!

34. a new commandment I give unto you, That ye love one another; as I have loved you, that ye also love one another – This was the *new* feature of it. Christ's love to His people in giving His life a ransom for them was altogether new,

and consequently as a Model and Standard for theirs to one another. It is not, however, something transcending the great moral law, which is 'the *old* commandment' (1Jo 2:7, and see Mr 12:28–33), but that law *in a new and peculiar form.* Hence it is said to be both *new* and *old* (1Jo 2:7,8).

35. By this shall all men know that ye are my disciples – the disciples of Him who laid down His life for those He loved.

if ye have love one to another – for My sake, and as one in Me; for to *such* love men outside the circle of believers know right well they are entire strangers. Alas, how little of it there is even within this circle!

36–38. Peter said – seeing plainly in these directions how to behave themselves, that He was indeed going from them.

Lord, whither goest thou? – having hardly a glimmer of the real truth.

Jesus answered, ... thou canst not follow me now, but thou shalt follow me afterwards – How different from what He said to the Jews: 'Whither I go *ye cannot come*' (Joh 8:21).

37. why not ... now? I will lay down my life for thy sake – He seems now to see that it was *death* Christ referred to as what would sever Him from them, but is not staggered at following Him thither. Jesus answered,

38. Wilt thou lay down thy life for my sake? – In this repetition of Peter's words there is deep though affectionate irony, and this Peter himself would feel for many a day after his recovery, as he retraced the painful particulars.

Verily ... The cock – See Lu 22:31–34.

Chapter 14

Joh 14:1–31.

Discourse at the table, after supper.

We now come to that portion of the evangelical history which we may with propriety call its *Holy of Holies.* Our Evangelist, like a consecrated priest, alone opens up to us the view into this sanctuary. It is the record of the last moments spent by the Lord in the midst of His disciples before His passion, when words full of heavenly thought flowed from His sacred lips. All that His heart, glowing with love, had still to say to His friends, was compressed into this short season. At first (from Joh 13:31) the intercourse took the form of conversation; sitting at table, they talked familiarly together. But when (Joh 14:31) the repast was finished, the language of Christ assumed a loftier strain; the disciples, assembled around their Master, listened to the words of life, and seldom spoke a word (only Joh 16:17,29). 'At length, in the Redeemer's sublime intercessory prayer, His full soul was poured forth in express petitions to His heavenly Father on behalf of those who were His own. It is a peculiarity of these last chapters, that they treat almost exclusively of the most profound relations – as that of the Son to the Father, and of both to the Spirit, that of Christ to the Church, of the Church to the world, and so forth. Moreover, a considerable portion of these sublime communications surpassed the point of view to which the disciples had at that time attained; hence the Redeemer frequently repeats the same sentiments in order to impress them more deeply upon their minds, and, because of what they still did not understand, points them to the Holy Spirit, who would remind them of all His sayings, and lead them into all truth (Joh 14:26)' [OLSHAUSEN].

1. Let not your heart be troubled – What myriads of souls have not these opening words cheered, in deepest gloom, since first they were uttered!

ye believe in God – absolutely.

believe also in me – that is, Have the *same trust* in Me. What less, and what else, can these words mean? And if so, what a demand to make by one sitting familiarly with them at the supper table! Compare the saying in Joh 5:17, for which the Jews took up stones to stone Him, as 'making himself equal with God' (Joh 14:18). But it is no *transfer of our trust from its proper Object*; it is but *the concentration of our trust in the Unseen and Impalpable One upon His Own Incarnate Son*, by which that trust, instead of the distant, unsteady, and too often cold and scarce real thing it otherwise is, acquires a conscious reality, warmth, and power, which makes all things new. *This is Christianity in brief.*

2. In my Father's house are many mansions – and so room for all, and a place for each.

if not, I would have told you – that is, I would tell you so at once; I would not deceive you.

I go to prepare a place for you – to obtain for you a right to be there, and to possess your 'place.'

3. I will come again and receive you unto myself – *strictly*, at His Personal appearing; but in a secondary and comforting sense, to each individually. Mark again the claim made: – to come again to receive His people *to Himself*, that where *He* is there they may be also. *He thinks it ought to be enough to be assured that they shall be where He is and in His keeping.*

4–7. whither I go ye know ... Thomas saith, Lord, we know not whither thou goest ... Jesus saith, I am the way – By saying this, He meant rather to draw out their inquiries and reply to them. Christ is 'THE WAY' to the Father – 'no man cometh unto the Father but by Me'; He is 'THE TRUTH' of all we find in the Father when we get to Him, 'For in Him dwelleth all the fulness of the Godhead bodily' (Col 2:9), and He is

all 'THE LIFE' that shall ever flow to us and bless us from the Godhead thus approached and thus manifested in Him – 'this is the true God and eternal life' (1Jo 5:20).

7. from henceforth – now, or from this time, understand.

8–12. The substance of this passage is that the Son is the ordained and perfect manifestation of the Father, that His own word for this ought to His disciples to be enough; that if any doubts remained His works ought to remove them (see on Joh 10:37); but yet that these works of His were designed merely to aid weak faith, and would be repeated, nay exceeded, by His disciples, in virtue of the power He would confer on them after His departure. His miracles the apostles wrought, though wholly in His name and by His power, and the 'greater' works – not in degree but in kind – were the conversion of thousands in a day, by His Spirit accompanying them.

13, 14. whatsoever ye ... ask in my name – as Mediator.

that will I do – as Head and Lord of the kingdom of God. This comprehensive promise is emphatically repeated in Joh 14:14.

15–17. If ye love me, keep my commandments. And I will pray the Father – This connection seems designed to teach that the proper temple for the indwelling Spirit of Jesus is a heart filled with that love to Him which lives actively for Him, and so this was the fitting preparation for the promised gift.

he shall give you another Comforter – a word used only by John; in his *Gospel* with reference to the Holy Spirit, in his *First Epistle* (1Jo 2:1), with reference to Christ Himself. Its proper sense is an 'advocate,' 'patron,' 'helper.' In this sense it is plainly meant of Christ (1Jo 2:1), and in this sense it comprehends all the *comfort* as well as *aid* of the Spirit's work. The Spirit is here promised as One who would *supply Christ's own place* in His absence.

that he may abide with you for ever – never go away, as Jesus was going to do in the body.

17. whom the world cannot receive – (See 1Co 2:14.)

he dwelleth with you, and shall be in you – Though the proper fulness of both these was yet future, our Lord, by using both the present and the future, seems plainly to say that they *already* had the germ of this great blessing.

18–20. I will not leave you comfortless – in bereaved and desolate condition; or (as in *Margin*) 'orphans.'

I will come to you – 'I come' or 'am coming' to you; that is, plainly *by the Spirit*, since it was to make His departure to be *no bereavement*.

19. world seeth – beholdeth.

me no more, but ye see – behold.

me – His bodily presence, being all the sight of Him which 'the world' ever had, or was capable of, it 'beheld Him no more' after His departure to the Father; but by the coming of the Spirit, the presence of Christ was not only *continued* to His spiritually enlightened disciples, but rendered *far more efficacious and blissful* than His bodily presence had been before the Spirit's coming.

because I live – not '*shall* live,' only when raised from the dead; for it is His unextinguishable, divine life of which He speaks, in view of which His *death and resurrection* were but as shadows passing over the sun's glorious disk. (Compare Lu 24:5 Re 1:18, 'the Living One'). And this grand saying Jesus uttered *with death immediately in view*. What a brightness does this throw over the next clause, 'ye shall live also!' 'Knowest thou not,' said LUTHER to the King of Terrors, 'that thou didst devour the Lord Christ, but wert obliged to give Him back, and wert devoured of Him? So thou must leave me undevoured because I abide in Him, and live and suffer for His name's sake. Men may hunt me out of the world – that I care not for – but I shall not on that account abide in death. I shall live with my Lord Christ, since I know and believe that *He liveth!*' (quoted in STIER).

20. At that day – of the Spirit's coming. **ye shall know that I am in my Father, ye in me, I in you** – (See on Joh 17:22,23.)

21. He that hath my commandments and keepeth them. – (See on Joh 14:15.)

my Father and I will love him – Mark the sharp line of distinction here, not only between the Divine Persons but the actings of love in Each respectively, towards true disciples.

22. Judas saith ... not Iscariot – Beautiful parenthesis this! The traitor being no longer present, we needed not to be told that this question came not from *him*. But it is as if the Evangelist had said, 'A very different Judas from the traitor, and a very different question from any that he would have put. Indeed [as one in STIER says], we never read of Iscariot that he entered in any way into his Master's words, or ever put a question even of rash curiosity (though it may be he did, but that nothing from *him* was deemed fit for immortality in the Gospels but his name and treason).'

how ... manifest thyself to us, and not to the world – a most natural and proper question, founded on Joh 14:19, though interpreters speak against it as *Jewish.*

23. we will come and make our abode with him – Astonishing statement! In the Father's 'coming' He 'refers to the revelation of Him *as a Father* to the soul, which does not take place till the Spirit comes into the heart, teaching it to cry, *Abba*, Father' [OLSHAUSEN]. The 'abode' means

a permanent, eternal stay! (Compare Le 26:11,12 Eze 37:26,27 2Co 6:16; and *contrast* Jer 14:8.)

25, 26. he shall teach you all things, and bring all to ... remembrance, whatsoever I have said unto you – (See on Joh 14:15; Joh 14:17.) As the Son came in *the Father's* name, so the Father shall send the Spirit *in My name*, says Jesus, that is, with like divine *power* and *authority* to 'reproduce in their souls what Christ taught them, 'bringing to living consciousness what lay like slumbering germs in their minds' [OLSHAUSEN]. On this rests the credibility and ultimate divine authority of THE GOSPEL HISTORY. The whole of what is here said of THE SPIRIT is decisive of His divine *personality.* 'He who can regard all the *personal* expressions, applied to the Spirit in these three chapters ("teaching," "reminding," "testifying," "coming," "convincing," "guiding," "speaking," "hearing," "prophesying," "taking") as being no other than a long drawn-out figure, deserves not to be recognized even as an interpreter of intelligible words, much less an expositor of Holy Scripture' [STIER].

27. Peace I leave with you, my peace I give unto you – If Joh 14:25,26 sounded like a note of preparation for drawing the discourse to a close, this would sound like a farewell. But oh, how different from ordinary adieus! It *is* a parting word, but of richest import, the customary 'peace' of a parting friend sublimed and transfigured. As 'the Prince of Peace' (Isa 9:6) He brought it into flesh, carried it about in His Own Person ('My peace') died to make it ours, left it as the heritage of His disciples upon earth, implants and maintains it by His Spirit in their hearts. Many a legacy is 'left' that is never 'given' to the legatee, many a gift destined that never reaches its proper object. But Christ is the Executor of His own Testament; the peace He 'leaves' He '*gives*'; Thus all is secure. **not as the world giveth** – in contrast with the world, He gives *sincerely, substantially, eternally.*

28. If ye loved me, ye would rejoice, because I said, I go unto the Father, for my Father is greater than I – These words, which Arians and Socinians perpetually quote as triumphant evidence against the proper Divinity of Christ, really yield no intelligible sense on their principles. Were a holy *man* on his deathbed, beholding his friends in tears at the prospect of losing him, to say, 'Ye ought rather to joy than weep for me, and would if ye really loved me, 'the speech would be quite natural. But if they should ask him, *why* joy at his departure was more suitable than sorrow, would they not start back with astonishment, if not horror, were he to reply, '*Because my Father is greater than I*?' Does not this strange speech from Christ's lips, then, *presuppose such teaching* on His part as would make it extremely difficult for them to think He could gain anything by departing to the Father, and make it necessary for Him to say expressly that there was a sense in which He *could* do so? Thus, this startling explanation seems plainly intended to correct such misapprehensions as might arise from the emphatic and reiterated teaching of *His proper equality with the Father* – as if so Exalted a Person were incapable of any accession by transition from this dismal scene to a cloudless heaven and the very bosom of the Father – and by assuring them that this was *not* the case, to make them forget their own sorrow in His approaching joy.

30, 31. Hereafter I will not talk much with you – 'I have a little more to say, but My work hastens apace, and the approach of the adversary will cut it short.'

for the prince of this world – (See on Joh 12:31.)

cometh – with hostile intent, for a last grand attack, having failed in His first formidable assault (Lu 4:1–13) from which he 'departed [only] *for a season*' (Joh 14:13).

and hath nothing in me – *nothing of His own* – *nothing to fasten on.* Glorious saying! The *truth* of it is, that that which makes the Person and Work of Christ the life of the world (Heb 9:14 1Jo 3:5 2Co 5:21).

31. But that the world may know that I love the Father – The sense must be completed thus: 'But to the Prince of the world, though he has nothing in Me, I shall yield Myself up even unto death, that the world may know that I love and obey the Father, whose commandment it is that I give My life a ransom for many.'

Arise, let us go hence – Did they then, at this stage of the discourse, leave the supper room, as some able interpreters conclude? If so, we think our Evangelist would have mentioned it: see Joh 18:1, which seems clearly to intimate that they then only left the upper room. But what do the words mean if not this? We think it was the dictate of that saying of earlier date, 'I have a baptism to be baptized with, and *how am I straitened till it be accomplished!*' – a spontaneous and irrepressible expression of the deep eagerness of His spirit to get into the conflict, and that if, as is likely, it was responded to somewhat too literally by the guests who hung on His lips, in the way of a movement to depart, a wave of His hand, would be enough to show that He had yet more to say ere they broke up; and that disciple, whose pen was dipped in a love to his Master which made *their* movements of small consequence save when essential to the illustration of *His* words, would record this little outburst of the Lamb hastening to the slaughter, in the very midst of His lofty discourse; while the effect of it, if any, upon His hearers, as of no consequence, would naturally enough be passed over.

Chapter 15

Joh 15:1–27.
Discourse at the supper table continued.

1–8. *The spiritual oneness of Christ and His people, and His relation to them as the Source of all their spiritual life and fruitfulness,* are here beautifully set forth by a figure familiar to Jewish ears (Isa 5:1).

I am the true vine – of whom the vine of *nature* is but a shadow.

my Father is the husbandman – the great Proprietor of the vineyard, the Lord of the spiritual kingdom. (It is surely unnecessary to point out the claim to *supreme divinity* involved in this.)

2. Every branch in me that beareth not fruit … every branch that beareth fruit – As in a fruit tree, some branches may be *fruitful*, others quite *barren*, according as there is a *vital connection* between the branch and the stock, or *no vital connection*; so the disciples of Christ may be spiritually fruitful or the reverse, according as they are *vitally* and *spiritually connected* with Christ, or but *externally* and *mechanically attached* to Him. The fruitless He 'taketh away' (see on Joh 15:6); the fruitful He 'purgeth' (cleanseth, pruneth) – *stripping it,* as the husbandman does, *of what is rank* (Mr 4:19), 'that it may bring forth more fruit'; a process often painful, but no less needful and beneficial than in the natural husbandry.

3. Now – rather, 'Already.'

ye are clean through – by reason of.

the word I have spoken to you – already in a purified, fruitful condition, in consequence of the long action upon them of that searching 'word' which was 'as a refiner's fire' (Mal 3:2,3).

4. Abide in me, and I in you; as the branch cannot bear fruit of itself, except it abide in the vine – As all spiritual fruitfulness had been ascribed to the mutual *inhabitation*, and living, active *interpenetration* (so to speak) of Christ and His disciples, so here the keeping up of this vital connection is made essential to continued fruitfulness.

5. without me – apart, or vitally disconnected from Me.

ye can do nothing – spiritually, acceptably.

6. If a man abide not in me, he is cast forth as a branch … withered … cast into the fire … burned – The one proper use of the vine is to *bear fruit;* failing this, it is good for one other thing – *fuel.* (See Eze 15:1–5.) How awfully striking the figure, in this view of it!

7. If ye abide in me, and my words … in you – Mark the change from the inhabitation of *Himself* to that of His *words,* paving the way for the subsequent exhortations (Joh 15:9,10).

ask what ye will, and it shall be done unto you – because this indwelling of His words in them would secure the harmony of their askings with the divine will.

8. glorified that ye bear much fruit – not only from His delight in it for its own sake, but as from 'the juices of the Living Vine.'

so shall ye be my disciples – *evidence* your discipleship.

9–11. continue ye in my love – not, 'Continue to love Me,' but, 'Continue in the possession and enjoyment of My love to you'; as is evident from the next words.

10. If ye keep my commandments, ye shall abide in my love – the obedient spirit of true discipleship cherishing and attracting the continuance and increase of Christ's love; and this, He adds, was the secret even of His own abiding in His Father's love!

12–16. That ye love one another – (See on Joh 13:34,35.)

13. Greater love hath no man than this, that a man lay down his life for his friends – The emphasis lies not on 'friends,' but on '*laying down his life*' for them; that is, 'One can show no greater regard for those dear to him than to give his life for them, and this is the love ye shall find in Me.'

14. Ye are my friends, if ye do whatsoever I command you – hold yourselves in absolute subjection to Me.

15. Henceforth I call you not servants – that is, *in the sense explained* in the next words; for servants He still calls them (Joh 15:20), and they delight to call themselves so, in the sense of being 'under law to Christ' (1Co 9:20).

the servant knoweth not what his lord doeth – knows nothing of his master's *plans* and *reasons,* but simply receives and executes his orders.

but … friends, for all things that I have heard of my Father I have made known unto you – admitted you to free, unrestrained fellowship, keeping back nothing from you which I have received to communicate. (Compare Ge 18:17 Ps 25:14 Isa 50:4.)

16. Ye have not chosen me, but I … you – a wholesale memento after the lofty things He had just said about their mutual indwelling, and the unreservedness of the friendship they had been admitted to.

ordained – appointed.

you, that ye should go and bring forth fruit – that is, give yourselves to it.

and that your fruit should remain – showing itself to be an imperishable and ever growing principle. (Compare Pr 4:18 2Jo 1:8.)

that whatsoever ye shall ask – (See on Joh 15:7.)

17–21. The substance of these important verses has occurred more than once before. (See on Mt 10:34–36; Lu 12:49–53.)

22–25. (See on Joh 9:39–41.)

If I had not come and spoken unto them, they had not had sin – *comparatively* none; all other sins being light compared with the rejection of the Son of God.

now they have no cloak for their sin – rather, 'pretext.'

24. If I had not done … the works which none other … did – (See on Joh 12:37.)

25. that the word might be fulfilled … They hated me without a cause – quoted from the Messianic Ps 69:4, applied also in the same sense in Joh 2:17 Ac 1:20 Ro 11:9,10 15:3.

26, 27. (See on Joh 14:15; Joh 14:17).

27. ye also shall bear witness – rather, 'are witnesses'; with reference indeed to their *future* witness-bearing, but putting the emphasis upon their *present* ample opportunities for acquiring their qualifications for that great office, inasmuch as they had been 'with Him from the beginning.' (See Lu 1:2.)

Chapter 16

Joh 16:1–33.

Discourse at the supper table concluded.

1–5. These things have I spoken unto you, that ye should not be offended – both the *warnings* and the *encouragements* just given.

2. They shall put you out of the synagogue – (Joh 9:22 12:42.)

the time cometh, that whosoever killeth you will think that he doeth God service – The words mean *religious service* – 'that he is offering a service to God.' (So Saul of Tarsus, Ga 1:13,14 Php 3:6.)

4. these things I said not … at – from.

the beginning – He *had* said it pretty early (Lu 6:22), but not quite as in Joh 16:2.

because I was with you.

5. But now I go my way to him that sent me – While He was with them, the world's hatred was directed chiefly against Himself; but His departure would bring it down upon them as His representatives.

and none of you asketh me, Whither goest thou? – They *had* done so in a sort (Joh 13:36 14:5); but He wished more intelligent and eager inquiry on the subject.

6, 7. But because I have said these things … sorrow hath filled your heart – Sorrow had too much paralysed them, and He would rouse their energies.

7. It is expedient for you that I go away –

> My Saviour, can it ever be
> That I should gain by losing thee?
> KEBLE

Yes.

for if I go not away, the Comforter will not come unto you, but if I depart, I will send him unto you – (See on Joh 7:39; Joh 14:15.)

8. And when he is come, he will – This is one of the passages most pregnant with thought in the profound discourses of Christ; with a few great strokes depicting all and every part of the ministry of the Holy Ghost in the world – His operation with reference to individuals as well as the mass, on believers and unbelievers alike [OLSHAUSEN].

he will reprove – This is too weak a word to express what is meant. *Reproof* is indeed implied in the term employed, and doubtless the word begins with it. But *convict* or *convince* is the thing intended; and as the one expresses the work of the Spirit on the *unbelieving* portion of mankind, and the other on the *believing*, it is better not to restrict it to either.

9. Of sin, because they believe not on me – As all sin has its root in unbelief, so the most aggravated form of unbelief is the rejection of Christ. The Spirit, however, in fastening this truth upon the conscience, does not *extinguish*, but, on the contrary, does *consummate and intensify, the sense of all other sins.*

10. Of righteousness, because I go to my Father, and ye see me no more – Beyond doubt, it is *Christ's personal righteousness* which the Spirit was to bring home to the sinner's heart. The evidence of this was to lie in the great *historical fact,* that He had 'gone to His Father and was no more visible to men': – for if His claim to be the Son of God, the Saviour of the world, had been a lie, how should the Father, who is 'a jealous God,' have raised such a blasphemer from the dead and exalted him to His right hand? But if He was the 'Faithful and True Witness,' the Father's 'Righteous Servant,' 'His Elect, in whom His soul delighted,' then was His departure to the Father, and consequent disappearance from the view of men, but the fitting consummation, the August reward, of all that He did here below, the seal of His mission, the glorification of the testimony which He bore on earth, by the reception of its Bearer to the Father's bosom. This triumphant vindication of Christ's *rectitude* is to us divine evidence, bright as heaven, that He is indeed the Saviour of the world, God's Righteous Servant to justify many, because He bare their iniquities (Isa 53:11). Thus the Spirit, in this clause, is seen convincing men that there is in Christ perfect relief under the sense of *sin* of which He had before convinced them; and so far from mourning over His absence from us, as an irreparable loss, we learn to glory in it, as the evidence of His perfect acceptance on our behalf, exclaiming with one who understood this point, 'Who shall lay anything to the charge of God's elect? It is God that justifieth: Who is he that condemneth? It is Christ that died; *yea, rather, that is risen again, who is even at the right hand of God,*' (Ro 8:33,34).

11. Of judgment, because the prince of this world is judged – By supposing that the *final judgment* is here meant, the point of this clause is, even by good interpreters, quite missed. The statement, 'The prince of this world is *judged,*' means, beyond all reasonable doubt, the same as that in Joh 12:31, 'Now shall the prince of this world be *cast out*'; and both mean that his dominion over men, or his power to enslave and so to ruin them, is destroyed. The death of Christ 'judged' or judicially overthrew him, and he was thereupon 'cast out' or expelled from his usurped dominion (Heb 2:14 1Jo 3:8 Col 2:15). Thus, then, the Spirit shall bring home to men's conscience: (1) the sense of *sin,* consummated in the rejection of Him who came to 'take away the sin of the world'; (2) the sense of perfect relief in the *righteousness* of the Father's Servant, now fetched from the earth that spurned Him to that bosom where from everlasting He had dwelt; and (3) the sense of emancipation from the fetters of Satan, whose *judgment* brings to men liberty to be holy, and transformation out of servants of the devil into sons and daughters of the Lord Almighty. To one class of men, however, all this will carry *conviction* only; they 'will not come to Christ' – revealed though He be to them as the life-giving One – that they may have life. Such, abiding voluntarily under the dominion of the prince of this world, are *judged in his judgment,* the visible consummation of which will be at the great day. To another class, however, this blessed teaching will have another issue – translating them out of the kingdom of darkness into the kingdom of God's dear Son.

12–15. when he, the Spirit of truth, is come … he shall not speak of himself – that is, *from* Himself, but, like Christ Himself, 'what He hears,' what is given Him to communicate.

he will show you things to come – referring specially to those revelations which, in the Epistles partially, but most fully in the Apocalypse, open up a vista into the Future of the Kingdom of God, whose horizon is the everlasting hills.

14. He shall glorify me; for he shall receive of mine and show it unto you – Thus the whole design of the Spirit's office is to glorify Christ – not in His own Person, for this was done by the Father when He exalted Him to His own right hand – but in the view and estimation of men. For this purpose He was to '*receive of Christ*' – *all the truth relating to Christ* – '*and show it unto them,*' or make them to discern it in its own light. The *subjective* nature of the Spirit's teaching – the discovery to the souls of men of what is Christ *outwardly* – is here very clearly expressed; and, at the same time, the vanity of looking for revelations of the Spirit which shall do anything beyond throwing light in the soul upon what Christ Himself is, and taught, and did upon earth.

15. All things that the Father hath are mine – a plainer expression than this of *absolute community* with the Father in all things cannot be conceived, though the 'all things' here have reference to the things of the Kingdom of Grace, which the Spirit was to receive that He might show it to us. We have here a wonderful glimpse into the *inner relations of the Godhead.*

16–22. A little while, and ye shall not see me; and again a little while, and ye shall see me, because I go to the Father – The joy of the world at their not seeing Him seems to show that His removal from them by *death* was what He meant; and in that case, their joy at again seeing Him points to their transport at His reappearance amongst them on His *Resurrection,* when they could no longer doubt His identity. At the same time the sorrow of the widowed Church in the absence of her Lord in the heavens, and her transport at His personal return, are certainly here expressed.

23–28. In that day – of the dispensation of the Spirit (as in Joh 14:20).

ye shall ask – inquire of

me nothing – by reason of the fulness of the Spirit's teaching (Joh 14:26 16:13; and compare 1Jo 2:27).

24. Hitherto have ye asked nothing in my name – for 'prayer *in the name of* Christ, and prayer to Christ, presuppose His *glorification*' [OLSHAUSEN].

ask – when I am gone, 'in My name.'

25. in proverbs – in obscure language, opposed to 'showing plainly' – that is, by the Spirit's teaching.

26. I say not ... I will pray the Father for you – as if He were not of *Himself* disposed to aid you: Christ does pray the Father for His people, but not for the purpose of inclining an *unwilling* ear.

27. For the Father himself loveth you, because ye have loved me – This love of theirs is that which is called forth by God's eternal love in the gift of His Son *mirrored* in the hearts of those who believe, and resting on His dear Son.

28. I came forth from the Father – that is, 'And ye are right, for I have indeed so come forth, and shall soon return whence I came.' This echo of the truth, alluded to in Joh 16:27, seems like *thinking aloud,* as if it were grateful to His own spirit on such a subject and at such an hour.

29, 30. His disciples said, ... now speakest thou plainly, and speakest no proverb – hardly more so than before; the time for perfect plainness was yet to come; but having caught a glimpse of His meaning (it was nothing more), they eagerly express their satisfaction, as if glad to make anything of His words. How touchingly does this show both the simplicity of their hearts and the infantile character of their faith!

31–33. Jesus answered ... Do ye now believe? – that is, 'It is well ye do, for it is soon to be tested, and in a way ye little expect.'

the hour cometh, yea, is now come, that ye shall be scattered, every man to his own, and shall leave me alone; and yet I am not alone – A deep and awful sense of *wrong* experienced is certainly expressed here, but how lovingly! That He was not to be utterly deserted, that there was One who would not forsake Him, was to Him matter of ineffable support and consolation; but that He should be without all *human* countenance and cheer, who as Man was exquisitely sensitive to the law of sympathy, would fill themselves with as much *shame,* when they afterwards recurred to it, as the Redeemer's heart in His hour of need with pungent *sorrow.* 'I looked for some to take pity, but there was none; and for comforters, but I found none' (Ps 69:20).

because the Father is with me – how near, and with what sustaining power, who can express?

33. These things I have spoken unto you – not the immediately preceding words, but this whole discourse, of which these were the very last words, and which He thus winds up.

that in me ye might have peace – in the sublime sense before explained. (See on Joh 14:27.)

In the world ye shall have tribulation – specially arising from its deadly opposition to those who 'are not of the world, but chosen out of the world.' So that the 'peace' promised was far from an unruffled one.

I have overcome the world – not only *before* you, but *for* you, that ye may be able to do the same (1Jo 5:4,5).

Chapter 17

Joh 17:1–26.

The intercessory prayer.

(See on Joh 14:1.) Had this prayer *not* been recorded, what reverential reader would not have exclaimed, Oh, to have been within hearing of such a prayer as that must have been, which wound up the whole of His past ministry and formed the point of transition to the dark scenes which immediately followed! But here it is, and with such signature of the Lips that uttered it that we seem rather to hear it from Himself than read it from the pen of His faithful reporter.

1–3. These words spake Jesus, and lifted up his eyes – 'John very seldom depicts the gestures or looks of our Lord, as here. But this was an occasion of which the impression was indelible, and the upward look could not be passed over' [ALFORD].

Father, the hour is come – (See on Joh 13:31,32.)

glorify thy Son – Put honour upon Thy Son, by countenancing, sustaining, and carrying Him through that 'hour.'

2. **given** – gavest **him power over all flesh** – (See Mt 11:27; Mt 28:18–20).

give eternal life to as many as – literally, 'to all that which thou hast given him.' (See on Joh 6:37–40.)

3. **this is** – that.

life eternal, that they might – may.

know – This life eternal, then, is not mere conscious and unending existence, but a life of acquaintance with God in Christ (Job 22:21).

thee, the only true God – the sole personal living God; in glorious contrast equally with heathen *polytheism*, philosophic *naturalism*, and mystic *pantheism*.

and Jesus Christ whom thou hast sent – This is the only place where our Lord gives Himself this compound name, afterwards so current in apostolic preaching and writing. Here the terms are used in their strict signification – 'JESUS,' because He '*saves* His people from their sins'; 'CHRIST,' as *anointed* with the measureless fulness of the Holy Ghost for the exercise of His saving offices (see Mt 1:16); 'WHOM THOU HAST SENT,' in the plenitude of Divine Authority and Power, to save. 'The very juxtaposition here of *Jesus Christ* with *the Father* is a proof, by implication, of our Lord's Godhead. The knowledge of *God and a creature* could not be eternal life, and such an association of the one with the other would be inconceivable' [ALFORD].

4, 5. **I have glorified thee on the earth** – rather, 'I glorified' (for the thing is conceived as now *past*).

I have finished – I finished.

the work which thou gavest me to do – It is very important to preserve in the translation the *past* tense, used in the original, otherwise it might be thought that the work already '*finished*' was only what He had done *before uttering that prayer;* whereas it will be observed that our Lord speaks throughout as already beyond this present scene (Joh 17:12), and so must be supposed to include in His 'finished work' the 'decease which He was to accomplish at Jerusalem.'

5. **And now** – in return.

glorify thou me – The '*I Thee*' and '*Thou Me*' are so placed in the original, each beside its fellow, as to show that A PERFECT RECIPROCITY OF SERVICES of the Son to the Father first, and then of the Father to the Son in return, is what our Lord means here to express.

with the glory which I had with thee before the world was – when 'in the beginning the Word was *with God*' (Joh 1:1), 'the only-begotten Son *in the bosom of the Father*' (Joh 1:18). With this pre-existent glory, which He veiled on earth, He asks to be reinvested, the design of the veiling being accomplished – not, however, simply as before, but *now in our nature.*

6–8. From praying for Himself He now comes to pray for His disciples.

I have manifested – I manifested.

thy name – His whole character towards mankind.

to the men thou gavest me out of the world – (See on Joh 6:37–40.)

8. **they ... have known surely that I came out from thee** – (See on Joh 16:29; Joh 16:31.)

9–14. **I pray for them** – not as individuals merely, but as representatives of all such in every succeeding age (see on Joh 17:20).

not for the world – for they had been given Him '*out of* the world' (Joh 17:6), and had been already transformed into the very *opposite* of it. The things sought for them, indeed, are applicable only to such.

10. **all mine are thine, and thine are mine** – literally, 'All My things are Thine and Thy things are Mine.' (On this use of the *neuter* gender, see on Joh 6:37–40.) Absolute COMMUNITY OF PROPERTY between the Father and the Son is here expressed as nakedly as words can do it. (See on Joh 17:5.)

11. **I am no more in the world** – (See on Joh 17:4.)

but these are in the world – that is, Though My struggles are at an end, theirs are not; though I have gotten beyond the scene of strife, I cannot sever Myself in spirit from them, left behind and only just entering on their great conflict.

Holy Father – an expression He nowhere else uses. '*Father*' is His wonted appellation, but '*Holy*' is here prefixed, because His appeal was to that perfection of the Father's nature, to 'keep' or preserve them from being tainted by the unholy atmosphere of 'the world' they were still in.

keep through thine own name – rather, 'in thy name'; in the exercise of that gracious and holy character for which He was known.

that they may be one – (See on Joh 17:21.)

12. **I kept** – guarded.

them in thy name – acting as Thy Representative on earth.

none of them is lost, but the son of perdition – It is not implied here that the son of perdition was one of those whom the Father had given to the Son, but rather the contrary (Joh 13:18) [WEBSTER and WILKINSON]. It is just as in Lu 4:26,27, where we are not to suppose that the woman of *Sarepta* (in Sidon) was one of the widows of *Israel,* nor Naaman the *Syrian* one of the lepers in *Israel,* though the language – the same as here – might *seem* to express it.

son of perdition – doomed to it (2Th 2:3 Mr 14:21).

13. I speak in the world, that they might have my joy fulfilled in themselves – that is, Such a strain befits rather the upper sanctuary than the scene of conflict; but I speak so '*in the world,*' that My joy, the joy I experience in knowing that such intercessions are to be made for them by their absent Lord, may be tasted by those who now hear them, and by all who shall hereafter read the record of them,

15–19. I pray not that thou shouldest take them out of the world – for that, though it would secure their own safety, would leave the world unblessed by their testimony.

but … keep them from the evil – all evil in and of the world.

16. They are not of the world, even as I am not of the world – (See Joh 15:18,19.) This is reiterated here, to pave the way for the prayer which follows.

17. Sanctify them – As the former prayer, '*Keep* them,' was 'negative,' asking *protection* for them from the poisonous element which surrounded and pressed upon their renewed nature, so this prayer, '*Sanctify* them,' is positive, asking the *advancement and completion* of their begun sanctification.

through – in.

thy truth – God's revealed truth, as the medium or element of sanctification; a statement this of immense importance.

thy word is truth – (Compare Joh 15:3 Col 1:5 Eph 1:13.)

18. As thou hast sent – sentest.

me into the world, even so have I also sent them – sent I also them.

into the world – As their mission was to carry into effect the purposes of their Master's mission, so our Lord speaks of the *authority* in both cases as *co-ordinate.*

19. And for their sakes I sanctify – consecrate.

myself that they also might – may.

be sanctified – consecrated. The only difference between the application of the same term to Christ and the disciples is, as applied to Christ, that it means *only* to 'consecrate'; whereas, in application to the disciples, it means to consecrate with the *additional idea* of previous sanctification, since nothing but what is holy can be presented as an offering. The whole self-sacrificing work of the disciples appears here as a mere *result* of the offering of Christ [OLSHAUSEN].

through – in.

the truth – Though the article is wanting in the original here, we are not to translate, as in the *Margin,* '*truly* sanctified'; for the reference seems plainly to be 'the truth' mentioned in Joh 17:17. (See on Joh 17:17.)

20–23. Neither pray I for these alone – This very important explanation, uttered in condescension to the hearers and readers of this prayer in all time, is meant not merely of what follows, but of the whole prayer.

them also which shall believe – The majority of the best manuscripts read 'which believe,' all future time being viewed as *present,* while the present is viewed as past and gone.

21. that they all may be one, as thou, Father, art in me, and I in thee, that they may be one in us – The indwelling Spirit of the Father and the Son is the one perfect bond of union, knitting up into a living unity, first all believers amongst themselves; next, this unity into one still higher, with the Father and the Son. (Observe, that Christ *never mixes Himself up with His disciples as He associates Himself with the Father,* but says I in THEM and THEY in US).

that the world may believe that thou hast sent me – sentest me. So the grand impression upon the world at large, that the mission of Christ is divine, is to be made by *the unity of His disciples.* Of course, then, it must be something that shall be *visible* or perceptible to the world. What is it, then? Not certainly a merely formal, mechanical unity of ecclesiastical machinery. For as that may, and to a large extent does, exist in both the Western and Eastern churches, with little of the Spirit of Christ, yea much, much with which the Spirit of Christ cannot dwell so instead of convincing the world *beyond its own pale* of the divinity of the Gospel, it generates infidelity to a large extent within its own bosom. But the Spirit of Christ, illuminating, transforming, and reigning in the hearts of the genuine disciples of Christ, drawing them to each other as members of one family, and prompting them to loving co-operation for the good of the world – this is what, when sufficiently glowing and extended, shall force conviction upon the world that Christianity is divine. Doubtless, the more that differences among Christians disappear – the more they can agree even in minor matters – the impression upon the world may be expected to be greater. But it is not *dependent* upon this; for living and loving oneness in Christ is sometimes more touchingly seen even amidst and in spite of minor differences, than where no such differences exist to try the strength of their deeper unity. Yet till this living brotherhood in Christ shall show itself strong enough to destroy the sectarianism, selfishness, carnality, and apathy that eat out the heart of Christianity in all the visible sections of it, in vain shall we expect the world to be overawed by it. It is when 'the Spirit shall be poured upon us from on high,' as a Spirit of truth and love, and upon all parts of the Christian territory alike, melting down differences and heart burnings, kindling astonishment and shame at past unfruitfulness, drawing forth longings of catholic affection, and yearnings over a world lying in wickedness, embodying themselves in palpable forms and active measures – it is then that we may expect the effect here announced to be produced, and then it will be irresistible. *Should not Christians ponder these things? Should not the same mind be in them which was also in Christ Jesus about this matter? Should not His prayer be theirs?*

22. And the glory which thou gavest – hast given.

me I have given them, that they may be one, even as we are one – The last clause shows the meaning of the first. It is not the *future* glory of the heavenly state, but the secret of that *present* unity just before spoken of; *the glory*, therefore, *of the indwelling Spirit of Christ;* the glory of an accepted state, of a holy character, of every grace.

23. I in them, and thou in me, that they may be made perfect in one – (See on Joh 17:21.)

24–26. Father, I will – The majesty of this style of speaking is quite transparent. No petty criticism will be allowed to fritter it away in any but superficial or perverted readers.

be with me where I am – (See on Joh 14:3.)

that they may behold my glory which thou hast given me – (See on Joh 17:5.) Christ regards it as glory enough for us to be admitted to see and gaze for ever upon *His* glory! This is 'the beatific vision'; but it shall be no mere vision, for 'we shall be like Him, because we shall see Him as He is' (1Jo 3:2).

25. O righteous Father, the world hath not known thee – knew thee not.

but I have known thee – knew thee.

and these have known – knew.

that thou hast sent – sentest

me – As before He said '*Holy* Father,' when desiring the display of that perfection on His disciples (Joh 17:11), so here He styles Him '*Righteous* Father,' because He is appealing to His righteousness or justice, to make a distinction between those two diametrically opposite classes – '*the world*,' on the one hand, which would not know the Father, though brought so nigh to it in the Son of His love, and, on the other, *Himself*, who recognized and owned Him, *and even His disciples*, who owned His mission from the Father.

26. And I have declared – I made known or communicated.

thy name – in His past ministry.

and will declare it – in yet larger measure, by the gift of the Holy Ghost at Pentecost and through all succeeding ages.

that the love wherewith thou hast loved – lovedst.

me may be in them, and I in them – This eternal love of the Father, resting first on Christ, is by His Spirit imparted to and takes up its permanent abode in all that believe in Him; and 'He abiding in them and they in Him' (Joh

15:5), they are '*one Spirit.*' 'With this lofty thought the Redeemer closes His prayer for His disciples, and in them for His Church through all ages. He has compressed into the last moments given Him for conversation with His own the most sublime and glorious sentiments ever uttered by mortal lips. But hardly has the sound of the last word died away, when He passes with the disciples over the brook Kedron to Gethsemane – and the bitter conflict draws on. The seed of the new world must be sown in Death, that thence Life may spring up' [OLSHAUSEN].

Chapter 18

Joh 18:1–13.

Betrayal and apprehension of Jesus.

1–3. over the brook Kedron – a deep, dark ravine, to the northeast of Jerusalem, through which flowed this small storm brook or winter torrent, and which in summer is dried up.

where was a garden – at the foot of the Mount of Olives, 'called Gethsemane; that is, olive press' (Mt 26:30,36).

2. Judas … knew the place, for Jesus ofttimes – see Joh 8:1 Lu 21:37.

resorted thither with his disciples – The baseness of this abuse of knowledge in Judas, derived from admission to the closest privacies of his Master, is most touchingly conveyed here, though nothing beyond bare narrative is expressed. Jesus, however, knowing that in this spot Judas would expect to find Him, instead of avoiding it, hies Him thither, as a Lamb to the slaughter. 'No man taketh My life from Me, but I lay it down of Myself' (Joh 10:18). Besides, the scene which was to fill up the little breathing-time, the awful interval, between the Supper and the Apprehension – like the 'silence in heaven for about the space of half an hour' between the breaking of the Apocalyptic Seals and the peal of the Trumpets of war (Re 8:1) – the AGONY – would have been too terrible for the upper room; nor would He cloud the delightful associations of the *last Passover* and the *first Supper* by pouring out the anguish of His soul there. The garden, however, with its amplitude, its shady olives, its endeared associations, would be congenial to His heart. Here He had room enough to retire – first, from eight of them, and then from the more favoured three; and here, when that mysterious scene was over, the stillness would only be broken by the tread of the traitor.

3. Judas then – 'He that was called Judas, one of the Twelve,' says Luke (Lu 22:47), in language which brands him with peculiar infamy, as *in* the sacred circle while in no sense *of* it.

a band of men – 'the *detachment* of the Roman cohort on duty at the festival for the purpose of maintaining order' [WEBSTER and WILKINSON].

officers from the chief priests and Pharisees – captains of the temple and armed Levites.

lanterns and torches – It was full moon, but in case He should have secreted Himself somewhere in the dark ravine, they bring the means of exploring its hiding-places – little knowing whom they had to do with. 'Now he that betrayed Him had given them a sign, saying, Whomsoever I shall kiss, that same is He, hold Him fast' (Mt 26:48). The cold-bloodedness of this speech was only exceeded by the deed itself. 'And Judas went before them [Lu 22:47], and forthwith he came to Jesus, and said, Hail, Master, and kissed Him' (Mt 26:49; compare Ex 4:27 18:7 Lu 7:45). The impudence of this atrocious deed shows how thoroughly he had by this time mastered all his scruples. If the dialogue between our Lord and His captors was *before* this, as some interpreters think it was, the kiss of Judas was purely gratuitous, and probably to make good his right to the money; our Lord having presented Himself unexpectedly before them, and rendered it unnecessary for any one to point Him out. But a comparison of the narratives seems to show that our Lord's 'coming forth' to the band was *subsequent* to the interview of Judas. 'And Jesus said unto him, Friend' – not the endearing term 'friend' (in Joh 15:15), but 'companion,' a word used on occasions of remonstrance or rebuke (as in Mt 20:13 22:12) – 'Wherefore art thou come?' (Mt 26:50). 'Betrayest thou the Son of man with a kiss' – imprinting upon the foulest act the mark of tenderest affection? What *wounded feeling* does this express! Of this Jesus showed Himself on various occasions keenly susceptible – as all generous and beautiful natures do.

4–9. Jesus … knowing all things that should come – were coming.

upon him, went forth – from the shade of the trees, probably, into open view, indicating His sublime preparedness to meet His captors.

Whom seek ye? – partly to prevent a rush of the soldiery upon the disciples [BENGEL]; and see Mr 14:51,52, as showing a tendency to this: but still more as part of that courage and majesty which so overawed them. He would not wait to be *taken*.

5. They answered … Jesus of Nazareth – just the sort of blunt, straight forward reply one expects from military men, simply acting on their instructions.

I am He – (See on Joh 6:20.)

Judas … stood with them – No more is recorded here of *his* part of the scene, but we have found the gap painfully supplied by all the other Evangelists.

6. As soon then as he said unto them, I am He, they went backward – recoiled.

and fell to the ground – struck down by a power such as that which smote Saul of Tarsus and his companions to the earth (Ac 26:14). It was the glorious effulgence of the majesty of Christ which overpowered them. 'This, occurring before His surrender, would show His *power* over His enemies, and so the *freedom* with which He gave Himself up' [MEYER].

7. Then asked he them again, Whom seek ye? – Giving them a door of escape from the guilt of a deed which *now* they were able in some measure to understand.

Jesus of Nazareth – The stunning effect of His first answer wearing off, they think only of the necessity of executing their orders.

8. I have told you that I am He: if therefore ye seek me, let these go their way – Wonderful self-possession, and consideration for others, in such circumstances!

9. That the saying might be fulfilled which he spake, Of them which thou gavest me have I lost none – The reference is to such sayings as Joh 6:39 17:12; showing how conscious the Evangelist was, that in reporting his Lord's former sayings, he was giving them not in *substance* merely, but in *form* also. Observe, also, how the preservation of the disciples on this occasion is viewed as part that *deeper preservation* undoubtedly intended in the saying quoted.

10, 11. Then Simon Peter, having a sword, drew it, and smote the high priest's servant, and cut off his right ear. The servant's name was Malchus – None of the other Evangelists mention the name either of the ardent disciple or of his victim. John being 'known to the high priest' (Joh 18:15), the mention of the servant's name by *him* is quite natural, and an interesting mark of truth in a small matter. As to the *right* ear, specified both here and in Luke (Lu 22:50), the man was 'likely foremost of those who advanced to seize Jesus, and presented himself in the attitude of a combatant; hence his right side would be exposed to attack. The blow of Peter was evidently aimed vertically at his head' [WEBSTER and WILKINSON].

11. Then said Jesus – 'Suffer ye thus far' (Lu 22:51).

Put up thy sword into the sheath: the cup which my Father hath given me, shall I not drink it? – This expresses *both the feelings* which struggled in the Lord's breast during the Agony in the garden – *aversion to the cup* viewed *in itself,* but, *in the light of the Father's will,* perfect *preparedness to drink it.* (See Lu 22:39–46.) Matthew adds to the address to Peter the following: – 'For all they that take the sword shall perish by the sword' (Mt 26:52) – that is, 'Those who take the sword must run all the risks of human warfare; but Mine is a warfare whose weapons, as they are not carnal, are attended with no such hazards, but carry certain victory.'

'Thinkest thou that I cannot now' – even after things have proceeded so far – 'pray to My Father, and He shall presently give Me' – rather, 'place at My disposal' – 'more than twelve legions of angels'; with allusion, possibly, to the one angel who had, in His agony, 'appeared to Him from heaven strengthening Him' (Lu 22:43); and in the precise number, alluding to the *twelve* who needed the help, Himself and His eleven disciples. (The full complement of a legion of Roman soldiers was six thousand). 'But how then shall the scripture be fulfilled that thus it must be?' (Mt 26:53,54). He could not suffer, according to the Scripture, if He allowed Himself to be delivered from the predicted death. 'And He touched his ear and healed him' (Lu 22:51); for 'the Son of man came not to destroy men's lives, but to save them' (Lu 9:56), and, even while they were destroying His, to save theirs.

12. Then the band ... took Jesus – but not till He had made them feel that 'no man took His life from Him, but that He laid it down of Himself.'

13. And led him away – 'In that hour,' says Matthew (Mt 26:55,56), and probably now, on the way to judgment. when the crowds were pressing upon Him, 'said Jesus to the multitudes, Are ye come out as against a thief, with swords and staves, for to take Me' – expressive of the indignity which He felt to be thus done to Him – 'I sat daily with you in the temple, and ye laid no hold on Me. But this' (adds Lu 22:53) 'is your hour and the power of darkness.' Matthew continues – 'But all this was done that the scriptures of the prophets might be fulfilled. Then all the disciples forsook Him and fled' (Mt 26:56) – thus fulfilling His prediction (Mr 14:27 Joh 16:32).

Joh 18:13–27.
Jesus before Annas and Caiaphas – fall of Peter.

13, 14. And led him away to Annas first – (See Lu 3:2, and Mt 26:57)

14. Now Caiaphas was he, which gave counsel to the Jews, that it was expedient that one man should die for the people – (Also see Mr 14:53.)

15–18. Simon Peter followed Jesus – Natural though this was, and safe enough, had he only 'watched and prayed that he enter not into temptation,' as his Master bade him (Mt 26:41), it was, in his case, a fatal step.

and ... another disciple – Rather, 'the other disciple' – our Evangelist himself, no doubt.

known unto the high priest – (See on Joh 18:10.)

went in with Jesus into the palace of the high priest.

16. But Peter stood at the door without – by preconcerted arrangement with his friend till he should get access for him.

Then went out that other ... and spake to her that kept the door, and brought in Peter – The *naturalness* of these small details is not unworthy of notice. This other disciple first made good his own entrance on the score of acquaintance with the high priest; this secured, he goes forth again, now as a privileged person, to make interest for Peter's admission. But thus our poor disciple is in the coils of the serpent. The next steps will best be seen by *inverting* Joh 18:17 and Joh 18:18.

17. Then saith the damsel that kept the door – 'one of the maids of the high priest,' says Mark (Mr 14:66). 'When she saw Peter warming himself, she looked upon him and said' (Mr 14:67). Luke is more graphic (Lu 22:56) – She 'beheld him as he sat by the fire (literally, 'the light'), and earnestly looked on him (fixed her gaze upon him), and said.' 'His demeanor and timidity, which must have vividly showed themselves, as it so generally happens, leading to the recognition of him' [OLSHAUSEN].

Art thou not also one of this man's disciples? – that is, thou as well as 'that other disciple,' whom she knew to be one, but did not challenge, perceiving that he was a privileged person.

He saith, I am not – 'He denied before them all, saying, I know not what thou sayest' (Mt 26:70) – a common form of point blank denial; 'I know [supply 'Him'] not, neither understand I what thou sayest' (Mr 14:68); 'Woman, I know Him not' (Lu 22:57). This was THE FIRST DENIAL. 'And he went out into the porch [thinking, perhaps, to steal away], *and the cock crew*,' (Mr 14:68).

18. And the servants and officers – the menials and some of the 'band' that 'took Jesus.'

stood there, who had made – 'having made.'

a fire of coals, for it was cold, and they warmed themselves – 'John alone notices the material (charcoal) of which the fire was made, and the reason for a fire – the coldness of the night' [WEBSTER and WILKINSON]. 'Peter went in and sat with the servants to see the end (Mt 26:58), and warmed himself at the fire' (Mr 14:54). These two statements are extremely interesting. His wishing to 'see the end,' or issue of these proceedings, was what led him into the palace, for he evidently feared the worst. But once in, the serpent coil is drawn closer; it is a cold night, and why should not he take advantage of the fire as well as others? Besides, in the talk of the crowd about the all-engrossing topic, he may pick up something which he would like to hear. 'And as Peter was beneath in the palace' (Mr 14:66). Matthew (Mt 26:69) says, 'sat *without* in the palace.' According to Oriental architecture, and especially in large buildings, as here, the street door – or heavy folding gate through which single persons entered by a wicket kept by a porter – opened by a passage or 'porch' (Mr 14:68) into a quadrangular *court*, here called the 'palace' or *hall*, which was *open above*, and is frequently *paved* with flagstones. In the centre of this court the 'fire' would be kindled (in a brazier). At the upper end of it, probably, was the chamber in which the trial was held, *open to the court and not far from the fire* (Lu 22:61), but on a higher level; for Mark (Mr 14:66) says the court was '*beneath*' it. The ascent was, perhaps, by a short flight of steps. This explanation will make the intensely interesting details more intelligible.

19–21. The high priest … asked Jesus of his disciples, and of his doctrine – probably to entrap Him into some statements which might be used against Him at the trial. From our Lord's answer it would seem that 'His disciples' were understood to be some secret party.

20. I spake – have spoken.

openly to the world – See Joh 7:4.

I ever taught in the synagogues and in the temple, whither the Jews always resort – courting publicity, though with sublime noiselessness.

in secret have I said – spake I.

nothing – that is, nothing of any different nature; all His private communications with the Twelve being but explanations and developments of His public teaching. (Compare Isa 45:19 48:16.)

21. Why askest thou me? ask them which heard me … they know what I … said – This seems to imply that He saw the attempt to draw Him into self-crimination, and resented it by falling back upon the right of every accused party to have some charge laid against Him by competent witnesses.

22. struck Jesus with the palm … Answerest Thou the high priest so – (See Isa 50:6; and compare Ac 23:2.)

23. If I have spoken – 'if I spoke' evil, in reply to the high priest.

if well – He does not say 'If *not*' evil, as if His reply were merely unobjectionable: '*well*' seems to challenge more than this as due to His remonstrance. This shows that Mt 5:39 is not to be taken to the letter.

24–27. Now Annas had sent him bound unto Caiaphas – Our translators so render the words, understanding that the foregoing interview took place before *Caiaphas;* Annas, declining to meddle with the case, having sent Him to Caiaphas *at once.* But the words here literally are, 'Annas sent Him [not '*had* sent Him'] to Caiaphas' – and the 'now' being of doubtful authority. Thus read, the verse affords no evidence that He was sent to Caiaphas *before* the interview just recorded, but implies rather the contrary. We take this interview, then, with some of the ablest interpreters, to be a preliminary and non-official one with *Annas*, at an hour of the night

when Caiaphas' Council could not convene; and one that ought not to be confounded with that solemn one recorded by the other Evangelists, when all were assembled and witnesses called. But *the building in which both met with Jesus appears to have been the same, the room only being different, and the court, of course, in that case, one.*

25. And Simon Peter was standing and warming himself. They said therefore … Art thou not also one of his disciples? – In Mt 26:71 the *second* charge was made by 'another maid, when he was gone out into the porch,' who 'saw him, and said unto them that were there, This [fellow] was also with Jesus of Nazareth.' So also Mr 14:69. But in Lu 22:58 it is said, 'After a little while' (from the time of the first denial), 'another [*man*] saw him, and said, Thou art also of them.' Possibly it was thrown at him by more than one; but these circumstantial variations only confirm the truth of the narrative.

He denied it, and said, I am not – in Mt 26:72, 'He denied with an oath, I do not know the man.' This was THE SECOND DENIAL.

26. One of the servants of the high priest, being his kinsman, whose ear Peter cut off, saith, Did not I see thee in the garden with him – No doubt his relationship to Malchus drew attention to the man who smote him, and this enabled him to identify Peter. 'Sad reprisals!' [BENGEL]. The other Evangelists make his detection to turn upon his *dialect.* 'After a while ["about the space of one hour after" (Lu 22:59)] came unto him they that stood by and said to Peter, Surely thou also art one of them, for thy speech betrayeth thee' (Mt 26:73). 'Thou art a Galilean, and thy speech agreeth thereto' (Mr 14:70; and so Lu 22:59). The Galilean dialect had a more *Syrian* cast than that of Judea. *If Peter had held his peace*, this peculiarity had not been observed; but hoping, probably, to put them off the scent by joining in the *fireside talk,* he only thus revealed himself.

27. Peter then denied again – But, if the challenge of Malchus' kinsman was made simultaneously with this on account of his Galilean dialect, it was no simple denial; for Mt 26:74 says, 'Then began he to *curse and to swear,* saying, I know not the man.' So Mr 14:71. This was THE THIRD DENIAL.

and immediately – 'while he yet spake' (Lu 22:60).

the cock crew – As Mark is the only Evangelist who tells us that our Lord predicted that the cock should crow *twice* (Mr 14:30), so he only mentions that it *did* crow twice (Mr 14:72). The other Evangelists, who tell us merely that our Lord predicted that 'before the cock should crow he would deny Him thrice' (Mt 26:34 Lu 22:34 Joh 13:38), mention only *one actual* crowing, which was Mark's last. This is something affecting in this Evangelist – who, according to the earliest tradition (confirmed by internal evidence), derived his materials so largely from Peter as to have been styled his '*interpreter*,' being the *only one* who gives both the sad prediction and its still sadder fulfilment *in full*. It seems to show that Peter himself not only retained through all his after-life the most vivid recollection of the circumstances of his fall, but that he was willing that others should know them too. The immediately *subsequent* acts are given in full only in Luke (Lu 22:61,62): 'And the Lord turned and looked upon Peter,' from the hall of judgment to the court, in the way already explained. But who can tell what lightning flashes of wounded love and piercing reproach shot from that 'look' through the eye of Peter into his heart! 'And Peter remembered the word of the Lord, how He had said unto him, Before the cock crow, thou shalt deny Me thrice. And Peter went out and wept bitterly.' How different from the sequel of Judas' act! Doubtless the hearts of the two men towards the Saviour were perfectly different from the first; and the treason of Judas was but the consummation of the wretched man's resistance of the blaze of light in the midst of which he had lived for three years, while Peter's denial was but a momentary obscuration of the heavenly light and love to his Master which ruled his life. But the immediate cause of the revulsion, which made Peter 'weep bitterly,' was, beyond all doubt, this heart-piercing 'look' which his Lord gave him. And remembering the Saviour's own words at the table, 'Simon, Simon, Satan hath desired to have you that he may sift you as wheat, *but I have prayed* [rather, "I prayed"] *for thee that thy faith fail not*' (see Lu 22:31,32), may we not say that *this prayer fetched down all that there was in that "look"* to pierce and break the heart of Peter, to keep it from despair, to work in it 'repentance unto salvation not to be repented of and at length, under other healing touches, to 'restore his soul?' (See Mr 16:7).

Joh 18:28–40.
Jesus before Pilate.

Note. – Our Evangelist, having given the interview with Annas, omitted by the other Evangelists, here omits the trial and condemnation before Caiaphas, which the others had recorded.(See Mr 14:53–65.)

28. **Then led they Jesus from Caiaphas to the hall of judgment** – but not till 'in the morning the chief priests held a consultation with the elders and scribes and the whole council against Him to put Him to death, and bound Him' (Mt 27:1; and see Mr 15:1). The word here rendered 'hall of judgment' is from the *Latin*, and denotes 'the palace of the governor of a Roman province.'

they themselves went not into the judgment hall lest they should be defiled – by contact with ceremonially unclean Gentiles.

but that they might eat the Passover – If this refer to the principal part of the festival, the eating of the lamb, the question is, how our Lord and His disciples came to eat it the night before; and, as it was an *evening* meal, how ceremonial defilement contracted in the *morning* would unfit them for partaking of it, as after six o'clock it was reckoned a new day. These are questions which have occasioned immense research and learned treatises. But as the usages of the Jews appear to have somewhat varied at different times, and our present knowledge of them is not sufficient to clear up all difficulties, they are among the not very important questions which probably will never be entirely solved.

29–32. **Pilate went out to them, and said, What accusation bring ye against this man?** – State your charge.

30. **If he were not a malefactor, we would not have delivered him up unto thee** – They were conscious they *had no case* of which Pilate could take cognizance, and therefore insinuate that they had already found Him worthy of death by their own law; but not having the power, under the Roman government, to carry their sentence into execution, they had come merely for his sanction.

32. **That the saying … might be fulfilled which he spake, signifying what death he should die** – that is, by *crucifixion* (Joh 12:32,33 Mt 20:19); which being a Roman mode of execution, could only be carried into effect by order of the governor. (The Jewish mode in such cases as this was by *stoning*.)

33–38. **Pilate … called Jesus, and said … Art thou the King of the Jews?** – In Lu 23:2 they charge our Lord before Pilate with 'perverting the nation, and forbidding to give tribute to Cæsar, saying that He Himself is Christ a king.' Perhaps this was what occasioned Pilate's question.

34. **Jesus answered … Sayest thou this of thyself, or did others tell it thee of me?** – an important question for our Lord's case, to bring out whether the word '*King*' were meant in a *political* sense, with which Pilate had a right to deal, or whether He were merely *put up* to it by His accusers, who had no claims to charge Him but such as were of a purely *religious* nature, with which Pilate had nothing to do.

35. **Pilate answered, Am I a Jew? Thine own nation and the chief priests delivered thee to me: What hast thou done?** – that is, 'Jewish questions I neither understand nor meddle with; but Thou art here on a charge which, though it *seems* only Jewish, *may* yet involve treasonable matter: As *they* state it, I cannot decide the point; tell me, then, what procedure of Thine has brought Thee into this position.' In

modern phrase, Pilate's object in this question was merely to determine the *relevancy* of the charge.

36. Jesus answered, My kingdom is not of this world – He does not say 'not *over*,' but 'not of this world' – that is, in its *origin* and *nature;* therefore 'no such kingdom as need give thee or thy master the least alarm.'

if my kingdom were of this world, then would my servants fight, that I should not be delivered to the Jews – 'A very convincing argument; for if His servants did not fight to prevent their King from being delivered up to His enemies, much less would they use force for the establishment of His kingdom' [WEBSTER and WILKINSON].

but now – but the fact is.

is my kingdom not from hence – Our Lord only says whence His kingdom is *not* – first simply affirming it, next giving proof of it, then reaffirming it. This was all that Pilate had to do with. The *positive* nature of His kingdom He would not obtrude upon one who was as little able to comprehend it, as entitled officially to information about it. (It is worthy of notice that the 'MY,' which occurs *four* times in this one verse – *thrice* of His *kingdom,* and *once* of His *servants* – is put in the emphatic form).

37. Art thou a king then? – There was no sarcasm or disdain in this question (as THOLUCK, ALFORD, and others, allege), else our Lord's answer would have been different. Putting emphasis upon '*thou*,' his question betrays a mixture of *surprise* and *uneasiness,* partly at the possibility of there being, after all, something dangerous under the claim, and partly from a certain awe which our Lord's demeanor probably struck into him.

Thou sayest that I am a king – It is even so.

To this end was I – 'have I been.'

born and for this cause came I – am I come.

into the world, that I may bear witness to the truth – His *birth* expresses His manhood; His *coming into the world,* His existence before assuming humanity: The truth, then, here affirmed, though Pilate would catch little of it, was that *His Incarnation was expressly in order to the assumption of Royalty in our nature.* Yet, instead of saying, He came to be a King, which is His meaning, He says He came to *testify to the truth.* Why this? Because, in such circumstances it required a noble courage not to flinch from His royal claims; and our Lord, *conscious that He was putting forth that courage,* gives a turn to His confession expressive of it. It is to this that Paul alludes, in those remarkable words to Timothy: 'I charge thee before God, who quickeneth all things, and before Christ Jesus, who, *in the presence* of Pontius Pilate, witnessed *the good confession*' (1Ti 6:13). This one act of our Lord's life, His courageous witness-bearing before the governor, was selected as an encouraging example of the *fidelity* which Timothy ought to display. As the Lord (says OLSHAUSEN beautifully) owned Himself *the Son of God* before the most exalted theocratic council, so He confessed His *regal dignity* in presence of the representative of the highest political authority on earth.

Every one that is of the truth heareth my voice – Our Lord here not only affirms that His word had in it a self-evidencing, self-recommending power, but gently insinuated the *true secret of the growth and grandeur of His kingdom* – as A KINGDOM OF TRUTH, in its highest sense, into which all souls who have learned to live and count all things but loss for the truth are, by a most heavenly attraction, drawn as into their proper element; THE KING of whom Jesus is, fetching them in and ruling them by His captivating power over their hearts.

38. Pilate saith unto him, What is truth? – that is, 'Thou stirrest the question of questions, which the thoughtful of every age have asked, but never man yet answered.'

And when he had said this – as if, by putting such a question, he was getting into interminable and unseasonable inquiries, when this business demanded rather prompt action.

he went out again unto the Jews – thus missing a noble opportunity for himself, and giving utterance to that consciousness of the want of all intellectual and moral certainty, which was the feeling of every thoughtful mind at that time. 'The only certainty,' says the elder PLINY, 'is that nothing is certain, nor more miserable than man, nor more proud. The fearful laxity of morals at that time must doubtless be traced in a great degree to this skepticism. The revelation of the eternal truth alone was able to breathe new life into ruined human nature, and that in the apprehension of complete redemption' [OLSHAUSEN].

and saith unto them – in the hearing of our Lord, who had been brought forth.

I find in him no fault – no crime. This so exasperated 'the chief priests and elders' that, afraid of losing their prey, they poured forth a volley of charges against Him, as appears from Lu 23:4,5: on Pilate's affirming His innocence, 'they were *the more fierce,* saying, He stirreth up the people, teaching throughout all Jewry, beginning from Galilee to this place.' They see no hope of getting Pilate's sanction to His death unless they can fasten upon Him a charge of conspiracy against the government; and as *Galilee* was noted for its turbulence (Lu 13:1 Ac 5:37), and our Lord's ministry lay chiefly there, they artfully introduce it to give colour to their charge. 'And the chief priests accused Him of *many things,* but He answered nothing (Mr 15:3). Then said Pilate unto Him, Hearest Thou not how many things they witness against Thee?

And He answered him to never a word, insomuch that the governor marvelled greatly' (Mt 27:13,14). See Mr 15:3–5. In his perplexity, Pilate, hearing of Galilee, bethinks himself of the expedient of sending Him to Herod, in the hope of thereby further shaking off responsibility in the case. See Mr 15:6; Lu 23:6–12. The return of the prisoner only deepened the perplexity of Pilate, who, 'calling together the chief priests, rulers, and people,' tells them plainly that not one of their charges against 'this man' had been made good, while even Herod, to whose jurisdiction he more naturally belonged, had done nothing to Him: He 'will therefore chastise and release him' (Lu 23:13–16).

39. But ye have a custom that I should release one unto you at the Passover. – See Mr 15:7–11. 'On the typical import of the choice of Christ to suffer, by which Barabbas was set free, see the sixteenth chapter of Leviticus, particularly Le 16:5–10, where the subject is the *sin offering* on the great day of atonement' [KRAFFT in LUTHARDT].

Chapter 19
Joh 19:1–16.
Jesus before Pilate – scourged – treated with other severities and insults – delivered up, and led away to be crucified.

1–3. Pilate took Jesus and scourged him – in hope of appeasing them. (See Mr 15:15.) 'And the soldiers led Him away into the palace, and they call the whole band' (Mr 15:16) – the body of the military cohort stationed there – to take part in the mock coronation now to be enacted.

2. the soldiers platted a crown of thorns, and put it on his head – in mockery of a regal *crown*.

and they put on him a purple robe – in mockery of the *imperial purple;* first 'stripping him' (Mt 27:28) of His own outer garment. The robe may have been the 'gorgeous' one in which Herod arrayed and sent Him back to Pilate (Lu 23:11). 'And they put a reed into His right hand' (Mt 27:29) – in mockery of the regal *sceptre.* 'And they bowed the knee before Him' (Mt 27:29).

3. And said, Hail, King of the Jews! – doing Him derisive homage, in the form used on approaching the emperors. 'And they spit upon Him, and took the reed and smote Him on the head' (Mt 27:30). The best comment on these affecting details is to *cover the face.*

4, 5. Pilate ... went forth again, and saith ... Behold, I bring him forth to you – am bringing, that is, going to bring him forth to you.

that ye may know I find no fault in him – and, by scourging Him and allowing the soldiers to make sport of Him, have gone as far to meet your exasperation as can be expected from a judge.

5. Then Jesus came forth, wearing the crown of thorns, and the purple robe. And Pilate saith unto them, Behold the man! – There is no reason to think that *contempt* dictated this speech. There was clearly a struggle in the breast of this wretched man. Not only was he reluctant to surrender to mere clamour an innocent man, but a feeling of anxiety about His mysterious claims, as is plain from what follows, was beginning to rack his breast, and the object of his exclamation seems to have been to *move their pity.* But, be *his* meaning what it may, those three words have been eagerly appropriated by all Christendom, and enshrined for ever in its heart as a sublime expression of its calm, rapt admiration of its suffering Lord.

6, 7. When the chief priests ... saw him, they cried out – their fiendish rage kindling afresh at the sight of Him.

Crucify him, crucify him – (See Mr 15:14.)

Pilate saith unto them, Take ye him, and crucify him; for I find no fault in him – as if this would relieve *him* of the responsibility of the deed, who, by surrendering Him, incurred it all!

7. The Jews answered him, We have a law, and by our law he ought to die, because he made himself the Son of God – Their criminal charges having come to nothing, they give up that point, and as Pilate was throwing the whole responsibility upon them, they retreat into their own Jewish law, by which, as claiming equality with God (see Joh 5:18 and Joh 8:59), He ought to die; insinuating that it was Pilate's duty, even as civil governor, to protect their law from such insult.

8–11. When Pilate ... heard this saying, he was the more afraid – the name 'SON OF GOD,' the lofty sense evidently attached to it by His Jewish accusers, the dialogue he had already held with Him, and the dream of his wife (Mt 27:19), all working together in the breast of the wretched man.

9. and went again into the judgment hall, and saith to Jesus, Whence art thou? – beyond all doubt a question relating not to His *mission* but to His personal *origin.*

Jesus gave him no answer – He had said enough; the time for answering such a question was past; the weak and wavering governor is already on the point of giving way.

10. Then saith Pilate unto him, Speakest thou not to me? – The 'me' is the emphatic word in the question. He falls back upon the *pride of office,* which doubtless tended to blunt the workings of his conscience.

knowest thou not that I have power to crucify thee, and have power to release thee? – said to work upon Him at once by *fear* and by *hope.*

11. Thou couldest – rather, 'shouldst.'

have no power at all against me – neither to crucify nor to release, nor to do anything whatever against Me [BENGEL].

except it were – 'unless it had been.'

given thee from above – that is, 'Thou think-est too much of thy power, Pilate: against Me that power is none, save what is meted out to thee by special divine appointment, for a special end.'

therefore he that delivered me unto thee – Caiaphas, to wit – but he only as representing the Jewish authorities as a body.

hath the greater sin – as having better oppor-tunities and more knowledge of such matters.

12–16. And from thenceforth – particularly this speech, which seems to have filled him with awe, and redoubled his anxiety.

Pilate sought to release him – that is, to gain their *consent* to it, for he could have done it at once on his authority.

but the Jews cried – seeing their advantage, and not slow to profit by it. If thou let this man go, thou art not Cæsar's friend – 'This was equivalent to a threat of *impeachment,* which we know was much dreaded by such officers as the procurators, especially of the character of Pilate or Felix. It also consummates the treachery and disgrace of the Jewish rulers, who were willing, for the purpose of destroying Jesus, to affect a zeal for the supremacy of a foreign prince' [WEBSTER and WILKINSON]. (See Joh 19:15.)

When Pilate … heard that, … he brought Jesus forth, and sat down in – 'upon'

the judgment seat – that he might pronounce sentence against the Prisoner, on this charge, the more solemnly.

in a place called the Pavement – a tesselated pavement, much used by the Romans.

in the Hebrew, Gabbatha – from its being *raised.*

14. It was the preparation – that is, the day before the Jewish Sabbath.

and about the sixth hour – The true reading here is probably, 'the *third* hour' – or nine A.M. – which agrees best with the whole series of events, as well as with the other Evangelists.

he saith to the Jews, Behold your King! – Having now made up his mind to yield to them, he takes a sort of quiet revenge on them by this irony, which he knew would sting them. This only reawakens their cry to despatch Him.

15. crucify your King? … We have no king but Cæsar – 'Some of those who thus cried died miserably in rebellion against Cæsar forty years afterwards. But it suited their present purpose' [ALFORD].

16. Then delivered he him therefore unto them to be crucified. – (See Mr 15:15.)

Joh 19:17–30.
Crucifixion and death of the Lord Jesus.

17. And he bearing his cross – (See Lu 23:26.)

went forth – Compare Heb 13:11–13, 'with-out the camp'; 'without the gate.' On arriving at the place, 'they gave Him vinegar to drink min-gled with gall [wine mingled with myrrh, Mr 15:23], and when He had tasted thereof, He would not drink' (Mt 27:34). This potion was stupefying, and given to criminals just before execution, to deaden the sense of pain.

Fill high the bowl, and spice it well, and pour
The dews oblivious: for the Cross is sharp,
The Cross is sharp, and He
Is tenderer than a lamb.
                                    KEBLE.

But our Lord would die with every faculty clear, and in full sensibility to all His sufferings.

Thou wilt feel all, that Thou may'st pity all;
And rather would'st Thou wrestle with strong pain
    Than overcloud Thy soul,
So clear in agony,
Or lose one glimpse of Heaven before the time,
O most entire and perfect Sacrifice,
    Renewed in every pulse.
                                    KEBLE

18. they crucified him, and two others with him – 'malefactors' (Lu 23:33), 'thieves' (rather 'robbers,' Mt 27:38 Mr 15:27).

on either side one and Jesus in the midst – a hellish expedient, to hold Him up as the worst of the three. But in this, as in many other of their doings, 'the scripture was fulfilled, which saith (Isa 53:12), *And he was numbered with the transgressors'* – (Mr 15:28) – though the predic-tion reaches deeper. 'Then said Jesus' – ['proba-bly while being nailed to the cross,'] [OLSHAUSEN], 'FATHER, FORGIVE THEM, FOR THEY KNOW NOT WHAT THEY DO' (Lu 23:34) – and again the Scripture was fulfilled which said, 'And He made intercession for the transgressors' (Isa 53:12), though this also reaches deeper. (See Ac 3:17 13:27; and compare 1Ti 1:13.) Often have we occasion to observe how our Lord is the first to fulfil His own precepts – thus furnishing the right interpretation and the perfect Model of them. (See Mt 5:44.) How quickly was it seen in 'His martyr Stephen,' that though He had left the earth in Person, His Spirit remained behind, and Himself could, in some of His brightest lin-eaments, be reproduced in His disciples! (Ac 7:60). And what does the world in every age owe to these few words, spoken *where* and *as* they were spoken!

19–22. Pilate wrote a title, and put it on the cross … Jesus of Nazareth, the King of the Jews … and it was written in Hebrew – or *Syro-Chaldaic,* the language of the country.

and Greek – the current language.

and Latin – the official language. These were the chief languages of the earth, and this secured that all spectators should be able to read it. Stung by this, the Jewish ecclesiastics entreat that it may be so altered as to express, not His real dignity, but His false claim to it. But Pilate thought he had yielded quite enough to them; and having intended expressly to spite and insult them by this title, for having got him to act against his own sense of justice, he peremptorily refused them. And thus, amidst the conflicting passions of men, was proclaimed, in the chief tongues of mankind, from the Cross itself and in circumstances which threw upon it a lurid yet grand light, the truth which drew the Magi to His manger, and will yet be owned by all the world!

23, 24. Then the soldiers, when they had crucified Jesus, took his garments, and made four parts; to every soldier – the four who nailed Him to the cross, and whose perquisite they were.

a part, and also his coat – the Roman *tunic*, or close-fitting vest.

without seam, woven from the top throughout – 'perhaps denoting considerable skill and labor as necessary to produce such a garment, the work probably of one or more of the women who ministered in such things unto Him, Lu 8:3' [WEBSTER and WILKINSON].

24. Let us not rend it, but cast lots … whose it shall be, that the scripture might be fulfilled which saith, They parted my raiment among them; and for my vesture they did cast lots – (Ps 22:18). That a prediction so exceedingly specific – distinguishing one piece of dress from others, and announcing that while *those* should be parted amongst several, *that* should be given by lot to one person – that such a prediction should not only be fulfilled to the letter, but by a party of heathen military, without interference from either the friends or the enemies of the Crucified One, is surely worthy to be ranked among the wonders of this all-wonderful scene. Now come the *mockeries,* and from four different quarters: – (1) 'And *they that passed by* reviled Him, wagging their heads' in ridicule (Ps 22:7 109:25; compare Jer 18:16 La 2:15). 'Ah!' – 'Ha,' an exclamation here of derision. 'Thou that destroyest the temple, and buildest it in three days, save Thyself and come down from the cross' (Mt 27:39,40 Mr 15:29,30). 'It is evident that our Lord's saying, or rather this *perversion* of it (for He claimed not to *destroy,* but to *rebuild* the temple destroyed by them) had greatly exasperated the feeling which the priests and Pharisees had contrived to excite against Him. It is referred to as the principal fact brought out in evidence against Him on the trial (compare Ac 6:13,14), as an offense for which He deserved to suffer. And it is very remarkable that now *while it was receiving its real fulfilment,* it should be made more public and more

impressive by the insulting proclamation of His enemies. Hence the importance attached to it after the resurrection, Joh 2:22' [WEBSTER and WILKINSON]. (2) 'Likewise also the *chief priests,* mocking Him, *with the scribes and elders,* said, He saved others, Himself He cannot save' (Mt 27:41,42). There was a deep truth in this, as in other taunts; for *both* He could not do, having 'come to give *His* life a ransom for *many*' (Mt 20:28 Mr 10:45). No doubt this added an unknown sting to the reproach. 'If He be the king of Israel, let Him now come down from the cross, and we will believe Him' (Mt 27:42). *No, they would not;* for those who resisted the evidence from the resurrection of Lazarus, and from His own resurrection, were beyond the reach of any amount of merely *external* evidence. 'He trusted in God that He would deliver him; let Him deliver Him now if He will have Him [or "delight in Him," compare Ps 18:19 De 21:14]; for He said, I am the Son of God' (Mt 27:41–43). We thank you, O ye chief priests, scribes, and elders, for this triple testimony, unconsciously borne by you, to our Christ: first to *His habitual trust in God,* as a feature in His character so marked and palpable that even ye found upon it your impotent taunt; next, *to His identity with the Sufferer of the twenty-second Psalm,* whose very words (Ps 22:8) ye unwittingly appropriate, thus *serving yourselves heirs* to the dark office and impotent malignity of Messiah's enemies; and again, to the true sense of that august title which He took to Himself, 'THE SON OF GOD,' which He rightly interpreted at the very first (see Joh 5:18) as a claim to that *oneness of nature* with Him, and *dearness to Him,* which a son has to his father. (3) 'And the *soldiers* also mocked Him, coming to Him and offering Him vinegar, and saying, If thou be king of the Jews, save Thyself' (Lu 23:36,37). They insultingly offer to share with Him their own vinegar, or sour wine, the usual drink of Roman soldiers, it being about the time of their midday meal. In the taunt of the soldiers we have one of those *undesigned coincidences* which so strikingly verify these historical records. While the ecclesiastics deride Him for calling Himself, 'the *Christ,* the *King of Israel,* the *Chosen,* the *Son of God,*' the soldiers, to whom all such phraseology was mere Jewish jargon, make sport of Him as a pretender to *royalty* ('KING of the Jews'), an office and dignity which it belonged to them to comprehend. '*The thieves* also, which were crucified with Him, cast the same in His teeth' (Mt 27:44 Mr 15:32). Not *both* of them, however, as some commentators unnaturally think we must understand these words; as if some sudden change came over the *penitent* one, which turned him from an unfeeling railer into a trembling petitioner. The plural 'thieves' need not denote more than the *quarter* or *class* whence came this last and cruelest taunt – that is, 'Not only did scoffs proceed from the *passers-by,* the *ecclesiastics,* the *soldiery,* but even from His *fellow-sufferers,*' a mode of speaking which no one would think necessarily meant both of them. Compare Mt 2:20, '*They* are dead which sought the child's life,' meaning *Herod;* and Mr 9:1, 'There be *some* standing here,' where it is next to certain that only John, the youngest and last survivor of the apostles, is meant. And is it conceivable that this penitent thief should have first himself reviled the Saviour, and then, on his views of Christ suddenly changing, he should have turned upon his fellow sufferer and fellow reviler, and rebuked him not only with dignified sharpness, but in the language of *astonishment* that he should be capable of such conduct? Besides, there is a deep calmness in all that he utters, extremely unlike what we should expect from one who was the subject of a mental revolution so sudden and total. On the scene itself, see Lu 23:29–43.

25–27. Now there stood by the cross of Jesus his mother, and his mother's sister, Mary, wife of Cleophas – This should be read, as in the *Margin,* 'Clopas,' the same as 'Alpheus' (Mt 10:3). The 'Cleopas' of Lu 24:18 was a different person.

26, 27. When Jesus … saw his mother, and the disciple whom he loved, standing by, he saith to his mother, WOMAN, BEHOLD THY SON! Then saith he to the disciple, BEHOLD THY MOTHER! – What forgetfulness of self, what filial love, and to the 'mother' and 'son' what parting words!

from that hour … took her to his own home – or, home with him; for his father Zebedee and his mother Salome were both alive, and the latter here present (Mr 15:40). See Mt 13:55. Now occurred the supernatural *darkness,* recorded by all the other Evangelists, but not here. 'Now from the sixth hour (twelve o'clock, noon) there was darkness over all the land unto the ninth hour' (Mt 27:45). No ordinary eclipse of the sun could have occurred at this time, it being then *full moon,* and this obscuration lasted about *twelve times* the length of any ordinary eclipse. (Compare Ex 10:21,23). Beyond doubt, the divine intention of the portent was to invest this darkest of all tragedies with a gloom expressive of its real character. 'And about the ninth hour Jesus cried, ELI, ELI, LAMA SABACHTHANI … My God, My God, why hast Thou forsaken Me?' (Mt 27:46). As the darkness commenced at the sixth hour, the second of the Jewish hours of prayer, so it continued till the ninth hour, *the hour of the evening sacrifice,* increasing probably in depth, and *reaching its deepest gloom at the moment of this mysterious cry,* when the flame of

the one great 'Evening Sacrifice' was burning fiercest. The words were made to His hand. They are the opening words of a Psalm (Ps 22:1) full of the last 'sufferings of Christ and the following glories' (1Pe 1:11). 'FATHER,' was the cry in the first prayer which He uttered on the cross, for matters had not then come to the worst. 'Father' was the cry of His last prayer, for matters had then passed their worst. But at this crisis of His sufferings, 'Father' does not issue from His lips, for the light of a Father's countenance was then mysteriously eclipsed. He falls back, however, on a title expressive of His *official* relation, which, though lower and more distant in itself, yet when grasped in pure and naked faith was mighty in its claims, and rich in psalmodic associations. And what deep earnestness is conveyed by the redoubling of this title! But as for the cry itself, it will never be fully comprehended. An absolute desertion is not indeed to be thought of; but a total eclipse of the *felt* sense of God's presence it certainly expresses. It expresses *surprise,* as under the experience of something not only *never before known,* but *inexplicable* on the footing which had till then subsisted between Him and God. *It is a question which the lost cannot utter.* They are forsaken, but they know why. Jesus is forsaken, but *does not know and demands to know why.* It is thus *the cry of conscious innocence, but of innocence* unavailing to draw down, at that moment, the least token of approval from the unseen Judge – innocence whose only recognition at that moment lay in the thick surrounding gloom which but reflected the horror of great darkness that invested His own spirit. *There was indeed a cause for it,* and He knew it too – the 'why' must not be pressed so far as to exclude this. *He must taste this bitterest of the wages of sin 'who did no sin'* (1Pe 2:22). But that is not the point now. In Him there was no cause at all (Joh 14:30) and He takes refuge in the glorious fact. When no ray from above shines in upon Him, He strikes a light out of His own breast. If God will not own Him, He shall own Himself. On the rock of His unsullied allegiance to Heaven He will stand, till the light of Heaven returns to His spirit. And it is near to come. While He is yet speaking, the fierceness of the flame is beginning to abate. One incident and insult more, and the experience of one other predicted element of suffering, and the victory is His. The incident, and the insult springing out of it, is the misunderstanding of the cry, for we can hardly suppose that it was anything else. 'Some of them that stood there, when they heard that, said, This man calleth for Elias' (Mt 27:47).

28–30. After this, Jesus knowing that all things were now accomplished – that is, the moment for the fulfilment of the last of them;

for there was one other small particular, and the time was come for that too, in consequence of the burning thirst which the fevered state of His frame occasioned (Ps 22:15).

that the scripture – (Ps 69:21.) **might be fulfilled saith, I thirst.** Now there was set a vessel full of vinegar – on the offer of the soldiers' vinegar, see on Joh 19:24.

and they – 'one of them,' (Mt 27:48).

29. filled a sponge with vinegar, and put it upon – a stalk of

hyssop, and put it to his mouth – Though a stalk of this plant does not exceed eighteen inches in length, it would suffice, as the feet of crucified persons were not raised high. 'The rest said, Let be' – [that is, as would seem, "Stop that officious service"] 'let us see whether Elias will come to save Him' (Mt 27:49). This was the last cruelty He was to suffer, but it was one of the most unfeeling. 'And when Jesus had cried with a loud voice' (Lu 23:46). This *'loud voice,'* noticed by three of the Evangelists, does not imply, as some able interpreters contend, that our Lord's strength was so far from being exhausted that He needed not to die then, and surrendered up His life sooner than Nature required, merely because it was the appointed time. It was indeed the appointed time, but time that He should be 'crucified *through weakness'* (1Co 13:4), and Nature was now reaching its utmost exhaustion. But just as even His own dying saints, particularly the martyrs of Jesus, have sometimes had such gleams of coming glory immediately before breathing their last, as to impart to them a strength to utter their feelings which has amazed the by-standers, so this *mighty voice* of the expiring Redeemer was nothing else but the exultant spirit of the Dying Victor, receiving the fruit of His travail just about to be embraced, and nerving the organs of utterance to an ecstatic expression of its sublime feelings (not so much in the *immediately* following words of tranquil surrender, in Luke, as in the *final* shout, recorded only by John): 'FATHER, INTO THY HANDS I COMMEND MY SPIRIT!' (Lu 23:46). Yes, the darkness is past, and the true light now shineth. His soul has emerged from its mysterious horrors; *'My God'* is heard no more, but in unclouded light He yields sublime into His *Father's* hands the infinitely precious spirit – using here also the words of those matchless Psalms (Ps 31:5) which were ever on His lips. 'As the Father receives the spirit of Jesus, so Jesus receives those of the faithful' (Ac 7:59) [BENGEL]. And now comes the expiring mighty shout.

30. It is finished! and he bowed his head and gave up the ghost – What is finished? The Law is fulfilled as never before, nor since, in His 'obedience unto death, even the death of the cross';

Messianic prophecy is accomplished; Redemption is completed; 'He hath finished the transgression, and made reconciliation for iniquity, and brought in everlasting righteousness, and sealed up the vision and prophecy, and anointed a holy of holies'; He has inaugurated the kingdom of God and given birth to a new world.

Joh 19:31–42.
Burial of Christ.

31–37. the preparation – Sabbath eve.

that the bodies should not remain – over night, against the Mosaic law (De 21:22,23).

on the Sabbath day, for that Sabbath day was an high day – or 'great' day – the first day of unleavened bread, and, as concurring with an ordinary Sabbath, the most solemn season of the ecclesiastical year. Hence their peculiar jealousy that the law should be infringed.

besought Pilate that their legs might be broken – to hasten their death, which was done in such cases with clubs.

33. But when they came to Jesus, and saw that he was dead already – there being in *His* case elements of suffering, unknown to the malefactors, which might naturally hasten His death, lingering though it always was in such cases, not to speak of His *previous* sufferings.

they brake not his legs – a fact of vast importance, as showing that the *reality* of His death was visible to those whose business it was to see to it. The *other* divine purpose served by it will appear presently.

34. But one of the soldiers – to make assurance of the fact doubly sure.

with a spear pierced his side – making a wound deep and wide, as indeed is plain from Joh 20:27,29. Had life still remained, it must have fled now.

and forthwith came there out blood and water – 'It is now well known that the effect of long-continued and intense agony is frequently to produce a secretion of a colourless lymph within the pericardium (the membrane enveloping the heart), amounting in many cases to a very considerable quantity' [WEBSTER and WILKINSON].

35. And he that saw it bare record – hath borne witness.

and his witness is true, and he knoweth that he saith true, that ye might believe – This solemn way of referring to his own testimony in this matter has no reference to what he says in his Epistle about Christ's 'coming by water and blood' (see 1Jo 5:6), but is intended to call attention both to the fulfilment of Scripture in these particulars, and to the undeniable evidence he was thus furnishing of the *reality* of Christ's death, and consequently of His resurrection; perhaps also to meet the growing tendency, in the Asiatic churches, to deny the reality of our Lord's body, or that 'Jesus Christ is come in the flesh' (1Jo 4:1–3).

36. that the scripture should be fulfilled, A bone of him shall not be broken – The reference is to the paschal lamb, as to which this ordinance was stringent (Ex 12:46 Nu 9:12. Compare 1Co 5:7). But though we are to see here the fulfilment of a very definite typical ordinance, we shall, on searching deeper, see in it *a remarkable divine interposition to protect the sacred body of Christ from the last indignity after He had finished the work given Him to do.* Every imaginable indignity had been permitted *before that,* up to the moment of His death. But no sooner is that over than an Unseen hand is found to have provided against the clubs of the rude soldiers coming in contact with that temple of the Godhead. Very different from such violence was that *spear-thrust,* for which not only doubting Thomas would thank the soldier, but intelligent believers in every age, to whom the certainty of their Lord's death and resurrection is the life of their whole Christianity.

37. And again another scripture saith, They shall look on him whom they pierced – The quotation is from Zec 12:10; not taken as usual from the *Septuagint* (the current *Greek* version), which here is all wrong, but direct from the *Hebrew.* And there is a remarkable nicety in the choice of the words employed both by the prophet and the Evangelist for 'piercing.' The word in Zechariah means to *thrust through* with spear, javelin, sword, or any such weapon. In that sense it is used in all the ten places, besides this, where it is found. How suitable this was to express the action of the Roman soldier, is manifest; and our Evangelist uses the exactly corresponding word, which the *Septuagint* certainly does not. Very *different is the other word* for 'pierce' in Ps 22:16, '*They pierced my hands and my feet.*' The word there used is one signifying to *bore* as with an awl or hammer. How striking are these small niceties!

38–40. Joseph of Arimathea – 'a rich man' (Mt 27:57), thus fulfilling Isa 53:9; 'an honourable counsellor,' a member of the Sanhedrim, and of good condition, 'which also waited for the kingdom of God' (Mr 15:43), a devout expectant of Messiah's kingdom; 'a good man and a just, the same had not consented to the counsel and deed of them' (Lu 23:50,51 – he had gone the length, perhaps, of dissenting and protesting in open council against the condemnation of our Lord); 'who also himself was Jesus' disciple,' (Mt 27:57).

being a disciple of Jesus, but secretly, for fear of the Jews – 'He went in boldly unto Pilate' (Mr 15:43) – literally, 'having taken courage went in,' or 'had the boldness to go in.' Mark alone, as his manner is, notices the *boldness* which this required. The act would without doubt identify him *for the first time* with the disciples of Christ. Marvellous it certainly is, that one who while Jesus was yet alive merely refrained from condemning Him, not having the courage to espouse His cause by one positive act, should, now that He was dead, and His cause apparently dead with Him, summon up courage to go in personally to the Roman governor and ask permission to take down and inter the body. But if this be the first instance, it is not the last, that *a seemingly dead Christ has wakened a sympathy which a living one had failed to evoke. The heroism of faith is usually kindled by desperate circumstances, and is not seldom displayed by those who before were the most timid, and scarce known as disciples at all.* 'And Pilate marvelled if he were already dead' (Mr 15:44) – rather 'wondered that he was already dead.' 'And calling the centurion, he asked him whether He had been any while dead' (Mr 15:44) – Pilate could hardly credit what Joseph had told him, that He had been dead 'some time,' and, before giving up the body to His friends, would learn how the fact stood from the centurion, whose business it was to oversee the execution. 'And when he knew it of the centurion' (Mr 15:45), that it was as Joseph had said, 'he gave' – rather 'made a gift of' – 'the body to Joseph'; struck, possibly, with the rank of the petitioner and the dignified boldness of the petition, in contrast with the spirit of the other party and the low rank to which he had been led to believe all the followers of Christ belonged. Nor would he be unwilling to show that he was not going to carry this black affair any farther. But, whatever were Pilate's motives, two most blessed objects were thus secured: (1) *The reality of our Lord's death was attested* by the party of all others most competent to decide on it, and certainly free from all bias – the officer in attendance – in full reliance on whose testimony Pilate surrendered the body: (2) The dead Redeemer, thus delivered out of the hands of His enemies, and committed by the supreme political authority to the care of His friends, was thereby protected from all further indignities; a thing most befitting indeed, now that His work was done, but impossible, so far as we can see, if His enemies had been at liberty to do with Him as they pleased. How wonderful are even the minutest features of this matchless History!

39. also Nicodemus, which at the first came to Jesus by night – 'This remark corresponds to the secrecy of Joseph's discipleship, just noticed, and calls attention to the similarity of their previous character and conduct, and the remarkable change which had now taken place' [WEBSTER and WILKINSON].

brought ... myrrh and aloes, about an hundred pounds weight – an immense quantity, betokening the greatness of their love, but part of it probably intended as a layer for the spot on which the body was to lie. (See 2Ch 16:14) [MEYER].

40. Then took they the body of Jesus, and wound it in linen clothes with the spices, as the manner of the Jews is to bury – the mixed and pulverized myrrh and aloes shaken into the folds, and the entire body, thus swathed, wrapt in an outer covering of 'clean linen cloth' (Mt 27:59). Had the Lord's own friends had the least reason to think that the spark of life was still in Him, would *they* have done this? But even if one could conceive them mistaken, could anyone have lain thus enveloped for the period during which He was in the grave, and life still remained? Impossible. When, therefore, He walked forth from the tomb, we can say with the most absolute certainty, 'Now is Christ *risen from the dead,* and become the first-fruits of them that slept' (1Co 15:20). No wonder that the learned and the barbarians alike were prepared to die for the name of the Lord Jesus; for such evidence was to the unsophisticated resistless. (No mention is made of *anointing* in this operation. No doubt it was a hurried proceeding, for fear of interruption, and because it was close on the Sabbath, the women seem to have set this as their proper task 'as soon as the Sabbath should be past' [Mr 16:1]. But as the Lord graciously held it as undesignedly anticipated by Mary at Bethany [Mr 14:8], so this was probably all the anointing, in the strict sense of it, which He received.)

41, 42. Now in the place where he was crucified there was a garden, and in the garden a new sepulchre – The choice of this tomb was, on *their* part, dictated by the double circumstance that it was so near at hand, and by its belonging to a friend of the Lord; and as there was need of haste, even they would be struck with the providence which thus supplied it. 'There laid they Jesus therefore, because of the Jew's preparation day, for the sepulchre was nigh at hand.' But there was one recommendation of it which probably would not strike them; but God had it in view. Not its being 'hewn out of a rock' (Mr 15:46), accessible only at the entrance, which doubtless would impress them with its security and suitableness. But it was 'a *new* sepulchre' (Joh 19:41), '*wherein never man before was laid*' (Lu 23:53): and Matthew (Mt 27:60) says that Joseph laid Him 'in *his own new tomb,* which he had hewn out in the rock' – doubtless for his own use, though the Lord had higher use for it. Thus as He rode into Jerusalem on an ass '*whereon never man before had sat*' (Mr 11:2), so now He shall lie in a tomb *wherein never man before had lain,* that from these specimens it

may be seen that in all things He was 'SEPARATE FROM SINNERS' (Heb 7:26).

Chapter 20

Joh 20:1–18.

Mary's visit to the sepulchre, and return to it with Peter and John – her risen Lord appears to her.

1, 2. The first day ... cometh Mary Magdalene early. – (See Mr 16:1–4; and Mt 28:1,2.)

she runneth and cometh to Simon Peter, and to the other disciple whom Jesus loved, and saith unto them, They have taken away the Lord out of the sepulchre – Dear disciple! thy dead Lord is to thee 'the Lord' still.

3–10. Peter therefore went forth, and that other disciple, and came first to the sepulchre – These particulars have a singular air of artless truth about them. Mary, in her grief, runs to the two apostles who were soon to be so closely associated in proclaiming the Saviour's resurrection, and they, followed by Mary, hasten to see with their own eyes. The younger disciple outruns the older; love haply supplying swifter wings. He stoops, he gazes in, but enters not the open sepulchre, held back probably by a reverential fear. The bolder Peter, coming up, goes in at once, and is rewarded with bright evidence of what had happened.

6–7. seeth the linen clothes lie – lying.

And the napkin, that was about his head, not lying with the linen clothes – not loosely, as if hastily thrown down, and indicative of a hurried and disorderly removal.

but wrapped – folded.

together in a place by itself – showing with what grand tranquillity 'the Living One' had walked forth from 'the dead' (Lu 24:5). 'Doubtless the two attendant angels (Joh 20:12) did this service for the Rising One, the one disposing of the linen clothes, the other of the napkin' [BENGEL].

8. Then went in ... that other disciple which came first to the sepulchre – The repetition of this, in connection with his not having gone in till after Peter, seems to show that at the moment of penning these words the advantage which each of these loving disciples had of the other was present to his mind.

and he saw and believed – Probably he means, though he does not say, that he believed in his Lord's resurrection more immediately and certainly than Peter.

9. For as yet they knew – that is, understood.

not the scripture that he must rise again from the dead – In other words, they believed in His resurrection at first, not because they were prepared by Scripture to expect it; but *facts* carried resistless conviction of it in the first instance to their minds, and furnished a key to the Scripture predictions of it.

11–15. But Mary stood without at the sepulchre weeping – Brief was the stay of those two men. But Mary, arriving perhaps by another direction after they left, lingers at the spot, weeping for her missing Lord. As she gazes through her tears on the open tomb, she also ventures to stoop down and look into it, when lo! 'two angels in white' (as from the world of light, and see Mt 28:3) appear to her in a 'sitting' posture, 'as having finished some business, and awaiting some one to impart tidings to' [BENGEL].

12. one at the head, and the other at the feet where the body of Jesus had lain – not merely proclaiming silently the *entire* charge they had had of the body, of Christ [quoted in LUTHARDT], but rather, possibly, calling mute attention to the narrow space within which the Lord of glory had contracted Himself; as if they would say, Come, see within what limits, marked off by the interval here between us two, *the Lord* lay! But she is in tears, and these suit not the scene of so glorious an Exit. They are going to point out to her the incongruity.

13. Woman, why weepest thou? – You would think the vision too much for a lone woman. But absorbed in the one Object of her affection and pursuit, she speaks out her grief without fear.

Because – that is, Can I choose but weep, when 'they have taken away,' repeating her very words to Peter and John. On this she turned herself and saw Jesus Himself standing beside her, but took Him for the gardener. Clad therefore in some such style He must have been. But if any ask, as too curious interpreters do, whence He got those habiliments, we answer [with OLSHAUSEN and LUTHARDT] where the two angels got theirs. Nor did the voice of His first words disclose Him to Mary – 'Woman, why weepest thou? whom seekest thou?' He will *try* her ere he *tell* her. She answers not the stranger's question, but comes straight to her point with him.

15. Sir, if thou have borne him hence – borne *whom*? She says not. She can think only of One, and thinks others must understand her. It reminds one of the question of the Spouse, 'Saw ye him whom my soul loveth?' (So 3:3).

tell me where thou hast laid him, and I will take him away – Wilt thou, dear fragile woman? But it is the language of sublime affection, that thinks itself fit for anything if once in possession of its Object. It is enough. Like Joseph, He can no longer restrain Himself (Ge 45:1).

16, 17. Jesus saith unto her, Mary – It is not now the distant, though respectful, 'Woman.' It is the oft-repeated name, uttered, no doubt, with all the wonted manner, and bringing a rush of unutterable and overpowering associations with it.

She turned herself, and saith to him, Rabboni! – But that single word of transported recognition was not enough for woman's full heart. Not knowing the change which had passed upon Him, she hastens to express by her action what words failed to clothe; but she is checked.

7. Jesus saith unto her, Touch me not, for I am not yet ascended to my Father – Old familiarities must now give place to new and more awful yet sweeter approaches; but for these the time has not come yet. This seems the spirit, at least, of these mysterious words, on which much difference of opinion has obtained, and not much that is satisfactory said.

but go to my brethren – (Compare Mt 28:10 Heb 2:11,17.) That He had still our Humanity, and therefore 'is not ashamed to call us brethren,' is indeed grandly evidenced by these words. But it is worthy of most reverential notice, that *we nowhere read of anyone who presumed to call Him Brother.* 'My brethren: Blessed Jesus, who are these? Were they not Thy followers? yea, Thy forsakers? How dost Thou raise these titles with Thyself! At first they were Thy *servants*; then *disciples*; a little before Thy death, they were Thy *friends*; now, after Thy resurrection, they were Thy *brethren.* But oh, mercy without measure! how wilt Thou, how canst Thou call *them* brethren whom, in Thy last parting, Thou foundest fugitives? Did they not run from Thee? Did not one of them rather leave his inmost coat behind him than not be quit of Thee? And yet Thou sayest, "Go, tell My brethren! It is not in the power of the sins of our infirmity to unbrother us"' [BISHOP HALL].

I ascend unto my Father and your Father, and to my God and your God – words of incomparable glory! Jesus had called God habitually His *Father*, and on one occasion, in His darkest moment, His *God.* But both are here united, expressing that full-orbed relationship which embraces in its vast sweep at once Himself and His redeemed. Yet, note well, He says not, *Our* Father and *our* God. All the deepest of the Church fathers were wont to call attention to this, as expressly designed to distinguish between what God is to Him and to us – *His Father essentially, ours not so: our God essentially, His not so: His God only in connection with us: our God only in connection with Him.*

18. Mary Magdalene came and told the disciples that she had seen the Lord, and that he had spoken these things unto her – To a woman was this honour given to be the first that saw the risen Redeemer, and that woman was not His mother. (See Mr 16:9.)

Joh 20:19–23.
Jesus appears to the assembled disciples.

19–23. the same day at evening, the first day of the week, the doors being shut where the disciples were assembled for fear of the Jews, came Jesus – plainly not by the ordinary way of entrance.

and saith unto them Peace be unto you – not the mere *wish* that even His own exalted peace might be theirs (Joh 14:27), but conveying it into their hearts, even as He 'opened their understandings to understand the scriptures' (Lu 24:45).

20. And when he had so said, he showed them his hands and his side – not only as *ocular* and *tangible* evidence of the *reality* of His resurrection (See Lu 24:37–43), but as through 'the *power* of that resurrection' dispensing all His peace to men.

Then were the disciples glad when they saw the Lord.

21. Then said Jesus – prepared now to listen to Him in a new character.

Peace be unto you. As my Father hath sent me, so send I you – (See on Joh 17:18.)

22. he breathed on them – a symbolical conveyance to them of the Spirit.

and saith, Receive ye the Holy Ghost – an earnest and first-fruits of the more copious Pentecostal effusion.

23. Whose soever sins ye remit, they are remitted unto them. – In any *literal* and *authoritative* sense *this power was never exercised by one of the apostles*, and plainly *was never understood by themselves as possessed by them or conveyed to them*. (See Mt 16:19.) The power to intrude upon the relation between men and God cannot have been given by Christ to His ministers in any but a *ministerial* or *declarative* sense – as the authorized interpreters of His word, while in the *actings* of His ministers, the real nature of the power committed to them is seen in the exercise of *church discipline.*

Joh 20:24–29.
Jesus again appears to the assembled disciples.

24, 25. But Thomas – (See on Joh 11:16).

was not with them when Jesus came – why, we know not, though we are loath to think (with STIER, ALFORD and LUTHARDT) it was *intentional,* from sullen despondency. The fact merely is here stated, as a loving apology for his slowness of belief.

25. We have seen the Lord – This way of speaking of Jesus (as Joh 20:20 and Joh 21:7), so suited to His resurrection-state, was soon to become the prevailing style.

Except I see in his hands the print of the nails, and put my finger into the print of the nails, and thrust my hand into his side, I will not believe – The very form of this speech betokens the strength of the unbelief. 'It is not, *If I shall see I shall believe,* but, *Unless I shall see I will not believe;* nor does he expect to see, although the others tell him they had' [BENGEL]. How Christ Himself viewed this state of mind, we know from Mr 16:14, 'He upbraided them with their unbelief and hardness of heart because they believed not them which had seen Him after He was risen.' But whence sprang this pertinacity of resistance in *such* minds? Not certainly from reluctance to believe, but as in Nathanael (see on Joh 1:46) from mere dread of mistake in so vital a matter.

26–29. And after eight days – that is, on the eighth, or first day of the preceding week. They probably met every day during the preceding week, but their Lord designedly reserved His second appearance among them till the recurrence of His resurrection day, that He might thus inaugurate the delightful sanctities of THE LORD'S DAY (Re 1:10).

disciples were within, and Thomas with them … Jesus … stood in the midst, and said, Peace be unto you.

27. Then saith he to Thomas, Reach hither … behold … put it into my side, and be not faithless, but believing – 'There is something rhythmical in these words, and they are purposely couched in the words of Thomas himself, to put him to shame' [LUTHARDT]. But with what condescension and gentleness is this done!

28. Thomas answered and said unto him, My Lord and my God – That Thomas did *not* do what Jesus invited him to do, and what he had made the condition of his believing, seems plain from Joh 20:29 ('Because thou hast *seen* Me, thou hast believed'). He is overpowered, and the glory of Christ now breaks upon him in a flood. His exclamation surpasses all that had been yet uttered, nor can it be surpassed by anything that ever will be uttered in earth or heaven. On the striking parallel in Nathanael, see on Joh 1:49. The Socinian invasion of the supreme divinity of Christ here manifestly taught – as if it were a mere call upon God in a fit of astonishment – is beneath notice, save for the profanity it charges upon this disciple, and the straits to which it shows themselves reduced.

29. because thou hast seen me, thou hast believed – words of measured commendation, but of indirect and doubtless painfully-felt rebuke: that is, 'Thou hast indeed believed; it is well: it is only on the evidence of thy senses, and after peremptorily refusing all evidence short of that.'

blessed they that have not seen, and yet have believed – 'Wonderful indeed and rich in blessing for us who have not seen Him, is this closing word of the Gospel' [ALFORD].

Joh 20:30, 31.
First close of this Gospel.

The connection of these verses with the last words of Joh 20:29 is beautiful: that is, And indeed, as the Lord pronounced them blessed who not having seen Him have yet believed, so for that one end have the whole contents of this Gospel been recorded, that all who read it may believe on Him, and believing, have life in that blessed name.

30. **many other signs** – miracles.

31. **But these are written** – as sufficient specimens.

the Christ, the Son of God – the one His *official*, the other His *personal*, title.

believing … may have life – (See on Joh 6:51–54.)

Chapter 21

Joh 21:1–23. Supplementary particulars.

1, 2. **Jesus showed himself again** – manifested himself again.

and on this wise he manifested himself – This way of speaking shows that after His resurrection He appeared to them but *occasionally, unexpectedly,* and in a way quite *unearthly,* though yet *really* and *corporeally.*

2. **Nathanael** – (See Mt 10:3.)

3–6. **Peter saith unto them, I go a fishing** – (See Lu 5:11.)

that night … caught nothing – as at the first miraculous draught (see Lu 5:5); no doubt so ordered that the miracle might strike them the more by contrast. The same principle is seen in operation throughout much of Christ's ministry, and is indeed a great law of God's spiritual procedure with His people.

4. **Jesus stood** – (Compare Joh 20:19,26.)

but the disciples knew not it was Jesus – Perhaps there had been some considerable interval since the last manifestation, and having agreed to betake themselves to their secular employment, they would be unprepared to expect Him.

5. **Children** – This term would not necessarily identify Him, being not unusual from any superior; but when they did recognize Him, they would feel it sweetly like Himself.

have ye any meat? – provisions, supplies, meaning *fish.*

They answered … No – This was in His wonted style, making them *tell* their case, and so the better prepare them for what was coming.

6. **he said unto them, Cast the net on the right side of the ship** – no doubt, by this very specific direction, intending to reveal to them His knowledge of the deep and power over it.

7–11. **that disciple whom Jesus loved, said, It is the Lord** – again having the advantage of his brother in quickness of recognition (see on Joh 20:8), to be followed by an alacrity in Peter *all his own.*

he was naked – his vest only on, worn next the body.

cast himself into the sea – the shallow part, not more than a hundred yards from the water's edge (Joh 21:8), not meaning therefore to swim, but to get sooner to Jesus than in the full boat which they could hardly draw to shore.

8. **the other disciples came in a little ship** – by ship.

9. **they saw** – 'see.'

a fire of coals, and fish laid thereon, and bread – By comparing this with 1Ki 19:6, and similar passages, the unseen agency by which Jesus made this provision will appear evident.

10. **Jesus saith unto them, Bring of the fish ye have now caught** – Observe the double supply thus provided – His and theirs. The meaning of this will perhaps appear presently.

11. **Peter went up** – into the boat; went aboard.

and drew the net to land full of great fishes, an hundred and fifty and three; and for all there were so many, yet was not the net broken – The manifest reference here to the former miraculous draught (Lu 5:1–11) furnishes the key to this scene. There the draught was *symbolical* of the success of their future ministry: While 'Peter and all that were with him were astonished at the draught of the fishes which they had taken, Jesus said unto him, Fear not, from henceforth thou shalt catch men.' Nay, when first called, in the act of 'casting their net into the sea, for they were fishers,' the same *symbolic* reference was made to their secular occupation: 'Follow Me, and I will make you fishers of men' (Mt 4:18,19). Here, then, if but the same symbolic reference be kept in view, the design of the whole scene will, we think, be clear. The *multitude* and the *size* of the fishes *they* caught symbolically foreshadowed the vast success of their now fast approaching ministry, and this only as a beginning of successive draughts, through the agency of a Christian ministry, till, 'as the waters cover the sea, the earth should be full of the knowledge of the Lord.' And whereas, at the first miraculous draught, the net 'was breaking' through the weight of what it contained – expressive of *the difficulty with which, after they had "caught men," they would be able to retain, or keep them from escaping back into the world* – while here, 'for all they were so many, yet was not the net broken,' are we not reminded of such sayings as these (Joh 10:28): 'I give unto My sheep eternal life, and they shall never perish, neither shall any pluck them out of My hand' [LUTHARDT]? But it is not through the agency of a Christian ministry that all true disciples are gathered. Jesus Himself, by unseen methods, gathers some, who afterwards are recognized by the constituted fishers of men, and mingle with the fruit of their labours. And are not these symbolized by that portion of our Galilean repast which the fishers found, in some unseen way, made ready to their hand?

12–14. none … durst ask him, Who art thou, knowing it was the Lord – implying that they *would* have liked Him just to say, 'It is I'; but having such convincing *evidence* they were afraid of being 'upbraided for their unbelief and hardness of heart' if they ventured to put the question.

13. Jesus … taketh bread – the bread.

and giveth them, and *the* **fish likewise** – (See Lu 24:30.)

14. This is the third time that Jesus showed himself – was manifested.

to his disciples – His *assembled* disciples; for if we reckon His appearances to individual disciples, they were more.

15–17. when they had dined, Jesus saith – Silence appears to have reigned during the meal; unbroken on *His* part, that by their mute observation of Him they might have their assurance of His identity the more confirmed; and on *theirs*, from reverential shrinking to speak till He did.

Simon, son of Jonas, lovest thou me more than these? – referring lovingly to those sad words of Peter, shortly before denying his Lord, 'Though *all men* shall be offended because of Thee, *yet will I never* be offended' (Mt 26:33), and intending by this allusion to bring the whole scene vividly before his mind and put him to shame.

Yea, Lord; thou knowest that I love thee – He adds not, 'more than these,' but prefixes a touching appeal to the Saviour's own omniscience for the truth of his protestation, which makes it a totally different kind of speech from his former.

He saith unto him, Feed my lambs – It is surely wrong to view this term as a mere diminutive of affection, and as meaning the same thing as 'the sheep' [WEBSTER and WILKINSON]. It is much more according to usage to understand by the 'lambs,' *young and tender* disciples, whether in age or Christian standing (Isa 40:11 1Jo 2:12,13), and by the 'sheep' the more *mature*. Shall we say (with many) that Peter was here reinstated in office? Not exactly, since he was not actually excluded from it. But after such conduct as his, the deep wound which the honour of Christ had received, the stain brought on his office, the damage done to his high standing among his brethren, and even his own comfort, in prospect of the great work before him, required some such renewal of his call and re-establishment of his position as this.

16. He saith to him … the second time … lovest thou me – In this repetition of the question, though the wound was meant to be reopened, the words '*more than these*' are not repeated; for Christ is a *tender* as well as *skilful* Physician, and Peter's silence on that point was confession enough of his sin and folly. On Peter's repeating his protestation in the same words, our Lord rises higher in the manifestation of His restoring grace.

Feed – keep.

my sheep – It has been observed that the word here is studiously changed, from one signifying simply to *feed*, to one signifying to *tend* as a shepherd, denoting the *abiding* exercise of that vocation, and in its highest functions.

17. He saith unto him the third time, Simon, son of Jonas, lovest thou me? Peter was grieved because he said the *third* **time** – This was the Physician's deepest incision into the wound, while yet smarting under the two former probings. Not till now would Peter discern the object of this succession of thrusts. The third time reveals it all, bringing up such a rush of dreadful recollections before his view, of his 'thrice denying that he knew Him,' that he feels it to the quick. It was fitting that he should; it was meant that he should. But this accomplished, the painful dialogue concludes with a delightful 'Feed My sheep'; as if He should say, 'Now, Simon, the last speck of the cloud which overhung thee since that night of nights is dispelled: Henceforth thou art to Me and to My work as if no such scene had ever happened.'

18, 19. When thou wast young – embracing the whole period of life to the verge of old age.

thou girdedst thyself, and walkedst whither thou wouldest – wast thine own master.

when … old thou shalt stretch forth thine hands – to be bound for execution, though not necessarily meaning *on a cross*. There is no reason, however, to doubt the very early tradition that Peter's death was by crucifixion.

19. This spake he, signifying by what death he should glorify God – not, therefore, a mere prediction of the manner of his *death,* but of the *honour* to be conferred upon him by dying for his Master. And, indeed, beyond doubt, this prediction was intended to follow up his triple restoration: – 'Yes, Simon, thou shalt not only feed My lambs, and feed My sheep, but after a long career of such service, shalt be counted worthy to die for the name of the Lord Jesus.'

And when he had spoken this, he saith unto him, Follow me – By thus connecting the utterance of this prediction with the invitation to follow Him, the Evangelist would indicate the deeper sense in which the call was understood, not merely to go along with Him at that moment, but to come after Him, '*taking up his cross*.'

20, 21. Peter, turning about – showing that he followed immediately as directed.

seeth the disciple whom Jesus loved following; which also leaned on Jesus' breast at supper, and said, Lord, which is he that betrayeth thee? – The Evangelist makes these allusions to the peculiar familiarity to which he had been admitted on the most memorable of all occasions, perhaps lovingly to account for Peter's somewhat forward question about him to Jesus; which is the rather probable, as it was at Peter's suggestion that he put the question about the traitor which he here recalls (Joh 13:24,25).

21. Peter … saith to Jesus, Lord, and what shall this man do? – What of this man? or, How shall it fare with him?

22, 23. Jesus saith to him, If I will that he tarry till I come, what is that to thee? follow thou me – From the fact that John alone of the Twelve survived the destruction of Jerusalem, and so witnessed the commencement of that series of events which belongs to 'the last days,' many good interpreters think that this is a virtual prediction of fact, and not a mere supposition. But this is very doubtful, and it seems more natural to consider our Lord as intending to give *no positive indication* of John's fate at all, but to signify that this was a matter which belonged to the Master of both, who would disclose or conceal it as He thought proper, and that Peter's part was to mind his own affairs. Accordingly, in 'follow thou Me,' the word '*thou*' is emphatic. Observe the absolute disposal of human life which Christ claims: '*If I will* that he tarry till I come.'

23. Then went this saying abroad among the brethren, that that disciple should not die – into which they the more easily fell from the prevalent expectation that Christ's second coming was then near at hand.

yet Jesus said not unto him, He shall not die – The Evangelist is jealous for His Master's honour, which his death might be thought to compromise if such a misunderstanding should not be corrected.

Joh 21:24, 25.
Final close of this Gospel.

24. This is the disciple which testifieth of these things, and wrote these things – thus identifying the author of this book with all that it says of this disciple.

we know that his testimony is true – (Compare Joh 19:35.)

25. And there are many other things which Jesus did – (Compare Joh 20:30,31.)

if … written every one, I suppose – an expression used to show that what follows is not to be pressed too far.

even the world itself would not hold the books – not a *mere* hyperbolical expression, unlike the sublime simplicity of this writer, but intended to let his reader know that, even now that he had done, he felt his materials so far from being exhausted, that he was still running over, and could multiply 'Gospels' to almost any extent within the strict limits of what 'Jesus did.' But in the *limitation* of these matchless histories, in point of number, there is as much of that divine wisdom which has presided over and pervades the living oracles, as in their *variety* and *fulness*.

ACTS

Matthew Henry

Introduction

This book unites the Gospels to the Epistles. It contains many particulars concerning the apostles Peter and Paul, and of the Christian church from the ascension of our Saviour to the arrival of St. Paul at Rome, a space of about thirty years. St. Luke was the writer of this book; he was present at many of the events he relates, and attended Paul to Rome. But the narrative does not afford a complete history of the church during the time to which it refers, nor even of St. Paul's life.

The object of the book has been considered to be:

1. To relate in what manner the gifts of the Holy Spirit were communicated on the day of Pentecost, and the miracles performed by the apostles, to confirm the truth of Christianity, as showing that Christ's declarations were really fulfilled.
2. To prove the claim of the Gentiles to be admitted into the church of Christ. This is shown by much of the contents of the book. A large portion of the Acts is occupied by the discourses or sermons of various persons, the language and manner of which differ, and all of which will be found according to the persons by whom they were delivered, and the occasions on which they were spoken. It seems that most of these discourses are only the substance of what was actually delivered. They relate nevertheless fully to Jesus as the Christ, the anointed Messiah.

Contents

See *Outlines of the New Testament Books*, p. 895

Chapter 1

Proofs of Christ's resurrection (1–5)

Christ's ascension (6–11)

The apostles unite in prayer (12–14)

Matthias chosen in the place of Judas (15–26)

Proofs of Christ's resurrection (1–5)

Our Lord told the disciples the work they were to do. The apostles met together at Jerusalem; Christ having ordered them not to depart thence, but to wait for the pouring out of the Holy Spirit. This would be a baptism by the Holy Ghost, giving them power to work miracles, and enlightening and sanctifying their souls. This confirms the Divine promise, and encourages us to depend upon it, that we have heard it from Christ; for in Him all the promises of God are yea and amen.

Christ's ascension (6–11)

They were earnest in asking about that which their Master never had directed or encouraged them to seek. Our Lord knew that his ascension and the teaching of the Holy Spirit would soon end these expectations, and therefore only gave them a rebuke; but it is a caution to his church in all ages, to take heed of a desire of forbidden knowledge. He had given his disciples instructions for the discharge of their duty, both before his death and since his resurrection, and this knowledge is enough for a Christian. It is enough that he has engaged to give believers strength equal to their trials and services; that under the influence of the Holy Spirit they may, in one way or other, be witnesses for Christ on earth, while in heaven he manages their concerns with perfect wisdom, truth, and love. When we stand gazing and trifling, the thoughts of our Master's second coming should quicken and awaken us: when we stand gazing and trembling, they should comfort and encourage us. May our expectation of it be stedfast and joyful, giving diligence to be found of him blameless.

The apostles unite in prayer (12–14)

God can find hiding-places for his people. They made supplication. All God's people are praying people. It was now a time of trouble and danger with the disciples of Christ; but if any is afflicted, let him pray; that will silence cares and fears. They had now a great work to do, and before they entered upon it, they were earnest in prayer to God for his presence. They were waiting for the descent of the Spirit, and abounded in prayer. Those are in the best frame to receive spiritual blessings, who are in a praying frame. Christ had promised shortly to send the Holy Ghost; that promise was not to do away prayer, but to quicken and encourage it. A little company united in love, exemplary in their conduct, fervent in prayer, and wisely zealous to promote the cause of Christ, are likely to increase rapidly.

Matthias chosen in the place of Judas (15–26)

The great thing the apostles were to attest to the world, was, Christ's resurrection; for that was the great proof of his being the Messiah, and the foundation of our hope in him. The apostles were ordained, not to wordly dignity and dominion, but to preach Christ, and the power of his resurrection. An appeal was made to God; 'Thou, Lord, who knowest the hearts of all men,' which we do not; and better than they know their own. It is fit that God should choose his own servants; and so far as he, by the disposals of his providence, or the gifts of his Spirit, shows whom he was chosen, or what he has chosen for us, we ought to fall in with his will.

Let us own his hand in the determining everything which befalls us, especially in those by which any trust may be committed to us.

Chapter 2

The descent of the Holy Spirit at the day of Pentecost (1–4)

We cannot forget how often, while their Master was with them there were strifes among the disciples which should be the greatest; but now all these strifes were at an end. They had prayed more together of late. Would we have the Spirit poured out upon us from on high, let us be all of one accord. And notwithstanding differences of sentiments and interests, as there were among those disciples, let us agree to love one another; for where brethren dwell together in unity, there the Lord commands his blessing. A rushing mighty wind came with great force. This was to signify the powerful influences and working of the Spirit of God upon the minds of men, and thereby upon the world. Thus the convictions of the Spirit make way for his comforts; and the rough blasts of that blessed wind, prepare the soul for its soft and gentle gales. There was an appearance of something like flaming fire, lighting on every one of them, according to John Baptist's saying concerning Christ; He shall baptize you with the Holy Ghost, and with fire. The Spirit, like fire, melts the heart, burns up the dross, and kindles pious and devout affections in the soul; in which, as in the fire on the altar, the spiritual sacrifices are offered up. They were all filled with the Holy Ghost, more than before. They were filled with the graces of the Spirit, and more than ever under his sanctifying influences; more weaned from this world, and better acquainted with the other. They were more filled with the comforts of the Spirit, rejoiced more than ever in the love of Christ and the hope of heaven: in it all their griefs and fears were swallowed up. They were filled with the gifts of the Holy Ghost; they had miraculous powers for the furtherance of the gospel. They spake, not from previous thought or meditation, but as the Spirit gave them utterance.

The apostles speak in divers languages (5–13)

The difference in languages which arose at Babel, has much hindered the spread of knowledge and religion. The instruments whom the Lord first employed in spreading the Christian religion, could have made no progress without this gift, which proved that their authority was from God.

Peter's address to the Jews (14–36)

Peter's sermon shows that he was thoroughly recovered from his fall, and thoroughly restored to the Divine favour; for he who had denied Christ, now boldly confessed him. His account of the miraculous pouring forth of the Spirit, was designed to awaken the hearers to embrace the faith of Christ, and to join themselves to his church. It was the fulfilling the Scripture, and the fruit of Christ's resurrection and ascension, and proof of both. Though Peter was filled with the Holy Ghost, and spake with tongues as the Spirit gave him utterance, yet he did not think to set aside the Scriptures. Christ's scholars never learn above their Bible; and the Spirit is given, not to do away the Scriptures, but to enable us to understand, approve, and obey them. Assuredly none will escape the condemnation of the great day, except those who call upon the name of the Lord, in and through his Son Jesus Christ, as the Saviour of sinners, and the Judge of all mankind.

From this gift of the Holy Ghost, Peter preaches unto them Jesus: and here is the history of Christ. Here is an account of his death and sufferings, which they witnessed but a few weeks before. His death is considered as God's act; and of wonderful grace and wisdom. Thus Divine justice must be satisfied, God and man brought together again, and Christ himself glorified, according to an eternal counsel, which could not be altered. And as the people's act; in them it was an act of awful sin and folly. Christ's resurrection did away the reproach of his death; Peter speaks largely upon this. Christ was God's Holy One, sanctified and set apart to his service in the work of redemption. His death and sufferings should be, not to him only, but to all his, the entrance to a blessed life for evermore. This event had taken place as foretold, and the apostles were witnesses. Nor did the resurrection rest upon this alone; Christ had poured upon his disciples the miraculous gifts and Divine influences, of which they witnessed the effects. Through the Saviour, the ways of life are made known; and we are encouraged to expect God's presence, and his favour for evermore. All this springs from assured belief that Jesus is the Lord, and the anointed Saviour.

Three thousand souls converted (37–41)

From the first delivery of that Divine message, it appeared that there was Divine power going with it; and thousands were brought to the obedience of faith. But neither Peter's words, nor the miracle they witnessed, could have produced such effects, had not the Holy Spirit been given. Sinners, when their eyes are opened, cannot but be pricked to the heart for sin, cannot but feel an inward uneasiness. The apostle exhorted them to repent of their sins, and openly to avow their belief in Jesus as the Messiah, by being baptized in his name. Thus professing their faith in Him, they would receive remission of their sins, and partake of the gifts and graces of the Holy Spirit. To separate from wicked people, is the only way to save ourselves from them. Those who repent of their sins, and give up themselves to Jesus Christ, must prove their sincerity by breaking off from the wicked. We must save ourselves from them; which denotes avoiding them with dread and holy fear. By God's grace three thousand persons accepted the gospel invitation. There can be no doubt that the gift of the Holy Ghost, which they all received, and from which no true believer has ever been shut out, was that Spirit of adoption, that converting, guiding, sanctifying grace, which is bestowed upon all the members of the family of our heavenly Father. Repentance and remission of sins are still preached to the chief of sinners, in the Redeemer's name; still the Holy Spirit seals the blessing on the believer's heart; still the encouraging promises are to us and our children; and still the blessings are offered to all that are afar off.

The piety and affection of the disciples (42–47)

In these verses we have the history of the truly primitive church, of the first days of it; its state of infancy indeed, but, like that, the state of its greatest innocence. They kept close to holy ordinances, and abounded in piety and devotion; for Christianity, when admitted in the power of it, will dispose the soul to communion with God in all those ways wherein he has appointed us to meet him, and has promised to meet us. The greatness of the event raised them above the world, and the Holy Ghost filled them with such love, as made every one to be to another as to himself, and so made all things common, not by destroying property, but doing away selfishness, and causing charity. And God who moved them to it, knew that they were quickly to be driven from their possessions in Judea. The Lord, from day to day, inclined the hearts of more to embrace the gospel; not merely professors, but such as were actually brought into a state of acceptance with God, being made partakers of regenerating grace. Those whom God has designed for eternal salvation, shall be effectually brought to Christ, till the earth is filled with the knowledge of his glory.

Chapter 3

A lame man healed by Peter and John (1–11)

Peter's address to the Jews (12–26)

A lame man healed by Peter and John (1–11)

The apostles and the first believers attended the temple worship at the hours of prayer. Peter and John seem to have been led by a Divine direction, to work a miracle on a man above forty years old, who had been a cripple from his birth. Peter, in the name of Jesus of Nazareth, bade him rise up and walk. Thus, if we would attempt to good purpose the healing of men's souls, we must go forth in the name and power of Jesus Christ, calling on helpless sinners to arise and walk in the way of holiness, by faith in Him. How sweet the thought to our souls, that in respect to all the crippled faculties of our fallen nature, the name of Jesus Christ of Nazareth can make us whole! With what holy joy and rapture shall we tread the holy courts, when God the Spirit causes us to enter therein by his strength!

Peter's address to the Jews (12–26)

Observe the difference in the manner of working the miracles. Our Lord always spoke as having Almighty power, never hesitated to receive the greatest honour that was given to him on account of his Divine miracles. But the apostles referred all to their Lord, and refused to receive any honour, except as his undeserving instruments. This shows that Jesus was one with the Father, and co-equal with Him; while the apostles knew that they were weak, sinful men, and dependent for every thing on Jesus, whose power effected the cure. Useful men must be very humble. Not unto us, O Lord, not unto us, but to thy name, give glory. Every crown must be cast at the feet of Christ. The apostle showed the Jews the greatness of their crime, but would not anger or drive them to despair. Assuredly, those who reject, refuse, or deny Christ, do it through ignorance; but this can in no case be an excuse.

The absolute necessity of repentance is to be solemnly charged upon the consciences of all who desire that their sins may be blotted out, and that they may share in the refreshment which nothing but a sense of Christ's pardoning love can afford. Blessed are those who have felt this. It was not needful for the Holy Spirit to make known the times and seasons of these dispensations. These subjects are still left obscure. But when sinners are convinced of their sins, they will cry to the Lord for pardon; and to the penitent, converted, and believing, times of refreshment will come from the presence of the Lord. In a state of trial and probation, the glorified Redeemer will be out of sight, because we must live by faith in him.

Here is a powerful address to warn the Jews of the dreadful consequences of their unbelief, in the very words of Moses, their favourite prophet, out of pretended zeal for whom they were ready to reject Christianity, and to try to destroy it. Christ came into the world to bring a blessing with him. And he sent his Spirit to be the great blessing. Christ came to bless us, by turning us from our iniquities, and saving us from our sins. We, by nature cleave to sin; the design of Divine grace is to turn us from it, that we may not only forsake, but hate it. Let none think that they can be happy by continuing in sin, when God declares that the blessing is in being turned from all iniquity. Let none think that they understand or believe the gospel, who only seek deliverance from the punishment of sin, but do not expect happiness in being delivered from sin itself. And let none expect to be turned from their sin, except by believing in, and receiving Christ the Son of God, as their wisdom, righteousness, sanctification, and redemption.

Chapter 4

Peter and John imprisoned (1–4)

The apostles boldly testify to Christ (5–14)

Peter and John refuse to be silenced (15–22)

The believers unite in prayer and praise (23–31)

The holy charity of the Christians (32–37)

Peter and John imprisoned (1–4)

The apostles preached through Jesus the resurrection from the dead. It includes all the happiness of the future state; this they preached through Jesus Christ, to be had through him only. Miserable is their case, to whom the glory of Christ's kingdom is a grief; for since the glory of that kingdom is everlasting, their grief will be everlasting also. The harmless and useful servants of Christ, like the apostles, have often been troubled for their work of faith and labour of love, when wicked men have escaped. And to this day instances are not wanting, in which reading the Scriptures, social prayer, and religious conversation meet with frowns and checks. But if we obey the precepts of Christ, he will support us.

The apostles boldly testify to Christ (5–14)

Peter being filled with the Holy Ghost, would have all to understand, that the miracle had been wrought by the name, or power, of Jesus of Nazareth, the Messiah, whom they had crucified; and this confirmed their testimony to his resurrection from the dead, which proved him to be the Messiah. These rulers must either be saved by that Jesus whom they had crucified, or they must perish for ever. The name of Jesus is given to men of every age and nation, as that whereby alone believers are saved from the wrath to come. But when covetousness, pride, or any corrupt passion, rules within, men shut their eyes, and close their hearts, in enmity against the light; considering all as ignorant and unlearned, who desire to know nothing in comparison with Christ crucified. And the followers of Christ should act so that all who converse with them, may take knowledge that they have been with Jesus. That makes them holy, heavenly, spiritual, and cheerful, and raises them above this world.

Peter and John refuse to be silenced (15–22)

All the care of the rulers is, that the doctrine of Christ spread not among the people, yet they cannot say it is false or dangerous, or of any ill tendency; and they are ashamed to own the true reason; that it testifies against their hypocrisy, wickedness, and tyranny. Those who know how to put a just value upon Christ's promises, know how to put just contempt upon the world's threatenings. The apostles look with concern on perishing souls, and know they cannot escape eternal ruin but by Jesus Christ, therefore they are faithful in warning, and showing the right way. None will enjoy peace of mind, nor act uprightly, till they have learned to guide their conduct by the fixed standard of truth, and not by the shifting opinions and fancies of men. Especially beware of a vain attempt to serve two masters, God and the world; the end will be, you can serve neither fully.

The believers unite in prayer and praise (23–31)

Christ's followers do best in company, provided it is their own company. It encourages God's servants, both in doing work, and suffering work, that they serve the God who made all things, and therefore has the disposal of all events; and the Scriptures must be fulfilled. Jesus was anointed to be a Saviour, therefore it was determined he should be a sacrifice, to make atonement for sin. But sin is not the less evil for God's bringing good out of it. In threatening times, our care should not be so much that troubles may be prevented, as that we may go on with cheerfulness and courage in our work and duty. They do not pray, Lord let us go away from our work, now that it is become dangerous, but, Lord, give us thy grace to go on stedfastly in our work, and not to fear the face of man. Those who desire Divine aid and encouragement, may depend upon having them, and they ought to go forth, and go on, in the strength of the Lord God. God gave a sign of acceptance of their prayers. The place was shaken, that their faith might be established and unshaken. God gave them greater degrees of his Spirit; and they were all filled with the Holy Ghost, more than ever; by which they were not only encouraged, but enabled to speak the word of God with boldness. When they find the Lord God help them by his Spirit, they know they shall not be confounded, Isaiah 1:7.

The holy charity of the Christians (32–37)

The disciples loved one another. This was the blessed fruit of Christ's dying precept to his disciples, and his dying prayer for them. Thus it was then, and it will be so again, when the Spirit shall be poured upon us from on high. The doctrine preached was the resurrection of Christ; a matter of fact, which being duly explained, was a summary of all the duties, privileges, and comforts of Christians. There were evident fruits of Christ's grace in all they said and did. They were dead to this world. This was a great evidence of the grace of God in them. They did not take away others' property, but they were indifferent to it. They did not call it their own; because they had, in affection, forsaken all for Christ, and were expecting to be stripped of all for cleaving to him. No marvel that they were of one heart and soul, when they sat so loose to the wealth of this world. In effect, they had all things common; for there was not any among them who lacked, care was taken for their supply. The money was laid at the apostles' feet. Great care ought to be taken in the distribution of public charity, that it be given to such as have need, such as are not able to procure a maintenance for themselves; those who are reduced to want for well-doing, and for the testimony of a good conscience, ought to be provided for. Here is one in particular mentioned, remarkable for this generous charity; it was Barnabas. As one designed to be a preacher of the gospel, he disentangled himself from the affairs of this life. When such dispositions prevail, and are exercised according to the circumstances of the times, the testimony will have very great power upon others.

Chapter 5

The death of Ananias and Sapphira (1–11)

The power which accompanied the preaching of the gospel (12–16)

The apostles imprisoned, but set free by an angel (17–25)

The apostles testify to Christ before the council (26–33)

The advice of Gamaliel. The council let the apostles go (34–42)

The death of Ananias and Sapphira (1–11)

The sin of Ananias and Sapphira was, that they were ambitious of being thought eminent disciples, when they were not true disciples. Hypocrites may deny themselves, may forego their worldly advantage in one instance, with a prospect of finding their account in something else. They were covetous of the wealth of the world, and distrustful of God and his providence. They thought they might serve both God and mammon. They thought to deceive the apostles. The Spirit of God in Peter discerned the principle of unbelief reigning in the heart of Ananias. But whatever Satan might suggest, he could not have filled the heart of Ananias with this wickedness had he not been consenting. The falsehood was an attempt to deceive the Spirit of truth, who so manifestly spoke and acted by the apostles. The crime of Ananias was not his retaining part of the price of the land; he might have kept it all, had he pleased; but his endeavouring to impose upon the apostles with an awful lie, from a desire to make a vain show, joined with covetousness. But if we think to put a cheat upon God, we shall put a fatal cheat upon our own souls. How sad to see those relations who should quicken one another to that which is good, hardening one another in that which is evil! And this punishment was in reality mercy to vast numbers. It would cause strict self-examination, prayer, and dread of hypocrisy, covetousness, and vain-glory, and it should still do so. It would prevent the increase of false professors. Let us learn hence how hateful falsehood is to the God of truth, and not only shun a direct lie, but all advantages from the use of doubtful expressions, and double meaning in our speech.

The power which accompanied the preaching of the gospel (12–16)

The separation of hypocrites by distinguishing judgments, should make the sincere cleave closer to each other and to the gospel ministry. Whatever tends to the purity and reputation of the church, promotes its enlargement; but that power alone which wrought such miracles by the apostles, can rescue sinners from the power of sin and Satan, and add believers to His worshippers. Christ will work by all his faithful servants; and every one who applies to him shall be healed.

The apostles imprisoned, but set free by an angel (17–25)

There is no prison so dark, so strong, but God can visit his people in it, and, if he pleases, fetch them out. Recoveries from sickness, releases out of trouble, are granted, not that we may enjoy the comforts of life, but that God may be honoured with the services of our life. It is not for the preachers of Christ's gospel to retire into corners, as long as they can have any opportunity of preaching in the great congregation. They must preach to the lowest, whose souls are as precious to Christ as the souls of the greatest. Speak to all, for all are concerned. Speak as those who resolve to stand to it, to live and die by it. Speak all the words of this heavenly, divine life, in comparison with which the present earthly life does not deserve the name. These words of life, which the Holy Ghost puts into your mouth. The words of the gospel are the words of life; words whereby we may be saved. How wretched are those who are vexed at the success of the gospel! They cannot but see that the word and power of the Lord are against them; and they tremble for the consequences, yet they will go on.

The apostles testify to Christ before the council (26–33)

Many will do an evil thing with daring, yet cannot bear to hear of it afterward, or to have it charged upon them. We cannot expect to be redeemed and healed by Christ, unless we give up ourselves to be ruled by him. Faith takes the Saviour in all his offices, who came, not to save us in our sins, but to save us from our sins. Had Christ been exalted to give dominion to Israel, the chief priests would have welcomed him. But repentance and remission of sins are blessings they neither valued nor saw their need of; therefore they, by no means, admitted his doctrine. Wherever repentance is wrought, remission is granted without fail. None are freed from the guilt and punishment of sin, but those who are freed from the power and dominion of sin; who are turned from it, and turned against it. Christ gives repentance, by his Spirit working with the word, to awaken the conscience, to work sorrow for sin, and an effectual change in the heart and life. The giving of the Holy Ghost, is plain evidence that it is the will of God that Christ should be obeyed. And He will surely destroy those who will not have Him to reign over them.

The advice of Gamaliel. The council let the apostles go (34–42)

The Lord still has all hearts in his hands, and sometimes directs the prudence of the worldly wise, so as to restrain the persecutors. Common sense tells us to be cautious, while experience and observation show that the success of frauds in matters of religion has been very short. Reproach for Christ is true preferment, as it makes us conformable to his pattern, and serviceable to his interest. They rejoiced in it. If we suffer ill for doing well, provided we suffer it well, and as we should, we ought to rejoice in that grace which enabled us so to do. The apostles did not preach themselves, but Christ. This was the preaching that most offended the priests. But it ought to be the constant business of gospel ministers to preach Christ: Christ, and him crucified; Christ, and him glorified; nothing beside this, but what has reference to it. And whatever is our station or rank in life, we should seek to make Him known, and to glorify his name.

Chapter 6

The appointment of deacons (1–7)

Stephen falsely accused of blasphemy (8–15)

The appointment of deacons (1–7)

Hitherto the disciples had been of one accord; this often had been noticed to their honour; but now they were multiplied, they began to murmur. The word of God was enough to take up all the thoughts, cares, and time of the apostles. The persons chosen to serve tables must be duly qualified. They must be filled with gifts and graces of the Holy Ghost, necessary to rightly managing this trust; men of truth, and hating covetousness. All who are employed in the service of the church, ought to be commended to the Divine grace by the prayers of the church. They blessed them in the name of the Lord. The word and grace of God are greatly magnified, when those are wrought upon by it, who were least likely.

Stephen falsely accused of blasphemy (8–15)

When they could not answer Stephen's arguments as a disputant, they prosecuted him as a criminal, and brought false witnesses against him. And it is next to a miracle of providence, that no greater number of religious persons have been murdered in the world, by the way of perjury and pretence of law, when so many thousands hate them, who make no conscience of false oaths. Wisdom and holiness make a

man's face to shine, yet will not secure men from being treated badly. What shall we say of man, a rational being, yet attempting to uphold a religious system by false witness and murder! And this has been done in numberless instances. But the blame rests not so much upon the understanding, as upon the heart of a fallen creature, which is deceitful above all things and desperately wicked. Yet the servant of the Lord, possessing a clear conscience, cheerful hope, and Divine consolations, may smile in the midst of danger and death.

Chapter 7

Stephen's defence (1–50)

Stephen reproves the Jews for the death of Christ (51–53)

The martyrdom of Stephen (54–60)

Stephen's defence (1–50)

1–16. Stephen was charged as a blasphemer of God, and an apostate from the church; therefore he shows that he is a son of Abraham, and values himself on it. The slow steps by which the promise made to Abraham advanced toward performance, plainly show that it had a spiritual meaning, and that the land intended was the heavenly. God owned Joseph in his troubles, and was with him by the power of his Spirit, both on his own mind by giving him comfort, and on those he was concerned with, by giving him favour in their eyes. Stephen reminds the Jews of their mean beginning as a check to priding themselves in the glories of that nation. Likewise of the wickedness of the patriarchs of their tribes, in envying their brother Joseph; and the same spirit was still working in them toward Christ and his ministers. The faith of the patriarchs, in desiring to be buried in the land of Canaan, plainly showed they had regard to the heavenly country. It is well to recur to the first rise of usages, or sentiments, which have been perverted. Would we know the nature and effects of justifying faith, we should study the character of the father of the faithful. His calling shows the power and freeness of Divine grace, and the nature of conversion. Here also we see that outward forms and distinctions are as nothing, compared with separation from the world, and devotedness to God.

17–29. Let us not be discouraged at the slowness of the fulfilling of God's promises. Suffering times often are growing times with the church. God is preparing for his people's deliverance, when their day is darkest, and their distress deepest. Moses was exceeding fair, 'fair toward God;' it is the beauty of holiness which is in God's sight of great price. He was wonderfully preserved in his infancy; for God will take special care of those of whom he designs to make special use. And did he thus protect the child Moses? Much more will he secure the interests of his holy child Jesus, from the enemies who are gathered together against him. They persecuted Stephen for disputing in defence of Christ and his gospel: in opposition to these they set up Moses and his law. They may understand, if they do not wilfully shut their eyes against the light, that God will, by this Jesus, deliver them out of a worse slavery than that of Egypt. Although men prolong their own miseries, yet the Lord will take care of his servants, and effect his own designs of mercy.

30–41. Men deceive themselves, if they think God cannot do what he sees to be good any where; he can bring his people into a wilderness, and there speak comfortably to them. He appeared to Moses in a flame of fire, yet the bush was not consumed; which represented the state of Israel in Egypt, where, though they were in the fire of affliction, yet they were not consumed. It may also be looked upon as a type of Christ's taking upon him the nature of man, and the union between the Divine and human nature. The death of Abraham, Isaac, and Jacob, cannot break the covenant relation between God and them. Our Saviour by this proves the future state, Matthew 22:31. Abraham is dead, yet God is still his God, therefore Abraham is still alive. Now, this is that life and immortality which are brought to light by the gospel. Stephen here shows that Moses was an eminent type of Christ, as he was Israel's deliverer. God has compassion for the troubles of his church, and the groans of his persecuted people; and their deliverance takes rise from his pity. And that deliverance was typical of what Christ did, when, for us men, and for our salvation, he came down from heaven. This Jesus, whom they now refused, as their fathers did Moses, even this same has God advanced to be a Prince and Saviour. It does not at all take from the just honour of Moses to say, that he was but an instrument, and that he is infinitely outshone by Jesus. In asserting that Jesus should change the customs of the ceremonial law, Stephen was so far from blaspheming Moses, that really he honoured him, by showing how the prophecy of Moses was come to pass, which was so clear. God who gave them those customs by his servant Moses, might, no doubt, change the custom by his Son Jesus. But Israel thrust Moses from them, and would have returned to their bondage; so men in general will not obey Jesus, because they love this present evil world, and rejoice in their own works and devices.

42–50. Stephen upbraids the Jews with the idolatry of their fathers, to which God gave them up as a punishment for their early forsaking him. It was no dishonour, but an honour to God, that the tabernacle gave way to the temple; so it is now, that the earthly temple gives way to the spiritual one; and so it will be when, at last, the spiritual shall give way to the eternal one. The whole world is God's temple, in which he is every where present, and fills it with his glory; what occasion has he then for a temple to manifest himself in? And these things show his eternal power and Godhead. But as heaven is his throne, and the earth his footstool, so none of our services can profit Him who made all things. Next to the human nature of Christ, the broken and spiritual heart is his most valued temple.

Stephen reproves the Jews for the death of Christ (51–53)

Stephen was going on, it seems, to show that the temple and the temple service must come to an end, and it would be the glory of both to give way to the worship of the Father in spirit and in truth; but he perceived they would not bear it. Therefore he broke off, and by the Spirit of wisdom, courage, and power, sharply rebuked his persecutors. When plain arguments and truths provoke the opposers of the gospel, they should be shown their guilt and danger. They, like their fathers, were stubborn and wilful. There is that in our sinful hearts, which always resists the Holy Ghost, a flesh that lusts against the Spirit, and wars against his motions; but in the hearts of God's elect, when the fulness of time comes, this resistance is overcome. The gospel was offered now, not by angels, but from the Holy Ghost; yet they did not embrace it, for they were resolved not to comply with God, either in his law or in his gospel. Their guilt stung them to the heart, and they sought relief in murdering their reprover, instead of sorrow and supplication for mercy.

The martyrdom of Stephen (54–60)

Nothing is so comfortable to dying saints, or so encouraging to suffering saints, as to see Jesus at the right hand of God: blessed be God, by faith we may see him there. Stephen offered up two short prayers in his dying moments. Our Lord Jesus is God, to whom we are to seek, and in whom we are to trust and comfort ourselves, living and dying. And if this has been our care while we live, it will be our comfort when we die. Here is a prayer for his persecutors. Though the sin was very great, yet if they would lay it to their hearts, God would not lay it to their charge. Stephen died as much in a hurry as ever any man did, yet, when he died, the words used are, he fell asleep; he applied himself to his dying work with as much composure as if he had been going to sleep. He shall awake again in the morning of the resurrection, to be received into the presence of the Lord, where is fulness of joy, and to share the pleasures that are at his right hand, for evermore.

Chapter 8

Saul persecutes the church (1–4)

Philip's success at Samaria. Simon the sorcerer baptized (5–13)

The hypocrisy of Simon detected (14–25)

Philip and the Ethiopian (26–40)

Saul persecutes the church (1–4)

Though persecution must not drive us from our work, yet it may send us to work elsewhere. Wherever the established believer is driven, he carries the knowledge of the gospel, and makes known the preciousness of Christ in every place. Where a simple desire of doing good influences the heart, it will be found impossible to shut a man out from all opportunities of usefulness.

Philip's success at Samaria. Simon the sorcerer baptized (5–13)

As far as the gospel prevails, evil spirits are dislodged, particularly unclean spirits. All inclinations to the lusts of the flesh which war against the soul are such. Distempers are here named, the most difficult to be cured by the course of nature, and most expressive of the disease of sin. Pride, ambition, and desire after grandeur have always caused abundance of mischief, both to the world and to the church. The people said of Simon, This man is the great power of God. See how ignorant and thoughtless people mistake. But how strong is the power of Divine grace, by which they were brought to Christ, who is Truth itself! The people not only gave heed to what Philip said, but were fully convinced that it was of God, and not of men, and gave up themselves to be directed thereby. Even bad men, and those whose hearts still go after covetousness, may come before God as his people come, and for a time continue with them. And many wonder at the proofs of Divine truths, who never experience their power. The gospel preached may have a common operation upon a soul, where it never produced inward holiness. All are not savingly converted who profess to believe the gospel.

The hypocrisy of Simon detected (14–25)

The Holy Ghost was as yet fallen upon none of these coverts, in the extraordinary powers conveyed by the descent of the Spirit upon the day of Pentecost. We may take encouragement from this example, in praying to God to give the renewing graces of the Holy Ghost to all for whose spiritual welfare we are concerned; for that includes all blessings. No man can give the Holy Spirit by the laying on of his hands; but we should use our best endeavours to instruct those for whom we pray. Simon Magus was ambitious to have the honour of an apostle, but cared not at all to have the spirit and disposition of a Christian. He was more desirous to gain honour to himself, than to do good to others. Peter shows him his crime. He esteemed the wealth of this world, as if it would answer for things relating to the other life, and would purchase the pardon of sin, the gift of the Holy Ghost, and eternal life. This was such a condemning error as could by no means consist with a state of grace. Our hearts are what they are in the sight of God, who cannot be deceived. And if they are not right in his sight, our religion is vain, and will stand us in no stead. A proud and covetous heart cannot be right with God. It is possible for a man to continue under the power of sin, yet to put on a form of godliness. When tempted with money to do evil, see what a perishing thing money is, and scorn it. Think not that Christianity is a trade to live by in this world. There is much wickedness in the thought of the heart, its false notions, and corrupt affections, and wicked projects, which must be repented of, or we are undone. But it shall be forgiven, upon our repentance. The doubt here is of the sincerity of Simon's repentance, not of his pardon, if his repentance was sincere. Grant us, Lord, another sort of faith than that which made Simon wonder only, and did not sanctify his heart. May we abhor all thoughts of making religion serve the purposes of pride or ambition. And keep us from that subtle poison of spiritual pride, which seeks glory to itself even from humility. May we seek only the honour which cometh from God.

Philip and the Ethiopian (26–40)

Philip was directed to go to a desert. Sometimes God opens a door of opportunity to his ministers in very unlikely places. We should study to do good to those we come into company with by travelling. We should not be so shy of all strangers as some affect to be. As to those of whom we know nothing else, we know this, that they have souls. It is wisdom for men of business to redeem time for holy duties; to fill up every minute with something which will turn to a good account. In reading the word of God, we should often pause, to inquire of whom and of what the sacred writers spake; but especially our thoughts should be employed about the Redeemer. The Ethiopian was convinced by the teaching of the Holy Spirit, of the exact fulfilment of the Scripture, was made to understand the nature of the Messiah's kingdom and salvation, and desired to be numbered among the disciples of Christ. Those who seek the truth, and employ their time in searching the Scriptures, will be sure to reap advantages. The avowal of the Ethiopian must be understood as expressing simple reliance on Christ for salvation, and unreserved devotion to Him. Let us not be satisfied till we get faith, as the Ethiopian did, by diligent study of the Holy Scriptures, and the teaching of the Spirit of God; let us not be satisfied till we get it fixed as a principle in our hearts. As soon as he was baptized, the Spirit of God took Philip from him, so that he saw him no more; but this tended to confirm his faith. When the inquirer after salvation becomes acquainted with Jesus and his gospel, he will go on his way rejoicing, and will fill up his station in society, and discharge his duties, from other motives, and in another manner than heretofore. Though baptized in the name of the Father, Son, and Holy Ghost, with water, it is not enough without the baptism of the Holy Ghost. Lord, grant this to every one of us; then shall we go on our way rejoicing.

Chapter 9

The conversion of Saul (1–9)

Saul converted preaches Christ (10–22)

Saul is persecuted at Damascus, and goes to Jerusalem (23–31)

Cure of Eneas (32–35)

Dorcas raised to life (36–43)

The conversion of Saul (1–9)

So ill informed was Saul, that he thought he ought to do all he could against the name of Christ, and that he did God service thereby; he seemed to breathe in this as in his element. Let us not despair of renewing grace for the conversion of the greatest sinners, nor let such despair of the pardoning mercy of God for the greatest sin. It is a signal token of Divine favour, if God, by the inward working of his grace, or the outward events of his providence, stops us from prosecuting or executing sinful purposes. Saul saw that Just One, ch. 26:13. How near to us is the unseen world! It is but for God to draw aside the veil, and objects are presented to the view, compared with which, whatever is most admired on earth is mean and contemptible. Saul submitted without reserve, desirous to know what the Lord Jesus would have him to do. Christ's discoveries of himself to poor souls are humbling; they lay them very low, in mean thoughts of themselves. For three days Saul took no food, and it pleased God to leave him for that time without relief. His sins were now set in

order before him; he was in the dark concerning his own spiritual state, and wounded in spirit for sin. When a sinner is brought to a proper sense of his own state and conduct, he will cast himself wholly on the mercy of the Saviour, asking what he would have him to do. God will direct the humbled sinner, and though he does not often bring transgressors to joy and peace in believing, without sorrows and distress of conscience, under which the soul is deeply engaged as to eternal things, yet happy are those who sow in tears, for they shall reap in joy.

Saul converted preaches Christ (10–22)

A good work was begun in Saul, when he was brought to Christ's feet with those words, Lord, what wilt thou have me to do? And never did Christ leave any who were brought to that. Behold, the proud Pharisee, the unmerciful oppressor, the daring blasphemer, prayeth! And thus it is even now, and with the proud infidel, or the abandoned sinner. What happy tidings are these to all who understand the nature and power of prayer, of such prayer as the humbled sinner presents for the blessings of free salvation! Now he began to pray after another manner than he had done; before, he said his prayers, now, he prayed them. Regenerating grace sets people on praying; you may as well find a living man without breath, as a living Christian without prayer. Yet even eminent disciples, like Ananias, sometimes stagger at the commands of the Lord. But it is the Lord's glory to surpass our scanty expectations, and show that those are vessels of his mercy whom we are apt to consider as objects of his vengeance. The teaching of the Holy Spirit takes away the scales of ignorance and pride from the understanding; then the sinner becomes a new creature, and endeavours to recommend the anointed Saviour, the Son of God, to his former companions.

Saul is persecuted at Damascus, and goes to Jerusalem (23–31)

When we enter into the way of God, we must look for trials; but the Lord knows how to deliver the godly, and will, with the temptation, also make a way to escape. Though Saul's conversion was and is a proof of the truth of Christianity, yet it could not, of itself, convert one soul at enmity with the truth; for nothing can produce true faith, but that power which new-creates the heart. Believers are apt to be too suspicious of those against whom they have prejudices. The world is full of deceit, and it is necessary to be cautious, but we must exercise 1 Corinthians 13 towards true believers; and he will bring them to his people, and often gives them opportunities of bearing testimony to his truth, before those who once witnessed their hatred to it.

Christ now appeared to Saul, and ordered him to go quickly out of Jerusalem, for he must be sent to the Gentiles: see ch. 22:21. Christ's witnesses cannot be slain till they have finished their testimony. The persecutions were stayed. The professors of the gospel walked uprightly, and enjoyed much comfort from the Holy Ghost, in the hope and peace of the gospel, and others were won over to them. They lived upon the comfort of the Holy Ghost, not only in the days of trouble and affliction, but in days of rest and prosperity. Those are most likely to walk cheerfully, who walk circumspectly.

Cure of Eneas (32–35)

Christians are saints, or holy people; not only the eminent ones, as Saint Peter and Saint Paul, but every sincere professor of the faith of Christ. Christ chose patients whose diseases were incurable in the course of nature, to show how desperate was the case of fallen mankind. When we were wholly without strength, as this poor man, he sent his word to heal us. Peter does not pretend to heal by any power of his own, but directs Eneas to look up to Christ for help. Let none say, that because it is Christ, who, by the power of his grace, works all our works in us, therefore we have no work, no duty to do; for though Jesus Christ makes thee whole, yet thou must arise, and use the power he gives thee.

Dorcas raised to life (36–43)

Many are full of good words, who are empty and barren in good works; but Tabitha was a great doer, no great talker. Christians who have not property to give in charity, may yet be able to do acts of charity, working with their hands, or walking with their feet, for the good of others. Those are certainly best praised whose own works praise them, whether the words of others do so or not. But such are ungrateful indeed, who have kindness shown them, and will not acknowledge it, by showing the kindness that is done them. While we live upon the fulness of Christ for our whole salvation, we should desire to be full of good works, for the honour of his name, and for the benefit of his saints. Such characters as Dorcas are useful where they dwell, as showing the excellency of the word of truth by their lives. How mean then the cares of the numerous females who seek no distinction but outward decoration, and who waste their lives in the trifling pursuits of dress and vanity! Power went along with the word, and Dorcas came to life. Thus in the raising of dead souls to spiritual life, the first sign of life is the opening of the eyes of the mind. Here we see that the Lord can make up every loss; that he overrules

every event for the good of those who trust in him, and for the glory of his name.

Chapter 10

Cornelius directed to send for Peter (1–8)

Peter's vision (9–18)

He goes to Cornelius (19–33)

His discourse to Cornelius (34–43)

The gifts of the Holy Spirit poured out (44–48)

Cornelius directed to send for Peter (1–8)

Hitherto none had been baptized into the Christian church but Jews, Samaritans, and those converts who had been circumcised and observed the ceremonial law; but now the Gentiles were to be called to partake all the privileges of God's people, without first becoming Jews. Pure and undefiled religion is sometimes found where we least expect it. Wherever the fear of God rules in the heart, it will appear both in works of charity and of piety, neither will excuse from the other. Doubtless Cornelius had true faith in God's word, as far as he understood it, though not as yet clear faith in Christ. This was the work of the Spirit of God, through the mediation of Jesus, even before Cornelius knew him, as is the case with us all when we, who before were dead in sin, are made alive. Through Christ also his prayers and alms were accepted, which otherwise would have been rejected. Without dispute or delay Cornelius was obedient to the heavenly vision. In the affairs of our souls, let us not lose time.

Peter's vision (9–18)

The prejudices of Peter against the Gentiles, would have prevented his going to Cornelius, unless the Lord had prepared him for this service. To tell a Jew that God had directed those animals to be reckoned clean which were hitherto deemed unclean, was in effect saying, that the law of Moses was done away. Peter was soon made to know the meaning of it. God knows what services are before us, and how to prepare us; and we know the meaning of what he has taught us, when we find what occasion we have to make use of it.

He goes to Cornelius (19–33)

When we see our call clear to any service, we should not be perplexed with doubts and scruples arising from prejudices or former ideas. Cornelius had called together his friends, to partake with him of the heavenly wisdom he expected from Peter. We should not covet to eat our spiritual morsels alone. It ought to be both given and taken as kindness and respect to our kindred and friends, to invite them to join us in religious exercises. Cornelius declared the direction God gave him to send for Peter. We are right in our aims in attending a gospel ministry, when we do it with regard to the Divine appointment requiring us to make use of that ordinance. How seldom ministers are called to speak to such companies, however small, in which it may be said that they are all present in the sight of God, to hear all things that are commanded of God! But these were ready to hear what Peter was commanded of God to say.

His discourse to Cornelius (34–43)

Acceptance cannot be obtained on any other ground than that of the covenant of mercy, through the atonement of Christ; but wherever true religion is found, God will accept it without regarding names or sects. The fear of God and works of righteousness are the substance of true religion, the effects of special grace. Though these are not the cause of a man's acceptance, yet they show it; and whatever may be wanting in knowledge or faith, will in due time be given by Him who has begun it. They knew in general the word, that is, the gospel, which God sent to the children of Israel. The purport of this word was, that God by it published the good tidings of peace by Jesus Christ. They knew the several matters of fact relating to the gospel. They knew the baptism of repentance which John preached. Let them know that this Jesus Christ, by whom peace is made between God and man, is Lord of all; not only as over all, God blessed for evermore, but as Mediator. All power, both in heaven and in earth, is put into his hand, and all judgment committed to him. God will go with those whom he anoints; he will be with those to whom he has given his Spirit. Peter then declares Christ's resurrection from the dead, and the proofs of it. Faith has reference to a testimony, and the Christian faith is built upon the foundation of the apostles and prophets, on the testimony given by them. See what must be believed concerning him. That we are all accountable to Christ as our Judge; so every one must seek his favour, and to have him as our Friend. And if we believe in him, we shall all be justified by him as our Righteousness. The remission of sins lays a foundation for all other favours and blessings, by taking that out of the way which hinders the bestowing of them. If sin be pardoned, all is well, and shall end well for ever.

The gifts of the Holy Spirit poured out (44–48)

The Holy Ghost fell upon others after they were baptized, to confirm them in the faith; but upon these Gentiles before they were baptized, to show that God does not confine himself to outward signs. The Holy Ghost fell upon those who were neither circumcised nor baptized; it is the Spirit that quickeneth, the flesh profiteth nothing. They magnified God, and spake of Christ and the benefits of redemption. Whatever gift we are endued with, we ought to honour God with it. The believing Jews who were present, were astonished that the gift of the Holy Ghost was poured out upon the Gentiles also. By mistaken notions of things, we make difficult for ourselves as to the methods of Divine providence and grace. As they were undeniably baptized with the Holy Ghost, Peter concluded they were not to be refused the baptism of water, and the ordinance was administered. The argument is conclusive; can we deny the sign to those who have received the things signified? Those who have some acquaintance with Christ, cannot but desire more. Even those who have received the Holy Ghost, must see their need of daily learning more of the truth.

Chapter 11

Peter's defence (1–18)

The success of the gospel at Antioch (19–24)

The disciples named Christians. Relief sent to Judea (25–30)

Peter's defence (1–18)

The imperfect state of human nature strongly appears, when godly persons are displeased even to hear that the word of God has been received, because their own system has not been attended to. And we are too apt to despair of doing good to those who yet, when tried, prove very teachable. It is the bane and damage of the church, to shut out those from it, and from the benefit of the means of grace, who are not in every thing as we are. Peter stated the whole affair. We should at all times bear with the infirmities of our brethren; and instead of taking offence, or answering with warmth, we should explain our motives, and show the nature of our proceedings. That preaching is certainly right, with which the Holy Ghost is given. While men are very zealous for their own regulations, they should take care that they do not withstand God; and those who love the Lord will glorify him, when made sure that he has given repentance to life to any fellow-sinners. Repentance is God's gift; not only his free grace accepts it, but his mighty grace works it in us, grace takes away the heart of stone, and gives us a heart of flesh. The sacrifice of God is a broken spirit.

The success of the gospel at Antioch (19–24)

The first preachers of the gospel at Antioch, were dispersed from Jerusalem by persecution; thus what was meant to hurt the church, was made to work for its good. The wrath of man is made to praise God. What should the ministers of Christ preach, but Christ? Christ, and him crucified? Christ, and him glorified? And their preaching was accompanied with the Divine power. The hand of the Lord was with them, to bring that home to the hearts and consciences of men, which they could but speak to the outward ear. They believed; they were convinced of the truth of the gospel. They turned from a careless, carnal way of living, to live a holy, heavenly, spiritual life. They turned from worshipping God in show and ceremony, to worship him in the Spirit and in truth. They turned to the Lord Jesus, and he became all in all with them. This was the work of conversion wrought upon them, and it must be wrought upon every one of us. It was the fruit of their faith; all who sincerely believe, will turn to the Lord, When the Lord Jesus is preached in simplicity, and according to the Scriptures, he will give success; and when sinners are thus brought to the Lord, really good men, who are full of faith and of the Holy Ghost, will admire and rejoice in the grace of God bestowed on them. Barnabas was full of faith; full of the grace of faith, and full of the fruits of the faith that works by love.

The disciples named Christians. Relief sent to Judea (25–30)

Hitherto the followers of Christ were called disciples, that is, learners, scholars; but from that time they were called Christians. The proper meaning of this name is, a follower of Christ; it denotes one who, from serious thought, embraces the religion of Christ, believes his promises, and makes it his chief care to shape his life by Christ's precepts and example. Hence it is plain that multitudes take the name of Christian to whom it does not rightly belong. But the name without the reality will only add to our guilt. While the bare profession will bestow neither profit nor delight, the possession of it will give both the promise of the life that now is, and of that which is to come. Grant, Lord, that Christians may forget other names and distinctions, and love one another as the followers of Christ ought to do. True Christians will feel for their brethren under afflictions. Thus will fruit be brought forth to the praise and glory of God. If all mankind were true Christians, how cheerfully would they help one another! The whole earth would be like one large family, every member of which would strive to be dutiful and kind.

Chapter 12

The martyrdom of James, and the imprisonment of Peter (1–5)

He is delivered from prison by an angel (6–11)

Peter departs, Herod's rage (12–19)

The death of Herod (20–25)

The martyrdom of James, and the imprisonment of Peter (1–5)

James was one of the sons of Zebedee, whom Christ told that they should drink of the cup that he was to drink of, and be baptized with the baptism that he was to be baptized with, Mt 20:23. Now the words of Christ were made good in him; and if we suffer with Christ, we shall reign with him. Herod imprisoned Peter: the way of persecution, as of other sins, is downhill; when men are in it, they cannot easily stop. Those make themselves an easy prey to Satan, who make it their business to please men. Thus James finished his course. But Peter, being designed for further services, was safe; though he seemed now marked out for a speedy sacrifice. We that live in a cold, prayerless world, can hardly form an idea of the earnestness of these holy men of old. But if the Lord should bring on the church an awful persecution like this of Herod, the faithful in Christ would learn what soul-felt prayer is.

He is delivered from prison by an angel (6–11)

A peaceful conscience, a lively hope, and the consolations of the Holy Spirit, can keep men calm in the full prospect of death; even those very persons who have been most distracted with terrors on that account. God's time to help, is when things are brought to the last extremity. Peter was assured that the Lord would cause this trial to end in the way that should be most for his glory. Those who are delivered out of spiritual imprisonment must follow their Deliverer, like the Israelites when they went out of the house of bondage. They knew not whither they went, but knew whom they followed. When God will work salvation for his people, all difficulties in their way will be overcome, even gates of iron are made to open of their own accord. This deliverance of Peter represents our redemption by Christ, which not only proclaims liberty to the captives, but brings them out of the prison-house. Peter, when he recollected himself, perceived what great things God had done for him. Thus souls delivered out of spiritual bondage, are not at first aware what God has wrought in them; many have the truth of grace, that want evidence of it. But when the

Comforter comes, whom the Father will send, sooner or later, he will let them know what a blessed change is wrought.

Peter departs, Herod's rage (12–19)

God's providence leaves room for the use of our prudence, though he has undertaken to perform and perfect what he has begun. These Christians continued in prayer for Peter, for they were truly in earnest. Thus men ought always to pray, and not to faint. As long as we are kept waiting for a mercy, we must continue praying for it. But sometimes that which we most earnestly wish for, we are most backward to believe. The Christian law of self-denial and of suffering for Christ, has not done away the natural law of caring for our own safety by lawful means. In times of public danger, all believers have God for their hiding-place; which is so secret, that the world cannot find them. Also, the instruments of persecution are themselves exposed to danger; the wrath of God hangs over all that engage in this hateful work. And the range of persecutors often vents itself on all in its way.

The death of Herod (20–25)

Many heathen princes claimed and received Divine honours, but it was far more horrible impiety in Herod, who knew the word and worship of the living God, to accept such idolatrous honours without rebuking the blasphemy. And such men as Herod, when puffed with pride and vanity, are ripening fast for signal vengeance. God is very jealous for his own honour, and will be glorified upon those whom he is not glorified by. See what vile bodies we carry about with us; they have in them the seeds of their own dissolution, by which they will soon be destroyed, whenever God does but speak the word. We may learn wisdom from the people of Tyre and Sidon, for we have offended the Lord with our sins. We depend on him for life, and breath, and all things; it surely then behoves us to humble ourselves before him, that through the appointed Mediator, who is ever ready to befriend us, we may be reconciled to him, lest wrath come upon us to the utmost.

Chapter 13

The mission of Paul and Barnabas (1–3)

Elymas the sorcerer (4–13)

Paul's discourse at Antioch (14–41)

He preaches to the Gentiles, and is persecuted by the Jews (42–52)

The mission of Paul and Barnabas (1–3)

What an assemblage was here! In these names we see that the Lord raises up instruments for his work, from various places and stations in life; and zeal for his glory induces men to give up flattering connexions and prospects to promote his cause. It is by the Spirit of Christ that his ministers are made both able and willing for his service, and taken from other cares that would hinder in it. Christ's ministers are to be employed in Christ's work, and, under the Spirit's guidance, to act for the glory of God the Father. They are separated to take pains, and not to take state. A blessing upon Barnabas and Saul in their present undertaking was sought for, and that they might be filled with the Holy Ghost in their work. Whatever means are used, or rules observed, the Holy Ghost alone can fit ministers for their important work, and call them to it.

Elymas the sorcerer (4–13)

Satan is in a special manner busy with great men and men in power, to keep them from being religious, that their example will influence many. Saul is here for the first time called Paul, and never after Saul. Saul was his name as he was a Hebrew; Paul was his name as he was a citizen of Rome. Under the direct influence of the Holy Ghost, he gave Elymas his true character, but not in passion. A fulness of deceit and mischief together, make a man indeed a child of the devil. And those who are enemies to the doctrine of Jesus, are enemies to all righteousness; for in it all righteousness is fulfilled. The ways of the Lord Jesus are the only right ways to heaven and happiness. There are many who not only wander from these ways themselves, but set others against these ways. They commonly are so hardened, that they will not cease to do evil. The proconsul was astonished at the force of the doctrine upon his own heart and conscience, and at the power of God by which it was confirmed. The doctrine of Christ astonishes; and the more we know of it, the more reason we shall see to wonder at it. Those who put their hand to the plough and look back, are not fit for the kingdom of God. Those who are not prepared to face opposition, and to endure hardship, are not fitted for the work of the ministry.

Paul's discourse at Antioch (14–41)

14–31. When we come together to worship God, we must do it, not only by prayer and praise, but by the reading and hearing of the word of God. The bare reading of the Scriptures in public assemblies is not enough; they should be expounded, and the people exhorted out of them. This is helping people in doing that which is necessary to make the word profitable, to apply it to themselves. Every thing is touched upon in this sermon, which might best prevail with Jews to receive and embrace Christ as the promised Messiah. And every view, however short or faint, of the Lord's dealings with his church, reminds us of his mercy and long-suffering, and of man's ingratitude and perverseness. Paul passes from David to the Son of David, and shows that this Jesus is his promised Seed; a Saviour to do that for them, which the judges of old could not do, to save them from their sins, their worst enemies. When the apostles preached Christ as the Saviour, they were so far from concealing his death, that they always preached Christ crucified. Our complete separation from sin, is represented by our being buried with Christ. But he rose again from the dead, and saw no corruption: this was the great truth to be preached.

32–37. The resurrection of Christ was the great proof of his being the Son of God. It was not possible he should be held by death, because he was the Son of God, and therefore had life in himself, which he could not lay down but with a design to take it again. The sure mercies of David are that everlasting life, of which the resurrection was a sure pledge; and the blessings of redemption in Christ are a certain earnest, even in this world. David was a great blessing to the age wherein he lived. We were not born for ourselves, but there are those living around us, to whom we must study to be serviceable. Yet here is the difference; Christ was to serve all generations. May we look to Him who is declared to be the Son of God by his resurrection from the dead, that by faith in him we may walk with God, and serve our generation according to his will; and when death comes, may we fall asleep in him, with a joyful hope of a blessed resurrection.

38–41. Let all that hear the gospel of Christ, know these two things: 1. That through this Man, who died and rose again, is preached unto you the forgiveness of sins. Your sins, though many and great, may be forgiven, and they may be so without any injury to God's honour. 2. It is by Christ only that those who believe in him, and none else, are justified from all things; from all the guilt and stain of sin, from which they could not be justified by the law of Moses. The great concern of convinced sinners is, to be justified, to be acquitted from all their guilt, and accepted as righteous in God's sight, for if any is left charged upon the sinner, he is undone. By Jesus Christ we obtain a complete justification; for by him a complete atonement was made for sin. We are justified, not only by him as our Judge but by him as the Lord our Righteousness. What the law could not do for us, in that it was weak, the gospel of Christ does. This is the most needful blessing, bringing in every other. The threatenings are warnings; what we are told will come upon impenitent sinners, is designed to awaken us to beware lest it come upon us. It ruins many, that they despise religion. Those that will not wonder and be saved, shall wonder and perish.

He preaches to the Gentiles, and is persecuted by the Jews (42–52)

The Jews opposed the doctrine the apostles preached; and when they could find no objection, they blasphemed Christ and his gospel. Commonly those who begin with contradicting, end with blaspheming. But when adversaries of Christ's cause are daring, its advocates should be the bolder. And while many judge themselves unworthy of eternal life, others, who appear less likely, desire to hear more of the glad tidings of salvation. This is according to what was foretold in the Old Testament. What light, what power, what a treasure does this gospel bring with it! How excellent are its truths, its precepts, its promises! Those came to Christ whom the Father drew, and to whom the Spirit made the gospel call effectual, Romans 8:30. As many as were disposed to eternal life, as many as had concern about their eternal state, and aimed to make sure of eternal life, believed in Christ, in whom God has treasured up that life, and who is the only Way to it; and it was the grace of God that wrought it in them. It is good to see honourable women devout; the less they have to do in the world, the more they should do for their own souls, and the souls of others: but it is sad, when, under colour of devotion to God, they try to show hatred to Christ. And the more we relish the comforts and encouragements we meet with in the power of godliness, and the fuller our hearts are of them, the better prepared we are to face difficulties in the profession of godliness.

Chapter 14

Paul and Barnabas at Iconium (1–7)

A cripple healed at Lystra, The people would have sacrificed to Paul and Barnabas (8–18)

Paul stoned at Lystra, The churches visited again (19–28)

Paul and Barnabas at Iconium (1–7)

The apostles spake so plainly, with such evidence and proof of the Spirit, and with such power; so warmly, and with such concern for the souls of men; that those who heard them could not but say, God was with them of a truth. Yet the success was not to be reckoned to the manner of their preaching, but to the Spirit of God who used that means. Perseverance in doing good, amidst dangers and hardships, is a blessed evidence of grace. Wherever God's servants are driven, they should seek to declare the truth. When they went on in Christ's name and strength, he failed not to give testimony to the word of his grace. He has assured us it is the word of God, and that we may venture our souls upon it. The Gentiles and Jews were at enmity with one another, yet united against Christians. If the church's enemies join to destroy it, shall not its friends unite for its preservation? God has a shelter for his people in a storm; he is, and will be their Hiding-place. In times of persecution, believers may see cause to quit a spot, though they do not quit their Master's work.

A cripple healed at Lystra, The people would have sacrificed to Paul and Barnabas (8–18)

All things are possible to those that believe. When we have faith, that most precious gift of God, we shall be delivered from the spiritual helplessness in which we were born, and from the dominion of sinful habits since formed; we shall be made able to stand upright and walk cheerfully in the ways of the Lord. When Christ, the Son of God, appeared in the likeness of men, and did many miracles, men were so far from doing sacrifice to him, that they made him a sacrifice to their pride and malice; but Paul and Barnabas, upon their working one miracle, were treated as gods. The same power of the god of this world, which closes the carnal mind against truth, makes errors and mistakes find easy admission. We do not learn that they rent their clothes when the people spake of stoning them; but when they spake of worshipping them; they could not bear it, being more concerned for God's honour than their own. God's truth needs not the services of man's falsehood. The servants of God might easily obtain undue honours if they would wink at men's errors and vices; but they must dread and detest such respect more than any reproach. When the apostles preached to the Jews, who hated idolatry, they had only to preach the grace of God in Christ; but when they had to do with the Gentiles, they must set right their mistakes in natural religion. Compare their conduct and declaration with the false opinions of those who think the worship of a God, under any name, or in any manner, is equally acceptable to the Lord Almighty. The most powerful arguments, the most earnest and affectionate addresses, even with miracles, are scarcely enough to keep men from absurdities and abominations; much less can they, without special grace, turn the hearts of sinners to God and to holiness.

Paul stoned at Lystra, The churches visited again (19–28)

See how restless the rage of the Jews was against the gospel of Christ. The people stoned Paul, in a popular tumult. So strong is the bent of the corrupt and carnal heart, that as it is with great difficulty that men are kept back from evil on one side, so it is with great ease they are persuaded to

evil on the other side. If Paul would have been Mercury, he might have been worshipped; but if he will be a faithful minister of Christ, he shall be stoned, and thrown out of the city. Thus men who easily submit to strong delusions, hate to receive the truth in the love of it. All who are converted need to be confirmed in the faith; all who are planted need to be rooted. Ministers' work is to establish saints as well as to awaken sinners. The grace of God, and nothing less, effectually establishes the souls of the disciples. It is true, we must count upon much tribulation, but it is encouragement that we shall not be lost and perish in it. The Person to whose power and grace the converts and the newly-established churches are commended, clearly was the Lord Jesus, 'on whom they had believed.' It was an act of worship. The praise of all the little good we do at any time, must be ascribed to God; for it is He who not only worketh in us both to will and to do, but also worketh with us to make what we do successful. All who love the Lord Jesus, will rejoice to hear that he has opened the door of faith wide, to those who were strangers to him and to his salvation. And let us, like the apostles, abide with those who know and love the Lord.

Chapter 15

The dispute raised by Judaizing teachers (1–6)

Some from Judea taught the Gentile converts at Antioch, that they could not be saved, unless they observed the whole ceremonial law as given by Moses; and thus they sought to destroy Christian liberty. There is a strange proneness in us to think that all do wrong who do not just as we do. Their doctrine was very discouraging. Wise and good men desire to avoid contests and disputes as far as they can; yet when false teachers oppose the main truths of the gospel, or bring in hurtful doctrines, we must not decline to oppose them.

The council at Jerusalem (7–21)

We see from the words 'purifying their hearts by faith,' and the address of St. Peter, that justification by faith, and sanctification by the Holy Ghost, cannot be separated; and that both are the gift of God. We have great cause to bless God that we have heard the gospel. May we have that faith which the great Searcher of hearts approves, and attests by the seal of the Holy

Spirit. Then our hearts and consciences will be purified from the guilt of sin, and we shall be freed from the burdens some try to lay upon the disciples of Christ. Paul and Barnabas showed by plain matters of fact, that God owned the preaching of the pure gospel to the Gentiles without the law of Moses; therefore to press that law upon them, was to undo what God had done. The opinion of James was, that the Gentile converts ought not to be troubled about Jewish rites, but that they should abstain from meats offered to idols, so that they might show their hatred of idolatry. Also, that they should be cautioned against fornication, which was not abhorred by the Gentiles as it should be, and even formed a part of some of their rites. They were counselled to abstain from things strangled, and from eating blood; this was forbidden by the law of Moses, and also here, from reverence to the blood of the sacrifices, which being then still offered, it would needlessly grieve the Jewish converts, and further prejudice the unconverted Jews. But as the reason has long ceased, we are left free in this, as in the like matters. Let converts be warned to avoid all appearances of the evils which they formerly practised, or are likely to be tempted to; and caution them to use Christian liberty with moderation and prudence.

The letter from the council (22–35)

Being warranted to declare themselves directed by the immediate influence of the Holy Ghost, the apostles and disciples were assured that it seemed good unto God the Holy Spirit, as well as to them, to lay upon the converts no other burden than the things before mentioned, which were necessary, either on their own account, or from present circumstances. It was a comfort to hear that carnal ordinances were no longer imposed on them, which perplexed the conscience, but could not purify or pacify it; and that those who troubled their minds were silenced, so that the peace of the church was restored, and that which threatened division was removed. All this was consolation for which they blessed God. Many others were at Antioch. Where many labour in the word and doctrine, yet there may be opportunity for us: the zeal and usefulness of others should stir us up, not lay us asleep.

Paul and Barnabas separate (36–41)

Here we have a private quarrel between two ministers, no less than Paul and Barnabas, yet made to end well. Barnabas wished his nephew John Mark to go with them. We should suspect ourselves of being partial, and guard against this in putting our relations forward. Paul did not think him worthy of the honour, nor fit for the

service, who had departed from them without their knowledge, or without their consent: see ch. 13:13. Neither would yield, therefore there was no remedy but they must part. We see that the best of men are but men, subject to like passions as we are. Perhaps there were faults on both sides, as usual in such contentions. Christ's example alone, is a copy without a blot. Yet we are not to think it strange, if there are differences among wise and good men. It will be so while we are in this imperfect state; we shall never be all of one mind till we come to heaven. But what mischief the remainders of pride and passion which are found even in good men, do in the world, and do in the church! Many who dwelt at Antioch, who had heard but little of the devotedness and piety of Paul and Barnabas, heard of their dispute and separation; and thus it will be with ourselves, if we give way to contention. Believers must be constant in prayer, that they may never be led by the allowance of unholy tempers, to hurt the cause they really desire to serve. Paul speaks with esteem and affection both of Barnabas and Mark, in his epistles, written after this event. May all who profess thy name, O loving Saviour, be thoroughly reconciled by that love derived from thee which is not easily provoked, and which soon forgets and buries injuries.

Chapter 16

Paul takes Timothy to be his assistant (1–5)

Paul proceeds to Macedonia, The conversion of Lydia (6–15)

An evil spirit cast out, Paul and Silas scourged and imprisoned (16–24)

The conversion of the jailer at Philippi (25–34)

Paul and Silas released (35–40)

Paul takes Timothy to be his assistant (1–5)

Well may the church look for much service from youthful ministers who set out in the same spirit as Timothy. But when men will submit in nothing, and oblige in nothing, the first elements of the Christian temper seem to be wanting; and there is great reason to believe that the doctrines and precepts of the gospel will not be successfully taught. The design of the decree being to set aside the ceremonial law, and its carnal ordinances, believers were confirmed in the Christian faith, because it set up a spiritual way of serving God, as suited to the nature both of God and man. Thus the church increased in numbers daily.

Paul proceeds to Macedonia, The conversion of Lydia (6–15)

The removals of ministers, and the dispensing the means of grace by them, are in particular under Divine conduct and direction. We must follow Providence: and whatever we seek to do, if that suffer us not, we ought to submit and believe to be for the best. People greatly need help for their souls, it is their duty to look out for it, and to invite those among them who can help them. And God's calls must be complied with readily. A solemn assembly the worshippers of God must have, if possible, upon the sabbath day. If we have not synagogues, we must be thankful for more private places, and resort to them; not forsaking the assembling together, as our opportunities are. Among the hearers of Paul was a woman, named Lydia. She had an honest calling, which the historian notices to her praise. Yet though she had a calling to mind, she found time to improve advantages for her soul. It will not excuse us from religious duties, to say, We have a trade to mind; for have not we also a God to serve, and souls to look after? Religion does not call us from our business in the world, but directs us in it. Pride, prejudice, and sin shut out the truths of God, till his grace makes way for them into the understanding and affections; and the Lord alone can open the heart to receive and believe his word. We must believe in Jesus Christ; there is no coming to God as a Father, but by the Son as Mediator.

An evil spirit cast out, Paul and Silas scourged and imprisoned (16–24)

Satan, though the father of lies, will declare the most important truths, when he can thereby serve his purposes. But much mischief is done to the real servants of Christ, by unholy and false preachers of the gospel, who are confounded with them by careless observers. Those who do good by drawing men from sin, may expect to be reviled as troublers of the city. While they teach men to fear God, to believe in Christ, to forsake sin, and to live godly lives, they will be accused of teaching bad customs.

The conversion of the jailer at Philippi (25–34)

The consolations of God to his suffering servants are neither few nor small. How much more happy are true Christians than their prosperous enemies! As in the dark, so out of the depths, we may cry unto God. No place, no time is amiss for prayer, if the heart be lifted up to God. No trouble, however grievous, should hinder us from praise. Christianity proves itself to be of God, in that it obliges us to be just to our own lives. Paul cried aloud to make the jailer

hear, and to make him heed, saying, Do thyself no harm. All the cautions of the word of God against sin, and all appearances of it, and approaches to it, have this tendency. Man, woman, do not ruin thyself; hurt not thyself, and then none else can hurt thee; do not sin, for nothing but that can hurt thee. Even as to the body, we are cautioned against the sins which do harm to that. Converting grace changes people's language of and to good people and good ministers. How serious the jailer's inquiry! His salvation becomes his great concern; that lies nearest his heart, which before was furthest from his thoughts. It is his own precious soul that he is concerned about. Those who are thoroughly convinced of sin, and truly concerned about their salvation, will give themselves up to Christ. Here is the sum of the whole gospel, the covenant of grace in a few words; Believe in the Lord Jesus Christ, and thou shalt be saved, and thy house. The Lord so blessed the word, that the jailer was at once softened and humbled. He treated them with kindness and compassion, and, professing faith in Christ, was baptized in that name, with his family. The Spirit of grace worked such a strong faith in them, as did away further doubt; and Paul and Silas knew by the Spirit, that a work of God was wrought in them. When sinners are thus converted, they will love and honour those whom they before despised and hated, and will seek to lessen the suffering they before desired to increase. When the fruits of faith begin to appear, terrors will be followed by confidence and joy in God.

Paul and Silas released (35–40)

Paul, though willing to suffer for the cause of Christ, and without any desire to avenge himself, did not choose to depart under the charge of having deserved wrongful punishment, and therefore required to be dismissed in an honourable manner. It was not a mere point of honour that the apostle stood upon, but justice, and not to himself so much as to his cause. And when proper apology is made, Christians should never express personal anger, nor insist too strictly upon personal amends. The Lord will make them more than conquerors in every conflict; instead of being cast down by their sufferings, they will become comforters of their brethren.

Chapter 17

Paul at Thessalonica (1–9)

The noble conduct of the Bereans (10–15)

Paul at Athens (16–21)

He preaches there (22–31)

The scornful conduct of the Athenians (32–34)

Paul at Thessalonica (1–9)

The drift and scope of Paul's preaching and arguing, was to prove that Jesus is the Christ. He must needs suffer for us, because he could not otherwise purchase our redemption for us; and he must needs have risen again, because he could not otherwise apply the redemption to us. We are to preach concerning Jesus that he is Christ; therefore we may hope to be saved by him, and are bound to be ruled by him. The unbelieving Jews were angry, because the apostles preached to the Gentiles, that they might be saved. How strange it is, that men should grudge others the privileges they will not themselves accept! Neither rulers nor people need be troubled at the increase of real Christians, even though turbulent spirits should make religion the pretext for evil designs. Of such let us beware, from such let us withdraw, that we may show a desire to act aright in society, while we claim our right to worship God according to our consciences.

The noble conduct of the Bereans (10–15)

The Jews in Berea applied seriously to the study of the word preached unto them. They not only heard Paul preach on the sabbath, but daily searched the Scriptures, and compared what they read with the facts related to them. The doctrine of Christ does not fear inquiry; advocates for his cause desire no more than that people will fully and fairly examine whether things are so or not. Those are truly noble, and likely to be more and more so, who make the Scriptures their rule, and consult them accordingly. May all the hearers of the gospel become like those of Berea, receiving the word with readiness of mind, and searching the Scriptures daily, whether the things preached to them are so.

Paul at Athens (16–21)

Athens was then famed for polite learning, philosophy, and the fine arts; but none are more childish and superstitious, more impious, or more credulous, than some persons, deemed eminent for learning and ability. It was wholly given to idolatry. The zealous advocate for the cause of Christ will be ready to plead for it in all companies, as occasion offers. Most of these learned men took no notice of Paul; but some, whose principles were the most directly contrary to Christianity, made remarks upon him. The apostle ever dwelt upon two points, which are indeed the principal doctrines of Christianity, Christ and a future state; Christ our way, and heaven our end. They looked on this as very different from the knowledge for many ages taught and professed at Athens; they desire to know more of it, but only because it was new and strange. They led him to the place where judges sat who inquired into such matters. They asked about Paul's doctrine, not because it was good, but because it was new. Great talkers are always busy-bodies. They spend their time in nothing else, and a very uncomfortable account they have to give of their time who thus spend it. Time is precious, and we are concerned to employ it well, because eternity depends upon it, but much is wasted in unprofitable conversation.

He preaches there (22–31)

Here we have a sermon to heathens, who worshipped false gods, and were without the true God in the world; and to them the scope of the discourse was different from what the apostle preached to the Jews. In the latter case, his business was to lead his hearers by prophecies and miracles to the knowledge of the Redeemer, and faith in him; in the former, it was to lead them, by the common works of providence, to know the Creator, and worship Him. The apostle spoke of an altar he had seen, with the inscription, 'TO THE UNKNOWN GOD.' This fact is stated by many writers. After multiplying their idols to the utmost, some at Athens thought there was another god of whom they had no knowledge. And are there not many now called Christians, who are zealous in their devotions, yet the great object of their worship is to them an unknown God? Observe what glorious things Paul here says of that God whom he served, and would have them to serve. The Lord had long borne with idolatry, but the times of this ignorance were now ending, and by his servants he now commanded all men every where to repent of their idolatry. Each sect of the learned men would feel themselves powerfully affected by the apostle's discourse, which tended to show the emptiness or falsity of their doctrines.

The scornful conduct of the Athenians (32–34)

The apostle was treated with more outward civility at Athens than in some other places; but none more despised his doctrine, or treated it with more indifference. Of all subjects, that which deserves the most attention gains the least. But those who scorn, will have to bear the consequences, and the word will never be useless. Some will be found, who cleave to the Lord, and listen to his faithful servants. Considering the judgement to come, and Christ as our Judge, should urge all to repent of sin, and turn to Him. Whatever matter is used, all discourses must lead to Him, and show his authority; our salvation, and resurrection, come from and by Him.

Chapter 18

Paul at Corinth, with Aquila and Priscilla
(1–6)

He continues to preach at Corinth
(7–11)

Paul before Gallio (12–17)

He visits Jerusalem (18–23)

Apollos teaches at Ephesus and in Achaia
(24–28)

Paul at Corinth, with Aquila and Priscilla (1–6)

Though Paul was entitled to support from the churches he planted, and from the people to whom he preached, yet he worked at his calling. An honest trade, by which a man may get his bread, is not to be looked upon with contempt by any. It was the custom of the Jews to bring up their children to some trade, though they gave them learning or estates. Paul was careful to prevent prejudices, even the most unreasonable. The love of Christ is the best bond of the saints; and the communings of the saints with each other, sweeten labour, contempt, and even persecution. Most of the Jews persisted in contradicting the gospel of Christ, and blasphemed. They would not believe themselves, and did all they could to keep others from believing. Paul hereupon left them. He did not give over his work; for though Israel be not gathered, Christ and his gospel shall be glorious. The Jews could not complain, for they had the first offer. When some oppose the gospel, we must turn to others. Grief that many persist in unbelief should not prevent gratitude for the conversion of some to Christ.

He continues to preach at Corinth (7–11)

The Lord knows those that are his, yea, and those that shall be his; for it is by his work upon them that they become his. Let us not despair concerning any place, when even in wicked Corinth Christ had much people. He will gather in his chosen flock from the places where they are scattered. Thus encouraged, the apostle continued at Corinth, and a numerous and flourishing church grew up.

Paul before Gallio (12–17)

Paul was about to show that he did not teach men to worship God contrary to law; but the judge would not allow the Jews to complain to him of what was not within his office. It was right in Gallio that he left the Jews to themselves in matters relating to their religion, but yet would not let them, under pretence of that,

persecute another. But it was wrong to speak slightly of a law and religion which he might have known to be of God, and which he ought to have acquainted himself with. In what way God is to be worshipped, whether Jesus be the Messiah, and whether the gospel be a Divine revelation, are not questions of words and names, they are questions of vast importance. Gallio spoke as if he boasted of his ignorance of the Scriptures, as if the law of God was beneath his notice. Gallio cared for none of these things. If he cared not for the affronts of bad men, it was commendable; but if he concerned not himself for the abuses done to good men, his indifference was carried too far. And those who see and hear of the sufferings of God's people, and have no feeling with them, or care for them, who do not pity and pray for them, are of the same spirit as Gallio, who cared for none of these things.

He visits Jerusalem (18–23)

While Paul found he laboured not in vain, he continued labouring. Our times are in God's hand; we purpose, but he disposes; therefore we must make all promises with submission to the will of God; not only if providence permits, but if God does not otherwise direct our motions. A very good refreshment it is to a faithful minister, to have for awhile the society of his brethren. Disciples are compassed about with infirmity; ministers must do what they can to strengthen them, by directing them to Christ, who is their Strength. Let us earnestly seek, in our several places, to promote the cause of Christ, forming plans that appear to us most proper, but relying on the Lord to bring them to pass if he sees good.

Apollos teaches at Ephesus and in Achaia (24–28)

Apollos taught in the gospel of Christ, as far as John's ministry would carry him, and no further. We cannot but think he had heard of Christ's death and resurrection, but he was not informed as to the mystery of them. Though he had not the miraculous gifts of the Spirit, as the apostles, he made use of the gifts he had. The dispensation of the Spirit, whatever the measure of it may be, is given to every man to profit withal. He was a lively, affectionate preacher; fervent in spirit. He was full of zeal for the glory of God and the salvation of precious souls. Here was a complete man of God, thoroughly furnished for his work. Aquila and Priscilla encouraged his ministry, by attendance upon it. They did not despise Apollos themselves, or undervalue him to others; but considered the disadvantages he had laboured under. And having themselves got knowledge in the truths of the gospel by their long intercourse with Paul, they told what they knew to him. Young scholars may gain a great deal by converse with old Christians. Those who do believe through grace, yet still need help. As long as they are in this world, there are remainders of unbelief, and something lacking in their faith to be perfected, and the work of faith to be fulfilled. If the Jews were convinced that Jesus is Christ, even their own law would teach them to hear him. The business of ministers is to preach Christ. Not only to preach the truth, but to prove and defend it, with meekness, yet with power.

Chapter 19

Paul instructs the disciples of John at Ephesus (1–7)

He teaches there (8–12)

The Jewish exorcists disgraced. Some Ephesians burn their evil books (13–20)

The tumult at Ephesus (21–31)

The tumult appeased (32–41)

Paul instructs the disciples of John at Ephesus (1–7)

Paul, at Ephesus, found some religious persons, who looked to Jesus as the Messiah. They had not been led to expect the miraculous powers of the Holy Ghost, nor were they informed that the gospel was especially the ministration of the Spirit. But they spake as ready to welcome the notice of it. Paul shows them that John never design that those he baptized should rest there, but told them that they should believe on Him who should come after him, that is, on Christ Jesus. They thankfully accepted the discovery, and were baptized in the name of the Lord Jesus. The Holy Ghost came upon them in a surprising, overpowering manner; they spake with tongues, and prophesied, as the apostles and the first Gentile coverts did. Though we do not now expect miraculous powers, yet all who profess to be disciples of Christ, should be called on to examine whether they have received the seal of the Holy Ghost, in his sanctifying influences, to the sincerity of their faith. Many seem not to have heard that there is a Holy Ghost, and many deem all that is spoken concerning his graces and comforts, to be delusion. Of such it may properly be inquired, 'Unto what, then, were ye baptized?' for they evidently know not the meaning of that outward sign on which they place great dependence.

He teaches there (8–12)

When arguments and persuasions only harden men in unbelief and blasphemy, we must separate ourselves and others from such unholy company. God was pleased to confirm the teaching of these holy men of old, that if their hearers believed them not, they might believe the works.

The Jewish exorcists disgraced. Some Ephesians burn their evil books (13–20)

It was common, especially among the Jews, for persons to profess or to try to cast out evil spirits. If we resist the devil by faith in Christ, he will flee from us; but if we think to resist him by the using of Christ's name, or his works, as a spell or charm, Satan will prevail against us. Where there is true sorrow for sin, there will be free confession of sin to God in every prayer and to man whom we have offended, when the case requires it. Surely if the word of God prevailed among us, many lewd, infidel, and wicked books would be burned by their possessors. Will not these Ephesian converts rise up in judgement against professors, who traffic in such works for the sake of gain, or allow themselves to possess them? If we desire to be in earnest in the great work of salvation, every pursuit and enjoyment must be given up which hinders the effect of the gospel upon the mind, or loosens its hold upon the heart.

The tumult at Ephesus (21–31)

Persons who came from afar to pay their devotions at the temple of Ephesus, bought little silver shrines, or models of the temple, to carry home with them. See how craftsmen make advantage to themselves of people's superstition, and serve their worldly ends by it. Men are jealous for that by which they get their wealth; and many set themselves against the gospel of Christ, because it calls men from all unlawful crafts, however much wealth is to be gotten by them. There are persons who will stickle for what is most grossly absurd, unreasonable, and false; as this, that those are gods which are made with hands, if it has but worldly interest on its side. The whole city was full of confusion, the common and natural effect of zeal for false religion. Zeal for the honour of Christ, and love to the brethren, encourage zealous believers to venture into danger. Friends will often be raised up among those who are strangers to true religion, but have observed the honest and consistent behaviour of Christians.

The tumult appeased (32–41)

The Jews came forward in this tumult. Those who are thus careful to distinguish themselves from the servants of Christ now, and are afraid of being taken for them, shall have their doom accordingly in the great day. One, having authority, at length stilled the noise. It is a very good rule at all times, both in private and public affairs, not to be hasty and rash in our motions, but to take time to consider; and always to keep our passions under check. We ought to be quiet, and to do nothing rashly; to do nothing in haste, of which we may repent at leisure. The regular methods of the law ought always to stop popular tumults, and in well-governed nations will do so. Most people stand in awe of men's judgments more than of the judgement of God. How well it were if we would thus quiet our disorderly appetites and passions, by considering the account we must shortly give to the Judge of heaven and earth! And see how the overruling providence of God keeps the public peace, by an unaccountable power over the spirits of men. Thus the world is kept in some order, and men are held back from devouring each other. We can scarcely look around but we see men act like Demetrius and the workmen. It is as safe to contend with wild beasts as with men enraged by party zeal and disappointed covetousness, who think that all arguments are answered, when they have shown that they grow rich by the practices which are opposed. Whatever side in religious disputes, or whatever name this spirit assumes, it is worldly, and should be discountenanced by all who regard truth and piety. And let us not be dismayed; the Lord on high is mightier than the noise of many waters; he can still the rage of the people.

Chapter 20

Paul's journeys (1–6)
Eutychus restored to life (7–12)
Paul travels towards Jerusalem (13–16)
Paul's discourse to the elders of Ephesus (17–27)
Their farewell (28–38)

Paul's journeys (1–6)

Tumults or opposition may constrain a Christian to remove from his station or alter his purpose, but his work and his pleasure will be the same, wherever he goes. Paul thought it worth while to bestow five days in going to Troas, though it was but for seven days' stay there; but he knew, and so should we, how to redeem even journeying time, and to make it turn to some good account.

Eutychus restored to life (7–12)

Though the disciples read, and meditated, and prayed, and sung apart, and thereby kept up communion with God, yet they came together to worship God, and so kept up their communion with one another. They came together on the first day of the week, the Lord's day. It is to be religiously observed by all disciples of Christ. In the breaking of the bread, not only the breaking of Christ's body for us, to be a sacrifice for our sins, is remembered, but the breaking of Christ's body to us, to be food and a feast for our souls, is signified. In the early times it was the custom to receive the Lord's supper every Lord's day, thus celebrating the memorial of Christ's death. In this assembly Paul preached. The preaching of the gospel ought to go with the sacraments. They were willing to hear, he saw they were so, and continued his speech till midnight. Sleeping when hearing the word, is an evil thing, a sign of low esteem of the word of God. We must do what we can to prevent being sleepy; not put ourselves to sleep, but get our hearts affected with the word we hear, so as to drive sleep far away. Infirmity requires tenderness; but contempt requires severity. It interrupted the apostle's preaching; but was made to confirm his preaching. Eutychus was brought to life again. And as they knew not when they should have Paul's company again, they made the best use of it they could, and reckoned a night's sleep well lost for that purpose. How seldom are hours of repose broken for the purposes of devotion! but how often for mere amusement or sinful revelry! So hard is it for spiritual life to thrive in the heart of man! so naturally do carnal practices flourish there!

Paul travels towards Jerusalem (13–16)

Paul hastened to Jerusalem, but tried to do good by the way, when going from place to place, as every good man should do. In doing God's work, our own wills and those of our friends must often be crossed; we must not spend time with them when duty calls us another way.

Paul's discourse to the elders of Ephesus (17–27)

The elders knew that Paul was no designing, self-seeking man. Those who would in any office serve the Lord acceptably, and profitably to others, must do it with humility. He was a plain preacher, one that spoke his message so as to be understood. He was a powerful preacher; he preached the gospel as a testimony to them if they received it; but as a testimony against them if they rejected it. He was a profitable preacher; one that aimed to inform their judgments, and reform their hearts and lives. He was a painful preacher, very industrious in his work. He was a faithful preacher; he did not keep back reproofs when necessary, nor keep back the preaching of the cross. He was a truly Christian, evangelical preacher; he did not preach notions or doubtful matters; nor affairs of state or the civil government; but he preached faith and repentance. A better summary of these things, without which there is no salvation, cannot be given: even repentance towards God, and faith towards our Lord Jesus Christ, with their fruits and effects. Without these no sinner can escape, and with these none will come short of eternal life. Let them not think that Paul left Asia for fear of persecution; he was in full expectation of trouble, yet resolved to go on, well assured that it was by Divine direction. Thanks be to God that we know not the things which shall befall us during the year, the week, the day which has begun. It is enough for the child of God to know that his strength shall be equal to his day. He knows not, he would not know, what the day before him shall bring forth. The powerful influences of the Holy Spirit bind the true Christian to his duty. Even when he expects persecution and affliction, the love of Christ constrains him to proceed. None of these things moved Paul from his work; they did not deprive him of his comfort. It is the business of our life to provide for a joyful death. Believing that this was the last time they should see him, he appeals concerning his integrity. He had preached to them the whole counsel of God. As he had preached to them the gospel purely, so he had preached it to them entire; he faithfully did his work, whether men would bear or forbear.

Their farewell (28–38)

If the Holy Ghost has made ministers overseers of the flock, that is, shepherds, they must be true to their trust. Let them consider their Master's concern for the flock committed to their charge. It is the church he has purchased with his own blood. The blood was his as Man; yet so close is the union between the Divine and human nature, that it is there called the blood of God, for it was the blood of him who is God. This put such dignity and worth into it, as to ransom believers from all evil, and purchase all good. Paul spake about their souls with affection and concern. They were full of care what would become of them. Paul directs them to look up to God with faith, and commends them to the word of God's grace, not only as the foundation of their hope and the fountain of their joy, but as the rule of their walking. The most advanced Christians are capable of growing, and will find the word of grace help their growth. As those cannot be welcome guests to the holy God who are unsanctified; so heaven would be no heaven to them; but to all who are born again, and on whom the image of God is renewed, it is sure, the almighty power and eternal truth make it so. He recommends himself to them as an example of not caring as to things of the present world; this they would find help forward their comfortable

passage through it. It might seem a hard saying, therefore Paul adds to it a saying of their Master's, which he would have them always remember; 'It is more blessed to give than to receive:' it seems they were words often used to his disciples. The opinion of the children of this world, is contrary to this; they are afraid of giving, unless in hope of getting. Clear gain, is with them the most blessed thing that can be; but Christ tell us what is more blessed, more excellent. It makes us more like to God, who gives to all, and receives from none; and to the Lord Jesus, who went about doing good. This mind was in Christ Jesus, may it be in us also. It is good for friends, when they part, to part with prayer. Those who exhort and pray for one another, may have many weeping seasons and painful separations, but they will meet before the throne of God, to part no more. It was a comfort to all, that the presence of Christ both went with him and stayed with them.

Chapter 21

Paul's voyage towards Jerusalem (1–7)

Paul at Cesarea. The prophecy of Agabus, Paul at Jerusalem (8–18)

He is persuaded to join in ceremonial observances (19–26)

Being in danger from the Jews, he is rescued by the Romans (27–40)

Paul's voyage towards Jerusalem (1–7)

Providence must be acknowledged when our affairs go on well. Wherever Paul came, he inquired what disciples were there, and found them out. Foreseeing his troubles, from love to him, and concern for the church, they wrongly thought it would be most for the glory of God that he should continue at liberty; but their earnestness to dissuade him from it, renders his pious resolution the more illustrious. He has taught us by example, as well as by rule, to pray always, to pray without ceasing. Their last farewell was sweetened with prayer.

Paul at Cesarea. The prophecy of Agabus, Paul at Jerusalem (8–18)

Paul had express warning of his troubles, that when they came, they might be no surprise or terror to him. The general notice given us, that through much tribulation we must enter into the kingdom of God, should be of the same use to us. Their weeping began to weaken and slacken his resolution. Has not our Master told us to take up our cross? It was a trouble to him, that they should so earnestly press him to do that in which he could not gratify them without wronging his conscience. When we see trouble coming, it becomes us to say, not only, The will of the Lord must be done, and there is no remedy; but, Let the will of the Lord be done; for his will is his wisdom, and he doeth all according to the counsel of it. When a trouble is come, this must allay our griefs, that the will of the Lord is done; when we see it coming, this must silence our fears, that the will of the Lord shall be done; and we ought to say, Amen, let it be done. It is honourable to be an old disciple of Jesus Christ, to have been enabled by the grace of God to continue long in a course of duty, stedfast in the faith, growing more and more experienced, to a good old age. And with these old disciples one would choose to lodge; for the multitude of their years shall teach wisdom. Many brethren at Jerusalem received Paul gladly. We think, perhaps, that if we had him among us, we should gladly receive him; but we should not, if, having his doctrine, we do not gladly receive that.

He is persuaded to join in ceremonial observances (19–26)

Paul ascribed all his success to God, and to God they gave the praise. God had honoured him more than any of the apostles, yet they did not envy him; but on the contrary, glorified the Lord. They could not do more to encourage Paul to go on cheerfully in his work. James and the elders of the church at Jerusalem, asked Paul to gratify the believing Jews, by some compliance with the ceremonial law. They thought it was prudent in him to conform thus far. It was great weakness to be so fond of the shadows, when the substance was come. The religion Paul preached, tended not to destroy the law, but to fulfil it. He preached Christ, the end of the law for righteousness, and repentance and faith, in which we are to make great use of the law. The weakness and evil of the human heart strongly appear, when we consider how many, even of the disciples of Christ, had not due regard to the most eminent minister that even lived. Not the excellence of his character, nor the success with which God blessed his labours, could gain their esteem and affection, seeing that he did not render the same respect as themselves to mere ceremonial observances. How watchful should we be against prejudices! The apostles were not free from blame in all they did; and it would be hard to defend Paul from the charge of giving way too much in this matter. It is vain to attempt to court the favour of zealots, or bigots to a party. This compliance of Paul did not answer, for the very thing by which he hoped to pacify the Jews, provoked them, and brought him into trouble. But the all-wise God overruled both their advice and Paul's compliance with it, to serve a better purpose than was intended. It was in vain to think of pleasing men who would be pleased with nothing but the rooting out of Christianity. Integrity and uprightness will be more likely to preserve us than insincere compliances. And it should warn us not to press men to doing what is contrary to their own judgment to oblige us.

Being in danger from the Jews, he is rescued by the Romans (27–40)

In the temple, where Paul should have been protected as in a place of safety, he was violently set upon. They falsely charged him with ill doctrine and ill practice against the Mosaic ceremonies. It is no new thing for those who mean honestly and act regularly, to have things laid to their charge which they know not and never thought of. It is common for the wise and good to have that charged against them by malicious people, with which they thought to have obliged them. God often makes those a protection to his people, who have no affection to them, but only have compassion for sufferers, and regard to the public peace. And here see what false, mistaken notions of good people and good ministers, many run away with. But God seasonably interposes for the safety of his servants, from wicked and unreasonable men; and gives them opportunities to speak for themselves, to plead for the Redeemer, and to spread abroad his glorious gospel.

Chapter 22

Paul's account of his conversion (1–11)

Paul directed to preach to the Gentiles (12–21)

The rage of the Jews. Paul pleads that he is a Roman citizen (22–30)

Paul's account of his conversion (1–11)

The apostle addressed the enraged multitude, in the customary style of respect and good-will. Paul relates the history of his early life very particularly; he notices that his conversion was wholly the act of God. Condemned sinners are struck blind by the power of darkness, and it is a lasting blindness, like that of the unbelieving Jews. Convinced sinners are struck blind as Paul was, not by darkness, but by light. They are for a time brought to be at a loss within themselves, but it is in order to their being enlightened. A simple relation of the Lord's dealings with us, in bringing us, from opposing, to profess and promote his gospel, when delivered in a right spirit and manner, will sometimes make more impression than laboured speeches, even though it amounts not to the full proof of the truth, such as was shown in the change wrought in the apostle.

Paul directed to preach to the Gentiles (12–21)

The apostle goes on to relate how he was confirmed in the change he had made. The Lord having chosen the sinner, that he should know his will, he is humbled, enlightened, and brought to the knowledge of Christ and his blessed gospel. Christ is here called that Just One; for he is Jesus Christ the righteous. Those whom God has chosen to know his will, must look to Jesus, for by him God has made known his good-will to us. The great gospel privilege, sealed to us by baptism, is the pardon of sins. Be baptized, and wash away thy sins; that is, receive the comfort of the pardon of thy sins in and through Jesus Christ, and lay hold on his righteousness for that purpose; and receive power against sin, for the mortifying of thy corruptions. Be baptized, and rest not in the sign, but make sure of the thing signified, the putting away of the filth of sin. The great gospel duty, to which by our baptism we are bound, is, to seek for the pardon of our sins in Christ's name, and in dependence on him and his righteousness. God appoints his labourers their day and their place, and it is fit they should follow his appointment, though it may cross their own will. Providence contrives better for us than we do for ourselves; we must refer ourselves to God's guidance. If Christ send any one, his Spirit shall go along with him, and give him to see the fruit of his labours. But nothing can reconcile man's heart to the gospel, except the special grace of God.

The rage of the Jews. Paul pleads that he is a Roman citizen (22–30)

The Jews listened to Paul's account of his conversion, but the mention of his being sent to the Gentiles, was so contrary to all their national prejudices, that they would hear no more. Their frantic conduct astonished the Roman officer, who supposed that Paul must have committed some great crime. Paul pleaded his privilege as a Roman citizen, by which he was exempted from all trials and punishments which might force him to confess himself guilty. The manner of his speaking plainly shows what holy security and serenity of mind he enjoyed. As Paul was a Jew, in low circumstances, the Roman officer questioned how he obtained so valuable a distinction; but the apostle told him he was free born. Let us value that freedom to which all the children of God are born; which no sum of money, however large, can purchase for those who remain unregenerate. This at once put a stop to his trouble. Thus many are kept from evil practices by the fear of man, who would not be held back from them by the fear of God. The apostle asks, simply, Is it lawful? He knew that the God

whom he served would support him under all sufferings for his name's sake. But if it were not lawful, the apostle's religion directed him, if possible, to avoid it. He never shrunk from a cross which his Divine Master laid upon his onward road; and he never stept aside out of that road to take one up.

Chapter 23

Paul's defence before the council of the Jews (1–5)

Paul's defence. He receives a Divine assurance that he shall go to Rome (6–11)

The Jews conspire to kill Paul. Lysias sends him to Cesarea (12–24)

Lysias's letter to Felix (25–35)

Paul's defence before the council of the Jews (1–5)

See here the character of an honest man. He sets God before him, and lives as in his sight. He makes conscience of what he says and does, and, according to the best of his knowledge, he keeps from whatever is evil, and cleaves to what is good. He is conscientious in all his words and conduct. Those who thus live before God, may, like Paul, have confidence both toward God and man. Though the answer of Paul contained a just rebuke and prediction, he seems to have been too angry at the treatment he received in uttering them. Great men may be told of their faults, and public complaints may be made in a proper manner; but the law of God requires respect for those in authority.

Paul's defence. He receives a Divine assurance that he shall go to Rome (6–11)

The Pharisees were correct in the faith of the Jewish church. The Sadducees were no friends to the Scripture or Divine revelation; they denied a future state; they had neither hope of eternal happiness, nor dread of eternal misery. When called in question for his being a Christian, Paul might truly say he was called in question for the hope of the resurrection of the dead. It was justifiable in him, by this profession of his opinion on that disputed point, to draw off the Pharisees from persecuting him, and to lead them to protect him from this unlawful violence. How easily can God defend his own cause! Though the Jews seemed to be perfectly agreed in their conspiracy against religion, yet they were influenced by very different motives. There is no true friendship among the wicked, and in a moment, and with the utmost ease, God can turn their union into open enmity. Divine consolations stood Paul in the most stead; the chief captain rescued him out of the hands of cruel men, but the event he could not tell. Whoever is against us, we need not fear, if the Lord stand by us. It is the will of Christ, that his servants who are faithful, should be always cheerful. He might think he should never see Rome; but God tells him, even in that he should be gratified, since he desired to go there only for the honour of Christ, and to do good.

The Jews conspire to kill Paul. Lysias sends him to Cesarea (12–24)

False religious principles, adopted by carnal men, urge on to such wickedness, as human nature would hardly be supposed capable of. Yet the Lord readily disappoints the best concerted schemes of iniquity. Paul knew that the Divine providence acts by reasonable and prudent means; and that, if he neglected to use the means in his power, he could not expect God's providence to work on his behalf. He who will not help himself according to his means and power, has neither reason nor revelation to assure him that he shall receive help from God. Believing in the Lord, we and ours shall be kept from every evil work, and kept to his kingdom. Heavenly Father, give us by thy Holy Spirit, for Christ's sake, this precious faith.

Lysias's letter to Felix (25–35)

God has instruments for every work. The natural abilities and moral virtues of the heathens often have been employed to protect his persecuted servants. Even the men of the world can discern between the conscientious conduct of upright believers, and the zeal of false professors, though they disregard or understand not their doctrinal principles. All hearts are in God's hand, and those are blessed who put their trust in him, and commit their ways unto him.

Chapter 24

The speech of Tertullus against Paul (1–9)

Paul's defence before Felix (10–21)

Felix trembles at the reasoning of Paul (22–27)

The speech of Tertullus against Paul (1–9)

See here the unhappiness of great men, and a great unhappiness it is, to have their services praised beyond measure, and never to be faithfully told of their faults; hereby they are hardened and encouraged in evil, like Felix. God's prophets were charged with being troublers of the land, and our Lord Jesus Christ, that he perverted the nation; the very same charges were brought against Paul. The selfish and evil passions of men urge them forward, and the graces

and power of speech, too often have been used to mislead and prejudice men against the truth. How different will the characters of Paul and Felix appear at the day of judgement, from what they are represented in the speech of Tertullus! Let not Christians value the applause, or be troubled at the revilings of ungodly men, who represent the vilest of the human race almost as gods, and the excellent of the earth as pestilences and movers of sedition.

Paul's defence before Felix (10–21)

Paul gives a just account of himself, which clears him from crime, and likewise shows the true reason of the violence against him. Let us never be driven from any good way by its having an ill name. It is very comfortable, in worshipping God, to look to him as the God of our fathers, and to set up no other rule of faith or practice but the Scriptures. This shows there will be a resurrection to a final judgment. Prophets and their doctrines were to be tried by their fruits. Paul's aim was to have a conscience void of offence. His care and endeavour was to abstain from many things, and to abound in the exercises of religion at all times; both towards God, and towards man. If blamed for being more earnest in the things of God than our neighbours, what is our reply? Do we shrink from the accusation? How many in the world would rather be accused of any weakness, nay, even of wickedness, than of an earnest, fervent feeling of love to the Lord Jesus Christ, and of devotedness to his service! Can such think that He will confess them when he comes in his glory, and before the angels of God? If there is any sight pleasing to the God of our salvation, and a sight at which the angels rejoice, it is, to behold a devoted follower of the Lord, here upon earth, acknowledging that he is guilty, if it be a crime, of loving the Lord who died for him, with all his heart, and soul, and mind, and strength. And that he will not in silence see God's word despised, or hear his name profaned; he will rather risk the ridicule and the hatred of the world, than one frown from that gracious Being whose love is better than life.

Felix trembles at the reasoning of Paul (22–27)

The apostle reasoned concerning the nature and obligations of righteousness, temperance, and of a judgment to come; thus showing the oppressive judge and his profligate mistress, their need of repentance, forgiveness, and of the grace of the gospel. Justice respects our conduct in life, particularly in reference to others; temperance, the state and government of our souls, in reference to God. He who does not exercise himself in these, has neither the form nor the power of godliness, and must be overwhelmed with the Divine wrath in the day of God's appearing. A prospect of the judgment to come, is enough to make the stoutest heart to tremble. Felix trembled, but that was all. Many are startled by the word of God, who are not changed by it. Many fear the consequences of sin, yet continue in the love and practice of sin. In the affairs of our souls, delays are dangerous. Felix put off this matter to a more convenient season, but we do not find that the more convenient season ever came. Behold now is the accepted time; hear the voice of the Lord to-day. He was in haste to turn from hearing the truth. Was any business more urgent than for him to reform his conduct, or more important than the salvation of his soul! Sinners often start up like a man roused from his sleep by a loud noise, but soon sink again into their usual drowsiness. Be not deceived by occasional appearances of religion in ourselves or in others. Above all, let us not trifle with the word of God. Do we expect that as we advance in life our hearts will grow softer, or that the influence of the world will decline? Are we not at this moment in danger of being lost for ever? Now is the day of salvation; tomorrow may be too late.

Chapter 25

Paul before Festus, he appeals to Caesar (1–12)

Festus confers with Agrippa respecting Paul (13–27)

Paul before Festus, he appeals to Caesar (1–12)

See how restless malice is. Persecutors deem it a peculiar favour to have their malice gratified. Preaching Christ, the end of the law, was no offence against the law. In suffering times the prudence of the Lord's people is tried, as well as their patience; they need wisdom. It becomes those who are innocent, to insist upon their innocence. Paul was willing to abide by the rules of the law, and to let that take its course. If he deserved death, he would accept the punishment. But if none of the things whereof they accused him were true, no man could deliver him unto them, with justice. Paul is neither released nor condemned. It is an instance of the slow steps which Providence takes; by which we are often made ashamed, both of our hopes and of our fears, and are kept waiting on God.

Festus confers with Agrippa respecting Paul (13–27)

Agrippa had the government of Galilee. How many unjust and hasty judgments the Roman maxim, ver. 16, condemn! This heathen, guided

only by the light of nature, followed law and custom exactly, yet how many Christians will not follow the rules of truth, justice, and charity, in judging their brethren! The questions about God's worship, the way of salvation, and the truths of the gospel, may appear doubtful and without interest, to worldly men and mere politicians. See how slightly this Roman speaks of Christ, and of the great controversy between the Jews and the Christians. But the day is at hand when Festus and the whole world will see, that all the concerns of the Roman empire were but trifles and of no consequence, compared with this question of Christ's resurrection. Those who have had means of instruction, and have despised them, will be awfully convinced of their sin and folly. Here was a noble assembly brought together to hear the truths of the gospel, though they only meant to gratify their curiosity by attending to the defence of a prisoner. Many, even now, attend at the places of hearing the word of God with 'great pomp,' and too often with no better motive than curiosity. And though ministers do not now stand as prisoners to make a defence for their lives, yet numbers affect to sit in judgment upon them, desirous to make them offenders for a word, rather than to learn from them the truth and will of God, for the salvation of their souls. But the pomp of this appearance was outshone by the real glory of the poor prisoner at the bar. What was the honour of their fine appearance, compared with that of Paul's wisdom, and grace, and holiness; his courage and constancy in suffering for Christ! It is no small mercy to have God clear up our righteousness as the light, and our just dealing as the noon-day; to have nothing certain laid to our charge. And God makes even the enemies of his people to do them right.

Chapter 26

Paul's defence before Agrippa (1–11)

His conversion and preaching to the Gentiles (12–23)

Festus and Agrippa convinced of Paul's innocence (24–32)

Paul's defence before Agrippa (1–11)

Christianity teaches us to give a reason of the hope that is in us, and also to give honour to whom honour is due, without flattery or fear of man. Agrippa was well versed in the Scriptures of the Old Testament, therefore could the better judge as to the controversy about Jesus being the Messiah. Surely ministers may expect, when they preach the faith of Christ, to be heard patiently. Paul professes that he still kept to all the good in which he was first educated and trained up. See here what his religion was. He was a moralist, a man of virtue, and had not learned the arts of the crafty, covetous Pharisees; he was not chargeable with any open vice and profaneness. He was sound in the faith. He always had a holy regard for the ancient promise made of God unto the fathers, and built his hope upon it. The apostle knew very well that all this would not justify him before God, yet he knew it was for his reputation among the Jews, and an argument that he was not such a man as they represented him to be. Though he counted this but loss, that he might win Christ, yet he mentioned it when it might serve to honour Christ. See here what Paul's religion is; he has not such zeal for the ceremonial law as he had in his youth; the sacrifices and offerings appointed by that, are done away by the great Sacrifice which they typified. Of the ceremonial cleansings he makes no conscience, and thinks the Levitical priesthood is done away in the priesthood of Christ; but, as to the main principles of his religion, he is as zealous as ever. Christ and heaven, are the two great doctrines of the gospel; that God has given to us eternal life, and this life is in his Son. These are the matter of the promise made unto the fathers. The temple service, or continual course of religious duties, day and night, was kept up as the profession of faith in the promise of eternal life, and in expectation of it.

The prospect of eternal life should engage us to be diligent and stedfast in all religious exercises. Yet the Sadducees hated Paul for preaching the resurrection; and the other Jews joined them, because he testified that Jesus was risen, and was the promised Redeemer of Israel. Many things are thought to be beyond belief, only because the infinite nature and perfections of Him that has revealed, performed, or promised them, are overlooked. Paul acknowledged, that while he continued a Pharisee, he was a bitter enemy to Christianity. This was his character and manner of life in the beginning of his time; and there was every thing to hinder his being a Christian. Those who have been most strict in their conduct before conversion, will afterwards see abundant reason for humbling themselves, even on account of things which they then thought ought to have been done.

His conversion and preaching to the Gentiles (12–23)

Paul was made a Christian by Divine power; by a revelation of Christ both to him and in him; when in the full career of his sin. He was made a minister by Divine authority: the same Jesus who appeared to him in that glorious light, ordered him to preach the gospel to the Gentiles. A world that sits in darkness must be enlightened; those must be brought to know the things that belong to their everlasting peace, who are yet ignorant of them. A world that lies in wickedness must be sanctified and reformed; it is not enough for them to have their eyes opened, they must have their hearts renewed; not enough to be turned from darkness to light, but they must be turned from the power of Satan unto God. All who are turned from sin to God, are not only pardoned, but have a grant of a rich inheritance. The forgiveness of sins makes way for this. None can be happy who are not holy; and to be saints in heaven we must be first saints on earth. We are made holy, and saved by faith in Christ; by which we rely upon Christ as the Lord our Righteousness, and give up ourselves to him as the Lord our Ruler; by this we receive the remission of sins, the gift of the Holy Ghost, and eternal life. The cross of Christ was a stumbling-block to the Jews, and they were in a rage at Paul's preaching the fulfilling of the Old Testament predictions. Christ should be the first that should rise from the dead; the Head or principal One. Also, it was foretold by the prophets, that the Gentiles should be brought to the knowledge of God by the Messiah; and what in this could the Jews justly be displeased at? Thus the true convert can give a reason of his hope, and a good account of the change manifest in him. Yet for going about and calling on men thus to repent and to be converted, vast numbers have been blamed and persecuted.

Festus and Agrippa convinced of Paul's innocence (24–32)

It becomes us, on all occasions, to speak the words of truth and soberness, and then we need not be troubled at the unjust censures of men. Active and laborious followers of the gospel often have been despised as dreamers or madmen, for believing such doctrines and such wonderful facts; and for attesting that the same faith and diligence, and an experience like their own, are necessary to all men, whatever their rank, in order to their salvation. But apostles and prophets, and the Son of God himself, were exposed to this charge; and none need be moved thereby, when Divine grace has made them wise unto salvation. Agrippa saw a great deal of reason for Christianity. His understanding and judgment were for the time convinced, but his heart was not changed. And his conduct and temper were widely different from the humility and spirituality of the gospel. Many are almost persuaded to be religious, who are not quite persuaded; they are under strong convictions of their duty, and of the excellence of the ways of God, yet do not pursue their convictions. Paul urged that it was the concern of every one to become a true Christian; that there is grace enough in Christ for all. He expressed his full conviction of the truth of the gospel, the absolute necessity of faith in Christ in order to salvation. Such salvation from such bondage, the gospel of Christ offers to the Gentiles; to a lost world. Yet it is with much difficulty that any person can be persuaded he needs a work of grace on his heart, like that which was needful for the conversion of the Gentiles. Let us beware of fatal hesitation in our own conduct; and recollect how far the being almost persuaded to be a Christian, is from being altogether such a one as every true believer is.

Chapter 27

Paul's voyage towards Rome (1–11)

Paul and his companions endangered by a tempest (12–20)

He receives a Divine assurance of safety (21–29)

Paul encourages those with him (30–38)

They are shipwrecked (39–44)

Paul's voyage towards Rome (1–11)

It was determined by the counsel of God, before it was determined by the counsel of Festus, that Paul should go to Rome; for God had work for him to do there. The course they steered, and the places they touched at, are here set down. And God here encourages those who suffer for him, to trust in him; for he can put it into the hearts of those to befriend them, from whom they least expect it. Sailors must make the best of the wind: and so must we all in our passage over the ocean of this world. When the winds are contrary, yet we must be getting forward as well as we can. Many who are not driven backward by cross providences, do not get forward by favourable providences. And many real Christians complain as to the concerns of their souls, that they have much ado to keep their ground. Every fair haven is not a safe haven. Many show respect to good ministers, who will not take their advice. But the event will convince sinners of the vanity of their hopes, and the folly of their conduct.

Paul and his companions endangered by a tempest (12–20)

Those who launch forth on the ocean of this world, with a fair gale, know not what storms they may meet with; and therefore must not easily take it for granted that they have obtained their purpose. Let us never expect to be quite safe till we enter heaven. They saw neither sun nor stars for many days. Thus melancholy sometimes is the condition of the people of God as to their spiritual matters; they walk in

darkness, and have no light. See what the wealth of this world is: though coveted as a blessing, the time may come when it will be a burden; not only too heavy to be carried safely, but heavy enough to sink him that has it. The children of this world can be prodigal of their goods for the saving their lives, yet are sparing of them in works of piety and charity, and in suffering for Christ. Any man will rather make shipwreck of his goods than of his life; but many rather make shipwreck of faith and a good conscience, than of their goods. The means the sailors used did not succeed; but when sinners give up all hope of saving themselves, they are prepared to understand God's word, and to trust in his mercy through Jesus Christ.

He receives a Divine assurance of safety (21–29)

They did not hearken to the apostle when he warned them of their danger; yet if they acknowledge their folly, and repent of it, he will speak comfort and relief to them when in danger. Most people bring themselves into trouble, because they do not know when they are well off; they come to harm and loss by aiming to mend their condition, often against advice. Observe the solemn profession Paul made of relation to God. No storms or tempests can hinder God's favour to his people, for he is a Help always at hand. It is a comfort to the faithful servants of God when in difficulties, that as long as the Lord has any work for them to do, their lives shall be prolonged. If Paul had thrust himself needlessly into bad company, he might justly have been cast away with them; but God calling him into it, they are preserved with him. They are given thee; there is no greater satisfaction to a good man than to know he is a public blessing. He comforts them with the same comforts wherewith he himself was comforted. God is ever faithful, therefore let all who have an interest in his promises be ever cheerful. As, with God, saying and doing are not two things, believing and enjoying should not be so with us. Hope is an anchor of the soul, sure and stedfast, entering into that within the veil. Let those who are in spiritual darkness hold fast by that, and think not of putting to sea again, but abide by Christ, and wait till the day break, and the shadows flee away.

Paul encourages those with him (30–38)

God, who appointed the end, that they should be saved, appointed the means, that they should be saved by the help of these shipmen. Duty is ours, events are God's; we do not trust God, but tempt him, when we say we put ourselves under his protection, if we do not use proper means, such as are within our power, for our safety. But how selfish are men in general, often even ready to seek their own safety by the destruction of others! Happy those who have such a one as Paul in their company, who not only had intercourse with Heaven, but was of an enlivening spirit to those about him. The sorrow of the world works death, while joy in God is life and peace in the greatest distresses and dangers. The comfort of God's promises can only be ours by believing dependence on him, to fulfil his word to us; and the salvation he reveals must be waited for in use of the means he appoints. If God has chosen us to salvation, he has also appointed that we shall obtain it by repentance, faith, prayer, and persevering obedience; it is fatal presumption to expect it in any other way. It is an encouragement to people to commit themselves to Christ as their Saviour, when those who invite them, clearly show that they do so themselves.

They are shipwrecked (39–44)

The ship that had weathered the storm in the open sea, where it had room, is dashed to pieces when it sticks fast. Thus, if the heart fixes in the world in affection, and cleaving to it, it is lost. Satan's temptations beat against it, and it is gone; but as long as it keeps above the world, though tossed with cares and tumults, there is hope for it. They had the shore in view, yet suffered shipwreck in the harbour; thus we are taught never to be secure. Though there is great difficulty in the way of the promised salvation, it shall, without fail, be brought to pass. It will come to pass that whatever the trials and dangers may be, in due time all believers will get safely to heaven. Lord Jesus, thou hast assured us that none of thine shall perish. Thou wilt bring them all safe to the heavenly shore. And what a pleasing landing will that be! Thou wilt present them to thy Father, and give thy Holy Spirit full possession of them for ever.

Chapter 28

Paul kindly received at Melita (1–10)

He arrives at Rome (11–16)

His conference with the Jews (17–22)

Paul preaches to the Jews, and abides at Rome a prisoner (23–31)

Paul kindly received at Melita (1–10)

God can make strangers to be friends; friends in distress. Those who are despised for homely manners, are often more friendly than the more polished; and the conduct of heathens, or persons called barbarians, condemns many in civilized nations, professing to be Christians. The people thought that Paul was a murderer, and that the viper was sent by Divine justice, to be the avenger of blood. They knew that there is a God who governs the world, so that things do not come to pass by chance, no, not the smallest event, but all by Divine direction; and that evil pursues sinners; that there are good works which God will reward, and wicked works which he will punish. Also, that murder is a dreadful crime, one which shall not long go unpunished. But they thought all wicked people were punished in this life. Though some are made examples in this world, to prove that there is a God and a Providence, yet many are left unpunished, to prove that there is a judgment to come. They also thought all who were remarkably afflicted in this life were wicked people. Divine revelation sets this matter in a true light. Good men often are greatly afflicted in this life, for the trial and increase of their faith and patience. Observe Paul's deliverance from the danger. And thus in the strength of the grace of Christ, believers shake off the temptations of Satan, with holy resolution. When we despise the censures and reproaches of men, and look upon them with holy contempt, having the testimony of our consciences for us, then, like Paul, we shake off the viper into the fire. It does us no harm, except we are kept by it from our duty. God hereby made Paul remarkable among these people, and so made way for the receiving of the gospel. The Lord raises up friends for his people in every place whither he leads them, and makes them blessings to those in affliction.

He arrives at Rome (11–16)

The common events of travelling are seldom worthy of being told; but the comfort of communion with the saints, and kindness shown by friends, deserve particular mention. The Christians at Rome were so far from being ashamed of Paul, or afraid of owning him, because he was a prisoner, that they were the more careful to show him respect. He had great comfort in this. And if our friends are kind to us, God puts it into their hearts, and we must give him the glory. When we see those even in strange places, who bear Christ's name, fear God, and serve him, we should lift up our hearts to heaven in thanksgiving. How many great men have made their entry into Rome, crowned and in triumph, who really were plagues to the world! But here a good man makes his entry into Rome, chained as a poor captive, who was a greater blessing to the world than any other merely a man. Is not this enough to put us for ever out of conceit with worldly favour? This may encourage God's prisoners, that he can give them favour in the eyes of those that carry them captives. When God does not soon deliver his people out of bondage, yet makes it easy to them, or them easy under it, they have reason to be thankful.

His conference with the Jews (17–22)

It was for the honour of Paul that those who examined his case, acquitted him. In his appeal he sought not to accuse his nation, but only to clear himself. True Christianity settles what is of common concern to all mankind, and is not built upon narrow opinions and private interests. It aims at no worldly benefit or advantage, but all its gains are spiritual and eternal. It is, and always has been, the lot of Christ's holy religion, to be every where spoken against. Look through every town and village where Christ is exalted as the only Saviour of mankind, and where the people are called to follow him in newness of life, and we see those who give themselves up to Christ, still called a sect, a party, and reproached. And this is the treatment they are sure to receive, so long as there shall continue an ungodly man upon earth.

Paul preaches to the Jews, and abides at Rome a prisoner (23–31)

Paul persuaded the Jews concerning Jesus. Some were wrought upon by the word, and others hardened; some received the light, and others shut their eyes against it. And the same has always been the effect of the gospel. Paul parted with them, observing that the Holy Ghost had well described their state. Let all that hear the gospel, and do not heed it, tremble at their doom; for who shall heal them, if God does not? The Jews had afterwards much reasoning among themselves. Many have great reasoning, who do not reason aright. They find fault with one another's opinions, yet will not yield to truth. Nor will men's reasoning among themselves convince them, without the grace of God to open their understandings. While we mourn on account of such despisers, we should rejoice that the salvation of God is sent to others, who will receive it; and if we are of that number, we should be thankful to Him who hath made us to differ. The apostle kept to his principle, to know

and preach nothing but Christ and him crucified. Christians, when tempted from their main business, should bring themselves back with this question, What does this concern the Lord Jesus? What tendency has it to bring us to him, and to keep us walking in him? The apostle preached not himself, but Christ, and he was not ashamed of the gospel of Christ. Though Paul was placed in a very narrow opportunity for being useful, he was not disturbed in it. Though it was not a wide door that was opened to him, yet no man was suffered to shut it; and to many it was an effectual door, so that there were saints even in Nero's household, Philippians 4:22. We learn also from Philippians 1:13, how God overruled Paul's imprisonment for the furtherance of the gospel. And not the residents at Rome only, but all the church of Christ, to the present day, and in the most remote corner of the globe, have abundant reason to bless God, that during the most mature period of his Christian life and experience, he was detained a prisoner. It was from his prison, probably chained hand to hand to the soldier who kept him, that the apostle wrote the epistles to the Ephesians, Philippians, Colossians, and Hebrews; epistles showing, perhaps more than any others, the Christian love with which his heart overflowed, and the Christian experience with which his soul was filled. The believer of the present time may have less of triumph, and less of heavenly joy, than the apostle, but every follower of the same Saviour, is equally sure of safety and peace at the last. Let us seek to live more and more in the love of the Saviour; to labour to glorify Him by every action of our lives; and we shall assuredly, by his strength, be among the number of those who now overcome our enemies; and by his free grace and mercy, be hereafter among the blessed company who shall sit with Him upon his throne, even as He also has overcome, and is sitting on his Father's throne, at God's right hand for evermore.

THE PRINCIPAL EVENTS CONNECTED WITH THE APOSTLE PAUL'S LIFE

Put into chronological order by David Brown

Certainty in these dates is not to be had, as the notes of time in the Acts of the Apostles are few and vague. It is only by connecting those events of secular history which it records, and the dates of which are otherwise tolerably known to us – such as the famine under Claudius Caesar (Ac 11:28), the expulsion of the Jews from Rome by the same emperor (Ac 18:2), and the entrance of Porcius Festus upon his procuratorship (Ac 24:27), with the intervals specified between some occurrences in the apostle's life and others (such as Ac 20:31 24:27 28:30; and Ga 1:1–2:21) – that we can thread our way through the difficulties that surround the chronology of the apostle's life, and approximate to certainty. Immense research has been brought to bear upon the subject, but, as might be expected, the learned are greatly divided. Every year has been fixed upon as the probable date of the apostle's conversion from A.D. 31 [Bengel] to A.D. 42 [Eusebius]. But the weight of authority is in favour of dates ranging between 35 and 40, a difference of not more than five years; and the largest number of authorities is in favour of the year 37 or 38. Taking the former of these, to which opinion largely inclines, the following Table will be useful to the student of apostolic history:

A.D. 37	PAUL'S CONVERSION	Ac 9:1.
A.D. 40	First Visit to Jerusalem	Ac 9:26 Ga 1:18.
A.D. 42–44	First Residence at Antioch	Ac 11:25–30.
A.D. 44	Second Visit to Jerusalem	Ac 11:30 12:25.
A.D. 45–47	FIRST MISSIONARY JOURNEY	Ac 13:2 14:26.
A.D. 47–51	Second Residence at Antioch	Ac 14:28.
	Third Visit to Jerusalem	Ac 15:2–30 Ga 2:1–10.
A.D. 51,53, or 54	SECOND MISSIONARY JOURNEY	Ac 15:36,40 18:22.
A.D. 53 or 54	Fourth Visit to Jerusalem	Ac 18:21,22.
	Third Residence at Antioch	Ac 18:22,23.
A.D. 54–58	THIRD MISSIONARY JOURNEY	Ac 16:23 21:15.
A.D. 58	Fifth Visit to Jerusalem	

The principal events connected with the apostle Paul's life

A.D. 60 (Autumn)	Arrest and Imprisonment at Caesarea	Ac 21:15 23:35.
A.D. 61 (Spring)	Voyage to and Arrival in Rome	Ac 27:1 28:16.
A.D. 63	Release from Imprisonment	
	At Crete, Colosse, Macedonia, Corinth,	
	Nicopolis, Dalmatia, Troas	
	First and Second Timothy and Titus	Ac 28:30.
A.D. 63–65, or 66, or possibly as late as A.D. 66–68	Martyrdom at Rome	

ROMANS

John Wesley

Introduction

Many of the writings of the New Testament are written in the form of letters. Such are not only those of St. Paul, James, Peter, Jude, but also both the treatises of St. Luke, and all the writings of St. John. Nay, we have seven epistles herein which the Lord Jesus himself sent by the hand of John to the seven churches; yea, the whole Revelation is no other than an epistle from Him.

Concerning the epistles of St. Paul, we may observe, he writes in a very different manner to those churches which he had planted himself, and to those who had not seen his face in the flesh. In his letters to the former, a loving or sharp familiarity appears, as their behaviour was more or less suitable to the gospel. To the latter, he proposes the pure, unmixed gospel, in a more general and abstract manner.

Time of writing

As to the time wherein he wrote his epistles, it is probable he wrote about the year of Christ, according to the common reckoning,

A.D. DATE	WRITTEN FROM	NAME OF LETTER
48	Corinth	The Epistle to the Thessalonians.
49	From Phrygia	To the Galatians.
52	From Ephesus	The First to the Corinthians.
	From Troas	The First Epistle to Timothy.
	From Macedonia	The Second to the Corinthians.
		To Titus.
	From Corinth	To the Romans.
57	From Rome	To the Philippians.
		To Philemon.
		To the Ephesians.
		To the Colossians.
53	From Italy	To the Hebrews.
66	From Rome	The Second to Timothy.

As to the general epistles, it seems, St. James wrote a little before his death, which was A.D. 63. St. Peter, who was martyred in the year 67, wrote his latter epistle a little before his death, and not long after his former. St. Jude wrote after him, when the mystery of iniquity was gaining ground swiftly. St. John is believed to have wrote all his epistles a little before his departure. The Revelation he wrote A.D. 96. That St. Paul wrote this epistle from Corinth we may learn from his commending to the Romans Phebe, a servant of the church of Cenchrea, Rom 16:1, a port of Corinth; and from his mentioning the salutations of Caius and Erastus, Rom 16:23, who were both Corinthians. Those to whom he wrote seem to have been chiefly foreigners, both Jews and gentiles, whom business drew from other provinces; as appears, both by his writing in Greek, and by his salutations of several former acquaintance.

Intention

His chief design herein is to show:

1. That neither the gentiles by the law of nature, nor the Jews by the law of Moses, could obtain justification before God; and that therefore it was necessary for both to seek it from the free mercy of God by faith.

2. That God has an absolute right to show mercy on what terms he pleases, and to withhold it from those who will not accept it on his own terms.

To express the design and contents of this epistle a little more at large: The apostle labours throughout to fix in those to whom he writes a deep sense of the excellency of the gospel, and to engage them to act suitably to it. For this purpose, after a general salutation, Rom 1:1–7, and profession of his affection for them, Rom 1:8–15, he declares he shall not be ashamed openly to maintain the gospel at Rome, seeing it is the powerful instrument of salvation, both to Jews and gentiles, by means of faith, Rom 1:16,17. And, in order to demonstrate this, he shows:

1. That the world greatly needed such a dispensation, the gentiles being in a most abandoned state, Rom 1:18–32, and the Jews, though condemning others, being themselves no better, Rom 2:1–29; as, not withstanding some cavils, which he obviates, Rom 3:1–8, their own scriptures testify, Rom 3:9–19. So that all were under a necessity of seeking justification by this method, Rom 3:20–31.

2. That Abraham and David themselves sought justification by faith, and not by works, Rom 4:1–25.

3. That all who believe are brought into so happy a state, as turns the greatest afflictions into a matter of joy, Rom 5:1–11.

4. That the evils brought on mankind by Adam are abundantly recompensed to all that believe in Christ, Rom 5:12–21.

5. That, far from dissolving the obligations to practical holiness, the gospel increases them by peculiar obligations, Rom 6:1–23.

In order to convince them of these things the more deeply, and to remove their fondness for the Mosaic law, now they were married to Christ by faith in him, Rom 7:1–6, he shows how unable the motives of the law were to produce that holiness which believers obtain by a living faith in the gospel, Rom 7:7–25, 8:1,2, and then gives a more particular view of those things which rendered the gospel effectual to this great end, Rom 8:3–39.

That even the gentiles, if they believed, should have a share in these blessings, and that the Jews, if they believed not, should be excluded from them, being a point of great importance, the apostle bestows the ninth, tenth, and eleventh chapters in settling it. He begins the ninth chapter by expressing his tender love and high esteem for the Jewish nation, Rom 9:1–5, and then shows:

1. That God's rejecting great part of the seed of Abraham, yea, and of Isaac too, was undeniable fact, Rom 9:6–13.
2. That God had not chosen them to such peculiar privileges for any kind of goodness either in them or their fathers, Rom 9:14–24.
3. That his accepting the gentiles, and rejecting many of the Jews, had been foretold both by Hosea and Isaiah, Rom 9:25–33.
4. That God had offered salvation to Jews and gentiles on the same terms, though the Jews had rejected it, Rom 10:1–21.
5. That though the rejection of Israel for their obstinacy was general, yet it was not total; there being still a remnant among them who did embrace the gospel, Rom 11:1–10.
6. That the rejection of the rest was not final, but in the end all Israel should be saved, Rom 11:11–31.
7. That, meantime, even their obstinacy and rejection served to display the unsearchable wisdom and love of God, Rom 11:32–36.

The rest of the epistle contains practical instructions and exhortations. He particularly urges:

1. An entire consecration of themselves to God, and a care to glorify Him by a faithful improvement of their several talents, Rom 7:1–11.
2. Devotion, patience, hospitality, mutual sympathy, humility, peace, and meekness, Rom 7:12–21.
3. Obedience to magistrates, justice in all its branches, love the fulfilling of the law, and universal holiness, Rom 8:1–14.
4. Mutual candour between those who differed in judgment, touching the observance of the Mosaic law, Rom 14:1–23, 15:1–17; in enforcing which he is led to mention the extent of his own labours, and his purpose of visiting the Romans; in the mean time recommending himself to their prayers, Rom 15:18–33.
5. After many salutations, Rom 16:1–16, and a caution against those who caused divisions, he concludes with a suitable blessing and doxology, Rom 16:17–27.

Contents

Chapter 1

1. Paul, a servant of Jesus Christ – To this introduction the conclusion answers, Romans 15:15. **Called to be an apostle** – And made an apostle by that calling. While God calls, he makes what he calls. As the Judaizing teachers disputed his claim to the apostolical office, it is with great propriety that he asserts it in the very entrance of an epistle wherein their principles are entirely overthrown. And various other proper and important thoughts are suggested in this short introduction; particularly the prophecies concerning the gospel, the descent of Jesus from David, the great doctrines of his Godhead and resurrection, the sending the gospel to the gentiles, the privileges of Christians, and the obedience and holiness to which they were obliged in virtue of their profession. **Separated** – By God, not only from the bulk of other men, from other Jews, from other disciples, but even from other Christian teachers, to be a peculiar instrument of God in spreading the gospel.

2. Which he promised before – Of old time,

frequently, solemnly. And the promise and accomplishment confirm each other. De 18:18; Isa 9:6,7; 53:1; 61:1; Jer 23:5.

3. Who was of the seed of David according to the flesh – That is, with regard to his human nature. Both the natures of our Saviour are here mentioned; but the human is mentioned first, because the divine was not manifested in its full evidence till after his resurrection.

4. But powerfully declared to be the Son of God, according to the Spirit of Holiness – That is, according to his divine nature. By the resurrection from the dead – For this is both the fountain and the object of our faith; and the preaching of the apostles was the consequence of Christ's resurrection.

5. By whom we have received – I and the other apostles. Grace and apostleship – The favour to be an apostle, and qualifications for it. For obedience to the faith in all nations – That is, that all nations may embrace the faith of Christ. For his name – For his sake; out of regard to him.

6. Among whom – The nations brought to the obedience of faith. Are ye also – But St. Paul gives them no preeminence above others.

7. To all that are in Rome – Most of these were heathens by birth, Ro 1:13, though with Jews mixed among them. They were scattered up and down in that large city, and not yet reduced into the form of a church. Only some had begun to meet in the house of Aquila and Priscilla. Beloved of God – And from his free love, not from any merit of yours, called by his word and his Spirit to believe in him, and now through faith holy as he is holy. Grace – The peculiar favour of God. And peace – All manner of blessings, temporal, spiritual, and eternal. This is both a Christian salutation and an apostolic benediction. From God our Father, and the Lord Jesus Christ – This is the usual way wherein the apostles speak, 'God the Father,' 'God our Father.' Nor do they often, in speaking of him, use the word Lord, as it implies the proper name of God, Jehovah. In the Old Testament, indeed, the holy men generally said, 'The Lord our God;' for they were then, as it were, servants; whereas now they are sons: and sons so well know their father, that they need not frequently mention his proper name. It is one and the same peace, and one and the same grace, which is from God and from Jesus Christ. Our trust and prayer fix on God, as he is the Father of Christ; and on Christ, as he presents us to the Father.

8. I thank – In the very entrance of this one epistle are the traces of all spiritual affections; but of thankfulness above all, with the expression of which almost all St. Paul's epistles begin. He here particularly thanks God, that what otherwise himself should have done, was done at

Rome already. My God – This very word expresses faith, hope, love, and consequently all true religion. Through Jesus Christ – The gifts of God all pass through Christ to us; and all our petitions and thanksgivings pass through Christ to God. That your faith is spoken of – In this kind of congratulations St. Paul describes either the whole of Christianity, as Col 1:3; or some part of it, as 1Cor 1:5. Accordingly here he mentions the faith of the Romans, suitably to his design, Rom 1:12,17. Through the whole world – This joyful news spreading everywhere, that there were Christians also in the imperial city. And the goodness and wisdom of God established faith in the chief cities; in Jerusalem and Rome particularly; that from thence it might be diffused to all nations.

9. God, whom I serve – As an apostle. In my spirit – Not only with my body, but with my inmost soul. In the gospel – By preaching it.

10. Always – In all my solemn addresses to God. If by any means now at length – This accumulation of particles declares the strength of his desire.

11. That I may impart to you – Face to face, by laying on of hands, prayer, preaching the gospel, private conversation. Some spiritual gift – With such gifts the Corinthians, who had enjoyed the presence of St. Paul, abounded, 1Cor 1:7; 12:1; 14:1. So did the Galatians likewise, Gal 3:5; and, indeed, all those churches which had had the presence of any of the apostles had peculiar advantages in this kind, from the laying on of their hands, Acts 19:6; 8:17; 2Tim 1:6. But as yet the Romans were greatly inferior to them in this respect; for which reason the apostle, in the twelfth chapter also, says little, if any thing, of their spiritual gifts. He therefore desires to impart some, that they might be established; for by these was the testimony of Christ confirmed among them. That St. Peter had no more been at Rome than St. Paul, at the time when this epistle was wrote, appears from the general tenor thereof, and from this place in particular: for, otherwise, what St. Paul wishes to impart to the Romans would have been imparted already by St. Peter.

12. That is, I long to be comforted by the mutual faith both of you and me – He not only associates the Romans with, but even prefers them before, himself. How different is this style of the apostle from that of the modern court of Rome!

13. Brethren – A frequent, holy, simple, sweet, and yet grand, appellation. The apostles but rarely address persons by their names; 'O ye Corinthians,' 'O Timotheus.' St. Paul generally uses this appellation, 'Brethren;' sometimes in exhortation, 'My beloved,' or, 'My beloved brethren;' St. James, 'Brethren,' 'My brethren,' 'My beloved brethren;' St. Peter and Jude always,

'Beloved;' St. John frequently, 'Beloved;' once, 'Brethren;' oftener than once, 'My little children.' **Though I have been hindered hitherto** – Either by: business, see Rom 15:22; or persecution, 1Thes 2:2; or the Spirit, Acts 16:7. **That I might have some fruit** – Of my ministerial labours. Even as I have already had from the many churches I have planted and watered among the other gentiles.

14. **To the Greeks and the barbarians** – He includes the Romans under the Greeks; so that this division comprises all nations. **Both to the wise, and the unwise** – For there were unwise even among the Greeks, and wise even among the barbarians. **I am a debtor to all** – I am bound by my divine mission to preach the gospel to them.

16. **For I am not ashamed of the gospel** – To the world, indeed, it is folly and weakness, 1Cor 1:18; therefore, in the judgment of the world, he ought to be ashamed of it; especially at Rome, the head and theatre of the world. But Paul is not ashamed, knowing it is **the power of God unto salvation to every one that believeth** – The great and gloriously powerful means of saving all who accept salvation in God's own way. As St. Paul comprises the sum of the gospel in this epistle, so he does the sum of the epistle in this and the following verse. Both to the **Jew, and to the gentile (Greek)** – There is a noble frankness, as well as a comprehensive sense, in these words, by which he, on the one hand, shows the Jews their absolute need of the gospel; and, on the other, tells the politest and greatest nation in the world both that their salvation depended on receiving it, and that the first offers of it were in every place to be made to the despised Jews.

17. **The righteousness of God** – This expression sometimes means God's eternal, essential righteousness, which includes both justice and mercy, and is eminently shown in condemning sin, and yet justifying the sinner. Sometimes it means that righteousness by which a man, through the gift of God, is made and is righteous; and that, both by receiving Christ through faith, and by a conformity to the essential righteousness of God. St. Paul, when treating of justification, means hereby the righteousness of faith; therefore called the righteousness of God, because God found out and prepared, reveals and gives, approves and crowns it. In this verse the expression means, the whole benefit of God through Christ for the salvation of a sinner. **Is revealed** – Mention is made here, and Rom 1:18, of a twofold revelation, – of wrath and of righteousness: the former, little known to nature, is revealed by the law; the latter, wholly unknown to nature, by the gospel. That goes before, and prepares the way; this follows. Each, the apostle says, is revealed at the present time, in opposition to the times of ignorance. **From faith to**

faith – By a gradual series of still clearer and clearer promises. **As it is written** – St. Paul had just laid down three propositions:

1. Righteousness is by faith, Rom 1:17:
2. Salvation is by righteousness, Rom 1:16:
3. Both to the Jews and to the gentiles, Rom 1:16.

Now all these are confirmed by that single sentence, **The just shall live by faith** – Which was primarily spoken of those who preserved their lives, when the Chaldeans besieged Jerusalem, by believing the declarations of God, and acting according to them. Here it means, He shall obtain the favour of God, and continue therein by believing. Hab 2:4.

18. **For** – There is no other way of obtaining life and salvation. Having laid down his proposition, the apostle now enters upon the proof of it. His first argument is, The law condemns all men, as being under sin. None therefore is justified by the works of the law. This is treated of Rom 3:20. And hence he infers, Therefore justification is by faith. **The wrath of God is revealed** – Not only by frequent and signal interpositions of divine providence, but likewise in the sacred oracles, and by us, his messengers. **From heaven** – This speaks the majesty of Him whose wrath is revealed, his all-seeing eye, and the extent of his wrath: whatever is under heaven is under the effects of his wrath, believers in Christ excepted. **Against all ungodliness and unrighteousness** – These two are treated of, Rom 1:23. **Of men** – He is speaking here of the gentiles, and chiefly the wisest of them. **Who detain the truth** – For it struggles against their wickedness. **In unrighteousness** – The word here includes ungodliness also.

19. **For what is to be known of God** – Those great principles which are indispensably necessary to be known. **Is manifest in them; for God hath showed it to them** – By the light which enlightens every man that cometh into the world.

20. **For those things of him which are invisible, are seen** – By the eye of the mind. **Being understood** – They are seen by them, and them only, who use their understanding.

21. **Because, knowing God** – For the wiser heathens did know that there was one supreme God; yet from low and base considerations they conformed to the idolatry of the vulgar. **They did not glorify him as God, neither were thankful** – They neither thanked him for his benefits, nor glorified him for his divine perfection. **But became vain** – Like the idols they worshipped. **In their reasonings** – Various, uncertain, foolish. What a terrible instance have we of this in the writings of Lucretius! What vain reasonings, and how dark a heart, amidst so pompous professions of wisdom!

23. **And changed** – With the utmost folly. Here are three degrees of ungodliness and of

punishment: the first is described, Rom 1:21–24; the second, Rom 1:25–27; the third, in Rom 1:28, and following verses. The punishment in each case is expressed by God gave them up. If a man will not worship God as God, he is so left to himself that he throws away his very manhood. **Reptiles** – Or creeping things; as beetles, and various kinds of serpents.

24. Wherefore – One punishment of sin is from the very nature of it, as Rom 1:27; another, as here, is from vindictive justice. **Uncleanness** – Ungodliness and uncleanness are frequently joined, 1Thes 4:5 as are the knowledge of God and purity. **God gave them up** – By withdrawing his restraining grace.

25. Who changed the truth – The true worship of God. **Into a lie** – False, abominable idolatries. **And worshipped** – Inwardly. **And served** – Outwardly.

26. Therefore God gave them up to vile affections – To which the heathen Romans were then abandoned to the last degree; and none more than the emperors themselves.

27. Receiving the just recompense of their error – Their idolatry being punished with that unnatural lust, which was as horrible a dishonour to the body, as their idolatry was to God.

28. God gave them up to an undiscerning mind – Treated of, Rom 1:32. **To do things not expedient** – Even the vilest abominations, treated of verses Rom 1:29–31.

29. Filled with all injustice – This stands in the first place; unmercifulness, in the last. **Fornication** – Includes here every species of uncleanness. **Maliciousness** – The Greek word properly implies a temper which delights in hurting another, even without any advantage to itself.

30. Whisperers – Such as secretly defame others. **Backbiters** – Such as speak against others behind their back. **Haters of God** – That is, rebels against him, deniers of his providence, or accusers of his justice in their adversities; yea, having an inward heart-enmity to his justice and holiness. **Inventors of evil things** – Of new pleasures, new ways of gain, new arts of hurting, particularly in war.

31. Covenant-breakers – It is well known, the Romans, as a nation, from the very beginning of their commonwealth, never made any scruple of vacating altogether the most solemn engagement, if they did not like it, though made by their supreme magistrate, in the name of the whole people. They only gave up the general who had made it, and then supposed themselves to be at full liberty. **Without natural affection** – The custom of exposing their own new–born children to perish by cold, hunger, or wild beasts, which so generally prevailed in the heathen world, particularly among the Greeks and Romans, was an amazing instance of this; as is

also that of killing their aged and helpless parents, now common among the American heathens.

32. Not only do the same, but have pleasure in those that practise them – This is the highest degree of wickedness. A man may be hurried by his passions to do the thing he hates; but he that has pleasure in those that do evil, loves wickedness for wickedness' sake. And hereby he encourages them in sin, and heaps the guilt of others upon his own head.

Chapter 2

1. Therefore – The apostle now makes a transition from the gentiles to the Jews, till, at Rom 2:6, he comprises both. **Thou art inexcusable** – Seeing knowledge without practice only increases guilt. **O man** – Having before spoken of the gentile in the third person, he addresses the Jew in the second person. But he calls him by a common appellation, as not acknowledging him to be a Jew. See verses Rom 2:17,28. **Whosoever thou art that judgest** – Censurest, condemnest. **For in that thou judgest another** – The heathen. **Thou condemnest thyself; for thou doest the same things** – In effect; in many instances.

2. For we know – Without thy teaching – that the judgment of God – Not thine, who exceptest thyself from its sentence. **Is according to truth** – Is just, making no exception, Rom 2:5,6,11; and reaches the heart as well as the life, Rom 2:16.

3. That thou shalt escape – Rather than the gentile.

4. Or despisest thou – Dost thou go farther still, – from hoping to escape his wrath, to the abuse of his love?. **The riches** – The abundance. **Of his goodness, forbearance, and longsuffering** – Seeing thou both hast sinned, dost sin, and wilt sin. All these are afterwards comprised in the single word goodness. **Leadeth thee** – That is, is designed of God to lead or encourage thee to it.

5. Treasurest up wrath – Although thou thinkest thou art treasuring up all good things. O what a treasure may a man lay up either way, in this short day of life! **To thyself** – Not to him whom thou judgest. In the day of wrath, and revelation, and **righteous judgment of God** – Just opposite to 'the goodness and forbearance and longsuffering' of God. When God shall be revealed, then shall also be 'revealed' the secrets of men's hearts, Rom 2:16. Forbearance and revelation respect God, and are opposed to each other; longsuffering and righteous judgment respect the sinner; goodness and wrath are words of a more general import.

6. Prov 24:12.

7. To them that seek for glory – For pure love does not exclude faith, hope, desire, 1Cor 15:58.

8. **But to them that are contentious** – Like thee, O Jew, who thus fightest against God. The character of a false Jew is disobedience, stubbornness, impatience. **Indignation and wrath, tribulation and anguish** – Alluding to Psalm 78:49: 'He cast upon them,' the Egyptians. 'the fierceness of his anger, wrath, and indignation, and trouble;' and finely intimating, that the Jews would in the day of vengeance be more severely punished than even the Egyptians were when God made their plagues so wonderful.

9. **Of the Jew first** – Here we have the first express mention of the Jews in this chapter. And it is introduced with great propriety. Their having been trained up in the true religion, and having had Christ and his apostles first sent to them, will place them in the foremost rank of the criminals that obey not the truth.

10. **But glory** – Just opposite to 'wrath,' from the divine approbation. **Honour** – Opposite to 'indignation,' by the divine appointment; and peace now and for ever, opposed to tribulation and anguish.

11. **For there is no respect of persons with God** – He will reward every one according to his works. But this is well consistent with his distributing advantages and opportunities of improvement, according to his own good pleasure.

12. **For as many as have sinned** – He speaks as of the time past, for all time will be past at the day of judgment. **Without the law** – Without having any written law. **Shall also perish without the law** – Without regard had to any outward law; being condemned by the law written in their hearts. The word also shows the agreement of the manner of sinning, with the manner of suffering. **Perish** – He could not so properly say, Shall be judged without the law.

13. **For not the hearers of the law are, even now, just before God, but the doers of the law shall be justified** – Finally acquitted and rewarded a most sure and important truth, which respects the gentiles also, though principally the Jews. St. Paul speaks of the former, Rom 2:14; of the latter, Rom 2:17. Here is therefore no parenthesis; for the sixteenth verse also depends on the fifteenth, not on the twelfth. Rom 2:16,15,12.

14. **For when the gentiles** – That is, any of them. St. Paul, having refuted the perverse judgment of the Jews concerning the heathens, proceeds to show the just judgment of God against them. He now speaks directly of the heathens, in order to convince the heathens. Yet the concession he makes to these serves more strongly to convince the Jews. **Do by nature** – That is, without an outward rule; though this also, strictly speaking, is by preventing grace. **The things contained in the law** – The ten commandments being only the substance of the law of nature.

These, not having the written law, are a law unto themselves – That is, what the law is to the Jews, they are, by the grace of God, to themselves; namely, a rule of life.

15. **Who show** – To themselves, to other men, and, in a sense, to God himself. **The work of the law** – The substance, though not the letter, of it. **Written on their hearts** – By the same hand which wrote the commandments on the tables of stone. **Their conscience** – There is none of all its faculties which the soul has less in its power than this. **Bearing witness** – In a trial there are the plaintiff, the defendant, and the witnesses. Conscience and sin itself are witnesses against the heathens. Their thoughts sometimes excuse, sometimes condemn, them. **Among themselves** – Alternately, like plaintiff and defendant. **Accusing or even defending them** – The very manner of speaking shows that they have far more room to accuse than to defend.

16. **In the day** – That is, who show this in the day. Everything will then be shown to be what it really is. In that day will appear the law written in their hearts as it often does in the present life. **When God shall judge the secrets of men** – On secret circumstances depends the real quality of actions, frequently unknown to the actors themselves, Rom 2:29. Men generally form their judgments, even of themselves merely from what is apparent. **According to my gospel** – According to the tenor of that gospel which is committed to my care. Hence it appears that the gospel also is a law.

17. **But if thou art called a Jew** – This highest point of Jewish glorying, after a farther description of it interposed, Rom 2:17–20, and refuted, Rom 2:21–24, is itself refuted, Rom 2:25. The description consists of twice five articles; of which the former five, Rom 2:17,18, show what he boasts of in himself; the other five, Rom 2:19,20, what he glories in with respect to others. The first particular of the former five answers to the first of the latter; the second, to the second, and so on. **And restest in the law** – Dependest on it, though it can only condemn thee. **And gloriest in God** – As thy God; and that, too, to the exclusion of others.

19. **Blind, in darkness, ignorant, babes** – These were the titles which the Jews generally gave the gentiles.

20. **Having the form of knowledge and truth** – That is, the most accurate knowledge of the truth.

21. **Thou dost not teach thyself** – He does not teach himself who does not practise what he teaches. **Dost thou steal, commit adultery, commit sacrilege** – Sin grievously against thy neighbour, thyself, God. St. Paul had shown the gentiles, first their sins against God, then against themselves, then against their neighbours. He now inverts the order: for sins against God are

the most glaring in an heathen, but not in a Jew. **Thou that abhorrest idols** – Which all the Jews did, from the time of the Babylonish captivity. **Thou committest sacrilege** – Doest what is worse, robbing Him 'who is God over all' of the glory which is due to him. None of these charges were rashly advanced against the Jews of that age; for, as their own historian relates, some even of the priests lived by rapine, and others in gross uncleanness. And as for sacrilegiously robbing God and his altar, it had been complained of ever since Malachi; so that the instances are given with great propriety and judgment.

24. Isaiah 52:5.

25. **Circumcision indeed profiteth** – He does not say, justifies. How far it profited is shown in the third and fourth chapters. **Thy circumcision is become uncircumcision** – is so already in effect. Thou wilt have no more benefit by it than if thou hadst never received it. The very same observation holds with regard to baptism.

26. **If the uncircumcision** – That is, a person uncircumcised. **Keep the law** – Walk agreeably to it. **Shall not his uncircumcision be counted for circumcision** – In the sight of God?

27. **Yea, the uncircumcision that is by nature** – Those who are, literally speaking, uncircumcised. **Fulfilling the law** – As to the substance of it. **Shall judge thee** – Shall condemn thee in that day. **Who by the letter and circumcision** – Who having the bare, literal, external circumcision, transgressest the law.

28. **For he is not a Jew** – In the most important sense, that is, one of God's beloved people. Who is one in outward show only; neither is that the true, acceptable circumcision, which is apparent in the flesh.

29. **But he is a Jew** – That is, one of God's people. **Who is one inwardly** – In the secret recesses of his soul. **And the acceptable circumcision is that of the heart** – Referring to Deut 30:6; the putting away all inward impurity. This is seated in the spirit, the inmost soul, renewed by the Spirit of God. **And not in the letter** – Not in the external ceremony. **Whose praise is not from men, but from God** – The only searcher of the heart.

Chapter 3

1. **What then**, may some say, is the advantage of the Jew, or of the circumcision – That is, those that are circumcised, above the gentiles?

2. **Chiefly in that they were intrusted with the oracles of God** – The scriptures, in which are so great and precious promises. Other prerogatives will follow, Romans 9:4–5. St. Paul here singles out this by which, after removing

the objection, he will convict them so much the more.

3. **Shall their unbelief disannul the faithfulness of God** – Will he not still make good his promises to them that do believe?

4. Psalm 2:4.

5. **But,** it may be farther objected, **if our unrighteousness be subservient to God's glory, is it not unjust in him to punish us for it? I speak as a man** – As human weakness would be apt to speak.

6. **God forbid** – By no means. If it were unjust in God to punish that unrighteousness which is subservient to his own glory, **how should God judge the world** – Since all the unrighteousness in the world will then commend the righteousness of God.

7. **But,** may the objector reply, **if the truth of God hath abounded** – Has been more abundantly shown. **Through my lie** – If my lie, that is, practice contrary to truth, conduces to the glory of God, by making his truth shine with superior advantage. **Why am I still judged as a sinner** – Can this be said to be any sin at all? Ought I not to do what would otherwise be evil, that so much 'good may come?' To this the apostle does not deign to give a direct answer, but cuts the objector short with a severe reproof.

8. **Whose condemnation is just** – The condemnation of all who either speak or act in this manner. So the apostle absolutely denies the lawfulness of 'doing evil,' any evil, 'that good may come.'

9. **What then** – Here he resumes what he said, verse 1. Rom 3:1. **Under sin** – Under the guilt and power of it: the Jews, by transgressing the written law; the gentiles, by transgressing the law of nature.

10. **As it is written** – That all men are under sin appears from the vices which have raged in all ages. St. Paul therefore rightly cites David and Isaiah, though they spoke primarily of their own age, and expressed what manner of men God sees, when he 'looks down from heaven;' not what he makes them by his grace. **There is none righteous** – This is the general proposition. The particulars follow: their dispositions and designs, Rom 3:11,12; their discourse, Rom 3:13,14; their actions, Rom 3:16–18. Psalm 14:1.

11. **There is none that understandeth** – The things of God.

12. **They have all turned aside** – From the good way. **They are become unprofitable** – Helpless, impotent, unable to profit either themselves or others.

13. **Their throat** – Is noisome and dangerous as an open sepulchre. Observe the progress of evil discourse, proceeding out of the heart, through the throat, tongue, lips, till the whole mouth is filled therewith. **The poison of asps** –

Infectious, deadly backbiting, tale-bearing, evil-speaking, is under their lips. An asp is a venomous kind of serpent. Psalm 5:9; Psalm 140:3.

14. Cursing – Against God. **Bitterness** – Against their neighbour. Psalm 10:7.

15. Isaiah 59:7,8.

17. Of peace – Which can only spring from righteousness.

18. The fear of God is not before their eyes – Much less is the love of God in their heart. Psalm 36:1.

19. Whatsoever the law – The Old Testament. **Saith, it saith to them that are under the law** – That is, to those who own its authority; to the Jews, and not the gentiles. St. Paul quoted no scripture against them, but pleaded with them only from the light of nature. **Every mouth** – Full of bitterness, Rom 3:14, and yet of boasting, Rom 3:27. **May become guilty** – May be fully convicted, and apparently liable to most just condemnation. These things were written of old, and were quoted by St. Paul, not to make men criminal, but to prove them so.

20. No flesh shall be justified – None shall be forgiven and accepted of God. **By the works of the law** – On this ground, that he hath kept the law. St. Paul means chiefly the moral part of it, Rom 3:9,19 Rom 2:21,26; &c. which alone is not abolished, Rom 3:31. And it is not without reason, that he so often mentions the works of the law, whether ceremonial or moral; for it was on these only the Jews relied, being wholly ignorant of those that spring from faith. **For by the law is only the knowledge of sin** – But no deliverance either from the guilt or power of it.

21. But now the righteousness of God – That is, the manner of becoming righteous which God hath appointed. **Without the law** – Without that previous obedience which the law requires; without reference to the law, or dependence on it. **Is manifested** – In the gospel. **Being attested by the Law itself, and by the Prophets** – By all the promises in the Old Testament.

22. To all – The Jews. **And upon all** – The gentiles **That believe: for there is no difference** – Either as to the need of justification, or the manner of it.

23. For all have sinned – In Adam, and in their own persons; by a sinful nature, sinful tempers, and sinful actions. **And are fallen short of the glory of God** – The supreme end of man; short of his image on earth, and the enjoyment of him in heaven.

24. And are justified – Pardoned and accepted. **Freely** – Without any merit of their own. **By his grace** – Not their own righteousness or works. **Through the redemption** – The price Christ has paid. **Freely by his grace** – One of these expressions might have served to convey the apostle's meaning; but he doubles his

assertion, in order to give us the fullest conviction of the truth, and to impress us with a sense of its peculiar importance. It is not possible to find words that should more absolutely exclude all consideration of our own works and obedience, or more emphatically ascribe the whole of our justification to free, unmerited goodness.

25. Whom God hath set forth – Before angels and men. **A propitiation** – To appease an offended God. But if, as some teach, God never was offended, there was no need of this propitiation. And, if so, Christ died in vain. **To declare his righteousness** – To demonstrate not only his clemency, but his justice; even that vindictive justice whose essential character and principal office is, to punish sin. **By the remission of past sins** – All the sins antecedent to their believing.

26. For a demonstration of his righteousness – Both of his justice and mercy. **That he might be just** – Showing his justice on his own Son. And yet the merciful justifier of every one that believeth in Jesus. **That he might be just** – Might evidence himself to be strictly and inviolably righteous in the administration of his government, even while he is the merciful justifier of the sinner that believeth in Jesus. The attribute of justice must be preserved inviolate; and inviolate it is preserved, if there was a real infliction of punishment on our Saviour. On this plan all the attributes harmonize; every attribute is glorified, and not one superseded no, nor so much as clouded.

27. Where is the boasting then of the Jew against the gentile? It is excluded. By what law? of works? Nay – This would have left room for boasting. **But by the law of faith** – Since this requires all, without distinction, to apply as guilty and helpless sinners, to the free mercy of God in Christ. The law of faith is that divine constitution which makes faith, not works, the condition of acceptance.

28. We conclude then that a man is justified by faith – And even by this, not as it is a work, but as it receives Christ; and, consequently, has something essentially different from all our works whatsoever.

29. Surely of the gentiles also – As both nature and the scriptures show.

30. Seeing it is one God who – Shows mercy to both, and by the very same means.

31. We establish the law – Both the authority, purity, and the end of it; by defending that which the law attests; by pointing out Christ, the end of it; and by showing how it may be fulfilled in its purity.

Chapter 4

Having proved it by argument, he now proves by example, and such example as must have greater weight with the Jews than any other.

1. That justification is by faith:

2. That it is free for the gentiles.

1. That our father Abraham hath found – Acceptance with God. **According to the flesh** – That is, by works.

2. The meaning is, If Abraham had been justified by works, he would have had room to glory. But he had not room to glory. Therefore he was not justified by works.

3. Abraham believed God – That promise of God concerning the numerousness of his seed, Gen 15:5,7; but especially the promise concerning Christ, Gen 12:3, through whom all nations should be blessed. **And it was imputed to him for righteousness** – God accepted him as if he had been altogether righteous. Gen 15:6.

4. Now to him that worketh – All that the law requires, the reward is no favour, but an absolute debt. These two examples are selected and applied with the utmost judgment and propriety. Abraham was the most illustrious pattern of piety among the Jewish patriarchs. David was the most eminent of their kings. If then neither of these was justified by his own obedience, if they both obtained acceptance with God, not as upright beings who might claim it, but as sinful creatures who must implore it, the consequence is glaring. It is such as must strike every attentive understanding, and must affect every individual person.

5. But to him that worketh not – It being impossible he should without faith. **But believeth, his faith is imputed to him for righteousness** – Therefore God's affirming of Abraham, that faith was imputed to him for righteousness, plainly shows that he worked not; or, in other words, that he was not justified by works, but by faith only. Hence we see plainly how groundless that opinion is, that holiness or sanctification is previous to our justification. For the sinner, being first convinced of his sin and danger by the Spirit of God, stands trembling before the awful tribunal of divine justice; and has nothing to plead, but his own guilt, and the merits of a Mediator. Christ here interposes; justice is satisfied; the sin is remitted, and pardon is applied to the soul, by a divine faith wrought by the Holy Ghost, who then begins the great work of inward sanctification. Thus God justifies the ungodly, and yet remains just, and true to all his attributes! But let none hence presume to 'continue in sin;' for to the impenitent, God 'is a consuming fire.' **On him that justifieth the ungodly** – If a man could possibly be made holy before he was justified, it would entirely set his justification aside; seeing he could not, in the very nature of the thing, be justified if he were not, at that very time, ungodly.

6. So David also – David is fitly introduced after Abraham, because be also received and delivered down the promise. **Affirmeth** – A man is justified by faith alone, and not by works. **Without works** – That is, without regard to any former good works supposed to have been done by him.

7. Happy are they whose sins are covered – With the veil of divine mercy. If there be indeed such a thing as happiness on earth, it is the portion of that man whose iniquities are forgiven, and who enjoys the manifestation of that pardon. Well may he endure all the afflictions of life with cheerfulness, and look upon death with comfort. O let us not contend against it, but earnestly pray that this happiness may be ours! Psalm 32:1,2.

9. This happiness – Mentioned by Abraham and David. **On the circumcision** – Those that are circumcised only. **Faith was imputed to Abraham for righteousness** – This is fully consistent with our being justified, that is, pardoned and accepted by God upon our believing, for the sake of what Christ hath done and suffered. For though this, and this alone, be the meritorious cause of our acceptance with God, yet faith may be said to be 'imputed to us for righteousness,' as it is the sole condition of our acceptance. We may observe here, forgiveness, not imputing sin, and imputing righteousness, are all one.

10. Not in circumcision – Not after he was circumcised; for he was justified before Ishmael was born, Gen 15:1–21; but he was not circumcised till Ishmael was thirteen years old, Gen 17:25.

11. And – After he was justified. **He received the sign of circumcision** – Circumcision, which was a sign or token of his being in covenant with God. **A seal** – An assurance on God's part, that he accounted him righteous, upon his believing, before he was circumcised. **Who believe in uncircumcision** – That is, though they are not circumcised.

12. And the father of the circumcision – Of those who are circumcised, and believe as Abraham did. To those who believe not, Abraham is not a father, neither are they his seed.

13. The promise, that he should be the heir of the world – Is the same as that he should be 'the father of all nations,' namely, of those in all nations who receive the blessing. The whole world was promised to him and them conjointly. Christ is the heir of the world, and of all things; and so are all Abraham's seed, all that believe in him with the faith of Abraham.

14. If they only who are of the law – Who have kept the whole law. **Are heirs, faith is made void** – No blessing being to be obtained by it; and so the promise is of no effect.

15. Because the law – Considered apart from that grace, which though it was in fact mingled with it, yet is no part of the legal dispensation, is so difficult, and we so weak and sinful, that, instead of bringing us a blessing, it only worketh wrath; it becomes to us an occasion of wrath, and exposes us to punishment as transgressors. Where there is no law in force, there can be no transgression of it.

16. Therefore it – The blessing. **Is of faith, that it might be of grace** – That it might appear to flow from the free love of God, and that the promise might be firm, sure, and effectual, to all the spiritual seed of Abraham; not only Jews, but gentiles also, if they follow his faith.

17. Before God – Though before men nothing of this appeared, those nations being then unborn. **As quickening the dead** – The dead are not dead to him and even the things that are not, are before God. **And calling the things that are not** – Summoning them to rise into being, and appear before him. The seed of Abraham did not then exist; yet God said, 'So shall thy seed be.' A man can say to his servant actually existing, Do this; and he doeth it: but God saith to the light, while it does not exist, Go forth; and it goeth. Gen 17:5.

18–21. The Apostle shows the power and excellence of that faith to which he ascribes justification. **Who against hope** – Against all probability, believed and hoped in the promise. The same thing is apprehended both by faith and hope; by faith, as a thing which God has spoken; by hope, as a good thing which God has promised to us. **So shall thy seed be** – Both natural and spiritual, as the stars of heaven for multitude. Gen 15:5.

19. See note ... 'Ro 4:18'
20. See note ... 'Ro 4:18'
21. See note ... 'Ro 4:18'
23. On his account only – To do personal honour to him.

24. But on ours also – To establish us in seeking justification by faith, and not by works; and to afford a full answer to those who say that, 'to be justified by works means only, by Judaism; to be justified by faith means, by embracing Christianity, that is, the system of doctrines so called.' Sure it is that Abraham could not in this sense be justified either by faith or by works; and equally sure that David was justified by works, and not by faith. **Who raised up Jesus from the dead** – As he did in a manner both Abraham and Sarah. **If we believe on him who raised up Jesus** – God the Father therefore is the proper object of justifying faith. It is observable, that St. Paul here, in speaking both of our faith and of the faith of Abraham, puts a part for the whole. And he mentions that part, with regard to Abraham, which would naturally affect the Jews most.

25. Who was delivered – To death. **For our offences** – As an atonement for them. **And raised for our justification** – To empower us to receive that atonement by faith.

Chapter 5

1. Being justified by faith – This is the sum of the preceding chapters. **We have peace with God** – Being enemies to God no longer, Rom 5:10; neither fearing his wrath, Rom 5:9. We have peace, hope, love, and power over sin, the sum of the fifth, sixth, seventh, and eighth chapters. These are the fruits of justifying faith: where these are not, that faith is not.

2. Into this grace – This state of favour.

3. We glory in tribulations also – Which we are so far from esteeming a mark of God's displeasure, that we receive them as tokens of his fatherly love, whereby we are prepared for a more exalted happiness. The Jews objected to the persecuted state of the Christians as inconsistent with the people of the Messiah. It is therefore with great propriety that the apostle so often mentions the blessings arising from this very thing.

4. And **patience** works more **experience** of the sincerity of our grace, and of God's power and faithfulness.

5. Hope shameth us not – That is, gives us the highest glorying. We glory in this our hope, because the **love of God is shed abroad in our hearts** – The divine conviction of God's love to us, and that love to God which is both the earnest and the beginning of heaven. **By the Holy Ghost** – The efficient cause of all these present blessings, and the earnest of those to come.

6. How can we now doubt of God's love? **For when we were without strength** – Either to think, will, or do anything good. **In due time** – Neither too soon nor too late; but in that very point of time which the wisdom of God knew to be more proper than any other. **Christ died for the ungodly** – Not only to set them a pattern, or to procure them power to follow it. It does not appear that this expression, of dying for any one, has any other signification than that of rescuing the life of another by laying down our own.

7. A just man – One who gives to all what is strictly their due. The **good man** – One who is eminently holy; full of love, of compassion, kindness, mildness, of every heavenly and amiable temper. **Perhaps** – one – **would** – **even** – **dare to die** – Every word increases the strangeness of the thing, and declares even this to be something great and unusual.

8. But God recommendeth – A most elegant expression. Those are wont to be recommended to us, who were before either unknown to, or alienated from, us. **While we were sinners** – So far from being good, that we were not even just.

9. By his blood – By his bloodshedding. **We shall be saved from wrath through him** – That is, from all the effects of the wrath of God. But is there then wrath in God? Is not wrath a human passion? And how can this human passion be in God? We may answer this by another question: Is not love a human passion? And how can this human passion be in God? But to answer directly: wrath in man, and so love in man, is a human passion. But wrath in God is not a human passion; nor is love, as it is in God. Therefore the inspired writers ascribe both the one and the other to God only in an analogical sense.

10. If – As sure as; so the word frequently signifies; particularly in this and the eighth chapter. **We shalt be saved** – Sanctified and glorified. **Through his life** – Who 'ever liveth to make intercession for us.'

11. And not only so, but we also glory – The whole sentence, from the third to the eleventh verse, may be taken together thus: We not only 'rejoice in hope of the glory of God,' but also in the midst of tribulations we glory in God himself through our Lord Jesus Christ, by whom we have now received the reconciliation.

12. Therefore – This refers to all the preceding discourse; from which the apostle infers what follows. He does not therefore properly make a digression, but returns to speak again of sin and of righteousness. **As by one man** – Adam; who is mentioned, and not Eve, as being the representative of mankind. **Sin entered into the world** – Actual sin, and its consequence, a sinful nature. **And death** – With all its attendants. It entered into the world when it entered into being; for till then it did not exist. **By sin** – Therefore it could not enter before sin. **Even so** – Namely, by one man. **In that** – So the word is used also, 2Cor 5:4. **All sinned** – In Adam. These words assign the reason why death came upon all men; infants themselves not excepted, in that all sinned.

13. For until the law sin was in the world – All, I say, had sinned, for sin was in the world long before the written law; but, I grant, sin is not so much imputed, nor so severely punished by God, where there is no express law to convince men of it. Yet that all had sinned, even then, appears in that all died.

14. Death reigned – And how vast is his kingdom! Scarce can we find any king who has as many subjects, as are the kings whom he hath conquered. **Even over them that had not sinned after the likeness of Adam's transgression** – Even over infants who had never sinned, as Adam did, in their own persons; and over others who had not, like him, sinned against an express law. **Who is the figure of him that was to come** – Each of them being a public person, and a federal head of mankind. The one, the fountain of sin and death to mankind by his offence; the other, of righteousness and life by his free gift. Thus far the apostle shows the agreement between the first and second Adam: afterward he shows the differences between them. The agreement may be summed up thus: As by one man sin entered into the world, and death by sin; so by one man righteousness entered into the world, and life by righteousness. As death passed upon all men, in that all had sinned; so life passed upon all men, in that all are justified. And as death through the sin of the first Adam reigned even over them who had not sinned after the likeness of Adam's transgression; so through the righteousness of Christ, even those who have not obeyed, after the likeness of his obedience, shall reign in life. We may add, As the sin of Adam, without the sins which we afterwards committed, brought us death; so the righteousness of Christ, without the good works which we afterwards perform, brings us life: although still every good, as well as evil, work will receive its due reward.

15. Yet not – St. Paul now describes the difference between Adam and Christ; and that much more directly and expressly than the agreement between them. Now the fall and the free gift differ

1. In amplitude, Rom 5:15.

2. He from whom sin came, and He from whom the free gift came, termed also 'the gift of righteousness,' differ in power, Rom 5:16.

3. The reason of both is subjoined, Rom 5:17.

4. This premised, the offence and the free gift are compared, with regard to their effect, Rom 5:18, and with regard to their cause, Rom 5:19.

16. The sentence was by one offence to Adam's condemnation – Occasioning the sentence of death to pass upon him, which, by consequence, overwhelmed his posterity. **But the free gift is of many offences unto justification** – Unto the purchasing it for all men, notwithstanding many offences.

17. There is a difference between grace and the gift. Grace is opposed to the offence; the gift, to death, being the gift of life.

18. Justification of life – Is that sentence of God, by which a sinner under sentence of death is adjudged to life.

19. As by the disobedience of one man many (that is, all men) **were constituted sinners** – Being then in the loins of their first parent, the common head and representative of them all. **So by the obedience of one** – By his obedience unto death; by his dying for us. **Many** – All that believe. **Shall be constituted righteous** – Justified, pardoned.

20. The law came in between – The offence and the free gift. **That the offence might abound** – That is, the consequence of the law's coming in was, not the taking away of sin, but the increase of it. **Yet where sin abounded, grace did much more abound** – Not only in the remission of that sin which Adam brought on us, but of all our own; not only in remission of sins, but infusion of holiness; not only in deliverance from death, but admission to everlasting life, a far more noble and excellent life than that which we lost by Adam's fall.

21. That as sin had reigned – so **grace** also **might reign** – Which could not reign before the fall; before man had sinned. **Through righteousness to eternal life by Jesus Christ our Lord** – Here is pointed out the source of all our blessings, the rich and free grace of God. The meritorious cause; not any works of righteousness of man, but the alone merits of our Lord Jesus Christ. The effect or end of all; not only pardon, but life; divine life, leading to glory.

Chapter 6

1. The apostle here sets himself more fully to vindicate his doctrine from the consequence above suggested, Rom 3:7,8. He had then only in strong terms denied and renounced it: here he removes the very foundation thereof.

2. Dead to sin – Freed both from the guilt and from the power of it.

3. As many as have been baptized into Jesus Christ have been baptized into his death – In baptism we, through faith, are ingrafted into Christ; and we draw new spiritual life from this new root, through his Spirit, who fashions us like unto him, and particularly with regard to his death and resurrection.

4. We are buried with him – Alluding to the ancient manner of baptizing by immersion. **That as Christ was raised from the dead by the glory** – Glorious power. **Of the Father,** so we also, by the same power, should rise again; and as he lives a new life in heaven, so we should walk in newness of life. This, says the apostle, our very baptism represents to us.

5. For – Surely these two must go together; so that if we are indeed made conformable to his death, we shall also know the power of his resurrection.

6. Our old man – Coeval with our being, and as old as the fall; our evil nature; a strong and beautiful expression for that entire depravity and corruption which by nature spreads itself over the whole man, leaving no part uninfected. This in a believer is crucified with Christ, mortified, gradually killed, by virtue of our union with him. **That the body of sin** – All evil tempers, words, and actions, which are the 'members' of the 'old man,' Col 3:5, might be destroyed.

7. For he that is dead – With Christ. Is freed from the guilt of past, and from the power of present, sin, as dead men from the commands of their former masters.

8. Dead with Christ – Conformed to his death, by dying to sin.

10. He died to sin – To atone for and abolish it. **He liveth unto God** – A glorious eternal life, such as we shall live also.

12. Let not sin reign even in your mortal body – It must be subject to death, but it need not be subject to sin.

13. Neither present your members to sin – To corrupt nature, a mere tyrant. **But to God** – Your lawful King.

14. Sin shall not have dominion over you – It has neither right nor power. **For ye are not under the law** – A dispensation of terror and bondage, which only shows sin, without enabling you to conquer it. **But under grace** – Under the merciful dispensation of the gospel, which brings complete victory over it to every one who is under the powerful influences of the Spirit of Christ.

17. The form of doctrine into which ye have been delivered – Literally it is, The mould into which ye have been delivered; which, as it contains a beautiful allusion, conveys also a very instructive admonition; intimating that our minds, all pliant and ductile, should be conformed to the gospel precepts, as liquid metal, take the figure of the mould into which they are cast.

18. Being then set free from sin – We may see the apostles method thus far at one view:–

THEME	BIBLE REFERENCE
1. Bondage to sin	Ro 3:9
2. The knowledge of sin by the law; a sense of God's wrath; inward death	Ro 3:20
3. The revelation of the righteousness of God in Christ through the gospel	Ro 3:21
4. The centre of all, faith, embracing that righteousness	Ro 3:22
5. Justification, whereby God forgives all past sin, and freely accepts the sinner	Ro 3:24
6. The gift of the Holy Ghost; a sense of God's love new inward life	Ro 5:5; Ro 6:4 Ro 6:4
7. The free service of righteousness	Ro 6:12

19. I speak after the manner of men – Thus it is necessary that the scripture should let itself down to the language of men. **Because of the weakness of your flesh** – Slowness of understanding flows from the weakness of the flesh, that is, of human nature. **As ye have presented your members servants to uncleanness and iniquity unto iniquity, so now present your members servants of righteousness unto**

holiness – Iniquity is here opposed to righteousness; and unto iniquity is the opposite of unto holiness. Righteousness here is a conformity to the divine will; holiness, to the whole divine nature. Observe, they who are servants of righteousness go on to holiness; but they who are servants to iniquity get no farther. Righteousness is service, because we live according to the will of another; but liberty, because of our inclination to it, and delight in it.

20. When ye were the servants of sin, ye were free from righteousness – In all reason, therefore, ye ought now to be free from unrighteousness; to be as uniform and zealous in serving God as ye were in serving the devil.

21. Those things – He speaks of them as afar off.

23. Death – Temporal, spiritual, and eternal. Is the due wages of sin; **but eternal life is the gift of God** – The difference is remarkable. Evil works merit the reward they receive: good works do not. The former demand wages: the latter accept a free gift.

Chapter 7

1. The apostle continues the comparison between the former and the present state of a believer, and at the same time endeavours to wean the Jewish believers from their fondness for the Mosaic law. **I speak to them that know the law** – To the Jews chiefly here. **As long** – So long, and no longer. **As it liveth** – The law is here spoken of, by a common figure, as a person, to which, as to an husband, life and death are ascribed. But he speaks indifferently of the law being dead to us, or we to it, the sense being the same.

2. She is freed from the law of her husband – From that law which gave him a peculiar property in her.

4. Thus ye also – Are now as free from the Mosaic law as an husband is, when his wife is dead. **By the body of Christ** – Offered up; that is, by the merits of his death, that law expiring with him.

5. When ye were in the flesh – Carnally minded, in a state of nature; before we believed in Christ. **Our sins which were by the law** – Accidentally occasioned, or irritated thereby. **Wrought in our members** – Spread themselves all over the whole man.

6. Being dead to that whereby we were held – To our old husband, the law. **That we might serve in newness of spirit** – In a new, spiritual manner. **And not in the oldness of the letter** – Not in a bare literal, external way, as we did before.

7. What shall we say then – This is a kind of a digression, to the beginning of the next chapter, wherein the apostle, in order to show in the most lively manner the weakness and inefficacy of the law, changes the person and speaks as of himself, concerning the misery of one under the law. This St. Paul frequently does, when he is not speaking of his own person, but only assuming another character, Rom 3:5, 1Cor 10:30, 1Cor 4:6. The character here assumed is that of a man, first ignorant of the law, then under it and sincerely, but ineffectually, striving to serve God. To have spoken this of himself, or any true believer, would have been foreign to the whole scope of his discourse; nay, utterly contrary thereto, as well as to what is expressly asserted, Rom 8:2. **Is the law sin** – Sinful in itself, or a promoter of sin. **I had not known lust** – That is, evil desire. I had not known it to be a sin; nay, perhaps I should not have known that any such desire was in me: it did not appear, till it was stirred up by the prohibition.

8. But sin – My inbred corruption. **Taking occasion by the commandment** – Forbidding, but not subduing it, was only fretted, and wrought in me so much the more all manner of evil desire. **For while I was without the knowledge of the law, sin was dead** – Neither so apparent, nor so active; nor was I under the least apprehensions of any danger from it.

9. And I was once alive without the law – Without the close application of it. I had much life, wisdom, virtue, strength: so I thought. **But when the commandment** – That is, the law, a part put for the whole; but this expression particularly intimates its compulsive force, which restrains, enjoins, urges, forbids, threatens. **Came** – In its spiritual meaning, to my heart, with the power of God. **Sin revived, and I died** – My inbred sin took fire, and all my virtue and strength died away; and I then saw myself to be dead in sin, and liable to death eternal.

10. The commandment which was intended for life – Doubtless it was originally intended by God as a grand means of preserving and increasing spiritual life, and leading to life everlasting.

11. Deceived me – While I expected life by the law, sin came upon me unawares and slew all my hopes.

12. The commandment – That is, every branch of the law. **Is holy, and just, and good** – It springs from, and partakes of, the holy nature of God; it is every way just and right in itself; it is designed wholly for the good of man.

13. Was then that which is good made the cause of evil to me; yea, of death, which is the greatest of evil? Not so. But it was sin, which was made death to me, inasmuch as it wrought death in me even by that which is good – By the good law. **So that sin by the commandment became exceeding sinful** – The consequence of which was, that inbred sin, thus driving furiously in spite of the commandment, became exceeding sinful; the guilt thereof being greatly aggravated.

14. I am carnal – St. Paul, having compared together the past and present state of believers, that 'in the flesh,' Rom 7:5, and that 'in the spirit,' Rom 7:6, in answering two objections, (Is then the law sin? Rom 7:7, and, Is the law death? Rom 7:13,) interweaves the whole process of a man reasoning, groaning, striving, and escaping from the legal to the evangelical state. This he does from Rom 7:7, to the end of this chapter. **Sold under sin** – Totally enslaved; slaves bought with money were absolutely at their master's disposal.

16. It is good – This single word implies all the three that were used before, Rom 7:12, 'holy, just, and good.'

17. It is no more I that can properly be said to do it, but rather sin that dwelleth in me – That makes, as it were, another person, and tyrannizes over me.

18. In my flesh – The flesh here signifies the whole man as he is by nature.

21. I find then a law – An inward constraining power, flowing from the dictate of corrupt nature.

22. For I delight in the law of God – This is more than 'I consent to,' Rom 7:16. The day of liberty draws near. **The inward man** – Called the mind, Rom 7:23,25.

23. But I see another law in my members – Another inward constraining power of evil inclinations and bodily appetites. **Warring against the law of my mind** – The dictate of my mind, which delights in the law of God. **And captivating me** – In spite of all my resistance.

24. Wretched man that I am – The struggle is now come to the height; and the man, finding there is no help in himself, begins almost unawares to pray, **Who shall deliver me?** He then seeks and looks for deliverance, till God in Christ appears to answer his question. The word which we translate deliver, implies force. And indeed without this there can be no deliverance. **The body of this death** – That is, this body of death; this mass of sin, leading to death eternal, and cleaving as close to me as my body to my soul. We may observe, the deliverance is not wrought yet.

25. I thank God through Jesus Christ our Lord – That is, God will deliver me through Christ. But the apostle, as his frequent manner is, beautifully interweaves his assertion with thanksgiving; the hymn of praise answering in a manner to the voice of sorrow, 'Wretched man that I am!' **So then** – He here sums up the whole, and concludes what he began, Rom 7:7. **I myself** – Or rather that I, the person whom I am personating, till this deliverance is wrought. **Serve the law of God with my mind** – My reason and conscience declare for God. **But with** my flesh the law of sin – But my corrupt passions and appetites still rebel. The man is now utterly weary of his bondage, and upon the brink of liberty.

Chapter 8

1. There is therefore now no condemnation – Either for things present or past. Now he comes to deliverance and liberty. The apostle here resumes the thread of his discourse, which was interrupted, Rom 7:7.

2. The law of the Spirit – That is, the gospel. Hath freed me **from the law of sin and death** – That is, the Mosaic dispensation.

3. For what the law – Of Moses. **Could not do, in that it was weak through the flesh** – Incapable of conquering our evil nature. If it could, God needed not to have sent **his own Son in the likeness of sinful flesh** – We with our sinful flesh were devoted to death. But God sending his own Son, in the likeness of that flesh, though pure from sin, condemned that sin which was in our flesh; gave sentence, that sin should be destroyed, and the believer wholly delivered from it.

4. That the righteousness of the law – The holiness it required, described, Rom 8:11. **Might be fulfilled in us, who walk not after the flesh, but after the Spirit** – Who are guided in all our thoughts, words, and actions, not by corrupt nature, but by the Spirit of God. From this place St. Paul describes primarily the state of believers, and that of unbelievers only to illustrate this.

5. They that are after the flesh – Who remain under the guidance of corrupt nature. **Mind the things of the flesh** – Have their thoughts and affections fixed on such things as gratify corrupt nature; namely, on things visible and temporal; on things of the earth, on pleasure, (of sense or imagination,) praise, or riches. **But they who are after the Spirit** – Who are under his guidance. **Mind the things of the Spirit** – Think of, relish, love things invisible, eternal; the things which the Spirit hath revealed, which he works in us, moves us to, and promises to give us.

6. For to be carnally minded – That is, to mind the things of the flesh. **Is death** – The sure mark of spiritual death, and the way to death everlasting. **But to be spiritually minded** – That is, to mind the things of the Spirit. **Is life** – A sure mark of spiritual life, and the way to life everlasting. **And attended with peace** – The peace of God, which is the foretaste of life everlasting; and peace with God, opposite to the enmity mentioned in the next verse.

7. Enmity against God – His existence, power, and providence.

8. They who are in the flesh – Under the government of it.

9. **In the Spirit** – Under his government. **If any man have not the Spirit of Christ** – Dwelling and governing in him. **He is none of his** – He is not a member of Christ; not a Christian; not in a state of salvation. A plain, express declaration, which admits of no exception. He that hath ears to hear, let him hear!

10. **Now if Christ be in you** – Where the Spirit of Christ is, there is Christ. **The body indeed is dead** – Devoted to death. **Because of sin** – Heretofore committed. **But the Spirit is life** – Already truly alive. **Because of righteousness** – Now attained. From Rom 8:13, St. Paul, having finished what he had begun, Rom 6:1, describes purely the state of believers.

12. **We are not debtors to the flesh** – We ought not to follow it.

13. **The deeds of the flesh** – Not only evil actions, but evil desires, tempers, thoughts. **If ye mortify** – Kill, destroy these. **Ye shall live** – The life of faith more abundantly here, and hereafter the life of glory.

14. **For as many as are led by the Spirit of God** – In all the ways of righteousness. **They are the sons of God** – Here St. Paul enters upon the description of those blessings which he comprises, Ro 8:30, in the word glorified; though, indeed, he does not describe mere glory, but that which is still mingled with the cross. The sum is, through sufferings to glory.

15. **For ye** – Who are real Christians. **Have not received the spirit of bondage** – The Holy Ghost was not properly a spirit of bondage, even in the time of the Old Testament. Yet there was something of bondage remaining even in those who then had received the Spirit. **Again** – As the Jews did before. **We** – All and every believer. **Cry** – The word denotes a vehement speaking, with desire, confidence, constancy. **Abba, Father** – The latter word explains the former. By using both the Syriac and the Greek word, St. Paul seems to point out the joint cry both of the Jewish and gentile believers. The spirit of bondage here seems directly to mean, those operations of the Holy Spirit by which the soul, on its first conviction, feels itself in bondage to sin, to the world, to Satan, and obnoxious to the wrath of God. This, therefore, and the Spirit of adoption, are one and the same Spirit, only manifesting itself in various operations, according to the various circumstances of the persons.

16. **The same Spirit beareth witness with our spirit** – With the spirit of every true believer, by a testimony distinct from that of his own spirit, or the testimony of a good conscience. Happy they who enjoy this clear and constant.

17. **Joint heirs** – That we may know it is a great inheritance which God will give us for he hath given a great one to his Son. **If we suffer with him** – Willingly and cheerfully, for

righteousness' sake. This is a new proposition, referring to what follows.

18. **For I reckon** – This verse gives the reason why he but now mentioned sufferings and glory. When that glory 'shall be revealed in us,' then the sons of God will be revealed also.

19. **For the earnest expectation** – The word denotes a lively hope of something drawing near, and a vehement longing after it. **Of the creation** – Of all visible creatures, believers excepted, who are spoken of apart; each kind, according as it is capable. All these have been sufferers through sin; and to all these shall refreshment redound from the glory of the children of God. Upright heathens are by no means to be excluded from this earnest expectation: nay, perhaps something of it may at some times be found even in the vainest of men; who in their sober, quiet, sleepless, afflicted hours, pour forth many sighs in the ear of God.

20. **The creation was made subject to vanity** – Abuse, misery, and corruption. **By him who subjected it** – Namely, God, Gen 3:17, 5:29. Adam only made it liable to the sentence which God pronounced; yet not without hope.

21. **The creation itself shall be delivered** – Destruction is not deliverance: therefore whatsoever is destroyed, or ceases to be, is not delivered at all. Will, then, any part of the creation be destroyed? **Into the glorious liberty** – The excellent state wherein they were created.

22. **For the whole creation groaneth together** – With joint groans, as it were with one voice. **And travaileth** – Literally, is in the pains of childbirth, to be delivered of the burden of the curse. **Until now** – To this very hour; and so on till the time of deliverance.

23. **And even we, who have the first-fruits of the Spirit** – That is, the Spirit, who is the first-fruits of our inheritance. **The adoption** – Persons who had been privately adopted among the Romans were often brought forth into the forum, and there publicly owned as their sons by those who adopted them. So at the general resurrection, when the body itself is redeemed from death, the sons of God shall be publicly owned by him in the great assembly of men and angels. **The redemption of our body** – From corruption to glory and immortality.

24. **For we are saved by hope** – Our salvation is now only in hope. We do not yet possess this full salvation.

26. **Likewise the Spirit** – Nay, not only the universe, not only the children of God, but the Spirit of God also himself, as it were, groaneth, while he helpeth our infirmities, or weaknesses. Our understandings are weak, particularly in the things of God our desires are weak; our prayers are weak. **We know not** – Many times. **What we should pray for** – Much less are we able to pray for it as we ought: **but the Spirit**

maketh intercession for us – In our hearts, even as Christ does in heaven. **With groanings** – The matter of which is from ourselves, but the Spirit forms them; and they are frequently inexpressible, even by the faithful themselves.

27. But he who searcheth the hearts – Wherein the Spirit dwells and intercedes. **Knoweth** – Though man cannot utter it. **What is the mind of the Spirit, for he maketh intercession for the saints** – Who are near to God. **According to God** – According to his will, as is worthy of God. and acceptable to him.

28. And we know – This in general; though we do not always know particularly what to pray for. **That all things** – Ease or pain, poverty or riches, and the ten thousand changes of life. **Work together for good** – Strongly and sweetly for spiritual and eternal good. **To them that are called according to his purpose** – His gracious design of saving a lost world by the death of his Son. This is a new proposition. St. Paul, being about to recapitulate the whole blessing contained in justification, first goes back to the purpose or decree of God, which is frequently mentioned in holy writ.

To explain this, nearly in the words of an eminent writer, a little more at large: – When a man has a work of time and importance before him, he pauses, consults, and contrives; and when he has laid a plan, resolves or decrees to proceed accordingly. Having observed this in ourselves, we are ready to apply it to God also; and he, in condescension to us has applied it to himself.

The works of providence and redemption are vast and stupendous, and therefore we are apt to conceive of God as deliberating and consulting on them, and then decreeing to act according to 'the counsel of his own will;' as if, long before the world was made, he had been concerting measures both as to the making and governing of it, and had then writ down his decrees, which altered not, any more than the laws of the Medes and Persians. Whereas, to take this consulting and decreeing in a literal sense, would be the same absurdity as to ascribe a real human body and human passions to the ever-blessed God.

This is only a popular representation of his infallible knowledge and unchangeable wisdom; that is, he does all things as wisely as a man can possibly do, after the deepest consultation, and as steadily pursues the most proper method as one can do who has laid a scheme beforehand. But then, though the effects be such as would argue consultation and consequent decrees in man, yet what need of a moment's consultation in Him who sees all things at one view?

Nor had God any more occasion to pause and deliberate, and lay down rules for his own conduct from all eternity, than he has now. What was there any fear of his mistaking afterwards, if he had not beforehand prepared decrees, to direct him what he was to do? Will any man say, he was wiser before the creation than since? or had he then more leisure, that he should take that opportunity to settle his affairs, and make rules for himself, from which he was never to vary?

He has doubtless the same wisdom and all other perfections at this day which he had from eternity; and is now as capable of making decrees, or rather has no more occasion for them now than formerly: his understanding being always equally clear and bright, his wisdom equally infallible.

29. Whom he foreknew, he also predestinated conformable to the image of his Son – Here the apostle declares who those are whom he foreknew and predestinated to glory; namely, those who are conformable to the image of his Son. This is the mark of those who are foreknown and will be glorified, 2Tim 2:19. Php 3:10,21.

30. Them he – In due time. **Called** – By his gospel and his Spirit. **And whom he called** – When obedient to the heavenly calling, Acts 26:19. **He also justified** – Forgave and accepted. **And whom he justified** – Provided they 'continued in his goodness,' Rom 11:22, he in the end **glorified** – St. Paul does not affirm, either here or in any other part of his writings. that precisely the same number of men are called, justified, and glorified. He does not deny that a believer may fall away and be cut off between his special calling and his glorification, Rom 11:22. Neither does he deny that many are called who never are justified. He only affirms that this is the method whereby God leads us step by step toward heaven. **He glorified** – He speaks as one looking back from the goal, upon the race of faith. Indeed grace, as it is glory begun, is both an earnest and a foretaste of eternal glory.

31. What shall we say then to these things – Related in the third, fifth, and eighth chapters? As if he had said, We cannot go, think, or wish anything farther. **If God be for us** – Here follow four periods, one general and three particular. Each begins with glorying in the grace of God, which is followed by a question suitable to it, challenging all opponents to all which, 'I am persuaded,' &c., is a general answer. The general period is, If God be for us, who can be against us? The first particular period, relating to the past time, is, He that spared not his own Son, how shall he not freely give us all things? The second, relating to the present, is, It is God that justifieth. Who is he that condemneth? The third, relating to the future, is, It is Christ that died – Who shall separate us from the love of Christ?

32. He that – This period contains four sentences: He spared not his own Son; therefore he will freely give us all things. He delivered him up for us all; therefore, none can lay anything to our charge. **Freely** – For all that follows justification is a free gift also. **All things** – Needful or profitable for us.

33. God's elect – The above-cited author observes, that long before the coming of Christ the heathen world revolted from the true God, and were therefore reprobated, or rejected.

But the nation of the Jews were chosen to be the people of God, and were therefore styled: 'the children' or 'sons of God,' Deut 14:1; 'holy people,' Deut 7:6; 14:2; 'a chosen seed,' Deut 4:37; 'the elect,' Isaiah 41:8,9; 43:10; 'the called of God,' Isaiah 48:12. And these titles were given to all the nation of Israel, including both good and bad.

Now the gospel having the most strict connexion with the Books of the Old Testament, where these phrases frequently occur; and our Lord and his apostles being native Jews, and beginning to preach in the land of Israel, language in which they preached would of course abound with the phrases of the Jewish nation. And hence it is easy to see why such of them as would not receive him were styled reprobated. For they no longer continued to be the people of God; whereas this and those other honourable titles were continued to all such Jews as embraced Christianity. And the same appellations which once belonged to the Jewish nation were now given to the gentile Christians also together with which they were invested with all the privileges of 'the chosen people of God;' and nothing could cut them off from these but their own wilful apostasy.

It does not appear that even good men were ever termed God's elect till above two thousand years from the creation. God's electing or choosing the nation of Israel, and separating them from the other nations, who were sunk in idolatry and all wickedness, gave the first occasion to this sort of language. And as the separating the Christians from the Jews was a like event, no wonder it was expressed in like words and phrases only with this difference, the term elect was of old applied to all the members of the visible church; whereas in the New Testament it is applied only to the members of the invisible.

34. Yea rather, that is risen – Our faith should not stop at his death, but be exercised farther on his resurrection, kingdom, second coming. **Who maketh intercession for us** – Presenting there his obedience, his sufferings, his prayers, and our prayers sanctified through him.

35. Who shall separate us from the love of Christ – Toward us? **Shall affliction or distress** – He proceeds in order, from less troubles to greater: can any of these separate us from his protection in it; and, if he sees good, deliverance from it?

36. All the day – That is, every day, continually. **We are accounted** – By our enemies; by ourselves. Psa 44:22.

37. We more than conquer – We are not only no losers, but abundant gainers, by all these trials. This period seems to describe the full assurance of hope.

38. I am persuaded – This is inferred from the thirty-fourth verse. **Neither death** – Terrible as it is to natural men; a violent death in particular, Rom 8:36. **Nor life** – With all the affliction and distress it can bring, Rom 8:35; or a long, easy life; or all living men. **Nor angels** – Whether good (if it were possible they should attempt it) or bad, with all their wisdom and strength. **Nor principalities, nor powers** – Not even those of the highest rank, or the most eminent power. **Nor things present** – Which may befall us during our pilgrimage; or the whole world, till it passeth away. **Nor things to come** – Which may occur either when our time on earth is past, or when time itself is at an end, as the final judgment, the general conflagration, the everlasting fire. **Nor height, nor depth** – The former sentence respected the differences of times; this, the differences of places. How many great and various things are contained in these words, we do not, need not, cannot know yet. **The height** – In St. Paul's sublime style, is put for heaven. **The depth** – For the great abyss: that is, neither the heights, I will not say of walls, mountains, seas, but, of heaven itself, can move us; nor the abyss itself, the very thought of which might astonish the boldest creature. **Nor any creature** – Nothing beneath the Almighty; visible enemies he does not even deign to name. **Shall be able** – Either by force, Rom 8:35; or by any legal claim, Rom 8:33. **To separate us from the love of God in Christ** – Which will surely save, protect, deliver us who believe in, and through, and from, them all.

Chapter 9

In this chapter St. Paul, after strongly declaring his love and esteem for them, sets himself to answer the grand objection of his countrymen; namely, that the rejection of the Jews and reception of the gentiles was contrary to the word of God. That he had not here the least thought of personal election or reprobation is manifest:

1. Because it lay quite wide of his design, which was this, to show that God's rejecting the Jews and receiving the gentiles was consistent with his word;

2. Because such a doctrine would not only have had no tendency to convince, but would have evidently tended to harden, the Jews;

3. Because when he sums up his argument in the close of the chapter, he has not one word, or the least intimation, about it.

1. **In Christ** – This seems to imply an appeal to him. **In the Holy Ghost** – Through his grace.

2. **I have great sorrow** – A high degree of spiritual sorrow and of spiritual Joy may consist together, Rom 8:39. By declaring his sorrow for the unbelieving Jews, who excluded themselves from all the blessings he had enumerated, he shows that what he was now about to speak, he did not speak from any prejudice to them.

3. **I could wish** – Human words cannot fully describe the motions of souls that are full of God. As if he had said, I could wish to suffer in their stead; yea, to be an anathema from Christ in their place. In how high a sense he wished this, who can tell, unless himself had been asked and had resolved the question? Certainly he did not then consider himself at all, but only others and the glory of God. The thing could not be; yet the wish was pious and solid; though with a tacit condition, if it were right and possible.

4. **Whose is the adoption.** – He enumerates six prerogatives, of which the first pair respect God the Father, the second Christ, the third the Holy Ghost. **The adoption and the glory** – That is, Israel is the first-born child of God, and the God of glory is their God, Deut 4:7; Psalm 106:20. These are relative to each other. At once God is the Father of Israel, and Israel are the people of God. He speaks not here of the ark, or any corporeal thing. God himself is 'the glory of his people Israel.' **And the covenants, and the giving of the law** – The covenant was given long before the law. It is termed covenants, in the plural, because it was so often and so variously repeated, and because there were two dispositions of it, Gal 4:24, frequently called two covenants; the one promising, the other exhibiting the promise. **And the worship, and the promises** – The true way of worshipping God; and all the promises made to the fathers.

5. To the preceding, St. Paul now adds two more prerogatives. **Theirs are the fathers** – The patriarchs and holy men of old, yea, the Messiah himself. **Who is over all, God blessed for ever** – The original words imply the self-existent, independent Being, who was, is, and is to come. **Over all** – The supreme; as being God, and consequently blessed for ever. No words can more dearly express his divine, supreme majesty, and his gracious sovereignty both over Jews and, gentiles.

6. **Not as if** – The Jews imagined that the word of God must fail if all their nation were not saved. This St. Paul now refutes, and proves that the word itself had foretold their falling away. **The word of God** – The promises of God to Israel. **Had fallen to the ground** – This could not be. Even now, says the apostle, some enjoy the promises; and hereafter 'all Israel shall be saved.' This is the sum of the ninth, tenth, and eleventh chapters. **For** – Here he enters upon the proof of it. **All are not Israel, who are of Israel** – The Jews vehemently maintained the contrary; namely, that all who were born Israelites, and they only, were the people of God. The former part of this assertion is refuted here, the latter, Rom 9:24. The sum is, God accepts all believers, and them only; and this is no way contrary to his word. Nay, he hath declared in his word, both by types and by express testimonies, that believers are accepted as the 'children of the promise,' while unbelievers are rejected, though they are 'children after the flesh.' **All are not Israel** – Not in the favour of God. Who are lineally descended of Israel.

7. **Neither because they are lineally the seed of Abraham, will it follow that they are all children of God** – This did not hold even in Abraham's own family; and much less in his remote descendants. **But God then said, In Isaac shall thy seed be called** – That is, Isaac, not Ishmael, shall be called thy seed; that seed to which the promise is made.

8. **That is, Not the children** – As if he had said, This is a clear type of things to come; showing us, that in all succeeding generations, not the children of the flesh, the lineal descendants of Abraham, but the children of the promise, they to whom the promise is made, that is, believers, are the children of God. Gen 21:12.

9. **For this is the word of the promise** – By the power of which Isaac was conceived, and not by the power of nature. Not, Whosoever is born of thee shall be blessed, but, **At this time** – Which I now appoint. **I will come, and Sarah shall have a son** – And he shall inherit the blessing. Gen 18:10.

10–11. And that God's blessing does not belong to all the descendants of Abraham, appears not only by this instance, but by that of Esau and Jacob, who was chosen to inherit the blessing, before either of them had done good or evil. The apostle mentions this to show, that neither were their ancestors accepted through any merit of their own. **That the purpose of God according to election might stand** – Whose purpose was, to elect or choose the promised seed. **Not of works** – Not for any preceding merit in him he chose. **But of him that calleth** – Of his own good pleasure who called to that privilege whom he saw good.

12. **The elder** – Esau. **Shall serve the younger** – Not in person, for he never did; but in his posterity. Accordingly the Edomites were often brought into subjection by the Israelites. Gen 25:23.

13. **As it is written** – With which word in Genesis, spoken so long before, that of Malachi agrees. **I have loved Jacob** – With a peculiar love; that is, the Israelites, the posterity of Jacob. And **I have,** comparatively, **hated** Esau – That is,

the Edomites, the posterity of Esau. But observe:

1. This does not relate to the person of Jacob or Esau.

2. Nor does it relate to the eternal state either of them or their posterity.

Thus far the apostle has been proving his proposition, namely, that the exclusion of a great part of the seed of Abraham, yea, and of Isaac, from the special promises of God, was so far from being impossible, that, according to the scriptures themselves, it had actually happened. He now introduces and refutes an objection. Mal 1:2,3.

14–15. Is there injustice with God – Is it unjust in God to give Jacob the blessing rather than Esau? or to accept believers, and them only. **God forbid** – In no wise. This is well consistent with justice; for he has a right to fix the terms on which he will show mercy, according to his declaration to Moses, petitioning for all the people, after they had committed idolatry with the golden calf. **I will have mercy on whom I will have mercy** – According to the terms I myself have fixed. **And I will have compassion on whom I will have compassion** – Namely, on those only who submit to my terms, who accept of it in the way that I have appointed. See Ex 33:19.

16. It – The blessing. Therefore **is not of him that willeth, nor of him that runneth** – It is not the effect either of the will or the works of man, **but of the grace and power of God.** The will of man is here opposed to the grace of God, and man's running, to the divine operation. And this general declaration respects not only Isaac and Jacob, and the Israelites in the time of Moses, but likewise all the spiritual children of Abraham, even to the end of the world.

17. Moreover – God has an indisputable right to reject those who will not accept the blessings on his own terms. And this he exercised in the case of Pharaoh; to whom, after many instances of stubbornness and rebellion, he said, as it is recorded in scripture, **For this very thing have I raised thee up** – That is, Unless thou repent, this will surely be the consequence of my raising thee up, making thee a great and glorious king, **that my power will be shown upon thee,** (as indeed it was, by overwhelming him and his army in the sea,) **and my name declared through all the earth** – As it is at this day. Perhaps this may have a still farther meaning. It seems that God was resolved to show his power over the river, the insects, other animals, (with the natural causes of their health, diseases, life, and death,) over the meteors, the air, the sun, (all of which were worshipped by the Egyptians, from whom other nations learned their idolatry,) and at once over all their gods, by that terrible stroke of slaying all their priests, and their choicest victims, the firstborn

of man and beast; and all this with a design, not only to deliver his people Israel, (for which a single act of omnipotence would have sufficed,) but to convince the Egyptians, that the objects of their worship were but the creatures of Jehovah, and entirely in his power, and to draw them and the neighbouring nations, who should hear of all these wonders, from their idolatry, to worship the one God. For the execution of this design, (in order to the display of the divine power over the various objects of their worship, in variety of wonderful acts, which were at the same time just punishments for their cruel oppression of the Israelites,) God was pleased to raise to the throne of an absolute monarchy, a man, not whom he had made wicked on purpose, but whom he found so, the proudest, the most daring and obstinate of all the Egyptian princes; and who, being incorrigible, well deserved to be set up in that situation, where the divine judgments fell the heaviest. Ex 9:16.

18. So then – That is, accordingly he does show mercy on his own terms, namely, on them that believe. **And whom he willeth** – Namely, them that believe not. **He hardeneth** – Leaves to the hardness of their hearts.

19. Why doth he still find fault – The particle still is strongly expressive of the objector's sour, morose murmuring. **For who hath resisted his will** – The word his likewise expresses his surliness and aversion to God, whom he does not even deign to name.

20. Nay, but who art thou, O man – Little, impotent, ignorant man. **That repliest against God** – That accusest God of injustice, for himself fixing the terms on which he will show mercy? **Shall the thing formed say to him that formed it, Why hast thou made me thus** – Why hast thou made me capable of honour and immortality, only by believing?

21. Hath not the potter power over the clay – And much more hath not God power over his creatures, to appoint one vessel, namely, the believer, to honour, and another, the unbeliever, to dishonour?

If we survey the right which God has over us, in a more general way, with regard to his intelligent creatures, God may be considered in two different views, as Creator, Proprietor, and Lord of all; or, as their moral Governor, and Judge.

God, as sovereign Lord and Proprietor of all, dispenses his gifts or favours to his creatures with perfect wisdom, but by no rules or methods of proceeding that we are acquainted with. The time when we shall exist, the country where we shall live, our parents, our constitution of body and turn of mind; these, and numberless other circumstances, are doubtless ordered with perfect wisdom, but by rules that lie quite out of our sight. But God's methods of dealing with us, as our Governor and Judge, are dearly revealed and perfectly known; namely, that he will finally reward every man according to his works: 'He that believeth shalt be saved, and he that believeth not shall be damned.'

Therefore, though 'He hath mercy on whom he willeth, and whom he willeth he hardeneth,' that is, suffers to be hardened in consequence of their obstinate wickedness; yet his is not the will of an arbitrary, capricious, or tyrannical being. He wills nothing but what is infinitely wise and good; and therefore his will is a most proper rule of judgment. He will show mercy, as he hath assured us, to none but true believers, nor harden any but such as obstinately refuse his mercy. Jer 18:6,7.

22. What if God, being willing – Referring to Ro 9:18,19. That is, although it was now his will, because of their obstinate unbelief, **To show his wrath** – Which necessarily presupposes sin. **And to make his power known** – This is repeated from the seventeenth verse. **Yet endured** – As he did Pharaoh. **With much longsuffering** – Which should have led them to repentance. **The vessels of wrath** – Those who had moved his wrath by still rejecting his mercy. **Fitted for destruction** – By their own wilful and final impenitence. Is there any injustice in this?

23. That he might make known – What if by showing such longsuffering even to 'the vessels of wrath,' he did the more abundantly show the greatness of his glorious goodness, wisdom, and power, on the vessels of mercy; on those whom he had himself, by his grace, prepared for glory. Is this any injustice?

24. Even us – Here the apostle comes to the other proposition, of grace free for all, whether Jew or gentile. **Of the Jews** – This he treats of, Ro 9:25. **Of the gentiles** – Treated of in the same verse.

25. Beloved – As a spouse. **Who once was not beloved** – Consequently, not unconditionally elected. This relates directly to the final restoration of the Jews. Hosea 2:23.

26. There shall they be called the sons of God – So that they need not leave their own country and come to Judea. Hosea 1:10.

27. But Isaiah testifies, that (as many gentiles will be accepted, so) many Jews will be rejected; that out of all the thousands of Israel, **a remnant only shall be saved.** This was spoken originally of the few that were saved from the ravage of Sennacherib's army. Isa 10:22,23.

28. For he is finishing or cutting short his account – In rigorous justice, will leave but a small remnant. There will be so general a destruction, that but a small number will escape.

29. As Isaiah had said before – Namely, Isa 1:9, concerning those who were besieged in Jerusalem by Rezin and Pekah. **Unless the Lord**

had left us a seed – Which denotes:
1. The present paucity:
2. The future abundance.
We had been as Sodom – So that it is no unexampled thing for the main body of the Jewish nation to revolt from God, and perish in their sin.

30, 31. What shall we say then – What is to be concluded from all that has been said but this, **That the gentiles, who followed not after righteousness** – Who a while ago had no knowledge of, no care or thought about, it. **Have attained to righteousness** – Or justification. Even the righteousness which is by faith. This is the first conclusion we may draw from the preceding observations. The second is, **that Israel** – The Jews. **Although following after the law of righteousness** – That law which, duly used, would have led them to faith, and thereby to righteousness. **Have not attained to the law of righteousness** – To that righteousness or justification which is one great end of the law

32. And wherefore have they not? Is it because God eternally decreed they should not? There is nothing like this to be met with but agreeable to his argument the apostle gives us this good reason for it, **Because they sought not by faith** – Whereby alone it could be attained. **But as it were** – In effect, if not professedly, **by works. For they stumbled at that stumblingstone** – Christ crucified.

33. As it is written – Foretold by their own prophet. **Behold, I lay in Sion** – I exhibit in my church, what, though it is in truth the only sure foundation of happiness, yet will be in fact **a stumblingstone and rock of offence** – An occasion of ruin to many, through their obstinate unbelief. Isa 8:14; Isa 28:16.

Chapter 10

1. My prayer to God is, that they may be saved – He would not have prayed for this, had they been absolutely reprobated.

2. They have a zeal, but not according to knowledge – They had zeal without knowledge; we have knowledge without zeal.

3. For they being ignorant of the righteousness of God – Of the method God has established for the justification of a sinner. **And seeking to establish their own righteousness** – Their own method of acceptance with God. **Have not submitted to the righteousness of God** – The way of justification which he hath fixed.

4. For Christ is the end of the law – The scope and aim of it. It is the very design of the law, to bring men to believe in Christ for justification and salvation. And he alone gives that pardon and life which the law shows the want of, but cannot give. **To every one** – Whether Jew or gentile, treated of, Ro 10:11. **That believeth** – Treated of, Ro 10:5.

5. For Moses describeth the only **righteousness which is** attainable **by the law,** when he saith, **The man who doeth these things shall live by them** – that is, he that perfectly keeps all these precepts in every point, he alone may claim life and salvation by them. But this way of justification is impossible to any who have ever transgressed any one law in any point. Lev 18:5.

6–7. But the righteousness which is by faith – The method of becoming righteous by believing. Speaketh a very different language, and may be considered as expressing itself thus: (to accommodate to our present subject the words which Moses spake, touching the plainness of his law:) **Say not in thy heart, Who shall ascend into heaven, as if it were to bring Christ down: or, Who shall descend into the grave, as if it were to bring him again from the dead** – Do not imagine that these things are to be done now, in order to procure thy pardon and salvation. Deut 30:14.

8. But what saith he – Moses. Even these words, so remarkably applicable to the subject before us. All is done ready to thy hand. **The word is nigh thee** – Within thy reach; easy to be understood, remembered, practised. **This is eminently true of the word of faith** – The gospel. **Which we preach** – The sum of which is, If thy heart believe in Christ, and thy life confess him, thou shalt be saved.

9. If thou confess with thy mouth – Even in time of persecution, when such a confession may send thee to the lions.

10. For with the heart – Not the understanding only. **Man believeth to righteousness** – So as to obtain justification. **And with the mouth confession is made** – So as to obtain final salvation. Confession here implies the whole of outward, as believing does the root of all inward, religion.

11. Isa 28:16.

12. The same Lord of all is rich – So that his blessings are never to be exhausted, nor is he ever constrained to hold his hand. The great truth proposed in Ro 10:11 is so repeated here, and in Ro 10:13, and farther confirmed, Ro 10:14,15, as not only to imply, that 'whosoever calleth upon him shall be saved;' but also that the will of God is, that all should savingly call upon him.

13. Joel 2:32.

15. But how shall they preach, unless they be sent – Thus by a chain of reasoning, from God's will that the gentiles also should 'call upon him,' St. Paul infers that the apostles were sent by God to preach to the gentiles also. **The feet** – Their very footsteps; their coming. Isa 52:7.

16. Isa 53:1.

17. Faith, indeed, ordinarily **cometh by hearing;** even by hearing **the word of God.**

18. But their unbelief was not owing to the want of hearing For they have heard. **Yes verily** – So many nations have already heard the preachers of the gospel, that I may in some sense say of them as David did of the lights of heaven. Psa 29:4.

19. But hath not Israel known – They might have known, even from Moses and Isaiah, that many of the gentiles would be received, and many of the Jews rejected. **I will provoke you to jealousy by them that are not a nation** – As they followed gods that were not gods, so he accepted in their stead a nation that was not a nation; that is, a nation that was not in covenant with God. **A foolish nation** – Such are all which know not God. Deut 32:21.

20. But Isaiah is very bold – And speaks plainly what Moses but intimated. Isa 65:1,2.

21. An unbelieving and gainsaying people – Just opposite to those who believed with their hearts, and made confession with their mouths.

Chapter 11

1. Hath God rejected his whole **people** – All Israel? In no wise. Now there is 'a remnant' who believe, Rom 11:5; and hereafter 'all Israel will be saved,' Rom 11:26.

2. God hath not rejected that part of his people whom he foreknew – Speaking after the manner of men. For, in fact, knowing and foreknowing are the same thing with God, who knows or sees all things at once, from everlasting to everlasting. **Know ye not** – That in a parallel case, amidst a general apostasy, when Elijah thought the whole nation was fallen into idolatry, God 'knew' there was 'a remnant' of true worshippers.

3. 1 Kin 19:10.

4. To Baal – Nor to the golden calves.

5. According to the election of grace – According to that gracious purpose of God, 'He that believeth shall be saved.'

6. And if by grace, then it is no more of works – Whether ceremonial or moral. **Else grace is no longer grace** – The very nature of grace is lost. And if it be of works, then it is no more grace: **else work is no longer work** – But the very nature of it is destroyed. There is something so absolutely inconsistent between the being justified by grace, and the being justified by works, that, if you suppose either, you of necessity exclude the other. For what is given to works is the payment of a debt; whereas grace implies an unmerited favour. So that the same benefit cannot, in the very nature of things, be derived from both.

7. What then – What is the conclusion from the whole? It is this: that Israel in general hath not obtained justification; but those of them only who believe. **And the rest were blinded** – By their own wilful prejudice.

8. God hath at length withdrawn his Spirit, and so given them up to a spirit of slumber; which is fulfilled unto this day. Isa 29:10.

9. And David saith – In that prophetic imprecation, which is applicable to them, as well as to Judas. A recompense – Of their preceding wickedness. So sin is punished by sin; and thus the gospel, which should have fed and strengthened their souls, is become a means of destroying them. Psa 69:22,23.

11. Have they stumbled so as to fall – Totally and finally? No. But by their fall – Or slip: it is a very soft word in the original. Salvation is come to the gentiles – See an instance of this, Acts 13:46. To provoke them – The Jews themselves, to jealousy.

12. The first part of this verse is treated of, Rom 11:13 the latter, How much more their fulness, (that is, their full conversion,) Rom 11:23.

So many prophecies refer to this grand event, that it is surprising any Christian can doubt of it. And these are greatly confirmed by the wonderful preservation of the Jews as a distinct people to this day. When it is accomplished, it will be so strong a demonstration, both of the Old and New Testament revelation, as will doubtless convince many thousand Deists, in countries nominally Christian; of whom there will, of course, be increasing multitudes among merely nominal Christians. And this will be a means of swiftly propagating the gospel among Muslims and Pagans; who would probably have received it long ago, had they conversed only with real Christians.

13. I magnify my office – Far from being ashamed of ministering to the gentiles, I glory therein; the rather, as it may be a means of provoking my brethren to jealousy.

14. My flesh – My kinsmen.

15. Life from the dead – Overflowing life to the world, which was dead.

16. And this will surely come to pass. For if the first fruits be holy, so is the lump – The consecration of them was esteemed the consecration of all and so the conversion of a few Jews is an earnest of the conversion of all the rest. And if the root be holy – The patriarchs from whom they spring, surely God will at length make their descendants also holy.

17. Thou – O gentile. Being a wild olive tree – Had the graft been nobler than the stock, yet its dependance on it for life and nourishment would leave it no room to boast against it. How much less, when, contrary to what is practised among men, the wild olive tree is engrafted on the good!

18. Boast not against the branches – Do not they do this who despise the Jews? or deny their future conversion?

20. They were broken off for unbelief, and thou standest by faith – Both conditionally, not absolutely: if absolutely, there might have been

room to boast. By faith – The free gift of God, which therefore ought to humble thee.

21. Be not highminded, but fear – We may observe, this fear is not opposed to trust, but to pride and security.

22. Else shalt thou – Also, who now 'standest by faith,' be both totally and finally cut off.

24. Contrary to nature – For according to nature, we graft the fruitful branch into the wild stock; but here the wild branch is grafted into the fruitful stock.

25. St. Paul calls any truth known but to a few, a mystery. Such had been the calling of the gentiles: such was now the conversion of the Jews. Lest ye should be wise in your own conceits – Puffed up with your present advantages; dreaming that ye are the only church; or that the church of Rome cannot fail. Hardness in part is happened to Israel, till – Israel therefore is neither totally nor finally rejected. The fullness of the gentiles be come in – Till there be a vast harvest amongst the heathens.

26. And so all Israel shall be saved – Being convinced by the coming of the gentiles. But there will be a still larger harvest among the gentiles, when all Israel is come in. The deliverer shall come – Yea, the deliverer is come; but not the full fruit of his coming. Isa 59:20.

28. They are now enemies – To the gospel, to God, and to themselves, which God permits. For your sake: but as for the election – That part of them who believe, they are beloved.

29. For the gifts and the calling of God are without repentance – God does not repent of his gifts to the Jews, or his calling of the gentiles.

32. For God hath shut up all together in disobedience – Suffering each in their turn to revolt from him. First, God suffered the gentiles in the early age to revolt, and took the family of Abraham as a peculiar seed to himself. Afterwards he permitted them to fall through unbelief, and took in the believing gentiles. And he did even this to provoke the Jews to jealousy, and so bring them also in the end to faith. This was truly a mystery in the divine conduct, which the apostle adores with such holy astonishment.

33. O the depth of the riches, and wisdom, and knowledge of God – In the ninth chapter, St. Paul had sailed but in a narrow sea: now he is in the ocean. The depth of the riches is described, Ro 11:35; the depth of wisdom, Ro 11:34; the depth of knowledge, in the latter part of this verse. Wisdom directs all things to the best end; knowledge sees that end. How unsearchable are his judgments – With regard to unbelievers. His ways – With regard to believers. His ways are more upon a level; His judgments 'a great deep.' But even his ways we cannot trace.

34. Who hath known the mind of the Lord – Before or any farther than he has revealed it. Isa 40:13.

35. **Given to him** – Either wisdom or power? 36. **Of him** – As the Creator. **Through him** – As the Preserver. **To him** – As the ultimate end, are all things. To him be the **glory** of his riches, wisdom, knowledge. **Amen** – A concluding word, in which the affection of the apostle, when it is come to the height, shuts up all.

Chapter 12

1. **I exhort you** – St. Paul uses to suit his exhortations to the doctrines he has been delivering. So here the general use from the whole is contained in the first and second verses. The particular uses follow, from the third verse to the end of the Epistle. **By the tender mercies of God** – The whole sentiment is derived from Rom 1–5. The expression itself is particularly opposed to 'the wrath of God,' Rom 1:18. It has a reference here to the entire gospel, to the whole economy of grace or mercy, delivering us from 'the wrath of God,' and exciting us to all duty. **To present** – So Rom 6:13; 16:19; now actually to exhibit before God. **Your bodies** – That is, yourselves; a part is put for the whole; the rather, as in the ancient sacrifices of beasts, the body was the whole. These also are particularly named in opposition to that vile abuse of their bodies mentioned, Rom 1:24. Several expressions follow, which have likewise a direct reference to other expressions in the same chapter. **A sacrifice** – Dead to sin and **living** – By that life which is mentioned, Rom 1:17; 6:4. **Holy** – Such as the holy law requires, Rom 7:12. **Acceptable** – Rom 8:8. **Which is your reasonable service** – The worship of the heathens was utterly unreasonable, Rom 1:18, &c so was the glorying of the Jews, Rom 2:3. But a Christian acts in all things by the highest reason, from the mercy of God inferring his own duty.

2. **And be not conformed** – Neither in judgment, spirit, nor behaviour. **To this world** – Which, neglecting the will of God, entirely follows its own. **That ye may prove** – Know by sure trial; which is easily done by him who has thus presented himself to God. **What is that good, and acceptable, and perfect will of God** – The will of God is here to be understood of all the preceptive part of Christianity, which is in itself so excellently good, so acceptable to God, and so perfective of our natures.

3. **And I say** – He now proceeds to show what that will of God is. **Through the grace which is given to me** – He modestly adds this, lest he should seem to forget his own direction. **To every one that is among you** – Believers at Rome. Happy, had they always remembered this! **The measure of faith** – Treated of in the first and following chapters, from which all other gifts and graces flow.

5. **So we** – All believers. **Are one body** – Closely connected together in Christ, and

consequently ought to be helpful to each other.

6. **Having then gifts differing according to the grace which is given us** – Gifts are various: grace is one. **Whether it be prophecy** – This, considered as an extraordinary gift, is that whereby heavenly mysteries are declared to men, or things to come foretold. But it seems here to mean the ordinary gift of expounding scripture. **Let us prophesy according to the analogy of faith** – St. Peter expresses it, 'as the oracles of God;' according to the general tenor of them; according to that grand scheme of doctrine which is delivered therein, touching original sin, justification by faith, and present, inward salvation. There is a wonderful analogy between all these; and a close and intimate connexion between the chief heads of that faith 'which was once delivered to the saints.' Every article therefore concerning which there is any question should be determined by this rule; every doubtful scripture interpreted according to the grand truths which run through the whole.

7. **Ministering** – As deacons. **He that teacheth** – Catechumens; for whom particular instructers were appointed. **He that exhorteth** – Whose peculiar business it was to urge Christians to duty, and to comfort them in trials.

8. **He that presideth** – That hath the care of a flock. **He that showeth mercy** – In any instance. **With cheerfulness** – Rejoicing that he hath such an opportunity.

9. Having spoken of faith and its fruit, Rom 12:3, he comes now to **love**. The ninth, tenth, and eleventh verses refer to chapter the seventh; the twelfth verse to chapter the eighth; the thirteenth verse, of communicating to the saints, whether Jews or gentiles, to chapter the ninth. Part of the sixteenth verse is repeated from Rom 11:25. **Abhor that which is evil; cleave to that which is good** – Both inwardly and outwardly, whatever ill-will or danger may follow.

10. **In honour preferring one another** – Which you will do, if you habitually consider what is good in others, and what is evil in yourselves.

11. Whatsoever ye do, do it with your might. In every **business** diligently and fervently **serving the Lord** – Doing all to God, not to man.

12. **Rejoicing in hope** – Of perfect holiness and everlasting happiness. Hitherto of faith and love; now of hope also, see the fifth and eighth chapters; afterwards of duties toward others; saints, Ro 12:13 persecutors, Ro 12:14 friends, strangers, enemies, Ro 12:15.

13. **Distributing to the necessities of the saints** – Relieve all Christians that are in want. It is remarkable, that the apostle, treating expressly of the duties flowing from the communion of saints, yet never says one word about the dead. **Pursue hospitality** – Not only embracing those

that offer, but seeking opportunities to exercise it.

14. Curse not – No, not in your heart.

15. Rejoice – The direct opposite to weeping is laughter; but this does not so well suit a Christian.

16. Mind not high things – Desire not riches, honour, or the company of the great.

17. Provide – Think beforehand; contrive to give as little offence as may be to any.

19. Dearly beloved – So he softens the rugged spirit. Revenge not yourselves, but leave that to God. Perhaps it might more properly be rendered, leave room for wrath; that is, the wrath of God, to whom vengeance properly belongs. Deut 32:35.

20. Feed him – With your own hand: if it be needful, even put bread into his mouth. **Heap coals of fire upon his head** – That part which is most sensible. 'So artists melt the sullen ore of lead, By heaping coals of fire upon its head; In the kind warmth the metal learns to glow, And pure from dross the silver runs below.' See Prov 25:21.

21. And if you see no present fruit, yet persevere. Be not overcome with evil – As all are who avenge themselves. But overcome evil with good. Conquer your enemies by kindness and patience.

Chapter 13

1. St. Paul, writing to the Romans, whose city was the seat of the empire, speaks largely of obedience to magistrates: and this was also, in effect, a public apology for the Christian religion. **Let every soul be subject to the supreme powers** – An admonition peculiarly needful for the Jews. Power, in the singular number, is the supreme authority; powers are they who are invested with it. That is more readily acknowledged to be from God than these. The apostle affirms it of both. They are all from God, who constituted all in general, and permits each in particular by his providence. **The powers that be are appointed by God** – It might be rendered, are subordinate to, or, orderly disposed under, God; implying, that they are God's deputies or viceregents and consequently, their authority being, in effect, his, demands our conscientious obedience.

2. Whosoever resisteth the power – In any other manner than the laws of the community direct. **Shall receive condemnation** – Not only from the magistrate, but from God also.

3. For rulers are – In the general, notwithstanding some particular exceptions. **A terror to evil works** – Only. **Wouldest thou then not be afraid** – There is one fear which precedes evil actions, and deters from them: this should always remain. There is another fear which

follows evil actions: they who do well are free from this.

4. The sword – The instrument of capital punishment, which God authorizes him to inflict.

5. Not only for fear of wrath – That is, punishment from man. **But for conscience' sake** – Out of obedience to God.

6. For this cause – Because they are the ministers (officers) of God for the public good. **This very thing** – The public good.

7. To all – Magistrates. **Tribute** – Taxes on your persons or estates. **Custom** – For goods exported or imported. **Fear** – Obedience. **Honour** – Reverence. All these are due to the supreme power.

8. From our duty to magistrates he passes on to general duties. **To love one another** – An eternal debt, which can never be sufficiently discharged; but yet if this be rightly performed, it discharges all the rest. **For he that loveth another** – As he ought. **Hath fulfilled the** whole **law** – Toward his neighbour.

9. If there be any other – More particular. **Commandment** – Toward our neighbour; as there are many in the law. **It is summed up in this** – So that if you was not thinking of it, yet if your heart was full of love, you would fulfil it.

10. Therefore love is the fulfilling of the law – For the same love which restrains from all evil, incites us to all good.

11. And do this – Fulfil the law of love in all the instances above mentioned. **Knowing the season** – Full of grace, but hasting away. **That it is high time to awake out of sleep** – How beautifully is the metaphor carried on! This life, a night; the resurrection, the day; the gospel shining on the heart, the dawn of this day; we are to awake out of sleep; to rise up and throw away our night-clothes, fit only for darkness, and put on new; and, being soldiers, we are to arm, and prepare for fight, who are encompassed with so many enemies. The day dawns when we receive faith, and then sleep gives place. Then it is time to rise, to arm, to walk, to work, lest sleep steal upon us again. Final **salvation**, glory, **is nearer** to us now, **than when we first believed** – It is continually advancing, flying forward upon the swiftest wings of time. And that which remains between the present hour and eternity is comparatively but a moment.

13. Banqueting – Luxurious, elegant feasts.

14. But put ye on the Lord Jesus Christ – Herein is contained the whole of our salvation. It is a strong and beautiful expression for the most intimate union with him, and being clothed with all the graces which were in him. The apostle does not say, Put on purity and sobriety, peacefulness and benevolence; but he says all this and a thousand times more at once, in saying, Put on Christ. **And make not provision** – To raise foolish desires, or, when they are raised already, to satisfy them.

Chapter 14

1. Him that is weak – Through needless scruples. **Receive** – With all love and courtesy into Christian fellowship. **But not to doubtful disputations** – About questionable points.

2. All things – All sorts of food, though forbidden by the law.

3. Despise him that eateth not – As overscrupulous or superstitious. **Judge him that eateth** – As profane, or taking undue liberties. **For God hath received him** – Into the number of his children, notwithstanding this.

5. One day above another – As new moons, and other Jewish festivals. **Let every man be fully persuaded** – That a thing is lawful, before he does it.

6. Regardeth it to the Lord – That is, out of a principle of conscience toward God. **To the Lord he doth not regard it** – He also acts from a principle of conscience. **He that eateth not** – Flesh. **Giveth God thanks** – For his herbs.

7. None of us – Christians, in the things we do. **Liveth to himself** – Is at his own disposal; doeth his own will.

10. Or why dost thou despise thy brother – Hitherto the apostle as addressed the weak brother: now he speaks to the stronger.

11. As I live – An oath proper to him, because he only possesseth life infinite and independent. It is Christ who is here termed both Lord and God; as it is he to whom we live, and to whom we die. **Every tongue shall confess to God** – Shall own him as their rightful Lord; which shall then only be accomplished in its full extent. The Lord grant we may find mercy in that day; and may it also be imparted to those who have differed from us! yea, to those who have censured and condemned us for things which we have done from a desire to please him, or refused to do from a fear of offending him. Isa 45:23.

13. But judge this rather – Concerning ourselves. **Not to lay a stumblingblock** – By moving him to do as thou doest, though against his conscience. **Or a scandal** – Moving him to hate or judge thee.

14. I am assured by the Lord Jesus – Perhaps by a particular revelation. **That there is nothing** – Neither flesh nor herbs. **Unclean of itself** – Unlawful under the gospel.

15. If thy brother is grieved – That is, wounded, led into sin. **Destroy not him for whom Christ died** – So we see, he for whom Christ died may be destroyed. **With thy meat** – Do not value thy meat more than Christ valued his life.

16. Let not then your good and lawful liberty be evil spoken of – By being offensive to others.

17. For the kingdom of God – That is, true religion, does not consist in external observances. **But in righteousness** – The image of God stamped on the heart; the love of God and man, accompanied with the peace that passeth all understanding, and joy in the Holy Ghost.

18. In these – Righteousness, peace, and joy. **Men** – Wise and good men.

19. Peace and edification are closely joined. Practical divinity tends equally to peace and to edification. Controversial divinity less directly tends to edification, although sometimes, as they of old, we cannot build without it, Neh 4:17.

20. The work of God – Which he builds in the soul by faith, and in the church by concord. **It is evil to that man who eateth with offence** – So as to offend another thereby.

21. Thy brother stumbleth – By imitating thee against his conscience, contrary to righteousness. **Or is offended** – At what thou doest to the loss of his peace. **Or made weak** – Hesitating between imitation and abhorrence, to the loss of that joy in the Lord which was his strength.

22. Hast thou faith – That all things are pure? **Have it to thyself before God** – In circumstances like these, keep it to thyself, and do not offend others by it. **Happy is he that condemneth not himself** – By an improper use of even innocent things! and happy he who is free from a doubting conscience! He that has this may allow the thing, yet condemn himself for it.

23. Because it is **not of faith** – He does not believe it lawful and, in all these cases, **whatsoever is not of faith is sin** – Whatever a man does without a full persuasion of its lawfulness, it is sin to him.

Chapter 15

1. We who are strong – Of a clearer judgment, and free from these scruples. **And not to please ourselves** – Without any regard to others.

2. For his good – This is a general word: edification is one species of good.

3. But bore not only the infirmities, but **reproaches,** of his brethren; and so fulfilled that scripture. Psa 69:9.

4. Aforetime – In the Old Testament. **That we through patience and consolation of the scriptures may have hope** – That through the consolation which God gives us by these, we may have patience and a joyful hope.

5. According to the power of **Christ Jesus.**

6. That ye – Both Jews and gentiles, believing with one mind, and confessing with one mouth.

7. Receive ye one another – Weak and strong, with mutual love.

8. Now I say – The apostle here shows how Christ received us. **Christ Jesus** – Jesus is the name, Christ the surname. The latter was first known to the Jews; the former, to the gentiles. Therefore he is styled Jesus Christ, when the words stand in the common, natural order. When the order is inverted, as here, the office of Christ is more solemnly considered. **Was a servant** – Of his Father. **Of the circumcision** – For the salvation of the circumcised, the Jews. **For the truth of God** – To manifest the truth and fidelity of God.

9. **As it is written** – In the eighteenth psalm, here the gentiles and Jews are spoken of as joining in the worship of the God of Israel. Psa 18:49.

10. Deu 32:43.

11. Psa 117:1.

12. **There shall be the root of Jesse** – That kings and the Messiah should spring from his house, was promised to Jesse before it was to David. **In him shall the gentiles hope** – Who before had been 'without hope,' Eph 2:12. Isa 11:10.

13. **Now the God of hope** – A glorious title of God, but till now unknown to the heathens; for their goddess Hope, like their other idols, was nothing; whose temple at Rome was burned by lightning. It was, indeed, built again not long after, but was again burned to the ground.

14. There are several conclusions of this Epistle.

The first begins at this verse;

the second, Rom 16:1;

the third, Rom 16:17;

the fourth, Rom 16:21;

and the fifth, Rom 16:25;

Ye are full of goodness – By being created anew. **And filled with all knowledge** – By long experience of the things of God. **To admonish** – To instruct and confirm.

15. **Because of the grace** – That is, because I am an apostle of the gentiles.

16. **The offering up of the gentiles** – As living sacrifices.

17. **I have whereof to glory through Jesus Christ** – All my glorying is in and through him.

18. **By word** – By the power of the Spirit. **By deed** – Namely, through 'mighty signs and wonders.'

20. **Not where Christ had been named** – These places he generally declined, though not altogether, having an holy ambition (so the Greek word means) to make the first proclamation of the gospel in places where it was quite unheard of, in spite of all the difficulty and dangers that attended it. **Lest I should only build upon another man's foundation** – The providence of God seemed in a special manner, generally, to prevent this, though not entirely, lest the enemies of the apostle, who sought every occasion to set light by him, should have had room to say that he was behind other apostles, not being sufficient for planting of churches

himself, but only for preaching where others had been already; or that he declined the more difficult part of the ministry.

21. Isa 52:15.

22. **Therefore I have been long hindered from coming to you** – Among whom Christ had been named.

23. **Having no longer place in these parts** – Where Christ has now been preached in every city.

24. **Into Spain** – Where the gospel had not yet been preached. **If first I may be somewhat satisfied with your company** – How remarkable is the modesty with which he speaks! They might rather desire to be satisfied with his. **Somewhat satisfied** – Intimating the shortness of his stay; or, perhaps, that Christ alone can throughly satisfy the soul.

26. **The poor of the saints that are in Jerusalem** – It can by no means be inferred from this expression, that the community of goods among the Christians was then ceased. All that can be gathered from it is, that in this time of extreme dearth, Acts 11:28,29, some of the church in Jerusalem were in want; the rest being barely able to subsist themselves, but not to supply the necessities of their brethren.

27. **It hath pleased them; and they are their debtors** – That is, they are bound to it, in justice as well as mercy. **Spiritual things** – By the preaching of the gospel. **Carnal things** – Things needful for the body.

28. **When I have sealed to them this fruit** – When I have safely delivered to them, as under seal, this fruit of their brethren's love. **I will go by you into Spain** – Such was his design; but it does not appear that Paul went into Spain. There are often holy purposes in the minds of good men, which are overruled by the providence of God so as never to take effect. And yet they are precious in the sight of God.

30. **I beseech you by the love of the Spirit** – That is, by the love which is the genuine fruit of the Spirit. **To strive together with me in your prayers** – He must pray himself, who would have others strive together with him in prayer. Of all the apostles, St. Paul alone is recorded to desire the prayers of the faithful for himself. And this he generally does in the conclusions of his Epistles; yet not without making a difference. For he speaks in one manner to them whom he treats as his children, with the gravity or even severity of a father, such as Timothy, Titus, the Corinthians, and Galatians; in another, to them whom he treats rather like equals, such as the Romans, Ephesians, Thessalonians, Colossians, Hebrews.

31. **That I may be delivered** – He is thus urgent from a sense of the importance of his life to the church. Otherwise he would have rejoiced 'to depart, and to be with Christ.' **And that my**

service may be acceptable – In spite of all their prejudices; to the end the Jewish and gentile believers may be knit together in tender love.

32. That I may come to you – This refers to the former, **With joy** – To the latter, part of the preceding verse.

Chapter 16

1. I commend unto you Phebe – The bearer of this letter. **A servant** – The Greek word is a deaconess. **Of the church in Cenchrea** – In the apostolic age, some grave and pious women were appointed deaconesses in every church. It was their office, not to teach publicly, but to visit the sick, the women in particular, and to minister to them both in their temporal and spiritual necessities.

2. In the Lord – That is, for the Lord's sake, and in a Christian manner. St. Paul seems fond of this expression.

4. Who have for my life, as it were, **laid down their own necks** – That is, exposed themselves to the utmost danger. **But likewise all the churches of the gentiles** – Even that at Rome, for preserving so valuable a life.

5. Salute the church that is in their house – Aquila had been driven from Rome in the reign of Claudius, but was now returned, and performed the same part there which Caius did at Corinth, Rom 16:23. Where any Christian had a large house, there they all assembled together though as yet the Christians at Rome had neither bishops nor deacons. There does not appear to have been then in the whole city any more than one of these domestic churches. Otherwise there can be no doubt but St. Paul would have saluted them also. **Epenetus** – Although the apostle had never been at Rome, yet had he many acquaintance there. But here is no mention of Linus or Cemens; whence it appears, they did not come to Rome till after this. **The firstfruits of Asia** – The first convert in the proconsular Asia.

7. Who are of note among the apostles – They seem to have been some of the most early converts. **Fellowprisoners** – For the gospel's sake.

9. Our fellowlabourer – Mine and Timothy's, verse 21. Rom 16:21.

11. Those of the family of Aristobulus and Narcissus, who are in the Lord – It seems only part of their families were converted. Probably, some of them were not known to St. Paul by face, but only by character. Faith does not create moroseness, but courtesy, which even the gravity of an apostle did not hinder.

12. Salute Tryphena and Tryphosa – Probably they were two sisters.

13. Salute Rufus – Perhaps the same that is mentioned, Mark 15:21. **And his mother and mine** – This expression may only denote the tender care which Rufus's mother had taken of him.

14. Salute Asyncritus, Phlegon – He seems to join those together, who were joined by kindred, nearness of habitation, or any other circumstance. It could not but encourage the poor especially, to be saluted by name, who perhaps did not know that the apostle bad ever heard of them. It is observable, that whilst the apostle forgets none who are worthy, yet he adjusts the nature of his salutation to the degrees of worth in those whom he salutes.

15. Salute all the saints – Had St. Peter been then at Rome, St. Paul would doubtless have saluted him by name; since no one in this numerous catalogue was of an eminence comparable to his. But if he was not then at Rome, the whole Roman tradition, with regard to the succession of their bishops, fails in the most fundamental article.

16. Salute one another with an holy kiss – Termed by St. Peter, 'the kiss of love,' 1Pet 5:14. So the ancient Christians concluded all their solemn offices; the men saluting the men, and the women the women. And this apostolical custom seems to have continued for some ages in all Christian churches.

17. Mark them who cause divisions – Such there were, therefore, at Rome also. **Avoid them** – Avoid all unnecessary intercourse with them.

18. By good words – Concerning themselves, making great promises. **And fair speeches** – Concerning you, praising and flattering you. **The harmless** – Who, doing no ill themselves, are not upon their guard against them that do.

19. But I would have you – Not only obedient, but discreet also. **Wise with regard to that which is good** – As knowing in this as possible. **And simple with regard to that which is evil** – As ignorant of this as possible.

20. And the God of peace – The Author and Lover of it, giving a blessing to your discretion. **Shall bruise Satan under your feet** – Shall defeat all the artifices of that sower of tares, and unite you more and more together in love.

21. Timotheus my fellowlabourer – Here he is named even before St. Paul's kinsmen. But as he had never been at Rome, he is not named in the beginning of the epistle.

22. I Tertius, who wrote this epistle, salute you – Tertius, who wrote what the apostle dictated, inserted this, either by St. Paul's exhortation or ready permission.

23. Caius – The Corinthian, 1Cor 1:14. **Mine host, and of the whole church** – Who probably met for some time in his house.

23. The chamberlain of the city – Of Corinth.

25. Now to him who is able – The last words of this epistle exactly answer Ro 1:1–5: in particular, concerning the power of God, the gospel,

Jesus Christ, the scriptures, the obedience of faith, all nations. **To establish you** – Both Jews and gentiles. **According to my gospel, and the preaching of Jesus Christ** – That is, according to the tenor of the gospel of Jesus Christ, which I preach. **According to the revelation of the mystery** – Of the calling of the gentiles, which, as plainly as it was foretold in the Prophets, was still hid from many even of the believing Jews.

26. According to the commandment – The foundation of the apostolical office. **Of the eternal God** – A more proper epithet could not be. A new dispensation infers no change in God.

Known unto him are all his works, and every variation of them, from eternity. **Made known to all nations** – Not barely that they might know, but enjoy it also, through obeying the faith.

27. To the only wise God – Whose manifold wisdom is known in the church through the gospel, Eph 3:10. 'To him who is able,' and, to the wise God,' are joined, as 1Cor 1:24, where Christ is styled 'the wisdom of God,' and 'the power of God.' To him **be glory through Christ Jesus for ever** – And let every believer say, Amen!

1 CORINTHIANS

Charles Hodge

Introduction

Paul's relationship to the Corinthian church was special in some ways. He was not only the founder of the congregation, but he continued in the closest relation to it. It excited his care, called for his wisest management, tried his patience and forbearance, rewarded him at times with a special evidence of affection and obedience, and filled him with hopes of its extended and healthy influence. His love for that church was therefore of special intensity. It was analogous to that of a father for a promising son beset with temptations, whose character combined great excellencies with great defects. The letters to the Corinthians, therefore, reveal to us more of the personal character of the apostle than any of his other letters. They show him to us as a man, as a pastor, as a counsellor, as in conflict not only with heretics but with personal enemies. They reveal his wisdom, his zeal, his forbearance, his liberality of principle and practice in all matters not affecting salvation, his strictness in all matters of right and wrong, his humility, and perhaps above all his unwearied activity and wonderful endurance.

There is another consideration that gives a special interest to these letters. More clearly than any other part of the New Testament, they show Christianity in conflict with heathenism. We see what method Paul adopted in founding the church in the midst of a refined and corrupt people, and how he answered questions of conscience arising out of the relationships of Christians to the heathen around them. The cases may never occur again, but the principles involved in their decisions serve as lights to the church in all ages. Principles relating to church discipline, social relations, public worship, the nature of the church and of the sacraments are here unfolded not in an abstract form so much as in their application. These letters, therefore, in reference to all practical measures in the establishment of the church among the heathen and to its conduct in Christian lands, are among the most important parts of the Word of God.

Contents

See *Outlines of the New Testament Books*, p. 897

Chapter 1

Greetings (verses 1–3).

Introduction (verses 4–9).

The divisions which existed in the Corinthian church (verses 10–16).

Defence of the apostle's preaching (verses 17–31).

Introduction to the letter (verses 1–9).

Paul declares himself to be a divinely appointed messenger of Christ (verse 1). As such he addresses the Corinthian church as those who were **sanctified in Christ Jesus,** and called to be saints. He includes in his greeting all the worshippers of Christ in that vicinity (verse 2), and invokes upon them the blessings of **grace and peace** (verse 3).

In the introduction, he thanks God, as usual, for the favour shown to the Corinthians; for the various gifts through which the Gospel had been confirmed among them, and by which they were made fully equal with the most favoured churches (verse 4–7). He expresses his confidence, founded on God's faithfulness, that they would be preserved from apostasy until the day of the Lord (verses 8–9).

1. Paul was so called after his conversion and the commencement of his labours among the Gentiles. His Jewish name was Saul. It was common for the Jews to bear one name among their own people, and another among foreigners.

Called to be an apostle. That is, appointed to be an apostle. The apostleship being an office, it could not be assumed at pleasure. Appointment by competent authority was absolutely indispensable. The word **apostle** means literally a messenger, and then a missionary, or someone sent to preach the Gospel. In its strict official sense it is applied only to the immediate messengers of Christ, the infallible teachers of his religion and founders of his church. In calling himself an apostle, Paul claims divine authority derived immediately from Christ.

By the will of God. That is, by divine authority. Paul was made an apostle neither by popular election, nor by consecration by those who were apostles before him, but by immediate appointment from God. On this point, see his explicit declaration in Galatians 1:1.

And our brother Sosthenes. In the Greek it is *the* brother. He was a brother well known to the Corinthians, and probably one of the messengers sent by them to the apostle, or whom they knew to be with him.

2. To the church of God. The word 'church' is used in Scripture as a collective term for the people of God, considered as called out from the world. Sometimes it means all of God's people, as when it is said that 'Christ loved the church and gave himself up for her' (Ephesians 5:25). Sometimes it means the people of God as a class, as when Paul said that he 'was persecuting the church of God' (Galatians 1:13). Sometimes it means the professing Christians of any one place, as when mention is made of the church in Jerusalem, Antioch, or Corinth. Any number, however small, of professing Christians, considered collectively, may be called a church. Hence we hear of the church in the house of Philemon, and in the house of Aquila and Priscilla (Romans 16:5). It is called the church **of God** because it belongs to him. He selects and calls its members, and, according to Acts 20:28, it is his, because he has bought it with his blood.

Who are sanctified in Christ Jesus. This explains the preceding clauses, and teaches us the nature of the church. It consists of the **sanctified.** The Greek word translated 'to sanctify' means 'to cleanse.'

Called to be saints. That is, made holy by the effectual call of the Holy Spirit. 'The called' always means those effectually called, as distinguished from those who are merely invited externally. The original word for **saints** (*hagios*) sometimes signifies 'sacred,' set apart for a holy use. In this sense the temple, the altar, the priests, the prophets, and the whole theocratic people are called holy. In the New Testament the word commonly expresses inner purity, or consecration of the soul to God. Believers are **saints** in both senses of the word; they are inwardly renewed, and outwardly consecrated.

Together with all those who in every place call on the name of our Lord Jesus Christ. To call on someone's name is to invoke his aid. It is properly used for religious invocation. Compare Acts 9:14, 21; Acts 22:16; Romans 10:12–13; 2 Timothy 2:22. To **call on the name of our Lord Jesus Christ** is to invoke his aid as Christ, the Messiah predicted by the prophets, and as our almighty and sovereign possessor and ruler.

3. Grace is favour, and **peace** its fruits. The former includes all that is included in the love of God as exercised towards sinners; and the latter includes all the benefits which flow from that love.

4. In Christ Jesus. This limits and explains the kind of favours to which the apostle refers. He gives thanks for those gifts which God had bestowed on them in virtue of their union with Christ.

5. This verse explains the preceding one. Paul gives thanks for the grace which they had received, that is, that they have been **enriched** in him in every way.

In speech and knowledge of every kind. That is, with all the gifts of speaking and knowledge. Some were prophets, some were teachers, some had the gift of tongues. These were different forms of the gift of utterance.

Knowledge. That is, in every kind and degree of religious knowledge.

6. Just as. They were thus enriched, because the testimony about Christ, that is, the Gospel, was confirmed among them.

Has been strengthened among you. This may mean either 'was firmly established among you,' or 'was firmly established in your faith.' The Gospel was demonstrated by the Holy Spirit to be true, and was firmly settled in their conviction. This firm faith was then, as it is now, the necessary condition of the enjoyment of the blessings by which the Gospel is attended.

7. Such was the strength of that faith that the gifts of the Spirit were bestowed on them as abundantly as on any other church. This connection of faith with the divine blessing is often presented in Scripture. Our Lord said to the father who sought his aid on behalf of his child with the evil spirit, 'Everything is possible for him who believes.' See also Matthew 9:29.

As you wait for the revealing of our Lord Jesus Christ. As you wait means expecting (compare 1 Peter 3:20), or expecting with desire, that is, longing for (compare Romans 8:19–20, 23). The object of this patient and earnest expectation of believers is the coming, that is, the revelation **of our Lord Jesus Christ.** The second coming of Christ, so clearly predicted by himself and by his apostles, connected as it is with the promise of the resurrection of his people and the consummation of his kingdom, was the object of longing expectation to all the early Christians.

8. He will also strengthen you. God had not only enriched them with the gifts of the Spirit, but he would also confirm them. The one was an assurance of the other. Those to whom God gives the renewing influence of the Spirit, he thereby pledges himself to save; for 'the first fruits of the Spirit' are, of the nature of a pledge. They are an earnest, as the apostle says, of the future inheritance (see Ephesians 1:14 and 2 Corinthians 1:21–22). **He will keep also strengthen you,** that is, will make you steadfast, preserve you from falling.

Blameless. That is, not accused.

9. God is faithful; by him you were called into the fellowship of his Son, Jesus Christ our Lord.

God is faithful. He is one in whom we may confide; one who will fulfill all his promises. The apostle's confidence in the steadfastness and final perseverance of believers was founded neither on the strength of their purpose to persevere, nor on any assumption that the principle of religion in their hearts was indestructible, but simply on God's faithfulness.

Fellowship includes union and communion. The original word, *koinonia*, signifies participation, as in 10:16 ('sharing in the blood of Christ'). We are called to share in Christ; share in his life, as members of his body; and therefore, share his character, his sufferings here and his glory hereafter.

The divisions of the Corinthian church (verses 10–16).

As one of the principal objects of this letter was to correct the evils which had arisen in the Corinthian church, the apostle first mentions the divisions which existed there. He exhorts the members of that church to unity (verse 10). The reason for that exhortation was the information which he had received concerning their dissensions (verse 11). These divisions arose from their ranging themselves under different religious teachers as party leaders (verse 12). The sin and folly of such divisions are manifest, in the first place, because religious teachers are not centres of unity to the church. They had not redeemed it, nor did its members profess allegiance to them in baptism (verse 13). These divisions, therefore, arose, on the one hand, from a forgetfulness of the common relationship which all Christians bear to Christ; and, on the other, from a misapprehension of the relationship in which believers stand to their religious teachers. Paul expresses his gratitude that he had not given any occasion for such misapprehension. He had baptized so few among them that no one could suspect him of a desire to make himself the head of the church or the leader of a party (verses 14–16).

10. There is only one explanation in this verse, which is expressed first in general terms, **that all of you should be in agreement,** and is then explained in the negative form, **that there should be no divisions among you,** and then positively, **that you should be united in the same mind and the same purpose.**

12. This explains the nature of these quarrels. In almost all the apostolic churches there were quarrels between the Jewish and Gentile converts. It is plain from the contents of this and of the following letter that these quarrels were fomented by false teachers (2 Corinthians 11:13); that these teachers were Jewish (2 Corinthians 11:22); and that they endeavoured to undermine the authority of Paul as an apostle. The two principal parties in Corinth, therefore, were Gentiles calling themselves the disciples of Paul, and Jews claiming to be the followers of Peter.

13. The grounds of our allegiance to Christ are, first, that he is the Christ, the Son of the living God; second, that he has redeemed us; third, that we are consecrated to him in baptism. All these grounds are unique to Christ. To no other being in the universe do believers stand in the relationship which they all sustain to their common Lord. As, therefore, there is but one Christ, but one redeemer, but one baptism, Christians cannot be divided without violating the bond which binds them to Christ and to one another.

14–15. Although it was the duty of the apostles to baptize (Matthew 28:19), Paul rejoiced that it had so happened that he had administered that ordinance to only a few people in Corinth, so all pretext that he was making disciples to himself was taken away. Paul did not consider this a matter of chance, but of providential direction, and, therefore, a cause of gratitude. **Crispus** was the chief ruler of the synagogue in Corinth, whose conversion is recorded in Acts 18:8. **Gaius** is mentioned in Romans 16:23 as the host of the apostle.

16. Stephanas was one of the three messengers sent to inform the apostle of the state of the church in Corinth, and to deliver the letter to which reference is made in 7:1 (compare 16:15, 17). Paul says he baptized the **household** or family of Stephanas. Under the old dispensation, whenever anyone professed Judaism or entered into covenant with God as one of his people, all his children and dependants, that is, all whom he represented, were included in the covenant and received circumcision as its sign. In the same way, under the Gospel, when a Jew or Gentile joined the Christian church, his children received baptism and were recognized as members of the Christian church. Compare Acts 16:15, 33.

Paul's defence of his manner of preaching (verses 17–31).

The apostle having been led to mention incidentally that he had baptized very few people in Corinth, states that the reason for this is that his great official duty was to preach the Gospel. This naturally led him to speak of the manner of preaching. It was one of the objections urged against him that he did not preach 'with eloquent wisdom,' that is, that he did not preach the doctrines taught by human reason, which he calls the wisdom of the world. Through the remainder of this, and the whole of the following chapter, he assigns his reasons for thus renouncing the wisdom of the world – and resumes the subject of the divisions existing in the Corinthian church at the beginning of chapter 3.

1. His first reason for not teaching human wisdom is that God had pronounced all such wisdom to be folly (verses 19–20).

2. Experience had proved the insufficiency of human wisdom to lead people to a saving knowledge of God (verse 21).

3. God had ordained the Gospel to be the great means of salvation (verses 21–25).

4. The experience of the Corinthians themselves showed that it was not wisdom nor any other human distinction that secured the salvation of men. Human wisdom could neither discover the method of salvation, nor secure compliance with its terms when revealed. They were in Christ (that is, converted), not because they were wiser, better, or more distinguished than others, but simply because God had chosen to called them (verses 26–30). God's plan in all this was to humble people so that whoever glories should glory in the Lord (verse 31).

17. So that the cross of Christ might not be emptied of its power. That is, made powerless and inoperative. If Paul in preaching had either substituted human wisdom for the doctrine of the cross, or had so presented that doctrine as to turn it into a philosophy, his preaching would have been powerless. It would lose its divine element and become nothing more than human wisdom. Whatever obscures the cross deprives the Gospel of its power.

18. For the message about the cross is the doctrine of salvation through the crucifixion of the Son of God as a sacrifice for human sins. This doctrine, though it is **foolishness** to one group, namely, **to those who are perishing**, that is, those certainly to perish, yet to another group, namely, those certainly to be saved, it is the power of God. That is, it is that through which **the power of God** is manifested and exercised, and therefore it is divinely efficacious.

19. This is not to be considered as the citation of any one particular passage of the Old Testament, so much as an appeal to a doctrine clearly revealed in it. In a multitude of passages, and in various forms, God had taught by his prophets the insufficiency of human reason to lead people to the knowledge of the way of salvation. In Isaiah 29:14, nearly the same words are used, but with a more limited application. 'The wisdom of the wise' and '**the discernment of the discerning**' are parallel expressions for the same thing.

20. This is a challenge to the wise of every class and of every nation to disprove what he had said.

Where is the debater of this age? That is, the inquirer, questioner, sophist – the appropriate designation of the Greek philosopher.

Of this age. This qualification belongs to all the preceding terms. 'Where is the wise of this world, whether scribe or sophist?'

21. This and the following verses contain the apostle's second argument in support of the insufficiency of human wisdom. The argument is this: experience having shown the insufficiency of human wisdom to lead people to a saving knowledge of God, God set it aside, and declared it to be worthless, by adopting the foolishness of preaching as the means of salvation. This argument therefore includes two distinct arguments. First, that derived from experience; and secondly, that derived from God's having appointed the Gospel, as distinguished from human wisdom, to be the means of saving people.

22–23. This passage is parallel to the preceding one. Since human reason in all its developments (Jewish or Greek) had failed, we preach Christ.

But we proclaim Christ crucified. This doctrine met the demands of neither group. It satisfied neither the expectations of the Jews, nor the requirements of the Greeks. On the contrary, it was a stumbling-block to Jews. They had anticipated the Messiah as a glorious temporal prince, who would deliver and exalt their nation. To present as their Messiah someone crucified as a malefactor was the greatest possible insult. Therefore, to them he was 'a stone that will make people stumble, a rock that will make them fall' (Romans 9:33; 1 Peter 2:8). To the Greeks this doctrine was foolishness. Nothing in the apprehension of rationalists can be more absurd than that the blood of the cross can remove sin, promote virtue, and secure salvation; or that the preaching of that doctrine is to convert the world.

24. Those who are the called always means those called effectually, as distinguished from those who are merely externally invited. There is a double call of the Gospel: the one external, by the word; the other internal, by the Spirit. The subjects of the latter are designated the 'called' (see Romans 1:7; 8:28; Jude 1; Revelation 17:14; and compare Isaiah 48:12). The Jews wanted a display of power; the Greeks sought wisdom. Both are found in Christ, and in the highest degree. He is **the power of God and the wisdom of God.**

25. This is a confirmation of what precedes. The Gospel is thus efficacious, for the lowest manifestation of divine wisdom exceeds the highest results of human wisdom; and the lowest exercise of God's power is more effectual than all human strength.

26. The connection is not with the preceding verse but with the whole preceding context. The apostle introduces a new argument to demonstrate the uselessness of human wisdom. The argument is derived from their religious experience. 'You see, brothers, it is not the wise who are called.'

Not many were of noble birth. The converts to Christianity were not in general from the higher ranks in society. The things which elevate people in the world – knowledge, influence, rank – are not the things which lead to God and salvation. Human distinctions are insignificant and inefficacious in the sight of God, who is sovereign in the distribution of his grace.

27. In this and the following verses the apostle asserts positively what he had just stated negatively: 'God does not choose the wise, but he chooses the foolish.'

Foolish in the world. That is, the foolish part of mankind. In this and in the following clauses the neuter is used although people are meant, because the reference is indefinite. God has chosen the foolish, the weak, the insignificant, etc.

28. What is low. That is, the base, the ignoble, those without family, as opposed to the noble.

Despised in the world. That is, people in low condition, whom the rich and noble look upon with contempt.

Things that are not. That is, those who are entirely overlooked as though they had no existence. There is a climax here. God has chosen not only lowly people but those who were objects of contempt, and even those below contempt, too insignificant to be noticed at all. These, and such as these, God chooses to make kings and priests to himself.

To reduce to nothing things that are. This is a stronger term than that used in the preceding verse, and is specially appropriate here. God brings to nothing the **things that are,** that is, those who make their existence known and felt, as opposed to those who are nothing. It is apparent from the dispensations of grace that knowledge, rank, and power do not attract the favour of God, or secure for their possessors any preeminence or preference before him. This should make the exalted humble, and the humble content.

29. God's aim in dealing with us like this, calling the ignorant rather than the wise, the lowly instead of the great, is that no one should boast before him. No one can stand in his sight and attribute his conversion or salvation to his own wisdom, or birth, or station, or to anything else by which he is favourably distinguished from his fellow humans.

30. In Christ Jesus is to be united to him:

1. Representatively, as we were in Adam (Romans 5:12–21; 1 Corinthians 15:22);

2. Vitally, as a branch in the vine, or a part of the body (John 15:17);

3. Consciously and voluntarily by faith (Romans 8:1).

The effects of this union, as here stated, are that Christ is **from God.** He is the author, made for us:

1. **Wisdom.** Christ is the true wisdom. He is the *logos*, the Revealer, in whom dwells all the fullness of the Godhead, and all the treasures of wisdom and knowledge. 'No one knows the Father except the Son and anyone to whom the Son chooses to reveal him' (Matthew 11:27). Union with him, therefore, makes the believer truly wise. It secures the knowledge of God, whose glory is revealed in the face of Christ, and whom to know is eternal life. All true religious knowledge is derived from Christ, and it is only those who submit to his teaching who are wise for salvation.

2. The second effect of union with Christ is **righteousness** and **sanctification**. These are intimately united as different aspects of the same thing. **Righteousness** is what satisfies the demands of the law as a rule of justification; **sanctification** is what satisfies the law as a rule of duty. Christ is both to us. He is our righteousness, because by his obedience and death he has fully satisfied the demands of justice, so that we are 'the righteousness of God' in him (2 Corinthians 5:21). When we stand before God's judgment seat, Christ is our **righteousness**. He answers for us; he presents his own infinite merit as the all-sufficient reason for our justification (see Romans 3:21–22; 5:19; Philippians 3:9). He is also our **sanctification**. His Spirit lives in all his people as the Spirit of holiness, so that they are transformed into his likeness from glory to glory. Wherever the Spirit dwells, there are the fruits of the Spirit (Acts 26:18; Romans 8:9–10; Galatians 5:22; Ephesians 2:5, 10).

3. The third effect is **redemption**, that is, deliverance from evil. This term sometimes includes all the benefits received from Christ. When he is called our Redeemer he is presented as our deliverer from guilt, from hell, from sin, from the power of Satan, from the grave. But when redemption is distinguished from justification and sanctification, it refers to the final deliverance from evil. The 'day of redemption' is the day when the work of Christ will be consummated in the perfect salvation of his people as to soul and body (Romans 8:23; Ephesians 1:14; 4:30; Hebrews 9:12).

31. In order that. God's aim in making wisdom, righteousness, sanctification, and redemption dependent on union with Christ, and union with Christ dependent not on our merit, but on his own good pleasure, is that we should glory only in him; that is, that our confidence should be in him and not in ourselves, and that all the glory of our salvation should be ascribed to him and not to us.

Chapter 2

Paul continues his defence of his way of preaching.

He shows that he acted on the principles set out in the preceding paragraph (verses 1–5).

He shows that the Gospel is the true wisdom (verses 6–9).

The source of this knowledge, as externally revealed and as spiritually understood, is the Holy Spirit (verses 10–16).

Continuation of his defence of his way of preaching (verses 1–16).

As God had determined to save people not by human wisdom but by the Gospel, Paul, when he appeared in Corinth, came neither as an orator nor as a philosopher, but simply as a witness (verses 1–2). He had no confidence in himself, but relied for success exclusively on the demonstration of the Spirit (verses 3–4). The true foundation of faith is not reason, but the testimony of God (verse 5).

Though what he preached was not human wisdom, it was the wisdom of God, undiscoverable by human reason (verses 6–9). The revealer of this divine wisdom is the Holy Spirit, he alone being competent to make this revelation, because he only knows the secret purposes of God (verses 10–12). In communicating the knowledge thus derived from the Spirit, the apostle used words taught by the Spirit (verse 13). Though the knowledge communicated was divine, and although communicated in appropriate language, it was not received by the natural man, because the things of the Spirit can be discerned only by the spiritual (verses 14–16).

1. Lofty words or wisdom. As speech and wisdom are distinguished here, the former probably refers to the manner or form, and the latter to the matter of his preaching. It was neither as a rhetorician nor as a philosopher that Paul appeared among them.

2. Jesus Christ, and him crucified. Paul's only aim in going to Corinth was to preach Christ; and Christ not as a teacher, or as an example, or as a perfect man, or as a new starting point in the development of the race – all this would be mere philosophy; but Christ **crucified**, that is, as dying for our sins. Christ as a propitiation was the burden of Paul's preaching. It has been well remarked that **Jesus Christ** refers to the person of Christ, and **him crucified** to his work; which constitute the sum of the Gospel.

3. Fear, and in much trembling. That is, in anxiety, or solicitude of mind arising out of a sense of his insufficiency, and of the infinite importance of his work (2 Corinthians 7:15; Philippians 2:12; Ephesians 6:5).

4. Demonstration means 'setting forth,' exhibition of proof. Paul relied, therefore, for success, not on his skill in argument or persuasion, nor upon any of the resources of human wisdom, but on the testimony which the Spirit bore to the truth. The Holy Spirit demonstrated the Gospel to be true.

5. In these verses, we are taught:

1. The proper method to convert people in any community, Christian or pagan, is to preach or set forth the truth concerning the person and work of Christ. Whatever other means are used must be subordinate and auxiliary, designed to remove obstacles, and to gain access for the truth to the mind, just as the ground is cleared

of weeds and brambles in order to prepare it for the precious seed.

2. The proper state of mind in which to preach the Gospel is the opposite of self-confidence or carelessness. The Gospel should be preached with a sense of weakness and with great anxiety and solicitude.

3. The foundation of saving faith is not reason, that is, not arguments addressed to the understanding, but the power of God as exerted with and by the truth on the heart.

6. **Among the mature,** the full-grown, the competent. Among one group of people the doctrine which he preached was regarded as foolishness, but among another it was seen to be divine wisdom. Who are meant by the **mature?** There are two answers to this question. Some say they were the advanced or mature Christians as distinguished from babes in Christ. Others say they were believers as opposed to unbelievers; those taught by the Spirit and thus enabled to understand the truth, as opposed to the unrenewed.

7. **God's wisdom, secret and hidden.** That is, the wisdom derived from God; which he has revealed, as distinguished from any form of knowledge of human origin.

8. **Lord of glory** is a title of divinity. It means 'possessor of divine excellence.' 'Who is the King of glory? The LORD of hosts, he is the King of glory' (Psalm 24:10; compare also Acts 7:2; James 2:1; Ephesians 1:17). The person crucified, therefore, was a divine person.

10. **The depths of God.** That is, the inmost recesses, as it were, of God's being, perfections and purposes. The Spirit, therefore, is fully competent to reveal that wisdom which had for ages been hidden in God. This passage proves at once the personality and the divinity of the Holy Spirit. His personality, because intelligent activity is ascribed to him – he **searches;** his divinity, because omniscience is ascribed to him – he knows all that God knows.

11. This verses aims to illustrate two points: First, as no one knows the thoughts of a man except the man himself, so no one knows the thoughts of God, except God himself. Therefore no one but a divine person is competent to make a revelation of the thoughts and purposes of God. Second, as every man does know his own thoughts, so the Spirit of God knows the thoughts of God. His knowledge of what is in God is analogous to that which we have of the contents of our own consciousness. The analogies of Scripture, however, are not to be pressed beyond the point which they are intended to illustrate. The point to be illustrated here is the knowledge of the Spirit. He knows what is in God, as we know what is in ourselves. It is not to be inferred from this that the Spirit of God bears in other points the same relation to God that our spirits do to us.

12. The apostle has set forth two sources of knowledge: the human and the divine. One is the informing principle that is in man; the other is the informing principle that is in God.

13. **Interpreting spiritual things to those are spiritual.** The apostle had said that the truths which he taught were revealed by the Spirit; and that the words which he used were taught by the Spirit, which he sums up by saying that he explained spiritual truths in spiritual words.

14. **Because they are discerned spiritually.** That is, because they are discerned through the Spirit. Therefore those who have not the Spirit cannot discern them.

15. **They are themselves subject to no one else's scrutiny.** This again is limited by the context. He is appreciated by no one who does not have the Spirit. Paul afterwards says it was a small matter to him to be judged by human judgment (4:3). Here, he is not speaking of the legitimate subjection of the believer to his brothers; for elsewhere he teaches that those who have the Spirit may determine how far they are really led by the Spirit. And he gives the rule by which that judgment is to be directed (5:9–12; 12:3; Galatians 1:8). If anyone claims to be spiritual, and yet does what the Spirit in his Word forbids, or denies what the Spirit teaches, we know that he deceives himself, and that the truth is not in him.

16. This confirms what precedes. No one can judge a spiritual person, for that would be to judge the Lord. The Lord had revealed certain doctrines. The spiritual discern those doctrines to be true. For anyone to pronounce them false, and to judge those who held them, supposes he is able to teach the Lord.

Chapter 3

Transition from the defence of his way of preaching to the subject of their divisions (verses 1–5).

The true relationship of ministers to the church as servants, and not party leaders (verses 7–23).

Reproof of the Corinthians for their dissensions about their religious teachers (verses 1–23).

The apostle resumes the subject of the quarrels in the Corinthian church. He passes to that subject from the defence of his way of preaching by a natural association. One of the objections against him was that his preaching was too simple. He answers that he could not make it otherwise, because they were mere infants in Christ. The proof of their being in this infantile or carnal state was that quarrels and divisions existed among them; one saying, 'I belong to Paul,' and another, 'I belong to Apollos' (verses 1–4).

As their quarrels had no reference to their religious teachers, the apostle endeavours to correct the evil by presenting the ministerial office in its true light.

1. Ministers were not head of schools or rival sects as were the Greek philosophers, but mere servants, without any authority or power of their own. One may plant, and another water, but the whole growth is from God (verses 5–7).

2. Ministers are one. They have one master and one work. They may have different departments in that great work, but they are like fellow-labourers on the same farm, or fellow-builders on the same temple (verses 8–9).

3. In performing their respective duties they incur a great responsibility. If they attempt to build up the temple of God with the rubbish of their own wisdom, they will be severely punished. If they employ the materials which God has provided, they will be rewarded (verses 10–15).

4. It is because the church is the temple of God that ministers will be held to this strict account for the doctrines which they preach, and for the way in which they execute their office (verses 16–17).

5. No minister need deceive himself in this matter. He cannot preach a higher wisdom than the wisdom of God; and to learn that wisdom he must renounce his own (verses 18–20).

6. Therefore the people should not place their confidence in ministers, who belong to the church, and not the church to them. To the interests and consummation of the church, all things, visible and invisible, are made subservient (verses 21–23).

1. There were two kinds of opponents of the apostle in Corinth. The false teachers, some of whom he denounces as anti-Christian; and secondly, those members of the church who had been taken in by these false teachers.

2. As they were children, he had treated them accordingly. He had given them **milk**; literally, 'I gave you milk to drink and not meat' – a concise form of expression. What is this distinction between milk and meat? The true nature of the distinction is to be learnt partly from the meaning of the imagery, and partly from parallel passages. The meaning of the image leads to the conclusion that the difference is in the teaching method rather than in the things taught. The same truth in one form is **milk**, in another form strong meat. 'Christ,' says Calvin, 'is milk for infants, and strong meat for men.' Every doctrine which can be taught to theologians is taught to children. The important truth is that there are not two sets of doctrine, a higher and a lower form of faith, one for the learned and the other for the unlearned; there is no part of the

Gospel which we are authorized to keep back from the people. Everything which God has revealed is to be taught to everyone just so fast and so far as he has the capacity to receive it.

3. You are still of the flesh. That is, you are under the influence of the corrupt nature. They were imperfectly sanctified. Even Paul said of himself, 'I am of the flesh' (Romans 7:14). This term, therefore, may be applied even to the most advanced Christians. Its definite meaning depends on the context.

4. This confirms the fact that there were such divisions among them as proved them to be governed by unholy feelings, and also explains the nature of those divisions. There were in Corinth, as appears from 1:12, more than two parties; but the apostle confines himself to those mentioned here, because throughout the whole discussion he has referred to the opposition of the Greek element in the church; and because he could speak as freely of Apollos as of himself because of their intimacy. As the party spirit which disturbed the peace of the Corinthian church arose from wrong views of the relationship of ministers to the church, the apostle endeavours to correct the evil by presenting that relationship in its true light.

5. This passage may read, 'Who then is Paul, and who is Apollos? Ministers by whom you believed. …' Ministers are mere instruments in God's hands. The doctrines which they preach are not their own discoveries, and the power which makes their preaching successful is not in them. They are nothing; and therefore it is an entire perversion of their relationship to the church to make them party leaders.

Paul and Apollos, men of the highest office and of the highest gifts, are **servants**, waiters, attendants – so called not just from their relationship to God, as those who serve him, but also because of their relationship to the church, whose they are, to whom they belong, and whom they serve.

6. I planted, Apollos watered, but God gave the growth. This illustrates two points. First, the diversity of service on the part of ministers, spoken of in verse 5 – one plants and another waters. Secondly, the entirely subordinate and instrumental nature of their service. As in nature, planting and watering are not what makes plants grow, so in the church, ministerial acts are not what causes grace. In both cases God brings everything about. And as humans do not have to plant and water if plants are to grow, so in the church ministerial acts are not necessary for faith. On the other hand, however, as the farmer's work is the ordinary and appointed means of securing a harvest, so the work of the ministry is the ordinary means of conversion.

7. This is the conclusion. Ministers are nothing. They are the instruments in God's hands.

8. Have a common purpose. Ministers have the same job; they have the same work, they stand in the same relationship to God and to his church. They are fellow-labourers. To set one against another, therefore, is inconsistent with their relationship to each other and to the people they serve.

9. For we are God's servants. This is at once the reason why ministers are one, and why they are to be rewarded according to their labours. They are one because they are all co-workers with God in the same great enterprise; and they are to be rewarded according to their labour, because that is the rule according to which labourers are rewarded. The propriety of this representation is apparent, because the church is God's **field**, or farm, which he makes fruitful by the light of truth and the dew of his grace, and on which his servants labour.

10. According to the grace God given to me. Paul often speaks of his apostolic office as a **grace** or favour which he had received from God, but here, as in 15:10, the reference is more general. By **the grace** he means all the gifts and influences of the Spirit, which not only qualified him for his work, but made him so labourious and faithful. Here, as elsewhere, he attributes to God all he was, and all that he was enabled to do.

A skilled master builder. That is, skilful. The word is often used of craftsmen. Paul was not only a labourer, but an architect. The whole plan of the building was revealed to him, and he was inspired to develop that plan, and to prescribe the way in which it should be carried out. He laid the **foundation.** The same idea was expressed above by saying 'I planted, Apollos watered.' He began the work in Corinth. Those who came after him were to carry on the building which he had commenced. The building must be erected on the foundation and according to it. Therefore he adds, **Each builder must choose with care how to build on it.** In the whole context he is speaking about ministers, and therefore this clause must be considered as warning addressed to them. They are to take heed **how,** that is, with what materials, they carried on the building of this holy temple. Faithfulness as well as diligence is required in a minister.

11. For others can only carry on the work already begun, for the foundation cannot be changed. The foundation of the church is Christ (see Isaiah 28:16; Acts 4:11; Ephesians 2:20; 1 Peter 2:6). This may be understood either of the person or of the doctrine of Christ. In either way the sense is good.

12–13. The work of each builder will become visible. In this life it may be disputed whether a person's doctrines are true or false. He may have great confidence in their truth, and set himself above his brothers and even above the Bible. But his work hereafter will appear in its true character.

And the fire will test what sort of work each has done. The image is that of a building on which many workmen are engaged. Some use proper materials, others wood, hay, and straw. The building is to be subjected to the test of fire. The wood, hay, and straw will be burnt up; only the solid materials will stand. False doctrine can no more stand the test of the day of judgment than hay or straw can stand a raging conflagration.

14–15. This amplifies what precedes. If the materials used by a spiritual builder stand the test of the day of judgment, he will receive the reward of a faithful servant.

If the work is burned. That is, if the materials used by any builder do not stand the test of that day.

The builder will suffer loss. That is, he will lose his reward.

The builder will be saved. Just as someone who has built his house of combustible materials may escape when the fire comes, yet his property is lost, and all his labour comes to nothing. The apostle is speaking here about those teachers who, although they retain the fundamental doctrines of the Gospel, combine them with error. This is clear from verse 12: 'If anyone builds on the foundation.' It is not enough, therefore, for a minister to hold fast to fundamental truth; he must take heed what he teaches in connection with that truth.

17. And you are that temple. As the word for **temple** is not in the text, the reference may be to the word **sacred.** 'The temple is sacred, which you also are.' The same reason exists why the church cannot be defiled or injured, that there is that the temple could not be profaned. Both are sacred.

18. Do not deceive yourselves. 'Let no one doubt the truth of what I have said about the worthlessness of human wisdom, and of the danger of substituting it for God's wisdom. If he does, he will find himself mistaken.'

19–20. We must renounce our own wisdom because it is folly. The infinite mind sees that to be folly which we children think to be wisdom. To prove the assertion that human wisdom is foolishness with God, he quotes two passages of Scripture. The first is from Job 5:13, the second is from Psalm 94:11. The former is a fragment of a sentence containing no verb in the Greek. Our translation treats the particle as if it were a verb. Those passages clearly express the same sentiment which the apostle had uttered. They declare the impotency and insufficiency of human wisdom.

21. All things are yours. The amplification of these words, given in the next verse, shows that they are to be taken in their widest sense. The universe is yours. How unworthy it is, then, for you to boast about men. Paul often appeals to the dignity and destiny of the church as a motive to right action. 'Do you not know that the saints will judge the world?' (6:2).

23. Christ belongs to God. As the church is subject only to Christ, so Christ is subject only to God. The Scriptures speak about a threefold subordination of Christ:

1. A subordination of the second person of the Trinity to the first in mode of subsistence and operation. This is perfectly consistent with their identity of substance, and equality in power and glory.

2. The voluntary subordination of the Son in his humbling himself to be found in appearance as a man, and becoming obedient to death, and therefore subject to the limitations and infirmities of our nature.

3. The subordination of the incarnate Son of God, in the work of redemption and as the head of the church. He who is by nature equal with God becomes, as it were, subject to him.

The passages most directly parallel with this one are 11:3 and 15:28, but the same truth is taught in Philippians 2:5–11 and Hebrews 1:3, and in many other passages.

Chapter 4

Deduction from the preceding discussion, teaching the proper light in which the people should regard the ministry (verses 1–5).

Contrast between the apostles and the false teachers (verses 6–21).

Ministers, as stewards, should be faithful, as Paul had proved himself to be (verses 1–21).

It follows from what was said in the previous chapter that the people should regard their ministers as the servants of Christ, and dispensers of the truths which God had revealed (verse 1). The most important qualification of a dispenser is faithfulness (verse 2). It is a small matter how people may estimate the faithfulness of ministers. The only competent judge is the Lord; and, therefore, the decision of that question should be referred to his judgment (verses 3–6).

What the apostle had said about himself and Apollos, in the earlier explanation of the true nature of the ministerial office, was intended to apply to all ministers. The people should not esteem them unduly, and all emulous quarrels should be avoided (verses 6–7). The false teachers in Corinth, and the people under their influence, considered themselves to be in a high state of religious prosperity, and were disposed to

self-indulgence (verse 8). The apostles were in a very different condition, at least as to their external circumstances. They were despised, afflicted, and persecuted; while their adversaries were honoured, prosperous, and caressed (verses 9–13). Paul presented this contrast not to mortify, but to admonish his readers (verse 14). He, if anyone, had a right to admonish them, for he was their spiritual father (verse 15). They should therefore imitate him; and, to that end, he had sent Timothy to remind them of his instructions and example (verses 16–17). He himself intended to visit Corinth soon; and it depended on them whether he would come with a rod, or in the spirit of meekness (verses 18–21).

1. Servants of Christ. Literally the Greek means 'an under-rower,' or common sailor; and then, subordinate servant of any kind. It is generally and properly used of the lower sort of servants. This is not always the case, but here the idea of entire subjection is to be retained. Ministers are the mere servants of Christ; they have no authority of their own; their whole business is to do what they are commanded.

Stewards of God's mysteries. The Greek word means slaves appointed as managers or overseers. It was their business to direct the affairs of the household, and dispense the provisions. Ministers are to dispense the truths which God had revealed, and which are called **mysteries** because they cannot be discovered by human reason – people must be initiated into the knowledge of them.

2. The great thing required of ministers is faithfulness. Faithfulness to Christ as servants, not arrogating to themselves any power other than ministerial power, or venturing to go beyond his commands. Faithfulness also to the people, not failing to dispense to them the truths which God has revealed, nor mixing those truths with their own speculations, much less substituting for those doctrines human knowledge or wisdom.

3. That I should be judged by you. This does not refer to the judicial judgment of the church, but simply to the opinions which the Corinthians had of Paul. It mattered little to him whether they thought him faithful or unfaithful. His responsibility was not to them. They had not sent him; they had not told him what doctrines to preach. He was not their steward, but God's.

4. My conscience is clear. Paul is speaking about his faithfulness as a steward.

5. Before the Lord comes. That is, till Christ's second coming, which in the New Testament is constantly represented as contemporary with the resurrection of the dead and the general judgment. He is to come for judgment (Matthew 24:30, 46; 2 Peter 3:4, 12; Jude 14; Revelation 1:7). The reason why the Lord's coming is the appropriate time for judgment is that he will then do what cannot be done before, or by any creature. **Who will bring to light** (shed light upon) **the things now hidden in darkness.** This includes acts which are now unknown, and those principles of action which lie concealed in the recesses of the heart, where no human eye can reach them.

From God. He is the ultimate source of all good. He is in Christ; and Christ is in God. As the final judge, Christ is the representative of the Godhead, so his decisions and awards are the decisions and awards of God. As remarked on 2:15, what the apostle says about his independence of human judgment, and his command not to anticipate the judgment of the Lord, is consistent with his frequent recognition of the right and duty of the church to sit in judgment on the qualifications of her own members. Here he is speaking about the heart. The church cannot judge the heart. Whether someone is sincere or insincere in his professions, whether his experience is genuine or spurious, only God can decide. The church can only judge what is external. If anyone claims to be holy, and yet is immoral, the church is bound to reject him, as Paul clearly teaches in a later chapter. Or if someone professes to be a Christian and yet rejects Christianity, or any of its essential doctrines, he cannot be received (Titus 3:10). But only the Searcher of hearts can judge **the purposes of the heart.**

6. **'Nothing beyond what is written.'** That is, not to esteem minister above the scriptural standard. As Paul had been dealing with this subject, **'nothing beyond what is written'** might seem naturally to refer to what he himself had just written. But as the phrase elsewhere always refers to the Old Testament, which were the 'writings' recognized as of divine authority, that is probably what he is referring to here. He is not appealing to any one passage, but to the doctrine taught in the Scriptures concerning ministers of religion. The Corinthians were not to think of their ministers more highly than the Bible authorized them to think. Compare Jeremiah 9:23–24.

7. Paul was as much self-formed as any man ever was, and yet he said, 'By the grace of God I am what I am.'

8. **Already.** 'You have reached the goal of perfection very quickly; and you have reached it **apart from us.** You have left us poor apostles far behind.' The reference is to the benefits of redemption. Paul represents the Corinthians as thinking that they had already attained the full blessedness of the Messiah's reign; that they had already attained, and were already perfect. He therefore adds, **I wish that you had become kings.** 'I wish the consummation of Christ's kingdom had really come, for then I would share with you in its glories.'

9. **God has exhibited us.** He has made us conspicuous as the last, the lowest, the most afflicted people. The original does not allow the translation which many proposes – 'us the last apostles,' that is, those appointed last – referring to himself, who was, as he says, born our of due time. The emphasis, from the order of the words, is thrown on **apostles** and not on 'last.' What follows explains it.

As though sentenced to death. This does not merely mean that they were exhibited as men daily exposed to death – which indeed was true (15:30–31; 2 Corinthians 1:8–9 and 11:23); but also that they were treated like people condemned to death as convicts, men to whom all comforts were denied. 'We have become a spectacle' (literally 'a theatre,' here meaning a 'show' exhibited at a theatre) 'to the universe, to angels as well as to men.' Such were the sufferings of the apostles that men and angels gazed on them with wonder, as people gaze at a spectacle in a theatre.

10. **We are fools for the sake of Christ.** Our devotion to the cause of Christ is such that you and others regard us as fools.

But you are wise in Christ. Your union with Christ is such that you regard yourselves, and are regarded by others, as wise.

We are weak. We feel weak, and are thought weak.

You are strong. You regard yourselves as strong, and are regarded as strong.

You are held in honour. You are objects of respect, we are objects of contempt.

All this doubtless refers specially, though not exclusively, to the false teachers, whose state in Corinth he contrasts with his own.

12–13. **We have become like the rubbish of the world.** That is, we are regarded as the filthiest of mankind, and the refuse of society. One word means what is carried off by rinsing, and the other means what is scraped off. They both express the general idea of refuse.

14. **Admonish.** The Greek word is the one normally used to express parental admonition and instruction. His aim was to bring the truth to their minds, and let them see what they really were, as contrasted with what they imagined themselves to be.

15. **Guardians.** Among the Greeks these were usually slaves who were the constant attendants, rather than the teachers, of the boys of a family. However, they were in charge of their education, and therefore the word is used in the New Testament for instructors. Paul is contrasting his relationship to the Corinthians as their spiritual father, with that of their other teachers. The point of the contrast is not that he loved them, and they did not; or that they were disposed to arrogate too much authority, and he was not; but simply that he was the means of their

conversion, and they were not. His relationship to them preceded theirs and was more intimate and tender.

16. Imitators of me. He does not exhort them to become his followers or partisans, instead of being the followers of Apollos or of Cephas. But as he had spoken of himself as being humble, self-denying, and self-sacrificing in the cause of Christ, he beseeches them to follow his example. In 11:1 he says, 'Be imitators of me, as I am of Christ.' Compare 1 Thessalonians 1:6 and 2:14; Ephesians 5:1.

17. Faithful child. Not only the object of my love, but my child; one whom I have fathered through the Gospel. This is implied from the use of the word in verse 14. Compare 1 Timothy 1:2, where he speaks of him as 'my loyal child in the faith.' The fact that Timothy stood in this relationship to Paul was a reason for his sending him, and also a reason why they should receive him with confidence. He was, however, not only Paul's son, but **faithful child in the Lord.** And this was a further reason both for his mission and for their regard and confidence. **Faithful child in the Lord** means faithful in the service of Christ, or as a Christian.

18. His sending Timothy was not to be considered as any indication that he himself did not intend to visit Corinth, as some in their pride and self-confidence supposed.

19. And I will find out not the talk of these arrogant people but their power. That is, not what they can say, but what they can do.

20. For the kingdom of God depends not on talk but on power. The idea expressed by the phrase **kingdom of God** in the New Testament is very comprehensive and various, and therefore indefinite. The two senses under which most, if not all, its applications may be included are:

1. The royal authority or dominion exercised by God or Christ.

2. Those over whom that authority extends, or who recognize and submit to it.

21. Paul, so far from being afraid to go to Corinth, as his enemies imagined, was prepared to go there with authority. He was their spiritual father and ruler. He had the right and the ability to punish them. It depended on them whether he appeared among them as a punisher or as a comforter – whether in the exercise of discipline, or as a kind and tender parent.

Chapter 5

The case of the incestuous member of the church (verses 1–5).

Exhortation to purity, and to faithfulness in discipline (verses 6–13).

Reproof for retaining an unworthy member in the church (verses 1–13).

The second evil in the Corinthian church to which Paul directs his attention is allowing a man guilty of incest to remain in its communion. He says it was generally reported that fornication was tolerated among them, and even such fornication and was not heard of among the heathen (verse 1).

He reproves them for being inflated, instead of being humbled and penitent, and excommunicating the offender (verse 2). As they had neglected their duty, he determined, in the name of Christ, and as spiritually present in their assembly, to deliver the man guilty of incest to Satan (verses 3–5). He exhorts to purity, in language borrowed from the Mosaic law respecting the Passover. As during the feast of the Passover all leaven was to be removed from the Hebrews' homes, so that Christian's life should be a perpetual paschal feast, all malice and hypocrisy being banished from the hearts and from the assemblies of believers (verses 6–8). He corrects or guards against a misapprehension of his command not to associate with the immoral. He shows that the command referred to church communion, and not to social relationships; and therefore was limited in its application to members of the church. Those out of the church, it was neither his nor their prerogative to judge. They must be left to the judgment of God (verses 9–13).

1. Having dismissed the subject of the divisions in the Corinthian church, he takes up the case of the incestuous member of that church.

The term **sexual immorality** is used in a comprehensive sense, including all violations of the seventh commandment. Here, a particular case is distinguished as especially atrocious. The offense was that a man had married his step-mother. His **father's wife** is a scriptural periphrase for step-mother (see Leviticus 18:8). That it was a case of marriage is to be inferred from the uniform use of the phrase 'to have a woman' in the New Testament, which always means to marry (see Matthew 14:4; 22:28; 1 Corinthians 7:2, 29). Besides, although the connection continued, the offense is spoken of as past (verses 2–3). Such a marriage Paul says was unheard of among the Gentiles, that is, it was regarded by them with abhorrence. Cicero speaks of such a connection as an incredible crime, and as, with one exception, unheard of. It is probable from 2 Corinthians 7:12 that the father of the offender was still alive. The crime, however, was not adultery, but incest; for otherwise the apostle would not have spoken of it as an unheard of offense, and made the atrocity of it to arise out of the relationship between the woman and the offender's father.

2. Should you not rather have mourned, that is, grieved for yourselves. Your condition, instead of filling you with pride, should humble you and make you sad.

3–5. For though absent in body, I am present in spirit. Neither Paul's capacity nor his authority to judge, nor his power to execute his judgment, depended on his bodily presence. He was present in spirit. This does not mean simply that he was present in mind, thinking of them and interested in their welfare; but it was a presence of knowledge, authority, and power.

Hand this man over to Satan. From the earliest times, there have been two prevalent interpretations of this expression. According to one view, it means simple excommunication; according to the other, it includes a miraculous subjection of the person to the power of Satan. Those who regard it as merely excommunication say that 'to deliver to Satan' corresponds to 'removed from among you' in verse 2, and therefore means the same thing. The Corinthians had neglected to excommunicate this offender, and Paul says he had determined to do it. Besides, it is argued that excommunication is properly expressed by the phrase 'to deliver to Satan' because, as the world is the kingdom of Satan, to cast someone out of the church was to cast him from the kingdom of Christ into the kingdom of Satan. Compare Colossians 1:13. In favour of the idea of something more than excommunication, it may be argued:

1. It is clearly revealed in Scripture that bodily evils are often inflicted on people by the agency of Satan.

2. The apostles were invested with the power of miraculously inflicting such evils (Acts 5:1–11; 13:9–11; 2 Corinthians 10:8 and 13:10).

3. In 1 Timothy 1:20, the same formula occurs, probably in the same sense. There, Paul says he had delivered Hymenaeus and Alexander to Satan, that they might learn not to blaspheme.

4. There is no evidence that the Jews of that age ever expressed excommunication by this phrase, and therefore it would not, in all probability, be understood in that sense by Paul's readers.

5. Excommunication would not have the effect of destroying the flesh, in the sense in which that expression is used in the following clause.

Most commentators, therefore, agree in understanding the apostle to threaten the infliction of some bodily evil, when he speaks of delivering this offender to Satan.

6. A little yeast leavens the whole batch of dough. This proverbial expression is not intended here to express the idea that one corrupt member of the church depraves the whole, because, in the following verses, in which the image is continued, the yeast is not a person, but sin. The idea, therefore, is that it is the nature of

evil to diffuse itself. This is true with regard to individuals and communities.

7. Yeast. Yeast in this context is a figurative expression for sin. To say, therefore, that they were unleavened is to say that they were holy. This was their normal state – as Christians. A Christian is a new or holy person. The argument, therefore, is drawn from the acknowledged fact that Christians, as such, are holy. 'Purge out the yeast of wickedness, that you may be pure, for believers are holy.'

8. Sincerity is purity, transparent clearness; something through which the sun may shine without revealing any flaw.

Truth, in Scripture, is far more than veracity. In its subjective sense, it means that inner state which corresponds to the truth – that moral condition which is conformed to the law and character of God.

9. Not to associate with sexually immoral persons. Not to be mixed up together with. See 2 Thessalonians 3:14. This may refer either to relating socially or to church communion. Paul explains this indefinite command, first, by stating that he did not mean to forbid social relationships; and then saying he did intend to prohibit Christian fellowship with the wicked.

10. The world means mankind as distinguished from the church (Galatians 4:3; Ephesians 2:2; Colossians 2:8). The prohibition, such as it was, was not limited to any one sort of immoral people; it included all sorts. The **greedy,** those who want more; and especially those who defraud for the sake of gain. In the Scriptures the controlling love of gain is spoken of as a specially heinous sin in God's sight. It is called idolatry in Ephesians 5:5 because wealth becomes the object supremely loved and sought. Therefore someone who sacrifices duty to the acquisition of wealth, who makes gain the great object of his life, is a **greedy** person. He cannot be a Christian, and should not, according to the apostle, be recognized as such.

11. Do not even eat with such a one. This does not refer to the Lord's Supper, which is never designated as a meal. The meaning is that we are not to recognize such a person in any way as a Christian, even by eating with him.

13. 'Drive out.' This seems to have been borrowed from Deuteronomy 24:7. It is a simple imperative injunction, or necessary application of the principle of Christian communion just laid down. This passage is not inconsistent with the interpretation given to verses 3–5. In consequence of their neglect of duty, Paul determined to deliver the incestuous member of the Corinthian church to Satan. He calls upon them to recognize the validity of that sentence, and to carry it into effect. The sentence was pronounced; they, so far as it involved their communion, were to execute it.

Chapter 6

This chapter consists of two distinct paragraphs:

Lawsuits before heathen magistrates (verses 1–11).

The abuse which some people had made of the principle, 'All things are lawful' (verses 12–20).

On going to law before the heathen (verses 1–11).

Paul expresses surprise that any Christian should prosecute a fellow Christian before a heathen judge (verse 1). If Christians are destined to judge the world, and even angels, they may surely settle among themselves their worldly affairs (verses 2–3). If they had such lawsuits, must they appoint those whom the church could not esteem to decide them? Was there not one man among themselves able to act as a judge? (verses 4–6). It was a great evil that they had such lawsuits. It would be better to submit to injustice (verse 7). However, instead of submitting to wrong, they committed it (verse 8). He solemnly assures them that the unjust, or rapacious, or corrupt would not inherit the kingdom of God (verses 9–10). They had been like that, but as Christians they were washed from these defilements, and justified through Christ and by his Spirit (verse 11).

1. The third evil in the Corinthian church which the apostle endeavours to correct was taking lawsuits to heathen judges. There was no need for this. The Roman laws allowed the Jews to settle their disputes about property by arbitration among themselves. And the early Christians, who were not distinguished as a distinct class from the Jews, doubtless had the same privilege. It is not necessary, however, to assume that the apostle is referring to that privilege here. It was enough that these civil suits might be arranged without the disgraceful spectacle of Christian suing Christian before heathen magistrates. The Rabbis say, 'It is a statute which binds all Israelites, that if one Israelite has a case against another, it must not be brought before the Gentiles.'

2. The saints will judge the world. The context and spirit of the passage require that it should be understood of the future and final judgment. Saints are said to sit in judgment on that great day for two reasons; first, because Christ, who is to be the judge, is the head and representative of his people, in whom they reign and judge. The exaltation and dominion of Christ are their exaltation and dominion. This is what Scripture constantly says (Ephesians 2:6). In Hebrews 2:5–9, the declaration that all things

are subject to man is said to be fulfilled in all things being made subject to Christ. Secondly, because his people are to be associated with Christ in his dominion. They are joint heirs with him (Romans 8:17). If we suffer, we shall reign with him (2 Timothy 2:12). In Daniel 7:22 it was predicted that judgment (the right and power to judge) would be given to the saints of the Most High. Compare Matthew 19:28; Luke 22:30; Revelation 2:26,27.

4. Paul laments that there were litigations among them; but if they could not be avoided, Christians should act in reference to them in a manner consistent with their high destiny. Here the word translated **ordinary cases** seems so naturally to mean 'causes,' 'things tried,' that the sense of the word is almost universally assumed. It may, however, mean 'trials,' 'judicial processes,' which is more in accordance with the established use of the words.

5. Between one believer and another. Literally, 'between his brother'; that is, between his complaining brother and the person against whom the complaint was brought.

9–10. The tendency to divorce religion from morality has manifested itself in all ages of the world, and under all forms of religion. The pagan, the Jew, the Muslim, the nominal Christian, have all been exact in the performance of religious services, and zealous in the assertion and defence of what they regard as religious truth, while unrestrained in the indulgence of every evil passion. This arises from looking upon religion as an outward service, and God as a being to be feared and propitiated, but not to be loved and obeyed. According to the Gospel, all moral duties are religious services; and piety is the conformity of the soul to the image and will of God. So, to be religious and yet immoral is, according to the Christian system, as palpable a contradiction as to be good and wicked. It is evident that among the members of the Corinthian church there were some who retained their pagan notion of religion, and who professed Christianity as a system of doctrine and as a form of worship, but not as a rule of life. The apostle warned all such people of their fatal mistake. He assures them that no immoral man – no one who allows himself the indulgence of any known sin – can be saved. This is one of the first principles of the Gospel, and therefore the apostle asks, **Do you not know that wrongdoers will not inherit the kingdom of God?** Are you Christians at all, and yet ignorant of this first principle of the religion you profess? The **wrongdoers** in this immediate context means the 'unjust' – those who violate the principles of justice in their dealings with their fellow men. It is not the unjust alone, however, who are to be debarred from the Redeemer's kingdom like this; it is also those who break any of God's commandments, as this and other passages of Scripture distinctly teach.

11. And this is what some of you used to be. This is understood by many as equivalent to 'That is what you were,' the word 'some' being redundant, or the idea being, 'Some were impure, some drunkards, some violent, etc.' The natural explanation is that the apostle deliberately avoided charging the gross immoralities just referred to upon all the Corinthian Christians in their previous condition.

But you were washed. To 'wash' means to purify, and is frequently used in Scripture to express moral or spiritual purification. See Isaiah 1:16; Psalm 51:7; Jeremiah 4:14. In these and many other passages the word expresses general purification, without exclusive reference to guilt or to pollution. There is no reason why it should not be taken in this general sense here, and the phrase be translated either 'You have purified yourselves,' or, 'You are purified.' The reference which so many assume to be to baptism does not seem to be authorized by anything in the context.

You were sanctified. This is either an amplification of the previous one, expressing one aspect or effect of the washing, namely, their holiness; or it is to be understood of their separation and consecration. 'You have not only been purified, but also set apart as a special people.' In Scripture, anything is said to be sanctified that is devoted to God's service. Thus, God blessed the seventh day and sanctified it (Genesis 2:3). Moses sanctified the people (Exodus 19:14).

You were justified. As to justify in Scripture always means to pronounce righteous, or to declare just in the sight of the law, it must be understood in that way here. The Corinthians had not only been purified and consecrated, but also justified, that is, clothed in the righteousness of Christ, and on that account accepted as righteous in the sight of God. They were therefore under the highest possible obligation not to relapse into their former state of pollution and condemnation.

Abuse of the principle of Christian liberty (verses 12–20).

The principle of Christian liberty, or the doctrine that 'all things are lawful,' is to be limited in its application to things which do not affect salvation; first, by considerations of expediency; and secondly, by regard to our own spiritual freedom (verse 12). We may legitimately infer from the adaptation of the stomach to food, that all things suited for food are lawful. The one is obviously designed for the other, during the temporary condition of the present life. But

we cannot apply the same principle to sexual immorality, because the body is not designed for that end, but belongs to the Lord, and is indissolubly connected to him, so that he who raised him up will also raise up our bodies (verses 13–14). It is because of this intimate relationship of our bodies as parts of Christ that sexual immorality is so great a crime, inconsistent with our union to him as partakers of his Spirit (verses 15–17). It is, in a special way, a sin against the body, destructive of its very nature (verse 18). The body is a temple in which the Spirit dwells, but it ceases to be such if profaned by licentiousness (verse 19). Believers must remember that they, even their bodies, are the objects of redemption, having been purchased by the blood of Christ, and therefore they should be devoted to his glory (verse 20).

13. The body is ... for the Lord, and the Lord for the body. The one stands in intimate relationship to the other. The body is designed to be a part of Christ, and the place where his Spirit lives. And he regards it as such, redeeming it with his blood, uniting it to himself as a part of his mystical body, making it an instrument of righteousness for holiness. The sin in question is absolutely incompatible with this, and destroys the relationship which the body has with the Lord.

14. On this destiny of the body, compare 15:15, 20, 35–56; Philippians 3:21; Romans 8:11; 2 Corinthians 4:14; 1 Thessalonians 4:14.

15–16. Do you not know that your bodies are members of Christ? This is a conceded and familiar point of Christian doctrine, one with which they were supposed to be acquainted; and which proved all that the apostle had said of the relationship between the body and Christ.

18. This does not teach that sexual immorality is greater than any other sin; but it does teach that it is altogether unique in its effects on the body; not so much in its physical as in its moral and spiritual effects. The idea runs through the Bible that there is something mysterious in sexual intercourse, and in the effects which flow from it. Every other sin, however degrading and ruinous to the health, even drunkenness, is external to the body, that is, external to its life. But sexual immorality, involving as it does a community of life, is a sin against the body itself, because it is incompatible with the purpose of its creation, and with its immortal destiny.

19. Two things characterize a temple. First, it is sacred as a place where God lives, and therefore it cannot be profaned with impunity. Second, the temple is not owned by man but by God. Both these things are true of the believer's body.

20. You were bought. That is, delivered by purchase.

Chapter 7

Instructions concerning marriage
(verses 1–17).

The Gospel was not designed to interfere
with people's ordinary relationships
(verses 18–24).

Concerning virgins and widows
(verses 25–40).

Instructions concerning marriage and other social relationships (verses 1–24).

The Corinthians had written to the apostle, seeking his advice about the state of things in their church. It appears from this chapter that one of the subjects about which they were in difficulty, and about which they sought direction, was marriage. On this subject the apostle tells them, first, that, as they were situated, marriage was inexpedient to them. But as a general rule every man should have his own wife, and every woman her own husband (verses 1–2). Secondly, he tells them that the obligation of the parties to the marriage covenant is mutual; the one therefore has no right to desert the other. Temporary separation, for the purpose of devotion, is allowable; but nothing more (verses 3–5). Thirdly, he tells them that what he had said either about marriage or about temporary separation was not to be considered as anything more than advice. He could only tell them what, under the circumstances, was expedient; each one must act according to the grace given to him (verses 6–9).

Fourthly, he says that with regard to the married the Lord had already taught that divorce was unlawful; the husband could not put away his wife, nor the wife her husband (verses 10–11). Fifthly, as to the case not specially contemplated in our Lord's instructions, where one of the parties was a Christian and the other a Jew or pagan, the apostle teaches, first, that if the unbelieving party is willing to remain in the marriage relationship, it should not be dissolved. Secondly, that if the unbeliever left, and refused to continue in the marriage relationship, the marriage contract was thereby dissolved, and the believing part was at liberty (verses 12–15). Such separations, however, are, if possible, to be avoided, because the Gospel is a Gospel of peace. It was not designed to break up any of the lawful relationships of life.

As a general rule, therefore, every man should continue in the same condition in which he was called. If a man was circumcised when he was called, his becoming a Christian did not impose on him the obligation to become uncircumcised; and if he was uncircumcised when he was called, he was not required to be circumcised. Similarly, if a slave is called to be a Christian, he may remain a slave, because every slave is the Lord's free man, and every free man is the Lord's slave. These social distinctions do not affect our relationship to Christ, that is, making them all his property has raised them into a sphere where all earthly distinctions are insignificant. Therefore, let every man remain as he was when he was called (verses 16–24).

1. Evidently there were various opinions in the Corinthian church about marriage. Probably some of them of Jewish origin thought it obligatory, while other members of the church thought it undesirable, if not wrong. Paul says, It is good for a man not to marry. The word **well** here means expedient, profitable, as it does frequently elsewhere (for example, in Matthew 17:4 and 18:8–9). The apostle does not mean to teach either that marriage is morally an evil as compared with celibacy, or that as a general rule it is inexpedient.

2. As a general rule, says the apostle, let every man have his own wife, and every woman her own husband. Whatever exceptions there may be to this rule in particular cases, or in special conditions of society or of the church, the rule itself stands.

3–5. There is abundant evidence in the New Testament of the early manifestation of those principles of asceticism which soon produced such widespread effects, and which to so great a degree modified the reigning spirit of the church. The idea that marriage was a less holy state than celibacy naturally led to the conclusion that married people ought to separate, and it soon came to be regarded as evidence of great spirituality when such separation was final. The apostle teaches that neither party has the right to separate from the other; that no separation is to be allowed which is not with mutual consent, for a limited time, for the purpose of special devotion, and with the definite intention of reunion. Nothing can be more foreign to the mind of the apostle than the spirit which filled the monasteries and convents of the medieval church.

6–7. Marriage, in other words, is permitted, not commanded, for I **wish that were as I myself am.** The sense is not materially different if, with many editors, we read 'Marriage is not commanded, but I wish. …' The apostle did not take sides with the extreme Jewish party, who regarded marriage as obligatory. He admitted the expediency of all remaining single in those times of persecution, if God had given them the necessary grace.

8–9. The apostle writes to the Corinthians as he would do to an army about to enter on a most unequal conflict in an enemy's country, and for a protracted period. He tells them, 'This is no time for you to think of marriage. You have a right to marry. And in general it is best that all men should marry. But in your circumstances marriage can only lead to embarrassment and increase of suffering.' This is the only view of the matter by which we can reconcile the apostle with himself, or with the truth of Scripture and of fact. This must therefore be borne in mind in the interpretation of this whole chapter.

10–11. Paul tells the Corinthians that so far as the matter of divorce was concerned, they had no need to apply to him for instruction; Christ had already taught that the marriage bond could not be dissolved at the option of the parties. The wife had no right to leave her husband, nor had the husband the right to repudiate his wife. But although the marriage bond cannot be dissolved by any human authority, because it is, in virtue of the law of God, a covenant for life between one man and one woman, yet it can be annulled – not rightfully, but effectually. Adultery annuls it, because it is a breach of the specific contract involved in marriage. And so does wilful desertion, for the same reason – as the apostle teaches in a later verse.

12–13. To the rest. That is, to those married people not considered in the preceding group. The Christian husband is forbidden to divorce his heathen wife; and the Christian wife is forbidden to divorce her heathen husband.

14. The proof that such marriages may properly be continued is that the unbelieving party is sanctified by the believing; and the proof that such is the fact is that by common consent their children are holy; which could not be, unless the marriages they came from were holy; or unless it were correct that intimate communion with the holy makes people holy.

15. The command in the previous verse was based on the assumption that the unbelieving party consented to remain in the marriage relationship. If the unbeliever refused to remain, the believer was then free. The unbeliever was not to divorce the unbelieving husband or wife, but if the unbeliever broke up the marriage, that liberated the Christian partner from the contract.

16. Here the idea is, 'Who knows, O wife, but that you may save your husband?'

17. Paul was not only averse to breaking up the conjugal relationship, but it was a general ordinance of his that, after becoming Christians, men should remain in the same social position which they had occupied before.

18. This is the first application of the principle just laid down. Let every man remain as he is, circumcised or uncircumcised.

19. This is the reason why they should be treated with indifference. They are nothing; they have no influence either favourable or

unfavourable on our relationship to God. No man is either the better or the worse for being either circumcised or uncircumcised. The Gospel has raised men above all such things.

21. The general sense is plain. A man who is a slave, so far as his being a Christian is concerned, is a matter of no importance. It need give him no concern.

22. Is a slave of Christ. That is, is one whom the Lord has redeemed.

23. You (that is, all Christians, bond and free) **were bought with a price.** That is, purchased by Christ with his most precious blood (1 Peter 1:18–19). You belong to him; you are his slaves, and should therefore act accordingly; and not be **slaves of human masters.** The slave of one master cannot be the slave of another. Anyone who is redeemed by Christ, who feels that he belongs to him, that his will is the supreme rule of action, and who performs all his duties, not as a man-pleaser, but as if he is serving the Lord, not men (Ephesians 6:6–7), is inwardly free, whatever his external relations may be.

Of virgins and widows (verses 25–40).

In this part of the chapter the apostle deals mainly with the marriage of virgins – including, however, the young of both sexes. On this subject he says he was not authorized to speak with authority, but simply to advise (verse 25). His advice was that, because of the impending troubles, they should not marry (verses 26–27). It was not wrong to marry, but it would expose them to greater suffering (verse 28). Besides, they should consider the transitory nature of all earthly ties. The world in its present form was passing away (verses 29–31). Still further, a single life was freer from worldly cares. The unmarried could consecrate themselves without distraction to the service of the Lord (verses 32–35). To parents he says that, if circumstances make it desirable, they might without hesitation give their daughters in marriage (verse 36). But if they were free to act on their own judgment, his advice was to keep them unmarried (verses 37–38). Marriage can only be dissolved by death. After the death of her husband, a woman is at liberty to marry again; but she should intermarry only with a Christian; and in Paul's judgment, her happiness would be promoted by remaining single (verses 39–40).

25. Concerning virgins. The word strictly means 'maidens,' though as an adjective it is used of both sexes (Revelation 14:4).

I have no command of the Lord. That is, neither Christ himself, nor the Spirit of Christ, by whom Paul was guided, had commissioned him to do anything more than to counsel these people. In this matter he was inspired, or led by the Spirit, not to command but to advise. His advice, however, was worthy of great deference.

It was not merely the counsel of a wise and experienced man, but of one who by the Lord's mercy was **trustworthy**.

26. Here Paul expressly states the basis of his opinion that it was inexpedient for his readers to marry. It was because of **the impending crisis**, the distress standing near (whether actually present or impending depends on the context). See Luke 21:23; 2 Corinthians 6:4; 1 Thessalonians 3:7. In the present case the apostle is probably referring not so much to the troubles in which Christians were then involved as to those which he saw to be hanging over them. Paul here is not referring to the calamities which will precede the second coming, but rather to those which it was predicted would accompany the introduction of the Gospel.

27. In the church's present circumstances, marriage will prove a burden. Although this fact will not justify the dissolution of any marriage, it should dissuade Christians from getting married.

29–31. 'This is another reason why you should not marry. You will soon have to leave your wives. It is nothing relating to your permanent and eternal interests which I urged you to forego, but only something which pertains to the fleeting relations of this changing world.'

32–33. This is the third reason why Paul wanted the early Christians to remain unmarried. The first was the increased suffering marriage would probably bring with it. The second was the transitory nature of all earthly things. And the third is the comparative freedom from care connected with a single life.

34. What is true of men is also true of women. The Greek literally translated is, 'Divided is a wife and a virgin.' The difference is that the virgin may devote her whole time to the Lord; the wife must be involved in worldly cares for the sake of her husband. Their interests are diverse. The one has a husband to divide her attention; the other is free from such distraction.

36. This and the following verse are addressed to fathers, for with them according to the practice both of Jews and of Greeks, rested the disposal of the daughters of the family. Though the apostle regarded marriage at that time as inexpedient, he tells fathers that they were perfectly free to exercise their own judgment in giving their daughters in marriage or keeping them single.

38. As there is no sin in marriage, and no superior virtue in celibacy, it is merely a question of expediency, to be determined by the circumstances of each particular case.

39. The uniform doctrine of the New Testament is that marriage is a contract for life, between one man and one woman, indissoluble by the will of the parties or by any human authority; but that the death of either party leaves the survivor free to contract another marriage.

Chapter 8

Eating of sacrifices offered to idols is not in itself wrong (verses 1–7).

But it should be avoided if it gave offense (verses 8–13).

On eating sacrifices (verses 1–13).

The second subject on which the Corinthians had requested the apostle's advice was the lawfulness of eating of the sacrifices offered to idols. Chapters 8–10 of this letter are chiefly devoted to discussing the different aspects of that question. At the council of Jerusalem it was decided by the apostles, elders, and brothers that the Gentile converts should abstain 'from what has been sacrificed to idols and from blood and from what is strangled and from immorality' (Acts 15:29); and this decree was referred to the Holy Spirit as its author (verse 28). Yet Paul, though present in that council, not only does not refer to it, but goes directly against it. That decree forbade the eating of meat offered to idols; Paul, in chapter 10, tells the Corinthians that when exposed for sale in the market, or found on private tables, they might eat it without scruple. These facts do not prove any discrepancy between the apostles gathered in Jerusalem and Paul; nor that the decisions of that council were not obligatory on the church. They only serve to explain the true intention and meaning of those decisions. They show two things:

1. There was no permanent moral basis for the prohibition of meat offered to idols.

2. Since the basis for the prohibition was expediency, it was necessarily temporary and limited. It applied to Christians in the midst of those to whom eating such meat was an abomination. Therefore, it ceased to be binding whenever and wherever the basis of the prohibition did not exist. It is analogous to Paul's condemnation of women appearing in church without a veil.

The decisions of that council, therefore, were no barrier to Paul's discussing the question on its merits. In this chapter, two aspects of the subject are viewed: first, considered in itself; and secondly, in its bearing on the weaker or less enlightened sort of Christians. Most of the questions which disturbed the early church had their origin in the conflicting prejudices of the Jewish and Gentile converts; or at least, of the more and less enlightened of the Christian converts, for many of those who had been educated as heathens were probably among the weaker brothers. As a body, however, the Gentiles were disposed to latitudinarianism; and the Jews to superstitious scruples.

So far as general principles were concerned, Paul sided with the Gentile party. Their views about food and drink, and holy days, and ceremonies were derived from the apostle himself, and were therefore approved by him. But he severely condemns the spirit and practice of this party. Thus, in the present instance, he admits that an idol is nothing; that a sacrifice is nothing; that all enlightened Christians know this; that, consequently, eating the heathen sacrifices was a matter of no significance – it made the person neither better nor wore. Yet eating them might be, and in their case it was, sinful, because it harmed their weaker brothers.

He begins the chapter by admitting that all enlightened Christians have knowledge. He reminds them, however, that there is something higher than knowledge; that knowledge without love is, after all, only another form of ignorance. The main thing to be known is not apprehended (verses 1–3). He admits, however, that Christians know that the gods of the heathen are vanities and lies, that there is only one, the living and true God (verse 4). For although the heathen acknowledge a whole hierarchy of deities, celestial and terrestrial, Christians acknowledge only one God and one Mediator (verse 6). All this is admitted. Nevertheless, it is true that many Christians, though they know that there is only one God, are still not persuaded that the heathen deities are nothing, and therefore they stand in awe of them, and could not help believing that eating sacrifices offered to idols was an act of worship, or in some way defiling (verse 7).

The apostle also admits the second principle relied on by the Gentile converts, namely, that meat does not commend us to God, that it can have no influence on our spiritual state (verse 8). It is not enough, however, that an act should be in its own nature indifferent to justify us in performing it. If we do something that is innocent in itself, but that action leads others into sin, it is for that reason sinful for us (verse 9). If, therefore, a weak brother should be led, against the convictions of his own mind, to join his stronger brothers in eating such sacrifices, he would bring himself into condemnation. It was, therefore, a breach of charity and a sin against Christ, to eat of the heathen sacrifices under circumstances which made other people bold to sin (verses 10–12). The apostle avows his own determination never to eat meat at all, if by doing so he would cause his brothers to sin (verse 13).

1. The idolatry of the Greeks and Romans pervaded their whole life. Their social contacts, their feasts, the administration of justice, public entertainment, the offices and honours of government, were all more or less connected with religious services. Christians, therefore, were constantly exposed to the danger of being involved in some idolatrous homage without even knowing it. This gave rise to numerous perplexing questions of conscience, which were often decided differently by different groups of Christians.

Love builds up. The old word 'charity' was an inadequate and unhappy translation of the Greek word *agape* because, in keeping with its Latin derivation, it actually means the feeling which arises from seeing other people's needs and sufferings, and the consequent desire to relieve them. **Love** (*agape*, a word unique to Hellenistic Greek) is much more comprehensive than this, not only because it may have God for its object, but also because, when exercised towards men, it includes delight as well as benevolence. It is this comprehensive virtue that the apostle deals with at length in chapter 13 of this letter, and which here he says **builds up**. It does not end in itself, as knowledge does, but foes out of itself, and seeks its happiness in another, and lives and acts for others. It is, therefore, something incomparably higher than knowledge, when the two are separated and distinguished.

3. To love is to know and to be known. Compare 1 John 4:7–8. This is the precise sentiment of the text. Love is essential to knowledge. Whoever loves God, knows God.

4. To determine whether it was proper to eat from these sacrifices, it must first be determined what an idol is; and secondly, what effect the eating would have. As for idols, Paul says there is no idol (or **'no idol in the world really exists'**); and as for the eating, he says it could have no effect on our religious state – it could make us neither better nor worse (verse 8). Nevertheless, if our eating causes other people to sin, we ought not to eat.

6. **For us.** That is, to Christians.

There is one God. That is, only one being who is eternal, self-existing, and almighty. This one God is, first, **the Father**; not the first person of the Trinity, but our father. The word does not here express the relationship of the first to the second person in the Godhead, but the relationship of God as such to us as his children. When we say, 'Our Father in heaven,' the word Father designates the Supreme Being, the Triune Jehovah.

Through whom we exist. This does not mean we were created by him, for we Christians are included in the **all things**. It would be tautological to say, 'He created all things, and he created us.' The meaning is that we as Christians (not we as creatures, for that had been said before), we as the children of God are 'by him.' We were redeemed by him; we are brought to God by him.

7. Since their conscience is weak, it is defiled. A **weak** conscience is one which either regards as wrong what is not in fact so, or one which is not clear and decided in its judgments. According to the Scriptures, 'whatever does not proceed from faith is sin' (Romans 14:23); therefore whatever a person does, thinking it is wrong, or doubtful whether it is wrong or not, is sin to that person. Thus the person who eats an idol-sacrifice, uncertain whether it is right or not, defiles his conscience. The conscience is said to be defiled, either when it approves or cherishes sin, or when it is burdened by a sense of guilt. The latter form of pollution is the one intended here. The person who acts in this way feels guilty, and is really guilty.

8. It is admitted that food does not **bring us close to God.** Eating neither causes us to excel nor to come behind.

9. Admitting you have the right to eat from these sacrifices, take care lest your eating become an occasion of sin to your weaker brothers.

Stumbling-block. An occasion to sin, or which causes people to fall. In the same sense the word is used in Luke 17:1; Romans 14:13; 1 John 2:10.

10. This verse is designed to show how eating these sacrifices might be an occasion of sin to others.

Eating. Literally, 'lying down,' according to the ancient custom of reclining on a couch at table. The verb 'to lie up' is also used, as the couches were usually higher than the table.

11. For whom Christ died. There is great power and pathos in these words. Shall we, for the sake of eating one kind of food rather than another, endanger the salvation of those for whom the eternal Son of God laid down his life?

13. Matthew 18:6 shows how serious a matter our Lord considers it to be if we lead even the weakest Christian to sin. It is still worse to lead him into error, for error is the mother of many sins.

Chapter 9

The apostle illustrates the duty of foregoing the exercise of our rights for the good of others, by referring to his giving up his undoubted right to be supported by the church (verses 1–18).

He shows that in other ways he accommodated himself to the opinions and prejudices of others (verses 19–23).

He reminds his readers that nothing good or great could be attained without self-denial (verses 24–27).

The right of ministers to an adequate maintenance. The necessity of self-denial (verses 1–27).

In the preceding chapter, the apostle had urged the strong that it was their duty to forego their rights for the sake of the weaker brothers. Now he shows he had acted on that principle. He was an apostle, and therefore had all the rights of an apostle. His apostleship was abundantly clear, because he had seen the Lord Jesus and was his immediate messenger; and his divine mission had been confirmed, at least among the Corinthians, beyond dispute. They were the seal of his apostleship (verses 1–3). Being an apostle, he had the same right to be supported and to have his family supported, if he had chosen to marry, as Peter or any other apostle (verses 4–6). This right lies at the foundation of society, that the labourer is worthy of his reward (verse 7). Secondly, from the fact that this principle is recognized in the Old Testament, even in its application to animals (verses 8–10). Thirdly, from the principles of commutative justice (verse 11). Fourthly, from the fact that the Corinthians recognized this right in the case of other teachers (verse 12). Fifthly, from the universal recognition of the principle among all nations. Those who served the temple were supported from the temple (verse 13). Sixthly, from the express ordinance of Christ, who had ordained that those who preached the Gospel should live by the Gospel (verse 14).

Paul had not availed himself of this undoubted right, and he was determined, especially at Corinth, not to avail himself of it in the future. By doing so he forestalled any questioning of his motives, and have himself a ground of confidence in resisting his opponents which he was determined not to relinquish (verses 15–18). This was not, however, the only case in which he abstained from the exercise of his rights for the good of others. He accommodated himself to Jews and Gentiles in everything that was not intrinsically wrong, so that he might gain all the more (verses 19–23). The heathen exercised such self-denial to gain a corruptible crown – should not Christians do as much to gain a crown that is incorruptible? Without self-denial and effort the prize of their high calling could never be attained (verses 24–27).

1. Am I not free? That is, am I not a Christian, with all the liberties with which Christ has made his people free? Am I not as free as any other believer to regulate my conduct according to my own convictions of what is right – free from any obligation to conform to the opinions or prejudices of other people? This, however, is a freedom which I have not availed myself of.

Am I not an apostle? Besides the rights which belong to Christians, have I not all the prerogatives of an apostle? Am I not on a level with the chief of the apostles? Which of them can show a better title to the office?

2. If I am not an apostle to others, that is, in their opinion, **at least I am to you.** Whatever pretense others may have to question my apostleship, you certainly can have none.

For you are the seal of my apostleship in the Lord. Your conversion is the seal of God on my commission.

4. Having proved his apostleship, he proves his right to be supported, and then shows that he had not availed himself of that right. He could, therefore, with the greater freedom urge the Corinthians to forego their right to eat things offered to idols for the sake of their weaker brothers.

5. And Cephas. This is the name by which Peter is called whenever he is mentioned by Paul, except in the letter to the Galatians. That Peter was married is clear from Matthew 8:14 and Mark 1:30.

7. Here are three illustrations of the principle, taken from people's ordinary occupations. The soldier, the farmer, the shepherd all live by their labour; why should not the minister? His work is as engrossing, as labourious, and as useful as theirs; why should it not meet with a similar reward?

9. Is it for oxen that God is concerned? It is perfectly certain that God does care for oxen; for he feeds the young ravens when they call (Job 38:41; Psalm 147:9; Matthew 6:26; Luke 12:24). Therefore the apostle cannot intend to deny this. He only means that the law referred to something higher. Although the immediate purpose of the command was that the working animals should be treated fairly, its ultimate aim was to teach people the moral truth involved in this teaching. If God requires that even the ox, which spends its strength in our service, should not be defrauded of its reward, how must stricter will he be in enforcing the application of the same principle of justice to his rational creatures.

11. That is, if we have given you one sort of benefit, is it unreasonable that we should receive another sort from you?

12. This rightful claim on you. Undisputable as this right was in Paul's case, he did not exercise it, but **endure anything,** that is, endured all kinds of privations. The word means 'to bear in silence.'

14. As God had ordained under the Old Testament, so also the Lord (that is, Christ) had ordained under the New. Christ has made the same ordinance respecting the ministers of the Gospel that God made concerning the priests of the law.

16. The reason why it was so important to him to refuse all remuneration as a minister was that *although he preached the Gospel* that was no ground of boasting to him. He was bound to do that; indeed, he says **Woe betide me if I do not proclaim the gospel!** Nothing could be a ground of boasting unless it were something which he was free to do, or not to do. He was free to receive or to refuse remuneration for preaching; and therefore his refusing to do so was a ground of glorying, that is, a proof of integrity to which he could appeal with confidence.

18. To do what was commanded was no ground of reward; but to preach the Gospel without charge was something of which he could boast, that is, make a basis of confidence.

19. The apostle's self-denial and accommodation of himself to the weakness and prejudices of others was not confined to the point of which he had been speaking. He constantly acted on the principle of abstaining in things of no intrinsic importance, from insisting on his rights.

20. To the Jews I became as a Jew. That is, he acted as they acted, he conformed to their practices, observed the law, avowing at the same time that he did it as a matter of accommodation. Wherever it would fairly have been inferred from his compliance that he regarded these Jewish observances as necessary, he strenuously refused to comply.

22. To the weak he became like a weak person; he accommodated himself to their prejudices so that he might win them over to better views. And he wanted the Corinthians to do the same.

I have become all things to all people. This generalizes all that had been said. It was not to this or that group that he was conciliatory, but to all sorts, and as to all matters not intrinsically affecting salvation, so that he might **by any means save some.**

25. Exercise self-control. He controls himself in all things. He exercises self-denial in diet, in bodily indulgences, and by painful and protracted discipline. The ancient writers abound in rules of abstinence and exercise to be observed by competitors in preparation for the games.

26. Aimlessly. The Greek word may mean 'inconspicuously,' not like someone unseen but like someone on whom all eyes are fixed. Or more probably the idea is, not like someone running uncertain where or for what he is running. A man who runs uncertain as to his course of object runs without spirit or effort.

Chapter 10

A continuation of the exhortation to self-denial and caution (verses 1–13).

Express prohibition of joining in the sacrificial feasts of the heathen (verses 14–22).

Particular directions as to the use of meat sacrificed to idols (verses 23–33).

The necessity of self-denial argued from the case of the Israelites (verses 1–13).

At the close of the preceding chapter the apostle had exhorted his readers to self-denial and effort, in order to secure the crown of life. Here he enforces that exhortation, by showing how disastrous had been the lack of such self-control in the case of the Israelites. They had been highly favoured as well as we. They had been miraculously guided by the pillar of cloud; they had been led through the Red Sea; they had been fed with manna from heaven, and with water from the rock; and yet the great majority of them perished (verses 1–5). This is a solemn warning to Christians not to give way to temptation, as the Israelites did (verse 6). That is, not to be led into idolatry (verse 7), nor into fornication (verse 8), nor into tempting Christ (verse 9), nor into grumbling (verse 10). In all these points the experience of the Israelites was a warning to Christians; and therefore those who thought themselves secure should take heed lest they fall (verses 11–12). God is merciful, and would not let them be too severely tempted (verse 13).

1. Our ancestors. Abraham is our father, even though we are not his natural descendants. And the Israelites were the fathers of the Corinthian Christians, although most of them were Gentiles. Although this is true, it is probable that the apostle, although writing to a church whose members were mostly of heathen origin, is speaking as a Jew to Jews. He often addresses a congregation as a whole when what he says only refers to a part.

2. Baptized into Moses. That is, with reference to Moses, so as to be made his disciples by baptism. See 1:13; Romans 6:3.

3. The reference is here obviously to the manna, which the apostle calls **spiritual food.**

4. The water which they drank was **spiritual** because it was derived from the Spirit, that is, by the special intervention of God. They all drank from it once when it was first provided, and they continued to drink it, for it followed them.

5. The proof of God's displeasure was that their path through the desert could be traced by the bones of those who perished through the judgments of God.

6. As examples. Literally, as 'types.' They stand as warnings to us.

7. 'The people sat down to eat and drink.' That is, of the sacrifices offered to Jehovah in the presence of the golden calf, as a symbol of creative power.

8. Idolatry and sexual immorality have always been so intimately connected that the former seldom fails to lead to the latter.

9. Destroyed by serpents. See Numbers 21:6. The people provoked God by their grumbling and by their regret about being delivered from Egypt. Similar judgments were in store for the Corinthians if they exhausted the Lord's forbearance.

10. To complain is to grumble in a rebellious spirit. The reference is to Numbers 14:2.

Were killed by the destroyer. That is, by an angel commissioned by God to use the pestilence as an instrument of destruction. Hence sometimes the destruction is ascribed to the plague, as in Numbers 14:14; sometimes to the angel, as here; and sometimes both the agent and the instrument are combined, as in 2 Samuel 24:16. See Acts 12:23.

12. This indicates the apostle's aim in referring to the events in Israelite history. There is perpetual danger of falling. No degree of progress we may have already made, no amount of privilege which we may have enjoyed, can justify the lack of caution.

Proof that attendance on sacrificial feasts in a heathen temple is idolatry (verses 14–22).

This whole discussion arose out of the question whether it was permissible to eat the sacrifices offered to idols. Paul, while admitting that there was nothing wrong in eating such food, exhorts the Corinthians to abstain for the sake of their weaker brothers. There was another reason for this abstinence: they might be led into idolatry. By going to the verge of the allowable, they might be drawn into the sinful. There was great danger that the Corinthians, convinced that an idol was nothing, might be induced to join the sacrificial feasts within the precincts of the temples. The danger was the greater because such feasts, if held in a private house, lost their religious nature, and might be attended without scruple. The aim of this section is to convince his readers that, if the feast was held in a temple, attendance at it was an act of idolatry.

The apostle argues from analogy. Attending the Lord's Supper is an act of communion with Christ, the object of Christian worship, and with all those who unite with us in the service. From its very nature, it brings all who share the bread and wine into fellowship with Christ and with one another (verses 14–17). The same is true of Jewish sacrifices. Whoever eats those sacrifices is thereby brought into communion with the object of Jewish worship. The act is in its nature an act of worship (verse 18). The conclusion is too clear to need being stated – those who join in the sacrificial feasts of the heathen join in the worship of idols. Such is the meaning of the act, and no denial on the part of those who perform it can alter its nature. It is not to be inferred from this way of reasoning that he regarded Jupiter or Juno as being just as real as Christ is. Far from it. What the heathen sacrifice, they sacrifice to demons; and therefore, to partake of their sacrifices under circumstances which gave religious significance to the act brought them into communion with demons (verses 19–20). The two things are incompatible. A person cannot worship Christ and worship demons, or be in communion with one while in communion with the other. Going to the Lord's table is a renunciation of demons; and going to the table of demons is a renunciation of Christ (verse 21). By this conduct the jealousy of the Lord would be excited against them, as it was against the Jews who turned aside after false gods (verse 22).

14. Flee from the worship of idols. That is, avoid it by fleeing from it. This is the only safe way to avoid sin. Its presence is malarious. The only safety is keeping at a distance. This includes two things: first, avoiding what is questionable; that is, everything which lies on the border of what is allowable, or which approaches the confines of sin; keeping at a distance from everything which excites evil passion, or which tends to ensnare the soul.

16. The cup of blessing. So far as the meaning of the words is concerned, this phrase may be translated either 'the cup of thanksgiving' (the eucharistic cup) or 'the cup of blessing' (the consecrated cup). In the Paschal service the cup was called 'the cup of blessing,' because a benediction was pronounced over it. The idea of consecration is necessarily included. Wine, as wine, is not the sacramental symbol of Christ's blood, but only when it is solemnly consecrated for that purpose. Even our ordinary food is said to be 'sanctified by God's word and by prayer' (1 Timothy 4:5), because it is set apart by a religious service for the purpose for which it was appointed.

18. The people of Israel. That is, the Jews as a nation, not the spiritual Israel or true people of God.

20. And I do not want you to be partners with demons. By **partners** the apostle means here what he meant by the same term in the preceding verses. We are said to have fellowship with those between whom and us there are congeniality of mind, community of interest, and friendly relations. In this sense we have fellowship with our fellow-Christians, with God and with his

Son. And in this sense the worshippers of idols have fellowship with evil spirits. They are united to them so as to form one community, with a common character and a common destiny.

21. The table of the Lord is the table at which the Lord presides, and at which his people are his guests. **The table of demons** is the table at which demons preside, and at which all present are their guests. What the apostle means to say is that there is not merely an incongruity and inconsistency between a person being the guest and friend of Christ, and the guest and friend of evil spirits, but that the thing is impossible. It is as impossible as that the same man should be wicked and holy at the same time.

Under what circumstances it was lawful to eat meat offered to idols (verses 23–33).

In the previous paragraph the apostle had proved that eating the sacrifices offered to idols, under circumstances which gave a religious character to the act, was idolatry. Now he comes to state the circumstances under which those sacrifices might be eaten without scruple. He begins by reverting to the general law of Christian liberty, stated with the same limitations as in 6:12. The right to use things which in themselves are morally neutral is limited by expediency. This should be governed in this matter by regard for the good of others, and for our own edification (verses 23–24). If the meat of sacrifices is sold in the market (verse 25), or found at private tables, it may be eaten without any hesitation (verse 27). But if anyone at a private table, from scruples on the subject, should let us know that a certain dish contained art of a sacrifice, for his sake, and not for our own, we ought to abstain (verse 28). The general rule of action, not only as to meats and drinks, but as to all other things, is first to act with regard for God's glory (verse 31), and secondly to avoid giving offense (that is, occasion for sin) to anyone (verse 32). In this matter Paul presents himself as an example to his fellow believers (verse 33).

26. For, 'The earth and its fullness are the Lord's' This was what the Jews commonly said before meals. It was the recognition of God as the proprietor and giver of all things, and specially of the food provided for his children. The words are taken from Psalm 24:1.

27. The apostle did not prohibit the Christians from social relations with the heathen. If invited to their tables, they were at liberty to go.

32. Give no offence. That is, give no occasion to sin. The exhortation is to avoid being the cause of sin to others (see verses 8–9, and Romans 14:13, 21). They were to be careful in this way with respect to all sorts of people, Christians and non-Christians. The latter are divided into the two great classes, the Jews and the Gentiles.

11:1. Be imitators of me, as I am of Christ. This verse should belong to the tenth chapter, as it is the conclusion of the preceding discussion, and as a new subject is introduced with the next verse. Paul had referred to his own conciliatory conduct as an example to the Corinthians, and he exhorts them to imitate him, as he did Christ, who is the ultimate standard.

Chapter 11

The impropriety of women appearing unveiled in the public assemblies (verses 2–16).

The improper manner of celebrating the Lord's Supper which prevailed in the Corinthian church (verses 17–34).

On the impropriety of women appearing in public unveiled (verses 2–16).

Having corrected the more private abuses which prevailed among the Corinthians, Paul begins in this chapter to consider those which relate to the way they conducted public worship. The first of these is the habit of women appearing in public without a veil. Dress is in a great degree conventional. A costume which is proper in one country would be indecorous in another. The principle insisted on in this paragraph is that women should conform in matters of dress to all those practices which the public sentiment of the community in which they live demands. The veil in all eastern countries was, and to a great extent still is, the symbol of modesty and subjection. For a woman to discard the veil in Corinth, therefore, was to renounce her claim to modesty, and to refuse to recognize her subordination to her husband. The apostle's whole argument in this paragraph is based on the assumption of this significance in the use of the veil.

He begins by praising the Corinthians for their obedience in general to his instructions (verse 2). He then reminds them of the divinely constituted subordination of the woman to the man (verse 3). Consequently it was disgraceful in the man to assume the symbol of subordination, and disgraceful in the women to discard it (verses 4–5). If the veil were discarded as the symbol of subordination, it must also be discarded as the symbol of modesty. An unveiled woman, therefore, in Corinth proclaimed herself as not only insubordinate, but as immodest (verse 6). The man ought not to wear a veil because he represents the authority of God; but the woman is the glory of the man (verse 7). This subordination is proved by the very history of her creation. Eve was formed out of Adam,

and made for him (verses 8–9), and therefore women should, especially in the religious assemblies where angels are present, wear the conventional symbol of their relationship (verse 10). This subordination of the woman, however, is perfectly consistent with the essential equality and mutual dependence of the sexes. Neither is, or can be, without the other (verses 11–12). Next, the apostle appeals to their instinctive sense of propriety, which taught them that, as it is disgraceful in a man to appear in the costume of a woman, so it is disgraceful in a woman to appear in the costume of a man (verses 13–15). Finally he appeals to authority; the custom which he censured was contrary to the universal practice of Christians (verse 16).

2. I commend you because you remember me in everything and maintain the traditions just as I handed them on to you. The Corinthians, although backward in following the self-denial and conciliatory conduct of the apostle, were nevertheless in general mindful of the ordinances or rules which he had delivered to them. The word **traditions** (Greek *paradosis*,) is used not only for instructions transmitted orally but for any instruction, whether relating to faith or practice, and whether delivered orally or in writing (as in 2 Thessalonians 2:15 and 3:6). It is never used in the New Testament to refer to the rule of faith, except for the immediate instructions of inspired men.

3. The head of the man is Christ; the head of the woman is the man; the head of Christ is God. If this link is disturbed in any of its parts, ruin must be the result. The head is that on which the body is dependent, and to which it is subordinate. The obvious meaning of this passage is that the woman is subordinate to the man, the man is subordinate to Christ, and Christ is subordinate to God.

4. Prophesies. In the scriptural sense of the word, a prophet is one who speaks for another, as Aaron is called the prophet or spokesman of Moses (Exodus 4:15–16; 7:1). The prophets of God, therefore, were his spokesmen, into whose mouth the Lord put the words which they were to utter to the people. To 'prophesy' in Scripture, is accordingly to speak under divine inspiration; not merely to predict future events, but to deliver, as the organ of the Holy Spirit, the messages of God to men, whether in the form of doctrine, exhortation, consolation, or prediction. This public function, the apostle says, should not be exercised by a man **with something on his head;** literally, having something on his head downward.' Among the Greeks, the priests officiated bareheaded; the Romans had the head veiled; the Jews (at least soon after the apostolic age) also wore the Tallis or covering for the head in their public services. It is not to be inferred from what is said here that the Christian prophets (or inspired men) had introduced this custom into the church. The thing to be corrected was women appearing in public assemblies unveiled. The apostle says the veil is inconsistent with the position of the man, but is required by that of the women. Men are mentioned only for the sake of illustrating the principle.

6. That is, let her act consistently. If she wishes to be regarded as a reputable woman, let her conform to the established practice.

7. The woman, and the woman only, ought to be veiled; for the man ought not to cover his head.

10. By authority, the apostle means the sign or symbol of authority. He had asserted and proved that the woman is subordinate to the man, and he had assumed as granted that the veil was the conventional symbol of the man's authority. The inference is that the woman ought to wear the ordinary symbol of the authority of her husband. As it was proper in itself, and demanded by the common sense of propriety, that the woman should be veiled, it was specially proper in the worshipping assemblies, for there they were in the presence not merely of men but of angels. It was, therefore, not only out of deference to public opinion, but from reverence to those higher intelligences that the woman should conform to all the rules of decorum.

11. That is, although there is this subordination of the woman to the man, they are mutually dependent. The one cannot exist without the other.

16. The apostle has presented the arguments against the custom of women appearing in public unveiled, and now he says that if anyone, despite these arguments, wants to argue about the mater, we have only to say that we (the apostles) have no such custom, nor do the churches of God.

Celebration of the Lord's Supper (verses 17–34).

This section relates to the disorders connected with the celebration of the Lord's Supper. These disorders were of a kind which, according to our method of celebrating the sacrament, seems almost unaccountable. It was, however, the early custom to connect the Lord's Supper in the strict sense of the words with an ordinary meal. This sacrament was instituted by our Lord at the close of the Paschal supper, and it appears to have been customary at the beginning for the Christians to assemble for a common meal and to connect with it the commemoration of the Redeemer's death. Intimations of this practice may be found in such passages as Acts 2:42: 'They devoted themselves to the apostles' teach-

ing and fellowship, to the breaking of bread and the prayers.' In verse 46 it says that this breaking of bread was from house to house. In Acts 20:7 it says, 'On the first day of the week, when we met to break bread,' which, from the narrative which follows, appears to have been an ordinary meal. Whatever may be thought of these passages, it is clear from the paragraph before us that at Corinth at least, the sacrament of the Lord's Supper was connected with a regular meal. This may have arisen not so much from the original institution of the Eucharist in connection with the Paschal supper, as from the sacred festivals of both Jews and Greeks. Both had been accustomed to unite with their sacrifices a feast of a more or less public character. It is also evident that, in keeping with a familiar Greek custom, the people assembled brought their own provisions, which were placed on the table and formed a common stock. The rich brought plentifully, the poor brought little or nothing. It was, however, essential to the very idea of a Christian feast that it should be a communion; that all the guests at the table of their common Lord should be on terms of equality. Instead of this fraternal union, there were division among the Corinthians even at the Lord's table. The rich eating by themselves the provisions which they had brought, and leaving their poorer brothers mortified and hungry. It is to the correction of these disorders that the concluding part of this chapter is devoted.

It was no matter of praise that the assemblies of the Corinthians made them worse rather than better (verse 17). The prominent evil was that there were schisms even in their most sacred meetings; an evil necessary in the state in which they were, and which God permitted in order that the good might be made manifest (verses 18–19). The evil to which he referred was not merely that they had degraded the Lord's supper into an ordinary meal, but that in that meal they were divided into parties, some eating and drinking to excess, and others left without anything (verses 20–21). This was not only making the Lord's Supper a meal for satisfying hunger – contrary to its original design, but a cruel perversion of a feast of love into a means of humiliating and wounding their poorer brothers (verse 22). In order to show how inconsistent their conduct was with the nature of the service in which they professed to engage, the apostle recounts the original institution of the Lord's Supper (verses 23–25). From this account it follows, first, that the Lord's Supper was designed not as an ordinary meal, but as a commemoration of the death of Christ; secondly, that to participate in this ordinance in an unworthy manner was an offense against his body and blood, the symbols of which were so irreverently treated; thirdly, that no one ought to approach the Lord's table without self-examination, in order that with due preparation and with a proper understanding of the ordinance, he may receive the bread and wine as the symbols of Christ's body and blood (verses 26–29). In this way they would escape the judgments which the Lord had brought upon them on account of their profanation of his table (verses 30–32). In conclusion, he exhorts them to use their houses for their ordinary meals, and to make the Lord's supper a real communion (verses 33–34).

18. I hear that there are divisions among you. Literally, 'schisms.' For the meaning of that word, see 1:10. The nature of these schisms is described in what follows. They were cliques, not sects, but parties, separated from each other by alienation of feeling. It is clear that the rich formed one of these parties, as opposed to the poor.

19. Factions. What are called 'divisions' in one verse are called **factions** in the next; both words have the same general sense.

20. Eating the Lord's Supper is not the real purpose, though it is your professed purpose.

23. For I received from the Lord. Paul asserts that he received the account given here from the Lord. The whole context shows that he intends to claim the direct authority of the Lord himself for this narrative.

24. When he had given thanks. The act of consecration is expressed by a grateful acknowledgment of God's mercy and invocation of his blessing.

He broke it. This detail is included in all the accounts; in those of Matthew, Mark, and Luke, as well as in Paul's. This is one of the significant parts of the service, and ought not to be omitted.

'In remembrance of me.' That is, that I may be remembered as he who died for your sins. This is the specific, definite object of the Lord's Supper, to which all other ends must be subordinate, because this alone is stated in the words of institution. It is of course involved in this that we profess faith in him as the sacrifice for our sins; that we receive him as such; that we acknowledge the obligations which rest upon us as those who have been redeemed by his blood; and that we recognize ourselves as constituent members of his church and all believers as our brothers. We are thus, as taught in the preceding chapter, brought into a real communion with Christ and with all his people by the believing participation of this ordinance.

25. After supper. That is, after the conclusion of the Paschal supper.

'As often as you drink it.' This does not mean that every time Christians drink wine together they should do it in commemoration of Christ's death; but, 'whenever this ordinance is celebrated, do what I have done, to commemorate my death.' The Lord's Supper is a commemoration of Christ's death, not only because it was designed for that purpose, but also because the bread and wine are the significant symbols of his broken body and his outpoured blood. In this ordinance therefore Christ is presented as a sacrifice which at once makes expiation for sin and ratifies the covenant of grace.

27. To eat or drink **in an unworthy manner** is in general to come to the Lord's table in a careless, irreverent spirit, without the intention or desire to commemorate the death of Christ as the sacrifice for our sins, and intending to comply with the commitments which we undertake in that service. The way in which the Corinthians ate unworthily was that they treated the Lord's table as though it were their own; making no distinction between the Lord's Supper and an ordinary meal; coming together to satisfy their hunger, and not to feed on the body and blood of Christ; and refusing to commune with their poorer brothers.

28. Examine yourselves. In other words, he should ascertain whether he has correct views of the nature and purpose of the ordinance, and whether he has the proper state of mind. That is, whether he desires to commemorate the Lord's death in thankfulness, to share in the benefits of that death as a sacrifice for his sins, publicly to accept the covenant of grace with all its promises and obligations, and to signify his fellowship with his brothers as joint members with himself of the body of Christ.

30. Some have died. That is, have already died. As there is nothing in the context to intimate that these terms are being used figuratively of moral infirmities and spiritual decline, they should be taken in their literal sense. Paul knew that the prevailing sickness and frequent deaths among the Christians of Corinth were a judgment from God because of the irreverent way they had celebrated the Lord's Supper.

33–34. The two great evils connected with the observance of the Lord's Supper at Corinth were, first, that it was not a communion – one took his supper before another (verse 21); and secondly, that they came to the Lord's table to satisfy their hunger. That is, they made it an ordinary meal. They thus sinned against their brothers (verse 22), and they sinned against Christ (verse 27). In the conclusion, therefore, of the whole discussion, Paul exhorts them to correct these evils; to wait for each others, and make it a joint service; and to satisfy their hunger at home, and come together only to commemorate the Lord's death. Mildly as this exhortation is expressed, it is enforced by the solemn warning already given, that **it will not be**

for your condemnation, that is, so as to incur God's displeasure.

Chapter 12

Of spiritual gifts (verses 1–31).

The ancient prophets had clearly predicted that the Messianic period would be accompanied by a remarkable effusion of the Holy Spirit. 'And afterwards,' God says in Joel 2:28, 'I will pour out my spirit on all flesh; your sons and your daughters shall prophesy, your old men shall dream dreams, and your young men shall see visions.' Our Lord, before his crucifixion, promised to send the Comforter, who is the Holy Spirit, to instruct and guide his church (see John 14, etc.). And after his resurrection he said to his disciples, 'These signs will accompany those who believe: by using my name they will cast out demons; they will speak in new tongues; they will pick up snakes in their hands; and if they drink any deadly thing, it will not hurt them; they will lay their hands on the sick, and they will recover' (Mark 16:17–18). And immediately before his ascension he said to the disciples, 'You will be baptized by the Holy Spirit' (Acts 1:5). Accordingly, on the day of Pentecost, these promises and prophecies were literally fulfilled.

What was special about the new dispensation was that, first of all, these gifts were not confined to any one group of people but extended to all – male and female, young and old. Secondly, these supernatural endowments were wonderfully diverse.

Under such extraordinary circumstances it was unavoidable that many disorders should arise. Some people would claim to be organs of the Spirit, when they were deluded or impostors; some would be dissatisfied with the gifts which they had received, and envy those whom they regarded as more highly favoured; others would be puffed up, and make an ostentatious display of their extraordinary powers; and in the public meetings it might be expected that the greatest confusion would arise from so many people wanting to exercise their gifts at the same time. The apostle devotes this chapter and the next two to correcting these evils, all of which had manifested themselves in the Corinthian church.

It is impossible to read these chapters without being deeply impressed by the divine wisdom with which they are pervaded. After contrasting the condition of the Corinthians, as members of that body which was filled with the life-giving Spirit of God, with their former condition as the senseless worshippers of lifeless idols, Paul *first* of all lays down the criterion by which they might decide whether those who claimed to be organs of the Spirit were really under this influence. How do they speak of Christ? Do they blaspheme, or do they worship him? If they openly and sincerely recognize Jesus as the supreme Lord, then they are under the influence of the Holy Spirit (verses 1–3).

Secondly, these gifts, whether viewed as graces of the Spirit, or as forms of ministering to Christ, or the effects of God's power (that is, whether viewed in relation to the Spirit, to the Son, or to the Father), are only different manifestations of the Holy Spirit living in his people, and are all intended for the edification of the church (verses 4–7).

Thirdly, he arranges them under three headings:

1. The word of wisdom and the word of knowledge.

2. Faith, the gift of healing, the power of working miracles, prophesying, and the discerning of spirits.

3. The gift of tongues and the interpretation of tongues (verses 8–10).

Fourthly, these gifts are not only all the fruits of the Spirit, but they are distributed according to his sovereign will (verse 11).

Fifthly, there is therefore in this matter a striking analogy between the church and the human body:

1. As the body is one organic whole, because it is animated by one spirit, so the church is one because of the indwelling of the Holy Spirit as the principle of its life.

2. As the unity of life in the body is manifested in a diversity of organs and members, so the indwelling of the Spirit in the church is manifested by a diversity of gifts and functions.

3. As the very idea of the body as an organization supposes this diversity in unity, the same is true in regard to the church.

4. As in the human body the members are mutually dependent, and no one exists for itself alone but for the body as a whole, so also in the church there is the same dependence of its members on each other, and their various gifts are not designed for the exclusive benefit of those who exercise them, but for the edification of the whole church.

5. As in the body the position and function of each member is determined not by itself but by God, so also these spiritual gifts are distributed according to the good pleasure of their author.

6. In the body the least attractive parts are those which are indispensable to its existence, and so in the church it is not the most attractive gifts which are the most useful.

Sixthly, the apostle draws from this analogy the following inferences:

1. Everyone should be content with the gift which he has received from the Lord, just as the hand and foot are content with their position and function in the body.

2. There should be no exaltation of one member of the church over others, on the ground of the supposed superiority of his gifts.

3. There should, and must, be mutual sympathy between the members of the church, as there is between the members of the body. One cannot suffer without all the other suffering with it. No one lives, or acts, or feels for himself alone, but each in the rest (verses 12–27).

In conclusion, the apostle shows that what he had said with regard to these spiritual gifts applies in all its force to the various functions in the church, which are the organs through which the gifts of the Spirit are exercised (verses 28–31).

3. **Cursed.** That is, anathema. The word strictly means something consecrated to God. As among the Jews any living thing consecrated in this way could not be redeemed, but must be put to death (Leviticus 27:28–29), so the word was used to designate any person of thing devoted to destruction; and then with the added idea of the divine displeasure, something devoted to destruction as accursed. This last is always its meaning in the New Testament (Romans 9:3; Galatians 1:8–9; 1 Corinthians 16:22). Hence to say that Jesus is anathema is to say that he was a malefactor, someone justly condemned to death. This is what the Jews said when they invoked his blood on their heads.

4–6. The second thing which the apostle teaches concerning these gifts is their diversity in connection with the unity of their source and purpose. However, we are not to understand him here as dividing these gifts into three classes, under the heads of 'gifts,' 'service,' and 'works.' He is presenting three different aspects of each and all of them. Viewed in relation to the Spirit, they are gifts; in the relation to the Lord, they are acts of service; in relation to God, they are works, that is, effects worked by his power. And it is the same Spirit, the same Lord, and the same God who are concerned in them all. That is, the same Spirit is the giver; it is he who is the immediate author of all these various endowments. It is the same Lord in whose service and by whose authority these various gifts are exercised. They are all different forms in which he is served, or ministered to. And it is the same God the Father, who having exalted the Lord Jesus to the supreme headship of the church, and having sent the Holy Spirit, works all these effects in the minds of men.

7. **For the common good.** That is, for edification. This is the common object of all these gifts. They are not intended exclusively or mainly for the recipients' benefit, much less for their gratification; but for the good of the church. Just as the power of vision is not for the benefit of the eye, but for the whole person. When God's gifts, natural or supernatural, are perverted as means

of self-exaltation or aggrandizement, therefore, it is a sin against their giver, as well as against those for whose benefit they were intended.

8. **According to the same Spirit.** That is, according to his will, or as he sees fit; see verse 11. The Spirit is not only the author, but the distributor of these gifts. And therefore sometimes they are said to be given 'by,' and sometimes 'according to,' the Spirit.

9. **To another faith.** As faith is mentioned here as a special gift some Christians have, it cannot mean saving faith, which is common to all. It is generally supposed to mean the faith of miracles to which our Lord refers in Matthew 17:19–20, and which the apostle mentions in 13:2 (a faith 'to remove mountains'). In the absence of clear evidence for deciding what faith is meant here, it is safest, perhaps, to stick to the simple meaning of the word, and assume that it means a higher measure of the ordinary grace of faith. Such a faith enabled people to become confessors and martyrs, and is fully illustrated in Hebrews 11:33–40. This is something truly as wonderful as the gift of miracles.

To another gifts of healing. That is, gifts by which the sick were healed (Acts 4:30). This evidently refers to the miraculous healing of diseases.

10. **To another various kinds of tongues.** That is, the ability to speak in languages previously unknown to the speakers. The nature of this gift is determined by the account given in Acts 2:4–11, where it says that the apostles 'began to speak in other languages, as the Spirit gave them ability.' People of all the neighbouring countries asked with astonishment, 'Are not all these who are speaking Galileans? And how is it that we hear, each of us, in our own native language?' It is impossible to deny that the miracle recorded in Acts consisted in enabling apostles to speak in languages which they had never learnt.

12. **So it is with Christ.** That is, the body of Christ, or the church. As the body consists of many parts and yet is one, so it is with the church: it is one and yet consists of many members, each having its own gift and function. See Romans 12:4–5; Ephesians 1:23; 4:4, 16.

14. **The body does not consist of one member but of many.** This is a proof that diversity of gifts and members is necessary to the unity of the church. The church no more consist of people who all have the same gifts, than the body is all eye or all ear. As the body is not **one member**, but **many**, so the church is not one member, but many.

15–16. The first and most obvious conclusion from the view that Paul has given of the nature of the church is the duty of being content.

17. This verse means that the very existence

of the body depends on the union of members endowed with different function.

18. Instead of the body being all one member, God has arranged and disposed the parts each in its place so as to constitute one living, organic whole.

19–20. These verses are a repetition of the idea that diversity of organs in the body is essential to its nature as a body.

21. This verse emphasises the mutual dependence of the members of the church.

22–23. We infer from the apostle's teaching here that the least attractive gifts are the most important.

24. By making the less presentable parts of the body essential to the well-being of the rest, and by diffusing a common life through all the members, he has made the body a harmonious whole.

25–26. God has so constituted the body **that there may be no dissension** in it, that is, no diversity of feeling or interest. When **dissension** is in an organized body, or a society, it commonly includes the idea of alienation of feeling. Such was the case among the Corinthians (see 1:10; 11:18).

But the members may have the same care for one another. The body is so constituted that the eye is as solicitous for the welfare of the foot as it is for its own well-being. The consequence is that if one member suffers, all the members suffer with it; and if one member is honoured, all the members rejoice with it. This is the law of our physical nature. The body is really one. It has a common life and consciousness. The pain or pleasure of one part if common to the whole.

28. Gifts of healing. That is, people endowed with the power of healing diseases.

Forms of assistance. That is, people qualified and appointed to help the other officers of the church, probably in the care of the poor and the sick. These, according to the common understanding from Chrysostom to the present day, were deacons and deaconesses.

Forms of leadership. That is, people who had the gift and authority to rule. As this gift and office are distinguished from those of teachers, it cannot be understood to mean the presbyter or overseers who were required to be apt teachers (see 1 Timothy 3:2). It seems to refer clearly to a class of officers distinct from teacher, that is, rulers, or as they are called in the Reformed churches, 'ruling elders.'

Various kinds of tongues. That is, people having the gift of speaking in foreign languages. This is probably put last because it was so unduly valued and so ostentatiously displayed by the Corinthians.

31. And I will show you a more excellent way. Whether it is excellent compared to something else, or most excellent, depends on the context.

Here no comparison is implied. The idea is not that he intends to show them a way that is better than seeking gifts, but a way *par excellence* to obtain those gifts. Calvin and other do indeed adopt the other view, but it supposes the preceding imperative (**strive**) to be merely concessive, and is contrary to 14:1, where the command to seek the more useful gifts is repeated. The sense is, 'Seek the better gifts, and moreover I show you an excellent way to do it.'

Chapter 13

Christian love (verses 1–13).

Love is superior to all extraordinary gifts. It is better than the gift of tongues (verse 1); than the gifts of prophecy and knowledge (verse 2); and than the gift of miracles (verse 2). All outward works of charity without it are worthless (verse 3). Love has this superiority, first, because of its inherent excellence; and secondly, because of its perpetuity. As for superiority, it implies of secures all other excellence.

1. It includes all the forms of kindness.
2. It is humble and modest.
3. It is unselfish.
4. It sympathizes with all good (verses 4–7).

It is perpetual – all the extraordinary gifts mentioned in the preceding chapter were intended for the present state of existence, or were temporary. Love is never to cease (verse 8). Knowledge, as a special gift, and perhaps also in the form in which its exists in this world, is to pass away. It is now the apprehension of truth as through a mirror – hereafter it will be lost in immediate vision (verses 9–12). The permanent graces are faith, hope, and love, and the greatest of these is love (verse 13).

This chapter, although devoted to a single Christian grace, and therefore not to be compared with Romans 8, or with some chapters in the letter to the Ephesians, as an unfolding of the mysteries of redemption, still has always been considered as one of the jewels of Scripture. For moral elevation, for richness and comprehensiveness, for beauty and felicity of expression, it has been the admiration of the church in all ages.

With regard to the word **love,** the Greek word *agape* occurs about 116 times in the New Testament. It is not of heathen origin. The heathen had no conception of the grace which in the Scriptures is expressed by this word; neither the Greek *eros* nor *philia,* nor the Latin *amor* or *caritas* has the Scriptural sense of *agape.* It was the unsuitability of the word *amor* that led Jerome to adopt the Latin word *caritas* as the more elevated of the two. One properly expresses love based on sympathy; the latter came to mean love based on respect. Its English derivative, 'charity,' retains more of the original meaning of the Latin word.

Caritas (from *carus, carendo*, 'dear,' 'costly') is strictly dearness or costliness; and then it came to express the feeling arising from the sight of need and suffering. And this is the common meaning still attached to the English word, which makes it unsuitable for the comprehensive word 'love.' Many people have been led to think that almsgiving covers a multitude of sins, because charity is said to have that effect; and have thought that kindness to the poor and the sick is the sum of all religion, because in the King James Version Paul exalts charity above faith and hope. It is not of charity, but of love, that the Bible speaks.

Superiority of love to all other gifts.

1. But do not have love. The mere lack of love has reduced me, despite the gift in question, to a level with **a noisy gong or a clanging cymbal.** There were two kinds of cymbals, one small, worn on the thumb and middle finger, like modern castanets, the other large, broad plates, like our common cymbals. The illustration was probably adapted from the shrill, discordant noise made by the speakers with their tongues, each endeavouring to drown the voice of all the others, as seems from what follows to have been the case with the Corinthians. Paul say (14:23) that the meetings for worship in Corinth, if everybody spoke in tongues, would be soon confused as to make strangers think they were mad.

3. Here Paul advances one step further. All outward acts of benevolence are of no avail without love. Someone may give away his whole estate, or sacrifice himself, and be in no sense the gainer. He may do all this from vanity, or from the fear of perdition, or to purchase heaven, and only increase his condemnation. Religion is no such easy thing.

4. Love is patient; love is kind; love is not envious or boastful or arrogant. Almost all the instructions of the New Testament are suggested by some occasion, and are adapted to it. This chapter is not a methodical dissertation on Christian love, but shows that grace as contrasted with extraordinary gifts which the Corinthians valued inordinately. Therefore, the traits of love which are mentioned are those which contrasted with the Corinthians' use of their gifts. They were impatient, discontented, envious, puffed up, selfish, indecorous, unmindful of the feelings or interests of others, suspicious, resentful, censorious. The apostle personifies love, and places her before them and lists her graces, not in logical order but as they occurred to him in contrast to the deformities of character which they displayed.

5. It is not irritable or easily angered. That is, is not quick-tempered; or, does not allow itself to be roused to resentment.

7. It bears all things. The Greek word is really a military word, and means to sustain the assault of an enemy. Hence it is used in the New Testament to express the idea of sustaining the assaults of suffering or persecution, in the sense of bearing up under them, and enduring them patiently (2 Timothy 2:10; Hebrews 10:32; 12:2).

9–10. For we know only in part, and we prophesy only in part; but when the complete comes, the partial will come to an end This is the reason why knowledge and prophecy are to cease. They are partial of imperfect, and therefore suited only to an imperfect state of existence. The revelations granted to the prophets imparted mere glimpses of the mysteries of God; when those mysteries stand disclosed in the full light of heaven, what need will there be of those glimpses? A skilful teacher may use diagrams and models to give us some knowledge of the mechanism of the universe, but if the eye is strengthened to take in the whole at a glance, what need is there of a planetarium or of a teacher? The apostle uses two illustrations to teach us the difference between the present and the future. One is derived from the differed between childhood and maturity; the other from the difference between seeing a thing by imperfect reflection, or through an obscure medium, and seeing it directly.

11. When I became an adult, or, having become an adult, I have **put an end to childish ways,** that is, my former childish way of talking, feeling, and thinking.

12. Dimly. Literally, 'in an enigma.' This may be taken adverbially – 'we see enigmatically,' that is, obscurely; or the idea may be that we see divine things as it were wrapped up in enigmas. We do not see the things themselves, but those things as represented in symbols and words which express them imperfectly.

Then we will see face to face. That is, no longer through a mirror but immediately. Compare Genesis 32:30; Numbers 12:8. The Word of God is a mirror in which even now we see the glory of the Lord (2 Corinthians 3:18), but what is that to seeing him face to face!

13. The true explanation of this verse is to be found in the use which Paul makes of this word **greatest,** or the equivalent term 'better.' In 12:31 he exhorts his readers to seek the 'greater' gifts, that is, the more useful ones. And in 14:5 he says, 'One who prophesies is greater than one who speaks in tongues'; that is, he is more useful. Throughout that chapter the reason one gift is preferred to others consists in its superior usefulness. This is Paul's standard; and judged by this rule, love is greater than either faith or hope. Faith saves ourselves, but love benefits others.

Chapter 14

Superiority of the gift of prophecy to that
of tongues (verses 1–25).

Special directions for the conduct of public
worship (verses 26–40).

Superiority of the gift of prophecy to that of tongues (verses 1–25).

The superiority of the gift of prophecy to that of
tongues is based on the following considerations:

1. A person who speaks in tongues speaks to
God, whereas a person who prophesies speaks
to other people (verses 2–3).

2. A person who speaks in tongues edifies
only himself, whereas a person who prophesies
edifies the church (verses 4–5). This is proved in
the following ways

a. By an appeal to their own judgment and
experience. If Paul came to them speaking in a
way which they could not understand, what
good could it do them? But if, as a prophet, he
brought them a revelation from God, or as a
teacher, set before them a doctrine, they would
be edified (verse 6).

b. From the analogy of musical instruments.
It is only when the sounds are understood that
they produce the desired effect. If a person does
not know that a given note of the trumpet is a
signal for battle, he will not prepare himself for
the conflict (verses 7–9).

c. From their experience of dealing with
strangers. If someone comes to me speaking a
language which I do not understand, no matter
how polished or significant that language may
be, he is a foreigner to me, and I to him (verses
10–11).

In their zeal for spiritual gifts, therefore, they
should have regard to the edification of the
church (verse 12). Hence, anyone who had the
gift of tongues should pray for the gift of interpretation, as, without it, however devotional, his
prayers could not profit other people (verses
13–14). It was not enough that the prayers and
praises should be spiritual; they must be intelligible; otherwise those who were unlearned
could not join in them (verses 15–17). For himself, the apostle says, although more richly
endowed with the gift of tongues than any of his
readers, he would rather speak five words so as
to be understood than ten thousand words in an
unknown tongue (verses 18–19). It was mere
childishness in the Corinthians to be so delighted with a gift which they could not use in any
practical way (verse 20). They should learn wisdom from the experience of the Hebrews. It was
as a judgment that God sent among them teachers whom they could not understand. So long
as they were obedient, or there was hope of

bringing them to repentance, he sent them
prophets speaking their own language (verses
21–22). Their experience would not be dissimi-
lar. If they came together, each speaking in an
unknown tongue, the effect would be only evil.
But if, when they assembled, all the speakers
spoke so as to be understood, and under the
influence of the Spirit, then people would be
convinced and converted, and God glorified
(verses 23–25).

In the comment on 12:10, reasons have
already been presented for sticking to the common view that the gift of tongues was the gift
miraculously conferred of speaking in foreign
languages. Everyone must feel, however, the
truth of Chrysostom's remark in his commentary on this chapter: 'This whole passage is very
obscure; but the obscurity arises from our ignorance of the facts described, which, though
familiar to those to whom the apostle wrote,
have ceased to occur.' This gift is specially
connected with prophesying ('they spoke in
tongues and prophesied' Acts 19:6). This is
because all speaking under divine, supernatural
influence was included under the head of
prophesying; and all who spoke in tongues
spoke 'as the Spirit enabled them,' so they all
prophesied in the wide sense of the term. But it
is not so easy to understand why this gift should
have been so common, nor why it should so
often accompany conversion (see Acts 10:46;
19:6). There are many things also in this chapter
which it is not easy to understand on any theory
of the nature of the gift. Under these circumstances it is necessary to hold fast what is clear,
and to make what is certain our guide in
explaining what is obscure. It is clear –

1. That the word 'tongues' in this context, as
already proved, means languages.

2. That the speaker with tongues was in a
state of calm self-control. He could speak, or be
silent (14:28).

3. That what he said was intelligible to himself, and could be interpreted to others.

4. That the unintelligibleness of what was
said arose not from the sounds uttered being
inarticulate, but from the ignorance of the hearer. The interpretation of particular passages
must, therefore, be controlled by these facts.

**1. Pursue love and strive for spiritual gifts,
and especially that you may prophesy.**
In the preceding chapters Paul had taught the
following:

1. That all the extraordinary gifts of the Spirit
were proper objects of desire.

2. That they were of different relative
importance.

3. That love was of greater value than any
gift.

In accordance with these principles, the
apostle exhorts his readers to **pursue love**, that

is, to press forward towards it, as people do towards the goal in a race (Philippians 3:12, 14). Pursue it earnestly as the greatest good. But at the same time, **strive for spiritual gifts.** Because love is more important than miraculous gifts, it does not follow that the latter were not to be sought. The same word is used here as in 12:31.

Especially that you may prophesy. The two gifts specially in the apostle's mind were the gift of speaking in tongues and that of prophecy, that is, the gift of speaking as the organ of the Spirit in a way that would instruct and edify the hearer. Of these two gifts, he says, the latter is to be preferred.

2. For those who speak in a tongue do not speak to other people but to God; for nobody understands them, since they are speaking mysteries in the Spirit. This teaches:

1. That he who speaks in tongues speaks not to men, but to God.

2. That this means that men do not understand *him.*

3. That the reason he is not understood is in the medium of communication, not in the things communicated.

4. **Those who speak in a tongue build up themselves, but those who prophesy build up the church.** This follows from what had been said. The speaker in tongues did not edify the whole church, because he was not understood; he did edify himself, because he understood himself. This verse, therefore, proves that the understanding was not in abeyance, and that the speaker was not in an ecstatic trance.

5. I would like all of you to speak in tongues. It was not to be inferred from what he had said, that the apostle undervalued this gift. He admitted its importance as one of the manifestations of the Spirit, and in verse 18 he gives thanks that he himself possessed it in rich measure. From this it is evident that it was something of a higher nature than modern theories would represent it.

6. He who received revelations was a prophet, and he who had **teaching** was a teacher.

7–9. The point the apostle is making is not about the nature of the gift, but the folly of its use.

10. Calvin understands **many different kinds of sounds in the world** as referring to the voices or natural cries of animals.

11. That is, because the sounds uttered are significant, because the person is not making a mere senseless noise but is speaking a real language, therefore, I do not know the meaning of the language, I will be like a foreigner to him and he to me. Otherwise it would not be so. If someone utters incoherent, inarticulate sounds, which no one alive could understand, that would not make him **foreigner.** It might prove him to be deranged, but not a stranger.

12. As all such unintelligible speaking is worthless, the apostle exhorts them to seek to edify the church.

13. Therefore, one who speaks in a tongue should pray for the power to interpret. This is an inference not only from the preceding verse but from the whole preceding argument, which was intended to show how useless it is to speak in a language which no one present understands.

16–17. You may give thanks well enough. That is, in a way acceptable to God and profitable to yourself. This proves that the speaker must have understood what he said. For if the unintelligible is useless, it must be sot to the speaker as well as to the hearer. If it was necessary for them to understand in order to be edified, it was no less necessary that he should understand what he said in order to benefit. This verse is therefore decisive against all theories of the gift of tongues which assume that those who used them did not understand their own words. The Scriptures recognize no unintelligent worship of God, or any spiritual edification (in the case of adults) disconnected from the truth -whether that edification be sought by sounds or signs, whether by prayers or sacraments.

18–19. We cannot believe that Paul should **thank God** for the gift of tongues if that gift consisted in the ability to speak in languages which he himself did not understand, and which could therefore benefit neither himself nor others. It is equally clear from this verse that speaking in tongues was not speaking in a state of mental unconsciousness. The common doctrine of the nature of this gift is the only one consistent with this passage. Paul says that although he could speak in foreign languages more than the Corinthians, he would rather speak **five words with my mind** than ten thousand words in an unknown language.

20. Children have two characteristics: a disposition to be pleased with trifles, or to value things falsely; and comparative innocence. With regard to evil, there is a great difference between a little child and a full-grown man. The apostle wanted the Corinthians to lay aside the first characteristic. He wanted them to cultivate the second. They had shown themselves childish in valuing the gift of tongues above more useful gifts, and in using it when it could serve no good purpose. A little child, however, is something so lovely, and is so often held up in Scripture for imitation, that he could not say, without qualification, 'Stop being children.' He therefore says, **Stop** *thinking* **like children.** But in regard to **evil** (a comprehensive word for evil dispositions), they are to **be infants.**

21. From this the Corinthians might learn that it was no mark of the divine favour to have

teachers whose language they could not understand. They were turning a blessing into a curse. The gift of tongues was intended, among other things, to facilitate the propagation of the Gospel, by enabling Christians to address people of various nations in their own languages. Used for this purpose, it was a blessing; but to use it for the sake of display, in addressing those who could not understand the language used, was to make it a curse. The Spirit of God often confers gifts on people, and then holds them responsible for the way in which they exercise them.

22. The inference from the preceding verse is that tongues are a sign not to the believing but to the unbelieving, and prophesying just the reverse.

This verse does not imply any disparagement of the gift in question. When used aright – that is, when used to address those to whom the language was intelligible – it was prophecy.

The obscurity of this passage arises in a great measure from the ambiguity of the expression 'to speak in tongues.' It means to speak in foreign or unknown languages. But a language may be said to be unknown either by the speaker or by the hearer. It is said to be unknown to the speaker if it has not previously been acquired; and it is said to be unknown to the hearers if they do not understand it. The apostle uses the expression sometimes in one sense and sometimes in the other. When it says that the apostles, on the day of Pentecost, spoke in tongues, it means that they used languages which they had never learned; but when Paul says he would rather speak five intelligible words than ten thousand words in a tongue, he means in a language unknown to the hearers. Speaking in tongues in the one sense was a grace and a blessing; in the other sense, it was a folly and a curse. In these verses the apostle deals with speaking in tongues in the latter sense.

23. The inference from the preceding argument is that speaking in languages not understood by the people is undesirable and useless. To show how right this conclusion is, the apostle supposes the case which follows.

If, therefore, the whole church comes together. That is, if all the Christians of the place, or the whole congregation, is assembled. This is one of the conditions of the hypothesis. Another is that **all speak in tongues.** This does not necessarily imply either that all present had the gift of tongues, or that all who possessed the gift spoke at one and the same time, although from verses 27 and 30 it may be inferred that this was sometimes done. All that the words here require is that all who spoke used foreign languages. 'To speak in tongues' must mean to speak in languages unknown to the hearers. The third condition of the case supposed is

that **outsiders or unbelivers** should come into the meeting. The apostle asks what impression such people, in the case supposed, would receive. Would they not say **you are out of your mind?** See John 12:20; Acts 12:15; 26:24.

24–25. This is another part of the inference from what was said in verses 21–22. Speaking in languages unknown to the hearers is suitable for producing the happiest effects.

Special directions for the conduct of public worship (verses 26–40).

The apostle concludes this chapter with certain practical directions derived from the principles which he had laid down. He neither denied the reality of the extraordinary gifts the Corinthians had in such abundance, nor forbade them to exercise them. He only told them that mutual edification should be their aim (verse 26). With regard to those having the gift of tongues, he directed that not more than two, or at most three, should speak, and that in succession, while someone interpreted. But if no interpreter was present, there was to be no speaking in tongues (verses 27–28). Of the prophets also, only two or three were to speak, and the rest were to sit in judgment on what was said. If a new revelation was made to one of the prophets, he was not to interrupt the speaker, but wait until he had concluded; or the one was to give way to the other. Both were not to speak at the same time, for God did not approve of confusion. As the influence which the prophets were subject to did not destroy their self-control, there could be no difficulty in obeying their injunction (verses 29–33). Women were not to speak in public; but to seek instruction at home. This prohibition rests on the divinely established subordination of the women, and on the instinct of propriety (verses 34–35). The Corinthians were not to act in this matter as though they were the oldest or the only church (verse 36). The apostle requires everyone, no matter how gifted, to regard his directions as the commands of Christ (verses 37–38).

He sums up the chapter in two sentences.

1. Earnestly seek the gift of tongues.
2. Do everything with decency and order.

26. A hymn. A song of praise to God. This can hardly mean one of the psalms of the Old Testament; but something prepared or suggested for the occasion. One was impelled by the Spirit to pour out his heart in a song of praise. Compare verse 15.

A lesson. That is, comes prepared to expound some doctrine.

A revelation. That is, as a prophet he has received a revelation from God which he wants to communicate.

A tongue. That is, he is able and impelled to

deliver an address or to pray in an unknown tongue.

Or an interpretation. That is, is prepared to give the interpretation of some discourse previously delivered in an unknown tongue.

This passage, and indeed the whole chapter, presents a lively image of an early Christian meeting. Officers in every church were appointed to conduct the services and especially to teach, but the extraordinary gifts of the Spirit were not confined to them or to any particular group of people. Any member present who experienced the working of the Spirit in any of its extraordinary manifestations was authorized to use and exercise his gift. Under such circumstances confusion could hardly fail to ensue. That such disorder did prevail in the public meetings in Corinth is clear enough from this chapter. The apostle's purpose in this whole passage is to correct this evil.

27. Only two or three people with the gift of tongues should speak; they were not to speak together, but in succession; and someone should interpret what the others said.

28. If neither the speaker himself, nor anyone else present, has the gift of interpretation, he is to keep **silent in church**, that is, in the public meeting.

And speak to themselves and God. That is, let him commune silently with God in the exercise of his gift.

29–30. The number of prophets who were to speak at any one meeting was also limited to two or three.

31. This verse gives the reason why two prophets should not speak at the same time. They could all have the opportunity of speaking one by one. Not indeed at the same meeting, for he had already limited the number of speakers to two or three for any one occasion.

32. This verse gives another reason for the injunction in verse 31. 'You need not speak together, because you can all have the opportunity of speaking in turn, and you are not compelled to speak by any irresistible impulse.'

33. This is the reason why the spirits of prophets must be assumed to be subject to the prophets. They are from God; but God is not a God of disorder or of commotion, but of peace. Therefore every spirit which is from him must be capable of control.

34. **Women should keep silent in the churches** The speaking intended is public speaking, and especially in the church. In the Old Testament it had been predicted that your sons and daughters will prophesy (see Joel 2:28) – a prediction which Peter quotes as verified on the day of Pentecost (Acts 2:17); and Acts 21:9 mentions four daughters of Philip who prophesied. The apostle himself seems to take it for granted, in 11:5, that women could receive and exercise the gift of prophecy. It is therefore only the public exercise of the gift that is prohibited.

35. The desire for knowledge in women is not to be repressed, and the facilities for its acquisition are not to be denied them. The refinement and delicacy of their sex, however, should be carefully preserved. They may learn all they wish to know without appearing before the public.

36. Paul means to ask whether the Gospel took its rise in Corinth. The disregard which the people of that church showed for the customs of their sister churches seemed to indicate arrogance. They acted as though they were entitled to be independent, if not to prescribe the law to others. Paul takes the authority of the church for granted. He assumes that anything contrary to the general sentiment and practice of the people of God is wrong. This he does because he understands by the church the body of Christ, those in whom the Holy Spirit dwells, and whose character and conduct are controlled and governed by his influence.

37. That is, if any man, with or without good reason, takes it upon himself to be a **prophet**, that is inspired; or has **spiritual powers**, that is, the possessor of any gift of the Spirit, let him prove himself what he claims to be by submitting to my authority.

Is a command of the Lord. That is, Christ's, because he is the person known in the Christian church as Lord. The continued influence of Christ by the Spirit over the minds of his apostles, which is a divine prerogative, is assumed or asserted here.

38. That is, if anyone is ignorant or refuses to acknowledge the divine authority of my instructions, let him be ignorant. Paul would neither attempt to convince him, nor waste time in arguing the point. Where the evidence of any truth is abundant and has been clearly presented, those who reject it should be left to act on their own responsibility.

39. Prophecy and the gift of tongues are the two gifts dealt with in this chapter. We are to be **eager** for one; exercising the other, even in Christian meetings, is not to be prohibited, provided someone is present who possesses the gift of interpretation.

40. **In order.** Not tumultuously as in a mob, but as in a well-ordered army, where everyone keeps his place and acts at the proper time and in the proper way. So far as external matters are concerned, these are the two principles which should regulate the conduct of public worship. The apostle not only condemns any church acting independently of other churches, but also any members of a particular church acting from his own impulses, without regard to others. The

church as a whole, and in every separate congregation, should be a harmonious, well-organized body.

Chapter 15

The resurrection of the dead.

In dealing with this subject the apostle first proves the fact of Christ's resurrection (Verse 1–11).

From this he deduces, first, the possibility, and then the certainty of the resurrection of his people (verses 12–34).

He afterwards teaches the nature of the resurrection, so far as to show that the doctrine is not liable to the objections which had been brought against it (verses 35–58).

The resurrection of Christ as securing the resurrection of his people (verse 1–34).

Certain false teachers in Corinth denied the resurrection of the dead; this is clear not only from the course of argument adopted here but from the explicit statement in verse 12.

In 2 Timothy 2:17–18, Paul speaks of Hymenaeus and Philaenus as teaching that the resurrection has already happened, and it is probable that the people in Corinth also refused to acknowledge any other than a spiritual resurrection.

After reminding the Corinthians that the doctrine of the resurrection was a primary principle of the Gospel which he had preached to them, and on which their salvation depended (verses 1–3), he proceeds to assert and prove the fact that Christ rose from the dead on the third day. This event had been predicted in the Old Testament. Its actual occurrence is proved by his resurrection appearances:

1. After his resurrection he appeared first to Peter and then to the twelve.

2. He appeared to more than five hundred brothers at once, most of whom were still alive.

3. He appeared separately to James.

4. Then he appeared again to all the apostles.

5. Finally he appeared to Paul himself.

There never was a historical event established on surer evidence than that of the resurrection of Christ (verses 4–8). This fact, therefore, was included in the preaching of all the apostles, and in the faith of all Christians (verse 11). But if this is so, how can the doctrine of the resurrection be denied by anyone who claims to be a Christian? To deny the resurrection of the dead is to deny the resurrection of Christ, and to deny the resurrection of Christ is to subvert the Gospel (verses 12–14), and also to make the apostles false witnesses (verse 15). If Christ is not risen, out faith is futile, we are still in our sins, those dead in Christ are perished, and all the hopes of Christians are destroyed (verses 16–19). But if Christ is risen, then his people also will rise, because he rose as a pledge of their resurrection. As Adam was the cause of death, so Christ is the cause of life; Adam secured the death of all who are in him (verses 20–22).

Although the resurrection of Christ secures the resurrection of his people, the two events are not contemporaneous. Christ rose first; his people are to rise when he comes the second time. Then is to be the final consummation, when Christ as Mediator hands over his providential kingdom to the Father, after all his enemies are subdued (verses 23–24). It is necessary for Christ's dominion over the universe, to which he was exalted after his resurrection, should continue until his great work of subduing or restraining evil was accomplished. When that is done, then the Son (the God-man, the incarnate Logos) will be subject to the Father, and God as God, and not as Mediator, will reign supreme (verses 25–28).

Besides the arguments already urged, there are two other considerations which prove the truth or importance of the doctrine of the resurrection. The first is 'baptism on behalf of the dead' (whatever that means) prevailing in Corinth, assumed the truth of the doctrine (verse 29). The other is the intimate connection between this doctrine and that of a future state is such that if the one is denied, the other cannot, in a Christian sense, be maintained. If there is no resurrection, there is for Christians no hereafter, and the may act on the principle, 'Let us eat and drink, for tomorrow we die' (verses 30–32). The apostle concludes this part of the subject by warning his readers against the corrupting influence of bad company. From this it is probable that the denial of the doctrine had already produced the evil effects referred to among those who rejected it (verses 33–34).

1–2. If, as the people in Corinth taught, there is no resurrection, Paul says, our faith is vain (verse 14); it is an empty, worthless thing. So here he says, the Gospel secures salvation, unless faith is of no account.

3. Of first importance. Among the first or principal things. The death of Christ for our sins and his resurrection were therefore the great facts on which Paul insisted as the foundation of the Gospel.

That Christ died for our sins. That is, as a sacrifice or propitiation for our sins.

6. Some have died. Death to the believer is a sleep for his body; a period of rest to be followed by a glorious day.

14. Our proclamation has been in vain. That is, it is empty, void of all truth, reality, and power.

And your faith has been in vain. These consequences are inevitable, for if the apostles preached a risen and living Saviour, and made his power to save depend on the fact of his resurrection, of course, their whole preaching was false and worthless if Christ was still in the grave.

19. We have hoped in Christ. The Greek expresses not what we do but what we are: 'We are hopers.' This passage does not teach that Christians are more miserable in this life than other people. This is contrary to experience. Christians are unspeakably happier than other people. All that Paul means to say is that if you take Christ from Christians, you take their all. He is the source not only of their future, but of their present happiness. Without him they are still in their sins, under the curse of the law, unreconciled to God, having no hope, and without God in the world; and yet subject to all the special trials which come to Christians, which in the apostolic age often included the loss of everything.

26. The last enemy to be destroyed is death. Death will reign until the resurrection. Then people will never more be subject to his power. Then death will be swallowed up in victory (Luke 20:36; 2 Timothy 1:10; Revelation 20:14).

28. So that God may be all in all. Before the ascension of Christ, God reigned as God; after that event he reigned and still reigns through the God-man; when the end comes, the God-man will hand over this administrative kingdom, and God again will be all in all. This is the way Scripture puts it, and seems to be the simple meaning of this passage. When our Lord ascended, all power in heaven and earth was given to him. It was given to him then, so he did not possess it before. He as Mediator, as God-man, is to retain this delegated power until his enemies are put under his feet. Then he, the God-man, is to hand it over. And God as God will reign supreme.

31. Paul solemnly assures his readers that he was constantly in jeopardy, for, he says, **I die every day!** – that is, I am constantly exposed to death (2 Corinthians 4:10).

34. The call is to prompt exertion to shake off the delusion that they were safe.

Nature of the resurrection body (verses 35–58).

Having proved the fact of the resurrection, the apostle comes to illustrate its nature, or to teach with what kind of bodies the dead are to rise. It seems that the great objection against the doctrine in the minds of his readers rested on the assumption that our future bodies are to be of the same nature as those we have now; that is, natural bodies consisting of flesh and blood, and sustained by air, food and sleep. Paul says this is a foolish assumption. Our future bodies may be material and identical with our present bodies, and yet organized in a very different way. You plant a seed; it does not come up as a seed, but as a flower. Why then may not the future be to the present body what the flower is to the seed (verse 35–37)?

Matter can be organized in an indefinite variety of ways. There is not only immense diversity in the vegetable products of the earth, but even flesh is variously modified in the different order of animals (verses 38–39). This is true not only for the earth, for there are heavenly as well as earthly bodies. And even the sun, moon, and stars differ from each other in glory; why then may not our future differ from our present bodies in glory (verse 40–41)? This not only may be, but will be the case. The body deposited in the grave is corruptible, mean, weak, and, in a word, natural; as raised from the grave, it will be incorruptible, glorious, powerful, and spiritual (verses 42–44). This is according to Scripture. Adam was created with a natural body, adapted to an earthly state of existence; Christ, as a life-giving spirit, has a spiritual body. As Adam was before Christ, so our earthly tabernacles are before our heavenly ones. As we have borne the image of the earthly, we shall bear the image of the heavenly (verses 45–49).

It is freely admitted that flesh and blood, that is, bodies organized as ours now are, are unfit for heaven. Corruption cannot inherit incorruption (verse 50). But our bodies are to be changed. This change will be instantaneous and at the last day. It will embrace both the living and the dead. Corruption will put on incorruption, mortality will put on immortality (verses 51–53). When this is done, the original promise that death will be swallowed up in victory will be fulfilled (verse 54). Death, therefore, has lost its sting for the believer, and the grave is conquered. Death has no sting except sin; sin has no strength except from the law; the law has no power over those who are in Christ Jesus, therefore thanks be to God, who gives us the victory through Christ Jesus our Lord (verses 55–57)! Seeing then that we have such a glorious hereafter, we should be steadfast, unmoveable, always abounding in the work of the Lord (verse 58).

35. Having completed his discussion of the fact of the resurrection, the apostle comes to consider the manner of it. He imagines some objector asking, **'How are the dead raised?'** This may mean, 'How can a corrupted and disorganized body be restored to life?' And the next question, **With what kind of body do they come?**, may refer to the result of the process. What is to be the nature of our future bodies?

Or the second question may merely explain the first, so that only point is presented. **How, that is, with what kind of body are the dead raised?** There are, however, two distinct questions, for although the two are not connected by 'and,' the apostle actually answers both questions in what follows. The second difficulty was the main one, and therefore most of what follows refers to that. The great objection in the minds of the Corinthians to the doctrine of the resurrection was evidently the same as that of the Sadducees. Both imagined our future bodies to be like our present ones. Our Lord's answer to the Sadducees, therefore, is the same as the one Paul gives to the Corinthians. The future body is not to be like the present.

41. Not only do the heavenly bodies differ from the earthly bodies in glory, but there is great diversity among the heavenly bodies themselves. How different is the sun from the moon, the moon from the stars, and even one star from another. Standing, therefore, as we do in the midst of this wonderful universe, in which we see matter in every conceivable modification, from a clod of earth to a sunbeam, from dust to the luster of the human eye, how unutterably absurd it is to say that if we are to have bodies hereafter, they must be as gross, and heavy, and as corruptible as those which we have now.

42. So it is with the resurrection of the dead. That is, as the heavenly bodies differ from the earthly bodies, and as one star differs from another star, so the resurrection body will differ from our present body. The apostle does not mean that as one star differs from another star in glory, so one risen believer will differ from another. This, no doubt, is true; but it is not what Paul here says or intimates. His object is simply to show the absurdity of the objection founded on the assumption that the body hereafter must be what it is here. He shows that it may be a body and yet differ as much from what it is now as the light of the sun differs from a piece of clay.

50. Flesh and blood. Our body as now constituted, not sinful human nature. The phrase never has this latter sense. See Hebrews 2:14; Matthew 16:17; Galatians 1:16; Ephesians 6:12. It is indeed true that our unsanctified nature cannot inherit the kingdom of God. But that is not what the apostle is speaking about. He is speaking of the body and of its state after the resurrection.

57. The victory meant here, of course, is the victory over death and the grave. Thanks be to God, who delivers us from the power of death, redeeming even our bodies from the grave, and making us share in everlasting life. This is done through Jesus Christ our Lord, that is, our divine possessor and absolute ruler. It is through him,

and through him alone.

58. Such being the truth and importance of the doctrine of the resurrection, Christians should be firm in sticking to it, not letting themselves be moved by the specious objections of philosophy falsely so called. They should remember that if the dead do not rise, then Christ did not rise; and if Christ did not rise, their faith is in vain, and they are still in the power of sin. But as Christ has risen, and as his resurrection illustrates that of his people, and makes it certain, what is more natural and proper than that they should give themselves fully to the work of the Lord?

Chapter 16

The collection to be made for the saints in Jerusalem (verses 1–9).

Timothy and Apollos, whom the apostle commends to the confidence of the Corinthians (verses 10–14).

Exhortations and greetings (verse 15–20).

Greeting written with Paul's own hand (verses 21–24).

Concerning the collection for the saints at Jerusalem (verses 1–9).

For some reason which we cannot now ascertain, poverty prevailed in Jerusalem among the believers more than in any other part of the church. Almost all the special exhortations in Paul's letters to provide for the poor refer primarily to the poor in Jerusalem. He had exhorted the churches of Galatia to make a collection for their relief; and then those of Macedonia, and he now addresses the Corinthians on the subject. It is a very common opinion that the poverty of Christians in Jerusalem arose from the common ownership of goods introduced among them at the beginning – an error which arose from an excess of love over knowledge. Perfection in one thing requires perfection in all. Perfect equality in goods requires perfect freedom from selfishness and indolence. The collection made by the Syrian churches, as recorded in Acts 11:29, was in consequence of the dearth the Christian prophet Agabus warned his brothers was to come on all the world. Whatever the cause may have been, the fact is certain that the saints in Jerusalem stood in special need of help from their richer brothers. Paul, therefore, undervalued and suspected as he was by the Jewish Christians, worked hard on their behalf.

He exhorts the Corinthians to adopt the same arrangements as he had established in the church of Galatia. A contribution was to be made on the Lord's day every week, in proportion to their resources, so that the collection might be ready when he came (verses 1–2). He would either send it to Jerusalem by people approved by them, or if the sum were large enough to make it worthwhile he would himself accompany their messengers (verses 3–4). He announces his intention of visiting the Corinthians after passing over Macedonia, and perhaps to spend the winter with them. His prospects of usefulness in Ephesus would keep him in that city until Pentecost (verses 5–9).

As for Timothy and Apollos, he exhorts them to treat Timothy in such a way that he would be free from fear among them, for he was worthy of their confidence (verses 10–11). Of Apollos, he says that he had urged him to go to Corinth with the other brothers, but that he was unwilling to do so then, but would go when a suitable occasion offered (verses 12–14). He exhorts them to submit to the household of Stephanas, and to everyone who was labouring in the good cause (verses 15–16). He says how pleased he was to see the brothers from Corinth, and sends greetings from those around him to the Christians in Achaia (verses 17–20). The conclusion of the letter was written with his own hand as an authentication of the whole (verses 21–24).

2. On the first day of every week. Literally, 'upon one of the Sabbath,' according to the Jewish method of naming the days of the week.

10. In Acts we read that Paul sent two of his helpers, Timothy and Erastus, to Macedonia, while he stayed in the province of Asia a little longer. (See Acts 19:22). Timothy, therefore, at this time, was travelling through Macedonia, and expected to reach Corinth, where the apostle had sent him; see 4:17. Besides this mission of Timothy, there was another some time later, consisting of Titus and other brothers, whose return the apostle so anxiously awaited (2 Corinthians 2:12–13). Paul requests the Corinthians so to receive Timothy that he might have **nothing to fear.** It was not fear of personal violence, but the fear of not being regarded with respect and confidence. The reason by which he enforces his request shows the nature of the evil which he apprehended, **for he is doing the work of the Lord.** If they would recognize this, Timothy would be satisfied.

13–14. These concise exhortations form a fitting close to the letter, each being adapted to the special circumstances of the Corinthians, though of course they applied to Christians in their conflicts with the world.

1. He exhorts them to be on their guard – that is, to be wakeful, constantly on the alert, that their spiritual enemies might not gain advantage over them before they were aware of their danger.

2. Beset as they were with false teachers, who handled the Word of God deceitfully (2 Corinthians 4:2), he exhorts them to **stand firm in your faith.** Do not consider every point of doctrine an open question. Matters of faith, doctrines for which you have a clear revelation of God, such as the doctrine of the resurrection for example, are to be considered settled, and, as among Christians, no longer matters of dispute. There are doctrines embraced in the creeds of all orthodox churches, so clearly taught in Scripture that it is not only useless but hurtful to be always calling them in question.

3. Be courageous. The Corinthians' circumstances called for great courage. They had to withstand the contempt of the learned, and the persecutions of the powerful.

4. Be strong. Not only courage, but strength, was needed to withstand their enemies, and to bear up under the trials which were to come upon them.

5. Let all that you do be done in love. That is, let love prevail, in your hearts, in your families, in your meetings. The preceding parts of the letter show how much need there was for this exhortation; as the church was torn apart with factions, and even the Lord's Supper, which everywhere else was a feast of love, had become a fountain of bitterness in Corinth.

21. As Paul usually wrote through an amanuensis, he used to write the concluding sentences of his letters with his own hand as an authentication of them (Colossians 4:18; 2 Thessalonians 3:17). He remarks in Galatians 6:11 on his having written that letter with his own hand as something unusual, and as indicating a particular stress of feeling.

24. My love ... in Christ is my Christian love. Paul in conclusion assures them all, all the believers in Corinth, even those whom he had been called upon to reprove, of his sincere love.

2 CORINTHIANS

Charles Hodge

Introduction

See 1 Corinthians, *Introduction.*

Contents

Chapter 1

The greeting (verses 1–2).

Thanksgiving to God for the deliverance and consolation which the writer had experienced (verses 3–11).

Defence of himself against the charge of inconstancy and inconsistency (verses 12–24).

Paul's gratitude for the deliverance and consolation which he had experienced (verses 1–11).

After the apostle had written his first letter to the Corinthians, and had sent Titus either as the bearer of the letter or immediately after sending it by other hands, to see what effect it produced, he seems to have been in a state of unusual depression and anxiety. The persecutions to which he had been exposed in Asia placed him in continued danger of death (1:8), and his care for the church in Corinth allowed him no inner peace (7:5). After leaving Ephesus, he went to Troas; but although the most promising prospects of usefulness there presented themselves, he could not rest, but passed over into Macedonia hoping to meet Titus and obtain news of Corinth from him (2:12, 23). This letter is the outpouring of his heart occasioned by the

information which he received. More than any other of Paul's letters, it shows how strong his feelings were when he wrote it. The Corinthians had received his previous letter with a proper spirit; it had brought them to repentance, led them to excommunicate the incestuous person, and led the majority of the congregation to show the warmest affection for the apostle. All this relieved his mind of a load of anxiety, and filled his heart with gratitude to God.

On the other hand, the increased boldness and influence of the false teachers, the perverting errors which they inculcated, and the frivolous calumnies which they brought against him filled him with indignation. This accounts for the abrupt transitions from one subject to another, the sudden changes of tone and manner which characterize this letter. When writing to Corinthians as a church obedient, affectionate, and penitent, there is no limit to his tenderness and love. His great desire seems to be to heal the temporary breach which had occurred between them, and to assure his readers that all was forgiven and forgotten, and that his heart was entirely theirs. But when he turns to the wicked, designing corrupters of the truth among them, there is a severe tone which is not found in any other of his writings, even the letter to the Galatians. Erasmus compares this letter to a river which sometimes flows in a gentle stream, sometimes rushes down as a torrent bearing all before it; sometimes spreading out like a placid lake; sometimes losing itself, as it were, in the sand, and breaking out in its fullness in some unexpected place. Though it is perhaps the least methodical of Paul's writings, it is among the most interesting of his letters as bringing out the man before the reader and revealing his intimate relationship with the people for whom he laboured. The remark must be borne in mind which has often been made before, that the full play allowed to the peculiarities of mind and feeling of the sacred writers is in no way inconsistent with their plenary inspiration. The grace of God in conversion does not change the natural character of its subjects, but accommodates itself to all their peculiarities of disposition and temperament. And the same is true with regard to the influence of the Spirit in inspiration.

The greeting in this letter is nearly in the same words as in the previous letter (verses 1–2). Here also the introduction is a thanksgiving. As these expressions of gratitude are not mere forms, but genuine effusions of the heart, they vary according to the circumstances under which each letter was written. Here the thanksgiving was for consolation. Paul blesses God as the God of all mercy for the consolation which he had experienced. He associates, or rather identifies himself with the Corinthians, representing his afflictions as their and his consolation also as belonging to them (verses 37). He refers to the afflictions which came upon him in Asia, so that he despaired of life, but through their prayers God who had delivered, still delivered, and he was assured, would continue to deliver him (verses 8–11).

1–2. The sense which the word **apostle** has here, the meaning of the expression **by the will of God**, the scriptural meaning of the words **church** and **saints**, are all stated in the commentary on 1 Corinthians 1:1–2.

Including all the saints throughout Achaia. This letter was not intended exclusively for the Christians in Corinth, but also for all the believers scattered through the province who were connected with the church in Corinth. These believers were probably not collected into separate congregations, or the apostle would have used the plural form, as when writing to the 'churches' of Galatia (Galatians 1:2). **Achaia** was originally the name of the northern part of the Peloponnesus including Corinth and its isthmus.

3. The God of all consolation. This most compassionate Father is **the God**, that is, the author, **of all**, that is, of all possible, **consolation**. God is the author of comfort not only by delivering us from evil, or by ordering our external circumstances, but also, and chiefly, by his inner influence on the mind itself, assuaging its tumults and filling it with joy and peace in believing (Romans 15:13).

4. Us here refers to the apostle himself. Throughout this chapter he is speaking of his own personal trials and comforts. He blessed God as the author of comfort, because he had experienced his comfort. And, he adds, God's purpose in afflicting and comforting was to qualify him for the job of comforting the afflicted. Paul acquiesced in this plan; he was willing to be afflicted like this in order to bring comfort to others. A life of ease is commonly stagnant. It is those who suffer much and who experience much of the comfort of the Holy Spirit, who live much. Their life is rich in experience and in resources.

5. The sufferings of Christ. Not 'sufferings on account of Christ,' for the genitive case will not allow this meaning; nor sufferings which Christ endures in his own members; but such sufferings as Christ suffered, and which his people are called on to endure in virtue of their union with him and in order to be like him. See Matthew 20:23; Philippians 3:1; 1 Peter 4:13. Compare Romans 8:17; Colossians 1:24; Galatians 6:17.

10. Paul's trust in God was not disappointed. He did deliver him from **so deadly a peril**, that is, one so fearful and apparently inevitable. It is evident from the whole context that the apostle had not only been in imminent peril, but exposed to a more than ordinarily painful death. Whether this was from disease or from enemies is a matter of conjecture. The latter is the more probable.

The apostle's defence against the charge of inconstancy (verses 12–24).

Paul had informed the Corinthians that it was his purpose to go direct from Ephesus to Corinth, from there into Macedonia, and back again to Corinth (verse 16). He had had to modify this plan before the first letter was sent, as in 1 Corinthians 16:5 he tells them he would not visit them until he had passed through Macedonia. On this slight ground his enemies in Corinth complained that he said one thing and meant another. They also seem to have made this an occasion for charging him with similar inconsistency in doctrine. If his word could not be depended on in small matters, what dependence could be placed on his preaching? Paul shows there was no levity or insincerity involved in this change of his plans, and no inconsistency in his preaching; but that to spare them he had deferred his visit to Corinth (verses 12–24).

13–14. You boast … our boast. Paul believed that in the day of the Lord Jesus the Corinthians would rejoice over him as he would rejoice over them. In that day they would appreciate the blessedness of having had him for their teacher, as he would rejoice in having had them for his converts. The joy, however, was already theirs to some extent. 'We are, and shall be, your rejoicing, as you are and shall be ours, in the day of the Lord Jesus.'

18. That is, 'My preaching, or the doctrine which I preached, was not inconsistent and contradictory. I did not preach first one thing and then another.' This sudden transition from the question about his veracity as a man to his consistency as a preacher shows two things. First, that he enemies had brought both charges against him, basing the latter on the former; and secondly, that Paul was much more concerned for the Gospel than for his own reputation.

21–22. In the previous verse the apostle had spoken of Christ as the truth and substance of all the divine promises, and of the hearty assent which believers gave those promises; here he brings into view God as the author and preserver of their faith, who would assuredly grant them the salvation of which he had already given them the foretaste and pledge.

Anointed us. Kings, prophets, and priests were anointed when at their inauguration. To 'anoint' may therefore mean to qualify by divine influence, and thus to authorize anyone to discharge the duties of any office. In Luke 4:18 our Lord applies to himself the language of Isaiah 61:1, 'The Spirit of the Lord is on me, because he has anointed me to bring good news to the poor.' See also Acts 4:27 and 10:38. Similarly, Christians are described as anointed because by the Spirit they are consecrated to God and qualified for his service (1 John 2:20, 27). When Paul says here that God has **anointed us**, the **us** means all Christians, and of course the anointing to which he refers is that which is common to all believers.

Chapter 2

Paul's change of his plan of going to Corinth straightaway (verses 1–4).

The disciplinary case mentioned in his previous letter (verses 5–11).

Why he did not remain in Troas (verses 12–14).

He pours out his heart in gratitude to God for the continued triumph of the Gospel (verses 14–17).

The true reason why the apostle did not go to Corinth straightaway, and his views about the offender whose excommunication he had insisted on in his previous letter (verses 1–17).

There is no change of subject in this chapter. After defending himself from the charge of levity in conduct and inconsistency in doctrine, the apostle had said in 1:23 that he did not go to Corinth before giving the church time to comply with the injunctions contained in his previous letter, because he did not wish to appear among them as a judge. Here, he amplifies this and says that he had decided not to visit Corinth again under circumstances which could only give pain to the Corinthians and to himself. He knew that he could not give them sorrow without being grieved himself, and he was assured that if he was happy they would share in his joy (verses 1–4).

The sorrow occasioned by the incestuous person was not confined to the apostle, but shared by the church. He was satisfied with the course which the church had pursued regarding that case, and was willing for the offender to be restored to their fellowship if they were (verses 5–11). His anxiety about them was so great that not finding Titus, from whom he expected to receive news, he was unable to remain at Troas, but passed over into Macedonia to meet him on his way (verses 12–13). The news which he received from Titus was favourable, and the apostle expresses in strong terms his gratitude to God who always caused him to triumph (verses 15–17).

3. I am confident about all of you, that my joy would be the joy of all of you. In saying that he wanted all causes of painful collision to be removed before he went to Corinth, Paul was not isolating himself from the people, as though concerned only for his own peace of mind, but was satisfied that what made him happy would make them happy. 'My joy will be the joy of you all.' This does not just mean that it would give them pleasure to see him happy, but also that obedience on their part, and the consequent purity and prosperity of the church, were as necessary to their happiness as to his. Paul says he had this confidence in them **all**, though it is perfectly clear that there were people among them who were his bitter opponents. He leaves these people out of view here, and speaks of the majority, probably the great body, of the church as though it were the whole.

4. Distress and anguish refer to his inner feelings, not to his external circumstances, for both are qualified by **of heart**. It was out of a distressed, oppressed heart that he wrote.

With many tears. The Greek says '*through many tears*.' The combination of faithfulness and love which makes parental discipline uniquely effective also gives special power to ecclesiastical censure. When the offender is made to feel that, while his sin is punished, he himself is loved, and that the target is not his suffering but his good, he is more likely to be brought to repentance. Every pastor must see an instructive example for imitation here in the apostle's love for the Corinthians, and in the extreme sorrow with which he exercised discipline in the case of offenders.

7. So that he may not be overwhelmed by excessive sorrow. That is, so that he will not be driven to despair and thus destroyed. Undue severity is as much to be avoided as undue leniency. The character which Paul displays here reflects the image of our heavenly Father. His Word is filled with denunciations against impenitent sinners, and at the same time with assurances of unbounded pity and tenderness towards the penitent. He never breaks the bruised reed or quenches the smoking flax.

11. We are not ignorant of his designs. This and similar passages of the Word of God teach that Satan is a personal being; that he exerts great influence over people's minds; that although he is finite (and therefore not ubiquitous), he nevertheless works on people's mind generally, and not merely on those in any one place. His powers of intelligence and agency must therefore be unimaginable. No individual and no community can ever be sure that he is not plotting their destruction. Paul might have said to the Romans or the Ephesians, as he did to the Corinthians, that they must take heed lest Satan outwit them, and in some way secure them as his own.

12–13. A door was opened for me in the Lord. That is, a way of access, and opening to labour effectively. According to this interpretation, the words **the Lord** are linked with **door**. However, it is more in accordance with Paul's style to link them with the whole clause: 'There was an open door in the Lord.' Paul frequently uses these words in such expressions as 'work in the Lord,' 'temple in the Lord,' 'fellow-labourer in the Lord.' Thus he is indicating here the kind of door, or the sphere of labour. It was an opportunity for labouring successfully in the Lord's service.

Because I did not find my brother Titus there. He calls Titus his **brother** both because of his relationship to him as a fellow-Christian, and because he was a joint labourer with him in the Gospel. He expected to meet Titus at Troas, and to learn from him the state of things in Corinth, and especially the effect his previous letter had had. It seems that he regarded this as a turning point in the history of that church. If they submitted to his authority and corrected the abuses which he had pointed out, and especially if they excommunicated the member guilty of the unheard-of offense so often referred to in this chapter, then he had hopes of their stability in faith and progress in holiness. But if they disregarded what he told them, and persisted in the course they had started on, then he foresaw their speedy destruction. So much was at stake that he could not endure the state of suspense which he was in; therefore he **said**

farewell to them, that is, to the brothers in Troas, **and went on to Macedonia.** On his first visit to this city, Paul was prevented from remaining by a vision, from which he gathered that the Lord was calling him to preach the Gospel in Macedonia (Acts 16:8). And on his return from his present journey, we are told that he sailed from Philippi and came to Troas in five days, and stayed there for seven days (Acts 20:6). It is clear from the circumstances of this last visit that there was an established church in Troas at that time.

14. Spreads in every place the fragrance that comes from knowing him. This knowledge is compared to the aroma of a sacrifice (Genesis 8:21; Ephesians 5:2; Philippians 4:18), or to incense.

17. We are not peddlers of God's word. Greek writers frequently use the word to express the idea of adulterating, and of selling anything for gain. Both ideas may be combined here, for both are included in the apostle's disclaimer. He neither adulterated the Word of God by mixing it with Judaism or false philosophy (that is, with his own speculations), not used it for any selfish or mercenary purpose.

As persons sent from God. We have here, then, Paul's description of a faithful minister, one who is qualified for the fearful responsibility of being a fragrance of life or the smell of death. He does not corrupt the Word of God by mixing anything else with it, nor use it as a means of his own advancement by dispensing it so as to please men; but he is governed by pure motives, is of God, and speaks as in the presence of God, and as a true Christian.

Chapter 3

The apostle shows that he does not need to commend himself or to be commended by the Corinthians; that God had qualified him for the work of a minister of the new, and not of the old covenant (verses 1–11).

He exercised his ministry in accordance with the special character of the new dispensation (verses 12–18).

Proof of the Apostle's fitness for his work, and its nature (verses 1–11).

Although the concluding paragraph of chapter 2 contained a strong assertion of the apostle's integrity and faithfulness, he says it was not written for the purpose of commending himself. He needed no commendation from any source (verse 1). The Corinthians themselves were his commendation. Their conversion was a letter from Christ authenticating his mission and his faithfulness, which everyone could read (verses 2–3). His fitness for his work was not due to himself at all, but to God, who had endowed him with the qualifications of a minister of the new covenant (verses 4–6). This covenant and its ministry are far superior to the old covenant and the ministry of Moses, because the one was a ministry of death, the other of life; the one was of condemnation, the other of righteousness; the glory of the one was transient, the glory of the other is perpetual (verses 7–11).

1. Many of this letter's special features are due to the fact that at the time the apostle wrote it his mind was filled with conflicting feelings. On the one hand, he was filled with gratitude to God and love to the Corinthians because of their repentance and ready obedience; and on the other, with feelings of indignation at the perverse and wicked course adopted by the false teachers in Corinth. Hence even when he was expressing the first sort of feelings, he is interrupted or turned aside by the thought that his opponents were on the watch to turn everything to his disadvantage. Thus although there was nothing of a spirit of self-commendation in his thanking God for causing him to triumph, or in the assertion of his sincerity (1:15–17), he still knew that he enemies would put that construction on what he had said. He seems to hear them say, 'He is commending himself again.' It is clear from the use of the word again that the charge had been made against him before.

5. **Our competence is from God.** All our fitness for our work – all our knowledge, holiness, and power – are of God. They are neither acquired by ourselves nor sustained by ourselves. I am nothing, the apostle would say; God in me is everything. The same truth and feeling are expressed in 1 Corinthians 15:10.

6. **A new covenant.** The covenant formed between God and the Hebrews at Mount Sinai is called the Old Covenant; the Gospel dispensation as distinct from the Mosaic one is called the New Covenant (Matthew 26:28; 1 Corinthians 11:25; Hebrews 8:8–9; etc.). However, as the promises of the Gospel, and especially the great promise of redemption by the blood of Christ, underlay both the patriarchal and Mosaic dispensations, the plan of salvation or the covenant of grace is also called the New Covenant, although older than the Mosaic covenant, to distinguish it from the covenant of works formed with Adam. This gives rise to no little obscurity. It is not always easy to decide whether the words 'new covenant' refer to the Gospel dispensation introduced by Christ, or to the covenant of grace inaugurated in the first promise made to our fallen parents. Similarly, it is not always easy to decide whether the words 'old covenant' designate the Mosaic covenant or the covenant of works. In every case, the context

must be our guide in deciding these questions. In the present case it is clear that by **new covenant** the apostle means the Gospel as distinguished from the Law – the Christian as distinguished from the Mosaic dispensation. It was that covenant that he was made a minister of, and it is that which he contrasts with the Old Testament system.

7–8. The purpose and effect of the law was to kill. So far as the work of salvation is concerned, this is true of the law in all its forms, whether the moral law as revealed in the Scriptures, or as written in the heart, or as the Mosaic law. In all these forms it was designed to bring people to the knowledge of sin and helplessness; to produce a sense of guilt and misery, and a longing for redemption, and thus lead us to Christ (Galatians 3:24). This was something necessary, and therefore glorious. But how can it compare with the Gospel? How can that which only makes us know that we are sinful and condemned be compared with what delivers us from sin and condemnation? This is the idea which the apostle expands, and, as it were with exultation, turns over as though he could not let it go, in verses 7–11.

10. Because of the greater glory. The ministry of the Gospel so much excels the ministry of the law that the latter ceases to be glorious at all in comparison. This is the common and natural interpretation of the text. Two other explanations have been proposed. First, the words **what once had glory** refer to Moses' luminous face. This gives a very insignificant sense. The shining of Moses' face was not the glory of his ministry or of the old system. It was only a symbol of it. Second, Meyer and others keep the ordinary construction of the passage but make the apostle say that the general truth that the lesser glory is eclipsed by the greater was illustrated 'in this particular,' that is, in the case of Moses and his ministry. This brings out the same sense as that given by the ordinary interpretation, but in a less natural way. **What once had glory** naturally refers to the definite subject which the context deals with, which is the ministry of Moses.

The clarity and freedom of the Gospel as contrasted with the obscurity of the law (verses 12–18).

The apostle had referred to the transient brightness of Moses' face, as a symbol of the passing glory of his ministry. Here he uses the fact that Moses veiled his face as a symbol, in two ways. First, it symbolizes the obscurity of the revelation made under the old dispensation. As the brightness of Moses' face was covered, so spiritual or evangelical truth was previously covered under the types and foreshadowings of the Mosaic system. Secondly, it symbolizes the blindness which rested on the minds of the Jews, which prevented their seeing the true meaning of their own institutions (verses 12–15). Nevertheless, as Moses removed the veil from his face when he turned to the Lord, so both the obscurity of the law and the blindness of the Jew are dispelled when he turns towards Christ. The vision of his glory transforms the soul into his likeness (verses 16–18).

12. We act with great boldness. That is, outspoken. This is contrasted with all concealment, whether from timidity or from a desire to deceive; and also to all fear of consequences. It is a frank, open, courageous manner of speech.

14. That same veil. That is, the same obscurity. A veil was thrown over the truth as first revealed by Moses, and that same veil is there still. The Israelites of Paul's day understood their Scriptures as little as their fathers did. They remained satisfied with the external, ritual, and ceremonial, without penetrating to what was beneath, or asking the real meaning of the types and foreshadowings of the old system.

When they hear the reading of the old covenant. That is, when the Old Testament (covenant) is read. This use of the word **covenant**, for the books in which that covenant is contained, is perfectly familiar to our ears, as we are accustomed to calling the two great divisions of the Scriptures the Old and New Testaments or covenants; but this is the only instance of this use of the word in the New Testament.

17. The Spirit of the Lord, as a designation of the Holy Spirit, shows that the Spirit stands in the same relationship to the Son as he does to the Father. Therefore he is called the 'Spirit of Christ' (Romans 8:9) and 'Spirit of his Son' (Galatians 4:6). And, therefore, also the Son is said to send and give the Spirit (John 16:7). All this of course supposes the supreme divinity of our Lord.

Freedom. This freedom must be the freedom which results from the indwelling of the Holy Spirit; that is, which flows from the application to us of the redemption purchased by Christ. We have not received a spirit that makes us slaves again to fear, says Paul, but the Spirit of sonship (Romans 8:15). The freedom intended here is 'the freedom of the glory of the children of God' (Romans 8:21). It is the freedom for which Christ has made us free (Galatians 5:1). This includes:

1. Freedom from the law in all its forms, Mosaic and moral (Romans 6:14; 7:4); that is, freedom from the obligation to fulfill the law as the condition of our justification before God. This involves freedom from condemnation and from a legal, slavish spirit.

2. Freedom from the dominion of sin (Romans 7:6) and from the power of Satan (Hebrews 2:14–15).

3. Freedom from the bondage of corruption, not only as to the soul, but as to the body (Romans 8:21–23).

This freedom, therefore, includes all that is involved in being the children of God.

18. The glory of the Lord. That is (as the context evidently demands), Christ's glory. The glory of Christ is his divine excellence. The believer is enabled to see that Jesus is the Son of God, or God manifested in the flesh. This is conversion. Whoever acknowledges that Jesus is the Son of God, God lives in him, and he in God (1 John 4:15). The turning to the Lord mentioned in the previous verse is recognizing Christ as Jehovah. This is not only conversion, it is religion. It is the highest state of the human soul. It is eternal life (John 17:3). Hence our Lord prays that his disciples may see his glory, as the consummation of their blessedness (John 17:24). And the apostle John says of all who received Christ, that they saw 'his glory, the glory as of a father's only son' (John 1:14).

Chapter 4

The apostle resumes the theme of 3:12, namely the open and faithful manner in which he preached the Gospel (verses 1–6).

He shows that his own personal insufficiency and suffering revealed more clearly the power of God, who made such a feeble instrument the means of producing such great effects (verses 7–15).

Therefore, he was not discouraged or faint-hearted, but exultingly looked above the things seen to those unseen (verses 16–18).

As Paul had been made a minister of the new covenant, entrusted with the ministry of righteousness and life, he acted in keeping with his high commission. He was neither timid nor deceitful. He did not doubt the truth, the power, or the success of the Gospel which he preached; nor did he in any way corrupt of conceal the truth, but by openly proclaiming it he commended himself to everyone's conscience (verses 1–2). It, despite this clear display of the truth, the Gospel still remained hidden, that could only be explained by the god of this world blinding people's eyes. Nothing short of this can account for the fact; for, says the apostle, we preach Christ and not ourselves, and Christ is the likeness of God. In him there is a revelation of the glory of God; there is nothing like it except the original creation of light out of darkness (verses 3–6). This treasure, however, is in jars of clay. The Gospel is the revelation of God. It is to do for the world what the creation of light did for the chaotic earth. But we ministers are to have none of the glory of the work. We are nothing. The whole power is of God, who so orders events as to make his power apparent. I am so perplexed, persecuted, down-trodden and exposed to death, as to make it evident that a divine power is at work in preserving me and continuing to make me effective. My continuing to live and work with success is a proof that Jesus lives. Paul tells the Corinthians that this is for their benefit (verses 7–12). Having the same faith that David had, he spoke with equal confidence, being sure that God, who raised up Christ, would not only preserve him while in this world, but also raise him from the dead hereafter.

As all that Paul endured and did was for the benefit of the church, the people of God would give thanks for his preservation and success (verses 13–15). Therefore, adds this great apostle, I do not faint; although outwardly I am wasting away, inwardly I am renewed day by day; for I know that my present troubles are not only temporary, but are to be followed by an eternal glory that outweighs them all (verses 16–18).

1. We do not lose heart. 'We do not turn out bad.' That is, we do not fail to discharge our duty, either through weariness or cowardice.

2. We have renounced the shameful things that one hides. The Greek word means either shame as a feeling, or the cause of shame, anything disgraceful or scandalous. The phrase therefore may mean either the things which people conceal (or do in secret) because they are ashamed of them; or secret scandals or crimes. It may be taken in a general sense, as including any course of conduct which people conceal for fear of being disgraced; or in a specific sense for secret immoralities, or for secret machinations and manoeuvres. The last is probably the true view, because the emphasis is on **what one hides** rather than on **shameful**. It was secrecy or concealment, the opposite of openness and honest frankness, that the apostle accuses his opponents of. In the preceding context he had spoken of the openness of speech and conduct, and in the latter part of this verse he speaks of setting forth the truth – that is, proclaiming it openly. Therefore what he says he renounced, what he says is characteristic of false teachers, is the lack of openness adopting secret methods of achieving their ends, which they would be ashamed to admit openly.

We refuse to practise cunning or to falsify God's word. Not falsifying or corrupting the Word of God; that is, not adulterating it with human doctrines or traditions. Compare 2:17. The Gospel which Paul preached was the Word of God; something divinely revealed, and therefore having a divine and not merely human

authority. The apostles always speak in this way with the consciousness of being the mouth of God or organs of the Spirit, so that we cannot deny their inspiration without denying not only their authority but their integrity.

4. The god of this world. That is, Satan, who is called the god of this age because of the power which he exercises over people, and because of the servile obedience which they render to him. They are taken captive by him to do his will (2 Timothy 2:26). For people to serve Satan, and even worship him, it is not necessary that they should intend to do so, or even that they should know that such a being exists (1 Corinthians 10:20). It is enough that he actually controls them, and that they fulfill his purposes as implicitly as good people fulfill the will of God. Not to serve God, is to serve Satan. There is no help for it. If Jehovah is not our God, Satan is. He is therefore called the prince of this world (John 12:31; 14:30; compare Matthew 4:8–9; Ephesians 2:2; 6:12). This was one of the designations which the Rabbis applied to Satan. The true God, they said, is 'the first God'; Satan is 'the second God.' Or as Calovius said, the devil is the ape of God.

5. And ourselves as your slaves for Jesus' sake. Paul presented Christ as Lord; himself as a servant. A servant is someone who works, not for himself, but for someone else. Paul did not work for himself, but for the Corinthians.

For Jesus' sake. His motive in devoting himself to the service of the Corinthians was the love of Christ. Here again the wisdom of the world would say the proper motive would be a desire for their good. Paul always puts God before man. A regard for the glory of Christ is a far higher motive than regard for the good of men, and is its only true source. The ideal of a Christian minister, as presented in this passage, is that he is a preacher of Christ, and a servant of the church, governed and animated by the love of Jesus.

9. Struck down, but not destroyed. The allusion is still to a combat. Paul was not only persecuted or pursued by his enemies, but actually overtaken by them and cast to the ground, but not killed. When they seemed to have him in their power, God delivered him. This occurred so often, and in cases so extreme, as to make it manifest that the power of God was exerted on his behalf. No man from his own resources could have endured or escaped so much. There is in these verses an evident climax, which reaches its culmination in the next sentence. He compares himself to a combatant, first hard pressed, then hemmed in, then pursued, then actually thrown down. This was not an occasional experience, but his life was like that of Christ, an uninterrupted succession of indignities and suffering.

10. The death of Jesus. This corresponds to the life of Jesus in the next clause. The word **death** is used figuratively in Romans 4:19, 'the barrenness of Sarah's womb.' Here it is to be taken literally. Originally it meant a slaying or putting to death, and then violent death, or simply death. **The death of Jesus** does not mean death on his account, but such death as he suffered. Compare 1:5. Though it refers principally to the dying of Christ, and the climax begun in the previous verse is reached here, yet his other sufferings are not to be excluded. 'The mortification of Jesus,' says Calvin, 'includes everything which made him (that is, Paul) despicable before men.' Paul elsewhere refers to his constant exposure to death in terms as strong as those which he uses here. In Romans 8:36 he says, 'we are killed all day long,' and in 1 Corinthians 15:31, 'I die every day!' Compare also 1 Corinthians 4:9; 2 Corinthians 11:23. The death or sufferings of Christ were constantly, as it were, reproduced in the experience of the apostle. In the use of another figure he expresses the same idea in Galatians 6:17 – 'I carry the marks of Jesus branded on my body.' The scars which I bear in my body mark me as Christ's soldier, and as belonging to him as my divine Master, and as suffering in his cause.

14. This is to be understood of the literal resurrection, and not of a mere deliverance from dangers. This is evident for the following reasons:

1. Wherever a figurative sense is preferred to the literal meaning of a word or proposition, the context or nature of the passage must justify or demand it. Such is not the case here. There is nothing to forbid, but everything to favor the literal interpretation.

2. The figurative interpretation cannot be carried through without doing violence to the passage and to the analogy of Scripture. 'To present us with you' cannot be made to mean 'to exhibit us with you as rescued from danger.'

3. The figurative interpretation rests on false assumptions. It assumes that Paul confidently expected to survive the second coming of Christ, and therefore could not say he expected to be raised from the dead. In this very connection, however, he says he longs to be absent from the body and to be present with the Lord; as he said to the Philippians, at a later period of his career, that he had a desire to depart and to be with Christ. Again, it is said that according to the true reading of the passage, Paul says he knows we shall be raised up *with* (not *by*) Christ, and therefore he cannot be referring to the literal resurrection. But admitting the reading to be assumed, to be raised up *with* Christ does not mean to be raised contemporaneously with him, but in fellowship with him, and in virtue of union with him.

The resurrection of Christ here, as in other passages, is represented as the pledge of the resurrection of his people. 'The Spirit of him who raised Christ from the dead dwells in you' (Romans 8:11). 'And God raised the Lord and will also raise us up by his power' (1 Corinthians 6:14) See also 1 Corinthians 15:20–22; 1 Thessalonians 4:14; John 11:25; Ephesians 2:6; Colossians 2:12. In the view of the sacred writers, therefore, the glorious resurrection of believers is as certain as the resurrection of Christ, and that not simply because God who has raised up Jesus has promised to raise his followers, but because of the union between him and them. They are in him in such a sense as to be partakers of his life, so that his life of necessity secures theirs. If he lives, they will live too. Now as the fact of Christ's resurrection was no more doubted by the apostles, who had seen and heard and even handled him after he rose from the dead, than their own existence, we may see how assured was their confidence of their own resurrection to eternal life. And as to us, no event in the history of the world is better authenticated than the fact that Christ rose from the dead, we too have the same ground of assurance of the resurrection of those who are Christ's at his coming. If only we had the apostle's faith, we would have his constancy and his joy even in the midst of the greatest trials.

16. We do not lose heart. We do not become discouraged and give up the conflict. On the contrary, though his whole physical constitution was utterly worn out and wasted away by constant suffering and labour, his spiritual nature is **renewed**, that is, receives new life and vigor, **day by day**. This is not just his soul as opposed to his body, but his higher nature – his soul as the subject of the divine life (Romans 7:22; Ephesians 3:16). It could not be said of any unholy man in the apostle's sense that he was being renewed inwardly day by day. The apostle is not speaking about renewed supplies of animal spirits or of intellectual vigor, but about the renewal of spiritual strength to do and suffer. This constant renewal of strength is opposed to losing heart.

Day by day. This is a Hebraism (Genesis 39:10; Psalm 68:19), familiar to our ears but foreign to Greek usage. The supplies of strength came without fail and as they were needed.

18. Few passages in Paul's writings shows so clearly his inner exercises amidst sufferings and when death seems to be near. When he wrote this passage, he was in great trouble. He felt that his life was in constant and imminent danger, and that even if he was delivered from the violence of his enemies, his strength was gradually wearing away under the uninterrupted trials to which he was subjected. Under these circumstances we see him feeling suffering and sorrow keenly; he was very susceptible to the conduct and feelings of others towards him; he was well aware of his danger, and yet his confidence in his ultimate triumph was unshaken; he is firmly determined not to yield either to opposition or to suffering, but to persevere in faithfully and energetically doing the duty which had brought all his trials on him, and to exult heroically in the very troubles which tried him so sorely. He was sustained by the assurance that the life of Christ secured his life; that if Jesus rose, he would rise too; and by the firm conviction that the more he suffered for the sake of Christ, or in such a way as to honour his divine master, the more glorious he would be through all eternity. Suffering, therefore, became not just endurable for him, but a ground of great joy.

Chapter 5

The confidence expressed in the previous chapter is justified by showing that the apostle was assured of a dwelling in heaven, even if his earthly tent was destroyed (verses 1–10).

His object in what he had said about himself was not self-commendation. He laboured only for the good of the church, impelled by the love of Christ, whose ambassador he was, in exhorting people to be reconciled to God (verses 11–21).

The state of believers after death (verses 1–10).

Paul did not lose heart in the midst of his sufferings, because he knew that even if his earthly house was destroyed, he had a house in heaven – not like the present perishable tent, but one not made with hands, and eternal (verse 1). He looked forward to the unseen things, because in his present tent he groaned, desiring to enter his heavenly dwelling. He longed to be unclothed, so that he might be clothed with his house from heaven (verses 2–4). This confidence he owed to God, who had given him the Holy Spirit as a pledge of his salvation (verse 5). Having this indwelling of the Spirit, he was always in good courage, knowing that as soon as he was absent from the body, he would be present with the Lord (verses 6–8). Therefore his great desire was to please him before whose tribunal he and everyone else was to appear to receive what was due to their works (verses 9–10).

1. **The earthly tent we live in.** A frail, temporary abode, as opposed to a stable, permanent building. See 2 Peter 1:13–14.

A building from God. One provided by him, and of which he is the builder and maker

(Hebrews 11:10), and therefore is said to be **a house not made with hands**, that is, not like the buildings erected by man. Compare Hebrews 9:11 and Colossians 2:11. The latter passage refers to the circumcision of the heart as the immediate work of God; the soul therefore at death enters a house whose builder is God. This is said to exalt to the utmost our conceptions of its glory and excellence. Being made by God it is **eternal**. It is to last forever, and we are never to leave it. We dwell in our present bodies only for a little while, as in a tent; but heaven is an abode which, once entered, is retained forever.

4. **We groan under our burden.** That is, we groan because we are burdened. The burden may mean the trouble which Paul was overwhelmed by, or the body itself, or the longing for a better world. As this passage is intimately connected with the preceding chapter, in which the apostle had spoken so freely of his sufferings, and as his experience in view of death was determined by those sufferings, it is perfectly natural to understand him to refer to the burden of sorrow. It was because he suffered so much that he groaned to be delivered, that is, to be absent from the body and present with the Lord.

So that what is mortal may be swallowed up by life. That is, absorbed by it so that the one ceases to appear and the other becomes dominant. Compare 1 Corinthians 15:53–54. This is the elevated object of the apostle's longing desire. It was not death, not annihilation, nor mere exemption from suffering; but to be raised to that higher state of existence in which all that was mortal, earthly and corrupt about him would be absorbed in the life of God, that divine and eternal life arising from the beatific vision of God, and consisting in perfect knowledge, holiness, and blessedness.

9. **We make it our aim.** The Greek word means literally 'to love honour,' 'to be ambitious'; and then to make something a point of honour, or to set one's honour in doing or attaining something. So Paul says he made it a point of honour not to build on another man's foundation (Romans 15:20). And here he means that as ambitious people desire and strive after fame, so Christians long and labour to be acceptable to Christ. Love for him, the desire to please him, and to be pleasing to him, animates their hearts and governs their lives, and makes them do and suffer what heroes do for glory.

10. **For all of us must appear.** This means either nothing more than a judicial appearance, as when anyone is said to appear in court before a judge; or, as Bengel explains it, 'we must all stand revealed in our true character before the judgment-seat of Christ.' See 1 Corinthians 4:5; Colossians 3:4. As there can be no disguise, no deception before an omniscient judge, Paul was

assiduous in his efforts to be prepared to stand the scrutiny of an all-seeing eye.

Before the judgment seat of Christ. Literally, 'step'; then a raised platform, or seat; most frequently used of the elevated seat on which the Roman magistrates sat to administer justice, an object of reverence and fear to all the people. As Christ is to be the judge, as everyone is to appear before him, as the secrets of the heart are to be the basis of judgment, it is obvious that the sacred writers believed Christ to be a divine person, for nothing less than omniscience could qualify anyone for the office here ascribed to our Lord.

Paul's defence of himself against the charge of self-commendation (verses 11–21).

He declares that he acted under a solemn sense of his responsibility to God (verse 11). This was not said with the view of commending himself; but rather to give them the means of vindicating his character (verse 12). Whether his way of speaking of himself was extravagant or moderate, sane or insane, his motive in doing as he did was a sincere regard to the glory of God and the good of his church (verse 13). For the love of Christ constrained him to live, not for himself, but for him who died for him and rose again (verses 14–15).

Acting under the control of this elevated principle, he was raised above the influence of external things. He did not judge people by their external state. He was a new creature in virtue of his union with Christ (verses 16–17). This great change which he had experienced was not brought about by himself; it came from God, who is the author of the whole scheme of redemption. He is reconciled to the world through Jesus Christ, and he has commissioned his ministers to proclaim this great truth to everyone (verses 18–19). Therefore, the apostle, as an ambassador of God, exhorted people to accept this offer of reconciliation, for which the most abundant provision had been made, in that God had made Christ to be sin for us, in order that we might be made the righteousness of God in him (verses 20–21).

14. For the love of Christ urges us. That is, it controls and governs us. The Greek word also means 'to restrain,' a sense which many adopt here: 'The love of Christ restrains me from acting for myself.' This is a more limited sense, and is not required by the usage of the word, which if often used to express the idea of being pressed as by a crow, or figuratively, by calamity or sorrow. In this passage it coerces, or presses, and therefore impels. It is the governing influence which controls the life.

15. This is a continuation of the previous sentence, and is designed to express more fully the judgment or conviction which the apostle had formed of his relationship to his people, and that the purpose for which he died for them was that they might live for him. This idea is expressed in various forms in the Word of God. Sometimes our Lord is said to have died, the righteous for the unrighteous, to bring us to God (1 Peter 3:18); or that we might die to sins and live to righteousness (1 Peter 2:24); or to purify for himself a people that are his very own, eager to do what is good (Titus 2:14). In Romans 14:9, the mode of statement is exactly parallel to the passage before us. To say that Christ died that he might be the Lord of his people is to say that he died that they might be his servants, that is, belong to him and be devoted to him. The proximate purpose and effect of Christ's death is the expiation of sin and reconciliation with God, and the purpose and effect of reconciliation with God are devotion to his service. Hence the death of Christ is sometimes presented in reference to its proximate, and sometimes in reference to its ultimate purpose; that is, sometimes he is said to have died to make a propitiation for sin, and sometimes to bring us near to God. Here it is the latter. He died **that those who live might live no longer for themselves.**

20. Be reconciled to God. This does not mean, 'Reconcile yourselves to God.' The word is passive. **Be reconciled**, that is, embrace the offer of reconciliation. The reconciliation is effected by the death of Christ. God is now propitious. He can now be just, and yet justify the ungodly. All we have to do is not to refuse the offered love of God. Calvin remarks that this exhortation is not directed exclusively to the unconverted. The believer needs daily, and is allowed whenever he needs, to avail himself of the offer of peace with God through Jesus Christ. It is not the doctrine of the Scriptures that the merits of Christ avail only for the forgiveness of sins committed before conversion, while for post-baptismal sins, as they were called, there is no satisfaction except in the penances of the offender. Christ is always alive to make intercession for us, and for every shortcoming and renewed offense the penitent believer is offered renewed application of that blood which cleanses from all sin.

21. For our sake he made him to be sin who knew no sin. Christ was without sin. This was one of the indispensable conditions of his being made sin for us. If he had not been free from sin, he could not have taken the place of sinners. Under the old system the sacrifices were required to be without blemish, in order to teach the necessity of freedom from all sin in him who was to bear the sins of the world. See Hebrews 4:15; 1 Peter 2:22; 1 John 3:5.

Chapter 6

The apostle continues the vindication of himself (verses 1–10).

He asserts his strong love for the Corinthians, and exhorts them to keep themselves free from all contaminating alliances (verses 11–18).

The apostle's faithfulness and love (verses 1–18).

As the occasion of writing this letter was the false accusations of his opponents, a strain of self-vindication runs through the whole. In 5:12 he said he spoke of himself to enable his friends in Corinth to defend him against his enemies. He was governed by the love of Christ, and acted as his ambassador; as such he was a fellow-worker with God, and exhorted people not to fail of the grace of God (verses 1–2). In doing this, he avoided all offense (verse 3), proving his sincerity and faithfulness as a minister of God, by patiently enduring all kinds of trials (verses 4–5); by exercising all the grace and gifts of the Spirit (verses 6–7); and under all circumstances, whether of honour or dishonour, prosperity or adversity, whether understood or misunderstood by his fellow men (verses 8–10). He unburdened himself to the Corinthians in this way because his heart was enlarged. It was wide enough to take them all in. Whatever there was of the lack of love or of due appreciation between them and him, the fault was on their side, not on his (verses 11–12). He begs them to be as large-hearted towards him as he was towards them (verse 13), and not to allow themselves to be involved in any intimate alliances with the wicked (verses 13–18).

4–5. Through great endurance. That is, by patient endurance and constancy. Both ideas are expressed by the Greek word. Paul proved himself to be a true minister of Christ by the fortitude with which he endured sufferings, and by the constancy with which he stuck to his master under all these trials. In what follows in this verse and the next, he lists the trials to which he was subjected. The first group is general: **afflictions, hardships, calamities.** The second group is specific: **beatings, imprisonments, riots.** The third group is voluntary: **labours, sleepless nights, hunger.** His constancy was displayed in the cheerful endurance of all these kinds of trials.

6–7. Holiness of spirit. That is, by showing that the Holy Spirit is living in me. It is the doctrine of the Scriptures, and especially of Paul's writings, that the Spirit of God lives in all believers, and that besides those manifestations of his presence which are common to everyone, there is a special gift given to everyone, whether it be an ordinary or an extraordinary gift; to one

wisdom, to another knowledge, to another the gift of teaching, to another the working of miracles, etc. (1 Corinthians 12:7–11). To prove that he was a minister of God, Paul appeals to the evidence of the presence of the Spirit in him; this evidence was to be found in those graces and gifts of the Holy Spirit which he was full of; and in the divine power which accompanied his preaching and made it successful. He could appeal to his converts and say, 'You are the seal of my apostleship in the Lord' (1 Corinthians 9:2).

9. As dying, and see – we are alive. That is, regarded by others as certain to perish, **we are alive.** However, it is more in harmony with what follows to understand the apostle to be referring to actual facts. He was, as he says (4:11, and 1 Corinthians 15:31), constantly exposed to death. He died every day, and yet he lived. God always interposed to rescue him from destruction when it seemed inevitable, and to sustain him under calamities which it seemed no one could bear.

14. Do not be mismatched. The Greek means to be yoked with an animal of another kind, which evidently alludes to the Mosaic law which forbade the use of animals of different kinds in the same yoke (Deuteronomy 22:10). It is the combination of incongruous, uncongenial elements or people that is forbidden.

With unbelievers. The heathen – those who did not profess faith in the Gospel. The exhortation is reinforced by the questions which follow, which are designed to show the incongruity of such unions.

16. This and the following verses –

1. assert the incongruity between the temple of God and idols;

2. give the reason for presenting this incongruity (**For we are the temple of the living God**);

3. prove from Scripture that believers are God's temple;

4. show the duty which flows from this intimate relationship to God;

5. quote the gracious promise made to those who live in accordance with the relationship which they have with God.

18. The concluding verses of this chapter are an instructive illustration of the way the New Testament writers quote the Old.

1. They often quote a translation which does not strictly keep to the original.

2. They often quote according to the sense and not according to the letter.

3. The often blend together different passages of Scripture, so as to give the sense not of any one passage, but the combined sense of several.

4. They sometimes give the sense not of any particular passage or passages, but, so to speak, the general sense of Scripture. That is, they

quote the Scriptures as saying what is nowhere found in so many words, but what nevertheless, the Scriptures clearly teach. There is no such passage, for example, as that contained in this verse in the Old Testament, but the sentiment is often and clearly expressed in it.

5. They never quote as of authority any but the canonical books of the Old Testament.

Chapter 7

An exhortation founded on what is said in the preceding chapter (verse 1).

Paul's consolation derived from the favourable account which he had received from Corinth (verses 2–16).

The effect produced on the church in Corinth by the apostle's previous letter, and his consequent satisfaction and joy.

After exhorting them in verse 1 to live as befitted those to whom such precious promises had been given as he had just recited from the Word of God, in verses 2–3 he repeats his desire that they would reciprocate his ardent love (compare 6:13). So far as he was concerned there was nothing in the way of this cordial reconciliation. he had not injured them, nor was he alienated from them. He had great confidence in them. His apprehensions and anxiety had been to a great extent removed by the account which he had received from Titus of the feelings of the Corinthians towards him (verses 4–7).

It is true that he did at one time regret not having written that letter concerning the incestuous person; but he no longer regretted it, because he found that the sorrow which that letter occasioned was the sorrow of true repentance, redounding not to their injury but to their good (verses 8–9). It was not the sorrow of the world, but true godly sorrow, as was evident from its effects (verses 10–12). Therefore the apostle was comforted, and delighted to find how much Titus had been gratified by his visit to Corinth. All that the apostle had told him about the Corinthians' good disposition had proved to be true (verses 13–16).

1. Making holiness perfect. This expresses or indicates the way in which we are to purify ourselves. It is by perfecting holiness. The word translated perfect does not here mean simply 'to practise,' but to complete, to carry on to perfection. Compare 8:6, 11; Philippians 1:6. It is only by being completely or perfectly holy that we can attain the purity required of us as the temples of God. Holiness (see Romans 1:3; 1 Thessalonians 3:13) includes not only the negative idea of purity, or freedom from all defilement, but also, positively, that of moral excellence.

In the fear of God. This is the motive which is to determine our endeavours to purify ourselves. It is not regard for the good of others, nor our own happiness, but reverence for God. We are to be holy, because he is holy.

4. I often boast about you. The primary sense of the Greek word is 'freedom of speech,' but here, as in many other passages (Ephesians 3:12; Hebrews 3:6; 1 John 2:28; 3:21; 4:17; 5:14) expresses the idea of joyful confidence; that is, the state of mind from which freedom of utterance, or boldness of speech, flows. Paul means that so far from wishing to condemn the Corinthians, he had joyful confidence in them. And not only that, he adds, but I have great pride in you. The accounts which the apostle had just received of the state of things at Corinth, and especially of the effect produced by his first letter, had not only obliterated his feelings of anxiety and doubt concerning them, but made him boast of them. He gloried on their account. He was disposed to tell everyone how well his dear Corinthians behaved. He thus, as it were, unconsciously lays bare the throbbings of his warm and generous heart.

6. In the Greek, the word order is: 'He who comforts the downcast comforted us, even God, by the coming of Titus.' The fact that it is the characteristic work of God, or, so to speak, his office, to comfort the dejected, is thus made more prominent. All those who are miserable are thus encouraged, because they are miserable, to look to that God who proclaims himself as the comforter. It is notable that the objects of his compassion, those who call forth the exercise of his power as a consoler, are described not by a term which expresses moral excellence, but by a word which simply designates them as sufferers. The downcast are simply the low, those who are in depressed circumstances. As, however, it is the tendency of such circumstances to make people fearful, or meek, or humble, the word often expresses one or the other of these states of mind. In 10:1 it means 'timid' as opposed to 'bold'; in 1 Peter 5:5 it is the opposite of 'proud.' Here, however, it has it own, simple sense – those who are low, that is, cast down by suffering so as to be the proper objects of compassion. See Luke 1:52; James 1:9; Psalm 18:27. Paul says God comforted him by the coming of Titus, whom he had sent to Corinth to know the state of the church there.

9. Led to repentance. That is, change of mind, sometimes in the restricted sense of the word 'mind' (or 'purpose'), as in Hebrews 12:17; generally, in the comprehensive sense of the word as including the principles and affections, the whole soul, or inner life (Matthew 3:8; Luke

5:32; Acts 5:31). Repentance, therefore, in its religious sense, is not merely a change of purpose, but includes a change of heart which leads to a turning from sin with grief and hatred thereof unto God. Such is the repentance intended here, as appears from what follows. **For** (this shows their sorrow led to repentance) **you felt a godly grief** (that is, in a manner agreeable to the mind and will of God, so that God approved of their sorrow). He saw that it arose from right views of their past conduct.

11. Eagerness. The Greek word originally means 'haste'; then the feeling which leads to haste; then any outward manifestation of that earnestness of feeling. Here it means earnest solicitude as opposed both to indifference and neglect. The Corinthians had strangely allowed a grievous sin, committed by a church member, to pass unnoticed, as a matter of no importance. The first effect or manifestation of their godly sorrow was an earnest solicitude on the subject, and a desire to have the evil corrected; they very opposite of their former indifference. It is so in all cases of repentance. Sins which had been regarded as of little account are apprehended in their true character; and deep feeling takes the place of unconcern.

16. This is the conclusion of the whole matter. The first seven chapters of the letter are intimately linked. They all relate to the state of the congregation at Corinth and to Paul's relationship to the people there. The eighth and ninth chapters form a distinct division of the letter. Here, therefore, we have the conclusion of the whole preceding discussion. The result of the long conflict of feeling about the Corinthians as a church was the full restoration of confidence. I rejoice that I have confidence in you in all things.

Chapter 8

The extraordinary generosity of the Macedonians (verses 1–6).

Exhortation to the Corinthians to follow the example of their Macedonian brothers (verse 7–16).

Commendation of Titus for his zeal in promoting the collection of contributions for the poor, and of the other brothers who were to accompany him to Corinth (verses 17–24).

Exhortation to be generous to the poor.

The apostle devotes this and the following chapter to this subject. He begins by setting before the Corinthians the generosity of the churches in Macedonia. They, in the midst of great trou-bles and extreme poverty, had exceeded their ability in the contributions which they had made for the saints (verses 1–3). And this not by constraint or in obedience to earnest entreaties on the part of the apostle; on the contrary, it was they who urged him to receive and take charge of their alms (verse 4). Liberality to the poor was only a part of what they did; they devoted themselves to the Lord (verse 5). The conduct of the Macedonians led the apostle to exhort Titus, as he had already begun the work, to carry it on to completion in Corinth (verse 6).

He begs them, therefore, to add this to all their other graces (verse 7). This was a matter of advice, not of command. He was induced to give this exhortation because others had evinced so much zeal in this matter, and because he desired them to prove the sincerity of their love. What was all they could do for others, compared to what Christ had done for them (verse 8–9)? Being generous was something good for them, provided their feelings found expression in corresponding acts (verse 10–11). The disposition, not the amount of their contributions, was the main thing (verse 12). What the apostle wished was that there might be some approximation to equality among Christians, that the abundance of one may supply the needs of another (verses 13–15).

He thanks God who had inspired Titus with so much zeal on this subject (verses 16–17). With him he had sent a brother who had not only the approval of the churches, but had been chosen for the very purpose of taking charge of the contributions in connection with the apostle (verse 18–19). Paul was determined to avoid all occasion of reproach, and therefore he associated others with himself in the charge of the money entrusted to him (verse 20–21). With those already mentioned he sent another brother of approved character and great zeal (verse 22). Therefore if anyone inquired who Titus was, they might answer that he was Paul's companion and fellow worker; or who those brothers were, they might say that they were messengers of the churches, and the glory of Christ. Let the church therefore prove their love and justify his boasting of them (verses 23–24).

4. This ministry to the saints. The word *diakonia* ('ministry', 'service') is often used in the sense of 'aid' or 'relief' (9:1,13; Acts 6:1; 11:29).

6. Paul had urged the Corinthians (1 Corinthians 16:1) to make collections for the poor saints. Titus visited Corinth after that letter was written and made a beginning in this work. When Paul came to Macedonia and found how generously the churches there had contributed, he urged Titus to return to Corinth and complete what he had so successfully begun. Therefore the exhortation to Titus, which the apostle mentions here, was not the exhortation given him before the visit from which he had just returned, but the one he gave him in reference to a fresh visit yet to be made. So instead of translating it 'we urged Titus,' it would be clearer to say 'we have urged Titus.'

7. From this verse onward to verse 16 the apostle urges on the Corinthians the duty of generosity.

1. It was necessary to the completeness and harmony of their Christian character.

2. It would be a proof of their sincerity.

3. Christ had become poor for their sake.

4. It would redound to their own advantage, inasmuch as consistency required that having manifested the disposition, they should carry it out in action.

5. What was required of them was perfectly reasonable. They were asked to give only according to their means; and what they were called on to do for others, others under similar circumstances would be required to do for them.

10. Last year. If Paul, following the Jewish reckoning, began the year in October, he could write in November of an event which happened in the spring as having occurred last year. According to this view, an interval of little more than six months, from spring to autumn, intervened between the date of the first and second letters of Paul to the Corinthians.

14. The Greek refers not to reciprocity or equity but to fair balance as the illustration in verse 15 shows. We must give so as to produce equality. This is not community of goods. The New Testament teaching on this subject is as follows:

1. All giving is voluntary. A person's property is his own. It is in his own power to retain or give away; and if he gives, it is his prerogative to decide whether it will be much or little (Acts 5:4). This is the doctrine taught in this whole context. Giving must be voluntary. It is the fruit of love. It is of course obligatory as a moral duty, and the indisposition to give is proof of the absence of the love of God (1 John 3:17). Still it is one of those duties the performance of which others cannot enforce as a right belonging to them. It must remain at our own discretion.

2. The purpose of giving is relief of poverty. The equality aimed at, therefore, is not an equality as to the amount of property, but equal relief from the burden of want. This is taught in the remainder of this verse. 'At the present time,' says the apostle, 'let your abundance be imparted to their want, in order that their abundance may to your want, that there may be equality;' that is, an equal relief from want or destitution.

3. While all men are brothers, and the poor are proper objects of charity whether they are Christians or not, there is a special obligation resting on the members of Christ to relieve the needs of their fellow believers. We are to do good to everyone, says the apostle, especially to those who belong to the family of believers (Galatians 6:1). All the instructions in this chapter and the next refer to the duty of Christians to their fellow believers. There are two reasons for this. One is the common relationship of believers to Christ as member of his body, so that what is done to them is done to him; and their consequent intimate relationship to each other as being one body in Christ Jesus. The other is the assurance that the good done to them is pure good. There is no apprehension that the alms given will encourage idleness or vice.

4. A fourth rule is designed to prevent any abuse of the brotherhood of Christians. The poor have no right to depend on the gifts of the rich because they are brothers. The same apostle says, 'We gave you this command: "Anyone unwilling to work should not eat"' (2 Thessalonians 3:10). Thus the Scriptures avoid, on the one hand, the injustice and destructive evils of agrarian communism, by recognizing the right of property and making all almsgiving optional; and on the other, the heartless disregard of the poor by inculcating the universal brotherhood of believers, and the consequent duty of each to contribute out of his abundance to relieve the needs of the poor. At the same time they inculcate on the poor the duty of self-support to the extent of their ability. They are commanded 'to do their work quietly and to earn their own living' (2 Thessalonians 3:12). If these principles could be carried out, there would be among Christians neither idleness nor want.

19. While we are administering this generous undertaking. Paul had undertaken to administer the benefactions of the Gentile Christians among the brothers at Jerusalem, and the brother referred to had been chosen to travel with him and assist him in this service or ministry.

23. This is a recapitulation, or summary recommendation. The language in the original is very concise.

He is my partner. He is my associate, one who has a part with me in a common ministry.

Messengers of the churches. Literally, 'apostles of the churches'; the word is obviously used in its literal, not its official, sense. These men were surely not apostles in the sense in which Paul was. Similarly, in Philippians 2:5, Epaphroditus is called the apostle of the Philippians, because he was their messenger sent to minister to Paul at Rome. Both the brothers mentioned above, therefore, and not only the one of whom it is specifically said that he was chosen by the churches, were delegated by the people. They are further said to be the glory of Christ. As Christ alone, says Calvin, is the glory of believers, so he is glorified by them.

They reflect his glory. They by their holiness lead people to see the excellence of Christ whose image they bear.

24. Openly before the churches. That is, so that the churches by whom these brothers were sent may see the proof of your love. Instead of the received text, which has the imperative, some scholars follow the older manuscripts and translate it as, 'Exhibiting the evidence of your love, … (do it) in the presence of the churches.' This whole chapter proves how intimately the early Christians were bound together, not only from the dealings which we see here between the different churches, but from the influence which they exerted over each other, from their brotherly love and sympathy, and from the responsibility which each is assumed to owe to the judgment of the others.

Chapter 9

An exhortation to the Corinthians not to falsify his boasting of their generosity (verses 1–5).

An exhortation to give not only generously but cheerfully (verses 6–15).

Continuation of the discourse in the preceding chapter on making collections for the saints.

Although aware of their readiness, the apostle sent the brothers to bring the collection for the poor to an end, lest when the Macedonians who were to accompany him to Corinth arrived, they should find them unprepared, not so much to their disgrace, as to his mortification (verses 1–4). He sent the brothers, therefore, that everything they intended to do might be done in time, and be done cheerfully (verse 5). It was not only generosity, but cheerfulness in giving that the Lord required (verses 6–7). God who commanded them to give could and would supply their needs, and increase their graces. They would be the richer and the better for what they gave (verses 8–10). What he had at heart was not so much that the temporal sufferings of the poor should be relieved, as that God might be glorified by the gratitude and mutual love of believers, and by the display of their Christian graces (verses 10–14). What are our gifts to the poor compared to the gift of Christ to us (verse 15)?

1. To the saints. All believers are called **saints** in the sense of 'sacred,' that is, separated from the world and consecrated to God, and as inwardly renewed and purified by the Holy Spirit (8:4; Acts 9:13; Romans 1:7; 8:27). The saints referred to were of course the poor believers in Jerusalem for whose benefit Paul instituted this collection in the various churches which

he had founded (1 Corinthians 16:1–3).

2. That Achaia has been ready since last year. This was Paul's boast. All the Christians in Achaia belonged to the church in Corinth, although they did not all live in that city (see 1:1).

Has stirred up. The Greek word means to excite, whether the feeling called into exercise be good or bad. In Colossians 3:21 fathers are cautioned not to provoke their children. Here the meaning is that the enthusiasm of the Corinthians had excited that of others.

5. This bountiful gift. Literally, the 'blessing' – just as in English, the word can mean either a prayer for good or the good itself.

Not as an extortion. Literally, 'not as covetousness,' that is, not such a gift as betrays the greed of the giver.

7. Though he wishes them to give generously, he wanted them to do it freely.

As you have made up your mind. This is contrasted with what follows, and therefore is explained by it.

Not reluctantly. Not out of sorrow; that is, do not let the gift come from a reluctant state of mind, grieving after what is given as so much lost.

Or under compulsion. That is, compelled by circumstances to give, when you prefer not to do it. Many gifts are thus given sorrowfully, where the giver is induced to give by concern for public opinion, or under pressure of conscience. This reluctance spoils the gift. It loses all its fragrance when the incense of a free and joyful spirit is lacking.

For God loves a cheerful giver. A joyful giver – one to whom giving is a delight, who does it with hilarity. The passage is quoted from Proverbs 22:9, where the Hebrew means, 'A good eye will be blessed.' God blesses, loves, delights in, the joyous giver. Therefore, do not let those who give reluctantly, or under pressure of circumstances, or to secure merit, imagine that mere giving is acceptable to God. Unless we feel it is an honour and a joy to give, God does not accept the offering.

8. God is able. The sacred writers often appeal to God's power as a ground of confidence to his people (Romans 16:25; Ephesians 3:20; Jude 24). This is done especially when we are called upon to believe something which is contrary to the natural course of things. Giving is, to the natural eye, the way to lessen our store, not to increase it. The Bible says it is the way to increase it. To believe this it is only necessary to believe in the power, providence, and promise of God. God is able to make the paradox true that 'a generous person will be enriched' (Proverbs 11:24).

To provide you with every blessing. The Greek word may mean favour, gift (whether temporal or spiritual, or both, depends on the context). Here it clearly refers to earthly good; it means the kind of good or favour which enables those who receive it to give abundantly. The idea, therefore, obviously, is, 'God is able to increase your wealth.'

13. People will glorify God for your **confession of the gospel.** The Greek means 'on account of obedience to your confession' (the word 'confession' always in the New Testament means the profession, or confession, of Christianity – see 1 Timothy 6:12; Hebrew 3:1; 4:14; 10:23).

Chapter 10

Paul deprecates the necessity of asserting his authority and of exercising his power to punish the disobedient (verses 1–6).

He confronts his opposers with the assertion of divinely derived power (verses 9–11).

He shows that he claims authority only over those who were committed to his care (verses 12–18).

Paul's assertion of his authority and vindication of his apostolic prerogative (verses 1–18).

The remarkable change in the whole tone and style of this part of the letter, from the beginning of chapter 10 to near the end of chapter 13, has attracted the attention of every careful reader. The contrast between this and the preceding parts of the letter is so great that some have concluded they are separate letters, written at different time and under different circumstances. There is no external authority for this conjecture, and it is not only unnecessary but inconsistent with the facts of the case. The same topics are presented, and there is reference (in 12:18) to the mission of Titus spoken of in the earlier chapters. It is an adequate explanation of the change that, in chapter 1–9, Paul had in mind, and was really addressing, the faithful and obedient part of the church, whereas here he has in view the unreasonable and wicked false teachers and their adherents, who not only made light of his authority, but corrupted the Gospel, which he was appointed to propagate and defend. He therefore naturally assumes a tone of authority and severity.

Satisfied of his divine mission, and conscious of supernatural power, he cautioned them not to rely too much on his forbearance. He was indeed humble as a man, insignificant if you like; but there was an energy slumbering in him which they would do well not to provoke. He

had no desire to exercise in Corinth the authority with which Christ had invested him for the purpose of bringing down all opposition. He would give them a fair trial, and wait to see how far they would be obedient, before he punished their disobedience (verses 1–6). They should not judge by appearance, or set themselves up on the ground of their fancied advantages, because whatever they had, he had in larger measure (verse 7–8). He had no intention of frightening them by his letters – which they said were written in a tone he would not dare to assume when present – for they would find that, when occasion called for it, he could be as bold when present as when he was absent (verses 9–11).

They were subject to his apostolic authority. He usurped nothing in exercising the powers of his office over the churches which he had himself founded. He did not interfere with the jurisdiction of the other apostles, or undertake the special oversight of churches founded by others. Macedonia and Achaia were within the sphere of his operations, and he hoped to preach the Gospel far beyond those limits in regions where it had never been heard (verses 12–16). His confidence was not self-confidence, but confidence in God. His self-commendation amounted to nothing, unless the Lord commended him. Paul constantly felt that in himself he could do nothing, but in the Lord he could do all things (verses 17–18).

1. I myself, Paul, appeal to you by the meekness and gentleness of Christ. That is, the meekness and gentleness which belonged to Christ, and which, therefore, his disciples are bound to imitate. To appeal **by** is to appeal on account of, or out of regard to. The request is reinforced by referring to the obligation of Christians to be meek and gentle as their Lord was (Matthew 11:29; Isaiah 42:2). In Romans 12:1 we have a similar expression: 'I appeal to you therefore, brothers and sisters, by the mercies of God.' See Philippians 2:1. **Meekness** refers more to the inner virtue, **gentleness** to its outward expression. As Christians are bound to be meek and gentle, Paul begged the Corinthians not to force him to be severe.

3. Wage war. The war he is referring to is that which he wages against error and against everything opposed to the Gospel. He says he did not conduct this war **according to human standards** – that is, governed by the flesh, or relying on it. He was not guided by the principles of ordinary men, who act under the influence of their corrupt nature; nor did he depend for success on anything the flesh (that is, human nature) could afford. He was governed by the Spirit and relied on the Spirit. 'What Paul says of himself is true of all the faithful ministers of Christ,' comments Calvin. 'They bear about in incomparable treasure in clay jars. Therefore, although they are compassed with infirmities, nevertheless the spiritual power of God is resplendent in them.'

6. To punish every disobedience when your obedience is complete. The Gospel, being the Word of God, is divinely efficacious, and is certain ultimately to triumph over all opposition. This, however, does not imply that all will obey it. In the apostolic churches, there were those who corrupted the Word of God, Judaizing or philosophizing teachers and their followers, who refused to obey the truth. Paul announced his ability and his determination to punish such people.

8. Authority. The Greek word includes the ideas of power and authority. The apostle had authority (that is, the right to rule) and he had ability, inherent power, to enforce that authority. **The Lord gave for building you up.** The authority was given when he was constituted an apostle, with not only a commission to exercise dominion, but a grace, or inner gift of the Spirit, making him infallible as a teacher and investing him with supernatural power. The giver of this authority and power was the Lord, that is, Christ. Christ, therefore, as the author of supernatural gifts, is a divine person, for to give such gifts is a prerogative of God. The purpose for which Paul was not endowed was not his own exaltation, not the accomplishment of any worldly end, not, as he says, to 'pull them down,' that is, not that he might be able to put down his personal enemies, but **for building you up,** that is, building up the church in holiness and peace. Power in the church comes not from the civil magistrate, nor from the people, but only from Christ. He is, as Calvin says, the only Lord and Master. And this power can be legitimately exercised only for building up the church. When it is exercised for other purposes, or for the destruction of the church, then it would be disowned and resisted. Even an apostle, or angel from heaven, who preached any other gospel – teach or require anything contrary to the Word of God – would be accursed. And the people (that is, those who are required to believe and obey) are, at their peril, to be the judges of this: they must be, from the nature of the case and from the authority of Scripture. If they reject a true apostle, their sin is as great as if they listened to false teachers. Having the inner teaching of the Spirit, they know whether their doctrine comes from God.

13. The field that God has assigned. The Greek word refers to a rule, or measuring line, which, so to speak, God used in determining the apostle's gifts and sphere of activity. Paul's boasting, therefore, was not immoderate, but confined to just limits.

17. 'Boast in the Lord.' This means either to regard God as the ground of confidence and source of all good, and to ascribe everything we have, are, and hope to his grace; or, it is to exult in his approval. Instead of comforting ourselves with our own high estimate of our attainments and effectiveness, or allowing ourselves to be puffed up by human praise, we should be satisfied with nothing short of the divine approval. The context here favours the latter. 'Let him who boasts boast in the Lord; that is, he who rejoices should rejoice in the approval of God, not in his own good opinion of himself, nor in the praises of other; for it is not the person who commends himself who is really worthy of approval, but the one the Lord commends.' Paul did not commend himself; his claims were not based on the suggestions of self-conceit; nor did he rely on the commendation of other people. His eye was fixed on God. If he could secure his favour, it was a small matter to him to be judged by human judgment (1 Corinthians 4:3).

Chapter 11

The apostle apologizes for the self-commendation which was forced upon him (verses 1–15).

He contrasts himself and his labours with the assumptions of the false teachers (verses 15–33).

Reasons for his self-commendation (verses 1–15).

He had just condemned all self-commendation, yet he was forced to do what looked like praising himself. The Corinthians were in danger of being turned away from Christ by having their confidence in Paul undermined by the misrepresentations of his enemies. It was therefore unnecessary for him to present the grounds which he had for claiming authority over them, and for asserting his superiority over his opponents. Yet so repugnant was this task to his feelings that he not only humbly apologizes for speaking of himself in this way, but he finds it difficult to do what he felt must be done. He over and over begins what he calls his boasting, and immediately turns aside to something else. He begs them to bear with him while he proceeds to praise himself (verse 1), for his doing so sprang from the purest motive, love for them and anxiety for their welfare (verses 2–3). This anxiety was justified by the readiness with which they bore with those who preached another Gospel (verse 4).

He spoke like this because he was on a par with the chief apostles, and not behind those who among them claimed to be his superiors (verse 5). They might have higher claims as orators, but in knowledge and in everything that really pertained to the apostolic office he was abundantly manifest among them (verse 6). His refusal to avail himself of his right to be supported by those to whom he preached was no offense to them, and no renunciation of his apostleship (verses 7–9). He was determined to refuse any financial aid from the Christians in Achaia, not because he did not love them, but because he wished to cut off all occasion to question his sincerity from those who sought such occasion, and because he desired to put the false teachers to the same test of disinterestedness (verses 10–12). These teachers claimed to be apostles, though they had no more right to the office than Satan had to be regarded as an angel of light (verses 13–15).

2. I promised you in marriage to one husband. It was natural for the apostle to feel this jealousy over them, for he stood in a most intimate relationship to them. Their union with Christ was his work (1 Corinthians 4:15; 9:1). He may compare himself in this verse to a father who gives his daughter to the bridegroom.

4. Proclaims another Jesus than the one we proclaimed. Not another Saviour, but another person than the son of Mary whom we preached. That is, if he presents some other individual as the true deliverer from sin.

6. I may be untrained in speech. 'If, as is true, I am untrained or unskilful in speech.' The Greek word means one who is a private person, as opposed to one in an official position; a commoner as opposed to a patrician; an uneducated or unskilful man as opposed to those who were specially trained for any service or work, physical or mental. What Paul concedes is not the lack of eloquence – his writings give plenty of evidence of this – but of a Greek's special training. He spoke Greek as a Jew. It is not improbable that some of his opponents in Corinth, although themselves of Hebrew origin, prided themselves on their skill in the use of the Greek language, and made the apostle's deficiency in that respect a ground of disparagement.

But not in knowledge. Having been taught the Gospel by immediate revelation from Christ (Galatians 2:12), he had complete possession of that system of truth which it was the object of the apostleship to communicate to people. He therefore everywhere asserts his competence as a teacher instructed by God and entitled to full credence and implicit confidence (1 Corinthians 2:6–11; Ephesians 3:4–5).

7. Did I commit sin by humbling myself …? by renouncing a privilege which was my due? Compare Philippians 4:12. It was an act of self-humiliation that Paul, though entitled to be supported by the people, supported himself in great measure by the labour of his own hands. I humbled myself, he says, **so that you might be**

exalted – that is, for your good. It was to promote their spiritual interests that he worked at the trade of a tent-maker.

13. The reason given in this verse for the determination expressed in verse 12 is the unworthy character of his opponents. They were so unprincipled and unscrupulous that Paul was determined they should have no advantage over him.

False apostles are those who falsely claimed to be apostles, in the same way that 'false Christ' and 'false prophets' are those who falsely claimed to be Christ or prophets (Matthew 24:24; 11:15). An apostle was commissioned by Christ, endowed with the gifts of plenary inspiration and knowledge, and invested with supernatural powers. People in that age, and those who now claim to be apostles without this commission, these gifts, and these signs of the apostleship, are false apostles. They claim to be what they are not, and usurp an authority which does not belong to them.

Disguising themselves as apostles of Christ. Though their real object was not to advance the kingdom and glory of Christ, and although they were never commissioned for that work, they gave themselves out as Christ's messengers and servants, and even claimed to have a more intimate relationship to him, and to be more devoted to his service, than Paul himself.

15. If Satan can be changed like this, it is no great thing if his ministers undergo a similar transformation. If a bad angel can assume the appearance of a good angel, a bad man may put on the semblance of a good man.

Their end will match their deeds. Satan is none the less Satan when called by the name of good. God's judgments are according to the truth. He does not pass sentence on the external form we assume, but on our real character; not on the mask, but on the man. The end, that is, the reward of every person, will not be for appearances or human judgment, but for their works. If people really promote Christ's kingdom, they will be regarded and treated as his servants; if they increase the dominion of sin and error, they will be regarded and treated as the servants of Satan.

20. Preys upon you. That is, rapaciously consumes your substance, as our Lord describes the Pharisees as devouring widows' houses (Matthew 23:14).

Takes advantage of you. The Greek says, 'takes (you),' that is, captures of ensnares you, as a huntsman takes his prey. Our translation supplies an extra word, reading 'takes (of you),' which alters the sense, and makes this phrase express less than the previous one, since exploiting is a stronger expression than taking advantage.

Puts on airs. That is, proudly and insolently

lifts himself up against you.

Gives you a slap in the face. This was the highest indignity; as such it was offered to our Lord (Luke 22:64) and to Paul (Acts 23:2; see also 1 Kings 22:24; Matthew 5:39). Such was the treatment to which the Corinthians submitted from the hands of the false teachers; and such is always the tendency of unscriptural church authority. It assumes an absolute dependence of the people on the clergy – an inherent, as well as official, superiority of the clergy over the people, and therefore false teachers have, as a rule, been tyrants. The Gospel, and of course the evangelical system as opposed the high-church system, is incompatible with all undue authority, because it teaches the essential quality of believers and opens the way to grace and salvation to the people without the intervention of a priest.

24–25. These verses are a parenthesis designed to confirm the preceding statement that he worked and suffered more in the service of Christ than any of his opponents. In verse 26 the construction is resumed.

The apostle had at this period been scourged eight times; five times by the Jews and three by the Romans. Acts contains no record of this cruel ill-treatment at the hands of his own countrymen; and of the three occasions on which he was beaten with rods, the only one we have any account of elsewhere is that mentioned in Acts 16:22. In the law of Moses (Deuteronomy 25:3) it was forbidden to inflict more than forty lashes on an offender, and it appears that the Jews, in their punctilious observance of the letter of the law, were in the habit of inflicting only thirty-nine so as to be sure not to transgress the prescribed limit. The later Rabbis say that the scourge was made with three thongs, so that each blow inflicted three lashes; and that only thirteen strokes were given to make up the prescribed number of thirty-nine lashes.

Once I received a stoning. See Acts 14:19. On this occasion his enemies thought he was dead. He must therefore have been unconscious for a time.

Three times I was shipwrecked. We have no mention of this in Acts. The shipwreck in which Paul was involved on his journey to Rome was at a much later period.

For a night and a day I was adrift at sea. That is, he was tossed about by the waves, clinging to a fragment of a wreck, for a whole day of twenty-four hours. The Jews commenced their day at sunset.

26. It was voluntarily exposing himself to these dangers, and by the endurance of these sufferings, that the apostle proved his superior claim to be regarded as a devoted minister of Christ.

In danger from rivers. History shows that in the country which Paul travelled through great danger was often encountered in passing the rivers which crossed his path.

Danger from bandits. All travellers were exposed to these.

Danger from my own people. The Jews were, at least in most cases, the first to stir up opposition and to excite the mob against the apostle. This was the case at Damascus (Acts 9:23); at Jerusalem (Acts 9:29); at Antioch in Pisidia (Acts 13:50); at Iconium (Acts 14:5); at Lystra (Acts 14:19); at Thessalonica (Acts 17:5); at Berea (Acts 17:13); at Corinth (Acts 18:12).

Danger from Gentiles. As at Philippi and Ephesus.

Danger in the city. As in Damascus, Jerusalem, and Ephesus.

Danger in the country. The dangers of the desert are proverbial. Paul crossed Arabia, as well as the mountainous regions of Asia Minor, and was doubtless often exposed in these journeys to the dangers of robbers, as well as those arising from exposure, and hunger and thirst.

Danger at sea. Not only in the case of shipwreck mentioned before, but other and lesser perils.

Danger from false brothers and sisters. This probably refers to the treachery of those who falsely claimed to be his brothers in Christ, and yet tried to deliver him into the power of his enemies.

29. That is, he sympathized with his fellow Christians, who were his children in the faith, so that their sorrows and sufferings were his own. This was the consequence not only of the communion of saints, in virtue of which 'if one member suffers, all suffer together with it; if one member is honoured, all rejoice together with it' (1 Corinthians 12:26); it also shows the special relationship which Paul had with the churches which he himself had planted.

Who is weak … That is, in faith, or scrupulous through lack of knowledge (compare 1 Corinthians 9:22).

And am I not weak? That is, with whose infirmities of faith and knowledge do I not sympathize? He pitied their infirmities and bore with their prejudices. To the weak, he became as weak. There are people, says Calvin, who either despise the infirmities of their brothers, or trample them under their feet. Such people know little of their own hearts, and have little of the spirit of Paul or of Paul's master. God never snuffs out the smoldering wick.

Who is made to stumble, and I am not indignant? It was not a matter of indifference to Paul when any of the brothers, because of bad example or the seductions of false teachers, were led to depart from the truth or to act inconsistently with what they professed. Such events filled him not only with grief at the fall of the weak, but with indignation at those who had caused them to fall. Thus his mind was kept in a state of constant agitation by his numerous anxieties and his wide-hearted sympathy.

Chapter 12

The account of a remarkable vision granted to the apostle (verses 1–6).

The other evidence of his apostleship and his conduct and purposes in the exercise of his office (verses 7–21).

Paul's revelations and visions.

He would give up boasting, and refer not to what he had done, but to what God had done; not to scenes in which he was the agents, but to those in which he was merely the subject – to revelations and visions. He had been caught up to the third heavens, and received communications and revelations which he was not permitted to make known. This was to him, and to all who believed his word, a more reliable evidence of the favour of God to him as an apostle than anything he had yet mentioned (verses 1–6). With this extraordinary proof of the divine favour there was given him some painful bodily affection, from which he could not be delivered, in order to keep him duly humble (verses 7–10).

This reference to his personal experience was exceedingly painful to him. He had been forced by their unreasonable opposition to speak of himself as he had done; for the external signs of his apostleship should have convinced them that he was the immediate messenger of Christ (verses 11–12). They themselves were a standing proof that he was truly an apostle. They were not less richly endowed than other churches founded by other apostles. If inferior at all, it was only that he had refused to be supported by them. This he could not help. He was determined to pursue in the future the course in that matter which he had hitherto adopted; neither by himself nor by others, neither directly nor indirectly, would he receive anything from them (verses 13–18).

All this self-vindication was of little account. It was a small matter what they thought of him. God is the only competent and final judge. His fear was that when he reached Corinth he would be forced to appear as a judge; that not finding them what he desired them to be, he would be obliged to assume the form of a reprover (verses 19–21).

2. I knew a person. He speaks of himself in the third person. Why he does this is not clear. He narrates what had happened as though he had been a spectator of the scene, perhaps because his own activity was so completely in abeyance.

Fourteen years ago. The event referred to in this verse is not the same as that which occurred at the time of Paul's conversion. That was a vision of Christ to the apostle here on earth; this was a translation of the apostle into heaven; that occurred twenty years before the probable date of this letter. So the two agree neither in nature nor in the time they occurred.

7. To keep me from being too elated. Lifted up above what is right or proper. This clause expresses God's purpose in permitting the apostle to be afflicted in this way. He carried about with him a continued evidence of his weakness. However much he was exalted, although raised to the third heaven, he could not extract this rankling thorn. And the experience of God's people shows that bodily pain has a special part to play in the work of sanctification. In the unrenewed its tendency is to exasperate; when self-inflicted its tendency is to debase and fill the soul with grovelling ideas of God and religion, and with low self-conceit. But when inflicted by God on his own children, it more than anything teaches them their weakness and dependence, and calls them to submit when submission is most difficult. 'Though he slay me, yet will I hope in him' is the expression of the highest form of faith.

The exceptional character of the revelations. 'Excess, or exceeding abundance, of revelations.' This expression seems to refer not exclusively to the event mentioned above, but to other similar communications made to him at other times. That was not the only occasion on which God had unveiled to the apostle the treasures of divine knowledge.

A thorn was given to me in my flesh. The word Greek word translated **thorn** originally meant a sharpened stake, a palisade, then any piece of sharpened wood, and specifically a thorn. This last is the meaning best suited to this passage, and is the one commonly adopted.

A messenger of Satan. In the Bible the idea is often presented that bodily diseases are at times produced by the direct agency of Satan, so that they may be regarded as his messengers, something sent by him. The word **Satan** is used here probably as an indeclinable noun, as in one or two places in the Septuagint, but in the New Testament it is always, except in this instance, declined. For this reason many take the word here as in the nominative, and translate the phrase 'angel Satan,' that is, an angel (or messenger) who is Satan. But since **Satan** is at times indeclinable, and as Satan is never called an angel in the New Testament, the great majority of commentators give the same exposition as that given in the English version.

To torment me. In order that he (the angel or messenger) may torment me. The use of the present tense seems to imply that the 'thorn in the flesh' was a permanent affliction under which the apostle continued to suffer.

10. The difference between delighting in weaknesses and taking pleasure in them, is that the former phrase expresses the external sign of the feeling expressed by the latter. He delighted in weaknesses when he boasted of them, that is, referred to them as things which reflected honour on him and were a source of joy to him. As they were thus the occasions of revealing Christ's power, Paul was pleased with them and was glad that he was subjected to them.

12. This is the proof that he was not inferior to the 'super-apostles.'

The signs of a true apostle were the insignia of the apostleship; those things which by divine appointment were made the evidence of a mission from God. When these were present an obligation rested on all who witnessed them to acknowledge the authority of those who bore those insignia. When they were absent, it was, on the one hand, an act of sacrilege to claim the apostleship; and, on the other, an act of apostasy from God to admit its possession. To acknowledge the claims of those who said they were apostles and were not, was (and is) to turn from God to the creature, to receive as divine what was in fact human or Satanic. This is evidently Paul's view of the matter, as appears from 11:13–15, where he speaks of those who were the ministers of Satan and yet claimed to be the apostles of Christ. Compare Revelation 2:2. These signs of an apostle, as we learn from Scripture, were of different kinds. Some consisted in the manifestations of the inner gifts of the apostleship (that is, of those gifts whose possession made a man an apostle); such as plenary knowledge of the Gospel derive by immediate revelation from Jesus Christ (Galatians 1:12; 1 Corinthians 15:3); inspiration, or that influence of the Holy Spirit which made its possessor infallible in the communication of the truth (1 Corinthians 2:10–13; 12:8, in connection with 12:29 and 14:37). Other signs consisted in the external manifestations of God's favour sanctioning the claim to the apostleship (Galatians 2:8). To this class belongs faithfulness in teaching the truth, or conformity to the authenticated standard of faith (Galatians 1:8). To this class also belong success in preaching the Gospel (1 Corinthians 9:2; 2 Corinthians 3:2–3); the power of communicating the Holy Spirit by the imposition of hands (Acts 8:18; 19:6); the power of working miracles, as appears from the passage under consideration and from Romans 15:18–19 and many other passages (such as Hebrews 2:4; Mark 14:20; Acts 5:12; 14:3); and holy behaviour (2 Corinthians 6:4). Without these signs no one can be recognized and obeyed as an apostle without apostasy from God; without turning from the true apostles to those who are the servants of Satan.

Signs and wonders and mighty works. These are different names for the same thing. Miracles are called **signs** in reference to their purpose, which is to confirm the divine mission of those who perform them; miracles are called **wonders** because of the effect which they produced; and miracles are called **signs** because they are manifestations of divine power.

With utmost patience. This does not mean that the patient endurance of severe trials was one of the signs of his apostleship, but that those signs were performed under adverse circumstances requiring the exercise of the greatest constancy.

15. As I am your father, I will gladly act as such, spend and be spent for you; even though I forfeit your love by acting in a way which love forces me to act. This is the strongest expression of disinterested affection. Paul was willing not only to give his property but himself, his life and strength, for them (literally, 'for your souls'), not only without a recompense, but at the cost of their love.

20. He aimed at their edification, **for** he feared their state was not what he could desire. He feared lest they would not be acceptable to him, nor he to them. What he feared was that the evils to which frequent reference had already been made should be found still to exist. Those evils were:

Quarrelling, such as existed between the different factions into which the church was divided, some saying 'We belong to Paul,' others, 'We belong to Peter,' etc. (see 1 Corinthians 1:11).

Jealousy. Those feelings of jealousy and alienation which generally accompany quarrels.

Anger. Cabals. The word is from a Greek word meaning 'hireling,' and is often used of a factious spirit of party.

Slander, gossip. Backbiting and whisperings; that is, open detractions and secret calumnies.

Conceit. Examples of pride and insolence.

Disorder. That is, the disorder which necessarily follows the state of things described above.

This is a formidable list of evils, and it seems hard to reconcile what is said here with the glowing description of the repentance and obedience of the church found in chapter 7. To account for this discrepancy some suppose, as we have already seen, that the latter part of the letter, from chapter 10 to the end, formed a distinct letter written at a different time and under different circumstances from those under which the first part was written. Others, admitting that the two parts are one and the same letter sent at the same time, still assume that a considerable interval of time elapsed between the writing of the first and second parts of the letter; and that during that interval news had reached the apostle that the evils prevailing in the church had not been so thoroughly corrected as he had hoped. The common and sufficient explanation of the difficulty is that part of the congregation, probably the majority, were penitent and obedient, while another part were just the opposite. When the apostle was thinking of one group, he used the language of commendation; when he was thinking of the others, the language of censure. Examples of this kind are abundant in his letters. The first part of his first letter to the Corinthians is full of the strongest expressions of praise, but in what follows severe reproof fills most of its pages.

Chapter 13

Threatening of punishment to impenitent offenders; exhortation to self-examination and amendment; conclusion of the letter.

Paul's warnings and exhortations (verses 1–14).

Having previously admonished and warned, he now distinctly announces his intention of exercising his apostolic power in the punishment of offender (verses 1–2). As they sought evidence of his apostleship, he would show that although weak in himself, he was invested with supernatural power by Christ. As Christ appeared as weak in dying, but was none the less imbued with divine power, as was proved by his resurrection from the dead; so the apostle in one sense was weak, in another full of power (verses 3–4). Instead of exposing themselves to this exercise of judicial authority, he exhorts them to test themselves, since Christ lived in them unless they were reprobates (verse 5). He trusted that they would acknowledge him as an apostle, as he sought their good (verses 6–7). His power was given, and could be exercised, only for the truth. He rejoiced in his own weakness and in the prosperity of the Corinthians. The point of warning them was to avoid the need to exercise the power of judgment with which Christ had invested him (verses 8–10). Concluding exhortation and benediction (verses 11–13).

1. From this it is evident that Paul had already been in Corinth. He was about to make his third visit. The Acts of the Apostles does not contain a full record of all the journeys, labours and sufferings of the apostle. He may have visited Corinth repeatedly without its coming within the purpose of that book to mention the fact. 'The evidence of two or three witnesses.' The Old Testament expressly laid it down that no one should be condemned without the testimony of two or three witnesses: see Numbers 35:30 and Deuteronomy 17:6; 19:15. In this latter pas-

sage, the very words used by the apostle are to be found. This principle of justice was transferred by our Lord to the New Dispensation. See Matthew 18:16; see also John 8:17; Hebrews 10:28. In 1 Timothy 5:19 the apostle applies the rule specially to the case of elders. In the judgment of God, therefore, it is better that many offenders should go unpunished through lack of testimony, than that the security of reputation and life should be endangered by allowing a single witness to establish a charge against anyone. This principle, although thus clearly and repeatedly sanctioned in both Old and New Testaments, is not held sacred in civil courts. Even in criminal cases the testimony of one witness is often considered sufficient to establish the guilt of an accused person, no matter how pure his previous reputation may have been. Paul here announces his determination to stick strictly to the rule relating to testimony laid down in the Scriptures, when administering discipline.

3. He is not weak in dealing with you, but is powerful in you. The messenger of Christ was not to be rejected or offended with impunity, since Christ was not weak, but powerful. His power had been proved among them not only in the conversion of multitudes, but by signs and wonders, and by various manifestations of omnipotence.

4. In weakness. His weakness was the cause or necessary condition and evidence of his death; not of course as implying that his death was not voluntary, for our Lord said he laid down his life of his own accord; but the assumption of a weak human nature liable to death was of course necessary, in order that the eternal Son of God should be capable of death. Compare Philippians 2:9; Hebrews 2:14–15. His death, therefore, was the evidence of weakness, in the sense of having a weak, or mortal, nature.

But lives by the power of God. The same person who died now lives. That complex person, having a perfect human and a true divine nature united, rose from the dead, and lives forever, and therefore can manifest the divine power which the apostle attributed to him. The resurrection of Christ is sometimes ascribed to God (as in Romans 6:4; Ephesians 1:20; Philippians 2:9), and sometimes to himself (as in Matthew 26:61; Mark 14:58; John 2:19; 10:18). This is done on the same principle that the works of creation and providence are ascribed sometimes to the Father and sometimes to the Son. That principle is the unity of the divine nature, or the essential identity of the persons of the Trinity. They are the same in substance, and therefore the works of one are the works of the others also. It is not, however, the fact that the resurrection of Christ was effected by the power of God, but the fact that he is now alive and clothed with divine power, that the apostle urges as pertinent to his purpose.

5. Jesus Christ is in you. This does not mean 'Christ is among you as a people.' It refers to an indwelling of Christ in the individual believer, as is clear from such passages as Galatians 2:20; 4:19; Romans 8:10. Christ lives in his people by his Spirit. The presence of his Spirit is the presence of Christ. This is not a mere figurative expression, as when we say we have a friend in our heart – but a real truth. The Spirit of Christ, the Holy Spirit, is in the people of God collectively and individually, the ever-present source of a new kind of life, so that if anyone does not have the Spirit of God he is none of his (Romans 8:9).

Unless, indeed, you fail to pass the test! Those in whom Christ does not live cannot stand the test, and are proved to be Christians only in name, if at all.

9. That you may become perfect. That is, we are not only glad when you are strong, but we pray for your complete establishment. The Greek word translated **perfect** comes from a word meaning 'to put into complete order.' Paul prayed that they might be perfectly restored from the state of confusion, contention, and evil into which they had fallen.

10. The authority the Lord has given me. His authority was not self-assumed, and his power was not derived from himself. They were the gifts of the Lord, the only source of either in the church. **The Lord** is of course Christ, whose divine power and omnipresence are taken for granted. Paul everywhere assumes as much that the Lord Jesus is invested with divine attributes and entitled to divine worship, as God himself. Nothing can be more foreign to the whole spirit of the New testament than the idea that Christ, having finished his work on earth as a teacher and witness, has passed away so as to be no longer present with his people. The whole Scriptures, on the contrary, assume that he is everywhere present in knowledge and power, the source of all grace, strength, and consolation, the object of the religious affections, and of the acts of religious worship.

11. The severe rebukes contained in the preceding chapters are softened by the parental and apostolic tone assumed in these concluding verses. He addresses them as **brothers and sisters** – members of the family of God and of the body of Christ.

Farewell. Literally, 'rejoice,' or, 'joy to you.' It is often used in greetings. On account of what follows, it is better to take it as an exhortation to spiritual joy: 'Rejoice (that is, in the Lord)!' In Philippians 3:1 and 4:4 we have the same exhortation. Joy in redemption, rejoicing in our union and communion with the Lord is one of

our highest duties. Blessings as infinite as these should not be received with indifference. Joy is the atmosphere of heaven, and the more we have of it on earth, the more heavenly we shall be in character and temper.

Live in peace. One of the greatest evils prevailing in Corinth, as we learn from 1 Corinthians 1:10–12, was the quarrels of the various parties into which the church was divided.

And the God of love and peace will be with you. God is the author of love and peace. The existence of love and peace is the condition of the presence of the God of peace. He withdraws the manifestations of his presence from the soul disturbed by angry passions, and from a community torn by dissensions. We have here the familiar Christian paradox. God's presence produces love and peace, and we must have love and peace in order to have his presence. God gives what he commands. God gives, but we must cherish his gifts.

12. The kiss was the expression of fellowship and affection. It was and is in the East the common way friends greet each other. A **holy** kiss is a kiss which expresses Christian communion and love. It was the practice in Christian meetings for the men to kiss the minister and each other, especially at the celebration of the Lord's Supper. [Other Bible versions make a separate verse of the words, **All the saints greet you.**]

14. This comprehensive benediction closes the letter. It includes all the benefits of redemption.

The grace (or favour) **of our Lord Jesus Christ.** This is calling our blessed Saviour the God-man. It includes or indicates his divine nature, he is our Lord; his human nature, he is Jesus; his office, he is the Christ, the Messiah, the long-promised Redeemer. It is the favour, the unmerited love and all that springs from it, of this divine person clothed in our nature, and who as the God-man is invested with the office of Messiah, the headship over his own people and all power in heaven and earth, that the apostle invokes for all his believing readers. Every one feels that this is precisely what he, as a guilty, polluted, helpless sinner, needs. If this glorious, mysteriously constituted, exalted Saviour, Son of God and Son of man, makes us the object of his favour, then our present security and ultimate salvation is made certain.

And the communion of the Holy Spirit. The primary object of the death of Christ was the communication of the Holy Spirit. He redeemed us from the curse of the law, that we might receive the promise of the Spirit (Galatians 3:13–14). It is the gift of the Holy Spirit secured in the covenant of redemption by the death of Christ that applies to us the benefits of his mediation. As the gift of the Spirit is secured to all the people of God, they are joint partakers of the

Holy Spirit, and thereby made one body. This is the ground of the communion of saints in which the church universal professes her faith.

The distinct personality and the divinity of the Son, the Father, and the Holy Spirit, to each of whom prayer is addressed, is here taken for granted. And therefore this passage is a clear recognition of the doctrine of the Trinity, which is the fundamental doctrine of Christianity. For a Christian is one who seeks and enjoys the grace of the Lord Jesus, the love of God, and the communion of the Holy Spirit.

GALATIANS

Martin Luther

Introduction

St. Paul sets about establishing the doctrine of faith, grace, forgiveness of sins, or Christian righteousness. His purpose is that we may understand exactly the nature of Christian righteousness and its difference from all other kinds of righteousness. For there are various sorts of righteousness. There is a political or civil righteousness, which emperors, princes of the world, philosophers and lawyers deal with. There is also a ceremonial righteousness, which human traditions teach. This righteousness may be taught without danger by parents and schoolteachers, because they do not attribute to it any power to satisfy for sin, to please God, or to deserve grace; but they teach such ceremonies as are necessary simply for the correction of manners, and certain observations concerning this life. Besides these, there is another righteousness, called the righteousness of the law, or of the ten commandments, which Moses teaches. We too teach this, according to the doctrine of faith.

There is yet another righteousness which is above all these; namely, the righteousness of faith, or Christian righteousness, which we must carefully distinguish from the other sorts mentioned above, for they are quite contrary to this righteousness, both because they flow out of the laws of rulers, the traditions of the church, and the commands of God; and also because they consist in our works and may be performed by us either by our pure natural strength or else by God's gift. For these kinds of righteousness are also from God's gift, just as other good things are which we enjoy.

But this most excellent righteousness – that of faith, I mean – which God imputes to us through Christ, without works – is neither political nor ceremonial, nor is it the righteousness of God's law, nor does it consist in works. It is quite the opposite; that is to say, it is a mere passive righteousness, whereas the others are active. We do nothing in this matter; we give nothing to God, but simply receive and allow someone else to work in us – that is, God. Therefore it seems to me that this righteousness of faith, or Christian righteousness, can well be called the passive righteousness.

This is a righteousness hidden in a mystery, which the world does not know. Even Christians themselves do not thoroughly understand it, and can hardly grasp it in their temptations. Therefore it must be diligently taught and continually practised. And whoever does not understand this righteousness when afflicted and frightened in conscience must be overthrown. For nothing comforts our conscience so firmly and securely as this passive righteousness.

But human weakness and misery is so great that in the terrors of conscience and danger of death we see nothing but our works, our worthiness, and the law. And when we are shown our sin, in time we remember the evil of our past life. Then the poor sinner groans with great anguish of spirit, and thinks, 'Alas, what a dreadful life I have lived! Would to God I might live longer; then I would amend my life.' Thus human reason cannot restrain itself from the sight of this active or working righteousness, that is, our own righteousness; nor can it look up to see the passive or Christian righteousness, but relies altogether on the active righteousness – so deeply is this evil rooted in us.

On the other hand, Satan abuses our natural weakness and increases and aggravates these thoughts of ours. Then our poor conscience becomes more troubled, terrified, and confounded. For it is impossible for the human mind to conceive any comfort, or look only to grace in the feeling and horror of sin, or constantly reject all argument and reasoning about words. For this is far above human strength and ability, and indeed above the law of God as well. It is true that the law is the most excellent of all things in the world; yet it is not able to quieten a troubled conscience, but makes our terrors worse, and drives us to desperation – 'so that through the commandment sin might become utterly sinful' (Romans 7:13).

Therefore the afflicted and troubled conscience has no remedy against desperation and eternal death unless it takes hold of the forgiveness of sins by grace, freely offered in Christ Jesus, that is to say, this 'passive faith,' or Christian righteousness. If it can take hold of this, then it may be at rest, boldly say, 'I do not seek this active or working righteousness, although I know that I ought to have it, and also to fulfill it. But if I had it, and did actually fulfill it, I still could not place my trust in it, nor should I dare to set it against God's judgment. Thus I abandon all active righteousness, both of my own and of God's law, and embrace only that passive righteousness which is the righteousness of grace, mercy, and forgiveness of sins. Briefly, I rest only on that righteousness which is the righteousness of Christ and of the Holy Spirit.'

Just as the earth does not generate rain, and cannot of itself work to produce it but receives it by the mere gift of God from above, so this heavenly righteousness is given us by God without our working for or deserving it. See, then, how much the earth is able by itself to do in getting showers of rain to make it fruitful; that much, and no more, are we able to do by our own strength and works in winning this heavenly and eternal righteousness. We shall never be able to attain it unless God himself bestows it on us, imputing it to us by his gift beyond words. The greatest wisdom of Christians, then, is to have nothing to do with the law and works, and the whole of active righteousness, especially when the conscience wrestles with God's judgment. On the other hand, the quintessence of wisdom amongst those who are not among God's people is to know and earnestly follow the law and active righteousness.

It is very strange to the world to teach Christians to learn to be ignorant of the law, and to live before God as if there were no law, yet unless you are ignorant of the law and convinced in your heart that there is now no law nor wrath of God, but altogether grace and mercy for Christ's sake, you cannot be saved; for knowledge of sin comes through the law. On the contrary, works and keeping the law must be strictly required in the world, as if there were no promise or grace. This is because of the stubborn, proud and hard-hearted, before whose eyes nothing must be set but the law, that they may be terrified and humbled. For the law is given to terrify and kill such people, and to exercise the old nature, and both the word of grace and that of wrath must be properly taught, as the apostle teaches in 2 Timothy 2.

Here, then, we need a wise and faithful teacher of the Word of God, who can moderate the law so that it is kept within bounds. Anyone who teaches that people are justified before God by observing the law goes beyond the law, and muddled these two kinds of righteousness, active and passive, and is a poor logician, for he does not explain the law correctly. On the contrary, anyone who sets out the law and works to the old nature, and the promise and forgiveness of sins and God's mercy to the new nature, interprets the Word well. For the old nature must be coupled with the law and works; the spirit, or new nature, must be joined with the promise of God and his mercy. Therefore, when I see a person who is bruised enough already being oppressed with the law, terrified with sin, and thirsting for comfort, it is time for me to remove the law and active righteousness from his sight, and set before him, by the Gospel, the Christian and passive righteousness. This excludes Moses with his law, and offers the promise made in Christ, who came for the afflicted and for sinners. Here we are raised up again, and acquire hope; here we are no longer under the law, but under grace (see Romans 6:14). How is it that we are not under the law? According to the new nature, to whom the law does not appertain. As Paul says later on, 'Christ is the end of the law' (Romans 10:4); since he has come, Moses ceases with his law, circumcision, sacrifices, Sabbaths, and indeed all the prophets.

This is how we teach people to distinguish between these two kinds of righteousness, active and passive, so that manners and faith, works and grace, politics and religion, should not be confused with each other. Both are necessary, but both must be kept within their rightful place; Christian righteousness belongs to the new nature, and the righteousness of the law belongs to the old nature, which is born of flesh and blood. A burden must be laid on this old nature, as upon an ass; it will press down and the freedom of the spirit of grace will not be enjoyed unless we first put on the new nature, by faith in Christ (though this is not fully done in this life); when we do that, we may enjoy the kingdom and inestimable gift of grace.

I say this so that no one should think we reject or forbid good works. Those who know nothing but the righteousness of the law may still judge this doctrine which is far above the law, yet it is impossible for unspiritual people to be able to judge it. Of course such people take offense, for they can see no higher than the law. But imagine two worlds, the one heavenly and the other earthly. In these, there are two kinds of righteousness, quite separate from each other. The righteousness of the law is earthly, and has to do with earthly things, and by it we do good works. But as the earth can only produce fruit if it is first watered and made fertile from above, so by the righteousness of the law, in doing many things we do nothing, and in fulfilling the law we do not fulfill it, unless we are first made righteousness without any merit or work of ours, by the Christian righteousness, which has nothing to do with the righteousness of the law, or with the earthly and active righteousness. This righteousness is heavenly – we receive it from heaven, we do not have it of ourselves; it is worked in us by grace, and apprehended by faith, and by it we rise above all laws and works. Therefore, as St. Paul says in 1 Corinthians 15:49, 'just as we have borne the likeness of the earthly man, so shall we bear the likeness of the man from heaven,' which is the new man in a new world, where there is no law, no sin, no remorse or sting of conscience, no death, but perfect joy, righteousness, grace, peace, salvation and glory.

So, then, do we do nothing to obtain this righteousness? No, nothing at all. For perfect righteousness is to do nothing, to hear nothing, to know nothing of the law, or of works, but to know and believe only that Christ has gone to the Father, and is no longer visible; that he sits in heaven at the right hand of his Father, not as a judge, but made by God our wisdom, righteousness, holiness, and redemption; in short, that he is our high priest, entreating for us, and reigning over us and in us by grace. In this heavenly righteousness sin can have no place, for there is no law; and 'where there is no law there is no transgression' (Romans 4:15).

Seeing, then, that sin has no place here, there can be no anguish of conscience, no fear, no heaviness. That is why St. John says, 'anyone born of God does not continue to sin' (1 John 5:18). But if there is any fear or grief of conscience, it is a sign that this righteousness has been withdrawn, that grace is hidden, and that Christ is darkened and out of sight. But where Christ is truly visible there must be full and perfect joy in the Lord, and the conscience is at peace and thinks, 'Although I am a sinner by the law, and under condemnation of the law, I still do not despair and do not die, because Christ lives, and he is my righteousness and my everlasting life.' In that righteousness and life I have no sin, no fear, no sting of conscience, no worry about death. I am indeed a sinner, as far as this present life and righteousness are concerned, as I am child of Adam; where the law accuses me, death reigns over me, and wants to devour me finally. But I have another righteousness and life above this life, which is Christ the Son of God, who knows no sin or death but is righteousness and eternal life. By him, this body of mine which is dead will be raised up again, and delivered from the bondage of the law and sin, and will be sanctified together with the spirit.

So both these continue whilst we live here. The flesh is accused, tempted, oppressed with heaviness and sorrow, bruised by active righteousness of the law; but the spirit reigns, and is saved by this passive and Christian righteousness, because it knows that it has a Lord in heaven, at the right hand of his Father, who has abolished the law, sin, death, and has trodden underfoot all evils, led them captive, and triumphed over them in himself (Colossians 2:15).

Therefore St. Paul, in this letter, teaches us in order to comfort us and confirm us in the perfect knowledge of this most Christian and excellent righteousness. For if once we lose our belief in justification, then all true Christian doctrine is lost. There is no mean between the 'righteousness of the law' and 'Christian righteousness.' Anyone who strays from 'Christians righteousness' must fall into the 'righteousness of the law'; in other words, when people lose Christ, they slip back into reliance on their own works.

That is why we so earnestly repeat this doctrine of 'faith,' or 'Christian righteousness,' so that it may be continually exercised and may be plainly distinguished from the 'active righteousness of the law.' Otherwise we should never be able to believe the true theology. The church is founded on, and consists in, this doctrine alone. So, if we want to teach and lead other people, we need to pay careful attention to these matters, and to note well this distinction between the righteousness of the law and the righteousness of Christ. It is easy to describe in words, but hard to put into practice, for when we are near death or in other agonies of conscience these two sorts of righteousness come closer together than you would wish. So I warn you, especially those of you who will become teachers and guides of consciences, to exercise yourselves continually by study, reading, meditation on the Word, and prayer, so that in time of temptation you may be able to instruct and strengthen both your own conscience and that of other people, and bring them from the law to grace, from active and working righteousness to passive and received righteousness, from Moses to Christ. When we are afflicted, and our conscience suffers conflict, the devil makes us afraid by the law, and accuses us with the guilt of sin, our wicked past life, God's wrath and judgment, hell, and eternal death. Thus he drives us to desperation, makes us bondslaves to himself, and plucks us from Christ. Furthermore, he brings against us those passages of the Gospel in which Christ himself requires works of us, and clearly threatens those who do not perform them with damnation. Now, if we are unable to judge between these two kinds of righteousness – if we do not by faith take hold of Christ as he sits at God's right hand, interceding with the Father for us wretched sinners, then we are under the law and not under grace, and Christ is no more a Saviour, but a lawgiver. Then there will be no more salvation for us, but a certain desperation and everlasting death, unless repentance follows.

Let us then be careful to learn to discriminate between these two kinds of righteousness, so that we may know how far we should obey the law. We have already seen that the law in a Christian ought to have dominion only over the flesh. When it is so, the law is kept within bounds. But if it presumes to creep into your conscience, and try to reign there, you must make the right distinction. Give no more to the law than is right, but say, 'You want to climb up into the kingdom of my conscience, do you, Law? You want to reign over it and reprove sin, and take away the joy I have by faith in Christ, and drive me to desperation? This is beyond your remit; keep within your bounds, and exercise your power over the flesh, but do not touch my conscience. I am baptized, and by the Gospel I am called to share righteousness and everlasting life. I am called to Christ's kingdom, where my conscience is at rest and there is no law, but forgiveness of sins, peace, quietness, joy, health, and everlasting life. Do not trouble me in these matters; for I will not let an intolerable tyrant like you reign in my conscience, which is the temple of Christ, the Son of God. He is the king of righteousness and peace, and my sweet Saviour and Mediator; he will keep my conscience joyful and quiet in the sound and pure doctrine of the Gospel, and in the knowledge of this Christian and heavenly righteousness.'

When I have this righteousness reigning in my heart, I descend from heaven like the rain which makes the earth fertile. That is to say, I come out into another kingdom, and I do 'good works,' whenever I have a chance. If I am a minister of the Word, I preach, I comfort the broken-hearted, I administer the sacraments. If I am a householder, I am in charge of my house and my family, I bring up my children in the knowledge and fear of God. If I am a magistrate, I work hard at the job that heaven has given me. If I am a servant, I do my master's business faithfully. Whoever is convinced that Christ is his righteousness works cheerfully and well in his vocation, and also submits through love to the magistrates and their laws even if they are severe and cruel. If necessary, he will submit to all manner of burdens and dangers in this present life, because he knows that this is God's will, and that this obedience pleases him.

That is Paul's argument. He sets himself against the false teachers who had obscured this righteousness of faith among the Galatians, and he defends and commends his own authority and office.

Contents

See *Outlines of the New Testament Books,* p. 898

Chapter 1

The occasion of the letter

Paul had planted the pure teaching of the Gospel among the Galatians, and the righteousness of faith. But after he had left, certain false teachers crept in who overthrew all that he had taught. The devil cannot but argue furiously against this teaching or rest as long as he sees any spark of it remaining. We too, simply because we preach the Gospel, suffer from the world, the devil, and his ministers, all the mischief they can work against us on every hand.

The Gospel is a doctrine that teaches a far higher matter than the wisdom, righteousness, and religion of the world; it teaches free forgiveness of sins through Christ. But the world prefers these things to the Creator, and tries to get rid of sin, be delivered from death, and deserve everlasting life. The Gospel condemns this. On the other hand, the world cannot abide things being condemned when it values them highly and likes them best; and therefore it claims that the Gospel is a seditious doctrine, full of errors; that it overthrows government, countries, and empires, and therefore offends against God and the emperor; it abolishes laws, corrupts good manners, and sets everybody free to do what they want. Therefore, with what appears to be holy and righteous zeal, it persecutes this doctrine, and abhors its teachers and adherents as the greatest plague on earth.

Moreover, preaching this doctrine overthrows the devil, destroys his kingdom, and wrests out of his hand the law, sin, and death (by which he has subjugated all mankind). In short, the devil's prisoners are transferred from the kingdom of darkness into the kingdom of light and liberty. Will the devil permit all this? Will the father of lies not use all his force and ingenuity to obscure, to corrupt, and utterly to root out this doctrine of salvation and eternal life? Indeed, St. Paul complains in this and all his other letters that the devil showed himself skilful at this.

The Gospel is a doctrine which condemns all sorts of righteousness, and preaches the sole righteousness of Christ. To those who accept this, it brings peace of conscience and all good things; yet the world hates and persecutes it bitterly.

I have already said that the reason Paul wrote this letter was that after he left, false teachers among the Galatians had destroyed what he had built with much hard work. These false apostles were Pharisees – men of authority, highly esteemed – who boasted that they belonged to the chosen people, that they were Abraham's descendants (see Romans 4:4–6), that they had the promises and the fathers; and finally, that they were the ministers of Christ and scholars of the apostles, with whom they had been conversant, and whose miracles they had seen. Perhaps they had also performed some miracles themselves, for Christ says that they wicked do also perform miracles (see Matthew 7:22). Moreover, these false apostles defaced St. Paul's authority, saying, 'Why do you rate Paul so highly? Why do you have him is such great reverence? He was just the last of all those who were converted to Christ. But we are the disciples of the apostles; we knew them well. We saw Christ performing miracles, and heard him preach. Paul came after us, and is inferior to us, and it would be impossible for God to allow us to go wrong when we belong to his holy people, the ministers of Christ, and have received the Holy Spirit. Again, there are many of us, and Paul is one on his own, and neither knows the apostles nor has seen Christ. Indeed, for a long time he persecuted the church of Christ. Do you think God would allow so many churches to be deceived, just for Paul's sake?'

When people of such authority come into any country or city, people soon admire them, and they deceive not only the simple but also the learned with this apparent godliness. They even deceive people who seem to be pretty well established in the faith. Thus Paul lost his authority among the Galatians, and his doctrine was brought under suspicion.

Against this boasting of the false apostles, Paul firmly asserts his apostolic authority. And although he does not do anything like it elsewhere, he will not give way to anyone, even to the apostles themselves, much less to any of their followers. And to stop their pharisaical pride and shameless boldness, he mentions what happened at Antioch, where he withstood Peter himself. Besides this, he ignores any possible offense and plainly states that he was so bold as to accuse and reprove Peter himself, the chief of the apostles, who had seen Christ, and knew him really well. I am an apostle, he says, and was not afraid to chide the pillar of all the rest.

So, in the first two chapters, Paul sets out his calling, his office, and his Gospel, affirming that he had not received it from any human being, but by the revelation of Jesus Christ. Also, that if he, or even an angel from heaven, should bring any other Gospel than that which he has preached, he should be condemned.

The certainty of calling

What does Paul mean by this boasting? The answer is that every minister of God's Word should be sure of his calling, that he may preach the Gospel as one who is called and sent. A royal ambassador boasts that he does not come as a private person but as the king's ambassador, and is honoured because of this dignity. In the same way, the preacher of the Gospel should be certain that his calling is from God, and it is expedient that he should follow Paul's example and give honour to this calling, so that he may win credit and authority among the people. This is a necessary kind of glorying, because he is glorying not in himself but in the king who sent him, and whose authority he wants to be honoured.

Similarly, when Paul commends his calling so highly, he is not seeking praise for himself, but exalts his ministry with a necessary and a holy pride. As he says in Romans 11, 'Inasmuch as I am the apostle to the Gentiles, I make much of my ministry,' that is, I want people to receive me not as Paul of Tarsus but as Paul the apostle or ambassador of Jesus Christ. He has to do this in order to maintain his authority, so that the people are more willing to listen to him. In Paul they hear Christ himself, and God the Father, and they should reverently receive Christ and listen to his messengers.

This is a notable passage, therefore, for Paul is boasting of his calling, despising all others. If a person in a worldly way despised everyone else, he would really be a fool, and give great offense. But this kind of boasting is necessary, and refers not to Paul's glory but to God's, and it is by such boasting that the sacrifices of praise and thanksgiving are offered to him, as it tells the world about the name, the grace, and the mercy of God.

1. **Paul, an apostle – sent not from men nor by man.** Right at the beginning, he mentions those false teachers who boasted they were the apostles' disciples, and sent by them, but

despised Paul as someone who was neither of the apostles' school nor sent by anyone to preach the Gospel, but came in some other way, and thrust himself forward into that office on his own.

And God the Father, who raised him from the dead. Paul is here so inflamed with zeal that he cannot wait till he comes to the matter itself, but immediately, in the very title, bursts out and utters what is in his heart. His intention in this letter is to deal with the righteousness that comes by faith, and defend it; and to beat down the law, and the righteousness that comes by works. He is full of such thoughts, and this great burning fire of his heart cannot be hidden; it will not let him hold his tongue. Therefore he thought it insufficient to say that he was **an apostle** sent **by Jesus Christ** but also added **and God the Father, who raised him from the dead.**

3. **Grace and peace to you from God our Father and the Lord Jesus Christ.** The apostle's greeting is strange to the world, and was never heard of before the preaching of the Gospel. And these two words, **grace** and **peace**, include whatever belongs to Christianity. **Grace** releases sin, and **peace** makes the conscience quiet. The two fiends that torment us are sin and conscience. But Christ has vanquished these two monsters, and trodden them underfoot, both in this world and the world to come. The world does no know this, and therefore it can teach no certainty of the overcoming of sin, conscience, and death. Only Christians have this kind of teaching, and are armed with it to gain the victory against sin, despair, and everlasting death. It is a kind of teaching which neither comes of free-will, nor is invented by human wisdom or reason, but is given to us from above.

Grace contains the remission of sins, peace, a quiet and joyful conscience. But **peace** of conscience can never be had unless sin is forgiven first. But sin is not forgiven for fulfilling the law, for no one is able to satisfy the law. Rather, the law shows sin, accuses and terrifies the conscience, declares God's wrath, and drive people to desperation. Much less is sin taken away by human deeds and human ideas, such as wicked worship, strange religions, vows, and pilgrimages. Finally, there is no work that can take sin away: rather, sin is increased by works. For the merit-monger, the more they labour and sweat to bring themselves out of sin, the deeper they are plunged in it. There is no means to take sin away but **grace** alone. That is why Paul, in all the greetings of his letter, sets **grace and peace** against sin and a bad conscience. Note this most carefully. The words are simple. But, in temptation, it is the hardest thing that can be, to be convinced in our hearts that we have forgiveness of sins and peace with God by **grace** alone.

The world does not understand this teaching, and therefore it cannot abide it, and does not wish to; it condemns it as heretical and wicked. It brags about free-will, the light of reason, the soundness of the power and qualities of nature, and about good deeds as means whereby it could discern and attain **grace and peace**; that is, forgiveness of sins and a quiet conscience. But it is impossible for the conscience to be quiet and joyful unless it has **peace** through **grace** – that is, through the forgiveness of sins promised in Christ. Many people have conscientiously laboured to attain peace and quietness of conscience by seeking out various religious orders and exercises for the purpose; but by doing so, they have plunged themselves into more and greater miseries, for all such devices are only ways of increasing doubt and despair. Therefore there will be no rest for my bones or yours unless we listen to the Word of **grace**, and stick to it consistently and faithfully. Then our conscience will undoubtedly find grace and peace.

4. **Who gave himself for our sins.** In every word, Paul deals with the argument of this letter. Everything he says is to do with Christ; and therefore in every word there is a fervency of spirit and life. And notice how well and appositely he speaks. He does not say, 'who has received our works,' nor 'who has received the sacrifice of Moses' law, worship, religions, masses, vows, and pilgrimages,' but **who gave** – what? Not gold, or silver, or animals, or paschal lambs, or an angel, but **himself!** What for? Not a crown, or a kingdom, or our holiness and righteousness, but **for our sins.** These words are great thunderclaps from heaven against all kinds of righteousness. So also is this sentence of John: 'Look, the Lamb of God, who takes away the sin of the world!' (John 1:29).

The force and power of sin is made quite clear by these words: **who gave himself for our sins.** Here we must note the infinite price given for it, and then it will be clear that its power is so great that it could not be put away by any means except by the Son of God giving himself for it. Anyone who considers these things properly will understand that this one word 'sin' includes God's everlasting wrath and the whole kingdom of Satan, and that it is something more horrible than can be expressed; which ought indeed to move us and make us afraid. But we are careless and make light of sin, as if it were nothing. Although it brings with it the sting and remorse of conscience, we still think it is not so important but that we may get rid of it by some little work or merit.

So this sentence tells us that we are all servants and slaves to sin (compare Romans 7:14). It tells us that sin is a most cruel and mighty tyrant over everyone, and cannot be vanquished by the power of any creatures, whether they are angels or human beings, but only by the sovereign and infinite power of Jesus Christ, **who gave himself for our sins.**

Christ was given not only for other people' s sins but also for your own. Hold on to this, and by no means let yourself be drawn away from this very sweet definition of Christ, which makes even the angels in heaven rejoice – that Christ is no Moses, no lawgiver, no tyrant, but a mediator for sins, a free giver of grace, righteousness, and life; who **gave himself,** not for our merits, holiness, righteousness, and godly life, but **for our sins.** Christ does indeed interpret the law, but that is not his chief, or his own particular, job.

To rescue us from the present evil age. In these words Paul deals yet more effectually with the argument of this letter. He calls this whole world, past, present, and future, **the present evil age,** to distinguish between this and the everlasting world to come. Moreover, he calls it **evil** because whatever is in this world is subject to the malice of the devil reigning over the whole world. For there is in it nothing but ignorance, contempt, blasphemy, hatred of God, and disobedience against all God's words and works. We are in and under this kingdom of the world.

And if you are not in Christ's kingdom, you certainly belong to Satan's kingdom, which is **the present evil age.** Therefore all the gifts, either physical or mental, which you enjoy, such as wisdom, righteousness, holiness, eloquence, power, beauty, and riches, are only the slavish instruments of the devil, and you are compelled to serve him with all of them, and to advance his kingdom.

Evil. By this word, Paul shows that the kingdom of the world, or the devil's kingdom, is the kingdom of iniquity, ignorance, error, sin, death, blasphemy, desperation and everlasting damnation. On the other hand, the kingdom of Christ is the kingdom of equity, light, grace, forgiveness of sins, peace, consolation, saving health, and everlasting life, and we are brought into this world (Colossians 1:13) by our Lord Jesus Christ, to whom be glory, world without end. Amen.

5. To whom be the glory for ever and ever. The Jews mix praise and thanksgiving in their writings, and the apostles themselves follow this practice. It may often be seen in Paul. The name of the Lord should be greatly revered, and never named without praise and thanksgiving. Doing this is a certain kind of worship and service to God.

6. I am astonished. You see here how Paul treats his Galatians, who had fallen away and had been seduced by the false apostles. He does not at first set upon them with vehement and rigorous words, but in a very fatherly manner. Patiently he bears their fall, and in a way excuses it. Furthermore, he shows motherly affection

towards them, and speaks very gently to them, yet in such a way that he reproves them nonetheless. They are very appropriate words, however, and wisely framed to the purpose. Conversely, he is very hot and full of indignation against those false apostles, their seducers, upon whom he lays all the blame. Even at the beginning of his letter, he bursts out into loud thunder and lightning against them (see verse 8), and later he threatens them with damnation (Galatians 5:10). These are dreadful thunderclaps against the righteousness of the flesh or the law.

And are turning to a different gospel. Here we learn to see the devil's tricks. No heretic comes to us claiming the title of errors and of the devil, nor does the devil himself come as a devil in his own likeness, especially that white devil which we spoke about earlier. Even the black devil, which forces people to reveal wickedness, makes a cloak for them to cover the sin which they commit, or intend to commit. The murderer, in his rage, does not see that murder is as great and horrible a sin as it really is, for he has a cloak to cover it. Whoremongers, thieves, greedy people, drunkards, and so on, have something to flatter themselves with, and cover up their sins. The black devil too comes out disguised and counterfeit in all his actions and plots. But in spiritual matters, when Satan does not appear black but white, like an angel or God himself, he dissimulates in a most deadly way, and offers for sale his most deadly poison instead of the doctrine of grace, the Word of God, the Gospel of Christ. That is why Paul calls the doctrine of the false apostles, Satan's ministers, **a different gospel** – but derisively. It is like saying, 'You Galatians now have other evangelists, and another gospel; my Gospel is despised by you now; you no longer value it.'

7. Which is really no gospel at all. Evidently some people are throwing you into confusion. Here again he excuses the Galatians, and most bitterly reproves the false apostles. It is like saying, 'You Galatians are assured that the Gospel which you received from me is not the true and sincere Gospel, and therefore you think you are doing the right thing by accepting that new gospel, which the false apostles teach, and which seems to be better than mine. I do not so much accuse you of this fault as those disturbers who trouble your consciences, and pull you out of my hand.' Here you see once more how vehement he is against those deceivers, and with what harsh words he describes them, calling them troublers of the churches, who do nothing else but seduce and deceive innumerable poor consciences, occasioning horrible mischief and calamities in the congregations. We also see this great enormity today, to the great grief of our hearts, yet we are no more able to remedy it than Paul was at that time.

8. But even if we or an angel from heaven should preach a gospel other than the one we preached to you, let him be eternally condemned! Here Paul really throws out flames of fire, and his zeal if so fervent that he also begins almost to condemn the angels. Although we ourselves (he says) – I and my brothers Timothy and Titus, and everyone who teaches Christ purely with me (I am not now speaking about those seducers of consciences), or even if **an angel from heaven should preach …**, I would still rather that I myself, my brothers, and even the angels from heaven too should be **eternally condemned**, than that my Gospel should be overthrown.

The Greek word *anathema*, or Hebrew *herem*, means something accursed, execrable, and detestable, which has nothing to do with God, no communion with him. Thus Joshua says, 'Cursed before the Lord is the man who undertakes to rebuild this city, Jericho' (Joshua 6:26). And in Leviticus 27:28 it says, 'Nothing that a man owns and devotes to the Lord – whether man or animal or family land – may be sold or redeemed; everything so devoted is most holy to the Lord.' Thus God appointed Amalek, and certain other cities cursed by God's own sentence, to be utterly razed and destroyed. So Paul's though is: 'I would rather that myself, and my other brothers, and even an angel from heaven, were condemned than that we or others should preach any gospel other than that which we have already preached.' He begins by condemning himself, for clever workmen find fault with themselves first of all, in order to be free to reprove other people afterwards.

10. Or am I trying to please men? That is, am I serving men or God? He always has an eye to the false apostles. These people, he says, have to please and flatter men; for that is how they seek, so that they may glory in the flesh. Moreover, because they will not bear human hatred and persecution, they teach circumcision, simply to avoid the persecution of the cross, as follows in chapter 5.

11–12. I want you to know, brothers, that the gospel I preached is not something that man made up. I did not receive it from any man, nor was I taught it; rather, I received it by revelation from Jesus Christ. Here is the principal point of this matter, which contains a proof that his adversaries are wrong, and a defence of his doctrine, to the end of chapter 2. He stands on this, and urges it and confirms it with an oath: that he did not learn his Gospel from a man, but received it by the revelation of Jesus Christ. He is forced to swear, so that the Galatians may believe him, and also so that they will not listen to the false apostles – whom he reproves as liars, because they had said that he had learned and received his Gospel from the apostles.

When he says his Gospel is **not something that man made up**, he does not mean that his Gospel is not earthly, for that is obvious, and the false apostles too boasted that their doctrine was not earthly but heavenly. He means that he had not learned his Gospel from men's ministry, or received it by any earthly means, as we all learn it either by human ministry or else receive it by some earthly means (some by hearing, some by reading, and some by writing); but he received it only by the revelation of Jesus Christ.

13. For you have heard of my previous way of life in Judaism, how intensely I persecuted the church of God and tried to destroy it. There is no special doctrine in this verse. Paul instances his own case, saying, 'I have defended the traditions of the Pharisees, and the Jewish religion, more constantly than you and all your false teachers. So if the righteousness of the law had been worth anything, I would not have turned away from it. Before I knew Christ, I excelled many of my own nation in keeping the law. Moreover, I was so zealous in its defence that I greatly persecuted the church of God. I had the authority of the high priests, and I put many people in prison (Acts 26:10). When they were to be put to death, I pronounced the sentence, and punished them throughout all the synagogues. I made them blaspheme, and was so furious with them that I even followed them to foreign cities.'

14. I was advancing in Judaism beyond many Jews of my own age and was extremely zealous for the traditions of my fathers. In this verse he is not thinking of the traditions of the Pharisees, but of something far greater; **the traditions of my fathers** includes even the holy law of Moses. See also Philippians 3:6. It is like saying, 'Here I may compare with the whole of the Jewish nation, even with the best and holiest of all those who are circumcised. Let them show me, if they can, a more zealous and earnest defender of Moses' law than I have been. This should have persuaded you not to believe these deceivers who magnify the righteousness of the law as a matter of great importance. If there were any cause to glory in the righteousness of the law, I have more cause to glory than anybody else.'

15–17. This is Paul's first journey. Immediately after he was called by the grace of God to preach Christ among the Gentiles, he went to Arabia, without anyone's advice, to the work he was called to. This passage shows by whom he was taught, and by what means he came to the knowledge of the Gospel, and to his apostleship. It is like saying: 'I have not deserved it, because I was zealous for the law of God without judgment. Indeed, this foolish and wicked zeal stirred me up so that, God permitting, I fell headlong into more abominable and outrageous sins; I persecuted the church of God, I was an enemy to Christ, I blasphemed his Gospel, and finally I was the cause so much innocent blood was shed. This was what I deserved. In the midst of this cruel rage, I was called to such inestimable grace. Was it because of this outrageous cruelty? No indeed. But the abundant grace of God, who calls, and shows mercy to those he wants to, pardoned me and forgave me all those blasphemies; and for these horrible sins of mine, which I then thought to be perfect righteousness, and an acceptable service to God, he gave me his grace, the knowledge of his truth, and called me to be an apostle.'

15. **But when God …** It is like saying: 'It is the one inestimable favour of God that he not only has spared me, so wicked and cursed a wretch, such a blasphemer, persecutor, and a rebel against God, but also has given me the knowledge of salvation, his Spirit, Christ his Son, the role of an apostle, and everlasting life.' In the same way, God saw that we were guilty in sins like this, yet he has not only pardoned our impieties and blasphemies out of mere mercy for Christ's sake, but has also overwhelmed us with great benefits and spiritual gifts. But many of us are not only ungrateful to God for this inestimable grace, and forget we have been cleansed from our past sins (2 Peter 1:9), but also open a window to the devil again, beginning to loathe his Word. Many also pervert and corrupt it, and so become authors of new errors. 'The final condition of that man is worse than the first' (Matthew 12:45).

16. **So that I might preach him among the Gentiles.** It pleased God, says Paul, **to reveal his Son in me.** Why? Not only so that Paul himself should believe in the Son of God, but also so that he should **preach him among the Gentiles.** And why not among the Jews? Here we see that Paul is really the apostle of the Gentiles, although he preached Christ among the Jews too.

Here, as is his usual practice, Paul includes in a few words his whole theology, which is, to preach Christ among the Gentiles. It is like saying, 'I will not burden the Gentiles with the law, because I am the apostle and evangelist of the Gentiles, and not their lawgiver.' Thus he directs all his words against the false apostles, as though saying, 'You Galatians have not heard the righteousness of the law, or of works, taught by me; for this belongs to Moses, and not to me, Paul, being the apostle of the Gentiles. My office and ministry are to bring the Gospel to you, and to show you the same revelation that I myself have had. Therefore you should listen to no teacher that teaches the law.' Among the Gentiles, the law should not be preached, but the Gospel; not Moses, but the Son of God; not the righteousness of works, but the righteousness of faith.

I did not consult any man. Paul is not talking about the apostles, for he goes on to say, **nor did I go up to Jerusalem, to see those who were apostles before I was.** Paul means that once he had received the revelation of the Gospel from Christ, he **did not consult any man** in Damascus, much less desire to teach him the Gospel. He did not go to Jerusalem, to Peter and the other apostles, to learn the Gospel from them, but immediately he preached Jesus Christ in Damascus, where he received baptism from Ananias, and the imposition of hands; for it was necessary for him to have the outward sign and testimony of his calling. Luke says the same thing in Acts 9.

17. He went into Arabia before he saw the apostles, or consulted with them, and immediately took upon himself the office of preaching among the Gentiles; for that is what he was called for, and had also received a revelation from God. He did not, then, receive his Gospel from any man, or from the apostles themselves, but was content with his heavenly calling, and with the revelation of Jesus Christ alone.

18–19. **Then after three years, I went up to Jerusalem to get acquainted with Peter and stayed with him fifteen days. I saw none of the other apostles – only James, the Lord's brother.** Paul grants that he was with the apostles, but not with all the apostles. He says that he went up to Jerusalem to them; not at their command, but of his own accord; not to learn anything from them but to see Peter.

20. **I assure you before God that what I am writing you is no lie.** Why does he add an oath? Because he is reporting a story, and he wants the churches to believe him – and also so that the false apostles should not say, 'Who knows whether Paul s speaking the truth or not?' Here you see that Paul, God's chosen instrument, was in such great contempt among his own Galatians, to whom he had preached Christ, that it was necessary for him to swear that he was speaking the truth. If this happened to the apostles, it is hardly surprising that it happens to us today.

21. **Later I went to Syria and Cilicia.** These are countries close together. He is still trying to persuade his readers that he was always a teacher of the Gospel, before he had seen the apostles as well as afterwards; and that he had received it by the revelation of Christ, and was never any disciple of the apostles.

22–24. **I was personally unknown to the churches of Judea that are in Christ. They only heard the report: 'The man who formerly persecuted us is now preaching the faith he once tried to destroy.' And they praised God because of me.** He adds the sequel: that after he had seen Peter, he went to Syria and Cilicia, and preached there so that he won the testimony of all the churches in Judea. It is like saying: 'I appeal to the testimony of all the churches, even those in Judea. The churches witness, not only in Damascus, Arabia, Syria, and Cilicia, but also in Judea, that I have preached the same faith which I once withstood and persecuted. And they glorified God in me; not because I taught that circumcision and the law of Moses should be kept, but for preaching faith, and for edifying the churches by my ministry in the Gospel.'

Chapter 2

1. This time with Barnabas. I took Titus along also. Barnabas joined Paul in preaching to the Gentiles freedom from the servitude of the law. He was also a witness of everything Paul did, and had seen the Holy Spirit given to the Gentiles who were uncircumcised and free from Moses' law, simply by the preaching of faith in Jesus Christ. He was the only person who stuck with Paul in saying that it was not necessary for the Gentiles to be burdened with the law, but that it was enough for them to believe in Christ. So by his own experience he testified with Paul against the laws, saying that the Gentiles had become God's children, and were saved purely by faith in Jesus Christ, without the law of circumcision.

Titus was not only a Christian, but also chief overseer in Crete. Paul had committed to him the charge of governing the churches there (Titus 1:1), and this Titus was a Gentile.

2. I went in response to a revelation. If Paul had not been warned by a revelation, he would not have gone up to Jerusalem. He went in order to bridle, or at least, appease the Jews who believed, and yet obstinately argued about the keeping of the law, so that the truth of the Gospel might be all the more advanced and strengthened.

And set before them the gospel that I preach among the Gentiles. Among the Jews, he allowed the law and circumcision to remain for a time, as the other apostles did: 'I have become all things to all men,' he said (1 Corinthians 9:22). But he always held the true doctrine of the Gospel, which he rated above the law, circumcision, the apostles, and even an angel from heaven. This is what he said to the Jews: 'Through Jesus the forgiveness of sins is proclaimed to you.' And he adds very plainly: 'Through him everyone who believes is justified from everything you could not be justified from by the law of Moses' (Acts 13:38–39). This is why he teaches and defends the doctrine of the Gospel so diligently everywhere, and never lets it be endangered. Yet he did not suddenly insist on this at first, but had consideration for the weak. And because the weak should not be offended, there is no doubt he spoke to the Jews

something like this: 'If the unprofitable obedience to Moses' law, which does not help us attain righteousness, pleases you so much, you may keep it still, so long as the Gentiles who are not bound by this law are not told they must keep it.'

3. Yet not even Titus, who was with me, was compelled to be circumcised, even though he was a Greek. The word **compelled** indicates what the conclusion was: that the Gentiles should not be forced to be circumcised, but that circumcision should be permitted them for a time, not because it was necessary for righteousness, but in deference to the fathers, and for the sake of love to the weak, in case they should be offended, until they grew stronger in faith. It would have seemed very strange and unseemly if the law and traditions of the fathers were suddenly abandoned, when they had been given to this people from God with such great glory.

Paul, then, did not reject circumcision as a damnable thing, nor did he say or do anything to force the Jews to abandon it (see also 1 Corinthians 7:18). But he rejected circumcision, as something not necessary for righteousness, since the fathers themselves were not justified by it (see Romans 4:11). It was only a sign to them, or a seal of righteousness, by which they testified and exercised their faith.

4–5. Here Paul shows why he went to Jerusalem, and discussed his Gospel with the other apostles, and why he would not circumcise Titus. It was not in order to be more certain, or confirmed in the Gospel by the apostles, for he did not doubt it himself. Rather, it was so that **the truth of the gospel** might **remain** in the Galatian churches, and all the Gentile churches. So Paul's business was no small matter.

6–7. Paul gives the false apostles themselves no glorious title, but destroys their dignity, as it were, saying they **seemed to be great**, that is, in authority, in a position to decide everything. But the authority of the apostles was indeed very great in all the churches. Paul too did not seek to diminish their authority one whit, but he contemptuously answers the false apostles who set the authority and dignity of the apostles against Paul in all the churches, so that they might weaken his authority and bring his whole ministry into contempt. This Paul would not allow. So that the truth of the Gospel and liberty of conscience in Christ might continue among the Galatians, and in all the churches of the Gentiles, he answers the false apostles firmly that it did not matter how great the apostles were, or what they had been in the past. Whereas they claimed the authority of the apostles against him, but it did not affect him at all. He agrees that the apostles are something, and their authority is to be respected, but his Gospel and ministry should not be overthrown for anybody's authority, whoever they are, apostle, or angel from heaven.

7–8. Here Paul claims for himself the same authority that the false apostles ascribed to the true apostles. He turns their argument against themselves. 'The false apostles,' he says, 'support their case by referring to the authority of the great apostles; but I refer to the same authority in my defence, for the apostles are on my side. Do not believe these counterfeit apostles, who boast so much of the authority of the apostles. When the apostles saw that the Gospel had been committed to me for the Gentiles, and knew of the grace that had been given to me, they gave me and Barnabas the right hand of fellowship (verse 9), approving my ministry and giving thanks to God for the gifts which I had received.'

I had been entrusted with the task of preaching the gospel to the Gentiles, just as Peter had been to the Jews. There are examples in Acts both of Paul preaching to the Jews in their synagogues, and of Peter preaching to the Gentiles. Peter converted the centurion and his family, who were Gentiles (Acts 10:3), and wrote his first letter to the Gentiles. Paul entered the Jewish synagogues and preached the Gospel there (Acts 14:1). And our Saviour Christ commanded his apostles to go throughout the whole world and preach the Gospel to every creature (Matthew 28:20; Mark 16:15). Paul, again, says that the Gospel 'has been proclaimed to every creature under heaven' (Colossians 1:23). So why does he say he has been entrusted with preaching to the Gentiles, and Peter and the other apostles to the Jews?

Paul is referring to the fact that the other apostles remained in Jerusalem until God called them to other places. At the time, while the political state of the Jews still existed, the apostles remained in Judea. When the destruction of Jerusalem approached, they were dispersed throughout the whole world. But Paul was specially called to be the apostle of the Gentiles; he was sent out of Judea, and travelled through Gentile countries (Acts 13:2). Now the Jews were scattered through almost the whole world, and lived here and there in cities and other place among the Gentiles. When Paul came there, he used to go into the Jewish synagogues (Acts 14:1), bringing to them first, as children of the kingdom, the good news that the promises made to their ancestors were fulfilled in Jesus Christ. When they would not listen to this, he turned to the Gentiles: Luke tells us that Paul boldly said to the Jews, 'We had to speak the word of God to you first. Since you reject it and do not consider yourselves worthy of eternal life, we now turn to the Gentiles' (Acts 13:46; see also Acts 28:28). So Paul was specially sent to the Gentiles. But because he was obligated to all, and became all things to all people, he went into the Jewish synagogues as occasion offered, both Jews and Gentiles heard him preaching Christ there. Otherwise, he preached publicly in the marketplace, in houses, and by the riverside. So he was especially the apostle to the Gentiles, as Peter was to the Jews, even though Peter also preached Christ to the Gentiles when occasion offered.

9. 'When they heard that I had received my calling and charge from God, to preach the Gospel among the Gentiles, and that God had performed so many miracles through me, and moreover that so many of the Gentiles had come to a knowledge of Christ through my ministry, and that the Gentiles had received the Holy Spirit without the law and circumcision, but simply by the preaching of faith, they glorified God for his grace given to me.'

The right hand of fellowship. It was like saying: 'In preaching the Gospel we agree with you in everything, Paul. Therefore we are companions in doctrine, and have fellowship with each other in it; that is, we all have one doctrine, for we preach one Gospel, one baptism, one Christ, and one faith. We cannot teach you or tell you anything, since there is mutual agreement between us in everything. We do not teach anything different or better than what you teach; the same gifts we have, we see are in you as well, except that you have been entrusted with preaching the Gospel to the Gentiles as we preach it to the Jews. But we conclude that neither Jew nor Gentile should hinder our fellowship, since it is one Gospel which we both preach.'

10. After the preaching of the Gospel, the task of a true and faithful pastor is to remember the poor. Where the church is, there will be poor people, who, mostly, are the only true disciples of the Gospel (see Isaiah 66:1; Matthew 11:5; Luke 4:26). The world and the devil persecute the church, and reduce to poverty many people who are afterwards abandoned and despised by the world. Moreover, the world not only offends in this, but also is careless about the preservation of the Gospel, true religion, and the true service of God. True religion is always in need, and Christ complains that he is hungry, thirsty, homeless, naked, and sick (Matthew 25:42). Conversely, false religion and impiety flourishes and abounds with worldly wealth and prosperity. A true and faithful pastor, therefore, must care for the poor too; and Paul confesses that he cared for them.

11. Paul continues his refutation of the false apostles, saying that he has for his defence not only Peter's testimony, and the other apostles at Jerusalem, but also that he withstood Peter in the presence of the whole church of Antioch. He refers to something not done in a corner but in face of the whole church. He was dealing with the chief point of all Christian doctrine. Whoever properly values it will find everything else worthless. What is Peter? What is Paul? What is an angel from heaven? What are all other creatures to justification? If we know this, we are in the light; if we are ignorant of it, we are in most miserable darkness. Therefore, if we see this impugned, do not be afraid of resisting either Peter or an angel from heaven, following Paul's example. 'Anyone who loves his father or mother more than me is not worthy of me' (Matthew 10:37).

12. Before certain men came from James, he used to eat with the Gentiles. The converted Gentiles ate food which was forbidden by the law, and Peter, who knew the converted Gentiles, ate with them, and also drank wine which was forbidden; he knew that he was doing the right thing, and was therefore bold to transgress the law with the Gentiles. Paul says that he did the same, when he says that he 'became like a Jew, to win the Jews' and 'to those under the law ... like one under the law'; that is to say, with the Gentiles he ate and drank like a Gentile, and kept no law at all; with the Jews, according to the law, he abstained from everything forbidden in the law; for he tried to serve and please everyone, so that he might save them (see 1 Corinthians 9:19–22). Therefore Peter, in eating and drinking with the Gentiles, was not sinning, but doing the right thing, and he knew it was lawful for him to do so. By this transgression he showed that the law was not necessary for righteousness, and also set the Gentiles free from the observance of the law. If it was lawful for Peter to break the law in one matter, it was lawful for him to break it in all matters. Paul is not here reproving Peter for his transgression, but for his hypocrisy.

13. Here we see clearly that Paul charged Peter with hypocrisy. Peter knew perfectly well what the truth was.

14. When I saw that they were not acting in line with the truth of the gospel. This is a wonderful example of such excellent men and pillars of the church. Only Paul has his eyes open, and sees the offense of Peter, of Barnabas, and the other Jews who were hypocrites with Peter. On the other hand, they do not see their own offense; rather, they think they are right to bear with the weakness of the Jews. So it was very necessary for Paul to criticize them, and not hide their offense; so he accuses Peter, Barnabas, and others of swerving from the truth of the Gospel. It is significant that Peter is accused by Paul as someone who had fallen from the truth of the Gospel. He could not be more grievously reprehended, yet he suffered it patiently, and no doubt acknowledged his offense. I said before that many people have the Gospel, but not the truth of the Gospel. So Paul says here that Peter,

Barnabas, and other Jews had the Gospel, but were not walking uprightly according to it. Although they preached the Gospel, they established the law – but this is to abolish the Gospel.

15. We are born to the righteousness of the law, to Moses, and to circumcision, and even in our birth we bring the law with us. We have the righteousness of the law by nature, as Paul himself says in chapter 1 ('zealous for the traditions of my fathers,' verse 14). So if we are compared with the Gentiles, we are no sinners; we are not without the law, and without works, like the Gentiles; but we are born Jews, born righteous, and brought up in righteousness. Our righteousness begins with our birth, for the Jewish religion is natural to us. The law of circumcision, received from the fathers (Genesis 17:10), was afterwards confirmed by Moses. Yet although we have the privilege of being righteous by nature, born to the law and its observance, and are not sinners as the Gentiles are, yet we are not righteous before God because of this.

16. Know that a man is not justified by observing the law, but by faith in Jesus Christ. The phrase **the law** includes a lot. Whatever is not grace is **the law**, whether it be judicial, ceremonial, or the Ten Commandments. Therefore, if you could follow the law according to the commandment to 'love the Lord your God with all your heart' (which nobody has yet done, or can do), you would still not be justified before God, for we are not justified by **the law**.

Notice here that these three things – faith, Christ, and acceptance or imputation – must be joined together. Faith takes hold of Christ as a ring does a precious stone. Whoever has this confidence in Christ will be accounted righteousness by God. This is the means, and the merit, by which we attain the forgiveness of sins and righteousness. Because you believe in me, says the Lord, and your faith lays hold on Christ, whom I have freely given to you in order that he should be your mediator and high priest, therefore you are justified and righteousness. That is why God accepts or accounts us as righteous – simply for our faith in Christ.

This acceptance, or imputation, is very necessary: first, because we are not yet perfectly righteous – while we remain in this life, sin still remains in our bodies, and this remnant of sin God purges in us. Moreover, we are sometimes left by the Holy Spirit, and fall into sins, and did Peter, David, and other holy men. Yet we always have recourse to this belief, that our sins are covered, and that God will not hold them against us (see Romans 4). Not that there is no sin in us; sin is indeed always in us, and godly people feel it, but it is covered. For Christ's sake, God does not impute it to us, and because we take hold of Christ by faith, all our sins are now no sins. But where there is neither Christ nor faith, there is no remission or covering of sins, but mere imputation of sins and condemnation. Thus God will glorify his Son, and will be glorified himself in us through him.

17. If it is true, he says, that we are justified by Christ, then it is impossible for us to be sinners, or be justified by the law. On the contrary, if this is not true, but that we must be justified by observing the law, then it is impossible for us to be justified by Christ. One of these two must be false. Either we are not justified by Christ, or we are not justified by the law. But the truth is that we are justified by Christ; therefore we are not justified by the law. So Paul reasons like this: 'If while we seek to be made righteous by Christ. ...' That is, if we seek to be justified by Christ, and being justified in this way are still found to be sinners, and need the law to justify us, then Christ is nothing else but a lawgiver, and a minister of sin.

18. It is as if he is saying, 'I have not preached in order to rebuild what I once destroyed, for if I did that I would not only labour in vain but would make myself a lawbreaker too, and overthrow everything together, as the false apostles do. I would be taking grace, and Christ, and turning them into the law and Moses; and conversely, I would be taking the law and Moses and making them into grace and Christ. Now, by the ministry of the Gospel, I have abolished sin, heaviness of heart, wrath, and death. I have taught that the human conscience is subject to the law, sin, and death, and we cannot be set free from this by men or by angels. But now the Gospel comes and preaches remission of sins through Christ Jesus, who has abolished the law, and has destroyed sin and death. Believe in him, and you will be set free from the curse of the law, and from the tyranny of sin and death; you will become righteous, and have eternal life.

19. These are marvellous words, which human reason cannot understand at all. Although the words are few, they are uttered with great zeal and vehemence of spirit, and as if in great displeasure. It is like saying: 'Why do you boast so much of the law? In this case, I will remain ignorant of it. But if you must have the law, I also have the law.' Therefore, as though he were moved to indignation by the Holy Spirit, he calls grace itself the law, giving a new name to the effect and working of grace, in contempt of the law of Moses and the false apostles, who argued that the law was necessary for justification. And it is a beautiful way of putting it, and full of consolation, when the Scriptures (and especially Paul) set the law against the law, sin against sin, death against death, captivity against captivity, hell against hell, the altar against the altar, the lamb against the lamb, the Passover against the Passover. It is like saying:

'The law of Moses accuses and condemns me, but against that accusing and condemning law I have another law, which is grace and freedom' (see James 1:25). This law accuses the accusing law, and condemns the condemning law. So death killed death; but this killing death is life itself. But with vehement indignation of spirit it is called the death of death. Thus righteousness takes the name of sin, because it condemns sin, and this condemning of sin is true righteousness.

20. **I have been crucified with Christ.** He adds this to show that the law devours the law. Not only am I dead to the law through the law, he says, so that I may live to God, but also **I have been crucified with Christ.** But Christ is Lord over the law, because he has been crucified and is dead to the law; therefore I also am Lord over the law; for I likewise have been crucified and am dead to the law, forasmuch as I have been crucified and have died with Christ. How? By grace and faith. Through this faith, because I have now been crucified and am dead to the law, the law loses all the power which it had over me, just as it has lost all the power which it had over Christ. Therefore, just as Christ himself was crucified to the law, sin, death, and the devil, so that they have no further power over him, so also now that I through faith have been crucified with Christ in spirit, I have been crucified and am dead to the law, sin, death, and the devil, so that they have no further power over me, but are now crucified and dead to me.

21. **I do not set aside the grace of God.** Now he prepares for the second argument of this letter. Here we must carefully consider that to seek to be justified by the works of the law is to reject the grace of God. But what sin can be more horrible than to reject the grace of God, and to refuse the righteousness which comes through Christ? It is enough and too much already that we are wicked sinners and transgressors of all God's commands, yet we commit the most execrable sin of all sins as well, in contemptuously refusing the grace of God and forgiveness of sins offered to us by Christ. This is inexpressible blasphemy. There is no sin which Paul and the other apostles so much detested as the contempt of grace, and refusal of Christ, and yet there is no sin more common. That is why Paul, more than the others, so sharply inveighs against Antichrist, for despising the grace of God and refusing the benefit of Christ our high priest, who offered himself as a sacrifice for our sins. Denying Christ like this is to spit in his face, to tread him underfoot, and to set himself in his place, and to say, 'I will justify you, and I will save you.' The Antichrist teaches that faith is no good unless it is combined with works; instead of the grace of Christ and his kingdom, he has established the doctrine of works and

ceremonies. Thus we may understand what it means to reject God's grace: it is to seek righteousness through the law. Whoever heard of people rejecting grace by keeping the law? No, indeed. But we despise grace when we observe the law in order to be justified through it. The law is good, and holy, and profitable, yet it does not justify us.

Now follows the second argument. **For if righteousness could be gained through the law, Christ died for nothing.** Is it true that Christ suffered death or not? Did he suffer in vain or not? Unless we are quite mad, we have to answer that he did indeed suffer, not in vain or for himself, but for us. Therefore it follows that righteousness does not come through the law.

Chapter 3

1. **You foolish Galatians!** Here Paul shows his apostolic care, and burning zeal for the church. In arguing, he sometimes mixes gentle exhortation, and sometimes sharply criticizes, according to his own rule in 2 Timothy 4:2. Here the simple reader may perhaps be deceived, if he is not careful, into thinking that Paul is not following any plan in his teaching. And certainly he does not observe any plan in the rhetorical sense, but he has a good plan concerning the spirit.

Before your very eyes Jesus Christ was clearly portrayed. In effect he is saying, 'There is no painter that can depict Christ as vividly as I have painted him by my preaching, yet you are still most miserably bewitched.'

As crucified. Before, he had said that they sought righteousness by the law, rejecting the grace of God, and that to them Christ died in vain. Now he adds that they crucify Christ, who had lived and reigned in them before. It is like saying, 'You have now not only rejected God's grace – not only did Christ die in vain for you – but also he is most shamefully crucified by you.' In the same way, Hebrews 6:6 says, 'they are crucifying the Son of God all over again and subjecting him to public disgrace.'

2. 'If I had nothing else against you but your own experience,' says Paul indignantly, 'that is still enough. Tell me – I am your pupil, for you have become teachers all of a sudden – did you receive the Holy Spirit by obeying the law, or by hearing the Gospel preached?' With this argument he so convinces them that they have nothing more to say in reply. Their own experience is altogether against them; namely, that they had received the Holy Spirit, not through observing the law, but through believing the Gospel they heard preached.

Here again I warn you that Paul is not just speaking about the ceremonial law, but about the whole law. He bases his argument on the contrast between receiving the Holy Spirit by the law, or by believing. If it is by the law, then is not by believing what is preached. There is no middle way between the two. Everything that is not the Holy Spirit, or believing what is preached, is the law. To be justified, there is no other way but either the voice of the Gospel or the voice of the law. Therefore the law here is to be taken generally, as wholly separate from the Gospel. But it is not the ceremonial law that is separate from the Gospel, but also the moral law, or the law of the Ten Commandments. Therefore Paul here is speaking about the whole law. 'Tell, me,' he says: **Did you receive the Spirit by observing the law, or by believing what you heard?** You cannot say that this was done by the law, for whilst you were under the law, and observed it, you never received the Holy Spirit. Indeed, you taught and heard the law of Moses every Sabbath; but you have never seen the Holy Spirit given to anyone, either teacher or disciple, through the preaching of the law. Moreover, you have not only taught and heard the law, but also have laboured with all your power to obey it in your actions, by which you should most of all have received the Spirit if he had been given by the law, seeing you were not only teachers and hearers but also doers of the law. Yet you cannot show me that this was done at any time. But as soon as you heard the Gospel and believed, you received the Holy Spirit, before you had done anything or showed any fruit of the Gospel.' As Luke witnesses in Acts 10:44–46, Peter and Paul had only to preach and the Holy Spirit came upon those who heard their message, and through him they also received various gifts, so that they spoke in tongues.

3. Paul now begins to exhort and alarm them with a double danger. He says, in effect: 'You began in the Spirit – that is, your religion began excellently. But what have you gained by it? You will end up trying human effort!'

Paul here contrasts **the Spirit** with **human effort.** The **Spirit** means whatever we do according to the Spirit; **human effort** means whatever we do without the Spirit. So every Christian duty such as loving our spouse, bringing up our children, and so on is a fruit of the Spirit. But the righteousness of the law, which Paul here refers to as **trying to attain your goal by human effort,** is so far from justifying us that those who fall back on it again after receiving the Holy Spirit are utterly destroyed.

4. **Have you suffered so much for nothing?** This is the other danger. He says in effect, 'Consider not just how well you began and how miserably you have abandoned your good beginning and fallen into sin and death again, but also think how much you have suffered for the Gospel's sake, and for the name of Christ – namely, losing your possessions, being

reproached, suffering danger to life and limb, and so on. Everything was going well with you. You taught pure doctrine, you lived a holy life, and you endured many evils constantly for the name of Christ. But now all is lost, doctrine as well as faith, actions as well as suffering, the Spirit as well as its fruits.

5. Paul now repeats the same argument: the Galatians have not only received the Spirit by believing what they heard, but whatever they had known or done came about by believing what they had heard too. It is like saying, 'It was not enough for God to give you the Spirit once. The same God also enriched you with the gifts of the Spirit, and made them grow in you, so that once you had received the Spirit it would always grow, and be more and more effective in you.' Thus it is clear that the Galatians had performed miracles, or at least had shown such fruits of faith as the true disciples of the Gospel are accustomed to produce. In 1 Corinthians 4:20 Paul says that 'the kingdom of God is not a matter of talk but of power.' Now this power is not only to be able to speak of the kingdom of God, but actually to show that God through his Spirit is effective in us (see also Galatians 2:8).

6. Now Paul adds the example of Abraham, and quotes Genesis 15:6. He makes great use of this passage, as he does in Romans 4. Before God, Abraham has in him nothing but sin and wrath. Now he was justified before God, not because of anything he did, but because he believed. Paul makes faith in God the chief worship, the chief duty, the chief obedience, and the chief sacrifice. Faith is infinitely powerful, because it gives glory to God, which is the greatest service that can be offered him. To give glory to God is to believe in him, to regard him as true, wise, righteous, merciful, almighty – in short, to acknowledge him to be the author and giver of all goodness. This is not done by reason, but by faith. That is what makes us divine people, and it makes, so to speak, for a certain divinity in us. Without faith, God's glory, wisdom, righteousness, truth, and mercy are lost in us. No majesty or divinity remains in God where there is no faith. And the chief thing that God requires of us is that we give him his glory and divinity – that is, that we take him not for an idol, but for God, who watches us, listens to us, shows mercy to us, and helps us. When we have done this, God has his full and perfect divinity – that is, he has whatever a faithful heart can attribute to him. To be able to give that glory to God is the greatest wisdom, the greatest righteousness, the greatest religion, the greatest sacrifice. Thus we can see what an excellent righteousness faith is, and conversely what a horrible and grievous sin infidelity is.

7. It is Paul's whole argument against the Jews that the children of Abraham are not those who are his physical descendants but those who believe. He prosecutes this argument vigorously both here and in Romans 4 and 9. It was the Jews' greatest confidence and glory that they were the children of Abraham, who had been circumcised and kept the law. No one could deny that God spoke to the children of Abraham, but this prerogative did not bring the unbelieving Jews any advantage. That is why Paul, especially in this passage, fights strongly against this argument, and wrests from the Jews this strong faith in themselves. As the chosen instrument of Christ (Acts 9:15), he could do this above anyone else.

8. The Scripture foresaw that God would justify the Gentiles by faith. This belongs with the previous argument. It is like saying, 'You Jews glory in the law too much; you highly commend Moses because God spoke to him in the bush, and so on.' Paul's answer is this: 'Your proud boasting is to no purpose, for the Scripture anticipates it, and foresaw long before the law that the Gentiles would not be justified by the law, but by the blessing of Abraham's descendant, which was promised 430 years before the law was given. Now the law, being given so many years afterwards, could not hinder or abolish this promise of the blessing made to Abraham, but it has remained firm, and will remain forever.' What can the Jews answer to this?

9. When he says **Abraham, the man of faith**, it is as if he is making a distinction between two Abrahams, and saying there is a working Abraham and a believing Abraham. We have nothing to do with the working Abraham, for if he is justified by what he does, he has something to rejoice about, but not with God. The Jews may glory as much as they like about that ancestor who is circumcised, and keep the law; we glory in the Abraham of whom the Scripture says that he received the blessing of righteousness through his faith, not only for himself but also for all those who believe as he did; and so the world was promised to Abraham because he believed. Therefore all the world is blessed – that is, is credited with righteousness – if it believes as Abraham did.

10. All who rely on observing the law are under a curse. The curse is like a flood, swallowing up whatever is without Abraham – that is, without faith, and the promise of the blessing of Abraham. Now if the law itself, given by Moses at God's command, makes those who are under it subject to a curse, how much more so will laws and traditions of human devising? If we want to avoid the curse, we must lay hold on the promise of blessing, or on Abraham's faith; otherwise we shall remain under the curse. All nations, whether before Abraham, or in his time, or afterwards, are under a curse and will remain under the curse forever unless they are blessed in the faith of Abraham, to whom the promise of blessing was given that it might be proclaimed throughout the whole world by his descendants.

11. This is another argument based on Habakkuk (see Habakkuk 2:4). Paul says in effect, 'Why do we need any long argument? No one can argue with this clear statement of the prophet: 'The righteous will live by faith.' If they live by faith, then they do not live by the law, for the law is not faith.' Here Paul excludes the law as something contrary to faith.

It is corrupting the Scriptures to twist this to mean that the righteous live by a working faith, that is, formed and made perfect by love – so that if it is not formed with love, it does not justify us. The Holy Spirit could have said that the righteous will live by faith formed and beautified, or made perfect, by love. But he deliberately omits this and says plainly, 'The righteous will live by faith.' What God has called faith is a true and certain faith, which does not doubt God or his promises, nor the forgiveness of sins through Christ, that we may remain safe and secure in Christ and always hold before our eyes the passion and blood of the mediator and all his benefits. Faith alone, which lays hold on Christ, is the only way we stop those benefits being taken out of our sight.

12. **The law is not based on faith.** What is the law? Is it not a law of love? Yes, the law teaches nothing else but love (as we can see from Exodus 20:6; Deuteronomy 6:5; Matthew 22:37, 40). So if the law that commands love is contrary to faith, it must follow that love is not based on faith. The law is separate and set apart, and love is also set apart, with all that belongs to the law, and only faith is left, which justifies us and brings us to everlasting life.

Paul's argument here is that the only people who obtain justification and life before God are those who believe, who obtain righteousness and everlasting life without the law, and without love, by faith alone. The reason is because **the law is not based on faith** or anything belonging to faith, for it does not believe; nor are the works of the law faith, nor based on faith either. Faith is something as different from the law as the promise is different from the law. We claim the promise not by what we do but by believing. There is as great a difference between the promise and the law, and consequently between faith and works, as there is between heaven and earth.

13. Paul does not say that Christ was made a curse for himself, but **for us.** Christ is innocent as far as his own person is concerned, and therefore he ought not to have been hanged upon a tree; but because, under the law of Moses, every thief and criminal had to be hanged, Christ too had to be hanged, for he sustained the person of

a sinner and of a thief – not just one, but all sinners and thieves. For we are sinners and thieves, and therefore guilty of death and everlasting damnation. But Christ took all our sins upon him, and for them died upon the cross; therefore it was right for him to be 'numbered with the transgressors' (Isaiah 53:12).

14. **He redeemed us in order that the blessing given to Abraham might come to the Gentiles through Christ Jesus.** Paul is still thinking about Genesis 22:18, for the blessing promised to Abraham could not come to the Gentiles except through Christ, the seed of Abraham; he had to be made a curse so that this promise given to Abraham – 'Through your offspring all nations on earth will be blessed' – might be fulfilled. It could only be done by Jesus Christ becoming a curse and uniting himself with those who were cursed, so that he might take the curse away from them, and through his blessing might bring them righteousness and life. Note that the word **blessing** is not just a greeting; Paul is dealing with sin and righteousness, death and life before God. He is speaking about incomprehensible things.

15. Now Paul adds another argument, based on the parallel of a human covenant. This seems very weak, something the apostle should not use to confirm such an important matter. But where there is in the creature something ordained by God, an argument may well be applied to divine and heavenly things. And the civil law, which is ordained by God, says that it is unlawful to break or change a person's testament. It commands that a person's last will and testament be strictly kept, for it is one of the holiest and most laudable human customs. Now then, Paul argues as follows: How is it that we obey human commands but not God's? Civil ordinances concerning testaments and other things are kept diligently. Nothing in them is changed, nothing is added or taken away. But we change God's testament, that is, his promise concerning the spiritual blessing – concerning heavenly and everlasting things – which the whole world ought to accept enthusiastically and most religiously to reverence and honour. God's last will was given to Abraham and his seed after him, and when Christ died, it was confirmed in him, and after his death the writing of his last testament was opened; that is to say, the promised blessing of Abraham was preached among all nations dispersed throughout the world. This was God's last will and testament, confirmed by the death of Christ; therefore no one ought to change it or add anything to it, as is done by people who teach the law and human traditions. These people say you cannot be saved without being circumcised, keeping the law, doing many works, and suffering many things. This is not God's last will and testament. He did not say to

Abraham, 'If you do this or that you will obtain the blessing,' or, 'Those who are circumcised and keep the law will obtain it,' but, 'All nations of the world will be blessed through your seed.' It was like saying, 'I promise you, by pure mercy, that Christ will come from your seed, and will bring the blessing to all nations oppressed with sin and death, that is to say, he will deliver the nations from the everlasting curse, from sin and death, if they receive this promise by faith.'

16. The blessing is indeed a testament, not yet revealed but sealed up. Now, a testament is not a law, but a free gift. Heirs are not looking for laws, or any burden to be laid upon them by a testament; they are looking for the inheritance to be confirmed.

First of all, Paul expounds the words. Afterwards he applies the parallel, and concentrates on this word **seed**. No laws were given to Abraham, he says, but a testament was made and given to him; the promises were pronounced concerning the spiritual blessing, and therefore something was promised and given to him. If a human testament is kept, should God's testament not be kept? If we want to keep the signs, why do we not keep the things which they signify?

Now, the promises are made to him, not in all the Jews or in many seeds, but in one seed, which is Christ. The Jews will not accept this interpretation of Paul's, for they say that the singular number here means the plural, one standing for many. But we gladly accept this interpretation.

17. The Jews might object that God was not only content to give promises to Abraham, but also after 430 years he made the law. God, therefore, not trusting his own promises but thinking they were not enough to justify people, added something better, namely the law, so that when it came people who were not idle but obeyed the law might be made righteous by it. The law therefore abrogated the promise.

To this argument Paul answers very well. The law, he says, could not make the promise void and useless, for the promise of God's testament, confirmed by God himself, in Christ, so many years before the law. What God has once promised and confirmed, he does not revoke, but it remains ratified and sure forever.

Why then was the law added? It was not so that Abraham's descendants might obtain the blessing through it, for the role of the law is not to bless but to bring people under the curse. It was so that there might be in the world a certain people which would have the word and testimony of Christ, and out of which Christ might be born; and so that people, shut up under the law, might long for deliverance through the seed of Abraham, which is Christ, who alone could bless, that is, deliver all people from sin and

everlasting death. Moreover, the ceremonies commanded in the law foreshadowed Christ. Therefore the promise was not abolished either by the law or by the ceremonies of the law, but was for a time confirmed, as by certain seals, until the writing of the testament (that is, the promise) could be opened and by the preaching of the Gospel spread among all peoples.

18. **For if the inheritance depends on the law, then it no longer depends on a promise.** Similarly, in Romans 4:14 he says: 'If those who live by law are heirs, faith has no value and the promise is worthless.' And it must be so, for it is clear that the law is something quite different from the promise. Even natural reason, however blind, is compelled to admit that it is one thing to promise, and another to require; one thing to give, and another thing to take. The law requires us to do things; the promise of the seed offers us the spiritual and everlasting benefits of God, freely for Christ's sake. Therefore we obtain the inheritance or blessing through the promise, and not through the law. The promise says, 'All nations of the world will be blessed through your seed.' Therefore if you have the law you do not have enough, because you do not yet have the blessing, without which you are compelled to remain under the curse. The law therefore cannot justify, because the blessing is not combined with it. Moreover, if the inheritance came by the law, God would be a liar, and the promise would be in vain. And if the law could obtain the blessing, why did God make this promise about the seed? Why did he not rather say, 'Do this, and you will receive the blessing'? Or, 'By keeping the law, you will deserve everlasting life'? This argument is based on opposites: the inheritance is given by the promise, therefore not by the law.

19. **What, then, was the purpose of the law?** When we teach that people are justified without the law, the question necessarily follows: 'If the law does not justify, why was it given?' Also, why does God burden us with the law if it does not justify? Why are we so troubled with it, if those who work just one hour are made equal with us who have borne the heat and burden of the day? Once we are told of the grace that the Gospel sets out, there arises this great complaining – the Gospel cannot be preached without it. The Jews thought that if they kept the law they would be justified thereby. So when they heard that the Gospel was preached concerning Christ, who came into the world to save not the righteous but sinners, and that they would go into the kingdom of God before them (Matthew 20:12), they were most offended, complaining that they had born the heavy yoke of the law all these years with great labour, and that they were miserably oppressed with the tyranny of the law, without any benefit, and in fact to their

great hurt – and that the Gentiles, who were idolaters, obtained grace without any labour.

20. A mediator, however, does not represent just one party. Here Paul compares these two mediators, though we soon understand that he is speaking of the mediator generally, and not just of Moses. The word includes both the person offended and the offender; the latter needs intercession, the other does not. So a mediator does not just represent one party, but two, who are at variance with each other. So Moses, by a general definition, is a mediator because he mediates between the law and the people, who cannot bear the true and spiritual use of the law. The law therefore must have a new face, and its voice must be changed; that is, the voice of the law must be made spiritual, or the law must be brought to life internally, and must put on a veil so that it may be more tolerable. The people will be able to hear it through Moses' voice.

21. Is the law, therefore, opposed to the promises of God? Before, Paul had said that the law does not justify. It brings us to self-knowledge. It reveals and increases sin. Here there arises another objection: 'If the law does nothing but make people worse, then it is contrary to the promises of God, for it seems that God is only provoked to anger by the law, and therefore he does not fulfill his promises. We Jews have thought the contrary, namely, that we are restrained by this external discipline, so that God, being provoked by this, might hurry to fulfill his promise, and so that by this discipline we might deserve the promise.'

Paul answers that it is nothing of the sort. On the contrary, if you consider the law, the promise is hindered, for natural reason offends God, who makes such faithful promises, and it will not listen to his good and holy law. It says, 'Do not let the LORD speak to us.' How, then, can God fulfill his promise to those who not only do not accept his law and discipline, but also with a mortal hatred shun it and fly from it? Hence this objection, which Paul touches on and answers briefly.

22. The Scripture declares that the whole world is a prisoner of sin. Where? First, in the promises themselves, regarding Christ, such as Genesis 3:15 and 22:18. Wherever in the Scriptures a promise is made to the fathers concerning Christ, there the blessing is promised – that is, righteousness, salvation, and eternal life. Therefore, from the converse it is evident that those who are to receive the blessing are subject to the curse – that is, sin and eternal death; otherwise, why was the blessing promised?

Secondly, the Scripture says that the whole world is imprisoned by sin, and under the curse, especially the law, whose particular function it is to reveal sin and engender wrath (see especially verse 10 of this chapter). The apostle also

adduces Deuteronomy 27:26. These verses clearly say that sin imprisons not only those who sin blatantly against the law, or do not outwardly obey the law, but also those who are under the law, and try their best to obey it. Whatever is without Christ and his promise, whether it be God's law or human law, ceremonial or moral law, without any exception, it is **a prisoner of sin.** The policies and laws of all nations, however good and necessary, with all ceremonies and religions, without faith in Christ are and remain under sin, death, and eternal damnation.

23. Paul goes on to explain how the law profits us, and its necessity. He has already said that it was added because of transgressions – not that it was God's principal purpose to make a law that would bring death and damnation (see Romans 7:13). The law is a word that shows life, and drives people to it. Therefore it is not only given as a minister of death, but its chief purpose is to reveal death, so that it might be seen and known how horrible sin is. Still, it is not as though it served no other purpose but to kill and destroy; it reveals death in order that when people are terrified, and cast down, and humbled, they should fear God (Exodus 20:20). The function of the law is to kill, and yet in such a way that God may revive and bring to life again. Because people are proud, and dream that they are wise, righteous, and holy, it is necessary for them to be humbled by the law, so that the beast which is their high opinion of their righteousness might be slain; otherwise no one can obtain life.

24. So the law was put in charge to lead us to Christ. Here again the law and the Gospel are combined. The law is not **put in charge** forever, but only until it has led us **to Christ** (see also verses 19, 23). It does not justify hypocrites, for they remain without Christ in their presumption and complacency; conversely, it does not leave the contrite in death and damnation, but drives them to Christ. Those who remain in their wickedness and do not lay hold on Christ by faith eventually fall into despair. But those who are troubled and oppressed by the law know that these terrors and troubles will not continue forever, but that they are prepared in this way to come to Christ, and to receive the freedom of the spirit.

That we might be justified by faith. The law does not lead us to another lawgiver requiring good works, but to Christ our justifier and Saviour, so that we might be justified by faith in him, and not by works.

25. We are free from the law, from the prison, for when faith is revealed, the law does not terrify or torment us any more. Here Paul speaks of faith as it was preached to the world by Christ at the appointed time. For Christ, putting on our sinful nature, came into the world; he abolished the law with all its effects, and delivered from eternal death all those who receive his benefit by faith. If, therefore, you look to Christ, and what he has done, there is no law. He has come and taken it away. Now, since the law is gone, we are not kept under its tyranny any longer, but live in joy and safety under Christ, who now reigns in us by his Spirit. Now where the Lord reigns, there is liberty. Therefore, if we could perfectly lay hold on Christ, who has abolished the law by his death, and has reconciled us to his Father, the law would have no power over us at all. But the law of our members, rebelling against the law of the mind, stops us, so that we cannot perfectly lay hold on Christ. The lack, therefore, is not in Christ, but in us, who have not yet taken off this sinful nature to which sin clings for as long as we live. Therefore we are partly free from the law, and partly under the law. In our mind, we serve the law of God, but in our sinful nature, the law of sin (see Romans 7:21–23).

26. As a true and excellent teacher of faith, Paul is constantly saying **through faith in Christ Jesus**. He does not say, 'You are God's children because you are circumcised, because you have heard the law and have obeyed it,' but **through faith in Christ Jesus**. It is not the law, then, that makes us God's children, much less human traditions. It cannot give us new birth, but it sets before us the old birth, by which we were born to the kingdom of the devil; and so it prepares us for a new birth, which is **through faith in Christ Jesus** and not by the law. (See also John 1:12; Romans 8:16–17.)

27. To clothe ourselves with Christ can be taken in two ways: by the law, and by the Gospel. By the law, we clothe ourselves with Christ by following his example, doing what he did and suffering what he suffered (see Romans 13: 1 Peter 2). We see in Christ a singular patience, an inestimable mildness and love, and a wonderful modesty in all things. This goodly clothing we must put on – that is, follow these virtues.

28. Many more things might be added here which are ordained by God just like these. There is neither magistrate nor subject, teacher nor hearer, schoolmaster nor scholar, master nor servant, mistress nor maid, and so on, for in Christ Jesus all states, even those ordained by God, are nothing. Indeed, the male, the female, the slave, the free the Jew, the Gentile, the prince, the subject, are the good creatures of God, but in Christ – that is, in the matter of salvation – they are nothing, with all their wisdom, righteousness, religion, and power.

29. If you believe, and are baptized into Christ – if you believe that he is that promised Seed of Abraham which brought the blessing to all the Gentiles – then you are the children of Abraham, not by nature, but by adoption; for the Scripture attributes to him not only the physical children but also those of adoption and of the promise, and shows that they will receive the inheritance, whereas other people will be thrown out of the house.

Chapter 4

1–2. You see how forcefully Paul tries to call the Galatians back, and what strong arguments he uses. He takes examples from Abraham's experience, from the testimony of Scripture, and from the time, so that he often seems to go over the whole matter repeatedly. He had already more or less finished the argument concerning justification, concluding that people are justified before God by faith alone. But because he also thinks of the example of the heir who is a minor, he adds this to confirm the matter. Trying every means like this, he lies in wait, with a sort of holy cunning, to take the Galatians unawares; for ignorant people are more likely to be persuaded by examples than by deep and subtle argument. They prefer a picture well painted to a book well written. So Paul, having used the example of a person's will, also uses this example of an heir – something familiar to everyone – to move and persuade them. And surely it is very good to have examples; it is not just Paul who uses them, but also the prophets, and Christ himself.

3. Similarly, when we were little children, we were heirs, having the promise of the future inheritance to be given by the Seed of Abraham, that is to say, by Christ, in whom all nations would be blessed. But because the time had not yet arrived, Moses came, holding us in captivity so that we could bear no rule, nor possess our inheritance. Meanwhile, however, just as an heir is nourished and maintained in hope of future liberty, so Moses nourished us with the hope of the promise which was to be revealed at the appointed time; namely, when Christ came to put an end to the time of the law, and begin the time of grace.

4–5. When the time had fully come. That is, when Christ had been revealed and had delivered us from the law, and the promise had been proclaimed among all nations. **God sent his Son, born of a woman, born under law, to redeem those under law.** Note how Paul defines Christ's person and work. His person consists of his divine and human nature (**God sent his Son, born of a woman**). Christ, therefore, is truly God and truly human.

6. Because you are sons, God sent the Spirit of his Son into our hearts. The Holy Spirit is sent in two ways. In the early church he was sent in a visible way. Thus he came upon Christ at the Jordan, in the form of a dove (Matthew 3:16), and in the form of fire upon the apostles and other believers (Acts 2:3). This was the first sending of the Holy Spirit, and it was necessary in the early church because it was expedient that it should be established by many miracles, because of the unbelievers, as Paul witnesses in 1 Corinthians 14:23. But after the church had been gathered together, and confirmed with those miracles, it was not necessary for this visible sending of the Holy Spirit to continue any longer.

Secondly, the Holy Spirit is sent by the Word into the hearts of the believers, as is said here. This sending is invisible; it comes by the hearing of the external word, when we receive an inner fervency and light by which we are changed and become new creatures; by which also we receive a new judgment, a new feeling, and a new moving. This change, and this new judgment, is no work of reason, or of human power, but is the gift and operation of the Holy Spirit, who comes with the preached Word, which purifies our hearts by faith, and produces spiritual motions in us. Therefore there is a great different between us and those who persecute the Gospel teaching. By the grace of God, we judge surely, by the Word, what God wills for us, and also all laws and doctrines, our own life, and other people's lives. But without the Word, people cannot give any certain judgment of anything.

Who calls out, 'Abba, Father.' If we could believe this confidently, we would never be overcome by any affliction, however great.

7. So you are no longer a slave, but a son. This is the conclusion. It is like saying, 'Since it is true that we have received the Spirit by the Gospel, by which we cry, "Abba, Father," heaven decrees that there is no bondage any more, but only freedom and adoption.'

8–9. This is the conclusion of Paul's argument. From this point to the end of the letter he just gives precepts concerning manners. But first he reproves the Galatians, being very displeased that this divine and heavenly doctrine should be so suddenly and easily removed from their hearts. In effect he is saying, 'You have teachers who want to bring you back into slavery to the law. I did not do this, but by my teaching I called you out of darkness, and our of ignorance of God, into a wonderful light and knowledge of him. I brought you out of slavery, and set you in the freedom of the sons of God, not by preaching obedience to the law, or human merit, but the grace and righteousness of God, and the gift of heavenly and eternal blessings through Christ. Now why do you so quickly forsake the light, and return to darkness? Why do you let yourselves be brought so easily from grace to the law, from freedom to slavery?'

10. The Jews were commanded to keep holy the Sabbath day, the new moons the first and seventh months, the Passover, the Feast of Weeks, the Feast of Tabernacles, and the year of jubilee. The false apostles made the Galatians observe these as necessary for righteousness. That is why Paul says that they had turned back to serving weak and miserable principles, losing the grace and liberty which they had in Christ. Paul cannot allow people's consciences to be bound by the law of Moses (see Galatians 5:6; Colossians 2:16, and compare Luke 17:20). Much less, then, are our consciences to be burdened and snared with human traditions.

11. Paul shows that he is very troubled by the fall of the Galatians. He would reprove them more bitterly if he did not fear that he might offend them more, and so utterly alienate them. So he softens his words, as though all the harm redounded to himself; he says that it grieves him that he has preached the Gospel so diligently and faithfully amongst the Galatians, and sees no fruit. Yet although he shows them loving and fatherly affection, he still chides them rather sharply, though covertly. When he says that he has wasted his efforts (that is, that he had preached the Gospel among them without any fruit), he is covertly showing that either they were obstinate unbelievers, or else they had fallen from the doctrine of faith.

12. Up till now Paul has been occupied wholly in teaching. He is so incensed at the Galatians' revolt that he calls them fools, bewitched, not believing the truth, crucifers of Christ, and so on. Having finished most of his letter, he begins to realize that he has treated them too sharply. Therefore, being careful not to do more harm than good, he shows that his sharp chiding came from fatherly affection and a true apostolic heart. No doubt many people were offended by his words, but he qualifies the matter with gentle words to win them back.

13–14. Paul now declares what pleasures he had received from the Galatians. The greatest benefit, he says, was that when he began to preach the Gospel among them, they behaved so lovingly that they were not at all offended at his illness, at the temptation and afflictions which almost overwhelmed him. They loved him dearly, and received him as if he were **an angel of God,** or rather as if he were **Christ Jesus himself.** This is indeed a great thing to say that the Galatians received the Gospel from a man as contemptible and afflicted in every way as Paul was. Both Jews and Gentiles complained and fumed against him when he preached the Gospel to them. All powerful, wise, religious, and learned people hated and persecuted Paul. Yet the Galatians were not offended at all, but averted their eyes from his illness, simply listening to the poor, despised, wretched, and afflicted Paul, and acknowledged themselves to be his disciples. Paul does not say this of anyone else but the Galatians.

15. What has happened to all your joy? This is like saying, 'Not only were you blessed, but in everything you were most highly commended.' Thus Paul mitigates the bitter medicine of his sharp reproof. He knew how the false apostles would slander him, and interpret his words spitefully, for this is the nature of such snakes – they maliciously pervert the words uttered by a sincere heart, and twist them clean contrary to their true meaning. They are amazingly clever at this, for they are led by a wicked spirit, which so bewitches them that they are inflamed with devilish rage against the faithful, and cannot but interpret their words and writings maliciously. Paul tries to see that they have no occasion to slander and pervert his words, saying, 'Paul is treating you very harshly! He calls you foolish, bewitched, and disobedient to the truth! This is a sure sign that he is not seeking your salvation, but regards you as damned and rejected by Christ.'

16. Here Paul shows why he is speaking so gently to the Galatians. He suspects that they take him for their enemy because he had reproved them so sharply. 'I beg you,' he says, 'to put these rebukes on one side, and separate them from doctrine, and you will then find that my purpose was not to rebuke you but to teach you the truth. I admit that my letter is severe, but by being severe I am trying to recall you to the truth of the Gospel, from which you have fallen away, and to keep you in it. Apply this sharpness and this bitter medicine not to your persons but to your disease. Do not regard me as your enemy, but realize that I am your father. Unless I loved you dearly, as my children, and also knew that I am loved by you, I would not have reproved you so sharply.'

17. Those people are zealous to win you over, but for no good. Here he criticizes the flattery of the false apostles. Satan, through his servants, is very clever at beguiling simple people (Romans 16:18). First of all, they protest that they seek nothing but the advancement of God's glory; and that they are moved by the Spirit to teach the infallible truth (either because people are neglected, or because the truth is not taught purely by others), so that the chosen people may be delivered from error, and may come to the true light and knowledge of the truth. Moreover, they promise certain salvation to those who accept their teaching. If vigilant and faithful pastors do not withstand these ravening wolves, they will do great harm to the church, under this pretense of godliness. The Galatians might say, 'Why do you criticize our teachers so bitterly? They are zealous for us. What they do, they do purely out of zeal and love. This should not upset you.'

18. In effect Paul is saying, 'I commend you for loving me so entirely when I preached the Gospel to you in my weakness. You should have the same affection for me now, when I am absent, just as though I had never left you; for although I am absent in body, you have my doctrine, which you ought to keep and maintain, for you received the Holy Spirit through it. You should remember that Paul is always present with you as long as you have his doctrine. I do not, therefore, criticize your zeal, but I praise it; it is the zeal of God or of the Spirit, and not of the flesh.'

19. My dear children. All Paul's words are weighty and appropriate for moving the hearts of the Galatians and win back their favour.

For whom I am again in the pains of childbirth. This is an allegory. The apostles are in *loco parentis,* as schoolteachers are. Parents beget the bodily form, but teachers beget the form of the mind. Now the form of a Christian is faith, or laying hold upon Christ, and clinging to him alone. When the heart has this assurance – that for Christ's sake we are righteous – it has the true form of Christ. This form is given by the ministry of the Word: 'I became your father through the gospel' (1 Corinthians 4:15), that is to say, through the Spirit (see also 2 Corinthians 3:3). Thus, every godly teacher is a father, who engenders and forms the true shape of a Christian heart by the ministry of the Word.

20. How I wish I could be with you now and change my tone. These are the true cares of an apostle. It is often said that a letter is a dead messenger, for it can give no more than it has. And no letter is written so accurately that there is nothing lacking. Times, places, persons, manners, and feelings are all so varied that no letter can express them, and so a letter moves its readers in various ways, making them sad or happy as they themselves are disposed. But if anything is said sharply, or out of time, the living voice may explain, mitigate, or correct it. Therefore the apostle wishes he were with them, so that he might temper and change his tone as he sees necessary. If he saw any of them troubled, he could temper his words so that they would not be oppressed by them with more heaviness; conversely, if he saw others high-minded, he could reprehend them sharply, lest they should be too complacent and careless, and eventually despise God.

21. Paul would have finished his letter here, for he did not want to write any more, but rather to be present with the Galatians, and to speak to them himself. But in his perplexity and care he takes this allegory which came to his mind. People love allegories and parables – Christ himself often uses them. They are very good at persuading people, especially the simple and ignorant.

22–23. Paul says in effect: 'You forsake grace, faith, and Christ, and return to the law; you want to be under the law, and become wise through it; therefore I will talk to you about the law. Consider the law carefully and you will find that Abraham had two sons: Ishmael by Hagar and Isaac by Sarah. They were both the true sons of Abraham, Ishmael as much as Isaac. What was the difference? It was not that the mother of one was free and the other a slave, although that is relevant to the allegory; but that Ishmael, who was born of the slave woman, was born in the ordinary way, without the promise and the Word of God, but Isaac was not only born of the free woman but also as the result of a promise.' Nobody noticed this difference but Paul.

24. These things may be taken figuratively. Allegories are not very persuasive in theology, but, as certain pictures do, they beautify and set out the doctrine.

24–25. The women represent two covenants. One covenant is from Mount Sinai and bears children who are to be slaves: This is Hagar. Now Hagar stands for Mount Sinai in Arabia. Abraham is a figure of God, with two sons; that is to say, two sorts of people are represented by Ishmael and Isaac. These two are born to him by Hagar and Sarah, who signify the two covenants, the old and the new. The old is of Mount Sinai, begetting to slavery, which is Hagar. (In Arabic Hagar is the name for the mountain the Jews call Sinai; it seems to get this name from brambles and thorns.) Now it is very appropriate that Mount Sinai in Arabic means a handmaid, and I think the name gave Paul the opportunity to seek out this allegory. Just as Hagar the slave gave Abraham a son, yet not an heir but a servant, so Sinai, the allegorical Hagar, gave God a son, that is, a carnal people. Again, as Ishmael was the true son of Abraham, so the people of Israel had the true God as their Father, giving them his law, his oracles, religion, and true service, and the temple (Psalm 147:19). The only difference was that Ishmael had been born physically of a slave woman, without the promise, and could not therefore be the heir. So the mystical Hagar, that is, mount Sinai, where the law was given, and the old covenant ordained, gave God, the great Abraham, a people, but without the promise; that is to say, a carnal and a servile people, and not the heir of God. The promises concerning Christ, the giver of all blessing, and the deliverance from the curse of the law, from sin and death; and concerning the free forgiveness of our sins, righteousness, and everlasting life, are not added to the law, but the law says, 'The man who does these things will live by them' (Leviticus 18:5; Romans 10:5).

26. The spiritual Jerusalem corresponds to Sarah, the true lady and free woman who is the mother of us all, bringing us into liberty, and

not into slavery as Hagar does. The heavenly Jerusalem is the church, that is to say, the faithful scattered throughout the world, who have one and the same Gospel, one and the same faith in Christ, the same Holy Spirit, and the same sacraments.

28. We are not children physically, as Ishmael was, or as all the physical Israel, who boasted that they were the seed of Abraham and the people of God (John 8:31–42). We are not like children who remain servants, and eventually are thrown out of the house; we are children of the promise, as Isaac was; that is to say, of grace and of faith, born only of the promise. We are pronounced righteous not by the law, by works, or our own righteousness, but by the mere mercy and grace of God. Paul often repeats the promise which is received by faith alone, for he knew that it was very necessary to do so.

29. This verse contains singular consolation. Whoever is born and lives in Christ, and rejoices in the birth and inheritance of God, has Ishmael for an enemy and persecutor. We learn this today by experience, for we see all the world full of unrest, persecution, sects, and offenses. Therefore, if we did not arm ourselves with Paul's consolation and so on, and understand this doctrine of justification properly, we should never be able to withstand the violence and subtle tricks of Satan. But we must arms ourselves with the knowledge that the faithful must bear the reputation in the world of being seditious and schismatic, and the originators of innumerable evils. Hence our adversaries think they have a good case against us, and indeed that they perform a great service for God when they hate, persecute, and kill us (John 16:2). Ishmael has to persecute Isaac, but Isaac does not persecute Ishmael in return. Whoever does not want to be persecuted by Ishmael should not profess to be a Christian.

30. Sarah's word was very grievous to Abraham; and when he heard this sentence, he was moved with fatherly compassion towards his son Ishmael, who had been born of his flesh (Genesis 21:11). But God confirmed the sentence which Sarah had pronounced (Genesis 21:12–13).

Chapter 5

Paul now draws towards the end of his letter, and argues very forcefully in defence of the doctrine of faith and Christian freedom, against the false apostles, who are its enemies and destroyers. He thunders against them and exhorts the Galatians to shun their pernicious doctrine as a dangerous poison. He tries in every way to keep them in the freedom which Christ has purchased for them.

1. It is for freedom that Christ has set us free.

Stand firm, then. That is, be steadfast. Compare 1 Peter 5:8–9. Do not be careless, but steadfast and constant. Do not lie down and sleep, but stand up. It is like saying: It is best to be watchful and constant, so that you may keep and hold fast the freedom with which Christ has made you free. Those who are complacent and negligent cannot keep this freedom, for Satan has a deadly hatred of the light of the Gospel, that is to say, the doctrine of grace, liberty, consolation, and life. Therefore, once he sees it begin to appear, he fights against it with all his might and main, stirring up storms and tempests to hinder its course and overthrow it. Therefore Paul warns the believers not to sleep, not to be negligent, but constantly and valiantly to resist Satan, so that he does not spoil them of the freedom which Christ has purchased for them.

2. Paul here is wonderfully stirred up with zeal and fervency of spirit, and thunders against the law and circumcision. These thunderings are wrested from him by the Holy Spirit.

3. Paul says these words so earnestly and forcefully that he confirms them with an oath: **I declare**, that is, I swear by the living God. But these words may be expounded in two ways, negatively and positively. Negatively, like this: I declare to every man who is circumcised that he is bound to keep the whole law. In circumcision he is not circumcised, and even in fulfilling the law he does not fulfil it, but transgresses it. This seems to me to be Paul's simple and true meaning in this verse. Afterwards, he expounds himself, saying, 'Not even those who are circumcised obey the law' (Galatians 6:13); and he has already said, 'All who rely on observing the law are under a curse' (Galatians 3:13). In effect he says, 'Although you are circumcised, you are not righteous and free from the law; rather, by this act you are debtors and slaves of the law; and the more you try to satisfy the law, and be set free from it, the more you trap yourselves in its yoke, so that it has more power to accuse and condemn you. This is washing away dirt with dirt.'

4. Here Paul shows that is not speaking simply of the law, or the act of circumcision, but of the idea that people will be justified by it. In effect he is saying, 'I do not utterly condemn the law or circumcision (for it is legitimate for me to drink, to eat, and to keep company with the Jews, according to the law; it is lawful for me to circumcise Timothy), but to seek to be justified by the law, as if Christ had not yet come, or, now that it is here, that he alone were not able to justify – this is what I condemn, for this is to be separated from Christ. Therefore,' he says, 'you are abolished – you are utterly empty of Christ; Christ is not in you, he no longer works in you; you do not share in the knowledge, the Spirit, the fellowship, the favour, the liberty, the life, or the actions of Christ, but are utterly separate from him, so that he has no more to do with you, nor you with him.'

5. Paul here concludes the matter by saying, 'You seek to be justified by the law, by circumcision, and by your actions; but we do not seek to be justified by this means, lest Christ should be made completely worthless to us, and we have to perform the whole law, and so finally fall away from grace; but we wait in spirit, through faith, for the hope of righteousness.' Every word here is to be noted carefully, for every word is pithy and full of power. He is not just saying, as he usually does, that we are justified by faith, or in spirit by faith; he adds that we await 'the hope of righteousness.'

Hope, as the Scripture uses the term, has two meanings: the thing hoped for, and the feeling of the person who hopes. The meaning here is, first, that we wait in spirit, through faith, for the righteousness we hope for, which shall surely be revealed when the Lord chooses to give it; and second, that we wait in spirit, by faith, for righteousness, with hope and desire; that is to say, we are righteous, though our righteousness is not yet revealed, but remains in hope.

6. Faith which is not hypocritical, but true and lively, is what exercises and requires good works through love. Anyone who wants to be a true Christian, or one of Christ's kingdom, must be a true believer. We do not believe truly if loving actions do not follow on our faith. Paul excludes the Jews, and all those who want to work out their own salvation, saying, **In Christ Jesus neither circumcision** – that is to say, no acts, no service, no worshipping, no kind of life in the world, but faith, without any trust in works or merits, avails before God. On the other hand, he excludes all slothful and idle people, who say, 'If faith justifies us without works, then let us do nothing, but let us only believe and do what we like.' Paul says otherwise. Although it is true that only faith justifies, here he is speaking about faith in another respect: that after it has justified, it is not idle, but occupied and exercised in working through love.

7. Paul is teaching them the truth, the same as he had taught them before, and says that they were running well as long as they obeyed the truth, believing and living rightly; but now they were not doing this, since they were misled by the false apostles. Paul uses a new image here in calling the Christina life a **race**. In Hebrew, to run or to walk means the same as to live or to behave. The teachers run when they teach purely, and the listeners run when they receive the word with joy, and when the fruits of the Spirit follow. This happened as long as Paul was present.

8. The false apostles appeared to surpass Paul both in learning and in godliness. The Galatians

were deceived by this appearance, and thought that when they heard them, they were listening to Christ himself. However, Paul shows that this doctrine did not come from Christ, who had called them in grace, but from the devil; and thus he won many of them from this false idea.

9. The whole letter shows clearly enough how upset Paul was at the fall of the Galatians, and how, sometimes chiding and sometimes entreating, he beat into their heads the great and horrible enormities that would ensue upon their fall unless they repented. Some of them were not at all moved by this fatherly and apostolical care and admonition of Paul's, for many of them no longer acknowledged Paul as their teacher, but rated the false apostles far above him. They thought they had received the true doctrine from them and not from Paul. Moreover, the false apostles, no doubt, slandered Paul among the Galatians, saying that he was an obstinate and contentious fellow, who would break the unity of the churches for a mere trifle, just because he alone wanted to be thought wise, and be praised by them. With this false accusation they made Paul very odious to many people.

10. I am confident in the Lord that you will take no other view. Paul says, in effect, 'I have taught, admonished, and reproved you enough, so that you would listen to me; but I hope well of you in the Lord.' Faith trusts in God, and therefore it cannot be deceived; love believes in man, and therefore it is often deceived. Now, this faith that springs from love is so necessary to this present life that without it life cannot continue in the world. If one person should not believe and trust another, what life should we live on earth? True Christians are more ready to believe and give credit through love than the children of this world do, for faith in other people is a fruit of the Spirit, or of Christian faith in the godly. Thus Paul trusts the Galatians even though they had fallen away from his doctrine. It is like saying, 'I trust you so far as the Lord is in you, and you in him; that is to say, so far as you remain in the truth. If you are seduced by Satan's ministers and fall away from that, I will not trust you any more.'

11. Paul tries every way of bringing the Galatians back. Here he reasons from his own example. I have brought on myself the hatred and persecution of the priests and elders, he says (Acts 13:50), and of my whole nation, because I take away righteousness from circumcision. If I would attribute righteousness to circumcision, the Jews would not only stop persecuting me, they would love me and commend me highly. But I preach the Gospel of Christ and the righteousness of faith, abolishing the law and circumcision, and therefore I suffer persecution. The false apostles, on the other hand,

avoid the cross and this deadly hatred of the Jewish nation, preaching circumcision; thus they obtain and retain the Jews' favour (see Galatians 6:12). They would be glad to see that there was no dissension, but peace and agreement between the Gentiles and the Jews. But that is impossible without the loss of the doctrine of faith, which is the doctrine of the cross, and is full of offenses. Paul's meaning in this verse is that it would be quite wrong for the offense of the cross to cease – see also 1 Corinthians 1:17.

12. Here Paul is alluding to circumcision. The false apostles seemed on the surface to be men of great authority and holiness. We must not make little account of the leaven of doctrine, for however small it is, if it is neglected it will be the cause of truth and salvation being gradually lost, and God himself denied. When the word is corrupted, and God denied (which is what must follow, if the word is corrupted), there is no longer any hope of salvation. But for our part, if we are cursed and slain, there is still someone who can raise us up again, and deliver us from the curse, death, and hell.

13. There now follow exhortations and teachings about life and good works, for the apostles' custom, when they have taught faith and instructed people's consciences, is to add teaching about good works, exhorting faithful people to exercise the duties of love towards one another. Reason itself, in a way, teaches and understands this part of doctrine; but as for the doctrine of faith, it knows nothing at all. So, in order that we should see that Christian doctrine does not destroy good works or militate against civil ordinances, the apostles tells us to busy ourselves in good works, and in decent outward behaviour, and to love and be at peace with one another. The world cannot, therefore, justly accuse Christians of destroying good works, or of disturbing the peace. They teach good works and all other virtues better than all the philosophers and magistrates of the world, because they combine faith with their actions.

14. After laying the foundation of Christian doctrine, Paul builds gold, silver, and precious stones on it. There is no other foundation than Jesus Christ (1 Corinthians 3:11), or the righteousness of Christ. On this foundation he now builds good works, all of them comprehended in one command, to love our neighbors as ourself. Paul says, in effect: 'When I say that you must serve one another in love, I mean the same thing that the law says elsewhere – "Love your neighbors as yourself"' (Leviticus 19:18). This is the true way to interpret the Scripture and God's commands.

15. If the foundation – faith in Christ – is overthrown by wicked teachers, no peace can remain in the church, either in doctrine or in life, but there will be various opinions and dissensions from time to time, both in doctrine and life, and one person will bite and devour another, judging and condemning, until they are destroyed. This is proved not only by Scripture but by the example of all times. One sect gives rise to another, and one condemns another. When the unity of the Spirit is broken, it is impossible for there to be any agreement either in doctrine or life, but new errors will spring up every day, endlessly.

16. In effect, he says: 'I have not forgotten what I was saying earlier about faith, and I am not taking that back. So that you may understand me, I will now add this: Walk in the Spirit, and you will not gratify the desires of the sinful nature.'

17. **For the sinful nature desires what is contrary to the Spirit, and the Spirit what is contrary to the sinful nature.** Paul is warning us that we will inevitably feel pride, wrath, heaviness, impatience, unbelief, and so on. But he wants us to feel them in such a way that we do not consent to them, or carry them out – that is, that we do not think, speak, or do these things that our sinful nature provokes us to. If it moves us to anger, we should be angry in such a way that we do not sin (Psalm 4:4). If we abandon the Spirit's guidance, and follow our sinful nature, we shall fulfill the desires of our sinful nature, and we shall die (Romans 8).

18. Paul cannot forget the doctrine of faith, but still repeats it, and beats it into their heads, even when he is dealing with good works. Here someone may object: 'How can it be that we are not under the law? Paul teaches us that we have sinful natures, which lust against the Spirit, fight against us, torment us, and bring us into slavery.' We do indeed feel sin, and cannot be delivered from feeling it however much we want it; and what is this if it is not being under the law? But Paul says this must not trouble us; we must simply try to be led by the Spirit, showing ourselves willing to follow and obey the will that resists our sinful nature, and does not follow its desires. Then we are not under the law. So Paul speaks about himself: 'In my inner being I delight in God's law' (Romans 7:22), that is to say, in my inner being I am not subject to any sin, yet in my sinful nature I serve the law of sin. The faithful, then, are not under the law, that is to say, in spirit; for the law cannot accuse them or sentence them to death, although they feel sin and confess themselves to be sinners. The power and strength of the law is taken from it by Christ, who was 'born under law, to redeem those under law' (Galatians 4:4–5). Therefore the law cannot accuse something as sin in the faithful, although it is indeed sin and committed against the law.

19. **The acts of the sinful nature are obvious.** Paul teaches the very same thing that Christ taught (Matthew 7:16), that works and fruit witness whether the trees are good or evil: whether people follow the guidance of the sinful nature, or of the Spirit. 'In case people say they do not understand me when I talk about the battle between the sinful nature and the Spirit,' says Paul in effect, 'I will set out the works of the sinful nature, many of which are known even to the ungodly; and then also the works of the Spirit.'

20. **Idolatry.** All the highest religions, the holiness and most fervent devotions of those who reject Christ the Mediator, and worship God without his Word and commandment, are nothing but plain idolatry. And the more holy and spiritual it appears to be, the more dangerous and pernicious it is, for then it turns people away from faith in Christ, and leads them to trust in their own strength, acts, and righteousness. When people imagine themselves to be saints, and to be saved, not by Christ (whom they fear as a severe and cruel judge) but by observing their own rules, they think of God and of heavenly things according to their own reason, and not the Word of God. They hope to be rewarded by him for their good deeds and righteousness. But the Father is well pleased in Christ alone, and whoever listens to him, and does what he has commanded, is loved because of 'the beloved.' He commands us to believe his Word, and to be baptized, and so on, and not to devise any new worship of service of God. Adultery, fornication, and so on are clearly seen by everyone, but idolatry looks so spiritual that it is only the few, the faithful, who know it to be an act of the sinful nature.

Witchcraft. In the light of the Gospel, witchcraft is not so often heard of, for the Gospel thrusts the devil out of his seat, with all his illusions. But now he bewitches people much more horribly, namely with spiritual sorcery and witchcraft.

21. **Drunkenness, orgies.** Paul is not saying that to eat and drink are acts of the sinful nature, but to get drunk and to surfeit. Those who are given to this animal excess must realize that they are not spiritual, as they claim to be, but follow the sinful nature. The horrible sentence pronounced on them is that they **will not inherit the kingdom of God.** Paul wants Christians to fly from drunkenness and surfeiting, living soberly and moderately, without any excess, lest by pampering the flesh they should be provoked to wantonness. It is not enough merely to restrain this outrageous wantonness and lust of the flesh, which follows drunkenness and surfeiting, or any sort of excess. The flesh, when it is most sober and temperate, must be subdued and repressed, lest it give in to its desires. It often happens that even the most sober are tempted most of all. We must be aided

by the Spirit, that is, by meditating on God's Word, faith, and prayer. Certainly fasting represses the gross assaults of fleshly lust, but the desires of the sinful nature are not overcome by abstinence from food and drink, but only by the meditation on the Word of God and by calling on Christ.

22. The apostle does not say 'the acts of the spirit,' as he speaks of 'the acts of the sinful nature,' but honours these Christian virtues by calling them **the fruit of the Spirit**. Those who have them give glory to God, and attract other people by them, and provoke others to embrace the doctrine and faith of Christ.

Love. It would have been enough to have said love and no more, for love extends to all the fruit of the Spirit. And in 1 Corinthians 13 Paul attributes to love all the fruit which is done in the Spirit. But he wants to set it by itself here, amongst the rest of the fruit of the Spirit, and in the first place, so that he warns Christians that before everything else they should love one another, giving honour to one another (Romans 12:10), each thinking others better than themselves, and serving one another, and because of the Word, baptism, and other gifts of God, which Christians have.

Joy. This is the voice of the bridegroom and of the bride – sweet thoughts of Christ, wholesome exhortations, pleasant songs or psalms, praises, and thanksgivings, by which godly people instruct, stir up, and refresh themselves. God does not love depression and doubt; he hates doctrine that does not strengthen, and heavy and sorrowful thoughts, and he loves cheerful hearts. He sent his Son not to oppress us with heaviness and sorrow, but to cheer up our souls in him. That is why the prophets, the apostles, and Christ himself command us to rejoice and be glad. Where this joy of the spirit is, there the heart inwardly rejoices through faith in Christ, with full assurance that he is our Saviour. Outwardly, it expresses this joy with words and gestures. Also, the faithful rejoice when they see the Gospel spreading, many people being won to the faith, and the kingdom of Christ enlarged.

Peace. Both towards God and other people, that Christians may be peaceable and quiet – not contentious, nor hating one another, but bearing one another's burdens, through long-suffering or perseverance, without which peace cannot last, which is why Paul puts it after peace.

Patience. By which people not only bear adversity, injury, reproach, and so on, but also wait patiently for the amendment of those who have done them any wrong. When the devil cannot overcome by force those who are tempted, he seeks to overcome them by perseverance. He knows that we are earthen containers, which

cannot last long and hold out many knocks and violent blows, so he overcomes many people by long repeated temptations. To overcome these continual assaults we must be patient, looking not only for the amendment of those who wrong us, but also for the end of those temptations which the devil raises up against us.

Kindness. This is when people are gentle and tractable in their behaviour, and in their whole life. Those who want to be true followers of the Gospel must not be sharp and bitter, but gentle, mild, courteous, and fair spoken, which should encourage others to delight in their company. They should wink at other people's faults, or at least put them in the best light; they will be perfectly content to yield and give way to others; contented to bear with those who are froward and intractable. Such a person was our Saviour Christ, as we see everywhere in the Gospel. It is said of Peter that he wept every time he remembered the mildness of Christ, which he adopted in his daily life. It is an excellent virtue, and most necessary in every kind of life.

Goodness. This is when a person willingly helps others in the necessities, but giving, lending, and other such means.

Faithfulness. Clearly Paul is not speaking about faith in Christ, but of fidelity and humanity of one person towards another. In 1 Corinthians 13:7 he says that love 'always trusts'; those who have this faithfulness are not suspicious but mild, and take all things to the best; and although they may be deceived, and find that they have been mocked, they are patient and soft, so that they let it pass. They are ready to believe everyone, but do not trust all. On the contrary, where this virtue is lacking, there people are suspicious, froward, wayward, dogged, and will not believe anything or give way to anybody; they can suffer nothing; whatever a person says or does, however well, they cavil and slander it, so that whoever does not satisfy their whims can never please them. Therefore it is impossible for them to keep love, friendship, unity, and peace with people. But if these virtues are taken away, what is this life but biting and devouring of one another? Faithfulness, therefore, in this verse means when one person gives credit to another in things pertaining to this present life.

23. **Gentleness.** This is when a person is not lightly moved or provoked to anger. There are so many occasions in this life which provoke people to anger, but the godly overcome them by gentleness.

Self-control. This is a sobriety or modesty in the whole of human life, which Paul sets against the acts of the sinful nature. He want Christians to live soberly and chastely; he wants them to be no adulterers, fornicators, or wantons; and if they cannot live chastely he wants them to marry. Also, he wants them not to be contentious or quarrelers; he does not want them given to drunkenness or surfeiting, but abstaining from all these things. Self-control includes all these things.

Against such things there is no law. See 1 Timothy 1:9. Righteous people live in such a way that they have no need of any law to admonish or constrain them, but willingly do what the law requires. Therefore the law cannot accuse or condemn those who believe in Christ.

24. This whole passage shows that true believers are no hypocrites. The saints, inasmuch as they have not yet completely divested themselves of the corrupt and sinful nature, are inclined to sin, and neither fear nor love God as perfectly as they ought to do. Also, they are provoked to anger, to envy, to impatience, to unclean desires, and so on, though they do not actually perform them for they crucify the sinful nature, with all its desires.

25. The apostle earlier listed heresy and envy among the acts of the sinful nature, and pronounced sentence against those who are envious, and who are the authors of factions, saying that they would not inherit the kingdom of God. Now, as if he had forgotten what he had said earlier, he again reproves those who provoke and envy one another. Why does he do this? Was it not enough to have done it once? He does it purposely, for he takes occasion here to inveigh against the execrable vice of vainglory, which was the cause of the troubles that existed in all the churches of Galatia, and has always been most pernicious and hateful to the whole church of Christ. Therefore, in his letter to Titus, he says he does not want a proud person to be ordained, for pride (as Augustine truly says) is the mother of all heresies, or rather the headspring of all sin and confusion. Secular histories as well as sacred witness this.

26. **Let us not become conceited.** This is glorying not in God but in lies, in the high opinion of other people. This is no proper foundation for true glory, but a false foundation, and therefore it cannot last long. Anyone who praises a man as he is a man, is a liar; for there is nothing praiseworthy about him.

Chapter 6

1. **Brothers, if someone is caught in a sin, you who are spiritual should restore him gently.** The apostle is not speaking here about errors and offenses against doctrine, but about far lesser sins, into which people fall not deliberately but through weakness. The words **is caught in** imply being tricked by the devil, or by the sinful nature. The saints in this life now and then, through the enticement of the devil, fall into impatience, envy, wrath, error, doubt, distrust, and so on, for Satan always attacks the

purity of doctrine through sects and dissensions, as well as attacking the soundness of life with daily offenses. Paul therefore teaches how those who have fallen should be dealt with: namely, that those who are strong should raise them up and restore them gently.

2. This is a gentle command, with a great commendation attached. The law of Christ is the law of love. After Christ had redeemed us, renewed us, and made us his church, he gave us no other law but that of mutual love (John 13:34). And to love is not to wish one another well, but to carry one another's burden's, that is, things which are grievous to you, and which you would not willingly bear. Therefore, Christians must have strong shoulders and mighty bones, that they may carry their brothers' weakness, for Paul says that they have burdens and troubles. Love, therefore, is mild, courteous, patient, not in receiving, but in giving; for it is constrained to wink at many things, and to bear them (1 Corinthians 13:4). Faithful teachers see in the church many errors and offenses which they are compelled to bear. Citizens are never as obedient to the civil laws as they should be. Therefore, unless the magistrate can turn a blind eye in the right time and place, he will never be fit to rule the commonwealth. In household affairs many things are done which displease the master of the house. But if we can bear and wink at our own vices and offenses which we commit every day, let us also bear other people's faults.

3. Here again Paul criticizes the authors of sects, and depicts them in their right colours, saying that they are hard-hearted, merciless, and without compassion. They despise the weak, and will not carry their burdens, but require everything done strictly, like wayward husbands and severe schoolteachers. Nothing can please them but what they themselves do, and they will always be your bitter enemies, unless you commend whatever they say or do, and frame yourself according to their wishes in everything. They are the proudest of all people, and Paul says they think themselves to be something – that is, that they have the Holy Spirit, that they understand all the mysteries of the Scriptures, that they cannot go wrong, and so on.

4. Paul continues to depict those proud people. The desire of arrogance is an odious and cursed vice; it is the occasion of all evils, and troubles both communities and consciences, and especially in spiritual matters it is an incurable evil. Although this verse may be understood of the actions of this life, or of civil relationships, the apostle is mainly speaking about the work of the ministry, and inveighs against those who with their extraordinary ideas trouble well-instructed consciences.

5. It is quite mad to seek glory in someone else, and not in yourself; for in the agony of

death, and in the last judgment, it will be of no benefit to you that other people have praised you. Other people will not carry your load, but you will stand before the judgment-seat of Christ, and will carry your load alone. There your praises will not help you at all. When we die, these praises will end. And on that day, when the Lord judges the secrets of all hearts, the witness of your own conscience will stand either with you or against you (Romans 2:15). It will be against you if you glory in other people; with you if you take pride in yourself, that is, if your conscience tells you that you have done your duty in the ministry of the Word, or otherwise according to your calling, sincerely and faithfully, thinking only of God's glory and the salvation of souls.

6. Here he preaches to the disciples of hearers of the Word, commanding them to give all good things to those who have taught and instructed them in the Word. I have sometimes wondered why the apostles commanded the churches so diligently to look after their teachers, for I saw the clergy overflowing with wealth and riches. I thought people ought rather to be exhorted to withhold from giving, instead of encouraging them to give any more; for I saw that when people were excessively generous the greed of the clergy increased. But now I know why they had such abundance of good things before, and now the pastors and ministers of the Word are needy. Before, when errors and wicked doctrines were being taught, they had plenty of everything, but since the Gospel has been preached, its adherents are as rich as Christ and his apostles once were. Whenever I read Paul's exhortations to the churches to nourish their pastors, or give something for the relief of the poor Jewish saints, I am ashamed that such a great apostle should have to use so many words to obtain this from the congregations. Writing to the Corinthians, he deals with this matter in two whole chapters, 8 and 9. This is the lot of the Gospel when it is preached: not only is no one willing to give anything for the maintenance of ministers and scholars, but people begin to rob and steal, and trick one another with various subterfuges. People seem suddenly to grow into cruel beasts. Yet when the doctrine of devils was preached, people were liberal, and offered everything willingly to those who deceived them (1 Timothy 4:2). The prophets criticize the Jews for the same sin: they were reluctant to give anything to the godly priests and Levites, but gave everything to the wicked.

7. **Do not be deceived: God cannot be mocked.** Paul now adds a threat, touching to the quick the perverseness of those who proudly despise our ministry. They think it is just a game, and so they try to make their pastors subject to them, like servants and slaves. Paul horribly

threatens those who so proudly scorn the miserable preachers, and yet want to be thought to worship God very devoutly. God will not let himself be mocked through his ministers (Luke 10:16; 1 Samuel 8:7). He may delay his punishment for a while, but when he sees it is time, he will punish this contempt of his Word and hatred of his ministers. Therefore you are not deceiving God, but yourselves, and you will not laugh at God, but he will laugh at you (Psalm 2). Moreover, God will not let his ministers starve, but even when rich people suffer scarcity and hunger, he will feed them, and in the time of famine they will have enough (Psalm 37:19).

8. Paul applies the general sentence about owing to the particular matter of maintaining the ministers of the Word.

9. Intending to close his letter, the apostle passes from the particular to the general, with a general exhortation to good works. Let us be generous, he says, not only to ministers of the Word, but also to everyone else, without wearying; for it is easy to do good once or twice, but very hard to continue, and not be discouraged by the ingratitude or those to whom we have done good.

10. This concludes his exhortation to maintain ministers of the Word generously, and give charitably to all those in need. It is like John 9:4; and see John 12:35. Unless you continue in the sound doctrine you have received from me, says Paul, your good deeds, your suffering of many troubles, and so on, will be of no benefit to you (see also Galatians 3:4).

12. Before, he had cursed the false apostles. Now, as it were, saying the same thing again but in different words, he accuses them very sharply, so that he may turn the Galatians away from their doctrine, despite the great authority which they seemed to have. The teachers you have, says Paul, do not care for Christ's glory, and the salvation of your souls, but only seek their own glory. Secondly, they shun the cross. Thirdly, they do not understand what they teach.

13. These things serve to condemn the false apostles, so that the Galatians may be afraid to listen to them. It is as if Paul were saying, 'Look, I will show you the sort of teachers you have. First, they seek only their own benefit, and care for nothing but their own interests (Philippians 2:21). Secondly, they shun the cross. Finally, they teach no truth or certainty, but all they say and do is counterfeit and full of hypocrisy. So although they keep the law outwardly, they are not keeping it, for it cannot be kept without the Holy Spirit. But the Holy Spirit cannot be received without Christ; and where the Holy Spirit does not live, there is an unclean spirit, despising God and seeking his own gain and glory. Therefore, all that he does, concerning the law, is mere hypocrisy and double sin; for an unclean

heart does not fulfill the law, but only makes an outward show of doing so, and is all the more confirmed in wickedness and hypocrisy.'

14. May I never boast except in the cross of our Lord Jesus Christ. The apostle closes with indignation and great vehemence. 'The glory and ambition of the false apostles is so dangerous a poison that I wish it buried in hell,' he says, 'for it is the cause of many people's destruction. But let people glory in the flesh if that is what they want, and let them perish with their cursed glory; as for me, I desire no other glory but that of the cross of Christ.' (See also Romans 5:3; 2 Corinthians 12:10.) The glory and rejoicing of Christians is to be proud of tribulations, reproach, weakness, and so on.

15. It may seem that Paul should have said, 'Circumcision and uncircumcision mean two different things.' But he denies that either of them means anything. It is like saying, 'You must climb higher, for circumcision and uncircumcision are things of no such importance as to be able to obtain righteousness before God.' True, they are contrary to one another; but this does not affect Christian righteousness, which is not earthly, but heavenly. It does not consist in physical things. Therefore, whether you are circumcised or not, it is all the same, for in Christ Jesus neither the one nor the other makes any difference.

16. Peace and mercy to all who follow this rule. Paul adds this as a conclusion. this is the only true rule by which we should live: the new creature, which is neither circumcision nor uncircumcision, but the new person created in God's image in righteousness and true holiness (Ephesians 4:24), which inwardly is righteous in the spirit, and outwardly is holy and clean in the flesh.

17. Finally, let no one cause me trouble. He concludes his letter with a certain indignation. 'I have faithfully taught the Gospel as I have received it by the revelation of Jesus Christ,' he says in effect. 'Whoever will not follow it may follow what he likes, provided he does not trouble me any more. My censure is that Christ, whom I have preached, is the only high priest and saviour of the world. Therefore, the world must either live by the rule of which I have spoken throughout this letter, or else perish forever.'

For I bear on my body the marks of Jesus. The marks that are in my body show well enough whose servant I am. The wounds and sufferings which he bore in his body, he calls **marks.** The anguish and terror of spirit he calls the devil's flaming arrows. He mentions these sufferings everywhere in Acts, and in 1 Corinthians 4:9, 11–13 and 2 Corinthians 6:4–6; 11:23–26. These are the true marks and signs of which the apostle speaks in this passage. They are a seal and a sure sign of true doctrine and faith.

18. Paul ends his letter with the same words he began it with. In effect he is saying, 'I have taught you Christ purely, I have entreated you, I have criticized you, and I have not let anything pass which I thought profitable for you. I can say no more, but that I heartily pray that our Lord Jesus Christ will bless my labour and bring fruit from it, and govern you with his Holy Spirit forever.'

EPHESIANS

Charles Hodge

Introduction

The apostle addresses himself principally to Gentile Christians. His object was:

1. To bring them to a just appreciation of the plan of redemption, as a scheme devised from eternity by God, for the manifestation of the glory of his grace.

2. To make them aware of the greatness of the blessing which they enjoyed by sharing its benefits.

3. To lead them to enter into the spirit of the Gospel, as a system which ignored the distinction between Jews and Gentiles, and united all the members of the church in one living body, destined to be brought into full conformity to the image of Christ.

4. To induce them to live as suited a religion which had delivered them from the degradation of their heathen condition, and exalted them to the dignity of sons of God.

He begins, therefore, with the primal fountain of all spiritual blessings. He refers them to their predestination to sonship, and their consequent election to holiness, before the foundation of the world. From this flowed their actual redemption by the blood of Christ; and the revelation of the divine purpose to unite all the subjects of redemption in one body in Christ; in whom first the Jews, and then the Gentiles, had been made the heirs of eternal life (Ephesians 1:1–14).

He next earnestly prays that God would enable them to appreciate the hope which they were thus entitled to cherish; the glory of the inheritance in reserve for them; and the exceeding greatness of that power which had already wrought in them a change analogous to that effected in the resurrection and exaltation of Christ. For as Christ was dead and deposited in the tomb, so they were spiritually dead; and as Christ was raised an exalted above all creatures, so they also were quickened and exalted to a heavenly state in him (Ephesians 1:15–2:10).

He therefore calls on them to contrast their former condition as heathen, with their present state. Formerly they were without Christ, aliens from the commonwealth of Israel, without God, and without hope. But by the blood of Christ a two-fold reconciliation had been effected: the Jews and Gentiles are united as one body, and both are reconciled to God and have equally free access to his presence. The Gentiles, therefore, are now fellow citizens with the saints, members of the family of God, and living stones in that temple in which God dwells by his Spirit (Ephesians 2:11–22).

This great mystery of the union of Jews and Gentiles had been partially revealed under the old dispensation; but it was not then made known as clearly as it had since been revealed to the apostles and prophets of the new dispensation. It was their great vocation to preach the unsearchable riches of Christ, and to make everyone understand the plan of redemption, hidden for ages in God, but now revealed, that God's manifold wisdom might be made known to principalities and powers through the church (Ephesians 3:1–13).

The apostle, therefore, bows his knees before the common Father of the redeemed, and prays that Christ may dwell in their hearts by faith; that they, being rooted and grounded in love, might be able to apprehend the infinite love of Christ, and be filled with the fullness of God, who is able to do for us far more than we are able either to ask or to think (Ephesians 3:14–21).

The Gentiles, therefore, are bound to enter into the spirit of this great scheme – to remember that the church, composed of Jews and Gentiles, bond and free, wise and unwise, is one body, filled by one Spirit, subject to the same Lord, having one faith, one hope, one baptism, and one God and Father, who is in, through, and over all. They should also bear in mind that diversity in gifts and office was not inconsistent with this unity of the church, but essential to its edification. For the ascended Saviour had constituted some apostles, some prophets, some evangelists, some pastors and teachers, for the very purpose of building up the church; and through them, as the channels of the truth and grace of Christ, the church was to be brought to the end of its high calling (Ephesians 4:1–16).

They should not, therefore, live as the other Gentiles did, who, being in a state of darkness and alienation from God, gave themselves up to impurity and greed. On the contrary, having been taught by Christ, they should put off the old self, and be renewed in the image of God. Avoiding all falsehood, all undue anger, all dishonesty, all improper language, all malice, all impurity and covetousness, they should walk as children of the light, reproving evil, striving to do good, and expressing their joy by singing hymns to Christ, and giving thanks to God (Ephesians 4:17–5:20).

He impresses upon his readers reverence for the Lord Jesus Christ, as the great principle of Christian obedience. He applies this principle especially to people's domestic obligations. The marriage relationship is illustrated by a reference to the union between Christ and the church. The former is an obscure foreshadowing of the latter. Marriage is shown to be not merely a civil contract, not simply a voluntary compact between the parties, but a vital union producing a sacred identity. The violation of the marriage relationship is, therefore, presented as one of the greatest of crimes and one of the greatest of evils. Parents and children are bound together not only by natural ties but also by spiritual bonds; and, therefore, the obedience on the part of the child, and nurture on the part of the parent, should be religious. Masters and slaves, however different their condition in human eyes, stand on the same level before God – a consideration which exalts the slave, and humbles and restrains the master. Finally, the apostle teaches his readers the nature of that great spiritual conflict on which they have entered; a conflict, not with men, but with the powers of darkness. He tells them what armor they need, how it is to be used, and where they are to find strength to bring them off victorious (Ephesians 5:21–6:20).

Contents

Chapter 1

Verses 1–2: Greeting.

Verses 3–14: Thanksgiving for the blessings of redemption.

Verses 15–21: Prayer that the Ephesians might increase in the knowledge and experience of those blessings.

Verses 1–2

1. Paul, an apostle of Christ Jesus. The word **apostle** is used in three senses in the New Testament:

1. In its primary sense of 'messenger': John 13:16 (the messenger).

2. In the sense of missionaries, men sent by the church to preach the Gospel. In this sense Paul and Barnabas are called apostles, Acts 14:4, 14; and probably Andronicus and Junias, Romans 16:7.

3. In the sense of plenipotentiaries of Christ; men whom he personally selected and sent out invested with full authority to teach and rule in his name. In this sense it is always used when 'the apostles,' 'the twelve,' or 'the apostles of the Lord' are spoken of as a well-known, definite category of people. They were appointed as witnesses of Christ's miracles, doctrines, resurrection; and therefore it was necessary that they should not only have seen him after his resurrection, but that their knowledge of the Gospel should be immediately from Christ, John 15:26; Acts 1:22, 2:32, 3:15, 13:31, 26:16; 1 Corinthians 9:1; Galatians 1:12. They were not confined to any one territory, but had a general jurisdiction over the churches, as is manifest from their letters. To qualify for this office of authoritative teaching, organizing, and governing the church, they were made infallible by the inspiration of the Holy Spirit, and their divine mission was confirmed by miraculous powers. Their authority, therefore, rested, first, on their commission, and secondly on their inspiration. Hence, it is evident that no one can have the authority of an apostle who does not have apostolic gifts.

To the saints who are in Ephesus. The Israelites, under the old dispensation, were called **saints**, because they were separated from other nations and consecrated to God. In the New Testament the word is applied to believers, not merely as externally consecrated, but as reconciled to God and inwardly purified. The Greek word from which the word 'saint' is derived signifies 'to cleanse,' either from guilt by a propitiatory sacrifice, as in Hebrews 2:11 and 9:10, 14, or from inward pollution, and also to consecrate. Hence, **saints** are those who are cleansed by the blood of Christ, and by the

renewing of the Holy Spirit, and thus separated from the world and consecrated to God.

Are faithful in Christ Jesus. The faithful are believers.

2. This verse contains the usual apostolic blessing. Paul prays that grace and peace may be granted to his readers. **Grace** is unmerited favour; and the grace or favour of God is the source of all good. **Peace**, according to how the corresponding Hebrew word is used, means well-being in general. It includes all blessings flowing from the goodness of God.

Verses 3–14

Analysis

The apostle blesses God for the spiritual gifts bestowed on his people (verse 3). Of these the first in order and the source of all the others is election (verse 4). This election is; 1. Of individuals. 2. In Christ. 3. It is from eternity. 4. It is to holiness, and to the dignity of sons of God. 5. It is founded on the sovereign pleasure of God (verses 4–5). 6. Its final object is the glory of God, or the manifestation of his grace (verse 6).

The second blessing mentioned here is actual redemption through the blood of Christ; the free remission of sins according to the riches of his grace (verses 7–8).

The third blessing is the revelation of the divine purpose in relation to the system of redemption; which has for its object the reduction of all things to a harmonious whole under Jesus Christ (verses 9–10).

Through this Redeemer, the Jewish Christians, who had long looked for the Messiah, are made heirs of God, in accordance with the divine purpose (verses 11–12).

The Gentile converts are partakers of the same inheritance, because, having believed in Christ, they are assured of their redemption by the possession of the Holy Spirit, the pledge of the inheritance until its actual and complete enjoyment (verses 13–14).

Commentary

3. The Greek word used here, like its English equivalent, 'to bless,' signifies to praise, as when we bless God; to pray for blessings, as when we bless others; and to bestow blessings, as when God blesses us. 'Praise to the God who has blessed us' is then the expression of thanksgiving and praise to God on account of those special benefits which we receive from him through Christ.

In the heavenly places. The meaning is that these blessings pertain to that heavenly state into which the believer is introduced. Here on earth he is, as the apostle says in Ephesians 3:6, 'in the heavenly realms.' He is a citizen of heaven (Philippians 3:20). The word 'heaven,' in Scripture, is not confined to the place or state of future blessedness, but is sometimes nearly equivalent to 'kingdom of heaven.'

4. All these blessings have their source in the electing love of God. He blessed us – because he **chose us.** Election is the cause or source of all subsequent benefits.

If election is for holiness, as the apostle teachers here, it follows, first, that individuals, and not communities or nations, are the objects of election; secondly, that holiness cannot in any form be the ground of election. If men are chosen to be holy, they cannot be chosen because they are holy. And, thirdly, it follows that holiness is the only evidence of election. For one who lives in sin to claim to be elected for holiness is a contradiction.

5. The apostle says, God has chosen us for holiness, having predestinated us to sonship; that is, because he has thus predestinated us. Holiness, therefore, must be a necessary condition or prerequisite for the sonship here spoken of Sonship, in reference to God, includes:

1. Participation of his nature, or conformity to his image.

2. They enjoyment of his favour, or being the special objects of his love.

3. Heirship, or a participation of the glory and blessedness of God.

The ground of this predestination, and of the election founded on it, is expressed by the clause, **according to the good pleasure of his will.**

6. The final purpose of election is the glory of God. He has predestinated us to sonship, **to the praise of his glorious grace.** That is, in order that in the exaltation and blessedness of his people there might be abundant reason for celebrating his grace. It is worth noting that here, as in Ephesians 2:7, 1 Corinthians 1:27–29, and elsewhere, the specific purpose of redemption and of the way in which its blessings are dispensed, is declared to be the manifestation of the **grace** or unmerited favour of God. Nothing, therefore, can be more foreign to the nature of the Gospel than the doctrine of merit in any form. It is uncongenial with that great scheme of mercy whose principal purpose is to exhibit the grace of God.

7. In him we have redemption. In him, means not in ourselves. We are not self- redeemed. Christ is our Redeemer. The word 'redemption' sometimes means deliverance in the general, without reference to the way in which it is accomplished. When it refers to the work of Christ it is always to be understood in its strict sense, namely deliverance by ransom, because this particular way of redemption is always either expressed or implied. We are redeemed neither by power, nor truth, but by blood; that is, by the sacrificial death of the Lord Jesus. A sacrifice is a ransom, as to its effect. It delivers those for whom it is offered and accepted. The words

through his blood explain the words **in him. In him,** i.e., by means of his blood. They serve to explain the method by which Christ redeems.

The redemption which the apostle speaks about here is not the inner deliverance from sin, but it is an outer work, i.e., **the forgiveness of our trespasses.**

8. That he lavished on us. We are redeemed according to the riches of that grace which God has so freely exercised toward us.

9. God has caused this wisdom to abound, or has communicated it: **he has made known to us the mystery of his will,** in other words, by the revelation of the Gospel. The word **mystery** means a secret, something into which we must be initiated; something which we cannot discover ourselves and which can be known only as it is revealed. In this sense the Gospel is a mystery; and any fact or truth, however simple in itself, in the New Testament sense of the word, is a mystery, if it lies beyond the reach of our powers. Compare Romans 16:25; 1 Corinthians 2:7–10; Ephesians 3:9; Colossians 1:26. For the same reason, any doctrine imperfectly revealed is a mystery. It remains in a measure secret. Thus, in Ephesians 5:32, Paul calls the union of Christ and believers 'a great mystery'; and in 1 Timothy 3:16 he refers to the manifestation of God in the flesh, and writes, 'the mystery of religion is great.'

In the present case **the mystery of his will** means 'his secret purpose,' that purpose of redemption which was hidden for ages, but which he has now graciously revealed.

10. The general sense of this verse seems to be this. The purpose spoken of in the preceding verse had reference to the scheme of redemption, the design of which is to unite all the subjects of redemption, as one harmonious body, under Jesus Christ.

11. God having formed and revealed the purpose of gathering the redeemed as one body in Christ, it is in carrying out this purpose that, the apostle says, **in Christ we have also obtained an inheritance.** 'We,' in this clause, is not to be understood to refer either to the apostle individually, or believers indiscriminately, but **we** who first hoped in Christ; **we** as contrasted with 'you also' in verse 13; 'you' who were formerly Gentiles in the flesh (Ephesians 2:11). This clause, therefore, refers to the Jewish Christians.

According to his counsel and will means the purpose which has its origin in his will; neither suggested by others, nor determined by anything apart from him. It is therefore equivalent to his sovereign will.

12. So that we … might live for the praise of his glory, that is, that we should be the means of causing his divine majesty or excellence to be praised. Here, as in verse 6, the glory of God is declared to be the purpose of the plan of redemption, and of everything connected with its outworking. The people spoken about here are described as **the first to set our hope on Christ**. That is, who hoped in him of old, or before his coming; or, who hoped in him before others, mentioned in verse 13, had heard of him. In either case it designates not the first converts to Christianity, but the Jews who, before the Gentiles, had the Messiah as the object of their hopes. The expression **hope** used here does not mean simply 'to expect,' but to place one's hope or confidence in anyone. Compare 1 Corinthians 15:19. It is not, therefore, the Jews as such, but the believing Jews, who are spoken of here as those who are in Christ, the partakers of the inheritance which he has purchased.

13. The apostle having, in verse 10, declared that God's purpose is to bring all the subjects of redemption into one harmonious body, says in verse 11 that this purpose is realised in the conversion of the Jewish Christians; and here he adds that another group of people, namely the Gentile Christians, to whom his letter is specially addressed, are included in the same purpose.

Had believed in him, were marked with the seal of the promised Holy Spirit. This is more than a translation – it is an exposition of the original. In Christ, the Gentile Christians had obtained an inheritance, and in him, also, they were sealed, after having believed. Whatever is meant by sealing, it is something which follows faith.

There are several uses for a seal:

1. To authenticate or confirm as genuine and true.

2. To mark as one's property.

3. To make secure.

In all these senses believers are sealed. They are authenticated as the true children of God; they have the witness within themselves (1 John 5:10; Romans 8:16 and 5:5). They are thus assured of their reconciliation and acceptance. They are, moreover, marked as belonging to God (Revelation 7:3); that is, they show other people, by the seal impressed on them, that they are God's chosen ones. And, thirdly, they are sealed for salvation; i.e., they are certain of being saved. The sealing of God secures their safety. Thus believers were 'marked with a seal for the day of redemption' (Ephesians 4:30). See 2 Corinthians 1:21–22. So the sealing which this passage speaks about answers all these ends. It assures us of God's favour; it indicates who belong to him; and it makes their salvation certain.

The promised Holy Spirit; that is, by the Spirit who was promised, or who comes in virtue of the promise. This promise was given frequently through the ancient prophets, who predicted that when the Messiah came, and in

virtue of his mediation, God would pour his Spirit on all flesh. When on earth, Christ frequently repeated this promise, assuring his disciples that when he had gone to the Father, he would send them the Comforter, the Spirit of truth, to stay with them forever. After his resurrection he commanded the apostles to stay in Jerusalem until they had received 'the promise my Father promised' (Acts 1:4), meaning the gift of the Holy Spirit. Galatians 3:14 says it is the reason why Christ redeemed us from the curse of the law, that we should receive the promise of the Spirit. This, then, is the great gift which Christ secures for his people – the indwelling of the Holy Spirit, as the source of truth, holiness, consolation, and eternal life.

14. This Spirit is **the pledge of our inheritance**. It is both the foretaste and the pledge of all that is laid up for the believer in heaven. The word **pledge** is a Hebrew term, which passed into the Greek and then into the Latin vocabulary, retaining its original sense. It means, first, a part of the price of anything purchased, paid as a security for the full payment, and then more generally a pledge. Three times it refers to the Holy Spirit in the New Testament, in 2 Corinthians 1:22 and 5:5, and in the passage before us. In the same sense the Scriptures speak of 'the first fruits of the Spirit' (Romans 8:23). Those influences of the Spirit which believers now enjoy are both a foretaste of future blessedness, the same in kind though immeasurably less in degree, and a pledge of the certain enjoyment of that blessedness; just as the first fruits were a part of the harvest, and a guarantee of its ingathering. It is because the Spirit is a guarantee of our **inheritance** that his indwelling is a seal. It assures those in whom he dwells of their salvation, and renders that salvation certain. Hence it is a most precious gift, to be most religiously cherished.

Verses 15–23

Analysis

Having, in the preceding section, unfolded the nature of those blessings which the Ephesians had shared, the apostle gives thanks to God for their conversion, and assures them of his prayers (verses 15–16). He prays that God will give them that wisdom and knowledge of himself of which the Spirit is the author (verse 17); that their eyes might be enlightened properly to understand the nature and value of that hope which is founded in the call of God, and the glory of the inheritance to be enjoyed among the saints (verse 18); and the greatness of that power which had already been exercised in their conversion (verse 19). The power which effected their spiritual resurrection was the same as that which raised Christ from the dead, and exalted him above all created beings and associated him in the glory and dominion of God (verses 20–21). To him all things are made subject, and he is constituted the supreme head of the church, which is his body, the fullness or complement of the mystical person of him who fills the universe with his presence and power (verses 22–23).

Commentary

15. Your love towards all the saints, i.e., for those who are saints – those who have been cleansed, separated from the world, and consecrated to God. This love is founded on the character of its objects as the people of God, and therefore it embraces **all** the saints.

16. I do not cease to give thanks for you as I remember. … This does not mean, 'praying I give thanks,' but two things are mentioned: constant thanksgiving on their account, and intercession.

17. The burden of his prayer is contained in this and the following verses. The object of his prayer, or the person to whom it is addressed, is designated, first, as **the God of our Lord Jesus Christ,** i.e., the God whose work Christ came to do, by whom he was sent, of whom he testified, and to whom he has gone; and, secondly, **the Father of glory.**

18. With the eyes of your heart enlightened. The word 'heart' in Scripture is often used as we use the word 'soul,' to designate the whole spiritual nature in people. Romans 1:21; 2 Corinthians 4:6.

You may know what is the hope to which he has called you, i.e., the hope of which his calling is the source, or to which he has **called** you. The vocation spoken of here is not merely the external call of the Gospel, but the effectual call of God by the Spirit, to which the word 'calling' in the letters of Paul always refers. It is a great thing to know, or estimate aright, the value of a well-founded hope of salvation.

The riches of his glorious inheritance, i.e., what is the abundance and greatness of the excellence of that **inheritance** of which God is the author. The apostle labours here, and still more in the following verses, for language to express the greatness of his conceptions. This **inheritance** is not only divine, as it has God as its author; but it is a **glorious inheritance**; and not simply **glorious,** but the glory of it is inconceivably great.

19. And what is the immeasurable greatness of his power for us who believe. This is the third petition in the apostle's prayer. He prays that his readers may have right apprehensions of the greatness of the change which they had experienced. It was no mere moral reformation effected by rational considerations; nor was it a self-wrought change, but one due to the almighty power of God.

The prayer recorded in these verses is a very comprehensive one. In praying that the Ephesians might be enlightened with spiritual understanding of the truth, the apostle prays for their sanctification. In praying that they might have just conceptions of the inheritance to which they were called, he prayed that they might be elevated above the world. And in praying that they might know the exceeding greatness of the power exercised in their conversion he prayed that they might be at once humble and confident – humble, in view of the death of sin from which they had been raised; and confident, in view of the omnipotence of that God who had begun their salvation.

20. This power to work in Christ when he raised him from the dead. There are two things clearly intended in these words:

1. That the **power** which raises the believer from spiritual death is the same as that which **raised** Christ from the grave.

2. That there is a striking analogy between these events and an intimate connection between them. The one was not only the symbol, but the pledge and agency for the other. The resurrections of Christ is both the type and the cause of the spiritual resurrection of his people, as well of their future rising from the grave in his glorious likeness. The apostle speaks at length about this analogy and connection in Romans 6:1–10, and also in the following chapters of this letter. Therefore, as often as the believer contemplates Christ as risen and seated at the right hand of God, he has at once an illustration of the change which has been effected in his own spiritual state, and a pledge that the work commenced in regeneration will be consummated in glory.

And seated him at his right hand in the heavenly places. Kings place at their right hand those whom they wish to honour, or whom they associate with themselves in regal authority. No creature can be thus associated in honour and authority with God, and therefore to none of the angels has he ever said, 'Sit at my right hand' (Hebrews 1:13). That divine honour and authority are expressed by sitting at the right hand of God, is further seen from those passages which speak of the extent of that dominion and of the nature of that honour to which the exalted Redeemer is entitled. It is a universal dominion, Matthew 28:18; Philippians 2:9; 1 Peter 3:22; and it is an honour that is due to God alone, John 5:23.

The immediate subject under discussion in this chapter is the blessings of redemption conferred on believers. The resurrection and exaltation of Christ are introduced incidentally, by way of illustration. The apostle dwells for a moment on the nature of this exaltation, and on the relation of Christ, at the right hand of God, to his church; and then, at the beginning of the following chapter, reverts to his main topic.

21. To illustrate the exaltation of Christ mentioned in verse 20, the apostle says here that he is seated **far above all rule and authority and power and dominion**. That these terms refer to angels is plain from the context, and from such passages as Romans 8:38, Colossians 1:16, and Ephesians 3:10 and 6:12, where angels are either specifically mentioned, or they are opposed to 'flesh and blood,' i.e. mankind, as a different order of beings.

22. **And he placed all things under his feet.** Christ is not only exalted above all creatures, but he has dominion over them; all are placed in absolute subjection to him. They are under his feet. This passage is a quotation from Psalm 8:6. It is applied to Christ by this same apostle in 1 Corinthians 15:27 and Hebrews 2:8. In both of these passages the word 'all' is pressed to the full extent of its meaning. It is made to include all creatures, all capable of subjection; all beings except God alone are made subject to man in the person of Jesus Christ, the Lord of lords, and King of kings.

The sense in which Christ is the **head of the church** is, that he is the source of its life, its supreme ruler, ever present with it, sympathizing with it, and loving it as a man loves his own flesh. See Ephesians 4:15–16 and 5:23, 29; Romans 12:5; 1 Corinthians 12:27. Intimate union, dependence, and community of life, are the main ideas expressed by this metaphor.

23. **Which is his body.** This is the radical or formative idea of the church. It is the indwelling of the Spirit of Christ that constitutes the church **his body**. And, therefore, only those in whom the Spirit dwells are constituent members of the true church.

Chapter 2

Verses 1–10: The apostle contrasts the spiritual state of the Ephesians before their conversion with that into which they had been introduced by the grace of God.

Verses 11–22: He contrasts their previous condition as foreigners with that of fellow-citizens of the saints and members of the family of God.

Verses 1–10

Analysis

There are three principal topics treated in this section: First, the spiritual state of the Ephesians before their conversion. Second, the change which God had made in them. Third, the purpose for which that change had been made.

1. The state of the Ephesians before their conversion, and the natural state of mankind universally, is spiritual death, which includes (a) a state of sin; (b) a state of subjection to Satan and to our own corrupt affections; (c) a state of condemnation. (Verses 1–3.)

2. The change which they had experienced was a spiritual resurrection, concerning which the apostle teaches (a) that God is its author; (b) that it is a work of love and grace; (c) that it was through Christ, or in virtue of union with him; (d) that it involves great exaltation, even an association with Christ in his glory. (Verses 4–6.)

3. The purpose of this dispensation is to reveal God's grace through all coming ages. It reveals grace (a) because salvation, in general, is of grace; (b) because the fact that the Ephesian Christians believed or accepted this salvation was due not to themselves but to God – faith is his gift; (c) because good works are the fruits not of nature but of grace – we are created for good works. (Verses 7–10.)

Commentary

1. **You were dead through the trespasses and sins.** There is an intimate connection between this clause and the preceding paragraph. In Ephesians 1:19 the apostle prays that the Ephesians might duly appreciate the greatness of the power which had been exercised in their conversion. It was to be known from its effects. It was that power which was exercised in the resurrection and exaltation of Christ, and which had brought about an analogous change in them. The same power which brought Christ to life has brought you to life.

2. **In which you once lived.** Their former condition was briefly described in verse 1 as a state of spiritual death. In this and the following verses it is described in more detail. They walked in sin. They were daily conversant with it, and devoted to it. They were surrounded by it, and clothed with it. They lived according to the **course of this world**. In this clause is stated not only the character of their life, but the governing principle which controlled their conduct. They lived according to, and under the control of, the spirit of the world.

3. **We were by nature children of wrath.** The expression **children of wrath** agrees with the Hebrew 'sons of' idiom meaning those to be punished. This wrath is God's displeasure and, of course, the idea of ill-desert is necessarily implied.

4. Thus the apostle has described people's natural state; and in this and the following verses he unfolds the manner in which those to whom he wrote had been delivered from that dreadful condition. It was by a spiritual resurrection. God, and not themselves, was the

author of the change. It was not to be referred to any goodness in them, but to the abounding love of God. The objects of this love were not Jews, as opposed to Gentiles, nor the Gentiles as such, nor people in general, but *us*, i.e., Christians, the actual subjects of the life-giving power spoken of here. All this is included in this verse.

But God, i.e., notwithstanding our guilt and corruption, God, **who is rich in mercy,** 'because he is rich in mercy.' **Mercy** is 'the desire to succour the miserable.' **Love** is more than either pity or **mercy.** It was not merely **mercy,** which has all the miserable for its object; but **love,** which has definite individual people for its objects, which constrained this intervention of God for our salvation.

5. Made us alive together with Christ. The Greek word translated 'to make alive' means 'to impart life.' In the New Testament it almost always refers to the giving of the life of which Christ is the author.

6. And raised us up with him and seated us with him in the heavenly places in Christ Jesus. This is an amplification of what precedes. In its broadest sense the life, which in verse 5 is said to be given to us, includes the exaltation expressed in this verse. It is, therefore, only by way of amplification that the apostle, after saying we are made sharers of the life of Christ, adds that we are **raised ... up** and enthroned with him in heaven.

7. Why has God done all this? Why from eternity has he chosen us to be holy before him in love? Why has he made us accepted in the beloved? Why, when dead in trespasses and sins, has he made us alive, raised us up, and made us to sit together in heavenly realms with Christ? The answer to these questions is given in this verse. It was **so that in the ages to come he might show the immeasurable riches of his grace in kindness towards us in Christ Jesus.** The revelation of the **grace** of God, i.e., of his unmerited love, is declared to be the specific object of redemption. From this it follows that whatever clouds the grace of God, or clashes with the free nature of the blessings promised in the Gospel, must be inconsistent with its nature and purpose. If the salvation of sinners is intended as an exhibition of the grace of God, it has to be free.

8–9. These verses confirm the preceding declaration. The manifestation of the **grace** of God is the great end of redemption. This is plain, for salvation is entirely of grace. **For by grace you have been saved through faith, and this is not your own doing; it is the gift of God** (verse 8). So here we have a manifold assertion, affirmative and negative, of the free nature of salvation. It is not only said in general, 'You are saved by grace,' but further, that salvation is by **faith,** i.e.,

by simply receiving or apprehending the offered blessing. From the very nature of **faith,** as an act of assent and trust, it excludes the idea of merit. If it is by **faith,** it is of **grace;** if it is by works, it is earned by him; as the apostle argues in Romans 4:4–5. **Faith,** therefore, is the mere act of accepting, and not the ground on which salvation is bestowed.

Not the result of works (verse 9). The apostle says **works,** without qualification or limitation. It is not, therefore, ceremonial, as distinguished from good **works;** or legal, as distinguished from evangelical or gracious **works;** but **works** of all kinds, as distinguished from faith, which are excluded. Salvation is in no sense, and in no degree, of works; for the person who attains the reward has earned it. But salvation is of **grace,** and therefore not of **works,** lest any man should **boast.**

10. That salvation is thus entirely the work of God, and that good **works** cannot be the ground of our acceptance with him, is proved in this verse 1. By showing that we are God's workmanship – he, not we, has made us what we are. And 2. By the consideration that we are created for **good works.** As the fact that men are elected for holiness proves that holiness is not the ground of their election, so their being created for **good works** shows that **good works** are not the ground on which they are made the subjects of this new creation, which is itself incipient salvation.

The apostle has clearly taught in this paragraph that the natural state of man is one of condemnation and spiritual death; that from that condition believers are delivered by the grace of God in Christ Jesus; and the purpose of this deliverance is the manifestation, through all coming ages, of the exceeding riches of his grace.

Verses 11–22

Analysis
In the preceding paragraph the apostle set out:
1. The moral and spiritual condition of the Ephesians by nature.
2. The spiritual renovation and exaltation which they had experienced.
3. God's purpose in this dispensation.

In this paragraph he exhibits the corresponding change in their relationships. In doing this he sets out:
1. Their former relationship (verses 11–12).
(a) to the church: they were foreigners and aliens;
(b) to God: they were far off, without any saving knowledge of him, or interest in his promises.
2. The means by which this alienation from God and the church had been removed, namely, by the blood of Christ (verses 13–18). His death had a double effect:

(a) By satisfying the demands of justice, it secured reconciliation with God.

(b) By abolishing the law in the form of the Mosaic institutions, it removed the wall of partition between the Jews and Gentiles.

A double reconciliation was thus accomplished: the Jews and Gentiles are united in one body, and both are reconciled to God.

3. As a result of this double reconciliation, the Ephesians were intimately united with God and his people (verses 19–22). This idea is set out in three ways:

(a) They are represented as fellow-citizens of the saints.

(b) They are members of the family of God.

(c) They are constituent parts of that temple in which God dwells by his Spirit.

The idea of the church, which underlies this paragraph, is presented everywhere in the New Testament. The church is the body of Christ. It consists of those in whom he dwells by his Spirit. To be alien from the church, therefore, is to be an alien from God. It is to be without Christ and without hope. The church about which this is said is not the nominal, external, visible church as such, but the true people of God. As, however, the Scriptures always speak of people according to what they profess, calling those who profess faith 'believers' and those who confess Christ 'Christians,' so they speak of the visible church as the true church, and predicate of the former what is true only of the latter. The Gentiles while they were aliens were without Christ, without God, and without hope; when amalgamated with the church, they are lived in by God through the Spirit. Many of them were really like this, all of them professed to be like this, and they are therefore addressed in this way. But union with the visible church no more made them real partakers of the Spirit of Christ, than the profession of faith made them living believers.

Commentary

11. **So then, remember** – i.e., since God has done such great things for you, call to mind your former condition, as a motive both for humility and for gratitude. **That at one time you Gentiles by birth**, i.e., uncircumcised heathen. This gives, in a word, the description of their former state. All that follows, in this and the next verse, is merely an amplification of this idea. The context shows that the words **by birth** refer to circumcision, which is a sign in the flesh.

12. The sentence begun in verse 11 is resumed here: **Remember that you were at that time without Christ.** This means more than that they were, as heathen, destitute of the knowledge and expectation of the Messiah. As Christ is the only Redeemer of men, and the only

Mediator between God and man, to be without Christ was to be without redemption, and without access to God. To possess Christ, to be in him, is the sum of all blessedness; to be without Christ includes all evil.

13. **But now in Christ Jesus** – in virtue of union with Christ, **you who were once far off have been brought near.** As under the old dispensation God lived in the temple, those living near his dwelling place and having access to him were his people. Israel was near; the Gentiles were far away. They lived at a distance, and had no freedom of access to the place where God revealed his presence. Hence in the prophets, as in Isaiah 49:1 and 57:19, those who are near means the Jews, and those who are far away are the Gentiles. This expression came over to the New Testament writers: Acts 2:39, 'The promise is for you, for you children, and for all who are far away'; Ephesians 2:17, 'proclaimed peace to you who were far off and peace to those who were near.' Among the later Jews the act of receiving a proselyte was called 'making him near.' Being far from God included both separation from his people and spiritual distance or alienation from God himself; so to be **brought near** includes both introduction into the church and reconciliation with God.

14–15. These verses contain a confirmation and illustration of what precedes: 'You who once were far off have been brought near by the blood of Christ' (verse 13). **For he is our peace; in his flesh he has made both groups into one and has broken down the dividing wall ...** This he has accomplished by abolishing the law.

The breaking down of **the dividing wall** which the apostle speaks of, does not consist in setting the law aside, or suspending it by a sovereign, executive act. It is no longer active or binding. Its demands have been satisfied, so that we are judicially free from it; free not by the act of a sovereign, but by the sentence of a judge – not by mere pardon, but by justification. Who is he that condemns, when God justifies? (See Romans 8:34.)

16. The second part of Christ's purpose is expressed in this verse. It was that he **might reconcile** the two, united in **one body**, to God, by means of **the cross**, having thereby slain the enmity. The goal achieved was reconciliation with God; the subjects of this reconciliation are the church, the **one body** into which Jews and Gentiles are merged (they are member together of **one body**, Ephesians 4:4); the means of this reconciliation is **the cross**, because the crucifixion of our Lord removes the enmity which prevented the reconciliation spoken about here. **And might reconcile** is to effect peace and union between parties previously at variance.

17. **So he came and proclaimed peace to you who were far off and peace to those who were**

near. The preaching is the annunciation of the favour of God made by Christ, either in person, or through his apostles and his Spirit. Christ announced that peace with God had by the cross been secured for those who were far off, the Gentiles, as well as for the Jews, or those who were near.

18. The proof that peace has thus been obtained for both is that both have the same free **access** to God. If his wrath had not been removed (Romans 5:10) – the hostility put to death – we could never have had access to God just as the Jews do, on the same terms and in the same way. It follows that the peace procured by the death of Christ was designed for the one group of people as well as for the other.

Access is not mere liberty of approach; it is 'introduction.' Christ did not die simply to open the way of access to God, but actually to introduce us into his presence and favour.

19. The consequences of this reconciliation are that the Gentiles are now **citizens with the saints and also members of the household of God**, and part of that temple in which God dwells by his Spirit. Previously, they were **strangers and aliens**; now they are **citizens**. Previously the Gentiles stood in the same relation to the theocracy or commonwealth of Israel that we do to a foreign state. They had no share in its privileges, no participation in its blessings. Now they are **citizens with the saints**. The word **saints** does not refer to the Jews, nor the ancient patriarchs, but to the people of God. Christians have become, under the new dispensation, what the Jews once were, namely **saints**, people selected and separated from the world, and consecrated to God as his special people. They now constitute the theocracy, which is no longer confined to any one people or country, but embraces everyone in every country who has access to God by Christ Jesus.

In this spiritual kingdom the Gentiles now have the right of citizenship. They are on terms of perfect equality with all other members of that kingdom. And that kingdom is the kingdom of heaven. The same terms of admission are required, and neither more nor less, for membership in that kingdom, and for admission into heaven; all who enter the one enter the other; one leads to the other; we are now, says Paul, the citizens of heaven. It is not therefore to the participation of the privileges of the old, external, visible theocracy, nor simply to the pale of the visible Christian church, that the apostle here welcomes his Gentile brothers, but to the spiritual Israel, the communion of **saints**; to citizenship in that kingdom of which Christ is king, and membership in that body of which he is the head.

20. As the Greek word for a family and a house is the same, the apostle passes from one figure to the other. The Gentiles are members of the family of God, and they are parts of his house. They are **built upon the foundation of the apostles and prophets, with Christ Jesus himself as the cornerstone.**

21. Christ being the cornerstone, everything depends on union with him. Therefore the apostle adds, **In him the whole structure is joined together and grows into a holy temple in the Lord.** Christ is the principle both of support and of growth. He not only sustains the building, but carries it on to its consummation.

Into a holy temple – i.e., increasing so as to become **a holy temple.** A temple is a building in which God lives. Such a temple is holy, as sacred to him. It belongs to him, is consecrated to his use, and can neither be appropriated by anyone else nor used for anything except his service, without causing it to be profaned. This is true of the church as a whole, and of all its constituent members. The money-changers of the world cannot, with impunity, make the church a place of commerce, or use it in any way to answer their sordid or secular ends. The church does not belong to the state, and cannot lawfully be controlled by it. It is sacred, set apart for God. It is his house, in which he alone has any authority.

22. What was said about the whole body of believers is here affirmed of the Ephesian Christians: **In whom you also are built together spiritually into a dwelling-place for God.**

Chapter 3

Verses 1–13: The nature and purpose of Paul's commission.

Verses 14–21: His prayer for the Ephesians.

Verses 1–13

Analysis
The office which Paul had received was that of an apostle to the Gentiles (verses 1–2). For this office he was qualified by direct revelation from Jesus Christ, concerning the purpose of redemption – the preceding parts of the letter were sufficient evidence of this knowledge of his (verses 3–4). The special truth, now revealed more plainly than ever before, was the union of the Gentiles with the Jews as joint partakers of the promise of redemption, by means of the Gospel (verses 5–6). As the Gospel is the means of bringing the Gentiles to this fellowship with the saints, Paul was, by the special grace and almighty power of God, converted and made a minister of the Gospel (verses 7–8). The object of his ministry was to make known the unsearchable riches of Christ, and enlighten people about the purpose of redemption which had from eternity been hidden in the divine

mind (verse 9). And the object of redemption itself is the manifestation of God's wisdom to principalities and power in heaven (verse 10). This glorious purpose has been executed in Christ, in whom we, as redeemed, have free access to God. Afflictions endured in such a cause were no ground of depression, but rather of glory (verses 11–13).

Commentary

1. **This is the reason,** – because you Gentiles are fellow citizens with God's people, and especially because you Ephesians are included in the temple of God.

The expression **a prisoner for Christ** does not mean 'prisoner on account of Christ.' Those for whom he suffered chains are immediately said to be the Gentiles. It means Christ's prisoner. As he was Christ's servant, apostle, and minister, so he was Christ's prisoner **for the sake of you Gentiles.** It was preaching the Gospel to the Gentiles which brought down on him the hatred of his countrymen, and led them to accuse him before the Roman magistrates, and to him being sent as a prisoner to Rome.

2. The expression **the commission of God's grace that was given to me** is the designation of his office. It was a stewardship. A stewardship of the grace given means either a stewardship which is a grace or favour, or which flows from grace – i.e., was graciously conferred. Compare verse 8, in which he says, 'this grace was given to me.' Not infrequently the office itself is called a grace or favour: Romans 12:3 and 15:15; 1 Corinthians 3:10; Galatians 2:9. Paul esteemed the office of a messenger of Christ as a manifestation of the undeserved kindness of God towards him, and he always speaks of it with gratitude and humility. It was not its honours, nor its authority, which gave it value in his eyes; but the privilege which it involved of preaching the unsearchable riches of Christ.

3. **The mystery was made known to me by revelation** – i.e., a secret, something which cannot be discovered by human reason, which could only be attained by **revelation.** This **revelation** was a grace or favour conferred on the apostle himself.

4. **By reading** what he had written they could judge about his knowledge **of the mystery of Christ.** What he had written might be taken as the standard or evidence of his knowledge.

5. Through revelation, God had made known to Paul a **mystery,** or purpose, which was not **revealed** as it now was to the apostles. That the Gentiles were to partake of the blessings of the Messiah's reign, and to be united as one body with the Jews in his kingdom, is not only frequently predicted by the ancient prophets, but Paul himself repeatedly and at length quotes their declarations on this point, to prove that

what he taught was in accordance with the Old Testament; see Romans 9:25–33. The emphasis must therefore be placed on the word **as.** This doctrine was not formerly revealed **as,** i.e. not so fully or so clearly as under the Gospel.

As it has now been revealed to his holy apostles and prophets by the Spirit. The **apostles and prophets** of the new dispensation were the only types of inspired men; the former being the permanent, the latter the occasional organs of the Spirit. Therefore they were the only recipients of direct revelations. They are called **holy** here in the sense of 'sacred,' 'consecrated.' They were men set apart for God's special service. In the same sense the prophets of the old economy are called holy (Luke 1:70).

By the Spirit – i.e., revealed by the Spirit. **Spirit,** though without the article, refers to the Holy Spirit, the immediate author of these divine communications. It follows from the scriptural doctrine of the Trinity, which teaches the identity about the substance of the Father, Son, and Spirit, that the action of the one is the action of the others. Paul therefore refers the revelations which he received sometimes to God, as in verse 3; sometimes to Christ, as in Galatians 1:12; sometimes to the Spirit.

6. The mystery made known to the apostles and prophets of the new dispensation was that **the Gentiles** are to be heirs together, that the Gentiles *are,* in fact, **fellow-heirs of the same body, and sharers in the promise.** The way in which the calling of the Gentiles was predicted in the Old Testament led to the general impression that they were to take part in the blessings of the Messiah's reign by becoming Jews, by becoming proselytes merged into the old theocracy, which was to remain in all its peculiarities. It seems never to have occurred to anyone until the day of Pentecost that the theocracy itself would be abolished, and a new form of religion introduced, designed and adapted equally for all mankind, under which the distinction between Jew and Gentile was to be done away. It was this catholicity of the Gospel which was the expanding and elevating revelation made to the apostles, and which raised them from sectarians to Christians.

7. **I became a servant.** A servant, 'a runner,' 'minister.' A minister of the Gospel, meaning one whose business it is to preach the Gospel. This is his service, the work for which he is engaged, and to which he is bound to devote himself. There are two things which Paul here and in the following verse says about his introduction into the ministry: first, it was a great favour, and secondly, it involved the exercise of divine power.

8. **Although,** adds the apostle, **I am the very least of all the saints,** this grace was given to me to bring to the Gentiles the news of the boundless riches of Christ.

By the words **all the saints** we should understand, not the apostles, but the people of God, who are 'called to be saints' (1 Corinthians 1:2; Romans 1:7). **The very least of all** is a comparative formed from a superlative. It was not merely the sense of his sinfulness in general which weighed so heavily on the apostle's conscience; it was the sin of persecuting Christ, which he could never forgive himself.

The **boundless riches of Christ** are the fullness of the Godhead, the plenitude of all divine glories and perfections which dwell in him; the fullness of grace to pardon, to sanctify and save; everything, in short, which makes him satisfy the soul.

9. The words translated **to make everyone see** really means 'to shine,' as any luminous body does, and then 'to illuminate,' to impart light to, as a candle does to those on whom it shines, and as God does to people's minds, and as the Gospel does, which is like a light shining in a dark place, and hence the apostle in 2 Corinthians 4:4 speaks of the 'light of the gospel.' The church is compared to a candlestick, and ministers to stars. Their office is to dispense light. The light imparted by the Gospel was knowledge, and hence to illuminate is in fact to teach; which is the idea the word is intended to express here.

10. **The wisdom of God in its rich variety** refers to the various aspects under which the wisdom of God is displayed in redemption; in reconciling justice and mercy; in exalting the unworthy, while it effectually humbles them; in the person of the Redeemer, in his work; in the works of the Holy Spirit; in the varied dispensations of the old and new economy; and in the whole conduct of the work of mercy, and in its glorious consummation.

11. This exhibition of God's manifold wisdom was contemplated in the original conception of the plan of redemption; for the apostle adds that it was in **accordance with the eternal purpose that he has carried out in Christ Jesus our Lord.** The purpose of God to make provision for the redemption of mankind has been fulfilled in the incarnation and death of his Son.

12. Hence, as the consequence of this accomplished work, **we have access to God in boldness and confidence,** i.e., free and unrestricted access to God, as children to a father. We come with the assurance of being accepted, because our **confidence** does not rest on our own merit, but on the infinite merit of an infinite Saviour. It is **in him** we have this liberty. **We** have this free **access to God** – we believers; not any particular group, a priesthood among Christians to whom alone access is permitted, but all believers, without any priestly intervention other than that of one great High Priest who has passed through the heavens – Jesus, the Son of God. The word

confidence, as used in Scripture, is not 'frankness,' but 'fearlessness,' freedom from apprehension of rejection or of evil. This is what Christ has procured for us. Even the vilest may, in Christ, approach the Infinitely Holy, who is a consuming fire, with fearlessness. Nothing short of an infinite Saviour could effect such a redemption. The accumulation of substantives in this sentence – **boldness, confidence** – shows that there was no word which could express what Paul felt in view of the complete reconciliation of men to God through Jesus Christ.

13. **Therefore,** i.e., because we have this access to God, the sum of all good, we ought to be superior to all the afflictions of this life, and always maintain a joyful spirit. Being the subjects of such a redemption, and having this liberty of access to God, believers ought not to be discouraged by all the apparently adverse circumstances which come with the propagation of the Gospel.

Verses 14–21

Analysis

The apostle's prayer is addressed to the Father of our Lord Jesus Christ, who is also in him our Father. He offers only one petition, namely, that his readers might be strengthened by the Holy Spirit in the inner being; or that Christ might dwell in their hearts by faith. The consequence of this would be that they would be confirmed in love, and thus enabled, in some measure, to understand the infinite love of Christ, which would enlarge their capacity to the fullness of God; that is, ultimately render them, in their measure, as full of holiness and blessedness as God is in his.

Commentary

14. This verse follows on from verse 1. The prayer which the apostle commenced there he here begins afresh. **For this reason** is repeated from verse 1, and therefore the connection is the same here as there, i.e., 'Because you Ephesians are made partakers of the redemption purchased by Christ.'

I bow my knees. The posture of prayer, kneeling, means prayer itself.

15. **From whom every family in heaven and on earth takes its name.** The word **family** is a collective term for the descendants of the same father, immediate or remote. In Luke 2:4, we read of the house and family of David, and in Acts 3:25, of all the families of the earth.

16. This verse contains the apostle's prayer on behalf of the Ephesians. He prays that God, according to the riches of his glory, would strengthen them with might **through his Spirit** in the **inner being.**

The riches of his glory means the fullness of divine perfection. It is not his **power** to the exclusion of his mercy, nor his mercy to the exclusion of his **power**, but it is everything in God that makes him glorious, the proper object of adoration. The apostle prays that God would deal with his people according to that fullness of grace and **power** which constitutes his glory, and makes him the source of all good to his creatures.

17. That Christ may dwell in your hearts through faith. Christ dwells in his people; he dwells in their **hearts**; he dwells in them **through faith.** These are the truths contained in this passage.

18–19. The **love** in which we are to be rooted is not the love of God or of Christ for us, but either brotherly love or love as a Christian grace, without determining its object. It is that love which flows from faith, and which both God and the brothers are objects of. The apostle here prays for the increase and ascendancy of this grace through the indwelling of Christ, till it sustains and strengthens the whole inner being, so that the believer may stand like a firmly planted tree or like a building with firm foundations.

20–21. Paul's prayer had apparently reached a height beyond which neither faith, nor hope, nor even imagination could go, and yet he is not satisfied. Much still lay in the future. God was able to do not only what he had asked, but infinitely more than he knew how either to ask or think. Having exhausted all the forms of prayer, he casts himself on God's infinitude, in full confidence that he can and will do all that omnipotence itself can effect. His **power**, not our prayers nor our highest conceptions, is the measure of the apostle's anticipations and desires. This idea he weaves into a doxology, which has in it more of heaven than of earth.

Paul says, **now to him who by the power at work within us is able to accomplish abundantly far more than all we can ask or imagine.** God is not only unlimited in himself, but is unrestricted by our prayers or knowledge. No definite bounds, therefore, can be set on what people may expect in whom Christ dwells, and who are the objects of his infinite love.

Chapter 4:1–Chapter 5:2

Verses 1–16: An exhortation to unity.

Verses 17–32: An exhortation to holiness and to specific virtues.

Verses 1–16

Analysis
The apostle exhorts his readers to walk in a way that is worthy of their vocation. Such a walk should be characterized by humility, meekness,

longsuffering, and zeal, to promote spiritual unity and peace (verses 1–3.) The church is one, because it is one body, has one Spirit, one hope, one Lord, one faith, one baptism, and one God and Father, who is over, through, and in all its members (verses 4–6).

This unity, however, is consistent with great diversity of gifts, which Christ distributes according to his own will (verse 7). This is confirmed by a passage from the Psalms, which speaks of the Messiah giving gifts to men. This passage must refer to Christ, since it speaks of a divine person ascending to heaven, which necessarily implies a previous descent to the earth (verses 8–10). The gifts which Christ bestows on his church are the various categories of ministers, apostles, prophets, evangelists, and pastors, who are teachers (verse 11). The purpose of the ministry is the building up of the church, and to bring all its members to unity of faith and knowledge, and to the full stature of Christ; that they should no longer have the instability of children, but be a firm, compact, and growing body in living union with Christ its head (verses 12–16).

Commentary
1–3. I Therefore, the prisoner in the Lord, beg you. ... The exhortation is a general one; it flows from the preceding doctrines, and is enforced by the authority and the sufferings of the person who gave it. As you are partakers of the redemption bought by Christ, **I beg you.** 'I the prisoner, not of, but 'for' the Lord,' literally 'in' the Lord. He was a prisoner because he was in the Lord. It was as a Christian, and in the cause of Christ, that he suffered imprisonment.

The exhortation is, **to lead a life worthy of the calling to which you have been called.** That calling was to sonship (Ephesians 1:5). This includes three things: holiness, exaltation, and unity. They were called to be conformed to the image of Christ, to share in his exaltation and glory, and to constitute one family, since they are all God's children. A life fitting for such a **calling**, therefore, should be characterized by holiness, humility, and mutual forbearance and brotherly love. The apostle, therefore, immediately adds, **with all humility and gentleness.** Undeserved honour always produces these effects on the ingenuous.

Gentleness is 'softness,' 'mildness,' which, when united with strength, is one of the loveliest attributes of our nature. The blessed Saviour says of himself, 'I am gentle and humble in heart' (Matthew 11:29); and the apostle speaks of 'the meekness and gentleness of Christ' (2 Corinthians 10:1).

The third virtue which is becoming for this calling is **patience. Patience** leads to anger being suppressed (2 Corinthians 6:6; Galatians 5:22;

Colossians 3:12). **Patience** defers the infliction of punishment, and is therefore often attributed to God (Romans 2:4; 9:22; 1 Peter 3:20). **Patience** refers to forbearance towards our fellow human beings (2 Timothy 4:2; 1 Timothy 1:16). It is explained by what follows: **bearing with one another in love.** Or, rather, the three virtues, humility, gentleness, and patience are all illustrated and shown in this mutual forbearance.

4–5. Having urged the duty of preserving unity, the apostle proceeds to state both its nature and grounds. It is a unity which arises from the fact that there is and can be but **one body and one Spirit, … one hope, … one Lord, one faith, one baptism, one God.**

6. One God and Father of all, who is above all and through all and in all. As the church is one because it is pervaded by one Spirit, and because it is owned and governed by one Lord, so it is one because it has **one God and Father,** one glorious Being with whom it sustains the double relationship of creature and child. This God is not merely **above** us, from a distance, but **through all and in all,** i.e. pervading and filling all with his sustaining and life-giving presence. There are many passages where the doctrine of the Trinity gives a sacred rhythm, though the doctrine itself is not directly asserted. This is the case here. There is one Spirit, one Lord, one God and Father. The unity of the church is founded on this doctrine. It is one, because there is over us one God the Father, one Lord, one Spirit. It is a truly mystical union; not a mere union of opinion, of interest, or of feeling, but something supernatural arising from a common principle of life.

7. This unity of the church, although it involves the essential equality of all believers, is still consistent with great diversity as to gifts, influence, and honour. According to the apostle's favourite illustration, it is like the human body, which is composed of many parts with different functions. It is not all eye nor all ear. This diversity of gifts is not only consistent with unity, but is essential to it.

8. The position which the previous verse gives to the Lord Jesus as the source of all life and power in the church is so exalted that the apostle interrupts himself to show that this representation is in accordance with what the Scriptures had already taught on this subject. Verse 7 speaks about Christ giving gifts. As this was his office, the Scriptures speak of him as a conqueror laden with spoils, enriched by his victories, and giving gifts to men.

9–10. When he says, 'he ascended', what does it mean but that he had also descended into the lower parts of the earth? He who descended is the same one who ascended far above all the heavens, so that he might fill all things.

The obvious purpose of these verses is to show that the passage quoted from the Psalmist refers to Christ. The proof lies in the fact that ascension in the case of a divine person, a giver of spiritual gifts to men, implies a previous descent. It was Christ who **descended**, and therefore it is Christ who **ascended**. It is true the Old Testament often speaks of God's descending, and therefore they may speak of his ascending. But according to the apostle, the divine person intended in those representations was the Son, and no previous descent or ascent, no previous triumph over his enemies, included all that the Spirit or prophecy intended by such representations. And, therefore, the Psalmist must have included in his language the most conspicuous and illustrious of God's condescensions and exaltations. All other comings were only typical of his ascension from the grave.

The apostle, therefore, teaches here that God, the subject of Psalm 68, **descended into the lower parts of the earth,** and that he **ascended far above all the heavens, so that he might fill all things.**

11. The gifts he gave. He, the ascended Saviour, to whom all power and all resources have been given – he gift was that **some would be apostles, some prophets, some evangelists, some pastors and teachers.** These were among the gifts which Christ gave to his church; which, though implying diversity of grace and office, were necessary to its unity as an organized whole. These offices are mentioned in order of their importance:

1. The **apostles** – the immediate messengers of Christ; his witnesses concerning his doctrines, his miracles, and his resurrection; infallible as teachers, and absolute as rulers, because of the gift of inspiration and because of their commission. No man, therefore, could be an apostle unless

(a) he was appointed by Christ;

(b) he had seen him after his resurrection, and had received the knowledge of the Gospel by direct revelation;

(c) he was made infallible by the gift of inspiration.

These things constituted the office, and were essential to its authority. Those who claimed the office without having these gifts and qualifications are called 'false apostles.'

2. **Prophets.** A prophet is someone who speaks on behalf of someone else, a spokesman, as Aaron was the prophet of Moses. Those whom God spoke through to people were **prophets,** whether their communications were doctrinal, moral, or prophetic, in the restricted sense of the term. Everyone who spoke by inspiration was a prophet. The New Testament

prophets differed from the apostles in that their inspiration was occasional, and therefore their authority as teachers was subordinate. The nature of their office is taught in detail in 1 Corinthians 14:1–40. As the gift of infallibility was essential for the apostolic office, so the gift of occasional inspiration was essential for the prophetic office. It is inconceivable that God should invest any set of men with the authority claimed and exercised by the apostles and prophets of the New Testament, requiring everyone to believe their teaching and submit to their authority, on pain of perdition, without giving the inner gifts qualifying them for their work.

3. **Some evangelists.** Evangelists were itinerant preachers.

4. **Some pastors and teachers.** This refers to a twofold name for the same officers, who were both the guides and instructors of the people.

12. Having mentioned the officers Christ gave his church, the apostle states why this gift was conferred. It was **to equip the saints for the work of ministry, for building up the body of Christ may be built up.**

13. The ministry is not a temporary institution, it is to continue until the church has reached the goal of its high calling. This does not prove that all the offices mentioned above are permanent. By common consent the prophets were temporary officers. It is the ministry, and not those particular offices, that is to continue. The church's goal is described here in three equivalent forms: **unity of faith and of knowledge of the Son of God, to maturity, to the measure of the full stature of Christ.**

Until all of come to the unity in the faith. The **all** mentioned here is not all people, but all the people of Christ.

14. Children are not only unstable but are easily deceived. They fall easy prey to the deceitful and scheming. The apostle therefore adds, **by people's trickery. Trickery** comes from a word which means 'cube,' 'die,' which comes to mean 'dice-playing,' in which there are many deceptive tricks, and therefore the word is used for craft or deceit. It is explained by the next phrase, **by their craftiness in deceitful scheming. The craftiness** is that craft which is used by seducers or people in error. The preposition **in** may mean 'according to': 'Cunning according to the craft which error uses, or which is characteristic of error.' Or it may, in line with its usual meaning, indicate direction of tendency: :The cunning which is directed to the craft of error – i.e., that craft which is designed to seduce.' The sense is the same.

The word **deceitful** occurs only here and in Ephesians 6:11, where in the plural form it is translated 'wiles' – 'the wiles of the devil.' It is derived from a word which means 'to follow anyone,' 'to track him,' as a wild animal tracks its prey.

15. These remarks are relevant to the subject in hand; for the apostle, while condemning all instability in connection with faith, and while denouncing the cunning of false teachers, immediately adds the injunction to adhere to **the truth in love.** It is not mere stability in sound doctrine, but faith which is combined with **love** that God requires. The only saving, salutary faith is that which works by **love,** and purifies the heart.

16. **From whom the whole body, joined and knitted together by every ligament with which it is equipped, as each part is working properly, promotes the body's growth in building itself up in love.** The church is Christ's **body;** he is the head. The **body** grows. About this growth, the apostle says:

1. It is from him. He is the causal source, form whom all life and power are derived.

2. It depends on the intimate union of all the parts of the body with the head, by means of appropriate links.

3. It is symmetrical.

4. It is a growth in love.

Verses 4:17–5:2

Analysis

This section contains, first, a general exhortation to holiness (4:17–24); and, secondly, injunctions concerning specific duties (4:25–5:2). The exhortation to holiness is in keeping with the apostle's style, first in the negative form, not to walk as the heathen do (verses 17–19); and then positively, to walk as Christ had taught them (verses 20–24). The heathen walk in the futility of their thinking, i.e., in a state of moral and spiritual fatuity, not knowing what they are about, nor where they are going (verse 17); because they are in mental darkness, and are alienated from God's life through the ignorance that is in them, and through the hardness of their hearts (verse 18); as is shown as they give themselves over to sensuality (verse 19). The Christian walk is the opposite of this, because believers have been taught. Instead of ignorance, truth dwells in them, enlightening and purifying. Hence they are led to put off the old self, and to put on the new self, which is more and more conformed to the image of God (verses 20–24). Therefore, they must avoid lying and speak the truth (verse 25); abstain from anger, and guard against giving the devil a foothold (verses 26–27); avoid stealing, and work and share with those in need (verse 28); avoid all unwholesome talk, but build others up by what they say and so not grieve the Holy Spirit (verses 29–30); instead of malicious feelings, they should be kind, compassionate and forgiving, as God forgives them (4:31–5:2).

Commentary

17. In the preceding section, the apostle taught that Christ had destined his church to perfect conformity to himself, and made provision for that end. Now, as a natural consequence, Paul solemnly enjoins those who profess to be Christians to live in accordance with this high vocation: **Now this I affirm and insist on in the Lord: you must no longer live as the Gentiles live, in the futility of their minds.**

Insist, here, means to say solemnly, like a person who calls on God to bear witness to the truth and importance of what he says. **Insist** here means 'to invoke as a witness,' rather than 'to act as a witness.' **In the Lord** means in communion with the Lord. Paul speaks as one who had access to the mind of Christ, knew his will, and could therefore speak in his name. The exhortation is, **no longer live as the Gentiles live.** The word translated **live** literally means 'walk.' 'To walk,' in Scripture, includes all the manifestations of life, inner and outer, seen and unseen. It does not merely express the outer, visible action. People are said to walk with God, which refers to the secret fellowship of the soul with its Maker, more than to the outer life. So here the walk which the apostle tells us to avoid is not only the visible actions which characterize the Gentiles, but also the inner life which outer actions reveal.

18. They are darkened in their understanding, alienated from the life of God because of their ignorance and hardness of heart. This verse explains and confirms the preceding statement. The heathen live in futility, i.e., in intellectual and moral darkness, because their understanding is darkened, and because they are **alienated from the life of God.**

Alienated from the life of God means strangers to that life. **The life of God** means the **life** of which **God** is the author. It is spiritual life; that is, the life of which the indwelling Spirit is the principle or source.

19. The practical proof of their being in the state described is found in the fact that they live without feeling, they give themselves over to the sins which are mentioned.

They have lost all sensibility. Conscience ceases to upbraid us or to restrain them. Therefore, they **practise** themselves and indulge in all kinds of **impurity** – i.e. they are insatiable.

20. That is not the way you learned Christ! That is, your knowledge of Christ has not led you to live like the Gentiles. As we say we can learn a thing, but never 'learn' a person, the expression **you learned Christ** has no comparison. But as the Scriptures refer to preaching Christ, which does not just mean preaching his doctrines but preaching Christ himself, setting him out as the object of supreme love and confidence, so 'to learn Christ' does not just mean learning his doctrines, but attaining the knowledge of Christ as the Son of God – God in our nature, the Holy One of God, the Saviour from sin, whom to know is holiness and life. Anyone who has learned Christ like this cannot live in darkness and sin. Such knowledge is in its very nature light. Where it enters, the mind is irradiated, refined, and purified.

21. For surely you have heard about him. The Greek does not mean 'to hear about him.' In writing to Christians, the apostle could not express this in a hypothetical way. He knew that the Ephesian Christians had heard about Christ. To hear, in this context, implies intelligence and obedience, as in the frequently occurring phrase, 'He who has ears to hear, let him hear'; and, 'Today if you will hear his voice … ,' and in many other cases. To hear the voice of God or of Christ, therefore, is not merely to perceive with the outer ear, but to receive with the understanding and the heart. The apostle assumes that they were obedient to the truth: 'You have not so learned Christ that you live like the Gentiles do, if, as I assume, you have really heard his voice and have been taught by him.'

22. Sanctification includes dying to sin, or mortification of the flesh, and living to righteousness; or, as it says here, putting off the **old self** and putting on the new self. The obvious allusions is to a change of clothing. To put off is to renounce, to remove from us, like clothes that are set aside. To put on is to adopt, to make our own. We are called on to put off the works of darkness (Romans 13:12); to put away lying (Ephesians 4:25); to put off anger, wrath, malice, etc. (Colossians 3:8); to get rid of all moral filth (James 1:21). On the other hand, we are called on to put on the Lord Jesus Christ (Romans 13:14; Galatians 3:27); the armour of light (Romans 13:12); compassion (Colossians 3:12); and people are said to be clothed with power from on high (Luke 24:49); with the imperishable and with immortality (1 Corinthians 15:53).

23. In this verse and the following verse we have the positive part of sanctification, which is expressed by 'renewing' and 'putting on the new self.' The verb **to be renewed** is passive. This renewal is always represented as the work of God. 'For we are what he has made us, created in Christ Jesus for good works' (Ephesians 2:10). It is therefore called 'renewal by the Holy Spirit' (Titus 3:5). Both these phrases, **to be renewed** and 'clothe yourselves with the new self,' may express either the instantaneous act of regeneration or the gradual work of sanctification. Thus in Romans 12:2 we are told, 'Do not be conformed to this world, but be transformed by the renewing of your minds.' So, here and in the parallel passage in Colossians 3:9–10, these terms express the whole process by which the soul is restored to God's image. It is a process of renewal from the beginning to the end. The apostle says, 'our inner nature is being renewed day by day' (2 Corinthians 4:16).

24. And to clothe yourselves with the new self. As we are called to put off our corrupt nature as a ragged and filthy garment, so we are required to put on our new nature as a garment of light. And as the former was personified as an old self, decrepit, deformed, and tending to corruption, so the latter is personified as a **new self**, fresh, beautiful, and vigorous, like God, for it is **created according to the likeness of God in true righteousness and holiness.**

25. Having enforced the general duty of holiness, or of being conformed to the image of God, the apostle insists on specific duties. It will be noted that in almost every case there is first a negative, then a positive statement of the duty, and then a motive. Thus here: **Putting away falsehood, let all of us speak the truth … for we are members of one another.**

26–27. His next exhortation refers to **anger**, about which he teaches that we are not to allow anger to be an occasion of **sin**; we are not to cherish it; we are not to give Satan any advantage over us when we are angry.

Do not let the sun go down on your anger. The word **anger** here is 'paroxysm' or 'excitement.' Anger, even when justifiable, is not to be cherished. The wise man says, 'Anger lodges in the bosom of fools' (Ecclesiastes 7:9).

28. The next exhortation relates to theft. We are not to steal, but to labour, that we may not only honestly support ourselves, but be able also to give to those who are in need.

29–30. These verses forbid corrupt communication, enjoin profitable discourse, assign as a motive the good of others, and reverence for the Holy Spirit.

31. Put away from you all bitterness and wrath and anger and wrangling and slander, together with all malice. These are intimately related evils. **Bitterness** is a word transferred from the sphere of sensations to that of the mind. The adjective 'bitter' means sharp, like an arrow; then pungent to the taste, disagreeable; and then venomous. The poisonous water given to the women suspected of adultery (Numbers 5:18) is called the 'water of bitterness.' The word **bitterness**, therefore, in its figurative sense, means what is corroding, as grief, or anything which acts on the mind as poison does on the body, or on the minds of others, as venom does on their bodies. The venom of the serpent lies harmless in his fang; but all evil feelings are poison to the subject of them, as well as venom to their object. The command, therefore, to lay aside all **bitterness**, is a command to lay aside everything which corrodes our own minds or wounds the feelings of others. Under this heading are the particulars which follow: **Wrath** (from the word 'to burn') means the mind itself, and the seat of emotions and desires; then the mind in the work of passion. **Anger** is the passion itself, i.e., the manifestation of **wrath**, as **wrangling** and **slander** are the outward expression of **anger**. The context shows that **slander** is neither blasphemy against God nor merely slander against men, but any form of speech springing from anger, and designed either to wound or to injure others.

With all malice. Malice is a general term for 'badness' or 'depravity' of any kind. Here the context shows that it means 'malevolence,' the desire to injure. We are to lay aside not only **wrath** and **anger**, but all other forms of malevolent feelings.

32. This is an exhortation to the opposite virtues. We are required to be **kind**. The word correctly means 'useful'; then 'disposed to do good.' Thus, God is said to be 'kind' to the grateful and the evil (Luke 6:35). **Tender-hearted** is also translated 'compassion' (that is, pity, compassion towards the suffering) in the parallel passage, Colossians 3:12. **Forgiving one another:** the verb means to give as a matter of favour, then to forgive, to pardon freely. **As God, in Christ has forgiven you.** This is the motive which should make us forgive others. God's forgiveness towards us is free; it precedes even our repentance, and is the cause of it. It is exercised despite the number and enormity of our sins, and the long period of time we have sinned our sins. He forgives us far more than we can ever be called on to forgive others. God forgives us **in Christ.** Out of Christ, he is, in virtue of his holiness and justice, a consuming fire; but in him, he is long-suffering, abundant in mercy, and ready to forgive.

5:1–2. As God has placed us under such a great obligation, **therefore be imitators of God.** The exhortation is enlarged. We are not only to imitate God in being forgiving, but also as becomes **beloved loved children.** We are to **live in love.** As God is live, and as we, by regeneration and adoption, are his **children**, we are bound to exercise love habitually. Our whole walk should be characterized by it.

As Christ loved us. This is the reason why we should love one another. We should be like Christ, which is being like God, for Christ is God. The apostle makes no distinction between our being the objects of God's love, and our being the objects of Christ's love. We are to be **imitators of God** in **love**, for **Christ** has **loved** us. He **gave himself up for us.** Here, as elsewhere, the great evidence of divine love is the death of Christ. See verse 25; Ephesians 3:19; John 15:13, 'no one has greater love than this, to lay down one's life for one's friends'; Galatians 2:20, 'Who loved me and gave himself for me.' See also 1 John 3:16.

Chapter 5

Verses 3–20: Specific exhortations.

Verses 21–33: Relative duties of husbands and wives.

Verses 3–20

Analysis

It becomes saints to avoid not only the sins of uncleanness and covetousness, but also all impropriety of conduct and frivolity of language (verses 3–4); because uncleanness and covetousness not only exclude us from heaven, but, whatever people may say, bring down the wrath of God (verses 5–6). Christians, therefore, should not participate in those sins, seeing they have been divinely enlightened and made the recipients of that light whose fruits are goodness, righteousness, and truth. They are bound to exemplify this in their conduct, avoiding and reproving the deeds of darkness (verses 7–10). Those deeds are too shameful to be named, but they may still be corrected by the power of that light which it is the prerogative of believers to disseminate; therefore the Scriptures speak of the light which flows from Christ as reaching even the dead (verses 12–14). Christians, therefore, should be wise, making the most of every occasion for good, in the midst of the evils by which they are surrounded (verses 13–16). They should seek exhilaration not from wine, but from the Holy Spirit, and give expression to their gladness in psalms and hymns, praising and thanking God through Jesus Christ (verses 17–20).

Commentary

3. **But fornication and impurity of any kind, or greed, must not even be mentioned among you, as is proper among saints.** In the preceding section the apostle had spoken about sins against our neighbors; here, from verse 3 to verse 20, he talks mainly about sins against ourselves. Not only **fornication** but everything of the same nature, or which leads to it, is to be avoided – and not only avoided, but not even mentioned among believers. The inconsistency of all such sins with the character of Christians, as **saints**, people selected from the world and consecrated to God, is such as should forbid the very mention of them in a Christian society. With the sins of uncleanness the apostle here, as in Ephesians 4:19, connects **greed.**

4. **Entirely out of place is obscene, silly, and vulgar talk.** The word here for **obscene** includes whatever is morally hateful. The adjective derived from this word means 'deformed,' 'revolting,' what causes disgust, physical or moral. It is the opposite of 'good,' which means both beautiful and good.

5. The apostle reverts to what he said in verse 3, and enforces the exhortation given there: **Be sure of this, that no fornicator, or impure person, or one who is greedy (that is an idolater), has any inheritance in the kingdom of Christ and of God.**

6. It is common not only among the Gentiles, but among the mass of humanity in all ages and nations, to extenuate the particular sins which the apostle refers to here. It is urged that they have their origin in the very constitution of our nature; that they are not malignant; that they may coexist with amiable tempers; and that they are not harmful to others; that no one is the worse for them, if no one knows about them, etc. Paul, therefore, cautions his readers in every age of the church not to be deceived by such vain words, assuring them that on these things (immorality and greed) that their **wrath of God comes** on the children of **disobedience.**

Empty words are words which contain no truth, and are therefore both false and fallacious, as people will discover who trust in them.

God's wrath. This expression is a fearful one, because human wrath is the disposition to inflict evil, limited by human feebleness; whereas **God's wrath** is the determination to punish in a being whose presence and power are unlimited.

7. God is determined to punish the impure and the greedy, so the apostle says, **Therefore do not be associated with them**; that is, do not be their partners in these sins, which would necessarily expose you to the penalty threatened against them.

8. This is enforced by a reference to their conversion from a previous state of sin and misery, to one of holiness and blessedness. **For once you were darkness.** As **light** stands for knowledge, and as knowledge, in the scriptural sense of the word, produces holiness, and holiness happiness; so **darkness** stands for ignorance, such ignorance inevitably produces sin, and sin misery. Therefore, the expression **once you were darkness** means, 'you were ignorant, polluted, and wretched.' **But now in the Lord you are light,** – i.e., in virtue of union with the Lord, you are enlightened, sanctified, and blessed. **Live as children of light,** i.e., as the children of holiness and truth. **Children of light** means 'enlightened.'

10. Verse 9 is a parenthesis, as verse 10 is grammatically connected with verse 8. **Live as children of light – . ...** **Find out** is to try, to put to the test, to examine, then to judge or estimate, and then to approve. Thus it is said, 'The fire shall try every man's work'; God is said 'to try the heart'; we are said to 'discern what is the will of God' (Romans 12:2), that is, to examine and determine what the will of God is. And so in this passage believers are required to walk as

children of light, examining and determining what is acceptable to the Lord. They are to regulate their conduct by thinking what pleases him.

11. The apostle, having in the previous verse insisted on the duty of Christians to walk in such a way as to show by their works that they were the subjects of divine illumination, adds here a statement about their duty with reference to the sins of those still in **darkness**. Those sins he calls **unfruitful works of darkness**. By **unfruitful** is meant not merely 'barren' or 'worthless,' but positively evil. **Works of darkness** are those works which spring from darkness, i.e., from ignorance of God, as works of light are those deeds which light or divine knowledge produces.

12. These works of darkness should be exposed like this, **for it is shameful even to mention what such people do secretly**. There are two reasons why sins are called 'works of darkness.' The first and principal one is, as has been stated, because they spring from darkness or ignorance of God; and the second is, because they are committed in darkness. They shun the light. The great turpitude of these sins is the apostle's reason why they should be reproved.

13. However, vile as those sins are, they are capable of being corrected. They are not beyond cure. Reprove them. Let in the **light** of divine truth on them, and they will be corrected or healed, for the truth is divinely efficacious.

14. As **light** is thus efficacious, and as it is accessible, or may be obtained, therefore the Scriptures call even on the sleeping and the **dead** to wake up and meet its life-giving beams.

15. Believers, as children of light, are required to have no fellowship with the works of darkness, but rather to reprove them. **Be careful**, i.e. take heed therefore, **how you live**, in what manner. 'See in what manner you render your deportment accurate.' **Careful … live** is to walk strictly by rule, so as not to deviate by a hair's breadth. **Not as unwise people but as wise.** Paul often uses the word **wise** for divine truth. The **wise** are those who possess this truth, which he had earlier called light, and the **unwise** are those who do not have it. So **wise** and **unwise** here are equivalent to the 'enlightened' and 'those in darkness.' His exhortation, therefore, is that believers should take care how they live, not as the heathen and unrenewed, who do not have the divine light of which he had been speaking, but as those who are enlightened from above, and are therefore **wise**.

16. **Making the most of the time.** This is one manifestation of wisdom, one method in which their Christian character as the children of light should be exhibited.

17. **So**, i.e., either 'because the days are evil,' or 'because you are bound to walk as wise people.' The latter is to be preferred, because the reference is to the main idea of verses 15–16, and not to a subordinate clause. Compare Luke 11:40.

18. **Do not get drunk on wine.** This is an example of folly, a lack of sense, especially inconsistent with the intelligence of the true believer. The person who has correct discernment will not seek refreshment of excitement from wine, but from the Holy Spirit. Therefore, the apostle adds, **but be filled with the Spirit.** In drunkenness, he says, there is **debauchery**, 'revelry,' 'riot,' whatever tends to destruction; for the word is derived from a word which means 'what cannot be saved,' one given up to a destructive course of life. Compare Titus 1:6; 1 Peter 4:4.

People are said to be filled with wine when they are completely under its influence; so they are said to **be filled with the Spirit** when he controls all their thoughts, feelings, words, and actions. The expression is a common one in Scripture. Of our Lord himself it was said that he was 'full of the Holy Spirit' (Luke 4:1); and of Stephen, that he was 'full of faith and the Holy Spirit' (Acts 6:5); and of Barnabas (Acts 11:24), etc. To the Christians, therefore, the source of strength and joy is not **wine**, but the blessed Spirit of God. And as drunkenness produces rioting and debauchery, so the Holy Spirit produces a joy which expresses itself in psalms, and hymns, and spiritual songs.

19. **Among yourselves** – as in Ephesians 4:32 and elsewhere – not 'to yourselves.' Compare Colossians 3:16, where it is 'teach and admonish one another.' Speaking and singing **among yourselves** signifies the interchange of thoughts and feelings expressed in the **psalms** and **hymns** used.

The early use of the words for **psalms and hymns**, and **spiritual songs** appears to have been as loose as that of the corresponding English terms.

20. Therefore the apostle connects the two: 'Be filled with the Spirit, singing hymns to Christ, and giving thanks to God the Father.' The Spirit dictates the one as naturally as the other. We are to give thanks **at all times.** It is not a duty to be performed once for all, nor merely when new mercies are received; but always, because we are under obligation for blessings temporal and spiritual already received, which calls for perpetual acknowledgment. We are to give thanks **for everything** – afflictions as well as for our joys, say the ancient commentators. This is not in the text, though Paul, as we learn from other passages, gloried in his afflictions.

Verses 21–33

Analysis

The apostle enjoins mutual obedience as a Christian duty (verse 21). Under this heading he treats the relative duties of husbands and wives, parents and children, masters and servants. The remainder of this chapter is devoted to the duties of husbands and wives. As the married relationship is analogous to that which Christ sustains to the church, the one serves to illustrate the other. The apostle, therefore, combines the two subjects throughout the paragraph.

Wives should submit to their husbands, as the church does to Christ. The motive for this submission is a regard for the Lord (verse 22). The ground for it is that the husband is the head of the wife, as Christ is the head of the church (verse 23). This subjection is not confined to any one sphere, but extends to all (verse 24).

Husbands should love their wives. 1. The extent of this love is Christ's love for the church, for whose redemption he died (verses 25–27). 2. The ground of love is in both cases the same. The wife is flesh of her husband's flesh and bone of his bone; so the church is flesh of Christ's flesh, and bone of his bone. Husband and wife are one flesh; so are Christ and the church. What is true of the one is true of the other (verses 29–31). 3. The union between Christ and his church is indeed of a higher order than that between husband and wife; nevertheless, the analogy between the two cases is such as to render it obligatory on the husband to love his wife as being himself and on the wife to reverence her husband (verses 32–33).

Commentary

21. This command to submit to one another is found in other passages of the New Testament, as in 1 Peter 5:5, 'accept the authority of the elders. And all of you must clothe yourselves with humility in your dealings with one another.' See also Romans 12:10 and Philippians 2:3. The scriptural teaching on this subject is that people are not isolated individuals, each one independent of everyone else. No one lives to himself, and no one dies to himself. People's essential equality and their mutual dependence lay the foundation for the obligation of mutual subjection. The apostle, however, is here speaking about the duties of Christians. Therefore, this passage is about the Christian duty of mutual submission.

22. Wives, be subject to your husbands as you are to the Lord. The general duty of mutual submission includes the specific duty of wives to be subject to their husbands, and this leads the apostle to speak about the relative duties of husbands and wives. And as the marriage relation is analogous to the relation between Christ and his church, he is thus led to illustrate the one by the other. As the relationship is the same, the duties flowing from it are the same: obedience on the part of the wife, and love on the part of the husband.

23. The scriptural doctrine, while it lays the foundation for order in requiring wives to obey their husbands, at the same time exalts the wife to be the companion and ministering angel to her husband. The man, therefore, so far as this particular point is concerned, stands in the same relation to his wife that Christ does to the church.

24. Just as – i.e., notwithstanding this peculiarity in the relationship of Christ to the church which has no parallel in the relationship of wife to husband, 'nevertheless, as the husband is the head of the wife, let the wife be subject to her husband **in everything,** just as the church is subject to Christ her head.'

25. As the special duty of the wife is submission, the special duty of the husband is **love.** With regard to this, the apostle teaches its measure and its ground. In its measure, it should be analogous to the love which Christ has for his church. Its ground is the intimate and mysterious union which exists between a man and his wife.

Husbands, love your wives, just as Christ loved the church and gave himself up for her. Husbands should love their wives **just as,** i.e., both 'because' and 'as.' As their relationship to their wives is analogous to that of Christ to his **church,** it imposes the obligation to love them as he loves **the church.** But **Christ loved the church** so much that he died for her. Husbands, therefore, should be willing to die for their wives.

26–27. As the apostle unites with his purpose of teaching the duties arising from the marriage relationship, in order to illustrate the nature of the union between Christ and his **church,** these verses relate to the latter point and not to the former. They set out the purpose of Christ's death. Its overall purpose was to gain the church for himself, as an object of delight. Its immediate purpose was to prepare it for that high destiny. These ideas are presented figuratively. The **church** is regarded as the bride of Christ.

27. The ultimate end for which Christ gave himself for the church, and for which he sanctifies it, is to present it to himself, i.e., to gain it for himself as his special possession.

28. In this same way, husbands should love their wives as they do their own bodies. As Christ loves the church and gave himself for it, and as the church is his body, **in this same way,** and in keeping with the analogous relationship between them, husbands should love their wives, **as,** i.e., as being, or because they are, **their own bodies.** Christ loves his church because it is his body. Husbands should love their wives because they are their **bodies. In this same way** is not comparative, but argumentative. It does not indicate the measure of the husband's love, as if it meant he should love his wife as much as he loves his own body; but it indicates the nature of the relationship which is the ground of his love. He should love his wife because she is his body.

So also it is a fact which the apostle declares, when he says, **He who loves his wife loves himself.**

29. Married love, therefore, is as much a dictate of nature as self-love; and it is just as unnatural for a man to hate his wife as it would be for him to hate himself or his own body.

Just as Christ does for the church, i.e., Christ also nourishes and cherishes the church as a man does his own body. The relationship between a man and his wife is analogous to that between a man and his own body; and the relationship between Christ and his church is analogous to that between a husband and his wife: therefore, Christ nourishes and cherishes the church as man does his own body.

30. This verse assigns the reason of the preceding declaration. Christ acts towards his church as a man does towards his body, **because we are members of his body.** This might mean, simply, that we stand before him in the same intimate and vital union that a man's body sustains to the man himself.

31. 'For this reason a man will leave his father and mother and be joined to his wife, and the two will become one flesh. That is, because the relationship between husband and wife is more intimate than any other, even than that between parents and children, therefore a man shall consider all other relationships subordinate to that which he has with his wife, with whom he is connected in the bonds of a common life.

32. **This is a great mystery.** The word **mystery** does not refer to the passage in Genesis 2:24, as though the apostle intended to say that that passage had a mystical sense, which he had just unfolded by applying it to the relationship between Christ and his church. It is the union between Christ and his people, the fact that they are 'one flesh,' that he declares to be a great mystery. The word **mystery** is used here, as it is everywhere else, for something hidden, something beyond the reach of human knowledge.

33. **Each of you, however, should love his wife as himself.** The meaning is the same as in verse 28. The husband is to love his wife as being himself.

Chapter 6

Verses 1–9: Relative duties of parent and children and of masters and servants.

Verses 10–20: Exhortations and directions as to the spiritual conflict.

Verses 21–24: Conclusion.

Verses 1–9

Analysis

Children should obey their parents. This obedience should be in the Lord, determined and regulated by a regard for Christ (verse 1). The basis for the obligation is, first, that it is right in itself; and secondly, that it is enforced by an express command in the Ten Commandments, to which a special promise is added (verses 1–3).

Parents should do nothing to cherish evil feelings in the minds of their children, but bring them up in the disciplines of Christianity (verses 4–5).

Servants should be obedient to their masters. This obedience should be rendered (1) with solicitude; (2) with singleness of mind; (3) as part of their obedience to Christ (verse 5). Therefore, not only when observed by men, or from the desire to please men, but as serving Christ, and desiring to please him; rendering their services with readiness, as to the Lord, and not to men, because they know that at his bar all men, whether slave or free, will be treated according to their works (verses 6–8).

Masters are to act on the same principles of regard for the authority of Christ, and of their responsibility to him in their conduct towards their slaves, avoiding all harshness, because master and slave have a common Master in heaven, with whom there is no respect of persons (verse 8).

Commentary

1. **Children, obey your parents.** The nature of character of this obedience is expressed by the words **in the Lord.** It should be religious, arising out of the conviction that such obedience is the will of **the Lord.**

2–3. This consideration is enforced by a reference to the express command of God. The duty is so important that it is included in that brief summary of the moral law given by God on Mount Sinai. It was engraved by God's finger on the tablets of stone, '**Honour your father and mother.**' Any flagrant breach of this command was, according to the Mosaic law, punished with death. To **Honour** is to reverence; and, therefore, the command refers to the inner feeling as well as to outer behaviour. This precept is said to be **the first commandment with a promise.**

4. The duty of parents, who are here represented by the father, is stated in a negative and positive form. **Fathers, do not provoke your children.** This is what they are not to do. They are not to excite the bad passions of their children by severity, injustice, partiality, or unreasonable exercise of authority. A parent would do

better to sow weeds in a field from which he expects to derive food for himself and his family, than by his own bad behaviour to nurture evil in the heart of his child.

5. The five following verses deal with the duties of masters and servants. **Slaves** and **masters** are relative terms here, although in Greek the antithetical term to 'slave' is used in 1 Timothy 6:1 and Titus 2:9; compare also 1 Peter 2:18. The word for 'slave' comes from the word 'to bind,' and means a slave as distinguished from a hired servant. We can see that this meaning is clearly contrasted here because of the normal use of the word, and also from the antithesis between 'slave' and 'free' in verse 8.

The word here for 'master' means 'possessor' or 'owner.' It implies the relationship which a man may have both with people and with things.

6. The apostle explains in the two following verses what he means by **from the heart** or sincere obedience. It is not **only while being watched, in order to please them** that is, such service as is only given when the eye of the master sees what is done, as though the only object was to please men. Servants are required to act as the **slaves of Christ**, whose eyes are everywhere; and, therefore, if their desire is to please him, they must be as faithful in their master's absence as in his presence.

7. The whole character of the obedience of the slave is summed up in this verse: **Render service with enthusiasm, as to the Lord and not to men and women.** This, as the Scriptures teach, is not peculiar to the obedience of the slave to his master, but applies to all other cases in which obedience is required from one person to another.

The word **enthusiams** qualifies **service**. This is contrasted with the sullenness and inner indignation with which a service extorted by fear of punishment is often given. No service given to Christ can be like that; it is given with alacrity and cheerfulness.

8. This verse presents, for the encouragement of the slave, the elevating truth that everyone stands on equal ground before the bar of Christ. In him and before him there is neither Jew nor Greek, bond nor free, male nor female (see Galatians 3:28), but, so far as these external distinctions are concerned, all are alike. The apostle, therefore, says to slaves, 'Give this cheerful obedience **knowing that whatever good we do, we will receive the same again from the Lord, whether we are slaves or free.** 'In this world some people are masters and some are slaves. In the next, these distinctions will cease.

9. Having enjoined on slaves their special duties, the apostle turns to masters: **And, masters.** The force of **and** here is, 'Not only do slaves have their duties; you masters have your special

obligations.' Masters are to act towards their slaves with the same regard for God's will, with the same recognition of Christ's authority, with the same sincerity and good feeling, which had been enjoined on the slaves themselves.

Verses 10–24

Analysis
Directions about the spiritual conflict. As such a conflict is inevitable, the believer should (1) muster strength for the struggle. (2) He should seek that strength from Christ. (3) Since his enemies are not human, but superhuman, Satan and all the powers of darkness, the believer needs not only more than human strength, but also divine armour. He should, therefore, take the armour of God, that he may be able to stand in the evil day. That armour consists (1) in the knowledge and reception of the truth; (2) in the righteousness of Christ; (3) in the alacrity which flows from the peace of the Gospel; (4) in the consciousness of salvation; (5) in faith; (6) in the Word of God, which is the sword of the Spirit.

To obtain strength to use this armour correctly, and to secure victory for ourselves and for the army of which we are a part, we should pray. These prayers should be (1) of all kinds; (2) on every occasion; (3) importunate and persevering; (4) with the help of the Holy Spirit; (5) for all saints.

Believing in the efficacy of such prayers, the apostle begs the Ephesians believers to pray for him, that God would enable him to preach the Gospel in a suitable way.

To relieve their anxiety, he had sent Tychicus to inform them of his circumstances and of his health.

He invokes the Father and Son to bestow on the brothers the blessings of divine peace and love, united with faith; and implores the special favour of God for all who love the Lord Jesus Christ with a love that cannot die.

Commentary
10. Though the redemption purchased by Christ, as described in this letter, is so complete and so free, yet between the beginning and the end of the work there is a protracted conflict. This is not a figure of speech. It is something real and arduous. Salvation, however gratuitous, is not to be obtained without great effort. The Christian conflict is not only real, it is difficult and dangerous. It is one in which true believers are often grievously wounded, and multitudes of reputed believers entirely succumb.

Finally, be strong in the Lord. He concludes his letter, so full of elevated views, and so rich in disclosures of the mysteries of redemption, with directions about the struggle necessary to secure salvation. His first exhortation is to muster strength for the inevitable conflict, and to seek that strength from the right source. We are to be **strong in the Lord**. A Christian separated from Christ is like a branch separated from the vine, or like a limb severed from the body. Therefore, whoever rushes into this conflict without thinking of Christ, without putting his trust in him, and without continually looking to him for strength, and regarding himself as a member of his body, deriving all life and vigour from him, is demented. He does not know what he is doing. He has not strength even to reach the field. With him the whole conflict is a sham.

The words **in the strength of his power** mean, 'in the vigour derived from his strength.' The vigour of a man's arm is derived from the strength of his body. It is only as members of Christ's body that we have either life or power.

11. The second direction refers to the weapons necessary for the successful conduct of this conflict: **put on the whole armour of God**. In this verse, **armour** includes both the defensive and the offensive armour of the soldier. The believer has not only to defend himself, but also to attack his spiritual enemies; and the latter is as necessary for his safety as the former.

The whole armour of God means that armour which God has provided, and which he gives. Thus we are taught from the outset that as the strength we need is not from ourselves.

12. For our struggle is not against enemies of blood and flesh, **but against rulers, against the authorities, against the cosmic powers of this present darkness, against the spiritual forces of evil in the heavenly places**. The significance of the terms used here, the context, and the analogy of Scripture, make it certain that the reference is to evil spirits. In Scripture they are called 'demons,' who are declared to be fallen angels (2 Peter 3:4; Jude 6), and are now subject to Satan, their prince. They are called **rulers**, those who are first or high in rank; and **authorities**, those invested with authority. These terms probably refer to the relationship of the spirits among themselves. The designation **powers of this present darkness** expresses the power or authority which they exercise over the world. Mankind is subject to them. Compare 2 Corinthians 4:4; John 16:11. The word **world** correctly refers only to those rulers whose dominion is universal. These evil spirits are the rulers of this darkness. The meaning is either that they reign over the existing state of ignorance and alienation from God, i.e., the world in its apostasy is subject to their control; or **this present darkness** is equivalent to 'kingdom of darkness.' Rulers of the kingdom of darkness – which, Scripture teaches us, includes the world as distinguished from the true people of God. The word 'dark' is used elsewhere, the abstract for the concrete, for those in darkness, i.e., for those who belong to

or constitute the kingdom of darkness: see Luke 22:53 and Colossians 1:13. Our struggle, therefore, is with the potentates who are rulers of the kingdom of darkness as it now is.

13. Therefore, 'because you have such formidable enemies, and because the conflict is inevitable, not only arm yourselves, but **put on the whole armour of God**; no other is adequate for the emergency.' **You may be able to withstand,** i.e., 'successfully to resist,' **on that evil day.** The **evil day** is the day of trial.

14. With the flowing garments of the East, the first thing to be done in preparing for any active work was to gird the loins. The apostle therefore says, **Stand therefore, and fasten your belt of truth around your waist.** In this verse **truth** is not here to be understood as divine truth, as objectively revealed, i.e., the Word of God; for that is mentioned in the following verse as the **sword**. Nor does it mean 'sincerity of mind,' for that is a natural virtue, and does not belong to God's armour; which, according to the context, consists of supernatural gifts and graces. But it means **truth** subjectively considered; that is, the knowledge and belief of the truth. This is the first and indispensable qualification for a Christian soldier. To enter on this spiritual conflict ignorant or doubting would be to enter battle blind and lame.

As the **belt** gives strength and freedom of action, and therefore confidence, so does the **truth** when spiritually apprehended and believed. Truth alone, as abiding in the mind in the form of divine knowledge, can give strength of confidence even in the ordinary conflicts of the Christian life, much more in any really **evil day**.

Put on the breastplate of righteousness. The **breastplate** was the armour covering the body from the neck to the thighs, consisting of two parts, one covering the front and the other the back. A warrior without his **breastplate** was naked, exposed to every thrust of his enemy, and even to every random spear. In such a state flight or death is inevitable. In Isaiah 59:17, Jehovah is described as putting on 'righteousness like a breastplate, and a helmet of salvation on his head'; as in Isaiah 11:5, it refers to the Messiah, 'Righteousness shall be the belt around his waist, and faithfulness the belt around his waist.'

15. In ancient warfare, which was most often hand to hand combat, swiftness of foot was one of the most important qualifications for a good soldier. So the apostle says, **as shoes for your feet put on whatever will make you ready to proclaim the gospel of peace.**

16. With all of these. Not 'above all,' as of greatest importance. Besides the parts of armour already mentioned, they were to take **the shield of faith**. In this verse **shield** means, literally, a door, and then came to mean a large oblong shield, like a door. Being four feet long and two and a half feet broad, it completely covered the body, and was essential for the safety of the combatant. Hence the appropriateness of the apostle's metaphor. Such a protection, and thus essential, is **faith**. The more ways in which a **shield** is used, the more suitable is the illustration. The **faith** intended here is that through which we are justified, and reconciled to God through the blood of Christ.

17. The most ornamental part of ancient armour, and scarcely less important than the breastplate or the shield, was the **helmet**. The Christian, therefore, is exhorted to take **the helmet of salvation**. According to the analogy of the preceding expressions, 'the breastplate of righteousness' and 'shield of faith,' salvation is itself the **helmet**. What adorns and protects the Christian, which enables him to hold up his head with confidence and joy, is the fact that he is saved. He is one of the redeemed, translated from the kingdom of darkness into the kingdom of God's dear Son. If still under condemnation, if still estranged from God, a foreigner, and alien, without God and without Christ, he could have no courage to enter into this conflict. It is because he is a fellow citizen of the saints, a child of God, a partaker of the salvation of the Gospel, that he can face event the most potent enemies with confidence, knowing that he will become more than a conqueror through him that loved him (see Romans 8:37).

Up until now, the armour mentioned is defensive. The only offensive weapon of the Christian is **the sword of the Spirit**. Here **of the Spirit** cannot be the genitive of apposition. The Spirit is not the sword; this would be incongruous, as the sword is something which the soldier wields, but the Christian cannot control the Spirit. Besides, the explanation immediately follows, **which is the word of God**. **The sword of the Spirit** means the sword which the Spirit gives. The **word of God** does not mean the divine precepts, nor the threatenings of God against his enemies. There is nothing to limit the expression. It is what God has spoken, his Word, the Bible. This is sharper than any double edged sword (see Galatians 4:12). It is the wisdom of God and the power of God. It has a self-authenticating light. It commends itself to the reason and conscience.

18. It is not armour or weapons which make the warrior. There must be courage and strength – and even then he often needs help. As the Christian has no resources of strength in himself, and can succeed only as helped from above, the apostle urges the duty of prayer. The believer is to avail himself of all kinds of **prayer**;

he is to **pray** on every suitable occasion; he is to **pray in the Spirit;** he is to be alert and persevering in the discharge of this duty; and he is to pray **for all the saints,** and the Ephesians were urged by the apostle to **pray** for him.

19. The importance which the apostle attributed to intercessory prayer, and his faith in its efficacy, are evident from the frequency with which he enjoins the duty, and from the earnestness with which he solicits such prayers for himself. What the apostle wishes the Ephesians to **pray** for was not any temporal blessing, not even his deliverance from prison so that he might be at liberty to preach the Gospel more freely, but that God would enable him to preach with the freedom and boldness with which he ought to preach. The literal translation is, 'that utterance may be given me in opening my mouth, with boldness to make known. …' What Paul desired was divine assistance in preaching. He begs his reader to **pray** that **a message may be given to me,** 'that the power of speech,' or 'freedom of utterance,' might be given to him, when he opened his mouth.

20. **For which I am an ambassador in chains.** An **ambassador** is one through whom a sovereign speaks. 'So we are ambassadors for Christ, since God is making his appeal through us; we entreat you on behalf of Christ, be reconciled to God' (2 Corinthians 5:20). The apostles, as sent by Christ with authority to speak in his name, and to negotiate with men, proposing the terms of reconciliation, and urging their acceptance, were in an eminent sense his ambassadors. As all ministers are sent by Christ, and are commissioned by him to propose the terms of salvation, they too are entitled to the same honourable designation. Paul was **an ambassador in chains,** and yet he did not lose his courage, but preached with as much boldness as ever.

21. In conclusion, the apostle informs the Ephesians that he had sent **Tychicus** to them to reliever their anxiety concerning him. **So that you also may know** – i.e., you as well as other Christian friends who had shown concern about me in my chains – **how I am and what I am doing,** – i.e., my circumstances. His health, as well as his situation, was a matter of anxiety to his friends.

24. True to the last, as a needle to the pole, the apostle turns to Christ, and implores the divine favour on **all who have an undying love for our Lord Jesus Christ.** Love for Christ includes adoring admiration of his person, desire for his presence, zeal for his glory, and devotion to his service. It need not be ecstatic, but it must control us.

PHILIPPIANS

A.R. Faussett

Introduction

Internal evidence

The internal evidence for the authenticity of this Epistle is strong. The style, manner of thought, and doctrine, accord with Paul's. The incidental allusions also establish his authorship. PALEY [*Horæ Paulinæ*, ch. 7] instances the mention of the object of Epaphroditus' journey to Rome, the Philippian contribution to Paul's wants, Epaphroditus' sickness (Php 1:7 2:25–30 4:10–18), the fact that Timothy had been long with Paul at Philippi (Php 1:1 2:19), the reference to his being a prisoner at Rome now for a long time (Php 1:12–14 2:17–28), his willingness to die (compare Php 1:23, with 2Co 5:8), the reference to the Philippians having *seen* his maltreatment at Philippi (Php 1:29,30 2:1,2).

External evidence

The external evidence is equally decisive: Philippi was *the first* (that is, the farthest from Rome, and first which met Paul in entering Macedonia) Macedonian *city of the district*, called *Macedonia Prima* (so called as lying *farthest eastward*). The *Greek* (Ac 16:12) should not be translated 'the *chief* city,' as *English Version*, but as above [ALFORD]. Not it, but Thessalonica, was the *chief* city of the province, and Amphipolis, of the district called Macedonia Prima. It was a *Roman* 'colony' (Ac 16:12), made so by Augustus, to commemorate his famous victory over Brutus and Cassius. A *colony* was in fact a portion of Rome itself transplanted to the provinces, an offshoot from Rome, and as it were a portrait of the mother city on a small scale [AULUS GELLIUS, *Attic Nights*, 16.13]. Its inhabitants were Roman citizens, having the right of voting in the Roman tribes, governed by their own senate and magistrates, and not by the governor of the province, with the Roman law and *Latin* language.

Paul, with Silas and Timothy, planted the Gospel there (Ac 16:12), in his second missionary journey, A.D. 51. Doubtless he visited it again on his journey from Ephesus into Macedonia (Ac 20:1); and Ac 20:3,6, expressly mentions his third visit on his return from Greece (Corinth) to Syria by way of Macedonia. His sufferings at Philippi (Ac 16:19) strengthened the Christian bond of union between him and his Philippian converts, who also, like him, were exposed to trials for the Gospel's sake (1Th 2:2). They alone sent supplies for his temporal wants, *twice* shortly after he had left them (Php 4:15,16), and again a third time shortly before writing this Epistle (Php 4:10,18 2Co 11:9). This fervent attachment on their part was, perhaps, also in part due to the fact that few Jews were in Philippi, as in other scenes of his labours, to sow the seeds of distrust and suspicion. There was no synagogue, but merely a Jewish *Proseucha,* or oratory, by the riverside. So that there only do we read of his meeting no opposition from Jews, but only from the masters of the divining damsel, whose gains had been put an end to by her being dispossessed.

Though the Philippian Church was as yet free from Judaizing influence, yet it needed to be forewarned of that danger which might at any time assail it from without (Php 3:2); even as such evil influences had crept into the Galatian churches. In Php 4:2,3 we find a trace of the fact recorded in the history (Ac 16:13,14), that *female* converts were among the first to receive the Gospel at Philippi.

The state of the church

As to the state of the Church, we gather from 2Co 8:1,2 that its members were *poor,* yet most *liberal*; and from Php 1:28–30, that they were undergoing persecution. The only blemish referred to in their character was, on the part of some members, a tendency to dissension. Hence arise his admonitions against disputings (Php 1:27 2:1–4,12,14 4:2).

The object of the Epistle is general: not only to thank the Philippians for their contribution sent by Epaphroditus, who was now in returning to take back the apostle's letter, but to express his Christian love and sympathy, and to exhort them to a life consonant with that of Christ, and to warn them against existing dissensions and future possible assaults of Judaizers from without. It is remarkable in this Epistle alone, as compared with the others, that, amidst many commendations, there are no express censures of those to whom it is addressed. No doctrinal error, or schism, has as yet sprung up; the only blemish hinted at is, that some of the Philippian Church were somewhat wanting in lowliness of mind, the result of which want was disputation. Two women, Euodias and Syntyche, are mentioned as having erred in this respect (Php 4:2,3). The Epistle may be divided into *three* parts: (1) Affectionate address to the Philippians; reference to his own state as a prisoner at Rome, and to theirs, and to his mission of Epaphroditus to them (the first and second chapters). Epaphroditus probably held a leading office in the Philippian Church, perhaps as a presbyter. After Tychicus and Onesimus had departed (A.D. 62), carrying the Epistles to the Ephesians, Colossians, and Philemon, Paul was cheered in his imprisonment by the arrival of Epaphroditus with the Philippian contribution. That faithful 'brother, companion in labour, and fellow soldier' (Php 2:25), had brought on himself by the fatigues of the journey a dangerous sickness (Php 2:26,30). But now that he was recovered, he 'longed' (Php 2:26) to return to his Philippian flock, and in person to relieve their anxiety on his behalf, in respect to his sickness; and the apostle gladly availed himself of the opportunity of writing to them a letter of grateful acknowledgments and Christian exhortations. (2) Caution against Judaizing teachers, supported by reference to his own former and present feeling towards Jewish legalism (Php 3:1–21). (3) Admonitions to individuals, and to the Church in general, thanks for their seasonable aid, and concluding benedictions and salutations (Php 4:1–23).

This Epistle was written from Rome during the imprisonment, the beginning of which is related in Ac 28:16,20,30,31. The reference to 'Cæsar's household' (Php 4:22), and to the 'palace' (Php 1:13, *Greek,* 'Prætorium,' probably, *the barrack of the Prætorian bodyguard,* attached to the palace of Nero) confirms this. It must have been during his *first* imprisonment at Rome, for the mention of the Prætorium agrees with the fact that it was during his first imprisonment he was in the custody of the Prætorian Prefect, and his situation, described in Php 1:12–14, agrees with his situation in the first two years of his imprisonment

(Ac 28:30,31). The following reasons show, moreover, that it was written towards *the close* of that imprisonment: (1) He, in it, expresses his expectation of the immediate decision of his cause (Php 2:23). (2) Enough time had elapsed for the Philippians to hear of his imprisonment, to send Epaphroditus to him, to hear of Epaphroditus' arrival and sickness, and send back word to Rome of their distress (Php 2:26). (3) It must have been written after the three other Epistles sent from Rome, namely, Colossians, Ephesians, and Philemon; for Luke is no longer with him (Php 2:20); otherwise he would have been specified as saluting them, having formerly laboured among them, whereas he is mentioned as with him, Col 4:14 Phm 1:24. Again, in Eph 6:19,20, his freedom to preach is implied: but in Php 1:13-18, his bondage is dwelt on, and it is implied that, *not himself*, but *others*, preached, and made his imprisonment known. Again, in Phm 1:22, he confidently anticipates his release, which contrasts with the more depressed anticipations of this Epistle. (4) A considerable time had elapsed since the beginning of his imprisonment, for 'his bonds' to have become so widely known, and to have produced such good effects for the Gospel (Php 1:13). (5) There is evidently an increase in the rigour of his imprisonment implied now, as compared with the early stage of it, as described in Ac 28:1–31; compare Php 1:29,30 2:27. History furnishes a probable clue to account for this increase of vigour. In the second year of Paul's imprisonment (A.D. 62), Burrus, the Prætorian Prefect, to whose custody he had been committed (Ac 28:16, 'the captain of the guard'), died; and Nero the emperor having divorced Octavia, and married Poppoea, a Jewish proselytess (who then caused her rival, Octavia, to be murdered, and gloated over the head of her victim), exalted Tigellinus, the chief promoter of the marriage, a monster of wickedness, to the Prætorian Prefecture. It was then he seems to have been removed from his own house into the Prætorium, or barrack of the Prætorian guards, attached to the palace, for stricter custody; and hence he writes with less hopeful anticipations as to the result of his trial (Php 2:17 3:11). Some of the Prætorian guards who had the custody of him before, would then naturally make known his 'bonds,' in accordance with Php 1:13; from the smaller Prætorian bodyguard at the palace the report would spread to the general permanent Prætorian camp, which Tiberius had established north of the city, outside of the walls. He had arrived in Rome, February, 61; the 'two whole years (Ac 20:30) in his own hired house' ended February, 63, so that the date of this Epistle, written shortly after, evidently while the danger was imminent, would be about spring or summer, 63. The providence of God averted the danger. He probably was thought beneath the notice of Tigellinus, who was more intent on court intrigues. The death of Nero's favourite, Pallas, the brother of Felix, this same year, also took out of the way another source of danger.

Style

The style is abrupt and discontinuous, his fervour of affection leading him to pass rapidly from one theme to another (Php 2:18,19–24,25–30 3:1,2,3,4–14,15). In no Epistle does he use so warm expressions of love. In Php 4:1 he seems at a loss for words sufficient to express all the extent and ardour of his affection for the Philippians: 'My brethren dearly beloved and longed for, my joy and crown, so stand fast in the Lord, my dearly beloved.' The mention of bishops and deacons in Php 1:1 is due to the late date of the Epistle, at a time when the Church had begun to assume that order which is laid down in the Pastoral Epistles, and which continued the prevalent one in the first and purest age of the Church.

Contents

See *Outlines of the New Testament Books*, p. 899

Chapter 1

Php 1:1–30. Inscription. Thanksgiving and prayers for the flourishing spiritual state of the Philippians. His own state at Rome, and the result of his imprisonment in spreading the gospel. Exhortation to Christian consistency.

1. Timotheus – mentioned as being well known to the Philippians (Ac 16:3,10–12), and now present with Paul. Not that Timothy had any share in writing the Epistle; for Paul presently uses the first person singular, 'I,' not 'we' (Php 1:3). The mention of his name implies merely that Timothy joined in affectionate remembrances to them.

servants of Jesus Christ – The oldest manuscripts read the order, 'Christ Jesus.' Paul does not call himself 'an apostle,' as in the inscriptions of other Epistles; for the Philippians needed not to be reminded of his apostolic authority. He writes rather in a tone of affectionate familiarity.

all – so Php 1:4,7,8,25 Php 2:17,26. It implies comprehensive affection which desired not to forget any one among them 'all.'

bishops – synonymous with 'presbyters' in the apostolical churches; as appears from the same persons being called 'elders of the Church' at Ephesus (Ac 20:17), and 'overseers' (Ac 20:28), Greek, 'bishops.' And Tit 1:5, compare with Php 1:7. This is the earliest letter of Paul where bishops and deacons are mentioned, and the only one where they are separately addressed in the salutation. This accords with the probable course of events, deduced alike from the letters and history. While the apostles were constantly visiting the churches in person or by messengers, regular pastors would be less needed; but when some were removed by various causes, provision for the permanent order of the churches would be needed. Hence the three pastoral letters, subsequent to this Epistle, give instruction as to the due appointment of bishops and deacons. It agrees with this new want of the Church, when other apostles were dead or far away, and Paul long in prison, that bishops and deacons should be prominent for the first time in the opening salutation. The Spirit thus intimated that the churches were to look up to their own pastors, now that the miraculous gifts were passing into God's ordinary providence,

and the presence of the inspired apostles, the dispensers of those gifts, was to be withdrawn [PALEY, 'Horæ Paulinæ']. 'Presbyter,' implied the *rank*; 'bishop,' *the duties of the office* [NEANDER]. Naturally, when the apostles who had the chief supervision were no more, one among the presbyters presided and received the name 'bishop,' in the more restricted and modern sense; just as in the Jewish synagogue one of the elders presided as 'ruler of the synagogue.' Observe, the apostle addresses the Church (that is, the congregation) more directly than its presiding ministers (Col 4:17 1Th 5:12 Heb 13:24 Re 1:4,11). The bishops managed more the internal, the deacons the external, affairs of the Church. The plural number shows there was more than one bishop or presbyter, and more than one deacon in the Church at Philippi.

2. Grace … peace – The very form of this salutation implies the union of Jew, Greek, and Roman. The Greek salutation was 'joy' (*chairein*), akin to the *Greek* for 'grace' (*charis*). The Roman was 'health,' the intermediate term between *grace* and *peace*. The *Hebrew* was 'peace,' including both temporal and spiritual prosperity. *Grace* must come first if we are to have true *peace*.

from … from – Omit the second 'from': as in the *Greek*, 'God our Father' and 'the Lord Jesus Christ,' are most closely connected.

3. Translate, 'In all my remembrance of you.'

4. making request – Translate, 'making *my* request.'

for you all – The frequent repetition in this Epistle of 'all' with 'you,' marks that Paul desires to declare his love for *all* alike, and will not recognize any divisions among them.

with joy – the characteristic feature in this Epistle, as *love* is in that to the Ephesians (compare Php 1:18 Php 2:2,19,28 3:1 4:1,4). *Love* and *joy* are the two first-fruits of the Spirit. *Joy* gives especial animation to prayers. It marked his high opinion of them, that there was almost everything in them to give him *joy*, and almost nothing to give him pain.

5. Ground of his 'thanking God' (Php 1:3): 'For your (continued) fellowship (that is, real spiritual participation) in (literally, "in regard to") the Gospel from the first day (of your becoming *partakers* in it) until now.' Believers have the fellowship of the Son of God (1Co 1:9) and of the Father (1Jo 1:3) in the Gospel, by becoming partakers of 'the fellowship of the

Holy Ghost' (2Co 13:14), and exercise that fellowship by acts of communion, not only the communion of the Lord's Supper, but holy liberality to brethren and ministers (Php 4:10,15, 'communicated ... concerning giving'; 2Co 9:13 Ga 6:6 Heb 13:16, 'To communicate forget not').

6. confident – This confidence nerves prayers and thanksgivings (Php 1:3,4).

this very thing – *the very thing* which he prays for (Php 1:4) is the matter of his believing confidence (Mr 11:24 1Jo 5:14,15). Hence the result is sure.

he which hath begun – God (Php 2:13).

a good work – Any work that God begins, He will surely finish (1Sa 3:12). Not even men begin a work at random. Much more the fact of His beginning the work is a pledge of its completion (Isa 26:12). So as to the particular work here meant, the *perfecting of their fellowship in the Gospel* (Php 1:5 Ps 37:24 89:33 138:8 Joh 10:28,29 Ro 8:29,35–39 11:1,2 Heb 6:17–19 Jas 1:17 Jude 1:24). As God cast not off Israel for ever, though chastening them for a time, so He will not cast off the spiritual Israel (De 33:3 Isa 27:3 1Pe 1:5).

perform it until – 'perfect it up to' [ALFORD, ELLICOTT, and others].

the day of ... Christ – (Php 1:10). The Lord's coming, designed by God in every age of the Church to be regarded as near, is to be the goal set before believers' minds rather than their own death.

7. meet – *Greek*, 'just.'

to think this – to have the prayerful confidence I expressed (Php 1:4-6).

of you – literally, '*in behalf of* you.' Paul's confident prayer *in their behalf* was that God would perfect His own good work of grace in them.

because – Punctuate and translate, 'Because I have you in my heart (so Php 1:8; otherwise the *Greek* and the words immediately following in the verse, favour the *Margin*, "Ye have *me* in *your* heart ... being partakers of my grace") (both, in my bonds, and in *my* defence and confirmation of the Gospel), you (I say) all being fellow partakers of my grace.' This last clause thus assigns the reason why he has them *in his heart* (that is, cherished in his love, 2Co 3:2 7:3), even in his bonds, and in his defence and confirmation of the Gospel (such as he was constantly making in private, Ac 28:17–23; his self-defence and confirmation of the Gospel being necessarily conjoined, as the *Greek* implies; compare Php 1:17), namely, 'inasmuch as ye are fellow partakers of my grace': inasmuch as ye share with me in 'the fellowship of the Gospel' (Php 1:5), and have manifested this, both by suffering as I do for the Gospel's sake (Php 1:28–30), and by imparting to me of your substance (Php 4:15). It is natural and right for me thus confidently to pray in your behalf. (ELLICOTT, and others translate,

'To be thus minded for you all'), because of my having you in my warmest remembrances even in my bonds, since you are sharers with me in the Gospel grace. Bonds do not bind love.

8. Confirmation of Php 1:7.

record – that is, *witness*.

in the bowels of Jesus Christ – 'Christ Jesus' is the order in the oldest manuscripts. My *yearning love* (so the *Greek* implies) to you is not merely from natural affection, but from devotedness to Christ Jesus. 'Not Paul, but Jesus Christ lives in Paul; wherefore Paul is not moved in the bowels (that is, the tender love, Jer 31:20) of Paul, but of Jesus Christ' [BENGEL]. All real spiritual love is but a portion of Christ's love which yearns in all who are united to Him [ALFORD].

9. The subject of his prayer for them (Php 1:4).

your love – to Christ, producing love not only to Paul, Christ's minister, as it did, but also to one another, which it did not altogether as much as it ought (Php 2:2 4:2).

knowledge – of doctrinal and practical truth.

judgment – rather, 'perception'; 'perceptive sense.' Spiritual perceptiveness: spiritual sight, spiritual hearing, spiritual feeling, spiritual taste. Christianity is a vigorous plant, not the hotbed growth of enthusiasm. 'Knowledge' and 'perception' guard love from being ill-judged.

10. Literally, '*With a view to* your *proving* (and so approving and embracing) *the things that excel*' (Ro 2:18); not merely things not bad, but the things best among those that are good; the things of more advanced excellence. Ask as to things, not merely, Is there no harm, but is there any good, and which is the best?

sincere – from a *Greek* root. *Examined in the sunlight and found pure.*

without offence – not stumbling; running the Christian race without falling through any stumbling-block, that is, temptation, in your way.

till – rather, 'unto,' 'against'; so that when the day of Christ comes, ye may be found pure and without offense.

11. which are – 'which *is* by (*Greek*, "*through*") Jesus Christ.' Through His sending to us the Spirit from the Father. 'We are wild and useless olive trees till we are grafted into Christ, who, by His living root, makes us fruit-bearing branches' [CALVIN].

12. understand – *Greek*, 'know.' The Philippians probably had feared that his imprisonment would hinder the spread of the Gospel; he therefore removes this fear.

the things which happened unto me – *Greek*, 'the things concerning me.'

rather – so far is my imprisonment from hindering the Gospel. Faith takes in a favourable light even what seems adverse [BENGEL] (Php 1:19,28 Php 2:17).

13. my bonds in Christ – rather as *Greek,* 'So that my bonds *have become manifest in Christ,*' that is, known, as endured in Christ's cause.

palace – literally, 'Prætorium,' that is, the barrack of the Praetorian guards attached to the palace of Nero, on the Palatine hill at Rome; not the general Prætorian camp outside of the city; for this was not connected with 'Cæsar's household,' which Php 4:22 shows the Prætorium here meant was. The emperor was 'Praetor,' or Commander-in-Chief; naturally then the barrack of his bodyguard was called the Prætorium. Paul seems now not to have been at large in his own hired house, though chained to a soldier, as in Ac 28:16,20,30,31, but in strict custody in the Prætorium; a change which probably took place on Tigellinus becoming Prætorian Prefect. See *Introduction.*

in all other places – so Chrysostom. Or else, 'To all the rest,' that is, 'manifest to all the other' Prætorian soldiers stationed elsewhere, through the instrumentality of the Prætorian household guards who might for the time be attached to the emperor's palace, and who relieved one another in succession. Paul had been now upwards of two years a prisoner, so that there was time for his cause and the Gospel having become widely known at Rome.

14. Translate as *Greek,* 'And *that* (Php 1:13) *most* of the brethren in the Lord.' 'In the Lord,' distinguishes them from 'brethren after the flesh,' Jewish fellow countrymen. Ellicott translates, '*Trusting in the Lord.*'

by my bonds – encouraged by my patience in bearing my bonds.

much more bold – Translate as *Greek,* 'are more abundantly bold.'

15. 'Some indeed *are preaching* Christ even *for* envy, that is, to carry out the *envy* which they felt towards Paul, on account of the success of the Gospel in the capital of the world, owing to his steadfastness in his imprisonment; they wished through envy to transfer the credit of its progress from him to themselves. Probably Judaizing teachers (Ro 14:1–23 1Co 3:10–15 9:1, 2Co 11:1–4).

good will – answering to 'the brethren' (Php 1:14); some being *well disposed* to him.

16, 17. The oldest manuscripts transpose these verses, and read, '*These* (last) *indeed out of love* (to Christ and me), knowing (the opposite of "thinking" below) that I am set (that is, appointed by God, 1Th 3:3) for the defence of the Gospel (Php 1:7, not on my own account). But the others *out of* contention (or rather, "a factious spirit"; "cabal"; a spirit of intrigue, using unscrupulous means to compass their end; "self-seeking" [Alford]) *proclaim* (the *Greek* is not the same as that for "preach," but, "*announce*") Christ, not sincerely (answering to "but of a spirit of intrigue," or "self-seeking").

Literally, "not purely"; not with a pure intention; the Jewish leaven they tried to introduce was in order to *glorify themselves* (Ga 6:12,13; however, see on Php 1:18), thinking (but in vain) *to raise up* (so the oldest manuscripts read) *tribulation* to my bonds.' Their *thought* was, that taking the opportunity of my being laid aside, they would exalt themselves by their Judaizing preaching, and depreciate me and my preaching, and so cause me trouble of spirit in my bonds; they thought that I, like themselves, sought my own glory, and so would be mortified at their success over mine. But they are utterly mistaken; 'I rejoice' at it (Php 1:18), so far am I from being *troubled* at it.

18. What follows from this? Does this trouble me as they thought it would? 'Notwithstanding' their unkind *thought* to me, and self-seeking intention, the cause I have at heart is furthered 'every way' of preaching, 'whether in pretense (with a by motive, Php 1:16) or in truth (out of true "love" to Christ, Php 1:17), Christ is *proclaimed;* and therein I do rejoice, yea, and I will rejoice.' From this it would seem that these self-seeking teachers in the main 'proclaimed Christ,' not 'another Gospel,' such as the Judaizers in Galatia taught (Ga 1:6-8); though probably having some of the Jewish leaven (see on Php 1:15,16), their *chief* error was their self-seeking envious *motive,* not so much error of doctrine; had there been *vital* error, Paul would not have *rejoiced.* The *proclamation of* Christ,' however done, roused attention, and so was sure to be of service. Paul could thus rejoice at the good result of their bad intentions (Ps 76:10 Isa 10:5,7).

19. turn to my salvation – 'turn out *to me for,* (or *unto*) salvation.' This proclamation of Christ every way will turn out to *my spiritual good.* Christ, whose interests are my interests, being glorified thereby; and so the coming of His kingdom being furthered, which, when it does come, will bring completed 'salvation' (Heb 9:28) to me and all whose 'earnest expectation' (Php 1:20) is that Christ may be magnified in them. So far is their preaching from causing me, as they thought, *tribulation in my bonds* (Php 1:16). Paul plainly quotes and applies to himself the very words of the *Septuagint* (Job 13:16), 'This shall turn out to my salvation,' which belong to all God's people of every age, in their tribulation (compare Job 13:15).

through your prayer and the supply – The *Greek* intimately joins the two nouns together, by having but one preposition and one article: 'Through your prayer and (*the consequent*) supply of the Spirit of Jesus Christ (obtained for me through your prayer).'

20. According to my earnest expectation – The *Greek* expresses, 'expectation *with uplifted head* (Lu 21:28) *and outstretched neck.*' Ro 8:19

is the only other place in the New Testament that the word occurs. TITTMANN says, in both places it implies not mere *expectation,* but *the anxious desire of an anticipated prosperous issue in afflictive circumstances.* The subject of his earnest expectation which follows, answers to 'my salvation' (Php 1:19).

in nothing I shall be ashamed – in nothing have reason to be ashamed of 'my work for God, or His work in me' [ALFORD]. Or, 'in nothing be *disappointed* in my *hope,* but that I may fully obtain it' [ESTIUS]. So 'ashamed' is used in Ro 9:33.

all boldness – 'all' is opposed to 'in nothing,' as 'boldness' is the opposite to 'ashamed.'

so now also – when 'my body' is 'in bonds' (Php 1:17).

Christ – not Paul, 'shall be magnified.'

life, or by death – Whatever be the issue, I cannot lose; I must be the gainer by the event. Paul was not omniscient; in the issue of things pertaining to themselves, the apostles underwent the same probation of faith and patience as we.

21. For – in either event (Php 1:20) I must be the gainer, 'For to me.'

to live is Christ – whatever life, time, and strength, I have, is Christ's; Christ is the sole object for which I live (Ga 2:20).

to die is gain – not the act of dying, but as the Greek ('to have died') expresses, *the state after death.* Besides the glorification of Christ by my death, which is my primary object (Php 1:20), the change of state caused by death, so far from being a matter of *shame* (Php 1:20) or loss, as my enemies suppose, will be a positive 'gain' to me.

22. Rather as *Greek,* 'But if to live in the flesh (if), this (I say, the continuance in life which I am undervaluing) be the fruit of my labour (that is, be the condition in which the fruit of my ministerial labour is involved), *then* what I shall choose I know not (I cannot determine with myself, if the choice were given me, both alternatives being great goods alike).' So ALFORD and ELLICOTT. BENGEL takes it as *English Version,* which the *Greek* will bear by supposing an ellipsis, 'If to live in the flesh (be my portion), this (continuing to live) is the fruit of my labour,' that is, this continuance in life will be the occasion of my bringing in 'the fruit of labour,' that is, will be the occasion of 'labours' which are their own 'fruit' or reward; or, this my continuing 'to live' will have this 'fruit,' namely, 'labours' for Christ. GROTIUS explains 'the fruit of labour' as an idiom for 'worthwhile'; If I live in the flesh, this is worth my while, for thus Christ's interest will be advanced, 'For to me to live is Christ' (Php 1:21; compare Php 2:30 Ro 1:13). The second alternative, namely, dying, is taken up and handled,

Php 2:17, 'If I be offered.'

23. For – The oldest manuscripts read, 'But.' 'I know not (Php 1:22), BUT am in a strait (am perplexed) betwixt *the* two (namely, "to live" and "to die"), having the desire *for* departing (literally, "*to loose* anchor," 2Ti 4:6) and being with Christ; FOR (so the oldest manuscripts) it is by far better'; or as the *Greek,* more forcibly, 'by far *the more preferable*'; a double comparative. This refutes the notion of the soul being dormant during its separation from the body. It also shows that, while he regarded the Lord's advent as at all times near, yet that his death before it was a very possible contingency. The *partial* life eternal is in the interval between death and Christ's second advent; the *perfectional,* at that advent [BISHOP PEARSON]. *To depart* is better than to remain in the flesh; *to be with Christ is far, far better;* a New Testament hope (Heb 12:24), [BENGEL].

24. to abide – to continue somewhat longer.

for you – *Greek,* 'on your account'; 'for your sake.' In order to be of service to *you,* I am willing to forego my entrance a little sooner into blessedness; heaven will not fail to be mine at last.

25. I know – by prophetical intimations of the Spirit. He did not yet know the issue, as far as *human appearances* were concerned (Php 2:23). He doubtless returned from his first captivity to Philippi (Heb 13:19 Phm 1:22).

joy of faith – *Greek,* 'joy in your faith.'

26. Translate, 'That your matter of glorying (or *rejoicing*) may abound in Christ Jesus in me (that is, in my case; *in respect to me,* or *for me* who have been granted to your prayers, Php 1:19) through my presence again among you.' ALFORD makes the 'matter of glorying,' *the possession of the Gospel,* received from Paul, which would abound, be assured and increased, by his presence among them; thus, 'in me,' implies that Paul is the worker of the material of abounding in Christ Jesus. But 'my *rejoicing* over you' (Php 2:16), answers plainly to 'your *rejoicing* in respect to me' here.

27. Only – Whatever happens as to my coming to you, or not, make this your one only care. By supposing this or that future contingency, many persuade themselves they will be such as they ought to be, but it is better always without evasion to perform present duties under present circumstances [BENGEL].

let your conversation be – (Compare Php 3:20). The *Greek* implies, 'Let your *walk as citizens* (namely, of the heavenly state; "the city of the living God," Heb 12:22, "the heavenly Jerusalem," "fellow citizens of the saints," Eph 2:19) be.'

I ... see ... hear – so Php 1:30. 'Hear,' in order to include both alternatives, must include the meaning *know.*

your affairs – your state.

in one spirit – the fruit of partaking of the Holy Spirit (Eph 4:3,4).

with one mind – rather as *Greek*, '*soul*,' the sphere of the affections; subordinate to the 'Spirit,' man's higher and heavenly nature. 'There is sometimes natural antipathies among believers; but these are overcome, when there is not only unity of spirit, but also of *soul*' [BENGEL].

striving together – with united effort.

28. terrified – literally, said of horses or other animals startled or suddenly scared; so of sudden *consternation* in general.

which – your not being terrified.

evident token of perdition – if they would only perceive it (2Th 1:5). It attests this, that in contending hopelessly against you, they are only rushing on to their own perdition, not shaking your united faith and constancy.

to you of salvation – The oldest manuscripts read, 'of *your* salvation'; not merely *your temporal safety*.

29. it is given – *Greek*, 'it *has been* granted *as a favour*,' or 'gift of grace.' Faith is the gift of God (Eph 2:8), not wrought in the soul by the will of man, but by the Holy Ghost (Joh 1:12,13).

believe on him – 'To believe *Him*,' would merely mean to believe He speaks the truth. 'To believe *on Him*,' is to believe in, and trust through, Him to obtain eternal salvation. *Suffering for Christ* is not only not a mark of God's anger, but *a gift of His grace*.

30. ye saw in me – (Ac 16:12,19, 1Th 2:2). I am 'in nothing terrified by mine adversaries' (Php 1:29), so ought not ye. The words here, 'ye saw … and … hear,' answer to 'I come and *see* you, or else … *hear*' (Php 1:27).

Chapter 2

Php 2:1–30. Continued exhortation: to unity: to humility after Christ's example, whose glory followed his humiliation: to earnestness in seeking perfection, that they may be his joy in the day of Christ: his joyful readiness to be offered now by death, so as to promote their faith. His intention to send Timothy: his sending Epaphroditus meantime.

1. The 'therefore' implies that he is here expanding on the exhortation (Php 1:27), 'In one Spirit, with one mind (soul).' He urges *four influencing motives* in this verse, to inculcate the four Christian duties corresponding respectively to them (Php 2:2). 'That ye be *like-minded*, having the same *love*, of *one accord*, of one mind'; (1) 'If there be (with you) *any consolation in Christ*,' that is, any *consolation of which Christ is the source*, leading you to wish *to console me* in my afflictions borne for Christ's sake, ye owe it to me to grant my request 'that ye be like-minded' [CHRYSOSTOM and ESTIUS]: (2) 'If there be any comfort of (that is, flowing from) love,' the adjunct of 'consolation in Christ'; (3) 'If any fellowship of (communion together as Christians, flowing from joint participation in) the Spirit' (2Co 13:14). As *Pagans* meant literally those who were of one village, and *drank of one fountain*, how much greater is the union which conjoins those who drink of the same Spirit! (1Co 12:4,13) [GROTIUS]: (4) 'If any bowels (tender emotions) and mercies (compassions),' the adjuncts of 'fellowship of the Spirit.' The opposites of the two pairs, into which the four fall, are reprobated, Php 2:3,4.

2. Fulfil – that is, Make full. I have joy in you, *complete* it by that which is still wanting, namely, *unity* (Php 1:9).

likeminded – literally, 'that ye be of the same mind'; more general than the following 'of one mind.'

having the same love – equally disposed to love and be loved.

being of one accord – literally, 'with united souls.' This pairs with the following clause, thus, 'With united souls, being of one mind'; as the former two also pair together, 'That ye be like-minded, having the same love.'

3. *Let* nothing *be done* – The italicized words are not in the *Greek*. Perhaps the ellipsis had better be supplied from the *Greek* (Php 2:2), '*Thinking* nothing in the way of strife' (or rather, 'factious intrigue,' 'self-seeking,' see on Php 1:16). It is the *thought* which characterizes the action as good or bad before God.

lowliness of mind – The *direct* relation of this grace is to God alone; it is the sense of dependence of the creature on the Creator as such, and it places all created beings in this respect on a level. The man 'lowly of mind' as to his spiritual life is independent of men, and free from all slavish feeling, while sensible of his continual dependence on God. Still it INDIRECTLY affects his behaviour toward his fellow men; for, conscious of his entire dependence on God for all his abilities, even as they are dependent on God for theirs, he will not pride himself on his abilities, or exalt self in his conduct toward others (Eph 4:2 Col 3:12) [NEANDER].

let each esteem – Translate as *Greek*, 'esteeming each other superior to *yourselves*.' Instead of fixing your eyes on those points in which you excel, fix them on those in which your neighbors excels you: this is true 'humility.'

4. The oldest manuscripts read, 'Not *looking each of you* (plural, *Greek*) on his own things (that is, not *having regard* solely to them), but *each of you* on the things of others' also. Compare Php 2:21; also Paul's own example (Php 1:24).

5. The oldest manuscripts read, 'Have this mind in you.' He does not put forward himself (see on Php 2:4, and Php 1:24) as an example, but Christ, THE ONE pre-eminently who sought not His own, but 'humbled Himself' (Php 2:8), first in taking on Him our nature, secondly, in humbling Himself further in that nature (Ro 15:3).

6. Translate, 'Who *subsisting* (or *existing,* namely, originally: the *Greek* is not the simple substantive verb, "*to be*") in the form of God (the divine *essence* is not meant: but the *external self-manifesting characteristics of God,* the *form* shining forth from His glorious essence). The divine nature had infinite BEAUTY in itself, even without any creature contemplating that beauty: that beauty was "the form of God"; as "the *form* of a servant" (Php 2:7), which is in contrasted opposition to it, takes for granted the *existence* of His human nature, so "the form of God" takes for granted His divine nature [BENGEL], compare Joh 5:37 17:5 Col 1:15, "Who is the IMAGE of the invisible God" at a time *before* "every creature," 2Co 4:4, *esteemed* (the same *Greek* verb as in Php 2:3) His being *on an equality* with God no (act of) robbery' or *self-arrogation;* claiming to one's self what does not belong to him. ELLICOTT, WAHL, and others have translated, '*A thing* to be grasped at,' which would require the *Greek* to be *harpagma,* whereas *harpagmos* means the *act* of seizing. So *harpagmos* means in the only other passage where it occurs, PLUTARCH [*On the Education of Children,* 120]. The same insuperable objection lies against ALFORD's translation, 'He regarded not as *self-enrichment* (that is, an *opportunity for self-exaltation*) His equality with God.' His argument is that the antithesis (Php 2:7) requires it, 'He used His equality with God as *an opportunity, not for self-exaltation,* but for self-abasement, or *emptying Himself.*' But the antithesis is not between His *being on an equality with God,* and His *emptying Himself;* for He never emptied Himself of the fulness of His Godhead, or His 'BEING on an equality with God'; but between His being 'in the FORM (that is, the outward glorious self-manifestation) of God,' and His 'taking on Him *the form of a servant,*' whereby He in a great measure emptied Himself of His precedent 'form,' or outward self-manifesting glory as God. Not 'looking on His own things' (Php 2:4), He, though existing in the form of God, He esteemed it no robbery to be on an equality with God, yet made Himself of no reputation. 'Being on an equality with God, is not identical with subsisting in the form of God'; the latter expresses the *external characteristics,* majesty, and beauty of the Deity, which 'He emptied Himself of,' to assume 'the *form* of a servant'; the former, 'HIS BEING,' or NATURE, His already existing STATE OF EQUALITY with God, both the

Father and the Son having the same ESSENCE. A glimpse of Him 'in the form of God,' previous to His incarnation, was given to Moses (Ex 24:10,11), Aaron.

7. made himself of no reputation, and ... and – rather as the *Greek,* '*emptied* Himself, *taking* upon him the form of a servant, *being* made in the likeness of men.' The two latter clauses (there being no conjunctions, 'and ... and,' in the *Greek*) expresses *in what* Christ's 'emptying of Himself' consists, namely, in 'taking the form of a servant' (see on Heb 10:5; compare Ex 21:5,6, and Ps 40:6, proving that it was at the time when He assumed a *body,* He took 'the form of a *servant*'), and in order to explain *how* He took 'the form of a servant,' there is added, by 'being made in the likeness of men.' His subjection to the law (Lu 2:21 Ga 4:4) and to His parents (Lu 2:51), His low state as a carpenter, and carpenter's reputed son (Mt 13:55 Mr 6:3), His betrayal for the price of a bond-servant (Ex 21:32), and slave-like death to relieve us from the slavery of sin and death, finally and chiefly, *His servant-like dependence as man on God,* while His divinity was not outwardly manifested (Isa 49:3,7), are all marks of His 'form as a servant.' This proves: (1) He was in the form of a servant as soon as He was made man. (2) He was 'in the form of God' *before* He was 'in the form of a servant.' (3) He did as really subsist in the divine nature, as in the form of a servant, or in the nature of man. For He was as much 'in the form of God' as 'in the form of a servant'; and was so in the form of God as 'to be on an equality with God'; He therefore could have been none other than God; for God saith, 'To whom will ye liken Me and make Me equal?' (Isa 46:5), [BISHOP PEARSON]. His *emptying Himself* presupposes His previous *plenitude of Godhead* (Joh 1:14 Col 1:19 2:9). He remained full of this; yet He bore Himself as if He were *empty.*

8. being found in fashion as a man – *being already, by His* 'emptying Himself,' *in the form of a servant,* or likeness of man (Ro 8:3), 'He humbled Himself (still further by) *becoming* obedient *even* unto death (not as *English Version,* "He humbled Himself *and became,*" &c.; the *Greek* has no "and," and has the *participle,* not the verb), and that the death of the cross.' 'Fashion' expresses that He had the *outward guise, speech,* and *look.* In Php 2:7, in the Greek, the emphasis is on Himself (which stands before the *Greek* verb), 'He emptied *Himself,*' His divine self, viewed in respect to what He had heretofore been; in Php 2:8 the emphasis is on '*humbled*' (which stands before the *Greek* 'Himself'); He not only 'emptied Himself' of His previous 'form of God,' but submitted to *positive* HUMILIATION. He 'became obedient,' namely, to God, as His 'servant' (Ro 5:19 Heb 5:8). Therefore '*God*' is said to 'exalt' Him (Php 2:9), even as it was God to whom He became voluntarily 'obedient.' 'Even unto death' expresses the climax of His obedience (Joh 10:18).

9. Wherefore – as the just consequence of His self-humiliation and obedience (Ps 8:5,6 110:1,7 Mt 28:18 Lu 24:26 Joh 5:27 10:17 Ro 14:9 Eph 1:20–22 Heb 2:9). An intimation, that if we would hereafter be exalted, we too must, after His example. now humble ourselves (Php 2:3,5 Php 3:21 1Pe 5:5,6). Christ emptied Christ; God exalted Christ as man to equality with God [BENGEL].

highly exalted – Greek, 'super-eminently exalted' (Eph 4:10).

given him – Greek, 'bestowed on Him.'

a name – along with the corresponding reality, glory and majesty.

which – Translate, namely, 'that which is above every name.' The name 'JESUS' (Php 2:10), which is even now in glory His name of honour (Ac 9:5). 'Above' not only men, but angels (Eph 1:21).

10. at the name – rather as Greek, 'in the name.'

bow – rather, 'bend,' in token of worship. Referring to Isa 45:23; quoted also in Ro 14:11. To worship 'in the name of Jesus,' is to worship Jesus Himself (compare Php 2:11 Pr 18:10), or God in Christ (Joh 16:23 Eph 3:14). Compare 'Whosoever shall call upon the name of the Lord (that is, whosoever shall call on the Lord in His revealed character) shall be saved' (Ro 10:13 1Co 1:2); 'all that call upon the name of Jesus Christ our Lord' (compare 2Ti 2:22); 'call on the Lord'; Ac 7:59, 'calling upon … and saying, Lord Jesus' (Ac 9:14,21 22:16).

of things in heaven – angels. They worship Him not only as God, but as the ascended God-man, 'Jesus' (Eph 1:21 Heb 1:6 1Pe 3:22).

in earth – men; among whom He tabernacled for a time.

under the earth – the dead; among whom He was numbered once (Ro 14:9,11 Eph 4:9,10 Re 5:13). The demons and the lost may be included indirectly, as even they give homage, though one of fear, not love, to Jesus (Mr 3:11 Lu 8:31 Jas 2:19, see on Php 2:11).

11. every tongue – Compare 'every knee' (Php 2:10). In every way He shall be acknowledged as Lord (no longer as 'servant,' Php 2:7). As none can fully do so 'but by the Holy Ghost' (1Co 12:3), the spirits of good men who are dead, must be the class directly meant, Php 2:10, 'under the earth.'

to the glory of God the Father – the grand end of Christ's mediatorial office and kingdom, which shall cease when this end shall have been fully realized (Joh 5:19–23,30 17:1,4–7 1Co 15:24–28).

12. Wherefore – Seeing that we have in Christ such a specimen of glory resulting from

'obedience' (Php 2:8) and humiliation, see that ye also be 'obedient,' and so 'your salvation' shall follow your obedience.

as ye have … obeyed – 'even as ye have been obedient,' namely, to God, as Jesus was 'obedient' unto God (see on Php 2:8).

not as – 'not as if it were a matter to be done 'in my presence only, but now (as things are) much more (with more earnestness) in my absence (because my help is withdrawn from you)' [ALFORD].

work out – carry out to its full perfection. 'Salvation' is 'worked in' (Php 2:13 Eph 1:11) believers by the Spirit, who enables them through faith to be justified once for all; but it needs, as a progressive work, to be 'worked out' by obedience, through the help of the same Spirit, unto perfection (2Pe 1:5–8). The sound Christian neither, like the formalist, rests in the means, without looking to the end, and to the Holy Spirit who alone can make the means effectual; nor, like the fanatic, hopes to attain the end without the means.

your own – The emphasis is on this. Now that I am not present to further the work of your salvation, 'work out your own salvation' yourselves the more carefully. Do not think this work cannot go on because I am absent; 'for (Php 2:13) it is God that worketh in you.' In this case adopt a rule different from the former (Php 2:4), but resting on the same principle of 'lowliness of mind' (Php 2:3), namely, 'look each on his own things,' instead of 'disputings' with others (Php 2:14).

salvation – which is in 'Jesus' (Php 2:10), as His name (meaning God-Saviour) implies.

with fear and trembling – the very feeling enjoined on 'servants,' as to what ought to accompany their 'obedience' (Eph 6:5). So here: See that, as 'servants' to God, after the example of Christ, ye be so 'with the fear and trembling' which becomes servants; not slavish fear, but trembling anxiety not to fall short of the goal (1Co 9:26,27 Heb 4:1, 'Let us fear, lest a promise being left us of entering into His rest, any should come short of it'), resulting from a sense of our human insufficiency, and from the consciousness that all depends on the power of God, 'who worketh both to will and to do' (Ro 11:20). 'Paul, though joyous, writes seriously' [J. J. WOLF].

13. For – encouragement to work: 'For it is God who worketh in you,' always present with you, though I be absent. It is not said, 'Work out your own salvation, though it is God,' but, 'because it is God who.' The will, and the power to work, being first instalments of His grace, encourage us to make full proof of, and carry out to the end, the 'salvation' which He has first 'worked,' and is still 'working in' us, enabling us to 'work it out.' 'Our will does nothing thereunto without grace; but grace is inactive without our will' [St. Bernard]. Man is, in different senses, entirely active, and entirely passive: *God producing all, and we acting all.* What He produced is our own acts. It is not that God does some, and we the rest. God does all, and we do all. God is the only proper author, we the only proper actors. Thus the same things in Scripture are represented as from God, and from us. God makes a new heart, and we are commanded to make us a new heart; not merely because we must use the means in order to the effect, but the effect itself is our act and our duty (Eze 11:19 18:31 36:26) [Edwards].

worketh – rather as *Greek,* 'worketh *effectually.'* We cannot of ourselves embrace the Gospel of grace: 'the will' (Ps 110:3 2Co 3:5) comes solely of God's gift to whom He will (Joh 6:44,65); so also the power 'to do' (rather, '*to work effectually,'* as the *Greek* is the same as that for 'worketh in'), that is, effectual perseverance to the end, is wholly of God's gift (Php 1:6 Heb 13:21).

of his good pleasure – rather as *Greek,* 'FOR His good pleasure'; *in order to carry out* His sovereign gracious purpose towards you (Eph 1:5,9).

14. murmurings – *secret murmurings* and complaints against your fellow men arising from selfishness: opposed to the example of Jesus just mentioned (compare the use of the word, Joh 7:12,13 Ac 6:1 1Pe 4:9 Jude 1:16).

disputings – The *Greek* is translated 'doubting' in 1Ti 2:8. But here referring to profitless 'disputings' with our fellow men, in relation to whom we are called on to be 'blameless and harmless' (Php 2:15): so the *Greek* is translated, Mr 9:33,34. These disputings flow from 'vain glory' reprobated (Php 2:3); and abounded among the Aristotelian philosophers in Macedon, where Philippi was.

15. blameless and harmless – without either the repute of mischief, or the inclination to do it [Alford].

sons – rather as *Greek,* 'the children of God' (Ro 8:14–16). Imitation of our heavenly Father is the instinctive guide to our duty as His children, more than any external law (Mt 5:44,45,48).

without rebuke – 'without (giving handle for) *reproach.'* The whole verse tacitly refers by contrast to De 32:5, 'Their *spot* ... not ... of His *children ... a perverse* and *crooked* generation' (compare 1Pe 2:12).

ye shine – literally, 'appear' [Trench]. 'Show yourselves' (compare Mt 5:14–16 Eph 5:8–13).

as lights in the world – The *Greek* expresses 'as *luminaries* in the world,' as the sun and moon, 'the lights,' or 'great lights,' in the *material* world or in the firmament. The *Septuagint* uses the very same *Greek* word in the passage,

Ge 1:14,16; compare *Note,* see on Re 21:11.

16. Holding forth – to them, and so *applying* it (the common meaning of the *Greek;* perhaps here including also the other meaning, 'holding *fast').* The image of *light-bearers* or *luminaries* is carried on from Php 2:15. As the heavenly luminaries' *light* is closely connected with the *life* of animals, so ye hold forth the light of Christ's 'word' (received from me) which is the 'life' of the Gentiles (Joh 1:4 1Jo 1:1,5–7). Christ is 'the Light of the world' (Joh 8:12); believers are only 'light-bearers' reflecting His light.

that I may rejoice in – literally, 'with a view to (your being) *a subject of rejoicing* to me *against* the day of Christ' (Php 4:1 2Co 1:14 1Th 2:19).

that I have not run in vain – that it was not in vain that I laboured for your spiritual good.

17. Yea, and if – rather as *Greek,* 'Yea, if even'; implying that he regarded the contingency as not unlikely: He had assumed the *possibility* of his being found alive at Christ's coming (for in every age Christ designed Christians to stand in preparedness for His coming as at hand): he here puts a supposition which he regards as more likely, namely, his own death before Christ's coming.

I be offered – rather as *Greek,* 'I am poured out.' 'I am made a libation.' Present, not future, as the danger is threatening him *now.* As in sacrifices libations of wine were '*poured* upon' the offerings, so he represents his Philippian converts, offered through faith (or else their *faith* itself), as the sacrifice, and *his blood as the libation* 'poured upon' it (compare Ro 15:16 2Ti 4:6).

service – *Greek,* 'priest's ministration'; carrying out the image of a sacrifice.

I joy – for myself (Php 1:21,23). His expectation of release from prison is much fainter, than in the Epistles to Ephesians, Colossians, and Philemon, written somewhat earlier from Rome. The appointment of Tigellinus to be Prætorian Prefect was probably the cause of this change. See *Introduction.*

rejoice with you all – Alford translates, '*I congratulate* you all,' namely on the honour occurring to you by my blood being poured out on the sacrifice of your faith. If *they rejoiced* already (as *English Version* represents), what need of his urging them, 'Do ye *also* joy.'

18. 'Do ye also rejoice' at this honour to you, 'and congratulate me' on my blessed 'gain' (Php 1:21).

19. Php 2:22, 'ye know the proof of him ... that ... he hath served with me,' implies that Timothy had been long with Paul at Philippi; Accordingly, in the history (Ac 16:1–4 17:10,14), we find them *setting out* together from Derbe in Lycaonia, and together again at Berea in Macedonia, near *the conclusion* of Paul's missionary journey: an *undesigned* coincidence between the Epistle and history, a mark of genuineness [PALEY]. From Php 2:19–30, it appears Epaphroditus was to set out at once to allay the anxiety of the Philippians on his account, and at the same time bearing the Epistle; Timothy was to follow after the apostle's liberation was decided, when they could arrange their plans more definitely as to *where* Timothy should, on his return with tidings from Philippi, meet Paul, who was designing by a wider circuit, and slower progress, to reach that city. Paul's reason for sending Timothy so soon after having heard of the Philippians from Epaphroditus was that they were now suffering persecutions (Php 1:28–30); and besides, Epaphroditus' delay through sickness on his journey to Rome from Philippi, made the tidings he brought to be of less recent date than Paul desired. Paul himself also hoped to visit them shortly.

But I trust – Yet my death is by no means certain; yea, 'I *hope* (*Greek*) in the Lord (that is, by the Lord's help)'

unto you – literally, '*for* you,' that is, to your satisfaction, not merely motion, *to* you.

I also – that not only you 'may be of good *courage*' (so *Greek*) on hearing of me (Php 2:23), but 'I also, when I know your state.'

20. His reason for sending Timothy above all others: I have none so 'like-minded,' literally, 'like-*souled*,' with myself as is Timothy. Compare De 13:6, 'Thy friend which is as thine own *soul*' (Ps 55:14). Paul's second self.

naturally – *Greek*, 'genuinely'; 'with *sincere* solicitude.' A case wherein the Spirit of God so changed man's nature, that to be *natural* was with him to be *spiritual*: the great point to be aimed at.

21. Translate as *Greek*, '*They* all' (namely, who are now with me, Php 1:14,17 Php 4:21: such Demas, then with him, proved to be, Col 4:14; compare 2Ti 4:10 Phm 1:24).

seek their own – opposed to Paul's precept (Php 2:4 1Co 10:24,33 13:5). This is spoken, by comparison with Timothy; for Php 1:16,17 implies that some of those with Paul at Rome were genuine Christians, though not so self-sacrificing as Timothy. Few come to the help of the Lord's cause, where ease, fame, and gain have to be sacrificed. Most help only when Christ's gain is compatible with their own (Jud 5:17,23).

22. Rare praise (Ne 7:2).

as a son with the father – Translate, 'as a *child (serveth) a father.*'

served with me – When we might expect the sentence to run thus. 'As a child *serveth a father,* so he *served me*'; he changes it to 'served *with* me' in modesty; as Christians are not *servants* TO *one another*,' but *servants of God* WITH *one another* (compare Php 3:17).

in the gospel – *Greek*, '*unto*,' or '*for* the Gospel.'

23. so soon as I shall see – that is, so soon *as I shall have known for certain.*

24. also myself – as well as Timothy.

25. I supposed – 'I thought it necessary.'

to send – It was properly a *sending* Epaphroditus *back* (Php 4:18). But as he had come intending to stay some time with Paul, the latter uses the word 'send' (compare Php 2:30).

fellow soldier – in the 'good fight' of faith (Php 1:27,30 2Ti 2:3 4:7).

your messenger – literally, 'apostle.' The 'apostles' or 'messengers *of the churches*' (Ro 16:7 2Co 8:23), were distinct from the 'apostles' specially commissioned *by Christ,* as the Twelve and Paul.

ministered to my wants – by conveying the contributions from Philippi. The *Greek* '*leitourgon,*' literally, implies *ministering in the ministerial office.* Probably Epaphroditus was a presbyter or else a deacon.

26. For – reason for thinking it 'necessary to send' Epaphroditus. Translate as *Greek,* '*Inasmuch as* he *was longing* after you all.'

full of heaviness – The *Greek* expresses the being *worn out and overpowered with heavy grief.*

because that ye had heard that he had been sick – rather, 'that he was sick.' He felt how exceedingly saddened you would be in hearing it; and he now is hastening to relieve your minds of the anxiety.

27. Epaphroditus' sickness proves that the apostles had not ordinarily the *permanent* gift of miracles, any more than of inspiration: both were vouchsafed to them only for each particular occasion, as the Spirit thought fit.

lest I should have sorrow upon sorrow – namely, the sorrow of losing him by death, in addition to the sorrow of my imprisonment. Here only occurs anything of a sorrowful tone in this Epistle, which generally is most joyous.

29. Receive him – There seems to be something behind respecting him. If extreme affection had been the sole ground of his 'heaviness,' no such exhortation would have been needed [ALFORD].

in reputation – 'in honour.'

30. for the work of Christ – namely, the bringing of a supply to me, the minister of Christ. He was probably in a delicate state of health in setting out from Philippi; but at all hazards he undertook this service of Christian love, which cost him a serious sickness.

not regarding his life – Most of the oldest manuscripts read, 'hazarding.'

to supply your lack of service – Not that Paul would imply, they lacked the *will:* what they 'lacked' was the '*opportunity*' by which to send their accustomed bounty (Php 4:10). 'That which ye would have done if you could (but which you could not through absence), he did for you; therefore receive him with all joy' [ALFORD].

Chapter 3

Php 3:1–21. Warning against Judaizers: he has greater cause than they to trust in legal righteousness, but renounced it for Christ's righteousness, in which he presses after perfection: warning against carnal persons: contrast of the believer's life and hope.

1. Finally – rather, not with the notion of time, but making a transition to another general subject.

the same things – concerning 'rejoicing,' the prevailing feature in this Epistle (Php 1:18,25 2:17 4:4, where, compare the 'again I say,' with 'the same things' here).

In the Lord – marks the true ground of joy, in contrast with 'having confidence in the flesh,' or in any outward sensible matter of boasting (Php 3:3).

not grievous – 'not irksome.'

for you it is safe – Spiritual *joy* is the best safety against error (Php 3:2 Ne 8:10, end).

2. Beware – *Greek,* 'Have your eye on' so as to beware of. Contrast 'mark,' or 'observe,' namely, so as to follow Php 3:17.

dogs – *Greek,* 'the dogs,' namely, those impure persons 'of whom I have told you often' (Php 3:18,19); 'the abominable' (compare Re 21:8, with Re 22:15 Mt 7:6 Tit 1:15,16): 'dogs' in filthiness, unchastity, and snarling (De 23:18 Ps 59:6,14,15 2Pe 2:22): especially 'enemies of the cross of Christ' (Php 3:18 Ps 22:16,20). The Jews regarded the Gentiles as 'dogs' (Mt 15:26); but by their own unbelief they have ceased to be the true Israel, and are become 'dogs' (compare Isa 56:10,11).

evil workers – (2Co 11:13, 'deceitful workers.' Not simply 'evildoers' are meant, but men who 'worked,' indeed, ostensibly for the Gospel, but worked for evil: 'serving not our Lord, but their own belly' (Php 3:19; compare Ro 16:18). Translate, '*The* evil *workmen,*' that is, bad *teachers* (compare 2Ti 2:15).

concision – *Circumcision* had now lost its spiritual significance, and was now become to those who rested on it as any ground of justification, a senseless mutilation. Christians have the only true *circumcision,* namely, that of the heart; legalists have only 'concision,' that is, *the cutting off of the flesh.* To make 'cuttings in the flesh' was expressly prohibited by the law (Le 21:5): it was a Gentile-heathenish practice (1Ki 18:28); yet this, writes Paul indignantly, is what these *legalists* are virtually doing in violation of the law. There is a remarkable gradation, says Birks [*Horæ Apostolicæ*] in Paul's language as to circumcision. In his first recorded discourse (Ac 13:39), circumcision is not named, but implied as included in the law of Moses which cannot justify. Six or seven years later, in the

Epistle to Galatians (Ga 3:3), the first Epistle in which it is named, its spiritual inefficiency is maintained against those Gentiles who, beginning in the Spirit, thought to be perfected in the flesh. Later, in Epistle to Romans (Ro 2:28,29), he goes farther, and claims the substance of it for every believer, assigning the shadow only of it to the unbelieving Jew. In Epistle to Colossians (Col 2:11 3:11), still later, he expounds more fully the true circumcision as the exclusive privilege of the believer. Last of all here, the very name is denied to the legalist, and a term of reproach is substituted, 'concision,' or *flesh-cutting.* Once obligatory on all the covenant-people, then reduced to a mere national distinction, it was more and more associated in the apostle's experience with the open hostility of the Jews, and the perverse teaching of false brethren.

3. 'We are the (real) circumcision' (Ro 2:25–29 Col 2:11).

worship God in the Spirit – The oldest manuscripts read, 'worship *by the Spirit of God*'; our religious *service* is rendered by the Spirit (Joh 4:23,24). Legal worship was outward, and consisted in outward acts, restricted to certain times and places. Christian worship is *spiritual,* flowing from the in workings of the Holy Spirit, not relating to certain isolated acts, but embracing the whole life (Ro 12:1). In the former, men trusted in something human, whether descent from the theocratic nation, or the righteousness of the law, or mortification of 'the flesh' ('Having confidence,' or 'glorying in the flesh') [Neander] (Ro 1:9).

rejoice in Christ Jesus – 'make our *boast* in Christ Jesus,' not in the law: the ground of their boasting.

have no confidence in the flesh – but in the Spirit.

4. 'Although I (emphatic) might have confidence *even* in the flesh.' Literally, 'I *having,*' but not using, 'confidence in the flesh.'

I more – have more 'whereof I might *have confidence* in the flesh.'

5. In three particulars he shows how he 'might have confidence in the flesh' (Php 3:4): (1) His pure Jewish blood. (2) His legal preciseness and high status as such. (3) His zeal for the law. The *Greek* is literally, 'Being in circumcision an eighth day person,' that is, not one circumcised in later life as a proselyte, but on the eighth day after birth, as the law directed in the case of Jew-born infants.

of **the tribe of Benjamin** – son of Rachel, not of the maid-servant [Bengel].

Hebrew of the Hebrews – neither one or other parent being Gentile. The 'Hebrew,' wherever he dwelt, retained the *language* of his fathers. Thus Paul, though settled in Tarsus, a Greek city, calls himself a Hebrew. A 'Grecian' or

Hellenist, on the other hand, in the New Testament, is the term used for a 'Greek-speaking' Jew [TRENCH].

touching the law – that is, as to legal status and strictness.

a Pharisee – 'of the straitest sect' (Ac 26:5).

6. Concerning – Translate as before and after, 'As touching Zeal' (compare Ac 22:3 26:9).

blameless – Greek, 'having become blameless' as to ceremonial righteousness: having attained in the eyes of man blameless legal perfection. As to the holiness before God, which is the inner and truest spirit of the law, and which flows from 'the righteousness of God by faith,' he on the contrary declares (Php 3:12–14) that he has not attained perfection.

7. gain – rather as Greek, 'gains'; including all possible advantages of outward status, which he had heretofore enjoyed.

I counted – Greek, 'I have counted for Christ's sake loss.' He no longer uses the plural as in 'gains'; for he counts them all but one great 'loss' (Mt 16:26 Lu 9:25).

8. Yea doubtless – The oldest manuscripts omit 'doubtless' (Greek, 'ge'): translate, 'nay more.' Not only 'have I counted' those things just mentioned 'loss for Christ's sake, but, moreover, I even DO count ALL things but loss.'

for the excellency – Greek, 'On account of the surpassing excellency (the super-eminence above them all) of the knowledge of Christ Jesus.'

my Lord – believing and loving appropriation of Him (Ps 63:1 Joh 20:28).

for whom – 'on account of whom.'

I have suffered the loss – not merely I 'counted' them 'loss,' but have actually lost them.

all things – The Greek has the article, referring to the preceding 'all things'; 'I have suffered the loss of them all.'

dung – Greek, 'refuse (such as excrements, dregs, dross) cast to the dogs,' as the derivation expresses. A 'loss' is of something having value; but 'refuse' is thrown away as not worthy of being any more touched or looked at.

win – Translate, to accord with the translation, Php 3:7, 'gain Christ.' A man cannot make other things his 'gain' or chief confidence, and at the same time 'gain Christ.' He who loses all things, and even himself, on account of Christ, gains Christ: Christ is His, and He is Christ's (So 2:16 6:3 Lu 9:23,24 1Co 3:23).

9. be found in him – 'be found' at His coming again, living spiritually 'in Him' as the element of my life. Once lost, I have been 'found,' and I hope to be perfectly 'found' by Him (Lu 15:8).

own righteousness … of the law – (Php 3:6 Ro 10:3,5). 'Of,' that is, from.

righteousness … of God by faith – Greek, 'which is from God (resting) upon faith.' Paul was transported from legal bondage into Christian freedom at once, and without any gradual transition. Hence, the bands of Pharisaism were loosed instantaneously; and opposition to Pharisaic Judaism took the place of opposition to the Gospel. Thus God's providence fitly prepared him for the work of overthrowing all idea of legal justification. 'The righteousness of faith,' in Paul's sense, is the righteousness or perfect holiness of Christ appropriated by faith, as the objective ground of confidence for the believer, and also as a new subjective principle of life. Hence it includes the essence of a new disposition, and may easily pass into the idea of sanctification, though the two ideas are originally distinct. It is not any arbitrary act of God, as if he treated as sinless a man persisting in sin, simply because he believes in Christ; but the objective on the part of God corresponds to the subjective on the part of man, namely, faith. The realization of the archetype of holiness through Christ contains the pledge that this shall be realized in all who are one with Him by faith, and are become the organs of His Spirit. Its germ is imparted to them in believing although the fruit of a life perfectly conformed to the Redeemer, can only be gradually developed in this life [NEANDER].

10. That I may know him – experimentally. The aim of the 'righteousness' just mentioned. This verse resumes, and more fully explains, 'the excellency of the knowledge of Christ' (Php 3:8). To know HIM is more than merely to know a doctrine about Him. Believers are brought not only to redemption, but to the Redeemer Himself.

the power of his resurrection – assuring believers of their justification (Ro 4:25 1Co 15:17), and raising them up spiritually with Him, by virtue of their identification with Him in this, as in all the acts of His redeeming work for us (Ro 6:4 Col 2:12 3:1). The power of the Divine Spirit, which raised Him from literal death, is the same which raises believers from spiritual death now (Eph 1:19,20), and shall raise their bodies from literal death hereafter (Ro 8:11).

the fellowship of his sufferings – by identification with Him in His sufferings and death, by imputation; also, in actually bearing the cross whatever is laid on us, after His example, and so 'filling up that which is behind of the afflictions of Christ' (Col 1:24); and in the will to bear aught for His sake (Mt 10:38 16:24 2Ti 2:11). As He bore all our sufferings (Isa 53:4), so we participate in His.

made conformable unto his death – 'conformed to the likeness of His death,' namely, by continued sufferings for His sake, and mortifying of the carnal self (Ro 8:29 1Co 15:31 2Co 4:10–12 Ga 2:20).

11. If by any means – not implying uncertainty of the issue, but the earnestness of the struggle of faith (1Co 9:26,27), and the urgent need of jealous self-watchfulness (1Co 10:12).

attain unto the resurrection of the dead – The oldest manuscripts read, 'the resurrection *from* (out of) the dead,' namely, the first resurrection; that of believers at Christ's coming (1Co 15:23 1Th 4:15 Re 20:5,6). The *Greek* word occurs nowhere else in the New Testament. 'The power of Christ's resurrection' (Ro 1:4), ensures the believer's attainment of the 'resurrection from the (rest of the) dead' (compare Php 3:20,21). Compare 'accounted worthy to *obtain the resurrection from the dead*' (Lu 20:35). 'The resurrection of the just' (Lu 14:14).

12. Translate, 'Not *that* I.' (I do *not* wish to be understood as saying *that*).

attained – 'obtained,' namely, a perfect knowledge of Christ, and of the power of His death, and fellowship of His sufferings, and a conformity to His death.

either were already perfect – 'or *am* already perfected,' that is, *crowned* with the garland of victory, my course *completed*, and *perfection absolutely reached*. The image is that of a *race course* throughout. See 1Co 9:24 Heb 12:23. See TRENCH [*Greek Synonyms of the New Testament*].

I follow after – 'I press on.'

apprehend … apprehended – 'If *so be* that I may *lay hold on* that (namely, the *prize*, Php 3:14) for which also *I was laid hold on* by Christ' (namely, at my conversion, So 1:4 1Co 13:12). Jesus – omitted in the oldest manuscripts. Paul was close to 'apprehending' the prize (2Ti 4:7,8). Christ the Author, is also the Finisher of His people's 'race.'

13. **I** – whatever others count as to themselves. He who counts himself perfect, must deceive himself by calling sin infirmity (1Jo 1:8); at the same time, each must *aim* at perfection, to be a Christian at all (Mt 5:48).

forgetting those things … behind – *Looking back* is sure to end in *going back* (Lu 9:62): So Lot's wife (Lu 17:32). If in stemming a current we cease pulling the oar against it, we are carried back. God's word to us is as it was to Israel, 'Speak unto the children of Israel that they go forward' (Ex 14:15). The Bible is our landmark to show us whether we are progressing or retrograding.

reaching forth – with hand and foot, like a runner in a race, and the body bent forward. The Christian is always humbled by the contrast between what he is and what he desires to be. The eye reaches before and draws on the hand, the hand reaches before and draws on the foot [BENGEL].

unto – towards (Heb 6:1).

14. **high calling** – literally, 'the calling that is *above*' (Ga 4:26 Col 3:1): 'the *heavenly* calling' (Heb 3:1). 'The prize' is 'the crown of righteous-

ness' (1Co 9:24 2Ti 4:8). Re 2:10, 'crown of life.' 1Pe 5:4, 'a crown of glory that fadeth not away.' 'The high,' or 'heavenly calling,' is not restricted, as ALFORD thinks, to Paul's own calling as an apostle by the summons of God from heaven; but *the common calling of all Christians to salvation in Christ*, which coming from heaven invites us to heaven, whither accordingly our minds ought to be uplifted.

15. **therefore** – resuming Php 3:3. 'As many of us then, as are perfect,' that is, *full grown* (no longer 'babes') in the Christian life (Php 3:3, 'worshipping God in the Spirit, and having no confidence in the flesh'), 1Co 2:6, fully established in things of God. Here, by 'perfect,' he means one *fully fit for running* [BENGEL]; knowing and complying with the *laws* of the course (2Ti 2:5). Though 'perfect' in this sense, he was not yet 'made perfect' (*Greek*) in the sense intended in Php 3:12, namely, 'crowned with *complete* victory,' and having attained *absolute perfection*.

thus minded – having the mind which he had described, Php 3:7–14.

otherwise minded – having too high an opinion of yourselves as to your attainment of Christian *perfection*. 'He who thinks that he has attained everything, hath nothing' [CHRYSOSTOM]. Probably, too, he refers to those who were tempted to think to attain to *perfection* by the law (Ga 3:3): who needed the warning (Php 3:3), 'Beware of the concision,' though on account of their former piety, Paul hopes confidently (as in Ga 5:10) that God will reveal the path of right-mindedness to them. Paul taught externally God 'reveals' the truth internally by His Spirit (Mt 11:25 16:17 1Co 3:6).

unto you – who sincerely strive to do God's will (Joh 7:17 Eph 1:17).

16. The expectation of a new revelation is not to make you less careful in walking according to whatever degree of knowledge of divine things and perfection you have already attained. God makes further revelations to those who walk up to the revelations they already have (Ho 6:3).

rule, let us mind the same thing – omitted in the oldest manuscripts. Perhaps partly inserted from Ga 6:16, and Php 2:2. Translate then, 'Whereunto we have attained, let us walk on (a military term, *march in order*) in the same (the measure of knowledge already attained).'

17. **followers** – *Greek*, 'imitators together.'

of me – as I am an *imitator of Christ* (1Co 11:1): Imitate me no farther than as I imitate Christ. Or as BENGEL 'My fellow imitators of God' or 'Christ'; 'imitators of Christ together with me' (see on Php 2:22; Eph 5:1).

mark – for imitation.

which walk so as ye have us for an ensample – In *English Version* of the former clause, the translation of this clause is, 'those who are walking so as ye have an example in us.' But in BENGEL's translation, 'inasmuch as,' or 'since,' instead of 'as.'

18. many walk – in such a manner. Follow not evildoers, because they are 'many' (Ex 23:2). Their numbers are rather a presumption against their being Christ's 'little flock' (Lu 12:32).

often – There is need of constant warning.

weeping – (Ro 9:2). A hard tone in speaking of the inconsistencies of professors is the very opposite of Paul's spirit, and David's (Ps 119:136), and Jeremiah's (Jer 13:17). The Lord and His apostles, at the same time, speak more strongly against empty professors (as the Pharisees), than against open scoffers.

enemies of the cross of Christ – in their *practice*, not in doctrine (Ga 6:14 Heb 6:6 10:29).

19. destruction – everlasting at Christ's coming. Php 1:28, 'perdition'; the opposite word is 'Saviour' (Php 3:20).

end – fixed doom.

whose god is their belly – (Ro 16:18); hereafter to be destroyed by God (1Co 6:13). In contrast to our 'body' (Php 3:21), which *our God*, the Lord Jesus, shall 'fashion like unto His glorious body.' Their belly is now pampered, our body now wasted; then the respective states of both shall be reversed.

glory is in their shame – As 'glory' is often used in the Old Testament for *God* (Ps 106:20), so here it answers to 'whose God,' in the parallel clause; and 'shame' is the Old Testament term contemptuously given to an idol (Jud 6:32, *Margin*). Ho 4:7 seems to be referred to by Paul (compare Ro 1:32). There seems no allusion to circumcision, as no longer *glorious*, but a *shame* to them (Php 3:2). The reference of the immediate context is to sensuality, and carnality in general.

mind earthly things – (Ro 8:5). In contrast to Php 3:20 Col 3:2.

20. our conversation – rather, 'our state' or 'country'; *our citizenship: our life as citizens.* We are but *pilgrims* on earth; how *then* should we 'mind earthly things?' (Php 3:19 Heb 11:9,10,13–16). Roman citizenship was then highly prized; how much more should the heavenly citizenship (Ac 22:28; compare Lu 10:20)?

is – *Greek,* 'has its existence.'

in heaven – *Greek,* 'in the heavens.'

look for the Saviour, the Lord Jesus Christ – 'We wait for (so the same *Greek* is translated, Ro 8:19) the Lord Jesus as a (that is, in the capacity of a) Saviour' (Heb 9:28). That He is 'the Lord,' now exalted above every name, assures our expectation (Php 2:9–11). Our High Priest is gone up into the Holy of Holies not made with hands, there to atone for us; and as the Israelites stood outside the tabernacle, expecting Aaron's return (compare Lu 1:21), so must we look unto the heavens expecting Christ thence.

21. *Greek,* 'Who shall *transfigure* the body *of our humiliation* (namely, in which our humiliation has place, 2Co 4:10 Eph 2:19 2Ti 2:12), that it may be *conformed* unto the body *of His glory* (namely, in which His glory is manifested), according to the *effectual working* whereby.' Not only shall He come as our 'Saviour,' but also as our *Glorifier.*

even – not only to make *the body* like His own, but 'to subdue *all things,*' even death itself, as well as Satan and sin. He gave a sample of the coming *transfiguration* on the mount (Mt 17:1). Not a change of *identity,* but of *fashion* or *form* (Ps 17:15 1Co 15:51). Our spiritual resurrection now is the pledge of our bodily resurrection to glory hereafter (Php 3:20 Ro 8:11). As Christ's glorified body was essentially identical with His body of humiliation; so our resurrection bodies as believers, since they shall be like His, shall be identical essentially with our present bodies, and yet 'spiritual bodies' (1Co 15:42–44). Our 'hope' is, that Christ, by His rising from the dead, hath obtained the power, and is become the pattern, of our resurrection (Mic 2:13).

Chapter 4

Php 4:1–23. Exhortations: thanks for the supply from Philippi: greeting; and closing benediction.

1. 'Wherefore'; since we have such a glorious hope (Php 3:20,21).

dearly beloved – repeated again at the close of the verse, implying that his great love to them should be a motive to their obedience.

longed for – 'yearned after' in your absence (Php 1:8).

crown – in the day of the Lord (Php 2:16 1Th 2:19).

so – as I have admonished you.

stand fast – (Php 1:27).

2. Euodia and Syntyche were two women who seem to have been at variance; probably deaconesses of the church. He repeats, 'I beseech,' as if he would admonish each separately, and with the utmost impartiality.

in the Lord – the true element of Christian union; for those 'in the Lord' by faith to be at variance, is an utter inconsistency.

3. true yoke-fellow – yoked with me in the same Gospel yoke (Mt 11:29,30; compare 1Ti 5:17,18).

help those women – rather, as *Greek,* 'help *them,*' namely, Euodia and Syntyche.

which laboured with me – 'inasmuch as they laboured with me.' At Philippi, women were the first hearers of the Gospel, and Lydia the first convert. It is a coincidence which marks genuineness, that in this Epistle alone, special instructions are given to women who laboured with Paul in the Gospel. In selecting the first teachers, those first converted would naturally be fixed on. Euodia and Syntyche were doubtless two of 'the women who resorted to the riverside, where prayer was wont to be made' (Ac 16:13), and being early converted, would naturally take an active part in teaching other women called at a later period; of course not in public preaching, but in a less prominent sphere (1Ti 2:11,12).

Clement – bishop of Rome shortly after the death of Peter and Paul. His Epistle from the Church of Rome to the Church of Corinth is extant. It makes no mention of the supremacy of the See of Peter. He was the most eminent of the apostolical fathers. ALFORD thinks that the Clement here was *a Philippian,* and not necessarily Clement, bishop of Rome.

in the book of life – the register-book of those whose 'citizenship is in heaven' (Lu 10:20 Php 3:20). Anciently, free cities had a roll book containing the names of all those having the right of citizenship (compare Ex 32:32 Ps 69:28 Eze 13:9 Da 12:1 Re 20:12 21:27).

4. (Isa 61:10.)
alway – even amidst the afflictions now distressing one (Php 1:28–30).

again – as he had already said, 'Rejoice' (Php 3:1). Joy is the predominant feature of the Epistle.

I say – *Greek,* rather, 'I *will* say.'
5. moderation – from a *Greek* root, 'to yield,' whence *yieldingness* [TRENCH]; or from a root, 'it is fitting,' whence *'reasonableness of dealing'* [ALFORD], that considerateness for others, *not urging one's own rights to the uttermost,* but waiving a part, and thereby rectifying the injustices of justice. The archetype of this grace is God, who presses not the strictness of His law against us as we deserve (Ps 130:3,4); though having exacted the fullest payment for us from our Divine Surety. There are included in 'moderation,' *candour* and *kindliness. Joy in the Lord* raises us above rigorism towards others (Php 4:5), and carefulness (Php 4:6) as to one's own affairs. Sadness produces *morose harshness* towards others, and a troublesome spirit in ourselves.

Let … be known – that is, in your conduct to others, let nothing inconsistent with 'moderation' be seen. Not a precept to make a *display* of moderation. Let this grace 'be known' to men in *acts;* let 'your requests be made to God' in word (Php 4:6).

unto all men – even to the 'perverse' (Php 2:15), that so ye may win them. Exercise 'forbearance' even to your persecutors. None is so ungracious as not to be kindly to someone, from some motive or another, on some occasion; the believer is to be so 'unto all men' at all times.

The Lord is at hand – The Lord's coming again speedily is the grand motive to every Christian grace (Jas 5:8,9). Harshness to others (the opposite of 'moderation') would be taking into our own hands prematurely the prerogatives of judging, which belongs to the Lord alone (1Co 4:5); and so provoking God to judge us by the strict letter of the law (Jas 2:12,13).

6. Translate, 'Be anxious about nothing.' Care and prayer are as mutually opposed as fire and water [BENGEL].

by prayer and supplication – *Greek,* 'by *the* prayer and *the* supplication' appropriate to each case [ALFORD]. *Prayer* for blessings; and the general term. *Supplication,* to avert ills; a special term, *suppliant entreaty* (see on Eph 6:18).

thanksgiving – for every event, prosperity and affliction alike (1Th 5:18 Jas 5:13). The Philippians might remember Paul's example at Philippi when in the innermost prison (Ac 16:25). Thanksgiving gives effect to prayer (2Ch 20:21), and frees from *anxious carefulness* by making all God's dealings matter for *praise,* not merely for *resignation,* much less *murmuring.* 'Peace' is the companion of 'thanksgiving' (Php 4:7 Col 3:15).

let your requests be made known unto God – with generous, filial, unreserved confidence; not keeping aught back, as too great, or else too small, to bring before God, though you might feel so as to your fellow men. So Jacob, when fearing Esau (Ge 32:9–12); Hezekiah fearing Sennacherib (2Ki 19:14 Ps 37:5).

7. And – The inseparable consequence of thus laying everything before God in 'prayer with thanksgiving.'

peace – the dispeller of 'anxious care' (Php 4:6).

of God – coming from God, and resting in God (Joh 14:27 16:33 Col 3:15).

passeth – *surpasseth,* or *exceedeth,* all man's notional powers of understanding its full blessedness (1Co 2:9,10 Eph 3:20; compare Pr 3:17).

shall keep – rather, 'shall *guard*'; shall keep as a well-garrisoned stronghold (Isa 26:1,3). The same *Greek* verb is used in 1Pe 1:5. There shall be peace secure within, whatever outward troubles may besiege.

hearts and minds – rather, 'hearts (the *seat* of the thoughts) and *thoughts*' or purposes.

through – rather as *Greek,* 'in Christ Jesus.' It is in Christ that we are 'kept' or 'guarded' secure.

8. Summary of all his exhortations as to relative duties, whether as children or parents, husbands or wives, friends, neighbors, men in the intercourse of the world.

true – sincere, *in words.*

honest – *Old* English for 'seemly,' namely, *in action;* literally, *grave, dignified.*

just – towards *others.*

pure – 'chaste,' in relation to *ourselves.*

lovely – lovable (compare Mr 10:21 Lu 7:4,5).

of good report – referring to the *absent* (Php 1:27); as 'lovely' refers to what is lovable *face to face.*

if there be any virtue – 'whatever virtue there is' [ALFORD]. 'Virtue,' the standing word in heathen ethics, is found once only in Paul's Epistles, and once in Peter's (2Pe 1:5); and this in uses different from those in heathen authors. It is a term rather earthly and human, as compared with the names of the spiritual graces which Christianity imparts; hence the rarity of its occurrence in the New Testament. Piety and true morality are inseparable. Piety is love with its face towards God; morality is love with its face towards man. Despise not anything that is good in itself; only let it keep its due place.

praise – whatever is *praiseworthy;* not that Christians should make man's praise their aim (compare Joh 12:43); but they should live so as to *deserve* men's praise.

think on – have a continual regard to, so as to 'do' these things (Php 4:9) whenever the occasion arises.

9. both – rather, 'The things *also* which ye have learned ... these *practice*'; the things which besides recommending them in words, have been *also* recommended *by my example,* carry into practice.

heard – though ye have not yet sufficiently 'received' them.

seen – though ye have not as yet sufficiently 'learned' them [BENGEL].

and – 'and then,' as the necessary result (Php 4:7). Not only 'the peace of God,' but 'the God of peace' Himself 'shall be with you.'

10. But – transitional conjunction. But 'now' to pass to another subject.

in the Lord – He views everything with reference to Christ.

at the last – 'at last'; implying he was expecting their gift, not from a selfish view, but as a 'fruit' of their faith, and to 'abound' to their account (Php 4:11,17). Though long in coming, owing to Epaphroditus' sickness and other delays, he does not imply their gift was too late.

your care ... hath flourished again – Greek, 'Ye have flourished again (*revived,* as trees sprouting forth *again* in spring) in your care *for* me.'

wherein ye were also careful – in respect to which (*revival,* namely, the sending of a supply to me) 'ye were also (all along) careful, but ye lacked opportunity'; whether from want of means or want of a messenger. Your 'lack of service' (Php 2:30), was owing to your having 'lacked opportunity.'

11. I have learned – The *I* in Greek is emphatic. I leave it to others if they will, to be discontented. *I,* for my part, have learned, by the teaching of the Holy Spirit, and the dealings of Providence (Heb 5:8), to be content in every state.

content – The *Greek,* literally expresses 'independent of others, and having *sufficiency in one's self.*' But Christianity has raised the term above the haughty *self-sufficiency* of the heathen Stoic to the *contentment* of the Christian, whose *sufficiency* is not in *self,* but in *God* (2Co 3:5 1Ti 6:6,8 Heb 13:5; compare Jer 2:36 45:5).

12. abased – in low circumstances (2Co 4:8 6:9,10).

everywhere – rather, 'in each, and in all things' [ALFORD].

instructed – in the secret. Literally, 'initiated' in a secret teaching, which is a *mystery* unknown to the world.

13. I can do all things – Greek, 'I have strength for all things'; not merely 'how to be abased and how to abound.' After special instances he declares his *universal* power – how triumphantly, yet how humbly! [MEYER].

through Christ which strengtheneth me – The oldest manuscripts omit 'Christ'; then translate, 'In *Him* who giveth me *power,*' that is, by virtue of my living union and identification with Him, who is my strength (Ga 2:20). Compare 1Ti 1:12, whence probably, 'Christ' was inserted here by transcribers.

14. He here guards against their thinking from what he has just said, that he makes light of their bounty.

ye did communicate with my affliction – that is, ye made yourselves *sharers with* me in my present affliction, namely, by sympathy; of which sympathy your *contribution* is the proof.

15. Now – 'Moreover.' Arrange as *Greek,* 'Ye also know (as well as I do myself).'

in the beginning of the gospel – dating from the *Philippian* Christian era; at the first preaching of the Gospel at Philippi.

when I departed from Macedonia – (Ac 17:14). The Philippians had followed Paul with their bounty when he left Macedonia and came to Corinth. 2Co 11:8,9 thus accords with the passage here, the dates assigned to the donation in both Epistles agreeing; namely, 'in the *beginning* of the Gospel' here, and there, at the time of his *first* visit to Corinth [PALEY, *Horæ Paulinæ*]. However, the supply meant here is not that which he received at Corinth, but the supply sent to him when 'in Thessalonica, once and again' (Php 4:16), [ALFORD].

as concerning giving and receiving – In the account between us, 'the giving' was all on your part; 'the receiving' all on mine.

ye only – We are not to wait for others in a good work, saying, 'I will do so, when others do it.' We must go forward, though *alone.*

16. even in Thessalonica – 'even' as early as when I had got no further than Thessalonica, ye sent me supplies for my necessities more than once.

17. a gift – *Greek,* '*the* gift.' Translate, 'It is not that *I seek after* the gift, but *I do seek after the* fruit that *aboundeth* to your account'; what I do seek is your spiritual good, in the abounding of fruits of your faith which shall be put down to your account, against the day of reward (Heb 6:10).

18. But – Though 'the gift' is not what I chiefly 'seek after' (Php 4:17), *yet* I am grateful for the gift, and hereby acknowledge it as ample for all my needs. Translate, 'I have all' that I want, 'and more than enough.' Literally, as *English Version,* 'I abound' over and above my needs.

I am full – *Greek,* 'I am filled full.'

the odour of a sweet smell – (See on Eph 5:2). The figure is drawn from the sweet-smelling incense which was burnt along with the sacrifices; their gift being in faith was not so much to Paul, as *to God* (Mt 25:40), before whom it 'came up for a memorial' (Ac 10:4), sweet-smelling in God's presence (Ge 8:21 Re 8:3,4).

sacrifice acceptable – (Heb 13:16).

19. my – Paul calls God here 'my God,' to imply that God would reward their bounty to HIS servant, by 'fully supplying' (translate so, literally, *fill to the full*) their every 'need' (2Co 9:8), even as they had 'fully' supplied his 'need' (Php 4:16,18). My Master will fully repay you; I cannot. The Philippians invested their bounty well since it got them such a glorious return.

according to his riches – The measure of His supply to you will be the immeasurable 'riches of His grace' (Eph 1:7).

in glory – These words belong to the whole sentence. 'Glory' is the element in which His rich grace operates; and it will be the element IN which He will 'supply fully all your need.'

by Christ Jesus – by virtue of your being 'IN' (so *Greek,* not 'by') Christ Jesus, the Giver and Mediator of all spiritual blessings.

20. God and our Father – Translate, 'Unto *our God and Father.*'

be glory – rather as the *Greek,* 'be *the* glory.' Not to us, but to Him be '*the* glory' alike of your gift, and of His gracious recompense to you.

21. Salute every saint – *individually.*

greet – salute you.

The brethren which are with me – Perhaps Jewish believers are meant (Ac 28:21). I think Php 2:20 precludes our thinking of 'closer friends,' 'colleagues in the ministry' [ALFORD]; he had only one close friend with him, namely, Timothy.

22. they that are of Cæsar's household – the slaves and dependents of Nero who had been probably converted through Paul's teaching while he was a prisoner in the Prætorian barrack attached to the palace. Philippi was a Roman 'colony,' hence there might arise a tie between the citizens of the mother city and those of the colony; especially between those of both cities who were Christians, converted as many of them were by the same apostle, and under like circumstances, he having been imprisoned at Philippi, as he now is at Rome.

23. (Ga 6:18).

be with you all. Amen – The oldest manuscripts read, 'Be with your spirit,' and omit 'Amen.'

COLOSSIANS

J.B. Lightfoot

Introduction

Character and contents of the letter

Only when we have once grasped the nature of the teaching which St. Paul is combating do we perceive that every sentence is vibrant with life and meaning.

The errors though twofold sprang from one root

The error of the heretical teachers was twofold. They had a false conception in theology, and they had a false basis of morals. These two were closely linked together, and had their root in the same fundamental error, the idea of matter as the abode of evil and thus antagonistic to God.

The answer to both is the same truth. As the two elements of the heretical teaching were derived from the same source, so the reply to both was sought by the apostle in the same idea, the conception of the Person of Christ as the one absolute mediator between God and man, the true and only reconciler of heaven and earth.

But though they are thus ultimately linked, it is still necessary for a better appreciation of St. Paul's position to deal with them separately, and to consider first the theological and then the ethical teaching of the letter.

1. The theological error of the heretics

This Colossian heresy was no coarse and vulgar development of falsehood. It soared far above the Pharisaic Judaism which St. Paul refutes in the letter to the Galatians. The question in which it was interested lies at the very root of our religious consciousness. The impulse was given to its speculations by an overwhelming sense of the unapproachable majesty of God, but an instinctive recognition of the chasm which separates God from man, God from the world, and God from matter. Its energy was sustained by the intense yearning after some mediation which might span the gap, and establish communion between the finite and the Infinite. Up to this point it was deeply religious in the best sense of the term.

The answer which it gave to these questions failed signally in two respects. On the one hand it was drawn from the atmosphere of mystical speculation. It had no foundation in history, and made no appeal to experience. On the other hand, notwithstanding its complexity, it was unsatisfactory in its results; for in this plurality of mediators none was competent to meet the requirements of the case. God here and man there – no angel or spirit, whether one or more, being neither God nor man, could truly reconcile the two.

St. Paul's answer is in the Person of Christ

The apostle pointed out to the Colossians a more excellent way. It was the great purpose of Christianity to satisfy those very yearnings which were working in their hearts, to solve that very problem which had exercised their minds. In Christ they would find the answer which they sought. His life – his cross and resurrection – was the guarantee; his Person – the Word incarnate – was the solution. He alone filled up, he alone could fill up, the void which lay between God and man, spanning the gulf which separated the Creator and creation. This solution offered by the gospel is as simple as it is adequate. To their cosmical speculations, and to their religious yearnings alike, Jesus Christ is the true answer. In the world, as in the church, Christ is the one and only mediator, the one and only reconciler. This twofold idea runs like a double thread through the fabric of the apostle's teaching in those passages of the letter where he is describing the Person of Christ.

It is convenient, in order to better understand St, Paul's teaching, to consider these two aspects of Christ's mediation separately – its function in the natural and in the spiritual order respectively.

a. In the universe

The heresy of the Colossian teachers came from their cosmical speculations. Therefore, it was natural for the apostle, in his reply, to stress the function of the Word in the creation and rule of the world. This is the aspect of Christ's work most prominent in the first of the two distinctly Christological passages (1:15–20). Everything was created by him, is sustained by him, and leads to him. Thus Christ is the beginning, the middle and the end of creation. He is this because he is the very image of the invisible God, because in him dwells the plenitude of Deity.

b. In the church

But, if Christ's mediatorial office in the physical creation was the starting point of the apostle's teaching, his mediatorial office in the spiritual creation is its principal theme. The cosmogonies of the false teachers were framed not so much in the interests of philosophy as in the interests of religion; and the apostle replies to them in the same spirit and with the same motive. If the function of Christ is unique in the universe, so is it also in the church. He is the sole and absolute link between God and humanity. Nothing short of his personality would suffice as medium of reconciliation between the two. Nothing short of his life and work in the flesh, as consummated in his person, would serve as an assurance of God's love and pardon. His cross is the atonement of mankind with God. He is the Head with whom all the living members of the body are in direct and immediate communication, who suggests their many activities to each other, who directs their different functions in subordination to the healthy working of the whole, from whom they individually receive their inspiration and their strength.

So angelic mediations are fundamentally wrong

Since Christ is all this he cannot consent to share his prerogative with others. He absorbs in himself the whole function of mediation. Through him alone, without any interposing link, the human soul has access to the Father. Here was the true answer to those deep yearnings after spiritual communion with God, which sought, and could not find, satisfaction in the many and fantastic creations of a dreamy mysticism. The worship of angels might give the appearance of humility; but it was in reality a contemptible defiance of the fundamental idea of the gospel, a flat denial of the absolute character of Christ's Person and office. It was a severance of the correct link with the Head, an amputation of the disordered limb, which was thus cut off from the source of life and left to perish for lack of spiritual nourishment.

2. The ethical error of the heretics

When we turn from the theology of these Colossian heretics to their ethical teaching, we find it characterized by the same earnestness. Of them it might indeed be said that they did 'hunger and thirst after righteousness.' Escape from impurity, immunity from evil, was a passion with them. But it was no less true that notwithstanding all their sincerity they 'went astray in the wilderness'; 'hungry and thirsty, their soul fainted within them.' By their fatal transference of the abode of sin from the human heart within to the material world without, they had incapacitated themselves from finding the true antidote. Where they placed the evil, there they necessarily sought the remedy. Hence they attempted to fence themselves around, and to purify their lives by a code of rigorous prohibitions. Their energy was expended on battling with the physical conditions of human life. Their whole mind was absorbed in the struggle with imaginary forms of evil. So their characters were moulded by the thoughts which habitually engaged them. Where the 'basic principles of this world,' the things that are 'all destined to perish with use' (1:20,22), engrossed all their attention, it could not fail but that they should be dragged down from the serene heights of the spiritual life into the cloudy atmosphere which shrouds this lower earth.

St. Paul substitutes a principle for ordinances

St. Paul sets himself to combat this false tendency. For negative prohibitions he substitutes a positive principle; for special enactments, a comprehensive motive. He tells them that all their scrupulous restrictions are vain, because they fail to touch the springs of action. If they would overcome the evil, they must strike at the root of the evil. Their point of view must be entirely changed. They must transfer themselves into a wholly new sphere of energy. This transference is nothing less than a journey from earth to heaven – from the region of the external and transitory to the region of the spiritual and eternal (3:1ff.). For a code of rules they must substitute a principle of life, which is one in its essence but infinite in its application, which will meet every emergency, will control every action, will resist every form of evil.

This principle is the heavenly life in Christ

This principle they have in Christ. With him they have died to the world; with him they have risen to God. Christ, the revelation of God's holiness, of God's righteousness, of God's love, is light, is life, is heaven. With him they have been translated into a higher sphere, have been brought face to face with the eternal Presence. Let them only realize this translation. It involves new insight, new motives, new energies. They will no more waste themselves on vexatious special restrictions. For they will be furnished with a higher inspiration which will cover all the minute details of action. They will not exhaust their energies in crushing this or that rising desire, but they will kill the whole body (2:11; 3:5,9) of their earthly passions through the strong arm of this personal communion with God in Christ.

St. Paul's teaching about faith and deeds considered in the light of this principle

When we once grasp this idea, which lies at the root of St. Paul's ethical teaching, the moral difficulty which is supposed to attach to his doctrine of faith and deeds has vanished. It is simply an impossibility that faith should exist without deeds. Though in form he states his doctrine as a relation of contrast between the two, in substance it resolves itself into a question of precedence. Faith and deeds are related as principle and practice. Faith – the repose in the unseen, the recognition of eternal principles of truth and right, the sense of personal obligations to an eternal Being who vindicates these principles – must come first. Faith is not an intellectual assent, nor merely a sympathetic sentiment. It is the absolute surrender of self to the will of a Being who has a right to command this surrender. It is this which puts people into a personal relationship with God, which (in St. Paul's language) justifies them before God. For it touches the springs of their actions; it fastens not on this or that detail of conduct, but extends throughout the whole sphere of moral activity; and thus it determines their character as responsible beings in the sight of God.

The style of this letter

While the hand of St. Paul is unmistakable throughout this letter, we miss the flow and the versatility of the apostle's earlier letters. A comparison with the letters to the Corinthians and to the Philippians will show the difference. It is distinguished from them by a certain ruggedness of expression. The divergence of style is not greater than will appear in the letters of any active-minded person, written at different times and under different circumstances. The letters which I have selected for contrast suggest that the absence of all personal link with the Colossian church will partially, if not wholly, explain the diminished fluency of this letter. At the same time none of St. Paul's letters are more vigorous in conception or more full of meaning. It is the very compression of the thoughts which creates the difficulty. If there is a lack of fluency, there is not lack of force. Feebleness is the last charge which can be brought against this letter.

Analysis

The following is an analysis of the letter

1. Introductory (1:1–13)

a. 1:1,2. Opening salutation
b. 1:3–8. Thanksgiving for the progress of the Colossians so far
c. 1:9–13. Prayer for their future advance in knowledge and well-doing through Christ.
(This leads the apostle to speak of Christ as the only path of progress.)

2. Doctrinal (1:13–2:3)

The Person and Office of Christ
a. 1:13,14. Through the Son we have our deliverance, our redemption
b. 1:15–19. The preeminence of the Son
    i) As the Head of the natural creation, the universe (1:15–17);
    ii) As the Head of the new moral creation, the church (1:18).
Thus he is the first in all things; and this, because the *pleroma* has its abode in him (1:19).
c. 1:20–2:3. The work of the Son – a work of reconciliation;
    i) Described generally (1:20)
    ii) Applied specially to the Colossians (1:21–23)
    iii) St. Paul's own part in carrying out this work. His sufferings and preaching. The 'mystery' with which he is charged (1:24–27).
His anxiety on behalf of all (1:28,29): and more especially of the Colossian and neighbouring churches (2:1–3).
(This expression of concern leads him straight on to the next division of the letter.)

3. Polemical (2:4–3:4)

Warning against errors.

a. 2:4–8. The Colossians charged to abide in the truth of the gospel as they received it at first, and not to be led astray by a strange philosophy which the new teachers offer.

b. 2:9–15. The truth stated first positively and then negatively.

(In the passage which follows (2:9–23) it will be observed how St. Paul alternates between the theological and practical bearings of the truth, marked (a) and (b) respectively.)

   i) Positively.

  (a) The *pleroma* dwells wholly in Christ and is communicated through him (2:9,10).

  (b) The true circumcision is a spiritual circumcision (2:11,12).

   ii) Negatively. Christ has

  (b) annulled the law of ordinances (2:14);

  (a) triumphed over all spiritual agencies, however powerful (2:15).

c. 2:1–3:4. Obligations which follow.

   i) Consequently the Colossians must not

  (a) either submit to ritual prohibitions (2:16,17),

  (b) or substitute the worship of inferior beings for allegiance to the Head (2:18,19).

   ii) On the contrary this must henceforth be their rule:

  1. They have died with Christ; and with him they have died to their old life, to earthly ordinances (2:20–23).

  2. They have risen with Christ; and with him they have risen to a new life, to heavenly principles (3:1–4).

4. Hortatory (3:5–4:6)

Practical application of this death and this resurrection.

a. 3:15–17. Comprehensive rules

   i) What vices are to be put off, being mortified in this death (3:5–11).

   ii) What graces are to be put on, being quickened through his resurrection (3:12–17).

b. 3:18–4:6. Special precepts

   i) The obligations

    Of wives and husbands (3:18,19);

    Of children and parents (3:20,21);

    Of slaves and masters (3:22–4:1).

   ii) The duty of prayer and thanksgiving; with special intercession on the apostle's behalf (4:2-4).

   iii) The duty of propriety in behaviour towards the unconverted (4:5,6).

5. Personal (4:7–18)

a. 4.7–9. Explanations relating to the letter itself.

b. 4:10–14. Greetings from various people.

c. 4:15–17. Greetings to various people. A message about Laodicea.

d. 4:18. Farewell.

Contents

See also *Outlines of the New Testament Books*, pp. 899–900, by John Wesley

---

Chapter 1

Opening greeting (1:1–2)

1. Apostle. On the exceptional omission of this title in some of St. Paul's letters see Philippians 1:1. Though there is no reason for supposing that his authority was directly impugned in the Colossian church, yet he interposes by virtue of his apostolic commission and therefore uses his authoritative title.

By the will of God. As in 1 Corinthians 1:1; 2 Corinthians 1:1; Ephesians 1:1–2; 2 Timothy 1:1. These passages show that the words cannot have a polemical bearing. If they had been directed against those who questioned his apostleship, they would probably have taken a stronger form. The expression must therefore be regarded as a renunciation of all personal worth, and a declaration of God's unmerited grace.

Timothy. The name of this disciple is attached to the apostle's own in the heading of the Philippian letter, which was probably written at an earlier stage in his Roman captivity. It appears also in the same connection in the letter to Philemon, but not in the letter to the Ephesians, though these two letters were contemporaneous with one another and with the Colossian letter. For an explanation of the omission, see the introduction of that letter.

In the letters to the Philippians and to Philemon the presence of Timothy is forgotten at once (see Philippians 1:1). In this letter the plural is maintained throughout the thanksgiving (1:3,4,7,8,9), but later dropped, when the apostle begins to speak in his own person (1:23,24), and so he continues to the end.

Brother. As some designation for Timothy seemed to be required, and as Timothy could not be called an apostle, this, as the simplest title, would naturally suggest itself.

2. The saints. That is, the people consecrated to God, the Israel of the new covenant. This mode of address marks the later letters of St. Paul. In his earlier letters (1 and 2 Thessalonians, 1 and 2 Corinthians and Galatians) he writes 'the church.' The change begins with the letter to the Romans, and from then on the apostle always uses 'holy' in various combinations in addressing churches (Romans, Philippians, Colossians and Ephesians). For a similar phenomenon, serving as a chronological mark.

And faithful brothers. This unusual addition is full of meaning. Some members of the Colossian church were shaken in their allegiance, even if they had not fallen from it. The apostle makes it plain that when he speaks about the holy brothers, saints, he means the true and steadfast members of the brotherhood. In this way he obliquely hints at the defection. So the words **and faithful brothers** are a supplementary explanation of **saints**. He does not directly exclude any, but he indirectly warns all. The epithet **faithful** cannot mean simply 'believing'; for then it would add nothing which is not already contained in **saints** and **brothers**.

In Christ. Most naturally connected with both words **faithful brothers**, though referring chiefly to **faithful**. Their state thus contrasts with the description of the heretical teacher, who (2:19) is 'not holding fast to the head.'

Our Father. This is the only instance in St. Paul's letters where the name of the **Father** stands alone in the opening benediction without the addition of Jesus Christ.

Thanksgiving for the Progress of the Colossians so far (1:3–8)

3. Father. If the word 'and' is omitted, as the balance of the authorities appears to suggest, the form of words here is quite exceptional. Elsewhere it runs, 'the God and Father of our Lord Jesus Christ' (see Romans 15:6; 2 Corinthians 1:3; 11:31; Ephesians 1:3; 1 Peter 1:3; compare Revelation 1:6). In Colossians 3:17 we have the words 'God the Father' which is also an unusual expression.

4. We have heard. Having heard from Epaphras (verse 8); for the apostle had no direct personal knowledge of the Colossian church.

In Christ Jesus. This links with **your faith**. The preposition **in** here and in the parallel passage, Ephesians 1:15, denotes the sphere in which their faith moves, rather than the object to which it is directed (compare 1 Corinthians 3:5).

5. The hope. 'For the hope,' that is, looking to the **hope**. The hope here is identified with the object of the **hope**. The sense of **hope**, as of the corresponding words in any language, oscillates between the subjective feeling and the objective realization.

Laid up for you. This is the word used in the gospels; see Matthew 6:20,21; Luke 12:34; 18:22.

The word of the truth, the gospel. 'The truth of the gospel,' that is, the true and genuine gospel as taught by Epaphras, and not the spurious substitute of these later pretenders.

6. In the whole world. For a similar hyperbole see Romans 1:8, and compare 1 Thessalonians 1:8 and 2 Corinthians 2:14. More is hidden under these words than appears on the surface. The true gospel, the apostle seems to say, proclaims its truth by its universality. The false gospels are the outgrowths of local circumstances, of special idiosyncrasies; the true gospel is the same everywhere. The false gospels address themselves to limited circles; the true gospel proclaims itself boldly throughout the world. Heresies are at best ethnic: truth is essentially universal. (See verse 23.)

Bearing fruit. 'Is constantly bearing fruit.' The fruit, which the gospel bears without fail in all soils and under every climate, is its credential, its verification, as against the pretensions of spurious counterfeits.

The use of the middle [tense] **bearing fruit** no other instance has been found. The use of the middle points to the force of the word here. The middle is intensive, the active extensive. The middle denotes the inherent energy, the active the external diffusion. The gospel is essentially a reproductive organism, a plant whose seed is in itself.

The grace of God. St. Paul's synonym for the gospel. For God's power and goodness it substituted self-mortification and self-exaltation. The gospel is called **the grace of God** again in 2 Corinthians 6:1 and 8:9, with reference to the same leading characteristic which the apostle delights to dwell on (see Romans 3:24; 5:15; Ephesians 2:5,8), and which he here tacitly contrasts with the teachings of the later intruders.

7. You learned. 'Even as you were instructed in it'.

Fellow-servant. See 4:7. The word does not occur elsewhere in St. Paul.

8. He has made known to us. 'As he preached to you from us, so also he brought back to us from the tidings, etc.'

In the Spirit. To be linked with **your love.** 'The fruit of the Spirit is love' (Galatians 5:22).

Prayer for their future advance in knowledge and well-doing through Christ (1:9–14)

9. The knowledge. A favourite word in the later letters of St. Paul. In all four letters of the first Roman captivity it is an element in the apostle's opening prayer for his correspondents' well-being (Philippians 1:9; Ephesians 1:17; Philemon 6; and here).

The compound translated **knowledge** (literally 'full knowledge') is used especially of the knowledge of God and of Christ, as being the perfection of knowledge (see Proverbs 2:5; Hosea 4:1 and 6:6; Ephesians 1:17 and 4:13; 2 Peter 1:2, 8 and 2:20).

Wisdom and understanding. The two words **wisdom** and **understanding** are frequently found together: Exodus 31:3; Deuteronomy 4:6; 1 Chronicles 22:12; 2 Chronicles 1:10; Isaiah 11:2 and 29:14; Daniel 2:20; 1 Corinthians 1:19.

Spiritual. The word is emphatic from its position in the Greek [where it is the last word in the sentence]. The false teachers also offered a **wisdom**, but it had only a show of wisdom (see 2:23); it was an empty counterfeit calling itself philosophy (2:8); it was the offspring of vanity nurtured by the unspiritual mind (2:18). (Also see 2 Corinthians 1:12, where a similar contrast is implied, and 1 Corinthians 1:20; 2:5,6,13; 3:19, where it is directly expressed.)

10. Lead lives worthy. See 1 Thessalonians 2:12 and Ephesians 4:1, and compare Philippians 1:27.

Pleasing. That is, 'to please God in all ways'; compare 1 Thessalonians 4:1. As this word for **pleasing** was commonly used to describe the correct attitude of men towards God, the addition of 'God' would not be necessary.

In every. That is, 'not only showing the fruits of your faith before men (Matthew 7:16), but yourselves growing meanwhile in moral stature (Ephesians 4:13).'

The knowledge of God. The simple instrumental dative represents the knowledge of God as the dew or the rain which nurtures the growth of the plant (Deuteronomy 32:2; Hosea 14:5).

11. Made strong. This word is not found elsewhere in the New Testament, except in Hebrews 11:34.

Endure everything with patience. The two words occur in the same context in 2 Corinthians 6:4, 6; 2 Timothy 3:10; James 5:10,11. The difference between their meanings is best seen in their opposites. While **endure** is the temper which does not easily succumb under suffering, **patience** is the self-restraint which does not hastily retaliate a wrong. The one is opposed to cowardice or despondency, the other to wrath or revenge (see Proverbs 15:18; 16:32). While **endure** is closely allied to hope (1 Thessalonians 1:3), **patience** is often connected with mercy (Exodus 34:6). This distinction however, though it applies generally, is not true universally (see Isaiah 57:15).

Joyfully. See James 1:2–3 and compare 1 Peter 4:13.

12. Giving thanks. The duty of thanksgiving is more than once laid on them later in this letter (2:7; 3:17; 4:2: compare 1 Thessalonians 5:18.)

To share in the inheritance. 'The portion

which consists in the lot.' The inheritance of Canaan, the allotment of the promised land, here presents an analogy to, and supplies a metaphor for, the higher hopes of the new dispensation, as in Hebrews 3:7–4:11. This is not won by us but is allotted to us.

Light. The inheritance of the saints is situated in the kingdom of light. For the whole context compare St. Paul's narrative in Acts 26:18 where all the ideas and many of the expressions recur. See also Acts 20:32, in another of St. Paul's later speeches.

13. 'We were slaves in the land of darkness. God rescued us from this thralldom. He transplanted us from there, and settled us as free colonists and citizens in the kingdom of his Son, in the realms of light.'

Rescued us. – By his strong arm, as a mighty conqueror: compare 2:15 'triumphing.'

Of his dear Son. Not of inferior angels, as the false teachers would have it (2:18), but of his own Son. The same contrast between a dispensation of angels and a dispensation of the Son underlies the words here, which is explicitly brought out in Hebrews 1:1–2:8; see especially Hebrews 1:2, compared with Hebrews 2:5.

14. Redemption The image of a captive and enslaved people is still continued. The metaphor, however, has changed from the victor who rescues the captive by force of arms 'rescued' (verse 13), to the philanthropist who releases him by the payment of a ransom.

The forgiveness of sins. In the parallel passage in Ephesians 1:7 the apostle defines redemption as the forgiveness of sins.

The Preeminence of the Son (1:15–19)

In the passage which follows St. Paul defines the Person of Christ, claiming for him the absolute supremacy:

first, in relation to the universe, the natural creation (verses 15–17);

second, in relation to the church, the new moral creation (verse 18).

He then combines the two, explaining this twofold sovereignty by the absolute indwelling of the *pleroma* (fullness) in Christ, and showing how, as a consequence, the reconciliation and harmony of all things must be effected in him (verses 19,20).

15.The image. This expression is used repeatedly by Philo, as a description of the Logos. St. Paul applies the term to our Lord in an earlier letter, 2 Corinthians 4:4 'Christ, who is the image of God'; compare 2 Corinthians 3:18.

Beyond the very obvious notion of 'likeness,' the word **image** involves two other ideas.

First, representation. **Image** implies the archetype of which it is a copy. The **image** might be the result of direct imitation like the head of a sovereign on a coin, or it might be due to

natural causes like the parental features in the child, but in any case it was derived from its prototype. The word itself, however, does not necessarily imply perfect representation. Thus man is said to be the image of God (1 Corinthians 11:7).

Second, manifestation. The underlying idea of **image** is the manifestation of the hidden. The Word, whether preincarnate or incarnate, is the revelation of the unseen Father (compare John 1:18; 14:9–10).

The firstborn of all creation. The word **firstborn** has a twofold parentage.

First, like **image** it is closely connected with and taken from the Alexandrian vocabulary of the Logos. Among the early Christian fathers Justin Martyr again and again recognizes the application of the term **firstborn** to the Word.

Second, the word **firstborn** used absolutely, became a recognized title of Messiah (Psalm 89:27).

As the Person of Christ was the divine response alike to the philosophical questionings of the Alexandrian Jew and to the patriotic hopes of the Palestinian, those two currents of thought meet in the term **firstborn** as applied to our Lord, who is both the true Logos and the true Messiah. The main ideas then which the word **firstborn** involves are twofold: the one more directly linked with the Alexandrian conception of the Logos, the other more closely allied to the Palestinian conception of the Messiah.

First, priority to all creation. In other words it declares the absolute preexistence of the Son.

Second, sovereignty over all creation. God's **firstborn** is the natural ruler, the acknowledged head, of God's household.

16. For in him. The apostolic doctrine of the Logos teaches us to regard the eternal Word as having the same relation to the universe which the incarnate Christ holds to the church. He is the source of its life, the centre of all its developments, the mainspring of all its motions. The use of this preposition **in** to describe his relationship to the church abounds in St. Paul (Romans 8:1,2; 12:5; 16:3,7,9; 1 Corinthians 1:30; 4:15,17; 7:39; 15:18, 22), and more especially in the letters to the Colossians (2:7,10) and Ephesians. In the present passage, as in Colossians 1:17, the same preposition is applied to the universe (compare John 1:4).

Were created. The aorist tense is used here, which describes the definite historical act of creation.

All things. 'The universe of things,' not 'all things severally,' but 'all things collectively.' With very few exceptions, wherever this phrase occurs elsewhere, it stands in a similar connection (Colossians 1:17,20; 3:11; Romans 11:36; 1 Corinthians 8:6; 11:12; 12:6; 15:27,28; 2 Corinthians 5:18; Ephesians 1:10,11,23; 4:10; Hebrews

1:3; 2:8; Revelation 4:11). Thus it is seen that **all things** is almost equivalent to 'the universe.'

Thrones belonged to the highest grade of angelic beings, whose place is in the immediate presence of God. The meaning of the name, however, is doubtful. First, it may signify the occupants of thrones which surround the throne of God; as in the imagery of Revelation 4:4. The imagery there is taken from the court of an earthly king (see Jeremiah 52:32).

All things have been created through him and for him. 'As all creation passed out from him, so does it all converge again towards him.' He is not only the alpha but also the omega, not only the beginning but the end of creation, not only the first but also the last in the history of the universe (Revelation 23:13). For this double relation of Christ to the universe, as both the initial and the final cause, see Hebrews 2:10.

17. He himself is before all things. Compare John 8:58. The imperfect tense might have sufficed, but the present **is** declares that this preexistence is absolute existence. The **he** is as necessary for the completeness of the meaning, as the **is**. The one emphasized the personality, as the other declares the preexistence. For this emphatic **he** see again verse 18 (compare Ephesians 2:14; 4:10,11; 1 John 2:2, and especially Revelation 19:15).

All things hold together. 'Hold together, cohere.' He is the principle of cohesion in the universe. He impresses on creation that unity and solidarity which makes it a cosmos instead of a chaos.

18. The head. The inspiring, ruling, guiding, combining, sustaining power, the mainspring of its activity, the centre of its unity, and the seat of its life. In his earlier letters the relationship of the church to Christ is described in the same way (1 Corinthians 12:12–27; compare Romans 12:4); but the apostle there takes as his starting point the various functions of the members, the originating and controlling power of the Head. Compare 1:24; 2:19; Ephesians 1:22; 2:16; 4:4, 12,15; 5:23,30.

The church. This is in apposition with **the body**; compare 1:24; Ephesians 1:23.

He is the beginning. 'The origin.' The term is here applied to the incarnate Christ in his relationship to the church, because it is applicable to the eternal Word in relationship to the universe (Revelation 3:14). The parallelism of the two relationships is kept in view throughout. The word 'beginning' here involves two ideas. First, priority in time. Christ was the first-fruits of the dead (1 Corinthians 15:20,23). Second, originating power. Christ was also the source of life (Acts 3:14, compare Acts 5:31; Hebrews 2:10). He rose first from the dead, that others might rise through him.

In everything. Not in the universe only but in the church also.

19. All the fullness. 'The plenitude' [Greek: *pleroma*], a recognized technical term in theology, denoting the totality of the divine powers and attributes; compare 2:9.

Dwell. 'Should have its permanent abode.' The word occurs again in the same context at 2:9. The false teachers probably, like their later counterparts, maintained only a partial and transient connection of *pleroma* with the Lord.

The Work of the Son – a work of reconciliation (1:20–2:3)

20. The false teachers aimed at effecting a partial reconciliation between God and man through the interposition of angelic mediators. The apostle speaks of an absolute and complete reconciliation of universal nature to God, effected through the mediation of the incarnate Word. Their mediators were ineffective, because they were neither human nor divine. The true mediator must be both human and divine. It was necessary that in him all the plenitude of the Godhead should dwell. It was necessary also that he should be born into the world and should suffer as a man.

To reconcile. The corresponding word used in Ephesians 2:16 implies a restitution to a state from which they had fallen, or which was potentially theirs, or for which they were destined.

All things. The whole universe of things, material as well as spiritual, will be restored to harmony with God. How far this restoration of universal nature may be subjective, as involved in the changed perceptions of man thus brought into harmony with God, and how far it may have an objective and independent existence, it were vain to speculate.

To himself. The reconciliation is always represented as made to the Father. The reconciler is sometimes the Father (2 Corinthians 5:18–19), sometimes the Son (Ephesians 2:16: compare Romans 5:10,11).

21. Estranged. 'Alienated,' not strangers; compare Ephesians 2:12; 4:18.

Hostile. Enemies of God, as the consequence of being **estranged**, not 'hateful to God,' as it is taken by some. The active rather than the passive sense of 'enemies' is required by the context, which (as commonly in the New Testament) speaks of the sinner as reconciled to God, not of God as reconciled to the sinner: compare Romans 5:10. It is the mind of man, not the mind of God, which must undergo a change, that a reunion may be effected.

22. Before him. Does this refer to God's future judgment or his present approbation? The latter seems more probable as it has this meaning in the parallel passage in Ephesians 1:4. Where the future judgment is intended, a different expression is found (2 Corinthians 5:10).

23. To every creature. In fulfilment of the Lord's last command, (see Mark 16:15). The expression **to every creature** must not be limited to man. The statement is given in the broadest form, all creation animate and inanimate being included, as in Revelation 5:13. For the hyperbole **to every creature** compare 1 Thessalonians 1:8. To demand statistical exactness in such a context would be to require what is never required in similar cases. The apostle's motive here is to emphasize the universality of the genuine gospel, which has been offered without reserve to all alike, and to appeal to its publicity, as the credential and guarantee of its truth.

I, Paul, became a servant of this gospel. Why does St. Paul introduce himself here so abruptly? His motive can hardly be the assertion of his apostolic authority, for it does not appear that this was questioned; otherwise he would have declared his commission in stronger terms. We can only answer that impressed with the dignity of his office, as involving the offer of grace to the Gentiles, he cannot refrain from magnifying it. At the same time this mention enables him to link himself in ties of closer sympathy with the Colossians, and he passes on at once to his relationship with them: compare Ephesians 3:2–9; 1 Timothy 1:11, in which latter passage the introduction of his own name is equally abrupt.

24. I am now rejoicing. A sudden outburst of thanksgiving, that he, who was less than the least, who was not worthy to be called an apostle, should be allowed to share and even to supplement the sufferings of Christ.

The thought underlying **now** seems to be this: 'If ever I have been disposed to repine at my lot, if ever I have felt my cross almost too heavy to bear, yet now – now, when I contemplate the lavish wealth of God's mercy – now when I see all the glory of bearing a part in this magnificent work – my sorrow is turned to joy.'

In my flesh I am completing. Single compounds of this verb (1 Corinthians 14:16; 16:17; Galatians 6:2) and double compounds of this verb (2 Corinthians 9:12; 11:9) occur, but the Greek word for **I am completing** without any compounds occurs only here in the Septuagint or New Testament. This Greek word signifies that the supply comes from an opposite quarter to the deficiency. The point of the apostle's boast is that Christ the sinless Master should have left something for Paul the unworthy servant to suffer.

What is lacking. See 1 Corinthians 16:17; Philippians 2:30; 2 Corinthians 8:13,14; compare Luke 21:4.

For the sake of his body. An antithesis of the apostle's own flesh and Christ's body. This antithetical form of expression obliges St. Paul to explain what he means by the body of Christ, **that is, the church**; compare verse 18.

25. Fully known. That is, 'to preach fully,' 'to give its complete development to' (see Romans 15:19). Thus **the word of God** is here 'the gospel,' as in most places (1 Corinthians 14:36; 2 Corinthians 2:17; 4:2), though not always (Romans 9:6), in St. Paul, and also in the Acts.

26. The mystery. This is not the only term borrowed from the ancient mysteries, which St. Paul employs to describe the teaching of the gospel. The word 'mature' (verse 28) seems to be an extension of the same metaphor. But, whereas the heathen mysteries were strictly confined to a narrow circle, the Christian mysteries are freely communicated to all. There is therefore the intentional paradox in the use of the image by St. Paul.

Thus the idea of secrecy or reserve disappears when **mystery** is adopted into the Christian vocabulary by St. Paul: and the word signifies simply 'a truth which was once hidden but now is revealed,' 'a truth which without special revelation would have been unknown.' Of the nature of the truth itself the word says nothing. It may be transcendental, incomprehensible, mystical, mysterious, in the modern sense of the word (1 Corinthians 15:51; Ephesians 5:32): but this idea is quite accidental, and must be gathered from the special circumstances of the case, for it cannot be inferred from the word itself. Hence **mystery** is almost universally found in connection with words denoting revelation or publication (see Romans 16:25–26; Ephesians 3:3,5; 2 Thessalonians 2:7; 1 Timothy 3:16; 1 Corinthians 2:7; 14:2; 15:51).

But the one special **mystery** which absorbs St. Paul's thoughts in the letters to the Colossians and Ephesians is the free admission of the Gentiles on equal terms to the privileges of the covenant. For this he is a prisoner; this he is bound to proclaim fearlessly (4:3; Ephesians 6:19); this, though hidden from all time, was communicated to him by a special revelation (Ephesians 3:3); in this had God most signally displayed the lavish wealth of his goodness (verse 27; 2:2; Ephesians 1:6; 3:8). In one passage only throughout these two letters is **mystery** applied to anything else (Ephesians 5:32). The same idea of the **mystery** appears very prominently also in the thanksgiving at the end of Romans (Romans 16:25).

27. Riches. The 'wealth' of God as manifested in his dispensation of grace, is a prominent idea in these letters: compare 2:2; Ephesians 1:7,18; 3:8, 16.

Glory. That is, 'of the glorious manifestation.' This word **glory** in Hellenistic Greek is frequently used of a bright light (Luke 2:9; Acts 22:11; 1 Corinthians 15:41; 2 Corinthians 3:7). Hence it is applied generally to a divine disclosure, even where there is no physical accompaniment of light; and more especially to the revelation of God in Christ (John 1:14; 2 Corinthians 4:4).

Among the Gentiles. That is, 'as exhibited among the Gentiles.' It was just here that this **mystery,** this dispensation of grace, achieved its greatest triumphs and displayed its transcendent glory. Here too it was **riches;** for it overflowed all barriers of caste or race.

Christ in you. That is, 'you Gentiles.' Not Christ, but Christ given freely to the Gentiles, is the **mystery** of which St. Paul speaks.

28. We. The preachers. The apostle hastens, as usual, to speak of the part which he was privileged to bear in this glorious dispensation. He is constrained to magnify his office.

Warning. The two words **warning** and **teaching** present complementary aspects of the preacher's duty. For the two functions of the preacher's office, corresponding respectively to the two words, see Paul's own language in Acts 20:21.

Everyone. Three times repeated for the sake of emphasizing the universality of the gospel. This great truth, for which St. Paul gave his life, was now again endangered by the doctrine of an intellectual exclusiveness taught by the Gnosticizers, as before it had been endangered by the doctrine of a ceremonial exclusiveness taught by the Judaizers in Galatia.

In all wisdom. The Gnostic spoke of a blind faith for the many, of a higher 'knowledge' for the few. St. Paul declares that the fullest wisdom is offered to all alike. The character of the teaching is as free from restriction as are the qualifications of the recipients.

Mature. See 1 Corinthians 2:6–7. In both these passages the epithet **mature** is probably a metaphor borrowed from the ancient mysteries, where it seems to have been applied to the fully instructed, as opposed to the novices. While using the favourite Gnostic term, the apostle strikes at the root of the Gnostic doctrine. The language descriptive of the heathen mysteries is transferred by him to the Christian dispensation, that he may thus more effectively contrast the things signified. The true gospel also has its mysteries, its initiation: but these are open to all alike. In Christ every believer is **mature** for he has been admitted into its secrets.

29. For this. That is, 'that I may initiate all mankind in the fullness of this mystery,' 'that I may preach the gospel to all without reserve.' If St. Paul had been content to preach an exclusive gospel, he might have saved himself from more than half the troubles of his life.

Struggle. This word is used especially of the labour undergone by the athlete in his training, and therefore fitly introduces the metaphor 'striving' (compare 1 Timothy 4:10).

Chapter 2

1. Those in Laodicea. The Laodiceans were exposed to the same doctrinal perils as the Colossians.

2. Encouraged. 'Comforted' in the older and wider meaning of the word, but not with its modern and restricted sense (see Philippians 2:1).

3. All. These repetitions serve to emphasize the character of the gospel, which is as complete in itself, as it is universal in its application.

Wisdom and knowledge. The two words occur together again in Romans 11:33 and 1 Corinthians 12:8. While **knowledge** is simply intuitive, **wisdom** is the process of reasoning also. While **knowledge** applies mainly to the understanding of truths, **wisdom** is additionally the power of reasoning about them and seeing what else they link up with.

Abide in the truth of the gospel (2:4–8)

4. I am saying this. 'I say all this to you, lest you should be led astray by those false teachers who speak of another knowledge, of other mysteries.'

The reference in **I am saying this** extends over verses 1–3, and involves two statements: first, the declaration that all knowledge is comprehended in Christ (verses 2–3); second, the expression of his own personal anxiety that they should remain steadfast in this conviction (verses 1–2). This last point explains the language which follows, 'for though I am absent in body' (verse 5).

Firmness. 'Solid front, close phalanx,' a continuation of the metaphor. Compare 1 Peter 5:9, Acts 16:5.

6. As you therefore have received Christ Jesus as Lord. That is, 'Let your conviction and conduct be in perfect accordance with the doctrines and precepts of the gospel as it was taught to you.' For this use of **received,** that is, 'you received from your teachers, were instructed in,' compare 1 Corinthians 15:1, 3; Galatians 1:9; Philippians 4:9; 1 Thessalonians 2:13; 4:1,2; 2 Thessalonians 3:6. The word **received** implies either 'to receive as transmitted,' or 'to receive for transmission'.

Christ. Christ rather than the gospel, because the central point in the Colossian heresy was the subversion of the true idea of the Christ.

Jesus the Lord. 'Even Jesus the Lord,' in whom the true conception of the Christ is realized, compare Ephesians 4:20–21, where the same idea is more directly expressed. The true teaching of Christ consists of, firstly, the recognition of the historical person Jesus, and, secondly, the acceptance of him as the Lord. This teaching was put at serious risk by the mystic theosophy of the false teachers.

7. Built up in him. 'Being built up,' as in 1 Corinthians 3:10–14. **In him,** because in this letter Christ is represented as the binding element rather than as the foundation of the building. The repetition of **in him** emphasizes the main idea of the passage, and indeed of the whole letter.

In the faith. Faith is, as it were, the cement of the building.

As you were taught. That is, 'remaining true to the lessons which you received from Epaphras, and not led astray by any later pretenders'; compare 1:6–7.

8. Takes you captive. 'Makes you his prey, carries you off body and soul.' The Colossians had been rescued from the bondage of darkness; they had been transferred to the kingdom of light; they had been settled there as free citizens (1:12,13); and now there was danger that they should fall into a state worse than their former slavery, that they should be carried off as so much booty. Compare 2 Timothy 3:6.

Through philosophy and empty deceit. 'Through his philosophy which is an empty and deceptive deceit.' It should be remembered that in this later age, owing to Roman influence, the term **philosophy** was used to describe practical not less than speculative systems, so that it would cover the ascetic life as well as the mystic theosophy of these Colossian heretics. Hence the apostle is here flinging back at these false teachers a favourite term of their own, 'their vaunted philosophy, which is hollow and misleading.'

Tradition. Other systems, like the ceremonial *Mishnah* of the Pharisees, might correctly be described in this way (Matthew 15:2ff.; Mark 7:3ff.), but this description was peculiarly appropriate to a mystic theosophy like this of the Colossian false teachers. The teaching might be oral or written, but it was essentially esoteric, essentially traditional. It could not appeal to sacred books which were in front of the world for centuries.

Of the universe. That is, 'belonging to the sphere of material and external things.'

According to Christ. The apostle seems to say, 'you have attained the liberty and the intelligence of manhood; do not submit yourselves again to a rudimentary discipline fit only for children. In Christ you have been exalted into the sphere of the Spirit: do not plunge yourselves again into the atmosphere of material and sensuous things.'

The truth stated, positively and negatively (2:9–15)

9–15. In explaining the true teaching which is 'after Christ,' St. Paul condemns the two false principles which lay at the root of this heretical

teaching: first, the theological error of substituting inferior and created beings, angelic mediators, for the divine head himself (verses 9,10); and, secondly, the practical error of insisting on ritual and ascetic observances as the foundation of their moral teaching (verses 11–14). Their theological speculations and their ethical code alike were at fault.

9. For in him … The apostle justifies the foregoing charge that this doctrine was not according to Christ. 'In Christ dwells the whole *pleroma*, the entire fullness of the Godhead, whereas they represent it to you as dispersed among several spiritual agencies. Christ is the one fountain-head of all spiritual life, whereas they teach you to seek it in communion with inferior creatures.' The same truths have been stated before (1:14ff.) more generally, and they are now restated, with direct and immediate reference to the heretical teaching.

The whole fullness. 'The totality of the divine powers and attributes.'

Bodily. 'Bodily-wise,' 'corporeally,' that is, 'assuming a bodily form, becoming incarnate.' The indwelling of the *pleroma*, **fullness,** refers to the eternal Word, and not to the incarnate Christ: but **bodily** is added to show that the Word, in whom the *pleroma* thus had its abode from all eternity, crowned his work by the incarnation. Thus while the main statement **in him dwelleth all the fullness of the Godhead bodily** of St. Paul corresponds to the opening sentence of St. John 'In the beginning was the Word, and the Word was with God, and the Word was God,' the subsidiary adverb **bodily** of St. Paul has its counterpart in the additional statement of St. John, 'The Word was made flesh' (John 1:14). All other meanings which have been assigned to **bodily** here, such as 'wholly,' or 'really,' or 'essentially,' are unsupported by usage. Nor again can the body be thought of as anything else but Christ's human body; as for instance of the created world.

10. In him. True life consists in union with him, and not in dependence on any inferior being.

You have come to fullness in him. 'Your fulness comes from his fulness; his *pleroma* is transfused into you by virtue of your incorporation in him.' See John 1:16; Ephesians 3:19; 4:13.

The head. The image expresses much more than the idea of sovereignty: the head is also the centre of vital force, the source of all energy and life.

Of every ruler and authority. And therefore of those angelic beings whom the false teachers adopted as mediators, thus transferring to the inferior members the allegiance due to the Head: compare verse 18.

11. The previous verses have dealt with the

theological tenets of the false teachers. The apostle now turns to their practical errors: 'You do not need the circumcision of the flesh; for you have received the circumcision of the heart. There are three distinguishing features of this higher circumcision. First, it is not external but internal, not made with hands but by the Spirit. Second, it divests not of a part only of the flesh, but of the whole body of evil human desires. Third, it is the circumcision not of Moses, or of the patriarchs, but of Christ.' Thus it is distinguished, as regards first its character, secondly its extent, and thirdly its author.

Putting off the body of the flesh. 'The whole body which consists of the flesh,' that is, 'the body with all its corrupt and carnal affections,' as in 3:5. See also Romans 6:6; 7:24; Philippians 3:21.

12. Baptism is the grave of the old man, and the birth of the new. As he sinks beneath the baptismal waters, the believer buries there all his corrupt affections and past sins; as he emerges from there, he rises regenerate, quickened to new hopes and a new life. This it is, because it is not only the crowning act of his own faith but also the seal of God's adoption and the earnest of God's Spirit. Thus baptism is an image of his participation both in the death and in the resurrection of Christ. For this twofold image, as it presents itself to St. Paul; see especially Romans 6:3ff.

In baptism. 'In the act of baptism.' A distinction seems to be observed elsewhere in the New Testament between **baptism** correctly called by this name, and 'washing' of different kinds, of 'cups, pitchers and kettles' in Mark 7:4 and 'ceremonial washings' in Hebrews 9:10. Doubtless the form **baptism** was more appropriate to describe the one final and complete act of Christian

13. And when you. That is, 'you Gentiles.' This will appear from a study of the parallel passages 3:7–8; 1:13, 2:1ff.; 11,13,17,22; 3:2; 4:17.

Dead in trespasses. 'Sins' are the actual definite transgressions, while 'uncircumcision of your flesh' is the impure cardinal disposition which prompts them.

The uncircumcision of your flesh. The external fact is here mentioned, not for its own sake but for its symbolical meaning. The outward uncircumcision of the Gentiles is a type of their unchastened carnal mind. In other words, though the literal meaning is not excluded, the spiritual reference is most prominent, as appears from verse 11.

He forgave. As in Luke 6:42ff.; 2 Corinthians 2:7,10; 12:13; Ephesians 4:32. The idea of sin as a debt incurred to God (Matthew 6:12) underlies this expression. The image is carried out in the cancelled written code, verse 14.

14. Nailing it to his cross. 'The abrogation was even more emphatic. Not only was the writing erased, but the document itself was torn up and thrown aside.' By **nailing** is meant that the law of ordinances was nailed to the cross, torn with Christ's body, and destroyed with his death. It has been supposed that in some cities the abrogation of a decree was signified by running a nail through it and hanging it up in public. The image would thus gain force, but there is no distinct evidence of such a custom.

15. Having disarmed. This word appears not to occur at all before St. Paul, and rarely, if ever, after his time. The occurrence of this word here and in 3:9 and of 'putting off' verse 11 is remarkable. The choice of an unusual, if not a wholly new word must have been prompted by the desire to emphasize the completeness of the action. The Greek fathers translated this verse: 'having stripped off and put away the powers of evil,' making 'disarmed' govern 'the powers and authorities.' (See Chrysostom, Severianus, Theodore of Mopsuestia, and Theodoret.)

The meaning then will be as follows. Christ took upon himself our human nature with all its temptations (Hebrews 4:15) the powers of evil gathered about him. Again and again they assailed him; but each fresh assault ended in a new defeat. In the wilderness he was tempted by Satan; but Satan retired for the time baffled and defeated (Luke 4:13). Through the voice of his chief disciple the temptation was renewed, and he was entreated to decline his appointed sufferings and death. Satan was again driven off (Matthew 16:23). Then the last hour came. This was the great crisis of all, when 'darkness' reigned (Luke 22:53), when the prince of this world asserted his tyranny (John 12:31). The final act in the conflict began with the agony in Gethsemane; it ended with the cross of Calvary. The victory was complete. The enemy of mankind was defeated. The powers of evil, which had clung like a Nessus robe about his humanity, were torn off and thrown aside for ever. And the victory of mankind is involved in the victory of Christ. In his cross we too are divested of the poisonous clinging garments of temptation and sin and death. For the image of the garments compare Isaiah 64:6, but especially Zechariah 3:1ff. In this prophetic passage the image is used of his type and namesake, the Jesus of the Restoration, not in his own person, but as the high-priest and representative of a guilty but cleansed and forgiven people, with whom he is identified.

Triumphing over them. 'Leading them in triumph,' the same metaphor as in 2 Corinthians 2:14, where it is wrongly translated in the KJV 'causeth us to triumph.' Here, however, it is the defeated powers of evil, there the people who have submitted to Christ are led in public, chained to Christ's triumphal carriage. This is the correct meaning of 'triumph,' as found elsewhere.

Obligations which follow (2:16–3:4)

16ff. The two main tendencies of the Colossian heresy are discernible in this warning (verses 16–19), as they were in the previous statement (verses 9–15). Here, however, the order is reversed. The practical error, an excessive ritualism and ascetic rigour, is first dealt with (verses 16–17); the theological error, the interposition of angelic mediators, follows (verses 18–19). The first is the substitution of a shadow for the substance; the second is the preference of an inferior member to the head. The reversal of order is due to the link between the paragraphs; the opening subject in the second paragraph being a continuation of the concluding subject in the first, by the figure called chiasm: compare Galatians 4:5.

16. Condemn you. That is 'take you to task'; as in Romans 14:3ff. The judgment may or may not end in an acquittal; but in any case it is wrong, since these matters ought not to be taken as the basis of a judgment.

In matters of food or drink. See Romans 14:17; Hebrews 9:10; 1 Corinthians 8:8. The first indication that the Mosaic distinctions of things clean and unclean should be abolished is given by our Lord himself (Mark 7:14ff.). They were later formally annulled by the vision which St. Peter had (Acts 10:11ff.). The ordinances of the mosaic law applied almost exclusively to meats. It contained no prohibitions about drinks, except in a few cases; e.g., of priests ministering in the tabernacle (Leviticus 10:9), of liquids contained in unclean vessels etc. (Leviticus 11:34,36), and of Nazarite vows (Numbers 6:3).

The rigour of the Colossian false teachers, however, like that of their Jewish prototypes the Essenes, doubtless went far beyond the injunctions of the law. It is probable that they forbad wine and animal food altogether. For allusions in St. Paul to similar observances not required by the law; see Romans 14:2, 21; Titus 1:14; 1 Timothy 4:2–3.

Of observing festivals, new moons, or Sabbaths. The same three words occur together, as an exhaustive enumeration of the sacred times among the Jews, in 1 Chronicles 23:31; 2 Chronicles 2:4; 31:3; Ezekiel 45:17 and Hosea 2:11. See also Galatians 4:10, where the first three words correspond to the three words used here, though the order is reversed.

17. Two ideas are prominent in this image. First, the contrast between the ordinances of the law and the teaching of the gospel, as the shadow and the substance respectively; second, the conception of the shadow as thrown before the substance. Thus it implies both the unsubstantiality

and the supersession of the Mosaic ritual.

The substance belongs to of Christ. As the shadow belonged to Moses, so 'the substance belongs to Christ'; that is, the reality, the antitype, in each case is found in the Christian dispensation. Thus the Passover typifies the atoning sacrifice; the unleavened bread, the purity and sincerity of the true believer; the Pentecostal feast, the ingathering of the first fruits; the Sabbath, the rest of God's people.

18. The Christian's career is the contest of the stadium (Acts 20:24; 2 Timothy 4:7); Christ is the umpire, the dispenser of the rewards (2 Timothy 4:8); eternal life is the bay wreath, the victor's prize (1 Corinthians 9:24; Philippians 3:14). The Colossians were in a good position to win this prize; they had entered the competitions; they were running well: but the false teachers, thrusting themselves in the way, attempted to trip them up or otherwise impede them in the race, and thus to rob them of their just reward.

Disqualify you. 'Rob of the prize.' The false teachers at Colosse are not regarded as umpires nor as successful rivals but simply as people frustrating those who otherwise would have won the prize.

And worship of angels. There was an official parade of humility in selecting these lower beings as intercessors, rather than appealing directly to the throne of grace. The word refers to the external rites of religion, and signifies an over-scrupulous devotion to external forms.

Puffed up. Their profession of humility was a cloak for excessive pride (see 1 Corinthians 8:1).

By a human way of thinking. 'The mind of the flesh,' that is, unenlightened by the Spirit (compare Romans 8:7). It would seem that the apostle is here taking up some watchword of the false teachers. They doubtless boasted that they were directed 'by the mind.' Yes, he answers, but it is 'the mind of the flesh.'

19. The head. The supplication and worship of angels is a substitution of inferior members for the head, which is the only source of spiritual life and energy.

From God. That is, 'which partakes of God, which belongs to God, which has its abode in God.' Thus the finite is truly united with the Infinite; the end which the false teachers strove in vain to compass is attained; the gospel vindicates itself as the true theanthropism, after which the human heart is yearning and the human intellect is feeling.

20. From the theological tenets of the false teachers the apostle turns to the ethical – from the objects of their worship to the principles of their conduct. The baptism of Christ, he argues, is the death to the world. The Christian has passed away to another sphere of existence. Mundane ordinances have ceased to have any value for him, because his mundane life has ended. They belong to the category of the perishable; he has been translated to the region of the eternal. It is therefore a denial of his Christianity to subject himself again to their tyranny, to return once more to the dominion of the world.

If with Christ you died. For this link between baptism and death see 2:12 and 3:3. This death has many aspects in Paul's teaching. It is not only a dying with Christ (2 Timothy 2:11), but it is also a dying to or from something. This is sometimes represented as sin, (Romans 6:2), sometimes as self (2 Corinthians 5:14–15), sometimes as the law (Romans 7:6; Galatians 2:19).

To the elemental spirits of the universe. That is, 'from the rudimentary, disciplinary, ordinances, whose sphere is the mundane and sensuous.'

21. **'Do not handle.'** The apostle disparagingly repeats the prohibitions of the false teachers in their own words, '**Do not taste, Do not touch.'**

These prohibitions relate to defilement contracted in different ways by contact with impure objects. Some were doubtless reenactments of the Mosaic law; while others would be exaggerations or additions of a rigorous asceticism, such as we find among the Essene prototype of these Colossian heretics, for example, the avoidance of oil, of wine, or of flesh-meat, the shunning of contact with a stranger or a religious inferior, and the like.

22. Only consider what is the real import of this scrupulous avoidance. Why, you are attributing an inherent value to things which are fleeting; you yourselves are citizens of eternity, and yet your thoughts are absorbed in the perishable.

That perish with use. 'In the consuming.' The unusual word here was chosen for its expressiveness. The things could not be used without making them unfit for further use. The subtlety of the expression in the original cannot be reproduced by any translation.

They are simply human commands and teachings. The coincidences in St. Paul's language here with our Lord's words in Matthew 15:1–20 and Mark 7:1–23 are striking and suggest that the apostle had this discourse in his mind. First, both argue against these vexatious ordinances from the perishableness of meats. Second, both insist on the indifference of such things in themselves. In Mark 7:19 the evangelist emphasizes the importance of our Lord's words on this occasion, as practically abolishing the Mosaic distinction of meats by declaring all alike to be clean. Third, both link such ordinances with the practices condemned in the prophetic denunciation of Isaiah.

Chapter 3

1. **So if you have been raised with Christ.** The sacrament of baptism, as administered in the apostolic age, involved a twofold symbolism, a death or burial and a resurrection. In the rite itself these were represented by two distinct acts, the disappearance beneath the water and the emergence from the water: but in the changed typified by the rite they are two aspects of the same thing, 'like the concave and convex in a circle,' to use an old simile. The negative side – the death and burial – implies the positive side – the resurrection.

The change involved in baptism, if truly realized, must pervade a man's whole nature. It affects not only his practical conduct, but his intellectual conceptions also. It is nothing less than a removal into a new sphere of being. He is translated from earth to heaven; and with this translation his point of view is altered, his standard of judgment is wholly changed. Matter is to him no longer the great enemy; his position towards it is one of absolute neutrality. Ascetic rules, ritual ordinances, have ceased to have any absolute value, irrespective of their effects. All these things are of the earth, earthly. The material, the transitory, the mundane, has given place to the moral, the eternal, the heavenly.

Seek the things that are above. Cease to concentrate your energies, your thoughts on mundane ordinances, and realize your new and heavenly life, of which Christ is the pole-star.

Where Christ is seated on the right hand of God. Because Christ is seated this implies that the believer is also seated. See Ephesians 2:4–6; compare Revelation 3:21.

2. **Things that are above.** The same expression is repeated for emphasis; 'You must not only seek heaven; you must also think heaven.'

Hidden. 'Is hidden, is buried out of sight, to the world.' The apostle's argument is this: 'When you sank under the baptismal water, you disappeared forever to the world. You rose again, it is true, but you rose only to God. The world from then on knows nothing of your new life, and (as a consequence) your new life must know nothing of the world.'

4. **Christ.** A fourth occurrence of the name of Christ in this context; compare verse 1 'with Christ' and 'where Christ,' verse 3 'with Christ.' A pronoun would have been more natural, but less emphatic.

Then you also will be revealed with him. The veil which now shrouds your higher life from others, and even partly from yourselves, will then be withdrawn. The world which persecutes, despises, ignores now, will then be blinded with the dazzling glory of the revelation. Compare 1 John 3:1–2.

In glory. See John 17:22; Romans 8:17.

Comprehensive rules (3:5–17)

5. The false teachings of the Gnostics had failed to check sensual indulgence (2:23). The true teaching of the apostle has power to kill the whole carnal man. The substitution of a comprehensive principle for special precepts – of the heavenly life in Christ for a code of minute ordinances – eventually achieves the goal which the Gnostic teachers have striven, and striven in vain.

Put to death. 'Carry out this principle of death to the world (2:20; 3:3), and kill everything that is mundane and carnal in your being.'

Whatever in you is earthly. Each person has a twofold moral personality. There is in him the 'old self,' and there is in him also 'the new self' (verses 9–10). The old self with all his members must be pitilessly slain.

Fornication, impurity … The general order is from the less comprehensive to the more comprehensive.

And greed. 'And (especially) covetousness.' Impurity and greed may be said to include between them nearly the whole realm of human selfishness and vice.

(Which is idolatry.) Compare Ephesians 5:5. The covetous person sets up another object of worship besides God. There is a sort of religious purpose, devotion of the soul, to greed, which makes the sin of the miser so hateful.

7. These are the ways you also once followed. When you lived in this atmosphere of sin, when you had not yet died to the world.

8. All such things. 'Not only those vices which have been specially named before (verse 5) but all vices, of whatever kind.' The apostle accordingly goes on to specify sins of a wholly different type from those already mentioned, sins of uncharitableness, such as anger, rage, malice and the like.

Anger, wrath. The one denotes a more or less settled feeling of hatred, the other a tumultuous outburst of passion.

Malice. Or 'malignity,' as it may be translated in default of a better word. It is not (at least in the New Testament) vice generally, but the vicious nature which is bent on doing harm to others. This is clear from the context in which it comes in Romans 1:29; Ephesians 4:31 and Titus 3:3.

9. Old self. As in Romans 6:6; Ephesians 4:22. With this expression compare Romans 7:22; 2 Corinthians 4:16; Ephesians 3:16; 1 Peter 3:4.

10. The new self. Compare Ephesians 4:24. The **new self** in these passages is not Christ himself, but the regenerate person formed after Christ.

In knowledge. 'Unto perfect knowledge,' the true knowledge in Christ, as opposed to the false knowledge of the heretical teachers.

To the image of its creator. The reference is to Genesis 1:26. See also Ephesians 4:24. This reference, however, does not imply an identity of the creation here mentioned with the creation of Genesis, but only an analogy between the two. The spiritual man in each believer's heart, like the primal man in the beginning of the world, was created after God's image. The new birth was a recreation of God's image; the subsequent life must be a deepening of this image thus stamped on the man.

11. No longer Greek and Jew. Comparing the enumeration here with the parallel passage in Galatians 3:28, we note the difference. In Galatians the abolition of all distinctions is stated in the broadest way by the selection of three typical instances; religious prerogative ('neither Jew nor Greek'), social caste ('slave nor free'), gender ('male nor female'). In Colossians, on the other hand, the examples are chosen with special reference to the immediate circumstances of the Colossian church. First, the Judaism of the Colossian heretics is met by **no longer Greek and Jew**, and as it manifested itself especially in enforcing circumcision, this is further emphasized by **circumcised and uncircumcised.** Second, their Gnosticism again is met by **barbarian, Scythian.** They laid special stress on intelligence and knowledge. The apostle offers the full privileges of the gospel to barbarians. Third, special circumstances, connected with the eminent member of the church of Colosse, had directed his attention at this moment to the relationship between masters and slaves. Hence he cannot leave the subject without adding **slave and free,** though this has no special bearing on the Colossian heresy.

Barbarian. To the Jew the whole world was divided into 'Jews' and 'Greeks,' the privileged and unprivileged sections of mankind, religious prerogative being taken as the line of demarcation. To the Greek and Roman it was similarly divided into 'Greeks' and 'Barbarians,' again the privileged and unprivileged sections of the human race, civilization and culture being now the criterion and distinction. Thus from the one point of view the 'Greek' is contrasted disadvantageously with the 'Jew,' while from the other he is contrasted advantageously with the **Barbarian.** Both distinctions are equally antagonistic to the spirit of the gospel. The apostle declares both null and void in Christ. The twofold character of the Colossian heresy enables him to strike at these two opposite forms of error with one blow.

The word **Barbarian** correctly denoted one who spoke an inarticulate stammering, unintelligible language. 'Not till that word "barbarian,"' writes Professor Max Müller, 'was struck out of the dictionary of mankind and replaced by "brother," not until the right of all nations of the world to be classed as members of one genus or kind was recognized, can we look even for the first beginnings of our civilization. This change was effected by Christianity. ... "Humanity" is a word which you look for in vain in Plato or Aristotle; the idea of mankind as one family, as the children of one God, is an idea of Christian growth: and the science of mankind, and of the languages of mankind, is a science which, without Christianity, would never have sprung into life. When people had been taught to look on all men as brethren, then and only then, did the variety of human speech present itself as a problem that called for a solution in the eyes of thoughtful observers: and I therefore date the real beginning of the science of language from the first day of Pentecost.'

St. Paul was the great exponent of the fundamental principle in the Christian church which was symbolized on the day of Pentecost, when he declared, as here, that in Christ there is neither **Greek** nor **Barbarian**, or as in Romans 1:14 that he himself was a debtor equally to 'Greeks, and to Barbarians.'

Scythian. The lowest type of Barbarian. The savageness of the Scythians was proverbial.

But Christ is all, and in all! Christ has dispossessed and obliterated all distinctions of religious prerogative and intellectual preeminence and social caste. Christ has substituted himself for all these. Christ occupies the whole sphere of human life and permeates all its developments: compare Ephesians 1:23.

12. As. As people to whom Christ has become all in all. The incidental mention of Christ (verse 11) as superseding all other relationships gives occasion to this argumentative **As.** Compare 3:1.

As God's chosen ones. 'As elect ones of God.' Compare Romans 8:3; Titus 1:1. With St. Paul the same people are 'called' to Christ, and 'chosen out' from the world. St. Paul speaks of an individual Christian as 'elect,' or 'chosen' (see Romans 16:13; 1 Corinthians 1:26–27; 1 Peter 1:1; 2 Peter 1:10).

Elect denotes election by God not only to final salvation, but to any special privilege or work, whether it be, firstly, to church membership (Romans 1:6–7); secondly, to the work of preaching (Acts 9:15); thirdly, the Messiahship (1 Peter 2:4,6); fourthly, the Fatherhood of the chosen people (Romans 9:11); fifthly, the faithful remnant under the theocracy (Romans 11:5, 7,28).

Kindness, humility. The two words **kindness** and **humility** describe disposition of the Christian mind in general. It affects either our relationship to others (**kindness**), or our estimate of self (**humility**).

Meekness, and patience. These next two words denote the exercise of the Christian temper in its outer bearing towards others. They are best distinguished by their opposites.

Meekness is the opposite of rudeness or harshness, while **patience** is the opposite of resentment, revenge or wrath.

14. Above all. 'Over and above all these,' compare Luke 3:20. Love is the outer garment which holds the others in their places.

Which binds everything together. 'The bond of perfection,' that is, the power, which unites and holds together all those graces and virtues, which together make up perfection.

15. Rule. 'Be umpire'. Where there is a conflict of motives or desires, the peace of Christ must step in and decide which is to prevail.

16. The word of Christ. In this verse **Of Christ** is the subjunctive genitive, so that Christ is the speaker. Though 'the word of the Lord' and 'the word of God' occur frequently, **the word of Christ** is found here only. There seems to be no direct reference in this expression to any definite body of truths either written or oral, but **the word of Christ** denotes the presence of Christ in the heart, as an inner monitor: compare 1 John 2:14.

Psalms, hymns, and spiritual songs to God. The main idea of **psalms** is a musical accompaniment, and that of **hymns** praise to God, while **spiritual songs** is the general word for a song, whether accompanied or unaccompanied, whether of praise or on any other subject. Thus it was quite possible for the same song to be at the same time a 'psalm,' a 'hymn,' and a 'spiritual song.'

In the text the reference to **psalms**, we may suppose, is specially, though not exclusively (1 Corinthians 14:26), to the psalms of David, which would have in early times have formed part of the religious worship of the Christian brotherhood. On the other hand, **hymns** would more appropriately designate those hymns of praise which were composed by the Christians themselves on distinctly Christian themes, being either set forms of words or spontaneous effusions of the moment. The third term, **spiritual songs**, gathers up the other two, and extends the precept to all forms of song, with the limitation however that they must be **spiritual**.

Psalmody and hymnody were highly developed in the religious services of the Jews at this time. They would thus find their way into the Christian church from the very beginning. For instances of singing hymns or psalms in the apostolic age see Acts 4:24; 16:25; 1 Corinthians 14:15,26. Hence even in St. Paul's letters, more especially his later letters, fragments of such hymns appear to be quoted; for example, Ephesians 5:14.

The reference in the text is not solely or chiefly to public worship as such.

Singing ... in your hearts to the Lord. This external manifestation must be accompanied by the inner emotion. There must be the thanksgiving of the heart, as well as of the lips; compare Ephesians 5:19.

17. In the name of the Lord Jesus. This is the great practical lesson which flows from the theological teaching of the letter. Hence the reiteration of **Lord** in verses 18,20,22,23,24.

Special precepts (3:18–4:6)

1. The obligations of wives and husbands, children and parents.

18ff. These precepts, providing for the conduct of Christians in private households, should be compared with Ephesians 5:22–6:9; 1 Peter 2:18–3:7; Titus 2:1ff.

20. In everything. As verse 22. The rule is stated absolutely, because the exceptions are so few that they may be disregarded.

21. Do not provoke your children. Irritation is the first result of being too exacting with children, and irritation leads to moroseness ('discouragement').

Or they may lose heart. 'Become spiritless,' that is, 'go about their task in a listless, moody, sullen frame of mind.'

2. The obligations of slaves and masters

22. Slaves. The relationship of masters and slaves, both here and in the companion letter (Ephesians 6:5–9), are treated at greater length than is usual with St. Paul. Here especially the expansion of this topic, compared with the brief space assigned to the duties of wives and husbands (verses 18–19), or of children and parents (verses 20–21), deserves to be noticed. The fact is explained by a contemporary incident in the apostle's private life. His connections with Onesimus had turned his thoughts in this direction.

Not only while being watched. See Ephesians 6:6. This happy expression would seem to be the apostle's own coinage. At least there are no traces of it earlier.

24. From the Lord. 'However you may be treated by your earthly masters, you have still a Master who will recompense you.'

Chapter 4

1. Have a Master. As Ephesians 6:9; compare 1 Corinthians 7:22.

The duty of prayer and thanksgiving and right behaviour towards the unconverted (4:2–6)

2. Keeping alert. Long continuance in prayer is apt to produce listlessness. Hence the additional charge that the heart must be awake, if the prayer is to have any value. The word is not to be taken literally here, but metaphorically.

Thankgiving. As the crown of all prayer.

3. Pray for us. Here **us** is the apostles and preachers of the gospel, with reference more especially to Timothy (1:1) and Epaphras (4:12–13).

Open to us a door for the word. 'A door of admission for the word,' that is, 'an opportunity of preaching the gospel,' as 1 Corinthians 16:9, and 2 Corinthians 2:12.

The mystery of Christ. That is, the teaching of the free admission of the Gentiles. This is the leading idea which St. Paul in these letters attaches to **the mystery** of the gospel, see 1:26.

For which. St. Paul might have been still at large, if he had been content to preach a Judaic gospel. It was because he contended for Gentile liberty, and thus offended Jewish prejudices, that he found himself a prisoner. See Acts 21:28; 22:21–22; 24:5–6; 25:6,8.

In prison. See 2 Timothy 2:9 and Philemon 9.

4. So that I may reveal. The immediate purport of the Colossians' prayers must be that the apostle should have all opportunities of preaching the gospel: the ulterior object, that he should use these opportunities boldly.

5. Towards outsiders. 'Those outside the pale' of the church, the unbelievers; as in 1 Corinthians 5:12–13 and 1 Thessalonians 4:12. See also 1 Timothy 3:7. The believers on the other hand are 'those who are inside' (1 Corinthians 5:12).

Making the most of the time. 'Buying up the opportunity for yourselves,' letting no opportunity slip you, of saying and doing what may further the cause of the God.

6. Always be gracious. 'With grace, favour,' that is, 'acceptableness,' 'pleasingness'; compare Ecclesiastes 10:12.

Seasoned with salt. Compare Mark 9:50. The salt has two uses. First, it give a flavour to the discourse and recommend it to the palate: compare Job 6:6. This is the primary idea of the metaphor here, as the word **seasoned** seems to indicate. Secondly, salt preserves from corruption and renders wholesome.

Everyone. The apostle's precept was enforced by his own example, for he made it a rule to 'become all things to all people, so that I might by any means save some' (1 Corinthians 9:22).

Explanations about the letter (4:7–9)

7. Tychicus. Tychicus was charged by St. Paul at this same time with a more extended mission. He was entrusted with copies of the circular letter, which he was told to deliver in the principal churches of proconsular Asia. This mission would bring him to Laodicea, which was one of these great centres of Christianity; and, as Colosse was only a few miles away, the apostle would naturally engage him to pay a visit to the Colossians. At the same time the presence of an authorized delegate of St. Paul, as Tychicus was known to be, would serve to recommend Onesimus, who owing to his former conduct stood in every need of such a recommendation.

Tychicus was born in proconsular Asia (Acts 20:4) and perhaps of Ephesus (2 Timothy 4:12). He is found with St. Paul at three different epochs of his life. First, he accompanied him when on his way eastward at the close of the third missionary journey A.D. 58 (Acts 20:4), and probably like Trophimus (Acts 21:29) went with him to Jerusalem. It is probably indeed that Tychicus, together with others mentioned among St. Paul's numerous retinue on this occasion, was a delegate appointed by his own church according to the apostle's injunctions (1 Corinthians 16:3–4) to bear the contributions of his brethren to the poor Christians of Judea; and if so, he may possibly be the person recommended as the brother 'who is praised by all the churches for his service to the gospel' (2 Corinthians 8:18): but this will depend on the interpretation of Acts 20:5.

Second, we find Tychicus again in St. Paul's company at the time with which we are immediately concerned, when this letter was written, probably towards the end of the first Roman captivity. Third, we find Tychicus at the close of St. Paul's life (about A.D. 67), he appears again to have associated himself with the apostle, when his name is mentioned in connection with a mission to Crete (Titus 3:12) and another to Ephesus (2 Timothy 4:12).

Minister. But to whom? To the churches, or to St. Paul himself? The following **fellow-servant** suggests the latter as the prominent idea here. So in Acts 19:22 Timothy and Erastus are described as 'two of them that ministered unto him.' Tychicus himself also was one of several who ministered to St. Paul about that time (Acts 20:4). It is not probable, however, that **minister** has here its strict official sense, 'a deacon,' as in Romans 16:1; Philippians 1:1; 1 Timothy 3:8, 12.

Fellow-servant. The word does not occur elsewhere in St. Paul, except in 1:7, where it is said of Epaphras. It is probably owing to the fact of St. Paul's applying the term in both these passages to people whom he calls 'ministers', that **fellow-servant** seems to have been adopted as a customary form of address in the early church on the part of a bishop, when speaking of a deacon.

8. Encourage your hearts. That is, 'encourage you to persevere by his tidings and exhortations.' The phrase occurs again in Ephesians 6:22 and 2 Thessalonians 2:17. The prominent idea in all these passages is not comfort or consolation but perseverance in the right way.

9. The faithful and beloved brother. The man whom the Colossians had only known up to then, if they knew him at all, as a worthless

runaway slave, is thus commended to them as no more a slave but a brother, no more dishonest and faithless but trustworthy, no more an object of contempt but of love; compare Philemon 11,16.

Greetings to different people (4:10–14)

10. The greetings to Philemon (Philemon 23–24) are sent from the same people as to the Colossians, except that in the former case the name Jesus Justus is omitted.

Aristarchus. The Thessalonian. He started with St. Paul on his voyage from Jerusalem to Rome, but probably had parted from the apostle at Myra. If so, he must have rejoined him at Rome at a later date. He would be well known in proconsular Asia, which he had visited from time to time (Acts 19:29; 20:4; 27:2).

Fellow-prisoner. In Philemon 23 this honourable title is withheld from Aristarchus and given to Epaphras. In Romans 16:7 St. Paul's relatives, Andronicus and Junias, are called by this name.

Mark. Doubtless John Mark, who has been associated with St. Paul in his earlier missionary work; Acts 12:25; 15:37ff. This commendatory notice is especially interesting as being the first mention of him since the separation some twelve years before, Acts 15:39. In the later years of the apostle's life he entirely effaced the unfavourable impression left by his earlier desertion (2 Timothy 4:11).

Barnabas. Whenever St. Paul mentions Barnabas after the collision at Antioch (Galatians 2:11ff.), and the separation of missionary spheres (Acts 15:39), he does so in affectionate tones.

11. Jesus. He is not mentioned elsewhere. Even in the letter to Philemon his name is omitted. Probably he was not a man of any prominence in the church, but his personal devotion to the apostle prompted this honourable mention.

Justus. A common name or surname of Jews and proselytes, denoting obedience and devotion to the law. It is applied to two people in the New Testament, besides this Justus; first, to Joseph Barsabbas (Acts 1:23); second, to a proselyte at Corinth (Acts 18:7).

12. Epaphras. His full name would have been Epaphroditus, but he is always called by the shortened form Epaphras, and must not be confused with the Philippian Epaphroditus who also was with St. Paul at one period of his Roman captivity.

Who is one of you. 'Who belongs to you,' that is, born at Colosse, or at least living at Colosse, as in the case of Onesimus (verse 9); compare Acts 4:6; 21:8; Romans 16:10–11; 1 Corinthians 12:16; Philippians 4:22.

A servant of Christ. This title, which the apostle uses several times of himself, is not elsewhere conferred on any other individual, except once on Timothy (Philippians 1:1), and probably points to the exceptional services in the cause of the gospel on the part of Epaphras.

13. And for those in Laodicea and in Hierapolis. The neighbouring cities are taken in the geographical order, starting from Colosse. Epaphras, though a Colossian, may have been the evangelist of the two larger cities also.

14. Luke. St. Luke had travelled with St. Paul on his last journey to Jerusalem (Acts 21:1ff.). He had also accompanied him two years later from Jerusalem to Rome (Acts 27:2ff.). And now again, probably after another interval of two years, we find him in the apostle's company. It is not probable that he remained with St. Paul in the meanwhile, and this will account for his name not occurring in the letter to the Philippians. He was at the apostle's side in his second captivity (2 Timothy 4:11).

The beloved physician. Indications of medical knowledge have been traced both in the third gospel and in the Acts of the Apostles. It has been observed also that St. Luke's first appearance in company with St. Paul (Acts 16:10) nearly synchronizes with an attack of the apostle's constitutional illness (Galatians 4:13–14); so that he may have joined him partly in a professional capacity.

Demas. Demas alone is dismissed with a bare mention and without any epithet of commendation.

A message to Laodicea (4:15–17)

15. Nympha. As the context shows, an inhabitant of Laodicea. The name in full would probably be Nymphodorus, as Artemas (Titus 3:12) for Artemidorus, Zenas (Titus 3:13) for Zenodorus, Theudas (Acts 5:16) for Theodorus, Olympas (Romans 16:15) for Olympiodorus, and probably Hermas (Romans 16:14) for Hermodorus.

The church in her house. The same expression is used of Prisca and Aquila both at Rome (Romans 16:5) and at Ephesus (1 Corinthians 16:19), and also of Philemon, whether at Colosse or at Laodicea is somewhat uncertain (Philemon 2). The Christians were first recognized by the Roman government as 'collegia' or burial clubs, and protected by this recognition doubtless held their meetings for religious worship. There is no clear example of a separate building set apart for Christian worship within the limits of the Roman empire before the third

century, though apartments in private houses might be specially devoted to this purpose.

16. This letter. The letter which has just been concluded, for these greetings have the character of a postscript; compare Romans 16:22 and 2 Thessalonians 3:14.

Have it read also in the church of the Laodiceans. A similar charge is given in 1 Thessalonians 5:27. The precaution here is probably suggested by the distastefulness of the apostle's warnings, which might led to the suppression of the letter.

17. The task. From the emphasis that is put on this word, the **task** here would seem to refer, as in the case of Tychicus (verse 7), to some higher function than the diaconate. In Acts 12:25 the same phrase is used of a temporary ministry, the collection and transporting of the alms for the poor of Jerusalem (Acts 11:29); but the solemnity of the warning here points to a continuous office, rather than an immediate service.

Farewell (4:18)

18. Greeting. The letter was evidently written by an amanuensis (compare Romans 16:22). The final greeting along, with the accompanying sentence **Remember my chains …,** was in the apostle's own handwriting. This seems to have been the apostle's general practice, even where he does not call attention to his own signature. In 2 Thessalonians 3:17ff. and 1 Corinthians 16:21, as here, he directs his readers' notice to the fact, but in other letters he is silent. In some cases, however, he writes much more than the final sentence. Thus the whole letter to Philemon is apparently in his own handwriting (see Philemon 19), and in the letter to the Galatians he writes a long paragraph at the close.

Chains. His chains establish an additional claim to hearing. He who is suffering for Christ has a right to speak on behalf of Christ. The appeal is similar in Ephesians 3:1, which is resumed again (after a long digression) in Ephesians 4:1, so, too, Philemon 9. These passages seem to show that the appeal here is not for himself, but for his teaching – not for sympathy with his sufferings but for obedience to the gospel. His bonds were not his own; they were 'for the gospel' (Philemon 13). See also Galatians 6:17.

Grace be with you. This very short form of the final benediction appears only here and in 1 Timothy 6:21, 2 Timothy 4:22. In Titus 3:15 'all' is inserted, and so in Hebrews 13:25.

1 THESSALONIANS

A.R. Faussett

Introduction

The object of the epistle

Thessalonica was at this time capital of the Roman second district of Macedonia. It lay on the bay of Therme, and has always been, and still is, under its modern name Saloniki, a place of considerable commerce. After his imprisonment and scourging at Philippi, Paul (1Th 2:2) passed on to Thessalonica; and in company with Silas (Ac 17:1–9) and Timotheus (Ac 16:3 17:14, compare with 1Th 1:1 3:1–6 2Th 1:1) founded the Church there. The Jews, as a body, rejected the Gospel when preached for three successive Sabbaths (Ac 17:2); but some few 'believed and consorted with Paul and Silas, and of the devout (that is, proselytes to Judaism) Greeks a great multitude, and of the chief women not a few.' The believers received the word joyfully, notwithstanding trials and persecutions (1Th 1:6 2:13) from their own countrymen and from the Jews (1Th 2:14–16). His stay at Thessalonica was doubtless not limited to the three weeks in which were the three Sabbaths specified in Ac 17:2; for his labouring there with his hands for his support (1Th 2:9 2Th 3:8), his receiving supplies there more than once from Philippi (Php 4:16), his making many converts from the Gentiles (1Th 1:9; and as two oldest manuscripts read, Ac 17:4, 'of the devout *and* of the Greeks a great multitude,' Ac 17:4), and his appointing ministers – all imply a longer residence. Probably as at Pisidian Antioch (Ac 13:46), at Corinth (Ac 18:6,7), and at Ephesus (Ac 19:8,9), having preached the Gospel to the Jews, when they rejected it, he turned to the Gentiles. He probably thenceforth held the Christian meetings in the house of Jason (Ac 17:5), perhaps 'the kinsman' of Paul mentioned in Ro 16:21.

His great subject of teaching to them seems to have been the coming and kingdom of Christ, as we may infer from 1Th 1:10 2:12,19 3:13 4:13–18 5:1–11,23,24; and that they should walk worthy of it (1Th 2:12 4:1). And it is an undesigned coincidence between the two Epistles and Ac 17:5,9, that the very charge which the assailants of Jason's house brought against him and other brethren was, 'These do contrary to the decrees of Cæsar, saying that there is another *king*, one Jesus.' As in the case of the Lord Jesus Himself (Joh 18:33–37 19:12; compare Mt 26:64), they perverted the doctrine of the coming kingdom of Christ into a ground for the charge of treason against Cæsar. The result was, Paul and Silas were obliged to flee under the cover of night to Berea; Timothy had probably preceded him (Ac 17:10,14). But the Church had been planted, and ministers appointed; nay, more, they virtually became missionaries themselves for which they possessed facilities in the extensive commerce of their city, and both by word and example were extending the Gospel in Macedonia, Achaia, and elsewhere (1Th 1:7,8). From Berea, also. Paul, after having planted a Scripture-loving Church, was obliged to flee by the Thessalonian Jews who followed him thither. Timothy (who seems to have come to Berea separately from Paul and Silas, compare Ac 17:10, with Ac 17:14) and Silas remained there still, when Paul proceeded by sea to Athens. While there he more than once longed to visit the Thessalonians again, and see personally their spiritual state, and 'perfect that which was lacking in their faith' (1Th 3:10); but (probably using the Thessalonian Jews as his instruments, Joh 13:27) 'Satan hindered' him (1Th 2:18; compare Ac 17:13). He therefore sent Timotheus, who seems to have followed him to Athens from Berea (Ac 17:15), immediately on his arrival to Thessalonica (1Th 3:1); glad as he would have been of Timothy's help in the midst of the cavils of Athenian opponents, he felt he must forego that help for the sake of the Thessalonian Church. Silas does not seem to have come to Paul *at Athens* at all, though Paul had desired him and Timothy to 'come to him with all speed' (Ac 17:15); but seems with Timothy (who from Thessalonica called for him at Berea) to have joined Paul *at Corinth* first; compare Ac 18:1,5, 'When Silas and Timothy were come from *Macedonia.*' The Epistle makes no mention of Silas *at Athens,* as it does of Timothy (1Th 3:1).

Timothy's account of the Thessalonian Church was highly favourable. They abounded in faith and charity and reciprocated his desire to see them (1Th 3:6–10). Still, as nothing human on earth is perfect, there were some defects. Some had too exclusively dwelt on the doctrine of Christ's coming kingdom, so as to neglect the sober-minded discharge of present duties (1Th 4:11,12). Some who had lost relatives by death, needed comfort and instruction in their doubts as to whether they who died before Christ's coming would have a share with those found alive in His kingdom then to be revealed. Moreover, also, there had been committed among them sins against chastity and sobriety (1Th 5:5–7), as also against charity (1Th 4:3–10 5:13,15). There were, too, symptoms in some of want of respectful love and subordination to their ministers; others treated slightingly the manifestations of the Spirit in those possessing His gifts (1Th 5:19). To give spiritual admonition on these subjects, and at the same time commend what deserved commendation, and to testify his love to them, was the object of the Epistle.

The place of writing

The place of writing was doubtless Corinth, where Timothy and Silas rejoined him (Ac 18:5) soon after he arrived there (compare 1Th 2:17) in the autumn of A.D. 52.

The time of writing

The time of writing was evidently immediately after having received from Timothy the tidings of their state (1Th 3:6) in the winter of A.D. 52, or early in 53. For it was written not long after the conversion of the Thessalonians (1Th 1:8,9), while Paul could speak of himself as only *taken from them for a short season* (1Th 2:17). Thus this Epistle was *first in date of all Paul's extant Epistles.* The Epistle is written in the joint names of Paul, Silas, and Timothy, the three founders of the Thessalonian Church. The plural first person 'we,' is used everywhere, except in 1Th 2:18 3:5 5:27.

The style of writing

The style is calm and equable, in accordance with the subject matter, which deals only with Christian duties in general, taking for granted the great doctrinal truths which were not as yet disputed. There was no deadly error as yet to call forth his more vehement bursts of feeling and impassioned argument. The earlier Epistles, as we should expect, are moral and practical. It was not until Judaistic and legalizing errors arose at a later period that he wrote those Epistles (for example, Romans and Galatians) which unfold the cardinal doctrines of grace and justification by faith. Still, later the Epistles from his Roman prison confirm the same truths. And last of all, the Pastoral Epistles are suited to the more developed ecclesiastical constitution of the Church, and give directions as to bishops and deacons, and correct abuses and errors of later growth.

The prevalence of the Gentile element in this Church is shown by the fact that these two Epistles are among the very few of Paul's writings in which no quotation occurs from the Old Testament.

Contents

See *Outlines of the New Testament Books*, p.900

Chapter 1

1Th 1:1–10. Address: salutation: his prayerful thanksgiving for their faith, hope, and love. Their first reception of the gospel, and their good influence on all around.

1. **Paul** – He does not add 'an apostle,' because in their case, as in that of the Philippians his apostolic authority needs not any substantiation. He writes familiarly as to faithful friends, not but that his apostleship was recognized among them (1Th 2:6). On the other hand, in writing to the Galatians, among whom some had called in question his apostleship, he strongly asserts it in the superscription. An undesigned propriety in the Epistles, evincing genuineness.

Silvanus – a 'chief man among the brethren' (Ac 15:22), and a 'prophet' (Ac 15:32), and one of the deputies who carried the decree of the Jerusalem council to Antioch. His age and position cause him to be placed before 'Timothy,' then a youth (Ac 16:1 1Ti 4:12). Silvanus (the Gentile expanded form of 'Silas') is called in 1Pe 5:12, 'a faithful brother' (compare 2Co 1:19). They both aided in planting the Thessalonian Church, and are therefore included in the address. This, the first of Paul's Epistles, as being written before various evils crept into the churches, is without the censures found in other Epistles. So realizing was their Christian faith, that they were able hourly to look for the Lord Jesus.

unto the church – not merely as in the Epistles to Romans, Ephesians, Colossians, Philippians, 'to the saints,' or 'the faithful at Thessalonica.' Though as yet they do not seem to have had the *final* Church organization under *permanent* 'bishops' and deacons, which appears in the later Epistles. Yet he designates them by the honourable term 'Church,' implying their status as not merely isolated believers, but a corporate body with spiritual rulers (1Th 5:12 2Co 1:1 Ga 1:2).

in – implying *vital union*.

God the Father – This marks that they were no longer *heathen*.

the Lord Jesus Christ – This marks that they were not *Jews*, but Christians.

Grace be unto you, and peace – that ye may have in God that *favour and peace* which men withhold [ANSELM]. This is the salutation in all the Epistles of Paul, except the three pastoral ones, which have 'grace, mercy, and peace.' Some of the oldest manuscripts support, others omit the clause following, 'from God our Father and the Lord Jesus Christ.' It may have crept in from 1Co 1:3 2Co 1:2.

2. (Ro 1:9 2Ti 1:3.) The structure of the sentences in this and the following verses, each successive sentence repeating with greater fulness the preceding, characteristically marks Paul's abounding love and thankfulness in respect to his converts, as if he were seeking by words heaped on words to convey some idea of his exuberant feelings towards them.

We – I, Silvanus, and Timotheus. Ro 1:9 supports ALFORD in translating, 'making mention of you in our prayers without ceasing' (1Th 1:3). Thus, 'without ceasing,' in the second clause, answers in parallelism to 'always,' in the first.

3. **work of faith** – *the working reality of your faith; its alacrity in receiving the truth, and in*

evincing itself by its fruits. Not an otiose assent; but a *realizing, working faith;* not 'in word only,' but in *one* continuous chain of 'work' (singular, not plural, *works*), 1Th 1:5–10 Jas 2:22. So 'the work of faith' in 2Th 1:11 implies its *perfect development* (compare Jas 1:4). The other governing substantives similarly mark respectively the characteristic manifestation of the grace which follows each in the genitive. *Faith, love,* and *hope,* are the three great Christian graces (1Th 5:8 1Co 13:13).

labour of love – The *Greek* implies *toil,* or *troublesome labour,* which we are stimulated by love to bear (1Th 2:9 Re 2:2). For instances of self-denying *labours of love,* see Ac 20:35 Ro 16:12. Not here *ministerial* labours. Those who shun trouble for others, love little (compare Heb 6:10).

patience – Translate, '*endurance* of hope'; the *persevering endurance* of trials which flows from 'hope.' Ro 15:4 shows that 'patience' also nourishes 'hope.'

hope in our Lord Jesus – literally, 'hope *of* our Lord Jesus,' namely, of His coming (1Th 1:10): a hope that looked forward beyond all present things for the manifestation of Christ.

in the sight of God and our Father – Your 'faith, hope, and love' were not merely such as would pass for genuine *before men,* but 'in the sight of God,' the Searcher of hearts [GOMARUS]. Things are really what they are before God. BENGEL takes this clause with 'remembering.' Whenever we *pray,* we *remember before God* your faith, hope, and love. But its separation from 'remembering' in the order, and its connection with 'your … faith,' make me to prefer the former view.

and, – The *Greek* implies, 'in the sight of *Him who* is [at once] God and our Father.'

4. Knowing – Forasmuch as we know.

your election of God – The *Greek* is rather, 'beloved by God'; so Ro 1:7 2Th 2:13. 'Your election' means that *God has elected you* as individual believers to eternal life (Ro 11:5,7 Col 3:12 2Th 2:13).

5. our gospel – namely, the Gospel which we preached.

came – *Greek,* 'was made,' namely, by God, its Author and Sender. God's having made our preaching among you to be attended with such 'power,' is the proof that you are 'elect of God' (1Th 1:4).

in power – in the efficacy of the Holy Spirit clothing us with power (see end of verse; Ac 1:8 4:33 6:5,8) in preaching the Gospel, and making it in you the power of God unto salvation (Ro 1:16). As 'power' produces *faith;* so 'the Holy Ghost,' *love;* and 'much assurance' (Col 2:2, *full persuasion*), *hope* (Heb 6:11), resting on faith (Heb 10:22). So *faith, love,* and *hope* (1Th 1:3).

as ye know – answering to the 'knowing,' that

is, *as* WE *know* (1Th 1:4) your character as *the elect of God,* so YE *know* ours as *preachers.*

for your sake – The purpose herein indicated is not so much that of the apostles, as that of God. 'You know what *God enabled us to be … how mighty in preaching the word … for your sakes …* thereby proving that He had *chosen* (1Th 1:4) you for His own' [ALFORD]. I think, from 1Th 2:10–12, that, in 'what manner of men we were among you,' besides the *power in preaching,* there is included also Paul's and his fellow missionaries' whole *conduct* which confirmed their preaching; and in this sense, the 'for your sake' will mean 'in order to win you.' This, though not the sole, yet would be a strong, motive to holy circumspection, namely, so as to win those without (Col 4:5; compare 1Co 9:19–23).

6. And ye – answering to '*For our Gospel,*' 1Th 1:5.

followers – *Greek,* 'imitators.' The Thessalonians in their turn became 'ensamples' (1Th 1:7) for others to *imitate.*

of the Lord – who was the apostle of the Father, and taught the word, which He brought from heaven, under adversities [BENGEL]. This was the point in which they imitated Him and His apostles, *joyful* witness for *the word in much affliction:* the second proof of their *election of God* (1Th 1:4).

received the word in much affliction – (1Th 2:14 3:2–5 Ac 17:5–10).

joy of – that is, *wrought* by 'the Holy Ghost.' 'The oil of gladness' wherewith the Son of God was 'anointed above His fellows' (Ps 45:7), is the same oil with which He, by the Spirit, anoints His fellows too (Isa 61:1,3 Ro 14:17 1Jo 2:20,27).

7. ensamples – So some of the oldest manuscripts read. Others, 'ensample' (singular), the whole Church being regarded as *one.* The *Macedonian* Church of Philippi was the only one in Europe converted before the Thessalonians. Therefore he means their past conduct is an ensample to all believers now; of whom he specifies those 'in Macedonia' because he had been there since the conversion of the Thessalonians, and had left Silvanus and Timotheus there; and those in 'Achaia,' because he was now at Corinth in Achaia.

8. from you sounded … the word of the Lord – not that they actually became missionaries: but they, by the *report* which spread abroad of their 'faith' (compare Ro 1:8), and by Christian merchants of Thessalonica who travelled in various directions, bearing 'the word of the Lord' with them, were *virtually* missionaries, recommending the Gospel to all within reach of their influence by word and by example (1Th 1:7). In 'sounded,' the image is that of a trumpet filling with its clear-sounding echo all the surrounding places.

to God-ward – no longer directed to idols.

so that we need not to speak any thing – to them in praise of your faith; 'for (1Th 1:9) they themselves' (the people in Macedonia, Achaia, and in every place) know it already.

9. Strictly there should follow, 'For they themselves show of you'; but, instead, he substitutes that which was the instrumental cause of the Thessalonians' conversion and faith, 'for they themselves show of us what manner of entering in we had *unto you*'; compare 1Th 1:5, which corresponds to this former clause, as 1Th 1:6 corresponds to the latter clause. 'And how ye turned from idols to serve the living ... God.' Instead of *our* having 'to speak any thing' to them (in Macedonia and Achaia) in your praise (1Th 1:8), 'they *themselves* (have the start of us in speaking of you, and) *announce concerning* (so the *Greek* of "show of" means) us, what manner of (how effectual an) entrance we had unto you' (1Th 1:5 2:1).

the living and true God – as opposed to the *dead* and *false* gods from which they had 'turned.' In the *English Version* reading, Ac 17:4, 'of *the devout Greeks* a great multitude,' no mention is made, as here, of the conversion of *idolatrous* Gentiles at Thessalonica; but the reading of some of the oldest manuscripts and *Vulgate* singularly coincides with the statement here: 'Of the devout AND of Greeks (namely, *idolaters*) a great multitude'; so in 1Th 1:17, 'the devout persons,' that is, Gentile proselytes to Judaism, form a separate class. PALEY and LACHMANN, by distinct lines of argument, support the 'AND.'

10. This verse distinguishes them from the *Jews*, as 1Th 1:9 from the *idolatrous* Gentiles. To wait for the Lord's coming is a sure characteristic of a true believer, and was prominent amidst the graces of the Thessalonians (1Co 1:7,8). His *coming* is seldom called his *return* (Joh 14:3); because the two advents are regarded as different phases of the same coming; and the second coming shall have features altogether new connected with it, so that it will not be a mere repetition of the first, or a mere coming *back again.*

his Son ... raised from the dead – the grand proof of His divine *Sonship* (Ro 1:4).

delivered – rather as *Greek,* 'who *delivereth us.*' Christ has once for all *redeemed* us; He is our *Deliverer* ALWAYS.

wrath to come – (1Th 5:9 Col 3:6).

Chapter 2

1Th 2:1–20. His manner of preaching, and theirs of receiving, the Gospel; his desire to have revisited them frustrated by Satan.

1. For – confirming 1Th 1:9. He discusses the manner of his fellow missionaries' preaching among them (1Th 1:5, and former part of 1Th

2:9) at 1Th 2:1–12; and the Thessalonians' reception of the word (compare 1Th 1:6,7, and latter part of 1Th 2:9) at 1Th 2:13–16.

yourselves – Not only do strangers report it, but *you* know it to be true [ALFORD] 'yourselves.'

not in vain – *Greek,* 'not vain,' that is, it was full of 'power' (1Th 1:5). The *Greek* for 'was,' expresses rather 'hath been and is,' implying the *permanent* and continuing character of his preaching.

2. even after that we had suffered before – at Philippi (Ac 16:11-40): a circumstance which would have deterred mere natural, unspiritual men from further preaching.

shamefully entreated – ignominiously scourged (Ac 16:22,23).

bold – (Ac 4:29 Eph 6:20).

in our God – The ground of our boldness in speaking was the realization of God as 'OUR God.'

with much contention – that is, literally, as of *competitors in a contest:* striving earnestness (Col 1:29 2:1). But here *outward* conflict with persecutors, rather than *inward* and mental, was what the missionaries had to endure (Ac 17:5,6 Php 1:30).

3. For – The ground of his 'boldness' (1Th 2:2), his freedom from all 'deceit, uncleanness, and guile'; *guile,* before God, *deceit* (*Greek,* 'imposture'), towards men (compare 2Co 1:12 2:17 Eph 4:14); *uncleanness,* in relation to one's self (impure motives of carnal self-gratification in gain, 1Th 2:5), or lust; such as actuated false teachers of the Gentiles (Php 1:16 2Pe 2:10,14 Jude 1:8 Re 2:14,15). So Simon Magus and Cerinthus taught [ESTIUS].

exhortation – The *Greek* means 'consolation' as well as 'exhortation.' The same Gospel which exhorts comforts. Its first lesson to each is that of peace in believing amidst outward and inward sorrows. It comforts them that mourn (compare 1Th 2:11 Isa 61:2,3 2Co 1:3,4).

of – *springing from – having its source in –* deceit.

4. as – according as; even as.

allowed – *Greek,* 'We have been approved on trial,' 'deemed fit.' This word corresponds to 'God which *trieth* our hearts' below. This approval as to sincerity depends solely on the grace and mercy of God (Ac 9:15 1Co 7:25 2Co 3:5 1Ti 1:11,12).

not as pleasing – not as persons who seek to please men; characteristic of false teachers (Ga 1:10).

5. used we flattering words – literally, 'become (that is, have we been found) in (the use of) language of flattery'; the resource of those who try to 'please men.'

as ye know – 'Ye know' as to whether I *flattered* you; as to 'covetousness,' GOD, the Judge of the heart, alone can be 'my witness.'

cloak of – that is, any specious guise under which I might cloak 'covetousness.'

6. Literally, 'Nor of men (have we been found, 1Th 2:5) seeking glory.' The 'of' here represents a different *Greek* word from 'of' in the clause '*of you … of* others.' ALFORD makes the former (*Greek*, '*ex*') express the *abstract ground* of the glory; the latter (*apo*) the *concrete object* from which it was to come. The former means 'originating from'; the latter means 'on the part of.' Many teach heretical novelties, though not for fain, yet for 'glory.' Paul and his associates were free even from this motive [GROTIUS], (Joh 5:44).

we might have been burdensome – that is, by claiming maintenance (1Th 2:9 2Co 11:9 12:16 2Th 3:8). As, however, 'glory' precedes, as well as 'covetousness,' the reference cannot be *restricted* to the latter, though I think it is not *excluded*. Translate, 'when we might have borne heavily upon you,' by pressing you *with the weight of self-glorifying authority*, and *with the burden* of our *sustenance*. Thus the antithesis is appropriate in the words following, 'But we were *gentle* (the opposite of *pressing weightily*) among you' (1Th 2:7). ALFORD's translation, which *excludes* reference to his right of claiming *maintenance* ('when we might have stood on our *dignity*'), seems to me disproved by 1Th 2:9, which uses *the same Greek word* unequivocally for 'chargeable.' Twice he received supplies from Philippi while at Thessalonica (Php 4:16).

as the apostles – that is, as being apostles.

7. we were – *Greek*, 'we were *made*' by God's grace.

gentle – *Greek*, '*mild* in bearing with the faults of others' [TITTMANN]; one, too, who is gentle (though firm) in reproving the erroneous opinions of others (2Ti 2:24). Some of the oldest manuscripts read, 'we became *little children*' (compare Mt 18:3,4). Others support the *English Version* reading, which forms a better antithesis to 1Th 2:6,7, and harmonizes better with what follows; for he would hardly, in the same sentence, compare himself both to the 'infants' or 'little children,' and to 'a nurse,' or rather, 'suckling mother.' *Gentleness* is the fitting characteristic of *a nurse*.

among you – *Greek*, 'in the midst of you,' that is, in our intercourse with you being *as one of yourselves*.

nurse – a suckling mother.

her – *Greek*, '*her own* children' (compare 1Th 2:11). So Ga 4:19.

8. So – to be joined to 'we were willing'; '*As a nurse cherisheth … so* we were willing,' [ALFORD]. But BENGEL, 'So,' that is, *seeing that we have such affection for you*.

being affectionately desirous – The oldest reading in the *Greek* implies, literally, *to connect one's self with another*; to be closely *attached* to another.

willing – The *Greek* is stronger, 'we were *well content*'; 'we would *gladly* have imparted,' 'even our own *lives*' (so the *Greek* for 'souls' ought to be translated); as we showed in the sufferings we endured in giving you the Gospel (Ac 17:1–34). As a nursing mother is ready to impart not only her milk to them, but her life for them, so we not only imparted gladly the spiritual milk of the word to you, but risked our own lives for your spiritual nourishment, imitating Him who laid down His life for His friends, the greatest proof of love (Joh 15:13).

ye were – *Greek*, 'ye were become,' as having become our spiritual children.

dear – *Greek*, 'dearly beloved.'

9. labour and travail – The *Greek* for 'labour' means *hardship in bearing*; that for 'travail,' *hardship in doing*; the former, toil with the utmost solicitude; the latter, the being wearied with fatigue [GROTIUS]. ZANCHIUS refers the former to *spiritual* (see 1Th 3:5), the latter to *manual* labour. I would translate, 'weariness (so the *Greek* is translated, 2Co 11:27) and travail' (hard labour, *toil*).

for – omitted in the oldest manuscripts.

labouring – *Greek*, 'working,' namely, at tent-making (Ac 18:3).

night and day – The Jews reckoned the day from sunset to sunset, so that 'night' is put before 'day' (compare Ac 20:31). Their labours with their hands for a scanty livelihood had to be engaged in not only by day, but by night also, in the intervals between spiritual labours.

because we would not be chargeable – *Greek*, '*with a view to* not *burdening* any of you' (2Co 11:9,10).

preached unto you – *Greek*, 'unto and among you.' Though but 'three Sabbaths' are mentioned, Ac 17:2, these refer merely to the time of his preaching *to the Jews in the synagogue*. When rejected by them as a body, after having converted a few Jews, he turned to the Gentiles; of these (whom he preached to in a place distinct from the synagogue) 'a great multitude believed' (Ac 17:4, where the oldest manuscripts read, 'of the devout [proselytes] and Greeks a great multitude'); then after he had, by labours continued *among the Gentiles* for some time, gathered in many converts, the Jews, provoked by his success, assaulted Jason's house, and drove him away. His receiving 'once and again' supplies from Philippi, implies a longer stay at Thessalonica than three weeks (Php 4:16).

10. Ye are witnesses – as to our outward conduct.

God – as to our inner motives.

holily – towards God.

justly – towards men.

unblameably – in relation to ourselves.

behaved ourselves – *Greek*, 'were made to be,' namely, by God.

among you that believe – rather, 'before (that is, in the eyes of) you that believe'; whatever we may have seemed in the eyes of the unbelieving. As 1Th 2:9 refers to their outward occupation in the world; so 1Th 2:10, to their character among believers.

11. exhorted and comforted – *Exhortation* leads one to do a thing willingly; *consolation,* to do it joyfully [BENGEL], (1Th 5:14). Even in the former term, 'exhorted,' the *Greek* includes the additional idea of *comforting* and *advocating* one's cause: 'encouragingly exhorted.' Appropriate in this case, as the Thessalonians were in sorrow, both through persecutions, and also through deaths of friends (1Th 4:13).

charged – 'conjured solemnly,' literally, 'testifying'; *appealing solemnly* to you before God. **every one of you** – in private (Ac 20:20), as well as publicly. The minister, if he would be useful, must not deal merely in generalities, but must individualize and particularize.

as a father – with mild gravity. The *Greek* is, 'his own children.'

12. worthy of God – 'worthy *of the Lord*' (Col 1:10); 'worthily *of the saints*' (Ro 16:2, *Greek*): '... *of the Gospel*' (Php 1:27) '... *of the vocation* wherewith ye are called' (Eph 4:1). Inconsistency would cause God's name to be 'blasphemed among the Gentiles' (Ro 2:24). The *Greek* article is emphatic, 'Worthy of THE God who is calling you.'

hath called – So one of the oldest manuscripts and *Vulgate.* Other oldest manuscripts, 'Who *calleth us.*'

his kingdom – to be set up at the Lord's coming.

glory – that ye may share His glory (Joh 17:22 Col 3:4).

13. For this cause – Seeing ye have had such teachers (1Th 2:10–12) [BENGEL], 'we also (as well as "all that believe" in Macedonia and Achaia) thank God without ceasing ("always" ... "in our prayers," 1Th 1:2), that when ye received the word of God which ye heard from us (literally, "God's word of hearing from us," Ro 10:16,17), ye accepted it not as the word of men, but, even as it is truly, the word of God.' ALFORD omits the 'as' of *English Version.* But the 'as' is required by the clause, 'even as it is truly.' 'Ye accepted it, not (*as*) the word of men (which it might have been *supposed* to be), but (as) the word of God, *even as it really is.*' The *Greek* for the first 'received,' implies simply the hearing of it; the *Greek* of the second is 'accepted,' or 'welcomed' it. The proper object of faith, it hence appears, is *the word of God,* at first oral, then for security against error, written (Joh 20:30,31 Ro 15:4 Ga 4:30). Also, that faith is *the work of divine grace,* is implied by Paul's *thanksgiving.*

effectually worketh also in you that believe – 'Also,' besides your accepting it with your hearts, it evidences itself in your lives. It shows its *energy* in its practical effects on you; for instance, working in you patient endurance in trial (1Th 2:14; compare Ga 3:5 5:6).

14. followers – *Greek,* 'imitators.' Divine *working* is most of all seen and felt in affliction.

in Judea – The churches of Judea were naturally the patterns to other churches, as having been the first founded, and that on the very scene of Christ's own ministry. Reference to them is specially appropriate here, as the Thessalonians, with Paul and Silas, had experienced from Jews in their city persecutions (Ac 17:5–9) similar to those which 'the churches in Judea' experienced from Jews in that country.

in Christ Jesus – not merely 'in God'; for the synagogues of the Jews (one of which the Thessalonians were familiar with, Ac 17:1) were also *in God.* But the Christian churches alone were not only *in God,* as the Jews in contrast to the Thessalonian idolaters were, but also *in Christ,* which the Jews were not.

of your own countrymen – including primarily the Jews settled at Thessalonica, from whom the persecution originated, and also the Gentiles there, instigated by the Jews; thus, 'fellow countrymen' (the *Greek* term, according to Herodian, implies, not the *enduring* relation of fellow citizenship, but sameness of country *for the time being*), including naturalized Jews and native Thessalonians, stand in contrast to the pure 'Jews' in Judea (Mt 10:36). It is an undesigned coincidence, that Paul at this time was suffering persecutions of the Jews at Corinth, whence he writes (Ac 18:5,6,12); naturally his letter would the more vividly dwell on Jewish bitterness against Christians.

even as they – (Heb 10:32–34). There was a *likeness* in respect to *the nation* from which both suffered, namely, Jews, and those *their own countrymen;* in the *cause* for which, and in the *evils* which, they suffered, and also in the steadfast *manner* in which they suffered them. Such sameness of fruits, afflictions, and experimental characteristics of believers, in all places and at all times, is a subsidiary evidence of the truth of the Gospel.

15. the Lord Jesus – rather as *Greek,* 'Jesus THE LORD.' This enhances the glaring enormity of their sin, that in killing Jesus they killed the LORD (compare Ac 3:14,15).

their own – omitted in the oldest manuscripts.

prophets – (Mt 21:33–41 23:31–37 Lu 13:33). **persecuted us** – rather as *Greek* (see *Margin*), 'By persecution drove us out' (Lu 11:49).

please not God – that is, they do not *make it their aim* to please God. He implies that with all their boast of being God's peculiar people, they all the while are 'no pleasers of God,' as certainly as, by the universal voice of the world, which even they themselves cannot contradict, they are declared to be perversely 'contrary to all men.' JOSEPHUS [*Against Apion*, 2.14], represents one calling them 'Atheists and Misanthropes, the dullest of barbarians'; and TACITUS [*Histories*, 5.5], 'They have a hostile hatred of all other men.' However, the *contrariety to all men* here meant is, *in that they* 'forbid us to speak to the Gentiles that they may be saved' (1Th 2:16).

16. Forbidding – *Greek*, 'Hindering us from speaking.'

to fill up their sins alway – Tending thus 'to the filling up (the full measure of, Ge 15:16 Da 8:23 Mt 23:32) their sins at all times,' that is, *now as at all former times*. Their hindrance of the Gospel preaching to the Gentiles was the last measure added to their continually accumulating iniquity, which made them fully ripe for vengeance.

for – *Greek*, 'but.' 'But,' they shall proceed no further, for (2Ti 3:8) 'the' divine 'wrath *has* (so the *Greek*) come upon (overtaken unexpectedly; the past tense expressing the speedy certainty of the divinely destined stroke) them to the uttermost'; not merely partial wrath, but wrath to its full extent, 'even to the finishing stroke' [EDMUNDS]. The past tense implies that the fullest visitation of wrath was already begun. Already in A.D. 48, a tumult had occurred at the Passover in Jerusalem, when about thirty thousand (according to some) were slain; a foretaste of the whole vengeance which speedily followed (Lu 19:43,44 21:24).

17. But we – resumed from 1Th 2:13; in contrast to *the Jews*, 1Th 2:15,16.

taken – rather as *Greek*, 'severed (violently, Ac 17:7–10) from you,' as parents bereft of their children. So 'I will not leave you comfortless,' *Greek*, 'orphanized' (Joh 14:18).

for a short time – literally, 'for the space of an hour.' 'When we had been severed from you but a very short time (perhaps alluding to the suddenness of his unexpected departure), we the more abundantly (the shorter was our separation; for the desire of meeting again is the more vivid, the more recent has been the parting) endeavoured.' (Compare 2Ti 1:4). He does not hereby, as many explain, anticipate a short separation from them, which would be a false anticipation; for he did not soon revisit them. The *Greek* past participle also forbids their view.

18. Wherefore – The oldest manuscripts read, 'Because,' or 'Inasmuch as.'

we would – *Greek*, 'we wished to come'; we intended to come.

even I Paul – My fellow missionaries as well as myself wished to come; I can answer for *myself* that I intended it more than once. His slightly distinguishing himself here from his fellow missionaries, whom throughout this Epistle he associates with himself in the plural, accords

with the fact that Silvanus and Timothy stayed at Berea when Paul went on to Athens; where subsequently Timothy joined him, and was thence sent *by Paul alone* to Thessalonica (1Th 3:1).

Satan hindered us – On a different occasion 'the Holy Ghost, the Spirit *of Jesus*' (so the oldest manuscripts read), Ac 16:6,7, forbad or hindered them in a missionary design; here it is *Satan*, acting perhaps by wicked men, some of whom had already driven him out of Thessalonica (Ac 17:13,14; compare Joh 13:27), or else by some more direct 'messenger of Satan – a thorn in the flesh' (2Co 12:7; compare 2Co 11:14). In any event, the Holy Ghost and the providence of God overruled Satan's opposition to further His own purpose. *We* cannot, in each case, define whence hindrances in good undertakings arise; *Paul* in this case, by inspiration, was enabled to say; the hindrance was from Satan. GROTIUS thinks Satan's mode of hindering Paul's journey to Thessalonica was by instigating the Stoic and Epicurean philosophers to cavil, which entailed on Paul the necessity of replying, and so detained him; but he seems to have left Athens leisurely (Ac 17:33,34 18:1). The *Greek* for 'hindered' is literally, 'to cut a trench between one's self and an advancing foe, to prevent his progress'; so Satan opposing the progress of the missionaries.

19. For – giving the reason for his earnest desire to see them.

Are not even ye in the presence of ... Christ – 'Christ' is omitted in the oldest manuscripts. Are not even ye (namely, among others; the 'even' or 'also,' implies that not *they alone* will be his crown) our hope, joy, and crown of rejoicing before Jesus, when He shall come (2Co 1:14 Php 2:16 4:1)? The 'hope' here meant is his hope (in a lower sense), that these his converts might be found in Christ at His advent (1Th 3:13). Paul's *chief* 'hope' was JESUS CHRIST (1Ti 1:1).

20. Emphatic repetition with increased force. Who but ye and our other converts are our *hope, hereafter,* at Christ's coming? For it is *ye who* ARE now our glory and joy.

Chapter 3

1Th 3:1–13. Proof of his desire after them in his having sent Timothy: his joy at the tidings brought back concerning their faith and charity: prayers for them.

1. Wherefore – because of our earnest love to you (1Th 2:17–20).

forbear – 'endure' the suspense. The *Greek* is literally applied to a watertight vessel. When we could no longer contain ourselves in our yearning desire for you.

left at Athens alone – See my *Introduction*. This implies that he sent Timothy *from Athens*, whither the latter had followed him. However, the 'we' favours ALFORD's view that the determination to send Timothy was formed during the hasty consultation of Paul, Silas, and Timothy, *previous to his departure from Berea,* and that then he with them 'resolved' to be 'left alone' at Athens, when he should arrive there: Timothy and Silas not accompanying him, but remaining at Berea. Thus the 'I,' 1Th 3:5, will express that the *act* of sending Timothy, when he arrived at Athens, was *Paul's,* while the determination that Paul should be left alone at Athens, was that of the brethren as well as himself, at Berea, whence he uses, 1Th 3:1, 'we.' The non-mention of Silas at Athens implies that he did not follow Paul to Athens as was at first intended; but Timothy did. Thus the history, Ac 17:14,15, accords with the Epistle. The word 'left behind' (*Greek*) implies that Timothy had been with him *at Athens.* It was an act of self-denial for their sakes that Paul deprived himself of the presence of Timothy at Athens, which would have been so cheering to him in the midst of philosophic cavillers; but from love to the Thessalonians, he is well content to be left all 'alone' in the great city.

2. minister of God and our fellow labourer – Some oldest manuscripts read, 'fellow workman with God'; others, 'minister of God.' The former is probably genuine, as copyists probably altered it to the latter to avoid the bold phrase, which, however, is sanctioned by 1Co 3:9 2Co 6:1. The *English Version* reading is not well supported, and is plainly compounded out of the two other readings. Paul calls Timothy 'our *brother*' here; but in 1Co 4:17, 'my *son.*' He speaks thus highly of one so lately ordained, both to impress the Thessalonians with a high respect for the delegate sent to them, and to encourage Timothy, who seems to have been of a timid character (1Ti 4:12 5:23). 'Gospel ministers do the work of God *with* Him, *for* Him, and *under* Him' [EDMUNDS].

establish – Greek, 'confirm.' In 2Th 3:3, GOD is said to 'stablish': He is the true establisher: ministers are His 'instruments.'

concerning – Greek, 'in behalf of,' that is, *for the furtherance* of your faith. The Greek for 'comfort' includes also the idea, 'exhort.' The Thessalonians in their trials needed both (1Th 3:3; compare Ac 14:22).

3. moved – 'shaken,' 'disturbed.' The Greek is literally said of dogs *wagging* the tail in fawning on one. Therefore TITTMANN explains it, 'That no man should, amidst his calamities, be *allured* by the *flattering* hope of a more pleasant life to abandon his duty.' So ELSNER and BENGEL, 'cajoled out of his faith.' In afflictions, relatives and opponents combine with the ease-loving heart itself in flatteries, which it needs strong faith to overcome.

yourselves know – We always candidly told you so (1Th 3:4 Ac 14:22). None but a religion from God would have held out such a trying prospect to those who should embrace it, and yet succeed in winning converts.

we – Christians.

appointed thereunto – by God's counsel (1Th 5:9).

4. that we should suffer – Greek, 'that we are about (we are sure) to suffer' according to the *appointment* of God (1Th 3:3).

even as – '*even* (exactly) as it *both* came to pass *and* ye know'; ye know *both* that it came to pass, *and* that we foretold it (compare Joh 13:19). The correspondence of the event to the prediction powerfully confirms faith: 'Forewarned, forearmed' [EDMUNDS]. The repetition of 'ye know,' so frequently, is designed as an argument, that being forewarned of coming affliction, they should be less readily 'moved' by it.

5. For this cause – Because I know of your 'tribulation' having actually begun (1Th 3:4).

when I – Greek, 'when I *also* (as well as Timothy, who, Paul delicately implies, was equally anxious respecting them, compare 'we,' 1Th 3:1), could no longer contain myself (*endure the suspense*).'

I sent – Paul was the actual sender; hence the 'I' here: Paul, Silas, and Timothy himself had agreed on the mission already, before Paul went to Athens: hence the 'we'.

to know – to learn the state of your faith, whether it stood the trial (Col 4:8).

lest ... have tempted ... and ... be – The indicative is used in the former sentence, the subjunctive in the latter. Translate therefore, 'To know ... *whether haply* the tempter *have* tempted you (the indicative implying that he supposed such was the case), and *lest* (in that case) our labour *may prove to be* in vain' (compare Ga 4:11). Our labour in preaching would in that case be vain, so far as *ye* are concerned, but not as concerns *us* in so far as *we* have sincerely laboured (Isa 49:4 1Co 3:8).

6. Join 'now' with 'come'; 'But Timotheus having *just now come* from you unto us' [ALFORD]. Thus it appears (compare Ac 18:5) Paul is writing from Corinth.

your faith and charity – (1Th 1:3; compare 2Th 1:3, whence it seems their faith subsequently increased still more). *Faith* was the solid foundation: *charity* the cement which held together the superstructure of their practice on that foundation. In that *charity* was included their 'good (kindly) remembrance' of their teachers.

desiring greatly – Greek, 'having a yearning desire for.'

we also – The desires of loving friends for one another's presence are reciprocal.

7. over you – in respect to you.

in – in the midst of: notwithstanding 'all our distress (*Greek*, "necessity") and affliction,' namely, external trials at Corinth, whence Paul writes (compare 1Th 3:6, with Ac 18:5–10).

8. now – as the case is; seeing ye stand fast.

we live – we flourish. It *revives us* in our affliction to hear of your steadfastness (Ps 22:26 2Jo 1:3:4).

if – implying that the vivid joy which the missionaries 'now' feel, *will continue* if the Thessalonians continue steadfast. They still needed exhortation, 1Th 3:10; therefore he subjoins the conditional clause, 'if ye,' (Php 4:1).

9. For what thanks – *what sufficient* thanks?

render ... again – in return for His goodness (Ps 116:12).

for you – 'concerning you.'

for all the joy – on account of all the joy. It was 'comfort,' 1Th 3:7, now it is more, namely, *joy*.

for your sakes – on your account.

before our God – It is a joy which will bear God's searching eye: a joy as in the presence of God, not self-seeking, but disinterested, sincere, and spiritual (compare 1Th 2:20 Joh 15:11).

10. Night and day – Night is the season for the saint's holiest meditations and prayers (2Ti 1:3).

praying – connected with, 'we joy'; we joy while we pray; or else as ALFORD, *What thanks can we render to God while we pray?* The *Greek* implies a *beseeching* request.

exceedingly – literally, 'more than exceeding abundantly' (compare Eph 3:20).

that which is lacking – Even the Thessalonians had points in which they needed improvement [BENGEL], (Lu 17:5). Their doctrinal views as to the nearness of Christ's coming, and as to the state of those who had fallen asleep, and their practice in some points, needed correction (1Th 4:1–9). Paul's method was to begin by commending what was praiseworthy, and then to correct what was amiss; a good pattern to all admonishers of others.

11. Translate, '*May* God Himself, *even* our Father (there being but one article in the *Greek*, requires this translation, "He who is at once God and our Father"), direct.' The 'Himself' stands in contrast with 'we' (1Th 2:18); *we* desired to come but could not through Satan's hindrance; but if God *Himself* direct our way (as we pray), none can hinder Him (2Th 2:16,17). It is a remarkable proof of *the unity of the Father and Son*, that in the *Greek* here, and in 2Th 2:16,17, the verb is *singular*, implying that the subject, the Father and Son, are but *one in essential Being*, not in mere unity of will. Almost all the chapters in both Epistles to the Thessalonians are sealed, each with its own prayer (1Th 5:23 2Th 1:11 2:16 3:5,16) [BENGEL]. Paul

does not think the prosperous issue of a journey an unfit subject for prayer (Ro 1:10 15:32) [EDMUNDS]. His prayer, though the answer was deferred, in about five years afterwards was fulfilled in his return to Macedonia.

12. The 'you' in the *Greek* is emphatically put *first*; 'But' (so the *Greek* for 'and') what concerns 'YOU,' whether we come or not, 'may the Lord make you to increase and abound in love.' The *Greek* for 'increase' has a more *positive* force; that for 'abound' a more *comparative* force, 'make you *full* (supplying "that which is lacking," 1Th 3:10) and even abound.' 'The Lord' may here be the Holy Spirit; so the Three Persons of the Trinity will be appealed to (compare 1Th 3:13), as in 2Th 3:5. So the Holy Ghost is called 'the Lord' (2Co 3:17). 'Love' is the fruit of the Spirit (Ga 5:22), and His office is 'to stablish in holiness' (1Th 3:13 1Pe 1:2).

13. your hearts – which are naturally the spring and seat of unholiness.

before God, even our Father – rather, 'before Him who is at once God and our Father.' Before not merely men, but Him who will not be deceived by the mere show of holiness, that is, may your holiness be such as will stand His searching scrutiny.

coming – *Greek*, 'presence,' or 'arrival.'

with all his saints – including both the holy angels and the holy elect of men (1Th 4:14 Da 7:10 Zec 14:5 Mt 25:31 2Th 1:7). The saints are 'His' (Ac 9:13). We must have 'holiness' if we are to be numbered with His holy ones or 'saints.' On 'unblameable,' compare Re 14:5. This verse (compare 1Th 3:12) shows that 'love' is the spring of true 'holiness' (Mt 5:44–48 Ro 13:10 Col 3:14). God is He who really 'stablishes'; Timothy and other ministers are but instruments (1Th 3:2) in 'stablishing.'

Chapter 4

1Th 4:1–18. Exhortations to chastity; brotherly love; quiet industry; abstinence from undue sorrow for departed friends, for at Christ's coming all his saints shall be glorified.

1. Furthermore – *Greek*, 'As to what remains.' Generally used towards the close of his Epistles (Eph 6:10 Php 4:8).

then – with a view to the *love* and *holiness* (1Th 3:12,13) which we have just prayed for in your behalf, we now give you exhortation.

beseech – 'ask' as if it were a personal favour.

by, – rather as *Greek*, 'IN the Lord Jesus'; in communion with the Lord Jesus, as Christian ministers dealing with Christian people [EDMUNDS].

as ye ... received – when we were with you (1Th 2:13).

how – Greek, the 'how,' that is, *the manner.*

walk and … please God – that is, 'and so please God,' namely, by your walk; in contrast to the Jews who 'please not God' (1Th 2:15). The oldest manuscripts add a clause here, 'even as also ye do walk' (compare 1Th 4:10 5:11). These words, which he was able to say of them with truth, conciliate a favourable hearing for the precepts which follow. Also the expression, 'abound *more and more,*' implies that there had gone before a recognition of their already in some measure *walking so.*

2. by the Lord Jesus – by His authority and direction, not by our own. He uses the strong term, 'commandments,' in writing to this Church not long founded, knowing that they would take it in a right spirit, and feeling it desirable that they should understand he spake with divine authority. He seldom uses the term in writing subsequently, when his authority was established, to other churches. 1Co 7:10 11:17 and 1Ti 1:5 (1Th 4:18, where the subject accounts for the strong expression) are the exceptions. 'The Lord' marks His paramount authority, requiring implicit obedience.

3. For – enforcing the assertion that his 'commandments' were 'by (the authority of) the Lord Jesus' (1Th 4:2). Since 'this is the will of God,' let it be your will also.

fornication – not regarded as a sin at all among the heathen, and so needing the more to be denounced (Ac 15:20).

4. know – by moral self-control.

how to possess his vessel – rather as Greek, 'how to *acquire* (get for himself) *his own* vessel,' that is, that each should have *his own wife* so as to avoid fornication (1Th 4:3 1Co 7:2). The emphatic position of 'his own' in the Greek, and the use of 'vessel' for *wife,* in 1Pe 3:7, and in common Jewish phraseology, and the correct translation 'acquire,' all justify this rendering.

in sanctification – (Ro 6:19 1Co 6:15,18). Thus, 'his own' stands in opposition to dishonouring his brother by lusting after *his* wife (1Th 4:6).

honour – (Heb 13:4) contrasted with '*dishonour* their own bodies' (Ro 1:24).

5. in the lust – Greek, 'passion'; which implies that such a one is unconsciously the *passive* slave of lust.

which know not God – and so know no better. Ignorance of true religion is the parent of unchastity (Eph 4:18,19). A people's morals are like the objects of their worship (De 7:26 Ps 115:8 Ro 1:23,24).

6. go beyond – transgress the bounds of rectitude in respect to his 'brother.'

defraud – 'overreach' [ALFORD]; 'take advantage of' [EDMUNDS].

in any matter – rather as Greek, 'in *the* matter'; a decorous expression for the matter now in question; the conjugal honour of his neighbors as a husband, 1Th 4:4; 1Th 4:7 also confirms this view; the word 'brother' enhances the enormity of the crime. It is your *brother* whom you wrong (compare Pr 6:27–33).

the Lord – the coming Judge (2Th 1:7,8).

avenger – the Righter.

of all such – Greek, 'concerning all *these things;*' in all such cases of wrongs against a neighbors's conjugal honour.

testified – Greek, 'constantly testified [ALFORD].

7. unto uncleanness – Greek, 'for the purpose of.'

unto – rather as Greek, 'in'; marking that 'holiness' is the element in which our calling has place; in a sphere of holiness. *Saint* is another name for *Christian.*

8. despiseth, – Greek, 'setteth at naught' such engagements imposed on him in his calling, 1Th 4:7; in relation to his 'brother,' 1Th 4:6. He who doth so, 'sets at naught not man (as for instance his brother), but God' (Ps 51:4) is used of *despising* or *rejecting* God's minister, it may mean here, 'He who despiseth' or 'rejecteth' these our ministerial precepts.

who hath also given unto us – So some oldest manuscripts read, but most oldest manuscripts read, 'Who (without "also") *giveth* (present) unto *you*' (not 'us').

his Spirit – Greek, 'His own Spirit, the *Holy* (One)'; thus emphatically marking 'holiness' (1Th 4:7) as the end for which the Holy (One) is being given. 'Unto you,' in the Greek, implies that the Spirit is being given *unto, into* (put 'into' your hearts), *and among* you (compare 1Th 2:9 Eph 4:30). 'Giveth' implies that sanctification is not merely a work once for all accomplished in the past, but a *present progressive* work. So the Church of England Catechism, '*sanctifieth* (present) all the elect people of God.' 'His own' implies that as He gives you that which is essentially identical with Himself, He expects you should become like Himself (1Pe 1:16 2Pe 1:4).

9. brotherly love – referring here to acts of brotherly kindness in relieving distressed brethren. Some oldest manuscripts support *English Version* reading, 'YE have'; others, and those the weightiest, read, 'WE have.' We need not write, as *ye yourselves* are taught, and that by God: namely, in the heart by the Holy Spirit (Joh 6:45 Heb 8:11 1Jo 2:20,27).

to love – Greek, 'with a view to,' or 'to the end of your loving one another.' Divine teachings have their confluence in love [BENGEL].

10. And indeed – Greek, 'For even.'

11. study to be quiet – Greek, '*make it your ambition* to be quiet, and to do *your own business.*' In direct contrast to the world's *ambition,* which is, 'to make a great stir,' and 'to be busybodies' (2Th 3:11,12).

work with your own hands – The Thessalonian converts were, it thus seems, chiefly of the *working* classes. Their expectation of the immediate coming of Christ led some enthusiasts among them to neglect their daily work and be dependent on the bounty of others. See end of 1Th 4:12. The expectation was right in so far as that the Church should be always looking for Him; but they were wrong in making it a ground for neglecting their daily work. The evil, as it subsequently became worse, is more strongly reproved in 2Th 3:6–12.

12. honestly – in the *Old* English sense, 'becomingly,' as becomes your Christian profession; not bringing discredit on it in the eyes of the outer world, as if Christianity led to sloth and poverty (Ro 13:13 1Pe 2:12).

them ... without – outside the Christian Church (Mr 4:11).

have lack of nothing – not have to beg from others for the supply of your wants (compare Eph 4:28). So far from needing to beg from others, we ought to work and get the means of supplying the need of others. Freedom from pecuniary embarrassment is to be desired by the Christian on account of the liberty which it bestows.

13. The leading topic of Paul's preaching at Thessalonica having been the coming *kingdom* (Ac 17:7), some perverted it into a cause for fear in respect to friends lately deceased, as if these would be excluded from the glory which those found alive alone should share. This error Paul here corrects (compare 1Th 5:10).

I would not – All the oldest manuscripts and versions have '*we* would not.' My fellow labourers (Silas and Timothy) and myself desire that ye should not be ignorant.

them which are asleep – The oldest manuscripts read *present tense*, 'them which are *sleeping*'; the same as 'the dead in Christ' (1Th 4:16), to whose bodies (Da 12:2, not their *souls*; Ec 12:7 2Co 5:8) death is a calm and holy sleep, from which the resurrection shall waken them to glory. The word 'cemetery' means *a sleeping-place*. Observe, the glory and chief hope of the Church are not to be realized at death, but at the Lord's coming; one is not to anticipate the other, but all are to be glorified together at Christ's coming (Col 3:4 Heb 11:40). Death affects the mere individual; but the coming of Jesus the whole Church; at death our souls are invisibly and individually with the Lord; at Christ's coming the whole Church, with all its members, in body and soul, shall be visibly and collectively with Him. As this is offered as a consolation to mourning relatives, *the mutual recognition of the saints* at Christ's coming is hereby implied.

that ye sorrow not, even as others – Greek, 'the rest'; all the rest of the world besides Christians. Not all natural *mourning* for dead friends is forbidden: for the Lord Jesus and Paul sinlessly gave way to it (Joh 11:31,33,35 Php 2:27); but sorrow as though there were 'no hope,' which indeed the heathen had not (Eph 2:12): the Christian *hope* here meant is that of *the resurrection*. Ps 16:9,11 17:15 73:24 Pr 14:32, show that the Old Testament Church, though not having the hope *so bright* (Isa 38:18,19), yet *had* this hope. Contrast CATULLUS [*Carmina* 5.4], 'When once our brief day has set, we must sleep one everlasting night.' The sepulchral inscriptions of heathen Thessalonica express the hopeless view taken as to those once dead: as AESCHYLUS writes, 'Of one once dead there is no resurrection.' Whatever glimpses some heathen philosophers, had of the existence of the soul after death, they had none whatever of the body (Ac 17:18,20,32).

14. For if – confirmation of his statement, 1Th 4:13, that the removal of *ignorance* as to the sleeping believers would remove undue grief respecting them. See 1Th 4:13, 'hope.' Hence it appears our *hope* rests on our *faith* ('if we believe'). 'As surely as we all believe that Christ died and rose again (the very doctrine specified as taught at Thessalonica, Ac 17:3), *so also* will God bring *those laid to sleep by Jesus* with Him (Jesus).' (So the order and balance of the members of the *Greek* sentence require us to translate.) Believers are laid in sleep by Jesus, and so will be brought back from sleep with Jesus in His train when He comes. The disembodied souls are not here spoken of; the reference is to the sleeping *bodies*. The facts of Christ's experience are repeated in the believer's. He died and then rose: so believers shall die and then rise with Him. But in His case *death* is the term used, 1Co 15:3,6; in theirs, *sleep;* because His death has taken for them the sting from death. The same Hand that shall raise them is that which *laid them to sleep*. 'Laid to sleep by Jesus,' answers to 'dead in Christ' (1Th 4:16).

15. by the word of the Lord – Greek, 'in,' that is, *in virtue* of a direct revelation from the Lord to me. So 1Ki 20:35. This is the 'mystery,' a truth once hidden, now revealed, which Paul shows (1Co 15:51,52).

prevent – that is, 'anticipate.' So far were the early Christians from regarding their departed brethren as *anticipating* them in entering glory, that they needed to be assured that those who remain to the coming of the Lord 'will not anticipate them that are asleep.' The 'we' means *whichever of us* are alive and remain unto the coming of the Lord. The Spirit designed that believers in each successive age should live in continued expectation of the Lord's coming, not knowing but that *they* should be among those found alive at His coming (Mt 24:42). It is a sad fall from this blessed hope, that *death* is looked for by most men, rather than the coming of our Lord. Each successive generation in its time and place represents the generation which shall actually survive till His coming (Mt 25:13 Ro 13:11 1Co 15:51 Jas 5:9 1Pe 4:5,6). The Spirit subsequently revealed by Paul that which is not inconsistent with the expectation here taught of the Lord's coming at any time; namely, that His coming would not be until there should be a 'falling away first' (2Th 2:2,3); but as symptoms of this soon appeared, none could say but that still this precursory event might be realized, and so the Lord come in his day. Each successive revelation fills in the details of the general outline first given. So Paul subsequently, while still looking mainly for the Lord's coming to clothe him with his body from heaven, looks for going to be with Christ in the meanwhile (2Co 5:1–10 Php 1:6,23 3:20,21 4:5). EDMUNDS well says, The 'we' is an affectionate identifying of ourselves with our fellows of all ages, as members of the same body, under the same Head, Christ Jesus. So Ho 12:4, 'God spake with *us* in Beth-el,' that is, with Israel. '*We* did rejoice,' that is, Israel at the Red Sea (Ps 66:6). Though neither Hosea, nor David, was alive at the times referred to, yet each identifies himself with those that were present.

16. himself – in all the Majesty of His presence in person, not by deputy.

descend – even as He ascended (Ac 1:11).

with – Greek, 'in,' implying one concomitant circumstance attending His appearing.

shout – Greek, 'signal shout,' 'war shout.' Jesus is represented as a victorious King, giving the word of command to the hosts of heaven in His train for the last onslaught, at His final triumph over sin, death, and Satan (Re 19:11–21).

the voice of ... archangel – distinct from the 'signal shout.' Michael is perhaps meant (Jude 1:9 Re 12:7), to whom especially is committed the guardianship of the people of God (Da 10:13).

trump of God – the trumpet blast which usually accompanies God's manifestation in glory (Ex 19:16 Ps 47:5); here the last of the three accompaniments of His appearing: as the trumpet was used to convene God's people to their solemn convocations (Nu 10:2,10 31:6), so here to summon God's elect together, preparatory to their glorification with Christ (Ps 50:1–5 Mt 24:31 1Co 15:52).

shall rise first – previously to the living being 'caught up.' The 'first' here has no reference to the *first* resurrection, as contrasted with that of 'the rest of the dead.' That reference occurs elsewhere (Mt 13:41,42,50 Joh 5:29 1Co 15:23,24 Re 20:5,6); it simply stands in opposition to 'then,' 1Th 4:17. FIRST, 'the *dead* in Christ' shall rise, THEN the *living* shall be caught up. The Lord's people alone are spoken of here.

17. we which are alive ... shall be caught up – after having been 'changed in a moment' (1Co 15:51,52). Again he says, 'we,' recommending thus the expression to Christians of all ages, each generation bequeathing to the succeeding one a continually increasing obligation to look for the coming of the Lord. [EDMUNDS].

together with them – all together: the raised dead, and changed living, forming one joint body.

in the clouds – Greek, 'in clouds.' The same honour is conferred on them as on their Lord. As He was taken in a cloud at His ascension (Ac 1:9), so at His return with clouds (Re 1:7), they shall be caught up in clouds. The clouds are His and their triumphal chariot (Ps 104:3 Da 7:13). ELLICOTT explains the Greek, 'robed round by upbearing clouds' [*Aids to Faith*].

in the air – rather, '*into* the air'; caught up *into* the region just above the earth, where the *meeting* (compare Mt 25:1,6) shall take place between them ascending, and their Lord descending towards the earth. Not that the air is to be the place of their *lasting abode* with Him.

and so shall we ever be with the Lord – no more parting, and no more going out (Re 3:12). His point being established, that the dead in Christ shall be on terms of equal advantage with those found alive at Christ's coming, he leaves undefined here the other events foretold elsewhere (as not being necessary to his discussion), Christ's reign on earth with His saints (1Co 6:2,3), the final judgment and glorification of His saints in the new heaven and earth.

18. comfort one another – in your mourning for the dead (1Th 4:13).

Chapter 5

1Th 5:1–28. The suddenness of Christ's coming a motive for watchfulness; various precepts: prayer for their being found blameless, body, soul, and spirit, at Christ's coming: conclusion.

1. times – the general and indefinite term for chronological periods.

seasons – the *opportune times* (Da 7:12 Ac 1:7). *Time* denotes quantity; *season*, quality. *Seasons* are parts of *times.*

ye have no need – those who watch do not need to be told *when* the hour will come, for they are always ready [BENGEL].

cometh – present: expressing its *speedy* and awful *certainty.*

2. as a thief in the night – The apostles in this image follow the parable of their Lord, expressing how the Lord's coming shall take men by surprise (Mt 24:43 2Pe 3:10). 'The *night* is wherever there is quiet unconcern' [BENGEL]. 'At midnight' (perhaps figurative: to some parts of the earth it will be *literal* night), Mt 25:6. The thief not only gives no notice of his approach but takes all precaution to prevent the household knowing of it. So the Lord (Re 16:15). *Signs* will precede the coming, to confirm the patient hope of the watchful believer; but the coming itself shall be sudden at last (Mt 24:32–36 Lu 21:25–32,35).

3. they – the men of the world. 1Th 5:5,6 4:13, 'others,' all the rest of the world save Christians.

Peace – (Jud 18:7,9,27,28 Jer 6:14 Eze 13:10).

then – *at the very moment* when they least expect it. Compare the case of Belshazzar, Da 5:1–5,6,9,26–28; Herod, Ac 12:21–23.

sudden – 'unawares' (Lu 21:34).

as travail – 'As *the* labour pang' comes in an instant on the woman when otherwise engaged (Ps 48:6 Isa 13:8).

shall not escape – *Greek,* 'shall not at all escape.' Another awful feature of their ruin: there shall be then no possibility of shunning it however they desire it (Am 9:2,3 Re 6:15,16).

4. not in darkness – not in darkness of understanding (that is, spiritual ignorance) or of the moral nature (that is, a state of sin), Eph 4:18.

that – *Greek,* 'in order that'; with God results are all purposed.

that day – *Greek,* 'THE day'; the *day* of the Lord (Heb 10:25, '*the* day'), in contrast to 'darkness.'

overtake – unexpectedly (compare Joh 12:35).

as a thief – The two oldest manuscripts read, 'as (the daylight overtakes) *thieves*' (Job 24:17).

5. The oldest manuscripts read, 'FOR ye are all.' Ye have no reason for fear, or for being taken by surprise, by the coming of the day of the Lord: '*For* ye are all sons (so the *Greek*) of light and sons of day'; a *Hebrew* idiom, implying that as *sons* resemble their fathers, so you are *in character* light (intellectually and morally illuminated in a spiritual point of view), Lu 16:8 Joh 12:36.

are not of – that is, *belong not to* night nor darkness. The change of person from 'ye' to 'we' implies this: Ye are sons of light because ye are Christians; and *we,* Christians, are not of night nor darkness.

6. others – *Greek,* 'the rest' of the world: the unconverted (1Th 4:13). 'Sleep' here is worldly apathy to spiritual things (Ro 13:11 Eph 5:14); in 1Th 5:7, ordinary *sleep*; in 1Th 5:10, death.

watch – for Christ's coming; literally, 'be wakeful.' The same *Greek* occurs in 1Co 15:34 2Ti 2:26.

be sober – refraining from carnal indulgence, mental or sensual (1Pe 5:8).

7. This verse is to be taken in the literal sense. Night is the time when sleepers sleep, and drinking men are drunk. To sleep by day would imply great indolence; to be drunken by day, great shamelessness. Now, in a spiritual sense, 'we Christians profess to be day people, not night people; therefore our work ought to be day work, not night work; our conduct such as will bear the eye of day, and such has no need of the veil of night' [EDMUNDS], (1Th 5:8).

8. *Faith, hope,* and *love,* are the three pre-eminent graces (1Th 1:3 1Co 13:13). We must not only be awake and sober, but also *armed;* not only watchful, but also guarded. The armour here is only *defensive;* in Eph 6:13–17, also *offensive.* Here, therefore, the reference is to the Christian means of being *guarded* against being surprised by the day of the Lord as a thief in the night. The *helmet* and *breastplate* defend the two vital parts, the head and the heart respectively. 'With head and heart right, the whole man is right' [EDMUNDS]. The head needs to be kept from error, the heart from sin. For 'the breastplate of righteousness,' Eph 6:14, we have here 'the breastplate of faith and love'; for the righteousness which is imputed to man for justification, is 'faith working by love' (Ro 4:3,22–24 Ga 5:6). 'Faith,' as the motive *within,* and 'love,' exhibited in *outward* acts, constitute the perfection of *righteousness.* In Eph 6:17 the helmet is 'salvation'; here, 'the *hope* of salvation.' In one aspect 'salvation' is a present possession (Joh 3:36 5:24 1Jo 5:13); in another, it is a matter of 'hope' (Ro 8:24,25). Our Head primarily wore the 'breastplate of righteousness' and 'helmet of salvation,' that we might, by union with Him, receive both.

9. For – assigning the ground of our 'hopes' (1Th 5:8).

appointed us – Translate, 'set' (Ac 13:47), in His everlasting purpose of love (1Th 3:3 2Ti 1:9). Contrast Ro 9:22 Jude 1:4.

to – that is, *unto* wrath.

to obtain – *Greek,* 'to the acquisition of salvation'; said, according to BENGEL, Of one saved out of a general wreck, when all things else have been lost: so of the elect saved out of the multitude of the lost (2Th 2:13,14). The fact of God's 'appointment' of His grace 'through Jesus Christ' (Eph 1:5), takes away the notion of our being able to 'acquire' salvation *of ourselves.* Christ 'acquired (so the *Greek* for "purchased") the Church (and its salvation) with His own blood' (Ac 20:28); each member is said to be appointed by God to the 'acquiring of salvation.' In the primary sense, God does the work; in the secondary sense, man does.

10. died for us – *Greek,* 'in our behalf.'

whether we wake or sleep – whether we be found at Christ's coming awake, that is, alive, or asleep, that is, in our graves.

together – *all* of us *together;* the living not preceding the dead in their glorification 'with Him' at His coming (1Th 4:13).

11. comfort yourselves – *Greek,* 'one another.' Here he reverts to the same consolatory strain as in 1Th 4:18.

edify one another – rather as *Greek,* 'edify (ye) the one the other'; 'edify,' literally, 'build up,' namely, in faith, hope, and love, by discoursing together on such edifying topics as the Lord's coming, and the glory of the saints (Mal 3:16).

12. beseech – 'Exhort' is the expression in 1Th 5:14; here, 'we beseech you,' as if it were a personal favour (Paul making the cause of the Thessalonian presbyters, as it were, his own).

know – to have a regard and respect for. Recognize their office, and treat them accordingly (compare 1Co 16:18) with reverence and with liberality in supplying their needs (1Ti 5:17). The Thessalonian Church having been newly planted, the ministers were necessarily novices (1Ti 3:6), which may have been in part the cause of the people's treating them with less respect. Paul's practice seems to have been to ordain elders in every Church soon after its establishment (Ac 14:23).

them which labour ... are over ... admonish you – not three classes of ministers, but one, as there is but one article common to the three in the *Greek.* 'Labour' expresses their labourious life; 'are over you,' their pre-eminence as presidents or superintendents ('bishops,' that is, *overseers,* Php 1:1; 'them that have rule over you,' literally, *leaders,* Heb 13:17; 'pastors,' literally, *shepherds,* Eph 4:11); 'admonish you,' one of their leading functions; the *Greek* is 'put in mind,' implying not arbitrary authority, but gentle, though faithful, admonition (2Ti 2:14,24,25 1Pe 5:3).

in the Lord – Their presidency over you is *in divine things;* not in worldly affairs, but in things appertaining to the Lord.

13. very highly – *Greek,* 'exceeding abundantly.'

for their work's sake – The high nature of their work alone, the furtherance of your salvation and of the kingdom of Christ, should be a sufficient motive to claim your reverential love. At the same time, the word 'work,' teaches ministers that, while claiming the reverence due to their office, it is not a sinecure, but a 'work'; compare '*labour*' (even to *weariness:* so the *Greek*), 1Th 5:12.

be at peace among yourselves – The 'and' is not in the original. Let there not only be peace between ministers and their flocks, but also no party rivalries among yourselves, one contending in behalf of some one favourite minister, another in behalf of another (Mr 9:50 1Co 1:12 4:6).

14. brethren – This exhortation to 'warn (*Greek,* "admonish," as in 1Th 5:12) the unruly (those "disorderly" persons, 2Th 3:6,11, who would not work, and yet expected to be maintained, literally, said of soldiers who will *not* remain *in their ranks,* compare 1Th 4:11; also

those insubordinate as to Church discipline, in relation to those "over" the Church, 1Th 5:12), comfort the feeble-minded (the *faint-hearted,* who are ready to sink "without hope" in afflictions, 1Th 4:13, and temptations),' applies to all clergy and laity alike, though primarily the duty of the clergy (who are meant in 1Th 5:12).

support – literally, 'lay fast hold on so as to support.'

the weak – spiritually. Paul practised what he preached (1Co 9:22).

be patient toward all men – There is no believer who needs not the exercise of patience 'toward' him; there is none to whom a believer ought not to show it; many show it more to strangers than to their own families, more to the great than to the humble; but we ought to show it 'toward *all men*' [BENGEL]. Compare 'the long-suffering of our Lord' (2Co 10:1 2Pe 3:15).

15. (Ro 12:17 1Pe 3:9.)

unto any *man* – whether unto a Christian, or a heathen, however great the provocation.

follow – as a matter of earnest pursuit.

16, 17. In order to 'rejoice evermore,' we must 'pray without ceasing' (1Th 5:17). He who is wont to thank God for all things as happening for the best, will have continuous joy [THEOPHYLACT]. Eph 6:18 Php 4:4,6, 'Rejoice *in the Lord* . . . by prayer and supplication with thanksgiving'; Ro 14:17, '*in the Holy Ghost*'; Ro 12:12, 'in *hope*'; Ac 5:41, '*in being counted worthy to suffer shame for Christ's name*'; Jas 1:2, *in falling* 'into divers temptations.'

17. The *Greek* is, 'Pray *without intermission*'; without allowing prayerless gaps to intervene between the times of prayer.

18. In every thing – even what *seems* adverse: for nothing is *really* so (compare Ro 8:28 Eph 5:20). See Christ's example (Mt 15:36 26:27 Lu 10:21 Joh 11:41).

this – That ye should 'rejoice evermore, pray without ceasing, (and) in every thing give thanks,' 'is the will of God in Christ Jesus (as the Mediator and Revealer of that will, observed by those who are *in Christ* by faith, compare Php 3:14) concerning you.' *God's will* is the believer's law. LACHMANN rightly reads commas at the end of the three precepts (1Th 5:16–18), making 'this' refer to all three.

19. Quench not – the Spirit being a holy *fire:* 'where the Spirit is, He burns' [BENGEL] (Mt 3:11 Ac 2:3; 7:51). Do not throw cold water on those who, under extraordinary inspiration of the Spirit, stand up to speak with tongues, or reveal mysteries, or pray in the congregation. The enthusiastic exhibitions of some (perhaps as to the nearness of Christ's coming, exaggerating Paul's statement, 2Th 2:2, By *spirit*), led others (probably the presiding ministers, who had not always been treated with due respect by enthusiastic novices, 1Th 5:12), from dread of enthusiasm, to discourage the free utterances of those really inspired, in the Church assembly. On the other hand, the caution (1Th 5:21) was needed, not to receive 'all' pretended revelations as divine, without 'proving' them.

20. prophesyings – whether exercised in inspired teaching, or in predicting the future. 'Despised' by some as beneath 'tongues,' which seemed most miraculous; therefore declared by Paul to be a greater gift than tongues, though the latter were more showy (1Co 14:5).

21, 22. Some of the oldest manuscripts insert 'But.' You ought indeed not to 'quench' the manifestations of 'the Spirit,' nor 'despise prophesyings'; 'but,' at the same time, do not take 'all' as genuine which professes to be so; 'prove (test) all' such manifestations. The means of testing them existed in the Church, in those who had the 'discerning of spirits' (1Co 12:10 14:29 1Jo 4:1). Another sure test, which we also have, is, to try the professed revelation whether it accords with Scripture, as the noble Bereans did (Isa 8:20 Ac 17:11 Ga 1:8,9). This precept negatives the Romish priest's assumption of infallibly laying down the law, without the laity having the right, in the exercise of private judgment, to test it by Scripture. LOCKE says, Those who are for laying aside reason in matters of revelation, resemble one who would *put out his eyes* in order to use a *telescope*.

hold fast that which is good – Join this clause with the next clause (1Th 5:22), not merely with the sentence preceding. As the result of your 'proving all things,' and especially all *prophesyings,* 'hold fast (Lu 8:15 1Co 11:2 Heb 2:1) the good, and *hold yourselves aloof from* every appearance of evil' ('*every evil species*' [BENGEL and WAHL]). Do not accept even a professedly spirit-inspired communication, if it be at variance with the truth taught you (2Th 2:2).

22. TITTMANN supports *English Version,* 'from every evil *appearance*' or 'semblance.' The context, however, does not refer to *evil appearances* IN OURSELVES which we ought to abstain from, but to *holding ourselves aloof from every evil appearance* IN OTHERS; as for instance, in the pretenders to spirit-inspired prophesyings. In many cases the Christian should *not* abstain from what has the *semblance* ('appearance') of evil, though really good. Jesus healed on the Sabbath, and ate with publicans and sinners, acts which wore the *appearance* of evil, but which were not to be abstained from on that account, being really good. I agree with TITTMANN rather than with BENGEL, whom ALFORD follows. The context favours this sense: However *specious* be the *form* or *outward appearance* of such would-be prophets and their prophesyings, hold yourselves aloof from every such form when it is evil, literally, 'Hold yourselves aloof from every evil appearance' or 'form.'

23. the very God – rather as the *Greek,* 'the God of peace *Himself*'; who can do for you by His own power what *I* cannot do by all my monitions, nor *you* by all your efforts (Ro 16:20 Heb 13:20), namely, keep you from all evil, and give you all that is good.

sanctify you – for *holiness* is the necessary condition of 'peace' (Php 4:6–9).

wholly – Greek, '(so that you should be) perfect in every respect' [TITTMANN].

and – that is, 'and so (omit "I pray God"; not in the *Greek*) may your ... spirit and soul and body be preserved.'

whole – A different *Greek* word from 'wholly.' Translate, 'entire'; with none of the integral parts wanting [TITTMANN]. It refers to man in his normal integrity, as originally designed; an ideal which shall be attained by the glorified believer. All three, spirit, soul, and body, each in its due place, constitute man 'entire.' The 'spirit' links man with the higher intelligences of heaven, and is that highest part of man which is receptive of the quickening Holy Spirit (1Co 15:47). In the unspiritual, the spirit is so sunk under the lower animal *soul* (which it ought to keep under) that such are termed 'animal' (*English Version.* 'sensual,' having merely the *body* of organized matter, and the *soul* the immaterial animating essence), having *not the Spirit* (compare 1Co 2:14). The unbeliever shall rise with an *animal* (soul-animated) *body,* but not like the believer with a *spiritual* (spirit-endued) *body* like Christ's (Ro 8:11).

blameless unto – rather as Greek, 'blamelessly (so as to be in a blameless state) at the coming of Christ.' In *Hebrew,* 'peace' and 'wholly' (perfect in every respect) are kindred terms; so that the prayer shows what the title 'God of peace' implies. BENGEL takes 'wholly' as *collectively,* all the Thessalonians without exception, so that no one should fail. And 'whole (entire),' *individually,* each one of them entire, with 'spirit, soul, and body.' The mention of the preservation of the *body* accords with the subject (1Th 4:16). TRENCH better regards 'wholly' as meaning, 'having perfectly attained the moral *end,*' namely, to be a full-grown man in Christ. 'Whole,' *complete,* with no grace which ought to be wanting in a Christian.

24. Faithful – to His covenant promises (Joh 10:27–29 1Co 1:9 10:23 Php 1:6).

he that calleth you – God, the caller of His people, will cause His calling not to fall short of its designed end.

do it – preserve and present you blameless at the coming of Christ (1Th 5:23 Ro 8:30 1Pe 5:10). You must not look at the foes before and behind, on the right hand and on the left, but to God's faithfulness to His promises, God's zeal for His honour, and God's love for those whom He calls.

25. Some oldest manuscripts read, 'Pray ye *also* for (literally, '*concerning*') us'; make us and our work the subject of your prayers, even as *we* have been just praying for you (1Th 5:23). Others omit the 'also.' The clergy need much the prayers of their flocks. Paul makes the same request in the Epistles to Romans, Ephesians, Philippians, Colossians, Philemon, and in Second Corinthians; not so in the Epistles to Timothy and Titus, whose intercessions, as his spiritual sons, he was already sure of; nor in the Epistles, I Corinthians, and Galatians, as these Epistles abound in rebuke.

26. Hence it appears this Epistle was first handed to the elders, who communicated it to 'the brethren.'

holy kiss – pure and chaste. 'A kiss of charity' (1Pe 5:14). A token of Christian fellowship in those days (compare Lu 7:45 Ac 20:37), as it is a common mode of salutation in many countries. The custom hence arose in the early Church of passing the kiss through the congregation at the holy communion [JUSTIN MARTYR, *Apology*, 1.65; *Apostolic Constitutions*, 2.57], the men kissing the men, and the women the women, in the Lord. So in the Syrian Church each takes his neighbors's right hand and gives the salutation, 'Peace.'

27. I charge – *Greek*, 'I adjure you.'

read unto all – namely, publicly in the congregation at a particular time. The *Greek* aorist tense implies a single act done at a particular time. The earnestness of his adjuration implies how solemnly important he felt this divinely inspired message to be. Also, as this was the FIRST of the Epistles of the New Testament, he makes this the occasion of a solemn charge, that so its being publicly read should be a sample of what should be done in the case of the others, just as the Pentateuch and the Prophets were publicly read under the Old Testament, and are still read in the synagogue. Compare the same injunction as to the public reading of the Apocalypse, the LAST of the New Testament canon (Re 1:3). The 'all' includes women and children, and especially those who could not read it themselves (De 31:12 Jos 8:33–35). What Paul commands with an adjuration, Rome forbids under a curse [BENGEL]. Though these Epistles had difficulties, the laity were all to hear them read (1Pe 4:11 2Pe 3:10; even the very young, 2Ti 1:5 3:15). 'Holy' is omitted before 'brethren' in most of the oldest manuscripts, though some of them support it.

28. Paul ends as he began (1Th 1:1), with 'grace.' The oldest manuscripts omit 'Amen,' which probably was the response of the Church after the public reading of the Epistle.

The subscription is a comparatively modern addition. The Epistle was not, as it states, written from Athens, but from Corinth; for it is written in the names of Silas and Timothy (besides Paul), who did not join the apostle before he reached the latter city (Ac 18:5).

2 THESSALONIANS

A.R. Faussett

Introduction

Purpose

The accounts from Thessalonica, after the sending of the first Epistle, represented the faith and love of the Christians there as on the increase; and their constancy amidst persecutions unshaken. One error of doctrine, however, resulting in practical evil, had sprung up among them. The apostle's description of Christ's sudden second coming (1Th 4:13, and 1Th 5:2), and the *possibility* of its being at any time, led them to believe it was *actually* at hand. Some professed to know by 'the Spirit' (2Th 2:2) that it was so; and others alleged that Paul had said so when with them. A letter, too, purporting to be from the apostle to that effect, seems to have been circulated among them. (That 2Th 2:2 refers to such a spurious letter, rather than to Paul's first Epistle, appears likely from the statement, 2Th 3:17, as to his autograph salutation being the mark whereby his genuine letters might be known.) Hence some neglected their daily business and threw themselves on the charity of others, as if their sole duty was to wait for the coming of the Lord. This error, therefore, needed rectifying, and forms a leading topic of the second Epistle. He in it tells them (2Th 2:1–17), that before the Lord shall come, there must first be a great *apostasy*, and *the Man of Sin* must be revealed; and that the Lord's sudden coming is no ground for neglecting daily business; that to do so would only bring scandal on the Church, and was contrary to his own practice among them (2Th 3:7–9), and that the faithful must withdraw themselves from such disorderly professors (2Th 3:6,10–15). Thus, there are *three* divisions of the Epistle:

(1) 2Th 1:1–12. Commendations of the Thessalonians' faith, love, and patience, amidst persecutions.

(2) 2Th 2:1–17. The error as to the immediate coming of Christ corrected, and the previous rise and downfall of the Man of Sin foretold.

(3) 2Th 3:1–16. Exhortations to orderly conduct in their whole walk, with prayers for them to the God of peace, followed by his autograph salutation and benediction.

Date of writing

As the Epistle is written in the joint names of Timothy and Silas, as well as his own, and as these were with him while at Corinth, and not with him for a long time subsequently to his having left that city (compare Ac 18:18, with Ac 19:22; indeed, as to Silas, it is doubtful whether he was ever subsequently with Paul), it follows, the *place* of writing must have been Corinth, and the *date,* during the one 'year and six months' of his stay there, Ac 18:11

(namely, beginning with the autumn of A.D. 52, and ending with the spring of A.D. 54), say about six months after his first Epistle, early in A.D. 53.

Style of writing

The style is not different from that of most of Paul's other writings, except in the prophetic portion of it (2Th 2:1–12), which is distinguished from them in subject matter. As is usual in his more solemn passages (for instance, in the denunciatory and prophetic portions of his Epistles, for example, compare Col 2:8,16, with 2Th 2:3; 1Co 15:24–28, with 2Th 2:8,9; Ro 1:18, with 2Th 2:8,10), his diction here is more lofty, abrupt, and elliptical. As the former Epistle dwells mostly on the second Advent in its aspect of glory to the sleeping and the living saints (1Th 4:1–5:28), so this Epistle dwells mostly on it in its aspect of everlasting destruction to the wicked and him who shall be the final consummation of wickedness, the Man of Sin. So far was Paul from laboring under an erroneous impression as to Christ's speedy coming, when he wrote his first Epistle (which rationalists impute to him), that he had distinctly told them, when he was with them, the same truths as to the apostasy being about first to arise, which he now insists upon in this second Epistle (2Th 2:5). Several points of coincidence occur between the two Epistles, confirming the genuineness of the latter. Thus, compare 2Th 3:2, with 1Th 2:15,16; again, 2Th 2:9, the Man of Sin 'coming after the working of Satan,' with 1Th 2:18 3:5, where Satan's incipient work as the *hinderer* of the Gospel, and the *tempter,* appears; again, mild *warning* is enjoined, 1Th 5:14; but, in this second Epistle, when the evil had grown worse, stricter discipline (2Th 3:6,14): 'withdraw from' the 'company' of such.

Paul probably visited Thessalonica on his way to Asia subsequently (Ac 20:4), and took with him thence Aristarchus and Secundus: the former became his 'companion in travel' and shared with him his perils at Ephesus, also those of his shipwreck, and was his 'fellow prisoner' at Rome (Ac 27:2 Col 4:10 Phm 1:24). According to tradition he became bishop of Apamea.

Contents

See *Outlines of the New Testament Books,* pp. 900–1

Chapter 1

2Th 1:1–12. Address and salutation: introduction: thanksgiving for their growth in faith and love, and for their patience in persecutions, which are a token for good everlasting to them, and for perdition to their adversaries at Christ's coming: prayer for their perfection.

1. in God our Father – still more endearing than the address, 1Th 1:1 'in God THE Father.'

2. from God our Father – So some oldest manuscripts read. Others omit 'our.'

3. We are bound – Greek, 'We owe it as a debt' (2Th 2:13). They had prayed for the Thessalonians (1Th 3:12) that they might 'increase and abound in love'; their prayer having been heard, it is a small but a bounden return for them to make, to thank God for it. Thus, Paul and his fellow missionaries practice what they preach (1Th 5:18). In 1Th 1:3, their thanksgiving was for the Thessalonians' 'faith, love, and patience'; here, for their *exceeding growth* in *faith,* and for their *charity abounding.* 'We are bound' expresses the duty of thanksgiving from its subjective side as an inward conviction. 'As it is meet,' from the *objective* side as something answering to the state of circumstances [ALFORD]. Observe the exact correspondence of the prayer (1Th 3:12, 'The Lord make you to abound in love') and the answer, 'The love of every one of you all toward each other aboundeth' (compare 1Th 4:10).

meet – right.

4. glory in you – make our boast of you, literally, 'in your case.' 'Ourselves' implies that not merely did they hear others speaking of the Thessalonians' faith, but they, the missionaries *themselves,* boasted of it. Compare 1Th 1:8, wherein the apostle said, their faith was so well known in various places, that he and his fellow missionaries had no need to speak of it; but here he says, so abounding is their love, combined with faith and patience, that he and his fellow missionaries *themselves,* make it a matter of glorying in the various churches elsewhere (he was now at Corinth in Achaia, and boasted there of the faith of the Macedonian churches, 2Co 10:15–17 8:1, at the same time giving the glory to the Lord), not only looking forward to glorying threat at Christ's coming (1Th 2:19), but doing so even now.

patience – in 1Th 1:3, 'patience *of hope.*' Here *hope* is tacitly implied as the ground of their patience; 2Th 1:5,7 state the object of their hope, namely, the kingdom for which they suffer.

tribulations – literally, 'pressures.' The Jews were the instigators of the populace and of the magistrates against Christians (Ac 17:6,8).

which ye endure – *Greek,* 'are (now) enduring.'

5. Which – Your *enduring* these tribulations is a 'token of the righteous judgment of God,' manifested in your being enabled to endure them, and in your adversaries thereby filling up the measure of their guilt. The judgment is even now begun, but its consummation will be at the Lord's coming. David (Ps 73:1–14) and Jeremiah (Jer 12:1–4) were perplexed at the wicked prospering and the godly suffering. But Paul, by the light of the New Testament, makes this fact a matter of consolation. It is a *proof* (so the *Greek*) of the future judgment, which will set to rights the anomalies of the present state, by rewarding the now suffering saint, and by punishing the persecutor. And even now 'the Judge of all the earth does right' (Ge 18:25); for the godly are in themselves sinful and need chastisement to amend them. What they suffer unjustly at the hands of cruel men they suffer justly at the hands of God; and they have their evil things here that they may escape condemnation with the world and have their good things hereafter (Lu 16:25 1Co 11:32) [EDMUNDS].

that ye may be counted worthy – expressing the purpose of God's 'righteous judgment' as regards you.

for which – *Greek,* 'in behalf of which ye are also suffering' (compare Ac 5:41 9:16 Php 1:29).

'Worthy' implies that, though men are justified by faith, they shall be judged 'according to their works' (Re 20:12; compare 1Th 2:12 1Pe 1:6,7 Re 20:4). The 'also' implies the connection between *the suffering for the kingdom* and *being counted worthy* of it. Compare Ro 8:17,18.

6. seeing it is a righteous thing – This justifies the assertion above of there being a 'righteous judgment' (2Th 1:5), namely, 'seeing that it is (literally, "if at least," "if at all events it is") a *righteous* thing with (that is, in the estimation of) God' (which, as we all feel, it certainly is). Our own innate feeling of what is just, in this confirms what is revealed.

recompense – requite *in kind,* namely, *tribulation* to them that trouble you (*affliction* to those that *afflict* you); and to you who are *troubled, rest from trouble.*

7. rest – governed by 'to recompense' (2Th 1:6). The *Greek* is literally, 'relaxation'; loosening of the *tension* which had preceded; *relaxing* the strings of endurance now so tightly drawn. The *Greek* word for 'rest,' Mt 11:28, is distinct, namely, *cessation* from labour. Also, Heb 4:9, 'A keeping of Sabbath.'

with us – namely, Paul, Silas, and Timothy, the writers, who are troubled like yourselves.

when – at the time when …; not sooner, not later.

with his mighty angels – rather as the *Greek,* 'with the angels of His might,' or 'power,' that is, the angels who are the ministers by whom He makes His might to be recognized (Mt 13:41,52). It is not *their* might, but His might, which is the prominent thought.

8. In flaming fire – *Greek,* 'In flame of fire'; or, as other oldest manuscripts read, '*in fire of flame.*' This *flame of fire* accompanied His manifestation in the bush (Ex 3:2); also His giving of the law at Sinai (Ex 19:18). Also it shall accompany His revelation at His advent (Da 7:9,10), symbolizing His own bright glory and His consuming vengeance against His foes (Heb 10:27 12:29 2Pe 3:7,10).

taking – literally, '*giving*' them, as their portion, 'vengeance.'

know not God – the Gentiles primarily (Ps 79:6 Ga 4:8 1Th 4:5); not of course those *involuntarily* not knowing God, but those *wilfully* not knowing Him, as Pharaoh, who might have known God if he would, but who boasted 'I know not the Lord' (Ex 5:2); and as the heathen persecutors who might have known God by the preaching of those whom they persecuted. Secondarily, all who 'profess to know God but in works deny Him' (Tit 1:16).

obey not the gospel – primarily the unbelieving Jews (Ro 10:3,16); secondarily, all who obey not the truth (Ro 2:8).

Christ – omitted by some of the oldest manuscripts, and retained by others.

9. Who – *Greek,* 'persons who.'

destruction from the presence of the Lord – driven *far from* His presence [ALFORD]. The sentence *emanating from Him* in person, sitting as Judge [BENGEL], and *driving them far from* Him (Mt 25:41 Re 6:16 12:14; compare 1Pe 3:12 Isa 2:10,19). 'The presence of the Lord' is the source whence the sentence goes forth; 'the glory of His power' is the instrument whereby the sentence is carried into execution [EDMUNDS]. But ALFORD better interprets the latter clause (see 2Th 1:10), driven 'from the manifestation of His power *in the glorification of His saints.*' *Cast out from the presence of the Lord* is the idea at the root of eternal death, the law of evil left to its unrestricted working, without one counteracting influence of the presence of God, who is the source of all light and holiness (Isa 66:24 Mr 9:44).

10. 'When He shall have come.'

glorified in his saints – as the element and mirror IN which His glory shall shine brightly (Joh 17:10).

admired in all them that believe – *Greek,* 'them that *believed.*' Once they *believed,* now they *see:* they had taken His word on trust. Now His word is made good and they need faith no longer. With *wonder* all celestial intelligences (Eph 3:10) shall see and *admire* the Redeemer on account of the excellencies which He has wrought in them.

because – Supply for the sense, among whom (namely, those who shall be found to have believed) *you,* too, shall be; 'because our testimony unto (so the *Greek* for "among") you was believed' (and was not rejected as by those 'who obey not the Gospel,' 2Th 1:8). The early preaching of the Gospel was not abstract discussions, but a *testimony* to facts and truths experimentally known (Lu 24:48 Ac 1:8). *Faith* is defined by BISHOP PEARSON as 'an assent unto truths, credible upon the testimony of God, delivered unto us by the apostles and prophets' (originally delivering their testimony orally, but now in their writings). 'Glorified in His saints' reminds us that *holiness* is *glory* in the bud; *glory* is *holiness* manifested.

11. Wherefore – *Greek,* 'With a view to which,' namely, His glorification in you as His saints.

also – We not only anticipate the coming glorification of our Lord *in His saints, but we also pray concerning* (so the *Greek*) YOU.

our God – whom we serve.

count you worthy – The prominent position of the 'You' in the *Greek* makes it the emphatic word of the sentence. May *you* be found among the saints whom God shall count worthy of their calling (Eph 4:1)! There is no dignity in us independent of God's calling of us (2Ti 1:9). *The calling* here is not merely the first actual call, but the whole of God's electing act, originating in His 'purpose of grace given us in Christ before the world began,' and having its consummation in glory.

the good pleasure of – on the part of God [BENGEL].

faith – on your part. ALFORD refers the former clause, 'good pleasure of his goodness,' also to *man,* arguing that the *Greek* for 'goodness' is never applied to God, and translates, 'All [that is, every possible] *right purpose of goodness.*' WAHL, 'All *sweetness* of goodness,' that is, impart in full to you all the refreshing delights of goodness. I think that, as in the previous and parallel clause, 'calling' refers to GOD's purpose; and as the *Greek* for 'good pleasure' mostly is used of *God,* we ought to translate, 'fulfil (His) *every gracious purpose* of goodness (*on your part*),' that is, fully perfect in you all goodness according to *His gracious purpose.* Thus, 'the grace of our God,' 2Th 1:12, corresponds to *God's* 'good pleasure' here, which confirms the *English Version,* just as 'the grace of the *Lord Jesus Christ*' is parallel to 'work of *faith,*' as Christ especially is the object of faith. 'The work of faith'; *Greek,* (no article; supply from the previous clause *all*) *work* of faith'; faith manifested by *work,* which is its perfected development (Jas 1:4). *Working reality of faith.*

with power – *Greek,* 'in power,' that is, '*powerfully fulfil in you*' (Col 1:11).

12. the name of our Lord Jesus – Our Lord Jesus *in His manifested personality* as the God-man.

in you, and ye in him – reciprocal glorification; compare Isa 28:5, '*The Lord of hosts* shall be … a crown of glory and … a diadem of beauty unto … His people,' with Isa 62:3, '*Thou* (Zion) shalt be a crown of glory in the hand of the Lord, and a royal diadem.' (Joh 21:10 Ga 1:24 1Pe 4:14). The believer's graces redound to Christ's glory, and His glory, as their Head, reflects glory on them as the members.

the grace of our God and the Lord Jesus Christ – There is but one *Greek* article to both, implying the inseparable unity of God and the Lord Jesus.

Chapter 2

2Th 2:1–17. Correction of their error as to Christ's immediate coming. The apostasy that must precede it. Exhortation to steadfastness, introduced with thanksgiving for their election by God.

1. Now – rather, 'But'; marking the transition from his prayers *for* them to entreaties *to* them.

we beseech you – or 'entreat you.' He uses affectionate entreaty, rather than stern reproof, to win them over to the right view.

by – rather, 'with respect to'; as the *Greek* for 'of' (2Co 1:8).

our gathering together unto him – the consummating or final gathering together of the saints to Him at His coming, as announced, Mt 24:31 1Th 4:17. The *Greek* noun is nowhere else found except in Heb 10:25, said of *the assembling together* of believers for *congregational* worship. Our instinctive fears of the judgment are dispelled by the thought of being gathered together UNTO HIM ('even as the hen gathereth her chickens under her wings'), which ensures our safety.

2. soon – on trifling grounds, without due consideration.

shaken – literally, 'tossed' as ships tossed by an agitated sea. Compare for the same image, Eph 4:14.

in mind – rather as the *Greek,* '*from* your mind,' that is, from your mental steadfastness on the subject.

troubled – This verb applies to *emotional* agitation; as 'shaken' to *intellectual.*

by spirit – by a *person professing* to have the *spirit* of prophecy (1Co 12:8–10 1Jo 4:1–3). The Thessalonians had been warned (1Th 5:20,21) to 'prove' such professed prophesyings, and to 'hold fast (only) that which is good.'

by word – *of mouth* (compare 2Th 2:5,15); some word or saying alleged to be that of Paul, orally communicated. If oral tradition was liable to such perversion in the apostolic age (compare a similar instance, Joh 21:23), how much more in our age!

by letter as from us – purporting to be from us, whereas it is a forgery. Hence he gives a test by which to know his genuine letters (2Th 3:17).

day of Christ – The oldest manuscripts read, 'day of *the Lord.*'

i s at hand – rather, 'is *immediately imminent,*' literally, 'is *present*'; 'is *instantly* coming.' Christ and His apostles always taught that the day of the Lord's coming *is at hand*; and it is not likely that Paul would imply anything contrary here; what he denies is, that it is so *immediately imminent, instant,* or *present,* as to justify the neglect of everyday worldly duties. CHRYSOSTOM, and after him ALFORD, translates, 'is (already) present' (compare 2Ti 2:18), a kindred error. But in 2Ti 3:1, the same *Greek* verb is translated 'come.' WAHL supports this view. The *Greek* is usually used of actual presence; but is quite susceptible of the translation, 'is all but present.'

3. by any means – *Greek,* 'in any manner.' Christ, in Mt 24:4, gives the same warning in connection with the same event. He had indicated three ways (2Th 2:2) in which they might be deceived (compare other ways, 2Th 2:9, and Mt 24:5,24).

a falling away – rather as the *Greek,* '*the* falling away,' or '*apostasy*,' namely, *the* one of

which 'I told you' before (2Th 2:5), 'when I was yet with you,' and of which the Lord gave some intimation (Mt 24:10–12 Joh 5:43).

that man of sin be revealed – The *Greek* order is, 'And there have been revealed the man of sin.' As Christ was first in *mystery,* and afterwards *revealed* (1Ti 3:16), so Antichrist (the term used 1Jo 2:18 4:3) is first in mystery, and afterwards shall be developed and revealed (2Th 2:7–9). As righteousness found its embodiment in Christ, 'the Lord our righteousness,' so 'sin' shall have its embodiment in 'the man of sin.' *The hindering* power meanwhile restrains its manifestation; when that shall be removed, then this manifestation shall take place. The articles, '*the* apostasy,' and '*the* man of sin,' may also refer to their being *well known as foretold* in Da 7:8,25, 'the little horn speaking great words against the Most High, and thinking to change times and laws'; and Da 11:36, the wilful king who 'shall exalt and magnify himself above every god, and shall speak marvellous things against the God of gods; neither shall he regard any god.'

the son of perdition – a title applied besides to Judas (the traitor, Joh 17:12), and to none else. Antichrist (the second 'beast' coming up out of the earth); therefore he shall at first be 'like a lamb, while he speaks as a dragon' (Re 13:11); 'coming in peaceably and by flatteries,' 'working deceitfully,' but 'his heart shall be against the holy covenant' (Da 11:21,23,28,30). Seeds of 'the falling away' soon appear (1Ti 4:1–3), but the full development and concentration of these anti-Christian elements in one person are still to appear. Contrast the King of Zion's coming as JESUS: (1) righteous or *just*; (2) having *salvation;* (3) *lowly*; whereas Antichrist is: (1) 'the man of (the embodiment of) *sin*; (2) the son of *perdition*; (3) *exalting himself* above all that is worshipped. He is *the son of perdition,* as consigning many to it, and finally doomed to it himself (Re 17:18,11). 'He whose essence and inheritance is perdition' [ALFORD]. As 'the *kingdom* of heaven' is first brought before us in the abstract, then in the concrete, the *King,* the Lord Jesus; so here, first we have (2Th 2:7) 'the mystery of *iniquity,*' then 'the *iniquitous one*' (2Th 2:8).

4. Da 11:36,37 is here referred to. The words used there as to Antiochus Epiphanes, Paul implies, shall even be more applicable to the man of sin, who is the New Testament actual Antichrist, as Antiochus was the Old Testament typical Antichrist. The previous world kingdoms had each one extraordinary person as its representative head and embodiment (thus Babylon had Nebuchadnezzar, Da 2:38, end; Medo-Persia had Cyrus; Greece had Alexander, and Antiochus Epiphanes, the forerunner of Antichrist); so the fourth and last world kingdom, under which we now live, shall have one final head, the concentrated embodiment of all the *sin* and *lawless iniquity* which have been in pagan and papal Rome. Rome's final phase will probably be an unholy alliance between idolatrous superstition and godless infidelity.

Who opposeth and exalteth himself – There is but one *Greek* article to both participles, implying that the reason why he *opposeth himself* is in order that he may *exalt himself above*. ALFORD takes the former clause absolutely, 'He that withstands (CHRIST),' that is, Antichrist (1Jo 2:18). As at the conclusion of the Old Testament period, Israel apostate allied itself with the heathen world power against Jesus and His apostles (Lu 23:12; and at Thessalonica, Ac 17:5–9), and was in righteous retribution punished by the instrumentality of the world power itself (Jerusalem being destroyed by Rome), Da 9:26,27; so the degenerate Church (become an 'harlot'), allying itself with the godless world power (the 'beast' of Revelation) against vital religion (that is, the harlot sitting on the beast), shall be judged by that world power which shall be finally embodied in Antichrist (Zec 13:8,9 14:2 Re 17:16,17). In this early Epistle, the apostate Jewish Church as the harlot, and pagan Rome as the beast, form the historical background on which Paul draws his prophetic sketch of the apostasy. In the Pastoral Epistles, which were later, this prophecy appears in connection with Gnosticism, which had at that time infected the Church. The harlot (the apostate Church) is first to be judged by the beast (the world power) and its kings (Re 17:16); and afterwards the beasts and their allies (with the personal Antichrist at their head, who seems to rise after the judgment on the harlot, or apostate Church) shall be judged by the coming of Jesus Himself (Re 19:20). Anti-Christian tendencies produce different Antichrists: these separate Antichrists shall hereafter find their consummation in an individual exceeding them all in the intensity of his evil character [AUBERLEN]. But judgment soon overtakes him. He is necessarily *a child of death*, immediately after his *ascent* as *the beast out of the bottomless pit going into perdition* (Re 17:8,11). *Idolatry of self, spiritual pride*, and *rebellion against God*, are his characteristics; as *Christ-worship, humility*, and *dependence on God*, characterize Christianity. He not merely *assumes* Christ's character (as the 'false Christs,' Mt 24:24), but 'opposes' Christ. The *Greek* implies one *situated on an opposite side* (compare 1Jo 2:22 2Jo 1:7). One who, on the destruction of every religion, shall seek to establish his own throne, and for God's great truth, 'God is man,' to substitute his own lie, 'Man is God' [TRENCH].

or that is worshipped – Antichrist shall exalt himself above *every* object of worship, whether on earth as the Cæsar, or in heaven as God. The various prefigurations of Antichrist, Mohammed, Rome, Napoleon, and modern infidel secularism, contain only *some*, not *all*, his characteristics. It is the union of all in some one person that shall form the full Antichrist, as the union in one Person, Jesus, of all the types and prophecies constituted the full Christ [OLSHAUSEN].

in the temple of God … that he is God – 'He will reign a time, times, and half a time' (Da 7:25), that is, three and a half years, and will sit *in the temple at Jerusalem:* then the Lord shall come from heaven and cast him into the take of fire and shall bring to the saints the times of their reigning, the seventh day of hallowed rest, and give to Abraham the promised inheritance' [IRENAEUS, *Against Heresies*, 30.4].

showing himself – with blasphemous and arrogant DISPLAY (Compare a type, Ac 12:21–23). The earliest Fathers unanimously looked for a personal Antichrist. An objection fatal to interpreting *the temple of God* here as *the Church* (1Co 3:16,17 6:19) is, the apostle would never designate the *apostate* anti-Christian Church 'the temple *of God*.' It is likely that, as Messiah was revealed among the Jews at Jerusalem, so Antimessiah shall appear among them when restored to their own land, and after they have rebuilt their *temple at Jerusalem*. Thus Da 11:41,45, corresponds, 'He shall enter the glorious land (Judea), and he shall plant the tabernacles of his palaces between the seas in *the glorious holy mountain*'; and then (Da 12:1) 'Michael, the great prince, shall stand up' to deliver God's people. Also the king of Assyria, type of Antichrist (Isa 14:12–14). 'Lucifer' (a title of Messiah, assumed by Antichrist, Re 22:16); 'I will exalt my throne above the stars of God.' 'I will sit upon the *mount of the congregation* (that is, God's place of meeting His people of old, the temple), *in the sides of the north* (Ps 48:2); I will be like the Most High.' Re 11:1,2, 'The temple of God … the holy city' (namely, Jerusalem, Mt 4:5), compare Ps 68:18,29, referring to a period since Christ's ascension, therefore not yet fulfilled (Isa 2:1–3 Eze 40:1–44:31 Zec 14:16–20 Mal 3:1). 'In the temple of God,' implies that it an *internal*, not an external, enemy which shall assail the Church. Antichrist shall, the first three and a half years of the prophetical week, keep the covenant, then break it and usurp divine honours in the midst of the week. Some think Antichrist will be a Jew. At all events he will, 'by flatteries,' bring many, not only of the Gentiles, but also of 'the tribes' of Israel (so the *Greek* for 'kindreds,' Re 11:8,9), to own him as their long-looked-for Messiah, in the same 'city where our Lord was crucified.' 'Sitteth' here implies his occupying the place of power and majesty in opposition to Him who 'sitteth on the right hand of the Majesty on high' (Heb 1:3), and who shall come to 'sit' there where the usurper had sat (Mt 26:64). Compare Eze 38:2,3,6,9,10,13,14,16, as to Tyre, the type of Antichrist, characterized by similar blasphemous arrogance.

5. Remember – confuting those who represent Paul as having laboured under error as to Christ's immediate coming when writing his first Epistle, and as now correcting that error.

I told you – more than once, literally, 'I was telling,' or 'used to tell.'

6. now ye know – by my having told you. The power must have been one 'known' to the Thessalonians.

what withholdeth – that which *holds* him *back;* 'keeps him in check': the power that has restrained the man of sin from his full and final development, is *the moral and conservative influence of political states* [OLSHAUSEN]: *the fabric of human polity* as a *coercive* power; as 'he who now letteth' refers to *those who rule that polity* by which the great upbursting of godlessness is kept down [ALFORD]. The 'what withholdeth' refers to the *general hindrance;* 'he who now letteth,' to *the person in whom that hindrance is summed up.* Romanism, as a forerunner of Antichrist, was thus kept in check by *the Roman emperor* (the then representative of the coercive power) until Constantine, having removed the seat of empire to Constantinople, the Roman bishop by degrees first raised himself to precedency, then to primacy, and then to sole empire above the secular power. The historical fact from which Paul starts in his prediction was probably the emperor Claudius' expulsion of the Jews, the representative of the anti-Christian adversary in Paul's day, from Rome, thus 'withholding' them in some degree in their attacks on Christianity; this suggested the principle holding good to the end of time, and about to find its final fulfilment in the removal of *the withholding person* or *authority,* whereupon Antichrist in his worst shape shall start up.

that he might be – Greek, 'in order that': ye know that which keeps him back, in God's purposes, from being sooner manifested, '*in order that* he *may* be revealed in *his own* time' (that is, the time appointed by God to him as his proper time for being manifested), not sooner (compare Da 11:35). The removal of the withholding power will be when the civil polity, derived from the Roman empire, which is to be, in its last form, divided into ten kingdoms (Re 17:3,11–13), shall, with its leading representative head for the time being ('he who now letteth,' Greek, 'withholdeth,' as in 2Th 2:6), yield to the prevalent godless 'lawlessness' with 'the lawless one' as its embodiment. *The elect Church* and *the Spirit* cannot well be, as DEBURGH suggests, the *withholding* power meant; for both

shall never be *wholly* 'taken out of the way' (Mt 28:20). However, the testimony of *the elect Church,* and *the Spirit* in her, are the great hindrance to the rise of the apostasy; and it is possible that, though the Lord shall have a faithful few even then, yet the full energy of the Spirit in *the visible* Church, counteracting the energy or 'working' of 'the mystery of lawlessness' by the testimony of the elect, shall have been so far 'taken out of the way,' or *set aside,* as to admit the manifestation of 'the lawless one'; and so DEBURGH's view may be right (Lu 18:8 Re 11:3–12). This was a power of which the Thessalonians might easily 'know' through Paul's instruction.

7. the mystery of iniquity – the counter work to 'the mystery of godliness' (1Ti 3:16). Anti-Christianity *latently* working, as distinguished from its final *open* manifestation. 'Mystery' in Scripture means, not what remains always a secret, but that which is for a while hidden, but in due time manifested (compare Eph 3:4,5). Satan will resort to a mode of opposition more conformed to the then imminent 'appearing' and 'presence' of the Saviour, and will anticipate Him with a last effort to maintain the dominion of the world [DEBURGH], just as at His first advent he rushed into open opposition, by taking possession of the bodies of men. 'Iniquity,' *Greek,* '*lawlessness*'; defiant rejection of God's *law*. 'Wickedness' (translated by the *Septuagint* by the same *Greek,* meaning 'lawlessness,' which Paul employs here), embodied there as a woman, answers to 'the mystery of iniquity,' here embodied finally in 'the man of sin': as the former was ultimately banished for ever from the Holy Land to her own congenial soil, Babylon, so iniquity and the man of sin shall fall before Michael and the Lord Himself, who shall appear as the Deliverer of His people (Da 12:1–3 Zec 14:3–9). Compare Mt 12:43. The Jewish nation dispossessed of the evil spirit, the demon of idolatry being cast out through the Babylonian captivity, receives ultimately a worse form of the evil spirit, Christ-opposing self-righteousness. Also, the Christian Church in course of time taken possession of by the demon of Romish idolatry, then dispossessed of it by the Reformation, then its house 'garnished' by hypocrisy, secularity, and rationalism, but 'swept empty' of living faith, then finally apostatizing and repossessed by 'the man of sin,' and *outwardly* destroyed for a brief time (though even then Christ shall have witnesses for Him among both the Jews, Zec 13:9, and Gentiles, Mt 28:20), when Christ shall suddenly come (Da 11:32–45 Lu 18:7,8).

already – (2Jo 1:9,10 Col 2:18–23 1Ti 4:1); compare 'even now already' (1Jo 2:18 4:3) as distinguished from 'in his own time' of being revealed *hereafter*. Antiquity, it appears from hence, is not a justification for unscriptural usages or dogmas, since these were 'already,' even in Paul's time, beginning to spring up: the written word is the only sure test. 'Judaism infecting Christianity is the fuel; the mystery of iniquity is the spark.' 'It is one and the same impurity diffusing itself over many ages' [BENGEL].

only he who now letteth *will let* – The italicized words are not in the *Greek*. Therefore, translate rather, 'only (that is, the continuance of *the* MYSTERY *of iniquity-working* will be *only*) until he who now *withholdeth* (the same *Greek* as in 2Th 2:6) be taken out of the way.' 'Only (*waiting*, Heb 10:13) until he.' Then it will work no longer in *mystery*, but in open manifestation.

8. Translate, 'the lawless one'; the embodiment of all the godless 'lawlessness' which has been working in 'mystery' for ages (2Th 2:7): 'the man of sin' (2Th 2:3).

whom the Lord – Some of the oldest manuscripts read, 'the Lord *Jesus*.' How awful that He whose very name means *God-Saviour*, should appear as the Destroyer; but the *salvation* of the Church requires the destruction of her foe. As the reign of Israel in Canaan was ushered in by judgments on the nations for *apostasy* (for the Canaanites were originally worshippers of the true God: thus Melchisedek, king of Salem, was the 'priest of the most high God,' Ge 14:18: Ammon and Moab came from righteous Lot), so the Son of David's reign in Zion and over the whole earth, is to be ushered in by judgments on the apostate Christian world.

consume … and … destroy – So Da 7:26, 'consume and destroy'; Da 11:45. He shall 'consume' him by His mere breath (Isa 11:4 30:33): the sentence of judgment being the sharp sword that goeth out of His mouth (Re 19:15,21). Antichrist's manifestation and destruction are declared in the same breath; at his greatest height he is nearest his fall, like Herod his type (Isa 1:24–27 Ac 12:20–23). As the advancing fire, while still at a distance consumes little insects [CHRYSOSTOM] by its mere heat, so Christ's mere approach is enough to consume Antichrist. The mere 'appearance of the coming' of the Lord of glory is sufficient to show to Antichrist his perfect nothingness. He is seized and 'cast alive into the take of fire' (Re 19:20). So the world kingdoms, and the kingdom of the beast, give place to that of the Son of man and His saints. The *Greek* for 'destroy' means 'abolish' (the same *Greek* is so translated, 2Ti 1:10); that is, cause every vestige of him to disappear. Compare as to Gog attacking Israel and destroyed by Jehovah (Eze 38:1–39:29), so as not to leave a vestige of him.

with the brightness of his coming – *Greek*, 'the *manifestation*, (or *appearance*) of His presence': the first outburst of His advent – the first gleam of His presence – is enough to *abolish* utterly all traces of Antichrist, as darkness disappears before the dawning day. Next, his adherents are 'slain with the sword out of His mouth' (Re 19:21). BENGEL's distinction between 'the appearance of His coming' and the 'coming' itself is not justified by 1Ti 6:14 2Ti 1:10 4:1,8 Tit 2:13, where the same *Greek* for 'appearing' (*English Version,* here 'the brightness') plainly refers to *the coming itself*. The expression, '*manifestation* (appearing) of His presence,' is used in awful contrast to the *revelation* of the wicked one in the beginning of the verse.

9. whose coming – The same *Greek* as was used for *the* Lord's coming (2Th 2:8) or personal 'presence.'

is – in its essential character.

after – *according to* the working ('energy') of Satan, as opposed to the *energy* or *working* of the Holy Spirit in the Church. As Christ is related to God, so is Antichrist to Satan, his visible embodiment and manifestation: Satan works through him. Re 13:2, 'The dragon gave him (the beast) his power … seat … great authority.'

lying wonders – literally, 'wonders' or 'prodigies of falsehood.' His 'power, signs, and wonders,' all have *falsehood* for their base, essence, and aim (Joh 8:44), [ALFORD]. In Mt 24:24 Jesus implies that the miracles shall be real, though demoniac, such mysterious effects of the powers of darkness as we read of in the case of the Egyptian sorcerers, not such as Jesus performed in their character, power, or aim; for they are against the revealed Word, and therefore not to be accepted as evidences of truth; nay, on the authority of that sure Word of prophecy (here, and Mt 24:24), to be known and rejected as wrought in support of *falsehood* (De 13:1–3,5 Ga 1:8,9 Re 13:11–15 19:20). The same three *Greek* words occur for *miracles of Jesus* (Ac 2:22 Heb 2:4); showing that as the Egyptian magicians imitated Moses (2Ti 3:1–8), so Antichrist will try to imitate Christ's works as a 'sign,' or *proof* of divinity.

10. deceivableness – rather as *Greek*, 'deceit of (to promote) unrighteousness' (2Th 2:12).

in – The oldest manuscripts and versions omit 'in.' Translate, '*unto* them that *are perishing*' (2Co 2:15,16 4:3): the victims of him whose very name describes his *perishing* nature, 'the son of perdition'; in contrast to *you* whom (2Th 2:13) 'God hath from the beginning chosen to *salvation* through *sanctification* of the Spirit and belief of the truth.'

because – literally, 'in requital for'; in just retribution for their having no *love* for the truth which was within their reach (on account of its putting a check on their bad passions), and for their having 'pleasure in unrighteousness' (2Th 2:12 Ro 1:18); they are *lost* because they loved not, but rejected, the truth which would have *saved* them.

received not – Greek, 'welcomed not'; admitted it not cordially.

love of the truth – not merely love of *truth,* but love of THE *truth* (and of, Jesus who is *the Truth,* in opposition to Satan's 'lie,' 2Th 2:9,11 Joh 8:42–44), can *save* (Eph 4:21). We are required not merely to assent to, but to *love* the truth (Ps 119:97). The Jews rejected Him who came in His divine Father's name; they will receive Antichrist coming in *his own* name (Joh 5:43). Their pleasant sin shall prove their terrible scourge.

11. for this cause – because 'they received not the love of the truth.' The best safeguard against error is 'the love of the truth.'

shall send – Greek, 'sends,' or 'is sending'; the 'delusion' is already beginning. God judicially sends hardness of heart on those who have rejected the truth, and gives them up in righteous judgment to Satan's delusions (Isa 6:9,10 Ro 1:24–26,28). They first cast off the love of the truth, then God gives them up to Satan's delusions, then they settle down into 'believing the lie': an awful climax (1Ki 22:22,23 Eze 14:9 Job 12:16 Mt 24:5,11 1Ti 4:1).

strong delusion – Greek, 'the powerful working of error,' answering to the energizing 'working of Satan' (2Th 2:9); the same expression as is applied to the Holy Ghost's operation in believers: 'powerful' or 'effectual (energizing) working' (Eph 1:19).

believe a lie – rather, '*the* lie' which Antichrist tells them, appealing to his miracles as proofs of it ... (2Th 2:9).

12. they all . . . damned – rather as Greek, 'that *all.*' He here states the general proposition which applies specially to Antichrist's adherents. Not all in the Church of Rome, or other anti-Christian systems, shall be damned, but only 'all who believed not the truth,' *when offered to them,* 'but had pleasure in unrighteousness' (Ro 1:32 2:8). Love of *unrighteousness* being the great obstacle to *believing the truth.*

13. But – In delightful contrast to the damnation of the lost (2Th 2:12) stands the 'salvation' of Paul's converts.

are bound – in duty (2Th 1:3).

thanks ... to God – not to ourselves, your ministers, nor to you, our converts.

beloved of the Lord – Jesus (Ro 8:37 Ga 2:20 Eph 5:2,25). Elsewhere *God the Father* is said to love us (2Th 2:16 Joh 3:16 Eph 2:4 Col 3:12). Therefore Jesus and the Father are one.

from the beginning – 'before the foundation of the world' (Eph 1:4; compare 1Co 2:7 2Ti 1:9); in contrast to those that shall 'worship the beast, whose names are not written in the book of life of the Lamb slain from the foundation of the world' (Re 13:8). Some of the oldest manuscripts

read as *English Version,* but other oldest manuscripts and *Vulgate* read, 'as *first-fruits.*' The Thessalonians were among the first converts in Europe (compare Ro 16:5 1Co 16:15). In a more general sense, it occurs in Jas 1:18 Re 14:4; so I understand it here including the more restricted sense.

chosen you – The *Greek,* is not the ordinary word for 'elected,' implying His eternal *selection;* but *taken for Himself,* implying His having *adopted* them in His eternal purpose. It is found in the *Septuagint* (De 7:7 10:15).

through – rather as Greek, 'in sanctification' as the element in which *the choice to salvation* had place (compare 1Pe 1:2), standing in contrast to the 'unrighteousness,' the element in which Antichrist's followers are given over by God to *damnation* (2Th 2:12).

of the Spirit – wrought by the Spirit who sanctifies all the elect people of God, first by eternally consecrating them to perfect holiness in Christ, once for all, next by progressively imparting it.

belief of the truth – contrasted with 'believed not the truth' (2Th 2:12).

14. you – The oldest manuscripts read, 'us.'

by our gospel – '*through*' the Gospel which we preach.

to ... glory – In 2Th 2:13 it was 'salvation,' that is, deliverance from all evil, of body and soul (1Th 5:9); here it is positive good, even 'glory,' and that 'the glory of our Lord Jesus' Himself, which believers are privileged to share with Him (Joh 17:22,24 Ro 8:17,29 2Ti 2:10).

15. Therefore – God's sovereign choice of believers, so far from being a ground for inaction on their part, is the strongest incentive to action and perseverance in it. Compare the argument, Php 2:12,13, 'Work out *your own* salvation, FOR it is God which worketh in you.' We cannot fully explain this in *theory;* but to the sincere and humble, the *practical* acting on the principle is plain. 'Privilege first, duty afterwards' [EDMUNDS].

stand fast – so as not to be 'shaken or troubled' (2Th 2:2).

hold – so as not to let go. Adding nothing, subtracting nothing [BENGEL]. The Thessalonians had not held fast his oral instructions but had suffered themselves to be imposed upon by pretended spirit-revelations, and words and letters pretending to be from Paul (2Th 2:2), to the effect that 'the day of the Lord was instantly imminent.'

traditions – truths *delivered* and *transmitted* orally, or in writing (2Th 3:6 1Co 11:2; *Greek,* 'traditions'). The *Greek* verb from which the noun comes, is used by Paul in 1Co 11:23 15:3. From the *three* passages in which 'tradition' is used in a good sense, Rome has argued for her accumulation of *uninspired* traditions, virtually overriding God's Word, while put forward as of co-ordinate authority with it. She forgets the *ten* passages (Mt 15:2,3,6 Mr 7:3,5,8,9,13 Ga 1:14 Col 2:8) stigmatizing *man's uninspired* traditions. Not even the apostles' sayings were all inspired (for example, Peter's dissimulation, Ga 2:11–14), but only when they claimed to be so, as in their words afterwards embodied in their canonical writings. Oral inspiration was necessary in their case, until the canon of the written Word should be complete; they proved their possession of inspiration by miracles wrought in support of the new revelation, which revelation, moreover, accorded with the existing Old Testament revelation; an additional test needed besides miracles (compare De 13:1–6 Ac 17:11). When the canon was complete, the infallibility of the living men was transferred to the written Word, now the sole unerring guide, interpreted by the Holy Spirit. Little else has come down to us by the most *ancient* and *universal* tradition save this, the all-sufficiency of Scripture for salvation. Therefore, by tradition, we are constrained to cast off all tradition not contained in, or not provable by, Scripture. The Fathers are valuable *witnesses to historical facts*, which give force to the *intimations* of Scripture: such as the Christian Lord's day, the baptism of infants, and the genuineness of the canon of Scripture. Tradition (in the sense of *human testimony*) cannot establish a *doctrine*, but can *authenticate a fact*, such as the facts just mentioned. Inspired tradition, in Paul's sense, is not a supplementary oral tradition completing *our* written Word, but it is identical with the written Word *now* complete; then the latter not being complete, the tradition was necessarily in part oral, in part written, and continued so until, the latter being complete before the death of St. John, the last apostle, the former was no longer needed. Scripture is, according to Paul, the complete and sufficient rule in all that appertains to making 'the man of God *perfect, throughly furnished* unto *all* good works' (2Ti 3:16,17). It is by leaving Paul's God-inspired tradition for human traditions that Rome has become the forerunner and parent of the Antichrist. It is striking that, from this very chapter denouncing Antichrist, she should draw an argument for her 'traditions' by which she fosters anti-Christianity. Because the apostles' oral word was as trustworthy as their written word, it by no means follows that the oral word of those *not apostles* is as trustworthy as the *written* word of those who were apostles or inspired evangelists. No tradition of the apostles except their written word can be *proved* genuine on satisfactory evidence. We are no more bound to accept implicitly the Fathers' interpretations of Scripture, because we accept the Scripture canon on their testimony, than we are bound to accept the Jews'

interpretation of the Old Testament, because we accept the Old Testament canon on their testimony.

our epistle – as distinguished from a 'letter AS from us,' 2Th 2:2, namely, that purports to be from us, but is not. He refers to his first Epistle to the Thessalonians.

16, 17. himself – by His own might, as contrasted with our feebleness; ensuring the efficacy of our prayer. Here *our Lord Jesus* stands first; in 1Th 3:11, 'God our Father.'

which … loved us – in the work of our redemption. Referring both to *our Lord Jesus* (Ro 8:37 Ga 2:20) and God *our Father* (Joh 3:16).

everlasting consolation – not transitory, as worldly consolations in trials (Ro 8:38,39). This for all time present, and then 'good hope' for the future [ALFORD].

through grace – rather as *Greek* 'IN grace'; to be joined to 'hath given.' Grace is the element in which the gift was made.

17. Comfort your hearts – unsettled as you have been through those who announced the immediate coming of the Lord.

good word and work – The oldest manuscripts invert the order, 'work and word.' *Establishment* in these were what the young converts at Thessalonica needed, not fanatical teaching (compare 1Co 15:58).

Chapter 3

2Th 3:1–18. He asks their prayers: his confidence in them: prayer for them: charges against disorderly idle conduct; his own example: concluding prayer and salutation.

1. Finally – literally, 'As to what remains.'

may have free course – literally, 'may run'; spread rapidly without a drag on the wheels of its course. That the new-creating word may 'run,' as 'swiftly' as the creative word at the first (Ps 147:15). The opposite is the word of God being 'bound' (2Ti 2:9).

glorified – by sinners accepting it (Ac 13:48 Ga 1:23,24). Contrast 'evil spoken of' (1Pe 4:14).

as it is with you – (1Th 1:6 4:10 5:11).

2. that we … be delivered from unreasonable … men – literally, men *out of place, inept,* unseemly: *out of the way bad:* more than ordinarily bad. An undesigned coincidence with Ac 18:5–9. Paul was now at Corinth, where the JEWS 'opposed themselves' to his preaching: in answer to his prayers and those of his converts at Thessalonica and elsewhere, 'the Lord, in vision,' assured him of exemption from 'the hurt,' and of success in bringing in 'much people.' On the unreasonable, out-of-the way perversity of the Jews, as known to the Thessalonians, see 1Th 2:15,16.

have not faith – or as *Greek,* 'the faith' of the Christian: the only antidote to what is 'unreasonable and wicked.' The Thessalonians, from their ready acceptance of the Gospel (1Th 1:5,6), might think 'all' would similarly receive it; but the Jews were far from having such a readiness to believe the truth.

3. faithful – alluding to 'faith' (2Th 3:2): though many will not believe, the Lord (other very old manuscripts read 'God') is still to be believed in as faithful to His promises (1Th 5:24 2Ti 2:13). *Faith* on the part of man answers to faithfulness on the part of God.

stablish you – as he had prayed (2Th 2:17). Though it was on himself that wicked men were making their onset, he turns away from asking the Thessalonians' prayers for HIS deliverance (2Th 3:2: so unselfish was he, even in religion), to express his assurance of THEIR establishment in the faith, and preservation from evil. This assurance thus exactly answers to his prayer for them (2Th 2:17), 'Our Lord ... *stablish* you in every good word and work.' He has before his mind the Lord's Prayer, 'Lead us not into temptation, but deliver us from evil'; where, as here, the translation may be, 'from the evil one'; the great hinderer of 'every good word and work.' Compare Mt 13:19, 'the wicked one.'

4. we have confidence in the Lord – as 'faithful' (2Th 3:3). Have confidence in no man when left to himself [BENGEL].

that ye both do – Some of the oldest manuscripts insert a clause, 'that ye both have done' before, 'and are doing, and will do.' He means the *majority* by 'ye,' not *all* of them (compare 2Th 3:11 1:3 1Th 3:6).

5. If 'the Lord' be here the Holy Ghost (2Co 3:17), the three Persons of the Trinity will occur in this verse.

love of God – love to God.

patient waiting for Christ – rather as *Greek,* 'the patience (endurance) of Christ,' namely, which Christ showed [ALFORD] (2Th 2:4 1Th 1:3). ESTIUS, however, supports *English Version* (compare Re 1:9 3:10). At all events, this grace, 'patience,' or *persevering endurance,* is connected with the 'hope' (1Th 1:3,10) of *Christ's coming.* In ALFORD's translation we may compare Heb 12:1,2, 'Run with *patience* (*endurance*) ... looking to JESUS ... who, for the joy that was before Him, *endured* the cross'; so WE are to endure, as looking for the hope to be realized at His coming (Heb 10:36,37).

6. we command you – Hereby he puts to a particular test their obedience in general to his *commands,* which obedience he had recognized in 2Th 3:4.

withdraw – literally, 'to furl the sails'; as we say, *to steer clear of* (compare 2Th 3:14). Some

had given up labour as though the Lord's day was immediately coming. He had enjoined mild censure of such in 1Th 5:14, 'Warn ... the unruly'; but now that the mischief had become more confirmed, he enjoins stricter discipline, namely, withdrawal from their company (compare 1Co 5:11 2Jo 1:10,11): not a formal sentence of excommunication, such as was subsequently passed on more heinous offenders (as in 1Co 5:5 1Ti 1:20). He says 'brother,' that is, professing Christian; for in the case of unprofessing heathen, believers needed not be so strict (1Co 5:10–13).

disorderly – Paul plainly would not have sanctioned the *order* of Mendicant Friars, who reduce such a 'disorderly' and lazy life to a system. Call it not an *order,* but a *burden* to the community (BENGEL, alluding to the *Greek,* 2Th 3:8, for 'be chargeable,' literally, 'be a burden').

the tradition – the oral instruction which he had given to them when present (2Th 3:10), and subsequently committed to writing (1Th 4:11,12).

which he received of us – Some oldest manuscripts read, '*ye* received'; others, '*they* received.' The *English Version* reading has no very old authority.

7. how ye ought to follow us – how ye ought to live so as to '*imitate* (so the *Greek* for "follow") *us*'.

8. eat any man's bread – *Greek,* 'eat bread *from* any man,' that is, live at anyone's expense. Contrast 2Th 3:12, '*eat* THEIR OWN *bread.*'

wrought – (Ac 20:34). In both Epistles they state they maintained themselves by labour; but in this second Epistle they do so in order to offer themselves herein as an example to the idle; whereas, in the first, their object in doing so is to vindicate themselves from all imputation of mercenary motives in preaching the Gospel (1Th 2:5,9) [EDMUNDS]. They preached gratuitously though they might have claimed maintenance from their converts.

labour and travail – 'toil and hardship'.

night and day – scarcely allowing time for repose.

chargeable – *Greek,* 'a burden,' or 'burdensome.' The Philippians did not regard it as a *burden* to contribute to his support (Php 4:15,16), sending to him while he was in this very Thessalonica (Ac 16:15,34,40). Many Thessalonians, doubtless, would have felt it a privilege to contribute, but as he saw some idlers among them who would have made a pretext of his example to justify themselves, he waived his right. His reason for the same course at Corinth was to mark how different were his aims from those of the false teachers who sought their own lucre (2Co 11:9,12,13). It is at the very time and place of writing these Epistles that Paul is expressly said to have *wrought at tent-making* with Aquila (Ac 18:3); an undesigned coincidence.

9. (1Co 9:4–6, Ga 6:6.)

10. For even – Translate, 'For *also*.' We not only set you the example, but gave a positive 'command.'

commanded – *Greek* imperfect, 'We were commanding'; we kept charge of you.

would not work – *Greek*, '*is unwilling* to work.' BENGEL makes this to be the argument: not that such a one is to have his food withdrawn from him by others; but he proves from the necessity of *eating* the necessity of *working*; using this pleasantry, Let him who will not work *show himself an angel*, that is, do without food as the angels do (but since he cannot do without food, then he ought to be not unwilling to work). It seems to me simpler to take it as a punishment of the idle. Paul often quotes good adages current among the people, stamping them with inspired approval. In the *Hebrew*, '*Bereshith Rabba*,' the same saying is found; and in the book *Zeror*, 'He who will not work before the Sabbath, must not eat on the Sabbath.'

11. busy bodies – In the *Greek* the similarity of sound marks the antithesis, 'Doing none of their own business, yet overdoing in the business of others.' Busy about everyone's business but their own. 'Nature abhors a vacuum'; so if not doing one's own business, one is apt to meddle with his neighbors's business. Idleness is the parent of busybodies (1Ti 5:13). Contrast 1Th 4:11.

12. by – The oldest manuscripts read, 'IN the Lord Jesus.' So the *Greek*, 1Th 4:1, implying the sphere wherein such conduct is appropriate and consistent. 'We exhort you thus, as *ministers* IN *Christ*, exhorting our people IN Christ.'

with quietness – quiet industry; laying aside restless, bustling, intermeddling officiousness (2Th 3:11).

their own – bread earned by themselves, not another's bread (2Th 3:8).

13. be not weary – The oldest manuscripts read, 'Be not cowardly in'; do not be wanting in strenuousness in doing well. EDMUNDS explains it: Do not *culpably* neglect to do well, namely, with patient industry do your duty in your several callings. In contrast to the 'disorderly, not-working busybodies' (2Th 3:11; compare Ga 6:9).

14. note that man – mark him in your own mind as one to be avoided (2Th 3:6).

that he may be ashamed – *Greek*, 'made to turn and look into himself, and so be put to shame.' Feeling himself shunned by godly brethren, he may become ashamed of his course.

15. admonish him as a brother – not yet excommunicated (compare Le 19:17). Do not shun him in contemptuous silence, but tell him why he is to be avoided (Mt 18:15 1Th 5:14).

16. Lord of peace – Jesus Christ. The same title is given to Him as to the Father, 'the GOD of peace' (Ro 15:33 16:20 2Co 13:11). An appropriate title in the prayer here, where the harmony of the Christian community was liable to interruption from the 'disorderly.' The *Greek* article requires the translation, 'Give you *the* peace' which it is 'His to give.' 'Peace' outward and inward, here and hereafter (Ro 14:17).

always – unbroken, not changing with outward circumstances.

by all means – *Greek*, 'in every way.' Most of the oldest manuscripts read, 'in every *place*'; thus he prays for their peace *in all times* ('always') *and places*.

Lord be with you all – May He bless you not only with *peace*, but also with His *presence* (Mt 28:20). Even the disorderly brethren (compare 2Th 3:15, 'a brother') are included in this prayer.

17. The Epistle was written by an amanuensis (perhaps Silas or Timothy), and only the closing salutation written by Paul's 'own hand' (compare Ro 16:22 1Co 16:21 Col 4:18). Wherever Paul does not subjoin this autograph salutation, we may presume he wrote the whole Epistle himself (Ga 6:11).

which – *which* autograph salutation.

the token – to distinguish genuine Epistles from spurious ones put forth in my name (2Th 2:2).

in every epistle – Some think he signed his name to every Epistle with his own hand; but as there is no trace of this in any manuscripts of *all* the Epistles, it is more likely that he alludes to *his writing with his own hand in closing every Epistle*, even in those Epistles (Romans, Second Corinthians, Ephesians, Philippians, First Thessalonians) wherein he does not specify his having done so.

so I write – so I sign my name: this is a specimen of my *handwriting*, by which to distinguish my genuine letters from forgeries.

18. He closes every Epistle by praying for GRACE to those whom he addresses.

Amen – omitted in the oldest manuscripts. It was doubtless the response of the congregation after hearing the Epistle read publicly; hence it crept into copies.

The Subscription is spurious, as the Epistle was written not 'from Athens,' but from *Corinth*.

1 TIMOTHY

John Calvin

Introduction

I believe that this letter was written for the sake of other people, and not just for Timothy himself. If you think about this carefully you will agree with me. Of course, I am not denying that Paul's aim was to teach and instruct Timothy as well. However, my point is that this letter contains many things which would have been excluded if the letter was only written for Timothy's benefit. Timothy was a young man without enough authority to curb the powerful people who opposed him. Paul makes it clear that at this time some people were so bent on making a name for themselves that they would not submit to anybody. If Timothy had not acted decisively, there is no telling what havoc he would have caused in the church, as they were so fired by their selfish ambitions. In addition to this, there were a number of things that needed to be put right in Ephesus with Paul's backing and authority. Paul wanted to instruct Timothy about many things, but he also wanted to advise many other people as well.

Contents

See *Outlines of the New Testament Books,* p. 901

Chapter 1

In this chapter Paul opposes the selfish people who were only interested in focussing attention on themselves as they discussed empty questions. You can deduce that these people were Jews, who made a show of being keen to uphold the law. They cared more about their futile debates than about building up Christians in the faith. Such abuse of God's law should not be tolerated. They only used God's law as a topic of empty discussion and as an excuse to burden the church with unnecessary and inconsequential matters. Paul promises that he will help Timothy to eradicate this false teaching. He does this by pointing to the most important lessons to be learned from the law, while at the same time pointing out that people who turn to the law with other motives are in reality polluting it.

Then Paul admits to his own unworthiness and says in glowing words how God has turned him into the man he is through the work of God's grace in him. Paul does this to ensure that no one rejects his authority. Paul concludes this chapter with a serious warning which is meant to strengthen Timothy with solid teaching and a good conscience. Paul also makes use of the example of Hymenaeus and Alexander as a warning to others.

Verses 1–4

1. Paul, an apostle of Christ Jesus. Had Paul been only writing to Timothy, he would not have needed to set out his credentials and highlight his apostolic appointment, as he does in this verse. Had he just been writing to Timothy, it would have been enough to say his name. Timothy did not need any evidence to convince him that Paul was **an apostle of Christ**. For a long time Timothy had been totally happy to acknowledge this. So Paul must be aiming at those who did not want to listen to him and were not so prepared to embrace what he said. For their sake Paul emphasizes that he is **an apostle of Christ Jesus**, so that they will not write him off as an unimportant nonentity.

By the command of God. Paul goes on to say he is an apostle due to the **command**, or appointment of God. For no one can make himself an apostle, but a person appointed by God to this office is a genuine apostle and should be held in honour. Paul does not say that God the Father alone was responsible for him being an apostle: he says that he is an apostle **by the command of God our Saviour and of Christ Jesus**. Paul adds the name of Christ. As the church is ordered and ruled, the Father does everything with the Son, so that the Father and the Son are united in this.

God our Saviour. Paul calls God **Saviour**, which is a title more often given to the Son. However, this title is entirely appropriate for the Father. The Father gave his Son to us, so it is correct to say the glory of our salvation comes from the Father. Our salvation only comes because the Father loved us so much that, through his will, he redeemed and saved us through the Son.

Christ Jesus our hope. This is a particularly apposite title for Christ, because we have hope as we look to Christ, as only in him do we find our salvation.

2. To Timothy, my loyal son. Paul heaps much praise on Timothy as he commends him in this way. Paul says that Timothy is **my loyal son**. He is not ashamed to be called his father. Paul also wants other people to acknowledge that Timothy is his son. Paul commends Timothy as if he were another Paul. We may wonder how this can be consistent with Christ's command, 'and call no one your father on earth' (Matthew 23:9), or with Paul's own assertion, 'for though you might have ten thousand guardians in Christ, you do not have many fathers. Indeed, in Christ, I became your father through the gospel' (1 Corinthians 4:15). I reply by pointing out that when Paul says that he is Timothy's father, he does not lessen God's honor in any way, or substitute glory for himself in God's place. Everyone knows that if one thing is subordinate to another, then they are not fighting each other. This is the way that Paul claims to be Timothy's father, while God himself remains Timothy's Father.

In the faith. God is only Father to all those who have **faith**. Through his Word and the power of his Spirit he regenerates all believers. He alone confers **faith**. He graciously allows ministers to share his honor without losing any of his honor himself. Strictly speaking, Timothy's spiritual Father was God, and only God; but Paul in a subordinate way, as God's minister, was Timothy's spiritual father as well.

Grace, mercy, and peace. Paul's usual order for these words is changed here, because **mercy** comes second and not first. This may be in deference to Timothy. **Grace** should really come second because **grace** comes from **mercy**. It is through God's mercy that we are welcomed into his grace, where he continues to love us. It is rather unusual to mention the result before the cause.

3. I urge you. Paul reminds Timothy why he had asked him to remain in Ephesus. It was with real reluctance, on account of a compelling need, that Paul was separated from his faithful helper whom he loved so much. Timothy had to stay, as Paul's deputy, as there was nobody else qualified enough to cope with such demanding duties. Timothy must have been greatly affected by this. It prevented him from dissipating his energies and helped him to rise to exceptional standards of behaviour.

So that you may instruct certain people not to teach any different doctrine. Paul also tells Paul to resist false teachers who were polluting pure teaching. Paul's concern for God to be honored is apparent in this instruction he gives to Timothy to carry out this duty at Ephesus. Paul never moved on from a church without appointing a minister there, no matter how busy he was in founding new churches. It is true, as one writer has said, 'It takes as much ability to keep what you have gained as it took to gain it.'

Instruct certain people. The word **instruct** implies authority. Paul wanted to furnish Timothy with authority to keep the others in check.

Not to teach any different doctrine. Literally, 'to teach differently.' This could mean 'to teach in a different way,' that is, using a different method, or 'to teach new doctrine.' I do not agree with Erasmus' translation, 'to follow a new doctrine,' as this could refer to hearers as well as teachers. We have a broader meaning here if we translate the words as, 'to teach in a different way.' This indicates that Paul wanted Timothy to stop people introducing new methods of teaching, which are not consistent with the true method he had given them. In Paul's second letter to Timothy Paul does not just tell Timothy to be faithful to the contents of the teaching, but he uses the word 'pattern' which means to keep a real likeness to his teaching. 'What you heard from me, keep as the pattern of sound teaching' (2 Timothy 1:13). Just as God's truth is one, so there is only one way to teach it. This is the way that has no pretense about it and is not characterized by a demonstration of human eloquence, but displays the majesty of the Spirit. Anyone who departs from this will be disfiguring the doctrine itself. So 'to teach differently' does refer to the form of the teaching.

4. By myths. I do not think he means errors that have been dreamed up, but silly stories that are without foundation. Something which is not false may still be an exaggerated story. This is the way that Suetonius spoke of 'history in fables' and Livy uses the verb 'to fable' to refer to silly and senseless talk. The word Paul uses here – **myths,** literally 'tales' – means trifles, and this is confirmed by the example of a fable which he gives.

Endless genealogies. Under the heading of fables Paul places arguments about **genealogies,** not because they are all untrue but because they are silly and lead nowhere. So this verse means that they are not to take any notice of fables which have the same character as **genealogies.** This is exactly what Suetonius meant by 'history in fables' which is something for which even the learned are rightly derided by sensible people. To devote one's life to tracing the family tree of Achilles or Ajax, or trying to calculate how many sons Priam had, must be termed a ridiculous occupation which ignores the quest for useful information. If this is out of place in a classroom, which is the place for making inquiry into things, how much more out of place it is in our quest for seeking knowledge about God. These genealogies can be **endless** because their convoluted paths never end.

That promote speculations. Paul judges teaching by its fruit. Anything that does not build up is discarded, even if there is nothing wrong with it in itself. Anything that fuels arguments should be condemned outright. Such were the intricate ideas to which these self-seekers devoted their clever minds. We must bear in mind the test by which all teaching should be tried.

Divine training that is known by faith. Intricate arguments of this kind flatter people's intellectual pride but they do not lead to a knowledge of God. Paul refers to the kind of teaching which is godly, either because God approves of it or because it is in line with God's will. This sort of teaching includes loving each other, showing reverence for God, and repentance, as these all stem from faith. Faith always promotes godliness. Paul realized that faith is the only basis for worshiping God so it was enough for him to mention **faith** on which everything else is built.

Verses 5–11

Timothy had to cope with people who had no principles, and who claimed support from the law for their ideas. Paul pre-empts them by demonstrating that the law, far from lending weight to their arguments, is in fact in total agreement with the Gospel he himself teaches. Their line of argument is similar to those who, in our own day, love to indulge in subtle arguments about theology. They accuse us of killing off sacred theology, as if they were the only ones who nurtured it in their hearts. Those who opposed Paul deliberately used the law to stir up opposition against him. How did Paul answer this attack? To crush their arguments, he anticipates their line of attack and points out that his teaching is in perfect accord with the law. They are the ones who are twisting the law for their own ends and totally abusing it in the process. In our own day we teach true theology and we have to attempt to restore something that has been crushed and twisted by trumped-up so-called theologians. In reality they can only offer feeble, hollow ideas. When Paul says **the law** (verses 8 and 9), he means the complete law, not an individual law.

5. But the aim of such instruction is love. If the goal of the law is that we should be taught about the **love** which flows from **faith** and **a good conscience,** the opposite results from those who pervert its teaching into idle questions. In this verse it does not matter whether we take **love** to refer to all of the Ten Commandments, or just to the second half of the Ten Commandments. We are commanded to love God with all our heart and to love our neighbors as ourselves. However, when love is mentioned in the Bible, it is most often restricted to loving our neighbors. If Paul had spoken of love by itself in this passage I would have immediately thought that he was referring to love of God and love of neighbor. But Paul adds **faith** and **a good conscience,** so my exposition suits this context well. The law can be summed up as saying that we should worship God with **a pure heart, a good conscience,** and that we should love each other. Anyone who moves away from this pollutes God's law and perverts it to serve some other strange purpose.

Love … faith. Someone may ask why Paul seems to put **love** before **faith.** I think this is a childish objection. Just because **love** is mentioned first does not mean that it is superior to what is mentioned after it. Paul clearly states that **love** flows from **faith.** Everyone knows that the cause of something determines the result. It is as if Paul is saying here, 'We have been given the law so that we can learn the faith, which is the mother of a good conscience and of love.' So we start with **faith** not love.

A pure heart, a good conscience. There is little difference between these two, as they are both fruits of faith. A pure heart is mentioned in the Acts of the Apostles: 'he purified their hearts by faith' (Acts 15:9). According to Peter a good conscience is based on Christ's resurrection: 'A good conscience, through the resurrection of Jesus Christ' (1 Peter 3:21). Here it is clear that genuine love is impossible without reverence for God and a clear conscience. Note how Paul describes each virtue.

6. Paul carries on with his theme that the goal of God's command is love and that everything else misses the mark. The word translated deviated from, literally 'missing aim,' means to turn away from, or to miss the target.

Meaningless talk. Note that Paul judges that all teaching which does not have this end in view is meaningless talk. He asserts that all other ideas and talents people may possess will fade into nothing. People do, however, applaud vain trifles, but Paul is adamant that whatever does not edify is meaningless talk. So we should take great care never to look for anything in God's holy Word which does not edify, in case God punishes us for misusing his Word.

7. Paul is not opposing those who publicly attack the teaching of the law, but those who falsely claim to be its teachers. Such people understand nothing as they spend all their time pondering idle curiosities.

About which they make assertions. He adds this rebuke concerning their arrogance. No other people push themselves forward as much as these teachers who rashly pontificate about things they know nothing about. In all this the ancient proverb, 'Ignorance is bold,' is fulfilled, according to the apostle. He says of these people that they are 'puffed up without cause by a human way of thinking' (Colossians 2:18).

8. Paul, again, pre-empts a false accusation. It is as if they say of him, 'Do you want to bury the law and rub it out for good?' This was their argument whenever Paul exposed their hollow theories. To rebut their false idea Paul affirms that the law is good but that it must be used legitimately. However, Paul also demonstrates that the law totally supports his teaching and so he turns the tables on his accusers.

9. The apostle's intention here is not to list all the functions of the law. Rather, he makes his attack a personal one, on those people he is dealing with. Often, the people who claim to have the highest regard for the law turn out to live lives which show that they are the greatest despisers of the law.

The lawless and disobedient, for the godless and sinful. The sinful here refers to those who live an immoral life.

Paul touches on different kinds of sin and briefly mentions all categories of transgressions.

These people are obstinate and rebellious and he describes them as lawless and disobedient. They are the root cause of sin. The unholy and profane may correspond to the first and second halves of the Ten Commandments. He then goes on to mention those who lead impure and dissolute lives, as there are three ways that people can harm their neighbor: through violence, dishonesty and lust – all of which Paul condemns. Those who kill their father or mother . . . murderers and the violent people Paul singles out.

10. Paul then mentions fornicators and sodomites, as people who indulge in lust; and then he mentions slave-traders and other dishonest practices, such as lying.

And whatever else is contrary to the sound teaching. Paul maintains that his Gospel supports the law and does not oppose it. He says it is in line with the Lord's pronouncement that whatever ... is contrary to sound teaching is against his law. So those who turn their backs on the Gospel are not embracing the law but chasing after shadows.

Sound teaching. This contrasts with the frivolous arguments which, as Paul makes clear elsewhere, shipwreck the faith of the false teachers and manage to lead others astray.

11. By describing the gospel as the glorious Gospel Paul emphasizes that God demonstrates his glory in the Gospel. This also served as a sharp rebuke to those who wanted to disparage it. Paul specifically stated that God had entrusted the Gospel to him, to underline that the Gospel he preached is God's only Gospel, and to emphasize that all the myths he had spoken against were at odds with both the Gospel and the law.

Verses 12–13

12. I am grateful to Christ Jesus our Lord. What is Paul giving thanks for? He has been given a role in serving Christ, and he deduces that Christ judged him faithful to do this work. Christ does not receive everyone indiscriminately. He chooses those who are suitable for the work, and so everyone Christ honors in this way, we know to be worthy to hold the office. Judas' brief rise to office, before his sudden fall, is consistent with this. As the psalmist says, 'May his days be few; may another seize his position' (Psalm 109:8). It was different in Paul's case, as he received his office for a different reason in a different set of circumstances. As Christ said of Paul, 'He is an instrument whom I have chosen' (Acts 9:15).

Who has strengthened me. Paul moves on to another blessing Christ has given him. Christ enabled him to hold this office, or, strengthened him so he could hold this office. From the start God's hand made him and qualified him for this office. But that is not all. The strength he was given includes that constant supply of grace he experienced while he held this office. He received his apostleship through Christ's grace. He continues in his apostleship through the same grace.

13. A blasphemer, a persecutor. Paul had blasphemed against God and had persecuted the church. Paul now owns up to what could easily have been held against him. He does not try to excuse his sins. By openly acknowledging his own unworthiness he highlights God's wonderful grace even more. Paul does not just say that he was a **persecutor** but adds that he was **a man of violence**, venting his anger on the church.

I had acted ignorantly in unbelief. Paul says, 'My **unbelief** was forgiven because I acted **ignorantly**.' The result of his **unbelief** resulted in persecution and violence. He is probably suggesting that he can only be forgiven because there were extenuating circumstances: his ignorance.

Verses 14–17

14. The grace of our Lord overflowed for me. Paul emphasizes again God's **grace** which **overflowed** on him. He does this not just to witness to his own gratitude but to defend against the slanderous and malicious attacks of his detractors who wanted to attack his apostleship. When Paul says that the Lord's grace **overflowed**, he means that his past offenses have been wiped away and forgotten so that they no longer drag him down at all or leave him in an inferior position against other good people who have received God's grace.

With the faith and love. Faith and love may be thought of as both referring to God. This would then mean that God has revealed himself to be a faithful God and shows us his love in Christ as he gives his grace to Paul. But I opt for a more straightforward exposition. **Faith and love** bear witness to God's grace that has just been referred to, so nobody will conclude that Paul is boasting for no good reason. **Faith** is contrasted with Paul's unbelief (verse 13); love in Christ is contrasted with the cruel persecution Paul had handed out to believers. It is as if he was now saying that God had transformed him and he was now a new person. So Paul revels in God's grace in him which wipes out all memory of his former way of life.

15. The saying is sure and worthy of full acceptance. Paul has just defended his ministry against false attacks. Now he turns the tables on his enemies and uses the arguments of his opponents to attack them. Paul says that the church benefits from him being a persecutor before he was called to be an apostle. It focusses on God's grace in Paul and so shows that Christ calls all sinners to confidently expect forgiveness of sins.

Christ Jesus came into the world to save sinners. Paul makes this general statement: **Christ Jesus came … to save sinners.** He gives a little introduction to this important topic, as he often did: **Jesus came into the world.** This is the major point in our religion, that the lost should find their salvation through Christ. We should never lose our sense of reverence and wonder about our salvation, no matter how many thousands of times Christ's salvation is offered to us by God the Father, and no matter how often Christ himself tells us of his saving work.

To save sinners. Sinners is the emphatic word here. People are willing to say that Christ's work is to save people, but reluctant to believe that salvation belongs to sinners. We are liable to focus on our own unworthiness, and as soon as we concentrate on this, our trust in God collapses. So the more a person is burdened by his sins the more he should confidently turn to Christ. He trusts in what is taught here, that **Christ Jesus came into the world to save sinners**, not righteous people. Note how Paul applies to himself the truth of Christ's work. He wanted people to know that what he had said about himself was nothing out of the ordinary.

Of whom I am the foremost. Paul was not speaking out of false modesty here. Paul acknowledged his sin with humility and truth, from the depths of his heart. But the question arises about why Paul should say he is **the foremost** sinner, since he acted in ignorance and the rest of his life seemed blameless to other people. This underlines how gravely God looks on the sin of unbelief, especially when it goes hand in hand with violence. People might easily overlook all that Paul said about himself as the actions of a zealous person. God, however, judges unbelief, deliberately persisted in, very seriously, as he holds the obedience of faith so highly.

16. Paul repeats that he is **the foremost** of sinners. From the start God showed his grace in Paul in a most obvious way. So, no one could entertain any doubt that he would be forgiven if he came to Christ in faith. Our doubts evaporate when we see that Paul is a type of the grace we want.

17. To the King of the ages. Paul's praise of God overflows with these expressions about God, as he sought words to express his gratitude to God. Paul is so overwhelmed with this that he interrupts his train of thought. Paul calls him **the King of the ages**, who never changes. He calls him **invisible** as he lives in inaccessible light – 'who dwells in unapproachable light' (1 Timothy 6:16).

Verses 18–20

18. I am giving you these instructions. Everything Paul has said about himself has been a digression from his main theme. His main aim was to give Timothy authority, to give him these **instructions**, literally 'charge.' Before he could do this had to make his own supreme authority totally secure, and defeat those who attacked his position. Paul had demonstrated that his apostleship should not be held in any less honor because he had once attacked Christ's kingdom. Paul had dealt with his detractors and now he returns to the main theme of his exhortation. The **instructions** mentioned here also comes in verse 5.

My child. Paul is showing both his affection for Timothy and also how much he recommends him to others.

In accordance with the prophecies made earlier about you, so that by following them. Paul further encourages Timothy by reminding him about the witness God's Spirit had given to him. Timothy derived much comfort from knowing that his ministry had God's approval. He had been called by God's revelation, before people had cast their vote in his favor. It is as if Paul was saying, 'While it may be terrible not to live up to human expectations, how much more shameful is it to ignore God's wishes?'

The prophecies. We need to understand what Paul means by these **prophecies**. Some commentators believe that, through some special revelation, Paul invested Timothy in this office. I agree with this, but must point out that others, in addition to Paul, were involved in this. For the word **prophecies** is in the plural. From this I deduce that there were a number of prophecies about Timothy commending him to the church.

You may fight the good fight. By adding this Timothy is reminded to rely on God's initial approval of him, so he can fight more strongly for him. What greater encouragement could we have, than to know that what we are doing we do, because God has specifically told us to do it? With this armor we will never lose. **Fight the good fight** indicates that a war is on. Paul relates this to all Christians, and especially to Christian teachers, who can be thought of as God's standard bearers in Christ's army. It is as if Paul had said, 'You have battles in your ministry, but remember that God's Word to you is your armor, and your victory is assured. May that give you renewed courage.' A **good** fight is fought under God's control and so is glorious.

19. Having faith. Here **faith** means sound doctrine, in the general sense. 'They must hold fast to the mystery of the faith with a clear conscience' (3:9). This is the teacher's top priority. He must stick to the pure truth of the Gospel. He should minister this with **a good conscience**, that is with a clear conscience, as well as with genuine zeal. Where **faith and a good conscience** are present, everything else will follow.

By rejecting conscience. Paul explains the necessity of having a **good conscience**, as well as **faith**; for a bad conscience ends in turning away from the right path. People who do not serve God in a pure and honest way, but allow evil ways to creep in, even though they may have started on the right track, will lose their way.

Have suffered shipwreck. This metaphor of a shipwreck is most apt. If we want to reach the port with our faith in one piece we should pilot our course with a good conscience, or else we are liable to **shipwreck**. Just as a storm at sea sinks a ship, so faith without a good conscience can sink without trace.

20. Hymenaeus and Alexander. Paul mentions **Hymenaeus** again in his letter to Timothy, where the type of shipwreck that befell him is seen. He maintained that the resurrection of the dead had already taken place. 'And their talk will spread like gangrene. Among them are Hymenaeus and Philetus, who have swerved from the truth by claiming that the resurrection has already taken place. They are upsetting the faith of some' (2 Timothy 2:17–18).

Whom I have turned over to Satan. I interpret this passage as referring to excommunication. For nobody believes that anything other than excommunication happened to the immoral person in the church at Corinth (1 Corinthians 5:1–5). So should this passage not have the same meaning? Christ sits on his throne in the church, so outside the church, is Satan's dominion. So, anybody who is cut off from the church will be under Satan's jurisdiction, until he is reconciled to the church and returns to Christ. I just need to qualify this. Because of the seriousness of the sin, it is possible that Paul issued a permanent excommunication against Hymenaeus and Alexander. However, I would not like to be dogmatic about this.

So that they may learn not to blaspheme. What does this mean? The person who has been thrown outside the church is no longer restrained by discipline and so is free to be totally insolent. I think that no matter what depths of evil they sink to, the door will remain bolted against them, and they will be unable to harm the flock. Men do more evil by worming their way into Christian fellowship, pretending to believe the same faith. So the power for excommunicated people to harm us is taken away from them. They are marked people and publicly disgraced, so that everyone knows that they are ungodly people to be avoided. Sometimes, people who are disgraced in this way, turn away from their evil. So, while excommunication can make people worse, it does sometimes overcome their fierceness.

Chapter 2

In this second chapter Paul directs that prayers should be offered in public for everyone, especially for 'kings and all who are in high positions.' This leads him into a digression about the benefits of civil government. Paul says that prayers should be offered for everyone, because God, in offering the Gospel and Christ as Mediator for everyone, demonstrates that he wants everyone to be saved. Paul supports this by pointing out that his own apostleship was particularly directed towards the Gentiles. So Paul invites all people, from every country and of every race to pray to God. He takes the opportunity to say that women should behave in a modest and subservient way when the church fellowship comes together.

Verses 1–4

1. **First of all, then, I urge.** The religious exercises Paul urges here keep and strengthen us in our sincere worship and fear of God and encourage the good conscience he has already spoken about. **Then,** is used appropriately here, since his instructions follow on from what he has just told Timothy.

First, Paul mentions public prayer. He says **prayers** should be offered not just for believers, but for everyone. Some might respond to this and say, 'Why do we need to worry about unbelievers, as they have nothing to do with us? Is it not enough for us to pray for our Christian brothers and sisters and to commend the whole church to God?' Paul opposes such a perverse idea and encourages the Ephesians to include everyone in their prayers and not to restrict them just to the body of the church.

2. **For kings and all who are in high positions.** Paul mentions these because Christians may have had good reason to hate them above everyone else. All the magistrates of those days were implacably opposed to Christ. They may have thought that they should not pray for people who used all their energies and money to oppose Christ's kingdom. For Christians, the one thing that mattered was that Christ's kingdom should be extended. Human depravity is not sufficient ground for not supporting something that God ordained. God appointed princes and magistrates to preserve mankind. No matter how much they fail to do this, we must not stop supporting what God willed.

So that we may lead a quiet and peaceful life. Paul gives another reason for praying for kings and magistrates. He says this is to our advantage and that many benefits can be derived from a well-ordered government. One benefit is **a quiet life.** Magistrates have the power of the sword to keep the peace.

In all godliness and dignity. Another advantage is that **godliness** is promoted. This happens when magistrates support religion, the worship of God and make sure sacred things are given due reverence.

3. **This is right and is acceptable in the sight of God our Saviour.** Paul has shown how expedient his argument is. He now uses a stronger basis for his argument, that it is **acceptable in the sight of God.** If we know that something is God's will that is the best reason we can have for doing it. **Acceptable** means right and lawful. God's will is the overall yardstick for everything we do, so Paul demonstrates that this is right because it pleases God.

4. **Who desires everyone to be saved.** This builds on the previous argument. For nothing could be more reasonable than that all our prayers are devoted to this goal. Paul is showing that God's central concern is everyone's salvation. He calls everyone to acknowledge his truth.

Our Saviour. Paul calls God **our Saviour** for the same reason. We only receive God's salvation from his kindness, which we do not deserve. The same God, who has already brought us to share in his salvation, may one day extend this grace to them. We have been drawn to God by his grace, and others may be added in the same way. Paul assumes that this will happen from all strata of society among all nations, as the prophets predicted.

Verses 5–7

5. **Paul talks about one mediator.** Just as there is one God, the Creator and Father of all, so there is one Mediator, through whom we have access to God. This is not for only one nation, or for a few men of a special class, but for everyone. For the benefit of the sacrifice, through which he has expiated for our sins, applies to everyone. At that time much of the world had cut itself off from God, so Paul specially mentions the Mediator, through whom people who are far away can come close. The word 'all' is a universal one which applies to groups of people, but never to individuals. It is as if Paul had said, 'Not only Jews, but Greeks also; not only people of humble rank but also rulers have been redeemed by Christ's death.' Therefore Christ intends that the benefit of his death should extend to everyone, so people who exclude anyone from this hope of salvation are do Christ a disservice.

Christ Jesus, himself human. Just because Paul calls Jesus **human** he is not denying that he is God. He is highlighting the bond between God and man, and so mentions his human nature rather than his divine nature. Whenever we pray to God, if the thought of his sublime, inaccessible glory floods our minds with awe, we must also remember the **human** Christ is gently inviting us, and taking us by the hand, so that the Father whom we had feared so much becomes our friend. This is the only key which opens the door of the kingdom of heaven, so that we may confidently come into God's presence.

6. Who gave himself a ransom for all. It is not irrelevant to mention redemption here as there is a link between Christ's sacrificial death and his continual intercession. 'It is Christ Jesus, who died, yes, who was raised, who is at the right hand of God, who indeed intercedes for us.' (Romans 8:34). There are two parts of his priestly work.

A ransom. By saying that Christ is our **ransom**, he rules out all other ways by which God might be satisfied.

This was attested at the right time. The refers to this grace which should be made known **at the right time.** The words **for all**, in the sentence, **who gave himself a ransom for all**, could make us ask why God chose one special people, if had planned to reveal himself as a reconciled Father to 'all' without distinction? Was there one redemption in Christ in which everyone had to share? Paul deals with such questions by saying that at the **proper time** for this revelation of grace was appointed by God's counsel.

7. I was appointed. Paul did not want people to think that he was pontificating about a subject he knew he did not fully understand. He states that God had appointed him to bring the Gentiles, who had previously been strangers to God's kingdom, into taking part in the Gospel. His own apostleship to the Gentiles was clear evidence that God was calling them. Therefore, Paul takes great care to defend this and to emphasize it, as so many people had such trouble in accepting it. Paul adds an oath, or protestation, to underline how important this is – (**I am telling the truth, I am not lying.**) He says he is **a teacher of the Gentiles in faith and truth.** **Faith and truth** reveals that Paul was assured about God's will in this matter, and that he had a good conscience about it. Paul is saying that he not only preaches the Gospel with a sincere heart, but also with a clear, upright conscience, since he does everything in response to God's commands.

Verses 8–10

8. This verse follows on in its thinking from what Paul has just said. We need to be given the Spirit of adoption before we can call upon God in the right way. 'But when the fullness of time had come, God sent his Son, born of a woman, born under the law, in order to redeem those under the law, so that we might receive adoption as children. And because you are children, God has sent the Spirit of his Son into our hearts, crying, "Abba! Father!"' (Galatians 4:5–6). Paul has explained that God's grace is for everyone; and he has touched on his own appointment as apostle to the Gentiles, and that Gentiles, as much as Jews, enjoyed the blessings of redemption. Now Paul invites everyone to pray in the same way.

In every place. This phrase means the same as it does in 1 Corinthians 1:2, 'To the church of God in Corinth, to those who are sanctified in Christ Jesus, called to be saints, together with all those who are in every place call on the name of our Lord Jesus Christ.' There should now be no difference between Gentile and Jew, between Greek and barbarian, since God is their common Father. 'For there is no distinction between Jew and Greek; the same Lord is Lord of all' (Romans 10:12); 'There is no longer Jew or Greek, there is no longer slave or free' (Galatians 3:28).

Men should pray, lifting up holy hands. It is as if Paul is saying, 'Nothing should stop all nations, everywhere, from calling on God, provided that they have a good conscience.' Paul is using an outward sign for an inner reality, as our hands stand for a clean heart.

9. As Paul had given instructions that men should **pray, lifting up holy hands**, so he now gives instructions about how women should pray. I believe that there is an implied contrast here between the external Jewish rites of purification and the virtues he commends. Paul says that nowhere is profane, and men and women have access to God everywhere, so long as they have no vices holding them back.

10. Is proper for women. A godly and honourable woman will undoubtedly dress differently from a prostitute. These are the distinctions which Paul is making here. If godliness is to be seen in good deeds, then it will be evident in the wearing of suitable clothes.

Verses 11–15

11. Paul moves on from how to dress to the sense of modesty women should display in the sacred assembly. First of all, he tells them to learn **in silence.** They should not allow themselves to speak in public, which is clear from his instruction that he goes on to give that they should not teach.

12. Paul is not saying that women should stop teaching their families at home, he is just excluding them from the office of teaching – an office which is only for men. On occasions there were women prophets and women teachers who held these offices under the direction of God's Spirit. God is above all laws and it is quite proper for him to act in this way, and this does not clash with his normal methods of working.

I permit no woman to teach or to have authority over a man. Paul moves on to a topic closely linked to the office of teaching. Women are forbidden to teach because this is incompatible with their being subject to men. To teach implies that the teacher has a superior authority and status over the pupil.

13. Paul gives two reasons for women being subject to men. First, God gave a law from the beginning that this should be so. Second, God made women live in this way as a punishment.

14. And Adam was not deceived. Paul is referring to the punishment the woman received because she listened to the serpent: 'your desire shall be for your husband, and he shall rule over you' (Genesis 3:16).

15. Paul, aiming to comfort them and make their condition bearable, reminds them that their hope of salvation is secure, even if they have to suffer punishment at the moment.

Through childbearing. There is no better comfort here, than knowing that the punishment itself is also, so to speak, the way of gaining salvation.

Provided they continue in faith. Faith applies to the women. To avoid giving the impression that all womanly virtues are tied up in marriage, Paul adds this list of virtues in which godly women should excel, and which should distinguish them from ungodly women. Even childbearing, as an obedient act, only pleases God if it springs from **faith** and **love.** To this Paul adds **holiness,** which describes the pure life which Christian women should live. Paul ends with **modesty.** This was mentioned in verse 9 – 'modesty and decency' – when Paul was talking about dress. Now this word applies to the whole of life.

Chapter 3

In this chapter Paul says how excellent the office of a bishop is and goes on to paint a picture of a true bishop, listing the characteristics he should possess. Then he lists the qualities a deacon should possess and those required of the wives of bishops and deacons. Paul reminds Timothy about what is involved in governing a church, which is God's house and a pillar of truth, so that Timothy may attend to these things the more diligently. Then Paul mentions the most important of all revealed teaching, the hinge of all teaching as it were, the manifestation of God's Son in the flesh. Everything else that Paul saw ambitious people absorbed in, pales into insignificance when compared with this.

Verses 1–7

1. Whoever aspires to the office of bishop. Paul had just said that the teaching office was not open to women, and he now takes the opportunity to talk about this office. So Paul affirms that this is no ordinary work which anyone can just go into.

A noble task. To prevent this boldness in seeking episcopal office, Paul says that this office is 'work.' It is not a sinecure.

Bishop. We should also take note of what Paul means by the office of a bishop here, especially since so many people, in the early generations of the church, were led astray here by the prevailing customs. Paul includes in this term **bishop** all pastors, but people have falsely taken this to mean just the one who was elected in each college of presbyters to rule over his brothers. We must remember that this word means 'minister,' 'pastor,' or 'presbyter.'

2. Above reproach. Paul wants a bishop to be **above reproach,** or, as he puts it in Titus 1:7, 'blameless.' Both words mean that he should not be tainted with any disgrace that might detract from his authority.

Married only once. Chrysostom's interpretation is the only correct one. He says this is a direct command that a bishop should not engage in polygamy, which was generally allowed among the Jews then.

Temperate. 'Sober-minded.' Erasmus translates this word 'watchful.' The Greek word has both meanings and so you may take your choice. I prefer 'temperate' to 'sober,' as temperance has a wider meaning than not becoming drunk. A **respectable** man is someone who behaves decently and honestly.

Hospitable. Hospitality was given to strangers and was practised much more in the early church, for it would have been a scandal for any honest person, especially a well-known person, to stay at an inn.

An apt teacher. Paul emphasizes teaching more in his letter to Titus (Titus 1:9; 2:1–10). Here Paul touches on the skill in teaching. It is not enough to be well known as a profound teacher if this is not accompanied with skill in teaching.

3. Not a drunkard. This word includes drinking too much wine, and well as outright drunkenness.

Not a lover of money. Lovers of money are covetous people. All covetousness is tainted with the evil characteristic which the apostle touches on here. Juvenal said, 'The man who desires to be rich wants to be rich quickly.'

Paul contrasts the **violent** person with the one who is **gentle, not quarrelsome. Gentle** is the opposite of being addicted to wine. It is a word used of a person who can bear injuries peacefully, who excuses many things, can absorb insults, and is not feared on account of his severity, and who does not exact everything that is owed to him. The person who is **not quarrelsome** avoids arguments and quarrels, for, as Paul says elsewhere, 'The Lord's servant must not be quarrelsome' (2 Timothy 2:24).

4. Paul does not insist that a bishop should have no experience in ordinary life, but he says that he should be an experienced family man.

Respectful in every way. Paul says what he means by **respectful** in the first chapter of his letter to Titus. Having said that a bishop's children should not be out of control and disobedient, he immediately adds that it should not be possible to accuse them of living a dissolute life.

6. He must not be a recent convert. During a time when people of outstanding ability and learning were being brought to the faith, Paul says that they should not be made bishops as soon as they profess Christ.

7. It seems strange that a godly man should have unbelievers witnessing about his integrity, since they are so keen to denigrate him. What the apostle means is that as far as external behaviour is concerned, even unbelievers should have to acknowledge that he is a good person.

Verses 8–13

8. Deacons. Clearly the apostle is speaking about men who hold public office in the church; this is in contrast with the view that **deacons** means domestic servants. The view that presbyters, a lesser form of bishops, are meant here is also without foundation, for it is clear from other passages that the title 'bishop' was held by all presbyters. This is universally acknowledged and is clear from Titus 1. I conclude that what is meant here by **deacons** is those people mentioned in Acts 6, people who were given the work of caring for the poor.

Note that he tells them to be **not double-tongued.** It is difficult to avoid this fault in this kind of work, and yet it should be absent from it more than from anything else.

9. It is as if Paul was saying, 'Hold the pure teaching of our religion from the heart, sincerely fearing God, so that people are correctly taught the faith, and know everything that a Christian needs to know.' Paul calls Christian teaching **the mystery of the faith** because through the Gospel God reveals to mortal men a wisdom that even the angels of heaven wonder at. It is hardly surprising if this is too much for humans to grasp.

With a clear conscience. Paul adds this to embrace all their life, but it particularly applies to their knowledge of serving God.

10. And let them first be tested. Paul wants people who are to be chosen as deacons to be men of experience whose integrity has been tested, just as it was for bishops. To **prove themselves blameless** means that they are free of any notorious fault. They need to be **tested** not just for an hour, but over a considerable period of time. So, deacons should not be appointed rashly or randomly.

11. Paul is referring here to the wives of both bishops and deacons. They are to help their husbands in their work, and they can only do this if their behaviour is better than other people's.

12. Having mentioned wives, Paul sets out what is required of deacons, just as he had done for bishops. Each should be content with his wife, should set an example of chaste and honourable family life and should rule over his children and household with holy discipline.

13. Those who serve well. Because of the practice of selecting presbyters from deacons, which happened in the first or second centuries after the apostles, this passage has been interpreted to refer to deacons being chosen for a higher status, as if Paul was saying that faithful deacons are called to the office of presbyters. I agree that the diaconate can be a training ground from which presbyters are chosen, but I prefer a simpler explanation of Paul's words. People who have been faithful in carrying out this ministry deserve to be honoured, for it is no menial task but a most honourable one. In this way Paul says how important it is for the church to have this carried out by men who have been carefully chosen, since carrying out these duties brings esteem and reverence with it.

Great boldness in the faith. 'Liberty in the faith.' Paul has a good reason for adding this. Nothing produces freedom like a good conscience and a life free from evil, just as a bad conscience induces timidity. While some people with bad consciences do seem to exult in their freedom it does not last as it is not build on any strong foundation. The kind of freedom he means he refers to as **great boldness in the faith that is in Christ Jesus**. This, says Paul, enables them to serve Christ with greater boldness. But those who have failed in their duty have closed mouths and tied hands and can do nothing well, so that nobody can depend on them and they are without any authority.

Verses 14–16

14. I hope to come to you soon. Paul gives Timothy hope about him coming soon, partly to encourage him, and partly to oppose those who were giving themselves over to laziness while he was absent.

I am writing you these instructions. Paul goes on to tell Timothy that he has written this letter, full of its instructions, in case he is delayed for longer than he hopes.

15. How one ought to behave in the household of God. Paul commends the importance of the pastoral office here, since pastors are like stewards to whom God has handed over the running of his house. God calls his church his **household** for good reasons. God has received us as his sons through the grace of adoption, and he himself lives in our midst.

16. Praise for God is amplified here. Paul declares that **the mystery of our religion is great**

to prevent God's truth from being demeaned through human ingratitude. This **mystery** does not deal with ordinary matters, but with the revelation of God's Son, 'in whom are hidden all the treasures of wisdom and knowledge' (Colossians 2:3).

Vindicated in Spirit. Just as the Son of God emptied himself as he took our nature on himself, so a spiritual power in him witnessed to the fact that he was God.

Seen by angels, proclaimed among Gentiles. These are wonderful and amazing statements. God honoured the Gentiles in doing this, even though up to that time they were blind to the revelation of God's Son, which had been hidden from the angels in heaven. When Paul says, **seen by angels**, he means that the angels were attracted to this because it was something new and excellent. It was new to the angels, because although they knew about the redemption of humanity, they did not then know how this was to be accomplished and was hidden from them so that the greatness of God's kindness would shine even more brightly when it was revealed.

Believed in throughout the world. The most wonderful thing of all was that God should make his revelation known equally to pagan Gentiles and to angels, who lived for ever in his kingdom. It was no ordinary miracle that, as a result of preaching the Gospel, Christ overcame all obstacles and won over to obey the faith those who, it seemed, would never submit. Every path to them seemed to be blocked so that nothing seemed as improbable as this. And yet faith won the day by an almost unbelievable victory.

Finally, Paul says that Christ was **taken up in glory**, after his earthly life of misery. So the world was wonderfully changed through obedience and faith and through the person of Christ. Christ was raised up from the status of a servant to the Father's right hand so that everyone would kneel before him.

Chapter 4

In chapter 4 Paul begins by roundly condemning false teaching about marriage and the prohibition of certain foods, and stupid ideas which were not included in his teaching. Then he says that the only enemies which he and godly men who hold on to the teaching of the Gospel have, are those who cannot tolerate people placing their hope in the living God. Paul ends this chapter by encouraging Timothy with an exhortation.

Verses 1–5

1. In later times. Nobody would have expected anyone to be led astray now that the clear light of the Gospel had arrived. But this is just

what Peter said would happen: see 2 Peter 3:3–5. Just as the false teachers had once disturbed the people of Israel, so they will always upset Christ's church. It is as if Paul says, 'The teaching of the Gospel is flourishing, but it will not be long before Satan becomes busy and tries to suffocate the good seed with weeds.'

Deceitful spirits. 'Seducing spirits.' Here Paul means prophets or teachers. He calls them this because they claim to possess God's Spirit so that they can impress people.

Paul further explains what he means by adding, **teachings of demons.** This is like saying, 'Do not listen to false prophets and their demonic teachings.' Once again it is clear that this is not a small error to be glossed over, as men's consciences were being chained by human inventions and, at the same time, the worship of God was being polluted.

3. They forbid marriage. Paul moves on from describing false teaching in general to two specific examples of false teaching, the prohibition of marriage and of certain foods.

Which God created. We should understand why we should be content with the freedom God has given us about using foods. God created them for this purpose – to be freely used.

God created food to be **received**, that is, so that we might enjoy it. And Paul adds, **with thanksgiving**, as the only way we can show our appreciation to God is by thanking him.

4. For everything created by God is good. How food should be used depends partly on what food it is and partly on the kind of person who is eating it. The apostle refers to both aspects here. Paul says food is pure because it was created by God and through faith and prayer we make use of it in the right way.

5. For it is sanctified. This underlines the previous verse, 'it is to be received with thanksgiving.' This is an argument which is based on contrasts, for holy and profane are opposite to each other. We now ask what kind of consecration he has in mind, for this consecration includes all the good things which sustain our present life. Paul declares that this consecration comes about by God's word and prayer. We also note that faith is needed if we are to understand the Word, so that we may benefit from it. God makes everything holy through the Spirit in his Word, but we only receive the blessing from this through faith. **Prayer** is added to this, as we not only ask for our daily bread as Christ commands, but we also offer thanksgiving for his goodness.

Verses 6–10

6. If you put these instructions before the brothers and sisters. Paul exhorts Timothy to remind them frequently about these things, and he says this again a second, and, a third time, as they are the things which must be remembered.

The words of the faith. Faith here means all Christian teaching. **sound teaching** is added to explain more clearly what faith is. Paul means that no matter how plausible other doctrines may be, they are not profitable. The phrase **that you have followed** indicates perseverance. Many people who learned about Christ in their childhood fall away later, but Paul says that Timothy is not like one of these.

7. Train yourself. After telling Timothy what kind of doctrine he should teach, he now tells him about the kind of example he should give to others. He says that he should train in **godliness**. When Paul says **train yourself** to Timothy, he means that this should be Timothy's constant occupation, his main concern and chief aim in life. It is as if Paul is saying, 'There is no reason why you should tire yourself with any other matters, which are all pointless. You will do the most valuable thing if you devote yourself only to godliness, using all your zeal and ability.' Godliness here means the spiritual worship of God which is only found in a pure conscience. This is made even clearer when godliness is contrasted with physical exercise.

8. But godliness is valuable in every way. The person who has **godliness** lacks nothing, even though he may not have the help of these ascetic practices, which are of such marginal help anyway. **Godliness** is the beginning, middle, and end of Christian living, where it is completed nothing is lacking. Christ, unlike John the Baptist, did not live an ascetic way of life, but that did not make him in any way inferior to John. We conclude that we should concentrate exclusively on **godliness**. Once we have attained this God requires nothing more from us. We should only spend times of physical exercises to the extent that they help or hinder the acquisition of **godliness**.

10. (For to this end we toil and strive.) Paul is here anticipating an objection. Are not believers, hard-pressed with all kinds of affliction, the most miserable of all people? In order to show that their real condition is not to be judged by outward appearances, Paul distinguishes them from others in relation to both the cause and the result of their sufferings. It follows from this that they do not lose any of these promises, even when they are surrounded by troubles. The conclusion of this matter is that believers are not miserable in their afflictions, because a good conscience sustains them and they know that a blessed and joyful end is waiting for them.

We have our hope set on the living God. This comfort refers to why we suffer, for as we suffer for righteousness, far from making us miserable, our sufferings give us grounds for praising God. In addition to this, in our sufferings **our hope** is **in the living God.** In fact hope is our

foundation and it will never make us ashamed.

Who is the Saviour of all people. This second comfort is dependent on the first comfort. For the deliverance he refers to is, so to speak, the fruit of **hope.** The argument here goes from the lesser to the greater.

Verses 11–16

11. These are the things you must insist on and teach. Even if somebody hears this teaching every day, they should not grow tired of listening to it.

12. Let no one despise your youth. This applies to other people, and not just to Timothy. They should respect Timothy, so long as he conducts himself correctly as a minister of Christ, and not despise him because of his age. By **set the believers an example** Paul means their words, deeds and their whole lives.

13. Until I arrive, give attention to the public reading of scripture. Paul knows how diligent Timothy is, but he still commands him to persevere in reading the Scripture. For how can pastors teach others if they themselves are not learning? Paul tells Timothy to concentrate on **exhorting** and **teaching.** It is as if Paul is advising Timothy to study so that he can pass on what he has learnt. Note that Paul says that Timothy should read before he preaches and teaches, as Scripture is the fountain of all wisdom and pastors should draw from it everything that they present to their flock.

14. Do not neglect the gift that is in you. Paul commands Timothy to use the grace he has been endowed with to edify the church. God does not want us to bury his talents but use them to bear fruit. To **neglect** a gift comes from sloth and carelessness in not making use of it, so that it becomes rusty and it degenerates. We should each reflect on what gift we have been given so that we can employ it fully.

Paul says that grace was given to Timothy **through prophecy.** How did this happen? Through a revelation, the Holy Spirit designated Timothy to enter the ranks of pastor. So Timothy was not chosen in the usual way, by being appointed by men, but was first appointed by the Holy Spirit.

With the laying on of hands by the council of elders. Paul says to Timothy, you received a **gift ... through prophecy with the laying on of hands by the council of elders.** This means that along with the ministry given to Timothy he was given a gift for this ministry. It was the normal practice of the apostles to ordain ministers through the laying on of hands. People who think that **elders** here is a collective term meaning the college of presbyters are, I believe, right. However, having reflected on this, I agree that another explanation also is possible, that it is the name of an office. Through the laying on of hands he shows the act of ordination to the presbyterate. So Paul means that Timothy, who has been called to the ministry through the voice of the prophets, and ordained to it through a solemn rite, was at the same time endued by the Holy Spirit with grace to carry out this work. So the ceremony was not held in vain, for God, through his Spirit, brought about that consecration, which men symbolized through the laying on of hands.

15. Devote yourself to them. The harder is it to minister to the church faithfully, the more earnestly would a pastor give himself to the work, not just for a short time, but all the time with unfailing perseverance. Paul reminds Timothy that this work requires great diligence and that slothfulness is totally out of place.

16. Pay close attention to yourself and to your teaching. A good pastor must take care about two things: first, being diligent about his teaching; second, taking care that he maintains his own integrity.

Save … yourself. A pastor is said to save himself when he carries out his calling faithfully. A pastor is said to **save** himself because it is usual to speak of believers winning their salvation when they persevere on the road that brings them God's grace.

Chapter 5

In this chapter Paul starts by telling people to be modest and to reprove people with gentleness; then he touches on the subject of widows who in those days were admitted into the service of the church. Paul tells them not to accept all widows indiscriminately, but to accept only those who have been approved of on account of their good way of life, who are sixty or over, and who do not have families of their own to support them. Paul then moves on to talk about presbyters, how they should behave themselves and how they should exercise discipline. Paul underlines this teaching with a solemn oath and again tells Timothy not to accept anyone into the presbyterate rashly. He tells Timothy to drink wine instead of water, for the sake of his health. He ends the chapter by telling Timothy to suspend judgment on hidden sins.

Verses 1–4

1. Do not speak harshly to an older man. Paul tells Timothy that faults should be corrected with gentleness. Correcting faults is always unpalatable. But because Timothy was a young man, it would have been intolerable to be told off by him, in a severe way. Paul tells Timothy to reprove older people as he would his own parents, and, he tells him not to rebuke him in a harsh way.

2. Absolute purity. This phrase refers to **younger women**, for no suggestion of wrong-doing must arise on account of their age. But Paul does not stop Timothy from taking strong action towards young men, for there was not need for this prohibition with them. He just tells Timothy not to give them any reason for complaining about him. So Paul suggests that Timothy has a serious demeanor with everyone, so that he can freely talk with young people without anybody raising an eyebrow.

3. Honour widows who are really widows. The word **honour** here does not mean give special deference, but rather the special care which bishops took of widows in the ancient church. Widows were taken under the church's protection and provided for out of common funds. It is as if Paul said, 'In choosing widows that you and your deacons look after you ought to carefully consider who really are widows.' Paul does not allow widows unless they are quite alone and without children, for it was in these situations that they dedicated themselves to the church, so as to withdraw from all private family concerns and be rid of all hindrances.

4. This is pleasing in God's sight. Everyone agrees that it is unnatural to be ungrateful to one's parents. It is universally agreed that the second part of godliness involves natural affection to one's parents, for even the stork teaches us how necessary this gratitude is. Paul is not content with this and declares that God has commanded this. It is as if he said, 'There are no good grounds for thinking that this comes from any human conviction, as God has commanded that it should happen.'

Verses 5–8

5. Paul is more specific about what he says here and explains that a true widow is one who is alone and without children. Such people, Paul says, have put their **hope on God.**

Continues in supplication and prayers night and day. This is a second reason for commending widows. They give themselves to pray, unceasingly. So it follows that they should be supported by the church. These two qualifications are also used to distinguish worthy widows from those who do not deserve to be called widows.

6. The widow who lives for pleasure. Having described the genuine widows, Paul now contrasts them with those widows who should not be accepted. The Greek word translated **lives for pleasure**, means one who indulges herself and lives a life of luxury.

8. Whoever does not provide. Paul says that those who do not care for their own, especially their own relatives, have **denied the faith.** This is true, as a person who has thrown out all positive feelings towards humanity has no reverence towards God. Paul goes further, and says that a person who neglects his relatives is **worse than**

an unbeliever. This is true in two ways. First, the more a person comes to know God, the less excuse he has in this matter. People who deliberately shut their eyes to God's light are more culpable than unbelievers. Second, this is an obligation that nature itself teaches. If unbelievers do this in response to what is natural, how are we to think of those who are unmoved by natural affections?

Verses 9–13

9. **Let a widow be put on the list.** Paul says even more explicitly than before what widows should be looked after by the church. They must be **not less than sixty years old.** Because they were to be supported by public funds it was right that they should be elderly.

10. **She must be well attested for her good works, as one who has brought up children, shown hospitality, washed the saints' feet, helped the afflicted, and devoted herself to doing good in every way.** These qualifications are designed to make sure that widows are honourable and hardworking.

Washing the saints' feet. This means all the good deeds done for saints, for it was customary then to wash a brother's feet. This was a duty usually performed by a servant, and Paul mentions it to show that these widows should be characterized by being diligent and not fastidious about their work.

Helped the afflicted. This is a way of saying that these widows should have a generous spirit.

Devoted herself to doing good in every way indicates that Paul has in mind acts of kindness in general.

11. **But refuse to put younger widows on the list.** Paul is not saying that **younger widows** should be excommunicated from the church or be treated as if they had done anything wrong, but just that they should not be included on this list of honourable widows he has been talking about.

For when their sensual desires alienate them from Christ. This means that they forget their calling and live a frivolous life. They should have restrained themselves and become people to whom others would look up.

12. **And so they incur condemnation.** Paul is warning them by reminding them about being condemned to eternal death. It is as if he was telling them off by saying that the excellent order which would have united them to Christ, brings them into condemnation instead.

13. **They learn to idle.** Nothing suits a woman more than looking after the home, so among the ancients a tortoise was the symbol of a good and honourable mother. But many women suffer from the opposite vice. They are never happier than when they are free to flit from one place to another, especially if they are

free from family responsibilities. Because the church was looking after these widows they were used to mixing with people. But they took advantage of this privilege, became lazy, and then indulged in gossip. Idleness is the mother of talkativeness.

Verses 14–16

14. When Paul says they are to **bear children,** he sums up in one phrase the whole business of bringing up a family. When he says that they are to **manage their households,** Paul is summarizing all that they do in caring for their homes as housewives.

So as to give the adversary no occasion to revile us. A husband is supposed to protect his wife. It is very hard for young widows who are still very attractive to act wisely when evil men slander them. If they want to silence such malicious people they should choose a state in life that is less open to attack. I think Paul is speaking in general terms here, about the common enemies of the Gospel, not just the individual attacks on women.

15. **For some have already turned away to follow Satan.** Nothing is so holy that is not liable to be attacked by human wickedness. However, certain essential things must remain in place, even if the heavens cave in. But there are other things about which we are free to make up our own minds, and in the light of experience it may be right to change our minds about what we were happy about, as in the present case.

To follow Satan. This expression should be noted, because it is impossible for anyone to turn away from Christ, even by a fraction, without following Satan.

16. **If any believing woman has relatives who are really widows, let her assist them; let the church not be burdened, so that it can assist those who are real widows.** All too often, people are all too pleased to shift their burdens on to the church. Paul specifically warns against this here. Paul tells believers that they should care for the widows in their own families.

Verses 17–21

17. **Let the elders who rule well be considered worthy of double honour, especially those who labour in preaching and teaching.**

It was important that presbyters should not be neglected, and that attention should be paid to them, if the good order of the church is to be maintained. **Elders,** 'presbyters' here describes an office. I do not object to Chrysostom's interpretation of **double honour** meaning support and reverence, and you are free to follow him. But I think that it is more probable elders and widows are being compared here. Paul had previously said that widows should be held in honour. Elders are more worthy than them of receiving honour, and, in comparison with widows, they should receive **double honour.** Paul excludes phony elders by restricting this double honour to those elders who **rule** the church well, that is to those who carry out their responsibilities diligently.

Especially those who labour in preaching and teaching. Paul gives priority to **those who work in preaching and teaching,** that is, to those who are diligent in teaching the Word. For the two expressions **preaching and teaching** amount to the same

18. For the scripture says, 'You shall not muzzle an ox while it is treading out the grain,' and 'The labourer deserves to be paid.' This is a 'political' precept, a general commendation of fairness. If we should not be unkind to brute beasts, how much kinder should we be to our fellow human beings? Paul means that they should not misuse the work that other people do on their behalf.

Paul's quotation, **'The labourer deserves to be paid,'** is not from the Scripture, but is a proverbial saying which common sense agrees with. When Christ said the same thing to his apostles he was expecting them to agree with him. From this it follows that those who allow hard-working cattle – let alone human beings – to go hungry are cruel and forget how animals and people deserve to be treated fairly. It is even more intolerable for people to deny a livelihood to pastors, who do something for them which it is impossible to repay.

19. Never accept any accusation against an elder except on the evidence of two or three witnesses. Paul moves on from saying how pastors should be remunerated, and now tells Timothy not to allow pastors to be exposed to slanderous attacks or to be burdened with unsubstantiated accusations.

20. As for those who persist in sin, rebuke them in the presence of all, so that the rest also may stand in fear. As soon as some action is taken to protect good men, bad men use it in a wrong way in order to stop themselves from being condemned. So Paul here qualifies what he has just said about unfounded accusations, so that nobody can use this as a pretext to escape being punished for their own sin.

21. Without prejudice. The Greek word translated **partiality** means, literally, 'prejudice' – a judgment that is made beforehand. But it means the excessive haste we show in rashly pronouncing judgment on a matter which we have not fully considered, or showing undue deference to people, or in preferring some people above others because we think that they are superior. In the eyes of a judge such decisions are wrong. Paul condemns here either lack of serious care, or respect for people. What follows

has a similar aim, that nothing should be done **on the basis of partiality.** It is impossible to overemphasize the difficulty judges have in remaining impartial, as they are bombarded with people trying to influence them.

Verses 22–25

22. Do not ordain anyone hastily. Paul undoubtedly wanted to protect Timothy from the endless complaints that are levelled against godly servants of Christ, when they refuse to give into the selfish requests that are constantly being made of them.

And do not participate in the sins of others. Paul means here that a bishop who assents to an illicit ordination becomes as guilty as the instigators of such an action.

Keep yourself pure. It is like saying, 'If other people do wrong things, see that you are not involved in it by giving it your assent. If you cannot stop them from polluting themselves, you should stay away from their counsels, so that you can keep yourself pure.'

23. No longer drink only water. What he says amounts to this, that Timothy should develop the habit of drinking a little wine for the sake of his health.

24. The sins of some people are conspicuous. There is nothing more upsetting for faithful ministers of the church than not to know how to correct evils, and to be forced to allow known hypocrites to carry on uncorrected, and to be unable to eject harmful people from the church, or even to be impotent to stop them spreading their poisonous ways. So Paul encourages Timothy here, and says that one day, in God's good time, these people will be publicly exposed.

The sins of others follow them. Paul has stated that some people's sins are quick to judge them; now he says, in contrast, that some people's sins come to light more slowly. He means that although some people's sins remain hidden for longer than we would wish, and are only exposed later, they will not remain hidden forever.

25. So also good works are conspicuous; and even when they are not, they cannot remain hidden. Here Paul means that sometimes godliness and other virtues win people's approval speedily and at the correct time, so that good people are honoured. But if this does not happen, the Lord will not allow innocence and uprightness to remain unnoticed forever.

Chapter 6

In this chapter Paul gives instruction about the duties of slaves, and then launches a strong attack on false teachers who argue over useless speculations and show that they are more concerned with personal gain than with building up other people's faith. Paul also points out the dead nature of covetousness. As he had done previously, Paul concludes with a solemn oath to make sure that his instructions to Timothy are not in vain. Paul makes passing reference to riches and then again instructs Timothy not to become entangled in vain teachings.

Verses 1–2a

It seems that in the early days of the Gospel slaves were eagerly anticipating their release, as if the signal for this had already been given; for Paul often had to restrain them. As slavery was such a terrible condition, it is little wonder that it was hated so much. It usually happens that people understand anything that is to their advantage. So when slaves were told that we are all brothers, they immediately drew the conclusion that they ought not to be slaves to any of the brothers. Even if none of this actually happened, it remains true that oppressed people are always in need of consolation to soothe their bitter conditions. In addition to this, it was a hard thing to persuade them to bend their necks cheerfully to the harsh yoke of slavery. But this is the aim behind Paul's teaching here.

1. **Let all who are under the yoke of slavery.** We all think, wrongly, that we are very good, so none of us willingly submits to someone else ruling over us. People who find themselves in this position grudgingly obey those who are over them, but are inwardly angry, as they feel they being trampled on. The apostle solves all such disputes in a single sentence, by insisting on voluntary submission from all those who are under the yoke of slavery.

When Paul tells them to **regard their masters as worthy of all honour,** he is saying that they should not only be faithful and diligent in carrying out their duties, but that they should sincerely respect their masters as people who have been placed in a higher position than them, to rule over them. Nobody gives to a ruler or master what is his due, unless he reflects on the fact that God has raised him to his eminent position, and thus honours him as one of his subjects.

Verses 2b–5

2. **Teach and urge these duties.** Paul means that these are the things Timothy should constantly emphasize in his teaching. It is as if he were saying that this sort of teaching should be given on a daily basis, and that people should not only be taught this but urged on with frequent exhortations.

3. **Whoever teaches otherwise.** Paul is condemning everyone who does not accept this kind of teaching, even if they are not openly opposed to godly teaching.

In accordance with godliness means the same as **sound words.** For **in accordance with godliness** is only consistent with godliness if it makes us reverence and worship God, if it builds up our faith, and if it trains us in patience and humility and in all the duties of love. So, anybody who does not try to teach in an edifying way is not teaching correctly. No matter what kind of display some teaching may give it is not **sound words** unless it benefits its hearers.

4. There is a veiled comparison here between the soundness of Christ's teaching and **a morbid craving for controversy.** After these subtle questioners have worn themselves out with their long-winded talk, what do they have to show for all their efforts except that their disease has been spread around? It follows from this that they are far from reaping from their teaching any of the benefit which Christ's disciples should.

Controversy and for disputes about words. Paul has good reason for mentioning **disputes about words.** They are contentious disputes about words, rather than about anything which has any substance. In short, Paul's aim is to condemn all such questions which involve us in heated debate about inconsequential things.

From these come envy. Paul shows from the results of being too curious about some matters that we should not become engrossed in them. For ambition is the mother of envy. Whenever **envy** rules, there will also be anger and strong disagreements, and the various things Paul lists here.

Paul adds that these things cause **dissension, slander, base suspicions.** It is quite clear here that he is telling off the sophists who have no thought for building people up.

5. **Imagining that godliness is a means of gain.** This means that **godliness** is equated with making money, as these people measure Christianity by how much profit they can derive from it. It is as if the oracles of the Holy Spirit had been given for the sole purpose of indulging their avarice.

Verses 6–10

6. Paul turns the tables on his opponents, using their own words but drawing a completely different conclusion from them. It is as if he said, 'They act wrongly and wickedly in profiting from Christ's teaching, as if godlessness brought wealth, and yet, correctly understood, it is true that godliness does bring great gain.' Paul says that godliness brings **great gain** because it brings us complete blessedness. People who devote their lives to making money and who use godliness in this quest are guilty of sacrilege. But godliness in itself is sufficient gain for us, because through it we not only inherit the world, but also enjoy Christ and all the riches he brings.

7. Paul adds, **we brought nothing into the world**, in order to emphasize what is useful for us. Our covetousness is a bottomless pit, unless it is restrained, and the best way to keep it in check is to desire nothing other than the necessities of life.

8. When Paul mentions **food and clothing**, he excludes luxury. For nature is content with a little and everything more than this is superfluous. Paul is not condemning here a generous use of possessions, as if that were evil in itself, but, rather, that the desire for possessions is evil.

9. **But those who want to be rich.** Paul has encouraged Timothy to be content and to despise riches, and now he warns him how dangerous it is for ministers of the church to desire them. It is not the riches themselves which cause the evil, but a desire for them, even in a person who is poor.

10. **For the love of money is a root of all kinds of evil.** Paul means that countless evils spring from covetousness, just as we say that arguments, or gluttony, or drunkenness, or any other vice, are responsible for every other kind of evil. This is especially true about the base greed for gain, that it is responsible for all kinds of evil every day. It is behind countless frauds, deceits, perjury, cheating, robbery, cruelty, judicial corruption, quarrels, hatred, poisoning people, murders, and nearly every other kind of crime.

In their eagerness to be rich some have wandered from the faith. It is clear what these words mean: from avarice springs the greatest evil of all – apostasy from the faith. People who suffer from this disease gradually degenerate until they completely renounce their faith.

Verses 11–16

11. By calling Timothy a **man of God**, Paul adds weight to his exhortation. For if it is correct that his call to pursue **righteousness, godliness, faith, love, endurance and gentleness** should be restricted to what he has just been talking about, then this is his answer to being greedy about money. Paul tells Timothy that he should follow spiritual desires. Everyone who is devoted to the pursuit of **righteousness**, who aims at **godliness, faith, love** and follows **endurance, gentleness**, will automatically hate avarice and all its fruits.

12. **Fight the good fight.** Paul exhorts Timothy to **fight** here so that he is free from too much concern for worldly matters. Self-indulgence springs from peoples' desire to serve Christ as if this will never bring them any difficulties, and as if this was a mere leisure activity. Christ, on the other hand, calls people to wage a war.

Take hold of the eternal life. It is as if Paul was saying, 'God calls you to eternal life, so you should despise the world and strive for this eternal life.' By telling them to **take hold** of it, Paul forbids them to give up or become weary in the middle of their struggle. It is as if he is saying, 'Nothing has been achieved until we have obtained the future life to which God invites us.' Paul says that he aims to keep on making progress until he achieves his goal.

For which you made the good confession. Paul encourages Timothy to persevere even more, by mentioning his earlier life. It brings greater shame on oneself to fail after one has made a good start, than never to have started in the first place. Paul makes use of this powerful argument as he tells Timothy that, up to now, he has lived courageously and has won praise, and that the finish should match up to his start. By **confession** I take it he means not spoken words, but actions; and not one instance, but his whole ministry.

14. **To keep the commandment.** The word **commandment** includes everything that Paul had said about Timothy's office, the most important point of which is that he should prove himself to be a minister who is faithful to Christ and the church.

Until the manifestation of our Lord Jesus Christ. It is impossible to overemphasize the need, then, for all godly people to have their minds focused exclusively on the day of Christ, as countless evils were taking place all over the world.

15. **Which he will bring about at the right time.** Sometimes we are too keen to specify the exact day or hour when God will come, fearing that he may delay in fulfilling his promise, so Paul takes this opportunity to curb uncontrolled expectations about Christ's coming. This is the force of his words, **which he will bring about at the right time**.

He who is the blessed and only Sovereign, the King of kings and Lord of lords. The honourable titles heaped on God demonstrate his kingly power, so that we may not be dazzled by the brilliance of worldly rulers. This instruction was particularly apposite then, when the greatness and power of all the kingdoms in the world were obscuring God's glory and majesty. **King of kings and Lord of lords.** By this Paul means that the powers of this world are subject to God's supreme dominion, and that they depend on him, and stand or fall at his will. Nothing can be compared with God's authority, because everything else fades away in front of his glory, and his authority which lasts for ever.

16. Paul takes great pains to demonstrate here that there is no happiness or life without God. He declares that God **alone … has immortality,** so that we may know that we and all his creatures have no life in ourselves, but that our lives are only on loan from God.

And dwells in unapproachable light. Paul means two things here. First that God is hidden from us; and, second, that it is not his fault that he is hidden, as if he was shrouded in darkness. The fault lies in us who are unable to approach his light, because of the weakness of our understanding. We take him to mean that he is **unapproachable** to any people who try to approach him in their own strength.

Whom no one has seen or can see. This gives a fuller explanation of the same point, that people may learn to look in faith to him whose face they cannot see with their eyes, or even understand with their minds. For I take this to refer not just to our physical eyes, but also the insight of our discerning minds.

Verses 17–21

17. As for those who in the present age are rich, command them not to be haughty. As so many Christians were poor and downtrodden, it is highly likely, as usually happens, that they were despised by the rich. This is especially likely to be the case in an opulent city like Ephesus, where pride is so often even worse than other places. From this we learn how dangerous material wealth can be. Paul has good reason for issuing such a warning, especially to the rich. He tries to correct the faults which nearly always accompany riches, just as our shadow stays with our body. Our depraved minds allow God's good gifts to become an opportunity for sin.

But rather on God. The person who understands this will find it easy not to trust riches any more. For God alone supplies everything that we need in life and we transfer his prerogative to riches, when we put our trust in them. Note the implied contrast where Paul says that God **richly provides us with everything.** Paul means that, even if we are overflowing with possessions, we have nothing that was not given us by God's kindness alone. Only he provides us so generously with everything that we need. So it is a great mistake to rely on riches and not to depend entirely on God's kindness, which supplies enough food and everything else we need.

18. They are to do good, to be rich in good works. Paul issues another command to the people he has already spoken about, in order to correct a depraved attachment to riches and to say how possessions should be used. Our opportunities to do good to others increase with the abundance of our riches.

19. The word **foundation** means something that is solid and lasting, for spiritual riches which we lay up for ourselves in heaven are not exposed to decay, theft, or fire, but remain permanently safe from all danger. In contrast with this, nothing on earth has such a solid foundation, for everything changes here.

20. Timothy, guard what has been entrusted to you. Paul exhorts Timothy to work hard to keep his conscience clear and to make proper use of what has been entrusted to him.

Avoid the profane chatter. The reason for this admonition is that we should devote ourselves to sound teaching. This can only happen if we turn away from everything that is ostentatious, for where the desire to please predominates, there is no longer the wish to edify. So when Paul mentions the thing that has been **entrusted,** it is very much to the point for him to add immediately this caution about turning away from **profane chatter.** This **profane chatter** does not so much refer to specific words, as to bombastic talk which pours out of ambitious people who are more concerned to gain recognition for themselves than they are about helping people in the church to make progress.

21. By professing it some have missed the mark. Paul points out how what harmful things result from following 'what is falsely called knowledge.' God punishes the arrogance of those who debase and corrupt the teaching of godliness, for the sake of their own reputations. They lose the ability to make sound judgments and become involved in many absurd errors.

Faith. Here, as in previous passages, this word means religion and sound teaching. We are warned here by the horrific possibility of wandering from the faith. We must stick close to the pure Word of God and hate sophistry and all clever philosophies which pollute godliness.

2 TIMOTHY

John Calvin

Introduction

It is not possible to determine with any certainty from Luke's account when Paul's first letter to Timothy was written. But I am sure that after that time Paul did have further personal contact with Timothy, and it may be, if we follow the generally accepted view, that Paul took him as his companion and assistant to many places. However, it is easy to conclude that Timothy was still in Ephesus when this second letter was written to him, as, towards the end of the letter, Paul sends greetings to Priscilla and Aquila and Onesiphorus. Onesiphorus lived in Ephesus, and Luke tells us that the other two stayed there when Paul sailed for Judea.

The main purpose of this letter is to strengthen Timothy both in the faith of the Gospel and in his pure and constant preaching of it. The particular circumstances of that time add special weight to these instructions. Paul faced imminent death, and was prepared to suffer as a witness to the Gospel. So everything that we read in this letter about Christ's kingdom, the hope of eternal life, the Christian warfare, confidence in confessing Christ, and the certainty of doctrine should be seen as written not merely in ink but in Paul's lifeblood. He is prepared to offer the pledge of his death for everything he writes about. So this letter may be seen as a solemn and urgent ratification of Paul's teaching.

It is important to remember, as we pointed out in the case of Paul's first letter to Timothy, that the apostle was not just writing for one man, but giving teaching which had a general application, and which Timothy could later pass on to others.

Contents

See *Outlines of the New Testament Books,* p. 902

Chapter 1

In this chapter Paul starts by praising Timothy for the faith in which he was brought up since his childhood. Paul exhorts him to persevere faithfully both in the doctrine he has been teaching and in the office entrusted to him. Timothy might have been upset by the news of Paul's imprisonment or by the apostasy of others, but Paul glories in his apostleship and in the reward that is waiting for him. He also praises Onesiphorus, so that other people may be encouraged by his example. Because followers of Christ will have a tough time, Paul uses metaphors from farming and warfare. Farmers think nothing of spending all their energies in cultivating the ground before it yields fruit; soldiers rid themselves of all other concerns so that they can devote themselves completely to fighting and to their commander's orders.

Verses 1–2

1. **Paul, an apostle.** These opening words show that Paul did not just have Timothy in mind, but other people as well. If the letter was only meant for Timothy, there would not have been any need for such a lofty assertion of his apostleship, and his strong language would not have been needed with somebody who was already completely convinced about the validity of his claims.

For the sake of the promise of life that is in Christ Jesus. In order to make his calling more certain, Paul links it with the promises of eternal life. It is like saying, 'As from the beginning God has promised eternal life in Christ, so now he had made me the minister appointed to spread that promise.' This reveals the purpose of his apostleship, that he should lead people to Christ, that they might find life in him.

2. **My beloved child.** By this phrase Paul not only expresses his affection for Timothy, but also secures for him a place of authority, for Paul wanted Timothy to be acknowledged as someone who had the right to be called his own son. Paul calls him **my dear son** as he had given birth to him in Christ. While the credit for this belongs wholly to God, it is transferred to those faithful ministers whose work God uses to regenerate us.

Grace, mercy, and peace from God the Father and Christ Jesus our Lord. The word **mercy** which Paul inserts here is not usually found in Paul's greetings and I think he puts it in here to express his special affection towards Timothy.

Verses 3–5

3. Prayer is a token of concern, and thanksgiving a token of joy. For Paul never thinks of Timothy without remembering the exceptional characteristics he was endowed with. From this springs his thanksgiving. Godly people always take delight in remembering God's gifts. Paul constantly remembers Timothy because he never forgets him in his prayers.

Whom I worship with a clear conscience, as my ancestors did. Paul mentions this to counter the well-known, slanderous accusations which the Jews levelled against him, saying that he had forsaken the religion of his people and had abandoned the law of Moses.

When I remember you constantly in my prayers. This shows how faithful Paul was in his praying.

5. Paul commends Timothy's faith and that of his mother and grandmother, more to encourage him than to praise him. For when anyone has started well his progress should be a spur for him to continue further, and these examples from his own family are strong incentives for him to press on. So Paul reminds him of his **mother Eunice**, and his **grandmother Lois**, who brought him up so that he could imbibe godliness along with his mother's milk. Because of this godly upbringing Timothy is commanded not to fall away from his past and his forebears.

Verses 6–12

6. **For this reason I remind you to rekindle the gift of God.** Paul means that the more grace Timothy has received, the more he should be keen to make progress every day. Notice how the words **for this reason** link up with the previous passage. This exhortation is necessary, for it often happens, and is most natural, that excellent gifts produce carelessness and sloth, and Satan uses this to remove everything that is of God from us.

That is within you through the laying on of my hands. It is undoubtedly true that Timothy was invited to become a minister through the votes of the church and was not just chosen by Paul on his own. But it is wholly understandable that Paul should say that he personally instigated Timothy's selection. Paul is dealing with Timothy's ordination, rather than with his election here – that is with the solemn rite of institution.

7. **For God did not give us a spirit of cowardice.** This confirms Paul's previous statement by which he continues to urge Timothy to demonstrate the power of the gifts he has received. Paul appeals to the fact that God governs his ministers through the **spirit of power**, which is opposite to the **spirit of cowardice**. From this it follows that they should not fall back into a state of laziness but should show themselves to be full of the Spirit's power.

Why does Paul add **love** and **self-discipline** after **power**? I think it is to distinguish the power of the Spirit from the intemperate zeal of fanatics who rush in recklessly, boasting that they have God's Spirit. Paul specifically says, therefore, that the powerful energy of the Spirit is tempered by **love** and **self-discipline** – that is, by a calm concern for edification. Paul is not denying that the same Spirit was given to prophets and teachers before the Gospel was preached, but he means that these two graces should be especially evident and powerful under Christ's reign.

8. **Do not be ashamed.** Paul says this because it was thought to be a disgraceful thing to confess the Gospel, so he tells Timothy not to let ambition, or fear of being badly thought of, hinder him in his confident preaching.

Do not be ashamed ... of me. By adding **of me** Paul tells Timothy not to refuse to be his companion in a common cause. When we begin to withdraw from those who are persecuted, we are attempting to make the Gospel free of all persecution. There were plenty of evil people who mocked Timothy and said, 'Don't you see what has happened to your master? Don't you know that the same reward is waiting for you? Why are you forcing teaching on us that makes the whole world wild?' Nevertheless, Timothy must have been cheered by Paul's exhortation. Paul says to him, 'You have not need to be ashamed about me, for I have nothing to be ashamed about, for I am the prisoner of Christ, I am in chains, not on account of committing any crime, but on account of Christ's name.'

9. From the greatness of the blessing he shows how much we owe to God, for the salvation he has given us more than compensates for all the evils we have to suffer in this world.

Not according to our works. Paul now concentrates on the source of our calling and on our whole salvation. We did not possess works so that we might be able to take the initiative out of God's hand, as our salvation depends entirely on his gracious purpose and election.

This grace was given to us. Paul argues that salvation was given to us by free grace, since we had done nothing before this to deserve it.

10. **But it has now been revealed.** Note how appropriately he links the faith we have from the Gospel with God's secret election and assigns to each its own place. God has called us through the Gospel, not because he has suddenly thought about our salvation, but because he has determined it from 'the beginning of time.'

To **life** Paul adds **immortality**, as if he were saying 'true and immortal life.' Our life is not made up of what we have in common with wild animals, but rather how we share God's image. But since the true nature of that life does not appear in this world, in order to explain it Paul correctly adds the word **immortality**, which is the revelation of that life which now lies concealed.

11. **For this Gospel I was appointed.** Paul has good reason to commend the Gospel so highly along with his own apostleship. Satan works hard above everything else to remove from our minds, through every possible means, faith in sound teaching, and because this cannot always be achieved through a direct attack on our faith, he creeps up on us unawares, using indirect ways, and in order to destroy faith in their teaching, he calls into question the calling of godly teachers. So Paul, who faces the prospect of death and knows all about old tricks of Satan, is determined to assert both the teaching of the Gospel in general and the genuineness of his own calling.

12. **And I am sure that he is able to guard.** The strength of the dangers ranged against us often make us despair or at least tempt us to distrust God. However, for our defence, we are armed with the knowledge that we have adequate protection in God's power.

Note how Paul describes eternal life as **what I have entrusted to him.** From this we learn that our salvation is in God's hand, just as we might entrust a trustee with holding property for us. If our salvation depended on ourselves, it would be constantly exposed to many dangers, but as it is entrusted with our Guardian it is out of danger.

Verses 13–18

13. **Sound teaching** is contrasted here not only with the teachings that are obviously godless, but with fruitless questions which are not healthy but lead to illness.

The faith and love. Paul adds this as a sign of sound teaching to show us what this contains, and how it may be summarized, and he does this by using the words he often used, **faith and love.** Both of these are founded **in Christ Jesus,** since knowledge about Christ largely consists in these two things. Paul declares that the whole of his teaching consists of **faith and love,** which have their source in knowing Christ.

14. **Guard the good treasure entrusted to you.** This instruction has a wider application than the previous one, for Paul is telling Timothy to reflect on what God has given him, and to give it the care and attention it deserves. When something has little value we do not think about it as much as something which we value highly. I think the phrase **that was entrusted to you** means the dignity of his ministerial office as well as all the other gifts showered on Timothy.

How are we to **guard** this **good treasure?** We must be careful that what God has given to us is not lost or taken away from us because of our laziness, ingratitude or through our abuse of it. Many people reject God's grace, and many more people, who, after they have received it, deprive themselves of it. Since we have not power in ourselves to protect it, he says we are to **guard the good treasure … with the help of the Holy Spirit.** It is as if he is saying, 'I do not ask from you more than you can give, for the Holy Spirit will give you what you lack.' So we must not judge God's commands by man's ability to obey them. For the words God commands he writes in our hearts and gives us the necessary strength to carry them out. What follows about **the Holy Spirit living in us** means that he is present to help believers, so long as they do not reject what God offers them.

15. **You are aware that all who are in Asia have turned away from me.** Many people might have been unsettled about these defections and made people suspect the worst. Paul faces these scandals with heroic courage. All good people can learn from this that they should loathe the treachery of those who have deserted Christ's servant when he was so isolated and feared for

the safety of his life. Good people are not to waver in their faith but must realize that Paul has not been deserted by God.

Including Phygelus and Hermogenes. Paul mentions by name two of his deserters, probably the best known of them, to stop these slanderous attacks. It is quite normal that deserters from the Christian war try to excuse their disgraceful behaviour by making accusations against faithful and upright ministers of the Gospel.

Phygelus and Hermogenes, realizing that they would rightly be held in such low esteem by the believers and that their treachery condemned them, would not hesitate to pile false accusations on to Paul and so shamelessly tarnish his innocence. So Paul singles them out in order to expose their deceit.

16. May the Lord grant mercy to the household of Onesiphorus. From this prayer we may deduce that good deeds done on behalf of Christians are not done in vain, even if such people are unable to repay them. For when Paul prays that God should reward them, it is equivalent to making a promise that this will happen. Paul also expresses his own gratitude by transferring to God the duty of paying back, since he himself is unable to repay the dept.

When Paul says that Onesiphorus was **not ashamed** of his **chains,** this is evidence not just of his generosity, but of his zeal, since he willingly exposed himself to danger and to the reproach of people in order to assist Paul. 'He eagerly searched for me and found me' (verse 17).

18. May the Lord grant that he will find mercy. This prayer shows that those who help Christians without expecting any earthly reward will receive a better reward than any they could receive from human hands. Note what Paul prays for – that Onesiphorus may **find mercy.** For the person who is merciful to his neighbors will receive mercy from God, and we would be foolish not to realize that this is meant to stimulate us to show kindness.

Chapter 2

In this chapter Paul gives a brief summary of his Gospel and instructs Timothy to hand it on to others. He touches on his own imprisonment and bursts into godly enthusiasm in order to help others to be courageous as well. He tells us all to reflect on the crown that waits for us in heaven. He also commands Timothy not to indulge in contentious arguments and pointless discussions, but rather to be keen to build people up in the faith. To underline how evil such disputes can be, he says that some people have ruined their faith because of them. He mentions two such people by name, Hymaenaeus and

Philetus, who went so far as to deny their faith in the resurrection and suffered a dreadful punishment because of their presumption. As lapses like that usually cause a great scandal, especially when people of high repute are involved, Paul says that godly people should not be disturbed by them, since not everyone who professes Christ's name is a genuine Christian. The church has to put up with this kind of opposition if it is to exist in the world of godless and evil people. But in case this should upset fearful people, Paul wisely softens this by saying that God will preserve to the end his own people, whom he has chosen.

Verses 1–7

1. You then, my child, be strong. As Paul has told Timothy previously to guard what was committed to him by the Spirit, so now he tells him to become strong in **grace.** By this he means that he should be shake off laziness, as the flesh is so sluggish that even those who are endowed with excellent gifts grow slack in the middle of what they are doing, if they are not frequently urged on to complete the task.

Paul adds the words **that is in Christ Jesus** for two reasons. First, to show that grace comes from Christ alone and from no one else; and, second, to show that no Christian is left without grace. Since the one Christ is common to everyone, it follows that everyone shares in his grace, and so the grace is said to be **in Christ Jesus** because all who are Christ's should have it.

The affectionate way in which Paul calls Timothy **my child** will allow a smoother passage for his teaching to enter his heart.

2. And what you have heard from me through many witnesses entrust to faithful people. Once again Paul reveals how keen he is to pass on sound teaching to the next generation. He exhorts Timothy not only, as he had done previously, to preserve its form and features, but also to hand it on to godly teachers, so that it might be proclaimed far and wide and take root in many hearts. Paul realized that the Gospel could easily die out if it was not spread widely by many ministers.

3. Share in suffering. Paul was bound to add this next exhortation. People who offer to be Christ's servants must be prepared to endure hardships patiently. Unless evils are endured there will never be any perseverance. This is why Paul adds the words **like a good soldier of Christ Jesus.** All who serve Christ are soldiers on active service, not so much inflicting evil on others, as in enduring evil patiently themselves. It is most important that we should consider these things.

4. No one serving in the army. Paul extends his military metaphor. Strictly speaking Paul was using this metaphor when he called

Timothy Christ's soldier, but now Paul proceeds to compare secular warfare with spiritual and Christian warfare. It is as if he is saying, 'The rule of military discipline is that as soon as a soldier has enrolled under a commander he leaves his home and all his affairs and concentrates only on the war. In the same way, we also can only be devoted to Christ if we are free from all the world's entanglements.'

5. And in the case of an athlete. Paul moves on to the subject of perseverance in case anybody thinks that he has done enough, by just being involved in one or two conflicts. This time Paul uses the metaphor of athletes, none of whom win the prize until they finish running their race. Christ wants us to strive every day, so the person who gives up half way through a race loses his honour, even though he may have set out bravely.

6. This verse means that the **farmer** does not gather his **crops** until he has worked hard in cultivating the earth by sowing and other work. If a farmer does not shrink from the hard work of obtaining fruit after a period of time, and if he waits patiently for the harvest, how much more absurd it is for us to refuse the work Christ sets on us, as we have the promise of such a great reward.

7. Think over what I say. Paul does not add this because his metaphors are hard to understand, but so that Timothy may ponder for himself how very much better is warfare under Christ's command, and how much richer is his reward.

Verses 8–13

8. Remember Jesus Christ, raised from the dead, a descendant of David. Paul now specifically mentions a part of his teaching which he particularly wanted to be passed on to posterity in its entirety, and uncorrupted.

A descendant of David. In this phrase, Paul not only asserts the reality of Christ's human nature but also claims for him the honour and name of Messiah. Some heretics deny that Christ was really man. Some imagine that he descended from heaven and only appeared to be a man. Paul counters this and says that he was **a descendant of David** and so undoubtedly asserts that Christ was really man, born of our humanity as the Son of Mary. This testimony is so clearly expressed that the attempts of heretics to evade it only showed up their own shamelessness. Jews and other enemies of Christ deny that he is the One who was promised for so long, but Paul says that Christ is David's Son and has his origin in that family from which the Messiah would be drawn.

9. For which I suffer hardship, even to the point of being chained like a criminal. But the word of God is not chained. Paul is anticipating

an objection at this point. For in the eyes of the ignorant his imprisonment distracted from the credibility of the Gospel. He acknowledges that to all outward appearances it looks as if he is in prison like any other common criminal, but Paul adds that this had not stopped the Gospel from having free rein. Indeed what he is suffering is for the benefit of the elect.

10. Therefore I endure. Paul shows that this imprisonment, far from resulting in reproach, was, in fact, most beneficial to the elect. When Paul says that he endures **everything for the sake of the elect**, he reveals how much more important the edification of the church is for him than his own safety. For Paul is not only prepared to die, but even to be known as a criminal, in order to promote the welfare of the church.

With eternal glory. This is the goal of the salvation we obtain in Christ. Our salvation is to live for God and this starts with our regeneration and is completed through our complete freedom from the miseries of this mortal life, when God takes us and brings us into his kingdom.

11. The saying is sure. Paul uses this to introduce what follows. There is nothing so opposed to the wisdom of human nature than believing that we must die in order to live and that death is the gateway to life. We gather from other passages that it is Paul's custom to use this preface before saying anything very difficult to believe or especially important. Paul means that the only way we can share Christ's life and glory is by sharing in first of all his death and humiliation. 'For those whom he foreknew he also predestined to be conformed to the image of his Son, in order that he might be the firstborn within a large family' (Romans 8:29). Paul taught that the elect would be conformed to Christ's likeness.

12. If we deny him. Paul adds this solemn warning to shake us out of our sloth. Paul aims this warning at those who have given up confessing Christ out of fear of persecution.

13. Paul's next statement, **he remains faithful**, seems, at first sight, to be incredible. But it means this, 'Our faithlessness cannot in any way detract from the Son of God and his glory. As he is all-sufficient in himself he does not need our confession.' It is as if Paul had said, 'Let everyone who wants to desert Christ, desert him; they will take nothing from him. For when they perish, Christ remains unchanged.' Paul then goes on to explain that Christ is not like us and does not deviate from his own truth. So it is clear that all who deny Christ are disowned by Christ.

Verses 14–18

14. Remind them of this. This is emphatic. Paul means that the summary of the Gospel which he has just given, along with the exhortations he has added, is so important that a good minister should never grow weary of dealing with them. On the negative side Paul tells Timothy not only to avoid useless questions himself but to prevent others from being led away by them. **Wrangling over words** (literally, 'fighting with words') means being earnestly engaged in contentious disputes and it usually springs out of a desire to be clever.

15. Do your best to present yourself to God as one approved. The source of all doctrinal disputes is that clever men wish to show off their abilities before the world, and Paul gives the best remedy for this by telling Timothy to keep his eyes fixed on God. It is as if Paul says, 'Some people seek popular applause, but it must be your aim to have God's approval on yourself and your ministry.' There is nothing that is better to check our foolish desire for display than to remember that it is God we have to deal with.

Rightly explaining the word of truth. This is a metaphor which accurately explains the main purpose in teaching. Paul assigns to teachers the duty of carving or dividing the Word, as a father cuts the bread into small pieces to feed his children. Paul advises Timothy to handle the Word correctly, in case he only succeeds in cutting the surface, as an unskilled man would, leaving the inner pith and marrow untouched. I think what is said here has a general application and refers to a judicious dispensing of the Word which is spoken for the benefit of the hearers. Some mutilate the Word, others dismember the Word, some distort the Word, some break it into little pieces, and some, as I have said, keep on the outside of it and never reach the heart of the matter. With all these faults he contrasts a correct handling of the Word, that is, a way of expounding it aimed at edifying people. This is the rule by which we should judge every interpretation of Scripture.

16. Avoid profane chatter, for it will lead people into more and more impiety. To deter Timothy from this profane and noisy speech he tells him that it is like a labyrinth, or, rather a deep whirlpool, from which there is no escape, and into which men plunge deeper and deeper.

17. Their talk will spread like gangrene. All the medical authorities agree that the nature of the disease is such that unless it is treated quickly it will spread to adjacent parts of the body and penetrate right into the bones and not stop spreading until it has killed the patient. As gangrene causes death so quickly, Paul aptly compares false teaching with this fatal disease. For once these people are allowed into the church they will spread until they destroy the church.

Among them are Hymenaeus and Philetus. Paul singles out these pests so that everyone may be on their guard against them, for if we allow people who are contriving to ruin the whole church to remain concealed, we only give them an opportunity to do real damage.

18. Having said that they have departed from the truth, Paul gives an example of their errors. They were telling people that **the resurrection** had **already taken place.** This means that they invented some kind of allegorical resurrection, as has been attempted in our day by some dirty dogs. Through this trick Satan overthrows the fundamental article of our faith concerning the resurrection of the body. Since this is such an old obsolete dream, which is so severely condemned by Paul, it should be less disturbing for us. But when we are told that from the very beginning of the Gospel that they destroyed the faith of some, such an example should arouse us to diligent watchfulness, so that we are quick to ward off such plagues from ourselves and from others.

Verses 19–21

19. But God's firm foundation stands. We know only too well how much scandal is produced by the defections of those who once professed the same faith as ourselves, and this is especially so in the case of people who are well known and have an outstanding reputation. If some ordinary people commit apostasy, we are hardly touched. But people with good reputations, who appeared to be pillars of the church, cannot fall without involving others in their ruin, at least, if their faith has no other support. This is Paul's concern here, and he says that this is no reason for godly people to lose heart, even if they see people falling whom once they thought to be very firm in the faith. To console them, Paul points out that human fickleness or infidelity cannot stop God from preserving his church to the end. First, Paul reminds them about God's election, which he calls, figuratively, a **foundation,** meaning that it is firm and endures. All this confirms the certainty of our salvation, provided that we belong to God's elect. It is like saying, 'God's elect do not depend on changing events, but rest on a solid and immovable foundation, for their salvation is in God's hand. Just as "Every plant that my heavenly Father has not planted will be uprooted" (Matthew 15:13), so the root which his hand has fixed cannot be injured by winds and storms.'

Bearing this inscription. The word **inscription** has been misunderstood, for some people thought it meant a mark or impression, so I prefer to use the word 'seal' to avoid any ambiguity. For Paul means that the salvation of the elect is kept privately by God, like a signet ring, for the Scripture declares that they are written in the book of life (see Psalm 69:28 and Philippians 4:3).

'Let everyone who calls on the name of the Lord turn away from wickedness.' Paul has faced the scandal caused by defection by saying that it should not make believers excessively alarmed, and now he goes on to say that we can learn from the example of hypocrites that we should not mock God with a similar pretense of professing Christianity. It is like saying, 'Since God punishes hypocrites by exposing their wickedness in this way, we must learn to fear him with a sincere conscience in case we meet the same fate.' So anyone who calls on God's name, that is, professes to belong to God's people and wants to be numbered among them, must be far from all ungodliness. For here confessing **the name of the Lord** means to boast in his title and to glory in belonging to his flock.

20. Paul moves on and introduces a comparison to show that when we see people fall away shamelessly who for a time had made a great show of piety and zeal, far from being disturbed by it, we should accept it as part of God's providence.

21. All who cleanse themselves of these things. If the reprobate are articles of dishonour, the dishonour is confined to themselves. They do not disfigure the house or bring any shame on the head of the family, who destines each article in his varied furnishings to the use for which it is suited. But we must learn, from their example, to make ourselves suitable for honourable and higher uses.

Will become special utensils, dedicated means one set apart for honourable and illustrious uses. A thing that is **useful** to the head of the family is something that is appropriate for being used in an honourable way.

Verses 22–26

22. Shun youthful passions. Paul advises Timothy to **shun youthful passions,** by which he does not mean sexual sins or other disgraceful desires or other licentious behaviour young men often indulge in, but rather those impetuous feelings and impulses which the excessive passion of youth make young men prone to. In arguments young people become more heated, more quickly than those of mature years; they become angry more easily, and they make more mistakes from lack of experience and rush into things with great rashness. So Paul has every reason to tell a young man to be on his guard against the faults which his age made him particularly prone to, or else he would easily be led into useless disputes.

Pursue righteousness. Paul recommends the qualities which are the opposites of youthful excess. It is as Paul had said, 'These are the things which you should give your complete attention to and which you should concentrate on.' First, Paul mentions **righteousness,** that is, a right way of living; and then, he adds **faith** and **love** which righteousness is made up of.

Peace is very relevant to his present concern, for those who delight in the topics he says should not be discussed are bound to be contentious and quarrelsome.

23. Have nothing to do with stupid and senseless controversies. Paul calls these arguments **foolish** because they do not instruct people, that is, they do not lead to increased godliness, no matter how good an opportunity the offer to display cleverness.

24. And the Lord's servant must not be quarrelsome. Paul's train of thought is as follows: 'God's servant must stand aloof from silly arguments; but foolish questions lead to silly arguments; therefore everyone who wants to be thought of as God's servant must shun them.' **But kindly to everyone, an apt teacher, patient.** In telling Christ's servant to be **kindly to everyone** Paul is emphasizing the virtue which is the opposite of polluted contentiousness. What comes next refers to the same point, that he should be **an apt teacher.** He will not be able to teach without moderation. For how far will a teacher go who is embroiled in a fight? The more qualified a person is to teach, the more he shuns disputes and controversies. The speed at which some people become irritated leads Paul to say that the Lord's servant should also be **not resentful.**

25. God may perhaps grant that they will repent. The phrase **may perhaps** 'if peradventure,' or, 'if sometime,' emphasizes how difficult this is, even to the point of being almost impossible. Paul means that gentleness should be shown even to those who least deserve it, and even if at first there is no apparent hope of making progress, still the challenge must be accepted. Paul reminds us that **God may … grant** this for the same reason. Since the conversion of a person is in God's hands, who can say whether those who today seem to be unteachable may be suddenly changed through God's power into different people?

26. Having been held captive by him to do his will. It is indeed a dreadful condition when the devil has such power over us that he drags us as captive slaves here and there at his pleasure. And yet this is the condition of all those whose overweening pride breaks their bond of obedience to God, and we see every day in the reprobate clear evidence of this tyrannical domination of Satan.

Chapter 3

In this chapter Paul returns to exhorting Timothy, so that he may persevere faithfully in carrying out his ministry. To make him more faithful, he predicts that dangerous times are in store for the good and godly and that destructive people will soon arise against them. But against all this Paul fortifies Timothy with the hope of a happy and successful outcome. More especially, he recommends him to engage in sound teaching all the time, pointing out how Scripture should be correctly used, so that Timothy may know that through it he will be fully equipped for the solid edification of the church.

Verses 1–7

1. **You must understand this.** Paul wants this warning to make Timothy even more diligent. When things turn out as we want them to we become careless; but necessity makes us more alert. So Paul warns Timothy that the church will be subject to terrible diseases which will mean that its pastors are especially faithful, diligent, careful, wise and constantly alert. It is as if Paul were warning Timothy to prepare himself for the arduous and deeply anxious struggles that awaited him. From this we learn not to be frightened in the face of difficulties but rather to strengthen our hearts to overcome them.

Under **the last days** Paul includes the universal condition of the Christian church. He is not comparing his own age with ours, but rather teaching what the future condition of Christ's kingdom will be. Many thought that there would be a blessed peace free from every trouble, but Paul means here that even under the Gospel there will not be any such state of perfection in which all vices are banished and every kind of virtue flourishes.

2. **People will be lovers of themselves.** We note what the danger will be in those days. In Paul's view it will not come from war, famine, disease, or any of the other disasters which happen to physical bodies, but it will come from the wickedness of depraved people. For good people who fear God, there is nothing more distressing than to see such moral corruption.

3–4. Paul here lists vices of a kind which are not immediately visible and which can accompany pretended holiness. For which hypocrite is not proud, or a lover of self, or a despiser of others, or harsh or cruel, or fraudulent? But all these are hidden from human eyes. There is no need to go through this list, item by item, as it does not need a detailed explanation. But readers should note that 'lovers of themselves,' which heads the list, can be regarded as the source from which spring all the others. For the person who loves himself claims superiority in everything, despises all other people, is cruel, indulges in covetousness, treachery, anger, disobedience against parents, neglect of good and all such things. As it was Paul's purpose to brand false prophets with such marks, that they might be seen and known by everyone, so it is our duty to open our eyes and see those who are thus pointed out.

5. **Avoid them!** From this instruction it is apparent that Paul is not speaking to some distant posterity, or prophesying what would happen many centuries later, but is pointing out existing evils and so applying to his own day what he has just said about the last days.

6. **For among them are those who make their way into households.** The characteristics by which Paul distinguishes false teachers from genuine teachers are sufficiently clear. They worm their way into families, being a trap for silly women, given over to mean flattery, imposing on people by various superstitions.

7. Immediately following this, it is stated that they are **always being instructed** but never learn to be really wise.

Verses 8–12

8. **Jannes and Jambres.** This comparison confirms what I have already said about the last days. Paul means that what is happening to us under the Gospel is the same as the church has experienced almost from its first beginning, and certainly since the promulgation of the law. It is generally agreed that the two men mentioned here were magicians in Pharaoh's court. We may suppose that two people are named here because God raised up for his people two leaders, Moses and Aaron, so Pharaoh decided to oppose them with two magicians.

9. **But they will not make much progress.** Paul encourages Timothy for the coming conflict by telling him that victory will be assured. For although false teachers will trouble him, Paul promises that in a short time they will be shamefully confounded.

10. **Now you have observed my teaching.** Here is another argument to spur Timothy on. He is no ignorant, raw recruit going into the arena, for Paul himself has already imparted to him a great deal of his own teaching. Paul refers not only to teaching, and the other things he mentions are also very important. In this verse he paints a vivid picture of a good teacher, as one who influences his pupils not only by his words, but, as it were, opens his own heart to them so that they may know that all his **teaching** is sincere. Paul adds other practical evidence of earnest sincerity: **my faith, my patience, my love, my steadfastness.** Such basic lessons have been given to Timothy in Paul's school. But Paul does not just remind Timothy about what he has taught him, but bears testimony to Timothy's past life to encourage him to persevere. He praises him as someone who has imitated his own virtues.

11. **Yet the Lord rescued me from all of them.** The fact that afflictions always end happily is most consoling and goes a long way to mitigating their bitterness. If anyone objects that the happy end he claims is not always obvious,

I agree that this is true as far as outward appearances are concerned, for Paul himself had not yet been set free from prison. But by delivering us often, God testifies that he is with us and will always be with us.

12. Indeed, all who want to live a godly life. The recollections of his own persecutions makes Paul add that everything that had happened to him will also come to all godly people.

Verses 13–17

13. It is the most bitter persecution of all when we see evil people with their sacrilegious boldness and their blasphemies and errors gaining strength. One worthless person will always be more effective in destroying people, than ten faithful teachers in building up, even though they toil with all their might.

14. Continue in what you have learned. Although ungodliness is increasing and making progress, Paul tells Timothy to stand firm. This is the acid test of our faith. With untiring zeal we should resist all the devil's schemes, and refuse to alter course with every wind that blows, and thus remain fixed on God's truth as on a sure anchor.

Knowing from whom you learned it. Paul's intention here is to commend the certainty of his teaching, for we should not persevere in things in which we have been wrongly instructed. If we wish to be Christ's disciples we must unlearn all that we have learnt that is not about him.

15. And how from childhood you have known the sacred writings. The fact that Timothy had been used to reading the Scriptures since his childhood was a powerful spur to keep him faithful, as this long established habit can make a person much more prepared to meet any kind of deception. They were wise in ancient times to make sure that those who were intended for the ministry of the Word should have been instructed in the solid teaching about godliness, and should have drunk deep from the sacred writings, so that when they came to fulfil their office they would not be inexperienced apprentices. So if anyone has acquired from his youth a knowledge of the Scriptures he should count it a special blessing from God.

That are able to instruct you for salvation. Scripture is commended very highly indeed when it is said that the wisdom necessary for salvation can only be found there, and the next verse explains this more fully. At the same time, Paul tells us what we should look for in Scripture itself.

16. All Scripture First, Paul commends the Scripture because of its authority, and then because of the benefit it brings. In order to assert its authority, Paul teaches that it is

inspired, for if that is so, it is beyond all question that people should receive it with reverence. This is the principle that distinguishes our religion from all others, that we know that God has spoken to us and that we are certain that the prophets did not just speak for their own time but as instruments of the Holy Spirit uttered only what they had been told to say from heaven. Anyone who wants to benefit from the Scriptures must first of all accept this as a settle principle, that the Law and the prophets are not teachings handed on at the whim of men or produced by human minds, but are dictated through the Holy Spirit. If anyone objects to this and asks how this can be, my answer is that it is through the revelation of the same Spirit both to students and to teachers that God is made known as its Author.

And is useful. The second part of Paul's commendation now follows. Scripture contains the perfect rule of a good and happy life. In saying this Paul means that Scripture is polluted by sinful abuse when this beneficial purpose is not sought in it. He is indirectly rebuking those who trifle with it, and who feed people empty speculations, like the wind. For the same reason we may condemn today all who abandon concern for edification and make much of ingenious but profitless questions. Whenever ingenious trifles of that kind are introduced, they should be warded of with this phrase, as with a shield, 'Scripture is useful.' It follows from this that it is wrong to use it to gratify our curiosity or satisfy our desire for ostentation or provide us with a chance for foolish conversation. God meant it for our good. So the correct use of Scripture will always benefit people.

For teaching. Here Paul enumerates, the many uses of Scripture. First of all he mentions **teaching**, since it takes precedence over all the others. But since **teaching** on its own is often cold and lifeless, Paul adds **for reproof** and **for correction.** It would take too long to set out here what we learn from Scripture, and Paul has already in the previous verse given a brief summary of it in the word 'faith.' This is indeed the biggest part of our knowledge – faith in Christ. Next follows instruction on the regulation of our lives, to which are added exhortations and reproofs. So the person who uses Scripture correctly lacks nothing either for salvation or for living in the right way. The only difference between **reproof** and **correction** is that the second is the result of the first. To acknowledge our sin and be convicted about God's judgment on it is the beginning of repentance. **Training in righteousness** means instruction in a godly and holy life.

17. Equipped for every good work means perfect. A person in whom there is nothing defective is such a person. Paul asserts, without any qualification, that the Scripture is sufficient to achieve perfection.

Chapter 4

In this chapter Paul reminds Timothy that his own death is approaching, but he does so as a conqueror looking forward to a glorious victory, which illustrates his amazing confidence. Lastly, having asked Timothy to come to him as soon as possible, he points out the need which arises from his present position. This is the main topic of the letter's concluding section.

Verses 1–4

1. **In the presence of God and of Christ Jesus, who is to judge the living and the dead.** This refers to those whom Christ will find still alive at his coming and also to those who have already died. Nobody will escape his judgment. **In view of his appearing and his kingdom. Appearing** and **kingdom** mean the same thing, for although Christ now rules in heaven and in earth, up until now his kingdom has not been made clearly visible; rather it lies in the shadow of the cross and is strongly opposed by his enemies.

2. **Be persistent whether the time is favourable or unfavourable.** Here Paul commends not merely perseverance but even aggressiveness in overcoming all barriers and difficulties. For, as we are naturally timid and lazy, we easily give up on the slightest pretext and we even sometimes welcome difficulties as an excuse for indolence.

Paul tells Timothy to be ever alert to **convince, rebuke, and encourage.** Here Paul is indicating that we need incentives if we are to hold to the true course. If we were as teachable as we should be, Christ's ministers could guide us merely by pointing out the right way. But, as things are, sane advice and mere moderate exhortations are not enough to shake us out of our lethargy. Thus there is need for stronger reproofs and exhortations.

With the utmost patience. This is a most necessary qualification. Rebukes either fail to have any effect because they are too violent or because they disappear into thin air, as they are not based on sound **teaching**. Exhortations are no more than supports to teaching, and without teaching they have little force. We see this in people who are very zealous but who have had little instruction.

3. **For the time is coming.** Human depravity shows just how careful pastors must be. For the Gospel would be quickly erased from people's memories, if godly people did not strive earnestly to preserve it. Paul is saying that we must make the most of the opportunities while some people still have reverence for Christ. It is

as if Paul says that when you see a storm approaching you must not take your time about your work, but you must work more diligently, because you will soon not have the opportunity for work.

When Paul says that **people will not put up with sound doctrine,** he means not only that they will not like it and will despise it, but also that they will actually hate it. Paul refers to it as **sound** because of its effect in instructing us in godliness. In the next verse he calls it 'truth,' meaning that **sound doctrine** is a pure and natural handling of God's Word, in contrast with those who 'wander away to myths' (verse 4). These 'myths' are useless ideas which corrupt the straightforward Gospel. We learn from this that the more determined people are to despise Christ's teaching, the more zealous godly ministers should be to assert it and guard it earnestly, and so ward off Satan's attacks.

They will accumulate for themselves teachers to suit their own desires. We should note the phrase **accumulate** which means that in their madness they will not be content with a few imposters, but will want a great crowd.

Verses 5–8

5. **As for you, always be sober.** Paul continues to say that the more terrible the trouble becomes, the more conscientiously Timothy must work to remedy them, and the more pressing the dangers are, the more he must keep watch.

To **do the work of an evangelist** is to do what evangelists should do.

6. **I am already being poured out as a libation.** Paul now says why he gave such a solemn charge. It is as if he was to say, 'As long as I was alive I could stretch out my hand and help you; you have never been without my constant exhortations, my advice has greatly assisted you and my example has been a great source of strength. Now the time is coming when you will have to teach and encourage yourself and begin to swim without support. Take care that nothing in you may be seen to be changed by my death.'

We should note the expressions Paul uses to describe his death. The word **departure** indicates that when we die we do not completely perish.

As a libation. A **libation** or sacrifice was a term specially suited to Paul's death, since he was dying in order to uphold Christ's truth. For although all godly people are sacrifices acceptable to God both in the obedience of their lives and in their deaths, martyrs are sacrificed in a more permanent way by shedding their blood for Christ's name. In addition, the phrase **poured out** which Paul uses here does not refer to just any kind of sacrifice but specifically to one used to ratify a covenant. Here Paul celebrates his death by commending it as the ratification of his teaching, that it might encourage believers to persevere rather than grow weary, as often happens.

The time for my departure has come. This phrase should also be noted because through it Paul rightly removes our excessive dread of death by focussing on its nature and effect. The only reason that people should be so greatly disturbed at the slightest mention of death is that they think that in death they will completely perish.

7. I have fought the good fight. Since it is normal to judge something by its result, Paul's fight could be condemned, since it had an unhappy ending. So Paul boasts here that, no matter what the world thinks, it has been a good fight. This is evidence of his exceptional faith, for not only did everyone think that Paul was in an extremely wretched situation, but that his death would also be shameful. So who would not say that he had struggled without success? But he himself does not depend on man's twisted judgments, but in his great courage he rises above every calamity, so that nothing can interfere with his happiness and glory. So Paul states that the **fight** he has **fought** has been a good and honourable one, and he can even rejoice at the prospect of death as this has been the goal he has been striving for.

8. From now on there is reserved for me. As Paul has gloried in his good fight, the course finished and the faith kept, so now he claims that his labours have not been in vain. It is possible to make a great effort and still fail to reach one's goal. But Paul says that he was certain of his reward. He derives this certainty from turning his eyes to the day of resurrection, and we should do the same. We see nothing but death all around us, so we should not concentrate on the appearances of the world, but should have Christ at the forefront of our minds. Then nothing can spoil our happiness.

And not only to me. So that all other believers may fight with the same courage, Paul invites them to share his crown. For his unbroken faithfulness could not serve as an example to us, if we did not have the same hope of a crown before us. Paul mentions an outstanding characteristic of believers when he calls them all **who have longed for his appearing.** For, wherever faith is strong it does not allow our heart to sleep in this world but lifts us up to hope in the final resurrection.

Verses 9–13

9. As Paul realized that his death was imminent, there were doubtless many matters about the welfare of the church that he wanted to discuss with Timothy. So Paul does not hesitate to ask him to travel across the sea to visit him.

Certainly there must have been very good reasons to justify asking him to leave the church he looked after in order to make such a long journey. From this we see how important meetings between people like this are, for what Timothy would in a brief time would be of lasting benefit to the churches, and the loss of six months or a year would be insignificant in comparison with the gain that would come from this meeting. But, from what follows, it appears that Paul is summoning Timothy for personal reasons as well, since he misses such a supporter so much. But Paul was not putting his own needs before the good of the church, for the Gospel itself was involved in this proposed meeting, and all believers would benefit as a result. Since Paul had to defend the Gospel from prison, he needed other people to work alongside him in this.

10. For Demas, in love with this present world, has deserted me and has gone to Thessalonica. It was disgraceful that a person could be more in love with this world than with Christ. But we do not have to suppose that he denied Christ completely and went over to a life of ungodliness and allowed the allurements of the world to take him over, but only that he cared more for his own convenience and safety than for Paul's life.

13. When you come, bring the cloak that I left with Carpus at Troas. Commentators disagree about the meaning of the word translated **cloak.** Some think that it is a chest or box for books, others that it is a kind of traveller's cloak which gave special protection against the cold and rain. I incline to interpret this word to mean 'chest' since that fits in with the **books, and above all the parchments** which the apostle goes on to mention. It is clear from this that although the apostle was preparing for death, he had not given up reading. Where are those who think that they have made so much progress that they do not need to make any more, and which of them can compare himself with Paul? This passage refutes the idiotic reasoning of the fanatics who condemn books and all reading and just boast about their private inspirations which God gives them.

Someone may ask why Paul was asking for a cloak if he expected to die so soon. This is another reason why I think the word means a chest, but there may have been another use for a cloak at that time which we do not know about today. I am not too concerned about this matter.

Verses 14–22

14. Alexander the coppersmith. This man was a terrible example of apostasy. He had professed some zeal in furthering Christ's kingdom, but later he attacked it publicly. This is the most dangerous and venomous kind of enemy. From the beginning the Lord determined that his church should not be exempt from this kind of evil lest our courage should fail when we are tried in the same way. We make note of the special evil which Paul condemns in **Alexander** – namely that he opposed his teaching. **Alexander** worked with his hands, and was not educated in debating skills. But enemies in one's own circle always do much damage. The wickedness which such people propagate is always believed by the world, so that sometimes ignorance creates more problems than the learning of clever people. In addition to this, when the Lord brings his servants into conflict with uneducated people like Alexander, the Lord deliberately conceals them from the world's view that they may not delight in pompous displays of cleverness.

17. But the Lord stood at me and gave me strength. Paul adds this to ensure that people did not use this event to dream up a baseless scandal. He acknowledges that God's hand has supported him, and it is enough for him that the inward grace of the Spirit was a shield against attacks. He adds the reason: **so that through me the message might be fully proclaimed.** This proclamation refers to the work of making the Gospel known among the Gentiles, which had been entrusted to Paul.

So I was rescued from the lion's mouth. Many people think that **the lion** was Nero. But I think that Paul uses this expression to indicate danger in general, as if he were saying 'out of the blazing fire,' or 'from the jaws of death.' Paul says that he escaped only through God's marvellous help, since the danger was so great that otherwise it would at once have swallowed him up.

18. Paul states that he is hoping for the same help in the future, not so that he may avoid death, but to avoid being overthrown by Satan, and to avoid veering from the right course. We should not make our safety our chief aim, but that we should rise above every trial, and be prepared to die a hundred times over rather than being infected by engaging in evil work.

This passage states that we have uninterrupted communion with God's grace. Some people acknowledge that salvation has its origin in God, but ascribe its continuation to our own free will, so that perseverance becomes a human achievement and not a divine gift. But Paul, by ascribing to God the work of leading us to heaven, openly asserts that we are ruled by God's hand throughout our lives, until we have engaged in the spiritual fight and achieve the victory. We have a clear warning about this in the person of Demas, whom Paul had just mentioned, for Demas went from being a noble athlete for Christ to becoming a base deserter.

TITUS

John Calvin

Introduction

Paul had only laid the foundations of the church in Crete when he had to hurry on elsewhere, since he was not just the pastor of one island but the apostle to the Gentiles. Paul therefore commissioned Titus as an evangelist to carry on his work. It is clear from this letter that, immediately after Paul left, Satan made great efforts not only to overthrow the government of the church, but also to corrupt its teaching.

Some people, out of selfish ambition, aspired to become pastors, and when Titus would not comply with their evil desires, they spoke ill of him to many people. There were also some Jews who tried to use the law of Moses as their pretext for introducing a great number of trifling regulations and observances, and they were being listened to attentively and very favourably. So Paul wrote to Titus to arm him with his authority to help him to bear such great burdens. Doubtless, some people openly scorned him, as being just an ordinary pastor. It is also possible that complaints were being circulated that he was taking upon himself more than he had a right to, since he refused to accept pastors until they had won his approval.

So we may conclude that this is not so much a private letter to Titus as a public letter to the people of Crete. Titus should probably not be blamed for being too ready to promote unworthy people to the office of bishop, or for having to have laid down for him what kind of doctrine he should teach the people, as if he were some ignorant novice. But since he was not receiving the honour due to him, Paul clothes him with his own personal authority both for ordaining ministers and in the whole government of the church. Because many people foolishly desired another kind of teaching from the one they received from Titus, Paul repudiates all others and grants his sole approval to Titus' teaching, encouraging him to continue as he has begun.

First of all, Paul teaches what kind of people should be chosen as ministers. Among other qualifications, he requires that a minister should be taught sound doctrine so that he can refute his adversaries. Here Paul takes the opportunity to censure the ways of the Cretans and especially rebukes the Jews, who made holiness consist of making distinctions between foods and other outward ceremonies. To refute their follies Paul contrasts with them the genuine practices of godliness and Christian living, and to impress this on them even more strongly, he describes the duties which belong to different vocations. He tells Titus to teach these carefully all the time, and he also tells the others not to become tired of listening to such teaching. Paul shows that this is the purpose of the redemption and salvation obtained through Christ. If anyone will not accept what he says, Paul tells Titus to have nothing more to do with him. We now see that Paul's single aim was to support Titus and to give him a helping hand in carrying out the Lord's work.

Contents

See *Outlines of the New Testament Books*, p. 902

Chapter 1

Verses 1–4

1. The long and detailed commendation of his apostleship shows that Paul was writing to the whole church, and not just to Titus. Titus had nothing against Paul's apostleship. Paul usually praised his calling when he wanted to assert and maintain his authority. So, depending on the disposition of the people to whom he is writing, he deals either briefly or at length with such matters. Since Paul's aim in this letter was to bring into line those who were rebelling, he extols his apostleship in the most lofty terms. Paul does not just write this letter so that Titus can read it in his own room, but so that it may be read in public.

Paul starts off by calling himself **a servant of God**, and then adds the particular designation of his ministry, **an apostle of Jesus Christ**. He moves from the general to the particular.

For the sake of the faith of God's elect. If anyone has doubts about Paul's apostleship, Paul gives a very strong reason for believing in it, by connecting it with the salvation **of God's elect**, as if he had said, 'there is a mutual relationship between my apostleship and the faith of God's elect, so that nobody can reject it without being a reprobate and a stranger to the true faith.' By the **elect** Paul does not just mean those who were alive when he wrote, but everyone who had been alive since the beginning of the world. Paul means that he teaches no doctrine that disagrees with the faith of Abraham and all the fathers.

When Paul calls faith **knowledge** he is not just distinguishing it from opinion but from what some people call unformed or implicit faith. By implicit faith they mean something devoid of all light of understanding. But it is of the essence of faith to know the truth, Paul clearly shows that there is definitely no faith without knowledge.

By the word **truth** Paul explains even more clearly the certainty which the nature of faith requires. For faith is not satisfied with probabilities but holds to what is true. Moreover, Paul is not speaking here about any kind of truth, but the truth which contrasts with the vanity of human understanding. For as God has revealed himself to us through that truth, it alone is worthy of the name **truth** – a name given to it in many parts of the Scripture.

The phrase that follows, **that is in accordance with godliness** qualifies the truth Paul has been speaking about, in a special way. At the same time Paul commends his teaching from its fruit and end, since its sole aim is to further the proper worship of God and protect pure religion among us.

2. In the hope of eternal life. Meditation on the life of heaven is the beginning both of true religion and of desire for godliness.

Who never lies. These words are not just added to glorify God but to strengthen our faith. Whenever the subject of our faith is dealt with, we should remember that it is founded on the Word of him who cannot deceive or lie. Indeed, the only foundation of all religion is the unchangeable truth of God.

3. In due time. This means the same as 'when the fullness of the time had come' (Galatians 4:4). Paul reminds us that the time that the Lord chose to do this must have been the most opportune time, and he maintains this to meet the temerity of those who dare to ask why it did not happen earlier, or why it is today rather than tomorrow.

He revealed his word. There was already some revelation about it when God of old spoke through the prophets. But since at his coming Christ openly manifested what they had dimly predicted, and because it was only then that Gentiles were received into the covenant, Paul says that what had been shown previously in part was now, in this sense, brought to light.

Through the proclamation. God has manifested life through his Word of life through the preaching of the Gospel. The **proclamation** Paul refers to is the spreading of the Gospel, and the most important part of this is that Christ has been given to us, and in him is life.

4. To Titus, my loyal child in the faith we share. Here we clearly see in what sense a minister of the Word is said to beget spiritually those whom he brings into obedience to Christ, namely, in such a way that he himself is also begotten. Paul calls himself the father of Titus in respect of his faith, but immediately adds that this faith is common to both of them, so that both of them share the same heavenly Father. Thus God in no way detracts from his own prerogative in allowing those through whose ministry he regenerates whoever he wants to be called spiritual fathers along with himself. For by themselves they do nothing, but only through the efficacy of the Spirit.

Verses 5–6

5. I left you behind in Crete for this reason. This opening shows clearly that Paul is not just advising Titus for his own sake but is commending him to others so that no one will stop his work. Paul states that he has appointed him to take his own place and so everyone should recognize him and receive him as Paul's own representative.

Appoint elders in every town. As the church is built up spiritually, the appointment of pastors to care for leading the church comes second only to sound teaching. So Paul mentions this before he mentions anything else. It must be noted most carefully that churches cannot safely be left without pastors. Wherever there is a large number of people, a pastor should be appointed over them. In saying that **every town** should have a pastor, Paul is not saying that no town should have more than one pastor, but that every town should have a pastor.

Elders or presbyters were not, of course, called by this name because of their age, for some men were still young – like Timothy – when they were chosen for this office. People who rule are called in all languages 'elders.' Although we may infer from 1 Timothy that there were two kinds of elders, it is clear that here teachers should be understood, that is, those who are ordained to teach, for almost immediately Paul will refer to the same people as presbyters.

6. To stop anyone from being angry with Titus for being too rigorous or severe in rejecting some people, Paul takes the whole blame on himself. He states that he has given explicit instructions that nobody should be admitted into this office who does not possess the qualifications he describes. So, as he has just declared that he had authorized Titus to preside as moderator at the appointment of pastors, so that other people would acknowledge his right in this matter, so now Paul describes the instructions he has given so that Titus may not be exposed to false accusations from evil or ignorant people. As this passage paints a picture of what an overseer should be like, we should note it carefully. But as I have already explained nearly everything here in my commentary on 1 Timothy 3, it will suffice to briefly mention the matter here.

By **blameless**, Paul does not mean that someone is free from every fault, for nobody is like that, but a person whose authority has not been undermined by some disgraceful action. An elder should have an unblemished reputation.

Married only once. Polygamy was so common among Jews that the depraved custom had almost become the rule. If anyone had married two wives before he became a Christian it would be almost inhuman to expect him to eject one of them. In this sense the apostles were prepared to tolerate a wrong, when they were unable to correct it. People who had already indulged in more than one marriage, even if they were now ready to demonstrate repentance by keeping only one wife, had already revealed their lack of self-control, which could tarnish their reputation. It is like saying that they should elect those who had lived in a chaste way, with just one wife, and exclude those whose lust had led them to have numerous wives. A person who was a widower because of his first wife's death, and who remarries, is to be thought of as a person who has one wife. Paul tells them to elect men who are at present husbands of one wife, not men who have been in this position.

Whose children are believers. Since prudence and earnestness are needed in a pastor, it is desirable that his family should share these qualities. For how can a man rule the church if he cannot control his own family?

Verses 7–9

7. For a bishop, as God's steward, must be blameless. Paul repeats that people who aspire to the office of overseer must have an untarnished reputation.

9. He must have a firm grip of the word that is trustworthy in accordance with the teaching. This is the first priority for a bishop who is especially chosen to teach, for the church cannot be governed unless it is through the word.

So that he may be able both to preach with sound doctrine and refute those who contradict it. A pastor needs two voices, one for gathering the sheep and the other for driving away wolves and thieves. The Scripture gives him the means for doing both, so that the person who has been correctly instructed in Scripture will be able to guide those who want to learn, and refute those who are enemies of the truth. Paul notes this double use of the Scripture when he says that he should be able to **encourage** and **refute**. This shows us what kind of knowledge a bishop should have, and how he should use it.

Verses 10–13a

10. Paul has laid down the general principle which is to be observed everywhere. To make Titus stick to it, Paul explains why it is essential and urgent for him to continue in this. Paul warns Titus that he has to cope with many obstinate and wild people, who may be puffed up with pride and idle talk, who deceive many people. So leaders need to be chosen who are qualified and well-equipped to deal with them. For if the children of this world are watchful in the face of danger, it would be disgraceful for us to sleep in false security, as if all was at peace, when Satan was gathering together all his forces against us.

11. They must be silenced. A good pastor should always be on the lookout in case his silence allows evil and dangerous teachings to creep in. He should not give wicked people any opportunity to spread them.

12. I am sure Paul is quoting here from Epimenides, who was a Cretan. For when Paul says **one of their own prophets** he is doubtless referring to someone who was born on Crete. Since the poet takes this from an old and well-known report, the apostle quotes it as if it is a proverbial saying. The Greek in question may be translated, 'A Cretan is a lying, lazy glutton, and always he will prove an evil brute.'

From this passage we deduce that there is no good reason not to make use of secular authors. Since all truth comes from God, if any ungodly person has said anything that is true, we should not reject it, for it also comes from God. Besides, since all things come from God, what is wrong with using to his glory everything that can be rightly used in that way? I refer the reader to Basil's essay on this subject, where he teaches young people about the benefit they can derive from ungodly authors.

13a. This testimony is true. However worthless the witness, Paul accepts the truth that he has spoken, for the Cretans undoubtedly were wicked people.

Verses 13b–16

13b. For this reason rebuke them sharply. One of the most important abilities required of a bishop is that he is able to adapt his teaching so that it applies to the people he addresses.

14. Paul now moves on to point out that sound faith is faith which is uncorrupted by any myths. And in guarding against the danger, Paul explains the remedy, not to listen to fables, for God wants us to be so absorbed in his Word that there will be no opportunity for empty trifles to force their way in. Once God's Word has gained entry, everything else will be so unattractive that it will have no place in our thinking. So if we want to keep our faith intact, we should learn to restrain our senses, so that they will not give way to such inventions. For as soon as a person begins to listen to fables, he will lose the purity of his faith.

Jewish myths. Paul calls all frivolous stories, myths, or, as we would say, trifles. For when Paul adds **to commandments of those who reject the truth** he is saying the same thing. Paul calls people who are not content with the pure teaching of Christ and who pollute it with their own corrupt thoughts, enemies of the truth. For everything that stems from human thought is to be thought of as a fable. Paul says that this fault is particularly true of the Jews, who were introducing superstitious ceremonies under the guise that they were obeying the divine law. The Gentiles realized that they had spent all their lives being deceived, so it was easier for them to forsake their way of life, but the Jews who had been brought up in true religion stubbornly defended the ceremonies they were used to, and could not be persuaded that the Law had been abrogated. In this way, they were upsetting all the churches, for as soon as the Gospel was planted in a particular place, they methodically begin to pollute it by adding their own leaven to it. So Paul singles out this pressing evil, so that they can be on their guard against it.

15. To the pure all things are pure. Paul touches on one example of their myths. The Jews still insisted that the distinctions between foods, and the purifications and washings that Moses had laid down for his day, were still essential for their own day. They derived most of their holiness from such practices. First, it enslaved people's consciences; and, second, people enslaved by these superstitions had a veil covering their eyes, which prevented them from progressing in their knowledge of Christ. If any Gentile refused to submit to this yoke, which was new to him, the Jews tried to force it on him, as they regarded it as the main article of faith. So Paul had good reason to set himself against such corruptions of the Gospel. In this passage, Paul not only refutes their error, but mocks their vanity in working so hard for no results, in their endeavour not to eat certain foods and so on.

16. Paul says these people are behaving like hypocrites who insist on minute observations, but flagrantly despise major parts of the Christian life. They expose their own vanity by showing their contempt for God in their public wrongdoing. People will draw attention to the fact that they are abstaining from a particular food, yet still indulge in great excesses, as if they were under no restraints whatsoever. Their behaviour is impure and full of wickedness, and their whole life has no virtue in it. By calling them **detestable,** Paul seems to be alluding to their pretense of being holy. Paul says that they achieve nothing, since they are still unholy and detestable. Paul has good reason to call them **disobedient,** for none are so proud as hypocrites, who wear themselves out with endless ceremonies so that they can break the chief requirements of the law with impunity. We may give the words **unfit for any good** an active meaning, as if Paul is saying that those who want to be thought of as being wise in trifling matters are devoid of judgment and understanding regarding good deeds.

Chapter 2

Verses 1–5

1. Paul points out how myths may be driven away, so that Titus can give himself over to edifying the church. Paul refers to **sound doctrine** as teaching which can build people up in godliness, for all trifles vanish when there is solid teaching. By telling him to **teach what is consistent with sound doctrine** Paul means that Titus must continually be teaching them. It would not be enough to mention these things just once or twice. Paul does not say that Titus should preach on one particular day, but that for as long as he holds the office of pastor Paul wants him to be preaching.

2. Paul starts with particular duties, in order to make his teaching relevant to the needs of his hearers – not just to suit what they could take in, but so that he could press home his teaching to every individual. General teaching is less effective, but when Paul reminds everyone about his own calling by citing a few examples, everyone becomes aware that the Lord has given him a clear enough command about what duty they should be engaged in. We must not look for any fixed scheme of teaching here, for Paul's aim was only to indicate briefly the topics godly teachers should deal with. Paul did not mean to go into each subject in detail.

Paul mentions **older men** first. He wants them **to be temperate**, as excessive drinking is an all too common fault in old age.

Serious. 'Gravity,' comes from well-regulated habits. There is nothing more disgraceful than for an old man to indulge in youthful lusts and through continuing to do this increase the shamelessness of the young. The life of an old man should engender respect from the young. From this self-control will naturally follow.

3. **Likewise, tell the older women to be reverent in behaviour.** We so often see elderly women either dressing with the frivolity of youth, or else wearing charms with their clothes; they rarely achieve the golden mean. Paul wanted to guard against both faults, and give a middle course suited both to decorum and to religious belief, or, to put it more simply, to show by the way they dressed that they were holy and godly.

4–5. To make them concentrate on their duties, Paul points out that it is not sufficient for them to lead decent lives themselves, unless they also **encourage the younger women** to live honourable and modest lives. So Paul tells them that through their example they should make these younger women sober in their minds, or else they will be carried away by the passions of youth.

Verses 6–10

6. Paul's only instruction to **the younger men** is that they should be taught how **to be self-controlled**, for self-control, as Plato teaches, sets right the whole human mind. It is as if Paul said, 'Let them be well regulated and obedient to reason.'

7. Teaching will have little authority unless its power and majesty shine in the life of a bishop, as in a mirror. Paul tells the teachers that they should set an example their pupils can follow.

8. **Sound speech** refers, in my view, to ordinary life and private conversation. It would be absurd to think it meant public instruction, since Paul's concern here is that Titus's behaviour should match his preaching. So Paul tells him that his words must be pure and free from all corruption.

9–10. **They are not to answer back, not to pilfer.** It may be observed that the apostle insists chiefly that those who are under the power of others should be obedient and submissive, and he has good reason to say this. For there is nothing more counter to man's natural disposition than submission.

10. **So that in everything they may be an ornament to the doctrine of God our Saviour.** This exhortation should spur us on greatly when we are told that through honourable behaviour we make the teaching about God attractive.

Verses 11–15

11. Paul bases his argument on God's purpose in redemption, which he shows to be zeal to live a godly and upright life. It follows on from this that it is the duty of a good teacher to exhort people to a holy life rather than to fill their minds with empty speculations. Zechariah said in his song, 'that we, being rescued from the hands of our enemies, might serve him without fear, in holiness and righteousness before him all our days' (Luke 1:74–75). In the same vein Paul says, 'the grace of God has appeared … instructing us.' Paul means that God's grace should instruct us so that we live the right sort of lives. Some are all too quick to use the preaching of God's mercy into an excuse for licentiousness, while carelessness keeps other people from thinking about the renewal of their lives. But the revelation of God's grace necessarily brings with it exhortations to a godly life.

12. **Training us to renounce.** Paul now lays down the rule by which we may live our lives rightly. He tells us that we should start by renouncing our former way of life, and he mentions two areas, **impiety and worldly passions.** Under **impiety** I include not only the superstitions in which they erred, but the neglect of God which exists among people until they have been enlightened by the knowledge of the truth.

Live lives that are self-controlled, upright and godly. Paul has already mentioned these three characteristics which give an overall summary of Christian living, and now he makes the same point again.

13. Paul finds a basis for his exhortation in the hope of future immortality, and certainly if that hope is firmly set in our minds, it will definitely lead us to devote ourselves wholly to God. On the other hand, those who continue to live for the world and the flesh have never really understood the importance of the promise of eternal life. For when the Lord calls us to heaven he takes away our desire for the world.

The manifestation of the glory of our great God and Saviour, Jesus Christ. I take **the manifestation of the glory** to mean not only the glory which God will have in himself, but also the glory which he will then spread everywhere so that all his elect share in it. Paul calls God **great** because his greatness, which people who are dazzled by the vanity of the world do not see, will be seen fully on the last day.

From this we learn, first, that our greatest incentive to increased activity and willingness to do good should be centred in the hope of a future resurrection. Second, believers should always have their eyes fixed on this, so that they will not become tired of following the right path, for, unless we depend wholly on this, we will always we swept away by the vanities of this world. But in case the Lord's coming frightens us, Christ is presented as the **Saviour**, and he is to be our future Judge.

14. Paul now appeals to the effect of Christ's death as the basis for his next exhortation. Christ offered himself for us so that he might redeem us from slavery to sin and purchase us for himself as his possession. New life comes with Christ's grace, for people who continue to serve sin make void the blessing of redemption. But we are now rescued from our slavery to sin so that we may serve God's righteousness.

15. This last verse is like an exhortation telling Titus to live all the time in this edifying teaching, and never to grow tired of it, as it cannot be emphasized enough. In addition to teaching, Paul says that Titus should use exhortations and reproofs, for people are not reminded about their duty enough, unless they are strongly urged to carry out their duties in this way. The person who understands everything that Paul has been saying, and always has it on his lips, will be able to correct as well as to teach.

With all authority. Paul tells Titus to claim for himself authority and respect in teaching these things. For people given over to curiosity and anger over trifles treat with contempt commands to live a godly and holy life. To overcome this antipathy, Titus is told to add the weight of his authority to his teaching. Paul adds the following words, **Let no one look down on you,** for the same reason.

Chapter 3

Verses 1–3

1. It is clear from many passages that the apostles had great difficulty in keeping the ordinary people in subjection to the authority of the **rulers and authorities.** By nature, we all want power and so no one wants to submit to anyone else. In addition to this, because nearly everyone in those days was opposed to Christ, they considered that his followers did not deserve to be noticed.

2. To speak evil of no one ... and to show every courtesy to everyone. Paul now states how they are to promote peace and friendship with everyone. We know that nothing is less congenial to human nature than to think less of ourselves than of others. Thus we boast about the gifts God has given us and go on to despise, and then insult, our brothers. So Paul tells them not to reproach other people, no matter how superior they believe they are to them. Paul is not condoning faults in ungodly people, he is only condemning the tendency people have to slander others.

3. For we ourselves were once foolish ... When we realize that the charges we level against others are true of us, we are prepared to keep our pride in check. The person who is trying to seek pardon for himself finds it easy to forgive others.

Verses 4–7

4. In this sentence either the principal clause is that God saved us by his mercy, or it is incomplete. If that is the case it would be better to understand it as saying that people are changed for the better and made new because God had mercy on them. It is as if Paul had said, 'You began to be different from others when God regenerated you by his Spirit.' But since Paul's words make sense as they stand, there is really no need to add to them. Paul includes himself along with the others so that his exhortation may be more efficacious.

The goodness and loving-kindness of God. God will never find in us anything worthy of his love, but he loves us because he is kind and merciful. Paul benefited from innumerable gifts of God before he was called to the faith of Christ, and he could have tasted God's fatherly kindness through these, as he had been brought up from infancy in the teachings of the Law. But Paul remained in darkness so that he had no sense of God's kindness until the Spirit enlightened his mind and Christ came as a witness and pledge of God the Father's grace. For without Christ we remain strangers to the Father's grace. So Paul is saying that God's loving kindness is revealed only by the light of faith.

5. He saved us, not because of any good works of righteousness that we had done, but according to his mercy, through the water of rebirth and renewal by the Holy Spirit. We must recall that Paul is talking to believers and is describing how they entered God's kingdom. Paul states that they have not in any way contributed to their own salvation. They have received this blessing solely through God's mercy. From these words we see that we can bring nothing to God, but that he goes before us, through the initiative of his pure grace, with no reference to any of our good deeds. For when he says **not because any works of righteousness that we have done** he means that until God regenerates us we can do nothing but sin.

He saved us. Paul speaks about faith and teaches that we have already received salvation. So although, since we are entangled in sin, we carry around a dead body, yet we are certain about our salvation, provided that we are engrafted into Christ through faith.

Through the water of rebirth. I am sure that there is at least an allusion here to baptism, and I do not object to this whole passage being explained in terms of baptism. But salvation is not obtained through the external symbol of water, but because baptism seals for us the salvation obtained by Christ. Paul is dealing with the manifestation of God's grace which, as we have said, consists of faith. As baptism is part of this revelation, in so far as it is meant to confirm faith, Paul is right to mention it here. Besides, since through baptism we enter into the church and since it is the symbol for being engrafted into Christ, it is appropriate for Paul to bring it in here, as he wants to show how God's grace has appeared to us. This is what this passage is saying: 'God saves us through his mercy, and he has given us a symbol and pledge of this salvation in baptism, through admitting us into his church, and engrafting us into the body of his Son.'

The apostles usually base an argument on the sacraments when they want to prove what is signified by them. It should be accepted as a fixed principle among godly people, that God does not tease us with empty symbols, but inwardly accomplishes through his own power what he shows us through the outward sign. Thus it is appropriate for baptism to be called **the washing of rebirth.** The power and use of the sacraments are correctly understood when we link the sign and the thing signified in such a way that the sign is not made useless in an inefficacious way, and when we do not, in an effort to exalt the sign, detract from what belongs to the Holy Spirit. Although ungodly people are neither washed nor renewed by baptism, it still retains its efficacy as far as God is concerned, for although they reject God's grace, it is still offered to them. But here, Paul is talking to believers in whom baptism is always efficacious and is therefore rightly spoken of in connection with its reality and effect. This way of speaking reminds us that if we do not want to make holy baptism null and void, we must prove its power by newness of life.

And renewal by the Holy Spirit. Although Paul mentions the sign to show God's grace to us very clearly, yet to stop us from focussing our whole attention on it, he quickly reminds us about the Spirit, so that we can understand that we are not washed by water but by God's power. 'I will sprinkle clean water upon you, and you will be clean from all your uncleannesses, and from all your idols ... I will put my Spirit within you, and make you follow my statutes' (Ezekiel 36:25, 27). Paul's words here agree completely with the prophet's. They are both saying the same thing. That is why I said at the beginning that, although Paul is dealing specifically with the Holy Spirit, he also alludes to baptism.

6. This Spirit he poured out on us richly. When Paul says **richly** he means that the more each of us excels in the greater gifts, the more we are indebted to God's mercy which alone enriches us, for in ourselves we are poor and devoid of anything good.

Through Jesus Christ. It is Christ alone in whom we are adopted. Thus it is through him that we participate in the Spirit who is the witness and guarantee of our adoption. Through this phrase Paul teaches that the Spirit of regeneration is given only to those who are members of Christ.

7. By his grace. This may refer to either Christ or to the Father, and we should not argue over this, because it always remains true that we have received righteousness by the grace of God through Christ.

We might become heirs according to the hope of eternal life. This clause is added like an explanatory note. Paul has said that we have been saved by God's mercy, but our salvation is still hidden, and he says now that we are heirs of life, not because we have yet attained this position, but because hope brings us full assurance about this. We may sum up what Paul says here, as follows: 'When we were dead we were restored to life through Christ's grace, when God the Father bestowed on us his Spirit, by whose power we are purified and renewed. This is our salvation. But because we are still in the world, we do not as yet enjoy eternal life, but receive it only through hoping.'

Verses 8–9

8. This saying is sure. This is how Paul introduces a solemn assertion. So Paul immediately adds, **I desires that you insist on these things.** The word **insist** means to affirm something strongly. Paul tells Titus here to ignore everything else and teach the things that are certain, and press them home, while other people are talking idly of things of little consequence. We conclude from this that a bishop should not be rash in asserting anything, but only those things which he has found out to be true. 'These,' says Paul, 'affirm, because they are true and deserve to be believed.' This reminds us that it is a bishop's duty to assert and strongly affirm things that are firmly established and which build up godliness.

Devote themselves to good works. Paul includes in this all the instructions he has given about the duties which belong to each individual.

9. But avoid stupid controversies, genealogies, dissensions, and quarrels about the law, for they are unprofitable and worthless. Paul contrasts **stupid controversies, genealogies, dissensions,** with sound teaching. For, while you have to seek in order to find, there is a limit to seeking in order that you may grasp what is worth knowing and hold firmly to the truth, once it is known. Those who inquire curiously into everything and are never at rest may truly be called 'questionarians.'

Paul mentions **genealogies** as one example of foolish questions. People forget to gather fruit from the sacred histories, and concentrate on the lineage of races and trifles of that kind. They tire themselves out with such things, but derive no profit from their labours.

Paul correctly adds **dissensions** because ambition is the motivating force behind controversies, and they are bound to end in quarrels, as everyone wants to win. This goes hand in hand with rash assertions about things which are not known about, which only provokes conflict.

Quarrels about the law. This is Paul's scornful description of the debates initiated by Jews who use the law as a pretext for debate. It is not that the law causes the quarrels but that these people, who pretend to defend the law, upset the church with absurd controversies about observing ceremonies, choosing foods, and such things.

These are unprofitable and worthless. When we teach, we should always be thinking about how useful the teaching is that we are giving. If it does not advance godliness, it should be cut out. Doubtless the sophists, in their ranting about useless things, boasted about them as if they were most worthwhile. But Paul does not allow anything which does not build up faith and a holy life.

Verses 10–15

10. After a first and second admonition, have nothing more to do with anyone who causes divisions. Paul had good reason to add this, as quarrels and altercations will never end if we desire to defeat obstinate people in argument. Such people never run out of words as they always have new strength from their wickedness, so they never tire of fighting. So, after telling Titus what kind of doctrine he should teach, Paul now tells him not to waste his time in debates with heretics, as one battle will always lead to another battle, and one dispute will give rise to a second. This is Satan's cunning strategy. He uses the evil talkativeness of such people to trap good and faithful pastors, in order to distract them from being devoted to their teaching. So we have to be alert not to allow ourselves becoming entangled in quarrelsome arguments, as we will then never be free to concentrate on the Lord's flock, and argumentative people will always hinder us.

When Paul told Titus to avoid such people, it is as if he said that he should not spend time in satisfying them, for they like nothing more than the opportunity to engage in a fight. This is a most necessary warning, as even people who are happy to take part in verbal battles are drawn into controversies, as they think they would lose face if they did not engage in battle in this way. But Paul does not want Christ's servants to become too involved in disputes with heretics.

After a first and second admonition. We have no right to decide that a person is a heretic or to reject him, unless we have first tried to restore his mind to a right way of thinking. When Paul talks about giving him a warning, he does not mean any kind of admonition, or one given to a private individual, but a warning given by a minister with the public authority of the church. These words amount to giving heretics a rebuke which consists of a public and severe censure.

11. Paul refers to such people as being **perverted** or 'ruined' when there is no hope of repentance for them. If there had been hope of restoring them through further efforts, we should certainly not withhold them. The metaphor is taken from a building which is not just partially destroyed, but completely demolished, so that it cannot be repaired.

13. Zenas the lawyer. We can deduce from what Paul says that **Zenas** was a poor man, in need of outside help. **See that they lack nothing.** From the context this means provide him with everything that is necessary for a journey.

14. To stop the Cretans complaining that this would be an extra burden for them to bear, Paul reminds them that they must not be unfruitful, and urges them to be zealous to engage in good deeds.

15. This concluding verse has already been explained in the other letters.

PHILEMON

J.B. Lightfoot

Introduction

The letter to Philemon holds a unique place among St. Paul's writings. It is the only strictly private letter which has been preserved. The Pastoral Letters indeed are addressed to individuals, but they discuss important matters of church discipline and government. Evidently they were intended to be read by others besides those to whom they are immediately addressed. On the other hand the letter to Philemon does not once mention any question of public interest. It is addressed apparently to a layman. It is wholly occupied with an incident of domestic life. The occasion which called it forth was altogether commonplace. It is only one sample of countless letters which must have been written to his many friends and disciples by one of St. Paul's eager temperament and warm affections, in the course of a long and chequered life. Yet, for us, this fragment, which has been rescued (we know not how) from the wreck of a large and varied correspondence, is infinitely precious. Nowhere is the social influence of the gospel more strikingly exerted; nowhere does the nobility of the apostle's character receive a more vivid illustration than in this accidental pleading on behalf of a runaway slave.

The people written to

The letter introduces us to an ordinary household in a small town in Phrygia. Four members of it are mentioned by name, the father, the mother, the son, and the slave.

1. Philemon

He was born, or at least, lived, in Colosse. This is seen by the fact that his slave is mentioned as belonging to that place. It may be added, to confirm this view, that in one of two letters written and sent at the same time St. Paul announces the restoration of Onesimus to his master, while in the other he speaks of this same person as revisiting Colosse (compare Corinthians 4:9 with Philemon 11ff.).

Philemon had been converted by St. Paul himself (verse 19). When and under what circumstances he received his first lessons in the gospel we do not know: but the apostle's long stay in Ephesus naturally suggests itself as the time when he was most likely to have met with a citizen of Colosse.

Philemon proved worthy of his spiritual heritage. Though to Epaphras belongs the chief glory of preaching the gospel at Colosse, his labours are well seconded by Philemon. The title of 'co-worker' (verse 1), conferred on him by the apostle, is a noble testimony to his evangelical zeal. Like Nymphas in the neighbouring church of Laodicea (Colossians 4:15), Philemon had placed his house at the disposal of the Christians at Colosse for their religious and social meetings (verse 2). Like Gaius (3 John 5ff.), to whom the only other private letter in the apostolic canon is written (assuming that 2 John is written to a church), he was generous with his hospitality. All those with whom he came into contact spoke with gratitude about his kindly attentions (verses 5, 7). Of his subsequent career we have no certain knowledge.

2. Apphia, the wife

It is a safe inference from the link between the names that Apphia was the wife of Philemon. From the overwhelming evidence of inscriptions, it is impossible to doubt that Apphia is a native Phrygian name. Of this Phrygian matron we know nothing more than can be gleaned from this letter.

3. Archippus, the son

With less confidence, but still with a reasonable degree of probability, we may infer that Archippus, who is also mentioned in the opening greeting, was a son of Philemon and Apphia.

4. Onesimus

But far more important to the history of Christianity than the parents or the son of the family is the servant. The name Onesimus was very common among slaves. Like other words meaning 'utility,' 'worth,' and so on, it naturally lent itself to this purpose. Onesimus represented the least respectable class in the social scale. He was regarded by philosophers as a live chattel, a living implement. He was treated in law as having no rights. He was now a thief and a runaway. Rome was the natural cesspool for these offscourings of humanity. In the dregs of the city rabble was his best hope of secrecy.

His encounter with St. Paul in Rome

But in Rome the apostle spread his net for him, and he was caught in its meshes. Whatever motive may have drawn him to the apostle's side – whether the pangs of hunger or the gnawings of conscience – when he was in his grip he could not escape. He listened, was impressed, was convinced, was baptized. The slave of Philemon became the freeman in Christ (1 Corinthians 7:22). St. Paul found not only a sincere convert but a devoted friend in his latest son in the faith. For St. Paul the conventional barrier between slave and free had completely vanished before the dissolving presence of an eternal truth (1 Corinthians 7:21ff.; Galatians 3:28; Colossians 3:11). St. Paul found in Onesimus something more than a slave, a beloved brother (verse 16). To take away Onesimus was to tear out St. Paul's heart (verse 12).

But there was a pressing reason for this sacrifice. Onesimus had repented, but he had not made restitution. He could only do this by submitting again to the servitude from which he had escaped. Philemon must be made to feel that when Onesimus was won for Christ, he was won back to his old master as well. But if the claim of duty demanded a great sacrifice from Paul, it demanded a greater still from Onesimus. By returning he would place himself entirely at the mercy of the master whom he had wronged. Roman law, more cruel than Athenian, gave limitless powers to a master over his slave. Life or death remained in Philemon's hands. Slaves were constantly crucified for far smaller offenses than his. As a thief and a runaway he had no claim to forgiveness.

Analysis of the letter

After the opening greetings to Philemon and the members of his family, St. Paul expresses his gratitude for the report which has reached his ears about his friend's charitable deeds. It is a great joy and encouragement to the apostle that so many brethren have had reason to bless his name. This widespread reputation for kindness makes him bold enough to reveal his purpose in writing. Though he has a right to command, he prefers to entreat. He has a petition to ask on behalf of a child of his own. This is none other than Onesimus, whom Philemon will remember only as a worthless creature, altogether untrue to his name, but who now is a reformed man. He wanted to keep Onesimus, for he can ill afford to dispense with his loving services. Indeed Philemon would doubtless have been glad thus to minister to the apostle's needs. But a benefit which has the appearance of being forced, whether truly so or not, loses all its value, and therefore he sends him back. Indeed, there may have been in this desertion a divine providence. Onesimus may have been withheld from Philemon for a time, that he might be restored to him forever. He may have left as a slave, that he might return more than a slave. To others – to the apostle himself especially – he is now a dearly beloved brother. Must he not be this and more than this to Philemon, whether in earthly things or in heavenly things? St. Paul therefore begs Philemon to receive Onesimus as he would receive himself. As for any injury that he may have done, as for any money that he may owe, the apostle makes himself responsible for this. The present letter may be accepted as a bond, a security for repayment. Yet at the same time he cannot refrain from reminding Philemon that he might fairly claim the remission of so small an amount. Does not his friend owe him his own soul? Yes, he has a right to look for some filial gratitude and duty from one to whom he stands as a spiritual father. Philemon will surely not refuse him this comfort in his many trials. St. Paul writes in the full confidence that he will be obeyed; he is quite sure that his friend will do more than is asked of him. At the same time he trusts to see him before very long, to talk over this and other matters. Philemon may provide him a lodging: for he hopes through their prayers that he may be liberated, and given back to them. Then follow the greetings, and the letter ends with the apostle's blessing.

Contents

See *Outlines of the New Testament Books,* p. 903

---

1. Prisoner. The authoritative title of 'apostle' is dropped, because throughout this letter St. Paul desires to entreat rather than to command (verses 8–9). In its place is put a designation which would touch his friend's heart. How could Philemon resist an appeal which was penned within prison walls and my a chained hand?

Timothy. Timothy seems to have been with St. Paul during a great part of his three years' stay in Ephesus (Acts 19:22), and could hardly have failed to make the acquaintance of Philemon.

Co-worker. It would probably be during St. Paul's long stay at Ephesus that Philemon had laboured with him.

2. Fellow-soldier. These spiritual campaigns, in which **Archippus** was his comrade, probably

took place while St. Paul was at Ephesus (A.D. 24–57).

4–7. The apostle's thanksgiving and intercessory prayer (verse 4) – the reason of his thanksgiving (verse 5) – the subject of his prayer (verse 6) – the joy and comfort which he has in Philemon's good deeds (verse 7) – this is the very simple order of topics in these verses.

5. Towards the Lord Jesus ... That is, 'the faith which you have towards the Lord Jesus Christ and the love which you show to all the saints.' The first and prominent thought is Philemon's love. This suggests the mention of his faith, as the source from which it springs. This again requires a reference to the object of faith. And then, at last, comes the deferred sequel to the first thought – the range and comprehensiveness of his love. The transition from the object of faith to the object of love is easier, because the love is represented as springing from faith.

6. The sharing of your faith … Of many interpretations which there have been two seem to deserve attention. First, 'Your friendly offices and sympathies, your kindly deeds of charity, which spring from your faith' (compare Philippians 1:5; Hebrews 13:16; Romans 15:26, 2 Corinthians 8:4; 9:13). Second, 'Your communion with God through faith': compare 1 Corinthians 1:9, and see also 2 Corinthians 13:13 and 1 John 1:3, 6–7. The parallel passages strongly support the former sense.

7. Refreshed. Compare verse 20. This compound expresses a temporary relief. Thus it implies 'relaxation, refreshment,' as a preparation for the renewal of labour or suffering.

Therefore. That is, 'Seeing that I have proofs of your love, I prefer to entreat, where I might command.'

9. On the basis of love. That is, 'having respect to the claims of love.' It is not Philemon's love (verses 5, 7), nor St. Paul's own love, but love absolutely, love regarded as a principle which demands a deferential respect.

I, Paul. The mention of his personal name involves an assertion of authority, as in Ephesians 3:1; compare Galatians 5:2.

A prisoner. Another title to respect. The mention of his bonds might suggest either an appeal for commiseration or a claim of authority. Here the addition of **Christ Jesus** invests it with the character of an official title, and so gives prominence to the latter idea.

10. I am appealing to you. So, too, 1 Corinthians 4:15. In Galatians 4:19 he speaks of himself as a mother's pangs for his children in the faith.

During my imprisonment. He was doubly dear to the apostle, as being the child of his sorrows.

13. So that he might be of service to me in your place. Compare Philippians 2:30 and 1 Corinthians 16:17. With a delicate tact the apostle assumes that Philemon would have wished to perform these friendly offices in person, if it had been possible.

15. For a while. 'For an hour,' 'for a short season': 2 Corinthians 7:8; Galatians 2:5. 'It was only a brief moment after all,' the apostle would say, 'compared with the magnitude of the work wrought in it.' He departed a reprobate; he returns a saved man. He departed for a few months; he returns to be with you for all time and for eternity! This sense of **for ever** [Greek: 'eternally'] must not be arbitrarily limited. Since he left, Onesimus had obtained eternal life, and eternal life involves eternal interchange of friendship. His services to his old master were no longer barred by the gates of death.

16. No longer as a slave. St. Paul does not say 'slave,' but **as a slave.** It was a matter of indifference whether he were outwardly 'slave' or outwardly 'free,' since both are one in Christ (Colossians 3:11). But though he might remain a slave, he could no longer be **as a slave.** A change had taken place in him, independently of his possible manumission: in Christ he had become a brother. The **no longer as a servant** is an absolute fact, whether Philemon chooses to recognize it or not.

17. If you consider me your partner. 'If you hold me to be a comrade, an intimate friend.' Those are 'partners' who have common interests, common feelings, common work.

18. If he has wronged you in any way. The case is stated hypothetically but the words doubtless describe the actual offense of Onesimus. He had done his master some injury, probably had robbed him; and he had fled to escape punishment.

19. I, Paul. The introduction of his own name gives it the character of a formal and binding signature: compare 1 Corinthians 16:21; Colossians 4:18; 2 Thessalonians 3:17. A signature to a deed in ancient or medieval times would commonly take this form – 'I – so and so.'

This incidental mention of his signature, occurring where it does, shows that he wrote the whole letter with his own hand. This procedure is quite exceptional, just as the reason for the letter is exceptional. In all other cases he appears to have employed an amanuensis, only adding a few words in his own handwriting at the close.

Even your own self. St. Paul was his spiritual father, who had given birth to him in the faith, and to whom therefore he owed his being.

20. Brother. It is the entreaty of a brother to a brother on behalf of a brother (verse 16).

21. You will do even more than I say. What was the uppermost thought in the apostle's mind when he penned these words? Did he contemplate the manumission of Onesimus? If so, the restraint which he imposes on himself is significant. Indeed throughout this letter the idea would seem to be present in his mind, though the word never passes his lips. This reserve is eminently characteristic of the gospel. Slavery is never directly attacked as such, but principles are inculcated which must prove fatal to it.

22. When St. Paul first contemplated visiting Rome, he had intended, after leaving the metropolis, to travel west to Spain; Romans 15:24, 28. But by this time he appears to have altered his plans, wishing first to revisit Greece and Asia Minor. Thus in Philippians 2:24 he looks forward to seeing the Philippians shortly; while here he contemplates a visit to the churches of the Lycus valley.

There is a gentle compulsion in this mention of a personal visit to Colosse. The apostle would thus be able to see for himself that Philemon had not disappointed his expectations.

23. Epaphras is mentioned first because he was a Colossian (Colossians 4:12) and, as the evangelist of Colosse, doubtless well known to Philemon. Of the four others, Aristarchus and Mark belonged to the Circumcision (Colossians 4:11) while Demas and Luke were Gentile Christians. All these were of Greek or Asiatic origin and would probably be well known to Philemon, at least by name. On the other hand Jesus Justus, who is honourably mentioned in the Colossian letter (Colossians 4:11), but passed over here, may have been a Roman Christian.

HEBREWS

John Wesley

Introduction

It is agreed by the general tenor of antiquity that this epistle was written by St. Paul, whose other epistles were sent to the gentile converts; this only to the Hebrews. But this improper inscription was added by some later hand. It was sent to the Jewish Hellenist Christians, dispersed through various countries. St. Paul's method and style are easily observed therein. He places, as usual, the proposition and division before the treatise, Heb 2:17; he subjoins the exhortatory to the doctrinal part, quotes the same scriptures, Heb 1:6; 2:8; 10:30,38,6; and uses the same expressions as elsewhere. But why does he not prefix his name, which, it is plain from Heb 13:19 was dear to them to whom he wrote? Because he prefixes no inscription, in which, if at all, the name would have been mentioned. The ardour of his spirit carries aim directly upon his subject (just like St. John in his First Epistle) and throws back his usual salutation and thanksgiving to the conclusion.

This epistle of St. Paul, and both those of St. Peter (one may add, that of St. James and of St. Jude also) were written both to the same persons, dispersed through Pontus, Galatia, and other countries, and nearly at the same time. St. Paul suffered at Rome, three years before the destruction of Jerusalem. Therefore this epistle likewise, was written while the temple was standing. St. Peter wrote a little before his martyrdom, and refers to the epistles of St. Paul; this in particular.

The scope of it is to confirm their faith in Christ; and this he does by demonstrating his glory. All the parts of it are full of the most earnest and pointed admonitions and exhortations; and they go on in one tenor, the particle therefore everywhere connecting the doctrine and the use.

Contents

See *Outlines of the New Testament Books,* pp. 903–4

Chapter 1

1. God, who at sundry times – The creation was revealed in the time of Adam; the last judgment, in the time of Enoch: and so at various times, and in various degrees, more explicit knowledge was given. **In divers manners** – In visions, in dreams, and by revelations of various kinds. Both these are opposed to the one entire and perfect revelation which he has made to us by Jesus Christ. The very number of the prophets showed that they prophesied only 'in part.' **Of old** – There were no prophets for a large tract of time before Christ came, that the great Prophet might be the more earnestly expected. **Spake** – A part is put for the whole; implying every kind of divine communication. **By the prophets** – The mention of whom is a virtual declaration that the apostle received the whole Old Testament, and was not about to advance any doctrine in contradiction to it. **Hath in these last times** – Intimating that no other revelation is to be expected. **Spoken** – All things, and in the most perfect manner. **By his Son** – Alone. The Son spake by the apostles.

The majesty of the Son of God is proposed:

1.Absolutely, by the very name of Son, verse 1, and by three glorious predicates, – 'whom he hath appointed,' 'by whom he made,' who 'sat down;' whereby he is described from the beginning to the consummation of all things, Heb 1:2,3.

2.Comparatively to angels, Heb 1:4. The proof of this proposition immediately follows: the name of Son being proved, Heb 1:5; his being 'heir of all things,' Heb 1:6–9; his making the worlds, Heb 1:10–12 his sitting at God's right hand, Heb 1:13, &c.

2. Whom he hath appointed heir of all things – After the name of Son, his inheritance is mentioned. God appointed him the heir long before he made the worlds, Eph 3:11; Prov 8:22, &c. The Son is the firstborn, born before all things: the heir is a term relating to the creation which followed, Heb 1:6. **By whom he also made the worlds** – Therefore the Son was before all worlds. His glory reaches from everlasting to everlasting, though God spake by him to us only 'in these last days.'

3. Who sat down – The third of these glorious predicates, with which three other particulars are interwoven, which are mentioned likewise, and in the same order, Col 1:15,17,20. **Who, being** – The glory which he received in his exaltation at the right hand of the Father no angel was capable of; but the Son alone, who likewise enjoyed it long before. **The brightness of his glory** – Glory is the nature of God revealed in its brightness. **The express image** – Or stamp. Whatever the Father is, is exhibited in the Son, as a seal in the stamp on wax. **Of his person** – Or substance. The word denotes the unchangeable perpetuity of divine life and power. **And sustaining all things** – Visible and invisible, in being. **By the word of his power** – That is, by his powerful word. **When he had by himself** – Without any Mosaic rites or ceremonies. **Purged our sins** – In order to which it was necessary he should for a time divest himself of his glory. In this chapter St. Paul describes his glory chiefly as he is the Son of God; afterwards, Heb 2:6, &c., the glory of the man Christ Jesus. He speaks, indeed, briefly of the former before his humiliation, but copiously after his exaltation; as from hence the glory he had from eternity began to be evidently seen. Both his purging our sins, and sitting on the right hand of God, are largely treated of in the seven following chapters. **Sat down** – The priests stood while they ministered: sitting, therefore, denotes the consummation of his sacrifice. This word, sat down, contains the scope, the theme, and the sum, of the epistle.

4.This verse has two clauses, the latter of which is treated of, Heb 1:5; the former, Heb 1:13. Such transpositions are also found in the other epistles of St. Paul, but in none so frequently as in this. The Jewish doctors were peculiarly fond of this figure, and used it much in all their writings. The apostle therefore, becoming all things to all men, here follows the same method. All the inspired writers were readier in all the figures of speech than the most experienced orators. **Being** – By his exaltation, after he had been lower than them, Heb 2:9. **So much higher than the angels** – It was extremely proper to observe this, because the Jews gloried in their law, as it was delivered by the ministration of angels. How much more may we glory in the gospel, which was given, not by the ministry of angels, but of the very Son of God! **As he hath by inheritance a more excellent name** – Because he is the Son of God, he inherits that name, in right whereof he inherits all things His inheriting that name is more ancient than all worlds; his inheriting all things, as ancient as all things. **Than they** – This denotes an immense pre-eminence. The angels do not inherit all things, but are themselves a portion of the Son's inheritance, whom they worship as their Lord.

5. Thou art my Son – God of God, Light of Light. **This day have I begotten thee** – I have begotten thee from eternity, which, by its unalterable permanency of duration, is one continued day. **I will be to him a Father, and he shall be to me a Son** – I will own myself to be his Father, and him to be my Son, by eminent tokens of my peculiar love The former clause relates to his natural Sonship, by an eternal, inconceivable generation; the other, to his Father's acknowledgment and treatment of him as his incarnate Son. Indeed this promise related immediately to Solomon, but in a far higher sense to the Messiah. Psa. 2:7; Sam. 7:14.

6. And again – That is, in another scripture. **He** – God. **Saith, when he Bridget in his first** – **begotten** – This appellation includes that of Son, together with the rights of primogeniture, which the first–begotten Son of God enjoys, in a manner not communicable to any creature. **Into the world** – Namely, at his incarnation. **He saith, Let all the angels of God worship him** – So much higher is he, when in his lowest estate, than the highest angel. Psa. 97:7.

7. Who maketh his angels – This implies, they are only creatures, whereas the Son is eternal, Heb 1:8; and the Creator himself, Heb 1:10. **Spirits and a flame of fire** – Which intimates not only their office, but also their nature; which is excellent indeed, the metaphor being taken from the most swift, subtle, and efficacious things on earth; but nevertheless infinitely below the majesty of the Son. Psa. 104:4.

8. O God – God, in the singular number, is never in scripture used absolutely of any but the supreme God. **Thy reign**, of which the sceptre is the ensign, is full of justice and equity. Psa. 45:6,7.

9. Thou hast loved righteousness and hated iniquity – Thou art infinitely pure and holy. **Therefore God** – Who, as thou art Mediator, is thy God. **Hath anointed thee with the oil of gladness** – With the Holy Ghost, the fountain of joy. **Above thy fellows** – Above all the children of men.

10. Thou – The same to whom the discourse is addressed in the preceding verse. Psa. 102:25,26.

12. As a mantle – With all ease. **They shall be changed** – Into new heavens and a new earth. But thou art eternally the same.

13. Psa. 110:1.

14. Are they not all – Though of various orders. **Ministering spirits, sent forth** – Ministering before God, sent forth to men. **To attend on them** – In numerous offices of protection, care, and kindness. **Who** – Having patiently continued in welldoing, shall inherit everlasting salvation.

Chapter 2

In this and the two following chapters the apostle sub-joins an exhortation, answering each head of the preceding chapter.

1. Lest we should let them slip – As water out of a leaky vessel. So the Greek word properly signifies.

2. In giving the law, God spoke by angels; but in proclaiming the gospel, by his Son. Steadfast – Firm and valid. **Every transgression** – Commission of sin. **Every disobedience** – Omission of duty.

3. So great a salvation – A deliverance from so great wickedness and misery, into so great holiness and happiness. This was first spoken of (before he came it was not known) by Him who is **the Lord** – of angels as well as men. And **was confirmed to us** – Of this age, even every article of it. **By them that had heard him** – And had been themselves also both eye-witnesses and ministers of the word.

4. By signs and wonders – While he lived. And various **miracles** and **distributions of the Holy Ghost** – Miraculous gifts, distributed after his exaltation. **According to his will** – Not theirs who received them.

5. This verse contains a proof of the third; the greater the salvation is, and the more glorious the Lord whom we despise, the greater will be our punishment. God hath not subjected the world to come – That is, the dispensation of the Messiah; which being to succeed the Mosaic was usually styled by the Jews, the world to come, although it is still in great measure to come. **Whereof we now speak** – Of which I am now speaking. In this last great dispensation the Son alone presides.

6. What is man – To the vast expanse of heaven, to the moon and the stars which thou hast ordained! This psalm seems to have been composed by David, in a clear, moonshiny, and starlight night, while he was contemplating the wonderful fabric of heaven; because in his magnificent description of its luminaries, he takes no notice of the sun, the most glorious of them all. The words here cited concerning dominion were doubtless in some sense applicable to Adam; although in their complete and highest sense, they belong to none but the second Adam. **Or the son of man, that thou visitest him** – The sense rises: we are mindful of him that is absent; but to visit, denotes the care of a present God. Psa. 8:4.

7. Thou hast made him – Adam. **A little lower than the angels** – The Hebrew is, a little lower than (that is, next to) God. Such was man as he came out of the hands of his Creator: it seems, the highest of all created beings. But these words are also in a farther sense, as the apostle here shows, applicable to the Son of God. It should be remembered that the apostles constantly cited the Septuagint translation, very frequently without any variation. It was not their business, in writing to the Jews, who at that time had it in high esteem, to amend or alter this, which would of consequence have occasioned disputes without end.

8. Now this putting all things under him, implies that there is nothing that is not put under him. But it is plain, this is not done now, with regard to man in general.

9. It is done only with regard to Jesus, God-Man, who is now **crowned with glory and**

honour – As a reward for his having suffered death. **He was made a little lower than the angels** – Who cannot either suffer or die. **That by the grace of God, he might taste death** – An expression denoting both the reality of his death, and the shortness of its continuance. **For every man** – That ever was or will be born into the world.

10. In this verse the apostle expresses, in his own words, what he expressed before in those of the Psalmist. **It became him** – It was suitable to all his attributes, both to his justice, goodness, and wisdom. **For whom** – As their ultimate end. **And by whom** – As their first cause. **Are all things, in bringing many adopted sons to glory** – To this very thing, that they are sons, and are treated as such **To perfect the captain** – Prince, leader, and author of their salvation, by his atoning sufferings for them. To perfect or consummate implies the bringing him to a full and glorious end of all his troubles, Heb 5:9. This consummation by sufferings intimates:

1. The glory of Christ, to whom, being consummated, all things are made subject.

2. The preceding sufferings.

Of these he treats expressly, Heb 2:11-18; having before spoken of his glory, both to give an edge to his exhortation, and to remove the scandal of sufferings and death. A fuller consideration of both these points he interweaves with the following discourse on his priesthood. But what is here said of our Lord's being made perfect through sufferings, has no relation to our being saved or sanctified by sufferings. Even he himself was perfect, as God and as man, before ever be suffered. By his sufferings, in his life and death, he was made a perfect or complete sin-offering. But unless we were to be made the same sacrifice, and to atone for sin, what is said of him in this respect is as much out of our sphere as his ascension into heaven. It is his atonement, and his Spirit carrying on 'the work of faith with power' in our hearts, that alone can sanctify us. Various afflictions indeed may be made subservient to this; and so far as they are blessed to the weaning us from sin, and causing our affections to be set on things above, so far they do indirectly help on our sanctification.

11. **For** – They are nearly related to each other. **He that sanctifieth** – Christ, Heb 13:12. **And all they that are sanctified** – That are brought to God; that draw near or come to him, which are synonymous terms. **Are all of one** – Partakers of one nature, from one parent, Adam.

12. **I will declare thy name to my brethren** – Christ declares the name of God, gracious and merciful, plenteous in goodness and truth, to all who believe, that they also may praise him. **In the midst of the church will I sing praise unto thee** – As the precentor of the choir. This he did literally, in the midst of his apostles, on the night before his passion. And as it means, in a more general sense, setting forth the praise of God, he has done it in the church by his word and his Spirit; he still does, and will do it throughout all generations. Psa. 22:22.

13. **And again** – As one that has communion with his brethren in sufferings, as well as in nature, he says, **I will put my trust in him** – To carry me through them all. **And again** – With a like acknowledgment of his near relation to them, as younger brethren, who were yet but in their childhood, he presents all believers to God, saying, Behold I and the children whom thou hast given me. Isa 8:17,18.

14. **Since then these children partake of flesh and blood** – Of human nature with all its infirmities. He also in like manner took part of the same; that through his own death he might destroy the tyranny of him that had, by God's permission, the power of death with regard to the ungodly. Death is the devil's servant and serjeant, delivering to him those whom he seizes in sin. **That is, the devil** – The power was manifest to all; but who exerted it, they saw not.

15. **And deliver them, as many as through fear of death were all their lifetime, till then, subject to bondage** – Every man who fears death is subject to bondage; is in a slavish, uncomfortable state. And every man fears death, more or less, who knows not Christ: death is unwelcome to him, if he knows what death is. But he delivers all true believers from this bondage.

16. **For verily he taketh not hold of angels** – He does not take their nature upon him. **But he taketh hold of the seed of Abraham** – He takes human nature upon him. St. Paul says the seed of Abraham, rather than the seed of Adam, because to Abraham was the promise made.

17. **Wherefore it behoved him** – It was highly fit and proper, yea, necessary, in order to his design of redeeming them. **To be made in all things** – That essentially pertain to human nature, and in all sufferings and temptations. **Like his brethren** – This is a recapitulation of all that goes before: the sum of all that follows is added immediately. **That he might be a merciful and faithful High Priest** – Merciful toward sinners; faithful toward God. A priest or high priest is one who has a right of approaching God, and of bringing others to him.

Faithful is treated of, Heb 3:2, &c., with its use;

merciful, Heb 4:14, &c., with the use also;

High Priest, Heb 5:4, &c., Heb 7:1, &c. The use is added from Heb 10:19.

In things pertaining to God, to expiate the sins of the people – Offering up their sacrifices and prayers to God; deriving God's grace, peace, and blessings upon them.

18. **For in that he hath suffered being tempted himself he is able to succour them that are tempted** – That is, he has given a manifest, demonstrative proof that he is able so to do.

Chapter 3

1. **The heavenly calling** – God calls from heaven, and to heaven, by the gospel. **Consider the Apostle** – The messenger of God, who pleads the cause of God with us. **And High Priest** – Who pleads our cause with God. Both are contained in the one word Mediator. He compares Christ, as an Apostle, with Moses; as a Priest, with Aaron. Both these offices, which Moses and Aaron severally bore, he bears together, and far more eminently. **Of our profession** – The religion we profess.

2. **His house** – The church of Israel, then the peculiar family of God. Num 12:7.

3. **He that hath builded it hath more glory than the house** – Than the family itself, or any member of it.

4. **Now Christ, he that built not only this house, but all things, is God** – And so infinitely greater than Moses or any creature.

5. **And Moses verily** – Another proof of the pre-eminence of Christ above Moses. **Was faithful in all his house, as a servant, for a testimony of the things which were afterwards to be spoken** – That is, which was a full confirmation of the things which he afterward spake concerning Christ.

6. **But Christ** was faithful **as a Son; whose house we are,** while we hold fast, and shall be unto the end, if we hold fast our confidence in God, and glorying in his promises; our faith and hope.

7. **Wherefore** – Seeing he is faithful, be not ye unfaithful. Psa. 95:7.

8. **As in the provocation** – When Israel provoked me by their strife and murmurings. **In the day of temptation** – When at the same time they tempted me, by distrusting my power and goodness. Exod 17:7.

9. **Where your fathers** – That hard–hearted and stiff-necked generation. So little cause had their descendants to glory in them. **Tempted me** – Whether I could and would help them. **Proved me** – Put my patience to the proof, even while they saw my glorious works both of judgment and mercy, and that for forty years.

10. **Wherefore** – To speak after the manner of men. **I was grieved** – Displeased, offended with **that generation, and said, They always err in their hearts** – They are led astray by their stubborn will and vile affections. **And** – For this reason, because wickedness has blinded their understanding. **They have not known my ways** – By which I would have led them like a flock. **Into my rest** – In the promised land.

12. **Take heed, lest there be in any of you** – As there was in them. **An evil heart of unbelief** – Unbelief is the parent of all evil, and the very essence of unbelief lies in **departing from God, as the living God** – The fountain of all our life, holiness, happiness.

13. **But,** to prevent it, **exhort one another, while it is called To-day** – This to-day will not last for ever. The day of life will end soon, and perhaps the day of grace yet sooner.

14. **For we are made partakers of Christ** – And we shall still partake of him and all his benefits, if we hold fast our faith unto the end. **If** – But not else; and a supposition made by the Holy Ghost is equal to the, strongest assertion. Both the sentiment and the manner of expression are the same as Heb 3:6.

16. **Were they not all that came out of Egypt** – An awful consideration! The whole elect people of God (a very few excepted) provoked God presently after their great deliverance, continued to grieve his Spirit for forty years, and perished in their sin!

19. **So we see they could not enter in** – Though afterward they desired it.

Chapter 4

2. **But the word which they heard did not profit them** – So far from it, that it increased their damnation. It is then only when it is mixed with faith, that it exerts its saving power.

3. **For we only that have believed enter into the rest** – The proposition is, There remains a rest for us. This is proved, Heb 4:3–11, thus: That psalm mentions a rest: yet it does not mean:

1. God's rest from creating; for this was long before the time of Moses. Therefore in his time another rest was expected, of which they who then heard fell short Nor is it;

2. The rest which Israel obtained through Joshua; for the Psalmist wrote after him. Therefore it is;

3. The eternal rest in heaven.

As he said – Clearly showing that there is a farther rest than that which followed the finishing of the creation. **Though the works were finished** – Before: whence it is plain, God did not speak of resting from them.

4. **For,** long after he had rested from his works, he speaks again. Gen 2:2.

5. In this psalm, of a rest yet to come.

7. **After so long a time** – It was above four hundred years from the time of Moses and Joshua to David. **As it was said before** – St. Paul here refers to the text he had just cited.

8. **The rest** – All the rest which God had promised.

9. **Therefore** – Since he still speaks of another day, there must remain a farther, even an eternal, rest for the people of God.

10. For they do not yet so rest. Therefore a fuller rest remains for them.

11. Lest any one should fall – Into perdition.

12. For the word of God – Preached, Heb 4:2, and armed with threatenings, Heb 4:3. **Is living and powerful** – Attended with the power of the living God, and conveying either life or death to the hearers. **Sharper than any two-edged sword** – Penetrating the heart more than this does the body. **Piercing** – Quite through, and laying open. **The soul and spirit, joints and marrow** – The inmost recesses of the mind, which the apostle beautifully and strongly expresses by this heap of figurative words. **And is a discerner** – Not only of the thoughts, but also of the intentions.

13. In his sight – It is God whose word is thus 'powerful:' it is God in whose sight every creature is manifest; and of this his word, working on the conscience, gives the fullest conviction. **But all things are naked and opened** – Plainly alluding to the sacrifices under the law which were first flayed, and then (as the Greek word literally means) cleft asunder through the neck and backbone; so that everything both without and within was exposed to open view.

14. Having therefore a great high priest – Great indeed, being the eternal Son of God, that is **passed through the heavens** – As the Jewish high priest passed through the veil into the holy of holies, carrying with him the blood of the sacrifices, on the yearly day of atonement; so our great high priest went once for all through the visible heavens, with the virtue of his own blood, into the immediate presence God.

15. He sympathizes with us even in our innocent infirmities, wants, weaknesses, miseries, dangers. **Yet without sin** – And, therefore, is indisputably able to preserve us from it in all our temptations.

16. Let us therefore come boldly – Without any doubt or fear. Unto the throne of God, our reconciled Father, even his **throne of grace** – Grace erected it, and reigns there, and dispenses all blessings in a way of mere, unmerited favour.

Chapter 5

1. For every high priest being taken from among men – Is, till he is taken, of the same rank with them. **And is appointed** – That is, is wont to be appointed. **In things pertaining to God** – To bring God near to men, and men to God. **That he may offer both gifts** – Out of things inanimate, and animal sacrifices.

2. Who can have compassion – In proportion to the offence: so the Greek word signifies. **On the ignorant** – Them that are in error. **And the wandering** – Them that are in sin. **Seeing himself also is compassed with infirmity** – Even with sinful infirmity; and so needs the compassion which he shows to others.

4. The apostle begins here to treat of the priesthood of Christ. The sum of what he observes concerning it is, Whatever is excellent in the Levitical priesthood is in Christ, and in a more eminent manner; and whatever is wanting in those priests is in him. **And no one taketh this honour** – The priesthood. **To himself, but he that is called of God, as was Aaron** – And his posterity, who were all of them called at one and the same time. But it is observable, Aaron did not preach at all; preaching being no part of the priestly office.

5. So also Christ glorified not himself to be an high priest – That is, did not take this honour to himself, but received it from him who said, **Thou art my Son, this day have I begotten thee** – Not, indeed, at the same time; for his generation was from eternity. Psa. 2:7.

6. Psa. 110:4.

7. The sum of the things treated of in the seventh and following chapters is contained, Heb 5:7–10; and in this sum is admirably comprised the process of his passion, with its inmost causes, in the very terms used by the evangelists. **Who in the days of his flesh** – Those two days, in particular, wherein his sufferings were at the height. **Having offered up prayers and supplications** – Thrice. **With strong crying and tears** – In the garden. **To him that was able to save him from death** – Which yet he endured, in obedience to the will of his Father. **And being heard in that which he** particularly **feared** – When the cup was offered him first, there was set before him that horrible image of a painful, shameful, accursed death, which moved him to pray conditionally against it: for, if he had desired it, his heavenly Father would have sent him more than twelve legions of angels to have delivered him. But what he most exceedingly feared was the weight of infinite justice; the being 'bruised' and 'put to grief' by the hand of God himself. Compared with this, everything else was a mere nothing; and yet, so greatly did he ever thirst to be obedient to the righteous will of his Father, and to 'lay down' even 'his life for the sheep,' that he vehemently longed to be baptized with this baptism, Lu 12:50. Indeed, his human nature needed the support of Omnipotence; and for this he sent up strong crying and tears: but, throughout his whole life, he showed that it was not the sufferings he was to undergo, but the dishonour that sin had done to so holy a God, that grieved his spotless soul. The consideration of its being the will of God tempered his fear, and afterwards swallowed it up; and he was heard not so that the cup should pass away, but so that he drank it without any fear.

8. Though he were a Son – This is interposed, lest any should be offended at all these instances of human weakness. In the garden, how frequently did he call God his Father! Mt 26:39,

&c. And hence it most evidently appears that his being the Son of God did not arise merely from his resurrection. **Yet learned he** – The word learned, premised to the word suffered, elegantly shows how willingly he learned. He learned obedience, when be began to suffer; when he applied himself to drink that cup: obedience in suffering and dying.

9. **And being perfected** – By sufferings, Heb 2:10; brought through all to glory. **He became the author** – The procuring and efficient cause. **Of eternal salvation to all that obey him** – By doing and suffering his whole will.

10. **Called** – The Greek word here properly signifies surnamed. His name is, 'the Son of God.' The Holy Ghost seems to have concealed who Melchisedec was, on purpose that he might be the more eminent type of Christ. **This only we know,** – that he was a priest, and king of Salem, or Jerusalem.

11. **Concerning whom** – The apostle here begins an important digression, wherein he reproves, admonishes, and exhorts the Hebrews. **We** – Preachers of the gospel. Have **many things to say, and hard to be explained** – Though not so much from the subject-matter, as from your slothfulness in considering, and dulness in apprehending, the things of God.

12. **Ye have need that one teach you again which are the first principles** of religion. Accordingly these are enumerated in the first verse of the ensuing chapter. **And have need of milk** – The first and plainest doctrines.

13. **Every one that useth milk** – That neither desires, nor can digest, anything else: otherwise strong men use milk; but not milk chiefly, and much less that only. **Is unexperienced in the word of righteousness** – The sublimer truths of the gospel. Such are all who desire and can digest nothing but the doctrine of justification and imputed righteousness.

14. **But strong meat** – These sublimer truths relating to 'perfection,' Heb 6:1. **Belong to them of full age, who by habit** – Habit here signifies strength of spiritual understanding, arising from maturity of spiritual age. By, or in consequence of, this habit they exercise themselves in these things with ease, readiness, cheerfulness, and profit.

Chapter 6

1. **Therefore leaving the principles of the doctrine of Christ** – That is, saying no more of them for the present. **Let us go on to perfection; not laying again the foundation of repentance from dead works** – From open sins, the very first thing to be insisted on. **And faith in God** – The very next point. So St. Paul in his very first sermon at Lystra, Acts 14:15, 'Turn from those vanities unto the living God.' And when they

believed, they were to be baptized with the baptism, not of the Jews, or of John, but of Christ. The next thing was, to lay hands upon them, that they might receive the Holy Ghost: after which they were more fully instructed, touching the resurrection, and the general judgment; called eternal, because the sentence then pronounced is irreversible, and the effects of it remain for ever.

3. **And this we will do** – We will go on to perfection; and so much the more diligently, because,

4. **It is impossible for those who were once enlightened** – With the light of the glorious love of God in Christ. **And have tasted the heavenly gift** – Remission of sins, sweeter than honey and the honeycomb. **And been made partakers of the Holy Ghost** – Of the witness and the fruit of he Spirit.

5. **And have tasted the good word of God** – Have had a relish for, and a delight in it. **And the powers of the world to come** – Which every one tastes, who has an hope full of immortality. Every child that is naturally born, first sees the light, then receives and tastes proper nourishment, and partakes of the things of this world. In like manner, the apostle, comparing spiritual with natural things, speaks of one born of the Spirit, as seeing the light, tasting the sweetness, and partaking of the things **of the world to come.**

6. **And have fallen away** – Here is not a supposition, but a plain relation of fact. The apostle here describes the case of those who have cast away both the power and the form of godliness; who have lost both their faith, hope, and love, Heb 6:10, and that wilfully, Heb 10:26. Of these wilful total apostates he declares, it is impossible to renew them again to repentance. (though they were renewed once) either to the foundation, or anything built thereon. **Seeing they crucify the Son of God afresh** – They use him with the utmost indignity. **And put him to an open shame** – Causing his glorious name to be blasphemed.

8. **That which beareth thorns and briers** – Only or chiefly. **Is rejected** – No more labour is bestowed upon it. **Whose end is to be burned** – As Jerusalem was shortly after.

9. **But, beloved** – in this one place he calls them so. He never uses this appellation, but in exhorting. **We are persuaded of you things that accompany salvation** – We are persuaded you are now saved from your sins; and that ye have that faith, love, and holiness, which lead to final salvation. **Though we thus speak** – To warn you, lest you should fall from your present steadfastness.

10. **For** – Ye give plain proof of your faith and love, which the righteous God will surely reward.

11. But we desire you may show the same diligence unto the end – And therefore we thus speak. To the full assurance of hope – Which you cannot expect, if you abate your diligence. The full assurance of faith relates to present pardon; the full assurance of hope, to future glory. The former is the highest degree of divine evidence that God is reconciled to me in the Son of his love; the latter is the same degree of divine evidence (wrought in the soul by the same immediate inspiration of the Holy Ghost) of persevering grace, and of eternal glory. So much, and no more, as faith every moment 'beholds with open face,' so much does hope see to all eternity But this assurance of faith and hope is not an opinion, not a bare construction of scripture, but is given immediately by the power of the Holy Ghost; and what none can have for another, but for himself only.

12. Inherited the promises – The promised rest; paradise.

13. For – Ye have abundant encouragement, seeing no stronger promise could be made than that great promise which God made to Abraham, and in him to us.

14. Gen 22:17.

15. After he had waited – Thirty years. He obtained the promise – Isaac, the pledge of all the promises.

16. Men generally swear by him who is infinitely greater than themselves, and an oath for confirmation, to confirm what is promised or asserted, usually puts an end to all contradiction. This shows that an oath taken in a religious manner is lawful even under the gospel: otherwise the apostle would never have mentioned it with so much honour, as a proper means to confirm the truth.

17. God interposed by an oath – Amazing condescension! He who is greatest of all acts as if he were a middle person; as if while he swears, he were less than himself, by whom he swears! Thou that hearest the promise, dost thou not yet believe?

18. That by two unchangeable things – His promise and his oath, in either, much more in both of which, it was impossible for God to lie, we might have strong consolation – Swallowing up all doubt and fear. Who have fled – After having been tossed by many storms. To lay hold on the hope set before us – On Christ, the object of our hope, and the glory we hope for through him.

19. Which hope in Christ we have as an anchor of the soul – Entering into heaven itself, and fixed there. Within the veil – Thus he slides back to the priesthood of Christ.

20. A forerunner uses to be less in dignity than those that are to follow him. But it is not so here; for Christ who is gone before us is infinitely superior to us. What an honour is it to believers, to have so glorious a forerunner, now appearing in the presence of God for them.

Chapter 7

1. The sum of this chapter is, Christ, as appears from his type, Melchisedec, who was greater than Abraham himself, from whom Levi descended, has a priesthood altogether excellent, new, firm, perpetual. Gen 14:18.

2. Being first – According to the meaning of his own name. King of righteousness, then – According to the name of his city. King of peace – So in him, as in Christ, righteousness and peace were joined. And so they are in all that believe in him.

3. Without father, without mother, without pedigree – Recorded, without any account of his descent from any ancestors of the priestly order. Having neither beginning of days, nor end of life – Mentioned by Moses. But being – In all these respects. Made like the Son of God – Who is really without father, as to his human nature; without mother, as to his divine; and in this also, without pedigree – Neither descended from any ancestors of the priestly order. Remaineth a priest continually – Nothing is recorded of the death or successor of Melchisedec. But Christ alone does really remain without death, and without successor.

4. The greatness of Melchisedec is described in all the preceding and following particulars. But the most manifest proof of it was, that Abraham gave him tithes as to a priest of God and a superior; though he was himself a patriarch, greater than a king, and a progenitor of many kings.

5. The sons of Levi take tithes of their brethren – Sprung from Abraham as well as themselves. The Levites therefore are greater than they; but the priests are greater than the Levites, the patriarch Abraham than the priests, and Melchisedec than him.

6. He who is not from them – The Levites blessed – Another proof of his superiority. Even him that had the promises – That was so highly favoured of God. When St. Paul speaks of Christ, he says, 'the promise;' promises refer to other blessings also.

7. The less is blessed – Authoritatively, of the greater.

8. And here – In the Levitical priesthood. But there – In the case of Melchisedec. He of whom it is testified that he liveth – Who is not spoken of as one that died for another to succeed him; but is represented only as living, no mention being made either of his birth or death.

9. And even Levi, who received tithes – Not in person, but in his successors, as it were, paid tithes – In the person of Abraham.

11. The apostle now demonstrates that the Levitical priesthood must yield to the priesthood

of Christ, because Melchisedec, after whose order he is a priest

1. Is opposed to Aaron, Heb 7:11–14.

2. Hath no end of life, Heb 7:15–19,

but 'remaineth a priest continually.' **If now perfection were by the Levitical priesthood** – If this perfectly answered all God's designs and man's wants. **For under it the people received the law** – Whence some might infer, that perfection was by that priesthood. **What further need was there, that another priest** – Of a new order, should be set up? From this single consideration it is plain, that both the priesthood and the law, which were inseparably connected, were now to give way to a better priesthood and more excellent dispensation.

12. **For** – One of these cannot be changed without the other.

13. But the priesthood is manifestly changed from one order to another, and from one tribe to another. **For he of whom these things are spoken** – Namely, Jesus. **Pertaineth to another tribe** – That of Judah. Of which no man was suffered by the law to attend on, or minister at, the altar.

14. **For it is evident that our Lord sprang out of Judah** – Whatever difficulties have arisen since, during so long a tract of time, it was then clear beyond dispute.

15. **And it is still far more evident, that** – Both the priesthood and the law are changed, because the priest now raised up is not only of another tribe, but of a quite different order.

16. **Who is made** – A priest. **Not after the law of a carnal commandment** – Not according to the Mosaic law, which consisted chiefly of commandments that were carnal, compared to the spirituality of the gospel. **But after the power of an endless life** – Which he has in himself, as the eternal Son of God.

18. For there is implied in this new and everlasting priesthood, and in the new dispensation connected therewith, a **disannulling of the preceding commandment** – An abrogation of the Mosaic law. **For the weakness and unprofitableness thereof** – For its insufficiency either to justify or to sanctify.

19. **For the law** – Taken by itself, separate from the gospel. **Made nothing perfect** – Could not perfect its votaries, either in faith or love, in happiness or holiness. **But the bringing in of a better hope** – Of the gospel dispensation, which gives us a better ground of confidence, does. **By which we draw nigh to God** – Yea, so nigh as to be one spirit with him. And this is true perfection.

20. **And** – The greater solemnity wherewith he was made priest, farther proves the superior excellency of his priesthood.

21. **The Lord sware and will not repent** – Hence also it appears, that his is an unchangeable priesthood.

22. **Of so much better a covenant** – Unchangeable, eternal. **Was Jesus made a surety** – Or mediator. The word covenant frequently occurs in the remaining part of this epistle. The original word means either a covenant or a last will and testament. St. Paul takes it sometimes in the former, sometimes in the latter, sense; sometimes he includes both.

23. **They were many priests** – One after another.

24. **He continueth for ever** – In life and in his priesthood. **That passeth not away** – To any successor.

25. **Wherefore he is able to save to the uttermost** – From all the guilt, power, root, and consequence of sin. **Them who come** – By faith. **To God through him** – As their priest. **Seeing he ever liveth to make intercession** – That is, he ever lives and intercedes. He died once; he intercedes perpetually.

26. **For such an high priest suited us** – Unholy, mischievous, defiled sinners: a blessed paradox! **Holy** – With respect to God. **Harmless** – With respect to men. **Undefiled** – With any sin in himself. **Separated from sinners** – As well as free from sin. And so he was when he left the world. **And made** – Even in his human nature. **Higher than the heavens** – And all their inhabitants.

27. **Who needeth not to offer up sacrifices daily** – That is, on every yearly day of expiation; for he offered once for all: not for his own sins, for he then offered up himself 'without spot to God.'

28. **The law maketh men high priests that have infirmity** – That are both weak, mortal, and sinful. **But the oath which was since the law** – Namely, in the time of David. **Maketh the Son, who is consecrated for ever** – Who being now free, both from sin and death, from natural and moral infirmity, remaineth a priest for ever.

Chapter 8

1. **We have such an high priest** – Having finished his description of the type in Melchisedec, the apostle begins to treat directly of the excellency of Christ's priesthood, beyond the Levitical. **Who is set down** – Having finished his oblation. **At the right hand of the Majesty** – Of God.

2. **A minister** – Who represents his own sacrifice, as the high priest did the blood of those sacrifices once a year. **Of the sanctuary** – Heaven, typified by the holy of holies. **And of the true tabernacle** – Perhaps his human nature, of which the old tabernacle was a type. **Which the Lord hath fixed** – Forever. **Not man** – As Moses fixed the tabernacle.

4. **But if he were on earth** – If his priesthood terminated here. **He could not be a priest** – At

all, consistently with the Jewish institutions. **There being other priests** – To whom alone this office is allotted.

5. Who serve – The temple, which was not yet destroyed. **After the pattern and shadow of heavenly things** – Of spiritual, evangelical worship, and of everlasting glory. **The pattern** – Somewhat like the strokes pencilled out upon a piece of fine linen, which exhibit the figures of leaves and flowers, but have not yet received their splendid colours and curious shades. **And shadow** – Or shadowy representation, which gives you some dim and imperfect idea of the body, but not the fine features, not the distinguishing air; none of those living graces which adorn the real person. Yet both the pattern and shadow lead our minds to something nobler than themselves: the pattern, to that holiness and glory which complete it; the shadow, to that which occasions it. Ex 25:40.

6. And now he hath obtained a more excellent ministry – His priesthood as much excels theirs, as the promises of the gospel (whereof he is a surety) excels those of the law. These better promises are specified, Heb 8:10,11: those in the law were mostly temporal promises.

7. For if the first had been faultless – If that dispensation had answered all God's designs and man's wants, if it had not been weak and unprofitable unable to make anything perfect, no place would have been for a second.

8. But there is; for finding fault with them – Who were under the old covenant he saith, I **make a new covenant with the house of Israel** – With all the Israel of God, in all ages and nations. It is new in many respects, though not as to the substance of it:

1. Being ratified by the death of Christ.

2. Freed from those burdensome rites and ceremonies.

3. Containing a more full and clear account of spiritual religion.

4. Attended with larger influences of the Spirit

5. Extended to all men. And, 6.Never to be abolished. Jer 31:31.

9. When I took them by the hand – With the care and tenderness of a parent. And just while this was fresh in their memory, they obeyed; but presently after they shook off the yoke. **They continued not in my covenant, and I regarded them not** – So that covenant was soon broken in pieces.

10. This is the covenant I will make after those days – After the Mosaic dispensation is abolished. **I will put my laws in their minds** – I will open their eyes, and enlighten their understanding, to see the true, full, spiritual meaning thereof. **And write them on their hearts** – So that they shall inwardly experience whatever I have commanded. **And I will be to them a God**

– Their all-sufficient portion, and exceeding great reward. **And they shall be to me a people** – My treasure, my beloved, loving, and obedient children.

11. And they who are under this covenant (though in other respects they will have need to teach each other to their lives' end, yet) **shall not need to teach every one his brother, saying, Know the Lord; for they shall all know me** – All real Christians. **From the least to the greatest** – In this order the saving knowledge of God ever did and ever will proceed; not first to the greatest, and then to the least. But 'the Lord shall save the tents,' the poorest, 'of Judah first, that the glory of the house of David,' the royal seed, 'and the glory of the inhabitants of Jerusalem,' the nobles and the rich citizens, 'do not magnify themselves,' Zec 12:7.

**12. For I will justify them, which is the root of all true knowledge of God. This, therefore, is God's method. First, a sinner is pardoned: then he knows God, as gracious and merciful then God's laws are written on his heart: he is God's, and God is his.

13. In saying, A new covenant, he hath antiquated the first – Hath shown that it is disannulled, and out of date. **Now that which is antiquated is ready to vanish away** – As it did quickly after, when the temple was destroyed.

Chapter 9

1. The first covenant had ordinances of outward worship, and a worldly – a visible, material sanctuary, or tabernacle. Of this sanctuary he treats, Heb 9:2–5. Of those ordinances, Heb 9:6–10.

2. The first – The outward tabernacle. **In which was the candlestick, and the table** – The showbread, shown continually before God and all the people, consisting of twelve loaves, according to the number of the tribes, was placed on this table in two rows, six upon one another in each row. This candlestick and bread seem to have typified the light and life which are more largely dispensed under the gospel by Him who is the Light of the world, and the Bread of life.

3. The second veil divided the holy place from the most holy, as the first veil did the holy place from the courts.

4. Having the golden censer – Used by the high priest only, on the great day of atonement. **And the ark,** or chest, **of the covenant** – So called from the tables of the covenant contained therein. **Wherein was the manna** – The monument of God's care over Israel. **And Aaron's rod** – The monument of the regular priesthood. **And the tables of the covenant** – The two tables of stone, on which the ten commandments were written by the finger of God the most venerable monument of all.

5. **And over it were the cherubim of glory** – Over which the glory of God used to appear. Some suppose each of these had four faces, and so represented the Three – One God, with the manhood assumed by the Second Person. With out-spread wings **shadowing the mercy-seat** – Which was a lid or plate of gold, covering the ark.

6. **Always** – Every day. **Accomplishing their services** – Lighting the lamps, changing the showbread, burning incense, and sprinkling the blood of the sin offerings.

7. **Errors** – That is, sins of ignorance, to which only those atonements extended.

8. **The Holy Ghost evidently showing** – By this token. **That the way into the holiest** – Into heaven. **Was not made manifest** – Not so clearly revealed. **While the first tabernacle, and its service, were still subsisting** – And remaining in force.

9. **Which** – Tabernacle, with all its furniture and services. **Is a figure** – Or type, of good things to come. **Which cannot perfect the worshipper** – Neither the priest nor him who brought the offering. **As to his conscience** – So that he should be no longer conscious of the guilt or power of sin. Observe, the temple was as yet standing.

10. They could not so perfect him, with all their train of precepts relating to meats and drinks, and carnal, gross, external ordinances; and were therefore **imposed only till the time of reformation** – Till Christ came.

11. **An high priest of good things to come** – Described, Heb 9:15. Entered through **a greater**, that is, a **more noble, and perfect tabernacle** – Namely, his own body. **Not of this creation** – Not framed by man, as that tabernacle was.

12. **The holy place** – Heaven. **For us** – All that believe.

13. **If the ashes of an heifer** – Consumed by fire as a sin-offering, being sprinkled on them who were legally unclean. **Purified the flesh** – Removed that legal uncleanness, and re-admitted them to the temple and the congregation. Nu 19:17,18,19.

14. **How much more shall the blood of Christ** – The merit of all his sufferings. **Who through the eternal Spirit** – The work of redemption being the work of the whole Trinity. Neither is the Second Person alone concerned even in the amazing condescension that was needful to complete it. The Father delivers up the kingdom to the Son; and the Holy Ghost becomes the gift of the Messiah, being, as it were, sent according to his good pleasure. **Offered himself** – Infinitely more precious than any created victim, and that without spot to God. **Purge our conscience** – Our inmost soul. **From dead works** – From all the inward and outward works of the devil, which spring from

spiritual death in the soul, and lead to death everlasting. **To serve the living God** – In the life of faith, in perfect love and spotless holiness.

15. **And for this end he is the Mediator of a new covenant, that they who are called** – To the engagements and benefits thereof. **Might receive the eternal inheritance** promised to Abraham: not by means of legal sacrifices, but of his meritorious death. **For the redemption of the transgressions that were under the first covenant** – That is, for the redemption of transgressors from the guilt and punishment of those sins which were committed in the time of the old covenant. The article of his death properly divides the old covenant from the new.

16. I say by means of death; **for where such a covenant is, there must be the death of him by whom it is confirmed** – Seeing it is by his death that the benefits of it are purchased. It seems beneath the dignity of the apostle to play upon the ambiguity of the Greek word, as the common translation supposes him to do.

17. **After he is dead** – Neither this, nor after men are dead is a literal translation of the words. It is a very perplexed passage.

18. **Whence neither was the first** – The Jewish covenant, originally transacted without the blood of an appointed sacrifice.

19. **He took the blood of calves** – Or heifers. **And of goats, with water, and scarlet wool, and hyssop** – All these circumstances are not particularly mentioned in that chapter of Exodus, but are supposed to be already known from other passages of Moses. **And the book** itself – Which contained all he had said. **And sprinkled all the people** – Who were near him. The blood was mixed with water to prevent its growing too stiff for sprinkling; perhaps also to typify that blood and water, John 19:34. Ex 24:7,8.

20. **Saying, This is the blood of the covenant which God hath enjoined me to deliver unto you** – By this it is established. Ex 24:8.

21. **And in like manner he ordered the tabernacle** – When it was made, and all its vessels, to be sprinkled with blood once a year.

22. **And almost all things** – For some were purified by water or fire. **Are according to the law purified with blood** – Offered or sprinkled. And according to the law, **there is no forgiveness of sins without shedding of blood** – All this pointed to the blood of Christ effectually cleansing from all sin, and intimated, there can be no purification from it by any other means.

23. **Therefore** – That is, it plainly appears from what has been said. **It was necessary** – According to the appointment of God. That the tabernacle and all its utensils, which were **patterns**, shadowy representations, **of things in heaven, should be purified by these** – Sacrifices and sprinklings. **But the heavenly things themselves** – Our heaven-born spirits: what more

this may mean we know not yet. **By better sacrifices than these** – That is, by a better sacrifice, which is here opposed to all the legal sacrifices, and is expressed plurally, because it includes the signification of them all, and is of so much more eminent virtue.

24. For Christ did not enter into the holy place made with hands – He never went into the holy of holies at Jerusalem, the figure of the true tabernacle in heaven, Heb 8:2. **But into heaven itself, to appear in the presence of God for us** – As our glorious high priest and powerful intercessor.

26. For then he must often have suffered from the foundation of the world – This supposes:

1. That by suffering once he atoned for all the sins which had been committed from the foundation of the world.

2. That he could not have atoned for them without suffering.

At the consummation of the ages – The sacrifice of Christ divides the whole age or duration of the world into two parts, and extends its virtue backward and forward, from this middle point wherein they meet to abolish both the guilt and power of sin.

27. After this, the judgment – Of the great day. At the moment of death every man's final state is determined. But there is not a word in scripture of a particular judgment immediately after death.

28. Christ having once died to bear the sins – The punishment due to them. **Of many** – Even as many as are born into the world. **Will appear the second time** – When he comes to judgment. **Without sin** – Not as he did before, bearing on himself the sins of many, but to bestow everlasting salvation.

Chapter 10

1. From all that has been said it appears that the law, the Mosaic dispensation, being a bare, unsubstantial shadow of good things to come, of the gospel blessings, and not the substantial, solid image of them, can never with the same kind of sacrifices, though continually repeated, make the comers thereunto perfect, either as to justification or sanctification. How is it possible, that any who consider this should suppose the attainments of David, or any who were under that dispensation, to be the proper measure of gospel holiness; and that Christian experience is to rise no higher than Jewish?

2. They who had been **once** perfectly **purged**, would have been no longer conscious either of the guilt or power of their sins.

3. There is a public commemoration of the sins both of the last and of all the preceding years; a clear proof that the guilt thereof is not perfectly purged away.

4. It is impossible the blood of goats should take away sins – Either the guilt or the power of them.

5. When he cometh into the world – In the fortieth psalm the Messiah's coming into the world is represented. It is said, into the world, not into the tabernacle, Heb 9:1; because all the world is interested in his sacrifice. **A body hast thou prepared for me** – That I may offer up myself. Psa. 40:6.

7. In the volume of the book – In this very psalm it is written of me. **Accordingly I come to do thy will** – By the sacrifice of myself.

8. Above when he said, Sacrifice thou hast not chosen – That is, when the Psalmist pronounced those words in his name.

9. Then said he – in that very instant he subjoined. Lo, I come to do Thy will – To offer a more acceptable sacrifice; and by this very act he taketh away the legal, that he may establish the evangelical, dispensation.

10. By which will – Of God, done and suffered by Christ. **We are sanctified** – Cleansed from guilt, and consecrated to God.

11. Every priest standeth – As a servant in an humble posture.

12. But he – The virtue of whose one sacrifice remains for ever. **Sat down** – As a son, in majesty and honour.

13. Psa. 110:1.

14. He hath perfected them for ever – That is, has done all that was needful in order to their full reconciliation with God.

15. In this and the three following verses, the apostle winds up his argument concerning the excellency and perfection of the priesthood and sacrifice of Christ. He had proved this before by a quotation from Jeremiah; which he here repeats, describing the new covenant as now completely ratified, and all the blessings of it secured to us by the one offering of Christ, which renders all other expiatory sacrifices, and any repetition of his own, utterly needless.

16. Jer 31:33.

19. Having finished the doctrinal part of his epistle, the apostle now proceeds to exhortation deduced from what has been treated of Heb 5:4, which he begins by a brief recapitulation. Having therefore liberty to enter –

20. By a living way – The way of faith, whereby we live indeed. **Which he hath consecrated** – Prepared, dedicated, and established for us. **Through the veil, that is, his flesh** – As by rending the veil in the temple, the holy of holies became visible and accessible; so by wounding the body of Christ, the God of heaven was manifested, and the way to heaven opened.

22. Let us draw near – To God. **With a true heart** – In godly sincerity. **Having our hearts sprinkled from an evil conscience** – So as to condemn us no longer. **And our bodies washed**

with pure water – All our conversation spotless and holy, which is far more acceptable to God than all the legal sprinklings and washings.

23. The profession of our hope – The hope which we professed at our baptism.

25. Not forsaking the assembling ourselves – In public or private worship. **As the manner of some is** – Either through fear of persecution, or from a vain imagination that they were above external ordinances. **But exhorting one another** – To faith, love, and good works. **And so much the more, as ye see the day approaching** – The great day is ever in your eye.

26. For when we – Any of us Christians. **Sin wilfully** – By total apostasy from God, termed 'drawing back,' Heb 10:38. After having received the experimental knowledge of the gospel truth, **there remaineth no more sacrifice for sins** – None but that which we obstinately reject.

28. He that, in capital cases, **despised** (presumptuously transgressed) **the law of Moses died without mercy** – Without any delay or mitigation of his punishment.

29. Of how much sorer punishment is he worthy, who – By wilful, total apostasy. It does not appear that this passage refers to any other sin. **Hath,** as it were, **trodden underfoot the Son of God** – A lawgiver far more honourable than Moses. And counted the blood wherewith the better covenant was established, an unholy, a common, worthless thing. **By which he hath been sanctified** – Therefore Christ died for him also, and he was at least justified once. **And done despite to the Spirit of grace** – By rejecting all his motions.

30. The Lord will judge his people – Yea, far more rigorously than the heathens, if they rebel against him. Deut 32:35.

31. To fall into the hands – Of his avenging justice.

32. Enlightened – With the knowledge of God and of his truth.

34. For ye sympathized with all your suffering brethren, and with me in particular; and received joyfully the loss of your own goods.

35. Cast not away therefore this your confidence – Your faith and hope; which none can deprive you of but yourselves.

36. The promise – Perfect love; eternal life.

37. He that cometh – To reward every man according to his works.

38. Now the just – The justified person. **Shall live** – In God's favour, a spiritual and holy life. **By faith** – As long as he retains that gift of God. **But if he draw back** – If he make shipwreck of his faith. **My soul hath no pleasure in him** – That is, I abhor him; I cast him off. Hab 2:3.

39. We are not of them who draw back to perdition – Like him mentioned Heb 10:38. **But of them that believe** – To the end, so as to attain eternal life.

Chapter 11

1. The definition of faith given in this verse, and exemplified in the various instances following, undoubtedly includes justifying faith, but not directly as justifying. For faith justifies only as it refers to, and depends on, Christ. But here is no mention of him as the object of faith; and in several of the instances that follow, no notice is taken of him or his salvation, but only of temporal blessings obtained by faith. And yet they may all be considered as evidences of the power of justifying faith in Christ, and of its extensive exercise in a course of steady obedience amidst difficulties and dangers of every kind.

Now faith is the subsistence of things hoped for, the evidence or conviction of things not seen – Things hoped for are not so extensive as things not seen. The former are only things future and joyful to us; the latter are either future, past, or present, and those either good or evil, whether to us or others. **The subsistence of things hoped for** – Giving a kind of present subsistence to the good things which God has promised: the divine supernatural evidence exhibited to, the conviction hereby produced in, a believer of things not seen, whether past, future, or spiritual; particularly of God and the things of God.

2. By it the elders – Our forefathers. This chapter is a kind of summary of the Old Testament, in which the apostle comprises the designs, labours, sojournings, expectations, temptations, martyrdoms of the ancients. The former of them had a long exercise of their patience; the latter suffered shorter but sharper trials. **Obtained a good testimony** – A most comprehensive word. God gave a testimony, not only of them but to them: and they received his testimony as if it had been the things themselves of which he testified, Heb 11:4,5,39. Hence they also gave testimony to others, and others testified of them.

3. By faith we understand that the worlds – Heaven and earth and all things in them, visible and invisible. **Were made** – Formed, fashioned, and finished. **By the word** – The sole command of God, without any instrument or preceding matter. And as creation is the foundation and specimen of the whole divine economy, so faith in the creation is the foundation and specimen of all faith. **So that things which are seen** – As the sun, earth, stars. **Were made of things which do not appear** – Out of the dark, unapparent chaos, Gen 1:2. And this very chaos was created by the divine power; for before it was thus created it had no existence in nature.

4. By faith – In the future Redeemer. **Abel offered a more excellent sacrifice** – The firstlings of his flock, implying both a confession of what his own sins deserved, and a desire of sharing in the great atonement. **Than Cain** – Whose offering testified no such faith, but a bare acknowledgment of God the Creator. By which faith he obtained both righteousness and a testimony of it: **God testifying** – Visibly that his gifts were accepted; probably by sending fire from heaven to consume his sacrifice, a token that justice seized on the sacrifice instead of the sinner who offered it. **And by it** – By this faith. **Being dead, he yet speaketh** – That a sinner is accepted only through faith in the great sacrifice.

5. **Enoch** was not any longer found among men, though perhaps they sought for him as they did for Elijah, 2Kin 2:17. **He had this testimony** – From God in his own conscience.

6. **But without faith** – Even some divine faith in God, it is impossible to please him. **For he that cometh to God** – in prayer, or another act of worship, must believe that he is.

7. **Noah being warned of things not seen as yet** – Of the future deluge. **Moved with fear, prepared an ark,** by which open testimony **he condemned the world** – Who neither believed nor feared.

8. Gen 12:1,4,5.

9. **By faith he sojourned in the land of promise** – The promise was made before, Gen 12:7. **Dwelling in tents** – As a sojourner. **With Isaac and Jacob** – Who by the same manner of living showed the same faith Jacob was born fifteen years before the death of Abraham. **The joint heirs of the same promise** – Having all the same interest therein. Isaac did not receive this inheritance from Abraham, nor Jacob from Isaac, but all of them from God. Gen 17:8.

10. **He looked for a city which hath foundations** – Whereas a tent has none. **Whose builder and former is God** – Of which God is the sole contriver, former, and finisher.

11. **Sarah also herself** – Though at first she laughed at the promise, Gen 18:12. Gen 21:2.

12. **As it were dead** – Till his strength was supernaturally restored, which continued for many years after.

13. **All these** – Mentioned Heb 11:7–11. **Died in faith** – In death faith acts most vigorously. **Not having received the promises** – The promised blessings. **Embraced** – As one does a dear friend when he meets him.

14. **They who speak thus show plainly that they seek their own country** – That they keep in view, and long for, their native home.

15. **If they had been mindful of** – Their earthly country, Ur of the Chaldeans, they might have easily returned.

16. **But they desire a better country, that is, an heavenly** – This is a full convincing proof that the patriarchs had a revelation and a promise of eternal glory in heaven. **Therefore God is not ashamed to be called their God: seeing he hath prepared for them a city** – Worthy of God to give.

17. **By faith Abraham** – When God made that glorious trial of him. **Offered up Isaac** – The will being accepted as if he had actually done it. **Yea, he that had received the promises** – Particularly that grand promise, 'In Isaac shall thy seed be called.' **Offered up** – This very son; the only one he had by Sarah. Gen 22:1.

18. **In Isaac shall thy seed be called** – From him shall the blessed seed spring. Gen 21:12.

19. **Accounting that God was able even to raise him from the dead** – Though there had not been any instance of this in the world. **From whence also** – To speak in a figurative way. **He did receive him** – Afterwards, snatched from the jaws of death.

20. **Blessed** – Gen 27:27,39; prophetically foretold the particular blessings they should partake of. **Jacob and Esau** – Preferring the elder before the younger.

21. **Jacob when dying** – That is, when near death. **Bowing down on the top of his staff** – As he sat on the side of his bed. Gen 48:16; Gen 47:31.

22. **Concerning his bones** – To be carried into the land of promise.

23. **They saw** – Doubtless with a divine presage of things to come.

24. **Refused to be called** – Any longer.

26. **The reproach of Christ** – That which he bore for believing in the Messiah to come, and acting accordingly. **For he looked off** – From all those perishing treasures, and beyond all those temporal hardships. **Unto the recompense of reward** – Not to an inheritance in Canaan; he had no warrant from God to look for this, nor did he ever attain it; but what his believing ancestors looked for – a future state of happiness in heaven.

27. **By faith he left Egypt** – Taking all the Israelites with him. **Not then fearing the wrath of the king** – As he did many years before, Ex 2:14. Ex 14:15.

28. **The pouring out of the blood** – Of the paschal lamb, which was sprinkled on the doorposts, lest the destroying angel should touch the Israelites. Ex 12:12–18.

29. **They** – Moses, Aaron, and the Israelites. **Passed the Red Sea** – It washed the borders of Edom, which signifies red. Thus far the examples are cited from Genesis and Exodus; those that follow are from the former and the latter Prophets.

30. By the faith of Joshua.

31. **Rahab** – Though formerly one not of the fairest character.

32. After Samuel, the prophets are properly mentioned. David also was a prophet; but he was a king too. **The prophets** – Elijah, Elisha, including likewise the believers who lived with them.

33, 34. David, in particular, **subdued kingdoms.** Samuel (not excluding the rest) **wrought** righteousness. The prophets, in general, obtained promises, both for themselves, and to deliver to others. Prophets also stopped the mouths of lions, as Daniel; and quenched the violence of fire, as Shadrach, Meshach, and Abednego. To these examples, whence the nature of faith clearly appears, those more ancient ones are subjoined (by a transposition, and in an inverted order) which receive light from these. Jephthah escaped the edge of the sword; Samson out of weakness was made strong; Barak became valiant in fight; Gideon put to flight armies of the aliens. Faith animates to the most heroic enterprises, both civil and military. Faith overcomes all impediments effects the greatest things; attains to the very best; and inverts, by its miraculous power the very course of nature. See 2Sa 8:1,&c.; 1Sa 8:9,&c.; 1Sa 13:3; Da 6:22; Da 3:27; Jud 12:3; Jud 15:19; Jud 16:28,&c.; Jud 4:14,&c.; Jud 7:21.

34. See note ... 'Heb 11:33'

35. Women – Naturally weak. **Received their dead** – Children. **Others were tortured** – From those who acted great things the apostle rises higher, to those who showed the power of faith by suffering. **Not accepting deliverance** – On sinful terms. **That they might obtain a better resurrection** – An higher reward, seeing the greater their sufferings the greater would be their glory. See 1Kin 17:22; 2Kin 4:35.

36. And others – The apostle seems here to pass on to recent examples.

37. They were sawn asunder – As, according to the tradition of the Jews, Isaiah was by Manasseh. **Were tempted** – Torments and death are mentioned alternately. Every way; by threatenings, reproaches, tortures, the variety of which cannot be expressed; and again by promises and allurements.

38. Of whom the world was not worthy – It did not deserve so great a blessing. **They wandered** – Being driven out from men.

39. And all these – Though they obtained a good testimony, Heb 11:2, yet did not receive the great promise, the heavenly inheritance.

40. God having provided some better thing for us – Namely, everlasting glory. **That they might not be perfected without us** – That is, that we might all be perfected together in heaven.

Chapter 12

1. Wherefore, being encompassed with a cloud – A great multitude, tending upward with a holy swiftness. **Of witnesses** – Of the power of faith. **Let us lay aside every weight** – As all who run a race take care to do. Let us throw off whatever weighs us down, or damps the vigour of our Soul. **And the sin which easily besetteth us** – As doth the sin of our constitution, the sin of our education, the sin of our profession.

2. Looking – From all other things. **To Jesus** – As the wounded Israelites to the brazen serpent. Our crucified Lord was prefigured by the lifting up of this; our guilt, by the stings of the fiery serpents; and our faith, by their looking up to the miraculous remedy. **The author and finisher of our faith** – Who begins it in us, carries it on, and perfects it. **Who for the joy that was set before him** – Patiently and willingly endured the cross, with all the pains annexed thereto. **And is set down** – Where there is fulness of joy.

3. Consider – Draw the comparison and think. The Lord bore all this; and shall his servants bear nothing? **Him that endured such contradiction from sinners** – Such enmity and opposition of every kind. **Lest ye be weary** – Dull and languid, and so actually faint in your course.

4. Unto blood – Unto wounds and death.

5. And yet ye seem already to have forgotten the exhortation – Wherein God speaketh to you with the utmost tenderness. **Despise not thou the chastening of the Lord** – Do not slight or make little of it; do not impute any affliction to chance or second causes but see and revere the hand of God in it. **Neither faint when thou art rebuked of him** – But endure it patiently and fruitfully. Pro 3:11.

6. For – All springs from love; therefore neither despise nor faint.

7. Whom his father chasteneth not – When he offends.

8. Of which all sons are partakers – More or less.

9. And we reverenced them – We neither despised nor fainted under their correction. **Shall we not much rather** – Submit with reverence and meekness. **To the Father of spirits** – That we may live with him for ever. Perhaps these expressions, fathers of our flesh, and Father of spirits, intimate that our earthly fathers are only the parents of our bodies, our souls not being originally derived from them, but all created by the immediate power of God; perhaps, at the beginning of the world.

10. For they verily for a few days – How few are even all our day on earth! **Chastened us as they thought good** – Though frequently they erred therein, by too much either of indulgence or severity. But he always, unquestionably, for our profit, that we may be **partakers of his holiness** – That is, of himself and his glorious image.

11. Now all chastening – Whether from our earthly or heavenly Father, Is **for the present grievous**, yet it **yieldeth the peaceable fruit of righteousness** – Holiness and happiness. **To them that are exercised thereby** – That receive this exercise as from God, and improve it according to his will.

12. Wherefore lift up the hands – Whether your own or your brethren's. **That hang down** –

Unable to continue the combat. **And the feeble knees** – Unable to continue the race. Isa 35:3.

13. **And make straight paths both for your own and for their feet** – Remove every hinderance, every offence. **That the lame** – They who are weak, scarce able to walk. **Be not turned out of the way** – Of faith and holiness.

14. **Follow peace with all men** – This second branch of the exhortation concerns our neighbours; the third, God. **And holiness** – The not following after all holiness, is the direct way to fall into sin of every kind.

15. **Looking diligently, lest any one** – If he do not lift up the hands that hang down. **Fall from the grace of God: lest any root of bitterness** – Of envy, anger, suspicion. **Springing up** – Destroy the sweet peace; lest any, not following after holiness, fall into fornication or profaneness. In general, any corruption, either in doctrine or practice, is a root of bitterness, and may pollute many.

16. **Esau** was profane for so slighting the blessing which went along with the birthright.

17. **He was rejected** – He could not obtain it. **For he found no place for repentance** – There was no room for any such repentance as would regain what he had lost. **Though he sought it** – The blessing of the birthright. **Diligently with tears** – He sought too late. Let us use the present time.

18. **For** – A strong reason this why they ought the more to regard the whole exhortation drawn from the priesthood of Christ: because both salvation and vengeance are now nearer at hand. **Ye are not come to the mountain that could be touched** – That was of an earthy, material nature.

19. **The sound of a trumpet** – Formed, without doubt, by the ministry of angels, and preparatory to the words, that is, the Ten Commandments, which were uttered with a loud voice, Deu 5:22.

20. **For they could not bear** – The terror which seized them, when they heard those words proclaimed, If even **a beast,** Exod 19:12.

21. **Even Moses** – Though admitted to so near an intercourse with God, who 'spake to him as a man speaketh to his friend.' At other times he acted as a mediator between God and the people. But while the ten words were pronounced, he stood as one of the hearers, Ex 19:25; Ex 20:19.

22. **But ye** – Who believe in Christ. **Are come** – The apostle does not here speak of their coming to the church militant, but of that glorious privilege of New Testament believers, their communion with the church triumphant. But this is far more apparent to the eyes of celestial spirits than to ours which are yet veiled. St. Paul here shows an excellent knowledge of the heavenly economy, worthy of him who had been caught up into the third heaven. **To mount Sion** – A spiritual mountain. **To the city of the living God, the heavenly Jerusalem** – All these glorious titles belong to the New Testament church. **And to an innumerable company** – Including all that are afterwards mentioned.

23. **To the general assembly** – The word properly signifies a stated convention on some festival occasion. **And church** – The whole body of true believers, whether on earth or in paradise. **Of the first-born** – The first-born of Israel were enrolled by Moses; but these are enrolled in heaven, as citizens there. It is observable, that in this beautiful gradation, these first-born are placed nearer to God than the angels. See Jam 1:18. **And to God the Judge of all** – Propitious to you, adverse to your enemies. **And to the spirits** – The separate souls. **Of just men** – It seems to mean, of New Testament believers. The number of these, being not yet large, is mentioned distinct from the innumerable company of just men whom their Judge hath acquitted. These are now made perfect in an higher sense than any who are still alive. Accordingly, St. Paul, while yet on earth, denies that he was thus made perfect, Php 3:12.

24. **To Jesus, the mediator** – Through whom they had been perfected. **And to the blood of sprinkling** – To all the virtue of his precious blood shed for you, whereby ye are sprinkled from an evil conscience. This blood of sprinkling was the foundation of our Lord's mediatorial office. Here the gradation is at the highest point. **Which speaketh better things than that of Abel** – Which cried for vengeance.

25. **Refuse not** – By unbelief. **Him that speaketh** – And whose speaking even now is a prelude to the final scene. The same voice which spake both by the law and in the gospel, when heard from heaven, will shake heaven and earth. **For if they escaped not** – His vengeance. **Much more shall not we** – Those of us who **turn from him that speaketh from heaven** – That is, who came from heaven to speak to us.

26. **Whose voice then shook the earth** – When he spoke from mount Sinai. **But now** – With regard to his next speaking. **He hath promised** – It is a joyful promise to the saints, though dreadful to the wicked. **Yet once more I will shake, not only the earth, but also the heaven** – These words may refer in a lower sense to the dissolution of the Jewish church and state; but in their full sense they undoubtedly look much farther, even to the end of all things. This universal shaking began at the first coming of Christ. It will be consummated at his second coming. Hag 2:6.

27. **The things which are shaken** – Namely, heaven and earth. **As being made** – And consequently liable to change. **That the things which are not shaken may remain** – Even 'the new heavens and the new earth,' Rev 21:1.

28. Therefore let us, receiving – By willing and joyful faith. **A kingdom** – More glorious than the present heaven and earth. Hold fast the **grace, whereby we may serve God** – In every thought, word, and work. **With reverence** – Literally, with shame. Arising from a deep consciousness of our own unworthiness. **And godly fear** – A tender, jealous fear of offending, arising from a sense of the gracious majesty of God.

29. For our God is a consuming fire – in the strictness of his justice, and purity of his holiness.

Chapter 13

1. Brotherly love is explained in the following verses.

2. Some – Abraham and Lot. **Have entertained angels unawares** – So may an unknown guest, even now, be of more worth than he appears, and may have angels attending him, though unseen. Gen 18:2; Gen 19:1.

3. Remember – In your prayers, and by your help. **Them that are in bonds, as being bound with them** – Seeing ye are members one of another. **And them that suffer, as being yourselves in the body** – And consequently liable to the same.

4. Marriage is honourable in, or for all sorts of men, clergy as well as laity. **And the bed undefiled** – Consistent with the highest purity; though many spiritual writers, so called, say it is only licensed whoredom. **But whoremongers and adulterers God will judge** – Though they frequently escape the sentence of men.

5. He – God. **Hath said** – To all believers, in saying it to Jacob, Joshua, and Solomon. Gen 28:15; Jos 1:5; 1Chr 28:20.

6. Psa. 118:6.

7. Remember them – Who are now with God, considering the happy end of their conversation on earth.

8. Men may die; but Jesus Christ, yea, and his gospel, is the same from everlasting to everlasting.

9. Be not carried about with various doctrines – Which differ from that one faith in our one unchangeable Lord. **Strange** – To the ears and hearts of all that abide in him. **For it is good** – It is both honourable before God and pleasant and profitable. **That the heart be stablished with grace** – Springing from faith in Christ. **Not with meats** – Jewish ceremonies, which indeed can never stablish the heart.

10. On the former part of this verse, the fifteenth and sixteenth depend; on the latter, the intermediate verses. **We have an altar** – The cross of Christ. **Whereof they have no right to eat** – To partake of the benefits which we receive therefrom. **Who serve the tabernacle** – Who adhere to the Mosaic law.

11. For – According to their own law, the sin-offerings were wholly consumed, and no Jew ever ate thereof. But Christ was a sin-offering. Therefore they cannot feed upon him, as we do, who are freed from the Mosaic law.

12. Wherefore Jesus also – Exactly answering those typical sin-offerings. **Suffered without the gate** – Of Jerusalem, which answered to the old camp of Israel. **That he might sanctify** – Reconcile and consecrate to God. **The people** – Who believe in him. **By his own blood** – Not those shadowy sacrifices, which are now of no farther use.

13. Let us then go forth without the camp – Out of the Jewish dispensation. **Bearing his reproach** – All manner of shame, obloquy, and contempt for his sake.

14. For we have here – On earth. **No continuing city** – All things here are but for a moment; and Jerusalem itself was just then on the point of being destroyed.

15. The sacrifice – The altar is mentioned, Heb 13:10; now the sacrifices:

1. Praise;
2. Beneficence;

with both of which God is well pleased.

17. Obey them that have the rule over you – The word implies also, that lead or guide you; namely, in truth and holiness. **And submit yourselves** – Give up (not your conscience or judgment, but) your own will, in all things purely indifferent. **For they watch over your souls** – With all zeal and diligence, they guard and caution you against all danger. **As they that must give account** – To the great Shepherd, for every part of their behaviour toward you. How vigilant then ought every pastor to be! How careful of every soul committed to his charge! **That they may do this** – Watch over you. **With joy and not with groans** – He is not a good shepherd, who does not either rejoice over them, or groan for them. The groans of other creatures are heard: how much more shall these come up in the ears of God! Whoever answers this character of a Christian pastor may undoubtedly demand this obedience.

20. The everlasting covenant – The Christian covenant, which is not temporary, like the Jewish, but designed to remain for ever. By the application of that blood, by which this covenant was established, may he make you, in every respect, inwardly and outwardly holy!

22. Suffer the word of exhortation – Addressed to you in this letter, which, though longer than my usual letters, is yet contained in few words, considering the copiousness of the subject.

23. If he come – To me.

25. Grace be with you all – St. Paul's usual benediction. God apply it to our hearts!

JAMES

A.R. Faussett

Introduction

This is called by Eusebius ([*Ecclesiastical History*, 2.23], about the year 330 A.D.) the first of the Catholic Epistles, that is, the Epistles intended for general circulation, as distinguished from Paul's Epistles, which were addressed to particular churches or individuals. In the oldest manuscripts of the New Testament extant, they stand *before* the Epistles of Paul. Of them, two only are mentioned by Eusebius as *universally acknowledged* (*Homologoumena*), namely, the First Epistle of Peter, and the First Epistle of John. *All*, however, are found in every existing manuscript of the whole New Testament.

Its history

It is not to be wondered at that Epistles not addressed to particular churches (and particularly one like that of James, addressed to the Israelite believers scattered abroad) should be for a time less known. The first mention of James' Epistle by name occurs early in the third century, in Origen [*Commentary* on John 1:19, 4.306], who was born about 185, and died A.D. 254. Clement of Rome ([*First Epistle to the Corinthians*, 10]; compare Jas 2:21,23; [*First Epistle to the Corinthians*, 11]; compare Jas 2:25 Heb 11:31) quotes it. So also Hermas [*Shepherd*] quotes Jas 4:7. Irenaeus [*Against Heresies*, 4.16.2] is thought to refer to Jas 2:23. Clement of Alexandria commented on it, according to Cassiodorus. Ephrem the Syrian [*Against the Greeks*, 3.51] quotes Jas 5:1. An especially strong proof of its authenticity is afforded by its forming part of the old *Syriac* version, which contains no other of *the disputed books* (*Antilegomena*, [Eusebius, *Ecclesiastical History*, 3.25]), except the Epistle to the Hebrews. None of the Latin fathers before the fourth century quote it; but soon after the Council of Nicea it was admitted as canonical both by the East and West churches, and specified as such in the Councils of Hippo and Carthage (A.D. 397). This is just what we might expect; a writing known only partially at first, when subsequently it obtained a wider circulation, and the proofs were better known of its having been recognized in apostolic churches, having in them men endowed with the discernment of spirits, which qualified them for discriminating between inspired and uninspired writings, was universally accepted. Though *doubted* for a time, at last the disputed books (James, Second Peter, Second and Third John, Jude, and Revelation) were universally and undoubtingly accepted, so that no argument for the Old Testament Apocrypha can be drawn from their case: as to *it* the Jewish Church had *no doubt*; it was *known not* to be inspired.

Luther's objection to it ('an Epistle of straw, and destitute of an evangelic character') was due to his mistaken idea that it (Jas 2:14–26) opposes the doctrine of justification by faith, and not by works, taught by Paul. But the two apostles, while looking at justification from distinct standpoints, perfectly harmonize and mutually complement the definitions of one another. Faith precedes love and the works of love; but without them it is dead. Paul regards faith in the justification of the sinner *before God;* James, in the justification of the believer *evidently before men.* The error which James meets was the Jewish notion that their possession and knowledge of the law of God would justify them, even though they disobeyed it (compare Jas 1:22 with Ro 2:17–25). Jas 1:3 4:1,12 seem plainly to allude to Ro 5:3 6:13 7:23 14:4. Also the tenor of Jas 2:14-26 on 'justification,' seems to allude to Paul's teaching, so as to correct false Jewish notions of a different kind from those which he combatted, though not unnoticed by him also (Ro 2:17).

Its author

Paul (Ga 2:9) arranges the names 'James, Cephas, John,' in the order in which their Epistles stand. James who wrote this Epistle (according to most ancient writers) is called (Ga 1:19), 'the Lord's brother.' He was son of Alpheus or Cleopas (Lu 24:13-18) and Mary, sister of the Virgin Mary. Compare Mr 15:40 with Joh 19:25, which seems to identify the mother of James the Less with the wife of Cleopas, not with the Virgin Mary, Cleopas' wife's sister. Cleopas is the *Hebrew,* Alpheus the *Greek* mode of writing the same name. Many, however, as HEGESIPPUUS [EUSEBIUS, *Ecclesiastical History,* 23.1], distinguish *the Lord's brother* from the son of Alpheus. But the Gospel according to the Hebrews, quoted by JEROME, represents James, the Lord's brother, as present at the institution of the Eucharist, and therefore identical with the apostle James. So the Apocryphal Gospel of James. In Acts, James who is put foremost in Jerusalem after the death of James, the son of Zebedee, is not distinguished from James, the son of Alpheus. He is not mentioned as one of the Lord's brethren in Ac 1:14; but as one of the 'apostles' (Ga 1:19). He is called 'the Less' (literally, 'the little,' Mr 15:40), to distinguish him from James, the son of Zebedee. ALFORD considers James, the brother of the Lord, the author of the Epistle, to have been the eldest of the sons of Joseph and Mary, after Jesus (compare Mt 13:55), and that James the son of Alpheus is distinguished from him by *the latter* being called 'the Less,' (that is, junior). His arguments against the Lord's brother, the bishop of Jerusalem, being the apostle, are: (1) The Lord's brethren did not believe on Jesus at a time when the apostles had been already called (Joh 7:3,5), therefore none of the Lord's brethren could be among the apostles (but it does not follow from Joh 7:3 that *no one* of them believed). (2) The apostles' commission was to preach the Gospel *everywhere,* not to be bishops in a particular locality (but it is unlikely that one not an apostle should be bishop of Jerusalem, to whom even apostles yield deference, Ac 15:13,19 Ga 1:19 2:9,12. The Saviour's last command to the apostles collectively to *preach the Gospel everywhere,* is not inconsistent with each having a particular sphere of labour in which he should be a missionary bishop, as Peter is said to have been at Antioch).

He was surnamed 'the Just.' It needed peculiar wisdom so to preach the Gospel as not to disparage the law. As bishop of Jerusalem writing to the twelve tribes, he sets forth the Gospel in its aspect of relation to the law, which the Jews so reverenced. As Paul's Epistles are a commentary on the doctrines flowing from the death and resurrection of Christ, so James's Epistle has a close connection with His teaching during His life on earth, especially His Sermon on the Mount. In both, the law is represented as fulfilled in love: the very language is palpably similar (compare Jas 1:2 with Mt 5:12; Jas 1:4 with Mt 5:48; Jas 1:5 5:15 with Mt 7:7–11; Jas 2:13 with Mt 5:7 6:14,15; Jas 2:10 with Mt 5:19; Jas 4:4 with Mt 6:24; Jas 4:11 with Mt 7:1,2; Jas 5:2 with Mt 6:19). The whole spirit of this Epistle breathes the same

Gospel-*righteousness* which the Sermon on the Mount inculcates as the highest realization of the law. James's own character as 'the Just,' or *legally righteous,* disposed him to this coincidence (compare Jas 1:20 2:10 3:18 with Mt 5:20). It also fitted him for presiding over a Church still zealous for the law (Ac 21:18–24 Ga 2:12). If any could win the Jews to the Gospel, he was most likely who presented a pattern of Old Testament righteousness, combined with evangelical faith (compare also Jas 2:8 with Mt 5:44,48). Practice, not profession, is the test of obedience (compare Jas 2:17 4:17 with Mt 7:2–23). Sins of the tongue, however lightly regarded by the world, are an offense against the law of love (compare Jas 1:26 3:2–18 with Mt 5:22; also any swearing, Jas 5:12; compare Mt 5:33–37).

The absence of the apostolic benediction in this Epistle is probably due to its being addressed, not merely to the believing, but also indirectly to unbelieving, Israelites. To the former he commends humility, patience, and prayer; to the latter he addresses awful warnings (Jas 5:7–11 4:9 5:1–6).

James was martyred at the Passover. This Epistle was probably written just before it. The destruction of Jerusalem foretold in it (Jas 5:1), ensued a year after his martyrdom, A.D. 69. HEGESIPPUS (quoted in EUSEBIUS [*Ecclesiastical History,* 2.23]) narrates that he was set on a pinnacle of the temple by the scribes and Pharisees, who begged him to restrain the people who were in large numbers embracing Christianity. 'Tell us,' said they in the presence of the people gathered at the feast, 'which is the door of Jesus?' James replied with a loud voice, 'Why ask ye me concerning Jesus the Son of man? He sitteth at the right hand of power, and will come again on the clouds of heaven.' Many thereupon cried, Hosanna to the Son of David. But James was cast down headlong by the Pharisees; and praying, 'Father, forgive them, for they know not what they do,' he was stoned and beaten to death with a fuller's club. The Jews, we know from Acts, were exasperated at Paul's rescue from their hands, and therefore determined to wreak their vengeance on James. The publication of his Epistle to the dispersed Israelites, to whom it was probably carried by those who came up to the periodical feasts, made him obnoxious to them, especially to the higher classes, because it foretold the woes soon about to fall on them and their country. Their taunting question, 'Which is the door of Jesus?' (that is, by what door will He come when He returns?), alludes to his prophecy, 'the coming of the Lord draweth nigh ... behold the Judge standeth before the *door*' (Jas 5:8,9). Heb 13:7 probably refers to the martyrdom of James, who had been so long bishop over the Jewish Christians at Jerusalem, 'Remember them which have (rather, "had") the rule (spiritually) over you, who have spoken unto you the word of God; whose faith follow, considering the end of their conversation.'

Inspiration

His inspiration as an apostle is expressly referred to in Ac 15:19,28, '*My sentence is*': 'It seemed good to *the Holy Ghost, and to us*'. His episcopal authority is implied in the deference paid to him by Peter and Paul (Ac 12:17 21:18 Ga 1:19 2:9). The Lord had appeared specially to him after the resurrection (1Co 15:7). Peter in his First Epistle (universally from the first received as canonical) tacitly confirms the inspiration of James's Epistle, by incorporating with his own inspired writings no less than ten passages from James. The 'apostle of the circumcision,' Peter, and the first bishop of Jerusalem, would naturally have much in common. Compare Jas 1:1 with 1Pe 1:1; Jas 1:2 with 1Pe 1:6 4:12,13; Jas 1:11 with 1Pe 1:24; Jas 1:18 with 1Pe 1:3; Jas 2:7 with 1Pe 4:14; Jas 3:13 with 1Pe 2:12; Jas 4:1 with 1Pe 2:11; Jas 4:6 with 1Pe 5:5,6; Jas 4:7 with 1Pe 5:6,9; Jas 4:10 with 1Pe 5:6; Jas 5:20 with 1Pe 4:6. Its being written in the purest *Greek* shows it was intended not only for the Jews at Jerusalem, but also for the Hellenistic, that is, Greek-speaking, Jews.

Style

The style is close, curt, and sententious, gnome following after gnome. A Hebraic character pervades the Epistle, as appears in the occasional poetic parallelisms (Jas 3:1–12). Compare 'assembly': *Greek*, 'synagogue', Jas 2:2, *Margin*. The images are analogical arguments, combining at once logic and poetry. Eloquence and persuasiveness are prominent characteristics.

The similarity to Matthew, the most Hebrew of the Gospels, is just what we might expect from the bishop of Jerusalem writing to Israelites. In it the higher spirit of Christianity is seen putting the Jewish law in its proper place. The law is enforced in its everlasting spirit, not in the letter for which the Jews were so zealous. The doctrines of grace, the distinguishing features of Paul's teaching to the Hellenists and Gentiles, are less prominent as being already taught by that apostle. James complements Paul's teaching, and shows to the Jewish Christians who still kept the legal ordinances down to the fall of Jerusalem, the spiritual principle of the law, namely, love manifested in obedience. To sketch 'the perfect man' *continuing* in the Gospel *law of liberty*, is his theme.

Contents

See *Outlines of the New Testament Books*, p. 904

Chapter 1

Jas 1:1–27. Inscription: exhortation on hearing, speaking, and wrath.
The last subject is discussed in Jas 3:13–4:17.

1. James – an apostle of the circumcision, with Peter and John, James in Jerusalem, Palestine, and Syria; Peter in Babylon and the East; John in Ephesus and Asia Minor. Peter addresses the dispersed *Jews of Pontus, Galatia, and Cappadocia;* James, the *Israelites of the twelve tribes scattered abroad.*

servant of God – not that he was not an *apostle;* for Paul, an apostle, also calls himself so; but as addressing the Israelites generally, including even indirectly the unbelieving, he in humility omits the title 'apostle'; so Paul in writing to the Hebrews; similarly Jude, an apostle, in his General Epistle.

Jesus Christ – not mentioned again save in Jas 2:1; not at all in his speeches (Ac 15:14,15 21:20,21), lest his introducing the name of Jesus oftener should seem to arise from vanity, as being 'the Lord's brother' [BENGEL]. His teaching being practical, rather than doctrinal, required less frequent mention of Christ's name.

scattered abroad – literally 'which are in the dispersion.' The dispersion of the Israelites, and their connection with Jerusalem as a centre of religion, was a divinely ordered means of propa-gating Christianity. The pilgrim troops of the law became caravans of the Gospel [WORDSWORTH].

greeting – found in no other Christian letter, but in James and the Jerusalem Synod's Epistle to the Gentile churches; an undesigned coincidence and mark or genuineness. In the original *Greek* (*chairein*) for 'greeting,' there is a connection with the 'joy' to which they are exhorted amidst their existing distresses from poverty and consequent oppression. Compare Ro 15:26, which alludes to their poverty.

2. My brethren – a phrase often found in James, marking community of nation and of faith.

all joy – cause for the highest joy [GROTIUS]. Nothing but joy [PISCATOR]. Count *all* 'divers temptations' to be *each* matter of *joy* [BENGEL].

fall into – unexpectedly, so as to be *encompassed by* them (so the original *Greek*).

temptations – not in the limited sense of allurements to sin, but *trials* or distresses of any kind which test and purify the Christian character. Compare 'tempt,' that is, try, Ge 22:1. Some of those to whom James writes were 'sick,' or otherwise 'afflicted' (Jas 5:13). Every possible trial to the child of God is a masterpiece of strategy of the Captain of his salvation for his good.

3. the trying – the *testing* or *proving* of your faith, namely, by 'divers temptations.' Compare Ro 5:3, *tribulation* worketh patience, and patience *experience* (in the original *dokime*, akin to *dokimion*, 'trying,' here; there it is *experience*: here the 'trying' or *testing*, whence experience flows).

patience – The original implies more; *persevering endurance* and *continuance* (compare Lu 8:15).

4. Let endurance have a perfect *work* (taken out of the previous '*worketh* patience' or endurance), that is, have its *full effect*, by showing the most perfect degree of endurance, namely, 'joy in bearing the cross' [MENOCHIUS], and enduring to the end (Mt 10:22) [CALVIN].

ye may be perfect – fully developed in all the attributes of a Christian character. For this there is required 'joy' [BENGEL], as part of the 'perfect work' of probation. The work of God in a man is the man. If God's teachings by patience have had a perfect work in you, *you* are perfect [ALFORD].

entire – that which has all *its parts complete, wanting no integral part;* 1Th 5:23, 'your whole (literally, "entire") spirit, soul, and body'; as 'perfect' implies *without a blemish in its parts.*

5. *English Version* omits 'But,' which the *Greek* has, and which is important. 'But (as this *perfect entireness wanting nothing* is no easy attainment) if any'.

lack – rather, as the *Greek* word is repeated after James's manner, from Jas 1:4, '*wanting nothing*,' translate, 'If any of you *want* wisdom,' namely, the wisdom whereby ye may 'count it all joy when ye fall into divers temptations,' and 'let patience have her perfect work.' This 'wisdom' is shown in its effects in detail, Jas 3:7. The highest wisdom, which governs patience alike in poverty and riches, is described in Jas 1:9,10.

ask – (Jas 4:2).

liberally – So the *Greek* is rendered by *English Version.* It is rendered *with simplicity,* Ro 12:8. God gives without adding aught which may take off from the graciousness of the gift [ALFORD]. God requires the same 'simplicity' in His children ('eye … single,' Mt 6:22, literally, 'simple').

upbraideth not – an illustration of God's giving *simply.* He gives to the humble suppliant without upbraiding him with his past sin and ingratitude, or his future abuse of God's goodness. The Jews pray, 'Let me not have need of the gifts of men, whose gifts are few, but their upbraidings manifold; but give me out of Thy large and full hand.' Compare Solomon's prayer for 'wisdom,' and God's gift above what he asked, though God foresaw his future abuse of His goodness would deserve very differently. James has before his eye the Sermon on the Mount (see my *Introduction*). God hears every true prayer and grants either the thing asked, or else something better than it; as a good physician consults for his patient's good better by denying something which the latter asks not for

his good, than by conceding a temporary gratification to his hurt.

6. ask in faith – that is, the persuasion that God can and will give. James begins and ends with *faith.* In the middle of the Epistle he removes the hindrances to faith and shows its true character [BENGEL].

wavering – between belief and unbelief. Compare the case of the Israelites, who seemed to partly believe in God's power, but leaned more to unbelief by 'limiting' it. On the other hand, compare Ac 10:20 Ro 4:20 ('*staggered not* … through unbelief,' literally, as here, '*wavered not*'); 1Ti 2:8.

like a wave of the sea – Isa 57:20 Eph 4:14, where the same *Greek* word occurs for 'tossed to and fro,' as is here translated, 'driven with the wind.'

driven with the wind – from without.

tossed – from within, by its own instability [BENGEL]. At one time cast on the shore of faith and hope, at another rolled back into the abyss of unbelief; at one time raised to the height of worldly pride, at another tossed in the sands of despair and affliction [WIESINGER].

7. For – resumed from 'For' in Jas 1:6.

that man – such a wavering self-deceiver.

think – Real *faith* is something more than a mere *thinking* or *surmise.*

anything – namely, of the things that he prays for: he does receive many things from God, food, raiment, but these are the general gifts of His providence: of the things specially granted in answer to prayer, the waverer shall not receive 'anything,' much less wisdom.

8. double-minded – literally, 'double-souled,' the one soul directed towards God, the other to something else. The *Greek* favours ALFORD's translation, 'He (the waverer, Jas 1:6) is a man double-minded, unstable'; or better, BEZA's. The words in this Jas 1:8 are in apposition with 'that man,' Jas 1:7; thus the 'us,' which is not in the original, will not need to be supplied, 'A man double-minded, unstable in all his ways!' The word for 'double-minded' is found here and in Jas 4:8, for the first time in Greek literature. It is not a *hypocrite* that is meant, but a *fickle,* 'wavering' man, as the context shows. It is opposed to *the single eye* (Mt 6:22).

9, 10. Translate, '*But let the brother*'; that is, the best remedy against *double-mindedness* is that Christian *simplicity* of spirit whereby the 'brother,' low in outward circumstances, may 'rejoice' (answering to Jas 1:2) 'in that he is exalted,' namely, by being accounted a son and heir of God, his very sufferings being a pledge of his coming glory and crown (Jas 1:12), and the rich may rejoice 'in that he is made low,' by being stripped of his goods for Christ's sake [MENOCHIUS]; or in that he is made, by sanctified trials, lowly in spirit, which is true matter for rejoicing [GOMARUS]. The design of the Epistle is to reduce all things to an equable footing (Jas 2:1 5:13). The 'low,' rather than the 'rich,' is here called 'the brother' [BENGEL].

10. So far as one is merely 'rich' in worldly goods, 'he shall pass away'; in so far as his predominant character is that of a 'brother,' he 'abideth for ever' (1Jo 2:17). This view meets all ALFORD's objections to regarding 'the rich' here as a 'brother' at all. To avoid making the rich a brother, he translates, 'But the rich glories in his humiliation,' namely, in that which is really his debasement (his rich state, Php 3:19), just as the low is told to rejoice in what is really his exaltation (his lowly state).

11. Taken from Isa 40:6–8.

heat – rather, 'the hot wind' from the (east or) south, which scorches vegetation (Lu 12:55). The 'burning heat' of the sun is not at its *rising*, but rather at noon; whereas the scorching *Kadim* wind is often at sunrise (Jon 4:8) [MIDDLETON, *The Doctrine of the Greek Article*]. Mt 20:12 uses the *Greek* word for 'heat.' Isa 40:7, 'bloweth upon it,' seems to answer to 'the hot *wind*' here.

grace of the fashion – that is of the external appearance.

in his ways – referring to the burdensome extent of the rich man's devices [BENGEL]. Compare 'his ways,' that is, his course of life, Jas 1:8.

12. Blessed – Compare the beatitudes in the Sermon on the Mount (Mt 5:4,10,11).

endureth temptation – not the 'falling into divers temptations' (Jas 1:2) is the matter for 'joy,' but the *enduring* of temptation 'unto the end.' Compare Job 5:17.

when he is tried – literally, 'when he has become tested' or 'approved,' when he has passed through the 'trying' (Jas 1:3), his 'faith' having finally gained the victory.

the crown – not in allusion to the crown or garland given to winners in the games; for this, though a natural allusion for Paul in writing to the heathen, among whom such games existed, would be less appropriate for James in addressing the Jewish Christians, who regarded Gentile usages with aversion.

of life – 'life' constitutes the crown, literally, *the* life, the only true life, the highest and eternal life. The crown implies a *kingdom* (Ps 21:3).

the Lord – not found in the best manuscripts and versions. The believer's heart fills up the omission, without the name needing to be mentioned. The 'faithful One who promised' (Heb 10:23).

to them that love him – In 2Ti 4:8, 'the crown of righteousness to them that love His appearing.' Love produces patient *endurance*: none attest their love more than they who suffer for Him.

13. when ... tempted – tried by *solicitation to evil*. Heretofore the 'temptation' meant was that of *probation by afflictions*. Let no one fancy that God lays upon him an inevitable necessity of sinning. God does not send trials on you in order to make you worse, but to make you better (Jas 1:16,17). Therefore do not sink under the pressure of evils (1Co 10:13).

of God – by agency proceeding *from* God. The *Greek* is not 'tempted *by*,' but, 'from,' implying indirect agency.

cannot be tempted with evil – 'Neither do any of our sins tempt God to entice us to worse things, nor does He tempt any *of His own accord*' (literally, 'of Himself'; compare the antithesis, Jas 1:18, '*Of His own will* He begat us' to holiness, so far is He from tempting us *of His own will*) [BENGEL]. God is said in Ge 22:1 to have 'tempted Abraham'; but there the *tempting* meant is that of *trying* or *proving*, not that of seducement. ALFORD translates according to the ordinary sense of the *Greek*, 'God is *unversed* in evil.' But as this gives a less likely sense, *English Version* probably gives the true sense; for ecclesiastical *Greek* often uses words in new senses, as the exigencies of the new truths to be taught required.

14. Every man, when tempted, is so through being drawn away of (again here, as in Jas 1:13, the *Greek* for 'of' expresses the actual *source*, rather than the agent of temptation) his own lust. The cause of sin is in ourselves. Even Satan's suggestions do not endanger us before they are made *our own*. Each one has *his own* peculiar (so the *Greek*) lust, arising from his own temperament and habit. Lust flows from the original birth-sin in man, inherited from Adam.

drawn away – the *beginning* step in temptation: drawn away from truth and virtue.

enticed – literally, 'taken with a bait,' as fish are. The *further progress*: the man *allowing himself* (as the *Greek* middle voice implies) *to be enticed* to evil [BENGEL]. 'Lust' is here personified as the harlot that allures the man.

15. The guilty union is committed by the will embracing the temptress. 'Lust,' the harlot, then, 'brings forth sin,' namely, of that kind to which the temptation inclines. Then the *particular sin* (so the *Greek* implies), 'when it is completed, brings forth death,' with which it was all along pregnant [ALFORD]. This 'death' stands in striking contrast to the 'crown of *life*' (Jas 1:12) which 'patience' or *endurance* ends in, when it has its 'perfect work' (Jas 1:4). He who will fight Satan with Satan's own weapons, must not wonder if he finds himself overmatched. Nip sin in the bud of lust.

16. Do not err in attributing to God temptation to evil; nay (as he proceeds to show), 'every good,' all that is good on earth, comes from God.

17. gift ... gift – not the same words in *Greek:* the first, *the act of giving,* or the gift in its *initiatory* stage; the second, *the thing given, the boon, when perfected.* As the 'good gift' stands in contrast to 'sin' in its initiatory stage (Jas 1:15), so the 'perfect boon' is in contrast to 'sin when it is finished,' bringing forth *death* (2Pe 1:3).

from above – (Compare Jas 3:15).

Father of lights – Creator *of the lights in heaven* (compare Job 38:28 [ALFORD]; Ge 4:20,21 Heb 12:9). This accords with the reference to the changes in the light of the heavenly bodies alluded to in the end of the verse. Also, Father of the spiritual lights in the kingdom of grace and glory [BENGEL]. These were typified by the supernatural lights on the breastplate of the high priest, the Urim. As 'God is light, and in Him is no darkness at all' (1Jo 1:5), He cannot in any way be the Author of sin (Jas 1:13), which is darkness (Joh 3:19).

no variableness ... shadow of turning – (Mal 3:6). None of the alternations of light and shadow which the physical 'lights' undergo, and which even the spiritual lights are liable to, as compared with God. 'Shadow of turning,' literally, the dark 'shadow-mark' cast *from* one of the heavenly bodies, arising from its 'turning' or revolution, for example, when the moon is eclipsed by the shadow of the earth, and the sun by the body of the moon. BENGEL makes a climax, 'no variation – not even the shadow of a turning'; the former denoting a change in the *understanding;* the latter, in the *will.*

18. (Joh 1:13). The believer's regeneration is the highest example of nothing but good proceeding from God.

Of his own will – Of his own good pleasure (which shows that it is God's essential nature to do good, not evil), not induced by any external cause.

begat he us – spiritually: a once-for-all accomplished act (1Pe 1:3,23). In contrast to 'lust when it hath conceived, *bringeth forth* sin, and sin ... *death*' (Jas 1:15). *Life* follows naturally in connection with *light* (Jas 1:17).

word of truth – the Gospel. The objective mean, as *faith* is the appropriating mean of regeneration by the Holy Spirit as the efficient agent.

a kind of first-fruits – Christ is, in respect to the resurrection, 'the first-fruits' (1Co 15:20,23): believers, in respect to regeneration, are, *as it were,* first-fruits (image from the consecration of the first-born of man, cattle, and fruits to God; familiar to the Jews addressed), that is, they are the first of God's regenerated creatures, and the pledge of the ultimate regeneration of the creation, Ro 8:19,23, where also the Spirit, the divine agent of the believer's regeneration, is termed 'the first-fruits,' that is, the earnest that the regeneration now begun in the soul, shall at

last extend to the body too, and to the lower parts of creation. Of all God's visible creatures, believers are the noblest part, and like the legal 'first-fruits,' sanctify the rest; for this reason they are much tried now.

19. Wherefore – as your evil is of yourselves, but your good from God. However, the oldest manuscripts and versions read thus: 'YE KNOW IT (so Eph 5:5 Heb 12:17), my beloved brethren; BUT (consequently) let every man be swift to hear,' that is, docile in receiving 'the word of truth' (Jas 1:18,21). The true method of hearing is treated in Jas 1:21–27, and Jas 2:1–26.

slow to speak – (Pr 10:19 17:27,28 Ec 5:2). A good way of escaping one kind of temptation arising from ourselves (Jas 1:13). Slow to speak authoritatively as a master or teacher of others (compare Jas 3:1): a common Jewish fault: slow also to speak such hasty things of God, as in Jas 1:13. Two ears are given to us, the rabbis observe, but only one tongue: the ears are open and exposed, whereas the tongue is walled in behind the teeth.

slow to wrath – (Jas 3:13,14 4:5). Slow in becoming heated by debate: another Jewish fault (Ro 2:8), to which much *speaking* tends. TITTMANN thinks not so much 'wrath' is meant, as an *indignant* feeling of *fretfulness* under the calamities to which the whole of human life is exposed; this accords with the 'divers temptations' in Jas 1:2. Hastiness of temper hinders hearing God's word; so Naaman, 2Ki 5:11 Lu 4:28.

20. Man's angry zeal in debating, as if jealous for the honour of God's righteousness, is far from working that which is really righteousness in God's sight. True 'righteousness is sown in peace,' not in wrath (Jas 3:18). The oldest and the received reading is 'worketh,' produceth not. best reading means 'worketh,' that is, *practiceth* not:

21. lay apart – 'once for all' (so the *Greek*): as a filthy garment. Compare Joshua's filthy garments, Zec 3:3,5 Re 7:14. 'Filthiness' is cleansed away by hearing the word (Joh 15:3).

superfluity of naughtiness – *excess* (for instance, the *intemperate* spirit implied in 'wrath,' Jas 1:19,20), which arises from *malice* (our natural, *evil disposition* towards one another). 1Pe 2:1 has the very same words in the *Greek.* So 'malice' is the translation, Eph 4:31 Col 3:8. '*Faulty* excess' [BENGEL] is not strong enough. Superfluous excess in *speaking* is also reprobated as 'coming of *evil*' (the *Greek* is akin to the word for 'naughtiness' here) in the Sermon on the Mount (Mt 5:37), with which James' Epistle is so connected.

with meekness – *in mildness* towards one ano-ther [ALFORD], the opposite to 'wrath' (Jas 1:20): answering to 'as new-born babes' (1Pe 2:2). *Meekness,* I think, includes also a childlike, *docile, humble,* as well as an uncontentious, spirit (Ps 25:9 45:4 Isa 66:2 Mt 5:5 11:28-30 18:3,4; contrast Ro 2:8). On 'receive,' applied to ground receiving seed, compare Mr 4:20. Contrast Ac 17:11 1Th 1:6 with 2Th 2:10.

engrafted word – the Gospel *word*, whose proper attribute is to be *engrafted* by the Holy Spirit, so as to be livingly incorporated with the believer, as the fruitful shoot is with the wild natural stock on which it is engrafted. The law came to man only from without, and admonished him of his duty. The Gospel is *engrafted* inwardly, and so fulfils the ultimate design of the law (De 6:6 11:18 Ps 119:11). ALFORD translates, 'The *implanted* word,' referring to the parable of the sower (Mt 13:1–23). I prefer *English Version.*

able to save – a strong incentive to correct our dulness in hearing the word: that word which we hear so carelessly, is able (instrumentally) to save us [CALVIN].

souls – your true selves, for the 'body' is now liable to sickness and death: but the soul being now saved, both soul and body at last shall be so (Jas 5:15,20).

22. Qualification of the precept, 'Be swift to *hear*': 'Be ye doers … not hearers only'; not merely '*Do* the word,' but '*Be* doers' systematically and continually, as if this was your regular business. James here again refers to the Sermon on the Mount (Mt 7:21–29).

deceiving your own selves – by the logical fallacy (the *Greek* implies this) that the mere hearing is all that is needed.

23. For – the logical self-deceit (Jas 1:22) illustrated.

not a doer – more literally, 'a not doer' [ALFORD]. The true disciple, say the rabbis, learns in order that he may do, not in order that he may merely know or teach.

his natural face – literally, 'the countenance of his birth': the face he was born with. As a man may behold his *natural face* in a mirror, so the hearer may perceive his *moral* visage in God's Word. This faithful portraiture of man's soul in Scripture, is the strongest proof of the truth of the latter. In it, too, we see mirrored God's glory, as well as our natural vileness.

24. beholdeth – more literally, 'he *contemplated* himself and hath *gone* his way,' that is, no sooner has he contemplated his image than he is gone his way (Jas 1:11). 'Contemplate' answers to hearing the word: 'goeth his way,' to relaxing the attention after hearing – letting the mind go elsewhere, and the interest of the thing heard pass away: then *forgetfulness* follows [ALFORD] (Compare Eze 33:31). 'Contemplate' here, and in Jas 1:23, implies that, though cursory, yet some knowledge of one's self, at least for the time, is imparted in hearing the word (1Co 14:24).

and … and – The repetition expresses hastiness joined with levity [BENGEL].

forgetteth what manner of man he was – in the mirror. Forgetfulness is no excuse (Jas 1:25 2Pe 1:9).

25. looketh into – literally, 'stoopeth down to take a close look into.' Peers into: stronger than 'beholdeth,' or 'contemplated,' Jas 1:24. A blessed curiosity if it be efficacious in bearing fruit [BENGEL].

perfect law of liberty – the Gospel rule of life, perfect and perfecting (as shown in the Sermon on the Mount, Mt 5:48), and making us truly walk at liberty (Ps 119:32, *Church of England Prayer Book Version*). Christians are to aim at a higher standard of holiness than was generally understood under the law. The *principle* of love takes the place of the letter of the law, so that by the Spirit they are free from the yoke of sin, and free to obey by spontaneous instinct (Jas 2:8,10,12 Joh 8:31–36 15:14,15; compare 1Co 7:22 Ga 5:1,13 1Pe 2:16). The law is thus *not made void,* but *fulfilled.*

continueth therein – contrasted with 'goeth his way,' Jas 1:24, continues both *looking into* the mirror of God's word, and doing its precepts.

doer of the work – rather, 'a doer of work' [ALFORD], an actual worker.

blessed in his deed – rather, 'in his *doing*'; in the very doing there is blessedness (Ps 19:11).

26, 27. An example of *doing work.*

religious … religion – The *Greek* expresses the *external service* or exercise *of religion,* 'godliness' being the internal soul of it. 'If any man *think himself to be* (so the Greek) religious, that is, *observant of the offices of religion,* let him know these consist not so much in outward observances, as in such acts of mercy and humble piety (Mic 6:7,8) as *visiting the fatherless,* and *keeping one's self unspotted from the world*' (Mt 23:23). James does not mean that these *offices* are the great essentials, or sum total of religion; but that, whereas the law service was merely ceremonial, the very *services* of the Gospel consist in acts of mercy and holiness, and it has light for its *garment,* its very *robe* being righteousness [TRENCH]. The *Greek* word is only found in Ac 26:5, 'after the straitest sect of our *religion* I lived a Pharisee.' Col 2:18, '*worshipping* of angels.'

bridleth not … tongue – Discretion in speech is better than fluency of speech (compare Jas 3:2,3). Compare Ps 39:1. God alone can enable us to do so. James, in treating of the law, naturally notices this sin. For they who are free from grosser sins, and even bear the outward show of sanctity, will often exalt themselves by detracting others under the pretense of zeal, while their real motive is love of evil-speaking [CALVIN].

heart – It and the tongue act and react on one another.

27. Pure … and undefiled – 'Pure' is that love which has in it *no foreign admixture,* as self-deceit and hypocrisy. 'Undefiled' is the means of its being 'pure' [TITTMANN]. 'Pure' expresses the *positive,* 'undefiled' the *negative* side of religious service; just as *visiting the fatherless and widow* is the active, *keeping himself unspotted from the world,* the passive side of religious duty. This is the nobler shape that our religious exercises take, instead of the ceremon-ial offices of the law.

before God and the Father – literally, 'before Him who is (our) God and Father.' God is so called to imply that if we would be like our Father, it is not by fasting, for He does none of these things, but in being 'merciful as our Father is merciful' [CHRYSOSTOM].

visit – in sympathy and kind offices to allevi-ate their distresses.

the fatherless – whose 'Father' is God (Ps 68:5); peculiarly helpless.

and – not in the *Greek;* so close is the connec-tion between active works of mercy to others, and the maintenance of personal unworldliness of spirit, word. and deed; no copula therefore is needed. Religion in its rise interests us about *our-selves* in its progress, about our *fellow creatures:* in its highest stage, about the honour of God.

keep himself – with jealous watchfulness, at the same time praying and depending on God as alone able to keep us (Joh 17:15 Jude 1:24).

Chapter 2

Jas 2:1–26. The sin of respect of persons: dead, unworking faith saves no man.

James illustrates 'the perfect law of liberty' (Jas 1:25) in one particular instance of a sin against it, concluding with a reference again to that law (Jas 2:12,13).

1. brethren – The equality of all Christians as 'brethren,' forms the groundwork of the admo-nition.

the faith of … Christ – that is, the Christian faith. James grounds Christian practice on Christian faith.

the Lord of glory – So 1Co 2:8. As all believ-ers, alike rich and poor, derive all their glory from their union with Him, 'the Lord of glory,' not from external advantages of worldly for-tune, the sin in question is peculiarly inconsis-tent with His 'faith.' BENGEL, making no ellipsis of 'the Lord,' explains 'glory' as in apposition with Christ who is THE GLORY (Lu 2:32); the true Shekinah glory of the temple (Ro 9:4). *English Version* is simpler. The glory of Christ resting on the poor believer should make him be regarded as highly by 'brethren' as his richer brother; nay, more so, if the poor believer has more of Christ's spirit than the rich brother.

with respect of persons – literally, 'in respect-ings of persons'; 'in' the practice of partial preferences of persons in various ways and on various occasions.

2, 3. 'If there chance to have come' [ALFORD].

assembly – literally, 'synagogue'; this, the latest honourable use, and the only *Christian* use of the term in the New Testament, occurs in James's Epistle, the apostle who maintained to the latest possible moment the bonds between the Jewish synagogue and the Christian Church. Soon the continued resistance of the truth by the Jews led Christians to leave the term to them exclusively (Re 3:9). The 'synagogue' implies a mere *assembly* or congregation not necessarily united by any common tie. 'Church,' a people bound together by mutual ties and laws, though often it may happen that the members are not assembled [TRENCH and VITRINGA]. Partly from James' Hebrew tendencies, partly from the Jewish Christian churches retaining most of the Jewish forms, this term 'synagogue' is used here instead of the Christian term 'Church' (*ecclesia,* derived from a root, 'called out,' implying the union of its members in spiritual bonds, inde-pendent of space, and called out into separation from the world); an undesigned coincidence and mark of truth. The people in the Jewish synagogue sat according to their rank, those of the same trade together. The introduction of this custom into Jewish Christian places of wor-ship is here reprobated by James. Christian churches were built like the synagogues, the holy table in the east end of the former, as the ark was in the latter; the *desk* and *pulpit* were the chief articles of furniture in both alike. This shows the error of comparing the Church to the temple, and the ministry to the priesthood; the temple is represented by the whole body of wor-shippers; the church building was formed on the model of the synagogue. See VITRINGA [*Synagogue and Temple*].

goodly apparel … gay clothing – As the *Greek,* is the same in both, translate both alike, 'gay,' or 'splendid clothing.'

3. have respect to him – though ye know not who he is, when perhaps he may be a heathen. It was the office of the deacons to direct to a seat the members of the congregation [CLEMENT OF ROME, *Apostolical Constitutions,* 2.57, 58].

unto him – not in the best manuscripts. Thus 'thou' becomes more demonstratively emphatic.

there – at a distance from where the good seats are.

here – near the speaker.

under my footstool – not literally so; but on the ground, down by my footstool. The poor man must either *stand,* or if he sits, *sit* in a degrading position. The speaker has a footstool as well as a good seat.

4. Are ye not … partial – literally, 'Have ye not made distinctions' or 'differences' (so as to prefer one to another)? So in Jude 1:22.

in yourselves – in your minds, that is, according to your carnal inclination [GROTIUS].

are become judges of evil thoughts – The Greek words for 'judges' and for 'partial,' are akin in sound and meaning. A similar translation ought therefore to be given to both. Thus, either for 'judges', translate, '*distinguishers* of (that is, *according to* your) evil thoughts'; or, do ye not *partially judge between* men, and are become *evilly-thinking judges* (Mr 7:21)? The 'evil thoughts' are in the judges themselves; as in Lu 18:6, the Greek, 'judge of injustice,' is translated, 'unjust judge.' ALFORD and WAHL translate, 'Did ye not *doubt*' (respecting your *faith*, which is inconsistent with the distinctions made by you between rich and poor)? For the Greek constantly means '*doubt*' in all the New Testament. So in Jas 1:6, 'wavering.' Mt 21:21 Ac 10:20 Ro 4:20, 'staggered not.' The same play on the same kindred words occurs in the Greek of Ro 14:10,23, 'judge ... doubteth.' The same blame of being a judge, when one ought to be an obeyer, of the law is found in Jas 4:11.

5. Hearken – James *brings to trial* the self-constituted 'judges' (Jas 2:4).

poor of this world – The best manuscripts read, 'those poor *in respect to the* world.' In contrast to 'the rich in this world' (1Ti 6:17). Not of course *all* the poor; but the poor, *as a class*, furnish more believers than the rich as a class. The rich, if a believer, renounces riches as his portion; the poor, if an unbeliever, neglects that which is the peculiar advantage of poverty (Mt 5:3 1Co 1:26,27,28).

rich in faith – *Their* riches consist *in faith*. Lu 12:21, 'rich toward God.' 1Ti 6:18, 'rich in good works' (Re 2:9; compare 2Co 8:9). Christ's poverty is the source of the believer's riches.

kingdom ... promised – (Lu 12:32 1Co 2:9 2Ti 4:8).

6. The world's judgment of the poor contrasted with God's.

ye – Christians, from whom better things might have been expected; there is no marvel that men of the world do so.

despised – literally, 'dishonoured.' To dishonour the poor is to dishonour those whom God honours, and so to invert the order of God [CALVIN].

rich – as a class.

oppress – literally, 'abuse their power against' you.

draw you – Translate, 'is it not *they* (those very persons whom ye partially prefer, Jas 2:1-4) that *drag* you (namely, with violence)' [ALFORD].

before ... judgment seats – instituting persecutions for religion, as well as oppressive lawsuits, against you.

7. 'Is it not they that blaspheme?' as in Jas 2:6 [ALFORD]. Rich heathen must here chiefly be meant; for none others would directly blaspheme the name of Christ. Only *indirectly* rich Christians can be meant, who, by their inconsistency, *caused* His name *to be blasphemed;* so Eze 36:21,22 Ro 2:24. Besides, there were few rich Jewish Christians at Jerusalem (Ro 15:26). They who dishonour God's name by wilful and habitual sin, 'take (or *bear*) the Lord's name in vain' (compare Pr 30:9, with Ex 20:7).

that worthy name – which is 'good before the Lord's saints' (Ps 52:9 54:6); which ye pray may be 'hallowed' (Mt 6:9), and 'by which ye are called,' literally, 'which was invoked' or, 'called upon by you' (compare Ge 48:16 Isa 4:1, *Margin*; Ac 15:17), so that at your baptism '*into* the name' (so the Greek, Mt 28:19) of Christ, ye became Christ's people (1Co 3:23).

8. The Greek may be translated, 'If, *however*, ye fulfil', that is, as ALFORD, after ESTIUS, explains, '*Still* I do not say, hate the rich (for their oppressions) and drive them from your assemblies; if you choose to observe the royal law ... well and good; but respect of persons is a breach of that law.' I think the translation is, 'If *in very deed* (or '*indeed on the one hand*') ye fulfil the royal law ... ye do well, but if (on the other hand) ye respect persons, ye practice sin.' The Jewish Christians boasted of, and rested in, the 'law' (Ac 15:1 21:18–24 Ro 2:17 Ga 2:12). To this the 'indeed' alludes. '(Ye rest in the law): If *indeed* (then) ye fulfil it, ye do well; but if'.

royal – the law that is king of all laws, being the sum and essence of the ten commandments. The great King, God, is love; His law is the royal law of love, and that law, like Himself, reigns supreme. He 'is no respecter of persons'; therefore to respect persons is at variance with Him and His royal law, which is at once a law of love and of liberty (Jas 2:12). The law is the 'whole'; 'the (particular) Scripture' (Le 19:18) quoted is a part. To break a part is to break the whole (Jas 2:10).

ye do well – being 'blessed in your deed' ('doing,' *Margin*) as a doer, not a forgetful hearer of the law (Jas 1:25).

9. *Respect of persons* violates the command to *love all alike* 'as thyself.'

ye commit sin – literally, 'ye work sin,' Mt 7:23, to which the reference here is probably, as in Jas 1:22. Your *works* are sin, whatever boast of the law ye make in words (see on Jas 2:8).

convinced – Old English for 'convicted.'

as transgressors – not merely of this or that particular command, but of the whole absolutely.

10. The best manuscripts read, 'Whosoever *shall have kept* the whole law, and yet *shall have offended* (literally, "stumbled"; not so strong as "fall," Ro 11:11) in one (point; here, the *respecting of persons*), is (hereby) become guilty of all.' The law is one seamless garment which is rent if you but rend a part; or a musical harmony

which is spoiled if there be one discordant note [TIRINUS]; or a golden chain whose completeness is broken if you break one link [GATAKER]. You thus break *the whole law,* though not the whole of the law, because you offend against *love,* which is the fulfilling of the law. If any part of a man be leprous, the whole man is judged to be a leper. God requires perfect, not partial, obedience. We are not to choose out parts of the law to keep, which suit our whim, while we neglect others.

11. He is One who gave the whole law; therefore, they who violate His will in one point, violate it all [BENGEL]. The law and its Author alike have a complete unity.

adultery ... kill – selected as being the most glaring cases of violation of duty towards one's neighbors.

12. Summing up of the previous reasonings.

speak – referring back to Jas 1:19,26; the fuller discussion of the topic is given Jas 3:5–12.

judged by the law of liberty – (Jas 1:25); that is, the Gospel law of love, which is not a law of external constraint, but of internal, *free,* instinctive inclination. The law of liberty, through God's mercy, frees us from the curse of the law, that henceforth we should be free to love and obey willingly. If we will not in turn practice the law of love to our neighbors, that law of grace condemns us still more heavily than the old law, which spake nothing but wrath to him who offended in the least particular (Jas 2:13). Compare Mt 18:32–35 Joh 12:48 Re 6:16, 'Wrath of the (merciful) Lamb.'

13. The converse of, 'Blessed are the merciful, for they shall obtain mercy' (Mt 5:7). Translate, '*The* judgment (which is coming on all of us) shall be without mercy to him who hath showed no mercy.' It shall be such toward every one as every one shall have been [BENGEL]. 'Mercy' here corresponds to 'love,' Jas 2:8.

mercy rejoiceth against judgment – Mercy, so far from fearing judgment in the case of its followers, actually *glorifieth against* it, knowing that it cannot condemn them. Not that *their* mercy is the ground of their acquittal, but the mercy of God in Christ towards them, producing mercy on their part towards their fellow men, makes them to *triumph over judgment,* which all in themselves otherwise deserve.

14. James here, passing from the particular case of 'mercy' or 'love' violated by 'respect of persons,' notwithstanding profession of the 'faith of our Lord Jesus' (Jas 2:1), combats the Jewish tendency (transplanted into their Christianity) to substitute a lifeless, inoperative acquaintance with the letter of the law, for change of heart to practical holiness, as if justification could be thereby attained (Ro 2:3,13,23). It seems hardly likely but that James had seen Paul's Epistles, considering that he uses the same phrases and examples (compare Jas 2:21,23,25, with Ro 4:3 Heb 11:17,31; and Jas 2:14,24, with Ro 3:28 Ga 2:16). Whether James individually designed it or not, the Holy Spirit by him combats not Paul, but those who abuse Paul's doctrine. The teaching of both alike is inspired, and is therefore to be received without wresting of words; but each has a different class to deal with; Paul, self-justiciaries; James, Antinomian advocates of a mere notional faith. Paul urged as strongly as James the need of works as evidences of faith, especially in the later Epistles, when many were abusing the doctrine of faith (Tit 2:14 3:8). 'Believing and doing are blood relatives' [RUTHERFORD].

What *doth it* profit – literally, 'What is the profit?'

though a man say – James' expression is not, 'If a man have faith,' but 'if a man *say* he hath faith'; referring to a mere *profession* of faith, such as was usually made at baptism. Simon Magus so 'believed and was baptized,' and yet had 'neither part nor lot in this matter,' for his 'heart,' as his words and works evinced, was not right in the sight of God. ALFORD wrongly denies that 'say' is emphatic. The illustration, Jas 2:16, proves it is: 'If one of you *say*' to a naked brother, 'Be ye warmed, notwithstanding ye give not those things needful.' The inoperative *profession* of sympathy answering to the inoperative *profession* of faith.

can faith save him – rather, 'can such a faith (literally, "the faith") save him?' – *the* faith you pretend to: the empty name of boasted faith, contrasted with true fruit-producing faith. So that which self-deceivers claim is called 'wisdom,' though not true wisdom, Jas 3:15. The 'him' also in the *Greek* is emphatic; the particular man who professes faith without having the works which evidence its vitality.

15. The *Greek* is, '*But if*': the 'But' taking up the argument against such a one as 'said he had faith, and yet had not works,' which are its fruits.

a brother – a *fellow Christian,* to whom we are specially bound to give help, independent of our general obligation to help all our fellow creatures.

be – The *Greek* implies, '*be found,* on your access to them.'

16. The habit of receiving passively sentimental impressions from sights of woe without carrying them out into active habits only hardens the heart.

one of you – James brings home the case to his hearers individually.

Depart in peace – as if all their wants were satisfied by the mere words addressed to them. The same words in the mouth of Christ, whose faith they said they had, were accompanied by efficient deeds of love.

be ... **warmed** – with clothing, instead of being as heretofore 'naked' (Jas 2:15 Job 31:20).

filled – instead of being 'destitute of food' (Mt 15:37).

what doth it profit – concluding with the same question as at the beginning, Jas 2:14. Just retribution: kind professions unaccompanied with corresponding acts, as they are of no 'profit' to the needy object of them, so are of no profit to the professor himself. So faith consisting in mere profession is unacceptable to God, the object of faith, and profitless to the possessor.

17. faith ... being alone – ALFORD joins 'is dead *in itself.*' So BENGEL, 'If the works which living faith produces have no existence, it is a proof that faith itself (literally, 'in respect to itself') has no existence; that is, that what one boasts of as faith, is *dead.*' 'Faith' is said to be 'dead *in itself,*' because when it has works it is *alive,* and it is discerned to be so, not in respect to its works, but in respect to *itself. English Version,* if retained, must not be understood to mean that faith can exist 'alone' (that is, severed from works), but thus: Even so *presumed* faith, if it have not works, is dead, being by itself 'alone,' that is, severed from works of charity; just as the body would be 'dead' if alone, that is, severed from the spirit (Jas 2:26). So ESTIUS.

18. '*But* some *one will* say': so the *Greek.* This verse continues the argument from Jas 2:14,16. One may *say* he has faith though he have not works. Suppose one were to *say* to a naked brother, 'Be warmed,' without giving him needful clothing. '*But* someone (entertaining views of the need of faith having works joined to it) will say (in opposition to the "say" of the professor).'

show me thy faith without thy works – if thou canst; but thou canst not SHOW, that is, *manifest* or *evidence* thy alleged (Jas 2:14, 'say') faith without works. 'Show' does not mean here to *prove* to me, but *exhibit* to me. Faith is unseen save by God. To *show* faith to man, works in some form or other are needed: we are justified judicially by God (Ro 8:33); meritoriously, by Christ (Isa 53:11); mediately, by faith (Ro 5:1); evidentially, by works. The question here is not as to the *ground* on which believers are justified, but about the *demonstration* of their faith: so in the case of Abraham. In Ge 22:1 it is written, God did *tempt* Abraham, that is, put to the *test of demonstration* the reality of his faith, not for the satisfaction of God, who already knew it well, but to *demonstrate* it before men. The offering of Isaac at that time, quoted here, Jas 2:21, formed no part of the *ground* of his justification, for he was justified previously on his simply believing in the promise of spiritual heirs, that is, believers, numerous as the stars. He was then justified: that justification was *showed* or manifested by his offering Isaac forty years after. That work of faith *demonstrated,* but

did not contribute to his justification. The tree *shows* its life by its fruits, but it was alive before either fruits or even leaves appeared.

19. Thou – emphatic. Thou self-deceiving claimant to faith without works.

that there is one God – rather, 'that God is one': God's *existence,* however, is also asserted. The fundamental article of the creed of Jews and Christians alike, and the point of faith on which especially the former boasted themselves, as distinguishing them from the Gentiles, and hence adduced by James here.

thou doest well – so far good. But unless thy faith goes farther than an assent to this truth, 'the evil spirits (literally, "demons": "devil" is the term restricted to *Satan,* their head) believe' so far in common with thee, 'and (so far from being saved by such a faith) shudder (so the Greek),' Mt 8:29 Lu 4:34 2Pe 2:4 Jude 1:6 Re 20:10. Their faith only adds to their torment at the thought of having to meet Him who is to consign them to their just doom: so thine (Heb 10:26,27, it is not the faith of love, but of fear, that hath torment, 1Jo 4:18).

20. wilt thou know – 'Vain' men are not *willing* to know, since they have no wish to 'do' the will of God. James beseeches such a one to lay aside his perverse *unwillingness* to know what is palpable to all who are willing to do.

vain – who deceivest thyself with a delusive hope, resting on an unreal faith.

without works – The *Greek,* implies *separate from the* works [ALFORD] which ought to flow from it if it were real.

is dead – Some of the best manuscripts read, 'is idle,' that is, unavailing to effect what you hope, namely, to save you.

21. Abraham ... justified by works – *evidentially,* and *before men* (see on Jas 2:18). In Jas 2:23, James, like Paul, recognizes the Scripture truth, that it was his *faith* that was counted to Abraham for righteousness in his justification before God.

when he had offered – rather, 'when he offered' [ALFORD], that is, brought as an offering at the altar; not implying that he actually offered him.

22. Or, 'thou seest.'

how – rather, 'that.' In the two clauses which follow, emphasize 'faith' in the former, and 'works' in the latter, to see the sense [BENGEL].

faith wrought with his works – for it was *by* faith he offered his son. Literally, 'was working (at the time) with his works.'

by works was faith made perfect – not was vivified, but attained its *fully consummated development,* and is *shown to be real.* So 'my strength is *made perfect* in weakness,' that is, *exerts itself most perfectly,* shows how great it is [CAMERON]: so 1Jo 4:17 Heb 2:10 5:9. The germ really, from the first, contains in it the full-grown tree, but its perfection is not attained till it is matured fully. So Jas 1:4, 'Let patience have her *perfect work*,' that is, have its *full effect* by showing the most perfect degree of endurance, 'that ye may be perfect,' that is, *fully developed* in the *exhibition* of the Christian character. ALFORD explains, 'Received its realization, was entirely exemplified and filled up.' So Paul, Php 2:12, 'Work out your own salvation': the salvation was already in germ theirs in their free justification through faith. It needed to be *worked out* still to fully developed perfection in their life.

23. scripture was fulfilled – Ge 15:6, quoted by Paul, as realized in Abraham's justification by *faith;* but by James, as realized subsequently in Abraham's *work* of offering Isaac, which, he says, *justified* him. Plainly, then, James must mean by *works* the same thing as Paul means by *faith,* only that he speaks of faith at its manifested development, whereas Paul speaks of it in its germ. Abraham's offering of Isaac was not a mere act of obedience, but an act of faith. Isaac was the subject of the promises of God, that in him Abraham's seed should be called. The same God calls on Abraham to slay the subject of His own promise, when as yet there was no seed in whom those predictions could be realized. Hence James' saying that Abraham was justified by *such* a work, is equivalent to saying, as Paul does, that he was justified by faith itself; for it was in fact *faith expressed in action,* as in other cases saving faith is expressed in words. So Paul states as the mean of salvation faith *expressed.* The 'Scripture' would not be 'fulfilled,' as James says it was, but contradicted by any interpretation which makes man's *works* justify him before God: for that Scripture makes no mention of works at all, but says that Abraham's *belief* was counted to him for righteousness. God, in the first instance, 'justifies the *ungodly*' through faith; subsequently the believer is justified *before the world* as righteous through faith manifested in words and works (compare Mt 25:35–37, 'the righteous,' Mt 25:40). The best authorities read, 'But Abraham believed'.

and he was called the Friend of God – He was not so *called* in his lifetime, though he *was* so even then from the time of his justification; but he was *called* so, being recognized as such by all on the ground of his works of faith. 'He was the *friend* (in an active sense), the *lover of God,* in reference to his works; and (in a passive sense) *loved by God* in reference to his justification by works. Both senses are united in Joh 15:14,15' [BENGEL].

24. justified and, not by faith only – that is, by 'faith without (*separated* from: *severed from*) works,' its proper fruits (see on Jas 2:20). Faith to justify must, from the first, include obedience in germ (to be developed subsequently), though the former alone is the ground of justification.

The scion must be grafted on the stock that it may live; it must bring forth fruit to prove that it does live.

25. It is clear from the nature of Rahab's act, that it is not quoted to prove justification by works as such. She *believed* assuredly what her other countrymen disbelieved, and this in the face of every improbability that an unwarlike few would conquer well-armed numbers. In this belief she hid the spies at the risk of her life. Hence Heb 11:31 names this as an example of *faith,* rather than of obedience. 'By *faith* the harlot Rahab perished not with them that *believed* not.' If an instance of obedience were wanting, Paul and James would hardly have quoted a woman of previously bad character, rather than the many moral and pious patriarchs. But as an example of free grace justifying men through an *operative,* as opposed to a mere verbal *faith,* none could be more suitable than a saved 'harlot.' As Abraham was an instance of an illustrious man and the father of the Jews, so Rahab is quoted as a woman, and one of abandoned character, and a Gentile, showing that justifying faith has been manifested in those of every class. The nature of the works alleged is such as to prove that James uses them only as *evidences of faith,* as contrasted with a mere verbal profession: not works of charity and piety, but works the value of which consisted solely in their being proofs of faith: they were faith expressed in act, synonymous with *faith* itself.

messengers – spies.

had received … had sent – rather, 'received … thrust them forth' (in haste and fear) [ALFORD].

another way – from that whereby they entered her house, namely, through the window of her house on the wall, and thence to the mountain.

26. Faith is a spiritual thing: works are material. Hence we might expect *faith* to answer to the *spirit, works* to the *body.* But James reverses this. He therefore does not mean that faith in all cases answers to the body; but the FORM *of faith* without *the working reality* answers to the *body* without the *animating spirit.* It does not follow that *living faith* derives its life from works, as the body derives its life from the animating spirit.

Chapter 3

Jas 3:1–18. Danger of eagerness to teach, and of an unbridled tongue: true wisdom shown by uncontentious meekness.

1. be not – literally, 'become not': taking the office too hastily, and of your own accord.

many – The office is a noble one; but few are fit for it. Few govern the tongue well (Jas 3:2), and only such as can govern it are fit for the office; therefore, 'teachers' ought not to be many.

masters – rather, 'teachers.' The Jews were especially prone to this presumption. The idea that faith (so called) without works (Jas 2:14-26) was all that is required, prompted 'many' to set up as 'teachers,' as has been the case in all ages of the Church. At first all were allowed to teach in turns. Even their inspired gifts did not prevent liability to abuse, as James here implies: much more is this so when self-constituted teachers have no such miraculous gifts.

knowing – as all might know.

we ... greater condemnation – James in a humble, conciliatory spirit, includes himself: if we teachers abuse the office, we shall receive greater condemnation than those who are mere hearers (compare Lu 12:42–46). CALVIN, like English Version, translates, 'masters' that is, self-constituted censors and reprovers of others Jas 4:12 accords with this view.

2. all – The Greek implies 'all without exception': even the apostles.

offend not – literally 'stumbleth not': is void of offence or 'slip' in word: in which respect one is especially tried who sets up to be a 'teacher.'

3. Behold – The best authorities read, 'but if,' that is, Now whensoever (in the case) of horses (such is the emphatic position of 'horses' in the Greek) we put the bits (so literally, 'the customary bits') into their mouths that they may obey us, we turn about also their whole body. This is to illustrate how man turns about his whole body with the little tongue. 'The same applies to the pen, which is the substitute for the tongue among the absent' [BENGEL].

4. Not only animals, but even ships.

the governor listeth – literally, 'the impulse of the steersman pleaseth.' The feeling which moves the tongue corresponds with this.

5. boasteth great things – There is great moment in what the careless think 'little' things [BENGEL]. Compare 'a world,' 'the course of nature,' 'hell,' Jas 3:6, which illustrate how the little tongue's great words produce great mischief.

how great a matter a little fire kindleth – The best manuscripts read, 'how little a fire kindleth how great a', ALFORD, for 'matter,' translates, 'forest.' But GROTIUS translates as English Version, 'material for burning': a pile of fuel.

6. Translate, 'The tongue, that world of iniquity, is a fire.' As man's little world is an image of the greater world, the universe, so the tongue is an image of the former [BENGEL].

so – omitted in the oldest authorities.

is – literally, 'is constituted.' 'The tongue is (constituted), among the members, the one which defileth' (namely, as fire defiles with its smoke).

course of nature – 'the orb (cycle) of creation.'

setteth on fire ... is set on fire – habitually and continually. While a man inflames others, he passes out of his own power, being consumed in the flame himself.

of hell – that is, of the devil. Greek, 'Gehenna'; found here only and in Mt 5:22. James has much in common with the Sermon on the Mount (Pr 16:27).

7. every kind – rather, 'every nature' (that is, natural disposition and characteristic power).

of beasts – that is, quadrupeds of every disposition; as distinguished from the three other classes of creation, 'birds, creeping things (the Greek includes not merely "serpents," as English Version), and things in the sea.'

is tamed, and hath been – is continually being tamed, and hath been so long ago.

of mankind – rather, 'by the nature of man': man's characteristic power taming that of the inferior animals. The dative in the Greek may imply, 'Hath suffered itself to be brought into tame subjection TO the nature of men.' So it shall be in the millennial world; even now man, by gentle firmness, may tame the inferior animal, and even elevate its nature.

8. no man – literally, 'no one of men': neither can a man control his neighbor's, nor even his own tongue. Hence the truth of Jas 3:2 appears.

unruly evil – The Greek, implies that it is at once restless and incapable of restraint. Nay, though nature has hedged it in with a double barrier of the lips and teeth, it bursts from its barriers to assail and ruin men [ESTIUS].

deadly – literally, 'death-bearing.'

9. God – The oldest authorities read, 'Lord.' 'Him who is Lord and Father.' The uncommonness of the application of 'Lord' to the Father, doubtless caused the change in modern texts to 'God' (Jas 1:27). But as Messiah is called 'Father,' Isa 9:6, so God the Father is called by the Son's title, 'Lord': showing the unity of the Godhead. 'Father' implies His paternal love; 'Lord,' His dominion.

men, which – not 'men who'; for what is meant is not particular men, but men genetically [ALFORD].

are made after ... similitude of God – Though in a great measure man has lost the likeness of God in which he was originally made, yet enough of it still remains to show what once it was, and what in regenerated and restored man it shall be. We ought to reverence this remnant and earnest of what man shall be in ourselves and in others. 'Absalom has fallen from his father's favour, but the people still recognize him to be the king's son' [BENGEL]. Man resembles in humanity the Son of man, 'the express image of His person' (Heb 1:3), compare Ge 1:26 1Jo 4:20. In the passage, Ge 1:26, 'image' and 'likeness' are distinct: 'image,' according to the Alexandrians, was something in which men were created, being common to all, and continuing to man after the fall, while the 'likeness' was something *toward* which man was created, to strive after and attain it: the former marks man's physical and intellectual, the latter his moral pre-eminence.

10. The tongue, says Aesop, is at once the best and the worst of things. So in a fable, a man with the same breath blows hot and cold. 'Life and death are in the power of the tongue' (compare Ps 62:4).

brethren – an appeal to their consciences by their *brotherhood* in Christ.

ought not so to be – a mild appeal, leaving it to themselves to understand that such conduct deserves the most severe reprobation.

11. **fountain** – an image of the *heart*: as the *aperture* (so the *Greek* for 'place' is literally) of the fountain is an image of man's *mouth*. The image here is appropriate to the scene of the Epistle, Palestine, wherein salt and bitter springs are found. Though 'sweet' springs are sometimes found near, yet 'sweet and bitter' (water) do not flow 'at the same place' (*aperture*). Grace can make the same mouth that 'sent forth the bitter' once, send forth the sweet for the time to come: as the wood (typical of Christ's cross) changed Marah's bitter water into sweet.

12. Transition from the mouth to the heart.

Can the fig tree – implying that it is an *impossibility*: as before in Jas 3:10 he had said it '*ought* not so to be.' James does not, as Matthew (Mt 7:16,17), make the question, 'Do men gather figs of *thistles*?' His argument is, No tree 'can' bring forth *fruit inconsistent with its nature*, as for example, the fig tree, olive berries: so if a man speaks bitterly, and afterwards speaks good words, the latter must be so only seemingly, and in hypocrisy, they *cannot* be real.

so can no fountain ... salt ... and fresh – The oldest authorities read, 'Neither can a salt (water spring) yield fresh.' So the mouth that emits cursing, cannot really emit also blessing.

13. **Who** – (Compare Ps 34:12,13). All wish to appear 'wise': few are so.

show – 'by works,' and not merely by profession, referring to Jas 2:18.

out of a good conversation his works – by *general* 'good conduct' manifested in *particular* 'works.' 'Wisdom' and 'knowledge,' without these being 'shown,' are as dead as faith would be without works [Alford].

with meekness of wisdom – with the meekness inseparable from true 'wisdom.'

14. **if ye have** – *as is the case* (this is implied in the *Greek* indicative).

bitter – Eph 4:31, 'bitterness.'

envying – rather, 'emulation,' or literally, 'zeal': kindly, generous emulation, or zeal, is not condemned, but that which is 'bitter' [Bengel].

strife – rather, 'rivalry.'

in your hearts – from which flow your words and deeds, as from a fountain.

glory not, and lie not against the truth – To *boast of your wisdom* is virtually a lying against the truth (the gospel), while your lives belie your glorying. Jas 3:15 Jas 1:18, 'The word of truth.' Ro 2:17,23, speaks similarly of the same contentious Jewish Christians.

15. **This wisdom** – in which ye 'glory,' as if ye were 'wise' (Jas 3:13,14).

descendeth not from above – literally, 'is not one descending': 'from the Father of lights' (true illumination and wisdom), Jas 1:17; through 'the Spirit of truth,' Joh 15:26.

earthly – opposed to *heavenly*. Distinct from 'earthy,' 1Co 15:47. *Earthly* is what is in the earth; *earthy*, what is of the earth.

sensual – literally, 'animal-like': the wisdom of the 'natural' (the same *Greek*) man, not born again of God; 'not having the Spirit' (Jude 1:19).

devilish – in its origin (from 'hell,' Jas 3:6; not from God, the Giver of true wisdom, Jas 1:5), and also in its character, which accords with its origin. Earthly, sensual, and devilish, answer to the three spiritual foes of man, the world, the flesh, and the devil.

16. **envying** – So *English Version* translates the Greek, which usually means 'zeal'; '*emulation*,' in Ro 13:13. 'The envious man stands in his own light. He thinks his candle cannot shine in the presence of another's sun. He aims directly at men, obliquely at God, who makes men to differ.'

strife – rivalry [Alford].

confusion – literally, 'tumultuous anarchy': both in society (translated 'commotions,' Lu 21:9; 'tumults,' 2Co 6:5), and in the individual mind; in contrast to the 'peaceable' composure of true 'wisdom,' Jas 3:17. James does not honour such effects of this earthly wisdom with the name 'fruit,' as he does in the case of the wisdom from above. Jas 3:18; compare Ga 5:19–22, '*works* of the flesh ... *fruit* of the Spirit.'

17. **first pure** – literally, 'chaste,' 'sanctified': pure from all that is 'earthly, sensual (animal), devilish' (Jas 3:15). This is put, '*first of all*,' before 'peaceable' because there is an unholy peace with the world which makes no distinction between clean and unclean. Compare 'undefiled' and 'unspotted from the world,' Jas 1:27 4:4,8, 'purify ... hearts'; 1Pe 1:22, '*purified ... souls*' (the same *Greek*). Ministers must not preach before a purifying change of heart, 'Peace,' where there is no peace. Seven (the perfect number) characteristic peculiarities of true wisdom are enumerated. *Purity* or *sanctity* is put first because it has respect both to God and to ourselves; the six that follow regard our fellow men. Our first concern is to have in ourselves sanctity; our second, to be at peace with men.

gentle – 'forbearing'; making allowances for others; lenient towards neighbors, as to the DUTIES they owe us.

easy to be entreated – literally, 'easily persuaded,' tractable; not harsh as to a neighbor's FAULTS.

full of mercy – as to a neighbor's MISERIES.

good fruits – contrasted with 'every evil work,' Jas 3:16.

without partiality – recurring to the warning against partial 'respect to persons,' Jas 2:1,4,9. ALFORD translates as the *Greek* is translated, Jas 1:6, 'wavering,' '*without doubting.*' But thus there would be an epithet referring to *one's self* inserted amidst those referring to one's conduct towards others. *English Version* is therefore better.

without hypocrisy – Not as ALFORD explains from Jas 1:22,26, 'Without deceiving yourselves' with the name without the reality of religion. For it must refer, like the rest of the six epithets, to our relations to others; our peaceableness and mercy towards others must be 'without dissimulation.'

18. 'The peaceable fruit of righteousness.' He says 'righteousness'; because it is itself the true wisdom. As in the case of the earthly wisdom, after the characteristic description came its *results*; so in this verse, in the case of the heavenly wisdom. There the results were present; here, future.

fruit … sown – Compare Ps 97:11 Isa 61:3, 'trees of righteousness.' Anticipatory, that is, the seed whose 'fruit,' namely, 'righteousness,' shall be ultimately reaped, is now 'sown in peace.' 'Righteousness,' now in germ, when fully developed as 'fruit' shall be itself the everlasting *reward* of the righteous. As 'sowing in peace' (compare '*sown in* dishonour,' 1Co 15:43) produces the 'fruit of righteousness,' so conversely 'the work' and 'effect of righteousness' is 'peace.'

of them that make peace – 'by (implying also that it is *for* them, and *to* their good) them that work peace.' They, and they alone, are 'blessed.' 'Peacemakers,' not merely they who reconcile others, but who *work peace.* 'Cultivate peace' [ESTIUS]. Those truly wise towards God, while peaceable and tolerant towards their neighbors, yet make it their chief concern to sow righteousness, not cloaking men's sins, but reproving them with such peaceable moderation as to be the physicians, rather than the executioners, of sinners [CALVIN].

Chapter 4

Jas 4:1–17. Against fightings and their source; worldly lusts; uncharitable judgments, and presumptuous reckoning on the future.

1. whence – The cause of quarrels is often sought in external circumstances, whereas internal lusts are the true origin.

wars – contrasted with the 'peace' of heavenly wisdom. 'Fightings' are the active carrying on of 'wars.' The best authorities have a second 'whence' before 'fightings.' Tumults marked the era before the destruction of Jerusalem when James wrote. He indirectly alludes to these. The members are the first seat of war; thence it passes to conflict between man and man, nation and nation.

***come they* not** – an appeal to their consciences.

lusts – literally, 'pleasures,' that is, the lusts which prompt you to 'desire' (see on Jas 4:2) *pleasures;* whence you seek self at the cost of your neighbors, and hence flow 'fightings.'

that war – 'campaign, as an army of soldiers encamped within' [ALFORD] the soul; tumultuously war against the interests of your fellow men, while lusting to advance self. But while warring thus against others they (without his knowledge) war against the soul of the man himself, and against the Spirit; therefore they must be 'mortified' by the Christian.

2. Ye lust – A different *Greek* word from that in Jas 4:1. 'Ye desire'; literally, 'ye set your *mind* (or heart) *on*' an object.

have not – The lust of desire does not ensure the actual possession. Hence 'ye kill' (not as *Margin,* without any old authority, 'envy') to ensure possession. Not probably in the case of professing Christians of that day in a literal sense, but 'kill and envy' (as the *Greek* for 'desire to have' should be translated), that is, harass and oppress through envy [DRUSIUS]. Compare Zec 11:5, 'slay'; *through envy, hate,* and desire to get out of your way, and so are 'murderers' in God's eyes [ESTIUS]. If literal murder [ALFORD] were meant, I do not think it would occur so early in the series; nor had Christians then as yet reached so open criminality. In the Spirit's application of the passage to all ages, literal *killing* is included, flowing from the desire to possess so David and Ahab. There is a climax: 'Ye desire,' the individual lust for an object; 'ye kill and envy,' the feeling and action of individuals against individuals; 'ye fight and war,' the action of many against many.

ye have not, because ye ask not – God promises to those who pray, not to those who fight. The petition of the lustful, murderous, and contentious is not recognized by God as *prayer.* If ye prayed, there would be no 'wars and fightings.' Thus this last clause is an answer to the question, Jas 4:1, 'Whence come wars and fightings?'

3. Some of them are supposed to say in objection, But we do 'ask' (pray); compare Jas 4:2. James replies, It is not enough to ask for good things, but we must ask with a good spirit and intention. 'Ye ask amiss, that ye may consume *it* (your object of prayer) upon (literally, "in") your lusts (literally, "pleasures")'; not that ye may have the things you need for the service of God. Contrast Jas 1:5 with Mt 6:31,32. If ye prayed aright, all your proper wants would be supplied; the improper cravings which produce 'wars and fightings' would then cease. Even believers' prayers are often best answered when their desires are most opposed.

4. The oldest manuscripts omit 'adulterers and,' and read simply, 'Ye adulteresses.' God is the rightful husband; the men of the world are regarded collectively as one *adulteress,* and individually as *adulteresses.*

the world – in so far as the men of it and their motives and acts are aliens to God, for example, its selfish 'lusts' (Jas 4:3), and covetous and ambitious 'wars and fightings' (Jas 4:1).

enmity – not merely 'inimical'; a state of enmity, and that enmity itself. Compare 1Jo 2:15, 'love ... the world ... the love of the Father.'

whosoever ... will be – The *Greek* is emphatic, 'shall *be resolved* to be.' Whether he succeed or not, if his *wish* be to be the friend of the world, he *renders himself, becomes* (so the *Greek* for 'is') by the very fact, 'the enemy of God.' Contrast 'Abraham the friend of God.'

5. in vain – No word of Scripture can be so. The quotation here, as in Eph 5:14, seems to be not so much from a particular passage as one gathered by James under inspiration from the general tenor of such passages in both the Old and New Testaments, as Nu 14:29 Pr 21:20 Ga 5:17.

spirit that dwelleth in us – Other manuscripts read, 'that God hath made to dwell in us' (namely, at Pentecost). If so translated, 'Does the (Holy) Spirit that God hath placed in us lust to (towards) envy' (namely, as ye do in your worldly 'wars and fightings')? Certainly not; ye are therefore walking in the flesh, not in the Spirit, while ye thus *lust towards,* that is, *with envy* against one another. The friendship of the world tends to breed *envy;* the Spirit produces very different fruit. ALFORD attributes the epithet 'with envy,' in the unwarrantable sense of *jealously,* to the Holy Spirit: 'The Spirit *jealously desires* us for His own.' In *English Version* the sense is, 'the (natural) spirit that hath its dwelling in us lusts with (literally, 'to,' or 'towards') envy.' Ye lust, and because ye have not what ye lust after (Jas 4:1,2), ye envy your neighbors who has, and so the *spirit of envy* leads you on to 'fight.' James also here refers to Jas 3:14,16.

6. But – 'Nay, rather.'

he – God.

giveth more grace – ever increasing grace; the farther ye depart from 'envy' [BENGEL].

he saith – The same God who causes His spirit to dwell in believers (Jas 4:5), by the Spirit also speaks in Scripture. The quotation here is probably from Pr 3:34; as probably Pr 21:10 was generally referred to in Jas 4:5. In *Hebrew* it is 'scorneth the scorners,' namely, those who think 'Scripture speaketh in vain.'

resisteth – literally, 'setteth Himself in array against'; even as they, like Pharaoh, set themselves against Him. God repays sinners in their own coin. 'Pride' is the mother of 'envy' (Jas 4:5); it is peculiarly satanic, for by it Satan fell.

the proud – The *Greek* means in derivation one who *shows himself above* his fellows, and so lifts himself against God.

the humble – the unenvious, uncovetous, and unambitious as to the world. Contrast Jas 4:4.

7. Submit to ... God – so ye shall be among 'the humble,' Jas 4:6; also Jas 4:10 1Pe 5:6.

Resist ... devil – Under his banner *pride* and *envy* are enlisted in the world; resist his temptations to these. Faith, humble prayers, and heavenly wisdom, are the weapons of resistance. The language is taken from warfare. 'Submit' as a good soldier puts himself in complete subjection to his captain. 'Resist,' stand bravely against.

he will flee – Translate, 'he *shall* flee.' For it is a promise of God, not a mere assurance from man to man [ALFORD]. He shall flee worsted as he did from Christ.

8. Draw nigh to God – So 'cleave unto Him,' De 30:20, namely, by prayerfully (Jas 4:2,3) 'resisting Satan,' who would oppose our access to God.

he will draw nigh – propitious.

Cleanse ... hands – the outward instruments of action. None but the clean-handed can ascend into the hill of the Lord (justified through Christ, who alone was perfectly so, and as such 'ascended' thither).

purify ... hearts – literally 'make chaste' of your spiritual *adultery* (Jas 4:4, that is, worldliness) 'your hearts': the inward source of all impurity.

double-minded – divided between God and the world. The 'double-minded' is at fault in *heart;* the *sinner* in his *hands* likewise.

9. Be afflicted – literally, 'Endure misery,' that is, mourn over your wretchedness through sin. *Repent with deep sorrow* instead of your present laughter. A blessed *mourning.* Contrast Isa 22:12,13 Lu 6:25. James does not add here, as in Jas 5:1, 'howl,' where he foretells the *doom of the impenitent* at the coming destruction of Jerusalem.

heaviness – literally, 'falling of the countenance,' casting down of the eyes.

10. in the sight of the Lord – as continually in the presence of Him who alone is worthy to be exalted: recognizing His presence in all your ways, the truest incentive to *humility.* The tree, to grow upwards, must strike its roots deep downwards; so man, to be exalted, must have his mind deep-rooted in humility. In 1Pe 5:6, it is, Humble yourselves under the mighty hand of God, namely, in His dealings of Providence: a distinct thought from that here.

lift you up – in part in this world, fully in the world to come.

11. Having mentioned sins of the tongue (Jas 3:5–12), he shows here that *evil-speaking* flows from the same spirit of exalting self at the expense of one's neighbors as caused the 'fightings' reprobated in this chapter (Jas 4:1).

Speak not evil – literally, 'Speak not against' one another.

brethren – implying the inconsistency of such depreciatory speaking of one another in *brethren*.

speaketh evil of the law – for the law in commanding, 'Love thy neighbors as thyself' (Jas 2:8), virtually condemns evil-speaking and judging [ESTIUS]. Those who superciliously condemn the acts and words of others which do not please themselves, thus aiming at the reputation of sanctity, put their own moroseness in the place of the law, and claim to themselves a power of censuring above the law of God, condemning what the law permits [CALVIN]. Such a one acts as though the law could not perform its own office of *judging,* but he must fly upon the office [BENGEL]. This is the last mention of the law in the New Testament. ALFORD rightly takes the 'law' to be the old moral law applied in its comprehensive spiritual fulness by Christ: 'the law of liberty.'

if thou judge the law, thou art not a doer ... but a judge – Setting aside the Christian *brotherhood* as all alike called to be *doers* of the law, in subjection to it, such a one arrogates the office of a *judge*.

12. **There is one lawgiver** – The best authorities read in addition, 'and judge.' Translate, 'There is One (alone) who is (at once) Lawgiver and Judge, (namely) He who is able to save and destroy.' Implying, God alone is Lawgiver and therefore Judge, since it is He alone who can execute His judgments; our inability in this respect shows our presumption in trying to act as judges, as though we were God.

who art thou – The order in the *Greek* is emphatic, 'But (inserted in oldest manuscripts) thou, who art thou that judgest another?' How rashly arrogant in judging thy fellows, and wresting from God the office which belongs to Him over thee and THEM alike!

another – The oldest authorities read, 'thy neighbors.'

13. **Go to now** – 'Come now'; said to excite attention.

ye that say – *boasting* of the morrow.

To-day or to-morrow – as if ye had the free choice of either day as a certainty. Others read, 'To-day *and* to-morrow.'

such a city – literally, 'this the city' (namely, the one present to the mind of the speaker). *This city here.*

continue ... a year – rather, 'spend one year.' Their language implies that when this one year is out, they purpose similarly settling plans for to come [BENGEL].

buy and sell – Their plans for the future are all worldly.

14. **what** – literally, 'of what nature' is your life? that is, how evanescent it is.

It is even – Some oldest authorities read, 'For ye are.' BENGEL, with other old authorities, reads, 'For it shall be,' the future referring to the 'morrow' (Jas 4:13–15). The former expresses, 'Ye yourselves are transitory'; so everything of yours, even your life, must partake of the same transitoriness. Received text has no old authority.

and then vanisheth away – 'afterwards vanishing as it came'; literally, 'afterwards (as it appeared), *so vanishing*' [ALFORD].

15. Literally, 'instead of your saying'. This refers to 'ye that say' (Jas 4:13).

we shall live – The best manuscripts read, 'We shall *both* live *and do*'. The boasters spoke as if *life, action,* and the particular kind of action were in their power, whereas all three depend entirely on the will of the Lord.

16. **now** – as it is. **rejoice in ... boastings** – 'ye boast in arrogant presumptions,' namely, vain confident fancies that the future is certain to you (Jas 4:13).

rejoicing – boasting [BENGEL].

17. The general principle illustrated by the particular example just discussed is here stated: knowledge without practice is imputed to a man as great and presumptuous sin. James reverts to the principle with which he started. Nothing more injures the soul than wasted impressions. Feelings exhaust themselves and evaporate, if not embodied in practice. As we will not act except we feel, so if we will not act out our feelings, we shall soon cease to feel.

Chapter 5

Jas 5:1–20. Woes coming on the wicked rich: believers should be patient unto the Lord's coming: various exhortations.

1. **Go to now** – Come now. A phrase to call solemn attention.

ye rich – who have neglected the true enjoyment of riches, which consists in doing good. James intends this address to rich Jewish unbelievers, not so much for themselves, as for the saints, that they may bear with patience the violence of the rich (Jas 5:7), knowing that God will speedily avenge them on their oppressors [BENGEL].

miseries that shall come – literally, 'that are coming upon you' unexpectedly and swiftly, namely, at the coming of the Lord (Jas 5:7); primarily, at the destruction of Jerusalem; finally, at His visible coming to judge the world.

2. corrupted – *about to be destroyed* through God's curse on your oppression, whereby your riches are accumulated (Jas 5:4). CALVIN thinks the sense is, Your riches perish without being of any use either to others or even to yourselves, for instance, your garments which are moth-eaten in your chests.

garments … moth-eaten – referring to Mt 6:19,20.

3. is cankered – 'rusted through' [ALFORD].

rust … witness against you – in the day of judgment; namely, that your riches were of no profit to any, lying unemployed and so contracting rust.

shall eat your flesh – The rust which once ate your riches, shall then gnaw your conscience, accompanied with punishment which shall prey upon your bodies for ever.

as … fire – not with the slow process of *rusting*, but with the swiftness of consuming *fire*.

for the last days – Ye have heaped together, not treasures as ye suppose (compare Lu 12:19), but wrath against the last days, namely, the coming judgment of the Lord. ALFORD translates more literally, '*In* these last days (before the coming judgment) ye laid up (worldly) treasure' to no profit, instead of repenting and seeking salvation (see on Jas 5:5).

4. Behold – calling attention to their coming doom as no vain threat.

labourers – literally 'workmen.'

of you kept back – So *English Version* rightly. Not as ALFORD, 'crieth out *from* you.' The 'keeping back of the hire' was, *on the part* OF the rich, virtually an act of '*fraud*,' because the poor labourers were not immediately paid. The phrase is therefore not, 'kept back *by* you,' but '*of* you'; the latter implying *virtual,* rather than overt, fraud. James refers to De 24:14,15, 'At this day … give his *hire,* neither shall the sun go down upon it, lest he CRY against thee unto the Lord, and it be sin unto thee.' Many sins 'cry' to heaven for vengeance which men tacitly take no account of, as unchastity and injustice [BENGEL]. Sins peculiarly offensive to God are said to 'cry' to Him. The rich ought to have given freely to the poor; their not doing so was sin. A still greater sin was their not paying their debts. Their greatest sin was not paying them to the poor, whose wages is their all.

cries of them – a double cry; both that of the hire abstractly, and that of the labourers hired.

the Lord of sabaoth – here only in the New Testament. In Ro 9:29 it is a quotation. It is suited to the Jewish tone of the Epistle. It reminds the rich who think the poor have no protector,

that the Lord of the whole hosts in heaven and earth is the guardian and avenger of the latter. He is identical with the 'coming Lord' Jesus (Jas 5:7).

5. Translate, 'Ye have luxuriated … and wantoned.' The former expresses *luxurious effeminacy;* the latter, *wantonness* and *prodigality.* Their luxury was at the expense of the defrauded poor (Jas 5:4).

on the earth – The same earth which has been the scene of your wantonness, shall be the scene of the judgment coming on you: instead of earthly delights ye shall have punishments.

nourished … hearts – that is glutted your bodies like beasts to the full extent of your hearts' desire; ye live to eat, not eat to live.

as in a day of slaughter – The oldest authorities omit 'as.' Ye are like beasts which eat to their hearts' content *on* the very day of their approaching slaughter, unconscious it is near. The phrase answers to 'the last days,' Jas 5:3, which favours ALFORD's translation there, 'in,' not 'for.'

6. Ye have condemned … the just – The Greek aorist expresses, 'Ye are *accustomed* to condemn … the just.' Their condemnation of Christ, 'the Just,' is foremost in James' mind. But all the innocent blood shed, and to be shed, is included, the Holy Spirit comprehending James himself, called 'the Just,' who was slain in a tumult. See my *Introduction.* This gives a peculiar appropriateness to the expression in this verse, the same 'as the righteous (*just*) man' (Jas 5:16). The justice or righteousness of Jesus and His people is what peculiarly provoked the ungodly great men of the world.

he doth not resist you – The very patience of the Just one is abused by the wicked as an incentive to boldness in violent persecution, as if they may do as they please with impunity. God doth 'resist the proud' (Jas 4:6); but Jesus as man, 'as a sheep is dumb before the shearers, so He opened not His mouth': so His people are meek under persecution. The day will come when God will resist (literally, 'set Himself in array against') His foes and theirs.

7. Be patient therefore – as judgment is so near (Jas 5:1,3), ye may well afford to be 'patient' after the example of the *unresisting Just one* (Jas 5:6).

brethren – contrasted with the 'rich' oppressors, Jas 5:1-6.

unto the coming of the Lord – Christ, when the trial of your patience shall cease.

husbandman waiteth for – that is, patiently bears toils and delays through hope of the harvest at last. Its 'preciousness' (compare Ps 126:6, 'precious seed') will more than compensate for all the past. Compare the same image, Ga 6:3,9.

hath long patience for it – 'over it,' *in respect to* it.

until he receive – 'until *it* receive' [ALFORD]. Even if *English Version* be retained, the receiving of the early and latter rains is not to be understood as the object of his hope, but *the harvest* for which those rains are the necessary preliminary. The early rain fell at sowing time, about November or December; the latter rain, about March or April, to mature the grain for harvest. The latter rain that shall precede the coming spiritual harvest, will probably be another Pentecost-like effusion of the Holy Ghost.

8. coming … draweth nigh – The *Greek* expresses present time and a settled state. 1Pe 4:7, 'is at hand.' We are to live in a continued state of expectancy of the Lord's coming, as an event *always* nigh. Nothing can more 'stablish the heart' amidst present troubles than the realized expectation of His speedy coming.

9. Grudge not – rather 'Murmur not'; 'grumble not.' The *Greek* is literally, 'groan': a half-suppressed murmur of impatience and harsh judgment, not uttered aloud or freely. Having exhorted them to patience in bearing wrongs from the wicked, he now exhorts them to a forbearing spirit as to the offenses given by brethren. Christians, who bear the former patiently, sometimes are impatient at the latter, though much less grievous.

lest … condemned – The best manuscript authorities read, 'judged.' James refers to Mt 7:1, 'Judge not lest ye be *judged*.' To 'murmur against one another' is virtually to *judge*, and so to become liable to be *judged*.

judge … before the door – referring to Mt 24:33. The *Greek* is the same in both passages, and so ought to be translated here as there, 'doors,' plural. The phrase means 'near at hand' (Ge 4:7), which in the oldest interpretations [Targums of *Jonathan* and *Jerusalem*] is explained, 'thy sin is reserved *unto the judgment of the world to come*.' Compare 'the everlasting doors' (Ps 24:7, whence He shall come forth). The Lord's coming to destroy Jerusalem is primarily referred to; and ultimately, His coming again visibly to judgment.

10. the prophets – who were especially persecuted, and therefore were especially 'blessed.'

example of suffering affliction – rather, simply, 'of affliction,' literally, 'evil treatment.'

11. count them happy – (Mt 5:10).

which endure – The oldest authorities read, 'which have endured,' which suits the sense better than *English Version*: 'Those who in past days, like the prophets and Job, have endured trials.' Such, not those who 'have lived in pleasure and been wanton on the earth' (Jas 5:5), are 'happy.'

patience – rather, 'endurance,' answering to 'endure': the *Greek* words similarly corresponding. Distinct from the *Greek* word for 'patience'

Jas 5:10. The same word ought to be translated, 'endurance,' Jas 1:3. He here reverts to the subject which he began with.

Job – This passage shows the history of him is concerning a real, not an imaginary person; otherwise his case could not be quoted as an example at all. Though he showed much of impatience, yet he always returned to this, that he committed himself wholly to God, and at last showed a perfect spirit of enduring submission.

and have seen – (with the eyes of your mind). ALFORD translates from the old and genuine reading, 'see also,' The old reading is, however, capable of being translated as *English Version*.

the end of the Lord – the end which the Lord gave. If Job had much to 'endure,' remember also Job's happy 'end.' Hence, learn, though much tried, to 'endure to the end.'

that – ALFORD and others translate, 'inasmuch as,' 'for.'

pitiful … of tender mercy – The former refers to the 'feeling'; the latter, to the *act*. His *pity* is shown in not laying on the *patient endurer* more trials than he is able to bear; His *mercy*, in His giving a happy 'end' to the trials [BENGEL].

12. But above all – as swearing is utterly alien to the Christian meek 'endurance' just recommended.

swear not – through impatience, to which trials may tempt you (Jas 5:10,11). In contrast to this stands the proper use of the tongue, Jas 5:13. James here refers to Mt 5:34

let your yea be yea – Do not use oaths in your everyday conversation, but let a simple affirmative or denial be deemed enough to establish your word.

condemnation – literally, 'judgment,' namely, of 'the Judge' who 'standeth before the doors' (Jas 5:9).

13. afflicted – referring to the 'suffering affliction' (Jas 5:10).

let him pray – not 'swear' in rash impatience.

merry – joyous in mind.

sing psalms – of praise. Paul and Silas sang psalms even in affliction.

14. let him call for the elders – not some *one* of the elders, as Roman Catholics interpret it, to justify their usage in *extreme unction*. The prayers of the elders over the sick would be much the same as though the whole Church which they represent should pray [BENGEL].

anointing him with oil – The usage which Christ committed to His apostles was afterwards continued with laying on of hands, as a token of the highest faculty of medicine in the Church, just as we find in 1Co 6:2 the Church's highest judicial function. Now that the miraculous gift of healing has been withdrawn for the most part, to use the sign where the reality is wanting would be unmeaning superstition. Compare other apostolic usages now discontinued rightly, 1Co 11:4–15 16:20. 'Let them use oil who can by their prayers obtain recovery for the sick: let those who cannot do this, abstain from using the empty sign' [WHITAKER]. Romish extreme unction is administered to those *whose life is despaired of*, to heal the *soul*, whereas James' unction was to heal the body. CARDINAL CAJETAN [*Commentary*] admits that James cannot refer to extreme unction. Oil in the East, and especially among the Jews (see the Talmud, *Jerusalem* and *Babylon*), was much used as a curative agent. It was also a sign of the divine grace. Hence it was an appropriate sign in performing miraculous cures.

in the name of the Lord – by whom alone the miracle was performed: men were but the instruments.

15. prayer – He does not say *the oil* shall save: it is but the symbol.

save – plainly not as Rome says, 'save' *the soul*, but heal 'the sick': as the words, 'the Lord shall raise him up,' prove. So the same *Greek* is translated, 'made (thee) whole,' Mt 9:21,22.

and if … sins – for not all who are sick are so because of some special sins. Here a case is supposed of one visited with sickness for special sins.

have committed – literally, '*be* in a state of *having committed* sins,' that is, be under the consequences of sins committed.

they – rather, '*it*': his *having committed sins* shall be forgiven him. The connection of sin and sickness is implied in Isa 33:24 Mt 9:2–5 Joh 5:14. The absolution of the sick, retained in the Church of England, refers to the sins which the sick man confesses (Jas 5:16) and repents of, whereby outward scandal has been given to the Church and the cause of religion; not to sins in their relation to God, the only Judge.

16. The oldest authorities read, 'Confess, THEREFORE', Not only in the particular case of sickness, but universally confess.

faults – your *falls* and *offenses*, in relation to one another. The word is not the same as *sins*. Mt 5:23,24 Lu 17:4, illustrate the precept here.

one to another – not to the priest, as Rome insists. The Church of England *recommends* in certain cases. Rome *compels* confession in all cases. Confession is desirable in the case of (1) *wrong* done to a neighbor; (2) when under a troubled conscience we ask *counsel* of a godly minister or friend as to how we may obtain God's forgiveness and strength to sin no more, or when we desire their intercessory prayers for us ('Pray for one another'): 'Confession may be made to anyone who can pray' [BENGEL]; (3) *open* confession of sin before the Church and the world, in token of penitence. Not *auricular* confession.

that ye may be healed – of your bodily sicknesses. Also that, if your sickness be the punishment of sin, the latter being forgiven on intercessory prayer, 'ye may be healed' of the former. Also, that ye may be healed spiritually.

effectual – intense and fervent, not 'wavering' (Jas 1:6), [BEZA]. 'When *energized*' by the Spirit, as those were who performed miracles [HAMMOND]. This suits the collocation of the *Greek* words and the sense well. A righteous man's prayer is always heard generally, but his particular request for the *healing* of another was then likely to be granted when he was one *possessing a special charism of the Spirit*. ALFORD translates, 'Availeth much *in its working*.' The 'righteous' is one himself careful to avoid 'faults,' and showing his faith by works (Jas 2:24).

17. Elias … like passions as we – therefore it cannot be said that he was so raised above us as to afford no example applicable to common mortals like ourselves.

prayed earnestly – literally, 'prayed with prayer': Hebraism for *prayed intensely*. Compare Lu 22:15, 'With desire I have desired,' that is, earnestly desired. ALFORD is wrong in saying, Elias' prayer that it might not rain 'is not even hinted at in the Old Testament history.' In 1Ki 17:1 it is plainly implied, 'As the Lord God of Israel liveth, *before whom I stand*, there shall not be dew nor rain these years, but *according to my word*.' His prophecy of the fact was according to a divine intimation given to him in answer to prayer. In jealousy for God's honour (1Ki 19:10), and being of one mind with God in his abhorrence of apostasy, he prayed that the national idolatry should be punished with a national judgment, drought; and on Israel's profession of repentance he prayed for the removal of the visitation, as is implied in 1Ki 18:39–42; compare Lu 4:25.

three years – Compare 1Ki 18:1, 'The third year,' namely, from Elijah's going to Zarephath; the prophecy (Jas 5:1) was probably about five or six months previously.

18. prayed … and – that is, 'and so.' Mark the connection between the prayer and its accomplishment.

her fruit – her usual and due fruit, heretofore withheld on account of sin. Three and a half years is the time also that the two witnesses prophesy who 'have power to shut and open heaven that it rain not.'

19. The blessing of reclaiming an erring sinner by the mutual consent and intercessory prayer just recommended.

do err – more literally, 'be led astray.'

the truth – the Gospel doctrine and precepts.

one – literally, 'any'; as '*any*' before. *Everyone* ought to seek the salvation of *everyone* [BENGEL].

20. Let him – the converted.

know – for his comfort, and the encouragement of others to do likewise.

shall save – future. The salvation of the one so converted shall be manifested hereafter.

shall hide a multitude of sins – not his own, but the sins of the converted. The *Greek* verb in the middle voice requires this. Pr 10:12 refers to charity 'covering' the sins of others *before men;* James refers to one's effecting by the conversion of another that that other's sins be covered *before God,* namely, with Christ's atonement. He effects this by making the convert partaker in the Christian covenant for the remission of all sins. Though this hiding of sins was included in the previous 'shall save,' James expresses it to mark in detail the greatness of the blessing conferred on the penitent through the converter's instrumentality, and to incite others to the same good deed.

1 PETER

A.R. Faussett

Introduction

Its genuineness

Its genuineness is attested by 2Pe 3:1. On the authority of Second Peter, see the *Introduction*. Also by POLYCARP (in EUSEBIUS [*Ecclesiastical History,* 4.14]), who, in writing to the Philippians, quotes many passages: in the second chapter he quotes 1Pe 1:13,21 3:9; in the fifth chapter, 1Pe 2:11. EUSEBIUS says of PAPIAS [*Ecclesiastical History,* 3.39] that he, too, quotes Peter's First Epistle. IRENAEUS [*Against Heresies,* 4.9.2] expressly mentions it; and in [4.16.5], 1Pe 2:16. CLEMENT OF ALEXANDRIA [*Miscellanies,* 1.3, p. 544], quotes 1Pe 2:11,12,15,16; and [p. 562], 1Pe 1:21,22; and [4, p. 584], 1Pe 3:14-17; and [p. 585], 1Pe 4:12–14. ORIGEN (in EUSEBIUS [*Ecclesiastical History,* 6.25]) mentions this Epistle; in [*Homily 7,* on Joshua, vol. 2, p. 63], he mentions *both* Epistles; and [*Commentary* on Psalm 3 and on John], he mentions 1Pe 3:18–21. TERTULLIAN [*Antidote to the Scorpion's Sting,* 12], quotes expressly 1Pe 2:20,21; and [*Antidote to the Scorpion's Sting,* 14], 1Pe 2:13,17. EUSEBIUS states it as the opinion of those before him that this was among *the universally acknowledged* Epistles.

The *internal evidence* is equally strong. The author calls himself the apostle Peter, 1Pe 1:1, and 'a witness of Christ's sufferings,' and an 'elder,' 1Pe 5:1. The energy of the style harmonizes with the warmth of Peter's character; and, as ERASMUS says, this Epistle is full of apostolic dignity and authority and is worthy of the leader among the apostles.

Peter's personal history

Simon, Or Simeon, was a native of Bethsaida on the Sea of Galilee, son of Jonas or John. With his father and his brother Andrew he carried on trade as a fisherman at Capernaum, his subsequent place of abode. He was a married man, and tradition represents his wife's name as *Concordia* or *Perpetua.* CLEMENT OF ALEXANDRIA says that she suffered martyrdom, her husband encouraging her to be faithful unto death, 'Remember, dear, our Lord.' His wife's mother was restored from a fever by Christ. He was brought to Jesus by his brother Andrew, who had been a disciple of John the Baptist, but was pointed to the Saviour as 'the Lamb of God' by his master (Joh 1:29). Jesus, on first beholding him, gave him the name by which chiefly he is known, indicative of his subsequent character and work in the Church, 'Peter' (*Greek*) or 'Cephas' (*Aramaic*), *a stone* (Mt 4:18). He did not join our Lord finally until a subsequent period. The leading incidents in his apostolic life are well known: his walking on the troubled waters to meet Jesus, but sinking through doubting (Mt 14:30);

his bold and clear acknowledgment of the divine person and office of Jesus (Mt 16:16 Mr 8:29 Joh 11:27), notwithstanding the difficulties in the way of such belief, whence he was then also designated as *the stone,* or *rock* (Mt 16:18); but his rebuke of his Lord when announcing what was so unpalatable to carnal prejudices, Christ's coming passion and death (Mt 16:22); his passing from one extreme to the opposite, in reference to Christ's offer to wash his feet (Joh 13:8,9); his self-confident assertion that *he* would never forsake his Lord, whatever others might do (Mt 26:33), followed by his base denial of Christ thrice with curses (Mt 26:75); his deep penitence; Christ's full forgiveness and prophecy of his faithfulness unto death, after he had received from him a profession of 'love' as often repeated as his previous denial (Joh 21:15–17). These incidents illustrate his character as zealous, pious, and ardently attached to the Lord, but at the same time impulsive in feeling, rather than calmly and continuously steadfast. Prompt in action and ready to avow his convictions boldly, he was hasty in judgment, precipitate, and too self-confident in the assertion of his own steadfastness; the result was that, though he abounded in animal courage, his moral courage was too easily overcome by fear of man's opinion. A wonderful change was wrought in him by his restoration after his fall, through the grace of his risen Lord. His zeal and ardour became sanctified, being chastened by a spirit of unaffected humility. His love to the Lord was, if possible, increased, while his mode of manifesting it now was in doing and suffering for His name, rather than in loud protestations. Thus, when imprisoned and tried before the Sanhedrim for preaching Christ, he boldly avowed his determination to continue to do so. He is well called 'the mouth of the apostles.' His faithfulness led to his apprehension by Herod Agrippa, with a view to his execution, from which, however, he was delivered by the angel of the Lord.

After the ascension he took the lead in the Church; and on the descent of the Holy Spirit at Pentecost, he exercised the designed power of 'the keys' of Christ's kingdom, by opening the door of the Church, in preaching, for the admission of thousands of Israelites; and still more so in opening (in obedience to a special revelation) an entrance to the 'devout' (that is, Jewish proselyte from heathendom) *Gentile,* Cornelius: the forerunner of the harvest gathered in from *idolatrous* Gentiles at Antioch. This explains in what sense Christ used as to him the words, 'Upon this rock I will build my Church' (Mt 16:18), namely, on the preaching of Christ, the true 'Rock', by connection with whom only he was given the designation: a title shared in common on the same grounds by the rest of the apostles, as the first founders of the Church on Christ, 'the chief corner-stone' (Eph 2:20). A name is often given in *Hebrew,* not that the person is actually the thing itself, but has some special relation to it; as Elijah means *Mighty Jehovah,* so Simon is called Peter 'the rock', not that he is so, save by connection with Jesus, the only true Rock (Isa 28:16 1Co 3:11). As subsequently he identified himself with 'Satan,' and is therefore *called so* (Mt 16:23), in the same way, by his clear confession of Christ, the Rock, he became identified with Him, and is accordingly so called (Mt 16:18). It is certain that there is no instance on record of Peter's having ever claimed or exercised supremacy; on the contrary, he is represented as *sent* by the apostles at Jerusalem to confirm the Samaritans baptized by Philip the deacon; again at the council of Jerusalem, not he, but James the president, or leading bishop in the Church of that city, pronounced the authoritative decision: Ac 15:19, 'My *sentence* is'. A kind of primacy, doubtless (though certainly not supremacy), was given him on the ground of his age, and prominent earnestness, and boldness in taking the lead on many important occasions. Hence he is called 'first' in enumerating the apostles. Hence, too, arise the phrases, 'Peter and the Eleven,' 'Peter and the rest of the apostles'; and Paul, in going up to Jerusalem after his conversion, went to see Peter in particular.

Once only he again betrayed the same spirit of vacillation through fear of man's reproach which had caused his denial of his Lord. Though at the Jerusalem council he advocated the exemption of Gentile converts from the ceremonial observances of the law, yet he, after having associated in closest intercourse with the Gentiles at Antioch, withdrew from them, through dread of the prejudices of his Jewish brethren who came from James, and timidly dissembled his conviction of the religious equality of Jew and Gentile; for this Paul openly withstood and rebuked him: a plain refutation of his alleged *supremacy* and *infallibility* (except where specially inspired, as in writing his Epistles). In all other cases he showed himself to be, indeed, as Paul calls him, 'a pillar' (Ga 2:9). Subsequently we find him in 'Babylon,' whence he wrote this First Epistle to the Israelite believers of the dispersion, and the Gentile Christians united in Christ, in Pontus, Galatia, Cappadocia, Asia, and Bithynia. JEROME [*On Illustrious Men,* 1] states that 'Peter, after having been bishop of Antioch, and after having preached to the believers of the circumcision in Pontus [plainly inferred from 1Pe 1:1], in the second year of Claudius went to Rome to refute Simon Magus, and for twenty-five years there held the episcopal chair, down to the last year of Nero, that is, the fourteenth, by whom he was crucified with his head downwards, declaring himself unworthy to be crucified as his Lord, and was buried in the Vatican, near the triumphal way.' EUSEBIUS [*Chronicles,* Anno 3], also asserts his episcopate at Antioch; his assertion that Peter founded that Church contradicts Ac 11:19–22. His journey to Rome to oppose Simon Magus arose from JUSTIN's story of the statue found at Rome (really the statue of the Sabine god, *Semo Sanctus,* or Hercules, mistaken as if Simon Magus were worshipped by that name, 'Simoni Deo Sancto'; found in the Tiber in 1574, or on an island in the Tiber in 1662), combined with the account in Ac 8:9–24. The twenty-five years' bishopric is chronologically impossible, as it would make Peter, at the interview with Paul at Antioch, to have been then for some years bishop of Rome! His crucifixion is certain from Christ's prophecy, Joh 21:18,19. DIONYSIUS OF CORINTH (in EUSEBIUS [*Ecclesiastical History,* 2.25]) asserted in an epistle to the Romans, that Paul and Peter planted both the Roman and Corinthian churches, and endured martyrdom in Italy at the same time. So TERTULLIAN [*Against Marcion,* 4.5, and *The Prescription Against Heretics,* 36, 38]. Also Caius, the presbyter of Rome, in EUSEBIUS [*Ecclesiastical History,* 2.25] asserts that some memorials of their martyrdom were to be seen at Rome on the road to Ostia. So EUSEBIUS [*Ecclesiastical History,* 2.25, and *Demonstration of the Gospel,* 3.116]. So LACTANTIUS [*Of the Manner in Which the Persecutors Died,* 2]. Many of the details are palpably false; whether the *whole* be so or not is dubious, considering the tendency to concentrate at Rome events of interest [ALFORD]. What is certain is, that Peter was not there before the writing of the Epistle to the Romans (A.D. 58), otherwise he would have been mentioned in it; nor during Paul's first imprisonment at Rome, otherwise he would have been mentioned in some one of Paul's many other Epistles written from Rome; nor during Paul's second imprisonment, at least when he was writing the Second Epistle to Timothy, just before his martyrdom. He *may* have gone to Rome after Paul's death, and, as common tradition represents, been imprisoned in the Mamertine dungeon, and crucified on the Janiculum, on the eminence of St. Pietro in Montorio, and his remains deposited under the great altar in the centre of the famous basilica of St. Peter. AMBROSE [*Epistles,* 33 (Edition Paris, 1586), p. 1022] relates that St. Peter, not long before his death, being overcome by the solicitations of his fellow Christians to save himself, was fleeing from Rome when he was met by our Lord, and on asking, 'Lord, whither goest Thou?' received the answer, 'I go to be crucified afresh.' On this he returned and joyfully went to martyrdom. The church called '*Domine quo vadis*' on the Appian Way, commemorates the legend. It is not unlikely that the whole tradition is built on the connection which existed between Paul and Peter. As Paul, 'the apostle of the uncircumcision,' wrote Epistles to Galatia, Ephesus, and Colosse, and to Philemon at Colosse, making the Gentile Christians the persons prominently addressed, and the Jewish Christians subordinately so; so, vice versa, Peter, 'the apostle of the circumcision', addressed the same churches, the Jewish Christians in them primarily, and the Gentile Christians also, secondarily.

To whom the epistle is addressed

The heading, 1Pe 1:1, 'to the elect strangers (spiritually *pilgrims*) of the dispersion' (*Greek*), clearly marks the Christians of the *Jewish* dispersion as prominently addressed, but still including also *Gentile* Christians as grafted into the Christian Jewish stock by adoption and faith, and so being part of the true Israel. 1Pe 1:14 2:9,10 3:6 4:3 clearly prove this. Thus he, the apostle of the circumcision, sought to unite in one Christ Jew and Gentile, promoting thereby the same work and doctrine as Paul the apostle of the uncircumcision. The provinces are named by Peter in the heading in the order proceeding from northeast to south and west. Pontus was the country of the Christian Jew Aquila. To Galatia Paul paid two visits, founding and confirming churches. Crescens, his companion, went there about the time of Paul's last imprisonment, just before his martyrdom. Ancyra was subsequently its ecclesiastical metropolis. Men of Cappadocia, as well as of 'Pontus' and 'Asia,' were among the hearers of Peter's effective sermon on the Pentecost whereon the Spirit decended on the Church; these probably brought home to their native land the first tidings of the Gospel. Proconsular 'Asia' included Mysia, Lydia, Caria, Phrygia, Pisidia, and Lyaconia. In LYACONIA were the churches of Iconium, founded by Paul and Barnabas; of Lystra, Timothy's birthplace, where Paul was stoned at the instigation of the Jews; and of Derbe, the birthplace of Gaius, or Caius. In Pisidia was Antioch, where Paul was the instrument of converting many, but was driven out by the Jews. In Caria was Miletus, containing doubtless a Christian Church. In Phrygia, Paul preached both times when visiting Galatia in its neighbourhood, and in it were the churches of Laodicea, Hierapolis, and Colosse, of which last Church Philemon and Onesimus were members, and Archippus and Epaphras leaders. In Lydia was the Philadelphian Church, favourably noticed in Re 3:7; that of Sardis, the capital, and of Thyatira, and of Ephesus, founded by Paul, and a scene of the labours of Aquila and Priscilla and Apollos, and subsequently of more than two whole years' labour of Paul again, and subsequently censured for falling from its first love in Re 2:4. Smyrna of Ionia was in the same quarter, and as one of the seven churches receives unqualified praise. In Mysia was Pergamos. Troas, too, is known as the scene of Paul's preaching and raising Eutychus to life (Ac 20:6–10), and of his subsequently staying for a time with Carpus (2Ti 4:13). Of 'Bithynia,' no Church is expressly named in Scripture elsewhere. When Paul at an earlier period 'assayed to go into Bithynia' (Ac 16:7), the Spirit suffered him not. But afterwards, we infer from 1Pe 1:1, the Spirit did impart the Gospel to that country, possibly by Peter's ministry, In government, these several churches, it appears from this Epistle (1Pe 5:1,2, 'Feed'), were much in the same states as when Paul addressed the Ephesian 'elders' at Miletus (Ac 20:17,28, 'feed') in very similar language; elders or presbyter-bishops ruled, while the apostles exercised the general superintendence. They were exposed to persecutions, though apparently not systematic, but rather annoyances and reproach arising from their not joining their heathen neighbors in riotous living, into which, however, some of them were in danger of falling. The evils which existed among themselves, and which are therefore reproved, were ambition and lucre-seeking on the part of the presbyters (1Pe 5:2,3), evil thoughts and words among the members in general, and a want of sympathy and generosity towards one another.

His object in writing

His object seems to be, by the prospect of their heavenly portion and by Christ's example, to afford consolation to the persecuted, and prepare them for a greater approaching ordeal, and to exhort all, husbands, wives, servants, presbyters, and people, to a due discharge of relative duties, so as to give no handle to the enemy to reproach Christianity, but rather to win them to it, and so to establish them in 'the true grace of God wherein they stand' (1Pe 5:12). However, see on 1Pe 5:12, on the oldest reading. ALFORD rightly argues that 'exhorting and testifying' there, refer to Peter's *exhortations* throughout the Epistle grounded on *testimony* which he bears *to the Gospel truth, already well known to his readers by the teaching of Paul in those churches.* They were already introduced 'into' (so the *Greek,* 1Pe 5:12) this *grace of God* as their safe *standing-ground.* Compare 1Co 15:1, 'I declare unto you the Gospel *wherein ye stand.*' Therefore he does not, in this Epistle, set forth a complete statement of this Gospel doctrine of grace, but falls back on it as already known. Compare 1Pe 1:8,18, 'ye know'; 1Pe 3:15 2Pe 3:1. Not that Peter servilely copies the style and mode of teaching of Paul, but as an independent witness in his own style attests the same truths. We may divide the Epistle into: (I) The inscription (1Pe 1:1,2). (II) The stirring-up of a pure feeling in believers as born again of God. By the motive of *hope* to which God has regenerated us (1Pe 1:3–12); bringing forth the fruit of *faith,* considering the costly price paid for our redemption from sin (1Pe 1:14–21). Being purified by the Spirit unto *love* of the brethren as begotten of God's eternal word, as spiritual priest-kings, to whom alone Christ is precious (1Pe 1:22 2:10); after Christ's example in suffering, maintaining a good *conversation* in every relation (1Pe 2:10 3:14), and a good *profession* of faith as having in view Christ's once-offered sacrifice, and His future coming to judgment (1Pe 3:15 4:11); and exhibiting *patience* in *adversity,* as looking for future glorification with Christ, (1) in general as Christians, 1Pe 4:12-19; (2) each in his own sphere, 1Pe 5:1–11. 'The title 'Beloved' marks the separation of the second part from the first, 1Pe 2:11; and of the third part from the second, 1Pe 4:12' [BENGEL]. (III). The conclusion.

Time and place of writing

It was plainly before the open and *systematic* persecution of the later years of Nero had begun. That this Epistle was written after Paul's Epistles, even those written during his imprisonment at Rome, ending in A.D. 63, appears from the acquaintance which Peter in this Epistle shows he has with them. Compare 1Pe 2:13 with 1Ti 2:2–4; 1Pe 2:18 with Eph 6:5; 1Pe 1:2 with Eph 1:4–7; 1Pe 1:3 with Eph 1:3; 1Pe 1:14 with Ro 12:2; 1Pe 2:6–10 with Ro 9:32,33; 1Pe 2:13 with Ro 13:1-4; 1Pe 2:16 with Ga 5:13; 1Pe 2:18 with Eph 6:5; 1Pe 3:1 with Eph 5:22; 1Pe 3:9 with Ro 12:17; 1Pe 4:9 with Php 2:14 Ro 12:13 Heb 13:2; 1Pe 4:10 with Ro 12:6–8; 1Pe 5:1 with Ro 8:18; 1Pe 5:5 with Eph 5:21 Php 2:3,5–8; 1Pe 5:8 with 1Th 5:6; 1Pe 5:14 with 1Co 16:20. Moreover, in 1Pe 5:13, Mark is mentioned as with Peter in Babylon. This must have been after Col 4:10 (A.D. 61-63), when Mark was with Paul at Rome, but intending to go to Asia Minor. Again, in 2Ti 4:11 (A.D. 67 or 68), Mark was in or near Ephesus, in Asia Minor, and Timothy is told to bring him to Rome. So that it is likely it was after this, namely, after Paul's martyrdom, that Mark joined Peter, and consequently that this Epistle was written. It is not likely that Peter would have entrenched on Paul's field of labour, the churches of Asia Minor, *during Paul's lifetime.* The death of the apostle of the uncircumcision, and the consequent need of someone to follow up his teachings, probably gave occasion to the testimony given by Peter to the same churches, collectively addressed, in behalf of the same truth. The relation in which the Pauline Gentile churches stood towards the apostles at Jerusalem favours this view. Even the Gentile Christians would naturally look to the spiritual fathers of the Church at Jerusalem, the centre whence the Gospel had emanated to them, for counsel wherewith to meet the pretensions of Judaizing Christians and heretics; and Peter, always prominent among the apostles in Jerusalem, would even when elsewhere feel a deep interest in them, especially when they were by death bereft of Paul's guidance. BIRKS [*Horæ Evangelicæ*] suggests that false teachers may have appealed from Paul's doctrine to that of James and Peter. Peter then would naturally write to confirm the doctrines of grace and tacitly show there was no difference between his teaching and Paul's. BIRKS prefers dating the Epistle A.D. 58, after Paul's second visit to Galatia, when Silvanus was with him, and so could not have been with Peter (A.D. 54), and before his imprisonment at Rome, when Mark was with him, and so could not have been with Peter (A.D. 62); perhaps when Paul was detained at Cæsarea, and so debarred from personal intercourse with those churches. I prefer the view previously stated. This sets aside the tradition that Paul and Peter suffered martyrdom together at Rome. ORIGEN's and EUSEBIUS' statement that Peter visited the churches of Asia in person seems very probable.

The PLACE OF WRITING was doubtless Babylon on the Euphrates (1Pe 5:13). It is most improbable that in the midst of writing matter-of-fact communications and salutations in a remarkably plain Epistle, the symbolical language of prophecy (namely, 'Babylon' for *Rome*) should be used. JOSEPHUS [*Antiquities*, 15.2.2; 3.1] states that there was a *great multitude of Jews* in the Chaldean Babylon; it is therefore likely that 'the apostle of the circumcision' (Ga 2:7,8) would at some time or other visit them. Some have maintained that the Babylon meant was in Egypt because Mark preached in and around Alexandria after Peter's death, and therefore it is likely he did so along with that apostle in the same region previously. But no mention elsewhere in *Scripture* is made of this Egyptian Babylon, but only of the Chaldean one. And though towards the close of Caligula's reign a persecution drove the Jews thence to Seleucia, and a plague five years after still further thinned their numbers, yet this does not preclude their return and multiplication during the twenty years that elapsed between the plague and the writing of the Epistle. Moreover, the order in which the countries are enumerated, from northeast to south and west, is such as would be adopted by one writing from the Oriental Babylon on the Euphrates, not from Egypt or Rome. Indeed, COSMAS INDICOPLEUSTES, in the sixth century, understood the Babylon meant to be *outside* the Roman empire. Silvanus, Paul's companion, became subsequently Peter's, and was the carrier of this Epistle.

Style

Fervour and practical truth, rather than logical reasoning, are the characteristics, of this Epistle, as they were of its energetic, warm-hearted writer. His familiarity with Paul's Epistles shown in the language accords with what we should expect from the fact of Paul's having 'communicated the Gospel which he preached among the Gentiles' (as revealed specially to him) to Peter among others 'of reputation' (Ga 2:2). Individualities occur, such as baptism, 'the answer of a good conscience toward God' (1Pe 3:21); 'consciousness of God' (*Greek*), 1Pe 2:19, as a motive for enduring sufferings; 'living hope' (1Pe 1:3); 'an inheritance incorruptible, undefiled, and that fadeth not away' (1Pe 1:4); 'kiss of charity' (1Pe 5:14). Christ is viewed less in relation to His past sufferings than as at present exalted and hereafter to be manifested in all His majesty. *Glory* and *hope* are prominent features in this Epistle (1Pe 1:8), so much so that WEISS entitles him 'the apostle of hope.' The realization of future bliss as near causes him to regard believers as but 'strangers' and 'sojourners' here. Chastened fervour, deep humility, and ardent love appear, just as we should expect from one who had been so graciously restored after his grievous fall. 'Being converted,' he truly does 'strengthen his brethren.' His fervour shows itself in often repeating the same thought in similar words.

In some passages he shows familiarity with the Epistle of James, the apostle of special weight with the Jewish legalizing party, whose inspiration he thus confirms (compare 1Pe 1:6,7 with Jas 1:2,3; 1Pe 1:24 with Jas 1:10; 1Pe 2:1 with Jas 1:21; 1Pe 4:8 with Jas 5:20, both quoting Pr 10:12 5:5 with Jas 4:6, both quoting Pr 3:34). In most of these cases Old Testament quotations are the common ground of both. 'Strong susceptibility to outward impressions, liveliness of feeling, dexterity in handling subjects, dispose natures like that of Peter to repeat afresh the thoughts of others' [STEIGER].

The diction of this Epistle and of his speeches in Acts is very similar: an undesigned coincidence, and so a mark of genuineness (compare 1Pe 2:7 with Ac 4:11; 1Pe 1:12 with Ac 5:32; 1Pe 2:24 with Ac 5:30 10:39; 1Pe 5:1 with Ac 2:32 3:15; 1Pe 1:10 with Ac 3:18 10:43; 1Pe 1:21 with Ac 3:15 10:40; 1Pe 4:5 with Ac 10:42; 1Pe 2:24 with Ac 3:19,26).

There is, too, a recurrence to the language of the Lord at the last interview after His resurrection, recorded in Joh 21:15–23. Compare 'the Shepherd … of … souls,' 1Pe 2:25; 'Feed the flock of God,' 'the chief Shepherd,' 1Pe 5:2,4, with Joh 21:15–17; 'Feed My lambs … sheep'; also 'Whom … ye *love*,' 1Pe 1:8 2:7, with Joh 21:15–17; 'lovest thou Me?' and 2Pe 1:14, with Joh 21:18,19. WIESINGER well says, 'He who in loving impatience cast himself into the sea to meet the Lord, is also the man who most earnestly testifies to the hope of His return; he who dated his own faith from the sufferings of his Master, is never weary in holding up the suffering form of the Lord before his readers to comfort and stimulate them; he before whom the death of a martyr is in assured expectation, is the man who, in the greatest variety of aspects, sets forth the duty, as well as the consolation, of suffering for Christ; as a rock of the Church he grounds his readers against the storm of present tribulation on the true Rock of ages.'

Contents

See *Outlines of the New Testament Books,* p. 905

Chapter 1

1Pe 1:1–25. Address to the elected of the Godhead: thanksgiving for the living hope to which we are begotten, producing joy amidst sufferings: this salvation an object of deepest interest to prophets and to angels: its costly price a motive to holiness and love, as we are born again of the ever-abiding word of God.

1. Peter – *Greek* form of Cephas, *man of rock.* **an apostle of Jesus Christ** – 'He who preaches otherwise than as a messenger of Christ, is not to be heard; if he preach as such, then it is all one as if thou didst hear Christ speaking in thy presence' [LUTHER].

to the strangers scattered – literally, 'sojourners *of the dispersion*'; only in Joh 7:35 and Jas 1:1, in New Testament, and the *Septuagint,* Ps 147:2, 'the outcasts of Israel'; the designation peculiarly given to *the Jews* in their dispersed state throughout the world ever since the Babylonian captivity. These he, as the apostle of the circumcision, primarily addresses, but not in the limited temporal sense only; he regards their temporal condition as a shadow of their spiritual calling to be *strangers* and pilgrims on earth, looking for the heavenly Jerusalem as their home. So the *Gentile* Christians, as the spiritual Israel, are included secondarily, as having the same high calling. He (1Pe 1:14 2:10 4:3) plainly refers to Christian *Gentiles* (compare 1Pe 1:17 1Pe 2:11). Christians, if they rightly consider their calling, must never settle themselves here, but feel themselves *travellers*. As the Jews in their *dispersion* diffused through the nations the knowledge of the one God, preparatory to Christ's first advent, so Christians, by their dispersion among the unconverted, diffuse the knowledge of Christ, preparatory to His second advent. 'The children of God scattered abroad' constitute one whole in Christ, who 'gathers them together in one,' now partially and in Spirit, hereafter perfectly and visibly. 'Elect,' in the *Greek* order, comes before 'strangers'; *elect*, in relation to heaven, *strangers*, in relation to the earth. The *election* here is that of individuals to eternal life by the sovereign grace of God, as the sequel shows. 'While each is certified of his own election by the Spirit, he receives no assurance concerning others, nor are we to be too inquisitive [Joh 21:21,22]; Peter numbers them among the *elect*, as they carried the appearance of having been regenerated' [CALVIN]. He calls the whole Church by the designation strictly belonging only to the better portion of them [CALVIN]. The election to *hearing*, and that to *eternal life*, are distinct. Realization of our election is a strong motive to holiness. The minister invites all, yet he does not hide the truth that in none but the elect will the preaching effect eternal blessing. As the chief fruit of exhortations, and even of threatenings, redounds to 'the elect'; therefore, at the outset, Peter addresses *them*. STEIGER translates, to 'the elect pilgrims who form the dispersion in Pontus.' The *order* of the provinces is that in which they would be viewed by one writing from the east from *Babylon* (1Pe 5:13); from northeast southwards to Galatia, southeast to Cappadocia, then Asia, and back to Bithynia, west of Pontus. Contrast the order, Ac 2:9. He now was ministering to those same peoples as he preached to on Pentecost: 'Parthians, Medes, Elamites, dwellers in Mesopotamia and Judea,' that is, the Jews now subject to the Parthians, whose capital was *Babylon*, where he laboured in person; 'dwellers in Cappadocia, Pontus, Asia, Phrygia, Bithynia,' the Asiatic dispersion derived from Babylon, whom he ministers to by letter.

2. foreknowledge – *foreordaining* love (1Pe 1:20), inseparable from God's *foreknowledge*, the origin *from* which, and pattern *according to* which, election takes place. Ac 2:23, and Ro 11:2, prove 'foreknowledge' to be *foreordination*. God's *foreknowledge* is not the perception of any ground of action out of Himself; still in it liberty is comprehended, and all absolute constraint debarred [ANSELM in STEIGER]. For so the Son of God was 'foreknown' (so the *Greek* for 'foreordained,' 1Pe 1:20) to be the sacrificial Lamb, not against, or without His will, but His will rested in the will of the Father; this includes self-conscious action; nay, even cheerful acquiescence. The *Hebrew* and *Greek* 'know' include *approval* and *acknowledging* as one's own. The *Hebrew* marks the oneness of *loving* and *choosing*, by having one word for both, *bachar* (*Greek*, '*hairetizo*,' Septuagint). Peter descends from the eternal 'election' of God through the *new birth*, to the believer's 'sanctification,' that from this he might again raise them through the consideration of their *new birth* to a 'living hope' of the heavenly 'inheritance' [HEIDEGGER]. The divine three are introduced in their respective functions in redemption.

through – *Greek*, 'in'; the element in which we are elected. The 'election' of God realized and manifested itself 'IN' their sanctification. Believers are 'sanctified through the offering of Christ once for all' (Heb 10:10). 'Thou must believe and know that thou art holy; not, however, through thine own piety, but through the blood of Christ' [LUTHER]. This is the true sanctification of the Spirit, to obey the Gospel, to trust in Christ [BULLINGER].

sanctification – the Spirit's setting apart of the saint as consecrated to God. The execution of God's *choice* (Ga 1:4). God the Father gives us salvation by gratuitous election; the Son earns it by His blood-shedding; the Holy Spirit applies the merit of the Son to the soul by the Gospel word [CALVIN]. Compare Nu 6:24–26, the Old Testament triple blessing.

unto obedience – the result or *end aimed at* by God as respects us, the *obedience* which consists in faith, and that which flows from faith; 'obeying the truth through the Spirit' (1Pe 1:22). Ro 1:5, 'obedience to the faith,' and obedience the fruit of faith.

sprinkling – not in justification through the atonement once for all, which is expressed in the previous clauses, but (as the order proves) *the daily being sprinkled by Christ's blood, and so cleansed from all sin*, which is the privilege of one already justified and 'walking in the light.'

Grace – the source of 'peace'.

be multiplied – still further than already. Da 4:1, 'Ye have now peace and grace, but still not in perfection; therefore, ye must go on increasing until the old Adam be dead' [LUTHER].

3. He begins, like Paul, in opening his Epistles with giving thanks to God for the greatness of the salvation; herein he looks forward (1) into the future (1Pe 1:3–9); (2) backward into the past (1Pe 1:10–12) [ALFORD].

Blessed – A distinct *Greek* word (*eulogetos,* 'Blessed BE') is used of God, from that used of man (*eulogemenos,* 'Blessed IS').

Father – This whole Epistle accords with the Lord's prayer; 'Father,' 1Pe 1:3,14,17,23 2:2; 'Our,' 1Pe 1:4, end; 'In heaven,' 1Pe 1:4; 'Hallowed be Thy name,' 1Pe 1:15,16 3:15; 'Thy kingdom come,' 1Pe 2:9; 'Thy will be done,' 1Pe 2:15 3:17 4:2,19; 'daily bread,' 1Pe 5:7; 'forgiveness of sins,' 1Pe 4:8,1; 'temptation,' 1Pe 4:12; 'deliverance,' 1Pe 4:18 [BENGEL]; Compare 1Pe 3:7 4:7, for allusions to *prayer.* '*Barak,*' *Hebrew* 'bless,' is literally 'kneel.' God, as the original source of blessing, must be blessed through all His works.

abundant – *Greek,* 'much,' 'full.' That God's 'mercy' should reach *us,* guilty and enemies, proves its fulness. 'Mercy' met our *misery;* 'grace,' our *guilt.*

begotten us again – of the *Spirit* by the *word* (1Pe 1:23); whereas we were children of wrath naturally, and *dead* in sins.

unto – so that we have.

lively – *Greek,* 'living.' It has life in itself, gives life, and looks for life as its object [DEWETTE]. *Living* is a favourite expression of Peter (1Pe 1:23 1Pe 2:4,5). He delights in contemplating *life* overcoming death in the believer. *Faith* and *love* follow *hope* (1Pe 1:8,21,22). '(Unto) a lively hope' is further explained by '(To) an inheritance incorruptible … fadeth not away,' and '(unto) salvation … ready to be revealed in the last time.' I prefer with BENGEL and STEIGER to join as in *Greek,* 'Unto a hope *living* (possessing life and vitality) *through* the resurrection of Jesus Christ.' Faith, the subjective means of the spiritual resurrection of the soul, is wrought by the same power whereby Christ was raised from the dead. Baptism is an objective means (1Pe 3:21). Its moral fruit is a new life. The connection of our sonship with the resurrection appears also in Lu 20:36 Ac 13:33. Christ's resurrection is the cause of ours, (1) as an efficient cause (1Co 15:22); (2) as an exemplary cause, all the saints being about to rise after the similitude of His resurrection. Our 'hope' is, Christ rising from the dead hath ordained the power, and is become the pattern of the believer's resurrection. The soul, born again from its natural state into the life of grace, is after that born again unto the life of glory. Mt 19:28, 'regeneration, when the Son of man shall sit in the throne of His glory'; the resurrection of our bodies is a kind of coming out of the womb of the earth and entering upon immortality, a nativity into another life [BISHOP PEARSON]. The four causes of our salvation are; (1) the primary cause, God's mercy; (2) the proximate cause, Christ's death and resurrection; (3) the formal cause, our regeneration; (4) the final cause, our eternal

bliss. As John is the disciple of *love,* so Paul of *faith,* and Peter of *hope.* Hence, Peter, most of all the apostles, urges the resurrection of Christ; an undesigned coincidence between the history and the Epistle, and so a proof of genuineness. Christ's resurrection was the occasion of his own restoration by Christ after his fall.

4. To an inheritance – the object of our 'hope' (1Pe 1:3), which is therefore not a *dead,* but a '*living*' hope. The inheritance is the believer's already by title, being actually assigned to him; the entrance on its possession is future, and hoped for as a certainty. Being 'begotten again' as a 'son,' he is an 'heir,' as earthly fathers *beget* children who shall *inherit* their goods. The *inheritance* is 'salvation' (1Pe 1:5,9); 'the grace to be brought at the revelation of Christ' (1Pe 1:13); 'a crown of glory that fadeth not away.'

incorruptible – not having within the germs of death. Negations of the imperfections which meet us on every side here are the chief means of conveying to our minds a conception of the heavenly things which 'have not entered into the heart of man,' and which we have not faculties now capable of fully knowing. Peter, sanguine, impulsive, and highly susceptible of outward impressions, was the more likely to feel painfully the deep-seated *corruption* which, lurking under the outward splendour of the loveliest of earthly things, dooms them soon to rottenness and decay.

undefiled – not stained as earthly goods by sin, either in the acquiring, or in the using of them; unsusceptible of any stain. 'The rich man is either a dishonest man himself, or the heir of a dishonest man' [JEROME]. Even Israel's inheritance was *defiled* by the people's sins. Defilement intrudes even on our holy things now, whereas God's service ought to be undefiled.

that fadeth not away – Contrast 1Pe 1:24. Even the most delicate part of the heavenly inheritance, its bloom, continues *unfading.* 'In *substance* incorruptible; in *purity* undefiled; in *beauty* unfading' [ALFORD].

reserved – *kept up* (Col 1:5, '*laid up* for you in heaven,' 2Ti 4:8); *Greek* perfect, expressing a *fixed and abiding state,* 'which has been and is reserved.' The inheritance is in security, beyond risk, out of the reach of Satan, though we for whom it is reserved are still in the midst of dangers. Still, if we be believers, we too, as well as the inheritance. are 'kept' (the same *Greek,* Joh 17:12) by Jesus safely (1Pe 1:5).

in heaven – *Greek,* 'in the heavens,' where it can neither be destroyed nor plundered. It does not follow that, because it is *now* laid up in *heaven,* it shall not *hereafter* be on *earth* also.

for you – It is secure not only in itself from all misfortune, but also from all alienation, so that no other can receive it in your stead. He had said us (1Pe 1:3); he now turns his address to the elect in order to encourage and exhort them.

5. kept – Greek, 'who are being guarded.' He answers the objection, Of what use is it that salvation is 'reserved' for us in heaven, as in a calm secure haven, when we are tossed in the world as on a troubled sea in the midst of a thousand wrecks? [CALVIN]. As the inheritance is 'kept' (1Pe 1:4) safely for the far distant 'heirs,' so must they be 'guarded' in their persons so as to be sure of reaching it. Neither shall it be wanting to them, nor they to it. 'We are *guarded in the world* as our inheritance is *kept in heaven.*' This defines the 'you' of 1Pe 1:4. The inheritance, remember, belongs only to those who 'endure unto the end,' being 'guarded' by, or IN 'the power of God, through *faith.*' Contrast Lu 8:13. God Himself is our sole *guarding power.* 'It is His *power* which saves us from our enemies. It is His *long-suffering* which saves us from ourselves' [BENGEL]. Jude 1:1, 'preserved in Christ Jesus'; Php 1:6 4:7, 'keep'; Greek, 'guard,' as here. This guarding is effected, on the part of God, by His 'power,' the efficient cause; on the part of man, 'through faith,' the effective means.

by – Greek, 'in.' The believer lives spiritually *in* God, and in virtue of His power, and God lives in him. 'In' marks that the cause is inherent in the means, working organically through them with living influence, so that the means, in so far as the cause works organically through them, exist also in the cause. The power of God which guards the believer is no external force working upon him from without with mechanical necessity, but the spiritual power of God in which he lives, and with whose Spirit he is clothed. It comes down on, and then dwells in him, even as he is in it [STEIGER]. Let none flatter himself he is being guarded by the power of God unto salvation, if he be not walking by *faith.* Neither speculative knowledge and reason, nor works of seeming charity, will avail, severed from faith. It is through faith that salvation is both received and kept.

unto salvation – the final end of the new birth. 'Salvation,' not merely accomplished for us in title by Christ, and made over to us on our believing, but *actually manifested, and finally completed.*

ready to be revealed – When Christ shall be revealed, it shall be revealed. The preparations for it are being made now, and began when Christ came: 'All things are now *ready*'; the salvation is already accomplished, and only waits the Lord's time to be manifested: He 'is ready to judge.'

last time – the last day, closing the day of grace; the day of judgment, of redemption, of the restitution of all things, and of perdition of the ungodly.

6. Wherein – in which prospect of final salvation.

greatly rejoice – 'exult with joy': 'are exuberantly glad.' *Salvation* is realized by faith (1Pe 1:9) as a thing so actually present as to cause exulting joy in spite of existing afflictions.

for a season – Greek, 'for a little time.'

if need be – 'if it be God's will that it should be so' [ALFORD], for not all believers are afflicted. One need not invite or lay a cross on himself, but only 'take up' the cross which God imposes ('his cross'); 2Ti 3:12 is not to be pressed too far. Not every believer, nor every sinner, is tried with afflictions [THEOPHYLACT]. Some falsely think that notwithstanding our forgiveness in Christ, a kind of atonement, or expiation by suffering, is needed.

ye are in heaviness – Greek, 'ye were grieved.' The 'grieved' is regarded as *past,* the 'exulting joy' present. Because the realized joy of the coming salvation makes the *present grief* seem as a thing of the *past.* At the first shock of affliction *ye were grieved,* but now *by anticipation ye rejoice,* regarding the present grief as past.

through – Greek, 'IN': the element in which the grief has place.

manifold – many and of various kinds (1Pe 4:12,13).

temptations – 'trials' testing your faith.

7. Aim of the 'temptations.'

trial – testing, proving. That your *faith so proved* 'may be found (aorist; *once for all,* as the result of its being proved on the judgment-day) unto (eventuating in) praise', namely, the praise to be bestowed by the Judge.

than that of gold – rather, 'than gold.'

though – 'which perisheth, YET is tried with fire.' If gold, though perishing (1Pe 1:18), is yet tried with fire in order to remove dross and test its genuineness, how much more does your faith, which shall never perish, need to pass through a fiery trial to remove whatever is defective, and to test its genuineness and full value?

glory – 'Honour' is not so strong as 'glory.' As 'praise' is in *words,* so 'honour' is in deeds: *honorary reward.*

appearing – Translate as in 1Pe 1:13, 'revelation.' At Christ's revelation shall take place also the revelation of the sons of God (Ro 8:19, 'manifestation,' Greek, 'revelation'; 1Jo 3:2, Greek, 'manifested ... manifested,' for 'appear ... appear').

8. not having seen, ye love – though in other cases it is *knowledge* of the person that produces *love* to him. They are more 'blessed that have not seen and yet have believed,' than they who believed because they have seen. On Peter's own love to Jesus, compare Joh 21:15–17. Though the apostles had seen Him, they now ceased to know Him merely after the flesh.

in whom – connected with 'believing': the result of which is 'ye rejoice' (*Greek*, 'exult').

now – *in the present state*, as contrasted with the *future* state when believers 'shall see His face.'

unspeakable – (1Co 2:9).

full of glory – *Greek*, 'glorified.' A joy now already *encompassed with glory*. The 'glory' is partly in present possession, through the presence of Christ, 'the Lord of glory,' in the soul; partly in assured anticipation. 'The Christian's *joy* is bound up with *love* to Jesus: its ground is *faith*; it is not therefore either self-seeking or self-sufficient' [STEIGER].

9. Receiving – in sure anticipation; 'the end of your faith,' that is, its crowning consummation, finally completed 'salvation' (Peter here confirms Paul's teaching as to *justification by faith*): also receiving *now* the title to it and the first-fruits of it. In 1Pe 1:10 the 'salvation' is represented as *already present*, whereas 'the prophets' had it not as yet present. It must, therefore, in this verse, refer to the present: *Deliverance now from a state of wrath:* believers even now 'receive salvation,' though its full 'revelation' is future.

of … souls – The immortal *soul* was what was lost, so 'salvation' primarily concerns the soul; the *body* shall share in redemption hereafter; the *soul* of the believer is saved already: an additional proof that 'receiving … salvation' is here a thing present.

10. The magnitude of this 'salvation' is proved by the earnestness with which 'prophets' and even 'angels' searched into it. Even from the beginning of the world this salvation has been testified to by the Holy Spirit.

prophets – Though there is no *Greek* article, yet *English Version* is right, 'the prophets' generally (including all the Old Testament *inspired* authors), as 'the angels' similarly refer to them in general.

inquired – perseveringly: so the *Greek*. Much more is manifested to us than by diligent inquiry and search the prophets attained. Still it is not said, they searched *after* it, but *concerning* (so the *Greek* for 'of') it. They were already certain of the redemption being about to come. They did not like us fully *see*, but they *desired* to see the one and the same Christ whom we fully see in spirit. 'As Simeon was anxiously desiring previously, and tranquil in peace only when he had seen Christ, so all the Old Testament saints saw Christ only hidden, and as it were absent – absent not in power and grace, but inasmuch as He was not yet manifested in the flesh' [CALVIN]. The prophets, as *private individuals*, had to reflect on the hidden and far-reaching sense of their own prophecies; because their words, *as prophets, in their public function*, were not so much their own as the Spirit's, speaking by and in them: thus Caiaphas. A striking testimony to verbal inspiration; the *words* which the inspired authors wrote are God's words expressing the mind of the Spirit, which the writers themselves searched into, to fathom the deep and precious meaning, even as the believing readers did. 'Searched' implies that they had determinate marks to go by in their search.

the grace that should come unto you – namely, the grace of the New Testament: an earnest of 'the grace' of perfected 'salvation … to be brought at the (second) revelation of Christ.' Old Testament believers also possessed the grace of God; they were children of God, but it was as children in their nonage, so as to be like servants; whereas we enjoy the full privileges of adult sons.

11. what – *Greek*, 'In reference to what, or what manner of time.' *What* expresses the *time* absolutely: what was to be the era of Messiah's coming; *what manner of time*; what events and features should characterize the time of His coming. The 'or' implies that some of the prophets, if they could not as individuals discover the exact *time*, searched into its characteristic features and events. The *Greek* for 'time' is *the season*, the epoch, the fit time in God's purposes.

Spirit of Christ … in them – (Ac 16:7, in oldest manuscripts, 'the Spirit of Jesus'; Re 19:10). So JUSTIN MARTYR says, 'Jesus was He who appeared and communed with Moses, Abraham, and the other patriarchs.' CLEMENT OF ALEXANDRIA calls Him 'the Prophet of prophets, and Lord of all the prophetical spirit.'

did signify – 'did give intimation.'

of – *Greek,* 'the sufferers (appointed) *unto* Christ,' or *foretold in regard to Christ.* 'Christ,' the anointed Mediator, whose *sufferings* are the price of our 'salvation' (1Pe 1:9,10), and who is the channel of 'the grace that should come unto you.'

the glory – *Greek*, 'glories,' namely, of His resurrection, of His ascension, of His judgment and coming kingdom, the necessary consequence of the sufferings.

that should follow – *Greek*, 'after these (sufferings),' 1Pe 3:18–22 5:1. Since the Spirit of Christ' is the *Spirit* of God, Christ is God. It is only because the Son of God was to become our Christ that He manifested Himself and the Father through Him in the Old Testament, and by the Holy Spirit, eternally proceeding from the Father and Himself, spake in the prophets.

12. Not only was the future revealed to them, but this also, that these revelations of the future were given them not for themselves, but for our good in Gospel times. This, so far from disheartening, only quickened them in unselfishly testifying in the Spirit for the partial good of their own generation (only of believers), and for the full benefit of posterity. Contrast in Gospel times, Re 22:10. Not that their prophecies were unattended with spiritual instruction as to the Redeemer to their own generation, but the full light was not to be given till Messiah should come; it was well that they should have this 'revealed' to them, lest they should be disheartened in not clearly discovering with all their *inquiry and search* the full particulars of the coming 'salvation.' To Daniel (Da 9:25,26) the 'time' was revealed. *Our* immense privileges are thus brought forth by contrast with theirs, notwithstanding that they had the great honour of Christ's Spirit speaking in them; and this, as an incentive to still greater earnestness on our part than even they manifested (1Pe 1:13).

us – The oldest manuscripts read 'you,' as in 1Pe 1:10. This verse implies that *we*, Christians, may understand the prophecies by the Spirit's aid in their most important part, namely, so far as they have been already fulfilled.

with the Holy Ghost sent down – on Pentecost. The oldest manuscripts omit *Greek* preposition *en*, that is, 'in'; then translate, 'by.' The Evangelists speaking by the Holy Spirit were infallible witnesses. 'The Spirit of Christ' was in the prophets also (1Pe 1:11), but not manifestly, as in the case of the Christian Church and its first preachers, 'SENT down from heaven.' How favoured are we in being ministered to, as to 'salvation,' by prophets and apostles alike, the latter now announcing the same things as actually fulfilled which the former foretold.

which things – 'the things now reported unto you' by the evangelistic preachers 'Christ's sufferings and the glory that should follow' (1Pe 1:11,12).

angels – still higher than 'the prophets' (1Pe 1:10). Angels do not any more than ourselves possess an INTUITIVE knowledge of redemption. 'To look into' in *Greek* is literally, 'to bend over so as to look deeply into and see to the bottom of a thing.' See on Jas 1:25, on same word. As the cherubim stood bending over the mercy seat, the emblem of redemption, in the holiest place, so the angels intently gaze upon and desire to fathom the depths of 'the great mystery of godliness, God manifest in the flesh, justified in the Spirit, *seen of angels*' (1Ti 3:16). Their 'ministry to the heirs of salvation' naturally disposes them to wish to penetrate this mystery as reflecting such glory on the love, justice, wisdom, and power of their and our God and Lord. They can know it only through its manifestation in the Church, as they personally have not the direct share in it that we have. 'Angels have only the contrast between good and evil, without the power of conversion from sin to righteousness: witnessing such conversion in the Church, they long to penetrate the knowledge of the means

whereby it is brought about' [HOFMAN in ALFORD].

13. Wherefore – Seeing that the prophets ministered unto you in these high Gospel privileges which they did not themselves fully share in, though 'searching' into them, and seeing that even angels 'desire to look into' them, how earnest you ought to be and watchful in respect to them!

gird up ... loins – referring to Christ's own words, Lu 12:35; an image taken from the way in which the Israelites ate the Passover with the loose outer robe girded up about the waist with a girdle, as ready for a journey. Workmen, pilgrims, runners, wrestlers, and warriors (all of whom are types of the Christians), so gird themselves up, both to shorten the garment so as not to impede motion, and to gird up the body itself so as to be braced for action. The believer is to have his mind (mental powers) collected and always ready for Christ's coming. 'Gather in the strength of your spirit' [HENSLER]. *Sobriety,* that is, spiritual *self-restraint,* lest one be overcome by the allurements of the world and of sense, and patient *hopeful* waiting for Christ's revelation, are the true ways of 'girding up the loins of the mind.'

to the end – rather, 'perfectly,' so that there may be nothing deficient in your hope, no *casting away of your confidence.* Still, there may be an allusion to the 'end' mentioned in 1Pe 1:9. Hope so perfectly (*Greek,* '*teleios*') as to reach unto *the end* (*telos*) of your faith and hope, namely, 'the grace that is being brought unto you in (so the *Greek*) the revelation of Christ.' As *grace* shall then be *perfected,* so you ought to *hope perfectly.* 'Hope' is repeated from 1Pe 1:3. The two appearances are but different stages of the ONE great revelation of Christ, comprising the New Testament from the beginning to the end.

14. From *sobriety of spirit* and *endurance of hope* Peter passes to *obedience, holiness,* and *reverential fear.*

As – marking their present actual character as 'born again' (1Pe 1:3,22).

obedient children – *Greek,* 'children of obedience': children to whom *obedience* is their characteristic and ruling nature, as a child is of the same nature as the mother and father. Contrast Eph 5:6, 'the children of disobedience.' Compare 1Pe 1:17, 'obeying the Father' whose 'children' ye are. Having the obedience of *faith* (compare 1Pe 1:22) and so of *practice* (compare 1Pe 1:16,18). 'Faith is the highest obedience, because discharged to the highest command' [LUTHER].

fashioning – The outward *fashion* (*Greek,* '*schema*') is fleeting, and merely on the surface. The 'form,' or *conformation* in the New Testament, is something deeper and more perfect and essential.

the former lusts in – which were characteristic of your state of ignorance of God: true of both Jews and Gentiles. The sanctification is first described negatively (1Pe 1:14, 'not fashioning yourselves'; the putting off the old man, even in the outward *fashion*, as well as in the inward *conformation*), then positively (1Pe 1:15, putting on the new man, compare Eph 4:22,24). 'Lusts' flow from the original birth-sin (inherited from our first parents, who by self-willed desire brought sin into the world), the *lust* which, ever since man has been alienated from God, seeks to fill up with earthly things the emptiness of his being; the manifold forms which the mother-lust assumes are called in the plural *lusts*. In the regenerate, as far as the *new man* is concerned, which constitutes his truest self, 'sin' no longer exists; but in the flesh or old man it does. Hence arises the conflict, uninterruptedly maintained through life, wherein the new man in the main prevails, and at last completely. But the natural man knows only the combat of his lusts with one another, or with the law, without power to conquer them.

15. Literally, 'But (rather) after the pattern of Him who hath called you (whose characteristic is that He is) holy, be (*Greek*, "become") ye yourselves also holy.' God is our grand model. God's *calling* is a frequently urged motive in Peter's Epistles. Every one that begets, begets an offspring resembling himself [Epiphanius]. 'Let the acts of the offspring indicate similarity to the Father' [Augustine].

conversation – deportment, course of life: one's way of going about, as distinguished from one's internal nature, to which it must outwardly correspond. Christians are already holy unto God by consecration; they must be so also in their *outward walk and behaviour in all respects*. The outward must correspond to the inward man.

16. Scripture is the true source of all authority in questions of doctrine and practice.

Be ye ... for I am – It is I with whom ye have to do. Ye are mine. Therefore abstain from Gentile pollutions. We are too prone to have respect unto men [Calvin]. As I am the fountain of holiness, being holy in My *essence*, be ye therefore zealous to be *partakers* of holiness, that ye may be as I also am [Didymus]. God is essentially holy: the creature is holy in so far as it is sanctified by God. God, in giving the command, is willing to give also the power to obey it, namely, through the sanctifying of the Spirit (1Pe 1:2).

17. if ye call on – that is, 'seeing that ye call on,' for all the regenerate pray as *children* of God, 'Our *Father* who art in heaven' (Mt 6:9 Lu 11:2).

the Father – rather, 'Call upon *as Father* Him who without acceptance of persons (Ac 10:34 Ro 2:11 Jas 2:1, not accepting the Jew above the Gentile, 2Ch 19:7 Lu 20:21; properly said of a judge not biassed in judgment by respect of persons) judgeth'. The Father judgeth by His Son, His Representative, exercising His delegated authority (Joh 5:22). This marks the harmonious and complete unity of the Trinity.

work – Each man's *work* is *one* complete whole, whether good or bad. The particular works of each are manifestations of the general character of his lifework, whether it was of faith and love whereby alone we can please God and escape condemnation.

pass – *Greek*, 'conduct yourselves during.'

sojourning – The outward state of the Jews in their *dispersion* is an emblem of the *sojourner-like* state of all believers in this world, away from our true Fatherland.

fear – reverential, not slavish. He who is your Father, is also your Judge – a thought which may well inspire reverential fear. *Fear* is not here opposed to *assurance*, but to carnal *security*: fear producing vigilant caution lest we offend God and backslide. '*Fear* and *hope* flow from the same fountain: *fear* prevents us from falling away from *hope*' [Bengel].

18. Another motive to reverential, vigilant *fear* (1Pe 1:17) of displeasing God, the consideration of the costly price of our redemption from sin. Observe, it is *we* who are bought by the blood of Christ, not heaven. The blood of Christ is not in Scripture said to buy heaven for us: heaven is the 'inheritance' (1Pe 1:4) given to us as sons, by the promise of God.

corruptible – Compare 1Pe 1:7, 'gold that perisheth,' 1Pe 1:23.

silver and gold – *Greek*, 'or.' Compare Peter's own words, Ac 3:6: an undesigned coincidence.

redeemed – Gold and silver being liable to corruption themselves, can free no one from spiritual and bodily death; they are therefore of too little value. Contrast 1Pe 1:19, Christ's '*precious* blood.' The Israelites were ransomed with half a shekel each, which went towards purchasing the *lamb* for the daily sacrifice (Ex 30:12–16; compare Nu 3:44–51). But the Lamb who redeems the spiritual Israelites does so 'without money or price.' Devoted by sin to the justice of God, the Church of the first-born is redeemed from sin and the curse with Christ's precious blood (Mt 20:28 1Ti 2:6 Tit 2:14 Re 5:9). In all these passages there is the idea of *substitution*, the giving of one for another by way of a ransom or equivalent. Man is 'sold under sin' as a slave; shut up under condemnation and the curse. The ransom was, therefore, paid to the righteously incensed Judge, and was accepted as a vicarious satisfaction for our sin by God, inasmuch as it was His own love as well as righteousness which appointed it. An Israelite sold as a bond-servant for debt might be redeemed by one of his brethren. As, therefore, we could not redeem ourselves, Christ assumed our nature in order to become our nearest of kin and brother, and so our God or Redeemer. Holiness is the natural fruit of redemption 'from our vain conversation'; for He *by* whom we are redeemed is also He *for* whom we are redeemed. 'Without the righteous abolition of the curse, either there could be found no deliverance, or, what is impossible, the grace and righteousness of God must have come in collision' [STEIGER]; but now, Christ having borne the curse of our sin, frees from it those who are made God's children by His Spirit.

vain – self-deceiving, unreal, and unprofitable: promising good which it does not perform. Compare as to the Gentiles, Ac 14:15 Ro 1:21 Eph 4:17; as to human philosophers, 1Co 3:20; as to the disobedient Jews, Jer 4:14.

conversation – course of life. To know what our sin is we must know what it cost.

received by tradition from your fathers – The Jews' traditions. 'Human piety is a vain blasphemy, and the greatest sin that a man can commit' [LUTHER]. There is only one Father to be imitated, 1Pe 1:17; compare Mt 23:9, the same antithesis [BENGEL].

19. precious – of inestimable value. The *Greek* order is, 'With precious blood, as of a lamb without blemish (*in itself*) and without spot (*contracted by contact with others*), (even the blood) of Christ.' Though very man, He remained pure *in Himself* ('without blemish'), and uninfected by any impression of sin *from without* ('without spot'), which would have unfitted Him for being our atoning Redeemer: so the Passover lamb, and every sacrificial victim; so too, the Church, the Bride, by her union with Him. As Israel's redemption from Egypt required the blood of the paschal lamb, so our redemption from sin and the curse required the blood of Christ; 'foreordained' (1Pe 1:20) from eternity, as the Passover lamb was taken up on the tenth day of the month.

20. God's eternal foreordination of Christ's redeeming sacrifice, and completion of it *in these last times for us*, are an additional obligation on us to our maintaining a holy walk, considering how great things have been thus done for us. Peter's language in the history corresponds with this here: an undesigned coincidence and mark of genuineness. Redemption was no afterthought, or remedy of an unforeseen evil, devised at the time of its arising. God's *foreordaining* of the Redeemer refutes the slander that, on the Christian theory, there is a period of four thousand years of nothing but an incensed God. God *chose us in Christ before the foundation of the world* (Eph 1:4).

manifest – in His incarnation in the fulness of the time. He existed from eternity before He was *manifested*.

in these last times – 1Co 10:11, 'the ends of the world.' This last dispensation, made up of 'times' marked by great changes, but still retaining a general unity, stretches from Christ's ascension to His coming to judgment.

21. by him – Compare 'the *faith* which is *by Him*,' Ac 3:16. *Through* Christ: His Spirit, obtained for us in His resurrection and ascension, enabling us to believe. This verse excludes all who do not 'by Him believe in God,' and includes all of every age and clime that do. Literally, '*are believers* in God.' '*To believe* IN (*Greek*, "*eis*") *God*' expresses an *internal* trust: 'by believing to love God, going INTO Him, and cleaving to Him, incorporated into His members. By this faith the ungodly is justified, so that *thenceforth* faith itself begins to work by love' [P. LOMBARD]. To *believe* ON (*Greek*, '*epi*,' or dative case) *God* expresses the confidence, which grounds itself *on* God, reposing on Him. 'Faith IN (*Greek*, "*en*") His blood' (Ro 3:25) implies that His blood is the element IN which faith has its proper and abiding place. Compare with this verse, Ac 20:21, 'Repentance toward (*Greek*, '*eis*,' 'into,' turning *towards* and *going into*) God and faith toward (*Greek*, '*eis*,' 'into') Christ': where, as there is but one article to both *repentance* and *faith*, the two are inseparably joined as together forming one truth; where 'repentance' is, there 'faith' is; when one knows God the Father spiritually, then he must know the Son by whom alone we can come to the Father. In Christ we have life: if we have not the doctrine of Christ, we have not God. The only living way to God is through Christ and His sacrifice.

that raised him – The raising of Jesus by God is the special ground of our 'believing': (1) because by it God declared openly His acceptance of Him as our righteous substitute; (2) because by it and His glorification He received power, namely, the Holy Spirit, to impart to His elect 'faith': the same power enabling us to believe as raised Him from the dead. Our faith must not only be IN Christ, but BY and THROUGH Christ. 'Since in Christ's resurrection and consequent dominion our safety is grounded, *there* "faith" and "hope" find their stay' [CALVIN].

that your faith and hope might be in God – the object and effect of *God's raising Christ*. He states what was the actual result and fact, not an exhortation, except *indirectly*. Your *faith* flows from His *resurrection;* your *hope* from God's having 'given Him glory' (compare 1Pe 1:11, 'glories'). Remember God's having raised and glorified Jesus as the anchor of your faith and hope in God, and so keep alive these graces. Apart from Christ we could have only feared, not *believed* and *hoped* in God. Compare 1Pe 1:3,7–9,13, on *hope* in connection with *faith; love* is introduced in 1Pe 1:22.

22. purified ... in obeying the truth – Greek, 'in *your* (or "*the*") obedience of (that is, "*to*") the truth (the Gospel way of salvation),' that is, in the fact of your *believing*. *Faith* purifies the heart as giving it the only pure motive, love to God (Ac 15:9 Ro 1:5, '*obedience* to the faith').

through the Spirit – omitted in the oldest manuscripts. The Holy Spirit is the purifier by bestowing the obedience of faith (1Pe 1:2 1Co 12:3).

unto – with a view to: the proper result of the *purifying* of your hearts by faith. 'For what end must we lead a chaste life? That we may thereby be saved? No: but for this, that we may serve our neighbour' [LUTHER].

unfeigned – 1Pe 2:1,2, 'laying aside ... *hypocrisies ... sincere*.'

love of the brethren – that is, of Christians. *Brotherly love* is distinct from common *love*. 'The Christian loves primarily those in Christ; secondarily, all who might be in Christ, namely, all men, as Christ as man died for all, and as he hopes that they, too, may become his Christian brethren' [STEIGER]. BENGEL remarks that as here, so in 2Pe 1:5–7, 'brotherly love' is preceded by the purifying graces, '*faith*, knowledge, and godliness'. Love to the brethren is the evidence of our regeneration and justification by faith.

love one another – When the *purifying by faith into love of the brethren* has formed the *habit*, then the *act* follows, so that the 'love' is at once *habit* and *act*.

with a pure heart – The oldest manuscripts read, '(love) from the heart.'

fervently – Greek, 'intensely': with all the powers *on the stretch* (1Pe 4:8). 'Instantly' (Ac 26:7).

23. Christian brotherhood flows from our new birth of an imperishable seed, the abiding word of God. This is the consideration urged here to lead us to exercise *brotherly love*. As natural relationship gives rise to natural affection, so spiritual relationship gives rise to spiritual, and therefore abiding love, even as the *seed* from which it springs is abiding, not transitory as earthly things.

of ... of ... by – 'The word of God' is not the material of the spiritual new birth, but its mean or medium. By means of the *word* the man receives the incorruptible *seed of the Holy Spirit*, and so becomes one 'born again': Joh 3:3–5, 'born *of water and the Spirit*': as there is but one Greek article to the two nouns, *the* close connection of the sign and the grace, or new birth signified is implied. The *word* is the remote and anterior instrument; *baptism*, the proximate and sacramental instrument. The word is the instrument in relation to the individual; baptism, in relation to the Church as a society (Jas 1:18). We are born again *of the Spirit*, yet not without the use of means, but by the word of God. The word is not the beggetting principle itself, but only that by which it works: the vehicle of the mysterious germinating power [ALFORD].

which liveth and abideth for ever – It is because the Spirit of God accompanies it that the word carries in it the germ of life. They who are so born again *live and abide for ever,* in contrast to those who sow to the flesh. 'The Gospel bears incorruptible fruits, not dead works, because it is itself incorruptible' [BENGEL]. The word is an eternal divine power. For though the voice or speech vanishes, there still remains the kernel, the truth comprehended in the voice. This sinks into the heart and is living; yea, it is God Himself. So God to Moses, Ex 4:12, 'I will be with thy mouth' [LUTHER]. The life is in *God,* yet it is communicated to us through the *word.* 'The *Gospel* shall never cease, though its ministry shall' [CALOVIUS]. The abiding *resurrection glory* is always connected with our *regeneration* by the Spirit. Regeneration beginning with renewing man's *soul* at the resurrection, passes on to the *body,* then to the whole world of nature.

24. Scripture proof that the word of God lives for ever, in contrast to man's natural frailty. If ye were born again of flesh, corruptible seed, ye must also perish again as the grass; but now that from which you have derived life remains eternally, and so also will render you eternal.

flesh – man in his mere earthly nature.

as – omitted in some of the oldest manuscripts.

of man – The oldest manuscripts read, 'of it' (that is, of the flesh). 'The glory' is the wisdom, strength, riches, learning, honour, beauty, art, virtue, and righteousness of the NATURAL man (expressed by 'flesh'), which all are transitory (Joh 3:6), not OF MAN (as *English Version* reads) absolutely, for the glory of *man, in his true ideal* realized in the believer, is eternal.

withereth – Greek, aorist: literally, 'withered,' that is, is withered as a thing of the past. So also the *Greek* for 'falleth' is '*fell* away,' that is, is fallen away; it no sooner is than it is gone.

thereof – omitted in the best manuscripts and versions. 'The grass' is the *flesh*: 'the flower' its *glory.*

25. (Ps 119:89.)

this is the word ... preached unto you – That is eternal which is born of incorruptible seed (1Pe 1:24): but ye have received the incorruptible seed, the word (1Pe 1:25); therefore ye are born for eternity, and so are bound now to live for eternity (1Pe 1:22,23). Ye have not far to look for the word; it is among you, even the joyful Gospel message which we preach. Doubt not that the Gospel *preached to you* by our brother Paul, and which ye have embraced, is the eternal truth.

Chapter 2

1Pe 2:1–25. Exhortations.

To guileless feeding on the word by the sense of their privileges as new-born babes, living stones in the spiritual temple built on Christ the chief corner-stone, and royal priests, in contrast to their former state: also to abstinence from fleshly lusts, and to walk worthily in all relations of life, so that the world without which opposes them may be constrained to glorify God in seeing their good works. Christ, the grand pattern to follow in patience under suffering for well-doing.

1. laying aside – once for all: so the *Greek* aorist expresses as a garment *put off.* The exhortation applies to Christians alone, for in none else is the new nature existing which, as 'the inward man' (Eph 3:16) can cast off the old as an outward thing, so that the Christian, through the continual renewal of his inward man, can also exhibit himself externally as a new man. But to unbelievers the demand is addressed, that *inwardly*, in regard to the *nous* (mind), they must become changed, *meta-noeisthai* (re-pent) [STEIGER]. The guileless knows no envy. Compare 1Pe 2:2, 'sincere,' *Greek*, 'guileless.' '*Malice* delights in another's hurt; *envy* pines at another's good; *guile* imparts duplicity to the heart; *hypocrisy* (flattery) imparts duplicity to the tongue; *evil-speakings* wound the character of another' [AUGUSTINE].

2. new-born babes – altogether without 'guile' (1Pe 2:1). As long as we are here we are 'babes,' in a specially tender relation to God (Isa 40:11). The childlike spirit is indispensable if we would enter heaven. 'Milk' is here not elementary truths in contradistinction to more advanced Christian truths, as in 1Co 3:2 Heb 5:12,13; but in contrast to 'guile, hypocrisies', (1Pe 2:1); the simplicity of *Christian doctrine in general* to the childlike spirit. The same 'word of grace' which is the instrument in regeneration, is the instrument also of *building up*. 'The mother of the child is also its natural nurse' [STEIGER]. The babe, instead of chemically analysing, instinctively desires and feeds on the milk; so our part is not self-sufficient rationalizing and questioning, but simply receiving the truth in the love of it (Mt 11:25).

desire – *Greek*, 'have a yearning desire for,' or 'longing after,' a natural impulse to the regenerate, 'for as no one needs to teach new-born babes what food to take, knowing instinctively that a table is provided for them in their mother's breast,' so the believer of himself thirsts after the word of God (Ps 119:1–176). Compare TATIUS' language as to Achilles.

sincere – *Greek*, 'guileless.' Compare 1Pe 2:1, 'laying aside *guile*.' IRENAEUS says of heretics. They mix chalk with the milk. The article, 'the',

implies that besides *the well-known pure milk, the* Gospel, there is no other pure, unadulterated doctrine; it alone can make us *guileless* (1Pe 2:1).

of the word – Not as ALFORD, 'spiritual,' nor 'reasonable,' as *English Version* in Ro 12:1. The *Greek* 'logos' in Scripture is not used of the *reason*, or *mind*, but of the WORD; the preceding context requires that 'the word' should be meant here; the adjective 'logikos' *follows* the meaning of the noun *logos*, 'word.' Jas 1:21, '*Lay apart* all filthiness … and receive with meekness *the engrafted* WORD,' is exactly parallel, and confirms *English Version* here.

grow – The oldest manuscripts and versions read, 'grow *unto salvation*.' Being BORN *again unto salvation*, we are also to *grow unto salvation*. The end to which growth leads is perfected *salvation*. 'Growth is the measure of the fulness of that, not only rescue from destruction, but positive blessedness, which is implied in *salvation*' [ALFORD].

thereby – *Greek*, '*in* it'; fed *on* it; *in its strength* (Ac 11:14). 'The word is to be desired with appetite as the cause of life, to be swallowed in the hearing, to be chewed as cud is by rumination with the understanding, and to be digested by faith' [TERTULLIAN].

3. Peter alludes to Ps 34:8. The first 'tastes' of God's goodness are afterwards followed by fuller and happier experiences. A taste whets the appetite [BENGEL].

gracious – *Greek*, 'good,' benignant, kind; as God is revealed to us in Christ, 'the Lord' (1Pe 2:4), we who are born again ought so to be *good* and *kind* to the brethren (1Pe 1:22). 'Whosoever has not tasted the word to him it is not sweet it has not reached the heart; but to them who have experienced it, who with the heart believe, "Christ has been sent *for me* and is become *my own*: my miseries are His, and His *life* mine," it tastes sweet' [LUTHER].

4. coming – *drawing near* (same Greek as here, Heb 10:22) by faith continually; present tense: not having come once for all at conversion.

stone – *Peter* (that is, *a stone*, named so by Christ) desires that all similarly should be *living stones* BUILT ON CHRIST, THE TRUE FOUNDATION-STONE; compare his speech in Ac 4:11. An undesigned coincidence and mark of genuineness. The Spirit foreseeing the Romanist perversion of Mt 16:18 (compare Mt 16:16, 'Son of the LIVING GOD,' which coincides with his language here, 'the LIVING stone'), presciently makes Peter himself to refuse it. He herein confirms Paul's teaching. Omit the *as unto* of *English Version*. Christ is positively termed the 'living stone'; *living*, as having life in Himself from the beginning, and as raised from the dead to live evermore (Re 1:18) after His rejection by men, and so the source of life to us. Like no earthly *rock,* He lives and gives life. Compare 1Co 10:4, and the type, Ex 17:6 Nu 20:11.

disallowed – rejected, reprobated; referred to also by Christ Himself: also by Paul; compare the kindred prophecies, Isa 8:14 Lu 2:34.

chosen of God – literally, 'with (or "*in the presence and judgment of*") God elect,' or, 'chosen out' (1Pe 2:6). Many are alienated from the Gospel, because it is not everywhere in favour, but is on the contrary rejected by most men. Peter answers that, though rejected by men, Christ is peculiarly the *stone* of salvation honoured by God, first so designated by Jacob in his deathbed prophecy.

5. Ye also, as lively stones – partaking of the name and life which is in 'THE LIVING STONE' (1Pe 2:4 1Co 3:11). Many names which belong to Christ in the singular are assigned to Christians in the plural. He is 'THE SON,' 'High Priest,' 'King,' 'Lamb'; they, 'sons,' 'priests,' 'kings,' 'sheep,' 'lambs.' So the Shulamite called from Solomon [BENGEL].

are built up – *Greek,* 'are being built up,' as in Eph 2:22. Not as ALFORD, 'Be ye built up.' Peter grounds his exhortations, 1Pe 2:2,11, on their conscious sense of their high privileges as *living stones in the course of being built up into a spiritual house* (that is, 'the habitation of the Spirit').

priesthood – Christians are both the spiritual *temple* and the *priests* of the temple. There are two *Greek* words for 'temple'; *hieron* (*the sacred place*), the whole building, including. the courts wherein the sacrifice *was killed;* and *naos* (*the dwelling,* namely, of God), the inner shrine wherein God peculiarly manifested Himself, and where, in the holiest place, the *blood* of the slain sacrifice was presented before Him. All believers alike, and not merely ministers, are now the dwelling of God (and are called the '*naos,' Greek,* not the *hieron*) and priests unto God (Re 1:6). The minister is not, like the Jewish priest (*Greek,* '*hiercus*'), admitted nearer to God than the people, but merely for order's sake leads the spiritual services of the people. *Priest* is the abbreviation of *presbyter* in the *Church of England Prayer Book,* not corresponding to the Aaronic *priest* (*hiereus,* who offered *literal* sacrifices). Christ is the only literal *hiereus-priest* in the New Testament through whom alone we may always draw near to God. Compare 1Pe 2:9, 'a royal priesthood,' that is, *a body of priest-kings,* such as was Melchisedec. The Spirit never, in New Testament, gives the name *hiereus,* or *sacerdotal* priest, to ministers of the Gospel.

holy – consecrated to God.

spiritual sacrifices – not the literal one of the mass, as the Romish self-styled disciples of Peter teach. Compare Isa 56:7, which compare with '*acceptable* to God' here; Ps 4:5 50:14 51:17,19

Ho 14:2 Php 4:18. 'Among spiritual sacrifices the first place belongs to the general oblation of ourselves. For never can we offer anything to God until we have offered ourselves (2Co 8:5) in sacrifice to Him. There follow afterwards prayers, giving of thanks, alms deeds, and all exercises of piety' [CALVIN]. Christian houses of worship are never called temples because the *temple* was a place for *sacrifice,* which has no place in the Christian dispensation; the Christian temple is the congregation of spiritual worshippers. The synagogue (where reading of Scripture and prayer constituted the worship) was the model of the Christian house of worship (compare *Note,* see on Jas 2:2, *Greek,* 'synagogue'; Ac 15:21). Our sacrifices are those of prayer, praise, and self-denying services in the cause of Christ (1Pe 2:9, end).

by Jesus Christ – as our mediating High Priest before God. Connect these words with 'offer up.' Christ is both *precious* Himself and makes us *accepted* [BENGEL].

6. Wherefore also – The oldest manuscripts read, 'Because that.' The statement above is so '*because* it is contained in Scripture.'

Behold – calling attention to the glorious announcement of His eternal counsel.

elect – so also believers (1Pe 2:9, 'chosen,' *Greek,* 'elect generation').

precious – in *Hebrew,* Isa 28:16, 'a corner-stone of preciousness.' See on Isa 28:16. So in 1Pe 2:7, Christ is said to be, to believers, 'precious,' *Greek,* 'preciousness'.

confounded – same *Greek* as in Ro 9:33 (Peter here as elsewhere confirming Paul's teaching. See *Introduction;* also Ro 10:11), 'ashamed.' In Isa 28:16, 'make haste,' that is, flee in sudden panic, covered with the *shame* of confounded hopes.

7. Application of the Scripture just quoted first to the believer, then to the unbeliever. On the opposite effects of the same Gospel on different classes, compare Joh 9:39 2Co 2:15,16.

precious – *Greek,* 'THE preciousness' (1Pe 2:6). To you believers belongs *the preciousness* of Christ just mentioned.

disobedient – to the faith, and so disobedient in practice.

the stone which … head of … corner – (Ps 118:22). Those who rejected the STONE were all the while in spite of themselves unconsciously contributing to its becoming Head of the corner. The same magnet has two poles, the one repulsive, the other attractive; so the Gospel has opposite effects on believers and unbelievers respectively.

8. stone of stumbling – quoted from Isa 8:14. Not merely they *stumbled,* in that their prejudices were offended; but their stumbling implies the *judicial punishment* of their reception of Messiah; they hurt themselves in stumbling over the corner-stone, as 'stumble' means in Jer 13:16 Da 11:19.

at the word – rather, join 'being disobedient to the word'; so 1Pe 3:1 4:17.

whereunto – to penal *stumbling;* to the judicial punishment of their unbelief. See above.

also – an additional thought; God's ordination; not that God ordains or *appoints* them to sin, but they are given up to 'the fruit of *their own* ways' according to the eternal counsel of God. The moral ordering of the world is altogether of God. God appoints the ungodly to be *given up unto* sin, and a *reprobate mind,* and its necessary penalty. The lost shall lay all the blame of their ruin on their own sinful perversity, not on God's decree; the saved shall ascribe all the merit of their salvation to God's electing love and grace.

9. Contrast in the privileges and destinies of believers. Compare the similar contrast with the preceding context.

chosen – 'elect' of God, even as Christ your Lord is.

generation – implying the unity of spiritual origin and kindred of believers as a class distinct from the world.

royal – kingly. Believers, like Christ, the antitypical Melchisedec, are at once *kings* and *priests.* Israel, in a spiritual sense, was designed to be the same among the nations of the earth. The full realization on earth of this, both to the literal and the spiritual Israel, is as yet future.

holy nation – antitypical to Israel.

peculiar people – literally, 'a people *for an acquisition,*' that is, whom God chose to be *peculiarly His:* Ac 20:28, 'purchased,' literally, 'acquired.' God's *peculiar treasure* above others.

show forth – *publish abroad.* Not *their own* praises but *His.* They have no reason to magnify themselves above others for once they had been in the same darkness, and only through God's grace had been brought to the light which they must henceforth *show forth* to others.

praises – Greek, 'virtues,' 'excellencies': His glory, *mercy* (1Pe 2:10), *goodness* (Greek, 1Pe 2:3 Nu 14:17,18 Isa 63:7). The same term is applied to believers, 2Pe 1:5.

of him who hath called you – (2Pe 1:3).

out of darkness – of heathen and even Jewish ignorance, sin, and misery, and so out of the dominion of the prince of darkness.

marvellous – Peter still has in mind Ps 118:23.

light – It is called 'His,' that is, God's. Only the (spiritual) *light* is created by God, not *darkness.* In Isa 45:7, it is physical darkness and evil, not moral, that God is said to *create,* the punishment of sin, not sin itself. Peter, with characteristic boldness, brands as *darkness* what all the world calls *light;* reason, without the Holy Spirit, in spite of its vaunted power, is spiritual

darkness. 'It cannot apprehend what faith is: there it is stark blind; it gropes as one that is without eyesight, stumbling from one thing to another, and knows not what it does' [LUTHER].

10. Adapted from Ho 1:9,10 2:23. Peter plainly confirms Paul, who quotes the passage as implying the call of the Gentiles to become spiritually that which Israel had been literally, 'the people of God.' Primarily, the prophecy refers to literal Israel, hereafter to be fully that which in their best days they were only partially, God's people.

not obtained mercy – literally, 'who were men not compassionated.' Implying that it was God's pure *mercy,* not their merits, which made the blessed change in their state; a thought which ought to kindle their lively *gratitude,* to be shown with their life, as well as their lips.

11. As heretofore he exhorted them to walk worthily of their calling, in contradistinction to their own former walk, so now he exhorts them to glorify God before unbelievers.

Dearly beloved – He gains their attention to his exhortation by assuring them of his love.

strangers and pilgrims – (1Pe 1:17). *Sojourners,* literally, settlers having a *house* in a city without being *citizens* in respect to the rights of citizenship; a picture of the Christian's position on earth; *and pilgrims,* staying for a time in a foreign land. FLACIUS thus analyses the exhortation: (1) Purify your souls (a) as *strangers* on earth who must not allow yourselves to be kept back by earthly lusts, and (b) because these lusts war against the soul's salvation. (2) Walk piously among unbelievers (a) so that they may cease to calumniate Christians, and (b) may themselves be converted to Christ.

fleshly lusts – enumerated in Ga 5:19. Not only the gross appetites which we have in common with the brutes, but all the thoughts of the unrenewed mind.

which – Greek, 'the which,' that is, inasmuch as being such as 'war,' &c. Not only do they impede, but they assail [BENGEL].

the soul – that is, against the regenerated soul; such as were those now addressed. The regenerated soul is besieged by sinful lusts. Like Samson in the lap of Delilah, the believer, the moment that he gives way to fleshly lusts, has the locks of his strength shorn, and ceases to maintain that spiritual separation from the world and the flesh of which the Nazarite vow was the type.

12. conversation – 'behaviour'; 'conduct'. There are two things in which 'strangers and pilgrims' ought to bear themselves well: (1) the *conversation* or conduct, as subjects (1Pe 2:13), servants (1Pe 2:18), wives (1Pe 3:1), husbands (1Pe 3:7), all persons under all circumstances (1Pe 2:8); (2) *confession* of the faith (1Pe 3:15,16). Each of the two is derived from *the will* of God. Our conversation should correspond to our Saviour's condition; this is in heaven, so ought that to be.

honest – honourable, becoming, proper (1Pe 3:16). Contrast 'vain conversation,' 1Pe 1:18. A good walk does not make us pious, but we must first be pious and believe before we attempt to lead a good course. Faith first receives from God, then love gives to our neighbour [LUTHER].

whereas they speak against you – *now* (1Pe 2:15), that they may, nevertheless, at some time or other *hereafter* glorify God. The *Greek* may be rendered, '*Wherein* they speak against you … that (*herein*) they may, by your good works, which *on a closer inspection they shall behold*, glorify God.' The very works 'which on more careful consideration, must move the heathen to praise God, are at first the object of hatred and raillery' [STEIGER].

evildoers – Because as Christians they could not conform to heathenish customs, they were accused of disobedience to all legal authority; in order to rebut this charge, they are told to *submit to every ordinance of man* (not sinful in itself).

by – owing to.

they shall behold – *Greek,* 'they shall be *eye-witnesses of*'; 'shall behold *on close inspection*'; as opposed to their 'ignorance' (1Pe 2:15) of the true character of Christians and Christianity, by judging on mere hearsay.

glorify – forming a high estimate of the God whom Christians worship, from the exemplary conduct of Christians themselves. We must do good, not with a view to *our own* glory, but to the glory *of God.*

the day of visitation – of God's grace; when God shall *visit* them *in mercy.*

13. every ordinance of man – 'every human institution' [ALFORD], literally, 'every human *creation.*' For though of divine appointment, yet in the mode of nomination and in the exercise of their authority, earthly governors are but human institutions, being *of men,* and *in relation to men.* The apostle speaks as one raised above all human things. But lest they should think themselves so ennobled by faith as to be raised above subordination to human authorities, he tells them to *submit themselves for the sake of Christ,* who desires you to be subject, and who once was subject to earthly rulers Himself, though having all things subject to Him, and whose honour is at stake in you as His earthly representatives. Compare Ro 13:5, 'Be subject for conscience' sake.'

king – The Roman emperor was 'supreme' in the Roman provinces to which this Epistle was addressed. The Jewish zealots refused obedience. The distinction between 'the king as supreme' and 'governors sent by him' implies that 'if the king command one thing, and the subordinate magistrate another, we ought rather to obey the superior' [AUGUSTINE in GROTIUS]. Scripture prescribes nothing upon the form of government, but simply subjects Christians to that everywhere subsisting, without entering into the question of the *right* of the rulers (thus the Roman emperors had by force seized supreme authority, and Rome had, by unjustifiable means, made herself mistress of Asia), because the *de facto* governors have not been made by chance, but by the providence of God.

14. governors – subordinate to the emperor, 'sent,' or delegated by Cæsar to preside over the provinces.

for the punishment – No tyranny ever has been so unprincipled as that some appearance of equity was not maintained in it; however corrupt a government be, God never suffers it to be so much so as not to be better than anarchy [CALVIN]. Although bad kings often oppress the good, yet that is scarcely ever done by public authority (and it is of what is done by public authority that Peter speaks), save under the mask of right. Tyranny harasses many, but anarchy overwhelms the whole state [HORNEIUS]. The only justifiable exception is in cases where obedience to the earthly king plainly involves disobedience to the express command of the King of kings.

praise of them that do well – Every government recognizes the excellence of truly Christian subjects. Thus PLINY, in his letter to the Emperor Trajan, acknowledges, 'I have found in them nothing else save a perverse and extravagant superstition.' The recognition in the long run mitigates persecution (1Pe 3:13).

15. Ground of his directing them to *submit themselves* (1Pe 2:13).

put to silence – literally, 'to muzzle,' 'to stop the mouth.'

ignorance – spiritual not having 'the knowledge of God,' and therefore ignorant of the children of God, and misconstruing their acts; influenced by mere appearances, and ever ready to open their mouths, rather than their eyes and ears. Their *ignorance* should move the believer's pity, not his anger. They judge of things which they are incapable of judging through unbelief (compare 1Pe 2:12). Maintain such a walk that they shall have no charge against you, except touching your faith; and so their minds shall be favourably disposed towards Christianity.

16. As free – as 'the Lord's freemen,' connected with 1Pe 2:15, *doing well as* being *free.* 'Well-doing' (1Pe 2:15) is the natural fruit of being *freemen* of Christ, made free by 'the truth' from the bondage of sin. Duty is enforced on us to guard against licentiousness, but the *way* in which it is to be fulfilled, is by love and the holy instincts of Christian liberty. We are given *principles*, not *details*.

not using – Greek, 'not *as having* your liberty for a veil (cloak) of *badness*, but as the servants of God,' and therefore bound to *submit to every ordinance of man* (1Pe 2:13) which is of God's appointment.

17. Honour all men – *according to whatever honour is due in each case.* Equals have a respect due to them. Christ has dignified our humanity by assuming it; therefore we should not dishonour, but be considerate to and honour our common humanity, even in the very humblest. The first 'honour' is in the *Greek* aorist imperative, implying, '*In every case render promptly* every man's due' [ALFORD]. The second is in the *present* tense, implying, *Habitually and continually* honour the king. Thus the first is the general precept; the three following are its three great divisions.

Love – present: *Habitually love* with the special and congenial affection that you ought to feel to brethren, besides the general *love* to all men.

Fear God … the king – The king is to be *honoured*; but God alone, in the highest sense, *feared*.

18. Servants – *Greek*, 'household servants': not here the *Greek* for 'slaves.' Probably including *freedmen* still remaining in their master's house. *Masters* were not commonly Christians; he therefore mentions only the duties of the *servants*. These were then often persecuted by their unbelieving masters. Peter's special object seems to be to teach them *submission*, whatever the character of the masters might be. Paul not having this as his prominent design, includes *masters* in his monitions.

be subject – *Greek*, 'being subject': the participle expresses a particular instance of the general exhortation to good conduct, 1Pe 2:11,12, of which the first particular precept is given 1Pe 2:13, 'Submit yourselves to every ordinance of man for the Lord's sake.' The general exhortation is taken up again in 1Pe 2:16; and so the participle 1Pe 2:18, 'being subject,' is joined to the hortatory imperatives going before, namely, 'abstain,' 'submit yourselves.' 'honour all men.'

with – Greek, 'in.'

all – all possible: under all circumstances, such as are presently detailed.

fear – the awe of one subject: God, however, is the ultimate object of the 'fear': *fear* 'for the Lord's sake' (1Pe 2:13), not merely slavish fear of masters.

good – kind.

gentle – indulgent towards errors: considerate: yielding, not exacting all which justice might demand.

froward – perverse: harsh. Those bound to obey must not make the disposition and behaviour of the superior the measure of the fulfilment of their obligations.

19. Reason for subjection even to froward masters.

thankworthy – (Lu 6:33). A course out of the common, and especially *praiseworthy* in the eyes of God: not as Rome interprets, earning merit, and so a work of supererogation (compare 1Pe 2:20).

for conscience toward God – literally, 'consciousness of God': from a conscientious regard to God, more than to men.

endure – *Greek*, 'patiently bear up under': as a superimposed burden [ALFORD].

grief – *Greek*, 'griefs.'

20. what – *Greek*, 'what kind of.'

glory – what peculiar *merit*.

buffeted – the punishment of slaves, and suddenly inflicted [BENGEL].

this is – Some oldest manuscripts read, 'for.' Then the translation is, 'But if when … ye take it patiently (it is a glory), *for* this is acceptable.'

acceptable – *Greek*, 'thankworthy,' as in 1Pe 2:19.

21. Christ's example a proof that patient endurance under undeserved sufferings is acceptable with God.

hereunto – to the patient endurance of unmerited suffering (1Pe 3:9). Christ is an example to servants, even as He was once in 'the form of a servant'.

called – with a heavenly calling, though slaves.

for us – His *dying for us* is the highest exemplification of 'doing well' (1Pe 2:20). Ye must patiently suffer, being innocent, as Christ also innocently suffered (not for Himself, but *for us*). The oldest manuscripts for 'us … us,' read, 'you … for you.' Christ's sufferings, while they are for an example, were also primarily sufferings '*for us*,' a consideration which imposes on us an everlasting obligation on us to please Him.

leaving – *behind*: so the *Greek*: on His departure to the Father, to His glory.

an example – *Greek*, 'a copy,' literally, 'a writing copy' set by masters for their pupils. Christ's precepts and sermons were the *transcript* of His life. Peter *graphically* sets before servants those features especially suited to their case.

follow – *close upon*: so the Greek.

his steps – *footsteps*, namely, of His *patience* combined with *innocence*.

22. Illustrating Christ's *well-doing* (1Pe 2:20) though suffering.

did – *Greek* aorist. 'Never in a single instance did' [ALFORD]. Quoted from Isa 53:9, end, *Septuagint*.

neither – nor yet: not even [ALFORD]. Sinlessness as to the *mouth* is a mark of *perfection*. *Guile* is a common fault of servants. 'If any boast of his innocency, Christ surely did not suffer as an evildoer' [CALVIN], yet He took it patiently (1Pe 2:20). On Christ's sinlessness, compare 2Co 5:21 Heb 7:26.

23. Servants are apt to 'answer again' (Tit 2:9). *Threats* of divine judgment against oppressors are often used by those who have no other arms, as for instance, slaves. Christ, who as Lord could have threatened with truth, never did so.

committed *himself* – or *His cause,* as man in His suffering. Compare the type, Jer 11:20. In this Peter seems to have before his mind Isa 53:8. Compare Ro 12:19, on our corresponding duty. Leave your case in His hands, not desiring to make Him executioner of your revenge, but rather praying for enemies. God's *righteous judgment* gives tranquillity and consolation to the oppressed.

24. his own self – there being *none other* but *Himself* who could have done it. His *voluntary* undertaking of the work of redemption is implied. The *Greek* puts in antithetical juxtaposition, OUR, and His OWN SELF, to mark the idea of *His substitution for us.* His 'well-doing' in His sufferings is set forth here as an example to servants and to us all (1Pe 2:20).

bare – to sacrifice: *carried and offered up:* a sacrificial term. Isa 53:11,12, 'He *bare* the sin of many': where the *idea of bearing on Himself* is the prominent one; here the *offering in sacrifice* is combined with that idea. So the same *Greek* means in 1Pe 2:5.

our sins – In *offering* or *presenting in sacrifice* (as the *Greek* for 'bare' implies) His body, Christ offered in it the *guilt* of our sins upon the cross, as upon the altar of God, that it might be expiated in Him, and so taken away from us. Compare Isa 53:10, 'Thou shalt make His soul an offering for sin.' Peter thus means by 'bare' what the *Syriac* takes two words to express, *to bear* and *to offer:* (1) He hath *borne* our sins laid upon Him [namely, their guilt, curse, and punishment]; (2) He hath so borne them that He *offered* them along with Himself on the altar. He refers to the animals upon which sins were first laid, and which were then *offered* thus laden [VITRINGA]. Sin or guilt among the Semitic nations is considered as a burden lying heavily upon the sinner [GESENIUS].

on the tree – the cross, the proper place for One on whom the *curse* was laid: this curse stuck to Him until it was legally (through His death as the guilt-bearer) destroyed in His body: thus the handwriting of the bond against us is cancelled by His death.

that we being dead to sins – the effect of His death to 'sin' in the aggregate, and to all particular 'sins,' namely, that we should be as entirely *delivered from* them, as a slave that is *dead* is delivered from service *to* his master. This is our spiritual *standing* through faith by virtue of Christ's death: our actual mortification of particular *sins* is in proportion to the degree of our effectually being made conformable to His death.

by whose stripes – *Greek,* 'stripe.'

ye were healed – a paradox, yet true. 'Ye servants (compare "buffeted," "the tree," 1Pe 2:20,24) often bear *the strife;* but it is not more than your Lord Himself bore; learn from Him patience in wrongful sufferings.

25. (Isa 53:6.)

For – Assigning their natural need of *healing* (1Pe 2:24).

now – Now that the atonement for all has been made, the foundation is laid for *individual conversion:* so '*ye* are *returned,*' or '*have become converted* to'.

Shepherd and Bishop – The designation of the *pastors* and *elders* of the Church belongs in its fullest sense to the great Head of the Church, 'the good Shepherd.' As the '*bishop*' oversees (as the *Greek* term means), so 'the *eyes of the Lord are over* the righteous' (1Pe 3:12). He gives us His spirit and feeds and guides us by His word.

Chapter 3

1Pe 3:1–22. Relative duties of husbands and wives: exhortations to love and forbearance: right conduct under persecutions for righteousness' sake, after Christ's example, whose death resulted in quickening to us through his being quickened again, of which baptism is the sacramental seal.

1. Likewise – *Greek,* 'In like manner,' as 'servants' in their sphere; compare the reason of the woman's subjection, 1Co 11:8–10 1Ti 2:11–14.

your own – enforcing the obligation: it is not strangers ye are required to *be subject to.* Every time that obedience is enjoined upon women to their husbands, the *Greek,* '*idios,*' 'one's own peculiarly,' is used, while the wives of men are designated only by *heauton,* 'of themselves.' Feeling the need of leaning on one stronger than herself, the wife (especially if joined to an *unbeliever*) might be tempted, though only spiritually, to enter into that relation with another in which she ought to stand to '*her own* spouse (1Co 14:34,35, 'Let them ask *their own* [*idious*] husbands at home'); an attachment to the person of the teacher might thus spring up, which, without being in the common sense spiritual adultery, would still weaken in its spiritual basis the married relation [STEIGER].

that, if – *Greek,* 'that even if.' *Even if* you have a husband that obeys not the word (that is, is an unbeliever).

without the word – *independently of hearing the word preached,* the usual way of *faith* coming. But BENGEL, 'without word,' that is, *without direct* Gospel *discourse* of the wives, 'they *may* (literally, in oldest manuscripts, 'shall,' which marks the almost objective *certainty* of the result) be won' indirectly. 'Unspoken acting is more powerful than unperformed speaking' [AECUMENIUS]. 'A soul converted is *gained* to itself, to the pastor, wife, or husband, who sought it, and to Jesus Christ; added to His treasury who thought not His own precious blood too dear to lay out for this gain' [LEIGHTON]. 'The discreet wife would choose first of all to persuade her husband to share with her in the things which lead to blessedness; but if this be impossible, let her then alone diligently press after virtue, in all things obeying him so as to do nothing at any time against his will, except in such things as are essential to virtue and salvation' [CLEMENT OF ALEXANDRIA].

2. behold – on narrowly looking into it, literally, 'having closely observed.'

chaste – pure, spotless, free from all impurity.

fear – *reverential*, towards your husbands. Scrupulously pure, as opposed to the noisy, ambitious character of worldly women.

3. Literally, 'To whom let there belong (namely, as their peculiar ornament) not the outward adornment (usual in the sex which first, by the fall, brought in the need of covering, see on 1Pe 5:5) of'.

plaiting – artificial braiding, in order to attract admiration.

wearing – literally, 'putting round,' namely, the head, as a diadem – the arm, as a bracelet – the finger, as rings.

apparel – showy and costly. 'Have the blush of modesty on thy face instead of paint, and moral worth and discretion instead of gold and emeralds' [MELISSA].

4. But – 'Rather.' The 'outward adornment' of jewels, is forbidden, in so far as woman loves such things, not in so far as she uses them from a sense of propriety, and does not *abuse* them. Singularity mostly comes from pride and throws needless hindrances to religion in the way of others. Under costly attire there may be a humble mind. 'Great is he who uses his earthenware as if it were plate; not less great is he who uses his silver as if it were earthenware' [SENECA in ALFORD].

hidden – *inner* man, which the Christian instinctively *hides* from public view.

of the heart – *consisting in the heart* regenerated and adorned by the Spirit. This 'inner man of the heart' is the subject of the verb 'be,' 1Pe 3:3, Greek: 'Of whom let the inner man be,' namely, the distinction or adornment.

in that – consisting or standing *in that* as its element.

not corruptible – not transitory, nor tainted with corruption, as all earthly adornments.

meek and quiet – *meek*, not creating disturbances: *quiet*, bearing with tranquillity the disturbances caused by others. *Meek* in affections and feelings; *quiet* in words, countenance, and actions [BENGEL].

in the sight of God – who looks to inward, not merely outward things.

of great price – The results of redemption should correspond to its costly price (1Pe 1:19).

5. after this manner – with the *ornament of a meek and quiet spirit* (compare the portrait of the godly wife, Pr 31:10–31).

trusted – Greek, 'hoped.' 'Holy' is explained by 'hoped in (so as to be "*united to*," Greek) God.' Hope in God is the spring of true holiness [BENGEL].

in subjection – Their ornament consisted in their subordination. Vanity was forbidden (1Pe 3:3) as being contrary to female *subjection*.

6. Sara – an example of *faith*.

calling him lord – (Ge 18:12).

ye are – Greek, 'ye have become': 'children' of Abraham and Sara by *faith*, whereas ye were Gentile aliens from the covenant.

afraid with any amazement – Greek, 'fluttering alarm,' 'consternation.' *Act well, and be not thrown into sudden panic* by any opposition from without.

7. dwell – Greek, 'dwelling': connected with the verb, 1Pe 2:17, 'Honour all.'

knowledge – Christian knowledge: appreciating the due relation of the sexes in the design of God, and acting with tenderness and forbearance accordingly: *wisely: with wise consideration.*

them ... giving honour to the wife – translate and punctuate the Greek rather, 'dwelling according to knowledge with the female (*Greek adjective*, qualifying "vessel"; not as *English Version*, a noun) as with the weaker vessel (see on 1Th 4:4. Both husband and wife are vessels in God's hand, and of God's making, to fulfil His gracious purposes. Both weak, the woman the *weaker*. The sense of his own weakness, and that she, like himself, is God's *vessel* and fabric, ought to lead him to act with tender and wise consideration towards her who is the *weaker fabric*), giving (literally, "*assigning*," "*apportioning*") honour as being also (besides being man and wife) heirs together'; or, as the Vatican manuscript reads, as to those who are also (besides being your wives) fellow heirs.' (The reason why the man should *give honour* to the woman is, because *God gives honour to both* as fellow heirs; compare the same argument, 1Pe 3:9). He does not take into account the case of an *unbelieving* wife, as she might yet believe.

grace of life – God's *gracious* gift of *life* (1Pe 1:4,13).

that your prayers be not hindered – by dissensions, which prevent *united* prayer, on which depends the blessing.

8. *General* summary of relative duty, after having detailed *particular* duties from 1Pe 2:18.

of one mind – as to the faith.

having compassion one of another – Greek, 'sympathizing' in the joy and sorrow of others.

love as brethren – *Greek,* 'loving the brethren.'

pitiful – towards the afflicted.

courteous – genuine Christian politeness; not the tinsel of the world's politeness; stamped with *unfeigned love* on one side, and *humility* on the other. But the oldest manuscripts read, 'humble-minded.' It is slightly different from 'humble,' in that it marks a *conscious effort* to be truly *humble.*

9. **evil** – in deed.

railing – in word.

blessing – your revilers; participle, not a noun after 'rendering.'

knowing that – The oldest manuscripts read merely, 'because.'

are – *Greek,* 'were called.'

inherit a blessing – not only passive, but also active; receiving spiritual blessing from God by faith, and in your turn blessing others from love [GERHARD in ALFORD]. 'It is not in order to inherit a blessing that we must bless, but because our portion is blessing.' No *railing* can injure you (1Pe 3:13). Imitate God who 'blesses' you. The first fruits of His *blessing* for eternity are enjoyed by the righteous even now (1Pe 3:10) [BENGEL].

10. **will love** – *Greek,* 'wishes to love.' He who *loves life* (present and eternal), and *desires to continue to do so,* not involving himself in troubles which will make this life a burden, and cause him to forfeit eternal life. Peter confirms his exhortation, 1Pe 3:9, by Ps 34:12–16.

refrain – curb, literally, 'cause to cease'; implying that our natural inclination and custom is to speak evil. 'Men commonly think that they would be exposed to the wantonness of their enemies if they did not strenuously vindicate their rights. But the Spirit promises a life of blessedness to none but those who are gentle and patient of evils' [CALVIN].

evil … guile – First he warns against sins of the *tongue,* evil-speaking, and deceitful, double-tongued speaking; next, against *acts* of injury to one's neighbour.

11. In oldest manuscripts, *Greek,* 'Moreover (besides his *words,* in *acts*), let him.'

eschew – 'turn from.'

ensue – *pursue* as a thing hard to attain, and that flees from one in this troublesome world.

12. Ground of the promised present and eternal life of blessedness to the meek (1Pe 3:10). The Lord's *eyes* are ever over them for good.

ears … unto their prayers – (1Jo 5:14,15).

face … against – The *eyes* imply *favourable* regard; the *face* of the Lord *upon* (not as *English Version,* 'against') them that do evil, implies that He narrowly observes them, so as not to let them really and lastingly hurt His people (compare 1Pe 3:13).

13. **who … will harm you** – This fearless confidence in God's protection from harm, Christ, the Head, in His sufferings realized; so His members.

if ye be – *Greek,* 'if ye have *become.*'

followers – The oldest manuscripts read 'emulous,' 'zealous of' (Tit 2:14).

good – The contrast in *Greek* is, 'Who will do you *evil,* if ye be zealous of *good?*'

14. **But and if** – 'But if even.' 'The promises of *this* life extend only so far as it is expedient for us that they should be fulfilled' [CALVIN]. So he proceeds to state the exceptions to the promise (1Pe 3:10), and how the truly wise will behave in such exceptional cases. 'If ye should *suffer*'; if it should so happen; 'suffer,' a milder, word than *harm.*

for righteousness – 'not the suffering, but the cause for which one suffers, makes the martyr' [AUGUSTINE].

happy – Not even can *suffering* take away your *blessedness,* but rather promotes it.

and – *Greek,* 'but.' Do not impair your blessing (1Pe 3:9) by *fearing* man's *terror* in your times of adversity. Literally, 'Be not terrified with their terror,' that is, with that which they try to strike into you, and which strikes themselves when in adversity. This verse and 1Pe 3:15 is quoted from Isa 8:12,13. God alone is to be feared; he that fears God has none else to fear.

neither be troubled – the threat of the law, Le 26:36 De 28:65,66; in contrast to which the Gospel gives the believer a heart assured of God's favour, and therefore unruffled, amidst all adversities. Not only be not *afraid,* but be not even *agitated.*

15. **sanctify** – *hallow; honour as holy,* enshrining Him *in your hearts.* So in the Lord's Prayer, Mt 6:9. God's holiness is thus glorified in our hearts as the dwelling-place of His Spirit.

the Lord God – The oldest manuscripts read 'Christ.' Translate, 'Sanctify *Christ as Lord.*'

and – *Greek,* 'but,' or 'moreover.' *Besides* this inward sanctification of God *in the heart,* be also *ready always to give*

answer – an apologetic answer defending your faith.

to every man that asketh you – The last words limit the universality of the 'always'; not to a roller, but to everyone among the heathen who inquires honestly.

a reason – a reasonable account. This refutes Rome's dogma, 'I believe it, because the Church believes it.' Credulity is believing without evidence; faith is believing on evidence. There is no repose for reason itself but in faith. This verse does not impose an obligation to bring forward a learned proof and logical defence of revelation. But as believers deny themselves, crucify the world, and brave persecution, they must be buoyed up by some strong 'hope'; men of the world, having no such hope themselves, are moved by curiosity to *ask* the secret of this hope; the believer must be *ready* to give an *experimental account* 'how this hope arose in him, what it contains, and on what it rests' [STEIGER].

with – The oldest manuscripts read, '*but* with.' Be ready, *but* with 'meekness.' Not pertly and arrogantly.

meekness – (1Pe 3:4). The most effective way; not self-sufficient impetuosity.

fear – due respect towards man, and reverence towards God, remembering His cause does not need man's hot temper to uphold it.

16. Having a good conscience – the secret spring of *readiness to give account* of our *hope*. So *hope* and *good conscience* go together in Ac 24:15,16. Profession without practice has no weight. But those who *have a good conscience* can afford to give an account of their hope 'with meekness.'

whereas – (1Pe 2:12).

they speak evil of you, as of evildoers – One oldest manuscript reads, 'ye are spoken against,' omitting the rest.

falsely accuse – 'calumniate'; the *Greek* expresses malice shown in deeds as well as in words. It is translated, 'despitefully use,' Mt 5:44 Lu 6:28.

conversation – life, conduct.

in Christ – who is the very element of your life as Christians. 'In Christ' defines 'good.' It is your good walk *as Christians,* not as citizens, that calls forth malice (1Pe 4:4,5,14).

17. better – One may object, I would not bear it so ill if I had deserved it. Peter replies, it is *better* that you did not deserve it, in order that doing well and yet being spoken against, you may prove yourself a true Christian [GERHARD].

if the will of God be so – rather as the optative is in the oldest manuscripts, 'if the will of God should will it so.' Those who honour God's will as their highest law (1Pe 2:15) have the comfort to know that suffering is God's appointment (1Pe 4:19). So Christ Himself; our inclination does not wish it.

18. Confirmation of 1Pe 3:17, by the glorious results of Christ's suffering innocently.

For – 'Because.' That is 'better,' 1Pe 3:17, means of which we are rendered more like to Christ in death and in life; for His death brought the best issue to Himself and to us [BENGEL].

Christ – the Anointed *Holy* One of God; the *Holy* suffered for *sins,* the *Just* for the *unjust.*

also – as well as yourselves (1Pe 3:17). Compare 1Pe 2:21; there His suffering was brought forward as an example to us; here, as a proof of the blessedness of suffering for well-doing.

once – for all; never again to suffer. It is 'better' for us also once to suffer with Christ, than for ever without Christ. We now are suffering our 'once'; it will soon be a thing of the past; a bright consolation to the tried.

for sins – as though He had Himself committed them. He exposed Himself to death by His 'confession,' even as we are called on to 'give an answer to him that asketh a reason of our hope.' This was 'well-doing' in its highest manifestation. As He suffered, 'The Just', so we ought willingly to suffer, for *righteousness'* sake (1Pe 3:14; compare 1Pe 3:12,17).

that he might bring us to God – together with Himself in His ascension to the right hand of God (1Pe 3:22). He brings us, 'the unjust,' justified together with Him into heaven. So the result of Christ's death is His *drawing men to Him;* spiritually now, in our having *access into the Holiest,* opened by Christ's ascension; literally hereafter.

put to death – the means of His *bringing us to God.*

in the flesh – that is, *in respect to* the life of *flesh* and blood.

quickened by the Spirit – The oldest manuscripts omit the *Greek* article. Translate with the preposition 'in,' as the antithesis to the previous 'in the flesh' requires, 'IN spirit,' that is, in respect to His Spirit. 'Put to death' in the former *mode of life;* 'quickened' in the other. Not that His Spirit ever died and was *quickened,* or made alive again, but whereas He had lived after the manner of mortal men in the flesh, He *began to live a spiritual* 'resurrection' (1Pe 3:21) *life,* whereby He has the power to bring us to God. Two ways of explaining 1Pe 3:18,19, are open to us: (1) 'Quickened in Spirit,' that is, *immediately* on His release from the 'flesh,' the energy of His undying spirit-life was 'quickened' by God the Father, into new modes of action, namely, 'in the Spirit He *went* down (as subsequently He *went* up to heaven, 1Pe 3:22, the same *Greek* verb) and heralded to the spirits (His *Spirit* speaking to the *spirits*) in prison (in Hades or Sheol, awaiting the judgment, 2Pe 2:4), which were of old disobedient when'. (2) The strongest point in favour of (1) is the position of 'sometime,' that is, *of old,* connected with 'disobedient'; whereas if the *preaching* or announcing were a thing long past, we should expect 'sometime,' or *of old,* to be joined to 'went and preached.' But this transposition may express that *their disobedience preceded His preaching.* The *Greek* participle expresses the reason of His preaching, '*inasmuch as* they were sometime disobedient' (compare 1Pe 4:6). Also 'went' seems to mean a *personal* going, as in 1Pe 3:22, not merely *in spirit.* But see the answer below. The objections are 'quickened' must refer to Christ's *body* (compare 1Pe 3:21, end), for as His *Spirit* never ceased to live, it cannot be said to be 'quickened.' Compare Joh 5:21 Ro 8:11, and other passages, where 'quicken' is used of the *bodily* resurrection. Also, not His *Spirit*, but His *soul*, went to Hades. His Spirit was commended by Him at death to His Father, and was thereupon 'in Paradise.' The theory – (1) would thus require that His descent to the spirits in prison should be *after* His resurrection! Compare Eph 4:9,10, which makes the *descent* precede the *ascent*. Also Scripture elsewhere is silent about such a heralding, though possibly Christ's death had immediate effects on the state of both the godly and the ungodly in Hades: the souls of the godly heretofore in comparative confinement, perhaps then having been, as some Fathers thought, translated to God's immediate and heavenly presence; but this cannot be *proved* from Scripture. Compare however, Joh 3:13 Col 1:18. *Prison* is always used in a *bad* sense in Scripture. 'Paradise' and 'Abraham's bosom,' the abode of good spirits in Old Testament times, are separated by a wide gulf from Hell or Hades, and cannot be called 'prison.' Compare 2 Co 12:2,4, where 'paradise' and the 'third heaven' correspond. Also, why should the antediluvian unbelievers in particular be selected as the objects of His preaching in Hades? Therefore explain: 'Quickened in spirit, in which (as distinguished from *in person*; the words 'in which,' that is, *in spirit*, expressly obviating the objection that 'went' implies a *personal going*) He went (in the person of Noah, 'a preacher of righteousness,' 2Pe 2:5; ALFORD's own *Note*, Eph 2:17, is the best reply to his argument from 'went' that a *local* going to Hades *in person* is meant. As 'He CAME and preached peace' *by His Spirit* in the apostles and ministers after His death and ascension: so before His incarnation He preached in Spirit through Noah to the antediluvians, Joh 14:18,28 Ac 26:23. 'Christ should show,' literally, '*announce* light to the Gentiles') and preached unto the spirits in prison, that is, the ante-diluvians, whose bodies indeed seemed free, but their spirits were in prison, shut up in the earth as one great condemned cell (exactly parallel to Isa 24:22,23 'upon the earth ... they shall be gathered together as *prisoners* are gathered in the pit, and shall be shut up *in the prison*', [just as the fallen angels are judicially regarded as 'in chains of darkness,' though for a time now at large on the earth, 1Pe 2:4], where 1Pe 3:18 has a plain allusion to the flood, 'the *windows from on high* are open,' compare Ge 7:11); from this prison the only way of escape was that preached by Christ in Noah. Christ, who in our times came in the flesh, in the days of Noah preached in Spirit by Noah to the spirits then in prison (Isa 61:1, end, 'the Spirit of the Lord God hath sent me to *proclaim* the opening of the *prison* to them that are bound'). So in 1Pe

1:11, 'the Spirit of Christ' is said to have testified in the prophets. As Christ suffered even to death by enemies, and was afterwards quickened in virtue of His 'Spirit' (or divine nature, Ro 1:3,4 1Co 15:45), which henceforth acted in its full energy, the first result of which was the raising of His body (1Pe 3:21, end) from the prison of the grave and His soul from Hades; so the same Spirit of Christ enabled Noah, amidst reproach and trials, to preach to the disobedient spirits fast bound in wrath. That Spirit in you can enable you also to suffer patiently now, looking for the resurrection deliverance.

20. once – not in the oldest manuscripts.

when ... the long-suffering of God waited in the days of Noah – Oldest manuscripts. *Greek*, '*was continuing to wait on*' (if haply men in the hundred twenty years of grace would repent) until the *end* of His waiting came in their death by the flood. This refutes ALFORD's idea of a second day of grace having been given in Hades. Noah's days are selected, as the ark and the destroying flood answer respectively to 'baptism' and the coming destruction of unbelievers by fire.

while the ark was a-preparing – (Heb 11:7). A long period of God's 'long-suffering and waiting,' as Noah had few to help him, which rendered the world's unbelief the more inexcusable.

wherein – literally, '(by having entered) *into* which.'

eight – seven (the sacred number) with ungodly Ham.

few – so now.

souls – As this term is here used of *living* persons, why should not 'spirits' also? Noah preached to their ears, but Christ *in spirit*, to their *spirits*, or spiritual natures.

saved by water – The same water which drowned the unbelieving, buoyed up the ark in which the eight were saved. Not as some translate, 'were brought safe *through* the water.' However, the sense of the preposition may be as in 1Co 3:15, 'they were safely preserved through the water,' though having to be *in the water*.

21. whereunto – The oldest manuscripts read, 'which': literally, 'which (namely, *water*, in general; being) the antitype (of the water of the flood) is now saving (the salvation being not yet fully realized by us, compare 1Co 1:2,5 Jude 1:5; *puts into a state of salvation*) us also (two oldest manuscripts read "*you*" for "us": You also, as well as Noah and his party), to wit, baptism.' Water saved Noah not of itself, but by sustaining the ark built in *faith*, resting on God's word: it was to him the sign and mean of a kind of *regeneration*, of the earth. The flood was for Noah a baptism, as the passage through the Red Sea was for the Israelites; by baptism in the flood he and his family were transferred from the old world to the new: from immediate destruction to lengthened probation; from the companionship of the wicked to communion with God; from the severing of all bonds between the creature and the Creator to the privileges of the covenant: so we by spiritual baptism. As there was a Ham who forfeited the privileges of the covenant, so many now. The antitypical water, namely, baptism, saves you also not of itself, nor the mere material water, but the spiritual thing conjoined with it, repentance and faith, of which it is the sign and seal, as Peter proceeds to explain. Compare the union of the sign and thing signified, Joh 3:5 Eph 5:26 Tit 3:5 Heb 10:22; compare 1Jo 5:6.

not the – 'flesh' bears the emphasis. 'Not the putting away of the filth of *the flesh*' (as is done by a mere water baptism, unaccompanied with the Spirit's baptism, compare Eph 2:11), but of the soul. It is the ark (Christ and His Spirit-filled Church), not the water, which is the instrument of salvation: the water only flowed round the ark; so not the mere water baptism, but the water when accompanied with the Spirit.

answer – *Greek*, 'interrogation'; referring to the *questions* asked of candidates for baptism; eliciting a confession of faith 'toward God' and a renunciation of Satan ([AUGUSTINE, *The Creed*, 4.1]; [CYPRIAN, *Epistles, 7, To Rogatianus*]), which, when flowing from 'a good conscience,' assure one of being 'saved.'

by the resurrection of Jesus – joined with 'saves you': In so far as baptism applies to us the power of Christ's resurrection. As Christ's death unto sin is the source of the believer's death unto, and so deliverance from, sin's penalty and power; so His resurrection life is the source of the believer's new spiritual life.

22. (Ps 110:1 Ro 8:34,38 1Co 15:24 Eph 1:21 3:10 Col 1:16 2:10–15). The fruit of His patience in His voluntary endured and undeserved sufferings: a pattern to us, 1Pe 3:17,18.

gone – (Lu 24:51). Proving against rationalists an actual material ascension. Literally, 'is on the right hand of God, *having gone* into heaven.'

Chapter 4

1Pe 4:1–19. Like the risen Christ, believers henceforth ought to have no more to do with sin.

As the end is near, cultivate self-restraint, watchful prayerfulness, charity, hospitality, scriptural speech, ministering to one another according to your several gifts to the glory of God: Rejoicing patience under suffering.

1. for us – supported by some oldest manuscripts and versions, omitted by others.

in the flesh – in His mortal body of humiliation.

arm – (Eph 6:11,13).

the same mind – of suffering with patient willingness what God *wills* you to suffer.

he that hath suffered – for instance, Christ first, and in His person the believer: a general proposition.

hath ceased – literally, 'has been made to cease,' *has obtained* by the very fact of His having suffered once for all, *a cessation from sin*, which had heretofore lain on Him (Ro 6:6–11, especially, 1Pe 4:7). The Christian is by faith one with Christ: as then Christ by death is judicially freed from sin; so the Christian who has in the person of Christ died, has no more to do with it judicially, and ought to have no more to do with it actually. 'The flesh' is the sphere in which sin has place.

2. That he – 'That he (the believer, who has once for all obtained cessation from sin by suffering, in the person of Christ, namely, in virtue of his union with the crucified Christ) should no longer live the rest of his time in the flesh to the lusts of men, but to the will of God' as his rule. '*Rest of his time in the flesh*' (the *Greek* has the preposition 'in' here, not in 1Pe 4:1 as to Christ) proves that the reference is here not to Christ, but to the believer, whose remaining time for glorifying God is short (1Pe 4:3). 'Live' in the truest sense, for heretofore he was *dead*. Not as ALFORD, 'Arm yourselves … with a view no longer to live the rest of *your* time.'

3. may suffice – *Greek*, 'is sufficient.' Peter takes the lowest ground: for not even the past time ought to have been wasted in lust; but since you cannot recall it, at least lay out the future to better account.

us – omitted in oldest manuscripts.

wrought – *Greek*, 'wrought out.'

Gentiles – heathen: which many of you were.

when – 'walking as ye have done [ALFORD] in *lasciviousness*'; the *Greek* means *petulant, immodest, wantonness*, unbridled conduct: not so much filthy lust.

excess of wine – 'wine-bibbings' [ALFORD].

abominable – 'nefarious,' 'lawless idolatries,' violating God's most sacred law; not that *all* Peter's readers (see on 1Pe 1:1) *walked* in these, but many, namely, the Gentile portion of them.

4. Wherein – In respect to which abandonment of your former *walk* (1Pe 4:3).

run not with them – eagerly, in troops [BENGEL].

excess – literally, 'profusion'; a sink: stagnant water remaining after an inundation.

riot – profligacy.

speaking evil – charging you with pride, singularity, hypocrisy, and secret crimes (1Pe 4:14 2Pe 2:2). However, there is no 'of you' in the *Greek*, but simply 'blaspheming.' It seems to me always to be used, either directly or indirectly, in the sense of *impious reviling against God, Christ,* or the Holy Spirit, and the Christian religion, not merely against men as such; Greek, 1Pe 4:14, below.

5. They who now call you to account falsely, shall have to give account themselves for this very evil-speaking (Jude 1:15), and be condemned justly.

ready – very speedily (1Pe 4:7 2Pe 3:10). Christ's coming is to the believer always near.

6. For – giving the reason for 1Pe 4:5, 'judge the dead.'

gospel preached also to … dead – as well as to them now living, and to them that shall be found alive at the coming of the Judge. 'Dead' must be taken in the same literal sense as in 1Pe 4:5, which refutes the explanation 'dead' in sins. Moreover, the absence of the Greek article does not necessarily restrict the sense of 'dead' to particular dead persons, for there is no Greek article in 1Pe 4:5 also, where 'the dead' is universal in meaning. The sense seems to be, Peter, as representing the true attitude of the Church in every age, expecting Christ at any moment, says, The Judge is ready to judge the quick and dead – the dead, I say, for they, too, in their lifetime, have had the Gospel preached to them, that so they might be judged at last in the same way as those living now (and those who shall be so when Christ shall come), namely, 'men in the flesh,' and that they might, having escaped condemnation by embracing the Gospel so preached, live unto God in the spirit (though death has passed over their flesh), Lu 20:38, thus being made like Christ in death and in life (see on 1Pe 3:18). He says, 'live,' not 'made alive' or quickened; for they are supposed to have been already 'quickened together with Christ' (Eph 2:5). This verse is parallel to 1Pe 3:18; compare Note, see on 1Pe 3:18. The Gospel, substantially, was 'preached' to the Old Testament Church; though not so fully as to the New Testament Church. It is no valid objection that the Gospel has not been preached to all that shall be found dead at Christ's coming. For Peter is plainly referring only to those within reach of the Gospel, or who might have known God through His ministers in Old and New Testament times. Peter, like Paul, argues that those found living at Christ's coming shall have no advantage above the dead who shall then be raised, inasmuch as the latter live unto, or 'according to,' God, even already in His purpose. ALFORD's explanation is wrong, 'that they might be judged according to men as regards the flesh,' that is, be in the state of the completed sentence on sin, which is death after the flesh. For 'judged' cannot have a different meaning in this verse from what 'judge' bears in 1Pe 4:5. 'Live according to God' means, live a life with God, such as God lives, divine; as contrasted with 'according to men in the flesh,' that is, a life such as men live in the flesh.

7. Resuming the idea in 1Pe 4:5.

the end of all things – and therefore also of the wantonness (1Pe 4:3,4) of the wicked, and of the sufferings of the righteous [BENGEL]. The nearness meant is not that of mere 'time,' but that before the Lord; as he explains to guard against misapprehension, and defends God from the charge of procrastination: We live in the last dispensation, not like the Jews under the Old Testament.

sober – 'self-restrained.' The opposite duties to the sins in 1Pe 4:3 are here inculcated. Thus 'sober' is the opposite of 'lasciviousness' (1Pe 4:3).

watch – Greek, 'be soberly vigilant'; not intoxicated with worldly cares and pleasures. Temperance promotes wakefulness or watchfulness, and both promote prayer. Drink makes drowsy, and drowsiness prevents prayer.

prayer – Greek, 'prayers'; the end for which we should exercise vigilance.

8. above all things – not that 'charity' or love is placed above 'prayer,' but because love is the animating spirit, without which all other duties are dead. Translate as Greek, 'Having your mutual (literally, "towards yourselves") charity intense.' He presupposes its existence among them; he urges them to make it more fervent.

charity shall cover the multitude – The oldest manuscripts have 'covereth.' Quoted from Pr 10:12; compare Pr 17:9. 'Covereth' so as not harshly to condemn or expose faults; but forbearingly to bear the other's burdens, forgiving and forgetting past offenses. Perhaps the additional idea is included, By prayer for them, love tries to have them covered by God; and so being the instrument of converting the sinner from his error, 'coAereth a (not "the," as English Version) multitude of sins'; but the former idea from Proverbs is the prominent one. It is not, as Rome teaches, 'coAereth' his own sins; for then the Greek middle voice would be used; and Pr 10:12 17:9 support the Protestant view. 'As God with His love covers my sins if I believe, so must I also cover the sins of my neighbour' [LUTHER].

9. (Ro 12:13 Heb 13:2.) Not the spurious hospitality which passes current in the world, but the entertaining of those needing it, especially those exiled for the faith, as the representatives of Christ, and all hospitality to whomsoever exercised from genuine Christian love.

without grudging – Greek, 'murmuring.' 'He that giveth, let him do it with simplicity,' that is, open-hearted sincerity; with cordiality. Not secretly speaking against the person whom we entertain, or upbraiding him with the favour we have conferred in him.

10. every – 'even as each man hath received,'

in whatever degree, and of whatever kind. The Spirit's *gifts* (literally, 'gift *of grace*,' that is, *gratuitously* bestowed) are the common property of the Christian community, each Christian being but a steward for the edifying of the whole, not receiving the gift merely for his own use.

minister the same – not discontentedly envying or disparaging *the gift of another.*

one to another – *Greek* as in 1Pe 4:8, 'towards yourselves'; implying that all form but one body, and in seeking the good of other members they are promoting the good of *themselves.*

stewards – referring to Mt 25:15; Lu 19:13–26.

11. If any … speak – namely, as a prophet, or divinely taught *teacher* in the Church assembly.

as the – The *Greek* has no article: 'as oracles of God.' This may be due to *Greek*: 'God,' having no article, it being a principle when a governed noun omits the *Greek* article that the governing noun should omit it, too. In Ac 7:38 also, the *Greek* article is wanting; thus *English Version*, 'as the oracles of God,' namely, *the Old Testament*, would be 'right,' and the precept be similar to Ro 12:6, 'prophesy according to *the analogy of the faith.*' But the context suits better thus, 'Let him speak as (becomes one speaking) *oracles* OF GOD.' His divinely inspired words are *not his own*, but *God's*, and as a *steward* (1Pe 4:10) having them committed to him, he ought so to speak them. Jesus was the pattern in this respect (Mt 7:29 Joh 12:49 14:10; compare Paul, 2 Co 2:17). Note, the very same term as is applied in the only other passages where it occurs (Ac 7:38 Ro 3:2 Heb 5:12), to the *Old Testament* inspired writings, is here predicated of the inspired *words* (the substance of which was afterwards committed to *writing*) of the *New Testament* prophets.

minister – in *acts;* the other sphere of spiritual activity besides *speaking.*

as of – 'out of' the store of his 'strength' (*Greek, physical* power in relation to outward service, rather than moral and intellectual 'ability'; so in Mr 12:30).

giveth – *Greek*, 'supplieth'; originally said of a *choragus*, who *supplied* the chorus with all necessaries for performing their several parts.

that God in all things may be glorified – the final end of all a Christian's acts.

through Jesus Christ – the mediator through whom all our blessings come down to us, and also through whom all our praises ascend to God. Through Christ alone can God be glorified in us and our sayings and doings.

to whom – Christ.

be – *Greek*, 'is.'

for ever and ever – *Greek*, 'unto the ages of the ages.'

12. strange – they might *think it strange* that God should allow His chosen children to be sore tried.

fiery trial – like the fire by which metals are tested and their dross removed. The *Greek* adds, 'in your case.'

which is to try you – *Greek*, 'which is taking place for a trial to you.' Instead of its '*happening* to you' as some strange and untoward *chance*, it 'is taking place' with the gracious *design* of trying you; God has a wise design in it – a consolatory reflection.

13. inasmuch as – The oldest manuscripts read, 'in proportion as'; 'in as far as' ye by suffering are partakers of Christ's sufferings, that is, by faith enter into realizing fellowship with them; willingly for His sake suffering as He suffered.

with exceeding joy – *Greek*, 'exulting joy'; now ye *rejoice* amidst sufferings; then ye shall EXULT, for ever free from sufferings (1Pe 1:6,8). If we will not bear suffering for Christ now, we must bear eternal sufferings hereafter.

14. for – *Greek*, 'IN the name of Christ,' namely, *as Christians* (1Pe 4:16 3:14, above); '*in My name*, because *ye belong to Christ.*' The emphasis lies on this: 1Pe 4:15, 'as a murderer, thief,' stands in contrast. Let your suffering be on account of Christ, not on account of evil-doing (1Pe 2:20).

reproached – *Reproach* affects noble minds more than loss of goods, or even bodily sufferings.

the spirit … upon you – the same Spirit as rested on Christ (Lu 4:18). 'The Spirit of glory' is *His* Spirit, for He is the 'Lord *of glory*' (Jas 2:1). Believers may well overcome the '*reproach*' (compare Heb 11:26), seeing that 'the Spirit of *glory*' rests upon them, as upon Him. It cannot prevent the happiness of the righteous, if they are reproached for Christ, because they retain before God their *glory* entire, as having the Spirit, with whom *glory* is inseparably joined [CALVIN].

and of God – *Greek*, 'and *the* (Spirit) of God'; implying that *the Spirit of glory* (which is Christ's Spirit) is at the same time also *the Spirit of God.*

on their part he is evil spoken of, but on your part he is glorified – omitted in the two oldest *Greek* manuscripts and *Syriac* and *Coptic* versions, but supported by one very old manuscript, *Vulgate, Sahidic*, CYPRIAN 'Evil spoken of,' literally, 'blasphemed'; not merely do they '*speak against you*,' as in 1Pe 3:16, but *blasphemously mock Christ* and Christianity itself.

15. But – *Greek*, 'For.' 'Reproached *in the name of Christ*' I say (1Pe 4:14), 'FOR *let none*' as … as … as … as – the 'as' twice in italics is not in the *Greek*. The second *Greek*, 'as,' distinguishes the class 'busybody in other men's matters,' from the previous class of delinquents. Christians, from mistaken zeal, under the plea of faithfulness, might readily step out of their own calling and make themselves judges of the acts of unbelievers. Literally, 'a bishop in what is (not his own, but) another's' province; an allusion to the existing *bishops* or overseers of the Church; a self-constituted bishop in others' concerns.

16. a Christian – the name given in contempt first at Antioch. Ac 11:26 26:28; the only three places where the term occurs. At first believers had no distinctive name, but were called among themselves 'brethren,' Ac 6:3; 'disciples,' Ac 6:1; 'those of the way,' Ac 9:2; 'saints,' Ro 1:7; by the Jews (who denied that Jesus was the CHRIST, and so would never originate the name *Christian*), in contempt, 'Nazarenes.' At Antioch, where first *idolatrous* Gentiles (Cornelius, Ac 10:1,2, was not an idolater, but a proselyte) were converted, and wide missionary work began, they could be no longer looked on as a *Jewish sect*, and so *the Gentiles* designated them by the new name 'Christians.' The rise of the new name marked a new epoch in the Church's life, a new stage of its development, namely, its missions to the Gentiles. The idle and witty people of Antioch, we know from heathen writers, were famous for inventing nicknames. The date of this Epistle must have been when this had become the generally recognized designation *among Gentiles* (*it is never applied by Christians to each other*, as it was in after ages – an undesigned proof that the New Testament was composed when it professes), and when the name exposed one to reproach and suffering, though not seemingly as yet to *systematic* persecution.

let him not be ashamed – though the world is ashamed of shame. To suffer for one's own faults is no honour (1Pe 4:15 1Pe 2:20), – for Christ, is no *shame* (1Pe 4:14 1Pe 3:13).

but let him glorify God – not merely glory in persecution; Peter might have said as the contrast, 'but let him esteem it an honour to himself'; but the honour is to be given *to God*, who counts him worthy of such an honour, involving exemption from the coming judgments on the ungodly.

on this behalf – The oldest manuscripts and *Vulgate* read, 'in this *name*,' that is, in respect of suffering for such a name.

17. Another ground of consolation to Christians. All must pass under the judgment of God; God's own household first, their chastisement being here, for which they should glorify Him as a proof of their membership in His family, and a pledge of their escape from the end of those whom the last judgment shall find disobedient to the Gospel.

the time – Greek, 'season,' 'fit time.'

judgment must begin at the house of God – the Church of living believers. Peter has in mind Eze 9:6; compare Am 3:2 Jer 25:29. Judgment is already begun, the Gospel word, as a 'two-edged sword,' having the double effect of saving some and condemning others, and shall be consummated at the last judgment. 'When power is given to the destroyer, he observes no distinction between the righteous and the wicked; not only so, but he begins first at the righteous' [WETSTEIN from *Rabbins*]. But God limits the destroyer's power over His people.

if ... at us, what shall the end *be* of them – If even the godly have chastening judgments now, how much more shall the ungodly be doomed to damnatory judgments at last.

gospel of God – the very God who is to judge them.

18. scarcely – Compare 'so as by fire,' 1Co 3:15; having to pass through trying chastisements, as David did for his sin. 'The righteous' man has always more or less of trial, but the issue is certain, and the entrance into the kingdom *abundant* at last. The 'scarcely' marks the severity of the ordeal, and the unlikelihood (in a mere human point of view) of the righteous sustaining it; but the righteousness of Christ and God's everlasting covenant make it all sure.

ungodly – having no regard for God; negative description.

sinner – loving sin; positive; the same man is at once God-forgetting and sin-loving.

appear – in judgment.

19. General conclusion from 1Pe 4:17,18. Seeing that the godly know that their sufferings are *by God's will*, to chasten them that they may not perish with the world, they have good reason to trust God cheerfully amidst sufferings, persevering *in well-doing*.

let them – Greek, 'let them *also*,' 'let *even* them,' as well as those not suffering. Not only under ordinary circumstances, but *also* in time *of suffering, let* believers *commit*. (Compare *Note*, see on 1Pe 3:14).

according to the will of God – (See on 1Pe 3:17). God's will that the believer should suffer (1Pe 4:17), is for his good. One oldest manuscript and *Vulgate* read, 'in *well-doings*'; contrast ill-doings, 1Pe 4:15. Our committing of ourselves to God is to be, not in indolent and passive quietism, but accompanied with active *well-doings*.

faithful – to His covenant promises.

Creator – who is therefore also our Almighty Preserver. He, not we, must *keep* our souls. Sin destroyed the original spiritual relation between creature and Creator, leaving that only of government. Faith restores it; so that the believer, living to *the will of God* (1Pe 4:2), rests implicitly on his *Creator's* faithfulness.

Chapter 5

1Pe 5:1–14. Exhortations to elders, juniors, and all in general. Parting prayer. Conclusion.

1. elders – alike in office and age (1Pe 5:5).

I ... also an elder – To put one's self on a level with those whom we exhort, gives weight to one's exhortations (compare 2Jo 1:1,2). Peter, in true humility for the Gospel's sake, does not put forward his *apostleship* here, wherein he *presided over the elders*. In the apostleship the apostles have no successors, for 'the signs of an apostle' have not been transmitted.

witness – an *eye-witness* of Christ's sufferings, and so qualified to exhort you to believing patience in *suffering for well-doing* after His example (1Pe 4:19 2:20). This explains the 'therefore' inserted in the oldest manuscripts, 'I therefore exhort', resuming exhortation from 1Pe 4:19. His higher dignity as an *apostle* is herein delicately implied, as *eye-witnessing* was a necessary qualification for apostleship: compare Peter's own speeches, Ac 1:21,22 2:32 10:39.

also – implying the righteous recompense corresponding to the sufferings.

partaker of the glory – according to Christ's promise; an earnest of which was given in the transfiguration.

2. Feed – Greek, 'Tend as a shepherd', by discipline and doctrine. Lead, feed, heed: by prayer, exhortation, government, and example. The dignity is marked by the term '*elder*'; the *duties* of the office, to *tend* or *oversee*, by '*bishop*.' Peter has in mind Christ's injunction to him, 'Feed (*tend*) My sheep ... Feed (*pasture*) My lambs' (Joh 21:16). He invites the elders to share with him the same duty (compare Ac 20:28). The flock is Christ's.

which is among you – While having a concern for *all* the Church, your special duty is to feed that portion of it 'which is among you.'

oversight – Greek, 'bishopric', or duty of bishops, that is, overseer.

not by constraint – Necessity is laid upon them, but willingness prevents it being felt, both in undertaking and in fulfilling the duty [BENGEL]. 'He is a true presbyter and minister of the counsel of God who doeth and teacheth the things of the Lord, being not accounted righteous merely because he is a presbyter, but because righteous, chosen into the presbytery' [CLEMENT OF ALEXANDRIA].

willingly – One oldest manuscript, *Vulgate*, *Syriac*, and *Coptic*, add, 'as God would have it to be done' (Ro 8:27).

not for filthy lucre – (Isa 56:11 Tit 1:7).

of a ready mind – promptly and heartily, without selfish motive of gain-seeking, as the Israelites gave their services *willing-heartedly* to the sanctuary.

3. being lords – Greek, 'lording it': implying pride and oppression. 'Not that we have dominion over your faith.'

God's heritage – Greek, 'the inheritances', that is, the *portions* of the Church committed severally to your pastoral charge [BENGEL]. It is explained by 'the flock' in the next clause. BERNARD OF CLAIRVAUX, wrote to Pope Eugene, 'Peter could not give thee what he had not: what he had he gave: the *care* over the Church, not *dominion*.'

being – Greek, 'becoming.'

ensamples – the most effective recommendation of precept (1Ti 4:12). Tit 2:7, 'patterns.' So Jesus. 'A monstrosity it is to see the highest rank joined with the meanest mind, the first seat with the lowest life, a grandiloquent tongue with a lazy life, much talking with no fruit' [BERNARD].

4. And – 'And so': as the result of 'being ensamples' (1Pe 5:3).

chief Shepherd – the title peculiarly Christ's own, not Peter's or the pope's.

when ... shall appear – Greek, 'be manifested' (Col 3:4). Faith serves the Lord while still unseen.

crown – Greek, '*stephanos*,' a garland of *victory*, the prize in the Grecian games, woven of ivy, parsley, myrtle, olive, or oak. Our crown is distinguished from *theirs* in that it is 'incorruptible' and 'fadeth not away', as the leaves of theirs soon did. 'The crown *of life*.' Not a *kingly* 'crown' (a different Greek word, *diadema*): the prerogative of the Lord Jesus (Re 19:12).

glory – Greek, 'the glory', namely, *to be* then *revealed* (1Pe 5:1 1Pe 4:13).

that fadeth not away – Greek, 'amaranthine' (compare 1Pe 1:4).

5. ye younger – The *deacons* were originally the younger men, the *presbyters* older; but subsequently as presbyter expressed the *office* of Church ruler or teacher, so Greek '*neoteros*' means not (as literally) *young men* in age, but *subordinate ministers* and servants of the Church. So Christ uses the term 'younger.' For He explains it by 'he that doth serve', literally, 'he that ministereth as a deacon'; just as He explains 'the greatness' by 'he that is chief', literally, 'he that *ruleth*,' the very word applied to the *bishops* or *presbyters*. So 'the young men' are undoubtedly the deacons of the Church of Jerusalem, of whom, as being all *Hebrews*, the Hellenistic Christians subsequently complained as neglecting their *Grecian* widows, whence arose the appointment of the seven others, *Hellenistic* deacons. So here, Peter, having exhorted the *presbyters*, or elders, not to lord it over those committed to them, adds, Likewise ye *neoters* or younger, that is, subordinate ministers and deacons, submit cheerfully to the command of the elders [MOSHEIM]. There is no Scripture sanction for 'younger' meaning *laymen* in general (as ALFORD explains): its use in this sense is probably of later date. The '*all* of you' that follows, refers to the *congregation* generally; and it is likely that, like Paul, Peter should notice, previous to the general congregation, the *subordinate ministers* as well as the *presbyters,* writing as he did to the same region (Ephesus), and to confirm the teaching of the apostle of the Gentiles.

Yea – to sum up all my exhortations in one.

be subject – omitted in the oldest manuscripts and versions, but TISCHENDORF quotes the *Vatican* manuscript for it. Then translate, 'Gird (1Pe 1:13 4:1) fast on humility (lowliness of mind) to one another.' The verb is literally, 'tie on with a fast *knot*' [WAHL]. Or, '*gird on* humility as *the slave dress (encomboma)*': as the Lord girded Himself with a towel to perform a servile office of humility and love, washing His disciples' feet, a scene in which Peter had played an important part, so that he would naturally have it before his mind.

God resisteth the proud – Quoted, as Jas 4:6, from Pr 3:34. Peter had James before his mind, and gives his Epistle inspired sanction. Compare 1Pe 5:9 with Jas 4:7, literally, 'arrayeth Himself against.' Other sins flee from God: pride alone opposeth itself to God; therefore, God also in turn *opposes Himself* to the proud [GERHARD in ALFORD]. Humility is the vessel of all graces [AUGUSTINE].

6. under the mighty hand – afflicting you (1Pe 3:15): 'accept' His chastisements, and turn to Him that smiteth you. He depresses the proud and exalts the humble.

in due time – Wait humbly and patiently for His own fit time. One oldest manuscript and *Vulgate* read, 'In the season of visitation,' namely, His visitation in mercy.

7. Casting – *once for all:* so the *Greek* aorist.

care – 'anxiety.' The advantage flowing from *humbling ourselves under God's hand* (1Pe 5:6) is confident reliance on His goodness. Exemption from care goes along with humble submission to God.

careth for you – literally '*respecting* you.' Care is a burden which faith casts off the man on his God. Compare Ps 22:10 37:5 55:22, to which Peter alludes; Lu 12:22,37 Php 4:6.

careth – not so strong a *Greek* word as the previous *Greek* 'anxiety.'

8. Peter has in mind Christ's warning to himself to *watch* against *Satan,* from forgetting which he fell. **Be sober ... vigilant** – 'Care,' that is, *anxiety,* will intoxicate the soul; therefore be sober, that is, self-restrained. Yet, lest this freedom from *care* should lead any to false security, he adds, 'Be vigilant' against 'your adversary.' Let this be your 'care.' God provides, therefore do not be anxious. The devil seeks, therefore watch [BENGEL].

because – omitted in the oldest manuscripts. The broken and disjointed sentences are more fervid and forcible. LUCIFER OF CAGLIARI reads as *English Version.*

adversary – literally, 'opponent in a court of justice' (Zec 3:1). 'Satan' means *opponent.* 'Devil,' *accuser* or *slanderer* (Re 12:10). 'The enemy' (Mt 13:39). 'A murderer from the beginning' (Joh 8:44). He counteracts the Gospel and its agents. 'The tempter'.

roaring lion – implying his violent and insatiable thirst for prey as a hungry lion. Through man's sin he got God's justice on his side against us; but Christ, our Advocate, by fulfilling all the demands of justice for us, has made our redemption altogether consistent with justice.

walketh about – (Job 1:7 2:2). So the children of the wicked one *cannot rest.* Evil spirits are in 2Pe 2:4 Jude 1:6, said to be already in chains of darkness and in hell. This probably means that this is their doom *finally:* a doom already begun in part; though for a time they are permitted to roam in the world (of which Satan is prince), especially in the dark air that surrounds the earth. Hence perhaps arises the miasma of the air at times, as physical and moral evil are closely connected.

devour – entangle in worldly 'care' (1Pe 5:7) and other snares, so as finally to destroy. Compare Re 12:15,16.

9. (Lu 4:13 Eph 6:11–17 Jas 4:7.)

steadfast – Compare established in the truth, 2Pe 1:12. Satan's power exists only in respect to the unbelieving; the faithful he cannot hurt (1Jo 5:18). Faith gives strength to prayer, the great instrument against the foe (Jas 1:6).

knowing – 'encouragement not to faint in afflictions': your brethren suffer the same; nothing beyond the common lot of Christians befalls you (1Co 10:13). It is a sign of God's favour rather than displeasure, that Satan is allowed to harass you, as he did Job. Your fellow Christians have the same battle of faith and prayer against Satan.

are – *are being accomplished* according to the appointment of God.

in the world – lying in the wicked one, and therefore necessarily the scene of 'tribulation' (Joh 16:33).

10. Comforting assurance that God will finally 'perfect' His work of 'grace' in them, after they have undergone the necessary previous suffering.

But – Only do you watch and resist the foe: God will perform the rest [BENGEL].

of all grace – (Compare 1Pe 4:10). The God to whom as its source all grace is to be referred; who in grace completes what in grace He began. He from the first 'called (so the oldest manuscripts read for 'us') unto (with a view to) glory.' He will not let His purpose fall short of completion. If He does so in punishing, much more in grace. The three are fitly conjoined: the *call*, the *glory* to which we are called, and the way (*suffering*); the fourth is the ground of the calling, namely, *the grace of God in Christ.*

by – *Greek*, 'in.' Christ is He *in virtue of* whom, and *in union with* whom, believers are called to glory. The opposite is 'in the world' (1Pe 5:9 Joh 16:33).

after that ye have suffered – Join to 'called you': *suffering,* as a necessary preliminary to *glory,* was contemplated in God's *calling.*

a while – short and inconsiderable, as compared with the *glory.*

perfect – The two oldest manuscripts, and *Vulgate* and *Coptic* versions, read, '*shall* perfect (so that there shall be nothing *defective* in you), stablish, strengthen,' and omit 'settle,' literally, 'ground,' or 'fix on a foundation.' ALFORD reads it in spite of the oldest manuscripts The authority of the latter I prefer; moreover the climax seems to require rather a verb of *completing* the work of grace, than, as the *Greek* means, *founding* it. The *Greek* has, 'shall HIMSELF perfect you': though you are called on to *watch* and *resist* the foe, God *Himself* must really do all in and through you. The same God who begins must *Himself* complete the work. The *Greek* for 'stablish' (so as to be 'steadfast in the faith,' 1Pe 5:9) is the same as 'strengthen,' Lu 22:32. Peter has in mind Christ's charge, 'When thou art converted, *strengthen* thy brethren.' His exhortation accords with his name *Peter,* 'Thou art *Peter,* and upon this *rock* I will build My Church.' 'Stablish,' so as not to waver. 'Strengthen' *with might in the inner man by His Spirit,* against the foe.

11. To him – emphatic. To Him and Him alone: not to ourselves. Compare 'Himself,' see on 1Pe 5:10.

glory and – omitted in the oldest manuscripts and versions.

dominion – *Greek,* 'the might' shown in so 'perfecting,' you, 1Pe 5:10.

12. Silvanus – *Silas,* the companion of Paul and Timothy: a suitable messenger by whom to confirm, as Peter here does, *Paul's* doctrine of 'the true grace of God' in the same churches (compare 2Pe 3:16). We never meet with Silvanus as Paul's companion after Paul's last journey to Jerusalem. His connection with Peter was plainly subsequent to that journey.

as I suppose – Join 'faithful unto you [STEIGER], as I suppose.' Silvanus may have stood in a close relation to the churches in Asia, perhaps having taken the oversight of them after Paul's departure, and had afterwards gone to Peter, by whom he is now sent back to them with this Epistle. He did not *know,* by positive observation, *Silvanus' faithfulness to them;* he therefore says, 'faithful *to you,* as I suppose,' from the accounts I hear; not expressing doubt.

ALFORD joins 'I have *written unto you*,' which the *Greek* order favours. The seeming uncertainty, thus, is not as to Silvanus' faithfulness, which strongly marked by the *Greek* article, but as to whether he or some other would prove to be the bearer of the letter, addressed as it was to five provinces, *all* of which Silvanus might not reach: 'By Silvanus, that faithful brother, as *expect,* I have Written to you' [BIRKS].

briefly – *Greek,* 'in few (words),' as compared with the importance of the subject (Heb 13:22).

exhorting – not so much formally *teaching doctrines,* which could not be done in so 'few words.'

testifying – bearing my testimony *in confirmation* (so the *Greek* compound verb implies) of that truth which ye have already heard from Paul and Silas (1Jo 2:27).

that this – of which I have just written, and of which Paul before testified to you (whose testimony, now that he was no longer in those regions, was called in question probably by some; compare 2Pe 3:15,16). 2Pe 1:12, 'the present truth,' namely, the grace formerly promised by the prophets, and *now* manifested to you. 'Grace' is the keynote of Paul's doctrine which Peter now confirms (Eph 2:5,8). Their sufferings for the Gospel made them to need some attestation and confirmation of the truth, that they should not fall back from it.

wherein ye stand – The oldest manuscripts read imperatively, '*Stand ye.*' Literally, '*into* which (having been already admitted, 1Pe 1:8,21 2:7,8,9) stand (therein).' Peter seems to have in mind Paul's words (Ro 5:2 1Co 15:1). 'The grace wherein we stand must be true, and our standing in it true also' [BENGEL]. Compare in 'He began his Epistle with grace (1Pe 1:2), he finishes it with grace, he has besprinkled the middle with grace, that in every part he might teach that the Church is not saved but by grace.'

13. The ... at Babylon – ALFORD, BENGEL, and others translate, 'She that is elected together with you in Babylon,' namely, *Peter's wife,* whom he *led about* with him in his missionary journeys. Compare 1Pe 3:7, 'heirs together' of the grace of life.' But why she should be called 'elected together with you *in Babylon,*' as if there had been no Christian woman in Babylon besides, is inexplicable on this view. In *English Version* the sense is clear: 'That portion of *the whole dispersion* (1Pe 1:1, *Greek*), or Church of Christianized Jews, with Gentile converts, which resides in Babylon.' As Peter and John were closely associated, Peter addresses the Church in John's peculiar province, Asia, and closes with 'your *co-elect* sister Church at *Babylon* saluteth you'; and John similarly addresses the 'elect lady,' that is, *the Church in Babylon,* and closes with 'the children of thine elect sister (the Asiatic Church) greet thee'. ERASMUS explains, 'Mark *who is in the* *place of a son* to me': compare Ac 12:12, implying Peter's connection with Mark; whence the mention of him in connection with *the Church* at Babylon, in which he laboured under Peter before he went to Alexandria is not unnatural. PAPIAS reports from the presbyter John [EUSEBIUS, *Ecclesiastical History,* 3.39], that Mark was interpreter of Peter, recording in his Gospel the facts related to him by Peter. Silvanus or Silas had been substituted for John Mark, as Paul's companion, because of Mark's temporary unfaithfulness. But now Mark restored is associated with Silvanus, Paul's companion, in Peter's esteem, as Mark was already reinstated in Paul's esteem. That Mark had a spiritual connection with the Asiatic' churches which Peter addresses, and so naturally salutes them, appears from 2Ti 4:11 Col 4:10.

Babylon – The Chaldean Babylon on the Euphrates. See *Introduction*, ON THE PLACE OF WRITING this Epistle, in proof that *Rome* is not meant as Papists assert. How unlikely that in a *friendly salutation* the enigmatical title of Rome given in *prophecy* (John, Re 17:5), should be used! Babylon was the centre from which the Asiatic *dispersion* whom Peter addresses was derived. PHILO [*The Embassy to Gaius,* 36] and JOSEPHUS [*Antiquities,* 15.2. 2 23.12] inform us that Babylon contained a great many Jews in the apostolic age (whereas those at Rome were comparatively few, about eight thousand [JOSEPHUS, *Antiquities,* 17.11]); so it would naturally be visited by the apostle of the circumcision. It was the headquarters of those whom he had so successfully addressed on Pentecost, Ac 2:9, Jewish 'Parthians … dwellers in Mesopotamia' (the Parthians were then masters of Mesopotamian Babylon); these he ministered to in *person.* His other hearers, the Jewish 'dwellers in Cappadocia, Pontus, Asia, Phrygia, Pamphylia,' he now ministers to by letter. The earliest distinct authority for Peter's martyrdom *at Rome* is DIONYSIUS, bishop of Corinth, in the latter half of the second century. The desirableness of representing Peter and Paul, the two leading apostles, as together founding the Church of the metropolis, seems to have originated the tradition. CLEMENT OF ROME [*First Epistle to the Corinthians,* 4.5], often quoted for, is really against it. He mentions Paul and Peter together, but makes it as a *distinguishing* circumstance of Paul, that he preached both in the East and West, implying that Peter never was in the West. In 2Pe 1:14, he says, 'I must *shortly* put off this tabernacle,' implying his martyrdom was near, yet he makes no allusion to Rome, or any intention of his visiting it.

14. kiss of charity – Ro 16:16, 'an *holy* kiss': the token of love to God and the brethren. *Love* and *holiness* are inseparable. Compare the instance, Ac 20:37.

Peace – Peter's closing salutation; as Paul's is, 'Grace be with you,' though he accompanies it with 'peace be to the brethren.' 'Peace' (flowing from *salvation*) was Christ's own salutation after the resurrection, and from Him Peter derives it.

be with you all that are in Christ Jesus – The oldest manuscripts omit 'Jesus.' In Eph 6:24, addressed to the same region, the same limitation of the salutation occurs, whence, perhaps, Peter here adopts it. Contrast, 'Be *with you all,*' Ro 16:24, 1Co 16:23.

2 PETER

A.R. Faussett

Introduction
Authenticity and genuineness

If not a gross imposture, *its own internal witness* is unequivocal in its favour. It has *Peter's* name and apostleship in its heading: not only his surname, but his original name *Simon*, or *Simeon*, he thus, at the close of his life, reminding his readers who he originally was before his call. Again, in 2Pe 1:16–18, he mentions *his presence at the Transfiguration,* and *Christ's prophecy of his death!* and in 2Pe 3:15, *his brotherhood with Paul.* Again, in 2Pe 3:1, the author speaks of himself as author of the former Epistle: it is, moreover, addressed so as to *include* (but not to be restricted to) the same persons as the first, whom he presupposes to be acquainted with the writings of Paul, by that time recognized as 'Scripture' (2Pe 3:15, 'the long-suffering of God,' compare Ro 2:4). This necessarily implies a *late date,* when Paul's Epistles (including Romans) already had become generally diffused and accepted as Scripture in the Church. The Church of the fourth century had, besides the testimony which we have of the *doubts* of the earlier Christians, other external evidence which we have not, and which, doubtless, under God's overruling providence, caused them to accept it. It is hard to understand how a book palpably false (as it would be if Peter be not the author) could have been accepted in the Canon as finally established in the Councils of Laodicea, A.D. 360 (if the fifty-ninth article be genuine), Hippo, and Carthage in the fourth century (393 and 397). The whole tone and spirit of the Epistle disprove its being an imposture. He writes as one not speaking of himself, but *moved by the Holy Ghost* (2Pe 1:21). An attempt at such a fraud in the first ages would have brought only shame and suffering, alike from Christians and heathen, on the perpetrator: there was then *no temptation to pious frauds* as in later times. That it must have been written in the earliest age is plain from the *wide gulf in style* which separates it and the other New Testament Scriptures from even the earliest and best of the post-apostolic period. Daille well says, 'God has allowed a fosse to be drawn by human weakness around the sacred canon to protect it from all invasion.'

It is not strange that *distinctive peculiarities* of style should mark each Epistle, the design of both not being the same. Thus the *sufferings* of Christ are more prominent in the First Epistle, the object there being to encourage thereby Christian sufferers; the *glory* of the exalted Lord is more prominent in the Second, the object being to communicate fuller 'knowledge' of Him as the antidote to the false teaching against which Peter warns his readers. Hence His title of redemption, 'Christ,' is the one employed in the First Epistle; but in the Second Epistle, 'the Lord.' *Hope* is characteristic of the First Epistle; *full knowledge,* of the Second Epistle. In the First Epistle he puts his *apostolic authority* less prominently forward than in the Second, wherein his design is to warn against false teachers. The same difference is observable in Paul's Epistles. Contrast 1Th 1:1 2Th 1:1 Php 1:1, with Ga 1:1 1Co 1:1. The reference to Paul's writings as already existing in numbers, and as then a recognized part of *Scripture* (2Pe 3:15,16), implies that this Epistle was written at a late date, just before Peter's death.

Striking verbal coincidences occur: compare 1Pe 1:19, end, with 2Pe 3:14, end; 2Pe 1:3, 'His own,' *Greek,* 2Pe 2:16 3:17 with 1Pe 3:1,5. The omission of the *Greek* article, 1Pe 2:13 with 2Pe 1:21,2:4,5,7. Moreover, two words occur, 2Pe 1:13, 'tabernacle,' that is, the body, and 2Pe 1:15, 'decease,' which at once remind us of the transfiguration narrative in the Gospel. Both Epistles refer to the deluge, and to Noah as the *eighth* that was saved. Though the First Epistle abounds in *quotations* of the Old Testament, whereas the Second contains none, yet *references* to the Old Testament occur often (2Pe 1:21 2:5–8,15 3:5,6,10,13). Compare *Greek,* 1Pe 3:21, 'putting away,' with 2Pe 1:14; 1Pe 1:17, *Greek,* 'pass the time,' with 2Pe 2:18; 1Pe 4:3, 'walked in,' with 2Pe 2:10 3:3; 'called you,' 1Pe 1:15 2:9 5:10, with 2Pe 1:3.

Moreover, more verbal coincidences with the speeches of Peter in Acts occur in this *Second,* than in the *First* Epistle. Compare *Greek,* 'obtained,' 2Pe 1:1 with Ac 1:17; 2Pe 1:6, *Greek,* 'godliness,' with Ac 3:12, the only passage where the term occurs, except in the Pastoral Epistles; and 2Pe 2:9 with Ac 10:2,7; 2Pe 2:9, 'punished,' with Ac 4:21, the only places where the term occurs; 2Pe 3:2, the double genitive, with Ac 5:32; 'the day of the Lord,' 2Pe 3:10, with Ac 2:20, where only it occurs, except in 1Th 5:2.

The testimony of Jude, Jude 1:17,18, is strong for its genuineness and inspiration, by adopting its very words, and by referring to it as received by the churches to which he, Jude, wrote, 'Remember the words which were spoken before of the *apostles* of our Lord Jesus Christ; how that they told you *there should be mockers in the last time, who should walk after their own ungodly lusts.'* Jude, therefore, must have written *after* Second Peter, to which he plainly refers; not before, as ALFORD thinks. No less than eleven passages of Jude rest on similar statements of Second Peter. Jude 1:2, compare 2Pe 1:2; Jude 1:4, compare 2Pe 2:1; Jude 1:6, compare 2Pe 2:4; Jude 1:7, compare 2Pe 2:6; Jude 1:8, compare 2Pe 2:10; Jude 1:9, compare 2Pe 2:11; Jude 1:11, compare 2Pe 2:15; Jude 1:12, compare 2Pe 2:17; Jude 1:16, compare 2Pe 2:18; Jude 1:18, compare 2Pe 2:1 3:3. Just in the same way Micah, Mic 4:1–4, leans on the somewhat earlier prophecy of Isaiah, whose inspiration he thereby confirms. ALFORD reasons that because Jude, in many of the passages akin to Second Peter, is fuller than Second Peter, he must be prior. This by no means follows. It is at least as likely, if not more so, that the briefer is the earlier, rather than the fuller. The dignity and energy of the style is quite consonant to what we should expect from the prompt and ardent foreman of the apostles. The difference of style between First and Second Peter accords with the distinctness of the subjects and objects.

Date of writing

The date, from what has been said, would be about A.D. 68 or 69, about a year after the first, and shortly before the destruction of Jerusalem, the typical precursor of the world's end, to which 2Pe 3:10–13 so solemnly calls attention, after Paul's ministry had closed (compare *Greek* aorist tense, 'wrote,' past time, 2Pe 3:15), just before Peter's own death. It was written to *include* the same persons, and perhaps in, or about the same place, as the first. Being without salutations of individuals, and entrusted to the care of no one church, or particular churches as the first is, but directed generally 'to them that have obtained like precious faith with us' (2Pe 1:1), it took a longer time in being recognized as canonical. Had Rome been the place of its composition or publication, it could hardly have failed to have had an early acceptance – an incidental argument against the tradition of Peter's martyrdom *at Rome*. The remote scene of its composition in Babylon, or else in some of the contiguous regions beyond the borders of the Roman empire, and of its circulation in Cappadocia, Pontus, will additionally account for its tardy but at last universal acceptance in the catholic Church. The former Epistle, through *its more definite address,* was earlier in its general acceptance.

Object in writing

In 2Pe 3:17,18 the twofold design of the Epistle is set forth; namely, to guard his readers against 'the error' of false teachers, and to exhort them to grow in experimental 'knowledge of our Lord and Saviour' (2Pe 3:18). The ground on which this *knowledge* rests is stated, 2Pe 1:12-21, namely, the inspired testimony of apostles and prophets. The danger now, as of old, was about to arise from false teachers, who soon were to come among them, as Paul also (to whom reference is made, 2Pe 3:15,16) testified in the same region. The grand antidote is 'the *full knowledge* of our Lord and Saviour,' through which we know God the Father, partake of His nature, escape from the pollutions of the world, and have entrance into Christ's kingdom. The aspect of Christ presented is not so much that of the past *suffering,* as of the future *reigning,* Saviour, His present *power,* and future new kingdom. This aspect is taken as best fitted to counteract the *theories* of the false teachers who should 'deny' His *Lordship* and His *coming* again, the two very points which, as an *apostle and eye-witness,* Peter attests (His 'power' and His 'coming'); also, to counteract *their evil example in practice,* blaspheming the way of truth, despising governments, slaves to covetousness and filthy lusts of the flesh, while boasting of Christian freedom, and, worst of all, apostates from the truth. The *knowledge of Christ,* as being the knowledge of 'the way of righteousness,' 'the right way,' is the antidote of their bad practice. Hence 'the preacher' of righteousness, Noah, and 'righteous Lot,' are instanced as escaping the destruction which overtook the 'unjust' or 'unrighteous'; and Balaam is instanced as exemplifying the awful result of 'unrighteousness' such as characterized the false teachers. Thus the Epistle forms one connected whole, the parts being closely bound together by mutual relation, and the end corresponding with the beginning; compare 2Pe 3:14,18 with 2Pe 1:2, in both 'grace' and 'peace' being connected with 'the knowledge' of our Saviour; compare also 2Pe 3:17 with 2Pe 1:4,10,12; and 2Pe 3:18, 'grow in grace and knowledge,' with the fuller 2Pe 1:5–8; and 2Pe 2:21; and 2Pe 3:13, 'righteousness,' with 2Pe 1:1; and 2Pe 3:1 with 2Pe 1:13; and 2Pe 3:2 with 2Pe 1:19.

The *germs* of Carpocratian and Gnostic heresies already existed, but the actual manifestation of these heresies is spoken of as *future* (2Pe 2:1,2): another proof that this Epistle was written, as it professes, in the apostolic age, before the *development* of the Gnostic heresies in the end of the first and the beginning of the second centuries. The description is too general to identify the heresies with any particular one of the subsequent forms of heresy, but applies generally to them all.

Though altogether distinct in aim from the First Epistle, yet a connection may be traced. The neglect of the warnings to circumspection in the walk led to the evils foretold in the Second Epistle. Compare the warning against the abuse of Christian *freedom,* 1Pe 2:16 with 2Pe 2:19, 'While they promise them *liberty,* they themselves are the *servants of corruption*'; also the caution against *pride,* 1Pe 5:5,6 with 2Pe 2:18, 'they speak great swelling words of vanity.'

Contents

See *Outlines of the New Testament Books,* pp. 905–6

Chapter 1

2Pe 1:1–21. Address: exhortation to all graces, as God has given us, in the knowledge of Christ, all things pertaining to life: confirmed by the testimony of apostles, and also prophets, to the power and coming of Christ.

1. Simon – the *Greek* form: in oldest manuscripts, 'Symeon' (*Hebrew,* that is, 'hearing'), as in Ac 15:14. His mention of his original name accords with the design of this Second Epistle, which is to warn against the coming false teachers, by setting forth the true 'knowledge' of Christ on the testimony of the *original apostolic eye-witnesses* like himself. This was not required in the First Epistle.

servant – 'slave': so Paul, Ro 1:1.

to them – He addresses a wider range of readers (*all* believers) than in the First Epistle, 2Pe 1:1, but means to include *especially* those addressed in the First Epistle, as 2Pe 3:1 proves.

obtained – by grace. Applied by *Peter* to the receiving of the apostleship, literally, 'by allotment': as the *Greek* is, Lu 1:9 Joh 19:24. They did not acquire it for themselves; the divine election is as independent of man's control, as the lot which is cast forth.

like precious – 'equally precious' to all: to those who believe, though not having seen Christ, as well as to Peter and those who have seen Him. For it lays hold of the same 'exceeding great and *precious* promises,' and the same 'righteousness of God our Saviour.' 'The *common* salvation ... the faith once delivered unto the saints' (Jude 1:3).

with us – apostles and eye-witnesses (2Pe 1:18). Though putting forward his *apostleship* to enforce his exhortation, he with true humility puts himself, as to 'the faith,' on a level with all other believers. The degree of faith varies in different believers; but *in respect to its objects,* present justification, sanctification, and future glorification, it is common alike to all. Christ is to all believers 'made of God wisdom, righteousness, sanctification, and redemption.'

through – *Greek,* 'in.' Translate, as the one article to both nouns requires, 'the righteousness of *Him who is* (at once) *our God and* (our) Saviour.' Peter, confirming Paul's testimony to the same churches, adopts Paul's inspired phraseology. The Gospel plan sets forth *God's*

righteousness, which is Christ's righteousness, in the brightest light. Faith has its sphere IN it as its peculiar element: God in redemption 'righteous,' and at the same time a 'Saviour'; compare Isa 45:21, 'a *just* God and a *Saviour.*

2. Grace ... peace – (1Pe 1:2).

through – *Greek,* 'in': the sphere IN which alone *grace* and *peace* can be multiplied.

knowledge – *Greek,* 'full knowledge.'

of God, and of Jesus our Lord – The *Father* is here meant by 'God,' but the *Son* in 2Pe 1:1: marking how entirely *one* the Father and Son are (Joh 14:7–11). The *Vulgate* omits 'of God and'; but oldest manuscripts support the words. Still the prominent object of Peter's exhortation is 'the knowledge *of Jesus our Lord*' (a phrase only in Ro 4:24), and, only secondarily, of the Father through Him (2Pe 1:8 2Pe 2:20 3:18).

3. According as – Seeing that [ALFORD]. '*As* He hath given us ALL things (needful) for life and godliness, (so) do you give us ALL diligence'. The oil and flame are given wholly of grace by God, and 'taken' by believers: their part henceforth is to 'trim their lamps' (compare 2Pe 1:3,4 with 2Pe 1:5).

life and godliness – Spiritual *life* must exist first before there can be true *godliness. Knowledge of God* experimentally is the first step to *life* (Joh 17:3). The child must have vital breath. first, and then cry to, and walk in the ways of, his father. It is not by *godliness* that we obtain *life,* but by *life, godliness.* To *life* stands opposed *corruption;* to *godliness, lust* (2Pe 1:4).

called us – (2Pe 1:10); 'calling' (1Pe 2:9).

to glory and virtue – rather, 'through (His) glory.' Thus *English Version* reads as one oldest manuscript. But other oldest manuscripts and *Vulgate* read, 'By His own (peculiar) glory and virtue'; being the explanation of 'His divine power'; *glory* and *moral excellency* (the same attribute is given to God in 1Pe 2:9, 'praises,' literally, 'virtues') characterize God's 'power.' 'Virtue,' the standing word in heathen ethics, is found only once in Paul (Php 4:8), and in Peter in a distinct sense from its classic usage; it (in the heathen sense) is a term too low and earthly for expressing the gifts of the Spirit [TRENCH, *Greek Synonyms of the New Testament*].

4. Whereby – By His *glory* and *virtue:* His glory making the 'promises' to be *exceeding great;* His *virtue* making them 'precious' [BENGEL]. *Precious promises* are the object of *precious faith.*

given – The *promises* themselves are a *gift:* for

God's *promises* are as sure as if they were fulfilled.

by these – *promises.* They are the object of
faith, and even now have a sanctifying effect on
the believer, assimilating him to God. Still more
so, when they shall be *fulfilled.*

might – *Greek,* 'that ye MAY become partakers
of the divine nature,' even now in part; hereafter
perfectly; 1Jo 3:2, 'We shall be like Him.'

the divine nature – not God's essence, but
His *holiness,* including His 'glory' and 'virtue,'
2Pe 1:3; the opposite to 'corruption through
lust.' Sanctification is the imparting to us of *God
Himself* by the Holy Spirit in the soul. We by
faith partake also of the material nature of Jesus
(Eph 5:30). The 'divine *power*' enables us to be
partakers of 'the divine *nature.*'

escaped the corruption – which involves in,
and with itself, *destruction* at last of soul and
body; on 'escaped' as from a condemned cell,
compare 2Pe 2:18–20 Ge 19:17 Col 1:13.

through – *Greek,* 'in.' 'The corruption in the
world' has its seat, not so much in the surrounding elements, as in the 'lust' or concupiscence of
men's hearts.

5. And beside this – rather, 'And for this very
reason,' namely, 'seeing that His divine power
hath given unto us all things that pertain to life
and godliness' (2Pe 1:3).

giving – literally, 'introducing,' side by side
with God's *gift,* on your part 'diligence.'
Compare an instance, 2Pe 1:10 2Pe 3:14 2Co
7:11.

all – all possible.

add – literally, 'minister additionally,' or,
abundantly (compare *Greek,* 2Co 9:10); said
properly of the one who *supplied* all the equip-
ments of a chorus. So accordingly, 'there will
be *ministered abundantly* unto you an entrance
into the everlasting kingdom of our Saviour'
(2Pe 1:11).

to – *Greek,* 'in'; '*in* the possession of *your
faith, minister virtue.* Their *faith* (answering to
'knowledge of Him,' 2Pe 1:3) is presupposed as
the gift of God (2Pe 1:3 Eph 2:8), and is not
required to be *ministered* by *us; in* its exercise,
virtue is to be, moreover, ministered. Each grace
being assumed, becomes the stepping stone to
the succeeding grace: and the latter in turn qualifies and completes the former. *Faith* leads the
band; *love* brings up the rear [BENGEL]. The
fruits of *faith* specified are *seven,* the perfect
number.

virtue – moral excellency; manly, strenuous
energy, answering to the *virtue* (energetic excellency) of God.

and to – *Greek,* 'in'; 'and in (the exercise of)
your virtue knowledge,' namely, practical discrimination of good and evil; intelligent appreciation of what is the will of God in each detail
of practice.

6. *Greek,* 'And in your knowledge self-
control.' In the exercise of Christian *knowledge*
or discernment of God's will, let there be the
practical fruit of *self-control* as to one's lusts and
passions. Incontinence weakens the mind; continence, or self-control, moves weakness and
imparts strength And in your self-control
patient endurance' amidst sufferings, so much
dwelt on in the First Epistle, second, third, and
fourth chapters. 'And in your patient endurance
godliness'; it is not to be mere stoical
endurance, but united to [and flowing from]
God-trusting [ALFORD].

7. 'And in your godliness brotherly kindness';
not suffering your godliness to be moroseness,
nor a sullen solitary habit of life, but kind, generous, and courteous [ALFORD]. Your natural
affection and *brotherly kindness* are to be sanctified by *godliness.* 'And in your brotherly kindness love,' namely, to *all* men, even to enemies,
in thought, word, and deed. From *brotherly
kindness* we are to go forward to *love.* Compare
1Th 3:12, 'Love one toward another (brotherly
kindness), and toward all men (charity).' So
charity completes the choir of graces in Col
3:14. In a retrograde order, he who has *love* will
exercise *brotherly kindness;* he who has *brotherly
kindness* will feel *godliness* needful; the *godly*
will mix nothing stoical with his *patience;* to
the patient, *temperance* is easy; the temperate
weighs things well, and so has *knowledge;*
knowledge guards against sudden impulse carrying away its *virtue* [BENGEL].

8. be – *Greek,* 'subsist' that is, supposing these
things to have an actual *subsistence* in you; 'be'
would express the mere matter-of-fact *being* (Ac
16:20).

abound – *more than in others;* so the *Greek.*

make – 'render,' 'constitute you,' habitually, by
the very fact of possessing these graces.

barren – 'inactive,' and, as a field lying fallow
and *unworked* (*Greek*), so *barren* and *useless.*

unfruitful in – rather, … *in respect to,* 'The
full knowledge (*Greek*) of Christ' is the goal
towards which all these graces tend. As their
subsisting in us constitutes us *not barren* or idle,
so their *abounding* in us constitutes us *not
unfruitful* in respect to it. It is through *doing* His
will, and so becoming like Him, that we grow in
knowing Him (Joh 7:17).

9. But – *Greek,* 'For.' Confirming the need of
these graces (2Pe 1:5-8) by the fatal consequences of the want of them.

he that lacketh – *Greek,* 'he to whom these
are not present.'

blind – as to the spiritual realities of the
unseen world.

and cannot see afar off – explanatory of
'blind.' He *closes his eyes* (*Greek*) as unable to see
distant objects (namely, heavenly things), and
fixes his gaze on present and earthly things

which alone he can see. Perhaps a degree of *wilfulness* in the blindness is implied in the *Greek*, 'closing the eyes,' which constitutes its culpability; hating and rebelling against the light shining around him.

forgotten – *Greek*, 'contracted forgetfulness,' wilful and culpable obliviousness.

that he was purged – The continually present sense of one's sins having been once for all forgiven, is the strongest stimulus to every grace (Ps 130:4). This once-for-all accomplished cleansing of unbelievers *at their* new birth is taught symbolically by Christ, Joh 13:10, *Greek*, 'He that has been *bathed* (once for all) needeth not save to *wash* his feet (of the soils contracted in the daily walk), but is clean every whit (in Christ our righteousness).' 'Once purged (with Christ's blood), we should have no more consciousness of sin (as condemning us, Heb 10:2, because of God's promise).' Baptism is the sacramental pledge of this.

10. Wherefore – seeking the blessed consequence of having, and the evil effects of not having, these graces (2Pe 1:8,9).

the rather – the more earnestly.

brethren – marking that it is affection for them which constrains him so earnestly to urge them. Nowhere else does he so address them, which makes his calling them so here the more emphatic.

give diligence – The *Greek* aorist implies *one lifelong effect* [ALFORD].

to make – *Greek* middle voice; to make *so far as it depends on you;* to do *your part* towards making. 'To make' absolutely and finally is God's part, and would be in the active.

your calling and election sure – by *ministering additionally in your faith virtue, and in your virtue knowledge* God must work all these graces in us, yet not so that we should be mere *machines,* but *willing instruments* in His hands in making His election of us 'secure.' The *ensuring* of our *election* is spoken of not in respect to God, whose counsel is steadfast and everlasting, but in respect to *our part.* There is no uncertainty on His part, but on ours the only security is our *faith* in His promise and the fruits of the Spirit (2Pe 1:5-7,11). Peter subjoins *election* to *calling,* because the *calling* is the effect and proof of God's *election,* which goes before and is the main thing (Ro 8:28,30,33, where God's *'elect'* are those *'predestinated,'* and election is 'His *purpose,' according to* which He 'called' them). We know His *calling* before His *election,* thereby *calling* is put first.

fall – *Greek,* 'stumble' and fall finally (Ro 11:11). Metaphor from one *stumbling* in a race (1Co 9:24).

11. an entrance – rather as *Greek,* 'the entrance' which ye look for.

ministered – the same verb as in 2Pe 1:5.

Minister in your faith virtue and the other graces, so shall there be *ministered to you* the entrance into that heaven where these graces shine most brightly. The reward of grace hereafter shall correspond to the work of grace here.

abundantly – *Greek,* 'richly.' It answers to 'abound,' 2Pe 1:8. If these graces *abound* in you, you shall have your entrance into heaven not merely 'scarcely' (as he had said, 1Pe 4:18), nor 'so as by fire,' like one escaping with life after having lost all his goods, but in triumph without 'stumbling and falling.'

12. Wherefore – as these graces are so necessary to your abundant entrance into Christ's kingdom (2Pe 1:10,11).

I will not be negligent – The oldest manuscripts read, '*I will be about* always to put you in remembrance' (an accumulated future: I will regard you as always needing to be reminded): compare 'I will endeavour,' 2Pe 1:15. 'I will be sure always to remind you' [ALFORD]. 'Always'; implying the reason why he writes the second Epistle so soon after the first. He feels *there is likely* to be more and more need of admonition on account of the increasing corruption (2Pe 2:1,2).

in the present truth – *the Gospel truth now present with you:* formerly promised to Old Testament believers as *about to be, now* in the New Testament *actually present* with, and in, believers, so that they are 'established' in it as a 'present' reality. Its importance renders frequent monitions never superfluous: compare Paul's similar apology, Ro 15:14,15.

13. Yea – *Greek,* 'But'; though 'you know' the truth (2Pe 1:12).

this tabernacle – soon to be taken down (2Co 5:1): I therefore need *to make the most of my short time* for the good of Christ's Church. The zeal of Satan against it, the more intense *as his time is short,* ought to stimulate Christians on the same ground.

by – *Greek,* 'in' (compare 2Pe 3:1).

14. shortly I must put off – *Greek,* 'the putting off (as a garment) of my tabernacle is speedy': implying a *soon approaching,* and also a *sudden* death (as a violent death is). Christ's words, Joh 21:18,19, 'When thou art old', were the ground of his 'knowing,' now that he was old, that his foretold martyrdom was near. Compare as to Paul, 2Ti 4:6. Though a violent death, he calls it a *departure* (*Greek* for 'decease,' 2Pe 1:15), compare Ac 7:60.

15. endeavour – 'use my diligence': the same *Greek* word as in 2Pe 1:10: this is the field in which my *diligence* has scope. Peter thus fulfils Christ's charge, 'Feed My sheep' (Joh 21:16,17).

decease – 'departure.' The very word ('exodus') used in the Transfiguration, Moses and Elias conversing about Christ's *decease (found nowhere else in the New Testament,* but Heb 11:22, 'the *departing* of Israel' out of Egypt, to which the saints' deliverance from the present bondage of corruption answers). 'Tabernacle' is another term found here as well as there (Lu 9:31,33): an undesigned coincidence confirming Peter's authorship of this Epistle.

that ye may be able – by the help of this written Epistle; and perhaps also of Mark's Gospel, which Peter superintended.

always – *Greek,* 'on each occasion': as often as occasion may require.

to have … in remembrance – *Greek,* 'to exercise remembrance of.' Not merely 'to remember,' as sometimes we do, things we care not about; but 'have them in (earnest) remembrance,' as momentous and precious truths.

16. For – reason why he is so earnest that the remembrance of these things should be continued after his death.

followed – out in detail.

cunningly devised – *Greek,* 'devised by (*man's*) *wisdom*'; as distinguished from what *the Holy Ghost* teaches (compare 1Co 3:13). But compare also 2Pe 2:3, 'feigned words.'

fables – as the heathen mythologies, and the subsequent Gnostic 'fables and genealogies,' of which the germs already existed in the junction of Judaism with Oriental philosophy in Asia Minor. A precautionary protest of the Spirit against the rationalistic theory of the Gospel history being *myth.*

when we made known unto you – not that Peter himself had *personally* taught the churches in Pontus, Galatia, but he was one of the apostles whose testimony was borne to them, and to *the Church in general,* to whom this Epistle is addressed (2Pe 1:1, *including,* but not *restricted, as First Peter,* to the churches in Pontus).

power – the opposite of 'fables'; compare the contrast of 'word' and 'power,' 1Co 4:20. A specimen of His *power* was given at the Transfiguration also of His '*coming*' again, and its attendant glory. The *Greek* for 'coming' is always used of His *second* advent. A refutation of the scoffers (2Pe 3:4): I, James and John, saw with our own eyes a mysterious sample of His coming glory.

were – *Greek,* 'were made.'

eye-witnesses – As initiated spectators of mysteries (so the *Greek*), we were admitted into His innermost secrets, namely, at the Transfiguration.

his – emphatic (compare *Greek*): 'THAT great ONE's majesty.'

17. received … honour – in the *voice* that spake to Him.

glory – in the *light* which shone around Him. *Greek,* 'was borne': the same phrase occurs only in 1Pe 1:13; one of several instances showing that the argument against the authenticity of this Second Epistle. from its dissimilarity of style as

compared with First Peter, is not well founded.

such a voice – as he proceeds to describe.

from the excellent glory – rather as *Greek,* 'by (that is uttered by) the magnificent glory (that is, by *God:* as His glorious manifested presence is often called by the Hebrews 'the Glory,' compare 'His Excellency,' De 33:26 Ps 21:5).'

in whom – *Greek,* '*in regard to* whom' (accusative case); but Mt 17:5, 'in whom' (dative case) centres and rests My good pleasure. Peter also omits, as not required by his purpose, 'hear Him,' showing his independence in his inspired testimony.

I am – *Greek* aorist, past time, 'My good pleasure *rested* from eternity.'

18. which came – rather as *Greek,* 'we heard borne from heaven.'

holy mount – as the Transfiguration mount came to be regarded, on account of the manifestation of Christ's divine glory there.

we – emphatic: we, James and John, as well as myself.

19. We – all believers.

a more sure – rather as *Greek,* 'we have *the* word of prophecy more sure (confirmed).' Previously we knew its *sureness* by faith, but, through that visible specimen of its hereafter entire fulfilment, assurance is made *doubly sure.* Prophecy assures us that Christ's *sufferings,* now past, are to be followed by Christ's *glory,* still future: the Transfiguration gives us a pledge to make our faith still stronger, that 'the day' of His glory will 'dawn' ere long. He does not mean to say that 'the word of prophecy,' or Scripture, is surer than *the voice of God* heard at the Transfiguration, as *English Version;* for this is plainly not the fact. The fulfilment of *prophecy* so far in Christ's history makes us the *surer* of what is yet to be fulfilled, His consummated glory. The word was the 'lamp (*Greek* for "light") heeded' by Old Testament believers, until a gleam of the 'day dawn' was given at Christ's first coming, and especially in His Transfiguration. So the word is *a lamp* to us still, until 'the day' burst forth fully at the second coming of 'the Sun of righteousness.' *The day,* when it dawns upon you, makes *sure* the fact that you saw correctly, though indistinctly, the objects revealed by *the lamp.*

whereunto – to which word of prophecy, primarily the Old Testament in Peter's *day;* but now also in our day the New Testament, which, though brighter than the Old Testament (compare 1Jo 2:8, end), is but a *lamp* even still as compared with the brightness of the eternal day (compare 2Pe 3:2). Oral teachings and traditions of ministers are to be tested by the written word (Ac 17:11).

dark – The *Greek* implies *squalid,* having neither water nor light: such spiritually is the world without, and the smaller world (microcosm) within, the heart in its natural state. Compare the '*dry* places' Lu 11:24 (namely, unwatered by the Spirit), through which the unclean spirit goeth.

dawn – bursting *through* the darkness.

day star – *Greek,* the morning star,' as Re 22:16. The Lord Jesus.

in your hearts – Christ's *arising in the heart* by His Spirit giving full assurance, creates spiritually full day in the heart, the means to which is prayerfully *giving heed to the word.* This is associated with the coming of *the day of the Lord,* as being the earnest of it. Indeed, even our *hearts* shall not *fully* realize Christ in all His unspeakable glory and felt presence, until He shall come (Mal 4:2).

20. 'Forasmuch as ye know this' (1Pe 1:18).

first – the *foremost* consideration in studying the word of prophecy. Laying it down as a *first principle* never to be lost sight of.

is – *Greek,* not the simple verb, *to be,* but *to begin to be,* 'proves to be,' 'becometh.' No prophecy is found to be the result of 'private (the mere individual writer's uninspired) *interpretation'* (*solution*), and so *origination.* The *Greek* noun *epilusis,* does not mean in itself *origination;* but that which the sacred writer could not always fully *interpret,* though being the speaker or writer (as 1Pe 1:10–12 implies), was plainly not of his own, but of God's *disclosure, origination,* and *inspiration,* as Peter proceeds to add, 'But holy men … spake (and afterwards *wrote*) … moved by the Holy Ghost': a reason why ye should 'give' all 'heed' to it. The parallelism to 2Pe 1:16 shows that '*private interpretation,*' contrasted with 'moved by the Holy Ghost,' here answers to 'fables *devised by* (*human*) *wisdom,*' contrasted with 'we were eye-witnesses of *His majesty,*' as attested by the 'voice from God.' The words of the prophetical (and so of all) Scripture writers were not mere words *of the individuals,* and therefore to be *interpreted by them,* but of 'the Holy Ghost' by whom they were 'moved.' 'Private' is explained, 2Pe 1:21, 'by the will of man' (namely, the individual writer). In a secondary sense the text teaches also, as the word is the *Holy Spirit's,* it cannot be *interpreted* by its *readers* (any more than by its *writers*) by their mere *private* human powers, but by the teaching of *the Holy Ghost* (Joh 16:14). 'He who is the author of Scripture is its supreme interpreter' [GERHARD]. ALFORD translates, 'springs not out of human interpretation,' that is, is not a prognostication made by a man *knowing what he means* when he utters it, but'. (Joh 11:49–52). Rightly: except that the verb is rather, *doth become,* or *prove to be.* It not being of private interpretation, you must '*give heed*' to it, looking for the *Spirit's* illumination 'in your hearts' (compare *Note,* see on 2Pe 1:19).

21. came not in old time – rather, 'was never at any time borne' (to us).

by the will of man – alone. Jer 23:26, 'prophets of the deceit *of their own heart.*' Compare 2Pe 3:5, 'willingly.'

holy – One oldest manuscript has, '*men* FROM *God*': the emissaries from God. 'Holy,' if read, will mean because they had the Holy Spirit.

moved – *Greek,* 'borne' (along) as by a mighty wind: Ac 2:2, '*rushing* (the same *Greek*) wind': rapt out of themselves: still not in fanatical excitement (1Co 14:32). The *Hebrew* '*nabi,*' 'prophet,' meant an *announcer* or interpreter of God: he, as *God's spokesman, interpreted* not his own 'private' will or thought, but God's 'Man *of the Spirit*' (Ho 9:7, *Margin*). 'Thou testifiedst by Thy Spirit in Thy prophets.' 'Seer,' on the other hand, refers to the *mode of receiving* the communications from God, rather than to the *utterance* of them to others. 'Spake' implies that, both in its original oral announcement, and now even when in writing, it has been always, and is, *the living voice* of God *speaking* to us through His inspired servants. *Greek,* 'borne (along)' forms a beautiful antithesis to 'was borne.' They were passive, rather than active instruments. The *Old Testament* prophets primarily, but including also *all* the inspired penmen, whether of the New or Old Testament (2Pe 3:2).

Chapter 2

2Pe 2:1–22. False teachers to arise: their bad practices and sure destruction, from which the godly shall be delivered, as Lot was.

1. But – in contrast to the prophets 'moved by the Holy Ghost' (2Pe 1:21).

also – as well as the true prophets (2Pe 1:19-21). Paul had already testified the entrance of false prophets into the same churches.

among the people – Israel: he is writing to believing *Israelites* primarily (see on 1Pe 1:1). Such a 'false prophet' was Balaam (2Pe 2:15).

there shall be – Already symptoms of the evil were appearing (2Pe 2:9–22 Jude 1:4–13).

false teachers – teachers of falsehood. In contrast to the true teachers, whom he exhorts his readers to give heed to (2Pe 3:2).

who – *such as* (literally, 'the which') shall.

privily – not at first openly and directly, but *by the way,* bringing in error *by the side* of the true doctrine (so the *Greek*): Rome objects, Protestants cannot point out the exact date of the beginnings of the false doctrines superadded to the original truth; we answer, Peter foretells us it would be so, that the first introduction of them would be stealthy and unobserved (Jude 1:4).

damnable – literally, 'of destruction'; entailing destruction (Php 3:19) on all who follow them.

heresies – *self-chosen* doctrines, not emanating from God (compare 'will-worship,' Col 2:23).

even – going *even* to such a length as to *deny* both in teaching and practice. *Peter* knew, by bitter repentance, what a fearful thing it is to deny the Lord (Lu 22:61,62).

denying – Him whom, above all others, they ought to *confess*.

Lord – 'Master and Owner' (*Greek*), compare Jude 1:4, *Greek*. Whom the true doctrine teaches to be their Owner *by* right of purchase. Literally, 'denying Him who bought them (that He should be thereby), their Master.'

bought them – Even the ungodly were bought by His 'precious blood.' It shall be their bitterest self-reproach in hell, that, as far as Christ's redemption was concerned, they might have been saved. The denial of His *propitiatory* sacrifice is included in the meaning (compare 1Jo 4:3).

bring upon themselves – compare 'God *bringing in* the flood *upon* the world,' 2Pe 2:5. Man brings upon himself the vengeance which God brings upon him.

swift – swiftly descending: as the Lord's coming shall be swift and sudden. As the ground swallowed up Korah and Dathan, and 'they went down *quick* into the pit.' Compare Jude 1:11, which is akin to this passage.

2. follow – out: so the *Greek*.

pernicious ways – The oldest manuscripts and *Vulgate* read, 'licentiousness' (Jude 1:4). False doctrine and immoral practice generally go together (2Pe 2:18,19).

by reason of whom – 'on account of whom,' namely, the followers of the false teachers.

the way of truth shall be evil spoken of – 'blasphemed' by those without, who shall lay on Christianity itself the blame of its professors' evil practice. Contrast 1Pe 2:12.

3. through – *Greek*, 'in covetousness' as their element (2Pe 2:14, end). Contrast 2Co 11:20 12:17.

of a long time – in God's eternal purpose. '*Before of old* ordained to condemnation' (Jude 1:4).

lingereth not – though sinners think it lingers; 'is not idle.'

damnation – *Greek*, 'destruction' (see on 2Pe 2:1). Personified.

slumbereth not – though sinners *slumber*.

4. if – The apodosis or consequent member of the sentence is not expressed, but is virtually contained in 2Pe 2:9. If God in past time has punished the ungodly and saved His people, He will be sure to do so also in our days (compare end of 2Pe 2:3).

angels – the highest of intelligent creatures

(compare with this verse, Jude 1:6), yet not spared when they sinned.

hell – *Greek*, '*Tartarus*': nowhere else in New Testament or the *Septuagint*: equivalent to the usual *Greek*, '*Gehenna*.' Not inconsistent with 1Pe 5:8; for though their final doom is *hell*, yet for a time they are permitted to roam beyond it in 'the darkness of this world.' Slaves of *Tartarus* (called 'the abyss,' or 'deep,' Lu 8:31; 'the bottomless pit,' Re 9:11) may also come upon earth. Step by step they are given to Tartarus, until at last they shall be wholly bound to it.

delivered – as the judge delivers the condemned prisoner to the officers (Re 20:2).

into chains – (Jude 1:6). The oldest manuscripts read, 'dens,' as ALFORD translates: the *Greek*, however, may, in Hellenistic *Greek*, mean 'chains,' as Jude expresses it. They are 'reserved' unto hell's 'mist of darkness' as their final 'judgment' or doom, and meanwhile their exclusion from the light of heaven is begun. So the ungodly were considered as virtually 'in prison,' though at large on the earth, from the moment that God's sentence went forth, though not executed till one hundred twenty years after.

5. eighth – that is, Noah, and seven others. Contrasted with the densely peopled 'world of the ungodly.'

preacher – not only 'righteous' himself (compare 2Pe 2:8), but also 'a preacher of righteousness': adduced by Peter against the *licentiousness* of the false teachers (2Pe 2:2) who have no prospect before them but destruction, even as it overtook the ungodly world in Noah's days.

6. with – 'TO overthrow' [ALFORD].

ensample – 'of (the fate that should befall) those who in after-time should live ungodly.' Compare Jude 1:7, 'set forth for an example.'

7. just – righteous.

filthy conversation – literally, 'behaviour in licentiousness' (Ge 19:5).

the wicked – *Greek*, 'lawless': who set at defiance the *laws* of nature, as well as man and God. The Lord reminds us of Lot's faithfulness, but not of his sin in the cave: so in Rahab's case.

8. vexed – *Greek*, 'tormented.'

9. knoweth how – He is at no loss for means, even when men see no escape.

out of – not actually *from*.

temptations – trials.

to be punished – *Greek*, 'being punished': as the fallen angels (2Pe 2:4), actually under sentence, and awaiting its final execution. Sin is already its own penalty; hell will be its full development.

10. chiefly – They *especially* will be punished (Jude 1:8).

after – following after.

lust of uncleanness – *defilement*: 'hankering after polluting and unlawful use of the flesh' [ALFORD].

government – *Greek,* 'lordship,' 'dominion' (Jude 1:8).

Presumptuous – *Greek,* 'Darers.' *Self-will* begets *presumption.* Presumptuously daring.

are not afraid – though they are so insignificant in *might; Greek,* 'tremble not' (Jude 1:8, end).

speak evil of – *Greek,* 'blaspheme.'

dignities – *Greek,* 'glories.'

11. which are – though they are.

greater – than these blasphemers. Jude instances *Michael* (Jude 1:9).

railing accusation – *Greek,* 'blaspheming judgment' (Jude 1:9).

against them – against 'dignities,' as for instance, the fallen angels: once exalted, and still retaining traces of their former power and glory.

before the Lord – In the presence of the Lord, *the Judge,* in reverence, they abstain from judgment [BENGEL]. Judgment belongs to God, not the angels. How great is the dignity of the saints who, as Christ's assessors, shall hereafter judge angels!

12. (Jude 1:19).

But – In contrast to the 'angels,' 2Pe 2:11.

brute – *Greek,* 'irrational.' In contrast to *angels* that 'excel in strength.'

beasts – *Greek,* 'animals' (compare Ps 49:20).

natural – transposed in the oldest manuscripts, 'born natural,' that is, born naturally so: being *in their very nature* (that is, naturally) as such (irrational animals), born to be taken and destroyed (*Greek,* 'unto capture and destruction,' or *corruption,* see on Ga 6:8; compare end of this verse, 'shall perish,' literally, 'shall be corrupted,' in their own *corruption.* Jude 1:10, *naturally … corrupt* themselves,' and so *destroy* themselves; for one and the same *Greek* word expresses *corruption,* the seed, and *destruction,* the developed fruit).

speak evil of – *Greek, 'in the case of* things which they understand not.' Compare the same presumption, the parent of subsequent Gnostic error, producing an opposite, though kindred, error, the worshipping of good angels': Col 2:18, *'intruding into those things which he hath not seen.'*

13. receive – 'shall carry *off* as their due.'

reward of – that is, *for* their 'unrighteousness' [ALFORD]. Perhaps it is implied, *unrighteousness* shall be its own *reward* or punishment. 'Wages of unrighteousness' (2Pe 2:15) has a different sense, namely, *the earthly gain to be gotten by* 'unrighteousness.'

in the daytime – Translate as *Greek,* 'counting the luxury' which is in the daytime (not restricted to *night,* as ordinary revelling. Or as *Vulgate* and CALVIN, 'the luxury which is *but for a day*': so Heb 11:25, 'the pleasures of sin *for a season*'; and Heb 12:16, Esau) 'to be pleasure,' that is, to be their chief good and highest enjoyment.

Spots – *in themselves.*

blemishes – disgraces: bringing *blame* (so the Greek) *on the Church and on Christianity* itself.

sporting themselves – *Greek,* 'luxuriating.'

with – *Greek,* 'in.'

deceivings – or else passively, 'deceits': *luxuries gotten by deceit.* Compare Mt 13:22, 'Deceitfulness of riches'; Eph 4:22, 'Deceitful lusts.' While deceiving others, they are deceived themselves. Compare with *English Version,* Php 3:19, 'Whose glory is in their shame.' 'Their own' stands in opposition to 'you': 'While partaking of the *love-feast* (compare Jude 1:12) with *you,*' they are at the same time 'luxuriating in *their own* deceivings,' or 'deceits' (to which latter clause answers Jude 1:12, end: Peter presents the positive side, 'they *luxuriate* in their own deceivings'; Jude, the negative, 'feeding themselves *without fear*'). But several of the oldest manuscripts, *Vulgate, Syriac,* and *Sahidic Versions* read (as Jude), 'In their own love-feasts': 'their own' will then imply that they pervert the *love-feasts* so as to make them subserve *their own* self-indulgent purposes.

14. full of adultery – literally, 'full of an adulteress,' as though they carried about adulteresses always dwelling in their eyes: the eye being the avenue of lust [HORNEIUS]. BENGEL makes the *adulteress* who fills their eyes, to be 'alluring desire.'

that cannot cease – 'that cannot *be made to cease* from sin.'

beguiling – 'laying baits for.'

unstable – not firmly established in faith and piety.

heart – not only the *eyes,* which are the channel, but the *heart,* the fountain head of lust. Job 31:7, 'Mine *heart* walked after mine *eyes.*'

covetous practices – The oldest manuscripts read singular, 'covetousness.'

cursed children – rather as *Greek,* 'children of curse,' that is, devoted to the curse. *Cursing* and *covetousness,* as in Balaam's case, often go together: the curse he designed for Israel fell on Israel's foes and on himself. True believers *bless,* and curse not, and *so are blessed.*

15. have – Some of the seducers are spoken of as *already come,* others as *yet to come.*

following – out: so the *Greek.*

the way – (Nu 22:23,32 Isa 56:11).

son of Bosor – the same as *Beor* (Nu 22:5). This word was adopted, perhaps, because the kindred word *Basar* means *flesh;* and Balaam is justly termed *son of carnality,* as covetous, and the enticer of Israel to lust.

loved the wages of unrighteousness – and therefore wished (in order to gain them from Balak) to curse Israel whom God had blessed, and at last gave the hellish counsel that the only way to bring God's curse on Israel was to entice them to *fleshly lust* and *idolatry,* which often go together.

16. was rebuked – *Greek*, 'had a rebuke,' or *conviction;* an *exposure* of his specious wickedness on his being *tested* (the root verb of the *Greek* noun means to 'convict on testing').

his – *Greek*, 'his own': his own beast convicted him of *his own* iniquity.

ass – literally, 'beast of burden'; the ass was the ordinary animal used in riding in Palestine.

dumb – *Greek*, 'voiceless-speaking *in* man's *voice*'; marking the marvellous nature of the miracle.

forbade – literally, 'hindered.' It was not the *words* of the ass (for it merely deprecated his beating it), but *the miraculous fact of its speaking at all*, which *withstood* Balaam's perversity in desiring to go after God had forbidden him in the first instance. Thus indirectly the ass, and directly the angel, *rebuked* his worse than asinine obstinacy; the ass *turned aside* at the sight of the angel, but Balaam, after God had plainly said, Thou shalt not go, persevered in wishing to go for gain; thus the ass, *in act, forbade* his madness. How awful a contrast – a *dumb* beast forbidding an *inspired prophet!*

17. (Jude 1:12,13.)

wells – 'clouds' in Jude; both *promising* (compare 2Pe 2:19) water, but yielding none; so their 'great swelling words' are found on trial to be but 'vanity' (2Pe 2:18).

clouds – The oldest manuscripts and versions read, 'mists,' *dark*, and not transparent and bright as 'clouds' often are, whence the latter term is applied sometimes to the saints; fit emblem of the children of darkness. 'Clouds' is a transcriber's correction from Jude 1:12, where it is appropriate, 'clouds … without water' (promising what they do not perform); but not here, 'mists driven along by a tempest'.

mist – *blackness;* the *chilling horror* accompanying *darkness*' [BENGEL].

18. allure – *Greek*, 'lay baits for.'

through – *Greek*, 'in'; the *lusts of the flesh* being the element IN which they lay their baits.

much wantonness – *Greek*, 'by licentiousness'; the bait which they lay.

clean escaped – *Greek*, 'really escaped.' But the oldest manuscripts and *Vulgate* read, 'scarcely,' or 'for but a little time'; scarcely have they escaped from them who live in error (the ungodly world), when they are allured by these seducers into sin again (2Pe 2:20).

19. promise … liberty – (Christian) – These promises are instances of their 'great swelling words' (2Pe 2:18). The *liberty* which they propose is such as fears not Satan, nor loathes the flesh. Pauline language, adopted by Peter here, and 1Pe 2:16; see on 1Pe 2:16; (compare 2Pe 3:15 Ro 6:16–22 8:15,21 Ga 5:1,13; compare Joh 8:34).

corruption – (See on 2Pe 2:12); 'destroyed … perish … corruption.'

of whom – 'by whatever … by the same'.

20. after they – *the seducers* 'themselves' *have escaped* (2Pe 2:19; see on Heb 6:4–6).

pollutions – which bring 'corruption' (2Pe 2:19).

through – *Greek*, 'in.'

knowledge – *Greek*, 'full and accurate knowledge.'

the Lord and Saviour Jesus Christ – solemnly expressing in full the great and gracious One from whom they fall.

latter end is worse … than the beginning – Peter remembers Christ's words. 'Worse' stands opposed to 'better' (2Pe 2:21).

21. the way of righteousness – 'the way of truth' (2Pe 2:2). Christian doctrine, and 'the knowledge of the Lord and Saviour.'

turn – back again; so the *Greek.*

from the holy commandment – the Gospel which enjoins *holiness;* in opposition to their *corruption.* 'Holy,' not that it makes holy, but because it ought to be kept *inviolate* [TITTMANN].

delivered – once for all; admitting no turning back.

22. But – You need not wonder at the event; for *dogs* and *swine* they were before, and dogs and swine they will continue. They 'scarcely' (2Pe 2:18) have escaped from their filthy folly, when they again are entangled in it. Then they seduce others who have in like manner 'for a little time escaped from them that live in error' (2Pe 2:18). Peter often quoted Proverbs in his First Epistle (1Pe 1:7 2:17 4:8,18); another proof that both Epistles come from the same writer.

Chapter 3

2Pe 3:1–18. Sureness of Christ's coming, and its accompaniments, declared in opposition to scoffers about to arise. God's long suffering a motive to repentance, as Paul's Epistles set forth; concluding exhortation to growth in the knowledge of Christ.

1. now – 'This now a second Epistle I write.' Therefore he had lately written the former Epistle. The seven Catholic Epistles were written by James, John, and Jude, shortly before their deaths; previously, while having the prospect of being still for some time alive, they felt it less necessary to write [BENGEL].

unto you – The Second Epistle, though more general in its address, yet *included* especially the same persons as the First Epistle was particularly addressed to.

pure – literally, 'pure when examined by sunlight'; 'sincere.' *Adulterated with no error.* Opposite to 'having the understanding *darkened.*' ALFORD explains, The mind, will, and affection, in relation to the outer world, being turned to God [the *Sun* of the soul], and not obscured by fleshly and selfish regards.

by way of – *Greek,* 'in,' '*in putting you in remembrance*' (2Pe 1:12,13). Ye already *know* (2Pe 3:3); it is only needed that I *remind* you (Jude 1:5).

2. prophets – of the Old Testament.

of us – The oldest manuscripts and *Vulgate* read, 'And of the commandment of the Lord and Saviour (declared) by YOUR apostles' (so '*apostle of the Gentiles,*' Ro 11:13) – the apostles *who live among you in the present time,* in contrast to the *Old Testament* 'prophets.'

3. Knowing this first – from the word of the apostles.

shall come – Their very *scoffing* shall confirm the truth of the prediction.

scoffers – The oldest manuscripts and *Vulgate* add, '(scoffers) *in* (that is, "with") *scoffing.*' As Re 14:2, 'harping with harps.'

walking after their own lusts – (2Pe 2:10 Jude 1:16,18). Their own pleasure is their sole law, unrestrained by reverence for God.

4. (Compare Ps 10:11 73:11.) Presumptuous skepticism and lawless lust, setting nature and its so-called laws above the God of nature and revelation, and arguing from the past continuity of nature's phenomena that there can be no future interruption to them, was the sin of the antediluvians, and shall be that of the scoffers in the last days.

Where – implying that it ought to have taken place before this, if ever it was to take place, but that it never will.

the promise – which you, believers, are so continually looking for the fulfilment of (2Pe 3:13). What becomes of the promise which you talk so much of?

his – Christ's; the subject of prophecy from the earliest days.

the fathers – to whom *the promise* was made, and who rested all their hopes on it.

all things – in the *natural world;* skeptics look not beyond this.

as they were – *continue as they do; as we see* them to continue. From the time of the promise of Christ's coming as Saviour and King being given to the fathers, down to the present time, all things continue, and have continued, *as they now are,* from 'the beginning of creation.' The 'scoffers' here are not necessarily atheists, nor do they maintain that the world existed from eternity. They are willing to recognize a God, but not the God *of revelation.* They reason from seeming delay against the fulfilment of God's word at all.

5. Refutation of their scoffing from Scripture history.

willingly – wilfully; they do not *wish* to know. Their ignorance is voluntary.

they … are ignorant of – in contrast to 2Pe 3:8, 'Be not ignorant of this.' Literally, in both verses, 'This escapes THEIR notice (sagacious philosophers though they think themselves)'; 'let this not escape YOUR notice.' They obstinately shut their eyes to the Scripture record of the creation and the deluge; the latter is the very parallel to the coming judgment by fire, which Jesus mentions, as Peter doubtless remembered.

by the word of God – not by a fortuitous concurrence of atoms [ALFORD].

of old – *Greek,* 'from of old'; from the first. beginning of all things. A confutation of their objection, 'all things continue as they were FROM THE BEGINNING OF CREATION.' Before the flood, the same objection to the possibility of the flood might have been urged with the same plausibility: The heavens (sky) and earth have been FROM OF OLD, how unlikely then that they should not *continue* so! But, replies Peter, the flood came in spite of their reasonings; so will the conflagration of the earth come in spite of the 'scoffers' of the last days, changing the whole order of things (the present 'world,' or as *Greek* means, 'order'), and introducing the new heavens and earth (2Pe 3:13).

earth standing out of – *Greek,* 'consisting of,' that is, 'formed out of the water.' The waters under the firmament were at creation gathered together into one place, and the dry land emerged *out of* and above, them.

in – rather, '*by means of* the water,' as a great instrument (along with *fire*) in the changes wrought on the earth's surface to prepare it for man. Held together BY the water. The earth arose *out of* the water *by the efficacy of the water* itself [TITTMANN].

6. Whereby – *Greek,* 'By which' (plural). *By means of which* heavens and earth (in respect to the WATERS which flowed together *from both*) *the then world perished* (that is, in respect to its *occupants,* men and animals, and its then existing *order:* not *was annihilated*); for in the flood 'the fountains of the great deep were broken up' from *the earth* (1) below, and 'the windows of *heaven*' (2) above 'were opened.' The earth was deluged by that water *out of* which it had originally risen.

7. (Compare Job 28:5, end).

which are now – 'the postdiluvian visible world.' In contrast to 'that *then was,*' 2Pe 3:6.

the same – Other oldest manuscripts read, 'His' (God's).

kept in store – *Greek,* 'treasured up.'

reserved – 'kept.' It is only God's constantly watchful providence which holds together the present state of things till His time for ending it.

8. be not ignorant – as those scoffers are (2Pe 3:5). Besides the refutation of them (2Pe 3:5–7) drawn from the history of the deluge, here he adds another (addressed more to believers than to the mockers): God's delay in fulfilling His promise is not, like men's delays, owing to inability or fickleness in keeping His word, but through 'long-suffering'.

this one thing – as the consideration *of chief importance* (Lu 10:42).

one day ... thousand years – (Ps 90:4): Moses there says, Thy *eternity,* knowing no distinction between a *thousand* years and a *day,* is the refuge of us creatures of a day. Peter views God's eternity in relation to the last day: that day seems to us, short-lived beings, long in coming, but *with the Lord* the interval is irrespective of the idea of long or short. His eternity exceeds all measures of time: to His divine knowledge all future things are present: His power requires not long delays for the performance of His work: His long-suffering excludes all impatient expectation and eager haste, such as we men feel. He is equally blessed in one day and in a thousand years. He can do the work of a thousand years in one day: so in 2Pe 3:9 it is said, 'He is not slack,' that is, 'slow': He has always the power to fulfil His 'promise'.

thousand years as one day – No delay which occurs is long to God: as to a man of countless riches, a thousand dollars are as a single penny. God's æonology (*eternal-ages* measurer) differs wholly from man's horology (*hour*-glass). His gnomon (dial-pointer) shows all the hours at once in the greatest activity and in perfect repose. To Him the hours pass away, neither more slowly, nor more quickly, than befits His economy. There is nothing to make Him need either to hasten or delay the end. The words, 'with the Lord' (Ps 90:4, 'In Thy sight'), silence all man's objections on the ground of his incapability of understanding this [BENGEL].

9. slack – slow, tardy, *late;* exceeding the due time, as though that time were already come. Heb 10:37, 'will not *tarry.*'

his promise – which the scoffers cavil at. 2Pe 3:4, 'Where is the promise?' It shall be surely fulfilled 'according to His promise' (2Pe 3:13).

some – the 'scoffers'.

count – His promise to be the result of 'slackness' (tardiness).

long-suffering – waiting until the full number of those appointed to 'salvation' (2Pe 3:15) shall be completed.

to us-ward – The oldest manuscripts, *Vulgate, Syriac* read, 'towards YOU.'

any – not desiring that any, yea, even that the scoffers, should perish, which would be the result if He did not give space for repentance.

come – *go and be received* to repentance: the *Greek* implies there is *room* for their being *received* to repentance (compare *Greek,* Mr 2:2 Joh 8:37).

10. The certainty, suddenness, and concomitant effects, of the coming of the day of the Lord. FABER argues from this that the millennium, must *precede* Christ's literal coming, not *follow* it. But 'the day of the Lord' comprehends the whole series of events, beginning with the pre-millennial advent, and ending with the destruction of the wicked, and final conflagration, and general judgment (which last intervenes between the conflagration and the renovation of the earth).

will – emphatic. But (in spite of the mockers, and notwithstanding the delay) *come and be present* the day of the Lord SHALL.

as a thief – Peter remembers and repeats his Lord's image (Lu 12:39,41) used in the conversation in which he took a part; so also Paul (1Th 5:2) and John (Re 3:3 16:15).

the heavens – which the scoffers say shall 'continue' as they are (2Pe 3:4 Mt 24:35 Re 21:1).

with a great noise – with a rushing noise, like that of a *whizzing* arrow, or the crash of a devouring flame.

elements – *the component materials of the world* [WAHL]. However, as 'the works' in the earth are mentioned separately from 'the earth,' so it is likely by 'elements,' mentioned after 'the heavens,' are meant 'the works therein,' namely, *the sun, moon, and stars* (as THEOPHILUS OF ANTIOCH [p. 22, 148, 228]; and JUSTIN MARTYR [*Apology,* 2.44], use the word 'elements'): these, as at creation, so in the destruction of the world, are mentioned [BENGEL]. But as 'elements' is not so used in Scripture *Greek,* perhaps it refers to *the component materials* of 'the heavens,' including *the heavenly bodies;* it clearly belongs to the former clause, 'the heavens,' not to the following, 'the earth'.

melt – be dissolved, as in 2Pe 3:11.

the works ... therein – of nature and of art.

11. Your duty, seeing that this is so, is to be ever eagerly expecting the day of God.

then – Some oldest manuscripts substitute 'thus' for 'then': a happy refutation of the 'thus' of the scoffers, 2Pe 3:4 (*English Version,* 'As they were,' *Greek,* 'thus').

shall be – *Greek, 'are being* (in God's appointment, soon to be fulfilled) dissolved'; the present tense implying *the certainty* as though it were actually present.

what manner *of men* – exclamatory. How watchful, prayerful, zealous!

to be – not the mere *Greek* substantive verb of existence (*einai*), but (*huparchein*) denoting a *state* or *condition* in which one is supposed to be [TITTMANN]. What holy men ye ought to be found to be, when the event comes! This is 'the holy commandment' mentioned in 2Pe 3:2.

conversation ... godliness – *Greek,* plural: *behaviours* (towards men), *godlinesses* (or *pieties* towards God) in their *manifold* modes of manifestation.

12. hasting unto – *with the utmost eagerness desiring* [WAHL], praying for, and contemplating, the coming Saviour as at hand. The *Greek may* mean 'hastening (that is, *urging onward* [ALFORD]) the day of God'; not that God's eternal appointment of the time is changeable, but God appoints *us* as instruments of accomplishing those events which must be first before the day of God can come. By praying for His coming, furthering the preaching of the Gospel for a witness to all nations, and bringing in those whom 'the long-suffering of God' waits to save, we *hasten the coming of the day of God*. The *Greek* verb is always in New Testament used as neuter (as *English Version* here), not active; but the *Septuagint* uses it *actively*. *Christ* says, 'Surely I come quickly. Amen.' *Our* part is to *speed forward* this consummation by praying, 'Even so, come, Lord Jesus' (Re 22:20).

the coming – *Greek*, '*presence*' of a *person*: usually, of the Saviour.

the day of God – God has given many myriads of days to *men*: one shall be the great 'day of God' Himself. **wherein** – rather as *Greek*, 'on account of (or *owing to*) which' day.

heavens – the upper and lower regions of the sky.

melt – Our igneous rocks show that they were once in a liquid state.

13. Nevertheless – 'But': in contrast to the destructive effects of the day of God stand its constructive effects. As the flood was the baptism of the earth, eventuating in a renovated earth, partially delivered from 'the curse,' so the baptism with fire shall purify the earth so as to be the renovated abode of regenerated man, wholly freed from the curse.

his promise – (Isa 65:17 66:22). The 'we' is not emphatic as in *English Version*.

new heavens – new atmospheric heavens surrounding the renovated earth.

righteousness – *dwelleth* in that coming world as its essential feature, all pollutions having been removed.

14. that ye … be found of him – 'in His sight' [ALFORD], at His coming; plainly implying a *personal* coming.

without spot – at the coming marriage feast of the Lamb, in contrast to 2Pe 2:13, 'Spots they are and blemishes while they feast,' not having on the King's pure wedding garment.

blameless – (1Co 1:8 Php 1:10 1Th 3:13 5:23).

in peace – in all its aspects, towards God, your own consciences, and your fellow men, and as its consequence eternal *blessedness*: 'the God of peace' will effect this for you.

15. account … the long-suffering … is salvation – is designed for the salvation of those yet to be gathered into the Church: whereas those scoffers 'count it (to be the result of) slackness' on the Lord's part (2Pe 3:9).

our beloved brother Paul – a beautiful instance of love and humility. Peter praises the very Epistles which contain his condemnation.

according to the wisdom given unto him – adopting Paul's own language, 1Co 3:10, '*According to the* grace of God which is *given unto* me as a *wise* master-builder.' Supernatural and inspired wisdom 'GIVEN' him, not acquired in human schools of learning.

hath written – *Greek* aorist, 'wrote,' as a thing wholly *past*: Paul was by this time either dead, or had ceased to minister to them.

to you – *Galatians, Ephesians, Colossians,* the same region as Peter addresses. Compare 'in peace,' 2Pe 3:14, a practical exhibition of which Peter now gives in showing how perfectly agreeing Paul (who wrote the Epistle to the *Galatians*) and he are, notwithstanding the event recorded (Ga 2:11–14). Col 3:4 refers to *Christ's second coming*. The Epistle to the Hebrews, too (addressed not only to the Palestinian, but also secondarily to the Hebrew Christians everywhere), may be referred to, as Peter primarily (though not exclusively) addresses in both Epistles the *Hebrew* Christians of the dispersion (see on 1Pe 1:1). Heb 9:27,28 10:25,37, 'speak of these things' (2Pe 3:16) which Peter has been handling, namely, the coming of the day of the Lord, delayed through His 'long-suffering,' yet near and sudden.

16. also in all his epistles – Ro 2:4 is very similar to 2Pe 3:15, beginning. The Pauline Epistles were by this time become the *common* property of all the churches. The 'all' seems to imply they were now completed. The subject of the Lord's coming is handled in 1Th 4:13 5:11; compare 2Pe 3:10 with 1Th 5:2. Still Peter distinguishes Paul's Epistle, or Epistles, 'TO YOU,' from '*all his* (*other*) Epistles,' showing that certain definite churches, or particular classes of believers, are meant by 'you'.

in which – *Epistles*. The oldest manuscripts read the feminine relative (*hais*); not as Received Text (*hois*), 'in which *things*.'

some things hard to be understood – namely, in reference to Christ's coming, for example, the statements as to the man of sin and the apostasy, before Christ's coming. 'Paul seemed thereby to delay Christ's coming to a longer period than the other apostles, whence some doubted altogether His coming' [BENGEL]. Though there be some things hard to be understood, there are enough besides, plain, easy, and sufficient for perfecting the man of God. 'There is scarce anything drawn from the obscure places, but the same in other places may be found most plain' [AUGUSTINE]. It is our own prejudice, foolish expectations, and carnal fancies, that make Scripture difficult [JEREMY TAYLOR].

unlearned – Not those wanting *human* learning are meant, but those *lacking the learning imparted by the Spirit*. The humanly *learned* have been often most deficient in spiritual learning, and have originated many heresies. Compare 2Ti 2:23, a different *Greek* word, 'unlearned,' literally, 'untutored.' When religion is studied as a science, nothing is more abstruse; when studied in order to know our duty and practice it, nothing is easier.

unstable – not yet established in what they have learned; shaken by every seeming difficulty; who, in perplexing texts, instead of waiting until God by His Spirit makes them plain in comparing them with other Scriptures, hastily adopt distorted views.

wrest – strain and twist (properly with a *hand screw*) what is straight in itself (for example, 2Ti 2:18).

other scriptures – Paul's Epistles were, therefore, by this time, recognized in the Church, as 'Scripture': a term never applied in any of the fifty places where it occurs, save to the Old and New Testament sacred writings. Men in each Church having miraculous *discernment of spirits* would have prevented any uninspired writing from being put on a par with the Old Testament word of God; the apostles' lives also were providentially prolonged, Paul's and Peter's at least to thirty-four years after Christ's resurrection, John's to thirty years later, so that fraud in the canon is out of question. The three first Gospels and Acts are included in 'the other Scriptures,' and perhaps all the New Testament books, save John and Revelation, written later.

unto their own destruction – not through Paul's fault (2Pe 2:1).

17. Ye – warned by the case of those 'unlearned and unstable' persons (2Pe 3:16).

knowing ... before – the event.

led away with – the very term, as Peter remembers, used by Paul of Barnabas' being 'carried,' *Greek*, 'led away with' Peter and the other Jews in their hypocrisy.

wicked – 'lawless,' as in 2Pe 2:7.

fall from – (*grace*, Ga 5:4: the true source of) 'steadfastness' or *stability* in contrast with the 'unstable' (2Pe 3:16): 'established' (2Pe 1:12): all kindred *Greek* terms. Compare Jude 1:20,21.

18. grow – Not only do not 'fall from' (2Pe 3:17), but *grow onward:* the true secret of not going backward. Eph 4:15, 'Grow up into Him, the Head, Christ.'

grace and ... knowledge of ... Christ – 'the grace and knowledge of Christ' [ALFORD rightly]: *the grace* of which *Christ* is the author, and *the knowledge* of which *Christ* is the object.

for ever – *Greek,* 'to the day of eternity': the day that has no end: 'the day of the Lord,' beginning with the Lord's coming.

1 JOHN

John Calvin

Introduction

This letter is altogether worthy of the spirit of that disciple who, above others, was loved by Christ, that he might exhibit him as a friend to us. But it contains doctrines mixed with exhortations; for he speaks of the eternal Deity of Christ, and at the same time of the incomparable grace which he brought with him when he appeared in the world, and generally of all his blessings; and he especially commends and extols the inestimable grace of divine adoption.

He grounds his exhortations on these truths; and at one time he admonishes us in generally to lead a pious and holy life, and at another time he expressly enjoins love. But he does none of these things in a regular order; for he mixes teaching with exhortation everywhere. But he particularly urges brotherly love; he also touches on other things, such as to beware of impostors, and similar things. But each detail will be dealt with in its own place.

Contents

See *Outlines of the New Testament Books*, p. 906

Chapter 1

1. What was from the beginning. These words doubtless refer to the divinity of Christ, for God did not appear in the flesh from the beginning; but he who always was life and the eternal Word of God appeared in the fullness of time as man. Again, what follows about looking at and touching with the hands refers to his human nature. But as the two natures constitute only one person, and Christ is one, because he came from the Father that he might put on our flesh, the apostle rightly declares that he is the same, and had been invisible, and afterwards became visible.

Let us then bear in mind that this doctrine of the Gospel is declared here: that he who in the flesh really proved himself to be the Son of God, and was acknowledged to be the Son of God, was always God's invisible Word, for he is not here referring to the beginning of the world, but ascends much higher.

What we have heard, what we have seen with our eyes. It was not hearing a report (to which little credit is usually given), but John means that he had faithfully learnt from his Master those things which he taught, so that he alleged nothing thoughtlessly and rashly. And, doubtless, no one is a fit teacher in the Church, who has not been the disciple of the Son of God, and rightly instructed in his school, since his authority alone ought to prevail.

With our eyes. This is no redundancy, but a fuller expression for the sake of amplifying. He was not satisfied with merely seeing, but added **what we have looked at and touched with our**

hands. By these words he shows that he taught nothing but what had been really made known to him.

The word of life. The genitive here is used adjectivally 'vivifying,' or 'life-giving'; for in him, as it says in the first chapter of John's Gospel, was life. At the same time, this distinction belongs to the Son of God on two accounts: because he has infused life into all creatures, and because he now restores life to us when we had perished, having been extinguished by Adam's sin. Moreover, the term **word** may be explained in two ways – either of Christ, or of the Gospel teaching, for that is how salvation is brought to us. But as its substance is Christ, and as it contains nothing other than that he, who had always been with the Father, at length appeared to us, the first view seems to me the simpler and more genuine. Moreover, it appears more fully from the Gospel that the wisdom which lives in God is called the Word.

2. This life was revealed. As though he had said, 'We testify of the life-giving Word, as life has appeared.' From this we learn that when Christ is preached to us, the kingdom of heaven is opened to us, so that being raised from death we may live the life of God.

That was with the Father. This is true not only from the time when the world was formed, but also from eternity, for he was always God, the fountain of life; and the power and the faculty of vivifying was possessed by his eternal wisdom; but he did not actually exercise it before the creation of the world, and from the time when God began to exhibit the Word, that power which before had been hidden, diffused itself over all created things. The apostle's object is to remove the idea of novelty, which might have lessened the dignity of the Gospel; he therefore says that life had not now at last begun to be, though it had only recently appeared, for it was always with the Father.

3. What we have seen. He now repeats the words **seen** and **heard** for the third time, so that nothing might be lacking as to the real certainty of his doctrine. And it ought to be carefully noticed that the heralds of the Gospel chosen by Christ were those who were fit and faithful witnesses of all those things which they were to declare.

John declares that, as the apostles were adopted by Christ as brothers, being gathered into one body so that they might be united together with God, so also he does with other colleagues: though they are many, they are made partakers of this holy and blessed union.

4. That our joy may be complete. By complete joy he expresses more clearly the complete and perfect happiness which we obtain through the Gospel; at the same time he reminds the faithful where they ought to fix all their affections.

5. He calls God light. Why Satan is called the prince of darkness is clear enough. When, therefore, God on the other hand is called the Father of light, and also **light**, we first understand that there is nothing in him but what is bright, pure, and unalloyed; and, secondly, that he makes all things so clear by his brightness, that he allows nothing vicious or perverted, no spots or filth, no hypocrisy or fraud, to remain hidden. So then, the sum of it all is that since there is no union between light and darkness, there is a separation between us and God as long as we walk in darkness; and the fellowship which he mentions cannot exist unless we also become pure and holy.

In him there is no darkness at all. This manner of speaking is commonly used by John to amplify what he has affirmed by a contrary negative. The meaning, then, is that God is such a light that no darkness belongs to him. Hence it follows that he hates an evil conscience, pollution, and wickedness, and everything that pertains to darkness.

7. But if we walk in the light. He now says that the proof of our union with God is certain if we conform to him; not that purity of life conciliates us to God, as the prior cause; but the apostle means that our union with God is made evident by the effect, that is, when his purity shines in us. And doubtless this is a fact; wherever God comes, all things are so imbued with his holiness that he washes away all filth; for without him we have nothing but filth and darkness. Hence it is evident that no one leads a holy life unless he is united to God.

And the blood of Jesus. After teaching what is the bond of our union with God, he now shows what fruit comes from it, namely that our sins are freely forgiven. And this is the blessedness which David describes in Psalm 32, in order that we may know that we are most miserable until, being renewed by God's Spirit, we serve him with a sincere heart. For who can be imagined more miserable than a person whom God hates and abominates, and over whose head is suspended both the wrath of God and eternal death?

This passage is remarkable; and from it we learn, first, that the expiation of Christ, effected by his death, really belongs to us when we do what is right and just, in uprightness of heart; for Christ is no redeemer except to those who turn from iniquity and lead a new life. If, then, we desire to have God propitious to us, so as to forgive our sins, we ought not to forgive ourselves. In short, remission of sins cannot be separated from repentance, nor can the peace of God be in those hearts where the fear of God does not prevail.

Secondly, this passage shows that the free pardon of sins is given us not just once, but is a benefit which always remains in the Church, and is offered to the faithful every day. For the apostle is writing to the faithful here; as doubtless no one has ever been, nor ever will be, who can please God in any other way, since all are guilty before him; for however strong a desire there may be in us to act rightly, we always go to God hesitatingly. Yet what is half done obtains no approval from God. In the meantime, by new sins we continually separate ourselves, as far as we can, from the grace of God. Thus it is that all the saints need daily forgiveness of sins; for this alone keeps us in the family of God.

8. And the truth is not in us. People are deceived if they glory in falsehood.

9. If we confess. Again he promises to the faithful that God will be propitious to them provided they acknowledge themselves to be sinners. It is important to be fully persuaded that when we have sinned, there is a reconciliation with God ready and prepared for us; otherwise, we shall always be carrying hell within us. Indeed, few people consider how miserable and wretched a doubting conscience is; but the truth is that hell reigns where there is no peace with God. So it becomes us all the more to receive with our whole hearts this promise which offers free pardon to all who confess their sins. Moreover, this is based on God's justice, because God who promises is true and just. Those who think that he is called **just** because he justifies us freely are being too refined, I think, for justice or righteousness here depends on faithfulness, and both are attached to the promise. God might have been just if he dealt with us with all the rigour of justice; but as he has bound himself to us by his Word, he would not have himself deemed just unless he forgives.

And cleanse us. The verb seems to be taken in a different sense than previously, for in verse 7 he had said that we are purified by the blood of Jesus, but here, having spoken of pardon, he also adds that God purifies us from all unrighteousness, so this second clause is different from the previous one. Thus he is telling us that a double fruit comes to us from confession – that God being reconciled by Christ's sacrifice forgives us, and that he renews and reforms us.

If anyone objects that, as long as we remain in the world, we are never cleansed from all unrighteousness, with regard to our reformation, this is indeed true; but John is not referring to what God now performs in us. He is faithful, he says, and will purify us, not today or tomorrow; for as long as we are surrounded with flesh, we ought to be in a continual state of progress; but what he has begun, he goes on to do every day, until at last he completes it. So Paul says that we are chosen to appear without blame before God (Colossians 1:22); and in another passage he says that the Church is

cleansed, that it might be without stain or wrinkle (Ephesians 5:27).

10. We make him a liar. Those who claim purity for themselves blaspheme God. For we see that he everywhere represents the whole human race as guilty of sin.

Whoever tries to escape this charge, then, carries on war with God, and accuses him of falsehood, as though he condemned people who did not deserve it. To confirm this, he adds **and his word is not in us** – which is like saying that we reject this great truth, that everyone is guilty.

Chapter 2

1. My little children. It is not only the sum and substance of the preceding doctrine, but the meaning of almost the whole Gospel, that we are to depart from sin; and yet, though we are always exposed to God's judgment, we are certain that Christ so intercedes by the sacrifice of his death that the Father is propitious to us. In the meantime, he also anticipates an objection, lest anyone should think that he gave license to sin when he spoke of God's mercy, and showed that it is presented to us all. So then, he joins together two parts of the Gospel, which unreasonable people separate, and thus lacerate and mutilate.

To obviate these calumnies, the apostle testifies first that the aim of his teaching was to keep people from sinning; for when he says **that you may not sin**, he simply means that they should abstain from sins, as far as human weakness allows.

Advocate. No small consolation comes to us when we hear that Christ not only died for us to reconcile us to the Father, but that he continually intercedes for us, so that an access in his name is open to us, that our prayers may be heard. We ought especially, then to beware lest this honour, which belongs uniquely to him, should be transferred to someone else.

2. Not for ours only. He added this by way of amplification, so that the faithful might be assured that the expiation made by Christ extends to all who by faith embrace the Gospel.

Here it may be asked how the sins of the whole world have been expiated. I will ignore the dotings of fanatics who say this means salvation extends to all the reprobate, and therefore to Satan himself. Such a monstrous thing deserves no refutation. People who seek to avoid this absurdity have said that Christ suffered sufficiently for the whole world, but efficiently only for the chosen. This solution has commonly prevailed among theologians. Though I admit that what has been said is true, I deny that it suits this passage; for John's purpose was none other than to make this benefit common to the whole Church. By the word **whole**, then, he does not mean to include the reprobate, but he means those who would believe as well as those who were then scattered through various parts of the world. For it really makes Christ's atoning sacrifice clear, as it should do, when it is declared to be the only true salvation of the world.

3. **If we obey his commandments.** But there is no one who keeps them in everything; there would thus be no knowledge of God in the world. To this I answer that the apostle is not being at all inconsistent, since he has already shown that all are guilty before God, so he does not mean that those who keep his commandments wholly satisfy the law – no such instance can be found in the world. He means those who strive, as much as human weakness allows, to shape their life in conformity to God's will. Whenever Scripture speaks of the righteousness of the faithful, it does not exclude the forgiveness of sins, but on the contrary begins with it.

But we are not to conclude from this that faith rests on works; for though everyone receives a testimony to his faith from his works, it does not follow that it is founded on them, since they are added as an evidence. So then, the certainty of faith depends on the grace of Christ alone; but piety and holiness of life distinguish true faith from that knowledge of God which is fictitious and dead; for the truth is that those who are in Christ, as Paul says, have taken off the old self (Colossians 3:9).

4. **Whoever says, 'I have come to know him.'** How does he prove that people are liars if they boast that they have faith without piety? He proves it by the contrary effect; for he has already said that the knowledge of God is efficacious. God is not known by mere imagination, since he reveals himself inwardly to our hearts by the Spirit. Besides, as many hypocrites vainly boast that they have faith, the apostle charges all of them with falsehood; for what he says would be superfluous if people made no false and vain profession of Christianity.

5. **But whoever keeps his word.** He now defines what a true keeping of God's law is, namely, to love God.

By this we may be sure that we are in him. He is referring to that fruit of the Gospel which he had mentioned – fellowship with the Father and the Son. Thus he confirms the previous sentence, by stating what follows as a consequence. If it is the purpose of the Gospel to hold communion with God, and no communion can be without love, then no one makes real progress in faith unless they hold fast to God with the heart.

6. **Whoever says, 'I abide in him.'** As he has already given as the example of God as light, he now calls us also to Christ, that we may imitate him. Yet he does not simply exhort us to imitate Christ, but from the union we have with him, he proves that we ought to be like him. A likeness

in life and deeds, he says, will prove that we are in Christ. But from these words he passes on to the next clause, which he immediately adds, respecting love to the brothers.

7. **Beloved, I am writing you no new commandment.** This is an explanation of the preceding doctrine, that to love God is to keep his commandments. He had good reason to dwell on this point. First, we know that novelty is disliked or suspected. Secondly, we do not easily undertake any yoke we are not used to. In addition to these things, when we have embraced any kind of doctrine, we dislike having anything changed or made new in it. For these reasons John reminds us that he was teaching nothing but what had been heard by the faithful concerning love from the beginning, and had become old through long usage.

8. **Yet I am writing you a new commandment.** He says *new* because God, as it were, renews it by daily suggesting it, so that the faithful may practise it through their whole life, for they can look for nothing more excellent.

That is true in him and in you. This proves what he had said; for this one command respecting love, about our conduct in life, constitutes the whole truth of Christ. Besides, what other greater revelation can be expected? No doubt Christ is the end and the completion of everything.

Because the darkness is passing away. He means that as soon as Christ brings light, we have the full brightness of knowledge: not that every one of the faithful becomes wise the first day as much as he ought to be but that the knowledge of Christ alone is sufficient to dissipate darkness. Hence, daily progress is necessary; and the faith of everyone has its dawn before it reaches the noon-day.

9. **Whoever says, 'I am in the light.'** He pursues the same metaphor: he said that love is the only true rule according to which our life is to be formed; he said that this rule or law is presented to us in the Gospel; he said, lastly, that it is there as the meridian light, which ought to be continually looked on.

11. **But whoever hates another believer.** Again he reminds us that whatever specious appearance of excellency you may show, there is still nothing but what is sinful if love is absent.

12. **Little children.** This is still a general declaration, for he is not addressing only those of tender age but people of all ages, as in verse 1, and also afterwards.

Your sins are forgiven. Without this assurance, religion would only be fading and shadowy; indeed, those who ignore the free forgiveness of sins, and dwell on other things, build without a foundation.

On account of his name. The material cause is mentioned, lest we should seek other means to reconcile us to God. For it would not be sufficient to know that God forgives us our sins unless we came directly to Christ, and to the price which he paid on the cross for us. And this ought to be observed all the more because we see that by Satan's craft and by wicked human fictions, this way is obstructed; for foolish people attempt to pacify God by various satisfactions and devise innumerable kinds of expiations for the purpose of redeeming themselves. Every means of deserving pardon which we intrude on God is another obstacle which prevents us from approaching him.

13. I am writing to you, fathers. Now he comes to list different ages, so that he can show that what he taught suited every one of them. He begins with the old, and says that the Gospel is right for them because from it they learned to know the eternal Son of God.

I am writing to you, young people. Though the Greek word is a diminutive, there is no doubt he is addressing all who were in the flower of their age. The apostle reminds them where true strength comes from, so that they might no longer exult as usual in the flesh. Doubtless the strength we ought to seek is spiritual.

14. I write to you, little children. They had to be addressed explicitly. The apostle concludes that the Gospel is well adapted to young children because they find the Father in it. We now see how diabolical it is to drive all ages away from the doctrine of the Gospel, while the Spirit of God so carefully addresses them all.

15. Do not love the world. He has already said that the only rule for living religiously is to love God; but when we are occupied with the vain love of the world, we turn away all our thoughts and affections another way, so this vanity must be torn away from us first, in order that the love of God may reign within us. Until our minds are cleansed, the former doctrine may be repeated a hundred times, but without effect.

The world means everything connected with the present life, apart from the kingdom of God and the hope of eternal life. So he includes in it corruptions of every kind, and the abyss of all evils. In the world are pleasures, delights, and all those attractions by which people are captivated so as to withdraw from God.

16. The desire of the flesh. John, who well knew the insubordination of the human heart, unhesitatingly condemns the desires of sinful nature, because they are always excessive, and never observe any due moderation. He afterwards comes gradually to grosser vices.

The desire of the eyes. I think he includes libidinous looks as well as the vanity which delights in pomp and empty splendour.

Lastly follows **the pride in riches** or haughtiness, with which is connected ambition, contempt of others, blind love of self, headstrong self-confidence.

The sum total is that as soon as the world presents itself, our lusts and desires, when our heart is corrupt, are captivated by it, like unbridled wild beasts; so that various lusts, all of them against God, rule in us.

17. And the world and its desire are passing away. As everything in the world is fading and ephemeral, he concludes that those who seek happiness from it make a wretched and miserable provision for themselves, especially when God calls us to the ineffable glory of eternal life. It is like saying, 'The true happiness which God offers to his children is eternal; it is then a shameful thing for us to be entangled with the world, which with all its benefits will soon vanish away.'

By saying that those who do God's will will live **for ever**, or perpetually, he means that those who seek God will be perpetually blessed.

18. It is the last hour! The apostle reminds them that the last hour had already come, and therefore he exhorts them to a greater vigilance. It is like saying, 'Whilst various errors arise, it is right for you to be awakened rather than to be overwhelmed; for we ought to conclude from this that Christ is not far off; let us then attentively look for him, lest he should come upon us suddenly.' We must understand the apostle's aim, that he calls **the last time** the time in which everything will be so completed that nothing will remain except the final revelation of Christ.

As you have heard that antichrist is coming. He speaks as though it is something well known, so we may conclude that the faithful had been taught and warned from the beginning about the future disorder of the church, in order that they might carefully keep themselves in the faith they professed, and also instruct posterity in the duty of watchfulness.

19. They went out from us. He anticipates another objection, that the church seemed to have produced these pests, and to have cherished them for a time. Certainly it serves more to disturb the weak when anyone among us, professing the true faith, falls away, than when a thousand aliens conspire against us. He then confesses that they had gone out from the heart of the church, but he denies that they were ever of the church. The way to remove this objection is to say that the church is always exposed to this evil, so that it is constrained to bear with many hypocrites who do not really know Christ, however much they may profess his name with their words.

For if they had belonged to us. He plainly declares that those who fell away had never been members of the church.

20. But you have been anointed. The apostle did not teach them as though they were ignorant, acquainted only with the rudiments of knowledge, but was reminding them of what they already knew, and was also exhorting them to rouse up the sparks of the Spirit so that a full brightness might shine in them.

By the Holy One. The oil by which the priests were anointed was obtained from the sanctuary, and Daniel mentions the coming of Christ as the proper time for anointing the Most Holy (Daniel 9:24). For he was anointed by the Father in order to pour out on us a great abundance from his own fullness. Hence it follows that people are not really made wise by the acumen of their own minds, but by the illumination of the Spirit; and further, that we do not share in the Spirit except through Christ, who is the true sanctuary and our only high priest.

21. No lie comes from the truth. He gives them a rule by which they could distinguish truth from falsehood. It is not the dialectic proposition that falsehood differs from truth, but what he says is applied to what is practical and useful. It is like saying that they not only held what was true, but were also so strengthened against the fallacies of ungodly people that they wisely took care of themselves.

22. Who is the liar? He does not assert that it was only those who denied that the Son of God appeared in the flesh who were liars, but that those people surpassed all others.

The one who denies that Jesus is the Christ? He is not speaking about the prince of defection who was to occupy God's seat, but about all those who seek to overthrow Christ. In order to magnify their crime, he asserts that the Father, no less than the Son, is denied by them. It is like saying that they no longer have any religion, because they throw God away completely. And he later confirms this by adding this reason, that the Father cannot be separated from the Son.

23. Everyone who confesses the Son has the Father also. There is no right confession of God without the Father being acknowledged in the Son.

24. Let what you have heard from the beginning abide in you. To the above doctrine he adds an exhortation and, so that it has more weight, he points out the fruit they would receive from obedience. He then urges them to persevere in the faith, so that what they had learned might remain fixed in their hearts.

Abide in you. Here is the fruit of perseverance: those in whom God's truth remains, remain in God.

26. I write these things to you. The apostle excuses himself again for having admonished people who had plenty of knowledge and judgment. But he did this so that they might ask for the Spirit's guidance, in case his warning was in vain. It was like saying, 'I indeed do my part, but still it is necessary for the Spirit of God to direct you in everything; for it is no good my voice sounding in your ears, or rather in the air, unless he speaks within you.'

27. Just as it has taught you, abide in him. He has said that the Spirit remained in them; he now exhorts them to remain in the revelation made by him, and he specifies what revelation it was. 'Remain in Christ,' he says, 'as the Spirit has taught you.'

29. If ye know that he is righteous. Again he passes on to exhortations, so that he mingles these continually with doctrine throughout the letter. But he proves by many arguments that faith is necessarily connected with a holy and pure life. The first argument is that we are spiritually born in the likeness of Christ; hence it follows that no one is born of Christ but those who live righteously. At the same time, it is uncertain whether he means Christ or God when he says that those who are born of him do what is right. It is certainly a manner of speaking used in Scripture, that we are born of God in Christ; but there is nothing wrong with the other interpretation, that those who are renewed by his Spirit are born of Christ.

Chapter 3

1. The second argument is from the dignity and excellence of our calling; for it was no common honour, he says, that the heavenly Father bestowed on us when he adopted us as his children. As this is such a great favour, it should kindle in us a desire for purity, so that we are conformed to his image. And it has to be that anyone who acknowledges himself to be one of God's children should purify himself. To reinforce this exhortation, he emphasizes God's favour; for when he says **see what love the Father has given us**, he means that from mere bounty and benevolence that God makes us his children. Where do we obtain such dignity, unless it is from God's love? Love, then, is declared here to be free. The language is, indeed, not quite right; but the apostle preferred to speak like this rather than not to express what had to be known. In short, he means that the more abundantly God's goodness has been revealed to us, the greater are our obligations to him, according to Paul's teaching when he urged the Romans in view of God's mercy to offer themselves as living sacrifices to him (Romans 12:1). At the same time, we are taught that the adoption of all godly people is free, and does not depend on any regard to works.

When he says that we are **called**, or named, the expression means that it is God himself who declares us to be his children, as he gave a name to Abraham according to what he was.

The world does not know us. It is a trial that grievously assaults our faith, that we are not so much regarded as God's children, or that no mark of such great excellence appears in us, but that, on the contrary, almost the whole world treats us with ridicule and contempt. Hence it can hardly be inferred from our present state that God is a Father to us, for the devil so contrives everything that it obscures this benefit. He obviates this offense by saying that we are not as yet acknowledged to be what we are, because the world does not know God.

2. We are God's children now. He now comes to what everyone knows and feels himself; for though the ungodly may not entice us to give up our hope, yet our present condition is very short of the glory of God's children; for as far as our body is concerned we are dust and a shadow, and death is always before our eyes; we are also subject to a thousand miseries, and the soul is exposed to innumerable evils; so that we always find a hell within us. It is all the more necessary that all our thoughts should be withdrawn from the present view of things, so that the miseries which surround and almost overwhelm us on every side do not shake our faith in the happiness which is as yet hidden. The apostle means that we act very foolishly when we estimate what God has bestowed upon us according to the present state of things, but that we ought with undoubting faith to hold on to what does not yet appear.

What we do know is this: when he is revealed. Our faith cannot stand in any other way but by looking to the coming of Christ. The reason God defers the manifestation of our glory is because Christ has not yet been revealed in the power of his kingdom. So then, this is the only way of sustaining our faith, so that we may wait patiently for the life promised to us. As soon as anyone turns away the least from Christ, he must necessarily fail.

We will be like him. He does not mean that we shall be equal to him; for there must be some difference between the head and the members; but we shall be like him because he will make our vile body like his glorious body, as Paul also teaches us in Philippians 3:21. The apostle intended to show that the final end of our adoption is that what has happened first of all with Christ will in the end be completed in us.

3. All who have this hope. He now draws this inference: that the desire for holiness should not grow cold in us because our happiness has not yet appeared, for that hope is enough; and we know that what is hoped for is hidden as yet. The meaning, then, is that though we do not have Christ present before our eyes now, if we hope in him our hope must excite and stimulate us to follow purity, for it leads us straight to Christ, whom we know to be a perfect pattern of purity.

4. Everyone who commits sin. The import of the passage is that the perverse life of those who indulge themselves in the liberty if sinning is hateful to God, and cannot be borne with by him, because it is contrary to his law. It does not follow, nor can it be inferred, from this that the faithful are iniquitous; because they desire to obey God, and abhor their own vices, and that in every instance; and they also form their own life, as far as they can, according to the law. But when there is a deliberate intention to sin, or a continued course in sin, then the law is transgressed.

5. You know that he was revealed. He shows by another argument how much sin and faith differ from one another; for it is Christ's function to take away sins, and for this purpose he was sent by the Father, and it is by faith we share in Christ's virtue. So then, anyone who believes in Christ necessarily cleansed from sins.

And in him there is no sin. He is not speaking about Christ personally but of his whole body. He denies that there is any more room for sin wherever Christ diffuses his efficacious grace. Therefore he immediately draws the inference that those who remain in Christ do not sin. For if he lives in us by faith, he performs his own work, that is, he cleanses us from sins. From this we see what it is to **sin**. Christ by his Spirit does not perfectly renew us at once, or in an instant, but he continues our renovation throughout life. It cannot be but that the faithful are exposed to sin as long as they live in the world, but as far as the kingdom of Christ prevails in them, sin is abolished. In the meantime they are designated according to the prevailing principle – that is, they are said to be righteous and to live righteously because they sincerely aspire to righteousness.

6. No one who abides in him. He says that the faithful live in Christ because we are united to him by faith, and made one with him.

No one who abides in him sins. They are said not to sin, because they do not consent to sin, though they labour under the infirmity of the flesh but, on the contrary, struggle with groaning, so that they can truly testify with Paul that they do the evil they do not want to do.

No one who sins has either seen him or known him. According to his usual manner he adds the opposite clause, so that we may know that it is in vain to claim faith in Christ and knowledge of him unless there is newness of life. For Christ is never dormant where he reigns, but the Spirit makes his power effective. It may rightly be said of him that he puts sin to flight, just as the sun drives darkness away by its own brightness. Again, this passage teaches us how strong and efficacious the knowledge of Christ is, for it transforms us into his image. So by seeing and knowing we are to understand nothing other than faith.

7. **Everyone who does what is right is righteous.** Here the apostle shows that newness of life is testified by good works. The likeness of which he has spoken (that is, between Christ and his members) appears only by the fruits they produce. It is like saying, 'Since it behoves us to be conformed to Christ, the truth and evidence of this must appear in our life.' Many people would gladly persuade themselves that they have this righteousness buried in their hearts, while iniquity evidently occupies their feet and hands and tongue and eyes.

8. **For the devil has been sinning from the beginning.** As before he did not speak about Christ personally, when he said that he is righteous, but mentioned him as the fountain and the cause of righteousness, so now, when he says that the Devil sins, he includes his whole body, even all the reprobate. It is like saying that it belongs to the devil to entice people to sin. Hence it follows that his members, and all who are ruled by him, give themselves up to commit sin. But the beginning which the apostle mentions is not from eternity, as when he says that the Word is from the beginning; for there is a great difference between God and creatures.

The Son of God has been revealed for this purpose. He repeats in other words what he had said before, that Christ came to take away sins. Hence two conclusions are to be drawn: that those in whom sin reigns cannot be reckoned among the members of Christ, and that they can by no means belong to his body; for wherever Christ exerts his own power, he puts the devil to flight as well as sin. And this is what John immediately adds; for the next sentence, where he says that those who do not sin are born of God (verse 9), is a conclusion from what has gone before.

9. **Those who have been born of God do not sin.** Now, we must consider whether God wholly regenerates us at once, or whether the remains of the old self continue in us until death. If regeneration is not as yet full and complete, it does not exempt us from the bondage of sin except in proportion to its own extent. Hence it appears that the God's children cannot be free from sins, and must sin every day, as far as they still have some remnants of their old nature. Nevertheless, what the apostle argues for stands unalterable, that the purpose of regeneration is to destroy sin, and that all who are born of God lead a righteous and a holy life, because the Spirit of God restrains the lusting of sin.

They cannot sin. Here the apostle ascends higher, for he plainly declares that the hearts of the godly are so effectually governed by the Spirit of God that through an inflexible disposition they follow his guidance. Some theologians, while confessing that the human will cannot desire what is right unless assisted by God's Spirit, imagine such a motion of the Spirit as leaves us the free choice of good and evil. Hence they draw out merits, because we willingly obey the influence of the Spirit, which it is in our power to resist. In short, they desire the grace of the Spirit to be only this, that we are thereby enabled to choose right if we will. John says something quite different here, for he not only shows that we cannot sin, but also that the power of the Spirit is so effectual that it necessarily keeps us in continual obedience to righteousness. Nor is this the only passage of Scripture which teaches us that the will is so formed that it cannot be otherwise than right. For God testifies that he gives a new heart to his children, and promises to do this so that they may walk in his commandments. Besides, John not only shows how efficaciously God works once in man, but plainly says that the Spirit continues his grace in us to the last, so that inflexible perseverance is added to newness of life. Let us not, then, imagine that it is some neutral movement, which leaves people free either to follow or to reject; but let us know that our own hearts are so ruled by God's Spirit that they constantly cling to righteousness.

10. **The children of God ... are revealed.** He sums up by concluding that it is wrong to claim a place and name among the children of God if we do not prove ourselves to be such by a pious and holy life, since this evidence shows that we differ from the children of the devil. But he does not mean that they are manifested in this way so that the whole world recognizes them. He only means that our fruit and adoption always appear in our life.

11. **All who do not do what is right.** To do what is right and to sin are here set in opposition to each other. John says that everyone who does not do what is right is not of God, because all those whom God calls, he regenerates by his Spirit. Hence newness of life is a perpetual evidence of divine adoption.

12–13. **We must not be like Cain.** This is another confirmation, taken from an opposite: in the reprobate and the children of the devil, hatred reigns, and as it were holds the chief place in their life; and John brings forward Cain as an instance. It also serves to console them, as he eventually concludes by saying, **Do not be astonished, brothers and sisters if the world hates you** (verse 13).

14. **We know.** He commends love to us by a remarkable eulogy, because it is evidence of a transition from death to life. From this it follows that if we love the brothers we are blessed, but that we are miserable if we hate them. There is no one who does not wish to be freed and delivered from death. So then, those who by cherishing hatred willingly give themselves up to death must be extremely stupid and senseless. But

when the apostle says that it is known by love that we have passed into life, he does not mean that we are our own deliverers, as though by loving the brothers we could rescue ourselves from death and procure life for ourselves; for he is not here dealing with the cause of salvation, but as love is the special fruit of the Spirit, it is also a sure symbol of regeneration. So then, the apostle is drawing an argument from the sign, and not from the cause. For as no one sincerely loves his brothers unless he is regenerated by the Spirit of God, John rightly concludes that the Spirit of God, who is life, lives in all who love the brothers. But it would be preposterous for anyone to infer from this that life is obtained by love, since love comes afterwards chronologically.

15. Are murderers. To stimulate us still more to love, John shows how detestable hatred is to God. There is no one who does not dread a murderer; we all execrate the very word. But the apostle declares that all who hate their brothers are murderers. He could have said nothing more atrocious; nor is what he says hyperbolical, for those we hate we wish to perish. It does not matter if we keep our hands from mischief; the very desire to do harm, as well as the attempt, is condemned before God. Indeed, when we do not ourselves seek to do an injury, but wish an evil to happen to our brother from someone else, we are murderers.

So then, the apostle defines the thing simply as it is when he ascribes murder to hatred. This proves the folly of people who pay no attention to the crime itself whilst they abominate the word. Why is this? It is because the external face of things engrosses our thoughts; but the inward feeling is called to account before God. Let no one, therefore, extenuate any longer such a grievous evil. Let us learn to refer our judgments to God's tribunal.

16. We know love by this. It would not have been enough to commend love unless its power is understood. As an instance of perfect love, he sets before us the example of Christ. By not sparing his own life, he testified how much he loved us. This, then, is the goal to which he calls them to advance. To sum up, our love is approved when we transfer the love of ourselves to our brothers, so that each of us, as we forget ourselves, seeks the good of others.

17. Anyone who has the world's goods. He speaks now about the common duties of love, which flow from that chief foundation that is, when we are prepared to serve our neighbors even to death. At the same time, he seems to be reasoning from the greater to the less; for anyone who refuses to use his own property to alleviate his brother's needs, while his own life is safe and secure, would be far less likely to put his own life in danger for him. So then, John denies that there is love in us if we withhold

help from our neighbors. But he recommends this external kindness so that he also very rightly expresses the proper way of doing good, and the sort of feeling we ought to have.

Let this be the first proposition, then: that no one truly loves to his brothers if he does not really show this whenever an opportunity occurs. The second is that a person must help his brothers as much as he is able, for the Lord gives us opportunity to exercise love in this way. The third is that each person's need should be attended to, for anyone who needs food and drink, or other things which we have plenty of, requires our help. The fourth is that no act of kindness pleases God unless it is accompanied with sympathy. There are many apparently generous people who do not feel for the miseries of their brothers. But the apostle requires that we have **compassion**, which happens when we feel sympathy with others in their distress just as if it were our own.

God's love. Here he speaks of loving the brothers; why, then, does he mention the love of God? It is because of the principle that the love of God necessarily generates love of the brothers in us. And thus God tests our love to him when he calls us to love people out of regard for himself.

18. Let us love, not in word or speech. The words must be explained like this: 'Let us not profess with our tongues that we love, but prove it by the deed; for this is the only true way of showing love.'

19. Why, does the apostle say, **will reassure our hearts before him?** In these words he is reminding us that faith does not exist without a good conscience; not that assurance arises from it or depends on it, but that we are only really and not falsely assured of our union with God, when he manifests himself in our love by the working of his Holy Spirit. It is always right and proper to consider what the apostle is dealing with; for as he condemns a false profession of faith, he says that we cannot have a genuine assurance before God unless his Spirit produces the fruit of love in us. Nevertheless, though a good conscience cannot be separated from faith, no one should conclude from this that we must look to our works in order that our conscience may be certain.

20. Whenever our hearts condemn us. He proves, on the other hand, that it is useless for people to be called Christians if they do not have the testimony of a good conscience. For if anyone is conscious of guilt, and is condemned by his own heart, much less can he escape God's judgment. Hence it follows that faith is subverted by the disquiet of an evil conscience.

God is greater than our hearts. This refers to judgment, that is, because he sees much more keenly than we do, and searches more minutely and judges more severely. For this reason, Paul says that though he was not conscious of wrong in himself, that did not mean he was justified (1 Corinthians 4:4), for he knew that however carefully he attended to his office, he went wrong in many ways, and through inadvertence was ignorant of mistakes which God perceived. What the apostle means, then, is that someone who is harassed and condemned by his own conscience cannot escape God's judgment.

21. If our hearts do not condemn. Here, arises a difficulty, which seems to leave no confidence in the whole world; for who can be found who does not feel guilty about something? To this I answer that godly people are reproved in this way, but may at the same time be absolved. It is indeed necessary for them to be seriously troubled inwardly for their sins, so that terror may lead them to humility and to a hatred of themselves; but they soon flee to the sacrifice of Christ, where they are sure of peace. Yet in another sense the apostle says that they are not condemned, because however deficient they may confess themselves to be in many things, they are still relieved by this testimony of conscience, so that they truly and from the heart fear God and desire to submit to his righteousness. All who possess this godly feeling, and at the same time know that all their endeavours, however far they may come short of perfection, still please God, are rightly said to have a calm or a peaceful heart, because there is no inward compunction to disturb their calm cheerfulness.

22. Whatever we ask. Confidence and prayer are connected. He has already shown that a bad conscience is inconsistent with confidence, and now he says that no one can really pray to God except those who fear and worship him properly, with a pure heart. The one follows from the other. It is a general truth taught in Scripture, that God does not listen to the ungodly, but that, on the contrary, their sacrifices and prayers are an abomination to him. Hence the door is shut to hypocrites, lest they rush into his presence in contempt of him.

Still, he does not mean that a good conscience must be brought, as though it obtained favour for our prayers. Woe to us if we rely on works, which have nothing in them but cause of fear and trembling. The faithful, then, cannot come to God's tribunal except by relying on Christ the Mediator. But as the love of God is always linked with faith, the apostle severely reproves hypocrites by depriving them of that unique privilege with which God favours his own children; that is, lest they should think that their prayers can reach God.

Because we obey his commandments. He does not mean that confidence in prayer is based on our works; he is only teaching that true religion and the sincere worship of God

cannot be separated from faith. Nor should it seem strange that he uses the word **because,** for an inseparable addition is sometimes mentioned as a cause – as when a person says, 'Because the sun shines on us at noon, there is more heat,' though it does not follow that heat comes from light.

23. And this is his commandment. Again he uses a general truth for his own purpose. The meaning is that such is the discord between us and God that we are kept away from him unless we are united to one another by love. At the same time he is not here commending love alone, as before, but as the companion and attendant of faith.

In the name of his Son. The **name** refers to preaching; and this link deserves to be noticed, for few people understand what it is to believe in Christ. From this manner of speaking we may easily see that the only true faith is that which embraces Christ as he is set forth in the Gospel. That is why there is no faith without preaching, as Paul also shows us in Romans 10:14. We must also notice that the apostle includes faith in the knowledge of Christ; for he is the living image of the Father, and in him are stored up all the treasures of wisdom and knowledge. As soon as we turn aside from him, then, we cannot do anything else but wander in error.

24. All who obey his commandments. John confirms that the union we have with God is evident when we entertain mutual love: not that our union begins by it, but that it cannot be fruitless or without effect whenever it begins to exist. And he proves this by adding a reason: because God does not remain in us unless his Spirit lives in us. But wherever the Spirit is, he necessarily reveals his power and efficacy. Hence we may readily conclude that the only people who remain in God and are united to him are those who keep his commands.

By the Spirit. The sum of what is said is that it is when God's Spirit rules and governs our life that we are clearly seen to be his children. John also teaches us that whatever good works are done by us proceed from the grace of the Spirit, and that the Spirit is not obtained by our righteousness, but is freely given to us.

Chapter 4

He returns to his earlier doctrine, which he had touched upon in the second chapter. As is usual with anything new, many people abused the name of Christ for the purpose of serving their own errors. Some people made a half profession of Christ; and when they obtained a place among his friends, they had more opportunity to injure his cause. Satan took the opportunity to disturb the church, especially through Christ himself; for he is the stumbling-block against whom everybody must stumble who does not keep on the right way, as shown to us by God.

What the apostle says consists of three parts. First, he points to an evil which is dangerous to the faithful, and therefore he urges them to beware. He prescribes how they were to beware, that is, by making a distinction between the spirits; and this is the second part. In the third place, he points out a particular error, the most dangerous to them; he therefore forbids them to listen to those who denied that the Son of God appeared in the flesh. We shall now consider each in order.

In the passage it adds that many false prophets had gone out into the world, and it is convenient to begin with this. The announcement contains a useful admonition, for if Satan had already seduced many people who, under the name of Christ, spread their errors around, then similar instances today need not terrify us. It is always the case with the Gospel that Satan attempts to pollute and corrupt its purity by a variety of errors. Our own age has brought forth some horrible and monstrous sects, and for this reason many people are confused and, not knowing where to turn, cast off all thought for religion because they cannot find any quicker way to extricate themselves from the danger of errors. Such a course is most foolish, for by shunning the light of truth they cast themselves into the darkness of errors. Therefore let this fact remain fixed in our minds, that from the time the Gospel began to be preached, false prophets immediately appeared; and this fact will strengthen us against such offenses.

The antiquity of errors keeps many people firmly tied up, as it were, so that they dare not emerge from them. But here John points out an internal evil which was then in the church. Now, if there were impostors then mixed with the apostles and other faithful teachers, what wonder is it that the doctrine of the Gospel has been suppressed for a long time, and that many corruptions have prevailed in the world? There is, then, no reason why we should not exercise our liberty in distinguishing between truth and falsehood just because the errors are long established.

1. **Do not believe every spirit.** When the church is disturbed by discord and contention, many people are frightened and depart from the Gospel. But the Spirit prescribes to us a very different remedy: the faithful should not accept any doctrine without thought or discrimination. We ought, then, to take heed lest, being offended at the variety of opinions, we should discard teachers, and, together with them, the Word of God. But it is sufficient precaution if we do not listen indiscriminately to every teacher.

I take the word **spirit** to mean someone who boasts that he is endowed with the gift of the Spirit to perform his office as a prophet. It was not permitted for anyone to speak in his own name, nor was credit given to speakers except insofar as they were the organs of the Holy Spirit, in order that prophets might have more authority. God honoured them with his name as though he had separated them from mankind in general. So then, the people who were called 'spirits' were those who represented the Holy Spirit by putting his oracles into words. They brought nothing of their own, nor did they speak on their own authority. But the point of this honourable title was that God's Word should not lose the respect due to it through the humble condition of the minister. For God wanted his Word always to be received from human mouths just as if he himself had appeared from heaven.

Here Satan interposed, sending false teachers to adulterate God's Word, and giving them this name, so that they might deceive people more easily. Thus false prophets have always boldly claimed for themselves whatever honour God had bestowed on his own servants. But the apostle deliberately made use of this name, lest those who falsely claim God's authority should deceive us by their masks.

We ought therefore to note this. The apostle might have said that every sort of person ought not to be believed; but false teachers claimed the Spirit, so he left them to do so. At the same time, he reminded people that their claim was frivolous and nugatory if they did not really exhibit what they professed. It was foolish for anyone to be overawed by the mere sound of such ah honourable name, and not dare to make any inquiry on the subject.

Test the spirits. As all were not true prophets, the apostle here declares that they ought to have been examined and tested. And he addresses not just the whole church, but every individual believer.

But you may ask where this discernment is to be obtained. Those who answer that the Word of God is the rule by which everything that people bring forward ought to be tested are giving some of the answer, but not the whole. I accept that doctrines ought to be tested by God's Word, but unless the Spirit of wisdom is present, having God's Word in our hands will avail little or nothing, for its meaning will not be apparent to us – as, for instance, gold is tested by fire or touchstone, but it can only be done by those who understand how to do it, for neither the touchstone nor fire can be of any use to anyone who does not have the skill. If we are to be fit to judge, we must have the Spirit of discernment to direct us. It would have been in vain for the apostle to command this if no power of judging were supplied, so we may conclude with certainty that godly people will never be left without the Spirit of wisdom as to what is necessary, provided they ask the Lord for him. But the Spirit will only thus guide us to a correct discrimination when we make all our thoughts subject to God's Word; for, it is like the touchstone: it should be regarded as most necessary to us, for it is only true doctrine that is drawn from it.

2. By this you know the Spirit of God. He lays down a special mark by which they might more easily distinguish between true and false prophets. Yet he only repeats here what we have already come across: just as Christ is the object at which faith aims, so also he is the stone on which all heretics stumble. As long as we remain in Christ, then, we are safe; but when we depart from him, faith is lost, and all truth is invalidated.

But let us consider what this confession includes; for when the apostle says that Christ **has come**, we conclude that he had previously been with the Father. This proves his eternal divinity. By saying that he has come **in the flesh**, John means that by putting on flesh he became a real man, with the same nature as we have, so that he might become our brother except that he was free from every sin and corruption. And lastly, by saying that he **has come**, the cause of his coming must be noticed, for it was not for nothing he was sent by the Father. So the office and merits of Christ depend on this.

The heretics in olden times departed from the faith, in one case, by denying the divine nature of Christ, and in another case by denying his human nature. And people who confess Christ to be God and man are still departing from the faith if they do not adhere to the confession which the apostle requires, because they rob Christ of his own merit. Where free-will, merits of works, fictitious modes of worship, satisfactions, the advocacy of saints are set up, how very little remains for Christ!

The apostle, then, meant that since the knowledge of Christ includes the sum and substance of the doctrine concerning true religion, we ought to fix our eyes on that so that we may not be deceived. And doubtless Christ is the end of the law and the prophets; nor do we learn anything else from the Gospel but his power and grace.

3. And this is the spirit of the antichrist. The apostle adds this to make us detest all the more any errors that lead us away from Christ. We have already said that the doctrine concerning the kingdom of Antichrist was well known, and the faithful had been warned about the future scattering of the church so that they might watch out. It was right, then, for them to dread the name as something base and ominous. The apostle now says that all those who reduced Christ were members of that kingdom.

4. You are from God. He had spoken about one antichrist; now he mentions many. But the many were the false prophets who had appeared before the head appeared. The apostle wanted to inspire the faithful to resist impostors courageously and boldly, for we are not too eager when the outcome of the contest is in doubt. Besides, it might have caused good people to be afraid when they saw that the kingdom of Christ had hardly been set up when enemies were ready to suppress it. So then, he says that although they must fight, they have conquered, because they will win. It is like saying that even in the middle of the battle they are already beyond danger, because they will certainly be conquerors.

5. They are from the world. It is no small consolation that those who dare to assail God in us have only the world to aid and help them. And by **the world** the apostle means that portion of which Satan is the prince. Another consolation is also added, when he says that the world embraces through the false prophets what it acknowledges as its own. We see how prone people are to vanity and falsehood. Hence false doctrines easily penetrate and spread far and wide. The apostle says that there is no reason for us to be disturbed because of this, for it is nothing new or unusual that the world, which is wholly fallacious, should readily listen to what is false.

6. We are from God. Though this really applies to all godly people, it refers strictly to the faithful ministers of the Gospel; for here the apostle, with the confidence imparted by the Spirit, is glorying that he and his fellow ministers served God in sincerity, and derived from him whatever they taught. It happens that false prophets boast of the same thing, for it is their custom to deceive under the mask of God; but faithful ministers are quite different from them, because of themselves they only declare what is really manifest in their conduct.

From this we know. The word **this** refers to the two preceding clauses. It is like saying, 'The truth is distinguished from falsehood because some people speak from God, others from the world.'

The spirit of truth and the spirit of error. I think he means simply that the test of doctrine must be whether it comes from God or from the world.

7. Beloved. He returns to the exhortation which he reinforces almost throughout the letter. We have, indeed, said that it is filled with the doctrine of faith and exhortation to love. On these two points he lingers so much that he continually passes from the one to the other.

Let us love one another. He does not mean that we discharge this duty when we love our friends, because they love us; but he is speaking to all the faithful together, so he had to say that they were to exercise mutual love. He confirms this sentence by a reason often adduced before, namely, that no one can prove himself to be a child of God without loving his neighbors; the true knowledge of God necessarily produces love in us.

He also sets in opposition to this, as is his custom, the contrary clause: that there is no knowledge of God when there is no love. And he takes for granted a general principle or truth, that God is love – that is, that his nature is to love us. I know that many people offer more complicated interpretations, and that the ancient writers especially perverted this passage in order to prove the divinity of the Spirit. But the apostle simply means that as God is the fountain of love, this effect flows from him, and is diffused wherever the knowledge of him comes, as he had started the letter by calling him light because there is nothing dark in him, but on the contrary he illuminates everything by his own brightness. Here, then, he is not speaking about God's essence, but showing what we find him to be.

9. God's love was revealed among us in this way. We have the love of God towards us testified also by many other proofs. If you ask why the world has been created, why we have been placed in it to rule over the earth, why we are preserved in life to enjoy innumerable blessings, why we are endued with light and understanding, no other reason can be given except the free love of God. But the apostle here has chosen the principal evidence of it, and what far surpasses everything else. It was not only an immeasurable love that God did not spare his own Son, that by his death he might restore us to life; but it was the most marvellous goodness, which should fill our minds with the greatest wonder and amazement. Christ, then, is so illustrious and remarkable a proof of divine love towards us that whenever we look at him he fully confirms the truth that God is love.

His only Son. He calls him this for the sake of amplifying. It showed more clearly how singularly he loved us, when he exposed his only Son to death for our sakes. He who is his only Son by nature, makes many sons by grace and adoption – all who, by faith, are united to his body. He expresses the purpose for which Christ has been sent by the Father, namely that we may live through him; for without him we are all dead, but by his coming he brought life to us; and unless our unbelief prevents the effect of his grace, we feel it in ourselves.

10. In this is love. He amplifies God's love by another reason: he gave us his own Son at the time when we were enemies, as Paul teaches us in Romans 5:8; but John uses different words – that God, induced by no love of ours, freely loved us. By these words John means to teach us that God's love towards us has been gratuitous.

And though it was the apostle's aim to show how God is an example to be imitated by us, the doctrine of faith which he mixes with it should not be overlooked. God freely loved us – how so? Because he loved us before we were born, and also when, through natural depravity, we had hearts turned away from him, and influenced by no right and pious feelings.

The atoning sacrifice for our sins. Again he points out the cause of Christ's coming and his function. And first, indeed, we are taught by these words that through sin we were all alienated from God, and that this alienation and discord remains until Christ intervenes to reconcile us. Secondly, we are taught that the beginning of our life is when God, having been pacified by the death of his Son, receives us into favour. We find, then, that this honour of expiating for the sins of the world, and of thus taking away the enmity between God and us, belongs only to Christ.

11. Beloved. The apostle now accommodates to his own purpose what he has just taught us about the love of God; for he urges us by God's example to **love one another.** Paul, too, sets Christ before us as offering himself to the Father as a fragrant sacrifice so that each of us might labour to benefit our neighbors (Ephesians 5:2). And John reminds us that our love ought not to be mercenary: he tells us to love our neighbors as **God so loved us;** for we ought to remember that we have been loved freely. And doubtless when we think about our own advantage, or do good things for our friends, it is self-love, and not love to others.

12. No one has ever seen God. The same words are found in the first chapter of John's Gospel; but there John the Baptist was not thinking of exactly the same thing, for he meant only that God could only be known as he has revealed himself in Christ. Here the apostle extends the same truth further, showing that the power of God is comprehended by us by faith and love, so as to know that we are his children and that he dwells in us.

However, he speaks first of love, when he says that God **lives in us** if we love one another; for his love is **perfected** or really proved to be, in us then. It is like saying that God shows himself as present when by his Spirit he forms our hearts so that they entertain brotherly love. For the same purpose he repeats what he had already said, that we know by the Spirit whom he has given us that he lives in us; for it is a confirmation of the previous sentence, because love is the effect or fruit of the Spirit.

So to sum up what has been said, since love is from the Spirit of God, we cannot truly and with a sincere heart love one another unless the Spirit gives us his power. In this way he testifies that he lives in us. But God lives in us by his

Spirit; so then, by love we prove that we have God remaining in us. On the other hand, whoever boasts that he has God and does not love the brothers, his falsehood is proved by this one thing, because he separates God from himself.

14. And we have seen. He now explains the other part of the knowledge of God, which we have referred to, that he communicates himself to us in his Son, and offers himself to be enjoyed by him. It follows from this that he is received by us by faith. For the apostle's purpose is to show that God is so united to us by faith and love that he really lives in us and makes himself in a way visible by the effect of his power, when otherwise he could not be seen by us.

When the apostle says **we have seen and do testify**, he is referring to himself and others. And by seeing he does not mean any sort of seeing, but what belongs to faith, by which they recognized the glory of God in Christ, according to what follows, that he was sent to be **the Saviour of the world**. This knowledge flows from the illumination of the Spirit.

15. Those who confess. He repeats the truth that we are united to God by Christ, and that we cannot be connected with Christ unless God remains in us. Acknowledgement means the same as faith, for though hypocrites boast falsely of faith, the apostle here means only those who believe truly and from the heart. Besides, when he says that **Jesus is the Son of God**, he includes in this brief statement the sum and substance of faith, for nothing is necessary for salvation which faith does not find in Christ.

16. So we have known and believe the love that God has to us. It is the same as saying, 'We have known by believing'; for such knowledge is only attained by faith. But from this we learn how different faith is from an uncertain or doubtful opinion. Besides, though as I have said he meant here to accommodate the last sentence to his readers, he still defines faith in various ways. He had already said that it is to acknowledge that Jesus is the Son of God; now he says that by faith we know God's love towards us. From this we see that God's fatherly love is found in Christ, and that nothing certain is known of Christ except by those who know themselves to be the children of God by his grace. For the Father sets his own Son before us each day in order that he may adopt us in him.

God is love. This is as it were the minor proposition in an argument; for he reasons from faith to love in this way: By faith God lives in us, and God is love; therefore, wherever God remains, love ought to be there. Hence it follows that love is necessarily connected with faith.

17. Love has been perfected among us in this. There are two clauses in this passage – that we share divine adoption when we resemble God as children resemble their father; and, sec-

ondly, that this confidence is invaluable, for without it we must be most miserable.

In the first place, then, he shows why God has embraced us in love, and how we enjoy that grace revealed to us in Christ. Then, God's love to us is what is to be understood here. He says it has been **perfected** because it is poured out abundantly and really given, so that it appears to be complete. But he asserts that the only people who share this blessing are those who, by being conformed to God, prove themselves to be his children. It is, then, an argument from what is an inseparable condition.

That we may have boldness. He now begins to show the fruit of divine love towards us, though afterwards he shows it more clearly from the contrary effect. However, it is an invaluable benefit that we can dare boldly to stand before God. By nature, indeed, we dread the presence of God, and quite rightly so; for, as he is the Judge of the world, and our sins make us guilty, death and hell must come to our minds whenever we think of God. Hence comes the dread which I have mentioned, which makes people shun God as much as they can. But John says that the faithful are not afraid when people mention the last judgment, but that on the contrary they go to God's tribunal confidently and cheerfully, because they feel assured of his fatherly love. Our proficiency in faith can be measured by how well we are prepared in our minds to look forward to the day of judgment.

18. There is no fear in love. John now commends the excellency of this blessing by stating the contrary effect, for he says that we are continually tormented until God delivers us from misery and anguish by the remedy of his own love towards us. The meaning is that just as there is nothing more miserable than to be harassed by continual unrest, the knowledge of God's love towards us brings us the benefit of a peaceful calmness beyond the reach of fear. Hence we see what a singular gift of God it is to be favoured with his love. Moreover, from this doctrine John presently draws an exhortation; but before he exhorts us to duty, he commends to us this gift of God, which by faith removes our fear.

You may ask when perfect love expels fear; for since we are endued only with a taste of divine love towards us, we can never be wholly freed from fear. To this I answer that although fear is not wholly shaken off, it is really expelled when we flee to God as to a quiet haven, safe and free from all danger of shipwreck and storms, for our fear gives way to faith. So then, fear may not be so far expelled that we are no longer assailed by it, but it is expelled sufficiently for it not to torment us or impede the peace which we obtain by faith.

Fear has to do with punishment. Here the apostle amplifies still further the greatness of the grace he is talking about; for as it is a most miserable condition to suffer continual torments, we want nothing more than to present ourselves before God with a quiet conscience and a calm mind.

19. We love. The Greek verb may be either in the indicative or the imperative mood; but the former is the more suitable here, for the apostle, I think, is repeating the preceding sentence, saying that as God has anticipated us by his free love, we ought in return to love him; for the apostle immediately infers that God ought to be loved in our brother, or that the love we have for God ought to be manifested towards our brother. However, if you prefer the imperative mood, the meaning would be nearly the same, that as God has freely loved us, we also ought to love him.

But this love cannot exist unless it generates brotherly love. Hence he says that people are liars if they boast that they love God whilst they hate their brothers.

But the reason he gives does not seem valid enough, for it is a comparison between the less and the greater: If, he says, we do not love our brothers whom we see, much less can we love God who is invisible. Now there are obviously two exceptions; for the love which God has to us is from faith and does not flow from sight, as we find in 1 Peter 1:8; and secondly, the love of God is quite different from the love of human beings; for while God leads his people to love him through his infinite goodness, human beings are worthy of hatred. To this I answer that the apostle here takes for granted what ought no doubt to appear evident to us, that God offers himself to us in those people who bear his image, and that he requires the duties which he does not want himself, to be performed to them. And surely the sharing of the same nature, the need of so many things, and mutual fellowship, must attract us to love, unless we are harder than iron. But John meant something else: he meant to show us how fallacious is the boast of every person who says that he loves God, and yet does not love God's image which is before his eyes.

21. The commandment we have from him is this. This is a stronger argument, drawn from the authority and doctrine of Christ; for he not only gave a command respecting the love of God, but also told us to love our brothers. We must therefore begin with God, so that there may also be a transition to human beings.

Chapter 5

1. Everyone who believes. He gives another reason confirming that faith and brotherly love are united; for since God regenerates us by faith, he must necessarily be loved by us as a Father;

and this love embraces all his children. Faith, then, cannot be separated from love.

That Jesus is the Christ. The first truth is that everyone who **has been born of God** believes that Jesus is the Christ; where, again, you see that Christ alone is set up as the object of faith, as in him it finds righteousness, life, and every blessing that can be desired, and God in all that he is. Hence the only true way of believing is when we direct our minds to him. Besides, to believe that he is the Christ is to hope from him everything that has been promised concerning the Messiah.

Christ. The title is not given here without reason, for it designates the office to which he was appointed by the Father. Under the law, the full restoration of all things, righteousness and happiness were promised through the Messiah; today, the whole of this is more clearly set out in the Gospel. So then, Jesus cannot be received as Christ if salvation is not sought from him, since this is why he was sent by the Father, and is offered to us every day.

Hence the apostle says that all those who really believe have been born of God; for faith is far above the reach of the human mind, so that we must be drawn to Christ by our heavenly Father; for none of us can ascend to him by our own strength. And this is what the apostle teaches us in his Gospel, when he says that those who believe in the name of the one and only Son were not born of natural descent (John 1:13).

2. By this we know. In these words John shows briefly what true love is, namely, that which is towards God. He has hitherto taught us that there is no true love unless our brothers are also loved; for this is always its effect. But now he teaches us that people are rightly and duly loved when God holds the primacy. And it is a necessary definition; for it often happens that we love people apart from God, as unholy and carnal friendships are only based on private advantage of some other evanescent goals. So, having first referred to the effect, he now refers to the cause; for his purpose is to show that mutual love should be cultivated in such a way that God may be honoured.

To the love of God he adds keeping the law, and rightly so; for when we love God as our Father and Lord, reverence must necessarily be connected with love. Besides, God cannot be separated from himself. As, then, he is the source of all righteousness and justice, anyone who loves him must necessarily have their heart prepared to obey righteousness. The love of God, then, is not idle or inactive.

But from this passage we also learn what keeping the law means. If we are only constrained by fear when we obey God by keeping his commands, we are very far from true obedience. So then, the first thing is that our hearts should be devoted to God in willing reverence, and then that our life should be formed according to the rule of the law.

3. His commandments are not burdensome. This has been added lest difficulties, as is usually the case, should damp or lessen our zeal. For those who have pursued a godly and holy life with a cheerful mind and great ardour afterwards grow weary, finding their strength inadequate. Therefore John, to rouse our efforts, says that God's commands are not burdensome.

4. This is the victory. John had said that **whatever is born of God conquers the world.** Now he sets out the way of overcoming it. For it might still be asked where this victory comes from. John makes the victory over the world dependent on faith.

This passage is remarkable, for though Satan continually repeats his dreadful and horrible onsets, the Spirit of God declares that we are beyond the reach of danger; he removes fear, and animates us to fight with courage. And the past time is more emphatic than the present or the future, for John says **this is the victory that conquers,** so that we might feel certain, as though the enemy had already been put to flight. Indeed, it is true that our warfare continues throughout life, that we are in conflicts every day, and that various new battles are stirred up against us on every side at every moment by the enemy; but God does not arm us just for one day, and faith is not that of just one day, but is the perpetual work of the Holy Spirit. We already share in victory, as though we had already conquered.

The world. This has a wide meaning here, for it includes whatever is against God's Spirit; thus, the corruption of our nature is a part of the world; all lusts, all Satan's crafts – in short, whatever leads us away from God. Having such a force to contend with, we have an immense war to carry on, and we would already have been conquered before coming to the contest, and conquered a hundred times a day, if God had not promised us the victory. But God encourages us to fight by promising us the victory. This promise secures for us God's invincible power for all time, and it annihilates all human strength. The apostle does not teach us here that God only brings some help to us, so that with his aid we may be able to resist; he makes victory dependent on faith alone, and faith receives from elsewhere what enables it to overcome. People who sing triumph to their own power, then, take away from God what is his own.

5. Who is it that conquers the world? If we are to conquer Satan and the world, and not succumb to our flesh, we must be diffident about ourselves and rely only on Christ's power.

The one who believes. He means a real apprehension of Christ, or an effectual laying hold on him, by which we apply his power to ourselves.

6. With the water and the blood. I have no doubt that this alludes to the ancient rites of the law. Moreover, the comparison is intended not only to teach us that the law of Moses was abolished by the coming of Christ, but that we may seek in him the fulfilment of those things which the ceremonies formerly typified. And though they were of various kinds, the apostle uses these two terms to denote the whole of holiness and righteousness: **water** washed all filth away, so that people might come before God pure and clean, and **blood** made expiation, and pledged a full reconciliation with God. The law only foreshadowed by external symbols what was to be really and fully achieved by the Messiah.

So then, John proves that Jesus is the Christ of the Lord who had previously been promised, because he brought with him that by which he sanctifies us wholly.

There is no doubt about the **blood** by which Christ reconciled God, but there may be some question about how he came **by water.** It is unlikely that the reference is to baptism. I am sure John here is referring to the fruit and effect of what he recorded in the Gospel story, for what he says there – that water and blood flowed from the side of Christ – is no doubt to be seen as a miracle. I know that such a thing does naturally happen to the dead; but it happened because God planned that Christ's side should become the fountain of blood and water so that the faithful may know that cleansing (of which the ancient baptisms were types) is found in him, and that they might know that what all the sprinklings of blood had indicated was fulfilled.

And the Spirit is the one that testifies. He shows in this clause how the faithful know and feel the power of Christ; it is because the Spirit makes them certain. And, so that their faith might not vacillate, he adds that a full and real firmness or stability is produced by the testimony of the Spirit. And he calls the Spirit **truth** because his authority cannot be doubted, and should be quite enough for us.

7. There are three that testify. God, in order to confirm our faith in Christ most abundantly, testifies in three ways that we ought to rest in him. For just as our faith acknowledges three person in the one divine essence, so it is called in three ways to Christ that it may rest on him.

8. These three. He applies what he had said about 'the water and the blood' to his own purpose, in order that those who reject Christ might have no excuse; for he proves, with very strong and clear testimonies, that it is he who had previously been promised. Water and blood, being the pledges and effects of salvation, really testify that he had been sent by God. He adds a third witness, **the Spirit.** The Holy Spirit has first place, for without him the water and blood would have flowed without any benefit; for it is he who seals on our hearts the testimony of the water and blood; it is he who by his power makes the fruit of Christ's death come to us; indeed, he makes the blood shed for our redemption penetrate into our hearts, or, to put it in a nutshell, he makes Christ with all his blessings become ours. Whatever signs of divine glory may shine in Christ, they would be obscure to us and escape our vision if the Holy Spirit did not open the eyes of faith for us.

9. If we receive human testimony. Reasoning from the less to the greater, he proves how ungrateful we are when we reject Christ, who has been approved by God; for if in worldly affairs we stand to people's words when they may lie and deceive, how unreasonable it is that God should have less credit given to him, when sitting as it were on his own throne, where he is the supreme judge. So then, our own corruption alone prevents us from receiving Christ, since he gives us every proof of his power. Besides, it is not just what the Spirit imprints on our hearts that he calls the testimony of God, but also what we derive from the water and the blood. For that power of cleansing and expiating was not earthly but heavenly. Hence the blood of Christ is not to be estimated according to the common human manner, but we must rather look to the intention of God, who ordained it for blotting out sins, and also to the divine efficacy which comes from it.

The testimony of God is greater. Having reminded us that God deserves to be believed much more than human beings, the apostle now adds that we can have no faith in God without believing in Christ, because God sets him alone before us and makes us stand in him. Hence he infers that we believe in Christ safely and with tranquil minds, because God by his authority warrants our faith. He does not say that God speaks outwardly, but that every one of the godly feels within that God is the author of his faith. Hence it appears how different faith is from a fading opinion dependent on something else.

10. Those who do not believe in God. As the faithful possess the benefit of knowing themselves to be beyond the danger of erring, because they have God as their foundation, so John makes the ungodly to be guilty of extreme blasphemy because they charge God with falsehood.

11. God has given us eternal life. Having now shown the benefit, he invites us to believe. It is, indeed, a reverence due to God, that we

immediately receive, as being beyond controversy, whatever he declares to us. But since he freely offers life to us, our ingratitude will be intolerable, unless we receive with prompt faith this sweet and lovely doctrine. Doubtless the apostle's words are intended to show that we should not only reverently obey the Gospel, lest we affront God, but also that we should love it because it brings us eternal life. From this we also learn what is especially to be sought in the Gospel, namely the free gift of salvation. In the Gospel, God exhorts us to repentance and fear, and this should not be separated from the grace of Christ.

But the apostle, in order to keep us altogether in Christ, repeats that life is found in him. It is like saying that no other way of obtaining life has been appointed for us by God the Father. And indeed the apostle briefly includes here three things. First, we are all given up to death until God in his unmerited favour restores us to life; for he clearly says that life is a gift from God; and hence also it follows that we are destitute of it, and that it cannot be acquired by merit. Secondly, he teaches us that this life is conferred on us by the Gospel, because there the goodness and fatherly love of God is made known to us. Lastly, he says that we cannot share in this life without believing in Christ.

12. Whoever does not have the Son. This confirms the last sentence. It should, indeed, have been enough that God made life to be in none but in Christ, so that it might be sought in him; but lest anyone should turn away to someone else, he excludes from the hope of life all who do not seek it in Christ. We know what it is to have Christ, for he is possessed by faith. So then, John shows that all who are separated from the body of Christ are without life.

13. I write these things to you. There should be daily progress in faith, and so he says that he was writing to those **who believe in the name of the Son of God,** so that they might believe more firmly and with greater certainty, and thus enjoy a fuller confidence as to eternal life. So then, the use of doctrine is not only to initiate the ignorant in the knowledge of Christ, but also to confirm more and more those who have already been taught. Therefore it becomes us to attend assiduously to the duty of learning, so that our faith may increase throughout our life. For there are still in us many remnants of unbelief, and our faith is so weak that what we believe is not yet really believed unless there is fuller confirmation.

But we should notice the way in which faith is confirmed. It is by having the office and power of Christ explained to us. The apostle says that he wrote these things (that is, that eternal life is to be sought only in Christ) in order that those who were already believers might believe, that is, make progress in believing. It is therefore the duty of a godly teacher, in order to confirm disciples in the faith, to extol the grace of Christ as much as possible, so that we may be satisfied with that and seek nothing else.

The apostle also teaches us in this passage that Christ is the unique object of faith, and that the hope of salvation is added to the faith which we have in his name. In this case the point of believing is that we become God's children and heirs.

14. This is the boldness. He commends the faith which he mentioned by its fruit, or he shows where our confidence is especially; namely, that godly people dare confidently to call on God.

Let us, then, bear in mind the apostle's declaration that calling on God is the chief test of our faith, and that we do not call on God truly or in faith unless we are sure that our prayers will not be in vain. The apostle denies that we are endued with faith if we are doubtful and hesitate.

According to his will. By this expression John wanted to remind us incidentally about the right way of praying, which is when people subject their own wishes to God. Although God has promised to do whatever his people may ask, he does not allow them an unbridled liberty to ask whatever may come into their heads. He has also prescribed for them a law according to which they are to pray. And doubtless nothing is better for us than this restriction; for if each of us was allowed to ask whatever we pleased, and if God were to indulge us in our wishes, it would be to provide very badly for us. We do not know what is expedient for us; we boil over with corrupt and harmful desires. But God supplies a double remedy, lest we should pray other than according to his own will; for he teaches us by his Word what he wants us to ask, and he has also set his Spirit over us as our guide and ruler, to restrain our feelings so as not to allow them to wander beyond due bounds. We do not know what or how to pray, says Paul, but the Spirit helps us in our weakness and excites in us groans that words cannot express (Romans 8:26). We should also ask the Lord to direct and guide our prayers; for, as I said, God in his promises has fixed the right way of praying.

15. And if we know. This is not a superfluous repetition, as it seems to be. What the apostle said generally about the success of prayer is now confirmed in a special manner: godly people pray to God only for what they obtain. But when he says that all the prayers of the faithful are heard, he is speaking about right and humble petitions, and such as are consistent with the rule of obedience. The faithful do not give free rein to their desires, or indulge in anything that pleases them, but always in their prayers consider what God commands.

16. If you see your brother or sister. The apostle extends the benefits of faith still further, so that our prayers may also help our brothers and sisters. It is a wonderful thing that as soon as we are oppressed, God kindly invites us to himself, and is ready to give us help; but his hearing us ask for others is no small confirmation to our faith, in order that we may be fully assured that we shall never meet with a repulse in our own case.

Committing what is not a mortal sin. In order that we do not give up all hope of the salvation of those who sin, he shows that God does not punish their falls so grievously as to repudiate them. Hence it follows that we should regard them as brothers, since God retains them in the number of his children. John denies that sins lead to death – not only those by which the saints offend every day, but even when it happens that God's wrath is grievously provoked by them. For as long as there is room for pardon, death does not entirely retain its dominion.

There is a sin that is mortal. I have already said that this refers to the sin to which no hope of forgiveness is left. But what is this? It must be very atrocious, when God punishes it as severely as this. It may be gathered from the context that it is not, as people say, a partial fall, or a transgression of a single commandment, but apostasy, by which people wholly alienate themselves from God. For the apostle later adds that the children of God do not continue to sin, that is, they do not forsake God and wholly surrender themselves to Satan, to be his slaves. No wonder such a defection leads to death, for God never deprives his own people of the grace of the Spirit, but they always have some spark of true religion. So then, people who fall away like this, and have no fear of God, must be reprobate and given up to destruction.

If anyone asks whether the door of salvation is closed against their repentance, the answer is obvious – as they are given up to a reprobate mind, and are destitute of the Holy Spirit, they cannot do anything other than obstinately become worse and worse, and add more and more sins. Moreover, as the sin and blasphemy against the Spirit always brings with it a defection of this kind, there is no doubt that it is pointed out here.

But again, you may ask what evidence tells us that someone's fall is fatal. If we could not be certain of this, the apostle would not have been able to say that they were not to pray for a sin of this kind. It is right, then, to decide sometimes whether there is still hope. This, indeed, I agree; and it is evident beyond dispute from this passage; but as this very seldom happens, and as God sets before us the infinite riches of his grace, and bids us be merciful according to his own example, we should not rashly conclude that anyone has brought the judgment of eternal death on himself. On the contrary, love should make us hope for good. But if some people's impiety does not appear to us anything other than hopeless, as though the Lord pointed it out by his finger, we should not argue with God's just judgment, or seek to be more merciful than he is.

17. **All wrongdoing is sin, but there is sin that is not mortal.** If you take it as a contrast, the sense would fit: 'Though all wrongdoing is sin, every sin does not lead to death.'

18. **The evil one does not touch them.** This means a deadly wound: God's children do not remain untouched by Satan's assaults, but they ward off his blows with the shield of faith, so that they do not penetrate the heart. Hence spiritual life is never extinguished in them. This is not to sin. Though the faithful do fall through the weakness of the flesh, they groan under the burden of sin, loathe themselves, and do not cease to fear God.

19. **We know that we are God's children.** He deduces an exhortation from his previous doctrine; for what he had declared was common to God's children he now applies to those he was writing to. He did this to stimulate them to beware of sin, and to encourage them to repel Satan's attacks.

The whole world lies under the power of the evil one. No doubt the apostle includes the whole human race. There is no reason why we should hesitate to shun the world, which holds God in contempt and gives itself up to the bondage of Satan; nor is there any reason why we should fear its enmity, because it is alienated from God. In short, since corruption pervades all nature, the faithful ought to study self-denial; and since nothing but wickedness and corruption is seen in the world, they have to disregard flesh and blood so that they may follow God. At the same time we should also add that God is the one who has called them, so that under his protection they may oppose all the machinations of the world and Satan.

20. **We know that the Son of God has come.** As the children of God are attacked on every side, he encourages and exhorts them to persevere in resisting their enemies. This is because they fight under God's banner, and know for certain that they are ruled by his Spirit; but now he reminds them where this knowledge is especially to be found.

And hath given us understanding. God has been made known to us in such a way that there is now no reason to doubt. It is not without

reason that the apostle dwells on this point; for unless our faith is really founded on God, we shall never stand firm in the battle. The apostle shows that we have obtained a sure knowledge of the true God through Christ, so that we may not fluctuate in uncertainty.

That we may know him who is true. By this he does not mean one who tells the truth, but him who is really God; and he calls him this to distinguish him from all idols. It is **true** as opposed to fictitious.

And Christ is said to have **given us understanding** not only because he shows us in the Gospel what sort of being the true God is, and also illuminates us by his Spirit, but because in Christ himself we have God manifested in the flesh, as Paul says, since in him all the fullness of the Deity lives, and in him are hidden all the treasures of knowledge and wisdom (Colossians 2:9). Thus it is that God's face in a way appears to us in Christ – not that there was no knowledge, or a doubtful knowledge, of God before the coming of Christ, but that now he reveals himself more fully and more clearly.

He is the true God and eternal life. Arians have attempted to escape this passage, but we have here a remarkable testimony to the divinity of Christ. The Arians apply this passage to the Father, as though the apostle was repeating that he is the true God. But nothing could be more cold than such a repetition. He has already said twice that the true God is he who has been made known to us in Christ; why should he add again, **He is the true God?** It applies most fitly to Christ; for after teaching us that Christ is the guide by whose hand we are led to God, he now, by way of amplification, affirms that Christ is that God, lest we should think that we are to look elsewhere. He confirms this by what is added: **and eternal life.** It is doubtless the same thing as being **the true God, and eternal life.** I say, then, that Christ is rightly called **eternal life**, and no one can deny that this manner of speaking occurs all the time in John.

The meaning is that when we have Christ, we enjoy the true and eternal God, for nowhere else is he to be sought; and, secondly, that how we come to share in eternal life, is because it is offered to us in Christ though it is hidden in the Father. The origin of life is indeed the Father; but the fountain from which we are to draw it is Christ.

21. **Keep yourselves from idols.** Although this is a separate sentence, it is a sort of appendix to the preceding doctrine. The life-giving light of the Gospel ought to scatter and dissipate not only darkness but also all mists from the minds of the godly. The apostle not only condemns idolatry, but commands us to beware of all images and idols. In this way he intimates that

the worship of God cannot continue uncorrupted and pure whenever people begin to be in love with idols or images. For superstition is so innate in us that the least occasion will infect us with its contagion. Dry wood will not burn so easily when coals are put under it, as idolatry will lay hold on and engross our minds when it is given the chance. And who does not see that images are the sparks? Or rather torches, which are sufficient to set the whole world on fire.

2 JOHN

Matthew Henry

Here we find a canonical letter written, principally, not only to a single person, but to a woman – to a heroine in the Christian religion, honoured by divine providence and distinguished by divine grace, and dignfied also by an apostle's letter.

Contents

See also *Outlines of the New Testament Books*, p. 906

The apostle greets an honourable lady and her children. (1–4)

He recommends to the faith and love. (5–6)

He warns them of deceivers, and to take care of themselves. (7–8)

He teaches how to treat those who do not bring the doctrine of Christ. (10–11)

Leaving other things for personal conversation, he concludes the letter. (12–13)

1. Ancient letters began, as here, with greeting and good wishes; as far as may be, religion consecrates old forms and turns compliments into real expressions of life and love. Here we have, as usual:

1. The person who is sending the greeting – not expressed by name, but by a chosen description, **the elder**. The expression, and style, and love indicate that the penman was the same as that of the previous letter; he is now **the elder**, emphatically and eminently so; possibly, the oldest apostle now living; the chief **elder** in the church of God.

2. The people who are being greeted – a noble Christian **the elect lady and her children**. A lady, a person eminent by birth, education, and estate – though usually not many of noble birth are called (see 1 Corinthians 1:26). Here is a pattern for high-ranking people of the same sex.

Elect lady: not only a choice one, but one chosen by God.

This **lady and her children** are further distinguished by the respect paid to them,

(a) By the apostle himself – **whom I love in the truth**, or 'in truth' – whom I sincerely and heartily love.

(b) By all her Christian acquaintance, all the religious people who knew her – **and not only I but also all who know the truth**.

2–4. Here we see, first, the greeting, which is indeed an apostolic benediction. Notice from whom these blessings are craved (1) **from God the Father**, the God of grace; (2) **from Jesus Christ**: he is the Author and Communicator of these heavenly blessings, and is distinguished by this emphatic description, **the Father's Son**.

From these divine persons the apostle craves (1) **Grace** – divine favour and goodwill, the spring of all good things. (2) **Mercy** – free pardon and forgiveness; those who are already rich in **grace** need continual forgiveness. (3) **Peace** – tranquillity of spirit and serenity of conscience, in an assured reconciliation with God, together with all safe and sanctified outward prosperity.

5–6.

We come now more into the design and substance of the letter.

The apostle's request

But now, dear lady, I ask you. Whether out of deference to her ladyship, or apostolic meekness, or both, he condescends to beseech.

What he requests

What the apostle requests of the chosen lady and her children is Christian sacred love – **let us love one another** (verse 5). Those who are eminent in any Christian virtue still have room to grow in it.

1. This love is recommended, first of all, as an obligation – it is a **commandment**. It is urged from the antiquity of the obligation – it is **not … a new commandment, but one we have had from the beginning** (verse 5). This command of mutual Christian love may be said to be a **new** one in that it had been newly enacted and sanctioned by the Lord Christ.

2. Then this love is illustrated by its fruitful nature: **And this is love, that we walk according to his commandments.** (verse 6). The test of our love to God is our obedience to him.

7–9.

The bad news

In the principal part of this letter we find, first of all, the bad news communicated to the lady – that seducers are about (verse 7). This report is introduced as giving a reason: 'You need to maintain your love, for there are destroyers of it in the world. Those who subvert the faith destroy this love. Secure your walk according to God's commands; this will secure you. Your stability is likely to be tried – for **many deceivers have gone out into the world.**'

1. Here is the description of the deceivers and their deceit: **those who do not confess that Jesus Christ has come in the flesh** (verse 7).

2. Here is the aggravation of the case: such a person is **the deceiver and the antichrist** (verse 7). He deludes souls and undermines the glory and kingdom of the Lord Christ.

The apostle's advice

Second, we find the counsel given to this chosen household concerning these deceivers. Now care and caution are needed: **Look to yourselves** (verse 8). Two things they must beware of:

1. They must **not lose** what **we have worked** (verse 8), what they have done or what they have gained.

2. They must not lose their reward, none of it, no part of that honour, or praise, or glory, that they once stood fair for. **May receive a full reward** (verse 8). The way to attain the full reward is to remain true to Christ, and constant in religion to the end.

The reason for this advice

The reason for the apostle's counsel, and of their care and caution about themselves, is twofold:

1. The danger and evil of departure from Gospel light and revelation: it is in effect and reality a departure from God himself (verse 9a).

2. The advantage and happiness of firm adherence to Christian truth is that it unites us to Christ. Thus it unites us also to the Father, for they are both one (verse 9b).

10–11.

How the deceivers should be treated

Due warning having been given concerning seducers, the apostle gives direction concerning their treatment. They are not to be entertained as the ministers of Christ. The Lord Christ will distinguish them from such, and wants his disciples to do the same. The direction is negative:

1. 'Do not support them.' **Do not receive into the house** (verse 10).

2. 'Do not bless their enterprises.' **Or welcome anyone who comes to you.** 'Do not give their service your prayers and good wishes.'

The reason for this prohibition

The reason the apostle forbids the support and patronage of the deceiver is that (verse 11).

12–13.

The apostle concludes this letter, first, by adjourning many things until he meets them personally (verse 12). He supposes that some things are better spoken than written.

Second, he presents the greetings of some near relatives of this lady (verse 13). Grace was abundant towards this family; here are two **elect** sisters, and probably their chosen **children**.

3 JOHN

Matthew Henry

Introduction

Christian communion is exerted and cherished by letter. Christians are to be commended in the practical proof of their professed subjection to the Gospel of Christ. The animating and countenancing of generous and public-spirited people is doing good to many. To this end, the apostle sends this encouraging letter to his friend Gaius, in which also he complains of the quite opposite spirit and practice of a certain minister, and confirms the good report concerning another who is more worthy to be imitated.

Contents

See also *Outlines of the New Testament Books,* p. 907

The apostle congratulates Gaius on the prosperity of his soul (1–2)

and upon the fame he had among good Christians (3–4)

and upon his charity and hospitality to Christ's servants. (5–6)

He complains of contemptuous treatment by an ambitious Diotrephes. (9–10)

He recommends Demetrius (12)

and hopes to visit Gaul shortly. (13–14)

1–2.

The sacred penman who writes and sends the letter
He is not, indeed, named here, but given a more general description – the elder. He is elder by years and by office: honour and deference are due to both. Some people have questioned whether this is John the apostle or not, but his style and spirit seem to shine in it.

The person greeted and honoured by the letter
The previous letter was directed to a chosen lady, this to a chosen gentleman. Such people are worthy of esteem and value. He is designated, first, by his name, **Gaius.** Then, he is designated by the kind expressions of the apostle to him – **beloved** and **whom I love in the truth.** Gaius is abiding and walking in **the truth,** as it is in Jesus.

The greeting
The greeting contains a prayer, and introduced by an affectionate compellation – **Beloved** one who is dear in Christ.

Here is his good wish for his friend, that his body **may go well** as well as his **soul.**

3–8.

In these verses we have, first, the good report that the apostle had received concerning this friend of his: **friends** came and **testified to your faithfulness to the truth** (verse 3). In this we may see:

1. The testimony or thing testified concerning the sincerity of his religion, and devotion to God; and this is evinced by his love, **your love** (verse 6), which includes his love to the brothers, kindness to the poor, hospitality to Christian strangers, and readiness to accommodate them for the service of the Gospel.

2. The audience, or judicatory, before which the report and testimony were given – **the church** (verse 6).

Second, we have the report which the apostle himself gives of him, introduced by an endearing appellation again – (verse 5).

1. He was hospitable, good to **friends**, even to **strangers**.

2. He was conscientious in what he did: **you do faithfully whatever you do.**

Third, we see the apostle's joy in the good report itself, and the good ground of it: **I was overjoyed when some of the friends arrived and testified …** (verse 3); **I have no greater joy than this, to hear that my children are walking in the truth,** in what the Christian religion teaches (verse 4). The best evidence for our having **the truth** is to be **walking in the truth.** Good people will greatly rejoice when other people's souls are getting along well.

Fourth, we see the direction the apostle gives his friend concerning further treatment of the brothers that were with him: **You will do well to send them on in a manner worthy of God** (verse 6). It seems to have been customary in those days of love to attend travelling ministers and Christians, at least some part of their way (see 1 Corinthians 16:6). It is a kindness to a stranger to be guided in his way; and a pleasure to travellers to meet with suitable company.

9–11.

Here is a very different example and character; an officer, a minister in the church, less generous, and communicative than the private Christians. Ministers may sometimes be out-shone, out-done.

In reference to this minister, we see, first, his name – a Gentile name – **Diotrephes** (verse 9), attended with an unchristian spirit.

Second, we see his temper and spirit – full of pride and ambition – he **likes to put himself first.** This ferment soon sprang up and got to work. It is an ill unbecoming character of Christ's ministers, to love to be first, to affect presidency and precedency in the church of God.

Third, we see his contempt of the apostle's authority and letter and friends:

1. His authority: **what he is doing** contrary to our instructions, **spreading false charges against us.** Strange that the contempt should be so great! But ambition will breed malice against those who oppose it.

2. His friends, the brothers he recommended: **he refuses to welcome the friends** (verse 10). Many people are thrown out of the church who should be received there with satisfaction and welcome. But woe to those who cast out the brothers whom the Lord Christ will take into his own communion and kingdom!

Then, in addition to Diotrephes' character, there is advice about it, dissuasion from copying such a pattern, and indeed any evil at all: **Beloved, do not imitate what is evil but imitate what is good** (verse 11). Do not imitate such unchristian, pernicious evil, but pursue the contrary good, in wisdom, purity, peace, and love.

12–14.

The character of another person

Demetrius (verse 12) is not much known otherwise, but here his name will live. A name in the Gospel, a fame in the churches, is better than that of sons and daughters. His character was his commendation.

1. His commendation was general: **Everyone has testified favourably about Demetrius.** Few are well spoken of by all; and sometimes it is ill to be so. But universal integrity and goodness are the way to (and sometimes obtain) the universal applause.

2. His commendation was deserved and well founded: **and so has the truth itself** (verse 12). Some people are well spoken of, but not by the truth itself.

The conclusion of the letter

1. Some things are left until they meet personally (verses 13–14). Many things may be more appropriately communicated directly than by letter.

2. Observe the blessing: **Peace to you.** May all happiness be with you. Those who are good and happy themselves wish other to be so as well.

3. A public greeting is sent to Gaius: **The friends send you their greetings.** A friend to the propagation of religion deserves a common remembrance. And these pious people show their friendship to religion as well as to Gaius.

4. The apostle particularly greets the Christians in Gaius's church or vicinity: **Greet the friends there, each by name.** I doubt if there were very many to be greeted personally, but we must learn humility as well as love. The lowest in the church of Christ should be greeted. And people may well greet one another on earth if they hope to live together in heaven. And the apostle who had reclined next to Jesus lays Christ's friends in his heart.

JUDE

A.R. Faussett

Introduction
Author

He calls himself in the address 'the servant of Jesus Christ, and brother of James.' See *Introduction to the Epistle of James,* in proof of James the *apostle,* and James *the Lord's brother,* the bishop of Jerusalem, being one and the same person. Ga 1:19 alone seems to me to prove this. Similarly, Jude the brother of our Lord, and Jude the apostle, seem to be one and the same. JEROME [*Against Helvidius*] rightly maintains that by the Lord's brethren are meant his cousins, children of Mary and Cleophas (the same as Alphæus). From 1Co 9:5 (as 'brethren of the Lord' stands between 'other apostles' and 'Cephas'), it seems natural to think that the *brethren of the Lord* are distinguished from the apostles only because *all* his brethren were not apostles, but only James and Jude. Jude's reason for calling himself 'brother of Jesus,' was that James, as bishop of Jerusalem, was better known than himself. Had he been, in the strict sense, *brother of our Lord,* he probably would have so entitled himself. His omission of mention of his *apostleship* is no proof that he was not an apostle; for so also James omits it in his heading; and Paul, in his Epistles to the Philippians, Thessalonians, and Philemon, omits it. Had the writer been a counterfeiter of the apostle Jude, he would doubtless have called himself an 'apostle.' He was called also Lebbæus and Thaddeus, probably to distinguish him from Judas Iscariot, the traitor. Lebbæus, from *Hebrew* 'leeb,' 'heart,' means *courageous.* Thaddeus is the same as Theudas, from *Hebrew* 'thad,' the 'breast.' Luke and John, writing later than Matthew, when there would be no confusion between him and Judas Iscariot, give his name Judas.

The only circumstance relating to him recorded in the Gospels occurs in Joh 14:22, 'Judas saith unto Him, not Iscariot, Lord, how is it that Thou wilt manifest Thyself unto us, and not unto the world?' JEROME [*Commentary on Matthew*] says that he was sent to Edessa, to Abgarus, king of Osroene, or Edessa, and that he preached in Syria, Arabia, Mesopotamia, and Persia, in which last country he suffered martyrdom. The story is told on EUSEBIUS' authority, that Abgarus, on his sickbed, having heard of Jesus' power to heal, sent to beg Him to come and cure him, to which the Lord replied, praising his faith, that though he had not seen the Saviour, he yet believed; adding, 'As for what thou hast written, that I should come to thee, it is necessary that all those things for which I was sent should be fulfilled by Me in this place, and that having filled them I should be received up to Him that sent Me. When, therefore, I shall be received into heaven, I will send unto thee some one of My disciples who shall both heal thy distemper and give life to thee and those with thee.' Thomas is accordingly said to have been inspired to send Thaddeus for the cure and baptism of

Abgarus. The letters are said to have been shown Thaddeus among the archives of Edessa. It is possible such a message was verbally sent. and the substance of it registered in writing afterwards (compare 2Ki 5:1-27; and Mt 15:22). Hegesippus (in Eusebius [*Ecclesiastical History,* 3.20]) states that when Domitian inquired after David's posterity, some grandsons of Jude, called the Lord's brother, were brought into his presence. Being asked as to their possessions, they said that they had thirty-nine acres of the value of nine thousand denarii, out of which they paid him taxes, and lived by the labour of their hands, a proof of which they gave by showing the hardness of their hands. Being interrogated as to Christ and His kingdom, they replied that it was not of this world, but heavenly; and that it would be manifested at the end of the world, when He would come in glory to judge the living and the dead.

Authenticity

Eusebius [*Ecclesiastical History,* 3.25], reckons it among the *Antilegomena* or *controverted* Scriptures, 'though recognized by the majority.' The reference to the contest of Michael, the archangel, with the devil, for the body of Moses, not mentioned elsewhere in the Old Testament, but found in the *apocryphal* 'Book of Enoch,' probably raised doubts as to its authenticity, as Jerome [*On Illustrious Men,* 4] says. Moreover, its not being addressed to one particular Church, or individual, caused it not to be so immediately recognized as canonical. A counterfeiter would have avoided using what did not occur in the Old Testament, and which might be regarded as apocryphal.

As to the book of Enoch, if quoted by Jude, his quotation of a passage from it gives an inspired sanction only to *the truth of that passage,* not to the whole book; just as Paul, by inspiration, sanctions particular sentiments from Aratus, Epimenides, and Menander, but not all their writings. I think, rather as there is some slight variation between Jude's statement and that of the book of Enoch, that Jude, though probably not ignorant of the book of Enoch, stamps with inspired sanction the current tradition of the Jews as to Enoch's prophecies; just as Paul mentions the names of the Egyptian magicians, 'Jannes and Jambres' (2Ti 3:8), not mentioned in the Old Testament. At all events, the prophecy ascribed to Enoch by Jude was really his, being sanctioned as such by this inspired writer. So also the narration as to the archangel Michael's dispute with Satan concerning the body of Moses, is by Jude's inspired authority (Jude 1:9) declared true. The book of Enoch is quoted by Justin Martyr, Irenaeus, Clement of Alexandria. Clement of Alexandria [*Adumbrations,* in *Epistle of Jude,* p. 1007] says, 'Jude, through reverential awe, did not call himself *brother,* but *servant,* of Jesus Christ, and brother of James.'

To whom addressed

The references to Old Testament history, Jude 1:5,7, and to Jewish tradition, Jude 1:14, make it likely that *Jewish* Christians are the readers to whom Jude mainly (though including also *all* Christians, Jude 1:1) writes, just as the kindred Epistle, Second Peter, is addressed primarily to the same class; compare *Introduction* to First Peter and *Introduction* to Second Peter. The persons stigmatized in it were not merely *libertines* (as Alford thinks), though no doubt that was one of their prominent characteristics, but heretics in *doctrine,* 'denying the only Lord God, and our Saviour Jesus Christ.' Hence he urges believers 'earnestly to contend for *the faith* once delivered unto the saints' (Jude 1:3). Insubordination, self-seeking, and licentiousness, the fruit of Antinomian teachings, were the evils against which Jude warns his readers; reminding them that, to build themselves in their most holy faith, and to pray in the Holy Ghost, are the only effectual safeguards. The same evils, along with mocking skepticism, shall characterize the last days before the final judgment, even as in the days when Enoch warned the ungodly of the coming flood. As Peter was in Babylon in writing 1Pe 5:13, and probably also in writing Second Peter (compare *Introduction* to First Peter and *Introduction* to Second Peter), Jude addressed his Epistle primarily to *the Jewish Christians in and about Mesopotamian Babylon* (a place of great resort to the Jews in that day), or else to *the Christian Jews dispersed in Pontus, Galatia, Cappadocia, Asia, and Bithynia* (1Pe 1:1), the persons addressed by Peter. For Jude is expressly said to have preached in *Mesopotamia* [JEROME, *Commentary on Matthew*], and his Epistle, consisting of only twenty-five verses, contains in them no less than eleven passages from Second Peter (see my *Introduction* to Second Peter for the list). Probably in Jude 1:4 he witnesses to the fulfilment of Peter's prophecy, 'There *are* certain men *crept in unawares,* who were before of old ordained (rather as *Greek,* 'forewritten,' that is, announced *beforehand* by the apostle Peter's *written* prophecy) to this *condemnation,* ungodly men *denying* the only Lord God, and our Lord Jesus Christ.' Compare 2Pe 2:1, 'There *shall* be false teachers among you who *privily* shall bring in *damnable* heresies, even *denying the Lord* that bought them, and bring upon themselves swift *destruction.*' Also Jude 1:17,18 plainly refers to *the very words* of 2Pe 3:3, 'Remember the words which were spoken before of the *apostles* of our Lord Jesus; how they told you there should be *mockers in the last time* who should *walk after their own* ungodly *lusts.*' This proves, in opposition to ALFORD, that Jude's Epistle is later than Peter's (whose inspiration he thus confirms, just as Peter confirms Paul's, 2Pe 3:15,16), not vice versa.

Time and place of writing

ALFORD thinks, that, considering Jude was writing to Jews and citing signal instances of divine vengeance, it is very unlikely he would have omitted to allude to the destruction of Jerusalem if he had written after that event which uprooted the Jewish polity and people. He conjectures from the tone and references that the writer lived in Palestine. But as to the former, negative evidence is doubtful; for neither does John allude in his Epistles, written after the destruction of Jerusalem, to that event. MILL fixes on A.D. 90, after the death of all the apostles save John. I incline to think from Jude 1:17,18 that some time had elapsed since the Second Epistle of Peter (written probably about A.D. 68 or 69) when Jude wrote, and, therefore, that the Epistle of Jude was written *after* the destruction of Jerusalem.

Contents

See also *Outlines of the New Testament Books,* p. 907

Jude 1:1–25. Address: greeting: his object in writing: warning against seducers in doctrine and practice from God's vengeance on apostates, Israel, the fallen angels, Sodom and Gomorrah. Description of these bad men, in contrast to Michael: like Cain, Balaam, and Core: Enoch's prophecy as to them: the apostles' forewarning: concluding exhortation as to preserving their own faith, and trying to save others: doxology.

1. servant of Jesus Christ – as His minister and apostle.

brother of James – who was more widely

known as bishop of Jerusalem and 'brother of the Lord' (that is, either *cousin,* or stepbrother, being son of Joseph by a former marriage; for ancient traditions universally agree that Mary, Jesus' mother, continued perpetually a virgin). Jude therefore calls himself modestly 'brother of James.' See my *Introduction.*

to them … sanctified by God the Father – The oldest manuscripts and versions, ORIGEN, LUCIFER, and others read, 'beloved' for *sanctified.* If *English Version* be read, compare Col 1:12 1Pe 1:2. The *Greek* is not 'by,' but 'in.' God the Father's *love* is the element IN which they are 'beloved.' Thus the conclusion, Jude 1:21, corresponds, 'Keep yourselves *in* the love of God.' Compare 'beloved of the Lord' 2Th 2:13.

preserved in Jesus Christ – 'kept.' Translate not 'in,' but as *Greek,* 'FOR Jesus Christ.' 'Kept *continually* (so the *Greek perfect* participle means) by God the Father for Jesus Christ,' against the day of His coming. Jude, beforehand, mentions the source and guarantee for the final accomplishment of believers' salvation; lest they should be disheartened by the dreadful evils which he proceeds to announce [BENGEL].

and called – predicated of 'them that are beloved in God the Father, and preserved in Jesus Christ: who are called.' God's effectual *calling* in the exercise of His divine prerogative, guarantees their eternal safety.

2. Mercy – in a time of wretchedness. Therefore *mercy* stands first; the mercy of *Christ* (Jude 1:21).

peace – in the *Holy Ghost* (Jude 1:20).

love – of *God* (Jude 1:21). The three answer to the divine Trinity.

be multiplied – in you and towards you.

3. Design of the Epistle (compare Jude 1:20,21).

all diligence – (2Pe 1:5). As the minister is to give *all diligence* to admonish, so the people should, in accordance with his admonition, give *all diligence* to have all Christian graces, and to make their calling sure.

the common salvation – wrought by Christ. Compare *Note,* see on 2Pe 1:1, 'obtained THIS precious faith,' This *community of faith,* and of the object of faith, *salvation,* forms the ground of mutual exhortation by appeals to common hopes and fears.

it was needful for me – rather, 'I felt it necessary to write (now *at once;* so the *Greek* aorist means; the *present* infinitive "to write," which precedes, expresses merely the general fact of writing) exhorting you.' The reason why he felt it necessary 'to write *with exhortation,*' he states, Jude 1:4, 'For there are certain men crept in.' Having intended to write generally of '*the common salvation,*' he found it necessary from the existing evils in the Church, to write specially that they should *contend for the faith against* those evils.

earnestly contend – Compare Php 1:27, 'striving together for the faith of the Gospel.'

once – *Greek,* 'once for all delivered.' No other faith or revelation is to supersede it. A strong argument for resisting heretical innovators (Jude 1:4). Believers, like Nehemiah's workmen (Ne 4:17), with one hand 'build themselves up in their most holy faith'; with the other they 'contend earnestly for the faith' against its foes.

the saints – all Christians, *holy* (that is, consecrated to God) by their calling, and in God's design.

4. certain men – implying disparagement.

crept in unawares – stealthily and unlawfully. See on 2Pe 2:1, '*privily* shall bring in damnable heresies.'

before … ordained – *Greek,* 'forewritten,' namely, in Peter's prophecy Jude 1:17,18; and in Paul's before that, 1Ti 4:1 2Ti 3:1; and by implication in the judgments which overtook the apostate angels. The disobedient Israelites, Sodom and Gomorrah, Balaam and Core, and which are *written* 'for an example' (Jude 1:7, and Jude 1:5,6,11). God's eternal character as the Punisher of sin, as set forth in Scripture 'of old,' is the ground on which such apostate characters are ordained to condemnation. Scripture is the reflection of God's book of life in which believers are 'written among the living.' 'Forewritten' is applied also in Ro 15:4 to the things written in Scripture. Scripture itself reflects God's character from everlasting, which is the ground of His decrees from everlasting. BENGEL explains it as an abbreviated phrase for, 'They were *of old foretold* by Enoch (Jude 1:14, who did not *write* his prophecies), and afterwards marked out by the *written* word.'

to this condemnation – Jude graphically puts their judgment as it were present before the eyes, 'THIS'. Enoch's prophecy comprises the 'ungodly men' of the last days before Christ's coming to judgment, as well as their forerunners, the 'ungodly men' before the flood, the type of the last judgment (Mt 24:37–39 2Pe 3:3–7). The disposition and the doom of both correspond.

the grace of our God – A phrase for the Gospel especially sweet to believers who appropriate God in Christ as '*our* God,' and so rendering the more odious the vile perversity of those who turn the Gospel state of grace and liberty into a ground of licentiousness, as if their exemption from the law gave them a license to *sin.*

denying the only Lord – The oldest manuscripts, versions, and Fathers omit 'God,' which follows in *English Version.* Translate as the *Greek,* 'the only Master'; here used of *Jesus Christ,* who is at once *Master* and 'Lord' (a different *Greek* word). See on 2Pe 2:1. By virtue of Christ's perfect oneness with the Father, He, as well as the Father, is termed 'the ONLY' God and 'MASTER.' *Greek*, 'Master,' implies God's *absolute ownership* to dispose of His creatures as He likes.

5. (Heb 3:16 4:13.)

therefore – Other oldest manuscripts and *Vulgate* read, 'But'; in contrast to the ungodly Jude 1:4.

though ye once – rather, 'once for all.' Translate, 'I wish to remind you, *as* knowing ALL (namely, *that I am referring to;* so the oldest manuscripts, versions, and Fathers) *once for all.*' As already they know all the facts once for all, he needs only to 'remind' them.

the Lord – The oldest manuscripts and versions read, 'Jesus.' So 'Christ' is said to have accompanied the Israelites in the wilderness; so perfectly is Jesus one with the God of the Israelite theocracy.

saved – brought safely, and into a state of safety and salvation.

afterward – *Greek*, 'secondly'; in the next instance 'destroyed them that believed not,' as contrasted with His *in the first instance* having *saved* them.

6. (2Pe 2:4.)

kept not their first estate – *Vulgate* translates, 'their own *principality,*' which the fact of angels being elsewhere called 'principalities,' favours: 'their own' implies that, instead of being content with the *dignity* once for all assigned to them under the Son of God, they aspired higher. ALFORD thinks the narrative in Ge 6:2 is alluded to, not the fall of the devil and his angels, as he thinks 'giving themselves over to fornication' (Jude 1:7) proves; compare *Greek*, 'in like manner *to these,*' namely, to the angels (Jude 1:6). It seems to me more natural to take 'sons of God' (Ge 6:2) of the Sethites, than of angels, who, as 'spirits,' do not seem capable of carnal connection. The parallel, 2Pe 2:4, plainly refers to the fall of the apostate angels. And 'in like manner *to these,*' Jude 1:7, refers to *the inhabitants of Sodom and Gomorrah,* 'the cities about them' sinning 'in like manner' as 'they' did [ESTIUS and CALVIN]. Even if *Greek* 'these,' Jude 1:7, refer to *the angels,* the sense of 'in like manner as these' will be, not that the angels carnally *fornicated* with the daughters of men, but that their ambition, whereby their affections went *away from* God and they fell, is in God's view a sin of like kind spiritually as Sodom's going *away* from God's order of nature after strange flesh; the sin of the apostate angels after their kind is analogous to that of the human Sodomites after their kind. Compare the somewhat similar spiritual connection of *whoremongers* and *covetousness.* The apocryphal book of Enoch interprets Ge 6:2 as ALFORD. But though Jude accords with it in some particulars, it does not follow that he accords with it in all.

The Hebrews name the fallen angels Aza and Azael.

left – on their own accord.

their own – *Greek*, 'their proper.'

habitation – heaven, all bright and glorious, as opposed to the '*darkness*' to which they now are doomed. Their ambitious designs seem to have had a peculiar connection with this earth, of which Satan before his fall may have been God's vice-regent, whence arises his subsequent connection with it as first the Tempter, then 'the prince of this world.'

reserved – As the *Greek* is the same, and there is an evident reference to *their* having '*kept not their first estate,*' translate, 'He hath kept.' Probably what is meant is, He hath kept them *in His purpose;* that is their sure doom; moreover, as yet, Satan and his demons roam at large on the earth. An earnest of their doom is their having been cast out of heaven, being already restricted to 'the darkness of this present world,' the 'air' that surrounds the earth, their peculiar element now. They lurk in places of gloom and death, looking forward with agonizing fear to their final torment in the bottomless pit. He means not literal chains and darkness, but figurative in this present world where, with restricted powers and liberties, shut out from heaven, they, like condemned prisoners, await their doom.

7. Even as – ALFORD translates, 'I wish to remind you (Jude 1:5) *that.*'

Sodom – (2Pe 2:6).

giving themselves over to fornication – following fornication *extraordinarily,* that is, *out of the* order of nature. On 'in like manner *to them*' (*Greek*), compare *Note,* see on Jude 1:6. Compare on spiritual fornication, 'go a *whoring from thee,*' Ps 73:27.

going after strange flesh – departing from the course of nature, and going after that which is unnatural. In later times the most enlightened heathen nations indulged in the sin of Sodom without compunction or shame.

are set forth – before our eyes.

suffering – undergoing *to this present time;* alluding to the marks of volcanic fire about the Dead Sea.

the vengeance – *Greek*, 'righteous retribution.'

eternal fire – The lasting marks of the fire that consumed the cities irreparably, is a type of the eternal fire to which the inhabitants have been consigned. BENGEL translates as the *Greek* will admit, '*Suffering (the) punishment* (which they endure) as an example or *sample of eternal fire* (namely, that which shall consume the wicked).' Eze 16:53–55 shows that Sodom's punishment, as a nation, is *not eternal.* Compare also 2Pe 2:6.

8. also – rather, 'In like manner nevertheless' (notwithstanding these warning examples) [ALFORD].

these … dreamers – The *Greek* has not *'filthy'* of *English Version*. The clause, 'these men dreaming' (that is, in their dreams), belongs to all the verbs, 'defile,' 'despise,' and 'speak evil.' All sinners are spiritually asleep, and their carnal activity is as it were a dream (1Th 5:6,7). Their *speaking evil of dignities* is because they are *dreaming*, and *know not what they are speaking evil of* (Jude 1:10). 'As a man dreaming seems to himself to be seeing and hearing many things, so the natural man's lusts are agitated by joy, distress, fear, and the other passions. But he is a stranger to self-command. Hence, though he bring into play all the powers of reason, he cannot conceive the true liberty which the sons of light, who are awake and in the daylight; enjoy' [BENGEL].

defile the flesh – (Jude 1:7).

dominion – 'lordship.'

dignities – literally, 'glories.' Earthly and heavenly *dignities*.

9. Michael, the archangel – Nowhere in Scripture is the plural used, 'archangels'; but only ONE, 'archangel.' The only other passage in the New Testament where it occurs, is 1Th 4:16, where Christ is distinguished from the archangel, with whose voice He shall descend to raise the dead; they therefore err who confound Christ with Michael. The name means, *Who is like God?* In Da 10:13 he is called 'One ("the first," *Margin*) of the chief princes.' He is the champion angel of Israel. In Re 12:7 the conflict between Michael and Satan is again alluded to.

about the body of Moses – his literal body. Satan, as having the power of death, opposed the raising of it again, on the ground of Moses' sin at Meribah, and his murder of the Egyptian. That Moses' body was raised, appears from his presence with Elijah and Jesus (who were in the body) at the Transfiguration: the sample and earnest of the coming resurrection kingdom, to be ushered in by Michael's standing up for God's people. Thus in each dispensation a sample and pledge of the future resurrection was given: Enoch in the patriarchal dispensation, Moses in the Levitical, Elijah in the prophetical. It is noteworthy that the same rebuke is recorded here as was used by the Angel of the Lord, or Jehovah the Second Person, in pleading for Joshua, the representative of the Jewish Church, against Satan, in Zec 3:2; whence some have thought that also here 'the body of Moses' means the Jewish Church accused by Satan, before God, for its filthiness, on which ground he demands that divine justice should take its course against Israel, but is rebuked by the Lord who has 'chosen Jerusalem': thus, as 'the body of Christ' is *the Christian Church*, so 'the body of Moses' is the Jewish Church. But the literal body is evidently here meant (though, secondarily, the Jewish Church is typified by Moses' body, as

it was there represented by Joshua the high priest); and Michael, whose connection seems to be so close with Jehovah-Messiah on the one hand, and with Israel on the other, naturally uses the same language as his Lord. As Satan (*adversary* in court) or the devil (*accuser*) accuses alike the Church collectively and 'the brethren' individually, so Christ pleads for us as our Advocate. Israel's, and all believers' full justification, and the accuser's being rebuked finally, is yet future. JOSEPHUS [*Antiquities*,4.8], states that God hid Moses' body, lest, if it had been exposed to view, it would have been made an idol of. Jude, in this account, either adopts it from the apocryphal 'assumption of Moses' (as ORIGEN [*Concerning Principalities,* 3.2] thinks), or else from the ancient tradition on which that work was founded. *Jude,* as inspired, could distinguish how much of the tradition was true, how much false. *We* have no such means of distinguishing, and therefore can be sure of no tradition, save that which is in the *written word*.

durst not – from reverence for Satan's former *dignity* (Jude 1:8).

railing accusation – *Greek,* 'judgment of blasphemy,' or *evil-speaking.* Peter said, Angels do not, in order to avenge themselves, rail at dignities, though ungodly, when they have to contend with them: Jude says that the archangel Michael himself did not rail even at the time when he fought with the devil, the prince of evil spirits – not from fear of him, but from reverence of God, whose delegated power in this world Satan once had, and even in some degree still has. From the word 'disputed,' or *debated in controversy,* it is plain it was a judicial contest.

10. (2Pe 2:12.)

those things which – *Greek,* 'all things *whatsoever* they *understand not,*' namely, the things of the spiritual world.

but what … naturally – Connect thus, 'Whatever (so the *Greek*) things naturally (by natural, blind instinct), as the unreasoning (so the *Greek*) animals, they know.' The *Greek* for the former 'know' implies deeper knowledge; the latter 'know,' the mere perception of the 'animal senses and faculties.'

11. Woe – See on 2Pe 2:14, '*cursed* children.'

Cain – the murderer: the root of whose sin was hatred and envy of the godly, as it is the sin of these seducers.

ran greedily – literally, 'have been poured forth' like a torrent that has burst its banks. Reckless of what it costs, the loss of God's favour and heaven, on they rush after gain like Balaam.

perished in the gainsaying of Core – When we read of Korah perishing by gainsaying, we read virtually also of these perishing in like manner through the same: for the same seed bears the same harvest.

1559

12. spots – So 2Pe 2:13, *Greek,* '*spiloi*'; but here the *Greek* is *spilades,* which elsewhere, in secular writers, means *rocks,* namely, on which the Christian *love-feasts* were in danger of being shipwrecked. The oldest manuscript prefixes the article emphatically, 'THE rocks.' The reference to 'clouds … winds … waves of the sea,' accords with this image of *rocks.* *Vulgate* seems to have been misled by the similar sounding word to translate, as *English Version,* 'spots'; compare however, Jude 1:23, which favours *English Version,* if the *Greek* will bear it. Two oldest manuscripts, by the transcriber's effort to make Jude say the same as Peter, read here 'deceivings' for 'love-feasts,' but the weightiest manuscript and authorities support *English Version* reading. The love-feast accompanied the Lord's Supper (1Co 11:17–34, end). Korah the Levite, not satisfied with his *ministry,* aspired to the *sacrificing priesthood* also: so ministers in the Lord's Supper have sought to make it a *sacrifice,* and themselves the *sacrificing* priests, usurping the function of our only Christian sacerdotal *Priest,* Christ Jesus. Let them beware of Korah's doom!

feeding themselves – *Greek,* 'pasturing (tending) themselves.' What they look to is the pampering of *themselves,* not the feeding of the flock.

without fear – Join these words not as *English Version,* but with 'feast.' Sacred feasts especially ought to be celebrated *with fear.* Feasting is not faulty in itself [BENGEL], but it needs to be accompanied with *fear* of forgetting God, as Job in the case of his sons' feasts.

clouds – from which one would expect refreshing rains. 2Pe 2:17, 'wells without water.' Professors without practice.

carried about – The oldest manuscripts have 'carried aside,' that is, out of the right course (compare Eph 4:14).

trees whose fruit withereth – rather, 'trees of the late (or *waning*) autumn,' namely, when there are no longer leaves or fruits on the trees [BENGEL].

without fruit – having no good fruit of knowledge and practice; sometimes used of what is positively *bad.*

twice dead – First when they cast their leaves in autumn, and seem during winter *dead,* but revive again in spring; secondly, when they are 'plucked up by the roots.' So these apostates, once dead in unbelief, and then by profession and baptism raised from the death of sin to the life of righteousness, but now having become *dead again* by apostasy, and so *hopelessly dead.* There is a climax. Not only *without leaves,* like *trees in late autumn,* but *without fruit:* not only so, but dead twice; and to crown all, 'plucked up by the roots.'

13. Raging – wild. Jude has in mind Isa 57:20.

shame – plural in *Greek,* 'shames' (compare Php 3:19).

wandering stars – instead of moving on in a regular orbit, as lights to the world, bursting forth on the world like erratic comets, or rather, meteors of fire, with a strange glare, and then doomed to fall back again into the blackness of gloom.

14. See *Introduction* on the source whence Jude derived this prophecy of Enoch. The Holy Spirit, by Jude, has sealed the truth of this much of the matter contained in the book of Enoch, though probably that book, as well as Jude, derived it from tradition. There are reasons given by some for thinking the book of Enoch copied from Jude rather than vice versa. It is striking how, from the first, prophecy hastened towards its consummation. The earliest prophecies of the Redeemer dwell on His second coming in glory, rather than His first coming in lowliness (compare Ge 3:15 with Ro 16:20). Enoch, in his translation without death, illustrated that truth which he all his life preached to the unbelieving world, the certainty of the Lord's coming, and the resurrection of the dead, as the only effectual antidote to their skepticism and self-wise confidence in nature's permanence.

And Enoch – *Greek,* 'Moreover, also Enoch.'

seventh from Adam – *Seven* is the sacred number. In Enoch, freedom from death and the sacred number are combined: for every seventh object is most highly valued. Jude thus shows the antiquity of the prophecies. Compare *Note,* see on Jude 1:4, 'of old.' There were only *five* fathers between Enoch and Adam. The *seventh* from Adam prophesied the things which shall close the *seventh age* of the world [BENGEL].

of these – in relation to these. The reference of his prophecies was not to the ante-diluvians alone, but to *all* the ungodly (Jude 1:15). His prophecy applied primarily indeed to the flood, but ultimately to the final judgment.

cometh – literally, 'came.' Prophecy regards the future as certain as if it were *past.*

saints – Holy angels (compare De 33:2 Da 7:10 Zec 14:5 Mt 25:31 Heb 12:22).

15. This verse and the beginning of Enoch's prophecy is composed in *Hebrew* poetic parallelism, the oldest specimen extant. Some think Lamech's speech, which is also in poetic parallelism, was composed in mockery of Enoch's prophecy: as Enoch foretold Jehovah's coming to judgment, so Lamech presumes on impunity in polygamy and murder (just as Cain the murderer seemed to escape with impunity).

convince – convict.

hard *speeches* – such as are noticed in Jude 1:8,10,16 Mal 3:13,14; contrast Ro 16:17.

ungodly sinners – not merely *sinners,* but proud *despisers of God: impious.*

against him – They who speak against God's children are regarded by God as speaking *against Himself.*

16. murmurers – in secret: *muttering murmurs* against God's ordinances and ministers in Church and state. Compare Jude 1:8, 'speak evil of dignities'; Jude 1:15, 'hard speeches'; against the Lord.

complainers – never satisfied with their lot (Nu 11:1; compare the penalty, De 28:47,48).

walking after their own lusts – (Jude 1:18). The secret of their *murmuring and complaining* is the restless insatiability of their desires.

great swelling words – (2Pe 2:18).

men's persons – their mere outward appearance and rank.

because of advantage – for the sake of what they may gain from them. While they *talk great swelling words,* they are really mean and fawning towards those of wealth and rank.

17. But; beloved … ye – in contrast to those reprobates, Jude 1:20, again.

remember – implying that his readers had been contemporaries of the apostles. For Peter uses the very same formula in reminding the contemporaries of himself and the other apostles.

spoken before – spoken already before now.

the apostles – Peter (see on 2Pe 3:2,3), and Paul before Peter (Ac 20:29 1Ti 4:1 2Ti 3:1). Jude does not exclude himself from the number of *the apostles* here, for in Jude 1:18, immediately after, he says, 'they told You,' not *us* (rather as *Greek,* 'used to tell you' implying that Jude's readers were contemporaries of the apostles, who *used to tell* them).

18. mockers – In the parallel, 2Pe 3:3, the same *Greek* is translated, 'scoffers.' The word is found nowhere else in the New Testament.

walk after their own ungodly lusts – literally, 'after (according to) their own lusts *of ungodliness.*'

19. These be they – showing that their characters are such as Peter and Paul had foretold.

separate themselves – from Church communion in its vital, spiritual reality: for outwardly they took part in Church ordinances (Jude 1:12). Some oldest manuscripts omit 'themselves': then understand it, 'separate,' cast out members of the Church by excommunication (Isa 65:5 66:5 Lu 6:22 Joh 9:34; compare 'casteth them out of the Church;' 3Jo 1:10). Many, however, understand 'themselves,' which indeed is read in some of the oldest manuscripts as *English Version* has it. Arrogant setting up of themselves, as having greater sanctity and a wisdom and peculiar doctrine, distinct from others, is implied.

sensual – literally, 'animal-souled': as opposed to the *spiritual,* or 'having the Spirit.' It is translated, 'the *natural* man,' 1Co 2:14. In the threefold division of man's being, *body, soul, and spirit,* the due state in God's design is, that 'the spirit,' which is the recipient of the Holy Spirit uniting man to God, should be first, and should rule the soul, which stands intermediate between *the body* and *spirit:* but in the *animal,* or *natural* man, the spirit is sunk into subserviency to the animal soul, which is earthly in its motives and aims. The 'carnal' sink somewhat lower, for in these *the flesh,* the lowest element and corrupt side of man's bodily nature, reigns paramount.

having not the Spirit – In the animal and natural man *the spirit,* his higher part, which ought to be the receiver of the Holy Spirit, is not so; and therefore, his spirit not being in its normal state, he is said *not to have the spirit* (compare Joh 3:5,6). In the completion of redemption the parts of redeemed man shall be placed in their due relation: whereas in the ungodly, *the soul* severed from *the spirit* shall have for ever animal life without union to God and heaven – a living death.

20. Resuming Jude 1:17.

building up yourselves – the opposite to the 'separate themselves' (Jude 1:19):as 'in the Holy Ghost' is opposed to 'having not the Spirit.'

on – as *on* a foundation. *Building on* THE FAITH is equivalent to building on *Christ,* the object of faith.

praying in the Holy Ghost – (Ro 8:26 Eph 6:18). The Holy Spirit teaches *what we* are to pray for, and *how.* None can pray aright save by being *in the Spirit,* that is, in the element of His influence. CHRYSOSTOM states that, among the charisms bestowed at the beginning of the New Testament dispensation, was *the gift of prayer,* bestowed on someone who prayed in the name of the rest, and taught others to pray. Moreover, their prayers so conceived and often used, were received and preserved among Christians, and out of them forms of prayer were framed. Such is the origin of liturgies [HAMMOND].

21. In Jude 1:20,21, Jude combines the Father, the Son, and the Holy Ghost: and *faith, hope,* and *love.*

Keep yourselves – not in your own strength, but 'in the love of God,' that is, *God's love to you* and all His believing children, the only guarantee for their being *kept* safe. Man's need of watching is implied; at the same time he cannot *keep* himself, unless God in His love keep him.

looking for – in hope.

the mercy of our Lord Jesus Christ – to be fully manifested at His coming. *Mercy* is usually attributed to the Father: here to the Son; so entirely one are they.

22, 23. None but those who 'keep themselves' are likely to 'save' others.

have compassion – So one oldest manuscript reads. But two oldest manuscripts, *Vulgate,* read, 'convict'; 'reprove to their conviction'; 'confute, so as to convince.'

making a difference – The oldest manuscripts and versions read the accusative for the nominative, 'when separating themselves' [WAHL], referring to Jude 1:19; or 'when contending with you,' as the *Greek* is translated, Jude 1:9.

23. save with fear – The oldest manuscripts do not read 'with fear' in this position: but after 'snatching them out of the fire' (with which, compare Am 4:11 1Co 3:15 Zec 3:2, said of a most narrow escape), they add the following words, forming a THIRD class, 'and others compassionate with (IN) fear.' Three kinds of patients require three kinds of medical treatment. Ministers and Christians are said to 'save' those whom they are made the instruments of saving; the *Greek* for 'save' is present, therefore meaning 'try to save.' Jude already (Jude 1:9) had reference to the same passage (Zec 3:1–3). The three classes are: (1) those who *contend with you* (accusative case in oldest manuscripts), whom you should *convict;* (2) those who are as brands already in the fire, of which hell-fire is the consummation: these you should *try to save by snatching them out;* (3) those who are objects of *compassion,* whom accordingly you should *compassionate* (and help if occasion should offer), but at the same time not let pity degenerate into connivance at their error. Your compassion is to be accompanied 'with fear' of being at all defiled by them.

hating – Even *hatred* has its legitimate field of exercise. Sin is the only thing which God hates: so ought we.

even the garment – a proverbial phrase: avoiding the most remote contact with sin, and hating that which borders on it. As *garments* of the apostles wrought miracles of good in healing, so the very *garment* of sinners metaphorically, that is, anything brought into contact with their pollution, is to be avoided. Compare as to lepers and other persons defiled, Le 13:52–57 15:4–17: the garments were held polluted; and anyone touching them was excluded, until purified, from religious and civil communion with the sanctified people of Israel. Christians who received at baptism the white garment in token of purity, are not to defile it by any approach to what is defiled.

24, 25. Concluding doxology.

Now – *Greek,* 'But.'

you – ALFORD, on inferior authority, reads, 'them.' *You* is in contradistinction to those *ungodly men* mentioned above.

keep … from falling – rather, 'guard … (so as to be) *without falling,*' or *stumbling.*

faultless – *Greek,* 'blameless.'

before the presence of his glory – that is, *before Himself,* when He shall be revealed in *glory.*

with exceeding joy – literally, 'with exultation' as of those who *leap* for joy.

25. To the only … God our Saviour – The oldest manuscripts add, 'through Jesus Christ our Lord.' The transcribers, fancying that 'Saviour' applied to Christ alone, omitted the words. The sense is, To the only God (the Father) who is our Saviour through (that is, by the mediation of) Jesus Christ our Lord.

dominion – *Greek,* 'might.'

power – *authority: legitimate power.* The oldest manuscripts and *Vulgate,* after 'power,' have 'before all the age,' that is, before all time as to the *past:* 'and now,' as to the present; 'and to all the ages,' that is, *for ever,* as to the time to come.

REVELATION

Matthew Henry

Introduction

The Book of the Revelation of St. John consists of two principal divisions.

1. Relates to 'the things which are,' that is, the then present state of the church, and contains the epistle of John to the seven churches, and his account of the appearance of the Lord Jesus, and his direction to the apostle to write what he beheld, ch. 1:9–20. Also the addresses or epistles to seven churches of Asia. These, doubtless, had reference to the state of the respective churches, as they then existed, but contain excellent precepts and exhortations, commendations and reproofs, promises and threatenings, suitable to instruct the Christian church at all times.

2. Contains a prophecy of 'the things which shall be hereafter,' and describes the future state of the church, from the time when the apostle beheld the visions here recorded. It is intended for our spiritual improvement; to warn the careless sinner, point out the way of salvation to the awakened inquirer, build up the weak believer, comfort the afflicted and tempted Christian, and, we may especially add, to strengthen the martyr of Christ, under the cruel persecutions and sufferings inflicted by Satan and his followers.

Contents

See *Outlines of the New Testament Books*, pp. 907–8

Chapter 1

The Divine origin, the design, and the importance of this book (1–3)

The apostle John salutes the seven churches of Asia (4–8)

Declares when, where, and how, the revelation was made to him (9–11)

His vision, in which he saw Christ appear (12–20)

The Divine origin, the design, and the importance of this book (1–3)

This book is the Revelation of Jesus Christ; the whole Bible is so; for all revelation comes through Christ, and all relates to him. Its principal subject is to discover the purposes of God concerning the affairs of the church, and of the nations as connected therewith, to the end of the world. These events would surely come to pass; and they would begin to come to pass very shortly. Though Christ is himself God, and has light and life in himself, yet, as Mediator between God and man, he receives instructions from the Father. To him we owe the knowledge of what we are to expect from God, and what he expects from us.

The subject of this revelation was, the things that must shortly come to pass. On all who read or hear the words of the prophecy, a blessing is pronounced. Those are well employed who search the Bible. It is not enough that we read and hear, but we must keep the things that are written, in our memories, in our minds, in our affections, and in practice, and we shall be blessed in the deed. Even the mysteries and difficulties of this book are united with discoveries of God, suited to impress the mind with awe, and to purify the soul of the reader, though he may not discern the prophetic meaning. No part of Scripture more fully states the gospel, and warns against the evil of sin.

The apostle John salutes the seven churches of Asia (4–8)

There can be no true peace, where there is not true grace; and where grace goeth before, peace will follow. This blessing is in the name of God, of the Holy Trinity, it is an act of adoration. The Father is first named; he is described as the Jehovah who is, and who was, and who is to come, eternal, unchangeable. The Holy Spirit is called the seven spirits, the perfect Spirit of God, in whom there is a diversity of gifts and operations. The Lord Jesus Christ was from eternity, a Witness to all the counsels of God. He is the First-born from the dead, who will by his own power raise up his people. He is the Prince of the kings of the earth; by him their counsels are overruled, and to him they are accountable. Sin leaves a stain of guilt and pollution upon the soul. Nothing can fetch out this stain but the blood of Christ; and Christ shed his own blood to satisfy Divine justice, and purchase pardon and purity for his people. Christ has made believers kings and priests to God and his Father. As such they overcome the world, mortify sin, govern their own spirits, resist Satan, prevail with God in prayer, and shall judge the world. He has made them priests, given them access to God, enabled them to offer spiritual and acceptable sacrifices, and for these favours they are bound to ascribe to him dominion and glory for ever.

He will judge the world. Attention is called to that great day when all will see the wisdom and happiness of the friends of Christ, and the madness and misery of his enemies. Let us think frequently upon the second coming of Christ. He shall come, to the terror of those who wound and crucify him by apostasy: he shall come, to the astonishment of the whole world of the ungodly. He is the Beginning and the End; all things are from him and for him; he is the Almighty; the same eternal and unchanged One. And if we would be numbered with his saints in glory everlasting, we must now willingly submit to him, receive him, and honour him as a saviour, who we believe will come to be our Judge. Alas, that there should be many, who

would wish never to die, and that there should not be a day of judgment!

Declares when, where, and how, the revelation was made to him (9–11)

It was the apostle's comfort that he did not suffer as an evil-doer, but for the testimony of Jesus, for bearing witness to Christ as the Immanuel, the Saviour; and the Spirit of glory and of God rested upon this persecuted apostle. The day and time when he had this vision was the Lord's day, the Christian sabbath, the first day of the week, observed in remembrance of the resurrection of Christ. Let us who call him 'Our Lord,' honour him on his own day. The name shows how this sacred day should be observed; the Lord's day should be wholly devoted to the Lord, and none of its hours employed in a sensual, worldly manner, or in amusements. He was in a serious, heavenly, spiritual frame, under the gracious influences of the Spirit of God. Those who would enjoy communion with God on the Lord's day, must seek to draw their thoughts and affections from earthly things. And if believers are kept on the Lord's holy day, from public ordinances and the communion of saints, by necessity and not by choice, they may look for comfort in meditation and secret duties, from the influences of the Spirit; and by hearing the voice and contemplating the glory of their beloved Saviour, from whose gracious words and power no confinement or outward circumstances can separate them. An alarm was given as with the sound of the trumpet, and then the apostle heard the voice of Christ.

His vision, in which he saw Christ appear (12–20)

The churches receive their light from Christ and the gospel, and hold it forth to others. They are golden candlesticks; they should be precious and pure; not only the ministers, but the members of the churches; their light should so shine before men, as to engage others to give glory to God. And the apostle saw as though of the Lord Jesus Christ appeared in the midst of the golden candlesticks. He is with his churches always, to the end of the world, filling them with light, and life, and love. He was clothed with a robe down to the feet, perhaps representing his righteousness and priesthood, as Mediator. This vest was girt with a golden girdle, which may denote how precious are his love and affection for his people. His head and hairs white like wool and as snow, may signify his majesty, purity, and eternity. His eyes as a flame of fire, may represent his knowledge of the secrets of all hearts, and of the most distant events. His feet like fine brass burning in a furnace, may denote the firmness of his appointments, and the excellence of his proceedings. His voice as the sound of many waters, may represent the power of his word, to remove or to destroy. The seven stars were emblems of the ministers of the seven churches to which the apostle was ordered to write, and whom Christ upheld and directed. The sword represented his justice, and his word, piercing to the dividing asunder of soul and spirit, Hebrews 4:12. His countenance was like the sun, when it shines clearly and powerfully; its strength too bright and dazzling for mortal eyes to behold. The apostle was overpowered with the greatness of the lustre and glory in which Christ appeared. We may well be contented to walk by faith, while here upon earth.

The Lord Jesus spake words of comfort; Fear not. Words of instruction; telling who thus appeared. And his Divine nature; the First and the Last. His former sufferings; I was dead: the very same whom his disciples saw upon the cross. His resurrection and life; I have conquered death, and am partaker of endless life. His office and authority; sovereign dominion in and over the invisible world, as the Judge of all, from whose sentence there is no appeal. Let us listen to the voice of Christ, and receive the tokens of his love, for what can he withhold from those for whose sins he has died? May we then obey his word, and give up ourselves wholly to him who directs all things aright.

Chapter 2

Epistles to the churches in Asia, with warnings and encouragements:

To the church at Ephesus (1–7)

To the church at Smyrna (8–11)

To the church at Pergamos (12—17)

To the church at Thyatira (18–29)

To the church at Ephesus (1–7)

These churches were in such different states as to purity of doctrine and the power of godliness, that the words of Christ to them will always suit the cases of other churches, and professors. Christ knows and observes their state; though in heaven, yet he walks in the midst of his churches on earth, observing what is wrong in them, and what they want.

The church of Ephesus is commended for diligence in duty. Christ keeps an account of every hour's work his servants do for him, and their labour shall not be in vain in the Lord. But it is not enough that we are diligent; there must be bearing patience, and there must be waiting patience. And though we must show all meekness to all men, yet we must show just zeal against their sins. The sin Christ charged this church with, is, not the having left and forsaken

the object of love, but having lost the fervent degree of it that at first appeared. Christ is displeased with his people, when he sees them grow remiss and cold toward him. Surely this mention in Scripture, of Christians forsaking their first love, reproves those who speak of it with carelessness, and thus try to excuse indifference and sloth in themselves and others; our Saviour considers this indifference as sinful. They must repent: they must be grieved and ashamed for their sinful declining, and humbly confess it in the sight of God. They must endeavour to recover their first zeal, tenderness, and seriousness, and must pray as earnestly, and watch as diligently, as when they first set out in the ways of God. If the presence of Christ's grace and Spirit is slighted, we may expect the presence of his displeasure. Encouraging mention is made of what was good among them. Indifference as to truth and error, good and evil, may be called charity and meekness, but it is not so; and it is displeasing to Christ. The Christian life is a warfare against sin, Satan, the world, and the flesh. We must never yield to our spiritual enemies, and then we shall have a glorious triumph and reward. All who persevere, shall derive from Christ, as the Tree of Life, perfection and confirmation in holiness and happiness, not in the earthly paradise, but in the heavenly. This is a figurative expression, taken from the account of the garden of Eden, denoting the pure, satisfactory, and eternal joys of heaven; and the looking forward to them in this world, by faith, communion with Christ, and the consolations of the Holy Spirit. Believers, take your wrestling life here, and expect and look for a quiet life hereafter; but not till then: the word of God never promises quietness and complete freedom from conflict here.

To the church at Smyrna (8–11)

Our Lord Jesus is the First, for by him were all things made; he was before all things, with God, and is God himself. He is the Last, for he will be the Judge of all. As this First and Last, who was dead and is alive, is the believer's Brother and Friend, he must be rich in the deepest poverty, honourable amidst the lowest abasement, and happy under the heaviest tribulation, like the church of Smyrna. Many who are rich as to this world, are poor as to the next; and some who are poor outwardly, are inwardly rich; rich in faith, in good works, rich in privileges, rich in gifts, rich in hope. Where there is spiritual plenty, outward poverty may be well borne; and when God's people are made poor as to this life, for the sake of Christ and a good conscience, he makes all up to them in spiritual riches. Christ arms against coming troubles. Fear none of these things; not only forbid slavish fear, but subdue it, furnishing the soul with strength and courage. It should be to try them, not to destroy them. Observe, the sureness of the reward; 'I will give thee:' they shall have the reward from Christ's own hand. Also, how suitable it is; 'a crown of life': the life worn out in his service, or laid down in his cause, shall be rewarded with a much better life, which shall be eternal. The second death is unspeakably worse than the first death, both in the agonies of it, and as it is eternal death: it is indeed awful to die, and to be always dying. If a man is kept from the second death and wrath to come, he may patiently endure whatever he meets with in this world.

To the church at Pergamos (12–17)

The word of God is a sword, able to slay both sin and sinners. It turns and cuts every way; but the believer need not fear this sword; yet this confidence cannot be supported without steady obedience. As our Lord notices all the advantages and opportunities we have for duty in the places where we dwell, so he notices our temptations and discouragements from the same causes. In a situation of trials, the church of Pergamos had not denied the faith, either by open apostasy, or by giving way so as to avoid the cross. Christ commends their stedfastness, but reproves their sinful failures. A wrong view of gospel doctrine and Christian liberty, was a root of bitterness from which evil practices grew. Repentance is the duty of churches and bodies of men, as well as of particular persons; those who sin together, should repent together. Here is the promise of favour to those that overcome. The influences and comforts of the Spirit of Christ, come down from heaven into the soul, for its support. This is hidden from the rest of the world. The new name is the name of adoption; when the Holy Spirit shows his own work in the believer's soul, this new name and its real import are understood by him.

To the church at Thyatira (18–29)

Even when the Lord knows the works of his people to be wrought in love, faith, zeal, and patience; yet if his eyes, which are as a flame of fire, observe them committing or allowing what is evil, he will rebuke, correct, or punish them. Here is praise of the ministry and people of Thyatira, by One who knew the principles from which they acted. They grew wiser and better. All Christians should earnestly desire that their last works may be their best works. Yet this church connived at some wicked seducers. God is known by the judgments he executes; and by this upon seducers, he shows his certain knowledge of the hearts of men, of their principles, designs, frame, and temper. Encouragement is given to those who kept themselves pure and undefiled. It is dangerous to despise the mystery of God, and as dangerous to receive the mysteries of Satan.

Let us beware of the depths of Satan, of which those who know the least are the most happy. How tender Christ is of his faithful servants! He lays nothing upon his servants but what is for their good. There is promise of an ample reward to the persevering, victorious believer; also knowledge and wisdom, suitable to their power and dominion. Christ brings day with him into the soul, the light of grace and of glory, in the presence and enjoyment of him their Lord and Saviour. After every victory let us follow up our advantage against the enemy, that we may overcome and keep the works of Christ to the end.

Chapter 3

Epistles to the churches in Asia, with warnings and encouragements:

To the church at Sardis (1–6)

To the church at Philadelphia (7–13)

To the church at Laodicea (14–22)

To the church at Sardis (1–6)

The Lord Jesus is He that hath the Holy Spirit with all his powers, graces, and operations. Hypocrisy, and lamentable decay in religion, are sins charged upon Sardis, by One who knew that church well, and all her works. Outward things appeared well to men, but there was only the form of godliness, not the power; a name to live, not a principle of life. There was great deadness in their souls, and in their services; numbers were wholly hypocrites, others were in a disordered and lifeless state. Our Lord called upon them to be watchful against their enemies, and to be active and earnest in their duties; and to endeavour, in dependence on the grace of the Holy Spirit, to revive and strengthen the faith and spiritual affections of those yet alive to God, though in a declining state. Whenever we are off our watch, we lose ground. Thy works are hollow and empty; prayers are not filled up with holy desires, alms-deeds not filled up with true charity, sabbaths not filled up with suitable devotion of soul to God. There are not inward affections suitable to outward acts and expressions; when the spirit is wanting, the form cannot long remain.

In seeking a revival in our own souls, or the souls of others, it is needful to compare what we profess with the manner in which we go on, that we may be humbled and quickened to hold fast that which remains. Christ enforces his counsel with a dreadful threatening if it should be despised. Yet our blessed Lord does not leave this sinful people without some encouragement. He makes honourable mention of the faithful remnant in Sardis, he makes a gracious promise to them. He that overcometh shall be clothed in white raiment; the purity of grace shall be rewarded with the perfect purity of glory. Christ has his book of life, a register of all who shall inherit eternal life; the book of remembrance of all who live to God, and keep up the life and power of godliness in evil times. Christ will bring forward this book of life, and show the names of the faithful, before God, and all the angels, at the great day.

To the church at Philadelphia (7–13)

The same Lord Jesus has the key of government and authority in and over the church. He opens a door of opportunity to his churches; he opens a door of utterance to his ministers; he opens a door of entrance, opens the heart. He shuts the door of heaven against the foolish, who sleep away their day of grace; and against the workers of iniquity, how vain and confident soever they may be. The church in Philadelphia is commended; yet with a gentle reproof. Although Christ accepts a little strength, yet believers must not rest satisfied in a little, but strive to grow in grace, to be strong in faith, giving glory to God. Christ can discover this his favour to his people, so that their enemies shall be forced to acknowledge it. This, by the grace of Christ, will soften their enemies, and make them desire to be admitted into communion with his people. Christ promises preserving grace in the most trying times, as the reward of past faithfulness; To him that hath shall be given. Those who keep the gospel in a time of peace, shall be kept by Christ in an hour of temptation; and the same Divine grace that has made them fruitful in times of peace, will make them faithful in times of persecution. Christ promises a glorious reward to the victorious believer. He shall be a monumental pillar in the temple of God; a monument of the free and powerful grace of God; a monument that shall never be defaced or removed. On this pillar shall be written the new name of Christ; by this will appear, under whom the believer fought the good fight, and came off victorious.

To the church at Laodicea (14–22)

Laodicea was the last and worst of the seven churches of Asia. Here our Lord Jesus styles himself, 'The Amen'; one steady and unchangeable in all his purposes and promises. If religion is worth anything, it is worth every thing. Christ expects men should be in earnest. How many professors of gospel doctrine are neither hot nor cold; except as they are indifferent in needful matters, and hot and fiery in disputes about things of lesser moment! A severe punishment is threatened. They would give a false opinion of Christianity, as if it were an unholy religion; while others would conclude it could afford no real satisfaction, otherwise its professors would not have been heartless in it, or so ready to seek pleasure or happiness from the world. One cause of this indifference and inconsistency in religion is, self-conceit and self-delusion; 'Because thou sayest.'

What a difference between their thoughts of themselves, and the thoughts Christ had of them! How careful should we be not to cheat our owns souls! There are many in hell, who once thought themselves far in the way to heaven. Let us beg of God that we may not be left to flatter and deceive ourselves. Professors grow proud, as they become carnal and formal. Their state was wretched in itself. They were poor; really poor, when they said and thought they were rich. They could not see their state, nor their way, nor their danger, yet they thought they saw it. They had not the garment of justification, nor sanctification: they were exposed to sin and shame; their rags that would defile them. They were naked, without house or harbour, for they were without God, in whom alone the soul of man can find rest and safety. Good counsel was given by Christ to this sinful people. Happy those who take his counsel, for all others must perish in their sins. Christ lets them know where they might have true riches, and how they might have them. Some things must be parted with, but nothing valuable; and it is only to make room for receiving true riches. Part with sin and self-confidence, that you may be filled with his hidden treasure. They must receive from Christ the white raiment he purchased and provided for them; his own imputed righteousness for justification, and the garments of holiness and sanctification. Let them give themselves up to his word and Spirit, and their eyes shall be opened to see their way and their end.

Let us examine ourselves by the rule of his word, and pray earnestly for the teaching of his Holy Spirit, to take away our pride, prejudices, and worldly lusts. Sinners ought to take the rebukes of God's word and rod, as tokens of his love to their souls. Christ stood without; knocking, by the dealings of his providence, the warnings and teaching of his word, and the influences of his Spirit. Christ still graciously, by his word and Spirit, comes to the door of the hearts of sinners. Those who open to him shall enjoy his presence. If what he finds would make but a poor feast, what he brings will supply a rich one. He will give fresh supplies of graces and comforts. In the conclusion is a promise to the overcoming believer. Christ himself had temptations and conflicts; he overcame them all, and was more than a conqueror. Those made like to Christ in his trials, shall be made like to him in glory. All is closed with the general demand of attention. And these counsels, while suited to the churches to which they were addressed, are deeply interesting to all men.

Chapter 4

A vision of God, as on his glorious throne, around which were twenty-four elders and four living creatures (1–8)

Whose songs, and those of the holy angels, the apostle heard (9–11)

A vision of God, as on his glorious throne, around which were twenty-four elders and four living creatures (1–8)

After the Lord Jesus had instructed the apostle to write to the churches 'the things that are,' there was another vision. The apostle saw a throne set in heaven, an emblem of the universal dominion of Jehovah. He saw a glorious One upon the throne, not described by human features, so as to be represented by a likeness or image, but only by his surpassing brightness. These seem emblems of the excellence of the Divine nature, and of God's awful justice. The rainbow is a fit emblem of that covenant of promise which God has made with Christ, as the Head of the church, and with all his people in him. The prevailing colour was a pleasant green, showing the reviving and refreshing nature of the new covenant.

Four-and-twenty seats around the throne, were filled with four-and-twenty elders, representing, probably, the whole church of God. Their sitting denotes honour, rest, and satisfaction; their sitting about the throne signifies nearness to God, the sight and enjoyment they have of him. They were clothed in white raiment; the imputed righteousness of the saints and their holiness: they had on their heads crowns of gold, signifying the glory they have with him. Lightnings and voices came from the throne; the awful declarations God makes to his church, of his sovereign will and pleasure.

Seven lamps of fire were burning before the throne; the gifts, graces, and operations of the Spirit of God in the churches of Christ, dispensed according to the will and pleasure of Him who sits upon the throne. In the gospel church, the laver for purification is the blood of the Lord Jesus Christ, which cleanses from all sin. In this all must be washed, to be admitted into the gracious presence of God on earth, and his glorious presence in heaven. The apostle saw four living creatures, between the throne and the circle of the elders, standing between God and the people. These seem to signify the true ministers of the gospel, because of their place between God and the people. This also is shown by the description given, denoting wisdom, courage, diligence, and discretion, and the affections by which they mount up toward heaven.

Whose songs, and those of the holy angels, the apostle heard (9–11)

All true believers wholly ascribe their redemption and conversion, their present privileges and future hopes, to the eternal and most holy God. Thus rise the for-ever harmonious, thankful songs of the redeemed in heaven. Would we on earth do like them, let our praises be constant, not interrupted; united, not divided; thankful, not cold and formal; humble, not self-confident.

Chapter 5

A book sealed with seven seals, which could be opened by none but Christ, who took the book to open it (1–7)

Upon which all honour is ascribed to him, as worthy to open it (8–14)

A book sealed with seven seals, which could be opened by none but Christ, who took the book to open it (1–7)

The apostle saw in the hand of Him that sat upon the throne, a roll of parchments in the form usual in those times, and sealed with seven seals. This represented the secret purposes of God about to be revealed. The designs and methods of Divine Providence, toward the church and the world, are stated, fixed, and made a matter of record. The counsels of God are altogether hidden from the eye and understanding of the creature. The several parts are not unsealed and opened at once, but after each other, till the whole mystery of God's counsel and conduct is finished in the world. The creatures cannot open it, nor read it; the Lord only can do so. Those who see most of God, are most desirous to see more; and those who have seen his glory, desire to know his will. But even good men may be too eager and hasty to look into the mysteries of the Divine conduct. Such desires, if not soon answered, turn to grief and sorrow. If John wept much because he could not look into the book of God's decrees, what reason have many to shed floods of tears for their ignorance of the gospel of Christ! of that on which everlasting salvation depends!

We need not weep that we cannot foresee future events respecting ourselves in this world; the eager expectation of future prospects, or the foresight of future calamities, would alike unfit us for present duties and conflicts, or render our prosperous days distressing. Yet we may desire to learn, from the promises and prophecies of Scripture, what will be the final event to believers and to the church; and the Incarnate Son has prevailed, that we should learn all that we need to know. Christ stands as Mediator between

God and both ministers and people. He is called a Lion, but he appears as a Lamb slain. He appears with the marks of his sufferings, to show that he pleads for us in heaven, in virtue of his satisfaction. He appears as a Lamb, having seven horns and seven eyes; perfect power to execute all the will of God, and perfect wisdom to understand it, and to do it in the most effectual manner. The Father put the book of his eternal counsels into the hand of Christ, and Christ readily and gladly took it into his hand; for he delights to make known the will of his Father; and the Holy Spirit is given by him to reveal the truth and will of God.

Upon which all honour is ascribed to him, as worthy to open it (8–14)

It is matter of joy to all the world, to see that God deals with men in grace and mercy through the Redeemer. He governs the world, not merely as a Creator, but as our Saviour. The harps were instruments of praise; the vials were full of odours, or incense, which signify the prayers of the saints: prayer and praise should always go together. Christ has redeemed his people from the bondage of sin, guilt, and Satan. He has not only purchased liberty for them, but the highest honour and preferment; he made them kings and priests; kings, to rule over their own spirits, and to overcome the world, and the evil one; and he makes them priests; giving them access to himself, and liberty to offer up spiritual sacrifices. What words can more fully declare that Christ is, and ought to be worshipped, equally with the Father, by all creatures, to all eternity! Happy those who shall adore and praise in heaven, and who shall for ever bless the Lamb, who delivered and set them apart for himself by his blood. How worthy art thou, O God, Father, Son, and Holy Ghost, of our highest praises! All creatures should proclaim thy greatness, and adore thy majesty.

Chapter 6

The opening of the seals,

The first, second, third, and fourth seals(1–8)

The fifth seal (9–11)

The sixth seal (12–17)

The first, second, third, and fourth seals (1–8)

Christ, the Lamb, opens the first seal: observe what appeared. A rider on a white horse. By the going forth of this white horse, a time of peace, or the early progress of the Christian religion, seems to be intended; its going forth in purity, at the time when its heavenly Founder sent his apostles to teach all nations, adding, Lo! I am with you alway, even to the end of the world. The Divine religion goes out crowned, having the Divine favour resting upon it, armed spiritually against its foes, and destined to be victorious in the end.

On opening the second seal, a red horse appeared; this signifies desolating judgments. The sword of war and persecution is a dreadful judgment; it takes away peace from the earth, one of the greatest blessings; and men who should love one another, and help one another, are set upon killing one another. Such scenes also followed the pure age of early Christianity, when, neglectful of charity and the bond of peace, the Christian leaders, divided among themselves, appealed to the sword, and entangled themselves in guilt.

On opening the third seal, a black horse appeared; a colour denoting mourning and woe, darkness and ignorance. He that sat on it had a yoke in his hand. Attempts were made to put a yoke of superstitious observances on the disciples. As the stream of Christianity flowed further from its pure fountain, it became more and more corrupt. During the progress of this black horse, the necessaries of life should be at excessive prices, and the more costly things should not be hurt. According to prophetic language, these articles signified that food of religious knowledge, by which the souls of men are sustained unto everlasting life; such we are invited to buy, Isaiah 55:1. But when the dark clouds of ignorance and superstition, denoted by the black horse, spread over the Christian world, the knowledge and practice of true religion became scarce. When a people loathe their spiritual food, God may justly deprive them of their daily bread. The famine of bread is a terrible judgment; but the famine of the word is more so.

Upon opening the fourth seal, another horse appeared, of a pale colour. The rider was Death, the king of terrors. The attendants, or followers of this king of terrors, hell, a state of eternal misery to all who die in their sins; and in times of general destruction, multitudes go down unprepared into the pit. The period of the fourth seal is one of great slaughter and devastation, destroying whatever may tend to make life happy, making ravages on the spiritual lives of men. Thus the mystery of iniquity was completed, and its power extended both over the lives and consciences of men. The exact times of these four seals cannot be ascertained, for the changes were gradual. God gave them power, that is, those instruments of his anger, or those judgments: all public calamities are at his command; they only go forth when God sends them, and no further than he permits.

The fifth seal (9–11)

The sight the apostle beheld at the opening the fifth seal was very affecting. He saw the souls of the martyrs under the altar; at the foot of the altar in heaven, at the feet of Christ. Persecutors can only kill the body; after that there is no more they can do; the soul lives. God has provided a good place in the better world, for those who are faithful unto death. It is not their own death, but the sacrifice of Christ, that gives them entrance into heaven. The cause in which they suffered, was for the word of God; the best any man can lay down his life for; faith in God's word, and the unshaken confession of that faith. They commit their cause to Him to whom vengeance belongs. The Lord is the comforter of his afflicted servants, and precious is their blood in his sight. As the measure of the sin of persecutors is filling up, so is the number of the persecuted, martyred servants of Christ. When this is fulfilled, God will send tribulation to those who trouble them, and unbroken happiness and rest to those that are troubled.

The sixth seal (12–17)

When the sixth seal was opened, there was a great earthquake. The foundations of churches and states would be terribly shaken. Such bold figurative descriptions of great changes abound in the prophecies of Scripture; for these events are emblems, and declare the end of the world and the day of judgment. Dread and terror would seize on all sorts of men. Neither grandeur, riches, valour, nor strength, can support men at that time. They would be glad to be no more seen; yea, to have no longer any being. Though Christ be a Lamb, he can be angry, and the wrath of the Lamb is exceedingly dreadful; for if the Redeemer himself, who appeases the wrath of God, be our enemy, where shall we find a friend to plead for us? As men have their day of opportunity, and their seasons of grace, so God has his day of righteous wrath. It seems that the overthrow of the paganism of the Roman empire is here meant.

The idolaters are described as hiding themselves in their dens and secret caves, and vainly seeking to escape ruin. In such a day, when the signs of the times show those who believe in God's word, that the King of kings is approaching, Christians are called to a decided course, and to a bold confession of Christ and his truth before their fellowmen. Whatever they may have to endure, the short contempt of man is to be borne, rather than that shame which is everlasting.

Chapter 7

A pause between two great periods (1–3)

The peace, happiness, and safety of the saints, as signified by an angel's sealing 144,000 (4–8)

A song of praise (9–12)

The blessedness and glory of those that suffered martyrdom for Christ (13–17)

A pause between two great periods (1–3)

In the figurative language of Scripture, the blowing of the four winds together, means a dreadful and general destruction. But the destruction is delayed. Seals were used to mark for each person his own possessions. This mark is the witness of the Holy Ghost, printed in the hearts of believers. And the Lord would not suffer his people to be afflicted before they were marked, that they might be prepared against all conflicts. And, observe, of those who are thus sealed by the Spirit, the seal must be on the forehead, plainly to be seen alike by friends and foes, but not by the believer himself, except as he looks stedfastly in the glass of God's word.

The peace, happiness, and safety of the saints, as signified by an angel's sealing 144,000 (4–8)

The number of those who were sealed, may be understood to stand for the remnant of people which God reserved. Though the church of God is but a little flock, in comparison with the wicked world, yet it is a society really large, and to be still more enlarged. Here the universal church is figured under the type of Israel.

A song of praise (9–12)

The first fruits of Christ having led the way, the Gentiles converted later follow, and ascribe their salvation to God and the Redeemer, with triumph. In acts of religious worship we come nigh to God, and must come by Christ; the throne of God could not be approached by sinners, were it not for a Mediator. They were clothed with the robes of justification, holiness, and victory; and they had palms in their hands, as conquerors used to appear in their triumphs. Such a glorious appearance will the faithful servants of God make at last, when they have fought the good fight of faith, and finished their course. With a loud voice they gave to God and the Lamb the praise of the great salvation. Those who enjoy eternal happiness must and will bless both the Father and the Son; they will do it publicly, and with fervour. We see what is the work of heaven, and we ought to begin it now, to have our hearts much in it, and to long for that world where our praises, as well as our happiness, will be made perfect.

The blessedness and glory of those that suffered martyrdom for Christ (13–17)

Faithful Christians deserve our notice and respect; we should mark the upright. Those who would gain knowledge, must not be ashamed to seek instruction from any who can give it. The way to heaven is through many tribulations; but tribulation, how great soever, shall not separate us from the love of God. Tribulation makes heaven more welcome and more glorious. It is not the blood of the martyrs, but the blood of the Lamb, that can wash away sin, and make the soul pure and clean in the sight of God; other blood stains, this is the only blood that makes the robes of the saints white and clean. They are happy in their employment; heaven is a state of service, though not of suffering; it is a state of rest, but not of sloth; it is a praising, delightful rest. They have had sorrows, and shed many tears on account of sin and affliction; but God himself, with his own gracious hand, will wipe those tears away. He deals with them as a tender father.

This should support the Christian under all his troubles. As all the redeemed owe their happiness wholly to sovereign mercy; so the work and worship of God their Saviour is their element; his presence and favour complete their happiness, nor can they conceive of any other joy. To Him may all his people come; from him they receive every needed grace; and to him let them offer all praise and glory.

Chapter 8

The seventh seal is opened and seven angels appear with seven trumpets, ready to proclaim the purposes of God (1–6)

Four sound them and another angel denounces greater woes to come (7–13)

The seventh seal is opened and seven angels appear with seven trumpets, ready to proclaim the purposes of God (1–6)

The seventh seal is opened. There was profound silence in heaven for a space; all was quiet in the church, for whenever the church on earth cries through oppression, that cry reaches up to heaven; or it is a silence of expectation. Trumpets were given to the angels, who were to sound them. The Lord Jesus is the High Priest of the church, having a golden censer, and much incense, fulness of merit in his own glorious person. Would that men studied to know the fulness that is in Christ, and endeavoured to be acquainted with his excellency. Would that they

were truly persuaded that Christ has such an office as that of Intercessor, which he now performs with deep sympathy. No prayers, thus recommended, were ever denied hearing and acceptance. These prayers, thus accepted in heaven, produced great changes upon earth. The Christian worship and religion, pure and heavenly in its origin and nature, when sent down to earth and conflicting with the passions and worldly projects of sinful men, produced remarkable tumults, here set forth in prophetical language, as our Lord himself declared, Luke 12:49.

Four sound them and another angel denounces greater woes to come (7–13)

The first angel sounded the first trumpet, and there followed hail and fire mingled with blood. A storm of heresies, a mixture of dreadful errors falling on the church, or a tempest of destruction. The second angel sounded, and a great mountain, burning with fire, was cast into the sea; and the third part of the sea became blood. By this mountain some understand leaders of the persecutions; others, Rome sacked by the Goths and Vandals, with great slaughter and cruelty. The third angel sounded, and there fell a star from heaven. Some take this to be an eminent governor; others take it to be some person in power who corrupted the churches of Christ. The doctrines of the gospel, the springs of spiritual life, comfort, and vigour, to the souls of men, are corrupted and made bitter by the mixture of dangerous errors, so that the souls of men find ruin where they sought refreshment.

The fourth angel sounded, and darkness fell upon the great lights of heaven, that give light to the world, the sun, and the moon, and the stars. The guides and governors are placed higher than the people, and are to dispense light, and kind influences to them. Where the gospel comes to a people, and has not proper effects on their hearts and lives, it is followed with dreadful judgments. God gives alarm by the written word, by ministers, by men's own consciences, and by the signs of the times; so that if people are surprised, it is their own fault. The anger of God makes all comforts bitter, and even life itself burdensome. But God, in this world, sets bounds to the most terrible judgments. Corruption of doctrine and worship in the church are great judgments, and also are the usual causes and tokens of other judgments coming on a people. Before the other three trumpets were sounded, there was solemn warning how terrible the calamities would be that should follow. If lesser judgments do not take effect, the church and the world must expect greater; and when God comes to punish the world, the inhabitants shall tremble before him. Let sinners take warning to flee from the wrath to come; let believers learn to value and to be thankful for their privileges; and let them patiently continue in well doing.

Chapter 9

The fifth trumpet is followed by a representation of another star as falling from heaven and opening the bottomless pit, out of which come swarms of locusts (1–12)

The sixth trumpet is followed by the loosing of four angels bound in the great river Euphrates (13–21)

The fifth trumpet is followed by a representation of another star as falling from heaven and opening the bottomless pit, out of which come swarms of locusts (1–12)

Upon sounding the fifth trumpet, a star fell from heaven to the earth. Having ceased to be a minister of Christ, he who is represented by this star becomes the minister of the devil; and lets loose the powers of hell against the churches of Christ. On the opening of the bottomless pit, there arose a great smoke. The devil carries on his designs by blinding the eyes of men, by putting out light and knowledge, and promoting ignorance and error. Out of this smoke there came a swarm of locusts, emblems of the devil's agents, who promote superstition, idolatry, error, and cruelty. The trees and the grass, the true believers, whether young or more advanced, should be untouched. But a secret poison and infection in the soul, should rob many others of purity, and afterwards of peace. The locusts had no power to hurt those who had the seal of God. God's all-powerful, distinguishing grace will keep his people from total and final apostasy. The power is limited to a short season; but it would be very sharp. In such events the faithful share the common calamity, but from the pestilence of error they might and would be safe. We learn from Scripture that this plainly refers to the first great host of corrupters who overspread the Christian church.

The sixth trumpet is followed by the loosing of four angels bound in the great river Euphrates (13–21)

The sixth angel sounded, and here the power of the Turks seems the subject. Their time is limited. They not only slew in war, but brought a poisonous and ruinous religion. The antichristian generation repented not under these dreadful judgments. From this sixth trumpet learn

that God can make one enemy of the church a scourge and a plague to another. The idolatry in the remains of the eastern church and elsewhere, and the sins of professed Christians, render this prophecy and its fulfilment more wonderful. And the attentive reader of Scripture and history, may find his faith and hope strengthened by events, which in other respects fill his heart with anguish and his eyes with tears, while he sees that men who escape these plagues, repent not of their evil works, but go on with idolatries, wickedness, and cruelty, till wrath comes upon them to the utmost.

Chapter 10

The Angel of the covenant presents a little open book, which is followed with seven thunders (1–4)

At the end of the following prophecies, time should be no more (5–7)

A voice directs the apostle to eat the book (8–10)

A voice tells the apostle to prophesy further (11)

The Angel of the covenant presents a little open book, which is followed with seven thunders (1–4)

The apostle saw another representation. The person communicating this discovery probably was our Lord and Saviour Jesus Christ, or it was to show his glory. He veils his glory, which is too great for mortal eyes to behold; and throws a veil upon his dispensations. A rainbow was upon his head; our Lord is always mindful of his covenant. His awful voice was echoed by seven thunders; solemn and terrible ways of discovering the mind of God. We know not the subjects of the seven thunders, nor the reasons for suppressing them. There are great events in history, perhaps relating to the Christian church, which are not noticed in open prophecy. The final salvation of the righteous, and the final success of true religion on earth, are engaged for by the unfailing word of the Lord.

At the end of the following prophecies, time should be no more (5–7)

Though the time may not be yet, it cannot be far distant. Very soon, as to us, time will be no more; but if we are believers, a happy eternity will follow: we shall from heaven behold and rejoice in the triumphs of Christ, and his cause on earth.

A voice directs the apostle to eat the book and to prophesy further (8–11)

Most men feel pleasure in looking into future events, and all good men like to receive a word from God. But when this book of prophecy was thoroughly digested by the apostle, the contents would be bitter; there were things so awful and terrible, such grievous persecutions of the people of God, such desolations in the earth, that the foresight and foreknowledge of them would be painful to his mind. Let us seek to be taught by Christ, and to obey his orders; daily meditating on his word, that it may nourish our souls; and then declaring it according to our several stations. The sweetness of such contemplations will often be mingled with bitterness, while we compare the Scriptures with the state of the world and the church, or even with that of our own hearts.

Chapter 11

The state of the church is represented under the figure of a temple measured (1, 2)

Two witnesses prophesy in sackcloth (3–6)

They are slain, after which they arise and ascend to heaven (7–13)

Under the seventh trumpet, all anti-Christian powers are to be destroyed and there will be a glorious state of Christ's kingdom upon earth (14–19)

The state of the church is represented under the figure of a temple measured (1, 2)

This prophetical passage about measuring the temple seems to refer to Ezekiel's vision. The design of this measuring seems to be the preservation of the church in times of public danger; or for its trial, or for its reformation. The worshippers must be measured; whether they make God's glory their end, and his word their rule, in all their acts of worship. Those in the outer court, worship in a false manner, or with dissembling hearts, and will be found among his enemies. God will have a temple and an altar in the world, till the end of time. He looks strictly to his temple. The holy city, the visible church, is trodden under foot; is filled with idolaters, infidels, and hypocrites. But the desolations of the church are limited, and she shall be delivered out of all her troubles.

Two witnesses prophesy in sackcloth (3–6)

In the time of treading down, God kept his faithful witnesses to attest the truth of his word and worship, and the excellence of his ways, The number of these witnesses is small, yet enough. They prophesy in sackcloth. It shows their afflicted, persecuted state, and deep sorrow for the abominations against which they protested. They are supported during their great and hard work, till it is done. When they had prophesied in sackcloth the greatest part of 1260 years, antiChrist, the great instrument of the devil, would war against them, with force and violence for a time. Determined rebels against the light rejoice, as on some happy event, when they can silence, drive to a distance, or destroy the faithful servants of Christ, whose doctrine and conduct torment them. It does not appear that the term is yet expired, and the witnesses are not at present exposed to endure such terrible outward sufferings as in former times; but such things may again happen, and there is abundant cause to prophesy in sackcloth, on account of the state of religion. The depressed state of real Christianity may relate only to the western church.

They are slain, after which they arise and ascend to heaven (7–13)

The Spirit of life from God, quickens dead souls, and shall quicken the dead bodies of his people, and his dying interest in the world. The revival of God's work and witnesses, will strike terror into the souls of his enemies. Where there is guilt, there is fear; and a persecuting spirit, though cruel, is a cowardly spirit. It will be no small part of the punishment of persecutors, both in this world, and at the great day, that they see the faithful servants of God honoured and advanced. The Lord's witnesses must not be weary of suffering and service, nor hastily grasp at the reward; but must stay till their Master calls them. The consequence of their being thus exalted was a mighty shock and convulsion in the anti-Christian empire. Events alone can show the meaning of this. But whenever God's work and witnesses revive, the devil's work and witnesses fall before him. And that the slaying of the witnesses in future, appears to be probable.

Under the seventh trumpet, all anti-Christian powers are to be destroyed and there will be a glorious state of Christ's kingdom upon earth (14–19)

Before the sounding of the seventh and last trumpet, there is the usual demand of attention. The saints and angels in heaven know the right of our God and Saviour to rule over all the world. But the nations met God's wrath with their own anger. It was a time in which he was beginning to reward his people's faithful services, and sufferings; and their enemies fretted against God, and so increased their guilt, and hastened their destruction. By the opening of the temple of God in heaven, may be meant, that there was a more free communication between heaven and earth; prayer and praises more freely and frequently going up, graces and blessings plentifully coming down. But it rather seems to refer to the church of God on earth. In the reign of antichrist, God's law was laid aside, and made void by traditions and decrees; the Scriptures were locked up from the people, but now they are brought to the view of all. This, like the ark, is a token of the presence of God returned to his people, and his favour toward them in Jesus Christ, as the Propitiation for their sins. The great blessing of the Reformation was attended with very awful providences; as by terrible things in righteousness God answered the prayers presented in his holy temple now opened.

Chapter 12

A description of the church of Christ and of Satan, under the figures of a woman and of a great red dragon (1-6)

Michael and his angels fight against the devil and his angels, who are defeated (7–12)

The dragon persecutes the church (13, 14)

His vain endeavours to destroy her; he renews his war against her seed (14–17)

A description of the church of Christ and of Satan, under the figures of a woman and of a great red dragon (1-6)

The church, under the emblem of a woman, the mother of believers, was seen by the apostle in vision, in heaven. She was clothed with the sun, justified, sanctified, and shining by union with Christ, the Sun of Righteousness. The moon was under her feet; she was superior to the reflected and feebler light of the revelation made by Moses. Having on her head a crown of twelve stars; the doctrine of the gospel, preached by the twelve apostles, is a crown of glory to all true believers. As in pain to bring forth a holy family; desirous that the conviction of sinners might end in their conversion. A dragon is a known emblem of Satan, and his chief agents, or those who govern for him on earth, at that time the pagan empire of Rome, the city built upon seven hills. As having ten horns, divided into ten kingdoms. Having seven crowns, representing seven forms of government. As drawing with his tail a third part of the stars in heaven,

and casting them down to the earth; persecuting and seducing the ministers and teachers. As watchful to crush the Christian religion; but in spite of the opposition of enemies, the church brought forth a manly issue of true and faithful professors, in whom Christ was truly formed anew; even the mystery of Christ, that Son of God who should rule the nations, and in whose right his members partake the same glory. This blessed offspring was protected of God.

Michael and his angels fight against the devil and his angels, who are defeated (7–12)

The attempts of the dragon proved unsuccessful against the church, and fatal to his own interests. The seat of this war was in heaven; in the church of Christ, the kingdom of heaven on earth. The parties were Christ, the great Angel of the covenant, and his faithful followers; and Satan and his instruments. The strength of the church is in having the Lord Jesus for the Captain of their salvation. Pagan idolatry, which was the worship of devils, was cast out of the empire by the spreading of Christianity. The salvation and strength of the church, are only to be ascribed to the King and Head of the church. The conquered enemy hates the presence of God, yet he is willing to appear there, to accuse the people of God. Let us take heed that we give him no cause to accuse us; and that, when we have sinned, we go before the Lord, condemn ourselves, and commit our cause to Christ as our Advocate. The servants of God overcame Satan by the blood of the Lamb, as the cause. By the word of their testimony: the powerful preaching of the gospel is mighty, through God, to pull down strong holds. By their courage and patience in sufferings: they loved not their lives so well but they could lay them down in Christ's cause. These were the warriors and the weapons by which Christianity overthrew the power of pagan idolatry; and if Christians had continued to fight with these weapons, and such as these, their victories would have been more numerous and glorious, and the effects more lasting. The redeemed overcame by a simple reliance on the blood of Christ, as the only ground of their hopes. In this we must be like them. We must not blend any thing else with this.

The dragon persecutes the church (13, 14)

The church and all her friends might well be called to praise God for deliverance from pagan persecution, though other troubles awaited her. The wilderness is a desolate place, and full of serpents and scorpions, uncomfortable and destitute of provisions; yet a place of safety, as well as where one might be alone. But being thus retired could not protect the woman.

The dragon's vain endeavours to destroy her. He renews his war against her seed (14-17)

The flood of water is explained by many to mean the invasions of barbarians, by which the western empire was overwhelmed; for the heathen encouraged their attacks, in the hope of destroying Christianity. But ungodly men, for their worldly interests, protected the church amidst these tumults, and the overthrow of the empire did not help the cause of idolatry. Or, this may be meant of a flood of error, by which the church of God was in danger of being overwhelmed and carried away. The devil, defeated in his designs upon the church, turns his rage against persons and places. Being faithful to God and Christ, in doctrine, worship, and practice, exposes to the rage of Satan; and will do so till the last enemy shall be destroyed.

Chapter 13

A wild beast rises out of the sea, to whom the dragon gives his power (1–10)

Another beast, which has two horns like a lamb, but speaks as a dragon (11–15)

It obliges all to worship its image, and receive its mark, as persons devoted to it (16–18)

A wild beast rises out of the sea, to whom the dragon gives his power (1–10)

The apostle, standing on the shore, saw a savage beast rise out of the sea; a tyrannical, idolatrous, persecuting power, springing up out of the troubles which took place. It was a frightful monster! It appears to mean that worldly, oppressing dominion, which for many ages, even from the times of the Babylonish captivity, had been hostile to the church. The first beast then began to oppress and persecute the righteous for righteousness' sake, but they suffered most under the fourth beast of Daniel (the Roman empire), which has afflicted the saints with many cruel persecutions. The source of this power was the dragon. It was set up by the devil, and supported by him. The wounding of the head may be the abolishing of pagan idolatry; and the healing of the wound, introducing popish idolatry, the same in substance, only in a new dress, but which as effectually answers the devil's design. The world admired its power, policy and success. They paid honour and subjection to the devil and his instruments. It exercised infernal power and policy, requiring men to

render that honour to creatures which belong to God alone. Yet the devil's power and success are limited. Christ has a chosen remnant, redeemed by his blood, recorded in his book, sealed by his Spirit; and though the devil and antichrist may overcome the body, and take away the natural life, they cannot conquer the soul, nor prevail with true believers to forsake their Saviour, and join his enemies. Perseverance in the faith of the gospel and true worship of God, in this great hour of trial and temptation, which would deceive all but the elect, is the character of those registered in the book of life. This powerful motive and encouragement to constancy, is the great design of the whole Revelation.

Another beast, which has two horns like a lamb, but speaks as a dragon (11–15)

Those who understand the first beast to denote a worldly power, take the second to be also a persecuting and assumed power, which acts under the disguise of religion, and of charity to the souls of men. It is a spiritual dominion, professing to be derived from Christ, and exercised at first in a gentle manner, but soon spake like the dragon. Its speech betrayed it; for it gives forth those false doctrines and cruel decrees, which show it to belong to the dragon, and not to the Lamb.

It obliges all to worship its image, and receive its mark, as persons devoted to it (16–18)

It exercised all the power of the former beast. It pursues the same design, to draw men from worshipping the true God, and to subject the souls of men to the will and control of men. The second beast has carried on its designs, by methods whereby men should be deceived to worship the former beast, in the new shape, or likeness made for it. By lying wonders, pretended miracles. And by severe censures. Also by allowing none to enjoy natural or civil rights, who will not worship that beast which is the image of the pagan beast. It is made a qualification for buying and selling, as well as for places of profit and trust, that they oblige themselves to use all their interest, power, and endeavour, to forward the dominion of the beast, which is meant by receiving his mark. To make an image to the beast, whose deadly wound was healed, would be to give form and power to his worship, or to require obedience to his commands. To worship the image of the beast, implies being subject to those things which stamp the character of the picture, and render it the image of the beast.

The number of the beast is given, so as to show the infinite wisdom of God, and to exercise the wisdom of men. The number is the number of a man, computed after the usual manner among men, and it is 666. What or who is intended by this, remains a mystery. To almost every religious dispute this number has yet been applied, and it may reasonably be doubted whether the meaning has yet been discovered. But he who has wisdom and understanding, will see that all the enemies of God are numbered and marked out for destruction; that the term of their power will soon expire, and that all nations shall submit to our King of righteousness and peace.

Chapter 14

Those faithful to Christ celebrate the praises of God (1–5)

Three angels; one proclaiming the everlasting gospel; another, the downfall of Babylon; and a third, the dreadful wrath of God on the worshippers of the beast. The blessedness of those who die in the Lord (6–13)

A vision of Christ with a sickle, and of a harvest ripe for cutting down (14–16)

The emblem of a vintage fully ripe, trodden in the wine-press of God's wrath (17–20)

Those faithful to Christ celebrate the praises of God (1–5)

Mount Sion is the gospel church. Christ is with his church, and in the midst of her in all her troubles, therefore she is not consumed. His presence secures perseverance. His people appear honourably. They have the name of God written in their foreheads; they make a bold and open profession of their faith in God and Christ, and this is followed by suitable actings. There were persons in the darkest times, who ventured and laid down their lives for the worship and truth of the gospel of Christ. They kept themselves clean from the wicked abominations of the followers of antichrist. Their hearts were right with God; and they were freely pardoned in Christ; he is glorified in them, and they in him. May it be our prayer, our endeavour, our ambition, to be found in this honourable company. Those who are really sanctified and justified are meant here, for no hypocrite, however plausible, can be accounted to be without fault before God.

Three angels; one proclaiming the everlasting gospel; another, the downfall of Babylon; and a third, the dreadful wrath of

God on the worshippers of the beast. The blessedness of those who die in the Lord (6–13)

The progress of the Reformation appears to be here set forth. The four proclamations are plain in their meaning; that all Christians may be encouraged, in the time of trial, to be faithful to their Lord. The gospel is the great means whereby men are brought to fear God, and to give glory to him. The preaching of the everlasting gospel shakes the foundations of antichrist in the world, and hastens its downfall. If any persist in being subject to the beast, and in promoting his cause, they must expect to be for ever miserable in soul and body. The believer is to venture or suffer any thing in obeying the commandments of God, and professing the faith of Jesus. May God bestow this patience upon us. Observe the description of those that are and shall be blessed: such as die in the Lord; die in the cause of Christ, in a state of union with Christ; such as are found in Christ when death comes. They rest from all sin, temptation, sorrow, and persecution; for there the wicked cease from troubling, there the weary are at rest. Their works follow them: do not go before as their title, or purchase, but follow them as proofs of their having lived and died in the Lord: the remembrance of them will be pleasant, and the reward far above all their services and sufferings. This is made sure by the testimony of the Spirit, witnessing with their spirits, and the written word.

A vision of Christ with a sickle, and of a harvest ripe for cutting down (14–16)

Warnings and judgments not having produced reformation, the sins of the nations are filled up, and they become ripe for judgments, represented by a harvest, an emblem which is used to signify the gathering of the righteous, when ripe for heaven, by the mercy of God. The harvest time is when the corn is ripe; when the believers are ripe for heaven, then the wheat of the earth shall be gathered into Christ's garner.

The emblem of a vintage fully ripe, trodden in the wine-press of God's wrath (17–20)

And by a vintage. The enemies of Christ and his church are not destroyed, till by their sin they are ripe for ruin, and then he will spare them no longer. The wine-press is the wrath of God, some terrible calamity, probably the sword, shedding the blood of the wicked. The patience of God towards sinners, is the greatest miracle in the world; but, though lasting, it will not be everlasting; and ripeness in sin is a sure proof of judgment at hand.

Chapter 15

A song of praise is sung by the church (1–4)

Seven angels with the seven plagues; and to them one of the living creatures gives seven golden vials full of the wrath of God (5–8)

A song of praise is sung by the church (1–4)

Seven angels appeared in heaven; prepared to finish the destruction of antichrist. As the measure of Babylon's sins was filled up, it finds the full measure of Divine wrath. While believers stand in this world, in times of trouble, as upon a sea of glass mingled with fire, they may look forward to their final deliverance, while new mercies call forth new hymns of praise. The more we know of God's wonderful works, the more we shall praise his greatness as the Lord God Almighty, the Creator and Ruler of all worlds; but his title of Emmanuel, the King of saints, will make him dear to us. Who that considers the power of God's wrath, the value of his favour, or the glory of his holiness, would refuse to fear and honour him alone? His praise is above heaven and earth.

Seven angels with the seven plagues; and to them one of the living creatures gives seven golden vials full of the wrath of God (5–8)

In the judgments God executes upon antichrist and his followers, he fulfils the prophecies and promises of his word. These angels are prepared for their work, clothed with pure and white linen, their breasts girded with golden girdles, representing the holiness, and righteousness, and excellence of these dealings with men. They are ministers of Divine justice, and do every thing in a pure and holy manner. They are armed with the wrath of God against his enemies. Even the meanest creature, when armed with the anger of God, will be too hard for any man in the world. The angels received the vials from one of the four living creatures, one of the ministers of the true church, as in answer to the prayers of the ministers and people of God. Antichrist could not be destroyed without a great shock to all the world, and even the people of God would be in trouble and confusion while the great work was doing. The greatest deliverances of the church are brought about by awful and astonishing steps of Providence; and the happy state of the true church will not begin till obstinate enemies shall be destroyed, and lukewarm or formal Christians are purified. Then, whatever is against Scripture being purged away, the whole church shall be spiritual, and the whole being brought to purity, unity, and spirituality, shall be firmly established.

Chapter 16

The first vial is poured out on the earth, the second on the sea, the third on the rivers and fountains (1–7)

The fourth on the sun, the fifth on the seat of the beast (8–11)

The sixth on the great river Euphrates (12–16)
And the seventh on the air, when shall follow the destruction of all anti-Christian enemies (17–21)

The first vial is poured out on the earth, the second on the sea, the third on the rivers and fountains (1–7)

We are to pray that the will of God may be done on earth as it is done in heaven. Here is a succession of terrible judgments of Providence; and there seems to be an allusion to several of the plagues of Egypt. The sins were alike, and so were the punishments. The vials refer to the seven trumpets, which represented the rise of antichrist; and the fall of the enemies of the church shall bear some resemblance to their rise. All things throughout their earth, their air, their sea, their rivers, their cities, all are condemned to ruin, all accursed for the wickedness of that people. No wonder that angels, who witness or execute the Divine vengeance on the obstinate haters of God, of Christ, and of holiness, praise his justice and truth; and adore his awful judgments, when he brings upon cruel persecutors the tortures they made his saints and prophets suffer.

The fourth on the sun, the fifth on the seat of the beast (8–11)

The heart of man is so desperately wicked, that the most severe miseries never will bring any to repent, without the special grace of God. Hell itself is filled with blasphemies; and those are ignorant of the history of human nature, of the Bible, and of their own hearts, who do not know that the more men suffer, and the more plainly they see the hand of God in their sufferings, the more furiously they often rage against him. Let sinners now seek repentance from Christ, and the grace of the Holy Spirit, or they will have the anguish and horror of an unhumbled, impenitent, and desperate heart; thus adding to their guilt and misery through all eternity. Darkness is opposed to wisdom and knowledge, and forebodes the confusion and folly of the idolaters and followers of the beast. It is opposed to pleasure and joy, and signifies anguish and vexation of spirit.

The sixth on the great river Euphrates (12–16)

This probably shows the destruction of the Turkish power, and of idolatry, and that a way will be made for the return of the Jews. Or, take it for Rome, as mystical Babylon, the name of Babylon being put for Rome, which was meant, but was not then to be directly named. When Rome is destroyed, her river and merchandise must suffer with her. And perhaps a way will be opened for the eastern nations to come into the church of Christ. The great dragon will collect all his forces, to make one desperate struggle before all be lost. God warns of this great trial, to engage his people to prepare for it. These will be times of great temptation; therefore Christ, by his apostle, calls on his professed servants to expect his sudden coming, and to watch that they might not be put to shame, as apostates or hypocrites. However Christians differ, as to their views of the times and seasons of events yet to be brought to pass, on this one point all are agreed, Jesus Christ, the Lord of glory, will suddenly come again to judge the world. To those living near to Christ, it is an object of joyful hope and expectation, and delay is not desired by them.

And the seventh on the air, when shall follow the destruction of all anti-Christian enemies (17–21)

The seventh and last angel poured forth his vial, and the downfall of Babylon was finished. The church triumphant in heaven saw it and rejoiced; the church in conflict on earth saw it and became triumphant. God remembered the great and wicked city; though for some time he seemed to have forgotten her idolatry and cruelty. All that was most secure was carried away by the ruin. Men blasphemed: the greatest judgments that can befall men, will not bring to repentance without the grace of God. To be hardened against God, by his righteous judgments, is a certain token of sure and utter destruction.

Chapter 17

One of the angels who had the vials, explains the meaning of the former vision of the anti-Christian beast that was to reign 1260 years, and then to be destroyed (1–6)

The interpretation of the mystery of the woman, and the beast that had seven heads and ten horns (7–18)

One of the angels who had the vials, explains the meaning of the former vision of the anti-Christian beast that was to reign 1260 years, and then to be destroyed (1–6)

Rome clearly appears to be meant in this chapter. Pagan Rome subdued and ruled with military power, not by art and flatteries. She left the nations in general to their ancient usages and worship. But it is well known that by crafty and politic management, with all kinds of deceit of unrighteousness, papal Rome has obtained and kept her rule over kings and nations. Here were allurements of worldly honour and riches, pomp and pride, suited to sensual and worldly minds. Prosperity, pomp, and splendour, feed the pride and lusts of the human heart, but are no security against the Divine vengeance. The golden cup represents the allurements, and delusions, by which this mystical Babylon has obtained and kept her influence, and seduced others to join her abominations. She is named, from her infamous practices, a mother of harlots; training them up to idolatry and all sorts of wickedness. She filled herself with the blood of the saints and martyrs of Jesus. She intoxicated herself with it; and it was so pleasant to her, that she never was satisfied. We cannot but wonder at the oceans of Christian blood shed by men called Christians; yet when we consider these prophecies, these awful deeds testify to the truth of the gospel. And let all beware of a splendid, gainful, or fashionable religion. Let us avoid the mysteries of iniquity, and study diligently the great mystery of godliness, that we may learn humility and gratitude from the example of Christ. The more we seek to resemble him, the less we shall be liable to be deceived by antichrist.

The interpretation of the mystery of the woman, and the beast that had seven heads and ten horns (7–18)

The beast on which the woman sat was, and is not, and yet is. It was a seat of idolatry and persecution, and is not; not in the ancient form, which was pagan: yet it is; it is truly the seat of idolatry and tyranny, though of another sort and form. It would deceive into stupid and blind submission all the inhabitants of the earth within its influence, except the remnant of the elect. This beast was seven heads, seven mountains, the seven hills on which Rome stands; and seven kings, seven sorts of government. Five were gone by when this prophecy was written; one was then in being; the other was yet to come. This beast, directed by the papacy, makes an eighth governor, and sets up idolatry again. It had ten horns, which are said to be ten kings who had as yet no kingdoms; they should not rise up till the Roman empire was broken; but should for a time be very zealous in her interest. Christ must reign till all enemies be put under his feet. The reason of the victory is, that he is the King of kings, and Lord of lords. He has supreme dominion and power over all things; all the powers of earth and hell are subject to his control. His followers are called to this warfare, are fitted for it, and will be faithful in it.

God so ruled the hearts of these kings, by his power over them, and by his providence, that they did those things, without intending it, which he purposed and foretold. They shall see their folly, and how they have been bewitched and enslaved by the harlot, and be made instruments in her destruction. She was that great city which reigned over the kings of the earth, when John had this vision; and every one knows Rome to be that city. Believers will be received to the glory of the Lord, when wicked men will be destroyed in a most awful manner; their joining together in sin, will be turned to hatred and rage, and they will eagerly assist in tormenting each other. But the Lord's portion is his people; his counsel shall stand, and he will do all his pleasure, to his glory, and the happiness of all his servants.

Chapter 18

Another angel from heaven proclaims the fall of mystical Babylon (1–3)

A voice from heaven admonishes the people of God, lest they partake of her plagues (4–8)

The lamentations over her (9–19)

The church called upon to rejoice in her utter ruin (20–24)

Another angel from heaven proclaims the fall of mystical Babylon (1–3)

The downfall and destruction of the mystical Babylon are determined in the counsels of God. Another angel comes from heaven. This seems to be Christ himself, coming to destroy his enemies, and to shed abroad the light of his gospel through all nations. The wickedness of this Babylon was very great; she had forsaken the true God, and set up idols, and had drawn all sorts of men into spiritual adultery, and by her wealth and luxury kept them in her interest. The spiritual merchandise, by which multitudes have wickedly lived in wealth, by the sins and follies of mankind, seems principally intended.

A voice from heaven admonishes the people of God, lest they partake of her plagues (4–8)

Fair warning is given to all that expect mercy from God, that they should not only come out of this Babylon, but assist in her destruction. God may have a people even in Babylon. But God's people shall be called out of Babylon, and called effectually, while those that partake with wicked men in their sins, must receive of their plagues.

The lamentations over her (9–19)

The mourners had shared Babylon's sensual pleasures, and gained by her wealth and trade. The kings of the earth, whom she flattered into idolatry, allowing them to be tyrannical over their subjects, while obedient to her; and the merchants, those who trafficked for her indulgences, pardons, and honours; these mourn. Babylon's friends partook her sinful pleasures and profits, but are not willing to share her plagues. The spirit of antichrist is a worldly spirit, and that sorrow is a mere worldly sorrow; they do not lament for the anger of God, but for the loss of outward comforts. The magnificence and riches of the ungodly will avail them nothing, but will render the vengeance harder to be borne. The spiritual merchandise is here alluded to, when not only slaves, but the souls of men, are mentioned as articles of commerce, to the destroying the souls of millions. Nor has this been peculiar to the Roman antichrist, and only her guilt. But let prosperous traders learn, with all their gains, to get the unsearchable riches of Christ; otherwise, even in this life, they may have to mourn that riches make to themselves wings and fly away, and that all the fruits their souls lusted after, are departed from them. Death, at any rate, will soon end their commerce, and all the riches of the ungodly will be exchanged, not only for the coffin and the worm, but for the fire that cannot be quenched.

The church called upon to rejoice in her utter ruin (20–24)

That which is matter of rejoicing to the servants of God on earth, is matter of rejoicing to the angels in heaven. The apostles, who are honoured and daily worshipped at Rome in an idolatrous manner, will rejoice in her fall. The fall of Babylon was an act of God's justice. And because it was a final ruin, this enemy should never molest them any more; of this they were assured by a sign. Let us take warning from the things which brought others to destruction, and let us set our affections on things above, when we consider the changeable nature of earthly things.

Chapter 19

The church in heaven and that on earth triumph, and praise the Lord for his righteous judgments (1–10)

A vision of Christ going forth to destroy the beast and his armies (11–21)

The church in heaven and that on earth triumph, and praise the Lord for his righteous judgments (1–10)

Praising God for what we have, is praying for what is yet further to be done for us. There is harmony between the angels and the saints in this triumphant song. Christ is the Bridegroom of his ransomed church. This second union will be completed in heaven; but the beginning of the glorious millennium (by which is meant a reign of Christ, or a state of happiness, for a thousand years on earth) may be considered as the celebration of his espousals on earth. Then the church of Christ, being purified from errors, divisions, and corruptions, in doctrine, discipline, worship, and practice, will be made ready to be publicly owned by him as his delight and his beloved. The church appeared; not in the gay, gaudy dress of the mother of harlots, but in fine linen, clean and white. In the robes of Christ's righteousness, imputed for justification, and imparted for sanctification. The promises of the gospel, the true sayings of God, opened, applied, and sealed by the Spirit of God, in holy ordinances, are the marriage-feast. This seems to refer to the abundant grace and consolation Christians will receive in the happy days which are to come. The apostle offered honour to the angel. The angel refused it. He directed the apostle to the true and only object of religious worship; to worship God, and him alone. This plainly condemns the practice of those who worship the elements of bread and wine, and saints, and angels; and of those who do not believe that Christ is truly and by nature God, yet pay him a sort of worship. They stand convicted of idolatry by a messenger from heaven. These are the true sayings of God; of Him who is to be worshipped, as one with the Father and the Holy Spirit.

A vision of Christ going forth to destroy the beast and his armies (11–21)

Christ, the glorious Head of the church, is described as on a white horse, the emblem of justice and holiness. He has many crowns, for he is King of kings, and Lord of lords. He is arrayed in a vesture dipped in his own blood, by which he purchased his power as Mediator; and in the blood of his enemies, over whom he always prevails. His name is 'The Word of God;' a name none fully knows but himself; only this we know, that this Word was God manifest in the flesh; but his perfections cannot be fully understood by any creature. Angels and saints follow, and are like Christ in their armour of purity and righteousness. The threatenings of the written word he is going to execute on his enemies. The ensigns of his authority are his name; asserting his authority and power, warning the most powerful princes to submit, or they must fall before him. The powers of earth and hell make their utmost effort. These verses declare important events, foretold by the prophets. These persons were not excused because they did what their leaders bade them. How vain will be the plea of many sinners at the great day! We followed our guides; we did as we saw others do! God has given a rule to walk by, in his word; neither the example of the most, nor of the chief, must influence us contrary thereto: if we do as the most do, we must go where the most go, even into the burning lake.

Chapter 20

Satan is bound for a thousand years (1–3)

The first resurrection; those are blessed that have part therein (4–6)

Satan loosed, Gog and Magog (7–10)

The last and general resurrection (11–15)

Satan is bound for a thousand years (1–3)

Here is a vision, showing by a figure the restraints laid on Satan himself. Christ, with Almighty power, will keep the devil from deceiving mankind as he has hitherto done. He never wants power and instruments to break the power of Satan. Christ shuts by his power, and seals by his authority. The church shall have a time of peace and prosperity, but all her trials are not yet over.

The first resurrection; those are blessed that have part therein (4–6)

Here is an account of the reign of the saints, for the same space of time as Satan is bound. Those who suffer with Christ, shall reign with him in his spiritual and heavenly kingdom, in conformity to him in his wisdom, righteousness, and holiness: this is called the first resurrection, with which none but those who serve Christ, and suffer for him, shall be favoured. The happiness of these servants of God is declared. None can be blessed but those that are holy; and all that are holy shall be blessed. We know something thing of what the first death is, and it is very awful; but we know not what this second death is. It must be much more dreadful; it is the death of the soul, eternal separation from God. May we never know what it is: those who have been made partakers of a spiritual resurrection, are saved from the power of the second death. We may expect that a thousand years will follow the destruction of the anti-Christian, idolatrous, persecuting powers, during which pure Christianity, in doctrine, worship, and holiness, will be made known over all the earth. By the all-powerful working of the Holy Spirit, fallen man will be new-created; and faith and holiness will as certainly prevail, as unbelief and unholiness now do. We may easily perceive what a variety of dreadful pains, diseases, and other calamities would cease, if all men were true and consistent Christians. All the evils of public and private contests would be ended, and happiness of every kind largely increased. Every man would try to lighten suffering, instead of adding to the sorrows around him. It is our duty to pray for the promised glorious days, and to do every thing in our public and private stations which can prepare for them.

Satan loosed, Gog and Magog (7–10)

While this world lasts, Satan's power in it will not be wholly destroyed, though it may be limited and lessened. No sooner is Satan let loose, than he again begins deceiving the nations, and stirring them up to make war with the saints and servants of God. It would be well if the servants and ministers of Christ were as active and persevering in doing good, as his enemies in doing mischief. God will fight this last and decisive battle for his people, that the victory may be complete, and the glory be to himself.

The last and general resurrection (11–15)

After the events just foretold, the end will speedily come; and there is no mention of any thing else, before the appearing of Christ to judge the world. This will be the great day: the Judge, the Lord Jesus Christ, will then put on majesty and terror. The persons to be judged are the dead, small and great; young and old, low and high, poor and rich. None are so mean, but they have some talents to account for; and none so great, as to avoid having to account for them. Not only those alive at the coming of Christ, but all the dead. There is a book of remembrance both for good and bad: and the book of the sinner's conscience, though formerly secret, will then be opened. Every man will recollect all his past actions, though he had long forgotten many of them. Another book shall be opened, the book of the Scriptures, the rule of life; it represents the Lord's knowledge of his people, and his declaring their repentance, faith, and good works; showing the blessings of the new covenant. By their works men shall be justified or condemned; he will try their principles by their practices. Those justified and acquitted by

the gospel, shall be justified and acquitted by the Judge, and shall enter into eternal life, having nothing more to fear from death, or hell, or wicked men; for these are all destroyed together. This is the second death; it is the final separation of sinners from God. Let it be our great concern to see whether our Bibles justify or condemn us now; for Christ will judge the secrets of all men according to the gospel. Who shall dwell with devouring flames?

Chapter 21

A new heaven, and new earth: the new Jerusalem where God dwells, and banishes all sorrow from his people (1–8)

Its heavenly origin, glory, and secure defence (9–21)

Its perfect happiness, as enlightened with the presence of God and the Lamb, and in the free access of multitudes, made holy (22–27)

A new heaven, and new earth: the new Jerusalem where God dwells, and banishes all sorrow from his people (1–8)

The new heaven and the new earth will not be separate from each other; the earth of the saints, their glorified, bodies, will be heavenly. The old world, with all its troubles and tumults, will have passed away. There will be no sea; this aptly represents freedom from conflicting passions, temptations, troubles, changes, and alarms; from whatever can divide or interrupt the communion of saints. This new Jerusalem is the church of God in its new and perfect state, the church triumphant. Its blessedness came wholly from God, and depends on him. The presence of God with his people in heaven, will not be interrupt as it is on earth, he will dwell with them continually. All effects of former trouble shall be done away. They have often been in tears, by reason of sin, of affliction, of the calamities of the church; but no signs, no remembrance of former sorrows shall remain. Christ makes all things new. If we are willing and desirous that the gracious Redeemer should make all things new in order, hearts, and nature, he will make all things new in respect of our situation, till he has brought us to enjoy complete happiness. See the certainty of the promise. God gives his titles, Alpha and Omega, the Beginning and the End, as a pledge for the full performance. Sensual and sinful pleasures are muddy and poisoned waters; and the best earthly comforts are like the scanty supplies of a cistern; when idolized, they become broken cisterns, and yield only vexation. But the joys which

Christ imparts are like waters springing from a fountain, pure, refreshing, abundant, and eternal. The sanctifying consolations of the Holy Spirit prepare for heavenly happiness; they are streams which flow for us in the wilderness. The fearful durst not meet the difficulties of religion, their slavish fear came from their unbelief; but those who were so dastardly as not to dare to take up the cross of Christ, were yet so desperate as to run into abominable wickedness. The agonies and terrors of the first death will lead to the far greater terrors and agonies of eternal death.

Its heavenly origin, glory, and secure defence (9–21)

God has various employments for his holy angels. Sometimes they sound the trumpet of Divine Providence, and warn a careless world; sometimes they discover things of a heavenly nature of the heirs of salvation. Those who would have clear views of heaven, must get as near to heaven as they can, on the mount of meditation and faith. The subject of the vision is the church of God in a perfect, triumphant state, shining in its lustre; glorious in relation to Christ; which shows that the happiness of heaven consists in intercourse with God, and in conformity to him. The change of emblems from a bride to a city, shows that we are only to take general ideas from this description. The wall is for security. Heaven is a safe state; those who are there, are separated and secured from all evils and enemies. This city is vast; here is room for all the people of God. The foundation of the wall; the promise and power of God, and the purchase of Christ, are the strong foundations of the safety and happiness of the church. These foundations are set forth by twelve sorts of precious stones, denoting the variety and excellence of the doctrines of the gospel, or of the graces of the Holy Spirit, or the personal excellences of the Lord Jesus Christ. Heaven has gates; there is a free admission to all that are sanctified; they shall not find themselves shut out. These gates were all of pearls. Christ is the Pearl of great price, and he is our Way to God. The street of the city was pure gold, like transparent glass. The saints in heaven tread gold under foot. The saints are there at rest, yet it is not a state of sleep and idleness; they have communion, not only with God, but with one another. All these glories but faintly represent heaven.

Its perfect happiness, as enlightened with the presence of God and the Lamb, and in the free access of multitudes, made holy (22–27)

Perfect and direct communion with God, will more than supply the place of gospel institutions. And what words can more full express the union and co-equality of the Son with the Father, in the Godhead? What a dismal world would this be, if it were not for the light of the sun! What is there in heaven that supplies its place? The glory of God lightens that city, and the Lamb is the Light thereof. God in Christ will be an everlasting Fountain of knowledge and joy to the saints in heaven. There is no night, therefore no need of shutting the gates; all is at peace and secure. The whole shows us that we should be more and more led to think of heaven as filled with the glory of God, and enlightened by the presence of the Lord Jesus. Nothing sinful or unclean, idolatrous, or false and deceitful, can enter. All the inhabitants are made perfect in holiness. Now the saints feel a sad mixture of corruption, which hinders them in the service of God, and interrupts their communion with him; but, at their entrance into the holy of holies, they are washed in the laver of Christ's blood, and presented to the Father without spot. None are admitted into heaven who work abominations. It is free from hypocrites, such as make lies. As nothing unclean can enter heaven, let us be stirred up by these glimpses of heavenly things, to use all diligence, and to perfect holiness in the fear of God.

Chapter 22

A description of the heavenly state, under the figures of the water and the tree of life, and of the throne of God and the Lamb (1–5)

The truth and certain fulfilling of all the prophetic visions, The Holy Spirit, and the bride, the church, invite, and say, Come (6–19)

The closing blessing (20, 21)

A description of the heavenly state, under the figures of the water and the tree of life, and of the throne of God and the Lamb (1–5)

All streams of earthly comfort are muddy; but these are clear, and refreshing. They give life, and preserve life, to those who drink of them, and thus they will flow for evermore. These point to the quickening and sanctifying influences of the Holy Spirit, as given to sinners through Christ. The Holy Spirit, proceeding from the Father and the Son, applies this salvation to our souls by his new-creating love and power. The trees of life are fed by the pure waters of the river that comes from the throne of God. The presence of God in heaven, is the health and happiness of the saints. This tree was an emblem of Christ, and of all the blessings of his salvation; and the leaves for the healing of the nations, mean that his favour and presence supply all good to the inhabitants of that blessed world. The devil has no power there; he cannot draw the saints from serving God, nor can he disturb them in the service of God. God and the Lamb are here spoken of as one. Service there shall be not only freedom, but honour and dominion. There will be no night; no affliction or dejection, no pause in service or enjoyment: no diversions or pleasures or man's inventing will there be wanted. How different all this from gross and merely human views of heavenly happiness, even those which refer to pleasures of the mind!

The truth and certain fulfilling of all the prophetic visions, The Holy Spirit, and the bride, the church, invite, and say, Come (6–19)

The Lord Jesus spake by the angel, solemnly confirming the contents of this book, particularly of this last vision. He is the Lord God faithful and true. Also by his messengers; the holy angels showed them to holy men of God. They are things that must shortly be done; Christ will come quickly, and put all things out of doubt. And by the integrity of that angel who had been the apostle's interpreter. He refused to accept religious worship from John, and reproved him for offering it. This presents another testimony against idolatrous worship of saints and angels. God calls every one to witness to the declarations here made. This book, thus kept open, will have effect upon men; the filthy and unjust will be more so, but it will confirm, strengthen, and further sanctify those who are upright with God. Never let us think that a dead or disobedient faith will save us, for the First and the Last has declared that those alone are blessed who do his commandments. It is a book that shuts out from heaven all wicked and unrighteous persons, particularly those who love and make lies, therefore cannot itself be a lie. There is no middle place or condition. Jesus, who is the Spirit of prophecy, has given his churches this morning-light of prophecy, to assure them of the light of the perfect day approaching. All is confirmed by an open and general invitation to mankind, to come and partake freely of the promises and of the privileges of the gospel. The Spirit, by the sacred word, and by convictions and influence in the sinner's conscience, says, Come to Christ for salvation; and the bride, or the whole church, on earth and in heaven, says, Come and share our happiness. Lest any should hesitate, it is added, Let whosoever will, or, is willing, come and take of the water of life freely. May every one who hears or reads these words, desire at once to accept the gracious invitation. All are condemned who should dare to corrupt or change the word of God, either by adding to it, or taking from it.

The closing blessing (20, 21)

After discovering these things to his people on earth, Christ seems to take leave of them, and return to heaven; but he assures them it shall not be long before he comes again. And while we are busy in the duties of our different stations of life; whatever labours may try us, whatever difficulties may surround us, whatever sorrows may press us down, let us with pleasure hear our Lord proclaiming, Behold, I come quickly; I come to put an end to the labour and suffering of my servants. I come, and my reward of grace is with me, to recompense, with royal bounty, every work of faith and labour of love. I come to receive my faithful, persevering people to myself, to dwell for ever in that blissful world. Amen, even so, come, Lord Jesus. A blessing closes the whole. By the grace of Christ we must be kept in joyful expectation of his glory, fitted for it, and preserved to it; and his glorious appearance will be joyful to those who partake of his grace and favour here. Let all add, Amen. Let us earnestly thirst after greater measures of the gracious influences of the blessed Jesus in our souls, and his gracious presence with us, till glory has made perfect his grace toward us. Glory be to the Father, and to the Son, and to the Holy Ghost; as it was in the beginning, is now, and ever shall be, world without end. Amen.